WEST ACADEMIC PUBLISHING'S LAW SCHOOL ADVISORY BOARD

AMERICAN CRIMINAL PROCEDURE

CASES AND COMMENTARY

Twelfth Edition

■ ■ ■

Stephen A. Saltzburg
Wallace and Beverley Woodbury University Professor of Law
Co-Director of the Litigation and Dispute Resolution Program
The George Washington University Law School

Daniel J. Capra
Reed Professor of Law
Fordham University School of Law

David C. Gray
Jacob A. France Professor of Law
University of Maryland, Carey School of Law

AMERICAN CASEBOOK SERIES®

WEST ACADEMIC PUBLISHING

444 Cedar Street, Suite 700
St. Paul, MN 55101
1-877-888-1330

Printed in the United States of America

ISBN: 978-1-64708-644-2

To the women we love,
Susan Lee, Anne Capra, & Stéphanie Gaillard

PREFACE

This Twelfth Edition plays to what we feel were the strengths of the first eleven editions. While the predominant focus is on Supreme Court jurisprudence, we have tried wherever possible to give the reader a sense of what the lower courts are doing with the interesting and exciting issues that abound in criminal procedure. The lower courts are where the day-to-day law is made, and where many of the most interesting fact situations arise. Since our topic is "American" Criminal Procedure, we have made an effort to include cases from all the circuits and state courts throughout the book. As with prior editions, extensive commentary and interesting fact situations are included to assist in doctrinal development. We have also added extensive academic commentary on some of the cutting-edge issues in criminal procedure. Finally, the book covers all problems of criminal investigation and adjudication. It is not limited to constitutional issues. Yet despite the breadth of the book, we have made a special effort to keep it to a manageable and readable length.

The format of the book is the same as the prior editions, although much of the material has been reorganized and updated. Specifically, we have reorganized the materials dealing with Fourth Amendment searches and seizures in an effort to put several of the Court's recent opinions in a useful analytic context. Citations to Supreme Court opinions are limited to United States Reports, unless the case is so recent that the U.S. cite is not available. Certiorari denied citations are omitted on the ground that they unnecessarily clutter a book that is primarily for classroom use. Citations included in cases are often omitted without so specifying. Lettered footnotes are from the original materials. Numbered footnotes are ours. Omissions from the text of original material are indicated by asterisks and brackets. We have added more than 1000 headnotes in an effort to make the book as user friendly as possible.

This Edition gives special treatment to some of the more active areas of criminal procedure in the past few years, including problems created by developing technology, such as GPS tracking, cellphone tracking and searches, and searches of computer hard-drives. Racially-based stops and encounters are discussed in Chapter 2. Important questions concerning the right to retained counsel and to counsel's role are also explored in Chapter 10. The fundamental changes wrought in sentencing under the Supreme Court's *Apprendi* line of cases, are explored in Chapters 10 and 11.

Because every criminal procedure teacher likes to cover different material, we have tried to divide the book into numerous subdivisions to enable teachers to pick and choose the subjects they most want to cover.

We think that an advanced criminal procedure course is a useful and popular addition to the curriculum. If an advanced course is contemplated, Chapters 9 through 13 could be reserved for that course. An alternative approach is to include Chapter 9 in the basic course and move Chapters 8 and 5 into the advanced course. A third approach is to cover parts of all, or almost all, chapters in the basic course, and to finish them in the advanced course. We believe and hope that the material lends itself to several different divisions that all work well in class and make either a single course or a tandem interesting for all students.

STEPHEN A. SALTZBURG
Washington, D.C.

DANIEL J. CAPRA
New York, NY

DAVID C. GRAY
Baltimore, MD

April, 2022

INTRODUCTION

Criminal procedure is one of the courses in law school that generates classroom excitement that continues from the first to the last day of class. Whether it is the opportunity to compare the Warren, Burger and Rehnquist Courts or to predict the likely course of the Roberts Court, criminal procedure as a subject of study is almost always on the cutting-edge of the law with significant cases on the Court's docket every term. It involves the fundamental constraints on government power that are core to our constitutional contract and traces the order of contest between governments and individuals in the criminal process. It is routinely one of the topics students and laypersons love to talk and argue about because it raises compelling questions of justice in the context of real human drama.

As excited as students of criminal procedure are, too often they leave their courses feeling somewhat frustrated. They have learned a lot of recent law and they know what the latest decisions of the Supreme Court are, but they do not feel comfortable in their understanding of the criminal justice system (to the extent that it is accurate to call the way criminal cases are handled a system) as a whole, their knowledge of the doctrinal roots of the numerous concepts that they have examined, or how to deploy what they know in practice. This book is an effort to remove some of that frustration, to clarify the way in which the parts of the criminal justice system relate to one another, to explain how we arrived where we now find ourselves, and to help students develop an organized analytic process.

To accomplish this task, the material in the book is organized with an eye toward assisting students in developing analytic roadmaps they can deploy when analyzing criminal procedure questions. Along the way, the book utilizes original text and scholarly commentary to trace the history of the rules discussed, to point out how judicial treatment of various concepts has changed over time, and to indicate the vices and the virtues of various approaches, past and present. An effort is made to provide students with citations to law journals, books and cases not presented in this book so that those who are interested can examine topics more fully on their own with easy access to the relevant literature.

When a subject is examined, an effort is made to point out inadequacies in judicial opinions or legislative reactions to judicial opinions. Sometimes our own views are stated, either explicitly or implicitly, in an effort to stimulate thinking about new approaches to familiar problems. Where appropriate, students are asked to think about the concepts they have learned in connection with problems that encourage them to develop their own ideas about how best to handle hard cases and close questions.

An effort has been made to reproduce in case form only those Supreme Court cases that are most important. Less important cases are discussed in the textual material. Some of the cases that are offered are not yesterday's Supreme Court decisions, but those of a more distant Court, because the important opinions may be those that were seminal.

The emphasis on the development of concepts over time indicates a bias that should be confessed here: We believe that the judiciary, including the Supreme Court, as well as legislatures and executive agencies, to the extent they become involved in establishing procedures for criminal cases, attempt to articulate and apply doctrines that will hold their own over time. We believe they struggle "to get it right" eventually, if not always at the first crack.

This is not to suggest that right answers are clear or easy to ascertain. In many instances, reasonable minds will differ on the proper solution to questions, and often reasonable minds will find proper solutions to be elusive. We suggest only that approaches that are plainly defective are almost always abandoned or changed, and that it seems that courts and legislatures do attempt to refine the procedures that govern criminal investigations and prosecutions as a result of experience.

Like most criminal procedure books, this one places much emphasis on constitutional rules. This hardly can be avoided, because the Constitution as now interpreted does set minimum standards for many parts of the criminal justice system. But an attempt is made to indicate when nonconstitutional rules may be more important or more useful than constitutional ones.

To sum up, this book combines elements of traditional casebooks with textual material that might more typically be found in a treatise or hornbook, and it intersperses problems in many chapters. Overall, the idea is to identify clearly the problems of criminal procedure, to offer various ideas about how to handle the problems, and to describe the work that still needs to be done if criminal cases are to be processed fairly.

Some comments on the particular chapters of the book may help to explain how we have approached various topics.

Chapter 1 begins with a development of the criminal justice system. The importance of constitutional rules is discussed, and the incorporation and retroactivity doctrines are examined, since they arise again and again in the cases that are discussed in the following chapters.

Chapter 2 examines all aspects of Fourth Amendment law. It begins with a brief history of its common law roots before engaging in a careful examination of the text—including the threshold requirement of "search" or "seizure"—and an exploration of the relationship between the warrant clause and the reasonableness clause. The concepts of probable cause, valid warrants, arrest, stop and frisk, and scrutiny by a detached magistrate are all covered at length. The chapter reserves an examination of the exclusionary rule until the end and attempts thereby to promote an understanding of what the rule is and what its true costs are. This is the longest chapter of the book, covering the many facets of search and seizure law.

Chapter 3 covers self-incrimination and confessions. More than usual attention is paid to traditional Fifth Amendment law and how it relates to the law of confessions. Much space is devoted to laying the historical foundation for present law. Only then are *Miranda, Thompkins, Massiah, Brewer, Henry* and other major cases discussed.

Identification evidence is scrutinized in Chapter 4. The major Supreme Court cases take up most of the chapter, but an attempt is made to point out the shortcomings in the Court's work and to suggest how identification procedures might be improved and how fairer trials might result. The chapter also discusses some of the scientific findings on what factors can render an identification unreliable, and analyzes some non-constitutional remedies for guaranteeing the reliability of identifications.

Chapter 5 is about the right to counsel. As the right to counsel may be important in connection with confessions and identifications, as well as later in the process, it might seem strange for this chapter to follow the previous ones. But we believe that the order works and that it is helpful to treat the counsel cases in one place—at the point at which counsel is likely to be involved for the remainder of the process. The doctrines of ineffective assistance and self-representation are not treated here, but are reserved for Chapter 10.

Chapter 6 looks at the decision whether or not to charge a suspect. The roles of the police, the prosecutor and the grand jury are examined, and an effort is made to show how interdependent they are. The current controversy over the utility of the grand jury as a screening device and the dangers of the grand jury serving as an arm of the executive are described and discussed. Preliminary hearings and their relationship to grand juries and charging decisions generally are considered in some detail.

Chapter 7 covers bail and pretrial release. Both constitutional and nonconstitutional rules, especially the 1984 Federal Bail Reform Act, are analyzed. The purposes of bail and the controversy over preventive detention are discussed. Some emphasis is placed on the traditional role of the bondsman and the need for bail reform.

Chapter 8 presents criminal discovery. After a general overview, attention is paid to what the defendant can get from the prosecutor and what the prosecutor can get from the defendant without violating the Constitution. Proposals for liberalizing discovery are considered.

Chapter 9 is devoted to guilty pleas and plea bargaining. An extensive excerpt from a comprehensive study of plea bargaining in the United States begins the chapter. It is followed by a scholarly debate about the merits of plea bargaining, and then by a discussion of the requirements of a valid plea and an analysis of the finality of a plea.

Trial and trial-related rights are treated in Chapter 10. Among the topics covered are speedy trial, joinder of defendants and charges, burdens of persuasion, jury trial, fair-trial—free press conflicts, and effective representation and self-representation. This is the second longest chapter in the book. It addresses in the context of criminal trials many issues that are considered in the context of civil trials in the typical course in Civil Procedure.

Sentencing is the exclusive concern of Chapter 11. Basic options in sentencing are described, as are the roles of judge and jury. The determinate versus indeterminate sentencing controversy is explored, and the Federal Sentencing Guidelines are carefully examined. Also, the procedures that are generally employed in sentencing, and the applicable constitutional rules are set forth.

Chapter 12 covers all aspects of double jeopardy. Most attention is paid to recent decisions of the Supreme Court that clarify (or further confuse, depending on how the decisions are read) a subject that has been puzzling criminal procedure students for years. Collateral estoppel and vindictive prosecutorial conduct also are discussed.

Finally, Chapter 13 focuses on post-trial motions, appeals, and collateral attacks on convictions. An effort is made to examine all important post-sentencing challenges that can be made to a conviction. The section on collateral attack endeavors to explain the development of habeas corpus by the Supreme Court and Congress and the high points of the debate over how much post-conviction attack is desirable in a criminal justice system.

It should be obvious that we have tried to cover all of the significant parts of the criminal justice system and to do so in a reasonable number of pages. To accomplish this, we have worked hard to make the textual portions of the book as informative as possible. This Edition cannot be called a short book, but criminal procedure is not a subject that is easily confined to a few pages. To make the length somewhat more tolerable, we have endeavored to use headnotes as well as several different type sizes, not only for purposes of emphasis, but also to break the monotony of the printed page. To make the book easier to read, we also delete most internal citations in material that we quote from other sources. Thus, most internal cites in the Supreme Court opinions found throughout the book are missing. Footnotes in quoted material generally are deleted also. When we leave internal citations and original footnotes in the quoted material, we do so in the belief that they make a contribution to the overall coverage of the materials. Footnotes that are taken from the original source all have small letters to identify them—i.e., a, b, c, etc. Our own footnotes are identified by number—i.e., 1, 2, 3, etc. We hope that these choices enhance the "readability" of the book, and that by choosing to delete unnecessary baggage in quoted material, we have been able to pay more attention to the important and interesting questions that make criminal procedure a joy to study.

STEPHEN A. SALTZBURG
Washington, D.C.

DANIEL J. CAPRA
New York, NY

DAVID C. GRAY
Baltimore, MD

April, 2022

SUMMARY OF CONTENTS

TABLE OF CONTENTS

TABLE OF CASES

The principal cases are in bold type.

TABLE OF AUTHORITIES

AMERICAN CRIMINAL PROCEDURE

CASES AND COMMENTARY

Twelfth Edition

CHAPTER 1

BASIC PRINCIPLES

■ ■ ■

I. A CRIMINAL CASE

This course covers rules and procedures employed in criminal cases. Whether these rules and procedures apply, and how, may depend on whether a particular process is "criminal." An answer frequently given is that criminal cases require proof beyond a reasonable doubt, whereas civil and administrative cases generally do not. But this answer is too circular to be helpful. Proof beyond a reasonable doubt is only required once a case is identified as criminal.

Another answer is that the label "criminal" implies jail and prison. But not always. It is generally true that if jail and prison are prescribed penalties for a violation of the law, then the law is criminal. But a person may be confined in jail or prison for civil contempt, and fines, restitution and other sanctions are also employed as criminal sanctions—many of which may also be available in civil cases.

If the existence or absence of jail and prison penalties does not determine whether or not a case is criminal, could the determinative factor be whether a penalty is a "punishment" or not? This would appear to be somewhat closer to the mark. Yet, individuals against whom punitive damages are awarded or who are hit with substantial civil fines for violating legal requirements might well feel they have been punished. Thus, the penalty aspect alone cannot identify a case as criminal rather than civil.

Legislative Designation

Something more is needed to identify criminal cases. That something is so obvious that it may appear unsatisfactory at first—it is the label that the legislature chooses to give a sanction. If the legislature calls something criminal, then it is "criminal," and the special procedures governing criminal cases apply. See generally Cheh, Constitutional Limits on Using Civil Remedies To Achieve Criminal Law Objectives: Understanding and Transcending the Criminal-Civil Law Distinction, 42 Hastings L.J. 1325 (1991) (proceeding is criminal where labeled as such by the legislature). But what about the obverse? Should a legislature's designation of a sanction as non-criminal be equally dispositive.

Civil Penalty: United States v. L.O. Ward

Usually it is a defendant who argues that his alleged violation is criminal in order to take advantage of certain constitutional rights that are only available in criminal prosecutions. In United States v. L.O. Ward, 448 U.S. 242 (1980), for example, the Supreme Court held that a penalty imposed upon persons discharging hazardous substances into navigable waters was a civil penalty and, therefore, a reporting requirement for violators did not violate the Fifth Amendment's privilege against compelled self-incrimination. The Court said that the question whether a penalty is criminal or civil is a matter of statutory construction.

> Our inquiry in this regard has traditionally proceeded on two levels. First, we have set out to determine whether Congress, in establishing the penalizing mechanism, indicated either expressly or impliedly a preference for one label or the other. Second, where Congress has indicated an intention to establish a civil penalty, we have inquired further whether the statutory scheme was so punitive either in purpose or effect as to negate that intention. In regard to this latter inquiry, we have noted that "only the clearest proof could suffice to establish the unconstitutionality of a statute on such a ground."

The Court accepted the congressional label of "civil," although Justice Stevens dissented.

Commitment of Sex Offenders: Allen v. Illinois and Kansas v. Hendricks

In Allen v. Illinois, 478 U.S. 364 (1986), the Court held that commitment proceedings under the Illinois Sexually Dangerous Persons Act were not criminal, and the Fifth Amendment self-incrimination clause therefore did not prevent the use of the defendant's compelled statements. In *Allen,* the Court found that the legislature's characterization of the statute as civil and treatment-oriented was crucial, even though persons committed under the Act were kept in a maximum security institution that also housed convicted prisoners in need of psychiatric care.

The Court relied heavily on *Allen* in Kansas v. Hendricks, 521 U.S. 346 (1997). Hendricks challenged a Kansas statute imposing involuntary civil commitment on sexual predators. Hendricks was committed under the Act just before he was to be released from prison, where he had been incarcerated after a series of sex crime convictions. Hendricks argued that the civil commitment violated his constitutional right against double jeopardy, and also that it operated as an ex post facto law (because the civil commitment statute was passed well after he committed his sexually abusive acts). Both of these constitutional claims are triggered only when the state imposes criminal "punishment" on the citizen. The case therefore boiled down to whether the involuntary commitment statute was civil or criminal in nature.

Justice Thomas, writing for five members of the Court, held that the statute was civil rather than criminal in nature. He wrote as follows:

> Here, Kansas' objective to create a civil proceeding is evidenced by its placement of the Sexually Violent Predator Act within the Kansas probate code, instead of the criminal code, as well as its description of the Act as creating a "civil commitment procedure." * * *
>
> Although we recognize that a civil label is not always dispositive, we will reject the legislature's manifest intent only where a party challenging the statute provides the clearest proof that the statutory scheme is so punitive either in purpose or effect as to negate the State's intention to deem it "civil." United States v. Ward. * * * Hendricks, however, has failed to satisfy this heavy burden.
>
> As a threshold matter, commitment under the Act does not implicate either of the two primary objectives of criminal punishment: retribution or deterrence. The Act's purpose is not retributive because it does not affix culpability for prior criminal conduct. Instead, such conduct is used solely for evidentiary purposes, either to demonstrate that a "mental abnormality" exists or to support a finding of future dangerousness. * * * In addition, the Kansas Act does not make a criminal conviction a prerequisite for commitment—persons absolved of criminal responsibility may nonetheless be subject to confinement under the Act. An absence of the necessary criminal responsibility suggests that the State is not seeking retribution for a past misdeed. * * *
>
> Nor can it be said that the legislature intended the Act to function as a deterrent. Those persons committed under the Act are, by definition, suffering from a "mental abnormality" or a "personality disorder" that prevents them from exercising adequate control over their behavior. * * *
>
> Where the State has "disavowed any punitive intent"; limited confinement to a small segment of particularly dangerous individuals; provided strict procedural safeguards; directed that confined persons be segregated from the general prison population and afforded the same status as others who have been civilly committed; recommended treatment if such is possible; and permitted immediate release upon a showing that the individual is no longer dangerous or mentally impaired, we cannot say that it acted with punitive intent. * * *

Justice Breyer, joined by Justices Stevens, Souter, and Ginsburg, dissented, contending that the Kansas procedure was punitive because Hendricks received no treatment for his illness.

Registration of Sex Offenders—Civil Regulation or Criminal Punishment?: Smith v. Doe

In Smith v. Doe, 538 U.S. 84 (2003), the Court upheld Alaska's version of a "Megan's Law" against a challenge that it violated the Ex Post Facto Clause (a clause that applies only to criminal punishment). Megan's Laws, adopted by legislatures throughout the country, require convicted sex offenders to register with their state of residence. Information about the offenders is then published over the internet. Alaska's version required sex offenders to register even if they were convicted before the date of the legislation. The Court, in an opinion by Justice Kennedy, held that the statutory scheme was civil rather than punitive, and therefore the Ex Post Facto Clause did not apply. Justice Kennedy relied on *Hendricks* and declared that "an imposition of restrictive measures on sex offenders adjudged to be dangerous is a legitimate nonpunitive governmental objective." The Court also noted that Alaska's law simply requires registration; it "imposes no physical restraint, and so does not resemble the punishment of imprisonment, which is the paradigmatic affirmative disability or restraint."

Criminal Procedure Issues in a Civil Context

Occasionally, constitutional guarantees covered in a criminal procedure course arise in a civil context. The most prevalent situation is an action for damages brought against a government agent under 42 U.S.C. § 1983 for violation of a plaintiff's constitutional rights. For example, if a plaintiff claims she was wrongly arrested or illegally searched, then she may sue for violations of her Fourth Amendment rights. Many such cases will be discussed throughout this book.

Some constitutional protections discussed in this book also apply outside the criminal context. As examples, the Fourth Amendment governs searches conducted by state agents for non-criminal purposes, including regulatory inspections; and the Eighth Amendment prohibition on excessive fines applies in civil contexts, such as forfeiture proceedings, where the government seeks sanctions that are at least partially "punitive" in nature. See Austin v. United States, 509 U.S. 602 (1993). By contrast, other constitutional protections, such as procedural guarantees afforded to criminal defendants by the Fifth and Sixth Amendments, apply only in criminal cases.

II. TWO SPECIAL ASPECTS OF CONSTITUTIONAL LAW: THE INCORPORATION DOCTRINE AND RETROACTIVE APPLICATION OF CONSTITUTIONAL DECISIONS

Most of the cases you will read in this course are decisions of the United States Supreme Court. Before discussing the constitutional law developed by the Supreme Court in these decisions, it is useful to analyze the practical *impact* of a constitutionally-based decision by the Supreme Court.

The impact of a Supreme Court decision is governed by two general principles—incorporation and retroactivity. Under the doctrine of incorporation, a constitutionally-based decision ordinarily will bind both the States and the Federal government. Retroactivity principles determine the extent to which the Court's decision will have an effect on official activity occurring before the date of the decision.

A. INCORPORATION

Few individual rights were guaranteed by the original Constitution. That was a point of contention during the ratification process. Most state constitutions at the time guaranteed individual rights, but anti-Federalist critics recognized that these state provisions offered no protection against potential Federal overreach. Many states therefore conditioned their ratification votes on a promise that the First Congress would draft, pass, and send to the States a slate of amendments designed to guarantee to citizens of the new nation rights familiar to them as citizens of their states. The First Congress fulfilled that promise, sending twelve proposed amendments to the States for ratification. Ten were ratified in 1791.[1]

In Barron v. Baltimore, 32 U.S. (7 Pet.) 243 (1833), Chief Justice Marshall, writing for the Court, concluded that the Bill of Rights applied only against the Federal government and not against the States. After the Civil War and the adoption of the Thirteenth, Fourteenth and Fifteenth Amendments, a new question arose: whether these Amendments, and particularly the Fourteenth Amendment's Privileges or Immunities Clause, incorporated Bill of Rights protections, making them applicable against the States. In the Slaughter-House Cases, 83 U.S. (16 Wall.) 36 (1872), the Court held that they did not. The question remained, however, whether the Fourteenth Amendment might make some provisions of the Bill of Rights applicable to the States, perhaps through the expansive language of the Fourteenth Amendment Due Process Clause.

---

[1] The original First Amendment, which would have governed proportional representation in the House of Representatives, was never ratified. The original Second Amendment, which governs the timing of changes to congressional compensation, was ratified in 1992 as the 27th Amendment.

For almost seventy years, it seemed that the answer was "no." In Hurtado v. California, 110 U.S. 516 (1884), the Court held that California could permit criminal proceedings to be instituted by information, rather than by grand jury indictment—that is, the Fifth Amendment right to be indicted by a grand jury did not apply to the States. And in 1908, the Court, in Twining v. New Jersey, 211 U.S. 78, held that the privilege against self-incrimination was not binding on the States. Then, there was a shift.

In Palko v. Connecticut, 302 U.S. 319 (1937), Justice Cardozo wrote for the Court to uphold a state procedure permitting a prosecutor to appeal an adverse trial court decision and to seek a new trial. Justice Cardozo assumed that the Double Jeopardy Clause of the Fifth Amendment would have invalidated such an appeal and retrial by the Federal government, but found that the States could take a different approach. Discussing the question whether the Bill of Rights was "absorbed" into the Fourteenth Amendment, Justice Cardozo wrote that the "specific pledges of particular amendments have been found to be implicit in the concept of ordered liberty, and thus, through the Fourteenth Amendment, become valid as against the States." But according to Justice Cardozo, the Double Jeopardy Clause was not among them.

A decade after *Palko*, a majority of the Court reaffirmed *Twining* in Adamson v. California, 332 U.S. 46 (1947).[2] Justice Black, joined by Justice Douglas, dissented. Justice Black argued that the Privileges or Immunities Clause of the Fourteenth Amendment was intended to assure that no state could deprive its citizens of protections guaranteed in the Bill of Rights—a position endorsed in recent years by Justices Thomas and Gorsuch. Also, Justice Black rejected what he called the "natural law" formula of *Palko,* which invited the Court to recognize rights "implicit in the concept of ordered liberty" and yet not found in the Bill of Rights.[3] Responding to the opinion by Justice Black and its appendix of constitutional history, Justice Frankfurter took vigorous exception to Black's argument.[4]

Justices Black and Frankfurter continued to disagree for years over the relationship of the Bill of Rights and the Fourteenth Amendment, with Justice Frankfurter generally prevailing on the theory that the Amendment did not make the Bill of Rights applicable to the states in its

---

[2] *Adamson* and *Twinning* were overruled by Griffin v. California, 380 U.S. 609 (1965), and Malloy v. Hogan, 378 U.S. 1 (1964).

[3] Justice Murphy, joined by Justice Rutledge, also dissented. Justice Murphy would have reserved the right to recognize procedural protections not explicitly recognized in the Bill of Rights. Later, Justice Douglas also would move to this position.

[4] Justice Frankfurter relied heavily on the historical analysis in Fairman, Does the Fourteenth Amendment Incorporate the Bill of Rights? The Original Understanding, 2 Stan.L.Rev. 5 (1949). Both Justice Black and Professor Fairman are criticized in Kelly, Clio and the Court: An Illicit Love Affair, 1965 Sup.Ct.Rev. 119. Professor Amar has written an important article that criticizes the Fairman view and concludes that the Fourteenth Amendment was designed to apply the Bill of Rights protections to the States. See Amar, The Bill of Rights and the Fourteenth Amendment, 101 Yale L.J. 1193 (1991).

entirety, but that it did incorporate such protections as were "implicit in the concept of ordered liberty." See, e.g., Wolf v. Colorado, 338 U.S. 25 (1949); Rochin v. California, 342 U.S. 165 (1952); Irvine v. California, 347 U.S. 128 (1954); Breithaupt v. Abram, 352 U.S. 432 (1957).

Matters changed in the 1960's as the Warren Court—without ever formally abandoning the fundamental fairness standard—began to incorporate more and more Bill of Rights protections under an approach referred to by Justice Black as "selective incorporation." Under this approach, the Court determined whether the right asserted was fundamental to the American system of justice. If so, it was incorporated through the Fourteenth Amendment and applied to the States. Moreover, the Court almost always held that, once incorporated, the scope of the Constitutional guarantee would be the same in state and federal cases: every detail of the incorporated provision was applicable "jot-for-jot" to the States.

The current approach of the Court, as well as the competing theories, are well illustrated by Duncan v. Louisiana. *Duncan* held that the right to jury trial, guaranteed by the Sixth Amendment, is binding on the states. That particular holding is not the subject of attention here [see Chapter 10 for that part of the case]; rather, the focus is on how the Court reached its result on incorporation. The change in the Court's analysis over time is well-described by the long footnote in the majority opinion.

DUNCAN V. LOUISIANA

Supreme Court of the United States, 1968.
391 U.S. 145.

JUSTICE WHITE delivered the opinion of the Court.

* * *

I

The Fourteenth Amendment denies the States the power to "deprive any person of life, liberty, or property, without due process of law." In resolving conflicting claims concerning the meaning of this spacious language, the Court has looked increasingly to the Bill of Rights for guidance; many of the rights guaranteed by the first eight Amendments to the Constitution have been held to be protected against state action by the Due Process Clause of the Fourteenth Amendment. That clause now protects the right to compensation for property taken by the State;[a] the rights of speech, press, and religion covered by the First Amendment;[b] the Fourth Amendment rights to be free from unreasonable searches and seizures and to have excluded from criminal trials any evidence illegally

---

[a] Chicago, B. & Q. R. Co. v. Chicago, 166 U.S. 226 (1897).

[b] See, e.g., Fiske v. Kansas, 274 U.S. 380 (1927).

seized;[c] the right guaranteed by the Fifth Amendment to be free of compelled self-incrimination;[d] and the Sixth Amendment rights to counsel,[e] to a speedy[f] and public[g] trial, to confrontation of opposing witnesses,[h] and to compulsory process for obtaining witnesses.[i]

The test for determining whether a right extended by the Fifth and Sixth Amendments with respect to federal criminal proceedings is also protected against state action by the Fourteenth Amendment has been phrased in a variety of ways in the opinions of this Court. The question has been asked whether a right is among those " 'fundamental principles of liberty and justice which lie at the base of all our civil and political institutions,' " Powell v. Alabama, 287 U.S. 45, 67 (1932); whether it is "basic in our system of jurisprudence," In re Oliver, 333 U.S. 257, 273 (1948); and whether it is "a fundamental right, essential to a fair trial," Gideon v. Wainwright, 372 U.S. 335, 343–344 (1963). The claim before us is that the right to trial by jury guaranteed by the Sixth Amendment meets these tests. The position of Louisiana, on the other hand, is that the Constitution imposes upon the States no duty to give a jury trial in any criminal case, regardless of the seriousness of the crime or the size of the punishment which may be imposed. Because we believe that trial by jury in criminal cases is fundamental to the American scheme of justice, we hold that the Fourteenth Amendment guarantees a right of jury trial in all criminal cases which—were they to be tried in a federal court—would come within the Sixth Amendment's guarantee.[j] Since we consider the appeal

[c] See Mapp v. Ohio, 367 U.S. 643 (1961).

[d] Malloy v. Hogan, 378 U.S. 1 (1964).

[e] Gideon v. Wainwright, 372 U.S. 335 (1963).

[f] Klopfer v. North Carolina, 386 U.S. 213 (1967).

[g] In re Oliver, 333 U.S. 257 (1948).

[h] Pointer v. Texas, 380 U.S. 400 (1965).

[i] Washington v. Texas, 388 U.S. 14 (1967).

[j] In one sense recent cases applying provisions of the first eight Amendments to the States represent a new approach to the "incorporation" debate. Earlier the Court can be seen as having asked, when inquiring into whether some particular procedural safeguard was required of a State, if a civilized system could be imagined that would not accord the particular protection. For example, Palko v. Connecticut, 302 U.S. 319, 325 (1937) stated: "The right to trial by jury and the immunity from prosecution except as the result of an indictment may have value and importance. Even so, they are not of the very essence of a scheme of ordered liberty * * *. Few would be so narrow or provincial as to maintain that a fair and enlightened system of justice would be impossible without them." The recent cases, on the other hand, have proceeded upon the valid assumption that state criminal processes are not imaginary and theoretical schemes but actual systems bearing virtually every characteristic of the common-law system that has been developing contemporaneously in England and in this country. The question thus is whether given this kind of system a particular procedure is fundamental—whether, that is, a procedure is necessary to an Anglo-American regime of ordered liberty. It is this sort of inquiry that can justify the conclusions that state courts must exclude evidence seized in violation of the Fourth Amendment, Mapp v. Ohio, 367 U.S. 643 (1961); that state prosecutors may not comment on a defendant's failure to testify, Griffin v. California, 380 U.S. 609 (1965); and that criminal punishment may not be imposed for the status of narcotics addiction, Robinson v. California, 370 U.S. 660 (1962). Of immediate relevance for this case are the Court's holdings that the States must comply with certain provisions of the Sixth Amendment, specifically that the States may not refuse a speedy trial, confrontation of witnesses, and the assistance, at state expense if necessary, of counsel. See

before us to be such a case, we hold that the Constitution was violated when appellant's demand for jury trial was refused.

* * * A criminal process, which was fair and equitable but used no juries is easy to imagine. It would make use of alternative guarantees and protections which would serve the purposes that the jury serves in the English and American systems. Yet no American State has undertaken to construct such a system. Instead, every American State, including Louisiana, uses the jury extensively, and imposes very serious punishments only after a trial at which the defendant has a right to a jury's verdict. In every State, including Louisiana, the structure and style of the criminal process—the supporting framework and the subsidiary procedures—are of the sort that naturally complement jury trial, and have developed in connection with and in reliance upon jury trial.

* * *

JUSTICE BLACK, with whom JUSTICE DOUGLAS joins, concurring.

* * *

All of these holdings making Bill of Rights' provisions applicable as such to the States mark, of course, a departure from the *Twining* doctrine holding that none of those provisions were enforceable as such against the States. The dissent in this case, however, makes a spirited and forceful defense of that now discredited doctrine. I do not believe that it is necessary for me to repeat the historical and logical reasons for my challenge to the *Twining* holding contained in my *Adamson* dissent and Appendix to it. What I wrote there in 1947 was the product of years of study and research. My appraisal of the legislative history followed 10 years of legislative experience as a Senator of the United States, not a bad way, I suspect, to learn the value of what is said in legislative debates, committee discussions, committee reports, and various other steps taken in the course of passage of bills, resolutions, and proposed constitutional amendments. My Brother Harlan's objections to my *Adamson* dissent history, like that of most of the objectors, relies most heavily on a criticism written by Professor Charles Fairman and published in the Stanford Law Review. 2 Stan.L.Rev. 5 (1949). * * * Professor Fairman's "history" relies very heavily on what was *not* said in the state legislatures that passed on the Fourteenth Amendment. Instead of relying on this kind of negative pregnant, my legislative experience has convinced me that it is far wiser to

---

cases cited supra. Of each of these determinations that a constitutional provision originally written to bind the Federal Government should bind the States as well it might be said that the limitation in question is not necessarily fundamental to fairness in every criminal system that might be imagined but is fundamental in the context of the criminal processes maintained by the American States.

rely on what *was* said, and most importantly, said by the men who actually sponsored the Amendment in the Congress. * * *

In addition to the adoption of Professor Fairman's "history," the dissent states that "the great words of the four clauses of the first section of the Fourteenth Amendment would have been an exceedingly peculiar way to say that 'The rights heretofore guaranteed against federal intrusion by the first eight Amendments are henceforth guaranteed against state intrusion as well.' " In response to this I can say only that the words "No State shall make or enforce any law which shall abridge the privileges or immunities of citizens of the United States" seem to me an eminently reasonable way of expressing the idea that henceforth the Bill of Rights shall apply to the States. What more precious "privilege" of American citizenship could there be than that privilege to claim the protections of our great Bill of Rights? I suggest that any reading of "privileges or immunities of citizens of the United States" which excludes the Bill of Rights' safeguards renders the words of this section of the Fourteenth Amendment meaningless. * * *

While I do not wish at this time to discuss at length my disagreement with Brother Harlan's forthright and frank restatement of the now discredited *Twining* doctrine, I do want to point out what appears to me to be the basic difference between us. His view * * * is that "due process is an evolving concept" and therefore that it entails a "gradual process of judicial inclusion and exclusion" to ascertain those "immutable principles * * * of free government which no member of the Union may disregard." Thus the Due Process Clause is treated as prescribing no specific and clearly ascertainable constitutional command that judges must obey in interpreting the Constitution, but rather as leaving judges free to decide at any particular time whether a particular rule or judicial formulation embodies an "immutable principl[e] of free government" or is "implicit in the concept of ordered liberty," or whether certain conduct "shocks the judge's conscience" or runs counter to some other similar, undefined and undefinable standard. Thus due process, according to my Brother Harlan, is to be a phrase with no permanent meaning, but one which is found to shift from time to time in accordance with judges' predilections and understandings of what is best for the country. If due process means this, the Fourteenth Amendment, in my opinion, might as well have been written that "no person shall be deprived of life, liberty or property except by laws that the judges of the United States Supreme Court shall find to be consistent with the immutable principles of free government." It is impossible for me to believe that such unconfined power is given to judges in our Constitution that is a written one in order to limit governmental power.

Another tenet of the *Twining* doctrine as restated by my Brother Harlan is that "due process of law requires only fundamental fairness." But the "fundamental fairness" test is one on a par with that of shocking the conscience of the Court. Each of such tests depends entirely on the particular judge's idea of ethics and morals instead of requiring him to depend on the boundaries fixed by the written words of the Constitution. * * *

Finally I want to add that I am not bothered by the argument that applying the Bill of Rights to the States, "according to the same standards that protect those personal rights against federal encroachment," interferes with our concept of federalism in that it may prevent States from trying novel social and economic experiments. I have never believed that under the guise of federalism the States should be able to experiment with the protections afforded our citizens through the Bill of Rights. * * *

In closing I want to emphasize that I believe as strongly as ever that the Fourteenth Amendment was intended to make the Bill of Rights applicable to the States. I have been willing to support the selective incorporation doctrine, however, as an alternative, although perhaps less historically supportable than complete incorporation. The selective incorporation process, if used properly, does limit the Supreme Court in the Fourteenth Amendment field to specific Bill of Rights' protections only and keeps judges from roaming at will in their own notions of what policies outside the Bill of Rights are desirable and what are not. And, most importantly for me, the selective incorporation process has the virtue of having already worked to make most of the Bill of Rights' protections applicable to the States.

JUSTICE HARLAN, whom JUSTICE STEWART joins, dissenting.

* * *

The Court's approach to this case is an uneasy and illogical compromise among the views of various Justices on how the Due Process Clause should be interpreted. The Court does not say that those who framed the Fourteenth Amendment intended to make the Sixth Amendment applicable to the States. And the Court concedes that it finds nothing unfair about the procedure by which the present appellant was tried. Nevertheless, the Court reverses his conviction: it holds, for some reason not apparent to me that the Due Process Clause incorporates the particular clause of the Sixth Amendment that requires trial by jury in federal criminal cases—including, as I read its opinion, the sometimes trivial accompanying baggage of judicial interpretation in federal contexts. I have raised my voice many times before against the Court's continuing undiscriminating insistence upon fastening on the States federal notions of criminal justice and I must do so again in this instance. With all respect, the Court's approach and its reading of history are altogether topsy-turvy.

* * * I believe I am correct in saying that every member of the Court for at least the last 135 years has agreed that our Founders did not consider the requirements of the Bill of Rights so fundamental that they should operate directly against the States. * * * The Bill of Rights was considered unnecessary by some but insisted upon by others in order to curb the possibility of abuse of power by the strong central government they were creating.

The Civil War Amendments dramatically altered the relation of the Federal Government to the States. The first section of the Fourteenth Amendment imposes highly significant restrictions on state action. But the restrictions are couched in very broad and general terms: citizenship; privileges and immunities; due process of law; equal protection of the laws. * * * Where does the Court properly look to find the specific rules that define and give content to such terms as "life, liberty, or property" and "due process of law"?

A few members of the Court have taken the position that the intention of those who drafted the first section of the Fourteenth Amendment was simply, and exclusively, to make the provisions of the first eight Amendments applicable to state action. This view has never been accepted by this Court. In my view, often expressed elsewhere, the first section of the Fourteenth Amendment was meant neither to incorporate, nor to be limited to, the specific guarantees of the first eight Amendments. The overwhelming historical evidence marshalled by Professor Fairman demonstrates, to me conclusively, that the Congressmen and state legislators who wrote, debated, and ratified the Fourteenth Amendment did not think they were "incorporating" the Bill of Rights[k] and the very breadth and generality of the Amendment's provisions suggest that its authors did not suppose that the Nation would always be limited to mid-19th century conceptions of "liberty" and "due process of law" * * *. In short, neither history, nor sense, supports using the Fourteenth Amendment to put the States in a constitutional straitjacket with respect to their own development in the administration of criminal or civil law.

* * *

Although I therefore fundamentally disagree with the total incorporation view of the Fourteenth Amendment, it seems to me that such

[k] Fairman, Does the Fourteenth Amendment Incorporate the Bill of Rights? The Original Understanding, 2 Stan.L.Rev. 5 (1949). Professor Fairman was not content to rest upon the overwhelming fact that the great words of the four clauses of the first section of the Fourteenth Amendment would have been an exceedingly peculiar way to say that "The rights heretofore guaranteed against federal intrusion by the first eight Amendments are henceforth guaranteed against state intrusion as well." He therefore sifted the mountain of material comprising the debates and committee reports relating to the Amendment in both Houses of Congress and in the state legislatures that passed upon it. He found that in the immense corpus of comments on the purpose and effects of the proposed amendment, and on its virtues and defects, there is almost no evidence whatever for "incorporation." * * *

a position does at least have the virtue, lacking in the Court's selective incorporation approach, of internal consistency: we look to the Bill of Rights, word for word, clause for clause, precedent for precedent because, it is said, the men who wrote the Amendment wanted it that way. * * *

Apart from the approach taken by the absolute incorporationists, I can see only one method of analysis that has any internal logic. That is to start with the words "liberty" and "due process of law" and attempt to define them in a way that accords with American traditions and our system of government. This approach * * * entails a gradual process of judicial inclusion and exclusion, seeking, with due recognition of constitutional tolerance for state experimentation and disparity, to ascertain those immutable principles of free government which no member of the Union may disregard. * * *

* * *

Today's Court still remains unwilling to accept the total incorporationists' view of the history of the Fourteenth Amendment. This, if accepted, would afford a cogent reason for applying the Sixth Amendment to the States. The Court is also, apparently, unwilling to face the task of determining whether denial of trial by jury in the situation before us, or in other situations, is fundamentally unfair. Consequently, the Court has compromised on the ease of the incorporationist position, without its internal logic. It has simply assumed that the question before us is whether the Jury Trial Clause of the Sixth Amendment should be incorporated into the Fourteenth, jot-for-jot and case-for-case, or ignored. Then the Court merely declares that the clause in question is "in" rather than "out."

The Court has justified neither its starting place nor its conclusion. * * *

NOTE ON INCORPORATION

The Court has never accepted Justice Black's view that the Fourteenth Amendment incorporates the entirety of the Bill of Rights. It has instead held fast to its selective approach, incorporating one-by-one most provisions of the Bill of Rights. Recent additions include Ramos v. Louisiana, 140 S.Ct. 1390 (2020), incorporating the Sixth Amendment jury unanimity requirement, and Timbs v. Indiana, 139 S.Ct. 682 (2019), incorporating the Eighth Amendment prohibition on excessive fines. Among the few rights that have not been incorporated are the Fifth Amendment right to indictment by grand jury, the Seventh Amendment right to jury trial in civil cases, and the Bail Clause of the Eighth Amendment.[5]

---

[5] Although the question was not squarely presented in *Timbs*, the Court seems to assume that the Eighth Amendment prohibition on excessive bail applies to the States. See Timbs v. Indiana, 139 S.Ct. 682, 686–87 (2019) ("Like the Eighth Amendment's proscriptions of 'cruel and

If Justice Black was wrong about the intent of the drafters of the Fourteenth Amendment and they did not intend incorporation, is there any rhyme or reason to the selective incorporation idea? If there is, it has to be that the Court has been willing to assume that the drafters of the Fourteenth Amendment wanted to enforce against the states only those portions of the Bill of Rights whose fundamentality remained evident many years after the first eight Amendments were adopted. Does that kind of prescience seem likely?

Justice Black argued that incorporation of the Bill of Rights is preferable to a case-by-case, fundamental fairness approach, because the latter gives rise to judicial subjectivity in applying the vague term "due process." Are the Bill of Rights protections less susceptible to judicial subjectivity? For instance, does the term "unreasonable searches and seizures" in the Fourth Amendment provide more limitation on judicial subjectivity than the term "due process"? Hundreds of pages of decisions covered in Chapter 2 will inform the answer to this question.

NOTE ON STATE CONSTITUTIONAL PROTECTIONS

The Supreme Court has the final say in interpreting federal constitutional protections concerning criminal procedure. But state courts have sometimes provided enhanced protections by relying on state constitutions. Of course, state courts cannot construe their own constitutions in order to provide *less* protection than is guaranteed by the Bill of Rights; but state courts, construing their own constitutions, can provide greater protections than those set by the Supreme Court's construction of the Bill of Rights. For an illuminating account of the often overlooked role of state constitutions, see Sutton, 51 Imperfect Solutions: States and the Making of American Constitutional Law (2008).

While some states have been more active than others, virtually every state has rejected at least one Supreme Court decision as insufficiently protective of the rights of citizens. Many of these decisions will be discussed in the context of particular Supreme Court rulings, *infra;* but advocates in state courts—where most criminal cases are adjudicated—are well-advised to consider making arguments on state constitutional grounds.

It must be remembered that if a state court explicitly relies on state constitutional law to provide more protection for its citizens than is guaranteed by the Federal Constitution, the state court's decision cannot be reviewed by the Supreme Court. This is because there is no federal question that would control the case. But the state court must be explicit that it is relying on state law. If it appears that the state court might have been relying in whole or part on Federal law, then the Supreme Court can take the case and reject the state court's construction of the Federal Constitution. See generally Michigan v.

---

unusual punishment' and '[e]xcessive bail,' the protection against excessive fines guards against abuses of government's punitive or criminal-law-enforcement authority. This safeguard, we hold, is 'fundamental to our scheme of ordered liberty,' with 'dee[p] root[s] in [our] history and tradition.' The Excessive Fines Clause is therefore incorporated by the Due Process Clause of the Fourteenth Amendment.").

Long, 463 U.S. 1032 (1983) (state court must place explicit reliance on state law in order to avoid Supreme Court review; otherwise it will be presumed that the state court was construing Federal constitutional law).

For extensive discussions about what has come to be called "state court activism," see Brennan, J., State Constitutions and the Protection of Individual Rights, 90 Harv.L.Rev. 489 (1977); Symposium on Emerging Issues in State Constitutional Law, 65 Temple L.Rev. 1119 (1992); Symposium, Independent State Grounds: Should State Courts Depart From the Fourth Amendment in Construing Their Own Constitutions, and if so, on What Basis Beyond Simple Disagreement With the United States Supreme Court's Result?, 77 Miss. L.Rev. 1 (2007). For a critical view, see Gardner, The Failed Discourse of State Constitutionalism, 90 Mich.L.Rev. 761 (1992).

B. RETROACTIVITY

1. The Impact of New Decisions

When the Supreme Court reviews the conduct of government officials in a criminal case, the legal rule it promulgates will obviously apply to all similar government conduct arising after the date of the decision—otherwise the decision would be advisory. But an important question is whether the legal rule should also be applied to government conduct occurring *before* the date of the decision. The question of retroactive application implicates competing policies and interests.

For example, when the Supreme Court overrules a prior decision that had permitted certain police behavior, the Court might be concerned that law enforcement officers, who relied on the case law existing at the time of their conduct acted as competent officers should. The Court might, therefore, be reluctant to see the government disadvantaged as a result of justifiable reliance by government agents. The Court also might be concerned that trial courts that relied on the old rule might be burdened with numerous retrials once the new decision is announced—assuming a retrial is even possible given the passage of time.

On the other hand, if a decision is important enough to be called a "constitutional decision," it is arguable that it ought to benefit all those who suffered the conduct later found to be unconstitutional.

For many years, the Supreme Court's position on retroactive application was complicated and often inconsistent. But one rule that the Court has followed is to give the benefit of the new rule to the litigant who establishes it—even though that constitutes retroactive application. The Court has done so for two reasons: 1) to provide litigants with incentives to improve past decisions of the Court, because few litigants would ask the Court to establish a new rule that they could not use; and 2) to assure that there is a concrete case or controversy before the Court. But, as we shall see, this practice is complicated by the distinction between rights and remedies, particularly in Fourth Amendment cases when the remedy sought is exclusion of evidence at trial.

2. Prior Supreme Court Law on Retroactivity, and the Harlan Approach

In Stovall v. Denno, 388 U.S. 293 (1967), and Desist v. United States, 394 U.S. 244 (1969), the Court refused to apply its decisions requiring counsel at certain lineups and its holding in an earlier Fourth Amendment case, Katz v. United States, 389 U.S. 347 (1967), to other cases still pending on direct review (i.e., appeals or petitions for review to a higher court, including all appellate activity up to and including the Supreme Court's denial of a writ of certiorari, have not been exhausted). Rather, the Court applied its earlier decisions to reach only the police activity that followed the announcement of the new rules. Essentially, the rulings were given only prospective effect, other than for the litigants in the cases in which the new rule was established.

Justice Harlan dissented in *Desist*, arguing that new constitutional rules must be applied, at a minimum, to all cases pending on direct review when the rules are handed down. Justice Harlan charged that a decision to apply a ruling on direct review of one case (i.e., the case before the Court), but not to other similarly situated cases, would be an assertion of legislative, not adjudicatory, power. Justice Harlan argued further that, as a general matter, a new rule should *not* be applied on post-conviction or collateral review (i.e., habeas corpus proceedings).[6]

Justice Harlan identified two situations in which the presumption of nonretroactivity of new rules to habeas corpus cases could be overcome. The first encompasses new rules that are fundamental and "implicit in the concept of ordered liberty" (quoting Justice Cardozo's opinion in *Palko*). The second exception covers petitioners challenging the constitutionality of a substantive rule of criminal law, such as a law criminalizing constitutionally protected speech. Justice Harlan's view is fully discussed and analyzed by the Court in Teague v. Lane, below.

3. Current Supreme Court Approach to Retroactivity

In a series of cases, the Court finally adopted the Harlan approach to retroactivity, with one slight modification to the "fundamental fairness" exception to non-retroactivity on habeas. In Griffith v. Kentucky, 479 U.S. 314 (1987), the Court held that its decision the previous term in Batson v. Kentucky, 476 U.S. 79 (1986) (defendant could establish a prima facie case

---

[6] Habeas corpus proceedings usually involve federal court review of a state judgment of conviction, and are brought after a defendant's direct appeals through the state appellate courts and the United States Supreme Court have been rejected or foregone; see the discussion in Chapter 13.

of racial discrimination based on the prosecution's use of peremptory challenges in a single case), would be applied retroactively to all cases still pending on direct review when the decision was announced. Although *Batson* overruled a decision that had withstood attack for more than twenty years, the Court declined to follow previous decisions barring some or all defendants on direct appeal from benefitting from recently announced decisions. The Court's analysis in *Griffith* is discussed in Teague v. Lane, immediately below.

TEAGUE V. LANE

Supreme Court of the United States, 1989.
489 U.S. 288.

JUSTICE O'CONNOR delivered the opinion of the Court.

In Taylor v. Louisiana, 419 U.S. 522 (1975), this Court held that the Sixth Amendment required that the jury venire be drawn from a fair cross section of the community. * * * The principal question presented in this case is whether the Sixth Amendment's fair cross section requirement should now be extended to the petit jury. Because we adopt Justice Harlan's approach to retroactivity for cases on collateral review, we leave the resolution of that question for another day.

* * *

Petitioner, a black man, was convicted by an all-white Illinois jury of three counts of attempted murder, two counts of armed robbery, and one count of aggravated battery. During jury selection for petitioner's trial, the prosecutor used all 10 of his peremptory challenges to exclude blacks. * * *

On appeal, petitioner argued that the prosecutor's use of peremptory challenges denied him the right to be tried by a jury that was representative of the community. The Illinois Appellate Court rejected petitioner's fair cross section claim. The Illinois Supreme Court denied leave to appeal, and we denied certiorari.

Petitioner then filed a petition for a writ of habeas corpus in the United States District Court for the Northern District of Illinois. Petitioner repeated his fair cross section claim * * *. [Both the District Court and the Court of Appeals en banc denied Teague's claim for habeas relief. The Court of Appeals held that the Constitution's fair cross-section requirement was limited to the jury venire—the pool from which the jury that sits in the case (the petit jury) is drawn].

* * *

Petitioner's * * * contention is that the Sixth Amendment's fair cross section requirement applies to the petit jury. * * * Petitioner * * * contends that the *ratio decidendi* of *Taylor* cannot be limited to the jury venire, and he urges adoption of a new rule. Because we hold that the rule urged by petitioner should not be applied retroactively to cases on collateral review, we decline to address petitioner's contention.

* * *

In the past, the Court has, without discussion, often applied a new constitutional rule of criminal procedure to the defendant in the case announcing the new rule, and has confronted the question of retroactivity later when a different defendant sought the benefit of that rule. In several cases, however, the Court has addressed the retroactivity question in the very case announcing the new rule. These two lines of cases do not have a unifying theme, and we think it is time to clarify how the question of retroactivity should be resolved for cases on collateral review.

* * *

In our view, the question "whether a decision [announcing a new rule should] be given prospective or retroactive effect should be faced at the time of [that] decision." Mishkin, Foreword: the High Court, the Great Writ, and the Due Process of Time and Law, 79 Harv. L. Rev. 56, 64 (1965). Retroactivity is properly treated as a threshold question, for, once a new rule is applied to the defendant in the case announcing the rule, evenhanded justice requires that it be applied retroactively to all who are similarly situated. Thus, before deciding whether the fair cross section requirement should be extended to the petit jury, we should ask whether such a rule would be applied retroactively to the case at issue. * * *

It is admittedly often difficult to determine when a case announces a new rule, and we do not attempt to define the spectrum of what may or may not constitute a new rule for retroactivity purposes. In general, however, a case announces a new rule when it breaks new ground or imposes a new obligation on the States or the Federal Government. To put it differently, a case announces a new rule if the result was not dictated by precedent existing at the time the defendant's conviction became final. Given [prior case law stating] that "[f]airness in [jury] selection has never been held to require proportional representation of races upon a jury," application of the fair cross section requirement to the petit jury would be a new rule.

Not all new rules have been uniformly treated for retroactivity purposes. Nearly a quarter of a century ago, in Linkletter v. Walker, 381 U.S. 618 (1965), the Court attempted to set some standards by which to determine the retroactivity of new rules. * * * The *Linkletter* retroactivity standard has not led to consistent results. Instead, it has been used to limit application of certain new rules to cases on direct review, other new rules only to the defendants in the cases announcing such rules, and still other new rules to cases in which trials have not yet commenced. * * *

Application of the *Linkletter* standard led to the disparate treatment of similarly situated defendants on direct review. For example, in * * * Johnson v. New Jersey, 384 U.S. 719, 733–735 (1966), the Court held, under the *Linkletter* standard, that *Miranda* would only be applied to trials commencing after that decision had been announced. Because the defendant in *Johnson*, like the defendants in *Miranda*, was on direct review of his conviction, the Court's refusal to give *Miranda* retroactive effect resulted in unequal treatment of those who were similarly situated. * * *

In Griffith v. Kentucky, 479 U.S. 314 (1987), we rejected as unprincipled and inequitable the *Linkletter* standard for cases pending on direct review at the time a new rule is announced, and adopted the first part of the retroactivity approach advocated by Justice Harlan. We agreed with Justice Harlan that "failure to apply a newly declared constitutional rule to criminal cases pending on direct review violates basic norms of constitutional adjudication." We gave two reasons for our decision. First, because we can only promulgate new rules in specific cases and cannot possibly decide all cases in which review is sought, "the integrity of judicial review" requires the application of the new rule to "all similar cases pending on direct review." * * * Second, because "selective application of new rules violates the principle of treating similarly situated defendants the same," we refused to continue to tolerate the inequity that resulted from not applying new rules retroactively to defendants whose cases had not yet become final. Although new rules that constituted clear breaks with the past generally were not given retroactive effect under the *Linkletter* standard, we held that "a new rule for the conduct of criminal prosecutions is to be applied retroactively to all cases, state or federal, pending on direct review or not yet final, with no exception for cases in which the new rule constitutes a 'clear break' with the past."

* * *

Justice Harlan believed that new rules generally should not be applied retroactively to cases on collateral review. * * * Given the "broad scope of constitutional issues cognizable on habeas," Justice Harlan argued that it is "sounder, in adjudicating habeas petitions, generally to apply the law prevailing at the time a conviction became final than it is to seek to dispose of [habeas] cases on the basis of intervening changes in constitutional interpretation." As he explained * * * "the threat of habeas serves as a necessary additional incentive for trial and appellate courts throughout the land to conduct their proceedings in a manner consistent with established constitutional standards. In order to perform this deterrence function, * * * the habeas court need only apply the constitutional standards that prevailed at the time the original proceedings took place."

Justice Harlan identified only two exceptions to his general rule of nonretroactivity for cases on collateral review. First, a new rule should be applied retroactively if it places "certain kinds of primary, private individual conduct beyond the power of the criminal law-making authority to proscribe." Second, a new rule should be applied retroactively if it requires the observance of "those procedures that . . . are 'implicit in the concept of ordered liberty.' "

* * *

We agree with Justice Harlan's description of the function of habeas corpus. "[T]he Court never has defined the scope of the writ simply by reference to a perceived need to assure that an individual accused of crime is afforded a trial free of constitutional error." Rather, we have recognized that interests of comity and finality must also be considered in determining the proper scope of habeas review. * * *

* * * Application of constitutional rules not in existence at the time a conviction became final seriously undermines the principle of finality which is essential to the operation of our criminal justice system. Without finality, the criminal law is deprived of much of its deterrent effect.

* * *

The "costs imposed upon the State[s] by retroactive application of new rules of constitutional law on habeas corpus * * * generally far outweigh the benefits of this application." In many ways the application of new rules to cases on collateral review may be more intrusive than the enjoining of criminal prosecutions, for it continually forces the States to marshal resources in order to keep in prison defendants whose trials and appeals conformed to then-existing constitutional standards. Furthermore, * * * "[s]tate courts are understandably frustrated when they faithfully apply existing constitutional law only to have a federal court discover, during a [habeas] proceeding, new constitutional commands."

We find these criticisms to be persuasive, and we now adopt Justice Harlan's view of retroactivity for cases on collateral review. Unless they fall within an exception to the general rule, new constitutional rules of criminal procedure will not be applicable to those cases which have become final before the new rules are announced.

* * *

Petitioner's conviction became final in 1983. As a result, the rule petitioner urges would not be applicable to this case, which is on collateral review, unless it would fall within an exception.

The first exception suggested by Justice Harlan—that a new rule should be applied retroactively if it places "certain kinds of primary, private individual conduct beyond the power of the criminal law-making authority to proscribe"—is not relevant here. Application of the fair cross section requirement to the petit jury would not accord constitutional protection to any primary activity whatsoever.

The second exception suggested by Justice Harlan—that a new rule should be applied retroactively if it requires the observance of "those procedures that * * * are 'implicit in the concept of ordered liberty,'" (quoting Palko v. Connecticut)—we apply with a modification. * * *

* * * Were we to employ the *Palko* test without more, we would be doing little more than importing into a very different context the terms of the debate over incorporation. Reviving the *Palko* test now, in this area of law, would be unnecessarily anachronistic. * * * [W]e believe that Justice Harlan's concerns about the difficulty in identifying both the existence and the value of accuracy-enhancing procedural rules can be addressed by limiting the scope of the second exception to those new procedures without which the likelihood of an accurate conviction is seriously diminished.

Because we operate from the premise that such procedures would be so central to an accurate determination of innocence or guilt, we believe it unlikely that many such components of basic due process have yet to emerge. * * *

* * * Because the absence of a fair cross section on the jury venire does not undermine the fundamental fairness that must underlie a conviction or seriously diminish the likelihood of obtaining an accurate conviction, we conclude that a rule requiring that petit juries be composed of a fair cross section of the community would not be a "bedrock procedural element" that would be retroactively applied under the second exception we have articulated.

Were we to recognize the new rule urged by petitioner in this case, we would have to give petitioner the benefit of that new rule even though it would not be applied retroactively to others similarly situated. * * *

If there were no other way to avoid rendering advisory opinions, we might well agree that the inequitable treatment described above is "an insignificant cost for adherence to sound principles of decision-making." But there is a more principled way of dealing with the problem. We can simply refuse to announce a new rule in a given case unless the rule would be applied retroactively to the defendant in the case and to all others similarly situated. We think this approach is a sound one. Not only does it eliminate any problems of rendering advisory opinions, it also avoids the inequity resulting from the uneven application of new rules to similarly situated defendants. We therefore hold that, implicit in the retroactivity approach we adopt today, is the principle that habeas corpus cannot be used as a vehicle to create new constitutional rules of criminal procedure unless those rules would be applied retroactively to all defendants on collateral review through one of the two exceptions we have articulated. * * *

[The opinion of JUSTICE WHITE, concurring in part and concurring in the judgment, is omitted.]

JUSTICE STEVENS, with whom JUSTICE BLACKMUN joins in relevant part, concurring in part and concurring in the judgment.

* * *

In general, I share Justice Harlan's views about retroactivity. * * * I am persuaded that the Court should adopt Justice Harlan's analysis of retroactivity for habeas corpus cases as well for cases still on direct review.

I do not agree, however, with the plurality's dicta proposing a "modification" of Justice Harlan's fundamental fairness exception. * * *

* * * I cannot agree that it is "unnecessarily anachronistic" to issue a writ of habeas corpus to a petitioner convicted in a manner that violates fundamental principles of liberty.

* * *

JUSTICE BRENNAN, with whom JUSTICE MARSHALL joins, dissenting.

* * * Out of an exaggerated concern for treating similarly situated habeas petitioners the same, the plurality would for the first time preclude the federal courts from considering on collateral review a vast range of important constitutional challenges; where those challenges have merit, it would bar the vindication of personal constitutional rights and deny society a check against further violations until the same claim is presented on direct review. * * *

* * *

[F]rom the plurality's exposition of its new rule, one might infer that its novel fabrication will work no great change in the availability of federal collateral review of state convictions. Nothing could be further from the truth. * * * Few decisions on appeal or collateral review are "dictated" by what came before. Most such cases involve a question of law that is at least debatable, permitting a rational judge to resolve the case in more than one way. Virtually no case that prompts a dissent on the relevant legal point, for example, could be said to be "dictated" by prior decisions. * * * The plurality's approach today can thus be expected to contract substantially the Great Writ's sweep.

* * *

Commentary on the Teague Rule

In Collins v. Youngblood, 497 U.S. 37 (1990), the Court held that the rule in *Teague,* prohibiting retroactive application or promulgation of new rules to habeas corpus cases, is not jurisdictional.

Note that under the Harlan-*Teague* view, defendants are subject to different treatment depending on the efficiency of the appellate courts in the state in which they are convicted. The slower the appellate system, the more likely that the defendant would benefit from new rules because it is more likely that the case will still be on direct review when the new rule is promulgated.

A different criticism of the Harlan approach, as applied to cases on direct review, is that if new rules are generally applicable to cases not finalized, the cost of a new rule will often be significant. That may deter the Court from promulgating new rules in the first place. See Jenkins v. Delaware, 395 U.S. 213 (1969) (non-retroactivity provides an impetus for the "implementation of long overdue reforms which otherwise could not be practicably effected."); People v. Mitchell, 80 N.Y.2d 519, 591 N.Y.S.2d 990 (1992) (rejecting the Harlan view as a matter of state law and holding that a new rule is not applicable to other cases on direct review: denying retroactive effect to new rules "permits this Court to expand the protection accorded defendants when we might otherwise hesitate to do so because retroactive application threatens to wreak more havoc in society that society's interest in stability will tolerate."). See also Heytens, Managing Transitional Moments in Criminal Cases, 115 Yale L.J. 922 (2006) (noting that the *Griffith* view of retroactivity to cases on direct review has led courts to counter by finding that defendants have forfeited their right to appeal by failing to raise the issue at trial—even though the trial was conducted before the new rule became law).

The academic commentary on *Teague's* limitation on habeas review has been almost uniformly negative. Examples include Liebman, More Than "Slightly Retro": The Rehnquist Court's Rout of Habeas Corpus Jurisdiction in Teague v. Lane, 18 N.Y.U. Rev. of Law & Social Change 537 (1991); Dubber, Prudence and Substance: How the Supreme Court's New Habeas Retroactivity Doctrine Mirrors and Affects Substantive Constitutional Law, 30 Am.Crim.L.Rev. 1 (1992); Meyer, "Nothing We Say Matters": *Teague* and New Rules, 61 Univ.Chi.L.Rev. 423 (1994).

What Is a "New Rule"?

After *Teague,* new rules are generally inapplicable to those whose convictions have been finalized—including the petitioner who initially brings the claim for a new rule on collateral review. However, Justice Harlan, whose views were generally adopted in *Teague,* emphasized that some "new" holdings are not "new" at all, but are merely applications of well-settled principles to different fact situations, and therefore these holdings must apply retroactively to all defendants.

The Court, following Justice Harlan's approach, has mandated that, when a decision merely applies settled precedent, it is not a "new" rule at all, and is thus completely retroactive. See Yates v. Aiken, 484 U.S. 211 (1988). The rationale is that if a constitutional rule is not "new," the state court should have applied it correctly, and therefore the failure to apply it is proper grounds for habeas relief. The difficulty is in determining if a rule is "new" or merely an old rule applied to a different fact situation. In *Teague,* the Court stated that a case announces a new rule when it was "not dictated by existing precedent."

In Butler v. McKellar, 494 U.S. 407 (1990), the Court expounded further on the *Teague* definition of a "new" rule. The issue was whether Arizona v. Roberson was a new rule or merely an application of Edwards v. Arizona[7] to a somewhat different fact situation. *Edwards* held that once a person in custody has requested counsel, the police may not conduct further interrogation unless counsel is provided or the suspect initiates communications. *Roberson* held that the *Edwards* rule applied even when the officer wants to question the suspect about a crime unrelated to that for which he has been arrested. When Butler was tried in state court, *Edwards* had been decided, but *Roberson* was not decided until Butler's conviction had been finalized. Butler, who confessed to a crime unrelated to that for which he was arrested, argued that the rule in *Roberson* should be retroactively applied to him, on the ground that the *Roberson* Court itself had stated that the rule was not new but merely an application of *Edwards.*

Chief Justice Rehnquist, writing for the majority, stated that a rule is "new" if reasonable minds could have differed about the result of the decision before it was rendered. The majority held that *Roberson* was a new rule, because reasonable-minded lower courts before *Roberson* had differed about whether *Edwards* would apply to questioning about unrelated investigations. The fact that the majority in *Roberson* characterized its decision as indistinguishable from *Edwards* and as a refusal to create an "exception" was not dispositive. According to the Chief Justice, "courts frequently view their decisions as being 'controlled' or 'governed' by prior opinions even when aware of reasonable contrary conclusions reached by lower courts." He stated that "[t]he 'new rule' principle * * * validates reasonable, good-faith interpretations of existing precedents made by state courts even though they are shown to be contrary to later decisions."

---

7 Both of these cases are discussed in the material on confessions in Chapter 3.

Justice Brennan, joined by Justices Marshall, Blackmun and Stevens, dissented in *Butler*.

Refusal to Promulgate a New Rule as a Decision on the Merits?

When the Court refuses to decide a question in a habeas case because to do so would result in the promulgation of a "new rule," has the Court given an opinion on the merits of the proposed rule itself? For example, in *Teague*, did the Court, by refusing to decide the issue of whether the fair cross section requirement applied to the petit jury, effectively signal to the lower courts its view about the merits of such a claim? If you were a lower court judge, would you be inclined to adopt a "new rule" in a direct review case after the Supreme Court had declined to adopt the rule in a habeas case?

The Supreme Court has given some indication that a refusal to render what would be a "new rule" on habeas is similar to a rejection of the proposed rule on the merits. In Johnson v. Texas, 509 U.S. 350 (1993), the Court considered a question of the constitutionality of a capital sentencing statute on direct review. This question was identical to that which the Court had, earlier in the same term, refused to consider on habeas review on the ground that granting relief would require promulgation of a "new rule." Acting on direct review "without the constraints of *Teague*," the Court rejected the constitutional claim on the merits, relying on "much of the reasoning" in the previous habeas case. Justice O'Connor, the author of *Teague*, wrote a dissent in *Johnson* for four Justices. She argued that "cases that reject a claim as requiring a new rule cannot constitute stare decisis on direct review," since a rejection on habeas means only that the issue is "susceptible to debate among reasonable minds."

Is it possible to separate the question of whether a proposed rule is "new" from the question whether a proposed rule is meritorious? See Arkin, The Prisoner's Dilemma: Life in the Lower Federal Courts After Teague v. Lane, 69 N.C.L.Rev. 371 (1991) (whether a rule is new requires a view into the merits of the rule).

Substantive Changes Are Fully Retroactive Under Teague v. Lane

The Supreme Court held in Miller v. Alabama, 567 U.S. 460 (2012), that the Eighth Amendment bars the government from imposing a sentence of life imprisonment without parole on a juvenile convicted of homicide, absent consideration of the juvenile's special circumstances in light of the principles and purposes of juvenile sentencing. In Montgomery v. Louisiana, 577 U.S. 190 (2016), Justice Kennedy wrote for the Court as it decided that *Miller* was a substantive decision, and thus fit within the exception provided by *Teague v. Lane* to the general rule that new rules are not applicable to finalized convictions. The complicating factor was that Montgomery sought relief by way of a post-conviction claim in a state court collateral proceeding, and was arguing that the *state* court was required to apply *Miller* retroactively. Louisiana argued that *Teague* was an application of habeas corpus principles that did not bind the States. Justice Kennedy sided with Montgomery, concluding that *Teague's* exception for full retroactivity of substantive decisions was required by the Constitution. He explained as follows:

> Substantive rules * * * set forth categorical constitutional guarantees that place certain criminal laws and punishments altogether beyond the State's power to impose. It follows that when a State enforces a proscription or penalty barred by the Constitution, the resulting conviction or sentence is, by definition, unlawful. Procedural rules, in contrast, are designed to enhance the accuracy of a conviction or sentence by regulating the manner of determining the defendant's culpability. Those rules merely raise the possibility that someone convicted with use of the invalidated procedure might have been acquitted otherwise. Even where procedural error has infected a trial, the resulting conviction or sentence may still be accurate; and, by extension, the defendant's continued confinement may still be lawful. For this reason, a trial conducted under a procedure found to be unconstitutional in a later case does not, as a general matter, have the automatic consequence of invalidating a defendant's conviction or sentence.

Justice Kennedy further found that the rule in *Miller* was in fact substantive:

> The Court now holds that *Miller* announced a substantive rule of constitutional law. The conclusion that *Miller* states a substantive rule comports with the principles that informed *Teague*. *Teague* sought to balance the important goals of finality and comity with the liberty interests of those imprisoned pursuant to rules later deemed unconstitutional. *Miller*'s conclusion that the sentence of life without parole is disproportionate for the vast majority of juvenile offenders raises a grave risk that many are being held in violation of the Constitution.

Justice Scalia, joined by Justices Thomas and Alito, dissented in *Montgomery*. He first argued that *Teague's* exception for substantive rules does not bind the States. He declared as follows:

> Neither *Teague* nor its exceptions are constitutionally compelled. Unlike today's majority, the *Teague*-era Court understood that cases on collateral review are fundamentally different from those pending on direct review because of considerations of finality in the judicial process. * * * A state court need only apply the law as it existed at the

> time a defendant's conviction and sentence became final. And once final, a new rule cannot reopen a door already closed. Any relief a prisoner might receive in a state court after finality is a matter of grace, not constitutional prescription.

Justice Scalia further concluded that *Miller* was a procedural rule, not a substantive one, because it did not completely bar imposition of life imprisonment but rather required the state to undertake procedures before doing so. He explained as follows:

> The majority * * * insists that *Miller* barred life-without-parole sentences "for all but the rarest of juvenile offenders, those whose crimes reflect permanent incorrigibility. * * * " The problem is that *Miller* stated, quite clearly, precisely the opposite: "Our decision does not categorically bar a penalty for a class of offenders or type of crime * * *. Instead, it mandates only that a sentencer *follow a certain process*—considering an offender's youth and attendant characteristics—before imposing a particular penalty."

Justice Thomas wrote a separate dissent in *Montgomery*. He stated that the majority's opinion "repudiates established principles of finality. It finds no support in the Constitution's text, and cannot be reconciled with our Nation's tradition of considering the availability of postconviction remedies a matter about which the Constitution has nothing to say."

Justice Thomas noted, however, that the States "have a modest path to lessen the burdens that today's decision will inflict on their courts. States can stop entertaining claims alleging that this Court's Eighth Amendment decisions invalidated a sentence, and leave federal habeas courts to shoulder the burden of adjudicating such claims in the first instance. Whatever the desirability of that choice, it is one the Constitution allows States to make."

In Welch v. United States, 578 U.S. 120 (2016), the Supreme Court considered the retroactive effect of a previous decision in which it held that a sentencing provision in a federal criminal statute was void for vagueness. (The decision was Johnson v. United States, 576 U.S. 591 (2015), invalidating the "residual clause" of the Armed Career Criminal Act under which defendants could be sentenced to 15 years to life in prison.) Welch was convicted in a federal court and sentenced under the statute's "residual clause," and after the Supreme Court decided *Johnson* he sought habeas relief. Welch argued that the new decision should be given full retroactive effect, because it was on a question of "substantive" law and essentially held that the defendant's conduct could not be sentenced under the statutory provision. The Supreme Court agreed with Welsh in an opinion by Justice Kennedy, and remanded the case for resentencing. Justice Kennedy provided the following analysis of how the *Johnson* decision required retroactive application even to cases on collateral review, under the exception provided in *Teague*:

> The normal framework for determining whether a new rule applies to cases on collateral review stems from the plurality opinion in Teague v. Lane. * * * The parties here assume that the *Teague* framework applies in a federal collateral challenge to a federal conviction as it does in a federal collateral challenge to a state conviction, and we proceed on that assumption.
>
> * * *
>
> A rule is substantive rather than procedural if it alters the range of conduct or the class of persons that the law punishes. This includes decisions that narrow the scope of a criminal statute by interpreting its terms, as well as constitutional determinations that place particular conduct or persons covered by the statute beyond the State's power to punish. Procedural rules, by contrast, regulate only the manner of determining the defendant's culpability. Such rules alter the range of permissible methods for determining whether a defendant's conduct is punishable. They do not produce a class of persons convicted of conduct the law does not make criminal, but merely raise the possibility that someone convicted with use of the invalidated procedure might have been acquitted otherwise.
>
> Under this framework, the rule announced in *Johnson* is substantive. By striking down the [statutory provision] as void for vagueness, *Johnson* changed the substantive reach of the Armed Career Criminal Act, altering the range of conduct or the class of persons that the Act punishes. * * *

Justice Thomas dissented in *Welch*.

The Teague Rule and Statutory Limitations on Habeas Corpus Relief

The result mandated by *Teague* and *Butler* largely has been codified as part of the substantive limitations imposed on habeas corpus relief by the 1996 Antiterrorism and Effective Death Penalty Act (AEDPA). The AEDPA severely limits federal habeas review over state court determinations of constitutional law, but the rule is now phrased as merit-based rather than retroactivity-based. The Act provides, in pertinent part:

> *(d) An application for a writ of habeas corpus on behalf of a person in custody pursuant to the judgment of a State court shall not be granted with respect to any claim that was adjudicated on the merits in State court proceedings unless the adjudication of the claim—*

> *(1) resulted in a decision that was contrary to, or involved an unreasonable application of, clearly established Federal law, as determined by the Supreme Court of the United States; or*
>
> *(2) resulted in a decision that was based on an unreasonable determination of the facts in light of the evidence presented in the State court proceeding.*

In Williams v. Taylor, 529 U.S. 362 (2000), the Court, in an opinion by Justice O'Connor, declared that the AEDPA essentially codified a standard of review of state court decisions that is equivalent to the "new rule" jurisprudence of *Teague*.

Under the AEDPA, a federal court cannot grant relief unless the state court decision is "contrary to, or involved an unreasonable application of, clearly established Federal law, as determined by the Supreme Court of the United States." In *Williams*, Justice O'Connor declared that "whatever would qualify as an old rule under our *Teague* jurisprudence will constitute 'clearly established Federal law, as determined by the Supreme Court of the United States' under § 2254(d)(1). The one caveat, as the statutory language makes clear, is that § 2254(d)(1) restricts the source of clearly established law to this Court's jurisprudence." Consequently, if a habeas petitioner is claiming that a state court misapplied constitutional law that was not clearly established by the United States Supreme Court at the time, the habeas petition must be denied—because the state court decision is not "contrary to" clearly established law as defined by the Supreme Court. It follows that the *Teague* "new rule" jurisprudence has been codified, for all practical purposes, by the AEDPA.

Note that in the AEDPA there are no exceptions provided comparable to the two limited exceptions permitting retroactive application in *Teague*, i.e., "watershed" rules of constitutional law, or rules that hold certain conduct beyond criminal proscription. The rationale for rejecting these exceptions, according to an official at the Justice Department who was instrumental in drafting the provision, is that the *Teague* exceptions are so narrow that they can never be invoked as a practical matter (although we know from the Court's decisions that at least one of the exceptions—for changes in substantive law—can be successfully invoked). The result under the AEDPA is that a habeas petitioner cannot seek to invoke a rule of law unless it was already clearly established at the time of the trial—and it makes no difference whether the rule of law proposed by the habeas claimant is a "watershed" rule or a rule that holds certain conduct beyond criminal proscription.

Teague continues to apply in cases where the AEDPA does not. One example is where a petitioner seeks the advantage of a substantive change in the law that occurred after direct review was completed, as in *Welch* and *Montgomery, supra*. Another possible example is where a state court never considered a defendant's claim on the merits, and so the standard of review set forth in the AEDPA is by its terms inapplicable. However, for habeas corpus relief to be granted in such a situation, the petitioner's claim must still be based on constitutional law as it existed at the time of his conviction. Any attempt to expand established rights will run into the "new rule" jurisprudence of *Teague* and its progeny. Thus, in Weeks v. Angelone, 176 F.3d 249 (4th Cir. 1999), the habeas petitioner claimed that his due process rights were denied by the state court's failure to provide him an expert in ballistics to assist in his defense. This claim was not covered by the AEDPA because the state court had never considered it on the merits, even though asked to do so. But the constitutional claim was still barred by *Teague* because the law existing at the time of the petitioner's conviction provided only that a defendant was entitled, upon a sufficient showing of need, to a state-appointed *psychiatrist* to assist in the defense. This precedent did not mandate appointment of *non-psychiatric* experts. Extending Supreme Court precedent to provide a guarantee of a non-psychiatric expert would constitute a "new rule," and therefore could not be entertained on habeas review.

Abandoning the Watershed Rule: Edwards v. Vannoy

The Court adopted the AEDPA's rejection of "watershed" exceptions in Edwards v. Vannoy, 141 S.Ct. 1547 (2021). Writing for the Court, Justice Kavanaugh pointed out that

> In practice, the exception has been theoretical, not real. The Court has identified only one pre-*Teague* procedural rule as watershed: the right to counsel recognized in the Court's landmark decision in *Gideon v. Wainwright*, 372 U.S. 335, 344–345 (1963). * * * The Court has never identified any other pre-*Teague* or post-*Teague* rule as watershed. None.

In light of that record, Justice Kavanaugh concluded "that the purported exception has become an empty promise," is "moribund," and "must be regarded as retaining no vitality." In so holding, the *Edwards* Court made clear that new substantive rules, which "alter the range of conduct or the class of persons that the law punishes" will continue to "apply to cases pending in trial courts and on direct review, and they also apply retroactively on collateral review." Justice Kagan, joined by Justices Breyer and Sotomayor, dissented.

Retroactivity of Fourth Amendment New Rules Does Not Justify Exclusion: Davis v. United States

In Davis v. United States, 564 U.S. 229 (2011), the defendant sought the application of a new rule that was handed down while his case was still on direct review. The new rule, if applied, would mean that a police search of the defendant's car—which was legal at the time—violated the Fourth Amendment. The Court held that, while the new rule of law applied to the search of Davis's car, that did not mean that the evidence should have been excluded. The Court ruled that the "good faith" exception to the exclusionary rule applied, and, therefore, the fruits of the illegal search were admissible at trial. Thus, the Court distinguished the law, which was applicable, and the remedy of exclusion, which was not. *Davis* is discussed more fully in the materials on the Fourth Amendment exclusionary rule, and its good faith exception, in Chapter 2. The doctrine of qualified immunity imposes similar limits on the availability of damages when plaintiffs allege violations of their constitutional rights in the civil context.

Can States Apply a New Supreme Court Rule Retroactively Even if the Supreme Court Does Not? Danforth v. Minnesota

In Danforth v. Minnesota, 552 U.S. 264 (2008), the Court held that *Teague* does not prevent states from giving *more* retroactive effect to new rules than would be given by the Supreme Court. *Danforth* involved a collateral attack under state (rather than federal habeas) law of a finalized conviction. After the conviction was final, the United States Supreme Court decided a case on the confrontation clause that, if applicable, would result in reversal of the state conviction. It was a new rule and so would not be applicable on federal habeas review. But Justice Stevens, writing for the Court, found that *Teague* "was tailored to the unique context of federal habeas and therefore had no bearing on whether States could provide broader relief in their own postconviction proceedings than required by that opinion." The Court reaffirmed this approach in *Edwards v. Vannoy*.

Retroactive Application Against the Defendant?: Lockhart v. Fretwell

The cases and statute discussed above deal with whether a defendant can, through retroactive application, receive a benefit from a change in law. But what about changes in law that are *detrimental* to a defendant?

In Lockhart v. Fretwell, 506 U.S. 364 (1993), a state court defendant convicted of capital murder and sentenced to death sought Federal habeas corpus relief, contending that his trial counsel was ineffective because counsel failed to raise an objection was supported by existing Federal circuit law (the sentence was invalid because it was based on an aggravating factor that duplicated an element of the underlying felony—murder in the course of a robbery). The circuit court overruled its earlier decision before the petition reached the Supreme Court.

The Supreme Court, in an opinion by Chief Justice Rehnquist, held that detrimental changes in the law must be applied retroactively against petitioners on habeas review.

The Chief Justice distinguished *Teague* and reasoned as follows:

> *Teague* stands for the proposition that new constitutional rules of criminal procedure will not be announced or applied on collateral review. * * * [T]his retroactivity rule was motivated by a respect for the States' strong interest in the finality of criminal convictions, and the recognition that a State should not be penalized for relying on the constitutional standards that prevailed at the time the original proceedings took place. The "new rule" principle therefore validates reasonable, good-faith interpretations of existing precedents made by state courts even though they are shown to be contrary to later decisions.
>
> A federal habeas petitioner has no interest in the finality of the state court judgment under which he is incarcerated: indeed, the very purpose of his habeas petition is to overturn that judgment. Nor does such a petitioner ordinarily have any claim of reliance on past judicial precedent as a basis for his actions * * *. The result of these differences is that the State will benefit from our *Teague* decision in some federal habeas cases, while the habeas petitioner will not.

Justice Stevens, joined by Justice Blackmun, dissented arguing that an "even-handed approach to retroactivity would seem to require that we continue to evaluate defendants' claims under the law as it stood at the time of trial." He reasoned that under *Teague*, a defendant may not take advantage of subsequent changes in the law when they are favorable to him, therefore "there is no self-evident reason why a State should be able to take advantage of subsequent changes in the law when they are adverse to his interests." The dissenters concluded that a "rule that generally precludes defendants from taking advantage of post-conviction changes in the law, but allows the State to do so, cannot be reconciled with this Court's duty to administer justice impartially."

CHAPTER 2

SEARCHES AND SEIZURES OF PERSONS AND THINGS

■ ■ ■

I. AN INTRODUCTION TO THE FOURTH AMENDMENT

The Fourth Amendment guarantees that:

> The right of the people to be secure in their persons, houses, papers and effects, against unreasonable searches and seizures shall not be violated, and no Warrants shall issue, but upon probable cause, supported by Oath or affirmation, and particularly describing the place to be searched, and the persons or things to be seized.

As Chief Justice Roberts explained in Riley v. California, 573 U.S. 373 (2014):

> [T]he Fourth Amendment was the founding generation's response to the reviled "general warrants" and "writs of assistance" of the colonial era, which allowed British officers to rummage through homes in an unrestrained search for evidence of criminal activity. Opposition to such searches was in fact one of the driving forces behind the Revolution itself. In 1761, the patriot James Otis delivered a speech in Boston denouncing the use of writs of assistance. A young John Adams was there, and he would later write that "[e]very man of a crowded audience appeared to me to go away, as I did, ready to take arms against writs of assistance." According to Adams, Otis's speech was "the first scene of the first act of opposition to the arbitrary claims of Great Britain. Then and there the child Independence was born."

Given this history, the Court has long looked to eighteenth century experiences with general warrants and writs of assistance to "ascertain the nature of the proceedings intended by the Fourth Amendment to the Constitution under the terms 'unreasonable searches and seizures.' " Boyd v. United States, 116 U.S. 616, 625 (1886). See also Carpenter v. United States, 138 S.Ct. 2206, 2214 (2018) ("We have kept this attention to Founding-era understandings in mind when applying the Fourth Amendment to innovations in surveillance tools."). That focus has intensified in recent years with the ascendancy of originalism as a mode of constitutional interpretation. The Court has not limited itself to this history, however. As we shall see, the Court also appeals to contemporary standards of privacy when elaborating the scope of Fourth Amendment protections, particularly when determining the application of the Fourth Amendment to new and emerging technologies.

We will spend considerable time in this Chapter tracing the Supreme Court's efforts to determine the meaning and scope of the Fourth Amendment, but it is useful to consider a few preliminary points.

The Fourth Amendment Protects "The People"

The Fourth Amendment guarantees a right of *the people*, not the rights of persons, as under the Fifth Amendment, or of an accused, as under the Sixth Amendment. The wording resembles that found in the First, Second, Ninth and Tenth Amendments. Professor Anthony Amsterdam has suggested that the choice of language might well be important in properly interpreting the Amendment. In his view, courts should focus on how to regulate or control the conduct of the government so that Fourth Amendment violations do not occur, rather than on fashioning remedies for only those individuals who have suffered a personal Fourth Amendment wrong. See Perspectives on the Fourth Amendment, 58 Minn.L.Rev. 349 (1974). See also Gray, The Fourth Amendment in an Age of Surveillance (2017) (describing how a collective rights reading of the Fourth Amendment can explain the warrant requirement and exclusionary rule). But the Supreme Court has instead invoked the term "the people" to narrow the class of those protected by the Fourth Amendment.

In United States v. Verdugo-Urquidez, 494 U.S. 259 (1990), the Supreme Court held that the Fourth Amendment does not apply to a search of property that is owned by a non-resident alien and located in a foreign country. Chief Justice Rehnquist, writing for the Court, reasoned that the Fourth Amendment's reference to "the people," as opposed to a particular person, was a "term of art." He asserted that the term was intended to refer only to "a class of persons who are part of a national community or who have otherwise developed sufficient connection with this country to be considered a part of that community." Looking to the history of the Amendment, he concluded that its purpose was "to protect the people of the United States against arbitrary action by their own Government; it was never suggested that the provision was intended to restrain the actions of the Federal Government against aliens outside of the United States territory."

The Court in *Verdugo-Urquidez* declined to decide whether an undocumented person who lives in the United States would be one of "the people" protected by the Fourth Amendment, but, in various opinions, Justices Brennan, Marshall, Blackmun, Stevens, and Kennedy indicated that they would hold the Fourth Amendment applicable to searches of undocumented persons conducted within the United States. The reasoning was that a person living in the United States would have the "connection" with this country required to be one of "the people" protected by the Fourth Amendment.

The Fourth Amendment Governs State Action

The Amendment plainly recognizes a right, but does not indicate against whom it applies. Arguably, the people have a right to be secure against all unreasonable searches and seizures, even if conducted by corporations or private persons. But the Fourth Amendment has been interpreted as providing protection only against the government and those acting in conjunction with it. This includes representatives of both the Federal government and the States (the Fourth Amendment has been incorporated in its entirety). We will see how this requirement applies in the cases discussed in this Chapter.

The Fourth Amendment Applies to "Searches" and "Seizures"

By its terms, the Fourth Amendment applies only to "searches" and "seizures." It is therefore essential to determine what kinds of activities constitute "searches" and "seizures." Intuitively, the answer may seem obvious. To "search" is to look for, look through, examine, seek, or try to find. To "seize" is to take possession, grasp, or hold. These intuitions are reflected in both modern and eighteenth-century dictionaries. Accordingly, entering a home to look for evidence, examining papers, taking possession of effects, or arresting a person would all seem to be activities subject to Fourth Amendment regulation. But what about other investigative techniques such as subpoenas for documents, interviewing witnesses, using undercover agents and confidential informants, or conducting human surveillance? Do these constitute "searches" or "seizures" in common parlance or according to dictionary meanings? And what about the use of technologies like wiretapping, electronic eavesdropping, video surveillance, GPS tracking, or heat detection devices? We will spend considerable time in this Chapter investigating the Court's efforts to answer these questions.

The Fourth Amendment Applies in Non-Criminal Cases

Some of the constitutional protections explored in this book apply only in the context of "criminal" cases. That is not the case when it comes to the Fourth Amendment. The Fourth Amendment regulates all government conduct constituting "searches" or "seizures." As we shall see in this Chapter, courts apply different rules when determining the reasonableness of searches and seizures conducted for purposes of detecting and prosecuting crimes and those conducted for purposes of advancing regulatory, administrative, or other "special needs."

The Fourth Amendment Is Composed of Two Clauses

The Fourth Amendment contains two clauses, the first dealing with unreasonable searches and seizures and the second with warrants. What is the relationship between these two clauses? The Court has long held that the "touchstone" of the Fourth Amendment is reasonableness. If that is true, then what role does the Warrant Clause play? Does it govern only where searches are conducted pursuant to warrants? If so, then why would a police officer ever subject herself to its demands? Or does the Warrant Clause imply a warrant requirement? One observer has suggested that this would stand "the amendment on its head" by making the subordinate clause dominant. T. Taylor, Two Studies in Constitutional Interpretation 23–24 (1969). Others find evidence for a warrant requirement in the common law history of the Fourth Amendment. See, e.g., Laura Donohue, *The Original Fourth Amendment*, 83 U. Chi. L. Rev. 1181 (2016). Whatever the source, the Court has adopted a strong preference for warrants in the context of criminal investigations. There are important exceptions, however. We will spend considerable time in this Chapter elaborating the scope and effect of this "warrant requirement."

From a textual point of view, "probable cause" is used in the Fourth Amendment to define the minimum showing necessary to support a warrant application. It is not used to demarcate reasonableness generally. Despite this textual arrangement, the Court requires probable cause for many searches and seizures that fall outside the warrant requirement. But what is "probable cause"? The definition is not altogether clear. The Amendment contains not a hint as to its meaning. This has left the courts to give meaning to the term. We shall analyze their efforts in this Chapter.

The Fourth Amendment Is Silent on Consequences

The Fourth Amendment reads as a commandment: "The right of the people to be secure in their persons, houses, papers, and effects against unreasonable searches and seizures *shall not* be violated." But how can that security be guaranteed? What happens if the commandment is violated? In the civil context, violations of the Fourth Amendment may provide grounds for injunctive relief or damages claims. The predominate consequence of Fourth Amendment violations in the criminal context is exclusion of illegally discovered evidence from the prosecutor's case-in-chief at trial. The wisdom of this "exclusionary rule" is hotly contested. Consider, for example, the following personal editorial by the late Judge Malcolm Wilkey of the United States Court of Appeals for the District of Columbia Circuit:

> Among nations of the civilized world we are unique in two respects: (1) We suffer the most extraordinary crime rate with firearms. (2) In

> criminal prosecutions, by a rule of evidence which exists in no other country, we exclude the most trustworthy and convincing evidence.
>
> These two aberrations are not unconnected. In fact, the "exclusionary rule" has made unenforceable the gun control laws we have and will make ineffective any stricter controls which may be devised. Its fetters particularly paralyze police efforts to prevent, detect and punish street crimes involving not only weapons but narcotics.

Why Suppress Valid Evidence, Wall Street Journal, Oct. 7, 1977, at 1, col. 1.

This is an argument by a distinguished jurist who pondered search and seizure problems for years. Yet, it is fundamentally flawed. "Probable cause" is a term found in the language chosen by the framers. If the Court correctly interprets the Fourth Amendment as requiring probable cause for particular police action, such as a search for guns, then it is the substance of the Fourth Amendment itself (as interpreted by the Court), not the remedy for a violation, that impairs the ability to enforce firearm laws. As one early interpreter of the Amendment put the point:

> It is true, that by insisting on an oath, felons may sometimes escape. This must have been very well known to the framers of our constitution; but they thought it better that the guilty should sometimes escape, than that every individual should be subject to vexation and oppression.

Connor v. Commonwealth, 3 Binney 38 (Pa. 1810).

Immediate abolition of the exclusionary rule would not free officers to search for guns in violation of the substance of the Amendment. They would remain bound by the Constitution.[1] So, by constitutional design, even with the demise of the exclusionary rule, some criminal laws still will be hard to enforce. Yet, the exclusionary rule casts a long shadow over Fourth Amendment doctrine and may have the effect of shrinking substantive rights.

The costs and benefits of the exclusionary rule are not discussed until late in the Chapter in order to provide an adequate opportunity to explore the substantive right. This delay does not imply that the exclusionary rule is plainly desirable or that the debate over it is not important. The debate is important for practical and symbolic reasons, and delay in reaching it is tantamount to deference to its significance. But it is true that even without the exclusionary rule, the basic problems of deciding what the Amendment means would remain. As you read the cases, keep in mind that, despite the fact that the issues usually are cast in terms of whether evidence should

---

[1] This point is made by another experienced jurist, Justice Stewart, in The Road to *Mapp v. Ohio* and Beyond: The Origins, Development, and Future of the Exclusionary Rule in Search-and-Seizure Cases, 83 Colum.L.Rev. 1365 (1989).

have been excluded at trial, the same issues could often arise in some form or other—perhaps in civil suits rather than criminal cases—even without an exclusionary rule. You cannot avoid grappling with the meaning and proper interpretation of the Fourth Amendment simply by doing away with the exclusionary rule.

II. THE STATE ACTION REQUIREMENT

The Supreme Court has held that the Fourth Amendment regulates state actors, not private persons or entities. In Burdeau v. McDowell, 256 U.S. 465 (1921), the Supreme Court held that private papers stolen from office safes that were blown open and a desk that was forced open could be presented to a grand jury by a government prosecutor because the search was conducted by private parties and so was not regulated by the Fourth Amendment. Justice Brandeis, joined by Justice Holmes, dissented. See also United States v. Stevenson, 727 F.3d 826 (8th Cir. 2013) (Internet service provider that scanned its users' emails for evidence of child pornography and turned over suspicious information to the government was a private actor and therefore the search did not violate the Fourth Amendment).

This does not mean that the Fourth Amendment applies only to police officers. It applies to any "representative of any branch or subdivision of the government." Gouled v. United States, 255 U.S. 298 (1921). Neither does it apply only to those who are in the direct employ of a government agency. Government officials may not avoid Fourth Amendment requirements by enlisting private individuals to do what government officials cannot. See United States v. Walther, 652 F.2d 788 (9th Cir. 1981) (airline employee acted as government agent when he expected a DEA reward for his actions and the agency had encouraged him).

In what circumstances is a private person considered a "state agent" for purposes of the Fourth Amendment? The Court provided some guidance in Skinner v. Railway Labor Executives' Ass'n, 489 U.S. 602 (1989). There, a Federal statute mandated that railroads not bargain away the drug-testing authority granted to them by Federal regulations, which made plain a strong preference for testing as well as the government's desire to have access to the results. The Court held that the Fourth Amendment governed drug testing performed by private rail carriers acting within this statutory regime even though the government did not actually direct or compel the search. The Court found "clear indices of the Government's encouragement, endorsement, and participation" sufficient to make the drug testing a government search regulated by the Fourth Amendment. See also United States v. Pierce, 893 F.2d 669 (5th Cir. 1990) (for a search by a private person to trigger Fourth Amendment protection, the government must have known about the search in advance, and the private party must be acting for law enforcement purposes). But see Coolidge v.

New Hampshire, 403 U.S. 443 (1971) (wife who "of her own accord" during a police interview at her home produced guns and clothing implicating her husband in a homicide was not acting as a "state agent" for purposes of the Fourth Amendment).

Foreign Officials

Courts have uniformly held that "[e]vidence obtained by foreign police officials from searches conducted in their country is generally admissible * * * regardless of whether the search complied with the Fourth Amendment." United States v. Behety, 32 F.3d 503 (11th Cir.1994). This is because searches by foreign officials do not constitute the kind of "state action" circumscribed by the Bill of Rights. There are, however, two very limited exceptions to this general rule. These exceptions are described by the court in United States v. Barona, 56 F.3d 1087 (9th Cir.1995):

> One exception * * * occurs if the circumstances of the foreign search and seizure are so extreme that they shock the judicial conscience, so that a federal appellate court in the exercise of its supervisory powers can require exclusion of the evidence. This type of exclusion is not based on our Fourth Amendment jurisprudence, but rather on the recognition that we may employ our supervisory powers when absolutely necessary to preserve the integrity of the criminal justice system.[2] * * *
>
> The second exception * * * applies when United States agents' participation in the investigation is so substantial that the action is a joint venture between United States and foreign officials.

A suggested approach for identifying foreign searches subject to American constitutional restraints is offered in Saltzburg, The Reach of the Bill of Rights Beyond the Terra Firma of the United States, 20 Va.J.Int'l L. 741 (1980).

Even if a search on foreign soil is conducted by or at the behest of American officials, it will not implicate the Fourth Amendment if the victim of the search is a non-resident alien. In United States v. Verdugo-Urquidez, 494 U.S. 259 (1990), discussed earlier in the Chapter, the Court held that non-resident aliens lack sufficient connection with the United States to be considered as part of "the people" covered by the Fourth Amendment when they are the targets of searches conducted in other countries.

---

[2] [Editors' Note: The extent to which federal courts may exercise this supervisory authority is explored in the materials on the exclusionary rule at the end of this Chapter.]

III. WHAT IS A "SEARCH"?

The Fourth Amendment prohibits unreasonable searches and seizures. If the government activity is neither a "search" nor a "seizure" it is not regulated by the Fourth Amendment. It has been argued that when deciding this threshold question one should err on the side of the citizen. The consequence of finding a search or seizure is merely that the government is required to act reasonably, whereas the consequence of not finding a search or seizure is that government officials can act unreasonably and arbitrarily. See Amsterdam, Perspectives on the Fourth Amendment, 58 Minn.L.Rev. 349 (1974). In fact, however, the Supreme Court has held that a variety of police investigative activity is neither a search nor a seizure, and is thus free from the strictures of the Fourth Amendment. These decisions have allowed government agents to expand the scope of their investigative activities by utilizing new means and methods of detecting crime and gathering evidence.

Faced with these expansions of state power, the Court has periodically modified its definitions of "search" and "seizure" to encompass some of these means and methods. Scholars have described this historical dynamic as a pendulum that swings back and forth, preserving a rough balance between individual rights and government interests over time. See, e.g., Orin Kerr, An Equilibrium-Adjustment Theory of the Fourth Amendment, 125 Harv.L.Rev. 476 (2011).

So, although the nominal focus in many of the cases that follow is a particular investigative means or method, there is much more at stake: the fundamental balance of rights and interests at the heart of our constitutional democracy. Those stakes have been evident since the days before the Fourth Amendment was adopted and continue to animate the Court's Fourth Amendment jurisprudence today. We therefore start with a bit of that history.

A. HISTORICAL FOUNDATIONS OF THE FOURTH AMENDMENT

The Fourth Amendment was adopted in response to founding-era concerns about general warrants and writs of assistance. Unlike the particularized warrants described in the Warrant Clause, general warrants and writs of assistance allowed "an officer or messenger . . . to search suspected places without evidence of a [crime] committed, or to seize any person or persons not named, or whose offense is not particularly described by evidence." Va. Const., Art. I, Sec. 10.

During the 1760's, general warrants and writs of assistance came under attack in both England and the colonies. The focus of the controversy in England was the General Warrants Cases, which famously included Wilkes v. Wood, 19 Howell's State Trials 1153 (C.P. 1763), and Entick v.

Carrington, 19 Howell's State Trials 1029 (1765). These cases involved efforts to identify and prosecute persons associated with the publication of the North Briton, a pamphlet sharply critical of King George III and his government. By authority of general warrants issued by Lord Halifax, who served as Privy Counsel and a Secretary of State, agents searched the homes and offices of John Wilkes, John Entick, and others, seizing their papers and property. Wilkes and Entick sued Halifax and his agents in trespass, winning substantial jury awards. The defendants challenged those verdicts, citing authority granted to them by the general warrants. In a series of opinions written in soaring prose, Charles Pratt, Lord Camden and Chief Justice of Common Pleas, rejected those efforts, condemning general warrants as granting "a discretionary power" for agents to "search wherever their suspicions may chance to fall" without specifying the things taken or the persons suspected. "If such a power is truly invested in the Secretary of State," Lord Camden concluded, "and he can delegate this power, it certainly may affect the person and property of every man in this kingdom, and is totally subversive of the liberty of the subject." As Justice Bradley reports in Boyd v. United States, 116 U.S. 616 (1886), "every American statesman, during our revolutionary and formative period as a nation, was undoubtedly familiar" with these cases and they were "in the minds of those who framed the fourth amendment to the constitution, and were considered as sufficiently explanatory of what was meant by unreasonable searches and seizures."

The locus of criticism for general warrants in the colonies was the Writs of Assistance Cases, including Paxton's Case. Writs of assistance were a special form of general warrant authorizing customs officials to search for smuggled goods. In Paxton's Case, a group of Boston merchants challenged the legality of writs of assistance. They were represented by James Otis who, in a fiery, hours-long speech, condemned writs of assistance as "the worst instrument of arbitrary power, the most destructive of English liberty and the fundamental principles of law," that placed "the liberty of every man in the hands of every petty officer." Otis railed that "by this writ, not only deputies, etc., but even their menial servants, are allowed to lord it over us." "It is a power," he continued, "that places the liberty of every man in the hands of every petty officer." "What is this," he lamented, "but to have the curse of Canaan with a witness on us; to be the servant of servants, the most despicable of God's creation?" The extent of that servitude, he explained, was virtually without limit, so that "Customhouse officers [and their] menial servants may enter, may break locks, bars, and everything in their way; and whether they break through malice or revenge, no man, no court, can inquire." Because writs of assistance were "directed to every subject in the king's dominions," he concluded "Everyone with this writ, may be a tyrant." Otis ultimately lost the case; but colonial fury over the abuse of search and seizure powers played a critical role in fomenting the American Revolution.

The founding generation's objections to general warrants and writs of assistance are evident in the constitutions adopted by the original states, eight of which specifically prohibited general warrants. Article XIV of the Massachusetts Declaration of Rights, which was drafted by John Adams, was particularly influential. It provided that:

> Every subject has a right to be secure from all unreasonable searches, and seizures of his person, his houses, his papers, and all his possessions. All warrants, therefore, are contrary to this right, if the cause or foundation of them be not previously supported by oath or affirmation; and if the order in the warrant to a civil officer, to make search in suspected places, or to arrest one or more suspected persons, or to seize their property, be not accompanied with a special designation of the persons or objects of search, arrest, or seizure: and no warrant ought to be issued but in cases, and with the formalities, prescribed by the laws.

During the ratification debates of 1787 and 1788, anti-Federalist critics pointed out that these and other rights guaranteed to citizens of the States by their state constitutions would not bind the federal government proposed by the Constitution. "[S]uppose for instance," the Maryland Farmer mused, "that an officer of the United States should force the house, the asylum of a citizen, by virtue of a general warrant, I would ask, are general warrants illegal by the constitution of the United States?" The answer, of course, was "no." In order to remedy this and other omissions, and in order to secure the ratification votes of several skeptical states, Federalists committed the First Congress to drafting and sending to the States for ratification a raft of rights protections. In fulfillment of that promise, a committee led by James Madison drafted twelve amendments, ten of which were ratified in 1791 as the Bill of Rights—the Fourth Amendment among them.

This brief history is valuable in its own right, but also provides important insight into what the founding generation had in mind when it elected to guarantee the "security of the people in their persons, houses, papers, and effects against unreasonable searches and seizures." As we shall see, the Supreme Court frequently refers to this history when elaborating the scope of the Fourth Amendment, both in terms of what kinds of government actions constitute "searches and seizures," and what kinds of searches and seizures are "unreasonable."

B. THE PHYSICAL INTRUSION TEST

For the first 100 years after ratification, the Supreme Court had few occasions to elaborate the scope of the Fourth Amendment. That is in large part because criminal law enforcement was a much more modest affair than it is now, particularly at the federal level. Professionalized, paramilitary law enforcement agencies with authority to investigate crimes did not appear in America until the middle decades of the nineteenth century and were not a significant feature of American society until the twentieth century. The progenitors of the Secret Service and Federal Bureau of Investigation were created in 1865 and 1908, respectively, but did not become a true national presence until Prohibition when efforts to enforce the Volstead Act led to a dramatic expansion of law enforcement agencies claiming authority to detect, investigate, and prosecute crime. See Lisa McGirr, The War on Alcohol: Prohibition and the Rise of the American State (2016).

As law enforcement agencies grew and expanded during the late nineteenth and early twentieth centuries, two things became inevitable. First, there were more, and more frequent, engagements between law enforcement and citizens. Second, law enforcement agencies experimented with a variety of investigative means and methods, often leveraging new and emerging technologies. These two phenomena jointly gave rise to cases challenging government action on constitutional grounds. It was in this context that the Court rendered its opinion in Olmstead v. United States, which both reviews the Court's major Fourth Amendment decisions to that point and establishes the test it would apply for the next forty years.

OLMSTEAD V. UNITED STATES

Supreme Court of the United States (1928).
277 U.S. 438.

CHIEF JUSTICE TAFT delivered the opinion of the Court.

These cases are here by certiorari from the Circuit Court of Appeals for the Ninth Circuit. They were granted with the distinct limitation that the hearing should be confined to the single question whether the use of evidence of private telephone conversations between the defendants and others, intercepted by means of wiretapping amounted to a violation of the Fourth and Fifth Amendments.[3]

The petitioners were convicted in the District Court for the Western District of Washington of a conspiracy to violate the National Prohibition Act by unlawfully possessing, transporting and importing intoxicating liquors and maintaining nuisances, and by selling intoxicating liquors. Seventy-two others in addition to the petitioners were indicted. Some were not apprehended, some were acquitted, and others pleaded guilty.

[3] [Editors' Note: At this point in its jurisprudence, the Supreme Court often read the Fourth and Fifth Amendments as [run]ning almost together" in cases where a defendant's papers or property were seized and then used as evidence against him. As we shall see later in this Chapter and in Chapter 3, the Court has shifted its views on both Amendments in important ways, setting them on distinct and separate doctrinal paths.]

The evidence in the records discloses a conspiracy of amazing magnitude to import, possess and sell liquor unlawfully.

It involved the employment of not less than fifty persons, of two seagoing vessels for the transportation of liquor to British Columbia, of smaller vessels for coastwise transportation to the State of Washington, the purchase and use of a ranch beyond the suburban limits of Seattle, with a large underground cache for storage and a number of smaller caches in that city, the maintenance of a central office manned with operators, the employment of executives, salesmen, deliverymen, dispatchers, scouts, bookkeepers, collectors and an attorney. In a bad month, sales amounted to $176,000; the aggregate for a year must have exceeded two millions of dollars. * * *

The information which led to the discovery of the conspiracy and its nature and extent was largely obtained by intercepting messages on the telephones of the conspirators by four federal prohibition officers. Small wires were inserted along the ordinary telephone wires from the residences of four of the petitioners and those leading from the chief office. The insertions were made without trespass upon any property of the defendants. They were made in the basement of the large office building. The taps from house lines were made in the streets near the houses.

The gathering of evidence continued for many months. Conversations of the conspirators, of which refreshing stenographic notes were currently made, were testified to by the government witnesses. They revealed the large business transactions of the partners and their subordinates. Men at the wires heard the orders given for liquor by customers and the acceptances; they became auditors of the conversations between the partners. All this disclosed the conspiracy charged in the indictment. Many of the intercepted conversations were not merely reports, but parts of the criminal acts. The evidence also disclosed the difficulties to which the conspirators were subjected, the reported news of the capture of vessels, the arrest of their men and the seizure of cases of liquor in garages and other places. It showed the dealing by Olmstead, the chief conspirator, with members of the Seattle police, the messages to them which secured the release of arrested members of the conspiracy, and also direct promises to officers of payments as soon as opportunity offered.

The Fourth Amendment provides:

> The right of the people to be secure in their persons, houses, papers, and effects against unreasonable searches and seizures shall not be violated, and no warrants shall issue but upon probable cause, supported by oath or affirmation and particularly describing the place to be searched and the persons or things to be seized. * * *

It will be helpful to consider the chief cases in this Court which bear upon the construction of [this Amendment].

[The Court discusses Boyd v. United States, 116 U. S. 616 (1886), (striking down on Fourth and Fifth Amendment grounds a New York statute that allowed for the compelled production of documents that might reveal efforts to avoid paying tariffs); Weeks v. United States, 232 U.S. 383 (1914) (holding that the "taking of papers by an official of the United States, acting under color of his office," from a home without a warrant "was in violation of the constitutional rights of the defendant" and could not be introduced at trial); Ex parte Jackson, 96 U. S. 727 (1878) (holding that a warrant is required to open and examine the contents of "sealed letters and packages in the mail"); Silverthorne Lumber Company v. United States, 251 U. S. 385 (1920) (excluding from trial evidence seized in violation of the Fourth Amendment along with investigative fruits of that violation); Amos v. United States, 255 U. S. 313 (1921) (extending the holding from *Weeks* to the "curtilage" of the home); Gouled v. United States, 255 U. S. 298 (1921) (holding that a government agent "pretending to make a friendly call," violated the Fourth Amendment when, without a warrant, he took advantage of that welcome to search defendant's office and seize papers); Agnello v. United States, 269 U. S. 20 (1925) (concluding that officers could not justify the warrantless search of defendant's home as incident to arrest when his home was "several blocks distant from the place of arrest, after his arrest").]

The well-known historical purpose of the Fourth Amendment, directed against general warrants and writs of assistance, was to prevent the use of governmental force to search a man's house, his person, his papers and his effects, and to prevent their seizure against his will. This phase of the misuse of governmental power of compulsion is the emphasis of the opinion of the Court in the *Boyd* case. This appears too in the *Weeks* case, in the *Silverthorne* case, and in the *Amos* case.

Gouled v. United States carried the inhibition against unreasonable searches and seizures to the extreme limit. Its authority is not to be enlarged by implication, and must be confined to the precise state of facts disclosed by the record. A representative of the Intelligence Department of the Army, having by stealth obtained admission to the defendant's office, seized and carried away certain private papers valuable for evidential purposes. This was held an unreasonable search and seizure within the Fourth Amendment. A stealthy entrance in such circumstances became the equivalent to an entry by force. There was actual entrance into the private quarters of defendant, and the taking away of something tangible. Here we have testimony only of voluntary conversations secretly overheard.

The Amendment itself shows that the search is to be of material things—the person, the house, his papers, or his effects. The description of the warrant necessary to make the proceeding lawful is that it must specify the place to be searched and the person or *things* to be seized.

It is urged that * * * *Ex parte Jackson* * * * offers an analogy to the interpretation of the Fourth Amendment in respect of wiretapping. But the analogy fails. The Fourth Amendment may have proper application to a sealed letter in the mail because of the constitutional provision for the Post Office Department and the relations between the Government and those who pay to secure protection of their sealed letters. * * * It is plainly within the words of the Amendment to say that the unlawful rifling by a government agent of a sealed letter is a search and seizure of the sender's papers or effects. The letter is a paper, an effect, and in the custody of a Government that forbids carriage except under its protection.

The United States takes no such care of telegraph or telephone messages as of mailed sealed letters. The Amendment does not forbid what was done here. There was no searching. There was no seizure. The evidence was secured by the use of the sense of hearing, and that only. There was no entry of the houses or offices of the defendants.

By the invention of the telephone fifty years ago and its application for the purpose of extending communications, one can talk with another at a far distant place. The language of the Amendment cannot be extended and expanded to include telephone wires reaching to the whole world from the defendant's house or office. The intervening wires are not part of his house or office any more than are the highways along which they are stretched.

This Court, in Carroll v. United States, 267 U. S. 132 [(1925)], declared:

> The Fourth Amendment is to be construed in the light of what was deemed an unreasonable search and seizure when it was adopted and in a manner which will conserve public interests as well as the interests and rights of individual citizens.

Justice Bradley, in the *Boyd* case, and Justice Clark in the *Gouled* case, said that the Fifth Amendment and the Fourth Amendment were to be liberally construed to effect the purpose of the framers of the Constitution in the interest of liberty. But that cannot justify enlargement of the language employed beyond the possible practical meaning of houses, persons, papers, and effects, or so to apply the words search and seizure as to forbid hearing or sight. * * *

Congress may, of course, protect the secrecy of telephone messages by making them, when intercepted, inadmissible in evidence in federal criminal trials by direct legislation, and thus depart from the common law of evidence. But the courts may not adopt such a policy by attributing an enlarged and unusual meaning to the Fourth Amendment. The reasonable view is that one who installs in his house a telephone instrument with connecting wires intends to project his voice to those quite outside, and that the wires beyond his house and messages while passing over them are not within the protection of the Fourth Amendment. Here, those who intercepted the projected voices were not in the house of either party to the conversation.

Neither the cases we have cited nor any of the many federal decisions brought to our attention hold the Fourth Amendment to have been violated as against a defendant unless there has been an official search and seizure of his person, or such a seizure of his papers or his tangible material effects, or an actual physical invasion of his house "or curtilage" for the purpose of making a seizure.

We think, therefore, that the wiretapping here disclosed did not amount to a search or seizure within the meaning of the Fourth Amendment. * * *

Affirmed.

JUSTICE BRANDEIS, dissenting:

* * * "We must never forget," said Mr. Chief Justice Marshall in McCulloch v. Maryland, "that it is a constitution we are expounding." Since then, this Court has repeatedly sustained the exercise of power by Congress, under various clauses of that instrument, over objects of which the Fathers could not have dreamed. We have likewise held that general limitations on the powers of Government, like those embodied in the due process clauses of the Fifth and Fourteenth Amendments, do not forbid the United States or the States from meeting modern conditions by regulations which, "a century ago, or even half a century ago, probably would have been rejected as arbitrary and oppressive." Clauses guaranteeing to the individual protection against specific abuses of power must have a similar capacity of adaptation to a changing world. It was with reference to such a clause that this Court said, in Weems v. United States:

> Legislation, both statutory and constitutional, is enacted, it is true, from an experience of evils, but its general language should not, therefore, be necessarily confined to the form that evil had theretofore taken. Time works changes, brings into existence new conditions and purposes. Therefore, a principle, to be vital, must be capable of wider application than the mischief which gave it birth. This is peculiarly true of constitutions. They are not ephemeral enactments, designed to meet passing occasions. They are, to use the words of Chief Justice Marshall "designed to approach immortality as nearly as human institutions can approach it." The future is their care, and provision for events of good and bad tendencies of which no prophecy can be made. In the application of a constitution, therefore, our contemplation cannot be only of what has been, but of what may be. Under any other rule, a constitution would indeed be as easy of application as it would be deficient in efficacy and power. Its general principles would have

little value, and be converted by precedent into impotent and lifeless formulas. Rights declared in words might be lost in reality.

When the Fourth and Fifth Amendments were adopted, "the form that evil had theretofore taken" had been necessarily simple. Force and violence were then the only means known to man by which a Government could directly effect self-incrimination. It could compel the individual to testify—a compulsion effected, if need be, by torture. It could secure possession of his papers and other articles incident to his private life—a seizure effected, if need be, by breaking and entry. Protection against such invasion of "the sanctities of a man's home and the privacies of life" was provided in the Fourth and Fifth Amendments by specific language. But "time works changes, brings into existence new conditions and purposes." Subtler and more far-reaching means of invading privacy have become available to the Government. Discovery and invention have made it possible for the Government, by means far more effective than stretching upon the rack, to obtain disclosure in court of what is whispered in the closet.

Moreover, "in the application of a constitution, our contemplation cannot be only of what has, been but of what may be." The progress of science in furnishing the Government with means of espionage is not likely to stop with wiretapping. Ways may someday be developed by which the Government, without removing papers from secret drawers, can reproduce them in court, and by which it will be enabled to expose to a jury the most intimate occurrences of the home. Advances in the psychic and related sciences may bring means of exploring unexpressed beliefs, thoughts and emotions. "That places the liberty of every man in the hands of every petty officer" was said by James Otis of much lesser intrusions than these. To Lord Camden, a far slighter intrusion seemed "subversive of all the comforts of society." Can it be that the Constitution affords no protection against such invasions of individual security? * * *

In *Ex parte Jackson*, it was held that a sealed letter entrusted to the mail is protected by the Amendments. The mail is a public service furnished by the Government. The telephone is a public service furnished by its authority. There is, in essence, no difference between the sealed letter and the private telephone message. As Judge Rudkin said below:

> True, the one is visible, the other invisible; the one is tangible, the other intangible; the one is sealed, and the other unsealed, but these are distinctions without a difference.

The evil incident to invasion of the privacy of the telephone is far greater than that involved in tampering with the mails. Whenever a telephone line is tapped, the privacy of the persons at both ends of the line is invaded and all conversations between them upon any subject, and, although proper, confidential and privileged, may be overheard. Moreover, the tapping of one man's telephone line involves the tapping of the telephone of every other person whom he may call or who may call him. As a means of espionage, writs of assistance and general warrants are but puny instruments of tyranny and oppression when compared with wiretapping. * * *

The makers of our Constitution undertook to secure conditions favorable to the pursuit of happiness. They recognized the significance of man's spiritual nature, of his feelings, and of his intellect. They knew that only a part of the pain, pleasure and satisfactions of life are to be found in material things. They sought to protect Americans in their beliefs, their thoughts, their emotions and their sensations. They conferred, as against the Government, the right to be let alone—the most comprehensive of rights, and the right most valued by civilized men. To protect that right, every unjustifiable intrusion by the Government upon the privacy of the individual, whatever the means employed, must be deemed a violation of the Fourth Amendment. * * * It is, of course, immaterial where the physical connection with the telephone wires leading into the defendants' premises was made. And it is also immaterial that the intrusion was in aid of law enforcement. Experience should teach us to be most on our guard to protect liberty when the Government's purposes are beneficent. Men born to freedom are naturally alert to repel invasion of their liberty by evil-minded rulers. The greatest dangers to liberty lurk in insidious encroachment by men of zeal, well meaning but without understanding. * * *

Decency, security and liberty alike demand that government officials shall be subjected to the same rules of conduct that are commands to the citizen. In a government of laws, existence of the government will be imperiled if it fails to observe the law scrupulously. Our Government is the potent, the omnipresent teacher. For good or for ill, it teaches the whole people by its example. Crime is contagious. If the Government becomes a lawbreaker, it breeds contempt for law; it invites every man to become a law unto himself; it invites anarchy. To declare that, in the administration of the criminal law, the end justifies the means—to declare that the Government may commit crimes in order to secure the conviction of a private criminal—would bring terrible retribution. Against that pernicious doctrine this Court should resolutely set its face.

JUSTICE HOLMES, dissenting:

[Although sympathetic with Justice Brandeis's views, Justice Holmes would have held that the wiretap violated state law, and that evidence from that wiretap should therefore be excluded at trial in order to avoid rewarding the agents' illegal conduct.]

JUSTICE BUTLER, dissenting:

[Justice Butler would have held that wiretapping falls within the compass of the Fourth Amendment, which "safeguards against all evils that are like and equivalent to those embraced within the ordinary meaning of its words." As he saw the facts,

> Telephones are used generally for transmission of messages concerning official, social, business and personal affairs, including communications that are private and privileged—those between physician and patient, lawyer and client, parent and child, husband and wife. The contracts between telephone companies and users contemplate the private use of the facilities employed in the service. The communications belong to the parties between whom they pass. During their transmission, the exclusive use of the wire belongs to the persons served by it. Wiretapping involves interference with the wire while being used. Tapping the wires and listening in by the officers literally constituted a search for evidence.]

JUSTICE STONE, dissenting:

[Justice Stone agreed with the substance of opinions written by Justices Brandeis, Holmes, and Butler.]

NOTE ON OLMSTEAD V. UNITED STATES

Olmstead is noteworthy both for the majority opinion and the expansive dissenting opinion of Justice Brandeis. In that contest we can see the blueprint for debates among the Justices that continue today. Chief Justice Taft's textualism leads him to the conclusion that the Fourth Amendment guards only against physical intrusions into constitutionally protected areas. Wiretapping and eavesdropping as they were conducted by the agents did not entail a physical trespass into Olmstead's person, house, paper, or effect, and therefore could not constitute a search. In reaching that holding, the Court resists Justice Brandeis's invitation to read the Fourth Amendment more expansively, looking beyond the particular "mischief" it was written to address in order to give full effect to its general principles in the face of new and emerging technologies capable of stealing away the "privacies of life."[4] Which view do you find more persuasive? If you favor Chief Justice Taft's narrow interpretation, then are you comfortable with the consequences? Do you find reassuring his suggestion that Congress is free to set limits on wiretapping and other eavesdropping techniques? If you favor Justice Brandeis's view, then how would you define "search" for purposes of the Fourth Amendment? How would you go about setting reasonable limits on the scope of Fourth Amendment

---

[4] Justice Brandeis's dissent in *Olmstead* is grounded in his longstanding concerns about privacy and technology, which he explores in an article co-authored with Samuel Warren. Samuel Warren & Louis Brandeis, The Right to Privacy, 4 Harv. L. Rev. 194 (1890).

regulation so as to provide reasonable latitude for officers to carry out their important public duties?

Continuing the Physical Intrusion Test

In the years after *Olmstead*, the Court continued to apply the physical intrusion test in Fourth Amendment cases. So, in Goldman v. United States, 316 U.S. 129 (1942), the Court concluded that the use of a detectaphone placed against the exterior of a party wall to eavesdrop on conversations next door did not violate the Fourth Amendment because there was no physical trespass into a constitutionally protected area. But, applying the same rule, the Court held in Silverman v. United States, 365 U.S. 505 (1961), that inserting a spike microphone through a party wall qualified as a search because it entailed an "intrusion into a constitutionally protected area." Likewise, the Court found that physical searches of cars, Carroll v. United States, 267 U.S. 132 (1925), persons, United States v. Di Re, 332 U.S. 581 (1948), and hotel rooms, Johnson v. United States, 333 U.S. 10 (1948), all constitute "searches" for purposes of the Fourth Amendment.

During this same period, the Court had several occasions to consider the use of eavesdropping devices carried by undercover agents. In On Lee v. United States, 343 U.S. 747 (1952), the Court held that the Fourth Amendment was not implicated when the government wired an undercover agent with a microphone that transmitted sounds to another officer outside the laundry in which the undercover agent was conversing with On Lee because the undercover agent was an invited guest, so there was no trespass. The Court reached the same result in Lopez v. United States, 373 U.S. 427 (1963), which involved an IRS agent who, having received an unsolicited bribe and reporting it to his superiors, concealed a wire recorder on his person, as directed by his superiors, when he met Lopez. Justice Harlan's majority opinion found no Fourth Amendment violation because "the device was used only to obtain the most reliable evidence possible of a conversation in which the Government's own agent was a participant and which that agent was fully entitled to disclose." The fact that the IRS agent falsely represented his interest in taking bribes was of no moment. So, too, in Lewis v. United States, 385 U.S. 206 (1966), where an undercover agent telephoned Lewis's home asking about the possibility of purchasing marijuana, arrangements were made, and a sale was consummated. Writing for the majority, Chief Justice Warren explained that:

> [W]hen, as here, the home is converted into a commercial center to which outsiders are invited for purposes of transacting unlawful business, that business is entitled to no greater sanctity than if it were carried on in a store, a garage, a car, or on the street. A government agent, in the same manner as a private person, may accept an

invitation to do business and may enter upon the premises for the very purposes contemplated by the occupant.

A similar result to that in *Lewis* was reached in Hoffa v. United States, 385 U.S. 293 (1966). Union leader James Hoffa was convicted for attempting to bribe jurors in a previous trial. Much of the government's case depended on the testimony of a local union official who, after being released from jail with federal and state charges pending against him, spent a great deal of time in the Hoffa camp at the time of the bribe attempts. Justice Stewart's majority opinion assumed that the witness had been an undercover agent from the first visit to Hoffa, but found that "no interest legitimately protected by the Fourth Amendment" was involved in the case. Justice Stewart wrote that "[w]hat the Fourth Amendment protects is the security a man relies upon when he places himself or his property within a constitutionally protected area." He concluded that the undercover agent invaded no protected area because he was invited into Hoffa's hotel room. Under these circumstances, Hoffa was not relying on the security of the hotel room but upon his "misplaced confidence" that the union official would not reveal his statements. Such a risk, according to Justice Stewart, is the kind "we necessarily assume whenever we speak."

Growing Discontent with the Physical Trespass Test

Although the Court applied the *Olmstead* rule in these cases, the results stirred unease among the Justices as police agencies expanded their roles in public life and made use of new means and methods of detecting, investigating, and prosecuting crime. In *Goldman*, Chief Justice Stone and Justice Frankfurter advertised their readiness to overturn *Olmstead*. So, too, did Justice Murphy, citing "the right of personal privacy guaranteed by the Fourth Amendment." Writing for the majority in *Di Re*, Justice Jackson worried about "too permeating police surveillance." Dissenting in *On Lee*, Justice Frankfurter lamented the result in *Olmstead* before concluding that "[t]he circumstances of the present case show how the rapid advances of science are made available for that police intrusion into our private lives against which the Fourth Amendment of the Constitution was set on guard." Justice Douglas also dissented in *On Lee*, noting the "increasing use of wiretapping by police" before aligning himself with Justice Brandeis's dissenting opinion in *Olmstead*. In 1963, Justices Brennan, Douglas, and Goldberg picked up this thread when they dissented in *Lopez*, arguing that *On Lee* "was error, in reason and authority, at the time it was decided; that subsequent decisions and subsequent experience have sapped whatever vitality it may once have had." Chief Justice Warren wrote separately in *Lopez* to share his view that *On Lee* should be overruled. Although not prepared to accept this invitation, a majority of the Court appeared to endorse a modest expansion of the *Olmstead* test in *Silverman* (the case involving the spike microphone inserted through a party wall) by discounting the implied requirement that a physical intrusion constitute a trespass. As Justice Stewart wrote for the Court:

> [T]he officers overheard the petitioners' conversations only by usurping part of the petitioners' house or office—a heating system which was an integral part of the premises occupied by the petitioners, a usurpation that was effected without their knowledge and without their consent. In these circumstances, we need not pause to consider whether or not there was a technical trespass under the local property law relating to party walls. Inherent Fourth Amendment rights are not inevitably measurable in terms of ancient niceties of tort or real property law. * * * [Our] decision here does not turn upon the technicality of a trespass upon a party wall as a matter of local law. It is based upon the reality of an actual intrusion into a constitutionally protected area. What the Court said long ago bears repeating now:
>
> "It may be that it is the obnoxious thing in its mildest and least repulsive form; but illegitimate and unconstitutional practices get their first footing in that way, namely, by silent approaches and slight deviations from legal modes of procedure." Boyd v. United States, 116 U.S. 6116, 635 (1886).

Despite this building discontent, the Court maintained its commitment to physical intrusion as the sine qua non of a search until its landmark decision in Katz v. United States, 389 U.S. 347 (1967).

C. THE REASONABLE EXPECTATION TEST

In the following landmark case, the Court established a new test for determining whether government investigative activity rises to the level of a search—the reasonable expectation of privacy test.

KATZ V. UNITED STATES

Supreme Court of the United States, 1967.
389 U.S. 347.

JUSTICE STEWART delivered the opinion of the Court.

The petitioner was convicted in the District Court for the Southern District of California under an eight-count indictment charging him with transmitting wagering information by telephone from Los Angeles to Miami and Boston, in violation of a Federal statute. At trial the Government was permitted, over the petitioner's objection, to introduce evidence of the petitioner's end of telephone conversations, overheard by FBI agents who had attached an electronic listening and recording device to the outside of the public telephone booth from which he had placed his calls. In affirming his conviction, the Court of Appeals rejected the contention that the recordings had been obtained in violation of the Fourth Amendment, because "[t]here was no physical entrance into the area occupied by [the petitioner]." We granted certiorari in order to consider the constitutional questions thus presented.

The petitioner has phrased those questions as follows:

> "A. Whether a public telephone booth is a constitutionally protected area so that evidence obtained by attaching an electronic listening recording device to the top of such a booth is obtained in violation of the right to privacy of the user of the booth.
>
> "B. Whether physical penetration of a constitutionally protected area is necessary before a search and seizure can be said to be violative of the Fourth Amendment to the United States Constitution."

We decline to adopt this formulation of the issues. In the first place, the correct solution of Fourth Amendment problems is not necessarily promoted by incantation of the phrase "constitutionally protected area." Secondly, the Fourth Amendment cannot be translated into a general constitutional "right to privacy." That Amendment protects individual privacy against certain kinds of governmental intrusion, but its protections go further, and often have nothing to do with privacy at all. Other provisions of the Constitution protect personal privacy from other forms of governmental invasion. But the protection of a person's *general* right to privacy—his right to be let alone by other people—is like the protection of his property and of his very life, left largely to the law of the individual States.

* * * The petitioner has strenuously argued that the booth was a "constitutionally protected area." The Government has maintained with equal vigor that it was not. But this effort to decide whether or not a given "area," viewed in the abstract, is "constitutionally protected" deflects attention from the problem presented by this case. For the Fourth Amendment protects people, not places. What a person knowingly exposes to the public, even in his own home or office, is not a subject of Fourth Amendment protection. But what he seeks to preserve as private, even in an area accessible to the public, may be constitutionally protected.

The Government stresses the fact that the telephone booth from which the petitioner made his calls was constructed partly of glass, so that he was as visible after he entered it as he would have been if he had remained outside. But what he sought to exclude when he entered the booth was not the intruding eye—it was the uninvited ear. He did not shed his right to do so simply because he made his calls from a place where he might be seen. No less than an individual in a business office, in a friend's apartment, or in a taxicab, a person in a telephone booth may rely upon the protection of the Fourth Amendment. One who occupies it, shuts the door behind him, and pays the toll that permits him to place a call is surely entitled to assume that the words he utters into the mouthpiece will not be broadcast to the world. * * *

The Government contends, however, that the activities of its agents in this case should not be tested by Fourth Amendment requirements, for the surveillance technique they employed involved no physical penetration of the telephone booth from which the petitioner placed his calls. It is true that the absence of such penetration was at one time thought to foreclose further Fourth Amendment inquiry, Olmstead v. United States, 277 U.S. 438, 457, 464, 466; Goldman v. United States, 316 U.S. 129, 134–136, for that Amendment was thought to limit only searches and seizures of tangible property. But the premise that property interests control the right of the Government to search and seize has been discredited. Thus, although a closely divided Court supposed in *Olmstead* that surveillance without any trespass and without the seizure of any material object fell outside the ambit of the Constitution, we have since departed from the narrow view on which that decision rested. Indeed, we have expressly held that the Fourth Amendment governs not only the seizure of tangible items, but extends as well to the recording of oral statements, overheard without any "technical trespass under * * * local property law." Silverman v. United States, 365 U.S. 505, 511. Once this much is acknowledged, and once it is recognized that the Fourth Amendment protects people—and not simply "areas"—against unreasonable searches and seizures, it becomes clear that the reach of that Amendment cannot turn upon the presence or absence of a physical intrusion into any given enclosure.

We conclude that the underpinnings of *Olmstead* and *Goldman* have been so eroded by our subsequent decisions that the "trespass" doctrine there enunciated can no longer be regarded as controlling. The Government's activities in electronically listening to and recording the petitioner's words violated the privacy upon which he justifiably relied while using the telephone booth and thus constituted a "search and seizure" within the meaning of the Fourth Amendment. The fact that the electronic device employed to achieve that end did not happen to penetrate the wall of the booth can have no constitutional significance.

The question remaining for decision, then, is whether the search and seizure conducted in this case complied with constitutional standards. In that regard, the Government's position is that its agents acted in an entirely defensible manner: They did not begin their electronic surveillance until investigation of the petitioner's activities had established a strong probability that he was using the telephone in question to transmit gambling information to persons in other States, in violation of Federal law. Moreover, the surveillance was limited, both in scope and in duration, to the specific purpose of establishing the contents of the petitioner's unlawful telephonic communications. The agents confined their surveillance to the brief periods during which he used the telephone booth, and they took great care to overhear only the conversations of the petitioner himself.

Accepting this account of the Government's actions as accurate, it is clear that this surveillance was so narrowly circumscribed that a duly authorized magistrate, properly notified of the need for such investigation, specifically informed of the basis on which it was to proceed, and clearly apprised of the precise intrusion it would entail, could constitutionally have authorized, with appropriate safeguards, the very limited search and seizure that the Government asserts in fact took place. * * *

* * * Yet the inescapable fact is that this restraint was imposed by the agents themselves, not by a judicial officer. They were not required, before commencing the search, to present their estimate of probable cause for detached scrutiny by a neutral magistrate. They were not compelled, during the conduct of the search itself, to observe precise limits established in advance by a specific court order. Nor were they directed, after the search had been completed, to notify the authorizing magistrate in detail of all that had been seized. In the absence of such safeguards, this Court has never sustained a search upon the sole ground that officers reasonably expected to find evidence of a particular crime and voluntarily confined their activities to the least intrusive means to that end * * *.

* * *

* * * Wherever a man may be, he is entitled to know that he will remain free from unreasonable searches and seizures. The government agents here ignored "the procedure of antecedent justification * * * that is central to the Fourth Amendment," a procedure that we hold to be a constitutional precondition of the kind of electronic surveillance involved in this case. Because the surveillance here failed to meet that condition, and because it led to the petitioner's conviction, the judgment must be reversed.

* * *

JUSTICE HARLAN, concurring.

I join the opinion of the Court, which I read to hold only (a) that an enclosed telephone booth is an area where, like a home, and unlike a field, a person has a constitutionally protected reasonable expectation of privacy; (b) that electronic as well as physical intrusion into a place that is in this sense private may constitute a violation of the Fourth Amendment; and (c) that the invasion of a constitutionally protected area by Federal authorities is, as the Court has long held, presumptively unreasonable in the absence of a search warrant.

As the Court's opinion states, "the Fourth Amendment protects people, not places." The question, however, is what protection it affords to those people. Generally, as here, the answer to that question requires reference to a "place." My understanding of the rule that has emerged from prior decisions is that there is a twofold requirement, first that a person have exhibited an actual (subjective) expectation of privacy and, second, that the expectation be one that society is prepared to recognize as "reasonable." Thus a man's home is, for most purposes, a place where he expects privacy, but objects, activities, or statements that he exposes to the "plain view" of outsiders are not "protected" because no intention to keep them to himself has been exhibited. On the other hand, conversations in the open would not be protected against being overheard, for the expectation of privacy under the circumstances would be unreasonable.

The critical fact in this case is that "[o]ne who occupies it, [a telephone booth] shuts the door behind him, and pays the toll that permits him to place a call is surely entitled to assume" that his conversation is not being intercepted. The point is not that the booth is "accessible to the public" at other times, but that it is a temporarily private place whose momentary occupants' expectations of freedom from intrusion are recognized as reasonable.

* * *

JUSTICE BLACK, dissenting.

* * *

My basic objection is twofold: (1) I do not believe that the words of the Amendment will bear the meaning given them by today's decision, and (2) I do not believe that it is the proper role of this Court to rewrite the Amendment in order "to bring it into harmony with the times" and thus reach a result that many people believe to be desirable.

* * *

The first clause protects "persons, houses, papers, and effects, against unreasonable searches and seizures * * *." These words connote the idea of tangible things with size, form, and weight, things capable of being searched, seized, or both. The second clause of the Amendment still further establishes its Framers' purpose to limit its protection to tangible things by providing that no warrants shall issue but those "particularly describing the place to be searched, and the persons or things to be seized." A conversation overheard by eavesdropping, whether by plain snooping or wiretapping, is not tangible and, under the normally accepted meanings of the words, can neither be searched nor seized. * * *

* * *

[Justice Marshall took no part in the consideration or decision of this case. Concurring opinions by Justice Douglas (joined by Justice Brennan) and by Justice White are omitted.]

Katz as a Two-Pronged Test

Katz has been read to set forth a two-pronged test for determining whether government conduct constitutes a search. First, the government conduct must offend the citizen's subjective manifestation of a privacy interest. Second, the privacy interest invaded must be one that society is prepared to accept as "reasonable" or "legitimate." This two-pronged test comes not from Justice Stewart's majority opinion but rather from Justice Harlan's concurring opinion. It is notable that in the later case of United States v. White, 401 U.S. 745 (1971) (holding that no search occurred where police electronically eavesdropped on a two-party conversation with the consent of one of the parties), Justice Harlan dissented and expressed misgivings about the test that he had promulgated in *Katz:*

> While these formulations represent an advance over the unsophisticated trespass analysis of the common law, they too have their limitations and can, ultimately, lead to the substitution of words for analysis. The analysis must, in my view, transcend the search for subjective expectations or legal attribution of assumptions of risk. Our expectations, and the risks we assume, are in large part reflections of laws that translate into rules the customs and values of the past and present.

Justice Harlan's concern was that the reasonableness of an expectation of privacy would be determined by existing laws and practices, and that this could result in the diminution of protected privacy interests; "expectation" of privacy could be based on what government allows us or conditions us to expect.

Should the Fourth Amendment threshold be dependent on what we should *expect* from government, or rather on what we can *demand* from government? Consider Professor Clancy's critique of *Katz:*

> The ability to exclude must extend to all invasions, tangible and intangible, and must protect both tangible and intangible aspects of the amendment's protected objects. That was the essential lesson of *Katz*. *Katz* and the privacy theory, however, failed to grasp the essence of the interest protected. Although it may have been Katz's *expectation* that his conversation was not being heard, it was his *right* to exclude others from hearing. It is not privacy which may motivate a person to assert his or her right. It is the right to prevent intrusions—to exclude—which affords personal security.

Clancy, What Does the Fourth Amendment Protect: Property, Privacy, or Security?, 33 Wake Forest L. Rev. 307, 367–8 (1998).

Did Katz Displace Olmstead?

The Court in *Katz* appeared to reject physical intrusion as a necessary condition for applying the Fourth Amendment. Does this mean that physical intrusion is no longer sufficient to trigger the Fourth Amendment? The Court addresses this question in the following case, clarifying the relationship between *Katz* and *Olmstead*.

UNITED STATES V. JONES

Supreme Court of the United States, 2012.
565 U.S. 400.

JUSTICE SCALIA **delivered the opinion of the Court.**

We decide whether the attachment of a Global Positioning-System (GPS) tracking device to an individual's vehicle, and subsequent use of that device to monitor the vehicle's movements on public streets, constitutes a search or seizure within the meaning of the Fourth Amendment.

* * *

In 2004 respondent Antoine Jones, owner and operator of a nightclub in the District of Columbia, came under suspicion of trafficking in narcotics and was made the target of an investigation by a joint FBI and Metropolitan Police Department task force. Officers employed various investigative techniques, including * * * installing a GPS tracking device on the undercarriage of [a Jeep regularly driven by Jones] while it was parked in a public parking lot. [The government conceded that its installation of this device was not authorized by a valid warrant.] Over the next 28 days, the Government used the device to track the vehicle's movements, and once had to replace the device's battery when the vehicle was parked in a different public lot in Maryland. By means of signals from multiple satellites, the device established the vehicle's location within 50 to 100 feet, and communicated that location by cellular phone to a Government computer. It relayed more than 2,000 pages of data over the 4-week period.

The Government ultimately obtained a multiple-count indictment charging Jones and several alleged coconspirators with, as relevant here, conspiracy to distribute and possess with intent to distribute five kilograms or more of cocaine and 50 grams or more of cocaine base * * *. Before trial, Jones filed a motion to suppress evidence obtained through the GPS device. The District Court granted the motion only in part, suppressing the data obtained while the vehicle was parked in the garage adjoining Jones's residence. It held the remaining data admissible, because " '[a] person traveling in an automobile on public thoroughfares has no reasonable expectation of privacy in his movements from one place to another.' " Jones's trial in October 2006 produced a hung jury on the conspiracy count.

In March 2007, a grand jury returned another indictment, charging Jones and others with the same conspiracy. The Government introduced at trial the same GPS-derived locational data admitted in the first trial, which connected Jones to the alleged conspirators' stash house that contained $850,000 in cash, 97 kilograms of cocaine, and 1 kilogram of cocaine base. The jury returned a guilty verdict, and the District Court sentenced Jones to life imprisonment.

The United States Court of Appeals for the District of Columbia Circuit reversed the conviction because of admission of the evidence obtained by warrantless use of the GPS device which, it said, violated the Fourth Amendment. * * * We granted certiorari.

The Fourth Amendment provides in relevant part that "[t]he right of the people to be secure in their persons, houses, papers, and effects, against unreasonable searches and seizures, shall not be violated." It is beyond dispute that a vehicle is an "effect" as that term is used in the Amendment. We hold that the Government's installation of a GPS device on a target's vehicle, and its use of that device to monitor the vehicle's movements, constitutes a "search."

It is important to be clear about what occurred in this case: The Government physically occupied private property for the purpose of obtaining information. We have no doubt that such a physical intrusion would have been considered a "search" within the meaning of the Fourth Amendment when it was adopted. Entick v. Carrington, 95 Eng. Rep. 807 (C. P. 1765), is a "case we have described as a 'monument of English freedom' 'undoubtedly familiar' to 'every American statesman' at the time the Constitution was adopted, and considered to be 'the true and ultimate expression of constitutional law' " with regard to search and seizure. In that case, Lord Camden expressed in plain terms the significance of property rights in search-and-seizure analysis:

> "[O]ur law holds the property of every man so sacred, that no man can set his foot upon his neighbour's close without his leave; if he does he is a trespasser, though he does no damage at all; if he will tread upon his neighbour's ground, he must justify it by law."

The text of the Fourth Amendment reflects its close connection to property, since otherwise it would have referred simply to "the right of the people to be secure against unreasonable searches and seizures"; the phrase "in their persons, houses, papers, and effects" would have been superfluous.

Consistent with this understanding, our Fourth Amendment jurisprudence was tied to common-law trespass, at least until the latter half of the 20th century. Thus, in Olmstead v. United States, we held that wiretaps attached to telephone wires on the public streets did not constitute a Fourth Amendment search because "[t]here was no entry of the houses or offices of the defendants."

Our later cases, of course, have deviated from that exclusively property-based approach. In Katz v. United States, we said that "the Fourth Amendment protects people, not places," and found a violation in attachment of an eavesdropping device to a public telephone booth. Our later cases have applied the analysis of Justice Harlan's concurrence in that case, which said that a violation occurs when government officers violate a person's "reasonable expectation of privacy."

The Government contends that the Harlan standard shows that no search occurred here, since Jones had no "reasonable expectation of privacy" in the area of the Jeep accessed by Government agents (its underbody) and in the locations of the Jeep on the public roads, which were visible to all. But we need not address the Government's contentions, because Jones's Fourth Amendment rights do not rise or fall with the *Katz* formulation. * * * As explained, for most of our history the Fourth Amendment was understood to embody a particular concern for government trespass upon the areas ("persons, houses, papers, and effects") it enumerates.[a] * * *

* * * *Katz* did not erode the principle that, when the Government does engage in physical intrusion of a constitutionally protected area in order to obtain information, that intrusion may constitute a violation of the Fourth Amendment. We have embodied that preservation of past rights in our very definition of "reasonable expectation of privacy" which we have said to be an expectation "that has a source outside of the Fourth Amendment, either by reference to concepts of real or personal property law or to understandings that are recognized and permitted by society." *Katz* did not narrow the Fourth Amendment's scope.[b]

---

[a] Justice Alito's concurrence * * * doubts the wisdom of our approach because "it is almost impossible to think of late-18th-century situations that are analogous to what took place in this case." But in fact it posits a situation that is not far afield—a constable's concealing himself in the target's coach in order to track its movements. There is no doubt that the information gained by that trespassory activity would be the product of an unlawful search—whether that information consisted of the conversations occurring in the coach, or of the destinations to which the coach traveled.

In any case, it is quite irrelevant whether there was an 18th-century analog. Whatever new methods of investigation may be devised, our task, at a minimum, is to decide whether the action in question would have constituted a "search" within the original meaning of the Fourth Amendment. Where, as here, the Government obtains information by physically intruding on a constitutionally protected area, such a search has undoubtedly occurred.

[b] The concurrence notes that post-*Katz* we have explained that "an actual trespass is neither necessary nor sufficient to establish a constitutional violation." That is undoubtedly true, and undoubtedly irrelevant. * * * Trespass alone does not qualify, but there must be conjoined with

[The majority distinguishes *Knotts* and *Karo*—two beeper-tracking cases discussed later in this Chapter, in which the Court found that the tracking was not a search—on the ground that *Knotts* did not challenge the placement of the beeper and *Karo* did not involve the government's trespass on private property.][c]

* * *

The concurrence begins by accusing us of applying "18th-century tort law." That is a distortion. What we apply is an 18th-century guarantee against unreasonable searches, which we believe must provide *at a minimum* the degree of protection it afforded when it was adopted. The concurrence does not share that belief. It would apply exclusively *Katz*'s reasonable-expectation-of-privacy test, even when that eliminates rights that previously existed. The concurrence faults our approach for "present[ing] particularly vexing problems" in cases that do not involve physical contact, such as those that involve the transmission of electronic signals. We entirely fail to understand that point. For unlike the concurrence, which would make *Katz* the exclusive test, we do not make trespass the exclusive test. Situations involving merely the transmission of electronic signals without trespass would remain subject to *Katz* analysis.

In fact, it is the concurrence's insistence on the exclusivity of the *Katz* test that needlessly leads us into "particularly vexing problems" in the present case. This Court has to date not deviated from the understanding that mere visual observation does not constitute a search. We accordingly held in *Knotts* that "[a] person traveling in an automobile on public thoroughfares has no reasonable expectation of privacy in his movements from one place to another." Thus, even assuming that the concurrence is correct to say that "[t]raditional surveillance" of Jones for a 4-week period "would have required a large team of agents, multiple vehicles, and perhaps aerial assistance," our cases suggest that such visual observation is constitutionally permissible. It may be that achieving the same result through electronic means, without an accompanying trespass, is an unconstitutional invasion of privacy, but the present case does not require us to answer that question.

---

that what was present here: an attempt to find something or to obtain information. Related to this, and similarly irrelevant, is the concurrence's point that, if analyzed separately, neither the installation of the device nor its use would constitute a Fourth Amendment search. Of course not. A trespass on "houses" or "effects," or a *Katz* invasion of privacy, is not alone a search unless it is done to obtain information; and the obtaining of information is not alone a search unless it is achieved by such a trespass or invasion of privacy.

[c] *Knotts* noted the "limited use which the government made of the signals from this particular beeper," and reserved the question whether "different constitutional principles may be applicable" to "dragnet-type law enforcement practices" of the type that GPS tracking made possible here.

And answering it affirmatively leads us needlessly into additional thorny problems. The concurrence posits that "relatively short-term monitoring of a person's movements on public streets" is okay, but that "the use of longer term GPS monitoring in investigations of most offenses" is no good. That introduces yet another novelty into our jurisprudence. There is no precedent for the proposition that whether a search has occurred depends on the nature of the crime being investigated. And even accepting that novelty, it remains unexplained why a 4-week investigation is "surely" too long and why a drug-trafficking conspiracy involving substantial amounts of cash and narcotics is not an "extraordinary offens[e]" which may permit longer observation. What of a 2-day monitoring of a suspected purveyor of stolen electronics? Or of a 6-month monitoring of a suspected terrorist? We may have to grapple with these "vexing problems" in some future case where a classic trespassory search is not involved and resort must be had to *Katz* analysis; but there is no reason for rushing forward to resolve them here.

* * *

JUSTICE SOTOMAYOR, concurring.

* * * [T]he trespassory test applied in the majority's opinion reflects an irreducible constitutional minimum: When the Government physically invades personal property to gather information, a search occurs. The reaffirmation of that principle suffices to decide this case.

Nonetheless, as Justice Alito notes, physical intrusion is now unnecessary to many forms of surveillance. With increasing regularity, the Government will be capable of duplicating the monitoring undertaken in this case by enlisting factory- or owner-installed vehicle tracking devices or GPS-enabled smartphones. In cases of electronic or other novel modes of surveillance that do not depend upon a physical invasion on property, the majority opinion's trespassory test may provide little guidance. * * * I agree with Justice Alito that, at the very least, "longer term GPS monitoring in investigations of most offenses impinges on expectations of privacy."

In cases involving even short-term monitoring, some unique attributes of GPS surveillance relevant to the *Katz* analysis will require particular attention. GPS monitoring generates a precise, comprehensive record of a person's public movements that reflects a wealth of detail about her familial, political, professional, religious, and sexual associations. The Government can store such records and efficiently mine them for information years into the future. And because GPS monitoring is cheap in comparison to conventional surveillance techniques and, by design, proceeds surreptitiously, it evades the ordinary checks that constrain abusive law enforcement practices: limited police resources and community hostility.

* * * The net result is that GPS monitoring—by making available at a relatively low cost such a substantial quantum of intimate information about any person whom the Government, in its unfettered discretion, chooses to track—may alter the relationship between citizen and government in a way that is inimical to democratic society. I would take these attributes of GPS monitoring into account when considering the existence of a reasonable societal expectation of privacy in the sum of one's public movements. I would ask whether people reasonably expect that their movements will be recorded and aggregated in a manner that enables the Government to ascertain, more or less at will, their political and religious beliefs, sexual habits, and so on. * * *

Resolution of these difficult questions in this case is unnecessary, however, because the Government's physical intrusion on Jones' Jeep supplies a narrower basis for decision. I therefore join the majority's opinion.

JUSTICE ALITO, with whom JUSTICE GINSBURG, JUSTICE BREYER, and JUSTICE KAGAN, join, concurring in the judgment.

This case requires us to apply the Fourth Amendment's prohibition of unreasonable searches and seizures to a 21st-century surveillance technique, the use of a Global Positioning System (GPS) device to monitor a vehicle's movements for an extended period of time. Ironically, the Court has chosen to decide this case based on 18th-century tort law. By attaching a small GPS device to the underside of the vehicle that respondent drove, the law enforcement officers in this case engaged in conduct that might have provided grounds in 1791 for a suit for trespass to chattels. And for this reason, the Court concludes, the installation and use of the GPS device constituted a search.

This holding, in my judgment, is unwise. It strains the language of the Fourth Amendment; it has little if any support in current Fourth Amendment case law; and it is highly artificial.

I would analyze the question presented in this case by asking whether respondent's reasonable expectations of privacy were violated by the long-term monitoring of the movements of the vehicle he drove.

* * * The Fourth Amendment prohibits "unreasonable searches and seizures," and the Court makes very little effort to explain how the attachment or use of the GPS device fits within these terms. The Court does not contend that there was a seizure. A seizure of property occurs when there is "some meaningful interference with an individual's possessory interests in that property," and here there was none. Indeed,

the success of the surveillance technique that the officers employed was dependent on the fact that the GPS did not interfere in any way with the operation of the vehicle, for if any such interference had been detected, the device might have been discovered.

The Court does claim that the installation and use of the GPS constituted a search, but this conclusion is dependent on the questionable proposition that these two procedures cannot be separated for purposes of Fourth Amendment analysis. If these two procedures are analyzed separately, it is not at all clear from the Court's opinion why either should be regarded as a search. It is clear that the attachment of the GPS device was not itself a search; if the device had not functioned or if the officers had not used it, no information would have been obtained. And the Court does not contend that the use of the device constituted a search either. * * *

The Court argues—and I agree—that we must assure preservation of that degree of privacy against government that existed when the Fourth Amendment was adopted. But it is almost impossible to think of late-18th-century situations that are analogous to what took place in this case. (Is it possible to imagine a case in which a constable secreted himself somewhere in a coach and remained there for a period of time in order to monitor the movements of the coach's owner?[e])

* * *

The Court's reasoning in this case is very similar to that in the Court's early decisions involving wiretapping and electronic eavesdropping, namely, that a technical trespass followed by the gathering of evidence constitutes a search. * * * This trespass-based rule was repeatedly criticized. * * * Katz v. United States finally did away with the old approach, holding that a trespass was not required for a Fourth Amendment violation. * * * Disharmony with a substantial body of existing case law is only one of the problems with the Court's approach in this case. I will briefly note four others. First, the Court's reasoning largely disregards what is really important (the use of a GPS for the purpose of long-term tracking) and instead attaches great significance to something that most would view as relatively minor (attaching to the bottom of a car a small, light object that does not interfere in any way with the car's operation). Attaching such an object is generally regarded as so trivial that it does not provide a basis for recovery under modern tort law. But under the Court's reasoning, this conduct may violate the Fourth Amendment. By contrast, if long term monitoring can be accomplished without committing a technical trespass—suppose, for example, that the Federal Government

---

[e] The Court suggests that something like this might have occurred in 1791, but this would have required either a gigantic coach, a very tiny constable, or both—not to mention a constable with incredible fortitude and patience.

required or persuaded auto manufacturers to include a GPS tracking device in every car—the Court's theory would provide no protection.

Second, the Court's approach leads to incongruous results. If the police attach a GPS device to a car and use the device to follow the car for even a brief time, under the Court's theory, the Fourth Amendment applies. But if the police follow the same car for a much longer period using unmarked cars and aerial assistance, this tracking is not subject to any Fourth Amendment constraints.

* * *

Third, under the Court's theory, the coverage of the Fourth Amendment may vary from State to State [according to their various approaches to the law of property and trespass].

Fourth, the Court's reliance on the law of trespass will present particularly vexing problems in cases involving surveillance that is carried out by making electronic, as opposed to physical, contact with the item to be tracked. For example, suppose that the officers in the present case had followed respondent by surreptitiously activating a stolen vehicle detection system that came with the car when it was purchased. Would the sending of a radio signal to activate this system constitute a trespass to chattels? Trespass to chattels has traditionally required a physical touching of the property. In recent years, courts have wrestled with the application of this old tort in cases involving unwanted electronic contact with computer systems, and some have held that even the transmission of electrons that occurs when a communication is sent from one computer to another is enough. * * * Assuming that what matters under the Court's theory is the law of trespass as it existed at the time of the adoption of the Fourth Amendment, do these recent decisions represent a change in the law or simply the application of the old tort to new situations?

* * *

The *Katz* expectation-of-privacy test avoids the problems and complications noted above, but it is not without its own difficulties. It involves a degree of circularity, and judges are apt to confuse their own expectations of privacy with those of the hypothetical reasonable person to which the *Katz* test looks. In addition, the *Katz* test rests on the assumption that this hypothetical reasonable person has a well-developed and stable set of privacy expectations. But technology can change those expectations. * * * New technology may provide increased convenience or security at the expense of privacy, and many people may find the tradeoff worthwhile. And even if the public does not welcome the diminution of privacy that new technology entails, they may eventually reconcile themselves to this development as inevitable.

On the other hand, concern about new intrusions on privacy may spur the enactment of legislation to protect against these intrusions. This is what ultimately happened with respect to wiretapping. After *Katz*, Congress did not leave it to the courts to develop a body of Fourth Amendment case law governing that complex subject. Instead, Congress promptly enacted a comprehensive statute, and since that time, the regulation of wiretapping has been governed primarily by statute and not by case law. * * *

B

* * *

In the pre-computer age, the greatest protections of privacy were neither constitutional nor statutory, but practical. Traditional surveillance for any extended period of time was difficult and costly and therefore rarely undertaken. The surveillance at issue in this case * * * would have required a large team of agents, multiple vehicles, and perhaps aerial assistance. Only an investigation of unusual importance could have justified such an expenditure of law enforcement resources. Devices like the one used in the present case, however, make long-term monitoring relatively easy and cheap. In circumstances involving dramatic technological change, the best solution to privacy concerns may be legislative. A legislative body is well situated to gauge changing public attitudes, to draw detailed lines, and to balance privacy and public safety in a comprehensive way.

To date, however, Congress and most States have not enacted statutes regulating the use of GPS tracking technology for law enforcement purposes. The best that we can do in this case is to apply existing Fourth Amendment doctrine and to ask whether the use of GPS tracking in a particular case involved a degree of intrusion that a reasonable person would not have anticipated.

Under this approach, relatively short-term monitoring of a person's movements on public streets accords with expectations of privacy that our society has recognized as reasonable. But the use of longer term GPS monitoring in investigations of most offenses impinges on expectations of privacy. For such offenses, society's expectation has been that law enforcement agents and others would not—and indeed, in the main, simply could not—secretly monitor and catalogue every single movement of an individual's car for a very long period. In this case, for four weeks, law enforcement agents tracked every movement that respondent made in the vehicle he was driving. We need not identify with precision the point at which the tracking of this vehicle became a search, for the line was surely crossed before the 4-week mark. * * * We also need not consider whether prolonged GPS monitoring in the context of investigations involving extraordinary offenses would similarly intrude on a constitutionally protected sphere of privacy. In such cases, long-term tracking might have been mounted using previously available techniques.

* * *

NOTE ON UNITED STATES V. JONES

Do even minor physical intrusions implicate the Fourth Amendment under the rationale in *Jones*? Consider Taylor v. City of Saginaw, 922 F.3d 328 (6th Cir. 2019) (making chalk marks on tires for purposes of parking enforcement constitutes a search).

In his concurring opinion, Justice Alito makes considerable hay over the majority's alleged linking of the Fourth Amendment to the law of trespass, which is both variable and ephemeral. Does this criticism hit its mark? Consider the following from Justice Scalia's majority opinion:

> It is important to be clear about what occurred in this case: The Government physically occupied private property for the purpose of obtaining information. We have no doubt that such a physical intrusion would have been considered a "search" within the meaning of the Fourth Amendment when it was adopted.

> This formulation appears as well in Justice Sotomayor's concurring opinion where she concludes that "[w]hen the Government physically invades personal property to gather information, a search occurs." Based on this language, it appears that the Fourth Amendment is concerned with physical intrusions into constitutionally protected "persons, houses, papers, and effects" for the purpose of gathering information, a category of conduct that may, but need not, also constitute a trespass.

The concurring opinions in *Jones* constitute what some analysts described as a "shadow majority" of five Justices willing to hold that the use of modern tracking technologies constitutes a "search" under *Katz*. Why? For Justices Alito, Ginsburg, Breyer, and Kagan, the key was the duration of the tracking. So, "relatively short-term monitoring of a person's movements on public streets accords with expectations of privacy that our society has recognized as reasonable," but the use of longer term GPS monitoring in investigations of most offenses impinges on expectations of privacy." Justice Sotomayor identifies some additional features of GPS tracking technologies that might raise Fourth Amendment concerns, even in "cases involving . . . short-term monitoring." Among these are:

1. the capacity to generate "a precise, comprehensive record of a person's public movements";
2. that comprehensive records of a person's movements may "reflect a wealth of detail about . . . familial, political, professional, religious, and sexual associations";
3. that location records can be "store[d] and efficiently mine[d] for information years into the future";

4. that the technology is "cheap in comparison to conventional surveillance techniques";
5. that the technology "by design, proceeds surreptitiously"; and
6. that deployment and use of the technology "evades the ordinary checks that constrain abusive law enforcement practices: 'limited police resources and community hostility.' "

In Justice Sotomayor's view, these features of GPS tracking technology, when deployed by law enforcement, raise the specter of what Professor Christopher Slobogin has dubbed "panvasive" surveillance. Christopher Slobogin, *Panvasive Surveillance, Political Process Theory and the Nondelegation Doctrine*, 102 Geo. L. Rev. 1721 (2014). She therefore worried about granting "unfettered discretion . . . to the Executive, in the absence of any oversight from a coordinate branch, a tool so amenable to misuse, especially in light of the Fourth Amendment's goal to curb arbitrary exercises of police power [and to] prevent 'a too permeating police surveillance,' " a result that "may 'alter the relationship between citizen and government in a way that is inimical to democratic society.' " As we shall see, Justice Sotomayor's framework provides a blueprint for the Court's application of the Fourth Amendment to 21st-century technologies. See Carpenter v. United States, 138 S.Ct. 2206 (2018); Riley v. California, 573 U.S. 373 (2014).

Property Interest Required to Invoke the Fourth Amendment Trespass Theory

There was no dispute in *Jones* that the defendant lawfully possessed the Jeep at the time it was trespassed upon. So the Court in *Jones* had no occasion fully to consider the nature of the property interest that is sufficient to establish a property-based Fourth Amendment claim. That question was explored in El-Nahal v. Yassky, 835 F.3d 248 (2d Cir. 2016), in which a taxi driver challenged a government mandate that all taxicabs install a GPS tracking device. The plaintiff argued that this requirement violated his Fourth Amendment rights under *Jones,* but the court rejected that argument because the plaintiff did not claim that he had a property interest in any particular taxi cab. The court stated that "to claim that the Government trespassed or physically intruded upon one's constitutionally protected area for the purposes of gathering information, a plaintiff must establish a property interest in the protected area at the time of intrusion."

D. APPLICATIONS OF THE PHYSICAL INTRUSION AND REASONABLE EXPECTATION OF PRIVACY TESTS

The cases discussed below illustrate the difficulty courts have had in applying the physical intrusion and reasonable expectation of privacy tests to evolving investigative techniques. It is important to keep in mind the consequences if a court does or does not find that police conduct is a search.

If police conduct is a "search," that just means that the Fourth Amendment applies. The activity will still be permissible if it is reasonable. On the other hand, if a court finds that police conduct is not a search, it means that the Fourth Amendment is completely inapplicable. As far as that Amendment is concerned, the police have complete, unfettered discretion.

It is worth noting that many of the cases featured in this section were decided during a time when many believed that the physical intrusion test had been displaced by *Katz*. As *Jones* makes clear, government conduct is subject to the strictures of the Fourth Amendment if it constitutes a "search" under either *Olmstead* or *Katz*. In *Jones*, Justice Scalia suggests that this was always the case, and that none of the cases decided under the *Katz* test would have come out differently under *Olmstead*. As we work through the cases in this section, ask yourself whether he is right. If he is, then what is gained by revitalizing the physical intrusion test? Justice Scalia claims that the answer is simplicity. If government conduct constitutes a "search" under *Olmstead*, then there is no reason to ask murkier questions relating to expectations of privacy. Does that suggest to advocates and courts an order of analysis in Fourth Amendment cases? Do you think that one test is more protective than the other?

1. Subjective Manifestation Under *Katz*

Individuals must take affirmative steps to protect their privacy interests; otherwise, a police inspection will not constitute a search due to failure to satisfy the "subjective manifestation" prong of *Katz*. See, e.g., United States v. Bellina, 665 F.2d 1335 (4th Cir.1981) (no search where officer used a step ladder to peer into the interior of a plane; the defendant made no attempt to cover the windows, and therefore did not sufficiently manifest a subjective interest in privacy).

In some cases, failure to manifest an expectation of privacy may also amount to disclaiming property interests. Many cases hold, for example, that abandonment of property is inconsistent with the retention of any subjective privacy or possessory interests, so police detention and investigation of abandoned property does not trigger Fourth Amendment protection under either the physical intrusion or *Katz* tests. Abandonment need not be explicit. "Whether abandonment has occurred is a question of intent that may be inferred from acts, words, and other objective facts." United States v. Cofield, 272 F.3d 1303 (11th Cir. 2001). Thus, in United States v. Hoey, 983 F.2d 890 (8th Cir.1993), police entered an apartment where Hoey had lived and discovered evidence later used against her at trial. The court held that the government activity did not constitute a search because the defendant had abandoned the apartment: at the time the police entered, the defendant was six weeks behind on her rent; she had held a moving sale; and she was seen leaving the apartment two days before the police entry and had not returned. See also United States v.

Nowak, 825 F.3d 946 (8th Cir. 2016) (defendant fled from police, abandoning his backpack in the process); United States v. Thomas, 451 F.3d 543 (8th Cir. 2006) (defendant abandoned the mail in his rented post office box; nobody had claimed the mail, or paid the rent on the mailbox, for a year; therefore a police officer's seizure and search of the mail in the box did not implicate the Fourth Amendment).

In contrast, in Smith v. Ohio, 494 U.S. 541 (1990), a defendant carrying a brown paper bag was approached by two plainclothes officers. When the officers identified themselves, the defendant threw the bag on the hood of his car. The officers asked what was in the bag and the defendant tried to grab it. One officer pushed the defendant's hand away and opened the bag. The Court declared that "a citizen who attempts to protect his private property from inspection after throwing it on a car to respond to a police officer's inquiry clearly has not abandoned that property."

Abandonment is often found when a person denies ownership of a container in the face of police inquiries. See, e.g., United States v. McDonald, 100 F.3d 1320 (7th Cir.1996) (police officers discovered contraband in a bag placed in the overhead bin of the passenger compartment of a bus; when the police asked the owner of the bag to claim it, McDonald did not come forward); United States v. Sanders, 196 F.3d 910 (8th Cir. 1999) ("statements to the officers that he did not own the bag were sufficient to constitute abandonment").

Often the issue of abandonment is considered as a question of whether the defendant has "standing" to assert a Fourth Amendment issue. See, e.g., United States v. Garzon, 119 F.3d 1446 (10th Cir. 1997) ("Abandonment is akin to the issue of standing because a defendant lacks standing to complain of an illegal search or seizure of property which has been abandoned.") The concept of "standing" under the Fourth Amendment is discussed in the materials on the exclusionary rule, *infra.*

2. Open Fields

Prior to *Katz,* the Court had established an "open fields" rule. In Hester v. United States, 265 U.S. 57 (1924), the Court distinguished open fields from constitutionally protected areas like houses, and held that a police entry into open fields was not regulated by the Fourth Amendment. In Oliver v. United States, 466 U.S. 170 (1984), the Court held that the "open fields" doctrine was still valid after *Katz* because a person does not have a legitimate expectation of privacy in an open field. The Court reaffirmed its commitment to the open fields doctrine in United States v. Jones, 565 U.S. 400, 410–11 (2012).

As the *Oliver* Court acknowledged, the term "open fields" is somewhat misleading in that "[a]n open field need be neither 'open' nor a 'field' as those terms are used in common speech." In *Oliver*, officers ignored a locked gate with a "No Trespassing" sign and walked several hundred yards onto fenced farmland before discovering a field of marijuana about a mile from Oliver's house. Despite this obvious trespass, the Court held that the officers had not intruded into Oliver's "house," inclusive of its curtilage and messuage. The distinction between the home and adjacent land is material, the Court concluded, because "[o]pen fields do not provide the setting for those intimate activities that the Amendment is intended to shelter from government interference or surveillance. There is no societal interest in protecting the privacy of those activities, such as the cultivation of crops, that occur in open fields."

The majority in *Oliver* rejected "the suggestion that steps taken to protect privacy establish that expectations of privacy in an open field are legitimate." Although it recognized that Oliver "planted the marijuana upon secluded land and erected fences and no trespassing signs around the property," the Court found that these efforts did not establish a constitutional expectation of privacy. Oliver manifested a *subjective* expectation of privacy by his efforts to cordon off his property; but it was not an expectation that society was prepared to accept as *reasonable*.

Justice Marshall, joined by Justices Brennan and Stevens, dissented in *Oliver*. He challenged the majority's reasoning that open fields are not protected by the language of the Fourth Amendment, observing that telephone booths and commercial establishments do not fit the language of the Amendment any more than open fields do, yet Supreme Court decisions have found them to be protected by the Fourth Amendment. He also noted that many private activities occur on property outside the curtilage of a home—including romantic activities, nature walks, and secret meetings.

QUESTIONS ABOUT OLIVER AND THE OPEN FIELDS DOCTRINE

Is it now the case that no one—scientist, naturalist, lover, or simply a private person who prefers outdoors to indoors—can rely on the Fourth Amendment to protect against police surveillance of land areas not immediately adjacent to a house? May the police trespass wherever they like so long as they do not invade the curtilage of a home? See United States v. Van Damme, 48 F.3d 461 (9th Cir.1995) (no search where police officer trespassed on the defendant's land in the middle of the night, walked through the defendant's forest, and climbed over his wire fence to conduct surveillance).

Suppose police officers jump over a property owner's fence and are traipsing through the owner's field when they come upon a barrel with a lid. If they pry open the lid and look into the barrel, is that a search? May officers in an "open field" lift up a tarpaulin to see what is beneath it? Does it make a difference if the tarpaulin is tied to the ground with stakes? If you would not be willing to let officers open barrels or lift up covers on objects, are you more willing to permit them to roam about and look at uncovered objects? Might the reason objects are uncovered be that landowners rely on their fences to keep out intruders?[5]

Defining "Curtilage": United States v. Dunn

"Open fields" are defined in the negative as areas located outside the curtilage of the home. But how far does the "curtilage" extend? The Court provides its best answer in United States v. Dunn, 480 U.S. 294 (1987), where it had to determine whether a barn on the defendant's ranch was within the curtilage of his home. The ranch was completely encircled by a perimeter fence and contained several interior barbed wire fences, including one around the house approximately 50 yards from the barn, and a wooden fence enclosing the front of the barn, which had an open overhang and locked, waist-high gates. Without a warrant, officers crossed the perimeter fence, several of the barbed wire fences, and the wooden fence in front of the barn. They did not enter the barn but stopped at the locked gate and shined a flashlight inside. From that position, they observed what looked like a drug laboratory.

Justice White's opinion for the Court declared that curtilage questions should be resolved with reference to four factors:

- the proximity of the area claimed to be curtilage to the home;
- whether the area is included within an enclosure surrounding the home;
- the nature of the uses to which the area is put; and
- "the steps taken by the resident to protect the area from observation by people passing by."

Justice White rejected the government's "invitation to adopt a 'bright-line' rule that the curtilage should extend no farther than the nearest fence surrounding a fenced house." He instead applied the four factors and found that the barn was outside the curtilage because it was 60 yards from the house itself, not within the area enclosed by the house fence, there was no objective indication that the barn was used for intimate activities associated with the home, and there was no protection from observation by those standing in open fields. The Court accepted arguendo, but did not decide, Dunn's contention that an *entry* into the barn would have been impermissible even though the barn itself was in an open field.

Justice Scalia concurred in the opinion, except for the portion that focused on whether law enforcement officials possessed objective data indicating that the barn was not being used for intimate activities of the

[5] The Supreme Court's open field cases are criticized in Saltzburg, Another Victim of Illegal Narcotics: The Fourth Amendment (As Illustrated By the Open Fields Doctrine) 48 U.Pitt.L.Rev. 1 (1986). See also Wilkins, Defining the "Reasonable Expectation of Privacy": An Emerging Tripartite Analysis, 40 Vand.L.Rev. 1077 (1987).

home. In his view, the significant point was that the barn was not being so used, not what law enforcement officers knew. Justice Brennan, joined by Justice Marshall, dissented.[6]

Even if property is within the curtilage, a visual inspection of that property from an open field or public space does not constitute a search. See United States v. Hatfield, 333 F.3d 1189 (10th Cir. 2003) ("[W]e hold that police observation of a defendant's curtilage from a vantage point in the defendant's open field is not a search under the Fourth Amendment. Even though we can conclude that Hatfield had a subjective expectation of privacy in the space immediately behind his house, this is not an expectation of privacy that society regards as reasonable, at least with respect to visual observations made from an adjoining open field.").

Implied Permission to Enter Curtilage

Oliver suggests that any physical intrusion into the curtilage of a home should be considered a "search" for purposes of the Fourth Amendment under either a physical intrusion or a reasonable expectation of privacy analysis. Does this mean that law enforcement officers must get a warrant before approaching a home to knock on the front door for the purpose of gathering information about a potential crime? The Court answers that question in the following case and, in so doing, introduces an important modification of the physical intrusion test from *Olmstead* and *Jones*.

FLORIDA V. JARDINES

Supreme Court of the United States, 2013.
569 U.S. 1.

JUSTICE SCALIA delivered the opinion of the Court.

We consider whether using a drug-sniffing dog on a homeowner's porch to investigate the contents of the home is a "search" within the meaning of the Fourth Amendment.[7]

---

[6] For lower court cases applying the *Dunn* factors, see Daughenbaugh v. City of Tiffin, 150 F.3d 594 (6th Cir.1998) (unattached garage was within curtilage of the house, where it was 50 yards away from the house, within natural boundaries of a river and trees that circled the property, set far back from the road, and the officers had no indication that the defendant was using the garage for any illegal activity); United States v. Traynor, 990 F.2d 1153 (9th Cir.1993) (workshop not within curtilage, where it was 70 feet from the house, and shop and house were not enclosed within a single fenced-in area); United States v. McKeever, 5 F.3d 863 (5th Cir.1993) (area not within curtilage where it was 50 feet from home and not within an immediate fenced-in area).

[7] [Editors' Note: As will be seen later in this section, the Court has held that a dog sniff to detect the presence of drugs does not, by itself, constitute a search but may trigger the Fourth Amendment if the dog physically intrudes into a constitutionally protected area for the purpose of gathering information absent permission, expressed or implied.]

* * *

In 2006, Detective William Pedraja of the Miami-Dade Police Department received an unverified tip that marijuana was being grown in the home of respondent Joelis Jardines. One month later, the Department and the Drug Enforcement Administration sent a joint surveillance team to Jardines' home. Detective Pedraja was part of that team. He watched the home for fifteen minutes and saw no vehicles in the driveway or activity around the home, and could not see inside because the blinds were drawn. Detective Pedraja then approached Jardines' home accompanied by Detective Douglas Bartelt, a trained canine handler who had just arrived at the scene with his drug-sniffing dog. The dog was trained to detect the scent of marijuana, cocaine, heroin, and several other drugs, indicating the presence of any of these substances through particular behavioral changes recognizable by his handler.

* * * As the dog approached Jardines' front porch, he apparently sensed one of the odors he had been trained to detect, and began energetically exploring the area for the strongest point source of that odor. * * * After sniffing the base of the front door, the dog sat, which is the trained behavior upon discovering the odor's strongest point. Detective Bartelt then pulled the dog away from the door and returned to his vehicle. He left the scene after informing Detective Pedraja that there had been a positive alert for narcotics.

On the basis of what he had learned at the home, Detective Pedraja applied for and received a warrant to search the residence. When the warrant was executed later that day, Jardines attempted to flee and was arrested; the search revealed marijuana plants, and he was charged with trafficking in cannabis.

[The question for the Court was whether the dog sniff on the porch of the house constituted a search within the meaning of the Fourth Amendment.]

* * *

The Fourth Amendment * * * establishes a simple baseline, one that for much of our history formed the exclusive basis for its protections: When "the Government obtains information by physically intruding" on persons, houses, papers, or effects, "a 'search' within the original meaning of the Fourth Amendment" has "undoubtedly occurred." United States v. Jones. By reason of our decision in Katz v. United States, property rights are not the sole measure of Fourth Amendment violations—but though *Katz* may add to the baseline, it does not subtract anything from the Amendment's protections when the Government does engage in a physical intrusion of a constitutionally protected area.

That principle renders this case a straightforward one. The officers were gathering information in an area belonging to Jardines and immediately surrounding his house—in the curtilage of the house, which we have held enjoys protection as part of the home itself. And they gathered that information by physically entering and occupying the area to engage in conduct not explicitly or implicitly permitted by the homeowner.

* * * The Fourth Amendment indicates with some precision the places and things encompassed by its protections: persons, houses, papers, and effects. The Fourth Amendment does not, therefore, prevent all investigations conducted on private property; for example, an officer may (subject to *Katz*) gather information in what we have called "open fields"—even if those fields are privately owned—because such fields are not enumerated in the Amendment's text. Hester v. United States, 265 U.S. 57 (1924).

But when it comes to the Fourth Amendment, the home is first among equals. At the Amendment's "very core" stands "the right of a man to retreat into his own home and there be free from unreasonable governmental intrusion." This right would be of little practical value if the State's agents could stand in a home's porch or side garden and trawl for evidence with impunity; the right to retreat would be significantly diminished if the police could enter a man's property to observe his repose from just outside the front window.

We therefore regard the area immediately surrounding and associated with the home—what our cases call the curtilage—as part of the home itself for Fourth Amendment purposes. That principle has ancient and durable roots. * * *

While the boundaries of the curtilage are generally clearly marked, the conception defining the curtilage is at any rate familiar enough that it is easily understood from our daily experience. Here there is no doubt that the officers entered it: The front porch is the classic exemplar of an area adjacent to the home and to which the activity of home life extends.

* * * Since the officers' investigation took place in a constitutionally protected area, we turn to the question of whether it was accomplished through an unlicensed physical intrusion. * * *

"A license may be implied from the habits of the country," notwithstanding the "strict rule of the English common law as to entry upon a close." We have accordingly recognized that "the knocker on the front door is treated as an invitation or license to attempt an entry, justifying ingress to the home by solicitors, hawkers and peddlers of all kinds." This implicit license typically permits the visitor to approach the home by the front path, knock promptly, wait briefly to be received, and then (absent invitation to linger longer) leave. Complying with the terms of that traditional invitation does not require fine-grained legal knowledge;

it is generally managed without incident by the Nation's Girl Scouts and trick-or-treaters. Thus, a police officer not armed with a warrant may approach a home and knock, precisely because that is no more than any private citizen might do.

But introducing a trained police dog to explore the area around the home in hopes of discovering incriminating evidence is something else. There is no customary invitation to do that. An invitation to engage in canine forensic investigation assuredly does not inhere in the very act of hanging a knocker. To find a visitor knocking on the door is routine (even if sometimes unwelcome); to spot that same visitor exploring the front path with a metal detector, or marching his bloodhound into the garden before saying hello and asking permission, would inspire most of us to—well, call the police. * * * Here, the background social norms that invite a visitor to the front door do not invite him there to conduct a search.

The State points to our decisions holding that the subjective intent of the officer is irrelevant. But those cases merely hold that a stop or search that is objectively reasonable is not vitiated by the fact that the officer's real reason for making the stop or search has nothing to do with the validating reason. Thus, the defendant will not be heard to complain that although he was speeding the officer's real reason for the stop was racial harassment. Here, however, the question before the court is precisely whether the officer's conduct was an objectively reasonable search. * * * Here, their behavior objectively reveals a purpose to conduct a search, which is not what anyone would think he had license to do.

* * * [W]e need not decide whether the officers' investigation of Jardines' home violated his expectation of privacy under *Katz*. One virtue of the Fourth Amendment's property-rights baseline is that it keeps easy cases easy. That the officers learned what they learned only by physically intruding on Jardines' property to gather evidence is enough to establish that a search occurred.

* * *

JUSTICE KAGAN, with whom JUSTICE GINSBURG and JUSTICE SOTOMAYOR join, concurring.

* * *

The Court today treats this case under a property rubric; I write separately to note that I could just as happily have decided it by looking to Jardines' privacy interests. A decision along those lines would have looked . . . well, much like this one. It would have talked about "the right of a man to retreat into his own home and there be free from unreasonable governmental intrusion." * * * It would have explained that "privacy expectations are most heightened" in the home and the surrounding area.

And it would have determined that police officers invade those shared expectations when they use trained canine assistants to reveal within the confines of a home what they could not otherwise have found there.

JUSTICE ALITO, with whom THE CHIEF JUSTICE, JUSTICE Kennedy, and JUSTICE BREYER join, dissenting.

The Court's decision in this important Fourth Amendment case is based on a putative rule of trespass law that is nowhere to be found in the annals of Anglo-American jurisprudence.

The law of trespass generally gives members of the public a license to use a walkway to approach the front door of a house and to remain there for a brief time. This license is not limited to persons who intend to speak to an occupant or who actually do so. (Mail carriers and persons delivering packages and flyers are examples of individuals who may lawfully approach a front door without intending to converse.) Nor is the license restricted to categories of visitors whom an occupant of the dwelling is likely to welcome; as the Court acknowledges, this license applies even to "solicitors, hawkers and peddlers of all kinds." And the license even extends to police officers who wish to gather evidence against an occupant (by asking potentially incriminating questions).

According to the Court, however, the police officer in this case * * * committed a trespass because he was accompanied during his otherwise lawful visit to the front door of respondent's house by his dog, Franky. Where is the authority evidencing such a rule? Dogs have been domesticated for about 12,000 years; they were ubiquitous in both this country and Britain at the time of the adoption of the Fourth Amendment; and their acute sense of smell has been used in law enforcement for centuries. Yet the Court has been unable to find a single case—from the United States or any other common-law nation—that supports the rule on which its decision is based. * * *

The Court's decision is also inconsistent with the reasonable-expectations-of-privacy test that the Court adopted in Katz v. United States. A reasonable person understands that odors emanating from a house may be detected from locations that are open to the public, and a reasonable person will not count on the strength of those odors remaining within the range that, while detectible by a dog, cannot be smelled by a human.

* * *

QUESTIONS ABOUT JARDINES

In contrast with his majority opinion in *Jones*, Justice Scalia studiously avoids using the word "trespass" in his opinion for the Court in

Jardines. He instead situates the Fourth Amendment "baseline" where "the Government obtains information by physically intruding on persons, houses, papers, or effects." But not always. Physical intrusion into a constitutionally protected area for purposes of gathering information does not require a warrant if it is pursuant to permission, either expressed or implied. In order to determine whether an implied permission to enter was granted, the Court looks to "the habits of the country." Although Justice Scalia denies that determining the extent of an implied license to enter requires "fine-grained legal knowledge," does he nevertheless link the Fourth Amendment to the law of trespass? Alternatively, does his reliance on cultural norms incorporate the same reasonable expectations that govern under *Katz*? If so, then is anything gained by adopting Justice Scalia's approach over Justice Kagan's?

What is the significance of implied permission to enter? If an officer conforms her behavior to the social expectations Justice Scalia describes, does that mean no search occurred, or does it mean that the search was reasonable? Does the answer change depending on which test is used, physical intrusion or reasonable expectation of privacy? Consider the "knock and talk"—in which an officer knocks on a person's door and asks to talk to them. This surely marks a physical intrusion for purposes of gathering information, but does it fall within the implied license of entry recognized in *Jardines*? The consensus among courts is that it does. See United States v. Perez-Diaz, 848 F.3d 33 (1st Cir. 2017) ("A police officer may approach and knock on a citizen's door, and request the opportunity to speak to the citizen, in what is known as a knock-and-talk."). Any observations officers make while engaged in an otherwise reasonable knock and talk are unlikely to raise any additional Fourth Amendment concerns. See United States v. Shuck, 713 F.3d 563 (10th Cir. 2013) (no Fourth Amendment violation where officers engaged in a knock and talk detected a marijuana smell emanating from a PVC pipe adjacent to an entry door to defendant's home while using "the normal route of access which would be used by anyone visiting this trailer").

Can property owners prevent officers from approaching their houses, even for a knock-and-talk, by posting no trespassing signs? This was a question addressed by then-Judge Gorsuch in United States v. Carloss, 818 F.3d 988 (10th Cir. 2016). Carloss posted a number of signs around his property stating "Private Property No Trespassing" while one sign, posted on the front door, stated more explicitly "Posted Private Property Hunting, Fishing, Trapping or Trespassing for Any Purpose Is Strictly Forbidden Violators Will Be Prosecuted." Judge Gorsuch found that these signs did not change the equation:

> As an initial matter, just the presence of a "No Trespassing" sign is not alone sufficient to convey to an objective officer, or member of the public, that he cannot go to the front door and knock. Such signs, by themselves, do not have the talismanic quality that Carloss attributes

> to them. * * * Carloss has not cited, nor can we find, any post-*Jardines* authority holding that a resident can invoke the implied license to approach his home and knock on the front door simply by posting a "No Trespassing" sign.

As to the more detailed sign on Carloss's front door, Judge Gorsuch noted that it referenced "activities that ordinarily do not take place in a home or its curtilage—hunting, fishing and trapping. Thus, on its face, this sign does not appear to be directed to people who desire to approach and speak directly with the occupants of the home in the ordinary course of socially accepted discourse."

It appears that Carloss, for all his efforts, was underinclusive in his asserted prohibition. He should have posted a sign that said "Do Not Knock On This Door For Any Purpose: I Revoke The Implied License To Do So." Would that have worked? *See* Andrew Ferguson & Stephen Henderson, *LAWn Signs: A Fourth Amendment for Constitutional Curmudgeons*, 13 Ohio St. J. Crim. L. (2016).

3. Information Voluntarily Shared with Third Parties

a. Consensual Electronic Surveillance: Misplaced Trust

Recall that in *On Lee*, *Lopez*, and *Hoffa*, the Court held that the use of confidential informants to report on their conversations does not implicate the Fourth Amendment even if the informant wears a recording or eavesdropping device. Those cases were decided before *Katz* under the physical intrusion test. Would the result in those cases have been different under a reasonable expectation of privacy analysis? The Court provided its answer in United States v. White, 401 U.S. 745 (1971), where a government informer carrying a radio transmitter engaged the defendant in conversations overheard by an agent listening-in through the receiver. Justice White's opinion for himself, Chief Justice Burger, Justice Stewart and Justice Blackmun concluded that *Katz* did not "disturb the result reached in the *On Lee*." The plurality stated that "the law permits the frustration of actual expectations of privacy by permitting authorities to use the testimony of those associates who for one reason or another have determined to turn to the police" and that "one contemplating illegal activities must realize and risk that his companions may be reporting to the police."

Justice Black concurred in the judgment on the grounds that there was no "search" under *Olmstead* and aural communications are not among the tangible things protected by the Fourth Amendment, which was also his position in *Katz*. Justice Douglas dissented, questioning whether a citizen must "live in fear that every word he speaks may be transmitted or recorded and later repeated to the entire world." Justice Harlan in dissent argued that the assumption of risk approach was not an adequate guide to controlling new threats to privacy. He did not think the Court "should impose on our citizens the risks of the electronic listener or observer without at least the protection of a warrant requirement" because doing so would "undermine that confidence and sense of security in dealing with another that is characteristic of individual relationships between citizens in a free society."[8] Justice Brennan concurred in the result because he thought *Katz* should not have retroactive effect, but indicated that a warrant is required when an informant secretly records a conversation with a suspect. Justice Marshall also dissented. The end result was that four Justices found no reasonable expectation of privacy, and four Justices disagreed. Justice Black stood alone in his view.

Courts have applied the *White* analysis to video surveillance as well. In United States v. Gonzalez, 328 F.3d 543 (9th Cir. 2003), Gonzalez and an associate arranged to receive a shipment of drugs in a package addressed to a hospital where one of them worked in the mailroom. Officers were tipped off to the shipment and obtained the consent of the hospital to install a hidden video camera in the mailroom. The video showed that when the package arrived, Gonzalez clapped his hands and acted "in a manner usually reserved for post-touchdown endzone celebrations." Gonzalez argued that the suspicious conduct on the video could not be used at trial because the video surveillance was an illegal search. But the court held that he had no reasonable expectation of privacy against visual surveillance because the mailroom was a large, "quasi-public" space at a public hospital that was accessed frequently by hospital employees and had large windows through which the room was visible.

b. Financial Records

In United States v. Miller, 425 U.S. 435 (1976), Justice Powell's opinion for the Court held that the Fourth Amendment was not implicated by a subpoena issued to a bank to obtain a depositor's records compiled by the bank. Over dissents by Justices Brennan and Marshall, the Court found that, because the depositor made the records accessible to the bank, there was no reasonable expectation that the government would not access these records through lawful means, such as a subpoena. See also California Bankers Assn. v. Shultz, 416 U.S. 21 (1974) (upholding bank record keeping and reporting law designed to combat money laundering). Although the Court did not base its holding on the physical intrusion test,

[8] Some state courts have sided with the dissenters. See, e.g., People v. Beavers, 393 Mich. 554, 227 N.W.2d 511 (1975); State v. Glass, 583 P.2d 872 (Alaska 1978). So, too, have some academics. *See, e.g.*, Maclin, Informants and the Fourth Amendment: a Reconsideration, 74 Wash.Univ.L.Q. 573 (1996) ("A home or private conversation should not lose its constitutional protection against promiscuous police intrusion merely because an individual has allowed a third party's presence. When it comes to Fourth Amendment rights, the difference between the police and everyone else matters.").

it is notable that the records in question where property of the bank, and were not Miller's "papers" or "effects."

c. *Pen Registers*

In Smith v. Maryland, 442 U.S. 735 (1979), police installed a pen register device in the phone company offices. This device recorded the numbers called by the defendant from his home telephone. This conduct clearly did not constitute a "search" under the physical intrusion test for the same reasons the tapping of a phone was not a search in *Olmstead*. But is the same true under *Katz*?

Justice Blackmun, writing for six members of the Court in *Smith*, held that the use of the pen register did not constitute a search because "a person has no legitimate expectation of privacy in information he voluntarily turns over to third parties" and that "when he used his phone, petitioner voluntarily conveyed numerical information to the telephone company." Justice Stewart, joined by Justice Brennan, dissented, arguing that because private telephone conversations were protected by *Katz,* the numbers dialed from a private telephone were also protected. Justice Marshall's dissent asserted that "privacy is not a discrete commodity, possessed absolutely or not at all" and those who disclose information for "a limited business purpose need not assume that this information will be released to other persons for other purposes."

After the Court's decision in *Smith,* Congress imposed statutory limitations on pen registers as part of the Electronic Communications Privacy Act of 1986, 18 U.S.C. § 3121 et seq. That statute prohibits the use of pen registers unless 1) the "provider" gives consent, or 2) a court order is obtained. A court is authorized to issue a pen register order based on a certified statement from a government official that the pen register is likely to uncover information relevant to an ongoing criminal investigation. Note that the government does not need to show probable cause, as it would have to do were the use of a pen register a search. Note also that the violation of the statutory requirement does not give rise to the exclusion of any evidence obtained. See United States v. German, 486 F.3d 849 (5th Cir. 2007) (pen register information obtained without court order was properly admitted because there was no search under *Katz* and Congress did not provide for exclusion as a remedy for violations of the pen register statute).

4. Government Investigative Activity Subsequent to Private and Other Legal Searches

Limits Imposed by the Initial Search: Walter v. United States

Difficult questions can arise when government agents follow up on a private search. Walter v. United States, 447 U.S. 649 (1980), divided the

Court on the question whether FBI agents, who received a package of films from a recipient to whom it was misdelivered by a private carrier, could view the films without a warrant. The recipient had opened the package but had not viewed the films. Justice Stevens's opinion, joined by Justice Stewart, concluded that "the unauthorized exhibition of the films constituted an unreasonable invasion of their owner's constitutionally protected interest in privacy," and that "an officer's authority to possess a package is distinct from his authority to examine its contents." So although the agents could receive the films, they could not view them without a warrant, even though a private person not covered by the Fourth Amendment had opened the package. These Justices reasoned that "[a] partial invasion of privacy cannot automatically justify a total invasion." Justice White, joined by Justice Brennan, concurred in part and disagreed with a footnote of Justice Stevens that left open the question "whether the Government projection of the films would have infringed any Fourth Amendment interest if private parties had projected the films before turning them over to the Government." Justice White agreed that a search by private persons could provide probable cause for a warrant, but said it could not excuse the government from the warrant requirement for its own search. Apparently, both opinions agreed that what the FBI observed in plain view was properly observed. Justice Marshall concurred in the judgment without opinion. Justice Blackmun's dissent, joined by Chief Justice Burger and Justices Powell and Rehnquist, argued "that, by the time the FBI received the films, these petitioners had no remaining expectation of privacy in their contents."

Reopening Permitted: United States v. Jacobsen

The extent to which government agents may search or seize evidence following searches by private individuals again divided the Court in United States v. Jacobsen, 466 U.S. 109 (1984). A Federal Express supervisor asked an office manager to examine a package that had been torn by a fork lift. Inside a cardboard outer container, the supervisor and manager found a ten-inch long tube wrapped with silver duct tape. They cut open the tube and found a number of zip-lock bags containing white powder. They then put the bags back into the tube and closed but did not reseal the tube. They notified the Drug Enforcement Administration of their finding. An agent arrived at the office, reopened the tube, opened the zip-lock bags, removed a trace of the powder from each, did a "field test," and discovered that the powder was cocaine.

The Court sustained the agent's actions. Justice Stevens's opinion commanded six votes. Noting that the Fourth Amendment is "wholly inapplicable to a search or seizure, even an unreasonable one, effected by a private individual not acting as an agent of the Government or with the participation or knowledge of any governmental official," and that "t[ ]he initial invasions of respondents' package were occasioned by private action," Justice Stevens concluded that "[w]hether those invasions were accidental or deliberate, and whether they were reasonable or unreasonable, they did not violate the Fourth Amendment because of their private character."

Fair enough. But what about the DEA agents' actions? Citing *Walter*, Justice Stevens determined that the salient Fourth Amendment question was whether and to what extent the agents' actions represented "additional invasions of respondents' privacy" by exceeding the scope of the private search. Citing *Miller*, the bank records case, Justice Stevens reasoned that Jacobsen's expectations of privacy had already "been frustrated" by the private search. He therefore did not have any reasonable expectation of privacy in information already revealed by the private search. Thus, there was no search insofar as the agents' actions did not result in any additional invasion of privacy.

Applying these principles, Justice Stevens concluded that the agents' reopening the package and "manual inspection of the tube and its contents" was not a search because it revealed "nothing that had not previously been learned during the private search." Justice Stevens allowed that the testing of the cocaine entailed a seizure, but that this intrusion was reasonable given the de minimus nature of possessory interests in the small samples used and the significant law enforcement interests at stake in determining the nature of a substance likely to be contraband.[9]

Justice White concurred in part and in the judgment, though he was very critical of the majority's analysis. He argued that the effect of the Court's decision was to permit police to break into a locked car, suitcase, or even a house, if a private person previously did so and reported what he found to the police. Justice White concluded that a warrant should be required in these cases. Justice Brennan, joined by Justice Marshall, dissented and agreed with Justice White's criticism of the majority opinion.

Do Justice White's concerns about officers breaking into locked cars and houses simply because a member of the public previously did so have more salience in light of the Court's decision in *Jones* revitalizing the physical intrusion test? No matter the prior conduct of private persons, didn't the agents in *Jacobsen* physically intrude into a constitutionally protected "effect" for the purpose of gathering information? Consider the majority's concession that "When the wrapped parcel involved in this case was delivered to the private freight carrier, it was unquestionably an 'effect' within the meaning of the Fourth Amendment" because "[l]etters and other sealed packages are in the general class of effects in which the

[9] Applying United States v. Place, 462 U.S. 696 (1983), which is discussed infra, Justice Stevens held that the use of the field test to determine whether the powder was cocaine did not constitute a "search" for purposes of the Fourth Amendment because it could only reveal illegal activity.

public at large has a legitimate expectation of privacy [and] warrantless searches of such effects are presumptively unreasonable."

Controlled Deliveries: Illinois v. Andreas

Jacobsen establishes that if an initial intrusion (at least into a container) is not covered by the Fourth Amendment, a later intrusion by police officers to the same extent is also free from Fourth Amendment constraints. While *Jacobsen* dealt with an initial search to which the Fourth Amendment did not apply, its principle has been held equally applicable when initial searches of containers are valid under the Fourth Amendment.

For example, in Illinois v. Andreas, 463 U.S. 765 (1983), government agents conducted a legal customs search of a wooden crate that was being shipped to an address in the United States, and found drugs hidden in a table therein. They then resealed the crate, and followed it to its destination using a surveillance process called a "controlled delivery." Surveilling police ultimately saw Andreas drag the container into his apartment; when he re-emerged with it 30 to 45 minutes later, the agents searched the container without a warrant. Chief Justice Burger, writing for the Court, reasoned that "the simple act of resealing the container to enable the police to make a controlled delivery does not operate to revive or restore the lawfully invaded privacy rights." Thus, the reopening of the container was not a search, because no legitimate expectation of privacy existed in the container at that time. Although the *Andreas* Court did not apply the physical intrusion test, it seems likely that, on the facts, the crate was in the constructive possession of government agents at all times after it was lawfully customs search revealed the presence of contraband.

What if Andreas came out with the crate two days later? If a customs official legally searches a suitcase, can government agents search the same suitcase without a warrant a year later? In *Andreas,* Chief Justice Burger recognized that there may be a gap in surveillance, during which "it is possible that the container will be put to other uses—for example, the contraband may be removed or other items may be placed inside." He concluded, however, that the Fourth Amendment would be applicable to a subsequent reopening only if there is "a substantial likelihood that the contents of the container have been changed during the gap in surveillance." Otherwise, "there is no legitimate expectation of privacy in the contents of a container previously opened under lawful authority." On the facts, the Court found that the re-opening did not implicate a revived privacy interest, due to the unusual size of the container, its specialized purpose, and the relatively short time that Andreas had the container in his apartment.

5. Exposure to Public View—the Public Observation Doctrine

Under both *Olmstead* and *Katz*, observing acts from a lawful public vantage is not a "search." There is no physical intrusion into a constitutionally protected area and there is no reason to expect that activities exposed to public view are private. But sometimes the question arises whether an area is truly "public" or conduct is actually exposed to public view. For example, is it a search if a police officer peers into a closed public bathroom stall? In United States v. White, 890 F.2d 1012 (8th Cir.1989), an officer surreptitiously observed the defendant in a bathroom stall by looking through the gap between the bathroom stall door and the wall of the stall. In this manner the officer saw the defendant engaged in criminal activity. The court held that the officer's conduct did not constitute a search. It stated that while the defendant "could reasonably expect a significant amount of privacy in the bathroom stall," that expectation was not violated "because the design of the stall allowed the officer to make her observations without placing herself in any position that would be unexpected by an occupant of the stall."

a. Tracking Public Movements: Radio Beepers

The Court first discussed the use of electronic beepers to track a person's public movements in United States v. Knotts, 460 U.S. 276 (1983). Investigators suspected that a purchaser of chemicals, Armstrong, might be using them to manufacture drugs, so they obtained the consent of the company selling the chemicals to install a radio beeper tracking device inside a 5 gallon container of chloroform before Armstrong picked it up. Armstrong placed the container in his car. The officers monitored the beeper signal and followed Armstrong to Petschen's house where the container was transferred to his car. Ultimately the signal became stationary at a location identified as a cabin belonging to Knotts. Along the way, "officers lost the signal from the beeper, but with the assistance of a monitoring device located in a helicopter the approximate location of the signal was picked up again." Knotts did not (and could not, for lack of standing) challenge the warrantless installation of the beeper in the container because it was not his "effect" when the beeper was installed. Justice Rehnquist's opinion for six Justices therefore focused on whether the officers had invaded any legitimate expectation of privacy held by Knotts when they tracked the container's movement using the beeper. The opinion reasoned as follows:

> Visual surveillance from public places along Petschen's route or adjoining Knotts' premises would have sufficed to reveal all of these facts to the police. The fact that the officers in this case relied not only on visual surveillance, but on the use of the beeper to signal the presence of Petschen's automobile to the police receiver, does not alter the situation. Nothing in the Fourth Amendment prohibited the police

from augmenting the sensory faculties bestowed upon them at birth with such enhancement as science and technology afforded them in this case.

Knotts argued that if tracking by beeper was not even a search, it would mean that unlimited surveillance of any citizen would be possible without judicial supervision. But the Court responded that "if such dragnet type law enforcement practices * * * should eventually occur, there will be time enough then to determine whether different constitutional principles may be applicable." It noted too that nothing in the record indicated that the beeper signal was used to monitor any activity in the cabin.

In United States v. Karo, 468 U.S. 705 (1984), officers tracked the movement of a beeper attached to a can of ether. Agents saw Karo pick up the ether from a government informant and followed him to his house. They used the beeper to determine that the ether was still in the house, and subsequently used it to determine that the ether had been moved to Horton's house. A third use of the beeper helped agents discover that the ether had been moved to Horton's father's house, and a fourth use revealed it had been taken to a commercial storage facility. Agents could smell the ether in a row of lockers at that facility and used the beeper a fifth time to discover its exact location. A sixth use led agents to another storage facility where they detected the smell of ether from a locker. They obtained consent to install a closed-circuit camera in the facility and observed a man and woman load the ether into Horton's pick-up truck. While undertaking to follow the truck to another house, the agents used the beeper a seventh time. The eighth use assured the agents that the ether remained in the house when the truck left. Finally, agents obtained a search warrant for the house. They found cocaine and laboratory equipment and made arrests.

Justice White wrote for the Court. He concluded first that no authorization was necessary to place a beeper in the can of ether.

> It is clear that the actual placement of the beeper into the can violated no one's Fourth Amendment rights. The can into which the beeper was placed belonged at the time to the DEA, and by no stretch of the imagination could it be said that respondents then had any legitimate expectation of privacy in it.

Justice White next concluded that the Fourth Amendment was not implicated by the fact that Karo received a can that contained an electronic tracking device.

> The mere transfer to Karo of a can containing an unmonitored beeper infringed no privacy interest. It conveyed no information that Karo wished to keep private, for it conveyed no information at all. To be sure, it created a *potential* for an invasion of privacy, but we have never held that potential, as opposed to actual, invasions of privacy constitute searches for purposes of the Fourth Amendment. A holding

> to that effect would mean that a policeman walking down the street carrying a parabolic microphone capable of picking up conversations in nearby homes would be engaging in a search even if the microphone were not turned on. It is the exploitation of technological advances that implicates the Fourth Amendment, not their mere existence.
>
> We likewise do not believe that the transfer of the container constituted a seizure. A "seizure" of property occurs when "there is some meaningful interference with an individual's possessory interests in that property." Although the can may have contained an unknown and unwanted foreign object, it cannot be said that anyone's possessory interest was interfered with in a meaningful way. * * *

Justice White reached a different conclusion as to the monitoring of the beeper when it was "in a private residence, a location not open to visual surveillance."

> The monitoring of an electronic device such as a beeper is, of course, less intrusive than a full-scale search, but it does reveal a critical fact about the interior of the premises that the Government is extremely interested in knowing and that it could not have otherwise obtained without a warrant. The case is thus not like *Knotts*, for there the beeper told the authorities nothing about the interior of Knotts' cabin.

Although the Court condemned warrantless monitoring of a beeper inside a private house, it nonetheless sustained the search warrant agents obtained at the end of their surveillance. The knowledge that the agents obtained without using the beeper, together with their proper use of the beeper in monitoring travel outside the house, provided sufficient independent information to justify the issuance of a search warrant. Thus, the illegally obtained information (i.e., that the can was inside a house for some period) had no effect on the Magistrate's issuance of the warrant.

Justice Stevens, joined by Justices Brennan and Marshall, dissented in part. Justice Stevens observed that "the character of the property is profoundly different when infected with an electronic bug than when it is entirely germ free." He concluded that agents asserted dominion and control over the can of ether when they inserted the beeper and that this amounted to a seizure of the property under the Fourth Amendment. He contended that "the private citizen is entitled to assume, and in fact does assume, that his possessions are not infected with concealed electronic devices." He found "little comfort in the Court's notion that no invasion of privacy occurs until a listener obtains some significant information by use of the device."

Justice O'Connor, joined by Justice Rehnquist, wrote a separate opinion in *Karo* concurring in most of the Court's opinion and in its judgment. She wrote separately to state her view that a homeowner might not be able to claim that his privacy rights are violated if he permits a third person to enter the home with property that contains a beeper. If, for example, a government undercover agent posing as a drug buyer entered a suspect's home and carried a beeper, the homeowner might not have a valid complaint, because he assumed the risk. Justice White responded in a footnote by saying that he did not necessarily disagree with this analysis. Justice White found it inapplicable to the instant case, where the defendant had purchased the beeper-infected can and brought it into the house.

b. Tracking Public Movements: Cell Site Location Information

If the Fourth Amendment does not regulate the use of radio beeper tracking devices to monitor public movements—at least where the installation of those devices does not involve a physical intrusion into a constitutionally protected person, house, paper, or effect—then is it equally uninterested in modern technologies such as cell site location information, which is gathered, aggregated, and stored by cellular service providers in the normal course of providing telephone services to their customers? The Court takes up this question in the following case.

CARPENTER V. UNITED STATES

Supreme Court of the United States, 2018.
138 S.Ct. 2206.

CHIEF JUSTICE ROBERTS **delivered the opinion of the Court.**

This case presents the question whether the Government conducts a search under the Fourth Amendment when it accesses historical cell phone records that provide a comprehensive chronicle of the user's past movements.

I

A

There are 396 million cell phone service accounts in the United States—for a Nation of 326 million people. Cell phones perform their wide and growing variety of functions by connecting to a set of radio antennas called "cell sites." Although cell sites are usually mounted on a tower, they can also be found on light posts, flagpoles, church steeples, or the sides of buildings. Cell sites have several directional antennas that divide the covered area into sectors.

Cell phones continuously scan their environment looking for the best signal, which generally comes from the closest cell site. Most modern devices, such as smartphones, tap into the wireless network several times a minute whenever their signal is on, even if the owner is not using one of the phone's features. Each time the phone connects to a cell site, it generates a time-stamped record known as cell-site location information (CSLI). The precision of this information depends on the size of the geographic area covered by the cell site. The greater the concentration of cell sites, the smaller the coverage area. As data usage from cell phones has increased, wireless carriers have installed more cell sites to handle the traffic. That has led to increasingly compact coverage areas, especially in urban areas.

Wireless carriers collect and store CSLI for their own business purposes, including finding weak spots in their network and applying "roaming" charges when another carrier routes data through their cell sites. In addition, wireless carriers often sell aggregated location records to data brokers, without individual identifying information of the sort at issue here. While carriers have long retained CSLI for the start and end of incoming calls, in recent years phone companies have also collected location information from the transmission of text messages and routine data connections. Accordingly, modern cell phones generate increasingly vast amounts of increasingly precise CSLI.

B

In 2011, police officers arrested four men suspected of robbing a series of Radio Shack and (ironically enough) T-Mobile stores in Detroit. One of the men confessed that, over the previous four months, the group (along with a rotating cast of getaway drivers and lookouts) had robbed nine different stores in Michigan and Ohio. The suspect identified 15 accomplices who had participated in the heists and gave the FBI some of their cell phone numbers; the FBI then reviewed his call records to identify additional numbers that he had called around the time of the robberies.

Based on that information, the prosecutors applied for court orders under the Stored Communications Act to obtain cell phone records for petitioner Timothy Carpenter and several other suspects. That statute, as amended in 1994, permits the Government to compel the disclosure of certain telecommunications records when it "offers specific and articulable facts showing that there are reasonable grounds to believe" that the records sought "are relevant and material to an ongoing criminal investigation." 18 U.S.C. § 2703(d). Federal Magistrate Judges issued two orders directing Carpenter's wireless carriers—MetroPCS and Sprint—to disclose "cell site sector [information] for [Carpenter's] telephone[ ] at call origination and at call termination for incoming and outgoing calls" during the four-month period when the string of robberies occurred. The first order sought 152 days of cell-site records from MetroPCS, which produced records spanning 127 days. The second order requested seven days of CSLI from Sprint, which produced two days of records covering the period when Carpenter's phone was "roaming" in northeastern Ohio. Altogether the Government obtained 12,898 location points cataloging Carpenter's movements—an average of 101 data points per day.

Carpenter was charged with six counts of robbery and an additional six counts of carrying a firearm during a federal crime of violence. See 18 U.S.C. §§ 924(c), 1951(a). Prior to trial, Carpenter moved to suppress the cell-site data provided by the wireless carriers. He argued that the Government's seizure of the records violated the Fourth Amendment because they had been obtained without a warrant supported by probable cause. The District Court denied the motion.

At trial, seven of Carpenter's confederates pegged him as the leader of the operation. In addition, FBI agent Christopher Hess offered expert testimony about the cell-site data. Hess explained that each time a cell phone taps into the wireless network, the carrier logs a time-stamped record of the cell site and particular sector that were used. With this information, Hess produced maps that placed Carpenter's phone near four of the charged robberies. In the Government's view, the location records clinched the case: They confirmed that Carpenter was "right where the . . . robbery was at the exact time of the robbery." Carpenter was convicted on all but one of the firearm counts and sentenced to more than 100 years in prison.

The Court of Appeals for the Sixth Circuit affirmed. The court held that Carpenter lacked a reasonable expectation of privacy in the location information collected by the FBI because he had shared that information with his wireless carriers. Given that cell phone users voluntarily convey cell-site data to their carriers as "a means of establishing communication," the court concluded that the resulting business records are not entitled to Fourth Amendment protection. (quoting Smith v. Maryland, 442 U.S. 735, 741 (1979)).

We granted certiorari.

II

A

The Fourth Amendment protects "[t]he right of the people to be secure in their persons, houses, papers, and effects, against unreasonable searches and seizures." The "basic purpose of this Amendment," our cases have recognized, "is to safeguard the privacy and security of individuals against arbitrary invasions by governmental officials." The Founding generation crafted the Fourth Amendment as a "response to the reviled 'general warrants' and 'writs of assistance' of the colonial era, which allowed British officers to rummage through homes in an unrestrained search for evidence of criminal activity." In fact, as John Adams recalled, the patriot James Otis's 1761 speech condemning writs of assistance was "the first act of opposition to the arbitrary claims of Great Britain" and helped spark the Revolution itself.

For much of our history, Fourth Amendment search doctrine was "tied to common-law trespass" and focused on whether the Government "obtains information by physically intruding on a constitutionally protected area." More recently, the Court has recognized that "property rights are not the sole measure of Fourth Amendment violations." In Katz v. United States, we established that "the Fourth Amendment protects people, not places," and expanded our conception of the Amendment to protect certain expectations of privacy as well. When an individual "seeks to preserve something as private," and his expectation of privacy is "one that society is prepared to recognize as reasonable," we have held that official intrusion into that private sphere generally qualifies as a search and requires a warrant supported by probable cause.

Although no single rubric definitively resolves which expectations of privacy are entitled to protection, the analysis is informed by historical understandings "of what was deemed an unreasonable search and seizure when [the Fourth Amendment] was adopted." On this score, our cases have recognized some basic guideposts. First, that the Amendment seeks to secure "the privacies of life" against "arbitrary power." Second, and relatedly, that a central aim of the Framers was "to place obstacles in the way of a too permeating police surveillance."

We have kept this attention to Founding-era understandings in mind when applying the Fourth Amendment to innovations in surveillance tools. As technology has enhanced the Government's capacity to encroach upon areas normally guarded from inquisitive eyes, this Court has sought to "assure[ ] preservation of that degree of privacy against government that existed when the Fourth Amendment was adopted." * * *

B

The case before us involves the Government's acquisition of wireless carrier cell-site records revealing the location of Carpenter's cell phone whenever it made or received calls. This sort of digital data—personal location information maintained by a third party—does not fit neatly under existing precedents. Instead, requests for cell-site records lie at the intersection of two lines of cases, both of which inform our understanding of the privacy interests at stake.

The first set of cases addresses a person's expectation of privacy in his physical location and movements. In United States v. Knotts, 460 U.S. 276 (1983), we considered the Government's use of a "beeper" to aid in tracking a vehicle through traffic. Police officers in that case planted a beeper in a container of chloroform before it was purchased by one of Knotts's co-conspirators. The officers (with intermittent aerial assistance) then followed the automobile carrying the container from Minneapolis to

Knotts's cabin in Wisconsin, relying on the beeper's signal to help keep the vehicle in view. The Court concluded that the "augment[ed]" visual surveillance did not constitute a search because "[a] person traveling in an automobile on public thoroughfares has no reasonable expectation of privacy in his movements from one place to another." Since the movements of the vehicle and its final destination had been "voluntarily conveyed to anyone who wanted to look," Knotts could not assert a privacy interest in the information obtained.

This Court in *Knotts,* however, was careful to distinguish between the rudimentary tracking facilitated by the beeper and more sweeping modes of surveillance. The Court emphasized the "limited use which the government made of the signals from this particular beeper" during a discrete "automotive journey." Significantly, the Court reserved the question whether "different constitutional principles may be applicable" if "twenty-four hour surveillance of any citizen of this country [were] possible."

Three decades later, the Court considered more sophisticated surveillance of the sort envisioned in *Knotts* and found that different principles did indeed apply. In United States v. Jones, FBI agents installed a GPS tracking device on Jones's vehicle and remotely monitored the vehicle's movements for 28 days. The Court decided the case based on the Government's physical trespass of the vehicle. At the same time, five Justices agreed that related privacy concerns would be raised by, for example, "surreptitiously activating a stolen vehicle detection system" in Jones's car to track Jones himself, or conducting GPS tracking of his cell phone. Since GPS monitoring of a vehicle tracks "every movement" a person makes in that vehicle, the concurring Justices concluded that "longer term GPS monitoring in investigations of most offenses impinges on expectations of privacy"—regardless of whether those movements were disclosed to the public at large.

In a second set of decisions, the Court has drawn a line between what a person keeps to himself and what he shares with others. We have previously held that "a person has no legitimate expectation of privacy in information he voluntarily turns over to third parties." Smith, 442 U.S., at 743–744. That remains true "even if the information is revealed on the assumption that it will be used only for a limited purpose." Miller, 425 U.S. 435, 443 (1976). As a result, the Government is typically free to obtain such information from the recipient without triggering Fourth Amendment protections.

This third-party doctrine largely traces its roots to *Miller*. While investigating Miller for tax evasion, the Government subpoenaed his banks, seeking several months of canceled checks, deposit slips, and monthly statements. The Court rejected a Fourth Amendment challenge to the records collection. For one, Miller could "assert neither ownership nor possession" of the documents; they were "business records of the banks." For another, the nature of those records confirmed Miller's limited expectation of privacy, because the checks were "not confidential communications but negotiable instruments to be used in commercial transactions," and the bank statements contained information "exposed to [bank] employees in the ordinary course of business." The Court thus concluded that Miller had "take[n] the risk, in revealing his affairs to another, that the information [would] be conveyed by that person to the Government."

Three years later, *Smith* applied the same principles in the context of information conveyed to a telephone company. The Court ruled that the Government's use of a pen register—a device that recorded the outgoing phone numbers dialed on a landline telephone—was not a search. Noting the pen register's "limited capabilities," the Court "doubt[ed] that people in general entertain any actual expectation of privacy in the numbers they dial." Telephone subscribers know, after all, that the numbers are used by the telephone company "for a variety of legitimate business purposes," including routing calls. And at any rate, the Court explained, such an expectation "is not one that society is prepared to recognize as reasonable." When Smith placed a call, he "voluntarily conveyed" the dialed numbers to the phone company by "expos[ing] that information to its equipment in the ordinary course of business." Once again, we held that the defendant "assumed the risk" that the company's records "would be divulged to police."

III

The question we confront today is how to apply the Fourth Amendment to a new phenomenon: the ability to chronicle a person's past movements through the record of his cell phone signals. Such tracking partakes of many of the qualities of the GPS monitoring we considered in *Jones*. Much like GPS tracking of a vehicle, cell phone location information is detailed, encyclopedic, and effortlessly compiled.

At the same time, the fact that the individual continuously reveals his location to his wireless carrier implicates the third-party principle of *Smith* and *Miller*. But while the third-party doctrine applies to telephone numbers and bank records, it is not clear whether its logic extends to the qualitatively different category of cell-site records. After all, when *Smith* was decided in 1979, few could have imagined a society in which a phone goes wherever its owner goes, conveying to the wireless carrier not just dialed digits, but a detailed and comprehensive record of the person's movements.

We decline to extend *Smith* and *Miller* to cover these novel circumstances. Given the unique nature of cell phone location records, the fact that the information is held by a third party does not by itself overcome the user's claim to Fourth Amendment protection. Whether the Government employs its own surveillance technology as in *Jones* or leverages the technology of a wireless carrier, we hold that an individual maintains a legitimate expectation of privacy in the record of his physical movements as captured through CSLI. The location information obtained from Carpenter's wireless carriers was the product of a search.

A

A person does not surrender all Fourth Amendment protection by venturing into the public sphere. To the contrary, "what [one] seeks to preserve as private, even in an area accessible to the public, may be constitutionally protected." A majority of this Court has already recognized that individuals have a reasonable expectation of privacy in the whole of their physical movements. [United States v. Jones, 565 U.S. 400, 430 (2012)] (Alito, J., concurring in judgment); id., at 415 (Sotomayor, J., concurring). Prior to the digital age, law enforcement might have pursued a suspect for a brief stretch, but doing so "for any extended period of time was difficult and costly and therefore rarely undertaken." Id., at 429 (opinion of Alito, J.). For that reason, "society's expectation has been that law enforcement agents and others would not—and indeed, in the main, simply could not—secretly monitor and catalogue every single movement of an individual's car for a very long period." Id.

Allowing government access to cell-site records contravenes that expectation. Although such records are generated for commercial purposes, that distinction does not negate Carpenter's anticipation of privacy in his physical location. Mapping a cell phone's location over the course of 127 days provides an all-encompassing record of the holder's whereabouts. As with GPS information, the time-stamped data provides an intimate window into a person's life, revealing not only his particular movements, but through them his "familial, political, professional, religious, and sexual associations." Id., at 415 (opinion of Sotomayor, J.). These location records "hold for many Americans the 'privacies of life.' " And like GPS monitoring, cell phone tracking is remarkably easy, cheap, and efficient compared to traditional investigative tools. With just the click of a button, the Government can access each carrier's deep repository of historical location information at practically no expense.

In fact, historical cell-site records present even greater privacy concerns than the GPS monitoring of a vehicle we considered in *Jones*. Unlike the bugged container in *Knotts* or the car in *Jones*, a cell phone—almost a "feature of human anatomy,"—tracks nearly exactly the movements of its owner. While individuals regularly leave their vehicles, they compulsively carry cell phones with them all the time. A cell phone faithfully follows its owner beyond public thoroughfares and into private residences, doctor's offices, political headquarters, and other potentially revealing locales. * * * Accordingly, when the Government tracks the location of a cell phone it achieves near perfect surveillance, as if it had attached an ankle monitor to the phone's user.

Moreover, the retrospective quality of the data here gives police access to a category of information otherwise unknowable. In the past, attempts to reconstruct a person's movements were limited by a dearth of records and the frailties of recollection. With access to CSLI, the Government can now travel back in time to retrace a person's whereabouts, subject only to the retention polices of the wireless carriers, which currently maintain records for up to five years. Critically, because location information is continually logged for all of the 400 million devices in the United States—not just those belonging to persons who might happen to come under investigation—this newfound tracking capacity runs against everyone. Unlike with the GPS device in *Jones*, police need not even know in advance whether they want to follow a particular individual, or when.

Whoever the suspect turns out to be, he has effectively been tailed every moment of every day for five years, and the police may—in the Government's view—call upon the results of that surveillance without regard to the constraints of the Fourth Amendment. Only the few without cell phones could escape this tireless and absolute surveillance.

The Government * * * [contends] that the collection of CSLI should be permitted because the data is less precise than GPS information. * * * [But] the rule the Court adopts "must take account of more sophisticated systems that are already in use or in development." While the records in this case reflect the state of technology at the start of the decade, the accuracy of CSLI is rapidly approaching GPS-level precision. As the number of cell sites has proliferated, the geographic area covered by each cell sector has shrunk, particularly in urban areas. In addition, with new technology measuring the time and angle of signals hitting their towers, wireless carriers already have the capability to pinpoint a phone's location within 50 meters.

Accordingly, when the Government accessed CSLI from the wireless carriers, it invaded Carpenter's reasonable expectation of privacy in the whole of his physical movements.

B

The Government's primary contention to the contrary is that the third-party doctrine governs this case. In its view, cell-site records are fair game because they are "business records" created and maintained by the wireless carriers. The Government * * * recognizes that this case features new technology, but asserts that the legal question nonetheless turns on a garden-variety request for information from a third-party witness.

The Government's position fails to contend with the seismic shifts in digital technology that made possible the tracking of not only Carpenter's location but also everyone else's, not for a short period but for years and years. Sprint Corporation and its competitors are not your typical witnesses. Unlike the nosy neighbor who keeps an eye on comings and goings, they are ever alert, and their memory is nearly infallible. There is a world of difference between the limited types of personal information addressed in *Smith* and *Miller* and the exhaustive chronicle of location information casually collected by wireless carriers today. The Government thus is not asking for a straightforward application of the third-party doctrine, but instead a significant extension of it to a distinct category of information.

The third-party doctrine partly stems from the notion that an individual has a reduced expectation of privacy in information knowingly shared with another. But the fact of "diminished privacy interests does not mean that the Fourth Amendment falls out of the picture entirely." *Smith* and *Miller,* after all, did not rely solely on the act of sharing. Instead, they considered "the nature of the particular documents sought" to determine whether "there is a legitimate 'expectation of privacy' concerning their contents." Miller, 425 U.S., at 442. *Smith* pointed out the limited capabilities of a pen register * * * telephone call logs reveal little in the way of "identifying information." Smith, 442 U.S., at 742. *Miller* likewise noted that checks were "not confidential communications but negotiable instruments to be used in commercial transactions." 425 U.S., at 442. In mechanically applying the third-party doctrine to this case, the Government fails to appreciate that there are no comparable limitations on the revealing nature of CSLI.

The Court has in fact already shown special solicitude for location information in the third-party context. In *Knotts,* the Court relied on *Smith* to hold that an individual has no reasonable expectation of privacy in public movements that he "voluntarily conveyed to anyone who wanted to look." But when confronted with more pervasive tracking, five Justices agreed that longer term GPS monitoring of even a vehicle traveling on public streets constitutes a search. Jones, 565 U.S., at 430 (Alito, J., concurring in judgment); id., at 415 (Sotomayor, J., concurring). * * * [This] case is not about "using a phone" or a person's movement at a particular time. It is about a detailed chronicle of a person's physical presence compiled every day, every moment, over several years. Such a chronicle implicates privacy concerns far beyond those considered in *Smith* and *Miller.*

Neither does the second rationale underlying the third-party doctrine—voluntary exposure—hold up when it comes to CSLI. Cell phone location information is not truly "shared" as one normally understands the term. In the first place, cell phones and the services they provide are "such a pervasive and insistent part of daily life" that carrying one is indispensable to participation in modern society. Second, a cell phone logs a cell-site record by dint of its operation, without any affirmative act on the part of the user beyond powering up. Virtually any activity on the phone generates CSLI, including incoming calls, texts, or e-mails and countless other data connections that a phone automatically makes when checking for news, weather, or social media updates. Apart from disconnecting the phone from the network, there is no way to avoid leaving behind a trail of location data. As a result, in no meaningful sense does the user voluntarily "assume[ ] the risk" of turning over a comprehensive dossier of his physical movements.

We therefore decline to extend *Smith* and *Miller* to the collection of CSLI. Given the unique nature of cell phone location information, the fact that the Government obtained the information from a third party does not overcome Carpenter's claim to Fourth Amendment protection. The Government's acquisition of the cell-site records was a search within the meaning of the Fourth Amendment.

* * *

Our decision today is a narrow one. We do not express a view on matters not before us: real-time CSLI or "tower dumps" (a download of information on all the devices that connected to a particular cell site during a particular interval). We do not disturb the application of *Smith* and *Miller* or call into question conventional surveillance techniques and tools, such as security cameras. Nor do we address other business records that might incidentally reveal location information. Further, our opinion does not consider other collection techniques involving foreign affairs or national security. * * *

IV

Having found that the acquisition of Carpenter's CSLI was a search, we also conclude that the Government must generally obtain a warrant supported by probable cause before acquiring such records. * * *

As Justice Brandeis explained in his famous dissent, the Court is obligated—as "[s]ubtler and more far-reaching means of invading privacy have become available to the Government"—to ensure that the "progress of science" does not erode Fourth Amendment protections. Olmstead v. United States, 277 U.S. 438, 473–474 (1928). Here the progress of science has afforded law enforcement a powerful new tool to carry out its important responsibilities. At the same time, this tool risks Government encroachment of the sort the Framers, "after consulting the lessons of history," drafted the Fourth Amendment to prevent.

We decline to grant the state unrestricted access to a wireless carrier's database of physical location information. In light of the deeply revealing nature of CSLI, its depth, breadth, and comprehensive reach, and the inescapable and automatic nature of its collection, the fact that such information is gathered by a third party does not make it any less deserving of Fourth Amendment protection. The Government's acquisition of the cell-site records here was a search under that Amendment.

JUSTICE KENNEDY, with whom JUSTICE THOMAS and JUSTICE ALITO join, dissenting.

This case involves new technology, but the Court's stark departure from relevant Fourth Amendment precedents and principles is, in my submission, unnecessary and incorrect, requiring this respectful dissent.

In concluding that the Government engaged in a search, the Court unhinges Fourth Amendment doctrine from the property-based concepts that have long grounded the analytic framework that pertains in these cases. In doing so it draws an unprincipled and unworkable line between cell-site records on the one hand and financial and telephonic records on the other. According to today's majority opinion, the Government can acquire a record of every credit card purchase and phone call a person makes over months or years without upsetting a legitimate expectation of privacy. But, in the Court's view, the Government crosses a constitutional line when it obtains a court's approval to issue a subpoena for more than six days of cell-site records in order to determine whether a person was within several hundred city blocks of a crime scene. That distinction is illogical and will frustrate principled application of the Fourth Amendment in many routine yet vital law enforcement operations. * * *

In general, the Court "risks error by elaborating too fully on the Fourth Amendment implications of emerging technology before its role in society has become clear." That judicial caution, prudent in most cases, is imperative in this one.

Technological changes involving cell phones have complex effects on crime and law enforcement. Cell phones make crimes easier to coordinate and conceal, while also providing the Government with new investigative tools that may have the potential to upset traditional privacy expectations. How those competing effects balance against each other, and how property norms and expectations of privacy form around new technology, often will be difficult to determine during periods of rapid technological change. In those instances, and where the governing legal standard is one of reasonableness, it is wise to defer to legislative judgments like the one embodied in § 2703(d) of the Stored Communications Act. In § 2703(d) Congress weighed the privacy interests at stake and imposed a judicial check to prevent executive overreach. The Court should be wary of upsetting that legislative balance and erecting constitutional barriers that foreclose further legislative instructions. The last thing the Court should do is incorporate an arbitrary and outside limit—in this case six days' worth of cell-site records—and use it as the foundation for a new constitutional framework. The Court's decision runs roughshod over the mechanism Congress put in place to govern the acquisition of cell-site records and closes off further legislative debate on these issues. * * *

This case should be resolved by interpreting accepted property principles as the baseline for reasonable expectations of privacy. Here the Government did not search anything over which Carpenter could assert ownership or control. Instead, it issued a court-authorized subpoena to a third party to disclose information it alone owned and controlled. That should suffice to resolve this case. * * *

JUSTICE THOMAS, dissenting.

This case should not turn on "whether" a search occurred. It should turn, instead, on *whose* property was searched. * * * By obtaining the cell-site records of MetroPCS and Sprint, the Government did not search Carpenter's property. He did not create the records, he does not maintain them, he cannot control them, and he cannot destroy them. Neither the terms of his contracts nor any provision of law makes the records his. The records belong to MetroPCS and Sprint.

The Court concludes that, although the records are not Carpenter's, the Government must get a warrant because Carpenter had a reasonable "expectation of privacy" in the location information that they reveal. I agree with Justice Kennedy, Justice Alito, Justice Gorsuch, and every Court of Appeals to consider the question that this is not the best reading of our precedents.

The more fundamental problem with the Court's opinion, however, is its use of the "reasonable expectation of privacy" test, which was first articulated by Justice Harlan in Katz v. United States, 389 U.S. 347, 360–361 (1967) (concurring opinion). The Katz test has no basis in the text or history of the Fourth Amendment. And it invites courts to make judgments about policy, not law. Until we confront the problems with this test, Katz will continue to distort Fourth Amendment jurisprudence.

I respectfully dissent. * * *

JUSTICE ALITO, with whom JUSTICE THOMAS joins, dissenting.

I share the Court's concern about the effect of new technology on personal privacy, but I fear that today's decision will do far more harm than good. The Court's reasoning fractures two fundamental pillars of Fourth Amendment law, and in doing so, it guarantees a blizzard of litigation while threatening many legitimate and valuable investigative practices upon which law enforcement has rightfully come to rely.

First, the Court ignores the basic distinction between an actual search (dispatching law enforcement officers to enter private premises and root through private papers and effects) and an order merely requiring a party to look through its own records and produce specified documents. The former, which intrudes on personal privacy far more deeply, requires probable cause; the latter does not. Treating an order to produce like an actual search, as today's decision does, is revolutionary. It violates both the original understanding of the Fourth Amendment and more than a century of Supreme Court precedent. Unless it is somehow restricted to the particular situation in the present case, the Court's move will cause upheaval. Must every grand jury subpoena *duces tecum* be supported by probable cause? If so, investigations of terrorism, political corruption, white-collar crime, and many other offenses will be stymied. And what about subpoenas and other document-production orders issued by administrative agencies?

Second, the Court allows a defendant to object to the search of a third party's property. This also is revolutionary. The Fourth Amendment protects "[t]he right of the people to be secure in *their* persons, houses, papers, and effects" (emphasis added), not the persons, houses, papers, and effects of others. Until today, we have been careful to heed this fundamental feature of the Amendment's text. This was true when the Fourth Amendment was tied to property law, and it remained true after Katz v. United States, 389 U.S. 347 (1967), broadened the Amendment's reach.

By departing dramatically from these fundamental principles, the Court destabilizes long-established Fourth Amendment doctrine. We will be making repairs—or picking up the pieces—for a long time to come. * * *

All of this is unnecessary. In the Stored Communications Act, Congress addressed the specific problem at issue in this case. The Act restricts the misuse of cell-site records by cell service providers, something that the Fourth Amendment cannot do. The Act also goes beyond current Fourth Amendment case law in restricting access by law enforcement. It permits law enforcement officers to acquire cell-site records only if they meet a heightened standard and obtain a court order. If the American people now think that the Act is inadequate or needs updating, they can turn to their elected representatives to adopt more protective provisions. Because the collection and storage of cell-site records affects nearly every American, it is unlikely that the question whether the current law requires strengthening will escape Congress's notice.

Legislation is much preferable to the development of an entirely new body of Fourth Amendment caselaw for many reasons, including the enormous complexity of the subject, the need to respond to rapidly changing technology, and the Fourth Amendment's limited scope. The

Fourth Amendment restricts the conduct of the Federal Government and the States; it does not apply to private actors. But today, some of the greatest threats to individual privacy may come from powerful private companies that collect and sometimes misuse vast quantities of data about the lives of ordinary Americans. If today's decision encourages the public to think that this Court can protect them from this looming threat to their privacy, the decision will mislead as well as disrupt. And if holding a provision of the Stored Communications Act to be unconstitutional dissuades Congress from further legislation in this field, the goal of protecting privacy will be greatly disserved.

The desire to make a statement about privacy in the digital age does not justify the consequences that today's decision is likely to produce.

JUSTICE GORSUCH, **dissenting**.

* * * From the founding until the 1960s, the right to assert a Fourth Amendment claim didn't depend on your ability to appeal to a judge's personal sensibilities about the "reasonableness" of your expectations or privacy. It was tied to the law. The Fourth Amendment protects "the right of the people to be secure in their persons, houses, papers and effects, against unreasonable searches and seizures." True to those words and their original understanding, the traditional approach asked if a house, paper or effect was *yours* under law. * * *

These ancient principles may help us address modern data cases too. Just because you entrust your data—in some cases, your modern-day papers and effects—to a third party may not mean you lose any Fourth Amendment interest in its contents. Whatever may be left of *Smith* and *Miller*, few doubt that e-mail should be treated much like the traditional mail it has largely supplanted—as a bailment in which the owner retains a vital and protected legal interest. * * *

I doubt that complete ownership or exclusive control of property is always a necessary condition to the assertion of a Fourth Amendment right. Where houses are concerned, for example, individuals can enjoy Fourth Amendment protection without fee simple title. Both the text of the Amendment and the common law rule support that conclusion. * * *

Another point seems equally true: just because you *have* to entrust a third party with your data doesn't necessarily mean you should lose all Fourth Amendment protections in it. Not infrequently one person comes into possession of someone else's property without the owner's consent. Think of the finder of lost goods or the policeman who impounds a car. The law recognizes that the goods and the car still belong to their true owners, for "where a person comes into lawful possession of the personal property of another, even though there is no formal agreement between the property's owner and its possessor, the possessor will become a constructive bailee when justice so requires." * * *

[P]ositive law may help provide detailed guidance on evolving technologies without resort to judicial intuition. State (or sometimes federal) law often creates rights in both tangible and intangible things. * * * Both the States and federal government are actively legislating in the area of third party data storage and the rights users enjoy. * * * If state legislators or state courts say that a digital record has the attributes that normally make something property, that may supply a sounder basis for judicial decision making than judicial guesswork about societal expectations. * * *

It seems to me entirely possible a person's cell-site data could qualify as *his* papers or effects under existing law. Yes, the telephone carrier holds the information. But 47 U.S.C. § 222 designates a customer's cell-site location information as "customer proprietary network information" (CPNI), § 222(h)(1)(A), and gives customers certain rights to control use of and access to CPNI about themselves. The statute generally forbids a carrier to "use, disclose, or permit access to individually identifiable" CPNI without the customer's consent, except as needed to provide the customer's telecommunications services. § 222(c)(1). It also requires the carrier to disclose CPNI "upon affirmative written request by the customer, to any person designated by the customer." § 222(c)(2). Congress even afforded customers a private cause of action for damages against carriers who violate the Act's terms. § 207. Plainly, customers have substantial legal interests in this information, including at least some right to include, exclude, and control its use. Those interests might even rise to the level of a property right. * * *

QUESTIONS AFTER CARPENTER

Carpenter answered one critical question: whether law enforcement officers need a warrant to access cell-site location information. It specifically declined to address the Fourth Amendment status of other records and other technologies. This has left lower courts to wonder whether *Carpenter* marks a watershed along the lines of *Katz* or is, instead, an application of *Katz* to a specific circumstance. Part of the challenge is that Chief Justice Roberts's majority opinion does not set forth a clear test for determining what kinds of data should be subject to Fourth Amendment protection and what kinds of surveillance technologies should be subject to Fourth Amendment restraints. Some courts and scholars have attempted to distill from his opinion a set of factors relevant to making those determinations, including the duration of surveillance, what kinds of personal and intimate information surveillance can reveal, the scope of threat to the right of "the people to be secure . . . against unreasonable searches and seizures," and whether people meaningfully consent to or can reasonably avoid surveillance. *See, e.g.*, Ohm, The Many

Revolutions of Carpenter, 32 Harv. J. L & Tech. 357 (2019); Gray, Collective Rights and the Fourth Amendment after Carpenter, 79 Md. L. Rev. 66 (2019); Freiwald & Smith, The Carpenter Chronicle: A Near Perfect Surveillance, 132 Harv. L. Rev. 205 (2018).

Advocates have cited some of these factors to challenge the warrantless deployment and use of a variety of surveillance technologies. Few of these efforts have succeeded, however. In the years after *Carpenter* was decided, lower courts largely declined to extend *Carpenter* beyond its facts. *See* Tokson, The Aftermath of Carpenter: An Empirical Study of Fourth Amendment Law, 2018–2021, 135 Harv.L.Rev. ___ (2022). But not always. There are notable exceptions.

In Commonwealth v. Mora, 485 Mass. 360, 150 N.E.3d. 297 (2020), the Supreme Judicial Court of Massachusetts held that using a camera installed on a utility pole to conduct continuous, long-term, targeted surveillance of a person's home constitutes a "search" under Article 14 of the Massachusetts Declaration of Rights—which guarantees security against unreasonable searches and seizures. Although the *Mora* court declined to base its holding on the Fourth Amendment, the Fifth Circuit Court of Appeals held in United States v. Cuevas-Sanchez, 821 F.2d 248 (5th Cir. 1987), that the use of a stationary camera to record activities in a target's backyard was a "search" for purposes of the Fourth Amendment. Other courts have reached a different conclusion, however. See, e.g., United States v. Tuggle, 4 F.4th 505 (7th Cir. 2021) (use of pole camera installed on public property used to surveil target's home was not a search, irrespective of duration); United States v. May-Shaw, 955 F.3d 563 (6th Cir. 2020) (23-day surveillance of apartment complex parking lot and carport not a search).

Cases challenging the use of pole cameras and other surveillance technologies are bound to reach the Supreme Court in the coming years. How do you think the Court should react? Do you think it should limit *Carpenter* to its facts, treating CSLI as *sui generis*? Or do you think the Court should apply the reasoning in *Carpenter* to bring other technologies within the compass of Fourth Amendment regulation? As you consider your views, you may find it interesting to review the opinions of the Court and Justice Brandeis in Olmstead v. United States.

In his concurring opinion in *Carpenter*, Justice Gorsuch wonders about what some scholars have called the "positive law" theory of the Fourth Amendment. See Baude & Stern, The Positive Law Model of the Fourth Amendment, 129 Harv. L. Rev. 1821 (2016). On this account, legislation can control the scope of Fourth Amendment protections by either grounding or denying claims or reasonable expectations of privacy. This proposal has been subject to considerable criticism. See Re, The Positive Law Floor, 129 Harv. L. Rev. F. 313 (2016). It is also in tension with cases where the Court has declined to bind Fourth Amendment protections to state law. See Virginia v. Moore, 553 U.S. 164 (2008); Atwater v. Lago Vista, 532 U.S. 318 (2001). Justice Alito cited some of these concerns in his criticism of the Court's return to the physical intrusion test in *Jones*. United States v. Jones, 565 U.S. 400, 425 (2012) (Alito, J., concurring) (noting that "under the Court's theory, the coverage of the Fourth Amendment may vary from State to State."). Nevertheless, with one potential advocate on the Court, and increasing public pressure for privacy legislation, the positive law may well become a significant factor for evaluating the reasonable expectations of privacy and property rights that ground Fourth Amendment claims.

The majority opinion in *Carpenter* does not identify, precisely, when the "search" occurred in that case and who did it. Was Carpenter's service provider conducting a "search" when it gathered and stored records of his location ("The location information obtained from Carpenter's wireless carriers was the product of a search.")? If so, then on what analysis was it acting as an agent of the state? Did the investigating agents conduct a search when they requested and accessed cell site location records ("The Government's acquisition of the cell-site records was a search within the meaning of the Fourth Amendment.")? Was the service provider conducting a "search" when it looked through its records in response to the government's request? Or did the "search" occur when the FBI agent analyzed the records to determine the location of Carpenter's phone on dates and times associated with the robberies ("From the 127 days of location data it received, the Government could, in combination with other information, deduce a detailed log of Carpenter's movements.")? The answers to these questions may matter quite a bit as courts wrestle with the Fourth Amendment status of other surveillance methods. For example, would it be a search if the government requested information about a suspect from a commercial data aggregator or used its own "Big Data" technologies to construct a detailed picture of a person's activities and associations based on information accessed through third parties?

c. *Aerial Surveillance*

The Court has applied the public observation doctrine to aerial surveillance of private property. In California v. Ciraolo, 476 U.S. 207 (1986), Chief Justice Burger wrote for the Court as it held, 5–4, that the Fourth Amendment was not violated by aerial observation of a fenced-in backyard, from an altitude of 1,000 feet, even though the officers were operating without a warrant or probable cause. Ciraolo had erected two fences, a six foot outer and a ten foot inner fence, to protect his backyard from observation on the ground. But the aerial overflight revealed the fact that Ciraolo was growing marijuana. The majority reasoned that because any member of the public flying in the public airspace could have peered into the yard, Ciraolo had no reasonable expectation of privacy against aerial surveillance by the police. The defendant argued that a flyover by members of the public would be different in character and purpose from a flyover by law enforcement officers. But the majority rejected any such distinction and had "difficulty understanding exactly how respondent's expectations of privacy from aerial observation might differ when two airplanes pass overhead at identical altitudes, simply for different purposes."

Justice Powell, joined by Justices Brennan, Marshall and Blackmun, dissented. Relying on *Katz*, he argued that the Court erred in relying solely on the manner of surveillance rather than "focusing on the interests of the individual and of a free society" and suggested that "[a]erial surveillance is nearly as intrusive on family privacy as physical trespass into the curtilage."

Dow Chemical Co. v. United States, 476 U.S. 227 (1986), was decided the same day by the same vote as *Ciraolo*. The Environmental Protection Agency engaged in aerial photographing of Dow Chemical Co.'s manufacturing plant in Michigan. Dow had maintained elaborate ground security that barred public views of its plant from the ground and had investigated low flights over the plant. It sued for injunctive relief against the EPA, arguing that its Fourth Amendment rights were violated by the aerial overflights. Chief Justice Burger's majority opinion concluded that "the taking of aerial photographs of an industrial plant complex from navigable airspace is not a search prohibited by the Fourth Amendment."

Again Justice Powell wrote for the four dissenters and again relied on *Katz*. He argued that trade secret laws demonstrate societal recognition of legitimate interests in business privacy, and distinguished *Ciraolo* on the ground that the EPA needed to use a sophisticated camera to discover the details revealed in its photographs.

The Court applied *Ciraolo* in Florida v. Riley, 488 U.S. 445 (1989), and held that surveillance from a helicopter hovering at 400 feet above Riley's backyard providing a view into a greenhouse located in his backyard was not a search. Justice White, writing for a plurality, noted that no law prohibited the public from hovering over Riley's property in a helicopter at that level; therefore the police could do so as well. Justice White relied on FAA regulations that allow helicopters to be operated at virtually any altitude so long as they do not pose a safety hazard. He added that there was no injury to the property or any dust or threat from the visual inspection, and that no intimate activities in the house or curtilage had been observed.

Justice O'Connor concurred in the judgment. She disagreed with the plurality's analysis and contended that the proper test for determining the reasonableness of an expectation of privacy was whether the public *ordinarily* had access to the information sought by the police, not whether it was legally possible for a member of the public to obtain it. Thus, for Justice O'Connor, the question was whether members of the public *ordinarily* hovered over Riley's property at 400 feet in helicopters—if not, the police conduct would be a search. Justice O'Connor nonetheless concurred, asserting that the burden was on Riley, the moving party, to show that members of the public did not regularly hover over his property in helicopters. Because Riley had offered no proof on this point in the lower court, she agreed that a search was not shown on the facts in *Riley*.

Justice Brennan wrote a dissenting opinion joined by Justices Marshall and Stevens. He agreed with Justice O'Connor that the reasonableness of a privacy expectation should be determined by whether the public ordinarily occupied the airspace over Riley's home, but urged that judicial notice could be taken of the infrequent nature of low flying helicopters, and that the burden should be placed upon the government to show that this type of overflight was so frequent as to render unreasonable a privacy expectation. Justice Blackmun also dissented arguing that a remand would give the government the opportunity to satisfy the burden.

How do the Court's opinions in *Jones* and *Carpenter* affect the constitutionality of aerial surveillance? Aerial surveillance does not entail a physical intrusion into a constitutionally protected area, so it appears to remain outside the scope of Fourth Amendment regulation under the physical intrusion test. But could police conducting overflights for a prolonged period trigger Fourth Amendment scrutiny under the Court's reasoning in *Carpenter*? In Leaders of a Beautiful Struggle v. Baltimore Police Dept., 2 F.4th 330 (4th Cir. 2021), the Fourth Circuit held that they could. There, the Baltimore Police Department collaborated with a private company to conduct aerial surveillance over the City of Baltimore during daylight hours. The program used small planes outfitted with powerful digital cameras operating in public airspace. The contractor stored images from those cameras in a database. In the context of an investigation, officers with supervisory approval could request access to images from the database. By tracking the movements of individuals before and after an incident, investigators could identify potential suspects and witnesses. They could also identify other potential investigative resources, such as closed circuit surveillance cameras operated by public and private entities. Writing for an en banc court, Chief Judge Gregory applied the factors outlined in *Carpenter*, finding that

> [The] program tracks every movement of every person outside in Baltimore. Because the data is retained for 45 days—at least—it is a detailed, encyclopedic, record of where everyone came and went within the city during daylight hours over the prior month-and-a-half. Law enforcement can travel back in time to observe a target's movements, forwards and backwards. Without technology, police can attempt to tail suspects, but [this] data is more like attaching an ankle monitor to every person in the city. Whoever the suspect turns out to be, they have effectively been tailed for the prior six weeks. Thus, the retrospective quality of the data enables police to retrace a person's whereabouts, granting access to otherwise "unknowable" information.

In light of the potential of this detailed location information to reveal the intimate details of individuals' lives, the court held that the warrantless operation of the program violated the Fourth Amendment.

d. Trash

In California v. Greenwood, 486 U.S. 35 (1988), police officers asked a neighborhood trash collector to pick up plastic garbage bags that Greenwood left on the curb in front of his house and turn the bags over to the police. The police rummaged through the bags and found items indicating narcotics use. This information was used to obtain warrants to search Greenwood's house. Greenwood challenged the warrants as the fruit of an illegal search of his trash. Justice White, writing for seven members of the Court, concluded that the officers' inspection of the trash was not a search and therefore was permissible without a warrant or probable cause. Relying on *Smith* (the pen register case) he asserted that

> respondents exposed their garbage to the public sufficiently to defeat their claim to Fourth Amendment protection. It is common knowledge that plastic garbage bags left on or at the side of a public street are readily accessible to animals, children, scavengers, snoops, and other members of the public * * * the police cannot be reasonably expected to avert their eyes from evidence of criminal activity that could have been observed by any member of the public.

The Court's ruling was not based on any claim that Greenwood abandoned the trash, because that would require some showing of a voluntary relinquishment—a challenge in light of local ordinances governing the disposal of garbage. Rather, the ruling was based squarely on the premise that Greenwood had no expectation of privacy in property to which members of the public had access.

Justice Brennan, joined by Justice Marshall, dissented. He argued that "scrutiny of another's trash is contrary to commonly accepted notions of civilized behavior" and that "society will be shocked to learn that the Court, the ultimate guarantor of liberty, deems unreasonable our expectation that the aspects of our private lives that are concealed safely in a trash bag will not become public." Justice Brennan concluded as follows:

> The mere *possibility* that unwelcome meddlers *might* open and rummage through the containers does not negate the expectation of privacy in its contents any more than the possibility of a burglary negates an expectation of privacy in the home; or the possibility of a private intrusion negates an expectation of privacy in an unopened package; or the possibility that an operator will listen in on a telephone conversation negates an expectation of privacy in the words spoken on the telephone.

QUESTIONS ABOUT GREENWOOD

Who more accurately captures societal expectations of the American people in *Greenwood*, Justice White or Justice Brennan?[10] Is a police officer rummaging through garbage more akin to a Girl Scout soliciting cookie sales or a nosy passerby lingering in the front garden? In a similar vein, should the question of reasonable expectations be determined empirically or in the abstract? In *Riley* five members of the Court agreed that the mere *possibility* of public access is not enough to render a privacy expectation unreasonable. Isn't that the same point that Justice Brennan made in dissent in *Greenwood*?

What if Greenwood had placed his garbage bags in a trash can just inside his fenced-in backyard? In United States v. Jackson, 728 F.3d 367 (4th Cir. 2013), the Fourth Circuit Court of Appeals, citing *Jardines*, suggested that it would make a difference, opining that "surely if bringing a drug-sniffing dog onto a home's front porch is beyond the scope of the implied license that invites a visitor to the front door, so too is rummaging through a trash can located within the home's curtilage."

Would it make a difference if Greenwood shredded documents and papers into tiny pieces before depositing them in the trash? The Court in United States v. Scott, 975 F.2d 927 (1st Cir.1992), held that it would not:

> What we have here is a failed attempt at secrecy by reason of underestimation of police resourcefulness, not invasion of constitutionally protected privacy. * * * The Fourth Amendment * * * does not protect appellee when a third party expends the effort and expense to solve the jigsaw puzzle created by shredding.

What if police went through Greenwood's trash every day for four weeks? Would that kind of long-term surveillance implicate the reasoning in *Carpenter*?

Finally, there is the question whether *Greenwood* might have been decided differently under the physical intrusion test. Presumably, garbage set on the curb is outside the curtilage of the home, but the can itself remains the homeowner's "effect." Even if a homeowner can be said to have disclaimed all property interests in the contents of a garbage can, do officers nevertheless conduct a "search" when physically intruding into the can itself for purposes of gathering information? If so, then does setting a garbage can out on the curb imply consent for members of the public, and therefore officers, to examine and even remove the contents?

---

[10] Professors Slobogin and Schumacher have argued, on the basis of some empirical research, that the Court's conclusions about societal expectations are often at odds with the actual views of most members of society. See Slobogin and Schumacher, Reasonable Expectations of Privacy and Autonomy in Fourth Amendment Cases: An Empirical Look at "Understandings Recognized and Permitted by Society," 42 Duke L.J. 727 (1993).

e. *Manipulation of Bags in Public Transit*

Officers use many techniques to halt the flow of drug traffic on interstate buses and trains. One method is for officers to enter a bus or train and examine, by touch, the outside of bags that have been placed in the overhead baggage rack. Soft bags are manipulated to determine whether they contain hard objects that could be guns or drugs. In Bond v. United States, 529 U.S. 334 (2000), the Court considered the question whether a law enforcement officer's physical manipulation of a bus passenger's carry-on luggage constitutes a search for purposes of the Fourth Amendment. The Court held that it did. The officer boarded a bus and squeezed a green canvas bag in the baggage area above Bond's seat. Chief Justice Rehnquist, writing for the Court, found that the officer's manipulation of the bag went beyond what would be expected by members of the public, and so constituted a search. He explained that "a bus passenger clearly expects that his bag may be handled," but "[h]e does not expect that other passengers or bus employees will, as a matter of course, feel the bag in an exploratory manner." Because the officer in *Bond* did not have probable cause to believe that Bond's bag contained weapons or contraband, the Court did not reach the question whether manipulating the outside of a bag requires a warrant.

Justice Breyer, joined by Justice Scalia, dissented in *Bond,* arguing that in modern travel other passengers often squeeze and handle the bags of others in an attempt to cram more bags into baggage compartments, and predicted that "[a]t best, this decision will lead to a constitutional jurisprudence of "squeezes."

Bond involved physical manipulation of a bag on a bus, but those traveling by air routinely have their persons and effects subject to both exploratory manipulation and revealing imaging. How do these practices square with the Fourth Amendment? Answers to this question might be found in the discussion of "special needs" searches and seizures, later in this Chapter.

6. Investigative Methods That Can Only Reveal Illegal Activity

Investigation that threatens to uncover innocent, private activity can constitute a search, because it invades a legitimate Fourth Amendment secrecy interest. In contrast, the Supreme Court has held that there is no legitimate expectation of privacy in illegal activity. Therefore—at least under the expectation of privacy test—an investigation is not a search if it can *only* reveal illegal activity. However, the use of methods that can only detect illegal activity may trigger Fourth Amendment protections if officers seize or physically intrude into a person, house, paper, or effects.

a. Canine Sniffs

In United States v. Place, 462 U.S. 696 (1983), the Supreme Court held that a canine sniff of closed luggage for drugs was not a search under the expectation of privacy test. Writing for the Court, Justice O'Connor had this to say about "canine sniffs":

> A "canine sniff' by a well-trained narcotics detection dog * * * does not require opening the luggage. * * * Thus, the manner in which information is obtained through this investigative technique is much less intrusive than a typical search. Moreover, the sniff discloses only the presence or absence of narcotics, a contraband item. Thus, despite the fact that the sniff tells the authorities something about the contents of the luggage, the information obtained is limited. This limited disclosure also ensures that the owner of the property is not subjected to the embarrassment and inconvenience entailed in less discriminate and more intrusive investigative methods.
>
> In these respects, the canine sniff is *sui generis*. We are aware of no other investigative procedure that is so limited both in the manner in which the information is obtained and in the content of the information revealed by the procedure. Therefore, we conclude that the particular course of investigation that the agents intended to pursue here—exposure of respondent's luggage, which was located in a public place, to a trained canine—did not constitute a "search" within the meaning of the Fourth Amendment.

While the dog sniff in *Place* was not a search, the Court nonetheless held that the cocaine found in Place's luggage was illegally obtained. This was because police did not have the dog ready when Place's luggage arrived at the airport; it took 90 minutes to bring the dog to the scene, and Place's luggage was detained for that time. This detention was an exercise of dominion and control constituting a seizure. The Court found the seizure unreasonable because the officers were not diligent in their investigation and did not have probable cause to detain the luggage.

So, how long may officers detain persons or property in order to bring a drug detection dog to the scene? The Court suggested an answer in Illinois v. Caballes, 543 U.S. 405 (2005). There, the defendant was legally stopped for speeding. While one officer was processing the speeding ticket, another officer came to the scene with a drug-detecting dog and walked the dog around Caballes's car. The officer had no justification for thinking that Caballes was carrying drugs. The dog alerted at the trunk. Based on that alert, the officers searched the trunk, found marijuana, and arrested Caballes. The entire incident lasted less than 10 minutes. Writing for the Court, Justice Stevens found no Fourth Amendment violation in the use of the dog. He relied on *Place* to conclude that the dog sniff did not violate any reasonable expectation of privacy and determined that the short seizure of

Caballes and his car was reasonable in light of the process of issuing a speeding ticket. He warned, however, that "[a] seizure that is justified solely by the interest in issuing a warning ticket to the driver can become unlawful if it is prolonged beyond the time reasonably required to complete that mission."

Chief Justice Rehnquist did not participate in the decision in *Caballes.* Justice Souter dissented, expressing concern that dog sniffs are fallible—he cited one dog with a 70% accuracy rate and another that gave false positives 38% of the time (the Court addressed these concerns in Florida v. Harris, 588 U.S. 237 (2013), discussed *infra*). Justice Ginsburg wrote a separate dissenting opinion in *Caballes.* She argued that the use of the dog changed the character of what began as a lawful traffic stop and expressed concern that "[u]nder today's decision, every traffic stop could become an occasion to call in the dogs, to the distress and embarrassment of the law-abiding population."

The Court had occasion to consider the extension of a stop to allow a drug dog to arrive in Rodriguez v. United States, 575 U.S. 348 (2015). In that case, a police officer stopped Rodriguez in order to issue a traffic ticket. He completed the ticketing process but continued to detain Rodriguez for five extra minutes in order to allow a drug dog to arrive on the scene. Writing for the Court, Justice Ginsburg held that the five-minute extension of the traffic stop constituted an unreasonable seizure.

As we saw in *Jardines*, the use of drug detection dogs may also constitute a search if a dog or its handler intrude into a constitutionally protected area in order to facilitate a sniff. But dog sniffs that do not entail a physical intrusion into a constitutionally protected area do not constitute a "search" under *Olmstead.*

b. *Chemical Testing for Drugs*

The Court applied the reasoning in *Place* when it upheld the warrantless chemical field-testing of a powder that a Federal agent obtained from a package opened by Federal Express employees in United States v. Jacobsen, 466 U.S. 109 (1984).[11] Justice Stevens's opinion for the Court stated that "[a] chemical test that merely discloses whether or not a particular substance is cocaine does not compromise any legitimate interest in privacy." Even if the results of the test are negative, the results reveal "nothing of special interest." Thus, "[h]ere, as in *Place,* the likelihood that official conduct * * * will actually compromise any legitimate interest in privacy seems much too remote to characterize the testing as a search subject to the Fourth Amendment."

[11] The portion of the Court's opinion upholding the visual examination and seizure of the plastic bags containing the powder is discussed in the section on mixed public and private searches, *supra.*

While the field test in *Jacobsen* was not a search, it did constitute a *seizure*, because the powder sample that was tested was destroyed in the process. Thus, the test affected "possessory interests protected by the Amendment, since by destroying a quantity of the powder it converted what had been only a temporary deprivation of possessory interests into a permanent one." However, Justice Stevens found that the seizure involved was reasonable under the Fourth Amendment because only a minimal amount was destroyed and the officer had a clear indication that the powder was some kind of contraband before he tested it.

Justice Brennan, joined by Justice Marshall, wrote a dissenting opinion in *Jacobsen*. He found it "most startling" that in this case and in *Place* the Court put "its exclusive focus on the nature of the information or item sought and revealed through the use of a surveillance technique, rather than on the context in which the information or item is concealed." Rather than hold that a technique either always or never violates reasonable expectations of privacy, Justice Brennan urged the Court to examine the private nature of the area or item subjected to intrusion.

Then-Judge Gorsuch questioned whether the *Jacobsen* holding needs to be reconsidered in light of the trespass analysis of *Jones*. Writing for a panel of the 10th Circuit in United States v. Ackerman, 831 F.3d 1292 (10th Cir. 2016), Judge Gorsuch ran the *Jacobsen* facts through the trespass-with-investigatory intent analysis and found as follows:

> Reexamining the facts of *Jacobsen* in light of *Jones*, it seems at least possible that the court today would find that a "search" did take place there. After all, the DEA agent who performed the drug test in *Jacobsen* took and destroyed a trace amount of private property, a seeming trespass to chattels. Neither is there any question that the purpose and effect of the agent's action was to obtain information.

In Skinner v. Railway Labor Executives' Ass'n, 489 U.S. 602 (1989), the Court unanimously held that drug testing of urine was a search. The Court noted that, unlike the field testing in *Jacobsen*, testing urine samples could uncover such innocent secret information as epilepsy, pregnancy, or the use of prescription drugs. Moreover, the process of collecting urine samples (including aural observation) was intrusive and embarrassing. The Court concluded that "the collection and testing of urine intrudes upon expectations of privacy that society has long recognized as reasonable."

7. Methods That Can Reveal Both Innocent and Illegal Activity

The methods used in *Place*, *Caballes*, and *Jacobsen* were not searches because they could only detect the presence of illegal activity. But what about methods aimed at detecting illegal activity that can also detect innocent activity? The Court offered its answer in *Skinner* where it concluded that "the collection and testing of urine intrudes upon expectations of privacy that society has long recognized as reasonable."

The Court applied this same logic in Kyllo v. United States, 533 U.S. 27 (2001), which asked whether the use of a thermal imaging device to determine the presence of infrared radiation emanating from a home constitutes a "search" for purposes of the Fourth Amendment. In that case, officers used an "Agema Thermovision 210" deployed on a public street to scan Kyllo's home to determine the presence of high-intensity lamps used to grow marijuana. Writing for the Court, Justice Scalia noted that:

> The *Katz* test—whether the individual has an expectation of privacy that society is prepared to recognize as reasonable—has often been criticized as circular, and hence subjective and unpredictable. While it may be difficult to refine *Katz* when the search of areas such as telephone booths, automobiles, or even the curtilage and uncovered portions of residences are at issue, in the case of the search of the interior of homes—the prototypical and hence most commonly litigated area of protected privacy—there is a ready criterion, with roots deep in the common law, of the minimal expectation of privacy that exists, and that is acknowledged to be reasonable. To withdraw protection of this minimum expectation would be to permit police technology to erode the privacy guaranteed by the Fourth Amendment.

In contrast with drug-sniffing dogs or chemical drug tests, granting law enforcement unfettered discretion to train thermal detection devices on homes would threaten these minimal expectations of privacy because they reveal both illegal and innocent activity. Some of these innocent activities may be quite intimate, and others quotidian, but Justice Scalia made clear that it is the home rather than the intimacy of the activity that warrants Fourth Amendment protection.

> The Fourth Amendment's protection of the home has never been tied to measurement of the quality or quantity of information obtained. In *Silverman*, for example, we made clear that any physical invasion of the structure of the home, "by even a fraction of an inch," was too much, and there is certainly no exception to the warrant requirement for the officer who barely cracks open the front door and sees nothing but the nonintimate rug on the vestibule floor. In the home, our cases show, all details are intimate details, because the entire area is held safe from prying government eyes. * * *
>
> Limiting the prohibition of thermal imaging to "intimate details" would not only be wrong in principle; it would be impractical in application * * *. To begin with, there is no necessary connection between the sophistication of the surveillance equipment and the "intimacy" of the details that it observes—which means that one cannot say (and the police cannot be assured) that use of the relatively

> crude equipment at issue here will always be lawful. The Agema Thermovision 210 might disclose, for example, at what hour each night the lady of the house takes her daily sauna and bath—a detail that many would consider "intimate"; and a much more sophisticated system might detect nothing more intimate than the fact that someone left a closet light on. We could not, in other words, develop a rule approving only that through-the-wall surveillance which identifies objects no smaller than 36 by 36 inches, but would have to develop a jurisprudence specifying which home activities are "intimate" and which are not. And even when (if ever) that jurisprudence were fully developed, no police officer would be able to know in advance whether his through-the-wall surveillance picks up "intimate" details—and thus would be unable to know in advance whether it is constitutional.

On this basis, the Court concluded that

> Where, as here, the Government uses a device that is not in general public use, to explore details of the home that would previously have been unknowable without physical intrusion, the surveillance is a "search" and is presumptively unreasonable without a warrant.

Joined by Chief Justice Rehnquist, Justice O'Conner, and Justice Kennedy, Justice Stevens dissented in *Kyllo*. Because the device used was purely passive, detected only heat that routinely emanates from buildings, and revealed no intimate details about the interior of Kyllo's home, he concluded that its use did not violate reasonable expectations of privacy. Justice Stevens also expressed concern about the Court's introduction of the idea that "common public use" should play a role in assessing Fourth Amendment interests. On his account,

> the contours of [this] new rule are uncertain because its protection apparently dissipates as soon as the relevant technology is "in general public use." Yet how much use is general public use is not even hinted at by the Court's opinion, which makes the somewhat doubtful assumption that the thermal imager used in this case does not satisfy that criterion. In any event, putting aside its lack of clarity, this criterion is somewhat perverse because it seems likely that the threat to privacy will grow, rather than recede, as the use of intrusive equipment becomes more readily available.

Although Justice Scalia draws on the idea of physical intrusion when evaluating the constitutionality of thermal detection devices, these technologies do not entail any actual physical intrusion. *Kyllo* therefore seems to mark another circumstance where the *Katz* test is more protective than the physical intrusion test.

What happens if the use of thermal imaging devices becomes commonplace among members of the public? Doesn't the majority in *Kyllo* admit that the use of the devices by police officers at that point will not be a search? If that is so, then how much has the Court done to protect citizens from technological advances in official investigations? What about drones? Lots of people have them. Does that mean that an officer can send a drone to hover and peek into Kyllo's house without triggering Fourth Amendment protection? How, if at all, might Federal Aviation Administration regulations or local laws governing the use of drones affect the analysis?

Note that, at least at this point, the Court's holding in *Kyllo* effectively puts an end to the law enforcement use of thermal imaging devices to scan homes. If an officer has the probable cause necessary to conduct a thermal imaging scan, then he has no need for the thermal imaging scan. He can just get a warrant to conduct a physical search of the home. Moreover, thermal imagers rely on a relative comparison of heat emanation. So typically—and as in *Kyllo*—an officer would need to scan other houses in the neighborhood to determine whether the suspect's house emanated heat more than those other houses. It is hard to see how an officer could show the probable cause necessary to scan these comparator homes.

8. Jails, Prison Cells, and Convicts

Chief Justice Burger wrote for the Court in Hudson v. Palmer, 468 U.S. 517 (1984), as it held that a prisoner has no constitutionally protected expectation of privacy in his prison cell or in papers or property in his cell. Therefore, the Fourth Amendment was not implicated when prison officials rummaged through Hudson's cell and personal effects and destroyed some of his property in the course of their conduct. The Court concluded that "[t]he uncertainty that attends random searches of cells renders these searches perhaps the most effective weapon of the prison administrator in the constant fight against the proliferation of knives and guns, illicit drugs, and other contraband." It added that prison officials must be free to seize any articles from cells when necessary to serve legitimate institutional interests.

Justice Stevens, joined by Justices Brennan, Marshall and Blackmun, dissented. He did not disagree that prison officials should be able to conduct random searches to protect prison security, but he took exception to the holding that "no matter how malicious, destructive or arbitrary a cell search and seizure may be, it cannot constitute an unreasonable invasion of any privacy or possessory interest that society is prepared to recognize as reasonable." In his opinion, "[t]o hold that a prisoner's possession of a letter from his wife, or a picture of his baby, has no protection against arbitrary or malicious perusal, seizure or destruction would not * * * comport with any civilized standard of decency."

Justice Stevens noted that the majority's holding was limited to a prisoner's papers and effects located in his cell, and that the Court apparently "believes that at least a prisoner's person is secure from unreasonable search and seizure." In Bell v. Wolfish, 441 U.S. 520 (1979), the Court stated that at best prisoners have a reasonable expectation of privacy "of diminished scope" and that strip searches and body cavity searches of pretrial detainees after contact visits were governed by the Fourth Amendment but were reasonable under the circumstances. As to when and whether searches of prisoners are reasonable under the Fourth Amendment, see the section on "special needs" searches later in this Chapter.

These cases were all decided before *Jones*. Does a physical intrusion test compel a different result? Probably not. The Fourth Amendment does not prohibit all searches and seizures. It only guarantees security against unreasonable searches and seizures. Given the weighty administrative, safety, and security interests at stake, suspicionless searches of effects belonging to incarcerated persons are reasonable under the special needs doctrine, which we discuss at length later in this Chapter.

9. Public Schools and Public Employees

In New Jersey v. T.L.O., 469 U.S. 325 (1985), the Court rejected a state's arguments that students have no legitimate expectation of privacy in their possessions that they take to a public school. Although the Court recognized the need for schools to maintain discipline, it declined to apply its decision in the prisoner case, *Hudson*, *supra*, to the school context. Justice White wrote for the Court and stated that "[w]e are not yet ready to hold that the schools and the prisons need be equated for purposes of the Fourth Amendment." His opinion also rejected the state's suggestion that a student is free to maintain any privacy interest in personal property simply by leaving the property at home. The opinion concluded that "schoolchildren may find it necessary to carry with them a variety of legitimate, noncontraband items, and there is no reason to conclude that they have necessarily waived all rights to privacy in such items merely by bringing them onto school grounds."

It is important to remember that a finding of a legitimate expectation of privacy is just the first step in the Fourth Amendment inquiry. If the citizen has a legitimate expectation of privacy or property interest, then the official intrusion is reviewed for its reasonableness. In *T.L.O.*, the Court held that the school official's inspection of a student's handbag was a search, but concluded that the search was reasonable because the official could reasonably suspect that the student had cigarettes in her bag. This holding on reasonableness is discussed further in the section on "special needs" searches, *infra*.

The Supreme Court in O'Connor v. Ortega, 480 U.S. 709 (1987), unanimously rejected an argument that governmental employees "can never have a reasonable expectation of privacy in their place of work," although the Justices could not agree on an opinion for the Court. State hospital officials, investigating various charges made against a psychiatrist, entered the psychiatrist's office and seized various items from his desk and file cabinets. The psychiatrist brought a civil rights action against the officials, claiming that they had violated his Fourth Amendment rights.

Justice O'Connor's plurality opinion, joined by Chief Justice Rehnquist and Justices White and Powell, declined to decide whether the psychiatrist had a reasonable expectation of privacy in his office, but found that he definitely had one in his desk and file cabinets. The plurality concluded "that public employers' intrusions upon the constitutionally protected privacy interests of government employees for noninvestigatory, work-related purposes, as well as for investigations of work-related misconduct should be judged by the standard of reasonableness under all the circumstances." Applying those reasonableness standards, Justice O'Connor found that the search of the public employee's office was permissible because investigating officials had reasonable suspicion to believe that the employee had stolen government property.

Justice Scalia concurred in the judgment. He objected to the vagueness of the plurality opinion and "would hold * * * that the offices of government employees, and *a fortiori* the drawers and files within those offices, are covered by the Fourth Amendment protections as a general matter. (The qualification is necessary to cover such unusual situations as that in which the office is subject to unrestricted public access * * *.)" But Justice Scalia also "would hold that government searches to retrieve work-related materials or to investigate violations of workplace rules—searches of the sort that are regarded as reasonable and normal in the private-employer context—do not violate the Fourth Amendment." He agreed with Justice O'Connor that the search in the instant case was reasonable because officials had reasonable suspicion to believe that the employee had stolen property.

Justice Blackmun, joined by Justices Brennan, Marshall, and Stevens, dissented in *Ortega*. The dissenters agreed with Justice Scalia's view that government employees had a reasonable expectation of privacy in their offices. But they argued that the reasonableness of the search should be judged by standards of probable cause rather than the lesser standards of reasonable suspicion. For further discussion on the reasonableness of searches of public employees, see the section on "special needs" searches later in this Chapter.

IV. WHAT IS A "SEIZURE"?

The Fourth Amendment guarantees security against both unreasonable searches and unreasonable seizures. In contrast with its search jurisprudence, the Court has adopted a fairly straightforward approach to defining "seizure." Broadly speaking, seizures of persons occur when government agents materially interfere with a person's interest in being free from physical disruption and inconvenience. Seizures of houses, papers, and effects occur when government agents exercise dominion and control over property or otherwise materially interfere with possessory interests. There are nuances, of course, which we will explore in the materials below.

It is worth noting that seizures will play a central role in our discussions of stops and frisks later in this Chapter. We will therefore have occasion to revisit some of the concepts discussed here when we turn to that material.

Seizures and Searches Implicate Different Interests

Note that a seizure may occur without a search, and a search may occur without a seizure. As Justice Stevens explained in his concurring opinion in Texas v. Brown, 460 U.S. 730, 747–48 (1983):

> The Amendment protects two different interests of the citizen—the interest in retaining possession of property and the interest in maintaining personal privacy. A seizure threatens the former, a search the latter. As a matter of timing, a seizure is usually preceded by a search, but when a container is involved the converse is often true. Significantly, the two protected interests are not always present to the same extent; for example, the seizure of a locked suitcase does not necessarily compromise the secrecy of its contents, and the search of a stopped vehicle does not necessarily deprive its owner of possession.

So, searches and seizures implicate different interests and the Fourth Amendment regulates searches and seizures independently. By way of application for this distinction, consider Soldal v. Cook County, 506 U.S. 56 (1992). The Soldal family lived in a trailer on a rented lot. The owner of the lot removed and towed the trailer prior to an eviction hearing while deputy sheriffs at the scene declined to intervene. The Soldals brought an action under 42 U.S.C. § 1983 claiming that their Fourth Amendment rights had been violated when their home was taken away and that their landlord had conspired with local police to unreasonably seize and remove their trailer.

The lower court dismissed the action, reasoning that the Fourth Amendment was not implicated because the removal and towing did not occur in the course of an investigation for evidence and did not involve invasion of the privacy interests in the trailer. Justice White, writing for the Court, rejected this position stating that, for Fourth Amendment purposes, a "seizure" of property occurs when "there is some meaningful interference with an individual's possessory interests in that property." He concluded: "[w]e fail to see how being unceremoniously dispossessed of one's home in the manner alleged to have occurred here can be viewed as anything but a seizure invoking the protection of the Fourth Amendment."

Justice White cited *Katz* for the proposition that privacy rights are not the sole measure of Fourth Amendment violations and noted that "seizures of property are subject to Fourth Amendment scrutiny even though no search within the meaning of the Amendment has taken place." He rejected the lower court's notion that the Fourth Amendment only applies to efforts to collect evidence.

After *Soldal,* the question of whether a seizure of property has occurred is usually obvious and is rarely contested, so we will cover these topics quickly. More difficult questions have arisen in the context of law enforcement engagements with citizens. We shall therefore take more time to consider when a *person* has been seized.

A. SEIZURES OF PERSONS

The Court offers a useful overview of the law defining seizures of persons[12] in the following case.

TORRES V. MADRID

Supreme Court of the United States, 2021.
141 S.Ct. 989.

CHIEF JUSTICE ROBERTS delivered the opinion of the Court.

The Fourth Amendment prohibits unreasonable "seizures" to safeguard "[t]he right of the people to be secure in their persons." Under our cases, an officer seizes a person when he uses force to apprehend her. The question in this case is whether a seizure occurs when an officer shoots someone who temporarily eludes capture after the shooting. The answer is yes: The application of physical force to the body of a person with intent to restrain is a seizure, even if the force does not succeed in subduing the person.

I

At dawn on July 15, 2014, four New Mexico State Police arrived at an apartment complex in Albuquerque to execute an arrest warrant for a woman accused of white collar crimes, but also "suspected of having been involved in drug trafficking, murder, and other violent crimes." * * *

The officers observed Torres standing with another person near a Toyota FJ Cruiser in the parking lot of the complex. Officer Williamson concluded that neither Torres nor her companion was the target of the warrant. As the officers approached the vehicle, the companion departed, and Torres—at the time experiencing methamphetamine withdrawal—got

---

[12] In Terry v. Ohio, 392 U.S. 1 (1968), the Court divided seizures of persons into two categories: stops and arrests. We will discuss in depth the rules governing stops and arrests in the materials on whether to apply or not apply the Warrant Clause.

into the driver's seat. The officers attempted to speak with her, but she did not notice their presence until one of them tried to open the door of her car.

Although the officers wore tactical vests marked with police identification, Torres saw only that they had guns. She thought the officers were carjackers trying to steal her car, and she hit the gas to escape them. Neither Officer Madrid nor Officer Williamson, according to Torres, stood in the path of the vehicle, but both fired their service pistols to stop her. All told, the two officers fired 13 shots at Torres, striking her twice in the back and temporarily paralyzing her left arm.

Steering with her right arm, Torres accelerated through the fusillade of bullets, exited the apartment complex, drove a short distance, and stopped in a parking lot. After asking a bystander to report an attempted carjacking, Torres stole a Kia Soul that happened to be idling nearby and drove 75 miles to Grants, New Mexico. The good news for Torres was that the hospital in Grants was able to airlift her to another hospital where she could receive appropriate care. The bad news was that the hospital was back in Albuquerque, where the police arrested her the next day. She pleaded no contest to aggravated fleeing from a law enforcement officer, assault on a peace officer, and unlawfully taking a motor vehicle.

Torres later sought damages from Officers Madrid and Williamson under 42 U.S.C. § 1983, * * *. She claimed that the officers applied excessive force, making the shooting an unreasonable seizure under the Fourth Amendment. The District Court granted summary judgment to the officers, and the Court of Appeals for the Tenth Circuit affirmed on the ground that "a suspect's continued flight after being shot by police negates a Fourth Amendment excessive-force claim." The court relied on Circuit precedent providing that "no seizure can occur unless there is physical touch or a show of authority," and that "such physical touch (or force) must terminate the suspect's movement" or otherwise give rise to physical control over the suspect.

We granted certiorari.

II

The Fourth Amendment protects "[t]he right of the people to be secure in their persons, houses, papers, and effects, against unreasonable searches and seizures." This case concerns the "seizure" of a "person," which can take the form of "physical force" or a "show of authority" that "in some way restrain[s] the liberty" of the person. The question before us is whether the application of physical force is a seizure if the force, despite hitting its target, fails to stop the person.

We largely covered this ground in *California v. Hodari D.*, 499 U.S. 621 (1991). * * *

Hodari D. articulates two pertinent principles. First, common law arrests are Fourth Amendment seizures. And second, the common law considered the application of force to the body of a person with intent to restrain to be an arrest, no matter whether the arrestee escaped. * * *

At the adoption of the Fourth Amendment, a "seizure" was the "act of taking by warrant" or "of laying hold on suddenly"—for example, when an "officer seizes a thief." A seizure did not necessarily result in actual control or detention. It is true that, when speaking of property, "[f]rom the time of the founding to the present, the word 'seizure' has meant [] 'taking possession.' " *Hodari D.*, 499 U.S., at 624 (quoting 2 Webster 67). But the Framers selected a term—seizure—broad enough to apply to all the concerns of the Fourth Amendment: "persons," as well as "houses, papers, and effects." As applied to a person, "[t]he word 'seizure' readily bears the meaning of a laying on of hands or application of physical force to restrain movement, even when it is ultimately unsuccessful." Then, as now, an ordinary user of the English language could remark: "She seized the purse-snatcher, but he broke out of her grasp." * * *

The common law rule identified in *Hodari D.*—that the application of force gives rise to an arrest, even if the officer does not secure control over the arrestee—achieved recognition to such an extent that English lawyers could confidently (and accurately) proclaim that "[a]ll the authorities, from the earliest time to the present, establish that a corporal touch is sufficient to constitute an arrest, even though the defendant do not submit." The slightest application of force could satisfy this rule. In *Genner v. Sparks*, 6 Mod. 173, 87 Eng. Rep. 928 (Q. B. 1704), the defendant did not submit to the authority of an arrest warrant, but the court explained that the bailiff would have made an arrest if he "had but touched the defendant even with the end of his finger." So too, if a "bailiff caught one by the hand (whom he had a warrant to arrest) as he held it out of a window," that alone would accomplish an arrest. The touching of the person—frequently called a laying of hands—was enough. Only later did English law grow to recognize arrest without touching through a submission to a show of authority. Even so, the traditional rule persisted that all an arrest required was "corporal seising or touching the defendant's body."

Early American courts adopted this mere-touch rule from England, just as they embraced other common law principles of search and seizure. Justice Baldwin, instructing a jury in his capacity as Circuit Justice, defined an arrest to include "touching or putting hands upon [the arrestee] in the execution of process." United States v. Benner, 24 F. Cas. 1084, 1086–1087 (No. 14,568) (CC ED Pa. 1830). State courts agreed that "any touching, however slight, is enough," provided the officer made his intent to arrest clear. Courts continued to hold that an arrest required only the application of force—not control or custody—through the framing of the

Fourteenth Amendment, which incorporated the protections of the Fourth Amendment against the States.

Stated simply, the cases "abundantly shew that the slightest touch [was] an arrest in point of law." Indeed, it was not even required that the officer have, at the time of such an arrest, "the power of keeping the party so arrested under restraint." The consequences would be "pernicious," an English judge worried, if the question of control "were perpetually to be submitted to a jury." * * *

This case, of course, does not involve "laying hands," but instead a shooting. Neither the parties nor the United States as *amicus curiae* suggests that the officers' use of bullets to restrain Torres alters the analysis in any way. And * * * we see no basis for drawing an artificial line between grasping with a hand and other means of applying physical force to effect an arrest. * * * The required "corporal seising or touching the defendant's body" can be as readily accomplished by a bullet as by the end of a finger. * * *

We stress, however, that the application of the common law rule does not transform every physical contact between a government employee and a member of the public into a Fourth Amendment seizure. A seizure requires the use of force with intent to restrain. Accidental force will not qualify. Nor will force intentionally applied for some other purpose satisfy this rule. In this opinion, we consider only force used to apprehend. We do not * * * opine on matters not presented here—pepper spray, flash-bang grenades, lasers, and more.

Moreover, the appropriate inquiry is whether the challenged conduct objectively manifests an intent to restrain, for we rarely probe the subjective motivations of police officers in the Fourth Amendment context. Only an objective test "allows the police to determine in advance whether the conduct contemplated will implicate the Fourth Amendment." While a mere touch can be enough for a seizure, the amount of force remains pertinent in assessing the objective intent to restrain. A tap on the shoulder to get one's attention will rarely exhibit such an intent.

Nor does the seizure depend on the subjective perceptions of the seized person. Here, for example, Torres claims to have perceived the officers' actions as an attempted carjacking. But the conduct of the officers—ordering Torres to stop and then shooting to restrain her movement—satisfies the objective test for a seizure, regardless of whether Torres comprehended the governmental character of their actions.

The rule we announce today is narrow. In addition to the requirement of intent to restrain, a seizure by force—absent submission—lasts only as long as the application of force. That is to say that the Fourth Amendment does not recognize any "continuing arrest during the period of fugitivity." *Hodari D.*, 499 U.S., at 625. The fleeting nature of some seizures by force undoubtedly may inform what damages a civil plaintiff may recover, and what evidence a criminal defendant may exclude from trial. But brief seizures are seizures all the same.

Applying these principles to the facts viewed in the light most favorable to Torres, the officers' shooting applied physical force to her body and objectively manifested an intent to restrain her from driving away. We therefore conclude that the officers seized Torres for the instant that the bullets struck her. * * *

* * *

We hold that the application of physical force to the body of a person with intent to restrain is a seizure even if the person does not submit and is not subdued. Of course, a seizure is just the first step in the analysis. The Fourth Amendment does not forbid all or even most seizures—only unreasonable ones. All we decide today is that the officers seized Torres by shooting her with intent to restrain her movement. We leave open on remand any questions regarding the reasonableness of the seizure, the damages caused by the seizure, and the officers' entitlement to qualified immunity.

JUSTICE BARRETT took no part in the consideration or decision of this case.

JUSTICE GORSUCH, with whom JUSTICE THOMAS and JUSTICE ALITO join, dissenting.

The majority holds that a criminal suspect can be simultaneously seized and roaming at large. On the majority's account, a Fourth Amendment "seizure" takes place whenever an officer "merely touches" a suspect. It's a seizure even if the suspect refuses to stop, evades capture, and rides off into the sunset never to be seen again. That view is as mistaken as it is novel.

Until today, a Fourth Amendment "seizure" has required taking possession of someone or something. To reach its contrary judgment, the majority must conflate a seizure with its attempt and confuse an arrest with a battery. * * *

NOTE ON TORRES: CALIFORNIA V. HODARI D.

The Court in *Torres* relies on California v. Hodari D., 499 U.S. 621 (1991). That case arose when officers encountered a group of youths who were huddled around a car and fled when they saw the officers. As officers pursued him, Hodari threw away a small rock of crack cocaine, which was later recovered. At a subsequent criminal trial, Hodari sought to suppress the cocaine claiming that the pursuit was an unreasonable seizure.

Justice Scalia, writing for the majority, separated seizures into two types: those in which the officer has physically touched the citizen and those in which the officer has used a non-physical show of authority. Predicting the Court's holding in *Torres*, Justice Scalia noted that "an arrest is effected by the slightest application of physical force" "whether or not it succeeded in subduing the arrestee." But what about non-physical shows of authority? If a suspect fails to submit to a police officer's commands, then has he been "seized"? The Court held that he has not.

As a matter of policy, Justice Scalia reasoned that the public should be encouraged to comply with police orders. It would not do to reward suspects like Hodari D. for noncompliance. Justice Scalia rejected the argument that police officers, having no justification to support a seizure, would routinely use non-physical displays of authority in the hope that suspects would disobey them, flee, and discard evidence. He reasoned that police do not issue orders expecting them to be ignored and would not take the risk of effecting unlawful seizures.

Justice Stevens, joined by Justice Marshall, dissented in *Hodari D.* He argued that the majority erred in focusing on a citizen's reaction to an officer's conduct rather than on the officer's conduct itself. He noted that, under the majority's test, police officers could take advantage of citizens by using all their conduct against them in the seconds before they actually submit to authority. For example, an officer could flash his lights to stop a car without adequate cause and then use any observations made before the car comes to a complete stop. Similarly, a drug enforcement agent could approach a group of passengers in an airport with a drawn gun, announce a baggage search, and then rely on the passengers' reaction to justify a subsequent investigative stop.

Justice Stevens concluded it was "anomalous, at best" to establish different rules for seizures effected by touching and those effected by a show of force. He argued that it was important for an officer to know in advance whether certain conduct would constitute a seizure and that the majority's test makes this impossible when the officer is using a non-physical show of force.

QUESTIONS AFTER TORRES AND HODARI D.

In his dissenting opinion in *Hodari D.*, Justice Stevens asks whether "a police officer may now fire his weapon at an innocent citizen and not implicate the Fourth Amendment—as long as he misses his target." Viewed as either a non-physical show of authority under *Hodari D.* or a failed attempt to achieve physical contact under *Torres*, the answer seems to be "yes." Is this a sensible result? See Saltzburg, The Fourth Amendment: Internal Revenue Code or Body of Principles? 74 Geo.Wash.L.Rev. 956 (2006) ("Apparently, Justice Scalia would hold that if an officer shot at a suspect to stop him from fleeing, but the bullet missed the suspect because he lunged away to avoid being shot, there would be no seizure. There is little logic to the result that the touch of a finger that fails to restrain a suspect is a seizure, while an unsuccessful attempt to shoot a suspect is not."). See also Mettler v. Whitledge, 165 F.3d

1197 (8th Cir.1999) (sending in an attack dog to subdue the suspect did not constitute an unreasonable seizure where the citizen shot the dog before the dog got to him).

Seizures by Displays of Authority: The Mendenhall "Free to Leave" Test

Police officers and other law enforcement officials routinely interact with citizens on the street and in other public spaces. Many of these engagements are quotidian—an exchanged greeting, a comment about the weather, or a gripe about the performance of a local sports franchise—and likely do not constitute "seizures" by any definition—they are akin to a "tap on the shoulder to get one's attention." Others are pointedly related to law enforcement activities. For example, an officer might ask a person loitering on a street corner what he is doing or approach a person matching the description of a suspect in a recent armed robbery to determine whether she is the perpetrator. None of these engagements involve a physical touching, but might they nevertheless constitute "seizures"?

One possible answer would be to ask whether the subject of police scrutiny in these cases had been arrested. In Terry v. Ohio, 392 U.S. 1 (1968), which is discussed later in this Chapter in the materials covering stops and frisks, the Court made clear "that the Fourth Amendment governs 'seizures' of the person which do not eventuate in a trip to the stationhouse and prosecution for crime—'arrests' in traditional terminology." According to the *Terry* Court, "whenever a police officer accosts an individual and restrains his freedom to walk away, he has 'seized' that person."

Justice Stewart relied on this language from *Terry* in United States v. Mendenhall, 446 U.S. 544 (1980). Mendenhall was observed by Drug Enforcement Administration agents at the Detroit Airport as she arrived on a flight from Los Angeles. The agents suspected she was a drug courier. They approached her as she was walking through the concourse, identified themselves as DEA agents, and asked to see her identification and airline ticket. The driver's license she produced was in her name, but her ticket was not. She became extremely nervous. The agents returned Mendenhall's license and ticket to her before asking her to accompany them to the airport DEA office for further questions. Without saying anything, she did so. In the office the agents asked Mendenhall if she would allow a search of her person and handbag. She said yes. During a subsequent strip search of her person, drugs were found. Mendenhall was arrested, prosecuted, and convicted.

Justice Stewart, joined only by Justice Rehnquist, addressed an argument the government had not made in the lower courts and concluded that, when Mendenhall was approached in the airport, no "seizure" had occurred, and therefore this initial police-citizen contact was outside the scope of the Fourth Amendment. Justice Stewart explained:

> The events took place in the public concourse. The agents wore no uniforms and displayed no weapons. They did not summon the respondent to their presence, but instead approached her and identified themselves as federal agents. They requested, but did not demand, to see the respondent's identification and ticket. Such conduct, without more, did not amount to an intrusion upon any constitutionally protected interest. * * *

This conclusion resulted from application of the following rule:

> A person has been "seized" within the meaning of the Fourth Amendment only if, in view of all the circumstances surrounding the incident, a reasonable person would have believed that he was not free to leave. Examples of circumstances that might indicate a seizure, even where the person did not attempt to leave, would be the threatening presence of several officers, the display of a weapon by an officer, some physical touching of the person of the citizen, or the use of language or tone of voice indicating that compliance with the officer's request might be compelled.

Note that Justice Stewart's test operates from the perspective of a reasonable person. It therefore does not "depend on the subjective perceptions of the seized person." Torres, supra. See United States v. Cardoza, 129 F.3d 6 (1st Cir.1997) ("police conduct, viewed from the totality of the circumstances, must objectively communicate that the officer is exercising his or her official authority to restrain the individual's liberty of movement before we can find that a seizure occurred.").

Justice Stewart's "free to leave" test did not command a majority of the Court in *Mendenhall*—seven Justices found that the question whether a seizure had occurred was not raised properly. But subsequent cases have established the "free to leave" test as the benchmark for determining whether a non-physical show of government authority is sufficient to constitute a "seizure" if the person targeted submits. Of course, even a show of authority sufficient to cause a reasonable person to believe she is not free to leave does not constitute a "seizure" absent submission.

Applying the "Free to Leave" Test: Florida v. Royer

A plurality of the Court applied the Stewart "free to leave" test in Florida v. Royer, 460 U.S. 491 (1983). Justice White, writing for himself and Justices Marshall, Powell, and Stevens, stated the facts:

> Royer was observed at Miami International Airport by two plain-clothes detectives * * *. Detectives Johnson and Magdalena believed that Royer's appearance, mannerisms, luggage, and actions fit the so-

called "drug courier profile." Royer, apparently unaware of the attention he had attracted, purchased a one-way ticket to New York City and checked his two suitcases, placing on each suitcase an identification tag bearing the name "Holt" and the destination, "LaGuardia". As Royer made his way to the concourse which led to the airline boarding area, the two detectives approached him, identified themselves as policemen working out of the sheriff's office, and asked if Royer had a "moment" to speak with them; Royer said "Yes."

Upon request, but without oral consent, Royer produced for the detectives his airline ticket and his driver's license. The airline ticket, like the baggage identification tags, bore the name "Holt," while the driver's license carried respondent's correct name, "Royer." When the detectives asked about the discrepancy, Royer explained that a friend had made the reservation in the name of "Holt." Royer became noticeably more nervous during this conversation, whereupon the detectives informed Royer that they were in fact narcotics investigators and that they had reason to suspect him of transporting narcotics.

The detectives did not return his airline ticket and identification but asked Royer to accompany them to a room, approximately forty feet away, adjacent to the concourse. Royer said nothing in response but went with the officers as he had been asked to do. The room was later described by Detective Johnson as a "large storage closet," located in the stewardesses' lounge and containing a small desk and two chairs. Without Royer's consent or agreement, Detective Johnson, using Royer's baggage check stubs, retrieved the "Holt" luggage from the airline and brought it to the room where respondent and Detective Magdalena were waiting. Royer was asked if he would consent to a search of the suitcases. Without orally responding to this request, Royer produced a key and unlocked one of the suitcases, which the detective then opened without seeking further assent from Royer. Drugs were found in that suitcase. According to Detective Johnson, Royer stated that he did not know the combination to the lock on the second suitcase. When asked if he objected to the detective opening the second suitcase, Royer said "no, go ahead," and did not object when the detective explained that the suitcase might have to be broken open. The suitcase was pried open by the officers and more marihuana was found. Royer was then told that he was under arrest. Approximately fifteen minutes had elapsed from the time the detectives initially approached respondent until his arrest upon the discovery of the contraband.

Justice White observed that Royer had testified that he believed he was not free to leave the officers' presence and that Detective Johnson stated that he did not believe he had probable cause to arrest until after he opened the suitcases. Justice White summarized some of the law regarding temporary seizures of persons, sometimes referred to as "stops."

> [L]aw enforcement officers do not violate the Fourth Amendment by merely approaching an individual on the street or in another public place, by asking him if he is willing to answer some questions, by putting questions to him if the person is willing to listen, or by offering in evidence in a criminal prosecution his voluntary answers to such questions. Nor would the fact that the officer identifies himself as a police officer, without more, convert the encounter into a seizure requiring some level of objective justification. The person approached, however, need not answer any question put to him; indeed, he may decline to listen to the questions at all and may go on his way. He may not be detained even momentarily without reasonable, objective grounds for doing so; and his refusal to listen or answer does not, without more, furnish those grounds. If there is no detention—no seizure within the meaning of the Fourth Amendment—then no constitutional rights have been infringed.

The plurality found that a seizure occurred when the officers took Royer's ticket and driver's license and started walking away:

> Here, Royer's ticket and identification remained in the possession of the officers throughout the encounter; the officers also seized and had possession of his luggage. As a practical matter, Royer could not leave the airport without them. In *Mendenhall,* no luggage was involved, the ticket and identification were immediately returned, and the officers were careful to advise that the suspect could decline to be searched. Here, the officers had seized Royer's luggage and made no effort to advise him that he need not consent to the search.

Justice Brennan concurred in the result. Four Justices dissented in *Royer* on the ground that, while Royer may have been seized, the seizure was reasonable and the police lawfully obtained Royer's consent. Thus, none of the Justices disagreed with the proposition that Royer was seized within the meaning of the Fourth Amendment when the officers retained his ticket and identification.

Factors Relevant to Finding a Seizure Under Mendenhall and Royer

Does the *Royer* Court give sufficient guidance to the police to determine what type of conduct constitutes a Fourth Amendment seizure? Lower courts have tried to impart some guidance. See United States v. Madden, 682 F.3d 920 (10th Cir. 2012) ("In this case, what began as a consensual encounter became an investigative detention when Officer Balderrama asked Madden to step out of the vehicle and then * * * directed Madden to sit in the back of his patrol car while he obtained Madden's personal information and ran it through the computer."); United States v. Espinoza, 490 F.3d 41 (1st Cir. 2007) (ordering a driver to turn off the engine of his car is a seizure); Johnson v. Campbell, 332 F.3d 199 (3d Cir. 2003) (motorist was stopped when officer persisted in telling him to roll his window down even after motorist refused: "At that time, Campbell made it clear that Johnson was not free to ignore him and would not be left alone until he complied."); United States v. High, 921 F.2d 112 (7th Cir.1990) (suggesting that officers "preface their questions with a statement that the encounter is consensual and that the citizen is free to go").

In United States v. Hernandez, 847 F.3d 1257 (10th Cir. 2017), the court "enumerated a non-exhaustive list of factors to be considered in determining whether a reasonable person would feel free to terminate his encounter with the police." Those factors are:

> the location of the encounter, particularly whether the defendant is in an open public place where he is within the view of persons other than law enforcement officers; whether the officers touch or physically restrain the defendant; whether the officers are uniformed or in plain clothes; whether their weapons are displayed; the number, demeanor and tone of voice of the officers; whether and for how long the officers retain the defendant's personal effects such as tickets or identification; and whether or not they have specifically advised defendant at any time that he had the right to terminate the encounter or refuse consent.

The court applied these factors to a case in which Hernandez was walking alone at night in a deserted area. Two uniformed, armed officers started following Hernandez in their patrol car. They began asking him questions, to which Hernandez responded without stopping. The officers then asked Hernandez to stop walking, which he did. The majority admitted that "this is a close case and there is a dearth of case law directly on point with the facts here" but found that a stop had been made. The dissenter argued that there was no indication of anything but a voluntary encounter. So how much help is a seven-factor test?

Factory Sweeps: INS v. Delgado

A majority of the Court adopted and applied the *Mendenhall* test in Immigration and Naturalization Service v. Delgado, 466 U.S. 210 (1984), which held that INS officers did not seize workers while surveying a factory in search of illegal aliens. Justice Rehnquist described the facts as follows:

> At the beginning of the surveys several agents positioned themselves near the buildings' exits, while other agents dispersed throughout the factory to question most, but not all, employees at their work stations. The agents displayed badges, carried walkie-talkies, and were armed, although at no point during any of the surveys was a

weapon ever drawn. Moving systematically through the factory, the agents approached employees and, after identifying themselves, asked them from one to three questions relating to their citizenship. If the employee gave a credible reply that he was a United States citizen, the questioning ended, and the agent moved on to another employee. If the employee gave an unsatisfactory response or admitted that he was an alien, the employee was asked to produce his immigration papers. During the survey, employees continued with their work and were free to walk around within the factory.

Four employees questioned in one of the surveys filed suit, claiming that the factory sweeps violated the Fourth Amendment and seeking declaratory and injunctive relief. The employees lost in the district court, prevailed in the court of appeals, and lost again in the Supreme Court.

Writing for the Court, Justice Rehnquist noted that "police questioning, by itself, is unlikely to result in a Fourth Amendment violation. While most citizens will respond to a police request, the fact that people do so, and do so without being told they are free not to respond, hardly eliminates the consensual nature of the response." He rejected the argument that the employees were seized during the entire sweep because guards were placed at the exits. Because the employees were at work and thus were not going to leave the factory in any event, Justice Rehnquist concluded that the guards at the exit could not have had a coercive or custodial effect. The majority reasoned that "[t]his conduct should have given [the employees] no reason to believe that they would be detained if they gave truthful answers to the questions put to them or if they simply refused to answer." And the majority also rejected an argument that individual employees were seized when they were questioned—because, generally, simple questions from a police officer do not amount to a seizure.

Justice Powell concurred in the result. Justice Brennan, joined by Justice Marshall, dissented from the holding that the individual interrogations were not seizures and argued that the testimony in the case "paints a frightening picture of people subjected to wholesale interrogation under conditions designed not to respect personal security and privacy, but rather to elicit prompt answers from completely intimidated workers."

Put yourself in the workers' place. Would you feel free to leave or to terminate the questioning? Would you assume the armed guards at the exits were placed there to keep you inside the factory? Would it affect you if, as is likely, all of the other factory members were "cooperating" by answering the officers' questions?

Bus Sweeps: Florida v. Bostick and United States v. Drayton

In the following case, the Court considers whether passengers on buses are "seized" when officers conduct a "bus sweep." The case discusses and applies the Court's first analysis of this subject in Florida v. Bostick.

UNITED STATES V. DRAYTON

Supreme Court of the United States, 2002.
536 U.S. 194.

JUSTICE KENNEDY delivered the opinion of the Court.

The Fourth Amendment permits police officers to approach bus passengers at random to ask questions and to request their consent to searches, provided a reasonable person would understand that he or she is free to refuse. Florida v. Bostick, 501 U.S. 429 (1991). This case requires us to determine whether officers must advise bus passengers during these encounters of their right not to cooperate.

* * * On February 4, 1999, respondents Christopher Drayton and Clifton Brown, Jr., were traveling on a Greyhound bus en route from Ft. Lauderdale, Florida, to Detroit, Michigan. The bus made a scheduled stop in Tallahassee, Florida. The passengers were required to disembark so the bus could be refueled and cleaned. As the passengers reboarded, the driver checked their tickets and then left to complete paperwork inside the terminal. As he left, the driver allowed three members of the Tallahassee Police Department to board the bus as part of a routine drug and weapons interdiction effort. The officers were dressed in plain clothes and carried concealed weapons and visible badges.

Once onboard Officer Hoover knelt on the driver's seat and faced the rear of the bus. He could observe the passengers and ensure the safety of the two other officers without blocking the aisle or otherwise obstructing the bus exit. Officers Lang and Blackburn went to the rear of the bus. Blackburn remained stationed there, facing forward. Lang worked his way toward the front of the bus, speaking with individual passengers as he went. He asked the passengers about their travel plans and sought to match passengers with luggage in the overhead racks. To avoid blocking the aisle, Lang stood next to or just behind each passenger with whom he spoke.

According to Lang's testimony, passengers who declined to cooperate with him or who chose to exit the bus at any time would have been allowed to do so without argument. In Lang's experience, however, most people are willing to cooperate. Some passengers go so far as to commend the police for their efforts to ensure the safety of their travel. Lang could recall five to six instances in the previous year in which passengers had declined to have their luggage searched. It also was common for passengers to leave the bus for a cigarette or a snack while the officers were on board. Lang sometimes informed passengers of their right to refuse to cooperate. On the day in question, however, he did not.

Respondents were seated next to each other on the bus. Drayton was in the aisle seat, Brown in the seat next to the window. Lang approached respondents from the rear and leaned over Drayton's shoulder. He held up his badge long enough for respondents to identify him as a police officer. With his face 12-to-18 inches away from Drayton's, Lang spoke in a voice just loud enough for respondents to hear:

> I'm Investigator Lang with the Tallahassee Police Department. We're conducting bus interdiction [sic], attempting to deter drugs and illegal weapons being transported on the bus. Do you have any bags on the bus?

Both respondents pointed to a single green bag in the overhead luggage rack. Lang asked, "Do you mind if I check it?," and Brown responded, "Go ahead." Lang handed the bag to Officer Blackburn to check. The bag contained no contraband.

Officer Lang noticed that both respondents were wearing heavy jackets and baggy pants despite the warm weather. In Lang's experience drug traffickers often use baggy clothing to conceal weapons or narcotics. The officer thus asked Brown if he had any weapons or drugs in his possession. And he asked Brown: "Do you mind if I check your person?" Brown answered, "Sure," and cooperated by leaning up in his seat, pulling a cell phone out of his pocket, and opening up his jacket. Lang reached across Drayton and patted down Brown's jacket and pockets, including his waist area, sides, and upper thighs. In both thigh areas, Lang detected hard objects similar to drug packages detected on other occasions. Lang arrested and handcuffed Brown. Officer Hoover escorted Brown from the bus.

Lang then asked Drayton, "Mind if I check you?" Drayton responded by lifting his hands about eight inches from his legs. Lang conducted a pat-down of Drayton's thighs and detected hard objects similar to those found on Brown. He arrested Drayton and escorted him from the bus. A further search revealed that respondents had duct-taped plastic bundles of powder cocaine between several pairs of their boxer shorts. Brown possessed three bundles containing 483 grams of cocaine. Drayton possessed two bundles containing 295 grams of cocaine.

[The defendants were charged with drug crimes. The trial court denied motions to suppress the drugs on the ground that the entire procedure was a consensual encounter.]

The Court of Appeals for the Eleventh Circuit reversed and remanded with instructions to grant respondents' motions to suppress. The court held that this disposition was compelled by its previous decisions [holding] that bus passengers do not feel free to disregard police officers' requests to search absent "some positive indication that consent could have been refused."

We granted certiorari. The respondents, we conclude, were not seized and their consent to the search was voluntary; and we reverse.

* * *

The Court has addressed on a previous occasion the specific question of drug interdiction efforts on buses. In *Bostick,* two police officers requested a bus passenger's consent to a search of his luggage. The passenger agreed, and the resulting search revealed cocaine in his suitcase. The Florida Supreme Court suppressed the cocaine. In doing so it adopted a *per se* rule that due to the cramped confines onboard a bus the act of questioning would deprive a person of his or her freedom of movement and so constitute a seizure under the Fourth Amendment.

This Court reversed. *Bostick* first made it clear that for the most part *per se* rules are inappropriate in the Fourth Amendment context. The proper inquiry necessitates a consideration of "all the circumstances surrounding the encounter." The Court noted next that the traditional rule, which states that a seizure does not occur so long as a reasonable person would feel free "to disregard the police and go about his business," is not an accurate measure of the coercive effect of a bus encounter. A passenger may not want to get off a bus if there is a risk it will depart before the opportunity to reboard. A bus rider's movements are confined in this sense, but this is the natural result of choosing to take the bus; it says nothing about whether the police conduct is coercive. The proper inquiry "is whether a reasonable person would feel free to decline the officers' requests or otherwise terminate the encounter." Finally, the Court rejected Bostick's argument that he must have been seized because no reasonable person would consent to a search of luggage containing drugs. The reasonable person test, the Court explained, is objective and "presupposes an *innocent* person."

In light of the limited record, *Bostick* refrained from deciding whether a seizure occurred. The Court, however, identified two factors "particularly worth noting" on remand. First, although it was obvious that an officer was armed, he did not remove the gun from its pouch or use it in a threatening way. Second, the officer advised the passenger that he could refuse consent to the search.

Relying upon this latter factor, the Eleventh Circuit has adopted what is in effect a *per se* rule that evidence obtained during suspicionless drug interdiction efforts aboard buses must be suppressed unless the officers have advised passengers of their right not to cooperate and to refuse consent to a search. * * *

The Court of Appeals erred in adopting this approach.

Applying the *Bostick* framework to the facts of this particular case, we conclude that the police did not seize respondents when they boarded the bus and began questioning passengers. The officers gave the passengers no reason to believe that they were required to answer the officers' questions. When Officer Lang approached respondents, he did not brandish a weapon or make any intimidating movements. He left the aisle free so that respondents could exit. He spoke to passengers one by one and in a polite, quiet voice. Nothing he said would suggest to a reasonable person that he or she was barred from leaving the bus or otherwise terminating the encounter.

* * * There was no application of force, no intimidating movement, no overwhelming show of force, no brandishing of weapons, no blocking of exits, no threat, no command, not even an authoritative tone of voice. It is beyond question that had this encounter occurred on the street, it would be constitutional. The fact that an encounter takes place on a bus does not on its own transform standard police questioning of citizens into an illegal seizure. Indeed, because many fellow passengers are present to witness officers' conduct, a reasonable person may feel even more secure in his or her decision not to cooperate with police on a bus than in other circumstances.

Respondents make much of the fact that Officer Lang displayed his badge. In * * * INS v. Delgado, the Court held that INS agents' wearing badges and questioning workers in a factory did not constitute a seizure. And while neither Lang nor his colleagues were in uniform or visibly armed, those factors should have little weight in the analysis. Officers are often required to wear uniforms and in many circumstances this is cause for assurance, not discomfort. Much the same can be said for wearing sidearms. That most law enforcement officers are armed is a fact well known to the public. The presence of a holstered firearm thus is unlikely to contribute to the coerciveness of the encounter absent active brandishing of the weapon.

Officer Hoover's position at the front of the bus also does not tip the scale in respondents' favor. Hoover did nothing to intimidate passengers, and he said nothing to suggest that people could not exit and indeed he left the aisle clear. * * *

Finally, the fact that in Officer Lang's experience only a few passengers have refused to cooperate does not suggest that a reasonable person would not feel free to terminate the bus encounter. * * * [B]us passengers answer officers' questions and otherwise cooperate not because of coercion but because the passengers know that their participation enhances their own safety and the safety of those around them. * * *

Drayton contends that even if Brown's cooperation with the officers was consensual, Drayton was seized because no reasonable person would feel free to terminate the encounter with the officers after Brown had been arrested. * * * The arrest of one person does not mean that everyone around him has been seized by police. If anything, Brown's arrest should have put Drayton on notice of the consequences of continuing the encounter by answering the officers' questions. * * *

JUSTICE SOUTER, with whom JUSTICE STEVENS and JUSTICE GINSBURG join, dissenting.

* * *

* * * [F]or reasons unexplained, the driver with the tickets entitling the passengers to travel had yielded his custody of the bus and its seated travelers to three police officers, whose authority apparently superseded the driver's own. The officers took control of the entire passenger compartment, one stationed at the door keeping surveillance of all the occupants, the others working forward from the back. With one officer right behind him and the other one forward, a third officer accosted each passenger at quarters extremely close and so cramped that as many as half the passengers could not even have stood to face the speaker. None was asked whether he was willing to converse with the police or to take part in the enquiry. Instead the officer said the police were "conducting bus interdiction," in the course of which they "would like . . . cooperation." The reasonable inference was that the "interdiction" was not a consensual exercise, but one the police would carry out whatever the circumstances; that they would prefer "cooperation" but would not let the lack of it stand in their way. * * *

It is very hard to imagine that either Brown or Drayton would have believed that he stood to lose nothing if he refused to cooperate with the police, or that he had any free choice to ignore the police altogether. No reasonable passenger could have believed that, only an uncomprehending one. * * *

Is the "Freedom to Walk Away" Test "Reasonable"

Professor Steinbock takes the Court's "freedom to walk away" test to task in The Wrong Line Between Freedom and Restraint: The Unreality, Obscurity, and Incivility of the Fourth Amendment Consensual Encounter Doctrine, 38 San Diego L.Rev. 507 (2001):

> There are legal fictions and there are legal fictions. One means of differentiating good from bad legal fictions is their relationship to reality * * *. By that measure, in light of the available evidence, the consensual encounter doctrine paints a false picture of reality as applied to encounters involving investigation of the individual being questioned. In so doing, it mislocates the dividing line between freedom and restraint, including on the "freedom" side of this line many people who are effectively restrained or—to put it another way—are restrained in all but the eyes of the law.
>
> * * * The consensual encounter doctrine virtually invites citizens, as an initial response, to question or rebuff police approaches. * * * Rudeness and confrontation by citizens, which are virtually required in order for citizens to determine whether they are free to go, stimulates rudeness and confrontation in response. This, in turn, poisons the relationship between citizens and their government, creating social friction and disunity.

Questions of decorum aside, does the "reasonable person" imagined by the Court in these cases reflect reality? Professor Nadler, in No Need to Shout: Bus Sweeps and the Psychology of Coercion, 2002 Sup.Ct. Rev. 153, has her doubts, arguing that the Court's "free to leave" test does line-up with the social science evidence concerning coercion and consent, particularly in the context of bus sweeps. She concludes as follows:

> [I]n its effort to be sensitive to the order-maintenance needs of the government, the Court has promulgated a standard to determining the bounds of consensual police-citizen encounters and voluntary searches that struggles against a wealth of social science evidence, that subjects many innocent people to suspicionless searches and seizures against their will, and that produces disagreement and confusion in the lower courts. It may be that large-scale, suspicionless searches of passengers on common carriers is a price that we ought to be willing to pay to stem the flow of illegal narcotics transported on intercity buses and trains. If this is the determination that underlies the decision in *Drayton*, then the Court should have explicitly stated it and justified it—rather than relying on the implausible assertion that bus passengers, when they are individually confronted by armed police officers who want to search them, feel free to ignore the police or outright refuse their requests.

But what is the alternative? Should it be considered a stop whenever a police officer approaches a citizen to ask questions? See Saltzburg, The Fourth Amendment: Internal Revenue Code or Body of Principles? 74 Geo.Wash.L.Rev. 956 (2006) ("A better approach is to focus on the conduct of law enforcement officers rather than on the reactions of individuals to law enforcement officers. This approach asks law enforcement officers to pay attention to their own actions, not to predict how reasonable civilians would respond to those actions.").

State of Mind Required for a Stop: Brower v. County of Inyo and Brendlin v. California

Must an officer have a certain state of mind in order to seize a person? Justice Scalia wrote for the Court in Brower v. County of Inyo, 489 U.S. 593 (1989), where officers set up a "blind" roadblock in an attempt to apprehend a fleeing suspect. The suspect, approaching the roadblock from around a curve, was not able to stop before crashing into it. The suspect died in the crash and a wrongful death action was brought alleging that the suspect had been illegally "seized" by the roadblock.

Justice Scalia agreed with the plaintiff that a seizure had occurred. He declared that "a Fourth Amendment seizure does not occur whenever there is a governmentally caused termination of an individual's freedom of movement * * *, nor even whenever there is a governmentally *desired* termination of an individual's freedom of movement * * *, but only when there is a governmental termination of freedom of movement *through means intentionally applied.*" In this case, the officers placed the roadblock with the intent to stop the suspect; and in fact the suspect was stopped by means of the roadblock. Therefore, the suspect was seized, even though he was not stopped in precisely the way that the officers intended for him to stop. The means used to stop him were intentionally applied.

Elaborating on this intent-based test, Justice Scalia posed the following hypothetical: suppose police officers park and leave their squad car on a hill, the parking brake accidentally disengages, the car rolls down the hill and just happens to pin a suspected criminal against a wall. Has the criminal been seized? Justice Scalia's answer was "no," because the officers never intentionally applied any means to stop the suspect's freedom of movement. They just got lucky.

Justice Stevens, joined by Justices Brennan, Marshall, and Blackmun, concurred in the judgment. He objected to Justice Scalia's emphasis on an intentional acquisition of physical control as marking the onset of a seizure, and suggested that, since it was clear in the instant case that the roadblock was intended to stop the deceased, "[d]ecision in the case before us is thus not advanced by pursuing a hypothetical inquiry concerning whether an unintentional act might also violate the Fourth Amendment."

Note that *Brower* does require courts to inquire into an officer's subjective state of mind. To the contrary, Justice Scalia observes that "we do not think it is practicable to conduct such an inquiry into subjective intent." In keeping with Chief Justice Roberts's discussion in *Torres*, the material question is one of objective purpose rather than subjective intent. The Court addressed this distinction in Brendlin v. California, 551 U.S. 249

(2007). There, evidence was found on a passenger in a car intentionally stopped by police. The government argued that the passenger was not seized by the mere stop of the car because the intent of the police was to stop *the driver*. The Court rejected this argument, stating that the intent that counts under the Fourth Amendment "is the intent that has been conveyed to the person confronted, and the criterion of willful restriction on freedom of movement is no invitation to look to subjective intent when determining who is seized." The Court concluded that the officers objectively intended to stop the car and a reasonable passenger would certainly think that he was not free to walk away.

When Does Submission Occur?

In California v. Hodari D., 499 U.S. 621 (1991), the Court held that a non-physical display of authority objectively calculated to effect a seizure that would lead a reasonable person to conclude they are not free to leave still does not constitute a "seizure" if the targeted person refuses to submit. This raises the question when, precisely, a suspect has submitted to a non-physical show of authority—i.e., when does the seizure begin. This is important when a citizen tries to dispose of evidence in response to a show of authority. Exemplary is United States v. Lender, 985 F.2d 151 (4th Cir. 1993). The court set forth the pertinent facts as follows:

> At approximately 12:50 a.m., [Officers Hill and Thornell] were patrolling an area in Kinston, North Carolina. The officers knew the area to be one where heavy drug traffic occurred. As they crossed an intersection, the officers observed a group of four or five men, including the defendant, huddled on a corner. The defendant had his hand stuck out with his palm up, and the other men were looking down toward his palm.
>
> Suspecting a drug transaction, the officers stopped their car, got out, and approached the men. * * * As the officers approached, the group began to disperse, and the defendant walked away from the officers with his back to them. Officer Hill called out for the defendant to stop, but the defendant refused. As he walked, the defendant turned and told Hill, "You don't want me; you don't want me."
>
> While Lender continued to walk away, both officers observed him bring his hands to the front of his waist as though reaching for or fumbling with something in that area. Officer Hill again called for the defendant to stop. At this point, the defendant stopped, and a loaded semi-automatic pistol fell from his waist to the ground. [Lender was convicted of possession of a firearm by a felon.]

Lender moved to suppress the gun, arguing that he had been seized when he dropped it. The court disagreed, concluding that Lender did not submit to the officer's order to stop.

> We do not believe * * * that Lender's momentary halt on the sidewalk with his back to the officers constituted a yielding to their authority. Between Officer Hill's first and second commands for the defendant to stop, both officers heard the defendant say, "You don't want me; you don't want me." They also observed him fumbling with his hands in the area of his waist as if reaching for or adjusting a weapon. Defendant asks us to characterize as capitulation conduct that is fully consistent with preparation to whirl and shoot the officers.
>
> The defendant's actions after he dropped the pistol indicate further that he had not yielded. Lender had stopped for at most an instant when the gun fell. Instead of stopping and standing still, the defendant quickly moved to pick up the weapon. Under the circumstances it cannot be said that the defendant had yielded, and therefore been seized, before the gun fell into the plain view of the officers.

See also United States v. Huertas, 864 F.3d 214 (2d Cir. 2017) (holding that defendant was not seized when he answered questions posed by an officer who was in a squad car but then ran when the officer got out of the car because his decision to answer questions reflected an effort "to quiet suspicion"); United States v. Griffin, 652 F.3d 793 (7th Cir. 2011) (holding that defendant who refused to pull over when directed by police to do so was not seized and rejecting defendant's argument that "a seizure does not necessarily occur at a discrete point in time but is better conceived of as a continuing event" that starts at the show of authority and ends with submission).

B. SEIZURES OF HOUSES

In Torres v. Madrid, 141 S.Ct. 989 (2021), Chief Justice Roberts reports that "when speaking of property" "the word 'seizure' [means] 'taking possession." As applied to houses, this definition certainly would include taking title—a form of seizure most often regulated by the Fifth Amendment. But what about lesser intrusions on property? For example, what if officers cordon-off a home, preventing residents from entering?

One circumstance where this question arises is when officers bar entry into a home in order to prevent the destruction of evidence. For example, in Segura v. United States, 468 U.S. 796 (1984), law enforcement agents entered petitioners' apartment, conducted a cursory search, observed evidence of illegal narcotics activity, removed all the occupants, and secured the premises for nineteen hours while they obtained a search warrant. Petitioners argued that the apartment and its contents were "seized" during that period because the apartment was under the exclusive control of the agents, who did not permit anyone to enter. The Court did not reach that question, holding instead that any seizure that may have occurred was reasonable under the circumstances. In so holding, however, the Court all but concluded that the agents had "seized" a home by "securing a dwelling, on the basis of probable cause, to prevent the destruction or removal of evidence . . . ."

In a dissenting opinion joined by Justices Brennan and Marshall, Justice Stevens was far less coy:

> A "seizure" occurs when there is some meaningful interference with an individual's possessory interests. There can be no doubt here that petitioners' possessory interests with respect to their apartment were subject to meaningful governmental interference. The agents not only excluded petitioners from access to their own apartment, and thereby prevented them from exercising any possessory right at all to the apartment and its contents, but they also exercised complete dominion and control over the apartment and its contents.

The Court appeared to adopt Justice Stevens's analysis in Illinois v. McArthur, 531 U.S. 326 (2001). There, officers prevented Charles McArthur from entering his home while they waited for a warrant to search the premises. Writing for the Court, Justice Breyer adopted without comment the lower court's determination that McArthur's home had been seized. See also Soldal v. Cook County, 506 U.S. 56 (1992) (trailer home was "seized" when owners were evicted and their home was forcibly detached from its moorings and water and sewer connections before being towed away; "the Soldals' domicile was not only seized, it literally was carried away * * *. We fail to see how being unceremoniously dispossessed of one's home in the manner alleged to have occurred here can be viewed as anything but a seizure invoking the protection of the Fourth Amendment.").

According to these precedents, government agents' securing a premises from the inside or the outside qualifies as a "seizure" because it materially interferes with a resident's possessory interests. By extension, physical searches of homes also constitute seizures. This means that courts assessing the constitutionality of physical searches conducted in homes must assess both the reasonableness of the search and the reasonableness of the seizure entailed by that search. We will have occasion to examine these issues at depth later in this Chapter in the context of our discussion of warranted searches.

C. SEIZURES OF PAPERS AND EFFECTS

When determining whether personal property, including papers and effects, have been "seized" for purposes of the Fourth Amendment, courts ask whether government activity has materially interfered with a claimant's possessory interests in that property. As the Court recognized in *Torres*, that usually entails taking possession. See, e.g., Texas v. Brown,

460 U.S. 730 (1983) (police effected a seizure when they took possession of personal property, including a small green balloon containing heroin); Coolidge v. New Hampshire, 403 U.S. 443 (1971) (car impounded by officers and towed to police station was "seized"). A frequently cited case on point is United States v. Jacobsen, 466 U.S. 109 (1984), which we discussed earlier in this Chapter with the materials on search.

Recall that in *Jacobsen* Federal Express employees opened a suspicious package revealing the presence of plastic bags containing a white powder. They summoned agents from the DEA who opened the bags, performed a field test on samples of their contents, and confirmed that the powder was cocaine. Writing for the Court, Justice Stevens pointed out that the Fourth Amendment "protects two types of expectations, one involving 'searches, the other 'seizures.' " "A 'seizure' of property," he continued, "occurs when there is some meaningful interference with an individual's possessory interests in that property." Applying that test to both the agents' taking custody of the package and their testing the cocaine, Justice Stevens concluded that the package, its contents, and the powder used for testing were all seized. As he explained, "the field test did affect respondents' possessory interests protected by the Amendment, since, by destroying a quantity of the powder, it converted what had been only a temporary deprivation of possessory interests into a permanent one."

As Justice Stevens suggests in *Jacobsen*, even temporary interference with possessory interests can constitute a seizure. For example, in United States v. Place, 462 U.S. 696 (1983), the Court held that officers seized Place's effects when they took possession of his luggage at an airport and moved it to another location where they used a drug detection dog to determine the presence of narcotics. Similarly, in United States v. Van Leeuwen, 397 U.S. 249 (1970), the Court recognized that the short-term detention of packages shipped through the mail while officers applied for warrants may constitute a seizure if those detentions interfere with possessory interests. See, e.g., United States v. Ramirez, 342 F.3d 1210 (10th Cir. 2003) (removing a package from the "mail stream" for 28 hours is a "seizure"); United States v. Dass, 849 F.2d 414 (9th Cir.1988) (detention of mail for 7–23 days is a "seizure").

Contrariwise, governmental assertions of possessory control over papers or effects may not constitute "seizures" if they are not adverse to a citizen's possessory interests. As an example, consider United States v. LaFrance, 879 F.2d 1 (1st Cir.1989). There, police had reasonable suspicion to believe that a Federal Express package, addressed to LaFrance, contained drugs. The package was guaranteed for delivery that day by noon. The officers arranged for a dog sniff, but the dog was several miles away. The sniff began at 1:15 p.m. and a positive result was obtained by 2:15. Officers then secured a warrant to search the package, which contained narcotics. LaFrance challenged the reasonableness of the detention of the package. He testified at the suppression hearing that, on the basis of prior experience, he expected to receive the package by 11:00 a.m. The court held that "LaFrance's anticipation that he would receive the goods soon after 11 a.m., though based on earlier experiences, is irrelevant. It is hornbook contract law that where a delivery time is agreed upon, a court should not intrude to imply a different reasonable time for delivery." The court recognized that "once noon arrived, the constitutional chemistry was altered" but that no seizure had occurred until the clock struck 12:00. See also United States v. Va Lerie, 424 F.3d 694 (8th Cir.2005) (en banc) (no seizure where officers removed checked luggage from the luggage compartment of a bus and transported it into the bus terminal in order to obtain consent to search; officer's removal of the luggage did not delay the passenger's travel or impact his freedom of movement); United States v. Terriques, 319 F.3d 1051 (8th Cir. 2003) (handling of package by mail clerk was not a seizure because it did not delay time of delivery).

As is the case with searches, seizures do not necessarily constitute Fourth Amendment violations. As Justice White stated in *Soldal*, "Whether the Amendment was in fact violated * * * requires determining if the seizure was reasonable." We turn to that question now.

V. THE TENSION BETWEEN THE REASONABLENESS AND THE WARRANT CLAUSES

A. THE IMPORTANCE OF THE WARRANT CLAUSE GENERALLY

By its terms, the Fourth Amendment guarantees to "the people" a right of security against "unreasonable searches and seizures." How does the Fourth Amendment guarantee that security? One answer is the warrant requirement, which holds that "searches conducted outside the judicial process, without prior approval by judge or magistrate are *per se* unreasonable under the Fourth Amendment—subject only to a few specifically established and well-delineated exceptions." Katz v. United States, 389 U.S. 347, 357 (1967). See also United States v. Place, 462 U.S. 696 (1983) ("In the ordinary case, the Court has viewed a seizure of personal property as *per se* unreasonable within the meaning of the Fourth Amendment unless it is accomplished pursuant to a judicial warrant issued upon probable cause and particularly describing the items to be seized.").

This vision of a tough, sweeping per se warrant rule yielding only to the most demanding claims for exceptions is at odds with reality. For example, it does not apply to arrests in public. And, as Justice Scalia stated in his concurring opinion in California v. Acevedo, 500 U.S. 565 (1991), the Court's jurisprudence with respect to the warrant requirement has "lurched back and forth between imposing a categorical warrant requirement and looking to reasonableness alone." According to Justice Scalia, the result is that the warrant requirement has become "so riddled with exceptions that it [is] basically unrecognizable."

As you work through the materials in this section, take note of when and in what circumstances the warrant requirement does and does not apply. From a practical point of view, are most searches and seizures subject to the warrant requirement or are most searches and seizures covered by an "exception"?

B. THE REASON FOR THE WARRANT REQUIREMENT

The following case is probably the Supreme Court's most thorough explication and justification of the warrant requirement. It lays the foundation of the current presumption that warrants are required for searches and seizures.

JOHNSON V. UNITED STATES

Supreme Court of the United States, 1948.
333 U.S. 10.

JUSTICE JACKSON delivered the opinion of the Court.

Petitioner was convicted of four counts charging violation of federal narcotic laws. The only question which brings the case here is whether it was lawful, without a warrant of any kind, to arrest petitioner and to search her living quarters.

Taking the Government's version of disputed events, decision would rest on these facts:

At about 7:30 p.m. Detective Lieutenant Belland, an officer of the Seattle police force narcotic detail, received information from a confidential informer, who was also a known narcotic user, that unknown persons were smoking opium in the Europe Hotel. The informer was taken back to the hotel to interview the manager, but he returned at once saying he could smell burning opium in the hallway. Belland communicated with federal narcotic agents and between 8:30 and 9 o'clock went back to the hotel with four such agents. All were experienced in narcotic work and recognized at once a strong odor of burning opium which to them was distinctive and unmistakable. The odor led to Room 1. The officers did not know who was occupying that room. They knocked and a voice inside asked who was there. "Lieutenant Belland," was the reply. There was a slight delay, some "shuffling or noise" in the room and then the defendant opened the door. The officer said, "I want to talk to you a little bit." She then, as he describes it, "stepped back acquiescently and admitted us." He said, "I want to talk to you about this opium smell in the room here." She denied that there was such a smell. Then he said, "I want you to consider yourself under arrest because we are going to search the room." The search turned up incriminating opium and smoking apparatus, the latter being warm, apparently from recent use. * * *

The defendant challenged the search of her home as a violation of the rights secured to her, in common with others, by the Fourth Amendment to the Constitution.

* * *

Entry to defendant's living quarters, which was the beginning of the search, was demanded under color of office. It was granted in submission to authority rather than as an understanding and intentional waiver of a constitutional right.

At the time entry was demanded the officers were possessed of evidence which a magistrate might have found to be probable cause for issuing a search warrant. * * * If the presence of odors is testified to before a magistrate and he finds the affiant qualified to know the odor, and it is one sufficiently distinctive to identify a forbidden substance, * * * it might very well be found to be evidence of most persuasive character.

The point of the Fourth Amendment, which often is not grasped by zealous officers, is not that it denies law enforcement the support of the usual inferences which reasonable men draw from evidence. Its protection consists in requiring that those inferences be drawn by a neutral and detached magistrate instead of being judged by the officer engaged in the often competitive enterprise of ferreting out crime. Any assumption that evidence sufficient to support a magistrate's disinterested determination to issue a search warrant will justify the officers in making a search without a warrant would reduce the Amendment to a nullity and leave the people's homes secure only in the discretion of police officers. Crime, even in the privacy of one's own quarters, is, of course, of grave concern to society, and the law allows such crime to be reached on proper showing. The right of officers to thrust themselves into a home is also a grave concern, not only to the individual but to a society which chooses to dwell in reasonable security and freedom from surveillance. When the right of privacy must reasonably yield to the right of search is, as a rule, to be decided by a judicial officer, not by a policeman or government enforcement agent.

There are exceptional circumstances in which, on balancing the need for effective law enforcement against the right of privacy, it may be contended that a magistrate's warrant for search may be dispensed with. But this is not such a case. No reason is offered for not obtaining a search warrant except the inconvenience to the officers and some slight delay necessary to prepare papers and present the evidence to a magistrate.

These are never very convincing reasons and, in these circumstances, certainly are not enough to by-pass the constitutional requirement. No suspect was fleeing or likely to take flight. The search was of permanent premises, not of a movable vehicle. No evidence or contraband was threatened with removal or destruction, except perhaps the fumes which we suppose in time would disappear. But they were not capable at any time of being reduced to possession for presentation to court. The evidence of their existence before the search was adequate and the testimony of the officers to that effect would not perish from the delay of getting a warrant.

If the officers in this case were excused from the constitutional duty of presenting their evidence to a magistrate, it is difficult to think of a case in which it should be required.

[The Court held that the officers had no probable cause to arrest the defendant until they entered the defendant's quarters, and reasoned that the search (entry and visual inspection) preceded the arrest. It was not possible, therefore, to justify the officers' conduct as a search incident to a valid arrest. Justices Black, Reed, and Burton, together with Chief Justice Vinson, dissented without opinion.]

NOTE ON JOHNSON

Johnson represents a victory for those who would have the police secure warrants. As the majority intimates, there almost certainly was enough evidence known to the police to justify a magistrate's issuance of a warrant. Yet, because no warrant was sought, the search is deemed presumptively "unreasonable" or invalid. Why is this the correct result? If you would answer that the Framers assumed that warrants generally would be required, you must recognize that the Warrant Clause is actually designed as a *limitation* on the issuance of warrants ("No warrant shall issue without probable cause . . .") and does not explicitly state a preference for warrants. How does the Court reason from a limitation on warrants to a warrant requirement?

The government did not argue in *Johnson* that the officers should have been excused from any requirement to obtain a warrant because of the risk that evidence would be destroyed while they sought a warrant. What if they had? See Kentucky v. King, 563 U.S. 452 (2011) (finding exigent circumstances in a similar case and distinguishing *Johnson* as a case in which the government did not argue exigent circumstances). *King* is discussed later in this Chapter in the section on the exigent circumstances exception to the warrant requirement.

C. THE FUNCTION OF THE WARRANT REQUIREMENT

For searches and seizures that are subject to the warrant requirement, probable cause represents the threshold of proof that must be satisfied before the power to search and seize is legitimated. That proof requirement means that the government must demonstrate a factually-based interest in people, places or things *before* using its power to disturb them. The proof requirement protects against *unreasonable* searches and seizures.

Related to the proof requirement are the "Oath or affirmation" and particularity provisions of the Amendment. Probable cause is to be shown by persons willing to swear to or affirm the truth of their statements and thus to be held accountable for their representations. In addition, the applicant for the warrant is committing to a public record the information that is known *before* the search so that, after the search takes place, there is no confusion between the ex-post and ex-ante positions of the applicant. Without an antecedent warrant requirement, an officer questioned about probable cause can work backwards from the search, and fill in the facts as if they were known beforehand.

The particularity requirement implies that the government can only interfere with those persons, places or things in which it has shown a valid interest. Here, too, the written record made in advance of the search may decrease the danger that after a search is completed, the police will claim that whatever is found is exactly what was sought. Also, the specification of objects sought to be seized may inform the magistrate's decision on whether the proposed search is reasonable or excessive. A showing of probable cause, then, does not mean that any search and seizure authorized by a warrant is valid; it means that any search and seizure directed by warrant at the people, places, or things to which the probable cause specifically relates satisfies the Warrant Clause of the Fourth Amendment. These limitations guard against *arbitrary* searches and seizures.

By placing a magistrate between the citizen and the police, the Amendment, in the words of the *Johnson* majority, establishes that a neutral observer is to decide whether the probable cause and particularity requirements have been satisfied. This is one way in which the Amendment operates to prevent unreasonable searches and seizures; the presumption is that a magistrate is better situated to determine whether there are good and sufficient reasons for a search than an "officer engaged in the often competitive enterprise of ferreting out crime."

By interposing the magistrate between the "competitors"—the police and the suspect—the Amendment may also serve another function. It gives the neutral magistrate an opportunity to refuse a warrant, even if the application is supported by oath, probable cause and specifics, on the ground that a search and seizure would be unreasonable under the circumstances. For example, if the police have probable cause to believe that A has marijuana cigarettes in his home, and if possession of small quantities of marijuana is punishable by fine only, a magistrate might be inclined to disapprove a warrant to search A's entire house on the ground that the scope of the search is unreasonably intrusive in light of the government's minimal interests at stake. The same magistrate might be persuaded to permit a search of A's briefcase. Similarly, if the police obtain a warrant to search A's house on Monday and execute the warrant that same day, but find nothing, a magistrate might hesitate to issue another warrant to search on Tuesday, and perhaps another to look again on Wednesday, even if the police still have probable cause. Or, in an income tax evasion case, if the police asked for authority to search for and seize everything found in a home as evidence of an income greater than that recorded on a tax return, a magistrate might balk at issuing such a warrant. However, the same magistrate might authorize an entry into the house to take photographs. By imposing limitations on searches, a magistrate may prevent *excessive* governmental intrusions.

Another important function of the warrant requirement was identified by the Court in Illinois v. Gates, discussed later in this Chapter. There, the Court states that "the possession of a warrant by officers conducting an arrest or search greatly reduces the perception of unlawful or intrusive police conduct, by assuring the individual whose property is searched or seized of the lawful authority of the executing officer, his need to search, and the limits of his power to search."

The Warrant Requirement in Reality

The above discussion articulates a number of theoretically sound reasons for the warrant requirement. But does the warrant process, in practice, serve these purposes? Consider these statistics compiled by the Administrative Office of the United States Courts reported in the New York Times:

> The figures show that Federal and state judges are largely rubber stamps for law enforcement when it comes to electronic surveillance, despite all the talk of the need for an independent review by the courts of bugs and wiretaps. The last time a court denied a wiretap application was in 1988; all told, only 7 applications out of 8,950 since 1983 have been turned down.

Labaton, Before the Explosion, Officials Saw Little Risk for Building in Oklahoma City, New York Times, May 2, 1995, p. A19. The data is similar for warrants to search for physical evidence.

What is the point of requiring a warrant if the warrant process is simply a formality as a practical matter? Could the almost-certain success of a warrant application be a reason for the Court's expansion of the exceptions to the warrant requirement? Is the Court attempting to focus the warrant requirement on those few areas in which a magistrate's determination might make a difference?

Could it be argued that the success rate for obtaining warrants is attributable not to lax review but to the care that is being put into warrant applications by police officers fearful that their applications will be rejected?

The exceptions to the warrant requirement will be considered shortly. Before reaching them, it is useful to understand what practical protections the warrant application procedure affords.

VI. OBTAINING A SEARCH WARRANT: CONSTITUTIONAL PREREQUISITES

As we explore the constitutional requirements for warranted searches in this Section, it is important to keep in mind some procedural realities. Foremost, warrant applications are ex parte proceedings and often occur in camera. Potential targets are neither present nor represented. Recording and taking of transcripts are uncommon.

In the normal course, a single investigator will present to the judge a written affidavit with a proposed warrant ready for signature. That affidavit may report the investigator's personal observations, refer to physical or documentary evidence, or report hearsay statements from other investigators, witnesses, or confidential informants. The investigator will be put under oath to swear to the truthfulness of the affidavit and to answer any questions the judge may have. If the judge is persuaded that probable cause is shown, then she will sign the warrant. Investigators are then left to serve the warrant according to its terms.

In most cases, those targeted by a search warrant do not have prior knowledge of the application or the search and therefore do not have the opportunity to contest the warrant or the search until after it has occurred. This is in contrast to subpoena processes, which allow targets the option to move to quash in an adversarial proceeding before complying.

A. DEMONSTRATING PROBABLE CAUSE

1. Source of Information on Which Probable Cause Is Based

The Fourth Amendment mandates a showing of probable cause as justification for a search warrant. Scant attention was paid to the term *probable cause* until the 1960's, when two major cases were decided, Aguilar v. Texas, 378 U.S. 108 (1964) and Spinelli v. United States, 393 U.S. 410 (1969). *Spinelli* is set forth below; the earlier *Aguilar* decision is discussed in the majority opinion. Both of these cases deal with regulation of the source of information on which probable cause is based. These cases must be read in light of the case that follows, Illinois v. Gates, which tempered the standards for determining probable cause on the basis of informants' tips.

SPINELLI V. UNITED STATES

Supreme Court of the United States, 1969.
393 U.S. 410.

JUSTICE HARLAN delivered the opinion of the Court.

William Spinelli was convicted * * * of traveling to St. Louis, Missouri, from a nearby Illinois suburb with the intention of conducting gambling activities proscribed by Missouri law. At every appropriate stage in the proceedings in the lower courts, the petitioner challenged the constitutionality of the warrant which authorized the FBI search that uncovered the evidence necessary for his conviction. * * *

In *Aguilar,* a search warrant had issued upon an affidavit of police officers who swore only that they had "received reliable information from a credible person and do believe" that narcotics were being illegally stored on the described premises. While recognizing that the constitutional requirement of probable cause can be satisfied by hearsay information, this Court held the affidavit inadequate for two reasons. First, the application failed to set forth any of the "underlying circumstances" necessary to enable the magistrate independently to judge of the validity of the informant's conclusion that the narcotics were where he said they were. Second, the affiant-officers did not attempt to support their claim that their informant was " 'credible' or his information 'reliable.' " The Government is, however, quite right in saying that the FBI affidavit in the present case is more ample than that in *Aguilar*. Not only does it contain a report from an anonymous informant, but it also contains a report of an independent FBI investigation which is said to corroborate the informant's tip. We are, then, required to delineate the manner in which *Aguilar's* two-pronged test should be applied in these circumstances.

In essence, the affidavit * * * contained the following allegations:[a]

1. The FBI had kept track of Spinelli's movements on five days during the month of August 1965. On four of these occasions, Spinelli was seen crossing one of two bridges leading from Illinois into St. Louis, Missouri, between 11 a.m. and 12:15 p.m. On four of the five days, Spinelli was also seen parking his car in a lot used by residents of an apartment house at 1108 Indian Circle Drive in St. Louis, between 3:30 p.m. and 4:45 p.m. On one day, Spinelli was followed further and seen to enter a particular apartment in the building.

---

[a] It is, of course, of no consequence that the agents might have had additional information which could have been given to the Commissioner. "It is elementary that in passing on the validity of a warrant, the reviewing court may consider *only* information brought to the magistrate's attention." Aguilar v. Texas, 378 U.S. 108, 109, n. 1 (emphasis in original). * * *

2. An FBI check with the telephone company revealed that this apartment contained two telephones listed under the name of Grace P. Hagen, and carrying the numbers WYdown 4–0029 and WYdown 4–0136.

3. The application stated that "William Spinelli is known to this affiant and to federal law enforcement agents and local law enforcement agents as a bookmaker, an associate of bookmakers, a gambler, and an associate of gamblers."

4. Finally, it was stated that the FBI "has been informed by a confidential reliable informant that William Spinelli is operating a handbook and accepting wagers and disseminating wagering information by means of the telephones which have been assigned the numbers WYdown 4–0029 and WYdown 4–0136."

There can be no question that the last item mentioned, detailing the informant's tip, has a fundamental place in this warrant application. Without it, probable cause could not be established. The first two items reflect only innocent-seeming activity and data. Spinelli's travels to and from the apartment building and his entry into a particular apartment on one occasion could hardly be taken as bespeaking gambling activity; and there is surely nothing unusual about an apartment containing two separate telephones. Many a householder indulges himself in this petty luxury. Finally, the allegation that Spinelli was "known" to the affiant and to other federal and local law enforcement officers as a gambler and an associate of gamblers is but a bald and unilluminating assertion of suspicion that is entitled to no weight in appraising the magistrate's decision.

So much indeed the Government does not deny. Rather, * * * the Government claims that the informant's tip gives a suspicious color to the FBI's reports detailing Spinelli's innocent-seeming conduct and that, conversely, the FBI's surveillance corroborates the informant's tip, thereby entitling it to more weight. It is true, of course that the magistrate is obligated to render a judgment based upon a common-sense reading of the entire affidavit. We believe, however, that the "totality of circumstances" approach taken by the Court of Appeals paints with too broad a brush. Where, as here, the informer's tip is a necessary element in a finding of probable cause, its proper weight must be determined by a more precise analysis.

The informer's report must first be measured against *Aguilar's* standards so that its probative value can be assessed. If the tip is found inadequate under *Aguilar,* the other allegations which corroborate the information contained in the hearsay report should then be considered. At this stage as well, however, the standards enunciated in *Aguilar* must inform the magistrate's decision. He must ask: Can it fairly be said that the tip, even when certain parts of it have been corroborated by independent sources, is as trustworthy as a tip which would pass *Aguilar's* tests without independent corroboration?

* * *

Applying these principles to the present case, we first consider the weight to be given the informer's tip when it is considered apart from the rest of the affidavit. * * * Though the affiant swore that his confidant was "reliable," he offered the magistrate no reason in support of this conclusion. Perhaps even more important is the fact that *Aguilar's* other test has not been satisfied. The tip does not contain a sufficient statement of the underlying circumstances from which the informer concluded that Spinelli was running a bookmaking operation. We are not told how the FBI's source received his information—it is not alleged that the informant personally observed Spinelli at work or that he had ever placed a bet with him. Moreover, if the informant came by the information indirectly, he did not explain why his sources were reliable. In the absence of a statement detailing the manner in which the information was gathered, it is especially important that the tip describe the accused's criminal activity in sufficient detail that the magistrate may know that he is relying on something more substantial than a casual rumor circulating in the underworld or an accusation based merely on an individual's general reputation.

The detail provided by the informant in Draper v. United States, 358 U.S. 307 (1959), provides a suitable benchmark. While Hereford, the Government's informer in that case, did not state the way in which he had obtained his information, he reported that Draper had gone to Chicago the day before by train and that he would return to Denver by train with three ounces of heroin on one of two specified mornings. Moreover, Hereford, went on to describe, with minute particularity, the clothes that Draper would be wearing upon his arrival at the Denver station. A magistrate, when confronted with such detail, could reasonably infer that the informant had gained his information in a reliable way.[b] Such an inference cannot be made in the present case. Here, the only facts supplied were that Spinelli was using two specified telephones and that these phones were being used in gambling operations. This meager report could easily have been obtained from an offhand remark heard at a neighborhood bar.

Nor do we believe that the patent doubts *Aguilar* raises as to the report's reliability are adequately resolved by a consideration of the allegations detailing the FBI's independent investigative efforts. At most, these allegations indicated that Spinelli could have used the telephones specified by the informant for some purpose. This cannot by itself be said

---

[b] While *Draper* involved the question whether the police had probable cause for an arrest without a warrant, the analysis required for an answer to this question is basically similar to that demanded of a magistrate when he considers whether a search warrant should issue.

to support both the inference that the informer was generally trustworthy and that he had made his charge against Spinelli on the basis of information obtained in a reliable way. Once again, *Draper* provides a relevant comparison. Independent police work in that case corroborated much more than one small detail that had been provided by the informant. There, the police, upon meeting the inbound Denver train on the second morning specified by informer Hereford, saw a man whose dress corresponded precisely to Hereford's detailed description. It was then apparent that the informant had not been fabricating his report out of whole cloth; since the report was of the sort which in common experience may be recognized as having been obtained in a reliable way, it was perfectly clear that probable cause had been established.

We conclude, then, that in the present case the informant's tip—even when corroborated to the extent indicated—was not sufficient to provide the basis for a finding of probable cause. This is not to say that the tip was so insubstantial that it could not properly have counted in the magistrate's determination. Rather, it needed some further support. When we look to the other parts of the application, however, we find nothing alleged which would permit the suspicions engendered by the informant's report to ripen into a judgment that a crime was probably being committed. As we have already seen, the allegations detailing the FBI's surveillance of Spinelli and its investigation of the telephone company records contain no suggestion of criminal conduct when taken by themselves—and they are not endowed with an aura of suspicion by virtue of the informer's tip. Nor do we find that the FBI's reports take on a sinister color when read in light of common knowledge that bookmaking is often carried on over the telephone and from premises ostensibly used by others for perfectly normal purposes. Such an argument would carry weight in a situation in which the premises contain an unusual number of telephones or abnormal activity is observed, but it does not fit this case where neither of these factors is present.[c]

* * *

JUSTICE MARSHALL took no part in the consideration or decision of this case.

[Justice White's concurring opinion is omitted.]

---

[c] A box containing three uninstalled telephones was found in the apartment, but only after execution of the search warrant.

JUSTICE BLACK, dissenting.

In my view, this Court's decision in Aguilar v. Texas, 378 U.S. 108 (1964), was bad enough. That decision went very far toward elevating the magistrate's hearing for issuance of a search warrant to a full-fledged trial, where witnesses must be brought forward to attest personally to all the facts alleged. But not content with this, the Court today expands *Aguilar* to almost unbelievable proportions. * * * Nothing in our Constitution * * * requires that the facts be established with that degree of certainty and with such elaborate specificity before a policeman can be authorized by a disinterested magistrate to conduct a carefully limited search.

* * *

JUSTICE FORTAS, dissenting.

* * *

A policeman's affidavit should not be judged as an entry in an essay contest. It is not "abracadabra." As the majority recognizes, a policeman's affidavit is entitled to common-sense evaluation. * * *

[Justice Stewart's dissenting opinion is omitted.]

Applying Spinelli

The majority in *Spinelli* appears to accept the following propositions:

- A police officer is presumed to be honest when making an affidavit.
- What may be questioned, however, is the source of the officer's information.
- If the officer avers that she has first-hand knowledge of the facts used to demonstrate probable cause, the only question is whether the sworn facts are sufficient to meet the threshold.
- If the officer is relying on someone else for part or all of the information, then it is necessary to make three additional determinations:

  (i.) Who is the source of the information, and is the source reliable? Reliability is the first prong of the *Spinelli* test.

  (ii.) What are the bases and details of the source's knowledge? Credible information is the second prong of the test.

  (iii.) Assuming reliability of the source, are the facts, either standing alone or taken together with other facts provided by the affiant, sufficient to show probable cause?

- If the source is not known to the police to be reliable, the police may be able to demonstrate reliability by corroborating the details provided by the informant. The Court in *Spinelli* required a substantial amount of corroboration in such circumstances. Corroborating the fact that Spinelli had two telephone lines in his apartment was not enough to eliminate the concerns about the informant's reliability.
- If the informant's basis of information is unclear, it may be sufficient that the information is so detailed that it could only have come from the informant's personal observation.
- If the information provided by the informant falls short of demonstrating probable cause, the police can gather other information to be included in the application for a warrant.
- When the magistrate looks at all the information provided to assess whether probable cause is shown, she is to take a common sense approach to the application and ask whether the government has shown "the probability" of criminal activity.

Spinelli does not impose a limitation where a *crime victim or eyewitness* reports an alleged crime immediately after he or she says it took place. It only addresses warrant applications in which the police rely on 1) tipsters who operate as paid informants or snitches; or 2) anonymous informants. It is these two categories of informants whose reliability is most questionable.

The *Spinelli* majority shows a mistrust of paid and anonymous informants. Is that justified? Consider an anecdote from Dallas, where informants were paid millions of dollars based on tips that certain people were carrying drugs. The informants would pick up migrant laborers, give them a backpack, and tell them to wait to be picked up at a certain corner, where they would be taken to a factory for employment for the day. The bag would contain a powdery substance with trace amounts of cocaine. Then the informants would "tip" the police that a person was standing at a street corner holding a backpack containing narcotics. The "tip" would include a detailed description of the person holding the bag. The scam was not uncovered until years later when the substances were retested and found to be largely ground up masonry, with only trace amounts of cocaine.

Spinelli was not well received by law enforcement officials. Generally speaking, law enforcement officers read *Spinelli* as prohibiting warrants based on information from paid or anonymous informants and setting a standard for corroboration of those tips that was equivalent to independent evidence of criminality approaching probable cause. But if officers had to corroborate with independent evidence approaching or equaling probable cause, it followed that the tip itself was all but irrelevant to the probable cause determination. Also, the decision may have appeared to be more complicated and even more hostile to police than it was intended to be.

2. Rejection of a Rigid Two-Pronged Test

In the following case, the Court holds that the two-pronged test of *Aguilar* and *Spinelli* would no longer control the determination of probable cause when police obtain information from paid, professional, or anonymous informants. Yet the Court took some pains to emphasize that the *Aguilar-Spinelli* structure still has continuing relevance when police rely in whole or in part on an informant's tip.

ILLINOIS V. GATES

Supreme Court of the United States, 1983.
462 U.S. 213.

JUSTICE REHNQUIST **delivered the opinion of the Court.**

Respondents Lance and Susan Gates were indicted for violation of state drug laws after police officers, executing a search warrant, discovered marijuana and other contraband in their automobile and home. Prior to trial the Gates' moved to suppress evidence seized during this search. The Illinois Supreme Court affirmed the decisions of lower state courts granting the motion. * * *

We granted certiorari to consider the application of the Fourth Amendment to a magistrate's issuance of a search warrant on the basis of a partially corroborated anonymous informant's tip. * * *

* * *

* * * Bloomingdale, Ill., is a suburb of Chicago located in DuPage County. On May 3, 1978, the Bloomingdale Police Department received by mail an anonymous handwritten letter which read as follows:

> "This letter is to inform you that you have a couple in your town who strictly make their living on selling drugs. They are Sue and Lance Gates, they live on Greenway, off Bloomingdale Rd. in the condominiums. Most of their buys are done in Florida. Sue his wife drives their car to Florida, where she leaves it to be loaded up with drugs, then Lance flys down and drives it back. Sue flys back after she drops the car off in Florida. May 3 she is driving down there again and Lance will be flying down in a few days to drive it back. At the time Lance drives the car back he has the trunk loaded with over $100,000.00 in drugs. Presently they have over $100,000.00 worth of drugs in their basement.
>
> They brag about the fact they never have to work, and make their entire living on pushers.

I guarantee if you watch them carefully you will make a big catch. They are friends with some big drugs dealers, who visit their house often.

Lance & Susan Gates Greenway in Condominiums"

The letter was referred by the Chief of Police of the Bloomingdale Police Department to Detective Mader, who decided to pursue the tip. Mader learned, from the office of the Illinois Secretary of State, that an Illinois driver's license had been issued to one Lance Gates, residing at a stated address in Bloomingdale. He contacted a confidential informant, whose examination of certain financial records revealed a more recent address for the Gates, and he also learned from a police officer assigned to O'Hare Airport that "L. Gates" had made a reservation on Eastern Airlines flight 245 to West Palm Beach, Fla., scheduled to depart from Chicago on May 5 at 4:15 p.m.

Mader then made arrangements with an agent of the Drug Enforcement Administration for surveillance of the May 5 Eastern Airlines flight. The agent later reported to Mader that Gates had boarded the flight, and that federal agents in Florida had observed him arrive in West Palm Beach and take a taxi to the nearby Holiday Inn. They also reported that Gates went to a room registered to one Susan Gates and that, at 7:00 a.m. the next morning, Gates and an unidentified woman left the motel in a Mercury bearing Illinois license plates and drove northbound on an interstate frequently used by travelers to the Chicago area. In addition, the DEA agent informed Mader that the license plate number on the Mercury registered to a Hornet station wagon owned by Gates. The agent also advised Mader that the driving time between West Palm Beach and Bloomingdale was approximately 22 to 24 hours.

Mader signed an affidavit setting forth the foregoing facts, and submitted it to a judge of the Circuit Court of DuPage County, together with a copy of the anonymous letter. The judge of that court thereupon issued a search warrant for the Gates' residence and for their automobile. The judge, in deciding to issue the warrant, could have determined that the *modus operandi* of the Gates had been substantially corroborated. As the anonymous letter predicted, Lance Gates had flown from Chicago to West Palm Beach late in the afternoon of May 5th, had checked into a hotel room registered in the name of his wife, and, at 7:00 a.m. the following morning, had headed north, accompanied by an unidentified woman, out of West Palm Beach on an interstate highway used by travelers from South Florida to Chicago in an automobile bearing a license plate issued to him.

At 5:15 a.m. on March 7th, only 36 hours after he had flown out of Chicago, Lance Gates, and his wife, returned to their home in Bloomingdale, driving the car in which they had left West Palm Beach some 22 hours earlier. The Bloomingdale police were awaiting them, searched the trunk of the Mercury, and uncovered approximately 350 pounds of marijuana. A search of the Gates' home revealed marijuana, weapons, and other contraband. The Illinois Circuit Court ordered suppression of all these items, on the ground that the affidavit submitted to the Circuit Judge failed to support the necessary determination of probable cause to believe that the Gates' automobile and home contained the contraband in question. This decision was affirmed in turn by the Illinois Appellate Court and by a divided vote of the Supreme Court of Illinois.

The Illinois Supreme Court concluded—and we are inclined to agree—that, standing alone, the anonymous letter sent to the Bloomingdale Police Department would not provide the basis for a magistrate's determination that there was probable cause to believe contraband would be found in the Gates' car and home. The letter provides virtually nothing from which one might conclude that its author is either honest or his information reliable; likewise, the letter gives absolutely no indication of the basis for the writer's predictions regarding the Gates' criminal activities. Something more was required, then, before a magistrate could conclude that there was probable cause to believe that contraband would be found in the Gates' home and car.

The Illinois Supreme Court also properly recognized that Detective Mader's affidavit might be capable of supplementing the anonymous letter with information sufficient to permit a determination of probable cause. In holding that the affidavit in fact did not contain sufficient additional information to sustain a determination of probable cause, the Illinois court applied a "two-pronged test," derived from our decision in Spinelli v. United States. The Illinois Supreme Court, like some others, apparently understood *Spinelli* as requiring that the anonymous letter satisfy each of two independent requirements before it could be relied on. According to this view, the letter, as supplemented by Mader's affidavit, first had to adequately reveal the "basis of knowledge" of the letter writer—the particular means by which he came by the information given in his report. Second, it had to provide facts sufficiently establishing either the "veracity" of the affiant's informant, or, alternatively, the "reliability" of the informant's report in this particular case.

The Illinois court, alluding to an elaborate set of legal rules that have developed among various lower courts to enforce the "two-pronged test," found that the test had not been satisfied. First, the "veracity" prong was not satisfied because, "there was simply no basis [for] * * * conclud[ing] that the anonymous person [who wrote the letter to the Bloomingdale Police Department] was credible." The court indicated that corroboration by police of details contained in the letter might never satisfy the "veracity" prong, and in any event, could not do so if, as in the present case, only "innocent" details are corroborated. In addition, the letter gave no indication of the basis of its writer's knowledge of the Gates' activities. * * * Thus, it concluded that no showing of probable cause had been made.

We agree with the Illinois Supreme Court that an informant's "veracity," "reliability" and "basis of knowledge" are all highly relevant in determining the value of his report. We do not agree, however, that these elements should be understood as entirely separate and independent requirements to be rigidly exacted in every case, which the opinion of the Supreme Court of Illinois would imply. Rather, as detailed below, they should be understood simply as closely intertwined issues that may usefully illuminate the commonsense, practical question whether there is "probable cause" to believe that contraband or evidence is located in a particular place.

* * * This totality of the circumstances approach is far more consistent with our prior treatment of probable cause than is any rigid demand that specific "tests" be satisfied by every informant's tip. Perhaps the central teaching of our decisions bearing on the probable cause standard is that it is a "practical, nontechnical conception." * * *

[P]robable cause is a fluid concept—turning on the assessment of probabilities in particular factual contexts—not readily, or even usefully, reduced to a neat set of legal rules. Informants' tips doubtless come in many shapes and sizes from many different types of persons. * * *

[T]he "two-pronged test" directs analysis into two largely independent channels—the informant's "veracity" or "reliability" and his "basis of knowledge." There are persuasive arguments against according these two elements such independent status. Instead, they are better understood as relevant considerations in the totality of circumstances analysis that traditionally has guided probable cause determinations: a deficiency in one may be compensated for, in determining the overall reliability of a tip, by a strong showing as to the other, or by some other indicia of reliability.

* * * Unlike a totality of circumstances analysis, which permits a balanced assessment of the relative weights of all the various indicia of reliability (and unreliability) attending an informant's tip, the "two-pronged test" has encouraged an excessively technical dissection of informants' tips, with undue attention being focused on isolated issues that cannot sensibly be divorced from the other facts presented to the magistrate.

* * * Finely-tuned standards such as proof beyond a reasonable doubt or by a preponderance of the evidence, useful in formal trials, have no place in the magistrate's decision. While an effort to fix some general, numerically precise degree of certainty corresponding to "probable cause" may not be helpful, it is clear that "only the probability, and not a prima facie showing, of criminal activity is the standard of probable cause." *Spinelli,* supra.

We have also recognized that affidavits are normally drafted by nonlawyers in the midst and haste of a criminal investigation. * * * The rigorous inquiry into the *Spinelli* prongs and the complex superstructure of evidentiary and analytical rules that some have seen implicit in our *Spinelli* decision, cannot be reconciled with the fact that many warrants are—quite properly—issued on the basis of nontechnical, common-sense judgments of laymen applying a standard less demanding than those used in formal legal proceedings.

* * *

If the affidavits submitted by police officers are subjected to the type of scrutiny some courts have deemed appropriate, police might well resort to warrantless searches, with the hope of relying on consent or some other exception to the warrant clause that might develop at the time of the search. In addition, the possession of a warrant by officers conducting an arrest or search greatly reduces the perception of unlawful or intrusive police conduct, by assuring the individual whose property is searched or seized of the lawful authority of the executing officer, his need to search, and the limits of his power to search. Reflecting this preference for the warrant process, the traditional standard for review of an issuing magistrate's probable cause determination has been that so long as the magistrate had a "substantial basis for * * * conclud[ing]" that a search would uncover evidence of wrongdoing, the Fourth Amendment requires no more. * * *

Finally, the * * * strictures that inevitably accompany the "two-pronged test" cannot avoid seriously impeding the task of law enforcement. If, as the Illinois Supreme Court apparently thought, that test must be rigorously applied in every case, anonymous tips would be of greatly diminished value in police work. Ordinary citizens * * * generally do not provide extensive recitations of the basis of their everyday observations. Likewise * * * the veracity of persons supplying anonymous tips is by hypothesis largely unknown, and unknowable. As a result, anonymous tips seldom could survive a rigorous application of either of the *Spinelli* prongs. Yet, such tips, particularly when supplemented by independent police investigation, frequently contribute to the solution of otherwise "perfect crimes." While a conscientious assessment of the basis for crediting such tips is required by the Fourth Amendment, a standard that leaves virtually no place for anonymous citizen informants is not.

For all these reasons, we conclude that it is wiser to abandon the "two-pronged test" established by our decisions in *Aguilar* and *Spinelli*. In its place we reaffirm the totality of the circumstances analysis that traditionally has informed probable cause determinations. The task of the issuing magistrate is simply to make a practical, common-sense decision whether, given all the circumstances set forth in the affidavit before him, including the "veracity" and "basis of knowledge" of persons supplying hearsay information, there is a fair probability that contraband or evidence of a crime will be found in a particular place. And the duty of a reviewing court is simply to ensure that the magistrate had a "substantial basis for * * * conclud[ing]" that probable cause existed. * * *

Our earlier cases illustrate the limits beyond which a magistrate may not venture in issuing a warrant. A sworn statement of an affiant that "he has cause to suspect and does believe that" liquor illegally brought into the United States is located on certain premises will not do. Nathanson v. United States, 290 U.S. 41 (1933). An affidavit must provide the magistrate with a substantial basis for determining the existence of probable cause, and the wholly conclusory statement at issue in *Nathanson* failed to meet this requirement. An officer's statement that "affiants have received reliable information from a credible person and believe" that heroin is stored in a home, is likewise inadequate. Aguilar v. Texas. As in *Nathanson,* this is a mere conclusory statement that gives the magistrate virtually no basis at all for making a judgment regarding probable cause. Sufficient information must be presented to the magistrate to allow that official to determine probable cause; his action cannot be a mere ratification of the bare conclusions of others. * * * But when we move beyond the "bare bones" affidavits present in cases such as *Nathanson* and *Aguilar,* this area simply does not lend itself to a prescribed set of rules, like that which had developed from *Spinelli.* Instead, the flexible, common-sense standard * * * better serves the purposes of the Fourth Amendment's probable cause requirement.

Justice Brennan's dissent suggests in several places that the approach we take today somehow downgrades the role of the neutral magistrate, because *Aguilar* and *Spinelli* "preserve the role of magistrates as independent arbiters of probable cause." Quite the contrary, we believe, is the case. * * * Nothing in our opinion in any way lessens the authority of the magistrate to draw such reasonable inferences as he will from the material supplied to him by applicants for a warrant; indeed, he is freer than under the regime of *Aguilar* and *Spinelli* to draw such inferences, or to refuse to draw them if he is so minded.

* * *

* * * Even standing alone, the facts obtained through the independent investigation of Mader and the DEA at least suggested that the Gateses were involved in drug trafficking. In addition to being a popular vacation site, Florida is well-known as a source of narcotics and other illegal drugs. Lance Gates' flight to Palm Beach, his brief, overnight stay in a motel, and apparent immediate return north to Chicago in the family car, conveniently awaiting him in West Palm Beach, is as suggestive of a pre-arranged drug run, as it is of an ordinary vacation trip.

In addition, the magistrate could rely on the anonymous letter which had been corroborated in major part by Mader's efforts—just as had occurred in *Draper*.[a] The Supreme Court of Illinois reasoned that *Draper* involved an informant who had given reliable information on previous occasions, while the honesty and reliability of the anonymous informant in this case were unknown to the Bloomingdale police. While this distinction might be an apt one at the time the police department received the anonymous letter, it became far less significant after Mader's independent investigative work occurred. The corroboration of the letter's predictions that the Gateses' car would be in Florida, that Lance Gates would fly to Florida in the next day or so, and that he would drive the car north toward Bloomingdale all indicated, albeit not with certainty, that the informant's other assertions also were true. "Because an informant is right about some things, he is more probably right about other facts"—including the claim regarding the Gateses' illegal activity. This may well not be the type of "reliability" or "veracity" necessary to satisfy some views of the "veracity prong" of *Spinelli,* but we think it suffices for the practical, common-sense judgment called for in making a probable cause determination. It is enough, for purposes of assessing probable cause, that "corroboration through other sources of information reduced the chances of a reckless or prevaricating tale," thus providing "a substantial basis for crediting the hearsay."

This is perfectly reasonable. As discussed previously, probable cause requires only a probability or substantial chance of criminal activity, not an actual showing of such activity. By hypothesis, therefore, innocent behavior frequently will provide the basis for a showing of probable cause; to require otherwise would be to *sub silentio* impose a drastically more rigorous definition of probable cause than the security of our citizens demands. * * * In making a determination of probable cause the relevant inquiry is not whether particular conduct is "innocent" or "guilty," but the degree of suspicion that attaches to particular types of non-criminal acts.

Finally, the anonymous letter contained a range of details relating not just to easily obtained facts and conditions existing at the time of the tip, but to future actions of third parties ordinarily not easily predicted. The letter writer's accurate information as to the travel plans of each of the Gateses' was of a character likely obtained only from the Gateses' themselves, or from someone familiar with their not entirely ordinary travel plans. If the informant had access to accurate information of this

[a] The Illinois Supreme Court thought that the verification of details contained in the anonymous letter in this case amounted only to "the corroboration of innocent activity," and that this was insufficient to support a finding of probable cause. We are inclined to agree, however with the observation of Justice Moran in his dissenting opinion that "In this case, just as in *Draper*, seemingly innocent activity became suspicious in the light of the initial tip." And it bears noting that *all* of the corroborating detail established in *Draper, supra,* was of entirely innocent activity * * *.

type a magistrate could properly conclude that it was not unlikely that he also had access to reliable information of the Gateses' alleged illegal activities.[b] Of course, the Gateses' travel plans might have been learned from a talkative neighbor or travel agent; under the "two-pronged test" developed from *Spinelli*, the character of the details in the anonymous letter might well not permit a sufficiently clear inference regarding the letter writer's "basis of knowledge." But, as discussed previously, probable cause does not demand the certainty we associate with formal trials. It is enough that there was a fair probability that the writer of the anonymous letter had obtained his entire story either from the Gateses or someone they trusted. And corroboration of major portions of the letter's predictions provides just this probability. * * *

JUSTICE WHITE, **concurring in the judgment.**

* * * [I]t is not at all necessary to overrule *Aguilar-Spinelli* in order to reverse the judgment below. Therefore, because I am inclined to believe that, when applied properly, the *Aguilar-Spinelli* rules play an appropriate role in probable cause determinations, * * * I am reluctant to approve any standard that does not expressly require, as a prerequisite to issuance of a warrant, some showing of facts from which an inference may be drawn that the informant is credible and that his information was obtained in a reliable way. * * *

JUSTICE BRENNAN, **with whom** JUSTICE MARSHALL **joins, dissenting.**

* * *

[O]ne can concede that probable cause is a "practical, nontechnical" concept without betraying the values that *Aguilar* and *Spinelli* reflect. *Aguilar* and *Spinelli* require the police to provide magistrates with certain crucial information. They also provide structure for magistrates' probable cause inquiries. In so doing, *Aguilar* and *Spinelli* preserve the role of magistrates as independent arbiters of probable cause, insure greater accuracy in probable cause determinations, and advance the substantive value of precluding findings of probable cause, and attendant intrusions, based on anything less than information from an honest or credible person who has acquired his information in a reliable way. Neither the standards

---

[b] Justice Stevens' dissent seizes on one inaccuracy in the anonymous informant's letter—its statement the Sue Gates would fly from Florida to Illinois, when in fact she drove—and argues that the probative value of the entire tip was undermined by this allegedly "material mistake." We have never required that informants used by the police be infallible, and can see no reason to impose such a requirement in this case. Probable cause, particularly when police have obtained a warrant, simply does not require the perfection the dissent finds necessary. * * *

nor their effects are inconsistent with a "practical, nontechnical" conception of probable cause. * * *

* * *

JUSTICE STEVENS, with whom JUSTICE BRENNAN joins, dissenting.

The fact that Lance and Sue Gates made a 22-hour nonstop drive from West Palm Beach, Florida, to Bloomingdale, Illinois, only a few hours after Lance had flown to Florida provided persuasive evidence that they were engaged in illicit activity. That fact, however, was not known to the magistrate when he issued the warrant to search their home.

What the magistrate did know at that time was that the anonymous informant had not been completely accurate in his or her predictions. The informant had indicated that "Sue drives their car to Florida *where she leaves it to be loaded up with drugs* * * *. *Sue flies back after she drops the car off in Florida.*" Yet Detective Mader's affidavit reported that she "left the West Palm Beach area driving the Mercury northbound."

The discrepancy between the informant's predictions and the facts known to Detective Mader is significant for three reasons. First, it cast doubt on the informant's hypothesis that the Gateses already had "over $100,000 worth of drugs in their basement." The informant had predicted an itinerary that always kept one spouse in Bloomingdale, suggesting that the Gateses did not want to leave their home unguarded because something valuable was hidden within. That inference obviously could not be drawn when it was known that the pair was actually together over a thousand miles from home.

Second, the discrepancy made the Gateses' conduct seem substantially less unusual than the informant had predicted it would be. It would have been odd if, as predicted, Sue had driven down to Florida on Wednesday, left the car, and flown right back to Illinois. But the mere facts that Sue was in West Palm Beach with the car, that she was joined by her husband at the Holiday Inn on Friday, and that the couple drove north together the next morning are neither unusual nor probative of criminal activity.

Third, the fact that the anonymous letter contained a material mistake undermines the reasonableness of relying on it as a basis for making a forcible entry into a private home.

* * * No one knows who the informant in this case was, or what motivated him or her to write the note. Given that the note's predictions were faulty in one significant respect, and were corroborated by nothing except ordinary innocent activity, I must surmise that the Court's evaluation of the warrant's validity has been colored by subsequent events.

* * *

NOTE ON GATES

Does *Gates* mean that the two-pronged test is no longer relevant? Or does it simply say that the prongs of the *Aguilar* and *Spinelli* are relevant but not necessarily independent or dispositive? See, e.g., United States v. Morales, 171 F.3d 978 (5th Cir.1999) (noting that the *Gates* totality of the circumstances test "includes four factors: (1) the nature of the information; (2) whether there has been an opportunity for the police to see or hear the matter reported; (3) the veracity and the basis of knowledge of the informant; (4) whether there has been any independent verification of the matters reported through police investigation."). See also United States v. Gagnon, 373 F.3d 230 (2d Cir. 2004) (after *Gates* "it is clear that the reliability or veracity of the informant and the basis for the informant's knowledge are but two of several relevant considerations when determining the existence of probable cause based on an informant's tip, and that a deficiency in one may be compensated for, in determining the overall reliability of a tip, by a strong showing as to the other, or by some other indicia of reliability.").

The New York Court of Appeals rejected *Gates* in the context of warrantless police activity in People v. Johnson, 66 N.Y.2d 398, 497 N.Y.S.2d 618, 488 N.E.2d 439 (1985). In so holding, the court followed the lead of the Washington Supreme Court in State v. Jackson, 102 Wash.2d 432, 688 P.2d 136 (1984). See also State v. Jacumin, 778 S.W.2d 430 (Tenn.1989) and State v. Jones, 706 P.2d 317 (Alaska 1985), both rejecting *Gates* in favor of the *Spinelli* two-pronged test. All of these decisions are based on a construction of the respective court's State constitution.

Strong Prong/Weak Prong

Does it make sense that a strong showing on one of the *Spinelli* prongs can make up for a weak showing on the other? For cases in which courts used this reasoning from *Gates* to uphold a finding of probable cause, see Carter v. United States, 729 F.2d 935 (8th Cir.1984) (no specific statement as to informant's basis of knowledge for stating that marijuana was growing on certain property; however, some detail concerning the location of the property was given, and any deficiency in basis of knowledge is compensated for by informant's prior track record of reliable tips); United States v. Phillips, 727 F.2d 392 (5th Cir.1984) (questionable veracity of informant, who hated defendant, overcome by wealth of detail in the tip).

The Function of Corroboration After Gates

Gates promotes corroboration as a means to shore up a defective tip. For a post-*Gates* example of the use of corroboration, consider United States v. Warner, 894 F.2d 957 (8th Cir.1990). A "confidential and reliable source" informed the Sheriff's office that he had seen Warner fire a machinegun at Warner's residence. The next day, an anonymous caller reported that Warner had shot a machinegun the previous day at Warner's residence. The officer checked firearms registrations and found that Warner had no registered firearms. On the basis of this information, a warrant was issued to search Warner's house for an unregistered firearm. The court of appeals upheld the magistrate's determination of probable cause, reasoning that the two tips were "mutually corroborative," and that the officer's check of firearms records provided further crucial corroboration. Would this corroboration have been sufficient under *Spinelli*? Did the officer's corroboration mean that Warner had an unlicensed gun, or that he had no gun? How did the court know that the "mutually corroborative" tips came from two different people?

The effect of *Gates* is apparent in cases like United States v. Peyko, 717 F.2d 741 (2d Cir.1983). An officer received an anonymous tip that Peyko was and would be receiving weekly deliveries of drugs by Federal Express. The officer investigated and found that Peyko had been using Federal Express to send and receive packages regularly. The court found that the tip, together with the corroboration, provided probable cause to seize a Federal Express package addressed to Peyko. While the corroboration was of completely innocent activity (regularly sending and receiving packages), it lent color to the tip, which lent color to the corroboration, which led to probable cause under the *Gates* totality of circumstances approach. In light of *Peyko*, is there any risk that an innocent person with enemies will be subject to a search of his house or possessions?

As seen in *Peyko*—and in *Gates* itself—it will be very important to a finding of probable cause if the informant's tip contains some prediction and that prediction bears out. When predictions are corroborated, a magistrate can draw the conclusion that the informant has some inside information about the defendant's activity, and that, because he got one activity correct, he is also correct about his assessment of criminal activity. See, e.g., United States v. Steppello, 664 F.3d 359 (2d Cir. 2011) (probable cause of drug activity existed where informant "predicted just what Steppello would do in response to his cryptic call.").

Insufficient Corroboration

There are a few reported cases finding that police corroboration was insufficient to shore up a defective tip, even under the *Gates* totality of the circumstances approach. One such case is United States v. Leake, 998 F.2d 1359 (6th Cir.1993). An anonymous informant phoned the police narcotics office and stated that he was a tradesman hired to do some work at 4825 Westport Road. While working, he smelled and saw marijuana in the basement. When questioned as to how he knew it was marijuana, he stated that in his "younger days" he had been a marijuana user, but that now he was older, with children, and was very "anti-drug." Surveillance was initiated at 4825 Westport Road. No undue amount of traffic was observed. It was confirmed that the house had a basement. Two vehicles were registered to the address, one owned by Leake. On the basis of the tip and the investigation, the magistrate issued a warrant to search the premises at 4825 Westport Road, and officers recovered over 300 pounds of marijuana in the basement.

The court in *Leake* held that the warrant lacked probable cause. The court first observed that unlike *Gates*, the anonymous caller in *Leake* had not provided much detail. No names of particular individuals were ever mentioned, no dates were provided, and "no planned future activity was described as in *Gates*." Nor was the corroboration sufficient to overcome the defective tip.

The *Leake* court found a moral in this story:

> Ultimately, this case demonstrates the importance of taking sufficient time to verify an anonymous tip before a warrant is requested. Detective Murphy's investigation of the caller's information was inadequate. More police work was needed. The supporting affidavit was too vague and Detective Murphy's limited two-night surveillance was insufficient to verify important elements of the anonymous caller's information.

See also United States v. Wilhelm, 80 F.3d 116 (4th Cir.1996), where the officer received information from a "reliable source" who observed marijuana in the defendant's home and provided directions to that home. The court found, understandably, that this barebones information was not sufficient to establish probable cause, but the government argued that the tip had been corroborated by the facts that: 1) the informant had given accurate directions to the defendant's home and 2) the informant, in describing the defendant's activity, had accurately described what marijuana looks like and how it is packaged and sold. The court found that this corroboration was not enough to cure the defect in the tip because "[a]lmost anyone can give directions to a particular house without knowing anything of substance about what goes on inside that house, and anyone who occasionally watches the evening news can make generalizations about what marijuana looks like and how it is packaged and sold."

The Gates Test Applied: Massachusetts v. Upton

The Court reiterated its "totality of the circumstances" test in Massachusetts v. Upton, 466 U.S. 727 (1984), a per curiam disposition reversing the state supreme court. The Court described the facts as follows:

At noon on September 11, 1980, Lt. Beland of the Yarmouth Police Department assisted in the execution of a search warrant for a motel room reserved by one Richard Kelleher at the Snug Harbor Motel in West Yarmouth. The search produced several items of identification, including credit cards, belonging to two persons whose homes had recently been burglarized. Other items taken in the burglaries, such as jewelry, silver and gold, were not found at the motel.

At 3:20 p.m. on the same day, Lt. Beland received a call from an unidentified female who told him that there was "a motor home full of stolen stuff" parked behind #5 Jefferson Ave., the home of respondent George Upton and his mother. She stated that the stolen items included jewelry, silver and gold. As set out in Lt. Beland's affidavit in support of a search warrant:

> She further stated that George Upton was going to move the motor home any time now because of the fact that Ricky Kelleher's motel room was raided and that George Upton had purchased these stolen items from Ricky Kelleher. This unidentified female stated that she had seen the stolen items but refused to identify herself because "he'll kill me," referring to George Upton. I then told this unidentified female that I knew who she was, giving her the name of Lynn Alberico, who I had met on May 16, 1980, at George Upton's repair shop off Summer St., in Yarmouthport. She was identified to me by George Upton as being his girlfriend, Lynn Alberico. The unidentified female admitted that she was the girl that I had named, stating that she was surprised that I knew who she was. She then told me that she'd broken up with George Upton and wanted to burn him. She also told me that she wouldn't give me her address or phone number but that she would contact me in the future, if need be.

Following the phone call, Lt. Beland went to Upton's house to verify that a motor home was parked on the property. Then, while other officers watched the premises, Lt. Beland prepared the application for a search warrant, setting out all the information noted above in an accompanying affidavit. He also attached the police reports on the two prior burglaries, along with lists of the stolen property. A magistrate issued the warrant, and a subsequent search of the motor home produced the items described by the caller and other incriminating evidence. The discovered evidence led to Upton's conviction on multiple counts of burglary, receiving stolen property, and related crimes.

The *Upton* Court explained why the state supreme court's invalidation of the warrant was inconsistent with *Gates*:

> [T]he Massachusetts court reasoned, first, that the basis of the informant's knowledge was not "forcefully apparent" in the affidavit. Although the caller stated that she had seen the stolen items and that they were in the motor home, she did not specifically state that she saw them in the motor home. Second, the court concluded that "[n]one of the common bases for determining the credibility of an informant or the reliability of her information is present here." The caller was not a "tried and true" informant, her statement was not against penal interest, and she was not an "ordinary citizen" providing information as a witness to a crime. "She was an anonymous informant, and her unverified assent to the suggestion that she was Lynn Alberico does not take her out of that category."
>
> Finally, the court felt that there was insufficient corroboration of the informant's tip to make up for its failure to satisfy the two-pronged test. The facts that tended to corroborate the informant's story were that the motor home was where it was supposed to be, that the caller knew of the motel raid which took place only three hours earlier, and that the caller knew the name of Upton and his girlfriend. But, much as the Supreme Court of Illinois did in the opinion we reviewed in *Gates*, the Massachusetts court reasoned that each item of corroborative evidence either related to innocent, nonsuspicious conduct or related to an event that took place in public. * * *

The Supreme Court took the Massachusetts Court to task in the following analysis:

> We think that the Supreme Judicial Court of Massachusetts misunderstood our decision in *Gates*. We did not merely refine or qualify the "two-pronged test." We rejected it as hypertechnical and divorced from "the factual and practical considerations of everyday life on which reasonable and prudent men, not legal technicians, act." * * *
>
> * * * The court did not consider Lt. Beland's affidavit in its entirety, giving significance to each relevant piece of information and balancing the relative weights of all the various indicia of reliability (and unreliability) attending the tip. Instead, the court insisted on judging bits and pieces of information in isolation against the artificial standards provided by the two-pronged test.
>
> The Supreme Judicial Court also erred in failing to grant any deference to the decision of the magistrate to issue a warrant. Instead of merely deciding whether the evidence viewed as a whole provided a "substantial basis" for the magistrate's finding of probable cause, the court conducted a de novo probable cause determination. We rejected just such after-the-fact, de novo scrutiny in *Gates*. * * *

The *Upton* Court then applied the *Gates* analysis to the facts and found that the warrant was supported by probable cause:

> Examined in light of *Gates*, Lt. Beland's affidavit provides a substantial basis for the issuance of the warrant. No single piece of evidence in it is conclusive. But the pieces fit neatly together and, so viewed, support the magistrate's determination that there was "a fair probability that contraband or evidence of crime" would be found in Upton's motor home. The informant claimed to have seen the stolen goods and gave a description of them which tallied with the items taken in recent burglaries. She knew of the raid on the motel room—which produced evidence connected to those burglaries—and that the room had been reserved by Kelleher. She explained the connection between Kelleher's motel room and the stolen goods in Upton's motor home. And she provided a motive both for her attempt at anonymity—fear of Upton's retaliation—and for furnishing the information—her recent breakup with Upton and her desire "to burn him."
>
> The Massachusetts court dismissed Lt. Beland's identification of the caller as a mere "unconfirmed guess." But "probable cause does not demand the certainty we associate with formal trials." Lt. Beland noted that the caller "admitted that she was the girl I had named, stating that she was surprised that I knew who she was." It is of course possible that the caller merely adopted Lt. Beland's suggestion as "a convenient cover for her true identity." But given the caller's admission, her obvious knowledge of who Alberico was and how she was connected with Upton, and her explanation of her motive in calling, Lt. Beland's inference appears stronger than a mere uninformed and unconfirmed guess. It is enough that the inference was a reasonable one and conformed with the other pieces of evidence making up the total showing of probable cause.[13]

On remand in *Upton,* the Massachusetts Supreme Judicial Court declined to follow *Gates* and reaffirmed its commitment to the two-pronged test under the state constitution. Commonwealth v. Upton, 394 Mass. 363, 476 N.E.2d 548 (1985). It reasoned that the two-pronged test "aids lay people, such as the police and certain lay magistrates, in a way that the 'totality of the circumstances' test never could." Did the state supreme court correctly apply the *Spinelli* test to the *Upton* facts?

3. The Citizen Informant

Under both *Spinelli* and *Gates,* the courts have distinguished police informants and anonymous informants from an ordinary citizen who identifies himself and reports a crime. The reason is that paid informants are presumptively unreliable given their dubious character and financial (or other) arrangements, and anonymous informants must be presumed

[13] Justice Stevens concurred in the judgment, expressing the opinion that the state supreme court should have indicated whether the warrant was valid under state law. Justices Brennan and Marshall dissented from the summary reversal of the state court.

unreliable because they may be using their anonymity for suspect reasons (e.g., to frame or harass an enemy). In contrast, identified citizen informants are considered reliable because they are presumed to be motivated by "concern for society or for [their] own safety." State v. Paszek, 50 Wis.2d 619, 184 N.W.2d 836 (1971). Are you persuaded that citizen informants should be presumed reliable?

4. Accomplices

In United States v. Patterson, 150 F.3d 382 (4th Cir.1998), the police arrested Greene after two masked men robbed a bank. Greene confessed and identified Patterson as his accomplice. On the basis of this statement, the officers searched Patterson's car and found incriminating evidence. Patterson challenged the search as lacking probable cause. But the court held that the confession of a co-participant is itself sufficient to establish probable cause—no corroboration is required. The court noted that a defendant can be *convicted* solely on the basis of the uncorroborated testimony of an accomplice, and reasoned that "it would be contradictory to allow a defendant to be convicted based on the uncorroborated testimony of his co-perpetrator while refusing to find that the same statement would be sufficient to support probable cause." But is the accomplice's testimony under oath at trial really the "same statement" as the accomplice's stationhouse, hearsay confession implicating another in the crime? Can any discrepancy be resolved by considering the different stakes and standards of persuasion at stake?

5. Quantity of Information Required for Probable Cause

Gates dealt with the *quality* of information that could be considered in the probable cause determination, i.e., whether the informant's tip is reliable enough to be considered as proof of probable cause. Assuming that all the information is reliable, another question arises: has the information submitted established a "fair probability" of criminal activity or the presence of evidence of a crime? This question arises not only with respect to affidavits submitted to magistrates, but also with warrantless searches and seizures; even if the search or seizure is conducted pursuant to an exception to the warrant requirement, the officer is ordinarily required to have probable cause.

Equivocal Activity

One circumstance in which a "fair probability" question is presented is where it is unknown whether a crime has been or is being committed. For example, what if the officer sees a person at 2:00 a.m. carrying a television and a stereo down the street in a shopping cart? There are many innocent explanations for this activity. Does that mean that there is no fair probability of criminal activity?

Consider United States v. Prandy-Binett, 995 F.2d 1069 (D.C.Cir.1993). Judge Randolph introduced the facts as follows:

> Detective John Centrella saw a small rectangular block wrapped in silver duct tape. To the uninitiated, the object's outward appearance said nothing about its contents. To Detective Centrella, the size, shape and wrapping of the object signified one kilogram of illegal narcotics. * * *
>
> Detective Centrella and another narcotics detective were on duty at Union Station, meeting trains arriving from New York City, a "source city" for drugs. As they watched departing passengers, their attention was drawn to an individual walking through the station faster than the others and trying to get around them. When the individual—Prandy-Binett—made eye contact with the detectives, who were in plain clothes, he moved even more quickly toward the exit. The detectives approached him and identified themselves. After telling the officers he had come from New Jersey, Prandy-Binett produced a one-way train ticket, purchased with cash, showing that his trip originated at Penn Station, New York City. After saying he lived in Washington, D.C., he handed the officers a driver's license showing Hyattsville, Maryland, as his residence. Detective Centrella's suspicions, aroused by these possible inconsistencies, were heightened by the cloth "tote" or "gym" bag Prandy-Binett carried on his shoulder. Prandy-Binett reported having spent a week working in New Jersey. Yet his only luggage was the small bag, which did not appear full. Asked whether the bag contained drugs or guns, Prandy-Binett said no. Detective Centrella then requested permission to search the bag. Prandy-Binett replied that he did not have to consent and that the bag contained only clothing. He took the bag from his shoulder, placed it on the ground, knelt down (as did the detective next to him), unzipped the bag and began pulling out a pair of blue jeans. This action uncovered a miniature shopping bag lying on its side, deep purple in color, a "perfume or a cologne bag" from Elizabeth Taylor Perfume. Unprompted, Prandy-Binett said, in evident reference to the perfume bag, "this is a gift." As Prandy-Binett continued to manipulate the blue jeans, a portion of a rectangular block, wrapped in silver duct tape, slid out of the perfume bag. Believing the block to contain illegal drugs, Detective Centrella handcuffed Prandy-Binett, examined the wrapped object further, and seized it and the gym bag. A later field test on the contents of the wrapped block revealed cocaine.

Judge Randolph concluded that, based on the totality of circumstances, there was a fair probability that the rectangular block contained drugs, and upheld the narcotics conviction on which the search and seizure were based. He analyzed the fair probability question as follows:

> Somewhere between "less than evidence which would justify conviction" and "more than bare suspicion," probable cause is satisfied. The precise point is indeterminate. * * * This is why the detectives' observations up to the time the block slipped out of the perfume bag cannot be disregarded. * * * Is the probability increased if the passenger moves quickly through the station after leaving the train? Greater if the passenger also gives apparently deceptive answers when the police question him? Greater still if the passenger opens his bag and refers to a package wrapped in duct tape inside a fancy perfume bag as a "gift?" Neither courts nor law enforcement officers, nor anyone else for that matter, can quantify any of this. * * * Still, we are convinced that, up to the sighting of the duct tape package, the conditional probability was low, much too low to have satisfied the Fourth Amendment in light of the interests it protects.
>
> The case thus comes down to the detectives' inference of narcotics from the appearance of the wrapped block, and on the extent to which that inference enhanced the probability of Prandy-Binett's possessing drugs. We put the question in these terms because "probable cause" is evaluated not only from the perspective of a "prudent man," but also from the particular viewpoint of the officer involved in the search or seizure. * * *

Judge Randolph concluded that the sighting of the rectangular block wrapped in duct tape added enough to the other facts to constitute a fair probability of criminal activity. He noted three factors bearing on this probability assessment:

> There was first the block's bulk. * * * Detective Centrella was quite familiar with the bulk of packages containing one kilogram of cocaine. * * * Detective Centrella * * * thus had good reason for believing that the wrapped block in Prandy-Binett's gym bag was about the size of a package containing one kilogram of cocaine or heroin.
>
> The second consideration was the rectangular shape of the object. The portion protruding from the perfume bag was consistent with what the detectives knew to be the standard configuration, the typical "kilo brick." * * * The brick-like shape of the object thus further alerted the detectives, in light of their training and experience, to the possible presence of narcotics.
>
> The third factor was wrapping—silver duct tape (over plastic). Duct tape is attractive to traffickers because fingerprints are difficult to lift from its surface and because some criminals believe—erroneously—that it masks the odor of the drugs from police dogs. * * *
>
> To Detective Centrella the wrapped block thus conveyed the message "one kilo of narcotics" just as surely as if the words were

> written on the tape. The circumstances leading up to the arrest and the incongruity of the crudely wrapped block inside the fancy perfume bag, together with Prandy-Binett's unsolicited disclaimer "This is a gift," must have confirmed what the detective saw in his mind's eye. * * * We cannot say exactly how probable it was that the block contained drugs, but we are convinced that it amounted, at the least, to a " 'fair probability' " Prandy-Binett was committing an offense.

Judge Edwards wrote a vigorous dissent in *Prandy-Binett.* He complained that the majority, "relying on a bizarre theory of 'conditional probabilities,' holds that probable cause can be based on the appearance of duct tape." He noted that Prandy-Binett was a person of color and argued that the officers were motivated more by racial profiling than by any assessment of probability:

> The circumstances that actually arouse police "suspicion" are obvious to anyone who bothers to look—individuals traveling through Union Station who are evidently poor, or people of color, are the individuals who are approached, questioned, stopped and searched. See Sheri Lynn Johnson, Race and the Decision to Detain a Suspect, 93 Yale L.J. 214, 225–37 (1983) (describing the varied uses of race as a motivation for police detention, and as an element in probable cause and reasonable suspicion analyses); Developments in the Law: Race and the Criminal Process, 101 Harv. L. Rev. 1472, 1496 (1988) (noting studies that reveal that "police use race as an independently significant, if not determinative, factor in deciding whom to follow, detain, search, or arrest").

Judge Edwards dismissed the supposed incongruity of carrying a package wrapped in duct tape as a gift in an expensive bag:

> The majority also finds suspicious the "incongruity" of the sight of a "crudely wrapped block inside the fancy perfume bag." Such comment reveals a distinct lack of empathy for some members of our society—those without much disposable income, for example—who readily find use for a discarded shopping bag and who might very well wrap a gift with whatever packaging material is on hand, including duct tape.

Judge Edwards concluded that the placement of a rectangular object wrapped in duct tape inside one's luggage was simply not enough to rise to a fair probability of criminal activity. He argued that the "brick-like shape of a package might provide the observer with a general hint about the size of its contents, but the shape of such a package is too generic to make reasonable the inference that the contents of the package are also brick-shaped."

Who has the better argument in *Prandy-Binett*? Of course it is true that Prandy-Binett might have wrapped some figurines into a rectangular mass of duct tape. But does that mean there wasn't a fair probability that the package contained contraband?

Regarding equivocal conduct, every circuit has decided cases on probable cause as applied to downloading or distributing child pornography on a computer. Most courts have held that probable cause can be found even without direct evidence that the defendant ever downloaded or distributed illegal images. Is that a proper application of the fair probability standard? See, e.g., United States v. Gourde, 440 F.3d 1065 (9th Cir. 2006) (en banc) (defendant's membership in a website that gave him unlimited access to child pornography on the site provided probable cause to believe that the defendant had actually downloaded illegal images); United States v. Martin, 426 F.3d 68 (2d Cir. 2005) (probable cause to search defendant's home existed on the basis of his membership in a chat group dedicated to child pornography; membership established a fair probability that the defendant did in fact exchange or download child pornography: it is "common-sense that one who voluntarily joins a child-pornography group and remains a member of that group * * * would download such pornography from the website and have it in his possession."). See also United States v. Perez, 484 F.3d 735 (5th Cir. 2007) (association between an IP address used for child pornography and a physical address constitutes a fair probability that criminal activity is occurring at that address: "though it was possible that the transmissions originated outside of the residence to which the IP address was assigned, it remained likely that the source of the transmissions was inside that residence.").

Probable Cause to Arrest

Although arrests in public usually do not require a warrant, the probable cause requirement still applies. Probable cause to search is determined by whether there is a fair probability that the area or object searched contains evidence of a crime. Probable cause to arrest is determined by whether there is a fair probability to believe that the person arrested has committed or is committing a crime. Often these two fair probability assessments are actually one. For example, if there was probable cause to believe that the rectangular object in Prandy-Binett's luggage contained contraband, then there was also probable cause to arrest Prandy-Binett on a narcotics offense. In some situations, however, there may be probable cause to arrest, but not probable cause to search. For example, there may be a fair probability that a person robbed a bank five years ago; but that does not mean there is a fair probability to believe that the defendant's briefcase contains evidence of the five year-old bank robbery. In other cases, there may be probable cause to search but not probable cause to arrest, such as where a criminal leaves a suitcase full of drugs in the home of an unsuspecting friend.

In the arrest context, the question of fair probability sometimes arises where police know that a crime has been committed, but they are not certain that a particular suspect is the perpetrator. Consider United States v. Valez, 796 F.2d 24 (2d Cir.1986), where the court set forth the following facts and analysis:

> At 4:30 p.m. on October 16, 1984, New York City Police Sergeant Albert Zarr and Officer James Allen were parked in a surveillance vehicle on West 48th Street between Eighth and Ninth Avenues in Manhattan. Zarr sat near the rear window watching the street with binoculars; Allen remained in the front seat. After observing what appeared to be a narcotics sale on the southeast corner of 48th and Ninth, Zarr sent one of his undercover police officers to make a drug buy.
>
> Zarr saw the undercover officer hand money to two men at the corner and in return receive two packets that later proved to contain cocaine. Zarr observed that one of the sellers was an Hispanic male in his twenties, wearing a black leather jacket, grey pants with a comb in the back pocket, and a white or off-white V-neck shirt with dark trim on the collar.
>
> Zarr described the sellers to Allen and radioed the description to the field team. At that point, the seller with the black jacket walked around the corner and disappeared from view. Zarr instructed Allen to follow the subject and make an arrest.
>
> Allen left the van immediately and proceeded west on 48th Street and then south on Ninth Avenue in search of the seller. Allen walked to the next corner, but did not see his subject. He decided to turn back on the hunch that the seller had ducked into one of the stores. When Allen returned to the corner of 48th and Ninth, he saw a man coming out of a Blimpie's fast food restaurant who matched the description that Zarr had given him. At 4:40 p.m., five to ten minutes after Allen left the surveillance van, he arrested the man. The person whom Allen had arrested was Valez. [Valez was brought to the station, and a search of his person uncovered packets of cocaine.]
>
> When Sergeant Zarr and the undercover officer who made the "buy" returned to the stationhouse, they realized that Allen had arrested the wrong man. [Valez moved to suppress the cocaine on the ground that the arrest was illegal for lack of probable cause.] Valez relied primarily on the fact that Zarr's description did not include any mention of facial hair, whereas Valez had a small goatee and a thick moustache. Valez also argued that Zarr's description of the seller was overly general and that the mistaken arrest resulted from the negligent and unorganized conduct of the surveillance team.

The *Valez* court held that the description of the perpetrator was not overly general, and that the officers had acted properly in arresting Valez, even though he was not in fact involved in the sale to the undercover officer:

> Given Zarr's detailed description of the seller's clothing, his failure to mention that the seller was clean-shaven does not constitute an unreasonable oversight. * * * [T]he police may justifiably place little reliance on the presence or absence of facial hair on a suspect who otherwise matches a description because facial hair may be worn or taken off as a disguise. * * *

Dissenting Judge Oakes argued that Officer Zarr's description was too general to support the conclusion that there was probable cause to arrest:

> By sending an officer into the area with a description only of race, approximate age, and clothing and, oh yes, of a comb in the hip pocket—but not mentioning facial hair or its absence, or the length of the suspect's haircut—Zarr was insufficiently distinguishing the person who made the sale from other Latin males of not uncommon appearance in the immediate area. It was the equivalent of "identifying" a suspect in the Wall Street area by describing him as a white, thirty-ish man with a button-down shirt and dark pinstripe suit, carrying a leather attaché case.

Who has the better of the argument on probable cause, the majority or the dissent? Would it have mattered if Zarr had arrested the real seller before Allen had arrested Valez?

Compare the result in *Valez* with that of United States v. Kithcart, 134 F.3d 529 (3d Cir. 1998). Officers received three radio transmissions reporting separate armed robberies. Two robberies were reported in Bensalem Township and one in the adjacent Bristol Township. The time and the exact location of the robbery in Bristol Township was not specified. The perpetrators were described as "two black males in a black sports car." One of the perpetrators might have been wearing white clothes, and the vehicle was described as a "possible Z-28, possible Camaro." Ten minutes after the last radio transmission, concerning the robbery in Bristol Township, Officer Nelson spotted a black Nissan 300ZX, about a mile from Bristol Township. The vehicle was being driven by a Black male, who appeared to be the only person in the car. Officer Nelson testified that since she had received the last radio transmission, this was the first time she had come upon either a black car or a Black driver. She signaled the car to pull over, and "saw two sets of arms raised toward the roof of the car, and she realized that there were two people in the car." Eventually the officer searched the car, and found firearms. Kithcart, the driver, was charged with being a felon in possession of a firearm. The trial court denied Kithcart's suppression motion, holding that Officer Nelson had probable cause to arrest Kithcart when she pulled him over, and therefore that the search of the car was a proper search incident to a valid arrest.

The court of appeals, however, held that Officer Nelson did not have probable cause to arrest Kithcart when she pulled him over. The court analyzed the probable cause standard, in light of the facts, as follows:

> The mere fact that Kithcart is black and the perpetrators had been described as two black males is plainly insufficient. * * * Moreover, the match between the description of the perpetrators' car (a black sports car, "possible Z-28, possible Camaro)" and the vehicle in which Kithcart was spotted (a black Nissan 300ZX) was far from precise. Although the Camaro Z-28 and the Nissan 300ZX could be considered "sports cars," there was no evidence offered at the suppression hearing that the shapes of the two cars were sufficiently similar so as to warrant an inference that a 300ZX could be mistaken for a Z-28.
>
> Nor is probable cause established by either the location or time of the stop. There was no evidence presented as to where in Bristol Township the final robbery occurred; nor was there evidence presented that the Bristol robbery occurred shortly before Officer Nelson stopped the car carrying Kithcart. * * * In other words, armed with information that two black males driving a black sports car were believed to have committed three robberies in the area some relatively short time earlier, Officer Nelson could not justifiably arrest any African-American man who happened to drive by in any type of black sports car.

What accounts for the different results in *Valez* and *Kithcart*? What more could the officer in *Kithcart* have offered to show probable cause?

Mistaken Arrests

As indicated by *Valez,* probable cause to arrest (or to search) can exist even though the police are mistaken in believing that the person arrested committed a crime. The question for probable cause is not accuracy but rather fair probability. See Hill v. California, 401 U.S. 797 (1971) (if police have probable cause to arrest Hill and have probable cause to believe that Miller is Hill, they act properly if they arrest Miller); Hirsch v. Burke, 40 F.3d 900 (7th Cir.1994) (police had probable cause to arrest a person for public drunkenness, even though the person was in fact a diabetic in a state of insulin shock).

Probabilities with Multiple Suspects

If a police officer finds drugs in a car, does he have probable cause to arrest everyone in the car? That is the question in the following case.

MARYLAND V. PRINGLE

Supreme Court of the United States, 2003.
540 U.S. 366.

CHIEF JUSTICE REHNQUIST delivered the opinion of the Court.

* * *

At 3:16 a.m. on August 7, 1999, a Baltimore County Police officer stopped a Nissan Maxima for speeding. There were three occupants in the car: Donte Partlow, the driver and owner, respondent Pringle, the front-seat passenger, and Otis Smith, the back-seat passenger. The officer asked Partlow for his license and registration. When Partlow opened the glove compartment to retrieve the vehicle registration, the officer observed a large amount of rolled-up money in the glove compartment. The officer returned to his patrol car with Partlow's license and registration to check the computer system for outstanding violations. The computer check did not reveal any violations. The officer returned to the stopped car, had Partlow get out, and issued him an oral warning.

After a second patrol car arrived, the officer asked Partlow if he had any weapons or narcotics in the vehicle. Partlow indicated that he did not. Partlow then consented to a search of the vehicle. The search yielded $763 from the glove compartment and five plastic glassine baggies containing cocaine from behind the back-seat armrest. * * *

The officer questioned all three men about the ownership of the drugs and money, and told them that if no one admitted to ownership of the drugs he was going to arrest them all. The men offered no information regarding the ownership of the drugs or money. All three were placed under arrest and transported to the police station.

Later that morning, Pringle waived his rights under Miranda v. Arizona, and gave an oral and written confession in which he acknowledged that the cocaine belonged to him, that he and his friends were going to a party, and that he intended to sell the cocaine or "use it for sex." Pringle maintained that the other occupants of the car did not know about the drugs, and they were released.

The trial court denied Pringle's motion to suppress his confession as the fruit of an illegal arrest, holding that the officer had probable cause to arrest Pringle. A jury convicted Pringle of possession with intent to distribute cocaine and possession of cocaine. * * * The Court of Appeals of Maryland, by divided vote, reversed, holding that, absent specific facts tending to show Pringle's knowledge and dominion or control over the drugs, "the mere finding of cocaine in the back armrest when [Pringle] was a front seat passenger in a car being driven by its owner is insufficient to establish probable cause for an arrest for possession." We granted certiorari, and now reverse.

* * *

It is uncontested in the present case that the officer, upon recovering the five plastic glassine baggies containing suspected cocaine, had probable cause to believe a felony had been committed. The sole question is whether the officer had probable cause to believe that Pringle committed that crime. Maryland law defines "possession" as "the exercise of actual or constructive dominion or control over a thing by one or more persons."

* * *

In this case, Pringle was one of three men riding in a Nissan Maxima at 3:16 a.m. There was $763 of rolled-up cash in the glove compartment directly in front of Pringle. Five plastic glassine baggies of cocaine were behind the back-seat armrest and accessible to all three men. * * *

We think it an entirely reasonable inference from these facts that any or all three of the occupants had knowledge of, and exercised dominion and control over, the cocaine. Thus a reasonable officer could conclude that there was probable cause to believe Pringle committed the crime of possession of cocaine, either solely or jointly.

Pringle's attempt to characterize this case as a guilt-by-association case is unavailing. His reliance on Ybarra v. Illinois [discussed in the section on stop and frisk, infra] * * * is misplaced. In *Ybarra*, police officers obtained a warrant to search a tavern and its bartender for evidence of possession of a controlled substance. Upon entering the tavern, the officers conducted patdown searches of the customers present in the tavern, including Ybarra. Inside a cigarette pack retrieved from Ybarra's pocket, an officer found six tinfoil packets containing heroin. * * * We held that the search warrant did not permit body searches of all of the tavern's patrons and that the police could not patdown the patrons for weapons, absent individualized suspicion.

This case is quite different from *Ybarra*. Pringle and his two companions were in a relatively small automobile, not a public tavern. * * * [A] car passenger—unlike the unwitting tavern patron in *Ybarra*—will often be engaged in a common enterprise with the driver, and have the same interest in concealing the fruits or the evidence of their wrongdoing. Here we think it was reasonable for the officer to infer a common enterprise among the three men. The quantity of drugs and cash in the car indicated the likelihood of drug dealing, an enterprise to which a dealer would be unlikely to admit an innocent person with the potential to furnish evidence against him.

* * *

QUESTIONS ON PRINGLE

Would the officers have had probable cause to arrest Pringle's 15 year-old son if he were a fourth occupant in the car? What about Pringle's 87 year-old great grandmother? Would the result in *Pringle* have been the same if the officer found no drugs in the car but obtained consent to search the trunk and found the drugs there?

Assume after *Pringle* that officers are in an area known for drug-trafficking and they know that at least one of every three residents is committing drug crimes. They just don't know which ones. Can they arrest every third person that comes walking down the street on the fair probability that they are involved in drug crimes? What about one out of every three residents in the area?

Dog Sniffs and Probable Cause: Florida v. Harris

A dog sniff of luggage is not a search under United States v. Place, supra, but what about the *opening* of the luggage after a positive dog sniff? That would be a search because it entails a physical intrusion into a constitutionally protected "effect" for purposes of gathering information without consent, either express or implied. Whether such an intrusion is reasonable would depend on whether there is probable cause to believe evidence of a crime will be found in the luggage, which raises the question whether that is sufficient to constitute probable cause.

The Supreme Court addressed that question in Florida v. Harris, 588 U.S. 237 (2013). During a lawful vehicle stop, "Aldo," a drug sniffing dog, alerted at the door of Harris's car. A search of the car revealed no drugs the dog was trained to detect but rather a number of substances used to make methamphetamine. Florida charged Harris with possessing pseudoephedrine for use in manufacturing methamphetamine. While he was released on bail, the same officer stopped him again, the same dog alerted at the same place, but this time nothing was found when the car was searched. A trial judge denied a motion to suppress, and the Florida Supreme Court reversed. Writing for the Court, Justice Kagan described the issue as follows: * * *

> The Florida Supreme Court * * * [held] that Wheetley [the officer] lacked probable cause to search Harris's vehicle under the Fourth Amendment. "[W]hen a dog alerts," the court wrote, "the fact that the dog has been trained and certified is simply not enough to establish probable cause." To demonstrate a dog's reliability, the State needed to produce a wider array of evidence:
>
> "[T]he State must present . . . the dog's training and certification records, an explanation of the meaning of the particular training and certification, field performance records (including any unverified alerts), and evidence concerning the experience and

training of the officer handling the dog, as well as any other objective evidence known to the officer about the dog's reliability."

* * *

Evidence of a dog's satisfactory performance in a certification or training program can itself provide sufficient reason to trust his alert. If a bona fide organization has certified a dog after testing his reliability in a controlled setting, a court can presume (subject to any conflicting evidence offered) that the dog's alert provides probable cause to search. The same is true, even in the absence of formal certification, if the dog has recently and successfully completed a training program that evaluated his proficiency in locating drugs. * * *

A defendant, however, must have an opportunity to challenge such evidence of a dog's reliability, whether by cross-examining the testifying officer or by introducing his own fact or expert witnesses. The defendant, for example, may contest the adequacy of a certification or training program, perhaps asserting that its standards are too lax or its methods faulty. So too, the defendant may examine how the dog (or handler) performed in the assessments made in those settings. Indeed, evidence of the dog's (or handler's) history in the field * * * may sometimes be relevant * * *. And even assuming a dog is generally reliable, circumstances surrounding a particular alert may undermine the case for probable cause—if, say, the officer cued the dog (consciously or not), or if the team was working under unfamiliar conditions.

In short, a probable-cause hearing focusing on a dog's alert should proceed much like any other. * * *

Justice Kagan found that the record "amply supported the trial court's determination that Aldo's alert gave Wheetley probable cause to search Harris's truck." The state produced "substantial evidence" of his training and efficiency having completed two recent drug-detection courses and maintained his proficiency through weekly training exercises. Moreover, Harris's cross-examination of the handler failed to rebut the State's showing of reliability. Justice Kagan explained as follows:

Harris principally contended in the trial court that because Wheetley did not find any of the substances Aldo was trained to detect, Aldo's two alerts must have been false. But * * * here we doubt that Harris's logic does justice to Aldo's skills. Harris cooked and used methamphetamine on a regular basis; so as Wheetley later surmised, Aldo likely responded to odors that Harris had transferred to the driver's-side door handle of his truck. A well-trained drug-detection dog *should* alert to such odors; his response to them might appear a mistake, but in fact is not. And still more fundamentally, we do not evaluate probable cause in hindsight, based on what a search does or does not turn up. For the reasons already stated, Wheetley had good cause to view Aldo as a reliable detector of drugs. And no special circumstance here gave Wheetley reason to discount Aldo's usual dependability or distrust his response to Harris's truck.

Probable Cause to Arrest for a Crime Different from the Charge on Which the Defendant Was Arrested: Devenpeck v. Alford

In Devenpeck v. Alford, 543 U.S. 146 (2004), Justice Scalia wrote for a unanimous Court (Chief Justice Rehnquist not participating) as it addressed "the question whether an arrest is lawful under the Fourth Amendment when the criminal offense for which there is probable cause to arrest is not 'closely related' to the offense stated by the arresting officer at the time of arrest." Alford had stopped to assist a disabled automobile before Washington State Patrol Officer Haner came to the scene and Alford left. Haney informed his supervisor, Devenpeck, that Alford appeared to be an impersonator or "wannabe cop." Haney pursued Alford and found that he was listening to a sheriff's office police frequency on a special radio, and that handcuffs and a hand-held police scanner were in the car.

Sergeant Devenpeck arrived at the scene where Haner stopped Alford, was told by Haner that he believed Alford had been impersonating a police officer. Devenpeck discovered that Alford had a tape recorder with the play and record buttons depressed on the passenger seat of his car and asked Alford about his wig-wag headlights. Devenpeck ordered Alford to play the recorded tape, found that Alford was taping his conversations with the officers, and arrested Alford for a violation of the state privacy act.

Haner booked Alford for violating the privacy act and issued a ticket for his flashing headlights. A state court dismissed both charges, and Alford filed suit against the officers for an unlawful arrest, claiming that there was no probable cause warranting arrest. A jury found for the officers despite the fact that it was instructed that at the time of Alford's arrest a state court of appeals had clearly held that the taping of the officers was not a crime.

The court of appeals rejected the argument that probable cause existed to arrest Alford for the offenses of impersonating a law-enforcement officer and obstructing a law-enforcement officer because those offenses were not "closely related" to the offense invoked by Devenpeck as he took Alford into custody.

The Supreme Court reversed. Justice Scalia explained:

> Our cases make clear that an arresting officer's state of mind (except for the facts that he knows) is irrelevant to the existence of probable cause. That is to say, his subjective reason for making the

arrest need not be the criminal offense as to which the known facts provide probable cause. * * *

The rule that the offense establishing probable cause must be "closely related" to, and based on the same conduct as, the offense identified by the arresting officer at the time of arrest is inconsistent with this precedent. Such a rule makes the lawfulness of an arrest turn upon the motivation of the arresting officer—eliminating, as validating probable cause, facts that played no part in the officer's expressed subjective reason for making the arrest, and offenses that are not "closely related" to that subjective reason. This means that the constitutionality of an arrest under a given set of known facts will vary from place to place and from time to time, depending on whether the arresting officer states the reason for the detention and, if so, whether he correctly identifies a general class of offense for which probable cause exists. An arrest made by a knowledgeable, veteran officer would be valid, whereas an arrest made by a rookie *in precisely the same circumstances* would not. We see no reason to ascribe to the Fourth Amendment such arbitrarily variable protection.

* * * Subjective intent of the arresting officer, *however* it is determined (and of course subjective intent is *always* determined by objective means), is simply no basis for invalidating an arrest. Those are lawfully arrested whom the facts known to the arresting officers give probable cause to arrest.

6. Collective Knowledge

In Whiteley v. Warden, 401 U.S. 560 (1971), the Supreme Court declared that "police officers called upon to aid other officers in executing arrest warrants are entitled to assume that the officers requesting aid offered the magistrate the information requisite to support an independent judicial assessment of probable cause." This approach means that once Officer A demonstrates to a magistrate probable cause to arrest a suspect, any other officer can make the arrest on the assumption that the warrant is valid. The arresting officer need not have independent knowledge of the arrestee's criminal activity. All that is required is collective knowledge in the police department that rises to the level of probable cause. The same rule applies in warrantless arrest cases. If Officer B makes an arrest pursuant to orders from Officer A, and the latter had probable cause for the order, the arrest is valid—Officer B need not be familiar with the facts supporting probable cause.

7. Staleness of Information

One problem that sometimes arises in assessing probable cause is that the officer's information is dated. For example, an officer may receive information from a reliable informant that the defendant had an ounce of marijuana in his home on January 1. Assuming that the informant's tip satisfies *Gates*, there is still a problem if the search of the defendant's home is conducted on July 1. Certainly, there is no fair probability that the same ounce of marijuana is still in the defendant's house six months later.

An example of a staleness problem arose in United States v. Harris, 20 F.3d 445 (11th Cir.1994). Police had probable cause to believe that Ford was involved in a narcotics conspiracy in 1988. However, the warrant to search Ford's house was not issued until 1990. Ford argued that the information supporting probable cause had become stale. The *Harris* Court had this to say about the staleness inquiry:

> When reviewing staleness challenges we do not apply some talismanic rule which establishes arbitrary time limitations * * *. In this case-by-case determination we may consider the maturity of the information, nature of the suspected crime (discrete crimes or ongoing conspiracy), habits of the accused, character of the items sought, and nature and function of the premises to be searched.

Applying these factors, the *Harris* Court found that the information provided to the magistrate established a fair probability that Ford was still involved in a narcotics conspiracy in 1990. The court noted that the conspiracy was "longstanding and protracted" and that the affidavit showed that Ford "had no visible source of income, yet owned a large house" and was still associated with some of his coconspirators. See also United States v. Spikes, 158 F.3d 913 (6th Cir.1998) (four-year-old information concerning drug activity was not stale where it was corroborated by more recent information leading to a fair conclusion that the defendant was engaged in continuous large-scale drug activity); United States v. Farmer, 370 F.3d 435 (4th Cir. 2004) (nine-month-old information about the defendant's large-scale counterfeiting operation was not stale because it was "unlikely to have been suddenly abandoned" and the information indicated that the operation had been going on for a long time).

8. First Amendment Concerns

In New York v. P.J. Video, 475 U.S. 868 (1986), Justice Rehnquist wrote for the Court as it held that warrants authorizing the seizure of "adult" tapes from a video store were supported by probable cause to believe that the tapes were pornographic. Justice Rehnquist first noted that "an application for a warrant authorizing the seizure of materials presumptively protected by the First Amendment should be evaluated under the same standard of probable cause used to review warrants generally." The Court found that supporting affidavits more than enough information to conclude there was a "fair probability" that the movies satisfied the statutory definition of obscenity (i.e., predominant appeal to prurient interest in sex, specific sexual conduct presented in patently offensive manner, and no serious redeeming social value).

Justice Marshall, joined by Justices Brennan and Stevens, dissented. He argued that the affidavits described only some excerpted scenes, and not the entirety of each film. In his view, the magistrate could not have determined that the sex acts pervaded the films or that the films as a whole lacked artistic value; while the *affidavits* were pervaded with sex acts, it did not necessarily follow that the *films* were obscene. The majority's response was that one of the affidavits described five hardcore sex scenes during a 93 minute film establishing at least a fair probability that there was no time left for the film to include anything of redeeming social value.

When *P.J. Video* returned to the state courts, the New York Court of Appeals held in New York v. P.J. Video, Inc., 68 N.Y.2d 296, 508 N.Y.S.2d 907, 501 N.E.2d 556 (1986), that the state constitution barred reliance on the totality of circumstances approach for warrants directed at allegedly obscene materials. It reasoned that all aspects of the statutory definition of obscenity are significant and that the Supreme Court's approach effectively ignored some of the statutory elements.

B. PROBABLE CAUSE, SPECIFICITY AND REASONABLENESS

1. The Things That Can Be Seized

Up until 1967, the Court had consistently held that the Fourth Amendment prohibited the government from searching for or seizing anything other than the "fruits and instrumentalities" of a crime. "Mere evidence" of a crime was considered beyond the scope of a permissible Fourth Amendment search. So for example, if officers had probable cause to believe that the defendant was a narcotics dealer, they could search for and seize narcotics and related paraphernalia, but they would not be permitted to look for phone records or storage locker rental agreements, because these things were "mere evidence" of the crime. Obviously, the mere evidence rule severely constricted the scope of a search that a magistrate could authorize.

In the following case, decided the same year as *Katz,* the Court rejected the "mere evidence" limitation, dramatically expanding the possibilities for law enforcement, both when searching pursuant to a warrant and when searching pursuant to an exception to the warrant requirement.

WARDEN V. HAYDEN

Supreme Court of the United States, 1967.
387 U.S. 294.

JUSTICE BRENNAN delivered the opinion of the Court.

We review in this case the validity of the proposition that there is under the Fourth Amendment a distinction between merely evidentiary materials, on the one hand, which may not be seized either under the authority of a search warrant or during the course of a search incident to arrest, and on the other hand, those objects which may validly be seized including the instrumentalities and means by which a crime is committed, the fruits of crime such as stolen property, weapons by which escape of the person arrested might be effected, and property the possession of which is a crime.

A Maryland court sitting without a jury convicted respondent of armed robbery. Items of his clothing, a cap, jacket, and trousers, among other things, were seized during a search of his home, and were admitted in evidence without objection. * * * The Court of Appeals believed that * * * respondent was correct in his contention that the clothing seized was improperly admitted in evidence because the items had "evidential value only" and therefore were not lawfully subject to seizure. * * * We reverse.

* * *

[The Court held that the search of Hayden's house, while without a warrant, was justified by exigent circumstances].

We come, then, to the question whether, even though the search was lawful, the Court of Appeals was correct in holding that the seizure and introduction of the items of clothing violated the Fourth Amendment because they are "mere evidence."

* * *

Nothing in the language of the Fourth Amendment supports the distinction between "mere evidence" and instrumentalities, fruits of crime, or contraband. On its face, the provision assures the "right of the people to be secure in their persons, houses, papers, and effects . . . ," without regard to the use to which any of these things are applied. This "right of the people" is certainly unrelated to the "mere evidence" limitation. Privacy is disturbed no more by a search directed to a purely evidentiary object than it is by a search directed to an instrumentality, fruit, or contraband. * * * Moreover, nothing in the nature of property seized as evidence renders it more private than property seized, for example, as an instrumentality; quite the opposite may be true. Indeed, the distinction is wholly irrational, since, depending on the circumstances, the same "papers and effects" may be "mere evidence" in one case and "instrumentality" in another.

* * *

The rationale most frequently suggested for the rule preventing the seizure of evidence is that "limitations upon the fruit to be gathered tend to limit the quest itself." But privacy would be just as well served by a restriction on search to the even-numbered days of the month. * * * And it would have the extra advantage of avoiding hair-splitting questions * * *. The "mere evidence" limitation has spawned exceptions so numerous and confusion so great, in fact, that it is questionable whether it affords meaningful protection. But if its rejection does enlarge the area of permissible searches, the intrusions are nevertheless made after fulfilling the probable cause and particularity requirements of the Fourth Amendment and after the intervention of "a neutral and detached magistrate." The Fourth Amendment allows intrusions upon privacy under these circumstances, and there is no viable reason to distinguish intrusions to secure "mere evidence" from intrusions to secure fruits, instrumentalities, or contraband.

The judgment of the Court of Appeals is reversed.

JUSTICE BLACK concurs in the result.

[The concurring opinion by Justice Fortas, joined by Chief Justice Warren, is omitted].

JUSTICE DOUGLAS, dissenting.

* * *

* * * The personal effects and possessions of the individual (all contraband and the like excepted) are sacrosanct from prying eyes, from the long arm of the law, from any rummaging by police. Privacy involves the choice of the individual to disclose or to reveal what he believes, what he thinks, what he possesses. * * * The Framers, who were as knowledgeable as we, knew what police surveillance meant and how the practice of rummaging through one's personal effects could destroy freedom.

* * *

* * * I would * * * leave with the individual the choice of opening his private effects (apart from contraband and the like) to the police or keeping their contents a secret and their integrity inviolate. The existence of that choice is the very essence of the right of privacy. * * *

NOTE ON THE MERE EVIDENCE RULE

By abrogating the mere evidence limitation, the Court dramatically expanded the search power of police officers. For example, without a mere evidence limitation, an innocent third party's home or office may be the legitimate object of a search; evidence that might be relevant to a crime can be spread far and wide, while the fruits and instrumentalities of a crime are more often kept with the perpetrators. As you proceed through this Chapter, try to determine how the cases discussed would have been resolved under a mere evidence limitation. You will undoubtedly conclude that Warden v. Hayden had a fundamental, pro-prosecution effect on Fourth Amendment law. Does this result comport with your impression of the Warren Court's criminal procedure jurisprudence? See Saltzburg, Criminal Procedure in the 1960s: A Reality Check, 42 Drake L.J. 179 (1993) (noting that the Warren Court's pro-defendant reputation is belied by cases like Warden v. Hayden). Do you ascribe any significance to the fact that *Warden* came months after the Court's decision in *Katz*?

2. Probable Cause as to Location of Evidence

Sometimes police have probable cause to believe that a suspect has committed a crime and is in control of certain evidence, but are less sure where the evidence is located. Can they obtain a search warrant for the premises where the suspect lives on the theory that it is the most likely place to search for evidence? The premises where the suspect works? The places the suspect frequents? In Zurcher v. Stanford Daily, 436 U.S. 547, 556 (1978), the majority stated that "[t]he critical element * * * is reasonable cause to believe that the specific 'things' to be searched for and seized are located on the property to which entry is sought." This will depend on "the type of crime, the nature of the items sought, the suspect's opportunity for concealment and normal inferences about where a criminal might hide" evidence of a crime. See United States v. Jones, 994 F.2d 1051 (3d Cir.1993) (sufficient nexus between robbery and defendants' homes, because items sought, such as cash, were the kinds of things "that criminals like to keep in secure places like their homes").

It follows that probable cause does not automatically exist to search a person's home—or any other particular location—simply because that person has been involved in a crime. For example, in United States v. Lalor, 996 F.2d 1578 (4th Cir.1993), the court held that a warrant to search Lalor's residence was invalid because it lacked probable cause. Investigation showed only that Lalor and others sold drugs on the street. The court reasoned that street sales did not raise a fair probability that Lalor kept evidence of drug activity at his house. The court emphasized that the government offered no information to the magistrate that linked the street sales with any activity at Lalor's house. The court, citing cases, declared that "residential searches have been upheld only where some information links the criminal activity to the defendant's residence." Compare United States v. Pitts, 6 F.3d 1366 (9th Cir.1993) (finding a sufficient nexus between defendant's narcotics activity and his home: "in the case of drug dealers, evidence is likely to be found where the dealers live"). See also United States v. McCoy, 483 F.3d 862 (8th Cir. 2007) (probable cause to believe that the defendant had child pornography in his house did not establish probable cause to search his car).

3. Searches of Non-Suspects' Premises

In some investigations, police may have probable cause to search a person's premises for evidence even though they are not suspected of a crime. That and several other problems arose in Zurcher v. Stanford Daily, 436 U.S. 547 (1978). Officers had probable cause to believe that a Stanford Daily photographer had taken pictures of demonstrators who attacked a group of police officers. A warrant was obtained to search the Daily's offices for negatives, film, and pictures taken at the demonstration. There was no allegation that members of the Daily staff were in any way involved in unlawful acts. The Daily's photographic laboratories, filing cabinets, desks, and wastepaper baskets were searched. Locked drawers and rooms were not opened. No evidence pertinent to the assault on the officers was uncovered. Thereafter, the Daily and some members of its staff brought a civil action seeking declaratory and injunctive relief, alleging that the entry, even though with a warrant, violated the Fourth Amendment.

The lower court in *Zurcher* held that the Fourth Amendment did not permit a warrant to search for materials in possession of one not suspected of a crime unless it was apparent that a subpoena and a court order would be futile. But the Supreme Court reversed and found the warrant and search valid. Writing for the Court, Justice White declared that there was nothing special about the search of a third party's premises:

> Under existing law, valid warrants may be issued to search *any* property, whether or not occupied by a third party, at which there is probable cause to believe that fruits, instrumentalities, or evidence of a crime will be found. Nothing on the face of the Amendment suggests that a third-party search warrant should not normally issue. * * *
>
> * * *
>
> The critical element in a reasonable search is not that the owner of the property is suspected of crime but that there is reasonable cause to believe that the specific "things" to be searched for and seized are located on the property to which entry is sought. * * *

Justice White intimated that the reasonableness clause of the Fourth Amendment might impose some limitations on the execution of a search of a third party's premises, even if the search was supported by a warrant issued upon probable cause. However, "the courts may not, in the name of Fourth Amendment reasonableness, forbid the States from issuing warrants to search for evidence simply because the owner or possessor of the place to be searched is not then reasonably suspected of criminal involvement."

Finally, Justice White rejected the argument that First Amendment concerns required a limitation on the use of warrants to search the office of a newspaper:

> There is no reason to believe * * * that magistrates cannot guard against searches of the type, scope, and intrusiveness that would actually interfere with the timely publication of a newspaper. Nor, if the requirements of specificity and reasonableness are properly applied, policed, and observed, will there be any occasion or opportunity for officers to rummage at large in newspaper files or to intrude into or to deter normal editorial and publication decisions. * * * Nor are we convinced * * * that confidential sources will disappear and that the press will suppress news because of fears of warranted searches.

Justice Stewart, joined by Justice Marshall, dissented in *Zurcher* arguing that the use of a warrant to search a newspaper constituted an infringement on First Amendment rights.

Justice Stevens wrote a separate dissent, in which he noted that the problem of third party searches had been created by "the profound change in Fourth Amendment law that occurred in 1967, when Warden v. Hayden was decided." He elaborated as follows:

> In the pre-*Hayden* era warrants were used to search for contraband, weapons, and plunder, but not for "mere evidence." The practical effect of the rule prohibiting the issuance of warrants to search for mere evidence was to narrowly limit not only the category of objects, but also the category of persons and the character of the privacy interests that might be affected by an unannounced police search.
>
> Just as the witnesses who participate in an investigation or a trial far outnumber the defendants, the persons who possess evidence that may help to identify an offender, or explain an aspect of a criminal transaction, far outnumber those who have custody of weapons or plunder. Countless law-abiding citizens—doctors, lawyers, merchants, customers, bystanders—may have documents in their possession that relate to an ongoing criminal investigation. The consequences of subjecting this large category of persons to unannounced police searches are extremely serious. The *ex parte* warrant procedure enables the prosecutor to obtain access to privileged documents that could not be examined if advance notice gave the custodian an opportunity to object. The search for the documents described in a warrant may involve the inspection of files containing other private matter. The dramatic character of a sudden search may cause an entirely unjustified injury to the reputation of the persons searched.

Justice Stevens concluded that "[t]he only conceivable justification for an unannounced search of an innocent citizen is the fear that, if notice were given, he would conceal or destroy the object of the search." As there was nothing in the warrant application to indicate that the Daily would destroy evidence, Justice Stevens contended that the search, even though pursuant to a warrant, was unreasonable.

Congress responded to *Zurcher* by enacting the Privacy Protection Act of 1980, 42 U.S.C. § 2000 aa-6(f), which limited searches of the media and the press.

4. Describing the Place to Be Searched

The Warrant Clause requires a particularized description of the place to be searched. The Colonial experience with general warrants was the major reason for including the Fourth Amendment in the Bill of Rights; the particularity requirement is designed to protect against the abuses of a general warrant, i.e., a warrant giving authority to an officer to search wherever the officer wants.

Function of the Particularity Requirement

The requirement of a particular description of the place to be searched provides at least three protections:

First, if the executing officer has no knowledge of the underlying facts, a particular description of the premises in the warrant operates as a necessary control on his discretion. We would not want an unknowing officer, armed with a single search warrant, to search every "house on Second Avenue," for example. See, e.g., United States v. Nafzger, 965 F.2d 213 (7th Cir.1992) ("By accepting 'the Western District of Wisconsin' as a particular description of the place the truck was to be found we would be giving the government carte blanche to search anywhere in that district that the truck might conceivably be found, condoning the use of the pernicious general warrant, and redacting the particularity requirement from the fourth amendment."). See also United States v. Stefonek, 179 F.3d 1030 (7th Cir.1999) (particularity requirement is necessary to "make sure that the law enforcement officer who executes the warrant stays within the bounds set by the issuer").

Second, a particular description in the warrant establishes a record of probable cause as to location *prior* to the search. The officer cannot, after the fact, construct a case supporting probable cause to search the place she eventually chose.

Finally, the particularity requirement prevents the officer from using the warrant as a blank check to search wherever she chooses by relying on an overly general description of the place to be searched. See, e.g., United States v. Cannon, 264 F.3d 875 (9th Cir. 2001) (warrant to search a house did not permit search of a building unconnected to the house).

Reasonable Particularity

The Fourth Amendment requires that the warrant must set forth the location of the place to be searched with reasonable particularity. Technical precision is not required in all cases. The degree of particularity that is reasonable depends on the nature of the place to be searched and on the information an officer could *reasonably* obtain about the location before a warrant is issued.

For example, it is well accepted that "two or more apartments in the same building stand on the same footing as two or more houses. A single warrant cannot describe an entire building when cause is shown for searching only one apartment." Moore v. United States, 461 F.2d 1236, 1238 (D.C.Cir.1972). But in Maryland v. Garrison, 480 U.S. 79 (1987), the Court upheld a warrant authorizing the search of a "third floor apartment" even though there were actually two apartments on the third floor. Baltimore police officers had probable cause to believe that illegal activity was being conducted in an apartment on the third floor of a converted brownstone. They conducted an investigation to determine whether there was more than one apartment on the floor. An officer obtained information from the utility company and telephone company that appeared to indicate that the entire third floor consisted of one apartment. The officer checked out the door buzzers outside the apartment building, but they did not indicate how many apartments were on any particular floor. The officers then obtained a warrant authorizing the search of the "third floor apartment." After entering the apartment building, the officers found that there were two apartments on the third floor, with one door to both apartments, and a shared entryway. McWebb, the suspect, occupied one of the apartments, and Garrison occupied the other. Before the officers realized that they were mistakenly in Garrison's apartment, they discovered contraband leading to Garrison's arrest and conviction.

Writing for the Court, Justice Stevens held that the description in the warrant of the place to be searched was sufficiently particular. Justice Stevens reasoned as follows:

> Plainly, if the officers had known, or even if they should have known, that there were two separate dwelling units on the third floor of 2036 Park Avenue, they would have been obligated to exclude [Garrison's] apartment from the scope of the requested warrant. But we must judge the constitutionality of their conduct in light of the information available to them at the time they acted. Those items of evidence that emerge after the warrant is issued have no bearing on whether or not a warrant was validly issued. * * * The validity of the warrant must be assessed on the basis of the information that the officers disclosed, or had a duty to discover and to disclose, to the issuing Magistrate. On the basis of that information, we agree with

> the conclusion of all three Maryland courts that the warrant, insofar as it authorized a search that turned out to be ambiguous in scope, was valid when it issued.[14]

Compare United States v. Johnson, 26 F.3d 669 (7th Cir.1994), where the warrant authorized the search of an entire duplex occupied by several members of a narcotics conspiracy. Even though the officer was aware that it was a multiple dwelling, the court upheld the warrant as sufficiently particular:

> The defendant argues that in "multiple dwelling" cases we must suppress all the evidence seized pursuant to the overbroad warrant. While that may be true when the warrant authorizes the search of an entire structure and the officers do not know which unit contains the evidence of illegal conduct, that analysis does not apply when (1) the officer knows that there are multiple units and believes there is probable cause to search each unit, or (2) the targets of the investigation have access to the entire structure.

Single family dwellings usually present less of a problem of particular description than the multi-family dwellings discussed above. In urban areas, a street address is considered sufficiently particular. In rural areas, alternative descriptions may be reasonable due to the absence of street addresses. See United States v. Dorrough, 927 F.2d 498 (10th Cir.1991) (warrant sufficiently particular where it describes a well-marked turnoff leading to the house, a quarter mile up a mountain, and defendant's house was the only one up the mountain). The ultimate question is "whether the place to be searched is described with sufficient particularity to enable the executing officer to locate and identify the premises with reasonable effort, and whether there is any reasonable probability that another premise might be mistakenly searched." United States v. Pelayo-Landero, 285 F.3d 491 (6th Cir. 2002) (trailer home sufficiently described where directions are given to the trailer park and the warrant describes the particular trailer by color, a certain exterior trim, and a wooden deck).

The Wrong Address

In some cases, warrants have misdescribed an address. These mistakes arise most often where a building is on a corner or is set back from a street. The fact that the warrant is for the wrong address will not be dispositive if the warrant sufficiently directs the officer to the correct premises. For example, in Lyons v. Robinson, 783 F.2d 737 (8th Cir.1985), the warrant listed the place to be searched as 325 Adkinson Street; Lyons'

---

[14] Of course, a validly issued warrant may be improperly executed. In *Garrison*, however, the Court found that the officers acted reasonably, though mistakenly, by searching Garrison's apartment, because the layout of the two apartments made it appear *as if it actually was a single apartment*. By the time the officers discovered that there were two separate apartments they had already discovered the evidence used against Garrison.

residence was actually 325 Short Street, on the corner of Short and Adkinson. The *Lyons* court stated that the description, though inaccurate, was sufficiently particular because it made it unlikely under the circumstances that another premises might be mistakenly searched.

The Breadth of the Place to Be Searched

The cases discussed above deal with whether the warrant sufficiently describes the location of the premises to be searched. A different particularity question may arise with respect to the premises described. For example, if the warrant authorizes the search of the "premises" at 1825 Elm Street, do the police have the authority to search a freestanding garage behind the house at that address?

In United States v. Earls, 42 F.3d 1321 (10th Cir.1994), the court held that a warrant to search "the premises" at a particular location covered a detached garage, a shed, and an office, each of which was located within the curtilage of the house described in the warrant. See also United States v. Kyles, 40 F.3d 519 (2d Cir.1994) (warrant to search an apartment authorized the agent to search the defendant's locked bedroom, even though the defendant was not named as a suspect—the room was not a separate residence outside the scope of the warrant).

One of the most difficult problems for the courts has been the scope of the search of property belonging to *persons* who happen to be on the premises of a warranted search. Most courts have held that *any* person's property is subject to search so long as the property could physically contain the items described in the warrant. United States v. Gonzalez, 940 F.2d 1413 (11th Cir.1991) (upholding the search of a visitor's briefcase capable of concealing evidence sought in the warrant).

All of these scope rulings are simply an application of the principle that a warrant permitting a search of a house or a building authorizes the police to search anywhere within the building (or curtilage) that is large enough to contain the evidence described in the warrant. The concept is set forth in colorful language by Judge Posner in United States v. Evans, 92 F.3d 540 (7th Cir.1996):

> If they are looking for a canary's corpse, they can search a cupboard, but not a locket. If they are looking for an adolescent hippopotamus, they can search the living room or garage but not the microwave oven. If they are searching for cocaine, they can search a container large enough to hold a gram, or perhaps less.

In *Evans,* the defendant objected to the search of the trunk of his car, which was parked in the detached garage of a house. The warrant authorized a search for drugs in both the house and detached garage. Evans complained, among other things, that he resided at the house (and parked his car there) only intermittently. But Judge Posner found no problem with the search:

> It seems to us that a car parked in a garage is just another interior container, like a closet or a desk. If, as in this case, the trunk or glove compartment is not too small to hold what the search warrant authorizes the police to look for, they can search the trunk and the glove compartment. * * * It does not matter whose [car] it is unless it obviously belonged to someone wholly uninvolved in the criminal activities going on in the house. If an innocent guest leaves a trunk in the host's house and the police obtain a search warrant to search the house for something small enough to fit in the trunk, then, unless it is apparent that the trunk does not belong to anyone connected with the illegal activity—a condition that will rarely be satisfied—the police can search the trunk and if it happens to contain evidence that the guest is a criminal after all, albeit innocent of any involvement in the criminal activities of his host, he is out of luck.

5. Particularity for Arrest Warrants

An arrest warrant must describe the person to be seized with sufficient particularity. Does the fact that the officers have probable cause to arrest a person mean that the person can be specifically described? Is a warrant authorizing the arrest of "John Doe a/k/a Ed" sufficiently particular? The court in United States v. Doe, 703 F.2d 745 (3d Cir.1983), held that such a warrant was overbroad, and held further that the insufficient description was not cured by the fact that the officer who executed the warrant had independent personal knowledge that the arrestee was the person for whom the warrant was intended. Why doesn't the officer's personal knowledge solve the problem? Would the warrant have been sufficiently particular if it described "John Doe, a/k/a Ed, a white male six feet tall and 200 pounds"?

6. Describing the Things to Be Seized

The Warrant Clause mandates that a warrant, to be valid, must particularly describe the things that the officers can look for and seize. This requirement operates to limit the possibility of a general search on a particular premises. The specific concern "is not that of intrusion per se, but of a general, exploratory rummaging in a person's belongings." Coolidge v. New Hampshire, 403 U.S. 443 (1971).

How does one determine whether a warrant's description of the things to be seized is sufficiently particular? As with particularity as to place, the question is one of reasonableness. As one court put it, "[t]he proper metric of sufficient specificity is whether it was reasonable to provide a more specific description of the items at that juncture of the investigation." United States v. Bass, 785 F.3d 1043 (6th Cir. 2015). The following case is the Supreme Court's major pronouncement on the particularity requirement as applied to the things to be seized.

ANDRESEN V. MARYLAND

Supreme Court of the United States, 1976.
427 U.S. 463.

JUSTICE BLACKMUN delivered the opinion of the Court.

* * *

In early 1972, a Bi-County Fraud Unit, acting under the joint auspices of the State's Attorneys' Offices of Montgomery and Prince George's Counties, Md., began an investigation of real estate settlement activities in the Washington, D.C., area. At the time, petitioner Andresen was an attorney who * * * specialized in real estate settlements in Montgomery County. During the Fraud Unit's investigation, his activities came under scrutiny, particularly in connection with a transaction involving Lot 13T in the Potomac Woods subdivision of Montgomery County. The investigation * * * disclosed that petitioner, acting as settlement attorney, had defrauded Standard-Young Associates, the purchaser of Lot 13T. Petitioner had represented that the property was free of liens and that, accordingly, no title insurance was necessary, when in fact, he knew that there were two outstanding liens on the property. In addition, investigators learned that the lienholders, by threatening to foreclose their liens, had forced a halt to the purchaser's construction on the property. When Standard-Young had confronted petitioner with this information, he responded by issuing, as an agent of a title insurance company, a title policy guaranteeing clear title to the property. By this action, petitioner also defrauded that insurance company by requiring it to pay the outstanding liens.

The investigators * * * applied for warrants to search petitioner's law office and the separate office of Mount Vernon Development Corporation, of which petitioner was incorporator, sole shareholder, resident agent, and director. The application sought permission to search for specified documents pertaining to the sale and conveyance of Lot 13T. A judge * * * concluded that there was probable cause and issued the warrants.

The searches of the two offices were conducted simultaneously during daylight hours on October 31, 1972. [The searches took a number of hours; approximately 4% of Andresen's files were seized.]

* * *

[Petitioner contends] that rights guaranteed him by the Fourth Amendment were violated because the descriptive terms of the search warrants were so broad as to make them impermissible "general" warrants * * *.

* * * Although petitioner concedes that the warrants for the most part were models of particularity, he contends that they were rendered fatally "general" by the addition, in each warrant, to the exhaustive list of particularly described documents, of the phrase "together with other fruits, instrumentalities and evidence of crime at this [time] unknown." The quoted language, it is argued, must be read in isolation and without reference to the rest of the long sentence at the end of which it appears. When read "properly," petitioner contends, it permits the search for and seizure of any evidence of any crime.

* * *

* * * [T]he challenged phrase must be read as authorizing only the search for and seizure of evidence relating to "the crime of false pretenses with respect to Lot 13T." The challenged phrase is not a separate sentence. Instead, it appears in each warrant at the end of a sentence containing a lengthy list of specified and particular items to be seized, all pertaining to Lot 13T.[a] We think it clear from the context that the term "crime" in the warrants refers only to the crime of false pretenses with respect to the sale of Lot 13T. The "other fruits" clause is one of a series that follows the colon after the word "Maryland." All clauses in the series are limited by what precedes that colon, namely, "items pertaining to * * * lot 13, block T." The warrants, accordingly, did not authorize the executing officers to conduct a search for evidence of other crimes but only to search for and seize evidence relevant to the crime of false pretenses and Lot 13T.[b]

Petitioner also suggests that the specific list of the documents to be seized constitutes a "general" warrant. We disagree. Under investigation was a complex real estate scheme whose existence could be proved only by piecing together many bits of evidence. Like a jigsaw puzzle, the whole "picture" of petitioner's false-pretense scheme with respect to Lot 13T could

[a] "[T]he following items pertaining to sale, purchase, settlement and conveyance of lot 13, block T, Potomac Woods subdivision, Montgomery County, Maryland:

> "title notes, title abstracts, title rundowns; contracts of sale and/or assignments from Raffaele Antonelli and Rocco Caniglia to Mount Vernon Development Corporation and/or others; lien payoff correspondence and lien payoff memoranda to and from lienholders and noteholders; correspondence and memoranda to and from trustees of deeds of trust; lenders instructions for a construction loan or construction and permanent loan; disbursement sheets and disbursement memoranda; checks, check stubs and ledger sheets indicating disbursement upon settlement; correspondence and memoranda concerning disbursements upon settlement; settlement statements and settlement memoranda; fully or partially prepared deed of trust releases, whether or not executed and whether or not recorded; books, records, documents, papers, memoranda and correspondence, showing or tending to show a fraudulent intent, and/or knowledge as elements of the crime of false pretenses, in violation of Article 27, Section 140, of the Annotated Code of Maryland, 1957 Edition, as amended and revised, together with other fruits, instrumentalities and evidence of crime at this [time] unknown."

[b] The record discloses that the officials executing the warrants seized numerous papers that were not introduced into evidence. Although we are not informed of their content, we observe that to the extent such papers were not within the scope of the warrants or were otherwise improperly seized, the State was correct in returning them voluntarily and the trial judge was correct in suppressing others.

be shown only by placing in the proper place the many pieces of evidence that, taken singly, would show comparatively little. The complexity of an illegal scheme may not be used as a shield to avoid detection when the State has demonstrated probable cause to believe that a crime has been committed and probable cause to believe that evidence of this crime is in the suspect's possession.

We recognize that there are grave dangers inherent in executing a warrant authorizing a search and seizure of a person's papers that are not necessarily present in executing a warrant to search for physical objects whose relevance is more easily ascertainable. In searches for papers, it is certain that some innocuous documents will be examined, at least cursorily, in order to determine whether they are, in fact among those papers authorized to be seized. Similar dangers, of course, are present in executing a warrant for the "seizure" of telephone conversations. In both kinds of searches, responsible officials, including judicial officials, must take care to assure that they are conducted in a manner that minimizes unwarranted intrusions upon privacy.

* * *

JUSTICE BRENNAN, **dissenting.**

* * * The overwhelming quantity of seized material that was either suppressed or returned to petitioner is irrefutable testimony to the unlawful generality of the warrants. The Court's attempt to cure this defect by *post hoc* judicial construction evades principles settled in this Court's Fourth Amendment decisions. * * *

[Justice Marshall also dissented, agreeing with Justice Brennan's Fourth Amendment analysis.]

The Particularity Requirement as Applied to Searches of Computers, Cellphones, etc.

The Court in *Andresen* notes that in a search for documents, it is all but inevitable that the police will be required to peruse innocuous private documents. That problem frequently arises when the police search for information stored in a computer or cellphone. The scope and amount of information contained in a computer or cellphone surely raises concerns about enforcing a particularity requirement. And yet, as in *Andresen,* officers with probable cause will often not have any specific information on where the incriminatory material is located in the electronic device, how it would be labeled, etc. So a requirement of reasonable particularity (based on what officers knew or should have known in advance) will not shield most information stored in a computer or cellphone from inspection where police have probable cause to believe that incriminating evidence is somewhere on the device.

Assume, for example, that an officer has a warrant to search for child pornography stored on a computer. In his search, he comes across a folder labeled "grocery lists." Can he open the folder? The answer generally given by the courts is, yes—otherwise a criminal could shield incriminating information from a warranted search simply by mislabeling the folder. But this means that the search of the computer will by necessity be extensive, potentially covering all files, including "cookies," history, deleted files, etc. See Guest v. Leis, 255 F.3d 325 (6th Cir. 2001) (officers with a warrant to a computer are permitted to seize the computer and conduct a thorough search of all files and to separate relevant files from unrelated files). As the court put it in United States v. Adjani, 452 F.3d 1140 (9th Cir. 2006), a case in which the defendant complained that the warrant should have restricted the search to a particular email program and specific search terms:

> Computer files are easy to disguise or rename, and were we to limit the warrant to such a specific search protocol, much evidence could escape discovery simply because of Adjani's * * * labeling of the files documenting Adjani's criminal activity. The government should not be required to trust the suspect's self-labeling when executing a warrant.

See also United States v. Giberson, 527 F.3d 882 (9th Cir. 2008) ("While officers ought to exercise caution when executing the search of a computer, just as they ought when sifting through documents that may contain personal information, the potential intermingling of materials does not justify an exception or heightened protection for computers beyond the Fourth Amendment's reasonableness requirement."); United States v. Hill, 459 F.3d 966 (9th Cir. 2006) ("Computer records are extremely susceptible to tampering, hiding, or destruction, whether deliberate or inadvertent. Images can be hidden in all manner of files, even word processing documents and spreadsheets. Criminals will do all they can to conceal contraband, including the simple expedient of changing the names and extensions of files to disguise their content from the casual observer."); United States v. Triplett, 684 F.3d 500 (5th Cir. 2012) ("Although officers should limit exposure to innocent files, in the end, there may be no practical substitute for actually looking in many (perhaps all) folders, and sometimes at the documents contained within those folders.").

Cellphones raise many of the same issues as computers, so courts have applied similar principles regarding particularity requirements. Consider as an example United States v. Bass, 785 F.3d 1043 (6th Cir. 2015), where officers had probable cause to search for evidence of credit card fraud on the defendant's cellphone. The warrant authorized the search for "any records of communication, indicia of use, ownership, or possession, including electronic calendars, address books, emails and chat logs." While that description sounded broad, the court found that "at the time of the search, . . . the officers could not have known where this information was located in the phone or in what format. Thus, the broad scope of the warrant was reasonable under the circumstances at that time."

One of the most helpful discussions of the particularity requirement as applied to computers is found in United States v. Richards, 659 F.3d 527 (6th Cir. 2011), a case involving the search of an entire server when there was probable cause to believe Richards was involved in child pornography:

> Courts that have addressed the permissible breadth of computer-related searches have grappled with how to balance two interests that are in tension with each other. On one hand, it is clear that because criminals can—and often do—hide, mislabel, or manipulate files to conceal criminal activity, a broad, expansive search of the hard drive may be required. On the other hand, granting the Government a *carte blanche* to search *every* file on the hard drive impermissibly transforms a limited search into a general one. * * * [G]iven the unique problem encountered in computer searches, and the practical difficulties inherent in implementing universal search methodologies, the majority of federal courts have eschewed the use of a specific search protocol and, instead, have employed the Fourth Amendment's bedrock principle of reasonableness on a case-by-case basis: "While officers must be clear as to what it is they are seeking on the computer and conduct the search in a way that avoids searching files of types not identified in the warrant, . . . a computer search may be as extensive as reasonably required to locate the items described in the warrant based on probable cause." United States v. Burgess, 576 F.3d 1078, 1092 (10th Cir. 2009). We agree with the Tenth Circuit in *Burgess* that it is folly for a search warrant to attempt to structure the mechanics of the search and a warrant imposing such limits would unduly restrict legitimate search objectives. One would not ordinarily expect a warrant to search filing cabinets for evidence of drug activity to prospectively restrict the search to "file cabinets in the basement" or to file folders labeled "Meth Lab" or "Customers." And there is no reason to so limit computer searches. But that is not to say methodology is irrelevant.
>
> A warrant may permit only the search of particularly described places and only particularly described things may be seized. As the description of such places and things becomes more general, the method by which the search is executed becomes more important—the search method must be tailored to meet allowed ends. And those limits must be functional. For instance, unless specifically authorized by the warrant there would be little reason for officers searching for evidence of drug trafficking to look at tax returns (beyond verifying the folder

> labeled "2002 Tax Return" actually contains tax returns and not drug files or trophy pictures).
>
> Respect for legitimate rights to privacy in papers and effects requires an officer executing a search warrant to first look in the most obvious places and as it becomes necessary to progressively move from the obvious to the obscure. That is the purpose of a search protocol which structures the search by requiring an analysis of the file structure, next looking for suspicious file folders, then looking for files and types of files most likely to contain the objects of the search by doing keyword searches.
>
> But in the end, there may be no practical substitute for actually looking in many (perhaps all) folders and sometimes at the documents contained within those folders, and that is true whether the search is of computer files or physical files. It is particularly true with image files.
>
> Consistent with this rule, the federal courts have not required a second warrant to search a properly seized computer where the evidence obtained in the search did not exceed the probable cause articulated in the original warrant.
>
> Applying a reasonableness analysis on a case-by-case basis, the federal courts have rejected most particularity challenges to warrants authorizing the seizure and search of entire personal or business computers. * * * In other words, in general, so long as the computer search is limited to a search for evidence explicitly authorized in the warrant, it is reasonable for the executing officers to open the various types of files located in the computer's hard drive in order to determine whether they contain such evidence.

In *Richards*, the defendant argued that the warrant to search the entire server was overbroad because he had set it up "in a neatly compartmentalized and segregated fashion, rendering it entirely unnecessary to search beyond the content maintained in the JustinsFriends file directory." But the court responded that "hindsight is 20/20" and also that a forensic evidence procedure could uncover "hidden, erased, compressed, password-protected or encrypted files." Therefore, "searching the entire server was necessary to look for child pornography related to the JustinsFriends websites because individuals often mislabel directory files, the server might contain related websites, and the unallocated server space might contain materials pertaining to those websites."

Protocols for Searching for Electronic Information

When it comes to electronic information, the concern is not so much about particularity per se but about rummaging through the device. Some have argued that the risk of abuse could be limited by requiring the government, in advance, to specify a search protocol it would follow when searching for the information. A search protocol might require officers to utilize IT personnel in the first instance, or might specify that a cursory inspection would be undertaken, with a more intensive search only of those areas which appear to be productive after the cursory inspection. For example, in searching a cellphone for evidence of drug activity, a cursory inspection of apps on the phone might be sufficient to convince a reasonable person that a more searching inspection of some apps (e.g., an intensive search of the Open Table app) may not be productive.

But most courts have declined to require a search protocol for searches of electronic devices, reasoning that "courts are better able to assess the reasonableness of search protocols ex post, in light of the totality of the circumstances, and where evidence and experts from both sides can be entertained and examined." United States v. Russian, 848 F. 3d 1239 (10th Cir. 2017). Professor Orin Kerr has argued that "the Fourth Amendment does not permit ex ante restrictions on the execution of computer warrants." Kerr, Ex Ante Regulation of Computer Search and Seizure, 96 Va. L.Rev. 1241 (2010).

Particularity as to Information in a Facebook Account

Are the particularity issues any different if officers serve a warrant on Facebook to turn over information about a particular user's account? In United States v. Blake, 868 F.3d 960 (11th Cir. 2017), officers had probable cause to believe that evidence of the defendant's sex trafficking would be found in his Facebook account. The warrant served on Facebook required disclosure of virtually every kind of data that could be found in a social media account. The court found that such a broad description of information was "unnecessary", explaining as follows:

> With respect to private instant messages, for example, the warrant could have limited the request to messages sent to or from persons suspected at that time of being prostitutes or customers. And the warrant should have requested data only from the period of time during which Moore was suspected of taking part in the prostitution conspiracy.

The government explained the breadth of the warrant by reference to the computer cases, and the possibility that users will mislabel, hide and manipulate the information so that broad searches are necessary. But the court found that this concern did not exist with regard to searches of Facebook accounts. It explained as follows:

> The means of hiding evidence on a hard drive—obscure folders, misnamed files, encrypted data—are not currently possible in the context of a Facebook account. Hard drive searches require time-consuming electronic forensic investigation with special equipment, and conducting that kind of search in the defendant's home would be impractical, if not impossible. By contrast, when it comes to Facebook account searches, the government need only send a request with the specific data sought and Facebook will respond with precisely that data. That procedure does not appear to be impractical for Facebook or for the government. Facebook produced data in response to over 9500 search warrants in the six-month period between July and December 2015.

The *Blake* court ultimately found it unnecessary to decide whether the warrant was overbroad, however, because even if it was, exclusion of evidence was not justified—under the good faith exception to the exclusionary rule, discussed later in this Chapter, officers could reasonably rely on the warrant. But the case does raise a distinction between Facebook accounts and computer hard drives insofar as particularity is concerned.

Reasonable Particularity

Ultimately, the particularity question with respect to items to be seized is one of reasonableness. "While a search warrant must describe items to be seized with reasonable particularity sufficient to prevent a general, exploratory rummaging in a person's belongings, it need only be reasonably specific, rather than elaborately detailed, and the specificity required varies depending on the circumstances of the case and the type of items involved." United States v. Bridges, 344 F.3d 1010 (9th Cir. 2003).

Some property may not be susceptible to anything more than a general description (e.g., "United States currency"). Other property may be reasonably susceptible to a detailed description (e.g., a description of a gun as a murder weapon ordinarily should include the caliber of the gun, whether it is a handgun or shotgun, etc.). The reasonableness inquiry takes into account how much an officer would be expected to know about the property in the course of obtaining probable cause to seize it. See United States v. Fuccillo, 808 F.2d 173 (1st Cir.1987) (warrant to seize "stolen clothing" held insufficiently particular where officers were given a detailed list of the articles stolen before applying for the warrant). Compare United States v. Upham, 168 F.3d 532 (1st Cir.1999) (in a child pornography case, a description of the property to be seized as "any and all visual depictions, in any format or media, of minors engaged in sexually explicit conduct" was sufficiently particular because the officers could not be expected to describe the materials with any more specificity).

In United States v. Strand, 761 F.2d 449 (8th Cir.1985), postal inspectors suspected that Strand, a mail carrier, was stealing items from the mail. They obtained a warrant authorizing the seizure of "stolen mail" from Strand's house. The court held that some items seized from Strand's home were legally obtained, others illegally obtained. The court explained:

> We believe that the term "stolen mail" is sufficiently definite to enable a postal inspector to identify and seize items which clearly fit within such a generic class, such as letters and parcels, neither addressed to nor sent by the person whose property is being searched, bearing postage stamps or marks. A search for "stolen mail" does not, however, permit the seizure of items which do not fit into the generic category. Many of the items seized in the present case under the rubric of stolen mail were not found in parcels of mail, and included items such as socks, a sweatshirt, cosmetics, a sweater, a thermometer, a china plate, and gloves; * * *

Has the court in *Strand* given the searching officers too much or too little discretion to determine whether an item constitutes "stolen mail"? See also United States v. Bridges, 344 F.3d 1010 (9th Cir. 2003) (warrant was overbroad where it did not specify the criminal activity that was being investigated, and yet set forth "a comprehensive laundry list of sundry goods and inventory that one would readily expect to discover in any small or medium-sized business in the United States").

Severability

Even if a clause in the warrant is overbroad, the defect will not ordinarily taint the entire search. Thus, in United States v. Brown, 984 F.2d 1074 (10th Cir.1993), a warrant to search a vehicle dismantling business described with particularity over forty items, including "bumpers, grills, fenders, hoods * * * blank registration forms", etc. But a catch-all clause was included to permit seizure of "[a]ny other item which the Officers determine or have reasonable belief is stolen while executing this search warrant." The Court held that the catch-all provision was overbroad. But this did not taint the evidence seized pursuant to the particular descriptions in the warrant. The Court stated:

> At least eight circuits have held that where a warrant contains both specific as well as unconstitutionally broad language, the broad portion may be redacted and the balance of the warrant considered valid. In such cases only those items confiscated under the overbroad portion of the warrant are suppressed.

7. Limitations on Warranted Searches

There are a few cases in which searches have been found unreasonable even though conducted with a warrant and probable cause. Most of these cases involve medical procedures. For example, in Winston v. Lee, 470 U.S. 753 (1985), the defendant had been wounded in the course of committing a robbery. The state obtained a court order forcing the defendant to undergo surgery under a general anesthetic to remove a bullet lodged at least 2.5 to 3 centimeters beneath the surface of his skin; the state clearly had probable cause that the search would uncover evidence, and had obtained a court order authorizing the procedure (tantamount to a warrant), but the defendant argued that the procedure was unreasonable under the Fourth Amendment. Justice Brennan, writing for the Court, agreed with the defendant. He noted that the medical risks of the operation were disputed and reasoned that the uncertainty militated against a finding that the operation was a reasonable search. The Commonwealth also failed to show a compelling need for the bullet. It had substantial other evidence tying the defendant to the robbery, including the location of the bullet in his body.

8. Anticipatory Warrants

Can government agents obtain an "anticipatory" search warrant conditioned upon future events that, if fulfilled, would create probable cause? In United States v. Grubbs, 547 U.S. 90 (2006), the Court held that a warrant is not invalid simply because it is contingent on a future occurrence. *Grubbs* involved an investigation into receipt of child pornography. Law enforcement officers obtained a search warrant for Grubbs's house on the basis of an affidavit explaining that the warrant would be executed only after a controlled delivery of child pornography to that location. Specifically, the affidavit stated:

> "Execution of this search warrant will not occur unless and until the parcel has been received by a person(s) and has been physically taken into the residence. . . . At that time, and not before, this search warrant will be executed by me and other United States Postal inspectors, with appropriate assistance from other law enforcement officers in accordance with this warrant's command."

The Magistrate Judge issued the warrant as requested. Two days later, an undercover postal inspector delivered the package. Then a search of the house was conducted pursuant to the warrant.

Justice Scalia, writing for the Court, had this to say about the use and constitutionality of anticipatory warrants:

> An anticipatory warrant is a warrant based upon an affidavit showing probable cause that at some future time (but not presently) certain evidence of crime will be located at a specified place. Most anticipatory warrants subject their execution to some condition precedent other

> than the mere passage of time—a so-called "triggering condition." * * * If the government were to execute an anticipatory warrant before the triggering condition occurred, there would be no reason to believe the item described in the warrant could be found at the searched location; by definition, the triggering condition which establishes probable cause has not yet been satisfied when the warrant is issued. Grubbs argues that for this reason anticipatory warrants contravene the Fourth Amendment's provision that "no Warrants shall issue, but upon probable cause."
>
> We reject this view, as has every Court of Appeals to confront the issue. Probable cause exists when there is a fair probability that contraband or evidence of a crime will be found in a particular place. Because the probable-cause requirement looks to whether evidence will be found *when the search is conducted*, all warrants are, in a sense, "anticipatory." In the typical case where the police seek permission to search a house for an item they believe is already located there, the magistrate's determination that there is probable cause for the search amounts to a prediction that the item will still be there when the warrant is executed. * * * Thus, when an anticipatory warrant is issued, the fact that the contraband is not presently located at the place described in the warrant is immaterial, so long as there is probable cause to believe that it will be there when the search warrant is executed.

Justice Scalia then set forth the requirements for a valid anticipatory warrant.

> Anticipatory warrants are, therefore, no different in principle from ordinary warrants. They require the magistrate to determine (1) that it is *now probable* that (2) contraband, evidence of a crime, or a fugitive *will be* on the described premises (3) when the warrant is executed. It should be noted, however, that where the anticipatory warrant places a condition (other than the mere passage of time) upon its execution, the first of these determinations goes not merely to what will probably be found *if* the condition is met. (If that were the extent of the probability determination, an anticipatory warrant could be issued for every house in the country, authorizing search and seizure *if* contraband should be delivered—though for any single location there is no likelihood that contraband will be delivered.) Rather, the probability determination for a conditioned anticipatory warrant looks also to the likelihood that the condition will occur, and thus that a proper object of seizure will be on the described premises. In other words, for a conditioned anticipatory warrant to comply with the Fourth Amendment's requirement of probable cause, two prerequisites of probability must be satisfied. It must be true not only that *if* the triggering condition occurs there is a fair probability that contraband

> or evidence of a crime will be found in a particular place, but also that there is probable cause to believe the triggering condition *will occur*. The supporting affidavit must provide the magistrate with sufficient information to evaluate both aspects of the probable-cause determination.

Justice Scalia then applied these requirements to the warrant issued in *Grubbs*.

> In this case, the occurrence of the triggering condition—successful delivery of the videotape to Grubbs' residence—would plainly establish probable cause for the search. In addition, the affidavit established probable cause to believe the triggering condition would be satisfied. Although it is possible that Grubbs could have refused delivery of the videotape he had ordered, that was unlikely. The Magistrate therefore had a substantial basis for concluding that probable cause existed.

Justice Souter, joined by Justices Stevens and Ginsburg, concurred in part and in the judgment. Justice Alito took no part in the decision.

9. "Sneak and Peek" Warrants

Fed.R.Crim.P. 41(f)(1)(C) requires that an officer executing a warrant must give a copy to the person whose premises is searched. Thus, secret searches are generally prohibited. But Rule 41(f)(3) provides that a judge may delay any notice "if the delay is authorized by statute." And in reaction to the events of 9/11, there is now statutory authority for secret searches in some circumstances.

Section 213 of Public Law 107–56, 115 Stat. 272, the "Uniting And Strengthening America By Providing Appropriate Tools Required To Intercept And Obstruct Terrorism (USA Patriot Act) Act of 2001," authorized so-called "sneak and peek" warrants in certain situations. These warrants permit federal agents to enter a person's home or office covertly. The government can delay notice of a search if it can show "reasonable cause to believe that providing immediate notification of the execution of the warrant may have an adverse result." "Adverse result" is defined as (1) endangering the life or physical safety of an individual, (2) flight from prosecution, (3) destruction of or tampering with evidence, (4) intimidation of potential witnesses, or (5) otherwise seriously jeopardizing an investigation or unduly delaying a trial. The government can also seize items without notice if it can show a "reasonable necessity" for the seizure.

Under what circumstances would it be necessary to employ a sneak and peek warrant?

C. EXECUTING THE WARRANT

Federal Rule of Criminal Procedure 41(e)(2)(A) sets forth the basic information that must be included in the warrant:

> [T]he warrant must identify the person or property to be searched, identify any person or property to be seized, and designate the magistrate judge to whom it must be returned. The warrant must command the officer to:
>
> (i) execute the warrant within a specified time no longer than 14 days;
>
> (ii) execute the warrant during the daytime, unless the judge for good cause expressly authorizes execution at another time; and
>
> (iii) return the warrant to the magistrate judge designated in the warrant.

Daytime means the hours from 6:00 a.m. to 10:00 p.m. according to local time. Fed.R.Crim.P. 41(a)(2)(B). Searches for narcotics, however, are covered by a specific statute that "requires no special showing for a nighttime search, other than a showing that the contraband is likely to be on the property or person to be searched at the time." Gooding v. United States, 416 U.S. 430 (1974) (citing 21 U.S.C. § 879). See also United States v. Rizzi, 434 F.3d 669 (4th Cir. 2006) (federal statute authorizing nighttime searches for narcotics was not unconstitutionally overbroad; the Fourth Amendment does not prohibit nighttime searches, and intrusion on privacy during daytime activities could be just as burdensome as a nighttime intrusion). Related questions regarding the knock and announce requirement and "no-knock warrants" are discussed below.

1. The Knock and Announce Requirement

Statutes throughout the country require that officers executing a warrant knock and announce their presence before attempting to enter a dwelling. Typical of these statutes is 18 U.S.C.A. § 3109.

> The officer may break open any outer or inner door or window of a house, or any part of a house, or anything therein, to execute a search warrant, if, after notice of his authority and purpose, he is refused admittance or when necessary to liberate himself or a person aiding him in the execution of the warrant.

The purposes of the knock and announce requirement are described in United States v. Contreras-Ceballos, 999 F.2d 432 (9th Cir.1993):

> The requirement that law enforcement officers give notice of their authority and purpose prior to forcing entry to execute a warrant serves three purposes: it protects citizens and law enforcement

officials from violence; it protects individual privacy rights; and it protects against needless destruction of private property.

In Wilson v. Arkansas, 514 U.S. 927 (1995), the Court considered whether the Fourth Amendment requires the police to announce their presence before entering a premises. Justice Thomas, writing for a unanimous Court, surveyed the common-law precedents and concluded as follows:

> Given the longstanding common-law endorsement of the practice of announcement, we have little doubt that the Framers of the Fourth Amendment thought that the method of an officer's entry into a dwelling was among the factors to be considered in assessing the reasonableness of a search or seizure. * * * [W]e hold that in some circumstances an officer's unannounced entry into a home might be unreasonable under the Fourth Amendment.

Justice Thomas stressed, however, that the announcement rule was not a rigid constitutional requirement, but rather a component of the Fourth Amendment reasonableness inquiry. He stated that the "Fourth Amendment's flexible requirement of reasonableness should not be read to mandate a rigid rule of announcement that ignores countervailing law enforcement interests." Among the countervailing circumstances that might permit an unannounced entry, the Court mentioned hot pursuit of a suspect, the risk of destruction of evidence, and the safety of officers. Justice Thomas concluded as follows:

> We need not attempt a comprehensive catalog of the relevant countervailing factors here. For now, we leave to the lower courts the task of determining the circumstances under which an unannounced entry is reasonable under the Fourth Amendment. We simply hold that although a search or seizure of a dwelling might be constitutionally defective if police officers enter without prior announcement, law enforcement interests may also establish the reasonableness of an unannounced entry.

"Refused Admittance"

An officer can break open premises if she has announced her authority and purpose and is refused admittance. Clearly, if the homeowner says "you can't come in", this will justify a forced entry with a warrant. But refused admittance may also be implied from the circumstances. Thus, in United States v. Knapp, 1 F.3d 1026 (10th Cir.1993), officers smashed down the defendant's door with a battering ram after announcing their presence and waiting in vain for twelve seconds for a response from the defendant, whom they knew was inside. The court found that the failure to respond within twelve seconds constituted a refusal of entry. The court noted that "the phrase 'refused admittance' is not restricted to an affirmative refusal, but encompasses circumstances that constitute constructive or reasonably inferred refusal." On the other hand, in United States v. Moore, 91 F.3d 96 (10th Cir.1996), the officers announced their presence, waited three seconds, and, when they got no response, entered the premises by force. The court found that the forced entry was "virtually instantaneous" with the announcement and that this "precluded any claim that the officers were constructively refused admittance."

Courts have held that occupants should be allowed more time to answer the door when the warrant is executed in the nighttime hours—and accordingly the time can be reduced during the day. See United States v. Jenkins, 175 F.3d 1208 (10th Cir.1999) (where officers waited for 14 seconds after twice announcing their presence, a forced entry was reasonable; the required waiting period "was somewhat reduced because the officers executed the warrant at 10:00 a.m., when most people are awake and engaged in everyday activities."). Another relevant factor is whether the premises is small or large. See United States v. Sargent, 319 F.3d 4 (1st Cir. 2003) (lack of response for five seconds was especially significant, and deemed to be refused admittance, given the small size of the defendant's apartment).

2. Exceptions to the Notice Rule

No "Breaking"

If the door to a residence is already open, police are not required to announce their presence before entering, because the prohibition is against a "breaking" of the door. See United States v. Mendoza, 281 F.3d 712 (8th Cir. 2002) (officers are not required to knock on the front door of a duplex because the door opened to a common hallway where the defendant had no legitimate expectation of privacy; and they were not required to knock before entering defendant's apartment because it did not have a door).

Courts have also held that if the officer can trick the homeowner into opening the door, there is no violation of the knock and announce requirement, because there is no "breaking." See United States v. Alejandro, 368 F.3d 130 (2d Cir. 2004) (officers pretended that they were employees of a utility company checking out a gas leak; when the defendant opened the door and the officers entered, there was no violation of the knock and announce requirement because there was no breaking).

Emergency Circumstances: Richards v. Wisconsin

As the Supreme Court stated in *Wilson v. Arkansas*, officers will be permitted to make an unannounced entry if announcement would create a risk of destruction of evidence or a risk of harm to the officers or others. In Richards v. Wisconsin, 520 U.S. 385 (1997), the Court considered this exigent circumstances exception to the knock and announce requirement. Justice Stevens, writing for the Court, set forth the facts of the case:

> On December 31, 1991, police officers in Madison, Wisconsin obtained a warrant to search Steiney Richards' hotel room for drugs and related paraphernalia. The search warrant was the culmination of an investigation that had uncovered substantial evidence that Richards was one of several individuals dealing drugs out of hotel rooms in Madison. The police requested a warrant that would have given advance authorization for a "no-knock" entry into the hotel room, but the magistrate explicitly deleted those portions of the warrant.
>
> The officers arrived at the hotel room at 3:40 a.m. Officer Pharo, dressed as a maintenance man, led the team. With him were several plainclothes officers and at least one man in uniform. Officer Pharo knocked on Richards' door and, responding to the query from inside the room, stated that he was a maintenance man. With the chain still on the door, Richards cracked it open. Although there is some dispute as to what occurred next, Richards acknowledges that when he opened the door he saw the man in uniform standing behind Officer Pharo. He quickly slammed the door closed and, after waiting two or three seconds, the officers began kicking and ramming the door to gain entry to the locked room. At trial, the officers testified that they identified themselves as police while they were kicking the door in. When they finally did break into the room, the officers caught Richards trying to escape through the window. They also found cash and cocaine hidden in plastic bags above the bathroom ceiling tiles.

The Wisconsin Supreme Court denied Richards relief, holding that the knock and announce requirement is automatically excused in any case in which the police were authorized to search for evidence of a felony drug crime. The Supreme Court rejected this bright line approach. Justice Stevens reasoned as follows:

> The Wisconsin court explained its blanket exception as necessitated by the special circumstances of today's drug culture, and the State asserted at oral argument that the blanket exception was reasonable in "felony drug cases because of the convergence in a violent and dangerous form of commerce of weapons and the destruction of drugs." But creating exceptions to the knock-and-announce rule based on the "culture" surrounding a general category of criminal behavior presents at least two serious concerns.
>
> First, the exception contains considerable overgeneralization. For example, while drug investigation frequently does pose special risks to officer safety and the preservation of evidence, not every drug investigation will pose these risks to a substantial degree. For example, a search could be conducted at a time when the only

> individuals present in a residence have no connection with the drug activity and thus will be unlikely to threaten officers or destroy evidence. Or the police could know that the drugs being searched for were of a type or in a location that made them impossible to destroy quickly. In those situations, the asserted governmental interests in preserving evidence and maintaining safety may not outweigh the individual privacy interests intruded upon by a no-knock entry. * * *
>
> A second difficulty with permitting a criminal-category exception to the knock-and-announce requirement is that the reasons for creating an exception in one category can, relatively easily, be applied to others. Armed bank robbers, for example, are, by definition, likely to have weapons, and the fruits of their crime may be destroyed without too much difficulty. If a per se exception were allowed for each category of criminal investigation that included a considerable—albeit hypothetical—risk of danger to officers or destruction of evidence, the knock-and-announce element of the Fourth Amendment's reasonableness requirement would be meaningless.
>
> Thus, the fact that felony drug investigations may frequently present circumstances warranting a no-knock entry cannot remove from the neutral scrutiny of a reviewing court the reasonableness of the police decision not to knock and announce in a particular case.

The Court's rejection of a per se exigent circumstances rule did not mean that the no-knock entry in *Richards* was unreasonable, however. Balancing the interests of the state and the individual, the Court set the standard of exigency that would be sufficient justify a no-knock entry:

> In order to justify a "no-knock" entry, the police must have a reasonable suspicion that knocking and announcing their presence, under the particular circumstances, would be dangerous or futile, or that it would inhibit the effective investigation of the crime by, for example, allowing the destruction of evidence. This standard—as opposed to a probable cause requirement—strikes the appropriate balance between the legitimate law enforcement concerns at issue in the execution of search warrants and the individual privacy interests affected by no-knock entries. Cf. Terry v. Ohio (requiring a reasonable and articulable suspicion of danger to justify a pat-down search). This showing is not high, but the police should be required to make it whenever the reasonableness of a no-knock entry is challenged.

Applying this standard to the facts of the case, the Court had little difficulty in determining that the no-knock entry in *Richards* was justified.

For other cases finding reasonable suspicion of exigent circumstances justifying a no-knock entry, see United States v. Sutton, 336 F.3d 550 (7th Cir. 2003) (information that pit bulls had been seen on the property and individuals with drug or weapons convictions had been seen entering the home, when added to the lack of cover for officers approaching the home, provided reasonable suspicion that compliance with the knock and announce requirement might place officers in danger); United States v. Weeks, 160 F.3d 1210 (8th Cir.1998) (no-knock entry of drug stash house justified where officers were informed that the residents answered the door with guns in their hands, one of the residents had been convicted of a firearms offense, and the front door was braced). Compare United States v. Nielson, 415 F.3d 1195 (10th Cir. 2005) (circumstances did not justify a no-knock entry to search for drugs at the residence of a defendant who 1) had no history of violence, 2) was not involved in trafficking drugs, and 3) had cooperated with police during a previous search).

No-Knock Warrants

The officers in *Richards* asked the magistrate for a no-knock warrant, i.e., a warrant that provided advance authorization excusing the knock and announce requirement. The magistrate refused to issue such a warrant, but that is not to say that such warrants can never be issued. If the officers make an advance showing of conditions at a premises that would excuse the knock and announce requirement, then a no-knock warrant can be valid as issued. As the Supreme Court stated in United States v. Banks, 540 U.S. 31 (2003): "When a warrant applicant gives reasonable grounds to expect futility or to suspect that one or another exigency already exists or will arise instantly upon knocking, a magistrate judge is acting within the Constitution to authorize a 'no-knock' entry."

Indeed it would seem that there should be a preference to have the magistrate determine in advance whether conditions exist that will excuse the knock and announce requirement—rather than leaving the question to the officers in the competitive enterprise of ferreting out crime. According to the courts, though, the preference is a mild one. There is no *requirement* that an officer obtain a no-knock warrant, even if she knows that the conditions at the premises would justify such a warrant at the time it is issued. However, "if police obtain a no-knock warrant prior to the search, the defendant bears the burden to show that the entry method was not justified. If, however, police execute a general search warrant without knocking and announcing, then the government is required to justify use of the no-knock entry." United States v. Esser, 451 F.3d 1109 (10th Cir. 2006).

No-Knock Entries and Destruction of Property: United States v. Ramirez

In United States v. Ramirez, 523 U.S. 65 (1998), officers had a no-knock warrant to search a house for a dangerous escaped prisoner. Approaching the house in the early morning hours, they announced over a loud speaker system that they had a search warrant. Simultaneously, they broke a single window in the garage and pointed a gun through the opening, hoping to prevent the occupants from rushing to the weapons stash that an informant told them was in the garage. Awakened by the noise, and fearful that his house was being burglarized, the owner of the house, Ramirez, grabbed a pistol and fired it into the garage ceiling. When the officers shouted "police," Ramirez surrendered and was taken into custody. Ramirez was indicted on federal charges of being a felon in possession of a firearm. As it turned out, the escaped prisoner was not on the premises. Ramirez challenged the forceable entry, arguing that a heightened degree of exigent circumstances is required if the police are going to destroy property during a no-knock warrant entry.

Chief Justice Rehnquist, writing for a unanimous Court, held that officers are not held to a higher standard when a no-knock entry results in the destruction of property. He declared: "Under *Richards*, a no-knock entry is justified if police have a 'reasonable suspicion' that knocking and announcing would be dangerous, futile, or destructive to the purposes of the investigation. Whether such a 'reasonable suspicion' exists depends in no way on whether police must destroy property in order to enter." The Chief Justice recognized that the general Fourth Amendment reasonableness requirement imposes some limitations on the destructiveness of a search. However, in this case, the very limited destruction of property was reasonable given that the officers were acting to prevent possible violent activity. Compare Mena v. City of Simi Valley, 226 F.3d 1031 (9th Cir. 2000) (Fourth Amendment violated where officers unnecessarily broke down doors that were unlocked and open, with one officer stating "I like to destroy these kind of materials, it's cool").

3. Exigent Circumstances After Knocking

In United States v. Banks, 540 U.S. 31 (2003), the Court discussed how and whether exigent circumstances can allow police to break a door down *after* knocking. Justice Souter, writing for a unanimous Court, described the pertinent facts as follows:

> With information that Banks was selling cocaine at home, [officers] got a warrant to search his two-bedroom apartment. As soon as they arrived there, about 2 o'clock on a Wednesday afternoon, officers posted in front called out "police search warrant" and rapped hard enough on the door to be heard by officers at the back door. There was no indication whether anyone was home, and after waiting for 15 to 20 seconds with no answer, the officers broke open the front door with a battering ram. Banks was in the shower and testified that he heard nothing until the crash of the door, which brought him out dripping to confront the police. The search produced weapons, crack cocaine, and other evidence of drug dealing.

The Court "granted certiorari to consider how to go about applying the standard of reasonableness to the length of time police with a warrant must wait before entering without permission after knocking and announcing their intent in a felony case." The Court found that exigent circumstances justified the officers' actions in knocking down the door and entering the premises. Justice Souter explained that, while the question was "a close one, we think that after 15 or 20 seconds without a response, police could fairly suspect that cocaine would be gone if they were reticent any longer."

Justice Souter noted that Banks was confusing two different concepts in his appeal: the time required to assume that a resident is refusing to answer the door, and the time required for a resident to destroy evidence:

> And the argument that 15 to 20 seconds was too short for Banks to have come to the door ignores the very risk that justified prompt entry. True, if the officers were to justify their timing here by claiming that Banks's failure to admit them fairly suggested a refusal to let them in, Banks could at least argue that no such suspicion can arise until an occupant has had time to get to the door, a time that will vary with the size of the establishment, perhaps five seconds to open a motel room door, or several minutes to move through a townhouse. In this case, however, the police claim exigent need to enter, and the crucial fact in examining their actions is not time to reach the door but the particular exigency claimed. On the record here, what matters is the opportunity to get rid of cocaine, which a prudent dealer will keep near a commode or kitchen sink. * * * And 15 to 20 seconds does not seem an unrealistic guess about the time someone would need to get in a position to rid his quarters of cocaine.

4. Does the Violation of the Knock and Announce Requirement Justify Exclusion of Evidence?

In Hudson v. Michigan, 547 U.S. 586 (2006), the Court in a 5–4 decision held that a violation of the knock and announce requirement does not justify exclusion of evidence found in the subsequent search of the premises. Justice Scalia, writing for the majority, explained as follows:

> The interests protected by the knock-and-announce requirement * * * do not include the shielding of potential evidence from the government's eyes.
>
> One of those interests is the protection of human life and limb, because an unannounced entry may provoke violence in supposed self-defense by the surprised resident. Another interest is the protection of property. * * * The knock-and-announce rule gives individuals the opportunity to comply with the law and to avoid the destruction of property occasioned by a forcible entry. And thirdly, the knock-and-announce rule protects those elements of privacy and dignity that can

be destroyed by a sudden entrance. It gives residents the opportunity to prepare themselves for the entry of the police. The brief interlude between announcement and entry with a warrant may be the opportunity that an individual has to pull on clothes or get out of bed. In other words, it assures the opportunity to collect oneself before answering the door.

What the knock-and-announce rule has never protected, however, is one's interest in preventing the government from seeing or taking evidence described in a warrant. Since the interests that *were* violated in this case have nothing to do with the seizure of the evidence, the exclusionary rule is inapplicable.

Justice Scalia found that the exclusionary rule was not necessary to deter violations of the knock and announce requirement, because victims of those violations could bring civil rights actions under 42 U.S.C. § 1983.

Justice Kennedy concurred in part and in the judgment. Justice Breyer, joined by Justices Stevens, Souter, and Ginsburg, dissented. He argued that without the threat of exclusion, officers have no reason to comply with the knock and announce rule. *Hudson* receives full-case treatment below in the section on the exclusionary rule.

5. Timing and Scope of Execution

Given the number of search and seizure cases that have been decided, it is surprising that few have discussed the permissible latitude that officers have in *executing* a warrant. Clearly they can only look in places where the objects specified might be found. As the Court stated in United States v. Ross, 456 U.S. 798 (1982): "A lawful search of fixed premises generally extends to the entire area in which the object of the search may be found and is not limited by the possibility that separate acts of entry or entry or opening may be required to complete the search." But beyond probable cause limits as to location, the manner of searching a premises has not received much treatment.

Destruction and Excessiveness

Does the authorization to search wherever evidence may be found mean that officers can break open walls, tear up floors and ceilings, and inflict other permanent damage? The case law, most of it old, offers little guidance. One case with a helpful discussion is Buckley v. Beaulieu, 104 Me. 56, 71 A. 70 (1908), where the court held that officers acted excessively and unreasonably when they searched unsuccessfully for liquor by tearing out the interior walls of a house. The court noted that the officers could have searched for any liquor concealed within the walls by using "some slender probe with comparatively little injury."

In contrast, the court in United States v. Weinbender, 109 F.3d 1327 (8th Cir.1997), found it reasonable for officers to remove a piece of drywall to search for clothes that would have tied the defendant to a crime. The officers found guns in the space behind the drywall. The court observed that the drywall was unfinished—it was a small square apparently covering a storage space—it was removed in a few seconds without tools; and the officers had been informed that Weinbender used hiding places in his home. The court observed that "the manner in which a warrant is executed is always subject to judicial review to ensure that it does not traverse the general Fourth Amendment proscription against reasonableness." In this case, the information possessed by the officers and the ease with which the drywall was removed led the court to conclude that the officers' actions were reasonable. Similarly it would be reasonable to break locks on briefcases and cabinets to search in areas where there is probable cause to believe that evidence exists. Otherwise, a person could stop a warranted search in its tracks simply by locking something up.

See also Bonney v. Wilson, 817 F.3d 703 (10th Cir. 2016), where the court upheld a search of an ice chest that involved destroying the inside liner because there was probable cause to believe there were drugs inside and "neither Defendant nor our imagination has suggested any nondestructive way to retrieve evidence from the chest's lining."

Unnecessarily Intrusive Searches

An example of an unreasonably intense search arose in Hummel-Jones v. Strope, 25 F.3d 647 (8th Cir.1994), a civil rights action brought by a husband (Jones) and wife (Hummel-Jones) after a 2:00 a.m. raid of the small birthing clinic at which they were staying. The court set forth the facts surrounding the search as follows:

> This dispute arises out of an investigation of the Country Cradle, a well-established and openly-operated alternative birthing clinic located in rural Missouri. A registered nurse operated the clinic. Evidently, the defendants' concern that the nurse might be practicing medicine without a license prompted the search at issue.
>
> Board of Healing Arts Inspector Kistler became convinced that the nurse was delivering a baby at the clinic, and thereby practicing medicine without a license. Kistler contacted Deputy Sheriff Popplewell about the possibility of an investigation or a search. As a result, a reserve deputy was sent to the clinic * * * at 10 P.M. The couple, their toddler, and their four-hour old newborn were the only occupants at the time the deputy knocked on the door. The [undercover] deputy told the family that he was a soldier on his way to the Gulf War. He claimed to be having car trouble, so the family admitted him to telephone for help. In reality, he was telephoning

> waiting officers to inform them that the Country Cradle was occupied by a family with a newborn infant.
>
> * * * The magistrate issued [a] warrant at approximately 1:00 A.M., and authorized a search for "video tapes, medical records, medical supplies, financial records, video equipment, medications or narcotics, sheets, [and] medical textbooks" being kept at the Country Cradle.
>
> At 2:00 A.M. four uniformed and armed officers, two prosecuting attorneys, and the inspector raided the Country Cradle. * * * Jones was ordered to sit on the waiting room couch and was questioned. Several others of the search party went into the separate bedroom where the pajama clad Hummel-Jones was attempting to nurse her newborn son, and began to question her. The couple declined to identify themselves. The searchers seized the couple and restricted them to the waiting room couch while the search was conducted. Whenever Hummel-Jones left the couch, an officer accompanied her. Inspector Kistler photographed the family as "evidence." Kistler also photographed Hummel-Jones's lingerie soaking in the bathroom sink. Popplewell searched Hummel-Jones's overnight bag against her wishes. The searchers seized one of the family's banking slips to establish their identity. The searchers also seized the couple's personal video-tape of Hummel-Jones's afterbirth experience, despite the couple's objections. The search lasted for three and a half hours, or, essentially, throughout the night.

The court held that the search was so excessive—even though conducted pursuant to a warrant and probable cause—as to be unreasonable.

> The primary justification the appellees put forth for performing this search of a well-established and openly-operating birthing clinic at 2:00 A.M. was to ensure that the mother and newborn would be present. Otherwise, we are told, items of evidence, to wit, the mother, newborn, and bloody sheets, might have been lost. Mothers and newborns at a birthing clinic are not "items of evidence." And, neither the warrant nor the warrant application mention either a mother or a newborn when particularly describing the "items" to be searched for and seized. In any case, the mother and newborn were not going to disappear. At worst, they were going to go home. Photographing the mother and her newborn on the clinic premises could not help establish whether or not there was unlicensed practice of medicine occurring at the clinic because it is not illegal to give birth wherever one happens to be when the moment arrives. Nor were the bloody sheets and lingerie attendant to a birth evidence of any illegality.

What should the officers have done in *Hummel-Jones* to make the search reasonable? Is the court simply saying that the crime at issue was not worth the havoc caused? Would the result have been the same if Hummel-Jones had been nursing her newborn during a search relating to suspected terrorism or narcotics trafficking?

When Is the Search Completed?

It is obvious that officers must terminate a search when all of the materials described in the warrant have been found. This standard works well if officers are looking for a discrete object, like a particular stolen television. But sometimes it is difficult to determine whether all the evidence described in the warrant has been found. For example, if officers have a warrant to search for narcotics, the search need not be terminated as soon as the officers find *some* narcotics. But does it follow that there is really no limitation on the scope and duration of a search for narcotics?

The courts do not seem very interested in imposing temporal or spatial limitations on searches for narcotics and related evidence. For example, in United States v. Stiver, 9 F.3d 298 (3d Cir.1993), officers armed with a search warrant for narcotics, paraphernalia, and proof of residency, entered Stiver's apartment. During the course of the search, which lasted about 80 minutes, the telephone rang many times. An officer answered the phone and pretended to be one of Stiver's associates taking 12 orders for drugs from the callers. Stiver argued that the officers exceeded their authority by answering the phone and taking orders from his customers. But the court held that this activity was within the scope of the search authorized by the warrant. The court noted that officers are not required to interpret narrowly the terms of the warrant, and reasoned as follows:

> [T]he warrant authorized the officers to search for and seize, among other things, "all drug paraphernalia." In ordinary usage, the term "paraphernalia" is defined to mean "equipment and apparatus used in or necessary for a particular activity." [quoting the Random House Dictionary]. In light of the fact that the officers had ample cause to believe that the defendant had been using the apartment for heroin sales, * * * the officers had an entirely reasonable basis for concluding that the defendant's telephone was a piece of "equipment" or "apparatus" that was used in [drug activity]. The officers therefore acted properly in "searching" the telephone, i.e., answering it.
>
> We also believe that the officers' conduct was authorized by the portion of the warrant permitting them to search for "any items to prove residency." Telephone calls for the defendant at the premises would provide evidence that he resided there.

Does the court's reasoning mean the officers could occupy Stiver's apartment for a week to take more calls from his customers? A year?

A question of when the search ends also arises when electronic devices are searched. As discussed above in the section on particularity, searches for information on a computer or cellphone can be very thorough because of the possibility that defendants are manipulating, hiding, and mislabeling electronic information. Moreover, the search of a computer or cellphone can take place over a long period of time, including a delayed search of the information after the electronic device is cloned. Rule 41(e)(2)(B) provides that a warrant seeking electronically stored information presumptively permits "a later review of the media or information" and that the time for executing the warrant "refers to the seizure or on-site copying of the media or information, and not to any later off-site copying or review."

6. Presence of the Warrant

Must the officer who executes a search warrant actually have the warrant in hand at the time of the search? Courts have held that while Fed.R.Crim.P. 41(f) requires the officer to serve upon the person searched a copy of the warrant, it does not require that this be done before the search takes place. See, e.g., United States v. Hepperle, 810 F.2d 836, 839 (8th Cir.1987) ("[w]hile it may be foolhardy to proceed in the absence of the physical presence of the warrant, it is not unconstitutional."). Considering that one reason for the warrant is to provide the executing officer with a lawful show of authority, does this result make sense?

7. Enlisting Private Citizens to Help Search

Compelling Assistance from Third Parties—Including Decryption

In United States v. New York Tel. Co., 434 U.S. 159 (1977), the Court, per Justice White, held that, upon a showing of probable cause, a district judge had power to order an unwilling telephone company to assist the government in installing pen registers. The All Writs Act, 28 U.S.C.A. § 1651(a) states: "The Supreme Court and all courts established by Act of Congress may issue all writs necessary or appropriate in aid of their respective jurisdictions and agreeable to the usages and principles of law." The Act was thought to be sufficient authority for a court to compel a private person to act. The Court emphasized that the burden imposed on the telephone company was not "unreasonable." Justice Stevens wrote for himself and Justices Brennan and Marshall in dissent. Their position was that Congress did not empower Federal courts to compel private parties to carry out this kind of surveillance. Justice Stewart, also in dissent, agreed with this point. Justice Stevens argued that the majority's decision provides a sweeping grant of authority without precedent in our Nation's history. Of course, there is precedent for such authority in the common law—the writ of assistance.

A similar question of unwilling assistance arises today with respect to encrypted and other secured electronic information on a person's cellphone or computer. For example, in United States v. Blake, 868 F.3d 960 (11th Cir. 2017), a magistrate judge issued an order requiring Apple to assist in bypassing the security features defendant had installed on his iPad. The court of appeals upheld the order as within the All Writs Act. It noted that the burden on Apple was not unreasonable: "To comply with the bypass order, Apple simply had to have an employee plug the iPad into a special computer and then transfer the iPad's data to a thumb drive."

It is notable that in *Blake,* Apple did not object to the bypass order's requirements. Other instances have arisen in which Apple has objected, including the case of the perpetrator of the 2015 terrorist attacks in San Bernadino, California. See "Apple Fights Order to Unlock San Bernardino Gunman's iPhone" NY Times, 2/17/16. In that case, Apple argued that the bypass order would actually require Apple to rewrite their encryption software, and that would be an "unreasonable" burden under *New York Telephone.* The case was eventually resolved when the FBI hired hackers to unlock the encrypted phone.

Willing Assistance

New York Telephone involved civilians who were unwilling to assist the government. Is the Fourth Amendment question different if an individual *agrees* to assist the government in conducting a search of another person's property? In Bellville v. Town of Northboro, 375 F.3d 25 (1st Cir. 2004), the court found no Fourth Amendment violation where an officer asked two corporate employees to assist him in a search of a premises where there was probable cause to believe that stolen electronic equipment was stored. The court noted that the civilians were "serving a legitimate investigative function" because they could assist the officer, who did not have the necessary technical expertise to identify the property that belonged to the company. The court noted that the employees did not participate in the search "to further their own personal ends." See also United States v. Bach, 310 F.3d 1063 (8th Cir. 2002) (no error for officers to allow Yahoo technicians to retrieve information from the defendant's Yahoo account in child pornography investigation because "the technical expertise of Yahoo's technicians far outweighs that of the officers").

In contrast, in Bills v. Aseltine, 958 F.2d 697 (6th Cir.1992), officers had a warrant to search for a stolen generator. They suspected that the Bills had other stolen property on the premises, but the warrant listed only the generator. The officers asked a General Motors official if he wanted to come along on the search to see if he could identify any property that might have been stolen from General Motors. During the search, the GM official took 231 photographs of various parts and equipment. The court declared:

> [The GM official] was present, not in aid of the officers or their mission, but for his own purposes, involving the recovery of stolen General Motors property not mentioned in any warrant. * * *
>
> * * * Officers * * * may * * * exceed the scope of * * * their warrant when they permit unauthorized invasions of privacy by third parties who have no connection to the search warrant or the officers' purposes for being on the premises.

8. Media Ride-Alongs

Are Fourth Amendment problems raised when officers invite the media along when they execute a search? This question was presented in Wilson v. Layne, 526 U.S. 603 (1999). Officers executing an arrest warrant for Dominic Wilson entered his parents' home late at night. They brought along a photographer and a reporter from the Washington Post. Dominic's father became upset, and was subdued on the floor. Dominic's mother came out of the bedroom and witnessed the confrontation in her nightgown. Numerous photographs were taken, but none were ever published.

The Wilsons brought a civil rights action against the officers contending that the "media ride-along" violated their Fourth Amendment rights. The Supreme Court, in an opinion by Chief Justice Rehnquist, unanimously agreed that the media presence in the Wilson's home constituted a Fourth Amendment violation.

The Chief Justice stated that police actions undertaken in execution of a warrant must be "related to the objectives of the authorized intrusion." In this case, "the presence of reporters inside the home was not related to the objectives of the authorized intrusion." The Chief Justice emphasized that this was not a case "in which the presence of the third parties directly aided in the execution of the warrant" and noted that when police enter a home to search for stolen property, "the presence of third parties for the purpose of identifying the stolen property has long been approved by this Court and our common-law tradition."

The officers cited a number of law enforcement objectives that might be met by a media ride-along. But the Court rejected these interests as insufficient. The Chief Justice elaborated in the following passage:

> Respondents argue that the presence of the Washington Post reporters in the Wilsons' home nonetheless served a number of legitimate law enforcement purposes. They first assert that officers should be able to exercise reasonable discretion about when it would "further their law enforcement mission to permit members of the news

media to accompany them in executing a warrant." But this claim ignores the importance of the right of residential privacy at the core of the Fourth Amendment. It may well be that media ride-alongs further the law enforcement objectives of the police in a general sense, but that is not the same as furthering the purposes of the search. * * *

Respondents next argue that the presence of third parties could serve the law enforcement purpose of publicizing the government's efforts to combat crime, and facilitate accurate reporting on law enforcement activities. * * * Surely the possibility of good public relations for the police is simply not enough, standing alone, to justify the ride-along intrusion into a private home. And even the need for accurate reporting on police issues in general bears no direct relation to the constitutional justification for the police intrusion into a home in order to execute a felony arrest warrant.

Finally, respondents argue that the presence of third parties could serve in some situations to minimize police abuses and protect suspects, and also to protect the safety of the officers. While it might be reasonable for police officers to themselves videotape home entries as part of a "quality control" effort to ensure that the rights of homeowners are being respected, or even to preserve evidence, such a situation is significantly different from the media presence in this case. The Washington Post reporters in the Wilsons' home were working on a story for their own purposes. * * *

Wilson was a civil action for damages, so the exclusionary rule was not operative. In a footnote, however, the Chief Justice took pains to note that with respect to media ride-alongs, "if the police are lawfully present, the violation of the Fourth Amendment is the presence of the media and not the presence of the police in the home." The Court had "no occasion here to decide whether the exclusionary rule would apply to any evidence discovered or developed by the media representatives." For a lower court answer to that question, see United States v. Duenas, 691 F.3d 1070 (9th Cir. 2012):

> Where the media were present, but did not discover or develop any of the evidence later used at trial, the evidence need not be excluded. Here, the media did not expand the scope of the search beyond the warrant's dictates; nor did the media assist the police, or touch, move, handle or taint the admitted evidence in any way. Because the [officers] complied with the terms of the warrant and the media did not disturb any evidence later admitted, the more appropriate remedy here * * * is a *Bivens* or a 42 U.S.C. § 1983 action.

The analysis in *Duenas* receives strong support from the Supreme Court's decision in Hudson v. Michigan, supra, where the Court held that a violation of the knock and announce requirement did not justify exclusion of evidence. Like the court in *Duenas,* the *Hudson* Court found no causal connection between the manner of entry and the obtaining of evidence.

D. THE SCREENING MAGISTRATE

1. Detached and Neutral

What is required for a magistrate to be considered detached and neutral? In Coolidge v. New Hampshire, 403 U.S. 443, 449–453 (1971), the Court invalidated a warrant issued by the state's Attorney General who was authorized by state law to act as a justice of the peace. The Court concluded that an executive officer, the head of law enforcement in the State, could not be the neutral and detached magistrate required by the Constitution. That holding is in-line with founding era concerns about general warrants and writs of assistance. Recall that Lord Halifax, King George III's secretary of state, issued the writs at issue in the general warrants cases. Justice Black, joined by Chief Justice Burger and Justice Blackmun, dissented in *Coolidge.*

In Connally v. Georgia, 429 U.S. 245 (1977), the Court was unanimous in holding that a magistrate who was paid a fee if he issued a warrant, and nothing if he denied an application, was not neutral because approving warrants advanced his personal monetary interests.

In United States v. McKeever, 906 F.2d 129 (5th Cir.1990), the magistrate who issued the warrant was formerly involved in law enforcement and retained reserve officer status; her husband was a deputy; and she visited the site of the search while it was being conducted. The court found these factors "troubling" but not enough to show a lack of neutrality. The court stated that a magistrate may retain certain law enforcement duties without losing neutrality; that no showing was made that the magistrate's husband participated in the issuance of the warrant or the search; and that the magistrate went to the site solely out of "curiosity" and did not assist in the search. Compare Lo-Ji Sales, Inc. v. New York, 442 U.S. 319 (1979) (magistrate loses neutral and detached status when he enthusiastically assists in the search).

Rubber Stamp

Of course, if the magistrate issues the warrant without even reading the application, he has become a rubber stamp and cannot be found neutral and detached. See United States v. Decker, 956 F.2d 773 (8th Cir.1992) (magistrate loses neutral and detached status when he fails to read a warrant because he was "intrigued" by the manner in which the officer became suspicious of the defendant). But it is difficult for a defendant to prove that the magistrate actually acted as a rubber stamp. For example, in United States v. Brown, 832 F.2d 991 (7th Cir.1987), the defendant sought to prove that the municipal judge who issued the warrant against him had acted as a rubber stamp. Brown submitted into evidence hundreds of search warrants issued by the judge. Most of these were based on form affidavits. The court stated that the volume of warrants issued, especially in comparison to lesser numbers issued by other judges, proved not that the judge was a rubber stamp, but rather that the judge had "extraordinary experience in reviewing warrant applications." The court noted, with considerable understatement, that "it might be difficult for a litigant to establish" that a judge has abandoned her neutral and detached role.

2. Who Qualifies as a Magistrate?: Legal Training

In Shadwick v. City of Tampa, 407 U.S. 345 (1972), the Court considered whether the Fourth Amendment requires a magistrate to have legal training. In Tampa, municipal clerks—who were not lawyers—were authorized to issue arrest warrants for minor offenses. Justice Powell, writing for a unanimous Court, held that the clerks qualified as neutral and detached magistrates despite their lack of legal training. Justice Powell found that the two standards of neutrality and competence were met by the Tampa municipal clerks:

> The clerk's neutrality has not been impeached: he is removed from prosecutor or police and works within the judicial branch subject to the supervision of the municipal court judge.
>
> Appellant likewise has failed to demonstrate that these clerks lack capacity to determine probable cause. The clerk's authority extends only to the issuance of arrest warrants for breach of municipal ordinances. We presume from the nature of the clerk's position that he would be able to deduce from the facts on an affidavit before him whether there was probable cause to believe a citizen guilty of impaired driving, breach of peace, drunkenness, trespass, or the multiple other common offenses covered by a municipal code. There has been no showing that this is too difficult a task for a clerk to accomplish.

Justice Powell emphasized that the Court was not making a categorical rule that the issuance of warrants by non-lawyers would always satisfy the Fourth Amendment requirements of neutrality and detachment. Rather, the Court simply rejected the categorical rule that non-lawyers could never act as neutral and detached magistrates. Justice Powell concluded: "States are entitled to some flexibility and leeway in their designation of magistrates, so long as all are neutral and detached and capable of the probable-cause determination required of them."

NOTE ON SHADWICK

Shadwick dealt with arrest warrants, not search warrants. But, the Court's disclaimers notwithstanding, it is clear that the Court was defining the term "magistrate" for Fourth Amendment purposes. The *Shadwick* Court cited arrest and search cases interchangeably. And in Illinois v. Gates, 462 U.S. 213 (1983), considered supra, the Court assumed that non-lawyers may issue search warrants. Do you believe that the Warrant Clause is meaningful when the magistrate is not a lawyer? What message, if any, does *Shadwick* send to magistrates about the importance of their screening function?

3. Records of Magistrate Decisions

There is no requirement that a magistrate give reasons for finding probable cause or for rejecting a warrant application. In the normal course, the magistrate simply signs the proposed warrant provided by the officers, with appropriate modifications, and attaches the affidavit. Is there an argument that magistrates should have to signify in writing their reasons for finding probable cause before issuing a warrant? Are you persuaded by the argument that it does not matter whether a magistrate reasons properly as long as the Fourth Amendment probable cause standard actually is satisfied by the warrant application? Can the Fourth Amendment be satisfied if magistrates issue warrants for the wrong reasons just because good and sufficient reasons appear in the record?

VII. TO APPLY OR NOT APPLY THE WARRANT CLAUSE

As stated previously, the Court has held that a search or seizure is presumptively unreasonable in the absence of a warrant based upon probable cause. However, the Court has found that the presumption of unreasonableness can be overcome in a variety of circumstances. Some of the circumstances excuse the officer from obtaining a warrant, but still require the officer to have probable cause. Other circumstances permit a search or seizure even though the officer has neither a warrant nor probable cause. As you read through the "exceptions" to the Warrant Clause discussed below, be sure to keep straight exactly what requirements the Court retains for each exception. In order to do this, it is helpful to begin with the justification for each exception.

A. ARRESTS IN PUBLIC

In light of the Court's view that warrants are necessary to search for property and seize it, it might seem that seizing a person would *a fortiori* require a warrant. But this is not the law when it comes to arrests in public. The following case sets forth the constitutional basis for this "exception."

UNITED STATES V. WATSON

Supreme Court of the United States, 1976.
423 U.S. 411.

JUSTICE WHITE delivered the opinion of the Court.

This case presents questions under the Fourth Amendment as to the legality of a warrantless arrest * * *.

* * *

The relevant events began on August 17, 1972, when an informant, one Khoury, telephoned a postal inspector informing him that respondent Watson was in possession of a stolen credit card and had asked Khoury to cooperate in using the card to their mutual advantage. On five to 10 previous occasions Khoury had provided the inspector with reliable information on postal inspection matters, some involving Watson. Later that day Khoury delivered the card to the inspector. On learning that Watson had agreed to furnish additional cards, the inspector asked Khoury to arrange to meet with Watson. * * * Khoury met with Watson at a restaurant designated by the latter. Khoury had been instructed that if Watson had additional stolen credit cards, Khoury was to give a designated signal. The signal was given, the officers closed in, and Watson was forthwith arrested. * * * A search having revealed that Watson had no credit cards on his person, the inspector asked if he could look inside Watson's car, which was standing within view. Watson said, "Go ahead," and repeated these words when the inspector cautioned that "[i]f I find anything, it is going to go against you." Using keys furnished by Watson, the inspector entered the car and found under the floor mat an envelope containing two credit cards in the names of other persons. * * *

Prior to trial, Watson moved to suppress the cards, claiming that his arrest was illegal for want of * * * an arrest warrant * * *. The motion was denied, and Watson was convicted of illegally possessing the two cards seized from his car.

[The court of appeals held that Watson's arrest was illegal because the officers had not obtained an arrest warrant, and there were no exigent circumstances to justify the absence of a warrant. The court of appeals further held that the credit cards should have been suppressed as the fruits of the illegal arrest.]

* * *

[T]here is nothing in the Court's prior cases indicating that under the Fourth Amendment a warrant is required to make a valid arrest for a felony. Indeed, the relevant prior decisions are uniformly to the contrary.

The usual rule is that a police officer may arrest without warrant one believed by the officer upon reasonable cause to have been guilty of a felony * * *. * * *

The cases construing the Fourth Amendment thus reflect the ancient common-law rule that a peace officer was permitted to arrest without a warrant for a misdemeanor or felony committed in his presence as well as for a felony not committed in his presence if there was reasonable ground for making the arrest. This has also been the prevailing rule under state constitutions and statutes. * * *

* * *

The balance struck by the common law in generally authorizing felony arrests on probable cause, but without a warrant, has survived substantially intact. It appears in almost all of the States in the form of express statutory authorization. * * *

This is the rule Congress has long directed its principal law enforcement officers to follow. Congress has plainly decided against conditioning warrantless arrest power on proof of exigent circumstances. Law enforcement officers may find it wise to seek arrest warrants where practicable to do so, and their judgments about probable cause may be more readily accepted where backed by a warrant issued by a magistrate. But we decline to transform this judicial preference into a constitutional rule when the judgment of the Nation and Congress has for so long been to authorize warrantless public arrests on probable cause rather than to encumber criminal prosecutions with endless litigation with respect to the existence of exigent circumstances, whether it was practicable to get a warrant, whether the suspect was about to flee, and the like.

Watson's arrest did not violate the Fourth Amendment, and the Court of Appeals erred in holding to the contrary.

* * *

[Justice Stevens took no part in the decision. Justice Stewart's one paragraph opinion concurring in the judgment is omitted.]

JUSTICE POWELL, concurring.

* * *

Since the Fourth Amendment speaks equally to both searches and seizures, and since an arrest, the taking hold of one's person, is quintessentially a seizure, it would seem that the constitutional provision should impose the same limitations upon arrests that it does upon searches. Indeed, as an abstract matter an argument can be made that the restrictions upon arrest perhaps should be greater. A search may cause only annoyance and temporary inconvenience to the law-abiding citizen, assuming more serious dimension only when it turns up evidence of criminality. An arrest, however, is a serious personal intrusion regardless of whether the person seized is guilty or innocent. * * *.

But logic sometimes must defer to history and experience. The Court's opinion emphasizes the historical sanction accorded warrantless felony arrests. * * *

[A] constitutional rule permitting felony arrests only with a warrant or in exigent circumstances could severely hamper effective law enforcement. Good police practice often requires postponing an arrest, even after probable cause has been established, in order to place the suspect under surveillance or otherwise develop further evidence necessary to prove guilt to a jury. Under the holding of the Court of Appeals such additional investigative work could imperil the entire prosecution. Should the officers fail to obtain a warrant initially, and later be required by unforeseen circumstances to arrest immediately with no chance to procure a last-minute warrant, they would risk a court decision that the subsequent exigency did not excuse their failure to get a warrant in the interim since they first developed probable cause. If the officers attempted to meet such a contingency by procuring a warrant as soon as they had probable cause and then merely held it during their subsequent investigation, they would risk a court decision that the warrant had grown stale by the time it was used. Law enforcement personnel caught in this squeeze could ensure validity of their arrests only by obtaining a warrant and arresting as soon as probable cause existed, thereby foreclosing the possibility of gathering vital additional evidence from the suspect's continued actions.

* * *

JUSTICE MARSHALL, with whom JUSTICE BRENNAN joins, dissenting.

By granting police broad powers to make warrantless arrests, the Court today sharply reverses the course of our modern decisions construing the Warrant Clause of the Fourth Amendment. * * *

* * *

The Government's assertion that a warrant requirement would impose an intolerable burden stems, in large part, from the specious supposition that procurement of an arrest warrant would be necessary as soon as probable cause ripens. There is no requirement that a search warrant be obtained the moment police have probable cause to search. The rule is only that present probable cause be shown and a warrant obtained before a search is undertaken. The same rule should obtain for arrest warrants, where it may even make more sense. Certainly, there is less need for prompt procurement of a warrant in the arrest situation. Unlike probable cause to search, probable cause to arrest, once formed, will continue to exist for the indefinite future, at least if no intervening exculpatory facts come to light.

* * *

It is suggested, however, that even if application of this rule does not require police to secure a warrant as soon as they obtain probable cause, the confused officer would nonetheless be prone to do so. If so, police "would risk a court decision that the warrant had grown stale by the time it was used." This fear is groundless. * * * Just as it is virtually impossible for probable cause for an arrest to grow stale between the time of formation and the time a warrant is procured, it is virtually impossible for probable cause to become stale between procurement and arrest. Delay by law enforcement officers in executing an arrest warrant does not ordinarily affect the legality of the arrest. In short, staleness should be the least of an arresting officer's worries.

* * *

Arrest for Minor Crimes

In 1791, when the Fourth Amendment was adopted, the prevalence of the death penalty and the incentive it provided offenders to escape might have justified seizing a person at the time he was charged with any felony. Then, and now, arresting someone who is committing an offense in the officer's presence, especially one who is disturbing the public peace, could be defended on the ground that officers should stop criminal activities before they are completed, if reasonably possible. See, e.g., Diaz v. City of Fitchburg, 176 F.3d 560 (1st Cir.1999) (not unreasonable to effect custodial arrest on persons who violated an ordinance that prohibits the obstruction of public passages: "If the officer always were obligated to allow the criminal obstruction to continue, he or she would be unable to satisfy the Ordinance's apparent purpose of assuring public convenience and safety."). But we now live in a world where criminal statutes cover a much broader range of conduct, including relatively minor misconduct that poses no immediate threat to the peace. Is it reasonable to license full custodial arrests for these kinds of crimes?

In Gustafson v. Florida, 414 U.S. 260, 267 (1973), Justice Stewart suggested that "a persuasive claim might have been made * * * that the custodial arrest of the petitioner for a minor traffic offense violated his rights under the Fourth and Fourteenth Amendments." But that suggestion has never become law.

To the contrary: in Atwater v. City of Lago Vista, 532 U.S. 318 (2001), the Court opted for a bright-line rule that a custodial arrest is *always* reasonable if the officer has probable cause of a criminal violation. Atwater was arrested for a minor traffic offense (a seat belt violation) that was punishable only by a fine. Yet, instead of getting a ticket that would operate as a notice to appear, Atwater was detained, brought to the police station and booked. She argued that these custodial actions were unreasonable for such a minor offense. But the Court reasoned, among other things, that it would be too difficult to distinguish among offenses that could justify custodial arrest and those that could not.

The Court went further in Virginia v. Moore, 553 U.S. 164 (2008). There, Moore was arrested for driving with a suspended license despite the fact that the state statute in question explicitly required issuance of a summons in lieu of arrest. Writing for the Court, Justice Scalia held that the officers had probable cause to believe Moore committed a crime, and therefore had constitutional authority to effect a full custodial arrest even if doing so contradicted state law.

We will discuss *Atwater* and *Moore* at greater depth in the section on the arrest-power rule, *infra*. For now, it is clear after these cases that the Fourth Amendment provides police with discretion to proceed by arrest or summons no matter the nature of the offense or constraints imposed by state law.

NOTE ON THE USE OF FORCE IN MAKING AN ARREST

The Supreme Court limited the use of deadly force to apprehend a suspect in Tennessee v. Garner, 471 U.S. 1 (1985). The Court held that under the Fourth Amendment, deadly force may not be used to prevent the escape of a felon unless it is necessary to prevent the escape *and* the officer has probable cause to believe that the suspect poses a significant threat of causing death or serious physical injury to the officer or others. The felon who was running from the police in *Garner* had committed a non-violent felony and was not known to be violent. The Court concluded that the felon's Fourth Amendment rights were violated when he was shot and killed by an officer who chased and could not catch him. Justice White wrote for six Justices that "[i]t is not better that all felony suspects die than that they escape."

Justice O'Connor, joined by Chief Justice Burger and Justice Rehnquist, dissented in *Garner*. She argued that "the Court effectively creates a Fourth Amendment right allowing a burglary suspect to flee unimpeded from a police officer who has probable cause to arrest, who has ordered the suspect to halt, and who has no means short of firing his weapon to prevent escape."

After *Garner*, the Supreme Court held in Graham v. Connor, 490 U.S. 386 (1989), that all claims of excessive force in the making of an arrest (whether deadly or not) are to be governed by Fourth Amendment standards of reasonableness. Chief Justice Rehnquist, writing for the Court, indicated that some of the relevant factors in the Fourth Amendment reasonableness inquiry "include the severity of the crime at issue, whether the suspect poses an immediate threat to the safety of the officers or others, and whether he is actively resisting arrest or attempting to evade arrest by flight." Consequently, while an officer may use non-deadly force in apprehending a fleeing or resistant felon, the manner in which the force is asserted might be unreasonable. For example, if the officer uses a police dog that is improperly trained, or fails to give a proper warning or instruction before letting the dog loose, this might be found to be an unreasonable use of force. See, e.g., Vathekan v. Prince George's County, 154 F.3d 173 (4th Cir.1998) (officer who releases an attack dog during a burglary investigation, without giving verbal warning to the suspect, would act unreasonably under the Fourth Amendment).

High-Speed Chases: Scott v. Harris

In Scott v. Harris, 550 U.S. 372 (2007), the Court held a law enforcement official can, consistent with the Fourth Amendment, attempt to stop a fleeing motorist from continuing a public-endangering flight by ramming the motorist's car from behind. Justice Scalia, writing for the Court, declared that officers were not required to avoid a risk to the public by simply stopping their pursuit of a suspect in a car. If that were the rule, drivers could avoid arrest simply by speeding away from the officers. Justice Scalia also noted that in determining reasonableness, it was appropriate to balance the risk to the suspect of ramming his car against the risk to the public of a continued chase. And in doing so, officers could consider the culpability of the suspect against the innocence of members of the public who could be put in danger.

Justice Scalia concluded, stating that "A police officer's attempt to terminate a dangerous high-speed car chase that threatens the lives of innocent bystanders does not violate the Fourth Amendment, even when it places the fleeing motorist at risk of serious injury or death."[15]

For other Supreme Court cases involving claims of excessive force under the Fourth Amendment, see, e.g., City of Tahlequah, Oklahoma v. Bond, 142 S.Ct. 9 (2021) (officers who used deadly force to subdue a hammer-wielding man during a domestic disturbance call were entitled to qualified immunity); County of Los Angeles v. Mendez, 137 S.Ct. 1539 (2017) (reasonableness of use of force is determined without regard to whether officers' Fourth Amendment precipitated a confrontation); Mullenix v. Luna, 577 U.S. 7 (2015) (lower court erred in denying qualified immunity where officer used deadly force in a high speed chase where the suspect stated he had a gun); Plumhoff v. Rickart, 572 U.S. 765 (2014) (deadly force used to terminate a high speed chase in which the party's flight imposed a grave public safety risk was reasonable).

---

[15] Justice Ginsburg wrote a short concurring opinion. Justice Stevens dissented.

B. THE ROLE OF MAGISTRATES IN ARRESTS

Watson holds that if an officer has probable cause to believe that a person has committed a felony, he can arrest the suspect in a public place without a warrant. As discussed earlier in this Chapter, the risk of a warrantless search or seizure is that an officer, in the competitive enterprise of ferreting out crime, may be mistaken in his assessment of probable cause. The Supreme Court has held that while a warrant is not required for a public arrest, certain post-arrest protections are necessary to minimize the intrusion on a person who is arrested without probable cause.

In Gerstein v. Pugh, 420 U.S. 103 (1975), the Court declared that, if a person is arrested without a warrant, then he is entitled to a "prompt" post-arrest assessment of probable cause by a magistrate. These hearings need not provide the adversary safeguards associated with a trial because, as the Court reasoned, the probable cause standard traditionally has been decided by a magistrate in a nonadversary hearing on the basis of hearsay and written testimony.

In County of Riverside v. McLaughlin, 500 U.S. 44 (1991), Justice O'Connor wrote for the Court in a class action by pretrial detainees as it defined what is "prompt" under *Gerstein*. She reasoned as follows:

> Given that *Gerstein* permits jurisdictions to incorporate probable cause determinations into other pretrial procedures, some delays are inevitable. * * * On weekends, when the number of arrests is often higher and available resources tend to be limited, arraignments may get pushed back even further. In our view, the Fourth Amendment permits a reasonable postponement of a probable cause determination while the police cope with the everyday problems of processing suspects through an overly burdened criminal justice system.
>
> But flexibility has its limits; *Gerstein* is not a blank check. A State has no legitimate interest in detaining for extended periods individuals who have been arrested without probable cause. * * *
>
> * * *
>
> Although we hesitate to announce that the Constitution compels a specific time limit, it is important to provide some degree of certainty so that States and counties may establish procedures with confidence that they fall within constitutional bounds. Taking into account the competing interests articulated in *Gerstein,* we believe that a jurisdiction that provides judicial determinations of probable cause within 48 hours of arrest will, as a general matter, comply with the promptness requirement of *Gerstein*. For this reason, such jurisdictions will be immune from systemic challenges.

This is not to say that the probable cause determination in a particular case passes constitutional muster simply because it is provided within 48 hours. Such a hearing may nonetheless violate *Gerstein* if the arrested individual can prove that his or her probable cause determination was delayed unreasonably. Examples of unreasonable delay are delays for the purpose of gathering additional evidence to justify the arrest, a delay motivated by ill will against the arrested individual, or delay for delay's sake. In evaluating whether the delay in a particular case is unreasonable, however, courts must allow a substantial degree of flexibility. Courts cannot ignore the often unavoidable delays in transporting arrested persons from one facility to another, handling late-night bookings where no magistrate is readily available, obtaining the presence of an arresting officer who may be busy processing other suspects or securing the premises of an arrest, and other practical realities.

Where an arrested individual does not receive a probable cause determination within 48 hours, the calculus changes. In such a case, the arrested individual does not bear the burden of proving an unreasonable delay. Rather, the burden shifts to the government to demonstrate the existence of a bona fide emergency or other extraordinary circumstance. * * * A jurisdiction that chooses to offer combined proceedings must do so as soon as is reasonably feasible, but in no event later than 48 hours after arrest.

* * *

Justice Scalia dissented in *Mclaughlin* arguing that "it is an unreasonable seizure * * * to delay a determination of probable cause for the arrest either (1) for reasons unrelated to arrangement of the probable-cause determination or completion of the steps incident to arrest, or (2) beyond 24 hours after the arrest."

Justice Marshall, joined by Justices Blackmun and Stevens also dissented and wrote that "I agree with Justice Scalia that a probable-cause hearing is sufficiently 'prompt' under *Gerstein* only when provided immediately upon completion of the 'administrative steps incident to arrest.' "

Detentions for Less than 48 Hours

The Court in *McLaughlin* noted that an individual detention might be unreasonable even if it is less than 48 hours. The court in United States v. Davis, 174 F.3d 941 (8th Cir. 1999), found a warrantless detention unreasonable even though it lasted only two hours. Officers arrested Davis for falsely reporting a theft. She was placed in a holding cell for two hours, and was then questioned about her boyfriend, who was suspected of illegally trafficking in firearms. She was released after agreeing to obtain evidence against her boyfriend. Booking procedures on the false report charge were never initiated and she was never taken before a magistrate to determine whether there was probable cause to arrest her on that charge. Under these circumstances, the court found that Davis had been detained illegally. The court read *McLaughlin* and subsequent lower court cases as having made clear "that a delay may be unreasonable if it is motivated by a desire to uncover additional evidence to support the arrest or to use the suspect's presence solely to investigate the suspect's involvement in other crimes." The court concluded that *McLaughlin* "does not * * * stand for the proposition that authorities may violate the Constitution as long as they do so for only a brief period of time."

Remedy for a McLaughlin Violation

What is the remedy for an unreasonable delay in presentment to a magistrate? Certainly there could be a possible damages recovery, but what about excluding evidence (most likely a confession) obtained from a defendant during an unreasonably excessive delay?

Courts have found that evidence can be excluded only if it was obtained as a result of an unreasonable detention. Thus, exclusion is not required if the magistrate would have found probable cause for the detention even if the hearing had been promptly conducted. See State v. Tucker, 137 N.J. 259, 645 A.2d 111 (1994) (confession made after 48 hour period was admissible where evidence against the defendant was so strong that he would not have been released had a hearing been held earlier). And exclusion would not be required if the evidence was obtained outside the context of an unreasonably lengthy detention. See United States v. Fullerton, 187 F.3d 587 (6th Cir. 1999) (even though the defendant was detained for 72 hours without a hearing, this did not result in exclusion of evidence obtained from him at the time of the arrest, as there was no causal connection between the *McLaughlin* violation and the seizure of the evidence).

C. ARRESTS IN THE HOME

Watson and *Gerstein* left open the question whether a warrant is necessary to enter a home to make an arrest. The Court took up that question in Payton v. New York, 445 U.S. 573 (1980), holding that the exception to the warrant requirement for public arrests did not extend to arrests in the home. The Court described the facts as follows:

> New York detectives * * * assembled evidence sufficient to establish probable cause to believe that Theodore Payton had murdered the manager of a gas station two days earlier. At about 7:30 a.m. on January 15, six officers went to Payton's apartment in the Bronx, intending to arrest him. They had not obtained a warrant.

Although light and music emanated from the apartment, there was no response to their knock on the metal door. They summoned emergency assistance and, about 30 minutes later, used crowbars to break open the door and enter the apartment. No one was there. In plain view, however, was a .30-caliber shell casing that was seized and later admitted into evidence at Payton's murder trial.

In due course Payton surrendered to the police, was indicted for murder, and moved to suppress the evidence taken from his apartment.

Justice Stevens's majority opinion emphasized that the home has always been viewed as an especially private place; set forth a history that indicated there were doubts at common law concerning authority to invade a home to make an arrest; conceded that a majority of state courts addressing the question had permitted warrantless arrests in the home, but observed a trend in the opposite direction in the previous decade; and finally decided that the home deserved special protection. Justice Stevens concluded that "the Fourth Amendment has drawn a firm line at the entrance to the house" and that "absent exigent circumstances, that threshold may not reasonably be crossed without a warrant."[16]

In its penultimate paragraph, the opinion addressed the kind of warrant required—specifically whether the officers needed a search warrant (with a magistrate's determination that there was probable cause to believe that the arrestee would be found in a particular place) or an arrest warrant (allowing the officers to make an arrest wherever the find the person named in the warrant):

> Finally, we note the State's suggestion that only a search warrant based upon probable cause to believe the suspect is at home at a given time can adequately protect the privacy interests at stake, and since such a warrant requirement is manifestly impractical, there need be no warrant of any kind. We find this ingenious argument unpersuasive. It is true that an arrest warrant requirement may afford less protection than a search warrant requirement [because it is not specific as to location], but it will suffice to interpose the magistrate's determination of probable cause between the zealous officer and the citizen. If there is sufficient evidence of a citizen's participation in a felony to persuade a judicial officer that his arrest is justified, it is constitutionally reasonable to require him to open his doors to the officers of the law. Thus, for Fourth Amendment purposes, an arrest warrant founded on probable cause implicitly carries with it

[16] If negative consequences could occur in the time it takes to obtain a warrant, the officers are excused from obtaining one under the doctrine of "exigent circumstances." This doctrine applies both to arrest warrants otherwise required by *Payton*, and to search warrants. See the discussion of exigent circumstances later in this Chapter.

the limited authority to enter a dwelling in which the suspect lives when there is reason to believe the suspect is within.[17]

An in-home arrest is no worse than a public arrest in terms of the seizure that occurs. Both arrestees end up in the same place. So the difference between an in-home arrest and one in public must be that, in conducting the arrest in the home, the officer also ends up *searching* the home. The Fourth Amendment interests at stake in *Payton* are therefore those attaching to the search that results from any arrest conducted in a home not those relating to the seizure of the person entailed by the arrest.

Reason to Believe the Suspect Is at Home

Does the Court in *Payton* mean that an arresting officer must have *probable cause* to believe the suspect is at home? Or does "reason to believe" mean something less than probable cause? Some courts have held that the "reason to believe" standard must mean less than probable cause, because the Court in *Payton* could have said "probable cause" if it wanted to do so. See United States v. Thomas, 429 F.3d 282 (D.C. Cir. 2005) (it is more likely that "the Supreme Court in *Payton* used a phrase other than 'probable cause' because it meant something other than probable cause"). Other courts have found that the "reason to believe" language in *Payton* was the Court's shorthand for probable cause and so the standards are the same. See United States v. Pruitt, 458 F.3d 477 (6th Cir. 2006) ("Despite some courts' attempt to distinguish between the two monikers, the 'reason to believe' standard directly echoes the underlying definition of probable cause."). See also United States v. Barrera, 464 F.3d 496 (the distinction between probable cause and reasonable belief is "more about semantics than substance"); United States v. Bohannon, 824 F.3d 242 (2d Cir. 2016) (noting the dispute among the courts and holding that "our reason-to-believe review does not demand probable cause").

Is the Arrest at Home or in Public?

In light of *Payton* and *Watson,* it becomes important to determine whether an arrest occurs in the home, where a warrant is generally required, or in public, where it is not. In United States v. Holland, 755 F.2d 253 (2d Cir.1985), the defendant was in his second-floor apartment in a two-family house when he heard someone ring the doorbell to his apartment. To answer the bell, he had to walk down a flight of stairs through a common hallway and open the door in the front of the building. There he was arrested without a warrant. The court found no intent in *Payton* to broaden the definition of "home" so as to include the main

[17] Justice Blackmun wrote a one paragraph concurring opinion. Justice White dissented and was joined by the Chief Justice and Justice Rehnquist. Justice Rehnquist also added a short dissent.

entranceway to a common hallway. Judge Newman in dissent noted that if Holland had been living in a modern building with a buzzer mechanism, the officer would have had to arrest him at the door to his apartment. He concluded that *Payton* should apply as well to the "humble surroundings" in which the defendant lived.

What if the officers announce their presence and order the citizen to open the door, the citizen opens the door to his home, and is then placed under arrest? Is that arrest made in the home or in public? Lower courts have split on this question. Some courts have stated that if the defendant is ordered to open the door under a lawful claim of authority, and is arrested upon opening the door, then the arrest occurs in the home and a warrant is required. See United States v. Flowers, 336 F.3d 1222 (10th Cir. 2003). Compare United States v. Vaneaton, 49 F.3d 1423 (9th Cir.1995) (no arrest warrant required where the defendant voluntarily opened the door, and thus "his actions were not taken in response to a claim of lawful authority"); United States v. Council, 860 F.3d 604 (8th Cir. 2017) (arrest was in public where the defendant came to a public place—his open doorway—"voluntarily, without coercion or deceit"). Other courts hold that if the officers remain outside the doorway and inform the defendant that he is under arrest, then the arrest is made in public (even though the defendant is responding to an order to open the door) because the officers never physically entered the home, and therefore did not conduct a search.

Hotels and Motels

The protections against warrantless intrusions into the home announced in *Payton* apply with equal force to a properly rented hotel or motel room during the rental period. See, e.g., United States v. Morales, 737 F.2d 761 (8th Cir.1984). However, this is only the case as long as the arrestee has rightful possession of the room. If the rental period has terminated, or if the person has been ejected from the premises, then the premises can no longer be considered a "home," and an arrest warrant is not required. See, e.g., United States v. Larson, 760 F.2d 852 (8th Cir.1985). See also United States v. Gooch, 6 F.3d 673 (9th Cir.1993) (arrest warrant required for an arrest inside a tent pitched in a public campground: "A guest in Yellowstone Lodge, a hotel on government park land, would have no less an expectation of privacy in his hotel room than a guest in a private hotel, and the same logic would extend to a campsite where the opportunity is extended to spend the night.").

Arrests in the Home of a Third Party

The Court in *Payton* held that an arrest warrant was sufficient to permit the search of a suspect's house to arrest him there. But what if the suspect is arrested in the home of a third person? Does the officer need a search warrant to search that house for the suspect? That was the question in Steagald v. United States, 451 U.S. 204 (1981). Officers obtained an arrest warrant for Ricky Lyons, a federal fugitive wanted on drug charges. They received information that Lyons was staying at a certain house for the next 24 hours. Armed with the arrest warrant, they searched the house. They did not find Lyons, but they did find drugs in the house. These drugs were offered against Steagald, the owner of the house. Steagald moved to suppress the drugs on the ground that the officers failed to secure a search warrant before entering his house to look for Lyons.

Justice Marshall's majority opinion in *Steagald* concluded that a search warrant must be obtained to look for a suspect in the home of a third party, absent exigent circumstances or consent. Drawing on the difference between an arrestee's Fourth Amendment interests against seizure and a homeowners Fourth Amendment interests against search, the majority held that an arrest warrant did not sufficiently protect the privacy and property interests of *the third party homeowner*. Justice Marshall noted that Steagald's only protection from an illegal search "was the agent's personal determination of probable cause" to believe that Lyons was in Steagald's house. The majority was concerned with the possibility of abuse akin to those licensed by general warrants: "Armed solely with an arrest warrant for a single person, the police could search all the homes of that individual's friends and acquaintances."

Justice Rehnquist's dissent was joined by Justice White. He focused on the mobility of fugitives—making probable cause determinations as to location quite difficult—and the likelihood of escape. He also observed that when a suspect lives in another's place for a significant period, this may convert the place into the suspect's home and thus justify a search for that suspect under an arrest warrant.

The majority in *Steagald* showed concern that a third party may be the victim of a search where there is no probable cause to believe that the arrestee is on the premises. But what about family members, roommates, or other third parties who live with the arrestee? See United States v. Litteral, 910 F.2d 547 (9th Cir.1990) ("if the suspect is a co-resident of the third party, then *Steagald* does not apply, and *Payton* allows both arrest of the subject of the arrest warrant and use of evidence found against the third party."). If an arrest warrant is sufficient to vindicate the privacy interests of an arrestee in his home, then it is also sufficient to protect the privacy interests of those who share the arrestee's living space. See United States v. Lovelock, 170 F.3d 339 (2d Cir. 1999) ("A person who occupies premises jointly with another has a reduced expectation of privacy since he assumes the risk that his housemate may engage in conduct that authorized entry into the premises.").

After *Steagald,* it is important for the officer to determine whether the suspect lives in the premises (in which case an arrest warrant is sufficient) or is merely a visitor (in which case a search warrant is required). What considerations should an officer take into account? See United States v. Pallais, 921 F.2d 684 (7th Cir.1990) (suspect who was staying in garage overseeing the renovation of his children's home was a resident, so an arrest warrant was sufficient). What if the officer wants to arrest a person in a third party's home, and knows that the suspect has a residence somewhere else? Does this prohibit the officer from reasonably believing that the suspect might reside in the third party's home as well? See United States v. Risse, 83 F.3d 212 (8th Cir.1996) (officer could enter defendant's home with an arrest warrant to arrest the defendant's girlfriend even though the officer knew that the girlfriend had her own apartment: "We have found no authority to support Risse's implicit assumption that a person can have only one residence for Fourth Amendment purposes.").

Who May Object to a Search

In *Steagald*, the officers entered Steagald's home to arrest Lyons. While trying to find Lyons, the officers discovered evidence that was used against Steagald at trial. The Court held that the evidence should have been suppressed because Steagald's Fourth Amendment rights against search were violated. Does that mean that Lyons, the suspect, could have objected to the search if the officers had found him in Steagald's home? The courts have answered in the negative, reasoning that *Steagald* was concerned with the privacy rights of the third-party homeowner, not with the visiting arrestee. See United States v. Bohannon, 824 F.3d 242 (2d Cir. 2016) (the subject of an arrest warrant may not invoke *Steagald* to claim that his Fourth Amendment rights are violated when officers search a third party's residence); United States v. Underwood, 717 F.2d 482 (9th Cir.1983) (*Steagald* addressed only the right of a third party not named in the arrest warrant to the privacy of his or her home; this right is personal and cannot be asserted vicariously by the person named in the arrest warrant). A contrary rule would be anomalous: the suspect would be entitled to demand a search warrant when arrested in the home of another, while under *Payton* he could demand only an arrest warrant when arrested in his own home. See United States v. Jackson, 576 F.3d 465 (7th Cir. 2009) ("Because it addresses only the Fourth Amendment rights of persons not named in an arrest warrant, *Steagald* did not hold that the subject of an arrest warrant has a higher expectation of privacy in another person's residence than he does in his own.").

What if an arrestee is not a mere visitor in the home of a third party? The Court concluded in Minnesota v. Olson, 495 U.S. 91 (1990), that a warrant was required under *Payton* to arrest a person who was an overnight guest in the home of a third party because he had a reasonable expectation of privacy in the premises. Justice White wrote the majority opinion. He stressed that a person's "status as an overnight guest is alone enough to show that he had an expectation of privacy in the home that society is prepared to accept as reasonable." The Court specifically rejected the State's argument that a place must be one's own home in order to have a legitimate expectation of privacy there. Chief Justice Rehnquist and Justice Blackmun dissented in *Olson* without opinion.

According to *Olson*, overnight guests have a sufficient expectation of privacy in the premises to invoke Fourth Amendment interests relating to search. What if the guest's connection with the premises is less substantial? In Minnesota v. Carter, 525 U.S. 83 (1998), Carter and Johns objected to a warrantless search of an apartment. Their connection with the apartment was that they were there for a couple of hours cutting-up cocaine. Chief Justice Rehnquist, writing for the Court, held that the defendants had no expectation of privacy in the premises and therefore could not complain about the search. The Chief Justice explained:

> If we regard the overnight guest in Minnesota v. Olson as typifying those who may claim the protection of the Fourth Amendment in the home of another, and one merely "legitimately on the premises" as typifying those who may not do so, the present case is obviously somewhere in between. But the purely commercial nature of the transaction engaged in here, the relatively short period of time on the premises, and the lack of any previous connection between respondents and the householder, all lead us to conclude that respondents' situation is closer to that of one simply permitted on the premises. We therefore hold that any search which may have occurred did not violate their Fourth Amendment rights.

D. MATERIAL WITNESSES

The power to arrest is usually applied to persons suspected of criminal activity. However, the police also have the power to arrest and detain a material witness to a crime under certain circumstances. The Federal material witness statute, 18 U.S.C.A. § 3144, provides as follows:

> If it appears from an affidavit filed by a party that the testimony of a person is material in a criminal proceeding, and if it is shown that it may become impracticable to secure the presence of the person by subpoena, a judicial officer may order the arrest of the person and treat the person [like an arrestee for a crime]. No material witness may be detained because of inability to comply with any condition of release if the testimony of such witness can adequately be secured by deposition, and if further detention is not necessary to prevent a failure of justice. Release of a material witness may be delayed for a reasonable period

of time until the deposition of the witness can be taken pursuant to the Federal Rules of Criminal Procedure.

In addition to the Federal statute, every state provides for detention of material witnesses. The Supreme Court has cited the practice with approval in Stein v. New York, 346 U.S. 156, 184 (1953) and Barry v. United States ex rel. Cunningham, 279 U.S. 597, 617 (1929).

There is no constitutional right to monetary compensation for time spent in confinement as a material witness. In Hurtado v. United States, 410 U.S. 578 (1973), the Court held that payment of one dollar per day as compensation did not constitute a "taking" without just compensation or a denial of equal protection.

The expansiveness of the power to arrest a material witness was shown in United States v. Awadallah, 349 F.3d 42 (2d Cir. 2003). A few days after 9/11, Awadallah was detained without probable cause that he was involved in terrorist activity. The detention was instead based on his purported knowledge of persons so involved. His detention as a material witness lasted for 20 days. Bail was denied. Awadallah eventually testified before a grand jury that he did not know the suspected terrorists named by the government. The government then indicted Awadallah for lying to the grand jury when he denied knowing the suspected terrorists. The court upheld the material witness detention as reasonable, and refused to dismiss the indictment, stating that detention of a witness during a grand jury investigation was permissible because a grand jury proceeding was a "criminal proceeding" within the meaning of section 3144. Five years after his initial detention, Awadallah was acquitted of all perjury charges and finally released.

Pretextual Use of Material Witness Detention: Ashcroft v. Al-Kidd

The dangers of material witness detention, especially after 9/11, are emphasized by Studnicki and Apol in Witness Detention and Intimidation: The History and Future of Material Witness Law, 76 St. John's L.Rev. 483 (2002):

> Material witness law is unique because of the potential *carte blanche* it provides to the government and law enforcement officials who may abuse it. In the aftermath of the September 11, 2001 terrorist attacks, the FBI has been accused of misusing the material witness law to detain people while investigating their backgrounds and activities. Indeed, the United States Attorney General announced that the "aggressive detention" of material witnesses in the wake of September 11th would be the norm. The secrecy surrounding the detention of material witnesses adds to the potential of misuse of this authority as an investigatory tool, rather than a legitimate means of

obtaining testimony or protecting a witness. Further, it is easier to arrest an individual as a material witness than as a criminal defendant since there is no required showing of probable cause that the witness has committed a crime.

In Ashcroft v. Al-Kidd, 563 U.S. 731 (2011), the Supreme Court reviewed *Bivens* claims brought against former Attorney General Ashcroft and other officials. The plaintiff alleged that the defendants suspected him of terrorist activity and employed the Material Witness statute to subject him to a long-term detention even though they had no intent to use him as a witness in any case. Thus, the plaintiff argued that the use of a statute was a pretext to detain him as a suspect rather than a material witness.

The Court, in an opinion by Justice Scalia, noted first that Al-Kidd "does not assert that Government officials would have acted unreasonably if they had used a material-witness warrant to arrest him for the purpose of securing his testimony for trial. He contests * * * the reasonableness of using the warrant to detain him as a suspected criminal." Justice Scalia rejected Al-Kidd's Fourth Amendment pretext argument the reasonableness of government activity in the criminal context is determined objectively, without regard to an official's subjective state of mind. The Court conceded that the subjective intent of a police officer has been considered in cases where searches were justified as promoting "special needs" beyond ordinary criminal law enforcement. [See the section on "special needs" searches later in this Chapter.] But the "special needs" cases were not applicable to Al-Kidd's detention, as Justice Scalia explained in the following passage:

> Needless to say, warrantless, suspicionless intrusions pursuant to a general scheme are far removed from the facts of this case. A warrant issued by a neutral Magistrate Judge authorized al-Kidd's arrest. The affidavit accompanying the warrant application (as al-Kidd concedes) gave individualized reasons to believe that he was a material witness and that he would soon disappear. The existence of a judicial warrant based on individualized suspicion takes this case outside the domain of ["special needs" suspicionless searches and seizures].

On the question of pretext, Justice Scalia concluded as follows:

> Because al-Kidd concedes that individualized suspicion supported the issuance of the material-witness arrest warrant; and does not assert that his arrest would have been unconstitutional absent the alleged pretextual use of the warrant; we find no Fourth Amendment violation. Efficient and evenhanded application of the law demands that we look to whether the arrest is objectively justified, rather than to the motive of the arresting officer.

Justice Kennedy, joined by Justices Ginsburg, Breyer, and Sotomayor, wrote a concurring opinion emphasizing that the Court had not decided "whether the Government's use of the Material Witness statute in this case was lawful." That is, Al-Kidd challenged only the pretextual use of the statute, and conceded for argument that detaining a material witness upon satisfying the statutory criteria was a reasonable seizure under the Fourth Amendment. On that broader Fourth Amendment question, Justice Kennedy noted his reservations:

> The scope of the statute's lawful authorization is uncertain. For example, a law-abiding citizen might observe a crime during the days or weeks before a scheduled flight abroad. It is unclear whether those facts alone might allow police to obtain a material witness warrant on the ground that it "may become impracticable" to secure the person's presence by subpoena. The question becomes more difficult if one further assumes the traveler would be willing to testify if asked; and more difficult still if one supposes that authorities delay obtaining or executing the warrant until the traveler has arrived at the airport. These possibilities resemble the facts in this case.
>
> In considering these issues, it is important to bear in mind that the Material Witness Statute might not provide for the issuance of warrants within the meaning of the Fourth Amendment's Warrant Clause. The typical arrest warrant is based on probable cause that the arrestee has committed a crime; but that is not the standard for the issuance of warrants under the Material Witness Statute. If material witness warrants do not qualify as "Warrants" under the Fourth Amendment, then material witness arrests might still be governed by the Fourth Amendment's separate reasonableness requirement for seizures of the person.

Justice Ginsburg wrote a separate opinion concurring in the judgment, joined by Justices Breyer and Sotomayor. Justice Sotomayor wrote a separate opinion concurring in the judgment, joined by Justices Ginsburg and Breyer.

E. STOP AND FRISK

There are numerous situations in which the police recognize that they do not have probable cause to act, but want to stop a suspicious person for preliminary questioning to determine whether a crime has or is about to occur. From the police perspective, if officers have to wait for probable cause to develop before conducting these preliminary investigations, they would be severely hampered in their efforts to prevent and detect crime. In their view, a standard of proof less demanding than probable cause is needed to nip a crime problem in the bud. Following the adoption in 1964 of a New York statute that became known as the "stop and frisk" law and the conclusion of several important studies of what police do in the real world, the United States Supreme Court placed its first imprimatur on searches and seizures of persons and things on a standard of proof less than probable cause.

1. Stop and Frisk Established

TERRY V. OHIO

Supreme Court of the United States, 1968.
392 U.S. 1.

CHIEF JUSTICE WARREN delivered the opinion of the Court.

This case presents serious questions concerning the role of the Fourth Amendment in the confrontation on the street between the citizen and the policeman investigating suspicious circumstances.

Petitioner Terry was convicted of carrying a concealed weapon and sentenced to the statutorily prescribed term of one to three years in the penitentiary. Following the denial of a pretrial motion to suppress, the prosecution introduced in evidence two revolvers and a number of bullets seized from Terry and a codefendant, Richard Chilton, by Cleveland Police Detective Martin McFadden. At the hearing on the motion to suppress this evidence, Officer McFadden testified that while he was patrolling in plain clothes in downtown Cleveland at approximately 2:30 in the afternoon of October 31, 1963, his attention was attracted by two men, Chilton and Terry, standing on the corner of Huron Road and Euclid Avenue. He had never seen the two men before, and he was unable to say precisely what first drew his eye to them. However, he testified that he had been a policeman for 39 years and a detective for 35 and that he had been assigned to patrol this vicinity of downtown Cleveland for shoplifters and pickpockets for 30 years. He explained that he had developed routine habits of observation over the years and that he would "stand and watch people or walk and watch people at many intervals of the day." He added: "Now, in this case when I looked over they didn't look right to me at the time."

His interest aroused, Officer McFadden took up a post of observation in the entrance to a store 300 to 400 feet away from the two men. * * * He saw one of the men leave the other one and walk southwest on Huron Road, past some stores. The man paused for a moment and looked in a store window, then walked on a short distance, turned around and walked back toward the corner, pausing once again to look in the same store window. He rejoined his companion at the corner, and the two conferred briefly. Then the second man went through the same series of motions, strolling down Huron Road, looking in the same window, walking on a short distance, turning back, peering in the store window again, and returning to confer with the first man at the corner. The two men repeated this ritual alternately between five and six times apiece—in all, roughly a dozen trips.

At one point, while the two were standing together on the corner, a third man approached them and engaged them briefly in conversation. This man then left the two others and walked west on Euclid Avenue. Chilton and Terry resumed their measured pacing, peering, and conferring. After this had gone on for 10 to 12 minutes, the two men walked off together, heading west on Euclid Avenue, following the path taken earlier by the third man.

By this time Officer McFadden had become thoroughly suspicious. He testified that after observing their elaborately casual and oft-repeated reconnaissance of the store window on Huron Road, he suspected the two men of "casing a job, a stick-up," and that he considered it his duty as a police officer to investigate further. He added that he feared "they may have a gun." Thus, Officer McFadden followed Chilton and Terry and saw them stop in front of Zucker's store to talk to the same man who had conferred with them earlier on the street corner. Deciding that the situation was ripe for direct action, Officer McFadden approached the three men, identified himself as a police officer and asked for their names. * * * When the men "mumbled something" in response to his inquiries, Officer McFadden grabbed petitioner Terry, spun him around so that they were facing the other two, with Terry between McFadden and the others, and patted down the outside of his clothing. In the left breast pocket of Terry's overcoat Officer McFadden felt a pistol. He reached inside the overcoat pocket, but was unable to remove the gun. At this point, keeping Terry between himself and the others, the officer ordered all three men to enter Zucker's store. As they went in, he removed Terry's overcoat completely, removed a .38-caliber revolver from the pocket and ordered all three men to face the wall with their hands raised. Officer McFadden proceeded to patdown the outer clothing of Chilton and the third man, Katz. He discovered another revolver in the outer pocket of Chilton's overcoat, but no weapons were found on Katz. The officer testified that he only patted the men down to see whether they had weapons, and that he did not put his hands beneath the outer garments of either Terry or Chilton until he felt their guns. So far as appears from the record, he never placed his hands beneath Katz' outer garments. Officer McFadden seized Chilton's gun, asked the proprietor of the store to call a police wagon, and took all three men to the station, where Chilton and Terry were formally charged with carrying concealed weapons.

On the motion to suppress the guns the prosecution took the position that they had been seized following a search incident to a lawful arrest. The trial court rejected this theory, stating that it "would be stretching the facts beyond reasonable comprehension" to find that Officer McFadden had probable cause to arrest the men before he patted them down for weapons. However, the court denied the defendants' motion on the ground that Officer McFadden, on the basis of his experience, "had reasonable cause to believe * * * that the defendants were conducting themselves suspiciously, and some interrogation should be made of their action." Purely for his own protection, the court held, the officer had the right to patdown the outer clothing of these men, who he had reasonable cause to believe might be armed. The court distinguished between an investigatory "stop" and an arrest, and between a "frisk" of the outer clothing for weapons and a full-blown search for evidence of crime. The frisk, it held, was essential to the proper performance of the officer's investigatory duties, for without it "the answer to the police officer may be a bullet, and a loaded pistol discovered during the frisk is admissible."

* * *

We would be less than candid if we did not acknowledge that this question thrusts to the fore difficult and troublesome issues regarding a sensitive area of police activity—issues which have never before been squarely presented to this Court. Reflective of the tensions involved are the practical and constitutional arguments pressed with great vigor on both sides of the public debate over the power of the police to "stop and frisk"—as it is sometimes euphemistically termed—suspicious persons.

* * *

In this context we approach the issues in this case mindful of the limitations of the judicial function in controlling the myriad daily situations in which policemen and citizens confront each other on the street. The State has characterized the issue here as "the right of a police officer * * * to make an on-the-street stop, interrogate and patdown for weapons (known in street vernacular as 'stop and frisk')." But this is only partly accurate. For the issue is not the abstract propriety of the police conduct, but the admissibility against petitioner of the evidence uncovered by the search and seizure. [The Court suggests that the exclusionary rule may not deter all Fourth Amendment violations. For example, where an officer is bent on harassment, and doesn't care about whether he finds evidence, the exclusionary rule cannot deter the officer because the exclusionary rule is dependent on litigation-oriented disincentives.]

* * *

Proper adjudication of cases in which the exclusionary rule is invoked demands a constant awareness of these limitations. The wholesale harassment by certain elements of the police community, of which minority groups, particularly Negroes, frequently complain, will not be stopped by the exclusion of any evidence from any criminal trial. Yet a rigid and unthinking application of the exclusionary rule, in futile protest against practices which it can never be used effectively to control, may exact a high toll in human injury and frustration of efforts to prevent crime. * * *

* * *

Our first task is to establish at what point in this encounter the Fourth Amendment becomes relevant. That is, we must decide whether and when Officer McFadden "seized" Terry and whether and when he conducted a "search." There is some suggestion in the use of such terms as "stop" and "frisk" that such police conduct is outside the purview of the Fourth Amendment because neither action rises to the level of a "search" or "seizure" within the meaning of the Constitution. We emphatically reject this notion. It is quite plain that the Fourth Amendment governs "seizures" of the person which do not eventuate in a trip to the station house and prosecution for crime—"arrests" in traditional terminology. It must be recognized that whenever a police officer accosts an individual and restrains his freedom to walk away, he has "seized" that person. And it is nothing less than sheer torture of the English language to suggest that a careful exploration of the outer surfaces of a person's clothing all over his or her body in an attempt to find weapons is not a "search." Moreover, it is simply fantastic to urge that such a procedure performed in public by a policeman while the citizen stands helpless, perhaps facing a wall with his hands raised, is a "petty indignity." It is a serious intrusion upon the sanctity of the person, which may inflict great indignity and arouse strong resentment, and it is not to be undertaken lightly.

* * *

In this case there can be no question, then, that Officer McFadden "seized" petitioner and subjected him to a "search" when he took hold of him and patted down the outer surfaces of his clothing. We must decide whether at that point it was reasonable for Officer McFadden to have interfered with petitioner's personal security as he did. And in determining whether the seizure and search were "unreasonable" our inquiry is a dual one—whether the officer's action was justified at its inception, and whether it was reasonably related in scope to the circumstances which justified the interference in the first place.

* * *

If this case involved police conduct subject to the Warrant Clause of the Fourth Amendment, we would have to ascertain whether "probable cause" existed to justify the search and seizure which took place. However, that is not the case. We do not retreat from our holdings that the police must, whenever practicable, obtain advance judicial approval of searches and seizures through the warrant procedure or that in most instances failure to comply with the warrant requirement can only be excused by exigent circumstances. But we deal here with an entire rubric of police conduct—necessarily swift action predicated upon the on-the-spot observations of the officer on the beat—which historically has not been, and as a practical matter could not be, subjected to the warrant procedure.

Instead the conduct involved in this case must be tested by the Fourth Amendment's general proscription against unreasonable searches and seizures.

Nonetheless, the notions which underlie both the warrant procedure and the requirement of probable cause remain fully relevant in this context. In order to assess the reasonableness of Officer McFadden's conduct as a general proposition, it is necessary "first to focus upon the governmental interest which allegedly justifies official intrusion upon the constitutionally protected interests of the private citizen," for there is "no ready test for determining reasonableness other than by balancing the need to search [or seize] against the invasion which the search [or seizure] entails." Camara v. Municipal Court, 387 U.S. 523, 534–535, 536–537 (1967). And in justifying the particular intrusion the police officer must be able to point to specific and articulable facts which, taken together with rational inferences from those facts, reasonably warrant that intrusion. * * * And in making that assessment it is imperative that the facts be judged against an objective standard: would the facts available to the officer at the moment of the seizure or the search "warrant a man of reasonable caution in the belief" that the action taken was appropriate? Anything less would invite intrusions upon constitutionally guaranteed rights based on nothing more substantial than inarticulate hunches, a result this Court has consistently refused to sanction. * * *

Applying these principles to this case, we consider first the nature and extent of the governmental interests involved. One general interest is of course that of effective crime prevention and detection; it is this interest which underlies the recognition that a police officer may in appropriate circumstances and in an appropriate manner approach a person for purposes of investigating possibly criminal behavior even though there is no probable cause to make an arrest. It was this legitimate investigative function Officer McFadden was discharging when he decided to approach petitioner and his companions. He had observed Terry, Chilton, and Katz go through a series of acts, each of them perhaps innocent in itself, but which taken together warranted further investigation. There is nothing unusual in two men standing together on a street corner, perhaps waiting for someone. Nor is there anything suspicious about people in such circumstances strolling up and down the street, singly or in pairs. Store windows, moreover, are made to be looked in. But the story is quite different where, as here, two men hover about a street corner for an extended period of time, at the end of which it becomes apparent that they are not waiting for anyone or anything; where these men pace alternately along an identical route, pausing to stare in the same store window roughly 24 times; where each completion of this route is followed immediately by a conference between the two men on the corner; where they are joined in one of these conferences by a third man who leaves swiftly; and where the two men finally follow the third and rejoin him a couple of blocks away. It would have been poor police work indeed for an officer of 30 years' experience in the detection of thievery from stores in this same neighborhood to have failed to investigate this behavior further.

The crux of this case, however, is not the propriety of Officer McFadden's taking steps to investigate petitioner's suspicious behavior, but rather, whether there was justification for McFadden's invasion of Terry's personal security by searching him for weapons in the course of that investigation. * * * Certainly it would be unreasonable to require that police officers take unnecessary risks in the performance of their duties. American criminals have a long tradition of armed violence, and every year in this country many law enforcement officers are killed in the line of duty, and thousands more are wounded. * * *

In view of these facts, we cannot blind ourselves to the need for law enforcement officers to protect themselves and other prospective victims of violence in situations where they may lack probable cause for an arrest. When an officer is justified in believing that the individual whose suspicious behavior he is investigating at close range is armed and presently dangerous to the officer or to others, it would appear to be clearly unreasonable to deny the officer the power to take necessary measures to determine whether the person is in fact carrying a weapon and to neutralize the threat of physical harm.

* * *

Our evaluation of the proper balance that has to be struck in this type of case leads us to conclude that there must be a narrowly drawn authority to permit a reasonable search for weapons for the protection of the police officer, where he has reason to believe that he is dealing with an armed and dangerous individual, regardless of whether he has probable cause to arrest the individual for a crime. The officer need not be absolutely certain that the individual is armed; the issue is whether a reasonably prudent man in the circumstances would be warranted in the belief that his safety or that of others was in danger. And in determining whether the officer acted reasonably in such circumstances, due weight must be given, not to his inchoate and unparticularized suspicion or "hunch," but to the specific reasonable inferences which he is entitled to draw from the facts in light of his experience.

* * *

We need not develop at length in this case * * * the limitations which the Fourth Amendment places upon a protective seizure and search for weapons. These limitations will have to be developed in the concrete factual circumstances of individual cases. Suffice it to note that such a search, unlike a search without a warrant incident to arrest, is not justified by any need to prevent the disappearance or destruction of evidence of crime. The sole justification of the search in the present situation is the protection of the police officer and others nearby, and it must therefore be confined in scope to an intrusion reasonably designed to discover guns, knives, clubs, or other hidden instruments for the assault of the police officer.

The scope of the search in this case presents no serious problem in light of these standards. * * *

V

We conclude that the revolver seized from Terry was properly admitted in evidence against him. At the time he seized petitioner and searched him for weapons, Officer McFadden had reasonable grounds to believe that petitioner was armed and dangerous, and it was necessary for the protection of himself and others to take swift measures to discover the true facts and neutralize the threat of harm if it materialized. The policeman carefully restricted his search to what was appropriate to the discovery of the particular items which he sought. Each case of this sort will, of course, have to be decided on its own facts. We merely hold today that where a police officer observes unusual conduct which leads him reasonably to conclude in light of his experience that criminal activity may be afoot and that the persons with whom he is dealing may be armed and presently dangerous, where in the course of investigating this behavior he identifies himself as a policeman and makes reasonable inquiries, and where nothing in the initial stages of the encounter serves to dispel his reasonable fear for his own or others' safety, he is entitled for the protection of himself and others in the area to conduct a carefully limited search of the outer clothing of such persons in an attempt to discover weapons which might be used to assault him. Such a search is a reasonable search under the Fourth Amendment, and any weapons seized may properly be introduced in evidence against the person from whom they were taken.

JUSTICE HARLAN, concurring.

* * *

[I]f the frisk is justified in order to protect the officer during an encounter with a citizen, the officer must first have constitutional grounds to insist on an encounter, to make a *forcible* stop. Any person, including a policeman, is at liberty to avoid a person he considers dangerous. If and when a policeman has a right instead to disarm such a person for his own protection, he must first have a right not to avoid him but to be in his presence. That right must be more than the liberty (again, possessed by every citizen) to address questions to other persons, for ordinarily the person addressed has an equal right to ignore his interrogator and walk away; he certainly need not submit to a frisk for the questioner's protection.

I would make it perfectly clear that the right to frisk in this case depends upon the reasonableness of a forcible stop to investigate a suspected crime.

Where such a stop is reasonable, however, the right to frisk must be immediate and automatic if the reason for the stop is, as here, an articulable suspicion of a crime of violence. Just as a full search incident to a lawful arrest requires no additional justification, a limited frisk incident to a lawful stop must often be rapid and routine. There is no reason why an officer, rightfully but forcibly confronting a person suspected of a serious crime, should have to ask one question and take the risk that the answer might be a bullet.

* * *

JUSTICE WHITE, concurring.

* * * I think an additional word is in order concerning the matter of interrogation during an investigative stop. There is nothing in the Constitution which prevents a policeman from addressing questions to anyone on the street. Absent special circumstances, the person approached may not be detained or frisked but may refuse to cooperate and go on his way. However, given the proper circumstances, such as those in this case, it seems to me the person may be briefly detained against his will while pertinent questions are directed to him. * * *

JUSTICE DOUGLAS, dissenting.

I agree that petitioner was "seized" within the meaning of the Fourth Amendment. I also agree that frisking petitioner and his companions for guns was a "search." But it is a mystery how that "search" and that "seizure" can be constitutional by Fourth Amendment standards, unless there was "probable cause" to believe that (1) a crime had been committed or (2) a crime was in the process of being committed or (3) a crime was about to be committed.

* * *

The infringement on personal liberty of any "seizure" of a person can only be "reasonable" under the Fourth Amendment if we require the police to possess "probable cause" before they seize him. Only that line draws a meaningful distinction between an officer's mere inkling and the presence of facts within the officer's personal knowledge which would convince a reasonable man that the person seized has committed, is committing, or is about to commit a particular crime. * * *

To give the police greater power than a magistrate is to take a long step down the totalitarian path. Perhaps such a step is desirable to cope with modern forms of lawlessness. But if it is taken, it should be the deliberate choice of the people through a constitutional amendment. * * *

NOTE ON THE IMPACT OF TERRY

It would be hard to overestimate the effect of *Terry* on Fourth Amendment jurisprudence. The Court not only permitted stops and frisks on less than probable cause; it also explicitly invoked the reasonableness clause over the Warrant Clause as the governing standard. Perhaps the Court intended to limit use of the reasonableness clause and its balancing approach to the area of stop and frisk; but once that balancing process was launched in one area, it became difficult to prevent its application to other searches and seizures. See Sundby, A Return to Fourth Amendment Basics: Undoing the Mischief of *Camara* and *Terry,* 72 Minn.L.Rev. 383 (1988) (noting that *Terry* has led, in time, to a general diminution of Fourth Amendment protection).

Critique of Terry

Professor Maclin provides a critique on *Terry*, and assesses its impact on minorities, in Terry v. Ohio's Fourth Amendment Legacy: Black Men and Police Discretion, 72 St.John's L.Rev. 1271, 1278 (1998):

> After *Terry*, police intrusions would be controlled by a malleable "reasonableness" standard that gave enormous discretion to the police. When this reasonableness norm was applied to street encounters between the police and urban residents, the result was predictable—expanded police powers and diminished individual freedom. One of the flaws of *Terry* was that this shift in constitutional doctrine was implemented without a full examination of the consequences for Blacks and other disfavored persons most affected by police investigatory methods. Moreover, the result in *Terry* provided a springboard for modern police methods that target Black men and others for arbitrary and discretionary intrusions. For some, the *Terry* Court made the right choice. The need for police safety justified the loss of Fourth Amendment freedom. But those that have been the most vocal defenders of *Terry* tend to come from socioeconomic and racial backgrounds that are predominantly free from police harassment. For many Blacks and other disfavored groups, however, the *Terry* Court wrongly subordinated their Fourth Amendment rights to police safety. The Court's failure to treat as dispositive the clear correlation between stop and frisk and the violation of their Fourth Amendment rights only served to remind Blacks and other minorities of their second-class status in America.

Stop and frisk programs have come under considerable scrutiny in recent years. Those investigations tend to support Professor Maclin's concerns. For example, data gathered on police practices in New York City reveal that NYPD officers reported conducting 685,724 stops in 2011, only 12% of which resulted in arrests or criminal charges. See http://www.nyclu.org/content/stop-and-frisk-data. 87% of those subjected to these seizures were Black or Latino. In the face of public criticism, the NYPD has reduced significantly the overall number of stops reported in subsequent years while also achieving modest improvements in success rates, but dramatic racial disparities have persisted. Id.

New York is not an outlier. Public data and investigations conducted by the Department of Justice reveal similar numbers in terms of the numbers of stops and frisks conducted, rates of success, and racial disparities among those targeted.[18]

Do these results raise questions about *Terry*, policies and practices implementing *Terry*, or both? How might you address low success rates and racial disparities?

An Early Application of Terry—Adams v. Williams

The *Terry* decision with its companion cases—Sibron v. New York, and Peters v. New York, 392 U.S. 40 (1968)—was only the first step in the articulation of what the Fourth Amendment permits police to do without probable cause. The Supreme Court's first post-*Terry* effort was Adams v. Williams, 407 U.S. 143 (1972). Williams was convicted of illegal possession of a handgun and possession of heroin after unsuccessfully challenging a stop and frisk. Justice Rehnquist, writing for the Court, set forth the facts surrounding the stop and frisk as follows:

> Police Sgt. John Connolly was alone early in the morning on car patrol duty in a high-crime area of Bridgeport, Connecticut. At approximately 2:15 a.m. a person known to Sgt. Connolly approached his cruiser and informed him that an individual seated in a nearby vehicle was carrying narcotics and had a gun at his waist.

[18] *See, e.g.*, United States Department of Justice, Civil Rights Division, *Investigation of the Baltimore City Police Department*, Aug. 10, 2016, www.justice.gov/opa/file/883366/download; Chicago Police Accountability Task Force, Recommendations for Reform: Restoring Trust between the Chicago Police and the Communities They Serve, April 2016, https://chicagopatf.org/wp-content/uploads/2016/04/PATF_Final_Report_4_13_16-1.pdf; Los Angeles Police Department, Office of the Inspector General, Review of Suspicious Activity Reports, Fiscal Year 2013/2014, Jan. 23, 2015, https://www.oig.lacity.org/audit-and-complaint-reports; American Civil Liberties Union of Illinois, Stop and Frisk in Chicago, March 2015, www.aclu-il.org/wp-content/uploads/2015/03/ACLU_StopandFrisk_6.pdf; United States Department of Justice, Civil Rights Division, *Investigation of the Newark Police Department*, July 22, 2014, www.justice.gov/sites/default/files/crt/legacy/2014/07/22/newark_findings_7-22-14.pdf; American Civil Liberties Union of Massachusetts, *Black, Brown and Targeted*, Oct. 2014, https://www.aclum.org/sites/default/files/wp-content/uploads/2015/06/reports-black-brown-and-targeted.pdf; Plaintiffs' Fifth Report to Court and Monitor on Stop and Frisk Practices, Bailey v. City of Philadelphia (2013) (C.A. No. 10-5952), https://www.aclupa.org/sites/default/files/field_documents/bailey_fifth_report_2-24-15.pdf; United States Department of Justice, *Civil Rights Division, Investigation of the Seattle Police Department*, Dec. 16, 2011, www.justice.gov/sites/default/files/crt/legacy/2011/12/16/spd_findletter_12-16-11.pdf.

After calling for assistance on his car radio, Sgt. Connolly approached the vehicle to investigate the informant's report. Connolly tapped on the car window and asked the occupant, Robert Williams, to open the door. When Williams rolled down the window instead, the sergeant reached into the car and removed a fully loaded revolver from Williams' waistband. The gun had not been visible to Connolly from outside the car, but it was in precisely the place indicated by the informant. Williams was then arrested by Connolly for unlawful possession of the pistol. A search incident to that arrest was conducted after other officers arrived. They found substantial quantities of heroin on Williams' person and in the car, and they found a machete and a second revolver hidden in the automobile.

Williams argued that the informant's tip was not a reliable basis on which to conduct the initial stop. But Justice Rehnquist disagreed:

> [W]e believe that Sgt. Connolly acted justifiably in responding to his informant's tip. The informant was known to him personally and had provided him with information in the past. This is a stronger case than obtains in the case of an anonymous telephone tip. The informant here came forward personally to give information that was immediately verifiable at the scene. Indeed, under Connecticut law, the informant might have been subject to immediate arrest for making a false complaint had Sgt. Connolly's investigation proved the tip incorrect. Thus, while the Court's decisions indicate that this informant's unverified tip may have been insufficient for a narcotics arrest or search warrant, the information carried enough indicia of reliability to justify the officer's forcible stop of Williams.
>
> In reaching this conclusion, we reject respondent's argument that reasonable cause for a stop and frisk can only be based on the officer's personal observation rather than on information supplied by another person. Informants' tips, like all other clues and evidence coming to a policeman on the scene, may vary greatly in their value and reliability.

Justice Rehnquist also held that the search of Williams's person was permissible in light of the safety risks presented to the officer:

> While properly investigating the activity of a person who was reported to be carrying narcotics and a concealed weapon and who was sitting alone in a car in a high-crime area at 2:15 in the morning, Sgt. Connolly had ample reason to fear of his safety. When Williams rolled down his window, rather than complying with the policeman's request to step out of the car so that his movements could more easily be seen, the revolver allegedly at Williams' waist became an even greater threat. Under these circumstances the policeman's action in reaching to the spot where the gun was thought to be hidden constituted a

limited intrusion designed to insure his safety, and we conclude that it was reasonable.

Finally, Justice Rehnquist concluded that the search of the passenger compartment of the car, which led to discovery of the heroin, was permissible as a search incident to arrest.

Justice Douglas, joined by Justice Marshall, dissented in *Williams*. He argued that Williams was illegally arrested because there was no indication at the time of arrest that it was illegal for him to possess a gun.

Justice Brennan wrote a separate dissent arguing that *Terry* should not be applicable to crimes like narcotics possession because "[t]here is too much danger that, instead of the stop being the object and the protective frisk an incident thereto, the reverse will be true."

Justice Marshall, joined by Justice Douglas, also wrote a separate dissent in *Williams*. He observed that the informant had no track record of giving reliable information. He concluded as follows:

> The Court explains what the officer knew about respondent before accosting him. But what is more significant is what he did not know. With respect to the scene generally, the officer had no idea how long respondent had been in the car, how long the car had been parked, or to whom the car belonged. With respect to the gun, the officer did not know if or when the informant had ever seen the gun, or whether the gun was carried legally, as Connecticut law permitted, or illegally. And with respect to the narcotics, the officer did not know what kind of narcotics respondent allegedly had, whether they were legally or illegally possessed, what the basis of the informant's knowledge was, or even whether the informant was capable of distinguishing narcotics from other substances.
>
> Unable to answer any of these questions, the officer nevertheless determined that it was necessary to intrude on respondent's liberty. I believe that his determination was totally unreasonable. As I read *Terry*, an officer may act on the basis of *reliable* information short of probable cause to make a stop, and ultimately a frisk, if necessary; but the officer may not use unreliable, unsubstantiated, conclusory hearsay to justify an invasion of liberty. *Terry* never meant to approve the kind of knee-jerk police reaction that we have before us in this case.

Bright Line Rules Under Terry—Pennsylvania v. Mimms

Another case in the Court's early development of the *Terry* doctrine was the per curiam decision in Pennsylvania v. Mimms, 434 U.S. 106 (1977). There, the Court held that officers in the course of a legal stop of an automobile have an *automatic* right under *Terry* to order the driver out of the vehicle. The Court came to its bright line rule in the following analysis:

> We think it too plain for argument that the State's proffered justification—the safety of the officer—is both legitimate and weighty. * * * According to one study, approximately 30% of police shootings occurred when a police officer approached a suspect seated in an automobile. We are aware that not all these assaults occur when issuing traffic summons, but we have before expressly declined to accept the argument that traffic violations necessarily involve less danger to officers than other types of confrontations. * * *
>
> The hazard of accidental injury from passing traffic to an officer standing on the driver's side of the vehicle may also be appreciable in some situations. Rather than conversing while standing exposed to moving traffic, the officer prudently may prefer to ask the driver of the vehicle to step out of the car and off onto the shoulder of the road where the inquiry may be pursued with greater safety to both.
>
> Against this important interest we are asked to weigh the intrusion into the driver's personal liberty occasioned not by the initial stop of the vehicle, which was admittedly justified, but by the order to get out of the car. We think this additional intrusion can only be described as *de minimis*. The driver is being asked to expose to view very little more of his person than is already exposed. * * * What is at most a mere inconvenience cannot prevail when balanced against legitimate concerns for the officer's safety.

Justice Marshall dissented. He argued that *Terry* requires a nexus between the reason for the stop and additional intrusion. He found no nexus between the traffic violation and the order to get out of the car.

Justice Stevens, joined by Justices Brennan and Marshall, wrote a separate dissent in *Mimms*. He argued that the bright-line rule chosen by the Court could not be supported by safety concerns:

> [Ordering the suspect out of the car] could actually aggravate the officer's danger because the fear of a search might cause a serious offender to take desperate action that would be unnecessary if he remained in the vehicle while being ticketed. Whatever the reason, it is significant that some experts in this area of human behavior strongly recommend that the police officer "never allow the violator to get out of the car * * *."

Justice Stevens also strenuously objected to the Court's adoption of a bright line rule to cover all vehicle stops, regardless of the circumstances:

> Until today the law applicable to seizures of a person has required individualized inquiry into the reason for each intrusion, or some comparable guarantee against arbitrary harassment. * * * [T]o eliminate any requirement that an officer be able to explain the reasons for his actions signals an abandonment of effective judicial supervision

of this kind of seizure and leaves police discretion utterly without limits. Some citizens will be subjected to this minor indignity while others—perhaps those with more expensive cars, or different bumper stickers, or different-colored skin—may escape it entirely.

QUESTIONS ABOUT MIMMS

Are the safety concerns cited by the *Mimms* majority likely to arise so often that the Court is justified in adopting a bright line rule? The dissenters considered the safety concerns overstated; but they did not argue that the Court's assessment of the individual rights at stake was understated. Given the minimal nature of the intrusion, why were the dissenters so upset?

What if the driver of the car *wants to get out,* and the officer (perhaps thinking it the safest procedure) *wants the driver to stay in the car*? Is this an additional seizure for Fourth Amendment purposes? Is the dissenters' position that the driver can do whatever she wants? What if the officer permits the driver to remain in the car, but says "keep your hands where I can see them"? Does the officer have the automatic right to issue this kind of order?

Mimms and Passengers

In Maryland v. Wilson, 519 U.S. 408 (1997), the Court extended the automatic rule established in *Mimms* to passengers. Writing for the Court, Chief Justice Rehnquist balanced the factors discussed in *Mimms*:

> On the public interest side of the balance, the same weighty interest in officer safety is present regardless of whether the occupant of the stopped car is a driver or passenger. Regrettably, traffic stops may be dangerous encounters. In 1994 alone, there were 5,762 officer assaults and 11 officers killed during traffic pursuits and stops. In the case of passengers, the danger of the officer's standing in the path of oncoming traffic would not be present except in the case of a passenger in the left rear seat, but the fact that there is more than one occupant of the vehicle increases the possible sources of harm to the officer.
>
> On the personal liberty side of the balance, the case for the passengers is in one sense stronger than that for the driver. There is probable cause to believe that the driver has committed a minor vehicular offense, but there is no such reason to stop or detain the passengers. But as a practical matter, the passengers are already stopped by virtue of the stop of the vehicle. The only change in their circumstances which will result from ordering them out of the car is that they will be outside of, rather than inside of, the stopped car.

Justice Stevens, joined by Justice Kennedy, dissented. He argued that police officers are rarely at risk from passengers during routine automobile stops and that any "limited additional risk to police officers must be weighed against the unnecessary invasion that will be imposed on innocent citizens under the majority's rule in the tremendous number of routine stops that occur each day." He asserted that "the aggregation of thousands upon thousands of petty indignities has an impact on freedom that I would characterize as substantial, and which in my view clearly outweighs the evanescent safety concerns pressed by the majority."

Justice Kennedy wrote a separate dissent in which he stated that officers should be able to order a passenger out of a car only if necessary under the circumstances to investigate a crime or to protect the officer.

Protective Frisks During Traffic Stops: Arizona v. Johnson

In Arizona v. Johnson, 555 U.S. 323 (2009), the Court declined to endorse a bright line rule when it comes to frisks conducted during lawful traffic stops. The Court instead held that "officers who conduct routine traffic stops may perform a patdown of a driver and any passengers upon reasonable suspicion that they may be armed and dangerous."

Mimms Applied: New York v. Class

The Court authorized a limited investigative entry into a car during the course of a stop in New York v. Class, 475 U.S. 106 (1986). Class was stopped for a traffic violation. Officers peered through the windshield of Class's car to obtain the vehicle identification, but the number was covered by papers on the dashboard. One officer entered the car to move the papers away, and, at that point, discovered a gun, which was admitted against Class at his trial for firearms violations. The Court, in a 6–3 opinion by Justice O'Connor, relied on *Mimms* and held that the officer acted reasonably. The Court held that "in order to observe a Vehicle Identification Number (VIN) generally visible from outside an automobile, a police officer may reach into the passenger compartment of a vehicle to move papers obscuring the VIN after its driver has been stopped for a traffic violation and has exited the car." Justice O'Connor reasoned that "[t]he VIN is a significant thread in the web of regulation of the automobile" and that "[a] motorist must surely expect that such regulation will on occasion require the State to determine the VIN of his or her vehicle, and the individual's reasonable expectation of privacy in the VIN is thereby diminished," especially for a driver who has committed a traffic violation.

Justice O'Connor noted that the Court's holding "does not authorize a police officer to enter a vehicle to obtain a dashboard-mounted VIN when the VIN is visible from outside the automobile," because "[i]f the VIN is in the plain view of someone outside the vehicle, there is no justification for governmental intrusion into the passenger compartment to see it."

Justice Powell, joined by Chief Justice Burger, concurred in *Class*, emphasizing the important governmental interest in the VIN, and concluding that "the Fourth Amendment question may be stated simply as whether the officer's efforts to inspect the VIN were reasonable." Justice Brennan, joined by Justices Marshall and Stevens, dissented. He argued that "the mere fact that the state utilizes the VIN in conjunction with regulations designed to promote highway safety does not give the police a reason to *search* for such information every time a motorist violates a traffic law." Justice White, joined by Justice Stevens, also dissented, based on his doubts that "the governmental interest in obtaining the VIN by entering a protected area is sufficient to outweigh the owner's privacy interest in the interior of the car."

Car manufacturers now place a second VIN plate somewhere secret in the interior of the car—this is a response to the fact that car thieves often replace the visible VIN plate with a fake. Under *Class,* can an officer conduct a search of the car's interior to look for that second VIN plate?

Detention of Occupants of a Residence During Legal Law Enforcement Activity: Note on Michigan v. Summers, Muehler v. Mena, and Bailey v. United States

In Michigan v. Summers, 452 U.S. 692 (1981), the Court held, 6–3, that police officers with a search warrant for a home can require occupants of the premises, even if leaving when the police arrive, to remain while the search warrant is executed. The Court held that such a seizure would *always* be reasonable, given the state's interest in preventing flight, and the risk that persons leaving the premises would attempt to destroy evidence. The Court noted that the detention in *Summers* was less serious than the street stops sanctioned in *Terry* because the occupant was being detained inside his home. The Court also observed that the search warrant provided protection against overreaching by police officers. Does *Mimms* lend support to the result in *Summers*?

The Court applied *Summers* in Muehler v. Mena, 544 U.S. 93 (2005), to uphold a more serious detention—including handcuffing—of a person during the warranted search of the home of a suspected gang member. The Court also found it permissible for the officers to question the detainee about her alienage during the time it took to conduct the search. Officers obtained a search warrant for a premises after a gang-related drive-by shooting based on information that at least one of the gang members lived there. The warrant authorized a search for deadly weapons and evidence of gang membership. Due to the violent gang connection, a SWAT team was used to secure the premises during the search.

The proceedings started at 7 a.m.. Officers found Mena asleep in her bed. After rousing her, officers handcuffed Mena and moved her to a partially furnished garage. While the search proceeded, officers guarded Mena and three other handcuffed residents in the garage for between two and three hours. An INS officer accompanied the officers executing the warrant. During Mena's detention in the garage, she was asked her name, date and place of birth, and immigration status. The INS officer later asked for her immigration documentation. Mena's status as a permanent resident was confirmed by her papers. The officers found some ammunition, a gun, and some gang paraphernalia, but did not find the gang members they were looking for. Mena was released at the end of the search. She brought a § 1983 suit against the officers alleging that she was detained "for an unreasonable time and in an unreasonable manner" in violation of the Fourth Amendment.

Chief Justice Rehnquist, writing for the Court, relied on *Summers* to conclude that Mena's Fourth Amendment rights were not violated by her detention and interrogation.

> Inherent in *Summers*' authorization to detain an occupant of the place to be searched is the authority to use reasonable force to effectuate the detention. Indeed, *Summers* itself stressed that the risk of harm to officers and occupants is minimized "if the officers routinely exercise unquestioned command of the situation."

The Court noted that while the detention in handcuffs was "more intrusive than that which we upheld in *Summers*" it was nonetheless reasonable given the facts at hand.

> [T]his was no ordinary search. The governmental interests in not only detaining, but using handcuffs, are at their maximum when, as here, a warrant authorizes a search for weapons and a wanted gang member resides on the premises. In such inherently dangerous situations, the use of handcuffs minimizes the risk of harm to both officers and occupants. Though this safety risk inherent in executing a search warrant for weapons was sufficient to justify the use of handcuffs, the need to detain multiple occupants made the use of handcuffs all the more reasonable.
>
> * * * The duration of a detention can, of course, affect the balance of interests * * *. However, the 2- to 3-hour detention in handcuffs in this case does not outweigh the government's continuing safety interests.

Chief Justice Rehnquist found Mena's interrogation to be reasonable as well, explaining that it was not necessary for the officers to have independent reasonable suspicion in order to question Mena concerning her immigration status. He noted that the Court had "held repeatedly that mere police questioning does not constitute a seizure." Because the detention was not prolonged by the questioning, "there was no additional seizure within the meaning of the Fourth Amendment."

Justice Kennedy wrote a concurring opinion in *Mena.* Justice Stevens, joined by Justices Souter, Ginsburg and Breyer, wrote an opinion concurring in the judgment.

There are differences between *Summers* and *Mena.* Arguably *Mena* states an overbroad principle. See Saltzburg, The Fourth Amendment: Internal Revenue Code or Body of Principles? 74 Geo.Wash.L.Rev. 956 (2006) ("Suppose that police officers have a search warrant to search a house for a gun belonging to X. They arrive and discover that a Lamaze birthing class is being conducted in a den by X's spouse. According to *Mena,* the officers executing the warrant have a per se right to detain all of the pregnant mothers-to-be and their coaches while the warrant is executed. This is indefensible.").

For a case applying *Summers* and *Mena,* see Los Angeles County v. Rettele, 550 U.S. 609 (2007) (detention at gunpoint of two people found in bed held reasonable even though those detained did not fit the description of those to be arrested: "The deputies needed a moment to secure the room and ensure that other persons were not close by or did not present a danger. Deputies were not required to turn their backs to allow Rettele and Sadler to retrieve clothing or to cover themselves with the sheets.").

In Bailey v. United States, 568 U.S. 106 (2013), the Court set important limits on *Summers.* There, police officers were preparing to conduct a warranted search of an apartment when they saw Bailey leave the apartment and get into a car. They stopped him a mile away from the apartment and brought him back to the apartment while the search was being conducted. The lower court relied on the categorical *Summers* rule—which does not require reasonable suspicion that a resident is involved in a crime—to justify the seizure and detention. But the Supreme Court, in an opinion by Justice Kennedy, concluded that the reasons for the *Summers* rule—to preserve the integrity of the search by detaining the residents—did not apply to a resident who had left the premises and was a mile away when the search began. He also noted that the seizure of Bailey was more intrusive than in *Summers,* where the resident was merely forced to stay on the premises. In contrast, Bailey was stopped in public, placed in a police car, and driven back to the premises. Justice Kennedy summed up as follows:

> Limiting the rule in *Summers* to the area in which an occupant poses a real threat to the safe and efficient execution of a search warrant ensures that the scope of the detention incident to a search is confined to its underlying justification. Once an occupant is beyond the immediate vicinity of the premises to be searched, the search-related law enforcement interests are diminished and the intrusiveness of the detention is more severe.

The *Bailey* Court found it unnecessary to decide how far beyond the premises the *Summers* power to detain residents could extend. Justice Kennedy explained as follows:

> Here, petitioner was detained at a point beyond any reasonable understanding of the immediate vicinity of the premises in question; and so this case presents neither the necessity nor the occasion to further define the meaning of immediate vicinity. In closer cases courts can consider a number of factors to determine whether an occupant was detained within the immediate vicinity of the premises to be searched, including the lawful limits of the premises, whether the occupant was within the line of sight of his dwelling, the ease of reentry from the occupant's location, and other relevant factors.

Justice Scalia, joined by Justices Ginsburg and Kagan, wrote a concurring opinion in *Bailey*. He emphasized the categorical nature of the *Summers* rule. Justice Breyer, joined by Justices Thomas and Alito, dissented, preferring a more fact-intensive approach "based on realistic considerations related to basic Fourth Amendment concerns such as privacy, safety, evidence destruction, and flight."

2. The Reasonable Suspicion Standard

The degree of suspicion required to make a stop is referred to as "reasonable suspicion" by the courts. See United States v. Brignoni-Ponce, 422 U.S. 873 (1975). But what constitutes "reasonable suspicion"? How does it relate to probable cause? What sources of information might officers cite in order to establish reasonable suspicion?

a. *Quantum of Suspicion*

The Supreme Court in United States v. Cortez, 449 U.S. 411 (1981), set forth the following oft-cited test for determining whether reasonable suspicion exists in a given set of circumstances:

> [T]he totality of the circumstances—the whole picture—must be taken into account. Based upon that whole picture the detaining officers must have a particularized and objective basis for suspecting the particular person stopped of criminal activity. * * * [P]articularized suspicion contains two elements, each of which must be present before a stop is permissible. First, the assessment must be based upon all the circumstances. The analysis proceeds with various objective observations, information from police reports, if such are available, and considerations of the modes or patterns of operation of certain kinds of lawbreakers. From these data, a trained officer draws inferences and makes deductions—inferences and deductions that might well elude an untrained person.

The process does not deal with hard certainties, but with probabilities. Long before the law of probabilities was articulated as such, practical people formulated certain common sense conclusions about human behavior; * * *.

The second element contained in the idea that an assessment of the whole picture must yield a particularized suspicion is the concept that the process just described must raise a suspicion that the particular individual being stopped is engaged in wrongdoing.

Comparison to Probable Cause

The Court in *Terry* reasoned that, because a stop was less intrusive than an arrest, it could be justified upon a lesser showing of proof than the probable cause required for an arrest. Courts have struggled with the meaning of reasonable suspicion and with how the reasonable suspicion standard differs from that of probable cause. It is clear, however, that the standards are materially different. There are many cases in which the courts have held that reasonable suspicion existed but probable cause did not. See Florida v. Royer, 460 U.S. 491 (1983) (consent tainted where it was obtained while Royer was under arrest and officers had only reasonable suspicion but not probable cause to believe that Royer was involved in drug activity); United States v. Anderson, 981 F.2d 1560 (10th Cir.1992) (reasonable suspicion but not probable cause existed where the defendant was twice seen leaving a house in which narcotics were sold and parked his car a few blocks from the house, near a truck where narcotics were stored; because the defendant was arrested rather than stopped, the evidence obtained as a result of the detention should have been suppressed).

The analytical framework used by courts in assessing reasonable suspicion is similar to that employed in assessing probable cause. Thus, a court will undertake a common sense analysis of the facts presented. It will give deference to the expertise of law enforcement officers, who may know through experience that certain facts are indicative of criminal activity (e.g., that drug dealers often carry beepers or cellular phones, or speak in code), and will not expect them to be infallible. The court will consider the totality of the circumstances because, while each fact may seem innocent if considered individually, the factors considered in their totality may not be so easily explained away.

The most important difference between reasonable suspicion and probable cause is that reasonable suspicion is a *less demanding standard of proof*—a stop is permissible upon something less than the fair probability/reason to believe standard that defines probable cause. Some courts have defined reasonable suspicion as a fair *possibility* (as opposed to probability) of criminal activity. It is appropriate to think of reasonable suspicion as "possible cause."

A probability-based example of the difference between reasonable suspicion and probable cause is presented by the facts of United States v. Winsor, 846 F.2d 1569 (9th Cir.1988). Officers chased suspected bank robbers fleeing from the bank into a hotel. The hotel had approximately 40 guest rooms, and the officers had no idea where in the hotel the robbers were hiding. The question was whether there was probable cause to search each of the hotel rooms for the suspects. The court found that a one-in-forty probability was too small to support probable cause, but that the low probability did amount to reasonable suspicion: "The odds on discovering the suspect in the first room upon whose door the police knocked were high enough to support a founded suspicion. The odds favoring discovery increase as rooms are searched. At some point, perhaps at the last two or three unsearched rooms, probable cause may be said to exist." Conversely, at some point of improbability, reasonable suspicion would not have existed—for example, if the hotel had 600 rooms.

Because there was only reasonable suspicion and not probable cause in *Winsor*, the court held that the search of the hotel room in which the suspects were actually found was illegal. A search for law enforcement purposes requires probable cause and cannot be justified under *Terry*. What should the police do in a case like Winsor where suspects might be in any of 40 rooms?

Probability, Alternative Explanations, and Common Sense: Assessing Reasonable Suspicion

In *United States v. Arvizu*, 534 U.S. 266 (2002), the Supreme Court rejected as contrary to its teachings a rigid, formalistic, and almost quantitative approach to assessing reasonable suspicion. In that case, the Ninth Circuit identified ten facts in the record that might have provided grounds for a border patrol officer to stop a minivan traveling unmarked dirt roads near the border with Mexico, analyzed each of them individually, found that seven were ambiguous, because susceptible to innocent explanation, and then concluded that the remaining three were insufficient to provide the officer with reason to suspect that the occupants of the minivan might be engaged in illegal activity. Writing for the Court, Chief Justice Rehnquist held that this approach to assessing reasonable suspicion "departs sharply from" the Court's teachings, which instead counsel assessing the "totality of the circumstances" to determine whether "the detaining officer has a 'particularized and objective basis' for suspecting legal wrongdoing." In making that assessment, the Court licensed officers to "make inferences and deductions about the cumulative information available to them that 'might elude an untrained person.' " Conceding that "the concept of reasonable suspicion is somewhat abstract," the *Arvizu* Court steadfastly refused to "reduc[e] it to a neat set of legal rules," echoing then-Justice Rehnquist's description of probable cause in

Illinois v. Gates, 462 U.S. 213 (1983), as a "fluid concept—turning on the assessment of probabilities in particular factual contexts—not readily, or even usefully, reduced to a neat set of legal rules."

The *Arvizu* Court roundly rejected the Ninth Circuit's rigid, atomistic approach to analyzing individual facts giving rise to reasonable suspicion. While clarifying that reasonable suspicion requires much less than 50% certainty, the Court also declined to specify a probabilistic threshold for reasonable suspicion. Nevertheless, the Court allowed that both innocent explanations and probabilities are relevant when assessing the totality of circumstances. This left lower courts and commentators to wonder about the analytic role these considerations can and should play when determining whether a set of facts provides reason to suspect that a person is engaged in criminal wrongdoing. The Court provides useful guidance in the following case.

KANSAS V. GLOVER

Supreme Court of the United States, 2020.
140 S.Ct. 1183.

JUSTICE THOMAS delivered the opinion of the Court.

This case presents the question whether a police officer violates the Fourth Amendment by initiating an investigative traffic stop after running a vehicle's license plate and learning that the registered owner has a revoked driver's license. We hold that when the officer lacks information negating an inference that the owner is the driver of the vehicle, the stop is reasonable.

I

Kansas charged respondent Charles Glover, Jr., with driving as a habitual violator after a traffic stop revealed that he was driving with a revoked license. Glover filed a motion to suppress all evidence seized during the stop, claiming that the officer lacked reasonable suspicion. Neither Glover nor the police officer testified at the suppression hearing. Instead, the parties stipulated to the following facts:

1. Deputy Mark Mehrer is a certified law enforcement officer employed by the Douglas County Kansas Sheriff's Office.

2. On April 28, 2016, Deputy Mehrer was on routine patrol in Douglas County when he observed a 1995 Chevrolet 1500 pickup truck with Kansas plate 295ATJ.

3. Deputy Mehrer ran Kansas plate 295ATJ through the Kansas Department of Revenue's file service. The registration came back to a 1995 Chevrolet 1500 pickup truck.

4. Kansas Department of Revenue files indicated the truck was registered to Charles Glover, Jr. The files also indicated that Mr. Glover had a revoked driver's license in the State of Kansas.

5. Deputy Mehrer assumed the registered owner of the truck was also the driver, Charles Glover, Jr.

6. Deputy Mehrer did not observe any traffic infractions, and did not attempt to identify the driver [of] the truck. Based solely on the information that the registered owner of the truck was revoked, Deputy Mehrer initiated a traffic stop.

7. The driver of the truck was identified as the defendant, Charles Glover, Jr.

The District Court granted Glover's motion to suppress. The Court of Appeals reversed, holding that "it was reasonable for [Deputy] Mehrer to infer that the driver was the owner of the vehicle" because "there were specific and articulable facts from which the officer's common-sense inference gave rise to a reasonable suspicion." The Kansas Supreme Court reversed. According to the court, Deputy Mehrer did not have reasonable suspicion because his inference that Glover was behind the wheel amounted to "only a hunch" that Glover was engaging in criminal activity. The court further explained that Deputy Mehrer's "hunch" involved "applying and stacking unstated assumptions that are unreasonable without further factual basis," namely, that "the registered owner was likely the primary driver of the vehicle" and that "the owner will likely disregard the suspension or revocation order and continue to drive." We granted Kansas' petition for a writ of certiorari and now reverse.

II

Under this Court's precedents, the Fourth Amendment permits an officer to initiate a brief investigative traffic stop when he has "a particularized and objective basis for suspecting the particular person stopped of criminal activity." "Although a mere 'hunch' does not create reasonable suspicion, the level of suspicion the standard requires is considerably less than proof of wrongdoing by a preponderance of the evidence, and obviously less than is necessary for probable cause." Because it is a "less demanding" standard, "reasonable suspicion can be established with information that is different in quantity or content than that required to establish probable cause." The standard "depends on the factual and practical considerations of everyday life on which reasonable and prudent men, not legal technicians, act." Courts "cannot reasonably demand scientific certainty . . . where none exists." Rather, they must permit officers to make "commonsense judgments and inferences about human behavior."

III

We have previously recognized that States have a "vital interest in ensuring that only those qualified to do so are permitted to operate motor vehicles [and] that licensing, registration, and vehicle inspection requirements are being observed." With this in mind, we turn to whether the facts known to Deputy Mehrer at the time of the stop gave rise to reasonable suspicion. We conclude that they did.

Before initiating the stop, Deputy Mehrer observed an individual operating a 1995 Chevrolet 1500 pickup truck with Kansas plate 295ATJ. He also knew that the registered owner of the truck had a revoked license and that the model of the truck matched the observed vehicle. From these three facts, Deputy Mehrer drew the commonsense inference that Glover was likely the driver of the vehicle, which provided more than reasonable suspicion to initiate the stop.

The fact that the registered owner of a vehicle is not always the driver of the vehicle does not negate the reasonableness of Deputy Mehrer's inference. Such is the case with all reasonable inferences. The reasonable suspicion inquiry "falls considerably short" of 51% accuracy, for, as we have explained, "[t]o be reasonable is not to be perfect." Glover's revoked license does not render Deputy Mehrer's inference unreasonable either. Empirical studies demonstrate what common experience readily reveals: Drivers with revoked licenses frequently continue to drive and therefore to pose safety risks to other motorists and pedestrians. * * *

Although common sense suffices to justify this inference, Kansas law reinforces that it is reasonable to infer that an individual with a revoked license may continue driving. The State's license-revocation scheme covers drivers who have already demonstrated a disregard for the law or are categorically unfit to drive. The Division of Vehicles of the Kansas Department of Revenue (Division) "shall" revoke a driver's license upon certain convictions for involuntary manslaughter, vehicular homicide, battery, reckless driving, fleeing or attempting to elude a police officer, or conviction of a felony in which a motor vehicle is used. Reckless driving is defined as "driv[ing] any vehicle in willful or wanton disregard for the safety of persons or property." The Division also has discretion to revoke a license if a driver "[h]as been convicted with such frequency of serious offenses against traffic regulations governing the movement of vehicles as to indicate a disrespect for traffic laws and a disregard for the safety of other persons on the highways," "has been convicted of three or more moving traffic violations committed on separate occasions within a 12-month period," "is incompetent to drive a motor vehicle," or "has been convicted of a moving traffic violation, committed at a time when the person's driving privileges were restricted, suspended[,] or revoked." Other reasons include violating license restrictions, being under house arrest, and being a habitual violator, which Kansas defines as a resident or nonresident who has been convicted three or more times within the past five years of certain enumerated driving offenses. The concerns motivating the State's various grounds for revocation lend further credence to the inference that a registered owner with a revoked Kansas driver's license might be the one driving the vehicle.

IV

Glover and the dissent respond with two arguments as to why Deputy Mehrer lacked reasonable suspicion. Neither is persuasive.

A

First, Glover and the dissent argue that Deputy Mehrer's inference was unreasonable because it was not grounded in his law enforcement training or experience. Nothing in our Fourth Amendment precedent supports the notion that, in determining whether reasonable suspicion exists, an officer can draw inferences based on knowledge gained only through law enforcement training and experience. We have repeatedly recognized the opposite. In *Navarette*, we noted a number of behaviors—including driving in the median, crossing the center line on a highway, and swerving—that as a matter of common sense provide "sound indicia of drunk driving." In *Wardlow*, we made the unremarkable observation that "[h]eadlong flight—wherever it occurs—is the consummate act of evasion" and therefore could factor into a police officer's reasonable suspicion determination. And in *Sokolow*, we recognized that the defendant's method of payment for an airplane ticket contributed to the agents' reasonable suspicion of drug trafficking because we "fe[lt] confident" that "[m]ost business travelers . . . purchase airline tickets by credit card or check" rather than cash. So too here. The inference that the driver of a car is its registered owner does not require any specialized training; rather, it is a reasonable inference made by ordinary people on a daily basis.

The dissent reads our cases differently, contending that they permit an officer to use only the common sense derived from his "experiences in law enforcement." Such a standard defies the "common sense" understanding of common sense, i.e., information that is accessible to people generally, not just some specialized subset of society. More importantly, this standard appears nowhere in our precedents. In fact, we have stated that reasonable suspicion is an "abstract" concept that cannot be reduced to "a neat set of legal rules," and we have repeatedly rejected courts' efforts to impose a rigid structure on the concept of reasonableness. This is precisely what the dissent's rule would do by insisting that officers must be treated as bifurcated persons, completely precluded from drawing factual inferences based on the commonly held knowledge they have acquired in their everyday lives.

The dissent's rule would also impose on police the burden of pointing to specific training materials or field experiences justifying reasonable suspicion for the myriad infractions in municipal criminal codes. And by removing common sense as a source of evidence, the dissent would considerably narrow the daylight between the showing required for probable cause and the "less stringent" showing required for reasonable suspicion. Such requirements are inconsistent with our Fourth Amendment jurisprudence, and we decline to adopt them here.

In reaching this conclusion, we in no way minimize the significant role that specialized training and experience routinely play in law enforcement investigations. We simply hold that such experience is not required in every instance.

B

Glover and the dissent also contend that adopting Kansas' view would eviscerate the need for officers to base reasonable suspicion on "specific and articulable facts" particularized to the individual, because police could instead rely exclusively on probabilities. Their argument carries little force. As an initial matter, we have previously stated that officers, like jurors, may rely on probabilities in the reasonable suspicion context. Moreover, as explained above, Deputy Mehrer did not rely exclusively on probabilities. He knew that the license plate was linked to a truck matching the observed vehicle and that the registered owner of the vehicle had a revoked license. Based on these minimal facts, he used common sense to form a reasonable suspicion that a specific individual was potentially engaged in specific criminal activity—driving with a revoked license. Traffic stops of this nature do not delegate to officers "broad and unlimited discretion" to stop drivers at random. Nor do they allow officers to stop drivers whose conduct is no different from any other driver's. Accordingly, combining database information and commonsense judgments in this context is fully consonant with this Court's Fourth Amendment precedents.

V

This Court's precedents have repeatedly affirmed that "the ultimate touchstone of the Fourth Amendment is reasonableness." Under the totality of the circumstances of this case, Deputy Mehrer drew an entirely reasonable inference that Glover was driving while his license was revoked.

We emphasize the narrow scope of our holding. Like all seizures, "[t]he officer's action must be 'justified at its inception.' " "The standard takes into account the totality of the circumstances—the whole picture." As a result, the presence of additional facts might dispel reasonable suspicion. For example, if an officer knows that the registered owner of the vehicle is in his mid-sixties but observes that the driver is in her mid-twenties, then the totality of the circumstances would not "raise a suspicion that the particular individual being stopped is engaged in wrongdoing." Here,

Deputy Mehrer possessed no exculpatory information—let alone sufficient information to rebut the reasonable inference that Glover was driving his own truck—and thus the stop was justified.

* * *

For the foregoing reasons, we reverse the judgment of the Kansas Supreme Court, and we remand the case for further proceedings not inconsistent with this opinion.

It is so ordered.

JUSTICE KAGAN, with whom JUSTICE GINSBURG joins, concurring.

When you see a car coming down the street, your common sense tells you that the registered owner may well be behind the wheel. Not always, of course. Families share cars; friends borrow them. Still, a person often buys a vehicle to drive it himself. So your suspicion that the owner is driving would be perfectly reasonable.

Now, though, consider a wrinkle: Suppose you knew that the registered owner of the vehicle no longer had a valid driver's license. That added fact raises a new question. What are the odds that someone who has lost his license would continue to drive? The answer is by no means obvious. You might think that a person told not to drive on pain of criminal penalty would obey the order—so that if his car was on the road, someone else (a family member, a friend) must be doing the driving. Or you might have the opposite intuition—that a person's reasons for driving would overcome his worries about violating the law, no matter the possible punishment. But most likely (let's be honest), you just wouldn't know. Especially if you've not had your own license taken away, your everyday experience has given you little basis to assess the probabilities. Your common sense can therefore no longer guide you.

Even so, Deputy Mark Mehrer had reasonable suspicion to stop the truck in this case, and I join the Court's opinion holding as much. Crucially for me, Mehrer knew yet one more thing about the vehicle's registered owner, and it related to his proclivity for breaking driving laws. As the Court recounts, Mehrer learned from a state database that Charles Glover, the truck's owner, had had his license revoked under Kansas law. And Kansas almost never revokes a license except for serious or repeated driving offenses. Crimes like vehicular homicide and manslaughter, or vehicular flight from a police officer, provoke a license revocation; so too do multiple convictions for moving traffic violations within a short time. In other words, a person with a revoked license has already shown a willingness to flout driving restrictions. That fact, as the Court states, provides a "reason[ ] to infer" that such a person will drive without a license—at least often enough to warrant an investigatory stop. And there is nothing else here to call that inference into question. * * *

But as already suggested, I would find this a different case if Kansas had barred Glover from driving on a ground that provided no similar evidence of his penchant for ignoring driving laws. Consider, for example, if Kansas had suspended rather than revoked Glover's license. Along with many other States, Kansas suspends licenses for matters having nothing to do with road safety, such as failing to pay parking tickets, court fees, or child support. Indeed, several studies have found that most license suspensions do not relate to driving at all; what they most relate to is being poor. So the good reason the Court gives for thinking that someone with a revoked license will keep driving—that he has a history of disregarding driving rules—would no longer apply. * * *

And even when, as under the revocation scheme here, a starting presumption of reasonable suspicion makes sense, the defendant may show that in his case additional information dictates the opposite result. The Court is clear on this point, emphasizing that under the applicable totality-of-the-circumstances test, "the presence of additional facts might dispel reasonable suspicion" even though an officer knows that a car on the road belongs to a person with a revoked license. * * * The Court offers a clear example of observational evidence dispelling reasonable suspicion: if the officer knows the registered owner of a vehicle is an elderly man, but can see the driver is a young woman. Similarly (if not as cut-and-dry), when the officer learns a car has two or more registered owners, the balance of circumstances may tip away from reasonable suspicion that the one with the revoked license is driving. And so too, the attributes of the car may be relevant. Consider if a car bears the markings of a peer-to-peer carsharing service; or compare the likelihoods that someone other than the registered owner is driving (1) a family minivan and (2) a Ferrari. The officer himself may have a wealth of accumulated information about such matters, and the defendant may probe what that knowledge suggests about the stop at issue.

Such a challenge may also use statistical evidence, which is almost daily expanding in sophistication and scope. States or municipalities often keep information about "hit rates" in stops like this one—in other words, the frequency with which those stops discover unlicensed drivers behind the wheel. * * * Here too, defendants may question testifying officers about such information. Indeed, an officer may have his own hit rate, which if low enough could itself negate reasonable suspicion.

* * * [I]n more fully litigated cases, the license-revocation alert does not (as it did here) end the inquiry. It is but the first, though no doubt an important, step in assessing the reasonableness of the officer's suspicion.

JUSTICE SOTOMAYOR, dissenting.

In upholding routine stops of vehicles whose owners have revoked licenses, the Court ignores key foundations of our reasonable-suspicion jurisprudence and impermissibly and unnecessarily reduces the State's burden of proof. I therefore dissent.

I

I begin with common ground. The Fourth Amendment permits "brief investigatory" vehicle stops on "facts that do not constitute probable cause." To assess whether an officer had the requisite suspicion to seize a driver, past cases have considered the "totality of the circumstances—the whole picture," and analyzed whether the officer assembled "fact on fact and clue on clue."

The stop at issue here, however, rests on just one key fact: that the vehicle was owned by someone with a revoked license. The majority concludes—erroneously, in my view—that seizing this vehicle was constitutional on the record below because drivers with revoked licenses (as opposed to suspended licenses) in Kansas "have already demonstrated a disregard for the law or are categorically unfit to drive." This analysis breaks from settled doctrine and dramatically alters both the quantum and nature of evidence a State may rely on to prove suspicion.

A

The State bears the burden of justifying a seizure. This requires the government to articulate factors supporting its reasonable suspicion, usually through a trained agent. While the Court has not dictated precisely what evidence a government must produce, it has stressed that an officer must at least "articulate more than an 'inchoate and unparticularized suspicion or "hunch"' of criminal activity. That articulation must include both facts and an officer's "rational inferences from those facts." A logical "gap as to any one matter" in this analysis may be overcome by " 'a strong showing' " regarding " 'other indicia of reliability.' " But gaps may not go unfilled.

Additionally, reasonable suspicion eschews judicial common sense in favor of the perspectives and inferences of a reasonable officer viewing "the facts through the lens of his police experience and expertise." It is the reasonable officer's assessment, not the ordinary person's—or judge's—judgment, that matters.

Finally, a stop must be individualized—that is, based on "a suspicion that the particular [subject] being stopped is engaged in wrongdoing." This does not mean that the officer must know the driver's identity. But a seizure must rest on more than the "likelihood that [a] given person" or particular vehicle is engaged in wrongdoing. The inquiry ordinarily involves some observation or report about the target's behavior—not merely the class to which he belongs.

B

Faithful adherence to these precepts would yield a significantly different analysis and outcome than that offered by the majority.

For starters, the majority flips the burden of proof. It permits Kansas police officers to effectuate roadside stops whenever they lack "information negating an inference" that a vehicle's unlicensed owner is its driver. This has it backwards: The State shoulders the burden to supply the key inference that tethers observation to suspicion. The majority repeatedly attributes such an inference to Deputy Mehrer. But that is an after-the-fact gloss on a seven-paragraph stipulation. Nowhere in his terse submission did Deputy Mehrer indicate that he had any informed belief about the propensity of unlicensed drivers to operate motor vehicles in the area—let alone that he relied on such a belief in seizing Glover.

The consequence of the majority's approach is to absolve officers from any responsibility to investigate the identity of a driver where feasible. But that is precisely what officers ought to do—and are more than capable of doing. Of course, some circumstances may not warrant an officer approaching a car to take a closer look at its occupants. But there are countless other instances where officers have been able to ascertain the identity of a driver from a distance and make out their approximate age and gender. Indeed, our cases are rife with examples of officers who have perceived more than just basic driver demographics. The majority underestimates officers' capabilities and instead gives them free rein to stop a vehicle involved in no suspicious activity simply because it is registered to an unlicensed person. That stop is based merely on a guess or a "hunch" about the driver's identity.

With no basis in the record to presume that unlicensed drivers routinely continue driving, the majority endeavors to fill the gap with its own "common sense." But simply labeling an inference "common sense" does not make it so, no matter how many times the majority repeats it. Whether the driver of a vehicle is likely to be its unlicensed owner is "by no means obvious." And like the concurrence, I "doubt" that our collective judicial common sense could answer that question, even if our Fourth Amendment jurisprudence allowed us to do so.

Contrary to the majority's claims, the reasonable-suspicion inquiry does not accommodate the average person's intuition. Rather, it permits reliance on a particular type of common sense—that of the reasonable officer, developed through her experiences in law enforcement. This approach acknowledges that what may be "common sense" to a layperson may not be relevant (or correct) in a law enforcement context. Indeed, this case presents the type of geographically localized inquiry where an officer's "inferences and deductions that might well elude an untrained person" would come in handy. By relying on judicial inferences instead, the majority promotes broad, inflexible rules that overlook regional differences.

Allowing judges to offer their own brand of common sense where the State's proffered justifications for a search come up short also shifts police work to the judiciary. Our cases—including those the majority cites—have looked to officer sensibility to establish inferences about human behavior, even though they just as easily could have relied on the inferences "made by ordinary people on a daily basis." There is no reason to depart from that practice here.

Finally, to bolster its conclusion as grounded in "common experience," the majority cites "empirical studies." But its use of statistics illustrates the danger of relying on large-scale data to carry out what is supposed to be a particularized exercise. Neither of the referenced reports tells us the percentage of vehicle owners with revoked licenses in Kansas who continue to drive their cars. Neither report even offers a useful denominator: One lumps drivers with suspended and revoked licenses together, while the other examines the license status of only motorists involved in fatal collisions. The figures say nothing about how the behavior of revoked drivers measures up relative to their licensed counterparts—whether one group is more likely to be involved in accidents, or whether the incidences are comparable—which would inform a trooper's inferences about driver identity.

As the concurrence recognizes, while statistics may help a defendant challenge the reasonableness of an officer's actions, they "cannot substitute for the individualized suspicion that the Fourth Amendment requires." If courts do not scrutinize officer observation or expertise in the reasonable-suspicion analysis, then seizures may be made on large-scale data alone—data that say nothing about the individual save for the class to which he belongs. That analytical approach strays far from "acting upon observed violations" of law—which this Court has said is the "foremost method of enforcing traffic and vehicle safety regulations."

The majority today has paved the road to finding reasonable suspicion based on nothing more than a demographic profile. Its logic has thus made the State's task all but automatic. That has never been the law, and it never should be.

* * *

Vehicle stops "interfere with freedom of movement, are inconvenient, and consume time." Worse still, they "may create substantial anxiety" through an "unsettling show of authority." Before subjecting motorists to this type of investigation, the State must possess articulable facts and officer inferences to form suspicion. The State below left unexplained key components of the reasonable-suspicion inquiry. In an effort to uphold the conviction, the Court destroys Fourth Amendment jurisprudence that requires individualized suspicion. I respectfully dissent.

QUESTIONS AFTER KANSAS V. GLOVER

There are a number of important takeaways from the Court's opinion in *Kansas v. Glover*. Foremost is that reasonable suspicion, like probable cause, is fundamentally indeterminate. It is neither quantifiable nor amenable to assessments based on abstract rules. It is, instead, a context-sensitive, qualitative, commonsense assessment. This does not mean that reasonable suspicion is a free-flying balloon, immune from rational constraint. Rather, as Justice Thomas and Justice Kagan describe it, common sense is grounded in logic. In this case, for example, Justice Thomas posits a simple syllogism:

1. If a car is registered in a person's name, then it is likely that he is driving it.

2. The pickup truck was registered to Charles Glover, Jr.

3. Therefore, it is likely that Charles Glover, Jr., was driving the pickup truck.

The Court divides on the validity of the major premise. For Justice Thomas and the majority, the major premise is obviously true; so an officer would only be denied the conclusion if she stumbled on evidence defeating the inference (e.g., that the car is registered to a middle aged man, but the driver is a young woman). Statistical data and details about state law provide helpful, but unnecessary, support for the obvious.

By contrast, Justice Kagan appears unwilling to rely solely on the intuitive appeal of the major premise. She is only persuaded that it holds in this case because of the substantive law in Kansas.

Justice Sotomayor would require that the major premise be subjected to empirical testing because common intuitions may prove to be wrong or unfounded. In her view, a Fourth Amendment intrusion is only reasonable if it *actually* serves legitimate law enforcement interests. Whether a particular intrusion actually serves legitimate law enforcement interests is an empirical question that can only be answered by reliable data and salient experience applied to a particular circumstance.

Who do you think has the better part of the argument? When you go to the doctor, do you expect her to make diagnostic and treatment decisions based on common sense; or do you instead expect her to use her best professional judgment informed by reliable science and relevant clinical experience? Is this an apt analogy?

The Court also appears to divide on whether officers confronted with circumstances that might support reasonable suspicion have a duty to engage in less intrusive investigative measures to confirm or dispel that suspicion before resorting to a stop. The majority does not seem to believe that is necessary at all. If an officer has reasonable suspicion, then she may engage in a stop and has no obligation to choose less intrusive alternatives. By contrast, Justice Sotomayor seems to favor a rule requiring that officers conduct additional, non-intrusive, investigative measures such as gaining visual confirmation that the driver of a car roughly matches the profile of the registered owner. Which view best reflects the text of the Fourth Amendment? The Court's jurisprudence? For some additional thoughts on the potential impact of *Glover*, see Stephen A. Saltzburg, Response, Kansas v. Glover: Just Common Sense?, Geo. Wash. L. Rev. On the Docket (Apr. 13, 2020), https://www.gwlr.org/kansas-v-glover-just-common-sense/.

Glover seems to virtually cast aside quantitative analysis when assessing reasonable suspicion. So long as an officer can cite specific facts and a plausible logical narrative explaining her suspicions, her decision to conduct a stop in order to confirm or dispel her suspicions is likely to clear the low hurdle erected by *Terry*. In a world where data and sophisticated means of data analysis are increasingly available, do you agree with the majority that common intuitions are sufficient to ground decisions to stop, or should we instead require quantitative, data-driven decisions? *See* Kiel Brennan Marquez, *Plausible Cause: Explanatory Standards in the Age of Powerful Machines*, 70 Vand.L.Rev. 1249 (2017).

In their *Glover* opinions, Justices Sotomayor and Kagan suggest that law enforcement agents and agencies should subject their stated grounds for stops to recursive review, discarding those that too often yield negative results. Might this approach provide an avenue to resolve problems with the scope of stop and frisk programs or racial disparities in stop and frisk practices? If data reveals that stops justified by "furtive movements" routinely fail to reveal criminal activity, then are stops based on "furtive movements" unreasonable insofar as they entail significant intrusions on liberty and privacy while failing to advance law enforcement interests? *See* Shima Baradaran Baughman, *Rebalancing the Fourth Amendment*, 102 Geo.L.Rev. 1 (2013). Do you agree with Justices Sotomayor and Kagan that this kind of critical inquiry is what Fourth Amendment reasonableness requires? If so, then who bears the burden of conducting these inquiries? What are the responsibilities of officers on the street?

b. Source of Information

In order to justify a stop, an officer must point to specific, articulable facts, that, in combination with reasonable inferences based on common sense or a police officer's training and experience, are sufficient to provide reason to suspect that the target has committed, is committing, or is about to commit a crime. For a frisk, facts and inferences must provide reason to suspect that the target possesses a weapon and poses a danger to the officer or the public. The facts cited in support of reasonable suspicion may come from an officer's own observations, but must they? Or can an officer rely on other sources of information when developing the reasonable suspicion necessary to justify a stop or frisk?

Anonymous Tips

In Adams v. Williams, supra, the Court held that the informant's tip could be credited toward reasonable suspicion. *Adams* did not consider, however, whether reasonable suspicion could be based on a tip from an *anonymous* informant.

The Court relied heavily on *Adams* and Illinois v. Gates (discussed in the material on probable cause) in Alabama v. White, 496 U.S. 325 (1990), holding that an anonymous tip that was "significantly corroborated" by a police officer's investigation provided reasonable suspicion for a stop. Police received an anonymous tip that White would be leaving a particular apartment in a brown Plymouth station wagon with the right taillight broken, and would be driving to Dobey's Motel with a brown attaché case containing cocaine. The officers went to the apartment, and saw White enter a brown Plymouth station wagon with a broken right taillight. She was not carrying an attaché case. They followed the station wagon as it took the most direct route toward Dobey's Motel. White was stopped just short of Dobey's Motel, and consented to the search of a brown attaché case that was in the car. The officers found marijuana in the attaché case, and three milligrams of cocaine in White's purse, which was searched during processing at the station. White argued that the stop was illegal because the officers did not have reasonable suspicion, and the evidence should therefore have been excluded as a product of the illegal stop.

Justice White, writing for the Court, held that the stop was supported by reasonable suspicion, derived from the informant's tip and the officers' corroboration of that tip. He noted that, under the *Gates* "totality of the circumstances" approach to probable cause, an informant's veracity and basis of knowledge remain "relevant in the reasonable suspicion context, although allowance must be made in applying them for the lesser showing required to meet that standard."

Even given the lesser showing required, Justice White acknowledged that the anonymous tip did not itself provide reasonable suspicion because it failed to show that the informant was reliable and it gave no indication of the informant's basis for concluding that White was involved in a drug transaction. But the majority stated: "As there was in *Gates,* however, in this case there is more than the tip itself." Justice White determined that the corroboration in *White* (i.e., the car was accurately identified and White was going *toward* Dobey's Motel) was not as substantial as that in *Gates.* Yet this was not fatal because reasonable suspicion is a less stringent standard than probable cause. Justice White explained as follows:

> Reasonable suspicion is a less demanding standard than probable cause not only in the sense that reasonable suspicion can be established with information that is different in quantity or content than that required to establish probable cause, but also in the sense that reasonable suspicion can arise from information that is less reliable than that required to show probable cause.

The Court found that reasonable suspicion existed even though the corroboration of the tip was not complete, and even though the tip was not correct in some details. Justice White acknowledged that the officer's corroboration of the existence of the car was insignificant, since "anyone could have predicted that fact because it was a condition presumably existing at the time of the call." However, the caller's ability to predict White's future behavior (i.e., getting in the car and driving toward Dobey's Motel) was "important" because:

> [I]t demonstrated inside information—a special familiarity with respondent's affairs. The general public would have had no way of knowing that respondent would shortly leave the building, get in the described car, and drive the most direct route to Dobey's Motel. Because only a small number of people are generally privy to an individual's itinerary, it is reasonable for police to believe that a person with access to such information is likely to also have access to reliable information about that individual's illegal activities. * * * When significant aspects of the caller's predictions were verified, there was reason to believe not only that the caller was honest but also that he was well informed, at least well enough to justify the stop.

Justice Stevens wrote a short dissenting opinion, joined by Justices Brennan and Marshall. The dissenters argued that the activity predicted by the informant and corroborated by the police (leaving an apartment and driving toward a motel) was completely innocent, and therefore could not provide reasonable suspicion of criminal activity.

The Court applied *Adams* and *White* in Florida v. J.L., 529 U.S. 266 (2000), to hold that an anonymous tip that a person is carrying a gun is not, without more, sufficient to justify a stop and frisk of that person. In that case, police received a tip from an anonymous caller that "a young black male standing at a particular bus stop and wearing a plaid shirt was carrying a gun." Officers responded to the scene, saw J.L., who fit the description from the tip, and on that basis alone conducted a stop and frisk, which produced a firearm from J.L.'s pocket. Charged with illegal possession of a firearm, J.L. successfully moved to suppress the gun as fruits of an illegal stop. That result was affirmed by the Supreme Court of Florida and again by the United States Supreme Court.

Writing for the Court in *J.L.*, Justice Ginsburg, pointed out that the tip came "from an unknown location" and was made "by an unknown caller." This made the tip less reliable than information coming from "a known informant whose reputation can be assessed and who can be held responsible if her allegations turn out to be fabricated." Citing *White*, Justice Ginsburg recognized that anonymous tips may provide a basis for reasonable suspicion if "suitably corroborated," but found no such corroboration in the record. She wrote:

> The anonymous call concerning J.L. provided no predictive information and therefore left the police without means to test the informant's knowledge or credibility. * * * All the police had to go on in this case was the bare report of an unknown, unaccountable informant who neither explained how he knew about the gun nor supplied any basis for believing he had inside information about J.L.

Justice Ginsburg also rejected the government's suggestion that tips involving firearms always provide grounds for a frisk in light of the public safety concerns at stake. While acknowledging "the serious threat that armed criminals pose to public safety," Justice Ginsburg concluded that "an automatic firearm exception to our established reliability analysis would rove too far." She reasoned as follows:

> Such an exception would enable any person seeking to harass another to set in motion an intrusive, embarrassing police search of the targeted person simply by placing an anonymous call falsely reporting the target's unlawful carriage of a gun. Nor could one securely confine such an exception to allegations involving firearms. Several Courts of Appeals have held it per se foreseeable for people carrying significant amounts of illegal drugs to be carrying guns as well. If police officers may properly conduct *Terry* frisks on the basis of bare-boned tips about guns, it would be reasonable to maintain under the above-cited decisions that the police should similarly have discretion to frisk based on bare-boned tips about narcotics. * * *

Justice Kennedy, joined by Chief Justice Rehnquist, concurred in *J.L.* to opine on potential means of corroborating anonymous tips, such as predicting a target's future conduct, prior provision of still-anonymous reliable tips, in-person delivery of a tip, the increased prevalence of caller-identification technologies, and knowledge that making false reports is a criminal offense.

In-Person Anonymous Tips

In United States v. Heard, 367 F.3d 1275 (11th Cir. 2004), an officer saw Heard and a woman having a loud argument at a train station. The woman accused Heard of owing her money. The officer intervened; Heard admitted owing the woman money, and the officer encouraged Heard to pay her. Heard did so and walked away. The officer walked off in the same direction as the woman. The woman then told the officer that Heard was carrying a weapon. The officer then proceeded back toward Heard, telling the woman to remain at the station to make a statement. She instead jumped on a waiting train and was never seen again. The officer stopped Heard, frisked him, and found a weapon.

Appealing his conviction for possession of a firearm by a felon, Heard argued that under *J.L.*, that the tip did not provide reasonable suspicion to stop or frisk him. The government argued that the woman's tip was more reliable than the purely anonymous tip in *J.L.*, because she spoke face-to-face with the officer. The court agreed, explaining as follows:

> A face-to-face anonymous tip is presumed to be inherently more reliable than an anonymous telephone tip because the officers receiving the information have an opportunity to observe the demeanor and perceived credibility of the informant.
>
> In this case, [Officer] Gore had an opportunity to judge the demeanor and credibility of the unknown woman. Gore stated that the woman seemed frightened when she reported Heard's weapon, and Gore reasonably presumed that Heard and the unidentified woman had some sort of relationship—they were arguing over money and Heard paid the woman the amount she demanded. Thus, reasoning that Heard knew the woman, Gore could reasonably conclude that she would have reliable information about whether Heard possessed a weapon.

Heard argued that whatever assurance of reliability was obtained by a face-to-face report, it was lost when the informant jumped on the train and fled the scene. But the court rejected this argument as well:

> The reliability of a tip is considered in light of all relevant circumstances * * *. In this case, although the unknown woman fled the MARTA station, because she and Heard apparently knew each other, she may have subjected herself to reprisal from Heard based on the tip she gave to Gore—which makes her more reliable. Considering the totality of the circumstances in this case, Gore reasonably concluded that the unknown woman's tip was reliable.

See also United States v. Brown, 496 F.3d 1070 (10th Cir. 2007) ("An unnamed [911 caller] who divulges enough distinguishing characteristics to limit his possible identity to only a handful of people may be nameless, but he is capable of being identified and thus is not anonymous."); United States v. Chavez, 660 F.3d 1215 (10th Cir. 2011) (caller "stated that he was a Wal-Mart employee at a specific Wal-Mart store and thereby provided the police with information to discover his identity.").

Inferring Reliability and Basis of Knowledge

In the following case, the Court provides useful guidance on how anonymous tips should be evaluated under the totality of the circumstances approach to evaluating reasonable suspicion. Notice how Justice Thomas's opinion for the Court sets the stage for his elaboration of the reasonable suspicion standard in *Kansas v. Glover*.

NAVARETTE V. CALIFORNIA

Supreme Court of the United States, 2014.
572 U.S. 393.

JUSTICE THOMAS delivered the opinion of the Court.

After a 911 caller reported that a vehicle had run her off the road, a police officer located the vehicle she identified during the call and executed a traffic stop. We hold that the stop complied with the Fourth Amendment because, under the totality of the circumstances, the officer had reasonable suspicion that the driver was intoxicated.

* * *

On August 23, 2008, a Mendocino County 911 dispatch team for the California Highway Patrol (CHP) received a call from another CHP dispatcher in neighboring Humboldt County. The Humboldt County dispatcher relayed [an anonymous] tip from a 911 caller, which the Mendocino County team recorded as follows: "Showing southbound Highway 1 at mile marker 88, Silver Ford 150 pickup. Plate of 8-David-94925. Ran the reporting party off the roadway and was last seen approximately five [minutes] ago." The Mendocino County team then broadcast that information to CHP officers at 3:47 p.m.

A CHP officer heading northbound toward the reported vehicle responded to the broadcast. At 4:00 p.m., the officer passed the truck near mile marker 69. At about 4:05 p.m., after making a U-turn, he pulled the truck over. A second officer, who had separately responded to the broadcast, also arrived on the scene. As the two officers approached the truck, they smelled marijuana. A search of the truck bed revealed 30 pounds of marijuana. The officers arrested the driver, petitioner Lorenzo Prado Navarette, and the passenger, petitioner José Prado Navarette.

[The Navarettes moved unsuccessfully to suppress the evidence on the ground that the stop was invalid because the officers had no reasonable suspicion. They were convicted, and the California Court of Appeal affirmed on the ground that the officers had a right to rely on a tip by an apparent eyewitness victim of reckless driving that was corroborated by the vehicle's location when the officers found it.]

* * * The "reasonable suspicion" necessary to justify * * * a stop "is dependent upon both the content of information possessed by police and its degree of reliability." The standard takes into account "the totality of the circumstances—the whole picture." Although a mere "hunch" does not create reasonable suspicion, the level of suspicion the standard requires is considerably less than proof of wrongdoing by a preponderance of the evidence, and obviously less than is necessary for probable cause.

* * *

These principles apply with full force to investigative stops based on information from anonymous tips. * * * Of course, an anonymous tip alone seldom demonstrates the informant's basis of knowledge or veracity. That is because "ordinary citizens generally do not provide extensive recitations of the basis of their everyday observations," and an anonymous tipster's veracity is "by hypothesis largely unknown, and unknowable." *White, supra.* But under appropriate circumstances, an anonymous tip can demonstrate sufficient indicia of reliability to provide reasonable suspicion to make an investigatory stop.

Our decisions in Alabama v. White and Florida v. J.L. are useful guides. [Justice Thomas discusses the facts and holdings of *White* and *J.L.*]

* * *

The initial question in this case is whether the 911 call was sufficiently reliable to credit the allegation that petitioners' truck "ran the [caller] off the roadway." * * * [Even though] the 911 call was anonymous, we conclude that the call bore adequate indicia of reliability for the officer to credit the caller's account. The officer was therefore justified in proceeding from the premise that the truck had, in fact, caused the caller's car to be dangerously diverted from the highway.

By reporting that she had been run off the road by a specific vehicle—a silver Ford F-150 pickup, license plate 8D94925—the caller necessarily claimed eyewitness knowledge of the alleged dangerous driving. That basis of knowledge lends significant support to the tip's reliability. [Citing *Gates* and *Spinelli*]. This is in contrast to *J. L.*, where the tip provided no basis for concluding that the tipster had actually seen the gun. * * * A driver's claim that another vehicle ran her off the road * * * necessarily implies that the informant knows the other car was driven dangerously.

There is also reason to think that the 911 caller in this case was telling the truth. Police confirmed the truck's location near mile marker 69 (roughly 19 highway miles south of the location reported in the 911 call) at 4:00 p.m. (roughly 18 minutes after the 911 call). That timeline of events suggests that the caller reported the incident soon after she was run off the road. That sort of contemporaneous report has long been treated as especially reliable. In evidence law, we generally credit the proposition that statements about an event and made soon after perceiving that event are especially trustworthy because "substantial contemporaneity of event and statement negate the likelihood of deliberate or conscious misrepresentation." Advisory Committee's Notes on Fed. Rule Evid. 803(1) (describing the rationale for the hearsay exception for "present sense impressions"). A similar rationale applies to a "statement relating to a startling event"—such as getting run off the road—"made while the declarant was under the stress of excitement that it caused." Fed. Rule Evid. 803(2) (hearsay exception for "excited utterances"). Unsurprisingly, 911 calls that would otherwise be inadmissible hearsay have often been admitted on those grounds. * * * There was no indication that the tip in *J. L.* (or even in *White*) was contemporaneous with the observation of criminal activity or made under the stress of excitement caused by a startling event, but those considerations weigh in favor of the caller's veracity here.

Another indicator of veracity is the caller's use of the 911 emergency system. * * * As this case illustrates, 911 calls can be recorded, which provides victims with an opportunity to identify the false tipster's voice and subject him to prosecution * * *. The 911 system also permits law enforcement to verify important information about the caller. In 1998, the Federal Communications Commission (FCC) began to require cellular carriers to relay the caller's phone number to 911 dispatchers. * * * None of this is to suggest that tips in 911 calls are *per se* reliable. Given the foregoing technological and regulatory developments, however, a reasonable officer could conclude that a false tipster would think twice before using such a system.

* * *

Even a reliable tip will justify an investigative stop only if it creates reasonable suspicion that "criminal activity may be afoot." We must therefore determine whether the 911 caller's report of being run off the roadway created reasonable suspicion of an ongoing crime such as drunk driving as opposed to an isolated episode of past recklessness. We conclude that the behavior alleged by the 911 caller, viewed from the standpoint of an objectively reasonable police officer, amounts to reasonable suspicion of drunk driving. The stop was therefore proper.[a]

Reasonable suspicion depends on "the factual and practical considerations of everyday life on which reasonable and prudent men, not legal technicians, act." Under that commonsense approach, we can appropriately recognize certain driving behaviors as sound indicia of drunk driving. * * * Of course, not all traffic infractions imply intoxication. Unconfirmed reports of driving without a seatbelt or slightly over the speed

[a] Because we conclude that the 911 call created reasonable suspicion of an ongoing crime, we need not address under what circumstances a stop is justified by the need to investigate completed criminal activity. *Cf.* United States v. Hensley, 469 U.S. 221, 229 (1985).

limit, for example, are so tenuously connected to drunk driving that a stop on those grounds alone would be constitutionally suspect. But a reliable tip alleging the dangerous behaviors discussed above generally would justify a traffic stop on suspicion of drunk driving.

The 911 caller in this case reported more than a minor traffic infraction and more than a conclusory allegation of drunk or reckless driving. Instead, she alleged a specific and dangerous result of the driver's conduct: running another car off the highway. That conduct bears too great a resemblance to paradigmatic manifestations of drunk driving to be dismissed as an isolated example of recklessness. Running another vehicle off the road suggests lane-positioning problems, decreased vigilance, impaired judgment, or some combination of those recognized drunk driving cues. And the experience of many officers suggests that a driver who almost strikes a vehicle or another object—the exact scenario that ordinarily causes running another vehicle off the roadway—is likely intoxicated. As a result, we cannot say that the officer acted unreasonably under these circumstances in stopping a driver whose alleged conduct was a significant indicator of drunk driving.

Petitioners' attempts to second-guess the officer's reasonable suspicion of drunk driving are unavailing. It is true that the reported behavior might also be explained by, for example, a driver responding to "an unruly child or other distraction." But we have consistently recognized that reasonable suspicion "need not rule out the possibility of innocent conduct."

Nor did the absence of additional suspicious conduct, after the vehicle was first spotted by an officer, dispel the reasonable suspicion of drunk driving. It is hardly surprising that the appearance of a marked police car would inspire more careful driving for a time. Extended observation of an allegedly drunk driver might eventually dispel a reasonable suspicion of intoxication, but the 5-minute period in this case hardly sufficed in that regard. Of course, an officer who already has such a reasonable suspicion need not surveil a vehicle at length in order to personally observe suspicious driving. Once reasonable suspicion of drunk driving arises, the reasonableness of the officer's decision to stop a suspect does not turn on the availability of less intrusive investigatory techniques. This would be a particularly inappropriate context to depart from that settled rule, because allowing a drunk driver a second chance for dangerous conduct could have disastrous consequences.

* * *

* * * Under the totality of the circumstances, we find the indicia of reliability in this case sufficient to provide the officer with reasonable suspicion that the driver of the reported vehicle had run another vehicle off the road. That made it reasonable under the circumstances for the officer to execute a traffic stop. We accordingly affirm.

JUSTICE SCALIA, with whom JUSTICE GINSBURG, JUSTICE SOTOMAYOR, and JUSTICE KAGAN join, dissenting.

* * *

Law enforcement agencies follow closely our judgments on matters such as this, and they will identify at once our new rule: So long as the caller identifies where the car is, anonymous claims of a single instance of possibly careless or reckless driving, called in to 911, will support a traffic stop. This is not my concept, and I am sure would not be the Framers', of a people secure from unreasonable searches and seizures. I would reverse the judgment of the Court of Appeal of California.

* * *

The tipster said the truck had "[run her] off the roadway," but the police had no reason to credit that charge and many reasons to doubt it, beginning with the peculiar fact that the accusation was anonymous. Eliminating accountability is ordinarily the very purpose of anonymity. * * * Anonymity is especially suspicious with respect to the call that is the subject of the present case. When does a victim complain to the police about an arguably criminal act (running the victim off the road) without giving his identity, so that he can accuse and testify when the culprit is caught?

* * *

The Court says that "[b]y reporting that she had been run off the road by a specific vehicle . . . the caller necessarily claimed eyewitness knowledge." So what? The issue is not how she claimed to know, but whether what she claimed to know was true. The claim to "eyewitness knowledge" of being run off the road supports *not at all* its veracity * * * .

The Court finds "reason to think" that the informant "was telling the truth" in the fact that police observation confirmed that the truck had been driving near the spot at which, and at the approximate time at which, the tipster alleged she had been run off the road. According to the Court, the statement therefore qualifies as a "present sense impression" or "excited utterance," kinds of hearsay that the law deems categorically admissible given their low likelihood of reflecting "deliberate or conscious misrepresentation." So, the Court says, we can fairly suppose that the accusation was true.

No, we cannot. To begin with, it is questionable whether either the "present sense impression" or the "excited utterance" exception to the hearsay rule applies here. The classic "present sense impression" is the recounting of an event that is occurring before the declarant's eyes, as the declarant is speaking ("I am watching the Hindenburg explode!"). And the classic "excited utterance" is a statement elicited, almost involuntarily, by the shock of what the declarant is immediately witnessing ("My God, those people will be killed!"). It is the immediacy that gives the statement some credibility; the declarant has not had time to dissemble or embellish. There is no such immediacy here. The declarant had time to observe the license number of the offending vehicle, 8D94925 (a difficult task if she was forced off the road and the vehicle was speeding away), to bring her car to a halt, to copy down the observed license number (presumably), and (if she was using her own cell phone) to dial a call to the police from the stopped car. Plenty of time to dissemble or embellish.

* * *

Finally, and least tenably, the Court says that another "indicator of veracity" is the anonymous tipster's mere "use of the 911 emergency system." * * * But assuming the Court is right about the ease of identifying 911 callers, it proves absolutely nothing in the present case unless the anonymous caller was *aware* of that fact. It is the tipster's *belief* in anonymity, not its *reality*, that will control his behavior. There is no reason to believe that your average anonymous 911 tipster is aware that 911 callers are readily identifiable.

* * *

All that has been said up to now assumes that the anonymous caller made, at least in effect, an accusation of drunken driving. But in fact she did not. She said that the petitioners' truck "[r]an [me] off the roadway." That neither asserts that the driver was drunk nor even raises the *likelihood* that the driver was drunk. The most it conveys is that the truck did some apparently nontypical thing that forced the tipster off the roadway * * * . * * *

I fail to see how reasonable suspicion of a *discrete instance* of irregular or hazardous driving generates a reasonable suspicion of *ongoing intoxicated driving*. What proportion of the hundreds of thousands—perhaps millions—of careless, reckless, or intentional traffic violations committed each day is attributable to drunken drivers? I say 0.1 percent. I have no basis for that except my own guesswork. But unless the Court has some basis in reality to believe that the proportion is many orders of magnitude above that—say 1 in 10 or at least 1 in 20—it has no grounds for its unsupported assertion that the tipster's report in this case gave rise to a *reasonable suspicion* of drunken driving.

Bear in mind that that is the only basis for the stop that has been asserted in this litigation. The stop required suspicion of an ongoing crime, not merely suspicion of having run someone off the road earlier. * * * In other words, in order to stop the petitioners the officers here not only had to assume without basis the accuracy of the anonymous accusation but also had to posit an unlikely reason (drunkenness) for the accused behavior.

In sum, at the moment the police spotted the truck, it was more than merely "*possible*" that the petitioners were not committing an ongoing traffic crime. It was overwhelmingly likely that they were not.

* * *

It gets worse. Not only, it turns out, did the police have no good reason *at first* to believe that Lorenzo was driving drunk, they had very good reason *at last* to know that he was not. * * * They followed the truck for five minutes, presumably to see if it was being operated recklessly. And *that* was good police work. * * * But the pesky little detail left out of the Court's reasonable-suspicion equation is that, for the five minutes that the truck was being followed (five minutes is a *long* time), Lorenzo's driving was irreproachable. Had the officers witnessed the petitioners violate a single traffic law, they would have had cause to stop the truck, and this case would not be before us. And not only was the driving *irreproachable*, but the State offers no evidence to suggest that the petitioners even did anything *suspicious*, such as suddenly slowing down, pulling off to the side of the road, or turning somewhere to see whether they were being followed. Consequently, the tip's suggestion of ongoing drunken driving (if it could be deemed to suggest that) not only went uncorroborated; it was affirmatively undermined.

* * *

Resisting this line of reasoning, the Court curiously asserts that, since drunk drivers who see marked squad cars in their rearview mirrors may evade detection simply by driving "more careful[ly]," the "absence of additional suspicious conduct" is "hardly surprising" and thus largely irrelevant. Whether a drunk driver drives drunkenly, the Court seems to think, is up to him. That is not how I understand the influence of alcohol. I subscribe to the more traditional view that the dangers of intoxicated driving are the intoxicant's impairing effects on the body—effects that no mere act of the will can resist. Consistent with this view, I take it as a fundamental premise of our intoxicated-driving laws that a driver soused enough to swerve once can be expected to swerve again—and soon. If he does not, and if the only evidence of his first episode of irregular driving is a mere inference from an uncorroborated, vague, and nameless tip, then the Fourth Amendment requires that he be left alone.

* * *

The Court's opinion serves up a freedom-destroying cocktail consisting of two parts patent falsity: (1) that anonymous 911 reports of traffic violations are reliable so long as they correctly identify a car and its location, and (2) that a single instance of careless or reckless driving necessarily supports a reasonable suspicion of drunkenness. All the malevolent 911 caller need do is assert a traffic violation, and the targeted car will be stopped, forcibly if necessary, by the police. If the driver turns out not to be drunk (which will almost always be the case), the caller need fear no consequences, even if 911 knows his identity. After all, he never alleged drunkenness, but merely called in a traffic violation—and on that point his word is as good as his victim's.

* * * After today's opinion all of us on the road, and not just drug dealers, are at risk of having our freedom of movement curtailed on suspicion of drunkenness, based upon a phone tip, true or false, of a single instance of careless driving. I respectfully dissent.

QUESTIONS AFTER NAVARETTE

Consider the following facts as recited by the court in United States v. Trullo, 809 F.2d 108 (1st Cir. 1987):

> At 1:00 p.m. two Boston police detectives in an unmarked car were patrolling that portion of Boston known as the "Combat Zone." The Combat Zone is a high crime area known for prostitution and drug-dealing. As the officers were stopped at a light, they noticed a grey Thunderbird automobile stopped on the curb of Washington Street with a man at the wheel. As the officers watched, a second man approached the Thunderbird from the sidewalk and engaged the driver in a twenty second conversation through the open passenger-side window. The second man got into the car and had an additional five or ten second conversation with the driver. The car then pulled out and proceeded for two blocks until it made a right turn onto Hayward Place, a short street which connects Washington Street and Harrison Avenue. The officers followed in their unmarked car. Hayward Place was deserted. The Thunderbird parked on Hayward Place, and the officers parked well behind it with an unobstructed view. The officers observed the driver and passenger engaged in a thirty second discussion with their heads inclined toward each other. The passenger then got out of the car and walked back toward Washington Street. One officer approached the car, ordered the driver out, noticed a bulge, and pursuant to a pat-down frisk uncovered a spring-activated knife. The officer arrested the driver for carrying an illegal weapon, and in a search incident to arrest eleven grams of cocaine were uncovered.

The *Trullo* court held that the officer acted reasonably, citing the high crime area, the officers' expertise in determining whether drug activity was afoot, the short nature of the conversation between the driver and passenger, and the fact that the passenger walked back toward the place where he had met the car (it was "unlikely that the man was seeking transportation."). The court concluded that while it would be possible to "hypothesize some innocent explanation" for the conduct, the test for a stop is whether there is reasonable suspicion of criminal activity, and not whether the facts can be construed as innocent.

Judge Bownes, in dissent, asked the following question: "If a citizen lets another person into his car on Washington Street, where must he let him off to avoid an armed stop by the police?" Judge Bownes claimed that the majority "seems to allow armed stops of individuals who meet in the Combat Zone on the basis of unlimited deference to police discretion." Who has the better of the argument? Do you think Justice Scalia in *Navarrete* and Judge Bownes in *Trullo* are right to deploy concerns akin to those raised by general warrants?

Consider United States v. Rodriguez, 976 F.2d 592 (9th Cir.1992). Officers sitting in a marked car alongside Interstate 8 in California saw Rodriguez drive toward them in a 1976 Ford Ranchero. They noticed that he looked Hispanic, sat up straight, kept both hands on the wheel, and looked straight ahead. He did not "acknowledge" the agents' presence, which they thought suspicious because all the other traffic passing by had acknowledged the presence of the officers. The agents testified that Interstate 8 is a "notorious route for alien smugglers" and that Ford Rancheros have a space behind the seat where illegal aliens can be concealed. The agents followed Rodriguez. They testified that his car responded sluggishly when it went over a bump, as if heavily loaded, rather than with a "crisp, light movement" that was typical of a Ford Ranchero. They also noted that, while being followed, Rodriguez looked often into his rear view mirror and swerved slightly within his lane. On the basis of this information, the officers stopped Rodriguez's vehicle. A subsequent search pursuant to consent yielded 168 pounds of marijuana. Rodriguez argued that the consent was tainted as a product of an unlawful stop.

The court held that reasonable suspicion did not exist to stop Rodriguez, and therefore the evidence was illegally obtained. It first noted that the testimony of the officers at the suppression hearing was eerily similar to that provided in other cases, so similar that "an inquiring mind may wonder about the recurrence of such fortunate parallelism in the experiences of the arresting agents." The court stated that it could not accept "what has come to appear to be a prefabricated or recycled profile of suspicious behavior very likely to sweep many ordinary citizens into a generality of suspicious appearance merely on hunch." According to the court, the factors cited by the agents "describe too many individuals to create a reasonable suspicion that this particular defendant was engaged in criminal activity." The court concluded as follows:

> In short, the agents in this case saw a Hispanic man cautiously and attentively driving a 16 year-old Ford with a worn suspension, who glanced in his rear view mirror while being followed by agents in a marked Border Patrol car. This profile could certainly fit hundreds or thousands of law abiding daily users of the highways of Southern California.

See also United States v. Peters, 10 F.3d 1517 (10th Cir.1993) (where two Nigerians in a Ryder truck were pulled over for a traffic violation, and consented to a search that uncovered no evidence, they could not be stopped later on down the road, on the basis that they appeared nervous when being followed by another marked police car).

In United States v. Manzo-Jurado, 457 F.3d 928 (9th Cir. 2006), the officer saw a group of six Hispanic men and became suspicious that they were in the country illegally. The men were attending a high school football game. The officer testified that he was suspicious because "the group members appeared out of place at the football game." Specifically, "they did not mingle with other attendees, did not appear associated with either high school, and were not familiar to" the officer. The court found that the officer's "unsupported intuition that a group of men keeping to themselves at a football game is indicative of the men's illegal status in this country is not a rational inference that helps establish reasonable suspicion." Is it ever suspicious that a person or group appears "out of place"? What if an obviously destitute person is walking on the street in a wealthy neighborhood?

Reasonable Suspicion of a Completed Crime: United States v. Hensley

Most of the cases discussed above evaluated whether the officer had reasonable suspicion that the suspect was either committing a crime or about to commit a crime. Can a *Terry* stop be made on the basis of reasonable suspicion to believe that the suspect has *already* committed a crime? In United States v. Hensley, 469 U.S. 221 (1985), the Court held that *Terry* was not confined to prospective crimes; the power granted by *Terry* may also be exercised to investigate completed crimes.

Relevance of the Race of the Suspect

The court in *Rodriguez, supra,* expressed concern that an overly broad test of reasonable suspicion could result in a dragnet for Hispanics. Can the suspect's race *ever* be taken into account explicitly in determining whether reasonable suspicion exists?

When the question is whether a suspect matches the description of a perpetrator, then race is frequently relevant. For example, if a bank teller describes a robber as an white male in his 40's, then an officer assessing reasonable suspicion must necessarily consider race when determining whether to stop a person for that crime.

More difficult questions arise when race factors into an assessment of suspiciousness. In these circumstances, stops based on race likely indulge racial bias and may ignore empirics. For example, race should not play a role in assessing whether a man walking down the street of an affluent suburb at 11 p.m. is "suspicious." We should likewise challenge claims that certain crimes are more commonly committed by members of particular racial groups.

The following facts present an example of an officer finding a person's race to be a suspicious factor:

> A St. Paul police officer observed Uber's vehicle at about 2:15 a.m. The officer saw the vehicle again about 30 minutes later in the same area. At that time the officer ran a check on the license number and determined that the vehicle was registered to a person in Moundsview, Minnesota, a suburb about 20 miles from St. Paul. Upon learning this information, the officer decided to stop the vehicle, because he thought the driver was seeking to solicit a prostitute. The Summit-University area, in which Uber's car was spotted, is well known as one where prostitution flourishes. The officer did not at that time see prostitutes in the area, nor had Uber slowed down or talked to anyone.

The court in City of St. Paul v. Uber, 450 N.W.2d 623 (Minn.App.1990), held that this information did not create reasonable suspicion to support a stop. The court stated as follows:

> We know of no authority that requires a resident of the State of Minnesota to have any reason to be on the public streets of another town * * *. No one from any suburb needs to justify his or her lawful presence on a public street in Minneapolis or St. Paul. * * * The officer's assumption that [Uber] was seeking prostitution was an inadvertent, but nevertheless invidious, form of discrimination. We would not tolerate the blatant discriminatory proposition that any member of a minority group found on a public street in Edina [an affluent suburb] had better live there, or be required to stop and justify his or her presence to the authorities. * * * Once we clear away the smoke from this case, it is clear that the stop of [Uber] is premised on the belief that after midnight, Caucasian males from the suburbs are only in the Summit-University area for no good, and that after midnight, no good is all the Summit-University area has to offer. Neither the residents of Summit-University nor the residents of Moundsview deserve the implications of this case. * * * Simply being on a public street in an area where one "might" find a prostitute or a drug dealer does not, without more, meet any constitutional standard for a stop by the authorities. See e.g. Brown v. Texas, 443 U.S. 47 (1979) (defendant's mere presence in a neighborhood frequented by drug users held insufficient to justify a stop).

While a person's race, or the existence of a high crime area, may not "without more" constitute reasonable suspicion, how much more is required? What if Uber had been driving ten miles below the speed limit and looking out along the street? Would such conduct be sufficiently suspicious, given the neighborhood, regardless of the suspect's race?[19] For a case consistent with *Uber*, see State v. Barber, 118 Wn.2d 335, 823 P.2d 1068 (1992) ("racial incongruity, i.e., a person of any race being allegedly out of place in a particular geographic area," could not be considered in the reasonable suspicion inquiry).

Some courts, in contrast to *Uber*, have found it permissible for an officer to consider the race of a person in determining whether the person's conduct is suspicious. These courts hold that, while the suspect's race cannot be the *only* factor supporting a stop, it can be considered together with other suspicious factors. In other words, these courts appear to permit a form of racial profiling, so long as race is not the only basis for the stop. As the court put it in United States v. Weaver, 966 F.2d 391 (8th Cir.1992), a case in which the only African-American male on a flight from Los Angeles to Kansas City was stopped on suspicion of drug trafficking:

> Had [Officer] Hicks relied solely on Weaver's race as a basis for his suspicions, we would have a different case before us. As it is, however, facts are not to be ignored simply because they may be unpleasant—and the unpleasant fact in this case is that Hicks had knowledge * * * that young black Los Angeles gangs were flooding the Kansas City area with cocaine. To that extent, then, race, when coupled with the other factors Hicks relied upon, [i.e., that Weaver came from a source city for drugs, had no identification, and appeared unusually nervous when encountered by police officers] was a factor in the decision to approach and ultimately detain Weaver. We wish it were otherwise, but we take the facts as they are presented to us, and not as we would like them to be.

Should the court in *Weaver* have taken the facts as they would have liked them to be instead of how they were presented? Would it be worth it to hold a person's race to be non-suspicious as a matter of law? Would that encourage the police to be more "race-blind" in their use of the *Terry* power, to subject their "common-sense" to empirical testing, or to conduct addition, non-intrusive, investigation before engaging in a seizure?

What about considering a suspect's Middle Eastern appearance as relevant to terrorism? The court in United States v. Ramos, 629 F.3d 60 (1st Cir. 2010), a case in which the defendants were seized while parked in a van outside a Boston train station, held that officers could take into account that the occupants of the van appeared to be Middle Eastern. The

---

[19] Professor Harris, in Factors for Reasonable Suspicion: When Black and Poor Means Stopped and Frisked, 69 Ind.L.J.659 (1994), argues that *Terry* stops have a disproportionate effect on minorities, even if race is not explicitly taken into account in determining reasonable suspicion. This is because in many courts "an individual's presence in a high crime location plus evasion of the police equals suspicion reasonable enough to allow a stop under *Terry*." Professor Harris argues that minorities, because of where they usually live and how they understandably react toward police, are more likely to trigger these two "suspicious" factors.

stop was made shortly after bombing attacks on trains in Madrid. The court reasoned as follows:

> While in other situations there may be merit to the argument that a description of ethnic appearance is irrelevant and nothing more than impermissible profiling, the argument fails on the facts here. The MBTA attempted to learn from the lessons of Madrid and had so trained its employees. * * * [E]xplicit warnings * * * of future strikes by the same groups in the United States, meant it was material for the officers to consider, among other facts, the risk of terrorist attacks on train stations in major urban centers and that the persons they were investigating had a Middle Eastern appearance. This is not a case about stereotyping or selective prosecution.

The *Ramos* court emphasized that its holding on ethnic-based stops could not be taken too far:

> We wish to be very clear. Just as it cannot be said that the appearance, even ethnic appearance, of a suspect is never relevant, it certainly cannot be said that it is always or even generally relevant. If the events in this case took place at a different time or place or under other circumstances, an attribution of "Middle Eastern" appearance may not necessarily be as relevant a fact.

The *Ramos* court also emphasized that the van occupants' Middle Eastern appearance was not the only basis for suspicion. Other factors included the fact that they were in a van, that they were in a commuter parking lot for an extended period of time without dropping anyone off or picking anyone up, that the van had tinted windows, and that it had a temporary, paper license plate from Texas. Would you have found reasonable suspicion on the basis of the facts independent of ethnicity? The court's reasoning in *Ramos* appears to turn on specific terrorist alerts. Do you think the results would or should have been different in the absence of those threats? What is the predominate racial profile of domestic terrorists in the United States?

Can an officer stop a Hispanic person on suspicion that he is undocumented? In Melendres v. Arpaio, 695 F.3d 990 (9th Cir.2012), the court found that Latino motorists were entitled to a preliminary injunction prohibiting Arizona police officers from detaining individuals based solely on reasonable suspicion that an individual was unlawfully present in the United States. The court noted that "unlike illegal reentry, mere unauthorized presence in the United States is not a crime." Because *Terry* is based on reasonable suspicion of crime, it followed that officers could not conduct a *Terry* stop solely on the basis of suspicion that a Hispanic person is undocumented.

Use of Profiles

Officers often use profiles to determine whether the conduct of citizens is sufficiently suspicious to justify a stop. A profile is a list of characteristics compiled by a law enforcement agency that have been found through experience to be common characteristics of those engaged in certain types of criminal activity. The most common example is a drug courier profile, but officers also employ profiles for other criminal activity, including terrorism. See United States v. Malone, 886 F.2d 1162 (9th Cir.1989) (officer stops the defendant on the basis of a gang member profile).

The use of drug courier profiles was discussed extensively in United States v. Berry, 670 F.2d 583 (5th Cir.1982) (en banc):

> * * * We conclude that the profile is nothing more than an administrative tool of the police. The presence or absence of a particular characteristic on any particular profile is of *no* legal significance in the determination of reasonable suspicion.
>
> Two consequences stem from this holding. First, a match between certain characteristics listed on the profile and characteristics exhibited by a defendant does not automatically establish reasonable suspicion. * * * Any checklist of suspicious characteristics cannot be mechanically applied by a court to determine whether a particular search or seizure meets the Supreme Court's standards. * * *
>
> The second consequence of our holding flows from the first. Although a match between a defendant's characteristics and some of the characteristics on a drug courier profile does not automatically support a finding of reasonable suspicion, the fact that a characteristic of a defendant also happens to appear on the profile does not preclude its use as a justification providing reasonable suspicion for a stop.

The Supreme Court has essentially adopted the *Berry* approach toward profiles. Thus, in United States v. Sokolow, 490 U.S. 1 (1989). DEA agents stopped Sokolow after they learned that he paid $2100 for two airplane tickets from a roll of $20 bills, he traveled under a name that did not match the name under which his telephone was listed, he traveled to Honolulu from Miami and stayed only 48 hours even though a round-trip flight takes 20 hours, he appeared nervous during the trip, and he checked no luggage. Chief Justice Rehnquist wrote for the majority, which found that the above facts, taken together, amounted to reasonable suspicion. The Chief Justice reviewed the facts known to the officers concerning Sokolow, and recognized that "any one of these factors is not by itself proof of any illegal conduct and is quite consistent with innocent travel." But he stated that the relevant inquiry "is not whether particular conduct is innocent or guilty, but the degree of suspicion that attaches to particular types of noncriminal acts."

The Chief Justice rejected Sokolow's argument that the officer's use of a drug courier profile tainted the stop:

> A court sitting to determine the existence of reasonable suspicion must require the agent to articulate the factors leading to that conclusion, but the fact that these factors may be set forth in a "profile" does not somehow detract from their evidentiary significance as seen by a trained agent.

The Court also rejected Sokolow's argument that agents were obliged to use the least intrusive means available to verify or dispel their suspicions—by, say, engaging in an encounter rather than a stop. The majority reasoned that any rule requiring a least intrusive alternative approach would hamper the police in making on-the-spot decisions.

Justice Marshall, joined by Justice Brennan, dissented. He wrote:

> Reflexive reliance on a profile of drug courier characteristics runs a far greater risk than does ordinary, case-by-case police work, of subjecting innocent individuals to unwarranted police harassment and detention. This risk is enhanced by the profile's chameleon-like way of adapting to any particular set of observations.

Overbroad Profile Factors

It is clear that some profile factors relied on by police are far too broad to support reasonable suspicion in the courts. For example, in United States v. Beck, 140 F.3d 1129 (8th Cir.1998), an officer sought to justify the stop of a motorist in part because he was driving through Arkansas in a car from California, and California was a "source state" for drugs. The criteria for considering the entire state of California to be a profile factor was unexplained. Indeed, the officer testified that he considered not only California to be a drug source state, but also Arizona, Texas, New Mexico, Florida, and Louisiana. The court held that the profile factor was far too broad to be useful in a consideration of reasonable suspicion.

> While we do not suggest that geography is an entirely irrelevant factor, we do not think that the entire state of California, the most populous state in the union, can properly be deemed a source of illegal narcotics such that mere residency in that state constitutes a factor supporting reasonable suspicion.

Note that the *Beck* court does not prevent the officer from using the California profile factor in *deciding* whether to stop a motorist. He simply cannot justify the stop by this factor. If the officer had reasonable suspicion to stop the car on other grounds, the use of the California profile factor would not raise a Fourth Amendment issue.

Reasonable Suspicion and Flight from the Police: Illinois v. Wardlaw

If a person runs upon seeing the police, is this enough to justify a stop of that person? This was a question presented in Illinois v. Wardlow, 528 U.S. 119 (2000). Wardlow fled upon seeing a caravan of police vehicles converge on an area of Chicago known for heavy narcotics trafficking. When Officers Nolan and Harvey caught up with him on the street, Nolan stopped him and conducted a protective pat-down search for weapons citing his experience that there were usually weapons in the vicinity of narcotics transactions. Discovering a handgun, the officers arrested Wardlow. The Illinois appellate courts reversed Wardlow's conviction for a firearm violation, reasoning that his flight from the police in a high crime area did not constitute reasonable suspicion. The Supreme Court, in an opinion by Chief Justice Rehnquist for five Justices, found that the officers did have reasonable suspicion under the circumstances, and reinstated Wardlow's conviction.

The Chief Justice analyzed the relevance of Wardlow's flight in a high crime area in the following passage:

> An individual's presence in an area of expected criminal activity, standing alone, is not enough to support a reasonable, particularized suspicion that the person is committing a crime. But officers are not required to ignore the relevant characteristics of a location in determining whether the circumstances are sufficiently suspicious to warrant further investigation. Accordingly, we have previously noted the fact that the stop occurred in a high crime area among the relevant contextual considerations in a Terry analysis. Adams v. Williams.
>
> In this case, moreover, it was not merely respondent's presence in an area of heavy narcotics trafficking that aroused the officers' suspicion but his unprovoked flight upon noticing the police. * * * Headlong flight—wherever it occurs—is the consummate act of evasion: it is not necessarily indicative of wrongdoing, but it is certainly suggestive of such. In reviewing the propriety of an officer's conduct, courts do not have available empirical studies dealing with inferences drawn from suspicious behavior, and we cannot reasonably demand scientific certainty from judges or law enforcement officers where none exists. Thus, the determination of reasonable suspicion must be based on commonsense judgments and inferences about human behavior. We conclude Officer Nolan was justified in suspecting that Wardlow was involved in criminal activity, and, therefore, in investigating further.
>
> Such a holding is entirely consistent with our decision in Florida v. Royer, where we held that when an officer, without reasonable suspicion or probable cause, approaches an individual, the individual

has a right to ignore the police and go about his business. And any refusal to cooperate, without more, does not furnish the minimal level of objective justification needed for a detention or seizure. But unprovoked flight is simply not a mere refusal to cooperate. Flight, by its very nature, is not going about one's business; in fact, it is just the opposite. * * * Respondent and amici also argue that there are innocent reasons for flight from police and that, therefore, flight is not necessarily indicative of ongoing criminal activity. This fact is undoubtedly true, but does not establish a violation of the Fourth Amendment. * * * *Terry* accepts the risk that officers may stop innocent people.

In an opinion joined by Justices Souter, Ginsburg and Breyer. Justice Stevens concurred in part and dissented in part. He agreed with the majority that a per se rule was not appropriate and that the relevance of flight in the reasonable suspicion inquiry depends on the circumstances. He dissented, however, from the Court's ruling that Wardlow's flight in a high crime area was sufficiently suspicious to justify a *Terry* stop under the circumstances. Justice Stevens emphasized why flight from the police might not be suspicious, particularly in minority communities and high crime neighborhoods:

> Among some citizens, particularly minorities and those residing in high crime areas, there is * * * the possibility that the fleeing person is entirely innocent, but, with or without justification, believes that contact with the police can itself be dangerous, apart from any criminal activity associated with the officer's sudden presence. For such a person, unprovoked flight is neither "aberrant" nor "abnormal." * * *

Reasonable Suspicion and Bad Answers to Police Questions

Officers can, in the course of an encounter, approach a suspect and ask preliminary questions. It follows that, if a citizen voluntarily gives an answer that is suspicious, then this will raise the level of suspicion under the totality of the circumstances. For example, if an officer sees a person with a lead pipe walking through a parking lot and looking into cars, the officer can approach and ask him where he is going. If he says "I am going to a museum" and yet can't provide the name or the location of the museum, then the answer raises the level of suspicion; and under the circumstances stated, there is probably reasonable suspicion of a planned breaking and entering of a car. Essentially, the suspect has "flunked" the encounter.

Sometimes, though, officers might think an answer is suspicious and a reviewing court will disagree. For example, in United States v. Hernandez, 784 F.3d 1257 (10th Cir. 2017), officers saw Hernandez walking near a construction zone, at night, in a high crime area, dressed in black clothing and wearing two backpacks. Officers pulled up in a cruiser and asked Hernandez where he was coming from and where he was going. Hernandez answered that he was coming from his grandmother's house and was just trying to go home. One officer asked Hernandez for his grandmother's address, but Hernandez said that he could not remember it. The officer then stopped Hernandez and eventually a gun was uncovered. In supporting the seizure, the government relied heavily on the fact that it was suspicious that Hernandez couldn't remember his grandmother's address. But the court stated that this fact was "not worthy of much weight in determining whether the officers had reasonable suspicion." The court stated that "ordinary experience tells us that a grandchild who knows the familiar way to his grandmother's house may well not know her exact street address." Does ordinary experience really teach us that?

The *Hernandez* court relied on United States v. Santos, 403 F.3d 1120 (10th Cir. 2005), in which the court found that a suspect's failure to remember his mother's telephone number was not entitled to much weight in a reasonable suspicion analysis. Is there any difference, suspicion-wise, between not remembering a phone number of a family member and not remembering their address?

c. *Can a Mistake of Law Give Rise to Reasonable Suspicion? Heien v. North Carolina*

In the following case, the Court considers the Fourth Amendment significance of police officers' mistakes of fact and mistakes of law.

HEIEN V. NORTH CAROLINA

Supreme Court of the United States, 2014.
574 U.S. 54.

CHIEF JUSTICE ROBERTS delivered the opinion of the Court.

The Fourth Amendment prohibits "unreasonable searches and seizures." Under this standard, a search or seizure may be permissible even though the justification for the action includes a reasonable factual mistake. An officer might, for example, stop a motorist for traveling alone in a high-occupancy vehicle lane, only to discover upon approaching the car that two children are slumped over asleep in the back seat. The driver has not violated the law, but neither has the officer violated the Fourth Amendment.

But what if the police officer's reasonable mistake is not one of fact but of law? In this case, an officer stopped a vehicle because one of its two brake lights was out, but a court later determined that a single working brake light was all the law required. The question presented is whether such a mistake of law can nonetheless give rise to the reasonable suspicion necessary to uphold the seizure under the Fourth Amendment. We hold that it can. Because the officer's mistake about the brake-light law was reasonable, the stop in this case was lawful under the Fourth Amendment.

* * *

* * * On the morning of April 29, 2009, Sergeant Matt Darisse of the Surry County Sheriff's Department sat in his patrol car near Dobson, North Carolina, observing northbound traffic on Interstate 77. Shortly before 8 a.m., a Ford Escort passed by. Darisse thought the driver looked "very stiff and nervous," so he pulled onto the interstate and began following the Escort. A few miles down the road, the Escort braked as it approached a slower vehicle, but only the left brake light came on. Noting the faulty right brake light, Darisse activated his vehicle's lights and pulled the Escort over.

[After the car was stopped for having only one working brake light, the officer obtained consent to search, and cocaine was found in the car. Heien argued that the cocaine should be suppressed because it was the fruit of an illegal stop. The trial judge rejected this argument, but the North Carolina Court of Appeal found that the stop was not valid, because driving with only one working brake light was permitted under North Carolina law.]

The relevant provision of the vehicle code provides that a car must be

> "equipped with a stop lamp on the rear of the vehicle. The stop lamp shall display a red or amber light visible from a distance of not less than 100 feet to the rear in normal sunlight, and shall be actuated upon application of the service (foot) brake. The stop lamp may be incorporated into a unit with one or more other rear lamps." N.C. Gen. Stat. Ann. § 20–129(g) (2007).

Focusing on the statute's references to "a stop lamp" and "[t]he stop lamp" in the singular, the [Court of Appeals] concluded that a vehicle is required to have only one working brake light—which Heien's vehicle indisputably did. [The state Supreme Court reversed on the ground that the officer could have reasonably read the state law to require that both brake lights be in good working order. The court reasoned that a nearby code provision requires that "all originally equipped rear lamps" be functional.]

II

* * *

The question here is whether reasonable suspicion can rest on a mistaken understanding of the scope of a legal prohibition. We hold that it can.

* * * We have recognized that searches and seizures based on mistakes of fact can be reasonable. The warrantless search of a home, for instance, is reasonable if undertaken with the consent of a resident, and remains

lawful when officers obtain the consent of someone who reasonably appears to be but is not in fact a resident. By the same token, if officers with probable cause to arrest a suspect mistakenly arrest an individual matching the suspect's description, neither the seizure nor an accompanying search of the arrestee would be unlawful. The limit is that "the mistakes must be those of reasonable men."

But reasonable men make mistakes of law, too, and such mistakes are no less compatible with the concept of reasonable suspicion. Reasonable suspicion arises from the combination of an officer's understanding of the facts and his understanding of the relevant law. The officer may be reasonably mistaken on either ground. Whether the facts turn out to be not what was thought, or the law turns out to be not what was thought, the result is the same: the facts are outside the scope of the law. * * *

Heien * * * contends that the reasons the Fourth Amendment allows some errors of fact do not extend to errors of law. Officers in the field must make factual assessments on the fly, Heien notes, and so deserve a margin of error. In Heien's view, no such margin is appropriate for questions of law: The statute here either requires one working brake light or two, and the answer does not turn on anything "an officer might suddenly confront in the field." But Heien's point does not consider the reality that an officer may "suddenly confront" a situation in the field as to which the application of a statute is unclear—however clear it may later become. A law prohibiting "vehicles" in the park either covers Segways or not, but an officer will nevertheless have to make a quick decision on the law the first time one whizzes by.

* * * [O]ur decision does not discourage officers from learning the law. The Fourth Amendment tolerates only *reasonable* mistakes, and those mistakes—whether of fact or of law—must be *objectively* reasonable. We do not examine the subjective understanding of the particular officer involved. * * * Thus, an officer can gain no Fourth Amendment advantage through a sloppy study of the laws he is duty-bound to enforce.

Finally, Heien and *amici* point to the well-known maxim, "Ignorance of the law is no excuse," and contend that it is fundamentally unfair to let police officers get away with mistakes of law when the citizenry is accorded no such leeway. Though this argument has a certain rhetorical appeal, it misconceives the implication of the maxim. The true symmetry is this: Just as an individual generally cannot escape criminal liability based on a mistaken understanding of the law, so too the government cannot impose criminal liability based on a mistaken understanding of the law. If the law required two working brake lights, Heien could not escape a ticket by claiming he reasonably thought he needed only one; if the law required only one, Sergeant Darisse could not issue a valid ticket by claiming he reasonably thought drivers needed two. But just because mistakes of law cannot justify either the imposition or the avoidance of criminal liability, it does not follow that they cannot justify an investigatory stop. And Heien is not appealing a brake-light ticket; he is appealing a cocaine-trafficking conviction as to which there is no asserted mistake of fact or law. * * *

* * * Here we have little difficulty concluding that the officer's error of law was reasonable. Although the North Carolina statute at issue refers to "a stop lamp," suggesting the need for only a single working brake light, it also provides that "[t]he stop lamp may be incorporated into a unit with one or more *other* rear lamps." N.C. Gen. Stat. Ann. § 20–129(g) (emphasis added). The use of "other" suggests to the everyday reader of English that a "stop lamp" is a type of "rear lamp." And another subsection of the same provision requires that vehicles "have all originally equipped rear lamps or the equivalent in good working order," § 20–129(d), arguably indicating that if a vehicle has multiple "stop lamp[s]," all must be functional.

The North Carolina Court of Appeals concluded that the "rear lamps" discussed in subsection (d) do not include brake lights, but, given the "other," it would at least have been reasonable to think they did. * * * It was thus objectively reasonable for an officer in Sergeant Darisse's position to think that Heien's faulty right brake light was a violation of North Carolina law. And because the mistake of law was reasonable, there was reasonable suspicion justifying the stop.

[The concurring opinion of Justice Kagan, joined by Justice Ginsburg, is omitted.]

JUSTICE SOTOMAYOR, dissenting.

* * *

I would hold that determining whether a search or seizure is reasonable requires evaluating an officer's understanding of the facts against the actual state of the law. * * *

[W]hen we have talked about the leeway that officers have in making probable-cause determinations, we have focused on their assessments of facts * * * based on the recognition that officers are generally in a superior position, relative to courts, to evaluate those facts and their significance as they unfold. * * *

The same cannot be said about legal exegesis. After all, * * * it is courts, not officers, that are in the best position to interpret the laws.

* * *

Departing from this tradition means further eroding the Fourth Amendment's protection of civil liberties in a context where that protection has already been worn down. Traffic stops like those at issue here can be annoying, frightening, and perhaps humiliating. * * * Giving officers license to effect seizures so long as they can attach to their reasonable view of the facts some reasonable legal interpretation (or misinterpretation) that suggests a law has been violated significantly expands this authority. One wonders how a citizen seeking to be law-abiding and to structure his or her behavior to avoid these invasive, frightening, and humiliating encounters could do so.

In addition to these human consequences—including those for communities and for their relationships with the police—permitting mistakes of law to justify seizures has the perverse effect of preventing or delaying the clarification of the law. Under such an approach, courts need not interpret statutory language but can instead simply decide whether an officer's interpretation was reasonable. * * * This result is bad for citizens, who need to know their rights and responsibilities, and it is bad for police, who would benefit from clearer direction.

* * *

3. Searches for Police Protection Under the *Terry* Doctrine

Terry and *Adams* indicate that an officer can frisk a suspect, and pull out objects found on the suspect, if there is reasonable suspicion to believe that the search is necessary to protect the officer or others from bodily harm during the course of an otherwise legal stop. See United States v. Preston, 685 F.3d 685 (8th Cir. 2012) ("Officers may conduct a protective pat-down search for weapons during a valid stop when they have objectively reasonable suspicion that a person with whom they are dealing might be armed and presently dangerous."). One obvious concern is that an officer may use the *Terry* frisk doctrine as a pretext to search for evidence of a crime. Thus, the officer may testify that he felt a fear of bodily harm, when in fact he was looking for evidence without having probable cause. Is there an easy way to distinguish *Terry* frisks from impermissible searches for evidence?

Frisk Cannot Be Used to Search for Evidence: Minnesota v. Dickerson

In Minnesota v. Dickerson, 508 U.S. 366 (1993), the Court reaffirmed the principle that *Terry* frisks are justified only for protective purposes and that a search for evidence is not permitted under *Terry*. The officer in *Dickerson*, suspecting drug activity, conducted a lawful stop and patdown, and felt a small, hard object in Dickerson's pocket. The officer determined that it was not a weapon, but nonetheless continued to squeeze and prod the object. This additional investigation led him to the conclusion that the object was crack cocaine. The officer then pulled the object out from Dickerson's pocket and found that his conclusion was correct. Justice

White, writing for the Court, declared that "the police officer in this case overstepped the bounds of the strictly circumscribed search for weapons allowed under *Terry*." He concluded as follows:

> Here, the officer's continued exploration of respondent's pocket after having concluded that it contained no weapon was unrelated to the sole justification of the search under *Terry*: the protection of the police officer and others nearby. It therefore amounted to the sort of evidentiary search that *Terry* expressly refused to authorize, and that we have condemned in subsequent cases.

See also United States v. Miles, 247 F.3d 1009 (9th Cir. 2001) (officer exceeded scope of *Terry* frisk by shaking a small box found in the outer pocket of the suspect's clothing, where the box clearly could not have contained a weapon); United States v. Askew, 529 F.3d 1119 (D.C. Cir. 2008) (en banc) (unzipping a suspect's jacket, in order to facilitate of show-up identification, was not justified by *Terry* because it was not a search for self-protection but rather was done to obtain information about a crime; therefore the gun found inside the suspect's jacket was illegally obtained).

Suspicion Required to Support the Right to Frisk

Evaluate the following facts in light of *Terry* and *Adams.*

> The officer received a radio report of an anonymous 911 call in which the informant stated that he had seen a woman in a blue car with a white top parked in front of 123 West 112th Street, a high crime area in New York City. The woman had passed a handgun to a man seated in the car with her. Finding defendant in a car meeting the description at the specific location indicated by the informant, the officer ordered the defendant out of the car, frisked her, and took a pistol from the area of her waistband.

The New York Court of Appeals held that while the stop was permissible, the frisk was not. The court reasoned as follows:

> A frisk requires reliable knowledge of facts providing reasonable basis for suspecting that the individual to be subjected to that intrusion is armed and may be dangerous. Here, there was no such predicate either in the information received, which indicated that defendant had given a gun to the man but provided no basis for inferring that she had another or that it had been returned to her, or in what occurred during the officer's encounter with defendant. No inquiry was made of defendant so she neither refused to answer nor answered evasively; no suspicious bulge was perceived in her clothing; no furtive movements were made by her; her appearance and movements were not concealed by darkness.

People v. Russ, 61 N.Y.2d 693, 472 N.Y.S.2d 601 (1984). If you were a police officer, would you have found it superfluous to frisk Russ for a gun after she had already passed a gun in a high crime area?

Most courts have given considerably more deference to police concerns about the risk of harm involved in making a stop. Consider United States v. Rideau, 969 F.2d 1572 (5th Cir.1992) (en banc). Two officers were on patrol in a high crime area of Beaumont, Texas, "where people often carried weapons and transacted drug deals on the street, and where public drunkenness was a recurrent problem." The officers saw a man standing in the road. They flashed a bright light at him. The man turned to step up to the curb and he stumbled. Officer Ellison, suspecting that the man was drunk, got out of his car and approached. Ellison asked the man his name. The man appeared nervous, did not answer, and began to back away. Ellison "immediately closed the gap and reached out to pat the man's outer clothing." The first place he touched was the man's right front pants pocket, where he felt a gun. The officer put the man up against the patrol car, removed the gun, and arrested him. The man, subsequently identified as Rideau, was convicted for illegal possession of a firearm.

Judge Higginbotham, writing for the majority of the en banc court of appeals, held that the frisk was justified because Officer Ellison had reasonable cause to believe that Rideau posed a threat of harm:

> Rideau's specific moves took place after a detention, at night, in a high crime area where the carrying of weapons is common. * * * Stripped from their context, the backward steps offer no threat, but to a police officer in Ellison's situation, they become very significant in the matrix of the general facts. * * * Of course, that an individual is in a high crime neighborhood at night is not in and of itself enough to support an officer's decision to stop and frisk him. But when someone engages in suspicious activity in a high crime area, where weapons and violence abound, police officers must be particularly cautious in approaching and questioning him.

Judge Smith, together with four other judges of the en banc panel, dissented in *Rideau*. He argued that under the majority's permissive approach, Rideau could have been frisked no matter what he did when Officer Ellison approached: if he had moved forward, this would have been deemed threatening as well; if he had moved to the side, this would have been deemed nervousness or flight; if he had remained motionless, it would have been viewed as "abnormal behavior caused by drugs or alcohol." Judge Smith concluded as follows:

> Perhaps if Rideau had graduated from charm school and had been taught how to look "cool and collected" in the face of approaching uniformed officers, he could have managed to avoid the patdown. Otherwise, he was doomed to the intrusion that in fact occurred. * * *

> * * * Rideau was searched not because of anything he did but because of his *status*—a person in a "bad part of town" where, presumably, people do not belong late at night, on the street, unless they are "up to no good." By that measure, almost any person in the vicinity of Martin Luther King Boulevard and Bonham Street that night could have been stopped and frisked.

Arguably, the New York court in *Russ* gave too little credence to an officer's concern for his safety in making a stop explicitly on a weapons charge. Did the majority in *Rideau* give too much?

The Effect of Concealed Gun Permits on the Right to Frisk for Weapons

Terry allows a frisk if there is reasonable suspicion to believe that a suspect is armed *and dangerous.* What if the suspect is armed, but he is legally entitled to carry a weapon? Is the risk to the officer eliminated if state law authorizes the suspect to carry a firearm? The Fourth Circuit, in United States v. Robinson, 846 F.3d 694 (4th Cir. 2017) (en banc), held that it makes no difference whether possession of a firearm is legal, because "[t]he danger justifying a protective frisk arises from the combination of a forced police encounter and the presence of a weapon, not from any illegality of the weapon's possession." The court noted that in *Terry,* the Supreme Court stated that the frisk was lawful because the officer had reasonable suspicion that Terry was "armed and thus dangerous." It stated that the Court's use of "thus" "recognizes the risk of danger is created simply because the person, who was forcibly stopped, is armed."

The dissenters in *Robinson* argued that there is no justification for thinking that a person is dangerous if their possession of a gun is legal under local law. The dissenters recognized that police officers would have a difficult job in assessing dangerousness when a person is legally armed, but argued that the solution would lie in state laws imposing on the citizen a "duty to inform" the police that they have a permit whenever they are stopped—and if a person failed to provide that information, this could give rise to a reasonable suspicion of dangerousness.

The firearm at issue in *Robinson* was concealed, so the question presented related to possession of a concealed weapon. Does the calculus change if a firearm is carried openly in a state where open carry is permitted with a license? Without a license?

Frisking Based on the Type of Crime for Which the Person Is Suspected

The justification for a frisks may relate to the suspected crime that justified a stop. If there is reasonable suspicion to believe that a person is going to commit a crime of violence with a weapon, then there will automatically be reasonable suspicion to frisk that person. On the other hand, if the citizen is suspected of a financial crime, then that fact alone will not justify a frisk. See Leveto v. Lapina, 258 F.3d 156 (3d Cir. 2001) (frisk of person suspected of tax offense was illegal because there was no reason to think that the person was armed and dangerous); United States v. McKoy, 428 F.3d 38 (1st Cir. 2005) (no reasonable suspicion for a pat-down, even though the defendant was in a high crime area, where the basis for the stop was a parking and license plate violation).

Courts have expanded the assumption that certain crimes are weapons-related beyond those crimes that by definition require a weapon (like armed robbery). Thus, in United States v. Snow, 656 F.3d 498 (7th Cir. 2011), officers frisked a person suspected of burglary, even though the person was completely cooperative during the stop and even though the stop occurred during the day in a low-crime area. The court stated that "[b]ecause the facts known to the officers supported a *Terry* stop to investigate whether he in fact had attempted a residential burglary, and because burglary is the type of offense that likely involves a weapon, Andrews' decision to order Snow out of the truck for purposes of a protective frisk was reasonable despite the absence of additional facts suggesting that Snow in particular might be armed." Snow argued that because he was being cooperative, the officers could have simply questioned him about whether he was carrying anything rather than resorting to a frisk. The court rejected that suggestion stating that there was no requirement that officers must take a less onerous alternative in conducting a stop when they have reasonable suspicion that the suspect is armed and dangerous in light of the crime for which he is suspected.

Protective Searches Beyond the Suspect's Person: Michigan v. Long

The Court held in Michigan v. Long, 463 U.S. 1032 (1983), that the power to search under *Terry* can extend to protective examinations of areas beyond the person of the suspect. Long was stopped by officers who saw him driving erratically before he swerved into a ditch. When the officers stopped him, Long was out of his car and he appeared to be under the influence of drugs or alcohol. Long failed to respond to initial requests that he produce a license and registration and then began to walk toward the passenger compartment of his car. An officer flashed a light into the car and saw a hunting knife. A protective search for weapons was conducted in the passenger compartment and marijuana was found and seized.

Justice O'Connor's opinion for the Court reasoned that *Terry* permits a limited examination of an area from which a person, who police reasonably believe is dangerous, might gain control of a weapon. While

Long may not have been able to reach a weapon *during* the stop, Justice O'Connor explained that because a stop is only a temporary intrusion, the suspect "will be permitted to reenter his automobile, and he will then have access to any weapons inside." Thus the officers had a legitimate concern that Long might gain access to a weapon, and use it on the officers, *once he returned to his car after the stop was completed*. Accordingly, it was permissible under the circumstances for the officers to do a cursory inspection of areas in the car from which a weapon could be quickly obtained after the stop was over.[20] Thus while the doctrine is called "stop and frisk", *Long* permits a protective search beyond the suspect's person. After *Long* the more accurate description of *Terry* is "stop and protective search."

The New York Court of Appeals, in People v. Torres, 74 N.Y.2d 224, 544 N.Y.S.2d 796 (1989), rejected the reasoning in *Long* as a matter of state constitutional law. The *Torres* court declared:

> [I]t is unrealistic to assume, as the Supreme Court did in Michigan v. Long, that having been stopped and questioned without incident, a suspect who is about to be released and permitted to proceed on his way would, upon reentry into his vehicle, reach for a concealed weapon and threaten the departing police officer's safety. Certainly, such a far-fetched scenario is an insufficient basis upon which to predicate the substantial intrusion that occurred here.

Is it "far-fetched" to believe that a suspect could present a risk of harm to the officer in a post-stop situation? Would you think it far-fetched if you were a police officer?

Applying Michigan v. Long

Is it reasonable to assume that those suspected of drug dealing *always* present a risk of harm to the officer when stopped, justifying a protective search of areas that the suspect could reach after a stop? In United States v. Brown, 913 F.2d 570 (8th Cir.1990), the court relied on *Long* to uphold a search of a locked glove compartment when the officers had reasonable suspicion of drug activity. The court concluded that "since weapons and violence are frequently associated with drug transactions, the officers reasonably believed that the individuals with whom they were dealing were armed and dangerous." Is there now a per se rule that a search of a passenger compartment for weapons can be conducted upon reasonable suspicion to believe the driver is a drug dealer? See also United States v. Sakyi, 160 F.3d 164 (4th Cir.1998) (finding it permissible to frisk all

---

[20] Justice Blackmun concurred in part and in the judgment. Justice Brennan, joined by Justice Marshall, and Justice Stevens filed dissenting opinions.

occupants of a car after a cigar box of marijuana was found in the car; court reasons that "guns often accompany drugs").

For interesting questions about the scope of a search under *Long,* see United States v. McGregor, 650 F.3d 813 (1st Cir. 2011). Officers had reasonable suspicion that gang members in a car were going to commit an act of reprisal after one of their members was shot. The officers pulled the car over, frisked the suspects, but found nothing. Nor was there any weapon lying about in the car. But Officer Feeney saw a magnet that he had been trained to suspect as part of a weapons "hide"—which is a series of programmed signals that will open up a secret compartment where a weapon could be hidden. The officer, using his expertise, figured out how the "hide" worked, described by the court as follows:

> Put the key in the ignition, fasten a seatbelt, switch on the cruise control, turn on the rear-window defroster, tug on the emergency brake, move the ceiling-light switch to the middle position, move a magnet around a spot on the dashboard (which would trigger a magnetic switch behind the dashboard), and press the sunroof button—doing this activates a series of switches, which starts up a motor under the center console, which opens up the hide so one can reach right through the bottom of the console and into a secret compartment. Feeney did the steps and found [a] round of ammo tucked inside the hide.

The court held that Officer Feeney's inspection of the car and finding of the "hide" was permissible under *Long* because "McGregor and his buddies could have grabbed the weapon from the console hide in a flash had they gotten back into the car." Feeney had testified that the process took about 20 seconds. Is that within the post-stop parameters of *Long*?

The *Long* rationale is not limited to protective searches of cars. Thus, in United States v. Johnson, 932 F.2d 1068 (5th Cir.1991), the court upheld a cursory inspection of a pair of overalls located a few feet away from a suspect who appeared to be attempting to burglarize a house. The court found that merely separating the suspect from his effects during the stop would not provide sufficient protection to the officers, because if the stop was terminated without an arrest, the officers would have to return the property to the suspect.

Protective Searches of Persons Other than the Suspect

In the course of detaining suspects either by a stop or an arrest, officers are often confronted with whether they can frisk persons other than the suspect. In Ybarra v. Illinois, 444 U.S. 85 (1979), the Court refused to uphold the frisk of a patron of a bar who happened to be present when the police arrived to conduct a search of the bar pursuant to a valid search warrant. The Court noted that the patron's mere presence in the bar was not enough to provide a reasonable belief that he posed a risk of harm to the officers, and that no specific facts were shown to indicate that Ybarra was armed and dangerous.

How much information does an officer need, other than mere presence, to support a frisk of a person in the vicinity of an arrest? See United States v. Reid, 997 F.2d 1576 (D.C.Cir.1993) (defendant could be frisked after officers saw him exit from a suspected crack house that they were about to search: "Common sense suggests that there is a much greater likelihood that a person found in a small private residence containing drugs will be involved in the drug activity occurring there than an individual who happens to be in a public tavern where the bartender is suspected of possessing drugs.").

Inspecting Objects During the Course of a Protective Frisk

Assume that an officer has properly stopped a person and has reasonable suspicion to believe that the person is armed and dangerous. The officer then conducts a pat-down and feels an object inside the suspect's coat. Can the officer pull the object out and inspect it? Under *Dickerson*, the answer is that the officer can inspect the object only if it is reasonably likely to be a weapon—*Terry* does not justify a search for evidence. But sometimes there is a dispute about whether an object felt by the officer during a pat-down could reasonably be a weapon.

A case in point is United States v. Swann, 149 F.3d 271 (4th Cir.1998). Officers responded to a report of a theft of a wallet in an office building. Witness reports indicated that the thief had been detained by employees, but broke free and tossed the wallet in the direction of three black males standing near the elevator. One of the men retrieved the wallet and all three men fled the scene. An officer spotted two black males in the basement parking garage. According to the officer, they appeared "really nervous and uneasy and kind of edgy; didn't want to hang around." When the officer told them that he needed to speak with them, one of them tried to circle around him to get behind his back. The officer felt threatened by this action and called for back-up. When another officer arrived, the men were patted down. The officer patting down Swann found a hard object in Swann's left sock. The officer pulled it out and it turned out to be five credit cards belonging to the victim of the theft.

Swann moved to suppress the credit cards on the ground that *Terry* did not permit the officer to inspect the object found in his sock. But the court disagreed, concluding that a reasonable officer "could justifiably have believed that the item was a weapon." The court elaborated:

> [T]he object in Swann's sock was approximately the same size and shape as a box cutter with a sharp blade, which is often used as a weapon.

> The location of the object in the sock, as well as its hard character and its shape, made it suspicious. A similarly shaped hard object in Swann's pocket surely would have raised no alarms, as there could be innumerable innocent explanations for it. And a hard rectangular object in one's sock might not be suspicious on a jogger or someone similarly dressed. But these men were both fully dressed, and Swann's pants had pockets that could have contained an item of that size and shape.
>
> * * * Officers making *Terry* stops must make quick decisions as to how to protect themselves and others from possible danger. Were we to disapprove of Officer Martin's actions, we would require an officer to allow a suspicious object to remain within easy reach of demonstrably nervous and potentially aggressive subjects. Our respect for the privacy rights of citizens does not require such an increase in the danger that police officers must face.

Why is it relevant that Swann had pockets and yet decided to use his sock as a storage space? Does that fact indicate that he was trying to hide a weapon? Or rather that he was trying to hide evidence of a crime? Would the result in *Swann* change if the object in Swann's sock was soft to the touch?

Protective Sweeps: Maryland v. Buie

In Maryland v. Buie, 494 U.S. 325 (1990), the Court considered the legality of a "protective sweep," which it defined as a "quick and limited search of a premises, incident to an arrest and conducted to protect the safety of police officers or others." Officers had probable cause to believe that Buie and an associate committed an armed robbery. They arrested Buie at his home, and conducted a protective sweep of the premises. During the sweep, the officers discovered clothing that tied Buie to the robbery. At the time of the sweep, the officers had reasonable suspicion, but not probable cause, to believe that a dangerous person such as Buie's associate might be hiding in the premises. Buie argued that a protective sweep could not be conducted in the absence of probable cause to believe that there were individuals on the premises who would harm the officers or others. But the Court, by a 7–2 vote, rejected Buie's argument. Justice White, writing for the majority, relied heavily on *Terry* and *Long* to find that a protective sweep could be justified by an officer's reasonable suspicion "that the area swept harbored an individual posing danger to the officer or others." According to Justice White, the reasonable suspicion standard was an appropriate balance between the arrestee's remaining privacy interest in the home and the officer's interest in safety. Justice White emphasized that a protective sweep is a relatively limited intrusion because it "may extend only to a cursory inspection of those spaces where a person may be found," and the sweep can last "no longer than is necessary to dispel the reasonable suspicion of danger." Justice Stevens concurred to emphasize that a protective sweep could only be conducted for safety purposes, not to prevent destruction of evidence.[21] Justice Brennan, joined by Justice Marshall, dissented and noted his continuing criticism "of the emerging tendency on the part of the Court to convert the *Terry* decision from a narrow exception into one that swallows the general rule that searches are 'reasonable' only if based upon probable cause."

Compare *Buie* with United States v. Colbert, 76 F.3d 773 (6th Cir.1996), where the court found that a protective sweep after an arrest was not permitted where there was no indication that anyone other than the arrestee was on the premises: "The facts upon which officers may justify a *Buie* protective sweep are those facts giving rise to a suspicion of danger from attack by a third party during the arrest, not the dangerousness of the arrested individual."

Note that the protective sweep allows a search for *people*, not evidence. Therefore it is limited in scope to areas in which a person could reasonably be. See United States v. Alatorre, 863 F.3d 810 (8th Cir. 2017) ("The Task Force conducted its protective sweep in a constitutional manner because it lasted only two minutes and was confined to places large enough to hide a person.").

Protective Sweep Other than During an Arrest

Courts have held that the self-protective principles of *Buie* and *Terry* can permit a protective sweep *even when no arrest is involved.* That is, if officers are lawfully on a premises and have reasonable suspicion to believe there are persons on the scene who may pose a danger, then they may be permitted to conduct a protective sweep. See, e.g., United States v. Gould, 364 F.3d 578 (5th Cir. 2004) (en banc), in which officers were given consent to search a particular room in a home. They were concerned, under the circumstances, that they might be walking into a trap, so conducted a cursory sweep of the entire house. The court found this to be reasonable.

> We decline to adopt any across-the-board rule that a protective sweep can never be valid where the initial entry to the home is pursuant to consent, even where the consent does not of itself legally authorize the entry into the area swept. Any such rule either would require officers to forego any and all consent entries or would prevent them, once having so entered, from taking reasonable, minimally intrusive, means for self-protection when reasonable suspicion of danger of

[21] See United States v. Hogan, 38 F.3d 1148 (10th Cir.1994) ("[I]t appears that once inside Hogan's property, officers went on a fishing expedition for evidence linking Hogan to the murder. This greatly exceeded the permissible scope of a protective sweep.").

ambush arises. * * * [W]e hold that the Fourth Amendment imposes no such Hobson's choice.

4. Brief and Limited Detentions: The Line Between "Stop" and "Arrest"

The line between a casual encounter outside the scope of Fourth Amendment regulation and the seizure of a person is marked by the "freedom to leave" test from *Mendenhall* or the physical contact test from *Torres*. But *Terry* teaches us that seizures of persons can take two forms: stops and arrests. These two forms of Fourth Amendment seizure are distinguished by the degree of suspicion required (reasonable suspicion versus probable cause), the degree of intrusion licensed (brief detention versus full custody), and whether review by a magistrate is mandated ("no" in the case of stops versus "yes" in the case of arrests).[22] Given these differences, it is important to know where the line between stops and arrests is drawn. When must an officer be able to show probable cause rather than reasonable suspicion to justify a seizure? Looking forward a bit, when can an officer conduct a search incident to arrest? When does a person seized have the right to a *Gerstein* hearing?

Some cases are clear. If a suspect is handcuffed, told he is under arrest, read his *Miranda* rights, taken to a police station in the back of a patrol car, and put through a standard booking process, then he most likely has been arrested. The arresting officers would therefore be required to show probable cause and the arrestee would be entitled under *Gerstein* to a prompt hearing before a magistrate. By contrast, if an officer hails someone whose conduct suggests that he may be reconnoitering a location in contemplation of a robbery, asks him his business, receives a perfectly plausible and innocent response, and then bids him a good day, then we are probably looking at a mere stop, which requires only reasonable suspicion and does not trigger a right to magisterial review. But what about cases in the middle? What if an officer uses physical force to detain a suspect? What if she draws her gun? Can forced movement or the length of detention convert a stop into an arrest? This section considers these and other factors that may be relevant when determining whether a seizure is a stop or an arrest.

a. *Applications of Physical Force*

A traditional arrest is sometimes accompanied by the officer's use of physical force including holds or handcuffs. Might the use of physical force and other coercive tactics mark the line between stop and arrest? Torres v. Madrid, 141 S.Ct. 989 (2021), which we discussed earlier in this Chapter,

[22] As we shall see in Chapter 3, the line between stops and arrests may also matter when determining whether a person is in "custody" for purposes of *Miranda v. Arizona*, 384 U.S. 436 (1966).

might be read as suggesting that the answer is "yes." Recall that, in that case, the Court relied on common law arrest cases to hold that the application of physical force to the body of a person with the objective intent to restrain constitutes a "seizure" for purposes of the Fourth Amendment. Does this mean that all seizures accomplished by the application of physical force are "arrests" and that "stops" are limited to seizures by non-physical shows of authority?

Although the *Torres* Court does not squarely address this question, the answer must be "no." Courts have long held that officers may use reasonable physical force in the context of a stop. See, e.g., United States v. Merkley, 988 F.2d 1062 (10th Cir.1993) ("because safety may require the police to freeze temporarily a potentially dangerous situation, both the display of firearms and the use of handcuffs may be part of a reasonable *Terry* stop"; use of such tactics was found permissible in this case where the defendant was suspected of threatening to kill someone). Many, if not most, stops entail some degree of force, even if it is only a firm hand on the arm—as was the case in *Terry*. A substantial proportion of stops also include frisks, which by their nature entail the application of physical force with intent to restrain. Yet, the vast majority of stops and frisks result in neither criminal charges nor the discovery of evidence, and the person targeted walks away. There is no indication in *Torres* that the Court meant to reclassify literally millions of such interactions as "arrests." Still, the use of coercive methods, including physical force, is a factor to consider when marking the line between stops and arrests. Where should that line be drawn?

In United States v. Alexander, 907 F.2d 269 (2d Cir.1990), the court held that officers acted reasonably under *Terry* when they unholstered their guns to detain two men suspected of purchasing drugs. The two men were in a Jaguar at 6:00 p.m., parked in an area known for drug activity. The court emphasized the "dangerous nature of the drug trade and the genuine need of law enforcement agents to protect themselves from the deadly threat it may pose." Has the court established a per se rule for those who are reasonably suspected of drug activity? Compare United States v. Novak, 870 F.2d 1345 (7th Cir.1989), where nine law enforcement officers working in an airport stopped two suspected drug couriers. One officer drew her gun and pointed it directly at one suspect's head at close range. The court found that an arrest had occurred. The action was clearly excessive given the fact that the suspects had just deplaned and could not have been carrying weapons.

b. Forced Movement of the Suspect to a Custodial Area

In Florida v. Royer, supra, Royer was taken from the public area of an airport into a small room, where the officers sought and obtained Royer's consent to search his luggage. The plurality in *Royer* held that the consent was invalid because it was obtained as the result of an arrest without probable cause. Justice White, writing for the plurality, explained:

> [A]t the time Royer produced the key to his suitcase, the detention to which he was then subjected was a more serious intrusion on his personal liberty than is allowable on mere suspicion of criminal activity.
>
> By the time Royer was informed that the officers wished to examine his luggage, he had identified himself when approached by the officers and had attempted to explain the discrepancy between the name shown on his identification and the name under which he had purchased his ticket and identified his luggage. The officers were not satisfied, for they informed him they were narcotics agents and had reason to believe that he was carrying illegal drugs. They requested him to accompany them to the police room. Royer went with them. He found himself in a small room—a large closet—equipped with a desk and two chairs. He was alone with two police officers who again told him that they thought he was carrying narcotics. He also found that the officers, without his consent, had retrieved his checked luggage from the airlines. What had begun as a consensual inquiry in a public place had escalated into an investigatory procedure in a police interrogation room, where the police, unsatisfied with previous explanations, sought to confirm their suspicions. The officers had Royer's ticket, they had his identification, and they had seized his luggage. Royer was never informed that he was free to board his plane if he so chose, and he reasonably believed that he was being detained. * * * As a practical matter, Royer was under arrest. * * *

Justice White noted that some forced movements of a suspect might be justifiable during a *Terry* stop; he emphasized, however, that probable cause is required if the officer forces the suspect to move in order to further the investigation or to place more pressure on the suspect:

> [T]here are undoubtedly reasons of safety and security that would justify moving a suspect from one location to another during an investigatory detention, such as from an airport concourse to a more private area. There is no indication in this case that such reasons prompted the officers to transfer the site of the encounter from the concourse to the interrogation room. It appears, rather, that the primary interest of the officers was not in having an extended conversation with Royer but in the contents of his luggage, a matter which the officers did not pursue orally with Royer until after the encounter was relocated to the police room.

Justice Blackmun dissented, arguing that Royer was only detained for 15 minutes, the officers were polite, and the intrusion was minimal. He concluded that Royer was only stopped, not arrested, when he gave consent to the luggage search.

Justice Rehnquist, joined by Chief Justice Burger and Justice O'Connor, also dissented, arguing as follows:

> Would it have been more "reasonable" to interrogate Royer about the contents of his suitcases, and to seek his permission to open the suitcases when they were retrieved, in the busy main concourse of the Miami Airport, rather than to find a room off the concourse where the confrontation would surely be less embarrassing to Royer? If the room had been large and spacious, rather than small, if it had possessed three chairs rather than two, would the officers' conduct have been made reasonable by these facts?

Is Justice Rehnquist asking the right question here? Are the factors he cites relevant to assessing the reasonableness of the officers' conduct or do they instead bear on the degree and nature of the intrusion and the objective purpose of the officers? See United States v. Ricardo D., 912 F.2d 337 (9th Cir.1990) (taking person by the arm and placing him in squad car for questioning held impermissible under *Terry*, where there was no showing that the police procedure was "necessary for safety or security reasons"); United States v. Wrensford, 866 F.3d 76 (3d Cir. 2017) ("The line between an investigative stop and a de facto arrest was certainly crossed when the police forcibly removed Wrensford from a place he was entitled to be and transported him to a police station * * * to question him.").

c. *Forced Movement for Identification Purposes*

In *Royer*, the Court held that an arrest occurred when Royer was forcibly moved to a custodial atmosphere for purposes of extracting consent to search for evidence of a crime. The Court noted, however, that an officer can, within the confines of a *Terry* stop, force the suspect to move for purposes of safety and security. Are there any other legitimate reasons to force a suspect to move without probable cause to arrest? Many courts have found that if reasonable suspicion exists, it is permissible to transport the suspect a short distance for purposes of identification by witnesses. In People v. Hicks, 68 N.Y.2d 234, 508 N.Y.S.2d 163 (1986), the New York Court of Appeals found that coercive movement to the crime scene for purposes of identification was within the confines of a permissible *Terry* stop. It explained as follows:

> There were witnesses within a quarter mile of the place of inquiry—approximately one minute away by car—who had just seen the perpetrators and would either identify defendant (in which event he would be arrested) or not identify him (in which event he would be released). A speedy on-the-scene viewing thus was of value both to law enforcement authorities and to defendant, and was appropriate here.

See also United States v. Benson, 686 F.3d 498 (8th Cir. 2012) ("The exigencies were such that the officers could not dispel their suspicions that had prompted the *Terry* stop until they transported [the suspect] to the bank for the show-up identification.").

d. Investigative Techniques That Are Permissible Within the Confines of a Terry Stop

The purpose of a *Terry* stop is to permit an officer to investigate the facts on which reasonable suspicion is based, in order to determine whether the suspect is involved in criminal activity. It therefore follows that some preliminary investigation, objectively designed to confirm or dispel that suspicion, is permissible within the confines of a stop.

The most common investigative technique permitted in a *Terry* stop is investigating the suspect's identity and recent whereabouts. See United States v. Guzman, 864 F.2d 1512 (10th Cir.1988) ("An officer conducting a routine traffic stop may request a driver's license and vehicle identification."). The officer may also verify the information obtained from the suspect by communicating with others or by conducting preliminary investigations such as a vehicle registration check, license check, or a computer search for outstanding warrants. See United States v. Mendez, 118 F.3d 1426 (10th Cir.1997) ("An officer conducting a routine traffic stop may run computer checks on the driver's license, the vehicle registration papers, and on whether the driver has any outstanding warrants or the vehicle has been reported stolen"). And of course officers are permitted to question the suspect about the circumstances that supported the stop in the first place.

Courts have also permitted officers to detain suspects on reasonable suspicion in order to conduct a canine sniff or to conduct a preliminary investigation of other suspicious circumstances. See United States v. Bloomfield, 40 F.3d 910 (8th Cir.1994) (where officers had reasonable suspicion that drugs were in a car, it was proper to detain the suspects while a dog was brought to the scene to sniff the vehicle because the investigation was "reasonably related in scope to the circumstances that justified the interference in the first place").

Criminalizing the Refusal to Provide Identification During a Terry Stop: Hiibel v. Sixth Judicial District Court of Nevada

In Hiibel v. Sixth Judicial District Court of Nevada, 542 U.S. 177 (2004), Hiibel was stopped on reasonable suspicion of being involved in a domestic assault. He refused to provide identification. He did not contest the stop, but contended that the state had no power to criminalize his refusal to provide identification during the stop. The Court, in an opinion by Justice Kennedy, upheld the conviction and stressed that an officer has a right to demand identification as part on an investigation during a *Terry* stop. Justice Kennedy explained as follows:

> Our decisions make clear that questions concerning a suspect's identity are a routine and accepted part of many *Terry* stops. Obtaining a suspect's name in the course of a *Terry* stop serves important government interests. Knowledge of identity may inform an officer that a suspect is wanted for another offense, or has a record of violence or mental disorder. On the other hand, knowing identity may help clear a suspect and allow the police to concentrate their efforts elsewhere. * * *
>
> The principles of *Terry* permit a State to require a suspect to disclose his name in the course of a *Terry* stop. The request for identity has an immediate relation to the purpose, rationale, and practical demands of a *Terry* stop. The threat of criminal sanction helps ensure that the request for identity does not become a legal nullity. On the other hand, the Nevada statute does not alter the nature of the stop itself: it does not change its duration, or its location.

Justice Breyer, joined by Justices Souter and Ginsburg, dissented in *Hiibel,* arguing that, while an officer can demand identification during a *Terry* stop, it is unreasonable to criminalize refusals.

e. Overly Intrusive Investigation Techniques

Some investigative techniques are themselves so intrusive or extensive as to require probable cause. The most obvious example is a search for evidence, which, as stated above, goes beyond the scope of both a *Terry* stop and frisk. Also, some courts have held that probable cause is required before a suspect can be subjected to a series of demanding physical tests to determine whether he is intoxicated. See People v. Carlson, 677 P.2d 310 (Colo.1984) (holding that the full battery of tests employed was so intrusive as to constitute an arrest). Roadside sobriety tests that are less demanding may be permissible under *Terry*, however. See State v. Wyatt, 67 Haw. 293, 687 P.2d 544 (1984) (limited field sobriety test permissible on reasonable suspicion). By contrast, breathalyzer tests and blood tests used to determine a driver's blood alcohol concentration require probable cause. See Birchfield v. North Dakota, 579 U.S. 438 (2016) (discussed infra).

f. Investigation of Matters Other than the Reasonable Suspicion That Supported the Stop: Stop After a Stop

A *Terry* stop must end when the reason for the stop has come to an end. If the reasonable suspicion supporting the stop has been cleared up (e.g., an identification checks out) or the person has been processed (e.g., the traffic ticket has been issued), then the stop is at an end and the suspect must be released. See United States v. Jenson, 462 F.3d 399 (5th Cir. 2006) (when a traffic stop was completed, an officer was not permitted to ask the defendant where he worked, and then rely on an implausible answer to justify continuing the stop).

In Rodriguez v. United States, 575 U.S. 348 (2015), an officer had probable cause to believe that Rodriguez had committed a traffic offense. He issued a ticket, but continued to detain Rodriguez because he wanted to do a canine sniff of the car and the dog had not yet arrived. It took five more minutes for the dog to arrive, at which point he alerted to the presence of drugs. Rodriguez argued that the drugs had to be suppressed because, by the time the dog arrived, the stop was over. The Court of Appeals found no violation because the post-stop detention was "de minimis."

The Court, in an opinion by Justice Ginsburg, agreed with Rodriguez. Justice Ginsburg stated that:

> the tolerable duration of police inquiries in the traffic-stop context is determined by the seizure's mission—to address the traffic violation that warranted the stop, and attend to related safety concerns. Because addressing the infraction is the purpose of the stop, it may last no longer than is necessary to effectuate that purpose. Authority for the seizure thus ends when tasks tied to the traffic infraction are—or reasonably should have been—completed.

Justice Ginsburg distinguished Illinois v. Caballes, discussed earlier in this Chapter. In *Caballes* officers conducted a canine sniff *before* the ticket was issued. Therefore, there was no Fourth Amendment violation because the dog sniff was not a search and Caballes was properly detained.

Justice Ginsburg noted that a traffic stop could be permissibly lengthened by conducting such procedures as checking the driver's license, determining whether there are outstanding warrants against the driver, and inspecting the automobile's registration and proof of insurance. She stated that "[t]hese checks serve the same objective as enforcement of the traffic code: ensuring that vehicles on the road are operated safely and responsibly." In contrast, a dog sniff is an attempt to obtain information and evidence unrelated to the grounds for the traffic stop.

Justice Thomas, joined by Justices Alito and Kennedy in pertinent part, argued that the majority completely ignored the fact that Rodriguez had not been subject to a *Terry* stop. Rodriguez conceded that the officer had probable cause to arrest Rodriguez for the traffic violation. While the officer did not do so, Justice Thomas concluded that the fact that he could have done so allowed for a more elastic consideration of the duration of the seizure. Justice Thomas concluded as follows:

> Because Rodriguez does not dispute that Officer Struble had probable cause to stop him, the only question is whether the stop was

otherwise executed in a reasonable manner. I easily conclude that it was. Approximately 29 minutes passed from the time Officer Struble stopped Rodriguez until his narcotics-detection dog alerted to the presence of drugs. That amount of time is hardly out of the ordinary for a traffic stop by a single officer of a vehicle containing multiple occupants even when no dog sniff is involved. During that time, Officer Struble conducted the ordinary activities of a traffic stop—he approached the vehicle, questioned Rodriguez about the observed violation, asked Pollman about their travel plans, ran serial warrant checks on Rodriguez and Pollman, and issued a written warning to Rodriguez. And when he decided to conduct a dog sniff, he took the precaution of calling for backup out of concern for his safety.

[The majority] renders the difference between probable cause and reasonable suspicion virtually meaningless in this context. That shift is supported neither by the Fourth Amendment nor by our precedents interpreting it. And it results in a constitutional framework that lacks predictability. Had Officer Struble arrested, handcuffed, and taken Rodriguez to the police station for his traffic violation, he would have complied with the Fourth Amendment. But because he made Rodriguez wait for seven or eight extra minutes until a dog arrived, he evidently committed a constitutional violation. Such a view of the Fourth Amendment makes little sense.

Justice Thomas also argued that under the majority's rule, an officer would have fewer options the more efficient the officer was.

Justice Alito, in a separate dissenting opinion, argued that the majority had ignored the fact that the officer delayed the dog sniff because he was concerned for his own security and so spent time calling for backup and waiting for another officer to arrive:

If he had chosen [a] riskier sequence of events, the dog sniff would have been completed before the point in time when, according to the Court's analysis, the authority to detain for the traffic stop ended. Thus, an action that would have been lawful had the officer made the *unreasonable* decision to risk his life became unlawful when the officer made the *reasonable* decision to wait a few minutes for backup. Officer Struble's error—apparently—was following prudent procedures motivated by legitimate safety concerns. The Court's holding therefore makes no practical sense.

Reasonable Suspicion as to Another Crime

Note that, in *Rodriguez*, officers had no reasonable suspicion to investigate any matter other than the traffic violation. If, however, in the course of a stop to investigate crime "A," the officer obtains reasonable suspicion to investigate crime "B," then the detention can be extended to investigate crime "B" even though the initial justification for the stop no longer exists. There will then be a *permissible* "stop after a stop." Thus, in United States v. Erwin, 155 F.3d 818 (6th Cir.1998) (en banc), officers pulled Ervin over because they had reason to suspect he was driving while intoxicated. While going through the drill of the traffic stop, it became apparent that Ervin was not intoxicated. But this investigation also uncovered evidence indicating that Ervin was a drug dealer. The court analyzed the situation as follows:

> After the deputies satisfied themselves that Erwin was not drunk or otherwise impaired, they were justified in continuing to detain Erwin if, by then, they had reasonable and articulable suspicion that Erwin was engaged in other criminal activity. We think, as the district court did, that the deputies were reasonably entitled to conclude that Erwin may have been a drug dealer, based on the facts that he (1) was nervous, (2) seemed to try to avoid being questioned by attempting to leave, (3) seemed to have used or was preparing to use a pay telephone to make a call when a cellular telephone was available, (4) seemed to have drug paraphernalia in his vehicle, (5) had a large amount of cash, (6) had no registration or proof of insurance, (7) had a criminal record of drug violations, and (8) had an out-of-place backseat cushion. Although many of these facts are consistent with innocence, all that is required is that the deputies' suspicion be "reasonable" and "articulable," as determined by the totality of the circumstances. We find this standard was met.

See also United States v. Estrada, 459 F.3d 627 (5th Cir. 2006) (continued detention of occupants of a vehicle stopped for a traffic violation was permissible; while waiting for the license check to clear, the officer noticed fresh marks and scratches around the fuel tank, as well as other information raising a reasonable suspicion to believe that the gas tank had a hidden compartment).

Consensual Encounters After a Stop Has Ended: Ohio v. Robinette

A suspect cannot be detained for investigation of matters different from those which support a stop, in the absence of reasonable suspicion as to those other matters. But what if the suspect is simply *asked* about another crime while the initial stop is ending? Can there be a permissible *encounter* after a stop? The Supreme Court addressed this question in Ohio v. Robinette, 519 U.S. 33 (1996). Robinette was legally stopped for speeding and given a verbal warning. When the officer returned Robinette's license, he said: "One question before you get gone: Are you carrying any illegal contraband in your car? Any weapons of any kind, drugs, anything like that?" Robinette answered "no" to these questions, after which the officer asked if he could search the car. Robinette consented. The officer found drugs and arrested Robinette.

Robinette argued that before valid consent could be obtained, the officer had to tell him that he was free to leave. Otherwise, the detention would still be continuing, and would amount to an illegal seizure because it was a continuing investigation on a matter other than that which gave rise to the initial stop. Chief Justice Rehnquist, in an opinion for seven members of the Court, disagreed. The Court held that Robinette voluntarily consented to the search and rejected any bright-line requirement that the suspect be told that the stop is over and he is free to go. The test for whether the continuing discussion was a consensual encounter was based on a totality of the circumstances and not on any one factor—therefore it was not dispositive that Robinette was never specifically told that the stop was over and he was free to go. Justice Ginsburg concurred in the judgment. Justice Stevens dissented.

g. *Interrogations Beyond the Confines of Terry*

In Dunaway v. New York, 442 U.S. 200 (1979), the Court distinguished *Terry* stops from cases in which the police detain a suspect for sustained interrogation. The Court emphasized that *Terry* was a narrow decision and concluded that police cannot detain a suspect and transport him to the stationhouse for questioning without probable cause, even if the detention is not deemed to be an arrest under state law (and there would be no arrest record or formal booking procedure). Justice Brennan, writing for the Court, concluded that "detention for custodial interrogation—regardless of its label—intrudes so severely on interests protected by the Fourth Amendment as necessarily to trigger the traditional safeguards against illegal arrest."[23]

h. *Fingerprinting*

In Davis v. Mississippi, 394 U.S. 721 (1969), the Court held that a round-up of twenty-five African-American youths for questioning and fingerprinting—in an effort to match prints found around a window entered by a rape suspect—violated the Fourth Amendment. Justice Brennan wrote for the Court that "[i]t is arguable * * * that because of the unique nature of the fingerprinting process, such detentions might, under narrowly defined circumstances, be found to comply with the Fourth Amendment even though there is no probable cause in the traditional sense." He explained that fingerprinting is less serious an intrusion on liberty than other searches, and that it can be done at a convenient time and does not offer opportunities for harassment. In this case, however, the fingerprinting did not comply with the Fourth Amendment because, among

[23] Justice White wrote a short opinion concurring in the judgment. Justice Stevens also wrote a brief concurring opinion. Justice Rehnquist, joined by Chief Justice Burger, dissented.

other things, "petitioner was unnecessarily required to undergo two fingerprinting sessions; and petitioner was not merely fingerprinted * * * but also subjected to interrogation."

Isn't fingerprinting simply a means of identification; and isn't investigation of the suspect's identity permitted in a *Terry* stop? If there is reasonable suspicion but not probable cause, and the officer who makes a stop knows that there were fingerprints found at the scene of a crime, is it permissible for the officer to take fingerprints and delay the suspect long enough to obtain a match?

Justice White addressed some of these questions as he wrote for the Court in Hayes v. Florida, 470 U.S. 811 (1985). Police officers who were investigating a series of rapes had reasonable suspicion, but not probable cause to believe, that Hayes was the perpetrator. The officers took Hayes to the stationhouse, without his consent, to be fingerprinted. Justice White concluded that this procedure amounted to an arrest. He indicated that the Court adhered to the view that when police forcibly remove a person to the stationhouse, they are making a seizure that must be considered an arrest, requiring probable cause. Justice White added, however, that the Court's reasoning did not imply "that a brief detention in the field for the purpose of fingerprinting, where there is only reasonable suspicion not amounting to probable cause, is necessarily impermissible under the Fourth Amendment." He relied on *Davis* and noted that fingerprinting in itself is a relatively minimal intrusion and a means of identification not unlike other methods of identification permitted under *Terry*.[24]

i. Time Limits on Terry Stops

The Supreme Court rejected an absolute time limit for *Terry* stops in United States v. Sharpe, 470 U.S. 675 (1985). The facts were as follows:

> A Drug Enforcement agent was on patrol in an unmarked car on a coastal road in North Carolina at approximately 6:30 a.m. when he saw a blue pickup truck with an attached camper "traveling in tandem with a blue Pontiac Bonneville." The agent saw that the truck was riding low, the camper did not bounce or sway appreciably around turns, and that a quilted material covered the rear and side windows of the camper. The agent followed the vehicles for 20 miles into South Carolina where he decided to make an "investigative stop." He radioed the highway patrol for help and a trooper in a marked patrol car responded to the call. Almost immediately after the trooper caught up with the vehicles, the Pontiac and the pickup turned off the highway onto a campground road. The agent and trooper followed the two

[24] Justice Brennan, joined by Justice Marshall, concurred in the judgment. He objected to "the Court's strained effort to reach the question" of "[t]he validity of on-site fingerprinting." Justice Blackmun concurred in the judgment without opinion. Justice Powell did not participate.

vehicles as they sped along the road at double the legal speed until they returned to the main road. The trooper pulled alongside the Pontiac, which was in the lead, turned on his flashing light and motioned for the driver to pull over. As the Pontiac moved to the side, the pickup truck cut between it and the trooper's car, nearly hitting the latter. The trooper pursued the truck while the agent approached the Pontiac and requested identification.

The agent examined the driver's license. After unsuccessfully attempting to radio the trooper, he radioed the local police for assistance. Two local officers arrived and the agent asked them to "maintain the situation" while he went to find the trooper. The trooper had stopped the pickup, removed the driver from the truck, examined his license and a bill of sale for the truck, and patted him down. When the trooper told the driver that he would be held until a DEA agent arrived, the driver became nervous, stated that he wanted to leave, and asked for the return of the driver's license. Approximately 15 minutes after the truck was stopped, the DEA agent arrived and learned that the name on the registration was the same as the name on the driver's license of the Pontiac's driver. The driver of the pickup denied two requests for permission to search the truck before the agent examined the truck and stated that he could smell marijuana. Without asking again for permission, he removed the keys from the ignition, opened the rear of the camper, and observed a large number of burlap-wrapped bales resembling marijuana. The agent arrested the driver and returned to the Pontiac to arrest its occupants. The total time between his initial stop of the Pontiac and the arrests of its occupants was between 30 and 40 minutes.

The defendants in *Sharpe* argued that the evidence was illegally obtained because the officers had only reasonable suspicion and not probable cause and by the time of the search of the camper, the defendants had been detained beyond the time limit of a *Terry* stop.

Chief Justice Burger wrote for the Court and held that the detention did not exceed the time limits of a permissible *Terry* stop; therefore the search of the camper was permissible because, by that time, the officer had smelled the marijuana. The Chief Justice noted the "difficult line drawing problems in distinguishing an investigative stop from a de facto arrest." He recognized that "if an investigative stop continues indefinitely, at some point it can no longer be justified as an investigative stop." Defendants suggested a bright-line time limit on *Terry* stops of 20 minutes. But the Court rejected a "hard-and-fast time limit" and concluded that it was "appropriate to examine whether the police diligently pursued a means of investigation that was likely to confirm or dispel their suspicions quickly, during which time it was necessary to detain the defendant." The officers satisfied that test, because there was no delay that was "unnecessary to the legitimate investigation of the law enforcement officers"; in part this was because the suspects contributed to the delay through their own actions, by refusing to pull over.

Justice Marshall concurred in the judgment because the evasive actions of the suspects turned a brief encounter with the officers into an extended one. He emphasized, however, that *Terry* stops must be brief "no matter what the needs of law enforcement in the particular case."

Justice Brennan dissented. He objected to treating the brevity limitation upon a stop as an "accordion-like concept that may be expanded outward depending on the law enforcement purposes to be served by the stop." He criticized the officers' handling of the investigation and found that the stop was unduly and unnecessarily lengthy. Justice Stevens dissented without reaching the merits.

QUESTIONS AFTER SHARPE

After *Sharpe* what kind of conduct, if any, will be considered impermissible delay, as opposed to diligent investigation? See United States v. Davies, 768 F.2d 893 (7th Cir.1985) (reasonable to detain suspects for an additional thirty minutes to await advice from superiors, where detaining officers were inexperienced); Embody v. Ward, 695 F.3d 577 (6th Cir. 2012) (after Embody was found with a loaded gun in a state park, a two-and-a-half hour detention was not unreasonable under *Terry;* Embody "points to no lack of diligence by [the officer] in trying to confirm (or allay) his suspicions. The officers took the time they needed to determine whether the AK-47 was a handgun, whether Embody had a permit for it, whether he had illegally modified it and whether he posed any other safety threats. A good part of the detention, moreover, came at the beck and call of Embody, who asked to speak to the police supervisor, even after being told it would delay his release.").

5. Limited Searches for Evidence by Law Enforcement Officers Under *Terry*

Terry allows limited investigative seizures of the person or property on the basis of reasonable suspicion. *Terry* also allows limited searches *for self-protection* on the basis of reasonable suspicion. Does *Terry* permit limited, cursory inspections by law enforcement officers searching for *evidence* on the basis of reasonable suspicion rather than probable cause? This was one question encountered by the Court in Arizona v. Hicks, 480 U.S. 321 (1987). Police lawfully entered premises from which a weapon had been fired and noticed two sets of expensive stereo components in an otherwise squalid apartment. Suspecting that the components were stolen, one officer moved a turntable in order to read the serial number that was on the underside of the unit. The serial number matched that of a turntable that had been reported stolen. The State did not argue that probable cause existed to move the turntable, but rather that the movement and inspection was a "cursory" search that was justified by reasonable suspicion.

Justice Scalia, writing for the Court, rejected the State's argument that a search for evidence could be justified upon reasonable suspicion. He declared that probable cause was required for the search of the turntable, even though it was cursory and minimally intrusive. Justice Scalia stated that "a search is a search, even if it happens to disclose nothing but the bottom of a turntable." He concluded that "we are unwilling to send police and judges into a new thicket of Fourth Amendment law, to seek a creature of uncertain description that is neither a plain-view inspection nor yet a full-blown search. Nothing in the prior opinions of this Court supports such a distinction." Why doesn't the prior opinion of the Court in *Terry* support the distinction that Justice Scalia rejected?

Justice O'Connor, joined by Chief Justice Rehnquist and Justice Powell, dissented. She argued that police officers who have reasonable, articulable suspicion that an object they come across in a lawful search is evidence of crime may make a cursory inspection of the object to verify their suspicion. Justice Powell added a dissenting opinion, joined by the Chief Justice and Justice O'Connor, that suggested that the majority's distinction between observing a serial number while searching (permissible) and moving an object to read a serial number (impermissible) trivialized the Fourth Amendment and would cause uncertainty. See also Minnesota v. Dickerson, 508 U.S. 366 (1993) (*Terry* protective search can be conducted if the officer has reasonable suspicion that the suspect poses a risk of harm to the officer or others; however, a search for contraband is outside the *Terry* doctrine and requires probable cause).

QUESTIONS AFTER HICKS

The State in *Hicks* did not argue that the presence of two new stereos in a squalid apartment constituted probable cause to believe they were stolen. Should this argument have been made?

The holding in *Hicks* has not prevented the government from arguing that cursory inspections can be conducted on reasonable suspicion. In United States v. Winsor, 846 F.2d 1569 (9th Cir.1988) (en banc), officers chased suspected bank robbers fleeing from the crime into a hotel. Given the large number of rooms in the hotel, the court found that there was reasonable suspicion, but not probable cause, to believe that the robbers were in any particular room. At each room, the officers knocked on the door and announced "Police, open the door." After checking a few rooms, they knocked on a door answered by Dennis Winsor. They recognized him as the robber. At this point, the police had probable cause to enter, whereupon they found Peter Winsor, the other robber, as well as incriminating evidence. The Winsors argued that, under *Hicks,* the police conducted a search of their room when they knocked on the door, commanded that it be opened, and looked inside. The government argued that the officers had not conducted a full-blown search for evidence, but rather only a cursory inspection that was justified by reasonable suspicion. The court held that the evidence the officers discovered when the door was opened (and all evidence found in the room thereafter) was illegally obtained:

> We refuse the government's invitation to decide this case by balancing the competing interests at stake. Instead, we adhere to the bright-line rule that *Hicks* appears to have announced: The Fourth Amendment prohibits searches of dwellings without probable cause.

Other courts have taken the contrary view and held, despite *Hicks*, that a minimally intrusive search for evidence is permissible if supported by reasonable suspicion. For example, in United States v. Concepcion, 942 F.2d 1170 (7th Cir.1991), officers took a key found on the defendant and inserted it into a lock on a door to an apartment in which drugs had been found. The court held that this was a search because the use of the key in the lock gave the officers information they did not otherwise have, i.e., that the defendant had a key to the apartment. But the search was upheld even though, at the time they used the key, the officers had only reasonable suspicion and not probable cause to connect the defendant with the apartment. The court reasoned that the search was minimally intrusive. It distinguished *Hicks* on the ground that the information uncovered in *Hicks* was more private and the officers in *Concepcion* could have connected the defendant with the apartment in a variety of ways. Is this a meaningful distinction?

6. Detention of Property Under *Terry*

Terry concerned seizures of the person, but its principles have been applied to seizures of property as well. The Court in United States v. Van Leeuwen, 397 U.S. 249 (1970), held that some detentions of property could occur upon reasonable suspicion. Officers, acting upon reasonable suspicion, detained a mailed package for more than a day while an investigation was made for purposes of developing probable cause and obtaining a warrant. A unanimous Court recognized that detention of mail could at some point become an unreasonable seizure, but found that in the instant case the investigation was conducted promptly and diligently. The Court concluded that "[d]etention for this limited time was, indeed, the prudent act rather than letting the packages enter the mails and then, in case the initial suspicions were confirmed, trying to locate them en route."

Unreasonably Lengthy Detention of Property: United States v. Place

The Court in United States v. Place, 462 U.S. 696 (1983), noted that it is often necessary to seize property upon reasonable suspicion while an investigation of criminal activity continues. The Court recognized, however, that if a person is traveling with his property, then a seizure of that property "intrudes on both the suspect's possessory interest in his luggage as well as his liberty interest in proceeding with his itinerary." It concluded that "the limitations applicable to investigative detentions of the person should define the permissible scope of an investigative detention of the person's luggage on less than probable cause.."

On the facts, the Court held that the officers detained Place's luggage for such a long period that probable cause was required to support the detention. Because the officers had only reasonable suspicion, the detention was illegal. Police officers seized Place's luggage as he arrived at LaGuardia Airport on a flight from Miami. 90 minutes later, they subjected the luggage to a canine sniff. Justice O'Connor, writing for the Court, stated that the 90 minute detention was unreasonable in the absence of probable cause because the delay was caused by the failure to transport the drug detecting dog from one New York metropolitan airport to another. She reasoned that the dog could have been transported while Place was in the air en route to New York since the officers had reasonable suspicion during that time. She concluded that the officers had not diligently pursued the investigation, and that "we have never approved a seizure of the person for the prolonged 90-minute period involved here." Finally, the Court noted that the Fourth Amendment violation was "exacerbated by the failure of the agents to inform the respondent of the place to which they were transporting his luggage, of the length of time he might be dispossessed, and of what arrangements would be made for return of the luggage if the investigation dispelled the suspicion." Under these circumstances, the detention of Place's luggage was tantamount to a detention of Place himself.

Justice Brennan, joined by Justice Marshall, concurred in the result. He argued that the *Terry* balancing approach "should not be conducted except in the most limited circumstances." Justice Blackmun also concurred in the result, similarly expressing concern "with what appears to me to be an emerging tendency on the part of the Court to convert the *Terry* decision into a general statement that the Fourth Amendment requires only that any seizure be reasonable."

QUESTIONS AFTER PLACE

Does *Place* mean that a 90-minute detention of luggage in transit is *always* unreasonable in the absence of probable cause? The Court in United States v. $191,910.00 in Currency, 16 F.3d 1051 (9th Cir.1994) held that a two-hour detention of a traveler's luggage, pending a dog sniff, violated the Fourth Amendment solely because of its length. Even if "an unforeseeable canine virus" had suddenly afflicted all the available drug-sniffing dogs, that court would have invalidated the two-hour seizure of the person's luggage. Do you agree, or should an officer's diligence in pursuing the investigation be the only factor for determining the reasonableness of the length of the seizure?

Does *Place* mean that officers must have the drug sniffing dog on the premises at the time the luggage is seized? See United States v. Frost, 999 F.2d 737 (3d Cir.1993) (80-minute detention of luggage pending dog sniff was reasonable: "It does not demonstrate a lack of diligence on the part of the detectives that a drug-sniffing unit was not on duty that day, so that he had to be summoned to the airport"; *Place* distinguished because officers in that case had substantial time to bring the dog to the airport before the luggage arrived).

7. Application of the *Terry* Reasonableness Analysis Outside the Stop and Frisk Context—to Probationers and Parolees

The *Terry* analysis balances the nature of the individual interest at stake in a search and seizure against the interest of the government in investigating and preventing crime. *Terry* applied this reasonableness analysis in the context of the limited intrusion known as stop and frisk. But it is possible that the balancing analysis could be applied in a wide variety of contexts to allow intrusions on less than probable cause, and without a warrant. To do so, however, would raise tension with the Court's position in *Hicks* and *Dickerson* that searches for evidence of a crime, even if not particularly intrusive, require probable cause.

In United States v. Knights, 534 U.S. 112 (2001), Chief Justice Rehnquist wrote for the Court as it held that no more than reasonable suspicion is required to search a probationer's home. He reasoned that "[j]ust as other punishments for criminal convictions curtail an offender's freedoms, a court granting probation may impose reasonable conditions that deprive the offender of some freedoms enjoyed by law-abiding citizens." The Court appeared to apply a reasonableness balancing approach even though the search was for evidence of a crime (as opposed to a *Terry* frisk for the protection of the officer). The Chief Justice declared as follows:

> [W]e conclude that the search of Knights was reasonable under our general Fourth Amendment approach of "examining the totality of the circumstances," with the probation search condition being a salient circumstance.
>
> The touchstone of the Fourth Amendment is reasonableness, and the reasonableness of a search is determined by assessing, on the one hand, the degree to which it intrudes upon an individual's privacy and, on the other, the degree to which it is needed for the promotion of legitimate governmental interests. Knights's status as a probationer subject to a search condition informs both sides of that balance. * * * Inherent in the very nature of probation is that probationers do not enjoy the absolute liberty to which every citizen is entitled. Just as other punishments for criminal convictions curtail an offender's freedoms, a court granting probation may impose reasonable conditions that deprive the offender of some freedoms enjoyed by law-

abiding citizens * * * Although the Fourth Amendment ordinarily requires the degree of probability embodied in the term "probable cause," a lesser degree satisfies the Constitution when the balance of governmental and private interests makes such a standard reasonable. See, e.g., Terry v. Ohio. Those interests warrant a lesser than probable-cause standard here. When an officer has reasonable suspicion that a probationer subject to a search condition is engaged in criminal activity, there is enough likelihood that criminal conduct is occurring that an intrusion on the probationer's significantly diminished privacy interests is reasonable.

QUESTIONS ABOUT KNIGHTS

Does the result in *Knights* mean that the reasonableness of *every* search—and accordingly the necessary standard of proof—is based on a balance of the needs of the state and the privacy interests of the individual? If so, what is left of its declaration in *Hicks* that "a search is a search" that requires probable cause even though the particular search is cursory and relatively unintrusive? And what is left of the *Terry* Court's statement that officers during a stop can conduct a search upon reasonable suspicion, but only for self-protection and not to search for evidence?

Suspicionless Searches of Parolees Found Reasonable: Samson v. California

In Samson v. California, 547 U.S. 843 (2006), the Court answered a question it left open in *Knights*: whether a condition of a parolee's release can so diminish or eliminate his reasonable expectation of privacy that a *suspicionless* search by a law enforcement officer would be permissible under the Fourth Amendment. The case involved a California statute providing that every prisoner eligible for release on state parole "shall agree in writing to be subject to search or seizure by a parole officer or other peace officer at any time of the day or night, with or without a search warrant and with or without cause." Samson so agreed and was paroled. While on parole he was searched without suspicion and was found in possession of drugs. The Court, in an opinion by Justice Thomas, found that the search was reasonable.

Justice Thomas relied heavily on *Knights,* emphasizing that the parolee's expectation of privacy is substantially diminished because his very liberty is conditional. In contrast, the state's interest in conducting a suspicionless search was found "substantial" because "parolees are more likely to commit future criminal offenses." He explained that, "most parolees require intense supervision" and that "a requirement that searches be based on individualized suspicion would undermine the State's ability to effectively supervise parolees and protect the public from criminal acts by reoffenders." In Justice Thomas's view, a reasonable suspicion standard "would give parolees greater opportunity to anticipate searches and conceal criminality."

Justice Thomas emphasized that the Court did not "address whether California's parole search condition is justified as a special need," [see the discussion of "special needs" searches later in this Chapter] because "our holding under general Fourth Amendment principles renders such an examination unnecessary."

Justice Stevens, joined by Justices Souter and Breyer, dissented in *Samson.* He noted that the search at issue could not possibly have been justified as a "special needs" search, because it was done for criminal law enforcement purposes. Yet the majority, in Justice Stevens's view, unaccountably found a suspicionless search to be reasonable.

> Ignoring just how closely guarded is that category of constitutionally permissible suspicionless searches, the Court for the first time upholds an entirely suspicionless search unsupported by any special need. And it goes further: In special needs cases we have at least insisted upon programmatic safeguards designed to ensure evenhandedness in application; if individualized suspicion is to be jettisoned, it must be replaced with measures to protect against the state actor's unfettered discretion. Here, by contrast, there are no policies in place—no standards, guidelines, or procedures—to rein in officers and furnish a bulwark against the arbitrary exercise of discretion that is the height of unreasonableness.

Can the Knights/Samson Balancing Test Be Extended Beyond Probationers and Parolees?

Knights and *Samson* could be broadly read to allow searches for evidence on less than probable cause whenever the state interest supporting the search outweighs the individual's interest in preventing it—in other words, a free-form balancing test that would allow any number of searches that would, under traditional Fourth Amendment theory (as applied in *Hicks* and *Dickerson, supra*) require probable cause.

The lower courts have generally read *Knights* and *Samson* narrowly, and even then have required something in the probation/parole conditions authorizing a search on less than probable cause. *See, e.g.,* United States v. Freeman, 479 F.3d 743 (10th Cir. 2007) ("We interpret the *Knights-Samson* line of cases as resting on the parolee's diminished expectation of privacy stemming from his own parole agreement and the state regulations applicable to his case.").

F. SEARCH INCIDENT TO ARREST: THE ARREST POWER RULE

A warrantless search incident to a valid arrest was an accepted practice when the Bill of Rights was adopted. While the principle was and is well-accepted, the application of the arrest power rule to various fact situations, and even the rationale underlying the exception, have been subject to dispute and inconsistent application by courts. In the following case, the Court clarifies the rationale for searches incident to arrest and explains how that rationale sets limits on the scope of these searches.

1. Spatial Limitations

CHIMEL V. CALIFORNIA

Supreme Court of the United States, 1969.
395 U.S. 752.

JUSTICE STEWART **delivered the opinion of the Court.**

This case raises basic questions concerning the permissible scope under the Fourth Amendment of a search incident to a lawful arrest.

The relevant facts are essentially undisputed. Late in the afternoon of September 13, 1965, three police officers arrived at the Santa Ana, California, home of the petitioner with a warrant authorizing his arrest for the burglary of a coin shop. The officers knocked on the door, identified themselves to the petitioner's wife, and asked if they might come inside. She ushered them into the house, where they waited 10 or 15 minutes until the petitioner returned home from work. When the petitioner entered the house, one of the officers handed him the arrest warrant and asked for permission to "look around." The petitioner objected, but was advised that "on the basis of the lawful arrest," the officers would nonetheless conduct a search. No search warrant had been issued.

Accompanied by the petitioner's wife, the officers then looked through the entire three-bedroom house, including the attic, the garage, and a small workshop. * * * After completing the search, they seized numerous items—primarily coins, but also several medals, tokens, and a few other objects. The entire search took between 45 minutes and an hour.

At the petitioner's subsequent state trial on two charges of burglary, the items taken from his house were admitted into evidence against him, over his objection that they had been unconstitutionally seized. * * *

[W]e proceed on the hypothesis that the California courts were correct in holding that the arrest of the petitioner was valid under the Constitution. This brings us directly to the question whether the warrantless search of the petitioner's entire house can be constitutionally justified as incident to that arrest. The decisions of this Court bearing upon that question have been far from consistent, as even the most cursory review makes evident.

* * *

[The Court describes its erratic decisions beginning with dictum in Weeks v. United States, 232 U.S. 383 (1914), and continuing through Harris v. United States, 331 U.S. 145 (1947), Trupiano v. United States, 334 U.S. 699 (1948), and United States v. Rabinowitz, 339 U.S. 56 (1950).]

Rabinowitz has come to stand for the proposition, *inter alia,* that a warrantless search "incident to a lawful arrest" may generally extend to the area that is considered to be in the "possession" or under the "control" of the person arrested. And it was on the basis of that proposition that the California courts upheld the search of the petitioner's entire house in this case. That doctrine, however, at least in the broad sense in which it was applied by the California courts in this case, can withstand neither historical nor rational analysis.

* * *

* * * When an arrest is made, it is reasonable for the arresting officer to search the person arrested in order to remove any weapons that the latter might seek to use in order to resist arrest or effect his escape. Otherwise, the officer's safety might well be endangered, and the arrest itself frustrated. In addition, it is entirely reasonable for the arresting officer to search for and seize any evidence on the arrestee's person in order to prevent its concealment or destruction. And the area into which an arrestee might reach in order to grab a weapon or evidentiary items must, of course, be governed by a like rule. A gun on a table or in a drawer in front of one who is arrested can be as dangerous to the arresting officer as one concealed in the clothing of the person arrested. There is ample justification, therefore, for a search of the arrestee's person and the area "within his immediate control"—construing that phrase to mean the area from within which he might gain possession of a weapon or destructible evidence.

There is no comparable justification, however, for routinely searching any room other than that in which an arrest occurs—or, for that matter, for searching through all the desk drawers or other closed or concealed areas in that room itself. Such searches, in the absence of well-recognized exceptions, may be made only under the authority of a search warrant. The "adherence to judicial processes" mandated by the Fourth Amendment requires no less.

* * *

It is argued in the present case that it is "reasonable" to search a man's house when he is arrested in it. But that argument is founded on little more than a subjective view regarding the acceptability of certain sorts of police conduct, and not on considerations relevant to Fourth Amendment interests. Under such an unconfined analysis, Fourth Amendment protection in this area would approach the evaporation point. It is not easy to explain why, for instance, it is less subjectively "reasonable" to search a man's house when he is arrested on his front lawn—or just down the street—than it is when he happens to be in the house at the time of arrest. * * *

It would be possible, of course, to draw a line between *Rabinowitz* and *Harris* on the one hand, and this case on the other. For *Rabinowitz* involved a single room, and *Harris* a four-room apartment, while in the case before us an entire house was searched. But such a distinction would be highly artificial. The rationale that allowed the searches and seizures in *Rabinowitz* and *Harris* would allow the searches and seizures in this case. No consideration relevant to the Fourth Amendment suggests any point of rational limitation, once the search is allowed to go beyond the area from which the person arrested might obtain weapons or evidentiary items. The only reasoned distinction is one between a search of the person arrested and the area within his reach on the one hand, and more extensive searches on the other.

The petitioner correctly points out that one result of decisions such as *Rabinowitz* and *Harris* is to give law enforcement officials the opportunity to engage in searches not justified by probable cause, by the simple expedient of arranging to arrest suspects at home rather than elsewhere. We do not suggest that the petitioner is necessarily correct in his assertion that such a strategy was utilized here, but the fact remains that had he been arrested earlier in the day, at his place of employment rather than at home, no search of his house could have been made without a search warrant. * * *

[The concurring opinion of Justice Harlan is omitted.]

JUSTICE WHITE, with whom JUSTICE BLACK joins, dissenting.

* * *

The justifications which make [a search incident to arrest] reasonable obviously do not apply to the search of areas to which the accused does not have ready physical access. This is not enough, however, to prove such searches unconstitutional. The Court has always held, and does not today deny, that when there is probable cause to search and it is "impracticable" for one reason or another to get a search warrant, then a warrantless search may be reasonable. This is the case whether an arrest was made at the time of the search or not.

This is not to say that a search can be reasonable without regard to the probable cause to believe that seizable items are on the premises. But when there are exigent circumstances, and probable cause, then the search may be made without a warrant, reasonably. An arrest itself may often create an emergency situation making it impracticable to obtain a warrant before embarking on a related search. Again assuming that there is probable cause to search premises at the spot where a suspect is arrested, it seems to me unreasonable to require the police to leave the scene in order to obtain a search warrant when they are already legally there to make a valid arrest, and when there must almost always be a strong possibility that confederates of the arrested man will in the meanwhile remove the items for which the police have probable cause to search. This must so often be the case that it seems to me as unreasonable to require a warrant for a search of the premises as to require a warrant for search of the person and his very immediate surroundings.

* * *

Application of Chimel's Case-by-Case Approach to the Permissible Scope of a Search Incident to Arrest

What are the precise spatial limitations on the arrest power rule after *Chimel*? Is the permissible scope of the search determined by where the suspect was arrested or by where the search occurred? Does it make a difference that the suspect is handcuffed? Infirm? Consider United States v. Lucas, 898 F.2d 606 (8th Cir.1990), where the defendant was convicted of bank robbery based in part upon evidence found in the following search incident to arrest:

> The magistrate found that Lucas was seated at a kitchen table with two other men as the officers stood in the front doorway of the apartment in which he was arrested. As Lucas began to get up from the table, the officers entered the apartment and ran into the kitchen. Two officers attempted to apprehend Lucas, and one officer monitored the other two men seated at the table. By the time the officers reached Lucas, his hand was within inches of the handle on a cabinet door. During the ensuing struggle, which lasted for approximately forty seconds, Lucas and the two officers slid around on the slick floor. At one point, Lucas fell to the floor, and the skirmish continued until Lucas was handcuffed. As an officer pulled Lucas from the floor and moved him toward the living room, another officer immediately stood up, opened the cabinet door that Lucas had been attempting to reach, and found a chrome automatic pistol inside the cabinet. The two men seated at the kitchen table were not handcuffed until after the gun was discovered.

The court upheld the search under *Chimel:*

> Lucas argues that *Chimel* does not justify the search here because he was being escorted, handcuffed, from the kitchen when the search

> occurred. While relevant under *Chimel,* this is not a determinative factor. * * * [A] warrantless search incident to an arrest may be valid even though a court, operating with the benefit of hindsight in an environment well removed from the scene of the arrest, doubts that the defendant could have reached the items seized during the search. The officers in this case searched a cabinet in a small kitchen immediately after handcuffing Lucas and while removing him from the kitchen. Moreover, two of Lucas' friends who had not been handcuffed were still at the kitchen table when the search took place. On these facts, we conclude that this was a valid warrantless search incident to Lucas' arrest.

Does the court in *Lucas* show too much or just enough concern for the safety of the officers? Compare United States v. Blue, 78 F.3d 56 (2d Cir.1996) (search of an area between a mattress and a box spring could not be justified under the arrest power rule; the suspects were on the floor, handcuffed with their hands behind their backs, and many officers were controlling them); United States v. Neely, 345 F.3d 366 (5th Cir. 2003) (officers could not seize the clothing of a suspect who was brought to the hospital and was in surgery: "there are no indications that he could have attempted to destroy the clothing" at the time of the seizure).

In United States v. Currence, 446 F.3d 554 (4th Cir. 2006), the defendant was arrested while on his bicycle. He was suspected of dealing drugs. Officers searched the inside of the handlebars of the bike and found cocaine. The court upheld that search under *Chimel*:

> We believe that because [the officer] was able to remove the handlebar end cap by simply sliding it off * * * there is no basis under *Chimel* to treat the handlebar differently from other items within the immediate control of an arrestee that may be opened in a search incident to an arrest. Just as an arrestee's ability to reach into, for example, a closed container or a locked bag makes those items searchable incident to an arrest, Currence's ability to reach into the easily accessible handlebar likewise makes it searchable.

The court did note, however, that "there are limits to the scope of a search incident to arrest" and that its opinion "should not be construed as a holding that all areas of a bicycle can automatically be searched in every case." So what areas on a bike could not be searched incident to arrest?

Timing of Grab Area Determination

Should the scope of the grab area be determined by where the arrestee is at the time of the *search*, or rather by where the arrestee *was* at the time of *arrest*? In Davis v. Robbs, 794 F.2d 1129 (6th Cir.1986), the court upheld the seizure of a rifle that had been in close proximity to the arrestee at the time of the arrest. Judge Wellford dissented on this point, noting that the search and seizure occurred after the arrestee was put in the squad car:

> The rationale justifying the search incident to arrest exception is that some exigency exists at the time of the search or seizure, not arrest. * * * The actual exigency at the time of arrest would become fictional through transplantation to the time of the search and seizure. At the time the police seized the rifle in the present case, [the arrestee] was handcuffed and in the squad car. He no longer had access to the gun nor posed any danger to the police. * * * Thus, the rationale justifying the exception does not support the seizure of the rifle. The danger had passed.

The court in United States v. Abdul-Saboor, 85 F.3d 664 (D.C.Cir.1996) agreed with the majority in *Davis* that the grab area should be determined as of the time of the arrest, not the time of the search. Thus, an officer's search of an area after the arrestee had been taken out of the room was permissible. The court reasoned that "if the courts were to focus exclusively upon the moment of the search, we might create a perverse incentive for an arresting officer to prolong the period during which the arrestee is kept in an area where he could pose a danger to the officer." Do you think this is a realistic possibility?

Since the above cases were decided, the Supreme Court in Arizona v. Gant—discussed infra—held that when a person in a *car* is arrested, the grab area is to be determined as of the time of the *search*—so if at the time of the search the arrestee has been placed in the squad car, the passenger compartment of his vehicle is no longer within the grab area. The Court in *Gant* specifically limited its holding to searches of vehicles incident to arrest. But some courts have relied on *Gant* to hold that *whenever* a person is arrested, the grab area must be determined as of the time of the search, not what it was at the time the person was arrested. An example is United States v. Shakir, 616 F.3d 315 (3d Cir. 2010). Shakir challenged the search of a bag that he was carrying when arrested. He argued that, at the time of the search of the bag, he was already handcuffed. The government responded by citing several circuit court decisions that assessed the grab area as of the time of the arrest; the defendant conceded that he had access to the bag at the time he was arrested. The court rejected the government's argument that the *Gant* time of search rule applied only to vehicle searches. It found "no plausible reason" to limit *Gant* to vehicle searches, as opposed to "any situation where the item searched is removed from the suspect's control between the time of the arrest and the time of the search." The court read *Gant* as "refocusing our attention on a suspect's ability (or inability) to access weapons or destroy evidence at the time a search incident to arrest is conducted."

It is notable, though, that the *Shakir* court upheld the search of the defendant's bag under the arrest-power rule. Even as assessed at the time of the search, the search of the bag was reasonably directed to protecting against destruction of evidence and harm to police officers. The court stated that handcuffs are "not fail-safe" and reasoned as follows:

> Although he was handcuffed and guarded by two policemen, Shakir's bag was literally at his feet, so it was accessible if he had dropped to the floor. Although it would have been more difficult for Shakir to open the bag and retrieve a weapon while handcuffed, we do not regard this possibility as remote enough to render unconstitutional the search incident to arrest. This is especially true when we consider that Shakir was subject to an arrest warrant for armed bank robbery, and that he was arrested in a public area near some 20 innocent bystanders, as well as at least one suspected confederate who was guarded only by unarmed hotel security officers.

Arrest Power Can Be Invoked for Any Custodial Arrest and Can Cover Post-Arrest Movements: Washington v. Chrisman

Does the rationale of *Chimel,* allowing search incident to arrest to protect the officer and preserve the evidence, apply to every arrest? Does it apply even if the arrestee is allowed to move about? In Washington v. Chrisman, 455 U.S. 1 (1982), Chief Justice Burger, writing for the Court, declared that "the absence of an affirmative indication that an arrested person might have a weapon available or might attempt to escape does not diminish the arresting officer's authority to maintain custody over the arrested person" and to conduct an automatic search for evidence and weapons within the grab area. The Court stated that "every arrest must be presumed to present a risk of danger to the arresting officer," because "there is no way for an officer to predict reliably how a particular subject will react to arrest of the degree of potential danger."

The Court in *Chrisman* upheld a search and seizure incident to arrest under the following circumstances: A police officer saw Chrisman, who appeared to be underage, carrying liquor. He asked for identification and Chrisman said it was in his dormitory room. At that point he was placed under arrest and the officer accompanied him to the dorm room to retrieve the identification. As Chrisman entered the room the officer remained in the open doorway, from where he saw Chrisman's roommate become nervous. The officer entered the room and noticed seeds and a small pipe that he concluded were used in marijuana smoking. After warning both roommates of their rights, the officer asked about other drugs and was given additional marijuana. The officer subsequently obtained consent to search the room and found LSD.

Chief Justice Burger reasoned that once the officer placed his suspect under arrest before returning to the suspect's room "[t]he officer had a right to remain literally at the suspect's elbow at all times." This was true even though the officer admitted that he did not think Chrisman was going up to the room to destroy evidence or get a weapon. The Chief Justice concluded that because the officer had a valid right to enter the room at any time to monitor the movements of the arrested person, he had a right to be where he was when he first saw the seeds and the pipe.

Justice White, joined by Justices Brennan and Marshall, dissented. The thrust of the dissent was that an officer "should not be permitted to invade living quarters any more than is necessary to maintain control and protect himself," which were not the reasons for the invasion in this case.[25]

Arrest Leading to Exigent Circumstances

Justice White, dissenting in *Chimel,* argues that when a person is arrested, the fact of the arrest itself will in almost all cases give rise to exigent circumstances to search beyond the grab area of the arrestee. He reasoned that friends, family, or business associates of the arrestee will almost always become aware of an arrest and will almost always try to destroy evidence (or police officers) when they learn about the arrest. Justice White does not contend that exigent circumstances will arise after *every* arrest, nor could he: if Chimel was a hermit, there could be no threat that upon his arrest one of his associates would immediately destroy evidence or raise a weapon. Rather, Justice White argues that exigent circumstances will arise *so often* upon an arrest that it makes sense to establish a bright line rule permitting a search of the whole premises if probable cause exists to believe evidence will be found so as to avoid the negative effects of ad hoc judgments by officers and the judicial costs of a case-by-case approach.

Why did Justice White's argument for a bright-line rule not persuade the majority? If, as *Chrisman* states, we presume that the arrestee will destroy evidence or harm the officer even if that is not so in a particular case, then why do we not presume that the arrestee's *associates* will learn about the arrest and destroy evidence or harm the officer? Do officers facing these circumstances have alternatives? What about a temporary seizure of the premises pending a warrant application?

We will discuss the exigent circumstances exception to the warrant requirement later in this Chapter, but for now it is important to note that the Court requires a showing of exigency on the particular facts of the case;

---

25 Although the Supreme Court reversed the Washington Supreme Court in *Chrisman,* it was the state supreme court that was to have the last word. On remand, it held that the officer violated the state constitution, which it interpreted to prohibit warrantless entry into a private dwelling by an officer unless he has specific articulable facts justifying the entry. State v. Chrisman, 100 Wash.2d 814, 676 P.2d 419 (1984).

the arrest of a person, while certainly relevant, is not dispositive of whether there is a risk of destruction of evidence or harm to the officers or public that would excuse the warrant requirement. Illustrative is Vale v. Louisiana, 399 U.S. 30 (1970). Officers observing Vale had probable cause to believe he had engaged in a drug transaction outside his house. When they approached, Vale walked quickly toward the house. He was arrested on his front steps. The officers searched the house and found narcotics in a bedroom. Three minutes after the officers entered the house, Vale's mother and brother came home carrying groceries. Justice Stewart wrote for the Court as it held that the officers' warrantless search of the bedroom violated the Fourth Amendment. The Court found that the State had not met its burden of showing that exigent circumstances existed and rejected the argument that "an arrest on the street can provide its own exigent circumstance so as to justify a warrantless search of the arrestee's house."[26]

Notwithstanding *Vale,* in many cases an arrest *will* create exigent circumstances due to the risk that the arrestee's friends, family, or criminal associates will destroy evidence or use weapons. In United States v. Socey, 846 F.2d 1439 (D.C.Cir.1988), the court set forth the following standard for determining whether exigent circumstances arise after an arrest:

> Consistent with *Vale,* we believe that a police officer can show an objectively reasonable belief that contraband is being, or will be, destroyed within a home if he can show 1) a reasonable belief that third persons were inside a private dwelling and 2) a reasonable belief that these third persons are aware of an * * * arrest of a confederate outside the premises so that they might see a need to destroy evidence.

The court in *Socey* found that exigent circumstances existed where an arrest was made outside a house in which a large-scale drug operation was being conducted. The court stated that it was not unreasonable for the officers to believe "that such an operation would have some type of look-out system." The court also emphasized the fact that drugs are easily destroyed.

Protective Sweep Incident to an Arrest: Maryland v. Buie

Even in the absence of exigent circumstances, police may have the authority, pursuant to the *Terry* doctrine, to search beyond the *Chimel* spatial limitations in order to conduct a "protective sweep" of the place where an arrest is made. As discussed in the section on *Terry,* in Maryland v. Buie, 494 U.S. 325 (1990), the Court defined a "protective sweep" as a "quick and limited search of a premises, incident to an arrest and conducted to protect the safety of police officers or others." The Court held that a protective sweep could be justified by reasonable suspicion "that the area

[26] Justice Blackmun did not take part. Justice Black, joined by Chief Justice Burger, dissented. He concluded that the State's burden of showing exigent circumstances was met.

swept harbored an individual posing a danger to the officer or others." Probable cause was not necessary for such a sweep.

Justice White, writing for the Court, concluded that the spatial limitations of *Chimel* were not undermined by allowing a protective sweep on reasonable suspicion. Unlike a search incident to arrest, the protective sweep is limited to areas where persons may be hidden. Nor does the officer have an automatic right to conduct a protective sweep (unlike the automatic right to conduct a search incident to arrest).

Justice Stevens concurred to emphasize that a protective sweep could not be conducted to root out those who might destroy evidence but who would not present a safety risk to the officers or others. That is, the protective sweep is a safety-based and not an evidence-based doctrine. Justice Brennan, joined by Justice Marshall dissented.

2. Temporal Limitations

Sequence of Search and Arrest

Generally, a search incident to arrest takes place immediately after the arrest itself. But courts will not overly concern themselves with the technicality of which came first—the arrest or the search—when both are nearly simultaneous and probable cause to arrest existed before the search was conducted. As the Court stated in Rawlings v. Kentucky, 448 U.S. 98 (1980): "Where the formal arrest followed quickly on the heels of the challenged search of petitioner's person, we do not believe it particularly important that the search preceded the arrest rather than vice versa." See also United States v. Cutchin, 956 F.2d 1216 (D.C.Cir.1992) ("The sequence makes no difference since police did not need the fruits of the search to establish probable cause.").

While a search can precede the arrest, a search cannot be used to provide the probable cause necessary to make the arrest. As the Court stated in the per curiam opinion in Smith v. Ohio, 494 U.S. 541 (1990): "That reasoning, * * * justifying the arrest by the search and at the same time * * * the search by the arrest, just will not do."

Removal from the Arrest Scene

The term "incident to" implies that if the search is too far removed from the arrest, it will not qualify for the exception. But how removed is too removed? In Chambers v. Maroney, 399 U.S. 42 (1970), officers searched an automobile that had been impounded and brought to the police station after the arrest of its occupants. The Court held that this search could not be justified as incident to the arrests, stating that "once an accused is under arrest and in custody, then a search made at another place, without a warrant, is simply not incident to the arrest." The Court concluded that the reasons for a search incident to arrest "no longer obtain when the accused is safely in custody at the station house." The Court applied the same principle in United States v. Chadwick, 433 U.S. 1 (1977), where a footlocker was searched at the police station, 90 minutes after the arrest of its owner. The Court stated that the search "cannot be viewed as incidental to the arrest or as justified by any other exigency."

In United States v. Edwards, 415 U.S. 800 (1974), the Court held that a suspect, who was arrested and jailed around, could be searched incident to arrest the next morning. Justice White, writing for the majority, declared that "searches and seizures that could be made on the spot at the time of arrest may legally be conducted later when the accused arrives at the place of detention" at least where "the normal processes incident to arrest and custody had not yet been completed." Justice White left open the possibility that a warrant might be required for some post-seizure searches of arrestees, but strongly implied that most searches of an arrestee's person are reasonable. After all, in contrast with cars and footlockers, arrestees always have access to themselves. Justice Stewart, joined by Justices Douglas, Brennan and Marshall dissented, taking the view that "the considerations that typically justify a warrantless search incident to a lawful arrest were wholly absent here." See also United States v. Johnson, 445 F.3d 793 (5th Cir. 2006) (testing defendant's hands for gunpowder residue at the police station was a permissible search incident to the arrest because the defendant, or time, could have destroyed the evidence).

3. Comparing Searches Incident to Arrest to Frisks

UNITED STATES V. ROBINSON

Supreme Court of the United States, 1973.
414 U.S. 218.

JUSTICE REHNQUIST delivered the opinion of the Court.

Respondent Robinson was convicted in United States District Court for the District of Columbia of the possession and facilitation of concealment of heroin * * *. [T]he Court of Appeals en banc reversed the judgment of conviction, holding that the heroin introduced in evidence against respondent had been obtained as a result of a search which violated the Fourth Amendment to the United States Constitution. * * *

* * * Officer Richard Jenks, a 15-year veteran of the District of Columbia Metropolitan Police Department, observed the respondent driving a 1965 Cadillac near the intersection of 8th and C Streets, N.E., in the District of Columbia. Jenks, as a result of previous investigation following a check of respondent's operator's permit four days earlier, determined there was reason to believe that respondent was operating a

motor vehicle after the revocation of his operator's permit. This is an offense defined by statute in the District of Columbia which carries a mandatory minimum jail term, a mandatory minimum fine, or both.

Jenks signaled respondent to stop the automobile, which respondent did, and all three of the occupants emerged from the car. At that point Jenks informed respondent that he was under arrest for "operating after revocation and obtaining a permit by misrepresentation." It is * * * conceded by the respondent here, that Jenks had probable cause to arrest respondent, and that he effected a full-custody arrest.

In accordance with procedures prescribed in police department instructions, Jenks then began to search respondent. * * * During this patdown, Jenks felt an object in the left breast pocket of the heavy coat respondent was wearing, but testified that he "couldn't tell what it was" and also that he "couldn't actually tell the size of it." Jenks then reached into the pocket and pulled out the object, which turned out to be a "crumpled up cigarette package." Jenks testified that at this point he still did not know what was in the package. * * *

The officer then opened the cigarette pack and found 14 gelatin capsules of white powder which he thought to be, and which later analysis proved to be, heroin. * * * The heroin seized from the respondent was admitted into evidence at the trial which resulted in his conviction in the District Court.

* * * We conclude that the search conducted by Jenks in this case did not offend the limits imposed by the Fourth Amendment, and we therefore reverse the judgment of the Court of Appeals.

* * *

It is well settled that a search incident to a lawful arrest is a traditional exception to the warrant requirement of the Fourth Amendment. This general exception has historically been formulated into two distinct propositions. The first is that a search may be made of the *person* of the arrestee by virtue of the lawful arrest. The second is that a search may be made of the area within the control of the arrestee.

Examination of this Court's decisions shows that these two propositions have been treated quite differently. The validity of the search of a person incident to a lawful arrest has been regarded as settled from its first enunciation, and has remained virtually unchallenged until the present case. The validity of the second proposition, while likewise conceded in principle, has been subject to differing interpretations as to the extent of the area which may be searched. * * *

Throughout the series of cases in which the Court has addressed the second proposition relating to a search incident to a lawful arrest—the permissible area beyond the person of the arrestee which such a search may cover—no doubt has been expressed as to the unqualified authority of the arresting authority to search the person of the arrestee.

* * * Since the statements in the cases speak not simply in terms of an exception to the warrant requirement, but in terms of an affirmative authority to search, they clearly imply that such searches also meet the Fourth Amendment's requirement of reasonableness.

* * *

In its decision of this case, the Court of Appeals decided that even after a police officer lawfully places a suspect under arrest for the purpose of taking him into custody, he may not ordinarily proceed to fully search the prisoner. He must, instead, conduct a limited frisk of the outer clothing and remove such weapons that he may, as a result of that limited frisk, reasonably believe and ascertain that the suspect has in his possession. While recognizing that Terry v. Ohio dealt with a permissible "frisk" incident to an investigative stop based on less than probable cause to arrest, the Court of Appeals felt that the principles of that case should be carried over to this probable-cause arrest for driving while one's license is revoked. Since there would be no further evidence of such a crime to be obtained in a search of the arrestee, the court held that only a search for weapons could be justified.

* * *

The justification or reason for the authority to search incident to a lawful arrest rests quite as much on the need to disarm the suspect in order to take him into custody as it does on the need to preserve evidence on his person for later use at trial. The standards traditionally governing a search incident to lawful arrest are not, therefore, commuted to the stricter *Terry* standards by the absence of probable fruits or further evidence of the particular crime for which the arrest is made.

Nor are we inclined, on the basis of what seems to us to be a rather speculative judgment, to qualify the breadth of the general authority to search incident to a lawful custodial arrest on an assumption that persons arrested for the offense of driving while their licenses have been revoked are less likely to possess dangerous weapons than are those arrested for other crimes. It is scarcely open to doubt that the danger to an officer is far greater in the case of the extended exposure which follows the taking of a suspect into custody and transporting him to the police station than in the case of the relatively fleeting contact resulting from the typical *Terry*-type stop. This is an adequate basis for treating all custodial arrests alike for purposes of search justification.

But quite apart from these distinctions, our more fundamental disagreement with the Court of Appeals arises from its suggestion that there must be litigated in each case the issue of whether or not there was present one of the reasons supporting the authority for a search of the person incident to a lawful arrest. * * * A police officer's determination as to how and where to search the person of a suspect whom he has arrested is necessarily a quick *ad hoc* judgment which the Fourth Amendment does not require to be broken down in each instance into an analysis of each step in the search. The authority to search the person incident to a lawful custodial arrest, while based upon the need to disarm and to discover evidence, does not depend on what a court may later decide was the probability in a particular arrest situation that weapons or evidence would in fact be found upon the person of the suspect. A custodial arrest of a suspect based on probable cause is a reasonable intrusion under the Fourth Amendment; that intrusion being lawful, a search incident to the arrest requires no additional justification. It is the fact of the lawful arrest which establishes the authority to search, and we hold that in the case of a lawful custodial arrest a full search of the person is not only an exception to the warrant requirement of the Fourth Amendment, but is also a "reasonable" search under that Amendment.

* * *

JUSTICE POWELL, concurring.

* * * I believe that an individual lawfully subjected to a custodial arrest retains no significant Fourth Amendment interest in the privacy of his person. Under this view the custodial arrest is the significant intrusion of state power into the privacy of one's person. If the arrest is lawful, the privacy interest guarded by the Fourth Amendment is subordinated to a legitimate and overriding governmental concern. * * *

JUSTICE MARSHALL, with whom JUSTICE DOUGLAS and JUSTICE BRENNAN join, dissenting.

* * *

The majority opinion fails to recognize that the search conducted by Officer Jenks did not merely involve a search of respondent's person. It also included a separate search of effects found on his person. And even were we to assume, *arguendo,* that it was reasonable for Jenks to remove the object he felt in respondent's pocket, clearly there was no justification consistent with the Fourth Amendment which would authorize his opening the package and looking inside.

To begin with, after Jenks had the cigarette package in his hands, there is no indication that he had reason to believe or did in fact believe that the package contained a weapon. More importantly, even if the crumpled-up cigarette package had in fact contained some sort of small weapon, it would have been impossible for respondent to have used it once the package was in the officer's hands. Opening the package, therefore, did not further the protective purpose of the search. * * *

The Government argues that it is difficult to see what constitutionally protected "expectation of privacy" a prisoner has in the interior of a cigarette pack. One wonders if the result in this case would have been the same were respondent a businessman who was lawfully taken into custody for driving without a license and whose wallet was taken from him by the police. Would it be reasonable for the police officer, because of the possibility that a razor blade was hidden somewhere in the wallet, to open it, remove all the contents, and examine each item carefully? * * *

4. The Arrest Power Rule Applied to Automobiles

Assume that an officer has probable cause to believe that the driver of an automobile has committed a crime for which a custodial arrest is authorized. The officer pulls over the car and places the driver under arrest, handcuffs the driver, and places him in a squad car. Can the officer then search the car incident to the arrest?

The Belton Rule

In New York v. Belton, 453 U.S. 454 (1981), the Court held that the passenger compartment of an automobile constituted the grab area of the car, and therefore officers arresting someone in the car were permitted to search the car incident to the arrest, and also to open any containers that are found in the passenger compartment. (The Court dropped a footnote indicating that the passenger compartment did not include the trunk of the car.) The precise scope of *Belton* was unclear, but most courts treated *Belton* as affording officers an *automatic right* to search the passenger compartment and all containers therein, even if the arrestee had no way to reach into the car for evidence or weapons at the time of the search.

The *Belton* Court styled its rule as being nothing more than an application of the *Chimel* grab area rule to the specific situation of cars. But it seemed hard to argue that the *Belton* search had anything to do with preserving evidence or protecting officers—the underlying reasons for permitting a search incident to arrest under *Chimel.*

Thereafter in Thornton v. United States, 541 U.S. 615 (2004), the Court held that the search power granted by *Belton* applied whenever the person arrested was a "recent occupant" of the car to be searched. Officers thought that Thornton was driving a stolen car, but before they could pull him over, Thornton parked the car and got out of the vehicle. Thornton was subjected to a *Terry* frisk that uncovered narcotics. He was arrested a few feet away from the car, and a search of the passenger compartment incident to arrest turned up a gun. The *Thornton* Court held that the search was permissible under *Belton* because Thornton was a recent occupant and any other rule would only encourage drivers to pop out of a car when they saw police coming, in order to avoid a search of the passenger compartment.

Justice Scalia, joined by Justice Ginsburg, concurred in the judgment in *Thornton*, but took the opportunity to question the wisdom and rationale of the *Belton* rule. He argued as follows:

> I see three reasons why the search in this case might have been justified to protect officer safety or prevent concealment or destruction of evidence. None ultimately persuades me.
>
> The first is that, despite being handcuffed and secured in the back of a squad car, petitioner might have escaped and retrieved a weapon or evidence from his vehicle—a theory that calls to mind Judge Goldberg's reference to the mythical arrestee "possessed of the skill of Houdini and the strength of Hercules." * * *
>
> The second defense of the search in this case is that, since the officer could have conducted the search at the time of arrest (when the suspect was still near the car), he should not be penalized for having taken the sensible precaution of securing the suspect in the squad car first. * * * The weakness of this argument is that it assumes that, one way or another, the search must take place. But conducting a *Chimel* search is not the Government's right; it is an exception—justified by necessity * * *.
>
> The third defense of the search is that, even though the arrestee posed no risk here, *Belton* searches in general are reasonable, and the benefits of a bright-line rule justify upholding that small minority of searches that, on their particular facts, are not reasonable. The validity of this argument rests on the accuracy of *Belton*'s claim that the passenger compartment is "in fact generally, even if not inevitably," within the suspect's immediate control. By the United States' own admission, however, "the practice of restraining an arrestee on the scene before searching a car that he just occupied is so prevalent that holding that *Belton* does not apply in that setting would . . . largely render *Belton* a dead letter." Reported cases involving this precise factual scenario—a motorist handcuffed and secured in the back of a squad car when the search takes place—are legion.

So in Justice Scalia's view, an automatic search of the passenger compartment incident to arrest cannot be supported by the reasons cited by *Chimel* for the search power incident to arrest, i.e., the need to protect against the arrestee's destruction of evidence or use of a weapon. Justice Scalia argued, however, that the power to search after an arrest might be justified on another ground. He explained as follows:

If *Belton* searches are justifiable, it is not because the arrestee might grab a weapon or evidentiary item from his car, but simply because the car might contain evidence relevant to the crime for which he was arrested. * * *

Numerous earlier authorities support this approach, referring to the general interest in gathering evidence related to the crime of arrest with no mention of the more specific interest in preventing its concealment or destruction. [Citing cases.] Only in the years leading up to *Chimel* did we start consistently referring to the narrower interest in frustrating concealment or destruction of evidence.

There is nothing irrational about broader police authority to search for evidence when and where the perpetrator of a crime is lawfully arrested. The fact of prior lawful arrest distinguishes the arrestee from society at large, and distinguishes a search for evidence of *his* crime from general rummaging. Moreover, it is not illogical to assume that evidence of a crime is most likely to be found where the suspect was apprehended.

* * *

Belton cannot reasonably be explained as a mere application of *Chimel*. Rather, it is a return to the broader sort of search incident to arrest that we allowed before *Chimel*—limited, of course, to searches of motor vehicles, a category of "effects" which give rise to a reduced expectation of privacy, and heightened law enforcement needs.

Limitations on Arrest-Power Rule as Applied to Automobile Searches: Arizona v. Gant

In the following case, the Court rejected the *Belton* rule, insofar as that rule was read to allow the automatic search of the passenger compartment of a car after a recent occupant of the car was arrested. But it also embraces the situation-based approach we saw in some of the court opinions discussed above as well as Justice Scalia's evidence-based view of the arrest power in the context of cars from *Thornton*.

ARIZONA V. GANT

Supreme Court of the United States, 2009.
556 U.S. 332.

JUSTICE STEVENS delivered the opinion of the Court.

After Rodney Gant was arrested for driving with a suspended license, handcuffed, and locked in the back of a patrol car, police officers searched his car and discovered cocaine in the pocket of a jacket on the backseat. Because Gant could not have accessed his car to retrieve weapons or evidence at the time of the search, the Arizona Supreme Court held that the search-incident-to-arrest exception to the Fourth Amendment's warrant requirement, as defined in Chimel v. California, and applied to vehicle searches in New York v. Belton, did not justify the search in this case. We agree with that conclusion.

[W]e hold that *Belton* does not authorize a vehicle search incident to a recent occupant's arrest after the arrestee has been secured and cannot access the interior of the vehicle. Consistent with the holding in Thornton v. United States, and following the suggestion in Justice Scalia's opinion concurring in the judgment in that case, we also conclude that circumstances unique to the automobile context justify a search incident to arrest when it is reasonable to believe that evidence of the offense of arrest might be found in the vehicle.

[During an earlier identification check, officers learned that Gant's driver's license was suspended. Later that day, officers observed Gant drive up to a house, park, and exit his car. Officers arrested Gant for driving on a suspended license, handcuffed him, and locked him in the back of a squad car. The officers then searched the passenger compartment of Gant's car and found a plastic bag containing cocaine.]

Gant was charged with two offenses—possession of a narcotic drug for sale and possession of drug paraphernalia (i.e., the plastic bag in which the cocaine was found). He moved to suppress the evidence seized from his car on the ground that * * * *Belton* did not authorize the search of his vehicle because he posed no threat to the officers after he was handcuffed in the patrol car and because he was arrested for a traffic offense for which no evidence could be found in his vehicle. When asked at the suppression hearing why the search was conducted, Officer Griffith responded: "Because the law says we can do it." * * *

* * *

In *Belton*, we considered *Chimel*'s application to the automobile context. [The Court discusses the facts and arguments of the parties in *Belton*.]

* * * [W]e held that when an officer lawfully arrests "the occupant of an automobile, he may, as a contemporaneous incident of that arrest, search the passenger compartment of the automobile" and any containers therein. That holding was based in large part on our assumption "that articles inside the relatively narrow compass of the passenger compartment of an automobile are in fact generally, even if not inevitably, within the area into which an arrestee might reach."

The Arizona Supreme Court read our decision in *Belton* as merely delineating "the proper scope of a search of the interior of an automobile" incident to an arrest. That is, when the passenger compartment is within an arrestee's reaching distance, *Belton* supplies the generalization that the entire compartment and any containers therein may be reached. On that view of *Belton*, the state court concluded that the search of Gant's car was unreasonable because Gant clearly could not have accessed his car at the time of the search.

* * *

Despite the textual and evidentiary support for the Arizona Supreme Court's reading of *Belton*, our opinion has been widely understood to allow a vehicle search incident to the arrest of a recent occupant even if there is no possibility the arrestee could gain access to the vehicle at the time of the search. * * *

Under this broad reading of *Belton*, a vehicle search would be authorized incident to every arrest of a recent occupant notwithstanding that in most cases the vehicle's passenger compartment will not be within the arrestee's reach at the time of the search. To read *Belton* as authorizing a vehicle search incident to every recent occupant's arrest would thus untether the rule from the justifications underlying the *Chimel* exception * * *. Accordingly, we reject this reading of *Belton* and hold that the *Chimel* rationale authorizes police to search a vehicle incident to a recent occupant's arrest only when the arrestee is unsecured and within reaching distance of the passenger compartment at the time of the search.[a]

Although it does not follow from *Chimel*, we also conclude that circumstances unique to the vehicle context justify a search incident to a lawful arrest when it is "reasonable to believe evidence relevant to the crime of arrest might be found in the vehicle." *Thornton* (Scalia, J., concurring in judgment). In many cases, as when a recent occupant is arrested for a traffic violation, there will be no reasonable basis to believe the vehicle contains relevant evidence. But in others, including *Belton* and *Thornton*, the offense of arrest will supply a basis for searching the passenger compartment of an arrestee's vehicle and any containers therein.

Neither the possibility of access nor the likelihood of discovering offense-related evidence authorized the search in this case. Unlike in *Belton*, which involved a single officer confronted with four unsecured arrestees, the five officers in this case outnumbered the three arrestees, all of whom had been handcuffed and secured in separate patrol cars before the officers searched Gant's car. Under those circumstances, Gant clearly was not within reaching distance of his car at the time of the search. An evidentiary basis for the search was also lacking in this case. Whereas

[a] Because officers have many means of ensuring the safe arrest of vehicle occupants, it will be the rare case in which an officer is unable to fully effectuate an arrest so that a real possibility of access to the arrestee's vehicle remains. * * * But in such a case a search incident to arrest is reasonable under the Fourth Amendment.

Belton and Thornton were arrested for drug offenses, Gant was arrested for driving with a suspended license—an offense for which police could not expect to find evidence in the passenger compartment of Gant's car. * * *

The State does not seriously disagree with the Arizona Supreme Court's conclusion that Gant could not have accessed his vehicle at the time of the search, but it nevertheless asks us to uphold the search of his vehicle under the broad reading of *Belton* discussed above. The State argues that *Belton* searches are reasonable regardless of the possibility of access in a given case because that expansive rule correctly balances law enforcement interests, including the interest in a bright-line rule, with an arrestee's limited privacy interest in his vehicle.

For several reasons, we reject the State's argument. First, the State seriously undervalues the privacy interests at stake. Although we have recognized that a motorist's privacy interest in his vehicle is less substantial than in his home, the former interest is nevertheless important and deserving of constitutional protection. It is particularly significant that *Belton* searches authorize police officers to search not just the passenger compartment but every purse, briefcase, or other container within that space. A rule that gives police the power to conduct such a search whenever an individual is caught committing a traffic offense, when there is no basis for believing evidence of the offense might be found in the vehicle, creates a serious and recurring threat to the privacy of countless individuals. * * * At the same time as it undervalues these privacy concerns, the State exaggerates the clarity that its reading of *Belton* provides. Courts that have read *Belton* expansively are at odds regarding how close in time to the arrest and how proximate to the arrestee's vehicle an officer's first contact with the arrestee must be to bring the encounter within *Belton*'s purview and whether a search is reasonable when it commences or continues after the arrestee has been removed from the scene. The rule has thus generated a great deal of uncertainty, particularly for a rule touted as providing a "bright line."

Contrary to the State's suggestion, a broad reading of *Belton* is also unnecessary to protect law enforcement safety and evidentiary interests. Under our view, *Belton* and *Thornton* permit an officer to conduct a vehicle search when an arrestee is within reaching distance of the vehicle or it is reasonable to believe the vehicle contains evidence of the offense of arrest. Other established exceptions to the warrant requirement authorize a vehicle search under additional circumstances when safety or evidentiary concerns demand. For instance, Michigan v. Long, 463 U.S. 1032 (1983), permits an officer to search a vehicle's passenger compartment when he has reasonable suspicion that an individual, whether or not the arrestee, is "dangerous" and might access the vehicle to "gain immediate control of weapons." If there is probable cause to believe a vehicle contains evidence of criminal activity, United States v. Ross, 456 U.S. 798 (1982), authorizes a search of any area of the vehicle in which the evidence might be found. Unlike the searches permitted by Justice Scalia's opinion concurring in the judgment in *Thornton*, which we conclude today are reasonable for purposes of the Fourth Amendment, *Ross* allows searches for evidence relevant to offenses other than the offense of arrest, and the scope of the search authorized is broader. * * *

These exceptions together ensure that officers may search a vehicle when genuine safety or evidentiary concerns encountered during the arrest of a vehicle's recent occupant justify a search. Construing *Belton* broadly to allow vehicle searches incident to any arrest would serve no purpose except to provide a police entitlement, and it is anathema to the Fourth Amendment to permit a warrantless search on that basis. * * *

Our dissenting colleagues argue that the doctrine of stare decisis requires adherence to a broad reading of *Belton* even though the justifications for searching a vehicle incident to arrest are in most cases absent. The doctrine of stare decisis is of course "essential to the respect accorded to the judgments of the Court and to the stability of the law," but it does not compel us to follow a past decision when its rationale no longer withstands "careful analysis."

* * *

Police may search a vehicle incident to a recent occupant's arrest only if the arrestee is within reaching distance of the passenger compartment at the time of the search or it is reasonable to believe the vehicle contains evidence of the offense of arrest. When these justifications are absent, a search of an arrestee's vehicle will be unreasonable unless police obtain a warrant or show that another exception to the warrant requirement applies. The Arizona Supreme Court correctly held that this case involved an unreasonable search. Accordingly, the judgment of the State Supreme Court is affirmed.

JUSTICE SCALIA, concurring.

To determine what is an "unreasonable" search within the meaning of the Fourth Amendment, we look first to the historical practices the Framers sought to preserve; if those provide inadequate guidance, we apply traditional standards of reasonableness. Since the historical scope of officers' authority to search vehicles incident to arrest is uncertain, traditional standards of reasonableness govern. It is abundantly clear that those standards do not justify what I take to be the rule set forth in New York v. Belton, and *Thornton*: that arresting officers may always search an arrestee's vehicle in order to protect themselves from hidden weapons. When an arrest is made in connection with a roadside stop, police virtually always have a less intrusive and more effective means of ensuring their safety—and a means that is virtually always employed: ordering the arrestee away from the vehicle, patting him down in the open, handcuffing him, and placing him in the squad car.

* * *

Justice STEVENS acknowledges that an officer-safety rationale cannot justify all vehicle searches incident to arrest, but asserts that that is not the rule *Belton* and Thornton adopted. * * * Justice STEVENS would therefore retain the application of Chimel v. California in the car-search context but would apply in the future what he believes our cases held in the past: that officers making a roadside stop may search the vehicle so long as the "arrestee is within reaching distance of the passenger compartment at the time of the search." I believe that this standard fails to provide the needed guidance to arresting officers and also leaves much room for manipulation, inviting officers to leave the scene unsecured (at least where dangerous suspects are not involved) in order to conduct a vehicle search. In my view we should simply abandon the *Belton-Thornton* charade of officer safety and overrule those cases. I would hold that a vehicle search incident to arrest is ipso facto "reasonable" only when the object of the search is evidence of the crime for which the arrest was made, or of another crime that the officer has probable cause to believe occurred. Because respondent was arrested for driving without a license (a crime for which no evidence could be expected to be found in the vehicle), I would hold in the present case that the search was unlawful.

Justice Alito insists that the Court must demand a good reason for abandoning prior precedent. That is true enough, but it seems to me ample reason that the precedent was badly reasoned and produces erroneous (in this case unconstitutional) results. We should recognize *Belton's* fanciful reliance upon officer safety for what it was: a return to the broader sort of [evidence-gathering] search incident to arrest that we allowed before *Chimel*.

* * *

No other Justice, however, shares my view that application of *Chimel* in this context should be entirely abandoned. It seems to me unacceptable for the Court to come forth with a 4-to-1-to-4 opinion that leaves the governing rule uncertain. I am therefore confronted with the choice of either leaving the current understanding of *Belton* and *Thornton* in effect, or acceding to what seems to me the artificial narrowing of those cases adopted by Justice STEVENS. The latter, as I have said, does not provide the degree of certainty I think desirable in this field; but the former opens the field to what I think are plainly unconstitutional searches—which is the greater evil. I therefore join the opinion of the Court.

JUSTICE BREYER, dissenting.

I agree with Justice Alito that New York v. Belton is best read as setting forth a bright-line rule that permits a warrantless search of the passenger compartment of an automobile incident to the lawful arrest of an occupant-regardless of the danger the arrested individual in fact poses. I also agree with Justice Stevens, however, that the rule can produce results divorced from its underlying Fourth Amendment rationale. For that reason I would look for a better rule—were the question before us one of first impression.

The matter, however, is not one of first impression, and that fact makes a substantial difference. The *Belton* rule has been followed not only by this Court in Thornton v. United States, but also by numerous other courts. Principles of stare decisis must apply, and those who wish this Court to change a well-established legal precedent—where, as here, there has been considerable reliance on the legal rule in question—bear a heavy burden. I have not found that burden met. * * *

JUSTICE ALITO, with whom THE CHIEF JUSTICE and JUSTICE KENNEDY join, and with whom JUSTICE BREYER joins except as to Part II-E, dissenting.

I

Although the Court refuses to acknowledge that it is overruling *Belton* and *Thornton*, there can be no doubt that it does so.

* * *

The precise holding in *Belton* could not be clearer. The Court stated unequivocally: "[W]e hold that when a policeman has made a lawful custodial arrest of the occupant of an automobile, he may, as a contemporaneous incident of that arrest, search the passenger compartment of that automobile."

* * *

II

* * *

Abandonment of the *Belton* rule cannot be justified on the ground that the dangers surrounding the arrest of a vehicle occupant are different today than they were 28 years ago. The Court claims that "[w]e now know that articles inside the passenger compartment are rarely within the area into which an arrestee might reach," but surely it was well known in 1981 that a person who is taken from a vehicle, handcuffed, and placed in the back of a patrol car is unlikely to make it back into his own car to retrieve a weapon or destroy evidence.

* * * The *Belton* rule has not proved to be unworkable. On the contrary, the rule was adopted for the express purpose of providing a test that would be relatively easy for police officers and judges to apply. * * *

E

* * * The Court is harshly critical of *Belton*'s reasoning, but the problem that the Court perceives cannot be remedied simply by overruling *Belton*. *Belton* represented only a modest—and quite defensible—extension of *Chimel*, as I understand that decision.

* * *

Unfortunately, *Chimel* did not say whether "the area from within which [an arrestee] might gain possession of a weapon or destructible evidence" is to be measured at the time of the arrest or at the time of the search, but unless the *Chimel* rule was meant to be a specialty rule, applicable to only a few unusual cases, the Court must have intended for this area to be measured at the time of arrest.

This is so because the Court can hardly have failed to appreciate the following two facts. First, in the great majority of cases, an officer making an arrest is able to handcuff the arrestee and remove him to a secure place before conducting a search incident to the arrest. Second, because it is safer for an arresting officer to secure an arrestee before searching, it is likely that this is what arresting officers do in the great majority of cases. * * * Thus, if the area within an arrestee's reach were assessed, not at the time of arrest, but at the time of the search, the *Chimel* rule would rarely come into play.

Moreover, if the applicability of the *Chimel* rule turned on whether an arresting officer chooses to secure an arrestee prior to conducting a search, rather than searching first and securing the arrestee later, the rule would create a perverse incentive for an arresting officer to prolong the period during which the arrestee is kept in an area where he could pose a danger to the officer. * * *

I do not think that this is what the *Chimel* Court intended. Handcuffs were in use in 1969. The ability of arresting officers to secure arrestees before conducting a search—and their incentive to do so—are facts that can hardly have escaped the Court's attention. I therefore believe that the *Chimel* Court intended that its new rule apply in cases in which the arrestee is handcuffed before the search is conducted.

The *Belton* Court, in my view, proceeded on the * * * assumption that the *Chimel* rule was to be applied at the time of arrest. Viewing *Chimel* as having focused on the time of arrest, *Belton*'s only new step was to eliminate the need to decide on a case-by-case basis whether a particular person seated in a car actually could have reached the part of the passenger compartment where a weapon or evidence was hidden. For this reason, if we are going to reexamine *Belton*, we should also reexamine the reasoning in *Chimel* on which *Belton* rests.

F

The Court, however, does not reexamine *Chimel* and thus leaves the law relating to searches incident to arrest in a confused and unstable state. The first part of the Court's new two-part rule—which permits an arresting officer to search the area within an arrestee's reach at the time of the search—applies, at least for now, only to vehicle occupants and recent occupants, but there is no logical reason why the same rule should not apply to all arrestees.

The second part of the Court's new rule, which the Court takes uncritically from Justice Scalia's separate opinion in *Thornton*, raises doctrinal and practical problems that the Court makes no effort to address. Why, for example, is the standard for this type of evidence-gathering search "reason to believe" rather than probable cause? And why is this type of search restricted to evidence of the offense of arrest? * * * [I]f reason-to-believe is the governing standard for an evidence-gathering search incident to arrest, it is not easy to see why an officer should not be able to search when the officer has reason to believe that the vehicle in question possesses evidence of a crime other than the crime of arrest.

Nor is it easy to see why an evidence-gathering search incident to arrest should be restricted to the passenger compartment. The *Belton* rule was limited in this way because the passenger compartment was considered to be the area that vehicle occupants can generally reach, but since the second part of the new rule is not based on officer safety or the preservation of evidence, the ground for this limitation is obscure.

QUESTIONS AFTER GANT

As Justice Alito predicted, the lower courts after *Gant* are now trending toward a time-of-search rule for *all* searches incident to arrest. See the discussion of *Shakir* earlier in this section. Doesn't this mean, as Justice Alito believes, that the arrest-power rule provides little if any utility for officers—because at the time of the search the officer will ordinarily have put the arrestee in custody so that he no longer presents any risk of destroying evidence or getting a weapon? Is Justice Alito correct that the Court in *Chimel* could not have been going to so much trouble to craft a rule that would seldom if ever be used?

Perhaps, though, a time-of-search rule might still lead to a finding that a passenger car was in the grab area in a particular case. For example, suppose a single officer arrests a driver of a car in which there are five tough-looking occupants, and it is late at night in a high crime area. If the officer searches the passenger compartment before securing all the occupants, would such a search be valid under *Gant*? See United States v. Salamasina, 615 F.3d 925

(8th Cir. 2010) (search of passenger compartment permissible under *Gant*; while the defendant was secured, his wife was not, and she was repeatedly entering and exiting the vehicle to tend to her children, and was communicating to the defendant in a foreign language despite the officers' direction not to talk to him).

What is the meaning of *Gant's* "reason to believe" test? The Court is clear that the test is not derived from *Chimel*. The Court likewise suggests that the test provides authority to search separate from the "car exception" to the warrant requirement, which we will discuss later in this Chapter. It therefore seems that, secondary to the lawful arrest of a driver, a search of the passenger compartment of a car is permitted upon proof less than probable cause. See United States v. Vinton, 594 F.3d 14 (D.C. Cir. 2010) ("Presumably, the 'reason to believe' standard requires less than probable cause, because otherwise *Gant's* evidentiary rationale would merely duplicate the automobile exception, which the Court in *Gant* specifically identified as a distinct exception to the warrant requirement."). Not surprisingly, the lower courts after *Gant* have interpreted "reason to believe" as equivalent to the reasonable suspicion standard established in *Terry*. Id. But what is the constitutional basis for justifying a search for evidence on less than probable cause? Does this rule rely to some degree on the rationale for the automobile exception? If so, then why create a separate rule for searches secondary to arrests?

Even as so construed, the "reason to believe" standard appears to be of marginal use to officers because it is specifically limited to evidence of the offense for which the suspect has been arrested. See United States v. Paige, 870 F.3d 693 (7th Cir. 2017) (officer arrested the defendant for driving while impaired, and smelled marijuana; this gives reason to believe that there is evidence of impairment in the car). Thus, in a case involving a traffic violation, like *Gant,* the "reason to believe" test will not be useful because there will rarely be evidence of the traffic violation in the passenger compartment. And for arrests on evidence-based crimes, such as drug offenses, the "reason to believe" test will be of little utility because if there is probable cause to arrest the defendant there will, in all but a few cases, be probable cause to believe that there is evidence of that crime in his car—and so the evidence could be found through the automobile exception.

If the "reason to believe" test somehow becomes untethered from the crime for which the person is arrested—as Justice Alito suggests is a logical result—*then* it could be a different matter. For example, if officers have only reasonable suspicion that the defendant is dealing drugs, and arrest him for a traffic offense, then the "reason to believe" prong of *Gant*—if it applied—would be very useful to the police. It would come close to the arrest power rules that were granted by *Belton*.

One thing about the "reason to believe" exception in *Gant* is clear: it is independent of the "access by the suspect" exception. For example, in United States v. Stegall, 850 F.3d 981 (8th Cir. 2017), officers responded to a road rage incident in which a driver brandished a gun. Eventually they arrested Stegall in his vehicle, charged him with terroristic threats, and placed him with restraints in the back of the patrol car. Then they searched the vehicle and found an unregistered gun. The court found that there was a "reasonable basis to believe Stegall's SUV contained evidence relevant to the terroristic threat charge—the gun." Stegall argued that the second *Gant* exception could not apply because he was secured in the squad car at the time of the search. But the court found that this argument "fails to appreciate the distinct rationales underlying the two *Gant* exceptions." One is based on the *Chimel* safety and security interests, while the other is based on evidentiary interests as described by Justice Scalia in *Thornton*.

5. Searches of Cellphones and Other Electronics Incident to Arrest

Robinson held that the officer could thoroughly search the cigarette pack even without any showing on the facts that there was evidence or a weapon in that container. Thus under *Robinson* there would appear to be an automatic right to search any container found on a person subject to a custodial arrest. But in the following case, the Court refuses to extend the automatic search rule of *Robinson* to searches of cellphones found on an arrestee. It is worth noting that this case falls in time between the Court's decisions in United States v. Jones, 565 U.S. 400 (2012), the GPS tracking case, and Carpenter v. United States, 138 S.Ct. 2206 (2018), the cell site location case.

RILEY V. CALIFORNIA

Supreme Court of the United States, 2014.
573 U.S. 373.

CHIEF JUSTICE ROBERTS delivered the opinion of the Court.

These two cases raise a common question: whether the police may, without a warrant, search digital information on a cell phone seized from an individual who has been arrested.

* * *

In the first case, petitioner David Riley was stopped by a police officer for driving with expired registration tags. In the course of the stop, the officer also learned that Riley's license had been suspended. The officer impounded Riley's car, pursuant to department policy, and another officer conducted an inventory search of the car. Riley was arrested for possession of concealed and loaded firearms when that search turned up two handguns under the car's hood.

An officer searched Riley incident to the arrest and found items associated with the "Bloods" street gang. He also seized a cell phone from Riley's pants pocket. * * * [T]he phone was a "smart phone," a cell phone with a broad range of other functions based on advanced computing capability, large storage capacity, and Internet connectivity. The officer accessed information on the phone and noticed that some words (presumably in text messages or a contacts list) were preceded by the letters "CK"—a label that, he believed, stood for "Crip Killers," a slang term for members of the Bloods gang.

At the police station about two hours after the arrest, a detective specializing in gangs further examined the contents of the phone. The detective testified that he "went through" Riley's phone "looking for evidence, because . . . gang members will often video themselves with guns or take pictures of themselves with the guns." Although there was "a lot of stuff" on the phone, particular files that "caught [the detective's] eye" included videos of young men sparring while someone yelled encouragement using the moniker "Blood." The police also found photographs of Riley standing in front of a car they suspected had been involved in a shooting a few weeks earlier. [Riley's motion to suppress the evidence found on his cellphone was denied and he was convicted of weapons-related and gang-related crimes. The lower courts affirmed the trial court's ruling that the search of the cellphone incident to arrest did not violate the Fourth Amendment.]

* * *

In the second case, a police officer performing routine surveillance observed respondent Brima Wurie make an apparent drug sale from a car. Officers subsequently arrested Wurie and took him to the police station. At the station, the officers seized two cell phones from Wurie's person. The one at issue here was a "flip phone," a kind of phone that is flipped open for use and that generally has a smaller range of features than a smart phone. Five to ten minutes after arriving at the station, the officers noticed that the phone was repeatedly receiving calls from a source identified as "my house" on the phone's external screen. A few minutes later, they opened the phone and saw a photograph of a woman and a baby set as the phone's wallpaper. They pressed one button on the phone to access its call log, then another button to determine the phone number associated with the "my house" label. They next used an online phone directory to trace that phone number to an apartment building.

When the officers went to the building, they saw Wurie's name on a mailbox and observed through a window a woman who resembled the woman in the photograph on Wurie's phone. They secured the apartment while obtaining a search warrant and, upon later executing the warrant, found and seized 215 grams of crack cocaine, marijuana, drug paraphernalia, a firearm and ammunition, and cash.

[The trial court found that the search of the phone was permissible as incident to arrest, but the First Circuit disagreed].

* * *

The two cases before us concern the reasonableness of a warrantless search incident to a lawful arrest. In 1914, this Court first acknowledged in dictum "the right on the part of the Government, always recognized under English and American law, to search the person of the accused when legally arrested to discover and seize the fruits or evidences of crime." Since that time, it has been well accepted that such a search constitutes an exception to the warrant requirement. * * *

Although the existence of the exception for such searches has been recognized for a century, its scope has been debated for nearly as long. That debate has focused on the extent to which officers may search property found on or near the arrestee. Three related precedents set forth the rules governing such searches.

[The Court describes and discusses *Chimel, Robinson,* and *Gant.*]

* * *

These cases require us to decide how the search incident to arrest doctrine applies to modern cell phones, which are now such a pervasive and insistent part of daily life that the proverbial visitor from Mars might conclude they were an important feature of human anatomy. A smart phone of the sort taken from Riley was unheard of ten years ago; a significant majority of American adults now own such phones. Even less sophisticated phones like Wurie's, which have already faded in popularity since Wurie was arrested in 2007, have been around for less than 15 years. Both phones are based on technology nearly inconceivable just a few decades ago, when *Chimel* and *Robinson* were decided.

Absent more precise guidance from the founding era, we generally determine whether to exempt a given type of search from the warrant requirement by assessing, on the one hand, the degree to which it intrudes upon an individual's privacy and, on the other, the degree to which it is needed for the promotion of legitimate governmental interests. Such a balancing of interests supported the search incident to arrest exception in *Robinson*, and a mechanical application of *Robinson* might well support the warrantless searches at issue here.

But while *Robinson*'s categorical rule strikes the appropriate balance in the context of physical objects, neither of its rationales has much force with respect to digital content on cell phones. On the government interest side, *Robinson* concluded that the two risks identified in *Chimel*—harm to officers and destruction of evidence—are present in all custodial arrests. There are no comparable risks when the search is of digital data. In addition, *Robinson* regarded any privacy interests retained by an individual after arrest as significantly diminished by the fact of the arrest itself. Cell phones, however, place vast quantities of personal information literally in the hands of individuals. A search of the information on a cell phone bears little resemblance to the type of brief physical search considered in *Robinson.*

We therefore decline to extend *Robinson* to searches of data on cell phones, and hold instead that officers must generally secure a warrant before conducting such a search.

* * *

We first consider each *Chimel* concern in turn. In doing so, we do not overlook *Robinson*'s admonition that searches of a person incident to arrest, "while based upon the need to disarm and to discover evidence," are reasonable regardless of "the probability in a particular arrest situation that weapons or evidence would in fact be found." Rather than requiring the "case-by-case adjudication" that *Robinson* rejected, we ask instead whether application of the search incident to arrest doctrine to this particular category of effects would "untether the rule from the justifications underlying the *Chimel* exception," *Gant.*

* * *

Digital data stored on a cell phone cannot itself be used as a weapon to harm an arresting officer or to effectuate the arrestee's escape. Law enforcement officers remain free to examine the physical aspects of a phone to ensure that it will not be used as a weapon—say, to determine whether there is a razor blade hidden between the phone and its case. Once an officer has secured a phone and eliminated any potential physical threats, however, data on the phone can endanger no one.

Perhaps the same might have been said of the cigarette pack seized from Robinson's pocket. Once an officer gained control of the pack, it was unlikely that Robinson could have accessed the pack's contents. But unknown physical objects may always pose risks, no matter how slight, during the tense atmosphere of a custodial arrest. The officer in *Robinson* testified that he could not identify the objects in the cigarette pack but knew they were not cigarettes. Given that, a further search was a reasonable protective measure. No such unknowns exist with respect to digital data. As the First Circuit explained, the officers who searched Wurie's cell phone "knew exactly what they would find therein: data. They also knew that the data could not harm them."

The United States and California both suggest that a search of cell phone data might help ensure officer safety in more indirect ways, for example by alerting officers that confederates of the arrestee are headed to the scene. There is undoubtedly a strong government interest in warning officers about such possibilities, but neither the United States nor California offers evidence to suggest that their concerns are based on actual experience. The proposed consideration would also represent a broadening of *Chimel*'s concern that an *arrestee himself* might grab a weapon and use it against an officer "to resist arrest or effect his escape." * * * To the extent dangers to arresting officers may be implicated in a particular way in a particular case, they are better addressed through consideration of case-specific exceptions to the warrant requirement, such as the one for exigent circumstances.

* * *

The United States and California focus primarily on the second *Chimel* rationale: preventing the destruction of evidence.

Both Riley and Wurie concede that officers could have seized and secured their cell phones to prevent destruction of evidence while seeking a warrant. That is a sensible concession. And once law enforcement officers have secured a cell phone, there is no longer any risk that the arrestee himself will be able to delete incriminating data from the phone.

The United States and California argue that information on a cell phone may nevertheless be vulnerable to two types of evidence destruction unique to digital data—remote wiping and data encryption. * * *

As an initial matter, these broader concerns about the loss of evidence are distinct from *Chimel*'s focus on a defendant who responds to arrest by trying to conceal or destroy evidence within his reach. With respect to remote wiping, the Government's primary concern turns on the actions of third parties who are not present at the scene of arrest. And data encryption is even further afield. There, the Government focuses on the ordinary operation of a phone's security features, apart from *any* active attempt by a defendant or his associates to conceal or destroy evidence upon arrest.

We have also been given little reason to believe that either problem is prevalent. The briefing reveals only a couple of anecdotal examples of remote wiping triggered by an arrest. Similarly, the opportunities for officers to search a password-protected phone before data becomes encrypted are quite limited. Law enforcement officers are very unlikely to come upon such a phone in an unlocked state because most phones lock at the touch of a button or, as a default, after some very short period of inactivity. * * *

In any event, as to remote wiping, law enforcement is not without specific means to address the threat. Remote wiping can be fully prevented by disconnecting a phone from the network. There are at least two simple ways to do this: First, law enforcement officers can turn the phone off or remove its battery. Second, if they are concerned about encryption or other potential problems, they can leave a phone powered on and place it in an enclosure that isolates the phone from radio waves. Such devices are commonly called "Faraday bags," after the English scientist Michael

Faraday. They are essentially sandwich bags made of aluminum foil: cheap, lightweight, and easy to use. They may not be a complete answer to the problem, but at least for now they provide a reasonable response. * * *

To the extent that law enforcement still has specific concerns about the potential loss of evidence in a particular case, there remain more targeted ways to address those concerns. If the police are truly confronted with a "now or never situation,"—for example, circumstances suggesting that a defendant's phone will be the target of an imminent remote-wipe attempt—they may be able to rely on exigent circumstances to search the phone immediately. Or, if officers happen to seize a phone in an unlocked state, they may be able to disable a phone's automatic-lock feature in order to prevent the phone from locking and encrypting data.

* * *

The search incident to arrest exception rests not only on the heightened government interests at stake in a volatile arrest situation, but also on an arrestee's reduced privacy interests upon being taken into police custody. * * * Put simply, a patdown of Robinson's clothing and an inspection of the cigarette pack found in his pocket constituted only minor additional intrusions compared to the substantial government authority exercised in taking Robinson into custody.

The fact that an arrestee has diminished privacy interests does not mean that the Fourth Amendment falls out of the picture entirely. * * * To the contrary, when privacy-related concerns are weighty enough a search may require a warrant, notwithstanding the diminished expectations of privacy of the arrestee. One such example, of course, is *Chimel*. * * * Because a search of the arrestee's entire house was a substantial invasion beyond the arrest itself, the Court concluded that a warrant was required.

Robinson is the only decision from this Court applying *Chimel* to a search of the contents of an item found on an arrestee's person. * * * Lower courts applying *Robinson* and *Chimel*, however, have approved searches of a variety of personal items carried by an arrestee. See, *e.g.*, United States v. Carrion, 809 F.2d 1120, 1123, 1128 (CA5 1987) (billfold and address book); United States v. Watson, 669 F.2d 1374, 1383–1384 (CA11 1982) (wallet); United States v. Lee, 501 F.2d 890, 892 (CADC 1974) (purse).

The United States asserts that a search of all data stored on a cell phone is "materially indistinguishable" from searches of these sorts of physical items. That is like saying a ride on horseback is materially indistinguishable from a flight to the moon. Both are ways of getting from point A to point B, but little else justifies lumping them together. Modern cell phones, as a category, implicate privacy concerns far beyond those implicated by the search of a cigarette pack, a wallet, or a purse. A conclusion that inspecting the contents of an arrestee's pockets works no substantial additional intrusion on privacy beyond the arrest itself may make sense as applied to physical items, but any extension of that reasoning to digital data has to rest on its own bottom.

* * *

Cell phones differ in both a quantitative and a qualitative sense from other objects that might be kept on an arrestee's person. The term "cell phone" is itself misleading shorthand; many of these devices are in fact minicomputers that also happen to have the capacity to be used as a telephone. * * *

One of the most notable distinguishing features of modern cell phones is their immense storage capacity. Before cell phones, a search of a person was limited by physical realities and tended as a general matter to constitute only a narrow intrusion on privacy. Most people cannot lug around every piece of mail they have received for the past several months, every picture they have taken, or every book or article they have read—nor would they have any reason to attempt to do so. And if they did, they would have to drag behind them a trunk of the sort held to require a search warrant * * *, rather than a container the size of the cigarette package in *Robinson*.

But the possible intrusion on privacy is not physically limited in the same way when it comes to cell phones. * * * We expect that the gulf between physical practicability and digital capacity will only continue to widen in the future.

The storage capacity of cell phones has several interrelated consequences for privacy. First, a cell phone collects in one place many distinct types of information—an address, a note, a prescription, a bank statement, a video—that reveal much more in combination than any isolated record. Second, a cell phone's capacity allows even just one type of information to convey far more than previously possible. The sum of an individual's private life can be reconstructed through a thousand photographs labeled with dates, locations, and descriptions; the same cannot be said of a photograph or two of loved ones tucked into a wallet. Third, the data on a phone can date back to the purchase of the phone, or even earlier. A person might carry in his pocket a slip of paper reminding him to call Mr. Jones; he would not carry a record of all his communications with Mr. Jones for the past several months, as would routinely be kept on a phone.

Finally, there is an element of pervasiveness that characterizes cell phones but not physical records. * * * A decade ago police officers searching an arrestee might have occasionally stumbled across a highly personal item such as a diary. But those discoveries were likely to be few and far between. Today, by contrast, it is no exaggeration to say that many of the more than

90% of American adults who own a cell phone keep on their person a digital record of nearly every aspect of their lives—from the mundane to the intimate. Allowing the police to scrutinize such records on a routine basis is quite different from allowing them to search a personal item or two in the occasional case.

Although the data stored on a cell phone is distinguished from physical records by quantity alone, certain types of data are also qualitatively different. An Internet search and browsing history, for example, can be found on an Internet-enabled phone and could reveal an individual's private interests or concerns—perhaps a search for certain symptoms of disease, coupled with frequent visits to WebMD. Data on a cell phone can also reveal where a person has been. Historic location information is a standard feature on many smart phones and can reconstruct someone's specific movements down to the minute, not only around town but also within a particular building.

Mobile application software on a cell phone, or "apps," offer a range of tools for managing detailed information about all aspects of a person's life. There are apps for Democratic Party news and Republican Party news; apps for alcohol, drug, and gambling addictions; apps for sharing prayer requests; apps for tracking pregnancy symptoms; apps for planning your budget; apps for every conceivable hobby or pastime; apps for improving your romantic life. * * * There are over a million apps available in each of the two major app stores; the phrase "there's an app for that" is now part of the popular lexicon. The average smart phone user has installed 33 apps, which together can form a revealing montage of the user's life.

* * * Indeed, a cell phone search would typically expose to the government far *more* than the most exhaustive search of a house: A phone not only contains in digital form many sensitive records previously found in the home; it also contains a broad array of private information never found in a home in any form—unless the phone is.

* * *

To further complicate the scope of the privacy interests at stake, the data a user views on many modern cell phones may not in fact be stored on the device itself. Treating a cell phone as a container whose contents may be searched incident to an arrest is a bit strained as an initial matter. But the analogy crumbles entirely when a cell phone is used to access data located elsewhere, at the tap of a screen. That is what cell phones, with increasing frequency, are designed to do by taking advantage of "cloud computing." * * *

The United States concedes that the search incident to arrest exception may not be stretched to cover a search of files accessed remotely—that is, a search of files stored in the cloud. Such a search would be like finding a key in a suspect's pocket and arguing that it allowed law enforcement to unlock and search a house. But officers searching a phone's data would not typically know whether the information they are viewing was stored locally at the time of the arrest or has been pulled from the cloud.

Although the Government recognizes the problem, its proposed solutions are unclear. It suggests that officers could disconnect a phone from the network before searching the device—the very solution whose feasibility it contested with respect to the threat of remote wiping. Alternatively, the Government proposes that law enforcement agencies "develop protocols to address" concerns raised by cloud computing. Probably a good idea, but the Founders did not fight a revolution to gain the right to government agency protocols. The possibility that a search might extend well beyond papers and effects in the physical proximity of an arrestee is yet another reason that the privacy interests here dwarf those in *Robinson*.

* * *

Apart from their arguments for a direct extension of *Robinson*, the United States and California offer various fallback options for permitting warrantless cell phone searches under certain circumstances. Each of the proposals is flawed and contravenes our general preference to provide clear guidance to law enforcement through categorical rules. * * *

The United States first proposes that the *Gant* standard be imported from the vehicle context, allowing a warrantless search of an arrestee's cell phone whenever it is reasonable to believe that the phone contains evidence of the crime of arrest. But *Gant* relied on "circumstances unique to the vehicle context" to endorse a search solely for the purpose of gathering evidence. Justice Scalia's *Thornton* opinion, on which *Gant* was based, explained that those unique circumstances are "a reduced expectation of privacy" and "heightened law enforcement needs" when it comes to motor vehicles. For reasons that we have explained, cell phone searches bear neither of those characteristics.

At any rate, a *Gant* standard would prove no practical limit at all when it comes to cell phone searches. In the vehicle context, *Gant* generally protects against searches for evidence of past crimes. In the cell phone context, however, it is reasonable to expect that incriminating information will be found on a phone regardless of when the crime occurred. Similarly, in the vehicle context *Gant* restricts broad searches resulting from minor crimes such as traffic violations. That would not necessarily be true for cell phones. It would be a particularly inexperienced or unimaginative law enforcement officer who could not come up with several reasons to suppose evidence of just about any crime could be found on a cell phone. Even an individual pulled over for something as basic as speeding might well have locational data dispositive of guilt on his phone. An individual pulled over for reckless driving might have evidence on the phone that shows whether he was texting while driving. The sources of potential pertinent information are virtually unlimited, so applying the *Gant* standard to cell phones would in effect give police officers unbridled discretion to rummage at will among a person's private effects.

The United States also proposes a rule that would restrict the scope of a cell phone search to those areas of the phone where an officer reasonably believes that information relevant to the crime, the arrestee's identity, or officer safety will be discovered. This approach would again impose few meaningful constraints on officers. The proposed categories would sweep in a great deal of information, and officers would not always be able to discern in advance what information would be found where.

We also reject the United States' final suggestion that officers should always be able to search a phone's call log, as they did in Wurie's case. The Government relies on Smith v. Maryland, 442 U.S. 735 (1979), which held that no warrant was required to use a pen register at telephone company premises to identify numbers dialed by a particular caller. The Court in that case, however, concluded that the use of a pen register was not a "search" at all under the Fourth Amendment. There is no dispute here that the officers engaged in a search of Wurie's cell phone. Moreover, call logs typically contain more than just phone numbers; they include any identifying information that an individual might add, such as the label "my house" in Wurie's case.

Finally, at oral argument California suggested a different limiting principle, under which officers could search cell phone data if they could have obtained the same information from a pre-digital counterpart. But the fact that a search in the pre-digital era could have turned up a photograph or two in a wallet does not justify a search of thousands of photos in a digital gallery. * * * And to make matters worse, such an analogue test would allow law enforcement to search a range of items contained on a phone, even though people would be unlikely to carry such a variety of information in physical form. In Riley's case, for example, it is implausible that he would have strolled around with video tapes, photo albums, and an address book all crammed into his pockets. But because each of those items has a pre-digital analogue, police under California's proposal would be able to search a phone for all of those items—a significant diminution of privacy.

* * *

We cannot deny that our decision today will have an impact on the ability of law enforcement to combat crime. Cell phones have become important tools in facilitating coordination and communication among members of criminal enterprises, and can provide valuable incriminating information about dangerous criminals. Privacy comes at a cost.

Our holding, of course, is not that the information on a cell phone is immune from search; it is instead that a warrant is generally required before such a search, even when a cell phone is seized incident to arrest. Our cases have historically recognized that the warrant requirement is an important working part of our machinery of government, not merely "an inconvenience to be somehow weighed against the claims of police efficiency. Recent technological advances similar to those discussed here have, in addition, made the process of obtaining a warrant itself more efficient.

Moreover, even though the search incident to arrest exception does not apply to cell phones, other case-specific exceptions may still justify a warrantless search of a particular phone. One well-recognized exception applies when the exigencies of the situation make the needs of law enforcement so compelling that a warrantless search is objectively reasonable under the Fourth Amendment. * * *

In light of the availability of the exigent circumstances exception, there is no reason to believe that law enforcement officers will not be able to address some of the more extreme hypotheticals that have been suggested: a suspect texting an accomplice who, it is feared, is preparing to detonate a bomb, or a child abductor who may have information about the child's location on his cell phone. The defendants here recognize—indeed, they stress—that such fact-specific threats may justify a warrantless search of cell phone data. The critical point is that, unlike the search incident to arrest exception, the exigent circumstances exception requires a court to examine whether an emergency justified a warrantless search in each particular case.

Our cases have recognized that the Fourth Amendment was the founding generation's response to the reviled general warrants and writs of assistance of the colonial era, which allowed British officers to rummage through homes in an unrestrained search for evidence of criminal activity. Opposition to such searches was in fact one of the driving forces behind the Revolution itself. * * *

Modern cell phones are not just another technological convenience. With all they contain and all they may reveal, they hold for many Americans the privacies of life. The fact that technology now allows an individual to carry such information in his hand does not make the information any less worthy of the protection for which the Founders fought. Our answer to the question of what police must do before searching a cell phone seized incident to an arrest is accordingly simple—get a warrant.

* * *

JUSTICE ALITO, concurring in part and concurring in the judgment.

I agree with the Court that law enforcement officers, in conducting a lawful search incident to arrest, must generally obtain a warrant before searching information stored or accessible on a cell phone. I write separately to address two points.

* * *

First, I am not convinced at this time that the ancient rule on searches incident to arrest is based exclusively (or even primarily) on the need to protect the safety of arresting officers and the need to prevent the destruction of evidence. This rule antedates the adoption of the Fourth Amendment by at least a century. * * *

[Justice Alito cites and discusses state cases and treatises from the 1800's.]

The idea that officer safety and the preservation of evidence are the sole reasons for allowing a warrantless search incident to arrest appears to derive from the Court's reasoning in Chimel v. California, a case that involved the lawfulness of a search of the scene of an arrest, not the person of an arrestee. As I have explained [in *Gant*] *Chimel*'s reasoning is questionable, and I think it is a mistake to allow that reasoning to affect cases like these that concern the search of the person of arrestees.

* * *

Despite my view on the point discussed above, I agree that we should not mechanically apply the rule used in the predigital era to the search of a cell phone. Many cell phones now in use are capable of storing and accessing a quantity of information, some highly personal, that no person would ever have had on his person in hard-copy form. This calls for a new balancing of law enforcement and privacy interests.

* * *

This brings me to my second point. While I agree with the holding of the Court, I would reconsider the question presented here if either Congress or state legislatures, after assessing the legitimate needs of law enforcement and the privacy interests of cell phone owners, enact legislation that draws reasonable distinctions based on categories of information or perhaps other variables.

* * * [I]t would be very unfortunate if privacy protection in the 21st century were left primarily to the federal courts using the blunt instrument of the Fourth Amendment. Legislatures, elected by the people, are in a better position than we are to assess and respond to the changes that have already occurred and those that almost certainly will take place in the future.

NOTE ON RILEY

Does *Riley* establish special rules for cellphones across the board, given the privacy interests in cellphones emphasized by the Court? Or does *Riley* apply special protection only when a cellphone is searched incident to arrest? We will consider the applicability of *Riley* to other kinds of warrantless searches, such as searches at the border, under the automobile exception, under the inventory exception, etc. For now it might be said that the government interest supporting each of these exceptions will be different from those supporting the arrest-power rule.

In addition to being noteworthy for its holding, *Riley* represents an important part of the Court's evolving Fourth Amendment jurisprudence in the context of new and emerging technologies. With *Jones* and *Carpenter*, that jurisprudence takes seriously the "quantitative and qualitative" differences between both law enforcement technologies and consumer technologies. How do you think the Court's reasoning in these cases might apply to other technologies such as connected devices inhabiting the internet of things, geofencing, pole cameras, networked surveillance systems, and "Big Data"? As you think through these questions, consider the Court's reasoning in Birchfield v. North Dakota, which is discussed in the next section.

6. Breathalyzers and Blood Tests Incident to Arrest

The Court in *Riley* noted that, while the arrest power rule leads to bright-line rules (as opposed to a case-by-case approach), a balance of interests determines which bright line rule to apply—warrant or no warrant. In the following case, the Supreme Court follows that construct to determine whether the arrest power rule justifies breathalyzers and blood tests incident to arrest of a driver for driving while impaired.

BIRCHFIELD V. NORTH DAKOTA

Supreme Court of the United States, 2016.
579 U.S. 438.

JUSTICE ALITO delivered the opinion of the Court.

Drunk drivers take a grisly toll on the Nation's roads * * * . To fight this problem, all States have laws that prohibit motorists from driving with a blood alcohol concentration (BAC) that exceeds a specified level. But determining whether a driver's BAC is over the legal limit requires a test, and many drivers stopped on suspicion of drunk driving would not submit to testing if given the option. So every State also has long had what are termed "implied consent laws." These laws impose penalties on motorists who refuse to undergo testing when there is sufficient reason to believe they are violating the State's drunk-driving laws.

In the past, the typical penalty for noncompliance was suspension or revocation of the motorist's license. The cases now before us involve laws that go beyond that and make it a crime for a motorist to refuse to be tested after being lawfully arrested for driving while impaired. The question presented is whether such laws violate the Fourth Amendment's prohibition against unreasonable searches.

[Justice Alito discusses the history of state regulation of drunk driving, and the development of breath testing machines and blood tests.]

Measurement of BAC [blood alcohol content] based on a breath test requires the cooperation of the person being tested. The subject must take a deep breath and exhale through a mouthpiece that connects to the machine. * * *

Because the cooperation of the test subject is necessary when a breath test is administered and highly preferable when a blood sample is taken, the enactment of laws defining intoxication based on BAC made it necessary for States to find a way of securing such cooperation. * * *

To combat the problem of test refusal, some States have begun to enact laws making it a crime to refuse to undergo testing. Minnesota has taken this approach for decades. And that may partly explain why its refusal rate now is below the national average. * * * North Dakota adopted a similar law, in 2013. * * *

[Justice Alito describes the facts of the three consolidated cases.]

* * * [S]uccess for all three petitioners depends on the proposition that the criminal law ordinarily may not compel a motorist to submit to the taking of a blood sample or to a breath test unless a warrant authorizing such testing is issued by a magistrate. If, on the other hand, such warrantless searches comport with the Fourth Amendment, it follows that a State may criminalize the refusal to comply with a demand to submit to the required testing, just as a State may make it a crime for a person to obstruct the execution of a valid search warrant. * * * We therefore begin by considering whether the searches demanded in these cases were consistent with the Fourth Amendment.

* * *

We have previously had occasion to examine whether one such exception—for "exigent circumstances"—applies in drunk-driving investigations. * * * [W]e have held that the natural dissipation of alcohol from the bloodstream does not *always* constitute an exigency justifying the warrantless taking of a blood sample. That was the holding of Missouri v. McNeely, [569 U.S. 141] (2013), where the State of Missouri was seeking a *per se* rule that "whenever an officer has probable cause to believe an individual has been driving under the influence of alcohol, exigent circumstances will necessarily exist because BAC evidence is inherently evanescent." We disagreed, emphasizing that [the Court] had adopted a case-specific analysis depending on "all of the facts and circumstances of the particular case." * * *

While emphasizing that the exigent-circumstances exception must be applied on a case-by-case basis, the *McNeely* Court noted that other exceptions to the warrant requirement "apply categorically" rather than in a "case-specific" fashion. One of these * * * is the long-established rule that a warrantless search may be conducted incident to a lawful arrest. * * *

The search-incident-to-arrest doctrine has an ancient pedigree. Well before the Nation's founding, it was recognized that officers carrying out a lawful arrest had the authority to make a warrantless search of the arrestee's person. [Justice Alito discusses *Chimel* and *Robinson*.]

Our decision two Terms ago in Riley v. California reaffirmed "*Robinson*'s categorical rule" and explained how the rule should be applied in situations that could not have been envisioned when the Fourth Amendment was adopted. * * * "Absent more precise guidance from the founding era," the Court wrote, "we generally determine whether to exempt a given type of search from the warrant requirement by assessing, on the one hand, the degree to which it intrudes upon an individual's privacy and, on the other, the degree to which it is needed for the promotion of legitimate governmental interests."

Blood and breath tests to measure blood alcohol concentration are not as new as searches of cell phones, but here, as in *Riley*, the founding era does not provide any definitive guidance as to whether they should be allowed incident to arrest. Lacking such guidance, we engage in the same mode of analysis as in *Riley*: we examine "the degree to which [they] intrud[e] upon an individual's privacy and . . . the degree to which [they are] needed for the promotion of legitimate governmental interests."

* * *

We begin by considering the impact of breath and blood tests on individual privacy interests, and we will discuss each type of test in turn.

* * *

Years ago we said that breath tests do not implicate significant privacy concerns. That remains so today.

First, the physical intrusion is almost negligible. Breath tests do not require piercing the skin and entail a minimum of inconvenience. [T]he process requires the arrestee to blow continuously for 4 to 15 seconds into a straw-like mouthpiece that is connected by a tube to the test machine. * * * The effort is no more demanding than blowing up a party balloon.

Petitioner Bernard argues, however, that the process is nevertheless a significant intrusion because the arrestee must insert the mouthpiece of the machine into his or her mouth. But there is nothing painful or strange about this requirement. The use of a straw to drink beverages is a common practice and one to which few object.

Nor, contrary to Bernard, is the test a significant intrusion because it "does not capture an ordinary exhalation of the kind that routinely is exposed to the public" but instead requires a sample of "alveolar" (deep lung) air. Humans have never been known to assert a possessory interest in or any emotional attachment to *any* of the air in their lungs. * * * Humans cannot hold their breath for more than a few minutes, and all the air that is breathed into a breath analyzing machine, including deep lung air, sooner or later would be exhaled even without the test.

* * *

Second, breath tests are capable of revealing only one bit of information, the amount of alcohol in the subject's breath. [Justice Alito contrasts DNA swabbing.]

Finally, participation in a breath test is not an experience that is likely to cause any great enhancement in the embarrassment that is inherent in any arrest. The act of blowing into a straw is not inherently embarrassing, nor are evidentiary breath tests administered in a manner that causes embarrassment. Again, such tests are normally administered in private at a police station, in a patrol car, or in a mobile testing facility, out of public view. Moreover, once placed under arrest, the individual's expectation of privacy is necessarily diminished.

* * *

Blood tests are a different matter. They require piercing the skin and extract a part of the subject's body. And while humans exhale air from their lungs many times per minute, humans do not continually shed blood. It is true, of course, that people voluntarily submit to the taking of blood samples as part of a physical examination, and the process involves little pain or risk. Nevertheless, for many, the process is not one they relish. It is significantly more intrusive than blowing into a tube. * * *

In addition, a blood test, unlike a breath test, places in the hands of law enforcement authorities a sample that can be preserved and from which it is possible to extract information beyond a simple BAC reading. Even if the law enforcement agency is precluded from testing the blood for any purpose other than to measure BAC, the potential remains and may result in anxiety for the person tested.

* * *

Having assessed the impact of breath and blood testing on privacy interests, we now look to the States' asserted need to obtain BAC readings for persons arrested for drunk driving.

* * *

The States and the Federal Government have a paramount interest in preserving the safety of public highways. * * * Alcohol consumption is a leading cause of traffic fatalities and injuries. * * *

Justice Sotomayor's partial dissent suggests that States' interests in fighting drunk driving are satisfied once suspected drunk drivers are arrested, since such arrests take intoxicated drivers off the roads where they might do harm. But of course States are not solely concerned with neutralizing the threat posed by a drunk driver who has already gotten behind the wheel. They also have a compelling interest in creating effective deterrents to drunken driving so such individuals make responsible decisions and do not become a threat to others in the first place.

* * *

Petitioners and Justice Sotomayor contend that the States and the Federal Government could combat drunk driving in other ways that do not have the same impact on personal privacy. Their arguments are unconvincing.

The chief argument on this score is that an officer making an arrest for drunk driving should not be allowed to administer a BAC test unless the officer procures a search warrant or could not do so in time to obtain usable test results. * * * This argument contravenes our decisions holding that the legality of a search incident to arrest must be judged on the basis of categorical rules. In *Robinson,* for example, no one claimed that the object of the search, a package of cigarettes, presented any danger to the arresting officer or was at risk of being destroyed in the time that it would have taken to secure a search warrant. The Court nevertheless upheld the constitutionality of a warrantless search of the package, concluding that a categorical rule was needed to give police adequate guidance * * * .

* * *

In advocating the case-by-case approach, petitioners and Justice Sotomayor cite language in our *McNeely* opinion. But *McNeely* concerned an exception to the warrant requirement—for exigent circumstances—that always requires case-by-case determinations. * * *

Petitioners and Justice Sotomayor next suggest that requiring a warrant for BAC testing in every case in which a motorist is arrested for drunk driving would not impose any great burden on the police or the courts. But of course the same argument could be made about searching through objects found on the arrestee's possession, which our cases permit even in the absence of a warrant. * * *

If a search warrant were required for every search incident to arrest that does not involve exigent circumstances, the courts would be swamped. * * * The number of arrests every year for driving under the influence is enormous—more than 1.1 million in 2014. Particularly in sparsely populated areas, it would be no small task for courts to field a large new influx of warrant applications that could come on any day of the year and at any hour. In many jurisdictions, judicial officers have the authority to issue warrants only within their own districts, and in rural areas, some districts may have only a small number of judicial officers.

* * *

In light of this burden and our prior search-incident-to-arrest precedents, petitioners would at a minimum have to show some special need for warrants for BAC testing. It is therefore appropriate to consider the benefits that such applications would provide. Search warrants protect privacy in two main ways. First, they ensure that a search is not carried out unless a neutral magistrate makes an independent determination that there is probable cause to believe that evidence will be found. Second, if the magistrate finds probable cause, the warrant limits the intrusion on privacy by specifying the scope of the search—that is, the area that can be searched and the items that can be sought.

How well would these functions be performed by the warrant applications that petitioners propose? In order to persuade a magistrate that there is probable cause for a search warrant, the officer would typically recite the same facts that led the officer to find that there was probable cause for arrest, namely, that there is probable cause to believe that a BAC test will reveal that the motorist's blood alcohol level is over the limit. As these three cases suggest, * * * the facts that establish probable cause are largely the same from one drunk-driving stop to the next and consist largely of the officer's own characterization of his or her observations—for example, that there was a strong odor of alcohol, that the motorist wobbled when attempting to stand, that the motorist paused when reciting the alphabet or counting backwards, and so on. A magistrate would be in a poor position to challenge such characterizations.

As for the second function served by search warrants—delineating the scope of a search—the warrants in question here would not serve that function at all. In every case the scope of the warrant would simply be a BAC test of the arrestee. * * *

Petitioner Bernard objects to the whole idea of analyzing breath and blood tests as searches incident to arrest. * * * On his reading, this Court's precedents permit a search of an arrestee solely to prevent the arrestee from obtaining a weapon or taking steps to destroy evidence. * * * Stopping an arrestee from destroying evidence, Bernard argues, is critically different from preventing the loss of blood alcohol evidence as the result of the body's metabolism of alcohol, a natural process over which the arrestee has little control.

The distinction that Bernard draws between an arrestee's active destruction of evidence and the loss of evidence due to a natural process makes little sense. In both situations the State is justifiably concerned that evidence may be lost, and Bernard does not explain why the cause of the loss should be dispositive. * * *

Nor is there any reason to suspect that *Chimel*'s use of the word "destruction," was a deliberate decision to rule out evidence loss that is mostly beyond the arrestee's control. The case did not involve any evidence that was subject to dissipation through natural processes, and there is no sign in the opinion that such a situation was on the Court's mind.

* * *

Having assessed the effect of BAC tests on privacy interests and the need for such tests, we conclude that the Fourth Amendment permits warrantless breath tests incident to arrests for drunk driving. The impact of breath tests on privacy is slight, and the need for BAC testing is great.

We reach a different conclusion with respect to blood tests. Blood tests are significantly more intrusive, and their reasonableness must be judged in light of the availability of the less invasive alternative of a breath test. Respondents have offered no satisfactory justification for demanding the more intrusive alternative without a warrant.

Neither respondents nor their *amici* dispute the effectiveness of breath tests in measuring BAC. Breath tests have been in common use for many years. Their results are admissible in court and are widely credited by juries, and respondents do not dispute their accuracy or utility. What, then, is the justification for warrantless blood tests?

One advantage of blood tests is their ability to detect not just alcohol but also other substances that can impair a driver's ability to operate a car safely. A breath test cannot do this, but police have other measures at their disposal when they have reason to believe that a motorist may be under the influence of some other substance (for example, if a breath test indicates that a clearly impaired motorist has little if any alcohol in his blood). Nothing prevents the police from seeking a warrant for a blood test when there is sufficient time to do so in the particular circumstances or from relying on the exigent circumstances exception to the warrant requirement when there is not.

* * *

It is true that a blood test, unlike a breath test, may be administered to a person who is unconscious (perhaps as a result of a crash) or who is unable to do what is needed to take a breath test due to profound intoxication or injuries. But we have no reason to believe that such situations are common in drunk-driving arrests, and when they arise, the police may apply for a warrant if need be.

A breath test may also be ineffective if an arrestee deliberately attempts to prevent an accurate reading by failing to blow into the tube for the requisite length of time or with the necessary force. But courts have held that such conduct qualifies as a refusal to undergo testing, and it may be prosecuted as such. And again, a warrant for a blood test may be sought.

Because breath tests are significantly less intrusive than blood tests and in most cases amply serve law enforcement interests, we conclude that a breath test, but not a blood test, may be administered as a search incident to a lawful arrest for drunk driving. As in all cases involving reasonable searches incident to arrest, a warrant is not needed in this situation.

* * *

JUSTICE SOTOMAYOR, with whom JUSTICE GINSBURG joins, concurring in part and dissenting in part.

[Justice Sotomayor agreed with the majority that criminalizing refusal to undergo a blood test without a warrant was a violation of the Fourth Amendment. She disagreed, however, with the majority's holding that a warrantless breath test was permissible as a search incident to arrest—and therefore that the state could criminalize refusal. Excerpts from her opinion follow.]

[T]he Court cites the governmental interest in protecting the public from drunk drivers. But it is critical to note that once a person is stopped for drunk driving and arrested, he no longer poses an immediate threat to the public. Because the person is already in custody prior to the administration of the breath test, there can be no serious claim that the time it takes to obtain a warrant would increase the danger that drunk driver poses to fellow citizens.

* * *

[T]he Court and the States cite a governmental interest in minimizing the costs of gathering evidence of drunk driving. But neither has demonstrated that requiring police to obtain warrants for breath tests would impose a sufficiently significant burden on state resources to justify the elimination of the Fourth Amendment's warrant requirement. * * * The Court finds a categorical exception to the warrant requirement because each of a State's judges and magistrate judges would need to issue less than one extra warrant a week.

* * *

Without even considering the comparative effectiveness of case-by-case and categorical exceptions, the Court reaches for the categorical search-incident-to-arrest exception and enshrines it for all breath tests. * * *

The search-incident-to-arrest exception is applied categorically precisely because the needs it addresses could arise in every arrest. But the government's need to conduct a breath test is present only in arrests for drunk driving. And the asserted need to conduct a breath test without a warrant arises only when a warrant cannot be obtained during the significant built-in delay between arrest and testing. The conditions that require warrantless breath searches, in short, are highly situational and defy the logical underpinnings of the search-incident-to-arrest exception and its categorical application.

* * *

JUSTICE THOMAS, concurring in the judgment in part and dissenting in part.

* * *

Today's decision chips away at a well-established exception to the warrant requirement. * * * Under our precedents, a search incident to lawful arrest required no additional justification. Not until the recent decision in Riley v. California did the Court begin to retreat from this categorical approach because it feared that the search at issue, the "search of the information on a cell phone," bore "little resemblance to the type of brief physical search" contemplated by this Court's past search-incident-to-arrest decisions. I joined *Riley*, however, because the Court resisted the temptation to permit searches of some kinds of cellphone data and not others, and instead asked more generally whether that entire "category of effects" was searchable without a warrant.

Today's decision begins where *Riley* left off. The Court purports to apply *Robinson* but further departs from its categorical approach by holding that warrantless breath tests to prevent the destruction of BAC evidence are constitutional searches incident to arrest, but warrantless blood tests are not. That hairsplitting makes little sense. Either the search-incident-to-arrest exception permits bodily searches to prevent the destruction of BAC evidence, or it does not.

* * *

7. Custodial Arrests for Minor Offenses

The Court in *Robinson* was not called upon to address whether Robinson's custodial arrest was reasonable under the Fourth Amendment. Robinson challenged only the search and not the validity of the arrest for a traffic offense. But is it reasonable to impose the serious intrusion of a custodial arrest and the consequent intrusion of a search incident to arrest upon a person who has done nothing more than commit a minor offense? The Court addresses this question in the following case.

ATWATER V. CITY OF LAGO VISTA

Supreme Court of the United States, 2001.
532 U.S. 318.

JUSTICE SOUTER delivered the opinion of the Court.

The question is whether the Fourth Amendment forbids a warrantless arrest for a minor criminal offense, such as a misdemeanor seatbelt violation punishable only by a fine. We hold that it does not.

* * * In Texas, if a car is equipped with safety belts, a front-seat passenger must wear one, and the driver must secure any small child riding in front. Violation of either provision is a misdemeanor punishable by a fine not less than $25 or more than $50. Texas law expressly authorizes "[a]ny peace officer [to] arrest without warrant a person found committing a violation" of these seatbelt laws, although it permits police to issue citations in lieu of arrest.

In March 1997, Petitioner Gail Atwater was driving her pickup truck in Lago Vista, Texas, with her 3-year-old son and 5-year-old daughter in the front seat. None of them was wearing a seatbelt. Respondent Bart Turek, a Lago Vista police officer at the time, observed the seatbelt violations and pulled Atwater over. According to Atwater's complaint (the allegations of which we assume to be true for present purposes), Turek approached the truck and "yelled" something to the effect of "we've met before" and "you're going to jail." [Turek had previously stopped Atwater for what he had thought was a seatbelt violation, but then had realized that Atwater's son, although seated on the vehicle's armrest, was in fact belted in. Atwater acknowledged that her son's seating position was unsafe, and Turek had issued a verbal warning.] He then called for backup and asked to see Atwater's driver's license and insurance documentation, which state law required her to carry. When Atwater told Turek that she did not have the papers because her purse had been stolen the day before, Turek said that he had "heard that story two-hundred times." Atwater asked to take her "frightened, upset, and crying" children to a friend's house nearby, but Turek told her, "you're not going anywhere." As it turned out, Atwater's friend learned what was going on and soon arrived to take charge of the children. Turek then handcuffed Atwater, placed her in his squad car, and drove her to the local police station, where booking officers had her remove her shoes, jewelry, and eyeglasses, and empty her pockets. Officers took Atwater's "mug shot" and placed her, alone, in a jail cell for about one hour, after which she was taken before a magistrate and released on $310 bond. Atwater was charged with driving without her seatbelt fastened, failing to secure her children in seatbelts, driving without a license, and failing to provide proof of insurance. She ultimately pleaded no contest to the misdemeanor seatbelt offenses and paid a $50 fine; the other charges were dismissed.

* * * Atwater and her husband * * * filed suit * * * under 42 U.S.C. § 1983 against Turek and respondents City of Lago Vista and Chief of Police Frank Miller. So far as concerns us, petitioners (whom we will simply call Atwater) alleged that respondents (for simplicity, the City) had violated Atwater's Fourth Amendment "right to be free from unreasonable seizure," and sought compensatory and punitive damages. * * * Given Atwater's admission that she had "violated the law" * * * the District Court ruled the Fourth Amendment claim "meritless" and granted the City's summary judgment motion. [The Fifth Circuit ultimately agreed with the lower court.]

* * * Atwater's specific contention is that "founding-era common-law rules" forbade peace officers to make warrantless misdemeanor arrests except in cases of "breach of the peace," a category she claims was then understood narrowly as covering only those nonfelony offenses "involving or tending toward violence." Although her historical argument is by no means insubstantial, it ultimately fails.

* * * [Justice Souter engages in an extensive and detailed analysis of pre-founding English common law and concludes that, "the common-law commentators (as well as the sparsely reported cases) reached divergent conclusions with respect to officers' warrantless misdemeanor arrest power. Moreover, in the years leading up to American independence, Parliament repeatedly extended express warrantless arrest authority to cover misdemeanor-level offenses not amounting to or involving any violent breach of the peace."]

* * * An examination of specifically American evidence is to the same effect. Neither the history of the framing era nor subsequent legal development indicates that the Fourth Amendment was originally understood, or has traditionally been read, to embrace Atwater's position.

[Justice Souter engages in another extensive and detailed analysis of American practice with respect to arrests, both pre-and post-founding. He concludes that there was a basic assumption that a custodial arrest was reasonable for nonviolent misdemeanors.]

* * * Small wonder, then, that today statutes in all 50 States and the District of Columbia permit warrantless misdemeanor arrests by at least some (if not all) peace officers without requiring any breach of the peace, as do a host of congressional enactments. * * * Atwater does not wager all on history. * * * Atwater * * * argues for a modern arrest rule * * * forbidding custodial arrest, even upon probable cause, when conviction

could not ultimately carry any jail time and when the government shows no compelling need for immediate detention.

If we were to derive a rule exclusively to address the uncontested facts of this case, Atwater might well prevail. She was a known and established resident of Lago Vista with no place to hide and no incentive to flee, and common sense says she would almost certainly have buckled up as a condition of driving off with a citation. In her case, the physical incidents of arrest were merely gratuitous humiliations imposed by a police officer who was (at best) exercising extremely poor judgment. * * *

But we have traditionally recognized that a responsible Fourth Amendment balance is not well served by standards requiring sensitive, case-by-case determinations of government need, lest every discretionary judgment in the field be converted into an occasion for constitutional review. Often enough, the Fourth Amendment has to be applied on the spur (and in the heat) of the moment, and the object in implementing its command of reasonableness is to draw standards sufficiently clear and simple to be applied with a fair prospect of surviving judicial second-guessing months and years after an arrest or search is made. * * *

At first glance, Atwater's argument may seem to respect the values of clarity and simplicity, so far as she claims that the Fourth Amendment generally forbids warrantless arrests for minor crimes not accompanied by violence or some demonstrable threat of it (whether "minor crime" be defined as a fine-only traffic offense, a fine-only offense more generally, or a misdemeanor). But the claim is not ultimately so simple, nor could it be, for complications arise the moment we begin to think about the possible applications of the several criteria Atwater proposes for drawing a line between minor crimes with limited arrest authority and others not so restricted.

One line, she suggests, might be between "jailable" and "fine-only" offenses * * *. The trouble with this distinction, of course, is that an officer on the street might not be able to tell. It is not merely that we cannot expect every police officer to know the details of frequently complex penalty schemes, but that penalties for ostensibly identical conduct can vary on account of facts difficult (if not impossible) to know at the scene of an arrest. Is this the first offense or is the suspect a repeat offender? Is the weight of the marijuana a gram above or a gram below the fine-only line? Where conduct could implicate more than one criminal prohibition, which one will the district attorney ultimately decide to charge? And so on. * * *

* * * Atwater's rule therefore would not only place police in an almost impossible spot but would guarantee increased litigation over many of the arrests that would occur. For all these reasons, Atwater's various distinctions between permissible and impermissible arrests for minor

crimes strike us as very unsatisfactory lines to require police officers to draw on a moment's notice. * * *

* * * The very fact that the law has never jelled the way Atwater would have it leads one to wonder whether warrantless misdemeanor arrests need constitutional attention, and there is cause to think the answer is no. So far as such arrests might be thought to pose a threat to the probable-cause requirement, anyone arrested for a crime without formal process, whether for felony or misdemeanor, is entitled to a magistrate's review of probable cause within 48 hours, and there is no reason to think the procedure in this case atypical in giving the suspect a prompt opportunity to request release. Many jurisdictions, moreover, have chosen to impose more restrictive safeguards through statutes limiting warrantless arrests for minor offenses. It is of course easier to devise a minor-offense limitation by statute than to derive one through the Constitution, simply because the statute can let the arrest power turn on any sort of practical consideration without having to subsume it under a broader principle. It is, in fact, only natural that States should resort to this sort of legislative regulation, for * * * it is in the interest of the police to limit petty-offense arrests, which carry costs that are simply too great to incur without good reason. Finally, and significantly, under current doctrine the preference for categorical treatment of Fourth Amendment claims gives way to individualized review when a defendant makes a colorable argument that an arrest, with or without a warrant, was conducted in an extraordinary manner, unusually harmful to his privacy or even physical interests. The upshot of all these influences, combined with the good sense (and, failing that, the political accountability) of most local lawmakers and law-enforcement officials, is a dearth of horribles demanding redress. * * *

Accordingly, we confirm today what our prior cases have intimated: * * * If an officer has probable cause to believe that an individual has committed even a very minor criminal offense in his presence, he may, without violating the Fourth Amendment, arrest the offender.

* * * Atwater's arrest satisfied constitutional requirements. There is no dispute that Officer Turek had probable cause to believe that Atwater had committed a crime in his presence. * * * Turek was accordingly authorized (not required, but authorized) to make a custodial arrest without balancing costs and benefits or determining whether or not Atwater's arrest was in some sense necessary.

Nor was the arrest made in an "extraordinary manner, unusually harmful to [her] privacy or * * * physical interests." * * * Atwater's arrest was surely "humiliating," * * * but it was no more "harmful to privacy or physical interests" than the normal custodial arrest. * * *

JUSTICE O'CONNOR, with whom JUSTICE STEVENS, JUSTICE GINSBURG, and JUSTICE BREYER join, dissenting.

* * *

The per se rule that the Court creates has potentially serious consequences for the everyday lives of Americans. A broad range of conduct falls into the category of fine-only misdemeanors. In Texas alone, for example, disobeying any sort of traffic warning sign is a misdemeanor punishable only by fine, as is failing to pay a highway toll, and driving with expired license plates. Nor are fine-only crimes limited to the traffic context. In several States, for example, littering is a criminal offense punishable only by fine. * * * Under today's holding, when a police officer has probable cause to believe that a fine-only misdemeanor offense has occurred, that officer may stop the suspect, issue a citation, and let the person continue on her way. Or, if a traffic violation, the officer may stop the car, arrest the driver, search the driver, * * * and impound the car and inventory all of its contents. * * * Such unbounded discretion carries with it grave potential for abuse. * * * Indeed, as the recent debate over racial profiling demonstrates all too clearly, a relatively minor traffic infraction may often serve as an excuse for stopping and harassing an individual. After today, the arsenal available to any officer extends to a full arrest and the searches permissible concomitant to that arrest. An officer's subjective motivations for making a traffic stop are not relevant considerations in determining the reasonableness of the stop. But it is precisely because these motivations are beyond our purview that we must vigilantly ensure that officers' post stop actions—which are properly within our reach—comport with the Fourth Amendment's guarantee of reasonableness.

* * *

Arrests for Minor Offenses After Atwater

The *Atwater* majority relies in part of a "dearth of horribles"—few if any examples of full custodial arrests for fine-only offenses. After *Atwater* there have indeed been real-life examples of such arrests; one such instance was reviewed by then-Judge Roberts in Hedgepeth v. Washington Metro Area Transit Auth., 386 F.3d 1148 (D.C. Cir. 2004). Judge Roberts described the facts:

> No one is very happy about the events that led to this litigation. A twelve-year-old girl was arrested, searched, and handcuffed. Her shoelaces were removed, and she was transported in the windowless rear compartment of a police vehicle to a juvenile processing center, where she was booked, fingerprinted, and detained until released to her mother some three hours later—all for eating a single french fry in a Metrorail station. The child was frightened, embarrassed, and crying throughout the ordeal.

The arrest was the result of WMATA's "zero-tolerance" policy for violations of the rule prohibiting eating on the subway. The arrest was made by an undercover officer, whose job that day was to pose as a passenger and look for people eating on the subway. Judge Roberts found that, while the arrest was the result of bad policy—a policy subsequently suspended due to public outcry—it was not unreasonable under the Fourth Amendment. The court concluded: "Given the undisputed existence of probable cause, *Atwater* precludes further inquiry into the reasonableness" of the arrest.

Could the *Atwater* Court take comfort in the fact that, after the student's arrest, the public outcry was so great that the WMATA ended its policy of arresting people for violating the no-eating rule?

8. The Arrest Power Rule Where No Custodial Arrest Takes Place

What if an officer issues a ticket or summons rather than effecting a full custodial arrest? Does the arrest-power rule still permit a search of the person and the grab area? In Knowles v. Iowa, 525 U.S. 113 (1998), the Court held that the arrest-power rule is limited to situations in which the person is subjected to a custodial arrest. Chief Justice Rehnquist, writing for a unanimous Court, noted that the threat to officer safety from issuing a traffic citation "is a good deal less than in the case of a custodial arrest." Moreover, the threat of destruction of evidence of a traffic stop was nonexistent. In Knowles's case, he was stopped for speeding, and "[n]o further evidence of excessive speed was going to be found either on the person of the offender or in the passenger compartment of the car." The Court also noted that the *Terry* doctrine was in place to protect the interests of officers, should circumstances warrant.

QUESTION ON KNOWLES

By denying the right to a search in the absence of a custodial arrest, isn't the Court providing police officers with an incentive to use a custodial arrest rather than a ticket or summons for minor offenses? How does encouraging police officers to act more intrusively further Fourth Amendment values?

9. The Arrest Power Rule Where the Arrest Violates State Law

In Virginia v. Moore, 553 U.S. 164 (2008), the Court considered whether a police officer violates the Fourth Amendment by searching a person incident to a custodial arrest based on probable cause, when the custodial arrest was not authorized by state law. Moore was arrested for driving with a suspended license. Officers searched him incident to the arrest and found drugs. State law, however, did not permit a custodial arrest for driving with a suspended license. But the Court, in an opinion by

Justice Scalia for eight Justices, held that the search was valid under the Fourth Amendment. Justice Scalia reasoned as follows:

> [L]inking Fourth Amendment protections to state law would cause them to vary from place to place and from time to time. Even at the same place and time, the Fourth Amendment's protections might vary if federal officers were not subject to the same statutory constraints as state officers. * * * It would be strange to construe a constitutional provision that did not apply to the States at all when it was adopted to now restrict state officers more than federal officers, solely because the States have passed search-and-seizure laws that are the prerogative of independent sovereigns.
>
> We conclude that warrantless arrests for crimes committed in the presence of an arresting officer are reasonable under the Constitution, and that while States are free to regulate such arrests however they desire, state restrictions do not alter the Fourth Amendment's protections.

Because the arrest was valid, the Court also found the search of Moore's person to be valid under *Robinson*.[27]

QUESTION AFTER VIRGINIA V. MOORE

Recall that, in his dissenting opinion in Carpenter v. United States, the cell site location case, Justice Gorsuch discusses the possibility of referencing positive law when assessing whether law enforcement activities violate reasonable expectations of privacy or intrude upon constitutionally protected property interests. Based on his analysis in *Moore*, do you think that Justice Scalia would endorse this approach to defining "search"?

G. PRETEXTUAL STOPS AND ARRESTS

The authority we have discussed this far, such as *Terry* and *Robinson,* give police officers the right to conduct certain searches on the basis of a stop or arrest for a minor offense, such as a traffic offense. Is it possible that these investigatory powers as to minor crimes can be used to search for evidence of a more serious crime for which probable cause or reasonable suspicion does not exist? Is it possible that the right to stop/arrest/search pursuant to a minor traffic offense could be used by police as a tool for harassing citizens, particularly minorities? Does the Fourth Amendment protect a citizen from pretextual stops, arrests and searches if the citizen has in fact committed a minor offense? The Supreme Court considered these questions in the following case.

---

[27] Justice Ginsburg concurred in the judgment.

WHREN V. UNITED STATES

Supreme Court of the United States, 1996.
517 U.S. 806.

JUSTICE SCALIA delivered the opinion of the Court.

In this case we decide whether the temporary detention of a motorist who the police have probable cause to believe has committed a civil traffic violation is inconsistent with the Fourth Amendment's prohibition against unreasonable seizures unless a reasonable officer would have been motivated to stop the car by a desire to enforce the traffic laws.

* * *

On the evening of June 10, 1993, plainclothes vice-squad officers of the District of Columbia Metropolitan Police Department were patrolling a "high drug area" of the city in an unmarked car. Their suspicions were aroused when they passed a dark Pathfinder truck with temporary license plates and youthful occupants waiting at a stop sign, the driver looking down into the lap of the passenger at his right. The truck remained stopped at the intersection for what seemed an unusually long time—more than 20 seconds. When the police car executed a U-turn in order to head back toward the truck, the Pathfinder turned suddenly to its right, without signaling, and sped off at an "unreasonable" speed. The policemen followed, and in a short while overtook the Pathfinder when it stopped behind other traffic at a red light. They pulled up alongside, and Officer Ephraim Soto stepped out and approached the driver's door, identifying himself as a police officer and directing the driver, petitioner Brown, to put the vehicle in park. When Soto drew up to the driver's window, he immediately observed two large plastic bags of what appeared to be crack cocaine in petitioner Whren's hands. Petitioners were arrested, and quantities of several types of illegal drugs were retrieved from the vehicle.

Petitioners were charged in a four-count indictment with violating various federal drug laws, * * *. At a pretrial suppression hearing, they challenged the legality of the stop and the resulting seizure of the drugs. They argued that the stop had not been justified by probable cause to believe, or even reasonable suspicion, that petitioners were engaged in illegal drug-dealing activity; and that Officer Soto's asserted ground for approaching the vehicle—to give the driver a warning concerning traffic violations—was pretextual. [The defendants were convicted and the Court of Appeals affirmed.]

* * *

Petitioners accept that Officer Soto had probable cause to believe that various provisions of the District of Columbia traffic code had been violated. They argue, however, that "in the unique context of civil traffic regulations" probable cause is not enough. Since, they contend, the use of automobiles is so heavily and minutely regulated that total compliance with traffic and safety rules is nearly impossible, a police officer will almost invariably be able to catch any given motorist in a technical violation. This creates the temptation to use traffic stops as a means of investigating other law violations, as to which no probable cause or even articulable suspicion exists. Petitioners, who are both black, further contend that police officers might decide which motorists to stop based on decidedly impermissible factors, such as the race of the car's occupants. To avoid this danger, they say, the Fourth Amendment test for traffic stops should be, not * * * whether probable cause existed to justify the stop; but rather, whether a police officer, acting reasonably, would have made the stop for the reason given.

* * * Petitioners contend that the standard they propose is consistent with our past cases' disapproval of police attempts to use valid bases of action against citizens as pretexts for pursuing other investigatory agendas. We are reminded that in Florida v. Wells, 495 U.S. 1 (1990), we stated that "an inventory search must not be used as a ruse for a general rummaging in order to discover incriminating evidence"; * * * and that in New York v. Burger, 482 U.S. 691 (1987), we observed, in upholding the constitutionality of a warrantless administrative inspection, that the search did not appear to be "a 'pretext' for obtaining evidence of . . . violation of . . . penal laws." But * * * [i]n each case we were addressing the validity of a search conducted * * * for the purpose of inventory or administrative regulation * * *.

* * *

Not only have we never held, outside the context of inventory search or administrative inspection * * * that an officer's motive invalidates objectively justifiable behavior under the Fourth Amendment; but we have repeatedly held and asserted the contrary. * * * In United States v. Robinson, we held that a traffic-violation arrest (of the sort here) would not be rendered invalid by the fact that it was "a mere pretext for a narcotics search," and that a lawful postarrest search of the person would not be rendered invalid by the fact that it was not motivated by the officer-safety concern that justifies such searches. * * *

We think these cases foreclose any argument that the constitutional reasonableness of traffic stops depends on the actual motivations of the individual officers involved. We of course agree with petitioners that the Constitution prohibits selective enforcement of the law based on considerations such as race. But the constitutional basis for objecting to intentionally discriminatory application of laws is the Equal Protection Clause, not the Fourth Amendment. Subjective intentions play no role in ordinary, probable-cause Fourth Amendment analysis.

* * * Recognizing that we have been unwilling to entertain Fourth Amendment challenges based on the actual motivations of individual officers, petitioners disavow any intention to make the individual officer's subjective good faith the touchstone of "reasonableness." They insist that the standard they have put forward—whether the officer's conduct deviated materially from usual police practices, so that a reasonable officer in the same circumstances would not have made the stop for the reasons given—is an "objective" one.

But although framed in empirical terms, this approach is plainly and indisputably driven by subjective considerations. Its whole purpose is to prevent the police from doing under the guise of enforcing the traffic code what they would like to do for different reasons. Petitioners' proposed standard may not use the word "pretext," but it is designed to combat nothing other than the perceived "danger" of the pretextual stop, albeit only indirectly and over the run of cases. Instead of asking whether the individual officer had the proper state of mind, the petitioners would have us ask, in effect, whether (based on general police practices) it is plausible to believe that the officer had the proper state of mind.

Why one would frame a test designed to combat pretext in such fashion that the court cannot take into account actual and admitted pretext is a curiosity that can only be explained by the fact that our cases have foreclosed the more sensible option. If those cases were based only upon the evidentiary difficulty of establishing subjective intent, petitioners' attempt to root out subjective vices through objective means might make sense. But they were not based only upon that, or indeed even principally upon that. Their principal basis—which applies equally to attempts to reach subjective intent through ostensibly objective means—is simply that the Fourth Amendment's concern with "reasonableness" allows certain actions to be taken in certain circumstances, whatever the subjective intent. But even if our concern had been only an evidentiary one, petitioners' proposal would by no means assuage it. Indeed, it seems to us somewhat easier to figure out the intent of an individual officer than to plumb the collective consciousness of law enforcement in order to determine whether a "reasonable officer" would have been moved to act upon the traffic violation. While police manuals and standard procedures may sometimes provide objective assistance, ordinarily one would be reduced to speculating about the hypothetical reaction of a hypothetical constable—an exercise that might be called virtual subjectivity.

Moreover, police enforcement practices, even if they could be practicably assessed by a judge, vary from place to place and from time to time. We cannot accept that the search and seizure protections of the Fourth Amendment are so variable, and can be made to turn upon such trivialities. The difficulty is illustrated by petitioners' arguments in this case. Their claim that a reasonable officer would not have made this stop is based largely on District of Columbia police regulations which permit plainclothes officers in unmarked vehicles to enforce traffic laws "only in the case of a violation that is so grave as to pose an immediate threat to the safety of others." This basis of invalidation would not apply in jurisdictions that had a different practice. And it would not have applied, even in the District of Columbia, if Officer Soto had been wearing a uniform or patrolling in a marked police cruiser.

* * *

Petitioners urge as an extraordinary factor in this case that the "multitude of applicable traffic and equipment regulations" is so large and so difficult to obey perfectly that virtually everyone is guilty of violation, permitting the police to single out almost whomever they wish for a stop. But we are aware of no principle that would allow us to decide at what point a code of law becomes so expansive and so commonly violated that infraction itself can no longer be the ordinary measure of the lawfulness of enforcement. And even if we could identify such exorbitant codes, we do not know by what standard (or what right) we would decide, as petitioners would have us do, which particular provisions are sufficiently important to merit enforcement.

For the run-of-the-mine case, which this surely is, we think there is no realistic alternative to the traditional common-law rule that probable cause justifies a search and seizure.

Here the District Court found that the officers had probable cause to believe that petitioners had violated the traffic code. That rendered the stop reasonable under the Fourth Amendment, the evidence thereby discovered admissible, and the upholding of the convictions by the Court of Appeals for the District of Columbia Circuit correct.

QUESTIONS ABOUT WHREN

Professor Maclin, in Race and the Fourth Amendment, 51 Vand.L.Rev. 333 (1998), cites statistics that might give some perspective on the impact of *Whren* on Fourth Amendment protections. These statistics were compiled in two separate actions in Maryland and New Jersey, each alleging that State Troopers were engaged in racial profiling of Black motorists. The New Jersey Turnpike data revealed the following:

> A count of the traffic indicated that 13.5% of the automobiles carried a black occupant. A count of the traffic surveyed for speeding indicated that 98.1% of the vehicles on the road exceeded the speed limit. Fifteen percent of the speeding vehicles had a black occupant. Fifteen percent of the automobiles that both violated the speed limit and committed some other moving violation also had a black occupant. * * * [W]hile automobiles with black occupants represented only 15% of the motorists

> who violated the speeding laws, * * * 35.6% of the race identified stops * * * involved vehicles with black occupants.

In the Maryland case, Wilkins v. Maryland State Police, a state trooper stopped an automobile with four black occupants for speeding in April 1992 in Allegheny County. One of the occupants was Robert Wilkins, an attorney in the office of the Public Defender Service for the District of Columbia, who, with his family, was returning to Washington after attending a funeral in Chicago. He was detained for more than 30 minutes and a drug-sniffing dog was brought to the scene. The canine sniff revealed no narcotics; the officer then permitted Wilkins and his family to leave after writing out a speeding ticket.

With the assistance of the ACLU, Wilkins filed a class action lawsuit alleging Maryland troopers were illegally stopping black motorists because of their race. In addition to the police data, the plaintiffs' expert designed a statistical plan to determine whether Maryland troopers stop and search black motorists at a rate disproportionate to their numbers on the roads. The expert's data indicated that

> 93.3% of the drivers on Interstate 95 "were violating traffic laws and thus were eligible to be stopped by State Police. Of the violators, 17.5% were black, and 74.7% were white." * * * 72.9% of the motorists stopped and searched were black; 80.3% of the motorists searched were black, Hispanic or some other racial minority group; 19.7% of those searched were white. * * * [T]hirteen troopers conducted 85.4% of the searches.
>
> * * * Troopers recovered contraband from 28.4% of the black motorists searched and from 28.8% of the white motorists searched. Thus, seventy percent of the searches uncovered no contraband.

The plaintiff's expert in *Wilkins* concluded that "the probability that black Interstate 95 drivers are subjected to searches at so high a rate by chance is less than one in one quintillion. It is wildly significant by statistical measures."

The *Wilkins* litigation resulted in a landmark consent decree that required the Maryland State Police to record and report data relating traffic stops including the race of those stopped.[28]

In light of the statistics indicating that traffic stops are used as a pretext to search minorities, did the Court reach the right result in *Whren* when it held that probable cause of a traffic violation ends the Fourth Amendment inquiry? If that is the wrong result, what should the Court have done? Should it have held that officers cannot make stops or arrests for traffic violations? Should it have held that officers can make stops for traffic violations, but that any evidence they find of some other violation cannot be admitted at trial? Would excluding the evidence, even though "legally" found, be justified? Would it deter police officers from stopping for traffic violations simply to harass minority drivers? Or is the problem a function of the myopic nature of most

---

[28] After a career in public service and private practice, Robert Wilkins was confirmed to the federal district bench and then to a seat on the United States Court of Appeals for the District of Columbia Circuit.

Fourth Amendment litigation, which focuses atomistically on the facts of a particular case rather than addressing the sweep of law enforcement practices, which we noted in our discussion of stop and frisk polices?

For other critiques of *Whren,* see O'Neill, Beyond Privacy, Beyond Probable Cause, Beyond the Fourth Amendment: New Strategies for Fighting Pretext Arrests, 69 Colo.L.Rev. 693 (1998) (arguing that instead of focusing on privacy, the Court in *Whren* should have focused on whether the police officer's conduct in *Whren* was abusive and arbitrary); Fan, The Police Gamesmanship Dilemma in Criminal Procedure, 44 U.C. Davis L.Rev. 1407 (2011) ("*Whren* stands as a controversial landmark of noninquiry and a license to make racial distinctions. *Whren* is a lightning rod for controversy because the Court took a don't ask, don't tell approach allowing police to do whatever it takes—without examining the accuracy of police beliefs about what it takes, basing deference on noninquiry rules rather than data."); Nancy Leong, The Open Road and the Traffic Stop: Narratives and Counter-Narratives of the American Dream, 64 Fla L. Rev. 305 (2012) (noting that after *Whren,* "the police are free to pick a car they wish to stop, follow it until the driver inevitably violates one of the vehicle code's myriad obscure provisions, and subsequently pull it over.").

Atwater and *Whren* make a powerful combination. See Saltzburg, The Fourth Amendment: Internal Revenue Code or Body of Principles? 74 Geo.Wash.L.Rev. 956 (2006) ("*Atwater* and *Whren* clearly empower police departments to direct officers who see any traffic violation for which an arrest can be made, no matter how minor, to arrest the driver for the specific purpose of searching the car, even though the officer lacks reasonable suspicion that the car contains contraband or evidence of a crime.").

Testilying?

The police officer in *Whren* testified that when he stopped the suspects' vehicle and approached the car, he observed two large plastic bags of crack cocaine in Whren's hands. Does this sound plausible? Professor Maclin, in Race and the Fourth Amendment, supra, comments on this aspect of *Whren:*

> After reviewing so many cases where police officers testify that they discovered illegal drugs in plain view or after a consent search, judges may begin to wonder why drug dealers are so stupid. * * * Of course, there is an alternative explanation other than drug dealers' desire to cooperate with the police for the type of police testimony seen in *Whren* and other cases where drugs are claimed to be found in plain view or after a consent search: police perjury. As Joseph D. McNamara, the former Police Chief of Kansas City and San Jose, has explained:
>
>> (H)undreds of thousands of police officers swear under oath that the drugs were in plain view or that the defendant gave consent to a search. This may happen occasionally but it defies belief that so many drug users are careless enough to leave illegal drugs

where the police can see them or so dumb as to give cops consent to search them when they possess drugs.

* * * We can suppose that criminals are not rocket scientists and that Freud's insights apply to criminals no less than to anyone else. But even if a self-destructive error of the sort posited by the police is possible, it is not probable.

Equal Protection Issues

The Court in *Whren* cited the Equal Protection Clause as a constraint on police officers in cases where the stop or arrest is reasonable under the Fourth Amendment but the officers are acting in a discriminatory manner. But it is extremely difficult to prove an equal protection violation when it comes to a discrete action of a police officer on the street. Professor Maclin, in Race and the Fourth Amendment, supra, elaborates:

> Before a black motorist can * * * prevail on the merits of an equal protection claim, he will have to show that he was singled out because of his race or ethnicity, and that similarly situated white motorists were not stopped. In the typical case, this means that a black defendant must show a specific intent or purpose by either the officer or his department to target blacks for traffic stops. * * * Unless an officer were to testify that the motorist was stopped because he was black or Hispanic, the specific intent standard will doom the typical pretextual traffic stop case involving a black motorist. In the atypical case involving a defense able to conduct a systematic study of the enforcement practices of a particular police department, there is a better chance of success if statistics suggest that officers are targeting black motorists. But even where statistics show a strong correlation between race and a particular outcome, the Court has still required the individual criminal defendant to prove that the government officials in his case were motivated by a discriminatory intent.
>
> Finally, even if a black defendant challenging a pretextual traffic stop is able to obtain discovery and prevail on the merits of an equal protection claim, there is the question of remedy. The Court has shown no sign that it interprets the Equal Protection Clause to embody an exclusionary rule remedy, or that the Clause even requires the dismissal of criminal charges in a case involving a race-based prosecution. * * *
>
> For these reasons, successful equal protection challenges to pretextual traffic stops by minority motorists will be rare. Thus, the *Whren* Court's apparent accord with the constitutional challenge in that case ("We of course agree with petitioners that the Constitution prohibits selective enforcement of the law based on considerations such as race."), seems hollow.

For cases rejecting equal protection challenges to police searches and seizures after *Whren*, see, e.g., Johnson v. Crooks, 326 F.3d 995 (8th Cir. 2003) (even though officer followed a black motorist 11 miles before making a traffic stop, there was no showing of an equal protection violation, as the plaintiff "offered no evidence that Crooks does not stop non-African Americans under similar circumstances."); Bingham v. City of Manhattan Beach, 329 F.3d 723 (9th Cir. 2003) ("Essentially, Bingham argues that because he is African-American, the officer is white, and they disagree about the reasonableness of the traffic stop, these circumstances are sufficient to raise an inference of discrimination. We disagree that this is sufficient to state an equal protection claim."); Bradley v. United States, 299 F.3d 197 (3d Cir. 2002) (the fact that the plaintiff, an African-American, was thoroughly searched at a Customs checkpoint while several white males were allowed to pass does not show discriminatory intent).

Moreover, as predicted by Professor Maclin, courts have held that even if there is an equal protection violation, the evidence obtained is not excluded. See United States v. Nichols, 512 F.3d 789 (6th Cir. 2008) ("we are aware of no court that has ever applied the exclusionary rule for a violation of the Fourteenth Amendment's Equal Protection Clause, and we decline Nichols's invitation to do so here. Rather, we believe the proper remedy for any alleged violation is a 42 U.S.C. § 1983 action against the offending officers.").

An exceptional case in which an equal protection violation was found is Floyd v. City of New York, 959 F.Supp.2d 540 (S.D.N.Y., 2013), where Judge Scheindlin concluded that the New York City stop-and-frisk program targeted minorities and therefore that searches conducted pursuant to that program violated the Equal Protection Clause. It is crucial to note, though, that the plaintiffs in that case were challenging a formal program that was established by the NYPD, and presented evidence that the *purpose of the program* was to target young men of color on the streets and stop and frisk them. *Floyd* was not challenging a particular stop or frisk except insofar as the plaintiffs purported to represent the class.

First Amendment Issues

In *Nieves v. Bartlett*, 139 S.Ct. 1715 (2019), the Court held that the existence of probable cause provided a defense to a claim of retaliation against the exercise of First Amendment rights. Russell Bartlett was arrested for disorderly conduct and resisting arrest during "Arctic Man," a raucous winter sports festival held in a remote part of Alaska. Bartlett was shouting at police officers and other attendees. The confrontation escalated, resulting in Bartlett's arrest. He subsequently sued under 42 U.S.C. § 1983, claiming that the officers violated his First Amendment rights by arresting him in retaliation for his speech.

Chief Justice Roberts wrote for the Court and concluded that the existence of probable cause to arrest provided a defense to any First Amendment claim for retaliatory arrest. He reasoned that Bartlett was required to show that the arrest was caused by an intent to retaliate for exercise of First Amendment rights, and when there is probable cause to make the arrest anyway, such causation cannot be shown. The Chief Justice rejected Bartlett's argument that the primary focus should be on the officer's subjective intent. Chief Justice Roberts did recognize a potential exception "where officers have probable cause to make arrests, but typically exercise their discretion not to do so." In such cases, "an unyielding requirement to show the absence of probable cause could pose a risk that some police officers may exploit the arrest power as a means of suppressing speech."

Justice Thomas, concurring in part and concurring in the judgment, disagreed with this "qualification," warning that "[t]his overbroad exception thus is likely to encourage protracted litigation about which individuals are 'similarly situated.' "

Justice Gorsuch, concurring in part and dissenting in part, reasoned that simply because a practice passes muster under the Fourth Amendment does not mean that it does not violate another constitutional provision—e.g., racial discrimination in violation of the Fourteenth Amendment.

Justice Ginsburg, concurring in the judgment in part and dissenting in part, argued that "[t]he plaintiff bears the burden of demonstrating that unconstitutional animus was a motivating factor for an adverse action; the burden then shifts to the defendant to demonstrate that, even without any impetus to retaliate, the defendant would have taken the action complained of."

Justice Sotomayor, dissenting, argued that "[t]here is no basis in § 1983 or in the Constitution to withhold a remedy for an arrest that violated the First Amendment solely because an officer could point to probable cause that some offense, no matter how trivial or obviously pretextual, has occurred."

Probable Cause of a Traffic Violation

The Court's decision in *Whren* assumes that Officer Soto and his partner had grounds to effect a traffic stop in the first place. But what if an officer makes a mistake when assessing whether a motorist has, in fact, violated the law?

When assessing probable cause or reasonable suspicion, officers' reasonable mistakes of fact are excused. Thus, in United States v. Flores-Sandoval, 366 F.3d 961 (8th Cir. 2004), the defendant was stopped for not having a front license plate, in violation of the state traffic law. After the stop (and recovery of evidence) it was determined that the car did in fact have a front license plate that was partially obscured from view because it had been mounted below the standard plate bracket. The court analyzed the officer's mistake as follows:

> Officer Lippold testified that he relied on a regular practice of observing oncoming traffic-via his rear view mirror-and observing the light that bounced off of the reflective surface on the front license plate of the approaching vehicle. His observation of the Toyota led him to conclude—after seeing no reflection from the front of the vehicle and an empty plate bracket—that the vehicle did not have a front license plate. These perceptions, although flawed, were sufficiently reasonable to provide probable cause to stop the vehicle in which Flores-Sandoval was traveling.

But what about a mistake of law? The Supreme Court, in Heien v. North Carolina, 574 U.S. 54 (2014), held that a stop can be valid even though there is no violation under the law, so long as the law is ambiguous and could be reasonably read as having been violated.

In *Heien,* the defendant was pulled over for having one brake light out. In the course of the subsequent stop, officers discovered drugs in the car. The North Carolina statute was ambiguous on whether there was a violation if one brake light was still working. The Supreme Court, in an opinion by Chief Justice Roberts, upheld the stop, finding that the officer's interpretation of the ambiguous statute, while wrong, was reasonable. The Court found no analytical distinction between reasonable mistakes of fact and reasonable mistakes of law. The Court emphasized that it wasn't sanctioning ignorance of the law, and that an officer who simply didn't know what the law was would not be making a reasonable mistake in stopping someone on the basis of the officer's unknowing misconception. In *Heien,* the officer was not ignorant of the law—the law was ambiguous and was susceptible to two reasonable interpretations.

Justice Sotomayor, in a lone dissent, decried the fact that the Court's decision would expand the possibilities of pretextual searches and arrests under *Whren.*

Heien is set forth in full in the section on reasonable suspicion earlier in this Chapter.

H. PLAIN VIEW AND PLAIN TOUCH SEIZURES

The concept of plain view underlies much of the law and practice under the *Terry* doctrine and the arrest-power rule, and it applies as well during searches conducted pursuant to a warrant or another exception to the warrant requirement. For example, the officer in *Robinson* seized narcotics in plain view (in the cigarette pack) during the course of a search incident to arrest; the officers in *Long* seized weapons in plain view in Long's car during the course of a search for self-protection under *Terry;* the officer in *Whren* seized evidence that he saw in Whren's hands after making a lawful traffic stop. As the Court put it in Texas v. Brown, 460 U.S. 730, 739 (1983), the plain view doctrine is best understood "not as an independent exception to the Warrant Clause, but simply as an extension of whatever the prior justification for an officer's access to an object may be."

In Coolidge v. New Hampshire, 403 U.S. 443 (1971), Justice Stewart's plurality opinion stated that, if officers have a right to be in a particular place and come upon evidence that they have probable cause to believe is subject to seizure, then they may seize it. See also Texas v. Brown, *supra* ("if, while lawfully engaged in an activity in a particular place, police officers perceive a suspicious object, they may seize it immediately"). In the following case, the Court explains the plain view doctrine in detail, and revisits some of the problems of applying that doctrine that divided the Court in *Coolidge.*

HORTON V. CALIFORNIA

Supreme Court of the United States, 1990.
496 U.S. 128.

JUSTICE STEVENS delivered the opinion of the Court.

In this case we revisit an issue that was considered, but not conclusively resolved, in Coolidge v. New Hampshire: Whether the warrantless seizure of evidence of crime in plain view is prohibited by the Fourth Amendment if the discovery of the evidence was not inadvertent. We conclude that even though inadvertence is a characteristic of most legitimate "plain view" seizures, it is not a necessary condition.

* * * Petitioner was convicted of the armed robbery of Erwin Wallaker, the treasurer of the San Jose Coin Club. * * *

Sergeant LaRault, an experienced police officer, investigated the crime and determined that there was probable cause to search petitioner's home for the proceeds of the robbery and for the weapons used by the robbers. His affidavit for a search warrant referred to police reports that described the weapons as well as the proceeds, but the warrant issued by the Magistrate only authorized a search for the proceeds, including three specifically described rings.

Pursuant to the warrant, LaRault searched petitioner's residence, but he did not find the stolen property. During the course of the search, however, he discovered the weapons in plain view and seized them. * * * LaRault testified that while he was searching for the rings, he also was interested in finding other evidence connecting petitioner to the robbery. Thus, the seized evidence was not discovered "inadvertently."

* * *

The right to security in person and property protected by the Fourth Amendment may be invaded in quite different ways by searches and seizures. A search compromises the individual interest in privacy; a seizure deprives the individual of dominion over his or her person or property. The "plain view" doctrine is often considered an exception to the general rule that warrantless searches are presumptively unreasonable, but this characterization overlooks the important difference between searches and seizures. If an article is already in plain view, neither its observation nor its seizure would involve any invasion of privacy. A seizure of the article, however, would obviously invade the owner's possessory interest. If "plain view" justifies an exception from an otherwise applicable warrant requirement, therefore, it must be an exception that is addressed to the concerns that are implicated by seizures rather than by searches.

The criteria that generally guide "plain view" seizures were set forth in Coolidge v. New Hampshire. The Court held that the seizure of two automobiles parked in plain view on the defendant's driveway in the course of arresting the defendant violated the Fourth Amendment. Accordingly, particles of gun powder that had been subsequently found in vacuum sweepings from one of the cars could not be introduced in evidence against the defendant. The State endeavored to justify the seizure of the automobiles, and their subsequent search at the police station, on four different grounds, including the "plain view" doctrine. * * *

* * *

It is, of course, an essential predicate to any valid warrantless seizure of incriminating evidence that the officer did not violate the Fourth Amendment in arriving at the place from which the evidence could be plainly viewed. There are, moreover, two additional conditions that must be satisfied to justify the warrantless seizure. First, not only must the item be in plain view, its incriminating character must also be "immediately apparent." * * * Second, not only must the officer be lawfully located in a place from which the object can be plainly seen, but he or she must also have a lawful right of access to the object itself. * * *

* * *

[In his plurality opinion in *Coolidge*,] Justice Stewart concluded that [an additional] inadvertence requirement was necessary to avoid a violation of the express constitutional requirement that a valid warrant must particularly describe the things to be seized. He explained:

> "The rationale of the exception to the warrant requirement, as just stated, is that a plain-view seizure will not turn an initially valid (and therefore limited) search into a 'general' one, while the inconvenience of procuring a warrant to cover an inadvertent discovery is great. But

where the discovery is anticipated, where the police know in advance the location of the evidence and intend to seize it, the situation is altogether different. The requirement of a warrant to seize imposes no inconvenience whatever, or at least none which is constitutionally cognizable in a legal system that regards warrantless searches as '*per se* unreasonable' in the absence of 'exigent circumstances.' "

* * *

We find two flaws in this reasoning. First, evenhanded law enforcement is best achieved by the application of objective standards of conduct, rather than standards that depend upon the subjective state of mind of the officer. The fact that an officer is interested in an item of evidence and fully expects to find it in the course of a search should not invalidate its seizure if the search is confined in area and duration by the terms of a warrant or a valid exception to the warrant requirement. If the officer has knowledge approaching certainty that the item will be found, we see no reason why he or she would deliberately omit a particular description of the item to be seized from the application for a search warrant. Specification of the additional item could only permit the officer to expand the scope of the search. On the other hand, if he or she has a valid warrant to search for one item and merely a suspicion concerning the second, whether or not it amounts to probable cause, we fail to see why that suspicion should immunize the second item from seizure if it is found during a lawful search for the first.

* * *

Second, the suggestion that the inadvertence requirement is necessary to prevent the police from conducting general searches, or from converting specific warrants into general warrants, is not persuasive because that interest is already served by the requirements that no warrant issue unless it "particularly describ[es] the place to be searched and the persons or things to be seized," and that a warrantless search be circumscribed by the exigencies which justify its initiation. Scrupulous adherence to these requirements serves the interests in limiting the area and duration of the search that the inadvertence requirement inadequately protects. * * *

* * *

In this case, the scope of the search was not enlarged in the slightest by the omission of any reference to the weapons in the warrant. Indeed, if the three rings and other items named in the warrant had been found at the outset—or if petitioner had them in his possession and had responded to the warrant by producing them immediately—no search for weapons could have taken place. * * *

* * * The prohibition against general searches and general warrants serves primarily as a protection against unjustified intrusions on privacy.

But reliance on privacy concerns that support that prohibition is misplaced when the inquiry concerns the scope of an exception that merely authorizes an officer with a lawful right of access to an item to seize it without a warrant.

* * *

[Based on the above reasoning, the Court rejects the implication in *Coolidge* that a plain view seizure must be inadvertent.]

JUSTICE BRENNAN, with whom JUSTICE MARSHALL joins, dissenting.

* * *

[T]here are a number of instances in which a law enforcement officer might deliberately choose to omit certain items from a warrant application even though he has probable cause to seize them, knows they are on the premises, and intends to seize them when they are discovered in plain view. For example, the warrant application process can often be time-consuming, especially when the police attempt to seize a large number of items. An officer interested in conducting a search as soon as possible might decide to save time by listing only one or two hard-to-find items, such as the stolen rings in this case, confident that he will find in plain view all of the other evidence he is looking for before he discovers the listed items. Because rings could be located almost anywhere inside or outside a house, it is unlikely that a warrant to search for and seize the rings would restrict the scope of the search. An officer might rationally find the risk of immediately discovering the items listed in the warrant—thereby forcing him to conclude the search immediately—outweighed by the time saved in the application process.

* * * It is true that the inadvertent discovery requirement furthers no privacy interests. * * * But it does protect possessory interests. * * * The Court today eliminates a rule designed to further possessory interests on the ground that it fails to further privacy interests. I cannot countenance such constitutional legerdemain.

* * *

Inadvertence and Computer and Cellphone Searches

Recall, from the discussion of particularity requirements, that broad searches of electronic devices are allowed on probable cause to believe that evidence will be found on such a device because a user might hide the information by mislabeling it. What happens if an officer comes across information about a crime different from the one that justified the search—such as finding child pornography while searching for evidence of tax fraud? As the court stated in United States v. Galpin, 720 F.3d 436 (2d Cir. 2013): "Once the government has obtained authorization to search the hard drive, the government may claim that the contents of every file it chose to open were in plain view and, therefore, admissible even if they implicate the defendant in a crime not contemplated by the warrant. Thus there is a serious risk that every warrant for electronic information will become, in effect, a general warrant."

A few courts have addressed the combination of broad searches of electronic devices together with the plain view requirement by essentially holding that plain view discovery of evidence relating to a different crime must be inadvertent. For example, in United States v. Carey, 172 F.3d 1268 (10th Cir. 1999), an officer had a warrant to search Carey's computer for evidence of drug activity. The officer came upon a jpeg file, opened it, and it was child pornography. Then the officer viewed many more jpeg files, finding more child pornography, but nothing indicating drug activity. The court found that the search of the first jpeg file was permissible because the discovery of child pornography was "inadvertent." But this could not be said of the subsequent jpeg files. As to those files, the officer knew he was going to find child pornography, not evidence of drug activity, so the content of those files was not in plain view.

The *Carey* approach is designed to limit computer searches, but does it really? Why couldn't the officer argue that he was still looking for evidence of drug activity in the subsequent jpeg files? Wouldn't it be plausible to believe that one of the pictures might show evidence of drug activity? Isn't that what gave the officer the authority to search the first jpeg file? If all the officer has to say is that he was still looking for drug-related evidence, then it is hard to see how an inadvertence requirement will impose any meaningful limit on a computer search.

Would it make a difference if "inadvertence" looked at the objective purpose of investigative activities rather than the subjective intent of a particular officer? Consider United States v. Williams, 592 F.3d 511 (4th Cir. 2010), where a warranted search of a computer for evidence of illegal gun activity uncovered files containing child pornography. The court addressed a potential limitation on plain view in the following passage:

> Williams, relying on the Tenth Circuit's opinion in United States v. Carey, advances an argument that the plain-view exception cannot apply to searches of computers and electronic media when the evidence indicates that it is the officer's *purpose* from the outset to use the authority of the warrant to search for unauthorized evidence because the unauthorized evidence would not then be uncovered "inadvertently."
>
> This argument, however, cannot stand against the principle, well-established in Supreme Court jurisprudence, that the scope of a search

conducted pursuant to a warrant is defined *objectively* by the terms of the warrant and the evidence sought, not by the *subjective* motivations of an officer. * * *

While Williams relies accurately on *Carey,* which effectively imposes an "inadvertence" requirement, such a conclusion is inconsistent with *Horton.* Inadvertence focuses incorrectly on the subjective motivations of the officer in conducting the search and not on the objective determination of whether the search is authorized by the warrant or a valid exception to the warrant requirement.

In this case, because the scope of the search authorized by the warrant included the authority to open and cursorily view each file, the observation of child pornography within several of these files did not involve an intrusion on Williams' protected privacy interests beyond that already authorized by the warrant, regardless of the officer's subjective motivations. * * * At bottom, we conclude that the sheer amount of information contained on a computer does not distinguish the authorized search of the computer from an analogous search of a file cabinet containing a large number of documents.

Probable Cause to Seize an Item in Plain View: Arizona v. Hicks

One of the difficult plain view issues is how closely the police may examine an object to decide whether it is subject to seizure. In Arizona v. Hicks, 480 U.S. 321 (1987), Justice Scalia wrote for the Court as it emphasized the plain view requirement that officers have lawful authority to be in the place from which they observe evidence. Arizona police entered Hicks' apartment after a bullet was fired through its floor into the apartment below, injuring a man. The officers looked for the shooter, other victims and weapons. One officer noticed two sets of expensive stereo components that seemed out of place in an "ill-appointed four-room apartment." The officer moved some of the components in order to find serial numbers, telephoned in the numbers, and learned that one turntable he had moved was stolen. He seized the turntable immediately. Later it was learned that other equipment was stolen, and a warrant was obtained.

Justice Scalia rejected the state's argument that the officer's inspection of the underside of the turntable did not amount to a search: "A search is a search, even if it happens to disclose nothing but the bottom of a turntable." He also rejected the argument that the officer had sufficient cause to justify his actions. The state conceded that the officer lacked probable cause for a search, but sought to justify his actions on the basis of reasonable suspicion. Justice Scalia described the plain view doctrine as resting on the "desirability of sparing police, whose viewing of the object in the course of a lawful search is as legitimate as it would have been in a public place, the inconvenience and the risk—to themselves or to preservation of the evidence—of going to get a warrant." He further observed that "[n]o reason is apparent why an object should routinely be seizable on lesser grounds, during an unrelated search and seizure, than would have been needed to obtain a warrant for that same object if it had been known to be on the premises." Justice O'Connor, joined by Chief Justice Rehnquist and Justice Powell, dissented.

After *Hicks*, an officer must have probable cause to seize an item that he views during the course of legal activity. And that probable cause must be *readily apparent*—meaning that probable cause must exist without the necessity of a further search. For cases discussing the probable cause requirement for plain view seizures after *Hicks*, see United States v. Conlan, 786 F.3d 380 (5th Cir. 2015) (laptop and cellphone were properly seized from the defendant's motel room under the plain view doctrine, where officers entered the premises with probable cause to believe that the defendant was sending out harassing electronic communications); United States v. Cooper, 19 F.3d 1154 (7th Cir.1994) (probable cause to seize an empty ammunition box was immediately apparent, where it was found together with drugs and weapons: "The ammunition box, unlike a cigar box, is probative of weapons possession and drug dealing."); United States v. Pindell, 336 F.3d 1049 (D.C. Cir. 2003) (probable cause to seize a notebook was immediately apparent, as the victim of a robbery had told the officer that the perpetrator had been disguised as a police officer and had recorded information in a notebook during the robbery; the officer found the notebook lying next to a police uniform in the defendant's car).

Plain View, Probable Cause, and Legalized Marijuana

What if the officer in the course of legal activity sees a user-amount of marijuana? When a jurisdiction decriminalizes possession of small amounts of marijuana, the fact that an officer sees a person in possession of marijuana in plain view does not necessarily amount to probable cause. For example, in Commonwealth v. Sheridan, 470 Mass. 752, 25 N.E.3d 875 (Mass. 2015), the Massachusetts Supreme Judicial Court held that state officers who observe what appears to be a legally possessed amount of marijuana in a car during a traffic stop do not have probable cause to search the vehicle or any other justification to enter the vehicle to seize the drug. But where federal law criminalizes possession of marijuana, federal officers with probable cause to believe that an individual possesses marijuana have authority to arrest the individual and to search a car if they see marijuana—even user amounts—in plain view. And in some jurisdictions where possession of small amounts of marijuana has been decriminalized, but remains a civil offense, courts have preserved the right of officers to search vehicles based on probable cause to believe that marijuana is present because it is still considered "contraband." See

Robinson v. State, 451 Md. 94 (2017). Compare Pacheco v. State, 465 Md. 311 (2019) (custodial arrest was not justified based on probable cause to believe that suspect was guilty of possessing a small amount of marijuana constituting only a civil offense).

The Plain Touch Doctrine

If an officer, acting in the course of lawful activity, can determine *by touch* that an object is evidence or contraband, can he seize the object? That was the question in Minnesota v. Dickerson, 508 U.S. 366 (1993), where an officer, in the course of a stop and frisk permitted by the *Terry* doctrine, patted-down the suspect and felt a small, hard, pea-shaped object in the suspect's shirt pocket. At the suppression hearing, the officer testified that he examined the object with his fingers "and it slid and it felt to be a lump of crack cocaine in cellophane." Because the suspect had left a house known to be a place for drug activity, the officer concluded that there was probable cause to believe that the pea-shaped object was contraband, and he pulled the object from the suspect's pocket; the object turned out to be a small plastic bag containing crack cocaine.

The state in *Dickerson* argued that the seizure was permissible because the officer obtained probable cause by "plain touch" during a lawful frisk, which was analogized to obtaining probable cause by plain view during a lawful search. The Supreme Court, in an opinion by Justice White, stated that the plain view doctrine "has an obvious application by analogy to cases in which an officer discovers contraband through the sense of touch during an otherwise lawful search."

While the Court found that the Fourth Amendment permits the seizure of evidence discovered through the sense of touch in the course of a lawful search, it also found that the plain touch exception *did not justify the search* under the facts of *Dickerson*. This was because the officer did more than merely touch the object; he pushed and prodded it after concluding that it was not a weapon with the objective purpose of determining whether it was contraband. That constituted a search for evidence beyond the scope of a *Terry* frisk. Justice White concluded:

> Although the officer was lawfully in a position to feel the lump in respondent's pocket, because *Terry* entitled him to place his hands upon respondent's jacket, the court below determined that the incriminating character of the object was not immediately apparent. Rather, the officer determined that the item was contraband only after conducting a further search, one not authorized by *Terry* or any other exception to the warrant requirement. Because the further search of respondent's jacket was constitutionally invalid, the seizure of the cocaine that followed is likewise unconstitutional.

Justice Scalia wrote a short concurring opinion. Chief Justice Rehnquist wrote a short dissenting opinion joined by Justices Blackmun and Thomas. He agreed with the majority's position on the plain touch exception, but argued that a remand was necessary to allow the Minnesota court to apply the exception to the facts of the case.

How much more information would have been required for the officer to find probable cause to believe that a hard, pea-shaped object in Dickerson's pocket was crack cocaine? See United States v. Yamba, 506 F.3d 251 (3d Cir. 2007) (officer properly frisking for weapons felt a "soft, squishy substance" and what felt like "small buds or seeds" inside the suspect's coat pocket; at that point the officer had probable cause to believe the suspect possessed marijuana); United States v. Williams, 139 F.3d 628 (8th Cir.1998) (officer who conducted *Terry* frisk and felt a package, had probable cause to seize it because the suspect had just been observed taking part in a drug transaction).

I. AUTOMOBILES AND OTHER MOVABLE OBJECTS

One of the well-recognized exceptions to the warrant requirement is the "automobile exception." Under this exception, the police may search an automobile without a warrant so long as they have probable cause to believe it contains evidence of criminal activity. The Court first recognized the exception in Carroll v. United States, 267 U.S. 132 (1925), and it is sometimes called "the *Carroll* Doctrine." As you study the following material, consider two questions: whether the rationale for the exception can withstand analysis; and whether acceptance of the rationale might logically require its extension to objects other than cars.

1. The *Carroll* Doctrine

Carroll v. United States involved a violation of the National Prohibition Act. In December 1921, Carroll and a cohort were driving westward on a highway between Detroit and Grand Rapids when they were stopped by federal prohibition agents who were patrolling the road. Bootlegging traffic was known to be heavy in the area, due to its proximity to Canada. The officers knew the men had been previously involved in transporting liquor. Carroll's car was searched, without a warrant, and 68 quarts of whiskey and gin were found behind the upholstering of the seats. The defendants were convicted of illegal transportation of intoxicating liquor, a misdemeanor.

In a 7–2 decision written by Chief Justice Taft, the Court found the search to be constitutional. The major contention was not probable cause, but whether a warrant was required for the search. Justice Taft declared that a warrant could not reasonably have been demanded in light of the mobility of the vehicle:

> [There is] a necessary difference between a search of a store, dwelling house or other structure in respect of which a proper official warrant readily may be obtained, and a search of a ship, motor boat, wagon or automobile, for contraband goods, where it is not practicable to secure a warrant because the vehicle can be quickly moved out of the locality or jurisdiction in which the warrant must be sought.

Taft further noted that the right to search and the validity of the seizure were not dependent on the right to arrest, thus clearly distinguishing this search from that of an automobile incident to the arrest of the driver.

2. The Progeny of *Carroll*

In the following case, the Court considered whether the *Carroll* doctrine applies to a car that is has been impounded. A car impounded by the police is hardly mobile within the meaning of *Carroll*. So what can justify a warrantless search of an immobile car?

CHAMBERS V. MARONEY

Supreme Court of the United States, 1970.
399 U.S. 42.

JUSTICE WHITE delivered the opinion of the Court.

The principal question in this case concerns the admissibility of evidence seized from an automobile, in which petitioner was riding at the time of his arrest, after the automobile was taken to a police station and was there thoroughly searched without a warrant. The Court of Appeals for the Third Circuit found no violation of petitioner's Fourth Amendment rights. We affirm.

[Petitioner was riding in a blue station wagon that matched the description of a vehicle associated with a robbery when it was stopped by police. Secondary to that stop, officers observed other details linking the car and some of its occupants to the robbery, including items of clothing. Petitioner and his associates were arrested and the car was driven to the police station. In the course of a thorough search of the car at the station, the police found weapons and evidence linking petitioner to the robbery.]

[The Court holds that the police had probable cause to make an arrest, but that the search of the car at the police station was too removed from the arrest to be justified as a search incident to arrest. It then turned to the question whether the search was justified under *Carroll*.]

* * *

* * * *Carroll* holds a search warrant unnecessary where there is probable cause to search an automobile stopped on the highway; the car is movable, the occupants are alerted, and the car's contents may never be

found again if a warrant must be obtained. Hence an immediate search is constitutionally permissible.

Arguably, because of the preference for a magistrate's judgment only the immobilization of the car should be permitted until a search warrant is obtained; arguably, only the "lesser" intrusion is permissible until the magistrate authorizes the "greater." But which is the "greater" and which the "lesser" intrusion is itself a debatable question and the answer may depend on a variety of circumstances. For constitutional purposes, we see no difference between on the one hand seizing and holding a car before presenting the probable cause issue to a magistrate and on the other hand carrying out an immediate search without a warrant. Given probable cause to search, either course is reasonable under the Fourth Amendment.

On the facts before us, the blue station wagon could have been searched on the spot when it was stopped since there was probable cause to search and it was a fleeting target for a search. The probable-cause factor still obtained at the station house and so did the mobility of the car unless the Fourth Amendment permits a warrantless seizure of the car and the denial of its use to anyone until a warrant is secured. In that event there is little to choose in terms of practical consequences between an immediate search without a warrant and the car's immobilization until a warrant is obtained.[a] The same consequences may not follow where there is unforeseeable cause to search a house. Compare Vale v. Louisiana [discussed in the section on exigent circumstances]. But as *Carroll,* supra, held, for the purposes of the Fourth Amendment there is a constitutional difference between houses and cars.

* * *

[Justice Blackmun took no part in the decision.]

JUSTICE HARLAN, concurring in part and dissenting in part.

* * *

The Court concedes that the police could prevent removal of the evidence by temporarily seizing the car for the time necessary to obtain a warrant. It does not dispute that such a course would fully protect the interests of effective law enforcement; rather it states that whether temporary seizure is a "lesser" intrusion than warrantless search "is itself a debatable question and the answer may depend on a variety of circumstances."[b] I believe it clear that a warrantless search involves the

---

[a] It was not unreasonable in this case to take the car to the station house. All occupants in the car were arrested in a dark parking lot in the middle of the night. A careful search at that point was impractical and perhaps not safe for the officers, and it would serve the owner's convenience and the safety of his car to have the vehicle and the keys together at the station house.

[b] The Court, unable to decide whether search or temporary seizure is the "lesser" intrusion, in this case authorizes both. * * * At all times the car and its contents were secure against removal

greater sacrifice of Fourth Amendment values . . . [and] in the circumstances in which this problem is likely to occur, the lesser intrusion will almost always be the simple seizure of the car for the period—perhaps a day—necessary to enable the officers to obtain a search warrant.

* * *

QUESTIONS AFTER CHAMBERS

What implications does *Chambers* have for searches of parked cars, where the police do not make an initial stop? Does it matter where the car is parked, or whether the initial police-vehicle encounter is deliberate or by chance? The Court considered these questions in Coolidge v. New Hampshire, 403 U.S. 443 (1971), in which the police seized the defendant's car from his driveway, shortly after his arrest, and searched it two days later at the police station, and twice more in the following months. Justice Stewart, writing for the plurality, found no exigency based on mobility, because Coolidge had been arrested, his wife had been removed from the premises, and the police had control of the car as it was parked outside Coolidge's house.

Justice Stewart distinguished *Chambers* on the ground that the *initial* intrusion was unjustified without a warrant. That is, the officers did not obtain a proper warrant even though they knew precisely where Coolidge's car was parked at all times and had been investigating him for weeks. This was unlike the situation in *Chambers*, where the officers were on patrol and happened to *come upon* a car that fit the description of one seen at a gas station robbery; there was no way in which the officers in *Chambers* could have been expected to obtain a warrant *before* they even seized the car. And because they could seize it without a warrant, under the rationale of *Chambers*, they could also search it without a warrant.

Subsequently, the Supreme Court has narrowed *Coolidge* to its facts—it does not stand for the proposition that the car must be actually mobile before officers can search without a warrant. In one post-*Coolidge* case, Cardwell v. Lewis, 417 U.S. 583 (1974), a plurality of the Court explicitly rejected the contention that mobility of the car before it is seized makes a difference: "The fact that the car in *Chambers* was seized after being stopped on a highway, whereas Lewis' car was seized from a public parking lot, has little, if any, legal significance." Similarly, in Texas v. White, 423 U.S. 67 (1975), the Court upheld the warrantless search of an automobile that had been towed to the police department's impound lot. The Court rejected the argument of the dissenters that the police should have been required to provide a justification for removing the car to the stationhouse rather than searching it on the scene. See also Michigan v. Thomas, 458 U.S. 259 (1982) (holding "that the justification to conduct such a warrantless search does not vanish once the car has been immobilized"). An impatient Supreme Court summarily reversed a

---

or destruction. Nevertheless, the Court approves the searches without even an inquiry into the officers' ability promptly to take their case before a magistrate.

Florida intermediate appellate court in Florida v. Meyers, 466 U.S. 380 (1984) (per curiam), and, as in Michigan v. Thomas, reiterated the *Chambers* holding that a warrantless search of an automobile may be conducted after it has been immobilized, as long as there is probable cause to believe that the automobile contains evidence of criminal activity.

In light of *White* and *Thomas,* some lower courts have interpreted *Coolidge* to mean that a warrant is required only if the officers had a clear opportunity to obtain a warrant before *seizing* the car. Under this view, *Chambers* is based on the rationale that, due to its mobility, a car can be seized pending the obtaining of a warrant; and a search without a warrant is permitted because the search of a car is no more intrusive than would be the seizure of the car pending a warrant. But if the original seizure itself could have been preceded by a warrant, then the premise of *Chambers* is missing and the car exception ought not to apply. This explanation is consistent with the facts of *Chambers,* where the officers clearly could not have obtained a warrant before seizing the car, and with the facts of *Coolidge,* where the officers could have obtained a valid warrant before seizing the car. See, e.g., United States v. Moscatiello, 771 F.2d 589 (1st Cir.1985) (*Coolidge* distinguished where officers seized car after pursuing it in a rapidly developing situation); United States v. Reed, 26 F.3d 523 (5th Cir.1994) (warrantless search of car permitted; *Coolidge* distinguished because the officers "did not know where the car was, nor that it contained the money, until they completed their tracking upon arrival at the house").

The Diminished Expectation of Privacy Rationale: California v. Carney

In California v. Carney, 471 U.S. 386 (1985), the Court re-evaluated the automobile exception to the warrant requirement and concluded that "the reasons for the vehicle exception are twofold." Chief Justice Burger, writing for the Court, explained as follows:

> The capacity to be quickly moved was clearly the basis of the holding in *Carroll,* and our cases have consistently recognized ready mobility as one of the principal bases of the automobile exception. * * *
>
> However, although ready mobility alone was perhaps the original justification for the vehicle exception, our later cases have made clear that ready mobility is not the only basis for the exception. * * * Besides the element of mobility, less rigorous warrant requirements govern because the expectation of privacy with respect to one's automobile is significantly less than that relating to one's home or office.
>
> Even in cases where an automobile was not immediately mobile, the lesser expectation of privacy resulting from its use as a readily mobile vehicle justified application of the vehicular exception.

See also United States v. Howard, 489 F.3d 484 (2d Cir. 2007) (Sotomayor, J.) ("Thus, even if the vehicles searched in the case at hand were not 'readily mobile' within the meaning of the automobile exception, a warrantless search of them would be justified based on the diminished expectation of privacy enjoyed by the drivers and passenger while traveling on the Thruway.").

Why do citizens have a diminished expectation of privacy with respect to their automobiles? The Chief Justice in *Carney* explained that these reduced expectations "derive not from the fact that the area to be searched is in plain view, but from the pervasive regulation of vehicles capable of traveling on the public highways." He stressed that automobiles are "subjected to pervasive and continuing governmental regulation and controls."

Thereafter, in Maryland v. Dyson, 527 U.S. 465 (1999) (per curiam), the Court found that the warrantless search of a car upon probable cause was permissible even in the absence of any exigency. The Court stated categorically that "the automobile exception has no separate exigency requirement" and that the probable cause finding "alone satisfies the automobile exception to the Fourth Amendment's warrant requirement."

Motor Homes

The Court in *Carney* considered whether the dual justification for the automobile exception (inherent mobility and diminished expectation of privacy) applied to the warrantless search of a motor home. A six-person majority held that police officers validly searched a "Dodge Mini Motor Home" with probable cause but no warrant when the motor home was parked in a lot in a downtown area. Officers had received information that the motor home was used by a person who exchanged marijuana for sex. They watched a youth enter the motor home and remain there for more than an hour. When he left, the officers stopped him and learned that he had received marijuana in exchange for sexual contacts. The officers knocked on the door and Carney stepped out. They identified themselves as officers and entered the motor home where they saw marijuana and related paraphernalia.

Chief Justice Burger rejected the argument that the motor home was different from other vehicles because it was capable of functioning as a home as well as a vehicle. He reasoned that "[t]o distinguish between respondent's motor home and an ordinary sedan for purposes of the vehicle exception would require that we apply the exception depending upon the size of the vehicle and the quality of its appointments" and "to fail to apply the exception to vehicles such as a motor home ignores the fact that a motor home lends itself easily to use as an instrument of illicit drug traffic and other illegal activity." Thus, the Court declined "to distinguish between 'worthy' and 'unworthy' vehicles which are either on the public roads and highways, or situated such that it is reasonable to conclude that the vehicle is not being used as a residence." In a footnote, the Court noted that it did not "pass on the application of the vehicle exception to a motor home that is situated in a way or place that objectively indicates that it is being used as a residence." It suggested, however, some factors that might be relevant in determining whether a warrant would be required: "its location, whether the vehicle is licensed, whether it is connected to utilities, and whether it has convenient access to a public road."[29]

Justice Stevens, joined by Justices Brennan and Marshall, dissented. He argued that the Court "accorded priority to an exception rather than to the general rule." He concluded that because a motor home was a combination of home and car, the general preference for a warrant should govern a close case.

Vehicles on Private Property: Collins v. Virginia

If police may search a car based on probable cause alone, but face a presumption of unreasonableness if they search a home without first securing a warrant, then what are their obligations if they want to search a car located in a home? This was the question presented to the Court in Collins v. Virginia, 138 S.Ct. 1663 (2018). In that case, a motorcyclist riding a distinctive orange and black motorcycle had, on several occasions, eluded officers who tried to stop him for speeding and other traffic violations. An investigation pointed to Collins as the likely culprit. When officers visited Collins's Facebook page, they saw pictures of the motorcycle parked next to his house. From the street in front of Collins's home, officers could see what appeared to be the motorcycle parked under a tarp on the driveway next to the house. In order "to investigate further," one of the officers walked up the driveway, pulled back the tarp, took pictures of the motorcycle, its license plate, and its vehicle identification number, and used this information to establish that the motorcycle was stolen. Collins later admitted that he had acquired the motorcycle without a title.

At a subsequent criminal trial where he was charged with receiving stolen property, Collins argued unsuccessfully that the investigating officer violated the Fourth Amendment by physically intruding into the curtilage of his home to gather information without first securing a warrant. The Supreme Court of Virginia affirmed, holding that the search of the motorcycle was justified by the automobile exception. In an opinion written by Justice Sotomayor, the Court reversed.

[29] See United States v. Navas, 597 F.3d 492 (2d Cir. 2010) (warrantless search of a trailer unattached to a vehicle upheld: "the trailer bore no objective indicia of residential use that might give rise to elevated privacy expectations in its contents").

After determining that the location where the motorcycle was found was part of the curtilage of Collins's home, Justice Sotomayor reasoned that the officers had no more authority to search the motorcycle where it was parked on the driveway than they would have if it was parked in Collins's living room. To reach the opposite conclusion would, she explained, erase the distinction between looking and going.

> Just as an officer must have a lawful right of access to any contraband he discovers in plain view in order to seize it without a warrant, and just as an officer must have a lawful right of access in order to arrest a person in his home, so, too, an officer must have a lawful right of access to a vehicle in order to search it pursuant to the automobile exception. The automobile exception does not afford the necessary lawful right of access to search a vehicle parked within a home or its curtilage because it does not justify an intrusion on a person's separate and substantial Fourth Amendment interest in his home and curtilage.
>
> * * * [T]he rationales underlying the automobile exception are specific to the nature of a vehicle and the ways in which it is distinct from a house. The rationales thus take account only of the balance between the intrusion on an individual's Fourth Amendment interest in his vehicle and the governmental interests in an expedient search of that vehicle; they do not account for the distinct privacy interest in one's home or curtilage. To allow an officer to rely on the automobile exception to gain entry into a house or its curtilage for the purpose of conducting a vehicle search would unmoor the exception from its justifications, render hollow the core Fourth Amendment protection the Constitution extends to the house and its curtilage, and transform what was meant to be an exception into a tool with far broader application. Indeed, its name alone should make all this clear enough: It is, after all, an exception for automobiles.

On similar grounds, Justice Sotomayor rejected the government's proposal to allow searches of cars parked outside but not those parked in "an enclosed structure" such as a garage. Reiterating the Court's established view that "curtilage is afforded [full] constitutional protection," she maintained that the "ability to observe inside curtilage from a lawful vantage point is not the same as the right to enter curtilage without a warrant for the purpose of conducting a search to obtain information not otherwise accessible." "So long as it is curtilage," she concluded "a parking patio or carport into which an officer can see from the street is no less entitled to protection from trespass and a warrantless search than a fully enclosed garage."

Justice Thomas joined the majority opinion in *Collins*, but wrote separately to express his doubts about the exclusionary rule. Portions of his opinion are reproduced later in this Chapter with the materials on the exclusionary rule.

Justice Alito dissented. In his view, the investigative steps taken by the officer were perfectly reasonable in light of the minimal nature of the intrusion and the significant law enforcement interests at stake.

3. Movable Containers—in and out of Cars

Is there any way to distinguish mobile containers, such as suitcases, from automobiles on privacy grounds? The Supreme Court did just that in United States v. Chadwick, 433 U.S. 1 (1977), where it held that the mobility of a footlocker justified its *seizure* upon probable cause, but that a warrant was required to *search* the footlocker, unless emergency circumstances rendered a seizure insufficient to protect the state interest (e.g., if the footlocker was ticking). Chief Justice Burger, writing for the Court, distinguished mobile containers from cars on the following grounds:

> The factors which diminish the privacy aspects of an automobile do not apply to respondents' footlocker. Luggage contents are not open to public view, except as a condition to a border entry or common carrier travel; nor is luggage subject to regular inspections and official scrutiny on a continuing basis. Unlike an automobile, whose primary function is transportation, luggage is intended as a repository of personal effects. In sum, a person's expectations of privacy in personal luggage are substantially greater than in an automobile.

Because of the higher expectation of privacy in the footlocker, it could not be said, as it could in *Chambers,* that an immediate search would be no more intrusive than a seizure pending a warrant. As the Chief Justice explained in a footnote:

> A search of the interior [of the footlocker] was therefore a far greater intrusion into Fourth Amendment values than the impoundment of the footlocker. Though surely a substantial infringement of respondents' use and possession, the seizure did not diminish respondents' legitimate expectation that the footlocker's contents would remain private.

It was the greatly reduced expectation of privacy in the automobile that made the Court in *Chambers* unwilling to decide whether an immediate search of an automobile constituted a greater intrusion than its seizure pending a warrant. But because there is a higher expectation of privacy in luggage than cars, a search of that luggage was found to be a greater intrusion than seizure pending a warrant.

QUESTIONS AFTER CHADWICK

The crux of the majority's argument in *Chadwick* is that one has a lesser expectation of privacy in one's car than in movable containers such as luggage. Is the lesser expectation of privacy surrounding autos simply the result of the Supreme Court having said so?

Does the fact that vehicles are used essentially for transportation demand, or even allow, the conclusion that they are seldom used as repositories for personal effects? Would that assertion hold true in the case of a traveling salesman who lives out of his car for several days each week? Do the particular facts of any case make a difference in light of the Court's categorical "diminished expectation" analysis?

Mobile Containers in the Car

With a warrant required for the search of a mobile container, but not required for the search of an automobile, it was only a matter of time before the Court was presented with cases in which the two rules would collide. Which rule applies when an officer finds a mobile container when searching a car without a warrant? In Arkansas v. Sanders, 442 U.S. 753 (1979), the Court held that a warrant was required to search a suitcase that had been placed in the trunk of a taxi. Thereafter, in United States v. Ross, 456 U.S. 798 (1982), the Court upheld the warrantless search of a paper bag and pouch found during the search of a car. Justice Marshall, joined by Justice Brennan in dissent in *Ross,* emphasized the anomalous results that could occur due to the fine lines drawn between *Ross* and *Sanders.* For example, if officers were informed that a person has drugs in a bag in the trunk, it would appear that probable cause is localized in the bag, and hence *Sanders* would apply. But if they are more generally informed that there are drugs in the trunk, *Ross* would apply.

Sanders, Ross, and *Chadwick* are extensively discussed in the next case, in which the Court again tries to resolve the question of whether a warrant is required to search a container placed in a car.

CALIFORNIA V. ACEVEDO

Supreme Court of the United States, 1991.
500 U.S. 565.

JUSTICE BLACKMUN delivered the opinion of the Court.

This case requires us once again to consider the so-called "automobile exception" to the warrant requirement of the Fourth Amendment and its application to the search of a closed container in the trunk of a car.

* * * On October 28, 1987, Officer Coleman of the Santa Ana, Cal., Police Department received a telephone call from a federal drug enforcement agent in Hawaii. The agent informed Coleman that he had

seized a package containing marijuana which was to have been delivered to the Federal Express office in Santa Ana and which was addressed to J.R. Daza at 805 West Stevens Avenue in that city. The agent arranged to send the package to Coleman instead. Coleman then was to take the package to the Federal Express office and arrest the person who arrived to claim it.

* * * At about 10:30 a.m. on October 30, a man, who identified himself as Jamie Daza, arrived to claim the package. He accepted it and drove to his apartment on West Stevens. He carried the package into the apartment.

* * *

At 12:30 p.m., respondent Charles Steven Acevedo arrived. He entered Daza's apartment, stayed for about 10 minutes, and reappeared carrying a brown paper bag that looked full. The officers noticed that the bag was the size of one of the wrapped marijuana packages sent from Hawaii. Acevedo walked to a silver Honda in the parking lot. He placed the bag in the trunk of the car and started to drive away. Fearing the loss of evidence, officers in a marked police car stopped him. They opened the trunk and the bag, and found marijuana.

* * *

The California Court * * * concluded that the marijuana found in the paper bag in the car's trunk should have been suppressed. The court concluded that the officers had probable cause to believe that the paper bag contained drugs but lacked probable cause to suspect that Acevedo's car, itself, otherwise contained contraband. Because the officers' probable cause was directed specifically at the bag, the court held that the case was controlled by United States v. Chadwick rather than by United States v. Ross. Although the court agreed that the officers could seize the paper bag, it held that, under *Chadwick,* they could not open the bag without first obtaining a warrant for that purpose. The court then recognized "the anomalous nature" of the dichotomy between the rule in *Chadwick* and the rule in *Ross.* That dichotomy dictates that if there is probable cause to search a car, then the entire car—including any closed container found therein—may be searched without a warrant, but if there is probable cause only as to a container in the car, the container may be held but not searched until a warrant is obtained.

* * *

In United States v. Ross, we held that a warrantless search of an automobile under the *Carroll* doctrine could include a search of a container or package found inside the car when such a search was supported by probable cause. * * * Thus, "[i]f probable cause justifies the search of a lawfully stopped vehicle, it justifies the search of every part of the vehicle and its contents that may conceal the object of the search." In *Ross,* therefore, we clarified the scope of the *Carroll* doctrine as properly including a "probing search" of compartments and containers within the automobile so long as the search is supported by probable cause.

In addition to this clarification, *Ross* distinguished the *Carroll* doctrine from the separate rule that governed the search of closed containers. The Court had announced this separate rule, unique to luggage and other closed packages, bags, and containers, in United States v. Chadwick. In *Chadwick,* federal narcotics agents had probable cause to believe that a 200-pound double-locked footlocker contained marijuana. The agents tracked the locker as the defendants removed it from a train and carried it through the station to a waiting car. As soon as the defendants lifted the locker into the trunk of the car, the agents arrested them, seized the locker, and searched it. In this Court, the United States did not contend that the locker's brief contact with the automobile's trunk sufficed to make the *Carroll* doctrine applicable. Rather, the United States urged that the search of movable luggage could be considered analogous to the search of an automobile.

The Court rejected this argument because, it reasoned, a person expects more privacy in his luggage and personal effects than he does in his automobile. * * *

In Arkansas v. Sanders, the Court extended *Chadwick's* rule to apply to a suitcase actually being transported in the trunk of a car. In *Sanders,* the police had probable cause to believe a suitcase contained marijuana. They watched as the defendant placed the suitcase in the trunk of a taxi and was driven away. The police pursued the taxi for several blocks, stopped it, found the suitcase in the trunk, and searched it. Although the Court had applied the *Carroll* doctrine to searches of integral parts of the automobile itself, (indeed, in *Carroll,* contraband whiskey was in the upholstery of the seats) it did not extend the doctrine to the warrantless search of personal luggage "merely because it was located in an automobile lawfully stopped by the police." * * *

In *Ross,* the Court endeavored to distinguish between *Carroll,* which governed the *Ross* automobile search, and *Chadwick* * * *. It held that the *Carroll* doctrine covered searches of automobiles when the police had probable cause to search an entire vehicle but that the *Chadwick* doctrine governed searches of luggage when the officers had probable cause to search only a container within the vehicle. Thus, in a *Ross* situation, the police could conduct a reasonable search under the Fourth Amendment without obtaining a warrant, whereas in a *Sanders* situation, the police had to obtain a warrant before they searched.

* * *

* * * We now must decide the question deferred in *Ross:* whether the Fourth Amendment requires the police to obtain a warrant to open the sack

in a movable vehicle simply because they lack probable cause to search the entire car. We conclude that it does not.

* * * Dissenters in *Ross* asked why the suitcase in *Sanders* was "more private, less difficult for police to seize and store, or in any other relevant respect more properly subject to the warrant requirement, than a container that police discover in a probable-cause search of an entire automobile?" We now agree that a container found after a general search of the automobile and a container found in a car after a limited search for the container are equally easy for the police to store and for the suspect to hide or destroy. In fact, we see no principled distinction in terms of either the privacy expectation or the exigent circumstances between the paper bag found by the police in *Ross* and the paper bag found by the police here. Furthermore, by attempting to distinguish between a container for which the police are specifically searching and a container which they come across in a car, we have provided only minimal protection for privacy and have impeded effective law enforcement.

The line between probable cause to search a vehicle and probable cause to search a package in that vehicle is not always clear, and separate rules that govern the two objects to be searched may enable the police to broaden their power to make warrantless searches and disserve privacy interests. * * * At the moment when officers stop an automobile, it may be less than clear whether they suspect with a high degree of certainty that the vehicle contains drugs in a bag or simply contains drugs. If the police know that they may open a bag only if they are actually searching the entire car, they may search more extensively than they otherwise would in order to establish the general probable cause required by *Ross*.

* * * We cannot see the benefit of a rule that requires law enforcement officers to conduct a more intrusive search in order to justify a less intrusive one.

To the extent that the *Chadwick-Sanders* rule protects privacy, its protection is minimal. Law enforcement officers may seize a container and hold it until they obtain a search warrant. *Chadwick*. Since the police, by hypothesis, have probable cause to seize the property, we can assume that a warrant will be routinely forthcoming in the overwhelming majority of cases. And the police often will be able to search containers without a warrant, despite the *Chadwick-Sanders* rule, as a search incident to a lawful arrest.

* * *

Finally, the search of a paper bag intrudes far less on individual privacy than does the incursion sanctioned long ago in *Carroll*. In that case, prohibition agents slashed the upholstery of the automobile. This Court nonetheless found their search to be reasonable under the Fourth Amendment. If destroying the interior of an automobile is not unreasonable, we cannot conclude that looking inside a closed container is. In light of the minimal protection to privacy afforded by the *Chadwick-Sanders* rule, and our serious doubt whether that rule substantially serves privacy interests, we now hold that the Fourth Amendment does not compel separate treatment for an automobile search that extends only to a container within the vehicle.

* * * The *Chadwick-Sanders* rule not only has failed to protect privacy but it has also confused courts and police officers and impeded effective law enforcement. * * *

The discrepancy between the two rules has led to confusion for law enforcement officers. For example, when an officer, who has developed probable cause to believe that a vehicle contains drugs, begins to search the vehicle and immediately discovers a closed container, which rule applies? The defendant will argue that the fact that the officer first chose to search the container indicates that his probable cause extended only to the container and that *Chadwick* and *Sanders* therefore require a warrant. On the other hand, the fact that the officer first chose to search in the most obvious location should not restrict the propriety of the search. The *Chadwick* rule, as applied in *Sanders,* has devolved into an anomaly such that the more likely the police are to discover drugs in a container, the less authority they have to search it. We have noted the virtue of providing "clear and unequivocal guidelines to the law enforcement profession." The *Chadwick-Sanders* rule is the antithesis of a "clear and unequivocal guideline."

* * *

Although we have recognized firmly that the doctrine of stare decisis serves profoundly important purposes in our legal system, this Court has overruled a prior case on the comparatively rare occasion when it has bred confusion or been a derelict or led to anomalous results. * * * [T]he existence of the dual regimes for automobile searches that uncover containers has proved as confusing as the *Chadwick* and *Sanders* dissenters predicted. We conclude that it is better to adopt one clear-cut rule to govern automobile searches and eliminate the warrant requirement for closed containers set forth in *Sanders.*

* * *

Until today, this Court has drawn a curious line between the search of an automobile that coincidentally turns up a container and the search of a container that coincidentally turns up in an automobile. The protections of the Fourth Amendment must not turn on such coincidences. We therefore interpret *Carroll* as providing one rule to govern all automobile searches. The police may search an automobile and the containers within it where they have probable cause to believe contraband or evidence is contained.

* * *

JUSTICE SCALIA, concurring in the judgment.

I agree with the dissent that it is anomalous for a briefcase to be protected by the "general requirement" of a prior warrant when it is being carried along the street, but for that same briefcase to become unprotected as soon as it is carried into an automobile. On the other hand, I agree with the Court that it would be anomalous for a locked compartment in an automobile to be unprotected by the "general requirement" of a prior warrant, but for an unlocked briefcase within the automobile to be protected. I join in the judgment of the Court because I think its holding is more faithful to the text and tradition of the Fourth Amendment, and if these anomalies in our jurisprudence are ever to be eliminated that is the direction in which we should travel.

* * *

Although the Fourth Amendment does not explicitly impose the requirement of a warrant, it is of course textually possible to consider that implicit within the requirement of reasonableness. For some years after the (still continuing) explosion in Fourth Amendment litigation that followed our announcement of the exclusionary rule in Weeks v. United States, our jurisprudence lurched back and forth between imposing a categorical warrant requirement and looking to reasonableness alone. (The opinions preferring a warrant involved searches of structures.) See generally Chimel v. California. By the late 1960's, the preference for a warrant had won out, at least rhetorically. See *Chimel;* Coolidge v. New Hampshire.

The victory was illusory. Even before today's decision, the "warrant requirement" had become so riddled with exceptions that it was basically unrecognizable. * * * Our intricate body of law regarding "reasonable expectation of privacy" has been developed largely as a means of creating these exceptions, enabling a search to be denominated not a Fourth Amendment "search" and therefore not subject to the general warrant requirement.

Unlike the dissent, therefore, I do not regard today's holding as some momentous departure, but rather as merely the continuation of an inconsistent jurisprudence that has been with us for years. * * *

JUSTICE WHITE, dissenting.

Agreeing as I do with most of Justice Stevens' opinion and with the result he reaches, I dissent and would affirm the judgment below.

JUSTICE STEVENS, with whom JUSTICE MARSHALL joins, dissenting.

* * *

To the extent there was any "anomaly" in our prior jurisprudence, the Court has "cured" it at the expense of creating a more serious paradox. For, surely it is anomalous to prohibit a search of a briefcase while the owner is carrying it exposed on a public street yet to permit a search once the owner has placed the briefcase in the locked trunk of his car. One's privacy interest in one's luggage can certainly not be diminished by one's removing it from a public thoroughfare and placing it—out of sight—in a privately owned vehicle. * * *

* * *

To support its argument that today's holding works only a minimal intrusion on privacy, the Court suggests that "[i]f the police know that they may open a bag only if they are actually searching the entire car, they may search more extensively than they otherwise would in order to establish the general probable cause required by *Ross.*" * * * [T]his fear is unexplained and inexplicable. Neither evidence uncovered in the course of a search nor the scope of the search conducted can be used to provide post hoc justification for a search unsupported by probable cause at its inception.

* * *

* * * No impartial observer could criticize this Court for hindering the progress of the war on drugs. On the contrary, decisions like the one the Court makes today will support the conclusion that this Court has become a loyal foot soldier in the Executive's fight against crime.

* * *

Probable Cause Issues After Acevedo

Professor Green has pointed out that the rule in *Acevedo* does not eliminate all the uncertainty of the previous law. There will still be difficult questions of whether there is probable cause to search a certain part of the car. See Green, "Power, Not Reason": Justice Marshall's Valedictory and the Fourth Amendment in the Supreme Court's 1990–91 Term, 70 N.C.L.Rev. 373 (1992). Not surprisingly, the lower courts have reached divergent results on the probable cause/location question after *Acevedo*. Compare United States v. McSween, 53 F.3d 684 (5th Cir.1995) (when officer smelled burnt marijuana, he had probable cause to search under the hood of the defendant's car, even though a search of the passenger compartment had turned up nothing), with United States v. Nielsen, 9 F.3d 1487 (10th Cir.1993) (when officer smelled burnt marijuana and a search of the passenger compartment turned up nothing, his search of the trunk was illegal: "We do not believe under the circumstances that there was a fair probability that the *trunk* contained marijuana, or that a disinterested magistrate would so hold if asked to issue a search warrant.").

Delayed Search of Containers: United States v. Johns

In United States v. Johns, 469 U.S. 478 (1985), the Court considered whether there are any temporal limitations on the power to search containers in cars without a warrant. Customs agents removed packages from a trunk, placed them in a Drug Enforcement Agency warehouse, and searched the packages three days later. The officers had probable cause, but no warrant. Writing for the Court, Justice O'Connor reasoned that *Ross* would have authorized a warrantless search of the packages when they were removed from the trunk; that previous cases—e.g., Chambers v. Maroney and Texas v. White—authorized a delayed search of the trunk; and that "searches of containers discovered in the course of a vehicle search are [not] subject to temporal restrictions not applicable to the vehicle search itself." The Court indicated that it did not intend to authorize indefinite retention of vehicles or "to foreclose the possibility that the owner of a vehicle or its contents might attempt to prove that delay in the completion of a vehicle search was unreasonable because it adversely affected a privacy or possessory interest." The Court also rejected the defendant's argument that the automobile exception was inapplicable because the agents had taken the packages from the trunk before searching them. Justice O'Connor saw no reason to require officers to keep a container in a car while the search of that container is conducted. Justice Brennan, joined by Justice Marshall, dissented and argued that no exigency precluded reasonable efforts to obtain a warrant.

Search of a Cellphone Found in a Car

Suppose officers have probable cause to believe that a suspect is dealing drugs out of his car. Under the automobile exception and *Ross*, that means they can search, without a warrant, any place in the car that the magistrate could authorize. Suppose they do such a search and find a cellphone. Can they search the cellphone for evidence of drug activity? Almost certainly there would be probable cause to believe that evidence of drug activity could be found on a cellphone, if there is probable cause to search the car itself, and so a magistrate could have authorized a search of the cellphone.

The Court in California v. Riley held that the search of a cellphone required a warrant, but the Court was evaluating a search incident to arrest. Is it different if the authority for the search lies in the automobile exception? It could be argued that the *Riley* court emphasizes that the reason for the arrest power rule—preserving evidence and protecting officers—were not present in a cellphone search. In contrast, the reason for the automobile exception lies in the diminished expectation of privacy in automobiles—and under *Acevedo,* that diminished expectation of privacy extends to everything that the person puts in the car. On the other hand, one could argue that a doctrine based on diminished expectation of privacy cannot justify a warrantless cellphone search because, as the Court emphasizes in *Riley*, cellphones—unlike other things that can be put in a car—carry gigabytes of private information.

The court in United States v. Camou, 773 F.3d 932 (9th Cir. 2014), held that the car exception does *not* authorize the warrantless search of a cellphone found in a car. The court reasoned as follows:

> Given the [*Riley*] Court's extensive analysis of cell phones as "containers" and cell phone searches in the vehicle context, we find no reason not to extend the reasoning in *Riley* from the search incident to arrest exception to the vehicle exception. Just as "[c]ell phones differ in both a quantitative and a qualitative sense from other objects that might be kept on an arrestee's person," so too do cell phones differ from any other object officers might find in a vehicle. Today's cell phones are unlike any of the container examples the Supreme Court has provided in the vehicle context. Whereas luggage, boxes, bags, clothing, lunch buckets, orange crates, wrapped packages, glove compartments, and locked trunks are capable of physically "holding another object," "[m]odern cell phones, as a category, implicate privacy concerns far beyond those implicated by the search of a cigarette pack, a wallet, or a purse." * * *
>
> We further note that the privacy intrusion of searching a cell phone without a warrant is of particular concern in the vehicle exception context because the allowable scope of the search is broader than that of an exigency search, or a search incident to arrest. Whereas exigency searches are circumscribed by the specific exigency at hand and searches incident to arrest are limited to areas within the arrestee's immediate control or to evidence relevant to the crime of arrest, vehicle exception searches allow for evidence relevant to criminal activity broadly. If cell phones are considered containers for purposes of the vehicle exception, officers would often be able to sift through all of the data on cell phones found in vehicles because they would not be restrained by any limitations of exigency or relevance to a specific crime.
>
> We therefore conclude that cell phones are *non*-containers for purposes of the vehicle exception to the warrant requirement, and the search of Camou's cell phone cannot be justified under that exception.

Search of Passengers' Property: Wyoming v. Houghton

In *Ross* and *Acevedo*, the Court upheld warrantless searches of containers that were clearly owned by the driver of the car, when there was probable cause to believe that they contained evidence of a crime. Should the situation change if the officer conducts a warrantless search of a passenger's property? The Supreme Court considered that question in Wyoming v. Houghton, 526 U.S. 295 (1999). Justice Scalia, writing for the Court, set forth the facts:

> In the early morning hours of July 23, 1995, a Wyoming Highway Patrol officer stopped an automobile for speeding and driving with a faulty brake light. There were three passengers in the front seat of the car: David Young (the driver), his girlfriend, and respondent. While questioning Young, the officer noticed a hypodermic syringe in Young's shirt pocket. He left the occupants under the supervision of two backup officers as he went to get gloves from his patrol car. Upon his return, he instructed Young to step out of the car and place the syringe on the hood. The officer then asked Young why he had a syringe; with refreshing candor, Young replied that he used it to take drugs.
>
> At this point, the backup officers ordered the two female passengers out of the car and asked them for identification. Respondent falsely identified herself as "Sandra James" and stated that she did not have any identification. Meanwhile, in light of Young's admission, the officer searched the passenger compartment of the car for contraband. On the back seat, he found a purse, which respondent claimed as hers. He removed from the purse a wallet containing respondent's driver's license, identifying her properly as Sandra K. Houghton. When the officer asked her why she had lied about her name, she replied: "In case things went bad."
>
> Continuing his search of the purse, the officer found a brown pouch and a black wallet-type container. Respondent denied that the former was hers, and claimed ignorance of how it came to be there; it was found to contain drug paraphernalia and a syringe with 60 ccs of methamphetamine. Respondent admitted ownership of the black container, which was also found to contain drug paraphernalia, and a syringe (which respondent acknowledged was hers) with 10 ccs of methamphetamine—an amount insufficient to support the felony conviction at issue in this case. The officer also found fresh needle-track marks on respondent's arms. He placed her under arrest.

The Wyoming Supreme Court found that the search of Houghton's purse violated the Fourth Amendment because the officer "knew or should have known that the purse did not belong to the driver, but to one of the passengers," and because "there was no probable cause to search the passengers' personal effects and no reason to believe that contraband had been placed within the purse."

Justice Scalia disagreed with the Wyoming Court's assumption that a passenger's property is subject to greater protection than that of the driver. He concluded that the search of the purse was permissible because there was probable cause to believe that drugs were in the car in which the purse was located. Under *Ross,* "[i]f probable cause justifies the search of a lawfully stopped vehicle, it justifies the search of every part of the vehicle and its contents that may conceal the object of the search." Justice Scalia stated that "the critical element in a reasonable search is not that the owner of the property is suspected of crime but that there is reasonable cause to believe that the specific things to be searched for and seized are located on the property to which entry is sought." Justice Scalia concluded as follows:

> When there is probable cause to search for contraband in a car, it is reasonable for police officers—like customs officials in the Founding era—to examine packages and containers without a showing of individualized probable cause for each one. A passenger's personal belongings, just like the driver's belongings or containers attached to the car like a glove compartment, are "in" the car, and the officer has probable cause to search for contraband in the car.
>
> * * * Passengers, no less than drivers, possess a reduced expectation of privacy with regard to the property that they transport in cars, which travel public thoroughfares, seldom serve as the repository of personal effects, are subjected to police stop and examination to enforce pervasive governmental controls as an everyday occurrence, and, finally, are exposed to traffic accidents that may render all their contents open to public scrutiny.

Houghton relied on United States v. Di Re, 332 U.S. 581 (1948), in which the Court had held that probable cause to search a car did not justify a body search of a passenger. But Justice Scalia distinguished *Di Re* on the basis of "the unique, significantly heightened protection afforded against searches of one's person." Quoting *Terry,* he observed that the search of one's person "must surely be an annoying, frightening, and perhaps humiliating experience" and concluded that "[s]uch traumatic consequences are not to be expected when the police examine an item of personal property found in a car."

In contrast to a passenger's minimal privacy expectations in property placed in a car, Justice Scalia found the government interests at stake in the search to be "substantial." This was because "[e]ffective law enforcement would be appreciably impaired without the ability to search a passenger's personal belongings when there is reason to believe contraband or evidence of criminal wrongdoing is hidden in the car." Justice Scalia explained that a passenger "will often be engaged in a common enterprise with the driver, and have the same interest in concealing the fruits or the evidence of their wrongdoing. A criminal might be able to hide contraband in a passenger's belongings as readily as in other containers in the car—perhaps even surreptitiously, without the passenger's knowledge or permission." Justice Scalia elaborated:

> To be sure, these factors favoring a search will not always be present, but the balancing of interests must be conducted with an eye to the generality of cases. To require that the investigating officer have positive reason to believe that the passenger and driver were engaged in a common enterprise, or positive reason to believe that the driver had time and occasion to conceal the item in the passenger's belongings, surreptitiously or with friendly permission, is to impose requirements so seldom met that a "passenger's property" rule would dramatically reduce the ability to find and seize contraband and evidence of crime. * * * [O]nce a "passenger's property" exception to car searches became widely known, one would expect passenger-confederates to claim everything as their own. And one would anticipate a bog of litigation—in the form of both civil lawsuits and motions to suppress in criminal trials—involving such questions as whether the officer should have believed a passenger's claim of ownership, whether he should have inferred ownership from various objective factors, whether he had probable cause to believe that the passenger was a confederate, or to believe that the driver might have introduced the contraband into the package with or without the passenger's knowledge.
>
> * * *
>
> We hold that police officers with probable cause to search a car may inspect passengers' belongings found in the car that are capable of concealing the object of the search.

Justice Breyer wrote a short concurring opinion in *Houghton,* reasoning that "[i]f the police must establish a container's ownership prior to the search of that container (whenever, for example, a passenger says 'that's mine'), the resulting uncertainty will destroy the workability of the bright-line rule set forth in United States v. Ross. At the same time, police officers with probable cause to search a car for drugs would often have probable cause to search containers regardless. Hence a bright-line rule will authorize only a limited number of searches that the law would not otherwise justify."

Justice Stevens, joined by Justices Souter and Ginsburg, dissented in *Houghton*. He argued that the Court had gone further than it had in *Ross* because it upheld the search of Houghton's purse even though the officer did not actually have probable cause to believe that there was contraband in the purse.

QUESTIONS AFTER HOUGHTON

Assume the following facts: the officer properly stops the car driven by Young. Young admits that he is a drug user and that syringes and drugs are in the car. He also says that Houghton, his passenger, is accompanying him to a drug counseling center. Houghton explains that she is a drug counselor fiercely opposed to drug use. Houghton produces identification and a business card that supports her statement. The officer searches under the driver's seat and finds drugs. Can he now search Houghton's purse? The answer appears to be yes under the Court's bright-line rule, because the officer has probable cause to search the car and therefore "may inspect passengers' belongings found in the car that are capable of concealing the object of the search." Does this result make sense under these facts? Are these facts so unlikely that it makes sense to have a bright line rule?

J. EXIGENT CIRCUMSTANCES

1. Exigent Circumstances Generally

It takes time to obtain a warrant. In some cases where police have probable cause to search or arrest, they have to work quickly, because delay could 1) give a suspect the opportunity to escape; 2) give the suspect, or others, an opportunity to take up and use weapons, or hurt others (such as family members during a violent argument); or 3) give the suspect or others the opportunity to destroy evidence. Relatedly, officers may have good reason to believe that someone on a premises is in immediate danger of death or bodily harm. The exigent circumstance exception to the warrant requirement allows warrantless entries into constitutionally protected areas when the balance of competing interests at stake in rapidly developing circumstances show that immediate action is necessary to prevent flight, to safeguard the police or public, or to preserve evidence.

The exigent circumstances exception excuses officers from having to obtain a magistrate's determination that probable cause exists. It does not permit a search in the absence of probable cause. Besides needing probable cause to search, the officer must demonstrate reason to believe that delay would unreasonably compromise legitimate law enforcement interests.

2. Hot Pursuit

If officers are in "hot pursuit" of a suspect when he enters a constitutionally protected premises, then the officers may be permitted to continue their pursuit without first securing a warrant. The rationale is that it is unrealistic to expect police officers to stop in the middle of a chase in order to apply for a warrant. To do so could allow the suspect to get away and thus render the warrant meaningless. Delaying the chase to apply for a warrant could also allow the suspect to destroy evidence or to create a dangerous situation for police officers or members of the public. On the other hand, officers have both probable cause to believe that the person pursued has committed a crime and probable cause to believe that they will be found on the premises to be searched. On balance, then, an unwarranted entry effected in the course of a hot pursuit is likely to be reasonable.

The Court's leading hot pursuit case is Warden v. Hayden, 387 U.S. 294 (1967). Officers pursued a robbery suspect into what was subsequently determined to be his home. The officers knocked, the suspect's wife answered the door, and officers then entered the house to search for the suspect. The Court held that the warrantless search was justified by the "hot pursuit" exception.

The "hot pursuit" doctrine is based on the premise that the suspect, knowing that he is being pursued, may seek to escape, destroy evidence or create a threat to public safety. It follows that the "hot pursuit" doctrine cannot apply where the suspect is unaware that he is being pursued by police officers. Thus, in Welsh v. Wisconsin, 466 U.S. 740 (1984), officers were notified that a car had been driven into a ditch. Eyewitnesses told the officers that the driver had been driving erratically, and had walked away from the scene. The officers quickly went to the address listed on the vehicle registration and arrested Welsh in his home for driving while intoxicated. The Court held that the "hot pursuit" doctrine could not apply in these circumstances because Welsh was not aware that he was being pursued by police officers until he was arrested. If the "hot pursuit" doctrine were determined only by how expeditiously the police were pursuing the suspect, then it would exist in virtually every case.

On the other hand, the "hot pursuit" doctrine can cover situations significantly short of high speed car chases. For example, in United States v. Santana, 427 U.S. 38 (1976), officers approached Santana while she was standing in the doorway of her home. They had probable cause to arrest her. When Santana saw the officers, she quickly retreated into her house. The officers told her she was under arrest and then followed her into the house to catch her and place her in custody. The Court, in an opinion by Justice Rehnquist, held that the police officers were permitted to follow Santana into her house under the doctrine of "hot pursuit." Justice Rehnquist noted that the hot pursuit doctrine serves to ensure that "a suspect may not defeat an arrest which has been set in motion in a public place * * * by the expedient of escaping into a private place." He concluded: "the fact that the pursuit here ended almost as soon as it began did not render it any the less a 'hot pursuit' sufficient to justify the warrantless entry."

The Court's holding in *Santana* raises the question whether warrantless entries into homes are always justified in cases of hot pursuit. In *Lange v. California*, 141 S.Ct. 2011 (2021), the Court held that no such categorical rule exists in cases where the crime suspected is a misdemeanor. Citing the significant privacy interests attaching to homes, and the wide range of law enforcement interests at stake in misdemeanor offenses, some of which may be weighty, and others less so, the Court opted for a case-by-case approach aimed at determining whether, on "the totality of circumstances," the facts in a particular case demonstrate a law enforcement emergency. Among the factors officers should consider are "imminent harm to others, a threat to the officer himself, destruction of evidence, or escape from the home." Attempted escape is certainly relevant, the Court allowed, "[b]ut the need to pursue a misdemeanant does not trigger a categorical rule allowing home entry, even absent a law enforcement emergency."

Lange left unanswered the question whether hot pursuit in felony cases might be more amenable to a categorical rule. Although the Court generally prefers a case-by-case approach in cases involving claims of exigency, Justice Kagan, writing for the majority in *Lange*, cited substantial evidence that eighteenth century common law allowed for warrantless entry into homes in all cases of hot pursuit involving felonies. She noted, however, that this historical record is muddied by the fact that "[t]he felony category then was a good deal narrower than now" and "[m]any modern felonies were classified as misdemeanors at common law, with the felony label mostly reserved for crimes punishable by death." Given this, and the Court's general reluctance to adopt bright line rules in Fourth Amendment cases, there is room for the Court to opt for a case-by-case approach in cases involving hot pursuit of felony suspects.

3. Police and Public Safety

A warrant is excused if the delay in obtaining it would result in a significant risk of harm to the police or to members of the public. See, e.g., United States v. Salava, 978 F.2d 320 (7th Cir.1992) (risk to public safety excuses warrant where the defendant was found outside his home with blood on his clothes, and stated that he shot someone inside the home; while it was subsequently discovered that the defendant had wounded himself in a fight with an imaginary opponent, the court must evaluate the risk to public safety from the point of view of the officer at the time of the search). See also United States v. Black, 466 F.3d 1143 (9th Cir.2006) (it was reasonable for police to enter an apartment without a warrant after receiving reports of a serious domestic disturbance, even though the house was quiet when they arrived, because someone inside may have been injured or in danger). Compare United States v. Williams, 354 F.3d 497 (6th Cir. 2003) (public safety not at stake, and warrant not excused, where officers entered a premises to check out a water leak: "Danger of water damage to a carpet is certainly not urgent within the meaning of the 'risk of danger' exigency.").

Public Safety and the Relevance of a Law Enforcement Objective: Brigham City v. Stuart

The following case applies the "public safety" exception and considers whether it can apply even though the officer is subjectively pursuing law enforcement (rather than public safety) objectives.

BRIGHAM CITY V. STUART

Supreme Court of the United States, 2006.
547 U.S. 398.

CHIEF JUSTICE ROBERTS delivered the opinion of the Court.

In this case we consider whether police may enter a home without a warrant when they have an objectively reasonable basis for believing that an occupant is seriously injured or imminently threatened with such injury. We conclude that they may.

* * *

This case arises out of a melee that occurred in a Brigham City, Utah, home in the early morning hours of July 23, 2000. At about 3 a.m., four police officers responded to a call regarding a loud party at a residence. Upon arriving at the house, they heard shouting from inside, and proceeded down the driveway to investigate. There, they observed two juveniles drinking beer in the backyard. They entered the backyard, and saw—through a screen door and windows—an altercation taking place in the kitchen of the home. According to the testimony of one of the officers, four adults were attempting, with some difficulty, to restrain a juvenile. The juvenile eventually "broke free, swung a fist and struck one of the adults in the face." The officer testified that he observed the victim of the blow spitting blood into a nearby sink. The other adults continued to try to restrain the juvenile, pressing him up against a refrigerator with such force that the refrigerator began moving across the floor. At this point, an officer opened the screen door and announced the officers' presence. Amid the tumult, nobody noticed. The officer entered the kitchen and again cried out, and as the occupants slowly became aware that the police were on the scene, the altercation ceased.

The officers subsequently arrested respondents and charged them with contributing to the delinquency of a minor, disorderly conduct, and intoxication. In the trial court, respondents filed a motion to suppress all evidence obtained after the officers entered the home, arguing that the warrantless entry violated the Fourth Amendment. [The Utah courts found that exigent circumstances did not support a warrantless entry, relying on the fact that the officers were primarily motivated in prosecuting crime rather than protecting the public.]

* * *

One exigency obviating the requirement of a warrant is the need to assist persons who are seriously injured or threatened with such injury. * * * Accordingly, law enforcement officers may enter a home without a warrant to render emergency assistance to an injured occupant or to protect an occupant from imminent injury.

Respondents do not take issue with these principles, but instead advance two reasons why the officers' entry here was unreasonable. First, they argue that the officers were more interested in making arrests than quelling violence. They urge us to consider, in assessing the reasonableness of the entry, whether the officers were "indeed motivated primarily by a desire to save lives and property." * * *

Our cases have repeatedly rejected this approach. An action is "reasonable" under the Fourth Amendment, regardless of the individual officer's state of mind, as long as the circumstances, viewed *objectively*, justify the action. The officer's subjective motivation is irrelevant. See Whren v. United States. It therefore does not matter here—even if their subjective motives could be so neatly unraveled—whether the officers entered the kitchen to arrest respondents and gather evidence against them or to assist the injured and prevent further violence.

* * *

Respondents further contend that their conduct was not serious enough to justify the officers' intrusion into the home. They rely on Welsh v. Wisconsin, 466 U.S. 740, 753 (1984), in which we held that "an important factor to be considered when determining whether any exigency exists is the gravity of the underlying offense for which the arrest is being made." This contention, too, is misplaced. *Welsh* involved a warrantless entry by officers to arrest a suspect for driving while intoxicated. There, the "only potential emergency" confronting the officers was the need to preserve evidence (*i.e.*, the suspect's blood-alcohol level)—an exigency that we held insufficient under the circumstances to justify entry into the suspect's home. Here, the officers were confronted with *ongoing* violence occurring *within* the home. *Welsh* did not address such a situation.

We think the officers' entry here was plainly reasonable under the circumstances. The officers were responding, at 3 o'clock in the morning, to complaints about a loud party. As they approached the house, they could hear from within "an altercation occurring, some kind of a fight." * * * The officers heard "thumping and crashing" and people yelling "stop, stop" and "get off me." * * * The noise seemed to be coming from the back of the house;

after looking in the front window and seeing nothing, the officers proceeded around back to investigate further. * * * From there, they could see that a fracas was taking place inside the kitchen. A juvenile, fists clenched, was being held back by several adults. As the officers watch, he breaks free and strikes one of the adults in the face, sending the adult to the sink spitting blood.

In these circumstances, the officers had an objectively reasonable basis for believing both that the injured adult might need help and that the violence in the kitchen was just beginning. Nothing in the Fourth Amendment required them to wait until another blow rendered someone "unconscious" or "semi-conscious" or worse before entering. The role of a peace officer includes preventing violence and restoring order, not simply rendering first aid to casualties; an officer is not like a boxing (or hockey) referee, poised to stop a bout only if it becomes too one-sided.

* * *

Accordingly, we reverse the judgment of the Supreme Court of Utah, and remand the case for further proceedings not inconsistent with this opinion.

[The concurring opinion of Justice Stevens is omitted.]

Application of Brigham City v. Stuart: Michigan v. Fisher

In Michigan v. Fisher, 558 U.S. 45 (2009), the Court, in a per curiam opinion, applied its analysis in *Brigham City* to uphold the warrantless search of a house by an officer responding to a complaint about a domestic disturbance. Upon arriving in response to the complaint, officers found a house "in considerable chaos: a pickup truck in the driveway with its front smashed, damaged fenceposts along the side of the property, and three broken house windows, the glass still on the ground outside. The officers also noticed blood on the hood of the pickup and on clothes inside of it, as well as on one of the doors to the house. * * * Through a window, the officers could see Fisher inside the house screaming and throwing things. The officers knocked, but Fisher refused to answer. They saw that Fisher had a cut on his hand, and they asked him whether he needed medical attention. Fisher ignored these questions and demanded, with accompanying profanity, that the officers go to get a search warrant." The officers entered and saw Fisher pointing a long gun. Fisher was charged with a firearms offense and challenged the warrantless entry into his house. The Court found that the public safety interest under the facts was every bit as strong as in *Brigham City*. It elaborated as follows:

> Officers do not need ironclad proof of "a likely serious, life-threatening" injury to invoke the emergency aid exception. The only injury police could confirm in *Brigham City* was the bloody lip they

> saw the juvenile inflict upon the adult. Fisher argues that the officers here could not have been motivated by a perceived need to provide medical assistance, since they never summoned emergency medical personnel. This would have no bearing, of course, upon their need to assure that Fisher was not endangering someone else in the house. Moreover, even if the failure to summon medical personnel conclusively established that [Officer] Goolsby did not subjectively believe, when he entered the house, that Fisher or someone else was seriously injured (which is doubtful), the test, as we have said, is not what Goolsby believed, but whether there was an objectively reasonable basis for believing that medical assistance was needed, or persons were in danger. * * * It sufficed to invoke the emergency aid exception that it was reasonable to believe that Fisher had hurt himself (albeit nonfatally) and needed treatment that in his rage he was unable to provide, or that Fisher was about to hurt, or had already hurt, someone else. * * *

Justice Stevens, joined by Justice Sotomayor, dissented in *Fisher*.

Pinging a Cellphone for Public Safety

Suppose officers have probable cause to believe that a suspect is going to commit a murder, do not know where he is, but do know he has a cellphone. One possibility is to get a warrant for historic cell-site location information from the suspect's provider, but securing the warrant takes time; obtaining the information from the provider takes time; the information is historic, not in real time; and the information may not reveal exact locations.

Another option is to determine where the cellphone is by GPS location, which is generated by triangulating the cell phone's position by reference to three or more network satellites. By contrast with cell-site data, this information is generated only at the specific command of a cellphone provider's operator—an action called "pinging"—and is quite precise. The "pinging" however is a search because it is seeking information from the phone, and that information is not in the hands of a third party.

In United States v. Caraballo, 831 F.3d 95 (2d Cir. 2016), officers had probable cause that Caraballo was in his car on his way to hurt or kill people. They contacted Sprint and Sprint agreed to ping Caraballo's cellphone, allowing the officers to identify his precise location. But no warrant was obtained. The court found that the warrantless pinging procedure was justified by exigent circumstances because people might have been killed during the time it would have taken to obtain a warrant. The court also noted that the pinging was "strictly circumscribed" because it was only two hours in duration; consequently the defendant could not claim that the officers were trying to obtain a "mosaic" of his life.

The *Carballo* court determined that exigent circumstances existed and thereby avoided the question whether obtaining real time location information by pinging a cellphone constitutes a search. Do you think this investigative method implicates the Fourth Amendment? On what grounds? Does pinging a phone entail an intrusion into the phone? Does it implicate the privacy concerns elaborated by the Court in Carpenter v. United States, supra? The *Carpenter* Court specifically declined to reach this question, but other courts have weighed-in. See, e.g., United States v. Skinner, 690 F.3d 772 (2012) (no reasonable expectation of privacy in real time location data generated by pinging a cellphone); Commonwealth v. Almonor, 482 Mass. 35 (2019) (pinging a cellphone to obtain real time location information violates reasonable expectations of privacy); State v. Muhammad, 194 Wash2d 577 (2019) (same).

4. The Risk of Destruction of Evidence

If evidence will be destroyed in the time it takes to obtain a warrant, then the warrant requirement is excused. The question usually disputed in the cases is whether there was really an imminent risk of destruction of evidence under the facts presented. Although this is a highly fact-dependent inquiry, Dorman v. United States, 435 F.2d 385 (D.C.Cir.1970) (in banc), describes a number of factors often relevant to the inquiry. The *Dorman* factors have been summarized as follows:

> (1) the gravity or violent nature of the offense with which the suspect is to be charged; (2) whether the suspect "is reasonably believed to be armed"; (3) "a clear showing of probable cause . . . to believe that the suspect committed the crime"; (4) "strong reason to believe that the suspect is in the premises being entered"; (5) "a likelihood that the suspect will escape if not swiftly apprehended"; and (6) the peaceful circumstances of the entry.

United States v. MacDonald, 916 F.2d 766 (2d Cir.1990).

The *MacDonald* court applied these factors to endorse an unwarranted entry into a home in circumstances where officers had probable cause to believe that narcotics, numerous firearms, and several coconspirators were on the premises. Because the officers had announced their presence by knocking on the door, they also had good reason to fear that those on the premises might try to destroy evidence or arm themselves in order to harm officers. By contrast, in Vale v. Louisiana, 399 U.S. 30 (1970), the Court held that exigent circumstances did not exist when Vale was arrested outside his home for engaging in a drug transaction and there was no indication that anyone was inside who could destroy evidence. See also United States v. Purcell, 526 F.3d 953 (6th Cir. 2008) (no imminent risk of destruction of evidence despite officers' claim that they thought the defendant was operating a methamphetamine lab in a hotel room; that assumption was based only on the defendant's prior meth lab activities, and not on any real indication that methamphetamine cooking was going on when the officers arrived).

The Seriousness of the Offense

In assessing whether there is a risk of destruction of evidence sufficient to excuse a warrant, the *Dorman* factors take into account not only the destructibility of the evidence but also the seriousness of the offense—the more serious the offense, the greater the incentive for destroying evidence, and the greater the government interest in protecting against its loss. For example, the serious nature of a narcotics offense was central to the *MacDonald* Court's finding of exigent circumstances.

The "seriousness" factor raises two questions: 1) Could an offense be so serious that exigency should be deemed automatic, without regard to the actual risk of destruction of evidence? and 2) Could an offense be so minor that a warrant should be required regardless of the actual risk of destruction of evidence? The Supreme Court has had something to say about both of these questions.

Murder Scene

As to the first question, the Court in Mincey v. Arizona, 437 U.S. 385 (1978), considered the government's argument that there should be a "murder scene" exception to the warrant requirement. Mincey shot and killed an officer during a drug bust. Mincey himself was seriously wounded. A protective sweep of the premises resulted in the detention of Mincey's associates. Ten minutes later, homicide detectives entered the premises without a warrant and began a search for evidence that lasted four days. Every item in the apartment was closely examined and inventoried, and two to three hundred objects were seized.

Justice Stewart wrote for a unanimous Court. He rejected a categorical "scene of the homicide" exception to the warrant requirement in favor of a fact-centered exigency analysis. Justice Stewart wrote as follows:

> All the persons in Mincey's apartment had been located before the investigating homicide officers arrived there and began their search. And a four-day search that included opening dresser drawers and ripping up carpets can hardly be rationalized in terms of the legitimate concerns that justify an emergency search.
>
> * * * [T]he State points to the vital public interest in the prompt investigation of the extremely serious crime of murder. No one can doubt the importance of this goal. But the public interest in the investigation of other serious crimes is comparable. If the warrantless search of a homicide scene is reasonable, why not the warrantless search of the scene of a rape, a robbery, or a burglary? No consideration

relevant to the Fourth Amendment suggests any point of rational limitation of such a doctrine.

What would be wrong with a rule that automatically allowed searches at the scene of a homicide, rape, or robbery, even the day after the crime occurred? Won't a search warrant be issued automatically for these kinds of crimes? If the warrant application is perfunctory, what is gained by having the police, who are already on the scene, seek a warrant?

Minor Offenses

The Court in Welsh v. Wisconsin, 466 U.S. 740 (1984), considered whether an offense could be so minor as not to justify an exception to the warrant requirement even given an imminent risk of destruction of evidence. Officers arrested Welsh in his home shortly after receiving a report from an observer that Welsh had been driving his car while being intoxicated or very sick. After seeing Welsh driving erratically and ultimately swerving off the road into a ditch, the observer blocked Welsh's car with his own car and saw Welsh walk away from the ditch after being refused a ride. Police came to the scene and discovered a motor vehicle registration in Welsh's abandoned car. The police went to the address listed on the registration and arrested Welsh in his home for driving while under the influence of an intoxicant. Welsh subsequently refused to submit to a breathalyzer test. The state revoked his license due to his refusal, and Welsh challenged this action, arguing that his refusal came about as a result of an illegal warrantless in-home arrest. The state argued that the warrantless arrest was legal because, among other things, the delay in obtaining a warrant would have resulted in the loss of evidence—specifically the loss of proof of Welsh's intoxication.

Justice Brennan's opinion for six members of the Court rejected the destruction of evidence argument and found the warrantless arrest in the home to be illegal. Justice Brennan declared that "it is difficult to conceive of a warrantless home arrest that would not be unreasonable under the Fourth Amendment when the underlying offense is extremely minor." He held that "an important factor to be considered when determining whether any exigency exists is the gravity of the underlying offense for which the arrest is being made" and declared that "application of the exigent-circumstances exception in the context of a home entry should rarely be sanctioned when there is probable cause to believe that only a minor offense, such as the kind at issue in this case, has been committed."

Applying these principles to the facts of the case, Justice Brennan noted that "[t]he State of Wisconsin has chosen to classify the first offense for driving while intoxicated as a noncriminal, civil forfeiture offense for which no imprisonment is possible," and that "[g]iven this expression of the state's interest, a warrantless home arrest cannot be upheld simply because evidence of the petitioner's blood-alcohol level might have dissipated while the police obtained a warrant."

Justice White, joined by Justice Rehnquist, dissented. He reasoned that a warrantless home entry is no more intrusive for a minor offense than a major one and that the majority's approach would force officers who must make quick decisions to assess whether a violation is major or minor for purposes of making an exigency determination.

Drawing Blood in a DUI Arrest to Prevent the Loss of Evidence: Missouri v. McNeely

In Schmerber v. California, 384 U. S. 757 (1966), the Court upheld a warrantless blood test of an individual arrested for driving under the influence of alcohol because the officer "might reasonably have believed that he was confronted with an emergency, in which the delay necessary to obtain a warrant, under the circumstances, threatened the destruction of evidence." But in Missouri v. McNeely, 569 U.S. 141 (2013), the Court held 5–4 that its decision in *Schmerber* did not establish a per se rule that exigent circumstances always exist to allow a warrantless seizure of blood in all drunk-driving cases.[30] The court held that exigency must be established case-by-case based on the totality of the circumstances.

An officer stopped McNeely's truck in the early morning hours for speeding and repeatedly crossing the center line. McNeely did badly on field-sobriety tests and declined to use a portable breath-test device to measure his blood alcohol concentration (BAC). The officer arrested him and, when McNeely indicated on the way to the station that he would refuse to provide a breath sample, the officer transported him to a hospital. McNeely refused to consent to a blood test even after being warned that under state law refusal to submit voluntarily to the test would lead to the immediate revocation of his driver's license for one year and could be used against him in a future prosecution. The officer directed a hospital lab technician to take a blood sample, and the sample showed a blood alcohol level almost double the legal limit.

McNeely moved to suppress the results of the test when prosecuted for driving while intoxicated. The trial judge granted the motion, reasoning that there was no exigency excusing a warrant apart from the fact that "[a]s in all cases involving intoxication, [McNeely's] blood alcohol was being metabolized by his liver." Justice Sotomayor, writing for the Court, agreed with the state court.

Justice Sotomayor explained that, in *Schmerber*, the Court "considered all of the facts and circumstances of the particular case and carefully based

[30] In Birchfield v. North Dakota, 579 U.S. 438 (2016), the Court addressed the application of the search incident to arrest doctrine to blood and breathalyzer tests in the DUI context. *Birchfield* is discussed earlier this Chapter with the materials on searches incident to arrest.

our holding on those specific facts." She recognized that "the alcohol level in a person's blood begins to dissipate once the alcohol is fully absorbed and continues to decline until the alcohol is eliminated," but reasoned that this reality did not establish an exigency in every drunk driving case, and that "where police officers can reasonably obtain a warrant before a blood sample can be drawn without significantly undermining the efficacy of the search, the Fourth Amendment mandates that they do so."

Justice Sotomayor rejected an alternative test offered by Chief Justice Roberts (and joined in by Justices Breyer and Alito) in an opinion concurring in part and dissenting in part "under which a warrantless blood draw is permissible if the officer could not secure a warrant (or reasonably believed he could not secure a warrant) in the time it takes to transport the suspect to a hospital or similar facility and obtain medical assistance." One example she offered to explain the problem with that test was a police officer's chance stop of a suspect near an emergency room. In that example, the test would "enable the officer to conduct a nonconsensual warrantless blood draw even if all agree that a warrant could be obtained with very little delay under the circumstances (perhaps with far less delay than an average ride to the hospital in the jurisdiction)."

The Court returned to the topic of blood tests in Mitchell v. Wisconsin, 139 S.Ct. 2525 (2019). Writing for the plurality in that case, Justice Alito maintained the Court's commitment to fact-based assessments, but held that "the exigent-circumstances rule almost always permits a blood test without a warrant" in cases where the arrestee is unconscious. In reaching that holding, Justice Alito noted that officers cannot administer a breathalyzer test to an unconscious suspect, that blood tests are medically indicated in most cases of unconsciousness, and that taking the time to secure a warrant would compromise officers' abilities to attend to important safety and investigative duties. He nevertheless allowed "that in an unusual case a defendant [might] be able to show that his blood would not have been drawn if police had not been seeking BAC information, and that police could not have reasonably judged that a warrant application would interfere with other pressing needs or duties." The Court remanded the case to allow Mitchell the opportunity to make this showing.

Justice Thomas concurred in *Mitchell* and would have established a categorical rule. In a dissenting opinion joined by Justices Ginsburg and Kagan, Justice Sotomayor objected to any departure from the Court's holding in *McNeely*. Justice Gorsuch also filed a dissenting opinion because certiorari was granted to consider whether implied consent rather than exigency justified testing Mitchell's blood.

5. When Police Provoke an Exigent Circumstance

In some cases suspects are alerted to the presence of police activity, and at that point there is little dispute about the risk of destruction of evidence or other danger when the officers make an entry. Instead, defendants argue that the police acted impermissibly in revealing their presence—for example, by knocking on a door and yelling "police"—and thus *manufacturing* the exigent circumstances. Does manufacturing exigency bar reliance on the exigent circumstances exception? That question is answered in the following case.

KENTUCKY V. KING

Supreme Court of the United States, 2011.
563 U.S. 452.

JUSTICE ALITO delivered the opinion of the Court.

It is well established that exigent circumstances, including the need to prevent the destruction of evidence, permit police officers to conduct an otherwise permissible search without first obtaining a warrant. In this case, we consider whether this rule applies when police, by knocking on the door of a residence and announcing their presence, cause the occupants to attempt to destroy evidence. The Kentucky Supreme Court held that the exigent circumstances rule does not apply in the case at hand because the police should have foreseen that their conduct would prompt the occupants to attempt to destroy evidence. We reject this interpretation of the exigent circumstances rule. The conduct of the police prior to their entry into the apartment was entirely lawful. They did not violate the Fourth Amendment or threaten to do so. In such a situation, the exigent circumstances rule applies.

* * *

This case concerns the search of an apartment in Lexington, Kentucky. Police officers set up a controlled buy of crack cocaine outside an apartment complex. Undercover Officer Gibbons watched the deal take place from an unmarked car in a nearby parking lot. After the deal occurred, Gibbons radioed uniformed officers to move in on the suspect. He told the officers that the suspect was moving quickly toward the breezeway of an apartment building, and he urged them to hurry up and get there before the suspect entered an apartment.

In response to the radio alert, the uniformed officers drove into the nearby parking lot, left their vehicles, and ran to the breezeway. Just as they entered the breezeway, they heard a door shut and detected a very strong odor of burnt marijuana. At the end of the breezeway, the officers saw two apartments, one on the left and one on the right, and they did not know which apartment the suspect had entered. * * * Because they smelled marijuana smoke emanating from the apartment on the left, they approached the door of that apartment.

Officer Steven Cobb * * * testified that the officers banged on the left apartment door as loud as they could and announced, "This is the police" or "Police, police, police." Cobb said that as soon as the officers started banging on the door, they could hear people inside moving, and it sounded as though things were being moved inside the apartment. These noises, Cobb testified, led the officers to believe that drug-related evidence was about to be destroyed.

At that point, the officers announced that they were going to make entry inside the apartment. Cobb then kicked in the door, the officers entered the apartment, and they found three people in the front room: respondent Hollis King, respondent's girlfriend, and a guest who was smoking marijuana. The officers performed a protective sweep of the apartment during which they saw marijuana and powder cocaine in plain view. In a subsequent search, they also discovered crack cocaine, cash, and drug paraphernalia.

Police eventually entered the apartment on the right. Inside, they found the suspected drug dealer who was the initial target of their investigation.

[The Supreme Court of Kentucky found that the entry violated the Fourth Amendment because the officers deliberately created the exigent circumstances.]

* * *

Over the years, lower courts have developed an exception to the exigent circumstances rule, the so-called police-created exigency doctrine. Under this doctrine, police may not rely on the need to prevent destruction of evidence when that exigency was created or manufactured by the conduct of the police. In applying this exception for the creation or manufacturing of an exigency by the police, courts require something more than mere proof that fear of detection by the police caused the destruction of evidence. An additional showing is obviously needed because * * * in some sense the police always create the exigent circumstances. That is to say, in the vast majority of cases in which evidence is destroyed by persons who are engaged in illegal conduct, the reason for the destruction is fear that the evidence will fall into the hands of law enforcement. Consequently, a rule that precludes the police from making a warrantless entry to prevent the destruction of evidence whenever their conduct causes the exigency would unreasonably shrink the reach of this well-established exception to the warrant requirement.

* * *

[T]he answer to the question presented in this case follows directly and clearly from the principle that permits warrantless searches in the first place. As previously noted, warrantless searches are allowed when the circumstances make it reasonable, within the meaning of the Fourth Amendment, to dispense with the warrant requirement. Therefore, the answer to the question before us is that the exigent circumstances rule justifies a warrantless search when the conduct of the police preceding the exigency is reasonable in the same sense. Where, as here, the police did not create the exigency by engaging or threatening to engage in conduct that violates the Fourth Amendment, warrantless entry to prevent the destruction of evidence is reasonable and thus allowed.[a]

We have taken a similar approach in other cases involving warrantless searches. For example, we have held that law enforcement officers may seize evidence in plain view, provided that they have not violated the Fourth Amendment in arriving at the spot from which the observation of the evidence is made. * * *

Similarly, officers may seek consent-based encounters if they are lawfully present in the place where the consensual encounter occurs. If consent is freely given, it makes no difference that an officer may have approached the person with the hope or expectation of obtaining consent.

* * *

Some lower courts have adopted a rule that is similar to the one that we recognize today. See United States v. MacDonald, 916 F.2d 766 (C.A.2 1990) (en banc) (law enforcement officers do not impermissibly create exigent circumstances when they act in an entirely lawful manner). But others, including the Kentucky Supreme Court, have imposed additional requirements that are unsound and that we now reject.

Bad faith. Some courts, including the Kentucky Supreme Court, ask whether law enforcement officers deliberately created the exigent circumstances with the bad faith intent to avoid the warrant requirement. This approach is fundamentally inconsistent with our Fourth Amendment jurisprudence. Our cases have repeatedly rejected a subjective approach, asking only whether the circumstances, viewed *objectively,* justify the action. * * *

The reasons for looking to objective factors, rather than subjective intent, are clear. Legal tests based on reasonableness are generally objective, and this Court has long taken the view that evenhanded law enforcement is best achieved by the application of objective standards of conduct, rather than standards that depend upon the subjective state of mind of the officer.

---

[a] There is a strong argument to be made that, at least in most circumstances, the exigent circumstances rule should not apply where the police, without a warrant or any legally sound basis for a warrantless entry, threaten that they will enter without permission unless admitted. In this case, however, no such actual threat was made, and therefore we have no need to reach that question.

Reasonable foreseeability. Some courts * * * hold that police may not rely on an exigency if it was reasonably foreseeable that the investigative tactics employed by the police would create the exigent circumstances. Courts applying this test have invalidated warrantless home searches on the ground that it was reasonably foreseeable that police officers, by knocking on the door and announcing their presence, would lead a drug suspect to destroy evidence.

* * *

Adoption of a reasonable foreseeability test would * * * introduce an unacceptable degree of unpredictability. For example, whenever law enforcement officers knock on the door of premises occupied by a person who may be involved in the drug trade, there is *some* possibility that the occupants may possess drugs and may seek to destroy them. * * *

Probable cause and time to secure a warrant. Some courts, in applying the police-created exigency doctrine, fault law enforcement officers if, after acquiring evidence that is sufficient to establish probable cause to search particular premises, the officers do not seek a warrant but instead knock on the door and seek either to speak with an occupant or to obtain consent to search. This approach unjustifiably interferes with legitimate law enforcement strategies. There are many entirely proper reasons why police may not want to seek a search warrant as soon as the bare minimum of evidence needed to establish probable cause is acquired. Without attempting to provide a comprehensive list of these reasons, we note a few.

First, the police may wish to speak with the occupants of a dwelling before deciding whether it is worthwhile to seek authorization for a search. They may think that a short and simple conversation may obviate the need to apply for and execute a warrant. Second, the police may want to ask an occupant of the premises for consent to search because doing so is simpler, faster, and less burdensome than applying for a warrant. A consensual search also may result in considerably less inconvenience and embarrassment to the occupants than a search conducted pursuant to a warrant. Third, law enforcement officers may wish to obtain more evidence before submitting what might otherwise be considered a marginal warrant application. Fourth, prosecutors may wish to wait until they acquire evidence that can justify a search that is broader in scope than the search that a judicial officer is likely to authorize based on the evidence then available. And finally, in many cases, law enforcement may not want to execute a search that will disclose the existence of an investigation because doing so may interfere with the acquisition of additional evidence against those already under suspicion or evidence about additional but as yet unknown participants in a criminal scheme.

We have said that law enforcement officers are under no constitutional duty to call a halt to criminal investigation the moment they have the minimum evidence to establish probable cause. Faulting the police for failing to apply for a search warrant at the earliest possible time after obtaining probable cause imposes a duty that is nowhere to be found in the Constitution.

Standard or good investigative tactics. Finally, some lower court cases suggest that law enforcement officers may be found to have created or manufactured an exigency if the court concludes that the course of their investigation was contrary to standard or good law enforcement practices (or to the policies or practices of their jurisdictions). This approach fails to provide clear guidance for law enforcement officers and authorizes courts to make judgments on matters that are the province of those who are responsible for federal and state law enforcement agencies.

* * * Respondent argues for a rule that differs from those discussed above, but his rule is also flawed. Respondent contends that law enforcement officers impermissibly create an exigency when they engage in conduct that would cause a reasonable person to believe that entry is imminent and inevitable. In respondent's view, relevant factors include the officers' tone of voice in announcing their presence and the forcefulness of their knocks. But the ability of law enforcement officers to respond to an exigency cannot turn on such subtleties.

Police officers may have a very good reason to announce their presence loudly and to knock on the door with some force. A forceful knock may be necessary to alert the occupants that someone is at the door. Furthermore, unless police officers identify themselves loudly enough, occupants may not know who is at their doorstep. Officers are permitted indeed, encouraged to identify themselves to citizens, and in many circumstances this is cause for assurance, not discomfort. Citizens who are startled by an unexpected knock on the door or by the sight of unknown persons in plain clothes on their doorstep may be relieved to learn that these persons are police officers. Others may appreciate the opportunity to make an informed decision about whether to answer the door to the police.

If respondent's test were adopted, it would be extremely difficult for police officers to know how loudly they may announce their presence or how forcefully they may knock on a door without running afoul of the police-created exigency rule. And in most cases, it would be nearly impossible for a court to determine whether that threshold had been passed. The Fourth Amendment does not require the nebulous and impractical test that respondent proposes.[b]

---

[b] Contrary to respondent's argument, Johnson v. United States, 333 U.S. 10 (1948), does not require affirmance in this case. In *Johnson*, officers noticed the smell of burning opium emanating from a hotel room. They then knocked on the door and demanded entry. Upon seeing that Johnson was the only occupant of the room, they placed her under arrest, searched the room, and discovered opium and drug paraphernalia. Defending the legality of the search, the Government attempted to justify the warrantless search of the room as a valid search incident to a lawful arrest. The

* * *

For these reasons, we conclude that the exigent circumstances rule applies when the police do not gain entry to premises by means of an actual or threatened violation of the Fourth Amendment. This holding provides ample protection for the privacy rights that the Amendment protects. When law enforcement officers who are not armed with a warrant knock on a door, they do no more than any private citizen might do. And whether the person who knocks on the door and requests the opportunity to speak is a police officer or a private citizen, the occupant has no obligation to open the door or to speak. When the police knock on a door but the occupants choose not to respond or to speak, the investigation will have reached a conspicuously low point, and the occupants will have the kind of warning that even the most elaborate security system cannot provide. And even if an occupant chooses to open the door and speak with the officers, the occupant need not allow the officers to enter the premises and may refuse to answer any questions at any time.

Occupants who choose not to stand on their constitutional rights but instead elect to attempt to destroy evidence have only themselves to blame for the warrantless exigent-circumstances search that may ensue.

[The Court finds no evidence that the officers violated or threatened to violate the Fourth Amendment.]

* * *

JUSTICE GINSBURG, dissenting.

The Court today arms the police with a way routinely to dishonor the Fourth Amendment's warrant requirement in drug cases. In lieu of presenting their evidence to a neutral magistrate, police officers may now knock, listen, then break the door down, never mind that they had ample time to obtain a warrant. I dissent from the Court's reduction of the Fourth Amendment's force.

* * *

The existence of a genuine emergency depends not only on the state of necessity at the time of the warrantless search; it depends, first and foremost, on actions taken by the police *preceding* the warrantless search. Wasting a clear opportunity to obtain a warrant, therefore, disentitles the

---

Government did not contend that the officers entered the room in order to prevent the destruction of evidence. Although the officers said that they heard a shuffling noise inside the room after they knocked on the door, the Government did not claim that this particular noise was a noise that would have led a reasonable officer to think that evidence was about to be destroyed. Thus, *Johnson* is simply not a case about exigent circumstances.

officer from relying on subsequent exigent circumstances. S. Saltzburg & D. Capra, American Criminal Procedure 376 (8th ed.2007).

* * *

I * * * would not allow an expedient knock to override the warrant requirement. Instead, I would accord that core requirement of the Fourth Amendment full respect. When possible, a warrant must generally be secured, the Court acknowledges. There is every reason to conclude that securing a warrant was entirely feasible in this case, and no reason to contract the Fourth Amendment's dominion.

Kentucky v. King and the Relevance of a Prior Opportunity to Obtain a Warrant

If the police can foresee that an exigency would arise at a certain time in the future, have a strong case of probable cause, and also ample time to obtain a warrant well before that exigency occurs, then it could be argued that the opportunity to obtain a warrant should prohibit later invocation of the exigent circumstances exception. For example, assume that an officer knows that a suspect has his house cleaned every Wednesday morning and that this would destroy relevant forensic evidence. Assume further that the officer learned this information on Thursday and had ample grounds for probable cause to search the premises. There is a good argument that he should not be able to wait almost a week in order to invoke the exigent circumstances exception rather than applying for a warrant.

The decided cases do not usually present such clean facts, however. In the typical case, the state argues that the officer *did not* have clear probable cause until the exigency arose, and therefore had no prior opportunity to obtain a warrant. The defendant then makes the anomalous argument that the officer *had* probable cause well before that. The state also argues that the officer should not be required to go to the magistrate at the very first moment that probable cause exists—they should have the right to take their time and strengthen their case. The state also argues that a rule requiring immediate warrant applications could jeopardize undercover activity and ongoing investigations. See, e.g., United States v. Samboy, 433 F.3d 154 (1st Cir. 2005) (warrantless search upheld, where officers "reasonably delayed not from a desire to avoid seeking a warrant, but because the circumstances of the investigation demanded first caution and then an immediate response."). Of course, Kentucky v. King casts substantial doubt on whether a warrantless search based on exigent circumstances could ever be found illegal on the ground that officers had an opportunity to obtain a warrant before the exigency arose.

6. Electronic Warrants

Procedures in most jurisdictions allow officers to apply for warrants without appearing in person before a magistrate. For example, Fed.R.Crim.P. 41(d)(3)(A) provides that a magistrate judge "may issue a warrant based on information communicated by telephone or other reliable electronic means." The language "other reliable electronic means" is intended to allow for the use of email or fax. The rule does not mean that warrants can be obtained immediately, however. Under Rule 41, a duplicate original warrant must be prepared by the officer and must be read or sent in written form verbatim to the magistrate, who must prepare an original warrant for the record. These recording requirements are considered necessary to prevent post hoc reconstructions of probable cause and particularity. It must also be remembered that, at certain times (e.g., late at night or on the weekend), it may be difficult to reach a magistrate, by telephone or otherwise.

While not instantaneous, the time involved in obtaining an electronic warrant can be significantly less than it would take to obtain a warrant in person. In *McNeely, supra,* the Court held that the time it takes to obtain an electronic warrant is relevant when assessing exigency. See also United States v. Patino, 830 F.2d 1413 (7th Cir.1987) (agent who observed fugitive in defendant's yard had adequate opportunity to obtain an electronic warrant during 30-minute wait for back-up assistance). Compare United States v. Berick, 710 F.2d 1035 (5th Cir.1983) (risk of destruction of evidence resulting from arrest of drug seller was so imminent that recourse to even an electronic warrant was unavailable).

7. Seizing Premises in the Absence of Exigent Circumstances

If exigent circumstances do not exist to search a house or other premises, then officers must obtain a search warrant. But can officers take any protective action to preserve the status quo while a warrant is being obtained? In Segura v. United States, 468 U.S. 796 (1984), officers had probable cause to believe that two individuals, Segura and Luz Colon, were trafficking in cocaine from their New York apartment. They established surveillance and arrested Segura as he entered the lobby of his apartment building. The agents took Segura to his apartment, and knocked on the door. Luz Colon answered the door. The agents entered without receiving permission, placed Luz Colon under arrest, and conducted a limited security sweep. In the process of the sweep, they saw evidence of drug activity. Luz Colon and Segura were incarcerated and two officers waited in Segura's apartment while a search warrant was being obtained. Due to "administrative delay" it was 19 hours before the search of the apartment was eventually conducted.

A majority of the Court found it unnecessary to reach the question of whether the officers acted illegally. The majority reasoned that, even if the warrantless entry of the premises was illegal, the later search conducted pursuant to a warrant was based on an independent legal source, i.e., the information the officers already had before they seized the premises. [The "independent source" aspect of the opinion will be discussed later in this Chapter in the materials on the exclusionary rule.] Chief Justice Burger, joined by Justice O'Connor, went further, however, and declared that the seizure of the premises pending a warrant was reasonable, even in the absence of exigent circumstances.

Chief Justice Burger's argument in *Segura* was adopted by a majority of the Court in Murray v. United States, 487 U.S. 533 (1988). Thus it is permissible to seize premises for a reasonable period of time while diligent efforts are being made to obtain a warrant. See also United States v. Veillette, 778 F.2d 899 (1st Cir.1985) (48 hour seizure of premises, pending a warrant, held reasonable under *Segura*).

Prohibiting Entry While a Warrant Is Being Obtained: Illinois v. McArthur

In the following case, the Court expanded upon the analysis in *Segura* and firmly established the authority of police officers to maintain the status quo while a warrant is being obtained.

ILLINOIS V. MCARTHUR

Supreme Court of the United States, 2001.
531 U.S. 326.

JUSTICE BREYER delivered the opinion of the Court.

Police officers, with probable cause to believe that a man had hidden marijuana in his home, prevented that man from entering the home for about two hours while they obtained a search warrant. We must decide whether those officers violated the Fourth Amendment. We conclude that the officers acted reasonably. They did not violate the Amendment's requirements. And we reverse an Illinois court's holding to the contrary.

* * * On April 2, 1997, Tera McArthur asked two police officers to accompany her to the trailer where she lived with her husband, Charles, so that they could keep the peace while she removed her belongings. The two officers, Assistant Chief John Love and Officer Richard Skidis, arrived with Tera at the trailer at about 3:15 p.m. Tera went inside, where Charles was present. The officers remained outside.

When Tera emerged after collecting her possessions, she spoke to Chief Love, who was then on the porch. She suggested he check the trailer because "Chuck had dope in there." She added (in Love's words) that she had seen Chuck "slid[e] some dope underneath the couch."

Love knocked on the trailer door, told Charles what Tera had said, and asked for permission to search the trailer, which Charles denied. Love then sent Officer Skidis with Tera to get a search warrant.

Love told Charles, who by this time was also on the porch, that he could not reenter the trailer unless a police officer accompanied him. Charles subsequently reentered the trailer two or three times (to get cigarettes and to make phone calls), and each time Love stood just inside the door to observe what Charles did.

Officer Skidis obtained the warrant by about 5 p.m. He returned to the trailer and, along with other officers, searched it. The officers found under the sofa a marijuana pipe, a box for marijuana (called a "one-hitter" box), and a small amount of marijuana. They then arrested Charles.

* * *

Illinois subsequently charged Charles McArthur with unlawfully possessing drug paraphernalia and marijuana (less than 2.5 grams), both misdemeanors. McArthur moved to suppress the pipe, box, and marijuana on the ground that they were the "fruit" of an unlawful police seizure, namely, the refusal to let him reenter the trailer unaccompanied, which would have permitted him, he said, to "have destroyed the marijuana."

* * * We granted certiorari to determine whether the Fourth Amendment prohibits the kind of temporary seizure at issue here.

* * *

We conclude that the restriction at issue was reasonable, and hence lawful, in light of the following circumstances, which we consider in combination. First, the police had probable cause to believe that McArthur's trailer home contained evidence of a crime and contraband, namely, unlawful drugs. The police had had an opportunity to speak with Tera McArthur and make at least a very rough assessment of her reliability. They knew she had had a firsthand opportunity to observe her husband's behavior, in particular with respect to the drugs at issue. And they thought, with good reason, that her report to them reflected that opportunity.

Second, the police had good reason to fear that, unless restrained, McArthur would destroy the drugs before they could return with a warrant. * * *

Third, the police made reasonable efforts to reconcile their law enforcement needs with the demands of personal privacy. They neither searched the trailer nor arrested McArthur before obtaining a warrant. Rather, they imposed a significantly less restrictive restraint, preventing

McArthur only from entering the trailer unaccompanied. They left his home and his belongings intact—until a neutral Magistrate, finding probable cause, issued a warrant.

Fourth, the police imposed the restraint for a limited period of time, namely, two hours. As far as the record reveals, this time period was no longer than reasonably necessary for the police, acting with diligence, to obtain the warrant. Compare United States v. Place (holding 90-minute detention of luggage unreasonable based on nature of interference with person's travels and lack of diligence of police), with United States v. Van Leeuwen (holding 29-hour detention of mailed package reasonable given unavoidable delay in obtaining warrant and minimal nature of intrusion). Given the nature of the intrusion and the law enforcement interest at stake, this brief seizure of the premises was permissible.

* * *

* * * The Appellate Court of Illinois * * * found negatively significant the fact that Chief Love, with McArthur's consent, stepped inside the trailer's doorway to observe McArthur when McArthur reentered the trailer on two or three occasions. McArthur, however, reentered simply for his own convenience, to make phone calls and to obtain cigarettes. Under these circumstances, the reasonableness of the greater restriction (preventing reentry) implies the reasonableness of the lesser (permitting reentry conditioned on observation).

In sum, the police officers in this case had probable cause to believe that a home contained contraband, which was evidence of a crime. They reasonably believed that the home's resident, if left free of any restraint, would destroy that evidence. And they imposed a restraint that was both limited and tailored reasonably to secure law enforcement needs while protecting privacy interests. In our view, the restraint met the Fourth Amendment's demands.

* * *

[Justice Souter, concurring, noted that the law "can hardly raise incentives to obtain a warrant without giving the police a fair chance to take their probable cause to a magistrate and get one."]

[The dissenting opinion of Justice Stevens is omitted.]

K. ADMINISTRATIVE SEARCHES AND OTHER SEARCHES AND SEIZURES BASED ON "SPECIAL NEEDS"

The Fourth Amendment applies to searches and seizures conducted by state agents whether for purposes of investigating and prosecuting crime or for purposes of vindicating administrative regulatory interests. These "special needs" searches generally do not require a warrant. The Court has reasoned that these searches vindicate important public interests but are not amenable to the regulatory framework described in the Warrant Clause. For example, an inspection regime designed to assess the cleanliness of commercial kitchens vindicates important public health concerns, but could not achieve its goals if officials had to secure a probable cause warrant from a judicial officer before conducting a routine inspection. This does not mean that special needs searches are immune from Fourth Amendment review and regulation. Courts instead seek to strike a reasonable balance among competing interests when determining what safeguards must apply. Legislatures and executive or administrative agencies often take the lead by promulgating and enforcing regulations governing special needs searches.

Special needs searches sometimes intersect with criminal law enforcement. Strictly speaking, if the purpose of a search is to obtain evidence for purposes of criminal law enforcement, then probable cause and a warrant are presumptively required. See Arizona v. Hicks, 480 U.S. 321 (1987) (holding that, absent "special operational necessities," probable cause is required for a search for evidence). An abiding question in special needs cases is whether the primary purpose of a search regime is to vindicate government interests separate from criminal law enforcement or is, instead, little more than an effort by law enforcement officials to circumnavigate the rules governing searches and seizures in the criminal law context. As we shall see, the answer is not always clear.

1. Safety Inspections of Homes

In Camara v. Municipal Court, 387 U.S. 523 (1967), a homeowner claimed the right to refuse a warrantless entry by a health and safety official charged with inspecting the house as provided for in the San Francisco housing code. The Court held that the Fourth Amendment covered these administrative searches. But Justice White's majority opinion held that government safety inspectors were not required to have probable cause to believe that a particular dwelling was in violation of the code—though that kind of particularized concern certainly would justify a search. Instead, the question was whether an inspection complied with a reasonable administrative scheme that was itself calculated to vindicate a demonstrated public health or safety concern. That structure, Justice White reasoned, would be sufficient to vindicate the "probable cause" requirement:

> Having concluded that the area inspection is a "reasonable" search of private property within the meaning of the Fourth Amendment, it is obvious that "probable cause" to issue a warrant to inspect must exist if reasonable legislative or administrative standards for conducting an area inspection are satisfied with respect to a particular dwelling. Such standards, which will vary with the municipal program being

enforced, may be based upon the passage of time, the nature of the building (*e.g.*, a multi-family apartment house), or the condition of the entire area, but they will not necessarily depend upon specific knowledge of the condition of the particular dwelling.

In a companion case, See v. City of Seattle, 387 U.S. 541 (1967), the Court, per Justice White, applied the *Camara* requirements—i.e., a warrant based on either probable cause or demonstrated compliance with some reasonable administrative inspection scheme—to inspections of non-residential commercial structures. But the Court did "not in any way imply that business premises may not reasonably be inspected in many more situations than private homes."

Justice Clark, joined by Justices Harlan and Stewart, dissented in both *Camara* and *See.* They argued that the special rules endorsed by the Court would degrade the Fourth Amendment.

The Assessment of Cause for a Safety Inspection

An official who issues an inspection order under *Camara* necessarily performs a different function than the magistrate assessing a search warrant application in a criminal investigation. This is because individualized suspicion is not required. The officer need only decide whether an established inspection policy exists and whether a particular inspection fits within that program.

What dangers do these orders guard against? What would be wrong with a rule prohibiting safety inspectors from entering a house without probable cause to believe that there was a safety violation? How would a safety inspector obtain enough information to constitute probable cause? Is a safety inspection of a home less intrusive than a search of a home by law enforcement officers investigating a crime?

Warrants Without Probable Cause?

The *Camara* Court couched its holding in the language of warrants, appearing to hold in the process that some warrants may be issued upon some objective standard other than probable cause. In Griffin v. Wisconsin, 483 U.S. 868 (1987), the Court had occasion to clarify. Griffin, a probationer, challenged the search of his home by his probation officer. One argument in the case was that, even if probable cause was not required for the search of a probationer's home (due to a probationer's diminished expectation of privacy and the state's administrative interest in regulating a probationer), the Court should nonetheless require a warrant. Justice Scalia, writing for the Court, contended that the Fourth Amendment could not be read to provide for such a warrant. He reasoned that a warrant based on something other than probable cause would violate the specific language in the Fourth Amendment that "no warrant shall issue, but upon probable cause." He distinguished *Camara* as a case where the Court "arguably came to permit an exception to that prescription for administrative search warrants, which may but do not necessarily have to be issued by courts." Justice Scalia emphasized that the general rule for judicial search warrants is that they can only be issued upon particularized probable cause. Thus, the Court refused to accept the solution of a warrant based on less than probable cause as a means of balancing state and individual interests. For purposes of clarity, then, it may be most useful to prefer "orders" or similar alternative language to "warrants" in the special needs context.

2. Administrative Searches of Businesses

The Court applied the *Camara* protections to businesses in *See,* but it is apparent that administrative searches of businesses involve different issues from searches of residences. For one thing, some entries into business premises may not be searches at all. For example, if a fire inspector walks through a hotel lobby and looks for fire exits, no reasonable expectation of privacy is implicated because it is an area open to the public. See Donovan v. Lone Steer, Inc., 464 U.S. 408 (1984). Neither would this activity constitute a search under the physical intrusion test because there is explicit consent to public access for these areas of a hotel. Also, an administrative search of a business implicates more complex regulatory concerns: the state has an administrative interest not only in whether the business *structure* is safe, but also in whether the business is being safely and properly conducted. Moreover, the businessperson may have a diminished expectation of privacy given the nature of the business conducted. But on the other hand, the risk of an arbitrary use of official power to conduct a regulatory search of a business must be a cause for special concern. It is no secret that businesspersons have occasionally been subject to harassment and extortion by unscrupulous investigators. Moreover, it might be difficult to distinguish between a search done for "administrative" purposes and a search to obtain evidence of a criminal violation. The Court discusses these considerations, and the special rules applicable to special needs searches, in the following case.

NEW YORK V. BURGER

Supreme Court of the United States, 1987.
482 U.S. 691.

JUSTICE BLACKMUN delivered the opinion of the Court.

This case presents the question whether the warrantless search of an automobile junkyard, conducted pursuant to a statute authorizing such a search, falls within the exception to the warrant requirement for administrative inspections of pervasively regulated industries. The case also presents the question whether an otherwise proper administrative inspection is unconstitutional because the ultimate purpose of the regulatory statute pursuant to which the search is done—the deterrence of criminal behavior—is the same as that of penal laws, with the result that the inspection may disclose violations not only of the regulatory statute but also of the penal statutes.

* * * Respondent Joseph Burger is the owner of a junkyard in Brooklyn, N.Y. His business consists, in part, of the dismantling of automobiles and the selling of their parts. * * * At approximately noon on November 17, 1982, Officer Joseph Vega and four other plainclothes officers, all members of the Auto Crimes Division of the New York City Police Department, entered respondent's junkyard to conduct an inspection pursuant to N.Y.Veh. & Traf.Law § 415–a5 (McKinney 1986).[a] On any given day, the Division conducts from 5 to 10 inspections of vehicle dismantlers, automobile junkyards, and related businesses.

Upon entering the junkyard, the officers asked to see Burger's license and his "police book"—the record of the automobiles and vehicle parts in his possession. Burger replied that he had neither a license nor a police book. The officers then announced their intention to conduct a § 415–a5 inspection. * * * In accordance with their practice, the officers copied down the Vehicle Identification Numbers (VINs) of several vehicles and parts of vehicles that were in the junkyard. After checking these numbers against a police computer, the officers determined that respondent was in possession of stolen vehicles and parts. Accordingly, Burger was arrested and charged with five counts of possession of stolen property and one count of unregistered operation as a vehicle dismantler, in violation of § 415–a1.

[The trial court denied a motion to suppress, but the New York Court of Appeals reversed, holding that the statute authorizing the warrantless inspection was unconstitutional.]

The Court long has recognized that the Fourth Amendment's prohibition on unreasonable searches and seizures is applicable to commercial premises, as well as to private homes. See v. City of Seattle. An owner or operator of a business thus has an expectation of privacy in commercial property, which society is prepared to consider to be

---

[a] This statute reads in pertinent part:

"Records and identification. (a) * * * Every person required to be registered pursuant to this section shall maintain a record of all motor vehicles, trailers, and major component parts thereof, coming into his possession together with a record of the disposition of any such motor vehicle, trailer or part thereof and shall maintain proof of ownership for any motor vehicle, trailer or major component part thereof while in his possession. * * * Upon request of an agent of the commissioner or of any police officer and during his regular and usual business hours, a vehicle dismantler shall produce such records and permit said agent or police officer to examine them and any vehicles or parts of vehicles which are subject to the record keeping requirements of this section and which are on the premises. . . . The failure to produce such records or to permit such inspection on the part of any person required to be registered pursuant to this section as required by this paragraph shall be a class A misdemeanor."

reasonable, see Katz v. United States (Harlan, J., concurring). This expectation exists not only with respect to traditional police searches conducted for the gathering of criminal evidence but also with respect to administrative inspections designed to enforce regulatory statutes. An expectation of privacy in commercial premises, however, is different from, and indeed less than, a similar expectation in an individual's home. This expectation is particularly attenuated in commercial property employed in "closely regulated" industries. * * *

The Court first examined the "unique" problem of inspections of "closely regulated" businesses in two enterprises that had "a long tradition of close government supervision." In Colonnade Corp. v. United States, 397 U.S. 72 (1970), it considered a warrantless search of a catering business pursuant to several federal revenue statutes authorizing the inspection of the premises of liquor dealers. Although the Court disapproved the search because the statute provided that a sanction be imposed when entry was refused, and because it did not authorize entry without a warrant as an alternative in this situation, it recognized that "the liquor industry [was] long subject to close supervision and inspection." We returned to this issue in United States v. Biswell, 406 U.S. 311 (1972), which [upheld] a warrantless inspection of the premises of a pawnshop operator, who was federally licensed to sell sporting weapons pursuant to the Gun Control Act of 1968. * * * We observed: "When a dealer chooses to engage in this pervasively regulated business and to accept a federal license, he does so with the knowledge that his business records, firearms, and ammunition will be subject to effective inspection."

The *"Colonnade-Biswell"* doctrine, stating the reduced expectation of privacy by an owner of commercial premises in a "closely regulated" industry, has received renewed emphasis in more recent decisions. In Marshall v. Barlow's, Inc., 436 U.S. 307 (1978), we noted its continued vitality but declined to find that warrantless inspections, made pursuant to the Occupational Safety and Health Act of 1970, of *all* businesses engaged in interstate commerce fell within the narrow focus of this doctrine. However, we found warrantless inspections made pursuant to the Federal Mine Safety and Health Act of 1977, proper because they were of a "closely regulated" industry. Donovan v. Dewey, 452 U.S. 594 (1981).

* * *

Because the owner or operator of commercial premises in a "closely regulated" industry has a reduced expectation of privacy, the warrant and probable-cause requirements, which fulfill the traditional Fourth Amendment standard of reasonableness for a government search, have lessened application in this context. Rather, we conclude that, as in other situations of "special need" where the privacy interests of the owner are weakened and the government interests in regulating particular businesses are concomitantly heightened, a warrantless inspection of commercial premises may well be reasonable within the meaning of the Fourth Amendment.

This warrantless inspection, however, even in the context of a pervasively regulated business, will be deemed to be reasonable only so long as three criteria are met. First, there must be a "substantial" government interest that informs the regulatory scheme pursuant to which the inspection is made. See Donovan v. Dewey ("substantial federal interest in improving the health and safety conditions in the Nation's underground and surface mines").

Second, the warrantless inspections must be necessary to further the regulatory scheme. For example, in *Dewey* we recognized that forcing mine inspectors to obtain a warrant before every inspection might alert mine owners or operators to the impending inspection, thereby frustrating the purposes of the Mine Safety and Health Act—to detect and thus to deter safety and health violations.

Finally, the statute's inspection program, in terms of the certainty and regularity of its application, must provide a constitutionally adequate substitute for a warrant." In other words, the regulatory statute must perform the two basic functions of a warrant: it must advise the owner of the commercial premises that the search is being made pursuant to the law and has a properly defined scope, and it must limit the discretion of the inspecting officers. To perform this first function, the statute must be sufficiently comprehensive and defined that the owner of commercial property cannot help but be aware that his property will be subject to periodic inspections undertaken for specific purposes. In addition, in defining how a statute limits the discretion of the inspectors, we have observed that it must be "carefully limited in time, place, and scope."

* * * Searches made pursuant to § 415–a5, in our view, clearly fall within this established exception to the warrant requirement for administrative inspections in "closely regulated" businesses. First, the nature of the regulatory statute reveals that the operation of a junkyard, part of which is devoted to vehicle dismantling, is a "closely regulated" business in the State of New York. The provisions regulating the activity of vehicle dismantling are extensive. An operator cannot engage in this industry without first obtaining a license, which means that he must meet the registration requirements and must pay a fee. Under § 415–a5(a), the operator must maintain a police book recording the acquisition and disposition of motor vehicles and vehicle parts, and make such records and inventory available for inspection by the police or any agent of the Department of Motor Vehicles. The operator also must display his registration number prominently at his place of business, on business documentation, and on vehicles and parts that pass through his business.

Moreover, the person engaged in this activity is subject to criminal penalties, as well as to loss of license or civil fines, for failure to comply with these provisions. * * *

* * * The automobile junkyard is closely akin to the secondhand shop or the general junkyard. * * * As such, vehicle dismantlers represent a modern, specialized version of a traditional activity. In New York, general junkyards and secondhand shops long have been subject to regulation. * * *

Accordingly, in light of the regulatory framework governing his business and the history of regulation of related industries, an operator of a junkyard engaging in vehicle dismantling has a reduced expectation of privacy in this "closely regulated" business.

* * * The New York regulatory scheme satisfies the three criteria necessary to make reasonable warrantless inspections pursuant to § 415–a5. First, the State has a substantial interest in regulating the vehicle-dismantling and automobile-junkyard industry because motor vehicle theft has increased in the State and because the problem of theft is associated with this industry. * * *

Second, regulation of the vehicle-dismantling industry reasonably serves the State's substantial interest in eradicating automobile theft. * * * Automobile junkyards and vehicle dismantlers provide the major market for stolen vehicles and vehicle parts. Thus, the State rationally may believe that it will reduce car theft by regulations that prevent automobile junkyards from becoming markets for stolen vehicles and that help trace the origin and destination of vehicle parts.

Moreover, the warrantless administrative inspections pursuant to § 415–a5 "are necessary to further [the] regulatory scheme." Donovan v. Dewey. * * * We explained in *Biswell:*

> "[I]f inspection is to be effective and serve as a credible deterrent, unannounced, even frequent, inspections are essential. In this context, the prerequisite of a warrant could easily frustrate inspection; and if the necessary flexibility as to time, scope, and frequency is to be preserved, the protections afforded by a warrant would be negligible."

* * * Because stolen cars and parts often pass quickly through an automobile junkyard, "frequent" and "unannounced" inspections are necessary in order to detect them. In sum, surprise is crucial if the regulatory scheme aimed at remedying this major social problem is to function at all.

Third, § 415–a5 provides a "constitutionally adequate substitute for a warrant." The statute informs the operator of a vehicle dismantling business that inspections will be made on a regular basis. Thus, the vehicle dismantler knows that the inspections to which he is subject do not constitute discretionary acts by a government official but are conducted pursuant to statute. Section 415–a5 also sets forth the scope of the inspection and, accordingly, places the operator on notice as to how to comply with the statute. In addition, it notifies the operator as to who is authorized to conduct an inspection.

Finally, the "time, place, and scope" of the inspection is limited to place appropriate restraints upon the discretion of the inspecting officers. The officers are allowed to conduct an inspection only "during [the] regular and usual business hours."[b] The inspections can be made only of vehicle-dismantling and related industries. And the permissible scope of these searches is narrowly defined: the inspectors may examine the records, as well as "any vehicles or parts of vehicles which are subject to the record keeping requirements of this section and which are on the premises."

* * * The Court of Appeals, nevertheless, struck down the statute as violative of the Fourth Amendment because, in its view, the statute had no truly administrative purpose but was "designed simply to give the police an expedient means of enforcing penal sanctions for possession of stolen property." The court rested its conclusion that the administrative goal of the statute was pretextual and that § 415–a5 really "authorize[d] searches undertaken solely to uncover evidence of criminality" particularly on the fact that, even if an operator failed to produce his police book, the inspecting officers could continue their inspection for stolen vehicles and parts. The court also suggested that the identity of the inspectors—police officers—was significant in revealing the true nature of the statutory scheme.

In arriving at this conclusion, the Court of Appeals failed to recognize that a State can address a major social problem *both* by way of an administrative scheme *and* through penal sanctions. Administrative statutes and penal laws may have the same *ultimate* purpose of remedying the social problem, but they have different subsidiary purposes and prescribe different methods of addressing the problem. An administrative statute establishes how a particular business in a "closely regulated" industry should be operated, setting forth rules to guide an operator's conduct of the business and allowing government officials to ensure that those rules are followed. Such a regulatory approach contrasts with that of the penal laws, a major emphasis of which is the punishment of individuals for specific acts of behavior.

* * * The New York penal laws address automobile theft by punishing it or the possession of stolen property, including possession by individuals in the business of buying and selling property. In accordance with its

[b] Respondent contends that § 415–a5 is unconstitutional because it fails to limit the number of searches that may be conducted of a particular business during any given period. While such limitations, or the absence thereof, are a factor in an analysis of the adequacy of a particular statute, they are not determinative of the result so long as the statute, as a whole, places adequate limits upon the discretion of the inspecting officers. * * *

interest in regulating the automobile-junkyard industry, the State also has devised a regulatory manner of dealing with this problem. Section 415–a, as a whole, serves the regulatory goals of seeking to ensure that vehicle dismantlers are legitimate businesspersons and that stolen vehicles and vehicle parts passing through automobile junkyards can be identified. * * *

If the administrative goals of § 415–a5 are recognized, the difficulty the Court of Appeals perceives in allowing inspecting officers to examine vehicles and vehicle parts even in the absence of records evaporates. The regulatory purposes of § 415–a5 certainly are served by having the inspecting officers compare the records of a particular vehicle dismantler with vehicles and vehicle parts in the junkyard. The purposes of maintaining junkyards in the hands of legitimate businesspersons and of tracing vehicles that pass through these businesses, however, *also* are served by having the officers examine the operator's inventory even when the operator, for whatever reason, fails to produce the police book. Forbidding inspecting officers to examine the inventory in this situation would permit an illegitimate vehicle dismantler to thwart the purposes of the administrative scheme and would have the absurd result of subjecting his counterpart who maintained records to a more extensive search.

Nor do we think that this administrative scheme is unconstitutional simply because, in the course of enforcing it, an inspecting officer may discover evidence of crimes, besides violations of the scheme itself. * * * The discovery of evidence of crimes in the course of an otherwise proper administrative inspection does not render that search illegal or the administrative scheme suspect.[c]

Finally, we fail to see any constitutional significance in the fact that police officers, rather than "administrative" agents, are permitted to conduct the § 415–a5 inspection. * * * It is, however, important to note that state police officers, like those in New York, have numerous duties in addition to those associated with traditional police work. As a practical matter, many States do not have the resources to assign the enforcement of a particular administrative scheme to a specialized agency. So long as a regulatory scheme is properly administrative, it is not rendered illegal by the fact that the inspecting officer has the power to arrest individuals for violations other than those created by the scheme itself. In sum, we decline to impose upon the States the burden of requiring the enforcement of their regulatory statutes to be carried out by specialized agents.

* * *

[c] The legislative history of § 415–a, in general, and § 415–a5, in particular, reveals that the New York Legislature had proper regulatory purposes for enacting the administrative scheme and was not using it as a "pretext" to enable law enforcement authorities to gather evidence of penal law violations. There is, furthermore, no reason to believe that the instant inspection was actually a "pretext" for obtaining evidence of respondent's violation of the penal laws. It is undisputed that the inspection was made solely pursuant to the administrative scheme. * * *

JUSTICE BRENNAN, with whom JUSTICE MARSHALL joins, and with whom JUSTICE O'CONNOR joins in pertinent part, dissenting.

* * *

The provisions governing vehicle dismantling in New York simply are not extensive. A vehicle dismantler must register and pay a fee, display the registration in various circumstances, maintain a police book, and allow inspections. Of course, the inspections themselves cannot be cited as proof of pervasive regulation justifying elimination of the warrant requirement; that would be obvious bootstrapping. Nor can registration and recordkeeping requirements be characterized as close regulation. * * * Few substantive qualifications are required of an aspiring vehicle dismantler; no regulation governs the condition of the premises, the method of operation, the hours of operation, the equipment utilized, etc. This scheme stands in marked contrast to, e.g., the mine safety regulations relevant in Donovan v. Dewey.

In sum, if New York City's administrative scheme renders the vehicle-dismantling business closely regulated, few businesses will escape such a finding. * * *

Even if vehicle dismantling were a closely regulated industry, I would nonetheless conclude that this search violated the Fourth Amendment. * * *

* * *

The fundamental defect in § 415–a5 is that it authorizes searches intended solely to uncover evidence of criminal acts. * * *

Here the State has * * * circumvented the requirements of the Fourth Amendment by altering the label placed on the search. This crucial point is most clearly illustrated by the fact that the police copied the serial numbers from a wheelchair and a handicapped person's walker that were found on the premises, and determined that these items had been stolen. * * * The scope of the search alone reveals that it was undertaken solely to uncover evidence of criminal wrongdoing.

Moreover, it is factually impossible that the search was intended to discover wrongdoing subject to administrative sanction. Burger stated that he was not registered to dismantle vehicles as required by § 415–a1, and that he did not have a police book, as required by § 415–a5(a). At that point he had violated every requirement of the administrative scheme. There is no administrative provision forbidding possession of stolen automobiles or automobile parts. The inspection became a search for evidence of criminal acts when all possible administrative violations had been uncovered.

* * *

The Court thus implicitly holds that if an administrative scheme has certain goals and if the search serves those goals, it may be upheld even if no concrete administrative consequences could follow from a particular search. This is a dangerous suggestion, for the goals of administrative schemes often overlap with the goals of the criminal law. * * * If the Fourth Amendment is to retain meaning in the commercial context, it must be applied to searches for evidence of criminal acts even if those searches would also serve an administrative purpose, unless that administrative purpose takes the concrete form of seeking an administrative violation.

* * *

A Narrower Definition of "Closely Regulated" Businesses: City of Los Angeles v. Patel

In his dissent in *Burger,* Justice Brennan complained—with some merit—that under the standards employed in *Burger,* virtually every business could be found to be "closely regulated" and so subject to warrantless administrative inspections. In City of Los Angeles v. Patel, 576 U.S. 409 (2015), the Court described some limits. The case involved a Los Angeles ordinance that required hotel operators to produce guest lists to inspectors—no warrant was required. The City argued that the hotel operators had no complaint because the hotel industry was heavily regulated. But the Court, in an opinion by Justice Sotomayor, found that the regulations on hotels were not sufficiently pervasive and intrusive to render the hotel industry "closely regulated." Justice Sotomayor analyzed the "closely regulated" question as follows:

> Over the past 45 years, the Court has identified only four industries that have such a history of government oversight that no reasonable expectation of privacy could exist for a proprietor over the stock of such an enterprise. Simply listing these industries refutes petitioner's argument that hotels should be counted among them. Unlike liquor sales, Colonnade Catering Corp. v. United States, 397 U.S. 72 (1970), firearms dealing, United States v. Biswell, 406 U.S. 311, 311–312 (1972), mining, Donovan v. Dewey, 452 U.S. 594 (1981), or running an automobile junkyard, New York v. Burger, 482 U.S. 691 (1987), nothing inherent in the operation of hotels poses a clear and significant risk to the public welfare.
>
> Moreover, the clear import of our cases is that the closely regulated industry is the exception. To classify hotels as pervasively regulated would permit what has always been a narrow exception to swallow the rule. The City wisely refrains from arguing that [the recordkeeping provision] itself renders hotels closely regulated. Nor do any of the other regulations * * *—requiring hotels to, *inter alia,*

> maintain a license, collect taxes, conspicuously post their rates, and meet certain sanitary standards—establish a comprehensive scheme of regulation that distinguishes hotels from numerous other businesses. * * * If such general regulations were sufficient to invoke the closely regulated industry exception, it would be hard to imagine a type of business that would not qualify.
>
> * * * History is relevant when determining whether an industry is closely regulated. * * * But laws obligating inns to provide suitable lodging to all paying guests are not the same as laws subjecting inns to warrantless searches. * * *
>
> The City claims that affording hotel operators any opportunity for precompliance review would fatally undermine the scheme's efficacy by giving operators a chance to falsify their records. The Court has previously rejected this exact argument, which could be made regarding any recordkeeping requirement. See *Barlow's, Inc.*, 436 U.S., at 320 ("[It is not] apparent why the advantages of surprise would be lost if, after being refused entry, procedures were available for the [Labor] Secretary to seek an *ex parte* warrant to reappear at the premises without further notice to the establishment being inspected"). We see no reason to accept it here. * * * [N]othing in our decision today precludes an officer from conducting a surprise inspection by obtaining an *ex parte* warrant or, where an officer reasonably suspects the registry would be altered, from guarding the registry pending a hearing on a motion to quash.

Justice Scalia, joined in dissent by Chief Justice Roberts and Justice Thomas, accused the majority of recalibrating the test for "closely regulated" businesses that the Court had established in *Burger:*

> [T]he regulatory tradition governing motels is not only longstanding, but comprehensive. And the tradition continues in Los Angeles. The City imposes an occupancy tax upon transients who stay in motels, and makes the motel owner responsible for collecting it. It authorizes city officials to enter a motel, free of charge, during business hours in order to inspect and examine them to determine whether these tax provisions have been complied with. It requires all motels to obtain a "Transient Occupancy Registration Certificate," which must be displayed on the premises. State law requires motels to post in a conspicuous place a statement of rate or range of rates by the day for lodging, and forbids any charges in excess of those posted rates. Hotels must change bed linens between guests, and they must offer guests the option not to have towels and linens laundered daily. "Multiuse drinking utensils" may be placed in guest rooms only if they are "thoroughly washed and sanitized after each use" and "placed in protective bags." And state authorities, like their municipal

counterparts, "may at reasonable times enter and inspect any hotels, motels, or other public places" to ensure compliance.

The regulatory regime at issue here is thus substantially *more* comprehensive than the regulations governing junkyards in *Burger,* where licensing, inventory-recording, and permit-posting requirements were found sufficient to qualify the industry as closely regulated. * * *

This copious evidence is surely enough to establish that "[w]hen a [motel operator] chooses to engage in this pervasively regulated business . . . he does so with the knowledge that his business records . . . will be subject to effective inspection." United States v. Biswell, 406 U.S. 311, 316 (1972). And *that* is the relevant constitutional test * * *.

The Court's observation that "[o]ver the past 45 years, the Court has identified only four industries" as closely regulated, is neither here nor there. * * * The Court's statistic * * * tells us more about how this Court exercises its discretionary review than it does about the number of industries that qualify as closely regulated. At the same time, lower courts, which do not have the luxury of picking the cases they hear, have identified many more businesses as closely regulated under the test we have announced: pharmacies, United States v. Gonsalves, 435 F.3d 64, 67 (C.A.1 2006); massage parlors, Pollard v. Cockrell, 578 F.2d 1002, 1014 (C.A.5 1978); commercial-fishing operations, United States v. Raub, 637 F.2d 1205, 1208–1209 (C.A.9 1980); day-care facilities, Rush v. Obledo, 756 F.2d 713, 720–721 (C.A.9 1985); nursing homes, People v. Firstenberg, 92 Cal.App.3d 570, 578–580, 155 Cal.Rptr. 80, 84–86 (1979); jewelers, People v. Pashigian, 150 Mich.App. 97, 100–101, 388 N.W.2d 259, 261–262 (1986) (per curiam); barbershops, Stogner v. Kentucky, 638 F.Supp. 1, 3 (W.D.Ky.1985); and yes, even rabbit dealers, Lesser v. Espy, 34 F.3d 1301, 1306–1307 (C.A.7 1994). Like automobile junkyards and catering companies that serve alcohol, many of these businesses are far from "intrinsically dangerous." This should come as no surprise. The reason closely regulated industries may be searched without a warrant has nothing to do with the risk of harm they pose; rather, it has to do with the expectations of those who enter such a line of work.

Substitute for a Warrant

In order to satisfy *Burger's* requirement of a constitutionally adequate substitute for a warrant for a closely regulated industry, a regulatory regime must 1) advise the owner of the regulated business that the inspection is being made pursuant to law; and 2) impose some meaningful limitation on the officer's discretion to search (e.g., time, place and manner restrictions). In *Burger*, discretion was found sufficiently limited by the provision in the statute requiring that the search be made during daytime hours. Is this enough limitation on discretion, given that *Burger* authorizes a suspicionless search? See United States v. Castelo, 415 F.3d 407 (5th Cir. 2005) (holding that an administrative scheme allowing weighing and inspection of commercial trucks imposed sufficient limits on officer discretion because only commercial vehicles could be inspected, and only when they were operating on the highways of the state: "These limitations are markedly similar to the limits on officer discretion in *Burger*.").

Although a statute authorizing administrative searches may be constitutional, actual searches purportedly conducted under that authority may not. If a search clearly goes beyond the statutory limitations that substitute for a warrant, it will be found unreasonable under the Fourth Amendment. See Bruce v. Beary, 498 F.3d 1232 (11th Cir. 2007) (search of vehicle dismantling business would be unreasonable if the owner could prove that it lasted 8 hours and involved both a display of automatic weapons by the officers and detention of shop employees: such a search would be "far beyond the statutory authorization" and "hardly seems to be what the Supreme Court in *Burger* had in mind when it held that the Constitution is not offended by * * * the regular, routine inspection of books and records required to be kept by auto salvagers."). See also Turner v. Dammon, 848 F.2d 440 (4th Cir. 1988) (disapproving officers' conduct in performing over 100 administrative inspections of a particular bar, where there was no evidence to support the need for such repeated searches).

The Element of Surprise

The Court justified the warrantless search in *Burger* partly because surprise was necessary. The concern was that the officer would go to Burger's business without a warrant, would be refused admission, and then, when the officer went to get a warrant, Burger would destroy or cover up evidence of an administrative violation. The Court held that Burger had no right to refuse a warrantless inspection because to permit such refusal would deprive the inspector of the element of surprise that is often necessary to further regulatory interests in heavily regulated industries.

But concern about loss of the element of surprise does not really explain why an officer shouldn't have to get a warrant *before* approaching Burger's business the first time around. Then the officer could conduct a surprise inspection *with a warrant*. (Indeed, that is the solution that the Court provided in *Patel*.)

The court in Lesser v. Espy, 34 F.3d 1301 (7th Cir.1994), confronted the question about the element of surprise for searching closely regulated businesses discussed in *Burger*, and proffered an explanation. *Lesser* involved the constitutionality of a warrantless inspection of a farm that raised rabbits to be used as laboratory animals. The court discussed the surprise element as follows:

> In rabbit farming many of the potential deficiencies that would violate the [Animal Welfare] Act can be quickly concealed. See, e.g., 9 C.F.R. §§ 3.50(c) (improper storage of food); 3.50(d) (improper waste disposal); 3.50(e) (unclean washrooms); 3.56(a) (unsanitary primary enclosures). Thus the Department correctly observes that preserving the element of surprise and the possibility of frequent inspections is necessary in order to detect violators. In response the Lessers rightly point out that the element of surprise may be easily maintained even with a warrant requirement—a warrant may be issued ex parte and executed without prior notice. Nevertheless, we believe a warrant requirement for the most routine inspection would interfere with the Department's ability to function and unnecessarily increase the cost of the Secretary's operations without a significant increase in privacy, especially since all licensed suppliers of research animals have a reasonable expectation of at least a couple of regular inspections * * * each year.

Thus, the need for surprise is really a false issue—the question is whether officials who undoubtedly need to make surprise inspections should be burdened with a warrant requirement. The *Lesser* court, following *Burger*, determined that the minimal privacy interest protected by a warrant requirement was outweighed by the inconvenience of having to obtain a warrant before every single administrative inspection, especially when the business is so heavily regulated to start with.

Is the *Lesser* court's reasoning based on the fact that most businesspersons would find it in their interest to consent to an administrative inspection anyway, which would mean that administrative inspectors would be obtaining warrants that they would by and large never have to use? Is that a legitimate reason for dispensing with the warrant requirement for those business owners who don't consent?

By the way, what would be wrong with having the rabbit farmer "cover up" his violations during the period after his refusal when the administrative inspector would have to go and get a warrant (assuming the inspector did not get one in the first instance)? Doesn't "cover up" mean "fix" in this circumstance? Isn't the goal of the administrative inspection to get the owner to repair the premises?

Administrative Inspections by Law Enforcement Officers

The Court in *Burger* held that the administrative nature of an inspection was not negated simply because the inspector was a law enforcement officer. Nonetheless, courts after *Burger* have been dubious when reviewing administrative searches conducted by law enforcement officers—the concern being that the "administrative" search is simply a pretext to evade the warrant and probable cause requirements that apply to searched for criminal law enforcement. For example, in United States v. Johnson, 994 F.2d 740 (10th Cir.1993), an FBI agent received information (not amounting to probable cause) that Johnson, a taxidermist, was involved in the illegal smuggling of protected animals. He called a state administrative officer, who agreed to accompany the federal agent, ostensibly to conduct an administrative taxidermy inspection. The applicable statute authorized warrantless administrative inspections of taxidermists, but only when performed by state agents. The federal agent drove 300 miles to Johnson's taxidermy shop in order to be present for the inspection; he also participated actively in the search of the business. The investigators discovered several specimens of illegally imported animals. The court held that "the administrative search was employed solely as an instrument of criminal law enforcement." Consequently, all of the evidence was illegally obtained. The court reasoned as follows:

> The presence and active participation of the federal agent during the search of Mr. Johnson's shop, and the federal agent's insistence that the state agent accompany him establish as a matter of law that the federal agent used the state regulatory inspection as a pretext for an investigatory search. Federal agents may not cloak themselves with the authority granted by state inspection statutes in order to seek evidence of criminal activity and avoid the Fourth Amendment's warrant requirement.

Recall the discussion of pretext earlier in this Chapter. Was the inspection in *Johnson* really pretextual, given the fact that the state agent had the right to conduct a warrantless administrative inspection? Or can it be argued that *Whren* permits otherwise pretextual searches and arrests only when there is probable cause? If that is so, then courts can still regulate for pretext when police officers seek to conduct a suspicionless "administrative" search that is really for purposes of criminal law enforcement. See also United States v. Knight, 306 F.3d 534 (8th Cir. 2002) (police officer's search of a truck, purportedly pursuant to a state safety inspection program, became illegal when it was extended to the trucker's briefcase: "We believe that, as a general matter, rummaging through a person's belongings is more likely to serve the purpose of crime control than the enforcement of a regulatory scheme."). Note that the Court in *Burger*, in upholding the inspection, specifically noted that there was "no reason to believe that the instant inspection was actually a 'pretext' for obtaining evidence of respondent's violation of the penal laws."

"Special Needs" Search of Text Messages of a Public Employee: City of Ontario v. Quon

In City of Ontario v. Quon, 560 U.S. 476 (2010), a police officer was given a pager with a monthly text allotment. He exceeded that allotment in a number of consecutive months. This led his supervisors to review his text messages, in order to determine whether they were work-related and whether a greater monthly allotment was required. The review indicated that many of Quon's texts were not work-related, and some were sexually explicit. The supervisors concluded that Quon had violated Department rules about use of the department-issued pagers, and Quon was disciplined. Quon challenged the review of his text messages as an unreasonable search. But the Court found no such violation, relying on the "special needs" exception.

Justice Kennedy, writing for eight members of the Court, found that the "there were reasonable grounds for suspecting that the search was necessary for a non-investigatory work-related purpose"—specifically the supervisors were trying to determine whether the character limit under the monthly plan with the provider was sufficient to meet the City's needs. The City and the Police Department "had a legitimate interest in ensuring that employees were not being forced to pay out of their own pockets for work-related expenses, or on the other hand that the City was not paying for extensive personal communications."

Justice Kennedy also found that the review of the text messages was reasonable in scope "because it was an efficient and expedient way to determine whether Quon's overages were the result of work-related messaging or personal use." Moreover, Quon's expectation of privacy, if any, was at least diminished by the fact that the Department had made Quon aware that his text messages were subject to auditing. Justice Kennedy noted that the audit of messages on an employer-provided pager "was not nearly as intrusive as a search of his personal e-mail account or pager, or a wiretap on his phone line, would have been. That the search did reveal intimate details of Quon's life does not make it unreasonable, for under the circumstances a reasonable employer would not expect that such a review would intrude on such matters."

The lower court had found the search of the texts unreasonable because the supervisors could have issued Quon a warning about overages, or they could have had Quon provide the messages to them in redacted form. But Justice Kennedy emphasized that the Supreme Court "has refused to declare that only the 'least intrusive' search practicable can be reasonable under the Fourth Amendment . . . because judges engaged in post-hoc evaluations of government conduct can always imagine some alternative means by which the objectives of the government might have been accomplished."

It should be noted that the *Quon* Court assumed arguendo that the review of the text messages was a search. The City contended that Quon had *no* expectation of privacy in his text messages because the Department gave him the pager and he was aware of the possibility of monitoring. Justice Kennedy cautioned that it was necessary to "proceed with care when considering the whole concept of privacy expectations in communications made on electronic equipment owned by a government employer. The judiciary risks error by elaborating too fully on the Fourth Amendment implications of emerging technology before its role in society has become clear."

Justice Stevens wrote a concurring opinion in *Quon*. Justice Scalia wrote an opinion concurring in part and concurring in the judgment.

3. "Special Needs" Searches and Seizures of Individuals

The Court has used its special needs balancing analysis in a series of cases upholding warrantless searches of individuals. These cases fall into two broad categories. The first encompasses suspicion-based searches, where the government had reasonable suspicion—but not probable cause—to justify a search. The second includes searches conducted in the absence of any suspicion at all.

a. Searches and Seizures on the Basis of Reasonable Suspicion Rather than Probable Cause

In New Jersey v. T.L.O., 469 U.S. 325 (1985), a school official searched the handbag of a student. The official had reasonable suspicion, but not probable cause, to believe that cigarettes were in the student's purse. In the absence of probable cause, the search could not be justified as a criminal-based search for evidence. Nor could the search be justified under the *Terry* doctrine, because *Terry* searches are limited to cursory searches for weapons and the school official had no basis for suspecting that the student possessed a weapon. Nonetheless, the Court upheld the search. The Court reasoned that the search served "special needs" separate from ordinary criminal law enforcement—specifically the state's need to assure a safe and healthy learning environment. This finding of special needs permitted the Court to balance the state interests at stake in the search against the student's interest in privacy and bodily security.

The *T.L.O.* Court noted that school officials have special responsibilities to guarantee the health and safety of students and to enforce disciplinary standards. In light of these responsibilities, and the fact that schools stand *in loco parentis* for students under their care, the Court held that students have a diminished expectation of privacy when they are on school grounds. Given these features of the school environment, the Court concluded that a reasonable suspicion standard would be sufficient to protect students' diminished expectations of privacy in the school environment while also permitting teachers and administrators the discretion and authority they need to maintain a safe and orderly environment. Writing for the Court, Justice White reasoned that, if probable cause were required, school officials would be unable to address disciplinary problems at an early stage before they became serious and intractable. That is, while waiting for probable cause to develop, the state's interests would already be undermined. Finally, the Court held that school officials could not be expected to obtain a judicial warrant before taking reasonable steps to enforce school disciplinary standards.

The *T.L.O.* analysis was used by the Court to uphold warrantless searches of the office of a government official, and of the house of a probationer. O'Connor v. Ortega, 480 U.S. 709 (1987); Griffin v. Wisconsin, supra. In both *O'Connor* and *Griffin,* as in *T.L.O.*, the Court found that conditioning searches on probable cause would unreasonably compromise state interests and that the reasonable suspicion standard struck an appropriate balance between state and (diminished) individual interests in privacy.

Limitations on Searches of Students: Safford Unified School District v. Redding

In *T.L.O.*, the Court sanctioned the search of a student's handbag based on reasonable suspicion by striking a balance among the competing interests at stake. Implicit in that analysis is the possibility that some searches would be unreasonable, and therefore unconstitutional, because they fail to strike a reasonable balance between the interests of school officials and students. The Court confronted this circumstance in Safford Unified School District #1 v. Redding, 577 U.S. 364 (2009). In his last opinion for the Court, Justice Souter described the issue presented:

> whether a 13-year-old student's Fourth Amendment right was violated when she was subjected to a search of her bra and underpants by school officials acting on reasonable suspicion that she had brought forbidden prescription and over-the-counter drugs to school.

The Court held that "[b]ecause there were no reasons to suspect the drugs presented a danger or were concealed in her underwear, * * * the search did violate the Constitution, but because there is reason to question the clarity with which the right was established, the official who ordered the unconstitutional search is entitled to qualified immunity from liability."

Justice Souter reasoned that Assistant Principal Wilson's suspicion that "Savana" was distributing over-the-counter drugs to other students was enough to justify a search of her backpack and outer clothing, but that this suspicion could not justify the more intrusive search conducted:

Here, the content of the suspicion failed to match the degree of intrusion. Wilson knew beforehand that the pills were prescription-strength ibuprofen and over-the-counter naproxen, common pain relievers equivalent to two Advil, or one Aleve. He must have been aware of the nature and limited threat of the specific drugs he was searching for, and while just about anything can be taken in quantities that will do real harm, Wilson had no reason to suspect that large amounts of the drugs were being passed around, or that individual students were receiving great numbers of pills.

Nor could Wilson have suspected that Savana was hiding common painkillers in her underwear. * * * [N]ondangerous school contraband does not raise the specter of stashes in intimate places, and there is no evidence in the record of any general practice among Safford Middle School students of hiding that sort of thing in underwear. * * *

In sum, what was missing from the suspected facts that pointed to Savana was any indication of danger to the students from the power of the drugs or their quantity, and any reason to suppose that Savana was carrying pills in her underwear. We think that the combination of these deficiencies was fatal to finding the search reasonable.

Justices Stevens and Ginsburg wrote separate concurrences. Justice Thomas concurred in part and dissented in part.

b. Suspicionless Searches of Persons on the Basis of "Special Needs"

Drug-Testing of Employees: Skinner v. Railway Labor Executives

T.L.O. permitted "special needs" searches on the basis of reasonable suspicion rather than probable cause. The *T.L.O.* Court did not decide whether a "special needs" search could be conducted *without any suspicion* that evidence would be found. Subsequently the Court, in companion cases, considered the constitutionality of suspicionless drug-testing of public employees. In Skinner v. Railway Labor Executives' Ass'n, 489 U.S. 602 (1989), the Court upheld a program mandating drug tests for all railroad personnel involved in certain train accidents. Failing the test could result in disciplinary action. Justice Kennedy, writing for the Court, made the following points:

1. The testing was essentially required by federal regulations. Thus, even though the tests were administered by a private employer, it was acting as a state agent for Fourth Amendment purposes.

2. Drug testing of urine is a search within the meaning of the Fourth Amendment, because it can reveal private information (such

as pregnancy or epilepsy), and because the process of monitoring the employee's act of urination implicates privacy interests.

3. The government's interest in regulating the conduct of railroad employees to ensure safety "presents 'special needs' beyond normal law enforcement that may justify departures from the usual warrant and probable-cause requirements."

4. A warrant was not required to subject the railroad employees to drug-testing, because, "in light of the standardized nature of the tests and the minimal discretion vested in those charged with administering the program, there are virtually no facts for a neutral magistrate to evaluate." Moreover, the railroad supervisors responsible for administering the testing program "are not in the business of investigating violations of the criminal laws or enforcing administrative codes, and otherwise have little occasion to become familiar with the intricacies of this Court's Fourth Amendment jurisprudence."

5. The drug-testing program was reasonable even though it provided for testing in the absence of any individualized suspicion of drug use. Justice Kennedy reasoned that "where the privacy interests implicated by the search are minimal, and where an important governmental interest furthered by the intrusion would be placed in jeopardy by a requirement of individualized suspicion, a search may be reasonable despite the absence of such suspicion." The urine testing was found not very intrusive, because "[t]he regulations do not require that samples be furnished under the direct observation of a monitor, despite the desirability of such a procedure to ensure the integrity of the sample. The sample is also collected in a medical environment, by personnel unrelated to the railroad employer, and is thus not unlike similar procedures encountered often in the context of a regular physical examination." Furthermore, the expectations of privacy of covered employees was "diminished by reason of their participation in an industry that is regulated pervasively to ensure safety, a goal dependent, in substantial part, on the health and fitness of covered employees." On the other side of the balancing equation, the Court found that the state interests at stake were "compelling," and could not be accommodated by a requirement of individualized suspicion. Employees subject to the tests "discharge duties fraught with such risks of injury to others that even a momentary lapse of attention can have disastrous consequences." Drug-testing provides an effective means of deterring drug use, because employees in safety-sensitive positions "know they will be tested upon the occurrence of a triggering event, the timing of which no employee can predict with certainty." Also, drug-testing will "help railroads obtain invaluable information

about the causes of major accidents, and to take appropriate measures to safeguard the general public."

6. The state's interest in a suspicionless testing plan was strengthened by the fact that there was a documented drug problem among railroad employees. Thus, the government was not simply enforcing some hypothetical interest.

7. A requirement of particularized suspicion of drug use would "seriously impede an employer's ability to obtain this information, despite its obvious importance." This is because "[o]btaining evidence that might give rise to the suspicion that a particular employee is impaired, a difficult endeavor in the best of circumstances, is most impracticable in the aftermath of a serious accident."

8. There was no indication that the suspicionless testing was a pretextual means of enforcing the criminal law.

Justice Stevens concurred in part and in the judgment in *Skinner*. He was dubious about the deterrent effect of drug-testing in the railroad context. He noted that the testing was undertaken *after* an accident, not before. He reasoned that workers would "not go to work with the expectation that they may be involved in a major accident," and that "if the risk of serious personal injury does not deter their use of these substances, it seems highly unlikely that the additional threat of loss of employment would have any effect on their behavior."

Justice Marshall, joined by Justice Brennan, dissented in *Skinner*. He criticized the Court for rejecting the probable cause requirement in favor of "a manipulable balancing inquiry under which, upon the mere assertion of a 'special need,' even the deepest dignitary and privacy interests become vulnerable to governmental incursion."

Drug-Testing of Employees: National Treasury Employees v. Von Raab

In National Treasury Employees Union v. Von Raab, 489 U.S. 656 (1989), a case decided the same day as *Skinner*, the Court upheld compelled urinalysis of certain Customs Service employees. Drug tests were made a condition of obtaining employment for three types of positions in the Customs Service: those involving drug interdiction, those requiring the employee to carry a firearm, and those in which the employee would handle "classified documents." The employee was allowed to produce the sample privately, but to protect against adulteration, "a monitor of the same sex as the employee remains close at hand to listen for the normal sounds of urination." Customs employees who tested positive for drugs and who could offer no satisfactory explanation were subject to dismissal from the Service;

but the testing results could not be turned over to a criminal prosecutor without the employee's consent.

Justice Kennedy again wrote the opinion for the Court. He found that the drug-testing served special needs beyond criminal law enforcement, specifically the need for safety and to ensure that customs employees responsible for controlling the flow of drugs into the country are not on drugs themselves. Balancing the state and individual interests, Justice Kennedy concluded that a warrant was not required for the testing, because the event that triggered the testing was "the employee's decision to apply for a covered position." There was thus no factual question similar to probable cause for a magistrate to decide.

The *Von Raab* Court found that suspicionless testing was reasonable as applied to two of the three covered types of employees—those involved in drug interdiction and those carrying handguns. Justice Kennedy noted that "the Government has a compelling interest in ensuring that front-line personnel are physically fit, and have unimpeachable integrity and judgment," and that the public interest "likewise demands effective measures to prevent the promotion of drug users to positions that require the incumbent to carry a firearm." The majority asserted that these two classes of employees had a diminished expectation of privacy, because the positions depended uniquely on the employees' "judgment and dexterity." Justice Kennedy also emphasized that the testing procedures were designed to minimize the intrusion involved, to the extent possible without sacrificing the reliability of the test.

The Court in *Von Raab* found itself unable to assess the reasonableness of suspicionless testing as applied to the third category of employees, those handling classified documents. The Court remanded this aspect of the case, and explained as follows:

> It is not clear * * * whether the category defined by the Service's testing directive encompasses only those Customs employees likely to gain access to sensitive information. Employees who are tested under the Service's scheme include those holding such diverse positions as "Accountant," "Accounting Technician," "Animal Caretaker," "Attorney (All)," "Baggage Clerk," "Co-op Student (All)," "Electric Equipment Repairer," "Mail Clerk/Assistant," and "Messenger." * * * [I]t is not evident that those occupying these positions are likely to gain access to sensitive information, and this apparent discrepancy raises in our minds the question whether the Service has defined this category of employees more broadly than is necessary to meet the purposes of the Commissioner's directive.

What if There Is No Record of Drug Abuse?

The most difficult issue for the majority in *Von Raab* was that the Customs Service had implemented the drug-testing program even though there was no documented drug problem among Customs employees. This was unlike the situation in *Skinner,* where the drug problem among railroad employees, and the risk therefrom, was well-documented. Those who challenged the plan in *Von Raab* argued that suspicionless drug-testing was unreasonable unless it could be justified as responsive to and effective against a documented drug problem. Justice Kennedy rejected this argument in the following analysis:

> Detecting drug impairment on the part of employees can be a difficult task, especially where, as here, it is not feasible to subject employees and their work product to the kind of day-to-day scrutiny that is the norm in more traditional office environments. * * * In light of the extraordinary safety and national security hazards that would attend the promotion of drug users to positions that require the carrying of firearms or the interdiction of controlled substances, the Service's policy of deterring drug users from seeking such promotions cannot be deemed unreasonable.
>
> The mere circumstance that all but a few of the employees tested are entirely innocent of wrongdoing does not impugn the program's validity. * * * The Service's program is designed to prevent the promotion of drug users to sensitive positions as much as it is designed to detect those employees who use drugs. Where, as here, the possible harm against which the Government seeks to guard is substantial, the need to prevent its occurrence furnishes an ample justification for reasonable searches calculated to advance the Government's goal.

In a footnote, Justice Kennedy compared suspicionless drug-testing to suspicionless searches at airports.

> As Judge Friendly explained in a leading case upholding such searches:
>
> > "When the risk is the jeopardy to hundreds of human lives and millions of dollars of property inherent in the pirating or blowing up of a large airplane, that danger *alone* meets the test of reasonableness, so long as the search is conducted in good faith for the purpose of preventing hijacking or like damage and with reasonable scope and the passenger has been given advance notice of his liability to such a search so that he can avoid it by choosing not to travel by air." United States v. Edwards, 498 F.2d 496, 500 (C.A.2 1974) (emphasis in original).
>
> * * * [W]e would not suppose that, if the validity of these searches be conceded, the Government would be precluded from conducting them

absent a demonstration of danger as to any particular airport or airline. It is sufficient that the Government have a compelling interest in preventing an otherwise pervasive societal problem from spreading to the particular context.

Justice Marshall, joined by Justice Brennan, dissented in *Von Raab* for the reasons stated in *Skinner*.

Justice Scalia, joined by Justice Stevens, both of whom found suspicionless drug-testing to be reasonable in *Skinner*, dissented in *Von Raab*. Justice Scalia explained as follows:

> I joined the Court's opinion [in *Skinner*] because the demonstrated frequency of drug and alcohol use by the targeted class of employees, and the demonstrated connection between such use and grave harm, rendered the search a reasonable means of protecting society. I decline to join the Court's opinion in the present case because neither frequency of use nor connection to harm is demonstrated or even likely. In my view the Customs Service rules are a kind of immolation of privacy and human dignity in symbolic opposition to drug use.

Justice Scalia rejected the majority's generalization that no American workplace is free from the drug problem. He responded that such a generalization could perhaps suffice "if the workplace at issue could produce such catastrophic social harm that no risk whatever is tolerable—the secured areas of a nuclear power plant for example." Justice Scalia noted that suspicionless testing for nuclear power plant employees in sensitive jobs had been upheld even without a showing of a drug problem. See Rushton v. Nebraska Public Power District, 844 F.2d 562 (8th Cir.1988). See also Thomson v. Marsh, 884 F.2d 113 (4th Cir.1989) (suspicionless testing of personnel in chemical weapons plant upheld). He responded, however, that if the majority considered that the threat posed by drug-addicted Customs officials was comparable to that found in *Rushton*, "then the Fourth Amendment has become frail protection indeed." He noted that this reasoning would extend approval of suspicionless drug testing to vast numbers of public employees, including "automobile drivers, operators of other potentially dangerous equipment, construction workers, school crossing guards."

Drug-Testing of Schoolchildren

The Supreme Court has taken up the question of suspicionless testing of schoolchildren in two cases after *Von Raab*: Vernonia School District 47J v. Acton, 515 U.S. 646 (1995), and Board of Education of Independent School District No. 2 v. Earls, 536 U.S. 822 (2002). In *Vernonia*, the Court upheld (6–3) the suspicionless drug testing of athletes, reasoning that there was a demonstrated problem of drug use among athletes, student athletes have lesser expectations of privacy—both for reasons cited in *T.L.O.* and because they dress and shower in close proximity to each other and submit themselves to close physical scrutiny—and student athletes tend to be social leaders. Justice Scalia wrote for the Court. Justice O'Connor, joined by Justices Stevens and Souter, dissented. In *Earls*, the Court expanded its holding to uphold (5–4) suspicionless drug testing of all students engaged in extracurricular activities. Justice Thomas, writing for the Court in *Earls*, relied heavily on *Vernonia*. He wrote as follows:

> A student's privacy interest is limited in a public school environment where the State is responsible for maintaining discipline, health, and safety. Schoolchildren are routinely required to submit to physical examinations and vaccinations against disease. Securing order in the school environment sometimes requires that students be subjected to greater controls than those appropriate for adults.
>
> Respondents argue that because children participating in nonathletic extracurricular activities are not subject to regular physicals and communal undress, they have a stronger expectation of privacy than the athletes tested in *Vernonia*. This distinction, however, was not essential to our decision in *Vernonia*, which depended primarily upon the school's custodial responsibility and authority.
>
> In any event, students who participate in competitive extracurricular activities voluntarily subject themselves to many of the same intrusions on their privacy as do athletes. Some of these clubs and activities require occasional off-campus travel and communal undress. All of them have their own rules and requirements for participating students that do not apply to the student body as a whole. * * * This regulation of extracurricular activities further diminishes the expectation of privacy among schoolchildren. We therefore conclude that the students affected by this Policy have a limited expectation of privacy.
>
> * * *
>
> Under the Policy, a faculty monitor waits outside the closed restroom stall for the student to produce a sample and must "listen for the normal sounds of urination in order to guard against tampered specimens and to insure an accurate chain of custody." The monitor then pours the sample into two bottles that are sealed and placed into a mailing pouch along with a consent form signed by the student. This procedure is virtually identical to that reviewed in *Vernonia*, except that it additionally protects privacy by allowing male students to produce their samples behind a closed stall. Given that we considered the method of collection in *Vernonia* a "negligible" intrusion, the method here is even less problematic.

In addition, the Policy clearly requires that the test results be kept in confidential files separate from a student's other educational records and released to school personnel only on a "need to know" basis. * * * Moreover, the test results are not turned over to any law enforcement authority. Nor do the test results here lead to the imposition of discipline or have any academic consequences. Rather, the only consequence of a failed drug test is to limit the student's privilege of participating in extracurricular activities.

* * *

Given the minimally intrusive nature of the sample collection and the limited uses to which the test results are put, we conclude that the invasion of students' privacy is not significant.

* * * Finally, this Court must consider the nature and immediacy of the government's concerns and the efficacy of the Policy in meeting them. This Court has already articulated in detail the importance of the governmental concern in preventing drug use by schoolchildren. The drug abuse problem among our Nation's youth has hardly abated since *Vernonia* was decided in 1995. * * * The health and safety risks identified in *Vernonia* apply with equal force to Tecumseh's children. Indeed, the nationwide drug epidemic makes the war against drugs a pressing concern in every school.

Additionally, the School District in this case has presented specific evidence of drug use at Tecumseh schools. Teachers testified that they had seen students who appeared to be under the influence of drugs and that they had heard students speaking openly about using drugs. A drug dog found marijuana cigarettes near the school parking lot. Police officers once found drugs or drug paraphernalia in a car driven by a Future Farmers of America member. And the school board president reported that people in the community were calling the board to discuss the "drug situation." We decline to second-guess the finding of the District Court that "[v]iewing the evidence as a whole, it cannot be reasonably disputed that the [School District] was faced with a 'drug problem' when it adopted the Policy."

* * *

Furthermore, this Court has not required a particularized or pervasive drug problem before allowing the government to conduct suspicionless drug testing. For instance, in *Von Raab* the Court upheld the drug testing of customs officials on a purely preventive basis, without any documented history of drug use by such officials. * * * Likewise, the need to prevent and deter the substantial harm of childhood drug use provides the necessary immediacy for a school testing policy. Indeed, it would make little sense to require a school district to wait for a substantial portion of its students to begin using drugs before it was allowed to institute a drug testing program designed to deter drug use.

* * *

Respondents also argue that the testing of nonathletes does not implicate any safety concerns, and that safety is a "crucial factor" in applying the special needs framework. * * * Respondents are correct that safety factors into the special needs analysis, but the safety interest furthered by drug testing is undoubtedly substantial for all children, athletes and nonathletes alike. We know all too well that drug use carries a variety of health risks for children, including death from overdose.

Justice Thomas challenged the argument that a program requiring reasonable suspicion would be a less intrusive alternative to suspicionless drug testing:

> [W]e question whether testing based on individualized suspicion in fact would be less intrusive. * * * A program of individualized suspicion might unfairly target members of unpopular groups. The fear of lawsuits resulting from such targeted searches may chill enforcement of the program, rendering it ineffective in combating drug use. In any case, this Court has repeatedly stated that reasonableness under the Fourth Amendment does not require employing the least intrusive means, because the logic of such elaborate less-restrictive-alternative arguments could raise insuperable barriers to the exercise of virtually all search-and-seizure powers.

Justice Breyer wrote a short concurring opinion that emphasized the fact that "the school board provided an opportunity for the airing of these differences at public meetings designed to give the entire community the opportunity to be able to participate" in developing the drug policy. The board used this "democratic, participatory process to uncover and to resolve differences, giving weight to the fact that the process, in this instance, revealed little, if any, objection to the proposed testing program." He also argued that "a contrary reading of the Constitution, as requiring individualized suspicion in this public school context, could well lead schools to push the boundaries of individualized suspicion to its outer limits, using subjective criteria that may unfairly target members of unpopular groups, or leave those whose behavior is slightly abnormal stigmatized in the minds of others."

Justice Ginsburg, joined by Justices Stevens, O'Connor, and Souter, dissented in *Earls*. She argued that "*Vernonia* cannot be read to endorse invasive and suspicionless drug testing of all students upon any evidence of drug use, solely because drugs jeopardize the life and health of those who use them." She further noted that the Court's reliance on voluntary participation in extracurricular activities was misplaced:

> While extracurricular activities are "voluntary" in the sense that they are not required for graduation, they are part of the school's educational program * * *. Participation in such activities is a key component of school life, essential in reality for students applying to college, and, for all participants, a significant contributor to the breadth and quality of the educational experience. Students "volunteer" for extracurricular pursuits in the same way they might volunteer for honors classes: They subject themselves to additional requirements, but they do so in order to take full advantage of the education offered them.

Justice Ginsburg concluded as follows:

> At the margins, of course, no policy of *random* drug testing is perfectly tailored to the harms it seeks to address. * * * Notwithstanding nightmarish images of out-of-control flatware, livestock run amok, and colliding tubas disturbing the peace and quiet of Tecumseh, the great majority of students the School District seeks to test in truth are engaged in activities that are not safety sensitive to an unusual degree. There is a difference between imperfect tailoring and no tailoring at all.

QUESTIONS AFTER EARLS

Can a school district now mandate random drug-testing of *all* public school students, whether or not they wish to participate in extracurricular activities? If not, why not?

What about suspicionless searches of student property? See Doe v. Little Rock School Dist., 380 F.3d 349 (8th Cir. 2004) (random suspicionless searches of students belongings were unreasonable; generalized concerns about the presence of weapons and drugs was not sufficient to justify such intrusive searches, even after *Earls*, especially because evidence obtained in the searches was routinely turned over to the police: "Rather than acting *in loco parentis,* with the goal of promoting the students welfare, the government officials conducting the searches are in large part playing a law enforcement role with the goal of ferreting out crime and collecting evidence to be used in prosecuting students.").

Drug-Testing Politicians

In Chandler v. Miller, 520 U.S. 305 (1997), the Court considered a Georgia statute providing that "each candidate seeking to qualify for nomination or election to a state office shall as a condition of such qualification be required to certify that such candidate has tested negative for illegal drugs." Within 30 days of qualifying for nomination or election, candidates were required to submit a certificate from an approved laboratory documenting negative urinalysis results. Candidates were permitted to provide a sample directly or through a personal physician.

Writing for the Court, Justice Ginsburg determined that the testing scheme was unconstitutional. After reviewing the Court's holdings in *Skinner, Von Raab*, and *Vernonia,* she noted that:

> Our precedents establish that the proffered special need for drug testing must be substantial—important enough to override the individual's acknowledged privacy interest, sufficiently vital to suppress the Fourth Amendment's normal requirement of individualized suspicion.

"Georgia," she concluded, had "failed to show * * * a special need of that kind." Justice Ginsburg reasoned as follows:

> * * * The statute is justified, respondents contend, because the use of illegal drugs draws into question an official's judgment and integrity; jeopardizes the discharge of public functions, including antidrug law enforcement efforts; and undermines public confidence and trust in elected officials. The statute, according to respondents, serves to deter unlawful drug users from becoming candidates and thus stops them from attaining high state office. Notably lacking in respondents' presentation is any indication of a concrete danger demanding departure from the Fourth Amendment's main rule.
>
> Nothing in the record hints that the hazards respondents broadly describe are real and not simply hypothetical for Georgia's polity. * * * A demonstrated problem of drug abuse, while not in all cases necessary to the validity of a testing regime would shore up an assertion of special need for a suspicionless general search program. Proof of unlawful drug use may help to clarify—and to substantiate—the precise hazards posed by such use.

In addition to noting Georgia's failure to identify clearly and convincingly the public interests at stake, Justice Ginsburg was skeptical that the testing regime would be effective in identifying or reducing drug use by aspirants to public office. She wrote:

> In contrast to the effective testing regimes upheld in *Skinner, Von Raab*, and *Vernonia*, Georgia's certification requirement is not well designed to identify candidates who violate antidrug laws. Nor is the scheme a credible means to deter illicit drug users from seeking election to state office. The test date—to be scheduled by the candidate anytime within 30 days prior to qualifying for a place on the ballot—is no secret. As counsel for respondents acknowledged at oral argument, users of illegal drugs, save for those prohibitively addicted, could abstain for a pretest period sufficient to avoid detection. * * * Moreover, respondents have offered no reason why ordinary law

enforcement methods would not suffice to apprehend such addicted individuals, should they appear in the limelight of a public stage. * * *

In contrast with *Von Raab*, where "it was not feasible to subject employees and their work product to the kind of day-to-day scrutiny that is the norm in more traditional office environments," Justice Ginsburg pointed out that public officials "are subject to relentless scrutiny—by their peers, the public, and the press."

Given the absence of clear public interest, and the ineffectual nature of the testing regime, Justice Ginsburg concluded that the statute was little more than a public relations stunt, which could not pass Fourth Amendment scrutiny.

> What is left, after close review of Georgia's scheme, is the image the State seeks to project. By requiring candidates for public office to submit to drug testing, Georgia displays its commitment to the struggle against drug abuse. The suspicionless tests, according to respondents, signify that candidates, if elected, will be fit to serve their constituents free from the influence of illegal drugs. But Georgia asserts no evidence of a drug problem among the State's elected officials, those officials typically do not perform high-risk, safety-sensitive tasks, and the required certification immediately aids no interdiction effort. The need revealed, in short, is symbolic, not "special," as that term draws meaning from our case law.
>
> * * *
>
> * * * However well-meant, the candidate drug test Georgia has devised diminishes personal privacy for a symbol's sake. The Fourth Amendment shields society against that state action.

Chief Justice Rehnquist dissented in *Chandler*, and would have deferred to the political judgment of Georgia's elected officials.

Drug-Testing Cases After Chandler

It should come as no surprise that drug-testing cases are all over the map after *Chandler*. In *Chandler*, the Court second-guessed whether a drug-testing plan would be effective in controlling drug abuse—such second-guessing was missing in the Court's previous cases. In *Chandler*, the Court held that people with minimal privacy interests could not be subject to drug-testing that was relatively non-intrusive. The emphasis in the previous cases was to the contrary.

For a taste of the differing results after *Chandler*, see, e.g., 19 Solid Waste Dept. Mech. v. City of Albuquerque, 156 F.3d 1068 (10th Cir.1998) (invalidating suspicionless searches of trash truck mechanics as not justified by a "special need"; stating that after *Chandler*, "even if the privacy interest is virtually non-existent, the special need requirement prevents suspicionless searches where the government has failed to show either that it has a real interest in testing or that its test will further its proffered interest."); Krieg v. Seybold, 481 F.3d 512 (7th Cir. 2007) (random drug-testing of sanitation workers found reasonable, because they performed a safety-sensitive job and used large and dangerous vehicles); Knox County Educ. Assoc. v. Knox County Board of Education, 158 F.3d 361 (6th Cir.1998) (random testing of all teachers permitted, even though no showing of a drug problem was made; *Chandler* distinguished on the grounds that teachers are more important than politicians, and teachers "are not subject to the same day-to-day scrutiny as are candidates for public office"); United Teachers v. School Bd. Through Holmes, 142 F.3d 853 (5th Cir.1998) (suspicionless testing of all teachers injured in the course of employment violates the Fourth Amendment; the court concluded that "there is an insufficient nexus between suffering an injury at work and drug impairment"); Lanier v. City of Woodburn, 518 F.3d 1147 (9th Cir. 2008) (drug testing of applicants for position of library worker was not reasonable; there was no evidence of a drug problem in the targeted population, and library workers do not perform high-risk or safety-sensitive tasks).

In *19 Solid Waste Dept.,* supra, the court found it necessary after *Chandler* to inquire into the effectiveness of the drug-testing plan. It held the plan ineffective (thus not furthering a "special need") in part because the employees were tested only once every four years. It therefore concluded that "this program is not at all well-designed to detect drug use among its employees and lacks deterrent effect." Would the court have been happier with a plan that required employees to be tested every day? Does the court mean that the more pervasive (and intrusive) the testing plan, the more it is likely to fulfill a special need and thus be reasonable? Can't the same perverse argument be found in *Chandler*, where the Court says that the plan is unreasonable because candidates receive 30 days advance notice? Is the court saying that surprise inspections, though obviously more upsetting to the citizen, are more reasonable?

The Purpose of Drug-Testing: Ferguson v. City of Charleston

In Ferguson v. City of Charleston, 532 U.S, 67 (2001), the Court continued along the difficult path of distinguishing searches that serve special needs beyond ordinary criminal law enforcement from those that do not. In an opinion by Justice Stevens, the Court struck down a state hospital policy requiring drug testing of pregnant mothers suspected of cocaine use. The Court held that the drug tests were not "special needs" searches because "the central and indispensable feature of the policy" was fulfillment of the State's law enforcement goals.

The Medical University of South Carolina (MUSC) was concerned about the effect of drug use by mothers on their babies and instituted a policy that required the drug testing of urine samples from maternity patients suspected of using cocaine. A patient who tested positive was offered counseling and medical care and was also required to undergo subsequent tests. Expectant mothers who continued to test positive could be arrested and prosecuted.

Because the evidence was collected for the specific purpose of incriminating the patients, the Court held that the Fourth Amendment's prohibition against warrantless and suspicionless searches applied in the absence of consent. The Court did not reach the issue of the sufficiency of the evidence with regard to consent and assumed, for purposes of the decision, that the searches were conducted without the patient's consent.

The Court distinguished the facts in *Ferguson* from its previous special needs cases upholding drug tests because the test results were disseminated to the police and prosecutors and the program was developed with input from police and prosecutors. The Court found the most critical difference was that, in prior cases, the "special need" advanced was totally divorced from the State's general interest in criminal law enforcement, while the purpose of the MUSC policy was precisely to enforce criminal law. While the ultimate goal of the policy may have been to help addicted patients, the immediate objective was "to generate evidence for law enforcement purposes in order to reach that goal."

Justice Kennedy concurred in the result. Justice Scalia dissented, joined by the Chief Justice and Justice Thomas. Justice Scalia contended that the urine tests were not protected by the Fourth Amendment because they were obtained with the patient's consent and the sharing of results with law enforcement did not constitute a Fourth Amendment event .

On remand, the Fourth Circuit held that the mothers did not consent to use of the urine tests in a criminal prosecution. Ferguson v. City of Charleston, 308 F.3d 380 (4th Cir. 2002).

Suspicionless Safety Searches in Airports, Subways, Public Buildings, etc.

In *Von Raab, supra,* the Supreme Court cited favorably some lower court cases from the 1970's that upheld—as reasonable under the "special needs" doctrine—magnetometer searches of persons and carry-on luggage at airports. Those searches were found reasonable because: 1) the searches were safety-based and not primarily intended to enforce the criminal law; 2) the state interest in protecting the safety of air travel was high; 3) the state interest could not be accommodated by limiting the searches to those who were reasonably suspected of presenting a safety risk—suspicionless searches were required because some travelers may pose a safety risk even though they have no intent to violate the law (e.g., a security officer carrying a weapon that might be stolen on board by a hijacker), and because some people might not look suspicious on a cursory view, but in fact may be intending to highjack or blow up an airplane; and 4) the searches are minimally intrusive, because a) all travelers are searched (minimizing the humiliation), b) travelers are notified in advance, and c) travelers are free to refuse the search and choose some other form of travel.

In the decades after the terrorist attacks of September 11, 2001, suspicionless searches at airports and other public places have become commonplace. Air passengers are usually required to take their shoes, belts and coats off; at some airports, passengers are required to pass through a machine that tests for traces of explosive substances; at others, passengers must submit to full-body scans; luggage is scanned using sophisticated 3-D x-ray technologies that reveal contents in detail; some passengers are selected for a more thorough inspection, including the use of an electric wand, a thorough search of personal effects, and what is in effect a *Terry* patdown and frisk. The selection for a more intrusive search is ordinarily done without particularized suspicion; the agents' discretion is purportedly controlled by the use of neutral criteria—the searches are either on a random basis, or because of some factual trigger like purchasing a one-way ticket or setting off the magnetometer.

Are these more intrusive searches reasonable under the special needs line of cases, or are they just enforcement of criminal laws prohibiting terrorism? While the Supreme Court has not yet reviewed the reasonableness of contemporary airport security searches, lower courts have upheld these measures on a special needs analysis. For example, in United States v. Marquez, 410 F.3d 612 (9th Cir. 2005), the defendant was randomly selected for an airport wand search and a pat-down, and was found to have two kilograms of cocaine stashed in his pants. The court analyzed the search as follows:

> * * * The issue here is whether the random selection of Marquez to go to the selectee lane, where he would automatically be subjected to the wanding of his person with the handheld magnetometer in addition to the walkthrough magnetometer and the x-ray luggage scan, was reasonable. We conclude that it was.
>
> Airport screenings of passengers and their baggage constitute administrative searches and are subject to the limitations of the Fourth Amendment. United States v. Davis, 482 F.2d 893, 908 (9th Cir. 1973) (noting that airport screenings are considered to be administrative searches because they are "conducted as part of a general regulatory scheme" where the essential administrative purpose is "to prevent the carrying of weapons or explosives aboard aircraft"). Thus airport screenings must be reasonable. To judge

> reasonableness, it is necessary to balance the right to be free of intrusion with society's interest in safe air travel.
>
> * * *
>
> It is hard to overestimate the need to search air travelers for weapons and explosives before they are allowed to board the aircraft. As illustrated over the last three decades, the potential damage and destruction from air terrorism is horrifically enormous. The random, additional screening procedure in this case satisfies the *Davis* reasonableness test for airport searches. The procedure is geared towards detection and deterrence of airborne terrorism, and its very randomness furthers these goals. This was a limited search, confined in its intrusiveness (both in duration and scope) and in its attempt to discover weapons and explosives. Given the randomness, the limited nature of the intrusion, the myriad devices that can be used to bring planes down, and the absence of any indicia of improper motive, we hold that the random, more thorough screening involving scanning of Marquez's person with the handheld magnetometer was reasonable. The district court properly denied Marquez's motion to suppress the contraband found during TSA screening

See also United States v. Hartwell, 436 F.3d 174 (3d Cir. 2006) (Alito, J.) (when defendant set off the magnetometer, a wand inspection was reasonable; stating that the search is "less offensive" because air passengers "are on notice that they will be searched" and noting that "the events of September 11, 2001, only emphasize the heightened need to conduct searches" at airports).

Some courts have reasoned that the "voluntary" nature of air travel is relevant when assessing intrusiveness. But is air travel really voluntary? Is it just as essential to modern life as the cellphone? See Carpenter v. United States, supra.

The Ninth Circuit, in United States v. Aukai, 497 F.3d 955 (9th Cir. 2007), had to confront the relevance of "consent" as diminishing the traveler's expectation of privacy. Aukai checked in at his flight but did not produce an appropriate identification. His ticket was stamped "no ID" and he proceeded to security. He went through the magnetometer without incident, and presented his boarding pass to the TSA officer. Under TSA procedures, a person who has no ID is subjected to a secondary inspection with a wand, etc. During the secondary inspection, Aukai said he no longer wished to board a plane and wanted to leave the airport. But TSA continued the inspection and eventually the agent discovered a glass pipe and a small quantity of drugs. The TSA procedures called for a secondary inspection to continue even if the traveler decides at some point not to fly.

The *Aukai* court began by noting that its case law "has erroneously suggested that the reasonableness of airport screening searches is dependent upon consent, either ongoing consent or irrevocable implied consent." The court explained its "error" and justified the search of Aukai in the following passage:

> The constitutionality of an airport screening search, however, does not depend on consent, and requiring that a potential passenger be allowed to revoke consent to an ongoing airport security search makes little sense in a post-9/11 world. Such a rule would afford terrorists multiple opportunities to attempt to penetrate airport security by "electing not to fly" on the cusp of detection until a vulnerable portal is found. This rule would also allow terrorists a low-cost method of detecting systematic vulnerabilities in airport security, knowledge that could be extremely valuable in planning future attacks. Likewise, given that consent is not required, it makes little sense to predicate the reasonableness of an administrative airport screening search on an irrevocable implied consent theory.
>
> Rather, where an airport screening search is otherwise reasonable and conducted pursuant to statutory authority, 49 U.S.C. § 44901, all that is required is the passenger's election to attempt entry into the secured area of an airport. Under current TSA regulations and procedures, that election occurs when a prospective passenger walks through the magnetometer or places items on the conveyor belt of the x-ray machine. The record establishes that Aukai elected to attempt entry into the posted secured area of Honolulu International Airport when he walked through the magnetometer, thereby subjecting himself to the airport screening process.

Another factor used to support security searches is that the public is on notice that the searches are occurring. Does this mean that if the TSA announces a program of random body cavity searches of air travelers in order to combat terrorism that those searches are now reasonable because the public has been notified?

Does it make sense that the more intrusive searches are random? Some have suggested that the search plan would be more efficient and reasonable if it was targeted at Muslim men. See Charles Krauthammer, The Case for Profiling, Time Magazine, Mar. 18, 2002, at 104. Professor Maclin rejects the suggestion that racial profiling is necessary or reasonable in "Voluntary" Interviews and Airport Searches of Middle Eastern Men: The Fourth Amendment in a Time of Terror, 73 Miss. L.Rev. 471 (2003). Professor Maclin argues that the proposal for racial profiling of suspect air terrorists relies on the same invalid premise that justified the detention of Japanese citizens during World War II.

In New York City, the police established a search plan for the subway system shortly after the terrorist bombings of commuter trains in Madrid (2004) and London (2005). The plan called for daily inspection checkpoints at selected subway stations. Passengers were randomly selected for a search of their effects before they entered the subway. The targeted stations changed from day to day. The court in MacWade v. Kelly, 460 F.3d 260 (2d Cir. 2006), rejected a Fourth Amendment challenge to these searches brought by some subway passengers. The court first found that "preventing a terrorist from bombing the subways constitutes a special need that is distinct from ordinary post hoc criminal investigation." Under the special needs doctrine, the program of suspicionless searches of subway passengers was found reasonable, the court determining that:

> 1) the government interest in searching was "immediate and substantial" given terrorist threats on the system and actual bombings of commuter trains elsewhere;
>
> 2) the searches were minimally intrusive, because a) passengers receive notice "and may decline to be searched so long as they leave the subway", b) "police search only those containers capable of concealing explosives" and "inspect eligible containers only to determine whether they contain explosives", c) the searches last only a few seconds, and d) "uniformed personnel conduct the searches out in the open, which reduces the fear and stigma that removal to a hidden area can cause."

The citizens challenging the subway search plan argued that it was ineffective because any terrorist could avoid searches simply by refusing to submit to a search and walking a few blocks to an unmonitored subway station. In response, the court stated that it was not its place to conduct "a searching examination of effectiveness"; that officers combating terrorism are entitled to some deference as to the methods chosen; and that the apparent flaw was a strength because "we always have viewed notice and the opportunity to decline as beneficial aspects of a suspicionless search regime because those features minimize intrusiveness."

Is it odd that the citizens are essentially arguing that the plan would be more effective and thus reasonable if all passengers were searched? On the other hand, is it odd that the government is arguing that the plan is reasonable because people can easily avoid searches, and yet the plan is reasonably effective even though people can easily avoid searches?

For other cases upholding security searches, see, e.g., Cassidy v. Chertoff, 471 F.3d 67 (2d Cir. 2006) (upholding searches of persons, luggage and cars on Lake Ticonderoga ferry; noting that passengers receive ample notice, and that searches promote a special need of preventing terrorist attacks on large vessels engaged in mass transportation: "Although the plaintiffs may be correct that Lake Champlain ferries are a less obvious terrorist target than ferries in, for example, New York City or Los Angeles, the airline cases make it clear that the government, in its attempt to counteract the threat of terrorism, need not show that every airport or every ferry terminal is threatened by terrorism in order to implement a nationwide security policy that includes suspicionless searches."); Johnston v. Tampa Bay Sports Authority, 530 F.3d 1320 (11th Cir. 2008) (upholding pat-down security searches at the Super Bowl on grounds of implied consent).

Searching Beyond the Scope of Safety

A safety-based search must be conducted within the limits of protecting safety. If an officer engages in tactics that are not safety-related, it is possible that the search will be found unreasonable. Illustrative is United States v. McCarty, 648 F.3d 820 (9th Cir. 2011). McCarty was traveling from Hilo Airport to Honolulu. He checked bags that were screened by TSA. The screeners used a "CTX" superscanner machine. One of the bags set off an alarm for having a dense item requiring further inspection. Under TSA policy, dense items triggering a CTX alarm must be removed and inspected. In this case, the dense item turned out to be an envelope of photos and other papers. Because of the possibility of "sheet explosives"—which may be disguised as a piece of paper or cardboard—the TSA official is required to thumb through papers or photographs that trigger a CTX alarm. The TSA screeners saw in the envelope some photos of children that looked "improper." The screeners also found letters and newspaper clippings. A brief scan of these increased their suspicion of a child pornography violation. Eventually, local police were called, McCarty was arrested, and ultimately convicted for transportation and possession of child pornography.

The court noted that "because TSA screeners are limited to the single administrative goal of search for possible safety threats related to explosives, the constitutional bounds of an airport administrative search require that the individual screener's actions be no more intrusive that necessary to determine the existence or absence of explosives that could result in harm to the passengers and aircraft." In this case, the screeners conceded that, at the point when they read the content of the letters and newspaper clippings, they were no longer searching for explosives—rather they were searching to confirm their suspicion that the photos they had thumbed through were evidence of child pornography. The court therefore concluded that the review of the letters and newspaper clippings "clearly fell outside the permissible scope of the lawful administrative search and violated McCarthy's Fourth Amendment rights." In contrast, the screeners' review of the pictures in the envelope was found proper because it was "consistent with the TSA protocol requiring [screeners] to thumb through the photographs in order to clear the bag." The court remanded to determine whether the photographs alone established probable cause to support McCarty's arrest.

McCarty argued that the screeners, when looking through the photographs, were not motivated by safety but rather were looking for evidence of child pornography. The court found the screeners' motivation to be irrelevant, so long as the search was justified by the safety concerns attendant to sheet explosives. Why would the screeners' motivations be irrelevant?

Safety-Based Strip Searches of Detainees Without Reasonable Suspicion: Florence v. Board of Chosen Freeholders

In Florence v. Board of Chosen Freeholders, 566 U.S. 318 (2012), Justice Kennedy wrote for the Court as it upheld the reasonableness of a policy of strip-searching all jail detainees, even when they were arrested on minor offenses.

Florence was arrested for a minor offense and was placed in the Burlington County Detention Center and then in the Essex County Correctional Facility. Justice Kennedy described the procedures in the two facilities:

> Burlington County jail procedures required every arrestee to shower with a delousing agent. Officers would check arrestees for scars, marks, gang tattoos, and contraband as they disrobed. Petitioner claims he was also instructed to open his mouth, lift his tongue, hold out his arms, turn around, and lift his genitals. (It is not clear whether this last step was part of the normal practice.) Petitioner shared a cell with at least one other person and interacted with other inmates following his admission to the jail.
>
> The Essex County Correctional Facility, where petitioner was taken after six days, is the largest county jail in New Jersey. It admits more than 25,000 inmates each year and houses about 1,000 gang members at any given time. When petitioner was transferred there, all arriving detainees passed through a metal detector and waited in a group holding cell for a more thorough search. When they left the holding cell, they were instructed to remove their clothing while an officer looked for body markings, wounds, and contraband. Apparently without touching the detainees, an officer looked at their ears, nose, mouth, hair, scalp, fingers, hands, arms, armpits, and other body openings. This policy applied regardless of the circumstances of the arrest, the suspected offense, or the detainee's behavior, demeanor, or criminal history. Petitioner alleges he was required to lift his genitals, turn around, and cough in a squatting position as part of the process. After a mandatory shower, during which his clothes were inspected,

petitioner was admitted to the facility. He was released the next day, when the charges against him were dismissed.

Florence brought an action under 42 U.S.C. § 1983, contending that under the Fourth Amendment, a person arrested for a minor offense could not be required to remove his clothing and expose his most private areas to close visual inspection as a routine part of the intake process. The lower court granted summary judgment for Florence, reasoning that a policy of strip-searching those arrested for minor offenses without reasonable suspicion violates the Fourth Amendment. The court of appeals reversed. The Supreme Court affirmed the court of appeals.

After observing that the term "strip search" was imprecise in describing the jail procedures, Justice Kennedy noted that operating a detention center posed major challenges to officials that a court should not underestimate. He cited Bell v. Wolfish, 441 U.S. 520 (1979), which upheld a Federal Bureau of Prisons rule that detainees in any correctional facility were required "to expose their body cavities for visual inspection as a part of a strip search conducted after every contact visit with a person from outside the institution." Justice Kennedy reasoned that correctional officials must be permitted to devise reasonable search policies to detect and deter possession of contraband; to assure that lice and contagious infections were not introduced into the prison population; to discover gang tattoos that might indicate a need for special housing; and to find weapons.

Florence acknowledged that correctional officials had to conduct effective intake searches and this would include having at least some detainees lift their genitals or cough in a squatting position, but argued that there was little benefit in imposing such procedures on a new detainee who has been arrested for a minor crime not involving weapons or drugs. Justice Kennedy rejected the argument and stated that "[i]t is reasonable * * * for correctional officials to conclude that this standard would be unworkable." One reason is that "[p]eople detained for minor offenses can turn out to be the most devious and dangerous criminals." Another is that "[i]t * * * may be difficult, as a practical matter, to classify inmates by their current and prior offenses before the intake search"; and "[j]ails can be even more dangerous than prisons because officials there know so little about the people they admit at the outset." Justice Kennedy cited *Atwater* for the proposition that it was important that officials in charge of jails, like police officers, can rely on readily administrable rules. In the end, Justice Kennedy stated that "[t]his case does not require the Court to rule on the types of searches that would be reasonable in instances where, for example, a detainee will be held without assignment to the general jail population and without substantial contact with other detainees."

Chief Justice Roberts concurred and emphasized that the majority's opinion did not foreclose the possibility that particular searches might be unreasonable. Justice Alito concurred and emphasized "that the Court does not hold that it is always reasonable to conduct a full strip search of an arrestee whose detention has not been reviewed by a judicial officer and who could be held in available facilities apart from the general population."

Justice Breyer, joined by Justices Ginsburg, Sotomayor and Kagan, dissented and stated that "I have found no convincing reason indicating that, in the absence of reasonable suspicion, involuntary strip searches of those arrested for minor offenses are necessary in order to further the penal interests mentioned above [to detect injuries or diseases, to identify gang tattoos which might reflect a need for special housing, or to detect contraband]."

Monitoring Parolees and Sex Offenders

In Grady v. North Carolina, 575 U.S. 306 (2015), the Court held that compulsory use of GPS tracking devices to monitor parolees and recidivist sex offenders constitutes a "search" for purposes of the Fourth Amendment, but may be "reasonable" under a special needs analysis.

4. DNA Testing

When, if ever, is suspicionless DNA testing of individuals reasonable? Can taking DNA samples or comparing samples to a DNA database be justified as promoting "special needs" beyond ordinary criminal law enforcement? The Court considered these questions in the following case.

MARYLAND V. KING

Supreme Court of the United States, 2013.
569 U.S. 455.

JUSTICE KENNEDY delivered the opinion of the Court.

In 2003 a man concealing his face and armed with a gun broke into a woman's home in Salisbury, Maryland. He raped her. The police were unable to identify or apprehend the assailant based on any detailed description or other evidence they then had, but they did obtain from the victim a sample of the perpetrator's DNA.

In 2009 Alonzo King was arrested in Wicomico County, Maryland, and charged with first- and second-degree assault for menacing a group of people with a shotgun. [Pursuant to provisions of the Maryland DNA Collection Act, a sample of King's DNA] was taken by applying a cotton swab or filter paper—known as a buccal swab—to the inside of his cheeks. The DNA was found to match the DNA taken from the Salisbury rape victim. King was tried and convicted for the rape. * * *

The Court of Appeals of Maryland, on review of King's rape conviction, ruled that the DNA taken when King was booked for the 2009 charge was an unlawful seizure because obtaining and using the cheek swab was an unreasonable search of the person. It set the rape conviction aside. This Court granted certiorari and now reverses the judgment of the Maryland court.

* * *

The advent of DNA technology is one of the most significant scientific advancements of our era. The full potential for use of genetic markers in medicine and science is still being explored, but the utility of DNA identification in the criminal justice system is already undisputed. Since the first use of forensic DNA analysis to catch a rapist and murderer in England in 1986, law enforcement, the defense bar, and the courts have acknowledged DNA testing's unparalleled ability both to exonerate the wrongly convicted and to identify the guilty. * * *

The current standard for forensic DNA testing relies on an analysis of the chromosomes located within the nucleus of all human cells. The DNA material in chromosomes is composed of "coding" and "noncoding" regions. The coding regions are known as genes and contain the information necessary for a cell to make proteins. Non-protein-coding regions are not related directly to making proteins, and have been referred to as "junk" DNA. The adjective "junk" may mislead the layperson, for in fact this is the DNA region used with near certainty to identify a person. The term apparently is intended to indicate that this particular noncoding region, while useful and even dispositive for purposes like identity, does not show more far-reaching and complex characteristics like genetic traits.

* * * The [Maryland DNA Collection] Act authorizes Maryland law enforcement authorities to collect DNA samples from "an individual who is charged with . . . a crime of violence or an attempt to commit a crime of violence; or . . . burglary or an attempt to commit burglary." * * * Once taken, a DNA sample may not be processed or placed in a database before the individual is arraigned (unless the individual consents). It is at this point that a judicial officer ensures that there is probable cause to detain the arrestee on a qualifying serious offense. If all qualifying criminal charges are determined to be unsupported by probable cause the DNA sample [is] immediately destroyed. DNA samples are also destroyed if a criminal action begun against the individual does not result in a conviction, the conviction is finally reversed or vacated and no new trial is permitted, or the individual is granted an unconditional pardon.

The Act also limits the information added to a DNA database and how it may be used. Specifically, only DNA records that directly relate to the identification of individuals [may] be collected and stored. No purpose other than identification is permissible * * *. Tests for familial matches are also prohibited. The officers involved in taking and analyzing respondent's DNA sample complied with the Act in all respects.

Respondent's DNA was collected in this case using a common procedure known as a "buccal swab." Buccal cell collection involves wiping a small piece of filter paper or a cotton swab similar to a Q-tip against the inside cheek of an individual's mouth to collect some skin cells. The procedure is quick and painless. * * *

Respondent's identification as the rapist resulted in part through the operation of a national project to standardize collection and storage of DNA profiles. Authorized by Congress and supervised by the Federal Bureau of Investigation, the Combined DNA Index System (CODIS) connects DNA laboratories at the local, state, and national level. Since its authorization in 1994, the CODIS system has grown to include all 50 States and a number of federal agencies. CODIS collects DNA profiles provided by local laboratories taken from arrestees, convicted offenders, and forensic evidence found at crime scenes. * * *. In short, CODIS sets uniform national standards for DNA matching and then facilitates connections between local law enforcement agencies who can share more specific information about matched * * * profiles.

All 50 States require the collection of DNA from felony convicts, and respondent does not dispute the validity of that practice. Twenty-eight States and the Federal Government have adopted laws similar to the Maryland Act authorizing the collection of DNA from some or all arrestees. * * *

A buccal swab is a far more gentle process than a venipuncture to draw blood. It involves but a light touch on the inside of the cheek * * *. The fact that an intrusion is negligible is of central relevance to determining reasonableness, although it is still a search as the law defines that term.

* * *

In some circumstances, such as "[w]hen faced with special law enforcement needs, diminished expectations of privacy, minimal intrusions, or the like, the Court has found that certain general, or individual, circumstances may render a warrantless search or seizure reasonable." Illinois v. McArthur. * * * The need for a warrant is perhaps least when the search involves no discretion that could properly be limited by the "interpo[lation of] a neutral magistrate between the citizen and the law enforcement officer." Treasury Employees v. Von Raab.

The instant case can be addressed with this background. The Maryland DNA Collection Act provides that, in order to obtain a DNA sample, all arrestees charged with serious crimes must furnish the sample on a buccal swab applied, as noted, to the inside of the cheeks. The arrestee is already in valid police custody for a serious offense supported by probable cause. * * * [I]n light of the standardized nature of the tests and the minimal discretion vested in those charged with administering the program, "there are virtually no facts for a neutral magistrate to evaluate."

Skinner. Here, the search effected by the buccal swab of respondent falls within the category of cases this Court has analyzed by reference to the proposition that the "touchstone of the Fourth Amendment is reasonableness, not individualized suspicion." *Samson*.

* * * To say that no warrant is required is merely to acknowledge that rather than employing a per se rule of unreasonableness, we balance the privacy-related and law enforcement-related concerns to determine if the intrusion was reasonable. This application of traditional standards of reasonableness requires a court to weigh the promotion of legitimate governmental interests against the degree to which the search intrudes upon an individual's privacy. * * *

The legitimate government interest served by the Maryland DNA Collection Act is one that is well established: the need for law enforcement officers in a safe and accurate way to process and identify the persons and possessions they must take into custody. It is beyond dispute that probable cause provides legal justification for arresting a person suspected of crime, and for a brief period of detention to take the administrative steps incident to arrest. Also uncontested is the right on the part of the Government, always recognized under English and American law, to search the person of the accused when legally arrested. * * *

The routine administrative procedures at a police station house incident to booking and jailing the suspect derive from different origins and have different constitutional justifications than, say, the search of a place; for the search of a place not incident to an arrest depends on the fair probability that contraband or evidence of a crime will be found in a particular place. The interests are further different when an individual is formally processed into police custody. * * * When probable cause exists to remove an individual from the normal channels of society and hold him in legal custody, DNA identification plays a critical role in serving those interests.

First, in every criminal case, it is known and must be known who has been arrested and who is being tried. * * * It is a well-recognized aspect of criminal conduct that the perpetrator will take unusual steps to conceal not only his conduct, but also his identity. * * * An arrestee may be carrying a false ID or lie about his identity, and criminal history records can be inaccurate or incomplete.

A suspect's criminal history is a critical part of his identity that officers should know when processing him for detention. It is a common occurrence that people detained for minor offenses can turn out to be the most devious and dangerous criminals. Police already seek this crucial identifying information. They use routine and accepted means as varied as comparing the suspect's booking photograph to sketch artists' depictions of persons of interest, showing his mugshot to potential witnesses, and of course making a computerized comparison of the arrestee's fingerprints against electronic databases of known criminals and unsolved crimes. In this respect the only difference between DNA analysis and the accepted use of fingerprint databases is the unparalleled accuracy DNA provides.

The task of identification necessarily entails searching public and police records based on the identifying information provided by the arrestee to see what is already known about him. * * * A DNA profile is useful to the police because it gives them a form of identification to search the records already in their valid possession. In this respect the use of DNA for identification is no different than matching an arrestee's face to a wanted poster of a previously unidentified suspect; or matching tattoos to known gang symbols to reveal a criminal affiliation; or matching the arrestee's fingerprints to those recovered from a crime scene. * * * Second, law enforcement officers bear a responsibility for ensuring that the custody of an arrestee does not create inordinate risks for facility staff, for the existing detainee population, and for a new detainee. DNA identification can provide untainted information to those charged with detaining suspects and detaining the property of any felon. For these purposes officers must know the type of person whom they are detaining, and DNA allows them to make critical choices about how to proceed.

* * *

[L]ooking forward to future stages of criminal prosecution, the Government has a substantial interest in ensuring that persons accused of crimes are available for trials. A person who is arrested for one offense but knows that he has yet to answer for some past crime may be more inclined to flee the instant charges, lest continued contact with the criminal justice system expose one or more other serious offenses. * * * [A]n arrestee's past conduct is essential to an assessment of the danger he poses to the public, and this will inform a court's determination whether the individual should be released on bail. * * * DNA identification of a suspect in a violent crime provides critical information to the police and judicial officials in making a determination of the arrestee's future dangerousness. * * *

* * * Even if an arrestee is released on bail, development of DNA identification revealing the defendant's unknown violent past can and should lead to the revocation of his conditional release. * * *

Finally, in the interests of justice, the identification of an arrestee as the perpetrator of some heinous crime may have the salutary effect of freeing a person wrongfully imprisoned for the same offense. "[P]rompt [DNA] testing . . . would speed up apprehension of criminals before they commit additional crimes, and prevent the grotesque detention of . . . innocent people." J. Dwyer, P. Neufeld, & B. Scheck, Actual Innocence 245 (2000).

* * *

DNA identification represents an important advance in the techniques used by law enforcement to serve legitimate police concerns for as long as there have been arrests, concerns the courts have acknowledged and approved for more than a century. * * * Perhaps the most direct historical analogue to the DNA technology used to identify respondent is the familiar practice of fingerprinting arrestees. From the advent of this technique, courts had no trouble determining that fingerprinting was a natural part of the administrative steps incident to arrest. * * *

DNA identification is an advanced technique superior to fingerprinting in many ways, so much so that to insist on fingerprints as the norm would make little sense to either the forensic expert or a layperson. The additional intrusion upon the arrestee's privacy beyond that associated with fingerprinting is not significant, * * * and DNA is a markedly more accurate form of identifying arrestees. A suspect who has changed his facial features to evade photographic identification or even one who has undertaken the more arduous task of altering his fingerprints cannot escape the revealing power of his DNA.

The respondent's primary objection to this analogy is that DNA identification is not as fast as fingerprinting, and so it should not be considered to be the 21st-century equivalent. But rapid analysis of fingerprints is itself of recent vintage. The FBI's vaunted Integrated Automated Fingerprint Identification System (IAFIS) was only launched on July 28, 1999. Prior to this time, the processing of fingerprint submissions was largely a manual, labor-intensive process, taking weeks or months to process a single submission. * * * The question of how long it takes to process identifying information obtained from a valid search goes only to the efficacy of the search for its purpose of prompt identification, not the constitutionality of the search. Given the importance of DNA in the identification of police records pertaining to arrestees and the need to refine and confirm that identity for its important bearing on the decision to continue release on bail or to impose of new conditions, DNA serves an essential purpose despite the existence of delays such as the one that occurred in this case. Even so, the delay in processing DNA from arrestees is being reduced to a substantial degree by rapid technical advances. And the FBI has already begun testing devices that will enable police to process the DNA of arrestees within 90 minutes. An assessment and understanding of the reasonableness of this minimally invasive search of a person detained for a serious crime should take account of these technical advances. * * *

* * * In the balance of reasonableness required by the Fourth Amendment, therefore, the Court must give great weight both to the significant government interest at stake in the identification of arrestees and to the unmatched potential of DNA identification to serve that interest.

* * * By comparison to this substantial government interest and the unique effectiveness of DNA identification, the intrusion of a cheek swab to obtain a DNA sample is a minimal one. * * *

The expectations of privacy of an individual taken into police custody necessarily are of a diminished scope. * * *

In this critical respect, the search here at issue differs from the sort of programmatic searches of either the public at large or a particular class of regulated but otherwise law-abiding citizens that the Court has previously labeled as "special needs" searches. * * * Once an individual has been arrested on probable cause for a dangerous offense that may require detention before trial, however, his or her expectations of privacy and freedom from police scrutiny are reduced. DNA identification like that at issue here thus does not require consideration of any unique needs that would be required to justify searching the average citizen * * * [because] a detainee has a reduced expectation of privacy.

The reasonableness inquiry here considers two other circumstances in which the Court has held that particularized suspicion is not categorically required: diminished expectations of privacy and minimal intrusions. * * * This is not to suggest that any search is acceptable solely because a person is in custody. Some searches, such as invasive surgery, or a search of the arrestee's home, involve either greater intrusions or higher expectations of privacy than are present in this case. * * *

Here, by contrast to the approved standard procedures incident to any arrest detailed above, a buccal swab involves an even more brief and still minimal intrusion. * * * A brief intrusion of an arrestee's person is subject to the Fourth Amendment, but a swab of this nature does not increase the indignity already attendant to normal incidents of arrest.

* * * In addition the processing of respondent's DNA sample * * * did not intrude on respondent's privacy in a way that would make his DNA identification unconstitutional.

First, as already noted, the CODIS loci come from noncoding parts of the DNA that do not reveal the genetic traits of the arrestee. * * * It is undisputed that law enforcement officers analyze DNA for the sole purpose of generating a unique identifying number against which future samples may be matched. This parallels a similar safeguard based on actual practice in the school drug-testing context, where the Court deemed it "significant that the tests at issue here look only for drugs, and not for whether the student is, for example, epileptic, pregnant, or diabetic." *Vernonia School Dist. 47J.* If in the future police analyze samples to determine, for instance, an arrestee's predisposition for a particular disease or other hereditary factors not relevant to identity, that case would present additional privacy concerns not present here.

Finally, the Act provides statutory protections that guard against further invasion of privacy. As noted above, the Act requires that only DNA records that directly relate to the identification of individuals shall be collected and stored. No purpose other than identification is permissible. * * * The Court need not speculate about the risks posed by a system that [does] not contain comparable security provisions. In light of the scientific and statutory safeguards, once respondent's DNA was lawfully collected the * * * analysis of respondent's DNA pursuant to CODIS procedures did not amount to a significant invasion of privacy that would render the DNA identification impermissible under the Fourth Amendment.

* * * When officers make an arrest supported by probable cause to hold for a serious offense and they bring the suspect to the station to be detained in custody, taking and analyzing a cheek swab of the arrestee's DNA is, like fingerprinting and photographing, a legitimate police booking procedure that is reasonable under the Fourth Amendment. * * *

JUSTICE SCALIA, with whom JUSTICE GINSBURG, JUSTICE SOTOMAYOR, and JUSTICE KAGAN join, dissenting.

The Fourth Amendment forbids searching a person for evidence of a crime when there is no basis for believing the person is guilty of the crime or is in possession of incriminating evidence. That prohibition is categorical and without exception; it lies at the very heart of the Fourth Amendment. Whenever this Court has allowed a suspicionless search, it has insisted upon a justifying motive apart from the investigation of crime.

It is obvious that no such noninvestigative motive exists in this case. The Court's assertion that DNA is being taken, not to solve crimes, but to identify those in the State's custody, taxes the credulity of the credulous. And the Court's comparison of Maryland's DNA searches to other techniques, such as fingerprinting, can seem apt only to those who know no more than today's opinion has chosen to tell them about how those DNA searches actually work.

* * *

Although there is a "closely guarded category of constitutionally permissible suspicionless searches," that has never included searches designed to serve "the normal need for law enforcement." Even the common name for suspicionless searches—"special needs" searches—itself reflects that they must be justified, always, by concerns other than crime detection. We have approved random drug tests of railroad employees, yes—but only because the Government's need to "regulat[e] the conduct of railroad employees to ensure safety" is distinct from "normal law enforcement." So too we have approved suspicionless searches in public schools—but only because there the government acts in furtherance of its "responsibilities . . . as guardian and tutor of children entrusted to its care."

So while the Court is correct to note that there are instances in which we have permitted searches without individualized suspicion, in none of these cases did we indicate approval of a search whose primary purpose was to detect evidence of ordinary criminal wrongdoing. That limitation is crucial. It is only when a governmental purpose aside from crime-solving is at stake that we engage in the free-form "reasonableness" inquiry that the Court indulges at length today. To put it another way, both the legitimacy of the Court's method and the correctness of its outcome hinge entirely on the truth of a single proposition: that the primary purpose of these DNA searches is something other than simply discovering evidence of criminal wrongdoing. As I detail below, that proposition is wrong.

The Court alludes at several points to the fact that King was an arrestee, and arrestees may be validly searched incident to their arrest. But the Court does not really rest on this principle, and for good reason: The objects of a search incident to arrest must be either (1) weapons or evidence that might easily be destroyed, or (2) evidence relevant to the crime of arrest. Neither is the object of the search at issue here.

* * *

Sensing (correctly) that it needs more, the Court elaborates at length the ways that the search here served the special purpose of "identifying" King. But that seems to me quite wrong—unless what one means by "identifying" someone is "searching for evidence that he has committed crimes unrelated to the crime of his arrest." * * * If identifying someone means finding out what unsolved crimes he has committed, then identification is indistinguishable from the ordinary law-enforcement aims that have never been thought to justify a suspicionless search. * * * I will therefore assume that the Court means that the DNA search at issue here was useful to "identify" King in the normal sense of that word—in the sense that would identify the author of Introduction to the Principles of Morals and Legislation as Jeremy Bentham.

* * * The portion of the Court's opinion that explains the identification rationale is strangely silent on the actual workings of the DNA search at issue here. To know those facts is to be instantly disabused of the notion that what happened had anything to do with identifying King.

King was arrested on April 10, 2009, on charges unrelated to the case before us. That same day, April 10, the police searched him and seized the DNA evidence at issue here. What happened next? Reading the Court's opinion, particularly its insistence that the search was necessary to know "who [had] been arrested," one might guess that King's DNA was swiftly processed and his identity thereby confirmed—perhaps against some master database of known DNA profiles, as is done for fingerprints. After all, was not the suspicionless search here crucial to avoid "inordinate risks for facility staff" or to "existing detainee population"? Surely, then—surely—the State of Maryland got cracking on those grave risks immediately, by rushing to identify King with his DNA as soon as possible.

Nothing could be further from the truth. Maryland officials did not even begin the process of testing King's DNA that day. Or, actually, the next day. Or the day after that. And that was for a simple reason: Maryland law forbids them to do so. A "DNA sample collected from an individual charged with a crime . . . may not be tested or placed in the statewide DNA data base system prior to the first scheduled arraignment date." Md. Pub. Saf. Code Ann. § 2–504(d)(1). And King's first appearance in court was not until three days after his arrest. (I suspect, though, that they did not wait three days to ask his name or take his fingerprints.)

This places in a rather different light the Court's solemn declaration that the search here was necessary so that King could be identified at "every stage of the criminal process." Does the Court really believe that Maryland did not know whom it was arraigning? The truth, known to Maryland and increasingly to the reader: this search had nothing to do with establishing King's identity.

* * *

More devastating still for the Court's "identification" theory, the statute does enumerate two instances in which a DNA sample may be tested for the purpose of identification: "to help identify human remains" and "to help identify missing individuals." No mention of identifying arrestees. * * *

* * *

The Court also attempts to bolster its identification theory with a series of inapposite analogies.

Is not taking DNA samples the same, asks the Court, as taking a person's photograph? No—because that is not a Fourth Amendment search at all. It does not involve a physical intrusion onto the person, and we have never held that merely taking a person's photograph invades any recognized "expectation of privacy." * * *

* * *

It is on the fingerprinting of arrestees, however, that the Court relies most heavily. [But] law enforcement's post-arrest use of fingerprints could not be more different from its post-arrest use of DNA. Fingerprints of arrestees are taken primarily to identify them (though that process sometimes solves crimes); the DNA of arrestees is taken to solve crimes (and nothing else).

* * *

Today, it can fairly be said that fingerprints really are used to identify people—so well, in fact, that there would be no need for the expense of a separate, wholly redundant DNA confirmation of the same information. What DNA adds—what makes it a valuable weapon in the law-enforcement arsenal—is the ability to solve unsolved crimes, by matching old crime-scene evidence against the profiles of people whose identities are already known. That is what was going on when King's DNA was taken, and we should not disguise the fact. Solving unsolved crimes is a noble objective, but it occupies a lower place in the American pantheon of noble objectives than the protection of our people from suspicionless law-enforcement searches. The Fourth Amendment must prevail.

* * *

Today's judgment will, to be sure, have the beneficial effect of solving more crimes; then again, so would the taking of DNA samples from anyone who flies on an airplane (surely the Transportation Security Administration needs to know the "identity" of the flying public), applies for a driver's license, or attends a public school. Perhaps the construction of such a genetic panopticon is wise. But I doubt that the proud men who wrote the charter of our liberties would have been so eager to open their mouths for royal inspection.

I therefore dissent, and hope that today's incursion upon the Fourth Amendment * * * will some day be repudiated.

Questions After King: DNA Investigations

In the years after *King*, investigators have found new ways to use DNA evidence to solve crimes. One such strategy involves uploading DNA profiles taken from crime-scene samples into ancestry databases in the hope of identifying suspects or individuals whose profiles suggest familial relationships with a perpetrator. Investigators famously used this investigative strategy to identify the notorious "Golden Gate Killer" in 2018. Does this use of DNA raise Fourth Amendment concerns? See Natalie Ram, Genetic Privacy after *Carpenter*, 105 Va.L.Rev. 1357 (2019).

In his *King* dissent, Justice Scalia offers as a bête noir the possibility of large or even universal DNA databases that might facilitate both identification and criminal law enforcement. Though certainly unsettling, could these kinds of databases be developed and used in such a way so as to accommodate Fourth Amendment interests? See Arnold Loewy, A Proposal for the Universal Collection of DNA, 48 Tex.Tech.L.Rev. 261 (2015); Christopher Slobogin, Dangerousness, Disability, and DNA, 52 Tex.Tech.L.Rev. 149 (2019). Or, as Professor Ram warns in America's Hidden National DNA Database, 100 Tex.L.Rev. ___ (2022), might police one day soon turn to blood samples routinely collected from nearly all newborn babies to solve crimes?

5. Roadblocks, Checkpoints and Suspicionless Seizures

Individual Stops Without Suspicion

In Delaware v. Prouse, 440 U.S. 648 (1979), the Court held that an officer could not, in the absence of reasonable suspicion, stop an automobile and detain the driver in order to check his license and registration. The officer in *Prouse* made an ad hoc, suspicionless stop, and the Court expressed its concern with "the unconstrained exercise of discretion." The Court concluded that such an ad hoc stop was not "a sufficiently productive mechanism to justify the intrusion" and that there were other, better ways to effectuate the state interest in vehicle registration and safety, such as yearly inspections. The majority emphasized that it was not foreclosing as one possible alternative the "questioning of all oncoming traffic at roadblock-type stops." In response to the majority's roadblock alternative, Justice Rehnquist argued in dissent that the majority had "elevated the adage 'misery loves company' to a novel role in Fourth Amendment jurisprudence." Why is it better to stop everybody rather than anybody?

Permanent Checkpoints

The dictum in *Prouse* concerning the reasonableness of roadblock-type stops was supported by the Court's earlier decision in United States v. Martinez-Fuerte, 428 U.S. 543 (1976), where the Court, invoking *Terry* principles, approved suspicionless stops at permanent checkpoints removed from the border. The Court emphasized that suspicionless stops were necessary to implement the state interest in regulating the flow of undocumented individuals and noted that the fixed checkpoint was minimally intrusive. Justice Powell, writing for the Court, argued that motorists are not surprised by a fixed checkpoint; that such checkpoints limit the discretion of the officer; and that "the location of a fixed checkpoint is not chosen by officers in the field, but by officials responsible for making overall decisions as to the most effective allocation of limited enforcement resources." Justice Powell stressed that it was permissible to dispense with particularized suspicion because "we deal neither with searches nor with the sanctuary of private dwellings."

Temporary DUI Checkpoints: Michigan Department of State Police v. Sitz

The Court upheld suspicionless stops at temporary sobriety checkpoints in Michigan Department of State Police v. Sitz, 496 U.S. 444 (1990). The Michigan program allowed checkpoints to be set up by officers in the field according to a list of considerations including "safety of the location," "minimum inconvenience for the driver," and available space "to pull the vehicle off the traveled portion of the roadway for further inquiry if necessary." Under the program, all motorists passing through the checkpoint were stopped and briefly examined for signs of intoxication. If the driver appeared intoxicated, he or she was directed to another area where license and registration was checked and further sobriety tests were conducted if warranted. The only checkpoint operated under the program resulted in a stop of 126 vehicles, and one arrest for drunk driving. The challenge in the Supreme Court focused solely on the initial detention and associated preliminary investigation of motorists for signs of intoxication.

Chief Justice Rehnquist's opinion for five members of the Court relied heavily on *Martinez-Fuerte,* and applied the "misery loves company" rationale that then-Justice Rehnquist had criticized in *Prouse.*

Respondents in *Sitz* argued that a reasonableness balancing approach could not be employed to evaluate sobriety checkpoints, because there was no special need beyond criminal law enforcement at stake. They argued that sobriety checkpoints are simply used to enforce criminal laws prohibiting drunk driving.

The majority responded that a special need beyond criminal law enforcement was not required to support reasonableness balancing for stops at fixed checkpoints. The Chief Justice stated that the special needs analysis of *Skinner* et al. "was in no way designed to repudiate our prior cases dealing with police stops." Thus, the Court relied on the *Terry* line of cases rather than on the "special needs" line of cases.

Balancing the interests of the state and the individual, as permitted for law enforcement seizures by *Terry,* the Chief Justice quoted from *Martinez-Fuerte,* and concluded that the intrusiveness of a sobriety checkpoint was extremely limited:

> At traffic checkpoints the motorist can see that other vehicles are being stopped, he can see visible signs of the officers' authority, and he is much less likely to be frightened or annoyed by the intrusion. * * * Here, checkpoints are selected pursuant to the guidelines, and uniformed police officers stop every approaching vehicle. The intrusion resulting from the brief stop at the sobriety checkpoint is for constitutional purposes indistinguishable from the checkpoint stops we upheld in *Martinez-Fuerte.*

Against this limited intrusion, the Court balanced the State's heavy interest in eradicating drunk driving. Chief Justice Rehnquist rejected the argument that sobriety checkpoints did not effectively advance this undeniable state interest. He stated that references to effectiveness of searches and seizures in previous cases, such as *Prouse,* were not intended "to transfer from politically accountable officials to the courts the decision as to which among reasonable alternative law enforcement techniques should be employed to deal with a serious public danger." The Court concluded that "the choice among such reasonable alternatives remains with the government officials who have a unique understanding of, and a responsibility for, limited public resources." The majority faulted the lower court for its "searching examination" of the effectiveness of sobriety checkpoints.

Justice Stevens wrote a dissenting opinion joined in substantial part by Justices Brennan and Marshall. He argued that, unlike the permanent, fixed checkpoint in *Martinez-Fuerte,* the police operating a sobriety checkpoint "have extremely broad discretion in determining the exact timing and placement of the roadblock." Moreover, a temporary checkpoint is more intrusive because of the element of surprise that it presents:

> A driver who discovers an unexpected checkpoint on a familiar local road will be startled and distressed. She may infer, correctly, that the checkpoint is not simply "business as usual," and may likewise infer, again correctly, that the police have made a discretionary decision to focus their law enforcement efforts upon her and others who pass the chosen point.

QUESTIONS AFTER SITZ

The Court in *Sitz* chided the lower court for second-guessing the legislature's determination that roadblocks would be an effective means of investigating and deterring drunk driving. Yet in *Chandler*, supra, the Court second-guessed the legislature's determination that its drug-testing plan would be an effective means of detecting and deterring drug use in candidates for public office. How do you square the two cases?

Judge Boudin discusses problems relating to judicial assessments of effectiveness—and the consequent need to defer to policymakers—in United States v. William, 603 F.3d 66 (1st Cir. 2010), where the defendant was stopped at a sobriety checkpoint and drugs were eventually found in his car:

> William argues that * * * the data offered to support the use of this checkpoint at this location was inadequate and that the results in arrest numbers were unimpressive. Certainly one can imagine a purported sobriety checkpoint whose location or timing was demonstrably unlikely to be of use. But in *Sitz,* Chief Justice Rehnquist went out of his way to say that whether and where to establish a stop is primarily a judgment for state or local officials. In addition, using the number of drunk driving arrests resulting from a specific checkpoint has at least two problems: one is that the reasonableness of the effort is primarily a forward-looking exercise (in fact, the percentage of arrests in *Sitz* was very low); and the other is that sobriety checkpoints likely have a deterrent value apart from immediate detentions resulting from the stops.

If *Martinez-Fuerte* is the correct analogy, can *Sitz* stand for the proposition that checkpoints are permissible at *any* location? Can *Martinez-Fuerte* justify roving or moveable checkpoints? If so, who decides where checkpoints are placed? Does it make a difference that the location of the checkpoint in *Martinez-Fuerte* was chosen by high-level officials rather than officers in the field?

Drug Checkpoints

In the following case, the Court revisits its analysis in *Sitz* and distinguishes sobriety roadblocks from checkpoints designed to combat drug trafficking.

CITY OF INDIANAPOLIS V. EDMOND

Supreme Court of the United States, 2000.
531 U.S. 32.

JUSTICE O'CONNOR delivered the opinion of the Court.

In Michigan Dept. of State Police v. Sitz and United States v. Martinez-Fuerte we held that brief, suspicionless seizures at highway checkpoints for the purposes of combating drunk driving and intercepting illegal immigrants were constitutional. We now consider the constitutionality of a highway checkpoint program whose primary purpose is the discovery and interdiction of illegal narcotics.

* * *

In August 1998, the city of Indianapolis began to operate vehicle checkpoints on Indianapolis roads in an effort to interdict unlawful drugs. The city conducted six such roadblocks between August and November that year, stopping 1,161 vehicles and arresting 104 motorists. Fifty-five arrests were for drug-related crimes, while 49 were for offenses unrelated to drugs. The overall "hit rate" of the program was thus approximately nine percent.

The parties stipulated to the facts concerning the operation of the checkpoints by the Indianapolis Police Department (IPD) for purposes of the preliminary injunction proceedings instituted below. At each checkpoint location, the police stop a predetermined number of vehicles. * * * Pursuant to written directives issued by the chief of police, at least one officer approaches the vehicle, advises the driver that he or she is being stopped briefly at a drug checkpoint, and asks the driver to produce a license and registration. The officer also looks for signs of impairment and conducts an open-view examination of the vehicle from the outside. A narcotics-detection dog walks around the outside of each stopped vehicle.

The directives instruct the officers that they may conduct a search only by consent or based on the appropriate quantum of particularized suspicion. The officers must conduct each stop in the same manner until particularized suspicion develops, and the officers have no discretion to stop any vehicle out of sequence. * * * [C]heckpoint locations are selected weeks in advance based on such considerations as area crime statistics and traffic flow. The checkpoints are generally operated during daylight hours and are identified with lighted signs reading, "NARCOTICS CHECKPOINT ___ MILE AHEAD, NARCOTICS K-9 IN USE, BE PREPARED TO STOP." Once a group of cars has been stopped, other traffic proceeds without interruption until all the stopped cars have been processed or diverted for further processing. * * * [T]he average stop for a vehicle not subject to further processing lasts two to three minutes or less.

Respondents James Edmond and Joell Palmer were each stopped at a narcotics checkpoint in late September 1998. Respondents then filed a lawsuit on behalf of themselves and the class of all motorists who had been stopped or were subject to being stopped in the future at the Indianapolis drug checkpoints. Respondents claimed that the roadblocks violated the Fourth Amendment of the United States Constitution. * * * [The court of appeals held that the checkpoints violated the Fourth Amendment.]

* * * A search or seizure is ordinarily unreasonable in the absence of individualized suspicion of wrongdoing. While such suspicion is not an "irreducible" component of reasonableness, *Martinez-Fuerte*, we have recognized only limited circumstances in which the usual rule does not apply. For example, we have upheld certain regimes of suspicionless searches where the program was designed to serve "special needs, beyond the normal need for law enforcement." [The Court describes its drug-testing cases.] We have also allowed searches for certain administrative purposes without particularized suspicion of misconduct, provided that those searches are appropriately limited. See, *e.g.*, New York v. Burger (warrantless administrative inspection of premises of "closely regulated" business); Camara v. Municipal Court of City and County of San Francisco (administrative inspection to ensure compliance with city housing code).

* * *

In *Sitz*, we evaluated the constitutionality of a Michigan highway sobriety checkpoint program. The *Sitz* checkpoint involved brief suspicionless stops of motorists so that police officers could detect signs of intoxication and remove impaired drivers from the road. * * * This checkpoint program was clearly aimed at reducing the immediate hazard posed by the presence of drunk drivers on the highways, and there was an obvious connection between the imperative of highway safety and the law enforcement practice at issue. The gravity of the drunk driving problem and the magnitude of the State's interest in getting drunk drivers off the road weighed heavily in our determination that the program was constitutional.

In *Prouse*, we invalidated a discretionary, suspicionless stop for a spot check of a motorist's driver's license and vehicle registration. The officer's conduct in that case was unconstitutional primarily on account of his exercise of "standardless and unconstrained discretion." We nonetheless acknowledged the States' "vital interest in ensuring that only those qualified to do so are permitted to operate motor vehicles, that these vehicles are fit for safe operation, and hence that licensing, registration, and vehicle inspection requirements are being observed." Accordingly, we suggested that "[q]uestioning of all oncoming traffic at roadblock-type stops" would be a lawful means of serving this interest in highway safety.

We further indicated in *Prouse* that we considered the purposes of such a hypothetical roadblock to be distinct from a general purpose of investigating crime. * * * [T]he common thread of highway safety thus run[s] through *Sitz* and *Prouse* * * *.

It is well established that a vehicle stop at a highway checkpoint effectuates a seizure within the meaning of the Fourth Amendment. The fact that officers walk a narcotics-detection dog around the exterior of each car at the Indianapolis checkpoints does not transform the seizure into a search. See United States v. Place. * * * [W]hat principally distinguishes these checkpoints from those we have previously approved is their primary purpose.

As petitioners concede, the Indianapolis checkpoint program unquestionably has the primary purpose of interdicting illegal narcotics. In their stipulation of facts, the parties repeatedly refer to the checkpoints as "drug checkpoints" and describe them as "being operated by the City of Indianapolis in an effort to interdict unlawful drugs in Indianapolis." In addition, the first document attached to the parties' stipulation is entitled "DRUG CHECKPOINT CONTACT OFFICER DIRECTIVES BY ORDER OF THE CHIEF OF POLICE.". These directives instruct officers to "[a]dvise the citizen that they are being stopped briefly at a drug checkpoint." * * * Further, * * * the checkpoints are identified with lighted signs reading, "NARCOTICS CHECKPOINT ___ MILE AHEAD, NARCOTICS K-9 IN USE, BE PREPARED TO STOP." * * *

We have never approved a checkpoint program whose primary purpose was to detect evidence of ordinary criminal wrongdoing. * * * [E]ach of the checkpoint programs that we have approved was designed primarily to serve purposes closely related to the problems of policing the border or the necessity of ensuring roadway safety. Because the primary purpose of the Indianapolis narcotics checkpoint program is to uncover evidence of ordinary criminal wrongdoing, the program contravenes the Fourth Amendment.

Petitioners propose several ways in which the narcotics-detection purpose of the instant checkpoint program may instead resemble the primary purposes of the checkpoints in *Sitz* and *Martinez-Fuerte.* Petitioners state that the checkpoints in those cases had the same ultimate purpose of arresting those suspected of committing crimes. Securing the border and apprehending drunk drivers are, of course, law enforcement activities, and law enforcement officers employ arrests and criminal prosecutions in pursuit of these goals. If we were to rest the case at this high level of generality, there would be little check on the ability of the authorities to construct roadblocks for almost any conceivable law enforcement purpose. Without drawing the line at roadblocks designed primarily to serve the general interest in crime control, the Fourth Amendment would do little to prevent such intrusions from becoming a routine part of American life.

Petitioners also emphasize the severe and intractable nature of the drug problem as justification for the checkpoint program. There is no doubt that traffic in illegal narcotics creates social harms of the first magnitude. * * * But the gravity of the threat alone cannot be dispositive of questions concerning what means law enforcement officers may employ to pursue a given purpose. Rather, in determining whether individualized suspicion is required, we must consider the nature of the interests threatened and their connection to the particular law enforcement practices at issue. We are particularly reluctant to recognize exceptions to the general rule of individualized suspicion where governmental authorities primarily pursue their general crime control ends.

Nor can the narcotics-interdiction purpose of the checkpoints be rationalized in terms of a highway safety concern similar to that present in *Sitz.* The detection and punishment of almost any criminal offense serves broadly the safety of the community, and our streets would no doubt be safer but for the scourge of illegal drugs. Only with respect to a smaller class of offenses, however, is society confronted with the type of immediate, vehicle-bound threat to life and limb that the sobriety checkpoint in *Sitz* was designed to eliminate.

Petitioners also liken the anticontraband agenda of the Indianapolis checkpoints to the antismuggling purpose of the checkpoints in *Martinez-Fuerte.* Petitioners cite this Court's conclusion in *Martinez-Fuerte* that the flow of traffic was too heavy to permit "particularized study of a given car that would enable it to be identified as a possible carrier of illegal aliens," and claim that this logic has even more force here. The problem with this argument is that the same logic prevails any time a vehicle is employed to conceal contraband or other evidence of a crime. This type of connection to the roadway is very different from the close connection to roadway safety that was present in *Sitz* and *Prouse.* Further, the Indianapolis checkpoints are far removed from the border context that was crucial in *Martinez-Fuerte.* * * *

* * * We decline to suspend the usual requirement of individualized suspicion where the police seek to employ a checkpoint primarily for the ordinary enterprise of investigating crimes. We cannot sanction stops justified only by the generalized and ever-present possibility that interrogation and inspection may reveal that any given motorist has committed some crime.

Of course, there are circumstances that may justify a law enforcement checkpoint where the primary purpose would otherwise, but for some emergency, relate to ordinary crime control. For example * * * the Fourth Amendment would almost certainly permit an appropriately tailored roadblock set up to thwart an imminent terrorist attack or to catch a dangerous criminal who is likely to flee by way of a particular route. The exigencies created by these scenarios are far removed from the circumstances under which authorities might simply stop cars as a matter of course to see if there just happens to be a felon leaving the jurisdiction. While we do not limit the purposes that may justify a checkpoint program to any rigid set of categories, we decline to approve a program whose primary purpose is ultimately indistinguishable from the general interest in crime control.

Petitioners argue that our prior cases preclude an inquiry into the purposes of the checkpoint program. For example, they cite Whren v. United States, * * * to support the proposition that "where the government articulates and pursues a legitimate interest for a suspicionless stop, courts should not look behind that interest to determine whether the government's 'primary purpose' is valid." These cases, however, do not control the instant situation.

In *Whren*, we held that an individual officer's subjective intentions are irrelevant to the Fourth Amendment validity of a traffic stop that is justified objectively by probable cause to believe that a traffic violation has occurred. * * * In so holding, we expressly distinguished cases where we had addressed the validity of searches conducted in the absence of probable cause. * * *

Whren therefore reinforces the principle that, while "[s]ubjective intentions play no role in ordinary, probable-cause Fourth Amendment analysis," programmatic purposes may be relevant to the validity of Fourth Amendment intrusions undertaken pursuant to a general scheme without individualized suspicion. Accordingly, *Whren* does not preclude an inquiry into programmatic purpose in such contexts. It likewise does not preclude an inquiry into programmatic purpose here.

* * *

Petitioners argue that the Indianapolis checkpoint program is justified by its lawful secondary purposes of keeping impaired motorists off the road and verifying licenses and registrations. If this were the case, however, law enforcement authorities would be able to establish checkpoints for virtually any purpose so long as they also included a license or sobriety check. For this reason, we examine the available evidence to determine the primary purpose of the checkpoint program. While we recognize the challenges inherent in a purpose inquiry, courts routinely engage in this enterprise in many areas of constitutional jurisprudence as a means of sifting abusive governmental conduct from that which is lawful. As a result, a program driven by an impermissible purpose may be proscribed while a program impelled by licit purposes is permitted, even though the challenged conduct may be outwardly similar. While reasonableness under the Fourth Amendment is predominantly an objective inquiry, our special needs and administrative search cases demonstrate that purpose is often relevant when suspicionless intrusions pursuant to a general scheme are at issue.[a]

* * *

Our holding also does not affect the validity of border searches or searches at places like airports and government buildings, where the need for such measures to ensure public safety can be particularly acute. Nor does our opinion speak to other intrusions aimed primarily at purposes beyond the general interest in crime control. Our holding also does not impair the ability of police officers to act appropriately upon information that they properly learn during a checkpoint stop justified by a lawful primary purpose, even where such action may result in the arrest of a motorist for an offense unrelated to that purpose. Finally, we caution that the purpose inquiry in this context is to be conducted only at the programmatic level and is not an invitation to probe the minds of individual officers acting at the scene.

Because the primary purpose of the Indianapolis checkpoint program is ultimately indistinguishable from the general interest in crime control, the checkpoints violate the Fourth Amendment. * * *

CHIEF JUSTICE REHNQUIST, with whom JUSTICE THOMAS joins, and with whom JUSTICE SCALIA joins [in relevant part], dissenting.

* * *

* * * The only difference between this case and *Sitz* is the presence of the dog. We have already held, however, that a "sniff test" by a trained narcotics dog is not a "search" within the meaning of the Fourth Amendment because it does not require physical intrusion of the object

---

[a] Because petitioners concede that the primary purpose of the Indianapolis checkpoints is narcotics detection, we need not decide whether the State may establish a checkpoint program with the primary purpose of checking licenses or driver sobriety and a secondary purpose of interdicting narcotics. Specifically, we express no view on the question whether police may expand the scope of a license or sobriety checkpoint seizure in order to detect the presence of drugs in a stopped car.

being sniffed and it does not expose anything other than the contraband items. And there is nothing in the record to indicate that the dog sniff lengthens the stop.

* * *

[T]he Court's newfound non-law-enforcement primary purpose test is both unnecessary to secure Fourth Amendment rights and bound to produce wide-ranging litigation over the "purpose" of any given seizure. Police designing highway roadblocks can never be sure of their validity, since a jury might later determine that a forbidden purpose exists.

* * * [I]f the Indianapolis police had assigned a different purpose to their activity here, but in no way changed what was done on the ground to individual motorists, it might well be valid. [The Chief Justice cites the majority's footnote concerning the possible permissibility of a checkpoint whose secondary purpose is drug interdiction.] The Court's non-law-enforcement primary purpose test simply does not serve as a proxy for anything that the Fourth Amendment is, or should be, concerned about in the automobile seizure context.

* * *

JUSTICE THOMAS, dissenting.

Taken together, our decisions in Michigan Dept. of State Police v. Sitz and United States v. Martinez-Fuerte stand for the proposition that suspicionless roadblock seizures are constitutionally permissible if conducted according to a plan that limits the discretion of the officers conducting the stops. I am not convinced that *Sitz* and *Martinez-Fuerte* were correctly decided. Indeed, I rather doubt that the Framers of the Fourth Amendment would have considered "reasonable" a program of indiscriminate stops of individuals not suspected of wrongdoing.

Respondents did not, however, advocate the overruling of *Sitz* and *Martinez-Fuerte,* and I am reluctant to consider such a step without the benefit of briefing and argument. For the reasons given by The Chief Justice, I believe that those cases compel upholding the program at issue here. I, therefore, join his opinion.

NOTE ON EDMOND AND SECURITY CHECKPOINTS

The *Edmond* majority was concerned that checkpoints would become "a routine part of American life." In the decades after the terrorist attacks of September 11, 2001, security checkpoints have indeed become routine. Many entail not just seizures, but intrusive searches as well (e.g., airport checkpoints). But these checkpoints seem to fall within the majority's perhaps prophetic paragraph permitting security-related checkpoints. And if these checkpoints qualify as "special needs," then the additional step of a search can usually be justified by balancing security interests against individuals' diminished privacy interests.

Terrorism-related checkpoints after 9/11 have been upheld without much difficulty. An example is United States v. Green, 293 F.3d 855 (5th Cir. 2002), upholding a suspicionless roadblock check on an open military installation. The court declared as follows:

> We believe that this case differs substantially from *Edmond* in two respects. First, the protection of the nation's military installations from acts of domestic or international terrorism is a unique endeavor, akin to the policing of our borders, and one in which a greater degree of intrusiveness may be allowed. Second, those cases focusing not on unique, national challenges, but instead on road safety, are concerned with dangers specifically associated with vehicles and therefore justify suspicionless checkpoint seizures. Since we know from painful experience that vehicles are often used to transport and deliver explosives in the form of "car bombs," and that military installations have historically faced greater risk than civilian communities of such a bombing, vehicles pose a special risk.

The majority in *Edmond* also seemed to approve of emergency roadblocks to catch a dangerous criminal, such as were used during the Washington, D.C. area sniper attacks of 2002. See United States v. Arnold, 835 F.3d 833 (8th Cir. 2016) (upholding as reasonable a checkpoint to catch an armed robber). Where is the line, then, between criminal law enforcement and special needs? Or is the Court instead providing for a separate category of checkpoints established to deal exigent circumstances? Serious crimes?

Drug Interdiction as a Secondary Purpose

The majority in *Edmond* dropped a footnote to state that it was not deciding whether checkpoints are invalid if they have drug interdiction as a *secondary* purpose. Throughout the opinion, the Court emphasizes that the *primary* purpose of the Indianapolis checkpoint was drug interdiction, as opposed to a vehicle-related threat to public safety. After *Edmond,* courts have upheld checkpoints where the articulated primary purpose effectuates special needs beyond law enforcement—even though there is also a secondary purpose of drug interdiction. See, e.g., United States v. Davis, 270 F.3d 977 (D.C. Cir. 2001) (checkpoint not invalidated by secondary purpose of drug interdiction, noting that *Edmond* "more than suggests that if the 'primary purpose' had been for a purpose the Court endorsed—such as detecting drunk drivers, or checking licenses—the roadblock would be constitutional."); United States v. Moreno-Vargas, 315 F.3d 489 (5th Cir. 2002) (use of drug-detecting dogs at a permanent fixed immigration checkpoint does not invalidate the checkpoint stops; drug interdiction was a permissible secondary purpose of the checkpoint).

Assuming there is a constitutional distinction between primary and secondary purposes, how hard is it for the government to evade the Court's holding in *Edmond*? What prevents the government from labeling its checkpoint a "sobriety" or "registration" checkpoint, and keeping a drug detecting dog at the checkpoint as part of a specified "secondary" purpose?

Drug-Detection as a Vehicle-Related Safety Interest

The *Edmond* Court distinguished sobriety checkpoints from the Indianapolis drug interdiction checkpoint on the ground that drunk drivers present an immediate, vehicle-related safety threat while drug dealers do not raise a specific safety issue merely by driving. Does this mean that suspicionless drug checkpoints would be permitted if they are styled as an attempt to detect those who are driving *under the influence* of drugs? Might these checkpoints be more reasonable in states where the consumption of marijuana is legal?

What if the state can make a reasonable argument that drug dealers do indeed create a vehicle-related threat to safety? Are those engaged in illegal narcotics trafficking more likely to drive recklessly? In United States v. Davis, 270 F.3d 977 (D.C. Cir. 2001), the court upheld a checkpoint established in response to community complaints that drug dealers and buyers in cars were speeding, committing illegal U-turns, and causing traffic congestion. The Court noted that the primary purpose of the roadblock was to remedy the traffic problems caused by drug activity and "[w]hatever advantage was gained in drug enforcement was coincidental to the principal purpose of the traffic roadblocks." If this is correct, how much is left of the majority opinion in *Edmond*? Does the fact that there was a documented traffic problem in *Davis* make a difference?

Suspicionless Checkpoints to Obtain Information About a Crime: Illinois v. Lidster

In Illinois v. Lidster, 540 U.S. 439 (2004), Justice Breyer wrote for the Court as it upheld a highway checkpoint where motorists were stopped, without suspicion, so that police could ask them about a recent hit-and-run accident. The roadblock was established about a week after the accident on the same highway where the accident occurred and at about the same time of night. Lidster was driving a minivan as he approached the checkpoint, his van swerved and nearly hit one of the officers, and eventually Lidster was arrested for and convicted of driving under the influence.

Justice Breyer reasoned that the checkpoint stop was different from *Edmund* because the officers were not stopping cars to determine whether occupants were committing crimes and the objective of the Illinois roadblock was not to further a "general interest in crime control," He concluded that information-seeking highway stops are less likely to provoke anxiety or to prove intrusive than other stops and "citizens will often react positively when police simply ask for their help as responsible citizens to give whatever information they may have to aid law enforcement." Justice Breyer found that the roadblock was reasonable given that "[t]he relevant public concern was grave" in light of the fact that the accident has resulted in a death, "[t]he stop advanced this grave public concern to a significant degree," and "[t]he police appropriately tailored their checkpoint stops to fit important criminal investigatory needs."

Justice Stevens, joined by Justices Souter and Ginsburg, concurred in part and dissented in part. He agreed that *Edmunds* was not controlling, but found that the reasonableness of the checkpoint was a close question that justified a remand.

6. Inventory Searches

In most jurisdictions it is standard procedure for the police to inventory the contents of automobiles and other containers being held in their custody. An inventory search is not based on probable cause that evidence will be found, and *ostensibly* is unrelated to criminal investigation of any kind. As one court has put it, the police are allowed to conduct inventory searches without a warrant and without suspicion, in order "to protect the owner's property while it is in police custody, to protect the police against claims of lost or stolen property, and to protect the police and the public from potential danger." The traditional requirements of warrant and probable cause are excused because inventory searches serve a "caretaking" function and "are not designed to uncover evidence of criminal activity." United States v. Andrews, 22 F.3d 1328 (5th Cir.1994).

As with other "special needs" searches, the lack of any requirement for a warrant or particularized suspicion raises concerns about unregulated discretion that traces to founding-era objections to general warrants and writs of assistance. To control that discretion, the government must show that the officer was operating pursuant to established inventory procedures promulgated by their police department. See United States v. Petty, 367 F.3d 1009 (8th Cir. 2004) ("Some degree of standardized criteria or established routine must regulate these police actions * * * to ensure that impoundments and inventory searches are not merely a ruse for general rummaging in order to discover incriminating evidence.").

Community Caretaking Function

The Supreme Court has analyzed warrantless, suspicionless inventory searches in several instances. In Cady v. Dombrowski, 413 U.S. 433 (1973), the Court approved the search of a car towed to a private garage after an accident that resulted in the hospitalization of the driver. The driver was a Chicago policeman, and the officer who conducted the search testified that he was looking for the driver's service revolver, which he believed Chicago policemen were required to carry at all times. In the course of the search, blood-stained garments were discovered in the trunk, which were later used to convict the defendant of murder. In a 5–4 decision, Justice Rehnquist found that the initial intrusion to search for the gun was reasonable as a "community caretaking function," to protect the public from the possibility that it would fall into the hands of vandals. Therefore, the seizure of evidence found in plain view was also justified.

In *Caniglia v. Strom*, 141 S.Ct. 1596 (2021), a unanimous Court held that the "caretaking function" language in *Cady* does not create a "standalone doctrine that justifies warrantless searches and seizures in the home." In *Caniglia*, law enforcement officers responded to a report that Edward Caniglia was potentially suicidal. Caniglia agreed to go by ambulance to a hospital for evaluation, but denied officers' requests to search his home for firearms. After Caniglia left for the hospital, the officers entered his home, conducted a search, and seized two handguns. Caniglia sued alleging violations of his Fourth Amendment rights. In their defense, the officers cited *Cady* as grounds for conducting a search relating to their public caretaking function. Drawing a bright line between an "impounded vehicle" and a home, Justice Thomas, writing for the majority, concluded that "What is reasonable for vehicles is different from what is reasonable for homes," and declined to endorse a broad caretaking function that would justify warrantless intrusions into homes.

In a series of concurring opinions, Chief Justice Roberts (joined by Justice Breyer), Justice Alito, and Justice Kavanaugh made clear that the Court's holding in *Caniglia* left undisturbed established doctrines such as the exigency exception to the warrant requirement and the special needs doctrine, each of which might provide authority for law enforcement officers to enter a home to prevent a possible suicide or to determine the welfare of an elderly resident who may have suffered an injury. Because such circumstances were not presented to the Court by the facts in *Caniglia*, the Court left for another day the task of describing the contours of Fourth Amendment rules governing these kinds of cases.

Warrantless, Suspicionless Searches: South Dakota v. Opperman

Two years after *Cady,* the Court upheld the warrantless, suspicionless inventory search of a car impounded for a parking violation. Chief Justice Burger, writing for the Court in South Dakota v. Opperman, 428 U.S. 364 (1976), emphasized that the search was conducted pursuant to standard police procedures, which helped to guarantee that the intrusion "would be limited to the scope necessary to carry out the caretaking function." The majority found the search of Opperman's impounded car to be a reasonable means of protecting valuables, which could be seen in plain view on the dashboard. Opperman argued that it was unreasonable for the officers to break open the lock of his car and search the glove compartment, where they found marijuana. The Court held that these actions were reasonable because they were authorized, and indeed mandated, by local police regulations.

As in other special needs cases, the *Opperman* Court balanced the state interests at stake against the intrusiveness of the search to determine whether inventory searches were reasonable. The Court found that three legitimate state interests support an inventory search: 1) protection of the police department from false property claims; 2) protection of the property interests of the owner; and 3) protection of the police and public from dangerous items. The Court concluded that these state interests, which could only be effectuated by a suspicionless search, outweighed the owner's privacy interests, especially given the diminished expectation of privacy in automobiles.

In a concurring opinion, Justice Powell explained why the warrant requirement is inapposite when an inventory search is conducted pursuant to departmental regulations: First, there are no special facts for a neutral magistrate to evaluate so as to determine whether probable cause exists because inventory searches are non-criminal in nature. Second, there is no danger of discretionary searches or hindsight justifications when searches are conducted in accordance with standard procedures. Third, there is no danger of arbitrariness when all impounded cars are searched routinely.

Justice Marshall—in a dissent joined by Justices Brennan and Stewart, and in part by Justice White—argued that warrantless, suspicionless inventory searches could not be justified by any "special need." He found the safety rationale—i.e., that inventory searches protected the police and public from dangerous items—to be overbroad because every automobile and container poses at least some hypothetical threat to safety. Justice Marshall concluded that an "undifferentiated possibility of harm" cannot serve as a basis for an inventory search, and that the safety rationale was only implicated where specific circumstances indicate the possibility of a particular danger—such as in *Cady*, where the officers reasonably believed that the defendant had a gun in his car.

Next, Justice Marshall considered the assertion that inventories are necessary to protect the police against lost property claims. In this case, the concern was irrelevant because South Dakota law absolved police of responsibility as "gratuitous depositors" beyond inventorying objects in plain view and locking the car. Furthermore, an inventory does not discourage false claims that an item was stolen prior to the search, or was intentionally omitted from police records. Nor does it ensure that such police misconduct did not in fact occur.

Finally, Justice Marshall derided the assertion that impoundment and search of property is a reasonable means of protecting the owner's property interests. In his view, the property owner's interests are best known by the property owner himself; if the owner feels that impoundment and search are needed to protect his property, then he can simply consent.

Property Carried by an Arrestee: Illinois v. Lafayette

The Supreme Court relied on South Dakota v. Opperman in Illinois v. Lafayette, 462 U.S. 640 (1983), as it upheld the inventory search at the police station of a shoulder bag belonging to a man arrested for disturbing the peace. The search uncovered drugs. Chief Justice Burger reasoned that the government's interests in an inventory search at the stationhouse "may in some circumstances be even greater that those supporting a search incident to arrest" and that police conduct that might be embarrassingly intrusive on the street could be handled privately at the stationhouse. The Chief Justice asserted that the three interests supporting an inventory search were fully applicable to a stationhouse search of an arrestee's possessions: police need to protect the property of arrested persons, to protect themselves from claims of theft or damage to property, and to remove dangerous instrumentalities from arrestees.

The lower court in *Lafayette* had found the inventory search unreasonable on the ground that preservation of the property could have been achieved in a less intrusive manner—such as by storing the bag rather than investigating its contents. Chief Justice Burger rejected this "less intrusive alternative" reasoning, stating as follows:

> The reasonableness of any particular governmental activity does not necessarily or invariably turn on the existence of alternative less intrusive means. * * * Even if less intrusive means existed of protecting some particular types of property, it would be unreasonable to expect police officers in the everyday course of business to make fine and subtle distinctions in deciding which containers or items may be searched and which must be sealed as a unit.

In a footnote, the Court stated that the inventory search of Lafayette's bag might have been invalid if he was not going to be incarcerated after being booked for disturbing the peace.[31] If the arrestee is going to be released immediately, then the interests supporting an inventory search would not appear to be implicated. Justice Marshall, joined by Justice Brennan, concurred in the judgment.

---

[31] A number of courts have held that a preincarceration inventory search is improper if the arrestee, upon posting collateral, has a right to immediate release. See, e.g., United States v. Mills, 472 F.2d 1231 (D.C.Cir.1972); People v. Dixon, 392 Mich. 691, 222 N.W.2d 749 (1974).

Limits on Police Discretion: Colorado v. Bertine

Opperman and *Lafayette* supported the Supreme Court's decision in Colorado v. Bertine, 479 U.S. 367 (1987), holding that police officers could inventory the contents of a van, including a closed backpack and a nylon bag and other containers within it. Chief Justice Rehnquist's opinion for the Court rejected an argument that the impoundment of the car was unjustified because the driver could have been offered the opportunity to make arrangements for the safekeeping of his property. The Court concluded that "reasonable police regulations relating to inventory procedures administered in good faith satisfy the Fourth Amendment, even though courts might as a matter of hindsight be able to devise equally reasonable rules requiring a different procedure."

The *Bertine* Court also rejected the defendant's claim that the inventory was impermissible because departmental regulations gave police officers discretion to decide whether to impound the van or to park and lock it in a public parking lot. The Chief Justice noted that the regulations established several factors by which the officer was to determine whether to impound the vehicle or instead exercise a park and lock alternative. The regulations permitted impoundment only in two conditions: if leaving the car would present a real risk of damage or vandalism to the car; or if approval to leave the car could not be obtained from the owner. The majority held that these conditions were sufficiently concrete and understandable to reasonably limit the discretion of the officer—providing a satisfactory substitute to the proof requirements of probable cause or reasonable suspicion. The Court concluded that "nothing in *Opperman* or *Lafayette* prohibits the exercise of police discretion so long as that discretion is exercised according to standard criteria and on the basis of something other than suspicion of criminal activity."

Bertine also challenged the opening of the containers found in his car, on the ground that the inventorying officer did not properly weigh the privacy interest in the container against the risk that it might serve as a repository for dangerous or valuable items. The majority again rejected a less intrusive means analysis for opening containers in an inventory search. In a footnote, the Court emphasized that "the police department procedures mandated the opening of closed containers and the listing of their contents." Thus, the officer's discretion as to what to open was limited by the inventory rules that were in place.

Justice Blackmun, joined by Justices Powell and O'Connor, concurred and wrote separately "to underscore the importance of having such inventories conducted only pursuant to standardized police procedures." Justice Marshall, joined by Justice Brennan, dissented. He urged that the officers did not act according to standards that sufficiently controlled their discretion and he repeated the arguments he made in *Opperman* that the government's interests in conducting an inventory search did not outweigh the property owner's privacy interests.

Unlimited Police Discretion Invalidates an Inventory Search: Florida v. Wells

The Court revisited the subject of police discretion in conducting inventory searches in Florida v. Wells, 495 U.S. 1 (1990). A unanimous Court found that the opening of a locked suitcase could not be justified as an inventory search where the Florida Highway Patrol had *no policy whatever* concerning the opening of closed containers. Chief Justice Rehnquist, writing for the Court, found the search to be insufficiently regulated by standardized police procedures. However, the Chief Justice took issue with a statement by the Florida Supreme Court that "the police under *Bertine* must mandate either that all containers will be opened during an inventory search, or that no containers will be opened. There can be no room for discretion." According to the Court in *Wells*, the Fourth Amendment does allow the officer *some* latitude to decide whether a container may be opened in an inventory search. This discretion can be exercised, pursuant to departmental regulations, "in light of the nature of the search and the characteristics of the container itself." The Chief Justice concluded:

> While policies of opening all containers or of opening no containers are unquestionably permissible, it would be equally permissible, for example, to allow the opening of closed containers whose contents officers determine they are unable to ascertain from examining the contents' exteriors. The allowance of the exercise of judgment based on concerns related to the purpose of an inventory search does not violate the Fourth Amendment.

This dictum prompted sharp responses in opinions by Justice Brennan (joined by Justice Marshall), Justice Blackmun, and Justice Stevens, all of whom concurred in the judgment. These Justices generally argued that to allow the individual officer any discretion to determine whether a container should be opened would create an unacceptable risk of abuse. Justice Brennan noted that the *Bertine* Court had allowed the officer some discretion as to whether to impound a car, but no discretion as to whether to open a container therein. He concluded that "attempting to cast doubt on the vitality of the holding in *Bertine* in this otherwise easy case is not justified." In response to Justice Brennan's characterization of the *Bertine* "holding," the Chief Justice stated that, while the departmental rules at issue in *Bertine* called for opening all containers, the Court did not actually hold that an all-or-nothing rule was required by the Fourth Amendment.

After *Wells,* would a policy allowing police officers to open containers "if they reasonably appear to contain valuables" be upheld? See United

States v. Mundy, 621 F.3d 283 (3d Cir. 2010) ("Though the [police department's inventory policy] does not contain magic words [specific] to closed containers, its reference to 'any personal property of value' sufficiently regulated the scope of a permissible inventory search, and therefore authorized the opening of the shoebox in Mundy's trunk to determine if such property was contained therein."). See also United States v. Andrews, 22 F.3d 1328 (5th Cir.1994) (upholding search of a notebook pursuant to departmental regulations authorizing officers to search property when necessary "to protect the city from claims of lost property").

In the end, there may be no way to eliminate the exercise of discretion in an inventory seizure and search. Certainly a rule requiring the "impoundment of all cars" would not be practicable, given the various fact situations in which officers come upon cars that might be subject to impoundment. And an all-or-nothing rule as applied to opening containers, would still require discretion to determine whether a certain item is or is not a container. For example, if the inventorying officer finds a fountain pen in a car, must she open up the pen under a policy requiring the opening of all containers? What if she finds a teddy bear? See United States v. Petty, 367 F.3d 1009 (8th Cir. 2004) (impoundment and inventory regulations "may allow some latitude and exercise of judgment by a police officer when those decisions are based on concerns related to the purposes" of the impoundment or inventory; noting that it is "not feasible for a police department to develop a policy that provides clear cut guidance" in every potential impoundment or inventory situation).

The Problem of Pretext

The emphasis in *Opperman* and *Bertine* on standardized inventory procedures reflects concern that, guidelines, investigatory searches for evidence of crime may be conducted under the guise of inventories. As we have seen in other areas, however, the fact that the officer is guided by bright line, all-or-nothing, rules does not eliminate the possibility of pretextual searches. And, as in other areas, the fact that the officer may have a pretextual motive is usually held irrelevant if the search itself is objectively reasonable. See, e.g., United States v. Hawkins, 279 F.3d 83 (1st Cir. 2002) ("Appellant also challenges the search saying that the inventory was clearly a 'ruse' used to search for drugs. Regardless of what appellant suggests, the law is clear. The subjective intent of the officers is not relevant so long as they conduct a search according to a standardized inventory policy."); United States v. Kanatzar, 370 F.3d 810 (8th Cir.2004) ("The presence of an investigative motive does not invalidate an otherwise valid inventory search.").

On the other hand, if the officer is acting without guidelines, as in *Wells,* or if the officer *disregards guidelines to obtain evidence,* then the search cannot be justified as an inventory search. An example of the latter is where the officer opens only a few containers in an impounded automobile, or fails to file an inventory list where such a filing is required. See United States v. Parr, 716 F.2d 796 (11th Cir.1983) (search cannot be justified as an inventory search where items were selectively investigated). As the court put it in United States v. Rowland, 341 F.3d 774 (8th Cir. 2003), in finding an illegal search where officers inventoried the evidence of crime but not other items of value in the car:

> In sum, law enforcement had standardized procedures in place but failed to follow them here. Such failure, coupled with the fact the officers disregarded items without evidentiary value * * * suggests they did not search the vehicle in order to safeguard the vehicle's contents from loss, or to protect law enforcement personnel from harm, or even to guard the department and county against a possible lawsuit. Rather, it appears law enforcement sifted through the vehicle's contents searching only for and recording only incriminating evidence; something law enforcement may not do.

See also United States v. Proctor, 489 F.3d 1348 (D.C. Cir. 2007) ("Because the officers failed to follow the MPD standard procedure, the impoundment of Proctor's vehicle was unreasonable and thus violated the Fourth Amendment.").

Less Onerous Alternatives

The problem of pretextual inventory searches could be regulated by requiring police officers to use the least onerous alternative in effectuating the state interests involved. For example, impoundment of a car could be prohibited if someone who was not being arrested is on the scene and could simply drive it away—the "drive away" alternative would protect the police from false claims, protect the owner's interest, and protect against safety risks, without necessitating an intrusive seizure. Similarly, a search of the car and containers in the car could be prohibited if the officer could simply seal the car to prevent entry. A container might also be sealed or locked, thus protecting the owner's valuables and protecting the police from false claims, without the intrusion of a search.

However, these arguments are based on a less intrusive means analysis, which the Supreme Court has rejected in *Lafayette* and *Bertine*. According to those cases, the issue is not whether a less intrusive alternative exists that would equally effectuate state interests. Rather, the issue is whether the alternative chosen is a reasonable means of accommodating the interests of the state and the privacy interests of citizens. So, while police departments are free to use these less onerous alternatives, they are not required to do so under the Fourth Amendment. See United States v. Betterton, 417 F.3d 826 (8th Cir. 2005) ("Nothing in the Fourth Amendment requires a police department to allow an arrested person to arrange for another person to pick up his car to avoid impoundment and inventory.").

Why does the Supreme Court reject the less intrusive alternative arguments in the inventory cases? Professor Maclin points out that the Court has required the State to employ less intrusive means when other constitutional rights, such as First Amendment rights, are involved. He proffers the following explanation for this apparent disparity in constitutional standards.

> The Court is uninterested in placing the Fourth Amendment in the category of preferred constitutional rights, including the rights of free speech, freedom of religion, and freedom from racial discrimination, despite its specific placement in the Bill of Rights.
>
> * * *
>
> Why is the Fourth Amendment considered a second-class right? My guess is that the Court sees the typical Fourth Amendment claimant as a second-class citizen, and sees the typical police officer as being overwhelmed with the responsibilities and duties of maintaining law and order in our crime-prone society. This dual perception may explain the Court's reluctance to subject police conduct to vigorous judicial oversight.

Maclin, The Central Meaning of the Fourth Amendment, 35 Wm. & Mary L.Rev. 197, 237 (1993). Can you see any reason to distinguish between, for example, First and Fourth Amendment protections? Is the difference that the Fourth Amendment specifically emphasizes reasonableness, while the First Amendment is written in more absolute terms?

Searches and Seizures That Serve No Inventory Interest

An inventory search that effectuates state interests in securing property, guarding against theft claims, and protecting officers and the public must be distinguished from an impoundment or search that effectuates *none* of those state interests. For example, it might not be reasonable to impound a vehicle parked in a locked garage attached to an arrestee's home because a seizure in this circumstance is not necessary to effectuate the interests that support an impoundment in the first place. Likewise, it may not be reasonable to vacuum a car's interior to "inventory" carpet fibers because there is no safety risk, no chance of a claim for lost property, and no need to protect the owner from the chance that his carpet fibers will be stolen. For example, in United States v. Showalter, 858 F.2d 149 (3d Cir.1988), the government sought to justify the search of an entire *residence* under the inventory exception. The court stated that "none of the factors which have been used to justify the warrantless inventory search of an automobile are present * * * when generally applied to the home." Similarly, in United States v. Best, 135 F.3d 1223 (8th Cir.1998), in the course of an "inventory" search an officer pried open the door panel of a car and discovered drugs. The court held the search invalid because it "did not serve the purpose of protecting the car and its contents."

Inventory Searches of Cellphones

What if an officer, properly conducting an inventory search of a car, comes upon a cellphone? Can the officer search through the phone? Under California v. Riley, a search of a cellphone must at a minimum promote the interests supported by a particular exception. The inventory exception is based on protecting property, maintaining security, and defending against false claims. Are any of those interests promoted by the search of a cellphone? If so, then how would they be weighed against the considerable privacy interests afforded to the contents of cellphones under *Riley*?

7. Border Searches

Customs and immigration officials have broad authority to conduct warrantless searches at international borders. This authority is justified by the government's special interest in protecting American borders "in order to regulate the collection of duties and to prevent the introduction of contraband into this country." United States v. Johnson, 991 F.2d 1287 (7th Cir.1993). As the Court stated in United States v. Montoya de Hernandez, 473 U.S. 531 (1985):

> At the border, customs officials have more than merely an investigative law enforcement role. They are also charged, along with immigration officials, with protecting this Nation from entrants who may bring anything harmful into this country, whether that be communicable diseases, narcotics, or explosives.

Because the border search serves special needs, it is evaluated under the reasonableness clause of the Fourth Amendment. Given the heavy state interest just stated, as well as the diminished expectation of privacy attendant to a border crossing, border searches are ordinarily deemed reasonable without a warrant or probable cause, and often without any suspicion at all. See United States v. Robles, 45 F.3d 1 (1st Cir.1995) ("routine border searches, conducted for the purposes of collecting duties and intercepting contraband destined for the interior of the United States, do not require reasonable suspicion, probable cause, or a warrant").

Warrantless, Suspicionless Search of International Mail: United States v. Ramsey

In United States v. Ramsey, 431 U.S. 606 (1977), Customs officials opened eight envelopes sent to the United States from Thailand, as part of an investigation of a heroin-by-mail enterprise in the Washington, D.C. area. Ramsey argued that the envelopes could not be opened without a warrant and probable cause. Writing for the Court, Justice Rehnquist disagreed. He analyzed the constitutionality of border searches as follows:

> That searches made at the border, pursuant to the longstanding right of the sovereign to protect itself by stopping and examining persons and property crossing into this country, are reasonable simply by virtue of the fact that they occur at the border should, by now, require no extended demonstration. The Congress which proposed the Bill of Rights, including the Fourth Amendment, to the state legislatures on September 25, 1789, 1 Stat. 97, had, some two months prior to that proposal, enacted the first customs statute, Act of July 31, 1789, c. 5, 1 Stat. 29. Section 24 of this statute granted customs officials "full power and authority" to enter and search "any ship or vessel, in which they shall have reason to suspect any goods, wares or merchandise subject to duty shall be concealed * * *." The historical importance of the enactment of this customs statute by the same Congress which proposed the Fourth Amendment is, we think, manifest. * * *
>
> * * *
>
> Border searches, then, from before the adoption of the Fourth Amendment, have been considered to be "reasonable" by the single fact that the person or item in question had entered into our country from outside. There has never been any additional requirement that the reasonableness of a border search depended on the existence of probable cause. This longstanding recognition that searches at our borders without probable cause and without a warrant are nonetheless "reasonable" has a history as old as the Fourth Amendment itself. We reaffirm it now.

The defendant in *Ramsey* argued that the border search doctrine should not apply to international *mail*, because it is not carried across the border by a traveler. But Justice Rehnquist found nothing special about information (as opposed to people) crossing the border.

> The border-search exception is grounded in the recognized right of the sovereign to control, subject to substantive limitations imposed by the Constitution, who and what may enter the country. It is clear that there is nothing in the rationale behind the border-search exception which suggests that the mode of entry will be critical. It was

conceded at oral argument that customs officials could search, without probable cause and without a warrant, envelopes carried by an entering traveler, whether in his luggage or on his person. Surely no different constitutional standard should apply simply because the envelopes were mailed, not carried. The critical fact is that the envelopes cross the border and enter this country, not that they are brought in by one mode of transportation rather than another. It is their entry into this country from without it that makes a resulting search "reasonable."

Justice Stevens, joined by Justices Brennan and Marshall, dissented in *Ramsey*, arguing that Congress did not confer authority to open letters without probable cause. Justice Powell wrote a concurring opinion.

The Court in *Ramsey* says the "mode of transportation" into the country makes no difference. Does that mean that the government can search emails sent from abroad to someone in America? Can the government intercept telephone communications coming into America without a warrant or probable cause? What about examining the contents of cellphones or other electronic devices carried across the border?

"Routine" Border Searches

The court in United States v. Charleus, 871 F.2d 265 (2d Cir.1989), states that "routine border searches of the personal belongings and effects of entrants may be conducted without regard to probable cause or reasonable suspicion." Such searches are deemed reasonable because of the important state interest involved in regulating the border, the diminished expectation of privacy attendant to crossing the border, and the relatively limited intrusiveness of a "routine" border search. Does the lesser expectation of privacy in luggage carried into the country justify warrantless border searches, or does the existence of such searches reduce one's expectation of privacy?

While suspicionless border searches are generally reasonable, it is possible that "the rule as to nonroutine border searches is, however, different." United States v. Robles, 45 F.3d 1 (1st Cir.1995). Because they are more intrusive, "non-routine" border searches must be supported by some level of individualized suspicion.

In the following case, the Supreme Court criticizes the use of the labels "routine" and "non-routine"—at least as applied to searches of vehicles—and finds an unusual search reasonable even in the absence of suspicion.

UNITED STATES V. FLORES-MONTANO

Supreme Court of the United States, 2004.
541 U.S. 149.

CHIEF JUSTICE REHNQUIST delivered the opinion of the Court.

Customs officials seized 37 kilograms—a little more than 81 pounds—of marijuana from respondent Manuel Flores-Montano's gas tank at the international border. The Court of Appeals for the Ninth Circuit * * * held that the Fourth Amendment forbade the fuel tank search absent reasonable suspicion. We hold that the search in question did not require reasonable suspicion.

Respondent, driving a 1987 Ford Taurus station wagon, attempted to enter the United States at the Otay Mesa Port of Entry in southern California. A customs inspector conducted an inspection of the station wagon, and requested respondent to leave the vehicle. The vehicle was then taken to a secondary inspection station.

At the secondary station, a second customs inspector inspected the gas tank by tapping it, and noted that the tank sounded solid. Subsequently, the inspector requested a mechanic under contract with Customs to come to the border station to remove the tank. Within 20 to 30 minutes, the mechanic arrived. He raised the car on a hydraulic lift, loosened the straps and unscrewed the bolts holding the gas tank to the undercarriage of the vehicle, and then disconnected some hoses and electrical connections. After the gas tank was removed, the inspector hammered off Bondo (a putty-like hardening substance that is used to seal openings) from the top of the gas tank. The inspector opened an access plate underneath the Bondo and found 37 kilograms of marijuana bricks. The process took 15 to 25 minutes.

* * *

The Government advised the District Court that it was not relying on reasonable suspicion as a basis for denying respondent's suppression motion * * *.

* * * [T]he Court of Appeals * * * asked whether the removal and dismantling of the defendant's fuel tank is a "routine" border search for which no suspicion whatsoever is required. The Court of Appeals stated that "in order to conduct a search that goes beyond the routine, an inspector must have reasonable suspicion," and the "critical factor" in determining whether a search is "routine" is the "degree of intrusiveness."

The Court of Appeals seized on language from our opinion in United States v. Montoya de Hernandez, 473 U.S. 531 (1985), in which we used the word "routine" as a descriptive term in discussing border searches. ("Routine searches of the persons and effects of entrants are not subject to any requirement of reasonable suspicion, probable cause, or warrant"). The Court of Appeals took the term "routine," fashioned a new balancing test, and extended it to searches of vehicles. But the reasons that might support a requirement of some level of suspicion in the case of highly intrusive searches of the person—dignity and privacy interests of the person being searched—simply do not carry over to vehicles. Complex balancing tests to determine what is a "routine" search of a vehicle, as opposed to a more "intrusive" search of a person, have no place in border searches of vehicles.

The Government's interest in preventing the entry of unwanted persons and effects is at its zenith at the international border. Time and again, we have stated that "searches made at the border, pursuant to the longstanding right of the sovereign to protect itself by stopping and examining persons and property crossing into this country, are reasonable simply by virtue of the fact that they occur at the border." * * * It is axiomatic that the United States, as sovereign, has the inherent authority to protect, and a paramount interest in protecting, its territorial integrity.

That interest in protecting the borders is illustrated in this case by the evidence that smugglers frequently attempt to penetrate our borders with contraband secreted in their automobiles' fuel tank. Over the past 5 1/2 fiscal years, there have been 18,788 vehicle drug seizures at the southern California ports of entry. Of those 18,788, gas tank drug seizures have accounted for 4,619 of the vehicle drug seizures, or approximately 25%. In addition, instances of persons smuggled in and around gas tank compartments are discovered at the ports of entry of San Ysidro and Otay Mesa at a rate averaging 1 approximately every 10 days.

Respondent asserts two main arguments with respect to his Fourth Amendment interests. First, he urges that he has a privacy interest in his fuel tank, and that the suspicionless disassembly of his tank is an invasion of his privacy. But on many occasions, we have noted that the expectation of privacy is less at the border than it is in the interior. We have long recognized that automobiles seeking entry into this country may be searched. It is difficult to imagine how the search of a gas tank, which should be solely a repository for fuel, could be more of an invasion of privacy than the search of the automobile's passenger compartment.

Second, respondent argues that the Fourth Amendment "protects property as well as privacy," and that the disassembly and reassembly of his gas tank is a significant deprivation of his property interest because it may damage the vehicle. He does not, and on the record cannot, truly contend that the procedure of removal, disassembly, and reassembly of the fuel tank in this case or any other has resulted in serious damage to, or destruction of, the property.[a] According to the Government, for example, in

[a] Respondent's reliance on cases involving exploratory drilling searches is misplaced. See United States v. Rivas, 157 F.3d 364 (CA5 1998) (drilling into body of trailer required reasonable suspicion); United States v. Robles, 45 F.3d 1 (CA1 1995) (drilling into machine part required reasonable suspicion); United States v. Carreon, 872 F.2d 1436 (CA10 1989) (drilling into camper required reasonable suspicion). We have no reason at this time to pass on the reasonableness of

fiscal year 2003, 348 gas tank searches conducted along the southern border were negative (*i.e.*, no contraband was found), the gas tanks were reassembled, and the vehicles continued their entry into the United States without incident.

Respondent cites not a single accident involving the vehicle or motorist in the many thousands of gas tank disassemblies that have occurred at the border. A gas tank search involves a brief procedure that can be reversed without damaging the safety or operation of the vehicle. If damage to a vehicle were to occur, the motorist might be entitled to recovery. While the interference with a motorist's possessory interest is not insignificant when the Government removes, disassembles, and reassembles his gas tank, it nevertheless is justified by the Government's paramount interest in protecting the border.[b]

For the reasons stated, we conclude that the Government's authority to conduct suspicionless inspections at the border includes the authority to remove, disassemble, and reassemble a vehicle's fuel tank. While it may be true that some searches of property are so destructive as to require a different result, this was not one of them. * * *

JUSTICE BREYER, concurring.

I join the Court's opinion in full. I also note that Customs keeps track of the border searches its agents conduct, including the reasons for the searches. This administrative process should help minimize concerns that gas tank searches might be undertaken in an abusive manner.

QUESTIONS AFTER FLORES-MONTANO

The Court dropped a footnote in *Flores-Montano* indicating that it was leaving open whether drilling into a vehicle would be reasonable without suspicion of any crime or violation. Lower courts after *Flores-Montano* have taken that footnote as an invitation to uphold suspicionless drilling and other types of (limited) destruction of property at the border. For example, in United

---

drilling, but simply note the obvious factual difference that this case involves the procedure of removal, disassembly, and reassembly of a fuel tank, rather than potentially destructive drilling. We again leave open the question "whether, and under what circumstances, a border search might be deemed 'unreasonable' because of the particularly offensive manner it is carried out." United States v. Ramsey.

[b] Respondent also argued that he has some sort of Fourth Amendment right not to be subject to delay at the international border and that the need for the use of specialized labor, as well as the hour actual delay here and the potential for even greater delay for reassembly are an invasion of that right. Respondent points to no cases indicating the Fourth Amendment shields entrants from inconvenience or delay at the international border.

The procedure in this case took about an hour (including the wait for the mechanic). At oral argument, the Government advised us that, depending on the type of car, a search involving the disassembly and reassembly of a gas tank may take one to two hours. We think it clear that delays of one to two hours at international borders are to be expected.

States v. Chaudhry, 424 F.3d 1051 (9th Cir. 2005), the court upheld a suspicionless border search that included drilling a hole in the bed of a pickup truck. Relying on *Flores-Montano,* the court declared that "a single small diameter hole in a truck bed does not reduce the functionality, operation or safety of the vehicle." The defendant cited cases from other circuits holding that drilling requires reasonable suspicion, but the court noted that all of those cases were decided before *Flores-Montano*, and all of them relied on "the distinction between 'routine' and 'non-routine' searches, a distinction that was specifically limited to searches of the person by the Supreme Court." See also United States v. Cortez-Rocha, 383 F.3d 1093 (9th Cir. 2004) (border search of defendant's vehicle, which included cutting open the defendant's spare tire, did not require reasonable suspicion: "the search of the spare tire, which neither damages the vehicle nor decreases the safety of operation of the vehicle, is not so destructive as to be unreasonable").

In *Flores-Montano,* the government "advised the District Court that it was not relying on reasonable suspicion as a basis for denying respondent's suppression motion." This was so even though the defendant avoided eye contact during questioning at the border, his hands were shaking when he produced identification, the agent tapped on the gas tank and noticed that it sounded solid, and a narcotics detection dog alerted on the vehicle. Despite having an excellent case of reasonable suspicion on the facts, the government argued for the broader point that dismantling a gas tank is reasonable at the border, in all cases, even if a car is plucked at random or at the officer's whim.

Why did the government in *Flores-Montano* eschew the reasonable suspicion argument for the broader position that the dismantling was permissible on no suspicion at all? Judge Fletcher, in United States v. Chaudhry, 424 F.3d 1051 (9th Cir. 2005), criticized the government's litigation position in a case in which she concurred in the court's holding that drilling a hole in a flat bed of a pickup truck was permissible without any suspicion:

> I write separately to express my distaste for the government's game-playing in this case and in two others we heard on the same calendar. In each case there was reasonable and articulable suspicion of drug smuggling. But the government wanted confirmation that no suspicion is required for extensive, intrusive searches at the border.
>
> * * *
>
> I see two problems with such an approach to litigation. First, such appeals are essentially a request for an advisory opinion, as the dispute over whether or not a particular search may be conducted in the absence of any suspicion is an entirely fictional construct. * * * The only possible purposes are the government's desire to push the envelope to its limits: to find out just how much destruction it can do without any suspicion, and to avoid proving it uses reliable dogs. Second, because there is ample suspicion in each case, it is difficult for judges to consider the issue cleanly on an unencumbered record. Evidence of probable criminal activity, especially evidence of narcotics detector dog alerts, cannot help but color

judges' views of the facts. We inevitably think "harmless error." I must admit that I take comfort in knowing that the border agents in these cases did not rip apart the defendants' cars on a whim. However, were I to decide a case where there is truly no suspicion, and where five or ten exploratory holes are drilled in the exterior walls of a vehicle, I might reach a different result.

Border Searches and Seizures of Persons: United States v. Montoya de Hernandez

The Court addressed the question of the appropriate standard of proof for highly intrusive border intrusions in United States v. Montoya de Hernandez, 473 U.S. 531 (1985). Justice Rehnquist, writing for a six-person majority, stated that "the detention of a traveler at the border, beyond the scope of a routine customs search and inspection, is justified at its inception if customs agents, considering all the facts surrounding the traveler and her trip, *reasonably suspect* that the traveler is smuggling contraband in her alimentary canal." (emphasis added).

Montoya de Hernandez went through customs in Los Angeles after arriving on a plane from Colombia. Her eight recent trips to either Miami or Los Angeles caused agents to question her about the purpose for her trip. She carried $5,000 cash, mostly $50 bills, with no billfold and stated that she came to purchase goods for her husband's store in Colombia. Although she had no appointments with sellers and no hotel reservation, she stated that she planned to ride around the city visiting retail stores and that she planned to stay at a Holiday Inn. She could not recall how her airline ticket was purchased. In her valise inspectors found four changes of "cold weather" clothing.

These facts, the Court held, were sufficient to warrant the experienced inspectors to have a reasonable suspicion that Montoya de Hernandez was a "balloon swallower" attempting to smuggle drugs into the country. A strip search by a female inspector revealed a fullness in the suspect's abdomen. The inspector noticed that the suspect was wearing two pair of elastic underpants with a paper towel lining the crotch area. Upon receiving this information, the inspector in charge informed the suspect of his suspicion. The inspector gave her the option of returning to Colombia on the next available flight, agreeing to an x-ray, or remaining in detention until she produced a monitored bowel movement. She chose the first option, but inspectors were unable to arrange a flight. Sixteen hours later, the suspect had not defecated or urinated and had refused food or drink. It appeared that she was struggling to avoid use of the toilet. Inspectors sought and obtained a warrant authorizing a rectal examination and x-ray, provided that the physician consider the suspect's claim of pregnancy. A pregnancy test was negative, and a rectal examination produced a balloon containing a foreign substance. Investigators arrested the suspect. She later passed 88 cocaine-filled balloons through her system.

The Supreme Court upheld both the initial inspection and the detention, finding that the delay was attributable to the suspect's "heroic" efforts "to resist the call of nature" and that the detention was not unreasonably long even though it "undoubtedly exceed[ed] any other detention we have approved under reasonable suspicion." Justice Rehnquist emphasized not only the suspect-created delay, but also the heavy state interest and diminished expectation of privacy attendant to a border crossing. He noted that "alimentary canal smuggling cannot be detected in the amount of time in which other illegal activity may be investigated through brief *Terry*-type stops."

Justice Stevens concurred in the judgment on the ground that the prolonged detention was attributable to the suspect's choice not to consent to an x-ray. Justice Brennan, joined by Justice Marshall, described the facts as a "disgusting and saddening episode" involving a detention based upon a profile that justified at most reasonable suspicion, and he dissented. He argued that "[i]ndefinite involuntary *incommunicado* detentions 'for investigation' are the hallmark of a police state, not a free society."

The Consequences of Montoya

After *Montoya,* there are two types of intrusions at the border—a "routine" border intrusion that can be done without suspicion, and a "non-routine" border intrusion that requires reasonable suspicion. It could be argued that some intrusions at the border could be so severe as to require probable cause, but, given the facts of *Montoya* and the state interest supporting border searches, can you envision such an intrusion? Perhaps compelled surgery? See United States v. Adekunle, 2 F.3d 559 (5th Cir.1993) (reasonable suspicion sufficient for 100 hour incommunicado detention, forced use of laxatives, and monitored bowel movement); United States v. Odofin, 929 F.2d 56 (2d Cir.1991) (24 day detention before bowel movement; reasonable suspicion sufficient).

Depending on their intrusiveness, searches of *persons* at the border can fall on either side of the "routine" versus "non-routine" line. For example, in United States v. Sanders, 663 F.2d 1 (2d Cir.1981), customs officials forced the defendant to take off his artificial leg and inspected it, finding drugs. The court likened the police activity to a body cavity search, well-recognized as more intrusive than the routine border search. See also United States v. Alfaro-Moncada, 607 F.3d 720 (11th Cir. 2010) ("Even at the border, * * * reasonable suspicion is required for highly intrusive searches of a person's body such as a strip search or an x-ray examination."). In contrast, in United States v. Charleus, 871 F.2d 265 (2d Cir.1989), a customs inspector patted down the defendant, felt a hard lump under his clothing, and lifted the back of his shirt, whereupon he found packages of narcotics taped to the defendant's body. The court analyzed the intrusion as follows:

> The [intrusion] arguably straddles the line between the two categories of border searches—searching more than personal belongings or effects such as a purse, wallet, or even outer jacket was involved; but the search was not nearly as intrusive as a body cavity or full strip search. Since the potential indignity resulting from a pat on the back followed by a lifting of one's shirt simply fails to compare with the much greater level of intrusion associated with a body cavity or full strip search, we decline to hold that reasonable suspicion was here required.

See also United States v. Kelly, 302 F.3d 291 (5th Cir. 2002) (canine sniff of a person, including contact with the dog's nose, was permissible without reasonable suspicion: "Certainly, a canine sniff, even one involving some bodily contact, is no more intrusive than a frisk or a pat-down, both of which clearly qualify as routine border searches.").

Border Searches of Laptops, Video Cameras, Cellphones, etc.

If you are carrying an electronic device across the border into the United States, can an officer—without having any suspicion—turn on the device and peruse all the material on it? The court in United States v. Ickes, 393 F.3d 501 (4th Cir. 2005), upheld an inspection of the contents of a video camera, laptop, etc., as a routine border search. Ickes's van was stopped at a border checkpoint. Officers first turned on Ickes's video camera and saw that he had taken a video of a young ball boy at a tennis match. They then conducted a thorough inspection of his laptop hard drive and computer disks that were in his car. Officers found child pornography. Ickes moved to suppress that evidence based on the Fourth and First Amendments. The court quickly disposed of the Fourth Amendment claim, holding that the search was no more intrusive than any other search of a person's effects at the border: such thorough inspections are allowed without suspicion, and there was nothing approaching a strip search or body cavity search that could be labeled "non-routine."

Does the Supreme Court's decision in California v. Riley have any impact on border searches of cellphones and laptops? The Court in *Riley* could be interpreted as arguing that cellphones and laptops are *sui generis* given the amount and nature of the private information that can be accessed by a search of these items. But also critical to the *Riley* Court was that the justifications for the arrest power rule are not applicable to cellphones and laptops. In contrast, the justification for the border search is to protect against harm to the United States coming from abroad—could evidence of that harm not be found on a cellphone or laptop? This was the core of the Court's holding in *Ramsey*, which left the contents of mail open to border searches despite the fact that mail has been afforded full Fourth Amendment protection since Ex Parte Jackson, 96 U.S. 727 (1878). Is there a meaningful difference between the contents of a letter and the contents of an electronic device from an interest balancing point of view?

Searches that are especially intrusive—like the body cavity search in *Montoya*—require reasonable suspicion. Could it be argued that a thorough search of a cellphone or laptop, especially after *Riley*, is so intrusive that it requires reasonable suspicion? In United States v. Cotterman, 709 F.3d 952 (9th Cir. 2013) (en banc), Cotterman's laptop was seized at the border and a quick inspection was conducted; then the computer was transferred to a forensic inspection center where it was thoroughly searched, and evidence of child pornography was found. The court held that, while a quick look at a cellphone or laptop could be done without suspicion, a thorough forensic examination requires reasonable suspicion. The court reasoned:

> An exhaustive forensic search of a copied laptop hard drive intrudes upon privacy and dignity interests to a far greater degree than a cursory search at the border. It is little comfort to assume that the government—for now—does not have the time or resources to seize and search the millions of devices that accompany the millions of travelers who cross our borders. It is the potential unfettered dragnet effect that is troublesome.
>
> * * *
>
> International travelers certainly expect that their property will be searched at the border. What they do not expect is that, absent some particularized suspicion, agents will mine every last piece of data on their devices or deprive them of their most personal property for days (or perhaps weeks or even months, depending on how long the search takes). Such a thorough and detailed search of the most intimate details of one's life is a substantial intrusion upon personal privacy and dignity. We therefore hold that the forensic examination of Cotterman's computer required a showing of reasonable suspicion, a modest requirement in light of the Fourth Amendment.

Searches Away from the Border

The right to search at the actual border has been extended to its functional equivalent as well. For example, if a plane flies from Mexico City non-stop to Denver, a search by customs officials at the Denver airport is considered a border search. The same standard applies to searches of ships, where the port of call is not at the border itself. United States v. Tilton, 534 F.2d 1363 (9th Cir.1976). In Torres v. Puerto Rico, 442 U.S. 465 (1979), the Court unanimously agreed that a trip from the mainland to Puerto Rico did not result in the crossing of an *international* border and that the border search exception to the warrant requirement did not apply.

A more troubling problem has arisen in connection with searches of vehicles inside the border, pursuant to § 287(a) of the Immigration and Nationality Act [8 U.S.C.A. § 1357(a)], which allows searches for aliens "within a reasonable distance from any external boundary of the United States." A reasonable distance has been defined as 100 air miles from any external border, 8 CFR § 287.1(a). The Court in United States v. Martinez-Fuerte, 428 U.S. 543, 552–53 (1976), described the kinds of searches that were implemented pursuant to this legislation:

> The Border Patrol conducts three kinds of inland traffic-checking operations in an effort to minimize illegal immigration. Permanent checkpoints, such as those at San Clemente and Sarita, are maintained at or near intersections of important roads leading away from the border. They operate on a coordinated basis designed to avoid circumvention by smugglers and others who transport the illegal aliens. Temporary checkpoints, which operate like permanent ones, occasionally are established in other strategic locations. Finally, roving patrols are maintained to supplement the checkpoint system.

Beginning with Almeida-Sanchez v. United States, 413 U.S. 266 (1973), the Supreme Court decided a series of cases challenging the constitutionality of these law enforcement efforts in border areas. In *Almeida-Sanchez* the defendant was stopped by a roving Border Patrol on an east-west road in California about 25 air miles north of the Mexican border. The officers had no warrant and no suspicion for stopping the car. The officers searched the defendant's vehicle for illegal aliens, discovering instead a large quantity of marijuana. The Court held the stop and search unconstitutional. In a 5–4 decision, Justice Stewart wrote for the majority that a roving patrol away from the border was regulated by the same standards as any other police activity—meaning that suspicionless seizures and searches were not permitted. Justice White's dissent found the search to be a reasonable response to the unique problems of enforcing immigration laws in border areas. See also United States v. Brignoni-Ponce, 422 U.S. 873 (1975), holding that roving border patrols are subject to the same standards as other law enforcement stops under *Terry*.

The use of traffic checkpoints removed from the border was at issue in United States v. Ortiz, 422 U.S. 873 (1975), where the Court held that warrantless *searches* at *internal* checkpoints are unconstitutional unless based on probable cause. The Court found that, at least insofar as searches were concerned, the risk of official abuse of discretion was just as great at a checkpoint as it was at a roving patrol; officers at checkpoints decided which cars to search, and only 3% of stopped vehicles were searched.

The following year, the Court approved warrantless *stops* of vehicles at *permanent checkpoints* for limited questioning of the occupants. United States v. Martinez-Fuerte, 428 U.S. 543 (1976). No probable cause or reasonable suspicion was required to justify the stops. The Court reasoned that suspicionless checkpoint stops are necessary tools of law enforcement, and that the public interest in making these stops outweighed the constitutionally protected interests of private citizens. In addition, Justice Powell, writing for the Court, stated that motorists could be selectively referred to secondary inspection areas for further questioning, again without any articulable suspicion. He argued that the additional intrusion—although admittedly a seizure—was limited and inoffensive and that use of the questioning techniques tended to minimize the intrusion on the general motoring public, thus protecting other Fourth Amendment interests. However, if the secondary inspection was unduly offensive or intrusive, then individualized suspicion would be required. See also United States v. Machuca-Barrera, 261 F.3d 425 (5th Cir. 2001) (stop at immigration checkpoint can last no longer than necessary to fulfil its immigration-related purpose).

L. CONSENT SEARCHES

1. Voluntary Consent

Voluntariness Distinguished from Waiver: Schneckloth v. Bustamonte

A search based upon voluntary consent is reasonable even in the absence of a warrant or any articulable suspicion. The Supreme Court addressed the requirements for valid consent in Schneckloth v. Bustamonte, 412 U.S. 218 (1973). A California police officer at 2:40 a.m. stopped an automobile with a headlight and a license plate light burned out. Six men were in the car. The driver had no license. Only one passenger produced his license, and he explained that the car was his brother's. The officer asked the men to step out of the car, they complied, and after two additional officers arrived, the officer asked the person who produced the license if he could search the car. The man replied, "Sure, go ahead," and opened the trunk for the officer. The search produced three stolen checks. The court of appeals held that consent was not valid because the consenting party was never told that he had the right to refuse to give consent. The Supreme Court disagreed.

Justice Stewart's majority opinion cited voluntariness concepts developed in confession cases and concluded that

> the question whether a consent to a search was in fact voluntary or was the product of duress or coercion, express or implied, is a question of fact to be determined from the totality of the circumstances. While

knowledge of the right to refuse consent is one factor to be taken into account, the government need not establish such knowledge as the sine qua non of an effective consent.

The defendant argued that warnings of the right to refuse to permit a search—comparable to the *Miranda* warnings, which we shall examine in connection with police interrogation—should be required before consent can be sought. The majority responded that it would be impractical to give such warnings under the "informal and unstructured conditions" in which consent requests are usually made.

Justice Stewart distinguished the traditional concept of waiver of "the safeguards of a fair criminal trial" from consent to search. He concluded that a defendant was to be given "the greatest possible opportunity to utilize every facet of the constitutional model of a fair criminal trial," and that "[a]ny trial conducted in derogation of that model leaves open the possibility that the trial reached an unfair result." But, he found, that "[t]he protections of the Fourth Amendment are of a wholly different order." Justice Stewart concluded that the proper test in consent search cases is not whether there was a waiver of the defendant's Fourth Amendment rights, but whether consent to search was voluntary under the totality of circumstances. He concluded that the Fourth Amendment does not require that citizens be discouraged from cooperating with the police—which would occur if they were required to be informed of their right to refuse.

As applied to the facts of the case, Justice Stewart had no trouble in concluding that the suspect's consent was voluntary—the suspect was not under arrest; the officer used no force and made no threats; and the suspect expressed no unwillingness to consent.

Justice Brennan dissented, arguing that "[i]t wholly escapes me how our citizens can meaningfully be said to have waived something as precious as a constitutional guarantee without ever being aware of its existence." Justice Marshall also dissented. He argued that consent searches are permissible because we permit our citizens to choose not to exercise their constitutional rights, and that "consent cannot be considered a meaningful choice unless he knew that he could in fact exclude the police." His solution was to have the government bear the burden of showing knowledge, which burden could be satisfied by a warning before asking for consent.

Reaffirming Schneckloth: United States v. Drayton

The Court reaffirmed its totality of the circumstances analysis in United States v. Drayton, 536 U.S. 194 (2002), in which the Court upheld searches of bags and persons made during a bus sweep. The Court found that while the officer did not inform the suspects of their right to refuse consent, "he did request permission to search, and the totality of the circumstances indicates that their consent was voluntary, so the searches were reasonable." The *Drayton* Court concluded as follows:

> In a society based on law, the concept of agreement and consent should be given a weight and dignity of its own. Police officers act in full accord with the law when they ask citizens for consent. It reinforces the rule of law for the citizen to advise the police of his or her wishes and for the police to act in reliance on that understanding. When this exchange takes place, it dispels inferences of coercion.

The Court's opinion in *Drayton* is fully set forth in the section on stops and frisks, supra. See also United States v. Collins, 683 F.3d 697 (6th Cir. 2012) (borrower of car validly consented to search—"when requesting an individual's consent to search, police do not have to inform the individual that others [in this case the owner of the car] could object to the search.").

The Consequences of Refusing Consent

Is refusal to consent to a search suspicious? Can an officer conclude that a person who refuses to permit a search has something to hide? In United States v. Prescott, 581 F.2d 1343 (9th Cir.1978), the court held that a person cannot be penalized for exercising the right to refuse to permit a search, and that "passive refusal to consent to a warrantless search is privileged conduct which cannot be considered as evidence of criminal wrongdoing." The majority said that its reasoning was necessary "to protect the exercise of a constitutional right." Surprisingly, there was a dissenting opinion arguing that no harm would come if a citizen's decision to invoke Fourth Amendment rights were admissible in evidence against them. See also United States v. Torres, 65 F.3d 1241 (4th Cir.1995) ("Officers cannot use a traveler's refusal to consent to the search of his bags as support for the requisite reasonable, articulable suspicion.").

The Impact of Custody

In *Schneckloth,* consent was obtained from a person who was not in police custody, a fact emphasized by the Court in its conclusion that its decision was "a narrow one." But in United States v. Watson, 423 U.S. 411 (1976), the Court found that the absence of consent warnings or of proof that Watson knew he could withhold consent was not controlling where the defendant "had been arrested and was in custody, but his consent was given while on a public street, not in the confines of the police station." The majority added that "to hold that illegal coercion is made out from the fact of arrest and the failure to inform the arrestee that he could withhold consent would not be consistent with *Schneckloth.*" *Watson* made clear that *Schneckloth* was not as narrow as Justice Stewart had proclaimed. Justice Marshall, joined by Justice Brennan, adhered to his opinion in *Schneckloth,* but added that "even short of this position there are valid reasons for application of such a rule to consents procured from suspects held in custody."

Not surprisingly, *Watson* has been relied upon to uphold consent obtained in all types of custodial situations; while the person's custodial status is relevant to whether the consent was voluntary, it is only one in the totality of circumstances. See, e.g., United States v. Hidalgo, 7 F.3d 1566 (11th Cir.1993) (consent voluntary even though the defendant "was arrested by SWAT team members who broke into his home in the early morning, woke him, and forced him to the ground at gun point"); United States v. Duran, 957 F.2d 499 (7th Cir.1992) (consent voluntary even though the suspect was under arrest and in the police station).

Totality of the Circumstances

After *Schneckloth* the totality of the circumstances must be examined to determine whether a person has voluntarily consented to a search. In Bumper v. North Carolina, 391 U.S. 543 (1968), the Court placed the burden of proving that consent "was, in fact, freely and voluntarily given" on the government, and declared that "[t]his burden cannot be discharged by showing no more than acquiescence to a claim of lawful authority."

The Supreme Court applied *Schneckloth* and found a valid consent in United States v. Mendenhall, 446 U.S. 544 (1980). Officers encountered Mendenhall in an airport, suspected she was a drug courier, and asked her to accompany them to a private room. She agreed. After a series of polite questions, Mendenhall ultimately agreed to a strip search and a search of her purse. Narcotics were found in the purse and on her person. Although a majority of the Court did not agree on whether to treat Mendenhall as "seized" when federal agents first approached her, a majority did agree that she voluntarily consented to accompany the agents to their airport office and to have her purse and person searched. In deciding that Mendenhall voluntarily accompanied the agents to their office, the Court observed that she was simply asked to go and was not threatened or physically forced. In deciding that the searches in the office were consensual, the Court emphasized that Mendenhall was twice told that she was free to decline consent. Justice White's dissent for four members of the Court argued that the government failed to meet its burden of proving that Mendenhall consented to accompany the officers to their office. "[T]he Court's conclusion can only be based on the notion that consent can be assumed from the absence of proof that a suspect resisted police authority. This is a notion that we have squarely rejected."

In United States v. Gonzalez-Basulto, 898 F.2d 1011 (5th Cir.1990), the court set forth a non-exclusive list of six factors relevant to whether consent is voluntarily obtained.

> (1) the voluntariness of the defendant's custodial status; (2) the presence of coercive police procedures; (3) the extent and level of the defendant's cooperation with the police; (4) the defendant's awareness of his right to refuse consent; (5) the defendant's education and intelligence; and (6) the defendant's belief that no evidence will be found.

Obviously, none of these factors are dispositive. For example, *Watson* found a consent voluntary even though the defendant was under arrest, and *Schneckloth* found voluntary consent even though the defendant was unaware of his right to refuse. However, a weak showing by the government on several of the factors substantially increases the likelihood that consent will be found involuntary.

The facts and resolution of *Gonzalez-Basulto,* supra, are typical of consent cases after *Schneckloth.* Border patrol agents at a permanent checkpoint suspected that Gonzalez-Basulto was carrying drugs in a refrigerated tractor-trailer rig. He was referred to a secondary inspection area to verify his claim that he was an American citizen. Gonzalez produced immigration documentation, and looked nervously about at the drug sniffing dogs present at the checkpoint. The agent asked whether Gonzalez would mind opening the trailer for an inspection. Gonzalez replied "no problem" and unlocked and opened the trailer, which contained boxes of oranges and lemons. A drug-sniffing dog was hoisted into the trailer, and gave a positive alert. The agents opened many boxes, and finally found cocaine in boxes near the front of the trailer. The court found that Gonzalez voluntarily consented to the search.

> The agents did not brandish weapons or threaten Gonzalez in any way. Gonzalez was not placed under arrest until the search uncovered the cocaine. Gonzalez cooperated with the agent who requested permission to search by responding "no problem" to the request and by unlocking and opening the trailer doors. While the agent admitted that he did not inform Gonzalez of his right to refuse to consent, the agent emphasized that he did not put any kind of pressure on Gonzalez to get his consent. He merely asked for permission. Gonzalez was not well-educated but he exhibited a sufficient degree of understanding to indicate his "no problem" response was intelligent. Gonzalez may well have believed that no drugs would be found because the cocaine was hidden in boxes toward the front of the trailer and there was little crawl space in the trailer.

Compare United States v. Isiofia, 370 F.3d 226 (2d Cir. 2004) (consent not voluntary where the defendant was never informed of his right to refuse consent, the agents demanded consent, yelled at the defendant, used abusive language, and told him that he would be jailed and deported and never see his family again unless he consented to the search).

Consider the sixth factor discussed in *Gonzalez-Basulto,* i.e. the defendant's belief that no evidence would be found. In United States v. Mendenhall, *supra,* the Court categorically rejected the argument that Mendenhall could not have voluntarily consented to a strip search because it would disclose the drugs that she carried. The Court stated that, while the suspect may later regret having given consent, "the question is not whether she acted in her ultimate self-interest, but whether she acted voluntarily." Wouldn't the contrary view—that a person could not give voluntary consent if the search would be likely to uncover incriminating evidence—all but do away with consent searches?

Threats of Action if Consent Is Refused

Suppose an officer says, "If you don't consent I'll just come back a little later with a warrant." Does this threat render a subsequent consent involuntary? The court considered this question in United States v. Duran, 957 F.2d 499 (7th Cir.1992), in which Karen Duran consented to the search of an outbuilding after officers told her that they would obtain a warrant if she didn't consent. The court stated:

> This may have induced Karen to grant her consent, but it was not coercive under the fourth amendment. Although empty threats to obtain a warrant may at times render a subsequent consent involuntary, see United States v. Talkington, 843 F.2d 1041 (7th Cir.1988) (consent invalid when police lied in telling suspect that they were in the process of getting a search warrant); Dotson v. Somers, 175 Conn. 614, 402 A.2d 790 (1978) (consent invalid where police had insufficient grounds upon which to base a warrant application), the threat in this case was firmly grounded. Karen's admission that [her husband, the defendant] dealt marijuana would have provided the police probable cause had they sought a search warrant, so their threat to do so in the event she refused consent was entirely proper.

On the relevance of police threats of action, and the rationality of giving consent, consider United States v. Welch, 683 F.3d 1304 (9th Cir. 2012). Officers were conducting a lawful protective sweep and came upon Welch in his bedroom. The officers had guns drawn. They asked for consent to search the room and Welch said "no." One officer then said, "Fine, but we're going to have to get a search warrant." Welch said nothing. The officer then said, "it could take awhile." Welch then said "okay you can search." The search uncovered a gun and ammunition and Welch was charged with felon-firearm-possession. He argued that he had not voluntarily consented, but the court disagreed.

> The explicit threat here is that Welch might have to stand around with nothing to do for some substantial period of time, much as we all do whenever we are stuck in a line. It would be a delicate will indeed

that might be overborne by the threat of a period of idleness and wasted time. Yet that threat, "it would take a while," is what changed Welch's "no" to a "yes."

The district judge provided a persuasive explanation of why Welch changed his mind. Welch, the court found, "reasonably believed that the officers would eventually be able to obtain a search warrant" and that, because he would have to wait on the balcony while they did, he would not be able to go into the apartment, retrieve the pistol and ammunition, and somehow dispose of them before the police came back with a warrant. So "it made sense for [Welch] to agree to the search rather than wait for the warrant to be obtained and, because of where the items were hidden, hope for the best." That was a rational gamble, but one that Welch lost. Welch's consent was not coerced, just constrained, by having to place his bet on one of two poor alternatives. Maybe if he let them in, the police would want to get the search done quickly and fail to find his contraband. Or maybe if he put them to the trouble of getting a search warrant, they would search more thoroughly because he had inconvenienced them.

Must a Person Who Is Stopped Be Told He Is Free to Leave?

In Ohio v. Robinette, 519 U.S. 33 (1996), Robinette was lawfully stopped for speeding and given a warning. After the officer returned his license, he asked Robinette: "One question before you get gone: Are you carrying any illegal contraband in your car? Any weapons of any kind, drugs, anything like that?" Robinette answered in the negative, and when the officer asked to search the car, Robinette consented. The officer found drugs in the car.

The state court held that Robinette's consent could not be voluntary because the officer never informed him that the stop had ended and he was free to go. The Court, in an opinion by Chief Justice Rehnquist for seven Justices, found no such bright-line requirement in the Fourth Amendment. The Chief Justice reasoned as follows:

> We have previously rejected a per se rule very similar to that adopted by the Supreme Court of Ohio in determining the validity of a consent to search. In Schneckloth v. Bustamonte, it was argued that such a consent could not be valid unless the defendant knew that he had a right to refuse the request. We rejected this argument: "While knowledge of the right to refuse consent is one factor to be taken into account, the government need not establish such knowledge as the sine qua non of an effective consent." And just as it "would be thoroughly impractical to impose on the normal consent search the detailed requirements of an effective warning," so too would it be

unrealistic to require police officers to always inform detainees that they are free to go before a consent to search may be deemed voluntary.

Justice Ginsburg concurred in the judgment in *Robinette,* emphasizing that while a "tell-then-ask" rule made good sense, imposing it as a constitutional requirement was inconsistent with the totality of circumstances approach mandated by *Schneckloth.*

Justice Stevens dissented. He argued that, by asking whether Robinette had contraband, the officer was continuing the detention, even though the initial reason for the detention had ended. Justice Stevens concluded from this that the continued interrogation, in the absence of reasonable suspicion, constituted an illegal seizure, which tainted Robinette's consent.

Did the Person Consent?

In some cases, the question is not whether the defendant consented voluntarily, but whether he consented at all. For example, in United States v. Price, 54 F.3d 342 (7th Cir.1995), Officer Brown stopped Pierce's car, became suspicious, and asked whether there were any drugs in the car. Pierce replied in the negative. Officer Brown then asked Pierce, "Do you mind if I take a look?" and Pierce quickly replied "Sure." Brown searched the car, and Pierce looked on without objection. Narcotics were discovered. At the suppression hearing, Pierce testified that when he said "Sure" what he meant was "Sure, I *mind.*" The court of appeals responded to this argument as follows:

> Perhaps in the abstract one could say that given the phrasing of Brown's question, Pierce's response to it is ambiguous and thus capable of being interpreted as either "Go ahead" or "No way." But * * * [t]he only conclusion to be drawn from the totality of the evidence is that Pierce's immediate response "Sure" meant, "Sure, go ahead." The crucial fact is Pierce's failure to protest upon learning that Brown understood his response as a consent to the search. Had Pierce not agreed to the search, now was the time to make that clear. Yet when confronted with Brown's understanding of his response, Pierce offered no objection at all; instead, he submitted to a pat-down search and took a seat in Brown's patrol car in order to get out of the rain. Given these circumstances it was not clear error for the district court to find that Pierce's response "Sure" meant that he agreed to the search.

Assume you are in Pierce's situation and that you *really* mean "Sure, I mind," not "Sure, go ahead." What would your reaction be if Officer Brown ignores you and goes ahead with the search anyway? Would telling him to stop have a positive effect, do you think? See also United States v. Bautista, 362 F.3d 584 (9th Cir. 2004) (no consent where the occupant of a motel room opened the door after the police demanded entrance, and stepped back as officers proceeded into the room); United States v. Williams, 521 F.3d 902 (8th Cir. 2008) ("The precise question is not whether [the defendant] consented subjectively, but whether his conduct would have caused a reasonable person to believe that he consented.").

2. Third Party Consent

Can a third party consent to the search of an area in which a suspect has an expectation of privacy? Frazier v. Cupp, 394 U.S. 731 (1969), upheld the search of a defendant's duffle bag when his cousin, a joint user of the bag, voluntarily consented. The Court rejected the argument that because the cousin had authority to use only one compartment of the bag, he could not consent to a search of the remainder, stating that it would not "engage in such metaphysical subtleties," and that the defendant, who allowed his cousin to use the bag, must "have assumed the risk" he would consent to let others see inside.

Actual Authority: United States v. Matlock

The leading third-party consent case is United States v. Matlock, 415 U.S. 164 (1974). Matlock was arrested in the front yard of a house. Mrs. Graff admitted the police to the house and told them she shared the house with Matlock. She consented to a search. The Court found the search to be reasonable because Mrs. Graff had actual authority to consent to the search. The Court stated the rationale for permitting third-party consent searches in the following analysis:

> The authority which justifies the third-party consent does not rest upon the law of property, with its attendant historical and legal refinements, but rests rather on mutual use of the property by persons generally having joint access or control for most purposes, so that it is reasonable to recognize that any of the co-inhabitants has the right to permit the inspection in his own right and that the others have assumed the risk that one of their number might permit the common area to be searched.

See also United States v. Kimoana, 383 F.3d 1215 (10th Cir. 2004) (person who stayed overnight in a motel room, left his possessions there, and had a room key, had actual authority to consent to a search of the room even though he was not the registered guest who paid for the room).

Third-Party Consent to Search Cellphones and Computers

Should the third-party consent doctrine have special limits when it comes to computers and cellphones? That was one of the questions in United States v. Thomas, 818 F.3d 1230 (11th Cir. 2016). Thomas's wife called police after she found child pornography on a computer that she shared with her husband. When police came to the premises, the child pornography was not showing on the computer screen. Police obtained consent from the wife to conduct a thorough forensic examination of the computer. The court held that the wife had actual authority to consent to this search. It noted that, while Thomas typically deleted his Internet search history, his wife nonetheless had "joint access and control over the computer for most purposes, and Thomas did not isolate his Internet use in a manner that prevented [his wife] from accessing it all together." The court found it particularly important that Thomas did not maintain a separate login name and password.

Thomas argued that a heightened requirement for actual authority for a third-party search was required for searches of computers, relying heavily on Riley v. California. But the court stated that the *Riley* Court's concern about the volume of private information in a cellphone or computer "played a central role in the Supreme Court's analysis of the search-incident-to-arrest rule, we find it less critical to our analysis because the Supreme Court has already approved of exhaustive searches in the consent-based search context. In *Matlock* itself, for example, the Supreme Court upheld the consent-based search of a home, including the defendant's bedroom and closet." The court concluded that "the touchstone of the third-party consent rule is assumption of the risk, and a person sharing access to a computer, just as a person sharing access to a home, exposes himself to a police search based on another's consent."

Apparent Authority: Illinois v. Rodriguez

The Court in Illinois v. Rodriguez, 497 U.S. 177 (1990), considered whether a search is valid when based on the consent of a third party who has *apparent* but not *actual* authority. The third party in *Rodriguez* was Gail Fischer, who had lived in Rodriguez's apartment but had, unknown to the officers, moved out a month before the search and had retained a key. She reported to police that she had been assaulted by Rodriguez in the apartment. She traveled with officers to the apartment, produced a key, unlocked the door, and gave them permission to enter. During that engagement, she referred to the premises as "our apartment." Once in the apartment, officers observed drugs and drug paraphernalia in plain view.

Justice Scalia, writing for a six-person majority, agreed with the lower courts that the Ms. Fischer did not have actual authority to consent to a search of the apartment, in that she had no joint access or control of the premises after moving out. According to the majority, however, the entry was valid if the officers had reasonably believed that she had authority to consent. The Court rejected the defendant's argument that permitting a search on the basis of apparent but not actual authority would amount to an unauthorized waiver of the defendant's Fourth Amendment rights.

Justice Scalia relied on *Schneckloth* and distinguished a waiver of constitutional rights and voluntary consent to search. He explained that, while a waiver of a constitutional right must be personal, the validity of a consent search is determined by whether the search is reasonable.

Justice Scalia concluded that the question of authority to consent should be governed by the same standard of reasonableness—and allowance for reasonable mistakes—as had been applied in other areas of Fourth Amendment jurisprudence, such as probable cause, the execution of a warrant, and the existence of exigent circumstances. The Court remanded for a determination of whether the officers could have reasonably believed that Ms. Fischer had actual authority to consent to a search of the apartment. Justice Marshall, joined by Justices Brennan and Stevens, dissented.

Mistakes of Law

In Stoner v. California, 376 U.S. 483 (1964), the government argued that the officers relied on the apparent authority of the hotel desk clerk to consent to a search of Stoner's room. The Court rejected that argument, stating that "the rights protected by the Fourth Amendment are not to be eroded by unrealistic doctrines of apparent authority." What appeared to be "unrealistic" in *Stoner* is the officer's assumption that a hotel desk clerk would have the legal authority to consent to the search of a rented room. See, e.g., United States v. Brown, 961 F.2d 1039 (2d Cir.1992) (stating that "an investigator's erroneous belief that landladies are generally authorized to consent to a search of a tenant's premises could not provide the authorization necessary for a warrantless search").

It should be noted that the mistake of law in *Stoner* was not reasonable. Based on the Court's holding in Heien v. North Carolina, 574 U.S. 54 (2014), supra, the result might be different if the law is ambiguous or the officer's mistake of law is otherwise reasonable.

The Duty to Investigate Third Party Authority to Consent

Does *Rodriguez* mean that the police can presume third party consent upon the simple assertion of the third party that she has common authority? If a babysitter answers the door, and asserts that she has actually been granted authority over the entire premises, can police search the entire house upon the babysitter's consent? In United States v. Dearing, 9 F.3d 1428 (9th Cir.1993), the court held that a live-in childcare provider lacked apparent authority to consent to a search of his employer's bedroom. The court declared that "the police are not allowed to proceed on the theory that ignorance is bliss," and concluded that the officer should have inquired into the extent of the provider's authorized access into his employer's bedroom. See also United States v. Kimoana, 383 F.3d 1215

(10th Cir. 2004) (government's burden of proving valid third party consent "cannot be met if agents, faced with an ambiguous situation, nevertheless proceed without making further inquiry").

Third Party Consent Where the Defendant Is Present and Objecting: Georgia v. Randolph

In Georgia v. Randolph, 547 U.S. 103 (2006), the Court held that, even if one occupant consents, a physically present co-occupant's stated refusal to permit entry prevails, rendering the warrantless search unreasonable and invalid as to him.

Randolph and his wife had separated. She moved away with their son, and returned to the home to get some belongings. Thereafter, she complained to the police that, after a dispute, her husband took their son away. When officers reached the house she told them that her husband was a cocaine user whose habit had caused financial troubles. She stated there was evidence of drugs in the house. Eventually, officers went to the house and both Mr. and Mrs. Randolph answered the door. An officer asked for consent to search. Mr. Randolph unequivocally refused, but Mrs. Randolph readily gave consent. The police entered and found drugs.

Writing for the Court, Justice Souter noted "the great significance" given in consent cases "to widely shared social expectations, which are naturally enough influenced by the law of property, but not controlled by its rules." Looking to those expectations he reasoned as follows:

> [I]t is fair to say that a caller standing at the door of shared premises would have no confidence that one occupant's invitation was a sufficiently good reason to enter when a fellow tenant stood there saying, "stay out." Without some very good reason, no sensible person would go inside under those conditions. Fear for the safety of the occupant issuing the invitation, or of someone else inside, would be thought to justify entry, but the justification then would be the personal risk, the threats to life or limb, not the disputed invitation.
>
> The visitor's reticence without some such good reason would show not timidity but a realization that when people living together disagree over the use of their common quarters, a resolution must come through voluntary accommodation, not by appeals to authority. Unless the people living together fall within some recognized hierarchy, like a household of parent and child or barracks housing military personnel of different grades, there is no societal understanding of superior and inferior. * * * In sum, there is no common understanding that one co-tenant generally has a right or authority to prevail over the express wishes of another, whether the issue is the color of the curtains or invitations to outsiders.

Justice Souter explicitly stated that "this case has no bearing on the capacity of police to protect domestic victims" and "[t]he undoubted right of the police to enter in order to protect a victim * * * has nothing to do with the question in this case * * *." At the end of his opinion, he noted the State did not argue exigent circumstances or that Janet Randolph gave any indication of a need for protection inside the house.

Justice Souter then considered the limits of a rule prohibiting entry on third party consent when the defendant is present and objecting:

> Although the *Matlock* defendant was not present with the opportunity to object, he was in a squad car not far away; the *Rodriguez* defendant was actually asleep in the apartment, and the police might have roused him with a knock on the door before they entered with only the consent of an apparent co-tenant. If those cases are not to be undercut by today's holding, we have to admit that we are drawing a fine line; if a potential defendant with self-interest in objecting is in fact at the door and objects, the co-tenant's permission does not suffice for a reasonable search, whereas the potential objector, nearby but not invited to take part in the threshold colloquy, loses out.
>
> This is the line we draw, and we think the formalism is justified. So long as there is no evidence that the police have removed the potentially objecting tenant from the entrance for the sake of avoiding a possible objection, there is practical value in the simple clarity of complementary rules, one recognizing the co-tenant's permission when there is no fellow occupant on hand, the other according dispositive weight to the fellow occupant's contrary indication when he expresses it. * * * Better to accept the formalism of distinguishing *Matlock* from this case than to impose a requirement, time-consuming in the field and in the courtroom, with no apparent systemic justification.

Justice Stevens wrote a short concurring opinion. Justice Breyer wrote a concurring opinion emphasizing the narrowness of the majority's holding.

Chief Justice Roberts, joined by Justice Scalia, dissented. He argued as follows:

> A wide variety of often subtle social conventions may shape expectations about how we act when another shares with us what is otherwise private, and those conventions go by a variety of labels—courtesy, good manners, custom, protocol, even honor among thieves. The Constitution, however, protects not these but privacy, and once privacy has been shared, the shared information, documents, or places remain private only at the discretion of the confidant.
>
> * * *
>
> Just as the source of the majority's rule is not privacy, so too the interest it protects cannot reasonably be described as such. That

> interest is not protected if a co-owner happens to be absent when the police arrive, in the backyard gardening, asleep in the next room, or listening to music through earphones so that only his co-occupant hears the knock on the door. That the rule is so random in its application confirms that it bears no real relation to the privacy protected by the Fourth Amendment. What the majority's rule protects is not so much privacy as the good luck of a co-owner who just happens to be present at the door when the police arrive. Usually when the development of Fourth Amendment jurisprudence leads to such arbitrary lines, we take it as a signal that the rules need to be rethought. We should not embrace a rule at the outset that its *sponsors* appreciate will result in drawing fine, formalistic lines.

The Chief Justice expressed the view that the decision would have serious consequences in domestic abuse situations because "[t]he majority's rule apparently forbids police from entering to assist with a domestic dispute if the abuser whose behavior prompted the request for police assistance objects."

Justice Scalia and Justice Thomas also wrote dissenting opinions. Justice Alito did not participate.

What Does It Mean to Be "Present" and "Objecting" Under Randolph?

Randolph gives veto power over a third party's consent only when the defendant is present and objecting. On the question of "presence" the Supreme Court held, in Fernandez v. California, 571 U.S. 292 (2014), that the defendant's wife's consent to search the premises was valid even though the defendant had objected to the search when the officers initially approached his apartment. At the time of that approach, officers saw that Fernandez's wife appeared to be battered and bleeding. They arrested Fernandez, then *returned* to the apartment and obtained consent from his wife. Justice Alito, writing for six members of the Court, declared that the Court in *Randolph* "went to great lengths to make clear that its holding was limited to situations in which the objecting occupant is present" at the time the consent search is conducted. The Court held that the officers were justified in removing Fernandez and that the *Randolph* rule could not apply where officers are "objectively reasonable" in removing the objector from the premises. The Court also rejected the defendant's argument that the objection he made while he *was* present was enough to bar third party consent at a later point when he was not. Justice Alito reasoned that the objection could not last forever, and to limit its duration to a "reasonable" time would create a host of practical problems and would be inconsistent with the bright line rule established in *Randolph*. Justice Ginsburg, joined by Justices Sotomayor and Kagan, dissented in *Fernandez*.

For other cases on "presence" under *Randolph,* see, e.g., United States v. Alama, 486 F.3d 1062 (8th Cir. 2007) (where defendant refused to come to the door in order to avoid arrest, he was not present and objecting when third-party consent was granted); United States v. Lopez, 547 F.3d 397 (2d Cir. 2008) (officers arrested the defendant on the first floor of his house, then escorted his girlfriend to the second floor bedroom to get the defendant's clothes, and at that point sought consent from her to search the bedroom; third-party consent was valid because the defendant was not present and there was no indication that the marshals removed Lopez for the purpose of avoiding his potential objection: "the ease with which law enforcement officers might seek the defendant's permission to search when a co-occupant has already consented is irrelevant").

As to whether a defendant is *objecting* at the time third-party consent is given, see, e.g., United States v. Uscanga-Ramirez, 475 F.3d 1024 (8th Cir. 2007) (defendant denied that there was a gun in his house and said his girlfriend was lying about it, but he never explicitly objected when the girlfriend granted consent to search, therefore the gun that was found was properly admitted); United States v. Hicks, 539 F.3d 566 (7th Cir. 2008) (defendant who objected to his arrest and removal from the premises did not explicitly object to a search of the premises, so third-party consent was valid).

In United States v. Moore, 770 F.3d 809 (9th Cir. 2014), the defendant locked himself in his house. His wife was outside with police officers. They knocked on the door and announced their presence. Defendant did not answer. The wife then authorized officers to use a battering ram to knock the door down—which they did, and then searched the premises. The court found that the search did not violate *Randolph*, because the "facts at best show that Moore implicitly refused to allow the police to search the residence. However, *Randolph* requires an express, not implicit, refusal."

Does Randolph Apply Outside the Home?

Assume that two people are sharing a laptop in a public park, having purchased it together. An officer asks one of them for permission to search the laptop and that person says "yes." But the other owner is present and objects. Does *Randolph* prohibit the search? The lower courts are split. See United States v. King, 604 F.3d 125 (3d Cir. 2010) (finding that third-party consent to search a computer justifies a consent search even where the co-owner is present and objecting; noting that the *Randolph* majority "crafted its rule using terms that apply solely to dwellings" and that Justice Breyer's concurring opinion emphasizes the fact-specific nature of that holding); United States v. Murphy, 516 F.3d 1117 (9th Cir. 2008) (finding that *Randolph* applies to the search of a storage unit: "there is no reason that the rule in *Randolph* should be limited to residences").

3. Scope of Consent

Even if a person voluntarily gives consent, there may be a question about whether the consent extended to the areas actually searched by the officer. A search beyond the scope of the consent granted cannot be justified as a consent search. See United States v. Neely, 564 F.3d 346 (4th Cir. 2009) (defendant's consent to search his trunk did not extend to a search of the passenger compartment of the car). The question, of course, is whether a given search is beyond the scope of a given consent.

Scope Defined by the Object of the Search: Florida v. Jimeno

In Florida v. Jimeno, 500 U.S. 248 (1991), Chief Justice Rehnquist, writing for a majority of seven Justices, relied on *Rodriguez* and *Schneckloth* to conclude that the scope of a consent is determined by a standard of objective reasonableness. The Court held that an officer could reasonably conclude that when a suspect gave general consent to search his car, he also consented to a search of a paper bag lying on the floor of the car. The officer had informed Jimeno that he was looking for narcotics in the car and obtained consent to search. Jimeno did not place any explicit limitation on the scope of the search. The Chief Justice reasoned that the general consent to search the car included consent to search containers that might contain drugs. He stated that "the scope of a search is generally defined by its expressed object" and that "a reasonable person might be expected to know that narcotics are carried in some form of container." The Chief Justice distinguished the instant case from one in which an officer, given consent to search the trunk of a car, pried open a locked briefcase found inside the trunk. He explained that "it is very likely unreasonable to think that a suspect, by consenting to the search of his trunk, has agreed to the breaking open of a locked briefcase within the trunk, but it is otherwise with a paper bag."

The *Jimeno* majority rejected the defendant's argument that police officers should be required to request separate permission to search each container found in a car. The Chief Justice saw "no basis for adding this sort of superstructure to the Fourth Amendment's basic tenet of reasonableness." He noted that a container-by-container requirement would result in fewer consents being given—which would be contrary to the public's interest in encouraging citizens to cooperate with authorities.

Justice Marshall, joined by Justice Stevens, dissented. Justice Marshall noted that, at best, general consent is ambiguous, and police can avoid ambiguity by asking specifically at the outset for permission to search the contents of a car, or by asking for additional permission to search a container when it is found within a car. Justice Marshall concluded by attacking the majority's expressed interest in encouraging consent searches:

The majority's real concern is that if the police were required to ask for additional consent to search a closed container * * * an individual who did not mean to authorize such additional searching would have an opportunity to say no. In essence, then, the majority is claiming that the community has a real interest not in encouraging citizens to *consent* to investigatory efforts of their law enforcement agents, but rather in encouraging individuals to be *duped* by them. That is not the community that the Fourth Amendment contemplates.

Ambiguity Construed Against the Citizen

After *Jimeno,* it is up to the citizen rather than the officer to clarify any ambiguity concerning the scope of consent. See United States v. Berke, 930 F.2d 1219 (7th Cir.1991) (consent to officer's "looking" into bag allows a thorough search of the bag; defendant did not ask for clarification of what the officers meant when they said they wanted to "look"); United States v. Luken, 560 F.3d 741 (8th Cir. 2009) (forensic analysis of hard drive on defendant's computer did not exceed the scope of consent; before defendant gave consent, the officer explained that they would be able to recover deleted files and images, and defendant did not place any explicit limitations on the search); United States v. Beckman, 786 F.3d 672 (8th Cir. 2015) (consent to search of "your computer" authorizes a search of an external hard-drive that is connected to the computer, where the defendant placed no explicit limitations on the search and did not object when the officer started searching the external hard-drive).

Imagine you are in Jimeno's position and the officer asks if he can search your car. Assume further that you want to limit the scope of this search. Because it is up to you to clarify any ambiguity, how would you go about doing so? Would you be concerned that by limiting the scope of the search, you will direct the officer's attention to the very area that you want to exclude from the search? Does it make sense for Jimeno to say, "yes, you can search the car, but not that bag in the back seat"? Is the solution to simply refuse to give consent in the first place? If so, then how does that play against the Court's interest in encouraging consent searches?

While ambiguity is construed against the citizen, there are certainly situations where an officers' search will be beyond what could be reasonably contemplated by the consent. For example, in United States v. Turner, 169 F.3d 84 (1st Cir.1999), Turner's next door neighbor was attacked with a knife, and blood was found around Turner's window. Officers thought the assailant might be hiding in Turner's house and asked for consent to search. They also had thoughts that Turner might be the assailant. They asked to search for any signs that the suspect might have been inside Turner's apartment, or might have left evidence of his presence there. Turner consented. An officer saw a picture on Turner's computer screen that resembled the victim. This got him curious, and so he sat down and started searching through the computer's hard drive. He discovered files containing child pornography, and Turner was prosecuted for that offense. But the court held that the search exceeded the scope of consent, and therefore that the files were illegally obtained:

> We think that an objectively reasonable person assessing in context the exchange between Turner and these detectives would have understood that the police intended to search only in places where an intruder hastily might have disposed of any physical evidence of the Thomas assault immediately after it occurred; for example, in places where a fleeing suspect might have tossed a knife or bloody clothing. Whereas, in sharp contrast, it obviously would have been impossible to abandon physical evidence of this sort in a personal computer hard drive * * * .

It is also likely that a search will be beyond the scope of the consent if it involves *destructive activity*—as in the example given by the Court in *Jimeno* involving breaking open a locked briefcase. See United States v. Strickland, 902 F.2d 937 (11th Cir.1990) (consent to search a car does not extend to officer's slashing open a spare tire); United States v. Osage, 235 F.3d 518 (10th Cir. 2000) (consent to search a bag does not permit the opening of a sealed can labeled "Tamales in Gravy" found in the bag: "before an officer may actually destroy or render completely useless a container which would otherwise be within the scope of a permissive search, the officer must obtain explicit authorization, or have some other, lawful, basis upon which to proceed."). Compare United States v. Jackson, 381 F.3d 984 (10th Cir. 2004) (consent to search for narcotics allowed the officer to pry open the top of a baby powder container: "removing the lid of the baby powder container did not exceed the scope of Jackson's consent because it did not destroy or render the container useless").

4. Withdrawing Consent

Because there is a right to refuse consent initially, and a right to control the scope of consent, it follows that there is also a right to revoke a consent once given. Of course, consent cannot be revoked retroactively after the officer has found incriminating information. United States v. Dyer, 784 F.2d 812 (7th Cir.1986) (revocation must be made before the search is completed). Also, the revocation of consent must be *clear and explicit.* See United States v. Gray, 369 F.3d 1024 (8th Cir. 2004) (expression of impatience is not sufficient to terminate consent: "Withdrawal of consent need not be effectuated through particular magic words, but an intent to withdraw consent must be made by unequivocal act or statement.").

Suppose an officer obtains voluntary consent to search a home and then, when he is about to enter a closet, the defendant revokes consent and forbids entry to the closet. Can the officer consider the defendant's actions as proof that there is something incriminating in the closet? As one court put it: "The constitutional right to withdraw one's consent would be of little value if the very fact of choosing to exercise that right could serve as any part of the basis for finding the reasonable suspicion that makes consent unnecessary." United States v. Carter, 985 F.2d 1095 (D.C.Cir.1993).

This principle is fact-sensitive, however. For example, in *Carter,* the court upheld a search made after consent was revoked based on the following sequence of events: 1) Officers suspected Carter of drug trafficking based on various profile factors and suspicious answers to questions during their encounter; 2) Carter permitted the officer to look through his tote bag; 3) the officer pulled out a paper bag from the tote bag; 4) Carter snatched the paper bag from the officer and volunteered to show the officer the food he claimed was in the paper bag; 5) Carter put his hand inside the paper bag, felt around, withdrew his hand—which was empty; and 6) Carter rolled up the paper bag and stood looking at the officer.

The *Carter* court held that the officer could reasonably take Carter's conduct into account, "as part of the totality of the circumstances, regardless of whether it occurred before or, as here, after Carter had given and then withdrawn his consent to a search." This was because Carter's "peculiar" way of retracting consent could legitimately be considered suspicious, independent of the withdrawal of consent itself.

Judge Wald, in dissent, complained that under the majority's approach, Carter "was entitled to just say no to any further search of the bag, [but] he had to do so in a way that would not raise the detective's suspicion that he had something to hide; not an easy feat under the circumstances." She concluded as follows:

> Permitting the police to rely on the atmospherics of the refusal or withdrawal of consent to supply the reasonable suspicion necessary to objectively justify an otherwise unlawful search strips the legal right of withdrawal of all practical value. * * * If the right to withdraw consent for a "consensual" encounter is to have any meaning on the streets, as well as in the jurisprudence, it must encompass the manner as well as the fact of its exercise.

For a different perspective on "suspicious" withdrawal of consent, see United States v. Wilson, 953 F.2d 116 (4th Cir.1991) (angry refusal to allow search of coat, after consenting to search of luggage and person, should not have counted as a factor in the analysis of reasonable suspicion; except in extraordinary circumstances, officers must have evidence independent of the withdrawal of consent and the manner in which it is executed).

5. Credibility Determinations

Consent cases often come down to a credibility determination between an officer's and a defendant's accounts of what happened. Typically, officers testify that they acted politely, asked the defendant to consent, informed him of his right to refuse, and the defendant readily consented. In contrast, defendants testify that officers either never sought consent, or the defendant never consented, or that the officers obtained consent only after using threatening and coercive tactics. In the typical consent case, there is little evidence other than the testimony of the opposing sides that is or can be produced on the consent question. It is fair to state, at least by viewing the reported opinions, that courts routinely find officers to be more credible than defendants. See United States v. Dean, 550 F.3d 626 (7th Cir. 2008) ("it was perfectly rational for the district court to have believed that Dean's desire to avoid another conviction provided a greater motive for him to fabricate a story than any motive that could be attributed to the officers.").

In New York City, the Mollen Commission reviewed the activities of the NYPD and found that perjury is "prevalent enough in the department that it has its own nickname: 'testilying.'" Sexton, New York Police Often Lie Under Oath, Report Says, New York Times, April 22, 1994, p.1, col. 1. See also Slobogin, Testilying and What To Do About It, 67 Colo.L.Rev. 1037 (1996) (citing surveys of defense attorneys, prosecutors, and judges, estimating that police perjure themselves in as much as fifty percent of suppression hearings).

Professor Lassiter, in Eliminating Consent from the Lexicon of Traffic Stop Interrogations, 27 Cap. L.Rev. 79 (1998), argues that "testilying" goes hand in hand with racial profiling. Officers single out minorities for traffic and other stops, and then lie at the suppression hearing about things like consent. He considers whether a rule should be promulgated that a suspect cannot consent to a search without a lawyer present, but dismisses that solution as "impractical." He states that, in light of the twin problems of racial profiling and testilying, the possibility that citizens truly and voluntarily consent to a search that uncovers evidence is so remote that the *entire concept of voluntary consent should be rejected.*

Can you think of any other solutions to the problem of testilying? What about subjecting officers to polygraph tests before they testify that the defendant voluntarily consented to a search that uncovered incriminating evidence? See also McClurg, Good Cop, Bad Cop: Using Cognitive Dissonance Theory to Reduce Police Lying, 32 U.C. Davis L.Rev. 389 (1999) (suggesting changes in police training and mentoring to reduce testilying).

VIII. STATUTORY REGULATION OF SEARCHES AND SEIZURES

We have discussed at length the constitutional regulation of searches and seizures elaborated by the courts. But should the task of promulgating rules governing when searches and seizures are reasonable fall exclusively to the judiciary? Do legislatures and executive agents also have authority to set rules governing searches and seizures? If they take up this mantle, then what standard should courts apply when determining whether a regulatory regime promulgated by a coequal branch of government is sufficient to guarantee the "right of the people to be secure in their persons, houses, papers, and effects against unreasonable searches and seizures"?

A. THE FEDERAL STATUTORY RESPONSE TO BERGER AND KATZ: TITLE III AND ITS AMENDMENTS

One year after *Berger*, Congress enacted a new scheme of regulating wiretapping and electronic eavesdropping as part of the Omnibus Crime Control and Safe Streets Act of 1968. This legislation—which does not regulate eavesdropping conducted with the consent of one of the parties—is commonly known as "Title III." Title III was modified by Title I of the 1986 Electronic Communications Privacy Act, to account for technological advances and to correct perceived gaps in the statute. Other amendments were made by, *inter alia*, the Stored Communications Act. Title III was further amended by the USA PATRIOT ACT (2001), the Homeland Security Act of 2002, and the USA Freedom Act (2015).

As one court has put it, with the passage of Title III, "Congress authorized wiretapping as needed to allow effective investigation of criminal activities while at the same time ensuring meaningful judicial supervision and requiring specific procedures to safeguard privacy rights." United States v. Gordon, 871 F.3d 35 (1st Cir. 2017).

The basic provisions of Title III as amended (18 U.S.C. §§ 2510–2522) are as follows:

1. ***Coverage:*** The statute covers "wire, oral or electronic communication." It regulates any "intercept," defined as "the aural or other acquisition of the contents of any wire, electronic, or oral communication through the use of any electronic, mechanical, or other device."

2. ***Prohibition and Exclusion:*** Section 2511 prohibits the unauthorized willful interception, use, or disclosure of wire, oral, or electronic communications covered by the Act; but it does not apply to interception conducted with the consent of one of the parties.[32] Section 2515 states that no information obtained in violation of Title III, and no evidence derived therefrom, may be admitted in any proceeding.

[32] Inadvertent interceptions do not violate the Act. See Adams v. Sumner, 39 F.3d 933 (9th Cir.1994) (switchboard operator at hotel inadvertently hears an incriminating conversation; no error to admit at trial). See also United States v. Wuliger, 981 F.2d 1497 (6th Cir.1992) (attorney who uses intercepted conversations to cross-examine a witness cannot be convicted under the Act unless he knows or has reason to know that the communications were intercepted in violation of the Act).

3. ***Authorization:*** Title III provides that a court order may be obtained authorizing or approving the interception of wire or oral communications when such interception may provide or has provided evidence of—a long list of specified crimes. Title III was amended by the USA PATRIOT ACT to add to the list of crimes those related to computer fraud and abuse, use of chemical weapons, and terrorism.

4. ***Procedural Requirements for Application:*** To obtain an order authorizing interception of a wire, oral, or electronic communication, an officer must make a written filing under oath or affirmation to a judge of competent jurisdiction and must include, among other things:

"a full and complete statement of the facts and circumstances relied upon by the applicant, to justify his belief that an order should be issued, including details as to the particular offense that has been, is being, or is about to be committed";

unless the application is for a "roving" wiretap, "a particular description of the nature and location of the facilities from which or the place where the communication is to be intercepted";

"a particular description of the type of communications sought to be intercepted";

"the identity of the person, if known, committing the offense and whose communications are to be intercepted";

"a full and complete statement as to whether or not other investigative procedures have been tried and failed or why they reasonably appear to be unlikely to succeed if tried or to be too dangerous";

"a statement of the period of time for which the interception is required to be maintained"; and

a full and complete statement of any prior applications made with judges to intercept communications with any of the targets.

5. ***Order Issued by the Court:*** Upon a proper submission, the court "may enter an ex parte order * * * authorizing or approving interception of wire, oral or electronic communications" if the court finds that:

there is probable cause to believe that an individual is committing, has committed, or is about to commit an enumerated offense;

there is probable cause to believe that particular communications concerning that offense will be obtained through the interception;

"normal investigative procedures have been tried and have failed or reasonably appear to be unlikely to succeed if tried or to be too dangerous";[33] and

---

[33] The statute's reference to other available investigative methods is known as the "necessity" requirement. But it is not an "exhaustion" requirement. As the Court stated in United States v.

there is probable cause to believe that the place where the communications are coming from are being used, or are about to be used, in connection with the commission of the specified offense.

6. ***Particularity Requirements***: A court order authorizing interception of communications must provide the following particularized information:

"the identity of the person, if known, whose communications are to be intercepted";[34]

"the nature and location of the communications facilities as to which, or the place where, authority to intercept is granted";

"a particular description of the type of communication sought to be intercepted, and a statement of the particular offense to which it relates";[35]

"the identity of the agency authorized to intercept the communications, and of the person authorizing the application"; and

"the period of time during which such interception is authorized, including a statement as to whether or not the interception shall automatically terminate when the described communication has been first obtained."

7. ***Time Limits***: An order permitting interception of communications under Title III must be limited in duration. It cannot authorize interception "for any period longer than is necessary to achieve the objective of the authorization, nor in any event longer than thirty days." Extensions of an order may be granted, but only upon application for an extension establishing necessity. The period of extension can be no longer than the judge deems necessary to achieve the purposes for which it was granted and in no event for longer than thirty days.

8. ***Minimization:*** Every order under Title III must contain a provision that the interception "shall be conducted in such a way as to

---

Giordano, 416 U.S. 505 (1974), the statute was intended to ensure not that wiretaps are used only as a last resort, "but that they were not to be routinely employed as the initial step in a criminal investigation." Thus, the statute does not require that alternative investigative procedures have been tried and failed, "but only that the success of other methods of investigation appear unlikely." United States v. Rivera, 527 F.3d 891 (9th Cir.2008) (necessity requirement met where it was clear that officers did not use the wiretap as the initial step in the investigation but instead used numerous techniques, and considered using several others, over the course of a 19-month investigation, before applying for the wiretap); United States v. Gordon, 871 F.3d 35 (1st Cir. 2017) ("necessity is not an absolute" but "must be viewed through what is pragmatic and achievable in the real world").

[34] In United States v. Kahn, 415 U.S. 143 (1974), the Court held that where the government knew of the existence of a person but did not know she was using the phone for illegal purposes, she was not a person whose identity must be disclosed under this section.

[35] It is enough for the government to cite the statutory offenses. United States v. Gordon, 871 F.3d 35 (1st Cir. 2017) ("the enumeration of specific criminal statutes itself serves to identify particular offenses and, thus, satisfies this facet of the particularity requirement").

minimize the interception of communications not otherwise subject to interception." This "minimization" requirement means that officers must stop monitoring a conversation as soon as it becomes apparent that it is not about the criminal activity that justified the court's order.[36]

9. ***Exigent Circumstances:*** Officers with probable cause can intercept communications without a court order, for a period no more than 48 hours, if an emergency situation exists that involves "immediate danger of death or serious physical injury to any person, conspiratorial activities threatening the national security interest, or conspiratorial activities characteristic of organized crime."

10. ***Inventory:*** Within a reasonable time and in no case more than 90 days of the issuance of a court order, the party whose communications were intercepted must receive an inventory which must include among other things notice of the fact and date of the entry of the order, and the fact that communications were intercepted. The court may in its discretion make available for inspection "such portions of the intercepted communications, applications and orders as the judge determines to be in the interest of justice." On an ex parte showing of good cause the court may order that the delivery of the inventory be postponed.[37]

11. ***Remedies:*** Any "aggrieved person" may move to suppress the contents of any intercepted "wire or oral communication, or evidence derived therefrom," on the grounds that—

the communication was unlawfully intercepted;

the order of authorization or approval under which it was intercepted is insufficient on its face; or

the interception was not made in conformity with the order of authorization or approval.

12. ***Roving Wiretaps***: Title III allows for "roving" wiretaps, i.e., interception of communications that are not tied to a particular location. An order for a roving wiretap can be issued upon a detailed showing that a

---

[36] In Scott v. United States, 436 U.S. 128 (1978), the Court held it irrelevant that officers had no subjective intent to comply with the minimization requirement. What is controlling, said the Court, is whether the agents actually intercepted conversations that were not otherwise subject to interception under the Act.

The court in United States v. Gordon, 871 F.3d 35 (1st Cir. 2017) notes that blanket suppression is not a necessary remedy for a violation of the minimization requirement: "A minimization violation can often be cured through a less draconian remedy: suppression of only those calls that the court determines should have been minimized."

[37] In United States v. Donovan, 429 U.S. 413 (1977), the Court held that when the government inadvertently excluded persons from its list of those intercepted and thus deprived them of the inventory notice, suppression of evidence was not warranted because the requirements did not play a "substantive role" in the statutory scheme. The Court in United States v. Ojeda Rios, 495 U.S. 257 (1990), held that a failure to comply with the Title III requirement that tapes be immediately sealed would not result in suppression if the government's error was the result of a good faith, objectively reasonable misinterpretation of the statute.

stationary wiretap will not be a sufficient means for intercepting the targeted communications. See United States v. Oliva, 686 F.3d 1106 (9th Cir. 2012) (orders allowing surveillance of cellphones authorized the government to transform the cellphones into roving electronic bugs through the use of sophisticated technology; government needed to specifically request that authority in order to have it provided).

The constitutionality of the Title III Wiretap Act has never been seriously challenged. This is likely due to the fact that it imposes procedural and substantive limitations beyond those described by the Warrant Clause—a "super-warrant requirement." It and its legislative progeny have been targets for trenchant critique, however. See, e.g., Schwartz, The Legitimization of Electronic Eavesdropping: The Politics of "Law and Order," 67 Mich.L.Rev. 455 (1969). The Supreme Court's handling of important questions under the statute is criticized in Goldsmith, The Supreme Court and Title III; Rewriting the Law of Electronic Surveillance, 74 J.Crim.L. & Crim. 1 (1983).

For an article analyzing the changes wrought to Title III by the PATRIOT ACT, including the authorization of "roving wiretaps", see Orin Kerr, Internet Surveillance After the USA PATRIOT ACT: The Big Brother That Isn't, 97 Nw.U.L.Rev. 607 (2003).

B. THE FOREIGN INTELLIGENCE SURVEILLANCE ACT

Title III exempts interceptions of communications involving foreign intelligence, as Congress determined that matters of national security could not be accommodated by the strictures of Title III: it provides that "nothing contained [herein], shall be deemed to affect the acquisition by the United States Government of foreign intelligence information from international or foreign communications, or foreign intelligence activities conducted in accordance with otherwise applicable Federal law involving a foreign electronic communications system."

Interception of communications pertinent to foreign intelligence are governed by the Foreign Intelligence Surveillance Act of 1978, 50 U.S.C.A. § 1801 et seq. FISA differs from Title III in several important respects:

1) The government does not need to show traditional probable cause that a crime has been or will be committed. All that must be shown is that "the target of the electronic surveillance is a foreign power or agent of a foreign power." This includes a so-called "Lone Wolf" who is not directly affiliated but who engages in "international terrorism." See, e.g., United States v. Wen, 471 F.3d 777 (7th Cir. 2006) (probable cause to believe that a foreign agent was

communicating with his controllers outside the United States was sufficient to support a FISA warrant; if, while conducting this surveillance, agents discover evidence of a domestic crime, they may use it to prosecute for that offense).

2) Requests for an order are made to one of eleven federal district judges specially selected by the Chief Justice of the Supreme Court. In order to secure an order, the application must set forth the identity or description of the target, and a statement of facts or circumstances relied upon to justify the officer's belief that the target is a foreign power or agent of a foreign power and that each facility or location to be subjected to surveillance is being used or is about to be used by the target.

3) Notice and inventory requirements are much less stringent; in fact, a target need *never* be notified of FISA surveillance if the Attorney General determines that there is a national security interest in continuing to maintain the secrecy of the search.

4) If there is a motion to suppress, the government may withhold the application it submitted to the FISA court, as well as the court order, on grounds of national security.

5) The "exigent circumstances" exception allows interceptions without a court order for up to 72 hours for an individual and for up to a year for foreign governmental entities.

6) Court review of a FISA application is extremely limited: "[I]n the absence of a prima facie showing of a fraudulent statement by the certifying officer, procedural regularity is the only determination to be made if a non-United States person is the target." United States v. Campa, 529 F.3d 980 (11th Cir. 2008). If a United States person is a target, the review is only over whether "some of the certifications are clearly erroneous." Defendants have argued that FISA is invalid because it does not assure adequate judicial review. But these arguments have been rejected. See United States v. Stewart, 590 F.3d 93 (2d Cir. 2009) (upholding FISA surveillance of a lawyer representing a defendant charged with conspiracy to bomb the World Trade Center).

Up until 9/11/2001, FISA was used exclusively to conduct foreign counterintelligence investigations. But Section 218 of the PATRIOT ACT amended FISA to authorize electronic surveillance even in investigations whose primary purpose is criminal prosecution, so long as foreign surveillance remains a "significant" purpose. See United States v. Ning Wen, 477 F.3d 896 (7th Cir. 2007) (FISA now applies to interceptions that have international intelligence as a "significant purpose"); United States v. Stewart, 590 F.3d 93 (2d Cir. 2009) (reviewing and rejecting defendant's argument that the primary purpose for wiretapping her under FISA was to pursue a criminal investigation). "Since the passage of the PATRIOT ACT, the government has instituted a significant number of criminal prosecutions involving evidence gathered through FISA surveillance. In 2004, the Federal Government requested and obtained 1,754 FISA orders to conduct searches and surveillance, more than seven times the number of FISA orders issued in the year 2000." Siegler, The PATRIOT ACT's Erosion of Constitutional Rights, 32 Litigation 18 (2006). For a case finding that the FISA "significant purpose" test is reasonable under the Fourth Amendment, see United States v. Duka, 671 F.3d 329 (3d Cir. 2011).

Despite the very mild limitations on surveillance imposed by FISA, the George W. Bush Administration took the position that it needed more flexibility in monitoring suspected terrorist activity. Congress responded by enacting the FISA Amendments Act of 2008. The Amendment left much of FISA intact, but it established a new and independent source of intelligence collection authority, beyond that granted in traditional FISA. Section 702 of FISA, 50 U.S.C. § 1881a, which was enacted as part of the FISA Amendments Act, supplements pre-existing FISA authority by creating a new framework under which the Government may seek the FISA court's authorization of certain foreign intelligence surveillance targeting the communications of non-U.S. persons located abroad. Unlike traditional FISA surveillance, Section 702 does not require the Government to demonstrate probable cause that the target of the electronic surveillance is a foreign power or agent of a foreign power. And, unlike traditional FISA, Section 702 does not require the Government to specify the nature and location of each of the particular facilities or places at which the electronic surveillance will occur. All that is required in a showing to the court is that the surveillance is of non-U.S. "persons reasonably believed to be located outside the United States" and that the targeting concerns "foreign intelligence information." Surveillance under Section 702 may not be intentionally targeted at any person known to be in the United States or any U.S. person reasonably believed to be located abroad Additionally, acquisitions under Section 702 must comport with the Fourth Amendment. Moreover, surveillance under Section 702 is subject to congressional oversight and several types of Executive Branch review. Section 702 has a sunset provision and thus requires active renewal by Congress. It was last renewed in January, 2018.

Section 702 mandates that the Government obtain the Foreign Intelligence Surveillance Court's approval of "targeting" procedures, "minimization" procedures, and a governmental certification regarding proposed surveillance. Among other things, the Government's certification must attest that (1) procedures are in place "that have been approved, have been submitted for approval, or will be submitted with the certification for approval by the [FISC] that are reasonably designed" to ensure that an acquisition is "limited to targeting persons reasonably believed to be located outside" the United States; (2) minimization procedures adequately restrict the acquisition, retention, and dissemination of nonpublic information about unconsenting U.S. persons, as appropriate; (3) guidelines have been adopted to ensure compliance with targeting limits and the Fourth Amendment; and (4) the procedures and guidelines referred to above comport with the Fourth Amendment.

Data Mining Under—and Around—FISA

In 2013, information was leaked that the National Security Agency obtained FISA orders to engage in data mining of phone calls, emails, and internet activity of millions of Americans. The orders purportedly did not allow interception of content, but did allow bulk collection of metadata—i.e., the length of a call, the number called, the recipient of an email, the fact of access to an internet page, etc. The data-mining was intended to further foreign intelligence surveillance but captured domestic transmissions as well. NSA contended that the contents of purely domestic transmissions were not searched, but the metadata was collected.

On June 2, 2015, President Obama signed the USA Freedom Act, which put certain limits on the NSA's bulk data collection program. As stated by Congressman Sensenbrenner, who introduced the legislation, the purpose of the USA Freedom Act is "[t]o rein in the dragnet collection of data by the National Security Agency (NSA) and other government agencies, increase transparency of the Foreign Intelligence Surveillance Court (FISC), provide businesses the ability to release information regarding FISA requests, and create an independent constitutional advocate to argue cases before the FISC."

The Act eliminated NSA bulk data collection. Instead, phone companies retain the data and the NSA can obtain information about targeted individuals only with permission from the FISA court. The government does not need probable cause to obtain such an order, however. Rather, the government can get an order to require the following:

- production on an ongoing basis of call detail records created before, on, or after the date of the application relating to an authorized investigation to protect against international terrorism, in which case the specific selection term must specifically identify an individual, account, or personal device; or

- production of call detail records or other tangible things in any other manner, in which case the selection term must specifically identify an individual, a federal officer or employee, a group, an entity, an association, a corporation, a foreign power, an account, a physical or an electronic address, a personal device, or any other specific identifier but is prohibited from including, when not used as part of a specific identifier, a broad geographic region (including the United States, a city, county, state, zip code, or area code) or an electronic communication or remote computing service provider, unless the provider is itself a subject of an authorized investigation.

To get such an order, the government must show: (1) reasonable grounds to believe that the call detail records are relevant to such investigation; and (2) a reasonable, articulable suspicion that the specific selection term is associated with a foreign power or an agent of a foreign power engaged in international terrorism or activities in preparation for such terrorism.

The USA Freedom Act also purports to bring some sunlight into FISA court decision-making, and establishes a panel of civil libertarians that will have input into the policy-based decisions of FISA courts and provides for an adversarial contests before the FISC using court-assigned attorneys.

For a full description of the USA Freedom Act, go to https://www.congress.gov/bill/114th-congress/house-bill/2048. It should be noted, for the purposes of a course on Constitutional Criminal Procedure, that it has never been definitively held that the NSA's bulk data program was *unconstitutional.* The Freedom Act is a legislative response to what Congress saw as offensive practices undertaken as a result of the NSA's reading of the PATRIOT Act to allow bulk data collection of phone calls.

For more on the use of FISA procedures after 9/11, see Maclin, The Bush Administration's Terrorist Surveillance Program and the Fourth Amendment's Warrant Requirement: Lessons from Justice Powell and the *Keith* case, 41 U.C. Davis L. Rev. 1259 (2008).

IX. REMEDIES FOR FOURTH AMENDMENT VIOLATIONS

A. THE BACKGROUND OF THE EXCLUSIONARY RULE

The exclusionary rule provides that evidence obtained in violation of the Fourth Amendment must be excluded from trial. But the exclusionary rule was not born contemporaneously with the Fourth Amendment. The Bill of Rights is not explicit as to remedies. For over a century after the adoption of the Fourth Amendment, virtually the only remedies available to victims of illegal searches were suits in trespass for damages, or in replevin for return of the goods seized. The trespass alternative was usually impractical. Replevin had no chance of success if the goods seized were contraband or the fruits or instrumentalities of crime because these items were forfeited to the state regardless of the legality of the seizure.

Exclusionary Rule for the Federal Courts: Weeks v. United States

The Court in Weeks v. United States, 232 U.S. 383 (1914), held that evidence obtained in violation of the Fourth Amendment must be excluded in federal courts. Justice Day wrote for a unanimous Court that if evidence obtained in violation of the Fourth Amendment could be used against a criminal defendant, then "the protection of the Fourth Amendment declaring his right to be secure against such searches and seizures is of no value." The Court noted that the officers who obtained the evidence illegally were "doubtless prompted by the desire to bring further proof to the aid of the Government." It concluded that "[t]o sanction such proceedings would be to affirm by judicial decision a manifest neglect if not an open defiance of the prohibitions of the Constitution intended for the protection of the people against such unauthorized action."

Two themes articulated in *Weeks,* and finding recurrent expression in later cases dealing with the rationale for excluding evidence, are that the exclusionary rule is the only effective means of protecting Fourth Amendment rights and that an interest in judicial integrity requires that courts not sanction illegal searches by admitting the fruits of illegality into evidence. In Silverthorne Lumber Co. v. United States, 251 U.S. 385 (1920), these considerations were held to prohibit the copying and investigative use of illegally seized documents. The Court stressed that "[t]he essence of a provision forbidding the acquisition of evidence in a certain way is [not merely that] evidence so acquired shall not be used before the Court but that it shall not be used at all."

B. THE EXCLUSIONARY RULE AND THE STATES

Weeks was grounded in the Court's supervisory power over federal courts. The holding was limited to cases where the illegal search was conducted by federal officers and the evidence proffered in federal court. The *Weeks* Court explicitly rejected the notion that the exclusionary rule should apply to violations by state or local police acting on their own accord or must apply in state courts. These limitations reflected both the fact that the Supreme Court's supervisory authority did not extend to state courts and that the Fourth Amendment had not been incorporated, and therefore did not bind the States or their agents.

One of those barriers fell in Wolf v. Colorado, 338 U.S. 25 (1949). Writing for the Court, Justice Frankfurter held that "The security of one's privacy against arbitrary intrusion by the police—which is at the core of the Fourth Amendment—is basic to a free society. It is therefore implicit in 'the concept of ordered liberty' and as such enforceable against the States through the Due Process Clause." The Court made clear, however, that its holding did not impose the exclusionary rule on the States. As Justice Frankfurter wrote:

> [T]he immediate question is whether the basic right to protection against arbitrary intrusion by the police demands the exclusion of logically relevant evidence obtained by an unreasonable search and seizure because, in a federal prosecution for a federal crime, it would be excluded. As a matter of inherent reason, one would suppose this to be an issue as to which men with complete devotion to the protection of the right of privacy might give different answers. When we find that in fact most of the English-speaking world does not regard as vital to such protection the exclusion of evidence thus obtained, we must hesitate to treat this remedy as an essential ingredient of the right. The contrariety of views of the States is particularly impressive in view of the careful reconsideration which they have given the problem in the light of the *Weeks* decision. [In 1949, 31 states had rejected the exclusionary rule and 16 states had adopted it.]
>
> The jurisdictions which have rejected the Weeks doctrine have not left the right to privacy without other means of protection. Indeed, the exclusion of evidence is a remedy which directly serves only to protect those upon whose person or premises something incriminating has been found. We cannot, therefore, regard it as a departure from basic standards to remand such persons, together with those who emerge scatheless from a search, to the remedies of private action and such protection as the internal discipline of the police, under the eyes of an alert public opinion, may afford. Granting that in practice the exclusion of evidence may be an effective way of deterring unreasonable searches, it is not for this Court to condemn as falling below the minimal standards assured by the Due Process Clause a State's reliance upon other methods which, if consistently enforced, would be equally effective. We cannot brush aside the experience of States which deem the incidence of such conduct by the police too slight to call for a deterrent remedy not by way of disciplinary measures but by overriding the relevant rules of evidence.

In the next decade, the issue received the Court's attention twice more. In Rochin v. California, 342 U.S. 165 (1952), the shocking method used by the State to obtain incriminating evidence—pumping the defendant's stomach—was held to so offend "a sense of justice" as to require exclusion at a state trial. Two years later, in Irvine v. California, 347 U.S. 128 (1954), *Wolf* was reaffirmed, 5–4, and evidence was admitted where the search of a home by a local law enforcement officer, although illegal, did not involve a physical assault on the suspect's person.

The asymmetry between remedies available in federal and state courts created by *Weeks* and preserved in *Wolf* amounted to an arbitrage opportunity. State officers could obtain evidence illegally and then offer it to federal officers for use in federal prosecutions. So, too, federal agents who seized evidence illegally could hand that evidence to state investigators for use in state prosecutions. This "silver platter doctrine" survived until Elkins v. United States, 364 U.S. 206 (1960), where the Court, again exercising its "supervisory power over the administration of criminal justice in the federal courts," prohibited the admission in federal courts of evidence seized illegally by agents of the States.

Writing for the Court in *Elkins*, Justice Stewart postulated that the exclusionary rule "is calculated to prevent, not to repair. Its purpose is to deter—to compel respect for the constitutional guaranty in the only effectively available way—by removing the incentive to disregard it." Justice Stewart admitted to a paucity of empirical evidence demonstrating the effectiveness of the exclusionary rule as a deterrent, but noted a "seemingly inexorable" shift toward its adoption by state legislatures and courts. He highlighted in particular the experience in California where

> In 1955, the Supreme Court of that State resolutely turned its back on many years of precedent and adopted the exclusionary rule. People v. Cahan, 44 Cal. 2d 434, 282 P.2d 905.
>
>> "We have been compelled to reach that conclusion because other remedies have completely failed to secure compliance with the constitutional provisions on the part of police officers, with the attendant result that the courts under the old rule have been constantly required to participate in, and in effect condone, the lawless activities of law enforcement officers. . . . Experience has demonstrated, however, that neither administrative, criminal, nor civil remedies are effective in suppressing lawless searches and seizures. The innocent suffer with the guilty, and we cannot close our eyes to the effect the rule we adopt will have on the rights of those not before the court." 44 Cal. 2d 434, at 445, 447, 282 P.2d 905, at 911–912, 913.
>
> The chief law enforcement officer of California was quoted as having made this practical evaluation of the *Cahan* decision less than two years later:
>
>> "The over-all effects of the *Cahan* decision, particularly in view of the rules now worked out by the Supreme Court, have been excellent. A much greater education is called for on the part of all peace officers of California. As a result, I am confident they will be much better police officers. I think there is more cooperation with the District Attorneys and this will make for better administration of criminal justice."

Based on this and other apparently successful experiments with the exclusionary rule in the States, Justice Stewart concluded that, as a matter of federalism and judicial integrity, it would be inappropriate to preserve a safe harbor in federal courts for evidence seized illegally by state officials. He reasoned as follows:

> The very essence of a healthy federalism depends upon the avoidance of needless conflict between state and federal courts. Yet when a federal court sitting in an exclusionary state admits evidence lawlessly seized by state agents, it not only frustrates state policy, but frustrates that policy in a particularly inappropriate and ironic way. For, by admitting the unlawfully seized evidence, the federal court serves to defeat the state's effort to assure obedience to the Federal Constitution. In states which have not adopted the exclusionary rule, on the other hand, it would work no conflict with local policy for a federal court to decline to receive evidence unlawfully seized by state officers. * * * Even less should the federal courts be accomplices in the willful disobedience of a Constitution they are sworn to uphold.

Justice Stewart was clear, however, that the Court's holding was limited and "affects not at all the freedom of the states to develop and apply their own sanctions in their own way."

In Mapp v. Ohio, 367 U.S. 643 (1961), the Supreme Court once again considered the question whether to mandate the exclusionary rule in state proceedings. On the briefs and at oral argument, *Mapp* appeared to be exclusively a First Amendment case asking whether Miss Mapp had the right to possess "obscene" material in her home. The exclusionary rule issue was neither briefed nor argued. Yet, the Court overruled *Wolf* 5–3. The change is partly explained by the fact that six members of the *Wolf* Court were no longer on the Bench.

MAPP V. OHIO

Supreme Court of the United States, 1961.
367 U.S. 643.

JUSTICE CLARK delivered the opinion of the Court.

* * *

Some five years after *Wolf,* in answer to a plea made here Term after Term that we overturn its doctrine on applicability of the *Weeks* exclusionary rule, this Court indicated that such should not be done until the States had "adequate opportunity to adopt or reject the [*Weeks*] rule." Irvine v. California. * * *

* * * Today we once again examine *Wolf's* constitutional documentation of the right to privacy free from unreasonable state intrusion, and, after its dozen years on our books, are led by it to close the only courtroom door remaining open to evidence secured by official lawlessness in flagrant abuse of that basic right, reserved to all persons as

a specific guarantee against that very same unlawful conduct. We hold that all evidence obtained by searches and seizures in violation of the Constitution is, by that same authority, inadmissible in a state court.

* * * Since the Fourth Amendment's right of privacy has been declared enforceable against the States through the Due Process Clause of the Fourteenth, it is enforceable against them by the same sanction of exclusion as is used against the Federal Government. * * * [T]he admission of the new constitutional right by *Wolf* could not consistently tolerate denial of its most important constitutional privilege, namely, the exclusion of the evidence which an accused had been forced to give by reason of the unlawful seizure. To hold otherwise is to grant the right but in reality to withhold its privilege and enjoyment. * * *

Indeed, we are aware of no restraint, similar to that rejected today, conditioning the enforcement of any other basic constitutional right. The right to privacy, no less important than any other right carefully and particularly reserved to the people, would stand in marked contrast to all other rights declared as basic to a free society. This Court has not hesitated to enforce as strictly against the States as it does against the Federal Government the rights of free speech and of a free press, the rights to notice and to a fair, public trial, including, as it does, the right not to be convicted by use of a coerced confession, however logically relevant it be, and without regard to its reliability. * * * Why should not the same rule apply to what is tantamount to coerced testimony by way of unconstitutional seizure of goods, papers, effects, documents, etc.? * * *

* * *

There are those who say, as did Justice (then Judge) Cardozo, that under our constitutional exclusionary doctrine "[t]he criminal is to go free because the constable has blundered." People v. Defore, 242 N.Y. at 21. In some cases this will undoubtedly be the result. But * * * there is another consideration—the imperative of judicial integrity. The criminal goes free, if he must, but it is the law that sets him free. Nothing can destroy a government more quickly than its failure to observe its own laws, or worse, its disregard of the charter of its own existence. * * *

The ignoble shortcut to conviction left open to the States tends to destroy the entire system of constitutional restraints on which the liberties of the people rest. Having once recognized that the right to privacy embodied in the Fourth Amendment is enforceable against the States, and that the right to be secure against rude invasions of privacy by state officers is, therefore, constitutional in origin, we can no longer permit that right to remain an empty promise. Because it is enforceable in the same manner and to like effect as other basic rights secured by the Due Process Clause, we can no longer permit it to be revocable at the whim of any police officer who, in the name of law enforcement itself, chooses to suspend its enjoyment. Our decision, founded on reason and truth, gives to the individual no more than that which the Constitution guarantees him, to the police officer no less than that to which honest law enforcement is entitled, and, to the courts, that judicial integrity so necessary in the true administration of justice. * * *

* * *

[Justice Black concurred in a separate opinion, arguing that the Constitutional basis for the majority rule was the Fourth Amendment in conjunction with the Fifth Amendment's ban against compelled self-incrimination. The concurrences of Justices Douglas and Stewart have been omitted. Justice Stewart did not reach the Fourth Amendment question, preferring to decide the case on First Amendment grounds.]

JUSTICE HARLAN, whom JUSTICE FRANKFURTER and JUSTICE WHITTAKER join, dissenting.

* * *

I would not impose upon the States this federal exclusionary remedy. The reasons given by the majority for now suddenly turning its back on *Wolf* seem to me notably unconvincing.

* * *

[T]he majority now finds an incongruity in *Wolf's* discriminating perception between the demands of "ordered liberty" as respects the basic right of "privacy" and the means of securing it among the States. That perception, resting both on a sensitive regard for our federal system and a sound recognition of this Court's remoteness from particular state problems, is for me the strength of that decision.

* * *

NOTE ON MAPP

What is the basis for the majority's conclusion that the exclusionary rule is required by the Constitution? Obviously, the texts of the Fourth and Fourteenth Amendments lend no support to the proposition. The origins of the rule likewise throw no historical weight behind its acceptance. In the final analysis, isn't the majority implicitly deciding that the exclusion of evidence is the only effective sanction, and that the right to be free from unreasonable searches is "a dead letter" without a sanction? If other alternatives had proved effective in deterring violations, would the Court have found exclusion to be a constitutional requirement?

Would a showing that exclusion of evidence has no deterrent effect whatsoever have required a different result? Professor Dripps, in Living with *Leon,* 95 Yale L.J. 906 (1986), argues that if no sanction attaches to a Fourth

Amendment violation, the Amendment does not qualify as a *law*, thus betraying "the fundamental principle of constitutionalism, which is after all that the Constitution states the law." He argues that "even if the sanction does not deter, the refusal to apply it or anything else expresses the judgment that the underlying norm is of little importance."

As we will see in *Leon, infra,* the Court has held that, despite its decision in *Mapp,* the exclusionary rule *is not constitutionally required for all Fourth Amendment violations*, in part because the violation of a Fourth Amendment right occurs at the time of the original police intrusion. The argument is that later exclusion from the trial has nothing to do with the already completed violation, and that introduction of the evidence at trial is not a separate violation of privacy. For an argument that the Fourth Amendment violation is not complete at the time of the intrusion, and that the exclusionary rule is constitutionally required, see Heffernan, On Justifying Fourth Amendment Exclusion, 1989 Wis.L.Rev. 1193.

C. ARGUMENTS FOR AND AGAINST THE EXCLUSIONARY RULE

Many judges are not enamored of the exclusionary rule. For example, Judge Bowman had this to say about the exclusionary rule in United States v. Jefferson, 906 F.2d 346 (8th Cir.1990), a case in which the entire court agreed that evidence obtained during a stop without reasonable suspicion had to be excluded due to the exclusionary rule:

> This case vividly illustrates the perversity of the exclusionary rule. Here, an officer's educated hunch led to the discovery of evidence (nine kilograms of cocaine) of substantial criminal activity. This discovery occurred as a result of information the officer developed by asking questions and examining documents in the course of his routine check of a parked car and its occupants at a highway rest stop. The ordinary law-abiding citizen, I believe, would think the officer should be commended for his fine work, and the cocaine dealers punished. Instead, because we hold (as I agree, under the existing case law, we must) that a "seizure" within the meaning of the Fourth Amendment occurred before the officer had formed an objectively reasonable basis for suspecting the defendants of criminal activity, the exclusionary rule requires that the evidence be suppressed. The defendants thus exit unpunished, free to continue dealing illegal drugs to the pathetic addicts and contemptible scofflaws who comprise the national market for these substances. As for the officer, far from his being commended, it is judicially recorded that he blundered, and the point once again is driven home that legalistic observance of even the most technical of the judge-created rules of search and seizure—rules which, like the Fourth Amendment itself, seek to protect law-abiding citizens from intrusive conduct by officers of the state—is more important than

intelligent, courageous, and vigorous initiative to expose criminal activity and bring those responsible for it to the bar of justice.

It has been reported that since 1961, when [*Mapp* was decided], "the murder rate has doubled, rape has quadrupled and robbery has quintupled." Wall St.J., May 7, 1990, at A14, Col. 1. While it would be foolish to blame the exclusionary rule for all of this alarming increase in violent crime, I believe it is equally foolish to pretend that the exclusionary rule, and the *zeitgeist* it has created, is to blame for none of it.

Judge Bowman's comments prompted Chief Judge Lay to respond as follows:

If police are not deterred from illegal intrusions of privacy by excluding whatever evidence is seized, the Fourth Amendment will have no meaning or force. Surely an appreciation for the history and purpose of our basic freedoms will never allow emotional fear to justify an environment where there is no check on the abuse of police power.

The Fourth Amendment protects the good guy as well as the bad. It would mean very little to anyone if it did not. The argument that since 1961 murders have doubled, rapes quadrupled, and robbery quintupled in part because of the exclusionary rule is a statement more fitting for headlines of the National Enquirer. It is irrational hyperbole totally unsupported in fact or in law.

Supporters of the exclusionary rule generally make four points in its favor:

1. The rule preserves judicial integrity, by insulating the courts from tainted evidence;

2. The rule prevents the government from profiting from its own wrong;

3. The rule is not costly, because it only excludes what should never have been obtained in the first place; and

4. The rule is necessary to deter police misconduct.

See, e.g., Barnett, Resolving the Dilemma of the Exclusionary Rule: An Application of Restitutive Principles of Justice, 32 Emory L.J. 937 (1983).

Professor Amar, in Fourth Amendment First Principles, 107 Harv.L.Rev. 757 (1994), attacks each of these justifications. As to the judicial integrity rationale, Amar responds: "we must remember that integrity and fairness are also threatened by excluding evidence that will help the justice system to reach a true verdict. Thus, the courts best affirm their integrity not by closing their eyes to truthful evidence, but by opening their doors to any civil suit brought against wayward government officials, even one brought by a convict."

Professor Amar continues his critique of the exclusionary rule as follows:

> Consider next the nice-sounding idea that government should not profit from its own wrongdoing. Our society, however, also cherishes the notion that cheaters—or murderers or rapists, for that matter—should not prosper. When the murderer's bloody knife is introduced, it is not only the government that profits; the people also profit when those who truly do commit crimes against person and property are duly convicted on the basis of reliable evidence. * * *
>
> The classic response is that setting criminals free is a cost of the Fourth Amendment itself, and not of the much-maligned exclusionary rule. If the government had simply obeyed the Fourth Amendment it would never have found the bloody knife. Thus, excluding the knife simply restores the status quo ante and confers no benefit on the murderer. The classic response is too quick.
>
> In many situations, it is far from clear that the illegality of a search is indeed a but-for cause of the later introduction of an item found in the search. Suppose the police could easily get a warrant, but fail to do so because they think the case at hand falls into a judicially recognized exception to the warrant requirement. A court later disagrees—and so, under current doctrine, the search was unconstitutional. But if the court goes on to exclude the bloody knife, it does indeed confer a huge benefit on the murderer. The police could easily have obtained a warrant before the search, so the illegality is not a but-for cause of the introduction of the knife into evidence.
>
> * * *
>
> But even if a defendant could conclusively establish but-for causation, the bloody knife should still come in as evidence. Not all but-for consequences of an illegal search are legally cognizable. * * * [I]f an illegal search turns up a ton of marijuana, the government need not return the contraband even if the government's possession of the marijuana is clearly a but-for consequence of its illegal search. Indeed, the government may sell the marijuana (say, for legitimate medical uses) and use the proceeds to finance the continued war on drugs. In a very real way, the government *has* profited from its own wrong.

Finally, Professor Amar critiques the deterrence rationale of the exclusionary rule, and decries the fact that deterrence comes by way of benefit to criminal defendants.

> Deterrence is concerned with the government, it is concerned with systematic impact. It treats the criminal defendant merely as a surrogate for the larger public interest in restraining the government. The criminal defendant is a kind of private attorney general.

> But the worst kind. He is self-selected and self-serving. He is often unrepresentative of the larger class of law-abiding citizens. Indeed, he is often despised by the public, the class he implicitly is supposed to represent. He will litigate on the worst set of facts, heedless that the result will be a bad precedent for the Fourth Amendment generally. He cares only about the case at hand—his case—and has no long view. He is not a sophisticated repeat player. He rarely hires the best lawyer. He cares only about exclusion—and can get only exclusion—even if other remedies (damages or injunctions) would better prevent future violations. * * * He is, in short, an awkward champion of the Fourth Amendment.
>
> He is also overcompensated. * * * In a criminal case, if we insist on using criminal defendants as private attorneys general, why not give a defendant who successfully establishes a Fourth Amendment violation only a ten percent sentence discount—surely a tangible incentive—and substitute for the remaining ninety percent some other structural remedy, injunctive or damages, that will flow to the direct benefit of law-abiding citizens? * * *
>
> Put differently, if deterrence is the key, the idea is to make the government pay, in some way, for its past misdeeds, in order to discourage future ones. But why should that payment flow to the guilty? Under the exclusionary rule, the more guilty you are, the more you benefit. * * * In sum, when it comes to private attorneys general, the exclusionary rule's deterrence rationale looks in the wrong place—to paradigmatically guilty criminal defendants rather than to prototypically law-abiding civil plaintiffs.

Professor Slobogin, in Why Liberals Should Chuck the Exclusionary Rule, 1999 Univ. Ill. L.Rev. 363, argues that the exclusionary rule should be replaced by an effective remedy of monetary damages.

> [I]f optimal deterrence of illegal searches and seizures is the goal, the exclusionary rule is a poor solution. Changing or suppressing behavior is a complex and difficult task. It is especially difficult when, as is true with many types of illegal searches and seizures, the behavior is implicitly or explicitly endorsed by peers, superiors, and a large segment of the general public. Without a strong disincentive to engage in such conduct, it will continue. Thus, a regime that directly sanctions officers and their departments is preferable to the [exclusionary] rule. Although there are many versions of such a regime, it should have several core components: (1) a liquidated damages/penalty for all unconstitutional actions, preferably based on the average officer's salary; (2) personal liability, at the liquidated damages sum, of officers who knowingly or recklessly violate the Fourth Amendment; (3) entity liability, at the liquidated damages sum, for all other violations; (4)

state-paid legal assistance for those with Fourth Amendment claims; and (5) a judicial decisionmaker.

That such a regime is a better deterrent than the exclusionary rule does not establish that it should be adopted, of course. The exclusionary rule clearly does have some deterrent effect. If it proves to be considerably less costly than a damages regime, perhaps it should remain the sanction of choice. It is unlikely that the rule is significantly "cheaper," however, whether one looks at financial or other types of costs. * * * A conservative estimate is that approximately 10,000 felons and 55,000 misdemeanants evade punishment each year because of successful Fourth Amendment suppression motions. Other costs of the rule are more subtle. These include the threat to the Fourth Amendment posed by judges and prosecutors concerned with freeing criminals, the psychic and systemic costs of routine perjury by police officers, the distracting impact of suppression hearings on the quality of defense representation on other issues, and the damage to courts and government generally because of public outrage at the huge benefit criminals receive when the cases against them are dismissed or damaged by exclusion.

For more arguments about the value of the exclusionary rule and alternative remedies, see Stuntz, The Virtues and Vices of the Exclusionary Rule, 20 Harv.J.L & Pub.Pol. 443 (1997); Perrin et al., If It's Broken, Fix It: Moving Beyond the Exclusionary Rule—A New and Extensive Empirical Study of the Exclusionary Rule and a Call for a Civil Administrative Remedy to Partially Replace the Rule, 83 Iowa L.Rev. 669 (1998); Richard Myers, Fourth Amendment Small Claims Court, 10 Ohio St. J. Crim L. 571 (2013).

For a debate over the exclusionary rule by two titans of the law, see Calabresi and Kamisar, Debate on the Search and Seizure Exclusionary Rule, 26 Harv. J. L. & Pub. Pol. 4 (2003). Judge Calabresi proposes an alternative to the exclusionary rule: that defendants could object to illegally obtained evidence, but only at *sentencing*, and if the motion is successful the defendant would receive a sentence reduction. In addition, Judge Calabresi would impose direct administrative sanctions on police officers for illegal searches and seizures. Professor Kamisar expresses doubt that administrative sanctions on wrongdoing police officers will be imposed in practice.

D. ALTERNATIVES TO EXCLUSION

The most common argument in support of the exclusionary rule is the alleged absence of alternative means of enforcing Fourth Amendment protections. The efficacy of the alternatives is, however, as hotly debated as the rule itself. In this section, other possible remedies will be evaluated, both in terms of deterrent value and workability.

It should be noted at the outset that most of these remedies could be used as *supplements* to, rather than replacements for, suppression of evidence.

1. Civil Damages Recovery

At present several forms of damage actions are available to the victim of an illegal search or seizure. Common law tort actions include false arrest, false imprisonment and trespass. More importantly, a federal civil rights action under 42 U.S.C.A. § 1983 is available when state officers, acting under color of law, violate a constitutional right. In Bivens v. Six Unknown Named Agents of Federal Bureau of Narcotics, 403 U.S. 388 (1971), the Supreme Court created a federal common law counterpart to § 1983 for violations by *federal* officials.

The two major problems involved in civil actions against police for violation of constitutional rights are first, winning, and second, collecting on the judgment. Obstacles such as governmental immunity exist in many states. Magistrates who issue invalid warrants are immune from suit. Pierson v. Ray, 386 U.S. 547, 553–55 (1967). Police officers exercising discretion are entitled to qualified immunity, so that even if they violate the Fourth Amendment, the citizen does not recover unless the law was clearly established at the time of the conduct.[38] How much Fourth Amendment law can be considered clearly established? (See *Safford, supra,* in the section on *Terry*, in which a strip search of a middle school student was found illegal under the Fourth Amendment, but the official was found not liable because the law against such an action was not clearly established at the time of the search).

Besides the daunting prospect of overcoming qualified immunity, the "moral aspects of the case" make recovery in a jury trial difficult. Many victims of illegal police practices are not very sympathetic plaintiffs. In a false arrest action, for example, proof of the plaintiff's prior convictions often can be used to impeach his credibility or to show that probable cause existed for the arrest. "Respectable" persons have the greatest chance of recovering, because they will not be tainted by their past, but the "respectable" person is probably least likely to be subject to arbitrary arrest and harassment, and thus least likely to require a tort remedy.

If a plaintiff succeeds in proving liability, the next obstacle is proving—and collecting—damages adequate to make the suit worth the effort. In a

[38] In Malley v. Briggs, 475 U.S. 335 (1986), the Court states that the question to be asked on qualified immunity with respect to a search with an invalid warrant is "whether a reasonably well-trained officer * * * would have known that his affidavit failed to establish probable cause and that he should not have applied for the warrant."

trespass action, where damages are limited to actual property loss, the award is usually small except in the most extreme search cases. Nominal damages provide no incentive for an aggrieved citizen to sue, and thus prevent private persons from effectively enforcing the public policy against police illegality. A § 1983 action, which provides for attorney fees for the prevailing party, avoids some of the drawbacks of common law tort remedies. However, proof of the requisite intent and measuring the value of constitutional rights impose additional problems.

If the plaintiff receives a substantial damage award, the final problem is collecting on the judgment. In § 1983 actions, the governmental unit employing the officer is not liable simply because one of its officers has violated the plaintiff's Fourth Amendment rights. In order to hold the government entity liable, the plaintiff must show that his injury resulted from the entity's custom or policy; otherwise the plaintiff is left to recover against the individual officer. Monell v. Department of Social Services, 436 U.S. 658 (1978) (applying the custom or policy requirement for municipal liability in § 1983 actions).

Supreme Court View on Civil Damage Recovery as an Alternative to the Exclusionary Rule: Hudson v. Michigan

Despite all these limitations on civil damages recovery for a Fourth Amendment violation, the Supreme Court in Hudson v. Michigan, 547 U.S. 586 (2006), seemed to find § 1983 actions to be a viable alternative to the exclusionary rule. The Court in *Hudson* held that a violation of the knock-and-announce requirement does not justify exclusion of evidence found in the home.[39] The defendant argued that without the exclusionary rule, such violations would not be deterred. Justice Scalia, writing for the majority, responded to that argument, and more broadly to the argument that the exclusionary rule was necessary to deter other Fourth Amendment violations, in the following passage:

> We cannot assume that exclusion in this context is necessary deterrence simply because we found that it was necessary deterrence in different contexts and long ago. That would be forcing the public today to pay for the sins and inadequacies of a legal regime that existed almost half a century ago. Dollree Mapp could not turn to 42 U.S.C. § 1983 for meaningful relief; Monroe v. Pape, 365 U.S. 167 (1961), which began the slow but steady expansion of that remedy, was decided the same Term as *Mapp*. It would be another 17 years before the § 1983 remedy was extended to reach the deep pocket of municipalities, Monell v. New York City Dept. of Social Servs., 436 U.S. 658 (1978). Citizens whose Fourth Amendment rights were violated by federal officers could not bring suit until 10 years after

[39] *Hudson* is set forth in detail in the section on the fruit of causation and attenuation, *infra*.

Mapp, with this Court's decision in Bivens v. Six Unknown Fed. Narcotics Agents, 403 U.S. 388 (1971).

Hudson complains that "it would be very hard to find a lawyer to take a case such as this", but 42 U.S.C. § 1988(b) answers this objection. Since some civil-rights violations would yield damages too small to justify the expense of litigation, Congress has authorized attorney's fees for civil-rights plaintiffs. This remedy was unavailable in the heydays of our exclusionary-rule jurisprudence, because it is tied to the availability of a cause of action. For years after *Mapp*, "very few lawyers would even consider representation of persons who had civil rights claims against the police," but now "much has changed. Citizens and lawyers are much more willing to seek relief in the courts for police misconduct." M. Avery, D. Rudovsky, & K. Blum, Police Misconduct: Law and Litigation, p. v (3d ed. 2005).

Is the Court saying that the exclusionary rule is no longer necessary to deter *any* Fourth Amendment violation, because of the modern strength and viability of § 1983 actions? What about the limitations on § 1983 liability that Justice Scalia did not discuss in *Hudson*—such as defenses of qualified immunity, and the absence of respondeat superior liability? What about the fact that many victims of Fourth Amendment violations are people with whom a jury will have little sympathy?

Fortified Civil Damages Remedy

It should be noted that after *Hudson*, any talk of a fortified damages remedy may be hypothetical, because the Court seems to think that existing damages remedies provide a sufficiently effective alternative to exclusion. Nonetheless, Professor Amar, in Fourth Amendment First Principles, 107 Harv.L.Rev.757 (1994), recommends five steps that would strengthen the deterrent effects of the existing civil damages remedy for Fourth Amendment violations. He contends that if these steps are employed, the damages remedy will provide effective deterrence against illegal police activity; the exclusionary rule can then be abolished.

Professor Amar's suggestions are as follows: First, the government should be made liable for illegal police behavior—that is, the current bar on respondeat superior liability should be abrogated. Not only would this provide a financially responsible defendant, but it would apply the deterrent at the level where policy is made. Second, damage multipliers and punitive damages should be made available—with some of the excess recovery going to a "Fourth Amendment Fund to educate Americans about the Amendment and comfort victims of crime and police brutality." Third, claims for small damage amounts should be entitled to reasonable attorney's fees and the possibility of class action consolidation. Fourth, the procedural limitations on injunctive relief for Fourth Amendment violations should be liberalized. Fifth, administrative channels should be established so that claims can be processed quickly and efficiently without the need for a court action.

Would this fortified damages remedy be more effective than the exclusionary rule? Does it make more sense than the exclusionary rule because it potentially provides compensation to innocent people, whereas the exclusionary rule can by definition be invoked only by guilty people? Or is it a remedy that is better seen as *supplementing* the exclusionary rule?

Some have argued that one of the costs of the exclusionary rule is that it results in courts diminishing the Fourth Amendment's substantive protections—the argument is that courts, when they see the consequences of exclusion of evidence (letting the guilty go free), tend to hold that there is no Fourth Amendment violation in the first place. Would the courts be more prone to find Fourth Amendment violations if the only consequence was a monetary remedy, as opposed to allowing a guilty person to go free?

Proposals in Congress for Alternatives to the Exclusionary Rule

Members of Congress have from time to time proposed legislation that would abrogate the exclusionary rule and replace it with a fortified tort remedy. As of yet, no such proposal has been enacted. A typical example is a proposal providing that the United States would be liable for damages resulting from an illegal search or seizure of an investigative or law enforcement officer. Punitive damages are capped at $10,000; awards to anyone convicted of an offense in which the illegally obtained evidence was used would be limited to damages for actual physical injury and property damage; and attorney's fees and costs would be awarded to claimants who prevail.

The Committee on Federal Legislation of the Association of the Bar of the City of New York had this to say about tort recovery alternatives to the exclusionary rule:

> [E]ven if a tort remedy could be fashioned that would result in meaningful monetary recovery for the victims of Fourth Amendment violations, we would object to it as a replacement for (rather than a supplement to) the exclusionary rule. The tort remedy is based upon the premise that Fourth Amendment rights can and should be left to the marketplace—that the government can make an economic decision to violate a person's Fourth Amendment rights, so long as it is willing to pay its way out of it. We do not believe that Fourth Amendment rights are susceptible to such a market analysis. * * *
>
> * * * We find it troubling that the government could establish a budget line for Fourth Amendment violations as part of its war on

> crime. It cannot be the case that a Fourth Amendment violation is truly remedied simply because the government cuts a check.

Proposed Changes to the Exclusionary Rule, 50 The Record of the Association of the Bar of the City of New York 385 (1995).

Does Congress even have the power under the Constitution to abrogate the exclusionary rule and replace it with another remedy?

2. Criminal Prosecutions of Offending Officers

Criminal prosecution of offending officers is sometimes suggested as the only real deterrent to police misconduct. A federal statute has been in existence since 1921 that makes federal officers who participate in illegal searches guilty of a misdemeanor and subject to substantial fines. 18 U.S.C.A. § 2236. To our knowledge, however, no officer has ever been convicted under the statute. Many states have similar statutes that also remain dormant.

Why has there been such a dearth of prosecutions? The most likely answer is that prosecutors are reluctant to press charges against the police, except in the most extreme cases involving physical injury, because they rely heavily on cooperation with the department. In addition, juries are reluctant to convict policemen of crime.

More fundamentally, it can be argued that the threat of a direct criminal sanction on the officer who conducts an illegal search is an *over-deterrent*. It may lead to officers "second-guessing" in fast-developing situations, and deciding, for example, not to enter a premises, when to enter might be needed to protect a member of the public. Isn't the systemic deterrence provided by the exclusionary rule more appropriate in these circumstances?

3. Police Rulemaking and Other Administrative Solutions

A third alternative remedy for Fourth Amendment violations is police regulation, education, training and internal discipline. In Hudson v. Michigan, supra, the Court extolled the virtues of internal police regulations and training programs to comply with the Fourth Amendment—which programs generally did not exist at the time of *Mapp*—as an alternative to the exclusionary rule for deterring police misconduct.

> Another development over the past half-century that deters civil-rights violations is the increasing professionalism of police forces, including a new emphasis on internal police discipline. * * * [W]e now have increasing evidence that police forces across the United States take the constitutional rights of citizens seriously. There have been wide-ranging reforms in the education, training, and supervision of

police officers. Numerous sources are now available to teach officers and their supervisors what is required of them under this Court's cases, how to respect constitutional guarantees in various situations, and how to craft an effective regime for internal discipline. [Citing treatises and manuals used by police.] Failure to teach and enforce constitutional requirements exposes municipalities to financial liability. See Canton v. Harris, 489 U.S. 378, 388 (1989). Moreover, modern police forces are staffed with professionals; it is not credible to assert that internal discipline, which can limit successful careers, will not have a deterrent effect. There is also evidence that the increasing use of various forms of citizen review can enhance police accountability.

While police education, training and discipline on Fourth Amendment issues has surely increased dramatically since *Mapp,* couldn't it be argued that all of these innovations occurred *because* the exclusionary rule finally made the Fourth Amendment relevant, as a practical matter, to police departments? As Justice Stewart reported in *Elkins,* this appears to have been the experience in California. Why was there no significant training on Fourth Amendment standards in the state before *Mapp*? If the exclusionary rule were abolished, would there be the same incentive to train officers in Fourth Amendment law and discipline them when they violate it?

4. Sentence Reductions

Some of the commentary discussed above suggests that instead of excluding illegally obtained evidence from the trial, a more fair and balanced result would allow or require the sentencing court to reduce a defendant's sentence if illegally obtained evidence was used against the defendant at trial. It is argued that the sentencing alternative would limit the costs to society and avoid a windfall for the defendant.

Would the threat of a reduction of sentence deter illegal searches and seizures? Would officers and police departments take account of a sentencing discount in determining whether to conduct a search or seizure? Or would these actors be focused on convicting the guilty?

E. LIMITATIONS ON EXCLUSION

There are a number of important situations in which evidence has been illegally obtained, and yet it will not be excluded. This section considers those limitations on the exclusionary rule.

1. "Good Faith"—Reasonable Belief That Conduct Is Legal

In the following case, the Court adopted a "good faith" exception for searches conducted pursuant to a warrant that is later found to be invalid.

As you read the case, keep in mind that the Court is not promulgating an "absolute" exception. Rather, there are "exceptions to the exception," where a good faith argument will be rejected and the evidence excluded.

Also note that the Court clearly holds that the Constitution does not require exclusion of evidence as a remedy for a Fourth Amendment violation. Does this mean that *Mapp* is overruled? If so, are the States permitted to abolish the exclusionary rule entirely and admit *all* illegally obtained evidence, as they were before *Mapp*?

UNITED STATES V. LEON

Supreme Court of the United States, 1984.
468 U.S. 897.

JUSTICE WHITE delivered the opinion of the Court.

This case presents the question whether the Fourth Amendment exclusionary rule should be modified so as not to bar the use in the prosecution's case-in-chief of evidence obtained by officers acting in reasonable reliance on a search warrant issued by a detached and neutral magistrate but ultimately found to be unsupported by probable cause. * * *

[On the basis of information from an informant and other investigation, officers obtained a facially valid search warrant. The ensuing searches produced large quantities of drugs and related evidence. The district court, applying *Spinelli*, found that the warrant was issued without probable cause and granted defendants' motions to suppress. The court of appeals affirmed. The Government petitioned for certiorari.]

The Government's petition for certiorari expressly declined to seek review of the lower courts' determinations that the search warrant was unsupported by probable cause and presented only the question "[w]hether the Fourth Amendment exclusionary rule should be modified so as not to bar the admission of evidence seized in reasonable, good-faith reliance on a search warrant that is subsequently held to be defective." * * *

We have concluded that, in the Fourth Amendment context, the exclusionary rule can be modified somewhat without jeopardizing its ability to perform its intended functions. Accordingly, we reverse the judgment of the Court of Appeals.

* * *

Language in opinions of this Court and of individual Justices has sometimes implied that the exclusionary rule is a necessary corollary of the Fourth Amendment * * * . These implications need not detain us long. The * * * Fourth Amendment has never been interpreted to proscribe the introduction of illegally seized evidence in all proceedings or against all persons.

* * * The Fourth Amendment contains no provision expressly precluding the use of evidence obtained in violation of its commands, and an examination of its origin and purposes makes clear that the use of fruits of a past unlawful search or seizure works no new Fourth Amendment wrong. The wrong condemned by the Amendment is fully accomplished by the unlawful search or seizure itself, and the exclusionary rule is neither intended nor able to cure the invasion of the defendant's rights which he has already suffered. The rule thus operates as a judicially created remedy designed to safeguard Fourth Amendment rights generally through its deterrent effect, rather than a personal constitutional right of the party aggrieved.

Whether the exclusionary sanction is appropriately imposed in a particular case, our decisions make clear, is an issue separate from the question whether the Fourth Amendment rights of the party seeking to invoke the rule were violated by police conduct. Only the former question is currently before us, and it must be resolved by weighing the costs and benefits of preventing the use in the prosecution's case-in-chief of inherently trustworthy tangible evidence obtained in reliance on a search warrant issued by a detached and neutral magistrate that ultimately is found to be defective.

The substantial social costs exacted by the exclusionary rule for the vindication of Fourth Amendment rights have long been a source of concern. * * * An objectionable collateral consequence of this interference with the criminal justice system's truth-finding function is that some guilty defendants may go free or receive reduced sentences as a result of favorable plea bargains. Particularly when law enforcement officers have acted in objective good faith or their transgressions have been minor, the magnitude of the benefit conferred on such guilty defendants offends basic concepts of the criminal justice system. * * *

Close attention to those remedial objectives has characterized our recent decisions concerning the scope of the Fourth Amendment exclusionary rule.

[Justice White notes that the Court had by this time: confined the rule to criminal trials; required "standing" on the part of defendants who seek suppression; permitted use of illegally seized evidence to impeach the defendant; and allowed evidence to be admitted where its link to a violation is attenuated.]

As yet, we have not recognized any form of good-faith exception to the Fourth Amendment exclusionary rule. But the balancing approach that has evolved during the years of experience with the rule provides strong support for the modification currently urged upon us. * * *

Because a search warrant provides the detached scrutiny of a neutral magistrate, which is a more reliable safeguard against improper searches than the hurried judgment of a law enforcement officer "engaged in the often competitive enterprise of ferreting out crime," we have expressed a strong preference for warrants and declared that "in a doubtful or marginal case a search under a warrant may be sustainable where without one it would fail." Reasonable minds frequently may differ on the question whether a particular affidavit establishes probable cause, and we have thus concluded that the preference for warrants is most appropriately effectuated by according "great deference" to a magistrate's determination.

* * *

* * * To the extent that proponents of exclusion rely on its behavioral effects on judges and magistrates in these areas, their reliance is misplaced. First, the exclusionary rule is designed to deter police misconduct rather than to punish the errors of judges and magistrates. Second, there exists no evidence suggesting that judges and magistrates are inclined to ignore or subvert the Fourth Amendment or that lawlessness among these actors requires application of the extreme sanction of exclusion.

Third, and most important, we discern no basis, and are offered none, for believing that exclusion of evidence seized pursuant to a warrant will have a significant deterrent effect on the issuing judge or magistrate. * * * Judges and magistrates are not adjuncts to the law enforcement team; as neutral judicial officers, they have no stake in the outcome of particular criminal prosecutions. * * * Imposition of the exclusionary sanction is not necessary to inform judicial officers of their errors, and we cannot conclude that admitting evidence obtained pursuant to a warrant while at the same time declaring that the warrant was somehow defective will in any way reduce judicial officers' professional incentives to comply with the Fourth Amendment, encourage them to repeat their mistakes, or lead to the granting of all colorable warrant requests.

If exclusion of evidence obtained pursuant to a subsequently invalidated warrant is to have any deterrent effect, therefore, it must alter the behavior of individual law enforcement officers or the policies of their departments. One could argue that applying the exclusionary rule in cases where the police failed to demonstrate probable cause in the warrant application deters future inadequate presentations or "magistrate shopping" and thus promotes the ends of the Fourth Amendment. Suppressing evidence obtained pursuant to a technically defective warrant supported by probable cause also might encourage officers to scrutinize more closely the form of the warrant and to point out suspected judicial errors. We find such arguments speculative and conclude that suppression of evidence obtained pursuant to a warrant should be ordered only on a case-by-case basis and only in those unusual cases in which exclusion will further the purposes of the exclusionary rule.[a]

We have frequently questioned whether the exclusionary rule can have any deterrent effect when the offending officers acted in the objectively reasonable belief that their conduct did not violate the Fourth Amendment. * * * But even assuming that the rule effectively deters some police misconduct and provides incentives for the law enforcement profession as a whole to conduct itself in accord with the Fourth Amendment, it cannot be expected, and should not be applied, to deter objectively reasonable law enforcement activity. * * *[b]

This is particularly true, we believe, when an officer acting with objective good faith has obtained a search warrant from a judge or magistrate and acted within its scope. In most such cases, there is no police illegality and thus nothing to deter. It is the magistrate's responsibility to determine whether the officer's allegations establish probable cause and, if so, to issue a warrant comporting in form with the requirements of the Fourth Amendment. In the ordinary case, an officer cannot be expected to question the magistrate's probable cause determination or his judgment that the form of the warrant is technically sufficient. * * * Penalizing the officer for the magistrate's error, rather than his own, cannot logically contribute to the deterrence of Fourth Amendment violations.

* * * We conclude that the marginal or nonexistent benefits produced by suppressing evidence obtained in objectively reasonable reliance on a subsequently invalidated search warrant cannot justify the substantial costs of exclusion. We do not suggest, however, that exclusion is always inappropriate in cases where an officer has obtained a warrant and abided by its terms. * * * [T]he officer's reliance on the magistrate's probable-cause determination and on the technical sufficiency of the warrant he issues must be objectively reasonable, and it is clear that in some circumstances the officer[c] will have no reasonable grounds for believing that the warrant was properly issued.

---

[a] Our discussion of the deterrent effect of excluding evidence obtained in reasonable reliance on a subsequently invalidated warrant assumes, of course, that the officers properly executed the warrant and searched only those places and for those objects that it was reasonable to believe were covered by the warrant. * * *

[b] We emphasize that the standard of reasonableness we adopt is an objective one. Many objections to a good-faith exception assume that the exception will turn on the subjective good faith of individual officers. Grounding the modification in objective reasonableness, however, retains the value of the exclusionary rule as an incentive for the law enforcement profession as a whole to conduct themselves in accord with the Fourth Amendment. The objective standard we adopt, moreover, requires officers to have a reasonable knowledge of what the law prohibits.

[c] References to "officer" throughout this opinion should not be read too narrowly. It is necessary to consider the objective reasonableness, not only of the officers who eventually executed a warrant, but also of the officers who originally obtained it or who provided information material to the probable-cause determination. Nothing in our opinion suggests, for example, that an officer could obtain a warrant on the basis of a "bare bones" affidavit and then rely on colleagues who are ignorant of the circumstances under which the warrant was obtained to conduct the search.

Suppression therefore remains an appropriate remedy if the magistrate or judge in issuing a warrant was misled by information in an affidavit that the affiant knew was false or would have known was false except for his reckless disregard of the truth. The exception we recognize today will also not apply in cases where the issuing magistrate wholly abandoned his judicial role in the manner condemned in Lo-Ji Sales, Inc. v. New York [where the magistrate issued the warrant and then participated in the search]; in such circumstances, no reasonably well-trained officer should rely on the warrant. Nor would an officer manifest objective good faith in relying on a warrant based on an affidavit so lacking in indicia of probable cause as to render official belief in its existence entirely unreasonable. Finally, depending on the circumstances of the particular case, a warrant may be so facially deficient—i.e., in failing to particularize the place to be searched or the things to be seized—that the executing officers cannot reasonably presume it to be valid.

In so limiting the suppression remedy, we leave untouched the probable-cause standard and the various requirements for a valid warrant. * * *

Nor are we persuaded that application of a good-faith exception to searches conducted pursuant to warrants will preclude review of the constitutionality of the search or seizure, deny needed guidance from the courts, or freeze Fourth Amendment law in its present state. * * *

If the resolution of a particular Fourth Amendment question is necessary to guide future action by law enforcement officers and magistrates, nothing will prevent reviewing courts from deciding that question before turning to the good-faith issue. Indeed, it frequently will be difficult to determine whether the officers acted reasonably without resolving the Fourth Amendment issue. Even if the Fourth Amendment question is not one of broad import, reviewing courts could decide in particular cases that magistrates under their supervision need to be informed of their errors and so evaluate the officers' good faith only after finding a violation. In other circumstances, those courts could reject suppression motions posing no important Fourth Amendment questions by turning immediately to a consideration of the officers' good faith. * * *

When the principles we have enunciated today are applied to the facts of this case, it is apparent that the judgment of the Court of Appeals cannot stand. * * *

* * *

Officer Rombach's application for a warrant clearly was supported by much more than a "bare bones" affidavit. The affidavit related the results of an extensive investigation and, as the opinions of the divided panel of the Court of Appeals make clear, provided evidence sufficient to create disagreement among thoughtful and competent judges as to the existence of probable cause. Under these circumstances, the officers' reliance on the magistrate's determination of probable cause was objectively reasonable, and application of the extreme sanction of exclusion is inappropriate.

JUSTICE BLACKMUN, concurring.

* * * I believe that the rule announced today advances the legitimate interests of the criminal justice system without sacrificing the individual rights protected by the Fourth Amendment. I write separately, however, to underscore what I regard as the unavoidably provisional nature of today's decisions.

* * *

* * * By their very nature, the assumptions on which we proceed today cannot be cast in stone. To the contrary, they now will be tested in the real world of state and federal law enforcement, and this Court will attend to the results. If it should emerge from experience that, contrary to our expectations, the good faith exception to the exclusionary rule results in a material change in police compliance with the Fourth Amendment, we shall have to reconsider what we have undertaken here.

* * *

JUSTICE BRENNAN, with whom JUSTICE MARSHALL joins, dissenting.[40]

* * *

[A]s critics of the exclusionary rule never tire of repeating, the Fourth Amendment makes no express provision for the exclusion of evidence secured in violation of its commands. A short answer to this claim, of course, is that many of the Constitution's most vital imperatives are stated in general terms and the task of giving meaning to these precepts is therefore left to subsequent judicial decisionmaking. * * *

A more direct answer may be supplied by recognizing that the Amendment, like other provisions of the Bill of Rights, restrains the power of the government as a whole; * * *. The judiciary is responsible, no less than the executive, for ensuring that constitutional rights are respected.

* * * Because seizures are executed principally to secure evidence, and because such evidence generally has utility in our legal system only in the context of a trial supervised by a judge, it is apparent that the admission of illegally obtained evidence implicates the same constitutional concerns as the initial seizure of that evidence. Indeed, by admitting unlawfully

[40] The dissent addresses both *Leon* and the companion case, *Sheppard* discussed infra.

seized evidence, the judiciary becomes a part of what is in fact a single governmental action prohibited by the terms of the Amendment. * * *

[I]f the Amendment is to have any meaning, police and the courts cannot be regarded as constitutional strangers to each other; because the evidence-gathering role of the police is directly linked to the evidence-admitting function of the courts, an individual's Fourth Amendment rights may be undermined as completely by one as by the other.

* * *

[T]he Court has frequently bewailed the "cost" of excluding reliable evidence. In large part, this criticism rests upon a refusal to acknowledge the function of the Fourth Amendment itself. If nothing else, the Amendment plainly operates to disable the government from gathering information and securing evidence in certain ways. * * * Thus, some criminals will go free *not,* in Justice (then Judge) Cardozo's misleading epigram, "because the constable has blundered," but rather because official compliance with Fourth Amendment requirements makes it more difficult to catch criminals.

* * * The key to the Court's conclusion * * * is its belief that the prospective deterrent effect of the exclusionary rule operates only in those situations in which police officers, when deciding whether to go forward with some particular search, have reason to know that their planned conduct will violate the requirements of the Fourth Amendment. * * *

* * * But what the Court overlooks is that the deterrence rationale for the rule is not designed to be, nor should it be thought of as, a form of "punishment" of individual police officers for their failures to obey the restraints imposed by the Fourth Amendment. Instead, the chief deterrent function of the rule is its tendency to promote institutional compliance with Fourth Amendment requirements on the part of law enforcement agencies generally. * * *

If the overall educational effect of the exclusionary rule is considered, application of the rule to even those situations in which individual police officers have acted on the basis of a reasonable but mistaken belief that their conduct was authorized can still be expected to have a considerable long-term deterrent effect. If evidence is consistently excluded in these circumstances, police departments will surely be prompted to instruct their officers to devote greater care and attention to providing sufficient information to establish probable cause when applying for a warrant, and to review with some attention the form of the warrant that they have been issued, rather than automatically assuming that whatever document the magistrate has signed will necessarily comport with Fourth Amendment requirements.

* * *

Although the Court brushes these concerns aside, a host of grave consequences can be expected to result from its decision to carve this new exception out of the exclusionary rule. A chief consequence of today's decision will be to convey a clear and unambiguous message to magistrates that their decisions to issue warrants are now insulated from subsequent judicial review. * * *

Moreover, the good faith exception will encourage police to provide only the bare minimum of information in future warrant applications. The police will now know that if they can secure a warrant, so long as the circumstances of its issuance are not "entirely unreasonable," all police conduct pursuant to that warrant will be protected from further judicial review. * * *

[E]ven if one were to believe, as the Court apparently does, that police are hobbled by inflexible and hypertechnical warrant procedures, today's decision cannot be justified. This is because, given the relaxed standard for assessing probable cause established just last Term in Illinois v. Gates, the Court's newly fashioned good faith exception, when applied in the warrant context, will rarely, if ever, offer any greater flexibility for police than the *Gates* standard already supplies. * * * Given such a relaxed standard, it is virtually inconceivable that a reviewing court, when faced with a defendant's motion to suppress, could first find that a warrant was invalid under the new *Gates* standard, but then, at the same time, find that a police officer's reliance on such an invalid warrant was nevertheless "objectively reasonable" under the test announced today. * * *

* * * [T]he full impact of the Court's regrettable decision will not be felt until the Court attempts to extend this rule to situations in which the police have conducted a warrantless search solely on the basis of their own judgment about the existence of probable cause and exigent circumstances. When that question is finally posed, I for one will not be surprised if my colleagues decide once again that we simply cannot afford to protect Fourth Amendment rights.

* * *

JUSTICE STEVENS, concurring in the judgment in [*Sheppard*], and dissenting in [*Leon*].[41]

* * *

The Court assumes that the searches in these cases violated the Fourth Amendment, yet refuses to apply the exclusionary rule because the Court concludes that it was "reasonable" for the police to conduct them. In

41 Justice Stevens expressed the view that there was no constitutional violation in *Sheppard*.

my opinion an official search and seizure cannot be both "unreasonable" and "reasonable" at the same time.

* * *

Today's decisions do grave damage to [the exclusionary rule's] deterrent function. Under the majority's new rule, even when the police know their warrant application is probably insufficient, they retain an incentive to submit it to a magistrate, on the chance that he may take the bait. No longer must they hesitate and seek additional evidence in doubtful cases. * * *

* * * Today, for the first time, this Court holds that although the Constitution has been violated, no court should do anything about it at any time and in any proceeding. In my judgment, the Constitution requires more. * * * Nor should we so easily concede the existence of a constitutional violation for which there is no remedy. To do so is to convert a Bill of *Rights* into an unenforced honor code that the police may follow in their discretion. The Constitution requires more; it requires a *remedy*. If the Court's new rule is to be followed, the Bill of Rights should be renamed.

NOTE ON MASSACHUSETTS V. SHEPPARD

Massachusetts v. Sheppard, 468 U.S. 981 (1984), is the companion case to *Leon*. In the course of a murder investigation in Roxbury, Officer O'Malley obtained probable cause to arrest Sheppard and to search his residence. Officer O'Malley's affidavit described in detail the property to be seized in the search of Sheppard's house, e.g., the victim's clothing. Detective O'Malley showed the affidavit to the district attorney, the district attorney's first assistant, and a sergeant, who all concluded that it set forth probable cause for the search and the arrest, and that a warrant based on the affidavit would particularly describe the things to be seized. The *Sheppard* Court described what happened next:

> Because it was Sunday, the local court was closed, and the police had a difficult time finding a warrant application form. Detective O'Malley finally found a warrant form * * * entitled "Search Warrant—Controlled Substance G.L. c. 276 §§ 1 through 3A." Realizing that some changes had to be made before the form could be used to authorize the search requested in the affidavit, Detective O'Malley deleted the subtitle "controlled substance" with a typewriter. He also substituted "Roxbury" for the printed "Dorchester" and typed Sheppard's name and address into blank spaces provided for that information. However, the reference to "controlled substance" was not deleted in the portion of the form that constituted the warrant application and that, when signed, would constitute the warrant itself.
>
> Detective O'Malley then took the affidavit and the warrant form to the residence of a judge who had consented to consider the warrant application. The judge examined the affidavit and stated that he would

authorize the search as requested. Detective O'Malley offered the warrant form and stated that he knew the form as presented dealt with controlled substances. He showed the judge where he had crossed out the subtitles. After unsuccessfully searching for a more suitable form, the judge informed O'Malley that he would make the necessary changes so as to provide a proper search warrant. The judge then took the form, made some changes on it, and dated and signed the warrant. However, he did not change the substantive portion of the warrant, which continued to authorize a search for controlled substances; nor did he alter the form so as to incorporate the affidavit. The judge returned the affidavit and the warrant to O'Malley, informing him that the warrant was sufficient authority in form and content to carry out the search as requested. * * * The scope of the ensuing search was limited to the items listed in the affidavit, and several incriminating pieces of evidence were discovered. Sheppard was then charged with first degree murder.

The *Sheppard* Court stated that "[t]here is no dispute that the officers believed that the warrant authorized the search that they conducted." The Court found that there was an objectively reasonable basis for the officers' mistaken belief. If an error was made, the Court found that it was the judge who made it, and the Court therefore declined to suppress the evidence. The Court concluded that the officers "took every step that could reasonably be expected of them," and that O'Malley was not required "to disbelieve a judge who has just advised him, by word and by action, that the warrant he possesses authorizes him to conduct the search he has requested." The Court refused to decide whether the warrant was in fact invalid for lack of particularity. It stated that this was "a fact-bound issue of little importance since similar situations are unlikely to arise with any regularity." Justice Stevens argued in his opinion concurring in the judgment that there was no error of constitutional dimension and therefore no need to suppress evidence.

For cases like *Sheppard*, applying the good faith exception for warrants that are failing in certain procedural requisites, see United States v. Kelley, 140 F.3d 596 (5th Cir.1998) (officers could reasonably rely on the warrant even though it was defective because the magistrate hadn't signed it: "The rare occasion when a magistrate accidentally fails to sign a warrant cannot be eliminated by suppressing the evidence" and "it is unlikely that police will willfully and recklessly attempt to evade getting a warrant signed"); United States v. Russell, 960 F.2d 421 (5th Cir.1992) (warrant fails to include an attachment of the items to be seized, but the officer specifically described the items in an affidavit; judge committed the "clerical error" of failing to incorporate the affidavit in the warrant); United States v. Workman, 863 F.3d 1313 (10th Cir. 2017) (even if warrant to obtain information regarding child pornography on a computer in Colorado was defective because it was issued by a judge in Virginia, no exclusion was required; the officers acted with an objectively reasonable belief in the validity of the warrant because the software was installed in Virginia and the information would be retrieved in Virginia).

Reasonable Reliance on Unreasonable Warrants

The *Leon* Court rejects a good faith test that would depend on the subjective state of mind of the officer. Instead, the Court establishes a concept of "reasonable" reliance on an invalid warrant. Justices Stevens and Brennan contend that it is impossible to rely reasonably on an unreasonable warrant. But reasonable minds can and often do differ as to what is reasonable. For example, in a typical negligence trial both sides can make reasonable arguments about whether the defendant acted unreasonably—if there was no such thing as a reasonable argument about whether the defendant acted reasonably, then no negligence case would ever get to a jury. And in terms of warrants, one person might think that a warrant is valid while two others might think it defective; certainly there could be a reasonable disagreement when it comes to Fourth Amendment standards that are often ambiguous and fact-dependent.

What the *Leon* Court appears to mean is that in cases where a reviewing court finds that a warrant is invalid—for lack of probable cause, or particularity, or other procedural details—the good faith exception will apply so long as reasonable minds can differ on the point. Where no reasonable argument can be made that the warrant is valid, then the good faith exception will not apply because no reasonable officer could rely on the magistrate's determination. It is at that point an error by the *officer* to rely on the warrant—and officers can be deterred by the exclusionary rule.

Thus, the good faith exception is similar to the standard used for reviewing jury verdicts in civil cases—the standard is not whether the jury was correct or whether the reviewing court would have decided the case another way, but rather whether no reasonable person could have decided the way the jury did. So long as there is room for argument, then, the good faith exception will apply.

Another useful analogy comes from the qualified immunity cases decided under the civil rights statute, 42 U.S.C. § 1983. Even if the plaintiff's constitutional rights are violated, an official is not liable unless he violated clearly established law; if the law was not clearly established at the time of the officer's action, then there is room for argument as to whether the officer's conduct was lawful. The Supreme Court has equated the standards of qualified immunity with the objective reasonableness standard of the good faith exception to the exclusionary rule.

For example, in Messerschmidt v. Millender, 565 U.S. 535 (2012), the Supreme Court reversed the Ninth Circuit's denial of qualified immunity to two officers who executed a search warrant for firearms and gang-related material based solely on a violent altercation between the defendant and his girlfriend. The Court, in an opinion by Chief Justice Roberts, noted that the standard for qualified immunity in cases alleging

Fourth Amendment violations was the same as provided in the good-faith exception under *Leon*:

> Where the alleged Fourth Amendment violation involves a search or seizure pursuant to a warrant, the fact that a neutral magistrate has issued a warrant is the clearest indication that the officers acted in an objectively reasonable manner or, as we have sometimes put it, in "objective good faith." Nonetheless * * * the fact that a neutral magistrate has issued a warrant authorizing the allegedly unconstitutional search or seizure does not end the inquiry into objective reasonableness. Rather, we have recognized an exception allowing suit when "it is obvious that no reasonably competent officer would have concluded that a warrant should issue." The "shield of immunity" otherwise conferred by the warrant will be lost, for example, where the warrant was "based on an affidavit so lacking in indicia of probable cause as to render official belief in its existence entirely unreasonable."

Because the officers had obtained a warrant, the main question was whether that warrant was so lacking in probable cause as to a gang-related offense that it could not have been reasonably relied upon. The Chief Justice concluded as follows:

> The question in this case is not whether the magistrate erred in believing there was sufficient probable cause to support the scope of the warrant he issued. It is instead whether the magistrate so obviously erred that any reasonable officer would have recognized the error. * * * Even if the warrant in this case were invalid, it was not so obviously lacking in probable cause that the officers can be considered "plainly incompetent" for concluding otherwise.

Justice Breyer wrote a short concurring opinion. Justice Kagan wrote an opinion concurring in part and dissenting in part. Justice Sotomayor, joined by Justice Ginsburg, dissented, accusing the Court of sanctioning a "general warrant" based on the faulty premise that "four wrongs apparently make a right."

Leon, Gates and Warrants Clearly Lacking in Probable Cause

In Justice Brennan's view, the good faith standard and the *Gates* standard for probable cause overlap completely, so that if a warrant is lacking in probable cause under the permissible test of *Gates* it must be so deficient, so clearly lacking in probable cause, that it could not possibly be reasonably relied upon. This view has not been adopted by the courts after *Leon*, however. There are a number of cases in which courts have found the good faith exception applicable because reasonable minds could differ about whether the *Gates* standards were satisfied. These cases indicate that there is some grey area between the *Gates* standard and a warrant that clearly lacks probable cause. See, e.g., United States v. Gibson, 928 F.2d 250 (8th Cir.1991) (*Gates* standard not satisfied because police only corroborated a few "innocent details," but good faith exception applies because reasonable minds could differ on whether *Gates* standard is satisfied on such minimal corroboration); United States v. Brunette, 256 F.3d 14 (1st Cir. 2001) (it was error for the magistrate to issue a warrant to search for internet child pornography where the magistrate relied solely on the officer's conclusion that the pictures posted by the defendant were pornographic; however, "although we hold that the omission of images or a description of them was a serious defect in the warrant application, the uncertain state of the law at the time made reliance on the warrant objectively reasonable."); United States v. Paull, 551 F.3d 516 (6th Cir. 2009) (while information about the defendant's possession of child pornography was very dated, the warrant did not "clearly lack" probable cause because of this stale information; the officer had experience in child pornography investigations that caused her to believe the evidence was still on the premises: "even where an officer's experience provides too little evidence to establish probable cause, it suffices to make the affidavit not bare bones by providing a reasonable connection between the defendant and the alleged crime.").

There are also some of cases in which probable cause is found lacking under *Gates*, and the court further finds that the officer was *not* objectively reasonable in relying on the warrant. See, e.g., United States v. Doyle, 650 F.3d 460 (4th Cir. 2011) (warrant to search for child pornography clearly lacked probable cause where "[t]he bulk of the information supplied in the affidavit concerned allegations of sexual assault"; the court found that "evidence of child molestation alone does not support probable cause to search for child pornography"); United States v. Griffith, 867 F.3d 1265 (D.C. Cir. 2017) (probable cause to arrest a gang member does not give probable cause to issue a warrant to search the defendant's premises for a cellphone and all other electronic devices: the "failings as to probable cause and overbreadth bring the warrant beyond the good-faith exception's reach"); United States v. John, 654 F.3d 412 (3d Cir. 2011) (warrant to search the defendant's home for child pornography clearly lacked probable cause where it was based solely on the fact that the defendant had molested his students on school property and kept evidence of those crimes at his home); United States v. Baxter, 889 F.2d 731 (6th Cir.1989) (affidavit describing tip from anonymous informant, with corroboration only of defendant's address and prior conviction on drug charges is a barebones affidavit and officer was not objectively reasonable in relying on the warrant); United States v. Helton, 314 F.3d 812 (6th Cir. 2003) ("A reasonable officer knows that evidence of three calls a month to known drug dealers from a house, a description of that house, and an allegation that a drug dealer stores drug proceeds with his brother and his brother's girlfriend (neither of whom live at or are known to visit that house) falls well short of establishing probable cause that the house contains evidence of a crime.").

Leon and Warrants Lacking Particularity

It would appear that the good faith exception applies to a search pursuant to an overbroad or unparticularized warrant so long as reasonable minds could differ about whether the warrant is in fact overbroad. On the other hand, if all reasonable people would agree that the warrant is deficient, then the officer cannot reasonably rely upon it.

In United States v. Dahlman, 13 F.3d 1391 (10th Cir.1993), officers searching for narcotics obtained a warrant to search two "lots" in a subdivision. As conducted, the search encompassed a camping trailer and a cabin on one of the lots, as well as the lots themselves. The court found that the warrant was defective as applied to the cabin: "a warrant authorizing the search of a lot of land without a more precise definition of the scope of the search is inconsistent with the particularity requirement of the Fourth Amendment, and does not suffice to authorize a search of a residence located on the land." Still, the court held that the evidence obtained in the cabin was admissible under the good faith exception. It noted that two other circuits had held similar warrants to be sufficiently particular, and therefore that reasonable minds could differ about whether the warrant was in fact overbroad. See also United States v. Otero, 563 F.3d 1127 (10th Cir. 2009) (warrant to search computer was overbroad because it authorized the seizure of "any and all information" stored on the computer and the subject matter limitations were placed in a different part of the affidavit; but good faith exception applied because "one could see how a reasonable officer might have thought that the limitations in the first portion of Attachment B would be read to also apply to the second portion").

By contrast, in United States v. Fuccillo, 808 F.2d 173 (1st Cir.1987), officers searched a clothing warehouse and retail clothing store with search warrants authorizing the seizure of "women's clothing" believed to be stolen. They seized virtually all the clothing found at each of the premises (including men's clothing). The court ruled that the warrants were insufficiently particular because the officers "could have obtained specific information for presentment to the magistrate and placement in the warrant which would have enabled the agents [executing the warrants] to differentiate contraband cartons of women's clothing from legitimate ones." In fact the officers had a detailed list of the stolen clothing, but failed to include it in their application. The court further held that the good faith exception did not apply because the officers were "reckless in not including in the affidavit information which was known or easily accessible to them," and that the warrant was so overbroad that the executing officers could not reasonably presume it to be valid. See also United States v. Stubbs, 873

F.2d 210 (9th Cir.1989) (good faith exception unavailable where warrant authorized seizure of virtually all business documents but probable cause existed for only one transaction).

Leon and Untrue or Omitted Statements in the Warrant Application

An exception to the good faith exception arises if the officer includes material information in the application that he "knew was false or would have known was false except for his reckless disregard of the truth." *Leon.* Exclusion also occurs if the officer knowingly omits material information that would have resulted in the magistrate's refusing to issue the warrant. The good faith exception cannot apply in these instances because the error is the officer's, not the magistrate's. Determining whether the officer has made such an error is sometimes difficult, however.

Consider United States v. Johnson, 78 F.3d 1258 (8th Cir.1996). A police officer received a call from an anonymous informant who stated that he had been present when marijuana had been delivered to Johnson's residence. The officer verified Johnson's address and discovered that Johnson had been arrested previously for marijuana possession. The officer then prepared an affidavit to obtain a search warrant. The affidavit had a printed warrant form attached, This form had a section relating to whether the informant was anonymous or confidential, and a section with four printed reasons why the informant is reliable. The officer checked two reasons why the anonymous caller was reliable: "C. Information he has supplied has been corroborated by law enforcement personnel." and "D. He has not given false information in the past." The warrant was issued and a search turned up drugs. The government conceded that the tip was too conclusory and the corroboration too thin to support probable cause under *Gates*; but the government argued that the information provided was close enough that reasonable minds could differ about whether the *Gates* standards were satisfied.

Because the officer had corroborated at least some part of the informant's tip, the question was whether the officer had knowingly or recklessly disregarded the truth in checking the line stating that the informant had not given false information in the past. The Court held that the officer's assertion did not trigger the "officer misrepresentation" exception to *Leon.* The court reasoned as follows:

> The officer took the literal view of the phrase that the caller had not given false information in the past even though this was the informant's first call. We do not believe that checking this statement rises to the level of making a false statement knowingly or intentionally or with a reckless disregard for the truth. * * * [W]e do not subject law enforcement officers to absolute syllogistic precision.

Judge Arnold, in dissent, disagreed and argued that the affidavit was deceptive and outside the realm of *Leon* good faith:

> A statement that an informant had not previously given false information is clearly calculated to influence the magistrate to whom the application for warrant was to be submitted. The statement could hardly have been other than deliberate. To read the statement absolutely literally seems disingenuous to me, and certainly not the way one would understand the statement under the circumstances.

Why did the form affidavit have a "fill in the blank" for whether the informant had ever given *false* information in the past? Why wasn't the issue phrased as whether the informant had ever given *truthful* information in the past? Isn't that the important question under *Gates*? If it is the form itself that is deceptive, should *Leon* apply?

For a case in which *Leon* was found inapplicable due to officer misrepresentations in the warrant application consider United States v. Vigeant, 176 F.3d 565 (1st Cir.1999). Officers filed a detailed affidavit, based in large part on a tip from a confidential informant (CI) alleging that Vigeant was engaged in money-laundering resulting from sales of drugs. Among the allegations was that Vigeant was unemployed, and yet had purchased a "pleasure boat"—the inference being that he must have done so with laundered funds. One problem with the case, however, was that Vigeant filed a proper Currency Transaction Report (CTR) for each of his financial transactions, and made no attempt to disguise the electronic or paper trail of any transaction. The court reviewed the affidavit and found it insufficient to establish probable cause; it also found the good faith exception inapplicable due to the various misrepresentations and omissions in the affidavit. It elaborated as follows:

> We believe this is a case in which excluding the evidence will have a substantial deterrent effect on the police. * * * Officer Botelho's numerous omissions of material facts were at least reckless. An enumeration of Botelho's omissions follows.
>
> First, and most important, Botelho neglected to mention the CI's long criminal history, his numerous aliases, his recent plea agreement, and other indicia of his unreliability. Second, Botelho failed to note that Vigeant had filed the necessary CTR, yet Botelho included in the affidavit such minute details about the transaction as that it involved "small bills"—a fact he presumably obtained from the CTR. Filing a CTR, like failing to "structure" the transaction to avoid the reporting requirement, is evidence manifestly inconsistent with money laundering. Third, Botelho mentioned an additional deposit by cashier's check, but neglected to say that Vigeant's grandmother, who was above suspicion in this case, was the purchaser of the check. Fourth, Botelho could have (but did not) obtain Vigeant's employment

status from the probation office, apparently deciding instead to infer (without informing the magistrate that he had done so) Vigeant's present unemployment from a blank space marked "current employment" on a two-year-old bank application. Fifth, Botelho stated that "the evidence indicates that Robert Vigeant has created front companies," which implies the existence of underlying evidence not disclosed. Such evidence did not, in fact, exist. Sixth, the government failed to note that the supposed "pleasure boat" mentioned in the affidavit was, in fact, a stripped-down craft in poor condition in need of considerable repair and refurbishing before it could be sold at a profit. Seventh, the affidavit implies that the CI personally witnessed a marijuana transaction and personally received $10,000; neither is true. * * *

The government offers no rational explanation for these omissions and foundationless conclusions. Instead, the government argues in its brief—with information obtained after the search in question—that Vigeant is a bad person. Be that as it may, even unsavory persons have constitutional rights. We conclude that a reasonable officer in Botelho's position—that is, in possession of the omitted information—would have known that he should not have applied for the warrant, at least not without further investigation.

Leon and the Abdicating Magistrate

United States v. Decker, 956 F.2d 773 (8th Cir.1992), is a rare case in which the court held that *Leon* could not apply because the magistrate abdicated his neutral and detached role. Agents subjected a suspicious-looking UPS package to a canine sniff and the dog positively alerted to drugs. The agents then made a controlled delivery and followed the package to Decker's house. Decker was arrested when he received the package. A search of his person revealed a small amount of narcotics. An agent prepared an affidavit setting forth these facts and applying for permission to seize narcotics at Decker's house. The magistrate issued a warrant to search Decker's house, but the warrant failed to list any items to be seized other than the UPS package, which was already in the possession of the agents. The search warrant was a standard form relating to stolen property, not to drugs, and referred to the UPS package as "unlawfully stolen." The magistrate later admitted that the flaws in the warrant were his fault and attributed these errors "to the fact that he was intrigued by the manner in which Agent Hicks became suspicious of the package and the ensuing investigation and therefore did not focus on the language of the warrant." Pursuant to the warrant, the officers seized more than 300 items from Decker's house, including a clock radio, two lamps, a microwave oven, and a weed eater. The court found that the magistrate signed the warrant without reading it, so he acted as "a rubber stamp," and that the agents could not reasonably rely on the warrant. Compare United States v. Breckenridge, 782 F.2d 1317 (5th Cir.1986), where the court held that the good faith exception applied even though the judge who issued the warrant never read the officer's affidavit. The court reasoned that the officer could reasonably rely on the warrant because, while the judge did not read the affidavit, he "appeared to Agent Alexander to be doing so."

The good faith exception will not apply if the person who issues the warrant is affiliated with law enforcement. See, e.g., United States v. Lucas, 451 F.3d 492 (8th Cir. 2006) (officers could not reasonably rely on a warrant issued by the Director of Corrections, a member of the executive branch: "the good faith exception does not apply when the individual who issued the warrant is not neutral and detached.").

The Teaching Function

The *Leon* dissenters were concerned that appellate courts will routinely refuse to decide Fourth Amendment questions about the validity of a warrant, preferring instead to reach the easier holding that the officer was not totally unreasonable in relying on a magistrate's determination that the warrant was valid. Lower court decisions suggest that the dissenters' concerns were justified—many courts are avoiding decisions about substantive Fourth Amendment law and ruling instead on the easier question of good faith. For example, in United States v. Henderson, 746 F.2d 619 (9th Cir.1984), defendants convicted of drug offenses challenged an order authorizing beeper surveillance. Rather than rule on whether the order was valid, the court sustained the search by citing *Leon* and relying upon the good faith of the agents. Thus, in future cases, the agents have no guidance as to the validity of similar orders. Presumably, officers continue to act in good faith until a similar order actually is invalidated. See also United States v. Perez, 393 F.3d 457 (4th Cir. 2004) ("Assuming without deciding that the * * * search warrant was invalid for lack of probable cause, we exercise our discretion to proceed directly to the question of good faith."; even if that the warrant lacked probable cause, it was close enough for reasonable minds to differ).

In response to this trend, the Supreme Court appeared in Saucier v. Katz, 533 U.S. 194 (2001), to direct lower courts to decide substantive constitutional questions before turning to potential claims of good faith or qualified immunity. A few years later, in Pearson v. Callahan, 555 U.S. 223 (2009), the Court clarified that *Saucier* merely expressed a preference and that courts may decide cases based on good faith or qualified immunity without reaching underlying constitutional claims.

Despite the general trend to avoid Fourth Amendment questions after *Leon*, there are some courts that have taken their teaching function seriously. Illustrative is United States v. Dahlman, 13 F.3d 1391 (10th

Cir.1993), discussed above. The court had this to say about the teaching function after *Leon*:

> This court could have simply affirmed the trial court on the good faith issue without first discussing the underlying Fourth Amendment issue, i.e., the validity of the warrant. * * * However, a close reading of *Leon* reveals that, while the Supreme Court intended to vest lower courts with discretion, the preferred sequence is to address the Fourth Amendment issues before turning to the good faith issue unless there is no danger of "freezing" Fourth Amendment jurisprudence or unless the case poses "no important Fourth Amendment questions."
>
> * * * If we were to have avoided addressing the underlying Fourth Amendment question today, a magistrate could legitimately issue an identical warrant tomorrow and the officers could engage in the same conduct without consequence—since there would be no adverse ruling to guide the magistrate or the officers, the warrant would be issued and the search would once again be valid under principles of good faith. In effect, Fourth Amendment jurisprudence would be frozen on this issue because of this never-ending cycle. Thus, the policy of avoiding "freezing" Fourth Amendment jurisprudence, discussed by the Court in *Leon*, compels us in this case to resolve the constitutional issue so that magistrates and law enforcement officers do not continue to make the same mistake indefinitely.

Once a court, such as in *Dahlman*, declares a particular practice illegal—though without an attendant exclusion of evidence in that case—an officer who thereafter engages in the conduct is acting unreasonably, and the good faith exception will not apply. See United States v. Buck, 813 F.2d 588 (2d Cir.1987), where the court held that a warrant with a catch-all clause was insufficiently particular, but nonetheless applied the good faith exception because "what the officers failed to do was to anticipate our holding today * * *." However, the court stated in a footnote that "with respect to searches conducted hereafter, police officers may no longer invoke the reasonable-reliance exception to the exclusionary rule when they attempt to introduce as evidence the fruits of searches undertaken on the basis of warrants containing only a catch-all description of the property to be seized." And the court was true to its word. In United States v. George, 975 F.2d 72 (2d Cir.1992), the court invalidated a warrant similar to that in *Buck*, and refused to apply the good faith exception "in light of the settled nature of the law."

2. The Good Faith Exception and Warrantless Searches

The Court in *Leon* applied the good faith exception because an officer reasonably relied on the magistrate's decision. The Court reasoned that the magistrate, rather than the officer, made the error, and that magistrates cannot be deterred by the exclusionary rule. An important question is whether this reasoning can be applied to excuse illegal but "good faith," objectively reasonable—but illegal—searches *without a warrant.*

Reasonable Reliance on Legislative Acts: Illinois v. Krull

In Illinois v. Krull, 480 U.S. 340 (1987), Illinois had enacted a statute authorizing warrantless searches by state officials to inspect the records of dealers in motor vehicles, automobile parts, or automobile scrap metal. Officers searched Krull's premises without a warrant, under the authority of the statute. The statute was found unconstitutional after the search. The government argued that while the search was illegal, the error was that of the legislature, not the officer, and so exclusion was unwarranted.

Justice Blackmun's majority opinion reasoned that, as in *Leon,* the presence of an intermediary upon whom the officer could reasonably rely meant that the officer could not be deterred by the exclusionary rule. Justice Blackmun recognized that the legislature made a mistake by passing an unconstitutional statute, but reasoned that the legislature could not be deterred from passing unconstitutional laws by application of the exclusionary rule. According to the Court, legislators enact statutes for "broad programmatic purposes, not for the purpose of procuring evidence in particular criminal investigations."

The *Krull* Court decided, as in *Leon,* that a good faith claim must have an objective basis, so that "[a] statute cannot support objectively reasonable reliance if, in passing the statute, the legislature wholly abandoned its responsibility to enact constitutional laws," and "a law enforcement officer [cannot] be said to have acted in good-faith reliance upon a statute if its provisions are such that a reasonable officer should have known that the statute was unconstitutional." But neither of these exceptions were applicable to the facts of the case.

Justice O'Connor, joined by Justices Brennan, Marshall and Stevens, dissented. She distinguished legislators from magistrates, finding that "[t]he judicial role is particularized, fact-specific and nonpolitical," and argued that "[p]roviding legislatures a grace period during which the police may freely perform unreasonable searches in order to convict those who might have otherwise escaped creates a positive incentive to promulgate unconstitutional laws." See also United States v. Duka, 671 F.3d 329 (3d Cir. 2011) (finding that FISA amendment allowing domestic wiretapping was reasonable and even if it were not, officer's reliance on it was objectively reasonable and so exclusion was unwarranted).

Reliance on Court Clerical Personnel: Arizona v. Evans

The Court continued to adhere to the *Leon* framework in Arizona v. Evans, 514 U.S. 1 (1995), a case that arose from a clerical error attributed to the judicial branch. Evans was stopped for a traffic violation. The officer entered Evans's name in a computer data terminal, and the computer inquiry indicated that there was an outstanding misdemeanor warrant for Evans' arrest. On the basis of that information, the officer arrested Evans. In a search incident to the arrest the officer found marijuana. Subsequently, it was discovered that the arrest warrant had been quashed well before Evans had been stopped by the officer but that the computer database had not been updated. The Supreme Court assumed that the error was the result of a clerical error by court personnel.

Chief Justice Rehnquist, writing for a seven-person majority, held that the critical question under *Leon* was whether a government official who makes a mistake leading to an illegal search or seizure can be deterred by operation of the exclusionary rule. Applying this reasoning to errors made by court clerical personnel, the Chief Justice stated as follows:

> Because court clerks are not adjuncts to the law enforcement team engaged in the often competitive enterprise of ferreting out crime, they have no stake in the outcome of particular criminal prosecutions. The threat of exclusion of evidence could not be expected to deter such individuals from failing to inform police officials that a warrant had been quashed.

The Chief Justice further concluded that the officers could not be deterred because they reasonably relied in good faith on the representations of court personnel.

Justice O'Connor, joined by Justices Souter and Breyer, wrote a concurring opinion emphasizing that the exclusionary rule should be applicable if police officers rely on a court recordkeeping system that is known to be rife with error. She elaborated as follows:

> Surely it would not be reasonable for the police to rely, say, on a recordkeeping system, their own or some other agency's, that has no mechanism to ensure its accuracy over time and that routinely leads to false arrests, even years after the probable cause for any such arrest has ceased to exist (if it ever existed).
>
> In recent years, we have witnessed the advent of powerful, computer-based recordkeeping systems that facilitate arrests in ways that have never before been possible. The police, of course, are entitled to enjoy the substantial advantages this technology confers. They may not, however, rely on it blindly.

Justice Souter, joined by Justice Breyer, wrote a separate, short concurring opinion in which he left open the possibility that the exclusionary rule might be necessary as a last resort to combat erroneous computerized recordkeeping by non-police personnel.

Justice Stevens dissented. He contended that court clerical personnel often "work in the same building with police officers and may have more regular and direct contact with police than with judges or magistrates." Justice Stevens found it "outrageous" for a citizen to be "arrested, handcuffed, and searched on a public street simply because some bureaucrat has failed to maintain an accurate computer data base."

Justice Ginsburg wrote a separate dissent that was joined by Justice Stevens. She noted her concern with the risk to privacy that could result from errors in law enforcement databases:

> [C]omputerization greatly amplifies an error's effect, and correspondingly intensifies the need for prompt correction; for inaccurate data can infect not only one agency, but the many agencies that share access to the database. * * *
>
> Evans' case is not idiosyncratic. Rogan v. Los Angeles, 668 F.Supp. 1384 (C.D.Cal.1987), similarly indicates the problem. There, the Los Angeles Police Department, in 1982, had entered into the NCIC computer an arrest warrant for a man suspected of robbery and murder. Because the suspect had been impersonating Terry Dean Rogan, the arrest warrant erroneously named Rogan. Compounding the error, the Los Angeles Police Department had failed to include a description of the suspect's physical characteristics. During the next two years, this incorrect and incomplete information caused Rogan to be arrested four times, three times at gunpoint, after stops for minor traffic infractions in Michigan and Oklahoma.

Reliance on Law Enforcement Clerical Personnel: Herring v. United States

The Court's holding in *Arizona v. Evans* turned, in part, on the fact that the clerical database at issue was maintained by court personnel. Those facts paralleled those in *Leon*, allowing the Court to argue that the exclusionary rule had little, if any, deterrent value because members of the judiciary are not participants in the "competitive enterprise of ferreting out crime." But what if the clerical database is maintained by law enforcement personnel? The Court addresses that question in the following case.

HERRING V. UNITED STATES

Supreme Court of the United States, 2009.
555 U.S. 135.

CHIEF JUSTICE ROBERTS delivered the opinion of the Court.

What if an officer reasonably believes there is an outstanding arrest warrant, but that belief turns out to be wrong because of a negligent bookkeeping error by another police employee? The parties here agree that the ensuing arrest is still a violation of the Fourth Amendment, but dispute whether contraband found during a search incident to that arrest must be excluded in a later prosecution.

Our cases establish that such suppression is not an automatic consequence of a Fourth Amendment violation. Instead, the question turns on the culpability of the police and the potential of exclusion to deter wrongful police conduct. Here the error was the result of isolated negligence attenuated from the arrest. We hold that in these circumstances the jury should not be barred from considering all the evidence.

[Herring was arrested by Coffee County Officer Mark Anderson after Anderson sought and received information that there was an outstanding warrant for Herring's arrest in nearby Dale County. There had, however, been a mistake about the warrant. It had been quashed, but the database had not been changed to reflect that fact. Unlike in *Evans,* though, the clerical error was made by a law enforcement officer. By the time Anderson found out about the error, Herring had already been arrested, and evidence had been found in a search incident to arrest. The court of appeals found that the good faith exception applied and so the evidence was properly admitted.]

In analyzing the applicability of the [exclusionary] rule, *Leon* admonished that we must consider the actions of all the police officers involved. * * * The Coffee County officers did nothing improper. Indeed, the error was noticed so quickly because Coffee County requested a faxed confirmation of the warrant.

* * *

1. * * * [E]xclusion has always been our last resort, not our first impulse, and our precedents establish important principles that constrain application of the exclusionary rule. * * *

2. The extent to which the exclusionary rule is justified by these deterrence principles varies with the culpability of the law enforcement conduct. As we said in *Leon*, "an assessment of the flagrancy of the police misconduct constitutes an important step in the calculus" of applying the exclusionary rule. * * *

Anticipating the good-faith exception to the exclusionary rule, Judge Friendly wrote that "[t]he beneficent aim of the exclusionary rule to deter police misconduct can be sufficiently accomplished by a practice . . . outlawing evidence obtained by flagrant or deliberate violation of rights." The Bill of Rights as a Code of Criminal Procedure, 53 Calif. L.Rev. 929, 953 (1965).

Indeed, the abuses that gave rise to the exclusionary rule featured intentional conduct that was patently unconstitutional. In *Weeks*, a foundational exclusionary rule case, the officers had broken into the defendant's home (using a key shown to them by a neighbor), confiscated incriminating papers, then returned again with a U.S. Marshal to confiscate even more. Not only did they have no search warrant, which the Court held was required, but they could not have gotten one had they tried. * * * Equally flagrant conduct was at issue in Mapp v. Ohio, which * * * extended the exclusionary rule to the States. Officers forced open a door to Ms. Mapp's house, kept her lawyer from entering, brandished what the court concluded was a false warrant, then forced her into handcuffs and canvassed the house for obscenity. An error that arises from nonrecurring and attenuated negligence is thus far removed from the core concerns that led us to adopt the rule in the first place. * * *

3. To trigger the exclusionary rule, police conduct must be sufficiently deliberate that exclusion can meaningfully deter it, and sufficiently culpable that such deterrence is worth the price paid by the justice system. As laid out in our cases, the exclusionary rule serves to deter deliberate, reckless, or grossly negligent conduct, or in some circumstances recurring or systemic negligence. The error in this case does not rise to that level.[a]

We do not suggest that all recordkeeping errors by the police are immune from the exclusionary rule. In this case, however, the conduct at issue was not so objectively culpable as to require exclusion. * * * If the police have been shown to be reckless in maintaining a warrant system, or to have knowingly made false entries to lay the groundwork for future false arrests, exclusion would certainly be justified under our cases should such misconduct cause a Fourth Amendment violation. * * * Petitioner's fears that our decision will cause police departments to deliberately keep their officers ignorant, are thus unfounded.

* * * In a case where systemic errors were demonstrated, it might be reckless for officers to rely on an unreliable warrant system. But there is no evidence that errors in Dale County's system are routine or widespread. * * *

Petitioner's claim that police negligence automatically triggers suppression cannot be squared with the principles underlying the exclusionary rule, as they have been explained in our cases. In light of our repeated holdings that the deterrent effect of suppression must be substantial and outweigh any harm to the justice system, we conclude that when police mistakes are the result of negligence such as that described here, rather than systemic error or reckless disregard of constitutional

[a] We do not quarrel with Justice GINSBURG's claim that "liability for negligence . . . creates an incentive to act with greater care," and we do not suggest that the exclusion of this evidence could have no deterrent effect. But our cases require any deterrence to be weighed against the substantial social costs exacted by the exclusionary rule, and here exclusion is not worth the cost.

requirements, any marginal deterrence does not pay its way. In such a case, the criminal should not "go free because the constable has blundered." People v. Defore, 242 N.Y. 13, 21, 150 N.E. 585, 587 (1926) (opinion of the Court by Cardozo, J.).

JUSTICE GINSBURG, with whom JUSTICE STEVENS, JUSTICE SOUTER, and JUSTICE BREYER join, dissenting.

* * *

Electronic databases form the nervous system of contemporary criminal justice operations. * * * The risk of error stemming from these databases is not slim. Herring's amici warn that law enforcement databases are insufficiently monitored and often out of date. Government reports describe, for example, flaws in NCIC databases, terrorist watchlist databases, and databases associated with the Federal Government's employment eligibility verification system.

* * * The Court assures that "exclusion would certainly be justified" if "the police have been shown to be reckless in maintaining a warrant system, or to have knowingly made false entries to lay the groundwork for future false arrests." This concession provides little comfort.

First, by restricting suppression to bookkeeping errors that are deliberate or reckless, the majority leaves Herring, and others like him, with no remedy for violations of their constitutional rights. There can be no serious assertion that relief is available under 42 U.S.C. § 1983. The arresting officer would be sheltered by qualified immunity, and the police department itself is not liable for the negligent acts of its employees. Moreover, identifying the department employee who committed the error may be impossible.

Second, I doubt that police forces already possess sufficient incentives to maintain up-to-date records. The Government argues that police have no desire to send officers out on arrests unnecessarily, because arrests consume resources and place officers in danger. The facts of this case do not fit that description of police motivation. Here the officer wanted to arrest Herring and consulted the Department's records to legitimate his predisposition.

Third, even when deliberate or reckless conduct is afoot, the Court's assurance will often be an empty promise: How is an impecunious defendant to make the required showing? * * *

JUSTICE BREYER, with whom JUSTICE SOUTER joins, dissenting.

I agree with Justice GINSBURG and join her dissent. I write separately to note one additional supporting factor that I believe important. In Arizona v. Evans, * * *[t]he rationale for our decision was premised on a distinction between judicial errors and police errors * * *.

Distinguishing between police recordkeeping errors and judicial ones not only is consistent with our precedent, but also is far easier for courts to administer than The Chief Justice's case-by-case, multifactored inquiry into the degree of police culpability. I therefore would apply the exclusionary rule when police personnel are responsible for a recordkeeping error that results in a Fourth Amendment violation.

* * *

New Rules, Retroactivity, and Remedies: Davis v. United States

Justice Alito wrote for the Court in Davis v. United States, 564 U.S. 229 (2011), as it held that the exclusionary rule did not require suppression of evidence when police officers executed a search in compliance with binding judicial authority that was later overruled. In *Davis*, officers stopped a car, arrested the driver for driving under the influence and a passenger for giving a false name to the police, and searched the passenger compartment of the car in reliance on circuit court cases interpreting New York v. Belton, supra. They found a revolver in Davis's jacket pocket. Davis was prosecuted and convicted for being a felon in possession of the firearm. While his conviction was on appeal, the Court decided Arizona v. Gant, supra, which limited searches of automobiles following an arrest. The search in *Davis* would have been illegal if *Gant* were applicable at the time.

Justice Alito agreed that the new rule of *Gant* applied on direct review, given the Court's approach to direct and collateral review spelled out in Griffith v. Kentucky and Teague v. Lane (discussed in Chapter 1). Justice Alito concluded, however, that the question was not whether Davis could benefit from the right afforded by *Gant*, but whether suppression was required where "the police conduct in this case was in no way culpable." He reasoned that "this acknowledged absence of police culpability dooms Davis's claim." Justice Alito concluded that exclusion was unwarranted because officers were reasonably applying the law as it existed at the time of their conduct, and therefore could not have been deterred by the threat of exclusion. In fact, they had been deterred, as demonstrated by the fact that they had obeyed the law as it existed at the time of the search.

Justice Sotomayor concurred in the judgment and stated that "[i]n my view, whether an officer's conduct can be characterized as 'culpable' is not itself dispositive," but "an officer's culpability is relevant because it may inform the overarching inquiry whether exclusion would result in appreciable deterrence."

Justice Breyer, joined by Justice Ginsburg, dissented. He argued that under the majority's position, no defendant would have an incentive to seek a change in Fourth Amendment law because they would not get the benefit of its application.

Davis and the Applicability of the Supreme Court's New Fourth Amendment Rulings

Since *Davis*, the lower courts have consistently applied the good faith exception to deny relief to defendants seeking application of a new Supreme Court ruling on the Fourth Amendment. For example, in United States v. Pineda-Moreno, 688 F.3d 1087 (9th Cir. 2012), officers tracked the defendant's movements by attaching an electronic tracking device to the undercarriage of his car. This tracking occurred before the Supreme Court's decision in United States v. Jones, supra, where the Court held that physically installing a tracking device constituted a search. By the time of appeal to the Ninth Circuit, *Jones* had been decided. The court concluded that, while *Jones* was retroactive and therefore the tracking was illegal, the evidence should not be excluded, because, at the time of the tracking, "circuit precedent held that placing an electronic tracking device on the undercarriage of a car was neither a search nor a seizure under the Fourth Amendment."

What about applying the good faith exception to the party who actually *won* in the Supreme Court? That happened in United States v. Rodriguez, a case discussed in the section on *Terry*, where the Supreme Court held that officers violated the Fourth Amendment by detaining him in order to do a canine sniff of his car, even though they had completed issuing him a ticket for a traffic stop. On remand, 799 F.3d 1222 (8th Cir. 2015), the court applied *Davis* and held that officers reasonably relied on then-authoritative circuit law permitting cars to be detained for a limited period of time after a traffic ticket was issued. Rodriguez argued that the Court in *Davis* never intended to withhold the remedy of suppression from the party who won in the Supreme Court, but the court of appeals found that the *Davis* Court had actually considered the scenario, and had expressed no concern that litigants would have little incentive to bring claims to the Supreme Court, because "defendants in jurisdictions in which the question remains open will still have an undiminished incentive to litigate the issue." Accordingly, the court of appeals held that the exclusionary rule did not apply.

Good Faith Where the Arresting/Searching Officer Is at Fault?

The Supreme Court has not specifically addressed the question whether the good faith exception applies to illegal searches and seizures where the fault is that of the searching or seizing officer, i.e., where that officer is relying only his or her own mistaken judgment. Can the officer argue that he was wrong in thinking that there was, e.g., voluntary consent, exigent circumstances, etc., but reasonable minds could differ?

The rationale of *Leon, Krull,* and *Evans* does not easily extend to "good faith" errors by police officers who rely on their own mistaken judgment. In each of those cases, the Court held that mistakes of intermediary officials (such as magistrates and legislators) cannot be deterred by the exclusionary rule, but presumed that an officer in the competitive enterprise of ferreting out crime *can* be deterred by strict operation of the exclusionary rule. How could the Court then turn around and say that officers cannot be deterred by the exclusionary rule when they wrongly, but reasonably, interpret Fourth Amendment law?

That turnaround becomes a bit easier after *Herring. Herring* is the first case in which the good faith exception was applied to excuse an error by a police department official. (In *Davis* it is the court that has made the error, which it recognizes by overruling a prior case). The wrinkle in *Herring* is that the error, though by a police official, was not by the officer who actually made the arrest and conducted the search. As the Court put it, the error was "attenuated" from the arrest and search. There is much in *Herring,* however, that could lead to the conclusion that the good faith exception is to apply to *all* police errors, even those of the officer directly involved. The majority spends a good deal of time arguing that the exclusionary rule can only deter reckless or intentional misconduct. That analysis could be used by the government to argue that while the searching officer made a mistake and violated the Fourth Amendment, reasonable minds could differ about the illegality and therefore the evidence should not be excluded.

How exactly could an officer be deterred from violating the law if reasonable minds can differ about whether it is a violation? One possible response is that police departments, with the exclusionary rule in mind, will train officers to follow a *strict application* of Fourth Amendment law, and will instruct them not to "push the envelope" for fear that action on the frontier of Fourth Amendment reasonableness will result in exclusion. In contrast, if officers are entitled to good faith protection for their own mistakes, police departments will have an incentive to conduct searches that are of dubious legality, so long as reasonable minds can differ on whether the search is legal.

For a post-*Herring* case adopting the good-faith exception for officer error—and applying what Justice Breyer in dissent in *Herring* referred to as the majority's "case-by-case, multifactored inquiry" into the degree of police culpability required for exclusion, see United States v. Julius, 610 F.3d 60 (2d Cir. 2010). Julius had violated parole, and officers arrested him in his girlfriend's apartment where he was residing. The girlfriend consented to entry into the apartment, and the officers found Julius on the bed in a bedroom, with his son. Julius offered no resistance to the arrest. After he was taken out of the room, an officer noticed that the mattress of the bed hung over the box spring by about a foot. The officer lifted the mattress and found a gun. Julius was charged with felon-firearm possession. The lower court found that the search was illegal, because: 1) the officers had taken Julius out of the room so the search was not within his grab area for purposes of search incident to arrest; and 2) the officers did not have the reasonable suspicion required to support a search of a parolee's premises under cases like Samson v. California, discussed earlier in this Chapter. In a decision rendered before *Herring,* the lower court excluded the evidence because it was illegally obtained. On appeal, the Second Circuit remanded in light of the intervening decision in *Herring.* The Second Circuit did not read *Herring* as applying the good faith exception only when the error is attenuated from the illegal search—if it had, there would have been no need to remand, because the error in *Julius* was by the officer who *did* the search. The Second Circuit instead held that *Herring* mandates "a case-by-case, multifactored inquiry into the degree of police culpability." It provided the following analysis of how *Herring* might apply to the search that found the gun.

> Unlike in *Herring,* in which the alleged error was attenuated from the search, the error here was made by the searching officer. Also unlike *Herring,* this case involves a warrantless search, which entails different concerns about deterrence of police misconduct. * * * Wood, the officer who conducted the search, however, testified that he thought he had a right to search the area within the arrestee's reach at the time of the arrest regardless of the arrestee's status at the time of the search as long as it was within a reasonable amount of time after the arrest. The district court may consider whether the other circumstances of the search support a finding that the law enforcement officers had knowledge, or may properly be charged with knowledge, that the search was unconstitutional under the Fourth Amendment, requiring suppression [under] *Herring.* * * *
>
> [T]here is no question that the arrest of Julius was justified because it is undisputed that he was in violation of the terms of his special parole. The search itself was not prolonged; Officer Barry testified that "less than two minutes" had elapsed between the arrest of Julius and Deputy Wood's announcement that he had found a gun. Further, the court may also consider the issue of officer safety when deciding whether the conduct of the officers was "the result of . . .

> systemic error or reckless disregard of constitutional requirements." Deputy Wood articulated a concern for the safety of the officers and others. He explained there was minimal possibility that Julius could have obtained the gun "because he was restrained," but that there was a risk that the minor child "could have accessed the weapon accidently" or that [the girlfriend] could have obtained the weapon if allowed to get clothes for Julius. Additionally, immediately upon finding the firearm, Deputy Wood and his colleagues: (1) ceased searching; (2) obtained [the girlfriend's] permission to search the entire residence, permission that the district court found was properly obtained; and (3) contacted New Haven police officers for assistance. We do not conclude that any of these circumstances are necessarily dispositive.

How can an exclusionary rule deter officer misconduct where it is subject to a multifactor, case-by-case analysis? Do the consequent, and virtually endless, exceptions compromise the message of deterrence? Or is all this just code for telling the officer that everything will be okay so long as the violation of the Fourth Amendment is not egregious? And if that is the message, how much deterrent effect does the exclusionary rule have after *Herring?* See Gray, A Spectacular Non Sequitur: The Supreme Court's Contemporary Fourth Amendment Exclusionary Rule Jurisprudence, 50 Am. Crim. L. Rev. 1 (2013).

For a narrower view of *Herring,* see United States v. Camou, 773 F.3d 932 (9th Cir. 2014) (en banc), discussed in the section on the automobile exception to the warrant requirement. Officers argued that the search of a cellphone found in a car could be conducted without a warrant—and the court rejected that argument, relying on California v. Riley. The government next argued that under *Herring,* the evidence found in the cellphone search should not be excluded because the officers could have reasonably thought that a warrantless search was permissible, but the court held that *Herring* did not apply:

> The officer [in *Herring*] was not negligent himself; the negligence was two degrees removed from the officer and thus amounted to "isolated negligence attenuated from the arrest." In *Herring,* as in its prior good faith jurisprudence, the Supreme Court found the good faith exception was met because the officer *reasonably relied on* an external source, which turned out to be erroneous.
>
> The Supreme Court has never applied the good faith exception to excuse an officer who was negligent himself, and whose negligence directly led to the violation of the defendant's constitutional rights. Here, the government fails to assert that Agent Walla relied on anyone or anything in conducting his search of Camou's cell phone, let alone that any reliance was reasonable. The government instead only asserts that by searching the phone, Agent Walla was not acting

recklessly, or deliberately misbehaving. In this case, the good faith exception cannot apply.

Obviously, the viability of the exclusionary rule as any kind of deterrent depends critically on whether one takes a broad or narrow interpretation of *Herring's* application of the good faith exception.

3. Establishing a Violation of a Personal Fourth Amendment Right

Fourth Amendment rights are personal rights. It therefore follows that for a defendant to be entitled to exclusion of evidence, he must establish that his own personal rights were affected by the government's search or seizure. This has been characterized by many courts as a question of "standing"—though as will be seen below, the Supreme Court has chafed at this label. The question of "standing" is determined by whether the person seeking to suppress the evidence has had his own Fourth Amendment rights violated.

In the 1960's, the Court developed a generous view of a defendant's ability to invoke the exclusionary rule. Jones v. United States, 362 U.S. 257 (1960), held that a defendant had "automatic standing" to challenge the legality of the search that produced the very drugs that he was charged with possessing at the time of the search. The Court in *Jones* also stated that a search could be challenged by anyone "legitimately on the premises where a search occurs." In the following case the Court substantially cuts back on *Jones* and, more importantly, recharacterizes "standing" questions so that they are now resolved by substantive standards of Fourth Amendment law.

RAKAS V. ILLINOIS

Supreme Court of the United States, 1978.
439 U.S. 128.

JUSTICE REHNQUIST delivered the opinion of the Court.

[Officers received a radio call concerning a robbery and describing the getaway car. They stopped a vehicle which matched the description. Petitioners and two female companions were ordered out of the car. The officers searched the passenger compartment and found a box of rifle shells in the glove compartment and a sawed-off rifle under the front passenger seat. Petitioners had been passengers in the car; the owner of the car was driving when the car was stopped. The lower court denied the motion to suppress, reasoning that petitioners lacked standing, and the Illinois appellate courts affirmed. The Supreme Court found that petitioners had the burden of proof as to standing, and that they failed to meet their burden of showing ownership of the rifle or shells. The Court proceeded to consider whether standing could be established in the absence of ownership of the property seized].

* * *

Petitioners first urge us to relax or broaden the rule of standing enunciated in Jones v. United States, so that any criminal defendant at whom a search was "directed" would have standing to contest the legality of that search and object to the admission at trial of evidence obtained as a result of the search. Alternatively, petitioners argue that they have standing to object to the search under *Jones* because they were "legitimately on [the] premises" at the time of the search.

* * * Adoption of the so-called "target" theory advanced by petitioners would in effect permit a defendant to assert that a violation of the Fourth Amendment rights of a third party entitled him to have evidence suppressed at his trial. If we reject petitioners' request for a broadened rule of standing such as this, and reaffirm the holding of *Jones* and other cases that Fourth Amendment rights are personal rights that may not be asserted vicariously, we will have occasion to re-examine the "standing" terminology emphasized in *Jones*. For we are not at all sure that the determination of a motion to suppress is materially aided by labeling the inquiry identified in *Jones* as one of standing, rather than simply recognizing it as one involving the substantive question of whether or not the proponent of the motion to suppress has had his own Fourth Amendment rights infringed by the search and seizure which he seeks to challenge. * * *

We decline to extend the rule of standing in Fourth Amendment cases in the manner suggested by petitioners. * * * A person who is aggrieved by an illegal search and seizure only through the introduction of damaging evidence secured by a search of a third person's premises or property has not had any of his Fourth Amendment rights infringed. And since the exclusionary rule is an attempt to effectuate the guarantees of the Fourth Amendment, it is proper to permit only defendants whose Fourth Amendment rights have been violated to benefit from the rule's protections. There is no reason to think that a party whose rights have been infringed will not, if evidence is used against him, have ample motivation to move to suppress it. Even if such a person is not a defendant in the action, he may be able to recover damages for the violation of his Fourth Amendment rights, or seek redress under state law for invasion of privacy or trespass.

* * *

In Alderman v. United States, 394 U.S. 165 (1969) * * * Mr. Justice Harlan [dissenting] * * * identified administrative problems posed by the target theory:

> "[T]he [target] rule would entail very substantial administrative difficulties. In the majority of cases, I would imagine that the police plant a bug with the expectation that it may well produce leads to a large number of crimes. A lengthy hearing would, then, appear to be necessary in order to determine whether the police knew of an accused's criminal activity at the time the bug was planted and whether the police decision to plant a bug was motivated by an effort to obtain information against the accused or some other individual * * *"

When we are urged to grant standing to a criminal defendant to assert a violation, not of his own constitutional rights but of someone else's, we cannot but give weight to practical difficulties such as those foreseen by Mr. Justice Harlan in the quoted language.

Conferring standing to raise vicarious Fourth Amendment claims would necessarily mean a more widespread invocation of the exclusionary rule during criminal trials. * * * Each time the exclusionary rule is applied it exacts a substantial social cost for the vindication of Fourth Amendment rights. Relevant and reliable evidence is kept from the trier of fact and the search for truth at trial is deflected. * * *

* * * [H]aving rejected petitioners' target theory * * * the question necessarily arises whether it serves any useful analytical purpose to consider this principle a matter of standing, distinct from the merits of a defendant's Fourth Amendment claim. We can think of no decided cases of this Court that would have come out differently had we concluded, as we do now, that the type of standing requirement discussed in *Jones* and reaffirmed today is more properly subsumed under substantive Fourth Amendment doctrine. * * * The inquiry under either approach is the same. But we think the better analysis forthrightly focuses on the extent of a particular defendant's rights under the Fourth Amendment, rather than on any theoretically separate, but invariably intertwined concept of standing.

* * *

Analyzed in these terms, the question is whether the challenged search and seizure violated the Fourth Amendment rights of a criminal defendant who seeks to exclude the evidence obtained during it. That inquiry in turn requires a determination of whether the disputed search and seizure has infringed an interest of the defendant which the Fourth Amendment was designed to protect. * * *

* * *

Here petitioners, who were passengers occupying a car which they neither owned nor leased, seek to analogize their position to that of the defendant in Jones v. United States. In *Jones,* petitioner was present at the time of the search of an apartment which was owned by a friend. The friend had given Jones permission to use the apartment and a key to it, with which Jones had admitted himself on the day of the search. He had a suit and shirt at the apartment and had slept there "maybe a night," but his home was elsewhere. At the time of the search, Jones was the only occupant of the apartment because the lessee was away for a period of several days. Under these circumstances, this Court stated that * * * "anyone legitimately on premises where a search occurs may challenge its legality." Petitioners argue that their occupancy of the automobile in question was comparable to that of Jones in the apartment and that they * * * had their Fourth Amendment rights violated by the search.

We do not question the conclusion in *Jones* that the defendant in that case suffered a violation of his personal Fourth Amendment rights if the search in question was unlawful. Nonetheless, we believe that the phrase "legitimately on premises" coined in *Jones* creates too broad a gauge for measurement of Fourth Amendment rights. For example, applied literally, this statement would permit a casual visitor who has never seen, or been permitted to visit, the basement of another's house to object to a search of the basement if the visitor happened to be in the kitchen of the house at the time of the search. Likewise, a casual visitor who walks into a house one minute before a search of the house commences and leaves one minute after the search ends would be able to contest the legality of the search. * * *

We think that *Jones* on its facts merely stands for the unremarkable proposition that a person can have a legally sufficient interest in a place other than his own home so that the Fourth Amendment protects him from unreasonable governmental intrusion into that place. * * *

* * *

Judged by the foregoing analysis, petitioners' claims must fail. They asserted neither a property nor a possessory interest in the automobile, nor an interest in the property seized. And as we have previously indicated, the fact that they were "legitimately on [the] premises" in the sense that they were in the car with the permission of its owner is not determinative of whether they had a legitimate expectation of privacy in the particular areas of the automobile searched. * * *

JUSTICE POWELL, with whom CHIEF JUSTICE BURGER joins, concurring.

* * *

This is not an area of the law in which any "bright line" rule would safeguard both Fourth Amendment rights and the public interest in a fair and effective criminal justice system. The range of variables in the fact situations of search and seizure is almost infinite. Rather than seek facile solutions, it is best to apply principles broadly faithful to Fourth Amendment purposes.

JUSTICE WHITE, with whom JUSTICE BRENNAN, JUSTICE MARSHALL, and JUSTICE STEVENS join, dissenting.

* * * Insofar as passengers are concerned, the Court's opinion today declares an "open season" on automobiles. However unlawful stopping and searching a car may be, absent a possessory or ownership interest, no "mere" passenger may object, regardless of his relationship to the owner. * * *

More importantly, the ruling today undercuts the force of the exclusionary rule in the one area in which its use is most certainly justified—the deterrence of bad-faith violations of the Fourth Amendment. This decision invites police to engage in patently unreasonable searches every time an automobile contains more than one occupant. Should something be found, only the owner of the vehicle, or of the item, will have standing to seek suppression, and the evidence will presumably be usable against the other occupants. The danger of such bad faith is especially high in cases such as this one where the officers are only after the passengers and can usually infer accurately that the driver is the owner. * * *

NOTE ON RAKAS

The Rakas Court ties standing to the *Katz* reasonable expectation of privacy test. But after United States v. Jones—the landmark case on GPS tracking discussed earlier in this Chapter—the reasonable expectation of privacy test is not the only test for determining whether the Fourth Amendment applies. Because *Rakas* evaluates standing by whether a person has a Fourth Amendment right at all, it follows that if a person's Fourth Amendment right is triggered under *either Katz* or *Jones,* then that person will have "standing" to raise the Fourth Amendment claim. This is why Jones himself was allowed to raise the argument that his Fourth Amendment rights were violated. Even if he had no expectation of privacy in his public movements, officers physically intruded upon his "effect" for purposes of gathering information.

The picture was complicated further by the Court's decision in *Carpenter v. United States,* the cell site location case. There, the Court held that law enforcement's accessing cell-site location records is a "search" for purposes of the Fourth Amendment requiring a warrant. In a spirited dissenting opinion joined by Justices Thomas and Alito, Justice Kennedy wondered how a cellular phone customer like Carpenter could possibly have "standing" to challenge a government's request for business records belonging to a cellular service provider given that "Fourth Amendment rights . . . are personal" and that the

"Amendment protects '[t]he right of the people to be secure in their . . . persons, houses, papers, and effects'—not the persons, houses, papers, and effects of others."

Writing separately, Justice Thomas pressed the point further:

> It bears repeating that the Fourth Amendment guarantees "[t]he right of the people to be secure in *their* persons, houses, papers, and effects." (Emphasis added.) The Fourth Amendment does not confer rights with respect to the persons, houses, papers, and effects of others. Its language makes clear that "Fourth Amendment rights are personal," and as a result, this Court has long insisted that they "may not be asserted vicariously." It follows that a "person who is aggrieved only through the introduction of damaging evidence secured by a search of a third person's premises or property has not had any of his Fourth Amendment rights infringed."
>
> In this case, as Justice Kennedy cogently explains, the cell-site records obtained by the Government belong to Carpenter's cell service providers, not to Carpenter.

By way of response on behalf of the majority, Chief Justice Roberts claimed that this "position fails to contend with the seismic shifts in digital technology that made possible the tracking of not only Carpenter's location but also everyone else's, not for a short period but for years and years." Later, he chided the dissenters for failing to "recognize that CSLI is an entirely different species of business record something that implicates basic Fourth Amendment concerns about arbitrary government power much more directly than corporate tax or payroll ledgers."

How, if at all, does the argument that digital records are different resolve Justices Kennedy, Thomas, and Alito's concerns about standing? If it does not, then is Justice Thomas right in suggesting that the majority opinion implicitly endorses a different theory of Fourth Amendment "standing" that allows some litigants to assert Fourth Amendment rights in the "persons, houses, papers, and effects" of others? If so, then what is that theory? How might it apply in other cases?

Abolition of Automatic Standing: United States v. Salvucci

The Supreme Court relied on *Rakas* in United States v. Salvucci, 448 U.S. 83 (1980), which abolished the automatic standing doctrine. The notion of automatic standing was that possession of property gave a person an automatic right to complain about the search or seizure of that property. Justice Rehnquist's majority opinion concluded that possession of a seized good should not be used as a substitute for a factual finding that the owner of the good had a legitimate expectation of privacy in the area searched. The automatic standing rule had been based on fairness concerns—that it would be unfair for the government to argue at the suppression hearing that the defendant did not possess the property sought to be suppressed, and then to turn around and argue at trial that the defendant did possess the same property. According to the *Salvucci* majority, however, *Rakas* and other cases "clearly establish that a prosecutor may simultaneously maintain that a defendant criminally possessed the seized good, but was not subject to a Fourth Amendment deprivation, without legal contradiction." This was because, after *Rakas,* a "person in legal possession of a good seized during an illegal search has not necessarily been subject to a Fourth Amendment deprivation." Thus, there was no unfairness or inconsistency in arguing, for example, that the defendant constructively possessed a gun, but had no Fourth Amendment protection in the area that was searched to find the gun.

Ownership of Seized Property Does Not Necessarily Confer Standing: Rawlings v. Kentucky

Rawlings v. Kentucky, 448 U.S. 98 (1980), demonstrated the significance of *Salvucci.* Rawlings was convicted of trafficking in and possession of various controlled substances. These substances were seized from the purse of a woman who, along with Rawlings, was visiting the premises when police arrived. The Court held that ownership of the drugs was not enough to confer a right to object to the search because the question was whether Rawlings had a legitimate expectation of privacy in the area that was searched, i.e., the purse. As to this question, the Court held that Rawlings had no right to object to the search of the purse because he had no legitimate expectation of privacy in the purse. Justice Marshall, joined by Justice Brennan, dissented.

Although ownership of the property seized does not necessarily provide the right to object to a search, it does provide a right to object to *seizure* of that property—because a seizure is by definition an intrusion on an ownership interest. Of course, this did not help Rawlings, because he could not have a legitimate possessory interest in contraband drugs.

Targets Without Standing: United States v. Payner

United States v. Payner, 447 U.S. 727 (1980), shows the consequences of the Court's rejection of the "target" theory of standing in *Rakas.* An IRS investigation of American citizens doing business in the Bahamas focused on a certain Bahamian bank. When an official of that bank visited the United States, IRS agents stole his briefcase and removed and photographed hundreds of documents. Among those documents were papers documenting Payner's failure to report substantial income. Under *Rakas,* Payner had no right to object to the search of the briefcase, even though he was the target of the illegal search.

Payner argued that the federal district court should exercise its supervisory power to exclude the evidence and thus to deter such purposefully illegal tactics. The district court agreed with Payner and excluded the evidence given the officers' criminal conspiracy, but the Supreme Court held "that the supervisory power does not authorize a federal court to suppress otherwise admissible evidence on the ground that it was seized unlawfully from a third party not before the court." Justice Marshall, joined by Justices Brennan and Blackmun, dissented arguing that the government agents acted in bad faith by manipulating the standing rules in order to conduct an unconstitutional search; therefore, suppression of the illegally seized evidence was essential to protect the integrity of the judiciary whose rules were being manipulated.

Presence in the Home of Another: Minnesota v. Carter

Assume that you are at a party. Police officers enter, conduct a thorough search of the premises, and find evidence that is offered against you in a criminal trial. If the search of the premises is illegal, do you, as a partygoer, have the right to complain that the search was a violation of your Fourth Amendment rights? In Minnesota v. Carter, 525 U.S. 83 (1998), the defendants complained about a search of a premises in which they were visitors—bagging cocaine with the owner. Chief Justice Rehnquist, writing for the Court, held that persons who are temporarily on the premises for a commercial transaction have no Fourth Amendment rights at stake in a search of the premises. He accepted the fact that a person might have a reasonable expectation of privacy in the home of another—as did the overnight guest in Minnesota v. Olson, discussed earlier in this Chapter—but he concluded that "the purely commercial nature of the transaction engaged in here, the relatively short period of time on the premises, and the lack of any previous connection between respondents and the householder, all lead us to conclude that respondents' situation is closer to that of one simply permitted on the premises."

Justice Scalia, joined by Justice Thomas, wrote a concurring opinion in *Carter*. Justice Kennedy wrote a concurring opinion emphasizing that social guests might have expectations that business visitors do not. Justice Breyer wrote an opinion concurring in the judgment. Justice Ginsburg, joined by Justices Stevens and Souter, dissented.

Cars, Drivers, Passengers

Questions about standing arise quite frequently when vehicles are stopped and searched. It is clear that an owner who is also in possession of a car at the time of a search has standing to object, but complications may arise if the owner is not present, not in possession, or if someone else is driving the car. And what about passengers? And then there is the question whether the Fourth Amendment claim is based on search versus seizure.

Some of these questions are discussed in United States v. Carter, 14 F.3d 1150 (6th Cir.1994). Carter was a passenger in a van owned and operated by Locklear. The police stopped the car for a traffic violation, then illegally searched suitcases in the back of the van and found drugs. Locklear was able to suppress the evidence and was never tried. Carter sought, in turn, to suppress the evidence. Carter argued that he had standing because he was accompanying Locklear on a lengthy trip. But he had no ownership interest in the van and no control over it; he had no possessions in the van other than a change of clothes (a pair of jeans and a shirt) and a shaving kit found in the front of the vehicle; and he claimed no possessory or other interest in the suitcases filled with marijuana.

The court held that Carter had the right to challenge the *seizure* of his person that occurred when the van was searched, but the evidence could not be excluded as the fruit of Carter's seizure. It was the search of the car that uncovered the evidence, and that search was not connected to Carter's seizure. The court explained with a hypothetical:

> Suppose that at the time of the driver's arrest the police had summoned a taxi cab for Mr. Carter and told him he was free to leave. The marijuana would still have been discovered, because it was located in a van owned and controlled by Mr. Locklear (who was not going anywhere until his vehicle had been searched) and not in a vehicle controlled by Mr. Carter.

As to the search of the back of the van, the court held that the presence of the shaving kit and change of clothing in the front of the van did not give Carter a legitimate expectation that the police would not open the van's back door. Thus, Carter did not meet his burden of showing that his expectation of privacy was violated by the search. Similarly, he seems unlikely to have been able to argue that those areas of the van were part of his constitutionally protected "effects" under the physical intrusion test.

Would the result in *Carter* have been different if his shaving kit and change of clothing had been in the back of the van? What if he could show that he had been traveling in the van across country for a week before it was stopped by the police? What if he shared driving responsibilities during that trip? Consider United States v. Lopez, 474 F.Supp. 943 (C.D.Cal.1979) (defendants had been given keys to a truck, had permission to use it, and did use it, had the right to challenge a search of the truck); United States v. Tropiano, 50 F.3d 157 (2d Cir.1995) ("a defendant who knowingly possesses a stolen car has no legitimate expectation of privacy in the car"). In United States v. Powell, 929 F.2d 1190 (7th Cir.1991), the court held that where the owner of a car was absent at the time the car was stopped and searched, he had the right to object to the search but not to the stop. Does this make sense?

Disassociation from Property

If a person disassociates himself from certain property, then he loses standing to object to a search of that property, at least under the reasonable expectation of privacy theory of *Rakas*. United States v. Boruff, 909 F.2d 111 (5th Cir.1990), provides an example. A pick-up truck driven by Taylor and a rented car driven by Boruff were involved in a drug-smuggling scheme. The truck had been purchased by Boruff, but title, registration and insurance were put in Taylor's name. Boruff added improvements to the truck, and it was understood that if the truck were sold, the money would go to Boruff. The car was rented by Boruff's girlfriend in her own name. The standard rental agreement signed by the girlfriend stated that only she could drive the car and that the car would not be used for any illegal purpose. Boruff and Taylor drove to Mexico, loaded marijuana into the pick-up truck, and started back. They travelled 100 yards apart on the highway. When a suspicious Border Patrol agent began to pursue the pick-up truck, Boruff did two U-turns in an effort to divert the agent's attention. A second agent pursued Boruff, while the first agent stopped the truck, searched it, found drugs, and placed Taylor under arrest. The second agent stopped Boruff, searched the rented car and found incriminating evidence. Boruff argued that both searches were illegal and moved to suppress all the evidence. As to the truck, the court held that Boruff had failed to establish an expectation of privacy, even though he paid for it.

> Despite his asserted ownership interest, Boruff did everything he could to disassociate himself from the truck in the event it was stopped by law enforcement officials. [Besides placing all documentation in Taylor's name], during the smuggling operation, Taylor, not Boruff, drove the truck. Boruff travelled in a separate vehicle, * * * and left his position in front of the truck after spotting the Border Patrol vehicle. * * * In addition, Boruff was not present when the truck was stopped or searched. See Rakas v. Illinois (legitimate presence at time of search an important factor). * * * Boruff also disavowed any knowledge of the truck and its contents after his own vehicle was stopped.

For another case in which disavowal of ownership resulted in a loss of "standing" see United States v. Mangum, 100 F.3d 164 (D.C.Cir.1996). Mangum was a passenger in a car that was stopped by police. Mangum conceded that there was reasonable suspicion for the stop. A knapsack was removed from the trunk and Mangum, when asked, denied that it was his and said it belonged to the driver. The officer searched the bag and found that it contained a loaded handgun and Mangum's driver's license. The court held that because Mangum denied ownership, "he abandoned his property and waived any legitimate privacy interest in it. Courts have long held that, when a person voluntarily denies ownership of property in response to a police officer's question, he forfeits any privacy interest in the property; consequently, police may search it without a warrant."

Rental Cars

Did Boruff have an expectation of privacy in the rental car? The Supreme Court provided an answer in Byrd v. United States, 138 S.Ct. 1518 (2018). Terrence Byrd was transporting 49 bricks of heroin in a car rented by Latasha Reed. Byrd was not listed on the rental agreement as an authorized driver. Reed acknowledged by her signature that only persons authorized by the agreement were permitted to drive the car. The rental agreement further provided that allowing an unauthorized person to drive the car might void insurance coverage provided under the agreement. Immediately after taking possession of the car, Reed turned the car over to Byrd who soon after hit the road for Pittsburgh.

Byrd's road trip was interrupted by Pennsylvania State Troopers. who stopped him on Interstate 81. During the course of the stop, officers conducted a search of the car, which led to discovery of the heroin. Prior to trial, Byrd moved to suppress the heroin on Fourth Amendment grounds. The trial court denied the motion finding that Byrd did not have "standing" to challenge the search of the car. The Court of Appeals for the Third Circuit affirmed, noting a split among the circuits as to whether an unauthorized driver has a reasonable expectation of privacy in a rental car.

Writing for the Court in *Byrd*, Justice Kennedy rejected the notion that absence of authorization under a rental contract can ground a per se rule. Instead, the material question is whether Byrd had "lawful possession and control [of the car] and the attendant right to exclude." In answer to this question, the Court allowed that it was possible that Byrd was in lawful possession of the car, because he had Reed's permission to drive it, and also had the right to exclude others, including carjackers. On the other hand, Byrd's possession of the car might have been unlawful if it was the product of a conspiracy to defraud the rental car company. The Court therefore remanded the case for lower courts to determine whether Byrd was in lawful possession of the car. Justice Thomas, joined by Justice Gorsuch, wrote a brief concurring opinion suggesting that the Court revisit *Katz*. Justice Alito also concurred to emphasize the scope of the remand.

Coconspirator "Standing" Rejected: United States v. Padilla

A unanimous Supreme Court held in United States v. Padilla, 508 U.S. 77 (1993) (per curiam), that a person does not have an automatic right to challenge a search or seizure simply because he is a member of the conspiracy that controlled the property that was searched or seized. In *Padilla*, the lower court held that the defendants could contest the legality of the stop and search of a car that was being operated by a coconspirator, even though the defendants were not present during the stop and did not own the car. The Supreme Court reversed, explaining that a "coconspirator standing" rule "squarely contradicts" *Rakas*, under which each person must establish an individual expectation of privacy, or a legitimate possessory interest, that has been affected by the search or seizure.

4. The Requirement of Causation and the Exception for Attenuation

The exclusionary rule does not apply unless there is a substantial causal connection between the illegal activity and the evidence offered at trial. Deterrence is unjustified in the absence of that causal link. Determining whether a causal link exists is often a difficult inquiry.

Searches and Seizures That Produce No Evidence: The Ker-Frisbie Doctrine

The exclusionary rule cannot apply unless evidence is seized as a result of a search or arrest. See United States v. Occhipinti, 998 F.2d 791 (10th Cir. 1993) (legality of protective sweep need not be decided because no evidence was obtained, so there was nothing to exclude). In Ker v. Illinois, 119 U.S. 436 (1886), and Frisbie v. Collins, 342 U.S. 519 (1952), the Supreme Court held that an illegal arrest of a person did not deprive the court of jurisdiction to try that person. That is, the body of the person, as distinct from evidence, was not subject to exclusion. The *Ker-Frisbie* doctrine has been used in cases involving the abduction of suspects from foreign countries in order for them to be tried in the United States. See United States v. Alvarez-Machain, 504 U.S. 655 (1992).

Causal Connection: Evidence Found After a Fourth Amendment Violation

Wong Sun v. United States, 371 U.S. 471 (1963) and the following case, Brown v. Illinois, are the Court's leading cases on whether there is a sufficient causal connection between proffered evidence and an illegal search or seizure to justify exclusion. In these cases, the defendant asserts that there is a direct link between the illegality and the proffered evidence. The government, while admitting at least for argument's sake that there was an illegal search or seizure, nonetheless contends that the relationship between the illegality and the proffered evidence is too attenuated to justify exclusion. *Wong Sun* is discussed in detail in *Brown*.

BROWN V. ILLINOIS

Supreme Court of the United States, 1975.
422 U.S. 590.

JUSTICE BLACKMUN delivered the opinion of the Court.

* * *

As petitioner Richard Brown was climbing the last of the stairs leading to the rear entrance of his Chicago apartment in the early evening of May 13, 1968, he happened to glance at the window near the door. He saw, pointed at him through the window, a revolver held by a stranger who was inside the apartment. The man said: "Don't move, you are under arrest." Another man, also with a gun, came up behind Brown and repeated the statement that he was under arrest. It was about 7:45 p.m. The two men turned out to be Detectives William Nolan and William Lenz of the Chicago police force. * * * As both officers held him at gunpoint, the three entered the apartment. Brown was ordered to stand against the wall and was searched. No weapon was found. * * * Detective Lenz informed him that he was under arrest for the murder of Roger Corpus, handcuffed him, and escorted him to the squad car.

The two detectives took petitioner to the Maxwell Street police station. [While at the station, Brown was twice given *Miranda* warnings and twice confessed. The first confession occurred 90 minutes after the arrest, the second occurred seven hours after the arrest. Brown moved to suppress the confessions as having been caused by an arrest without probable cause. The trial court denied the motion, and Brown was convicted. The Illinois Supreme Court found that Brown had been arrested without probable cause, but nonetheless held that the motion to suppress was properly denied because the confessions were too attenuated from the illegal arrest to justify exclusion].

* * * The [Illinois] court appears to have held that the *Miranda* warnings in and of themselves broke the causal chain so that any subsequent statement, even one induced by the continuing effects of unconstitutional custody, was admissible so long as, in the traditional sense, it was voluntary and not coerced in violation of the Fifth and Fourteenth Amendments.

* * *

In *Wong Sun,* the Court pronounced the principles to be applied where the issue is whether statements and other evidence obtained after an illegal arrest or search should be excluded. In that case, * * * [Wong Sun was arrested unlawfully and, after arraignment] was released on his own recognizance. Several days later, he returned voluntarily to give an unsigned confession.

This Court * * * held that in the light of his lawful arraignment and release on his own recognizance, and of his return voluntarily several days later to make the statement, the connection between his unlawful arrest and the statement "had become so attenuated as to dissipate the taint." The Court said:

> "We need not hold that all evidence is 'fruit of the poisonous tree' simply because it would not have come to light but for the illegal actions of the police. Rather, the more apt question in such a case is whether, granting establishment of the primary illegality, the evidence to which instant objection is made has been come at by exploitation of that illegality or instead by means sufficiently distinguishable to be purged of the primary taint."

* * *

The Illinois courts refrained from resolving the question, as apt here as it was in *Wong Sun,* whether Brown's statements were obtained by exploitation of the illegality of his arrest. They assumed that the *Miranda* warnings, by themselves, assured that the statements (verbal acts, as contrasted with physical evidence) were of sufficient free will as to purge the primary taint of the unlawful arrest. *Wong Sun,* of course, preceded *Miranda.*

* * *

* * * In order for the causal chain, between the illegal arrest and the statements made subsequent thereto, to be broken, *Wong Sun* requires not merely that the statement meet the Fifth Amendment standard of voluntariness but that it be "sufficiently an act of free will to purge the primary taint." * * *

If *Miranda* warnings, by themselves, were held to attenuate the taint of an unconstitutional arrest, regardless of how wanton and purposeful the Fourth Amendment violation, the effect of the exclusionary rule would be substantially diluted. * * * Any incentive to avoid Fourth Amendment violations would be eviscerated by making the warnings, in effect, a "cure-all," and the constitutional guarantee against unlawful searches and seizures could be said to be reduced to "a form of words."

* * *

While we therefore reject the *per se* rule which the Illinois courts appear to have accepted, we also decline to adopt any alternative *per se* or "but for" rule. * * * The question whether a confession is the product of a free will under *Wong Sun* must be answered on the facts of each case. No single fact is dispositive. * * * The *Miranda* warnings are an important factor, to be sure, in determining whether the confession is obtained by exploitation of an illegal arrest. But they are not the only factor to be considered. The temporal proximity of the arrest and the confession, the presence of intervening circumstances, and, particularly, the purpose and flagrancy of the official misconduct are all relevant. * * * And the burden of showing admissibility rests, of course, on the prosecution.

* * * We conclude that the State failed to sustain the burden of showing that the evidence in question was admissible under *Wong Sun*.

Brown's first statement was separated from his illegal arrest by less than two hours, and there was no intervening event of significance whatsoever. * * *[a] We could hold Brown's first statement admissible only if we overrule *Wong Sun*. We decline to do so. And the second statement was clearly the result and the fruit of the first.

The illegality here, moreover, had a quality of purposefulness. The impropriety of the arrest was obvious; awareness of that fact was virtually conceded by the two detectives when they repeatedly acknowledged, in their testimony, that the purpose of their action was "for investigation" or for "questioning." The arrest, both in design and in execution, was investigatory. The detectives embarked upon this expedition for evidence in the hope that something might turn up. The manner in which Brown's arrest was effected gives the appearance of having been calculated to cause surprise, fright, and confusion.

* * *

[The concurring opinion of Justice White is omitted.]

JUSTICE POWELL, with whom JUSTICE REHNQUIST joins, concurring in part.

I join the Court insofar as it holds that the *per se* rule adopted by the Illinois Supreme Court for determining the admissibility of petitioner's two statements inadequately accommodates the diverse interests underlying the Fourth Amendment exclusionary rule. I would, however, remand the case for reconsideration under the general standards articulated in the Court's opinion and elaborated herein.

* * *

* * * If an illegal arrest merely provides the occasion of initial contact between the police and the accused, and because of time or other intervening factors the accused's eventual statement is the product of his own reflection and free will, application of the exclusionary rule can serve little purpose: the police normally will not make an illegal arrest in the hope of eventually obtaining such a truly volunteered statement. * * *

[a] The situation here is thus in dramatic contrast to that of Wong Sun himself. Wong Sun's confession, which the Court held admissible, came several days after the illegality, and was preceded by a lawful arraignment and a release from custody on his own recognizance.

I would require the clearest indication of attenuation in cases in which official conduct was flagrantly abusive of Fourth Amendment rights. * * * In such cases the deterrent value of the exclusionary rule is most likely to be effective * * *. I thus would require some demonstrably effective break in the chain of events leading from the illegal arrest to the statement, such as actual consultation with counsel or the accused's presentation before a magistrate for a determination of probable cause, before the taint can be deemed removed.

At the opposite end of the spectrum lie "technical" violations of Fourth Amendment rights * * *.

* * * [In "technical" violation cases], with the exception of statements given in the immediate circumstances of the illegal arrest * * * I would not require more than proof that effective *Miranda* warnings were given and that the ensuing statement was voluntary in the Fifth Amendment sense. * * *

Between these extremes lies a wide range of situations that defy ready categorization, and I will not attempt to embellish on the factors set forth in the Court's opinion other than to emphasize that the *Wong Sun* inquiry always should be conducted with the deterrent purpose of the Fourth Amendment exclusionary rule sharply in focus. * * *

Statements Tainted by an Illegal Arrest: Dunaway v. New York, Taylor v. Alabama, and Kaupp v. Texas

Brown is followed in Dunaway v. New York, 442 U.S. 200 (1979), where the defendant was arrested without probable cause, taken down to the station, and confessed after receiving *Miranda* warnings. The Court found that Dunaway's situation was "virtually a replica of the situation in *Brown*." As in *Brown*, the Court was concerned that officers would "violate the Fourth Amendment with impunity, safe in the knowledge that they could wash their hands in the procedural safeguards of the Fifth."

Brown and *Dunaway* were deemed to be dispositive in Taylor v. Alabama, 455 U.S. 1014 (1982). Police arrested Taylor for a grocery store robbery without probable cause, searched him, took him to the station for questioning and gave him *Miranda* warnings. At the station, he was fingerprinted, re-advised of his rights, questioned and placed in a lineup. Police told Taylor that his fingerprints matched those on some grocery items that had been handled by a participant in the robbery, and after a short visit with his girlfriend and a male companion, Taylor signed a *Miranda* waiver and confessed. Although the length of time between the illegal arrests and the confessions in *Brown* and *Dunaway* was two hours and in this case it was six hours, the Court said that "a difference of a few hours is not significant where, as here, petitioner was in police custody, unrepresented by counsel, and he was questioned on several occasions, fingerprinted and subjected to a line-up." Although Taylor was given *Miranda* warnings three times, the Court found that this was insufficient to break the connection with the illegal arrest and detention. Four dissenters agreed on the applicable law but disagreed on its application to the facts of the case.

The Court applied *Brown*, *Dunaway* and *Taylor* in Kaupp v. Texas, 538 U.S. 626 (2003) (per curiam) as it held that a suspect's confession was the fruit of an arrest without probable cause. Police officers suspected Kaupp, an adolescent, of involvement in a murder, but did not have probable cause to arrest him. The officers entered Kaupp's house at 3 a.m., went to his bedroom, woke him up, placed him in handcuffs, and took him in his underwear to a patrol car. They drove and stopped for 5 to 10 minutes at the site where the victim's body had been found, and then went on to the sheriff's headquarters, where they removed his handcuffs, gave him *Miranda* warnings, and told him that the victim's brother had confessed to the crime and implicated him as an accomplice. Kaupp then admitted to some part in the crime. The Court analyzed the situation as follows:

> [W]ell-established precedent requires suppression of the confession unless that confession was an act of freewill sufficient to purge the primary taint of the unlawful invasion. Demonstrating such purgation is, of course, a function of circumstantial evidence, with the burden of persuasion on the state. Relevant considerations include observance of *Miranda*, the temporal proximity of the arrest and the confession, the presence of intervening circumstances, and, particularly, the purpose and flagrancy of the official misconduct.
>
> The record before us shows that only one of these considerations, the giving of *Miranda* warnings, supports the state * * * . All other factors point the opposite way. There is no indication from the record that any substantial time passed between Kaupp's removal from his home in handcuffs and his confession after only 10 or 15 minutes of interrogation. In the interim, he remained in his partially clothed state in the physical custody of a number of officers, some of whom, at least, were conscious that they lacked probable cause to arrest. In fact, the state has not even alleged any meaningful intervening event between the illegal arrest and Kaupp's confession.

Statements Not Tainted by an Illegal Arrest: Rawlings v. Kentucky

Brown was distinguished in Rawlings v. Kentucky, 448 U.S. 98 (1980). The Court assumed that Rawlings and others were improperly detained in a house while police went to get a search warrant, but found that the improper detention did not require suppression of statements made by Rawlings after evidence was discovered. Justice Rehnquist's majority opinion observed that *Miranda* warnings were given (also true in *Brown*); that the 45 minute detention was in a congenial atmosphere; that the statements were apparently spontaneous reactions to the discovery of evidence rather than the product of the illegal detention; that the police action did not involve flagrant misconduct; and that no argument was made that the statements were involuntary. Justices White and Stewart would have remanded for consideration of the "fruit" question. Justices Marshall and Brennan thought that the statements "were obviously the fruit of the illegal detention."

Warrantless In-Home Arrest Is Not Causally Connected to a Subsequent Confession: New York v. Harris

Brown, Dunaway and *Taylor* each excluded confessions as the fruit of an arrest made without probable cause. In New York v. Harris, 495 U.S. 14 (1990), Harris confessed at the station after police arrested him in his home, with probable cause but without a warrant—and so the in-home arrest was in violation of Payton v. New York, *supra* (holding that an arrest warrant is necessary for an in-home arrest in the absence of exigent circumstances). The challenged confession was made at the station an hour after the arrest. Justice White concluded for the Court that there was no substantial causative connection between the *Payton* violation and the confession, because, unlike the prior cases, the defendant was not unlawfully in custody when he made the confession. Justice White reasoned that "the rule in *Payton* was designed to protect the physical integrity of the home; it was not intended to grant criminal suspects * * * protection for statements made outside their premises where the police have probable cause to arrest the suspect." Thus, a violation of *Payton* constitutes an illegal *search* of the home, but it does not result in an illegal arrest, so long as there is probable cause; and while evidence obtained in the warrantless search of the home is subject to exclusion, there is no automatic connection between that search and a subsequent confession outside the home.

Justice Marshall dissented in an opinion joined by Justices Brennan, Blackmun and Stevens. Justice Marshall contended that the rule adopted by the majority would give the police an incentive to violate *Payton*. He reasoned that the officer might find it beneficial to enter the arrestee's home illegally in order to save time, and perhaps to rattle the suspect and increase the likelihood of a confession. Excluding evidence found in the house would be no deterrent, because such suppression would make the officer no worse off than if he had waited outside to make the arrest.

In *Harris* the *Payton* violation turned up no evidence; nothing incriminating was seen in Harris's home. Would exclusion be required if the officers found incriminating evidence in Harris's house in the course of making a warrantless arrest, and subsequently used that evidence to obtain a stationhouse confession from Harris? In United States v. Beltran, 917 F.2d 641, 645 (1st Cir.1990), police arrested Beltran in her home without a warrant. During the arrest the police saw cocaine in plain view. They took the defendant to the stationhouse where she made incriminating statements. The court stated that "whether or the extent to which *Harris* applies may turn on questions of fact such as when the police seized the items in question or what motivated Ms. Beltran's statements" and remanded the case to the district court. Does this mean that if Beltran was rattled into a confession by the fact that the police saw the cocaine—rather than by the arrest—then the confession would be excluded?

Insufficient Causal Connection Between a Knock-and-Announce Violation and Evidence Found in the Home: Hudson v. Michigan

In Hudson v. Michigan, 547 U.S. 586 (2006), police had a warrant to search Hudson's house for drugs and firearms. They executed the warrant and found both, but violated the knock-and-announce rule in the process—the officers waited only a few seconds after announcing themselves before turning the doorknob and entering the house. The only question before the Court was whether the evidence should be excluded because the officers violated the knock-and-announce requirement.

Writing for the Court, Justice Scalia reasoned as follows:

> Our cases show that but-for causality is only a necessary, not a sufficient, condition for suppression. In this case, of course, the constitutional violation of an illegal *manner* of entry was *not* a but-for cause of obtaining the evidence. Whether that preliminary misstep had occurred *or not*, the police would have executed the warrant they had obtained, and would have discovered the gun and drugs inside the house. * * *
>
> Attenuation can occur, of course, when the causal connection is remote. Attenuation also occurs when, even given a direct causal connection, the interest protected by the constitutional guarantee that has been violated would not be served by suppression of the evidence obtained. * * *
>
> * * * Exclusion of the evidence obtained by a warrantless search vindicates that entitlement. The interests protected by the knock-and-announce requirement are quite different—and do not include the shielding of potential evidence from the government's eyes. * * *
>
> Quite apart from the requirement of unattenuated causation, the exclusionary rule has never been applied except where its deterrence benefits outweigh its substantial social costs. The costs here are

> considerable. In addition to the grave adverse consequence that exclusion of relevant incriminating evidence always entails (viz., the risk of releasing dangerous criminals into society), imposing that massive remedy for a knock-and-announce violation would generate a constant flood of alleged failures to observe the rule * * *. The cost of entering this lottery would be small, but the jackpot enormous: suppression of all evidence, amounting in many cases to a get-out-of-jail-free card. * * *
>
> * * *
>
> Next to these "substantial social costs" we must consider the deterrence benefits, existence of which is a necessary condition for exclusion. * * * To begin with, the value of deterrence depends upon the strength of the incentive to commit the forbidden act. Viewed from this perspective, deterrence of knock-and-announce violations is not worth a lot. Violation of the warrant requirement sometimes produces incriminating evidence that could not otherwise be obtained. But ignoring knock-and-announce can realistically be expected to achieve absolutely nothing except the prevention of destruction of evidence and the avoidance of life-threatening resistance by occupants of the premises—dangers which, if there is even "reasonable suspicion" of their existence, *suspend the knock-and-announce requirement anyway*. Massive deterrence is hardly required.
>
> * * *
>
> In sum, the social costs of applying the exclusionary rule to knock-and-announce violations are considerable; the incentive to such violations is minimal to begin with, and the extant deterrences against them are substantial * * *. Resort to the massive remedy of suppressing evidence of guilt is unjustified.

Justice Kennedy concurred in part and in the judgment, clarifying that:

> Today's decision does not address any demonstrated pattern of knock-and-announce violations. If a widespread pattern of violations were shown, and particularly if those violations were committed against persons who lacked the means or voice to mount an effective protest, there would be reason for grave concern. Even then, however, the Court would have to acknowledge that extending the remedy of exclusion to all the evidence seized following a knock-and-announce violation would mean revising the requirement of causation that limits our discretion in applying the exclusionary rule.

Justice Breyer, joined by Justices Stevens, Souter and Ginsburg, dissented and wrote that "the Court destroys the strongest legal incentive to comply with the Constitution's knock-and-announce requirement"; "the Court does so without significant support in precedent"; "[t]oday's opinion is thus doubly troubling"; "[i]t represents a significant departure from the Court's precedents"; and "it weakens, perhaps destroys, much of the practical value of the Constitution's knock-and-announce protection."

Consent as Breaking the Chain of Causation

Police often argue that an illegal search or seizure should not result in exclusion of evidence because the suspect voluntarily consented to the search that ultimately uncovered that evidence. For example, assume that the defendant is illegally pulled over while driving. After a short period, the officer asks nicely whether the defendant would permit a search of the trunk; the defendant is told of his right to refuse; the defendant consents and weapons are found in the trunk. The defendant argues that there is a direct causal link between the illegal stop and the discovery of the evidence. The government argues that the voluntary consent broke the chain of causation.

The question in such cases is whether the voluntary consent is enough to break the chain of causation running from the illegal police activity to the evidence ultimately uncovered. The answer is dependent on the circumstances, and the analysis is no different from that employed in *Brown* to determine whether an admittedly voluntary confession should be excluded as the fruit of an illegal arrest. As one court put it:

> To determine whether the defendant's consent was an independent act of free will, breaking the causal chain * * * we must consider three factors: 1) the temporal proximity of the illegal conduct and the consent; 2) the presence of intervening circumstances; and 3) the purpose and flagrancy of the initial misconduct.

United States v. Hernandez, 279 F.3d 302 (5th Cir. 2002). In *Hernandez*, the court found that the defendant voluntarily consented to a search of luggage, but that this voluntary act was not sufficient to break the chain of causation from the officer's initial illegal search. Hernandez was traveling on a bus when police seized her bag and manipulated it in such a way as to determine that a hard package was inside it. This manipulation constituted an illegal search under Bond v. United States, discussed earlier in this Chapter. The officer then immediately sought and obtained consent from Hernandez to open the suitcase. The court found that there were no intervening circumstances, and therefore the opening of the suitcase was a fruit of the *Bond* violation. The court stated that while the police misconduct was not flagrant, the officer exploited the illegality, as the officer's suspicions were aroused only after manipulating Hernandez's suitcase. As a result, "even though Hernandez voluntarily consented to Officer Ordaz's opening her suitcase and searching it, her consent did not cure the Fourth Amendment violation caused by Officer Ordaz's prior manipulation of the suitcase." For a contrary result, see United States v.

Becker, 333 F.3d 858 (8th Cir. 2003) (voluntary consent severed the chain of causation from an illegal detention to the evidence obtained: consent was removed in time from the detention, and the officers were not engaged in flagrant misconduct).

Witness Testimony After Illegal Arrests and Searches: United States v. Ceccolini

Courts are reluctant to suppress the testimony from a live witness that is alleged to be the product of an illegal search or arrest. The witness's decision to testify is ordinarily enough to break any causal connection between the illegality and the testimony. The leading case is United States v. Ceccolini, 435 U.S. 268 (1978), where an officer stopped to talk with a friend who was in Ceccolini's flower shop. While there, the officer illegally picked up and opened an envelope, and found money and gambling slips. He then learned from his friend, who did not know about this discovery, that the envelope belonged to Ceccolini. The officer relayed his information to detectives who in turn transmitted it to the FBI. Four months later, an FBI agent questioned the officer's friend who had been in the flower shop, without mentioning the illegally discovered gambling slips. The friend expressed a willingness to testify against Ceccolini, and did so before the grand jury and at Ceccolini's trial.

Justice Rehnquist, writing for the Court, declined to adopt a rule that the testimony of a live witness could never be excluded. But he stated that "the exclusionary rule should be invoked with much greater reluctance where the claim is based on a causal relationship between a constitutional violation and the discovery of a live witness than when a similar claim is advanced to support suppression of an inanimate object." The Court noted that the willingness of the witness to testify is very likely, if not certain, to break the chain of causation under *Wong Sun*. Justice Rehnquist also noted that exclusion of a live witness would have a serious cost because it would "perpetually disable a witness from testifying about relevant and material facts, regardless of how unrelated such testimony might be to the purpose of the originally illegal search or the evidence discovered thereby." Because of this cost, the Court concluded that the exclusionary rule could only apply if there is a very close and direct link between the illegality and the witness's testimony. The Court found no such close link under the facts in *Ceccolini,* where the witness was willing to testify, four months passed between the illegality and the agent's contact with the witness, and the witness was unaware of the illegality. Justice Marshall, in a dissent joined by Justice Brennan, found no meaningful distinction between live witnesses and inanimate evidence. He argued that "the same tree" cannot bear "two different kinds of fruit, with one kind less susceptible than the other to exclusion."

After *Ceccolini,* can you think of facts that would result in the exclusion of a live witness? See United States v. Akridge, 346 F.3d 618 (6th Cir. 2003) (stating that after *Ceccolini,* the question of causal connection between an illegality and witness testimony is determined by the following factors: "(a) the degree of free will exercised by the witnesses; (b) the role of the illegality in obtaining the testimony; (c) the time elapsed between the illegal behavior, the decision to cooperate, and the actual testimony at trial; and (d) the purpose and flagrancy of the officials' misconduct.").

Outstanding Warrants Breaking the Chain of Causation: Utah v. Strieff

UTAH V. STRIEFF

Supreme Court of the United States, 2016.
579 U.S. 232.

JUSTICE THOMAS delivered the opinion of the Court.

To enforce the Fourth Amendment's prohibition against "unreasonable searches and seizures," this Court has at times required courts to exclude evidence obtained by unconstitutional police conduct. But the Court has also held that, even when there is a Fourth Amendment violation, this exclusionary rule does not apply when the costs of exclusion outweigh its deterrent benefits. In some cases, for example, the link between the unconstitutional conduct and the discovery of the evidence is too attenuated to justify suppression. The question in this case is whether this attenuation doctrine applies when an officer makes an unconstitutional investigatory stop; learns during that stop that the suspect is subject to a valid arrest warrant; and proceeds to arrest the suspect and seize incriminating evidence during a search incident to that arrest. We hold that the evidence the officer seized as part of the search incident to arrest is admissible because the officer's discovery of the arrest warrant attenuated the connection between the unlawful stop and the evidence seized incident to arrest.

[Officer Fackrell received an anonymous tip reporting "narcotics activity" at a particular residence. For a week, he conducted intermittent surveillance of the home. He observed visitors who left a few minutes after arriving at the house. One of those visitors was Strieff. The Officer observed Strieff exit the house and walk toward a nearby convenience store. In the store's parking lot, Officer Fackrell detained Strieff, identified himself, and asked Strieff what he was doing at the residence. He asked for identification and Strieff produced his Utah identification card. The Officer relayed Strieff's information to a police dispatcher, who reported that Strieff had an outstanding arrest warrant for a traffic violation. Strieff was then arrested on that warrant, and a search incident to arrest uncovered a baggie of methamphetamine and drug paraphernalia. Strieff moved to suppress on grounds of an illegal stop. The state conceded that the stop was illegal because the Officer lacked reasonable suspicion. But the trial court found that the search was attenuated from the stop because of the outstanding warrant. The Utah Supreme Court reversed, reasoning that the taint could be erased only by a voluntary act by the defendant.]

* * * Evidence is admissible when the connection between unconstitutional police conduct and the evidence is remote or has been interrupted by some intervening circumstance, so that the interest protected by the constitutional guarantee that has been violated would not be served by suppression of the evidence obtained. * * * The attenuation doctrine evaluates the causal link between the government's unlawful act and the discovery of evidence, which often has nothing to do with a defendant's actions. And the logic of our prior attenuation cases is not limited to independent acts by the defendant.

It remains for us to address whether the discovery of a valid arrest warrant was a sufficient intervening event to break the causal chain between the unlawful stop and the discovery of drug-related evidence on Strieff's person. The three factors articulated in Brown v. Illinois guide our analysis. * * *

The first factor, temporal proximity between the initially unlawful stop and the search, favors suppressing the evidence. Our precedents have declined to find that this factor favors attenuation unless "substantial time" elapses between an unlawful act and when the evidence is obtained. Here, however, Officer Fackrell discovered drug contraband on Strieff's person only minutes after the illegal stop. As the Court explained in *Brown*, such a short time interval counsels in favor of suppression; there, we found that the confession should be suppressed, relying in part on the "less than two hours" that separated the unconstitutional arrest and the confession.

In contrast, the second factor, the presence of intervening circumstances, strongly favors the State. * * *

In this case, the warrant was valid, it predated Officer Fackrell's investigation, and it was entirely unconnected with the stop. And once Officer Fackrell discovered the warrant, he had an obligation to arrest Strieff. A warrant is a judicial mandate to an officer to conduct a search or make an arrest, and the officer has a sworn duty to carry out its provisions. Fackrell's arrest of Strieff thus was a ministerial act that was independently compelled by the pre-existing warrant. And once Officer Fackrell was authorized to arrest Strieff, it was undisputedly lawful to search Strieff as an incident of his arrest to protect Officer Fackrell's safety.

Finally, the third factor, "the purpose and flagrancy of the official misconduct," also strongly favors the State. The exclusionary rule exists to deter police misconduct. The third factor of the attenuation doctrine reflects that rationale by favoring exclusion only when the police misconduct is most in need of deterrence—that is, when it is purposeful or flagrant.

Officer Fackrell was at most negligent. In stopping Strieff, Officer Fackrell made two good-faith mistakes. First, he had not observed what time Strieff entered the suspected drug house, so he did not know how long Strieff had been there. Officer Fackrell thus lacked a sufficient basis to conclude that Strieff was a short-term visitor who may have been consummating a drug transaction. Second, because he lacked confirmation that Strieff was a short-term visitor, Officer Fackrell should have asked Strieff whether he would speak with him, instead of demanding that Strieff do so. * * * But these errors in judgment hardly rise to a purposeful or flagrant violation of Strieff's Fourth Amendment rights.

* * *

Moreover, there is no indication that this unlawful stop was part of any systemic or recurrent police misconduct. To the contrary, all the evidence suggests that the stop was an isolated instance of negligence that occurred in connection with a bona fide investigation of a suspected drug house. Officer Fackrell saw Strieff leave a suspected drug house. And his suspicion about the house was based on an anonymous tip and his personal observations.

Applying these factors, we hold that the evidence discovered on Strieff's person was admissible because the unlawful stop was sufficiently attenuated by the pre-existing arrest warrant. Although the illegal stop was close in time to Strieff's arrest, that consideration is outweighed by two factors supporting the State. The outstanding arrest warrant for Strieff's arrest is a critical intervening circumstance that is wholly independent of the illegal stop. The discovery of that warrant broke the causal chain between the unconstitutional stop and the discovery of evidence by compelling Officer Fackrell to arrest Strieff. And it is especially significant that there is no evidence that Officer Fackrell's illegal stop reflected flagrantly unlawful police misconduct.

* * *

Strieff argues that, because of the prevalence of outstanding arrest warrants in many jurisdictions, police will engage in dragnet searches if the exclusionary rule is not applied. We think that this outcome is unlikely. Such wanton conduct would expose police to civil liability. And in any event, the *Brown* factors take account of the purpose and flagrancy of police misconduct. Were evidence of a dragnet search presented here, the application of the *Brown* factors could be different. But there is no evidence that the concerns that Strieff raises with the criminal justice system are present in South Salt Lake City, Utah.

* * *

JUSTICE SOTOMAYOR, with whom JUSTICE GINSBURG joins as to parts I, II, and III, dissenting.

* * *

The Court today holds that the discovery of a warrant for an unpaid parking ticket will forgive a police officer's violation of your Fourth Amendment rights. Do not be soothed by the opinion's technical language: This case allows the police to stop you on the street, demand your identification, and check it for outstanding traffic warrants—even if you are doing nothing wrong. If the officer discovers a warrant for a fine you forgot to pay, courts will now excuse his illegal stop and will admit into evidence anything he happens to find by searching you after arresting you on the warrant.

* * *

II

* * *

[T]he officer in this case discovered Strieff's drugs by exploiting his own illegal conduct. The officer did not ask Strieff to volunteer his name only to find out, days later, that Strieff had a warrant against him. The officer illegally stopped Strieff and immediately ran a warrant check. The officer's discovery of a warrant was not some intervening surprise that he could not have anticipated. Utah lists over 180,000 misdemeanor warrants in its database, and at the time of the arrest, Salt Lake County had a "backlog of outstanding warrants" so large that it faced the "potential for civil liability." The officer's violation was also calculated to procure evidence. His sole reason for stopping Strieff, he acknowledged, was investigative—he wanted to discover whether drug activity was going on in the house Strieff had just exited.

The warrant check, in other words, was not an "intervening circumstance" separating the stop from the search for drugs. * * * Under our precedents, because the officer found Strieff's drugs by exploiting his own constitutional violation, the drugs should be excluded.

III

* * *

The majority also posits that the officer could not have exploited his illegal conduct because he did not violate the Fourth Amendment on purpose. Rather, he made "good-faith mistakes." Never mind that the officer's sole purpose was to fish for evidence. The majority casts his unconstitutional actions as "negligent" and therefore incapable of being deterred by the exclusionary rule.

But the Fourth Amendment does not tolerate an officer's unreasonable searches and seizures just because he did not know any better. Even officers prone to negligence can learn from courts that exclude illegally obtained evidence. Indeed, they are perhaps the most in need of the education, whether by the judge's opinion, the prosecutor's future guidance, or an updated manual on criminal procedure. If the officers are in doubt about what the law requires, exclusion gives them an incentive to err on the side of constitutional behavior.

* * *

Outstanding warrants are surprisingly common. * * * The States and Federal Government maintain databases with over 7.8 million outstanding warrants, the vast majority of which appear to be for minor offenses. * * * The county in this case has had a "backlog" of such warrants. The Department of Justice recently reported that in the town of Ferguson, Missouri, with a population of 21,000, 16,000 people had outstanding warrants against them.

Justice Department investigations across the country have illustrated how these astounding numbers of warrants can be used by police to stop people without cause. In a single year in New Orleans, officers "made nearly 60,000 arrests, of which about 20,000 were of people with outstanding traffic or misdemeanor warrants from neighboring parishes for such infractions as unpaid tickets." In the St. Louis metropolitan area, officers "routinely" stop people—on the street, at bus stops, or even in court—for no reason other than "an officer's desire to check whether the subject had a municipal arrest warrant pending." In Newark, New Jersey, officers stopped 52,235 pedestrians within a 4-year period and ran warrant checks on 39,308 of them. The Justice Department analyzed these warrant-checked stops and reported that "approximately 93% of the stops would have been considered unsupported by articulated reasonable suspicion."

* * *

The majority does not suggest what makes this case "isolated" from these and countless other examples. Nor does it offer guidance for how a defendant can prove that his arrest was the result of "widespread" misconduct. Surely it should not take a federal investigation of Salt Lake County before the Court would protect someone in Strieff's position.

IV

Writing only for myself, and drawing on my professional experiences, I would add that unlawful "stops" have severe consequences much greater than the inconvenience suggested by the name. This Court has given officers an array of instruments to probe and examine you. When we condone officers' use of these devices without adequate cause, we give them reason to target pedestrians in an arbitrary manner. We also risk treating members of our communities as second-class citizens.

Although many Americans have been stopped for speeding or jaywalking, few may realize how degrading a stop can be when the officer is looking for more. This Court has allowed an officer to stop you for whatever reason he wants—so long as he can point to a pretextual justification after the fact. * * * The officer does not even need to know which law you might have broken so long as he can later point to any possible infraction—even one that is minor, unrelated, or ambiguous.

The indignity of the stop is not limited to an officer telling you that you look like a criminal. The officer may next ask for your "consent" to inspect your bag or purse without telling you that you can decline. Regardless of your answer, he may order you to stand helpless, perhaps facing a wall with your hands raised. If the officer thinks you might be dangerous, he may then "frisk" you for weapons. This involves more than just a patdown. As onlookers pass by, the officer may "feel with sensitive fingers every portion of [your] body. A thorough search [may] be made of [your] arms and armpits, waistline and back, the groin and area about the testicles, and entire surface of the legs down to the feet."

The officer's control over you does not end with the stop. If the officer chooses, he may handcuff you and take you to jail for doing nothing more than speeding, jaywalking, or driving your pickup truck with your 3-year-old son and 5-year-old daughter without your seatbelt fastened. At the jail, he can fingerprint you, swab DNA from the inside of your mouth, and force you to shower with a delousing agent while you lift your tongue, hold out your arms, turn around, and lift your genitals. Even if you are innocent, you will now join the 65 million Americans with an arrest record and experience the "civil death" of discrimination by employers, landlords, and whoever else conducts a background check. And, of course, if you fail to pay bail or appear for court, a judge will issue a warrant to render you "arrestable on sight" in the future.

* * * The white defendant in this case shows that anyone's dignity can be violated in this manner. But it is no secret that people of color are disproportionate victims of this type of scrutiny. For generations, black and brown parents have given their children "the talk"—instructing them never to run down the street; always keep your hands where they can be seen; do not even think of talking back to a stranger—all out of fear of how an officer with a gun will react to them.

By legitimizing the conduct that produces this double consciousness, this case tells everyone, white and black, guilty and innocent, that an officer can verify your legal status at any time. It says that your body is subject to invasion while courts excuse the violation of your rights. It implies that you are not a citizen of a democracy but the subject of a carceral state, just waiting to be cataloged.

We must not pretend that the countless people who are routinely targeted by police are "isolated." They are the canaries in the coal mine whose deaths, civil and literal, warn us that no one can breathe in this atmosphere. They are the ones who recognize that unlawful police stops corrode all our civil liberties and threaten all our lives. Until their voices matter too, our justice system will continue to be anything but.

* * *

JUSTICE KAGAN, with whom JUSTICE GINSBURG joins, dissenting.

* * *

The majority chalks up Fackrell's Fourth Amendment violation to a couple of innocent "mistakes." But far from a Barney Fife-type mishap, Fackrell's seizure of Strieff was a calculated decision, taken with so little justification that the State has never tried to defend its legality. * * *

* * * Fackrell's discovery of an arrest warrant—the only event the majority thinks intervened—was an eminently foreseeable consequence of stopping Strieff. As Fackrell testified, checking for outstanding warrants during a stop is the "normal" practice of South Salt Lake City police. In other words, the department's standard detention procedures—stop, ask for identification, run a check—are partly designed to find outstanding warrants. And find them they will, given the staggering number of such warrants on the books. * * * So outstanding warrants do not appear as bolts from the blue. * * * In short, they are nothing like what intervening circumstances are supposed to be. * * *

The majority's misapplication of *Brown*'s three-part inquiry creates unfortunate incentives for the police—indeed, practically invites them to do what Fackrell did here. Consider an officer who, like Fackrell, wishes to stop someone for investigative reasons, but does not have what a court would view as reasonable suspicion. If the officer believes that any evidence he discovers will be inadmissible, he is likely to think the unlawful stop not worth making—precisely the deterrence the exclusionary rule is meant to achieve. But when he is told of today's decision? Now the officer knows that the stop may well yield admissible evidence: So long as the target is one of the many millions of people in this country with an outstanding arrest warrant, anything the officer finds in a search is fair game for use in a criminal prosecution. The officer's incentive to violate the Constitution thus increases: From here on, he sees potential advantage in stopping individuals without reasonable suspicion—exactly the temptation the exclusionary rule is supposed to remove. * * *

5. Independent Source

Evidence will not be excluded if it is obtained independently from and without reliance on any illegal police activity. The "independent source" doctrine allows "the introduction of evidence discovered initially during an unlawful search if the evidence is discovered later through a source that is untainted by the initial illegality." United States v. Markling, 7 F.3d 1309 (7th Cir.1993).

In Segura v. United States, 468 U.S. 796 (1984), and in the following case, Murray v. United States, the Court considered whether an illegal search of premises could be cured when the officers later obtained a warrant, and where the probable cause supporting the warrant was not derived from information obtained in the illegal search. *Segura* is discussed in detail in *Murray*.

MURRAY V. UNITED STATES

Supreme Court of the United States, 1988.
487 U.S. 533.

JUSTICE SCALIA delivered the opinion of the Court.

In Segura v. United States, we held that police officers' illegal entry upon private premises did not require suppression of evidence subsequently discovered at those premises when executing a search warrant obtained on the basis of information wholly unconnected with the initial entry. In these consolidated cases we are faced with the question whether, again assuming evidence obtained pursuant to an independently obtained search warrant, the portion of such evidence that had been observed in plain view at the time of a prior illegal entry must be suppressed.

* * * Based on information received from informants, federal law enforcement agents had been surveilling petitioner Murray and several of his co-conspirators. At about 1:45 p.m. on April 6, 1983, they observed Murray drive a truck and Carter drive a green camper, into a warehouse in South Boston. When the petitioners drove the vehicles out about 20 minutes later, the surveilling agents saw within the warehouse two individuals and a tractor-trailer rig bearing a long, dark container. Murray and Carter later turned over the truck and camper to other drivers, who were in turn followed and ultimately arrested, and the vehicles lawfully seized. Both vehicles were found to contain marijuana.

After receiving this information, several of the agents converged on the South Boston warehouse and forced entry. They found the warehouse unoccupied, but observed in plain view numerous burlap-wrapped bales that were later found to contain marijuana. They left without disturbing the bales, kept the warehouse under surveillance, and did not reenter it until they had a search warrant. In applying for the warrant, the agents did not mention the prior entry, and did not rely on any observations made during that entry. When the warrant was issued—at 10:40 p.m., approximately eight hours after the initial entry—the agents immediately reentered the warehouse and seized 270 bales of marijuana and notebooks listing customers for whom the bales were destined.

[The motion to suppress was denied and the Court of Appeals affirmed.]

* * *

Almost simultaneously with our development of the exclusionary rule, * * * we also announced what has come to be known as the "independent source" doctrine. That doctrine, which has been applied to evidence acquired not only through Fourth Amendment violations but also through Fifth and Sixth Amendment violations, has recently been described as follows:

> "[T]he interest of society in deterring unlawful police conduct and the public interest in having juries receive all probative evidence of a crime are properly balanced by putting the police in the same, not a *worse*, position than they would have been in if no police error or misconduct had occurred. . . . When the challenged evidence has an independent source, exclusion of such evidence would put the police in a worse position than they would have been in absent any error or violation." Nix v. Williams, 467 U.S. 431, 443 (1984).

The dispute here is over the scope of this doctrine. Petitioners contend that it applies only to evidence obtained for the first time during an independent lawful search. The Government argues that it applies also to evidence initially discovered during, or as a consequence of, an unlawful search, but later obtained independently from activities untainted by the initial illegality. We think the Government's view has better support in both precedent and policy.

* * *

Petitioners' asserted policy basis for excluding evidence which is initially discovered during an illegal search, but is subsequently acquired through an independent and lawful source, is that a contrary rule will remove all deterrence to, and indeed positively encourage, unlawful police searches. As petitioners see the incentives, law enforcement officers will routinely enter without a warrant to make sure that what they expect to be on the premises is in fact there. If it is not, they will have spared themselves the time and trouble of getting a warrant; if it is, they can get the warrant and use the evidence despite the unlawful entry. We see the incentives differently. An officer with probable cause sufficient to obtain a search warrant would be foolish to enter the premises first in an unlawful manner. By doing so, he would risk suppression of all evidence on the premises, both seen and unseen, since his action would add to the normal burden of convincing a magistrate that there is probable cause the much more onerous burden of convincing a trial court that no information gained from the illegal entry affected either the law enforcement officers' decision to seek a warrant or the magistrate's decision to grant it. Nor would the officer *without* sufficient probable cause to obtain a search warrant have any added incentive to conduct an unlawful entry, since whatever he finds cannot be used to establish probable cause before a magistrate.[a]

It is possible to read petitioners' briefs as asserting the more narrow position that the "independent source" doctrine does apply to independent acquisition of evidence previously derived *indirectly* from the unlawful search, but does not apply to what they call "primary evidence," that is, evidence acquired during the course of the search itself. In addition to finding no support in our precedent, this strange distinction would produce results bearing no relation to the policies of the exclusionary rule. It would mean, for example, that the government's knowledge of the existence and condition of a dead body, knowledge lawfully acquired through independent sources, would have to be excluded if government agents had previously observed the body during an unlawful search of the defendant's apartment; but not if they had observed a notation that the body was buried in a certain location, producing consequential discovery of the corpse.

* * *

To apply what we have said to the present cases: Knowledge that the marijuana was in the warehouse was assuredly acquired at the time of the unlawful entry. But it was also acquired at the time of entry pursuant to the warrant, and if that later acquisition was not the result of the earlier entry there is no reason why the independent source doctrine should not apply. Invoking the exclusionary rule would put the police (and society) not in the *same* position they would have occupied if no violation occurred, but in a *worse* one.

* * *

The ultimate question, therefore, is whether the search pursuant to warrant was in fact a genuinely independent source of the information and

---

a * * * To say that a district court must be satisfied that a warrant would have been sought without the illegal entry is not to give dispositive effect to police officers' assurances on the point. Where the facts render those assurances implausible, the independent source doctrine will not apply.

We might note that there is no basis for pointing to the present cases as an example of a "search first, warrant later" mentality. The District Court found that the agents entered the warehouse "in an effort to apprehend any participants who might have remained inside and to guard against the destruction of possibly critical evidence." While they may have misjudged the existence of sufficient exigent circumstances to justify the warrantless entry * * * there is nothing to suggest that they went in merely to see if there was anything worth getting a warrant for.

tangible evidence at issue here. This would not have been the case if the agents' decision to seek the warrant was prompted by what they had seen during the initial entry, or if information obtained during that entry was presented to the Magistrate and affected his decision to issue the warrant. * * * The District Court found that the agents did not reveal their warrantless entry to the Magistrate and that they did not include in their application for a warrant any recitation of their observations in the warehouse. It did not, however, explicitly find that the agents would have sought a warrant if they had not earlier entered the warehouse. * * * To be sure, the District Court did determine that the purpose of the warrantless entry was in part "to guard against the destruction of possibly critical evidence," and one could perhaps infer from this that the agents who made the entry already planned to obtain that "critical evidence" through a warrant-authorized search. That inference is not, however, clear enough to justify the conclusion that the District Court's findings amounted to a determination of independent source.

Accordingly, we vacate the judgment and remand these cases to the Court of Appeals with instructions that it remand to the District Court for determination whether the warrant-authorized search of the warehouse was an independent source of the challenged evidence in the sense we have described.

[Justices Brennan and Kennedy took no part in the decision.]

JUSTICE MARSHALL, with whom JUSTICE STEVENS and JUSTICE O'CONNOR join, dissenting.

* * * In holding that the independent source exception may apply to the facts of these cases, I believe the Court loses sight of the practical moorings of the independent source exception and creates an affirmative incentive for unconstitutional searches. * * *

* * * Obtaining a warrant is inconvenient and time consuming. Even when officers have probable cause to support a warrant application, therefore, they have an incentive first to determine whether it is worthwhile to obtain a warrant. Probable cause is much less than certainty, and many "confirmatory" searches will result in the discovery that no evidence is present, thus saving the police the time and trouble of getting a warrant. If contraband is discovered, however, the officers may later seek a warrant to shield the evidence from the taint of the illegal search. The police thus know in advance that they have little to lose and much to gain by forgoing the bother of obtaining a warrant and undertaking an illegal search.

Under the Court's view, today's decision does not provide an incentive for unlawful searches, because the officer undertaking the search would know that "his action would add to the normal burden of convincing a magistrate that there is probable cause the much more onerous burden of convincing a trial court that no information gained from the illegal entry affected either the law enforcement officers' decision to seek a warrant or the magistrate's decision to grant it." The Court, however, provides no hint of why this risk would actually seem significant to the officers. * * * [T]oday's decision makes the application of the independent source exception turn entirely on an evaluation of the officers' intent. It normally will be difficult for the trial court to verify, or the defendant to rebut, an assertion by officers that they always intended to obtain a warrant, regardless of the results of the illegal search. The testimony of the officers conducting the illegal search is the only direct evidence of intent, and the defendant will be relegated simply to arguing that the officers should not be believed. Under these circumstances, the litigation risk described by the Court seems hardly a risk at all; it does not significantly dampen the incentive to conduct the initial illegal search.

* * *

[The dissenting opinion of Justice Stevens is omitted.]

QUESTIONS ABOUT MURRAY

The majority in *Murray* expresses concern about a "confirmatory" search, and states that the subsequent search will be invalidated if the officer's testimony denying a confirmatory motivation is "implausible." The officer denying a confirmatory motivation must explain why he or she made the original search without a warrant, and after *Murray* this explanation must rise only to the level of plausibility. In *Murray,* the explanation found plausible was that the officers thought they had exigent circumstances, even though in fact they did not. (If they did have exigent circumstances, *Murray* would not be an exclusionary rule case, because the original search would have been legal). Recall the discussion of exigent circumstances earlier in the Chapter. Under what facts could the officers be *so wrong* about exigent circumstances that their explanation on that point would not even be plausible? Could that *ever* happen in a narcotics case?

Has the Court in *Murray* established a good faith exception for warrantless searches that are later sanitized by a warrant? As in *Leon,* discussed *infra,* the search, though illegal, does not result in exclusion so long as the officers are not totally unreasonable in believing that they were acting legally. For criticism of *Murray* on these points, see Bradley, Murray v. United States: The Bell Tolls for the Search Warrant Requirement, 64 Ind.L.J. 907 (1989). See also United States v. Johnson, 994 F.2d 980 (2d Cir.1993) (independent source doctrine applies where officers made an initial search under the mistaken impression that it was incident to an arrest; while mistaken, the officers were not totally unreasonable).

Is the primary purpose of the exclusionary rule to deter police misconduct or to restore the situation to what it was before the illegal search? If the primary purpose is deterrence, might it sometimes be necessary to place the government in a worse position than if the illegal search had not occurred?

6. Inevitable Discovery

The inevitable discovery exception has been termed the "hypothetical independent source" exception. See Forbes, The Inevitable Discovery Exception, Primary Evidence, and the Emasculation of the Fourth Amendment, 55 Fordham L.Rev. 1221 (1987). For the exception to apply, the government must show that the illegally obtained evidence *would have been* discovered through legitimate means independent of the official misconduct. Note that if the evidence is *actually* discovered through legitimate independent means, the independent source exception would apply. So the inevitable discovery exception is one step removed from the independent source exception.

Establishing the Exception: Nix v. Williams

The Supreme Court approved the inevitable discovery limitation upon the exclusionary rule for the first time in Nix v. Williams, 467 U.S. 431 (1984), which is discussed in *Murray*. Seven years earlier, the Court had held that Williams's conviction for murdering a 10-year-old girl was tainted when a police officer managed to obtain statements from Williams in violation of his Sixth Amendment right to counsel. Those statements led police to his victim's body. Although the Court held that the statements must be suppressed, it left open the question whether the body might be admissible in a new trial.

At Williams's second trial, the trial court found that the government proved by a preponderance of the evidence that a search party, which had suspended its activities once Williams agreed to lead the police to the body, would have found the body hours later and that the body would have been found in essentially the same condition as when Williams led the police to it. Thus, the judge admitted evidence concerning the body, its location, and its condition on the ground that it inevitably would have been discovered through legal means. A federal court on habeas review found that the inevitable discovery rule could not be invoked where a police officer acted in bad faith, as it found the officer had in securing Williams's statements.

Chief Justice Burger wrote for a majority as it reversed the federal court. He treated the independent source and inevitable discovery doctrines as related, reasoning that both doctrines limit the exclusionary rule so that the government is not denied evidence it would have had even without the officers' illegal activity. The Court indicated that the exclusionary rule works to assure that police do not benefit from constitutional violations, and that the inevitable discovery exception simply recognizes that the government actually obtains no advantage from illegal conduct *if* the government can prove that it would have obtained the evidence legally anyway.

The Court declined to restrict the inevitable discovery limitation to situations in which an officer acts in good faith. It found that a "good faith" requirement is not needed to deter officers from violating constitutional rules because officers seeking to gather evidence cannot know in advance whether the government will be able to prove that their evidence would have been discovered inevitably through legal means. The Chief Justice reasoned that excluding evidence that inevitably would have been discovered legally because officers acted in bad faith "would put the police in a *worse* position than they would have been if no unlawful conduct had transpired" and that the exclusionary rule therefore did not apply.

The Court in *Nix* held that to invoke the inevitable discovery exception, the government must prove by a *preponderance* that the challenged evidence would have been discovered through independent legal means. Chief Justice Burger rejected the more stringent clear and convincing evidence standard, stating that "we are unwilling to impose added burdens on the already difficult task of proving guilt in criminal cases by enlarging the barrier to placing evidence of unquestioned truth before juries." The Court agreed with the trial court that the government had met its burden.

Justice Stevens concurred in the judgment. He expressed concern, however, that the majority emphasized the "societal costs" of the exclusionary rule without also emphasizing the "societal costs" of unconstitutional police conduct.

Justice Brennan, joined by Justice Marshall, dissented in *Nix*. Justice Brennan accepted the doctrine but argued that the government should have to prove inevitability by clear and convincing evidence.

Although *Williams* was a case involving a Sixth Amendment violation, the Court discussed the exclusionary rules it has adopted to enforce Fourth, Fifth and Sixth Amendment standards. Both before and after *Nix,* lower courts have applied the inevitable discovery exception to Fourth Amendment violations. See, e.g., United States v. Jackson, 901 F.2d 83 (7th Cir.1990) (even if defendant did not give voluntary consent to a search of his person, officers would have inevitably conducted a *Terry* frisk and uncovered crack cocaine in defendant's pockets); United States v. Kennedy, 61 F.3d 494 (6th Cir.1995) (evidence discovered by airport police in an illegal search of lost luggage was properly admitted, because if the police had not searched the suitcase, they would have returned it to the airline, and the airline's policy was to open lost luggage to determine the identity of the owner).

Inevitable Discovery Through a Hypothetical Inventory Search

An oft-repeated example of inevitable discovery is presented in United States v. Andrade, 784 F.2d 1431 (9th Cir.1986), where officers searched Andrade's bag and found cocaine after he was arrested for a drug violation. The search did not occur until an hour after the arrest. The court held that even if the search could not be justified as incident to arrest and was thus unlawful, "the cocaine was admissible because it would have been inevitably discovered through a routine inventory search." The court noted that it was normal DEA procedure to inventory the contents of bags held by arrestees, and that such a procedure was valid under Illinois v. Lafayette, *supra*. Judge Reinhardt, concurring, agreed that the "confluence" of *Nix* and *Lafayette* required this result, but concluded that "the result we are required to reach will serve only to encourage illegal and unconstitutional searches." See also United States v. Babilonia, 854 F.3d 163 (2d Cir. 2017) ("where a search incident to arrest is not justified, evidence recovered * * * may be admissible nevertheless if the contents would inevitably have been discovered in a permissible inventory search").

If *Andrade* is correct that the existence of routine inventory procedures allows admission of the evidence obtained from the illegal search of a car or container, then why would an officer ever have to comply with the rules that still limit searches of cars or containers? For example, probable cause is required to search the trunk of a car of an arrestee. But does the probable cause requirement mean anything if the inevitable discovery exception applies by way of the (hypothetical) inventory search of anything found in the trunk? Is there any reason for an officer even to follow the standardized inventory procedures themselves, given the fact that standards are in place to permit an argument that such an inventory would have been conducted? See United States v. Martin, 982 F.2d 1236 (8th Cir.1993) (improper inventory excused because a proper one would have been conducted under police guidelines).

In United States v. $639,558.00 in United States Currency, 955 F.2d 712 (D.C.Cir.1992), the court refused to apply the inevitable discovery rule to situations in which the hypothetical independent source was an inventory search. The court reasoned as follows:

> If the evidence stemming from the violation is nevertheless admissible on the basis that the bags inevitably would have been opened when they were inventoried, the practical consequence is apparent. In the vast run of cases, there would be no incentive whatever for police to go to the trouble of seeking a warrant (or, we should add, of waiting for a lawful inventory to occur during normal processing).

Note that even if a court follows the "inevitable discovery through a hypothetical inventory" analysis, the government will have to prove that the search conducted would have been permissible under the inventory standards. Thus, if the officer searches the door panels of a car, the inevitable discovery exception will not work because a search of door panels cannot be justified under the inventory rules. See the discussion in United States v. Martinez, 512 F.3d 1268 (10th Cir. 2008) (noting cases excluding evidence found in door panels because "searching behind the door panel of a vehicle does not qualify as standard police inventory procedure").

"We Would Have Obtained a Warrant"

Under the inevitable discovery exception, what is to stop the government from making the following argument:

> "We realize that we conducted an illegal warrantless search. Sorry. However, we had probable cause, and we would have obtained a warrant on that basis. Because we had probable cause, the warrant inevitably would have issued, and we would have searched pursuant to the warrant (if we had bothered to obtain it). So all the evidence we obtained is admissible under the inevitable discovery exception."

Do *Nix* and *Murray* require that such an argument must be accepted? If so, is there anything left of the warrant requirement?

Most courts have rejected government arguments that the inevitable discovery exception is met on the simple assertion that the officers had probable cause and would have obtained a warrant. Judge Easterbrook rejected that argument in United States v. Brown, 64 F.3d 1083 (7th Cir.1995), stating that "what makes a discovery 'inevitable' is not probable cause alone, * * * but probable cause plus a chain of events that would have led to a warrant." He reasoned that if inevitability would be found whenever there was probable cause, "the requirement of a warrant for a residential entry will never be enforced by the exclusionary rule." See also United States v. Johnson, 22 F.3d 674 (6th Cir.1994) ("to hold that simply because the police could have obtained a warrant, it was therefore inevitable that they would have done so would mean that there is inevitable discovery and no warrant requirement whenever there is probable cause"); United States v. Echegoyen, 799 F.2d 1271 (9th Cir.1986) ("to excuse the failure to obtain a warrant merely because the officers had probable cause and could have inevitably obtained a warrant would completely obviate the warrant requirement of the fourth amendment").

Some decisions can be found, however that rely on *Nix* to hold that evidence found in an illegal warrantless search was admissible because a warrant could and would have been obtained. See, e.g., United States v. Goins, 437 F.3d 644 (7th Cir.2006) (excusing an illegal search because police inevitably would have sought a search warrant and a magistrate would have issued one).

Establishing Inevitability

Nix holds that the government must prove by a preponderance that the illegally obtained evidence inevitably would have been discovered by legal means. In United States v. Feldhacker, 849 F.2d 293 (8th Cir.1988), the court cautioned that in deciding whether the inevitable discovery exception applies, courts must focus on what the officers actually *would have done*, not on what they *could possibly have done*.

> There are reasonable limits to the scope that courts will impute to the hypothetical untainted investigation. An investigation conducted over an infinite time with infinite thoroughness will, of course, ultimately or inevitably turn up any and all pieces of evidence in the world. Prosecutors may not justify unlawful extractions of information post hoc where lawful methods present only a theoretical possibility of discovery. While the hypothetical discovery by lawful means need not be reached as rapidly as that actually reached by unlawful means, the lawful discovery must be inevitable through means that would actually have been employed.

Similar concerns arose in United States v. Allen, 159 F.3d 832 (4th Cir.1998). The government sought to avoid exclusion after Officer Tackett illegally searched a bag in a bus sweep. The government argued, and Officer Tackett testified, that if she hadn't opened the bag and discovered drugs, she would have called the K-9 unit and had a dog sniff the bag. The government presented testimony that a dog unit was at the bus terminal that day, and that the dog would have had no problem alerting to the drugs in Allen's bag. Officer Tackett testified that if the dog alerted, she would have sought a search warrant to search the bag. But the court found this scenario speculative.

> Our initial problem * * * lies in the lack of evidentiary support for the conclusion that Tackett would have used the dog. We have no doubt that Tackett *could* have used the dog, but whether she *would* have presents an entirely different question. Tackett testified specifically that if she had not conducted the illegal search and if she had thought the bag "could have been Allen's," she would have used the drug dog to sniff the bag. However, when Detective Kennedy (the dog's handler) testified, he did not so much as suggest that his dog had ever been used to sniff bags located inside the passenger compartment of a bus. Instead, he stated that his usual duty involved sending his dog into the undercarriage of the bus, as he had done that day. Furthermore, nothing in the record indicates that Tackett had ever previously called for a police dog to sniff baggage inside a bus, and Tackett conceded as much. * * *
>
> A finding of inevitable discovery necessarily rests on facts that did not occur. However, by definition the occurrence of these facts must

have been likely, indeed "inevitable," absent the government's misconduct. On the record here, * * * we cannot possibly conclude that the government inevitably would have discovered the cocaine by employing a drug dog to establish probable cause.

7. Use of Illegally Seized Evidence Outside the Criminal Trial Context

Where it applies, the exclusionary rule operates to exclude evidence at a criminal trial. But in a series of cases, the Court has held that the exclusionary rule generally does not apply outside the context of a criminal trial on the merits. This is because, according to the Court, exclusion from the criminal prosecution's case-in-chief is all that is necessary to deter Fourth Amendment violations. The cost of exclusion in other "collateral" contexts generally has been held to outweigh the benefits in deterrence that the rule provides.

Grand Jury Proceedings

In United States v. Calandra, 414 U.S. 338 (1974), the Supreme Court held that the exclusionary rule does not apply in grand jury proceedings. The Court concluded that the marginal deterrent effect of suppressing illegally seized evidence in the grand jury is outweighed by the disruption of the grand jury's investigative process. The Court declared that sufficient deterrence flowed from exclusion of the illegally obtained evidence at trial. Justice Brennan, joined by Justices Douglas and Marshall, dissented citing concerns about judicial integrity.

The fact that indictments can be based on illegally seized evidence is another arrow in the government's quiver. It means that the government will get some benefits from an illegal search. On the other hand, there is something to the *Calandra* Court's assertion that it will ordinarily be impractical to use tainted evidence to obtain an indictment. Because that evidence would not be admissible at trial, it seems that the chances of obtaining a conviction would be remote. See United States v. Puglia, 8 F.3d 478 (7th Cir.1993) ("Prosecutors will not waste their time seeking indictments of individuals against whom they do not have enough evidence to convict.").

Yet prosecutors have sometimes been quoted as saying that it is important to indict someone even if they are not convicted—that is, the indictment can be used as punishment in the public eye, and as a means of imposing inconvenience and distress on a suspected criminal. The threat of indictment, or an actual indictment, may also change the dynamics in plea negotiations, including efforts to secure a defendant's cooperation. If prosecutors can use an indictment as an end in itself, did the Court get it right in *Calandra* when it reasoned that sufficient deterrence flows from excluding illegally obtained evidence at trial?

Civil Tax Proceedings

The Court has held that evidence illegally seized by state police can be used by federal tax officials in civil tax litigation. United States v. Janis, 428 U.S. 433 (1976). The Court in *Janis* found the deterrent effect of the exclusionary rule "attenuated when the punishment imposed upon the offending criminal enforcement officer is the removal of that evidence from a civil suit by or against a different sovereign." This attenuation, coupled with the "existing deterrence" effected by exclusion of the evidence from both state and federal criminal trials, tilted the cost-benefit analysis in favor of admitting the evidence.

Civil Deportation Proceedings

In Immigration and Naturalization Service v. Lopez-Mendoza, 468 U.S. 1032 (1984), the Court held that illegally obtained statements can be used in deportation proceedings. Justice O'Connor reasoned as follows:

- no matter how an arrest is made, deportation will still be possible when evidence derived independently of the arrest is available, and evidence of alienage alone might be sufficient to warrant deportation—thus, the use of illegally obtained evidence will ordinarily be harmless;
- as a practical matter, it is highly unlikely that deportees will raise exclusionary rule claims and therefore it is equally unlikely that the rule would deter INS agents;
- the INS has its own scheme for deterring Fourth Amendment violations by its agents;
- declaratory relief is available to restrain institutional practices by the INS that violate the Fourth Amendment;
- deportation currently requires only a simple hearing, and it would be inappropriate to add complex issues of exclusion to these hearings;
- INS agents handle so many cases that they might have difficulty accounting for exactly how they handled each suspected alien; and
- exclusion could mean that a person who is committing a criminal offense *at the time of the proceeding* would be allowed to go free, "requir[ing] the courts to close their eyes to ongoing violations of the law."

Justice White dissented. He reasoned that INS agents seek to gather evidence specifically for use in deportation proceedings, that their activities are closely analogous to those of police officers who seek to obtain evidence for criminal trials, so the deterrent effect of the exclusionary rule would be the similar in both contexts. Justices Brennan, Marshall and Stevens each filed a short dissenting opinion.

Some courts have found that the exclusionary rule can apply to deportation proceedings under dicta in Justice O'Connor's opinion indicating that exclusion "might" be justified for "egregious violations of Fourth Amendment or other liberties that might transgress notions of fundamental fairness and undermine the probative value of the evidence obtained." For a case involving egregious circumstances, see Cotzojay v. Holder, 725 F.3d 172 (2d Cir. 2013)(forced entry into a home, made in pre-dawn hours in order to coerce consent by startling sleeping residents). By contrast, other courts have extended the reasoning in *Lopez-Mendoza* to allow into evidence at criminal trials evidence seized illegally by INS agents engaged in civil immigration enforcement. See United States v. Oscar-Torres, 507 F.3d 224 (4th Cir.2007) ("If illegally obtained evidence that law enforcement officers intend to use in civil deportation hearings cannot be suppressed because exclusion will not effectively deter unlawful arrests, as *Lopez-Mendoza* holds, then suppressing that evidence in an unanticipated and unforeseen criminal prosecution surely cannot provide any additional ex ante deterrence.").

Habeas Corpus Proceedings

In Stone v. Powell, 428 U.S. 465 (1976), the Court held that the exclusionary rule could not be invoked in habeas corpus proceedings. The Court stated that, in the context of habeas proceedings, "the contribution of the exclusionary rule, if any, to the effectuation of the Fourth Amendment is minimal and the substantial societal costs of application of the rule persist with special force." The deterrent effect of exclusion was considered low because habeas proceedings are collateral to criminal trials and therefore not something officers would think about in deciding whether to conduct an illegal search. And the costs of exclusion are especially high because reversing a state conviction on habeas review implicates serious federalism and finality interests.

Parole Revocation Proceedings

In Pennsylvania Board of Probation and Parole v. Scott, 524 U.S. 357 (1998), Scott's parole was revoked and he was returned to prison to serve the remainder of his sentence, on the basis of evidence uncovered during an illegal search. The Court upheld the revocation, concluding that the exclusionary rule was not applicable in parole revocation proceedings.

Writing for the Court, Justice Thomas found that the cost of applying the exclusionary rule in parole revocation proceedings outweighed the benefits in deterrence of official misconduct. He reasoned as follows:

> The costs of excluding reliable, probative evidence are particularly high in the context of parole revocation proceedings. * * * In most cases, the State is willing to extend parole only because it is able to condition it upon compliance with certain requirements. * * * The exclusion of evidence establishing a parole violation, however, hampers the State's ability to ensure compliance with these conditions by permitting the parolee to avoid the consequences of his noncompliance. * * *
>
> The exclusionary rule, moreover, is incompatible with the traditionally flexible, administrative procedures of parole revocation. * * * Most States * * * have adopted informal, administrative parole revocation procedures in order to accommodate the large number of parole proceedings. These proceedings generally are not conducted by judges, but instead by parole boards, members of which need not be judicial officers or lawyers. * * * Nor are these proceedings entirely adversarial, as they are designed to be predictive and discretionary as well as factfinding.
>
> Application of the exclusionary rule would significantly alter this process. The exclusionary rule frequently requires extensive litigation to determine whether particular evidence must be excluded. Such litigation is inconsistent with the nonadversarial, administrative processes established by the States. Although States could adapt their parole revocation proceedings to accommodate such litigation, such a change would transform those proceedings from a predictive and discretionary effort to promote the best interests of both parolees and society into trial-like proceedings less attuned to the interests of the parolee. We are simply unwilling so to intrude into the States' correctional schemes. Such a transformation ultimately might disadvantage parolees because in an adversarial proceeding, the hearing body may be less tolerant of marginal deviant behavior and feel more pressure to reincarcerate than to continue nonpunitive rehabilitation. And the financial costs of such a system could reduce the State's incentive to extend parole in the first place, as one of the purposes of parole is to reduce the costs of criminal punishment while maintaining a degree of supervision over the parolee.

On the other side of the scale, the Court saw little deterrence value to the exclusionary rule in the context of parole revocation proceedings:

> [A]pplication of the exclusionary rule to parole revocation proceedings would have little deterrent effect upon an officer who is unaware that the subject of his search is a parolee. * * * The likelihood that illegally

obtained evidence will be excluded from trial provides deterrence against Fourth Amendment violations, and the remote possibility that the subject is a parolee and that the evidence may be admitted at a parole revocation proceeding surely has little, if any, effect on the officer's incentives.

The Court further rejected the lower court's position that the exclusionary rule should at least be applicable when the government official conducts an illegal search *for the specific purpose* of using illegally obtained evidence in the parole revocation proceeding:

> We have never suggested that the exclusionary rule must apply in every circumstance in which it might provide marginal deterrence. Furthermore, such a piecemeal approach to the exclusionary rule would add an additional layer of collateral litigation regarding the officer's knowledge of the parolee's status.

Justice Stevens wrote a short dissenting opinion in *Scott* emphasizing his continuing position that the Constitution requires exclusion of illegally obtained evidence. Justice Souter, in a dissenting opinion joined by Justices Ginsburg and Breyer, took issue with the majority's assessment of the costs and benefits of the exclusionary rule in the parole revocation context. He argued that the costs of applying the exclusionary rule in parole revocation proceedings are certainly no greater than the costs of applying the rule in a criminal trial. As to the benefits of applying the rule, Justice Souter noted that the parole revocation proceeding often takes the place of a criminal trial. He reasoned as follows:

> [P]arole revocation will frequently be pursued instead of prosecution as the course of choice * * *. The reasons for this tendency to skip any new prosecution are obvious. If the conduct in question is a crime in its own right, the odds of revocation are very high. Since time on the street before revocation is not subtracted from the balance of the sentence to be served on revocation, the balance may well be long enough to render recommitment the practical equivalent of a new sentence for a separate crime. And all of this may be accomplished without shouldering the burden of proof beyond a reasonable doubt; hence the obvious popularity of revocation in place of new prosecution.
>
> The upshot is that without a suppression remedy in revocation proceedings, there will often be no influence capable of deterring Fourth Amendment violations when parole revocation is a possible response to new crime.

Sentencing Proceedings

The Supreme Court has not considered whether illegally obtained evidence can be used in sentencing proceedings. But lower courts have found the exclusionary rule inapplicable to sentencing hearings. United States v. Tejada, 956 F.2d 1256 (2d Cir.1992), is an example of the predominant approach. The *Tejada* court analyzed the costs and benefits of exclusion of illegally obtained evidence at sentencing as follows:

> [The defendants] posit that police and prosecutors with enough lawfully obtained evidence for a conviction of a relatively minor offense that has a broad sentencing range could guarantee a heavier sentence by seizing other evidence illegally and introducing it at sentencing. * * *
>
> Defendants * * * do not explain why this supposed incentive to violate the Fourth Amendment will prove incrementally stronger than the rewards that already exist. Illegally seized evidence long has played a role in our legal system, and many of its uses might motivate a police officer to violate the Fourth Amendment. [Citing *Lopez-Mendoza*, *Janis*, and *Calandra*]. The Supreme Court has held that these uses for illegally seized evidence do not diminish deterrence sufficiently to justify the exclusion of probative evidence. We see no reason why this additional use of illegally seized evidence justifies different treatment.

The *Tejada* court asserted that "[g]reat rewards still exist for following accepted police procedures." If evidence cannot be used at trial, the government may never get to the sentencing proceeding due to the weakness of its case. Against the perceived minimal deterrent effect of exclusion at the sentencing hearing, the court weighed the need for sentencing courts to have "as much information as possible at sentencing."

> We conclude that the benefits of providing sentencing judges with reliable information about the defendant outweigh the likelihood that allowing consideration of illegally seized evidence will encourage unlawful police conduct. Absent a showing that officers obtained evidence expressly to enhance a sentence, a district judge may not refuse to consider relevant evidence at sentencing, even if that evidence has been seized in violation of the Fourth Amendment.

Note that the *Tejada* court provided a possible exception for cases in which officials obtain evidence expressly to enhance a sentence. Presumably those are cases in which application of the exclusionary rule would have some deterrent effect. But *Tejad*a was written before the Supreme Court's decision in *Scott, supra,* in which the Court held that the exclusionary rule does not apply to parole revocation proceedings, even if it is clear that the officer conducted an illegal search for the specific purpose of using the evidence at the parole revocation proceeding. Presumably the rationale of *Scott* applies to the sentencing context as well, meaning that illegally obtained evidence can be considered even if it was obtained solely for purposes of using it at the sentencing proceeding.

The collection of these collateral use exceptions to the exclusionary rule has been criticized for rehabilitating the silver platter doctrine rejected by the Court in Elkins v. United States, 364 U.S. 206 (1960). See Gray, Cooper, & McAloon, The Supreme Court's Contemporary Silver Platter Doctrine, 91 Texas L.Rev. 7 (2012).

8. Use of Illegally Obtained Evidence for Impeachment Purposes

Opening the Door on Direct Examination: Walder v. United States

In Walder v. United States, 347 U.S. 62 (1954), Walder testified on direct examination in a trial on narcotics charges that he had never possessed or sold narcotics in his life. The Supreme Court held that he was properly impeached with evidence of heroin that had been illegally seized from his home in an earlier, unrelated case. The Court reasoned that Walder had "opened the door" to this evidence and that the exclusionary rule could not be used as a license for perjury.

Opening the Door on Cross-Examination: United States v. Havens

United States v. Havens, 446 U.S. 620 (1980), extended the impeachment exception from *Walder*. Officers stopped McLeroth and Havens coming off a flight. They illegally searched Havens's suitcase and found a shirt from which the pocket had been torn out. McLeroth was also searched, and officers found a pocket, matching the shirt found in Havens's bag, sewn into McLeroth's clothing. The officers found cocaine in the pocket. At his trial, Havens took the stand and denied being involved with McLeroth in the transportation of cocaine; he did not mention anything about the shirt or the pocket. On cross-examination, Havens was asked specifically whether he had been involved in sewing a pocket into McLeroth's clothing, and whether he had a shirt in his own suitcase from which that pocket had been torn out. Havens answered in the negative, and this testimony was impeached by introduction of the illegally seized shirt. The court of appeals held that the evidence was improperly admitted. It reasoned that *Walder* permitted impeachment only if the defendant opened the door—and Havens had not done so in this case because he hadn't mentioned the shirt on direct.

But in a 5–4 decision written by Justice White, the Supreme Court held that illegally obtained evidence can be used to impeach the defendant's testimony no matter when that testimony is elicited. Justice White argued that there was no difference of constitutional magnitude between impeachment of direct testimony and impeachment of testimony elicited on cross-examination so long as the questions put to the defendant on cross-examination "are plainly within the scope" of the direct. Justice White concluded as follows:

> [The incremental deterrence that occurs] by forbidding impeachment of the defendant who testifies was deemed [in *Walder*] insufficient to permit or require that false testimony go unchallenged, with the resulting impairment of the integrity of the fact-finding goals of the criminal trial.

Justice Brennan, joined by Justices Stewart, Marshall and Stevens, dissented. He complained that the majority had passed control of the impeachment exception to the government, "since the prosecutor can lay the predicate for admitting otherwise suppressible evidence with his own questioning." He argued that, after *Havens,* a defendant who has been the victim of an illegal search will have to forgo testifying on his own behalf because it is impossible for the defendant to testify to anything on direct that would not open him up to impeachment through illegally obtained evidence on cross-examination.

Impeachment of Defense Witnesses: James v. Illinois

In James v. Illinois, 493 U.S. 307 (1990), the Court refused to extend the impeachment exception to allow impeachment of defense *witnesses* (as opposed to the defendant) with illegally obtained evidence. James made a statement to police officers that he had changed his hair color and style the day after taking part in a shooting. The trial court suppressed this statement because it was the fruit of an arrest made without probable cause. Prosecution witnesses at trial identified James, though they conceded that his hair color at trial was different from that of the perpetrator at the time of the shooting. To rebut the identification testimony, James called a family friend, who testified that, just before the shooting, James's hair color and style was the same as it was at trial. The trial court, relying on the impeachment exception to the exclusionary rule, allowed the prosecution to introduce James's suppressed statement to impeach the witness—a mode of impeachment known as "contradiction."

The Supreme Court, in an opinion by Justice Brennan, held that the exclusionary rule barred impeachment of a defense witness with illegally obtained evidence. He acknowledged that, as applied to the defendant, the impeachment exception serves salutary purposes because it "penalizes defendants for committing perjury," and yet "leaves defendants free to testify truthfully on their own behalf." In contrast, Justice Brennan argued that the fear of impeachment of one's witnesses likely would discourage defendants from even presenting the testimony of others. He posited that the defendant could carefully limit his own truthful testimony to avoid reference to matters that could be impeached by illegally obtained evidence but the defendant's witnesses could not be so easily controlled. Justice Brennan also argued that impeachment was not needed to deter defense witnesses from offering perjurious testimony. Unlike the defendant, defense witnesses are sufficiently deterred by the threat of a perjury prosecution.

Justice Brennan concluded that the exclusionary rule would be robbed of significant deterrent effect if illegally obtained evidence could be used to impeach not only the defendant but the defendant's witnesses. He argued that illegally obtained evidence would have greater value to the government because it could be used to prevent defendants from calling witnesses to give truthful testimony. Justice Brennan asserted that a rule allowing impeachment of defense witnesses "would leave officers with little to lose and much to gain by overstepping constitutional limits on evidence gathering."

Justice Kennedy, joined by Chief Justice Rehnquist and Justices O'Connor and Scalia, dissented. The dissenters complained that the majority had granted the defendant "broad immunity to introduce whatever false testimony it can produce from the mouth of a friendly witness." Justice Kennedy argued that impeachment is even more vital for attacking untruthful testimony of a defense witness than it is for attacking the defendant's testimony:

> It is natural for jurors to be skeptical of self-serving testimony by the defendant. Testimony by a witness said to be independent has the greater potential to deceive. And if a defense witness can present false testimony with impunity, the jurors may find the rest of the prosecution's case suspect, for ineffective and artificial cross-examination will be viewed as a real weakness in the State's case. * * * The State must * * * suffer the introduction of false testimony and appear to bolster the falsehood by its own silence.

The majority in *James* based its decision on the assumption that the defendant can restrict his testimony to avoid impeachment, while the defendant's witnesses cannot be so controlled. After *Havens*—which allowed impeachment on cross-examination even though the direct testimony was carefully tailored to avoid any reference to the shirt—is it ever possible for the defendant to avoid impeachment with illegally obtained evidence? If not, isn't the majority's decision in *James* based on a faulty premise? Is Justice Brennan simply making the best of what he thinks is bad law?

F. PROCEDURAL ASPECTS OF THE EXCLUSIONARY RULE

1. Attacking the Warrant

If the search was pursuant to a warrant, the judge ruling on a motion to suppress will consider the sworn evidence presented to the magistrate who issued the warrant. The Fourth Amendment determination will be made on the basis of only this evidence. No after-acquired evidence can be considered because the issue is whether the magistrate properly issued the warrant on the basis of the information available to her. See generally Kaiser v. Lief, 874 F.2d 732 (10th Cir.1989) (magistrate may rely on affidavit, complaint, and other affidavits contemporaneously presented for other warrants).

Challenging the Truthfulness of the Warrant Application: Franks v. Delaware

In Franks v. Delaware, 438 U.S. 154 (1978), the Court held that a defendant has a limited right to attack the truthfulness of statements made in warrant applications. The Court emphasized that it is difficult for a defendant to mount a successful challenge because, in order to obtain a hearing, the defendant must make a case that the officers preparing the application engaged in deliberate falsification or reckless disregard for the truth that materially affected the showing of probable cause. The Court stated that "[t]he deliberate falsity or reckless disregard whose impeachment is permitted today is only that of the affiant, not of any nongovernmental informant." It also noted that a hearing will not be granted "if, when the material that is the subject of the alleged falsity or reckless disregard is set to one side, there remains sufficient content in the warrant affidavit to support a finding of probable cause." On the other hand, if the remaining content is insufficient, the defendant is entitled, under the Fourth Amendment, to his hearing. But "[w]hether he will prevail at that hearing is, of course, another issue."

Justice Rehnquist, joined by Chief Justice Burger, dissented in *Franks*, arguing that even if "some inaccurate or falsified information may have gone into the making of the determination" to issue a warrant, "I simply do not think the game is worth the candle in this situation." When you recall that the warrant application is made ex parte and the magistrate makes nothing like a credibility determination, what would become of the warrant requirement if Justice Rehnquist's view had prevailed?

United States v. Johns, 851 F.2d 1131 (9th Cir.1988), provides an example of a showing sufficient to warrant a *Franks* hearing. In *Johns*, probable cause was based in material part on the officer's averment that he had detected the odor of methamphetamine emanating from the defendant's premises. The defendant submitted affidavits from two experts stating that, in light of the way the methamphetamine was stored, it would have been impossible for the officer outside the premises to smell it. *Johns* was distinguished in United States v. Mueller, 902 F.2d 336 (5th Cir.1990), where the officer averred that he could smell methamphetamine emanating from the defendant's house while standing across the street. The defendant submitted an expert affidavit to the effect that it would have been unlikely to pick up such a smell given the officer's distance from the house and the prevailing winds. The court denied a *Franks* hearing, noting that Mueller's expert merely concluded that the officer's story was "unlikely," while the experts in *Johns* concluded that the officer's story was "impossible."

Materiality Requirement

To obtain relief under *Franks,* the defendant must show that the deliberate falsehood or reckless disregard for the truth had a material effect on the issuance of the warrant. An officer's misstatement is not material under *Franks* if probable cause would exist even without the misstatement. See United States v. Campbell, 878 F.2d 170 (6th Cir.1989), citing cases in every circuit applying this test. In *Campbell,* the court found the search warrant valid even though the affidavit included a statement attributed to an informant known by the affiant to be fictitious. The court held that untainted information in the affidavit from three reliable informants was sufficient to establish probable cause. Essentially, the officer's fabrication constituted harmless error.

2. Challenging a Warrantless Search

If no warrant was obtained, the government must prove by a preponderance of the evidence that an exception to the warrant requirement was satisfied. See United States v. Matlock, 415 U.S. 164 (1974) (government must prove voluntary consent by a preponderance of the evidence). This allocation of the burden of proof reflects the Court's preference for warrants. See generally Saltzburg, Standards of Proof and Preliminary Questions of Fact, 27 Stan.L.Rev. 271 (1975).

3. The Suppression Hearing and Judicial Review

At the hearing on the motion to suppress evidence, the government will have a privilege to protect the identity of informants. See McCray v. Illinois, 386 U.S. 300 (1967) (holding that it is constitutional to withhold informant's identity on issue of probable cause). But the judge may, in her discretion, require the prosecution, *in camera,* to disclose the identity of the informant or produce the informant for questioning.

In a suppression hearing, the ordinary rules of evidence are not applicable, with the exception of rules of privilege. See Federal Rule of Evidence 1101. A judge can, for example, rely on hearsay to determine the legality of a search or seizure "and give it such weight as his judgment and experience counsel." United States v. Matlock, 415 U.S. 164 (1974).

Limitations on Use of Suppression Hearing Testimony at Trial: Simmons v. United States

At the suppression hearing, the defendant may testify in support of his claim of a Fourth Amendment violation. Simmons v. United States, 390 U.S. 377 (1968), holds that when a defendant testifies on the question of "standing" (a subject discussed infra) at a suppression hearing, the government may not use his testimony against him on the question of guilt or innocence. Justice Harlan's opinion for the majority reasoned that defendants would be unduly inhibited from making Fourth Amendment claims absent protection against automatic use of suppression hearing testimony at trial. In light of the way the opinion is written, it is likely that it extends to all Fourth Amendment questions, not just "standing."

Although *Simmons* did not reach the issue, lower courts have held that suppression hearing testimony may be used for impeachment purposes if a defendant chooses to testify at trial. See, e.g., United States v. Beltran-Gutierrez, 19 F.3d 1287 (9th Cir.1994). Thus, a defendant who testifies at the suppression hearing that he owned a briefcase full of drugs will run into difficulty if the evidence is not suppressed and he takes the stand at trial to testify that the briefcase was not his. For what it is worth, he will be entitled to an instruction that the prior statement is admissible only for impeachment and not to be used as substantive evidence of possession.

If the defendant calls a witness to testify at the suppression hearing (e.g., a friend who testifies that the briefcase was the defendant's), the government is not precluded by *Simmons* from using that testimony against the defendant. This is because *Simmons* was designed to protect defendants from sacrificing one constitutional right (the Fifth Amendment right against self-incrimination) for another (the Fourth Amendment right). When the defendant calls a witness at the suppression hearing, the defendant's Fifth Amendment rights are not implicated.

Appellate Review

If a motion to suppress is granted, federal law allows the government immediate appellate review of the ruling subject to certain conditions. 18 U.S.C. § 3731. Most states are in accord. The federal statute provides that three conditions must be satisfied before the government can appeal from a suppression order: 1. The government cannot appeal if the defendant has been put in jeopardy, within the meaning of the Double Jeopardy Clause;

2. An appeal must not be taken for the purpose of delay; and 3. The suppressed evidence must be substantial proof of a fact material to the proceedings. See United States v. Gantt, 179 F.3d 782 (9th Cir.1999), for an application of these factors.

Most jurisdictions deny the defendant the right to an immediate appeal. This includes the federal courts, where an appeal from the denial of a suppression motion must await a judgment of conviction. It must be kept in mind that prosecutors cannot appeal the merits of an adverse judgment; only defendants can. Thus, prosecutors have to get an immediate appeal or none at all. If the defendant is convicted, the denial of a suppression motion may be a subject of the appeal.

Fed.R.Crim.P. 11(a)(2) permits a defendant, with the approval of the court and the consent of the government, to enter a conditional plea of guilty, reserving the right to appeal a court's denial of a motion to suppress. A defendant who prevails on appeal "may then withdraw the plea."

CHAPTER 3

SELF-INCRIMINATION AND CONFESSIONS

■ ■ ■

I. THE PRIVILEGE AGAINST COMPELLED SELF-INCRIMINATION

A. THE POLICIES OF THE PRIVILEGE AGAINST COMPELLED SELF-INCRIMINATION

1. The Need to Examine Policies

The Fifth Amendment provides that no person "shall be compelled in any criminal case to be a witness against himself * * *." Judge Friendly pointed out the need for careful examination of the policies supporting this privilege in his oft-cited article, The Fifth Amendment Tomorrow: The Case For Constitutional Change, 37 U.Cin.L.Rev. 671, 679–81, 698 (1968):

> It is still true, as Bentham wrote 140 years ago, that the main obstacle to rational discussion of the privilege is the *assumption of the propriety of the rule,* as a proposition too plainly true to admit of dispute * * *.
>
> A good way to start dissipating the lyricism now generally accompanying any reference to the privilege is to note how exceptional it is in the general setting of jurisprudence and morality. While it carries the burden of impeding ascertainment of the truth that is common to all testimonial privileges, it has uncommon burdens as well. Most other privileges, for example, communications between husband and wife, attorney and client, doctor and patient, priest and penitent, promote and preserve relationships possessing social value. * * * In contrast, the fifth amendment privilege extends, by hypothesis, only to persons who have been breakers of the criminal law or believe they may be charged as such.
>
> Again, while the other privileges accord with notions of decent conduct generally accepted in life outside the court room, the privilege against self-incrimination defies them. No parent would teach such a doctrine to his children; the lesson parents preach is that while a misdeed, even a serious one, will generally be forgiven, a failure to make a clean breast of it will not be. Every hour of the day people are being asked to explain their conduct to parents, employers and

teachers. Those who are questioned consider themselves to be morally bound to respond, and the questioners believe it proper to take action if they do not.

* * * The privilege not only stands in the way of convictions but often prevents restitution to the victim—of goods, of money, even of a kidnapped child. In contrast to the rare case where it may protect an innocent person, it often may do the contrary. A man in suspicious circumstances but not in fact guilty is deprived of official interrogation of another whom he knows to be the true culprit * * *.

One would suppose that such a collection of detriments would have led the Supreme Court to expound the basis for the privilege thoughtfully and carefully before asking the country to accept extensions in no way called for by the fifth amendment's words or history. It thus is strange how rarely one encounters in the Court's opinions on the privilege the careful weighing of *pros* and *cons,* the objective investigation of how rules of law actually work, and, above all, the consideration whether a less extreme position might not adequately meet the needs of the accused without jeopardizing other important interests, which ought to characterize constitutional adjudication before the Court goes beyond the ordinary meaning of the language.

See also Tague, The Fifth Amendment: If an Aid to the Guilty Defendant, an Impediment to the Innocent One, 78 Geo.L.J. 1 (1989) (Fifth Amendment "can shackle the innocent defendant from attempting to prove that another person committed the crime").

2. A Chart to Assist Analysis

The chart below lists the most commonly offered justifications for the privilege against self-incrimination, critical responses to those justifications, and sources in which these arguments are discussed.[1] As you study the chart, consider which of the asserted policies are valid rationales for the privilege. Which responses adequately dispose of the policy

---

[1] Sources that are referred to several times are cited in shorthand form. The full citations follow:

Murphy v. Waterfront Comm., 378 U.S. 52 (1964).

Fortas, The Fifth Amendment: Nemo Tenetur Prodere Seipsum, 25 Clev.Bar Assn.J. 91 (1954).

Friendly, The Fifth Amendment Tomorrow: The Case for Constitutional Change, 37 U.Cin.L.Rev. 671 (1968).

McKay, Self-Incrimination and the New Privacy, 1967 Sup.Ct.Rev. 193.

L. Mayers, Shall We Amend the Fifth Amendment (1959).

8 J. Wigmore, Evidence in Trials at Common Law (McNaughten rev. 1961).

The usual rationales for the privilege against self-incrimination are found wanting in Dolinko, Is There a Rationale for the Privilege Against Self-Incrimination, 33 U.C.L.A.L.Rev. 1063 (1986).

arguments? Are there convincing responses to any of the criticisms? To all of them?

1. *Protection of the Innocent:* The privilege protects the innocent defendant from convicting himself by a bad performance on the witness stand. *Murphy,* 378 U.S. at 55; Mayers, at 61.	1. There is no proof that it protects the innocent. In fact, juries are unlikely to give a defendant the benefit of an innocent explanation of his silence in the face of evidence against him. Mayers, at 26, 61–67. It is admittedly possible that an innocent defendant will invoke the privilege to avoid impeachment with prior convictions. However, the problem of threatened impeachment does not require a constitutionally-based solution protecting all defendants. A better solution is to impose appropriate limitations on the use of prior convictions. See Montana Rule of Evidence 609 (prior convictions not admissible to attack credibility). Finally, the privilege historically—and by hypothesis—protects the guilty, i.e., those whose testimony would implicate them of a crime. Fortas, at 98–100.
2. *The Cruel Trilemma:* We are unwilling to subject those suspected of crime to the cruel trilemma of self-accusation, perjury, or contempt. Brown v. Walker, 161 U.S. 591, 637 (1896)(Field, J., dissenting).	2. This problem is not peculiar to self-incrimination: it exists whenever a witness is reluctant to testify for whatever reason. Any such witness is subject to the trilemma of testifying despite an interest in not doing so, perjury, or contempt. We do subject friends, lovers, parents, teachers, and most people to the discomfort of having to testify against individuals about whom they might care the most. Why is the incrimination interest protected and other interests not? Wigmore, § 2251, at 316. Also, the Supreme Court has ridiculed the "cruel trilemma" analysis. See Brogan v. United States, 522 U.S. 398 (1998) (dismissing the "cruel trilemma" as a "bon mot" and noting that "an innocent person will not find himself in a similar quandary" because the innocent person "lacks even a lemma").

3. *Deter Perjury:* If there were no privilege, people compelled to testify would commit perjury rather than incriminate themselves. Rampant perjury would burden the courts. Wigmore, § 2251, at 311.	3. Perjury is prevalent despite the existence of the privilege. Silence is also a burden on the truth-finding function of the criminal process. Friendly, at 680. There is no reason to believe that a defendant who concludes that perjury will succeed will not attempt it. Nor is there reason to believe that a defendant who concludes that perjury will fail will attempt it or succeed if an attempt is made.
4. *Unreliability of Coerced Statements:* We do not trust self-deprecatory statements, particularly when they are the product of coercion. *Murphy,* 378 U.S. at 55.	4. If reliability is the primary concern, there is no need to exclude compelled testimony that can be independently corroborated. Moreover, testimony at trial is likely to be cast by the defense in its most favorable light. It will not always be self-deprecatory. Also, it is more likely to be reliable than statements obtained by police interrogation, which are admitted as evidence.
5. *Preference for Accusatorial System:* We prefer an accusatorial rather than inquisitorial system of criminal justice. *Murphy,* 378 U.S. at 55.	5. "Language like this, no matter how often repeated, no matter how eloquently intoned, is merely restatement of the privilege itself." McKay, at 209.
6. *Deter Improper Police Practices:* Self-incriminating statements are likely to be elicited by inhumane treatment and abuses. The privilege has historically protected against such forms of torture. *Murphy,* 378 U.S. at 55.	6. Torture is unacceptable on its own merits, regardless of the existence of a privilege. Wigmore, § 2251, at 315. The privilege is unnecessary to guard against objectionable police practices—adequate protection is afforded by the Due Process clauses of the Fifth and Fourteenth Amendments. Testimony in court is subject to the safeguards of the judicial process.
7. *Fair State-Individual Balance:* "The privilege contributes towards a fair state-individual balance by requiring the government to leave the individual alone until good cause is shown for disturbing him and by	7. First, the probable cause requirements for search and arrest provide adequate protection against unwarranted governmental disturbance. Second, the argument relies on a notion of the criminal trial as "a jousting contest where the rules bear equally on

requiring the government in its contest with the individual to shoulder the entire load." Wigmore, § 2251, at 317.	both participants and neither is expected to be of the slightest help to the other"—a concept that bears no relation to reality. Third, even assuming that the ideal balance between state and defendant could be determined, manipulating the scope of the privilege is not necessarily the best way to achieve that balance. Friendly, at 693–94. Finally, the fact is that the government is not required to "shoulder the entire load" in a criminal prosecution. For example, the government can compel the defendant to produce DNA samples, voice prints, and physical evidence. Compelled production of this evidence is not covered by the Fifth Amendment. So what is it about testimony that makes it free from compulsion?
8. *Preservation of Official Morality:* "Any system * * * which permits the prosecution to trust habitually to compulsory self-disclosure as a source of proof must itself suffer morally thereby. 8 J. Wigmore, § 2251 (3d ed. 1940).	8. Wigmore's statement was based on two debatable assumptions: First, he believed the privilege applied only in the courtroom. When extended to the stationhouse, this rationale would disallow most police questioning—an untenable proposition. Second, he assumed that the privilege developed historically because the balance struck by the English judicial system had become morally unacceptable. Friendly, at 691.
9. *Privacy Rationale:* "Our respect for the inviolability of the human personality and of the right of each individual 'to a private enclave where he may lead a private life' " justifies the privilege. *Murphy,* 378 U.S. at 55.	9. If the basis for the privilege is a general freedom of silence to protect one's privacy, it is inconsistent first with immunity statutes—which require testimony no matter how private the matter; second, with rules requiring information of a far more private nature in civil suits (e.g., annulment suits); and third, with the Fourth Amendment, which clearly does protect privacy, but only to the extent that intrusions are unreasonable. This privacy rationale enjoys historical support only when

	crimes of belief or association are involved. It is immoral to suggest that a murderer in a typical criminal case is justified in withholding his aid because he "prefers to remain in a 'private enclave.' " Friendly, at 689–90.
10. *First Amendment Rationale:* The privilege affords "a shelter against governmental snooping and oppression concerning political and religious beliefs." Friendly, at 696.	10. The First Amendment is the appropriate vehicle for dealing with this problem, as the Court implicitly recognized in cases such as NAACP v. Alabama, 357 U.S. 449 (1958). Furthermore, this justification, even if valid, would apply only in free speech, religion, or association situations, not in the typical criminal investigation and prosecution. Wigmore, § 2251, at 314.

Consider how one's choice of rationale necessarily affects one's view of the legitimate scope of the Amendment. For example, if the privilege is primarily intended to prevent "the cruel trilemma" and to deter perjury, then it should be applicable only when testimony under oath is involved.[2] If one is concerned that the government bear its burden of proof without assistance, then voice or handwriting exemplars and other physical evidence extracted from a defendant would be protected. In the cases that follow, try to determine which policies underlie the Supreme Court's analysis of the privilege.

In light of the ascendency of textualism generally, and originalism specifically, you might also consider whether inquiring into potential policy justifications for the privilege is a game worth the candle. From a historical point of view, the Court has noted that the bêtes noires of the Fifth Amendment privilege against compelled witnessing were the Star Chamber in England and the Inquisitions conducted across Europe. *See* Pennsylvania v. Muniz, 496 U.S. 582, 594–96 (1990); Doe v. United States, 487 U.S. 201, 210–13 (1988). If this is right, then perhaps it is enough to read the text as prohibiting what it plainly prohibits in light of that history.

Judge Friendly criticizes the Fifth Amendment as protecting only the guilty. Professors Seidmann and Stein argue to the contrary in The Right to Silence Helps the Innocent: A Game-Theoretic Analysis of the Fifth Amendment Privilege, 114 Harv. L.Rev. 430 (2000). The professors assume that, under the current law, guilty defendants will rely on the Fifth Amendment and choose not to testify. Therefore, an innocent person who

[2] As we shall see, suspects may face a similarly cruel trilemma outside of a magisterial setting if faced with the prospect of confessing, obstructing justice, or accepting an adverse inference during a custodial interrogation.

actually *does* have an alibi will testify and be believed by the jury. If there were no Fifth Amendment, juries would have difficulty distinguishing between all of the false and true defendant-testimony. Query, though, whether juries are aware of the game theory going on and savvy enough to draw the assumption that the defendant has thought through the game and therefore must be innocent because he is testifying.

Professor Bibas, in The Right to Remain Silent Helps Only the Guilty, 88 Iowa L.Rev.421 (2003), disagrees with Seidmann and Stein. He states that their "elegant game-theoretic construct avails them little" because their premises do not mirror reality. Bibas, who later became a judge on the United States Court of Appeals for the Third Circuit, points out that most guilty defendants *do* confess in an attempt to cooperate with the government, and very few go to trial. He also notes that juries are instructed to consider a witness's stake in the outcome in deciding their credibility, and so there is no working assumption that only innocent defendants testify.

B. SCOPE OF THE PRIVILEGE

1. Proceedings in Which the Privilege Applies

Read literally, the language of the Fifth Amendment would seem to indicate that the privilege against self-incrimination applies only to testimony sought to be compelled in a *criminal case*. However, the Supreme Court has consistently given the privilege a broader interpretation, holding that it

> not only protects the individual against being involuntarily called as a witness against himself in a criminal prosecution but also privileges him not to answer official questions put to him in any other proceeding, civil or criminal, formal or informal, where his answers might incriminate him in future criminal proceedings.

Lefkowitz v. Turley, 414 U.S. 70, 77 (1973).

Applicability to Non-Criminal Cases: Counselman v. Hitchcock

This policy of allowing invocation of the Fifth Amendment privilege outside a criminal case was developed in Counselman v. Hitchcock, 142 U.S. 547, 562 (1892). The issue in *Counselman* was whether a grand jury witness could claim the privilege. The Court held that a grand jury investigation of a criminal matter was a "criminal case," but the Court went further and declared that the privilege was available in *any* proceeding if the testimony sought from a party or witness might later be *used* in a criminal prosecution against that person.

> It is impossible that the meaning of the constitutional provision can only be, that a person shall not be compelled to be a witness against himself in a criminal prosecution against himself. * * * The object was to insure that a person should not be compelled, when acting as a witness in any investigation, to give testimony which might tend to show that he himself had committed a crime. The privilege is limited to criminal matters, but it is as broad as the mischief against which it seeks to guard.

Thus, *Counselman* established that a person called as a witness in any federal proceeding could invoke the privilege against self-incrimination to avoid testifying to matters that could possibly tend to be damaging in a *subsequent* criminal prosecution. That rule now binds the states as well as the federal government. See Malloy v. Hogan, 378 U.S. 1 (1964) (right to be free from compelled self-incrimination is incorporated by the Fourteenth Amendment to apply against the states).

2. Criminal Cases

While witnesses in civil cases can invoke the Fifth Amendment protection, the actual *use* of compelled testimony in a civil case does not itself violate the Fifth Amendment. Thus, in Minnesota v. Murphy, 465 U.S. 420 (1984), the Court held that a person has no right to refuse to answer questions on the ground that they might be used against him in subsequent probation revocation proceedings because those proceedings are civil and not criminal. See also Piemonte v. United States, 367 U.S. 556 (1961) (privilege does not prevent use of compelled testimony for purposes of private retribution).

What makes a proceeding in which compelled testimony is used a "criminal case" that triggers Fifth Amendment protection? The discussion here was foreshadowed in Chapter 1.

Civil Penalties: United States v. L.O. Ward

When incarceration is not available as a penalty, a legislative determination that a proceeding is "civil" is likely to be upheld. United States v. L.O. Ward, 448 U.S. 242 (1980), held, for example, that a statute imposing a "civil penalty" upon persons discharging hazardous material into navigable waters was not "quasi-criminal" so as to invalidate a reporting requirement imposed upon polluters. The Court distinguished Boyd v. United States, 116 U.S. 616 (1886)—which held that a forfeiture proceeding was a "criminal case" in which compelled testimony could not be used—suggesting that *Boyd* involved penalties that had no correlation with the damages sustained by society or the costs of enforcing the law. It also noted that in *Boyd* the forfeiture provision was listed along with fine and imprisonment as possible punishments for customs fraud. Justice Stevens dissented.

Detention for "Treatment"

In Allen v. Illinois, 478 U.S. 364 (1986), the Court held 5–4 that proceedings under the Illinois Sexually Dangerous Persons Act were not criminal for self-incrimination purposes. Thus, the state court properly relied upon statements made by Allen to psychiatrists who subjected him to compulsory examination to determine whether he should be committed for treatment under the Act. (Though of course the compelled statements could not have been used against Allen in a criminal trial for sexual assault). The argument for applying the privilege focused on the fact that the state could not file a petition under the Act unless it had already filed criminal charges; the Act provided some of the same safeguards found in criminal proceedings; and a person committed for treatment was kept in a maximum security institution that also housed prisoners in need of psychiatric care.

Justice Rehnquist's majority opinion dismissed these factors and stated that the question of whether a proceeding is criminal for Fifth Amendment purposes was "first of all a question of statutory construction." The majority relied heavily on the fact that the Illinois Legislature had expressly provided that proceedings under the Act would "be civil in nature." Justice Rehnquist concluded that the state's decision to limit proceedings under the Act to persons charged with criminal acts did not turn a civil proceeding into a criminal one. Nor did the presence of some safeguards also found in criminal cases do so. The majority found that the conditions of the institution were not incompatible with the state's interest in treatment. Finally, it held that due process did not require recognition of the privilege, because the privilege would decrease, not increase, the reliability of the fact finding.

Justice Stevens, joined by Justices Brennan, Marshall, and Blackmun, dissented. He argued that a treatment goal was insufficient to render the privilege inapplicable and that the Court was "permitting a State to create a shadow criminal law without the fundamental protection of the Fifth Amendment."

For a case applying *Allen*, see United States v. Phelps, 955 F.2d 1258 (9th Cir. 1992) (insanity acquittee who seeks release from involuntary commitment has no Fifth Amendment right to refuse to speak to state psychiatrist; release proceeding is civil because the emphasis is on treatment rather than punishment, the acquittee bears the burden of proof, and there is no right to a jury determination).

Invoking the Privilege in a Civil Case to Prevent Use of Statements in a Criminal Case

As noted earlier, the privilege can be invoked in almost any proceeding, whether judicial, administrative, or legislative, in order to protect against the use of incriminating statements in a subsequent criminal proceeding. So for example, Fifth Amendment claims have been upheld when asserted by a party in a bankruptcy case. McCarthy v. Arndstein, 266 U.S. 34 (1924). Fifth Amendment claims also can be asserted by the subject of an investigation into possible wrongdoing by public contractors, Lefkowitz v. Turley, 414 U.S. 70 (1973) (architect); by public employees, Garrity v. New Jersey, 385 U.S. 493 (1967) (policemen); by prisoners, Baxter v. Palmigiano, 425 U.S. 308 (1976); or by lawyers (in disbarment proceedings), Spevack v. Klein, 385 U.S. 511 (1967). In none of these cases, however, did the Court hold that the proceeding itself was a "criminal case," although substantial penalties—loss of professional status or even more severe incarceration in the case of prisoners—were often at stake.

3. Foreign Prosecution

As will be discussed below, a grant of use immunity allows the state to compel a witness's testimony. The immunity grant means that neither the statement nor its fruits can be used against the person in either a state or a federal prosecution. But what if there is a risk of *foreign* prosecution? A grant of use immunity by an American court or prosecutor has no binding effect on a foreign government. Can the witness refuse to testify, regardless of a grant of domestic immunity, on the ground that the compelled testimony could incriminate him in a foreign prosecution? Put another way—is a foreign prosecution a "criminal" case, so that the threat of use of a compelled statement in that case is prohibited by the Fifth Amendment?

In United States v. Balsys, 524 U.S. 666 (1998), the Court held that "concern with foreign prosecution is beyond the scope of the Self-Incrimination Clause." Justice Souter wrote the majority opinion that was joined in full by four other Justices, and joined in substantial part by Justices Scalia and Thomas. Balsys had refused to answer questions in a deportation proceeding in which the government alleged that he had committed atrocities during World War II. Balsys asserted the Fifth Amendment privilege on the ground that his testimony could be used against him in a criminal prosecution in either Israel or Lithuania.

Justice Souter analyzed the policies of the Fifth Amendment, as asserted by the Court in Murphy v. Waterfront Commission, 378 U.S. 52 (1964), to determine whether these policies demanded application of Fifth Amendment protection against the risk of foreign prosecution. In particular, *Murphy* had stated that the Fifth Amendment reflects

> our unwillingness to subject those suspected of crime to the cruel trilemma of self-accusation, perjury or contempt; our preference for an accusatorial rather than an inquisitorial system of criminal justice; our fear that self-incriminating statements will be elicited by inhumane treatment and abuses; our sense of fair play which dictates a fair state-individual balance by requiring the government to leave the individual alone until good cause is shown for disturbing him and by requiring the government in its contest with the individual to shoulder the entire load; our respect for the inviolability of the human personality and of the right of each individual to a private enclave where he may lead a private life, our distrust of self-deprecatory statements; and our realization that the privilege, while sometimes a shelter to the guilty, is often a protection to the innocent.

Applying this grounding of the privilege by the *Murphy* Court to the risk of foreign prosecution, Justice Souter found that the Fifth Amendment did not protect against that risk. He reasoned that the existence of immunity and the fact that an individual cannot reject a grant of immunity demonstrate that the Fifth Amendment does not provide as comprehensive protection as *Murphy* suggested. He concluded that "[s]ince the Judiciary could not recognize fear of foreign prosecution and at the same time preserve the Government's existing rights to seek testimony in exchange for immunity (because domestic courts could not enforce the immunity abroad), it follows that extending protection as Balsys requests would change the balance of private and governmental interests that has seemingly been accepted for as long as there has been Fifth Amendment doctrine."

Justice Stevens wrote a short concurring opinion in *Balsys*, emphasizing that the costs of extending the privilege to protect against the risk of foreign prosecutions were too great to bear. If a person could refuse to testify due to a risk of foreign prosecution, "we would confer power on foreign governments to impair the administration of justice in this country." Like the majority, Justice Stevens appears to be concerned that sophisticated lawbreakers could manufacture foreign contacts to bring domestic prosecutions to a halt. In the modern era of international transactions, it might be possible to make a credible argument that there is a risk of foreign prosecution for many individuals involved in organized crime. Justice Stevens wrote that "[a] law enacted by a foreign power making it a crime for one of its citizens to testify in an American proceeding against another citizen of that country would immunize those citizens from being compelled to testify in our courts."

Justice Ginsburg wrote a short dissenting opinion in *Balsys* and joined Justice Breyer's far more extensive opinion. Justice Breyer disagreed with the majority's assessment that applying the privilege to claims of foreign incrimination would substantially impair law enforcement:

> [T]hat fear is overstated. After all, "foreign application" of the privilege would matter only in a case where an individual could not be prosecuted domestically but the threat of foreign prosecution is substantial. * * * [R]elatively few witnesses face deportation or extradition, and a witness who will not be forced to enter a country disposed to prosecute him, cannot make the showing of "real and substantial" fear that the Fifth Amendment would require.

4. Compulsion of Statements Never Admitted at a Criminal Trial

In Chavez v. Martinez, 538 U.S. 760 (2003), the Court considered whether the Fifth Amendment is violated when police compel a statement from a suspect during interrogation but the statement *is never admitted* against the suspect in a criminal trial. Martinez brought a civil rights action under 42 U.S. C. § 1983 for violation of his Fifth Amendment rights. Chavez was a police officer who interrogated Martinez after Martinez was shot in a fight with police officers. The interrogation session occurred while Martinez was in the hospital being treated for bullet wounds. Martinez made some inculpatory statements. For purposes of the appeal, the Court assumed that the statements made by Martinez would have been excluded under the Fifth Amendment as compelled self-incrimination had the statements been offered at a criminal trial. However, Martinez was never charged with a crime, and the statements were never used against him in a criminal prosecution.

A majority found that the Fifth Amendment provides no relief when statements are compelled but are never admitted in a criminal case. However, there was no opinion for the Court on this question. Justice Thomas, joined by Chief Justice Rehnquist and Justices O'Connor and Scalia, provided the broadest opinion, declaring that the Fifth Amendment simply did not apply because Martinez's confession was ever admitted against him in a criminal case. Justice Thomas reasoned as follows:

> Although Martinez contends that the meaning of "criminal case" should encompass the entire criminal investigatory process, including police interrogations, we disagree. In our view, a "criminal case" at the very least requires the initiation of legal proceedings. * * * Here, Martinez was never made to be a "witness" against himself in violation of the Fifth Amendment's Self-Incrimination Clause because his statements were never admitted as testimony against him in a criminal case. Nor was he ever placed under oath and exposed to the cruel trilemma of self-accusation, perjury or contempt.

Justice Souter, joined by Justice Breyer, concurred in the judgment, agreeing with the general proposition that the Fifth Amendment does not protect against compulsion of statements that are never used in a criminal case. Justice Souter expressed concern over the stopping point for a rule of law providing that compelled confessions are actionable in themselves.

> If obtaining Martinez's statement is to be treated as a stand-alone violation of the privilege subject to compensation, why should the same not be true whenever the police obtain any involuntary self-incriminating statement, or whenever the government so much as threatens a penalty in derogation of the right to immunity, or whenever the police fail to honor *Miranda?* Martinez offers no limiting principle or reason to foresee a stopping place short of liability in all such cases.

Justice Kennedy, joined by Justices Stevens and Ginsburg, dissented. He argued as follows:

> The conclusion that the Self-Incrimination Clause is not violated until the government seeks to use a statement in some later criminal proceeding strips the Clause of an essential part of its force and meaning. * * * To tell our whole legal system that when conducting a criminal investigation police officials can use severe compulsion or even torture with no present violation of the right against compelled self-incrimination can only diminish a celebrated provision in the Bill of Rights. * * *

Justice Ginsburg added a separate dissenting opinion.

Chavez appears to establish only that a person cannot recover civil damages when police compel a statement from that person without using methods that are so coercive that they violate Fifth Amendment Due Process, at least where those statements are not introduced at a criminal trial.[3] Actions seeking damages for torture and unconstitutional coercion are not barred by *Chavez*. Maclin, The Prophylactic Fifth Amendment, 97 B.U. Law Rev. 1047 (2017), criticizes the *Martinez* decision.

C. WHAT IS COMPULSION?

The Fifth Amendment protects against self-incrimination only if it is *compelled* by the government. It is sometimes difficult to determine whether a particular pressure imposed by the government on a citizen rises to the level of compulsion.

1. Use of the Contempt Power

Use of the contempt power is the classic form of compulsion because it imposes a substantial punishment on the witness who is exercising the right to remain silent, and it presents the witness with a cruel trilemma:

---

[3] As of this writing, the Court has granted certiorari in Vega v. Tekoh, 142 S.Ct. 858 (2022), to determine whether 42 U.S.C. § 1983 provides a right of action against police officers who take statements in violation of *Miranda* that are later admitted at trial.

remain silent and face imprisonment; tell the truth and face imprisonment; or tell a lie and face imprisonment for perjury. Thus, a witness cannot be subjected to contempt for refusing to testify as long as the testimony could create a risk of self-incrimination in a criminal case.

2. Other State-Imposed Sanctions

The Supreme Court has extended the concept of compulsion well beyond its original grounding in the contempt power. For example, the Court in Miranda v. Arizona, discussed *infra,* found compulsion in the setting of custodial interrogation. The Court has also found other state-imposed sanctions for silence, of less severity than contempt, to constitute compulsion. The following case provides an example of the Court's approach.

LEFKOWITZ V. TURLEY

Supreme Court of the United States, 1973.
414 U.S. 70.

MR. JUSTICE WHITE delivered the opinion of the Court:

[New York statutes required public contracts to provide that if a contractor refused to waive immunity or to testify concerning state contracts, existing contracts could be canceled and future contracts could be denied for five years. Contractors in this case refused to answer questions that could incriminate them and were denied the right to future contracts under the statute.]

* * *

It is true that the State has a strong, legitimate interest in maintaining the integrity of its civil service and of its transactions with independent contractors furnishing a wide range of goods and services; and New York would have it that this interest is sufficiently strong to override the privilege. The suggestion is that the State should be able to interrogate employees and contractors about their job performance without regard to the Fifth Amendment, to discharge those who refuse to answer or to waive the privilege by waiving the immunity to which they would otherwise be entitled, and to use any incriminating answers obtained in subsequent criminal prosecutions. But claims of overriding interests are not unusual in Fifth Amendment litigation and they have not fared well.

* * *

[I]n almost the very context here involved, this court has only recently held that employees of the State do not forfeit their constitutional privilege and that they may be compelled to respond to questions about the performance of their duties but only if their answers cannot be used against them in subsequent criminal prosecutions. Garrity v. New Jersey, 385 U.S. 493 (1967); Gardner v. Broderick, 392

U.S. 273 (1968); Sanitation Men v. Sanitation Comm'r, 392 U.S. 280 (1968).

* * *

In Garrity v. New Jersey, certain police officers were summoned to an inquiry being conducted by the Attorney General concerning the fixing of traffic tickets. They were asked questions following warnings that if they did not answer they would be removed from office and that anything they said might be used against them in any criminal proceeding. No immunity of any kind was offered or available under state law. The questions were answered and the answers later used over their objections, in their prosecutions for conspiracy. The Court held that "protection of the individual under the Fourteenth Amendment against coerced statements prohibits use in subsequent criminal proceedings of statements obtained under threat of removal from office, and that it extends to all, whether they are policemen or other members of our body politic." * * *

The issue in Gardner v. Broderick, supra, was whether the State might discharge a police officer who, after he was summoned before a grand jury to testify about the performance of his official duties and was advised of his right against compulsory self-incrimination, then refused to waive that right as requested by the State. Conceding that appellant could be discharged for refusing to answer questions about the performance of his official duties, if not required to waive immunity, the Court held that the officer could not be terminated, as he was, for refusing to waive his constitutional privilege. * * *

The companion case, Sanitation Men v. Sanitation Com'r, supra, was to the same effect. * * *

These cases, and their predecessors, ultimately rest on a reconciliation of the well-recognized policies behind the privilege of self-incrimination, and the need of the State, as well as the Federal Government, to obtain information "to assure the effective functioning of government." Immunity is required if there is to be "rational accommodation between the imperatives of the privilege and the legitimate demands of government to compel citizens to testify." It is in this sense that immunity statutes have "become part of our constitutional fabric."

* * * *Garrity, Gardner,* and *Sanitation Men* control the issue now before us. The State sought to interrogate appellees about their transactions with the State and to require them to furnish possibly incriminating testimony by demanding that they waive their immunity and by disqualifying them as public contractors when they refused. It seems to us that the State intended to accomplish what *Garrity* specifically prohibited—to compel testimony that had not been immunized. The waiver sought by the State, under threat of loss of contracts, would have been no

less compelled than a direct request for the testimony without resort to the waiver device. A waiver secured under threat of substantial economic sanction cannot be termed voluntary.

* * *

The Function of Immunity

If the contractor in *Lefkowitz* had been given immunity from criminal prosecution, could he then be denied public contracts for refusing to testify? If he spoke pursuant to a grant of immunity, could he then be denied public contracts on the basis of incriminating statements made in his testimony? The court explained the relevant principles in National Federation of Federal Employees v. Greenberg, 983 F.2d 286 (D.C. Cir. 1993), a case in which government employees were subject to firing for refusing to answer questions, and relevant statutes prevented use of the compelled statements in a criminal prosecution:

> The government * * * may fire employees who refuse, on the basis of their Fifth Amendment privilege, to answer questions concerning the performance of their duties, so long as the employees' answers could not be used against them in a criminal prosecution. For purposes of the Fifth Amendment, the threat of firing or other economic sanctions may constitute compulsion. But the protection of the privilege extends only to criminal prosecutions. A government employee would not be incriminating himself within the meaning of the Fifth Amendment if his answers could not be used against him in a criminal case.

This means that a contractor could be denied public contracts on the basis of compelled testimony, so long as the statements could not be *used against him in a criminal case.* Denial of public contracts would not itself constitute a criminal case.

Threat of Disbarment as Compulsion

Spevack v. Klein, 385 U.S. 511 (1967), forbids disbarment of a lawyer for invoking the privilege during a bar investigation, where any statements could be used against the lawyer in a subsequent criminal prosecution. But can an applicant for the bar exam refuse to answer questions on an application and still insist on admission to the bar? This requires a look at the Court's approach to benefits and penalties.

The Benefit-Penalty Distinction

What if the government does not impose a penalty for silence, as in *Turley*, but instead conditions a benefit on the waiver of the privilege? Is this "compulsion" within the meaning of the Fifth Amendment? The basic answer is that denial of a benefit is not a penalty, and therefore is not compulsion.

The benefit/penalty distinction has often been applied when a defendant is required to provide incriminating information in order to receive a reduction in sentence. For example, in United States v. Cruz, 156 F.3d 366 (2d Cir. 1998), the defendant was subject to a mandatory minimum sentence of ten years for a drug crime. However, a federal statute provides for "safety valve" relief from mandatory minimums in some narcotics cases if, among other things, the defendant "has truthfully provided to the Government all information and evidence the defendant has concerning the offense or offenses that were part of the same course of conduct or of a common scheme or plan." The defendant in *Cruz* argued that this disclosure provision compelled him to incriminate himself, because, in order to receive the waiver of the mandatory minimum, he would have to implicate himself in other drug transactions for which he was not yet charged. But the court found no compulsion, noting that the penalty cases "have all involved some kind of loss or reduction from the status quo" such as the loss of public employment or disbarment. "A defendant facing a particular sentence, however, with the option of obtaining a lower sentence if he or she waives the Fifth Amendment privilege is not presented with the same 'negative' sanction as presented in the penalty cases." The court declared that "the choice confronting the defendant gives rise to no more compulsion than that present in a typical plea bargain." If the defendant had actually suffered an *enhanced* sentence for remaining silent, this would have amounted to compulsion. But conditioning a *reduction* of sentence on cooperation is permitted.

Self-Incrimination and Clemency Proceedings: Ohio Adult Parole Authority v. Woodard

The Supreme Court considered the benefit-penalty distinction in Ohio Adult Parole Authority v. Woodard, 523 U.S. 272 (1998). The Parole Authority commenced a clemency proceeding in accordance with state law, after Woodard's appeal from his capital murder conviction had been denied. Under Ohio law, the Parole Authority must conduct a clemency hearing within 45 days of the scheduled date of execution. Prior to the hearing, the inmate may request an interview with one or more parole board members. The Authority must hold the hearing, complete its clemency review, and make a recommendation to the Governor. Woodard did not request an interview. Instead, he brought a section 1983 action in federal court, arguing, among other things, that the clemency proceeding left him with a "Hobson's choice": to have any chance of clemency, he would have to subject himself to an interview, thereby opening himself up to incrimination both on the current charge (given the possibility of successful post-conviction proceedings) as well as on other charges.

The Supreme Court, in a unanimous opinion on this point, rejected Woodard's Fifth Amendment argument and held that the clemency procedure did not *compel* him to incriminate himself. Chief Justice Rehnquist, writing for the Court, reasoned as follows:

> It is difficult to see how a voluntary interview could "compel" respondent to speak. He merely faces a choice quite similar to the sorts of choices that a criminal defendant must make in the course of criminal proceedings, none of which has ever been held to violate the Fifth Amendment.
>
> Long ago we held that a defendant who took the stand in his own defense could not claim the privilege against self-incrimination when the prosecution sought to cross-examine him. Brown v. Walker, 161 U.S. 591 (1896). A defendant who takes the stand in his own behalf may be impeached by proof of prior convictions without violation of the Fifth Amendment privilege. Spencer v. Texas, 385 U.S. 554, 561 (1967). A defendant whose motion for acquittal at the close of the Government's case is denied must then elect whether to stand on his motion or to put on a defense, with the accompanying risk that in doing so he will augment the Government's case against him. McGautha v. California, 402 U.S. 183 (1971). In each of these situations, there are undoubted pressures—generated by the strength of the Government's case against him—pushing the criminal defendant to testify. But it has never been suggested that such pressures constitute "compulsion" for Fifth Amendment purposes.
>
> * * *
>
> Here, respondent has the same choice of providing information to the Authority—at the risk of damaging his case for clemency or for postconviction relief—or of remaining silent. But this pressure to speak in the hope of improving his chance of being granted clemency does not make the interview compelled.

The Benefit-Penalty Distinction and Penalties Imposed on Incarcerated Sex Offenders: McKune v. Lile

In McKune v. Lile, 536 U.S. 24 (2002), a divided Court considered whether the benefit-penalty distinction works when applied to a program for rehabilitating incarcerated sex offenders. The Court also considered whether certain inconveniences can be imposed on a prisoner for remaining silent without rising to the level of compulsion.

Lile was convicted in state court of rape, aggravated sodomy and aggravated kidnaping in 1982. In 1994, prison officials in Kansas ordered him to participate in a Sexual Abuse Treatment Program. Participating inmates are required to complete and sign an "Admission of Responsibility" form, in which they discuss and accept responsibility for the crimes of conviction. They are also required to complete a sexual history form in which they detail all prior sexual activities, regardless of whether such activities constitute uncharged criminal offenses. The veracity of their answers is checked by polygraph examination. The information that the participants disclose is not privileged and can be used in future criminal prosecutions.

Lile refused to participate on the ground that the required disclosures would violate his privilege against self-incrimination. Department officials responded that if he refused to participate in the SATP, his privilege status would be reduced from Level III to Level I and, as a result, his visitation rights, earnings, work opportunities, ability to send money to family, canteen expenditures, access to a personal television, and other privileges automatically would be curtailed. One other detriment for non-participation was a transfer to a maximum-security unit, where his movement would be more limited, he would be moved from a two-person to a four-person cell, and he would be in a potentially more dangerous environment. Believing that the threatened response was a penalty for his invocation of his privilege, Lile sued in federal court to enjoin the prison officials from withdrawing his privileges.

Justice Kennedy, writing for himself, Chief Justice Rehnquist, Justice Scalia, and Justice Thomas, declared that the program did not constitute compulsion within the meaning of the Fifth Amendment. With respect to the losses suffered by Lile for not participating, Justice Kennedy declared as follows:

> The consequences in question here—a transfer to another prison where television sets are not placed in each inmate's cell, where exercise facilities are not readily available, and where work and wage opportunities are more limited—are not ones that compel a prisoner to speak about his past crimes despite a desire to remain silent. The fact that these consequences are imposed on prisoners, rather than ordinary citizens, moreover, is important in weighing respondent's constitutional claim.

Justice Kennedy rejected Lile's attempt to claim that he was faced with penalties:

> Respondent is mistaken as well to concentrate on the so-called reward/penalty distinction and the illusory baseline against which a change in prison conditions must be measured. The answer to the question whether the government is extending a benefit or taking away a privilege rests entirely in the eye of the beholder. For this reason, emphasis of any baseline, while superficially appealing, would be an inartful addition to an already confused area of jurisprudence. * * *

> * * * Respondent's reasoning would provide States with perverse incentives to assign all inmates convicted of sex offenses to maximum security prisons until near the time of release, when the rehabilitation program starts. The rule would work to the detriment of the entire class of sex offenders who might not otherwise be placed in maximum-security facilities. And prison administrators would be forced, before making routine prison housing decisions, to identify each inmate's so-called baseline and determine whether an adverse effect, however marginal, will result from the administrative decision. * * *
>
> Respondent's analysis also would call into question the constitutionality of an accepted feature of federal criminal law: the downward adjustment for acceptance of criminal responsibility provided in § 3E1.1 of the United States Sentencing Guidelines. If the Constitution does not permit the government to condition the use of a personal television on the acceptance of responsibility for past crimes, it is unclear how it could permit the government to reduce the length of a prisoner's term of incarceration based upon the same factor. By rejecting respondent's theory, we do not, in this case, call these policies into question.

Justice O'Connor concurred in the judgment and stated that she did not believe that the consequences facing Lile were "serious enough to compel him to be a witness against himself."

Justice Stevens dissented and was joined by Justices Souter, Ginsburg and Breyer. He stated that "[u]ntil today the Court has never characterized a threatened harm as 'a minimal incentive.' Nor have we ever held that a person who has made a valid assertion of the privilege may nevertheless be ordered to incriminate himself and sanctioned for disobeying such an order. This is truly a watershed case."

Justice Stevens relied upon the distinction between benefits and penalties:

> We have recognized that the government can extend a benefit in exchange for incriminating statements, but cannot threaten to take away privileges as the cost of invoking Fifth Amendment rights. Based on this distinction, nothing that I say in this dissent calls into question the constitutionality of *downward* adjustments for acceptance of responsibility under the United States Sentencing Guidelines. Although such a reduction in sentence creates a powerful incentive for defendants to confess, it completely avoids the constitutional issue that would be presented if the Guidelines operated like the scheme here and authorized an *upward* adjustment whenever a defendant refused to accept responsibility. * * * By obscuring the distinction between penalties and incentives, it is the plurality that calls into question both the Guidelines and plea bargaining.

3. Comment on the Invocation of the Privilege

The Griffin Rule

In Griffin v. California, 380 U.S. 609 (1965), the Court held that adverse comment to the jury, by either the judge or the prosecutor, on the defendant's election not to testify constitutes punishment for the invocation of silence, which is tantamount to compulsion and therefore violates the Fifth Amendment. Thus, the fact that the defendant did not take the stand cannot be used as information against him.[4] Notably, *Griffin* also has the effect of resolving more fully the "cruel trilemma" by reducing further the consequences to a defendant of remaining silent at trial.

The Court extended *Griffin* in Carter v. Kentucky, 450 U.S. 288 (1981). Carter asked the trial judge to instruct the jurors that they were not to draw an adverse inference from the fact that Carter did not testify. The trial judge denied the request, reasoning that such an instruction would only draw attention to the fact that the defendant had not testified. The Supreme Court held that the trial judge was required to give the instruction upon request, "to minimize the danger that the jury will give evidentiary weight to a defendant's failure to testify."

Lakeside v. Oregon, 435 U.S. 333 (1978), presented the opposite situation from *Carter*. The trial judge instructed the jury not to draw an adverse inference from Lakeside's failure to testify, and Lakeside *objected* to the instruction presumably because he was concerned that an instruction would only highlight his failure to take the stand. He argued that he was being penalized for not testifying when the trial judge gave the instruction against his wishes. But the Court rejected Lakeside's argument. It reasoned that *Griffin* was concerned with "adverse comment," and the instruction in this case was anything but an adverse comment. The instruction was designed to *dispel* the compulsion that might otherwise exist due to the negative inferences that could be drawn from the defendant's failure to testify.

The Court distinguished *Griffin* in United States v. Robinson, 485 U.S. 25 (1988), and held that a prosecutor properly pointed out in closing argument that the defendant had an opportunity to testify. The prosecutor was responding to defense counsel's closing argument that the defendant had not been permitted to explain his side of the story. Thus the defendant had opened the door to a rebuttal.

---

[4] For a criticism of *Griffin*, see Ayer, The Fifth Amendment and the Inference of Guilt from Silence: Griffin v. California After Fifteen Years, 78 Mich.L.Rev. 841 (1980) (arguing that *Griffin* is an ill-advised exception to the rule that attorneys may draw any reasonable inference from the facts legitimately within the jury's knowledge). For a defense of *Griffin*, see Saltzburg, Foreword: The Flow and Ebb of Constitutional Criminal Procedure in the Warren and Burger Courts, 69 Geo.L.J. 151, 204 (1980).

How does an adverse inference "punish" a defendant who refuses to testify? Consider the assessment of Judge Posner, writing in United States v. Castillo, 965 F.2d 238 (7th Cir. 1992). He argued that the "punishment" found impermissible in *Griffin* was "slight, because juries are perfectly capable of drawing an adverse inference from a defendant's refusal to testify on their own, without having to be told to do so." Arguably Judge Posner failed to recognize that, before *Griffin*, prosecutors could make powerful arguments about the significance of a defendant's failure to testify that a jury might not consider on its own.

Adverse Inferences at Sentencing: Mitchell v. United States

The defendant in Mitchell v. United States, 526 U.S. 314 (1999), pleaded guilty to federal charges of conspiring to distribute five or more kilograms of cocaine and of distributing cocaine. But she reserved the right to contest at sentencing the drug quantity attributable to her under the conspiracy count. Before accepting her plea, the District Court told Mitchell that she faced a mandatory minimum of one year in prison for distributing cocaine, but a 10-year minimum for conspiracy if the Government could show that she was involved in a quantity more than 5 kilograms; and explained that by pleading guilty she would be waiving her right "at trial to remain silent." Indicating that she had done "some of" the proffered conduct, Mitchell confirmed her guilty plea. At her sentencing hearing, three codefendants testified that she had sold 1 1/2 to 2 ounces of cocaine twice a week for 1 1/2 years, and another person testified that Mitchell had sold her two ounces of cocaine. This was enough to take the quantity over the 5 kilogram threshold for an enhancement of Mitchell's sentence. Mitchell put on no evidence at the sentencing hearing, choosing instead to attack the credibility of the codefendant-witnesses. The sentencing court found that the codefendants' testimony put her over the 5-kilogram threshold, thus mandating the 10-year minimum, and noted specifically that Mitchell's failure to testify at sentencing was a factor in persuading the court to rely on the codefendants' testimony.

Thus, one question in *Mitchell* was whether the sentencing court was permitted to draw an adverse inference from Mitchell's silence. In a 5–4 opinion written by Justice Kennedy, the Court relied on *Griffin* and held that a defendant could not be subject to an adverse inference upon invoking the right to remain silent at a sentencing proceeding. Justice Kennedy's analysis of *Griffin*, and its applicability to sentencing, proceeded as follows:

> [A] sentencing hearing is part of the criminal case—the explicit concern of the self-incrimination privilege. In accordance with the text of the Fifth Amendment, we must accord the privilege the same protection in the sentencing phase of "any criminal case" as that which is due in the trial phase of the same case.

> The concerns which mandate the rule against negative inferences at a criminal trial apply with equal force at sentencing. Without question, the stakes are high: Here, the inference drawn by the District Court from petitioner's silence may have resulted in decades of added imprisonment.

Justice Kennedy reserved the question of whether the sentencing judge could take into account the defendant's silence on questions of remorse and acceptance of responsibility, as opposed to questions about the crime itself.

Justice Scalia, joined by Chief Justice Rehnquist and Justices O'Connor and Thomas in dissent, argued that an adverse inference "does not 'compel' anyone to testify." He launched into an extensive historical analysis, concluding, on the basis of common-law cases and the understanding of the Framers, that *Griffin's* "pedigree" is "dubious." He asserted that "the text and history of the Fifth Amendment give no indication that there is a federal constitutional prohibition on the use of the defendant's silence as demeanor evidence." He explained as follows:

> Our hardy forebears, who thought of compulsion in terms of the rack and oaths forced by the power of law, would not have viewed the drawing of a commonsensical inference as equivalent pressure. And it is implausible that the Americans of 1791, who were subject to adverse inferences for failing to give unsworn testimony, would have viewed an adverse inference for failing to give sworn testimony as a violation of the Fifth Amendment.

Justice Scalia also noted that the *Griffin* rule "runs exactly counter to normal evidentiary inferences: If I ask my son whether he saw a movie I had forbidden him to watch, and he remains silent, the import of the silence is clear."

Justice Scalia next contested the application of *Griffin* to sentencing proceedings:

> Our case law has long recognized a natural dichotomy between the guilt and penalty phases. The jury-trial right contained in the Sixth Amendment—whose guarantees apply "[i]n all criminal prosecutions," a term indistinguishable for present purposes from the Fifth Amendment's "in any criminal case"—does not apply at sentencing. Nor does the Sixth Amendment's guarantee of the defendant's right "to be confronted with the witnesses against him." (The sentencing judge may consider, for example, reports of probation officers and psychiatrists without affording any cross-examination.)

Justice Thomas wrote a separate dissenting opinion in *Mitchell*, in which he stated that he was prepared to revisit the *Griffin* rule *in toto*. He attacked the analysis in *Griffin* in the following passage:

Prosecutorial comments on a defendant's decision to remain silent at trial surely impose no greater "penalty" on a defendant than threats to indict him on more serious charges if he chooses not to enter into a plea bargain—a practice that this Court previously has validated. * * * [A]t bottom, *Griffin* constitutionalizes a policy choice that a majority of the Court found desirable at the time. * * * This sort of undertaking is not an exercise in constitutional interpretation but an act of judicial willfulness that has no logical stopping point.

Adverse Inferences Drawn in Civil Cases

In Baxter v. Palmigiano, 425 U.S. 308 (1976), the Court declared that "the Fifth Amendment does not forbid inferences against parties to civil actions when they refuse to testify in response to probative evidence offered against them: the Amendment does not preclude the inference where the privilege is claimed by a party to a civil cause." The *Baxter* Court explained that in ordinary civil cases, the party confronted with the invocation of the privilege by the opposing side has no capacity to avoid it, say, by offering immunity from prosecution. Thus the rule allowing invocation of the privilege—though at the risk of suffering an adverse inference and possibly an adverse civil judgment—accommodates the right not to be a witness against oneself while still permitting civil litigation to proceed. For a discussion of what courts should do when the privilege against self-incrimination is raised in civil cases, see Heidt, The Conjurer's Circle, The Fifth Amendment Privilege in Civil Cases, 91 Yale L.J. 1062 (1982).

4. Compulsion and the "Exculpatory No" Doctrine

The Court in Brogan v. United States, 522 U.S. 398 (1998), considered whether the Fifth Amendment prohibited the criminal punishment of a person who lies to government investigators during the course of a criminal investigation. Federal agents interviewed Brogan, a union officer, and asked him whether he had accepted cash payments from a real estate company whose employees were represented by the union. Brogan denied that he had, the agents then disclosed to him that a search of the company's headquarters showed the payments, and Brogan stuck to his denial. He was indicted for accepting unlawful cash payments from an employer and making a false statement within the jurisdiction of a federal agency in violation of 18 U.S.C. § 1001.

Section 1001, in essential part, imposes a criminal penalty on anyone who willfully makes a false statement to the government. Brogan admitted that his denial of involvement was covered by the statute, but argued that he could not be convicted because of lower court case law that had developed the "exculpatory no doctrine." The rationale of the doctrine is that section 1001 should not criminalize simple denials of guilt to government investigators, because to do so would violate the "spirit" of the Fifth Amendment.

Justice Scalia categorically rejected the "exculpatory no" doctrine, and the Court upheld the false statement conviction. Justice Scalia dismissed the Fifth Amendment argument by noting that Brogan was not *compelled*, in any sense, to deny criminal responsibility when he said "no" to the agents. He could simply have remained silent without penalty.

Justice Ginsburg, joined by Justice Souter, concurred only in the judgment in *Brogan*, inviting Congress to consider the possibility that section 1001 might be used for overreaching, i.e., to prosecute people who are not aware that denying criminal responsibility in a situation like Brogan's is in fact a criminal act. Justice Stevens, joined by Justice Breyer, dissented.

D. TO WHOM DOES THE PRIVILEGE BELONG?

The privilege against self-incrimination is a personal right, belonging only to the person who is himself incriminated by his own testimony. For example, an employer may not claim the privilege on the ground that his testimony might incriminate his employee; nor may the employee complain about the employer's compelled testimony. Which of the rationales for the privilege, discussed above, justify this limitation? Consider the Court's policy analysis in the following case.

FISHER V. UNITED STATES

Supreme Court of the United States, 1976.
425 U.S. 391.

MR. JUSTICE WHITE delivered the opinion of the Court.

[Taxpayers, who were under investigation for possible civil or criminal tax violations, obtained documents relating to the preparation of their tax returns from their accountants. Shortly thereafter, they transferred these documents to the lawyers handling their cases. The IRS served summonses on the attorneys directing them to produce the records, but the attorneys refused to comply on Fifth Amendment grounds.]

II

All of the parties in these cases and the Court of Appeals for the Fifth Circuit have concurred in the proposition that if the Fifth Amendment would have excused a *taxpayer* from turning over the accountant's papers had he possessed them, the *attorney* to whom they are delivered for the purpose of obtaining legal advice should also be immune from subpoena. Although we agree with this proposition * * * we are convinced that, under our decision in Couch v. United States, 409 U.S. 322 (1973), it is not the taxpayer's Fifth Amendment privilege that would excuse the *attorney* from production.

The relevant part of that Amendment provides:

> "No person * * * shall be *compelled* in any criminal case to be a *witness against himself.*" (Emphasis added.)

The taxpayer's privilege under this Amendment is not violated by enforcement of the summonses involved in these cases because enforcement against a taxpayer's lawyer would not "compel" the taxpayer to do anything—and certainly would not compel him to be a "witness" against himself. * * * In Couch v. United States, we recently ruled that the Fifth Amendment rights of a taxpayer were not violated by the enforcement of a documentary summons directed to her accountant and requiring production of the taxpayer's own records in the possession of the accountant. We did so on the ground that in such a case "the ingredient of personal compulsion against an accused is lacking."

Here, the taxpayers are compelled to do no more than was the taxpayer in *Couch.* The taxpayers' Fifth Amendment privilege is therefore not violated by enforcement of the summonses directed toward their attorneys. This is true whether or not the Amendment would have barred a subpoena directing the taxpayer to produce the documents while they were in his hands.

* * * In Hale v. Henkel, 201 U.S. 43, 69–70 (1906), the Court said that the privilege "was never intended to permit [a person] to plead the fact that some third person might be incriminated by his testimony, even though he were the agent of such person * * *. [T]he Amendment is limited to a person who shall be compelled in any criminal case to be a witness against *himself.*" (Emphasis in original.) "It is extortion of information from the accused himself that offends our sense of justice."

* * *

The Court of Appeals for the Fifth Circuit suggested that because legally and ethically the attorney was required to respect the confidences of his client, the latter had a reasonable expectation of privacy for the records in the hands of the attorney and therefore did not forfeit his Fifth Amendment privilege with respect to the records by transferring them in order to obtain legal advice. * * *

* * *

We cannot cut the Fifth Amendment completely loose from the moorings of its language, and make it serve as a general protector of privacy—a word not mentioned in its text and a concept directly addressed in the Fourth Amendment. We adhere to the view that the Fifth

Amendment protects against "compelled self-incrimination, not [the disclosure of] private information."

* * *

[In Part III, the Court held that the attorney-client privilege protects against disclosure of documents that would have been protected by the Fifth Amendment had they been in the taxpayer's possession. However, in Part IV it concluded that the documents in question would not be privileged even in the hands of the taxpayer. See infra for the Court's discussion of the latter issue.]

NOTE ON THE COLLECTIVE ENTITY RULE

The Fifth Amendment prevents the state from compelling a "person" to be a "witness against himself." The Court in Bellis v. United States, 417 U.S. 85 (1974), held that the textual limitation to a "person" meant that partnerships have no Fifth Amendment protection. The partnership in *Bellis* was a law firm with three partners and a handful of employees. Justice Marshall, writing for the Court, stated broadly that the privilege against compelled self-incrimination is a "purely personal" one, which applies "only to natural individuals." Therefore, "no artificial organization may utilize the personal privilege against compulsory self-incrimination." Justice Marshall concluded that the partnership in *Bellis* had "an established institutional identity independent of its individual partners." Therefore, the partnership could be placed in contempt for failing to comply with an order to produce information, even though that information could be used in a criminal case to impose a penalty on the partnership.

In United States v. Doe, 465 U.S. 605 (1984), the Court distinguished *Bellis* and held that a *sole proprietorship* was entitled to Fifth Amendment protection. A sole proprietorship was not considered an entity distinct from the individual. However, in Braswell v. United States, 487 U.S. 99 (1988), the Court held that a corporation—even one wholly owned and operated by a single individual—was not itself entitled to Fifth Amendment protection. Chief Justice Rehnquist, writing for the Court, distinguished *Doe* as follows:

> Had petitioner conducted his business as a sole proprietorship, *Doe* would require that he be provided the opportunity to show that his act of production would entail testimonial self-incrimination. But petitioner has operated his business through the corporate form, and we have long recognized that for purposes of the Fifth Amendment, corporations and other collective entities are treated differently from individuals.

See also In re Grand Jury Subpoena, 973 F.2d 45 (1st Cir. 1992) (trust established by two brothers for purposes of conducting real estate transactions held an entity not entitled to Fifth Amendment protection).

Corporations have Fourth Amendment rights (see Marshall v. Barlow's in Chapter 2); they have First Amendment rights (First National Bank v. Bellotti,

435 U.S. 765 (1978)); they have due process rights (International Shoe Co. v. Washington, 326 U.S. 310 (1945)); why don't they have Fifth Amendment rights? Why is it of constitutional importance that Braswell operated a business as a wholly owned corporation rather than as a sole proprietorship?

E. WHAT IS PROTECTED

The privilege only protects a person when that person is being compelled to be a "witness" against himself. Thus, it does not protect against *all* forms of compelled self-incrimination. If a person is forced to give information other than what a "witness" would provide, the privilege is inapplicable. In the cases that follow, the Court attempts to define the scope of information protected by the privilege by examining what it means to be a "witness."

1. Non-Testimonial Evidence

SCHMERBER V. CALIFORNIA

Supreme Court of the United States, 1966.
384 U.S. 757.

MR. JUSTICE BRENNAN delivered the opinion of the Court.

Petitioner was convicted in Los Angeles Municipal Court of the criminal offense of driving an automobile while under the influence of intoxicating liquor. He had been arrested at a hospital while receiving treatment for injuries suffered in an accident involving the automobile that he had apparently been driving. At the direction of a police officer, a blood sample was then withdrawn from petitioner's body by a physician at the hospital. The chemical analysis of this sample revealed a percent by weight of alcohol in his blood at the time of the offense which indicated intoxication, and the report of this analysis was admitted in evidence at the trial. Petitioner objected to receipt of this evidence of the analysis on the ground that the blood had been withdrawn despite his refusal, on the advice of his counsel, to consent to the test. He contended that in that circumstance the withdrawal of the blood and the admission of the analysis in evidence denied him * * * his privilege against self-incrimination under the Fifth Amendment * * *.

* * * We hold that the privilege protects an accused only from being compelled to testify against himself, or otherwise provide the State with evidence of a testimonial or communicative nature,[a] and that the

[a] A dissent suggests that the report of the blood test was "testimonial" or "communicative," because the test was performed in order to obtain the testimony of others, communicating to the jury facts about petitioner's condition. Of course, all evidence received in court is "testimonial" or "communicative" if these words are thus used. But the Fifth Amendment relates only to acts on the part of the person to whom the privilege applies, and we use these words subject to the same limitations. A nod or head-shake is as much a "testimonial" or "communicative" act in this sense as are spoken words. But the terms as we use them do not apply to evidence of acts

withdrawal of blood and use of the analysis in question in this case did not involve compulsion to these ends.

It could not be denied that in requiring petitioner to submit to the withdrawal and chemical analysis of his blood the State compelled him to submit to an attempt to discover evidence that might be used to prosecute him for a criminal offense. * * * The critical question, then, is whether petitioner was thus compelled "to be a witness against himself."

If the scope of the privilege coincided with the complex of values it helps to protect, we might be obliged to conclude that the privilege was violated. * * *

* * * [H]owever, the privilege has never been given the full scope which the values it helps to protect suggest. History and a long line of authorities in lower courts have consistently limited its protection to situations in which the State seeks to submerge those values by obtaining the evidence against an accused through "the cruel, simple expedient of compelling it from his own mouth. * * * In sum, the privilege is fulfilled only when the person is guaranteed the right 'to remain silent unless he chooses to speak in the unfettered exercise of his own will." * * *

It is clear that the protection of the privilege reaches an accused's communications, whatever form they might take * * *. On the other hand, both federal and state courts have usually held that it offers no protection against compulsion to submit to fingerprinting, photographing, or measurements, to write or speak for identification, to appear in court, to stand, to assume a stance, to walk, or to make a particular gesture. The distinction which has emerged, often expressed in different ways, is that the privilege is a bar against compelling "communications" or "testimony," but that compulsion which makes a suspect or accused the source of "real or physical evidence" does not violate it.

* * * Not even a shadow of testimonial compulsion upon or enforced communication by the accused was involved either in the extraction or in the chemical analysis. Petitioner's testimonial capacities were in no way implicated; indeed, his participation, except as a donor, was irrelevant to the results of the test, which depend on chemical analysis and on that alone. Since the blood test evidence, although an incriminating product of compulsion, was neither petitioner's testimony nor evidence relating to some communicative act or writing by the petitioner, it was not inadmissible on privilege grounds.

---

noncommunicative in nature as to the person asserting the privilege, even though, as here, such acts are compelled to obtain the testimony of others.

* * *

MR. JUSTICE BLACK with whom MR. JUSTICE DOUGLAS joins, dissenting.

* * * [I]t seems to me that the compulsory extraction of petitioner's blood for analysis so that the person who analyzed it could give evidence to convict him had both a "testimonial" and a "communicative nature." The sole purpose of this project which proved to be successful was to obtain "testimony" from some person to prove that petitioner had alcohol in his blood at the time he was arrested. And the purpose of the project was certainly "communicative" in that the analysis of the blood was to supply information to enable a witness to communicate to the court and jury that petitioner was more or less drunk.

* * *

[The concurring opinion of JUSTICES HARLAN and STEWART and the dissenting opinions of CHIEF JUSTICE WARREN and JUSTICE FORTAS are omitted.]

NOTE ON TESTIMONIAL VS. NON-TESTIMONIAL EVIDENCE

The holding of *Schmerber* has been reaffirmed and applied several times. One year after that decision, the Court held that requiring a suspect to participate in a police line-up did not violate the Fifth Amendment. In United States v. Wade, 388 U.S. 218 (1967), the defendant was arrested for robbing a bank. He was forced to stand in a line-up with several other prisoners, each of whom wore strips of tape on their faces, as had the actual robber. In addition, the defendant, for identification purposes, was required to utter the words allegedly spoken by the robber. The Court held:

> We have no doubt that compelling the accused merely to exhibit his person for observation by a prosecution witness prior to trial involves no compulsion of the accused to give evidence having testimonial significance. It is compulsion of the accused to exhibit his physical characteristics, not compulsion to disclose any knowledge he might have. It is no different from compelling Schmerber to provide a blood sample * * *. [C]ompelling Wade to speak within hearing distance of the witnesses, even to utter words purportedly uttered by the robber, was not compulsion to utter statements of a "testimonial" nature; he was required to use his voice as an identifying physical characteristic, not to speak his guilt.

Justice Black again dissented on the Fifth Amendment issue, because requiring a suspect to stand in a line-up and speak certain words is "forcing [that] person to supply proof of his own crime."

Justice Fortas filed a separate opinion challenging the constitutionality of forcing a suspect to speak in the line-up.

> *Schmerber,* which authorized the forced extraction of blood from the veins of an unwilling human being, did not compel the person actively to cooperate—to accuse himself by a volitional act which differs only in degree from compelling him to act out the crime, which, I assume, would be rebuffed by the Court. It is the latter feature which places the compelled utterance by the accused squarely within the history and noble purpose of the Fifth Amendment's commandment.

What other physical characteristics are exempt from Fifth Amendment protection? In Gilbert v. California, 388 U.S. 263 (1967), a companion case to *Wade,* the Court held that handwriting exemplars may be compelled from an unwilling defendant. In United States v. Dionisio, 410 U.S. 1 (1973), the same rule was applied to voice-prints. While one's voice and handwriting are means of communication, the Court's view is that the sample itself, in contrast to the content of the communication, is merely an identifying physical characteristic—outside the protection of the Fifth Amendment because it is not the kind of evidence that a witness would provide.

Of course, another view of voice and handwriting exemplars is that the suspect is saying "this is my real voice and handwriting." If, in fact, the suspect attempts to distort the exemplar, this may be considered as evidence of guilt. Viewed in this light, do the cases make sense? Note that your answer may depend upon the policy arguments that you accept as a valid basis for the privilege.

Is evidence about a tattoo testimonial? In United States v. Greer, 631 F.3d 608 (2d Cir. 2011), a police officer testified about Greer's physical appearance when he was arrested for being a felon in possession of a firearm. The officer testified that Greer had a tattoo that said "Tangela." That evidence was used to tie him to the car owned by a Tangela Hudson in which the gun was found. The defendant argued that the testimony regarding his tattoo violated his right against compelled self-incrimination. The government argued that the tattoo was not testimonial, but the court disagreed. It stated that in the context of the case, the tattoo was more than just a physical feature: the government relied on the tattoo not simply as an identifying physical characteristic, but rather for its expressive content, i.e., "I know Tangela." However, the court found no Fifth Amendment violation because, although the tattoo, in context, was testimonial, that testimony was not compelled by the government. The detective merely viewed the tattoo on Greer's arm after his arrest. The court concluded that the "voluntary tattooing of an incriminating word to Greer's arm was * * * not the product of government compulsion. In the absence of compulsion, Greer's Fifth Amendment claim fails."

Suppose an officer searches the defendant and finds a cellphone. Assume the cellphone contains evidence but the only way the information can be obtained is to have the defendant use his fingerprint to unlock the phone. Would it violate the Fifth Amendment for the court to order the defendant to press his thumb to the phone? Is this just physical evidence, like the voice identification in *Dionisio?* The answer given by courts so far is that the compelled unlocking of a phone by biometric means—fingerprints, facial recognition, etc.—does not trigger Fifth Amendment protections but that compelling a suspect to enter a passcode might, Whether the Fifth Amendment *prevents* the compulsion of the testimony is a different question, however, one that will be discussed in the section on acts of production, infra.

Testimonial Evidence and the Cruel Trilemma: Pennsylvania v. Muniz

The Court in Pennsylvania v. Muniz, 496 U.S. 582 (1990), finally articulated a rationale for understanding the *Schmerber* line of cases. It held that the line between testimonial and non-testimonial evidence must be determined by whether the witness faces the "cruel trilemma" in disclosing the evidence. Muniz was pulled over on suspicion of drunk driving. After he failed sobriety tests, police officers placed Muniz under arrest and transported him to a booking center. There, they asked Muniz, among other things, the date of his sixth birthday. The officers did not give Muniz *Miranda* warnings. Muniz responded with slurred speech, stumbled over his answers, and said that he did not know the date of his sixth birthday. Both the manner of speech and the content of Muniz's answers were used at trial as evidence that he was under the influence of alcohol. The Court assumed that Muniz was subjected to custodial interrogation without warnings, so the issue in dispute was whether the evidence compelled from him was *testimonial* and therefore protected by the Fifth Amendment.

Writing for eight members of the Court, Justice Brennan concluded that evidence relating to the slurred nature of Muniz's speech was not testimonial under *Schmerber* and its progeny because its relevance was divorced from the content of the words themselves. The Court stated that "[r]equiring a suspect to reveal the physical manner in which he articulates words, like requiring him to reveal the physical properties of the sound produced by his voice * * * does not, without more, compel him to provide a 'testimonial' response for purposes of the privilege." Only Justice Marshall dissented on this point.

The Court did not decide whether a performance on a sobriety test (e.g., standing on one leg for thirty seconds and counting) is testimonial because Muniz did not challenge the lower court's finding that it is not. The Court noted, however, that many lower courts have held that these tests measure physical capacity such as reflex, dexterity, and balance, and consequently do not compel testimony under *Schmerber.* See People v. Hager, 69 N.Y.2d 141, 512 N.Y.S.2d 794, 505 N.E.2d 237 (1987) ("physical performance tests do not reveal a person's subjective knowledge or thought processes but, rather, exhibit a person's degree of physical coordination.").

With respect to the answer to the sixth birthday question, Justice Brennan, writing on this point for five members of the Court, held that Muniz's response *was* testimonial, and therefore that the use of it as evidence at trial was error. The State argued that an answer to the sixth birthday question did not trigger Fifth Amendment protection because the only evidence derived would concern the physiological functioning of Muniz's brain. Justice Brennan rejected this argument, reasoning "that the 'fact' to be inferred might be said to concern the physical status of Muniz's brain merely describes the way in which the inference is incriminating. The correct question * * * is whether the incriminating inference of mental confusion is drawn from a testimonial act or from physical evidence." Thus, when facts about a person's physical condition are obtained through testimonial evidence, the Fifth Amendment applies. For example, if police had compelled Muniz to answer questions about the alcohol in his blood, his oral responses (e.g., "I am drunk") would be testimonial even though the fact proven would concern his physical condition.

Justice Brennan found that Muniz's answer to the sixth birthday question was protected by the "core meaning" of the self-incrimination clause. He explained as follows:

> Because the privilege was designed primarily to prevent a recurrence of the Inquisition and the Star Chamber * * * it is evident that a suspect is compelled to be a witness against himself at least whenever he must face the modern day analog of the historic trilemma. * * * Whenever a suspect is asked for a response requiring him to communicate an express or implied assertion of fact or belief, the suspect confronts the trilemma of truth, falsity or silence and hence the response (whether based on truth or falsity) contains a testimonial component.

The State argued that Muniz did not face the cruel trilemma in answering the sixth birthday question, because the State was not interested in the actual date of Muniz's sixth birthday. Justice Brennan concluded, however, that Muniz was indeed "confronted with the trilemma." He reasoned as follows:

> By hypothesis, the inherently coercive environment created by the custodial interrogation precluded the option of remaining silent. * * * Muniz was left with the choice of incriminating himself by admitting that he did not then know the date of his sixth birthday, or answering untruthfully by reporting a date that he did not then believe to be accurate (an incorrect guess would be incriminating as well as untruthful). The content of his truthful answer supported an inference that his mental faculties were impaired, because his assertion (he did not know the date of his sixth birthday) was different from the assertion (he knew the date was [correct date]) that the trier of fact

might reasonably have expected a lucid person to provide. Hence, the incriminating inference of impaired mental faculties stemmed, not just from the fact that Muniz slurred his response, but also from a testimonial aspect of that response.

Chief Justice Rehnquist, joined by Justices White, Blackmun, and Stevens, dissented from the Court's holding that the content of Muniz's answer to the sixth birthday question was testimonial. The Chief Justice argued that the question was designed to elicit the physical fact of Muniz's mental coordination. The dissenters reasoned that because the police could extract Schmerber's blood "to determine how much that part of his system had been affected by alcohol," the police could likewise "examine the functioning of Muniz's mental processes for the same purpose."

Express or Implied Assertions of Fact: Doe v. United States

Muniz does not stand for the proposition that *all* compelled oral statements are testimonial. To be testimonial, the communication must be an express or implied assertion of fact that can be true or false: otherwise there is no risk of perjury, and no cruel trilemma (of punishment for truth, falsity, or silence) is presented. For example, in Doe v. United States, 487 U.S. 201 (1988), the Court held that a person's compelled signature on a bank consent form, directing the release of bank records—*assuming* such records existed—was not testimonial because there was no assertion of fact that the records did or did not exist. A simple authorization is not an implied assertion of fact—it cannot be false, and therefore cannot expose the citizen to the truth-falsity-silence trilemma. See In re Grand Jury Subpoena, 826 F.2d 1166 (2d Cir. 1987) ("the directives here * * * do not contain any assertions by appellants regarding the existence of, or control over, foreign bank accounts. They authorize disclosure of records and information only if such accounts exist."). Compare United States v. Davis, 767 F.2d 1025 (2d Cir. 1985) (consent form may be testimonial if there is an implied assertion that bank records actually exist).

Psychological Evaluations

Estelle v. Smith, 451 U.S. 454 (1981), holds that a defendant who is to be interviewed by a government psychiatrist who will testify at sentencing (in this case the death penalty was involved) has a right to be warned that what he says may be used against him in the sentencing proceeding. Writing for the Court, Chief Justice Burger held that the psychiatrist's assessment was made on the basis of testimonial communications, not merely upon physical actions and demeanor. The Court found that the doctor based his testimony, at least in part, on the defendant's statements about the crime and omissions from his statements. Three Justices concurred in the judgment on right to counsel grounds.

Drawing an Adverse Inference for Refusing to Produce Non-Testimonial Evidence

When a suspect refuses to supply physical evidence or to participate in a line-up, what sanctions are available to the state? One possibility is an action for contempt. Contempt, while compulsion, is permissible because the suspect has no constitutional right to refuse production of non-testimonial evidence.

Another possibility is that an adverse inference could be drawn against the person who refuses to supply non-testimonial evidence. Justice O'Connor wrote for seven members of the Court in South Dakota v. Neville, 459 U.S. 553 (1983), and explained why an adverse inference could be drawn. Neville was stopped for drunken driving and was asked to submit to a blood-alcohol test. He refused, saying he was too drunk to pass the test. The state courts suppressed evidence of the refusal on self-incrimination grounds, but the Supreme Court reversed. It reasoned as follows: *Schmerber* authorized a state to force a person to take such a test; South Dakota, therefore, had the power to administer a test to Neville *without* his consent;[5] the state could therefore impose a qualification on Neville's refusal—use of his refusal to take the test as evidence against him at trial. Nor was the officer required to inform Neville that his refusal might be used as evidence against him. The Court found no "implicit promise to forego use of evidence that would unfairly 'trick' " a person.

2. Documents and Other Information Existing Before Compulsion

In Boyd v. United States, 116 U.S. 616 (1886), the Court held that a subpoena of one's private books and papers violates the Fifth Amendment, when the *content* of those papers are incriminating. In *Fisher*, supra, the Court found that the privilege cannot be asserted to prevent the government from obtaining evidence from third parties. The rationale was that the incriminated person has not been *compelled* to do anything when the evidence is gathered from third parties. The same rationale served as a basis for the holding in Andresen v. Maryland, 427 U.S. 463 (1976) (discussed in the previous chapter), that the use at trial of the defendant's business records, seized pursuant to a valid warrant, did not violate the Fifth Amendment. The Court explained:

> [I]n this case, petitioner was not asked to say or to do anything. The records seized contained statements that petitioner had voluntarily committed to writing. The search for and seizure of these

[5] After Birchfield v. North Dakota, 136 S.Ct. 2160 (2016), and Mitchell v. Wisconsin, 139 S.Ct. 2525 (2019), which are discussed in Chapter 2, a warrant is required before compelling a person arrested for driving under the influence to submit to a blood alcohol test unless that person is unconscious or there are other exigent circumstances.

records were conducted by law enforcement personnel. Finally, when these records were introduced at trial, they were authenticated by a handwriting expert, not by petitioner. Any compulsion of petitioner to speak, other than the inherent psychological pressure to respond at trial to unfavorable evidence, was not present.

The rationale of *Fisher* and *Andresen* is inconsistent with the *Boyd* holding that a person may rely on the privilege to resist a formal governmental demand for private papers in existence when the demand is made. If the document was prepared voluntarily and before the demand, then any testimonial content in the document was not compelled. However, as seen in the excerpt from *Fisher* immediately below, in some circumstances a person may refuse to respond to a subpoena if the *act of production itself* is testimonial and tends to incriminate the party producing the documents.

The act of production doctrine is easy to understand. Suppose a grand jury issues a subpoena duces tecum to a suspect that compels her "to appear before the grand jury on September 1 and to bring with you the gun you used to shoot J. Doe." If the suspect responds to the subpoena by bringing a gun to the grand jury, then she is essentially making the statement "this is the gun I used to shoot J. Doe." The act of producing the gun is the equivalent of an incriminating statement and is as damaging to the suspect as her spoken words.

FISHER V. UNITED STATES

Supreme Court of the United States, 1976.
425 U.S. 391.

* * *

It is also clear that the Fifth Amendment does not independently proscribe the compelled production of every sort of incriminating evidence but applies only when the accused is compelled to make a *testimonial* communication that is incriminating. * * *

A subpoena served on a taxpayer requiring him to produce an accountant's workpapers in his possession without doubt involves substantial compulsion. But it does not compel oral testimony; nor would it ordinarily compel the taxpayer to restate, repeat, or affirm the truth of the contents of the documents sought. Therefore, the Fifth Amendment would not be violated by the fact alone that the papers on their face might incriminate the taxpayer, for the privilege protects a person only against being incriminated by his own compelled testimonial communications.

* * * [T]he preparation of all of the papers sought in these cases was wholly voluntary, and they cannot be said to contain compelled testimonial

evidence, either of the taxpayers or of anyone else.[a] The taxpayer cannot avoid compliance with the subpoena merely by asserting that the item of evidence which he is required to produce contains incriminating writing, whether his own or that of someone else.

The act of producing evidence in response to a subpoena nevertheless has communicative aspects of its own, wholly aside from the contents of the papers produced. Compliance with the subpoena tacitly concedes the existence of the papers demanded and their possession or control by the taxpayer. It also would indicate the taxpayer's belief that the papers are those described in the subpoena. The elements of compulsion are clearly present, but the more difficult issues are whether the tacit averments of the taxpayer are both "testimonial" and "incriminating" for purposes of applying the Fifth Amendment. These questions perhaps do not lend themselves to categorical answers; their resolution may instead depend on the facts and circumstances of particular cases or classes thereof. In light of the records now before us, we are confident that however incriminating the contents of the accountant's workpapers might be, the act of producing them—the only thing which the taxpayer is compelled to do—would not itself involve testimonial self-incrimination.

It is doubtful that implicitly admitting the existence and possession of the papers rises to the level of testimony within the protection of the Fifth Amendment. The papers belong to the accountant, were prepared by him, and are the kind usually prepared by an accountant working on the tax returns of his client. Surely the Government is in no way relying on the "truthtelling" of the taxpayer to prove the existence of or his access to the documents. The existence and location of the papers are a foregone conclusion and the taxpayer adds little or nothing to the sum total of the Government's information by conceding that he in fact has the papers. Under these circumstances by enforcement of the summons no constitutional rights are touched. The question is not of testimony but of surrender.

* * *

As for the possibility that responding to the subpoena would authenticate the workpapers, production would express nothing more than the taxpayer's belief that the papers are those described in the subpoena. The taxpayer would be no more competent to authenticate the accountant's workpapers or reports by producing them than he would be to authenticate them if testifying orally. The taxpayer did not prepare the papers and could

[a] The fact that the documents may have been written by the person asserting the privilege is insufficient to trigger the privilege, and, unless the Government has compelled the subpoenaed person to write the document, the fact that it was written by him is not controlling with respect to the Fifth Amendment issue. Conversations may be seized and introduced in evidence under proper safeguards, if not compelled. In the case of a documentary subpoena the only thing compelled is the act of producing the document and the compelled act is the same as the one performed when a chattel or document not authored by the producer is demanded.

not vouch for their accuracy. The documents would not be admissible in evidence against the taxpayer without authenticating testimony. Without more, responding to the subpoena in the circumstances before us would not appear to represent a substantial threat of self-incrimination.

Whether the Fifth Amendment would shield the taxpayer from producing his own tax records in his possession is a question not involved here; for the papers demanded here are not his "private papers." We do hold that compliance with a summons directing the taxpayer to produce the accountant's documents involved in these cases would involve no incriminating testimony within the protection of the Fifth Amendment.

* * *

Application of the Fisher Analysis: United States v. Doe and the Act of Production

The Court applied *Fisher* in United States v. Doe, 465 U.S. 605 (1984), holding that the owner of several sole proprietorships properly invoked his privilege against self-incrimination in response to grand jury subpoenas for business documents and records. A district judge had found that the act of producing the documents would have required the owner to "admit that the records exist, that they are in his possession, and that they are authentic." Justice Powell's opinion for the Court stated that the privilege did not protect the content of records prepared voluntarily by Doe, because the government did not compel the owner to make incriminating records. Justice Powell recognized, however, that the privilege may be invoked when the *act of producing* documents involves "testimonial self-incrimination." All Justices agreed with him on this point. Justice O'Connor added a one paragraph concurring opinion stating "that the Fifth Amendment provides absolutely no protection for the contents of private papers of any kind." Justice Marshall, joined by Justice Brennan, offered a short opinion, arguing that the Court had not decided whether the content of some private papers might be protected by the privilege.

Private Papers

Fisher and *Doe* dealt with business papers. Does the rationale of those cases apply to private papers as well? For example, can the government compel a criminal defendant to turn over a diary in which the defendant has written an account of how he committed the crime? In such a case, the act of production itself is not incriminating, because by production the defendant is simply admitting that the diary exists, that he has it, and that it's the document the government demanded. The existence of a diary is not an incriminating fact; having custody of your own diary is not incriminating; and so long as the government can prove that the authenticity of the diary in some way other than the act of production (e.g., by testimony of someone familiar with the defendant's handwriting), the defendant's act of production itself is not incriminating. The only thing incriminating is the voluntarily prepared content of the diary.

Most courts have agreed with Justice O'Connor's concurring opinion in *Doe*, that the contents of voluntarily prepared documents are *never* protected by the Fifth Amendment. See In re Grand Jury Proceedings on February 4, 1982, 759 F.2d 1418 (9th Cir. 1985) (no distinction between business and personal records); In re Grand Jury Subpoena Duces Tecum, 1 F.3d 87 (2d Cir. 1993) ("Self-incrimination analysis now focuses on whether the creation of the thing demanded was compelled and, if not, whether the act of producing it would constitute compelled testimonial communication."). Other courts still draw a business/personal distinction, and hold that the contents of personal records are protected; this position obviously creates problems in determining which records are business and which are personal. United States v. Stone, 976 F.2d 909 (4th Cir. 1992) (affirming a lower court finding, after a hearing, that beach house utility records were business-related and not personal). Given the rationale of *Fisher* and *Doe*, how can one validly distinguish between voluntarily prepared business records and voluntarily prepared personal records?

When Is the Act of Production Incriminating?

In *Fisher*, the Court found that the *act of producing* documents is testimonial, independent of the content of the documents. By producing documents in response to a subpoena, the individual admits that the documents exist; that he has custody of the documents; and that the documents are those described in the subpoena. This last admission is pertinent to *authenticating* the documents. If the documents are to be admitted at a trial, the government would have to establish that they are authentic, meaning that the documents are what the government says they are, e.g., the defendant's diary and not a forgery. See Federal Rule of Evidence 901. One possible way of proving authenticity is through the defendant's own admission, by way of production in response to a subpoena, that the documents are those demanded by the subpoena—at least where the documents were prepared by him or are familiar to him.

While every production of documents in response to a subpoena admits existence, control, and authenticity, it does not follow that the Fifth Amendment prohibits *every* compelled act of document production. The Fifth Amendment applies only if the compelled testimonial act of production could *incriminate* the person responding to the subpoena. In *Fisher*, the testimonial aspects of the act of production were not incriminating, because existence and control of the documents was a "foregone conclusion"—the defendant's production was unnecessary to prove that the documents existed and he controlled them—and because the defendant was not competent to authenticate the accountant's workpapers. (The *contents* of the documents were incriminating, but the Fifth Amendment provided no protection as to content, because the documents were voluntarily prepared.) In *Doe,* the Court accepted the finding of the District Court that the act of production would have incriminated the taxpayer. So just when is the act of production, independent of the contents of the documents, incriminating?

A simple admission of the mere existence of documents is rarely incriminating. For example, it is not incriminating for a business to have inventory records, so when someone turns them over to the government, a compelled admission of their existence is not protected by the Fifth Amendment. See United States v. Stone, 976 F.2d 909 (4th Cir. 1992) (act of producing utility records for a beach house was not privileged, because there was nothing incriminating about the existence of such records). However, in certain unusual cases the fact that records exist can itself tend to incriminate. Thus, if a corporation has a *second set* of books and records, that fact is incriminating independent of the content of the records. See also United States v. Argomaniz, 925 F.2d 1349 (11th Cir. 1991) (existence of documents would show that taxpayer had income for a year when he claimed not to have any). Similarly admission of existence of a document would be incriminating if a person had previously testified, under oath, that a document did not exist. The act of production of that document would be an admission of perjury.

The producer of documents in response to a subpoena admits not only existence but also that he has custody of the documents. Again, however, it is ordinarily not incriminating to control documents, independent of their content. See United States v. Stone, 976 F.2d 909 (4th Cir. 1992)(act of producing utility records for a beach house was not privileged, because as the owner of the house, it was not incriminating for the defendant to have the utility bills for the house). For example, the fact that a records custodian has control of corporate records is not inherently incriminating. However, in some limited cases the admission of control creates an inference of affiliation with another person or business that itself tends to incriminate. Thus, in In re Sealed Case, 832 F.2d 1268 (D.C. Cir. 1987), a person allegedly involved in the Iran-Contra scandal was served with a subpoena to produce the records of eight foreign companies involved in covert and illegal activity. The court found that by producing the records, thus admitting custody of them, the person would be admitting that he was intimately involved with these corporations—you couldn't possess their records unless you were intimately involved with them. See also Smith v. Richert, 35 F.3d 300 (7th Cir. 1994) (defendant charged with not reporting income could be incriminated by act of production of W-2 forms: "by producing them Smith would have acknowledged having received them, foreclosing any defense of nonwilfulness").

Finally, while admission of authenticity is potentially incriminating, it is sometimes the case that the act of production is insufficient to authenticate the records. In *Fisher,* for example, the Court found that the taxpayer's admission could not be used to authenticate the documents, because they were prepared by the accountant. In such cases, there is no risk of an incriminating admission of authentication.

Even in the limited cases where the act of production would be incriminating, the Fifth Amendment will not apply if existence, control, and authentication are in *Fisher's* words, a "foregone conclusion." This will be the case when the government has substantial independent evidence that the records exist, that the witness controls them, and that the records produced are authentic. For example, existence and control can be shown through other witnesses, when the records have either been prepared by or shown to them. See United States v. Clark, 847 F.2d 1467 (10th Cir. 1988) (existence and control of records that the defendant had once given to his accountant to prepare his tax return is proven by subpoenaing the accountant to testify; existence and control of bank records can be proven through testimony of bank officials). Persons in similar situations can testify that, in their jobs, records such as those subpoenaed exist and they have custody over them. See S.E.C. v. First Jersey Securities, Inc., 843 F.2d 74 (2d Cir. 1988) (possession of parallel documents by other branch managers). Existence and control are often admitted, though perhaps unwittingly, by the witness at some time before the subpoena is served. See United States v. Rue, 819 F.2d 1488 (8th Cir. 1987) (dentist demurs to voluntary inspection on grounds that his records are too voluminous to produce); In re Grand Jury Subpoena Duces Tecum, 1 F.3d 87 (2d Cir. 1993) ("Since Doe produced a copy of the calendar to the SEC and testified about his possession and use of it, its existence and location are foregone conclusions, and his production of the original adds little or nothing to the sum total of the government's information."). Finally, authenticity can be shown in a variety of ways other than through the act of production, such as by handwriting exemplars, testimony by those who prepared the documents, and comparison to similar documents. See In re Grand Jury Subpoena Duces Tecum, 1 F.3d 87 (2d Cir. 1993) (noting that the defendant's "authentication is a foregone conclusion if someone else can verify that the records are in fact what they purport to be"); United States v. Stone, 976 F.2d 909 (4th Cir. 1992) (defendant's authentication of utility records for a beach house was unnecessary to the government's case, because authentication "could easily be obtained from the utilities involved").

The "foregone conclusion" limitation on Fifth Amendment protection has been applied to allow compelled decryption of cellphones and laptops, at least in certain circumstances. Recall that compelling a person to decrypt their phone or laptop by entering a passcode amounts to compelled witnessing. See In re Grand Jury Subpoena Duces Tecum, 670 F.3d 1335 (11th Cir. 2012) (compelling a person to decrypt the contents of a hard drive violated the Fifth Amendment because decryption "would require the use of the contents of Doe's mind"). Fifth Amendment objections in these circumstances may be overcome, however, if authorities have substantial proof, independent of any decryption, that a defendant controls the device in question. See United States v. Apple Macro Computer, 851 F.3d 238 (3d Cir. 2017) (no Fifth Amendment protection where the government has substantial information that the defendant owned the device and knew the access code).

Production of Corporate Documents: Braswell v. United States

Recall that in *Bellis* the Court held that business entities are not entitled to Fifth Amendment protection. But a business entity *itself* cannot be compelled to produce incriminating evidence—except through individual agents of the entity. If the act of production of an entity's documents would be personally incriminating to an agent of the entity, can the agent invoke his personal Fifth Amendment privilege? This was the question in Braswell v. United States, 487 U.S. 99 (1988). Braswell formed two corporations in which he was the sole shareholder. A grand jury issued a subpoena to him—in his capacity as agent—to produce the books and records of the two companies. Braswell invoked his personal privilege against self-incrimination on the ground that the act of production might incriminate him. Chief Justice Rehnquist, writing for the Court, relied on the "collective entity" rule to deny the Fifth Amendment claim. The Chief Justice described that rule as follows:

> The official records and documents of the organization that are held [by the agent] in a representative rather than in a personal capacity cannot be the subject of the personal privilege against self-incrimination, even though production of the papers might tend to incriminate [the agent] personally.

The Chief Justice explained the obligations of a corporate agent:

> The custodian of corporate or entity records holds those documents in a representative rather than a personal capacity * * * and a custodian's assumption of his representative capacity leads to certain obligations, including the duty to produce corporate records on proper demand by the Government. Under those circumstances, the custodian's act of production is not deemed a personal act, but rather an act of the corporation.

Braswell sought support from Curcio v. United States, 354 U.S. 118 (1957), where Curcio was served with a subpoena to testify in his capacity as a secretary-treasurer of a local union. Curcio refused to answer any questions as to the whereabouts of the books and records of the union. The

Court in *Curcio* held that the collective entity rule did not require "the giving of oral testimony by the custodian" where that testimony could incriminate him personally. The Chief Justice distinguished *Curcio* in *Braswell,* stating that a corporate agent assumes the risk of producing *documents* as part of the job, but not the risk of being compelled to give incriminating *oral testimony*.

The Chief Justice reasoned that recognizing a privilege on the part of records custodians would essentially render meaningless the prior cases holding that corporations do not have a Fifth Amendment privilege—corporations engaged in wrongdoing would effectively have a back-door privilege through the personal invocation by the corporate agent.

Although a custodian like Braswell is not permitted to claim the privilege in response to a subpoena for corporate records, the Court recognized that "certain consequences flow from the fact that the custodian's act of production is one in his representative rather than personal capacity." The Court noted that the government had conceded that "it may make no use of the 'individual act' against the individual," which means, "[f]or example, in a criminal prosecution the Government may not introduce into evidence before the jury the fact that the subpoena was served upon and the corporation's documents were delivered by one particular individual, the custodian."

This is not to say, however, that the government may not use the act of production as evidence; the *corporation's* act of production may be used as evidence against the custodian. The jury cannot be told that the individual defendant produced the records as a corporate agent, but it can be told that the corporation produced the records. The *Braswell* Court concluded that "the jury may draw from the corporation's act of production the conclusion that the records in question are authentic corporate records, which the corporation possessed, and which it produced in response to the subpoena, and if the defendant held a prominent position within the corporation that produced the records, the jury may, just as it would had someone else produced the documents, reasonably infer that he had possession of the documents or knowledge of their contents."

As a result of the limits on the use of the corporate agent's act of production, the Court concluded that Braswell was not incriminated by the fact of personal production, only by the fact of corporate production. The Court left open "the question whether the agency rationale supports compelling a custodian to produce corporate records when the custodian is able to establish, by showing for example that he is the sole employee and officer of the corporation, that the jury would inevitably conclude that he produced the records."

Justice Kennedy, joined by Justices Brennan, Marshall, and Scalia, dissented and argued that "[t]he Court today denies an individual his Fifth

Amendment privilege against self-incrimination in order to vindicate the rule that a collective entity which employs him has no privilege itself." He concluded that the majority's approach to the privilege—i.e., holding that it did not apply to a corporate custodian but that the custodian's act of production could not be used as evidence—"avoided and manipulated" basic Fifth Amendment principles. He asserted that the only way to obtain corporate documents from an agent whose act of production would be personally incriminating was to grant use immunity to the agent.

The Difference Between a Corporate Agent's Compelled Oral Testimony and Compelled Document Production

In *Curcio,* the Court held that the corporate agent had a privilege to refuse to testify on the whereabouts of corporate documents. But in *Braswell,* the Court held that the agent had no privilege to refuse their production. What is the difference between a corporate agent's compelled oral testimony and compelled document production? Judge Kravitch proffered this explanation in In re Grand Jury Subpoena Dated April 9, 1996 v. Smith, 87 F.3d 1198 (11th Cir. 1996):

> In drawing a line between acts of production and oral testimony, the Court appears to have relied on one fact that distinguishes these two types of testimony: the corporation owns the documents. In contrast, to the extent that one's thoughts and statements can be said to "belong" to anyone, they belong to the witness herself. A custodian has no personal right to retain corporate books. Because the documents belong to the corporation, the state may exercise its right to review the records. For Fifth Amendment analysis, oral statements are different. The government has no right to compel a person to speak the contents of her mind when doing so would incriminate that person.

The corporate agent in *Grand Jury Subpoena* did not refuse to produce corporate documents. Rather, she claimed not to possess them, and refused to testify as to their location. The court stated that this case was controlled by *Curcio,* because the government was demanding oral testimony, and the answer could have personally incriminated the defendant (the answer probably being, "I destroyed them, that's where they are"). Accordingly, the subpoena demanding oral testimony was quashed.

Production of a Person in Response to a Court Order: Baltimore City Dept. of Social Services v. Bouknight

In Baltimore City Dept. of Social Services v. Bouknight, 493 U.S. 549 (1990), the Court relied in part upon the collective entity rule to find the Fifth Amendment inapplicable to an act of production of a *child.* Suspecting child abuse, the Department of Social Services obtained a court order removing Maurice Bouknight from his mother's control. The Department obtained a further order declaring Maurice to be a "child in need of assistance" under Maryland law. That court order gave the Department jurisdiction over Maurice. Maurice was returned to his mother, but only under conditions imposed by a protective order. Ms. Bouknight did not comply with those conditions, and the Juvenile Court granted the Department's petition again to remove Maurice from his mother's control. Ms. Bouknight failed to produce Maurice, and Department officials feared that he might be dead. The case was referred to the police homicide division. The Juvenile Court directed that Ms. Bouknight be held in contempt for failing to produce Maurice. That court rejected her argument that the Fifth Amendment protected her from any incrimination that might result from the act of producing Maurice.

Justice O'Connor wrote the majority opinion for the Supreme Court. She assumed, without deciding, that Bouknight's act of producing Maurice could be potentially incriminating, as an "implicit communication of control over Maurice at the moment of production." However, Justice O'Connor concluded that Bouknight could not invoke the privilege "because she has assumed custodial duties related to production and because production is required as part of a noncriminal regulatory regime." Justice O'Connor found an analogy to *Braswell.* She argued that by "accepting care of Maurice subject to the custodial order's conditions," Bouknight accepted the consequent obligations of production.

Justice Marshall, joined by Justice Brennan, dissented. He rejected the analogy to the collective entity rule and *Braswell.* He reasoned that Bouknight "is not the agent for an artificial entity that possesses no Fifth Amendment privilege. Her role as Maurice's parent is very different from the role of a corporate custodian who is merely the instrumentality through whom the corporation acts."

Bouknight continued to refuse to disclose Maurice's location after the Court ruled against her. She remained in jail for contempt of court until 1995, when a Maryland judge determined that extending her confinement was futile.

3. Required Records

Even if documents are prepared under compulsion, their contents as well as the act of production will be unprotected by the Fifth Amendment if the *government requires the documents to be kept for a legitimate administrative purpose* that is not focused solely on those inherently suspected of criminal activity. This principle is embodied in the "required records" exception to the Fifth Amendment. Under the exception, the government can require records to be kept; it can punish those who do not keep the records; it can punish those who keep false records; and it can punish those who truthfully admit criminal activity in the compelled records. The justification is that the state has legitimate administrative functions that would be impaired by a strict application of the Fifth Amendment, because any citizen could simply refuse to comply with the recordkeeping requirement by claiming that keeping the records would tend to incriminate them.

In Shapiro v. United States, 335 U.S. 1 (1948), a 5–4 decision, Chief Justice Vinson wrote for the Court as it held that the compelled production of defendant's customary business records, which were required to be kept under the Emergency Price Control Act, did not implicate the Fifth Amendment:

> It may be assumed at the outset that there are limits which the Government cannot constitutionally exceed in requiring the keeping of records which may be inspected by an administrative agency and may be used in prosecuting statutory violations committed by the record-keeper himself. But no serious misgiving that those bounds have been overstepped would appear to be evoked when there is a sufficient relation between the activity sought to be regulated and the public concern so that the Government can constitutionally regulate or forbid the basic activity concerned, and can constitutionally require the keeping of particular records, subject to inspection by the Administrator. It is not questioned here that Congress has constitutional authority to prescribe commodity prices as a war emergency measure, and that the licensing and record-keeping requirements of the Price Control Act represent a legitimate exercise of that power. * * *

In a dissenting opinion, Justice Frankfurter expressed concern about the scope of the required records exception. He suggested that the government might use the exception to set up a recordkeeping scheme as a device to force criminal targets to incriminate themselves.

Limitations on the Required Records Exception

The majority opinion in *Shapiro* refers to "limits which the Government cannot constitutionally exceed" in requiring that records be kept or produced for inspection. What are those limits? In 1968, the Court decided several cases in which the scope of the required records doctrine was an issue. Marchetti v. United States, 390 U.S. 39 (1968), involved a defendant who had been convicted for willfully failing to register and to pay an occupational tax for engaging in the business of accepting unlawful gambling wagers. Marchetti claimed that he failed to register and pay because to do so would provide an incriminating admission that he was involved in illegal gambling. While acknowledging Congress's authority to tax unlawful activities, the Court reversed the convictions, stating that "those who properly assert the constitutional privilege as to these provisions may not be criminally punished for failure to comply with their requirements."

Justice Harlan, writing for the Court in *Marchetti*, distinguished *Shapiro* and explained why the required records doctrine did not apply:

> Each of the three principal elements of the [required records] doctrine, as it is described in *Shapiro*, is absent from this situation. First, petitioner Marchetti was not, by the provisions now at issue, obliged to keep and preserve records "of the same kind as he has customarily kept"; he was required simply to provide information, unrelated to any records which he may have maintained, about his wagering activities. This requirement is not significantly different from a demand that he provide oral testimony. Second, whatever "public aspects" there were to the records at issue in *Shapiro*, there are none to the information demanded from Marchetti. The Government's anxiety to obtain information known to a private individual does not without more render that information public; if it did, no room would remain for the application of the constitutional privilege. * * * Third, the requirements at issue in *Shapiro* were imposed in "an essentially non-criminal and regulatory area of inquiry" while those here are directed to a "selective group inherently suspect of criminal activities."

In Haynes v. United States, 390 U.S. 85 (1968), decided the same day as *Marchetti*, the Court reversed a conviction for failing to register a sawed-off shotgun as required by the National Firearms Act. Other sections of the Act provided that possession of a sawed-off shotgun was itself a criminal offense. The reversal was grounded on a finding that the registration statute created real and appreciable hazards of incrimination, because it was "directed principally at those persons who * * * are immediately threatened by criminal prosecution" under other sections of the Act.

How does one distinguish between legislation that has a noncriminal or regulatory purpose, such as the production of tax revenue, and one that is essentially targeted at criminals? If both require self-reporting that may be incriminating, what is the basis for differential application of the Fifth Amendment? See, e.g., In re Grand Jury Proceedings, 707 F.3d 1262 (11th Cir. 2013) (provisions of Bank Secrecy Act requiring person to keep and produce records concerning foreign bank accounts were within the required records exception: "That a statute relates both to criminal law and to civil regulatory matters does not strip the statute of its status as essentially regulatory * * * There is nothing inherently illegal about having or being a beneficiary of an offshore foreign banking account."). Is this a question similar to the one we discussed in Chapter Two, where courts were determining whether a search program was intended to promote "special needs" beyond ordinary criminal law enforcement? As you ponder these questions, ask yourself whether and how Congress might be able to modify the legislation at issue in *Haynes* in order to allow for the collection of information on sawed-off shotguns while still respecting the Fifth Amendment. Suppose, for example, that Congress required registration of sawed-off shotguns but provided that the information and fruits thereof could not be used in criminal proceedings against the person who registers the weapon (a form of *Kastigar* immunity discussed infra). If possession of these weapons is illegal, then the government could obtain a court order akin to civil forfeiture to seize the weapons, since that would be a permissible use of compelled information. Alternatively, what if Congress passed a bill requiring that all shotgun owners register their weapons?

Compelled Reporting of an Accident: California v. Byers

In California v. Byers, 402 U.S. 424 (1971), the constitutionality of California's "hit and run" statute was in issue. Byers was convicted of a misdemeanor for failing to stop at the scene of an accident and to leave his name and address. The Court found that the statute was valid under the required records exception—so the defendant could be convicted for failing to report, and his incriminatory statements could be used against him if he did report. In a plurality opinion, Chief Justice Burger stressed that the statutory scheme was essentially regulatory and noncriminal; it was directed to the motoring public at large, rather than to "a highly selective group inherently suspect of criminal activities;" and self-reporting was indispensable to fulfillment of its purposes. Even if incrimination was a danger, Chief Justice Burger argued, the Fifth Amendment was not implicated. The act of stopping at the scene of an accident was no more "testimonial" than standing in a line-up, and disclosure of identity "is an essentially neutral act." It would be an extravagant extension of the Fifth Amendment, the Chief Justice concluded, to hold that there is a constitutional right "to flee the scene of an accident in order to avoid the possibility of legal involvement."

Justice Harlan, in his opinion concurring in the result in *Byers,* disagreed with the Chief Justice's analysis. Like the four dissenting Justices, Justice Harlan was willing to call the information sought by the statute testimonial and to recognize it as potentially incriminating. But he argued that the state had legitimate regulatory interests in controlling dangerous driving.

Is the Target Group Inherently Suspect?

In Baltimore City Dept. of Social Services v. Bouknight, discussed supra, the Court relied in part upon the required records exception to find the Fifth Amendment inapplicable to an act of production of a child who was feared dead. The mother, upon whom the order to produce the child was served, claimed that the Fifth Amendment protected her from the incriminating aspects of the act of production. The Court held that the collective entity rule and the required records exception each applied, so that the mother was not protected from incrimination.

With regard to the required records exception, Justice O'Connor, writing for the majority, relied heavily on *Shapiro* and *Byers*. As in those cases, the State's demand for information was imposed in an "essentially non-criminal and regulatory area of inquiry" and was not "directed to a selective group inherently suspect of criminal activities." Justice O'Connor reasoned that the State's efforts to gain access to "children in need of assistance" did not focus solely on criminal conduct, and were motivated by the proper regulatory purpose of concern for the child's safety and welfare.

Justice Marshall, joined by Justice Brennan, dissented. He rejected the analogy to the required records exception. He noted that the State's scheme was "narrowly targeted at parents who through abuse or neglect deny their children the minimal reasonable level of care and attention," and argued that the State's goal of protecting children from abuse "inevitably intersects" with criminal provisions that serve the same goal.

In Bionic Auto Parts and Sales, Inc. v. Fahner, 721 F.2d 1072 (7th Cir. 1983), the court held that the privilege against self-incrimination barred a state from enforcing a regulation requiring a record of any serial number or identifying mark that was removed from an auto or an auto part. It said that "[a]lthough there is a fine line between a regulatory purpose and the specific effort to root out criminal activity, we are hard pressed to articulate a regulatory rationale for the record-keeping requirement in question." The recordkeeping scheme was directly solely at autos and parts that are likely to be stolen. Compare that same court's decision in United States v. Lehman, 887 F.2d 1328 (7th Cir. 1989), which held that a statute requiring buyers and sellers of livestock to keep records was within the required records exception. The court stated that "there is nothing ordinarily criminally suspect in buying and selling livestock." See also United States v. Garcia-Cordero, 610 F.3d 613 (11th Cir. 2010) (statute requiring that anyone transporting aliens must present them to immigration officials upon arrival was valid under the required records exception: "The 'bring and present' requirement is part of the federal regulatory scheme through which the government controls our national borders. * * * The statute imposes the bring and present requirement on all who transport aliens to this country—not just those who do so illegally.").

18 U.S.C. § 922(e) makes it a crime to knowingly fail to provide written notice to an airline before transporting firearms. Does a defendant who fails to comply have a Fifth Amendment defense? Courts have held that the statute is within the required records exception, as a legitimate exercise of regulatory activity. Therefore there is no privilege to refuse to

comply, even if the report would be incriminating. See, e.g., United States v. Alkhafaji, 754 F.2d 641 (6th Cir. 1985). The courts rely on the fact that transporting firearms on an airline is not always illegal, and therefore the statute does not focus on a group inherently suspected of criminal activity. Moreover there is a legitimate regulatory interest in knowing that firearms are being transported.

For a general approach to required records, see Saltzburg, The Required Records Doctrine: Its Lessons for the Privilege Against Self-Incrimination, 53 U.Chi.L.Rev. 6 (1986). See also Rajah v. Mukasey, 544 F.3d 427 (2d Cir. 2008) (Fifth Amendment did not protect aliens from having to file information concerning their immigration status as part of a special call-in registration program: "Just as a taxpayer's W-2 forms are required records not subject to the Fifth Amendment because they are a mandatory part of a civil regulatory regime, so too are the passports and [disclosure forms] in the current case.").

F. PROCEDURAL ASPECTS OF SELF-INCRIMINATION CLAIMS

1. Determining the Risk of Incrimination

If a criminal defendant decides not to take the stand, there is no need for the court to decide whether this exercise of the privilege is valid, for it clearly is. But when the privilege is invoked by someone who is *testifying* at a proceeding or otherwise producing information to the government, it must be decided whether the person, by answering a particular question, would subject herself to the risk of incrimination within the meaning of the Fifth Amendment. The risk of incrimination must of course be assessed without compelling the person to divulge the information that is claimed to be protected by the privilege. Thus, the task of determining the risk of incrimination is both delicate and murky—and in most cases the claim is sustained. The Supreme Court has stated that the risk of incrimination is determined by whether it is

> *perfectly clear,* from a careful consideration of all the circumstances in the case, that the witness is mistaken, and that the answers *cannot possibly* have such tendency to incriminate.

Hoffman v. United States, 341 U.S. 479, 488 (1951). The Court in *Hoffman* detailed the standards for determining whether testimony could tend to incriminate a witness within the meaning of the Fifth Amendment:

> If a person cannot possibly be prosecuted in the future—e.g., a complete pardon has been issued, double jeopardy clearly bars future prosecution, or immunity [as discussed infra] has been granted—then the privilege cannot be relied upon. [The privilege] extends to answers that would in themselves support a conviction * * * but likewise

> embraces those which would furnish a link in the chain of evidence needed to prosecute * * *. [I]f the witness, upon interposing his claim, were required to prove the hazard * * * he would be compelled to surrender the very protection which the privilege is designed to guarantee. To sustain the privilege, it need only be evident from the implications of the question, in the setting in which it is asked, that a responsive answer to the question or an explanation of why it cannot be answered might be dangerous because injurious disclosure could result.

See also Malloy v. Hogan, 378 U.S. 1 (1964) (even after Malloy was convicted and served a prison sentence for gambling activities, he could not be compelled to identify his associates in those activities, because disclosure of these names "might furnish a link in a chain of evidence sufficient to connect the petitioner with a more recent crime for which he might still be prosecuted"); Kastigar v. United States, 406 U.S. 441 (1972) (Fifth Amendment protects against compelled disclosures "that the witness reasonably believes could be used in a criminal prosecution or could lead to other evidence that might be so used.").

In sum, the threshold for "tendency" to incriminate is not high, and as a practical matter in most cases, it is self-executing. If a person says that providing the information will tend to incriminate him, or might lead to evidence that would do so, it is an unusual case in which a court will disagree and compel that person to testify. But as the following case illustrates, there are indeed some unusual situations in which a statement's tendency to incriminate is extremely doubtful.

Compelled Self-Identification and the Tendency to Incriminate

HIIBEL V. SIXTH JUDICIAL DISTRICT COURT OF NEVADA, HUMBOLDT COUNTY

Supreme Court of the United States, 2004.
542 U.S. 177.

JUSTICE KENNEDY delivered the opinion of the Court.

[The defendant was convicted for refusing to give his name to a police officer during a lawful *Terry* stop. The Court first holds that Hiibel's Fourth Amendment rights were not violated because officers are permitted to determine the suspect's identity during the course of a lawful *Terry* stop.]

Petitioner further contends that his conviction violates the Fifth Amendment's prohibition on compelled self-incrimination. * * *

In this case petitioner's refusal to disclose his name was not based on any articulated real and appreciable fear that his name would be used to incriminate him, or that it "would furnish a link in the chain of evidence needed to prosecute" him. Hoffman v. United States, 341 U.S. 479, 486 (1951). As best we can tell, petitioner refused to identify himself only because he thought his name was none of the officer's business. Even today, petitioner does not explain how the disclosure of his name could have been used against him in a criminal case. While we recognize petitioner's strong belief that he should not have to disclose his identity, the Fifth Amendment does not override the Nevada Legislature's judgment to the contrary absent a reasonable belief that the disclosure would tend to incriminate him.

The narrow scope of the disclosure requirement is also important. One's identity is, by definition, unique; yet it is, in another sense, a universal characteristic. Answering a request to disclose a name is likely to be so insignificant in the scheme of things as to be incriminating only in unusual circumstances. In every criminal case, it is known and must be known who has been arrested and who is being tried. Even witnesses who plan to invoke the Fifth Amendment privilege answer when their names are called to take the stand. Still, a case may arise where there is a substantial allegation that furnishing identity at the time of a stop would have given the police a link in the chain of evidence needed to convict the individual of a separate offense. In that case, the court can then consider whether the privilege applies, and, if the Fifth Amendment has been violated, what remedy must follow. We need not resolve those questions here.

JUSTICE STEVENS, dissenting.

* * * A name can provide the key to a broad array of information about the person, particularly in the hands of a police officer with access to a range of law enforcement databases. And that information, in turn, can be tremendously useful in a criminal prosecution. * * *

[The dissenting opinion of JUSTICE BREYER, joined by JUSTICES SOUTER and GINSBURG, is omitted.]

The Risk of Incrimination and Denial of Guilt: Ohio v. Reiner

Can a witness invoke the Fifth Amendment privilege if she denies guilt of any crime? This question was faced by the Court in Ohio v. Reiner, 532 U.S. 17 (2001) (per curiam). Reiner was charged with involuntary manslaughter in connection with the death of his infant son. He blamed it on the babysitter. The babysitter refused to testify, claiming a Fifth Amendment privilege. She was granted immunity, then testified as a prosecution witness that she had nothing to do with the infant's death or with other injuries to the infant's brother. Reiner was convicted but the state court reversed on the ground that the babysitter should not have been granted immunity. In the state court's view, the babysitter's testimony "did not incriminate her, because she denied any involvement in the abuse. Thus, she did not have a valid Fifth Amendment privilege."

The Supreme Court reinstated the conviction; it found that the babysitter faced a risk of self-incrimination even though she denied wrongdoing, and therefore the grant of immunity was not unlawful. The Court reasoned as follows:

> We have held that the privilege's protection extends only to witnesses who have reasonable cause to apprehend danger from a direct answer. That inquiry is for the court; the witness' assertion does not by itself establish the risk of incrimination. A danger of "imaginary and unsubstantial character" will not suffice. But we have never held, as the Supreme Court of Ohio did, that the privilege is unavailable to those who claim innocence. To the contrary, we have emphasized that one of the Fifth Amendment's "basic functions * * * is to protect innocent men * * * who otherwise might be ensnared by ambiguous circumstances." Grunewald v. United States, 353 U.S. 391, 421 (1957). In *Grunewald,* we recognized that truthful responses of an innocent witness, as well as those of a wrongdoer, may provide the government with incriminating evidence from the speaker's own mouth.
>
> The Supreme Court of Ohio's determination that Batt [the babysitter] did not have a valid Fifth Amendment privilege because she denied any involvement in the abuse of the children clearly conflicts with * * * *Grunewald.* Batt had "reasonable cause" to apprehend danger from her answers if questioned at respondent's trial. Batt spent extended periods of time alone with Alex [the infant]. She was with Alex within the potential timeframe of the fatal trauma. The defense's theory of the case was that Batt, not respondent, was responsible for Alex's death and his brother's uncharged injuries. In this setting, it was reasonable for Batt to fear that answers to possible questions might tend to incriminate her. Batt therefore had a valid Fifth Amendment privilege against self-incrimination.

2. Immunity

If a witness is guaranteed that no criminal prosecution having anything to do with statements given to the government will take place, then there is no possibility of incrimination. Thus, a person who receives immunity has no right to refuse to testify and may be punished by imprisonment for contempt for so refusing. A person who receives immunity is not subject to the cruel trilemma of punishment for truth, silence and falsity—because there is no punishment for telling the truth when immunized.

A broad guarantee against future prosecution is called *transactional immunity*, to signify that no transaction about which a witness testifies can be the subject of a future prosecution against the witness. The Federal immunity statute, 18 U.S.C. § 6002, provides for a more limited kind of immunity known as *use and derivative use* (or use-fruits) immunity. That statute provides:

> Whenever a witness refuses, on the basis of his privilege against self-incrimination, to testify or provide other information in a proceeding before or ancillary to [a Federal court, grand jury, agency proceeding, or Congressional proceeding], and the person presiding over the proceeding communicates to the witness an order issued under this part, the witness may not refuse to comply with the order on the basis of his privilege against self-incrimination; but no testimony or other information compelled under the order (or any information directly or indirectly derived from such testimony or other information) may be used against the witness in any criminal case, except a prosecution for perjury, giving a false statement, or otherwise failing to comply with the order.

The Constitutionality of Use Immunity: Kastigar v. United States

At one time, it appeared that the Supreme Court might require transactional immunity (i.e., immunity from prosecution for the acts that are the subject of the compelled testimony) as the cost to the government of forcing a witness to testify. In Counselman v. Hitchcock, 142 U.S. 547 (1892), the Court held that a statute, providing that no "evidence obtained from a party or witness by means of a judicial proceeding * * * shall be given in evidence; or in any matter used against him * * * in any court of the United States," was insufficient to supplant the privilege against self-incrimination.

But, in the landmark case of Kastigar v. United States, 406 U.S. 441 (1972),[6] the Court explained that *Counselman* did not require transactional immunity; what it required was use and "derivative use" or "use-fruits" immunity. The defect in the statute rejected in *Counselman* was that it did not "prevent the use of his testimony to search out other testimony to be used in evidence against him [the immunized witness]." In *Kastigar,* the Court upheld 18 U.S.C.A. § 6002 and stated that use-fruits immunity was "a rational accommodation between the imperatives of the privilege and the legitimate demands of government to compel citizens to testify." The Court concluded that use-fruits immunity "leaves the witness and the

---

[6] Prior to *Kastigar,* the Court had held in Murphy v. Waterfront Comm., 378 U.S. 52 (1964), that a state grant of immunity prevented the federal government from using the compelled testimony or its fruits, and that this protection was sufficient to supplant the Fifth Amendment privilege against self-incrimination. Until *Kastigar,* no one was sure whether the *Murphy* rule applied when the same sovereign granted the immunity and subsequently sought to bring a criminal charge against an immunized witness.

prosecutorial authorities in substantially the same position as if the witness had claimed the Fifth Amendment privilege. The immunity therefore is coextensive with the privilege and suffices to supplant it."

The *Kastigar* Court declared that after immunity is granted and a witness is compelled to testify, the burden is on the government "to prove that the evidence it proposes to use is derived from a legitimate source wholly independent of the compelled testimony."

Justice Marshall dissented in *Kastigar*, arguing that the burden placed on the government was not adequate protection for the witness, "[f]or the paths of information through the investigative bureaucracy may well be long and winding, and even a prosecutor acting in the best of faith cannot be certain that somewhere in the depths of his investigative apparatus, often including hundreds of employees, there was not some prohibited use of the compelled testimony."[7]

Proving That Immunized Testimony Was Not Used

When a witness gives immunized testimony and is later prosecuted, the question of whether the government has used the fruits of the immunized testimony inevitably arises. One way for the government to satisfy its burden of showing that its evidence is not the fruit of immunized testimony is to establish a "Wall of Silence" between the prosecutors exposed to the testimony and the prosecutors who bring the case against the witness. See United States v. Schwimmer, 882 F.2d 22 (2d Cir. 1989) (recommending the "Wall of Silence" approach); U.S. Dep't of Justice, U.S. Attorneys' Manual, § 1–11.–400 (to demonstrate that no use has been made of the compelled testimony, prosecution should be handled by an attorney unfamiliar with its substance). How likely is it that a "Wall of Silence" will be effective? See also United States v. Slough, 641 F.3d 544 (D.C. Cir. 2011) (noting difficulties in determining whether the government evidence is tainted when it only partially overlaps immunized information).

Impeachment, Perjury

The Supreme Court has made clear that once use immunity is granted, the testimony that is extracted from the immunized witness is coerced and cannot be used as evidence against the witness in a subsequent case against the witness, *even for impeachment purposes*. New Jersey v. Portash, 440 U.S. 450 (1979). However, the Court held in United States v.

---

[7] Justice Douglas also dissented. Justices Brennan and Rehnquist did not participate. States may still require transactional immunity as a matter of state constitutional or statutory law. See, e.g., Attorney General v. Colleton, 387 Mass. 790, 444 N.E.2d 915 (1982); N.Y.C.P.L. 190.40. Even though a state gives transactional immunity, the witness can still be prosecuted in a federal court or a court in another state, so long as the testimony and its fruits are not used. United States v. Gallo, 863 F.2d 185 (2d Cir. 1988).

Apfelbaum, 445 U.S. 115 (1980), that an immunized witness has no right to lie, and that evidence of lying under a grant of immunity could be used in a subsequent prosecution for perjury, false statements, or obstruction of justice. Justice Rehnquist, writing for the Court, noted that if a person could not be punished for lying while immunized, an option would be created that would make a mockery of conferring immunity on a witness because the very purpose of granting immunity would be defeated. Justice Brennan and Justice Blackmun, joined by Justice Marshall, concurred in the result. The court in United States v. Veal, 153 F.3d 1233 (11th Cir. 1998), put it this way:

> When an accused has been accorded immunity to preserve his right against self-incrimination, he must choose either to relinquish his Fifth Amendment right and testify truthfully, knowing that his statements cannot be used against him in a subsequent criminal prosecution regarding the matter being investigated, or continue to assert the privilege and suffer the consequences. There is no third option for testifying falsely without incurring potential prosecution for perjury or false statements.

For a discussion of *Apfelbaum* and *Portash,* see Hoffman, The Privilege Against Self-Incrimination and Immunity Statutes: Permissible Uses of Immunized Testimony, 16 Crim.L.Bull. 421 (1980).

Subsequent Statements: Pennsylvania v. Conboy

What happens if a witness testifies pursuant to a grant of immunity, then later makes a statement that is identical to the immunized statement? Can the later statement be used against the witness? Put another way, does a witness who testifies under a grant of immunity have a Fifth Amendment right to refuse to give an identical statement at a later point? In Pillsbury Co. v. Conboy, 459 U.S. 248 (1983), the Court upheld the right of a witness at a deposition in a civil case to claim the privilege against self-incrimination, even though he had previously been granted use immunity in related criminal proceedings. Conboy was a former executive of a company involved in an antitrust case. He testified before a grand jury after receiving use immunity. Subsequently, his grand jury testimony was provided to lawyers in related civil litigation. The lawyers decided to depose Conboy, and at the deposition, they read from the grand jury transcript in the course of asking questions. Conboy invoked his privilege against self-incrimination, but the district court found that the former immunity grant required him to answer and held him in contempt. A majority of the Court concluded that the prior grant of immunity was not sufficient protection to assure Conboy that nothing he said at the deposition could be used against him in later criminal proceedings. The Court held that a new immunity grant would be required before the witness could be forced to answer. Justice Marshall wrote a concurring opinion, and Justices Brennan and Blackmun concurred in the judgment. Justice Stevens, joined by Justice O'Connor, dissented.

3. Invoking the Privilege

The Requirement of Expressly Invoking the Privilege: Garner v. United States, Minnesota v. Murphy and Salinas v. Texas

When a person is compelled by the government to answer questions that might tend to incriminate that person in a subsequent criminal case, the person can refuse to answer and rely on the Fifth Amendment privilege against self-incrimination. However, if the person *does* answer, the privilege will be deemed waived and the answer can be used as evidence. For example, in Garner v. United States, 424 U.S. 648 (1976), the Court held that a taxpayer lost whatever privilege he might have had when he answered questions on a tax return rather than invoking the privilege.

In Minnesota v. Murphy, 465 U.S. 420 (1984), the Court reiterated its view that generally a person who is asked to answer questions must invoke his privilege against self-incrimination or lose its protection. It held that a probationer lost the protection of the privilege when he answered questions of his probation officer concerning crimes for which he had not yet been charged.

In Salinas v. Texas, 570 U.S. 178 (2013), Salinas was being questioned by police officers about a murder. He was not in custody and he did not receive *Miranda* warnings—as discussed later in this Chapter, *Miranda* warnings are required only if the police are engaged in custodial interrogation. Salinas answered a number of questions voluntarily but balked and did not answer when the officer asked whether a ballistics test of shell casings found at the crime scene would match his shotgun. He answered a few other questions when the officer moved on from the ballistics test. At trial, prosecutors argued that Salinas's silence regarding the outcome of a ballistics test constituted an admission of guilt, and the defendant claimed that the use of his silence violated his Fifth Amendment right.

The Supreme Court held that Salinas's Fifth Amendment right was not violated by the use of his silence, but there was no opinion for the Court. Justice Alito wrote an opinion for the plurality, joined by Chief Justice Roberts and Justice Kennedy. Justice Alito relied on Minnesota v. Murphy and other cases to conclude that Salinas could not rely on his Fifth Amendment right at trial because he had not invoked it at the time he was questioned. Justice Alito elaborated as follows:

> Petitioner's Fifth Amendment claim fails because he did not expressly invoke the privilege against self-incrimination in response

to the officer's question. It has long been settled that the privilege "generally is not self-executing" and that a witness who desires its protection "must claim it." Minnesota v. Murphy. Although no ritualistic formula is necessary in order to invoke the privilege, a witness does not do so by simply standing mute.

* * *

The privilege against self-incrimination is an exception to the general principle that the Government has the right to everyone's testimony. To prevent the privilege from shielding information not properly within its scope, we have long held that a witness who "desires the protection of the privilege . . . must claim it" at the time he relies on it. *Murphy*.

That requirement ensures that the Government is put on notice when a witness intends to rely on the privilege so that it may either argue that the testimony sought could not be self-incriminating, or cure any potential self-incrimination through a grant of immunity. The express invocation requirement also gives courts tasked with evaluating a Fifth Amendment claim a contemporaneous record establishing the witness' reasons for refusing to answer. In these ways, insisting that witnesses expressly invoke the privilege assures that the Government obtains all the information to which it is entitled.

Justice Alito noted two recognized exceptions to the invocation requirement: 1) Griffin v. California, supra, holding that a criminal defendant need not take the stand and assert the privilege at his own trial; and 2) "we have held that a witness' failure to invoke the privilege must be excused where governmental coercion makes his forfeiture of the privilege involuntary." For this latter exception, Justice Alito cited *Miranda* and the cases holding that threats to withdraw a government benefit for being silent constitute compulsion, e.g., Lefkowitz v. Turley, supra. Justice Alito concluded that Salinas could not come within the exceptions because the interview was voluntary and he was not in "custody" for purposes of *Miranda*.

Justice Alito rejected Salinas's argument that an invocation requirement was unfair to suspects who are not schooled in the law—and who might think that being silent is the best way to invoke the Fifth Amendment right to silence:

> [P]opular misconceptions notwithstanding, the Fifth Amendment * * * does not establish an unqualified "right to remain silent." A witness' constitutional right to refuse to answer questions depends on his reasons for doing so, and courts need to know those reasons to evaluate the merits of a Fifth Amendment claim.

> In any event, it is settled that forfeiture of the privilege against self-incrimination need not be knowing. Statements against interest are regularly admitted into evidence at criminal trials, see Fed. Rule of Evid. 804(b)(3), and there is no good reason to approach a defendant's silence any differently.

Finally, Justice Alito rejected the argument that an invocation requirement in the context of noncustodial police questioning would be too difficult to apply, because "invocation" might be fuzzy:

> Petitioner and the dissent suggest that our approach will "unleash complicated and persistent litigation" over what a suspect must say to invoke the privilege, but our cases have long required that a witness assert the privilege to subsequently benefit from it. That rule has not proved difficult to apply. * * * Notably, petitioner's approach would produce its own line-drawing problems, as this case vividly illustrates. When the interviewing officer asked petitioner if his shotgun would match the shell casings found at the crime scene, petitioner did not merely remain silent; he made movements that suggested surprise and anxiety. At precisely what point such reactions transform "silence" into expressive conduct would be a difficult and recurring question that our decision allows us to avoid.
>
> * * * Petitioner worries that officers could unduly pressure suspects into talking by telling them that their silence could be used in a future prosecution. But as petitioner himself concedes, police officers have done nothing wrong when they accurately state the law. * * * So long as police do not deprive a witness of the ability to voluntarily invoke the privilege, there is no Fifth Amendment violation.

Justice Thomas, joined by Justice Scalia, concurred in the judgment in *Salinas*, but used a completely different theory to get to the result. Justice Thomas declared that it didn't matter whether Salinas invoked his Fifth Amendment right because even if he had done so, "the prosecutor's comments regarding his precustodial silence did not compel him to give self-incriminating testimony." Justice Thomas repeated the position that he and Justice Scalia had previously taken regarding Griffin v. California, supra, in which the Court held that the Fifth Amendment prohibits a prosecutor or judge from commenting on a defendant's failure to testify. Justice Thomas wrote as follows:

> Salinas argues that we should extend *Griffin's* no-adverse-inference rule to a defendant's silence during a precustodial interview. I have previously explained that the Court's decision in *Griffin* "lacks foundation in the Constitution's text, history, or logic" and should not be extended. I adhere to that view today.

Justice Breyer, joined by Justices Ginsburg, Sotomayor and Kagan, dissented in *Salinas*. He argued that allowing the prosecutor to comment on pre-custodial silence puts the citizen "in an impossible predicament. He must either answer the question or remain silent. If he answers the question, he may well reveal, for example, prejudicial facts, disreputable associates, or suspicious circumstances—even if he is innocent. If he remains silent, the prosecutor may well use that silence to suggest a consciousness of guilt. And if the defendant then takes the witness stand in order to explain either his speech or his silence, the prosecution may introduce, say for impeachment purposes, a prior conviction that the law would otherwise make inadmissible." Justice Breyer concluded that under the circumstances of the police interview, there was "a reasonable inference that Salinas' silence derived from an exercise of his Fifth Amendment rights. * * * The nature of the surroundings, the switch of topic, the particular question—all suggested that the right we have and generally know we have was at issue at the critical moment here. Salinas, not being represented by counsel, would not likely have used the precise words 'Fifth Amendment' to invoke his rights because he would not likely have been aware of technical legal requirements, such as a need to identify the Fifth Amendment by name."

4. Waiver of the Privilege

Voluntary testimony waives the privilege for the simple reason that the person is by definition not being compelled to testify. But there are sometimes difficult questions about the scope of a waiver of the privilege.

Determining the Scope of a Waiver

If a witness elects to testify, has the witness waived the privilege completely? On direct examination, the witness ordinarily can control what she says, but not on cross-examination. The usual rule is that a witness who takes the stand waives the privilege as to any subject matter within the scope of the direct examination. The witness is subject to cross-examination only to the extent necessary to fairly test the statements made upon direct examination and inferences that might be drawn from such statements.

United States v. Hearst, 563 F.2d 1331 (9th Cir. 1977), involved the scope of a waiver in a famous criminal trial. The defendant was charged with bank robbery. She admitted participation, but testified that at the time of the robbery, she was under duress from members of the Symbionese Liberation Army. The court held that by so testifying she waived the privilege with respect to questions on cross-examination concerning a later period in which she allegedly lived with SLA members voluntarily. The court found that the government's questions were "reasonably related" to the subjects covered by the direct testimony. Consequently, it was not error to allow the jury to hear Hearst invoke a privilege against self-incrimination in response to the questions: *Griffin* was not violated because Hearst's invocation of the privilege was invalid.

Hearst unsuccessfully relied on Calloway v. Wainwright, 409 F.2d 59 (5th Cir. 1968), a case in which the defendant testified at trial that his confession was involuntarily obtained. The *Calloway* court held that, by challenging his confession, the defendant had not waived the privilege concerning the substance of the charges against him, and therefore that the prosecutor's reference to Calloway's failure to testify on these matters violated *Griffin*. *Calloway* was not helpful to Hearst because she addressed the merits of the government's case against her.

Waiver of the Privilege at a Guilty Plea Hearing? Mitchell v. United States

The defendant in Mitchell v. United States, 526 U.S. 314 (1999), pleaded guilty to federal charges of conspiring to distribute five or more kilograms of cocaine and of distributing cocaine. But she reserved the right to contest at sentencing the drug quantity attributable to her under the conspiracy count. One of the questions in *Mitchell* was whether the defendant had waived her Fifth Amendment privilege, insofar as sentencing was concerned, by pleading guilty and admitting to "some of" the conduct at her plea colloquy. If so, there would be no constitutional problem in penalizing her silence at sentencing. The Supreme Court, in an opinion by Justice Kennedy, held that Mitchell had not waived her privilege. Justice Kennedy's analysis of the waiver question distinguished a witness who voluntarily testifies about a subject, and therefore waives the privilege so that she can be questioned about the details, from a witness who pleads guilty and "puts nothing in dispute regarding the essentials of the offense." Justice Kennedy observed that the government sought to turn a plea inquiry, which is a shield against an unintelligent or involuntary plea, "into a prosecutorial sword by having the defendant relinquish all rights against compelled self-incrimination upon entry of a guilty plea, including the right to remain silent at sentencing." Justice Kennedy reasoned that since a defendant who pleads guilty is removing facts from dispute, "there is little danger that the court will be misled by selective disclosure."[8]

[8] Justice Scalia, joined by the Chief Justice and Justices O'Connor and Thomas, dissented in *Mitchell*. He agreed, however, with the majority's position that Mitchell could invoke her Fifth Amendment right to silence at the sentencing proceeding. In Justice Scalia's view, while Mitchell could invoke her privilege, there was nothing in the Fifth Amendment to prohibit the sentencing judge from drawing an adverse inference from her silence. This aspect of the decision in *Mitchell* is discussed *supra* in this Chapter.

Defenses Regarding Mental State

In Buchanan v. Kentucky, 483 U.S. 402 (1987), the Court found no Fifth Amendment violation in the use of a psychiatric evaluation of the defendant to rebut a psychiatric defense. Justice Blackmun wrote for the Court and stated that if the defendant presents psychiatric evidence in defense, "then, at the very least, the prosecution may rebut this presentation with evidence from the reports of the examination that the defendant requested." Thus, the Court found a waiver of Fifth Amendment rights in this circumstance. Justice Marshall, joined by Justice Brennan, dissented.

Justice Sotomayor wrote for a unanimous Court in Kansas v. Cheever, 571 U.S. 87 (2013), as it held that the state did not violate the defendant's privilege against self-incrimination when it used evidence from a court-ordered examination to rebut the defendant's presentation of expert testimony to support a voluntary intoxication defense. The defendant was charged with capital murder for shooting a sheriff who had come to a residence to arrest him and others for methamphetamine offenses. The defendant had cooked and smoked methamphetamine prior to the shooting and presented a pharmaceutical expert to testify that his use of the drug had rendered him incapable of premeditation. The prosecution presented testimony in rebuttal from the expert who had examined the defendant at the order of a federal judge when he was facing federal charges arising from the murder. Justice Sotomayor relied on *Buchanan* and reasoned that "[w]hen a defendant presents evidence through a psychological expert who has examined him, the government likewise is permitted to use the only effective means of challenging that evidence: testimony from an expert who has examined him." She concluded that the Kansas Supreme Court had erred in limiting *Buchanan* to cases in which the defendant relies on a mental disease or defect defense and observed that *Buchanan* addressed "mental status" and covered cases like this one regardless of whether the defense is based on a temporary state of mind.

II. CONFESSIONS AND DUE PROCESS

A. INTRODUCTION

The United States Supreme Court has relied on three constitutional provisions in regulating the admissibility of confessions:

(1) From 1936 to the present, the due process clauses of the Fifth and Fourteenth Amendments have been used to exclude *involuntary* confessions.

(2) From 1964 to the present, the Sixth Amendment *right to counsel* has been applied in determining the admissibility of a

confession obtained from a defendant who has been charged with a crime.

(3) From 1966 to the present, the Fifth Amendment's privilege against self-incrimination has been applied to statements made during *custodial interrogation*, unless the suspect, after receiving warnings, makes a knowing and voluntary waiver of the right.

These developments have not been as smooth as this brief description might suggest. The changing nature of claims to exclude confessions and of the Court's approach to them is an important part of the development of constitutionally-based criminal procedure. Thus, it warrants careful attention.

In 1884, the Court reviewed a federal criminal conviction in Hopt v. People of Territory of Utah, 110 U.S. 574.[9] It recognized that there was a common-law rule prohibiting the use of confessions obtained by inducements, promises and threats. The common-law rule was based on the premise that confessions resulting from promises or threats are unreliable—therefore they could not be admitted into evidence. The same desire to prevent erroneous convictions led the Court to cite treatises on evidence and to follow the common-law rule. (There is no indication that the Court was relying on any constitutional language.)

Thirteen years later, in Bram v. United States, 168 U.S. 532 (1897) (suspect in custody of police was stripped, searched, and questioned), the Court abruptly departed from an emphasis on the reliability of confessions, and relied on the self-incrimination clause of the Fifth Amendment to find that statements of an accused, which were introduced to establish his guilt, were made involuntarily and therefore admitting them at trial violated the constitutional prohibition against compelled incrimination. *Bram* was sharply criticized by a number of legal scholars as an erroneous union of the right against self-incrimination and the common-law confessions rule.[10]

The proposition that the Fifth Amendment is the proper basis on which to assess the admissibility of confessions "was not itself developed in subsequent decisions," Miranda v. Arizona, 384 U.S. 436, 506 (1966) (Harlan, J., dissenting). Although it did not overrule *Bram*, for two-thirds of a century the Court never explicitly and exclusively relied on the privilege against self-incrimination to suppress the use of a confession in another federal case. See generally, Developments in the Law: Confessions,

[9] This section on the background of confessions law draws heavily from O. Stephens, The Supreme Court and Confessions of Guilt 19–26 (1973).

[10] See, e.g., 3 J. Wigmore, Evidence § 823 (Chadbourn Rev. 1981). The significance of *Bram* to the Court's development of its *Miranda* law is explored in Saltzburg, *Miranda v. Arizona* Revisited: Constitutional Law or Judicial Fiat, 26 Washburn Law Journal 1–26 (1986).

79 Harv.L.Rev. 935, 959–61 (1966).[11] After *Bram* and until 1964, the Court turned to the Due Process Clause to decide coerced confession cases.

For an argument that the Fifth Amendment privilege against compelled witnessing, rather than the Due Process Clause, is the better source for regulating police-induced confessions, see Godsey, Rethinking the Involuntary Confessions Rule: Toward a Workable Test for Identifying Compelled Self-Incrimination, 93 Calif. L. Rev. 465 (2005).

B. THE DUE PROCESS CASES

The Involuntariness Test: Brown v. Mississippi

The Court made its first important decision on confessions under the Due Process Clause of the Fourteenth Amendment in Brown v. Mississippi, 297 U.S. 278 (1936). The facts surrounding the Brown case indicate why the Supreme Court found it necessary to invoke due process to regulate confessions. The facts below are quoted from the dissenting opinion of Judge Griffith in the Mississippi state court. Judge Griffith dissented from the majority's decision that a confession obtained through torture was admissible because the Fifth Amendment protection against compelled self-incrimination was not applicable to the States:

> The crime with which these defendants, all ignorant negroes, are charged, was discovered about one o'clock p.m. on Friday, March 30, 1934. On that night one Dial, a deputy sheriff, accompanied by others, came to the home of Ellington, one of the defendants, and requested him to accompany them to the house of the deceased, and there a number of white men were gathered, who began to accuse the defendant of the crime. Upon his denial they seized him, and with the participation of the deputy they hanged him by a rope to the limb of a tree, and having let him down, they hung him again, and when he was let down the second time, and he still protested his innocence, he was tied to a tree and whipped, and still declining to accede to the demands that he confess, he was finally released and he returned with some difficulty to his home, suffering intense pain and agony. The record of the testimony shows that the signs of the rope on his neck were plainly visible during the so-called trial. A day or two thereafter the said deputy, accompanied by another, returned to the home of the said defendant and arrested him, and departed with the prisoner towards the jail in an adjoining county, but went by a route which led into the State of Alabama; and while on the way, in that State, the deputy stopped and again severely whipped the defendant, declaring that he

[11] The Court could not rely on *Bram* in reviewing state confession cases until 1964 when the Fifth Amendment's self-incrimination clause was incorporated into the Fourteenth Amendment and thereby made applicable to the states.

would continue the whipping until he confessed, and the defendant then agreed to confess to such a statement as the deputy would dictate, and he did so, after which he was delivered to jail.

The other two defendants, Ed Brown and Henry Shields, were also arrested and taken to the same jail. On Sunday night, April 1, 1934, the same deputy, accompanied by a number of white men, one of whom was also an officer, and by the jailer, came to the jail, and the two last named defendants were made to strip and they were laid over chairs and their backs were cut to pieces with a leather strap with buckles on it, and they were likewise made by the said deputy definitely to understand that the whipping would be continued unless and until they confessed, and not only confessed, but confessed in every matter of detail as demanded by those present; and in this manner the defendants confessed the crime, and as the whippings progressed and were repeated, they changed or adjusted their confession in all particulars of detail so as to conform to the demands of their torturers. When the confessions had been obtained in the exact form and contents as desired by the mob, they left with the parting admonition and warning that, if the defendants changed their story at any time in any respect from that last stated, the perpetrators of the outrage would administer the same or equally effective treatment.

* * *

The defendants were brought to the courthouse of the county on * * * April 5th, and the so-called trial was opened, and was concluded on the next day, April 6, 1934, and resulted in a pretended conviction with death sentences. The evidence upon which the conviction was obtained was the so-called confessions. * * * The defendants were put on the stand, and by their testimony the facts and the details thereof as to the manner by which the confessions were extorted from them were fully developed, and it is further disclosed by the record that the same deputy, Dial, under whose guiding hand and active participation the tortures to coerce the confessions were administered, was actively in the performance of the supposed duties of a court deputy in the courthouse and in the presence of the prisoners during what is denominated, in complimentary terms, the trial of these defendants. This deputy was put on the stand by the state in rebuttal, and admitted the whippings. It is interesting to note that in his testimony with reference to the whipping of the defendant Ellington, and in response to the inquiry as to how severely he was whipped, the deputy stated, "Not too much for a negro; not as much as I would have done if it were left to me." Two others who had participated in these whippings were introduced and admitted it—not a single witness was introduced who denied it.

So the defendants in *Brown* were sentenced to death, within a week of the crime, on the basis of confessions obtained by torture. One would think that if due process is to mean anything, it must mean that it was violated under the facts of *Brown*. And that is how the Supreme Court saw it. The Court declared as follows:

> The rack and torture chamber may not be substituted for the witness stand. The State may not permit an accused to be hurried to conviction under mob domination—where the whole proceeding is but a mask—without supplying corrective process. * * * [The trial] is a mere pretense where the state authorities have contrived a conviction resting solely upon confessions obtained by violence. The due process clause requires that state action, whether through one agency or another, shall be consistent with the fundamental principles of liberty and justice which lie at the base of all our civil and political institutions. It would be difficult to conceive of methods more revolting to the sense of justice than those taken to procure the confessions of these petitioners, and the use of the confessions thus obtained as the basis for conviction and sentence was a clear denial of due process.

The Court decided thirty-five confession cases between *Brown* in 1936 and Massiah v. United States, 377 U.S. 201, in 1964. It struggled in these cases—which involved more subtle and less physical methods of obtaining confessions—to define appropriate constitutional limitations on the interrogation methods used by police. Case-by-difficult-case, the Court attempted to describe the reach of the Due Process Clause, and its role in controlling the methods by which government agents seek confessions.

Pre-Miranda Cases: Circumstances Relevant to Involuntariness

A summary, by no means exhaustive, might convey the breadth of circumstances—with none being dispositive—that the Court considered when it tried to determine the validity of confessions under the Due Process Clause:

- *The personal characteristics of the accused.* The Court was concerned not only with the youthfulness of the suspect, but also with the educational background of the accused in cases such as Payne v. Arkansas, 356 U.S. 560 (1958) (fifth grade education), and Fikes v. Alabama, 352 U.S. 191 (1957) (illiterate). In addition, the Court was sensitive to any mental deficiency of the defendant as illustrated by Culombe v. Connecticut, 367 U.S. 568, 620 (1961) (illiterate mental defective), and Blackburn v. Alabama, 361 U.S. 199, 207 (1960) (strong probability that the accused was insane at the time he allegedly confessed). Conversely, the Court was less likely to find undue coercion if the defendant was well-educated as in Crooker v. California, 357 U.S. 433 (1958) (accused had completed one year of law school), or was a hardened veteran of criminal proceedings as in Stein v. New York, 346 U.S. 156, 185 (1953) (defendants were not "young, soft, ignorant or timid").

- *Physical deprivation or mistreatment.* The Court not only disapproved of severe brutality like that found in *Brown,* supra, but also of the denial of food, *Payne,* supra (accused was given no food for twenty-four hours), or sleep, Ashcraft v. Tennessee, 322 U.S. 143 (1944) (defendant was not permitted to sleep for thirty-six hours). If the accused was permitted certain amenities, the Court responded favorably. In *Crooker,* supra, for instance, the confession was found admissible and the Court pointed out that the defendant was provided with food and was permitted to smoke during interrogations.

- *Psychological pressure.* Use of threats, humiliation, isolation, etc., was accorded great weight by the Court. Although the Court stated that a voluntary statement need not be volunteered, it refused to hold that only physical brutality was impermissible. In Watts v. Indiana, 338 U.S. 49, 53 (1949), the Court said that:

  > if [the confession] is the product of sustained pressure by the police it does not issue from a free choice. When a suspect speaks because he is overborne, it is immaterial whether he has been subjected to a physical or mental ordeal. Eventual yielding to questioning under such circumstances is plainly the product of the suction process of interrogation and therefore the reverse of voluntary.

  In *Watts,* as in Haley v. Ohio, 332 U.S. 596 (1948), the Court paid special attention to whether the accused was denied the aid of family, friends, or counsel. Incommunicado confinement consistently was viewed as an element of coercion. Another form of psychological influence was trickery, though this was only one factor in the due process calculus. See generally White, Police Trickery in Inducing Confessions, 127 U.Pa.L.Rev. 581 (1979).

  The Court recognized the pressure inherent in such psychological techniques as sustained interrogation, *Ashcraft,* supra, and the threat of mob violence, *Payne,* supra (defendant was told thirty to forty people would be waiting to get him unless he confessed). The Court also was concerned about rewards and inducements to confess, which had been condemned in *Hopt,* supra. New techniques as well as old were carefully scrutinized. For example, in Leyra v. Denno, 347 U.S. 556 (1954), the Court took exception to the use of a trained psychiatrist to extract a confession through skillful and suggestive questioning.

- *Warnings.* Finally, the Court considered—as one factor in the totality—whether the accused was aware or had been apprised of his right to remain silent and the possibility of obtaining legal counsel.

It should be apparent from this overview that the voluntariness standard required a case-by-case scrutiny of the circumstances surrounding a particular confession to determine if the methods by which it was obtained comported with due process. The Court considered both the police conduct in procuring the confession and the defendant's ability to withstand coercion; therefore, the "totality of the circumstances" was determinative of the voluntariness of the confession.

Criticism of the Involuntariness Test

Although the Court refined its analysis of the voluntariness test in the course of deciding over 30 full-length opinions under the due process standard, some members of the Court recognized the shortcomings of the totality-of-circumstances voluntariness approach. Justice Frankfurter, a supporter of the due process standard, noted in *Culombe* that "[n]o single litmus-paper test for constitutionally impermissible interrogations has been evolved." Because the Court could not possibly pass on all of the confession cases in which review was sought, usually certiorari was limited to death penalty cases or others of special concern. That the Justices themselves often disagreed on the proper application of the test compounded the problem.

The word "voluntary" hardly offered clear guidance to law enforcement officers and to lower court judges. For example, the instruction "don't overbear the will of the suspect" has little defined content outside the realm of physical force. Professor Schulhofer has criticized the indeterminacy of the involuntariness test in the following passage:

> In theory, brutality is ruled out by the due process test * * * but in operation the due process test sends police a fatally mixed message. The job of the interrogator, of course, is to get the reticent suspect to "come clean." When a tired, confused, or shaky prisoner shows signs of starting to "crack," is the interrogator supposed to keep up the pressure, or back off to avoid breaking the suspect's will? In effect, under the due process test, the officer is expected to do both. Instances of overbearing coercion are bound to occur under such a system, not because some officers will deliberately flout the law but because even the best of professionals will inevitably misjudge the elusive psychological line.

Schulhofer, *Miranda's* Practical Effect: Substantial Benefits and Vanishingly Small Costs, 90 Nw. Univ.L.Rev. 500 (1996) .

Increasing Emphasis on Assistance of Counsel: Spano v. New York

The growing dissatisfaction of certain members of the Court with the voluntariness standard became very apparent in Spano v. New York, 360 U.S. 315 (1959). Four concurring justices expressed more concern about the fact that the defendant Spano had been indicted and was refused permission to see his attorney than about the "voluntariness" of the confession under the totality of the circumstances. Spano, a 25-year old immigrant with a junior high school education, shot a person after a bar fight. He left the scene and disappeared for a week or so, and was indicted for murder during this period. The facts surrounding Spano's confession were set forth by Chief Justice Warren as follows:

> On February 3, 1957, petitioner called one Gaspar Bruno, a close friend of [Spano] who had attended school with him. Bruno was a fledgling police officer, having at that time not yet finished attending police academy. According to Bruno's testimony, petitioner told him "that he took a terrific beating, that the deceased hurt him real bad and he dropped him a couple of times and he was dazed; he didn't know what he was doing and that he went and shot at him." Petitioner told Bruno that he intended to get a lawyer and give himself up. Bruno relayed this information to his superiors.
>
> The following day, February 4, at 7:10 p.m., petitioner, accompanied by counsel, surrendered himself to the authorities * * *. His attorney had cautioned him to answer no questions, and left him in the custody of the officers. He was promptly taken to the office of the Assistant District Attorney and at 7:15 p.m. the questioning began, being conducted by Assistant District Attorney Goldsmith, Lt. Gannon, Detectives Farrell, Lehrer and Motta, and Sgt. Clarke. The record reveals that the questioning was both persistent and continuous. Petitioner, in accordance with his attorney's instructions, steadfastly refused to answer. * * * He asked one officer, Detective Ciccone, if he could speak to his attorney, but that request was denied. Detective Ciccone testified that he could not find the attorney's name in the telephone book. He was given two sandwiches, coffee and cake at 11 p.m.
>
> At 12:15 a.m. on the morning of February 5, after five hours of questioning in which it became evident that petitioner was following his attorney's instructions, on the Assistant District Attorney's orders petitioner was transferred to the 46th Squad, Ryer Avenue Police Station. The Assistant District Attorney also went to the police station and to some extent continued to participate in the interrogation. Petitioner arrived at 12:30 and questioning was resumed at 12:40. * * * But petitioner persisted in his refusal to answer, and again

requested permission to see his attorney, this time from Detective Lehrer. His request was again denied.

It was then that those in charge of the investigation decided that petitioner's close friend, Bruno, could be of use. * * * Although, in fact, his job was in no way threatened, Bruno was told to tell petitioner that petitioner's telephone call had gotten him "in a lot of trouble," and that he should seek to extract sympathy from petitioner for Bruno's pregnant wife and three children. Bruno developed this theme with petitioner without success, and petitioner, also without success, again sought to see his attorney, a request which Bruno relayed unavailingly to his superiors. After this first session with petitioner, Bruno was again directed by Lt. Gannon to play on petitioner's sympathies, but again no confession was forthcoming. But the Lieutenant a third time ordered Bruno falsely to importune his friend to confess, but again petitioner clung to his attorney's advice. Inevitably, in the fourth such session directed by the Lieutenant, lasting a full hour, petitioner succumbed to his friend's prevarications and agreed to make a statement. Accordingly, at 3:25 a.m. the Assistant District Attorney, a stenographer, and several other law enforcement officials entered the room where petitioner was being questioned, and took his statement in question and answer form with the Assistant District Attorney asking the questions. The statement was completed at 4:05 a.m.

But this was not the end. At 4:30 a.m. three detectives took petitioner to Police Headquarters in Manhattan. On the way they attempted to find the bridge from which petitioner said he had thrown the murder weapon. They crossed the Triborough Bridge into Manhattan, arriving at Police Headquarters at 5 a.m., and left Manhattan for the Bronx at 5:40 a.m. via the Willis Avenue Bridge. When petitioner recognized neither bridge as the one from which he had thrown the weapon, they reentered Manhattan via the Third Avenue Bridge, which petitioner stated was the right one, and then returned to the Bronx well after 6 a.m. During that trip the officers also elicited a statement from petitioner that the deceased was always "on [his] back," "always pushing" him and that he was "not sorry" he had shot the deceased. All three detectives testified to that statement at the trial.

Spano argued that his *Sixth Amendment* right to counsel was violated when he was interrogated, despite his repeated request for counsel, after he had been formally charged with the crime. Chief Justice Warren found it unnecessary to decide the Sixth Amendment's applicability, because the use of Spano's confessions was "inconsistent with the Fourteenth Amendment under traditional principles." The Chief Justice surveyed the law governing involuntary confessions:

> The abhorrence of society to the use of involuntary confessions does not turn alone on their inherent untrustworthiness. It also turns on the deep-rooted feeling that the police must obey the law while enforcing the law; that in the end life and liberty can be as much endangered from illegal methods used to convict those thought to be criminals as from the actual criminals themselves. * * * The facts of no case recently in this Court have quite approached the brutal beatings in Brown v. Mississippi, or the 36 consecutive hours of questioning present in Ashcraft v. Tennessee, 322 U.S. 143 (1944). But as law enforcement officers become more responsible, and the methods used to extract confessions more sophisticated, our duty to enforce federal constitutional protections does not cease. It only becomes more difficult because of the more delicate judgments to be made.

The Court found that the following factors in their totality constituted substantial police misconduct that caused an involuntary confession: 1) Spano was young, foreign-born, relatively uneducated, emotionally unstable, and inexperienced in the criminal justice system; 2) Spano "did not make a narrative statement, but was subject to the leading questions of a skillful prosecutor in a question and answer confession"; 3) he was questioned virtually incessantly by a number of officers, throughout the night; 4) the questioning "persisted in the face of his repeated refusals to answer on the advice of his attorney"; 5) the officers "ignored his reasonable requests to contact the local attorney whom he had already retained and who had personally delivered him into the custody of these officers"; and 6) the officers used Bruno, Spano's friend to extract the confession by using false statements.

Justice Douglas, joined by Justice Black and Justice Brennan, wrote a concurring opinion that emphasized the officers' denial of Spano's request for counsel:

> We have often divided on whether state authorities may question a suspect for hours on end when he has no lawyer present and when he has demanded that he have the benefit of legal advice. But here we deal not with a suspect but with a man who has been formally charged with a crime. The question is whether after the indictment and before the trial the Government can interrogate the accused *in secret* when he asked for his lawyer and when his request was denied. * * * Depriving a person, formally charged with a crime, of counsel during the period prior to trial may be more damaging than denial of counsel during the trial itself.

Justice Stewart, joined by Justice Douglas and Justice Brennan wrote a separate concurring opinion that also emphasized the right to counsel:

> Our Constitution guarantees the assistance of counsel to a man on trial for his life in an orderly courtroom, presided over by a judge,

open to the public, and protected by all the procedural safeguards of the law. Surely a Constitution which promises that much can vouchsafe no less to the same man under midnight inquisition in the squad room of a police station.

The Importance of Spano

The concurring Justices in *Spano* believed that once a person is formally charged by an indictment or information, his constitutional right to counsel begins, at least when counsel previously has been retained. Although the majority of the Court analyzed the confession under the traditional voluntariness standard, the majority did not reject the views expressed in the concurring opinions. It left the counsel question for another day, which was not long in coming, as we shall soon see. Thus, while *Spano* is a due process case, it provided a doctrinal bridge for the Court to consider the applicability of other constitutional limitations on police efforts to obtain confessions.

The Continuing Relevance of Due Process Protection

Despite the Court's eventual regulation of confessions through the Sixth Amendment in *Massiah* and through the Fifth Amendment in *Miranda* (both discussed later in this Chapter), the totality of the circumstances voluntariness test is in some cases a suspect's only protection from police coercion. The Sixth Amendment does not apply until the suspect has been formally charged (Moran v. Burbine, infra). *Miranda* applies only during "custodial interrogation," and that term does not cover all potentially coercive police practices. See United States v. Murphy, 763 F.2d 202 (6th Cir. 1985) (sending an attack dog to apprehend the suspect is not custodial interrogation, but confession made while dog was attacking held involuntary); United States v. Lall, 607 F.3d 1277 (11th Cir. 2010) ("Even if Lall was not in custody (and thus *Miranda* warnings were not required), we would still be required to address the voluntariness of his confession."). Moreover, *Miranda* and Sixth Amendment rights can be waived, while the right to be free from coercion cannot (nobody argues, for example, that the defendants in Brown v. Mississippi could have waived the right to be free from physical beating). Thus, if the defendant has made a valid waiver of *Miranda* (and, if applicable, Sixth Amendment) rights, his only protection from subsequent police pressure is the due process involuntariness test. See, e.g., United States v. Astello, 241 F.3d 965 (8th Cir. 2001) (court considers whether confession was involuntary after the defendant made a valid waiver of *Miranda* rights). Finally, the Court has found several exceptions to *Miranda*, so that a *Miranda*-defective confession can be used for impeachment (Harris v. New York, infra), the fruits of such a confession are generally admissible (Oregon v. Elstad, infra), and the confession itself can be admitted if obtained under emergency circumstances (New York v. Quarles, infra). However, even where *Miranda* and *Massiah* are inapplicable, the confession is still excluded under the Due Process Clause if obtained through police coercion. Thus, the due process involuntariness test retains vitality today, and cases are still being decided under that doctrine.

Modern Due Process Cases

It is the rare and extreme case, however, in which a court will find that a suspect confessed involuntarily. See White, Interrogation Without Questions, 78 Mich.L.Rev. 1209 (1980). Examples of cases denying involuntariness claims are Sumpter v. Nix, 863 F.2d 563 (8th Cir. 1988) (suspect with I.Q. of 89 and psychological problems, promised treatment, and interrogated for more than seven hours); McCall v. Dutton, 863 F.2d 454 (6th Cir. 1988) (defendant was wounded, and officers interrogated with guns drawn); Moore v. Dugger, 856 F.2d 129 (11th Cir. 1988) (suspect with an I.Q. of 62, who functioned at the level of an 11-year old, had been without food or sleep for 25 hours at the time he confessed); and United States v. Kelley, 953 F.2d 562 (9th Cir. 1992) (suspect confessed while handcuffed and suffering from heroin withdrawal).

Grano, Voluntariness, Free Will, and the Law of Confessions, 65 Va.L.Rev. 859 (1979), argues that an involuntary confession is "any confession produced by interrogation pressures that a person of reasonable firmness, with some of the defendant's characteristics, would not resist." How would *Spano* be resolved under this standard?

Others have argued that a confession is involuntary only where police tactics are such as would force an innocent person to confess. This is a reflection of the premise that "the Constitution seeks to protect the innocent." Amar, The Constitution and Criminal Procedure: First Principles 154 (1997). On this view, the goal of the voluntariness test is to protect against false confessions. This would mean that threats of harm, and physical violence would be prohibited, but tactics that could be used to trick a person into giving a reliable confession (e.g., false expressions of sympathy, or understating the significance of the crime) would be permitted.

Deception and False Promises by the Police

What effect does the use of police deception and similar psychological ploys have on the voluntariness inquiry? The Court in *Bram* stated that a confession induced by "any direct or implied promises, however slight" must be suppressed. But courts have not felt bound by that language.

For example, in Green v. Scully, 850 F.2d 894 (2d Cir. 1988), Green was taken to the station by two New York detectives to be interrogated as a murder suspect. He waived his *Miranda* rights. Thereafter, Detective Byrnes threatened him with the electric chair, even though there was at that time no capital punishment in New York. Then Byrnes left the room. During a lengthy interrogation, Detective Hazel consistently asserted that the police had all the evidence they needed to convict Green, stating that he had personally checked it out. This was false. When Green stated that he would never confess because he would not be able to face his and the victim's families, Hazel said he could help Green with that and suggested that Green must have been mentally ill when he committed the murder. Hazel referred to Green as "brother" and said that he would try to get psychiatric help for Green. Then Hazel took a different tack, appeared frustrated, and threatened to leave the interrogation over to the "bad cop," Byrnes. Byrnes then came in and stated that he had found Green's palm prints at the scene, with blood stains on them. This was not true. Byrnes told Green that he was lucky that Hazel was there, because Hazel cared about him while Byrnes did not. Green then began to consider cooperating, after again receiving assurance from Hazel that he would obtain psychiatric help and would avoid capital punishment. In the course of his confession, Green stated that he suffered from blackouts, that he was confessing out of fear that if he were not convicted of this crime he might kill someone else, and that confessing would be the only way to obtain psychiatric help.

The court held that the confession was voluntary. It concluded that despite *Bram*, "the presence of a direct or implied promise of help or leniency alone has not barred the admission of a confession" and that "promises do not require an analysis separate from or different than the totality of circumstances rule." The court found that Green was of above average intelligence and streetwise, that the interrogation session was only two hours long, and that Green was not handcuffed or in pain during that time. As to the psychological tactics, the court found the police conduct "troubling." But the use of these tactics was not enough to taint the confession, in part because Green had his own motivation for confessing.

> [T]he scare tactics, false representation as to the evidence, good cop/bad cop routine, and whatever hopes were instilled from the promises or fears from the reference to the "chair" considered together did not overbear Green's will and bring about his confession. He confessed—as he candidly admitted—because he was afraid that what he had done to the victims in a blackout would be something he was going to do to his own family—maybe even his mother.

Did the court overlook the fact that Green confessed not precisely to take himself "off the street," but because in doing so he would obtain psychiatric help? See generally White, Confessions Induced by Broken Government Promises, 43 Duke L.J. 947 (1994).

A leading interrogation manual, authored by Inbau, Reid and Buckley, argues the merits of deceptive interrogation techniques in leading to confessions. The methods they recommend, which often are referred to as the "Reid Technique," include:

- showing fake sympathy for the suspect by acting like his friend (e.g., by falsely telling a rape suspect that the officer himself had once "roughed it up" with a girl in an attempt to have intercourse with her);
- reducing the suspect's feelings of guilt through lies (e.g., by telling a person suspected of killing his wife that he was not as "lucky" as the officer, who at one time was just about to "pound" his wife when the doorbell rang);
- exaggerating the crime in an effort to get the suspect to negotiate, or in hopes of obtaining a denial which will indirectly inculpate the suspect (e.g., accusing the suspect of stealing $40,000 when only $20,000 is involved, or accusing the suspect of murder where the victim, while shot, survived the incident);
- lying that implies that "the game is up" because the evidence is so strong (e.g., stating that the suspect was identified at the scene when in fact he was not); and
- playing one codefendant against another (e.g., leading one to believe the other has confessed when no confession has occurred).

Inbau, Reid & Buckley, Criminal Interrogation and Confessions 98–132 (3d ed. 1986).

Tactics such as these are routinely permitted by the courts in applying the voluntariness test. See, e.g., Frazier v. Cupp, 394 U.S. 731 (1969) (use of "false friend" and "game is up" techniques, although relevant to the due process inquiry, were not sufficient to render the confession involuntary); United States v. Whitfield, 695 F.3d 288 (4th Cir. 2012) (officers' misrepresentation about the offenses they were investigating—allowing the defendant to believe that he was only being investigated for a minor crime—did not render the defendant's confession involuntary: "we are satisfied that Whitfield's capacity for self-determination was not critically impaired by Sergeant Reynolds's misrepresentations."); Miller v. Fenton, 796 F.2d 598 (3d Cir. 1986) (use of "false friend" technique, together with a ruse that the victim had not died when in fact she had, does not render confession involuntary). See also Young, Unnecessary Evil: Police Lying in Interrogations, 28 Conn. L.Rev. 425 (1996) (providing citations to lower court cases refusing to exclude confessions obtained after the suspect was exposed to lies about matters such as the strength of the case, fabricated evidence, suggestions that the suspect was not at fault, and lies about the identity of the interrogator).

Are deception techniques permitted because the courts tacitly assume that suspects are not naive enough to believe that police will tell them the absolute truth during an interrogation? After all, it is an interrogation, not a picnic, right? But if suspects anticipate police mendacity, what good are these deceptive practices? See Paris, Trust, Lies and Interrogation, 3 Va.J.Soc.Pol. & L. 3 (1995) (arguing for a rule prohibiting police from lying, on the ground that such a rule would lead to more reliable confessions: "suspects would be able to relax their guard if assured that lying interrogators would be punished" and will be more prone "to trust their interrogators and confess in situations in which confessions will serve their interests").

For a case where police deception was found to cause an involuntary confession, see Aleman v. Village of Hanover Park, 662 F.3d 897 (7th Cir. 2011), in which Aleman, who ran a day care home, sued police officers who extracted a confession from him about the death of a child. (Aleman was charged and incarcerated but eventually released—because the evidence actually showed that the child's mother had beaten the child severely before dropping him off at Aleman's day care home). Aleman had shaken the child in an attempt to revive him. During Aleman's interrogation, an officer falsely reported that a medical report indicated the child's death was caused by shaking—when in fact the medical doctors had not excluded other possibilities. Aleman responded that "if the only way to cause [the injuries] is to shake that baby, then, when I shook that baby, I hurt that baby." Judge Posner explained why this statement was involuntary:

> Courts have been reluctant to deem trickery by police a basis for excluding a confession on the ground that the tricks made the confession coerced and thus involuntary. * * * The confession must be excluded only if the government feeds the defendant false information that seriously distorts his choice * * * in other words, only if the false statement destroyed the information that he required for a rational choice.
>
> In this case a false statement did destroy the information required for a rational choice. Not being a medical expert, Aleman could not contradict what was represented to him as settled medical opinion. He had shaken Joshua, albeit gently; but if medical opinion excluded any other possible cause of the child's death, then, gentle as the shaking was, and innocently intended, it *must* have been the cause of death. Aleman had no rational basis, given his ignorance of medical science, to deny that he had to have been the cause.

What is the difference between falsely reporting medical evidence—found coercive in *Aleman*—and falsely reporting that eyewitnesses saw the defendant at the scene of the crime, which is a trick that is routinely permitted?

False Documentary Evidence

In Florida v. Cayward, 552 So.2d 971 (Fla.App.1989), police fabricated a scientific report for use as a ploy in interrogating the defendant. The report was prepared on stationery of Lifecodes, Inc., a DNA testing service, and it indicated that DNA testing showed that bodily fluids on the victim came from the defendant. The defendant confessed when shown the false report. The court found the resulting confession involuntary, reasoning as follows:

> The reporters are filled with examples of police making false verbal assertions to a suspect, but * * * we perceive an intrinsic distinction between verbal assertions and manufactured documentation. * * * It may well be that a suspect is more impressed and thereby more easily induced to confess when presented with tangible, official-looking reports as opposed to merely being told that some tests have implicated him. In addition to our spontaneous distaste for the conduct we have reviewed in this matter, we have practical concerns regarding the use of the false reports beyond the inducement of a confession. Unlike oral misrepresentations, manufactured documents have the potential of indefinite life and the facial appearance of authenticity. * * * Such reports have the potential of finding their way into the courtroom.

Do you agree that there is a material distinction between false verbal statements and false documentary evidence? Is the distinction that an innocent person may shrug off an officer's verbal statement that the suspect's DNA was found at the scene, whereas even an innocent person might have to think about confessing where the forensic test apparently incriminates him?

Honest Promises vs. False Promises

The fact that an interrogating officer makes a promise does not mean that it is necessarily a false promise. Judge Posner, in United States v. Baldwin, 60 F.3d 363 (7th Cir. 1995), had this to say about a confession obtained after a police officer's promise to the defendant that any cooperation by him would be brought to the prosecutor's attention:

> A false promise of lenience would be an example of forbidden tactics, for it would impede the suspect in making an informed choice as to whether he was better off confessing or clamming up. But government is not forbidden to buy information with honest promises of consideration. And as it is well known that the suspect's cooperation,

> by lightening the government's burdens of investigation and prosecution, is looked upon favorably by prosecutors and judges, what the agent told the defendant was very close to a truism; * * * and the defendant was not a tyro or ignoramus, but a 39-year-old with a long history of involvement in the criminal justice system.

See also United States v. Fraction, 795 F.2d 12 (3d Cir. 1986) (officer promises to relate the fact of the suspect's cooperation to the prosecutor, but does not represent that he has authority to affect the outcome of the case; confession voluntary). But as Judge Posner recognizes, there will be a due process concern when the officer makes a *specific* promise that the defendant's statement will not be used against him or that he will get a specific benefit for confessing, and then such a promise is not kept. See, e.g., United States v. Walton, 10 F.3d 1024 (3d Cir. 1993) (confession involuntary where the officer, a long-time friend of the defendant, promises to keep a conversation "off the record" and then does not do so); United States v. Lall, 607 F.3d 1277 (11th Cir. 2010) (officer stated that anything the defendant said would not be used to prosecute him; admission of defendant's confession in response violated the defendant's due process rights).

Threats of Physical Violence: Arizona v. Fulminante

Justice White wrote for a majority in Arizona v. Fulminante, 499 U.S. 279 (1991), as it found that a confession made by a prisoner to an informant—when made to ward off a threat of physical violence—was coerced and thus involuntary under the Fifth and Fourteenth Amendments. Fulminante was suspected of murdering his stepdaughter in Arizona, but had not been arrested or charged before he was incarcerated in New Jersey on an unrelated firearms conviction. He became friends with another inmate who was a paid informant for the FBI and masqueraded as an organized crime figure. When the informant learned that Fulminante was suspected of killing a child, he suggested to Fulminante that he could protect him from other inmates, who did not look kindly upon suspected child killers. But this protection would be provided only if Fulminante told him the truth about what had occurred. This offer resulted in the confession, which the informant related at Fulminante's trial.

Justice White observed that the *Bram* standard, which condemned any confession obtained by any direct or implied promises, however slight, or by the exertion of any improper influence, had been replaced by a *totality of the circumstances* test. In applying that test, he concluded that a credible threat of physical violence had existed, and that Fulminante confessed due to his misplaced hope for protection from that violence. Therefore the confession was involuntary. Justice White stressed that "a finding of coercion need not depend upon actual violence by a government agent; a credible threat is sufficient." The majority analogized Fulminante's plight to that of the defendant in Payne v. Arkansas, supra, where the Court found a confession to be coerced when an interrogating officer threatened that unless Payne confessed, the officer would leave him to an angry mob just outside the jailhouse door.

Chief Justice Rehnquist, joined by Justices O'Connor, Kennedy, and Souter, dissented. He emphasized that Fulminante offered no evidence that he believed his life was in danger or that he confessed to obtain protection.

After *Fulminante,* is a credible threat of physical violence a per se factor? If so, why is it different from a threat of the electric chair, as in *Green,* or an assertion that the suspect's fingerprints were found at the scene? Is the distinction that even an innocent person might confess to avoid a beating?

Focus on Police Misconduct: Colorado v. Connelly

The Supreme Court held in Colorado v. Connelly, 479 U.S. 157 (1986), that the due process focus is primarily on *police misconduct* rather than the suspect's state of mind. Connelly approached a uniformed officer on the street and stated that he had murdered someone and wanted to talk about it. The officer warned Connelly that he had the right to remain silent, that anything he said could be used against him in court, and that he had a right to an attorney before any questioning. Connelly stated that he understood his rights and wanted to talk about the murder. A homicide detective arrived and repeated the warnings. Connelly then stated that he needed to confess to the murder of a young girl whom he had killed months earlier. The officers took him to the police station, examined their records, discovered that an unidentified female body had been found, talked with Connelly concerning the murder, and took Connelly in a police car to point out the location of the crime. The next morning Connelly began to appear disoriented, and he stated that "voices" had told him to confess. He was initially found incompetent to assist in his own defense, but later was declared fit to proceed to trial.

An expert witness testified in support of Connelly's motion to suppress his statements on grounds that he was experiencing "command hallucinations" at the time of his confession, which interfered with his ability to make free and rational choices. The state courts suppressed the confessions on the ground that Connelly only confessed because the voices told him to, and therefore his confession was involuntary. But the Supreme Court reversed. Writing for the Court, Chief Justice Rehnquist reasoned that the *police* applied absolutely no pressure on Connelly to confess. The state courts failed "to recognize the essential link between coercive activity of the State, on the one hand, and a resulting confession by a defendant, on the other." The Court held that "coercive police activity is a necessary predicate to the finding that a confession is not 'voluntary' within the meaning of the Due Process Clause."

The Chief Justice asserted that suppressing a statement in the absence of police coercion "would serve absolutely no purpose in enforcing constitutional guarantees" because it would not deter future police conduct.

The Court concluded as follows:

> Only if we were to establish a brand new constitutional right—the right of a criminal defendant to confess to his crime only when totally rational and properly motivated—could respondent's present claim be sustained. * * * Respondent would now have us require sweeping inquiries into the state of mind of a criminal defendant who has confessed, inquiries quite divorced from any coercion brought to bear on the defendant by the State. We think the Constitution rightly leaves this sort of inquiry to be resolved by state laws governing the admission of evidence * * *. A statement rendered by one in the condition of respondent might be proved to be quite unreliable, but this is a matter to be governed by the evidentiary laws of the forum.

Justice Brennan, joined by Justice Marshall, dissented from this holding. He argued that the absence of police wrongdoing was not conclusive and "[t]he requirement that a confession be voluntary reflects a recognition of the importance of free will and of reliability in determining the admissibility of a confession, and thus demands an inquiry into the totality of the circumstances surrounding the confession."

The effect of *Connelly* can be seen in such cases as United States v. Erving L., 147 F.3d 1240 (10th Cir. 1998), where the suspect's mother coerced him into confessing to the authorities. The court relied on *Connelly* to find no due process violation. Courts have also held after *Connelly* that it is irrelevant that the suspect was drunk, on drugs, mentally impaired, emotionally vulnerable, etc., when he confessed. As one court put it, "*Connelly* makes it clear that personal characteristics of the defendant are constitutionally irrelevant absent proof of police coercion." United States v. Rohrbach, 813 F.2d 142 (8th Cir. 1987). See also United States v. Williamson, 706 F.3d 405 (4th Cir. 2013) (secretly recording the suspect's statement to an associate did not render statement involuntary because the statements were not the product of coercion).

Problems with a Test Based on Free Will

Is "free will" a workable standard for confession cases? Judge Posner in United States v. Rutledge, 900 F.2d 1127 (7th Cir. 1990), had this to say about the "overbearing of free will" test:

Taken seriously it would require the exclusion of virtually all fruits of custodial interrogation, since few choices to confess can be thought truly "free" when made by a person who is incarcerated and is being questioned by * * * officers without the presence of counsel or anyone else to give him moral support. The formula is not taken seriously. *Connelly* may have driven the stake through its heart by holding that a confession which is not a product of the defendant's free choice * * * is admissible so long as whatever it was that destroyed the defendant's power of choice was not police conduct. In any event, very few incriminating statements, custodial or otherwise, are held to be involuntary, though few are the product of a choice that the interrogators left completely free.

An alternative approach, which is implied by *Connelly* and may well describe the courts' actual as distinct from articulated standard, is to ask whether the government has made it impossible for the defendant to make a *rational* choice as to whether to confess—has made it in other words impossible for him to weigh the pros and cons of confessing and go with the balance as it appears at the time. This approach * * * implies, for example, that if the government feeds the defendant false information that seriously distorts his choice, by promising him that if he confesses he will be set free, or if the government drugs him so that he cannot make a conscious choice at all, then the confession must go out. * * * The police are allowed to play on a suspect's ignorance, his anxieties, his fears, and his uncertainties; they just are not allowed to magnify those fears, uncertainties and so forth to the point where rational decision becomes impossible.

Is Judge Posner saying that confessions are involuntary only when police tactics are such as would cause an innocent person to confess (e.g., a statement "if you confess you go free")? Is his analysis consistent with *Fulminante*?

The Involuntariness Test and False Confessions

Certainly one goal of the involuntariness test is to protect against the risk of false confessions. These concerns were at the fore in Dassey v. Dittman, 877 F.3d 297 (7th Cir. 2017) (en banc), wherein Brendan Dassey, one of the defendants featured in the documentary film "Making a Murderer," challenged the admission of a confession he gave during an interrogation conducted when he was sixteen years old.[12] At trial, the prosecution relied heavily on his confession, arguing that "innocent people do not confess." In a dissenting opinion joined by Chief Judge Wood and Judge Williams, Judge Rovner responded to this claim, noting that

[12] The confession was featured in an ABC Nightline story (https://www.youtube.com/watch?v=BsDrsQvCwa4).

"innocent people do in fact confess with shocking regularity." Judge Rovner reviewed data from the National Registry of Exonerations showing that, out of almost 2000 exonerations, 227 defendants had falsely confessed. "This research," Judge Rover noted "indicates that false confessions (defined as cases in which indisputably innocent individuals confessed to crimes they did not commit) occur in approximately 25% of homicide cases." The rate is higher among exonerated defendants who were under 18 at the time they confessed—42% of whom provided false confessions—and exonerated defendants suffering from mental illness or disability—75% of whom made false confessions. "Overall," Judge Rovner concluded, "one sixth of the exonerees [in the study] were juveniles, mentally disabled, or both, but they accounted for 59% of false confessions. Indeed, youth and intellectual disability are the two most commonly cited characteristics of suspects who confess falsely. Dassey suffered under the weight of both characteristics."

Given these statistics, what more should be done to assure that the involuntariness test is an effective protection against false confessions?

Coercive Interrogation of Suspected Terrorists

After 9/11, suspected terrorists detained abroad or at Guantanamo have been subject to interrogation techniques that would be found coercive under the due process test. Examples include "waterboarding" (simulated drowning); forcing Muslim men to wear women's clothing and to disrobe in front of women; simulated dog attacks; jarring music and lighting; extended isolation; prolonged sleep deprivation; exposure to excessive cold; and food deprivation. Supporters of "enhanced interrogation" techniques take the position that they do not allow "torture," and that coercive techniques are necessary to crack terrorists and save lives.

Note, however, that if a person is charged with a terrorism-related crime in a civilian court, the Due Process Clause is fully applicable. See United States v. Abu Ali, 528 F.3d 210 (4th Cir. 2008) (will of defendant was not overborne during interrogation in Saudi Arabia, where defendant had responded to his interrogators' questions in Arabic; officials provided defendant with a prayer rug and the Koran among other accommodations; defendant was confined under reasonable conditions, including three meals per day, a bed, blanket and pillow; and the defendant began to confess just two days after interrogation started); In re Terrorist Bombings of U.S. Embassies, 548 F.3d 237 (2d Cir. 2008) (confession was voluntary even though the defendant was detained incommunicado for 14 days; defendant was not abused, and he was motivated to confess by a desire to air his grievances in a United States court).

III. THE FIFTH AMENDMENT PRIVILEGE AGAINST COMPELLED SELF-INCRIMINATION

As discussed above, the Court became dissatisfied with the due process-totality of the circumstances test as an exclusive means of regulating interrogations. After *Spano*, the Court applied the Sixth Amendment right to counsel to exclude confessions taken during police interrogations in Massiah v. United States, 377 U.S. 201 (1964), and Escobedo v. Illinois, 378 U.S. 478 (1964). But Sixth Amendment protection does not begin until there is a "criminal prosecution"; and the Court came to doubt whether that Amendment's protections could apply to the *investigatory* stage, before the defendant has been formally accused of a crime.[13] It is during this investigatory stage that most police interrogation occurs and most confessions are obtained. The Court therefore began to shift to a different constitutional protection—the Fifth Amendment guarantee that no person "shall be compelled in any criminal case to be a witness against himself . . .".[14] The problem, of course, is that, by its text, this privilege appears to apply at trial. In what sense is a suspect who is interrogated in a police station "compelled" to be "a witness" in a "criminal case"? The Court answered that question in Miranda v. Arizona.

A. MIRANDA V. ARIZONA

MIRANDA V. ARIZONA

Supreme Court of the United States, 1966.
384 U.S. 436.

MR. CHIEF JUSTICE WARREN **delivered the opinion of the Court.**

The cases before us raise questions which go to the roots of our concepts of American criminal jurisprudence: the restraints society must observe consistent with the Federal Constitution in prosecuting individuals for crime. More specifically, we deal with the admissibility of statements obtained from an individual who is subjected to custodial police interrogation and the necessity for procedures which assure that the individual is accorded his privilege under the Fifth Amendment to the Constitution not to be compelled to incriminate himself.

* * *

Our holding will be spelled out with some specificity in the pages which follow but briefly stated it is this: the prosecution may not use statements,

---

[13] Eventually the Court was to return to the Sixth Amendment as an additional control over police interrogations. *Massiah* and its progeny are discussed after the materials on the *Miranda* doctrine.

[14] In Malloy v. Hogan, 378 U.S. 1 (1964), the Court held that the Fifth Amendment privilege against compelled self-incrimination is applicable to the states through the Fourteenth Amendment.

whether exculpatory or inculpatory, stemming from custodial interrogation of the defendant unless it demonstrates the use of procedural safeguards effective to secure the privilege against self-incrimination. By custodial interrogation, we mean questioning initiated by law enforcement officers after a person has been taken into custody or otherwise deprived of his freedom of action in any significant way. As for the procedural safeguards to be employed, unless other fully effective means are devised to inform accused persons of their right of silence and to assure a continuous opportunity to exercise it, the following measures are required. Prior to any questioning, the person must be warned that he has a right to remain silent, that any statement he does make may be used as evidence against him, and that he has a right to the presence of an attorney, either retained or appointed. The defendant may waive effectuation of these rights, provided the waiver is made voluntarily, knowingly and intelligently. If, however, he indicates in any manner and at any stage of the process that he wishes to consult with an attorney before speaking there can be no questioning. Likewise, if the individual is alone and indicates in any manner that he does not wish to be interrogated, the police may not question him. The mere fact that he may have answered some questions or volunteered some statements on his own does not deprive him of the right to refrain from answering any further inquiries until he has consulted with an attorney and thereafter consents to be questioned.

* * * The constitutional issue we decide in each of these cases is the admissibility of statements obtained from a defendant questioned while in custody or otherwise deprived of his freedom of action in any significant way. In each, the defendant was questioned by police officers, detectives, or a prosecuting attorney in a room in which he was cut off from the outside world. In none of these cases was the defendant given a full and effective warning of his rights at the outset of the interrogation process. In all the cases, the questioning elicited oral admissions, and in three of them, signed statements as well which were admitted at their trials. They all thus share salient features—incommunicado interrogation of individuals in a police-dominated atmosphere, resulting in self-incriminating statements without full warnings of constitutional rights.

An understanding of the nature and setting of this in-custody interrogation is essential to our decisions today. The difficulty in depicting what transpires at such interrogations stems from the fact that in this country they have largely taken place incommunicado. From extensive factual studies undertaken in the early 1930's, including the famous Wickersham Report to Congress by a Presidential Commission, it is clear that police violence and the "third degree" flourished at that time. * * *

* * *

[T]he modern practice of in-custody interrogation is psychologically rather than physically oriented. * * * Interrogation still takes place in privacy. Privacy results in secrecy and this in turn results in a gap in our knowledge as to what in fact goes on in the interrogation rooms. A valuable source of information about present police practices, however, may be found in various police manuals and texts which document procedures employed with success in the past, and which recommend various other effective tactics. These texts are used by law enforcement agencies themselves as guides. It should be noted that these texts professedly present the most enlightened and effective means presently used to obtain statements through custodial interrogation. By considering these texts and other data, it is possible to describe procedures observed and noted around the country.

The officers are told by the manuals that the "principal psychological factor contributing to a successful interrogation is *privacy*—being alone with the person under interrogation." * * *

To highlight the isolation and unfamiliar surroundings, the manuals instruct the police to display an air of confidence in the suspect's guilt and from outward appearance to maintain only an interest in confirming certain details. The guilt of the subject is to be posited as a fact. The interrogator should direct his comments toward the reasons why the subject committed the act, rather than court failure by asking the subject whether he did it. Like other men, perhaps the subject has had a bad family life, had an unhappy childhood, had too much to drink, had an unrequited desire for women. The officers are instructed to minimize the moral seriousness of the offense, to cast blame on the victim or on society. These tactics are designed to put the subject in a psychological state where his story is but an elaboration of what the police purport to know already—that he is guilty. Explanations to the contrary are dismissed and discouraged.

The texts thus stress that the major qualities an interrogator should possess are patience and perseverance. * * *

The manuals suggest that the suspect be offered legal excuses for his actions in order to obtain an initial admission of guilt. * * *

When the techniques described above prove unavailing, the texts recommend they be alternated with a show of some hostility. * * *

The interrogators sometimes are instructed to induce a confession out of trickery. The technique here is quite effective in crimes which require identification or which run in series. In the identification situation, the interrogator may take a break in his questioning to place the subject among a group of men in a line-up. "The witness or complainant (previously coached, if necessary) studies the line-up and confidently points out the subject as the guilty party." Then the questioning resumes "as though there were now no doubt about the guilt of the subject." A variation on this technique is called the "reverse line-up":

> "The accused is placed in a line-up but this time he is identified by several fictitious witnesses or victims who associated him with different offenses. It is expected that the subject will become desperate and confess to the offense under investigation in order to escape from the false accusations."

* * *

Even without employing brutality, the "third degree" or the specific stratagems described above, the very fact of custodial interrogation exacts a heavy toll on individual liberty and trades on the weakness of individuals. * * *

In the cases before us today, given this background, we concern ourselves primarily with this interrogation atmosphere and the evils it can bring. In No. 759, Miranda v. Arizona, the police arrested the defendant and took him to a special interrogation room where they secured a confession. In No. 760, Vignera v. New York, the defendant made oral admissions to the police after interrogation in the afternoon, and then signed an inculpatory statement upon being questioned by an assistant district attorney later the same evening. In No. 761, Westover v. United States, the defendant was handed over to the Federal Bureau of Investigation by local authorities after they had detained and interrogated him for a lengthy period, both at night and the following morning. After some two hours of questioning, the federal officers had obtained signed statements from the defendant. Lastly, in No. 584, California v. Stewart, the local police held the defendant five days in the station and interrogated him on nine separate occasions before they secured his inculpatory statement.

In these cases, we might not find the defendants' statements to have been involuntary in traditional terms. Our concern for adequate safeguards to protect precious Fifth Amendment rights is, of course, not lessened in the slightest. In each of the cases, the defendant was thrust into an unfamiliar atmosphere and run through menacing police interrogation procedures. The potentiality for compulsion is forcefully apparent, for example, in *Miranda,* where the indigent Mexican defendant was a seriously disturbed individual with pronounced sexual fantasies, and in *Stewart,* in which the defendant was an indigent Los Angeles Negro who had dropped out of school in the sixth grade. To be sure, the records do not evince overt physical coercion or patent psychological ploys. The fact remains that in none of these cases did the officers undertake to afford appropriate safeguards at the outset of the interrogation to insure that the statements were truly the product of free choice.

It is obvious that such an interrogation environment is created for no purpose other than to subjugate the individual to the will of his examiner. This atmosphere carries its own badge of intimidation. To be sure, this is not physical intimidation, but it is equally destructive of human dignity. The current practice of incommunicado interrogation is at odds with one of our Nation's most cherished principles—that the individual may not be compelled to incriminate himself. Unless adequate protective devices are employed to dispel the compulsion inherent in custodial surroundings, no statement obtained from the defendant can truly be the product of his free choice.

From the foregoing, we can readily perceive an intimate connection between the privilege against self-incrimination and police custodial questioning. It is fitting to turn to history and precedent underlying the Self-Incrimination Clause to determine its applicability in this situation.

[The Court briefly traces the roots of the Fifth Amendment and how the privilege against self-incrimination obtained constitutional status in the United States.]

The question in these cases is whether the privilege is fully applicable during a period of custodial interrogation. * * * We are satisfied that all the principles embodied in the privilege apply to informal compulsion exerted by law-enforcement officers during in-custody questioning. An individual swept from familiar surroundings into police custody, surrounded by antagonistic forces, and subjected to the techniques of persuasion described above cannot be otherwise than under compulsion to speak. As a practical matter, the compulsion to speak in the isolated setting of the police station may well be greater than in courts or other official investigations, where there are often impartial observers to guard against intimidation or trickery.

This question, in fact could have been taken as settled in federal courts almost 70 years ago, when, in Bram v. United States, 168 U.S. 532, 542 (1897), this Court held:

> "In criminal trials, in the courts of the United States, wherever a question arises whether a confession is incompetent because not voluntary, the issue is controlled by that portion of the Fifth Amendment * * * commanding that no person 'shall be compelled in any criminal case to be a witness against himself.' "

* * *

Today, then, there can be no doubt that the Fifth Amendment privilege is available outside of criminal court proceedings and serves to protect persons in all settings in which their freedom of action is curtailed in any significant way from being compelled to incriminate themselves. We have concluded that without proper safeguards the process of in-custody interrogation of persons suspected or accused of crime contains inherently compelling pressures which work to undermine the individual's will to resist and to compel him to speak where he would not otherwise do so freely. In order to combat these pressures and to permit a full opportunity to exercise the privilege against self-incrimination, the accused must be adequately and effectively apprised of his rights and the exercise of those rights must be fully honored.

It is impossible for us to foresee the potential alternatives for protecting the privilege which might be devised by Congress or the States in the exercise of their creative rule-making capacities. Therefore we cannot say that the Constitution necessarily requires adherence to any particular solution for the inherent compulsions of the interrogation process as it is presently conducted. Our decision in no way creates a constitutional straitjacket which will handicap sound efforts at reform, nor is it intended to have this effect. We encourage Congress and the States to continue their laudable search for increasingly effective ways of protecting the rights of the individual while promoting efficient enforcement of our criminal laws. However, unless we are shown other procedures which are at least as effective in apprising accused persons of their right of silence and in assuring a continuous opportunity to exercise it, the following safeguards must be observed.

At the outset, if a person in custody is to be subjected to interrogation, he must first be informed in clear and unequivocal terms that he has the right to remain silent. For those unaware of the privilege, the warning is needed simply to make them aware of it—the threshold requirement for an intelligent decision as to its exercise. More important, such a warning is an absolute prerequisite in overcoming the inherent pressures of the interrogation atmosphere. It is not just the subnormal or woefully ignorant who succumb to an interrogator's imprecations, whether implied or expressly stated, that the interrogation will continue until a confession is obtained or that silence in the face of accusation is itself damning and will bode ill when presented to a jury.[a] Further, the warning will show the individual that his interrogators are prepared to recognize his privilege should he choose to exercise it.

The Fifth Amendment privilege is so fundamental to our system of constitutional rule and the expedient of giving an adequate warning as to the availability of the privilege so simple, we will not pause to inquire in individual cases whether the defendant was aware of his rights without a warning being given. Assessments of the knowledge the defendant possessed, based on information as to his age, education, intelligence, or

[a] In accord with our decision today it is impermissible to penalize an individual for exercising his Fifth Amendment privilege when he is under police custodial interrogation. The prosecution may not, therefore, use at trial the fact that he stood mute or claimed his privilege in the face of accusation.

prior contact with authorities, can never be more than speculation; a warning is a clearcut fact. More important, whatever the background of the person interrogated, a warning at the time of the interrogation is indispensable to overcome its pressures and to insure that the individual knows he is free to exercise the privilege at that point in time.

The warning of the right to remain silent must be accompanied by the explanation that anything said can and will be used against the individual in court. This warning is needed in order to make him aware not only of the privilege, but also of the consequences of forgoing it. It is only through an awareness of these consequences that there can be any assurance of real understanding and intelligent exercise of the privilege. Moreover, this warning may serve to make the individual more acutely aware that he is faced with a phase of the adversary system—that he is not in the presence of persons acting solely in his interest.

The circumstances surrounding in-custody interrogation can operate very quickly to overbear the will of one merely made aware of his privilege by his interrogators. Therefore, the right to have counsel present at the interrogation is indispensable to the protection of the Fifth Amendment privilege under the system we delineate today. Our aim is to assure that the individual's right to choose between silence and speech remains unfettered throughout the interrogation process. A once-stated warning, delivered by those who will conduct the interrogation, cannot itself suffice to that end among those who most require knowledge of their rights. A mere warning given by the interrogators is not alone sufficient to accomplish that end. Prosecutors themselves claim that the admonishment of the right to remain silent without more "will benefit only the recidivist and the professional." Even preliminary advice given to the accused by his own attorney can be swiftly overcome by the secret interrogation process. Thus, the need for counsel to protect the Fifth Amendment privilege comprehends not merely a right to consult with counsel prior to questioning, but also to have counsel present during any questioning if the defendant so desires.

That presence of counsel at the interrogation may serve several significant subsidiary functions as well. If the accused decides to talk to his interrogators, the assistance of counsel can mitigate the dangers of untrustworthiness. With a lawyer present the likelihood that the police will practice coercion is reduced, and if coercion is nevertheless exercised the lawyer can testify to it in court. The presence of a lawyer can also help to guarantee that the accused gives a fully accurate statement to the police and that the statement is rightly reported by the prosecution at trial.

An individual need not make a pre-interrogation request for a lawyer. While such request affirmatively secures his right to have one, his failure to ask for a lawyer does not constitute a waiver. No effective waiver of the right to counsel during interrogation can be recognized unless specifically made after the warnings we here delineate have been given. The accused who does not know his rights and therefore does not make a request may be the person who most needs counsel. * * *

* * *

Accordingly we hold that an individual held for interrogation must be clearly informed that he has the right to consult with a lawyer and to have the lawyer with him during interrogation under the system for protecting the privilege we delineate today. As with the warnings of the right to remain silent and that anything stated can be used in evidence against him, this warning is an absolute prerequisite to interrogation. No amount of circumstantial evidence that the person may have been aware of this right will suffice to stand in its stead. Only through such a warning is there ascertainable assurance that the accused was aware of this right.

If an individual indicates that he wishes the assistance of counsel before any interrogation occurs, the authorities cannot rationally ignore or deny his request on the basis that the individual does not have or cannot afford a retained attorney. The financial ability of the individual has no relationship to the scope of the rights involved here. The privilege against self-incrimination secured by the Constitution applies to all individuals. The need for counsel in order to protect the privilege exists for the indigent as well as the affluent. In fact, were we to limit these constitutional rights to those who can retain an attorney, our decisions today would be of little significance. The cases before us as well as the vast majority of confession cases with which we have dealt in the past involve those unable to retain counsel. While authorities are not required to relieve the accused of his poverty, they have the obligation not to take advantage of indigence in the administration of justice. Denial of counsel to the indigent at the time of interrogation while allowing an attorney to those who can afford one would be no more supportable by reason or logic than the similar situation at trial and on appeal. * * *

In order fully to apprise a person interrogated of the extent of his rights under this system then, it is necessary to warn him not only that he has the right to consult with an attorney, but also that if he is indigent a lawyer will be appointed to represent him. Without this additional warning, the admonition of the right to consult with counsel would often be understood as meaning only that he can consult with a lawyer if he has one or has the funds to obtain one. The warning of a right to counsel would be hollow if not couched in terms that would convey to the indigent—the person most often subjected to interrogation—the knowledge that he too has a right to have counsel present. As with the warnings of the right to remain silent and of the general right to counsel, only by effective and express explanation to the indigent of this right can there be assurance that he was truly in a position to exercise it.[b]

Once warnings have been given, the subsequent procedure is clear. If the individual indicates in any manner, at any time prior to or during questioning, that he wishes to remain silent, the interrogation must cease.[c] At this point he has shown that he intends to exercise his Fifth Amendment privilege; any statements taken after the person invokes his privilege cannot be other than the product of compulsion, subtle or otherwise. Without the right to cut off questioning, the setting of in-custody interrogation operates on the individual to overcome free choice in producing a statement after the privilege has been once invoked. If the individual states that he wants an attorney, the interrogation must cease until an attorney is present. At that time, the individual must have an opportunity to confer with the attorney and to have him present during any subsequent questioning. If the individual cannot obtain an attorney and he indicates that he wants one before speaking to police, they must respect his decision to remain silent.

This does not mean, as some have suggested, that each police station must have a "station house lawyer" present at all times to advise prisoners. It does mean, however, that if police propose to interrogate a person they must make known to him that he is entitled to a lawyer and that if he cannot afford one, a lawyer will be provided for him prior to any interrogation. If authorities conclude that they will not provide counsel during a reasonable period of time in which investigation in the field is carried out, they may refrain from doing so without violating the person's Fifth Amendment privilege so long as they do not question him during that time.

If the interrogation continues without the presence of an attorney and a statement is taken, a heavy burden rests on the government to demonstrate that the defendant knowingly and intelligently waived his privilege against self-incrimination and his right to retained or appointed counsel. This Court has always set high standards of proof for the waiver of constitutional rights, and we reassert these standards as applied to in-custody interrogation. Since the State is responsible for establishing the isolated circumstances under which the interrogation takes place and has the only means of making available corroborated evidence of warnings

[b] While a warning that the indigent may have counsel appointed need not be given to the person who is known to have an attorney or is known to have ample funds to secure one, the expedient of giving a warning is too simple and the rights involved too important to engage in *ex post facto* inquiries into financial ability when there is any doubt at all on that score.

[c] If an individual indicates his desire to remain silent, but has an attorney present, there may be some circumstances in which further questioning would be permissible. In the absence of evidence of overbearing, statements then made in the presence of counsel might be free of the compelling influence of the interrogation process and might fairly be construed as a waiver of the privilege for purposes of these statements.

given during incommunicado interrogation, the burden is rightly on its shoulders.

An express statement that the individual is willing to make a statement and does not want an attorney followed closely by a statement could constitute a waiver. But a valid waiver will not be presumed simply from the silence of the accused after warnings are given or simply from the fact that a confession was in fact eventually obtained. * * *

* * * Moreover, where in-custody interrogation is involved, there is no room for the contention that the privilege is waived if the individual answers some questions or gives some information on his own prior to invoking his right to remain silent when interrogated.

Whatever the testimony of the authorities as to waiver of rights by an accused, the fact of lengthy interrogation or incommunicado incarceration before a statement is made is strong evidence that the accused did not validly waive his rights. In these circumstances the fact that the individual eventually made a statement is consistent with the conclusion that the compelling influence of the interrogation finally forced him to do so. It is inconsistent with any notion of a voluntary relinquishment of the privilege. Moreover, any evidence that the accused was threatened, tricked, or cajoled into a waiver will, of course, show that the defendant did not voluntarily waive his privilege. The requirement of warnings and waiver of rights is a fundamental with respect to the Fifth Amendment privilege and not simply a preliminary ritual to existing methods of interrogation.

The warnings required and the waiver necessary in accordance with our opinion today are, in the absence of a fully effective equivalent, prerequisites to the admissibility of any statement made by a defendant. No distinction can be drawn between statements which are direct confessions and statements which amount to "admissions" of part or all of an offense. The privilege against self-incrimination protects the individual from being compelled to incriminate himself in any manner; it does not distinguish degrees of incrimination. Similarly, for precisely the same reason, no distinction may be drawn between inculpatory statements and statements alleged to be merely "exculpatory." If a statement made were in fact truly exculpatory it would, of course, never be used by the prosecution. In fact, statements merely intended to be exculpatory by the defendant are often used to impeach his testimony at trial or to demonstrate untruths in the statement given under interrogation and thus to prove guilt by implication. These statements are incriminating in any meaningful sense of the word and may not be used without the full warnings and effective waiver required for any other statement. * * *

The principles announced today deal with the protection which must be given to the privilege against self-incrimination when the individual is first subjected to police interrogation while in custody at the station or otherwise deprived of his freedom of action in any significant way. * * * Under the system of warnings we delineate today or under any other system which may be devised and found effective, the safeguards to be erected about the privilege must come into play at this point.

Our decision is not intended to hamper the traditional function of police officers in investigating crime. When an individual is in custody on probable cause, the police may, of course, seek out evidence in the field to be used at trial against him. Such investigation may include inquiry of persons not under restraint. General on-the-scene questioning as to facts surrounding a crime or other general questioning of citizens in the fact-finding process is not affected by our holding. It is an act of responsible citizenship for individuals to give whatever information they may have to aid in law enforcement. In such situations the compelling atmosphere inherent in the process of in-custody interrogation is not necessarily present.

In dealing with statements obtained through interrogation, we do not purport to find all confessions inadmissible. Confessions remain a proper element in law enforcement. Any statement given freely and voluntarily without any compelling influences is, of course, admissible in evidence.

* * *

Because of the nature of the problem and because of its recurrent significance in numerous cases, we have to this point discussed the relationship of the Fifth Amendment privilege to police interrogation without specific concentration on the facts of the cases before us. We turn now to these facts to consider the application to these cases of the constitutional principles discussed above. In each instance, we have concluded that statements were obtained from the defendant under circumstances that did not meet constitutional standards for protection of the privilege.

* * *

MR. JUSTICE CLARK, dissenting in Nos. 759, 760, and 761, and concurring in the result in No. 584.

It is with regret that I find it necessary to write in these cases. However, I am unable to join the majority because its opinion goes too far on too little, while my dissenting brethren do not go quite far enough. Nor can I join in the Court's criticism of the present practices of police and investigatory agencies as to custodial interrogation. The materials it refers to as "police manuals" are, as I read them, merely writings in this field by professors and some police officers. * * *

* * * Such a strict constitutional specific inserted at the nerve center of crime detection may well kill the patient. Since there is at this time a paucity of information and an almost total lack of empirical knowledge on the practical operation of requirements truly comparable to those announced by the majority, I would be more restrained lest we go too far too fast.

MR. JUSTICE HARLAN, whom MR. JUSTICE STEWART and MR. JUSTICE WHITE join, dissenting.

I believe the decision for the Court represents poor constitutional law and entails harmful consequences for the country at large. How serious these consequences may prove to be only time can tell. But the basic flaws in the Court's justification seem to me readily apparent now once all sides of the problem are considered.

* * *

* * * The new rules are not designed to guard against police brutality or other unmistakably banned forms of coercion. Those who use third-degree tactics and deny them in court are equally able and destined to lie as skillfully about warnings and waivers. Rather, the thrust of the new rules is to negate all pressures, to reinforce the nervous or ignorant suspect, and ultimately to discourage any confession at all. The aim in short is toward "voluntariness" in a utopian sense, or to view it from a different angle, voluntariness with a vengeance.

* * *

[Justice Harlan surveys the limits on confessions the Court evolved under the Due Process Clause of the Fourteenth Amendment.]

I turn now to the Court's asserted reliance on the Fifth Amendment, an approach which I frankly regard as a *trompe l'oeil.* The Court's opinion in my view reveals no adequate basis for extending the Fifth Amendment's privilege against self-incrimination to the police station. Far more important, it fails to show that the Court's new rules are well supported, let alone compelled, by Fifth Amendment precedents. Instead, the new rules actually derive from quotation and analogy drawn from precedents under the Sixth Amendment, which should properly have no bearing on police interrogation.

The Court's opening contention, that the Fifth Amendment governs police station confessions, is perhaps not an impermissible extension of the law but it has little to commend itself in the present circumstances. Historically, the privilege against self-incrimination did not bear at all on the use of extra-legal confessions, for which distinct standards evolved. * * * Even those who would readily enlarge the privilege must concede some linguistic difficulties since the Fifth Amendment in terms proscribes only compelling any person "in any criminal case to be a witness against himself."

* * *

Having decided that the Fifth Amendment privilege does apply in the police station, the Court reveals that the privilege imposes more exacting restrictions than does the Fourteenth Amendment's voluntariness test. * * *

The more important premise is that pressure on the suspect must be eliminated though it be only the subtle influence of the atmosphere and surroundings. The Fifth Amendment, however, has never been thought to forbid *all* pressure to incriminate one's self in the situations covered by it. * * * This is not to say that short of jail or torture any sanction is permissible in any case; policy and history alike may impose sharp limits. However, the Court's unspoken assumption that *any* pressure violates the privilege is not supported by the precedents and it has failed to show why the Fifth Amendment prohibits that relatively mild pressure the Due Process Clause permits.

The Court appears similarly wrong in thinking that precise knowledge of one's rights is a settled prerequisite under the Fifth Amendment to the loss of its protections. * * * No Fifth Amendment precedent is cited for the Court's contrary view. * * *

MR. JUSTICE WHITE, with whom MR. JUSTICE HARLAN and MR. JUSTICE STEWART join, dissenting.

The proposition that the privilege against self-incrimination forbids in-custody interrogation without the warnings specified in the majority opinion and without a clear waiver of counsel has no significant support in the history of the privilege or in the language of the Fifth Amendment. As for the English authorities and the common-law history, the privilege, firmly established in the second half of the seventeenth century, was never applied except to prohibit compelled judicial interrogations. * * * Morgan, The Privilege Against Self-Incrimination, 34 Minn.L.Rev. 1, 18 (1949).

[Justice White surveyed the history of the Fifth Amendment and the Court's prior treatment of confession cases in support of this proposition.]

* * *

[E]ven if one assumed that there was an adequate factual basis for the conclusion that all confessions obtained during in-custody interrogation are the product of compulsion, the rule propounded by the Court would still be irrational, for, apparently, it is only if the accused is also warned of his right to counsel and waives both that right and the right against self-incrimination that the inherent compulsiveness of interrogation disappears. But if the defendant may not answer without a warning a question such as "Where were you last night?" without having his answer be a compelled one, how can the Court ever accept his negative answer to the question of whether he wants to consult his retained counsel or counsel whom the court will appoint? * * * The Court apparently realizes its dilemma of foreclosing questioning without the necessary warnings but at the same time permitting the accused, sitting in the same chair in front of the same policemen, to waive his right to consult an attorney. It expects, however, that the accused will not often waive the right; and if it is claimed that he has, the State faces a severe, if not impossible burden of proof.

All of this makes very little sense in terms of the compulsion which the Fifth Amendment proscribes. That amendment deals with compelling the accused himself. It is his free will that is involved. Confessions and incriminating admissions, as such, are not forbidden evidence; only those which are compelled are banned. I doubt that the Court observes these distinctions today. * * *

* * *

The obvious underpinning of the Court's decision is a deep-seated distrust of all confessions. As the Court declares that the accused may not be interrogated without counsel present, absent a waiver of the right to counsel, and as the Court all but admonishes the lawyer to advise the accused to remain silent, the result adds up to a judicial judgment that evidence from the accused should not be used against him in any way, whether compelled or not. This is the not so subtle overtone of the opinion—that it is inherently wrong for the police to gather evidence from the accused himself. And this is precisely the nub of this dissent. I see nothing wrong or immoral, and certainly nothing unconstitutional, in the police's asking a suspect whom they have reasonable cause to arrest whether or not he killed his wife or in confronting him with the evidence on which the arrest was based, at least where he has been plainly advised that he may remain completely silent * * *. Particularly when corroborated, as where the police have confirmed the accused's disclosure of the hiding place of implements or fruits of the crime, such confessions have the highest reliability and significantly contribute to the certitude with which we may believe the accused is guilty. * * *

Analysis of Miranda

Miranda brought the Fifth Amendment into the stationhouse by way of three critical insights. First, a person subject to police questioning is, in effect, testifying in a criminal case because anything he says can, and likely will, be put before the jury through the testimony of officers or in the defendant's own words if his statements are written or recorded. Second, any statements given in response to interrogations conducted by police agents in a custodial setting are "compelled" because custodial interrogation present suspects with an "inherently coercive atmosphere."[15] It follows, the Court concludes, that allowing the prosecution to admit into evidence at trial statements taken during custodial interrogation violates the Fifth Amendment privilege against compelled witnessing unless interrogators take steps to dispel that inherently coercive atmosphere.

This is *Miranda*'s fundamental constitutional holding. Importantly, the Court does not forbid custodial interrogation or bar the admission at trial of all statements taken during custodial interrogation. It instead offers law enforcement guidance as to how officers can dispel the inherently coercive atmosphere that attends custodial interrogation. This is the office of the prophylactic measures prescribed in *Miranda*, which track the constitutional holding. If a suspect subjected to custodial interrogation is, in effect, about to take the stand in his own criminal trial, then he must be apprised of this fact, just as he would be at trial. Having been made aware of this circumstance, the suspect must be further apprised that he has the absolute right not to testify, just as he would at trial. The decision whether to take the stand in one's own defense is heady indeed—perhaps one of the most fraught faced by any criminal defendant. At trial, criminal defendants have the right to consult counsel before making this important decision. In keeping with the Court's holding in Escobedo v. Illinois, 378 U.S. 478 (1964), which we will discuss with the materials on the Sixth Amendment, a suspect who is, in effect, being asked to testify against himself at his own trial should have the same opportunity to consult with counsel.[16] Having held that indigent defendants have a right to appointed counsel in Gideon v. Wainwright, 372 U.S. 335 (1963), the Court reasons that an indigent suspect facing the prospect of testifying against himself during a custodial interrogation should likewise have access to appointed counsel. And, finally, if a suspect is compelled to witness against himself during a custodial interrogation, then, by consequence of the privilege itself, his

[15] Suspects may also confront a version of the cruel trilemma during custodial interrogations—confess (and go to jail), lie and face charges for obstruction of justice or lying to investigators (and go to jail), or remain silent and risk an adverse inference (and go to jail). See Bram v. United States, 168 U.S. 532, 562 ("It cannot be doubted that, placed in the position in which the accused was when the statement was made to him that the other suspected person had charged him with crime, the result was to produce upon his mind the fear that, if he remained silent, it would be considered an admission of guilt, and therefore render certain his being committed for trial as the guilty person, and it cannot be conceived that the converse impression would not also have naturally arisen, that, by denying there was hope of removing the suspicion from himself.") By extending the Fifth Amendment privilege against compelled witnessing to the interrogation room, the Court resolves this trilemma by eliminating the threat of an adverse inference if a suspect remains silent in the face of police questioning.

[16] The Court would later reframe the holding in *Escobedo* as grounded in the Fifth Amendment privilege against self-incrimination rather than the Sixth Amendment right to counsel. *See* Kirby v. Illinois, 406 U.S. 682, 689 (1972) (noting that "the Court, in retrospect, perceived that the 'prime purpose' of *Escobedo* was not to vindicate the constitutional right to counsel as such, but, like *Miranda*, 'to guarantee full effectuation of the privilege against self-incrimination. . . .' ").

statements cannot be introduced as part of the prosecution's case-in-chief at trial (though, as we shall see, this exclusionary rule provides less protection than the absolute prohibition on compelled trial testimony and grants of immunity used to bypass that prohibition).

Of course, a criminal defendant can elect to take the stand at trial and may even proceed as his own counsel. The Court concludes that suspects facing custodial interrogation should have the same authority to waive their rights and answer questions. As Justice White suggests in his dissenting opinion, it may well be farcical to think that the minimal warnings prescribed by the Court are sufficient to underwrite a truly knowing, voluntary, and intelligent waiver of these important rights amidst the inherently coercive atmosphere of the interrogation room. After all, parallel waivers in the trial setting would be preceded by an extended colloquy with a neutral judicial officer. But the Court seems comfortable with the compromise between Fifth Amendment concerns and law enforcement interests in securing reliable, voluntary confessions.

Despite its logic, *Miranda* was viewed by many as a radical change in the law because the scope of the Fifth Amendment had been thought limited to protecting against formal modes of state compulsion—such as contempt of court. But the history of the privilege against self-incrimination is ambiguous enough that reasonable people easily may reach different conclusions as to whether it should reach into the modern day stationhouse. For a defense of the majority's approach, see Kamisar, A Dissent From the Miranda Dissents: Some Comments on the "New" Fifth Amendment and the Old "Voluntariness" Test, 65 Mich.L.Rev. 59 (1966).

Miranda's importation of the Fifth Amendment into the stationhouse, and the Court's rationale for doing so, is explained by Professor Schulhofer in *Miranda's* Practical Effect: Substantial Benefits and Vanishingly Small Social Costs, 90 Nw.U.L.Rev. 500 (1996):

> Police do not have to violate KGB standards in order to violate the Fifth Amendment. * * * [W]hatever one may think of *Miranda*, it is clear—and uncontroversial—that pressure need not rise to the level of overbearing physical or psychological coercion, in the due process sense, before it is sufficiently compelling to violate the Fifth Amendment. Outside the context of police interrogation, the law has long been settled, before *Miranda* and since, that the Fifth Amendment is violated by any pressure or penalty deliberately imposed for the purpose of getting a criminal suspect to speak. [citing cases such as *Lefkowitz* and *Griffin*, discussed earlier in this Chapter]. * * * The opposing view, pressed so hard by *Miranda's* critics—that Fifth Amendment compulsion and due-process coercion are identical concepts—would, if taken seriously and applied to contexts other than

police interrogation, make shreds of the entire fabric of Fifth Amendment doctrine and tradition.

Miranda's innovation was to hold that police interrogation could no longer be treated as a world apart. Prior to *Miranda*, the courts had uniformly held that police interrogation, because it imposed no formal penalty for silence, was immune from the Fifth Amendment limitations that apply in every other context. Because there was no formal legal obligation to speak, and thus no duty against which a formal privilege of silence could be applied, there simply was no privilege for the arrested suspect to waive * * *. *Miranda*, in a radical break with prior precedent, rejected that view. The Court's central holding was not the now-famous warnings, but the principle that Fifth Amendment standards would henceforth apply. And the two premises cited to support that conclusion, though hotly contested then, are surely uncontroversial now: that a formalistic showing of compulsion by legal process or official punishment cannot be essential, and that from every practical vantage point, once a suspect is isolated in police custody and deprived of his freedom to leave, interrogation involves pressures that can dwarf those that were decisive in cases like *Griffin* and *Lefkowitz*. The pressures are normally compelling in this practical sense, as even *Miranda's* most committed critics now acknowledge. * * * As a result, the typical custodial police interrogation, even if not brutally coercive in the due process sense, will readily (perhaps almost invariably) violate the Fifth Amendment bar on the use of compelling pressure, at least in the absence of safeguards sufficient to dispel that pressure.

In thinking about *Miranda*, it might be useful to ask whether a suspect who is compelled to undergo interrogation in the police station might believe that the police have the power to keep him in custody and to ask questions until he confesses. If so, the warnings simply clarify that the suspect may be confined against his will but not compelled to speak. See Saltzburg, Miranda v. Arizona Revisited: Constitutional Law or Judicial Fiat, 26 Washburn L.Rev. 1 (1986).

Judicial Review and Education of the Public

The Court in *Miranda* appears to have two distinct goals, and it is useful to consider them separately. First, the Court was clearly concerned that under the due process test it was impossible to have meaningful judicial review over police interrogation practices. It is difficult after an interrogation to determine how coercive it really was, especially when the usual witnesses are police officers and the suspect—none of whom are neutral observers. One purpose of *Miranda* is therefore to create a prophylactic rule to aid in judicial review: If the warnings are not given, then a confession in response to custodial interrogation is irrebuttably presumed to be tainted. If warnings are given, then the confession still may not be voluntary, but at least courts have some greater confidence in any confession that is obtained. But, to the extent that *Miranda* was intended to ease the task of judicial review of confessions, it is subject to attack on the ground that tape recording of interrogations and the placement of a heavy burden on the government to demonstrate voluntariness would have been a sufficient, and perhaps a better, way to promote effective review. The wisdom of the Court's approach also can be challenged on the ground that courts remain dependent on testimony (and perhaps "testilying") to determine whether and how the warnings were ever given and what happened afterwards.

Second, *Miranda* serves an important educational function. If our educational system taught criminal procedure alongside reading, writing, and arithmetic, *Miranda* might not have been necessary. But, prior to *Miranda*, it was the rare person who could articulate her constitutional rights to refuse cooperation to the police. Although the Court could not compel schools to teach criminal procedure, it could ensure timely education of suspects. Thus, part of *Miranda* involves educating suspects about the real choice they have to make in the interrogation process. See generally Thomas, Separated at Birth but Siblings Nonetheless: *Miranda* and the Due Process Notice Cases, 99 U. Mich. L.Rev. 1081 (2001).

The educational aspect of *Miranda* has its own problems, however. The Court was depending on the very police officers about whom it was concerned to give the warnings. How effective could the Court have expected police officers to be as teachers of constitutional rights to their adversaries? We do not rely on an officer "in the competitive enterprise of ferreting out crime" to protect our Fourth Amendment rights, but instead we impose a judicial officer as an intermediary. Why do we rely on a police officer to protect our Fifth Amendment rights? On the other hand, what is the alternative? That no custodial interrogation can occur until the suspect is brought before a magistrate and given warnings? How would that rule affect the state's ability to obtain confessions? See Kamisar, Kauper's "Judicial Examination of the Accused" Forty Years Later—Some Comments on a Remarkable Article, 73 Mich.L.Rev. 15 (1974) (suggesting that no custodial interrogation should be permitted until the suspect is presented to a judicial officer and told he has the right to remain silent).

Even as a set of warnings, *Miranda* is not wholly adequate. Despite the fact that Chief Justice Warren repeats the Court's holding in several places, it is arguable that there are subtle differences in different parts of the opinion. Test yourself on this by stating what you think the Court's required warnings are. Then ask someone else to do the same. Compare your warnings. You may find some significant differences. Also, ask yourself what you have *not* told the suspect. For example, have you communicated *what happens* if the suspect remains silent? Have you invited the person to ask questions to assure an understanding of the warnings? Have you informed the suspect that, if she wants to talk, then she can change her mind at any time? Have you told the suspect how long it will take to provide counsel if she wants counsel?

The Impact of Miranda

What effect has *Miranda* had? Some empirical evidence appears to indicate that the costs imposed by *Miranda* are limited. See generally Stephens, The Supreme Court and Confessions of Guilt 179–200 (1973), and authorities cited therein. See also Medalie, Leitz and Alexander, Custodial Police Interrogation in Our Nation's Capital: The Attempt to Implement *Miranda*, 66 Mich.L.Rev. 1347 (1968). Although in some places the absolute number of confessions may have fallen after *Miranda,* it does not appear that the conviction rates of law enforcement agencies has ever suffered. See Seeburger & Wettick, *Miranda* in Pittsburgh—A Statistical Study, 29 U.Pitt.L.Rev. 1 (1967). Certainly the published cases in which confessions are excluded and convictions reversed under *Miranda*—when the confessions would not have been excluded anyway under the involuntariness test—are few. See Guy and Huckabee, Going Free on a Technicality: Another Look at the Effect of the *Miranda* Decision on the Criminal Justice Process, 4 Crim.J.Res.Bull. 1 (1988) (*Miranda* issue raised in 9% of appeals, but only 5.6% of those claims were successful, resulting in a reversal rate of .51% of all criminal appeals).

Among the writings asserting that *Miranda* has hurt law enforcement are Office of Legal Policy, Report on the Law of Pretrial Interrogation (Feb. 12, 1986), defended in Markman, The Fifth Amendment and Custodial Questioning: A Response to "Reconsidering *Miranda*," 54 U.Chi.L.Rev. 938 (1987), and Caplan, Questioning *Miranda*, 38 Vand.L.Rev. 1417 (1985). An attempt to reevaluate the empirical data to consider all relevant costs, including lost cases and more lenient plea bargains, can be found in Cassell, *Miranda's* Social Costs: An Empirical Reassessment, 90 Nw.U.L.Rev. 387 (1996). Professor Cassell finds the costs of *Miranda* significant, especially in light of less onerous alternatives that he asserts are available to deal with the concerns of the *Miranda* majority. Cassell has argued that *Miranda* has imposed substantial harms on the innocent, including victims of criminals not caught due to the *Miranda* safeguards, and innocent people who are. accused of crime because police are not permitted to obtain a confession from another suspect. See Cassell, Protecting the Innocent From False Confessions and Lost Confessions—and From *Miranda*, 88 J.Crim.L. & Crim. 497 (1998). See also Cassell & Fowles, Still Handcuffing the Cops? A Review of Fifty Years of Empirical Evidence of *Miranda*'s Harmful Effects on Law Enforcement, 97 B.U. Law Rev. 685 (2017) (investigating crime clearance data, purportedly controlling for confounding factors, and concluding that there are "statistically significant reduction in crime clearance rates after *Miranda* for violent and property crimes.").

Contrary views are found in Schulhofer, The Fifth Amendment at Justice: A Reply, 54 U.Chi.L.Rev. 950 (1987); Schulhofer, Reconsidering *Miranda*, 54 U.Chi.L.Rev. 435 (1987); and White, Defending *Miranda*: A Reply to Professor Caplan, 39 Vand.L.Rev. 1 (1986). Professor White concludes that "the great weight of empirical evidence supports the conclusion that *Miranda's* impact on the police's ability to obtain confessions has not been significant." And a special committee of the ABA Criminal Justice Section reported that a "very strong majority of those surveyed—prosecutors, judges and police officers—agree that compliance with *Miranda* does not present serious problems for law enforcement." Special Committee on Criminal Justice in a Free Society, Criminal Justice Section, ABA, Criminal Justice In Crisis 28–29 (1988).

Professors Inbau and Manak assess another cost of *Miranda* in Miranda v. Arizona: Is It Worth the Cost? (A Sample Survey, with Commentary, of the Expenditure of Court Time and Effort), 24 Cal.Western L.Rev. 185 (1988). They conclude that *Miranda* questions take up a disproportionate amount of time in trial and appellate courts. They do not factor in, however, the amount of court time that would be expended if *Miranda* were overruled and the courts returned to the old case-by-case voluntariness test to regulate confessions.

If you agree with the supporters of *Miranda* that it has had no real effect on police officers' ability to obtain confessions, then you have to ask yourself, "what good is *Miranda* anyway?" Wasn't the point of *Miranda* to limit confessions? Professor Schulhofer addresses this question in *Miranda's* Practical Effect: Substantial Benefits and Vanishingly Small Social Costs, 90 Nw.U.L.Rev. 500 (1996):

> If *Miranda* really has so little impact on confession and conviction rates, why bother defending it? Isn't *Miranda* simply a hollow promise for civil libertarians and an inconvenient nuisance for law enforcement? If the *Miranda* Court's goal was to reduce or eliminate confessions, the decision was an abject failure. Plainly, however, the Warren Court had no such thought in mind; it explicitly structured *Miranda's* warning and waiver requirements to ensure that confessions could continue to be elicited and used. *Miranda's* stated objective was not to eliminate confessions, but to eliminate compelling pressure in the interrogation process.
>
> * * *
>
> For those concerned with the "bottom line," *Miranda* may appear to be a mere symbol. But the symbolic effects of criminal procedure

safeguards are important. Those guarantees help shape the self-conception and define the role of conscientious police professionals; they underscore our constitutional commitment to restraint in an area in which emotions easily run uncontrolled.

Miranda is, in any event, more than a mere symbol. In a constitutional system, procedure matters; the means to the end are never irrelevant. *Miranda* does not protect suspects from conviction but only from a particular method of conviction. The rate of confessions has not changed, but those confessions are now mostly the result of persuasion and the suspect's overconfidence, not of pressure and fear. That difference in method is crucial.

As you read further, you will see that evaluating the "costs" of *Miranda* is an ongoing process, as the Court has trimmed away much of the protection that the Court in 1966 clearly assumed would be present going forward. For various views on the first 50 years of experience with *Miranda*, see Symposium, The Fiftieth Anniversary of *Miranda v. Arizona*, 97 B.U. Law Rev. 681 (2017).

Miranda's Costs on Habeas Review: Withrow v. Williams

In Withrow v. Williams, 507 U.S. 680 (1993), the Court downplayed the costs of deciding *Miranda* issues, as it held that *Miranda* claims can be pursued on collateral review of a state court conviction. Justice Souter, writing for five Justices, concluded if *Miranda* claims were barred on habeas it "would not significantly benefit the federal courts." Justice Souter explained this assertion as follows:

> [E]liminating habeas review of *Miranda* issues would not prevent a state prisoner from simply converting his barred *Miranda* claim into a due process claim that his conviction rested on an involuntary confession. * * *
>
> We thus fail to see how abdicating *Miranda's* bright line (or, at least, brighter line) rules in favor of an exhaustive totality-of-circumstances approach on habeas would do much of anything to lighten the burdens placed on busy federal courts.[17]

Miranda's Impact on Review of Confessions for Voluntariness

If a defendant is interrogated while in custody, *Miranda* requires that he receive warnings before a confession is admissible. But it also provides that the suspect can waive his *Miranda* rights. But of course, if there is a waiver, this does not mean that officers can then beat or threaten the

[17] Justice O'Connor wrote a dissenting opinion joined by the Chief Justice, while Justice Scalia wrote a dissenting opinion joined by Justice Thomas.

suspect. Any confession made after *Miranda* warnings must still be voluntary.

Yet some have argued that *Miranda* has had a negative effect on the voluntariness inquiry. The argument is that once courts know that *Miranda* warnings have been given and the rights have been voluntarily waived, they tend to think that everything worked out fine. There is an indication in the case law that *Miranda* distracts judges from the propriety of the interrogation that follows the waiver of *Miranda* rights. For more on this point, see Stuntz, The Collapse of American Criminal Justice 235 (2011).

The Miranda Compromise

Part of the reason *Miranda* may not have much of an adverse effect on law enforcement is that the *Miranda* opinion is not as drastic as its opponents initially feared. *Miranda* does not put an end to confessions without counsel, nor does it prohibit stationhouse interrogation. *Miranda* does prescribe warnings, but these warnings are given by a police officer, not a judicial officer. *Miranda* provides a right to silence and to counsel, but the decision whether to *invoke* these rights (and conversely whether to waive them) is made by the suspect, *in the same coercive atmosphere* that the Court was so concerned about. *Miranda* does not impose a videotaping requirement, and so what goes on in the stationhouse can be as difficult to determine as under the old voluntariness test.

The Court in *Miranda* specifically rejected the suggestion—which would seem to flow from the premise that stationhouse interrogation is inherently coercive—that a suspect must have a nonwaivable right to an attorney before being interrogated. Thus, *Miranda* struck a compromise. See Benner, Requiem for *Miranda:* The Rehnquist Court's Voluntariness Doctrine in Historical Perspective, 67 Wash.U.L.Q. 59 (1989) ("confronted with the storm of controversy that *Escobedo* [implying an absolute right to counsel] created, the Court retreated in *Miranda,* and struck a compromise" that "transformed the debate about self-incrimination into a debate about waiver"); Saltzburg, Miranda v. Arizona Revisited: Constitutional Law or Judicial Fiat, 26 Washburn L.J. 1 (1986) ("*Miranda* is more of a compromise than most critics would care to admit").

For an argument that the *Miranda* Court did not go far enough and that "all suspects should have a nonwaivable right to consult with a lawyer before being interrogated by police," see Ogletree, Are Confessions Really Good for the Soul? A Proposal to Mirandize *Miranda,* 100 Harv.L.Rev. 1826 (1987). If *Miranda* had gone that far, would it have been overruled by now? Would a rule imposing an absolute right to counsel have garnered a majority of the *Miranda* Court?

Alternatives to Miranda

The *Miranda* Court emphasized that its system of warnings and waivers was not the only means possible for regulating the problem of custodial interrogation. According to Professor Cassell, however, the Court's invitation to alternatives "was in reality empty because it did not specify what alternatives would be deemed acceptable." Consequently, since *Miranda*, "reform efforts have been virtually nonexistent." In Cassell's view, the lack of experimentation results from the reluctance of the states to spend resources on alternatives that the Court might simply strike down. Cassell, *Miranda's* Social Costs: An Empirical Reassessment, 90 Nw.U.L.Rev. 387 (1996) . Undaunted, Professor Cassell proposes the following alternative to *Miranda*:

> Videotaping interrogations would be at least as effective as *Miranda* in preventing police coercion. The *Miranda* regime appears to have had little effect on what police misconduct exists. In contrast, videotaping, when it has been used, has often reduced claims of police coercion and probably real coercion as well. To be sure, police could conceivably alter tapes or deploy force off-camera. But if you were facing a police officer with a rubber hose, would you prefer a world in which he was required to mumble the *Miranda* warnings and have you waive your rights, all as reported by him in later testimony? Or a world in which the interrogation is videorecorded and the burden is on law enforcement to explain if it is not; where date and time are recorded on the videotape; where your physical appearance and demeanor during the interrogation are permanently recorded?

Do you agree that videotaping will be a better solution than *Miranda* to the problem of police coercion?[18] Does the proposal to videotape interrogations address the Court's concerns with compelled witnessing in *Miranda* or is it better understood as a way to detect and prevent involuntary confessions? Professor Schulhofer, in *Miranda's* Practical Effect: Substantial Benefits and Vanishingly Small Social Costs, 90 Nw.U.L.Rev. 500 (1996), argues that a videotaping requirement would be a valuable *supplement* to, but a problematic replacement for, the *Miranda* safeguards.

> In effect, the proposal to substitute videotaping for *Miranda* amounts to a police offer in the form, "We'll stop lying about what we do, if you allow us to do it." No doubt a videotaped record would often prevent

[18] Some state courts have relied on their own constitutions to mandate videotaping of all custodial interrogations. See, e.g., Kane, No More Secrets: Minnesota State Due Process Requirement that Law Enforcement Officers Electronically Record Custodial Interrogation and Confessions, 77 Minn.L.Rev.983 (1993). These requirements are, however, in addition to and not in replacement of the *Miranda* safeguards. See also Leonard Post, Illinois to Tape Police Questioning, Nat'l L.J., Aug. 4, 2003, p.1 (noting some police officers are critical of taping because "it absolutely hasn't shortened evidentiary hearings or the swearing contests" and that "When suspects have to go to the bathroom, we chase them with tape recorders.").

> police abuse and manipulation of the "swearing contest." But without clear substantive requirements against which to test the police behavior that the videotape will reveal, the objective record will lack any specific legal implications. * * * Thus, videotaping, though an excellent idea, does not meet the constitutional concerns about compulsion to which the *Miranda* safeguards are addressed. Videotaping could provide a useful complement to the *Miranda* protections, but it cannot replace them.

According to The Innocence Project, "[t]o date, Connecticut, Illinois, Maine, Maryland, Michigan, Missouri, Montana, Nebraska, New Mexico, North Carolina, Ohio, Oregon, Wisconsin, and the District of Columbia have enacted legislation regarding the recording of custodial interrogations. State supreme courts have taken action in Alaska, Indiana, Iowa, Massachusetts, Minnesota, New Hampshire, and New Jersey. Approximately 850 jurisdictions have recording policies."

In a Memorandum dated May 12, 2014, James M. Cole, Deputy Attorney General, announced a new Department of Justice policy, effective July 11, 2014, that establishes a presumption that federal prosecutors and law enforcement agents will record the entirety of custodial interrogations. There are exceptions. One is "where questioning is undertaken to gather national security-related intelligence or questioning concerning intelligence, sources, or methods, the public disclosure of which would cause damage to national security." There is a "residual exception" that applies "where the Special Agent in Charge and the United States Attorney, or their designees, agree that a significant and articulable law enforcement purpose requires setting [the presumption] aside."

The Memorandum opens with these paragraphs:

> This policy establishes a presumption that the Federal Bureau of Investigation (FBI), the Drug Enforcement Administration (DEA), the Bureau of Alcohol, Tobacco, Firearms, and Explosives (ATF), and the United States Marshals Service (USMS) will electronically record statements made by individuals in their custody in the circumstances set forth below.
>
> This policy also encourages agents and prosecutors to consider electronic recording in investigative or other circumstances where the presumption does not apply. The policy encourages agents and prosecutors to consult with each other in such circumstances.
>
> This policy is solely for internal Department of Justice guidance. It is not intended to, does not, and may not be relied upon to create any rights or benefits, substantive or procedural, enforceable at law or in equity in any matter, civil or criminal, by any party against the United States, its departments, agencies, or entities, its officers, employees, or agents, or any other person, nor does

it place any limitation on otherwise lawful investigative and litigative prerogatives of the Department of Justice.

Can you think of any other means by which police coercion can be controlled, without the loss of reliable evidence? Amar and Lettow, in Fifth Amendment First Principles: The Self-Incrimination Clause, 93 Mich.L.Rev. 857 (1995), suggest "a prophylactic rule that no police-station confession by a defendant is ever allowed in, unless volunteered by a suspect in the presence of an on-duty defense lawyer or ombudsman in the police station." In place of custodial interrogation, Amar and Lettow propose that at a pretrial hearing before a judge, the government would be permitted to compel a suspect to provide evidence against himself. The suspect would be given only "testimonial" immunity as opposed to use-fruits immunity, meaning that his statement could not be used as evidence against him, but the government could use the statement as a means of finding other information such as physical evidence and adverse witnesses. If the suspect refuses to make a statement at this pretrial hearing, Amar and Lettow propose that the suspect could be jailed for contempt, and that an adverse inference could be drawn at trial. Is this a better system than *Miranda*? Is this system possible given the Court's interpretation of the privilege against self-incrimination?

B. DID CONGRESS OVERRULE *MIRANDA*?

In 1968, Congress passed 18 U.S.C. § 3501, which provides, among other things, that a confession "shall be admissible in evidence if it is voluntarily given," and that voluntariness is to be determined on the basis of "all the circumstances surrounding the giving of the confession," including whether the defendant received warnings and counsel. Thus, warnings and counsel are simply factors in the voluntariness analysis—the absence of warnings or the failure to provide counsel do not themselves render a confession inadmissible under the statute. The expressed intent of Congress was to "overrule" *Miranda* in favor of a return to the due process "voluntariness" standard. The Supreme Court considered whether Congress had the power to overrule *Miranda* in the following case.

DICKERSON V. UNITED STATES

Supreme Court of the United States, 2000.
530 U.S. 428.

CHIEF JUSTICE REHNQUIST delivered the opinion of the Court.

In Miranda v. Arizona, we held that certain warnings must be given before a suspect's statement made during custodial interrogation could be admitted in evidence. In the wake of that decision, Congress enacted 18 U.S.C. § 3501, which in essence laid down a rule that the admissibility of such statements should turn only on whether or not they were voluntarily made. We hold that *Miranda*, being a constitutional decision of this Court, may not be in effect overruled by an Act of Congress, and we decline to overrule *Miranda* ourselves. We therefore hold that *Miranda* and its progeny in this Court govern the admissibility of statements made during custodial interrogation in both state and federal courts.

[Dickerson was charged with bank robbery and related offenses. He moved to suppress a confession on the ground that he didn't receive *Miranda* warnings. The Court of Appeals held that § 3501 was satisfied because Dickerson was not coerced. It then concluded that our decision in *Miranda* was not a constitutional holding, and that therefore Congress could reject the *Miranda* safeguards.].

* * *

Two years after *Miranda* was decided, Congress enacted § 3501. * * * Given § 3501's express designation of voluntariness as the touchstone of admissibility, its omission of any warning requirement, and the instruction for trial courts to consider a nonexclusive list of factors relevant to the circumstances of a confession, we agree with the Court of Appeals that Congress intended by its enactment to overrule *Miranda*. Because of the obvious conflict between our decision in *Miranda* and § 3501, we must address whether Congress has constitutional authority to thus supersede *Miranda*. If Congress has such authority, § 3501's totality-of-the-circumstances approach must prevail over *Miranda's* requirement of warnings; if not, that section must yield to *Miranda's* more specific requirements.

* * * Congress retains the ultimate authority to modify or set aside any judicially created rules of evidence and procedure that are not required by the Constitution. But Congress may not legislatively supersede our decisions interpreting and applying the Constitution. This case therefore turns on whether the *Miranda* Court announced a constitutional rule or merely exercised its supervisory authority to regulate evidence in the absence of congressional direction.

Recognizing this point, the Court of Appeals surveyed *Miranda* and its progeny to determine the constitutional status of the *Miranda* decision. Relying on the fact that we have created several exceptions to *Miranda's* warnings requirement and that we have repeatedly referred to the *Miranda* warnings as "prophylactic," New York v. Quarles, and "not themselves rights protected by the Constitution," Michigan v. Tucker, [cases discussed immediately infra in the section on exceptions to *Miranda*.] the Court of Appeals concluded that the protections announced in *Miranda* are not constitutionally required.

We disagree with the Court of Appeals' conclusion, although we concede that there is language in some of our opinions that supports the view taken by that court. But first and foremost of the factors on the other side—that *Miranda* is a constitutional decision—is that both *Miranda* and two of its companion cases applied the rule to proceedings in state courts—to wit, Arizona, California, and New York. Since that time, we have consistently applied *Miranda's* rule to prosecutions arising in state courts. It is beyond dispute that we do not hold a supervisory power over the courts of the several States.

The *Miranda* opinion itself begins by stating that the Court granted certiorari "to explore some facets of the problems . . . of applying the privilege against self-incrimination to in-custody interrogation, and to give concrete constitutional guidelines for law enforcement agencies and courts to follow." In fact, the majority opinion is replete with statements indicating that the majority thought it was announcing a constitutional rule. Indeed, the Court's ultimate conclusion was that the unwarned confessions obtained in the four cases before the Court in *Miranda* "were obtained from the defendant under circumstances that did not meet constitutional standards for protection of the privilege."

Additional support for our conclusion that *Miranda* is constitutionally based is found in the *Miranda* Court's invitation for legislative action to protect the constitutional right against coerced self-incrimination. After discussing the "compelling pressures" inherent in custodial police interrogation, the *Miranda* Court concluded that, "[i]n order to combat these pressures and to permit a full opportunity to exercise the privilege against self-incrimination, the accused must be adequately and effectively apprised of his rights and the exercise of those rights must be fully honored." However, the Court emphasized that it could not foresee "the potential alternatives for protecting the privilege which might be devised by Congress or the States," and it accordingly opined that the Constitution would not preclude legislative solutions that differed from the prescribed *Miranda* warnings but which were "at least as effective in apprising accused persons of their right of silence and in assuring a continuous opportunity to exercise it."

The Court of Appeals also relied on the fact that we have, after our *Miranda* decision, made exceptions from its rule in cases such as New York v. Quarles, and Harris v. New York, [also discussed immediately infra]. * * * These decisions illustrate the principle—not that *Miranda* is not a constitutional rule—but that no constitutional rule is immutable. No court laying down a general rule can possibly foresee the various circumstances in which counsel will seek to apply it, and the sort of modifications represented by these cases are as much a normal part of constitutional law as the original decision.

The Court of Appeals also noted that in Oregon v. Elstad, 470 U.S. 298 (1985), we stated that "[t]he Miranda exclusionary rule . . . serves the Fifth Amendment and sweeps more broadly than the Fifth Amendment itself."

Our decision in that case—refusing to apply the traditional "fruits" doctrine developed in Fourth Amendment cases—does not prove that *Miranda* is a nonconstitutional decision, but simply recognizes the fact that unreasonable searches under the Fourth Amendment are different from unwarned interrogation under the Fifth Amendment.

As an alternative argument for sustaining the Court of Appeals' decision, the court-invited amicus curiae contends that the section complies with the requirement that a legislative alternative to *Miranda* be equally as effective in preventing coerced confessions. * * * *Miranda* requires procedures that will warn a suspect in custody of his right to remain silent and which will assure the suspect that the exercise of that right will be honored. As discussed above, § 3501 explicitly eschews a requirement of pre-interrogation warnings in favor of an approach that looks to the administration of such warnings as only one factor in determining the voluntariness of a suspect's confession. The additional remedies cited by amicus do not, in our view, render them, together with § 3501 an adequate substitute for the warnings required by *Miranda*.

The dissent argues that it is judicial overreaching for this Court to hold § 3501 unconstitutional unless we hold that the *Miranda* warnings are required by the Constitution, in the sense that nothing else will suffice to satisfy constitutional requirements. But we need not go farther than *Miranda* to decide this case. In *Miranda*, the Court noted that reliance on the traditional totality-of-the-circumstances test raised a risk of overlooking an involuntary custodial confession, a risk that the Court found unacceptably great when the confession is offered in the case in chief to prove guilt. The Court therefore concluded that something more than the totality test was necessary. As discussed above, § 3501 reinstates the totality test as sufficient. Section 3501 therefore cannot be sustained if *Miranda* is to remain the law.

Whether or not we would agree with *Miranda's* reasoning and its resulting rule, were we addressing the issue in the first instance, the principles of stare decisis weigh heavily against overruling it now. * * *

We do not think there is such justification for overruling *Miranda*. *Miranda* has become embedded in routine police practice to the point where the warnings have become part of our national culture. While we have overruled our precedents when subsequent cases have undermined their doctrinal underpinnings, we do not believe that this has happened to the *Miranda* decision. If anything, our subsequent cases have reduced the impact of the *Miranda* rule on legitimate law enforcement while reaffirming the decision's core ruling that unwarned statements may not be used as evidence in the prosecution's case in chief.

The disadvantage of the *Miranda* rule is that statements which may be by no means involuntary, made by a defendant who is aware of his "rights," may nonetheless be excluded and a guilty defendant go free as a result. But experience suggests that the totality-of-the-circumstances test which § 3501 seeks to revive is more difficult than *Miranda* for law enforcement officers to conform to, and for courts to apply in a consistent manner. The requirement that *Miranda* warnings be given does not, of course, dispense with the voluntariness inquiry. But as we said in Berkemer v. McCarty, 468 U.S. 420 (1984), "[c]ases in which a defendant can make a colorable argument that a self-incriminating statement was 'compelled' despite the fact that the law enforcement authorities adhered to the dictates of *Miranda* are rare."

In sum, we conclude that *Miranda* announced a constitutional rule that Congress may not supersede legislatively. Following the rule of stare decisis, we decline to overrule *Miranda* ourselves. The judgment of the Court of Appeals is therefore

Reversed.

JUSTICE SCALIA, with whom JUSTICE THOMAS joins, dissenting.

* * *

It was once possible to characterize the so-called *Miranda* rule as resting (however implausibly) upon the proposition that what the statute here before us permits—the admission at trial of un-*Mirandized* confessions—violates the Constitution. That is the fairest reading of the *Miranda* case itself. * * *

So understood, *Miranda* was objectionable for innumerable reasons, not least the fact that cases spanning more than 70 years had rejected its core premise that, absent the warnings and an effective waiver of the right to remain silent and of the (hitherto unknown) right to have an attorney present, a statement obtained pursuant to custodial interrogation was necessarily the product of compulsion. Moreover, history and precedent aside, the decision in *Miranda*, if read as an explication of what the Constitution requires, is preposterous. There is, for example, simply no basis in reason for concluding that a response to the very first question asked, by a suspect who already knows all of the rights described in the *Miranda* warning, is anything other than a volitional act. And even if one assumes that the elimination of compulsion absolutely requires informing even the most knowledgeable suspect of his right to remain silent, it cannot conceivably require the right to have counsel present. * * * Thus, what is most remarkable about the *Miranda* decision—and what made it unacceptable as a matter of straightforward constitutional interpretation in the *Marbury* tradition—is its palpable hostility toward the act of confession per se, rather than toward what the Constitution abhors, compelled confession.

* * *

As the Court today acknowledges, since *Miranda* we have explicitly, and repeatedly, interpreted that decision as having announced, not the circumstances in which custodial interrogation runs afoul of the Fifth or Fourteenth Amendment, but rather only "prophylactic" rules that go beyond the right against compelled self-incrimination. * * * The Court has squarely concluded that it is possible—indeed not uncommon—for the police to violate *Miranda* without also "violating the Constitution."

[Justice Scalia discusses cases in which the Court stated that the *Miranda* warnings are prophylactic safeguards rather than constitutional rights, including New York v. Quarles and Oregon v. Elstad, discussed infra in this Chapter.]

In light of these cases, * * * it is simply no longer possible for the Court to conclude, even if it wanted to, that a violation of *Miranda's* rules is a violation of the Constitution. * * *

The Court seeks to avoid this conclusion in two ways: First, by misdescribing these post-*Miranda* cases as mere dicta. The Court concedes only "that there is language in some of our opinions that supports the view" that *Miranda's* protections are not "constitutionally required." It is not a matter of language; it is a matter of holdings. The proposition that failure to comply with *Miranda's* rules does not establish a constitutional violation was central to the holdings of *Tucker*, *Hass*, *Quarles*, and *Elstad*.

The second way the Court seeks to avoid the impact of these cases is simply to disclaim responsibility for reasoned decisionmaking. * * * [I]f confessions procured in violation of *Miranda* are confessions "compelled" in violation of the Constitution, the post-*Miranda* decisions I have discussed do not make sense. The only reasoned basis for their outcome was that a violation of *Miranda* is not a violation of the Constitution. * * *

* * *

Neither am I persuaded by the argument for retaining *Miranda* that touts its supposed workability as compared with the totality-of-the-circumstances test it purported to replace. *Miranda's* proponents cite ad nauseam the fact that the Court was called upon to make difficult and subtle distinctions in applying the "voluntariness" test in some 30-odd due process "coerced confessions" cases in the 30 years between Brown v. Mississippi and *Miranda*. It is not immediately apparent, however, that the judicial burden has been eased by the "bright-line" rules adopted in *Miranda*. In fact, in the 34 years since *Miranda* was decided, this Court has been called upon to decide nearly 60 cases involving a host of *Miranda* issues, most of them predicted with remarkable prescience by Justice White in his *Miranda* dissent. * * * But even were I to agree that the old totality-of-the-circumstances test was more cumbersome, it is simply not true that *Miranda* has banished it from the law and replaced it with a new test. Under the current regime, which the Court today retains in its entirety, courts are frequently called upon to undertake both inquiries.

* * *

I dissent from today's decision, and, until § 3501 is repealed, will continue to apply it in all cases where there has been a sustainable finding that the defendant's confession was voluntary.

NOTE ON DICKERSON

The Court in *Dickerson* seemed to be between a rock and a hard place: it had rendered decisions binding state courts, which it could only do if *Miranda* were a constitutional decision, and yet repeatedly referred to the *Miranda* prophylaxis as non-constitutional while elaborating limits on its accompanying exclusionary rule. Thus, the Court appeared to have treated the decision as both constitutional and non-constitutional. Court-watchers may have thought that the Court was finally going to choose. According to Justice Scalia, the Court instead decided to have its cake and eat it too by holding that the *Miranda* safeguards are constitutionally required, and yet all of the exceptions are retained, though now as exceptions to a constitutional rule. But is that a fair reading of *Dickerson*? Chief Justice Rehnquist clearly thinks it is not. In his view, the *Dickerson* Court goes no further than the Court did in *Miranda*.

Recall that *Miranda*'s core holding is that a suspect subjected to custodial interrogation is being compelled to bear witness against himself. *Miranda* does not displace the Court's due process jurisprudence, however. After *Miranda*, courts must ask both whether statements made during custodial interrogation have been "compelled" and whether they were given voluntarily. See Arizona v. Fulminate, 499 U.S. 279 (1991). These are separate questions. Each has constitutional dimension. To the extent § 3501 purports to render the Fifth Amendment privilege against compelled witnessing inapplicable in the context of custodial interrogations it is unconstitutional, and the Court so holds.

The *Miranda* Court did not hold that its curative prescription is constitutionally required. Chief Justice Warren makes clear that the prophylactic measures his Court prescribed are sufficient, but not necessary, to resolve concerns about compelled witnessing in the context of custodial interrogations. The *Miranda* Court explicitly leaves the door open to "other procedures" while recognizing that, as a practical matter, it is hard to imagine measures that would be both sufficient and less burdensome than its recommended procedure. *Dickerson* maintains that posture—the invitation for legislatures to innovate remains open—while affirming the *Miranda* Court's holding that ex post facto assessments of voluntariness based on a totality of the circumstances test are not sufficient to resolve Fifth Amendment concerns with compelled self-incrimination. Thus, the *Dickerson* Court's carefully crafted, and admittedly obscure, language (e.g., "*Miranda* was not a constitutional holding," but "*Miranda* is constitutionally based . . .").

For more on *Dickerson* and its effect on the *Miranda* exceptions, see Klein, *Miranda's* Exceptions in a Post-*Dickerson* World, 91 J.Crim.L. & Criminology 567 (2001).

Fed. R. Crim. P. 5

Before *Miranda*, the Supreme Court—exercising its supervisory power over federal courts—sought to protect suspects in custody by requiring their *prompt presentment before a magistrate*. The idea was that the magistrate would inform suspects of their rights to silence and counsel. If police did not comply with the prompt presentment requirement, statements made after the time at which the suspect should have been brought before a magistrate were held inadmissible. The "prompt presentment" requirement—and exclusion of confessions made in violation of it—became known as the *McNabb-Mallory* rule. That rule was, and still is, embodied in Fed. R. Crim.P. 5, which provides that a person making an arrest within the United States "must take the defendant without unnecessary delay before a magistrate judge."

18 U.S.C. § 3501 purports to limit *McNabb-Mallory* by providing that, in any federal prosecution, a confession made while under arrest "shall not be inadmissible solely because of delay in bringing such person before a magistrate judge * * * if such confession is found by the trial judge to have been made voluntarily * * * and if such confession was made * * * within six hours" of the arrest. The six-hour time limit is extended when further delay is "reasonable considering the means of transportation and the distance to be traveled to the nearest available" magistrate.

In Corley v. United States, 556 U.S. 303 (2009), Justice Souter wrote for the Court as it examined the effect of § 3501 on the *McNabb-Mallory* rule: "The question here is whether Congress intended 18 U.S.C. § 3501 to discard, or merely to narrow, the rule in McNabb v. United States, 318 U.S. 332 (1943), and Mallory v. United States, 354 U.S. 449 (1957), under which an arrested person's confession is inadmissible if given after an unreasonable delay in bringing him before a judge. We hold that Congress meant to limit, not eliminate, *McNabb-Mallory*."

Corley was arrested for bank robbery. He was detained and confessed about 9 hours after arrest. He was presented to a magistrate about 20 hours after that. Corley moved unsuccessfully to suppress his confessions under Rule 5(a) and *McNabb-Mallory*. The lower court that held that § 3501 entirely abrogated the *McNabb-Mallory* rule and replaced it with a pure voluntariness test. To that court, unreasonable delay was irrelevant as long as the confession was voluntary.

The Government's argument in the Supreme Court relied on § 3501(a), which provides that any confession "shall be admissible in evidence" in federal court "if it is voluntarily given." The government maintained that subsection (a) means that once a district court finds a confession voluntary it is admissible, regardless of *McNabb-Mallory*. Corley argued that § 3501(a) had no effect on *McNabb-Mallory*.

Justice Souter concluded for the Court that "Corley has the better argument." Justice Alito, joined by Chief Justice Roberts, and Justices Scalia and Thomas, dissented and argued that "[u]nless the unambiguous language of § 3501(a) is ignored, petitioner's confession may not be suppressed." Justice Alito also questioned whether the *McNabb-Mallory* rule retained its significance:

> [T]he need for the *McNabb-Mallory* exclusionary rule is no longer clear. * * * In the pre-*Miranda* era, the requirement of prompt presentment ensured that persons taken into custody would, within a relatively short period, receive advice about their rights. Now, however, *Miranda* ensures that arrestees receive such advice at an even earlier point, within moments of being taken into custody. * * * [I]t is certainly not clear that the *McNabb-Mallory* rule adds much protection beyond that provided by *Miranda*.

C. LIMITATIONS ON *MIRANDA* EXCLUSION

Miranda held that statements made during custodial interrogation must be excluded from a prosecutor's case-in-chief unless officers first take steps to dispel the coercive atmosphere. But what about other uses of those statements? Can statements obtained in violation of *Miranda* be used to impeach a defendant should he testify at trial? May officers exploit *Miranda* violations to advance their investigative efforts? Should the Fifth Amendment privilege against self-incrimination give way in some circumstances to important public and law enforcement interests? The Court addressed these questions in a series of cases decided in the years after *Miranda*.

1. Impeaching the Defendant-Witness

One of the most significant cases elaborating the limits of *Miranda* is Harris v. New York, 401 U.S. 222 (1971). Harris was charged with selling heroin to undercover police officers and took the stand in his own defense. On cross-examination, he was asked if he had made statements to the police immediately after his arrest that partially contradicted his direct testimony. The statements were not admissible as substantive evidence under *Miranda* because Harris was not warned of his right to counsel prior to his in-custody interrogation.

Writing for the Court, Chief Justice Burger held that using Harris's statements to impeach his credibility on cross examination did not implicate the constitutional rule announced in *Miranda*. That is because prior inconsistent statements used for purposes of impeachment are not offered for their contents, but instead, for the fact that they were made.[19] Thus, "[t]he trial judge instructed the jury that the statements attributed to [Harris] by the prosecution could be considered only in passing on petitioner's credibility, and not as evidence of guilt." Because his prior statements were not offered for the truth of the matter asserted, their admission did not cast Harris in the role of an out-of-court witness. The use of those statements for purposes of impeachment by prior inconsistent statements therefore did not constitute an act of testimonial witnessing.

By contrast, "having voluntarily taken the stand," Harris put his reliability and credibility as a witness at issue. He "was under an obligation to speak truthfully and accurately, and," the Chief Justice opined, "the prosecution here did no more than utilize the traditional truth-testing devices of the adversary process." "Had inconsistent statements been made by the accused to some third person," the Court continued, "it could hardly be contended that the conflict could not be laid before the jury by way of cross-examination and impeachment."

In reaching its holding, the Court made clear that Harris made "no claim that the statements made to the police were coerced or involuntary." Had officers secured his statements by torture, threats of violence, or other means rendering them involuntary for purposes of due process, then his statements would not have been admissible for any purpose, including impeachment. See Mincey v. Arizona, 437 U.S. 385 (1978).

In answer to concerns that its holding might encourage officers to violate *Miranda* in order to secure statements that might be used for impeachment purposes at a later trial, the *Harris*, Court reasoned as follows:

> * * * The impeachment process here undoubtedly provided valuable aid to the jury in assessing petitioner's credibility, and the benefits of this process should not be lost, in our view, because of the speculative possibility that impermissible police conduct will be encouraged thereby. Assuming that the exclusionary rule has a deterrent effect on proscribed police conduct, sufficient deterrence flows when the evidence in question is made unavailable to the prosecution in its case in chief.
>
> The shield provided by *Miranda* cannot be perverted into a license to use perjury by way of a defense, free from the risk of confrontation with prior inconsistent utterances. We hold, therefore, that petitioner's credibility was appropriately impeached by use of his earlier conflicting statements.

[19] The claim for relevance in this circumstance is that a witness who has previously made statements inconsistent with his testimony at trial is, by consequence of that inconsistency, less reliable as a witness, less credible, or both.

Justice Brennan, joined by Justices Douglas and Marshall, dissented in *Harris*. In his view, there is a constitutional distinction between impeachment using prior statements that bear directly on the question of guilt and those that bear on collateral matters. Even when technically offered for the fact that they were made rather than for their contents, Justice Brennan worried that allowing defendants to be impeached based on illegally obtained statements that relate directly to "the elements of the case," would place too great a burden on the decision to testify at trial because "[a]n incriminating statement is as incriminating when used to impeach credibility as it is when used as direct proof of guilt, and no constitutional distinction can legitimately be drawn."

Is it possible that the Court that decided *Miranda* would agree with *Harris*? Chief Justice Warren appeared to go out of his way to declare that statements obtained in violation of *Miranda* could not be used by the prosecution whether they were exculpatory or inculpatory. Is there any way to find that his Court did not intend to treat statements obtained in violation of *Miranda* as requiring the same remedies associated with other compelled statements—e.g., those made following a grant of *Kastigar* immunity, which cannot be used for impeachment after New Jersey v. Portash, 440 U.S. 450 (1979)?[20]

The Court reaffirmed *Harris* in Oregon v. Hass, 420 U.S. 714 (1975). In *Hass,* the defendant had received the full *Miranda* warnings and had said that he would like to call a lawyer. He was told that he could not telephone an attorney until he and the police officer reached the police station. Thereafter, the defendant made inculpatory statements before he was given an opportunity to call a lawyer. Thus the violation of *Miranda* was not in the failure to warn, but in the refusal of the police to respect the defendant's invocation of his *Miranda* rights. Finding that *Hass* was controlled by *Harris,* the Court held that the statements were admissible to impeach the defendant, who had taken the stand and offered direct testimony in conflict with his prior statements.[21]

The Court's decisions in *Harris* and *Hass* leave a defendant who has made a *Miranda*-defective confession with a practical problem. The defendant may not want to take the stand, because, if he does, the jury may learn about the confession. Even though the jury will be told that the confession can be used for impeachment purposes only, such an instruction is very difficult for a lay jury to follow. It is entirely possible that the jury

---

[20] The *Portash* Court distinguished *Harris* and *Hass* on grounds that in "*Harris* and *Hass,* the Court expressly noted that the defendant made no claim that the statements made to the police were coerced or involuntary." In contrast with statements taken in violation of *Miranda,* the Court concluded, "[t]estimony given in response to a grant of legislative immunity is the essence of coerced testimony . . . [it] may well be more reliable than information beaten from a helpless defendant, but it is no less compelled."

[21] Justice Brennan, joined by Justice Marshall, dissented on the same grounds he cited in *Harris.* Justice Douglas took no part in the decision.

will disregard the instruction and use the confession as evidence of guilt. That is precisely the concern underlying Justice Brennan's dissents in both *Harris* and *Hass*. On the other hand, if the defendant does not take the stand in order to avoid impeachment, the chance of conviction increases appreciably. See H. Kalven & H. Zeisel, The American Jury 160 (1960).

Was Chief Justice Burger right in *Tucker* to discount the possibility of strategic violations of the *Miranda* prophylaxis? Consider the police training tape entitled "Questioning Outside *Miranda*," which provides a lecture from an Assistant District Attorney suggesting options an officer might consider if the suspect, when given *Miranda* warnings, decides not to talk. The ADA suggests that the questioning continue "outside *Miranda*" because such questioning can help the police officer even if the confession is inadmissible at trial. The ADA notes, for example, that obtaining a confession "outside *Miranda*"

> forces the defendant to commit to a statement that will prevent him from pulling out some defense and using it at trial—that he's cooked up with some defense lawyer—that wasn't true. So if you get a statement "outside *Miranda*" and he tells you that he did it and how he did it or if he gives you a denial of some sort, he's tied to that, he's married to that, because * * * we can use statements outside *Miranda* to impeach or rebut. We can't use them for our case-in-chief. The D.A. can't trot them out to the jury before he says "I rest," but * * * we can use his "outside *Miranda*" statements to impeach him. * * * I mean we can't use them for any purpose if you beat them out of him, but if they're voluntary statements, the fact that they weren't Mirandized will mean that we cannot use them in the case-in-chief but it does not mean we can't use them to impeach or rebut. So you see you got all those legitimate purposes that could be served by statements taken "outside *Miranda*."

Given the value to the prosecution of a *Miranda*-defective confession after *Harris* and *Hass*, as emphasized in the police training video, do you think the Chief Justice was correct in asserting that sufficient deterrence flows from exclusion of the confession in the case-in-chief? Alternatively, do you think there is anything to deter? So long as statements taken in violation of *Miranda* are never admitted at trial for their contents, then is there ever a question of the defendant's being compelled to witness against himself? For a critique of *Harris*, see Weisselberg, Saving *Miranda*, 84 Cornell L.Rev. 109 (1998).

Impeachment with Prior Silence

Under standard evidentiary principles, a defendant can be impeached with prior silence if a reasonable person would have spoken at the time about the matter to which the defendant later testifies. For example, if Joe is sitting in his yard and his neighbor comes up, accuses him of stealing money from the neighbor's home, and Joe says nothing, then Joe can be impeached at trial with this silence if he later testifies that he did not steal the money. The silence is considered *inconsistent* with the later testimony—much as if Joe had said, "yes, I did steal the money."

Is it different if *Miranda* warnings are given? In Doyle v. Ohio, 426 U.S. 610 (1976), the defendant had been given *Miranda* warnings at the time of his arrest and chose to remain silent. At his trial, he took the stand and related an exculpatory story that he had not told to the police when Mirandized. On cross-examination, he was asked why he had not given the exculpatory explanation before; the jury was instructed that it could consider Doyle's silence as bearing on his credibility as a witness. Doyle appealed his conviction, arguing that the reference to post-*Mirandized* silence violated his constitutional rights.

The *Doyle* Court held that, after *Miranda* warnings are given, the Due Process Clause prohibits the government from using the defendant's silence against him, even for impeachment purposes.[22] In reaching this conclusion, the Court said that "while it is true that the *Miranda* warnings contain no express assurance that silence will carry no penalty, such assurance is implicit to any person who receives the warnings. In such circumstances, it would be fundamentally unfair and a deprivation of due process to allow the arrested person's silence to be used to impeach an explanation subsequently offered at trial."[23]

The Court later held that a person who *waived* his rights after receiving *Miranda* warnings and who spoke to the police could be asked at trial why his pretrial statement differed from his trial testimony, even if the question focused on a relevant omission in the pretrial statement. Anderson v. Charles, 447 U.S. 404 (1980). This is because the *Miranda* promise—that silence will not carry a penalty—is inoperative where the defendant chooses to speak.

---

[22] Justices Stevens, Blackmun, and Rehnquist dissented. Prior to *Doyle,* the Court had limited the use of silence upon arrest for impeachment, but as an evidentiary, not a constitutional, ruling. See United States v. Hale, 422 U.S. 171 (1975).

[23] The Supreme Court found no violation of *Doyle* in Greer v. Miller, 483 U.S. 756 (1987). When Miller took the stand in his trial for kidnaping, robbery, and murder, he testified that he had taken no part in the criminal activity and that two other defendants had come to his trailer and confessed to the crimes shortly after they occurred. The prosecutor asked Miller why he didn't tell his story to anyone after he was arrested. Miller's lawyer objected and moved for a mistrial. The trial judge denied the motion and instructed the jury to "ignore the question, for the time being." Justice Powell's opinion for the Court concluded that the trial judge in Miller's case, unlike the judge in *Doyle,* did not permit the inquiry into silence after receipt of warnings. Once objection was made, no further question or argument concerning silence was heard. Justice Stevens filed an opinion concurring in the judgment. Justice Brennan filed a dissenting opinion, in which Justices Marshall and Blackmun joined.

Pre-Arrest Silence

In Jenkins v. Anderson, 447 U.S. 231 (1980), the Court considered whether the use of *pre*-arrest silence for impeachment purposes was prohibited by *Doyle*. Jenkins stabbed and killed Redding. At his trial for murder, he contended that the killing was in self-defense. Jenkins waited until two weeks after the killing to turn himself in. On cross-examination and in closing argument, the prosecutor emphasized that Jenkins' two-week waiting period was inconsistent with his later claim of self-defense, i.e., if he had really acted in self-defense, then he would have come forward right away rather than remaining at large. Justice Powell, writing for the Court, found *Doyle* inapplicable, reasoning as follows:

> In this case, no governmental action induced petitioner to remain silent before arrest. The failure to speak occurred before the petitioner was taken into custody and given *Miranda* warnings. Consequently, the fundamental unfairness present in *Doyle* is not present in this case. We hold that impeachment by use of pre-arrest silence does not violate the Fourteenth Amendment.

Justice Stevens, joined by Justice Stewart, concurred in the judgment, stating that "the admissibility of petitioner's failure to come forward with the excuse of self-defense shortly after the stabbing raised a routine evidentiary question that turns on the probative significance of that evidence and presented no issue under the Federal Constitution." Justices Marshall and Brennan dissented.

Assume you are a criminal lawyer and a client comes to you and tells you facts that might indicate possible criminal activity. What do you advise? If you tell your client to tell the police everything she knows, you are a more effective agent for the government than the police can be under *Miranda*. If you tell your client to do nothing, *Jenkins* suggests that the client may suffer as a result. Could you tell your client to send an anonymous letter to the police stating that she is not guilty of criminal activity and that her failure to come forward represents a decision not to risk misinterpretation of the facts and concomitant incrimination? Would this bar use of silence as evidence under *Jenkins*?

For a criticism of *Jenkins*, see Saltzburg, Foreword: The Flow and Ebb of Constitutional Criminal Procedure in the Warren and Burger Courts, 69 Geo.L.J. 151, 203–05 (1980).

Post-Arrest, Pre-Miranda Silence

In Fletcher v. Weir, 455 U.S. 603 (1982), the Court considered whether *Doyle* prohibited the use of a suspect's *post-arrest* silence for impeachment purposes, when that silence *preceded* the giving of *Miranda* warnings. Weir testified at trial that he acted in self-defense, and the prosecutor asked why he did not offer this explanation when he was arrested. The Court, per curiam, held that "in the absence of the sort of affirmative assurances embodied in the *Miranda* warnings," impeachment with post-arrest silence was constitutionally permissible. The Court stated that the arrest by itself does not implicitly induce a suspect to remain silent.[24] See also United States v. Frazier, 394 F.3d 612 (8th Cir. 2005) (allowing the use of post-arrest, pre-*Miranda* silence in the government's *case-in-chief* because the defendant was under no compulsion to speak and therefore silence can be deemed an admission).

2. Admitting the Fruits of a *Miranda* Violation

By its terms (and even after *Harris*), *Miranda* requires that, if the police engage in custodial interrogation, and give no warnings or incomplete warnings, then the resulting confession must be excluded from the prosecution's case-in-chief. But what about the *fruits* of that confession? Some possible fruits of a *Miranda*-defective confession are: investigative leads pursued as a result of the confession; physical evidence; and a second confession by the suspect. In Michigan v. Tucker, 417 U.S. 433 (1974), and Oregon v. Elstad, 470 U.S. 298 (1985), the Court severely limited the exclusionary impact of *Miranda* on the fruits of confessions, relying on two propositions: 1) that exclusion of the fruit of a poisonous tree is only justified if a constitutional right is violated (i.e., the "poison" must be a constitutional violation); and 2) that a violation of *Miranda* is not by itself a violation of the Fifth Amendment privilege against compelled self-incrimination. That right is only violated if the statement itself is admitted for its contents at trial.

Leads to Witnesses: Michigan v. Tucker

In *Tucker,* the defendant was arrested for rape. Before he was interrogated, he was advised of his right to remain silent and his right to counsel, but was not told that he had the right to appointed counsel if he was indigent. The defendant told the police that he was with his friend Henderson at the time the crime was committed. The police then went to talk to Henderson. But Henderson gave information tending to incriminate the defendant. Before trial, the defendant moved to exclude Henderson's expected testimony because the defendant's *Miranda*-defective statement had led them to Henderson. In Tucker's view, Henderson's statement was the fruit of the poisonous tree. The motion was denied and the defendant was convicted.

The Court found that the failure to give the full *Miranda* warnings required exclusion of Tucker's confession, but not Henderson's testimony.

---

[24] Some state courts have rejected *Fletcher* as a matter of state law. See Nelson v. State, 691 P.2d 1056 (Alaska App.1984); State v. Davis, 38 Wash.App. 600, 686 P.2d 1143 (1984).

The Court found "no reason to believe that Henderson's testimony is untrustworthy simply because [Tucker] was not advised of *his* right to appointed counsel." Justice Rehnquist, writing for the majority, declared that exclusion of this reliable evidence was not required simply because it proceeded from Tucker's *Miranda*-defective confession. That is because *Miranda* warnings are "procedural safeguards" that are "not themselves rights protected by the Constitution but [are] instead measures to insure that the right against compulsory self-incrimination was protected." Although it is true, Justice Rehnquist continued, that "[t]his Court said in *Miranda* that statements taken in violation of the *Miranda* principles must not be used to prove the prosecution's case at trial. That requirement was fully complied with by the state court here: respondent's statements, * * * were not admitted against him at trial."

Because Tucker's Fifth Amendment interests were fully vindicated by exclusion of his statements from the prosecutor's case-in-chief, only prudential considerations could justify broader "judicially imposed consequences." Here, Justice Rehnquist considered whether the benefits of exclusion (deterring future *Miranda* violations) outweighed the costs of exclusion (the loss of reliable evidence). He reasoned that "[w]hatever deterrent effect on future police conduct the exclusion of [Tucker's] statements may have had, we do not believe it would be significantly augmented by excluding the testimony of the witness Henderson as well." Weighing this minimal incremental benefit against the cost of excluding Henderson's reliable testimony, the Court held that Henderson's testimony should not be excluded.

Justice Rehnquist noted, however, that if Tucker's confession had been *involuntary*, the Due Process Clause would require exclusion of the confession as well as its fruits. Justices Brennan and Marshall concurred in the judgment.

Subsequent Confessions: Oregon v. Elstad and Missouri v. Seibert

Justice O'Connor, writing for the Court in *Elstad,* extended the *Tucker* analysis to a case where a second confession resulted from a *Miranda*-defective confession. Justice O'Connor rejected the argument that the second confession had to be excluded because it was tainted by the first. Again, the Court relied on its view that violations of the *Miranda* safeguards do not constitute violations of the Fifth Amendment by themselves. So long as any statements taken in violation of *Miranda* are not admitted for their contents at trial, the Fifth Amendment privilege against compelled self-incrimination is vindicated ("We find that the dictates of *Miranda* and the goals of the Fifth Amendment proscription against use of compelled testimony are fully satisfied in the circumstances of this case by barring use of the unwarned statement in the case in chief."). As to the proposition that a broader exclusionary rule should apply, Justice O'Connor reasoned as follows:

> It is an unwarranted extension of *Miranda* to hold that a simple failure to administer the warnings, unaccompanied by any actual coercion or other circumstances calculated to undermine the suspect's ability to exercise his free will, so taints the investigatory process that a subsequent voluntary and informed waiver is ineffective for some indeterminate period. Though *Miranda* requires that the unwarned admission must be suppressed, the admissibility of any subsequent statement should turn in these circumstances solely on whether it is knowingly and voluntarily made.

By extension, Justice O'Connor recognized that, if Elstad's first confession was *involuntary* within the meaning of the Due Process Clause, then the second confession would be excluded if it was derived from the first. The fruits doctrine applies to due process violations, but not *Miranda* violations, because "[t]here is a vast difference between the direct consequences flowing from coercion of a confession by physical violence or other deliberate means calculated to break the suspect's will and the uncertain consequences of disclosure of a 'guilty secret' freely given in response to an unwarned but noncoercive question, as in this case."

Justice Brennan, dissenting in *Elstad,* argued that the majority had dealt a "crippling blow to *Miranda*" by allowing police officers to obtain an unwarned confession virtually secure in the knowledge that by giving warnings they could then obtain a second (admissible) confession "because the suspect knows that the authorities know of his earlier statements and most frequently will believe that those statements have already sealed his fate." That is precisely the circumstance presented to the Court in the following case.

MISSOURI V. SEIBERT

Supreme Court of the United States, 2004.
542 U.S. 600.

JUSTICE SOUTER announced the judgment of the Court and delivered an opinion, in which JUSTICE STEVENS, JUSTICE GINSBURG, and JUSTICE BREYER join.

This case tests a police protocol for custodial interrogation that calls for giving no warnings of the rights to silence and counsel until interrogation has produced a confession. Although such a statement is generally inadmissible, since taken in violation of Miranda v. Arizona, the interrogating officer follows it with *Miranda* warnings and then leads the suspect to cover the same ground a second time. The question here is the admissibility of the repeated statement. Because this midstream recitation of warnings after interrogation and unwarned confession could not effectively comply with *Miranda*'s constitutional requirement, we hold that a statement repeated after a warning in such circumstances is inadmissible.

* * *

Respondent Patrice Seibert's 12-year-old son Jonathan had cerebral palsy, and when he died in his sleep she feared charges of neglect because of bedsores on his body. In her presence, two of her teenage sons and two of their friends devised a plan to conceal the facts surrounding Jonathan's death by incinerating his body in the course of burning the family's mobile home, in which they planned to leave Donald Rector, a mentally ill teenager living with the family, to avoid any appearance that Jonathan had been unattended. Seibert's son Darian and a friend set the fire, and Donald died.

Five days later, the police awakened Seibert at 3 a.m. at a hospital where Darian was being treated for burns. In arresting her, Officer Kevin Clinton followed instructions from Rolla, Missouri, officer Richard Hanrahan that he refrain from giving *Miranda* warnings. After Seibert had been taken to the police station and left alone in an interview room for 15 to 20 minutes, Hanrahan questioned her without *Miranda* warnings for 30 to 40 minutes, squeezing her arm and repeating "Donald was also to die in his sleep." After Seibert finally admitted she knew Donald was meant to die in the fire, she was given a 20-minute coffee and cigarette break. Officer Hanrahan then turned on a tape recorder, gave Seibert the *Miranda* warnings, and obtained a signed waiver of rights from her. He resumed the questioning with "Ok, 'trice, we've been talking for a little while about what happened on Wednesday the twelfth, haven't we?," and confronted her with her prewarning statements:

> Hanrahan: "Now, in discussion you told us, you told us that there was an understanding about Donald."
>
> Seibert: "Yes."
>
> Hanrahan: "Did that take place earlier that morning?"
>
> Seibert: "Yes."
>
> Hanrahan: "And what was the understanding about Donald?"
>
> Seibert: "If they could get him out of the trailer, to take him out of the trailer."
>
> Hanrahan: "And if they couldn't?"
>
> Seibert: "I, I never even thought about it. I just figured they would."
>
> Hanrahan: " 'Trice, didn't you tell me that he was supposed to die in his sleep?"

Seibert: "If that would happen, 'cause he was on that new medicine, you know. . . ."

Hanrahan: "The Prozac? And it makes him sleepy. So he was supposed to die in his sleep?"

Seibert: "Yes."

After being charged with first-degree murder for her role in Donald's death, Seibert sought to exclude both her prewarning and postwarning statements. At the suppression hearing, Officer Hanrahan testified that he made a "conscious decision" to withhold *Miranda* warnings, thus resorting to an interrogation technique he had been taught: question first, then give the warnings, and then repeat the question "until I get the answer that she's already provided once." He acknowledged that Seibert's ultimate statement was "largely a repeat of information . . . obtained" prior to the warning.

The trial court suppressed the prewarning statement but admitted the responses given after the *Miranda* recitation. A jury convicted Seibert of second-degree murder. On appeal, the Missouri Court of Appeals affirmed, treating this case as indistinguishable from Oregon v. Elstad.

The Supreme Court of Missouri reversed, holding that "in the circumstances here, where the interrogation was nearly continuous, . . . the second statement, clearly the product of the invalid first statement, should have been suppressed." The court distinguished *Elstad* on the ground that warnings had not intentionally been withheld there * * *.

* * *

The technique of interrogating in successive, unwarned and warned phases raises a new challenge to *Miranda*. Although we have no statistics on the frequency of this practice, it is not confined to Rolla, Missouri. An officer of that police department testified that the strategy of withholding *Miranda* warnings until after interrogating and drawing out a confession was promoted not only by his own department, but by a national police training organization and other departments in which he had worked. Consistently with the officer's testimony, the Police Law Institute, for example, instructs that "officers may conduct a two-stage interrogation. . . . At any point during the pre-*Miranda* interrogation, usually after arrestees have confessed, officers may then read the *Miranda* warnings and ask for a waiver. If the arrestees waive their *Miranda* rights, officers will be able to repeat any *subsequent* incriminating statements later in court." Police Law Institute, Illinois Police Law Manual 83 (Jan.2001/Dec.2003). The upshot of all this advice is a question-first practice of some popularity, as one can see from the reported cases describing its use, sometimes in obedience to departmental policy.

* * * The object of question-first is to render *Miranda* warnings ineffective by waiting for a particularly opportune time to give them, after the suspect has already confessed.

* * * The threshold issue when interrogators question first and warn later is thus whether it would be reasonable to find that in these circumstances the warnings could function "effectively" as *Miranda* requires. Could the warnings effectively advise the suspect that he had a real choice about giving an admissible statement at that juncture? Could they reasonably convey that he could choose to stop talking even if he had talked earlier? For unless the warnings could place a suspect who has just been interrogated in a position to make such an informed choice, there is no practical justification for accepting the formal warnings as compliance with *Miranda*, or for treating the second stage of interrogation as distinct from the first, unwarned and inadmissible segment.[a]

* * * By any objective measure, applied to circumstances exemplified here, it is likely that if the interrogators employ the technique of withholding warnings until after interrogation succeeds in eliciting a confession, the warnings will be ineffective in preparing the suspect for successive interrogation, close in time and similar in content. * * * Upon hearing warnings only in the aftermath of interrogation and just after making a confession, a suspect would hardly think he had a genuine right to remain silent, let alone persist in so believing once the police began to lead him over the same ground again. * * * What is worse, telling a suspect that "anything you say can and will be used against you," without expressly excepting the statement just given, could lead to an entirely reasonable inference that what he has just said will be used, with subsequent silence being of no avail. Thus, when *Miranda* warnings are inserted in the midst of coordinated and continuing interrogation, they are likely to mislead and deprive a defendant of knowledge essential to his ability to understand the nature of his rights and the consequences of abandoning them. By the same token, it would ordinarily be unrealistic to treat two spates of integrated and proximately conducted questioning as independent interrogations

[a] Respondent Seibert argues that her second confession should be excluded from evidence under the doctrine known by the metaphor of the "fruit of the poisonous tree," developed in the Fourth Amendment context in Wong Sun v. United States, 371 U.S. 471 (1963): evidence otherwise admissible but discovered as a result of an earlier violation is excluded as tainted, lest the law encourage future violations. But the Court in *Elstad* rejected the *Wong Sun* fruits doctrine for analyzing the admissibility of a subsequent warned confession following "an initial failure . . . to administer the warnings required by *Miranda*." * * *. *Elstad* held that "a suspect who has once responded to unwarned yet uncoercive questioning is not thereby disabled from waiving his rights and confessing after he has been given the requisite *Miranda* warnings." In a sequential confession case, clarity is served if the later confession is approached by asking whether in the circumstances the *Miranda* warnings given could reasonably be found effective. If yes, a court can take up the standard issues of voluntary waiver and voluntary statement; if no, the subsequent statement is inadmissible for want of adequate *Miranda* warnings, because the earlier and later statements are realistically seen as parts of a single, unwarned sequence of questioning.

subject to independent evaluation simply because *Miranda* warnings formally punctuate them in the middle.

* * *

Missouri argues that a confession repeated at the end of an interrogation sequence envisioned in a question-first strategy is admissible on the authority of Oregon v. Elstad, 470 U.S. 298 (1985), but the argument disfigures that case. In *Elstad*, the police went to the young suspect's house to take him into custody on a charge of burglary. Before the arrest, one officer spoke with the suspect's mother, while the other one joined the suspect in a "brief stop in the living room," where the officer said he "felt" the young man was involved in a burglary. The suspect acknowledged he had been at the scene. This Court noted that the pause in the living room "was not to interrogate the suspect but to notify his mother of the reason for his arrest," and described the incident as having "none of the earmarks of coercion." The Court, indeed, took care to mention that the officer's initial failure to warn was an "oversight" that "may have been the result of confusion as to whether the brief exchange qualified as 'custodial interrogation' or . . . may simply have reflected . . . reluctance to initiate an alarming police procedure before [an officer] had spoken with respondent's mother." At the outset of a later and systematic station house interrogation going well beyond the scope of the laconic prior admission, the suspect was given *Miranda* warnings and made a full confession. * * *. Although the *Elstad* Court expressed no explicit conclusion about either officer's state of mind, it is fair to read *Elstad* as treating the living room conversation as a good-faith *Miranda* mistake, not only open to correction by careful warnings before systematic questioning in that particular case, but posing no threat to warn-first practice generally.

* * *

At the opposite extreme are the facts here, which by any objective measure reveal a police strategy adapted to undermine the *Miranda* warnings.[b] The unwarned interrogation was conducted in the station house, and the questioning was systematic, exhaustive, and managed with psychological skill. When the police were finished there was little, if anything, of incriminating potential left unsaid. The warned phase of questioning proceeded after a pause of only 15 to 20 minutes, in the same place as the unwarned segment. When the same officer who had conducted the first phase recited the *Miranda* warnings, he said nothing to counter the probable misimpression that the advice that anything Seibert said could be used against her also applied to the details of the inculpatory statement previously elicited. In particular, the police did not advise that

[b] Because the intent of the officer will rarely be as candidly admitted as it was here (even as it is likely to determine the conduct of the interrogation), the focus is on facts apart from intent that show the question-first tactic at work.

her prior statement could not be used.[c] Nothing was said or done to dispel the oddity of warning about legal rights to silence and counsel right after the police had led her through a systematic interrogation, and any uncertainty on her part about a right to stop talking about matters previously discussed would only have been aggravated by the way Officer Hanrahan set the scene by saying "we've been talking for a little while about what happened on Wednesday the twelfth, haven't we?" * * *

* * *

Because the question-first tactic effectively threatens to thwart *Miranda*'s purpose of reducing the risk that a coerced confession would be admitted, and because the facts here do not reasonably support a conclusion that the warnings given could have served their purpose, Seibert's postwarning statements are inadmissible. The judgment of the Supreme Court of Missouri is affirmed.

JUSTICE BREYER, concurring.

In my view, the following simple rule should apply to the two-stage interrogation technique: Courts should exclude the "fruits" of the initial unwarned questioning unless the failure to warn was in good faith. I believe this is a sound and workable approach to the problem this case presents. Prosecutors and judges have long understood how to apply the "fruits" approach, which they use in other areas of law. And in the workaday world of criminal law enforcement the administrative simplicity of the familiar has significant advantages over a more complex exclusionary rule.

I believe the plurality's approach in practice will function as a "fruits" test. The truly "effective" *Miranda* warnings on which the plurality insists will occur only when certain circumstances—a lapse in time, a change in location or interrogating officer, or a shift in the focus of the questioning—intervene between the unwarned questioning and any postwarning statement.

I consequently join the plurality's opinion in full. I also agree with Justice Kennedy's opinion insofar as it is consistent with this approach and makes clear that a good-faith exception applies.

JUSTICE KENNEDY, concurring in the judgment.

---

[c] We do not hold that a formal addendum warning that a previous statement could not be used would be sufficient to change the character of the question-first procedure to the point of rendering an ensuing statement admissible, but its absence is clearly a factor that blunts the efficacy of the warnings and points to a continuing, not a new, interrogation.

The interrogation technique used in this case is designed to circumvent Miranda v. Arizona. It undermines the *Miranda* warning and obscures its meaning. The plurality opinion is correct to conclude that statements obtained through the use of this technique are inadmissible. Although I agree with much in the careful and convincing opinion for the plurality, my approach does differ in some respects, requiring this separate statement.

* * * In my view, *Elstad* was correct in its reasoning and its result. *Elstad* reflects a balanced and pragmatic approach to enforcement of the *Miranda* warning. An officer may not realize that a suspect is in custody and warnings are required. The officer may not plan to question the suspect or may be waiting for a more appropriate time. Skilled investigators often interview suspects multiple times, and good police work may involve referring to prior statements to test their veracity or to refresh recollection. In light of these realities it would be extravagant to treat the presence of one statement that cannot be admitted under *Miranda* as sufficient reason to prohibit subsequent statements preceded by a proper warning. * * *

This case presents different considerations. The police used a two-step questioning technique based on a deliberate violation of *Miranda*. The *Miranda* warning was withheld to obscure both the practical and legal significance of the admonition when finally given. * * *

The technique used in this case distorts the meaning of *Miranda* and furthers no legitimate countervailing interest. The *Miranda* rule would be frustrated were we to allow police to undermine its meaning and effect. * * * When an interrogator uses this deliberate, two-step strategy, predicated upon violating *Miranda* during an extended interview, postwarning statements that are related to the substance of prewarning statements must be excluded absent specific, curative steps.

The plurality concludes that whenever a two-stage interview occurs, admissibility of the postwarning statement should depend on "whether the *Miranda* warnings delivered midstream could have been effective enough to accomplish their object" given the specific facts of the case. This test envisions an objective inquiry from the perspective of the suspect, and applies in the case of both intentional and unintentional two-stage interrogations. In my view, this test cuts too broadly. *Miranda's* clarity is one of its strengths, and a multifactor test that applies to every two-stage interrogation may serve to undermine that clarity. I would apply a narrower test applicable only in the infrequent case, such as we have here, in which the two-step interrogation technique was used in a calculated way to undermine the *Miranda* warning.

The admissibility of postwarning statements should continue to be governed by the principles of *Elstad* unless the deliberate two-step strategy was employed. If the deliberate two-step strategy has been used, postwarning statements that are related to the substance of prewarning statements must be excluded unless curative measures are taken before the postwarning statement is made. Curative measures should be designed to ensure that a reasonable person in the suspect's situation would understand the import and effect of the *Miranda* warning and of the *Miranda* waiver. For example, a substantial break in time and circumstances between the prewarning statement and the *Miranda* warning may suffice in most circumstances, as it allows the accused to distinguish the two contexts and appreciate that the interrogation has taken a new turn. Alternatively, an additional warning that explains the likely inadmissibility of the prewarning custodial statement may be sufficient. No curative steps were taken in this case, however, so the postwarning statements are inadmissible and the conviction cannot stand.

For these reasons, I concur in the judgment of the Court.

JUSTICE O'CONNOR, with whom THE CHIEF JUSTICE, JUSTICE SCALIA, and JUSTICE THOMAS join, dissenting.

* * *

I would analyze the two-step interrogation procedure under the voluntariness standards central to the Fifth Amendment and reiterated in *Elstad*. *Elstad* commands that if Seibert's first statement is shown to have been involuntary, the court must examine whether the taint dissipated through the passing of time or a change in circumstances * * *. In addition, Seibert's second statement should be suppressed if she showed that it was involuntary despite the *Miranda* warnings. Although I would leave this analysis for the Missouri courts to conduct on remand, I note that, unlike the officers in *Elstad*, Officer Hanrahan referred to Seibert's unwarned statement during the second part of the interrogation when she made a statement at odds with her unwarned confession. Such a tactic may bear on the voluntariness inquiry.

* * *

QUESTIONS AFTER SEIBERT

Notice that Justice O'Connor's dissent focuses on questions of voluntariness. Are these concerns salient in a case about *Miranda*? Or do they indulge the same non sequitur the *Dickerson* Court noted in its rejection of Congress's attempt to overrule *Miranda* by passing 18 U.S.C. § 3501?

Seibert was a 4–1–4 decision. With no majority opinion, how is it to be interpreted? Most lower courts have held that Justice Kennedy's opinion is controlling because it is the narrowest view on which five members of the Court could agree. This means that a confession made after a *Miranda*-defective confession will be admissible unless 1) the officers were in *bad faith* in not giving the warnings before the first confession; and 2) the second confession proceeded directly from the first. Justice Kennedy's approach was applied in United States v. Stewart, 388 F.3d 1079 (7th Cir. 2004) ("*Seibert* governs only where the police set out deliberately to withhold *Miranda* warnings until after a confession has been secured"; "[w]here the initial violation of *Miranda* was not part of a deliberate strategy to undermine the warnings, *Elstad* appears to have survived *Seibert*"), and United States v. Kiam, 432 F.3d 524 (3d Cir. 2006) ("Once we determine that the *Miranda* violation was not deliberate, we must fall back on *Elstad* as instructed by Justice Kennedy.").

So under Justice Kennedy's controlling view, the bad faith of the interrogating officer is the controlling factor. How can you tell if the officer's failure to give *Miranda* warnings was a bad faith attempt to engage in a two-step interrogation process with midstream warnings? In *Seibert* the officers *admitted* that they intended to evade *Miranda* by using a two-step interrogation process. How many officers are going to admit that?

For an application of the Justice Kennedy "bad faith" test see United States v. Terry, 400 F.3d 575 (8th Cir. 2005), where the defendant was convicted of violating a federal law prohibiting a person from possessing a firearm if that person has been previously convicted of a crime of domestic violence. Officers responded to a call about a domestic dispute and arrested Terry, who appeared drunk. At the station, an officer asked a single question without giving *Miranda* warnings—whether Terry had been previously convicted of domestic violence. Terry answered "yes" and seemed eager to talk further, but the officer stopped the conversation. Later he was given warnings and admitted that he had brandished a gun during the current domestic dispute. The court held that the confession made after warnings was admissible under *Seibert*. The court found "no evidence that the police engaged in a deliberate strategy to undermine the *Miranda* warnings. Accordingly, the concerns of Justice Kennedy * * * in *Seibert* are not present here." See also United States v. Williams, 681 F.3d 35 (2d Cir. 2012) ("public safety considerations plausibly account for [the officer's] limited questioning of Williams at the apartment in a way that militates against finding that the first interview was a premeditated attempt to evade *Miranda*"; officer asked only three questions about ownership and location of guns); United States v. Stewart, 536 F.3d 714 (7th Cir. 2008) (failure to give warnings was not in bad faith—officer was distracted because he was in a rush to release information on the defendant's accomplice, who was at large after a bank robbery). Compare United States v. Barnes, 713 F.3d 1200 (9th Cir. 2013) (court finds that warnings were deliberately delayed for fear that the suspect would be less willing to talk about another suspect that the agents were targeting; mid-stream warnings were ineffective where the subject of the interrogations was the same, there was no break in the interrogation, and the officers "treated the second round of interrogation as continuous with the first").

Is There a Seibert Violation if the Mirandized Statement Is Not Repetitive of the Unwarned Statement?: Bobby v. Dixon

In Bobby v. Dixon, 565 U.S. 23 (2011), the Court, in a unanimous per curiam opinion, reversed the Sixth Circuit, which had granted habeas relief because of a *Seibert* violation. The Court found that *Seibert* could not apply where the unwarned statement and the Mirandized statement are about different (even if related) crimes. Police had three encounters with the defendant. The first was when he came to the stationhouse to retrieve his car. When a detective issued *Miranda* warnings and asked him about the murder victim's disappearance, the defendant refused to answer questions without a lawyer. Later, as the investigation continued, the police determined that the defendant had forged the victim's name on a check the defendant received as a result of selling the victim's car. The police arrested the defendant and deliberately interrogated him without *Miranda* warnings. The defendant admitted obtaining an identification card in the victim's name and signing the victim's name on the check but claimed he had permission to sell the car and that he did not know where the victim was. The interrogation occurred intermittently for a total of 45 minutes over about four hours, and the police brought the defendant to a correctional facility where he was booked on a forgery charge. The same afternoon another suspect led police to the victim's body and said that the defendant had told him where the victim was buried. The police released the other suspect and had the defendant brought back to the stationhouse.

Upon arriving at the station, several hours after he had left it, the defendant said that he had heard the police had found a body and asked whether the other suspect was in custody. The police said "no," whereupon the defendant said that "I talked to my attorney, and I want to tell you what happened." The police provided *Miranda* warnings, the defendant talked, the police then used a tape recorder and, after again advising of *Miranda* warnings, taped the defendant's detailed confession of murder. At the defendant's trial, the confession of forgery was excluded from the trial but the confession to murder was admitted.

The Court found this case to be very different from *Seibert*. The Court described the result in *Seibert* and distinguished it in the following passage:

> In this case, no two-step interrogation technique of the type that concerned the Court in *Seibert* undermined the *Miranda* warnings Dixon received. In *Seibert*, the suspect's first, unwarned interrogation left "little, if anything, of incriminating potential left unsaid," making it "unnatural" not to "repeat at the second stage what had been said before." But in this case Dixon steadfastly maintained during his first, unwarned interrogation that he had "[n]othing whatsoever" to do with Hammer's disappearance. Thus, unlike in *Seibert*, there is no concern

here that police gave Dixon *Miranda* warnings and then led him to repeat an earlier murder confession, because there was no earlier confession to repeat. * * * Nor is there any evidence that police used Dixon's earlier admission to forgery to induce him to waive his right to silence later: Dixon declared his desire to tell police what happened to Hammer before the second interrogation session even began. * * *

The Court concluded as follows:

> The admission of Dixon's murder confession was consistent with this Court's precedents: Dixon received *Miranda* warnings before confessing to Hammer's murder; the effectiveness of those warnings was not impaired by the sort of "two-step interrogation technique" condemned in *Seibert*; and there is no evidence that any of Dixon's statements was the product of actual coercion. That does not excuse the detectives' decision not to give Dixon *Miranda* warnings before his first interrogation. But the Ohio courts recognized that failure and imposed the appropriate remedy: exclusion of Dixon's forgery confession and the attendant statements given without the benefit of *Miranda* warnings. Because no precedent of this Court required Ohio to do more, the Sixth Circuit was without authority to overturn the reasoned judgment of the State's highest court.

Physical Evidence Derived from Miranda-Defective Confessions

In United States v. Patane, 542 U.S. 630 (2004), the Court held that the exclusionary rule does not bar the admission of the physical fruits of a *Miranda*-defective confession as part of the prosecution's case-in-chief at trial. Patane was arrested for harassing his ex-girlfriend. He was released on bond subject to a restraining order, which he violated. Officers arrested him for violation of the order and began to give *Miranda* warnings before Patane interrupted and said he knew his rights. The officers had received a tip that Patane, a convicted felon, might have a firearm. They asked about it, and Patane told them where it was gave them permission to retrieve it.

The Justices did not address whether Patane's interruption justified the officers in failing to complete the warnings. Instead, they assumed that the officers violated *Miranda*. Justice Thomas's plurality opinion, joined by Chief Justice Rehnquist and Justice Scalia, reasoned as follows:

> [T]he *Miranda* rule is a prophylactic employed to protect against violations of the Self-Incrimination Clause. The Self-Incrimination Clause, however, is not implicated by the admission into evidence of the physical fruit of a voluntary statement. Accordingly, there is no justification for extending the *Miranda* rule to this context. And just as the Self-Incrimination Clause primarily focuses on the criminal trial, so too does the *Miranda* rule. The *Miranda* rule is not a code of

police conduct, and police do not violate the Constitution (or even the *Miranda* rule, for that matter) by mere failures to warn. For this reason, the exclusionary rule articulated in cases such as *Wong Sun* does not apply. * * *

* * * For present purposes, it suffices to note that the core protection afforded by the Self-Incrimination Clause is a prohibition on compelling a criminal defendant to testify against himself at trial. The Clause cannot be violated by the introduction of nontestimonial evidence obtained as a result of voluntary statements.

* * *

[I]n *Miranda*, the Court concluded that the possibility of coercion inherent in custodial interrogations unacceptably raises the risk that a suspect's privilege against self-incrimination might be violated. To protect against this danger, the *Miranda* rule creates a presumption of coercion, in the absence of specific warnings, that is generally irrebuttable for purposes of the prosecution's case in chief.

* * *

Our cases also make clear the related point that a mere failure to give *Miranda* warnings does not, by itself, violate a suspect's constitutional rights or even the *Miranda* rule. * * * This, of course, follows from the nature of the right protected by the Self-Incrimination Clause, which the *Miranda* rule, in turn, protects. It is a fundamental *trial* right.

It follows that police do not violate a suspect's constitutional rights (or the *Miranda* rule) by negligent or even deliberate failures to provide the suspect with the full panoply of warnings prescribed by *Miranda*. Potential violations occur, if at all, only upon the admission of unwarned statements into evidence at trial. And, at that point, the exclusion of unwarned statements is a complete and sufficient remedy for any perceived *Miranda* violation.

* * *

* * * [A]lthough it is true that the Court requires the exclusion of the physical fruit of actually coerced statements, it must be remembered that statements taken without sufficient *Miranda* warnings are presumed to have been coerced only for certain purposes and then only when necessary to protect the privilege against self-incrimination. For the reasons discussed above, we decline to extend that presumption further.

Justice Kennedy, joined by Justice O'Connor, concurred in the judgment and reasoned that "it is sufficient to note that the Government presents an even stronger case for admitting the evidence obtained as the result of Patane's unwarned statement" because "admission of nontestimonial physical fruits (the Glock in this case), even more so than the postwarning statements to the police in *Elstad* * * * does not run the risk of admitting into trial an accused's coerced incriminating statements against himself." He added that "I find it unnecessary to decide whether the detective's failure to give Patane the full *Miranda* warnings should be characterized as a violation of the *Miranda* rule itself, or whether there is 'anything to deter' so long as the unwarned statements are not later introduced at trial."

Justice Souter, joined by Justices Stevens and Ginsburg, dissented and argued that "[t]here is no way to read this case except as an unjustifiable invitation to law enforcement officers to flout *Miranda* when there may be physical evidence to be gained." He added that "[t]he incentive is an odd one, coming from the Court on the same day it decides Missouri v. Seibert."

Justice Breyer also dissented and, as in *Seibert*, concluded that courts should exclude the fruit of the poisonous tree "unless the failure to provide *Miranda* warnings was in good faith."

QUESTIONS AFTER PATANE

Patane and *Seibert* were decided the same day. One holds that the physical fruits of a *Miranda* violation are never excluded; the other holds that testimonial fruits of a *Miranda* violation must be excluded under certain circumstances. Is there a difference between physical and testimonial fruits that would justify such a difference in treatment? The Court holds that there is. In the course of explaining why, Justice Thomas's plurality opinion provides a refreshingly clear summary of the Court's *Miranda* jurisprudence.

In a few pithy paragraphs, Justice Thomas explains in frank fashion fundamental features of the Court's Fifth Amendment jurisprudence that sometimes are lost in opinions that can border on obscurity.[25] The *Miranda* Court, he reminds us, holds that the Fifth Amendment privilege against compelled self-incrimination is at risk during police interrogations because custodial interrogation presents suspects with an inherently coercive atmosphere. In recognition of this fact, *Miranda* erects a presumption that statements made during custodial interrogation are compelled. Admitting these statements at a subsequent criminal trial would violate the privilege because the now-defendant would, in effect, be compelled to testify against himself. But, if the contents of those statements are never put before the jury, then the privilege remains intact and there is no constitutional violation because the suspect is never a witness against himself. Unlike in the Fourth Amendment context, where the exclusion is justified as a tool to deter police misconduct, the *Miranda* exclusionary rule is inherent in the right itself.

[25] It is notable on this score that Chief Justice Rehnquist, who wrote the somewhat more elliptical majority opinion in *Dickerson*, joins Justice Thomas's plurality opinion in *Patane*.

Exclusion from the prosecutor's case-in-chief at trial perfects the right. No alternative remedy would suffice; and no additional remedy is required.[26]

The prophylactic measures prescribed by the Court in *Miranda* offer a constitutionally sufficient—and perhaps minimally sufficient—means of dispelling the coercive atmosphere inherent in custodial interrogation. Their constitutional status is tied to the privilege, however. If the privilege is perfected by exclusion of the statements at trial, then there is no residual constitutional concern and there is no remaining need for a remedy. There are no grounds for an action under 42 U.S.C. § 1983, see Chavez v. Martinez, 538 U.S. 760 (2003),[27] supra, and certainly no reason to exclude from the jury's consideration evidence that does not itself constitute testimony, including physical evidence. As *Seibert* recognizes, subsequent statements by a suspect are different precisely because they are testimony.

It is of course quite a different circumstance if "nontestimonial evidence [is] obtained as a result of [in]voluntary statements." In that case, due process rights are at stake, raising quite different questions relating to the role, justification, and scope of available remedies, including exclusion.

Justice Thomas's opinion does not command a majority of the Court. As noted, Justice Kennedy joins with Justice O'Connor to second Justice Thomas's proposed holding—that the physical fruits of a *Miranda* violation are not excluded—and his core rationale—because the "[a]dmission of nontestimonial fruits . . . does not run the risk of admitting into trial an accused's coerced incriminating statements against himself." Lower courts have treated Justice Kennedy's opinion as controlling. See United States v. Jackson, 506 F.3d 1358 (11th Cir. 2007) (noting that Justice Kennedy's opinion controls, and concluding that "the *Patane* plurality and concurrence agreed, at least, that *Miranda* does not require the exclusion of physical evidence that is discovered on the basis of a voluntary, although unwarned, statement. As several of our sister circuits have recognized, this narrow agreement is the holding of *Patane*.").

3. An Emergency Exception

New York v. Quarles

In New York v. Quarles, 467 U.S. 649 (1984), the Court concluded that "overriding considerations of public safety" can justify an officer's failure to provide *Miranda* warnings, and that an unwarned confession obtained under such circumstances is admissible *in the government's case-in-chief* despite *Miranda*. As Justice Kennedy makes clear in his *Seibert* opinion,

---

[26] The Court granted certiorari in City of Hays v. Vogt, 138 S.Ct. 720 (2018), to determine whether statements taken in violation of *Miranda* can be admitted into evidence at a probable cause hearing. The Court ultimately dismissed the case as improvidently granted.

[27] As of this writing, the Court has granted certiorari in Vega v. Tekoh, 142 S.Ct. 858 (2022), to determine whether 42 U.S.C. § 1983 provides a right of action against police officers who take statements in violation of *Miranda* that are later admitted at trial.

Dickerson "did not undermine" *Quarles*. See also United States v. Talley, 275 F.3d 560 (6th Cir. 2001) ("the *Dickerson* majority expressly incorporated existing decisions, like *Quarles*, into the 'constitutional' right to a *Miranda* warning").

Justice Rehnquist wrote for the majority in *Quarles* and stated the facts as follows:

> On September 11, 1980, at approximately 12:30 a.m., Officer Frank Kraft and Officer Sal Scarring were on road patrol in Queens, New York, when a young woman approached their car. She told them that she had just been raped by a black male, approximately six feet tall, who was wearing a black jacket with the name "Big Ben" printed in yellow letters on the back. She told the officers that the man had just entered an A & P supermarket located nearby and that the man was carrying a gun.
>
> The officers drove the woman to the supermarket, and Officer Kraft entered the store while Officer Scarring radioed for assistance. Officer Kraft quickly spotted respondent, who matched the description given by the woman, approaching a check-out counter. Apparently upon seeing the officer, respondent turned and ran toward the rear of the store, and Officer Kraft pursued him with a drawn gun. When respondent turned the corner at the end of an aisle, Officer Kraft lost sight of him for several seconds, and upon regaining sight of respondent, ordered him to stop and put his hands over his head.
>
> Although more than three other officers had arrived on the scene by that time, Officer Kraft was the first to reach respondent. He frisked him and discovered that he was wearing a shoulder holster which was then empty. After handcuffing him, Officer Kraft asked him where the gun was. Respondent nodded in the direction of some empty cartons and responded, "the gun is over there." Officer Kraft thereafter retrieved a loaded .38 caliber revolver from one of the cartons.

The Court noted that these facts did not raise any due process concerns, but agreed with the state courts that the facts demonstrated custodial interrogation and thus the confession would appear to fall within the exclusionary rule of *Miranda* because Quarles never received the warnings. But it explained the need for an exception for emergency circumstances as follows:

> The police in this case, in the very act of apprehending a suspect, were confronted with the immediate necessity of ascertaining the whereabouts of a gun which they had every reason to believe the suspect had just removed from his empty holster and discarded in the supermarket. So long as the gun was concealed somewhere in the supermarket, with its actual whereabouts unknown, it obviously posed

more than one danger to the public safety: an accomplice might make use of it, a customer or employee might later come upon it.

In such a situation, if the police are required to recite the familiar *Miranda* warnings before asking the whereabouts of the gun, suspects in Quarles' position might well be deterred from responding. Procedural safeguards which deter a suspect from responding were deemed acceptable in *Miranda* in order to protect the Fifth Amendment privilege; when the primary social cost of those added protections is the possibility of fewer convictions, the *Miranda* majority was willing to bear that cost. Here, had *Miranda* warnings deterred Quarles from responding to Officer Kraft's question about the whereabouts of the gun, the cost would have been something more than merely the failure to obtain evidence useful in convicting Quarles. Officer Kraft needed an answer to his question not simply to make his case against Quarles but to insure that further danger to the public did not result from the concealment of the gun in a public area.

* * * We decline to place officers such as Officer Kraft in the untenable position of having to consider, often in a matter of seconds, whether it best serves society for them to ask the necessary questions without the *Miranda* warnings and render whatever probative evidence they uncover inadmissible, or for them to give the warnings in order to preserve the admissibility of evidence they might uncover but possibly damage or destroy their ability to obtain that evidence and neutralize the volatile situation confronting them.

Although the Court recognized that it had "to some degree * * * lessen[ed] the desirable clarity of" the *Miranda* rule, it stated that "we recognize here the importance of a workable rule to guide police officers, who have only limited time and expertise to reflect on and balance the social and individual interests involved in the specific circumstances they confront." It expressed the belief that "the exception we recognize today lessens the necessity of that on-the-scene balancing process." The Court held that the both the gun and the statement revealing its location were therefore admissible despite the *Miranda* violation.

Justice O'Connor concurred in part and dissented in part. She dissented from the public safety exception created by the Court on the ground that it would be confusing and contrary to *Miranda's* bright line approach. While disagreeing with the majority's implementation of a public safety exception, and thus dissenting from the Court's ruling that Quarles's statement was admissible, Justice O'Connor concurred in the result as to the admission of the gun. In her view, the gun was admissible because *Miranda* does not require exclusion of the fruits of *Miranda*-defective confessions—a view eventually adopted by the Court in *Patane,* supra.

Justice Marshall dissented and was joined by Justices Brennan and Stevens. He found no emergency on the facts of the case:

> [C]ontrary to the majority's intimations, no customers or employees were wandering about the store in danger of coming across Quarles' discarded weapon. Although the supermarket was open to the public, Quarles' arrest took place during the middle of the night when the store was apparently deserted except for the clerks at the checkout counter. The police could easily have cordoned off the store and searched for the missing gun. Had they done so, they would have found the gun forthwith. The police were well aware that Quarles had discarded his weapon somewhere near the scene of the arrest.

Questions After Quarles

In contrast with cases like *Tucker*, *Harris*, and *Patane*, the *Quarles* Court creates a true exception to *Miranda* by providing for the admission as part of a prosecutor's case-in-chief statements that are presumptively compelled. It reaches that result by adopting a balancing of interests approach familiar from the Fourth Amendment context. Is that framework salient in the context of trial rights like the Fifth Amendment privilege against compelled self-incrimination? Do you find convincing the Court's assessments of the interests at stake? Or do you think Justice O'Connor has the better view? As you ponder these questions, you might consider some of the Court's Sixth Amendment jurisprudence. In Crawford v. Washington, 541 U.S. 36 (2004), the Court held that the Sixth Amendment right to confront witnesses bars the admission at trial of prior "testimonial statements" by witnesses who do not testify at trial absent a prior opportunity to cross-examine. The Court narrowed *Crawford* in Davis v. Washington, 547 U.S. 813 (2006), holding that statements made by out-of-court witnesses during law enforcement efforts to respond to an ongoing emergency are not "testimonial," and their admission at trial therefore does not violate the Sixth Amendment.

The Scope of the Public Safety Exception

How "exigent" must the circumstances be before the public safety exception applies? See United States v. Mobley, 40 F.3d 688 (4th Cir. 1994), where the court found that an officer's question concerning the location of a gun in a house was *not* within the public safety exception. The officers went to the defendant's house to arrest him for a narcotics violation, the defendant was naked when he answered the door, and before asking the question about the gun the officers had already conducted a protective sweep and found that no other persons were present. The court found no "immediate need" to ask about a gun and declared that "[t]here is nothing that separates these facts from those of an ordinary arrest scenario."

Therefore the defendant's statement about the location of the gun could not be admitted under *Miranda.* See also United States v. Jackson, 544 F.3d 351 (1st Cir. 2008) (public safety exception does not apply to unwarned statements the defendant made concerning the presence of a gun in the cereal box of his refrigerator; at the time of questioning, the defendant was outside the residence and surrounded by police officers, and the residence was unoccupied). Compare United States v. Liddell, 517 F.3d 1007 (8th Cir. 2008): where officers had already obtained a gun from the defendant's car, their question—"Is there anything else we need to know about?"—was within the public safety exception because officers "had good reason to believe that additional weapons might pose a threat to their safety when they searched Liddell's car incident to a late night arrest."

What kind of questions can be asked within the rubric of public safety? The Court in *Quarles* held that questions without warnings, to be permissible, must be addressed to the public safety risk. So for, example, it was permissible to ask Quarles about the location of the gun, but it would not have been within the public safety exception to ask whether he had committed the crime for which he was arrested. See United States v. Newton, 369 F.3d 659 (2d Cir. 2004) (asking the defendant about the location of a gun was within the public safety exception, but asking why he needed the gun was not).

Categorical Application of the Public Safety Exception

Can the public safety exception be applied categorically to certain arrest situations? Consider United States v. Carrillo, 16 F.3d 1046 (9th Cir. 1994). Carrillo was arrested after a narcotics transaction, and transported to a detention facility. At that point, Officer Weeks decided to search Carrillo. Before beginning the search, however, the officer asked Carrillo if he had any drugs or needles on his person. Carrillo responded, "No, I don't use drugs, I sell them." This statement was used against Carrillo as an admission at trial. Carrillo argued that the statement should have been suppressed because it was made before he had been given a *Miranda* warning. But the court held that the statement was properly admitted under the "public safety" exception to *Miranda.* The court noted that at the suppression hearing, Officer Weeks testified that during past searches he had been poked by needles and suffered headaches and skin irritation from contact with illegal drugs.

Does the *Carrillo* holding mean that "public safety" permits an officer to dispense with *Miranda* warnings and ask *any* arrestee (e.g., those arrested for theft or white collar crime) whether they are carrying drugs or syringes? See also United States v. Lackey, 334 F.3d 1224 (10th Cir. 2003) (it was proper, under the public safety exception, to ask an arrestee whether he was carrying any guns or sharp objects, before conducting a search incident to the arrest; the defendant's response, "no I am not, but there is a gun in the car" was properly admitted under *Quarles*).

Questioning Suspected Terrorists Under the Public Safety Exception

The FBI and the Department of Justice issued a memo in 2010 that instructs agents to question un-Mirandized suspected terrorists about anything "reasonably prompted by an immediate concern for the safety of the public or the arresting agents." That is a straightforward application of the public safety exception to *Miranda*. But the memo goes further, and advises that officers may ask questions beyond the immediate threat if "valuable and timely intelligence" may be recovered from the suspect. Is seeking broader intelligence about, say, the operations of a terrorist group within the public safety exception? One commentator opines that "[i]n practical terms, this memo authorizes FBI agents to ask almost anyone suspected of terrorism any question." Lonky, Revisiting the Public Safety Exception to *Miranda* for Suspected Terrorists: Dzokhar Tsarnaev and the Bombing of the 2013 Boston Marathon, 107 J. of L. & Crim. 393 (2017) (arguing that unwarned questioning of terrorists should be limited to questions attendant to an imminent and specific threat). Of course, as *Patane* makes clear, officers interested in intelligence gathering are always at liberty to engage in a custodial interrogation without providing *Miranda* warnings so long as they steer clear of conduct that might implicate due process concerns and understand that any statements made will not be admissible at trial.

D. OPEN QUESTIONS AFTER *MIRANDA*

What does it mean for the suspect to be "in custody"? When is a suspect being "interrogated"? Must the warnings be given pursuant to a standard and precise script? These and other important questions are discussed in this section.

1. What Is Custody?

If the defendant who confesses is not in custody, *Miranda* does not apply, and the admissibility of the confession depends on whether it was given voluntarily under the totality of the circumstances. As one court put it: "Because the presence of *both* a custodial setting and official interrogation is required to trigger the *Miranda* right * * * absent one or the other, *Miranda* is not implicated." Alston v. Redman, 34 F.3d 1237 (3d Cir. 1994). It follows that if the defendant is not in custody, it wouldn't matter if the suspect invokes his right to remain silent or his right to counsel—those invocations need not be respected because they are only triggered by custodial interrogation. See United States v. Infante, 701 F.3d

386 (1st Cir. 2012) (defendant was not in custody at the time of an interrogation, "obviating the need for *Miranda* warnings and for heeding Infante's invocation of his rights.").

Arrest Is Custody

According to *Miranda,* the test for custody is whether a person is deprived of his freedom of action in any significant way. In several cases subsequent to *Miranda,* the Court specifically addressed the custody question. In Orozco v. Texas, 394 U.S. 324 (1969), it held that the defendant was in custody when four armed policemen entered his bedroom at 4:00 a. m. and tried to elicit incriminating information from him. In so deciding, the Court noted that one of the four officers had testified that the defendant was under arrest and not free to leave his bedroom. If a person is arrested, he is in custody.

Conversely, in Beckwith v. United States, 425 U.S. 341 (1976), the Court found that the defendant was not in custody for purposes of receiving *Miranda* warnings where two I.R.S. agents arrived at his house at 8:00 p.m., were invited in, and sat with the defendant at his dining room table to discuss their investigation of his federal income tax returns. The agents were looking into the possibility of criminal tax fraud. The Court maintained that although Beckwith was the focus of a tax investigation, he was not in a custodial situation when he talked with the agents in his home. The Court stated that if the defendant is not in custody the inherently coercive atmosphere that triggers concerns about compelled self-incrimination and, therefore, the need for *Miranda* warnings is not present. See also United States v. Courtney, 463 F.3d 333 (5th Cir. 2006) (confession was not custodial where the agents met with the defendant in public, at a restaurant of her choice, agents were not in uniform and did not display weapons, she was not told that she had to meet with the agents, and she was allowed to leave after the interview).

Objective Test: Stansbury v. California

In Stansbury v. California, 511 U.S. 318 (1994) (per curiam), the Court held, "not for the first time, that an officer's subjective and undisclosed view concerning whether the person being interrogated is a suspect is irrelevant to the assessment whether the person is in custody." An officer questioned Stansbury about a murder, thinking that Stansbury was a potential witness. When the questioning began, the officer believed that another man was the prime suspect. But after Stansbury gave incriminating information in response to a few questions, it became clear to the officer that Stansbury was the perpetrator. At that point, the officer gave Stansbury *Miranda* warnings. There was no indication that the officer's initial lack of suspicion had been imparted to Stansbury.

The question for the Court was whether Stansbury's initial statements had been obtained in violation of *Miranda*. Stansbury argued that he was in custody during the period of initial questioning because he was questioned in the jail part of the police station by officers whose guns were visible. But the lower courts found that Stansbury was not in custody until the *officer's suspicions* shifted to him as a result of the initial questioning.

The Supreme Court unanimously held that the lower courts were incorrect in focusing on the officer's undisclosed state of mind. It reasoned as follows:

> It is well settled * * * that a police officer's subjective view that the individual under questioning is a suspect, if undisclosed, does not bear upon the question whether the individual is in custody for purposes of *Miranda*. The same principle obtains if an officer's undisclosed assessment is that the person being questioned is not a suspect. In either instance, one cannot expect the person under interrogation to probe the officer's innermost thoughts. * * *
>
> * * * [A]n officer's views concerning the nature of an interrogation, or beliefs concerning the potential culpability of the individual being questioned, may be one among many factors that bear upon the assessment whether that individual was in custody, but only if the officer's views or beliefs were somehow manifested to the individual under interrogation and would have affected how a reasonable person in that position would perceive his or her freedom to leave.

The Court remanded to the lower court to determine the question of custody without relying on the officer's subjective and undisclosed opinions. See also United States v. Panak, 552 F.3d 462 (6th Cir. 2009) (officer's knowledge about evidence incriminating the suspect "is relevant only if (1) it was somehow manifested to the individual under interrogation and (2) it would have affected how a reasonable person in that position would perceive his or her freedom to leave.").

The Relevance of the Suspect's Youth: J.D.B. v. North Carolina

In J.D.B. v. North Carolina, 564 U.S. 261 (2011), Justice Sotomayor wrote for the Court as it reasoned that

> [i]t is beyond dispute that children will often feel bound to submit to police questioning when an adult in the same circumstances would feel free to leave," and "[s]eeing no reason for police officers or courts to blind themselves to that commonsense reality, we hold that a child's age properly informs the *Miranda* custody analysis."

J.D.B. was a 13-year-old, seventh-grade student attending class at Smith Middle School in Chapel Hill, North Carolina when he was removed from his classroom by a uniformed police officer, escorted to a closed-door conference room, and questioned by police for at least half an hour regarding two home break-ins. After learning of the prospect of juvenile detention, J.D.B. confessed that he and a friend were responsible for the break-ins. The officer only then informed J.D.B. that he could refuse to answer the investigator's questions and that he was free to leave.

Justice Sotomayor concluded that "so long as the child's age was known to the officer at the time of police questioning, or would have been objectively apparent to a reasonable officer, its inclusion in the custody analysis is consistent with the objective nature of that test." Justice Alito, with whom The Chief Justice, Justice Scalia, and Justice Thomas joined, dissented. Justice Alito argued that the decision was "fundamentally inconsistent with one of the main justifications for the *Miranda* rule: the perceived need for a clear rule that can be easily applied in all cases."

Prisoners in Custody: Mathis v. United States and Howes v. Fields

In Mathis v. United States, 391 U.S. 1 (1968), the defendant was interrogated, while in jail, by I.R.S. agents about his alleged tax evasion. Those statements were introduced at a subsequent criminal trial where Mathis was convicted on tax-related charges. The Court found that, although the defendant was in jail for reasons unrelated to the tax investigation, and the investigators were not contemplating criminal charges at the time of the interrogation, he was in custody and subjected to interrogation. As a consequence, "the courts below were wrong in permitting the introduction of petitioner's self-incriminating evidence given without warning of his right to be silent and right to counsel."

Subsequent cases have refused to read *Mathis* as establishing a per se rule that prisoners are always in custody for *Miranda* purposes. Rather, the question is whether prison officials' conduct would cause "a reasonable person to believe his freedom of movement had been *further* diminished." Garcia v. Singletary, 13 F.3d 1487 (11th Cir. 1994).

In Howes v. Fields, 565 U.S. 499 (2012), the Supreme Court rejected the Sixth Circuit's categorical rule—purportedly based on *Mathis*—that interrogation is per se custodial when a prisoner is questioned in private about conduct occurring outside the prison. Justice Alito wrote the majority opinion for six Justices. While Fields was incarcerated, he was escorted to a conference room in the prison and interrogated, without *Miranda* warnings, about committing a crime unrelated to his incarceration. He confessed after an interrogation session that took between five and seven hours.

Justice Alito first stated that "our decisions do not clearly establish that a prisoner is always in custody for purposes of *Miranda* whenever a prisoner is isolated from the general prison population and questioned about conduct outside the prison." He went on to observe that a determination of custody must focus on all features of the interrogation, and incarceration is only one such feature. Justice Alito found that two factors pointed in favor of a finding of custody under the facts presented: the interrogation was lengthy (well past the time when the prisoners generally went to bed), and Fields was not informed of his right to refuse to speak to the deputies. However, Justice Alito found those factors were offset by others. Most importantly, Fields was told twice that he was free to leave and return to his cell. Further, Fields was not physically restrained and the door to the conference room was sometimes left open.

The Court also suggested that the interests protected by *Miranda* may apply with less force to prisoners. It identified three reasons this might be so: 1) questioning a person already in custody does not involve the "shock" that generally accompanies arrest; 2) a prisoner is unlikely to be lured into speaking based on the hope of prompt release; and 3) a prisoner knows that the law enforcement officers conducting the interrogation probably lack the authority to affect the duration of his sentence.

Justice Ginsburg, joined by Justices Breyer and Sotomayor, concurred in part and dissented in part. Justice Ginsburg recognized that the case law did not support an automatic rule that prison interrogation was always custodial. But she concluded that Fields was in custody at the time of his interrogation. She stated: "I would not train, as the Court does, on the question whether there can be custody within custody. Instead, I would ask, as *Miranda* put it, whether Fields was subjected to 'incommunicado interrogation . . . in a police-dominated atmosphere,' whether he was placed, against his will, in an inherently stressful situation, and whether his freedom of action was curtailed in any significant way. Those should be the key questions, and to each I would answer 'Yes.' "

Interrogation at the Police Station: Oregon v. Mathiason and California v. Beheler

In Oregon v. Mathiason, 429 U.S. 492 (1977), a per curiam opinion, the Court ruled that an individual questioned at a police station is not necessarily in custody. Mathiason was out on parole when an officer telephoned him to say that he wanted to discuss something with him and asked if they could meet somewhere. Mathiason had no preference, so the policeman asked if he could come down to the station house. Mathiason agreed, and arriving a short time later, was told that he was not under arrest. The officer ushered Mathiason into an office, closed the door, and the two sat across a desk. No *Miranda* warnings were given. The officer told Mathiason about the burglary he was investigating, that he believed Mathiason was involved, and that his fingerprints were found at the scene (which was not true). Mathiason confessed, and was then allowed to leave the police station.

The Court concluded that Mathiason's freedom was not restrained so as to render him in custody under *Miranda.* The Court stressed that Mathiason went down to the station voluntarily, was informed that he was not under arrest, and left the station without hindrance after he confessed. The dissenters, Justices Brennan, Marshall, and Stevens, stressed that Mathiason was a parolee and so it could not be truly said that he went down to the station of his own accord.

In California v. Beheler, 463 U.S. 1121 (1983), the Court extended *Mathiason* to find that the suspect was not in custody when he agreed to accompany police officers down to the station for questioning. He was told he was not under arrest and was released after confessing. Shouldn't there be a difference between going to the station unaccompanied and going to the station with police officers? See also Yarborough v. Alvarado, 541 U.S. 652 (2004), where the Court found that a teenager who was brought to the station by his parents, at the request of police, was not in custody when he was interrogated in the stationhouse for two hours.

Meetings with a Probation Officer: Minnesota v. Murphy

Justice White wrote for six Justices in Minnesota v. Murphy, 465 U.S. 420 (1984), as the Court held that the privilege against self-incrimination was not violated when a probation officer called Murphy, a probationer, to her office and questioned him about the rape and murder of a teenage girl. Murphy had admitted the offenses to a counselor as part of the treatment prescribed as a condition of probation. The Court held that *Miranda* did not require the officer to warn Murphy of his rights prior to asking questions about crimes he might have committed, because Murphy was not arrested or otherwise in custody even though he was required to meet with the officer. Although the Court recognized that the officer sought incriminating information, it declared that warnings are not required simply because an investigation has focused upon a suspect.

Justice Marshall, joined by Justice Stevens and in part by Justice Brennan, dissented. He argued that a reasonable man in Murphy's position would have believed that his duty to answer questions honestly as a condition of probation required him to respond to the questions put by the officer.

Terry Stops: Berkemer v. McCarty

If a police officer interrogates a suspect during a *Terry* stop, must the officer give *Miranda* warnings? As Chapter 2 made clear, a *Terry* stop occurs either when officers apply physical force to a person with intent to seize or when a person submits to a show of authority by officers that would lead a reasonable person to believe that she is not free to leave. Yet, in Berkemer v. McCarty, 468 U.S. 420 (1984), the Court in an opinion by Justice Marshall held that *Terry* stops are not custodial for *Miranda* purposes. Justice Marshall noted that *Terry* stops are typically of brief duration; questioning is limited, because the officer can ask only a "moderate number of questions to determine identity and to try to obtain information confirming or dispelling the officer's suspicions;" the detainee is not obliged to respond (though he must provide identification); and unless probable cause arises in a short time, the detainee must be released. Justice Marshall concluded that *Terry* stops were "comparatively nonthreatening" and hence unlike the custodial situations required to trigger *Miranda*. If the stop escalates to an arrest, however, *Miranda* will apply.

Thus, the law distinguishing *Terry* stops from arrests discussed in Chapter 2 (see, e.g., Dunaway v. New York, supra) also determines whether custody exists under *Miranda*. See Saltzburg, Foreword: The Flow and Ebb of Constitutional Criminal Procedure in the Warren and Burger Courts, 69 Geo.L.J. 151, 200–03 (1980). See also United States v. Ozuna, 170 F.3d 654 (6th Cir. 1999) (limited interrogation at customs checkpoint is not custodial within the meaning of *Miranda:* "All persons attempting to enter the United States must anticipate detention while answering a few basic questions and this cuts against the potentially coercive aspect of the Customs inquiry.").

Summary on Custody: Relevant Factors

One court has set forth six indicia for determining whether a suspect is in custody for *Miranda* purposes:

> (1) whether the suspect was informed at the time of questioning that the questioning was voluntary, that the suspect was free to leave or request the officers to do so, or that the suspect was not considered under arrest; (2) whether the suspect possessed unrestrained freedom of movement during questioning; (3) whether the suspect initiated contact with authorities or voluntarily acquiesced to official request to respond to questions; (4) whether strong arm tactics or deceptive stratagems were employed during questioning; (5) whether the atmosphere of the questioning was police dominated; and (6) whether the suspect was placed under arrest at the termination of the questioning.

United States v. Brown, 990 F.2d 397 (8th Cir. 1993). After *J.D.B.*, we must add to this list the age of the suspect. The *Brown* court stated that "[t]he presence of the first three indicia tends to mitigate the existence of custody at the time of questioning" while "the presence of the last three indicia aggravate the existence of custody."

How would the above six-factor test apply to the following facts?

On February 25, 1989, the Twin Cities Federal Savings and Loan Association (TCF) was robbed by two men armed with a shotgun and possibly a handgun. [Eyewitness descriptions and other information led the officers to focus on Griffin as a suspect. The officers telephoned Griffin's house].

* * * Griffin's stepfather answered the phone and informed the agents that Griffin would be home early that evening. Agents Waldie and Tremper proceeded to Griffin's home, arriving at 7 p.m., and were invited into the living room by Griffin's stepfather. The purpose of the interview was to determine what Griffin knew of the bank robbery. The officers did not intend to arrest him at that time. The agents waited in the living room until 8:15 p.m. when Griffin was heard approaching the house outside. The agents moved to the hall near the front door to meet Griffin as he entered the house. Waldie and Tremper identified themselves as F.B.I. agents investigating a bank robbery and informed Griffin that they needed to speak with him. At that point, before any other words were spoken, Griffin stated, "The gun wasn't loaded."

The agents explained to Griffin's parents that it was necessary for them to speak to Griffin in private and, accordingly, the three went into the dining room and sat down. The agents did not draw their guns, handcuff Griffin, or place him under formal arrest. Griffin's parents retired to the upstairs of the house where they remained throughout the course of the questioning.

Neither of the agents informed Griffin that he was not under arrest, that he was free to request the agents to leave without speaking to them, nor did they inform him of his *Miranda* rights. Twice during the two-hour interview Griffin asked to obtain cigarettes from other places in the house and each time Agent Waldie required that Agent Tremper escort him. Griffin was told he was to stay in their view at all times. The agents used this procedure to ensure their personal safety because a weapon had been used in the course of the robbery, although this was not explained to Griffin at the time.

During the interview, Griffin appeared nervous, "sort of choked up for words" and "fearful" of the agents. In the course of the questioning Griffin implicated himself and Chapman in the robbery. The agents questioned Griffin for approximately two hours. At the conclusion of the interview the agents placed Griffin under arrest. Griffin was then transported to the F.B.I. office where, three hours after his initial confrontation with the agents, he was advised of his *Miranda* rights for the first time.

In United States v. Griffin, 922 F.2d 1343 (8th Cir. 1990), the Court analyzed the above facts and held that Griffin was in custody when he confessed. Do you agree? Which of the factors cut most strongly in Griffin's favor? Which cut most strongly in the government's favor?

Most courts have found that the weightiest factor in the totality is whether the police informed the suspect that he is free to leave or to terminate the interrogation. That factor was lacking in *Griffin, supra.* In contrast, see United States v. Giboney, 863 F.3d 1022 (8th Cir. 2017), with basically the same facts as *Griffin,* the only difference being that Giboney was told several times that he was not under arrest and could terminate the interview whenever he wanted. The Court stated that "[w]here a suspect is questioned in the familiar surroundings of his home, and informed several times of his right to terminate the interview at will, we believe that strong evidence of restraint on freedom of movement of the degree associated with a formal arrest is necessary to overcome the natural inference that such questioning is non-custodial."

2. What Is Interrogation?

In addition to the custody requirement, the police must also be interrogating the individual before the need for *Miranda* warnings arises. Thus, volunteered statements or "threshold" confessions (where the defendant walks into the police station and immediately confesses) are not barred at trial by the fact that they were made without *Miranda* warnings.

The following case sets forth the Supreme Court's guidelines for determining when interrogation occurs.

RHODE ISLAND V. INNIS

Supreme Court of the United States, 1980.
446 U.S. 291.

JUSTICE STEWART delivered the opinion of the Court.

In Miranda v. Arizona, the Court held that, once a defendant in custody asks to speak with a lawyer, all interrogation must cease until a lawyer is present. The issue in this case is whether the respondent was "interrogated" in violation of the standards promulgated in the *Miranda* opinion.

[Innis was identified as the perpetrator in the shooting death of a cab driver. Some time later, Innis was seen on the street and arrested by Patrolman Lovell. He was unarmed. Lovell gave Innis *Miranda* warnings.]

Within minutes, Sergeant Sears arrived at the scene of the arrest, and he also gave the respondent the *Miranda* warnings. Immediately thereafter, Captain Leyden and other police officers arrived. Captain Leyden advised the respondent of his *Miranda* rights. The respondent stated that he understood those rights and wanted to speak with a lawyer. Captain Leyden then directed that the respondent be placed in a "caged wagon," a four-door police car with a wire screen mesh between the front and rear seats, and be driven to the central police station. Three officers, Patrolmen Gleckman, Williams, and McKenna, were assigned to accompany the respondent to the central station. They placed the respondent in the vehicle and shut the doors. Captain Leyden then instructed the officers not to question the respondent or intimidate or coerce him in any way. The three officers then entered the vehicle, and it departed.

While enroute to the central station, Patrolman Gleckman initiated a conversation with Patrolman McKenna concerning the missing shotgun. As Patrolman Gleckman later testified:

> "At this point, I was talking back and forth with Patrolman McKenna stating that I frequent this area while on patrol and [that because a school for handicapped children is located nearby,] there's a lot of handicapped children running around in this area, and God forbid one of them might find a weapon with shells and they might hurt themselves."

Patrolman McKenna apparently shared his fellow officer's concern:

> "I more or less concurred with him [Gleckman] that it was a safety factor and that we should, you know, continue to search for the weapon and try to find it."

While Patrolman Williams said nothing, he overheard the conversation between the two officers:

> "He [Gleckman] said it would be too bad if the little—I believe he said girl—would pick up the gun, maybe kill herself."

The respondent then interrupted the conversation, stating that the officers should turn the car around so he could show them where the gun was located. * * * At the time the respondent indicated that the officers should turn back, they had traveled no more than a mile, a trip encompassing only a few minutes.

The police vehicle then returned to the scene of the arrest where a search for the shotgun was in progress. There, Captain Leyden again advised the respondent of his *Miranda* rights. The respondent replied that he understood those rights but that he "wanted to get the gun out of the way because of the kids in the area in the school." The respondent then led the police to a nearby field, where he pointed out the shotgun under some rocks by the side of the road.

[A motion to suppress was denied by the trial court and Innis was convicted. But the state appellate court found that Innis had been subject to interrogation about the gun and so his statements should have been suppressed.]

* * *

In the present case, the parties are in agreement that the respondent was fully informed of his *Miranda* rights and that he invoked his *Miranda* right to counsel when he told Captain Leyden that he wished to consult with a lawyer. It is also uncontested that the respondent was "in custody" while being transported to the police station.

The issue, therefore, is whether the respondent was "interrogated" by the police officers in violation of the respondent's undisputed right under *Miranda* to remain silent until he had consulted with a lawyer.[a] In resolving this issue, we first define the term "interrogation" under *Miranda* before turning to a consideration of the facts of this case.

* * *

The starting point for defining "interrogation" in this context is, of course, the Court's *Miranda* opinion. There the Court observed that "[b]y custodial interrogation, we mean *questioning* initiated by law enforcement officers after a person has been taken into custody or otherwise deprived of his freedom of action in any significant way." This passage and other references throughout the opinion to "questioning" might suggest that the *Miranda* rules were to apply only to those police interrogation practices that involve express questioning of a defendant while in custody.

We do not, however, construe the *Miranda* opinion so narrowly. The concern of the Court in *Miranda* was that the "interrogation environment" created by the interplay of interrogation and custody would "subjugate the individual to the will of his examiner" and thereby undermine the privilege against compulsory self-incrimination. The police practices that evoked this concern included several that did not involve express questioning. * * *

This is not to say, however, that all statements obtained by the police after a person has been taken into custody are to be considered the product of interrogation. * * * It is clear therefore that the special procedural safeguards outlined in *Miranda* are required not where a suspect is simply taken into custody, but rather where a suspect in custody is subjected to interrogation. "Interrogation," as conceptualized in the *Miranda* opinion,

[a] Since we conclude that the respondent was not "interrogated" for *Miranda* purposes, we do not reach the question whether the respondent waived his right under *Miranda* to be free from interrogation until counsel was present.

must reflect a measure of compulsion above and beyond that inherent in custody itself.[b] * * *

We conclude that the *Miranda* safeguards come into play whenever a person in custody is subjected to either express questioning or its functional equivalent. That is to say, the term "interrogation" under *Miranda* refers not only to express questioning, but also to any words or actions on the part of the police (other than those normally attendant to arrest and custody) that the police should know are reasonably likely to elicit an incriminating response[c] from the suspect. The latter portion of this definition focuses primarily upon the perceptions of the suspect, rather than the intent of the police. This focus reflects the fact that the *Miranda* safeguards were designed to vest a suspect in custody with an added measure of protection against coercive police practices, without regard to objective proof of the underlying intent of the police. A practice that the police should know is reasonably likely to evoke an incriminating response from a suspect thus amounts to interrogation.[d] But, since the police surely cannot be held accountable for the unforeseeable results of their words or actions, the definition of interrogation can extend only to words or actions on the part of police officers that they *should have known* were reasonably likely to elicit an incriminating response.[e]

* * * Turning to the facts of the present case, we conclude that the respondent was not "interrogated" within the meaning of *Miranda*. It is undisputed that the first prong of the definition of "interrogation" was not satisfied, for the conversation between Patrolmen Gleckman and McKenna included no express questioning of the respondent. Rather, that

---

[b] There is language in the opinion of the Rhode Island Supreme Court in this case suggesting that the definition of "interrogation" under *Miranda* is informed by this Court's decision in Brewer v. Williams [discussed infra in the section on the Sixth Amendment]. This suggestion is erroneous. Our decision in *Brewer* rested solely on the Sixth and Fourteenth Amendment right to counsel. That right, as we held in *Massiah*, prohibits law enforcement officers from "deliberately eliciting" incriminating information from a defendant in the absence of counsel after a formal charge against the defendant has been filed. Custody in such a case is not controlling; * * *. By contrast, the right to counsel at issue in the present case is based not on the Sixth and Fourteenth Amendments, but rather on the Fifth and Fourteenth Amendments as interpreted in the *Miranda* opinion. The definitions of "interrogation" under the Fifth and Sixth Amendments, if indeed the term "interrogation" is even apt in the Sixth Amendment context, are not necessarily interchangeable, since the policies underlying the two constitutional protections are quite distinct.

[c] By "incriminating response" we refer to any response—whether inculpatory or exculpatory—that the *prosecution* may seek to introduce at trial. * * *

[d] This is not to say that the intent of the police is irrelevant, for it may well have a bearing on whether the police should have known that their words or actions were reasonably likely to evoke an incriminating response. In particular, where a police practice is designed to elicit an incriminating response from the accused, it is unlikely that the practice will not also be one which the police should have known was reasonably likely to have that effect.

[e] Any knowledge the police may have had concerning the unusual susceptibility of a defendant to a particular form of persuasion might be an important factor in determining whether the police should have known that their words or actions were reasonably likely to elicit an incriminating response from the suspect.

conversation was, at least in form nothing more than a dialogue between the two officers to which no response from the respondent was invited.

* * *

Moreover, it cannot be fairly concluded that the respondent was subjected to the "functional equivalent" of questioning. * * * There is nothing in the record to suggest that the officers were aware that the respondent was peculiarly susceptible to an appeal to his conscience concerning the safety of handicapped children, or that the police knew that the respondent was unusually disoriented or upset at the time of his arrest.

The case thus boils down to whether, in the context of a brief conversation, the officers should have known that the respondent would suddenly be moved to make a self-incriminating response. Given the fact that the entire conversation appears to have consisted of no more than a few off-hand remarks, we cannot say that the officers should have known that it was reasonably likely that Innis would so respond. This is not a case where the police carried on a lengthy harangue in the presence of the suspect. Nor does the record support the respondent's contention that, under the circumstances, the officers' comments were particularly "evocative."

* * *

[JUSTICE WHITE's concurring opinion, and CHIEF JUSTICE BURGER's opinion concurring in the judgment, are omitted].

JUSTICE MARSHALL, with whom JUSTICE BRENNAN joins, dissenting.

I am substantially in agreement with the Court's definition of "interrogation" within the meaning of Miranda v. Arizona. In my view, the *Miranda* safeguards apply whenever police conduct is intended or likely to produce a response from a suspect in custody. * * *

I am utterly at a loss, however, to understand how this objective standard as applied to the facts before us can rationally lead to the conclusion that there was no interrogation. * * *

One can scarcely imagine a stronger appeal to the conscience of a suspect—*any* suspect—than the assertion that if the weapon is not found an innocent person will be hurt or killed. And not just any innocent person, but an innocent child—a little girl—a helpless, handicapped little girl on her way to school. The notion that such an appeal could not be expected to have any effect unless the suspect were known to have some special interest in handicapped children verges on the ludicrous.

* * *

I firmly believe that this case is simply an aberration, and that in future cases the Court will apply the standard adopted today in accordance with its plain meaning.

JUSTICE STEVENS, **dissenting.**

* * * In my view any statement that would normally be understood by the average listener as calling for a response is the functional equivalent of a direct question, whether or not it is punctuated by a question mark. The Court, however, takes a much narrower view. It holds that police conduct is not the "functional equivalent" of direct questioning unless the police should have known that what they were saying or doing was likely to elicit an incriminating response from the suspect. This holding represents a plain departure from the principles set forth in *Miranda.*

* * *

Application of Innis: Arizona v. Mauro

Applying the *Innis* test, the Court found no interrogation when a suspect confessed to his wife in the presence of a police officer who recorded the statements. Arizona v. Mauro, 481 U.S. 520 (1987). Police received a telephone call stating that a man had entered a store claiming to have killed his son. When officers reached the store, Mauro freely admitted that he had killed his son and directed officers to the body. The police arrested Mauro and gave him two sets of *Miranda* warnings. After the second set, given at the police station, Mauro indicated that he wished to say nothing more without a lawyer. Mrs. Mauro, who was being questioned separately, asked to speak with her husband. The police were reluctant to permit her to do so, but ultimately agreed to her request. An officer told the Mauros, however, that they could speak together only if an officer were present to observe and hear what was said. The officer placed a tape recorder in plain view. During the conversation between husband and wife, Mrs. Mauro expressed despair, and Mr. Mauro consoled her by saying that "You tried to stop me as best you can." Mauro's defense at trial was insanity, and the prosecutor played the tape at trial in rebuttal, arguing that it demonstrated that Mauro was sane.

Justice Powell wrote for the majority, as it concluded that there was no evidence that the officers sent Mrs. Mauro in to see her husband for the purpose of eliciting statements. Even though the officers conceded that they recognized a *possibility* that Mauro would incriminate himself while talking with his wife, Justice Powell concluded that "officers do not interrogate a suspect simply by hoping that he will incriminate himself." Justice Powell determined that "Mauro was not subjected to compelling influences, psychological ploys, or direct questioning," and "his volunteered statements cannot properly be considered the result of police interrogation." He added that "[p]olice departments need not adopt inflexible rules barring suspects from speaking with their spouses, nor must they ignore legitimate security concerns by allowing spouses to meet in private."

Justice Stevens, joined by Justices Brennan, Marshall, and Blackmun, dissented. He concluded that "it was not only likely, but highly probable, that one of the suspects would make a statement that the prosecutor might seek to introduce at trial," and that "[i]t follows that the police conduct in this case was the functional equivalent of deliberate, direct interrogation."

Suppose the police officers refused to permit Mrs. Mauro to speak with her husband, and he had made a statement to the police. Wouldn't Mauro have argued that the refusal to permit contact was itself interrogation? If the dissenters are correct in *Mauro,* what advice would they give to police confronted with the *Mauro* facts? See also United States v. Swift, 623 F.3d 618 (8th Cir. 2010) (police officers' act of leaving two defendants alone in a monitored interrogation room was not the functional equivalent of interrogation; even though officers hoped that they would make incriminating statements when left alone, the conduct did not put pressure on the defendants). Even if the statements were deemed the product of a custodial interrogation, could they be admitted to rebut a claim of insanity under *Tucker*? If they were offered not for their contents, but to show that Mauro was lucid, would they qualify as being "testimonial" under *Muniz*?

Appeals to the Welfare of Others as Interrogation?

In *Innis*, the Court held that an average suspect would not likely be moved by an appeal based on a risk of harm to innocent children; the fact that Innis himself *was* so moved was not dispositive, because the test is whether an incriminating response would have been likely from an *average suspect*—and apparently an average suspect doesn't care about whether children could be harmed by a gun. Would an average suspect be affected by an appeal based on possible harm to a loved one? Consider United States v. Calisto, 838 F.2d 711 (3d Cir. 1988), where officers searched Calisto's home and found large quantities of drugs in a bedroom. Calisto was placed under arrest by Officer McKeefry and invoked his right to silence. The officers knew that Calisto lived with his adult daughter. One of the searching officers came up to McKeefry and said that he had found both men's and women's clothing in the bedroom where the drugs had been located. Officer McKeefry responded, "Well, then we'll have to get an arrest warrant for the daughter." Calisto, who was a few feet away from McKeefry, said "Don't lock my daughter up. She has nothing to do with that stuff. That's mine. I'm the one you want." The court found that McKeefry's statement concerning the daughter was not interrogation, reasoning that his remark "was not directed at Calisto, was the kind of remark that an officer would normally make in carrying out his duties under the circumstances that confronted him, and was not made in a provocative manner." The court concluded that "even if it could be said that reasonable officers might have expected a protest of some kind from Calisto upon his hearing of his daughter's possible arrest, we do not think it was reasonable to expect an *inculpatory* response from Calisto." (emphasis added).

The courts in *Innis* and *Calisto* appear to take a dim view of the character of an average suspect—i.e., the suspect's regard for others. Is there reason to believe that anyone suspected of crime has less regard for others than most people have?

Confronting the Suspect with Incriminating Evidence

In Edwards v. Arizona, 451 U.S. 477 (1981), the Court found that Edwards had been interrogated when officers played for him a recorded statement of his associate that implicated Edwards in the crime. See also People v. Ferro, 63 N.Y.2d 316, 482 N.Y.S.2d 237 (1984) (interrogation found where officers placed the fruits of Ferro's crime in front of his jail cell); United States v. Green, 541 F.3d 176 (3d Cir. 2008) ("we can hardly imagine a more prototypical example of the functional equivalent of interrogation than when a suspect is shown a video in which he is depicted as engaging in a criminal act").

Why does confronting the suspect with incriminating evidence constitute interrogation, while confronting the same suspect with a risk of harm to innocent children, as in *Innis*, does not?

It should be noted that, despite the holding in *Edwards,* courts have not been uniform in finding interrogation whenever a suspect in custody is confronted with incriminating evidence. See Shedelbower v. Estelle, 885 F.2d 570 (9th Cir. 1989) (lying to the defendant that he had just been identified by an eyewitness was not reasonably likely to elicit an incriminating response). The court in United States v. Payne, 954 F.2d 199 (4th Cir. 1992), argued that it would be inappropriate to apply *Miranda* to every instance in which a person in custody is told about incriminating evidence against them:

> That no comment on the evidence in a case will ever issue in the presence of a criminal suspect seems to us neither realistic nor desirable as an absolute rule derived from the Fifth Amendment. Indeed, it may even be in the interest of a defendant to be kept informed about matters relating to the charges against him. * * * Information about the evidence against a suspect may also contribute to the intelligent exercise of his judgment regarding what course of conduct to follow.

> * * * It simply cannot be said that all such statements are objectively likely to result in incriminating responses by those in custody. The inquiry mandated by *Innis* into the perceptions of the suspect is necessarily contextual, and whether descriptions of incriminating evidence constitute the functional equivalent of interrogation will depend on circumstances that are too numerous to catalogue.

Of course it is true, as the *Payne* court states, that a suspect may have an interest in being apprised of the evidence against him. But does that mean that *Miranda* is inapplicable? *Miranda* does not prevent an officer from speaking to a suspect, it just requires that a confession in response to the officer must be preceded by warnings and waiver in order for that confession to be admissible. Hasn't the *Payne* court overlooked the fact that an officer who is trying to "help" the defendant by keeping him informed, can also help him by providing the warnings? If there is no per se rule, how does one tell whether confronting a suspect with incriminating evidence will constitute interrogation?

Direct vs. Indirect Statements

One factor mentioned in *Innis* as cutting against a finding of interrogation was that the officers were ostensibly talking among themselves; they did not direct their comments at Innis. Likewise, the officer's statement in *Calisto*, supra—about arresting the defendant's daughter—was found not to be interrogation in part because it was not made in a "provocative" manner. The reasoning is that a comment not even directed at a suspect is less likely to produce an incriminating response.

Conversely, if an officer is addressing the suspect directly, an incriminating response is presumably more likely. Illustrative is United States v. Soto, 953 F.2d 263 (6th Cir. 1992). Soto was stopped for a traffic violation, gave suspicious answers to preliminary questions, and ultimately consented to a search of his car. The officer discovered narcotics in an opaque bag in the trunk, and Soto was placed under arrest. The officer continued to search the car, and came upon a photograph of Soto's wife and child. The officer pointed to the narcotics and said "What are you doing with crap like that when you have these two waiting for you at home?" Soto gave an incriminating answer. The court held that the officer's comment constituted impermissible interrogation. It reasoned that while the remark "was not couched in formal question and answer form, in substance it was a direct inquiry into Soto's reasons for committing the offense he appeared to have committed, and it elicited an incriminating response." Do you think the officer in *Soto* was trying to obtain an incriminating statement? Does that make any difference under *Innis*? See also United States v. Rambo, 365 F.3d 906 (10th Cir. 2004) (directly addressing the defendant to tell him that "most of the blame will fall on your shoulders" constitutes interrogation).

Clarifying Ambiguous, Voluntary Statements of the Suspect

Courts have often refused to find interrogation when the officer is responding to a voluntary, but ambiguous, statement of the suspect. For example, in United States v. Jones, 842 F.3d 1077 (8th Cir. 2016), the defendant was arrested after a suspicious fire in which his wife died. As he was being taken into the squad car, he said "You finally f***ing got me." The officer responded: "What do you mean?" and the defendant said "That's all you're getting. I hope I get the max." The court found that Jones's statement was admissible because it was not the product of interrogation. The court stated that "an officer's request for clarification of a spontaneous statement does generally not amount to interrogation." Why not? Is it because the suspect "opened the door"?

The Relevance of the Officer's Intent to Obtain an Incriminating Answer

The Court in *Innis* states that an officer's intent to elicit incriminating information is relevant only insofar as it makes it more likely that there will be an incriminating answer—i.e., if you intend to do something it makes it more likely that it happens than if you had no intent. That said, there are courts that will find interrogation if the officer had no plausible reason for asking a question other than to elicit incriminating information. For example, in United States v. Jackson, 852 F.3d 764 (8th Cir. 2017), the defendant was charged with murder and claimed self-defense. Officers had found that Jackson had his hair cut just before the killing. When Jackson was arrested he voluntarily stated he had taken drugs and hadn't slept, and then curled up in the fetal position. Officers asked if he took any prescription medications and to rate his health on a scale of one to ten. He made some statements about his condition that tended to contradict his testimony about the killing. Then an officer asked, "do you know when you last cut your hair?" and the defendant answered no. At trial, the prosecution challenged the defendant's memory of the killing, arguing that he couldn't even remember whether he had cut his hair just before the killing, so it was implausible that he could remember the killing. The court held that the statements asking about the defendant's health were not interrogation—their point was to assess his condition and the officers were not trying to elicit an incriminating response. In contrast, the question about the haircut "crossed the line into improper interrogation." It could not be justified as a question relating to health (despite the government's argument that the officers were only inquiring into the defendant's mental health) and that "[b]ecause the officers had prior knowledge about the murder suspect having recently cut his hair, they should have known that the question regarding Jackson's last haircut was reasonably likely to elicit an incriminating response."

But *objectively,* it seems difficult to understand what officers would reasonably have expected the defendant to say about the haircut that would be incriminating. The defendant's response "I don't remember" only became incriminating in an impeachment context at a much later trial. It seems clear that the focus is more on bad intent than on whether the officers really thought there was a reasonable likelihood of the defendant's saying something that would prove to be incriminating.

QUESTIONS ATTENDANT TO CUSTODY: PENNSYLVANIA V. MUNIZ

In *Innis,* the Court's definition of interrogation excludes questions "attendant to custody." Thus, officers can ask custody-related questions without *Miranda* warnings, and if the suspect's answer is incriminating, it is admissible at trial. This *"booking exception"* was further developed in Pennsylvania v. Muniz, 496 U.S. 582 (1990). Muniz was stopped on suspicion of drunk driving. He failed sobriety tests and was brought to a booking center, where he was asked, among other things, his name, address, height, weight, eye color, date of birth, and current age. Muniz stumbled over the answers and gave incorrect information on some points. His responses were admitted at his trial as evidence of drunkenness. Justice Brennan, writing for a plurality of four members of the Court, held that Muniz's answers to the questions were admissible, even though in response to custodial interrogation, because they fell within a "routine booking question exception which exempts from *Miranda's* coverage questions to secure the biographical data necessary to complete booking or pretrial services." The plurality noted that the booking exception would not apply if such questions were "designed to elicit incriminatory admissions."

Chief Justice Rehnquist, joined by Justices White, Blackmun, and Stevens, concurred in the result. The Chief Justice did not find it necessary to consider whether the questions to Muniz fell within a booking exception to *Miranda.* He found Muniz's answers to these questions to be non-testimonial, and hence not protected by the Fifth Amendment in the first place, because they were used at trial only to show that Muniz's mental processes were not operating properly. (This aspect of the case is discussed earlier in this Chapter in the section on the testimonial aspect of the privilege against self-incrimination). However, Chief Justice Rehnquist assumed that a booking exception to *Miranda* does exist.

Justice Marshall dissented. He argued that a booking exception would lead to difficult, time-consuming litigation concerning its scope and application, contrary to the *Miranda* bright-line approach.

Determining the Scope of the Booking Questions Exception

How is a court able to tell whether an officer's question about biographical information is, as *Muniz* puts it, "designed to elicit incriminatory admissions?" Lower courts have looked to objective factors such as whether there could be a proper administrative purpose for the question, whether the question is asked by an officer who routinely books suspects, and whether the officer would need to know the information for booking purposes. See, e.g., United States v. Pacheco-Lopez, 531 F.3d 420 (6th Cir. 2008): In a drug case, questions concerning when the suspect arrived at the house where drugs were sent and how he got there were not within the booking questions exception—questions did not serve an administrative purpose, questioning was done on the scene and not at the station, and no effort was made to document the suspect's answers in any arrest-related paperwork. Compare United States v. Washington, 462 F.3d 1124 (9th Cir. 2006) (questions about defendant's gang affiliation and gang moniker were proper booking questions: "agents routinely obtain gang moniker and gang affiliation information for the United States Marshals and Metropolitan Detention Center in order to ensure prisoner safety").

In United States v. Carmona, 873 F.2d 569 (2d Cir. 1989), officers arresting Carmona asked his name, even though they knew who he was. He answered with a false name, and this answer was used as evidence of consciousness of guilt at his trial. The court held that the question "what's your name?" is *always* within the booking exception, even if the officer knows the information in advance. The court noted that it is prudent practice for officers to make sure that the person arrested is the correct person. Was the question in *Carmona* "designed to elicit incriminating information?" What kind of answer were they expecting?

3. Does *Miranda* Apply to Undercover Activity?

What if a suspect in custody does not know that he is speaking to a police officer or agent? In Illinois v. Perkins, 496 U.S. 292 (1990), authorities suspected that Perkins was involved in a murder. Perkins was in prison on charges unrelated to the murder. An undercover officer was placed as Perkins's cellmate with the hope that he could obtain incriminating statements from Perkins about the murder. In the course of conversation concerning a planned escape, the undercover officer asked Perkins whether he had ever killed anybody. Perkins said yes and described the murder that was being investigated. For obvious reasons, Perkins had received no *Miranda* warnings. The Court held that Perkins's unwarned statement was admissible because "*Miranda* was not meant to protect suspects from boasting about their criminal activities in front of persons who they believe to be their cellmates." Justice Kennedy wrote the opinion for seven members of the Court. He reasoned that *Miranda* was concerned with the pressures upon a suspect in a police-dominated atmosphere. If the suspect does not even know he is talking to a police officer, the problems with which the Court was concerned in *Miranda* do not exist. Justice Kennedy explained as follows:

> It is the premise of *Miranda* that the danger of coercion results from the interaction of custody and official interrogation. * * * Questioning by captors, who appear to control the suspect's fate, may create mutually reinforcing pressures that the Court has assumed will weaken the suspect's will, but where a suspect does not know that he is conversing with a government agent, these pressures do not exist.

One of the virtues of *Miranda,* often recognized by the Court, is its bright-line character. Perkins argued that the creation of an "undercover investigations exception" to *Miranda* would destroy the clarity of the rule. But the majority rejected this argument, reasoning that the *Perkins* rule *itself* is a bright-line rule: if there is an undercover investigation (and it is easy to determine whether there is one) then *Miranda* is completely inapplicable. Justice Kennedy stated that "law enforcement officers will have little difficulty putting into practice our holding that undercover agents need not give *Miranda* warnings to incarcerated suspects."

Justice Brennan concurred in the judgment. He agreed that when a suspect does not know he is talking to a police agent, *Miranda* warnings are not required. Justice Brennan argued, however, that undercover activity constituted trickery, which could raise a "substantial claim that the confession was obtained in violation of the Due Process Clause."

Justice Marshall dissented. He argued that undercover questioning of an incarcerated suspect constituted both "custody" and "interrogation," and that the majority's opinion was thus an unjustified "exception" to *Miranda.* Justice Marshall also expressed concern that police would use the majority's decision to circumvent *Miranda* requirements by using undercover agents.

See also Cook v. Warden, 677 F.3d 1133 (11th Cir. 2012): admission of the defendant's custodial confession did not violate the Fifth Amendment where he was questioned by an FBI agent—who was his father. The father testified that he was not thinking of his job at the time and wanted to protect his son and convince him to cooperate for leniency. Under the circumstances, the defendant was not talking to a law enforcement officer within the meaning of *Miranda.*

4. Does *Miranda* Protection Depend on the Seriousness of the Offense?

The Court in Berkemer v. McCarty, 468 U.S. 420 (1984), established that there is no distinction between felonies and misdemeanors insofar as *Miranda* is concerned.

Writing for the Court, Justice Marshall rejected the felony-misdemeanor distinction on the ground that it would remove one of *Miranda's* principal advantages—the clarity of the rule.

> The exception to *Miranda* proposed * * * would substantially undermine this crucial advantage of the doctrine. The police often are unaware when they arrest a person whether he may have committed a misdemeanor or a felony. * * * Indeed, the nature of his offense may depend upon circumstances unknowable to the police, such as whether the suspect has previously committed a similar offense or has a criminal record of some other kind. It may even turn upon events yet to happen, such as whether a victim of the accident dies. It would be unreasonable to expect the police to make guesses as to the nature of the criminal conduct at issue before deciding how they may interrogate the suspect.
>
> Equally importantly, the doctrinal complexities that would confront the courts if we accepted [the misdemeanor-felony distinction] would be byzantine. Difficult questions quickly spring to mind: For instance, investigations into seemingly minor offenses sometimes escalate gradually into investigations into more serious matters; at what point in the evolution of an affair of this sort would the police be obliged to give *Miranda* warnings to a suspect in custody? * * * The litigation necessary to resolve such matters would be time-consuming and disruptive of law enforcement. And the end result would be an elaborate set of rules, interlaced with exceptions and subtle distinctions, discriminating between different kinds of custodial interrogations. Neither the police nor criminal defendants would benefit from such a development.

5. How Complete and Accurate Must the Warnings Be?

The Court in *Miranda* promulgated a set of detailed warnings. Yet it left unclear whether something less than a verbatim transcription of the Court's warnings would suffice. In California v. Prysock, 451 U.S. 1301 (1981), the Court concluded that police should be given some flexibility—so long as they provide the suspect with the gist of the warnings. Prysock was informed that he had "the right to talk to a lawyer before you are questioned, have him present while you are being questioned, and all during the questioning" and also that he had "the right to have a lawyer appointed to represent you at no cost to yourself." Prysock argued that he was never informed of his right to have an attorney appointed *before being questioned*. Thus, he was left with the impression that he could only have an attorney if he agreed to answer questions. The Court declared, however, that it had "never indicated that the rigidity of *Miranda* extends to the precise formulation of the warnings," and that "*Miranda* itself indicates that no talismanic incantation" is required. Under the circumstances, the warnings gave sufficient information, and were not misrepresentative. They didn't specifically say, for example, that Prysock had no right to an attorney unless he agreed to talk.

Chief Justice Rehnquist wrote for the Court in Duckworth v. Eagan, 492 U.S. 195 (1989), as it found no *Miranda* violation in a police officer's reading a printed waiver form to a suspect, which provided:

> "Before we ask you any questions, you must understand your rights. You have the right to remain silent. Anything you say can be used against you in court. *You have the right to talk to a lawyer for advice before we ask you any questions, and to have him with you during questioning.* You have this right to the advice and presence of a lawyer even if you cannot afford to hire one. We *have no way of giving you a lawyer, but one will be appointed for you, if you wish, if and when you go to court.* If you wish to answer questions now without a lawyer present, you have the right to stop answering questions at any time. You also have the right to stop answering at any time until you've talked to a lawyer." (emphasis added)

The Chief Justice noted that the Court has never insisted that *Miranda* warnings be given in the exact form described in Chief Justice Warren's opinion, and concluded that the inclusion of the "if and when you go to court" language accurately described state procedure and did not fail to apprise the defendant of his rights.

Justice Marshall, joined by Justices Brennan, Blackmun, and Stevens, dissented. He argued that the "if and when" language led the defendant to believe that a lawyer would not be appointed until some future time after questioning took place.

Ambiguity About the Right to Have an Attorney Present Throughout the Questioning: Florida v. Powell

In Florida v. Powell, 559 U.S. 50 (2010), Justice Ginsburg wrote for the Court as it held that advice that a suspect has "the right to talk to a lawyer before answering any of [the law enforcement officers'] questions," and that he can invoke this right "at any time . . . during th[e] interview," satisfies *Miranda*. Officers arrested Powell on suspicion of robbery and read warnings from the standard Tampa Police Department Consent and Release Form 310. The form states:

> "You have the right to remain silent. If you give up the right to remain silent, anything you say can be used against you in court. You have the right to talk to a lawyer before answering any of our questions. If you cannot afford to hire a lawyer, one will be appointed for you without cost and before any questioning. You have the right to use any of these rights at any time you want during this interview."

A Florida court found that the advice Powell received was misleading because it suggested that Powell could "only consult with an attorney before questioning" and did not convey Powell's entitlement to counsel's presence throughout the interrogation. Justice Ginsburg found this unpersuasive and emphasized that the warning that Powell had "the right to talk to a lawyer before answering any of [their] questions" communicated that Powell could consult with a lawyer before answering any particular question, and "the right to use any of [his] rights at any time [he] want[ed] during th[e] interview" confirmed that he could exercise that right while the interrogation was underway. She concluded that the combination reasonably conveyed Powell's right to have an attorney present, not only at the outset of interrogation, but at all times.

Justice Ginsburg reasoned that "[t]o reach the opposite conclusion, i.e., that the attorney would not be present throughout the interrogation, the suspect would have to imagine an unlikely scenario: To consult counsel, he would be obliged to exit and reenter the interrogation room between each query." She concluded that "[a] reasonable suspect in a custodial setting who has just been read his rights, we believe, would not come to the counterintuitive conclusion that he is obligated, or allowed, to hop in and out of the holding area to seek his attorney's advice," and "[i]nstead, the suspect would likely assume that he must stay put in the interrogation room and that his lawyer would be there with him the entire time."

Justice Ginsburg noted that all federal law enforcement agencies explicitly advise suspects of the full contours of each *Miranda* right, including the right to the presence of counsel during questioning. She identified the standard warnings used by the Federal Bureau of Investigation as exemplary: "You have the right to talk to a lawyer for advice before we ask you any questions. You have the right to have a lawyer with you during questioning." Although she recognized that "[t]his advice is admirably informative," she "decline[d] to declare its precise formulation necessary to meet *Miranda*'s requirements."

Justice Stevens, joined in part by Justice Breyer, dissented in *Powell.*

6. Do the *Miranda* Safeguards Apply to Custodial Interrogations of Foreigners Conducted Abroad?

Courts have struggled with whether and to what extent United States officials are bound by the *Miranda* requirements when interrogating suspects on foreign soil. See United States v. Mohammed, 693 F.3d 192 (D.C. Cir. 2012) ("We need not resolve the novel question whether *Miranda* applies to the overseas custodial interrogation of a person who is not a U.S. citizen" because any error in admitting the confession was harmless).

The question of *Miranda's* applicability to interrogations of foreigners on foreign soil arises most often in cases involving charges of terrorism.[28] For example, the court in In re Terrorist Bombings, U.S. Embassies, East Africa, 552 F.3d 177 (2d Cir. 2008), considered whether and how the *Miranda* safeguards applied to custodial interrogation of a suspected terrorist in Kenya. United States investigators[29] gave the suspect an Advice of Rights form, which stated that the suspect did not have to speak or answer any questions and that anything he said could be used against him "in a court in the United States or elsewhere." The Advice of Rights form then informed the suspect of his right to counsel *if he were being questioned in the United States.* It then proceeded as follows:

> Because we are not in the United States, we cannot ensure that you will have a lawyer appointed for you before any questioning.

The suspect was given a further oral warning, and eventually waived his rights and confessed. He complained at trial and on appeal that he did not receive the full panoply of *Miranda* protections. The court found no error in admitting the confession. It first addressed whether *Miranda* was applicable *at all* to a foreign interrogation in which United States officials participate. It proceeded on the assumption that *Miranda* was applicable, but noted that, even assuming *Miranda* was applicable, its "warning/waiver framework" has been applied by many courts "in a flexible fashion to accommodate the exigencies of local conditions."

Applying that flexible approach to the facts of the case, the court found that the Advice of Rights form and the subsequent oral warning presented the suspect with a "factually accurate" statement of the right to counsel, given the fact that there was no such right under Kenyan law—the controlling law under the circumstances. The court concluded as follows:

> In cases where a suspect has no entitlement to counsel under the law of the foreign land, it would be misleading to inform him falsely that the was guaranteed the presence or appointment of an attorney—and *Miranda* does not require the provision of false assurances.

The court also held that the United States officials had no affirmative obligation to urge local officials to provide counsel to the suspect. It declared that "*Miranda* requires government agents to be the conduits of *information* to detained suspects" but it does not "compel the police to serve

[28] Note that if a terrorism-related case is brought in a military commission proceeding, as opposed to a civilian judicial tribunal, the questions of the admissibility of any confession may be different. See the discussion in the section on voluntariness, supra.

[29] Note that foreign investigators questioning a suspect in a foreign jurisdiction are not bound by the *Miranda* requirements. In re Terrorist Bombings, 552 F.3d 177 (2d Cir. 2008) ("Recognizing that the threat of suppression in U.S. courts for failure to comply with *Miranda* holds little sway over foreign authorities, we have declined to suppress un-warned statements obtained overseas by foreign officials.")

as *advocates* for detainees before local authorities, endeavoring to expand the rights and privileges available under local law."

The court therefore concluded that the suspect was properly informed of his rights; it also found the waiver to be knowing and voluntary and therefore the confession was properly admitted under *Miranda*. The court did note, however, that the Advice of Rights form "created a needless risk of misunderstanding by stating, albeit accurately, what the right to counsel would have been had the interrogation occurred in the United States." According to the court, an advice of rights form "should state only what rights are available, not what rights would be available if circumstances were different."

E. WAIVER OF RIGHTS DURING CUSTODIAL INTERROGATION

1. Waiver and the Role of Counsel

In contrast with the right not to be subjected to treatment that produces involuntary confessions guaranteed by due process, the *Miranda* Court stated that the accused may waive the rights to silence and counsel during custodial interrogation, but only if, under all the circumstances, the rights are waived "voluntarily, knowingly, and intelligently." Thus, the validity of a waiver is a question of fact in any particular case. According to *Miranda,* a valid waiver will not be assumed from the silence of the accused after the warnings are given, nor merely from the fact that a confession is eventually obtained. However, the Court later held in North Carolina v. Butler, 441 U.S. 369 (1979), that neither an express statement of waiver nor a written waiver is required, so long as there is sufficient circumstantial evidence to indicate that the suspect understood his rights and voluntarily waived them. The *Butler* Court stated that "the question is not one of form, but rather whether the defendant in fact knowingly and voluntarily waived the rights delineated in the *Miranda* case." Although a written waiver is not required, it certainly supports the government's claim that a knowing and voluntary waiver was obtained.

For more on implied waivers, see the watershed case of Berghuis v. Thompkins, set forth in full in the section on invoking the right to silence, infra. There the Court found that a suspect who understood the warnings impliedly waived his rights when he confessed, even though he was silent for more than two hours while being interrogated.

Knowing and Voluntary

The Court in Moran v. Burbine, 475 U.S. 412 (1986), held that two requirements must be met before a suspect can be found to have waived his *Miranda* rights:

> First, the relinquishment of the right must have been voluntary in the sense that it was the product of a free and deliberate choice rather than intimidation, coercion, or deception. Second, the waiver must have been made with a full awareness both of the nature of the right being abandoned and the consequences of the decision to abandon it.

A waiver can be found if it reasonably appears from the giving of the warnings and the suspect's reaction that the suspect understood his *Miranda* rights and freely waived them. For example, in United States v. Frankson, 83 F.3d 79 (4th Cir. 1996), the officer read Frankson his rights, asked him if he understood those rights, and Frankson said "yes." Immediately after that, Frankson answered a number of questions posed by the officer, providing extensive details on how he evaded detection for drug activity: he would find a house where no one was ordinarily home during the day, instruct his drug supplier to send a package of drugs via UPS to that house, and then pick up the package when it was left on the home's doorstep. The court held that the circumstances indicated a knowing and voluntary waiver:

> A defendant's subsequent willingness to answer questions after acknowledging his *Miranda* rights is sufficient to constitute an implied waiver. * * * Even though Frankson never "formally" waived his *Miranda* rights, such cooperation, when coupled with his acknowledgment of his *Miranda* rights, constituted a valid waiver.

See also United States v. Banks, 78 F.3d 1190 (7th Cir. 1996) (waiver found, even though waiver form not signed, where defendant was familiar with the criminal justice system, and answered some questions and refused to answer others); United States v. Smith, 218 F.3d 777 (7th Cir. 2000) (waiver found where the defendant refused to sign a waiver form, but then immediately began to talk to police officers and continued to do so for an hour).

For more on applying the standards for knowing and voluntary waiver, see the Supreme Court's decision in Berghuis v. Thompkins, set forth in the section on invoking the right to silence, infra. There the Court held that after warnings are given, the police can continue to interrogate, and obtain a knowing and voluntary waiver, until the suspect explicitly invokes his right to remain silent. That is, a waiver need not be obtained *before* interrogation is conducted; rather, interrogation can be conducted until the suspect invokes his *Miranda* rights either explicitly or implicitly.

Relationship of Waiver Standards to the Test for Voluntary Confessions

Even after *Miranda* warnings are given, a confession can still be coerced under traditional due process standards. For example, the suspect may make a valid waiver of his rights, but the subsequent confession can be involuntary due to overbearing police pressure after the waiver of rights. See United States v. Syslo, 303 F.3d 860 (8th Cir. 2002) (statements were properly suppressed even though the defendant had voluntarily waived her *Miranda* rights, where after waiver the suspect had her young children at the police station and was informed that they could not be picked up by a relative until she confessed). Or it may be that warnings are given but the police pressure is so great that it cannot be said that the suspect voluntarily waived his *Miranda* rights. See, e.g., Commonwealth v. Perry, 475 Pa. 1, 379 A.2d 545 (1977) (a confession was involuntary even when warnings were given, because the statement was taken while the defendant was in the hospital and in a great deal of pain).

The Supreme Court held in Colorado v. Connelly, 479 U.S. 157 (1986)—the decision holding that coercive police activity is a prerequisite to a finding that a confession is involuntary—that "[t]here is obviously no reason to require more in the way of a 'voluntariness' inquiry in the *Miranda* waiver context than in the Fourteenth Amendment confession context." Thus, "[t]he voluntariness of a waiver of this privilege [against self-incrimination] has always depended on the absence of police overreaching, not on 'free choice' in any broader sense of the word." The Court found that a defendant voluntarily waived his *Miranda* rights because he decided to confess after receiving warnings, without the police engaging in any coercive behavior: "Respondent's perception of coercion flowing from the 'voice of God,' however important or significant such a perception may be in other disciplines, is a matter to which the United States Constitution does not speak." Chief Justice Rehnquist's majority opinion did not address the question whether Connelly actually understood the warnings and thus made a *knowing* waiver. That question was left for the state courts on remand.

Understanding the Miranda Warnings

Subsequent to *Connelly* and its remand on the issue of whether Connelly *understood* his rights as well as voluntarily waived them, several courts have held that persons who are deranged or mentally defective cannot knowingly and intelligently waive their *Miranda* rights. In Smith v. Zant, 887 F.2d 1407 (11th Cir. 1989) (en banc), the court concluded that "the *Connelly* Court addressed only voluntariness," and noted the "continued vitality of the knowing and intelligent requirement." The court found that the state did not satisfy its burden of showing that the defendant in that case was capable of understanding his *Miranda* rights; the defendant had an I.Q. of 65, he was under extreme stress, and the warnings were read to him only once, very quickly.

Similarly, courts have held that a waiver might not be "knowing and understanding" if the suspect could not understand the *Miranda* warnings due to some language barrier. Thus, in United States v. Garibay, 143 F.3d 534 (9th Cir. 1998), the suspect was given *Miranda* warnings in English and said he understood them. Nonetheless, the Court held that the government failed to satisfy its burden that Garibay *actually* understood the warnings. The court noted that Garibay's primary language was Spanish; that he received D+ grades in English in high school, and only passed because those classes were taught in Spanish; that he was "borderline retarded with extremely low verbal-English comprehension skills"; and that he had no previous experience with the criminal justice system, so that his "personal life experiences do not indicate that he was familiar with his *Miranda* rights and with his option to waive those rights." The court concluded that its result would have changed if Garibay either had been given the warnings in Spanish, or if he had signed a waiver form in English.

Conditional Waivers: Connecticut v. Barrett

Is it possible for the suspect to give a limited or conditional waiver of *Miranda* rights? In Connecticut v. Barrett, 479 U.S. 523 (1987), Barrett received *Miranda* warnings and then signed a form indicating that he would talk to the police about a sexual assault investigation. He stated he had "no problem" in talking about the assault, but that he would not give a written statement. He was given *Miranda* warnings several times, and eventually gave an oral confession which was admitted at trial. In an opinion by Chief Justice Rehnquist, the Court held that Barrett had knowingly and voluntarily waived his *Miranda* rights. The Chief Justice reasoned that the police had complied with Barrett's conditions, because they never sought to obtain a written statement. He emphasized that Barrett gave affirmative indications that he was willing to make an oral statement. The fact that Barrett's decision may have been "illogical" was held irrelevant, "for we have never embraced the theory that a defendant's ignorance of the full consequences of his decisions vitiates their voluntariness."

Justice Brennan concurred in the judgment. He argued that if Barrett was laboring under the misimpression that oral statements could not be admitted against him at trial, his waiver would have been invalid. However, Barrett's testimony at trial that he understood the warnings (to the effect that *any* statement could be used against him) demonstrated a valid waiver. Justice Stevens, joined by Justice Marshall, dissented.

Another question of limited waiver arises when a suspect says he will talk about "x" but not about "y." If the police then question him on "y," they have violated *Miranda* because the suspect never waived his rights with respect to "y." For example, in United States v. Soliz, 129 F.3d 499 (9th Cir. 1997), the defendant was arrested on suspicion of an immigration violation as well as smuggling activity. He agreed to talk to police officers about his citizenship. The police then began asking him about the smuggling and Soliz said "I thought this was just about my citizenship." The questioning continued about the smuggling and Soliz made admissions concerning the smuggling. The court held that those statements had to be excluded. It found that Soliz had made an unequivocal invocation of his right to remain silent on all issues other than citizenship. Accordingly, the officers were required to respect the conditions Soliz placed on his waiver.

Information Needed for an Intelligent Waiver: The Scope of the Interrogation—Colorado v. Spring

How much information must a suspect have to make a "knowing and intelligent" waiver of *Miranda* rights? This question arose in three Supreme Court cases, in each of which defendants argued that the *Miranda* warnings did not give them enough information. The Court rejected this argument in each case.

In Colorado v. Spring, 479 U.S. 564 (1987), Spring was arrested in Missouri when he tried to sell stolen firearms to an undercover agent. Agents also had information that Spring had been involved in a killing in Colorado. Spring was given warnings and signed a waiver form. He was first questioned about the firearms. Then the agents asked him whether he had ever shot anyone. He said that he had "shot another guy once." Eventually Spring gave a complete confession to the killing. Spring argued that he had not knowingly and intelligently waived his *Miranda* rights concerning the Colorado shooting because the agents had not warned him that he would be questioned about that matter. Justice Powell, writing for seven members of the Court, rejected Spring's argument that the warnings must be tied to the planned subject matter of the interrogation. Justice Powell reasoned as follows:

> Spring understood that he had the right to remain silent and that anything he said could be used as evidence against him. The Constitution does not require that a criminal suspect know and understand every possible consequence of a waiver of the Fifth Amendment privilege. * * * The *Miranda* warnings protect this privilege by ensuring that a suspect knows that he may choose not to talk to law enforcement officers, to talk only with counsel present, or to discontinue talking at any time. * * * [A] suspect's awareness of all the possible subjects of questioning in advance of interrogation is not relevant to determining whether the suspect voluntarily, knowingly, and intelligently waived his Fifth Amendment privilege.

Spring also argued that his waiver was invalid because the agents "tricked" him into believing that they were only concerned with the firearms charge. Justice Powell rejected this argument as well, stating that while trickery could vitiate the voluntariness of a waiver, trickery could not be found through "mere silence" on the part of the police. Here, the agents had not affirmatively misrepresented the intended scope of their questioning; they simply said nothing about it.

Justice Marshall, joined by Justice Brennan, dissented. He argued that a suspect's decision to waive the privilege will "necessarily be influenced by his awareness of the scope and seriousness of the matters under investigation." He claimed that the majority's rule would allow officers to take "unfair advantage of the suspect's psychological state."

Information Needed for an Intelligent Waiver: The Inadmissibility of a Previous Confession—Oregon v. Elstad

In Oregon v. Elstad, 470 U.S. 298 (1985), Elstad gave a *Miranda*-defective confession, then he received warnings, signed a waiver, and made a formal confession. Only this second confession was admitted at his trial. Elstad argued that the waiver he made before giving his second confession was not knowing and intelligent. Justice O'Connor described the argument, and rejected it, in the following passage:

> Respondent * * * has argued that he was unable to give a fully *informed* waiver of his rights because he was unaware that his prior statement could not be used against him. Respondent suggests that Deputy McAllister, to cure this deficiency, should have added an additional warning to those given him at the Sheriff's office. Such a requirement is neither practicable nor constitutionally necessary. In many cases, a breach of *Miranda* procedures may not be identified as such until long after full *Miranda* warnings are administered and a valid confession obtained. The standard *Miranda* warnings explicitly inform the suspect of his right to consult a lawyer before speaking. Police officers are ill equipped to pinch-hit for counsel, construing the murky and difficult questions of when "custody" begins or whether a given unwarned statement will ultimately be held admissible.
>
> This Court has never embraced the theory that a defendant's ignorance of the full consequences of his decisions vitiates their voluntariness. * * *

Information Needed for an Intelligent Waiver: Efforts of a Lawyer to Contact the Suspect—Moran v. Burbine

The Court in Moran v. Burbine, 475 U.S. 412 (1986), again considered whether the basic *Miranda* warnings were sufficient to establish the knowledge required for a knowing and intelligent waiver of *Miranda* rights. Justice O'Connor's majority opinion begins with a useful summary of the case:

> After being informed of his rights pursuant to Miranda v. Arizona, and after executing a series of written waivers, respondent confessed to the murder of a young woman. At no point during the course of the interrogation, which occurred prior to arraignment, did he request an attorney. While he was in police custody, his sister attempted to retain a lawyer to represent him. The attorney telephoned the police station and received assurances that respondent would not be questioned until the next day. In fact, the interrogation session that yielded the inculpatory statements began later that evening. The question presented is whether either the conduct of the police or respondent's ignorance of the attorney's efforts to reach him taints the validity of the waivers and therefore requires exclusion of the confessions.

Justice O'Connor concluded first that Burbine's waiver was valid despite the fact that he was not informed that an attorney sought to contact him. She reasoned as follows:

> The voluntariness of the waiver is not at issue. As the Court of Appeals correctly acknowledged, the record is devoid of any suggestion that police resorted to physical or psychological pressure to elicit the statements. * * * Nor is there any question about respondent's comprehension of the full panoply of rights set out in the *Miranda* warnings and of the potential consequences of a decision to relinquish them. * * *
>
> Events occurring outside of the presence of the suspect and entirely unknown to him surely can have no bearing on the capacity to comprehend and knowingly relinquish a constitutional right. [Accepting Burbine's argument would mean that] the same defendant, armed with the same information and confronted with precisely the same police conduct, would have knowingly waived his *Miranda* rights had a lawyer not telephoned the police station to inquire about his status. Nothing in any of our waiver decisions or in our understanding of the essential components of a valid waiver requires so incongruous a result. No doubt the additional information would have been useful to respondent; perhaps even it might have affected his decision to confess. But we have never read the Constitution to require that the police supply a suspect with a flow of information to help him calibrate his self interest in deciding whether to speak or stand by his rights. Once it is determined that a suspect's decision not to rely on his rights was uncoerced, that he at all times knew he could stand mute and request a lawyer, and that he was aware of the state's intention to use

his statements to secure a conviction, the analysis is complete and the waiver is valid as a matter of law.

State of Mind of Police Irrelevant

In the *Burbine* majority's view, the fact that the police acted *deliberately* to deprive the suspect of information concerning counsel's attempt to reach him did not affect the validity of the waiver. Justice O'Connor reasoned as follows:

> [W]hether intentional or inadvertent, the state of mind of the police is irrelevant to the question of the intelligence and voluntariness of respondent's election to abandon his rights. Although highly inappropriate, even deliberate deception of an attorney could not possibly affect a suspect's decision to waive his *Miranda* rights unless he were at least aware of the incident. Nor was the failure to inform respondent of the telephone call the kind of "trickery" that can vitiate the validity of a waiver. * * * Because respondent's voluntary decision to speak was made with full awareness and comprehension of all the information *Miranda* requires the police to convey, the waivers were valid.

The Role of Counsel Under Miranda

The defendant in *Burbine* argued that, apart from the waiver issue, *Miranda* should be read to prohibit the police from deliberately deceiving counsel, or from denying counsel's request to see the suspect. According to the defendant, *Miranda* should be read to provide some protection of the right to counsel *independent of the suspect's decision whether to invoke that right*. The majority, however, declined "to further extend *Miranda's* reach." Justice O'Connor explained the Court's position as follows:

> [W]hile we share respondent's distaste for the deliberate misleading of an officer of the court, reading *Miranda* to forbid police deception of an *attorney* would cut [the decision] completely loose from its own explicitly stated rationale. As is now well established, "[t]he . . . *Miranda* warnings are not themselves rights protected by the Constitution, but [are] instead measures to insure that the [suspect's] right against compulsory self-incrimination [is] protected.' " * * * Clearly, a rule that focuses on how the police treat an attorney—conduct that has no relevance at all to the degree of compulsion experienced by the defendant during interrogation—would ignore both *Miranda's* mission and its only source of legitimacy.

In other words, it is the suspect who has the right to counsel under *Miranda*; and counsel has a role *only after the suspect has invoked the right.*

Counsel had *no independent rights* to assert. His presence at the police station was irrelevant.

No Requirement to Inform the Suspect of Counsel's Efforts

Finally, the *Burbine* Court declined to "extend" *Miranda* to require the police to inform the suspect of an attorney's efforts to reach him. Such a requirement would be inconsistent with *Miranda's* bright-line approach. Justice O'Connor explained as follows:

> As we have stressed on numerous occasions, "[o]ne of the principal advantages" of *Miranda* is the ease and clarity of its application. We have little doubt that the approach urged by respondent * * * would have the inevitable consequence of muddying *Miranda's* otherwise relatively clear waters. The legal questions it would spawn are legion: To what extent should the police be held accountable for knowing that the accused has counsel? Is it enough that someone in the station house knows, or must the interrogating officer himself know of counsel's efforts to contact the suspect? Do counsel's efforts to talk to the suspect concerning one criminal investigation trigger the obligation to inform the defendant before interrogation may proceed on a wholly separate matter?

Justice O'Connor also argued that an extra warning requirement would be too costly to law enforcement interests, and thus was inconsistent with the *Miranda* compromise:

> * * * [R]eading *Miranda* to require the police in each instance to inform a suspect of an attorney's efforts to reach him would work a substantial and, we think, inappropriate shift in the subtle balance struck in that decision. Custodial interrogations implicate two competing concerns. On the one hand, the need for police questioning as a tool for effective enforcement of criminal laws cannot be doubted. Admissions of guilt are more than merely desirable, they are essential to society's compelling interest in finding, convicting and punishing those who violate the law. On the other hand, the Court has recognized that the interrogation process is "inherently coercive" and that, as a consequence, there exists a substantial risk that the police will inadvertently traverse the fine line between legitimate efforts to elicit admissions and constitutionally impermissible compulsion.
>
> *Miranda* attempted to reconcile these opposing concerns by giving the *defendant* the power to exert some control over the course of the interrogation. Declining to adopt the more extreme position that the actual presence of a lawyer was necessary to dispel the coercion inherent in custodial interrogation, the Court found that the suspect's Fifth Amendment rights could be adequately protected by less intrusive means. Police questioning, often an essential part of the

investigatory process, could continue in its traditional form, the Court held, but only if the suspect clearly understood that, at any time, he could bring the proceeding to a halt or, short of that, call in an attorney to give advice and monitor the conduct of his interrogators.

The position urged by respondent would upset this carefully drawn approach in a manner that is both unnecessary for the protection of the Fifth Amendment privilege and injurious to legitimate law enforcement. * * * Because neither the letter nor purposes of *Miranda* require this additional handicap on otherwise permissible investigatory efforts, we are unwilling to expand the *Miranda* rules to require the police to keep the suspect abreast of the status of his legal representation.

Dissent in Burbine

Justice Stevens, joined by Justices Brennan and Marshall, dissented in *Burbine.* He argued that the Court's holding "exalts incommunicado interrogation, sanctions police deception, and demeans the right to consult with an attorney." In his view, "[p]olice interference with communications between an attorney and his client is a recurrent problem." Justice Stevens responded to the majority's reliance on *Miranda's* careful balance with the observation that a rule requiring the police to inform a suspect of an attorney's call would serve *Miranda's* goal of dispelling the compulsion inherent in custodial interrogation. He responded to the majority's concern for clarity with the suggestion that no state that required the police to tell a suspect of an attorney's call had experienced problems. Justice Stevens argued that the police deliberately deceived the suspect's agent, his attorney, and that "as a matter of law, the police deception of Munson [the attorney] was tantamount to deception of Burbine himself."

Abstract Right to Counsel vs. Concrete Offer of Assistance

In Connecticut v. Stoddard, 206 Conn. 157, 537 A.2d 446 (1988), the court rejected *Burbine* as a matter of state constitutional law and held that a waiver could not be knowing if the suspect is unaware of a lawyer's attempt to contact him. The court reasoned as follows:

> *Miranda* warnings refer only to an abstract right to counsel. That a suspect validly waives the presence of counsel only means that for the moment the suspect is forgoing the exercise of that conceptual privilege. Faced with a concrete offer of assistance, however, a suspect may well decide to reclaim his or her continuing right to legal assistance. We cannot therefore conclude that a decision to forgo the abstract offer contained in *Miranda* embodies an implied rejection of a specific opportunity to confer with a known lawyer.

Has the *Stoddard* court effectively addressed the concerns of the majority in *Burbine?*

2. Waiver After Invocation of *Miranda* Rights—and Questions of Whether Those Rights *Have* Been Invoked

In all the above cases, the suspect had never invoked his *Miranda* rights, and the government argued that the suspect waived his rights and confessed. What if the suspect first invokes his *Miranda* rights and later confesses? It's obviously more difficult to argue waiver in such circumstances. If rights aren't invoked, then the suspect may have at all times wanted to speak with the police. But where the suspect has initially invoked his rights, *something* must have changed his mind. The government must show that this change of mind came from the suspect, and not from police harassment. Where the suspect has invoked his rights, the Supreme Court has shown greater sensitivity to the waiver issue than in cases where there was no invocation.

A suspect can invoke two rights in response to the *Miranda* warnings—the right to silence, and the right to counsel. The Court has held that the rules on waiver after invocation differ depending on which right is invoked. The Court has also made a number of rulings on *whether* the rights have been properly invoked under a variety of circumstances.

a. Invocation of the Right to Silence

Scrupulous Honor: Michigan v. Mosley

In Michigan v. Mosley, 423 U.S. 96 (1975), the defendant was arrested in connection with certain robberies. After receiving *Miranda* warnings, Mosley said he did not want to discuss the robberies and the detective refrained from questioning him further. Approximately two hours later, *Miranda* warnings were given again, and a different detective questioned Mosley about a murder that was not related to the robberies. Mosley signed a waiver form and made an incriminating statement, which was admitted at his subsequent murder trial, where he was convicted.

Justice Stewart, writing for the Court, found that the admission of the incriminating statements did not violate *Miranda.* In reaching this decision, the Court found it necessary to interpret the following language from *Miranda:*

> If the individual indicates in any manner, at any time prior to or during questioning, that he wishes to remain silent, the interrogation must cease. At this point he has shown that he intends to exercise his Fifth Amendment privilege; any statement taken after the person invokes his privilege cannot be other than the product of compulsion, subtle or otherwise.

The *Mosley* Court concluded that the *Miranda* Court could not have meant that interrogation is *forever barred* simply because the defendant invoked his right to silence at some point. Justice Stewart concluded that the only sensible reading of the above language was that the suspect's right to cut off questioning must be "*scrupulously honored.*" If the right to silence was scrupulously honored, then police interrogation could be permitted and a knowing and voluntary waiver could be found. Reviewing the circumstances of Mosley's second interrogation, the Court stated:

> This is not a case * * * where the police failed to honor a decision of a person in custody to cut off questioning, either by refusing to discontinue the interrogation upon request or by persisting in repeated efforts to wear down his resistance and make him change his mind. In contrast to such practices, the police here immediately ceased the interrogation, resumed questioning only after the passage of a significant period of time and the provision of a fresh set of warnings, and restricted the second interrogation to a crime that had not been a subject of the earlier interrogation.

Justice Stewart indicated that the Court would not tolerate repetitive and continuous attempts to interrogate a defendant who wanted to remain silent. But he concluded *Miranda* should not be a per se bar to resumption of questioning.

Scrupulously Honoring an Invocation of Silence

It may be wondered how an officer can "scrupulously honor" a suspect's right to remain silent and yet resume interrogation after the suspect invokes that right. Generally speaking, courts have found the most important factor to be whether the officers gave the suspect a "cooling off" period after he invoked the right to silence. See United States v. Rambo, 365 F.3d 906 (10th Cir. 2004) ("Whatever else *Mosley* might require, it is clear that some break in the interrogation must occur."); Charles v. Smith, 894 F.2d 718 (5th Cir. 1990) (waiver invalid where suspect was asked whether he owned a certain hat and coat, two minutes after invoking the right to silence); United States v. Ramsey, 992 F.2d 301 (11th Cir. 1993) (waiver invalid where defendant was given a last "opportunity to help himself," twenty minutes after invoking the right to silence); Grooms v. Keeney, 826 F.2d 883 (9th Cir. 1987) (waiver valid after four hour break in questioning).

Multiple attempts to get the suspect to speak are considered problematic. See Vujosevic v. Rafferty, 844 F.2d 1023 (3d Cir. 1988) (waiver invalid where suspect was approached four times to determine whether he had changed his mind about not talking, and where officers had no reason to believe he had changed his mind). If the officers give fresh *Miranda* warnings when they approach the suspect, this is evidence (though not dispositive) that they are scrupulously honoring the suspect's right to silence, as well as evidence that defendant knowingly and voluntarily waived his rights. See Otey v. Grammer, 859 F.2d 575 (8th Cir. 1988) (waiver found where warnings were given frequently and defendant was allowed to control the subject matter of the questioning).

What if the officers use a tactic designed to impress upon the defendant the seriousness of the situation? In United States v. Tyler, 164 F.3d 150 (3d Cir. 1998), the defendant was arrested for murdering a witness who was scheduled to testify at his brother's criminal trial. He invoked his right to silence and was placed in a room at the police station. The walls of the room contained a timeline of the murder investigation and crime scene photographs, including two photos of the body of the victim. Tyler remained in the room, alone, for hours. When the officers came to question him again, Tyler immediately confessed. The Court found that this confession had to be excluded under *Mosley*. Do you agree? See also United States v. Lafferty, 503 F.3d 293 (3d Cir. 2007) (officers did not scrupulously honor the right to remain silent when they put the suspect in an interrogation room with her alleged accomplice after he had agreed to give a confession).

Right to Silence Must Be Clearly Invoked; Waiver Can Be Implied from the Confession Itself; and Interrogation After Warnings Is Permissible So Long as Waiver Is Ultimately Found: Berghuis v. Thompkins

The *Mosley* standards presume that the suspect has invoked the right to silence after receiving *Miranda* warnings. If the suspect, in response to the warnings, says "I don't want to talk about anything," then he has clearly triggered the protections provided by *Mosley*. Not all invocations are so clear, however. What if the suspect says "If I knew what was good for me, I wouldn't be talking to you," or "I'd like to cooperate, but my brother would kill me if I did"? If it is unclear whether the suspect is invoking his right to silence, must the police stop the interrogation?

The following case takes up a number of important questions concerning waiver of *Miranda* rights. The case concerns specifically whether the *Miranda* right to silence is invoked by remaining silent. But the Court also provides important rules on when a waiver of *Miranda* rights can be found in the absence of an invocation.

BERGHUIS V. THOMPKINS

Supreme Court of the United States, 2010.
560 U.S. 370.

JUSTICE KENNEDY delivered the opinion of the Court.

* * *

On January 10, 2000, a shooting occurred outside a mall in Southfield, Michigan. Among the victims was Samuel Morris, who died from multiple gunshot wounds. The other victim, Frederick France, recovered from his injuries and later testified. Thompkins, who was a suspect, fled. About one year later he was found in Ohio and arrested there.

Two Southfield police officers traveled to Ohio to interrogate Thompkins, then awaiting transfer to Michigan. The interrogation began around 1:30 p.m. and lasted about three hours. The interrogation was conducted in a room that was 8 by 10 feet, and Thompkins sat in a chair that resembled a school desk * * *. At the beginning of the interrogation, one of the officers, Detective Helgert, presented Thompkins with a form derived from the *Miranda* rule. It stated:

"NOTIFICATION OF CONSTITUTIONAL RIGHTS AND STATEMENT

"1. You have the right to remain silent.

"2. Anything you say can and will be used against you in a court of law.

"3. You have a right to talk to a lawyer before answering any questions and you have the right to have a lawyer present with you while you are answering any questions.

"4. If you cannot afford to hire a lawyer, one will be appointed to represent you before any questioning, if you wish one.

"5. You have the right to decide at any time before or during questioning to use your right to remain silent and your right to talk with a lawyer while you are being questioned."

Helgert asked Thompkins to read the fifth warning out loud. Thompkins complied. Helgert later said this was to ensure that Thompkins could read, and Helgert concluded that Thompkins understood English. Helgert then read the other four *Miranda* warnings out loud and asked Thompkins to sign the form to demonstrate that he understood his rights. Thompkins declined to sign the form. The record contains conflicting evidence about whether Thompkins then verbally confirmed that he understood the rights listed on the form.

Officers began an interrogation. At no point during the interrogation did Thompkins say that he wanted to remain silent, that he did not want to talk with the police, or that he wanted an attorney. Thompkins was "[l]argely" silent during the interrogation, which lasted about three hours. He did give a few limited verbal responses, however, such as "yeah," "no," or "I don't know." And on occasion he communicated by nodding his head. Thompkins also said that he "didn't want a peppermint" that was offered to him by the police and that the chair he was "sitting in was hard."

About 2 hours and 45 minutes into the interrogation, Helgert asked Thompkins, "Do you believe in God?" Thompkins made eye contact with Helgert and said "Yes," as his eyes "well[ed] up with tears." Helgert asked, "Do you pray to God?" Thompkins said "Yes." Helgert asked, "Do you pray to God to forgive you for shooting that boy down?" Thompkins answered "Yes" and looked away. Thompkins refused to make a written confession, and the interrogation ended about 15 minutes later.

Thompkins was charged with first-degree murder * * *. He moved to suppress the statements made during the interrogation. He argued that he had invoked his Fifth Amendment right to remain silent, requiring police to end the interrogation at once, see Michigan v. Mosley, that he had not waived his right to remain silent, and that his inculpatory statements were involuntary. The trial court denied the motion. [Thompkins was convicted. His state appeals were rejected. The district court denied a writ of habeas corpus but the Sixth Circuit reversed.]

* * *

All concede that the warning given in this case was in full compliance with these requirements. The dispute centers on the response—or nonresponse—from the suspect.

Thompkins makes various arguments that his answers to questions from the detectives were inadmissible. He first contends that he invoked his privilege to remain silent by not saying anything for a sufficient period of time, so the interrogation should have ceased before he made his inculpatory statements.

This argument is unpersuasive. In the context of invoking the *Miranda* right to counsel, the Court in Davis v. United States [discussed infra in the section on invoking the right to counsel], held that a suspect must do so "unambiguously." If an accused makes a statement concerning the right to counsel "that is ambiguous or equivocal" or makes no statement, the police are not required to end the interrogation, or ask questions to clarify whether the accused wants to invoke his or her *Miranda* rights.

The Court has not yet stated whether an invocation of the right to remain silent can be ambiguous or equivocal, but there is no principled reason to adopt different standards for determining when an accused has invoked the *Miranda* right to remain silent and the *Miranda* right to counsel at issue in *Davis*. Both protect the privilege against compulsory self-incrimination, by requiring an interrogation to cease when either right is invoked.

There is good reason to require an accused who wants to invoke his or her right to remain silent to do so unambiguously. A requirement of an unambiguous invocation of *Miranda* rights results in an objective inquiry that avoids difficulties of proof and provides guidance to officers on how to proceed in the face of ambiguity. If an ambiguous act, omission, or statement could require police to end the interrogation, police would be required to make difficult decisions about an accused's unclear intent and face the consequence of suppression if they guess wrong. Suppression of a voluntary confession in these circumstances would place a significant burden on society's interest in prosecuting criminal activity. Treating an ambiguous or equivocal act, omission, or statement as an invocation of *Miranda* rights might add marginally to *Miranda's* goal of dispelling the compulsion inherent in custodial interrogation. But as *Miranda* holds, full comprehension of the rights to remain silent and request an attorney are sufficient to dispel whatever coercion is inherent in the interrogation process.

Thompkins did not say that he wanted to remain silent or that he did not want to talk with the police. Had he made either of these simple, unambiguous statements, he would have invoked his right to cut off questioning. Michigan v. Mosley. Here he did neither, so he did not invoke his right to remain silent.

* * *

We next consider whether Thompkins waived his right to remain silent. Even absent the accused's invocation of the right to remain silent, the accused's statement during a custodial interrogation is inadmissible at trial unless the prosecution can establish that the accused in fact knowingly and voluntarily waived *Miranda* rights when making the statement. The waiver inquiry has two distinct dimensions: waiver must be voluntary in the sense that it was the product of a free and deliberate choice rather than intimidation, coercion, or deception, and "made with a full awareness of both the nature of the right being abandoned and the consequences of the decision to abandon it." Moran v. Burbine.

Some language in *Miranda* could be read to indicate that waivers are difficult to establish absent an explicit written waiver or a formal, express oral statement. * * *

The course of decisions since *Miranda*, informed by the application of *Miranda* warnings in the whole course of law enforcement, demonstrates that waivers can be established even absent formal or express statements of waiver that would be expected in, say, a judicial hearing to determine if a guilty plea has been properly entered. * * *

One of the first cases to decide the meaning and import of *Miranda* with respect to the question of waiver was North Carolina v. Butler. The *Butler* Court, after discussing some of the problems created by the language in *Miranda*, established certain important propositions. *Butler* interpreted the *Miranda* language concerning the "heavy burden" to show waiver, in accord with usual principles of determining waiver, which can include waiver implied from all the circumstances. And in a later case, the Court stated that this "heavy burden" is not more than the burden to establish waiver by a preponderance of the evidence. Colorado v. Connelly.

The prosecution therefore does not need to show that a waiver of *Miranda* rights was express. * * * *Butler* made clear that a waiver of *Miranda* rights may be implied through "the defendant's silence, coupled with an understanding of his rights and a course of conduct indicating waiver." The Court in *Butler* therefore retreated from the language and tenor of the *Miranda* opinion, which suggested that the Court would require that a waiver be specifically made.

If the State establishes that a *Miranda* warning was given and the accused made an uncoerced statement, this showing, standing alone, is insufficient to demonstrate a valid waiver of *Miranda* rights. The prosecution must make the additional showing that the accused understood these rights. Where the prosecution shows that a *Miranda* warning was given and that it was understood by the accused, an accused's uncoerced statement establishes an implied waiver of the right to remain silent.

Although *Miranda* imposes on the police a rule that is both formalistic and practical when it prevents them from interrogating suspects without first providing them with a *Miranda* warning, it does not impose a formalistic waiver procedure that a suspect must follow to relinquish those rights. As a general proposition, the law can presume that an individual who, with a full understanding of his or her rights, acts in a manner inconsistent with their exercise has made a deliberate choice to relinquish the protection those rights afford. * * *

The record in this case shows that Thompkins waived his right to remain silent. * * * First, there is no contention that Thompkins did not understand his rights; and from this it follows that he knew what he gave up when he spoke. There was more than enough evidence in the record to conclude that Thompkins understood his *Miranda* rights. Thompkins received a written copy of the *Miranda* warnings; Detective Helgert determined that Thompkins could read and understand English; and Thompkins was given time to read the warnings. * * * Helgert, moreover, read the warnings aloud.

Second, Thompkins's answer to Detective Helgert's question about whether Thompkins prayed to God for forgiveness for shooting the victim is a "course of conduct indicating waiver" of the right to remain silent. *Butler*. If Thompkins wanted to remain silent, he could have said nothing in response to Helgert's questions, or he could have unambiguously invoked his *Miranda* rights and ended the interrogation. The fact that Thompkins made a statement about three hours after receiving a *Miranda* warning does not overcome the fact that he engaged in a course of conduct indicating waiver. Police are not required to rewarn suspects from time to time. Thompkins's answer to Helgert's question about praying to God for forgiveness for shooting the victim was sufficient to show a course of conduct indicating waiver. This is confirmed by the fact that before then Thompkins had given sporadic answers to questions throughout the interrogation.

Third, there is no evidence that Thompkins's statement was coerced. * * * Thompkins does not claim that police threatened or injured him during the interrogation or that he was in any way fearful. The interrogation was conducted in a standard-sized room in the middle of the afternoon. It is true that apparently he was in a straight-backed chair for three hours, but there is no authority for the proposition that an interrogation of this length is inherently coercive. Indeed, even where interrogations of greater duration were held to be improper, they were accompanied, as this one was not, by other facts indicating coercion, such as an incapacitated and sedated suspect, sleep and food deprivation, and threats. The fact that Helgert's question referred to Thompkins's religious beliefs also did not render Thompkins's statement involuntary. The Fifth Amendment privilege is not concerned with moral and psychological pressures to confess emanating from sources other than official coercion. In these circumstances, Thompkins knowingly and voluntarily made a statement to police, so he waived his right to remain silent.

* * *

Thompkins next argues that, even if his answer to Detective Helgert could constitute a waiver of his right to remain silent, the police were not allowed to question him until they obtained a waiver first. *Butler* forecloses this argument. The *Butler* Court held that courts can infer a waiver of *Miranda* rights "from the actions and words of the person interrogated." This principle would be inconsistent with a rule that requires a waiver at the outset. The *Butler* Court thus rejected the rule proposed by the *Butler* dissent, which would have "requir[ed] the police to obtain an express waiver of [*Miranda* rights] before proceeding with interrogation." This holding also makes sense given that the primary protection afforded suspects subjected to custodial interrogation is the *Miranda* warnings themselves. * * *

Interrogation provides the suspect with additional information that can put his or her decision to waive, or not to invoke, into perspective. As questioning commences and then continues, the suspect has the opportunity to consider the choices he or she faces and to make a more informed decision, either to insist on silence or to cooperate. When the suspect knows that *Miranda* rights can be invoked at any time, he or she has the opportunity to reassess his or her immediate and long-term interests. * * *

In order for an accused's statement to be admissible at trial, police must have given the accused a *Miranda* warning. If that condition is established, the court can proceed to consider whether there has been an express or implied waiver of *Miranda* rights. In making its ruling on the admissibility of a statement made during custodial questioning, the trial court, of course, considers whether there is evidence to support the conclusion that, from the whole course of questioning, an express or implied waiver has been established. Thus, after giving a *Miranda* warning, police may interrogate a suspect who has neither invoked nor waived his or her *Miranda* rights. On these premises, it follows the police were not required to obtain a waiver of Thompkins's *Miranda* rights before commencing the interrogation.

* * *

In sum, a suspect who has received and understood the *Miranda* warnings, and has not invoked his *Miranda* rights, waives the right to remain silent by making an uncoerced statement to the police. Thompkins did not invoke his right to remain silent and stop the questioning. Understanding his rights in full, he waived his right to remain silent by making a voluntary statement to the police. The police, moreover, were not required to obtain a waiver of Thompkins's right to remain silent before interrogating him.

JUSTICE SOTOMAYOR, with whom JUSTICE STEVENS, JUSTICE GINSBURG, and JUSTICE BREYER join, dissenting.

The Court concludes today that a criminal suspect waives his right to remain silent if, after sitting tacit and uncommunicative through nearly three hours of police interrogation, he utters a few one-word responses. The Court also concludes that a suspect who wishes to guard his right to remain silent against such a finding of "waiver" must, counterintuitively, speak—and must do so with sufficient precision to satisfy a clear-statement rule that construes ambiguity in favor of the police. Both propositions mark a substantial retreat from the protection against compelled self-incrimination that *Miranda* has long provided during custodial interrogation. * * *.

* * *

That Thompkins did not make the inculpatory statements at issue until after approximately 2 hours and 45 minutes of interrogation serves as strong evidence against waiver. *Miranda* and *Butler* expressly preclude the possibility that the inculpatory statements themselves are sufficient to establish waiver. * * *

Today's dilution of the prosecution's burden of proof to the bare fact that a suspect made inculpatory statements after *Miranda* warnings were given and understood takes an unprecedented step away from the high standards of proof for the waiver of constitutional rights this Court has long demanded. * * *

* * *

I cannot agree with the Court's * * * ruling that a suspect must clearly invoke his right to silence by speaking. Taken together with the Court's reformulation of the prosecution's burden of proof as to waiver, today's novel clear-statement rule for invocation invites police to question a suspect at length—notwithstanding his persistent refusal to answer questions—in the hope of eventually obtaining a single inculpatory response which will suffice to prove waiver of rights. * * *

I disagree with [the Court's] novel application of *Davis*. Neither the rationale nor holding of that case compels today's result. *Davis* involved the right to counsel, not the right to silence. * * *

* * *

In my mind, a more appropriate standard for addressing a suspect's ambiguous invocation of the right to remain silent is the constraint *Mosley* places on questioning a suspect who has invoked that right: The suspect's "right to cut off questioning" must be "scrupulously honored." Such a standard is necessarily precautionary and fact specific. * * *

To be sure, such a standard does not provide police with a bright-line rule. But * * * *Mosley* itself does not offer clear guidance to police about when and how interrogation may continue after a suspect invokes his rights. Given that police have for nearly 35 years applied *Mosley's* fact-specific standard in questioning suspects who have invoked their right to remain silent * * * I see little reason to believe today's clear-statement rule is necessary to ensure effective law enforcement.

Davis' clear-statement rule is also a poor fit for the right to silence. Advising a suspect that he has a "right to remain silent" is unlikely to convey that he must speak (and must do so in some particular fashion) to ensure the right will be protected. By contrast, telling a suspect he has the right to the presence of an attorney, and that if he cannot afford an attorney one will be appointed for him prior to any questioning if he so desires implies the need for speech to exercise that right. * * *

Conversely, the Court's concern that police will face "difficult decisions about an accused's unclear intent" and suffer the consequences of "guessing wrong," is misplaced. If a suspect makes an ambiguous statement or engages in conduct that creates uncertainty about his intent to invoke his right, police can simply ask for clarification. It is hardly an unreasonable burden for police to ask a suspect, for instance, "Do you want to talk to us?" * * *

Today's decision turns *Miranda* upside down. Criminal suspects must now unambiguously invoke their right to remain silent—which, counterintuitively, requires them to speak. At the same time, suspects will be legally presumed to have waived their rights even if they have given no clear expression of their intent to do so. Those results, in my view, find no basis in *Miranda* or our subsequent cases and are inconsistent with the fair-trial principles on which those precedents are grounded. * * *

Is Thompkins Consistent with Miranda?

Recall the following language from *Miranda*:

> An express statement that the individual is willing to make a statement and does not want an attorney, followed closely by a statement, could constitute a waiver. But a valid waiver will not be presumed simply from the silence of the accused after warnings are given, or simply from the fact that a confession was, in fact, eventually obtained. * * * Whatever the testimony of the authorities as to waiver of rights by an accused, the fact of lengthy interrogation or incommunicado incarceration before a statement is made is strong evidence that the accused did not validly waive his rights. In these circumstances the fact that the individual eventually made a statement is consistent with the conclusion that the compelling influence of the interrogation finally forced him to do so. It is inconsistent with any notion of a voluntary relinquishment of the privilege.

Does the Court in *Thompkins* adequately explain why the *Miranda* reasoning is no longer persuasive?

Custodial Interrogation Requirement

Mosley's requirement of "scrupulous honor" applies only if the defendant's explicit invocation of the right to silence occurs in the context of custodial interrogation. For example, in United States v. Kelly, 329 F.3d 624 (8th Cir. 2003), the defendant argued that his confession had to be excluded under *Mosley* because he had previously invoked his right to silence when he spoke to police officers in an initial interview, and then confessed when the officers interrogated him later. The court, however, noted that the defendant was not in custody during the initial interview; accordingly, he had no *Miranda* rights to invoke. The court concluded that "Kelly's termination of the voluntary encounter posed no independent barrier to later questioning."

b. Invocation of the Right to Counsel

Bright Line Rule: Edwards v. Arizona

In Edwards v. Arizona, 451 U.S. 477 (1981), the Court determined whether and under what circumstances a waiver can be found after the suspect invokes his right to *counsel*. The Court adopted a per se approach:

> [A]dditional safeguards are necessary when the accused asks for counsel; and we now hold that when an accused has invoked his right to have counsel present during custodial interrogation, a valid waiver of that right cannot be established by showing only that he responded to further police-initiated custodial interrogation even if he has been advised of his rights. We further hold that an accused, such as Edwards, having expressed his desire to deal with the police only through counsel, *is not subject to further interrogation by the authorities until counsel has been made available to him, unless the accused himself initiates further communication, exchanges or conversations with the police.*[30]

Relationship Between Edwards and Innis

Edwards holds that police must terminate and cannot re-initiate an interrogation of a suspect who has invoked his right to counsel. But if police-renewed contact does not rise to the level of custodial interrogation, *Miranda* itself is inapplicable to a resulting confession, and therefore so is *Edwards*. This is shown by the facts of *Innis*. Innis invoked his right to counsel, but the Court found it unnecessary to reach the question of waiver, because the officers never interrogated him after he invoked. They had *contact* with him—the officer's statement in the cruiser about the gun possibly being picked up by a handicapped child—but they did not interrogate him.

So if the suspect invokes his right to counsel, what *Edwards* holds is that police may not *interrogate* him while in *Miranda* custody unless the suspect initiates the conversation and then knowingly and voluntarily waives his *Miranda* rights. See, e.g., Van Hook v. Anderson, 444 F.3d 830

---

[30] Chief Justice Burger and Justices Powell and Rehnquist agreed with the result, but expressed concern about the seemingly per se aspects of the majority rule which they found to be an unnecessary embellishment on the standard knowing and intelligent waiver rule.

(6th Cir. 2006) (after defendant invoked his right to counsel, the officer spoke with the defendant's mother, then approached the defendant and said "I just spoke to your mother, we need to talk"; this was interrogation, so the subsequent confession was obtained in violation of *Edwards*).

Defining Initiation: Oregon v. Bradshaw

Edwards requires that a suspect "initiate" further communication before a waiver can be found. Whether a suspect has initiated reinterrogation is often a difficult question. In Oregon v. Bradshaw, 462 U.S. 1039 (1983), Oregon police were investigating the death of Lowell Reynolds, a minor who apparently died in the wreck of his pickup truck. Bradshaw was asked and agreed to come to the police station for questioning. Once there, he was advised of his rights and admitted providing liquor to Reynolds. He was arrested for furnishing liquor to a minor. When an officer suggested that Bradshaw might have been driving Reynolds' truck, Bradshaw invoked his right to an attorney. Questioning stopped. Thereafter, during or just before a 10 or 15 mile trip from the police station to the jail, Bradshaw asked, "Well, what is going to happen to me now?" An officer answered that Bradshaw had requested an attorney and that Bradshaw should not be talking with the officer unless he desired to do so. The two had a conversation concerning where Bradshaw was being taken and what the charges against him would be. The officer suggested that Bradshaw might help himself by taking a lie detector test, and Bradshaw agreed to take one. The next day, following new warnings, he took the test. The examiner expressed doubts that Bradshaw had told the truth and Bradshaw then admitted he was driving the vehicle in which Reynolds was killed. The trial court admitted Bradshaw's confession.

A plurality of the Supreme Court found that *Edwards* was satisfied because Bradshaw initiated contact with the police officer after invoking his right to counsel and then made a knowing and voluntary waiver of his *Miranda* rights. Justice Rehnquist's plurality opinion, joined by Chief Justice Burger and Justices White and O'Connor, found initiation by reasoning as follows:

> There can be no doubt in this case that in asking, "Well, what is going to happen to me now?" respondent "initiated" further conversation in the ordinary dictionary sense of that word. While we doubt that it would be desirable to build a superstructure of legal refinements around the word "initiate" in this context, there are undoubtedly situations where a bare inquiry by either a defendant or by a police officer should not be held to "initiate" any conversation or dialogue. There are some inquiries, such as a request for a drink of water or a request to use a telephone that are so routine that they cannot be fairly said to represent a desire on the part of an accused to

open up a more generalized discussion relating directly or indirectly to the investigation. Such inquiries or statements, by either an accused or a police officer, relating to routine incidents of the custodial relationship, will not generally "initiate" a conversation in the sense in which that word was used in *Edwards*.

> Although ambiguous, the respondent's question in this case as to what was going to happen to him evinced a willingness and a desire for a generalized discussion about the investigation; it was not merely a necessary inquiry arising out of the incidents of the custodial relationship. It could reasonably have been interpreted by the officer as relating generally to the investigation. That the police officer so understood it is apparent from the fact that he immediately reminded the accused that "you do not have to talk to me," and only after the accused told him that he "understood" did they have a generalized conversation. On these facts we believe that there was not a violation of the *Edwards* rule.

The plurality clarified that a finding of initiation by the suspect was not enough to constitute a waiver under *Edwards.* Justice Rehnquist stated that, even if the suspect initiates communication, "where reinterrogation follows, the burden remains upon the prosecution to show that subsequent events indicated a waiver of the Fifth Amendment right to have counsel present during the interrogation."

Thus, the Court uses a two-step analysis to determine whether a suspect waives his rights after invoking the right to counsel:

- The first step is the bright-line prophylactic safeguard of the suspect-initiation requirement.
- The second step is the familiar totality of circumstances test of a knowing and voluntary waiver.

The plurality in *Bradshaw* found that, after initiating communication, Bradshaw knowingly and voluntarily waived his *Miranda* rights, because he was given fresh warnings and it was clear he understood them and voluntarily waived them.

Justice Marshall, joined by Justices Brennan, Blackmun, and Stevens, dissented. The dissenters applied the same two-step approach as had the majority, but they differed as to the application of the threshold requirement of "initiation" to the facts. Justice Marshall argued that the plurality's definition of "initiation" was overbroad and "drastically undermined" the protection erected in *Edwards.* In Justice Marshall's view, initiation could not be found unless the suspect expresses a willingness to discuss the *specific subject matter of the investigation.* He argued that Bradshaw's question was merely a response to his custodial surroundings, rather than an expression of willingness to discuss his crime.

The deciding vote in *Bradshaw* was cast by Justice Powell, who concurred in the result. He expressed concern about the bright line initiation requirement. Justice Powell preferred to rely on the totality of the circumstances, which in this case indicated that Bradshaw had knowingly and voluntarily waived his *Miranda* rights.

Applications of Bradshaw

While the Court split 4–4 in *Bradshaw* as to the proper test for initiation, the lower courts have consistently followed Justice Rehnquist's view that any ambiguity in whether the suspect expressed an intent to reopen the dialogue should be construed in favor of finding an initiation. The court in United States v. Velasquez, 885 F.2d 1076 (3d Cir. 1989), relied on the *Bradshaw* plurality to hold that the suspect's statement "what is going to happen?" was an initiation under *Edwards.* The court stated that the plurality's test was a reasonable compromise between individual and state interests, and that Justice Marshall's test "might convert the prophylactic value of the initiation requirement * * * into an overly stringent substantive hurdle." The court felt it was unnecessary to apply the initiation requirement aggressively, because the government continues to have the burden of showing that the suspect knowingly and voluntarily waived his *Miranda* rights.

Even under the plurality's view of initiation in *Bradshaw,* however, it does not follow that every statement from a suspect's mouth evinces a desire to "talk generally about his case." See, e.g., United States v. Soto, 953 F.2d 263 (6th Cir. 1992) (indicating desire to keep belongings separate from those of co-defendant is not initiation); Jacobs v. Singletary, 952 F.2d 1282 (11th Cir. 1992) (asking officer "Where are my children?" is not initiation).

Ambiguous Invocation of the Right to Counsel: Davis v. United States

As with invocation of the right to silence, questions sometimes arise as to whether the suspect has *in fact* invoked a right to counsel. If there is no invocation, then there is no initiation requirement, and the analysis reverts to whether the defendant knowingly and voluntarily waived his *Miranda* rights.

In Davis v. United States, 512 U.S. 452 (1994), the Court held that a suspect must *clearly and unequivocally* invoke the right to counsel in order to trigger the protections of *Edwards.* If the invocation is ambiguous or equivocal, police questioning can continue; and such questioning need not be limited to that necessary to clarify the suspect's desire with respect to counsel. [As discussed above, the Court thereafter in Berghuis v.

Thompkins applied the *Davis* explicit invocation requirement to the right to silence.]

After waiving his *Miranda* rights, Davis answered questions about a killing; about 90 minutes into the interview, he said, "Maybe I should talk to a lawyer." The officers then asked clarifying questions to determine whether Davis wanted a lawyer. He said that he did not. A short break was taken, Davis was reminded of his rights, and the interview continued for another hour, until Davis said, "I think I want a lawyer before I say anything else." At that point, questioning ceased. In the Supreme Court, Davis argued that the statements he made after his first reference to counsel were improperly admitted at his trial.

The Supreme Court, in an opinion by Justice O'Connor for five Justices, rejected Davis's argument and held that the statements Davis made after referring to counsel were properly admitted at his trial. Justice O'Connor set forth the standards applicable to the invocation of the *Miranda* right to counsel, and the protections of *Edwards,* in the following analysis:

> [T]he suspect must unambiguously request counsel. Although a suspect need not "speak with the discrimination of an Oxford don," he must articulate his desire to have counsel present sufficiently clearly that a reasonable police officer in the circumstances would understand the statement to be a request for an attorney. If the statement fails to meet the requisite level of clarity, *Edwards* does not require that the officers stop questioning the suspect.
>
> We decline petitioner's invitation to extend *Edwards* and require law enforcement officers to cease questioning immediately upon the making of an ambiguous or equivocal reference to an attorney. The rationale underlying *Edwards* is that the police must respect a suspect's wishes regarding his right to have an attorney present during custodial interrogation. But when the officers conducting the questioning reasonably do not know whether or not the suspect wants a lawyer, a rule requiring the immediate cessation of questioning would * * * needlessly prevent the police from questioning a suspect in the absence of counsel even if the suspect did not wish to have a lawyer present. Nothing in *Edwards* requires the provision of counsel to a suspect who consents to answer questions without the assistance of a lawyer.

Davis argued that if police were permitted to continue interrogation in the face of an ambiguous invocation of counsel, they could take unfair advantage of inarticulate and overmatched suspects. But Justice O'Connor held that these concerns were not of sufficient weight to prevent the continuation of police questioning:

> We recognize that requiring a clear assertion of the right to counsel might disadvantage some suspects who—because of fear, intimidation, lack of linguistic skills, or a variety of other reasons—will not clearly articulate their right to counsel although they actually want to have a lawyer present. But the primary protection afforded suspects subject to custodial interrogation is the *Miranda* warnings themselves. * * * A suspect who knowingly and voluntarily waives his right to counsel after having that right explained to him has indicated his willingness to deal with the police unassisted. Although *Edwards* provides an additional protection—if a suspect subsequently requests an attorney, questioning must cease—it is one that must be affirmatively invoked by the suspect.

Justice O'Connor further declared that the continued questioning after a suspect's ambiguous reference to counsel need not be limited to questions clarifying whether the suspect really wants a lawyer:

> Of course, when a suspect makes an ambiguous or equivocal statement it will often be good police practice for the interviewing officers to clarify whether or not he actually wants an attorney. That was the procedure followed by the [officers] in this case. Clarifying questions help protect the rights of the suspect by ensuring that he gets an attorney if he wants one, and will minimize the chance of a confession being suppressed due to subsequent judicial second-guessing as to the meaning of the suspect's statement regarding counsel. But we decline to adopt a rule requiring officers to ask clarifying questions. If the suspect's statement is not an unambiguous or unequivocal request for counsel, the officers have no obligation to stop questioning him.

Finally, Justice O'Connor found no reason to disturb the rulings of the lower courts that Davis' statement—"Maybe I should talk to a lawyer"—was not a sufficiently explicit request for counsel.

Justice Souter, joined by Justices Blackmun, Stevens, and Ginsburg, concurred only in the judgment in *Davis.* He agreed with the Court that Davis's position—i.e., questioning must cease completely whenever the suspect invokes counsel, even if the invocation is ambiguous—was overprotective of suspects and too costly to law enforcement. He disagreed, however, with the Court's position that an ambiguous invocation was essentially irrelevant and placed no limits on subsequent questioning.

Justice Souter preferred the view taken by the majority of courts prior to *Davis*—that questioning could continue, but that the questions must be limited to clarifying whether or not the suspect wanted to invoke the right to counsel. Justice Souter expressed concern that the majority's explicit invocation test, without a safety valve requirement that officers ask only clarifying questions, would fall hard on many criminal suspects:

> [C]riminal suspects who may (in *Miranda's* words) be "thrust into an unfamiliar atmosphere and run through menacing police interrogation procedures," would seem an odd group to single out for the Court's demand of heightened linguistic care. A substantial percentage of them lack anything like a confident command of the English language; many are "woefully ignorant;" and many more will be sufficiently intimidated by the interrogation process or overwhelmed by the uncertainty of their predicament that the ability to speak assertively will abandon them.

QUESTIONS AFTER DAVIS

What is the difference between Davis's first statement—"Maybe I should talk to a lawyer"—and his second statement—"I think I want a lawyer before I say anything else"? Are you as convinced as the Court that the first one was an ambiguous statement that did not constitute a request for counsel, while the second one was a clear invocation of the right to counsel? The majority in *Davis* opted for the "clarity" of a bright-line rule. Are you convinced that the rule is as bright a line as the *Davis* Court suggests?

Here are three examples of statements that have been found insufficiently specific to constitute an invocation of the right to counsel after *Davis:*

- "My daddy wants me to get a lawyer"—held insufficiently specific in Hyatt v. Branker, 569 F.3d 162 (4th Cir. 2009).
- "My lawyer told me to keep my mouth shut"—held insufficiently specific in Sechrest v. Ignacio, 549 F.3d 789 (9th Cir. 2008).
- "I guess you better get me a lawyer, then"—held insufficiently specific (because "I guess" is defined as equivocal in the Oxford Dictionary) in United States v. Havlik, 710 F.3d 818 (8th Cir. 2013).

Compare Moore v. Berghuis, 700 F.3d 882 (6th Cir. 2012) ("Moore invoked his constitutional right to counsel by requesting that the police officer call his attorney's phone number."); United States v. Wysinger, 683 F.3d 784 (7th Cir. 2012) ("Do you think I should have a lawyer at this point?" is not an explicit invocation, but later question "Can I call one now?' was an explicit invocation).

Consequences of Explicit Invocation: Smith v. Illinois

In Smith v. Illinois, 469 U.S. 91 (1984), a suspect who was asked whether he understood his right to have a lawyer present stated, "Uh, yeah, I'd like that." The Court rejected the state's argument that this statement was too vague to be considered an invocation of counsel that triggered the protections of *Edwards*. It found that "with the possible exception of the word 'uh' the defendant's statement in this case was neither indecisive nor ambiguous." The Court concluded that "where nothing about the request for counsel or the circumstances leading up to the request would render it ambiguous, all questioning must cease."

When the officer questioned Smith after his "uh" response to the warnings, ostensibly to clarify the request, Smith did make ambiguous statements concerning his desire for counsel. But the Court dismissed this *later* ambiguity as irrelevant. It declared that "using an accused's subsequent responses to cast doubt on the adequacy of the initial request *itself* is * * * intolerable" and that a contrary rule would lead to abusive use of "clarifying" questions.[31]

Unrelated Crimes: Arizona v. Roberson

In Arizona v. Roberson, 486 U.S. 675 (1988), the Court held that an invocation of the right to counsel under *Edwards* was not offense-specific. Such an invocation extends to interrogation *about any crime.*

Roberson was arrested at the scene of a just-completed burglary. After he was given *Miranda* warnings, he stated that he wanted a lawyer before answering any questions. Three days later while the defendant remained in custody, a different officer, who was unaware of the previous request for a lawyer, gave new *Miranda* warnings and obtained a statement concerning another burglary. Justice Stevens wrote for the Court as it declared that "*Edwards* serves the purpose of providing clear and unequivocal guidelines to the law enforcement profession," and that "there is nothing ambiguous about the requirement that after a person in custody has expressed his desire to deal with the police only through counsel, he is not subject to further interrogation by the authorities until counsel has been made available to him, unless the accused himself initiates further communication, exchanges, or conversations with the police."

The Court concluded that "to a suspect who has indicated his inability to cope with the pressures of custodial interrogation by requesting counsel, any further interrogation without counsel having been provided will surely exacerbate whatever compulsion to speak the suspect may be feeling." The government argued that a suspect might have good reason to want to speak to police about a new investigation. But Justice Stevens responded that "[t]he simple answer is that the suspect, having requested counsel, can determine how to deal with the separate investigations with counsel's advice." He added that "even if the police have decided temporarily not to provide counsel, they are free to inform the suspect of the facts of the second investigation as long as such communication does not constitute interrogation."

---

[31] Justice Rehnquist, joined by Chief Justice Burger and Justice Powell, dissented. He argued that Smith's statement was ambiguous under the circumstances, and that the majority's rule preventing consideration of post-request statements was overbroad.

Justice Kennedy, joined by Chief Justice Rehnquist, dissented, complaining that the Court's ruling was unnecessary to protect a suspect's rights and unduly restricted legitimate investigations of crimes other than those for which a suspect has been arrested. He described the breadth of the Court's rule as follows:

> The rule announced today will bar law enforcement officials, even those from some other city or other jurisdiction, from questioning a suspect about an unrelated matter if he is in custody and has requested counsel to assist in answering questions put to him about the crime for which he was arrested.

Justice Kennedy attacked the Court's presumption "that a suspect has made the decision that he does not wish to talk about that [separate investigation] without counsel present, although that decision was made when the suspect was unaware of even the existence of a second investigation," and argued that "[a]llowing authorities who conduct a separate investigation to read the suspect his *Miranda* rights and ask him whether he wishes to invoke them strikes an appropriate balance."

Waiver After the Suspect Has Consulted with Counsel: Minnick v. Mississippi

Suppose the suspect invokes his *Miranda* right to counsel and then the police let him confer with counsel. After counsel leaves, can the police approach the suspect and ask him if he would *now* like to talk to them? This was the question in Minnick v. Mississippi, 498 U.S. 146 (1990). The Court in *Minnick* held that the protection of *Edwards* continues *even after the suspect has consulted with an attorney*. Justice Kennedy, who dissented in *Roberson,* wrote the majority opinion for six justices. Minnick committed murders in Mississippi and was apprehended in California. After making inculpatory statements at an FBI interview (which were excluded from Minnick's trial as violative of *Edwards*), an appointed attorney met with Minnick on two or three occasions. The attorney told Minnick not to say anything, and not to sign any waiver forms. After these consultations, a Mississippi Deputy Sheriff initiated an interrogation of Minnick. Minnick was given *Miranda* warnings, refused to sign a waiver of rights form, and confessed. The trial court held that the confession to the Deputy Sheriff was not excluded by *Edwards,* reasoning that *Edwards* was inapplicable once counsel had been made available to Minnick.

Justice Kennedy declared that, under *Edwards,* police-initiated interrogation after an invocation of counsel may occur only if counsel is *actually present* during the interrogation. The Court relied upon language in *Miranda* and *Edwards,* which stated that "the interrogation must cease until an attorney is present" and that the suspect has the right "to have counsel present during custodial interrogation." Justice Kennedy reasoned that two policies underlying *Edwards* rendered its application in this case "appropriate and necessary":

- the bright line *Edwards* rule provides clarity and certainty; and
- the rule guarantees that suspects will not be badgered by police officers and provides prophylactic protection against police coercion.

On the issue of clarity, the Court found that a rule allowing police-initiated interrogation after consultation with counsel "would undermine the advantages flowing from *Edwards'* clear and unequivocal character." Justice Kennedy observed that a rule denying *Edwards* protection after consultation with a lawyer would be vague because "consultation is not a precise concept, for it may encompass variations from a telephone call to say that the attorney is in route, to a hurried exchange, * * * to a lengthy in-person conference."

As to the *Edwards* policy of preventing badgering and coercion, the Court found that mere consultation with an attorney would be insufficient to protect against the risk of harassment and exploitation of the suspect by the police. Justice Kennedy stated that "a single consultation with an attorney does not remove the suspect from persistent attempts by officials to persuade him to waive his rights, or from the coercive pressures that accompany custody and that may increase as custody is prolonged."

In a vigorous dissent, Justice Scalia, joined by Chief Justice Rehnquist, attacked the Court's "irrebuttable presumption" that a suspect who has invoked his right to counsel "can never validly waive that right during any police-initiated encounter, even after the suspect has been provided multiple *Miranda* warnings and has actually consulted with his attorney." Justice Scalia contended that a suspect who has consulted with counsel knows "that he has an advocate on his side, and that the police will permit him to consult with that advocate. He almost certainly also has a heightened awareness (above what the *Miranda* warning itself will provide) of his right to remain silent."

Justice Scalia concluded with a broad attack on the prophylactic rules of *Edwards* and *Miranda* itself:

> Both holdings are explicable * * * only as an effort to protect suspects against what is regarded as their own folly. The procedural protections of the Constitution protect the guilty as well as the innocent, but it is not their objective to set the guilty free. That some clever criminals may employ those protections to their advantage is poor reason to allow criminals who have not done so to escape justice.
>
> Thus, even if I were to concede that an honest confession is a foolish mistake, I would welcome rather than reject it * * *. While every person is entitled to stand silent, it is more virtuous for the

wrongdoer to admit his offense and accept the punishment he deserves. * * * We should, then, rejoice at an honest confession, rather than pity the "poor fool" who has made it.

The Requirement of Continuous Custody for Edwards Protection: Maryland v. Shatzer

In Maryland v. Shatzer, 559 U.S. 98 (2010), the Court held that the prophylactic safeguards of *Edwards* do not apply if the suspect, after invoking his right to counsel, is released from *Miranda* custody for fourteen days. In that circumstance, the officers are free to take the suspect back into custody, initiate interrogation, provide *Miranda* warnings, and, if they secure a knowing, voluntary, and intelligent waiver, then a resulting confession is admissible.

Shatzer was serving time on a child sex abuse offense when officers sought to interrogate him about another crime—the abuse of his son. Shatzer invoked his right to counsel and was returned to the prison population. Two years and six months later, officers initiated a new interrogation on the abuse of his son. Shatzer, who was still incarcerated, waived his rights and confessed. All agreed that if *Edwards* applied, the confession would be inadmissible because Shatzer did not initiate the new interrogation.

Justice Scalia, writing for seven members of the Court, held that *Edwards* did not apply because he was released from *Miranda* custody during the extended period between his invocation and later waiver and confession. Justice Scalia explained as follows:

> It is easy to believe that a suspect may be coerced or badgered into abandoning his earlier refusal to be questioned without counsel in * * * a case in which the suspect has been arrested for a particular crime and is held in uninterrupted pretrial custody while that crime is being actively investigated. After the initial interrogation, and up to and including the second one, he remains cut off from his normal life and companions, "thrust into" and isolated in an "unfamiliar," "police-dominated atmosphere," *Miranda,* where his captors "appear to control [his] fate," Illinois v. Perkins. * * *
>
> When * * * a suspect has been released from his pretrial custody and has returned to his normal life for some time before the later attempted interrogation, there is little reason to think that his change of heart regarding interrogation without counsel has been coerced. He has no longer been isolated. He has likely been able to seek advice from an attorney, family members, and friends. And he knows from his earlier experience that he need only demand counsel to bring the interrogation to a halt; and that investigative custody does not last indefinitely. In these circumstances, it is far fetched to think that a

police officer's asking the suspect whether he would like to waive his *Miranda* rights will any more wear down the accused than did the first such request at the original attempted interrogation—which is of course not deemed coercive. His change of heart is less likely attributable to "badgering" than it is to the fact that further deliberation in familiar surroundings has caused him to believe (rightly or wrongly) that cooperating with the investigation is in his interest. Uncritical extension of *Edwards* to this situation would not significantly increase the number of genuinely coerced confessions excluded. The justification for a conclusive presumption disappears when application of the presumption will not reach the correct result most of the time.

At the same time that extending the *Edwards* rule yields diminished benefits, extending the rule also increases its costs: the in-fact voluntary confessions it excludes from trial, and the voluntary confessions it deters law enforcement officers from even trying to obtain. * * *

The only logical endpoint of *Edwards* disability is termination of *Miranda* custody and any of its lingering effects. Without that limitation—and barring some purely arbitrary time-limit—every *Edwards* prohibition of custodial interrogation of a particular suspect would be eternal. * * *

We conclude that such an extension of *Edwards* is not justified; we have opened its protective umbrella far enough. The protections offered by *Miranda*, which we have deemed sufficient to ensure that the police respect the suspect's desire to have an attorney present the first time police interrogate him, adequately ensure that result when a suspect who initially requested counsel is reinterrogated after a break in custody that is of sufficient duration to dissipate its coercive effects.

Justice Scalia addressed the possibility that police officers might seek to evade the *Edwards* protections by releasing suspects for only a short period of time, then putting them into custody and reinterrogating them:

We think it appropriate to specify a period of time to avoid the consequence that continuation of the *Edwards* presumption will not reach the correct result most of the time. It seems to us that period is 14 days. That provides plenty of time for the suspect to get reacclimated to his normal life, to consult with friends and counsel, and to shake off any residual coercive effects of his prior custody.

The 14-day limitation meets Shatzer's concern that a break-in-custody rule lends itself to police abuse. He envisions that once a suspect invokes his *Miranda* right to counsel, the police will release the suspect briefly (to end the *Edwards* presumption) and then

> promptly bring him back into custody for reinterrogation. But once the suspect has been out of custody long enough (14 days) to eliminate its coercive effect, there will be nothing to gain by such gamesmanship—nothing, that is, except the entirely appropriate gain of being able to interrogate a suspect who has made a valid waiver of his *Miranda* rights.

Finally, Justice Scalia addressed Shatzer's argument that he *was* in continuous custody—he was imprisoned the entire time between his invocation of the right to counsel and the reinterrogation (albeit on a different charge):

> Without minimizing the harsh realities of incarceration, we think lawful imprisonment imposed upon conviction of a crime does not create the coercive pressures identified in *Miranda*.
>
> Interrogated suspects who have previously been convicted of crime live in prison. When they are released back into the general prison population, they return to their accustomed surroundings and daily routine-they regain the degree of control they had over their lives prior to the interrogation. Sentenced prisoners, in contrast to the *Miranda* paradigm, are not isolated with their accusers. They live among other inmates, guards, and workers, and often can receive visitors and communicate with people on the outside by mail or telephone.

Justice Thomas concurred in part and concurred in the result in *Shatzer*. He objected to the Court's 14-day rule as arbitrary. Justice Stevens dissented. He contended that the majority had ignored "the compulsion caused by a second (or third, or fourth) interrogation of an indigent suspect who was told that if he requests a lawyer, one would be provided for him" and that if a suspect is reinterrogated without a lawyer "the suspect is likely to feel that the police lied to him and that he really does not have any right to a lawyer."

Which Constitutional Right to Counsel Is Invoked? McNeil v. Wisconsin

Besides the *Miranda* right to counsel, a defendant who has been formally charged with a crime (e.g., indicted) also has a Sixth Amendment right to counsel, as discussed later in this Chapter. When a formally charged defendant appears at an arraignment and invokes the right to counsel, is that an invocation of the *Miranda* right to counsel, the Sixth Amendment right to counsel, or both? Why would it make any difference?

The Court in McNeil v. Wisconsin, 501 U.S. 171 (1991), held that an accused who is arraigned and asks for counsel is invoking the Sixth Amendment, rather than the *Miranda*, right to counsel, and that there *is* a difference in the protections provided. As we will see, the *Edwards* protection against reinitiation is available only if *Miranda* rights are invoked. It is not available for invocations of the Sixth Amendment right to counsel.

McNeil was formally charged with armed robbery, and at his initial appearance before a judicial officer, he invoked his right to counsel. Police thereafter initiated questioning of McNeil. McNeil then waived his *Miranda* rights and confessed. McNeil argued that he was denied his protection under *Edwards* and *Roberson,* because the police had initiated interrogation after he had invoked his right to counsel. Justice Scalia, writing for a six-person majority, stated that McNeil had invoked his Sixth Amendment right, not his *Miranda* right. He explained as follows:

> To invoke the Sixth Amendment interest is, as a matter of fact, not to invoke the *Miranda-Edwards* interest. One might be quite willing to speak to the police without counsel present concerning many matters, but not the matter under prosecution. It can be said, perhaps, that it is likely that one who has asked for counsel's assistance in defending against a prosecution would want counsel present for all custodial interrogation, even interrogation unrelated to the charge. * * * But even if that were true, the likelihood that a suspect would wish counsel to be present is not the test for applicability of *Edwards.* The rule of that case * * * requires, at a minimum, some statement that can reasonably be construed to be expression of a desire for the assistance of an attorney in dealing with custodial interrogation by the police. Requesting the assistance of an attorney at a bail hearing does not bear that construction.

Can Edwards Protections Be Triggered in Advance of Interrogation?

McNeil holds that when a suspect is arraigned before a judicial officer and asks for counsel, he is invoking his Sixth Amendment right, not his *Miranda* right, and therefore gets no protection from *Edwards,* which is a prophylactic rule designed to safeguard *Miranda* rights. So if it is a Sixth Amendment invocation, officers are free to approach the person who has invoked and ask him if he has changed his mind. Then, if the person makes a knowing and voluntary waiver, the confession will be admissible.

This raises the question of whether someone in McNeil's position could find a way to invoke his *Miranda* right to counsel instead of, or in addition to, his Sixth Amendment right. Would it make a difference, for example, if at the arraignment, McNeil tells the judge that "I want a lawyer under *Miranda*" or in some other way specifically indicates that he wants a *Miranda* right to counsel?

Justice Stevens, dissenting in *McNeil*, argued that the case amounted to little because suspects being arraigned could simply specify that they want their *Miranda* right to counsel, and thereby get the protection of *Edwards* that the majority had denied to McNeil. Thus, Justice Stevens assumed that the *Miranda* right to counsel can be invoked *in advance of police interrogation*. But this assumption was challenged by Justice Scalia in a footnote in the *McNeil* majority opinion. Justice Scalia asserted that "we have never held that a person can invoke his *Miranda* rights anticipatorily, in a context other than custodial interrogation—which a preliminary hearing will not always, or even usually, involve." He stated that such reasoning would lead to the unacceptable conclusion that *Miranda* rights could be invoked "in a letter prior to arrest, or indeed even prior to identification as a suspect."

Subsequently the Court in Montejo v. Louisiana (infra in the section on Sixth Amendment waiver) expressly stated that the protections of *Edwards* can only be obtained by invoking the right to counsel "in the context of custodial interrogation." See also United States v. Wyatt, 179 F.3d 532 (7th Cir. 1999) (suspect could not invoke his *Miranda* right to counsel when he was not yet in custody; therefore there was no violation of *Edwards* when officers later initiated interrogation, gave warnings, and the defendant voluntarily confessed).

IV. CONFESSIONS AND THE SIXTH AMENDMENT RIGHT TO COUNSEL

A. THE *MASSIAH* RULE

In addition to the Fifth Amendment and the Due Process Clause, the Court has also extended the protections of the *Sixth* Amendment right to counsel to some police-induced confessions. Recall that in *Spano*, the concurring Justices heavily emphasized the fact that Spano had been formally charged with a crime, and yet was interrogated without his counsel being present. In the following case, the Supreme Court explicitly relies on the Sixth Amendment to exclude a confession.

MASSIAH V. UNITED STATES

Supreme Court of the United States, 1964.
377 U.S. 201.

MR. JUSTICE STEWART delivered the opinion of the Court.

* * *

[Massiah was a merchant seaman. Drugs were found on a ship and connected to Massiah. He was arrested, arraigned, and subsequently indicted for possession of narcotics aboard a United States vessel.

Thereafter, a superseding indictment was returned, charging Massiah and another man, Colson, with narcotics offenses and conspiracy. Massiah, who had retained a lawyer, pleaded not guilty and was released on bail, along with Colson.]

A few days later, and quite without the petitioner's knowledge, Colson decided to cooperate with the government agents in their continuing investigation of the narcotics activities in which the petitioner, Colson, and others had allegedly been engaged. Colson permitted an agent named Murphy to install a Schmidt radio transmitter under the front seat of Colson's automobile, by means of which Murphy, equipped with an appropriate receiving device, could overhear from some distance away conversations carried on in Colson's car.

On the evening of November 19, 1959, Colson and the petitioner held a lengthy conversation while sitting in Colson's automobile, parked on a New York street. By prearrangement with Colson, and totally unbeknown to the petitioner, the agent Murphy sat in a car parked out of sight down the street and listened over the radio to the entire conversation. The petitioner made several incriminating statements during the course of this conversation. At the petitioner's trial these incriminating statements were brought before the jury through Murphy's testimony, despite the insistent objection of defense counsel. The jury convicted the petitioner of several related narcotics offenses, and the convictions were affirmed by the Court of Appeals.

* * * [I]t is said that the petitioner's Fifth and Sixth Amendment rights were violated by the use in evidence against him of incriminating statements which government agents had deliberately elicited from him after he had been indicted and in the absence of his retained counsel.

[The Court discusses *Spano,* paying more attention to the concurring opinions than to the majority opinion. It also discusses right to counsel precedents, which are discussed in Chapter 5, infra. The Court ultimately finds the Sixth Amendment right to counsel to be determinative.]

* * * We hold that the petitioner was denied the basic protections of that [Sixth Amendment] guarantee when there was used against him at his trial evidence of his own incriminating words, which federal agents had deliberately elicited from him after he had been indicted and in the absence of his counsel. It is true that in the *Spano* case the defendant was interrogated in a police station, while here the damaging testimony was elicited from the defendant without his knowledge while he was free on bail. But, as Judge Hays pointed out in his dissent in the Court of Appeals, "if such a rule is to have any efficacy it must apply to indirect and surreptitious interrogations as well as those conducted in the jailhouse. In this case, Massiah was more seriously imposed upon * * * because he did not even know that he was under interrogation by a government agent."

The Solicitor General * * * has strenuously contended that the federal law enforcement agents had the right, if not indeed the duty, to continue their investigation of the petitioner and his alleged criminal associates even though the petitioner had been indicted. He points out that the Government was continuing its investigation in order to uncover not only the source of narcotics found on the S. S. *Santa Maria,* but also their intended buyer. He says that the quantity of narcotics involved was such as to suggest that the petitioner was part of a large and well-organized ring, and indeed that the continuing investigation confirmed this suspicion, since it resulted in criminal charges against many defendants. Under these circumstances the Solicitor General concludes that the government agents were completely "justified in making use of Colson's cooperation by having Colson continue his normal associations and by surveilling them."

* * * We do not question that in this case, as in many cases, it was entirely proper to continue an investigation of the suspected criminal activities of the defendant and his alleged confederates, even though the defendant had already been indicted. All that we hold is that the defendant's own incriminating statements, obtained by federal agents under the circumstances here disclosed, could not constitutionally be used by the prosecution as evidence against *him* at his trial.

MR. JUSTICE WHITE, with whom MR. JUSTICE CLARK and MR. JUSTICE HARLAN join, dissenting.

* * *

Massiah was not prevented from consulting with counsel as often as he wished. No meetings with counsel were disturbed or spied upon. Preparation for trial was in no way obstructed. It is only a sterile syllogism—an unsound one, besides—to say that because Massiah had a right to counsel's aid before and during the trial, his out-of-court conversations and admissions must be excluded if obtained without counsel's consent or presence. The right to counsel has never meant as much before, and its extension in this case requires some further explanation, so far unarticulated by the Court.

* * *

[T]he Court's newly fashioned exclusionary principle goes far beyond the constitutional privilege against self-incrimination, which neither requires nor suggests the barring of voluntary pre-trial admissions. * * *

At the time of the conversation in question, petitioner was not in custody but free on bail. He was not questioned in what anyone would call an atmosphere of official coercion.

* * *

The Rationale of Massiah

Massiah was certainly not pressured to confess in the same way that Spano was. Indeed, he suffered less pressure than Miranda, because he didn't even know that he was speaking with a government agent. So the Sixth Amendment protection established in *Massiah* must be directed toward something *other* than police-created pressure to confess. What is the rationale for Sixth Amendment regulation of confessions? Judge Higginbotham, in United States v. Johnson, 954 F.2d 1015 (5th Cir. 1992), explained it this way:

> [The Sixth Amendment] recognizes that once the government has brought formal charges against an individual the adversary relationship between the parties is cemented. Once an accused has chosen to retain an attorney to act as his representative in the adversary process, the government may not try to circumvent the protection afforded by the presence of counsel during questioning. The vice is not deprivation of privacy, but interference with the parity required by the Sixth Amendment.

Thus, the *Massiah* right is basically a constitutionalized version of a rule of professional (and litigation) ethics: that an adverse party, in advance of litigation, may be contacted only through her lawyer. This rule protects the attorney-client relationship and guards against overreaching by the adversary. See Model Rules of Professional Conduct 4.2. This is not to say that the ethics rules *define* the constitutional right. But it is to say that the principles behind the ethics rule of proceeding through counsel, once litigation has begun, are the same principles that animate the Sixth Amendment right to counsel.[32]

NOTE ON ESCOBEDO V. ILLINOIS

In Escobedo v. Illinois, 378 U.S. 478 (1964), the Court undertook a short-lived experiment to extend the Sixth Amendment right to counsel to suspects who have *not yet been formally charged*. Escobedo was taken into custody on suspicion of murder. He asked for a lawyer several times, but his request was denied. His mother retained a lawyer for him, and the lawyer went to the police station, but the police would not let the lawyer speak to Escobedo. Escobedo was confronted with incriminating evidence, while handcuffed in a standing position, and was given false promises that if he confessed he would be allowed to go home. While these facts established a strong case for holding Escobedo's confession involuntary, the Court, in this pre-*Miranda* case, relied explicitly on the Sixth Amendment to invalidate the confession. Justice Goldberg, writing for the Court, recognized that, unlike Spano and Massiah, Escobedo

[32] For an eloquent defense of the *Massiah* doctrine, in response to an attack on that doctrine by the Justice Department, see Tomkovicz, The Truth About *Massiah,* 23 U.Mich.J.L.Ref. 641 (1990).

had not been indicted at the time he confessed; but he argued that "in the context of this case, that fact should make no difference." This was because the police had *focused* on Escobedo as a *prospective* criminal defendant. Justice Goldberg stated that when Escobedo was denied his request for counsel, "the investigation had ceased to be a general investigation of an unsolved crime" and that Escobedo had become the "accused."

Justices Harlan, Stewart, White, and Clark dissented in *Escobedo*. The dissenters were concerned that the majority's "focus" test would result in an extravagant extension of the Sixth Amendment right to counsel, which by its terms applies to criminal "prosecutions," not criminal "investigations." As Justice Stewart put it:

> [T]he institution of formal, meaningful judicial proceedings, by way of indictment, information, or arraignment, marks the point at which a criminal investigation has ended and adversary litigative proceedings have commenced. * * * [T]he Court today converts a routine police investigation of an unsolved murder into a distorted analogue of a judicial trial. It imports into this investigation constitutional concepts historically applicable only after the onset of formal prosecutorial proceedings.

As a Sixth Amendment case, *Escobedo* has no continuing relevance. In Moran v. Burbine, 475 U.S. 412 (1986), discussed in the section on *Miranda*, Burbine was being interrogated as a suspect in a murder. His family retained counsel for him, but police officers denied counsel's request to see Burbine. Burbine had not been formally charged at the time he confessed, but he was certainly the focus of the police investigation. Burbine relied on *Escobedo* to argue that his Sixth Amendment rights were violated, but Justice O'Connor, writing for the majority, rejected that argument. She stated that "subsequent decisions foreclose any reliance on *Escobedo* * * * for the proposition that the Sixth Amendment right, in any of its manifestations, applies prior to the initiation of adversary criminal proceedings." She concluded that *Escobedo* is in retrospect best understood as a *Fifth* Amendment case, because the prime purpose of the Court in *Escobedo* was not to vindicate the right to counsel as such but rather to guarantee "the full effectuation of the privilege against self-incrimination."

While *Escobedo* is therefore mainly of historical note on the Court's road to *Miranda,* the Sixth Amendment right to counsel has contemporary relevance where information is sought from a person who *has* been formally charged. After the Court decided *Miranda,* it returned to *Massiah* in a number of cases. These cases are discussed immediately below.

B. OBTAINING INFORMATION FROM FORMALLY CHARGED DEFENDANTS

After *Massiah*, the Supreme Court for several years virtually ignored the Sixth Amendment as a means of regulating confessions. As you know, the Court turned to the Fifth Amendment in *Miranda*. However, in 1977, the Court unexpectedly returned to the Sixth Amendment as an additional source for excluding confessions. At the time of this decision, *Miranda* was unpopular and various state Attorneys General filed as amicus curiae asking that *Miranda* be overturned. The Court sidestepped the issue by focusing, as in *Massiah*, on the Sixth Amendment.

BREWER V. WILLIAMS

Supreme Court of the United States, 1977.
430 U.S. 387.

JUSTICE STEWART delivered the opinion of the Court.

* * *

On the afternoon of December 24, 1968, a 10-year-old girl named Pamela Powers went with her family to the YMCA in Des Moines, Iowa, to watch a wrestling tournament in which her brother was participating. When she failed to return from a trip to the washroom, a search for her began. The search was unsuccessful.

Robert Williams, who had recently escaped from a mental hospital, was a resident of the YMCA. Soon after the girl's disappearance Williams was seen in the YMCA lobby carrying some clothing and a large bundle wrapped in a blanket. He obtained help from a 14-year-old boy in opening the street door of the YMCA and the door to his automobile parked outside. When Williams placed the bundle in the front seat of his car the boy "saw two legs in it and they were skinny and white." Before anyone could see what was in the bundle Williams drove away. His abandoned car was found the following day in Davenport, Iowa, roughly 160 miles east of Des Moines. A warrant was then issued in Des Moines for his arrest on a charge of abduction.

On the morning of December 26, a Des Moines lawyer named Henry McKnight went to the Des Moines police station and informed the officers present that he had just received a long distance call from Williams, and that he had advised Williams to turn himself in to the Davenport police. Williams did surrender that morning to the police in Davenport, and they booked him on the charge specified in the arrest warrant and gave him the warnings required by Miranda v. Arizona. The Davenport police then telephoned their counterparts in Des Moines to inform them that Williams had surrendered. McKnight, the lawyer, was still at the Des Moines police headquarters, and Williams conversed with McKnight on the telephone. In the presence of the Des Moines chief of police and a police detective named Leaming, McKnight advised Williams that Des Moines police officers would be driving to Davenport to pick him up, that the officers would not interrogate him or mistreat him, and that Williams was not to talk to the officers about Pamela Powers until after consulting with McKnight upon his return to Des Moines. As a result of these conversations, it was agreed between McKnight and the Des Moines police officials that Detective Leaming and a fellow officer would drive to Davenport to pick up Williams, that they would bring him directly back to Des Moines, and that they would not question him during the trip.

In the meantime Williams was arraigned before a judge in Davenport on the outstanding arrest warrant. The judge advised him of his *Miranda* rights and committed him to jail. Before leaving the courtroom, Williams conferred with a lawyer named Kelly, who advised him not to make any statements until consulting with McKnight back in Des Moines.

Detective Leaming and his fellow officer arrived in Davenport about noon to pick up Williams and return him to Des Moines. Soon after their arrival they met with Williams and Kelly, who, they understood, was acting as Williams' lawyer. Detective Leaming repeated the *Miranda* warnings, and told Williams:

> "[W]e both know that you're being represented here by Mr. Kelly and you're being represented by Mr. McKnight in Des Moines, and * * * I want you to remember this because we'll be visiting between here and Des Moines."

Williams then conferred again with Kelly alone, and after this conference Kelly reiterated to Detective Leaming that Williams was not to be questioned about the disappearance of Pamela Powers until after he had consulted with McKnight back in Des Moines. When Leaming expressed some reservations, Kelly firmly stated that the agreement with McKnight was to be carried out—that there was to be no interrogation of Williams during the automobile journey to Des Moines. Kelly was denied permission to ride in the police car back to Des Moines with Williams and the two officers.

The two detectives, with Williams in their charge, then set out on the 160-mile drive. At no time during the trip did Williams express a willingness to be interrogated in the absence of an attorney. Instead, he stated several times that "[w]hen I get to Des Moines and see Mr. McKnight, I am going to tell you the whole story." Detective Leaming knew that Williams was a former mental patient, and knew also that he was deeply religious.

The detective and his prisoner soon embarked on a wide-ranging conversation covering a variety of topics, including the subject of religion. Then, not long after leaving Davenport and reaching the interstate highway, Detective Leaming delivered what has been referred to in the briefs and oral arguments as the "Christian burial speech." Addressing Williams as "Reverend," the detective said:

> "I want to give you something to think about while we're traveling down the road. * * * Number one, I want you to observe the weather

conditions, it's raining, it's sleeting, it's freezing, driving is very treacherous, visibility is poor, it's going to be dark early this evening. They are predicting several inches of snow for tonight, and I feel that you yourself are the only person that knows where this little girl's body is, that you yourself have only been there once, and if you get a snow on top of it you yourself may be unable to find it. And, since we will be going right past the area on the way into Des Moines, I feel that we could stop and locate the body, that the parents of this little girl should be entitled to a Christian burial for the little girl who was snatched away from them on Christmas [E]ve and murdered. And I feel we should stop and locate it on the way in rather than waiting until morning and trying to come back out after a snow storm and possibly not being able to find it at all."

Williams asked Detective Leaming why he thought their route to Des Moines would be taking them past the girl's body, and Leaming responded that he knew the body was in the area of Mitchellville—a town they would be passing on the way to Des Moines.[a] Leaming then stated: "I do not want you to answer me. I don't want to discuss it any further. Just think about it as we're riding down the road."

As the car approached Grinnell, a town approximately 100 miles west of Davenport, Williams asked whether the police had found the victim's shoes. When Detective Leaming replied that he was unsure, Williams directed the officers to a service station where he said he had left the shoes; a search for them proved unsuccessful. As they continued towards Des Moines, Williams asked whether the police had found the blanket, and directed the officers to a rest area where he said he had disposed of the blanket. Nothing was found. The car continued towards Des Moines, and as it approached Mitchellville, Williams said that he would show the officers where the body was. He then directed the police to the body of Pamela Powers.

Williams was indicted for first-degree murder. Before trial, his counsel moved to suppress all evidence relating to or resulting from any statements Williams had made during the automobile ride from Davenport to Des Moines. After an evidentiary hearing the trial judge denied the motion. * * * The jury found Williams guilty of murder. [The Iowa Supreme Court affirmed 4–3. But Williams was successful below in his federal habeas corpus action.]

* * *

[T]he District Court based its judgment in this case on three independent grounds. The Court of Appeals appears to have affirmed the

[a] The fact of the matter, of course, was that Detective Leaming possessed no such knowledge.

judgment on two of those grounds. We have concluded that only one of them need be considered here.

Specifically, there is no need to review in this case the doctrine of Miranda v. Arizona, a doctrine designed to secure the constitutional privilege against compulsory self-incrimination. It is equally unnecessary to evaluate the ruling of the District Court that Williams' self-incriminating statements were, indeed, involuntarily made. For it is clear that the judgment before us must in any event be affirmed upon the ground that Williams was deprived of a different constitutional right—the right to the assistance of counsel.

* * *

There can be no doubt in the present case that judicial proceedings had been initiated against Williams before the start of the automobile ride from Davenport to Des Moines. A warrant had been issued for his arrest, he had been arraigned on that warrant before a judge in a Davenport courtroom, and he had been committed by the court to confinement in jail. The State does not contend otherwise.

There can be no serious doubt, either, that Detective Leaming deliberately and designedly set out to elicit information from Williams just as surely as—and perhaps more effectively than—if he had formally interrogated him. Detective Leaming was fully aware before departing for Des Moines that Williams was being represented in Davenport by Kelly and in Des Moines by McKnight. Yet he purposely sought during Williams' isolation from his lawyers to obtain as much incriminating information as possible. Indeed, Detective Leaming conceded as much when he testified at Williams' trial:

> "Q. In fact, Captain, whether he was a mental patient or not, you were trying to get all the information you could before he got to his lawyer, weren't you?
>
> "A. I was sure hoping to find out where that little girl was, yes, sir.
>
> * * *
>
> "Q. Well, I'll put it this way: You was [*sic*] hoping to get all the information you could before Williams got back to McKnight, weren't you?
>
> "A. Yes, sir."

* * *

The circumstances of this case are thus constitutionally indistinguishable from those presented in Massiah v. United States. * * *

That the incriminating statements were elicited surreptitiously in the *Massiah* case, and otherwise here, is constitutionally irrelevant. Rather, the clear rule of *Massiah* is that once adversary proceedings have commenced against an individual, he has a right to legal representation when the government interrogates him.[b] It thus requires no wooden or technical application of the *Massiah* doctrine to conclude that Williams was entitled to the assistance of counsel guaranteed to him by the Sixth and Fourteenth Amendments.

* * *

The Iowa courts recognized that Williams had been denied the constitutional right to the assistance of counsel. They held, however, that he had waived that right during the course of the automobile trip from Davenport to Des Moines. * * *

[I]t was incumbent upon the State to prove "an intentional relinquishment or abandonment of a known right or privilege." That standard has been reiterated in many cases. We have said that the right to counsel does not depend upon a request by the defendant, and that courts indulge in every reasonable presumption against waiver. This strict standard applies equally to an alleged waiver of the right to counsel whether at trial or at a critical stage of pretrial proceedings.

* * * [J]udged by these standards, the record in this case falls far short of sustaining petitioner's burden. It is true that Williams had been informed of and appeared to understand his right to counsel. But waiver requires not merely comprehension but relinquishment, and Williams' consistent reliance upon the advice of counsel in dealing with the authorities refutes any suggestion that he waived that right. He consulted McKnight by long distance telephone before turning himself in. He spoke with McKnight by telephone again shortly after being booked. After he was arraigned, Williams sought out and obtained legal advice from Kelly. Williams again consulted with Kelly after Detective Leaming and his fellow officer arrived in Davenport. Throughout, Williams was advised not to make any statements before seeing McKnight in Des Moines, and was assured that the police had agreed not to question him. His statements while in the car that he would tell the whole story *after* seeing McKnight in Des Moines were the clearest expressions by Williams himself that he desired the presence of an attorney before any interrogation took place. But even before making these statements, Williams had effectively asserted his right to counsel by having secured attorneys at both ends of the automobile trip, both of whom, acting as his agents, had made clear to the police that no interrogation was to occur during the journey. Williams knew of that

[b] The only other significant factual difference between the present case and *Massiah* is that here the police had *agreed* that they would not interrogate Williams in the absence of his counsel. This circumstance plainly provides petitioner with no argument for distinguishing away the protection afforded by *Massiah*.

agreement and, particularly in view of his consistent reliance on counsel, there is no basis for concluding that he disavowed it.

Despite Williams' express and implicit assertions of his right to counsel, Detective Leaming proceeded to elicit incriminating statements from Williams. Leaming did not preface this effort by telling Williams that he had a right to the presence of a lawyer, and made no effort at all to ascertain whether Williams wished to relinquish that right. The circumstances of record in this case thus provide no reasonable basis for finding that Williams waived his right to the assistance of counsel.

The Court of Appeals did not hold, nor do we, that under the circumstances of this case Williams *could not,* without notice to counsel, have waived his rights under the Sixth and Fourteenth Amendments. It only held, as do we, that he did not.

* * *

The judgment of the Court of Appeals is affirmed.

[Evidence of the body, its condition, and location were admitted on retrial. See Nix v. Williams, in the materials on inevitable discovery, in Chapter 2.]

JUSTICE MARSHALL, concurring.

* * *

Leaming knowingly isolated Williams from the protection of his lawyers and during that period he intentionally "persuaded" him to give incriminating evidence. It is this intentional police misconduct—not good police practice—that the Court rightly condemns. * * *

* * *

JUSTICE POWELL, concurring.

* * *

I join the opinion of the Court which also finds that the efforts of Detective Leaming "to elicit information from Williams," as conceded by counsel for petitioner at oral argument, were a skillful and effective form of interrogation. Moreover, the entire setting was conducive to the psychological coercion that was successfully exploited. Williams was known by the police to be a young man with quixotic religious convictions and a history of mental disorders. The date was the day after Christmas, the weather was ominous, and the setting appropriate for Detective Leaming's talk of snow concealing the body and preventing a "Christian burial." * * *

JUSTICE STEVENS, concurring.

* * *

Underlying the surface issues in this case is the question, whether a fugitive from justice can rely on his lawyer's advice given in connection with a decision to surrender voluntarily. The defendant placed his trust in an experienced Iowa trial lawyer who in turn trusted the Iowa law enforcement authorities to honor a commitment made during negotiations which led to the apprehension of a potentially dangerous person. Under any analysis, this was a critical stage of the proceeding in which the participation of an independent professional was of vital importance to the accused and to society. * * * If, in the long run, we are seriously concerned about the individual's effective representation by counsel, the State cannot be permitted to dishonor its promise to this lawyer.

CHIEF JUSTICE BURGER, dissenting.

* * *

Williams is guilty of the savage murder of a small child; no member of the Court contends he is not. While in custody, and after no fewer than *five* warnings of his rights to silence and to counsel, he led police to the concealed body of his victim. The Court concedes Williams was not threatened or coerced and that he spoke and acted voluntarily and with full awareness of his constitutional rights. In the face of all this, the Court now holds that because Williams was prompted by the detective's statement—not interrogation but a statement—the jury must not be told how the police found the body.

* * *

The evidence is uncontradicted that Williams had abundant knowledge of his right to have counsel present and of his right to silence. Since the Court does not question his mental competence, it boggles the mind to suggest that Williams could not understand that leading police to the child's body would have other than the most serious consequences. All of the elements necessary to make out a valid waiver are shown by the record and acknowledged by the Court; we thus are left to guess how the Court reached its holding.

* * *

JUSTICE WHITE, with whom JUSTICE BLACKMUN and JUSTICE REHNQUIST join, dissenting.

* * *

Respondent relinquished his right not to talk to the police about his crime when the car approached the place where he had hidden the victim's clothes. Men usually intend to do what they do and there is nothing in the record to support the proposition that respondent's decision to talk was anything but an exercise of his own free will. * * * The statement by Leaming was not coercive; it was accompanied by a request that respondent not respond to it; and it was delivered hours before respondent decided to make any statement. Respondent's waiver was thus knowing and intentional.

* * *

JUSTICE BLACKMUN, with whom JUSTICE WHITE and JUSTICE REHNQUIST join, dissenting.

* * *

First, the police did not deliberately seek to isolate Williams from his lawyers so as to deprive him of the assistance of counsel. The isolation in this case was a necessary incident of transporting Williams to the county where the crime was committed.

Second, Leaming's purpose was not solely to obtain incriminating evidence. The victim had been missing for only two days, and the police could not be certain that she was dead. Leaming, of course, and in accord with his duty, was "hoping to find out where that little girl was," but such motivation does not equate with an intention to evade the Sixth Amendment.

* * *

In summary, it seems to me that the Court is holding that *Massiah* is violated whenever police engage in any conduct, in the absence of counsel, with the subjective desire to obtain information from a suspect after arraignment. Such a rule is far too broad.

* * *

Sixth Amendment Attaches at Formal Charge: United States v. Gouveia

Reaffirming that the Sixth Amendment right to counsel attaches only after adversarial proceedings have begun, the Supreme Court held in United States v. Gouveia, 467 U.S. 180 (1984), that prison officials did not violate the right to counsel of inmates suspected of two murders when the officials placed them in administrative detention for periods of 19 and 8 months prior to their being indicted. Justice Rehnquist's opinion for the Court stated that "both inside and outside the prison, it may well be true that in some cases pre-indictment investigation could help a defendant prepare a better defense. But, * * * our cases have never suggested that the purpose of the right to counsel is to provide a defendant with a pre-indictment private investigator, and we see no reason to adopt that novel interpretation of the right to counsel in this case." Justice Marshall dissented and argued that administrative detention was part of an accusatorial process.

The Supreme Court held in Moran v. Burbine, supra, that there was no violation of a suspect's Sixth Amendment right to counsel when police failed to disclose to him that a lawyer had called and had been falsely told that the suspect would not be interrogated until the next day. Justice O'Connor's majority opinion observed that the suspect had not been formally charged, cited *Gouveia* as well as *Massiah, Brewer,* and other cases drawing a line between pre-and post-charge situations, and declined to adopt a rule that would make the right to counsel depend "on the fortuity of whether the suspect or his family happens to have retained counsel prior to interrogation."

On the Meaning of "Deliberate" Elicitation

The Sixth Amendment prohibits a government agent from "deliberately eliciting" incriminating information from an "accused" in the absence of counsel or a waiver. This means, does it not, that the officer must be *trying* to obtain incriminating information from the accused? For example, the Court found deliberate elicitation in Brewer v. Williams because Leaming actually admitted that he was trying to pump Williams for information about the location of the body. But what if the officer can plausibly argue that he was not trying to obtain incriminating information? Can there still be a violation of the Sixth Amendment?

The court in Bey v. Morton, 124 F.3d 524 (3d Cir. 1997), considered this question. Bey was on death row. The only people he was permitted to talk to were corrections officers. Bey struck up a relationship with Officer Pearson, and they engaged in a number of conversations, covering many different topics, including sports, women and the news. In the course of their extensive discourse, Bey confessed to the murder of two women—the murders for which he was sitting on death row. Then his convictions were reversed and he had to be retried. At the retrials, the Officer testified and related Bey's confessions. Bey argued that these confessions had to be excluded because Officer Pearson had deliberately elicited these confessions from him in violation of his right to counsel. But the court disagreed. It analyzed the deliberate elicitation question as follows:

> The critical distinction between this case and the *Massiah* [line of cases] is that Pearson, while a state actor, was not a state actor deliberately engaged in trying to secure information from the defendant for use in connection with the prosecution that was the subject matter of counsel's representation. * * *
>
> * * * First, Pearson had no responsibility for eliciting or reporting information for use in the prosecution of Bey's case and was not working with anyone who had such responsibility. Second, and most importantly, Pearson did not behave like someone who intended to secure incriminating statements from Bey. The record lacks evidence of any questions designed to elicit the statement that Bey had raped and beaten a woman to death on the beach, and merely reveals Pearson's asking "why" Bey had committed the act and seeking clarification "if it was something [he] didn't understand." Pearson did not take any notes or compile any reports of his conversations with Bey. In fact, Pearson disclosed the confession to no one for five years. It was only through the systematic efforts of the investigator that the prosecutor's office uncovered Bey's statements. Even Pearson's testimony in Bey's case was "reluctantly given." Thus, the state's receipt of Bey's confession was not the result of any deliberate elicitation by Pearson for use in connection with Bey's prosecution, and the state's use of Bey's confession at trial did not violate the Sixth Amendment.

If the focus of the Sixth Amendment is on whether the officer is *trying* to get information from a person charged with a crime, won't it be difficult for a court to assess the intent of the officer?

Application of the Deliberate Elicitation Standard: Fellers v. United States

In Fellers v. United States, 540 U.S. 519 (2004), the Supreme Court, in an opinion by Justice O'Connor, found that the lower court had improperly applied *Miranda* rules to a *Massiah* case. A grand jury indicted Fellers on drug charges. Police went to his home to arrest him, knocked on the door, asked for entry, were admitted, and advised Fellers they had come to discuss his involvement in methamphetamine distribution. They informed Fellers that they had a federal warrant for his arrest and that a grand jury had indicted him for conspiracy to distribute methamphetamine that involved certain individuals, four of whom they named. Fellers then told the officers that he knew the four people and had used methamphetamine during his association with them. Fellers later made statements at the jailhouse after being warned of his rights. He moved to suppress both his statements at home and at the jail.

The Court of Appeals held that Fellers' Sixth Amendment rights were not violated by the post-charge discussion because "the officers did not interrogate [petitioner] at his home." It further held that later statements by Fellers, made at the jailhouse, could not be excluded as the fruits of an illegally obtained statement—even assuming, arguendo, that Fellers' first statement was illegally obtained. It relied on the *Miranda*-based decision of Oregon v. Elstad, which held that the testimonial fruits of a *Miranda*-defective confession are not subject to *Miranda's* exclusionary rule. In essence, the lower court looked at the case as one involving *Miranda* rather than the Sixth Amendment.

Justice O'Connor noted that the Sixth Amendment "deliberately elicited" standard was distinct from "interrogation" and found that "there is no question that the officers in this case deliberately elicited information" from Fellers. Accordingly, she concluded that the lower court erred in finding that Fellers' Sixth Amendment right to counsel was not violated in his house. But she also concluded that the Court had not decided whether *Elstad* applied to a Sixth Amendment violation and therefore remanded for further proceedings.

C. USE OF UNDERCOVER OFFICERS AND STATE AGENTS

In one respect, the Sixth Amendment is less protective in regulating confessions than is the Fifth: it applies only to those who have been formally charged, whereas *Miranda* applies to all suspects facing custodial interrogation. In another respect, however, the Sixth Amendment is more protective than the Fifth: as *Massiah* shows, it limits the use of undercover tactics, whereas (according to Illinois v. Perkins, supra) *Miranda* only applies when the suspect knows that he is speaking to a police officer.

Jailhouse Plant: United States v. Henry

The Court in United States v. Henry, 447 U.S. 264 (1980), considered the application of the Sixth Amendment right to counsel when charged and incarcerated defendants are questioned by informants. Henry's cellmate, Nichols, testified at Henry's bank robbery trial to incriminating statements that Henry had made. At the time of those statements, Henry had already been indicted and was incarcerated awaiting trial. Nichols was a prisoner who operated as a paid government informant. An FBI agent told Nichols, who was kept in the same jail as Henry, of the government's interest in several individuals who were housed in the jail, including Henry. The agent told Nichols not to initiate conversations with Henry, but to pay attention to anything Henry said about the robbery.

Citing both *Massiah* and *Brewer,* the Chief Justice wrote that "[t]he question here is whether * * * a government agent deliberately elicited incriminating statements from Henry within the meaning of *Massiah.*" The Chief Justice found "deliberate" elicitation even though the state denied that the officers had the intent to elicit a confession from Henry. On the question of "deliberateness," the court reasoned as follows:

> Three factors are important. First, Nichols was acting under instructions as a paid informant for the Government; second, Nichols was ostensibly no more than a fellow inmate of Henry; and third, Henry was in custody and under indictment at the time he was engaged in conversation by Nichols.
>
> * * * Even if the agent's statement that he did not intend that Nichols would take affirmative steps to secure incriminating information is accepted, he must have known that such propinquity would lead to that result.
>
> The Government argues that the federal agents instructed Nichols not to question Henry about the robbery. Yet according to his own testimony, Nichols was not a passive listener; rather, he had "some conversations with Mr. Henry" while he was in jail and Henry's incriminatory statements were "the product of this conversation." While affirmative interrogation, absent waiver, would certainly satisfy *Massiah,* we are not persuaded, as the Government contends, that Brewer v. Williams modified *Massiah's* "deliberately elicited" test. * * *
>
> The Government argues that this Court should apply a less rigorous standard under the Sixth Amendment [to undercover activity] than where the accused is speaking in the hearing of persons he knows to be Government officers. That line of argument, however, seeks to infuse Fifth Amendment concerns * * * into the Sixth Amendment protection * * *.
>
> Moreover, the concept of a knowing and voluntary waiver of Sixth Amendment rights does not apply in the context of communications with an undisclosed undercover informant acting for the Government. In that setting, Henry, being unaware that Nichols was a Government agent expressly commissioned to secure evidence, cannot be held to have waived his right to the assistance of counsel.
>
> Finally, Henry's incarceration at the time he was engaged in conversation by Nichols is also a relevant factor. * * * [T]he mere fact of custody imposes pressures on the accused; confinement may bring into play subtle influences that will make him particularly susceptible to the ploys of undercover Government agents.

The Court concluded that "[b]y intentionally creating a situation likely to induce Henry to make incriminating statements without the assistance of counsel, the government violated Henry's Sixth Amendment's right to counsel."

Justice Blackmun, joined by Justice White, dissented. He argued that the Court purported to retain the "deliberately elicited" test, but that in reality it was extending *Massiah* to "cover even a 'negligent' triggering of events resulting in reception of disclosures." He concluded that a deliberateness standard "imposes the exclusionary sanction on that conduct that is most culpable, most likely to frustrate the purpose of having counsel, and most susceptible to being checked by a deterrent." He went on to criticize the Court's application of its own test to the facts, which in his view did not reveal that anything the government agent did was " 'likely to induce' Nichols' successful prompting of Henry."

Justice Rehnquist filed a separate dissent. He urged another look at the doctrinal underpinnings of the *Massiah* doctrine. After observing that in cases like this one the government has done nothing to impair the defendant's ability to consult with an attorney, Justice Rehnquist observed:

> The role of counsel in an adversary system is to offer advice and assistance in the preparation of a defense and to serve as a spokesman for the accused in technical legal proceedings. And the Sixth Amendment, of course, protects the confidentiality of communications between the accused and his attorney. But there is no constitutional or historical support for concluding that an accused has a right to have his attorney serve as a sort of guru who must be present whenever an accused has an inclination to reveal incriminating information to anyone who acts to elicit such information at the behest of the prosecution. To the extent the accused is protected from revealing evidence that may be incriminatory, the focus must be on the Fifth Amendment privilege against compulsory self-incrimination.

The Listening Post: Kuhlmann v. Wilson

The Court distinguished *Henry* in Kuhlmann v. Wilson, 477 U.S. 436 (1986), as it held that the Sixth Amendment was not violated when police put a jailhouse informant in close proximity to a defendant and the defendant made statements to the informant without any serious effort on the informant's part to elicit the statements. The Court stated that, to prove a Sixth Amendment violation, a defendant must show that the police took some action, beyond merely listening, that was deliberately designed to elicit incriminating remarks. *No elicitation* was found on the facts of the case.

The basic facts were the following: Prior to the defendant's arrival at a jail following an arraignment for robbery and murder, an officer entered into an agreement with inmate Lee under which Lee would listen to the defendant's conversations and report them, but Lee would ask no questions and would simply "keep his ears open." The defendant, without prompting, told Lee that he had been present during the robbery but denied knowing the robbers. Lee responded that the explanation "didn't sound too good." The defendant changed details over the next few days. Finally, after a visit from his brother, the defendant, again without prompting, admitted to Lee that he and two other men had committed the robbery and murder.

Justice Powell, writing for the Court, distinguished *Henry* on the ground that the informant in *Henry* had "stimulated" the conversations with Henry and that Lee had not done so in the instant case. The Court stated that a defendant does not show a Sixth Amendment violation "simply by showing that an informant, either through prior arrangement or voluntarily, reported his incriminating statements to the police." Justice Powell found it insignificant that Lee had said that the defendant's version of the crimes didn't sound too good. Just that one remark did not bring the case out of the realm of the "passive recording device"; that single remark did not constitute "elicitation."

Chief Justice Burger filed a short concurring opinion stating that "[t]here is a vast difference between placing an 'ear' in the suspect's cell and placing a voice in the cell to encourage conversation for the 'ear' to record." Justice Brennan, joined by Justice Marshall, dissented in *Wilson* and found the case to be virtually indistinguishable on its facts from *Henry*. Justice Stevens also dissented briefly and agreed with Justice Brennan.

See also United States v. York, 933 F.2d 1343 (7th Cir. 1991): The court found no deliberate elicitation where the informant responded with neutral comments when incriminating topics were brought up by the defendant. The court observed that informants are not required to risk revealing their status by refusing to participate in the natural flow of conversation.

Is the Informant a State Agent?

Sixth Amendment protection under *Henry* requires that the informant must have been working for the government at the time the information was obtained from the accused—otherwise there is no state action implicated in the deliberate elicitation.

Whether the informant is a state agent, or is simply working on his own account, is often a difficult question. For example, in United States v. Watson, 894 F.2d 1345 (D.C. Cir. 1990), Watson argued that the jailhouse informant was working as a government agent at the time he elicited incriminating statements from Watson. The informant had worked for the DEA for two years and was in regular contact with the DEA while he was in jail. But the court found "no evidence that the DEA in any way encouraged" the informant to talk to Watson; that the informant was in contact with the DEA on unrelated cases, and did not mention Watson until after Watson made incriminating statements; and that the informant "was acting as an entrepreneur." The court stated that the informant "may have hoped to make a sale to the government when he spoke with Watson, but that does not make the government responsible for his actions, any more than a person who has bought an article from a salesman in the past is responsible if the salesman then steals something similar in the hope of making a second sale."

The court in Ayers v. Hudson, 623 F.3d 301 (10th Cir. 2010), has noted the dispute among the courts on what is necessary for an informant to be a government agent for Sixth Amendment purposes:

> Some of [the] circuits employ a bright-line rule, deciding that an informant becomes a government agent only when the informant has been instructed by the police to get information about the particular defendant. Other circuits, however, flatly reject this approach, [and consider] the facts and circumstances of each case. Embracing this broader approach, at least two of these circuits require only some evidence that an agreement, express or implied, between the individual and a government official existed at the time the elicitation took place. [citations omitted]

The *Ayers* court agreed with the broader, totality of circumstances approach, noting that under *Henry*, a Sixth Amendment violation can occur even if the State specifically instructs its informant *not* to initiate any conversation. Thus the court found the bright-line rule requiring a specific instruction to the informant to be inconsistent with *Henry*. The court also noted that if the State could avoid a finding of agency simply by not explicitly instructing the informant to get information from the defendant, this "would allow the State to accomplish with a wink and a nod what it cannot do overtly."

D. CONTINUING INVESTIGATIONS

A defendant who is formally charged has a right to be free from deliberate attempts by state agents to elicit incriminating information in the absence of defendant's counsel. But defendants who have been formally charged are often suspected of committing crimes in addition to those charged. Does the Sixth Amendment prohibit an officer from obtaining information from the defendant concerning *uncharged* crimes?

Maine v. Moulton

That was the question in Maine v. Moulton, 474 U.S. 159 (1985). Moulton and a codefendant, Colson, were charged with theft of automobiles and parts. Colson, along with his lawyer, informed the Chief of Police of threatening telephone calls to his house and of the fact that Moulton had spoken of killing a key witness. Colson cooperated with the police. The police wired Colson with a transmitter when he agreed to meet with Moulton. The codefendants, at their meeting, spoke of eliminating witnesses. Moulton rejected the idea, and Colson led Moulton into talking about their theft activities, as well as burglaries that were related to the thefts. Both the recorded telephone statements and the recorded meeting were used as evidence at trial. Moulton was convicted.

Justice Brennan wrote for the Court as it reversed Moulton's conviction. He found it irrelevant that the meeting with the informant was initiated by Moulton, concluding that "knowing exploitation by the State of an opportunity to confront the accused without counsel being present is as much a breach of the State's obligation not to circumvent the right to the assistance of counsel as is the intentional creation of such an opportunity."

Justice Brennan also rejected the argument that Moulton's statements should be admissible because the police were investigating new crimes, including threats to the safety of witnesses. Justice Brennan emphasized that police may investigate crimes separate from the crimes charged and may use statements made by a suspect in a *later trial* for those crimes. But he concluded that "incriminating statements pertaining to pending charges are inadmissible at the trial of those charges, notwithstanding the fact that the police were also investigating other crimes, if, in obtaining the evidence, the State violated the Sixth Amendment by knowingly circumventing the accused's right to the assistance of counsel." He stated that the Sixth Amendment guarantees the accused "the right to rely on counsel as a 'medium' between him and the State."

The government argued that the elicitation of information about the charged crime was not "deliberate" because the officers instructed the informant to limit the scope of discussion to the subject matter of killing witnesses. But the majority was unpersuaded. Justice Brennan stated that the agents should have known that despite their instructions, the conversation between the informant and Moulton would be likely to turn to the crime for which both were charged. Justice Brennan noted that "direct proof of the State's knowledge will seldom be available," but that "proof that the State must have known that its agent was likely to obtain incriminating statements" suffices to establish the "deliberate" elicitation prohibited by the Sixth Amendment.

Thus, the officer's actions in *Moulton* constituted "deliberate" elicitation even though there was no showing of specific intent on the part of the officers to obtain information about the charged crime. "Deliberate" elicitation is found whenever the officers "must have known" that their investigative tactic would lead to incriminating information from a charged defendant in the absence of counsel.

Chief Justice Burger dissented in *Moulton*, joined by Justices White and Rehnquist and in part by Justice O'Connor. The Chief Justice argued that the Sixth Amendment term "deliberate elicitation" focuses upon a bad purpose—to use statements in connection with pending charges—and that suppression should not be required unless police institute the investigation of separate charges in bad faith to avoid the dictates of *Massiah.*

In a Continuing Investigation, Which Crimes Are Related to the Crime Charged for Purposes of the Sixth Amendment?: Texas v. Cobb

Assume that a defendant is indicted for robbing a neighbor. This means he has a Sixth Amendment right to counsel, and officers cannot deliberately elicit information from him in the absence of a waiver. But assume also that officers, after further investigation of the incident, suspect the defendant of not only robbing but also kidnapping the neighbor. Does the Sixth Amendment protect against deliberate elicitation about the kidnapping? The Court in Texas v. Cobb, 532 U.S. 162 (2001), noted that the Sixth Amendment protects an accused only for the crime charged—and that the scope of the "crime charged" is to be determined by the definition of "same offense" under the Double Jeopardy Clause. Chief Justice Rehnquist, writing for the Court, explained as follows:

> Although it is clear that the Sixth Amendment right to counsel attaches only to charged offenses, we have recognized in other contexts that the definition of an "offense" is not necessarily limited to the four corners of a charging instrument. In Blockburger v. United States, 284 U.S. 299 (1932), we explained that "where the same act or transaction constitutes a violation of two distinct statutory provisions, the test to be applied to determine whether there are two offenses or only one, is whether each provision requires proof of a fact which the other does not." * * * We see no constitutional difference between the meaning of the term "offense" in the context of double jeopardy and of the right to counsel. Accordingly, we hold that when the Sixth Amendment right to counsel attaches, it does encompass offenses that, even if not formally charged, would be considered the same offense under the *Blockburger* test.

In *Cobb,* the Court found no Sixth Amendment violation where the defendant was charged with burglarizing a premises, and officers thereafter deliberately elicited information from him about a murder that he committed during the burglary. The Court reasoned that burglary requires proof of entering into a building—not required for proof of murder. And murder requires killing someone—not required for proof of burglary. Similarly, to return to our hypothetical, officers could deliberately elicit information about a kidnapping after the defendant was indicted for robbery—and this is so even if the kidnapping and robbery were part of the same factual transaction.

Justice Kennedy wrote a concurring opinion in *Cobb* and was joined by Justices Scalia and Thomas. Justice Breyer, joined by Justices Stevens, Souter, and Ginsburg, dissented.

E. WAIVER OF SIXTH AMENDMENT PROTECTIONS

Under what circumstances can an accused be held to have *waived* his Sixth Amendment right to counsel during questioning? Is the test for waiver similar or identical to that applied for waiver of *Miranda* rights? In the *Miranda* section, we noted two distinct waiver situations: 1) where the defendant receives warnings and waives his rights; and 2) where the defendant receives his warnings, invokes his rights, and then subsequently is argued to have waived his rights. Similar situations arise in the Sixth Amendment context.

Waiving Sixth Amendment Rights After Receiving Miranda Warnings: Brewer v. Williams, Berghuis v. Thompkins, and Patterson v. Illinois

When the defendant receives warnings and waives his rights, the question is simply whether the waiver was knowing and voluntary. The Court in Brewer v. Williams, supra, held that the government, to prove a waiver of Sixth Amendment rights, *must show more than simply that the defendant received warnings and elected to speak.* The majority in *Williams* found nothing to indicate that Williams had actually relinquished his rights. Analogizing from *Miranda,* evidence of relinquishment could be found in myriad ways, for example by the defendant's signing a waiver form; answering some questions but not others; showing a high level of cooperation; or providing an extremely detailed and lengthy confession. But none of this was shown to the majority's satisfaction in Brewer v. Williams.

Assuming that the government can show that the defendant voluntarily relinquished his Sixth Amendment rights, another question arises: whether the defendant was sufficiently informed of his rights to make a *knowing* waiver. In the *Miranda* context, the Court held that the *Miranda* warnings provide a suspect with all the information he needs to make a knowing waiver. Do the *Miranda* warnings provide sufficient information for a knowing waiver of the Sixth Amendment right to counsel?

The Court's answer to this question came in Patterson v. Illinois, 487 U.S. 285 (1988). Patterson was indicted, received *Miranda* warnings, and signed the waiver form and confessed. He had never invoked his Sixth Amendment right to counsel. He argued that his waiver, while voluntary, was not knowing and intelligent, because he received only the *Miranda* warnings, and these warnings did not adequately inform him of his Sixth

Amendment right to counsel. Justice White, writing for the Court, rejected this argument in the following analysis:

> By telling petitioner that he had a right to consult with an attorney, to have a lawyer present while he was questioned, and even to have a lawyer appointed for him if he could not afford to retain one on his own, [the officers] conveyed to petitioner the sum and substance of the rights that the Sixth Amendment provided him. * * * [The *Miranda*] warning also sufficed * * * to let petitioner know what a lawyer could do for him during the postindictment questioning; namely, advise petitioner to refrain from making any [incriminating] statements * * *
>
> Our conclusion is supported by petitioner's inability, in the proceedings before this Court, to articulate with precision what additional information should have been provided to him before he would have been competent to waive his right to counsel. * * * The State's decision to take an additional step and commence formal adversarial proceedings against the accused does not substantially increase the value of counsel to the accused at questioning, or expand the limited purpose that an attorney serves when the accused is questioned by authorities. With respect to this inquiry, we do not discern a substantial difference between the usefulness of a lawyer to a suspect during custodial interrogation, and his value to an accused at postindictment questioning. * * * Because the role of counsel at questioning is relatively simple and limited, we see no problem in having a waiver procedure at that stage which is likewise simple and limited.

Justice White distinguished Faretta v. California, 422 U.S. 806 (1975), where the Court required copious warnings to be conveyed to an accused before an informed waiver of the right to counsel *at trial* could be found.[33] Justice White explained that the "full dangers and disadvantages of self-representation during questioning are less substantial and more obvious to an accused than they are at trial." That is, counsel can do a lot for you at trial, and so extensive warnings are necessary so that you understand what you are giving up; in contrast, counsel's role during police questioning is less complex—if counsel is there, she will tell you to shut up. And the *Miranda* warnings give the necessary information of counsel's role in that context.

Justice Stevens, joined by Justices Brennan, Marshall, and Blackmun dissented in *Patterson*. Justice Stevens argued that the majority had underplayed the significance of the initiation of formal proceedings and the multifaceted role of counsel after an indictment. He noted that the lawyer might examine the indictment for legal sufficiency, or might be able to

[33] The breadth and detail of the required *Faretta* warnings are discussed in Chapter 10.

negotiate a plea bargain, and that the *Miranda* warnings did not apprise the accused of these possibilities. Therefore, he concluded the person indicted is not fully aware of the value of an attorney if he simply receives the *Miranda* warnings.

In a footnote in *Patterson*, Justice White stressed that:

> This does not mean, of course, that all Sixth Amendment challenges to the conduct of postindictment questioning will fail whenever the challenged practice would pass constitutional muster under *Miranda*. For example, we have permitted a *Miranda* waiver to stand where a suspect was not told that his lawyer was trying to reach him during questioning; in the Sixth Amendment context, this waiver would not be valid. Likewise a surreptitious conversation between an undercover police officer and an unindicted suspect would not give rise to any *Miranda* violation as long as the "interrogation" was not in a custodial setting, however, once the accused is indicted, such questioning would be prohibited.

Indictment Warnings

The Court in *Patterson* left open whether an indicted suspect is entitled to a warning that he has been indicted before a waiver of the Sixth Amendment right to counsel can be found; Patterson had been so informed. But the sweeping language in *Patterson*, to the effect that *Miranda* warnings impart the necessary information for a Sixth Amendment waiver, has led courts to hold that an "indictment warning" is not required. See United States v. Chadwick, 999 F.2d 1282 (8th Cir. 1993) ("law enforcement officers need not inform an accused that he has been indicted before seeking a waiver of his right to counsel").

Waiving the Sixth Amendment Right to Counsel After Invoking It: Michigan v. Jackson and Montejo v. Louisiana

In Michigan v. Jackson, 475 U.S. 625 (1986), the accused formally requested counsel at an arraignment. Later, he was interrogated by police officers about the crime for which he had been charged. Jackson did not initiate the contact, but he signed a waiver form, and confessed. Justice Stevens wrote for the Court as it held that Jackson had not knowingly and voluntarily waived his Sixth Amendment rights. He stated that, when an accused invokes his Sixth Amendment right to counsel, the standards of Edwards v. Arizona, supra, govern the waiver of Sixth Amendment rights. Accordingly, Jackson could only have waived his Sixth Amendment rights if he had initiated a later conversation and also knowingly and voluntarily waived his rights; this he had not done. Justice Stevens contended that "the reasons for prohibiting the interrogation of an uncounseled prisoner are even stronger after he has been formally charged with an offense than before."

In the following case, the Court reconsidered—and rejected—the extension of *Edwards* to the Sixth Amendment waiver context. This means that there is a major difference between Fifth and Sixth Amendment waiver after the right to counsel has been invoked. If a charged defendant invokes his Sixth Amendment right—typically, at an arraignment or other hearing—police officers remain free to approach him at any time and initiate questioning after they secure a knowing and voluntary waiver. In contrast, if the suspect invokes his *Miranda* right to counsel—which can only be done in the context of custodial interrogation—then there can be no waiver unless the defendant initiates a new conversation with the officers or has been released from *Miranda* custody for 14 days.

MONTEJO V. LOUISIANA

Supreme Court of the United States, 2009.
556 U.S. 778.

JUSTICE SCALIA delivered the opinion of the Court.

We consider in this case the scope and continued viability of the rule announced by this Court in Michigan v. Jackson, 475 U.S. 625 (1986), forbidding police to initiate interrogation of a criminal defendant once he has requested counsel at an arraignment or similar proceeding.

* * *

Petitioner Jesse Montejo was arrested on September 6, 2002, in connection with the robbery and murder of Lewis Ferrari, who had been found dead in his own home one day earlier. Suspicion quickly focused on Jerry Moore, a disgruntled former employee of Ferrari's dry cleaning business. Police sought to question Montejo, who was a known associate of Moore.

Montejo waived his rights under *Miranda v. Arizona*, and was interrogated at the sheriff's office by police detectives through the late afternoon and evening of September 6 and the early morning of September 7. During the interrogation, Montejo repeatedly changed his account of the crime, at first claiming that he had only driven Moore to the victim's home, and ultimately admitting that he had shot and killed Ferrari in the course of a botched burglary. These police interrogations were videotaped.

On September 10, Montejo was brought before a judge for what is known in Louisiana as a "72-hour hearing"—a preliminary hearing required under state law. [Montejo did not expressly state that he wanted a lawyer, but the court ordered that counsel be appointed for Montejo.]

Later that same day, two police detectives visited Montejo back at the prison and requested that he accompany them on an excursion to locate the murder weapon (which Montejo had earlier indicated he had thrown into a lake). * * * Montejo was again read his *Miranda* rights and agreed to go along; during the excursion, he wrote an inculpatory letter of apology to the victim's widow. Only upon their return did Montejo finally meet his court-appointed attorney, who was quite upset that the detectives had interrogated his client in his absence.

At trial, the letter of apology was admitted over defense objection. The jury convicted Montejo of first-degree murder, and he was sentenced to death.

[The lower court found that Montejo's waiver was knowing and voluntary and that *Jackson/Edwards* was not applicable because Montejo had never explicitly requested counsel. Justice Scalia rejected the Louisiana rule that the *Jackson/Edwards* protection was contingent on an explicit invocation of the Sixth Amendment right to counsel at an arraignment. He noted among other things that in almost half the states the appointment of counsel is automatic upon a finding of indigency and in others the court appoints counsel sua sponte. In these states, the affirmative invocation requirement would be unworkable.]

But if the Louisiana Supreme Court's application of *Jackson* is unsound as a practical matter, then Montejo's solution is untenable as a theoretical and doctrinal matter. Under his approach, once a defendant is represented by counsel, police may not initiate any further interrogation. Such a rule would be entirely untethered from the original rationale of *Jackson*.

* * *

Our precedents * * * place beyond doubt that the Sixth Amendment right to counsel may be waived by a defendant, so long as relinquishment of the right is voluntary, knowing, and intelligent. Patterson v. Illinois; Brewer v. Williams. The defendant may waive the right whether or not he is already represented by counsel; the decision to waive need not itself be counseled. And when a defendant is read his *Miranda* rights (which include the right to have counsel present during interrogation) and agrees to waive those rights, that typically does the trick, even though the *Miranda* rights purportedly have their source in the Fifth Amendment * * *.

The only question raised by this case, and the only one addressed by the *Jackson* rule, is whether courts must presume that such a waiver is invalid under certain circumstances. We created such a presumption in *Jackson* by analogy to a similar prophylactic rule established to protect the Fifth Amendment based *Miranda* right to have counsel present at any custodial interrogation. * * *

Jackson represented a wholesale importation of the *Edwards* rule into the Sixth Amendment. The *Jackson* Court decided that a request for counsel at an arraignment should be treated as an invocation of the Sixth Amendment right to counsel "at every critical stage of the prosecution," despite doubt that defendants "actually inten[d] their request for counsel to encompass representation during any further questioning," because doubts must be "resolved in favor of protecting the constitutional claim." Citing *Edwards*, the Court held that any subsequent waiver would thus be "insufficient to justify police-initiated interrogation." In other words, we presume such waivers involuntary "based on the supposition that suspects who assert their right to counsel are unlikely to waive that right voluntarily" in subsequent interactions with police.

With this understanding of what *Jackson* stands for and whence it came, it should be clear that Montejo's interpretation of that decision—that no represented defendant can ever be approached by the State and asked to consent to interrogation—is off the mark. * * * No reason exists to assume that a defendant like Montejo, who has done nothing at all to express his intentions with respect to his Sixth Amendment rights, would not be perfectly amenable to speaking with the police without having counsel present. And no reason exists to prohibit the police from inquiring. *Edwards* and *Jackson* are meant to prevent police from badgering defendants into changing their minds about their rights, but a defendant who never asked for counsel has not yet made up his mind in the first instance.

* * *

The upshot is that even on *Jackson's* own terms, it would be completely unjustified to presume that a defendant's consent to police-initiated interrogation was involuntary or coerced simply because he had previously been appointed a lawyer.

* * *

So on the one hand, requiring an initial "invocation" of the right to counsel in order to trigger the *Jackson* presumption is consistent with the theory of that decision, but * * * would be unworkable in more than half the States of the Union. On the other hand, eliminating the invocation requirement would render the rule easy to apply but depart fundamentally from the *Jackson* rationale.

We do not think that *stare decisis* requires us to expand significantly the holding of a prior decision—fundamentally revising its theoretical basis in the process—in order to cure its practical deficiencies. To the contrary, the fact that a decision has proved "unworkable" is a traditional ground for overruling it. * * *

Beyond workability, the relevant factors in deciding whether to adhere to the principle of *stare decisis* include the antiquity of the precedent, the reliance interests at stake, and of course whether the decision was well reasoned. The first two cut in favor of abandoning *Jackson*: the opinion is only two decades old, and eliminating it would not upset expectations. Any criminal defendant learned enough to order his affairs based on the rule announced in *Jackson* would also be perfectly capable of interacting with the police on his own. Of course it is likely true that police and prosecutors have been trained to comply with *Jackson*, but that is hardly a basis for retaining it as a constitutional requirement. If a State wishes to abstain from requesting interviews with represented defendants when counsel is not present, it obviously may continue to do so.

Which brings us to the strength of *Jackson's* reasoning. When this Court creates a prophylactic rule in order to protect a constitutional right, the relevant "reasoning" is the weighing of the rule's benefits against its costs. * * * We think that the marginal benefits of *Jackson* (viz., the number of confessions obtained coercively that are suppressed by its bright-line rule and would otherwise have been admitted) are dwarfed by its substantial costs (viz., hindering society's compelling interest in finding, convicting, and punishing those who violate the law).

What does the *Jackson* rule actually achieve by way of preventing unconstitutional conduct? Recall that the purpose of the rule is to preclude the State from badgering defendants into waiving their previously asserted rights. The effect of this badgering might be to coerce a waiver, which would render the subsequent interrogation a violation of the Sixth Amendment. Even though involuntary waivers are invalid even apart from *Jackson*, mistakes are of course possible when courts conduct case-by-case voluntariness review. A bright-line rule like that adopted in *Jackson* ensures that no fruits of interrogations made possible by badgering-induced involuntary waivers are ever erroneously admitted at trial.

But without *Jackson*, how many would be? The answer is few if any. The principal reason is that the Court has already taken substantial other, overlapping measures toward the same end. * * * Under *Miranda's* prophylactic protection of the right against compelled self-incrimination, any suspect subject to custodial interrogation has the right to have a lawyer present if he so requests, and to be advised of that right. Under *Edwards'* prophylactic protection of the *Miranda* right, once such a defendant "has invoked his right to have counsel present," interrogation must stop. And under *Minnick's* prophylactic protection of the *Edwards* right, no subsequent interrogation may take place until counsel is present, "whether or not the accused has consulted with his attorney."

These three layers of prophylaxis are sufficient. * * *

* * *

Under the *Miranda-Edwards-Minnick* line of cases (which is not in doubt), a defendant who does not want to speak to the police without counsel present need only say as much when he is first approached and given the *Miranda* warnings. At that point, not only must the immediate contact end, but "badgering" by later requests is prohibited. If that regime suffices to protect the integrity of a suspect's voluntary choice not to speak outside his lawyer's presence before his arraignment, it is hard to see why it would not also suffice to protect that same choice after arraignment, when Sixth Amendment rights have attached. And if so, then *Jackson* is simply superfluous.

* * *

On the other side of the equation are the costs of adding the bright-line *Jackson* rule on top of *Edwards* and other extant protections. The principal cost of applying any exclusionary rule is, of course, letting guilty and possibly dangerous criminals go free. *Jackson* not only operates to invalidate a confession given by the free choice of suspects who have received proper advice of their *Miranda* rights but waived them nonetheless, but also deters law enforcement officers from even trying to obtain voluntary confessions. The ready ability to obtain uncoerced confessions is not an evil but an unmitigated good. Without these confessions, crimes go unsolved and criminals unpunished. These are not negligible costs, and in our view the *Jackson* Court gave them too short shrift.

* * * Montejo expresses concern that courts will have to determine whether statements made at preliminary hearings constitute *Edwards* invocations—thus implicating all the practical problems of the Louisiana rule we discussed above. That concern is misguided. We have * * * never held that a person can invoke his *Miranda* rights anticipatorily, in a context other than custodial interrogation. What matters for *Miranda* and *Edwards* is what happens when the defendant is approached for interrogation, and (if he consents) what happens during the interrogation—not what happened at any preliminary hearing.

In sum, when the marginal benefits of the *Jackson* rule are weighed against its substantial costs to the truth-seeking process and the criminal justice system, we readily conclude that the rule does not "pay its way." Michigan v. Jackson should be and now is overruled.

* * *

Although our holding means that the Louisiana Supreme Court correctly rejected Montejo's claim under *Jackson*, we think that Montejo should be given an opportunity to contend that his letter of apology should still have been suppressed under the rule of *Edwards*. If Montejo made a clear assertion of the right to counsel when the officers approached him about accompanying them on the excursion for the murder weapon, then no interrogation should have taken place unless Montejo initiated it. Even if Montejo subsequently agreed to waive his rights, that waiver would have been invalid had it followed an unequivocal election of the right.

Montejo understandably did not pursue an *Edwards* objection, because *Jackson* served as the Sixth Amendment analogy to *Edwards* and offered broader protections. Our decision today, overruling *Jackson*, changes the legal landscape and does so in part based on the protections already provided by *Edwards*. Thus we think that a remand is appropriate so that Montejo can pursue this alternative avenue for relief. * * *

[The concurring opinion by JUSTICE ALITO, joined by JUSTICE KENNEDY, is omitted.]

JUSTICE STEVENS, with whom JUSTICE SOUTER and JUSTICE GINSBURG join, and with whom JUSTICE BREYER joins [in pertinent part] dissenting.

* * *

The majority's analysis flagrantly misrepresents *Jackson's* underlying rationale and the constitutional interests the decision sought to protect. While it is true that the rule adopted in *Jackson* was patterned after the rule in *Edwards*, the *Jackson* opinion does not even mention the anti-badgering considerations that provide the basis for the Court's decision today. Instead, *Jackson* relied primarily on cases discussing the broad protections guaranteed by the Sixth Amendment right to counsel—not its Fifth Amendment counterpart. *Jackson* emphasized that the purpose of the Sixth Amendment is to "protec[t] the unaided layman at critical confrontations with his adversary" by giving him "the right to rely on counsel as a 'medium' between him[self] and the State." * * *

Once *Jackson* is placed in its proper Sixth Amendment context, the majority's justifications for overruling the decision crumble. * * *

[The dissenting opinion of JUSTICE BREYER is omitted.]

QUESTIONS AFTER PATTERSON AND MONTEJO

The Court's holding in *Patterson v. Illinois* has come under renewed scrutiny in recent years as courts and scholars have come to terms with *Montejo* and the effective merger of Fifth and Sixth Amendment rights in the context of warnings, invocation, and waiver. *See, e.g.*, Arnold H. Loewy, *Distinguishing Confessions Obtained in Violation of the Fifth Amendment from Those Obtained in Violation of the Sixth Amendment*, 50 Tex. Tech L. Rev. 145 (2017); Wayne A. Logan, *The Case for Greater Transparency in*

Sixth Amendment Right to Pretrial Counsel Warnings, 52 Tex. Tech L. Rev. 23 (2019). Do you think that *Miranda* warnings are adequate to ensure that a defendant knowingly waives his Sixth Amendment right to counsel as well as his Fifth Amendment protection against self-incrimination? If not, then what measures do you think the Constitution requires?

F. SIXTH AMENDMENT EXCLUSION

Does the exclusionary rule apply to evidence obtained in violation of the Sixth Amendment? If so, then what is the scope of that exclusion?

In Brewer v. Williams, 430 U.S. 387 (1977), the "Christian burial" case, the Court concluded that "neither Williams' incriminating statements themselves nor any testimony describing his having led the police to the victim's body can constitutionally be admitted into evidence." But the Court allowed that "evidence of where the body was found and of its condition might well be admissible on the theory that the body would have been discovered in any event, even had incriminating statements not been elicited from Williams." It then invited the state to make that argument at retrial. It did, successfully, and Williams was convicted a second time. Williams then pursued appeals that led him again to the Supreme Court.

In Nix v. Williams, 467 U.S. 431 (1984), Williams argued that the investigative fruits of his statements taken in violation of the Sixth Amendment should have been excluded at his second trial. Writing for the Court, Chief Justice Burger allowed that the fruit of the poisonous tree doctrine familiar in Fourth Amendment cases may also apply in the Sixth Amendment context, but that the evidence against Williams was properly admitted under a doctrine of inevitable discovery. The Chief Justice explained as follows:

> The core rationale consistently advanced by this Court for extending the exclusionary rule to evidence that is the fruit of unlawful police conduct has been that this admittedly drastic and socially costly course is needed to deter police from violations of constitutional and statutory protections. This Court has accepted the argument that the way to ensure such protections is to exclude evidence seized as a result of such violations notwithstanding the high social cost of letting persons obviously guilty go unpunished for their crimes. On this rationale, the prosecution is not to be put in a better position than it would have been in if no illegality had transpired.
>
> By contrast, the derivative evidence analysis ensures that the prosecution is not put in a worse position simply because of some earlier police error or misconduct. The independent source doctrine allows admission of evidence that has been discovered by means wholly independent of any constitutional violation. That doctrine, although closely related to the inevitable discovery doctrine, does not

> apply here; Williams' statements to Leaming indeed led police to the child's body, but that is not the whole story. The independent source doctrine teaches us that the interest of society in deterring unlawful police conduct and the public interest in having juries receive all probative evidence of a crime are properly balanced by putting the police in the same, not a worse, position that they would have been in if no police error or misconduct had occurred. When the challenged evidence has an independent source, exclusion of such evidence would put the police in a worse position than they would have been in absent any error or violation. There is a functional similarity between these two doctrines in that exclusion of evidence that would inevitably have been discovered would also put the government in a worse position, because the police would have obtained that evidence if no misconduct had taken place. Thus, while the independent source exception would not justify admission of evidence in this case, its rationale is wholly consistent with, and justifies, our adoption of the ultimate or inevitable discovery exception to the exclusionary rule.
>
> * * * If the prosecution can establish by a preponderance of the evidence that the information ultimately or inevitably would have been discovered by lawful means—here, the volunteers' search—then the deterrence rationale has so little basis that the evidence should be received. Anything less would reject logic, experience, and common sense.

The *Nix* Court agreed with the state courts' determinations that a volunteer search party inevitably would have discovered the body of Williams's victim, Pamela Powers, in the course of their ongoing search. On that basis, the Court concluded that her body and related evidence were properly presented to the jury as part of the prosecutor's case-in-chief.

Justice Brennan dissented with Justice Marshall in *Nix*. They agreed with the Court's application of the inevitable discovery rule, but would have preferred a clear and convincing evidence standard.

In Kansas v. Ventris, 556 U.S. 586 (2009), the Court reiterated its view that the Sixth Amendment exclusionary rule is justified solely as a general deterrent and runs parallel to the Fourth Amendment exclusionary rule rather than the Fifth Amendment exclusionary rule. Police officers deliberately elicited information from Ventris in violation of the Sixth Amendment. In the Supreme Court, the government conceded a *Massiah* violation, but maintained that Ventris's statements were properly used to impeach his trial testimony. The Court, in an opinion by Justice Scalia for seven Justices, agreed. Justice Scalia reasoned as follows:

> Our precedents make clear that the game of excluding tainted evidence for impeachment purposes is not worth the candle. The interests safeguarded by such exclusion are "outweighed by the need

to prevent perjury and to assure the integrity of the trial process." Stone v. Powell. "It is one thing to say that the Government cannot make an affirmative use of evidence unlawfully obtained. It is quite another to say that the defendant can . . . provide himself with a shield against contradiction of his untruths." Walder v. United States. Once the defendant testifies in a way that contradicts prior statements, denying the prosecution use of "the traditional truth-testing devices of the adversary process," Harris v. New York, is a high price to pay for vindication of the right to counsel at the prior stage.

On the other side of the scale, preventing impeachment use of statements taken in violation of *Massiah* would add little appreciable deterrence. Officers have significant incentive to ensure that they and their informants comply with the Constitution's demands, since statements lawfully obtained can be used for all purposes rather than simply for impeachment. And the *ex ante* probability that evidence gained in violation of *Massiah* would be of use for impeachment is exceedingly small. An investigator would have to anticipate both that the defendant would choose to testify at trial (an unusual occurrence to begin with) and that he would testify inconsistently despite the admissibility of his prior statement for impeachment. Not likely to happen—or at least not likely enough to risk squandering the opportunity of using a properly obtained statement for the prosecution's case in chief.

In any event, even if "the officer may be said to have little to lose and perhaps something to gain by way of possibly uncovering impeachment material," we have multiple times rejected the argument that this "speculative possibility" can trump the costs of allowing perjurious statements to go unchallenged. Oregon v. Hass. We have held in every other context that tainted evidence—evidence whose very introduction does not constitute the constitutional violation, but whose obtaining was constitutionally invalid—is admissible for impeachment. We see no distinction that would alter the balance here.[34]

Accordingly, the Court appears to have imported much of it Fourth Amendment exclusionary rule jurisprudence into the Sixth Amendment context by way of the same deterrence rationale.

[34] Joined by Justice Ginsburg, Justice Stevens dissented in *Ventris*.

CHAPTER 4

IDENTIFYING SUSPECTS

■ ■ ■

I. INTRODUCTION

Even in the days of DNA matching, eyewitness identification is an important part of many criminal prosecutions. Many types of crimes cannot usually be solved by DNA evidence, e.g., bank robbery, fraud, drugs, etc. Indeed most cases in which identity is disputed will turn on whether witnesses are believed. Yet, it is well known that eyewitness evidence is often not very reliable and that police procedures may render identifications even less reliable than they otherwise would be.

The late Circuit Judge McGowan explained more than 50 years ago that many experts believe that erroneous identifications are "conceivably the greatest single threat to the achievement of our ideal that no innocent man shall be punished." Constitutional Interpretation and Criminal Identification, 12 Wm. & Mary L.Rev. 235, 238 (1970). There is growing evidence that suggestive law enforcement conduct may exacerbate the problems of securing accurate identifications from victims and witnesses who often experience crime in circumstances of stress and poor observation conditions. The Innocence Project offers a compelling statistic about the impact of eyewitness identification on wrongful convictions and some examples of mistaken identifications:

> Eyewitness misidentification is the single greatest cause of wrongful convictions nationwide, playing a role in more than 75% of convictions overturned through DNA testing. While eyewitness testimony can be persuasive evidence before a judge or jury * * * research shows that the human mind is not like a tape recorder; we neither record events exactly as we see them, nor recall them like a tape that has been rewound. Instead, witness memory is like any other evidence at a crime scene; it must be preserved carefully and retrieved methodically, or it can be contaminated.
>
> In case after case, DNA has proven what scientists already know—that eyewitness identification is frequently inaccurate. In the wrongful convictions caused by eyewitness misidentification, the circumstances varied, but judges and juries all relied on testimony that could have been more accurate if reforms proven by science had

been implemented. The Innocence Project has worked on cases in which:

- A witness made an identification in a "show-up" procedure from the back of a police car hundreds of feet away from the suspect in a poorly lit parking lot in the middle of the night.
- A witness in a rape case was shown a photo array where only one photo—of the person police suspected was the perpetrator—was marked with an "R."
- Witnesses substantially changed their description of a perpetrator (including key information such as height, weight and presence of facial hair) after they learned more about a particular suspect.
- Witnesses only made an identification after multiple photo arrays or lineups—and then made hesitant identifications (saying they "thought" the person "might be" the perpetrator, for example), but at trial the jury was told the witnesses did not waver in identifying the suspect.

[www.innocenceproject.org]

Another documented problem is that an identification may be more in accord with the witness's expectation than with reality. This may be particularly so where a witness of one race identifies a person of another race as the perpetrator. See Johnson, Cross-Racial Identification Errors in Criminal Cases, 69 Cornell L.Rev. 934 (1984). An American Bar Association Report prepared in 2008 explained the problem with cross-racial identification.

> Research results vary but they show a generally consistent pattern. Persons of one racial group may have greater difficulty distinguishing among individual faces of persons in another group than among faces of persons in own group. Persons who primarily interact within their own racial group, especially if they are in the majority group, will better perceive and process the subtlety of facial features of persons within their own racial group than persons of other racial groups. In terms of personal experience, who has never heard the phrase, "they all look alike to me"?

Indeed there is a substantial body of social science data indicating reliability problems with virtually every possible type of identification process. Problems include:

- Where the lineup administrator is involved in the investigation, "the overall probability that administrator expectations do not influence the subject is near zero." New Jersey v. Henderson, 208 N.J. 208, 27 A.3d 872 (2011) (citing analysis of 345 studies).

- Where a weapon is used in the crime, the identifying witness is likely to be impaired by "weapons focus" and thus less likely to reliably identify the perpetrator. Thus, "an analysis of 19 weapon-focus studies involving 2082 identifications found that, on average, identification accuracy decreased approximately 10 percent when a weapon was present." Young v. Conway, 698 F.3d 69 (2nd Cir. 2012).

- High levels of stress have been shown to "induce a defensive mental state that can result in a diminished ability accurately to process and recall events, leading to inaccurate identifications. For example, a review of 16 studies involving 1727 participants found that accurate identifications decreased 22.2% under high stress conditions." *Young,* supra.

- Use of disguises—even subtle ones like hats—can substantially impair accurate identifications. Cutler et. al., The Reliability of Eyewitness Identification: The Role of System and Estimator Variables, 11 Law & Hum. Behavior 233 (1987) (reporting results of an experiment showing that when the "perpetrator" wore a hat, only 27% of participants' identifications were accurate, as opposed to 45% accuracy when no hat was worn).

- Where a witness is instructed to "pick one" of the alternatives, this encourages the witness "to assume that the police have arrested the actual perpetrator and that it would be incorrect to respond that they do not recognize *any* of the individuals in the lineup." United States v. Owens, 682 F.3d 1358 (11th Cir. 2012) (Barkett, J.).

- Multiple viewings of a suspect "can have a powerful corrupting effect on that witness's memory. It creates a risk that the witness will merely identify a suspect based on her past views of him rather than her memory of the relevant event. Meta-analysis has revealed that while 15 percent of witnesses mistakenly identify an innocent person during the first viewing of a lineup, that percentage jumps to 37 percent if the witness previously viewed that innocent person's mug shot." Dennis v. Secretary, PA. Dept. of Corrections, 834 F.3d 263 (3rd Cir. 2016) (McKee, J.).

- Once a witness has made an identification—even an inaccurate one—they can suffer "unconscious transference" or a "mugshot exposure effect" that affects any subsequent identification. This occurs because "the witness is unable to partition his or her memory in such a way as to know that the suspect's increased familiarity is due to the [prior identification procedure] rather than the suspect's presence at the time of the crime." *Young,* supra.

In short, "scientific research reveals that, in particular circumstances, an eyewitness's testimony suffers from intrinsic flaws that are unknown to most jurors and undetectable through the typical modes of examining lay witnesses." *Owens, supra.* The extensive scientific research on the reliability problems inherent in eyewitness identifications has led the National Research Council to conclude that substantial procedures and guarantees should be employed before such identifications are admissible. Some of the suggestions for improvement will be discussed in a later section of this Chapter.

As you will see, the Supreme Court took an interest in eyewitness identification beginning in 1967 but over subsequent years has become more tolerant of suggestive police procedures. Indeed, although eyewitness identification mistakes continue to pose a major problem for American criminal justice, the Supreme Court has largely left the playing field since 1977. There is irony here, given the fact that the search and seizure rules discussed in Chapter 2 and the privilege against self-incrimination and confession cases discussed in Chapter 3 largely deal with attempts to suppress evidence by suspects who often are guilty of serious crime—while eyewitness identification rules deal with attempts to prevent innocent individuals from being convicted. Fortunately, conscientious prosecutors and courts in some jurisdictions have adopted non-constitutional measures—discussed later in this Chapter—to reduce the likelihood of erroneous identifications and the possibility that police suggestiveness will contribute to wrongful convictions. Some federal and state courts have also filled part of the void by giving jury instructions on identification testimony that cautions jurors to view such testimony with care.

As you consider ways of reducing eyewitness errors, be aware that it is not possible to legislate rules that would assure that criminal actors commit crimes in well-lit places and refrain from wearing disguises and using weapons. Thus, the reality is that clever criminals will take steps to make identifications by witnesses and victims more difficult. It is possible, however, to legislate rules that would help to assure that eyewitness errors are not exacerbated by suggestive police procedures.

II. THE JUDICIAL RESPONSE

A. IDENTIFICATIONS AND THE RIGHT TO COUNSEL

1. The *Wade-Gilbert* Rule

With so much evidence casting doubt on the identification techniques commonly used by the police, sooner or later the judiciary was going to have to examine them. One morning in June of 1967, the Court handed down three major opinions designed to protect those suspected and accused of crime from unfair identification tactics.

The first case was the following one:

UNITED STATES V. WADE

Supreme Court of the United States, 1967.
388 U.S. 218.

JUSTICE BRENNAN delivered the opinion of the Court.

The question here is whether courtroom identifications of an accused at trial are to be excluded from evidence because the accused was exhibited to the witnesses before trial at a post-indictment lineup conducted for identification purposes without notice to and in the absence of the accused's appointed counsel.

The federally insured bank in Eustace, Texas, was robbed on September 21, 1964. A man with a small strip of tape on each side on his face entered the bank, pointed a pistol at the female cashier and the vice president, the only persons in the bank at the time, and forced them to fill a pillowcase with the bank's money. The man then drove away with an accomplice who had been waiting in a stolen car outside the bank. On March 23, 1965, an indictment was returned against respondent, Wade, and two others for conspiring to rob the bank, and against Wade and the accomplice for the robbery itself. Wade was arrested on April 2, and counsel was appointed to represent him on April 26. Fifteen days later an FBI agent, without notice to Wade's lawyer, arranged to have the two bank employees observe a lineup made up of Wade and five or six other prisoners and conducted in a courtroom of the local county courthouse. Each person in the line wore strips of tape such as allegedly worn by the robber and upon direction each said something like "put the money in the bag," the words allegedly uttered by the robber. Both bank employees identified Wade in the lineup as the bank robber.

At trial, the two employees, when asked on direct examination if the robber was in the courtroom, pointed to Wade. The prior lineup identification was then elicited from both employees on cross-examination. * * *

[T]he confrontation compelled by the State between the accused and the victim or witnesses to a crime to elicit identification evidence is peculiarly riddled with innumerable dangers and variable factors which might seriously, even crucially, derogate from a fair trial. The vagaries of eyewitness identification are well-known; the annals of criminal law are rife with instances of mistaken identification. * * * A major factor contributing to the high incidence of miscarriage of justice from mistaken identification has been the degree of suggestion inherent in the manner in which the prosecution presents the suspect to witnesses for pretrial identification. * * * Suggestion can be created intentionally or unintentionally in many subtle ways. And the dangers for the suspect are particularly grave when the witness' opportunity for observation was insubstantial, and thus his susceptibility to suggestion the greatest.

Moreover, it is a matter of common experience that, once a witness has picked out the accused at the lineup, he is not likely to go back on his word later on, so that in practice the issue of identity may (in the absence of other relevant evidence) for all practical purposes be determined there and then, before the trial.

The pretrial confrontation for purpose of identification may take the form of a lineup, also known as an "identification parade" or "showup," as in the present case, or presentation of the suspect alone to the witness. * * * It is obvious that risks of suggestion attend either form of confrontation and increase the dangers inhering in eyewitness identification. But as in the case with secret interrogations, there is serious difficulty in depicting what transpires at lineups and other forms of identification confrontations. * * * [T]he defense can seldom reconstruct the manner and mode of lineup identification for judge or jury at trial. Those participating in a lineup with the accused may often be police officers; in any event, the participants' names are rarely recorded or divulged at trial. The impediments to an objective observation are increased when the victim is the witness. * * * [N]either witnesses nor lineup participants are apt to be alert for conditions prejudicial to the suspect. And if they were, it would likely be of scant benefit to the suspect since neither witnesses nor lineup participants are likely to be schooled in the detection of suggestive influences. Improper influences may go undetected by a suspect, guilty or not, who experiences the emotional tension which we might expect in one being confronted with potential accusers. Even when he does observe abuse, if he has a criminal record he may be reluctant to take the stand and open up the admission of prior convictions. Moreover, any protestations by the suspect of the fairness of the lineup made at trial are likely to be in vain; the jury's choice is between the accused's unsupported version and that of the police officers present. In short, the accused's inability effectively to reconstruct at trial any unfairness that occurred at the lineup may deprive him of his only opportunity meaningfully to attack the credibility of the witness' courtroom identification.

* * *

Insofar as the accused's conviction may rest on a courtroom identification in fact the fruit of a suspect pretrial identification which the accused is helpless to subject to effective scrutiny at trial, the accused is deprived of that right of cross-examination which is an essential safeguard to his right to confront the witnesses against him. And even though cross-examination is a precious safeguard to a fair trial, it cannot be viewed as an absolute assurance of accuracy and reliability. Thus in the present context, where so many variables and pitfalls exist, the first line of defense must be the prevention of unfairness and the lessening of the hazards of eyewitness identification at the lineup itself. The trial which might determine the accused's fate may well not be that in the courtroom but that at the pretrial confrontation, with the State aligned against the accused, the witness the sole jury, and the accused unprotected against the overreaching, intentional or unintentional, and with little or no effective appeal from the judgment there rendered by the witness—"that's the man."

Since it appears that there is grave potential for prejudice, intentional or not, in the pretrial lineup, which may not be capable of reconstruction at trial, and since presence of counsel itself can often avert prejudice and assure a meaningful confrontation at trial, there can be little doubt that for Wade the post-indictment lineup was a critical stage of the prosecution at which he was as much entitled to such aid of counsel as at the trial itself. Thus both Wade and his counsel should have been notified of the impending lineup, and counsel's presence should have been a requisite to conduct of the lineup, absent an "intelligent waiver." No substantial countervailing policy considerations have been advanced against the requirement of the presence of counsel. Concern is expressed that the requirement will forestall prompt identifications and result in obstruction of the confrontations. As for the first, we note that in the two cases in which the right to counsel is today held to apply, counsel had already been appointed and no argument is made in either case that notice to counsel would have prejudicially delayed the confrontations. Moreover, we leave open the question whether the presence of substitute counsel might not suffice where notification and presence of the suspect's own counsel would result in prejudicial delay. And to refuse to recognize the right to counsel for fear that counsel will obstruct the course of justice is contrary to the basic assumptions upon which this Court has operated in Sixth Amendment cases. * * * In our view counsel can hardly impede legitimate law enforcement; on the contrary, for the reasons expressed, law enforcement may be assisted by preventing the infiltration of taint in the prosecution's identification evidence.

* * *

We come now to the question whether the denial of Wade's motion to strike the courtroom identification by the bank witnesses at trial because of the absence of his counsel at the lineup required * * * the grant of a new trial at which such evidence is to be excluded. * * * Where, as here, the admissibility of evidence of the lineup identification itself is not involved, a *per se* rule of exclusion of courtroom identification would be unjustified. A rule limited solely to the exclusion of testimony concerning identification at the lineup itself, without regard to admissibility of the courtroom identification, would render the right to counsel an empty one. The lineup is most often used, as in the present case, to crystallize the witnesses' identification of the defendant for future reference. We have already noted that the lineup identification will have that effect. * * * Counsel is then in the predicament in which Wade's counsel found himself—realizing that possible unfairness at the lineup may be the sole means of attack upon the unequivocal courtroom identification, and having to probe in the dark in an attempt to discover and reveal unfairness, while bolstering the government witness' courtroom identification by bringing out and dwelling upon his prior identification. Since counsel's presence at the lineup would equip him to attack not only the lineup identification but the courtroom identification as well, limiting the impact of violation of the right to counsel to exclusion of evidence only of identification at the lineup itself disregards a critical element of that right.

We think it follows that the proper test to be applied in these situations is that quoted in Wong Sun v. United States, 371 U.S. 471, 488, "[W]hether, granting establishment of the primary illegality, the evidence to which instant objection is made has been come at by exploitation of that illegality or instead by means sufficiently distinguishable to be purged of the primary taint." Application of this test in the present context requires consideration of various factors; for example, the prior opportunity to observe the alleged criminal act, the existence of any discrepancy between any pre-lineup description and the defendant's actual description, any identification prior to lineup of another person, the identification by picture of the defendant prior to the lineup, failure to identify the defendant on a prior occasion, and the lapse of time between the alleged act and the lineup identification. It is also relevant to consider those facts which, despite the absence of counsel, are disclosed concerning the conduct of the lineup.

* * *

On the record now before us we cannot make the determination whether the in-court identifications had an independent origin. * * * We therefore think the appropriate procedure to be followed is to vacate the conviction pending a hearing to determine whether the in-court identifications had an independent source, or whether, in any event, the introduction of the evidence was harmless error * * *.

* * *

[Separate opinions by JUSTICE FORTAS (joined by CHIEF JUSTICE WARREN), JUSTICE BLACK, JUSTICE CLARK, and JUSTICE DOUGLAS are omitted.]

JUSTICE WHITE, whom JUSTICE HARLAN and JUSTICE STEWART join, dissenting in part and concurring in part.

The Court has again propounded a broad constitutional rule barring use of a wide spectrum of relevant and probative evidence, solely because a step in its ascertainment or discovery occurs outside the presence of defense counsel. This was the approach of the Court in Miranda v. Arizona. I objected then to what I thought was an uncritical and doctrinaire approach without satisfactory factual foundation. * * *

The Court's opinion is far-reaching. It proceeds first by creating a new *per se* rule of constitutional law: a criminal suspect cannot be subjected to a pretrial identification process in the absence of his counsel without violating the Sixth Amendment. * * *

* * * The Court apparently believes that improper police procedures are so widespread that a broad prophylactic rule must be laid down, requiring the presence of counsel at all pretrial identifications, in order to detect recurring instances of police misconduct. I do not share this pervasive distrust of all official investigations. None of the materials the Court relies upon supports it.

* * *

NOTE ON THE MEANING OF WADE

In *Wade* the lineup was held improper because of the absence of counsel, substitute counsel, or waiver of counsel. But, when Wade was tried, the lineup was not mentioned by the prosecution; its results were not a part of the evidence until brought up by the defense in cross-examination. Thus, the controlling question was whether the *in-court identification* was tainted by the unconstitutional lineup—i.e., whether the in-court identification, which the prosecutor used, would have been made had there been no counsel-free lineup.

Evidence of an out-of-court identification, offered for its truth, was hearsay not subject to any exception at the time of the federal trial in *Wade.* The prosecution could make no direct use of the prior identification unless the defense "opened the door" by attacking the identifying witness at trial. But a federal prosecutor would no longer be so constrained, because Rule 801(d)(1)(C) of the Federal Rules of Evidence provides for admissibility of prior identifications when the person who made the identification is "subject to cross-examination." Some state courts had evidence rules that were more liberal in their approach to admitting prior identifications than the federal rule in effect in *Wade.* One was California in which a companion case to *Wade* arose.

Evidence of the Prior Identification Itself: Gilbert v. California

In Gilbert v. California, 388 U.S. 263 (1967), one of the companion cases to *Wade,* the out-of-court identification made in the absence of counsel was actually admitted in the prosecution's case-in-chief, under a state hearsay exception. Gilbert was convicted of armed bank robbery and the murder of a police officer who entered the bank during the course of the robbery. At the time of the challenged identification procedure, Gilbert had been indicted for robbery. Justice Brennan, writing for the Court, noted that the lineup was on a stage behind bright lights, which prevented those in the line from seeing the audience. Upwards of 100 persons were in the audience, each an eyewitness to one of the several robberies charged to Gilbert. Doubtful witnesses were allowed to call Gilbert out of the lineup to make him repeat a phrase in a particular way or to walk in a particular way. The witnesses talked to each other and made their identifications in each other's presence.

The Supreme Court found a Sixth Amendment violation in *Gilbert* because Gilbert, like Wade, had been subjected to an identification procedure in the absence of counsel, substitute counsel, or waiver of counsel. As in *Wade,* the Court held that the in-court identifications would be excluded unless they proceeded from a source independent of the tainted identification, such as a substantial opportunity to view the perpetrator at the time of the crime. As in *Wade,* the Court remanded for an independent source determination. And as to the use of the out-of-court identifications as evidence, the Court adopted a per se rule of exclusion. Justice Brennan explained:

> Only a *per se* exclusionary rule as to such testimony can be an effective sanction to assure that law enforcement authorities will respect the accused's constitutional right to the presence of his counsel at the critical lineup. In the absence of legislative regulations adequate to avoid the hazards to a fair trial which inhere in lineups as presently conducted, the desirability of deterring the constitutionally objectionable practice must prevail over the undesirability of excluding relevant evidence. That conclusion is buttressed by the consideration that the witness' testimony of his lineup identification will enhance the impact of his in-court identification on the jury and seriously aggravate whatever derogation exists of the accused's right to a fair trial.

The fact that the lineup violated the Sixth Amendment did not assure Gilbert a reversal, because the Court recognized that on remand the state courts could consider whether the constitutional error was harmless.

If Wade and Gilbert were remanded to the trial courts, consider the almost impossible position that those courts would have been in trying to determine "whether, granting establishment of the primary illegality, the evidence to which instant objection is made has been come at by exploitation of that illegality or instead by means sufficiently distinguishable to be purged of the primary taint." Neither Wade nor Gilbert would know what witnesses were told by police or were saying to each other during a lineup. As long as witnesses testify that their identifications at trial were based on their observations of the criminal acts rather than on the invalid lineups, how is a trial court able to question such testimony?

The Role of a Lawyer at a Lineup

The Court in *Wade* and *Gilbert* was concerned about inadequate identification procedures and the lasting effect they may have in some cases. But did the Court, in imposing a counsel requirement, fashion a remedy that suited the problems it identified? The Court's counsel remedy is criticized in Read, Lawyers at Lineups: Constitutional Necessity or Avoidable Extravagance?, 17 U.C.L.A.L.Rev. 339, 362–67 (1969). Read makes the following arguments:

- *Wade* viewed counsel as essentially an observer, i.e., a passive participant.
- A passive observer is unlikely to be able to improve the quality of lineups.
- If the defendant is not a very good witness in a hearing on a lineup because of obvious bias, his lawyer is likely to be almost as biased and thus no better a witness.
- Recording devices would depict the lineup more effectively than testimony by participants.
- Counsel is no more schooled than other participants in psychology and may be insensitive to lineup conditions that might be prejudicial to a defendant.

The presence of a lawyer at a lineup might do *some* good, however. A lawyer who is used to bargaining with law enforcement officials—even though only an observer—might be able to persuade them as to the unfairness of some procedures at lineups. Moreover, knowledge that a lawyer is present may tend to make officials more careful—just like having lawyers present at polling places is thought to make elections fairer. Even without formal interdisciplinary training, lawyers should be careful listeners and should be able to identify certain forms of suggestiveness—e.g., leading questions to witnesses. Finally, cross-examination of identification witnesses is likely to be more effective when the lawyer has actually seen the identification process.

If the lawyer is only a passive observer at the lineup, could police permissibly dispense with a lawyer's presence by simply videotaping the identification and giving the tape to counsel? In United States v. LaPierre, 998 F.2d 1460 (9th Cir.1993), the court refused to decide whether videotaping could ever be a substitute for the presence of counsel. It found, however, that videotaping was inadequate under the facts because the videotape showed only the people in the lineup, and did not record anything that occurred in the witness room.

2. Limits on the Right to Counsel at Identification Procedures

The Sixth Amendment right to counsel invoked in *Wade* applies to all "criminal prosecutions." As seen in the discussion of *Massiah* and *Escobedo* in Chapter 3, the Court has held that a criminal prosecution within the meaning of the Sixth Amendment does not begin until the suspect has been *formally charged* with a crime. Both Wade and Gilbert had been formally charged, although the Court did not emphasize that in its discussion of the need for counsel when the identification might be the real "trial." In Kirby v. Illinois, 406 U.S. 682, the Court held, 5–4, that it would not "extend" its Sixth Amendment reasoning to identifications made before an individual was indicted or otherwise formally charged. Justice Stewart wrote a plurality opinion. Justice Powell concurred in the result.

The plurality opinion in *Kirby* states that "[t]he Due Process Clause of the Fifth and Fourteenth Amendments forbids a lineup that is unnecessarily suggestive and conducive to irreparable mistaken identification." The cases reviewing claims of "unnecessary suggestiveness" under the Due Process Clause are examined in the next section. The bottom line, though, is that the vast majority of identification procedures are conducted *before* a formal charge has been filed. Indeed lineups and other identifications are ordinarily conducted to obtain evidence with which to bring a formal charge. Thus, *Kirby* strips the *Wade* counsel requirement of significant practical effect.

As a practical matter, the Court in *Kirby* must have been concerned with the implications of extending the *Wade* right to counsel rule to all or virtually all identifications. Many identifications are made *on the street* only minutes after the event. Application of the *Wade* rule in these circumstances obviously presents problems; the delay resulting from waiting for counsel to arrive may perversely decrease the reliability of the identification due to the fading memory of witnesses. In light of these problems, the result in *Kirby* is understandable, so long as the Due Process Clause provides meaningful protection against mistaken identifications in cases where the *Wade* rule does not apply. As we will see, though, this has not always been the case.

Does *Kirby* create an incentive for the government to delay an indictment in order to conduct an identification procedure in the absence of counsel? Does a suspect have a constitutional right to be indicted at a certain point? Courts have stated that if adversary proceedings are "deliberately delayed" in order to evade the *Wade* rule, the resulting identification will be invalidated. See, e.g., United States ex rel. Burbank v. Warden, 535 F.2d 361 (7th Cir.1976). However, proving that an indictment was deliberately delayed is difficult, to say the least. See United States ex rel. Hall v. Lane, 804 F.2d 79 (7th Cir.1986) (no evidence that delay in obtaining indictment was caused by bad faith, therefore there was no right to counsel at the pre-indictment identification).

Post-Charge Photographic Identifications: United States v. Ash

In United States v. Ash, 413 U.S. 300 (1973), the Court again restricted the *Wade* rule, holding that a defendant has no right to counsel at a *photographic* identification, whether conducted before or after indictment or formal charge. Justice Blackmun's majority opinion described the right to counsel as a defendant's right to have a spokesperson or advisor while being subject to an identification procedure. The Court stated that "the accused himself is not present at the time of the photographic display and asserts no right to be present" and therefore "no possibility arises that the accused might be misled by his lack of familiarity with the law or overpowered by his professional adversary."

The *Ash* Court noted that photo arrays are unlike lineups, because an "accurate reconstruction" of a photographic array is possible at trial. It concluded that "the opportunity to cure defects at trial causes the pretrial confrontation to cease to be critical." The Court also saw photo displays as a mere preparatory step in the gathering of evidence where the defense counsel had an "equal ability * * * to seek and interview witnesses himself."

Professor Grano, in *Kirby, Biggers,* and *Ash*: Do Any Constitutional Safeguards Remain Against the Danger of Protecting the Innocent?, 72 Mich.L.Rev. 717 (1974), suggests that there are myriad possibilities of suggestiveness in photographic identifications. While it might be true that the photograph array itself can be reproduced at trial, what about the conditions surrounding the identification of the photo?—such as police suggestion as to whom to pick, whether the witness was completely certain in his choice, etc. Doesn't counsel need to know about all of these factors in order to effectively cross-examine the identifying witness? How can counsel know these factors if she wasn't there?

What if a charged defendant is identified in a *photograph of a lineup*? Does the lineup rule of *Wade* control, so that counsel is required? In United States v. Barker, 988 F.2d 77 (9th Cir.1993), the court held that *Ash* rather than *Wade* applied to such an identification. It explained as follows:

> This case is a hybrid: it involves a photograph of a lineup. The fact that the lineup is depicted in the photograph, though, does not call into question the reasoning behind the decision in *Ash*. Counsel must be present where there is a potential "that the accused might be misled by his lack of familiarity with the law or overpowered by his professional adversary," or where counsel would "produce equality in a trial-like adversary confrontation." Here, as in *Ash*, the defendant is not present when the photograph of the lineup is shown and thus cannot be "misled" or "overpowered," and the "adversary mechanism

remains as effective for a photographic display as for other parts of a pretrial interview" whether the photos concerned are of a lineup or an array of suspects.

While it is probably true that the rationale of *Ash* is applicable to all photographic identifications, did the Court in *Ash* adequately state the rationale of *Wade*? Was counsel required in *Wade* in order to keep the *defendant* from being misled or overpowered? Or did the Court think that counsel was required in order to guarantee adequate cross-examination of the identification witnesses? If adequate cross-examination was the goal, why would counsel's presence not be required at a photographic identification?

The significance of *Ash* should be clear. Fair lineups can be difficult to stage, since finding five or so people who resemble the accused sufficiently to be a fair test can be a challenge. Today, it is far simpler for police to create photo arrays. They can input descriptions provided by witnesses—e.g., hair and eye color, race, height, weight, etc.—and a computer can generate photos of suspects who have been previously booked. Since counsel need *never* be present during a photo identification procedure, what little was left of *Wade* after *Kirby* is rendered largely irrelevant.

B. DUE PROCESS LIMITATIONS ON IDENTIFICATION EVIDENCE

1. The Foundations of a Due Process Test

Stovall v. Denno

On the same day that it decided *Wade* and *Gilbert,* the Court ruled that those decisions applied prospectively only (which meant that only Wade and Gilbert would get the benefit of the decisions and that the counsel requirement would only apply to future lineups or showups). Stovall v. Denno, 388 U.S. 293 (1967) (applying retroactivity analysis that has since been rejected by the Court; see Chapter 1). The important point from *Stovall* today is not about retroactivity but rather about what protections exist for identification procedures where the right to counsel does not apply. The Court in *Stovall* held that a *due process-fundamental fairness* approach would be used in assessing identification procedures that are not governed by *Wade* and *Gilbert.* As stated above, after *Kirby* and *Ash,* the application of *Wade* and *Gilbert* is limited to post-indictment corporeal identifications. The due process test set forth in *Stovall,* and developed in later cases discussed below, therefore governs the admissibility of most identification evidence. Justice Brennan, again writing for the Court, described the relevant facts in *Stovall*:

> Dr. Paul Behrendt was stabbed to death in the kitchen of his home in Garden City, Long Island, about midnight August 23, 1961. Dr. Behrendt's wife, also a physician, had followed her husband to the kitchen and jumped at the assailant. He knocked her to the floor and stabbed her 11 times. The police found a shirt on the kitchen floor and keys in a pocket which they traced to petitioner. They arrested him on the afternoon of August 24. An arraignment was promptly held but was postponed until petitioner could retain counsel.
>
> Mrs. Behrendt was hospitalized for major surgery to save her life. The police, without affording petitioner time to retain counsel, arranged with her surgeon to permit them to bring petitioner to her hospital room about noon of August 25, the day after the surgery. Petitioner was handcuffed to one of five police officers who, with two members of the staff of the District Attorney, brought him to the hospital room. Petitioner was the only Negro in the room. Mrs. Behrendt identified him from her hospital bed after being asked by an officer whether he "was the man" and after petitioner repeated at the direction of an officer a "few words for voice identification." None of the witnesses could recall the words that were used. Mrs. Behrendt and the officers testified at the trial to her identification of the petitioner in the hospital room, and she also made an in-court identification of petitioner in the courtroom.
>
> Petitioner was convicted and sentenced to death. * * *

After holding that *Wade* and *Gilbert* would not be applied retroactively, the Court considered Stovall's contention that "in any event the confrontation conducted in this case was so unnecessarily suggestive and conducive to irreparable mistaken identification that he was denied due process of law." Justice Brennan analyzed this question by focusing on whether it was necessary for the police to act as they did.

> The practice of showing suspects singly to persons for the purpose of identification, and not as part of a lineup, has been widely condemned. However, a claimed violation of due process of law in the conduct of a confrontation depends on the totality of the circumstances surrounding it, and the record in the present case reveals that the showing of Stovall to Mrs. Behrendt in an immediate hospital confrontation was imperative.

Justice Brennan then quoted approvingly from the Court of Appeals' decision finding no due process violation:

> "Here was the only person in the world who could possibly exonerate Stovall. Her words, and only her words, 'He is not the man' could have resulted in freedom for Stovall. The hospital was not far distant from the courthouse and jail. No one knew how long Mrs. Behrendt might live. Faced with the responsibility of identifying the attacker, with the

need for immediate action and with the knowledge that Mrs. Behrendt could not visit the jail, the police followed the only feasible procedure and took Stovall to the hospital room. Under these circumstances, the usual police station lineup, which Stovall now argues he should have had, was out of the question."

Note that the Court in *Stovall* did not mention the possible unreliability of the identification, even though Stovall was handcuffed and was the only African-American man in the room. Does the Court mean that even *unreliable* identifications are constitutionally permissible so long as the police have a legitimate excuse for conducting a suggestive identification? Conversely, if the police had no good reason for acting as they did, would the Court then be concerned about whether the identification was reliable? These questions were taken up by the Court in such cases as Manson v. Brathwaite and Perry v. New Hampshire, discussed below.

Note also that Mrs. Behrendt, the witness who made the identification in *Stovall,* actually survived her attack and testified at trial. Of course, her survival was a happy event; but could this lead you to question whether there was really such an emergency as to excuse the suggestive activity in *Stovall?*

Part of the reason the hospital show-up was held permissible was that this was the only procedure that could have resulted in exoneration for Stovall. But if that is the case, why not let Stovall decide whether he wants to be subject to a show-up identification in handcuffs? If Stovall had been given the option to "exonerate" himself in this way, what do you think he would have done?

Permissible Suggestiveness?

Cases arise from time to time in which the government argues, as in *Stovall,* that there was a legitimate excuse for conducting a suggestive identification procedure. Sometimes these claims are rebuffed. For example, in Neil v. Biggers, 409 U.S. 188 (1972), Biggers was identified in a one-on-one showup by the victim of a rape. The government offered an excuse for conducting the one-on-one showup: the officers tried to conduct a lineup, but when they checked the city jail and the juvenile home for people who looked similar to Biggers, they found no one at either place fitting the suspect's "unusual physical description." The Court stated that it was "inclined to agree with the courts below that the police did not exhaust all possibilities in seeking persons physically comparable to respondent." Yet in *Biggers*, the unnecessarily suggestive identification was nonetheless held admissible, because the identification in *Biggers* preceded the *Stovall* decision in which the Court for the first time held that a *due process-fundamental fairness* approach would be used in assessing identification procedures not governed by *Wade* and *Gilbert*.

In assessing the necessity of suggestive procedures, most courts have held that street identifications held immediately after a crime are "necessarily" suggestive. Whenever a court finds necessary suggestiveness, it does not examine the reliability of the identification. A typical analysis is found in United States v. Bautista, 23 F.3d 726 (2nd Cir.1994), a case in which the suspects were presented, in handcuffs, for an identification by a confidential informant (CI) immediately after a drug raid:

> We find that the presentation of the suspects to the CI immediately following the raid was not *unnecessarily* suggestive. * * * [A] prompt showing of a detained suspect at the scene of arrest has a very valid function: to prevent the mistaken arrest of innocent persons. Indeed, this court has instructed law enforcement officials that where an officer has or should have doubts whether a detained suspect is in fact the person sought, the officer must make immediate reasonable efforts to confirm the suspect's identity.
>
> * * *
>
> The fact that the suspects were handcuffed, in the custody of law enforcement officers, and illuminated by flashlights * * * did not render the pre-trial identification procedure unnecessarily suggestive. In this case, handcuffs, custody, and flashlights were all necessary incidents of an on-the-scene identification immediately following a night-time narcotics raid. Because the on-the-scene identification was necessary to allow the officers to release the innocent, the incidents of that identification were also necessary.

See also United States v. Martinez, 462 F.3d 903 (8th Cir.2006) ("Police officers need not limit themselves to station house lineups when an opportunity for a quick, on-the-scene identification arises. Such identifications are essential to free innocent suspects and to inform the police if further investigation is necessary."); Brisco v. Ercole, 565 F.3d 80 (2nd Cir. 2009) (show-up immediately after the crime was not unnecessarily suggestive: "If no identification was made at the showup, the officers could resume their search for the offender"); United States v. Sanders, 708 F.3d 976 (7th Cir. 2013) (identification of the perpetrator from photos found in a car at the scene was not unnecessary: "It would have taken significantly more time for the police to leave the scene, go to the station house, locate photos similar to those found in the car, and return. A dangerous suspect could have used that extra time to facilitate his escape.").

2. Applying the Due Process Test

Simmons v. United States

In Simmons v. United States, 390 U.S. 377 (1968), a bank was robbed by two men. Andrews and Simmons were suspected. The FBI had shown the bank employees at least six pictures, mostly group photos of Andrews, Simmons, and others, and some individual snapshots of Simmons and Andrews. Simmons and Andrews were identified; the witnesses identified Simmons at his trial, but the prosecution made no mention of the pre-trial identification. Simmons challenged the identification procedures under the Due Process Clause. The Court stated that the due process test protects against identifications that are "so impermissibly suggestive as to give rise to a very substantial likelihood of irreparable misidentification." Applying that test to the facts, the Court emphasized the following factors: the officers had a pressing need for fast action; Simmons was readily identified by the witnesses, while Andrews was not, even though Andrews was in many of the same pictures as Simmons; the witnesses had an excellent opportunity to observe the robbery and the perpetrators; and the identification was made shortly after the robbery.

The *Simmons* Court found no due process violation "even though the identification procedure employed may have in some respects fallen short of the ideal." The Court concluded that the witnesses' bases for making the identification were so strong that their identifications were unaffected by any police suggestiveness.

Violation of Due Process: Foster v. California

In Foster v. California, 394 U.S. 440 (1969), the Court found for the first time—and so far the only time—that a police procedure was so impermissibly suggestive as to create a substantial risk of mistaken identification under the Due Process Clause. The eyewitness was called to the station to view a three-person lineup. Foster, who was six feet tall, was placed between two men who were both six inches shorter. Only Foster wore a jacket similar to that of the perpetrator. The witness could not positively identify Foster. Foster was then brought into an office for a one-on-one showup. The witness could still not make a positive identification. A week later, the witness viewed a second lineup. Only Foster remained from the first lineup. At this point, the witness positively identified Foster. This identification was admitted at trial pursuant to the California hearsay exception that also applied in *Gilbert*, and the witness also identified Foster at trial.

The Supreme Court stated that the "suggestive elements in this identification procedure made it all but inevitable that [the witness] would identify petitioner whether or not he was in fact the man," and that the procedure "so undermined the reliability of the eyewitness identification as to violate due process." The Court held that both the in-court and out-of-court identifications were improperly admitted, because both were tainted by the police suggestiveness.

3. Unnecessary Police Suggestiveness Is Not Enough

MANSON V. BRATHWAITE

Supreme Court of the United States, 1977.
432 U.S. 98.

MR. JUSTICE BLACKMUN delivered the opinion of the Court.

This case presents the issue as to whether the Due Process Clause of the Fourteenth Amendment compels the exclusion, in a state criminal trial, apart from any consideration of reliability, of pretrial identification evidence obtained by a police procedure that was both suggestive and unnecessary. This Court's decisions in Stovall v. Denno and Neil v. Biggers are particularly implicated.

* * *

Jimmy D. Glover, a full-time trooper of the Connecticut State Police, in 1970 was assigned to the Narcotics Division in an undercover capacity. On May 5 of that year, about 7:45 p.m., e.d.t., and while there was still daylight, Glover and Henry Alton Brown, an informant, went to an apartment building at 201 Westland, in Hartford, for the purpose of purchasing narcotics from "Dickie Boy" Cicero, a known narcotics dealer. Cicero, it was thought, lived on the third floor of that apartment building. Glover and Brown entered the building, observed by backup Officers D'Onofrio and Gaffey, and proceeded by stairs to the third floor. Glover knocked at the door of one of the two apartments served by the stairway. The area was illuminated by natural light from a window in the third floor hallway. The door was opened 12 to 18 inches in response to the knock. Glover observed a man standing at the door and, behind him, a woman. Brown identified himself. Glover then asked for "two things" of narcotics. The man at the door held out his hand, and Glover gave him two $10 bills. The door closed. Soon the man returned and handed Glover two glassine bags. While the door was open, Glover stood within two feet of the person from whom he made the purchase and observed his face. Five to seven minutes elapsed from the time the door first opened until it closed the second time.

Glover and Brown then left the building. This was about eight minutes after their arrival. Glover drove to headquarters where he described the seller to D'Onofrio and Gaffey. * * * He described him as being "a colored man, approximately five feet eleven inches tall, dark complexion, black hair, short Afro style, and having high cheekbones, and of heavy build. He was wearing at the time blue pants and a plaid shirt." D'Onofrio, suspecting from this description that respondent might be the seller, obtained a photograph of respondent from the Records Division of the Hartford Police Department. He left it at Glover's office. D'Onofrio was not acquainted with respondent personally, but did know him by sight and had seen him "[s]everal times" prior to May 5. Glover, when alone, viewed the photograph for the first time upon his return to headquarters on May 7; he identified the person shown as the one from whom he had purchased the narcotics. * * * No explanation was offered by the prosecution for the failure to utilize a photographic array or to conduct a lineup.

[The photo identification was admitted at trial, and Glover also identified the defendant at trial. The defendant was convicted, but the Second Circuit reversed the conviction on the ground that the officers engaged in impermissible suggestiveness during the identification procedure. It did not matter to the Second Circuit that the identification might have been made despite, rather than because of, the suggestive procedure.]

[The Court discusses its precedents, all of which have been discussed, supra.]

* * *

Petitioner at the outset acknowledges that "the procedure in the instant case was suggestive [because only one photograph was used] and unnecessary" [because there was no emergency or exigent circumstance]. The respondent, in agreement with the Court of Appeals, proposes a *per se* rule of exclusion that he claims is dictated by the demands of the Fourteenth Amendment's guarantee of due process. * * *

Since the decision in *Biggers,* the Courts of Appeals appear to have developed at least two approaches to [identification] evidence. The first, or *per se* approach, employed by the Second Circuit in the present case, focuses on the procedures employed and requires exclusion of the out-of-court identification evidence, without regard to reliability, whenever it has been obtained through unnecessarily suggestive confrontation procedures. The justifications advanced are the elimination of evidence of uncertain reliability, deterrence of the police and prosecutors, and the stated "fair assurance against the awful risks of misidentification."

The second, or more lenient, approach is one that continues to rely on the totality of the circumstances. It permits the admission of the confrontation evidence if, despite the suggestive aspect, the out-of-court identification possesses certain features of reliability. Its adherents feel that the *per se* approach is not mandated by the Due Process Clause of the Fourteenth Amendment. This second approach, in contrast to the other, is *ad hoc* and serves to limit the societal costs imposed by a sanction that excludes relevant evidence from consideration and evaluation by the trier of fact.

The respondent here stresses * * * the need for deterrence of improper identification practice, a factor he regards as pre-eminent. Photographic identification, it is said, continues to be needlessly employed. * * * He argues that a totality rule cannot be expected to have a significant deterrent impact; only a strict rule of exclusion will have direct and immediate impact on law enforcement agents. Identification evidence is so convincing to the jury that sweeping exclusionary rules are required. * * *

There are, of course, several interests to be considered and taken into account. The driving force behind United States v. Wade and Gilbert v. California (right to counsel at a post-indictment lineup), and *Stovall,* all decided on the same day, was the Court's concern with the problems of eyewitness identification. Usually the witness must testify about an encounter with a total stranger under circumstances of emergency or emotional stress. The witness' recollection of the stranger can be distorted easily by the circumstances or by later actions of the police. Thus, *Wade* and its companion cases reflect the concern that the jury not hear eyewitness testimony unless that evidence has aspects of reliability. It must be observed that both approaches before us are responsive to this concern. The *per se* rule, however, goes too far since its application automatically and peremptorily, and without consideration of alleviating factors, keeps evidence from the jury that is reliable and relevant.

The second factor is deterrence. Although the *per se* approach has the more significant deterrent effect, the totality approach also has an influence on police behavior. The police will guard against unnecessarily suggestive procedures under the totality rule, as well as the *per se* one, for fear that their actions will lead to the exclusion of identifications as unreliable.

The third factor is the effect on the administration of justice. Here the *per se* approach suffers serious drawbacks. Since it denies the trier reliable evidence, it may result, on occasion, in the guilty going free. Also, because of its rigidity, the *per se* approach may make error by the trial judge more likely than the totality approach. And in those cases in which the admission of identification evidence is error under the *per se* approach but not under the totality approach—cases in which the identification is reliable despite an unnecessarily suggestive identification procedure—reversal is a Draconian sanction. Certainly, inflexible rules of exclusion, that may frustrate rather than promote justice, have not been viewed recently by this Court with unlimited enthusiasm.

* * *

We therefore conclude that reliability is the linchpin in determining the admissibility of identification testimony for both pre-and post-*Stovall* confrontations. The factors to be considered are set out in *Biggers*. These include the opportunity of the witness to view the criminal at the time of the crime, the witness' degree of attention, the accuracy of his prior description of the criminal, the level of certainty demonstrated at the confrontation, and the time between the crime and the confrontation. Against these factors is to be weighed the corrupting effect of the suggestive identification itself.

V

We turn, then, to the facts of this case and apply the analysis:

1. *The opportunity to view.* Glover testified that for two to three minutes he stood at the apartment door, within two feet of the respondent. The door opened twice, and each time the man stood at the door. The moments passed, the conversation took place, and payment was made. Glover looked directly at his vendor. It was near sunset, to be sure, but the sun had not yet set, so it was not dark or even dusk or twilight. Natural light from outside entered the hallway through a window. There was natural light, as well, from inside the apartment.

2. *The degree of attention.* Glover was not a casual or passing observer, as is so often the case with eyewitness identification. Trooper Glover was a trained police officer on duty—and specialized and dangerous duty—when he called at the third floor of 201 Westland in Hartford on May 5, 1970. Glover himself was a Negro and unlikely to perceive only general features of "hundreds of Hartford black males," as the Court of Appeals stated. It is true that Glover's duty was that of ferreting out narcotics offenders and that he would be expected in his work to produce results. But it is also true that, as a specially trained, assigned, and experienced officer, he could be expected to pay scrupulous attention to detail, for he knew that subsequently he would have to find and arrest his vendor. In addition, he knew that his claimed observations would be subject later to close scrutiny and examination at any trial.

3. *The accuracy of the description.* Glover's description was given to D'Onofrio within minutes after the transaction. It included the vendor's race, his height, his build, the color and style of his hair, and the high cheekbone facial feature. It also included clothing the vendor wore. No claim has been made that respondent did not possess the physical characteristics so described. D'Onofrio reacted positively at once. Two days later, when Glover was alone, he viewed the photograph D'Onofrio produced and identified its subject as the narcotics seller.

4. *The witness' level of certainty.* There is no dispute that the photograph in question was that of respondent. Glover, in response to a question whether the photograph was that of the person from whom he

made the purchase, testified: "There is no question whatsoever." This positive assurance was repeated.

5. *The time between the crime and the confrontation.* Glover's description of his vendor was given to D'Onofrio within minutes of the crime. The photographic identification took place only two days later. We do not have here the passage of weeks or months between the crime and the viewing of the photograph.

These indicators of Glover's ability to make an accurate identification are hardly outweighed by the corrupting effect of the challenged identification itself. Although identifications arising from single-photograph displays may be viewed in general with suspicion, we find in the instant case little pressure on the witness to acquiesce in the suggestion that such a display entails. D'Onofrio had left the photograph at Glover's office and was not present when Glover first viewed it two days after the event. There thus was little urgency and Glover could view the photograph at his leisure. And since Glover examined the photograph alone, there was no coercive pressure to make an identification arising from the presence of another. The identification was made in circumstances allowing care and reflection. * * *

Surely, we cannot say that under all the circumstances of this case there is "a very substantial likelihood of irreparable misidentification." Short of that point, such evidence is for the jury to weigh. We are content to rely upon the good sense and judgment of American juries, for evidence with some element of untrustworthiness is customary grist for the jury mill. Juries are not so susceptible that they cannot measure intelligently the weight of identification testimony that has some questionable feature.

* * *

JUSTICE STEVENS, concurring.

* * * [I]n evaluating the admissibility of particular identification testimony it is sometimes difficult to put other evidence of guilt entirely to one side. Mr. Justice Blackmun's opinion for the Court carefully avoids this pitfall and correctly relies only on appropriate indicia of the reliability of the identification itself. Although I consider the factual question in this case extremely close, I am persuaded that the Court has resolved it properly.

JUSTICE MARSHALL, with whom JUSTICE BRENNAN joins, dissenting.

Today's decision can come as no surprise to those who have been watching the Court dismantle the protections against mistaken eyewitness testimony erected a decade ago * * *. But it is still distressing to see the Court virtually ignore the teaching of experience embodied in those decisions and blindly uphold the conviction of a defendant who may well be innocent.

* * *

[T]he Court gives passing consideration to the dangers of eyewitness identification recognized in the *Wade* trilogy. It concludes, however, that the grave risk of error does not justify adoption of the *per se* approach because that would too often result in exclusion of relevant evidence. In my view, this conclusion totally ignores the lessons of *Wade.* * * *

Finally, the Court errs in its assessment of the relative impact of the two approaches on the administration of justice. * * * [O]ther exclusionary rules have been criticized for preventing jury consideration of relevant and usually reliable evidence in order to serve interests unrelated to guilt or innocence, such as discouraging illegal searches or denial of counsel. Suggestively obtained eyewitness testimony is excluded, in contrast, precisely because of its unreliability and concomitant irrelevance.

* * *

[Justice Marshall applies the majority's "totality of circumstances" test to the facts of the case. He points out that the transaction occurred quickly and the opportunity for observation was brief, argues that the witness's degree of certainty is worthless as a guarantee of reliability, notes that the greatest memory loss occurs within hours after an event, and concluded that Glover's description "was actually no more than a general summary of the seller's appearance."]

QUESTIONS AFTER MANSON

In evaluating who has the better of the argument in *Manson* on whether exclusion should occur *solely* because of police suggestiveness, consider the following hypothetical. A victim of a kidnaping, who lived in close quarters with the perpetrator for six months, finally escapes. He contacts the police and describes the kidnapper in perfect detail, including a distinctive scar on the kidnapper's forehead. The defendant is apprehended, and the victim views him in a one-on-one show-up, while the defendant is in handcuffs and prison clothing. The defendant has the distinctive scar described by the victim. The victim immediately identifies the defendant with absolute certainty. The police had no reason for failing to conduct a lineup.

Under the per se rule rejected in *Manson,* this identification would be inadmissible; but the in-court identification would be admissible because it proceeded from an independent source. Does this make sense? One could argue that it does because otherwise police will not be deterred from conducting suggestive identifications. Moreover, the cost of exclusion to the state is not significant because the in-court identification will still be admissible, and the police could always conduct a lineup *after* this suggestive procedure. The identification from that subsequent lineup, like the in-court identification, would proceed from an independent source and would therefore be admissible. But if the rule of exclusion can be so easily evaded, is it worth having? Ultimately, the question is whether the *per se* rule would be a more effective deterrent than the totality of circumstances test chosen by the Court. There is certainly strong evidence that the *Manson* test, at least as applied by the courts, does little to deter the police from using suggestive identification procedures. For example, the Court has denounced the use of unnecessary show-ups in most of the cases arising between *Wade* and *Braithwaite*. Yet, in 1990, the court in Rodriguez v. Young, 906 F.2d 1153 (7th Cir.), noted with distress "that we continue to review cases both of showups and other suggestive procedures," and that "in few of these cases do we ever find an explanation, by the prosecution, for the failure to conduct a lineup." Of course, the court in *Rodriguez* held that the identification was admissible despite the police suggestiveness (because the witness had a good view of the suspect at the time of the crime), so it will continue to hear more such cases.

In thinking about *Manson*, it can be useful to focus on two things the Court said and ask which way they cut. First, "[t]he police will guard against unnecessarily suggestive procedures under the totality rule, as well as the *per se* one, for fear that their actions will lead to the exclusion of identifications as unreliable." This assertion assumes a meaningful totality review and a positive relationship between the *Manson* factors and reliability. As you examine more cases below, decide how meaningful the review seems to be and how likely the *Manson* factors are to lead to a sound decision on suggestiveness. Second, "the *per se* approach suffers serious drawbacks"; "[s]ince it denies the trier reliable evidence, it may result, on occasion, in the guilty going free." But is it not equally true that "it may result, on occasion, in the innocent going free" rather than being convicted because of unnecessarily suggestive identification procedures?

4. State Courts Reject *Manson*

Some state courts have called the reasoning of *Manson* into question and have required trial judges to take special care in assessing the reliability of eyewitness testimony. Two early cases are State v. Lawson, 352 Ore. 724, 291 P.3d 673 (2012); and State v. Henderson, 208 N.J. 208, 27 A.3d 872 (2011).

Among the state courts seizing the mantle of New Federalism in this context is the Supreme Court of New Mexico. In the following case, that court holds that the Due Process Clause of the New Mexico Constitution requires more than the minimalist protections afforded by *Manson*. The full opinion contains references to authorities (not included here) that will be of interest to anyone doing work on identifications.

STATE V. MARTINEZ

Supreme Court of New Mexico, 2018.
478 P.3d 880.

VIGIL, CHIEF JUSTICE.

Convicted of two counts of murder in the first degree, Defendant Ricardo Martinez seeks reversal and a new trial on grounds that the district court erred by denying his motion to suppress out-of-court and in-court identification testimony * * *.

* * * Defendant challenges the continued viability of the prevailing federal rule, as articulated in *Manson v. Brathwaite*, 432 U.S. 98 (1977), governing the admission of identification evidence. Under *Manson*, courts apply a two-part test to determine the admissibility of eyewitness identification evidence, addressing first whether police identification procedures were "unnecessarily suggestive" and, if so, weighing specified factors in deciding the "linchpin" issue of whether the eyewitness identification was nonetheless sufficiently reliable to satisfy federal due process requirements. Although the *Manson* reliability test has been widely adopted among state courts, including our own, it has come to face ever-increasing criticism from legal scholars as a result of major advances in scientific knowledge of eyewitness memory, perception, and recall, knowledge that contradicts many of the analytical assumptions underlying the rule.

In light of the significant, recurrent, and deeply troubling problems caused by unnecessarily suggestive, police-arranged identification procedures, we take this opportunity to consider our state constitutional jurisprudence as it relates to the admission of this type of powerful yet problematic evidence in New Mexico courts. We ultimately hold that the *Manson* test does not satisfy due process under Article II, Section 18 of the New Mexico Constitution, and we adopt standards that must be satisfied before such evidence is admissible.

* * *

II. Discussion

A. Admissibility of the Eyewitness Identification Evidence

* * *

4. Defendant's Argument under the New Mexico Constitution

* * *

a. The Scientific Research

The reliability and significance of post-*Manson* scientific studies addressing the psychological factors affecting eyewitness identifications are now widely acknowledged by the courts. * * *

Scientific research calls into serious question the continued efficacy of the legal framework established in *Manson* and currently applied in New Mexico. *See, e.g.*, Brandon L. Garrett, *Eyewitnesses and Exclusion*, 65 Vand. L. Rev. 451, 468–69 (2012) ("Eyewitness identifications are designed to be a test of a witness's memory."). However, since the *Manson* decision, "[a] now vast body of social science research has demonstrated that most of the five *Manson* 'reliability' factors do not correlate at all with the reliability of an eyewitness's identification." *Garrett, supra*, at 468–69. In addition, due to the powerful effect eyewitness identification has on juries, especially when stated in a confident manner, modern scholars now recognize that mistaken identification evidence is the most significant cause of wrongful convictions in the United States. * * *

The scientific literature demonstrates multiple reasons why eyewitness testimony can be erroneous despite the fact that a witness testifies "in good faith and with a high degree of confidence," as we now summarize. Robert A. Wise, Clifford S. Fishman & Martin A. Safer, *How to Analyze the Accuracy of Eyewitness Testimony in a Criminal Case*, 42 Conn. L. Rev. 435, 454–55 (2009). * * *

[The following paragraph is from the Wise, et al. article. The five paragraphs that follow it cite to the article.]

> [A]n eyewitness's memory of a crime is not stored like a videotape that the eyewitness can replay to produce an exact record of the crime. It frequently does not contain the degree of detail sought by criminal investigators. Instead, when an eyewitness recalls a crime, he or she unconsciously reconstructs his or her memory of the crime. In unconsciously reconstructing his or her memory of the crime, the eyewitness unknowingly fills in the gaps in his or her factual memory of the crime based on such factors as the eyewitness's expectations, attitude, beliefs, and knowledge of similar events. These different sources of information are automatically blended together in the eyewitness's memory to produce an account of the crime that is apparently seamless and coherent but that may contain inaccuracies.

In addition, eyewitnesses are biased. An eyewitness's biases influence not only what the eyewitness "recalls about a crime, but also what the eyewitness perceives" and encodes into memory about the crime. * * *

Eyewitness testimony may also be erroneous due to the "[m]isinformation [e]ffect." "Because an eyewitness's memory of a crime is a reconstructive process, it can be altered by information that the eyewitness learns after the crime from other sources such as other eyewitnesses, the police, the prosecutor, and the media." This kind of "post-event information not only affects an eyewitness's memory of the crime, but it may also impair his or her ability to identify the perpetrator of the crime."

A fourth reason for misidentification stems from "[s]ource [m]onitoring [e]rrors." This category of cognitive error occurs when eyewitnesses become "confused about where they learned information about a crime or where they saw an individual." These errors lead to misattribution of information that eyewitnesses believe they saw during the crime to other sources they encountered later. There is, in addition, "[h]indsight [b]ias," which refers to the cognitive error that occurs when an individual knows how an event turns out and this knowledge influences the individual's memory of what the individual believes about what actually occurred. It follows that when "an eyewitness learns that a suspect has been indicted and is going to be tried for a crime, this information alters an eyewitness's memory of the crime and what the eyewitness remembers . . . or . . . was thinking when the crime occurred."

"Eyewitness [o]verconfidence" and tendencies toward "[r]elative [j]udgment" in making identifications also contribute to erroneous misidentifications. In general, "[p]eople tend to overestimate the accuracy of their perceptions and memory[,]" and as such, "eyewitnesses are likely to be overconfident about the accuracy of their account of the crime and their identification of the suspect as the perpetrator of the crime." Like memory, confidence in a memory is malleable, and post event information can increase an eyewitness's confidence in a false memory. Similarly, in the context of a lineup or photo array, eyewitnesses are likely to make a relative judgment in identifying a perpetrator such that eyewitnesses will choose the person "who most closely resembles their memory of the perpetrator of the crime." Relative judgments stem from two assumptions frequently made by eyewitnesses: (1) "law enforcement would not conduct a lineup if they did not have a suspect," and (2) "eyewitnesses feel pressure from law enforcement, relatives, friends, and themselves to make an identification."

Often lineups are done in such a way that the eyewitness's attention is drawn to the suspect. * * * Just as accurate scientific data depends on application of a scientific method free of bias and other extraneous factors, * * * extracting reliable eyewitness identification evidence "depends in part on the use of proper scientific procedures." * * *

Apart from the foregoing summary, a brief overview of the existing science reveals a near consensus among experts that certain factors may inherently impair the ability of witnesses to accurately process what they observe. These factors, described as "variables," fall into two categories: (1) system variables—those surrounding the identification procedure itself—which largely lie within the exclusive control of law enforcement officers, and (2) estimator variables—those peculiar to the circumstances of the crime and a witness's observation of it—over which the criminal justice system lacks control. System variables bear on the suggestiveness of an identification procedure while estimator variables are used to evaluate an identification's reliability.

With respect to system variables, psychological studies provide valuable insights for developing best practices for the fair, proper, and nonsuggestive administration of identification procedures. The relevant science shows, for instance, that it is preferable for a lineup identification, whether photographic or corporeal, to be conducted by a "blind" administrator—referring to one who does not know the identity of the suspect or where the suspect is located during the procedure—so as to avoid influence over the witness regarding which person to select. * * *

* * *

Scientific research also offers important insights into the workings of a wide array of estimator variables that are prone to diminish the reliability of an eyewitness identification. Prominently discussed in the scientific literature are variables relating to the focus of a witness's attention during the commission of a crime, a factor which is often dependent on a witness's level of stress or distraction at the time. * * *

A frequently discussed aspect of the "[w]itness [a]ttention" variable is what the scientific literature and case law describe as the "weapon-focus effect," the empirically tested theory that "the visible presence of a weapon during an encounter negatively affects memory for faces and identification accuracy because witnesses tend to focus their attention on the weapon instead of on the face or appearance of the perpetrator, or on other details of the encounter." * * *

* * *

b. The legal literature

The legal literature is replete with discussions of the doctrinal and scientific shortcomings of the *Manson* reliability test and the significant threat posed to the integrity of our criminal justice system by misidentifications engendered by the Manson rule. * * *

As to the analytic weaknesses of the *Manson* rule, commentators have expressed the view that the United States Supreme Court's two-part test—which relegates unnecessary suggestiveness to a threshold inquiry and focuses primarily on five fixed "reliability" factors—is untethered to any sound scientific knowledge* * * . At a minimum, there appears to be broad consensus among commentators that three of the five *Manson* factors—view, attention, and certainty—are insufficiently independent from each other and from the suggestiveness of a given identification procedure to be accurate predictors of reliability and accuracy. * * *

These concerns have prompted commentators to call for the adoption of new, science-driven admissibility standards in place of the reliability-based formulation set out in *Manson** * * .

Based on the research, legal scholars in the field of eyewitness identification evidence now also advocate for state courts to adopt a per se exclusionary rule for suggestively obtained eyewitness testimony * * * . * * *

5. State court decisions modifying or departing from the *Manson* test

* * *

Some jurisdictions, though adhering to *Manson*'s reliability-based framework, have taken modest measures to refine or expand upon *Manson*'s reliability criteria to be more closely aligned with modern empirical realities. * * *

Other jurisdictions have undertaken more sweeping reforms. * * *

The developing case law of Massachusetts and New York is particularly useful in informing our analysis. Each of these jurisdictions has rejected outright *Manson*'s traditional two-pronged test—which inquires whether a pretrial identification is reliable in spite of the suggestive procedures under which it was made—in favor of a bright-line, per se exclusionary rule triggered on the basis of suggestiveness alone.

* * *

A significant feature of this Massachusetts jurisprudence is the Supreme Judicial Court's establishment of a protocol for the police to follow in conducting a photographic identification procedure, *see* Commonwealth v. Silva-Santiago, 906 N.E.2d 299, 312 (2009). The protocol was adopted as part of the court's "superintendence . . . authority to regulate the presentation of evidence in court proceedings" and reflects the court's "recognition that there is a near consensus in the relevant scientific community that the failure to follow such a protocol increases the risk of misidentification." Commonwealth v. Thomas, 68 N.E.3d 1161, 1168–69 (2017).

New York, for its part, has also adopted a per se exclusionary rule in lieu of the traditional *Manson* standard, based on concerns over the inherent frailties of eyewitness identification evidence that mirror the concerns expressed by Massachusetts courts* * * . In *People v. Adams*, 423 N.E.2d 379, 383–84 (1981), the Court of Appeals, New York's court of last resort, refused to adopt the *Manson* reliability test, finding it incompatible with the due process protections afforded by its state constitution. In concluding that evidence of the identification procedure there at issue—a police "station house" show-up—was improperly admitted at trial, the

Adams court relied solely on the inherent suggestiveness of the procedure * * *.

6. The New Mexico Accurate Eyewitness Identification Act

State courts are not alone in their responses to the scientific research. A number of state legislatures have also taken measures to ensure that current scientific standards are taken into account in regulating the manner in which identification procedures are administered. * * *

Our Legislature has recently joined those ranks in taking remedial action, by enacting the Accurate Eyewitness Identification Act (the Act), as part of a comprehensive criminal justice reform bill which became effective July 1, 2019. *See* 2019 N.M. Laws, ch. 211, §§ 12–15 (compiled as NMSA 1978, §§ 29–3B–1 to –4 (2019)).

* * *

7. The *Manson* rule violates due process under the New Mexico Constitution

The Massachusetts and New York case authorities discussed in section 5 highlight the importance of judicial flexibility in addressing shortcomings in existing law that develop during changing times and by reason of evolving science. In the face of emergent scientific consensus on a given issue, blind adherence to outdated precedent is a failing. This is particularly the case in the constitutional realm and is no less so in the context of eyewitness evidence where the risks of misidentification are great and the stakes including wrongful convictions are high.

The frequent criticisms levelled against the *Manson* decision and its progeny from social scientists and legal scholars alike reveal serious flaws in the assumptions and premises underlying *Manson*. These criticisms are apt and compel us to conclude that the federal reliability standard set forth in *Manson* is both scientifically and jurisprudentially unsound and hence flawed under our interstitial review. * * *

We therefore join Massachusetts and New York in departing from the *Manson* rule and adopting in its place a per se rule of exclusion. * * *

* * *

9. Elements of the per se rule of exclusion

Under the per se exclusionary rule we adopt herein, if a witness makes an identification of a defendant as a result of a police identification procedure that is unnecessarily suggestive and conducive to irreparable misidentification, the identification and any subsequent identification by the same witness must be suppressed. The question of whether the identification is *unnecessarily* suggestive focuses not only on the identification procedure itself but also on whether the police have a *good* *reason* to use a suggestive identification procedure in the first instance. This rule in part mirrors the Massachusetts approach to the admission of eyewitness identification evidence. * * *

We depart, however, from the Massachusetts burden-of-proof framework, which requires a defendant alleging an unnecessarily suggestive eyewitness identification procedure "to prove, by a preponderance of the evidence, that the witness was subjected by the [s]tate to a pretrial confrontation . . . so unnecessarily suggestive and conducive to irreparable mistaken identification as to deny the defendant due process of law." Under our approach, the initial burden falls on the accused to establish prima facie that some aspect of the identification procedure employed by the police was suggestive in nature. If the accused does not meet that burden, suppression is not required. However, if the accused demonstrates that the identification procedure contained one or more suggestive elements, the burden shifts to the state to prove by clear and convincing evidence *either* that (1) the procedure employed was not so suggestive as to materially taint the identification made by the eyewitness, which is to say that any departure from proper procedure could not have increased the risk of misidentification, *or* (2) good reason existed for the police to employ the suggestive procedure in the first instance. If the state fails to carry its responsive burden, the identification evidence and any subsequent in-court identification must be suppressed.

* * *

By our decision today, we only announce the broad contours of a new per se exclusionary rule for unnecessarily suggestive pretrial identification procedures and do not purport to fully address the myriad procedural and substantive questions that the rule's application may ultimately implicate.

* * *

NOTE ON THE NEW MEXICO LEGISLATION

The New Mexico legislation referred to in the opinion requires all law enforcement agencies conducting eyewitness identification procedures to adopt, no later than, January 1, 2020, and biennially review written policies for the administration of identification procedures. All such policies must include

> (1) having a blind administrator or blinded administrator perform the live lineup or photo lineup;
>
> (2) documenting a description of the suspect provided by the eyewitness, including a description of the circumstances under which the suspect was seen by the eyewitness, the time of day, the length of time the suspect was seen, the perceived or actual distance from the eyewitness to the suspect and the lighting conditions;

(3) providing the eyewitness with instructions that minimize the likelihood of an inaccurate identification, including that the perpetrator may or may not be in the identification procedure and that the investigation will continue regardless of whether an identification is made;

(4) composing the lineup so that the fillers generally resemble the eyewitness's description of the perpetrator so that the suspect does not unduly stand out from the fillers;

(5) using at least four fillers in a live lineup and at least five fillers in a photo lineup;

(6) ensuring, when practicable, that a photograph of the suspect used in a photo lineup is contemporary and resembles the suspect's appearance at the time of the offense;

(7) presenting separate photo lineups and live lineups when there are multiple eyewitnesses, ensuring that the same suspect is placed in a different position for each identification procedure;

(8) having the administrator seek and document a clear statement from the eyewitness, at the time of the identification and in the eyewitness's own words, as to the eyewitness's confidence level that the person identified is the person who committed the crime;

(9) minimizing factors at any point in time that influence an eyewitness to identify a suspect or affect the eyewitness's confidence level in identifying a suspect, including verbal or nonverbal statements by or reactions from the administrator;

(10) presenting lineup members one at a time;

(11) adopting relevant practices shown to enhance the reliability of an eyewitness participating in a show-up procedure, such as:

> (a) identifying the circumstances under which a show-up is warranted;
>
> (b) transporting the eyewitness to a neutral, non-law enforcement location where the detained suspect is being held;
>
> (c) removing the suspect from the law enforcement squad car;
>
> (d) removing restraints from the suspect when the suspect is being observed by the eyewitness; and
>
> (e) administering the show-up procedure close in time to the commission of the crime;

(12) video recording the entirety of the photo lineup and live lineup and, where practicable, the show-up procedure, unless the recording equipment is not reasonably available or the recording equipment fails and obtaining replacement equipment is not feasible; and

(13) preserving photographic documentation of all live lineup and photo lineup members and show-up suspects, as well as all descriptions provided by the eyewitness of the perpetrator.

The nonexhaustive list of system variables set forth in the legislation sets forth a minimum standard for the identification procedures used in lineups, show-ups, and photo arrays. The legislation operated prospectively and required law enforcement to comply with standards by January 1, 2020.

5. Unnecessary Police Suggestiveness Required for a Due Process Violation

In the following case, the court clarifies whether due process regulation of identifications is concerned only with regulating unreliability, or whether police misconduct is a threshold requirement.

PERRY V. NEW HAMPSHIRE

Supreme Court of the United States, 2012.
565 U.S. 228.

JUSTICE GINSBURG delivered the opinion of the Court.

* * *

An identification infected by improper police influence, our case law holds, is not automatically excluded. Instead, the trial judge must screen the evidence for reliability pretrial. If there is a very substantial likelihood of irreparable misidentification, the judge must disallow presentation of the evidence at trial. But if the indicia of reliability are strong enough to outweigh the corrupting effect of the police-arranged suggestive circumstances, the identification evidence ordinarily will be admitted, and the jury will ultimately determine its worth.

We have not extended pretrial screening for reliability to cases in which the suggestive circumstances were not arranged by law enforcement officers. Petitioner requests that we do so because of the grave risk that mistaken identification will yield a miscarriage of justice. Our decisions, however, turn on the presence of state action and aim to deter police from rigging identification procedures, for example, at a lineup, showup, or photograph array. When no improper law enforcement activity is involved, we hold, it suffices to test reliability through the rights and opportunities generally designed for that purpose, notably, the presence of counsel at postindictment lineups, vigorous cross-examination, protective rules of evidence, and jury instructions on both the fallibility of eyewitness identification and the requirement that guilt be proved beyond a reasonable doubt.

* * *

Around 3 a.m. on August 15, 2008, Joffre Ullon called the Nashua, New Hampshire, Police Department and reported that an African-American male was trying to break into cars parked in the lot of Ullon's apartment building. Officer Nicole Clay responded to the call. Upon arriving at the parking lot, Clay heard what "sounded like a metal bat hitting the ground." She then saw petitioner Barion Perry standing between two cars. Perry walked toward Clay, holding two car-stereo amplifiers in his hands. A metal bat lay on the ground behind him. Clay asked Perry where the amplifiers came from. "[I] found them on the ground," Perry responded.

Meanwhile, Ullon's wife, Nubia Blandon, woke her neighbor, Alex Clavijo, and told him she had just seen someone break into his car. Clavijo immediately went downstairs to the parking lot to inspect the car. He first observed that one of the rear windows had been shattered. On further inspection, he discovered that the speakers and amplifiers from his car stereo were missing, as were his bat and wrench. Clavijo then approached Clay and told her about Blandon's alert and his own subsequent observations.

By this time, another officer had arrived at the scene. Clay asked Perry to stay in the parking lot with that officer, while she and Clavijo went to talk to Blandon. Clay and Clavijo then entered the apartment building and took the stairs to the fourth floor, where Blandon's and Clavijo's apartments were located. They met Blandon in the hallway just outside the open door to her apartment.

Asked to describe what she had seen, Blandon stated that, around 2:30 a.m., she saw from her kitchen window a tall, African-American man roaming the parking lot and looking into cars. Eventually, the man circled Clavijo's car, opened the trunk, and removed a large box.[a]

Clay asked Blandon for a more specific description of the man. Blandon pointed to her kitchen window and said the person she saw breaking into Clavijo's car was standing in the parking lot, next to the police officer. Perry's arrest followed this identification. About a month later, the police showed Blandon a photographic array that included a picture of Perry and asked her to point out the man who had broken into Clavijo's car. Blandon was unable to identify Perry.

* * *

[The State courts rejected Perry's challenge to Blandon's identification. They found that the police had not engaged in any

---

[a] The box, which Clay found on the ground near where she first encountered Perry, contained car-stereo speakers.

unnecessarily suggestive tactics, and therefore found it unnecessary to decide whether the identification was reliable.]

The Constitution, our decisions indicate, protects a defendant against a conviction based on evidence of questionable reliability, not by prohibiting introduction of the evidence, but by affording the defendant means to persuade the jury that the evidence should be discounted as unworthy of credit. Constitutional safeguards available to defendants to counter the State's evidence include the Sixth Amendment rights to counsel, compulsory process, and confrontation plus cross-examination of witnesses. Apart from these guarantees, we have recognized, state and federal statutes and rules ordinarily govern the admissibility of evidence, and juries are assigned the task of determining the reliability of the evidence presented at trial. * * * Only when evidence is so extremely unfair that its admission violates fundamental conceptions of justice, have we imposed a constraint tied to the Due Process Clause. See, e.g., Napue v. Illinois, 360 U.S. 264, 269 (1959) (Due process prohibits the State's "knowin[g] use [of] false evidence," because such use violates "any concept of ordered liberty.").

Contending that the Due Process Clause is implicated here, Perry relies on a series of decisions involving police-arranged identification procedures. [The Court discusses Stovall v. Denno, Simmons v. United States, Foster v. California, Neil v. Biggers, and Manson v. Brathwaite.]

Perry concedes that, in contrast to every case in the *Stovall* line, law enforcement officials did not arrange the suggestive circumstances surrounding Blandon's identification. * * * He contends, however, that it was mere happenstance that each of the *Stovall* cases involved improper police action. The rationale underlying our decisions, Perry asserts, supports a rule requiring trial judges to prescreen eyewitness evidence for reliability any time an identification is made under suggestive circumstances. We disagree.

Perry's argument depends, in large part, on the Court's statement in *Brathwaite* that "reliability is the linchpin in determining the admissibility of identification testimony." If reliability is the linchpin of admissibility under the Due Process Clause, Perry maintains, it should make no difference whether law enforcement was responsible for creating the suggestive circumstances that marred the identification.

Perry has removed our statement in *Brathwaite* from its mooring, and thereby attributes to the statement a meaning a fair reading of our opinion does not bear. [T]he *Brathwaite* Court's reference to reliability appears in a portion of the opinion concerning the appropriate remedy *when the police use an unnecessarily suggestive identification procedure.* * * * The due process check for reliability, *Brathwaite* made plain, comes into play only after the defendant establishes improper police conduct. * * *

Perry's contention that improper police action was not essential to the reliability check *Brathwaite* required is echoed by the dissent. Both ignore a key premise of the *Brathwaite* decision: A primary aim of excluding identification evidence obtained under unnecessarily suggestive circumstances, the Court said, is to deter law enforcement use of improper lineups, showups, and photo arrays in the first place. Alerted to the prospect that identification evidence improperly obtained may be excluded, the Court reasoned, police officers will "guard against unnecessarily suggestive procedures." This deterrence rationale is inapposite in cases, like Perry's, in which the police engaged in no improper conduct.

* * *

Perry's argument, reiterated by the dissent, thus lacks support in the case law he cites. Moreover, his position would open the door to judicial preview, under the banner of due process, of most, if not all, eyewitness identifications. External suggestion is hardly the only factor that casts doubt on the trustworthiness of an eyewitness's testimony. As one of Perry's *amici* points out, many other factors bear on "the likelihood of misidentification,"—for example, the passage of time between exposure to and identification of the defendant, whether the witness was under stress when he first encountered the suspect, how much time the witness had to observe the suspect, how far the witness was from the suspect, whether the suspect carried a weapon, and the race of the suspect and the witness. There is no reason why an identification made by an eyewitness with poor vision, for example, or one who harbors a grudge against the defendant, should be regarded as inherently more reliable, less of a "threat to the fairness of trial," than the identification Blandon made in this case. To embrace Perry's view would thus entail a vast enlargement of the reach of due process as a constraint on the admission of evidence.

Perry maintains that the Court can limit the due process check he proposes to identifications made under "suggestive circumstances." Even if we could rationally distinguish suggestiveness from other factors bearing on the reliability of eyewitness evidence, Perry's limitation would still involve trial courts, routinely, in preliminary examinations. Most eyewitness identifications involve some element of suggestion. Indeed, all in-court identifications do. Out-of-court identifications volunteered by witnesses are also likely to involve suggestive circumstances. * * *

* * *

Our unwillingness to enlarge the domain of due process as Perry and the dissent urge rests, in large part, on our recognition that the jury, not the judge, traditionally determines the reliability of evidence. We also take account of other safeguards built into our adversary system that caution juries against placing undue weight on eyewitness testimony of questionable reliability. These protections include the defendant's Sixth

Amendment right to confront the eyewitness. Another is the defendant's right to the effective assistance of an attorney, who can expose the flaws in the eyewitness's testimony during cross-examination and focus the jury's attention on the fallibility of such testimony during opening and closing arguments. Eyewitness-specific jury instructions, which many federal and state courts have adopted, likewise warn the jury to take care in appraising identification evidence. See, e.g., United States v. Telfaire, 469 F.2d 552, 558–559 (CADC 1972) (per curiam) (D. C. Circuit Model Jury Instructions) ("If the identification by the witness may have been influenced by the circumstances under which the defendant was presented to him for identification, you should scrutinize the identification with great care."). * * * The constitutional requirement that the government prove the defendant's guilt beyond a reasonable doubt also impedes convictions based on dubious identification evidence.

State and federal rules of evidence, moreover, permit trial judges to exclude relevant evidence if its probative value is substantially outweighed by its prejudicial impact or potential for misleading the jury. See, e.g., Fed. Rule Evid. 403; N. H. Rule Evid. 403 (2011) . . . In appropriate cases, some States also permit defendants to present expert testimony on the hazards of eyewitness identification evidence. See, e.g., State v. Clopten, 2009 UT 84, P33, 223 P. 3d 1103, 1113 ("We expect . . . that in cases involving eyewitness identification of strangers or near-strangers, trial courts will routinely admit expert testimony [on the dangers of such evidence].").

Many of the safeguards just noted were at work at Perry's trial. During her opening statement, Perry's court-appointed attorney cautioned the jury about the vulnerability of Blandon's identification. (Blandon, "the eyewitness that the State needs you to believe[,] can't pick [Perry] out of a photo array. How carefully did she really see what was going on? . . . How well could she really see him?"). While cross-examining Blandon and Officer Clay, Perry's attorney constantly brought up the weaknesses of Blandon's identification. She highlighted: (1) the significant distance between Blandon's window and the parking lot, (2) the lateness of the hour, (3) the van that partly obstructed Blandon's view, (4) Blandon's concession that she was "so scared [she] really didn't pay attention" to what Perry was wearing, (5) Blandon's inability to describe Perry's facial features or other identifying marks, (6) Blandon's failure to pick Perry out of a photo array, and (7) Perry's position next to a uniformed, gun-bearing police officer at the moment Blandon made her identification. Perry's counsel reminded the jury of these frailties during her summation. (Blandon "wasn't able to tell you much about who she saw. . . . She couldn't pick [Perry] out of a lineup, out of a photo array. . . . [Blandon said] [t]hat guy that was with the police officer, that's who was circling. Again, think about the context with the guns, the uniforms. Powerful, powerful context clues.").

After closing arguments, the trial court read the jury a lengthy instruction on identification testimony and the factors the jury should consider when evaluating it. The court also instructed the jury that the defendant's guilt must be proved beyond a reasonable doubt, and specifically cautioned that "one of the things the State must prove [beyond a reasonable doubt] is the identification of the defendant as the person who committed the offense."

* * *

Finding no convincing reason to alter our precedent, we hold that the Due Process Clause does not require a preliminary judicial inquiry into the reliability of an eyewitness identification when the identification was not procured under unnecessarily suggestive circumstances arranged by law enforcement. * * *

JUSTICE THOMAS, concurring.

The Court correctly concludes that its precedents establish a due process right to the pretrial exclusion of an unreliable eyewitness identification only if the identification results from police suggestion. I therefore join its opinion. I write separately because I would not extend Stovall v. Denno and its progeny even if the reasoning of those opinions applied to this case. The *Stovall* line of cases is premised on a "substantive due process" right to "fundamental fairness." * * * In my view, those cases are wrongly decided because the Fourteenth Amendment's Due Process Clause is not a "secret repository of substantive guarantees against 'unfairness.' " * * * Accordingly, I would limit the Court's suggestive eyewitness identification cases to the precise circumstances that they involved.

JUSTICE SOTOMAYOR, dissenting.

Our due process concern * * * arises not from the act of suggestion, but rather from the corrosive effects of suggestion on the reliability of the resulting identification. By rendering protection contingent on improper police arrangement of the suggestive circumstances, the Court effectively grafts a *mens rea* inquiry onto our rule. The Court's holding enshrines a murky distinction—between suggestive confrontations intentionally orchestrated by the police and, as here, those inadvertently caused by police actions—that will sow confusion. It ignores our precedents' acute sensitivity to the hazards of intentional and unintentional suggestion alike and unmoors our rule from the very interest it protects, inviting arbitrary results. And it recasts the driving force of our decisions as an interest in police deterrence, rather than reliability. Because I see no warrant for declining to assess the circumstances of this case under our ordinary approach, I respectfully dissent.

* * *

As this case illustrates, police intent is now paramount. As the Court acknowledges, Perry alleges an "accidental showup." He was the only African-American at the scene of the crime standing next to a police officer. For the majority, the fact that the police did not intend that showup, even if they inadvertently caused it in the course of a police procedure, ends the inquiry. The police were questioning the eyewitness, Blandon, about the perpetrator's identity, and were intentionally detaining Perry in the parking lot—but had not intended for Blandon to identify the perpetrator from her window. Presumably, in the majority's view, had the police asked Blandon to move to the window to identify the perpetrator, that could have made all the difference.

* * *

[T]he majority emphasizes that we should rely on the jury to determine the reliability of evidence. But our cases are rooted in the assumption that eyewitness identifications upend the ordinary expectation that it is "the province of the jury to weigh the credibility of competing witnesses." As noted, jurors find eyewitness evidence unusually powerful and their ability to assess credibility is hindered by a witness' false confidence in the accuracy of his or her identification. That disability in no way depends on the intent behind the suggestive circumstances.

* * *

It would be one thing if the passage of time had cast doubt on the empirical premises of our precedents. But just the opposite has happened. A vast body of scientific literature has reinforced every concern our precedents articulated nearly a half-century ago, though it merits barely a parenthetical mention in the majority opinion. Over the past three decades, more than two thousand studies related to eyewitness identification have been published. * * *

* * * Study after study demonstrates that eyewitness recollections are highly susceptible to distortion by post-event information or social cues; that jurors routinely overestimate the accuracy of eyewitness identifications; that jurors place the greatest weight on eyewitness confidence in assessing identifications even though confidence is a poor gauge of accuracy; and that suggestiveness can stem from sources beyond police orchestrated procedures. The majority today nevertheless adopts an artificially narrow conception of the dangers of suggestive identifications at a time when our concerns should have deepened.

* * *

Independent Source for In-Court Identification?

If an out-of-court identification is excluded under the Due Process Clause, can the witness identify the defendant in court? Recall that under *Wade,* the witness could make an in-court identification if it was free from the taint of the lineup conducted in the absence of counsel. But if the prior identification was caused by *police suggestiveness,* as required for exclusion after *Perry*—and as distinguished from a counsel-free lineup which may not have changed the picture of the perpetrator in the witness's mind—there can by definition be no independent source for the in-court identification. If there were an independent source, then the out-of-court identification *itself* might be admissible. It follows that if the pretrial identification is excluded under the Due Process Clause, the in-court identification must be as well. See Young v. Conway, 698 F.3d 69 (2nd Cir. 2012) (where the prior identification was caused by police suggestiveness, there was no independent source that would allow the in-court identification to be admitted); Marsden v. Moore, 847 F.2d 1536 (11th Cir.1988) (single photograph procedure creates substantial risk of mistaken identification where witness had only a fleeting glimpse of the perpetrator two years before the identification; in-court identification must be excluded as well).

6. Determining Whether Unnecessary Suggestiveness Caused an Unreliable Identification

There are a lot of reported cases evaluating whether unnecessary police suggestiveness caused an unreliable identification to be made. It is fair to state that in most cases, the courts have refused to find causation, relying on the *Manson* factors.

As the New Mexico decision in *Martinez* discussed, the *Manson* factors have been challenged by the substantial social science that has developed since that case. The American Psychological Association, in a brief filed in *Perry,* urged the Court to revisit its assumptions in *Manson:*

> [M]ost of [the *Manson*] factors are indeed relevant to probable accuracy—with the notable exception of witness certainty. But given that notable exception, and given the plethora of other accuracy-related factors that researchers have identified since *Biggers* and *Manson,* APA urges the Court, in an appropriate case, to revisit the *Manson* framework so as to bring it in line with current scientific knowledge.

See also National Research Council, Identifying the Culprit: Assessing Eyewitness Identification (2014) ("Identifying the Culprit") (noting that since *Manson* more than 2000 scientific studies have been conducted that establish the reliability problems inherent in eyewitness identifications—

both system variables (problems in identification procedures) and estimator variables (inaccuracy of human perception and memory)).

It turns out that *Perry* was not an appropriate case in which to revisit *Manson,* because the Court held that in the absence of police misconduct, there is no call to review the identification for possible unreliability. As one court said, the Court "bypassed this topic in *Perry,* leaving to the future any inquiry into the *Biggers* framework." Phillips v. Allen, 668 F.2d 912 (7th Cir. 2012).

7. The Effect of Identification Procedures on Trials

Some of the defects in pre-trial lineups may even have an impact on trials aside from possibly tainting identification evidence. If the government uses "mug shots" in a photo identification, the suggestion to the witness will be that the mug shot reflects a prior criminal record of the person photographed. Although the courts will balance the need for the evidence against its possible prejudicial effect, in many cases the photos will be admitted because the circumstances of the identification procedure will be critical to the evidentiary weight to which it is entitled. See, e.g., United States v. Stevens, 935 F.2d 1380 (3d Cir.1991) (submitting "wanted board," with which defendant was identified, to the jury, was permissible under Federal Rule of Evidence 403, even though others on the board were violent felons and defendant had no record of violent activity: "Allowing the jury to inspect the board in its unaltered condition would permit the jurors to determine what, if anything, drew the victims' attention to Stevens"). Thus, the defendant identified by mug shot may have to choose between challenging the identification and protecting against disclosure of a prior record. United States v. McCoy, 848 F.2d 743 (6th Cir.1988) (introducing mug shots prohibited by Rule 403 where the defendant never challenged the suggestiveness of the identification, and therefore did not "open the door").

Can the defendant call *expert witnesses* to testify to the unreliability of identification evidence? How will that testimony help the jury? What kind of people have expertise on this subject? The National Research Council, in Identifying the Culprit, concluded that "[m]any scientifically established aspects of eyewitness memory are counterintuitive and may defy expectations, and jurors need assistance in understanding the factors that may affect the accuracy of an identification. In many cases this information can be most effectively conveyed by expert testimony. Judges should have the discretion to allow expert testimony explaining relevant research on eyewitness memory and identifications."

But most federal courts have been reluctant to allow expert testimony on the unreliability of identifications. Some have reasoned, counterintuitively, that jurors don't need assistance on the subject because they understand that identifications can be unreliable. United States v.

Smith, 122 F.3d 1355 (11th Cir. 1997) (expert testimony concerning the unreliability of identification procedures is inadmissible because it does not assist the jury; it is not needed, "because the jury [can] determine the reliability of identification with the tools of cross-examination."). Some older cases question whether there is sufficient scientific data to render any conclusions. See United States v. Rincon, 28 F.3d 921 (9th Cir.1994) (upholding trial court's exclusion of such evidence on the ground that the expert's testimony was not sufficiently scientific). But surely this is no longer the case given the plethora of studies on the subject over the last 20 years. Other courts have not been hostile, but do require the expert testimony to be specific to the facts of the case. United States v. Brien, 59 F.3d 274 (1st Cir.1995) (finding no abuse of discretion in the trial court's exclusion of the defense expert on the unreliability of identification evidence; the expert's proffered testimony was very general and did not fit with many of the circumstances underlying the identifications in this case; nor did the expert explicate the methodology by which he concluded that the identifications were unreliable). See also United States v. Jones, 689 F.3d 12 (1st Cir. 2012) (trial court did not abuse discretion in excluding expert testimony on identifications and choosing instead to instruct the jury on potential areas of unreliability).

8. The Unreliability of In-Court Identifications

Speaking of unreliable identifications, what can be more suggestive than an identification that occurs *at the trial* when the witness on the stand points accusingly at the defendant seated at counsel's table? Unfortunately for defendants, any challenge to an in-court identification does not rise to a constitutional argument. This is because, after *Perry,* the Due Process Clause regulates the reliability of identifications only if they have been caused by police misconduct. And there is no police misconduct in an in-court identification. See United States v. Whatley, 719 F.3d 1206 (11th Cir. 2013) (holding that the circuit's previous cases reviewing in-court identifications under the Due Process Clause had been overruled by *Perry*: "under *Perry,* the admission of the in-court identifications of Whatley cannot violate his right to due process because he cannot establish that the suggestive circumstances of the identifications were the result of improper police conduct.")

Can anything be done about the suggestiveness inherent in an identification at trial? Defense counsel in United States v. Brien, 59 F.3d 274 (1st Cir.1995), moved for permission to have the defendant seated in the spectator section of the courtroom and asked leave to "salt the audience with three or four individuals of the same general description as the bank robber." The trial judge responded that he would agree to a "fairly staged courtroom lineup" but that he was concerned about the risk of unfairness to the prosecution in defense counsel's open-ended proposal. Defense counsel did not take the judge up on his offer, and the defendant appealed the conviction as based on an unfair in-court identification. The court of appeals responded as follows:

> If Brien had presented the court with a detailed plan for a fair in-court lineup, and the court had rejected the plan without a plausible justification, then on the present facts we think that a significant issue would be presented. But Brien's motion is not within a country mile of such a proposal. As the trial court sensibly explained, Brien's plan left room for a scenario fully capable of misleading the jury. To alter the standard practice, it was up to Brien's counsel to propose a plan that would guard against unfairness to either side.

Why do you suppose Brien's counsel did not accept the trial judge's offer of a fairly staged courtroom lineup? Suppose witnesses picked Brien from the spectator section of the courtroom. After that, how likely is it that a jury would be willing to accept a defense claim of misidentification?

Why was it Brien's obligation to propose a plan that would guard against unfairness to both sides? Isn't it the prosecution's obligation to respond to a defendant's request with ideas about assuring that the government's interests are protected? See also United States v. Burdeau, 168 F.3d 352 (9th Cir.1999) (trial court has discretion to order an in-court lineup, but no obligation to do so).

9. Voice Identification

Do *voice* identifications raise problems that are different from those encountered in photograph identifications, lineups, show-ups, etc.? Courts use the *Manson* standards for voice identification. But as discussed above, the *Manson* test gives only minimal protection against police suggestiveness for any identification procedure, whether by sight or voice. For example, in United States v. Patton, 721 F.2d 159 (6th Cir.1983), the defendant was charged with making threatening phone calls. The witness identified the defendant's voice at a pretrial "show-up." The court held that the *Manson* test "applies with full force to aural identification." But then the court found that the show-up had not caused a mistaken identification. Applying the *Manson* factors, the court concluded that the witness had an opportunity to hear the defendant's voice during four phone calls; that the witness was attentive to these calls, as evidenced by her description of their content; that the time between the crime and the voice "show-up" was only three weeks; and that, upon hearing the defendant's voice at the "show-up" the witness "immediately recoiled, instantly recognizing the voice."

C. NON-CONSTITUTIONAL PROTECTIONS AGAINST UNRELIABLE IDENTIFICATIONS

The effect of police suggestiveness, and the unreliability of many pretrial identifications, are well-documented, as indicated in the material set forth at the beginning of this Chapter. It's also fair to state that the Supreme Court has not provided much in the way of constitutional protections that would guarantee the reliability of identification evidence. The lack of constitutional protection has led a number of actors in the criminal justice system in various parts of the country—lawyers, law enforcement officials, and courts included—to propose and to adopt a number of procedures designed to increase the reliability of pretrial identifications.

In 1999, the Justice Department published guidelines developed by the Office of Justice Programs for refining investigative practices dealing with eyewitness identifications. Eyewitness Evidence: A Guide For Law Enforcement (Nat'l Inst. of Justice, Office of Justice Programs, U.S. Dep't of Justice, Oct. 1999); see also Eyewitness Evidence: A Trainer's Manual For Law Enforcement (Nat'l Inst. of Justice, Office of Justice Programs, U.S. Dep't of Justice, Sept. 2003) (together "guidelines"). The guidelines emphasize: (1) the importance of selecting other subjects in arrays and lineups who resemble the suspect in respect to significant features described by the witnesses; (2) the dangers of simultaneous identification procedures—a number of people or photographs brought before the witness at one time—that encourage inaccurate relative judgments; and (3) the inherent suggestiveness of identifications in which only one individual is shown to a witness. The guidelines suggest, among other things, the following:

- Cautionary instructions to the witness that "the person who committed the crime may or may not be present" and that "it is just as important to clear innocent persons from suspicion as to identify guilty parties."
- Instructions to the witness that the procedure requires the investigator to state, in the witness's own words, how certain the witness is of any identification (designed to guard against post-identification inflation of certainty from the confirming feedback of police officers).
- Sequential presentation (designed to discourage a witness's tendency to engage in a relative judgment by identifying the person who looks more like the perpetrator than any of the other alternatives). (See Steblay et al., Eyewitness Accuracy Rates in Sequential and Simultaneous Lineup Presentations, 25 L. & Human Behavior 459 (2001)).

- Blind administration—meaning that the officer who conducts the procedure does not know who the suspect is—thus avoiding the threat of conscious or unconscious influence by the officer.

The National Research Council, in its 2014 report entitled "Identifying the Culprit" suggests the following safeguards for identification procedures: 1) "Police officers should be trained to ask open-ended questions, avoid suggestiveness, and efficiently manage scenes with multiple witnesses (for example, minimizing interactions among witnesses."; 2) Use of a double-blind procedure, in which neither the witness nor the administrator knows which person in the lineup is the suspect, is necessary to avoid bias; 3) The witness's confidence level should be documented at the time of identification, because the level of confidence at the time of trial is not a reliable predictor of accuracy; and 4) The identification procedures should be videotaped.

Jury Instructions

Federal and State courts throughout the country instruct juries to consider the potential unreliability of identification procedures. These instructions are of course tailored to the case, but they cover factors like the difference between a sequential identification and an identification in which all options are present at one time; the questionable validity of a witness being certain of an identification; problems of cross-racial identification; the effect of stress on the reliability of an identification; the threat to reliability if the administrator of the identification procedure is involved in the investigation; the phenomenon of weapons focus; and the impact of disguises and clothing on identifications. For a discussion of jury instructions provided by courts, see American Bar Association Policy 104D: Cross-Racial Identification, 37 Sw. U. L.Rev. 917 (2008).

In Commonwealth v. Gomes, 470 Mass. 352 (2015), the Massachusetts Supreme Judicial Court relied on research done by a Study Group and recognized five principles regarding identification evidence that it found to have achieved a "near consensus in the relevant scientific community"—and so would be included in a revised model jury instruction regarding eyewitness identification. The five principles are:

1. "Human memory does not function like a video recording but is a complex process that consists of three stages: acquisition, retention, and retrieval."

2. "An eyewitness's expressed certainty in an identification, standing alone, may not indicate the accuracy of the identification, especially where the witness did not describe that level of certainty when the witness first made the identification."

3. "High levels of stress can reduce an eyewitness's ability to make an accurate identification."

4. "Information that is unrelated to the initial viewing of the event, which an eyewitness receives before or after making an identification, can influence the witness's later recollection of the memory or of the identification."

5. "A prior viewing of a suspect at an identification procedure may reduce the reliability of a subsequent identification procedure in which the same suspect is shown."

The court offered a model instruction. Here are some of the pertinent provisions:

* * *

In evaluating eyewitness identification testimony, it is not essential that a witness be free from doubt as to the correctness of his or her identification of the defendant. However, you, the jury, must be satisfied beyond a reasonable doubt, based on all of the credible evidence, that this defendant is the person who committed [or participated in the commission of] the crime[s] before you may convict him/her.

* * *

Human beings have the ability to recognize other people from past experiences and to identify them at a later time, but research has shown that people sometimes make mistakes in identification. That research has focused on the factors that may affect the accuracy of an identification, including the nature of human memory.

Research has shown that human memory is not like a video recording that a witness need only replay to remember what happened. Memory is far more complex. The process of remembering consists of three stages: first, a person sees or otherwise acquires information about the original event; second, the person stores in the brain the information about the event for a period of time until, third, the person attempts to recall that stored information. At each of these stages, memory can be affected by a variety of factors.

Relying on some of the research that has been done in this area, I am going to list some specific factors you should consider in determining whether the identification testimony is accurate. By instructing you on the factors to consider, I am not expressing any opinion about the accuracy of any specific memory of any particular witness. You, the jury, must decide whether the witness's identification is accurate.

(1) *The witness's opportunity to view the event.* You should consider the opportunity the witness had to observe the offender at the time of the offense, how good a look the witness had of the offender, the degree of attention the witness was paying to the offender at that time, the distance between the witness and the offender, how good the lighting conditions were, and the length of time the witness had to observe the offender [with additional language addressing cases in which a disguise was involved, a face was obscured, the suspect had a distinctive face of feature, or a weapon was involved];

(2) *Characteristics of the witness.* You should also consider characteristics of the witness when the observation was made, such as the quality of the witness's eyesight, whether the witness knew the offender, and, if so, how well, and whether the witness was under a high degree of stress—high levels of stress, compared to low to medium levels, can reduce an eyewitness's ability to accurately perceive an event [with additional instructions if drugs or alcohol were involved, or the witness and offender are of different races];

(3) *The time elapsed.* You should consider how much time elapsed between the event observed and the identification. Generally, memory is most accurate right after the event and begins to fade thereafter.

(4) *Witness's expressed certainty.* Research shows that a witness's expressed certainty in an identification, standing alone, may not be a reliable indicator of the accuracy of the identification, especially where the witness did not describe that level of certainty when the witness first made the identification.

(5) *Exposure to identification information from others.* A person's memory may be affected by information the person received between the incident and the identification, as well as after the identification, and the person may not realize that his or her memory has been affected. You may consider whether the witness was exposed to identifications made by other witnesses, to opinions or descriptions given by others, including police officers, or to any other information or influence. Such exposure may affect the independence and reliability of a witness's identification, and may inflate the witness's confidence in the identification.

An identification that is the product of some suggestive conduct by the police or others should be scrutinized with special caution and care. The risk that suggestion will affect the identification is greater where the witness did not get so good a look at the offender, because a witness who got a good look is less likely to be influenced by suggestion [with an additional instruction if there was a photo array lineup, or showup; or if there were multiple viewings by the same witness].

(6) *Failure to identify or inconsistent identification.* You may take into account whether a witness ever tried and failed to make an identification of the defendant, or made an identification that was inconsistent with the identification that such witness made at trial.

(7) *Totality of the evidence.* You should consider all the relevant factors that I have discussed, viewed in the context of the totality of the evidence in this case, in evaluating the accuracy of a witness's identification testimony. Specifically, you should consider whether there was other evidence in the case, direct or circumstantial, that tends to support or not to support the accuracy of an identification. If you are not convinced beyond a reasonable doubt that the defendant was the person who committed [or participated in the commission of] the crime[s], you must find the defendant not guilty.

The Massachusetts Supreme Judicial Court has not made these instructions mandatory in all criminal cases. But state prosecutors report that trial judges generally give them when defendants request them, and prosecutors generally offer no objections.

The utility of jury instructions should be obvious. Instead of adversarial argument by counsel or conflicting expert testimony in courts that permit it, jury instructions are binding. They come to the jury from the judge who the jury regards as a neutral, respected source. They are the law that binds the jury. They are available to poor litigants as well as to wealthy ones. They offer some hope of improving jury understanding of the real problems associated with eyewitness testimony and, therefore, of reducing the number of wrongful convictions based upon such testimony. See Dennis v. Secretary, PA Dep't of Corrections, 834 F.3d 263 (3rd Cir. 2016) (McKee, J.) (arguing that "robust jury instructions can minimize the dangers associated with inaccurate witness identifications").

CHAPTER 5

THE RIGHT TO COUNSEL

■ ■ ■

I. THE BACKGROUND

The Sixth Amendment provides that "[i]n all criminal prosecutions, the accused shall enjoy the right * * * to have the Assistance of Counsel for his defence."[1] The right to counsel embodied in the Amendment differed from the English common-law practice at the time of the American Revolution. Under English law, an accused had a right to have counsel in misdemeanor but not felony cases. Although Parliament granted special treatment to those accused under the Treason Act of 1695 and required the court to appoint counsel upon the request of the accused, the defendant was not permitted to have counsel until 1836 in ordinary felony cases in England.[2]

When the Constitution was adopted, twelve of the thirteen original states had rejected the English common-law rule and had fully recognized the right to counsel in criminal prosecutions. Powell v. Alabama, 287 U.S. 45, 64–65 (1932). Adoption of the Sixth Amendment formalized this practice. As such, it conveyed the idea that the right to counsel was a grant of privilege—i.e., eliminating the prohibition on counsel—rather than a requirement that counsel be appointed. This can be contrasted with the Federal Crimes Act of 1790, which imposed a statutory *duty* on federal courts in capital cases to assign counsel. 1 Stat. 118 (1790). Although no statute required appointment of counsel in noncapital cases and no one

---

[1] The right to counsel is important in many stages of the criminal process. This is already apparent from the previous chapters. The *Massiah* rule, for example, governed attempts to elicit statements from an accused following an indictment or other formal charge. And the *Wade* and *Gilbert* rules governing lineups following a formal charge also involved a right to counsel. The chapters that follow this one involve the decision to bring formal charges against a suspect, the treatment of the suspect while charges are pending, trials and guilty pleas, sentencing and post-trial procedures. Counsel is important in most of the stages of the criminal process that will be examined. At some point it is useful to look at the *development* of the right to counsel. That look is provided in this Chapter. The discussion of counsel here is limited to establishing how the right to counsel developed and to examining the stages of the process to which the right extends. In Chapter 10, which covers trial rights, the right to counsel at trial is more extensively examined. The doctrine of effective assistance will be discussed there, along with the right of self-representation.

[2] See Faretta v. California, 422 U.S. 806, 821–826 (1975); W. Beaney, The Right to Counsel in American Courts 8–15 (1955); F. Heller, The Sixth Amendment (1951); Holtzoff, The Right of Counsel Under the Sixth Amendment, 20 N.Y.U.L.Rev. 1–22 (1944). Despite the absence of a right to counsel, in practice English courts frequently allowed counsel to argue points of law and to assume other defense functions. W. Beaney at 9–11.

originally read the Sixth Amendment as so requiring, the practice developed of appointing counsel for indigents in serious federal cases.

II. THE EARLY DEVELOPMENT OF THE RIGHT

In Johnson v. Zerbst, 304 U.S. 458 (1938), the Court held that the Sixth Amendment requires counsel in federal court in all criminal proceedings, unless the defendant waives the assistance of counsel. (At that point, the Sixth Amendment was not applicable to the States). The Court viewed counsel as a jurisdictional prerequisite to a federal court's authority to deprive an accused of life or liberty.

The right to counsel in state prosecutions for many years was determined exclusively by state law. In 1932, even before Johnson v. Zerbst, the famous "Scottsboro Case" raised the question of whether a failure of the state to make an effective appointment of counsel to indigent defendants in a capital case could deprive the defendants of their rights to due process.

The Right to Appointed Counsel in Felony Cases

POWELL V. ALABAMA

Supreme Court of the United States, 1932.
287 U.S. 45.

JUSTICE SUTHERLAND delivered the opinion of the Court.

* * *

The petitioners, hereinafter referred to as defendants, are negroes charged with the crime of rape, committed upon the persons of two white girls. The crime is said to have been committed on March 25, 1931. The indictment was returned in a state court of first instance on March 31, and the record recites that on the same day the defendants were arraigned and entered pleas of not guilty. * * *

There was a severance upon the request of the state, and the defendants were tried in three * * * groups * * *. Each of the three trials was completed within a single day. Under the Alabama statute the punishment for rape is to be fixed by the jury, and in its discretion may be from ten years imprisonment to death. The juries found defendants guilty and imposed the death penalty upon all.

* * *

The record shows that on the day when the offense is said to have been committed, these defendants, together with a number of other negroes, were upon a freight train on its way through Alabama. On the same train were seven white boys and the two white girls. A fight took place between the negroes and the white boys, in the course of which the white boys, with the exception of one named Gilley, were thrown off the train. A message was sent ahead, reporting the fight and asking that every negro be gotten off the train. The participants in the fight, and the two girls, were in an open gondola car. The two girls testified that each of them was assaulted by six different negroes in turn, and they identified the seven defendants as having been among the number. None of the white boys was called to testify, with the exception of Gilley, who was called in rebuttal.

Before the train reached Scottsboro, Alabama, a sheriff's posse seized the defendants and two other negroes. Both girls and the negroes then were taken to Scottsboro, the county seat. Word of their coming and of the alleged assault had preceded them, and they were met at Scottsboro by a large crowd. It does not sufficiently appear that the defendants were seriously threatened with, or that they were actually in danger of, mob violence; but it does appear that the attitude of the community was one of great hostility. The sheriff thought it necessary to call for the militia to assist in safeguarding the prisoners. * * * It is perfectly apparent that the proceedings, from beginning to end, took place in an atmosphere of tense, hostile and excited public sentiment. During the entire time, the defendants were closely confined or were under military guard. The record does not disclose their ages, except that one of them was nineteen; but the record clearly indicates that most, if not all, of them were youthful, and they are constantly referred to as "the boys." They were ignorant and illiterate. All of them were residents of other states, where all members of their families or friends resided.

* * *

[U]ntil the very morning of the trial no lawyer had been named or definitely designated to represent the defendants. Prior to that time, the trial judge had "appointed all the members of the bar" for the limited "purpose of arraigning the defendants." Whether they would represent the defendants thereafter if no counsel appeared in their behalf, was a matter of speculation only, or, as the judge indicated, of mere anticipation on the part of the court. Such a designation, even if made for all purposes, would, in our opinion, have fallen far short of meeting, in any proper sense, a requirement for the appointment of counsel. How many lawyers were members of the bar does not appear; but, in the very nature of things, whether many or few, they would not, thus collectively named, have been given that clear appreciation of responsibility or impressed with that individual sense of duty which should and naturally would accompany the appointment of a selected member of the bar, specifically named and assigned.

* * *

The defendants, young, ignorant, illiterate, surrounded by hostile sentiment, haled back and forth under guard of soldiers, charged with an atrocious crime regarded with especial horror in the community where they were to be tried, were thus put in peril of their lives within a few moments after counsel for the first time charged with any degree of responsibility began to represent them.

It is not enough to assume that counsel thus precipitated into the case thought there was no defense, and exercised their best judgment in proceeding to trial without preparation. Neither they nor the court could say what a prompt and thoroughgoing investigation might disclose as to the facts. No attempt was made to investigate. No opportunity to do so was given. Defendants were immediately hurried to trial. * * * Under the circumstances disclosed, we hold that defendants were not accorded the right of counsel in any substantial sense.

* * *

The Constitution of Alabama provides that in all criminal prosecutions the accused shall enjoy the right to have the assistance of counsel; and a state statute requires the court in a capital case, where the defendant is unable to employ counsel, to appoint counsel for him. The state supreme court held that these provisions had not been infringed, and with that holding we are powerless to interfere. The question, however, which it is our duty and within our power, to decide, is whether the denial of the assistance of counsel contravenes the due process clause of the Fourteenth Amendment to the federal Constitution.

[The Court discussed the historical development of the right to counsel in England and the colonies. One test for determining whether due process has been accorded is to examine whether the settled "usages and modes of proceeding" were followed. The Court concluded that the procedures employed in this case deviated from traditionally accepted practices.]

* * *

The right to be heard would be, in many cases, of little avail if it did not comprehend the right to be heard by counsel. Even the intelligent and educated layman has small and sometimes no skill in the science of law. If charged with crime, he is incapable, generally, of determining for himself whether the indictment is good or bad. He is unfamiliar with the rules of evidence. Left without the aid of counsel he may be put on trial without a proper charge, and convicted upon incompetent evidence, or evidence irrelevant to the issue or otherwise inadmissible. He lacks both the skill and knowledge adequately to prepare his defense, even though he have a perfect one. He requires the guiding hand of counsel at every step in the proceedings against him. Without it, though he be not guilty, he faces the danger of conviction because he does not know how to establish his innocence. If that be true of men of intelligence, how much more true is it of the ignorant and illiterate, or those of feeble intellect.

* * *

In the light of the facts outlined in the forepart of this opinion—the ignorance and illiteracy of the defendants, their youth, the circumstances of public hostility, the imprisonment and the close surveillance of the defendants by the military forces, the fact that their friends and families were all in other states and communication with them necessarily difficult, and above all that they stood in deadly peril of their lives—we think the failure of the trial court to give them reasonable time and opportunity to secure counsel was a clear denial of due process.

* * * [W]e are of opinion that, under the circumstances just stated, the necessity of counsel was so vital and imperative that the failure of the trial court to make an effective appointment of counsel was likewise a denial of due process within the meaning of the Fourteenth Amendment. Whether this would be so in other criminal prosecutions, or under other circumstances, we need not determine. All that it is necessary now to decide, as we do decide, is that in a capital case, where the defendant is unable to employ counsel, and is incapable adequately of making his own defense because of ignorance, feeble mindedness, illiteracy, or the like, it is the duty of the court, whether requested or not, to assign counsel for him as a necessary requisite of due process of law; and that duty is not discharged by an assignment at such a time or under such circumstances as to preclude the giving of effective aid in the preparation and trial of the case. * * *

* * *

[JUSTICE BUTLER dissented.]

NOTE ON POWELL AND BETTS V. BRADY

The Alabama Supreme Court affirmed the convictions and sentences in three separate opinions: Weems v. State, 224 Ala. 524 (1932); Patterson v. State, 224 Ala. 531 (1932); and Powell v. State, 224 Ala. 540 (1932). The vote in each case was 6–1. The negative reaction in parts of the country to the treatment of the Scottsboro defendants might have caused the Alabama Supreme Court to respond defensively by declaring that the defendants had received fair trials:

> The Alabama court's refusal to reverse convictions stemming from obviously unfair trials was plausibly attributable, at least in part, to the judges' defensive reaction to national criticism leveled against Alabama for its treatment of the Scottsboro defendants. The Communist International Labor Defense ("ILD"), which provided the Scottsboro Boys with defense counsel on their initial appeals and retrials, immediately

> converted Scottsboro into a national and international cause celebre, conducting mass protest meetings in northern cities as well as orchestrating demonstrations at United States consulates overseas in the spring and summer of 1931. The ILD consistently portrayed white Alabamians as "lynchers" for their treatment of the Scottsboro defendants. Sensitive to Yankee criticism in any context, Alabama whites were particularly enraged at Communists pillorying their state, especially at a time when the Communist Party was achieving some success at organizing rural Alabama farm workers in the midst of depression. Thousands of abusive and threatening protest letters from around the world were directed toward Alabama's governor and state supreme court justices. Those jurists were said to be "seething with anger at an avalanche of protests, demands, and threats." When Chief Justice Anderson opened the state court's session early in 1932, he expressly criticized these inflammatory messages, which had been made with "the evident intent to bulldoze the court." After the state court rejected the appeal in *Powell,* Anderson, the sole dissenter, explained in a letter to Walter White of the NAACP that his brethren had been swayed into denying a new trial by the ILD tactics, to which they did not wish to appear to be capitulating.

Klarman, The Racial Origins of Modern Criminal Procedure, 99 Mich. L. Rev. 48, 71–72 (2000). Professor Klarman observed that "[t]he Scottsboro Boys certainly were innocent of the crimes charged, as revealed in a subsequent recantation by one of the alleged victims. Their innocence should have been reasonably clear at the trial both from the medical evidence and from the conflicting testimony of the prosecution's witnesses."

Chief Justice Anderson's dissent in *Powell* was not well received in Alabama. He and his wife were ostracized by their community as a result of the dissent.

Although the Court found that the defendants' due process rights were violated in *Powell,* the Court did not require counsel in *all* state prosecutions. Ten years later, in fact, the Court held explicitly that the Due Process Clause of the Fourteenth Amendment did not incorporate the specific guarantees of the Sixth Amendment, i.e., an automatic right to counsel. Betts v. Brady, 316 U.S. 455 (1942). The Court endorsed a case-by-case inquiry into the fundamental fairness of the proceeding, in light of the totality of the facts in a given case. The Court considered the circumstances of the case in *Betts,* a prosecution for robbery, and concluded as follows:

> [T]he accused was not helpless, but was a man forty-three years old, of ordinary intelligence, and ability to take care of his own interests on the trial of this narrow issue [alibi defense]. He had once before been in a criminal court, pleaded guilty to larceny and served a sentence and was not wholly unfamiliar with criminal procedure. It is quite clear that in Maryland, if the situation had been otherwise and it had appeared that the petitioner was, for any reason, at a serious disadvantage by reason of

> the lack of counsel, a refusal to appoint would have resulted in the reversal of judgment of conviction. * * *

The Court in *Betts* held that the Due Process Clause required appointment of counsel only where "special circumstances" indicated that the defendant could not perform adequately on his own.

Between Betts and Gideon

The case-by-case, "special circumstances" approach to appointment of counsel in *Betts* was undermined by a number of cases decided before *Betts* was overruled in Gideon v. Wainwright, 372 U.S. 335 (1963), set forth infra. The Court faced difficult problems in deciding in what circumstances due process required appointment of counsel. In Hudson v. North Carolina, 363 U.S. 697 (1960), the Court held that the defendant needed a lawyer to protect against the prejudicial effect of his co-defendant's plea of guilty to a lesser charge in the presence of the jury. In Chewning v. Cunningham, 368 U.S. 443 (1962), the Court reversed the defendant's conviction under a recidivist statute. The defendant was denied due process because the difficult legal questions in the case presented too great a potential for prejudice to the defendant.

Although these cases were fact-specific, the Court held in Hamilton v. Alabama, 368 U.S. 52 (1961), that there was an unqualified right to counsel in state capital cases. The distinction between a case involving capital punishment, where counsel was mandated, and one involving a maximum punishment of life imprisonment, where counsel was not absolutely required, proved to be tenuous, at best under the Due Process Clause. By the time of *Gideon,* the *Betts* rule had been eroded to such an extent that it was ripe for a fall.

III. A NEW AND SWEEPING RIGHT AND ITS LIMITS

A. APPOINTED COUNSEL FOR INDIGENTS IN ALL FELONY PROSECUTIONS

GIDEON V. WAINWRIGHT

Supreme Court of the United States, 1963.
372 U.S. 335.

JUSTICE BLACK delivered the opinion of the Court.

Petitioner was charged in a Florida state court with having broken and entered a poolroom with intent to commit a misdemeanor. This offense is a felony under Florida law. Appearing in court without funds and without a lawyer, petitioner asked the court to appoint counsel for him, whereupon the following colloquy took place:

> "The Court: Mr. Gideon, I am sorry, but I cannot appoint Counsel to represent you in this case. Under the laws of the State of Florida, the only time the Court can appoint Counsel to represent a Defendant is when that person is charged with a capital offense. I am sorry, but I will have to deny your request to appoint Counsel to defend you in this case.
>
> "The Defendant: The United States Supreme Court says I am entitled to be represented by Counsel."

Put to trial before a jury, Gideon conducted his defense about as well as could be expected from a layman. He made an opening statement to the jury, cross-examined the State's witnesses, presented witnesses in his own defense, declined to testify himself, and made a short argument "emphasizing his innocence to the charge contained in the Information filed in this case." The jury returned a verdict of guilty, and petitioner was sentenced to serve five years in the state prison. * * * Since 1942, when Betts v. Brady was decided by a divided Court, the problem of a defendant's federal constitutional right to counsel in a state court has been a continuing source of controversy and litigation in both state and federal courts. To give this problem another review here, we granted certiorari.

[The Court discussed the facts of Betts v. Brady, which were virtually indistinguishable from those in *Gideon*. The Court noted that *Betts* addressed the circumstance of an indigent charged with a felony.]

* * * Upon full reconsideration we conclude that Betts v. Brady should be overruled.

* * *

We accept Betts v. Brady's assumption, based as it was on our prior cases, that a provision of the Bill of Rights which is "fundamental and essential to a fair trial" is made obligatory upon the States by the Fourteenth Amendment. We think the Court in *Betts* was wrong, however, in concluding that the Sixth Amendment's guarantee of counsel is not one of these fundamental rights. Ten years before Betts v. Brady, this Court, after full consideration of all the historical data examined in *Betts,* had unequivocally declared that "the right to the aid of counsel is of this fundamental character." Powell v. Alabama. While the Court at the close of its *Powell* opinion did by its language, as this Court frequently does, limit its holding to the particular facts and circumstances of that case, its conclusions about the fundamental nature of the right to counsel are unmistakable.

* * * The fact is that in deciding as it did—that "appointment of counsel is not a fundamental right, essential to a fair trial"—the Court in

Betts v. Brady made an abrupt break with its own well-considered precedents. In returning to these old precedents, sounder we believe than the new, we but restore constitutional principles established to achieve a fair system of justice. Not only these precedents but also reason and reflection require us to recognize that in our adversary system of criminal justice, any person haled into court, who is too poor to hire a lawyer, cannot be assured a fair trial unless counsel is provided for him. This seems to us to be an obvious truth. Governments, both state and federal, quite properly spend vast sums of money to establish machinery to try defendants accused of crime. Lawyers to prosecute are everywhere deemed essential to protect the public's interest in an orderly society. Similarly, there are few defendants charged with crime, few indeed, who fail to hire the best lawyers they can get to prepare and present their defenses. That government hires lawyers to prosecute and defendants who have the money hire lawyers to defend are the strongest indications of the widespread belief that lawyers in criminal courts are necessities, not luxuries. The right of one charged with crime to counsel may not be deemed fundamental and essential to fair trials in some countries, but it is in ours. From the very beginning, our state and national constitutions and laws have laid great emphasis on procedural and substantive safeguards designed to assure fair trials before impartial tribunals in which every defendant stands equal before the law. This noble ideal cannot be realized if the poor man charged with crime has to face his accusers without a lawyer to assist him. * * *

The Court in Betts v. Brady departed from the sound wisdom upon which the Court's holding in Powell v. Alabama rested. Florida, supported by two other States, has asked that Betts v. Brady be left intact. Twenty-two States, as friends of the Court, argue that *Betts* was "an anachronism when handed down" and that it should now be overruled. We agree.

The judgment is reversed and the cause is remanded to the Supreme Court of Florida for further action not inconsistent with this opinion.

[JUSTICES DOUGLAS, CLARK, and HARLAN wrote separate concurring opinions. JUSTICE HARLAN questioned whether *Betts* was an abrupt break with history. He viewed the *Betts* rule as one that did not work, but argued that it was "entitled to a more respectful burial than has been accorded."]

Establishing Indigency

Gideon requires the state to appoint counsel for indigents in felony cases, but what does it mean to be "indigent?" Consider Barry v. Brower, 864 F.2d 294 (3d Cir.1988), where the defendant was denied a request for the appointment of counsel on the ground that he and his wife had an $80,000 equity in their home and $7,500 in a money market fund. Barry claimed that his debts exceeded his assets, his wife opposed selling their property to pay for his legal expenses, and he had consulted six attorneys recommended by the public defender, all of whom had refused to represent him without a substantial "up-front" payment. The court held that Barry was entitled to appointed counsel. It stated that "indigence is not equivalent to destitution," and that "if by their nature an accused's assets cannot be timely reduced to cash and cash is required, the present financial inability to obtain counsel which defines indigence for Sixth Amendment purposes appears." The court noted that the state may require reasonable reimbursement if the defendant's indigency is temporary.

The federal standard for appointment of counsel "for any person financially unable to obtain adequate representation" is codified in the Criminal Justice Act, 18 U.S.C. § 3006A. For an application of the federal statute, see United States v. Bauer, 956 F.2d 693 (7th Cir.1992) ("It is not enough to claim inability to hire a lawyer and back up the claim with an affidavit. The statute provides for 'appropriate inquiry' into the veracity of that claim."). The court in *Bauer* held that it is the defendant's burden to establish indigency, and that the defendant has no right to appointed counsel at a hearing to establish indigency.

B. THE RIGHT TO APPOINTED COUNSEL IN MISDEMEANOR CASES

After *Gideon,* the Court was asked to determine whether a defendant charged with a misdemeanor was inherently more capable of self-representation than a felony defendant. The right to counsel grew with the answer.

ARGERSINGER V. HAMLIN

Supreme Court of the United States, 1972.
407 U.S. 25.

JUSTICE DOUGLAS delivered the opinion of the Court.

Petitioner, an indigent, was charged in Florida with carrying a concealed weapon, an offense punishable by imprisonment up to six months, a $1,000 fine, or both. The trial was to a judge, and petitioner was unrepresented by counsel. He was sentenced to serve 90 days in jail, and brought this habeas corpus action in the Florida Supreme Court, alleging that, being deprived of his right to counsel, he was unable as an indigent layman properly to raise and present to the trial court good and sufficient defenses to the charge for which he stands convicted. The Florida Supreme Court * * * in ruling on the right to counsel, followed the line we marked out in Duncan v. Louisiana, 391 U.S. 145, 159, as respects the right to trial by jury and held that the right to court-appointed counsel extends only to trials "for non-petty offenses punishable by more than six months imprisonment."

[The Court noted that the Sixth Amendment was binding on the states through the Fourteenth Amendment and proceeded to examine the Amendment's requirements of a public trial, the right to be informed of the nature and cause of the accusation, the right of confrontation, and the right of compulsory process. These rights have never been limited to felonies or to serious offenses. Although Duncan v. Louisiana limited the right to trial by jury to trials where the potential punishment was imprisonment for six months or more (as discussed in Chapter 10, infra), the Court concluded that "there is no support for a similar limitation on the right to assistance of counsel." The Court relied heavily on the rationale in *Powell* and *Gideon* and utilized lengthy quotations from both opinions.]

* * *

The requirement of counsel may well be necessary for a fair trial even in a petty-offense prosecution. We are by no means convinced that legal and constitutional questions involved in a case that actually leads to imprisonment even for a brief period are any less complex than when a person can be sent off for six months or more.

* * *

Beyond the problem of trials and appeals is that of the guilty plea, a problem which looms large in misdemeanor as well as in felony cases. Counsel is needed so that the accused may know precisely what he is doing, so that he is fully aware of the prospect of going to jail or prison, and so that he is treated fairly by the prosecution.

* * *

We must conclude, therefore, that the problems associated with misdemeanor and petty offenses often require the presence of counsel to insure the accused a fair trial. Mr. Justice Powell suggests that these problems are raised even in situations where there is no prospect of imprisonment. We need not consider the requirements of the Sixth Amendment as regards the right to counsel where loss of liberty is not involved, however, for here petitioner was in fact sentenced to jail. [T]he prospect of imprisonment for however short a time will seldom be viewed by the accused as a trivial or petty matter and may well result in quite serious repercussions affecting his career and his reputation. * * *

We hold, therefore, that absent a knowing and intelligent waiver, no person may be imprisoned for any offense, whether classified as petty, misdemeanor, or felony, unless he was represented by counsel at his trial.

* * *

[JUSTICE BRENNAN filed a concurring opinion. CHIEF JUSTICE BURGER concurred in the result, and JUSTICE POWELL filed an opinion concurring in the result, in which JUSTICE REHNQUIST joined. JUSTICE BRENNAN emphasized the availability of law students to assist indigents. THE CHIEF JUSTICE expressed concern that trial judges would have difficulty deciding whether to appoint counsel before hearing evidence in a case. He pointed out that the judge probably will rely on representations of the prosecutor. JUSTICE POWELL preferred an approach that, like Betts v. Brady, would have afforded counsel only when necessary to a fair trial. He was bothered by the fact that indigents would receive counsel in cases in which relatively poor non-indigents would be forced by circumstances to forego counsel. Also of concern to him was the lack of attorney resources available to courts in some areas and the increased burden that appointing counsel represented for overworked judges.]

NOTE ON ARGERSINGER

Argersinger appears to reflect a reluctance of the Court to move too quickly in imposing an obligation on states to provide counsel in the many thousands of misdemeanor cases processed each year. Only nine years had passed since the *Gideon* decision, and some states were slow to respond to that decision. The line the Court drew in *Argersinger* might at the time have been thought to buy time before states were required to provide indigent representation in all cases. But, as subsequent cases demonstrate, *Argersinger* remains the law.

The Actual Imprisonment Rule for Misdemeanor Cases: Scott v. Illinois

Argersinger was imprisoned after a trial in which he was forced to proceed without counsel. The Court did not decide whether the right to counsel extends to a misdemeanor defendant who is punished only with a fine. In Scott v. Illinois, 440 U.S. 367 (1979), the Court considered whether the Sixth Amendment requires appointed counsel when a defendant actually is fined, but the offense is *punishable* by fine or imprisonment. Scott was convicted of shoplifting and fined, after a trial in which he was denied the right to counsel. Shoplifting carried a sentence of either a fine or imprisonment of less than a year.

In *Scott,* the Court stated that there was a line drawn in *Argersinger* between actual imprisonment and other forms of punishment. Even though the statute under which Scott was convicted authorized a year of incarceration, he was not entitled to counsel because he was not sentenced to prison. The majority reasoned as follows:

> [W]e believe that the central premise of *Argersinger*—that actual imprisonment is a penalty different in kind from fines or the mere threat of imprisonment—is eminently sound and warrants adoption of actual imprisonment as the line defining the constitutional right to appointment of counsel. *Argersinger* has proved reasonably workable, whereas any extension would create confusion and impose

unpredictable, but necessarily substantial, costs on 50 quite diverse States. We therefore hold that the Sixth and Fourteenth Amendments to the United States Constitution require only that no indigent criminal defendant be sentenced to a term of imprisonment unless the State has afforded him the right to assistance of appointed counsel in his defense.

Justice Powell concurred, although he expressed reservations about the rule enunciated in *Argersinger* and reaffirmed in *Scott.* He argued that the Constitution does not mandate the rule in *Argersinger,* and preferred a more flexible due process approach to the appointment of counsel. Nevertheless, in *Scott* he recognized a need to provide clear guidance to lower courts.

Justice Brennan, joined by Justices Marshall and Stevens, dissented. The dissenters focused on the need for counsel to defend against a charge, and concluded that counsel should be furnished whenever imprisonment is *authorized* for an offense. They noted that public defender systems are economically feasible, and that many states actually require counsel where any imprisonment is authorized.

Justice Brennan argued in *Scott* that the actual imprisonment approach was unworkable because it forces the judge to consider sentencing factors before the case has even begun. He explained as follows:

> [T]he judge will be forced to decide in advance of trial—and without hearing the evidence—whether he will forego entirely his judicial discretion to impose some sentence of imprisonment and abandon his responsibility to consider the full range of punishments established by the legislature. His alternatives, assuming the availability of counsel, will be to appoint counsel and retain the discretion vested in him by law, or to abandon this discretion in advance and proceed without counsel.

Justice Brennan argued that another salutary effect of the authorized imprisonment approach would be to encourage state legislatures to update criminal statutes. As Justice Brennan put it, "a state legislature or local government might determine that it no longer desired to authorize incarceration for certain minor offenses in light of the expense of meeting the requirements of the Constitution. In my view, this re-examination is long overdue."

Justice Blackmun also dissented in *Scott.* He agreed that *Argersinger* did not decide this question, but would have held that an indigent defendant must be given counsel in any prosecution for an offense punishable by more than six months imprisonment (or, under *Argersinger,* when the defendant is actually subjected to a term of imprisonment). This approach would make the right to counsel co-extensive with the right to a jury trial, also guaranteed by the Sixth Amendment and discussed in Chapter 10, infra.

For a critical analysis of *Scott,* see Herman & Thompson, Scott v. Illinois and the Right to Counsel: A Decision in Search of a Doctrine?, 17 Am.Crim.L.Rev. 71 (1979).

One lower court had this to say about *Scott:*

> In essence, the *Scott* holding set up a trade-off whereby states could choose between providing indigent defendants with appointed counsel and foregoing jail time for convictions obtained without appointed counsel. *Scott* holds that, if the state wants to incarcerate an indigent defendant, the state must provide appointed counsel.

Moore v. Jarvis, 885 F.2d 1565 (11th Cir.1989). Does the "trade-off" approach described have anything to do with the Sixth Amendment right to counsel in "all criminal prosecutions?" Does it have anything to do with the right to due process, which extends to deprivations of both liberty and property?

Applying the Actual Imprisonment Approach

Recall that in Berkemer v. McCarty (Chapter 3) the Court held that the protections of Miranda v. Arizona applied to arrests for misdemeanors. Thus, an indigent person subject to custodial questioning for a misdemeanor has a right to appointed counsel during that questioning. But then at trial, he has no right to appointed counsel unless he receives a prison sentence. Is the *Miranda* right more important than the right to counsel at trial in misdemeanor cases?

If a defendant is not provided counsel at trial, can the court impose a suspended sentence and probation under *Scott*? The Court in Alabama v. Shelton, 535 U.S. 654 (2002), held in the negative. Justice Ginsburg, writing for the Court, declared that a suspended sentence is "a prison term imposed for the offense of conviction" upon the defendant's violation of probation and that once the prison term is triggered, "the defendant is incarcerated not for the probation violation, but for the underlying offense." Justice Scalia, joined by Chief Justice Rehnquist, Justice Kennedy, and Justice Thomas, dissented in *Shelton*. He argued that the threat of a suspended sentence could deter many probation violations.

Use of Uncounseled Convictions to Enhance a Sentence: Baldasar v. Illinois and Nichols v. United States

Suppose an indigent defendant is denied counsel and convicted of a misdemeanor. Under *Scott,* he can only be fined. Suppose further that the same defendant is later charged with another crime, given counsel, and convicted. Can the first uncounseled conviction be used to enhance his sentence for the second crime? In Baldasar v. Illinois, 446 U.S. 222 (1980), a divided Supreme Court held that a defendant was denied his right to counsel under *Argersinger* and *Scott* when his misdemeanor theft conviction was transformed into a felony because of a previous conviction for the same offense, where the defendant had not had counsel when previously convicted and fined. The Court reasoned that *Scott* was violated because Baldasar "was sentenced to an increased term of imprisonment *only* because he had been convicted in a previous prosecution in which he had *not* had the assistance of appointed counsel."

But the Court overruled *Baldasar* in Nichols v. United States, 511 U.S. 738 (1994). Nichols was sentenced under the Federal Sentencing Guidelines after pleading guilty to a federal drug felony. He had previously been convicted on a DUI offense, which was a misdemeanor for which he received no jail time; he was not provided counsel at that previous trial. The DUI conviction was used to place Nichols in a higher criminal history category for sentencing on the drug offense. As a consequence, Nichols received a sentence longer than he would otherwise have received. Chief Justice Rehnquist, in an opinion for five members of the Court, declared that "an uncounseled misdemeanor conviction, valid under *Scott* because no prison term was imposed, is also valid when used to enhance punishment at a subsequent conviction."

The Chief Justice reasoned that "[e]nhancement statutes, whether in the nature of criminal history provisions such as those contained in the Sentencing Guidelines, or recidivist statutes which are commonplace in state criminal laws, do not change the penalty imposed for the earlier conviction." To the contrary, enhancement statutes penalize "only the last offense committed by the defendant"—and Nichols had counsel for that offense. The Chief Justice also argued that the unrestricted use of valid uncounseled convictions was consistent with the "less exacting" standards applicable to the sentencing process. Under the Sentencing Guidelines, a defendant's prior bad acts can be taken into account as part of his criminal history, whenever the government can prove by a preponderance of the evidence that the defendant committed the acts. Thus, Nichols's DUI offense could have been used against him to enhance the sentence *even if he had never been convicted.* The Chief Justice concluded that "it must be constitutionally permissible to consider a prior uncounseled misdemeanor conviction based on the same conduct where that conduct must be proven beyond a reasonable doubt." Justice Souter concurred in the judgment.

Justice Blackmun, joined by Justices Stevens and Ginsburg, dissented. He contended that "a rule that an uncounseled conviction *never* can form the basis for a term of imprisonment is faithful to the principle born of *Gideon* and announced in *Argersinger* that an uncounseled misdemeanor, like an uncounseled felony, is not reliable enough to form the basis for the severe sanction of incarceration."[3]

IV. THE SCOPE OF THE RIGHT

A. CRITICAL STAGES

Gideon, Argersinger, and *Scott* analyze the right of an indigent to appointed trial counsel. But as we have already seen in connection with confessions and identification procedures, counsel may be needed *before* a trial starts. And counsel may be needed after it ends. Other "critical stages"—stages where the presence of counsel is critical—are so labeled when it is said that counsel is essential in order to protect against substantial prejudice to a defendant's rights.

Definition of a Critical Stage: United States v. Wade

The justification for and development of the "critical stage" analysis is expressed in United States v. Wade, 388 U.S. 218 (1967), a case examined in the preceding chapter on identification. The *Wade* Court wrote as follows:

> * * * When the Bill of Rights was adopted, there were no organized police forces as we know them today. The accused confronted the prosecutor and the witnesses against him, and the evidence was marshalled, largely at the trial itself. In contrast, today's law enforcement machinery involves critical confrontations of the accused by the prosecution at pretrial proceedings where the results might well settle the accused's fate and reduce the trial itself to a mere formality. In recognition of these realities of modern criminal prosecution, our cases have construed the Sixth Amendment guarantee to apply to "critical" stages of the proceedings. * * *

[The Court discusses *Powell, Escobedo, Massiah, Miranda,* and other cases.]

> In sum, the principle of Powell v. Alabama and succeeding cases requires that we scrutinize *any* pretrial confrontation of the accused to determine whether the presence of his counsel is necessary to preserve the defendant's basic right to a fair trial as affected by his right meaningfully to cross-examine the witnesses against him and to have effective assistance of counsel at the trial itself. It calls upon us to

---

[3] It must be remembered that Nichols' prior conviction, while uncounseled, was a *valid* conviction because Nichols received no jail time for it. In contrast, if the prior uncounseled conviction is invalid under *Gideon* and its progeny, the conviction cannot be used to enhance a later sentence. Thus, in Custis v. United States, 511 U.S. 485 (1994), the Court stated that, where a prior conviction is being used to enhance a sentence, the defendant can collaterally attack the prior conviction at the sentencing hearing if it was rendered in violation of *Gideon*.

analyze whether potential substantial prejudice to defendant's rights inheres in the particular confrontation and the ability of counsel to help avoid that prejudice.

The Court concluded, as Chapter 4 revealed, that there was great potential for suggestiveness in a lineup, and "the accused's inability effectively to reconstruct at trial any unfairness that occurred at the lineup may deprive him of his only opportunity meaningfully to attack the credibility of the witness' courtroom identification."

Preliminary Hearings: Coleman v. Alabama

Using this "critical stage" method of analysis, the Court found in Coleman v. Alabama, 399 U.S. 1 (1970), that Alabama's preliminary hearing was a critical stage requiring the appointment of counsel for the indigent defendant. Although preliminary hearings have not yet been examined, it is sufficient for present purposes to note that the major purpose of the preliminary hearing is to determine whether there is sufficient evidence against the accused to bind the defendant over for trial. The Court in *Coleman* declared as follows:

> Plainly the guiding hand of counsel at the preliminary hearing is essential to protect the indigent accused against an erroneous or improper prosecution. First, the lawyer's skilled examination and cross-examination of witnesses may expose fatal weaknesses in the State's case that may lead the magistrate to refuse to bind the accused over. Second, in any event, the skilled interrogation of witnesses by an experienced lawyer can fashion a vital impeachment tool for use in cross-examination of the State's witnesses at the trial, or preserve testimony favorable to the accused of a witness who does not appear at the trial. Third, trained counsel can more effectively discover the case the State has against his client and make possible the preparation of a proper defense to meet that case at the trial. Fourth, counsel can also be influential at the preliminary hearing in making effective arguments for the accused on such matters as the necessity for an early psychiatric examination or bail.

Other Pre-Trial Critical Stages

The right to counsel has not been extended to all pretrial phases of a criminal investigation. Kirby v. Illinois, 406 U.S. 682 (1972), for instance, provided a substantial temporal limitation on the Sixth Amendment right to counsel. Unless counsel is provided to safeguard an independent constitutional right, as in *Miranda,* generally one can say that adversary proceedings must be formally initiated before a particular phase of a prosecution can be considered a critical stage requiring counsel. (Recall Massiah v. United States, and Moran v. Burbine). Adversary criminal proceedings plainly can be initiated by formal charge, preliminary hearing, indictment, information, or arraignment. It is not clear what the Supreme Court means by "formal charge," but presumably the Court is focusing on the filing of some statement with the court that expresses the government's belief that the criminal process leading to conviction should begin against a suspect. Before this formal filing, an investigation generally does not trigger counsel rights. Thus, counsel is not constitutionally required at the grand jury stage, because no charges have yet been filed. See, e.g., In re Grand Jury Subpoenas, 906 F.2d 1485 (10th Cir.1990) (subpoenaing attorney to testify before the grand jury to give information against his client does not violate defendant's right to counsel, even though it may result in defense attorney's disqualification from representation; no Sixth Amendment rights attach prior to indictment).

Even where the criminal process has begun, there are limitations on the extension of the right to counsel to pre-trial proceedings. United States v. Ash, 413 U.S. 300 (1973), holding that a photographic identification at which the accused was not present was not a critical stage, illustrates this point. After reviewing the history and expansion of the Sixth Amendment counsel guarantee, the *Ash* Court redefined the approach used in extending the right to counsel: "[T]he test utilized by the Court has called for examination of the event in order to determine whether the accused required aid in coping with legal problems or assistance in meeting his adversary." The Court distinguished the lineup in *Wade* because in *Ash* there was no confrontation between the accused and the prosecution. After stating that there is no right to counsel because the accused has no right to be present at a photographic array, the Court went on to make the following argument:

> A substantial departure from the historical test would be necessary if the Sixth Amendment were interpreted to give Ash a right to counsel at the photographic identification in this case. Since the accused himself is not present at the time of the photographic display, and asserts no right to be present, no possibility arises that the accused might be misled by his lack of familiarity with the law or overpowered by his professional adversary. Similarly, the counsel guarantee would not be used to produce equality in a trial-like adversary confrontation. * * *

After *Ash*, what kind of post-charge, pre-trial situations will be deemed critical stages? See, e.g., Commonwealth v. Holzer, 480 Pa. 93, 389 A.2d 101 (1978) (indigent has right to appointed counsel at search and seizure suppression hearing).

B. POST-TRIAL STAGES

The right to counsel has been extended to certain stages of a criminal prosecution following trial. Generally speaking, extension appears to be based on whether counsel's presence is necessary to provide the defendant with a minimum level of fairness.

MEMPA V. RHAY

Supreme Court of the United States, 1967.
389 U.S. 128.

JUSTICE MARSHALL **delivered the opinion of the Court.**

These consolidated cases raise the question of the extent of the right to counsel at the time of sentencing where the sentencing has been deferred subject to probation.

Petitioner Jerry Douglas Mempa was convicted in the Spokane County Superior Court on June 17, 1959, of the offense of "joyriding." This conviction was based on his plea of guilty entered with the advice of court-appointed counsel. He was then placed on probation for two years on the condition, *inter alia,* that he first spend 30 days in the county jail, and the imposition of sentence was deferred * * *.

About four months later the Spokane County prosecuting attorney moved to have petitioner's probation revoked on the ground that he had been involved in a burglary on September 15, 1959. A hearing was held in the Spokane County Superior Court on October 23, 1959. Petitioner Mempa, who was 17 years old at the time, was accompanied to the hearing by his stepfather. He was not represented by counsel and was not asked whether he wished to have counsel appointed for him. Nor was any inquiry made concerning the appointed counsel who had previously represented him.

At the hearing Mempa was asked if it was true that he had been involved in the alleged burglary and he answered in the affirmative. A probation officer testified without cross-examination that according to his information petitioner had been involved in the burglary and had previously denied participation in it. * * * [T]he court immediately entered an order revoking petitioner's probation and then sentenced him to 10 years in the penitentiary, * * *.

* * *

In 1948 this Court held in Townsend v. Burke, 334 U.S. 736, that the absence of counsel during sentencing after a plea of guilty coupled with "assumptions concerning his criminal record which were materially untrue" deprived the defendant in that case of due process. Mr. Justice Jackson there stated in conclusion, "in this case, counsel might not have changed the sentence, but he could have taken steps to see that the conviction and sentence were not predicated on misinformation or misreading of court records, a requirement of fair play which absence of counsel withheld from this prisoner." [The Court discusses other pre-*Gideon* cases.]

There was no occasion in *Gideon* to enumerate the various stages in a criminal proceeding at which counsel was required, but [these earlier cases] clearly stand for the proposition that appointment of counsel for an indigent is required at every stage of a criminal proceeding where substantial rights of a criminal accused may be affected. * * *

The State, however, argues that the petitioners were sentenced at the time they were originally placed on probation and that the imposition of sentence following probation revocation is, in effect, a mere formality constituting part of the probation revocation proceeding. It is true that sentencing in Washington offers fewer opportunities for the exercise of judicial discretion than in many other jurisdictions. The applicable statute requires the trial judge in all cases to sentence the convicted person to the maximum term provided by law for the offense of which he was convicted. The actual determination of the length of time to be served is to be made by the Board of Prison Terms and Paroles within six months after the convicted person is admitted to prison.

On the other hand, the sentencing judge is required by statute, together with the prosecutor, to furnish the Board with a recommendation as to the length of time that the person should serve, in addition to supplying it with various information about the circumstances of the crime and the character of the individual. We were informed during oral argument that the Board places considerable weight on these recommendations, although it is in no way bound by them. Obviously to the extent such recommendations are influential in determining the resulting sentence, the necessity for the aid of counsel in marshaling the facts, introducing evidence of mitigating circumstances and in general aiding and assisting the defendant to present his case as to sentence is apparent.

Even more important in a case such as this is the fact that certain legal rights may be lost if not exercised at this stage. For one, Washington law provides that an appeal in a case involving a plea of guilty followed by probation can only be taken after sentence is imposed following revocation of probation. Therefore in a case where an accused agreed to plead guilty, although he had a valid defense, because he was offered probation, absence of counsel at the imposition of the deferred sentence might well result in loss of the right to appeal. * * *

Likewise the Washington statutes provide that a plea of guilty can be withdrawn at any time prior to the imposition of sentence, if the trial judge in his discretion finds that the ends of justice will be served. Without undertaking to catalog the various situations in which a lawyer could be of substantial assistance to a defendant in such a case, it can be reiterated that a plea of guilty might well be improperly obtained by the promise to have a defendant placed on the very probation the revocation of which furnishes the occasion for desiring to withdraw the plea. An uncounseled defendant might very likely be unaware of this opportunity.

The two foregoing factors assume increased significance when it is considered that * * * the eventual imposition of sentence on the prior plea of guilty is based on the alleged commission of offenses for which the accused is never tried.

In sum, we do not question the authority of the State of Washington to provide for a deferred sentencing procedure coupled with its probation provisions. Indeed, it appears to be an enlightened step forward. All we decide here is that a lawyer must be afforded at this proceeding whether it be labeled a revocation of probation or a deferred sentencing. We assume that counsel appointed for the purpose of the trial or guilty plea would not be unduly burdened by being requested to follow through at the deferred sentencing stage of the proceeding.

* * *

Limitations on Mempa

Today, it is likely to come as no surprise that sentencing is treated as part of the trial process and as requiring the assistance of counsel. However, courts have held that *Mempa* does not mean that every step in the sentencing process is "critical" within the meaning of the Sixth Amendment. In United States v. Johnson, 935 F.2d 47 (4th Cir.1991), the defendant was sentenced in part on the basis of *ex parte* communications between his probation officer and the sentencing judge. The court rejected the argument that the right to counsel attached to those meetings. It found the communications to be "nonadversarial," reasoning that under the Federal Sentencing Guidelines, the probation officer is an agent of the court and assists the court in arriving at a just sentence. Do you agree that a conference between the probation officer and the judge is not a critical stage?

Right to Counsel on Appeal: Douglas v. California and Ross v. Moffitt

Before *Mempa*, the Court had ruled in Douglas v. California, 372 U.S. 353 (1963), that an indigent defendant has a right to appointed counsel for his first appeal of right from a criminal conviction. The Court relied, for the first and only time, on an equal protection rationale for requiring provision of counsel: because a person with means would retain counsel for an appeal of right, the denial of counsel to an indigent was discrimination that violated the Equal Protection Clause.

The problem with an equal protection rationale is that there would appear to be no limits to it; stated broadly, *Douglas* appeared to endorse a form of wealth equalization. See Harris, The Constitution and Truth Seeking: A New Theory on Expert Services for Indigent Defendants, 83 J.Crim.L. and Crim. 469 (1992) ("While the equality principle surely represents an earnest and well-intentioned effort to deal with the effect of poverty on criminal defendants, it is, if nothing else, too open-ended.").

Over time, the Court switched from an equal protection rationale to a due process rationale in assessing whether indigents had a right to appointed counsel in the appeal process. Under this approach, the state has an obligation to appoint counsel for an indigent whenever counsel would be necessary for adequate access to court relief. Thus, in Ross v. Moffitt, 417 U.S. 600 (1974), the Court refused to extend the *Douglas* reasoning to require counsel for discretionary appeals. Ross received counsel for his first appeal to the state's intermediate appellate court. But he was denied counsel for his subsequent appeal to the state supreme court. Justice Rehnquist, writing for the court, declared that the Fourteenth Amendment "does not require absolute equality or precisely equal advantages, nor does it require the State to equalize economic conditions." Applying the due process test of *adequate access*, Justice Rehnquist found that counsel was not reasonably necessary for discretionary appeals:

> [P]rior to his seeking discretionary review in the State Supreme Court, [respondent's] claims had once been presented by a lawyer and passed upon by an appellate court. Douglas v. California. We do not believe it can be said, therefore, that a defendant in respondent's circumstances is denied meaningful access to the North Carolina Supreme Court simply because the State does not appoint counsel to aid him in seeking review in that court. At that stage he will have, at the very least, a brief on his behalf in the Court of Appeals setting forth his claims of error, and in many cases an opinion by the Court of Appeals disposing of his case. These materials, supplemented by whatever submission respondent may make *pro se,* would appear to provide the Supreme Court of North Carolina with an adequate basis on which to base its decision to grant or deny review. * * *
>
> This is not to say, of course, that a skilled lawyer * * * would not prove helpful to any litigant able to employ him. * * * [But] the fact that a particular service might be of benefit to an indigent defendant does not mean that the service is constitutionally required. The duty of the State under our cases is not to duplicate the legal arsenal that may be privately retained by a criminal defendant in a continuing

effort to reverse his conviction, but only to assure the indigent defendant an adequate opportunity to present his claims fairly in the context of the State's appellate process.

Applying Ross to Other Post-Trial Stages

Reasoning from Ross v. Moffitt, the Court held, in Wainwright v. Torna, 455 U.S. 586 (1982) (per curiam), that a defendant could not challenge his retained lawyer's failure to file a timely petition for discretionary review in the state supreme court. Torna argued that counsel had been ineffective. But under *Ross,* Torna had no right to counsel in his appeal to the state supreme court; so there could be no claim of ineffective counsel. Justice Marshall, dissenting, argued that the defendant was denied due process.

Chief Justice Rehnquist wrote for the Court in Pennsylvania v. Finley, 481 U.S. 551 (1987), as it relied on Ross v. Moffitt to hold that a defendant has no right to counsel in postconviction (habeas corpus) proceedings. Because such right is lacking, the Court held that a lawyer, who is appointed to represent a defendant in such a proceeding and who finds the defendant's claims to be frivolous, need not file a brief referring to anything in the record that would support the defendant's claims. Such a brief (or a similar showing by counsel) is required on direct appeal as of right under the Supreme Court's decision in Anders v. California, 386 U.S. 738 (1967), but the requirement is derived from the right to counsel itself. When the right is nonexistent, there is no requirement of an *Anders* brief or any other comparable effort by counsel. The Chief Justice also rejected due process and equal protection arguments made in support of a briefing requirement.

In Murray v. Giarratano, 492 U.S. 1 (1989), the Court relied on *Ross* and *Finley* to hold that the state was not required to provide counsel for death-row inmates pursuing post conviction habeas corpus remedies. The plurality opinion, written by Chief Justice Rehnquist, "declined to read either the Eighth Amendment or the Due Process Clause to require yet another distinction between the rights of capital case defendants and those in noncapital cases." The Chief Justice noted, however, that many states "automatically provide counsel to death-row inmates in state habeas corpus proceedings, as a matter of state law." Justice Kennedy concurred in the judgment "on the facts and record of this case" noting that "no prisoner on death row in Virginia has been unable to obtain counsel to represent him in postconviction proceedings." Justice Stevens, joined by Justices Blackmun, Marshall, and Brennan, dissented. He noted that under Virginia law, some claims that would ordinarily be brought on direct review are deferred until habeas corpus proceedings, such as claims concerning ineffective assistance of counsel. He concluded that review of those claims in a habeas proceeding is tantamount to a first appeal of right, as to which the defendant does have a right to counsel under *Douglas*. Justice Stevens also argued that capital litigation is more complex and subject to greater time pressure than the postconviction proceedings considered in *Finley*.[4]

In Halbert v. Michigan, 545 U.S. 605 (2005), the Court held that an indigent defendant had a constitutional right to the assistance of counsel in a first appeal of a conviction entered after a guilty plea. The Court likened that appeal to a first appeal of right from a conviction after trial, as to which the right to counsel is guaranteed under *Douglas*.

Parole and Probation Revocation Proceedings: Gagnon v. Scarpelli

Once the defendant has been properly convicted and sentenced, some constitutional protections diminish or disappear. A defendant has no absolute right to counsel at parole or probation revocation proceedings, for example. In Gagnon v. Scarpelli, 411 U.S. 778 (1973), the Court adopted a case-by-case approach to the appointment of counsel at these revocation hearings. Relying on Morrissey v. Brewer, 408 U.S. 471 (1972), which held that due process protections apply to parole revocation proceedings (in other words, that they have to be fundamentally fair because liberty interests are threatened), the *Gagnon* Court first determined that due process also applied to probation revocation hearings. However, the Court rejected the contention that states are under a constitutional duty to provide counsel for indigents in all probation and parole revocation cases. Acknowledging that its case-by-case approach to counsel is similar to the fundamental fairness approach of *Betts,* which was rejected in *Gideon,* the Court distinguished criminal trials from probation or parole revocation hearings, reasoning as follows:

> In a criminal trial, the State is represented by a prosecutor; formal rules of evidence are in force; a defendant enjoys a number of procedural rights which may be lost if not timely raised; and, in a jury trial, a defendant must make a presentation understandable to untrained jurors. In short, a criminal trial under our system is an adversary proceeding with its own unique characteristics. In a revocation hearing, on the other hand, the State is represented, not by a prosecutor, but by a parole officer with a different orientation; formal procedures and rules of evidence are not employed; and the members of the hearing body are familiar with the problems and practice of probation or parole. The need for counsel at revocation hearings

[4] 21 U.S C. § 848(q)(4)(B) entitles capital defendants to qualified legal representation in any "post conviction proceeding" brought under 28 U.S.C. § 2254 or § 2255, sections of the federal habeas corpus statute.

derives, not from the invariable attributes of those hearings, but rather from the peculiarities of particular cases.

The Court in *Gagnon* articulated the relevant considerations:

> * * * Presumptively, it may be said that counsel should be provided in cases where, after being informed of his right to request counsel, the probationer or parolee makes such a request, based on a timely and colorable claim (i) that he has not committed the alleged violation of the conditions upon which he is at liberty; or (ii) that, even if the violation is a matter of public record or is uncontested, there are substantial reasons which justified or mitigated the violation and make revocation inappropriate, and that the reasons are complex or otherwise difficult to develop or present. In passing on a request for the appointment of counsel, the responsible agency also should consider, especially in doubtful cases, whether the probationer appears to be capable of speaking effectively for himself.

Juvenile Proceedings: In re Gault

When guilt is adjudicated at a particular stage, the Court has shown a special sensitivity to the need for counsel. This helps to explain In re Gault, 387 U.S. 1 (1967), which involved a fifteen-year-old who was confined to a State Industrial School until he reached majority. Before being committed as a juvenile delinquent, he was given a hearing without counsel. In holding that due process required that he be appointed counsel, the Court focused on the juvenile's need for assistance of counsel to cope with the problems of law. Underlying the majority's opinion is the concern that the proceeding, though ostensibly civil in nature, involved the potential for incarceration that was as real as a similar threat in a criminal case.[5]

C. THE RIGHT EXTENDED TO EXPERTS

Using the principle of adequate access, the Court in Ake v. Oklahoma, 470 U.S. 68 (1985), held that an indigent defendant may in some cases be entitled to appointed expert assistance in addition to appointed counsel—but that appointment of an expert is by no means automatic. Ake was arrested and charged with murdering a couple and wounding their two children. He was hospitalized after initially being found incompetent to stand trial. Subsequently, he responded sufficiently well to medication that he was declared fit to stand trial. At the guilt stage of the capital proceeding, he raised an insanity defense. Defense counsel called and

---

[5] In contrast, in Middendorf v. Henry, 425 U.S. 25 (1976), the Court refused to hold, on the basis of *Argersinger,* that a summary court-martial is a criminal prosecution because it results in a loss of liberty. The peculiarities of the military setting and its procedures led the Court to distinguish the summary court-martial from the traditional criminal trial. The Court was concerned that counsel would alter the nature of the proceeding, which is informal and flexible.

questioned each psychiatrist who had examined Ake while he was hospitalized. But each doctor indicated on cross-examination that he had not diagnosed Ake's mental state at the time of the offense. The jury convicted. During the sentencing stage no new evidence was presented.

Justice Marshall's opinion for the Court reasoned that Ake should have had a psychiatrist appointed to assist his defense at both stages. The Court borrowed a procedural due process test it uses in civil cases to balance the defendant's need for help against the burden on the state of providing help. It found a strong "private interest" in life and liberty and the importance of avoiding an unjust conviction; no governmental interest in prevailing at trial if the result "is to cast a pall on the accuracy of the verdict obtained"; and a great value in providing expert assistance to a defendant when his sanity at the time of the offense is to be a significant factor at trial and when the government presents psychiatric evidence concerning future dangerousness in a capital sentencing proceeding. Thus, it held that Ake had been denied due process when he was not afforded access to a competent psychiatrist who might have conducted an appropriate examination and assisted in the evaluation, preparation, and presentation of the defense.

An indigent defendant's right to an appointed expert under *Ake* is only triggered when the defendant will be deprived of a fair opportunity to present his defense without the expert assistance. For example, in Caldwell v. Mississippi, 472 U.S. 320 (1985), the defendant sought the appointment of several experts, including a ballistics expert. As support for his request, he stated only that the expert "would be of great necessarius [sic] witness." The trial court denied the request. The Supreme Court affirmed and stated that Caldwell's "undeveloped assertions" were not sufficient to require appointment of an expert. See also Bowden v. Kemp, 767 F.2d 761 (11th Cir.1985) (appointment of psychiatrist not required where no showing was made that sanity would be a real issue at trial).

Ake Violation: McWilliams v. Dunn

The Court found that a capital defendant had a constitutional right to an appointed expert under *Ake*, and that the right was violated, in McWilliams v. Dunn, 137 S.Ct. 1790 (2017). Alabama charged McWilliams with rape and murder. Finding him indigent, the trial court appointed counsel who requested a psychiatric evaluation of McWilliams. The court granted the motion, and the State convened a panel of doctors. The panel concluded that McWilliams was competent to stand trial and had not been suffering from mental illness at the time of the alleged offense. A jury convicted McWilliams of capital murder and recommended a death sentence. Later, while the parties awaited McWilliams' judicial sentencing hearing, defense counsel asked for neurological and neuropsychological testing for his client. The court agreed and McWilliams was examined by Dr. Goff. Dr. Goff filed a report two days before the judicial sentencing hearing. He concluded that McWilliams was likely exaggerating his symptoms, but nonetheless appeared to have some genuine neuropsychological problems. Just before the hearing, counsel also received updated records from the commission's evaluation and previously subpoenaed mental health records from the Alabama Department of Corrections. At the hearing, defense counsel requested a continuance in order to evaluate all the new material, and asked for the assistance of someone with expertise in psychological matters to review the findings. The trial court denied defense counsel's requests. At the conclusion of the hearing, the court sentenced McWilliams to death.

Justice Breyer, writing for five members of the Court, noted that "no one denies that the conditions that trigger application of *Ake* are present. McWilliams is and was an indigent defendant. His mental condition was relevant to the punishment he might suffer. And, that mental condition, i.e., his sanity at the time of the offense, was seriously in question. Consequently, the Constitution, as interpreted in *Ake*, required the State to provide McWilliams with 'access to a competent psychiatrist who will conduct an appropriate examination and assist in evaluation, preparation, and presentation of the defense.' "

Justice Breyer concluded that the examination provided by the state through Dr. Goff was no substitute. He elaborated as follows:

> *Ake* does not require just an examination. Rather, it requires the State to provide the defense with access to "a competent psychiatrist who will conduct an appropriate [1] examination and assist in [2] evaluation, [3] preparation, and [4] presentation of the defense."
>
> We are willing to assume that Alabama met the examination portion of this requirement by providing for Dr. Goff's examination of McWilliams. But what about the other three parts? Neither Dr. Goff nor any other expert helped the defense evaluate Goff's report or McWilliams' extensive medical records and translate these data into a legal strategy. Neither Dr. Goff nor any other expert helped the defense prepare and present arguments that might, for example, have explained that McWilliams' purported malingering was not necessarily inconsistent with mental illness * * * . Neither Dr. Goff nor any other expert helped the defense prepare direct or cross-examination of any witnesses, or testified at the judicial sentencing hearing himself.
>
> Since Alabama's provision of mental health assistance fell so dramatically short of what *Ake* requires, we must conclude that the Alabama court decision affirming McWilliams's conviction and

sentence was "contrary to, or involved an unreasonable application of, clearly established Federal law." 28 U. S. C. § 2254(d)(1).

Justice Alito, joined by Chief Justice Roberts and Justice Thomas, dissented in *McWilliams.* He argued that there is no clearly established right under *Ake* to have a psychiatric expert who is a member of the defense team, as opposed to a neutral expert who is available to assist both the prosecution and the defense—and therefore the Alabama courts' determination that Dr. Goff's examination was sufficient under *Ake* could not be overturned on habeas review. Justice Gorsuch took no part in the case.

NOTE ON AKE

Generally speaking, the courts have read *Ake* narrowly and have refused to require appointment of an expert unless it is absolutely essential to the defense. See Harris, *Ake* Revisited: Expert Psychiatric Witnesses Remain Beyond Reach for the Indigent, 68 No.Car.L.Rev. 763 (1990).

Professor Giannelli contends that the limited right to expert assistance provided by *Ake* must be expanded in light of two important developments: 1) the government's substantially increased use of forensic expert testimony, most prominently DNA identification; and 2) the Supreme Court's opinion in *Daubert,* requiring district courts to act as gatekeepers in excluding unreliable expert testimony—including non-scientific expert testimony. See Giannelli, Ake v. Oklahoma: The Right to Expert Assistance in a Post-Daubert, Post-DNA World, 89 Cornell L. Rev. 1305 (2004). He concludes as follows:

> In 1985, the *Ake* Court could not have anticipated how the advent of DNA evidence would revolutionize forensic science or how [*Daubert*] would alter the judicial approach to scientific evidence. It could not have foreseen the scientific fraud cases or the expanded use of social science and modus operandi experts. All of these developments have increased the need for defense experts.
>
> While *Ake* settled the core issue by recognizing a right to expert assistance, significant issues were left unresolved. *Ake's* rationale extends to nonpsychiatric experts, to noncapital trials, and to other proceedings such as juvenile transfer hearings and sex offender commitments. Developing a useful standard for the appointment decision remains critical; courts have often applied a far too demanding standard. Finally, the role of the expert should be viewed as grounded in the right to counsel—i.e., a *defense* rather than neutral expert should be provided.

D. CIVIL CONTEMPT PROCEEDINGS

The Sixth Amendment right to counsel is limited by its terms to criminal prosecutions. In Turner v. Rogers, 564 U.S. 431 (2011), Justice Breyer's opinion for the Court examined how South Carolina's Family Court enforces its child support orders by threatening with incarceration for civil contempt those who are (1) subject to a child support order, (2) able to comply with that order, but (3) fail to do so. The Court held that "where as here the custodial parent (entitled to receive the support) is unrepresented by counsel, the State need not provide counsel to the noncustodial parent (required to provide the support)," but added "that the State must nonetheless have in place alternative procedures that assure a fundamentally fair determination of the critical incarceration-related question, whether the supporting parent is able to comply with the support order."

Justice Breyer relied upon factors set out in Mathews v. Eldridge, 424 U.S. 319, 335 (1976) (considering fairness of an administrative proceeding) in determining the Due Process requirements in a civil contempt proceeding. He reasoned that the risk of incarceration argued for a right to counsel in this case, but countervailing considerations of fairness to an unrepresented parent and delay of the proceedings cut against providing counsel. He concluded that alternative procedures could provide a parent with a fair hearing.

Justice Breyer identified the following safeguards that would increase the fairness and accuracy of proceedings: "(1) notice to the defendant that his "ability to pay" is a critical issue in the contempt proceeding; (2) the use of a form (or the equivalent) to elicit relevant financial information; (3) an opportunity at the hearing for the defendant to respond to statements and questions about his financial status (e.g., those triggered by his responses on the form); and (4) an express finding by the court that the defendant has the ability to pay."

Justice Thomas, joined by Justice Scalia, and in pertinent part by Chief Justice Roberts and Justice Alito, dissented. He agreed that there was no right to counsel for all indigent defendants facing incarceration in civil contempt proceedings but would not have addressed whether Due Process required safeguards other than counsel.

V. THE PROMISE OF *GIDEON*

In Gideon's Broken Promise: America's Continuing Quest for Equal Justice, A Report on the American Bar Association's Hearings on the Right to Counsel in Criminal Proceedings (December 2004), an ABA Committee reported on the results of hearings that it held in 2003 throughout the United States.

Part V of the Report outlined the principal findings of the Committee, which continue to have resonance:

- Despite *Gideon v. Wainwright*, indigent defense in the United States remains in a state of crisis, resulting in a system that lacks fundamental fairness and places poor persons at constant risk of wrongful conviction.

- Funding for indigent defense services is shamefully inadequate.
- Lawyers who provide representation in indigent defense systems sometimes violate their professional duties by failing to furnish competent representation.
- Lawyers are not provided in numerous proceedings in which a right to counsel exists in accordance with the Constitution and/or state law. Too often, prosecutors seek to obtain waivers of counsel and guilty pleas from unrepresented accused persons, while judges accept and sometimes even encourage waivers of counsel that are not knowing, voluntary, intelligent, and on the record.
- Judges and elected officials often exercise undue influence over indigent defense attorneys, threatening the professional independence of the defense function.
- Indigent defense systems frequently lack basic oversight and accountability, impairing the provision of uniform, quality services.
- Efforts to reform indigent defense systems have been most successful when they involve multi-faceted approaches and representatives from a broad spectrum of interests.
- The organized bar too often has failed to provide the requisite leadership in the indigent defense area.
- Model approaches to providing quality indigent defense services exist in this country, but these models often are not adequately funded and cannot be replicated elsewhere absent sufficient financial support.

Part VI of the Report sets forth seven recommendations to respond to the principal findings.

- State governments should provide increased funding for the delivery of indigent defense services in criminal and juvenile delinquency proceedings at a level that ensures the provision of uniform, quality legal representation. The funding for indigent defense should be in parity with funding for the prosecution function, assuming that prosecutors are funded and supported adequately in all respects.
- The federal government should provide substantial financial support for the provision of indigent defense services in state criminal and juvenile delinquency proceedings.

- State governments should establish oversight organizations that ensure the delivery of independent, uniform, quality indigent defense representation in all criminal and juvenile delinquency proceedings.
- Attorneys and defense programs should refuse to continue indigent defense representation, or to accept new cases for representation, when, in the exercise of their best professional judgment, workloads are so excessive that representation will interfere with the rendering of quality legal representation or lead to the breach of constitutional or professional obligations.
- Judges should fully respect the independence of defense lawyers who represent the indigent, but judges should also be willing to report to appropriate authorities defense lawyers who violate ethical duties to their clients. Judges also should report prosecutors who seek to obtain waivers of counsel and guilty pleas from unrepresented accused persons, or who otherwise give legal advice to such persons, other than the advice to secure counsel. Judges should never attempt to encourage persons to waive their right to counsel, and no waiver should ever be accepted unless it is knowing, voluntary, intelligent, and on the record.
- State and local bar associations should be actively involved in evaluating and monitoring criminal and juvenile delinquency proceedings to ensure that defense counsel is provided in all cases to which the right to counsel attaches and that independent and quality representation is furnished.
- In addition to state and local bar associations, many other organizations and individuals should become involved in efforts to reform indigent defense systems.

Anthony Lewis, former New York Times columnist and author of Gideon's Trumpet, described the importance of the Report in his Foreword to it:

> In recent years we have all read accounts of criminal proceedings that showed how far we were from realizing the promise of the *Gideon* case. There was the Texas defendant whose lawyer slept through parts of his trial—a trial for his life. A number of convicts on death row, awaiting execution, were belatedly found to be innocent; they had been convicted with lawyers who lacked the skill, determination or resources to defend them adequately.
>
> We knew the stories, the anecdotal evidence. Now we have a systematic exploration of the problem, thanks to the American Bar Association's Standing Committee on Legal Aid and Indigent Defendants. Its report, "*Gideon's* Broken Promise," is a challenge to

the country: to legislators, state and federal; to judges; and to lawyers. It asks all of us to think of our commitment to the very idea of law.

The United States Supreme Court can recognize a right to counsel and make it binding on both the federal government and the states. But, funding that right and making it a reality inevitably depends on legislatures. Spending on indigent defense is rarely popular. See Lucas, Reclaiming Equality to Reframe Indigent Defense Reform, 97 Minn. L. Rev. 1197 (2013); Bright, Legal Representation for the Poor: Can Society Afford This Much Injustice?, 75 Mo. L. Rev. 683 (2010).

On August 14, 2017, the American Bar Association passed a resolution urging Congress to enact legislation that would (1) authorize the U.S. Department of Justice to initiate and pursue civil action to obtain equitable relief for systemic violations of the constitutional right to the effective assistance of counsel, (2) deputize private litigants to file such actions in the name of the United States, and (3) recognize the rights of private litigants in their individual capacities or in class actions to seek the same equitable relief.

The challenge of *Gideon* is to make what the Supreme Court has promised a reality.

CHAPTER 6

THE SCREENING AND CHARGING PROCESS

■ ■ ■

I. CRIMINAL JUSTICE CHOICES

A. CONTROLLED AND UNCONTROLLED CHOICES

Choices must be made at all levels of our criminal justice system. The police must decide whether to arrest or to investigate. Prosecutors must decide whether to initiate cases, what charges to file, and whether to plea bargain. Magistrates issuing search and arrest warrants, or sitting in preliminary hearings, must decide whether probable cause exists or whether a suspect should be released on bail or pursuant to other conditions of pre-trial release. Grand juries must decide whether to indict, and prosecutors must decide whether to take cases to grand juries or to bring charges when grand jury indictments are not required. Trial judges must decide whether there is enough evidence for cases to go to petit juries, and petit juries must decide whether to convict or acquit. Judges or juries must determine the sentences to be imposed on convicted offenders. Correctional authorities must decide how to treat incarcerated offenders, and parole or pardon authorities must determine whether to release offenders before their formal sentences have been served.

Some of these choices are controlled by standards—e.g., whether probable cause exists, whether there is enough evidence to go to a jury, and how convinced the jury must be before it convicts—and the task of government officials or jurors is to apply the standards to particular facts. Other choices—sentencing is an example—might be controlled by minimum and maximum provisions but provide the decisionmaker some latitude in choosing where to settle within the permissible range. Still other choices are essentially discretionary. The screening and charging process involves many uncontrolled choices, and these are a cause of concern.

B. LESS THAN FULL ENFORCEMENT OF THE LAW

One of the realities of law enforcement is that not all crimes are investigated, not all criminals are prosecuted, and not all laws are enforced. Nowhere in the United States is there a full enforcement policy—i.e., one that seeks to impose a sanction on every criminal act that occurs.

There is no such thing as full enforcement because it would be too costly. We are not willing to pay for the police, the prosecutors, the public defenders, the judges, the courtrooms, and the penal institutions that would be required to punish all criminal acts that occur. But apart from economics, there are reasons why choices are made in the processing of cases. The notion of individualized justice runs deep in this country. Actions that technically fall under the same statutory proscription may not be equally reprehensible.

Moreover, legislative "overcriminalization" has resulted in criminal codes that, if they were fully enforced, might be intolerable. Laws are sometimes passed as "state-declared ideals," such as adultery statutes, which are "unenforced because we want to continue our conduct, and unrepealed because we want to preserve our morals."[1] Other laws like gambling laws might be drafted broadly for administrative convenience but never intended to be fully enforced because the legislature never really wanted to prohibit private poker games among friends. Outdated laws, which would cause public outrage were they enforced, remain unrepealed, sometimes because legislators do not want to go on record as having repealed *any* criminal law for fear of being labelled as "soft on crime."[2]

It seems, then, that legislatures pass and refuse to repeal statutes that invite choices by those who screen cases and make charging decisions. See Misner, note 2 supra (arguing that legislatures, "by creating too many policy choices, have effectively abdicated policy-making to the prosecutor since it is the prosecutor, and not the legislature, that has the final decision in determining which public policy, if any, is breached by an individual's conduct."). See also Richman and Stuntz, Al Capone's Revenge: An Essay on the Political Economy of Pretextual Prosecution, 105 Colum. L.Rev. 583 (2005) (arguing that the "overexpansion of the federal criminal code" has invited "pretextual enforcement" whereby a prosecutor who suspects a person of one crime can "charge and convict him of a different crime, unrelated to and less severe than the first.").

Some other countries purport to operate on the principle that the police and prosecutor have no discretion to exercise at all. If the case is one in which there is sufficient evidence to prosecute, it must be prosecuted. Whether these systems operate in practice as they are designed to in theory is questionable. Two observers make the following comment:

---

1 LaFave, The Prosecutor's Discretion in the United States, 18 J.Am.Comp.L. 532, 533 (1970).

2 An example of this problem is mentioned in Misner, Recasting Prosecutorial Discretion, 86 J.Crim.L. & Crim. 717 (1996). When the Arizona legislature adopted a revised criminal code, a majority of legislators refused to go on record as voting for a repeal of any of the old sex offense statutes, even if they had become outmoded or superfluous. So that left two sets of sex offense statutes, using different terminology and imposing different punishment—thus increasing prosecutorial discretion.

> The principle of compulsory prosecution which formally permeates the German and Italian systems, and informally the French, demands the impossible: full enforcement of the law in a time of rising crime and fierce competition for resources. Inevitably, adjustments must be made in the way in which the principle is to be applied; where formal law or ideology does not permit these adjustments, informal processes are created that do.[3]

This observation serves as a reminder that it may be more difficult to make a mandatory system of prosecutions work in practice than it is to posit such a system in theory.

Judge Miner, in The Consequences of Federalizing Criminal Law, 4 Crim.Just. 16 (1989) argues that a prosecutor's decision not to prosecute someone who is guilty of a crime invades the province of the jury and creates a public perception of unfairness. Professor Green, in "Hare and Hounds": The Fugitive Defendant's Constitutional Right to be Pursued, 56 Brooklyn L.Rev. 439 (1990), disagrees with Judge Miner and argues that it makes sense that the prosecutor enjoys "virtually unfettered discretion in deciding how to allocate investigative and prosecutorial resources." Professor Green contends that the prosecutor is in the "best position" to decide how to use the finite resources allocated to prosecuting crime.

II. SCREENING BY THE POLICE

A. THE NATURE OF POLICE CHOICES

In Chapter 2, we examined the restrictions on police investigations, arrests, and searches. The assumption there was that the police wanted to proceed against citizens, and the question was what limits, if any, should be placed on police activity. Sometimes, though, the police decide they do not want to take action against individuals, even though such action might be permissible under the rules previously discussed. When the police decide not to act, the effect is usually to screen cases from the criminal justice process. And it is of course extremely problematic if that decision is affected by racial considerations.

The Choice Not to Arrest

The first level of screening occurs when the police decide whom to arrest. Although a decision to make an arrest must be reviewed by an impartial magistrate, either before or after the arrest is made, a decision *not to arrest* is essentially unreviewable.

[3] Goldstein & Marcus, The Myth of Judicial Supervision in Three Inquisitorial Systems: France, Italy, and Germany, 87 Yale L.J. 240, 280 (1977).

The suggestion has been made that police cannot properly be given the choice whether or not to arrest, and that they must arrest when they have probable cause to do so.[4] In fact, police in all American jurisdictions make decisions not to arrest people whom they could arrest. Several explanations can be offered for this phenomenon.

Were the police to arrest every suspect who they reasonably believed committed a crime, an already overburdened judicial system would be further burdened. Thus, we tolerate choices by the police because we are not prepared to handle more cases. Actually, the police themselves are not prepared to handle more cases. If they spent more time in processing cases, they would have less time to spend on the street to deal with crimes that they view as more serious than the ones they now choose to ignore.

Also, police officers learn that courts and prosecutors will not proceed very far in processing certain kinds of cases. Rather than initiating a process that they know will be shortlived, the police may decide not to make arrests for certain crimes and to devote their energies to other activities. For an interesting discussion of the interrelationship between the police investigatory function and the prosecutor's function, see Richman, Prosecutors and Their Agents: Agents and Their Prosecutors, 103 Colum.L.Rev. 749 (2003).

Police also might refrain from an arrest when they are engaged in a community caretaking function, in which case they need to maintain good relations with community elements who might resent the filing of criminal charges in some instances. The police officer may approach a disruptive incident "not in terms of enforcing the law but in terms of handling the situation."[5] Arrest is only one of several tools that the officer may use to maintain order and protect the public. The officer may rely on personal qualities and an aura of authority, rather than the arrest power, to maintain and restore order.

Police officers are also aware that complete enforcement of certain crimes by arrest would create a public backlash. If police officers arrested every driver who drove 56 miles per hour in a 55 mile per hour zone, it is clear that the police would hear about it. Upset drivers might create a risk of violence during the arrest for such a minimal offense. (Witness Walter White's reaction to simply being ticketed for a cracked windshield in "Breaking Bad"). Requiring police officers to arrest whenever they have probable cause of a violation of any of the thousands of offenses that legislatures have enacted would simply be unworkable.

That said, there is an undeniable problem in the police having virtually unfettered discretion in determining whom to arrest and whom not to arrest. Professor Davis, in Prosecution and Race: The Power and

---

4 Hall, Police and Law in a Democratic Society, 28 Ind.L.J. 133, 155 (1953).

5 J. Wilson, Varieties of Police Behavior 33 (1968).

Privilege of Discretion, 67 Fordham L.Rev. 13 (1998), notes the *racial impact* that such discretion can have:

> Because police officers are not required to make an arrest when they observe conduct creating probable cause, their discretion may result in the failure to detain or arrest whites who commit acts for which their African American counterparts would often be detained or arrested.

As an illustration, Professor Davis notes an event in Prince George's County, Maryland, "where white officers observed three white adults smoking crack cocaine in a car with a baby and neither made arrest nor filed charges"—whereas the arrest of black people under the same conditions is surely more likely. If someone can prove that police arrest racial minorities but not white suspects for particular crimes, an equal protection violation may be established. But, as we shall see later in this Chapter, it is difficult to gather sufficient evidence to prove racial discrimination.

B. SOME TYPICAL CASES

Consider the following situations that a police officer might expect to confront, and in which a choice to arrest or not will be made.

1. An officer responds to a call from a woman who says her husband is going to beat her. When the officer arrives, the woman has a broken nose and several facial bruises, but she refuses to sign a complaint. Should the officer arrest the husband anyway? Should the officer suggest that the couple see a marriage counselor? Should the decision be affected by whether the couple has children who witnessed the beating?

2. Suppose two officers are operating a speed trap and a car whizzes by at 30 miles per hour over the speed limit. They usually make an arrest of anyone speeding more than 15 miles over the limit. Should they make an arrest if the driver is a parent rushing to the hospital to see an ill child? If the driver is an employee who is late to work and may be facing the loss of a job if tardy one more time? If the driver is from out of town and did not realize that he was speeding?

3. Officers enter a house without a warrant believing that they will find illegal narcotics. They find the drugs they were looking for but have grave reservations about whether they had exigent circumstances excusing the warrantless entry. Should the officers arrest the occupants and let the prosecution and the court figure it out? Or should they just seize and destroy the narcotics as an informal sanction? Does it matter if the officers believe that if they make an arrest, a motion to suppress will likely follow that will probably lead to a conclusion that the officers violated the Fourth Amendment and could be disciplined for the warrantless entry?

4. The U.S. Department of Justice at various time encourages and even insists that state and local law enforcement authorities assist in determining the immigration status of those who are stopped or arrested. The state and local authorities in many jurisdictions believe that if they appear to be an arm of immigration officials, potential witnesses and actual victims might be discouraged from reporting criminal acts and cooperating in bringing offenders to justice. See, e.g., Yee and Ruiz, Sessions Once Again Threatens Sanctuary Cities, N.Y. Times, July 26, 2017, https://www.nytimes.com/2017/07/26/us/politics/sessions-sanctuary-cities.html?_r=0.

The clash between the Department of Justice and some state and local jurisdictions raises constitutional issues that are beyond the scope of this course. Federal immigration officials believe they need help in doing their job, while law enforcement officials believe that by providing such help they make it more difficult to do their own jobs. So the questions in the end are which function is more important and who decides.

Is police rulemaking a means by which an officer's discretion to arrest or not to arrest can be limited? Would rulemaking make decisions easier in the first three examples set forth above? Ironically, if police departments contemplate adopting rules that would indicate circumstances in which an arrest could, but probably ought not be, made, they may be criticized. There would be no deterrent effect to a law that the police have advertised will not be enforced. Yet, without rules, decisions are left to individual officers at the lowest enforcement level.

III. THE PROSECUTORIAL DECISION WHETHER TO CHARGE

A. THE POWER OF THE PROSECUTOR

While discretion runs through the criminal justice system, it is the discretionary decisions made by the prosecutor that have the most impact. Professor Misner, supra note 2, notes the awesome authority granted to prosecutors—authority that has increased over time.

> The prosecutor's authority is evident in bail hearings, grants of immunity, and in trial strategy. But in the areas of charging, bargaining, and sentencing, it has become clear that the prosecutor plays the pivotal role in the criminal justice process. Despite criticism, plea bargaining continues unabated. While a few courts have rather unsuccessfully attempted to formulate "a common law of prosecutorial discretion," the authority of the prosecutor continues to grow.
>
> Three closely related trends have been at work to promote the authority of the prosecutor. First, current criminal codes contain so many overlapping provisions that the choice of how to characterize conduct as criminal has passed to the prosecutor. In many cases the

legislature has effectively delegated its prerogative to define the nature and severity of criminal conduct to the prosecutor. Legislative mandates regarding sentencing maxima, sentencing minima, and sentencing guidelines are dependent upon the substantive charge chosen by the prosecutor. In addition, prosecutors have the untrammeled authority to select the number of separate criminal acts for which the defendant will be charged. The prosecutors also determine whether to seek sentencing enhancements.

Second, the increase in reported crime without a concomitant increase in resources dedicated to the prosecution and defense of criminal conduct has resulted in a criminal process highly dependent upon plea bargaining. There are very few restraints placed upon the prosecutor in the bargaining process.

Third, the development of sentencing guidelines and a growth of statutes with mandatory minimum sentences have increased the importance of the charging decision since the since the charging decision can affect the range of sentences available to the court. * * *

The American Bar Association approved a resolution (10B) on August 15, 2017 expressing disapproval of mandatory minimum sentences and urging their repeal. In the report accompanying the resolution, the authors focus on the extent to which these sentences take discretion from judges and give it to prosecutors:

> Mandatory minimums undermine judicial discretion and disturb a just allocation of authority among the parties. In the United States adversarial criminal justice system, the judge serves as an impartial arbiter of the case, neither on the side of the prosecution nor the defense. Because of this, judges are entrusted to determine appropriate sentences. Mandatory minimum sentencing regimes, however, deprive judges of the discretion they need to fashion sentences tailored to the circumstances of the offense and the offender. And while judges are stripped of the discretion they need to do justice, at the same time, mandatory minimums often shift that discretion to prosecutors, who do not have the incentive, training or even the appropriate information to properly consider a defendant's mitigating circumstances at the initial charging stage of a case. To give prosecutors such unchecked authority dangerously disturbs the balance of power between the parties in an adversarial system, and deprives defendants of access to an impartial decision-maker in the all-important area of sentencing.

B. THE NATURE OF THE CHARGING DECISION

The prosecutor's decision whether to charge a suspect with a crime is of a different character than the officer's decision whether to arrest. While the officer usually must make an on-the-spot decision, the prosecutor has time, a fuller knowledge of the facts, and the opportunity to consult with colleagues. The consequences of a decision to charge are far greater than those of the decision to arrest. A decision to charge constitutes a finding that the suspect should bear the monetary and social costs of trial and, in some cases, that the suspect's freedom should either be conditioned on payment of bail or suspended as a means of preventive detention. That the defendant may reduce some of these costs by pleading guilty to a lesser charge only makes the prosecutor's decision more consequential.

Professor Davis, in Prosecution and Race: The Power and Privilege of Discretion, 67 Fordham L.Rev. 13 (1998), describes the importance of the prosecutor's decision to charge a person with a crime:

> The first and most important function exercised by a prosecutor is the charging decision. * * * This decision is entirely discretionary. Even if there is probable cause to believe the suspect has committed a crime, the prosecutor may decide to dismiss the case and release the suspect. She may also file a charge that is either more or less serious than that recommended by the police officer, as long as there is probable cause to believe the suspect committed the crime. Other than a constitutional challenge by a criminal defendant, there is very little process for review of these decisions.
>
> The charging decision is one of the most important decisions a prosecutor makes. In conjunction with the plea bargaining process, the charging decision almost predetermines the outcome of a criminal case, because the vast majority of criminal cases result in guilty pleas or guilty verdicts. The charge also often determines the sentence that the defendant will receive * * *.

At the outset, does it trouble you that the prosecutor's decision to charge, carrying the grave consequences that it does, is largely discretionary? If you think the prosecutor's unfettered discretion is a problem, what safeguards would you impose?

C. THE FACTORS THAT ARE CONSIDERED

The prosecutor must decide whether to charge and what crime to charge. The decision whether to charge depends on the prosecutor's belief that (1) the suspect is guilty, (2) the evidence is sufficient to secure conviction, and (3) it is in the community's best interest to prosecute the suspect. General criteria to be employed by the prosecutor are recommended in the ABA Standards for Criminal Justice: The Prosecution Function (4th edition).

Standard 3–4.4 Discretion in Filing, Declining, Maintaining, and Dismissing Criminal Charges

(a) In order to fully implement the prosecutor's functions and duties, including the obligation to enforce the law while exercising sound discretion, the prosecutor is not obliged to file or maintain all criminal charges which the evidence might support. Among the factors which the prosecutor may properly consider in exercising discretion to initiate, decline, or dismiss a criminal charge * * * are:

(i) the strength of the case;

(ii) the prosecutor's doubt that the accused is in fact guilty;

(iii) the extent or absence of harm caused by the offense;

(iv) the impact of prosecution or non-prosecution on the public welfare;

(v) the background and characteristics of the offender, including any voluntary restitution or efforts at rehabilitation;

(vi) whether the authorized or likely punishment or collateral consequences are disproportionate in relation to the particular offense or the offender;

(vii) the views and motives of the victim or complainant;

(viii) any improper conduct by law enforcement;

(ix) unwarranted disparate treatment of similarly situated persons;

(x) potential collateral impact on third parties, including witnesses or victims;

(xi) cooperation of the offender in the apprehension or conviction of others;

(xii) the possible influence of any cultural, ethnic, socioeconomic or other improper biases;

(xiii) changes in law or policy;

(xiv) the fair and efficient distribution of limited prosecutorial resources;

(xv) the likelihood of prosecution by another jurisdiction; and

(xvi) whether the public's interests in the matter might be appropriately vindicated by available civil, regulatory, administrative, or private remedies.

(b) In exercising discretion to file and maintain charges, the prosecutor should not consider:

(i) partisan or other improper political or personal considerations;

(ii) hostility or personal animus towards a potential subject, or any other improper motive of the prosecutor; * * *

(c) A prosecutor may file and maintain charges even if juries in the jurisdiction have tended to acquit persons accused of the particular kind of criminal act in question.

(d) The prosecutor should not file or maintain charges greater in number or degree than can reasonably be supported with evidence at trial and are necessary to fairly reflect the gravity of the offense or deter similar conduct.

(e) * * * A prosecutor should not use a civil waiver to avoid a bona fide claim of improper law enforcement actions, and a decision not to file criminal charges should be made on its merits and not for the purpose of obtaining a civil waiver.

(f) The prosecutor should consider the possibility of a noncriminal disposition, formal or informal, or a deferred prosecution or other diversionary disposition, when deciding whether to initiate or prosecute criminal charges. The prosecutor should be familiar with the services and resources of other agencies, public or private, that might assist in the evaluation of cases for diversion or deferral from the criminal process.

Professor Fairfax discusses a number of nonevidentiary factors that prosecutors usually consider in a charging decision, including:

> whether the defendant is a recidivist or is likely to offend again, whether the prosecutor has a heavy caseload at the time, whether the type of case is career-advancing, whether the investigating law enforcement agency is pleasant to work with, whether the case has jury appeal, whether a matter is more appropriately prosecuted by a different sovereign or handled as a civil matter, and whether the criminal conduct is a priority area for the prosecutor's superiors.

Fairfax, Grand Jury Discretion and Constitutional Design, 93 Cornell L. Rev. 703, 735 (2008). See also Green and Zacharias, Prosecutorial Neutrality, 2004 Wis. L.Rev. 837 (discussing criteria for a charging decision and the difficulty of crafting clear standards given the need for prosecutorial discretion in charging).

Sample Cases

Using the criteria from the standards set forth above, consider whether the prosecutor should have brought the following cases:

1. Congressman Mel Reynolds, an African-American, was charged and convicted of statutory rape and obstruction of justice. The evidence showed that he had a long-term sexual relationship with a teenage girl, and that he tried to cover-up the relationship when an investigation began. The relationship was consensual and the girl was at best a reluctant witness against him. In such a case, should the prosecutor take into account (a) the fact that Reynolds is an elected official, and (b) the attempted cover-up? If so, how important are these factors?

2. In the Southern District of New York, the U.S. Attorney promulgated a "Federal Tuesday" program, in which low-level drug dealers were arrested on the streets while making narcotics transactions. These low-level dealers were prosecuted under the federal narcotics laws, and given much harsher sentences than they would have received had they been prosecuted in the state system. Does deterrence justify prosecuting ordinary dealers caught on one week day in federal court while similarly situated dealers arrested every other day are prosecuted in state court?

3. Leona Helmsley was charged and convicted of tax fraud. The government proved that she evaded taxes by charging renovations to her home as business expenses. On balance, however, Ms. Helmsley paid millions of dollars a year in taxes—the amount of evasion was a rather small percentage of the amount she paid. Mrs. Helmsley was a well-known hotelier. Assuming that a prosecutor would not ordinarily bring a criminal prosecution for a relatively small amount of unjustified deductions, is a prosecution justifiable if it focuses public attention on tax evasion and the possible consequences?

4. Los Angeles police officers Stacy Koon and Lawrence Powell were convicted in federal court for violating the civil rights of Rodney King. The convictions arose out of the use of excessive force after the officers had lawfully pursued King in a high-speed chase and stopped and arrested him. The Rodney King beating was on videotape. A state prosecution had already been brought, resulting in acquittal on most of the counts and a hung jury on one count. The case was highly publicized and was widely watched both in Los Angeles and around the nation. Should a federal prosecutor consider filing federal charges if she believes that the acquittals were largely attributable to the fact that the entire jury was white while the victim in the case was black?

5. The accused snipers who tormented Maryland, Virginia and the District of Columbia for three weeks in October 2002, John Muhammad and Lee Malvo, were going to be tried in Maryland, where most of the sniper attacks occurred. But the Justice Department intervened to assure that the defendants would be prosecuted in Virginia. The apparent reason for this decision was that prosecutors could seek the death penalty for Malvo in Virginia but not in Maryland (because Malvo was a juvenile at

the time of the crimes, and Maryland does not permit the use of the death penalty when the crime is committed by a juvenile). Should the Department of Justice be deciding whether Maryland or Virginia has the better criminal justice policy when it comes to juveniles and the death penalty?

6. Arthur Anderson, the accounting firm, was indicted for destroying records that were pertinent to the SEC investigation of Enron. The indictment essentially resulted in the dissolution of the firm. The conviction, which was based on a single e-mail from a single lawyer concerning records destruction, was overturned by the Supreme Court, but by that time the firm was all but destroyed. Should a prosecutor consider the effects of a conviction on a partnership or corporation in deciding whether to charge the entity along with or in lieu of individuals? See Department of Justice Manual 9-28.200, Principles of Federal Prosecution of Business Organizations (declaring that "prosecutors should be aware of the public benefits that can flow from indicting a corporation in appropriate cases. For instance, corporations are likely to take immediate remedial steps when one is indicted for criminal misconduct that is pervasive throughout a particular industry, and thus an indictment can provide a unique opportunity for deterrence on a broad scale.").[6]

---

[6] See DOJ Guidelines on Charging Corporations, section 9-28.300, for special factors pertinent to charging business entities:

In conducting an investigation, determining whether to bring charges, and negotiating plea or other agreements, prosecutors should consider the following factors in reaching a decision as to the proper treatment of a corporate target:

1. the nature and seriousness of the offense, including the risk of harm to the public, and applicable policies and priorities, if any, governing the prosecution of corporations for particular categories of crime (*see* JM 9-28.400);
2. the pervasiveness of wrongdoing within the corporation, including the complicity in, or the condoning of, the wrongdoing by corporate management;
3. the corporation's history of similar misconduct, including prior criminal, civil, and regulatory enforcement actions against it (*see* JM 9-28.600);
4. the corporation's willingness to cooperate, including as to potential wrongdoing by its agents;
5. the adequacy and effectiveness of the corporation's compliance program at the time of the offense, as well as at the time of a charging decision;
6. the corporation's timely and voluntary disclosure of wrongdoing);
7. the corporation's remedial actions, including, but not limited to, any efforts to implement an adequate and effective corporate compliance program or to improve an existing one, to replace responsible management, to discipline or terminate wrongdoers, or to pay restitution;
8. collateral consequences, including whether there is disproportionate harm to shareholders, pension holders, employees, and others not proven personally culpable, as well as impact on the public arising from the prosecution;
9. the adequacy of remedies such as civil or regulatory enforcement actions, including remedies resulting from the corporation's cooperation with relevant government agencies;
10. the adequacy of the prosecution of individuals responsible for the corporation's malfeasance); and
11. the interests of any victims).

7. Beau Bergdahl was an army soldier stationed in Afghanistan when he left his post and was captured by the Taliban in 2009. President Obama announced his release in exchange for the release of five Guantanamo detainees in 2014. A Major General investigated why Bergdahl left his post, determined that he did so to call attention to poor leadership in his unit, and testified at a preliminary hearing that jail time would be inappropriate. The presiding officer at the preliminary hearing agreed and recommended that Bergdahl's case be handled by a special court martial with no jail time. But, the Commander of U.S. Army Forces Command rejected the recommendation and ordered Bergdahl's case to a general court-martial for trial on charges of desertion and misbehavior before the enemy. Then-candidate for President Donald Trump called Bergdahl a "dirty rotten traitor," and on Inauguration Day Bergdahl's lawyers moved to dismiss the charges on the ground that the President's earlier comments had made a fair trial impossible. The motion was denied, and ultimately Bergdahl elected a trial before a military judge. https://en.wikipedia.org/wiki/Bowe_Bergdahl. Ultimately, he pled guilty to desertion and misbehavior before the enemy and was sentenced to a dishonorable discharge but no prison time.

The Commander, almost certainly a non-lawyer who sent the case to a general court martial, had discretion to reject the recommendation of the presiding officer at the preliminary hearing. In the military justice system commanders have Judge Advocate General lawyers to advise them, but they have the ultimate decision-making power. There are those who believe that charging decisions should rest with lawyers, not commanders. See, e.g., Rustico, Note: Overcoming OverCorrection: Towards Holistic Military Sexual Assault Reform, 102 Va. L. Rev. 2027 (2016) (discussing proposals in Congress to shift the charging function from commanders to JAGs). Military commanders historically used the military justice system as a mechanism (a) to promote good order and discipline in the ranks and (b) to impose proper punishment for criminal acts. The question is whether these goals are complementary or conflicting. Should an exceptionally good soldier get more favorable consideration as to charges than an average soldier?

Politics, and the Chance of a Favorable Outcome

Of course, an important factor in a prosecutor's decision to prosecute is whether the prosecutor thinks a case can be won. A prosecutor with a high conviction rate is not only more likely to be successful in a reelection bid (in jurisdictions where prosecutors are elected), but also will have enhanced credibility when she does file charges. Therefore, she is likely to want to carry all the way to trial only those cases that are supported by a great deal of evidence to which the judge and jury will be sympathetic.

Problems can arise, however, if charging decisions are dominated by politics and the goal of maintaining high conviction rates. Prosecutors could become less concerned about the danger of convicting innocent persons. Conviction rates could be reached by offering very favorable plea bargains to people against whom the evidence is quite weak and who might well be acquitted at trial. Or, prosecutors could decline to pursue hard cases, which might lead to (a) wealthy litigants going free because prosecutors do not want to face well-paid defense counsel who will pull out all stops to defend their clients; and (b) serious offenses going unprosecuted despite sufficient evidence to support convictions because plausible defenses exist and prosecutors do not want to risk defeat. In short, it is not clear that a prosecutor's office should be judged on the basis of its rate of conviction. But the reality is that it often will be—largely because ordinary voters have few ways to assess the performance of prosecutors' offices.

D. THE DECISION NOT TO PROSECUTE

A prosecutor's decision not to prosecute a suspect is generally protected from judicial review. This means that the effect of a prosecutor's decision not to charge a suspect is a final resolution of the case in favor of the suspect. Of course, the prosecutor may change her mind and decide to charge the suspect within the time prescribed by the applicable statute of limitations, but few mechanisms exist that compel the prosecutor to pursue charges.

Even when statutory language appears to make prosecution of all violations of a statute mandatory, courts have been extremely reluctant to *require* prosecution where the prosecutor has decided against it. See, e.g., Inmates of Attica v. Rockefeller, 477 F.2d 375 (2d Cir.1973) (statutory language that prosecutor is "required" to institute prosecutions "has never been thought to exclude the exercise of prosecutorial discretion"). The court in *Attica* relied on separation of powers principles and refused to order the prosecutor to instigate prosecutions against state officials.

Refusing to Prosecute a Certain Type of Crime

In some situations, a prosecutor might decide that a certain type of crime will not be prosecuted. A prosecutor's decision not to prosecute a certain type of crime is often based on a judgment that the violation of law involved is simply not worth the resources that would have to be expended in a prosecution. Prosecutors might also be concerned about a public backlash in prosecuting certain crimes. Local and cultural conditions might be involved as well.

Kamin, Prosecutorial Discretion in the Context of Immigration and Marijuana Law Reform: The Search for a Limiting Principle, 14 Ohio St. J.

Crim. L. 183 (2016), discusses the Obama Administration's decision not to fully enforce particular federal laws:

> To the extent that marijuana and immigration policy are mentioned together on the national stage, it is usually in the context of pointing out that, despite the relaxation or elimination of many states' marijuana prohibitions, marijuana possession and manufacture can still be grounds for the deportation of migrants otherwise in the country lawfully. However, these two seemingly disparate policy arenas share one other important thing in common: in the enforcement of both federal marijuana law and immigration policy, the Obama administration has quite publicly promulgated a policy of limited and selective enforcement of federal law. * * *
>
> * * *
>
> Thus, we can imagine two extreme views of prosecutorial discretion, both of which are untenable. On the one hand, the power to completely invalidate a criminal statute by categorically refusing to enforce a validly enacted law is clearly beyond the authority of a prosecutor. Such a policy would be a clear usurpation of the legislative prerogative, tantamount to allowing a prosecutor to substitute her own views regarding the wisdom of criminal laws for those of a duly elected legislative body. On the other hand, the conception that prosecutorial discretion should, or even could, be completely legislated away is a fallacy. For better or for worse, and in a world of limited resources, any sensible criminal justice system will always rely in part on the wisdom and judgment of those charged with enforcing the laws.
>
> Of course, the trick lies in determining how far toward one of these extremes executive policy may stray in practice. * * *

Overriding the Grand Jury's Decision to Indict

No federal prosecutor can lawfully sign an indictment not approved by the grand jury, but he or she may *decline* to sign off on charges that the grand jury wishes to file. See, e.g., United States v. Navarro-Vargas, 408 F.3d 1184 (9th Cir. 2005) ("The prosecutor has no obligation to prosecute the [grand jury's] presentment, to sign the return of an indictment, or even to prosecute an indictment properly returned.").

It is unusual for prosecutors and the grand juries with which they work to be at odds, but it does happen. A dozen grand jurors in Colorado rebelled against a prosecutor's decision not to indict Rockwell International for polluting a site with nuclear waste. During its term, the grand jury heard from more than 100 witnesses and examined hundreds of thousands of documents. The evidence indicated that the cost of the clean-up at the site would be $2 billion. But the prosecutor pulled the plug on the grand jury by entering into a deal whereby Rockwell would pay an $18 million fine. The grand jurors made statements to the press that they wanted to indict Rockwell but were overruled by the prosecutor. They then wrote a report about their findings and sent it to a federal judge, requesting judicial intervention. The judge not only refused to intervene in the prosecutor's decision; he asked the U.S. Attorney General to determine whether criminal charges could be brought against the grand jurors for violation of grand jury secrecy. The foreman of the grand jury was quoted as saying: "The judge's instructions were very vivid and clear to us. He said that we were not to be a rubber stamp for the prosecutor. What we've done is in the best interest of the prosecutor and the nation." Subsequently the grand jurors brought a petition to release materials associated with the grand jury's investigation. See In re Special Grand Jury, 450 F.3d 1159 (10th Cir. 2006).

Explaining the Decision Not to Prosecute

The public is rarely made aware of a prosecutor's decision not to bring charges. In highly publicized cases, however, prosecutors may have to worry about public opinion. Some prosecutors have found it necessary to explain their decisionmaking process when they decide not to charge in a high profile case.

For example, U.S. Attorney Otto Obermaier decided not to bring charges against Salomon Brothers, a Wall Street Brokerage house, in connection with Salomon's admission of submitting false bids in treasury securities auctions. He made a public statement explaining why he decided not to seek charges. Obermaier singled out four pertinent factors: (1) Salomon's extensive cooperation with the authorities; (2) Salomon's replacement of those senior management officials who had failed to promptly report the offenses to the authorities after first learning of it; (3) heavy fines and other punishments imposed as part of Salomon's civil settlement with the SEC, the Federal Reserve Bank, and the Treasury Department; and (4) the "negative effect on the company's innocent employees and shareholders" that would have resulted from criminal charges against the corporation. Obermaier, Drafting Companies to Fight Crime, New York Times, May 24, 1992, sec. 3, p.11, col.2.

The most controversial example of an explanation of a decision not to prosecute arose when FBI Director James Comey (1) explained publicly in July 2016 why the government declined to prosecute former Secretary of State (and then Presidential candidate) Hillary Clinton for her use of a private e-mail server during her service as Secretary; (2) informed Congress shortly before the November 2016 election that the FBI was investigating whether any classified information was contained in e-mails on the computer of her assistant who shared a computer with her husband, former Congressman Anthony Weiner; and (3) a few days later—after the election—announced that the newly discovered e-mails were duplicates of e-mails the FBI had previously examined. Questions arose as to Director Comey's motives and judgment. McLean, The True Story of the Comey Letter Debacle, https://www.vanityfair.com/news/2017/02/james-comey-fbi-director-letter.

In Secretary Clinton's case the public was aware of an investigation into her handling of e-mails. In such circumstances is it proper to announce that no charges will be brought? Should a government representative explain the decision not to prosecute? Once the decision not to prosecute is made, is it fair to a candidate to have the electorate believe that the investigation is ongoing? What if the public is unaware of an investigation but it is possible that charges might be brought against a candidate after the election? Is it fair for a prosecutor to remain silent? Is it fair for the prosecutor to reveal the investigation before a decision to charge has been made?

E. PROSECUTORIAL RULEMAKING

Just as there have been numerous calls for rulemaking by the police, there have been a number of suggestions that chief prosecutorial officers should formulate regulations to govern the conduct of their offices. See, e.g., ALI Model Code of Pre-Arraignment Procedure § 10.3 (calling for regulations); ABA Standards, The Prosecution Function § 3–2.4 ("[e]ach prosecutor's office should seek to develop general policies to guide the exercise of prosecutorial discretion, and standard operating procedures for the office").

Some guidelines have been drafted, but they leave much room for individualized charging judgment on the part of particular prosecutors. See, e.g., U.S. Dept. of Justice, Materials Relating to Prosecutorial Discretion. See also Baker, A View to the Future of Judicial Federalism: "Neither Out Far Nor In Deep," 45 Case W. Res. L. Rev. 705, 749 (1995) (discussing the process by which "the Department of Justice and the typical U.S. Attorney's Office have written prosecution guidelines, often labeled 'declination policies,' that describe principles for informed exercise of federal prosecutorial discretion."). The arguments for prosecutorial rulemaking are similar to those made in favor of police rulemaking, but they are even stronger, because policy-making executive officials are likely to be trusted with greater power to make enforcement decisions than are lower level police officers.

Arguments against prosecutorial rulemaking have been made, however. They are the following:

- the application of rules in particular cases would be challenged, thus raising the costs of the criminal process;

- rules would reduce the deterrent effect of the criminal law by announcing which laws would not be vigorously enforced;
- individual treatment would be sacrificed in order to have uniformity;
- problems in law enforcement change rapidly (e.g., post-September 11) and rulemaking would inhibit a rapid prosecutorial response to new problems; and
- adequate rules cannot be devised because discretion cannot be controlled by any clear criteria.[7]

Are these arguments persuasive? For an argument that internal standards are critical to assure the public integrity of a prosecutor's decisions, see Green and Zacharias, Prosecutorial Neutrality, 2004 Wis. L.Rev. 837.

F. SELECTIVE ENFORCEMENT

Whether by rules or by ad hoc decisions, prosecutors operating in a world of partial enforcement must somehow choose whom to prosecute. The selection of a certain type of case or person for enforcement may raise questions of arbitrariness and even equal protection. Understandably, however, courts are reluctant to regulate the traditional discretion of the prosecutor to charge. As Judge Posner has stated:

> A judge in our system does not have the authority to tell prosecutors which crimes to prosecute or when to prosecute them. Prosecutorial discretion resides in the executive, not in the judicial, branch, and that discretion, though subject of course to judicial review, is not reviewable for a simple abuse of discretion.

United States v. Giannattasio, 979 F.2d 98 (7th Cir.1992).[8]

1. Charges on Collateral Matters

It should be no surprise that a disproportionate number of prosecutions are brought against career offenders, members of organized crime, and suspected terrorists. Often prosecutors hunt to bring a charge that will "stick," even if the crime charged might be considered collateral

[7] See generally, Beck, The Administrative Law of Criminal Prosecution: The Development of Prosecutorial Policy, 27 Am.U.L.Rev. 310, 337–80 (1978). See also, Vorenberg, Decent Restraint of Prosecutorial Discretion, 94 Harv.L.Rev. 1521 (1981), which suggests appropriate ways of controlling discretion. Frase, The Decision to File Federal Criminal Charges: A Quantitative Study of Prosecutorial Discretion, 47 U.Chi.L.Rev. 246 (1980), focuses on one United States Attorney's office and documents the tremendous discretion afforded federal prosecutors and the factors they most often consider in exercising it.

[8] In Imbler v. Pachtman, 424 U.S. 409 (1976), the Court held that a prosecutor has absolute immunity from liability for all claims concerning the initiation of charges and the trying of the case. See also Buckley v. Fitzsimmons, 509 U.S. 259 (1993) (prosecutor entitled to absolute immunity for charging decisions, but receives the lesser protection of qualified immunity for statements to the media and for actions taken during the preliminary investigation of an uncharged crime).

to the central criminal activity of the defendant. The classic example is the successful prosecution of Al Capone for tax violations. Should a prosecutor be able to tell law enforcement officials to "go after X who I believe is an organized crime official. Check his tax records, his business dealings, everything"? Professors Richman and Stuntz, in Al Capone's Revenge: An Essay on the Political Economy of Pretextual Prosecution, 105 Colum. L.Rev. 583 (2005), argue that pretextual decisions to charge create social costs:

> There is a strong social interest in non-pretextual prosecution, and that interest is much more important than the "fairness to defendants" argument that has preoccupied the literature on this subject. Criminal charges are not only a means of identifying and punishing criminal conduct. They are also a means by which prosecutors send signals to their superiors, including the voters to whom they are ultimately responsible. When a murderer is brought to justice for murder rather than for tax evasion, voters learn some important things about their community and about the justice system: that a given homicide has been committed in a particular way * * * ; that the crime has been solved; that the police and prosecution have done a good job of assembling evidence against the killer, and so forth. If there is a legislative body that oversees the relevant law enforcement agencies, those same signals are sent to the legislative overseers. When a prosecutor gets a conviction * * * for an unrelated lesser crime than the one that motivated the investigation, the signals are muddied. They may disappear altogether. * * *
>
> Another audience also gets a muddied signal: would-be criminals. Instead of sending the message that running illegal breweries and bribing local cops would lead to a term in a federal penitentiary, the Capone prosecution sent a much more complicated and much less helpful message: If you run a criminal enterprise, you should keep your name out of the newspapers and at least pretend to pay your taxes. * * * [T]he political economy of criminal law enforcement depends on a reasonably good match between the charges that motivate prosecution and the charges that appear on defendants' rap sheets. When crimes and charges do not coincide, no one can tell whether law enforcers are doing their jobs. The justice system loses the credibility it needs, and voters lose the trust they need to have in the justice system. Individual agents and prosecutors pay only a tiny fraction of that price, which is why they continue to follow the Capone strategy. The larger price is paid only over time—by crime victims, by law enforcement agencies, and (not least) by the voting public.

2. Constitutional Limitations on the Charging Decision

The following case sets forth a very high threshold for proving a constitutional claim of selective prosecution.

UNITED STATES V. ARMSTRONG

Supreme Court of the United States, 1996.
517 U.S. 456.

CHIEF JUSTICE REHNQUIST delivered the opinion of the Court.

In this case, we consider the showing necessary for a defendant to be entitled to discovery on a claim that the prosecuting attorney singled him out for prosecution on the basis of his race. We conclude that respondents failed to satisfy the threshold showing: They failed to show that the Government declined to prosecute similarly situated suspects of other races.

In April 1992, respondents were indicted in the United States District Court for the Central District of California on charges of conspiring to possess with intent to distribute more than 50 grams of cocaine base (crack) and conspiring to distribute the same, in violation of 21 U.S.C. §§ 841 and 846, and federal firearms offenses. * * * On seven separate occasions * * * informants had bought a total of 124.3 grams of crack from respondents and witnessed respondents carrying firearms during the sales. * * *

[R]espondents filed a motion for discovery or for dismissal of the indictment, alleging that they were selected for federal prosecution because they are black. In support of their motion, they offered only an affidavit [alleging] that, in every one of the 24 §§ 841 or 846 cases closed by the office during 1991, the defendant was black. Accompanying the affidavit was a "study" listing the 24 defendants, their race, whether they were prosecuted for dealing cocaine as well as crack, and the status of each case.

The Government opposed the discovery motion, arguing, among other things, that there was no evidence or allegation "that the Government has acted unfairly or has prosecuted non-black defendants or failed to prosecute them." The District Court granted the motion. It ordered the Government (1) to provide a list of all cases from the last three years in which the Government charged both cocaine and firearms offenses, (2) to identify the race of the defendants in those cases, (3) to identify what levels of law enforcement were involved in the investigations of those cases, and (4) to explain its criteria for deciding to prosecute those defendants for federal cocaine offenses.

The Government moved for reconsideration of the District Court's discovery order. With this motion it submitted affidavits and other evidence to explain why it had chosen to prosecute respondents and why respondents' study did not support the inference that the Government was singling out blacks for cocaine prosecution. The federal and local agents participating in the case alleged in affidavits that race played no role in their investigation. An Assistant United States Attorney explained in an affidavit that the decision to prosecute met the general criteria for prosecution, because

> "there was over 100 grams of cocaine base involved, over twice the threshold necessary for a ten year mandatory minimum sentence; there were multiple sales involving multiple defendants, thereby indicating a fairly substantial crack cocaine ring; . . . there were multiple federal firearms violations intertwined with the narcotics trafficking; the overall evidence in the case was extremely strong, including audio and videotapes of defendants; . . . and several of the defendants had criminal histories including narcotics and firearms violations."

The Government also submitted sections of a published 1989 Drug Enforcement Administration report which concluded that "large-scale, interstate trafficking networks controlled by Jamaicans, Haitians and Black street gangs dominate the manufacture and distribution of crack."

In response, one of respondents' attorneys submitted an affidavit alleging that an intake coordinator at a drug treatment center had told her that there are "an equal number of caucasian users and dealers to minority users and dealers." Respondents also submitted an affidavit from a criminal defense attorney alleging that in his experience many nonblacks are prosecuted in state court for crack offenses, and a newspaper article reporting that Federal "crack criminals . . . are being punished far more severely than if they had been caught with powder cocaine, and almost every single one of them is black," Newton, Harsher Crack Sentences Criticized as Racial Inequity, Los Angeles Times, Nov. 23, 1992, p. 1.

The District Court denied the motion for reconsideration. When the Government indicated it would not comply with the court's discovery order, the court dismissed the case.

A divided three-judge panel of the Court of Appeals for the Ninth Circuit reversed, holding that, because of the proof requirements for a selective-prosecution claim, defendants must "provide a colorable basis for believing that 'others similarly situated have not been prosecuted' " to obtain discovery. (Quoting United States v. Wayte, 710 F.2d 1385, 1387 (C.A.9 1983), aff'd, 470 U.S. 598 (1985)). * * * We granted certiorari to determine the appropriate standard for discovery for a selective-prosecution claim.

[The Court held that Federal Rule of Criminal Procedure 16 did not mandate disclosure of material supporting a selective prosecution claim. That Rule requires disclosure of documents "material to the preparation of the defendant's defense" and the Court construed that phrase to refer to a defense that was responsive to the government's case-in-chief (e.g., that the defendant is not guilty). A selective prosecution attack was not material to the "defense" in this sense. See the discussion of this aspect of the opinion in Chapter 8, infra.]

* * *

A selective-prosecution claim is not a defense on the merits to the criminal charge itself, but an independent assertion that the prosecutor has brought the charge for reasons forbidden by the Constitution. Our cases delineating the necessary elements to prove a claim of selective prosecution have taken great pains to explain that the standard is a demanding one.* * *

A selective-prosecution claim asks a court to exercise judicial power over a "special province" of the Executive. The Attorney General and United States Attorneys retain broad discretion to enforce the Nation's criminal laws. * * * In the ordinary case, so long as the prosecutor has probable cause to believe that the accused committed an offense defined by statute, the decision whether or not to prosecute, and what charge to file or bring before a grand jury, generally rests entirely in his discretion.

Of course, a prosecutor's discretion is subject to constitutional constraints. One of these constraints, imposed by the equal protection component of the Due Process Clause of the Fifth Amendment, is that the decision whether to prosecute may not be based on "an unjustifiable standard such as race, religion, or other arbitrary classification," Oyler v. Boles, 368 U.S. 448, 456 (1962). A defendant may demonstrate that the administration of a criminal law is "directed so exclusively against a particular class of persons . . . with a mind so unequal and oppressive" that the system of prosecution amounts to "a practical denial" of equal protection of the law. Yick Wo v. Hopkins, 118 U.S. 356, 373 (1886).

In order to dispel the presumption that a prosecutor has not violated equal protection, a criminal defendant must present "clear evidence to the contrary." We explained in *Wayte* why courts are "properly hesitant to examine the decision whether to prosecute." Judicial deference to the decisions of these executive officers rests in part on an assessment of the relative competence of prosecutors and courts. "Such factors as the strength of the case, the prosecution's general deterrence value, the Government's enforcement priorities, and the case's relationship to the Government's overall enforcement plan are not readily susceptible to the kind of analysis the courts are competent to undertake." It also stems from a concern not to unnecessarily impair the performance of a core executive constitutional function. "Examining the basis of a prosecution delays the criminal proceeding, threatens to chill law enforcement by subjecting the prosecutor's motives and decisionmaking to outside inquiry, and may undermine prosecutorial effectiveness by revealing the Government's enforcement policy."

The requirements for a selective-prosecution claim draw on ordinary equal protection standards. The claimant must demonstrate that the federal prosecutorial policy had a discriminatory effect and that it was motivated by a discriminatory purpose. To establish a discriminatory effect in a race case, the claimant must show that similarly situated individuals of a different race were not prosecuted. * * *

The similarly situated requirement does not make a selective-prosecution claim impossible to prove. [In Yick Wo v. Hopkins], we invalidated an ordinance, * * * adopted by San Francisco, that prohibited the operation of laundries in wooden buildings. The plaintiff in error successfully demonstrated that the ordinance was applied against Chinese nationals but not against other laundry-shop operators. The authorities had denied the applications of 200 Chinese subjects for permits to operate shops in wooden buildings, but granted the applications of 80 individuals who were not Chinese subjects to operate laundries in wooden buildings "under similar conditions."

* * *

Having reviewed the requirements to prove a selective-prosecution claim, we turn to the showing necessary to obtain discovery in support of such a claim. If discovery is ordered, the Government must assemble from its own files documents which might corroborate or refute the defendant's claim. Discovery thus imposes many of the costs present when the Government must respond to a prima facie case of selective prosecution. It will divert prosecutors' resources and may disclose the Government's prosecutorial strategy. The justifications for a rigorous standard for the elements of a selective-prosecution claim thus require a correspondingly rigorous standard for discovery in aid of such a claim.

The parties, and the Courts of Appeals which have considered the requisite showing to establish entitlement to discovery, describe this showing with a variety of phrases, like "colorable basis," "substantial threshold showing," "substantial and concrete basis," or "reasonable likelihood". However, the many labels for this showing conceal the degree of consensus about the evidence necessary to meet it. The Courts of Appeals "require some evidence tending to show the existence of the essential elements of the defense," discriminatory effect and discriminatory intent. United States v. Berrios, 501 F.2d 1207, 1211 (C.A.2 1974).

In this case we consider what evidence constitutes "some evidence tending to show the existence" of the discriminatory effect element. The Court of Appeals held that a defendant may establish a colorable basis for discriminatory effect without evidence that the Government has failed to prosecute others who are similarly situated to the defendant. We think it was mistaken in this view. The vast majority of the Courts of Appeals require the defendant to produce some evidence that similarly situated defendants of other races could have been prosecuted, but were not, and this requirement is consistent with our equal protection case law. As the three-judge panel explained, "selective prosecution implies that a selection has taken place."

The Court of Appeals reached its decision in part because it started "with the presumption that people of all races commit all types of crimes—not with the premise that any type of crime is the exclusive province of any particular racial or ethnic group." It cited no authority for this proposition, which seems contradicted by the most recent statistics of the United States Sentencing Commission. Those statistics show that: More than 90% of the persons sentenced in 1994 for crack cocaine trafficking were black; 93.4% of convicted LSD dealers were white.; and 91% of those convicted for pornography or prostitution were white (Table 13). Presumptions at war with presumably reliable statistics have no proper place in the analysis of this issue.

The Court of Appeals also expressed concern about the "evidentiary obstacles defendants face." But all of its sister Circuits that have confronted the issue have required that defendants produce some evidence of differential treatment of similarly situated members of other races or protected classes. In the present case, if the claim of selective prosecution were well founded, it should not have been an insuperable task to prove that persons of other races were being treated differently than respondents. For instance, respondents could have investigated whether similarly situated persons of other races were prosecuted by the State of California, were known to federal law enforcement officers, but were not prosecuted in federal court. We think the required threshold—a credible showing of different treatment of similarly situated persons—adequately balances the Government's interest in vigorous prosecution and the defendant's interest in avoiding selective prosecution.

In the case before us, respondents' "study" did not constitute "some evidence tending to show the existence of the essential elements of" a selective-prosecution claim. The study failed to identify individuals who were not black, could have been prosecuted for the offenses for which respondents were charged, but were not so prosecuted. This omission was not remedied by respondents' evidence in opposition to the Government's motion for reconsideration. The newspaper article, which discussed the discriminatory effect of federal drug sentencing laws, was not relevant to an allegation of discrimination in decisions to prosecute. Respondents' affidavits, which recounted one attorney's conversation with a drug treatment center employee and the experience of another attorney defending drug prosecutions in state court, recounted hearsay and reported personal conclusions based on anecdotal evidence. The judgment of the

Court of Appeals is therefore reversed, and the case is remanded for proceedings consistent with this opinion.

[The concurring opinions of JUSTICES SOUTER, GINSBURG and BREYER are omitted.]

JUSTICE STEVENS, **dissenting.**

* * *

[I]t is undisputed that the brunt of the elevated federal penalties [for crack cocaine] falls heavily on blacks. While 65% of the persons who have used crack are white, in 1993 they represented only 4% of the federal offenders convicted of trafficking in crack. Eighty-eight percent of such defendants were black.. * * *

The extraordinary severity of the imposed penalties and the troubling racial patterns of enforcement give rise to a special concern about the fairness of charging practices for crack offenses. * * * In my view, the District Judge, who has sat on both the federal and the state benches in Los Angeles, acted well within her discretion to call for the development of facts that would demonstrate what standards, if any, governed the choice of forum where similarly situated offenders are prosecuted.

Critique of Armstrong

Professor Davis, in Prosecution and Race: The Power and Privilege of Discretion, 67 Fordham L.Rev. 13 (1998), provides the following critique on the intent-based test of selective prosecution set forth by the Court in *Armstrong*:

> * * * Instead of focusing on the harm experienced by African Americans as a result of actions by state actors, the Court has focused on whether the act itself is inherently invidious and whether the actor intended to cause the harm. In addition, the Court has placed the burden of proving intent on the shoulders of the victim. * * *
>
> The main problem with this intent-focused analysis is that it is backward-looking. Although perhaps adequate in combating straightforward and explicit discrimination as it existed in the past, it is totally deficient as a remedy for the more complex and systemic discrimination that African Americans currently experience. When state actors openly expressed their racist views, it was easy to identify and label the invidious nature of their actions. But today, with some notable exceptions, most racist behavior is not openly expressed. More significantly, some racist behavior is committed unconsciously, and many who engage in this behavior are well-intentioned people who

would be appalled by the notion that they would be seen as behaving in a racist or discriminatory manner.

> Unconscious racism, although arguably less offensive than purposeful discrimination, is no less harmful. In fact, in many ways it is more perilous because it is often unrecognizable to the victim as well as the perpetrator. And the Court, by focusing on intent rather than harm, has refused to recognize, much less provide a remedy for, this most common and widespread form of racism. * * *

For another critique of the *Armstrong* standards, see McAdams, Race and Selective Prosecution: Discovering the Pitfalls of *Armstrong*, 73 Chicago-Kent L.Rev. 605 (1998).

Unprosecuted Similar Conduct

In United States v. Parham, 16 F.3d 844 (8th Cir.1994), the defendants were African-Americans who were convicted of voting more than once in the same Arkansas election. The defendants, pursuing selective prosecution claims, proffered evidence of numerous voter irregularities attributable to whites that went unprosecuted. These included episodes where African-American disabled or elderly voters were refused assistance while whites were helped, and cases of intimidation of African-American voters by whites brandishing guns. While the court found that these acts by whites warranted prosecution, they were held irrelevant to the defendants' selective prosecution claims. This is because the acts by whites were

> not sufficiently similar to the acts of voter fraud for which Parham and Johnson were prosecuted to constitute a prima facie case of selective prosecution. Parham and Johnson were in effect charged with forging names on absentee ballots. They presented no evidence that other's acts of absentee ballot forgery or fraud were tolerated without prosecution. Where a defendant cannot show anyone in a similar situation who was not prosecuted, he has not met the threshold point of showing that there has been selectivity in prosecution.

Judge Heaney dissented in *Parham*, reasoning that the defendant need only establish that unprosecuted crimes are *similar*, not that they are identical.

Example of a Case in Which Discovery Was Ordered on a Selective Prosecution Claim

United States v. Jones, 159 F.3d 969 (6th Cir.1998), is one of the rare cases in which discovery was ordered to permit investigation of a selective prosecution claim, after the defendant was convicted of drugs and weapons offenses. The shocking facts were related by the court as follows:

Jones argues on appeal that he was prosecuted based on his race, citing to the Government's decision to prosecute him in federal court instead of state court and the egregious and unprofessional conduct of the arresting local law enforcement officers, Kerry Nelson and Terry Spence.

The conduct of officers Nelson and Spence was undeniably shameful. Prior to the planned arrest of Jones and his wife, the two officers had t-shirts made with Jones's picture emblazoned on the front accompanied by the printed words, "See ya, wouldn't want to be ya" above the picture, and below, "going back to prison." On the back of the t-shirts appeared a picture of Jones's wife, a co-defendant, with the words, "wait on me, Slow, [Jones' nickname was "Slow Motion"] I am coming, too." The two officers were wearing the t-shirts when they arrested Jones in August of 1995. Over one year later, while on a Caribbean cruise, Officer Spence mailed a postcard purchased in Jamaica to Jones while he was in custody awaiting trial. Jones regards Spence's mailing of the postcard, that pictured a black woman with a basket of bananas on her head, as a racial insult. On the postcard, postmarked from Cozumel, Mexico on October 24, 1996, appeared the following handwritten message:

> Slow Motion. What's up? Haven't talked to you since you were in court and lost all your motions. Sorry, but life goes on. Just wanted to drop you a line and let you know that Cozumel, Mexico is beautiful. I'm on vacation and I'll be back Monday for trial, and chances are good you're going to jail for a long time. See ya, Officer Spence.

Spence testified that he sent the postcard to relieve "stress I was feeling while I was on the cruise." Regarding the t-shirts, Spence explained that "It was just—I took pride in arresting [Jones]." Nelson also testified that he wore the t-shirt to demonstrate "a great deal of pride in Mr. Jones's arrest."

In addition, there was testimony at the hearing with respect to Jones's claim that local law enforcement agents improperly referred his case for federal prosecution based on his race. [Federal prosecution subjected to the defendants to much harsher sentencing penalties]. The testimony showed that the Murfreesboro Police Department had referred fourteen defendants, including Jones and his Caucasian co-defendant, Donnie Billings, for federal prosecution in the preceding five years. Of those fourteen defendants, four were African-American, two were Columbian, two were Lebanese, one was Israeli and five were Caucasian. Of the cases referred for federal prosecution in the preceding five years, however, only Jones's and Billings's prosecutions involved crack cocaine. Further, Jones presented evidence of eight non-African-American defendants prosecuted for crack cocaine offenses who were not referred for federal prosecution.

The court found that Jones had established a prima facie case of discriminatory intent, which is the first part of the intent/impact test imposed by *Armstrong.*

The court found, however, that there was not enough evidence of discriminatory impact to require dismissal of the indictment. Yet there was enough to justify further discovery.

3. Choice of Forum

In the American system of dual sovereignty, the same criminal conduct is often prosecutable under either federal or state law. It is also possible for the choice of forum to be outcome-determinative. For example, in drug cases—as indicated in *Jones* above—the federal sentencing laws generally provide for much harsher sentences than could be given for the same conduct in a state prosecution. Suppose that the defendant can show that a federal prosecution was brought in order to trigger the harsher federal sentences—but unlike in *Jones, supra,* there is no allegation that the decision was based on racial or other discriminatory grounds. Is the defendant entitled to relief?

A typical response to a challenge to the prosecutor's choice of forum is found in United States v. Jacobs, 4 F.3d 603 (8th Cir.1993), a case in which the defendant would have received probation had he been convicted on state charges, but instead received a five-year prison sentence after being convicted in federal court. As the court noted:

> Prosecutors have broad discretion in making prosecutive decisions. So long as the prosecutor has probable cause to believe that the accused committed an offense defined by statute, the decision whether or not to prosecute, and what charge to file, generally rests entirely in his discretion. In exercising this discretion, the prosecutor may take into account the penalties available upon conviction. The prosecutor may not, of course, base the decision to prosecute upon impermissible factors such as race, religion, or other arbitrary and unjustifiable classifications. Likewise the prosecutor may not file charges out of vindictiveness nor in retaliation for a defendant's exercise of legal rights.
>
> The fact that the federal government prosecutes a federal crime in a federal court that could have been or has been prosecuted as a state crime in a state court does not itself violate due process. Choice of forum lies within the realm of prosecutorial discretion.

See also United States v. Dockery, 965 F.2d 1112 (D.C.Cir.1992) (it was permissible for the U.S. Attorney in the District of Columbia to terminate prosecutions in the D.C. Superior Court and reinstitute them in the U.S. District Court a block away to take advantage of the sterner penalties set by the federal sentencing law; defendant received a ten-year minimum sentence, which would have been 1–5 years in the Superior Court); United States v. Williams, 963 F.2d 1337 (10th Cir.1992) (defendant received 20 years under federal law, and would have received 5 years under state law: "prosecution in a federal rather than a state court does not violate due process despite the absence of guidelines for such referral"); United States v. Ucciferri, 960 F.2d 953 (11th Cir.1992) (it was irrelevant that a federal prosecution was motivated by a desire to avoid more rigorous state constitutional protections).

4. Choice of Crime to Charge

What if two criminal statutes cover the same conduct—does the prosecutor have the discretion to charge under the statute resulting in the longer prison sentence? In United States v. Batchelder, 442 U.S. 114 (1979), Justice Marshall wrote for the Court as it held that a defendant who was convicted of receiving a firearm that had traveled in interstate commerce could be sentenced to five years' imprisonment, the maximum term under the statute, and that he was not entitled to be sentenced under another statute that punished felons for transporting firearms with a maximum penalty of two years. Justice Marshall reasoned that a wrongdoer has notice that more than one statute covers his conduct. Thus, the fact that conduct violates two statutes does not require a prosecution under the more lenient of them. The Court emphasized the deference due to the prosecutor in making a charging decision and reiterated that a defendant's sole complaint is against invidious discrimination.

Prosecutors may, however, be limited in their ability to charge a defendant in a certain way as punishment for a defendant's exercise of constitutional rights. The subject of vindictive prosecutions is considered in Chapter 12, infra.

IV. THE GRAND JURY

The American criminal justice system, like the American political system, has checks and balances to prevent against too much centralized authority being placed in the hands of the executive. In some instances, depending on the jurisdiction and the seriousness of the crime, the grand jury operates as a check on the prosecutor's decision to charge. In other instances, the preliminary hearing serves this function. In some rare instances, both checks are available. Where a minor offense is charged, it is possible that no pretrial screening procedure will be utilized. This section will focus on the grand jury and how it operates.

A. BACKGROUND ON THE GRAND JURY

The Ninth Circuit, in United States v. Navarro-Vargas, 408 F.3d 1184 (9th Cir. 2005) provides a good summary of the history and purpose of the grand jury, and addresses critiques about its modern function. The court relies on an extensive list of sources, most of which are deleted from the entry below.

The Historical Role of the Grand Jury

1. The Early English Grand Jury: Quasi-Prosecutor

The modern grand jury is a direct descendant of the English grand jury first employed more than 800 years ago. Its origins belie its modern role as intermediary between the people and their government. The earliest grand juries were the tool of the Crown. In 1164, anxious to consolidate power held by the church and feudal barons, King Henry II signed the Constitutions of Clarendon, which created a jury to charge all laity who were to be tried in ecclesiastical courts. Two years later he established the Assize of Clarendon, which was composed of twelve men who would "present" those suspected of crimes to the royal courts. These acts reasserted the King's power over his subjects and filled his coffers with the proceeds from chattels confiscated after conviction.

During its first hundred years, * * * the English grand jury was somewhat like a quasi-prosecutor for the King. Indeed, grand juries were expected to bring charges based on their own knowledge, as well as consider charges brought by prosecutors. * * *

The first real evidence of the grand jury acting as a shield to protect the accused was in 1681 when two London grand juries refused to indict the Earl of Shaftesbury and his follower Stephen Colledge, the political enemies of King Charles II. The King wanted them held over for public proceedings before the grand jury, but the grand jury insisted on conducting its inquiry in private. Given its powerful influence, the Crown expected a quick indictment pursuant to its charges. However, the grand jury returned the equivalent of a no-bill in the matter, defying the Crown's will both in holding private proceedings and in its ultimate decision not to indict. The Shaftesbury and Colledge cases established grand jury secrecy, which continues to be a crucial element in grand juries serving as an independent screen. * * *

2. The Colonial Grand Jury: Quasi-Legislative, Quasi-Administrative

American colonists adopted the grand jury as integral to the common law system. * * * In America, the institution gained broad powers to propose legislation and perform various administrative tasks. Grand juries "exercised broad, unorthodox powers," inspecting roads, jails, and other public buildings; monitoring public works expenditures, construction and maintenance; proposing new legislation; and criticizing poor administration. The colonial grand jury still performed a quasi-prosecutorial role by accusing individuals suspected of crimes, but colonial grand juries demonstrated greater independence than their English counterparts, due in part to the relatively weak position of colonial governments. With their expanding quasi-legislative and quasi-administrative roles, grand juries acquired greater popularity because they were regarded as more representative of the people. * * * [T]he American grand jury in effect enjoyed a roving commission to ferret out official malfeasance or self-dealing of any sort and bring it to the attention of the public at large * * *. Following the English traditions established in the Shaftesbury and Colledge cases, grand jury secrecy remained an important part of grand jury proceedings in the colonies. Grand jurors pledged to an oath of secrecy, and its violation was both a contempt and a crime.

While Colonial grand juries continued to serve as accusatory bodies, they occasionally refused to return indictments in high-profile cases. The most celebrated example in American history is that of John Peter Zenger, a newspaper publisher charged with libel after criticizing the Governor of New York. Based on the jury instructions, it seems clear that Zenger was guilty of the crime of libel. Nevertheless, three grand juries refused to indict not because of insufficient evidence but rather because the jurors were politically opposed to the prosecutions. As the Revolutionary War drew closer, the grand jury became popular at least as much from its success as a political weapon as from its role in the criminal justice system. * * * Grand jurors, selected from the public, frustrated prosecutors loyal to the king by refusing to indict those charged under unpopular laws imposed by the Crown, often on the urging of colonial judges. Grand jury presentments served an additional function during this time: they became excellent mediums of propaganda as grand juries issued stinging denunciations of Great Britain and stirring defenses of their rights as Englishmen. * * *

* * * In early debates over the ratification of the Constitution, before the Bill of Rights had been written, some feared that "there is no provision ... to prevent the attorney-general from filing information against any person, whether he is indicted by the grand jury or not; in consequence of which the most innocent person in the commonwealth may be taken by virtue of a warrant issued in consequence of such information. . . ." Because of this fear, the Grand

Jury Clause, located in the Fifth Amendment, was adopted with little debate or discussion.

3. The Post-Revolutionary and Nineteenth Century Grand Jury: Screening Function

As they had in colonial times, nineteenth century grand juries occasionally asserted their independence by refusing to indict under unpopular laws, even when the grand jury was instructed to indict if the facts satisfied the law. Prominently, grand juries in Kentucky and Mississippi refused to indict former Vice President Aaron Burr, although he was finally indicted in Virginia; refused to indict Americans who aided French privateers in violation of the Neutrality Proclamation of 1793; and resisted indicting those accused of violating the controversial Alien and Sedition Acts. Throughout the nineteenth century, courts continued to recognize the necessity of secrecy in grand jury proceedings. This secrecy allowed grand juries to independently determine whether to indict, despite a judge's instructions.

* * *

The political potential in the screening function of the grand jury was * * * manifest during the Civil War era. Prior to the war, Southern grand juries readily indicted those involved in crimes related to abolition of the slave trade, while Northern grand juries were slow to indict those charged with violations of the fugitive slave laws. Following the Civil War, Southern grand juries frustrated enforcement of Reconstruction-era laws by refusing to indict Ku Klux Klan members and others accused of committing crimes against newly-freed blacks. * * *

4. The Modern Grand Jury

By the twentieth century, dramatic confrontations between prosecutors and jurors in grand jury proceedings had become rare. Currently, grand jurors no longer perform any other function but to investigate crimes and screen indictments, and they tend to indict in the overwhelming number of cases brought by prosecutors. Because of this, many criticize the modern grand jury as no more than a "rubber stamp" for the prosecutor. *See* Federal Justice Statistics Resource Center, Federal Justice Statistics Database (noting that federal grand juries returned only twenty-one no-bills in 2001). * * * As the grand jury's tendency to indict has become more pronounced, some commentators claim that the modern grand jury has lost its independence. * * * Against this criticism, the Supreme Court has steadfastly insisted that the grand jury remains as a shield against unfounded prosecutions.

So as a historical matter, the grand jury served two major functions. On one hand, it was a "buffer" protecting citizens from unjust prosecution by the state. On the other hand, it served an enforcement function by investigating incidents or offenses that the grand jurors thought suspicious. These functions were considered so important that they are expressed in the Fifth Amendment, which states in relevant part:

> No person shall be held to answer for a capital, or otherwise infamous crime, unless on a presentment or indictment of a Grand Jury, except in cases arising in the land or naval forces, or in the Militia, when in actual service in time of War or public danger; * * *.

The Supreme Court has stated that the grand jury's dual historic functions "survive to this day. Its responsibilities continue to include both the determination whether there is probable cause to believe a crime has been committed and the protection of citizens against unfounded criminal prosecutions." United States v. Calandra, 414 U.S. 338 (1974).

Many observers, however, see the modern grand jury as performing only the first (prosecutorial) function and ignoring the second (protective) function. For example, Hafetz and Pellettieri conclude that

> whatever its historic antecedents, the grand jury has long ceased to function as an independent entity acting both as shield for the citizenry as well as sword for the prosecutor. * * * [T]he grand jury functions as an investigative tool of the prosecutor. Employing the power of compulsory process in a secret proceeding the prosecutor investigates and determines with virtually no check by the grand jury who gets indicted and for what.

Time to Reform the Grand Jury, The Champion, at 12 (Jan. 1999).

As you read the materials in this Chapter, consider whether the assessment of the grand jury as only a tool for the prosecutor is correct, and if so, whether reforms can be instituted to return the grand jury to its role as protector of citizens from unfounded prosecutions.

A Right Not Incorporated

Unlike most other provisions of the Bill of Rights examined thus far, the right to a grand jury indictment does not extend to defendants accused of state crimes. In Hurtado v. California, 110 U.S. 516 (1884), the Supreme Court held that the right to a grand jury indictment is not incorporated in the Due Process Clause of the Fourteenth Amendment. Today, slightly less than half the states require prosecution by indictment for serious crimes as a matter of state constitutional or statutory law. The majority of the states use the alternatives of preliminary hearing and the filing of an information, methods of charging discussed later in this Chapter.

What Is an Infamous Crime?

The Fifth Amendment requires a grand jury indictment for the prosecution of an "infamous crime." Courts have held that a crime is "infamous" only if it can result in either hard labor or imprisonment in a penitentiary. Ex parte Wilson, 114 U.S. 417 (1885). Thus, the court in United States v. Armored Transport, Inc., 629 F.2d 1313 (9th Cir.1980), held that an indictment was not constitutionally required for a corporation to be convicted of an antitrust felony—a corporation is subject only to a fine and a fine is not an infamous punishment. See also United States v. Colt, 126 F.3d 981 (7th Cir.1997) (no right to grand jury indictment where statute authorized imprisonment in a federal prison camp, but not in a federal penitentiary: "The distinction between penitentiaries and other places of imprisonment survives in today's federal prison system. * * * Only eight of the Bureau of Prisons' institutions are designated as U.S. Penitentiaries, which feature the highest security and the closest control of prisoner actions.").

How the Grand Jury Works

The court in In re Motions of Dow Jones & Co., 142 F.3d 496 (D.C.Cir.1998), provided this summary of the operation of the grand jury:

> Grand juries summon witnesses and documents with subpoenas. Witnesses, including custodians of documents, report on the scheduled date not to a courtroom, but to a hallway outside the room where the grand jury is sitting. The witness must enter the grand jury room alone, without his or her lawyer. No judge presides and none is present. See Beale et al., Grand Jury Law and Practice § 4.10, at 4–44 (2d ed.1997). Inside the grand jury room are sixteen to twenty-three grand jurors, one or more prosecuting attorneys, and a court reporter. 18 U.S.C. § 3321; Fed.R.Crim.P. 6. The witness is sworn, and questioning commences, all to the end of determining whether "there is adequate basis for bringing a criminal charge." United States v. Williams, 504 U.S. 36 (1992). Other than witnesses, each person present in the grand jury room or otherwise assisting the prosecutor is forbidden from disclosing matters occurring before the grand jury, Fed.R.Crim.P. 6.

The court explained judicial oversight of the grand jury in the following paragraph:

> Although the grand jury normally operates, of course, in the courthouse and under judicial auspices, its institutional relationship with the Judicial Branch has traditionally been, so to speak, at arm's length. Still, at many points, from service of the subpoena through the completion of the witness's grand jury appearance, judicial

proceedings relating to the grand jury may take place. The judge may be called upon to decide a witness's motion to postpone the date of testimony or to quash the subpoena. If a witness refuses to answer questions on the basis of a testimonial privilege, * * * the grand jury may seek a court order compelling the witness to answer. This may be done forthwith, through an oral presentation to the court, or upon the filing of pleadings, followed by a hearing. A hearing will also be needed if a witness asserts his or her privilege against self-incrimination, and the prosecutor seeks an order from the court granting the witness immunity. See 18 U.S.C. § 6003(a).

B. THE CHARGE TO THE GRAND JURY

What follows are excerpts from the Model Grand Jury Charge approved by the Judicial Conference of the United States. It provides a useful introduction to the work of the grand jury and the expectations that the community has for this body. The charge is given by the judge who empanels and supervises the grand jury. https://cldc.org/wp-content/uploads/2012/10/model-gj-charge.pdf.

MODEL GRAND JURY CHARGE

Ladies and Gentlemen:

1. Now that you have been empaneled and sworn as a Grand Jury, it is the Court's responsibility to instruct you as to the law which should govern your actions and your deliberations as Grand Jurors.

2. * * * The purpose of the Grand Jury is to determine whether there is sufficient evidence to justify a formal accusation against a person—that is, to determine if there is "probable cause" to believe the person committed a crime. If law enforcement officials were not required to submit to an impartial grand jury proof of guilt as to a proposed charge against a person suspected of having committed a crime, they would be free to arrest a suspect and bring that suspect to trial no matter how little evidence existed to support the charge.

3. The Grand Jury is an independent body and does not belong to any branch of the government. As members of the Grand Jury, you, in a very real sense, stand between the government and the person being investigated by the government. A federal grand jury must never be made an instrument of private prejudice, vengeance, or malice. It is your duty to see to it that indictments are returned only against those who you find probable cause to believe are guilty and to see to it that the innocent are not compelled to go to trial.

4. A member of the Grand Jury who is related by blood or marriage to a person under investigation, or who knows that person well enough to have a biased state of mind as to that person, or is

biased for any reason, should not participate in the investigation of that person or in the return of the indictment. This does not mean that if you have an opinion you should not participate in the investigation. However, it does mean that if you have a fixed opinion before you hear any evidence, either on a basis of friendship or ill will or some other similar motivation, you should not participate in that investigation and in voting on the indictment.

5. Sixteen of the twenty-three members of the Grand Jury constitute a quorum and must be present for the transaction of any business. If fewer than this number are present, even for a moment, the proceedings of the Grand Jury must stop.

Limitation on the Power of the Grand Jury

6. Although as Grand Jurors you have extensive powers, they are limited in several important respects.

7. You can only investigate conduct which violates federal criminal laws. Criminal activity which violates state law is outside your inquiry. Sometimes, though, the same conduct violates both federal and state law, and this you may properly consider.

8. There is also a geographic limitation on the scope of your inquiries in the exercise of your power. You may inquire only to federal offenses committed in this district.

9. You cannot judge the wisdom of the criminal laws enacted by Congress, that is, whether or not there should or should not be a federal law designating certain activity as criminal. That is to be determined by Congress and not by you.[9]

10. Furthermore, when deciding whether or not to indict, you should not consider punishment in the event of conviction.

The Grand Jury Procedures

11. The cases which you will hear will come before you in various ways. Frequently, suspects are arrested during or shortly after the commission of an alleged crime, and they are taken before a Magistrate Judge, who then holds a preliminary hearing to determine whether there is probable cause to believe that the person has committed a crime. If the Magistrate Judge finds such probable cause, he or she will direct that the person be held for the action of the Grand Jury so that you can independently consider whether there should be an indictment.

---

[9] The court in United States v. Navarro-Vargas, 408 F.3d 1184 (9th Cir. 2005), rejected the defendants' claim that this charge unconstitutionally impinged upon the grand jury's independence. See the discussion on grand jury nullification later in this Chapter.

12. Other cases will be brought before you by a government attorney—the U.S. Attorney or an Assistant U.S. Attorney before an arrest but after an investigation has been conducted by a governmental agency such as the Federal Bureau of Investigation, the Treasury Department, the Drug Enforcement Administration, Postal Authorities, or other federal law enforcement officials.

13. Since the government attorney has the duty of prosecuting persons charged with the commission of federal crimes, the government attorney will present the matters which the government desires to have you consider. The government will point out to you the laws which it believes have been violated, and will subpoena for testimony before you such witnesses as the government attorney may consider important and necessary and also any other witnesses that you may request or direct be called before you.

14. If during the course of your hearings, a different crime other than the one you are investigating surfaces, you have the right to pursue this new crime. Although you can subpoena new witnesses and documents, you have no power to employ investigators or to expend federal funds for investigative purposes. If the government attorney refuses to assist you or if you believe he or she is not acting impartially, you may take it up with me or any Judge of this Court. You may use this power even over the active opposition of the government's attorneys, if you believe it is necessary to do so in the interest of justice.

Evidence

15. The evidence you will consider will normally consist of oral testimony of witnesses and written documents. Each witness will appear before you separately. When the witness first appears before you, the Grand Jury foreperson will administer the witness an oath or affirmation, to testify truthfully. After this has been accomplished, the witness may be questioned. Ordinarily, the government attorney questions the witness first. Next, the foreperson may question the witness, and then any other members of the Grand Jury may ask questions. In the event a witness does not speak or understand the English language, an interpreter may be brought into the Grand Jury room to assist in the questioning.

16. Witnesses should be treated courteously and questions put to them in an orderly fashion. If you have any doubt whether it is proper to ask a particular question, ask the government attorney for advice. If necessary, a ruling may be obtained from the court.

17. You alone decide how many witnesses you want to hear. You can subpoena witnesses from anywhere in the country, directing the government attorney to issue necessary subpoenas. However, persons should not ordinarily be subjected to disruption of their daily lives,

harassed, annoyed, or inconvenienced, nor should public funds be expended to bring in witnesses unless you believe they can provide meaningful evidence which will assist you in your investigation.

18. Every witness has certain rights when appearing before a Grand Jury. Witnesses have the right to refuse to answer any question if the answer would tend to incriminate them and the right to know that anything they say may be used against them. The Grand Jury should hold no prejudice against a witness who exercises the right against compulsory self-incrimination, and this can play no part in the return of any indictment.

19. Although witnesses are not permitted to have a lawyer present with them in the Grand Jury room, the law permits witnesses to confer with their lawyer outside of the Grand Jury room. Since an appearance before a Grand Jury may present complex legal problems requiring the assistance of a lawyer, you also can not hold it against a witness if a witness chooses to exercise this right and leaves the Grand Jury room to confer with an attorney.

20. Ordinarily, neither the person being investigated by the government nor any witnesses on behalf of that person will testify before the Grand Jury. Upon his or her request, preferably in writing, you may afford that person an opportunity to appear before you. Because the appearance of the person being investigated before you may raise complicated legal problems, you should seek the government attorney's advice and, if necessary, the Court's ruling before his or her appearance is permitted. Before that person testifies, he or she must be advised of his or her rights and required to sign a formal waiver. You should be completely satisfied that the person being investigated understands what he or she is doing. * * *

21. The determination of whether a witness is telling the truth is something that you must decide. * * * You may consider in that regard whether the witnesses are personally interested in the outcome of the investigation, whether their testimony has been corroborated or supported by other witnesses or circumstances, what opportunity they have had for observing or acquiring knowledge concerning the matters about which they testify, the reasonableness or probability of the testimony they relate to you, and their manner and demeanor in testifying before you.

22. Hearsay is testimony as to facts not known by the witness of the witness's own personal knowledge but which have been told or related to the witness by persons other than the person being investigated. Hearsay testimony, if deemed by you to be persuasive, may in itself provide a basis for returning an indictment. You must be satisfied only that there is evidence against the accused showing

probable cause, even if such evidence is composed of hearsay testimony that might or might not be admissible in evidence at a trial.

23. Frequently, charges are made against more than one person. It will be your duty to examine the evidence as it relates to each person, and to make your finding as to each person. In other words, where charges are made against more than one person, you may indict all of the persons or only those persons who you believe properly deserve indictment.

Deliberation and Vote

24. After you have heard all the evidence you wish to hear in a particular matter, you will then proceed to deliberate as to whether the person being investigated should be indicted. No one other than your own members or an interpreter necessary to assist a juror who is hearing or speech impaired is to be present while you are deliberating or voting.

25. To return an indictment charging an individual with an offense, it is not necessary that you find that individual guilty beyond a reasonable doubt. You are not a trial jury and your task is not to decide the guilt or innocence of the person charged. Your task is to determine whether the government's evidence as presented to you is sufficient to cause you to conclude that there is probable cause to believe that the person being investigated committed the offense charged. To put it another way, you should vote to indict where the evidence presented to you is sufficiently strong to warrant a reasonable person's belief that the person being investigated is probably guilty of the offense charged.

26. Each juror has the right to express his or her view of the matter under consideration. Only after all Grand Jurors have been given full opportunity to be heard will a vote be taken. You may decide after deliberation among yourselves that further evidence should be considered before a vote is taken. In such case you may direct to subpoena the additional documents or witnesses you desire to consider.

27. When you have decided to vote, the foreperson shall designate a juror as secretary who will keep a record of the vote, which shall be filed with the Clerk of Court. The record does not include the names of the jurors but only the number of those voting for the indictment. Remember, at least sixteen jurors must be present at all times, and at least twelve members must vote in favor of an indictment before one may be returned.

28. If twelve or more members of the Grand Jury, after deliberation, believe that an indictment is warranted, then you will

request the government attorney to prepare the formal written indictment if one has not already been prepared and presented to you. The indictment will set forth the date and place of the alleged offense, will assert the circumstances making the alleged conduct criminal, and will identify the criminal statute violated. The foreperson will sign the indictment as a true bill, in the space followed by the word "foreperson." It is the duty of the foreperson to sign every indictment, whether the foreperson voted for or against. If less than twelve members of the Grand Jury vote in favor of an indictment which has been submitted to you for your consideration, the foreperson will endorse the indictment "Not a True Bill" and return it to the Court and the Court will impound it.

29. Indictments which have been signed as a true bill will be presented to a Judge [or a Magistrate Judge] in open court by your foreperson at the conclusion of each deliberative session of the Grand Jury. In the absence of the foreperson, a deputy foreperson may act in place of the foreperson and perform all functions and duties of the foreperson.

Independence of the Grand Jury

30. It is extremely important for you to realize that * * * the Grand Jury is independent of the United States Attorney and is not an arm or agent of the Federal Bureau of Investigation, the Drug Enforcement Administration, the Internal Revenue Service, or any governmental agency charged with prosecuting a crime. Simply put, as I have already told you, the Grand Jury is an independent body and does not belong to any branch of the government.

31. However, as a practical matter you must work closely with the government attorneys. They will provide you with important service in helping you to find your way when confronted with complex legal matters. It is entirely proper that you should receive this assistance. If past experience is any indication of what to expect in the future, then you can expect candor, honesty and good faith in matters presented by the government attorneys.[10] However, ultimately, you must depend on your own independent judgment, never becoming an arm of the United States Attorney's office. The government attorneys are prosecutors. You are not. If the facts suggest that you should not indict, then you should not do so, even in the face of the opposition or statements of the government attorney. You would violate your oath if

[10] In United States v. Navarro-Vargas, 408 F.3d 1184 (9th Cir. 2005), the defendants challenged this instruction because it amounted to a "vote of confidence" by the judge on the honesty of government attorneys and therefore undermined the independence of the grand jury. The court rejected the defendants' argument by looking to the instruction as a whole, reasoning that the passage would be problematic if it stated that the Grand Jury was an agent of the U.S. Attorney—but it did not.

you merely "rubber-stamped" indictments brought before you by the government representatives.

* * *

The Obligation of Secrecy

33. Your proceedings are secret and must remain secret permanently unless and until the Court decrees otherwise. You cannot relate to your family, to the news or television reporters, or to anyone that which transpired in the Grand Jury room. There are several important reasons for this requirement. A premature disclosure of Grand Jury action may frustrate the ends of justice by giving an opportunity to the person being investigated to escape and become a fugitive or to destroy evidence. Also, if the testimony of a witness is disclosed, the witness may be subject to intimidation, retaliation, bodily injury, or other tampering before testifying at trial. Thirdly, the requirement of secrecy protects an innocent person who may have come under investigation but has been cleared by the actions of the Grand Jury. In the eyes of some, investigation by a Grand Jury alone carries with it a suggestion of guilt. Thus great injury can be done to a person's good name even though the person is not indicted. And fourth, the secrecy requirement helps to protect the members of the grand jury themselves from improper contacts by those under investigation. For all these reasons, therefore, the secrecy requirement is of the utmost importance and must be regarded by you as an absolute duty. If you violate your oath of secrecy, you may be subject to punishment.

34. To insure the secrecy of Grand Jury proceedings, the law provides that only authorized persons may be in the Grand Jury room while evidence is being presented. Only the members of the Grand Jury, the government attorney, the witness under examination, the court reporter, and an interpreter, if required, may be present.

* * *

C. THE PROCEDURES OF THE GRAND JURY

Rule 6 of the Federal Rules of Criminal Procedure illustrates typical procedures of the grand jury—providing for number of jurors (16 to 23), provisions on secrecy, and the process and requirements for handing down an indictment. State grand juries may have fewer members and operate somewhat differently. But, the limitations on who can be present in the grand jury room and other aspects of Rule 6 are common to most grand juries. See Fed.R.Crim.P. 6 in the Statutory Supplement.

Discriminatory Selection of Grand Jurors

The Equal Protection Clause prohibits racial or ethnic discrimination in the selection of grand jurors. See Rose v. Mitchell, 443 U.S. 545 (1979) (racial discrimination in the selection of grand jurors is a valid ground for setting aside a criminal conviction, even where the defendant has been found guilty beyond a reasonable doubt by a properly constituted petit jury at a trial that was free from other constitutional error). In Castaneda v. Partida, 430 U.S. 482 (1977), the Court established that statistics could be used to make out a prima facie case of discrimination against Mexican-Americans, even where a majority of a county's population were Mexican-Americans. Challenges under the Fourteenth Amendment are like all of the challenges to government action on the basis of suspect classifications. See also Jefferson v. Morgan, 962 F.2d 1185 (6th Cir.1992) (statistical evidence, adjusted by standard deviation, shows systematic exclusion of African-Americans from grand jury; conviction reversed and indictment dismissed; error was not harmless simply because the defendant was convicted at trial).

Discriminatory Selection of Grand Jury Forepersons

Chief Justice Burger wrote for the Court in Hobby v. United States, 468 U.S. 339 (1984), as it held that discrimination in the selection of grand jury forepersons and deputy forepersons in a federal district did not require reversal of a conviction. Chief Justice Burger condemned all discrimination in the selection of grand jurors, but found that the ministerial functions of the foreperson and the deputy added little to the role that any particular grand juror plays. Thus, as long as the grand jury itself was validly selected, discrimination in the selection of the two ministerial leaders did not prejudice the defendant.

Secrecy of Grand Jury Proceedings

The Supreme Court has consistently recognized the importance of grand jury secrecy:

> First, if preindictment proceedings were made public, many prospective witnesses would be hesitant to come forward voluntarily, knowing that those against whom they testify would be aware of that testimony. Moreover, witnesses who appeared before the grand jury would be less likely to testify fully and frankly, as they would be open to retribution as well as to inducements. There also would be the risk that those about to be indicted would flee, or would try to influence individual grand jurors to vote against indictment. Finally, by preserving the secrecy of the proceedings, we assure that persons who

are accused but exonerated by the grand jury will not be held up to public ridicule.

Douglas Oil Co. v. Petrol Stops N.W., 441 U.S. 211 (1979).

Grand Jury Witnesses and Secrecy

Note that Federal Rule 6 does not require grand jury witnesses to maintain secrecy as to their own testimony. The argument has been made that a secrecy requirement for the witness's own testimony would be impractical. Do you agree with this? If witnesses are free to talk, how effective do you think the secrecy rule is likely to be?

Exceptions to Grand Jury Secrecy

Other than the witness who testifies at the grand jury, exceptions to secrecy are very limited—basically Rule 6 allows disclosure to officials within the government (including other sovereignties under certain circumstances). But public disclosure is essentially prohibited.

Some courts have found that there is an exception allowing disclosure in cases of exceptional historical or public interest—the rationale being that there is no real danger in reaching back into history to determine how a particular grand jury proceeded, and the inquiry could provide an important source of historical research. But most courts have found that the exceptions to secrecy in Rule 6 are exclusive. See, e.g., United States v. McDougal, 559 F.3d 837, 840–41 (8th Cir. 2009) ("Because the grand jury is an institution separate from the courts, over whose functioning the courts do not preside, courts will not order disclosure absent a recognized exception to Rule 6(e) or a valid challenge to the original sealing order or its implementation."); In re Grand Jury 89-4-72, 932 F.2d 481, 488 (6th Cir. 1991) ("[W]ithout an unambiguous statement to the contrary from Congress, we cannot, and must not, breach grand jury secrecy for any purpose other than those embodied by the Rule."). A few courts hold that district courts retain inherent authority to release grand jury material in appropriate cases without an express exemption. See, e,g, Carlson v. United States, 837 F.3d 753, 766–67 (7th Cir. 2016). This authority is found sufficiently broad to include historical grand jury materials of exceptional importance in appropriate cases.

In 2021, the Advisory Committee on Criminal Rules discussed amending Rule 6 to allow for a specific exemption for cases of exceptional historical or public interest. The Committee ultimately decided not to propose an amendment. Basically, there were concerns about how to define "exceptional historic interest"—and an abiding notion that grand jury secrecy is of paramount importance.

D. THE RELATIONSHIP OF THE GRAND JURY TO THE PROSECUTOR AND TO THE COURT

The roles played by the prosecutor, the court, and the grand jury are not exactly the same in all jurisdictions. However, it is common for courts to view the prosecutor's relationship to the grand jury as subject to little, if any, judicial scrutiny. United States v. Chanen, 549 F.2d 1306 (9th Cir.1977), illustrates this. The government presented its case three times to a federal grand jury. The first time the government did not ask for an indictment, and no vote was taken before the grand jury was discharged. A second grand jury indictment was dismissed because no transcript was made, and the government failed to present the jury with the evidence presented to the first grand jury. On the third attempt, the government secured an indictment against defendants for statutory fraud. The government presented its evidence to the third grand jury by reading testimony from its first grand jury presentation. The district court quashed the indictment because the judge felt that where the first grand jury failed to indict on the basis of live testimony, a subsequent grand jury should hear live testimony as well. The court of appeals reversed. It held that the prosecutor's action was not "fundamentally unfair" and therefore did not constitute a basis for dismissal. It reasoned as follows:

> As a practical matter, the grand jury generally relies on the prosecutor to determine what witnesses to call. Also, in practice the prosecutor conducts the examination of the witnesses and otherwise determines what evidence to present before the grand jury. In addition, it is the prosecutor who normally prepares the indictment, although of course the grand jury must review the indictment and adopt it as its own. Some of these functions—such as initiating a criminal case by presenting evidence before the grand jury—qualifies as an executive function within the exclusive prerogative of the Attorney General.
>
> The court, on the other hand, exercises its power to summon witnesses to attend and to give testimony before the grand jury. Also, it is the court which must compel a witness to testify if, after appearing, he refuses to do so. In addition, the court exercises a form of authority over the grand jury when, for example, it dismisses an indictment for failure to charge all elements of the offense or to warn the defendant fairly of the charge against which he must defend. Likewise, the court exercises authority over the prosecutor when it dismisses an indictment because of prosecutorial misconduct. * * *
>
> Nevertheless, given the constitutionally-based independence of each of the three actors—court, prosecutor and grand jury—we believe a court may not exercise its "supervisory power" in a way which encroaches on the prerogatives of the other two unless there is a clear

> basis in fact and law for doing so. If the district courts were not required to meet such a standard, their "supervisory power" could readily prove subversive of the doctrine of separation of powers.
>
> Application of this standard to the present case requires reversal. The asserted legal basis for the district court's interference with a standard prosecutorial decision—what evidence to present to the grand jury and how to present it—is the need to preserve the integrity of the judicial process and to avoid any fundamental unfairness. But it is far from clear that the prosecutor's decision in this case regarding the presentation of evidence to the third grand jury implicates any of those interests.

See also United States v. Strouse, 286 F.3d 767 (5th Cir. 2002) (federal court does not have supervisory power to dismiss a grand jury indictment based on perjured testimony, unless it is shown that the prosecutor knew that the testimony was perjurious: "a rule allowing dismissal of an indictment without a showing of government misconduct would open the door to attacks on grand jury evidence for which there are large incentives including discovery by the accused").[11]

Role of the Prosecutor

The role of the prosecutor may vary somewhat from place to place in grand jury proceedings, but generally she serves the following functions:

(a) She is the legal advisor to the grand jury. Many critics maintain that the grand jury should have separate counsel at its disposal to reduce the prosecutor's control over the grand jury. But traditionally the prosecutor is also the grand jury's counsel. See Mogul Bent on Grand Jury Reform, Nat.L.J. July 27, 1998, p. A10 (discussing an "Open Letter" sent to grand jurors suggesting that grand jurors should retain their own counsel, as "a simple way to the Grand Jury to reclaim its legal independence").

(b) She presents evidence to the grand jury. The grand jury can hear any additional evidence that it requests, but as a practical matter grand juries usually rely on the prosecutor to explain criminal offenses and to present the evidence that the grand jury considers. The prosecutor can subpoena witnesses to attend grand jury hearings, and once the witnesses are present the grand jury will hear them.

(c) The prosecutor may negate a grand jury's decision to return an indictment by refusing to sign the indictment, or by nolle prosequi, which dismisses the charges. And a grand jury decision not to indict can be

---

[11] United States v. McKenzie, 678 F.2d 629 (5th Cir.1982), indicates that an indictment will be quashed because of prosecutorial misconduct before a grand jury "only when prosecutorial misconduct amounts to overbearing the will of the grand jury so that the indictment is, in effect, that of the prosecutor rather than the grand jury." The court indicated that a prosecutor could tell the grand jury that the evidence shows the defendant is guilty.

circumvented if the prosecutor resubmits the case to another grand jury. In some jurisdictions such action requires court approval.

E. THE GRAND JURY AS A PROTECTION AGAINST UNJUST PROSECUTION

The traditional view of the grand jury as a protection against unwarranted prosecution has been described by the Supreme Court as follows:

> Historically, this body has been regarded as a primary security to the innocent against hasty, malicious and oppressive persecution; it serves the invaluable function in our society of standing between the accuser and the accused, whether the latter be an individual, minority group, or other, to determine whether a charge is founded upon reason or was dictated by an intimidating power or by malice and personal ill will.

Wood v. Georgia, 370 U.S. 375, 390 (1962).

More recently this view has been challenged. Commentators and courts now see a grand jury indictment as little more than a rubber stamp for the prosecutor's decision to go forward. See Leipold, Why Grand Juries Do Not (And Cannot) Protect the Accused, 80 Cornell L.Rev.260 (1995) (noting that during 1984, federal grand juries returned 17,419 indictments and only sixty-eight no bills, a success rate of 99.6%). In Hawkins v. Superior Court, 22 Cal.3d 584, 150 Cal.Rptr. 435, 586 P.2d 916 (1978), the California Supreme Court expressed its somewhat cynical view of the modern grand jury:

> The prosecuting attorney is typically in complete control of the total process in the grand jury room: he calls the witnesses, interprets the evidence, states and applies the law, and advises the grand jury on whether a crime has been committed. The grand jury is independent only in the sense that it is not formally attached to the prosecutor's office; though legally free to vote as they please, grand jurors virtually always assent to the recommendations of the prosecuting attorney, a fact borne out by available statistical and survey data. * * * The contemporary grand jury investigates only those whom the prosecutor asks to be investigated, and by and large indicts those whom the prosecutor wants to be indicted. * * *
>
> The domination of grand jury proceedings by the prosecuting attorney no doubt derives at least in part from the grand jury's institutional schizophrenia: it is expected to serve two distinct and largely inconsistent functions—accuser and impartial factfinder. * * *

The high proportion of true bills (i.e., decisions to charge) compared to no bills is not surprising. The grand jury is a body that hears only one side of a case. And it reacts to that side. Moreover the relevant standard of proof for issuing an indictment—probable cause—is low.

The principal function of the grand jury today probably is not to refuse indictment, but rather to force the prosecution to gather and to offer evidence in some systematic way before a charge is brought. What often is overlooked in discussions of grand juries is the fact that when the evidence, once put together, turns out to be weak, prosecutors sometimes decide not to ask for indictments or to seek indictments on lesser offenses than they might have charged on their own.

F. THE EVIDENCE BEFORE THE GRAND JURY

One reason that the screening function of the grand jury does not work better than it otherwise could is that prosecutors are permitted to offer a good deal of evidence to grand juries that could not be offered at trials. The next case is an illustration.

COSTELLO V. UNITED STATES

Supreme Court of the United States, 1956.
350 U.S. 359.

JUSTICE BLACK delivered the opinion of the Court.

We granted certiorari in this case to consider a single question: "May a defendant be required to stand trial and a conviction be sustained where only hearsay evidence was presented to the grand jury which indicted him?"

Petitioner, Frank Costello, was indicted for wilfully attempting to evade payment of income taxes due the United States for the years 1947, 1948 and 1949. * * * Petitioner promptly filed a motion for inspection of the minutes of the grand jury and for a dismissal of the indictment. His motion was based on an affidavit stating that he was firmly convinced there could have been no legal or competent evidence before the grand jury which indicted him since he had reported all his income and paid all taxes due. The motion was denied. At the trial which followed the Government offered evidence designed to show increases in Costello's net worth in an attempt to prove that he had received more income during the years in question than he had reported. To establish its case the Government called and examined 144 witnesses and introduced 368 exhibits. * * * The prosecution concluded its case by calling three government agents. Their investigations had produced the evidence used against petitioner at the trial. They were allowed to summarize the vast amount of evidence already heard and to introduce computations showing, if correct, that petitioner and his wife had received far greater income than they had reported.

* * *

Counsel for petitioner asked each government witness at the trial whether he had appeared before the grand jury which returned the indictment. This cross-examination developed the fact that the three investigating officers had been the only witnesses before the grand jury. After the Government concluded its case, petitioner again moved to dismiss the indictment on the ground that the only evidence before the grand jury was "hearsay," since the three officers had no firsthand knowledge of the transactions upon which their computations were based. Nevertheless the trial court again refused to dismiss the indictment, and petitioner was convicted. * * *

* * * [N]either the Fifth Amendment nor any other constitutional provision prescribes the kind of evidence upon which grand juries must act. * * * There is every reason to believe that our constitutional grand jury was intended to operate substantially like its English progenitor. The basic purpose of the English grand jury was to provide a fair method for instituting criminal proceedings against persons believed to have committed crimes. Grand jurors were selected from the body of the people and their work was not hampered by rigid procedural or evidential rules. * * *

* * * If indictments were to be held open to challenge on the ground that there was inadequate or incompetent evidence before the grand jury, the resulting delay would be great indeed. The result of such a rule would be that before trial on the merits a defendant could always insist on a kind of preliminary trial to determine the competency and adequacy of the evidence before the grand jury. This is not required by the Fifth Amendment. An indictment returned by a legally constituted and unbiased grand jury, like an information drawn by the prosecutor, if valid on its face, is enough to call for trial of the charge on the merits. * * *

* * * In a trial on the merits, defendants are entitled to a strict observance of all the rules designed to bring about a fair verdict. Defendants are not entitled, however, to a rule which would result in interminable delay but add nothing to the assurance of a fair trial.

[JUSTICE CLARK and JUSTICE HARLAN took no part in the consideration or decision of this case.]

[The concurring opinion of JUSTICE BURTON is omitted.]

Analysis of Costello

Aside from historical justifications, several arguments can be offered in support of *Costello*. First, inadmissible evidence often has probative value, and the grand jury's function is *investigative,* not adjudicative. Second, many evidentiary rules are designed to ensure fairness in an *adversary proceeding*, and the grand jury is not adversarial. See Federal Rule of Evidence 1101 (providing that the Rules of Evidence, except those related to privilege, are not applicable in grand jury proceedings). Evidence rules operate by way of objection; a prosecutor cannot be expected to object to her own evidence. Third, any misleading effect of inadmissible evidence will be remedied at trial. Fourth, grand jury proceedings would be greatly burdened if the rules of evidence were applicable to them. The court would have to review decisions as to the admissibility of evidence, because defense counsel would not be there to object. In order to make relevance and other rulings, supervising courts would have to ask grand juries why they wanted certain evidence, and this might infringe upon the independence of the grand jury.

Note that the fact situation of *Costello* was rather unique because defense counsel was able, by questioning witnesses at trial, to determine that hearsay statements were the only evidence presented to the grand jury. More commonly, the defendant will never know the degree to which hearsay and other inadmissible evidence is considered by the grand jury. Grand jury minutes are exempt from disclosure under Fed.R.Crim.P. 6. And the witnesses who render hearsay and other inadmissible testimony might not, for that very reason, testify at trial. As long as a defendant is convicted at trial on the basis of admissible evidence, he cannot complain that what occurred before the grand jury somehow affecte the trial. See United States v. Mechanik, 475 U.S. 66 (1986) (challenge to indictment based upon prosecutorial misconduct was rendered moot by conviction at a fairly conducted trial).

Use of Illegally Obtained Evidence

In Chapter 2, we saw that illegally seized evidence can be used in the grand jury proceeding. United States v. Calandra, 414 U.S. 338 (1974). The Court in *Calandra* reasoned that applying the exclusionary rule "would unduly interfere with the effective and expeditious discharge of the grand jury's duties" and that sufficient deterrence of illegal police activity would flow from the fact that the tainted evidence could not be used at trial.

Warnings to Witnesses Testifying Before the Grand Jury

Witnesses can be called to testify before the grand jury without being told why they are being called, what the purpose of the inquiry is, or whether they are suspected of criminal wrongdoing. Ignorance of the nature of the inquiry is compounded by the absence of counsel for the witness in the federal grand jury room (as well as in many states). Because grand jurors and prosecutors can ask leading questions, a witness who might be a target of the grand jury has good reason to fear that a slip of the tongue may come back to haunt her. Yet, the witness will have difficulty in answering carefully without knowledge of what the investigation is all about. Without a lawyer present to assist, vague or confusing questions may be asked, and a witness may later discover that what she said to the grand jury can be cast in a more negative light than she would have supposed while testifying.

In response to concerns about the possible unfair treatment of grand jury witnesses, the Department of Justice has added to the guidelines for United States Attorneys, found in the United States Attorney's Manual,[12] sections that require that a witness be advised of several things before testifying: of the general subject matter of the grand jury's inquiry (to the extent that an investigation would not be compromised); that the witness may refuse to answer questions that would tend to incriminate; that any answers may be used against the witness; and that the witness may step outside the grand jury room to consult with counsel. The guidelines provide that a target of an investigation may be subpoenaed, but known targets should be advised that they are targets and should be invited to testify voluntarily; if they refuse, a subpoena should be issued only after the grand jury and the responsible prosecutor have approved the subpoena. The prosecutor is encouraged to offer a target an opportunity to testify before the grand jury hands down an indictment.

It is notable, however, that there is no private right of action for violation of the DOJ guidelines on warnings. If they are ignored by the prosecutor, the most that will occur is a referral by the court to the Justice Department for internal (and confidential) discipline. See United States v. Gillespie, 974 F.2d 796 (7th Cir.1992) (asserting that judicial enforcement might deter the DOJ from adopting such rules in the first place). It should also be noted that a witness before the grand jury is not entitled to *Miranda* warnings, even if he is a target or subject of the investigation; such a witness is not in custody within the meaning of *Miranda*. See United States v. Mandujano, 425 U.S. 564 (1976).

Exculpatory Evidence: United States v. Williams

Does the prosecutor have an obligation to present all relevant evidence to the grand jury—including evidence that would exculpate the accused? Justice Scalia wrote for the Court in United States v. Williams, 504 U.S. 36 (1992), as it rejected a Tenth Circuit supervisory rule that required prosecutors to present "substantial exculpatory evidence" to the grand jury. He concluded that a rule requiring the prosecutor to present all substantially exculpatory evidence exceeded the courts' supervisory authority, because "the grand jury is an institution separate from the courts, over whose functioning the courts [do] not preside."

---

[12] United States Department of Justice, United States Attorneys' Manual, Title 9, Ch.11, ¶ 9–11.50.

Justice Scalia stated that "any power federal courts may have to fashion, on their own initiative, rules of grand jury procedure is a very limited one, not remotely comparable to the power they maintain over their own proceedings." He asserted that the Tenth Circuit's rule was far from so limited, because it would result in the "judicial reshaping of the grand jury institution, substantially altering the traditional relationships between the prosecutor, the constituting court, and the grand jury itself." Justice Scalia reasoned that "requiring the prosecutor to present exculpatory as well as inculpatory evidence would alter the grand jury's historical role, transforming it from an accusatory to an adjudicatory body." He explained as follows:

> It is axiomatic that the grand jury sits not to determine guilt or innocence, but to assess whether there is adequate basis for bringing a criminal charge. That has always been so; and to make the assessment it has always been thought sufficient to hear only the prosecutor's side. * * *
>
> Imposing upon the prosecutor a legal obligation to present exculpatory evidence in his possession would be incompatible with this system. If a "balanced" assessment of the entire matter is the objective, surely the first thing to be done—rather than requiring the prosecutor to say what he knows in defense of the target of the investigation—is to entitle the target to tender his own defense. To require the former while denying (as we do) the latter would be quite absurd. It would also be quite pointless, since it would merely invite the target to circumnavigate the system by delivering his exculpatory evidence to the prosecutor, whereupon it would *have* to be passed on to the grand jury * * *

Justice Scalia observed that the grand jury itself might choose not to hear more evidence than that which suffices to support an indictment. That is, the grand jury is free on its own to refuse to consider evidence that exculpated the target. He reasoned that if "the grand jury has no obligation to consider all substantial exculpatory evidence, we do not understand how the prosecutor can be said to have a binding obligation to present it." The Court thus rejected "the attempt to convert a nonexistent duty of the grand jury itself into an obligation of the prosecutor."

Justice Stevens, joined by Justices Blackmun and O'Connor and in relevant part by Justice Thomas, dissented. Justice Stevens stated that he was "unwilling to hold that countless forms of prosecutorial misconduct must be tolerated—no matter how prejudicial they may be, or how seriously they may distort the legitimate function of the grand jury—simply because they are not proscribed by Rule 6 of the Federal Rules of Criminal Procedure or a statute that is applicable in grand jury proceedings."

As to the scope of the prosecutor's duty to disclose exculpatory evidence to the grand jury, the dissenters endorsed the position expressed in the Department of Justice's United States Attorneys' Manual, Title 9, ch. 7, par. 9–11.233,88: "When a prosecutor conducting a grand jury inquiry is personally aware of substantial evidence which directly negates the guilt of a subject of the investigation, the prosecutor must present or otherwise disclose such evidence to the grand jury before seeking an indictment against such a person."

G. THE GRAND JURY'S POWERS OF INVESTIGATION

The Supreme Court has emphasized that the role of the grand jury is to investigate any and all potential criminal conduct, and that the power to obtain information is broad. See, e.g., Branzburg v. Hayes, 408 U.S. 665 (1972) (grand jury has a right to disclosure of journalist's sources); United States v. Nixon, 418 U.S. 683 (1974) (communications protected by executive privilege must be disclosed to the grand jury). To understand how broadly the grand jury can sweep, it is helpful to think back to the search and seizure material in Chapter 2. You will recall that the government generally cannot search for evidence unless it has probable cause, and the government cannot arrest a person without probable cause. This is in sharp contrast with the standards used by a grand jury. The grand jury can call anyone to testify before it upon the hint of suspicion or on the basis of a prosecutor's speculation about possible criminal activity. People called before the grand jury can be directed to bring documents and other tangible objects with them. Although certain privileges (such as Fifth Amendment and attorney-client) can be raised before the grand jury, the burden is on the person called to raise them and sometimes to be willing to litigate in order to preserve them. Any aspect of a person's life that might shed light on some criminal activity by somebody is within the proper scope of a grand jury inquest. See, e.g., In re Grand Jury, 286 F.3d 153 (3d Cir. 2002) (grand jury has the power to demand the production of material even where it is covered by a protective order in a civil case).

Grand Jury Subpoena Power

The scope of the subpoena power of a federal grand jury is nationwide, which means that the burden of traveling to testify can be considerable. The state grand jury has no such nationwide reach, but it too can impose travel burdens on witnesses. When it is recognized that often the prosecutor subpoenas witnesses without prior consultation with the grand jurors, it is apparent that a prosecutor can call witnesses who are considerably burdened by the duty of responding to a subpoena but who might end up having little to tell the grand jury.

For example, one of the cases consolidated for hearing in Branzburg v. Hayes, supra, involved Earl Caldwell, a New York Times reporter who covered the Black Panther Party. Caldwell claimed that his appearance before the grand jury would compromise his relationship with the Party. The Supreme Court held that this risk of harm gave him neither the right to refuse to appear before the grand jury nor the right to refuse to answer questions based on information related to him in confidence. Under the Court's opinion, even if the grand jury did not have any significant need for answers to questions, and even if, by answering, Caldwell's ability to function as a reporter covering the Party would be destroyed, the grand jury had a right to the information.

The breadth of grand jury power was evidenced once again in the grand jury investigation into charges of impropriety by then-President Clinton. The grand jury subpoenaed information from a bookstore concerning a purchase made by Monica Lewinsky. Despite the First Amendment ramifications, the subpoena was found valid. See Stout, Lewinsky's Bookstore Purchases Are Now Subject of a Subpoena, N.Y. Times, March 26, 1998, at A16 (quoting a legal director for the ACLU as stating that "people in this country ought to have the right to buy books without government scrutiny").

In Blair v. United States, 250 U.S. 273 (1919), the Supreme Court established the appropriate degree of deference to be accorded grand jury subpoenas by judicial officers:

> [T]he giving of testimony and the attendance upon court or grand jury in order to testify are public duties which every person within the jurisdiction of the Government is bound to perform upon being properly summoned, and for performance of which he is entitled to no further compensation than that which the statutes provide. The personal sacrifice involved is a part of the necessary contribution of the individual to the welfare of the public. The duty, so onerous at times, yet so necessary to the administration of justice * * * is subject to mitigation in exceptional circumstances; there is a constitutional exemption from being compelled in any criminal case to be a witness against oneself, entitling the witness to be excused from answering anything that will tend to incriminate him; some confidential matters are shielded from considerations of policy, and perhaps in other cases for special reasons a witness may be excused from telling all that he knows.
>
> But, aside from exceptions and qualifications—and none such is asserted in the present case—the witness is bound not only to attend but to tell what he knows in answer to questions framed for the purpose of bringing out the truth of the matter under inquiry.

* * *

[The grand jury] is a grand inquest, a body with powers of investigation and inquisition, the scope of whose inquiries is not to be limited narrowly by questions of propriety or forecasts of the probable result of the investigation, or by doubts whether any particular individual will be found properly subject to an accusation of crime. As has been said before, the identity of the offender, and the precise nature of the offense, if there be one, normally are developed at the conclusion of the grand jury's labors, not at the beginning.

Grand Jury Cattle Call: United States v. Dionisio

An objection to the breadth of a grand jury investigation, and correspondingly to the broad use of its subpoena power, is ordinarily dismissed out of hand. A case in point is United States v. Dionisio, 410 U.S. 1 (1973). The next excerpt contains the Court's description of the facts and the Court's deferential approach to grand jury subpoenas.

A special grand jury was convened in the Northern District of Illinois in February 1971, to investigate possible violations of federal criminal statutes relating to gambling. In the course of its investigation, the grand jury received in evidence certain voice recordings that had been obtained pursuant to court orders.

The grand jury subpoenaed approximately 20 persons, including the respondent Dionisio, seeking to obtain from them voice exemplars for comparison with the recorded conversations that had been received in evidence. Each witness was advised that he was a potential defendant in a criminal prosecution. Each was asked to examine a transcript of an intercepted conversation, and to go to a nearby office of the United States Attorney to read the transcript into a recording device. * * * Dionisio and other witnesses refused to furnish the voice exemplars * * *.

* * *

The Court of Appeals found critical significance in the fact that the grand jury had summoned approximately 20 witnesses to furnish voice exemplars. We think that fact is basically irrelevant to the constitutional issues here. The grand jury may have been attempting to identify a number of voices on the tapes in evidence, or it might have summoned the 20 witnesses in an effort to identify one voice. But whatever the case, a grand jury's investigation is not fully carried out until every available clue has been run down and all witnesses examined in every proper way to find if a crime has been committed * * *. The grand jury may well find it desirable to call numerous witnesses in the course of an investigation. It does not follow that each witness may resist a subpoena on the ground that too many witnesses have been called.

In dissent, Justice Marshall argued that some protection against prosecutorial control of the grand jury is necessary. Justice Marshall urged that the government should have to make a showing of reasonableness before real evidence is gathered by the grand jury over the objection of a witness.

Minimal Limits on Grand Jury Subpoenas: United States v. R. Enterprises, Inc.

The Court in United States v. Nixon, 418 U.S. 683 (1974), held that a *trial* subpoena must satisfy a three pronged test of relevancy, admissibility, and specificity. However, in United States v. R. Enterprises, Inc., 498 U.S. 292 (1991), the Court rejected the application of the *Nixon* standards to grand jury subpoenas. Justice O'Connor, writing for a unanimous Court on this point, stressed the distinction between a grand jury investigation and a trial proceeding. She stated that "the Government cannot be required to justify the issuance of a grand jury subpoena by presenting evidence sufficient to establish probable cause because the very purpose of requesting the information is to ascertain whether probable cause exists." The Court also noted that the multifactor *Nixon* test would produce unacceptable procedural delays that would frustrate the grand jury's investigation.

Justice O'Connor noted, however, that the grand jury's investigatory powers are "not unlimited." Under Federal Rule of Criminal Procedure 17(c), subpoenas may be quashed if compliance would be "unreasonable or oppressive." The Court held that a subpoena would be unreasonable under Rule 17(c) only if "there is no reasonable possibility that the category of materials the Government seeks will produce information relevant to the general subject of the grand jury's investigation." Justice O'Connor recognized that this standard would be extraordinarily difficult to meet in practice, especially given the difficult position of subpoena recipients, who may have no knowledge of the government's purpose in seeking production of the requested information. The Court suggested that an *in camera* proceeding should be employed in cases where the recipient of the subpoena is unaware of the nature of the investigation.

State Grand Jury Investigations and Federal Interests: Trump v. Vance

The Supreme Court had occasion to revisit some of the rules and principles limiting the scope of a grand jury's investigative powers during the 2019 term when President Donald J. Trump sought broad immunity against subpoenas issued by the District Attorney for New York County on behalf of a grand jury conducting a criminal investigation. Although the Court was unanimous in rejecting President Trump's claim of absolute immunity, the Justices divided on the legal and constitutional standards that should apply when the President challenges a specific subpoena.

TRUMP V. VANCE

Supreme Court of the United States, 2020.
140 S.Ct. 2412.

CHIEF JUSTICE ROBERTS **delivered the opinion of the Court.**

In our judicial system, "the public has a right to every man's evidence." Since the earliest days of the Republic, "every man" has included the President of the United States. Beginning with Jefferson and carrying on through Clinton, Presidents have uniformly testified or produced documents in criminal proceedings when called upon by federal courts. This case involves—so far as we and the parties can tell—the first *state* criminal subpoena directed to a President. The President contends that the subpoena is unenforceable. We granted certiorari to decide whether Article II and the Supremacy Clause categorically preclude, or require a heightened standard for, the issuance of a state criminal subpoena to a sitting President.

I

[The New York County District attorney was investigating possible tax fraud charges against the Trump Organization. A grand jury issued a subpoena on Mazars, USA, which was the personal accounting firm off President Trump. Trump sought to quash the subpoena, arguing that under Article II and the Supremacy Clause, a sitting President enjoys absolute immunity from state criminal process. The lower courts denied Trump's claim.]

II

In the summer of 1807, all eyes were on Richmond, Virginia. Aaron Burr, the former Vice President, was on trial for treason. Fallen from political grace after his fatal duel with Alexander Hamilton, and with a murder charge pending in New Jersey, Burr followed the path of many down-and-out Americans of his day—he headed West in search of new opportunity. But Burr was a man with outsized ambitions. Together with General James Wilkinson, the Governor of the Louisiana Territory, he hatched a plan to establish a new territory in Mexico, then controlled by Spain. Both men anticipated that war between the United States and Spain was imminent, and when it broke out they intended to invade Spanish territory at the head of a private army.

But while Burr was rallying allies to his cause, tensions with Spain eased and rumors began to swirl that Burr was conspiring to detach States by the Allegheny Mountains from the Union. Wary of being exposed as the principal coconspirator, Wilkinson took steps to ensure that any blame would fall on Burr. He sent a series of letters to President Jefferson accusing Burr of plotting to attack New Orleans and revolutionize the Louisiana Territory.

Jefferson, who despised his former running mate Burr for trying to steal the 1800 presidential election from him, was predisposed to credit Wilkinson's version of events. The President sent a special message to Congress identifying Burr as the "prime mover" in a plot "against the peace and safety of the Union." * * * Jefferson acknowledged that his sources contained a "mixture of rumors, conjectures, and suspicions" but, citing Wilkinson's letters, he assured Congress that Burr's guilt was "beyond question."

The trial that followed was "the greatest spectacle in the short history of the republic," complete with a Founder-studded cast. * * * Chief Justice John Marshall, who had recently squared off with the Jefferson administration in *Marbury* v. *Madison*, presided as Circuit Justice for Virginia. Meanwhile Jefferson, intent on conviction, orchestrated the prosecution from afar, dedicating Cabinet meetings to the case, peppering the prosecutors with directions, and spending nearly $100,000 from the Treasury on the five-month proceedings.

In the lead-up to trial, Burr, taking aim at his accusers, moved for a subpoena *duces tecum* directed at Jefferson. The draft subpoena required the President to produce an October 21, 1806 letter from Wilkinson and accompanying documents, which Jefferson had referenced in his message to Congress. The prosecution opposed the request, arguing that a President could not be subjected to such a subpoena and that the letter might contain state secrets. Following four days of argument, Marshall announced his ruling to a packed chamber.

The President, Marshall declared, does not "stand exempt from the general provisions of the constitution" or, in particular, the Sixth Amendment's guarantee that those accused have compulsory process for obtaining witnesses for their defense. At common law the "single reservation" to the duty to testify in response to a subpoena was "the case of the king," whose "dignity" was seen as "incompatible" with appearing "under the process of the court." But, as Marshall explained, a king is born to power and can "do no wrong." The President, by contrast, is "of the people" and subject to the law. According to Marshall, the sole argument for exempting the President from testimonial obligations was that his "duties as chief magistrate demand his whole time for national objects." But, in Marshall's assessment, those demands were "not unremitting." And should the President's duties preclude his attendance at a particular time and place, a court could work that out upon return of the subpoena.

* * *

While the arguments unfolded, Jefferson, who had received word of the motion, wrote to the prosecutor indicating that he would—subject to the prerogative to decide which executive communications should be withheld—"furnish on all occasions, whatever the purposes of justice may require." His "personal attendance," however, was out of the question, for it "would leave the nation without" the "sole branch which the constitution requires to be always in function."

Before Burr received the subpoenaed documents, Marshall rejected the prosecution's core legal theory for treason and Burr was accordingly acquitted. Jefferson, however, was not done. Committed to salvaging a conviction, he directed the prosecutors to proceed with a misdemeanor (yes, misdemeanor) charge for inciting war against Spain. Burr then renewed his request for Wilkinson's October 21 letter, which he later received a copy of, and subpoenaed a second letter, dated November 12, 1806, which the prosecutor claimed was privileged. Acknowledging that the President may withhold information to protect public safety, Marshall instructed that Jefferson should "state the particular reasons" for withholding the letter. The court, paying "all proper respect" to those reasons, would then decide whether to compel disclosure. But that decision was averted when the misdemeanor trial was cut short after it became clear that the prosecution lacked the evidence to convict.

In the two centuries since the Burr trial, successive Presidents have accepted Marshall's ruling that the Chief Executive is subject to subpoena. * * *

The bookend to Marshall's ruling came in 1974 when the question he never had to decide—whether to compel the disclosure of official communications over the objection of the President—came to a head. That spring, the Special Prosecutor appointed to investigate the break-in of the Democratic National Committee Headquarters at the Watergate complex filed an indictment charging seven defendants associated with President Nixon and naming Nixon as an unindicted co-conspirator. As the case moved toward trial, the Special Prosecutor secured a subpoena *duces tecum* directing Nixon to produce, among other things, tape recordings of Oval Office meetings. Nixon moved to quash the subpoena, claiming that the Constitution provides an absolute privilege of confidentiality to all presidential communications. This Court rejected that argument in *United States* v. *Nixon*, 418 U.S. 683 (1974), a decision we later described as "unequivocally and emphatically endors[ing] Marshall's" holding that Presidents are subject to subpoena. *Clinton* v. *Jones*, 520 U.S. 681, 704 (1997).

The *Nixon* Court readily acknowledged the importance of preserving the confidentiality of communications "between high Government officials and those who advise and assist them." * * * Confidentiality * * * promoted the "public interest in candid, objective, and even blunt or harsh opinions in Presidential decisionmaking."

But * * * the Court recognized the countervailing interests at stake. Invoking the common law maxim that "the public has a right to every man's evidence," the Court observed that the public interest in fair and accurate judicial proceedings is at its height in the criminal setting and recognized that it was "imperative" that "compulsory process be available for the production of evidence needed either by the prosecution or the defense."

The Court thus concluded that the President's "generalized assertion of privilege must yield to the demonstrated, specific need for evidence in a pending criminal trial." Two weeks later, President Nixon dutifully released the tapes.

III

The history surveyed above all involved *federal* criminal proceedings. Here we are confronted for the first time with a subpoena issued to the President by a local grand jury operating under the supervision of a *state* court.

* * *

A.

* * *

Marshall's ruling in *Burr*, entrenched by 200 years of practice and our decision in *Nixon*, confirms that *federal* criminal subpoenas do not "rise to the level of constitutionally forbidden impairment of the Executive's ability to perform its constitutionally mandated functions." But the President * * * argues that *state* criminal subpoenas pose a unique threat of impairment and thus demand greater protection. To be clear, the President does not contend here that *this* subpoena, in particular, is impermissibly burdensome. Instead he makes a *categorical* argument about the burdens generally associated with state criminal subpoenas, focusing on three: diversion, stigma, and harassment. We address each in turn.

1

The President's primary contention * * * is that complying with state criminal subpoenas would necessarily divert the Chief Executive from his duties. He grounds that concern in *Nixon* v. *Fitzgerald*, [475 U.S. 731 (1982)] which recognized a President's "absolute immunity from damages liability predicated on his official acts." In explaining the basis for that immunity, this Court observed that the prospect of such liability could "distract a President from his public duties, to the detriment of not only the President and his office but also the Nation that the Presidency was designed to serve." * * *

But *Fitzgerald* did not hold that distraction was sufficient to confer absolute immunity. * * * [T]he "dominant concern" in *Fitzgerald* was not mere distraction but the distortion of the Executive's "decisionmaking process" with respect to official acts that would stem from "worry as to the possibility of damages." The Court recognized that Presidents constantly face myriad demands on their attention, "some private, some political, and some as a result of official duty." But, the Court concluded, "[w]hile such distractions may be vexing to those subjected to them, they do not ordinarily implicate constitutional . . . concerns."

The same is true of criminal subpoenas. Just as a "properly managed" civil suit is generally "unlikely to occupy any substantial amount of" a President's time or attention, two centuries of experience confirm that a properly tailored criminal subpoena will not normally hamper the performance of the President's constitutional duties. If anything, we expect that in the mine run of cases, where a President is subpoenaed during a proceeding targeting someone else, as Jefferson was, the burden on a President will ordinarily be lighter than the burden of defending against a civil suit.

The President, however, believes the district attorney is investigating him and his businesses. In such a situation, he contends, the "toll that criminal process . . . exacts from the President is even heavier" than the distraction at issue in *Fitzgerald* and *Clinton*, because "criminal litigation" poses unique burdens on the President's time and will generate a "considerable if not overwhelming degree of mental preoccupation."

But the President is not seeking immunity from the diversion occasioned by the prospect of future criminal *liability*. Instead he concedes—consistent with the position of the Department of Justice—that state grand juries are free to investigate a sitting President with an eye toward charging him after the completion of his term. The President's objection therefore must be limited to the *additional* distraction caused by the subpoena itself. But that argument runs up against the 200 years of precedent establishing that Presidents, and their official communications, are subject to judicial process, even when the President is under investigation.

2

The President next claims that the stigma of being subpoenaed will undermine his leadership at home and abroad. Notably, * * * we have twice denied absolute immunity claims by Presidents in cases involving allegations of serious misconduct. But even if a tarnished reputation were a cognizable impairment, there is nothing inherently stigmatizing about a President performing "the citizen's normal duty of . . . furnishing information relevant" to a criminal investigation. Nor can we accept that the risk of association with persons or activities under criminal investigation can absolve a President of such an important public duty. Prior Presidents have weathered these associations in federal cases, and there is no reason to think any attendant notoriety is necessarily greater in state court proceedings.

* * *

Additionally, while the current suit has cast the Mazars subpoena into the spotlight, longstanding rules of grand jury secrecy aim to prevent the very stigma the President anticipates. Of course, disclosure restrictions are not perfect. But those who make unauthorized disclosures regarding a grand jury subpoena do so at their peril. See, *e.g.*, N. Y. Penal Law Ann. § 215.70 (West 2010) (designating unlawful grand jury disclosure as a felony).

3

Finally, the President and the Solicitor General warn that subjecting Presidents to state criminal subpoenas will make them "easily identifiable target[s]" for harassment. * * * They caution that, while federal prosecutors are accountable to and removable by the President, the 2,300 district attorneys in this country are responsive to local constituencies, local interests, and local prejudices, and might "use criminal process to register their dissatisfaction with" the President. What is more, we are told, the state courts supervising local grand juries may not exhibit the same respect that federal courts show to the President as a coordinate branch of Government.

We recognize, as does the district attorney, that harassing subpoenas could, under certain circumstances, threaten the independence or effectiveness of the Executive. Even so, * * * the risk of harassment [is] not "serious" because federal courts have the tools to deter and, where necessary, dismiss vexatious civil suits. And, while we cannot ignore the possibility that state prosecutors may have political motivations, here again the law already seeks to protect against the predicted abuse.

First, grand juries are prohibited from engaging in "arbitrary fishing expeditions" and initiating investigations "out of malice or an intent to harass." *United States* v. *R. Enterprises, Inc.*, 498 U. S. 292, 299 (1991). * * * These protections, as the district attorney himself puts it, "apply with special force to a President, in light of the office's unique position as the head of the Executive Branch." And, in the event of such harassment, a President would be entitled to the protection of federal courts. The policy against federal interference in state criminal proceedings, while strong, allows intervention in those cases where the District Court properly finds that the state proceeding is motivated by a desire to harass or is conducted in bad faith.

Second, contrary to JUSTICE ALITO's characterization, our holding does not allow States to "run roughshod over the functioning of [the Executive Branch." The Supremacy Clause prohibits state judges and prosecutors from interfering with a President's official duties. Any effort to manipulate a President's policy decisions or to retaliate against a President for official acts through issuance of a subpoena, would thus be an unconstitutional attempt to influence a superior sovereign exempt from such obstacles. We generally assume that state courts and prosecutors will observe constitutional limitations. Failing that, federal law allows a President to challenge any allegedly unconstitutional influence in a federal forum, as the President has done here.

Given these safeguards and the Court's precedents, we cannot conclude that absolute immunity is necessary or appropriate under Article II or the Supremacy Clause. Our dissenting colleagues agree. JUSTICE THOMAS reaches the same conclusion based on the original understanding of the Constitution reflected in Marshall's decision in *Burr*. And JUSTICE ALITO, also persuaded by *Burr*, "agree[s]" that "not all" state criminal subpoenas for a President's records "should be barred." On that point the Court is unanimous.

B

We next consider whether a state grand jury subpoena seeking a President's private papers must satisfy a heightened need standard. The Solicitor General would require a threshold showing that the evidence sought is "critical" for "specific charging decisions" and that the subpoena is a "last resort," meaning the evidence is "not available from any other source" and is needed "now, rather than at the end of the President's term." JUSTICE ALITO, largely embracing those criteria, agrees that a state criminal subpoena to a President "should not be allowed unless a heightened standard is met."

We disagree, for three reasons. First, such a heightened standard would extend protection designed for official documents to the President's private papers. As the Solicitor General and JUSTICE ALITO acknowledge, their proposed test is derived from executive privilege cases that trace back to *Burr*. * * * But this * * * does not account for the relevant passage from *Burr*: "If there be a paper in the possession of the executive, which is *not of an official nature*, he must stand, as respects that paper, in nearly the same situation with any other individual." And it is only "nearly"—and not "entirely"—because the President retains the right to assert privilege over documents that, while ostensibly private, "partake of the character of an official paper."

Second, neither the Solicitor General nor JUSTICE ALITO has established that heightened protection against state subpoenas is necessary for the Executive to fulfill his Article II functions. * * * In effect, they argue that even if federal subpoenas to a President are warranted whenever evidence is material, state subpoenas are warranted "only when [the] evidence is essential." But that double standard has no basis in law. For if the state subpoena is not issued to manipulate, the documents themselves are not protected, and the Executive is not impaired, then nothing in Article II or the Supremacy Clause supports holding state subpoenas to a higher standard than their federal counterparts.

Finally, in the absence of a need to protect the Executive, the public interest in fair and effective law enforcement cuts in favor of comprehensive access to evidence. Requiring a state grand jury to meet a heightened standard of need would hobble the grand jury's ability to acquire "all information that might possibly bear on its investigation." And, even assuming the evidence withheld under that standard were preserved until the conclusion of a President's term, in the interim the State would be deprived of investigative leads that the evidence might yield, allowing memories to fade and documents to disappear. This could frustrate the identification, investigation, and indictment of third parties (for whom applicable statutes of limitations might lapse). More troubling, it could prejudice the innocent by depriving the grand jury of *exculpatory* evidence.

Rejecting a heightened need standard does not leave Presidents with "no real protection." To start, a President may avail himself of the same protections available to every other citizen. These include the right to challenge the subpoena on any grounds permitted by state law, which usually include bad faith and undue burden or breadth. And, as in federal court, the high respect that is owed to the office of the Chief Executive . . . should inform the conduct of the entire proceeding, including the timing and scope of discovery. * * *

Furthermore, although the Constitution does not entitle the Executive to absolute immunity or a heightened standard, he is not "relegate[d]" only to the challenges available to private citizens. * * * As previously noted, he can challenge the subpoena as an attempt to influence the performance of his official duties, in violation of the Supremacy Clause. This avenue protects against local political machinations "interposed as an obstacle to the effective operation of a federal constitutional power." In addition, the Executive can—as the district attorney concedes—argue that compliance with a particular subpoena would impede his constitutional duties. * * * At that point, a court should use its inherent authority to quash or modify the subpoena, if necessary to ensure that such interference with the President's duties would not occur.

* * *

Two hundred years ago, a great jurist of our Court established that no citizen, not even the President, is categorically above the common duty to produce evidence when called upon in a criminal proceeding. We reaffirm that principle today and hold that the President is neither absolutely immune from state criminal subpoenas seeking his private papers nor entitled to a heightened standard of need. The "guard[ ] furnished to this high officer" lies where it always has—in "the conduct of a court" applying established legal and constitutional principles to individual subpoenas in a manner that preserves both the independence of the Executive and the integrity of the criminal justice system. *Burr*, 25 F. Cas., at 34.

The arguments presented here and in the Court of Appeals were limited to absolute immunity and heightened need. The Court of Appeals, however, has directed that the case be returned to the District Court, where the President may raise further arguments as appropriate.

We affirm the judgment of the Court of Appeals and remand the case for further proceedings consistent with this opinion.

JUSTICE KAVANAUGH, with whom JUSTICE GORSUCH joins, concurring in the judgment.

The Court today unanimously concludes that a President does not possess absolute immunity from a state criminal subpoena, but also unanimously agrees that this case should be remanded to the District Court, where the President may raise constitutional and legal objections to the subpoena as appropriate. I agree with those two conclusions.

* * *

In our system of government, as this Court has often stated, no one is above the law. That principle applies, of course, to a President. At the same time, in light of Article II of the Constitution, this Court has repeatedly declared—and the Court indicates again today—that a court may not proceed against a President as it would against an ordinary litigant. * * *

The question here, then, is how to balance the State's interests and the Article II interests. The longstanding precedent that has applied to federal criminal subpoenas for official, privileged Executive Branch information is *United States* v. *Nixon*, 418 U. S. 683 (1974). That landmark case requires that a prosecutor establish a "demonstrated, specific need" for the President's information. * * *

The *Nixon* "demonstrated, specific need" standard is a tried-and-true test that accommodates both the interests of the criminal process and the Article II interests of the Presidency. The *Nixon* standard ensures that a prosecutor's interest in subpoenaed information is sufficiently important to justify an intrusion on the Article II interests of the Presidency. The *Nixon* standard also reduces the risk of subjecting a President to unwarranted burdens, because it provides that a prosecutor may obtain a President's information only in certain defined circumstances.

* * * In the end, much may depend on how the majority opinion's various standards are applied in future years and decades. It will take future cases to determine precisely how much difference exists between (i) the various standards articulated by the majority opinion, (ii) the overarching *Nixon* "demonstrated, specific need" standard that I would adopt, and (iii) JUSTICE THOMAS's and JUSTICE ALITO's other proposed standards. In any event, in my view, lower courts in cases of this sort involving a President will almost invariably have to begin by delving into why the State wants the information; why and how much the State needs the information, including whether the State could obtain the information elsewhere; and whether compliance with the subpoena would unduly burden or interfere with a President's official duties.

* * *

JUSTICE THOMAS, dissenting.

* * * I agree with the majority that the President is not entitled to absolute immunity from *issuance* of the subpoena. But he may be entitled to relief against its *enforcement*. I therefore agree with the President that the proper course is to vacate and remand. If the President can show that "his duties as chief magistrate demand his whole time for national objects," *United States* v. *Burr*, 25 F. Cas. 30, 34 (No. 14,692d) (CC Va. 1807) (Marshall, C. J.), he is entitled to relief from enforcement of the subpoena.

* * *

In *Burr*, after explaining that the President was not absolutely immune from issuance of a subpoena, Chief Justice Marshall proceeded to explain that the President might be excused from the enforcement of one. As he put it, "[t]he guard, furnished to this high officer, to protect him from being harassed by vexatious and unnecessary subpoenas, is to be looked for in the conduct of a court *after those subpoenas have issued*; not in any circumstance which is to precede their being issued." Chief Justice Marshall set out the pertinent standard: To avoid enforcement of the subpoena, the President must "sho[w]" that "his duties as chief magistrate demand his whole time for national objects."

* * *

The *Burr* standard places the burden on the President but also requires courts to take pains to respect the demands on the President's time. The Constitution vests the President with extensive powers and responsibilities, and courts are poorly situated to conduct a searching review of the President's assertion that he is unable to comply.

* * *

In sum, the demands on the President's time and the importance of his tasks are extraordinary, and the office of the President cannot be delegated to subordinates. A subpoena imposes both demands on the President's limited time and a mental burden, even when the President is not directly engaged in complying. This understanding of the Presidency should guide courts in deciding whether to enforce a subpoena for the President's documents.

* * *

I would vacate and remand to allow the District Court to determine whether enforcement of this subpoena should be enjoined because the President's "duties as chief magistrate demand his whole time for national objects." Accordingly, I respectfully dissent.

JUSTICE ALITO, dissenting.

* * *

The important point is * * * that we should not treat this subpoena like an ordinary grand jury subpoena and should not relegate a President to the meager defenses that are available when an ordinary grand jury subpoena is challenged. But that, at bottom, is the effect of the Court's decision.

The Presidency deserves greater protection. Thus, in a case like this one, a prosecutor should be required (1) to provide at least a general description of the possible offenses that are under investigation, (2) to outline how the subpoenaed records relate to those offenses, and (3) to explain why it is important that the records be produced and why it is necessary for production to occur while the President is still in office.

In the present case, the district attorney made a brief proffer, but important questions were left hanging. It would not be unduly burdensome to insist on answers before enforcing the subpoena.

* * *

The district attorney should also explain why it is important that the information in question be obtained from the President's records rather than another source. And the district attorney should set out why he finds it necessary that the records be produced now as opposed to when the President leaves office. At argument, respondent's counsel told us that his office's concern is the expiration of the statute of limitations, but there are potential solutions to that problem. Even if New York law does not automatically suspend the statute of limitations for prosecuting a President until he leaves office, it may be possible to eliminate the problem by waiver. And if the prosecutor's statute-of-limitations concerns relate to parties other than the President, he should be required to spell that out.

There may be other good reasons why immediate enforcement is important, such as the risk that evidence or important leads will be lost, but if a prosecutor believes that immediate enforcement is needed for such a reason, the prosecutor should be required to provide a reasonably specific explanation why that is so and why alternative means, such as measures to preserve evidence and prevent spoliation, would not suffice.

* * *

For all practical purposes, the Court's decision places a sitting President in the same unenviable position as any other person whose records are subpoenaed by a grand jury.

* * *

The subpoena at issue here is unprecedented. Never before has a local prosecutor subpoenaed the records of a sitting President. The Court's decision threatens to impair the functioning of the Presidency and provides no real protection against the use of the subpoena power by the Nation's 2,300+ local prosecutors. Respect for the structure of Government created by the Constitution demands greater protection for an institution that is vital to the Nation's safety and well-being.

I therefore respectfully dissent.

H. SUGGESTED REFORMS OF GRAND JURY PROCEDURES

Many commentators suggest that the abuses seen in grand jury practice can be eliminated by imposing reforms. The ABA Criminal Justice Section Committee on the Grand Jury proposed the following reforms:

1. A witness before the grand jury shall have the right to be accompanied by counsel in his or her appearance before the grand jury. Such counsel shall be allowed to be present in the grand jury room only during the questioning of the witness and shall be allowed to advise the witness. Such counsel shall not be permitted to address the grand jurors or otherwise take part in proceedings before the grand jury.

2. No prosecutor shall knowingly fail to disclose to the grand jury evidence which will tend substantially to negate guilt.

> 3. The prosecutor shall not present to the grand jury evidence which he or she knows to be constitutionally inadmissible at trial.
>
> 4. A target of a grand jury investigation shall be given the right to testify before the grand jury. Prosecutors shall notify such targets of their opportunity to testify unless notification may result in flight, endanger other persons, or obstruct justice, or unless the prosecutor is unable to notify said persons with reasonable diligence. A target of the grand jury may also contact the foreperson in writing to offer information or evidence to the grand jury.
>
> 5. Witnesses should have the right to receive a transcript (at their own expense) of grand jury testimony.
>
> 6. The grand jury shall not name a person in an indictment as an unindicted coconspirator to a criminal conspiracy.[13]

The Criminal Justice Section report, proposing the above reforms, was issued in 1977. Congress held hearings on the proposals, but did not act on them. It is easy to see why no action was taken. The reforms would overrule Supreme Court doctrine, and would create a sea-change in the historically-ingrained federal grand jury practice. The reform proposals were staunchly opposed by the Justice Department. It is unlikely that the political climate will ever warm up enough for these or similar proposals to be enacted. See, e.g., Rovella, Grand Jury Battle Begins, Nat'l L.J., May 29, 2000, p. A4 (discussing attempt by Congressman Delahunt to revive the 1977 proposals under the new title "Federal Grand Jury Bill of Rights"; no legislation resulted).

Counsel in the Grand Jury Room

As discussed above, under Federal practice, a witness has no right to counsel while in the grand jury room. The Supreme Court reaffirmed the nonexistence of any right to counsel in Conn v. Gabbert, 526 U.S. 286 (1999). The plaintiff in *Conn* was a criminal defense attorney. He sued prosecutors and others for subjecting him to a search while his client was testifying before a grand jury. Before the Supreme Court, the attorney did not press a Fourth Amendment claim. Rather, he argued that the search "interfered with his client's right to have him outside the grand jury room and available to consult with her." Chief Justice Rehnquist, writing for the Court, analyzed this claim in the following passage:

> A grand jury witness has no constitutional right to have counsel present during the grand jury proceeding, and no decision of this Court

[13] See United States v. Briggs, 514 F.2d 794 (5th Cir.1975) ("the grand jury that returns an indictment naming a person as an unindicted coconspirator does not perform its shielding function but does exactly the reverse. If the charges are baseless, the named person should not be subjected to public branding, and if supported by probable cause, he should not be denied a forum.").

has held that a grand jury witness has a right to have her attorney present outside the jury room. We need not decide today whether such a right exists, because Gabbert clearly had no standing to raise the alleged infringement of the rights of his client Tracy Baker.

Thus, the Court in *Conn* does not even concede that a grand jury witness has a right to have counsel *outside* the room, much less inside. In practice, counsel is permitted to park herself outside the grand jury room, and the witness can excuse himself for consultation.[14]

A number of states permit witnesses to be accompanied by counsel in the grand jury room. A subcommittee of the Judicial Conference Advisory Committee on Criminal Rules considered making such a change in federal procedure, and ultimately decided against it. The Report of the Subcommittee reasons that allowing counsel to be present before the grand jury would create the following problems:

> 1. Loss of spontaneity of testimony.
>
> 2. Transforming the grand jury investigation into an adversary proceeding.
>
> 3. Loss of secrecy with resultant chilling effect on witness cooperation.

The Subcommittee also notes a "potential ancillary issue. Would an indigent witness summoned to the grand jury be entitled to the appointment of counsel at the obvious cost to the Treasury?"

To these concerns, the head of the Criminal Division of the Justice Department added another:

> [A]llowing defense counsel to accompany a witness before a grand jury would have adverse consequences for investigations of serious crimes by organizations, such as organized crime groups, corporations, or unions where typically a single lawyer represents all or several members of the organization. Currently, if a member of the organization wishes to cooperate with the grand jury secretly, the member may do so by appearing alone before the grand jury. But if the law allowed the member to bring the attorney, failure to do so would be a tip-off that the witness was likely cooperating, which would deter cooperation in many instances (or result in retaliation).

Letter from James K. Robinson to Subcommittee on Grand Jury Proceedings, Judicial Conference Advisory Committee on Criminal Rules, Dec. 22, 1998.

---

[14] This limited opportunity to consult counsel probably reflects a practical consideration: if the witness refuses to answer, the grand jury would have to seek a contempt citation to make the witness answer; before going through that process, the grand jury may be better advised to let the witness discuss with counsel the question, because the witness may after consultation find that there is no Fifth Amendment or other privilege that is implicated.

Despite these dire predictions, the evidence from the States that permit counsel in the grand jury room indicates that counsel's presence can have a positive rather than negative effect. For example, Colorado passed a law in the late 1970's permitting a witness's counsel to be present in the grand jury room. Jeffrey Bayles, a former Denver deputy district attorney, explains the salutary effect of the law as follows:

> Not only does the new law speed the process by eliminating the walk outside the room on every question, but it also reduces the number of questions requiring conferences between the witness and counsel. The educational process, which of necessity accompanies having counsel in the grand jury room, promotes a better understanding of the grand jury within the bar. The more the processes are known, the less is the aura of mystery surrounding the grand jury. * * * The demand for abolition of the grand jury will decrease in direct proportion to the number of counsel who attend grand jury sessions with their clients.

Bales, Grand Jury Reform: The Colorado Experience, A.B.A.J., May, 1981, at 568. See also Hixson, Bringing Down the Curtain on the Absurd Drama of Entrances and Exits—Witness Representation in the Grand Jury Room, 15 Am.Cr.L.Rev. 307 (1978) (given that the witness is allowed to go in and out of the room to get advice of counsel, it is more efficient to permit counsel to be present in the grand jury room.).

Grand Jury Nullification

Professor Laurie Levinson suggests another reform for grand jury practice: that grand jurors be told that they have the right to nullify, i.e., that they do not have to return an indictment even when they find probable cause. She notes that the history of the grand jury is laced with important cases of nullification, such as the refusal to indict John Peter Zenger on charges of sedition (as discussed in the section on the history of the grand jury, supra). She argues that there are compelling modern justifications for the nullification power:

> Federal prosecutors are not directly accountable to the community in which they serve. Rather, their appointments are made in Washington, and line prosecutors are increasingly receiving direction from Department of Justice officials who set national policy. Whether it is the war on drugs, the war on white-collar crime, or the war on terrorism, the national agenda may not adequately consider the needs of a particular community. A grand jury can perform this role.
>
> * * *
>
> The grand jury process, unlike trial jury deliberations, lends itself to a more thoughtful evaluation of community priorities and an evaluation of whether prosecutors are using the law for improper

reasons, such as political grandstanding or witch-hunting of opponents.

If grand juries have the discretion to reject charges that they think are improperly motivated or unwise, prosecutors will actually benefit in the long run because there will be greater moral authority behind the charges that grand jurors do bring.

Levinson, Grand Jury Nullification, Nat'l L. J. June 14, 2004 at 14.

Yet as shown earlier in this Chapter, the model charge given to federal grand jurors does not inform them that they have the right to decline to bring charges when the prosecutor establishes probable cause. The model charge says that when probable cause is established, the grand jury "should" return an indictment; and it further states that it is not for the grand jurors to second-guess the wisdom of laws passed by Congress. These charges have withstood attack. Thus, in United States v. Navarro-Vargas, 408 F.3d 1184 (9th Cir. 2005), the court noted that the grand jury has the *power*, as a matter of practice, to nullify a law because there is no means to review a grand jury's refusal to return an indictment. But according to the court, that does not mean that grand jurors have the *right* to nullify laws—or that they should in effect be invited to nullify by an instruction of informing them of their power to do so. The court stated: "we cannot say that the grand jury's power to judge the wisdom of the laws is so firmly established that the district court must either instruct the jury on its power to nullify the laws or remain silent." The court wrote that the instructions as a whole "remind the grand jury of its independence from the federal government and leave room for it to refuse to indict." The court made clear that the word "should" does not mean "must."

Note that if the grand jury does nullify and refuses to return an indictment, all the prosecutor has to do is empanel another grand jury; it is not like petit jury nullification, which triggers double jeopardy protection. Given the fact that grand jury nullification can be so easily trumped, is there any reason to encourage it?

For a comprehensive discussion of grand jury nullification, see Fairfax, Grand Jury Discretion and Constitutional Design, 93 Cornell L. Rev. 703, 711–16 (2008).

V. THE PRELIMINARY HEARING AND ITS RELATIONSHIP TO INDICTMENTS AND INFORMATIONS

Federal Rule of Criminal Procedure 5 provides that when an arrest is made, the arrested person must be taken without unnecessary delay before the nearest available federal magistrate. You will recall that Gerstein v. Pugh, 420 U.S. 103 (1975), and County of Riverside v. McLaughlin, 500

U.S. 44(1991), discussed in Chapter 2, requires that, if there has been no previous probable cause determination, one must be made promptly. Fed.R.Crim.P. 5 provides for such a determination when the person arrested is brought before the magistrate. The rule provides that a defendant is entitled to a preliminary examination for any crime except a petty offense. Fed.R.Crim.P. 5.1 governs preliminary examinations.

Note that an indictment cuts off the right to a preliminary hearing, because probable cause is held to be validly established by the indictment itself. It is common in some federal districts for prosecutors to avoid preliminary hearings by indicting as many defendants as possible.

Virtually every state that requires felony prosecutions to commence by indictment establishes some right to a preliminary examination. In most, the filing of the indictment cuts off the right to a preliminary hearing, just as does Federal Rule 5. About half the states do not require indictments in felony cases. In these states, prosecutors can begin felony cases by filing informations. A typical information procedure is to require a magistrate's determination of probable cause following a preliminary examination. In special cases prosecutors may utilize grand jury indictments, but usually they will file the information, since it is a less burdensome way of beginning a case.

Most states that permit the filing of an information in a felony case make a magistrate's decision to bind the defendant over for trial a prerequisite to the filing of the information. A few states do allow the prosecutor to file the information directly, however. The Supreme Court has upheld the direct filing of an information in Lem Woon v. Oregon, 229 U.S. 586 (1913), and Ocampo v. United States, 234 U.S. 91 (1914). Of course, after Gerstein v. Pugh, supra, a magistrate will have to make a probable cause determination, if the accused is deprived of freedom. But the *Gerstein* opinion indicates that the limited hearing it requires is to protect against erroneous detention; it is not a screening device to check the validity of the prosecutor's charges against a defendant.

Procedural Requirements for a Preliminary Hearing

Most states have time limits in which the preliminary hearing must be held. But other aspects of the hearing are often not covered by any rule. Even the standard to be used by the magistrate who conducts the preliminary hearing often is unclear. It is apparent that different judges sitting in the same jurisdiction have different ideas about what screening function the hearing is to serve. Some judges believe that their function is to determine probable cause, with the evidence viewed in the light most favorable to the government, ignoring credibility questions. This is the standard set forth in the federal system. See Fed.R.Crim.P. 5.1. Others take the view that there must be enough evidence for a trier of fact to find guilt beyond a reasonable doubt. Some magistrates probably consider whether a defendant should be burdened by going to trial in some cases, even if there is enough evidence to warrant a bindover.

The standard that is chosen indicates how much screening a jurisdiction wants its magistrates to do. It probably is true that if a prosecutor presents all her evidence to the magistrate and the magistrate concludes that no reasonable jury could convict, it is silly to bind the defendant over for trial, even if technically there is probable cause. But it is burdensome to require the prosecutor to present all of her evidence to the magistrate as a prerequisite to bringing charges. The more thorough the screening at the preliminary hearing, the more it resembles a trial, and the more duplicative and costly it is.

Although some jurisdictions require magistrates to follow the usual rules of evidence at preliminary hearings, most others (including the federal system, see Fed. R. Evid. 1101) provide that trial evidence rules need not be followed—which means in most cases that hearsay evidence can be used, as it can be used before grand juries. Again, the approach to the question whether evidence rules should be followed at the preliminary hearing depends on the kind of hearing that is to be held. Obviously, the more closely the evidence rules resemble the rules that will be used at trial, the more screening the magistrate is able to do. But the more screening that is done, the more time-consuming and duplicative the procedure is likely to be.

Another obvious difference among jurisdictions is in their approach to the hearing as a discovery device. If the hearing is not intended to serve a discovery purpose—as under Fed.R.Crim.P. 5.1, which does not mention discovery as a proper subject for the hearing—then questions asked for discovery reasons are unlikely to be permitted over objection.[15] If, however, a jurisdiction recognizes a discovery purpose, the scope of questioning may be quite broad.

Preclusive Effect of a Preliminary Determination

If the case is a felony case that will begin by a grand jury indictment, a decision by the magistrate at a preliminary hearing that there is no cause for bindover generally is not determinative for a grand jury. The grand jury still can indict, because it is an institution independent from the judiciary. See Fed.R.Crim.P. 5.1(f) ("A discharge does not preclude the government from later prosecuting the defendant for the same offense."). Likewise, a decision by the magistrate that bindover should be limited to designated

[15] The preliminary hearing may be used as a device to preserve testimony, and to precipitate bargaining that will lead to a guilty plea.

offenses does not limit the grand jury in most jurisdictions. The grand jury can charge any offense for which it finds probable cause.

If the prosecution can begin by information, generally the prosecutor is limited by the bindover in the charges that can be brought. In some states only those charges designated by the magistrate can be brought. In other states the offense for which the defendant is bound over or others supported by the evidence at the preliminary hearing may be charged. Still others use a transactional test, which allows all crimes related to the same transactions and facts adduced at the examination to be charged. Under all these approaches, the defendant can challenge the information in the trial court, although it is likely that the trial court will defer to the preliminary hearing judge (and the absence of a formal record may make a challenge especially difficult). If the prosecutor is not satisfied with the bindover decision, she may drop the prosecution, file a new information and hope for a better bindover ruling from another magistrate, or take the case to a grand jury. Generally, the refusal to bind the defendant over is not appealable, although sometimes mandamus may be possible.

VI. NOTICE OF CHARGES, CONSTRUCTIVE AMENDMENT, AND VARIANCE

In Stirone v. United States, 361 U.S. 212 (1960), the Supreme Court reversed a conviction for violation of the Hobbs Act (interfering with interstate commerce) because the government's proof of the defendants' effect on interstate commerce involved shipments of steel from inside Pennsylvania to points outside the state, whereas the indictment charged that the effect was on shipments from outside the state into Pennsylvania. The Court said that it could not permit a defendant to be tried on charges not made in the indictment, because to do so would undermine the defendant's constitutional right to an indictment by grand jury, and also would deny the defendant his constitutional right to be notified of the charges against him.

An indictment, to be sufficient under the Grand Jury Clause, must sufficiently state all elements of the crime. See, e.g., United States v. Villarreal, 707 F.3d 942 (8th Cir. 2013) ("An indictment is fatally insufficient when an essential element of the crime is omitted.").

United States v. Pickett, 353 F.3d 62 (D.C. Cir. 2004), is a case involving a defective indictment. Pickett was a security guard in the Capitol building who was indicted for lying to a government official. The prosecution involved the scare that arose when several Senators received anthrax in the mail. The defendant, as part of a "bad joke," placed a white substance on a table in the Capitol, and then lied about doing it. But the statute (18 U.S.C.§ 1001) requires that the lie to the government official must be made during an "investigation or review." That element was not charged in the indictment. The court dismissed the indictment, noting that on the plain language of the statute, the conduct charged against Pickett, making false statements, "does not constitute an offense" unless it occurs during the course of and investigation or review. The court concluded that "it is a fundamental protection, which an indictment is intended to guarantee, that the indictment contain the elements of the offense intended to be charged and sufficiently apprise the defendant of what he must be prepared to meet."

In contrast, the Court in United States v. Miller, 471 U.S. 130 (1985), held that the Fifth Amendment's protection of indictment by grand jury is not violated "when a defendant is tried under an indictment that alleges a certain fraudulent scheme but is convicted based on trial proof that supports only a significantly narrower and more limited, though included, fraudulent scheme." The government had charged Miller with fraudulent acts in consenting to a burglary of his business and lying to the insurer about the value of his loss. The proof focused only on the value of the loss and Miller's lying about it. Justice Marshall wrote that "[a]s long as the crime and the elements of the offense that sustain the conviction are fully and clearly set out in the indictment, the right to a grand jury is not normally violated by the fact that the indictment alleges more crimes or other means of submitting the same crime." He distinguished *Stirone* on the ground that the offense proved at Stirone's trial was *not* fully charged in the indictment.

Constructive Amendments and Variance from Indictment at Trial

Besides an indictment that simply does not state all the elements of a crime, a situation might arise in which the indictment pleads elements that are different from the proof presented by the prosecution at trial. Courts have found two types of claims that arise when a grand jury indictment is allegedly altered during the trial. One claim is that the indictment was *constructively amended*; the other claim is that there has been a *variance* between the indictment and the proof elicited at trial. The court in Martin v. Kassulke, 970 F.2d 1539 (6th Cir.1992), discussed the difference between these two claims:

> An amendment of the indictment occurs when the charging terms of the indictment are altered, either literally or in effect, by prosecutor or court after the grand jury has last passed upon them. A variance occurs when the charging terms of an indictment are left unaltered, but the evidence offered at trial proves facts materially different from those alleged in the indictment. An amendment is per se prejudicial, as it directly infringes the defendant's right to know of the charges

against him by effectively allowing the jury to convict the defendant of a different crime than that for which he was charged. * * *

A variance, on the other hand, is not reversible error unless the accused has proved a prejudicial effect upon his defense, because it merely permits the prosecution to prove facts to establish the criminal charge materially different from the facts contained in the charging instrument. Although it is generally subject to the harmless error test, a variance infringes upon the apprisal function of the sixth amendment which requires that in all criminal prosecutions, the accused shall enjoy the right to be informed of the nature and cause of the accusation. If a variance infringes too strongly upon a defendant's sixth amendment rights, it is considered a constructive amendment, which is a variance that is accorded the per se prejudicial treatment of an amendment. * * * A constructive amendment occurs when the terms of an indictment are in effect altered by the presentation of evidence and jury instructions which so modify essential elements of the offense charged that there is a substantial likelihood that the defendant may have been convicted of an offense other than that charged in the indictment.

* * *

A variance is not material, or does not rise to the level of a constructive amendment, unless the variance misleads the accused in making her defense or exposes her to the danger of double jeopardy.

In *Martin*, the defendant was charged with rape by engaging in sexual intercourse "by forcible compulsion." The evidence showed, and the prosecutor argued, that the rape occurred while the victim was "physically helpless"—i.e., while unconscious. The pertinent rape statute criminalized sexual intercourse either by forcible compulsion or when the victim was physically helpless. The *Martin* court found that the difference between the proof at trial and the charging instrument constituted a variance, but did not rise to the level of a constructive amendment of the indictment. Under the statute, rape was a single crime, which could be committed by two alternative methods. The defendant was not prejudiced by the prosecution's proof of a method other than that charged, because his defense was that the victim was a willing participant in *whatever* sex occurred. This defense "clearly negates any possibility that the victim was physically helpless and that her helplessness meant that he was not guilty of the crime with which he was charged." See also United States v. Moore, 198 F.3d 793 (10th Cir. 1999) (defendant was not prejudiced by a variance where he was charged with carjacking, and the victim named in the indictment was Brent Beyers, whereas the government proved that the car was owned by his wife, Anne Byers).

A case that can be compared usefully with *Martin* is United States v. Lawton, 995 F.2d 290 (D.C.Cir.1993). Lawton was an official of a local union. He was charged with embezzling money from the Local. His defense was that he had an oral arrangement with the Local to write checks to himself to pay his salary. The federal labor embezzlement statute makes criminal only the embezzlement of the funds of a labor organization of which the defendant "is an officer, or by which he is employed, directly or indirectly." The trial court instructed the jury, however, that it could convict Lawton if it found that he embezzled the Local's funds, *or* the District Labor Council's funds, *or* the International Union's funds. It was clear that Lawton was neither an officer nor an employee of these latter two groups. The court found that the trial judge's charge constituted a constructive amendment of the indictment, which was per se reversible error:

> Under the Fifth Amendment, the infamous crimes on which a defendant must stand trial are limited by the charges contained in the grand jury's indictment. The district court's embezzlement instructions, however, allowed the petit jury to convict Lawton of additional charges. The trial court's instructions thus violated the Grand Jury Clause just as surely as if the court had written additional charges onto the grand jury's "true bill." Still worse, the instructions allowed the jury to convict on the basis of conduct that, on the face of the evidence, did not amount to a violation of [the labor embezzlement statute].

See also Lucas v. O'Dea, 169 F.3d 1028 (6th Cir.1999) (where the defendant was charged in the indictment with murder by shooting the victim with a pistol, it was a fatal variance for the jury to be instructed that the defendant could be convicted if his coconspirator fired the shot; the defendant was clearly prejudiced because his defense to the murder charge was that he was not the shooter: "Because it exposed Lucas to charges for which he had no notice and thus no opportunity to plan a defense, the variance from the indictment to the jury instruction constituted a constructive amendment that violated his Fifth Amendment rights."); Geboy v. Brigano, 489 F.3d 752 (6th Cir. 2007) (defendant was not prejudiced by variance between the indictment and the evidence as to the location of charged crimes).

Inspecific Charges

The concern of *Stirone* and its progeny is that an amendment or variance at trial will deprive the defendant of sufficient notice and so impair his ability to prepare a defense. But a notice problem can also arise when the indictment, though stating the elements of the crime, provides factual assertions so general that it is difficult or impossible to prepare a defense.[16] One remedy for inspecific factual assertions is provided by Fed.R.Crim.P. 7(f), which permits the court to direct the filing of a bill of particulars. The court in United States v. Salisbury, 983 F.2d 1369 (6th Cir.1993), described the function of a bill of particulars:

> A bill of particulars is meant to be used as a tool to minimize surprise and assist defendant in obtaining the information needed to prepare a defense and to preclude a second prosecution for the same crimes. * * * The decision to order a bill of particulars is within the sound discretion of the court. * * * A court does not abuse its discretion in light of a detailed indictment.

If the defendant moves for a bill of particulars and that motion is denied, the defendant is not entitled to relief on appeal unless he can show that he was "actually surprised at trial and suffered prejudice from the denial." United States v. Livingstone, 576 F.3d 881 (8th Cir. 2009) (no error in denying motion for bill of particulars where the defendant's strategy was to attack the credibility of government witnesses, and he could not show how a bill of particulars could have affected his defense).

Whether or not supplemented by a bill of particulars, it is at least possible for an indictment to be so vague as to provide constitutionally inadequate notice. The test for constitutional sufficiency was stated by Judge Easterbrook in Fawcett v. Bablitch, 962 F.2d 617 (7th Cir.1992): "[A] charge is sufficiently specific when it contains the elements of the crime, permits the accused to plead and prepare a defense, and allows the disposition to be used as a bar in a subsequent prosecution." The *Fawcett* court rejected the argument that an indictment is constitutionally defective whenever the prosecution could have provided more specific information in the indictment. It declared that "the prosecutor's ability to do better does not vitiate the conviction."

In *Fawcett*, the defendant was charged with two events of unlawful sexual contact with a minor "during the six months preceding December 1985." Fawcett argued that the time period was impermissibly broad, because it was impossible for him to provide an alibi for the entire six month period. The court rejected this contention, finding that sufficient notice had been given, and noting that Fawcett was free to attack the complainant's veracity and to deny participation. Do you agree that sufficient notice was given? Would the indictment have been sufficient if it charged one act of sexual misconduct within a ten-year period? Compare United States v. Salisbury, 983 F.2d 1369 (6th Cir.1993) (indictment insufficiently specific where it charges the defendant with "voting more than once," and that term is not defined in the criminal statute).

---

[16] Fed.R.Crim.P. 7(c)(1) requires the indictment to set out the essential facts constituting the offense charged, in order to inform the defendant of the offense against which he must defend.

The Elements of the Crime: Apprendi v. New Jersey

Under *Stirone* an indictment that does not set forth all of the elements of the crime charged is constitutionally deficient. Sometimes however it is difficult to determine just what *is* an element of the crime—as distinct from a sentencing factor that can be left for the judge. This issue is discussed in detail in Chapters 10 and 11. At this juncture, it is sufficient to note that in Apprendi v. New Jersey, 530 U.S. 466 (2000), the Court held that a factual determination authorizing an increase in sentencing beyond a statutory maximum is an element of the crime, and therefore is a question for the jury that must be proved beyond a reasonable doubt—and it must accordingly be set forth in the charging instrument. So for example, if the legislature has authorized a sentencing enhancement, beyond the statutory maximum sentence, for possession of a certain amount of drugs, the jury must determine the amount that the defendant possessed, and that amount must be set forth in the indictment. In states where no indictment is required, it should be sufficient for any charging instrument to allege all of the essential elements of an offense.

CHAPTER 7

BAIL AND PREVENTIVE DETENTION

■ ■ ■

I. INTRODUCTION TO THE PROBLEMS OF PRETRIAL RESTRAINT

A. THE SUSPECT'S CONCERNS

Many defendants are released or convicted and sentenced within 24 hours of their arrest.[1] The remaining defendants may await disposition of their cases for days, weeks, or months, depending on prosecutors' workloads, the gravity and complexity of the cases, the condition of court calendars, and the actions of defense attorneys. Under Federal law, the magistrate judge must determine which defendants may and should be released pending trial. See e.g., United States v. Briggs, 697 F.3d 98 (2nd Cir. 2012) (upholding detention without bail for two years while awaiting trial). States allocate a similar responsibility to magistrate judges or trial judges.

By the time the magistrate judge rules, the police have progressed sufficiently far in the investigatory process to have focused on an individual suspect. But it is possible that the suspect is innocent of all or most charges that are being considered or have been brought. The pretrial determination of probable cause, which forms the basis for arrest and detention pending trial, has the limited function of establishing only a fair probability that a suspect committed a crime. So there is a significant risk that an innocent person may be subject to detention before trial, and maybe the trial may not ever occur. For example, a defendant in Chicago was held for a year in advance of trial on the basis of a report by ShotSpotter that he fired a gun while in his car. ShotSpotter is a program designed to identify and locate gun shots. But after a year, the state admitted that ShotSpotter was not capable of determining the precise location of a gunshot. So the defendant was released—after a year's incarceration, because he could not make bail.

The suspect can certainly point to significant personal costs associated with pretrial detention. The consequences of incarceration include deprivation of contacts with friends and family, absence from employment and possibly loss of job or a house, diminished ability to support family and

---

[1] The Challenge of Crime in a Free Society, Report of the President's Commission on Law Enforcement and the Administration of Justice (1968).

to hire counsel, limitations on the ability to prepare a defense, and stigmatizing effects on the prisoner's reputation and future employment prospects. If the defendant is ultimately convicted, it can be argued that any unfairness arising from pretrial incarceration serving as punishment is *de minimis* because pretrial incarceration can be treated as time served on the sentence. But this only applies to those who are incarcerated. Anyone who has charges dismissed, is acquitted, is diverted into a treatment program or is sentenced to community service or probation never receives credit or compensation for time served, even if the length was substantial.

Moreover, studies indicate that pretrial imprisonment actually does prejudice the adjudication of guilt or innocence when it finally occurs, because a defendant who is incarcerated will find it harder to help prepare his defense.[2] In addition, prior detention erodes the rehabilitative prospects of the accused, placing him at a disadvantage both in conviction and sentencing. The defendant's demeanor, recognized as an essential element of the fact-finding determination, will reflect recent imprisonment: He is apt to be unshaven, unwashed, unkempt, and unhappy as he enters the courtroom under guard.[3] The hopelessness, the lowered self-esteem, and a decline in respect for the criminal justice system may cause detained suspects to lose their incentives to prolong the adjudication process and accordingly to plead guilty. There is evidence that a person who can't make bail is substantially more likely to plead guilty than one who can. See, e.g., Note, Detaining for Danger Under the Bail Reform Act of 1984: Paradoxes of Procedure and Proof, 35 Ariz.L. Rev. 1091, 1095 (1993) ("it is widely acknowledged that the government now commonly misuses the leverage of pretrial detention to extract premature guilty pleas and cooperation agreements in exchange for pretrial release"). Individuals sometimes challenge convictions on the ground that they only pleaded guilty because of pretrial confinement. See, e.g., Smith v. Oklahoma Co., 2013 U.S. Dist. Lexis 105754 (W. D. Okla. 2013) (habeas petitioner claims charges to which he pled were false and he only pled because of danger in pretrial confinement).

There are social costs to pretrial detention, as well. In addition to the significant costs of maintenance and support of the prisoners, society must often bear the secondary welfare costs incident to the imprisonment of a member of a household. See Colbert, Thirty-Five Years After *Gideon*: The Illusory Right to Counsel at Bail Proceedings, 1998 Univ.Ill.L.Rev. 1 (noting that pretrial incarceration imposes "a hefty price on society" in the form of job loss, family dislocation, and emotional turmoil, and that when

---

[2] See Kinney v. Lenon, 425 F.2d 209 (9th Cir.1970), where the court held that the defendant's release was necessary so that he might track down witnesses essential to his defense.

[3] See P. Wald, Pretrial Detention and Ultimate Freedom: A Statistical Study, 39 N.Y.U.L.Rev. 631, 632 (1964).

the charges are eventually dismissed or not prosecuted, "the economic, social, and emotional consequences incurred cannot be justified or remedied.").

The individual costs of pretrial incarceration fall most heavily, of course, on the underprivileged and indigent, often people of color. See https://www.aclu.org/issues/smart-justice/bail-reform:

> Poorer Americans and people of color often can't afford to come up with money for bail, leaving them stuck in jail awaiting trial, sometimes for months or years. Meanwhile, wealthy people accused of the same crime can buy their freedom and return home.
>
> Across the country, money bail is set at levels that are far too high for many people or their families to pay. Defendants face an impossible choice: sit in jail as the case moves through the system; pay a nonrefundable fee to a for-profit bail bonds company; or plead guilty and give up the right to defend themselves at trial. For poorer families, paying this fee can be a significant hardship. They won't ever get the money back regardless of the outcome of the case—even if the arrest was a case of mistaken identity and no charges were ever filed.

This circumstance is all the more worrisome given the high rates at which charges ultimately are dismissed. See Colin Starger, The Argument that cries *Wolfish*, https://law.mit.edu/pub/theargumentcrieswolfish/release/2 (reporting that "over the five-year period studied [in Maryland], just under 12,000 defendants spent a combined total of over 1485 years incarcerated pretrial before all the charges they faced were dropped, an average of 46 days in jail per person). A 1992 study by the Department of Justice indicated that about one-third of pretrial detainees throughout the country were jailed on bail of less than $2,500. Bureau of Justice Statistics Bulletin, Pretrial Release of Felony Defendants, 1992, at 4. And an NPR report stated that over 500,000 people have been incarcerated because they cannot make bail in amounts from $50–400. Talk of the Nation, January 26, 2010. The ability of a defendant to meet even a relatively small amount of bail depends on personal and family resources or the ability to post a 10% bail bond fee and the willingness of a bondsman to accept a defendant as a client.

Recently, attention has been paid in some places to another, often hidden, cost of pretrial detention. The following excerpt offers an example:

> An individual is arrested for a minor, nonviolent offense such as shoplifting, a traffic violation or possession of drugs. Bail is set at $500. The defendant is poor and does not have cash. She is then placed in jail for days or weeks until her court hearing, but all this time the dollar clock is ticking. Most states have what are known as "pay-to-stay" statutes. This means that the individual is being charged for her room and board a long as she is behind bars.

Mark R. Rank, *For Poor Defendants, Minor Crimes can Lead to Devastating Debts,* The Washington Post, December 26, 2021, at B5. Judges become debt collectors as individuals struggle to pay back the pay-to-stay costs as well as any fines and fees. For some, the cycle of falling behind, being re-incarcerated and incurring more pay-to-stay costs, being released and falling behind again, etc. is endless. The horrors of such systems are explored in Tony Messenger, Profit and Punishment: How America Criminalizes the Poor in the Name of Justice (St. Martin's Press 2021).

B. COUNTERVAILING CONCERNS

On the other hand, there are compelling societal interests that militate in favor of pretrial detention of some criminal suspects. One obvious justification for imprisonment pending trial is to guarantee the presence of the suspect in order to ensure proper judicial disposition of the case.

Pretrial detention also has a *preventive* aspect. The state has an interest in protecting the community that warrants imprisonment of at least some of those accused of criminal activity. In some cases there is a legitimate concern that pretrial release will simply give the suspect an opportunity to commit more criminal acts. And this concern is obviously ratcheted up in the post-9/11 environment when the government apprehends a person with suspected ties to terrorism. See, e.g., United States v. Hir, 517 F.3d 1081 (9th Cir. 2008) (upholding pretrial detention of a defendant who was the brother of a terrorist responsible for many bombings in Asia, where the evidence indicated that the defendant was sending money and electronic devices to his brother).

Courts, in determining whether a person should be released pending trial, are thus essentially balancing the individual's liberty interests against the legitimate interests of the state. What mechanism will operate to release those who pose no threat to the judicial process or the community at large, while detaining criminal suspects who are dangerous or likely to flee? How can the system protect the presumption of innocence and the right to be free pending adjudication, without hampering the law enforcement process or risking public safety? These are the questions posed in this Chapter as well as in the real world of processing criminal cases.

II. BAIL: ITS HISTORY AND THE CONSTITUTION

A. THE COMMON LAW ORIGINS OF BAIL

The traditional mechanism for pretrial release, the posting of bail, originated in medieval England, where prisoners could be confined in disease-ridden and insecure prisons for years awaiting trial by traveling justices, whose visits were infrequent.

Sheriffs welcomed the opportunity to place custodial responsibility in third parties. A prisoner would seek a friend or master, usually a property owner, who accepted custody or "bailment" of the accused, and promised to surrender himself if the defendant failed to appear. Of course, the law developed to permit the surety to forfeit property or money instead of his person, but the relationship remained a personal one. Eventually Parliament specified which offenses were bailable, and the Habeas Corpus Act of 1679 provided procedures to free prisoners who were bailable by law. Some judges still circumvented these requirements by setting prohibitive levels of bail; so in 1689, Parliament responded with a provision forbidding excessive bail.

B. THE CONSTITUTIONAL PROHIBITION AGAINST EXCESSIVE BAIL: THE EIGHTH AMENDMENT

The American Constitution incorporated the right of a person in custody to seek a writ of habeas corpus in Article I § 9, and the ban on excessive bail in the Eighth Amendment ("[e]xcessive bail shall not be required"). The third aspect of British law regarding bail, that is, the actual right to bail for specific offenses, was not included in the Constitution. Thus, the Amendment prohibits excessive bail, but it does not explicitly grant a right to bail. See Fields v. Henry County, 701 F.3d 180 (6th Cir. 2012) (the Eighth Amendment does not give a right to bail but rather "mandates that when bail is granted, it may not be unreasonably high in light of the government's purpose for imposing bail."). The Supreme Court described the provenance of the Bail Clause in Carlson v. Landon, 342 U.S. 524 (1952), a civil case, in which the Court upheld denial of bail to communists awaiting deportation hearings:

> The bail clause was lifted with slight changes from the Bill of Rights Act. In England that clause has never been thought to accord a right to bail in all cases, but merely to provide that bail shall not be excessive in those cases where it is proper to grant bail. When this clause was carried over in our Bill of Rights, nothing was said that indicated any different concept. The Eighth Amendment has not prohibited Congress from defining the classes of cases in which bail shall be allowed in this country. * * *

Critics of the holding point out that this interpretation would subsume the Constitution to some other law. "It requires one to believe that a basic human right would be deliberately inserted in the Constitution in a form which permitted Congress to restrict it at will, or even to render the eighth amendment entirely moot by enacting legislation denying the right to bail in all cases." Foote, The Coming Constitutional Crisis in Bail, 113 U.Pa.L.Rev. 959 (1965). Some states have resolved this dilemma by adding

a bail *requirement*, usually for all but capital crimes, to their state constitutions.[4]

See United States v. Salerno, infra, for a further discussion of the constitutional and policy issues surrounding bail. For a comprehensive and academic perspective, see Frase, Excessive Prison Sentences, Punishment Goals, and the Eighth Amendment: "Proportionality" Relevant to What?, 89 Minn. L. Rev. 571 (2005).

III. THE OPERATION OF A BAIL RELEASE SYSTEM

A. THE ADMINISTRATION OF BAIL: THE PROCEDURES

The most frequently used procedure for obtaining one's pretrial release has traditionally been through *cash bail.* Having learned of the bail figure, a defendant may raise the full amount of the bond through personal savings or those of his friends and family. If the defendant shows up for all required court appearances and complies with all conditions of release, the entire amount posted is usually refunded. See Fed.R.Crim.P. 46(g) (providing for release of bail when bond conditions have been satisfied). Conditions of release may include not only appearance at all court dates, but other conditions such as refraining from criminal activity, retaining employment, drug treatment, avoiding association with certain individuals, etc.

A defendant who can't come up with money to post bail may seek the assistance of a bail bondsman, who has complete discretion in selecting clients. The bondsman's usual fee is 10 percent of the bond amount; this fee is non-refundable. The bondsman places the entire bond with the court and the defendant gains pretrial freedom. If the defendant fails to comply with the conditions of pretrial release the bond is forfeited. It is therefore in the bondsman's interest to assure such compliance.

Personal bond is another method of release, which may be referred to as personal surety, nominal bond, or release on own recognizance. It is used when a judge determines that the defendant is sufficiently motivated to show up for his scheduled court appearance and can be released on his own signature without bail. But, if the defendant fails to appear, a monetary penalty may be imposed.

Defendants released on personal or surety bond by a nonjudicial officer, such as a police desk sergeant, have obtained freedom only until their first court appearance, which usually occurs shortly after the initial

[4] The Supreme Court has never held that the Eighth Amendment Bail Clause is binding on the states, though it has implied that a limitation on excessive bail is a fundamental right. Schilb v. Kuebel, 404 U.S. 357 (1971). Again, however, this does not establish a right to bail.

release. At that time, unless the case is disposed of then and there, the judge reviews the bail amount and may revise it upward or downward. Similarly, bail set by a lower court for those accused of felonies may be reviewed and revised by the higher court which conducts the actual trial.

Judges might also exercise discretion to release the defendant into a third party's custody. The magistrate in such cases charges the third party with the responsibility of assuring that the defendant will appear and will not violate specified conditions of the release. Common candidates for third party responsibility include the defendant's relatives or friends, or social service agencies or pretrial release programs.

The Bureau of Justice Statistics 2004 Large Urban County Study reported that in the 75 largest urban counties, 57% of defendants charged with felonies were released pre-trial and 43% were detained. Not surprisingly, defendants charged with murder were least likely to be released (12%). More surprising is the next category of defendants least likely to be released: motor vehicle theft (39%). The other defendants least likely to be released were the following: robbery (42%), burglary (45%) and rape (52%).

The Bureau of Justice Statistics Special Report, State Court Processing Statistics, 1990–2002 Violent Felons in Large Urban Counties (July 2006) reported the following statistics: "An estimated 38% of violent felons were released from custody pending disposition of the case that resulted in their conviction. Fifty percent were held on bail, and 11% were denied bail. Among violent felons who had a bail amount set, about two-thirds were released when their bail was set at under $5,000, compared to just 4% when it was set at $100,000 or more."

B. THE BONDSMAN

Free of most political and governmental restraints, the private bail bondsman is one of the most important players in the pretrial drama. When bail is set, the accused can pay a non-refundable premium—usually 10%—to a private bondsman, who then puts up the total amount of bail. The bondsman assumes the risk of forfeiture and has traditionally been given much discretion in establishing collateral for bail, and in tracking down and retrieving a fleeing accused. The legal right of a bondsman to surrender the defendant to the court and to cancel the bond and keep the fee gives the bondsman considerable leverage, especially when bail may be set anew at different stages of a trial. The threat of being "turned in" ties the defendant to his bondsman, who may demand new premiums as the trial progresses.

Proponents of the bond system point out that without the private bondsman, numerous defendants would remain in jail for lack of available assets.[5] Also, bondsmen are often on call 24 hours a day. The profit motive provides them with the incentive to enforce a defendant's appearance in court. Thus, the system encourages private enterprise to assume part of the cost of administering the pretrial process. In theory, the bondsmen reinforce the law enforcement system by preventing flight and helping to return fugitives.

Critics, however, argue that the private bond system undercuts the purposes of bail and contravenes the ideals of the criminal justice system. Once released on a commercial bond, the defendant loses the same amount to the bondsman whether or not the defendant appears at trial. Theoretically, the court aims to set bail at a level that will ensure the appearance of the accused, but the intervening role of the bondsman supersedes the judicial determination. Thus, magistrates may fix bail with knowledge that the defendant has found a bondsman to advance funds or has been unable to secure help. Discretion in choosing clients provides one explanation for the relatively low level of risk in the bonding business. Bondsmen consider principally the type of crime for which the defendant was arrested, not necessarily the seriousness of the offense. Thus, those accused of organized crime or professional gambling are good risks, while a first time offender is considered a bad risk: unsophisticated as to the intricacies of the court system and prone to panic and jump bail. Narcotic addicts are considered good risks, prostitutes are not.[6] Bondsmen are free to incorporate their own political or personal prejudices in the bonding decision. The result can be disturbing. For example, civil rights activists who were arrested in the South often were unable to obtain the services of a bondsman.[7]

On the other hand, there are numerous minor, non-dangerous offenders who simply would have to stay in jail in most states, were it not for the private bondsman. When the bondsmen in New York went on strike in 1961 and 1964, refusing to write bonds except on 100% collateral in bankbooks or real estate, the population of the city jails swelled. The strikes were in retaliation for tighter collection policies enforced on forfeitures.[8]

If the defendant flees, some bondsmen use a system of informants and "skip tracers"—modern day bounty hunters, who often carry arms and have criminal records—to locate the fugitive. Recapture has been held to

---

5 Though this argument assumes that incarceration before trial is the only alternative. Another alternative, discussed below, is to abolish the system of cash bail in favor of allowing more defendants to be free before trial.

6 See A. Marticz, The Ups and Downs of a Bail Bondsman, L.A. Times, 8/2/76, reprinted in J. Snortum and I. Hader, Criminal Justice Allies and Adversaries (1978).

7 R. Goldfarb, Ransom 2–3 (1965).

8 Bail or Jail, 19 Record of the Ass'n of the N.Y. City Bar 13 (1964). Again, this argument assumes that defendants should be detained pending trial—an assumption rejected by recent bail reform movements, discussed below.

be a private remedy, arising from a private action, and thus freed from the constraints of due process[9] and constitutional criminal procedure. For example, a bondsman can seize a fugitive in another jurisdiction and present him to authorities, while the state must await extradition proceedings.

Noting that "the methods often employed by bondsmen are hardly likely to promote respect for the administration of justice," the ABA Standards on Pretrial Release set forth a standard prohibiting, or at least severely limiting, private bonding:

> **§ 5.4 Prohibition of Compensated Sureties**
>
> Compensated sureties should be abolished. Pending abolition, they should be licensed and carefully registered. The amount which a compensated surety can charge for writing a bond should be set by law. No licensed surety should be permitted to reject an applicant willing to pay the statutory fee or insist upon additional collateral other than specified by law.

Forfeiture of the Bond

A bond can be forfeited if the terms of the release are violated. See Fed.R.Crim.P. 46(f)(1) ("The court must declare the bail forfeited if a condition of the bond is breached."). Forfeiture may occur even if the defendant appears for trial; this is because the bail bond can impose numerous obligations other than attendance. For example, in United States v. Vaccaro, 51 F.3d 189 (9th Cir.1995), the defendant was charged with racketeering. His pretrial release was secured by a $100,000 bond provided by Bell Bail Bonds. As one of the conditions of his release, Vaccaro agreed that he would "not violate any local, state or Federal laws or regulations." Vaccaro committed a crime while released, and the trial court ordered the bail bond forfeited. Bell argued that the forfeiture provision of Fed.R.Crim.P. 46(f)(1) was triggered only if the defendant failed to appear. But the court held that the "break no laws" provision was a material part of his release agreement, and reasoned that "a bail bond is a contract between the government and the defendant and his surety." See also United States v. Gigante, 85 F.3d 83 (2d Cir.1996) (upholding bail condition requiring forfeiture of bond if the defendant commits a Federal, state or local crime while released on bail).

Bail bondsmen have (so far unsuccessfully) appealed to Congress for an amendment to Rule 46 to allow forfeiture only "if the defendant fails to

---

[9] Bondsmen are not public officers and therefore are not bound by the constitutional restraints that were examined in Chapters 2 and 3. Although they are not restrained by the Constitution, bondsmen rely upon it to protest forfeitures. In Wilshire Ins. Co. v. State, 94 Nev. 546, 582 P.2d 372 (1978), the court held that due process requires that the bondsmen be given notice of bail forfeiture proceedings.

appear physically before the court." (This was the language of the proposed "Bail Bond Fairness Act of 2001," H.R. 2929). The Judicial Conference opposed the legislation, having surveyed magistrate judges who reported that it is often important to impose other conditions of release as part of the bail bond—for example a condition that the defendant refrain from drug use. Magistrate judges argued that if they are not permitted to impose extra conditions, they will be less likely to grant bail in the first place. The Judicial Conference, in a letter to Congress, concluded that Rule 46 as written "provides judges with the valuable flexibility to impose added safeguards ensuring a defendant's compliance with conditions of release."

C. THE BAIL SETTING DECISION

Judges are entrusted with vast discretion in implementing the controlling statutes or court rules pertaining to bail. Bail criteria are not self-executing; it is the application of general criteria to particular cases that effectively determines which defendants are released and under what conditions. Often courts can choose among criteria in making bail decisions, and the choice often reflects a court's view of the purposes of bail.

Amount of Bail Must Support the Purposes for Setting It: Stack v. Boyle

As stated previously, the Court has never held that bail or any form of pretrial release is constitutionally required. However, the Court in Stack v. Boyle, 342 U.S. 1 (1951) recognized that, *if* bail is set, then a court must set it at an amount that appropriately furthers the purposes of bail. The Court held that bail fixed in uniform amounts of $50,000 for each of twelve defendants charged with violations of the Smith Act could not be justified in the absence of evidence relating to the particular characteristics and circumstances of each defendant. The *Stack* Court declared as follows:

> [T]he fixing of bail for any individual defendant must be based upon standards relevant to the purpose of assuring the presence of that defendant. * * * Upon final judgment of conviction, petitioners face imprisonment of not more than five years and a fine of not more than $10,000. It is not denied that bail for each petitioner has been fixed in a sum much higher than that usually imposed for offenses with like penalties and yet there has been no factual showing to justify such action in this case. The Government asks the courts to depart from the norm by assuming, without the introduction of evidence, that each petitioner is a pawn in a conspiracy and will, in obedience to a superior, flee the jurisdiction. To infer from the fact of indictment alone a need for bail in an unusually high amount is an arbitrary act. Such conduct would inject into our own system of government the very principles of

totalitarianism which Congress was seeking to guard against in passing the statute under which petitioners have been indicted.

If bail in an amount greater than that usually fixed for serious charges of crimes is required in the case of any of the petitioners, that is a matter to which evidence should be directed in a hearing so that the constitutional rights of each petitioner may be preserved. In the absence of such a showing, we are of the opinion that the fixing of bail before trial in these cases cannot be squared with the statutory and constitutional standards for admission to bail.

Relevant Factors in Setting Bail

The most important factor in setting bail is the seriousness of the offense charged. The rationale is that the more serious the offense, the more likely that the defendant presents a risk of flight or harm to others.

A second factor in the bail-setting decision is the strength of the case against the defendant. This information is often relayed to the judge by prosecutors and police officers. Prosecutors may not be unbiased in their recommendations to judges. By suggesting a high bail amount with the expectation that the judge will lower it, prosecutors may seek to shield themselves from responsibility if the accused fails to appear in court or commits additional offenses while on release.

A third factor considered very relevant by the judiciary is the defendant's prior criminal record.

A fourth factor involves an assessment of the possibility that the defendant poses a flight risk. See, e.g., United States v. Leisure, 710 F.2d 422 (8th Cir. 1983) (finding bail of $2 million was excessive "when all of the evidence adduced before the magistrate indicated that appellants would appear at their trial").

Other factors are the defendant's background, such as community ties, financial status, and character references.

Of course if the defendant's counsel is present at the bail hearing, she tries to supply facts in attempting to secure the client's release on the best conditions possible.[10]

Despite the Supreme Court's reasoning in *Stack*, the reality is that bond schedules are used in many places and they establish a presumption as to what bail should be required for various offenses. Such schedules may fail to account for personal differences among defendants, but they make

---

[10] Federal Rule 44 provides that an indigent defendant has a right to counsel at the bail hearing. But the bail hearing has never been held to be a "critical stage" at which counsel must be provided as a matter of constitutional law. Twelve states do not guarantee indigents the right to counsel at bail hearings. See Colbert, Thirty-Five Years After *Gideon*: The Illusory Right to Counsel at Bail Proceedings, 1998 Univ.Ill.L.Rev. 1.

the magistrate's job easier and increase the predictability of a bail decision. See Fields v. Henry County, 701 F.3d 180 (6th Cir. 2012) (upholding bail set pursuant to a bond schedule). The movement away from these bail schedules is discussed later in this Chapter.

D. FOUR SAMPLE CASES

In the following fact situations, consider what arguments you see for and against recommending bail for the accused. As judge, would you set bail? What conditions would you set, if any, in addition to a promise to appear? As a private bondsman, whose general practice is either to accept 10% of the bond as a non-refundable premium or to refuse the client, would you take the risk?

1. The 39-year-old defendant was arrested 2 days ago for attempted murder and aggravated battery. He has a prior record of 10 armed robberies and one attempted jailbreak while awaiting an earlier trial. Yesterday, he threatened the life of a cellmate, and boasted that he always carried a loaded gun. He has an excellent record for his prior experience on parole, and a perfect attendance record while free on bond for a prior conviction. He has been working part-time, and for the past 6 months has lived with his mother. The maximum sentence is 10 years. Would your answer differ if he had no job, and no permanent address? If he were charged with burglary? With armed robbery? With vagrancy?

2. A 36-year-old defendant is charged with breaking and entering. She is a heroin addict, and has a record of seven prior convictions for breaking and entering within the last three years, as well as two convictions for possession of narcotics in the same time period. She lives with her three young children, and works part-time in the department store where she was arrested. Should she be released on bail? How much bail should be required?

3. A 65-year-old defendant is charged in an arson conspiracy. He owned and ran a diner in New York City for 25 years, until it burned to the ground. He has no passport and no family members who live in New York. He has a brother in Greece. This is his first offense. Should bail be set? How high? Would it make a difference if a person died in the fire? Would it make a difference if the defendant had a passport?

4. A Muslim student is charged with lying to the grand jury about knowing some of the individuals who took part in planning terrorist attacks in Los Angeles. He is not charged with taking part in the attacks. He traveled extensively in the Middle East before settling in San Diego and becoming an American citizen. He has a brother in the United States. He has traveled back to the Middle East on several occasions, and the prosecutor submits a statement from a State Department official that the defendant has contributed to Muslim charities "known to funnel monies to

Al Qaeda." Do you set bail? Are you worried about a public outcry? Would taking away his passport guarantee that he is no longer a flight risk?

IV. BAIL REFORM

A. THE FEDERAL BAIL REFORM ACTS

Congress, concerned about the arbitrariness and unfairness of a system of pretrial release that depended heavily on bail bondsmen, enacted the Bail Reform Act of 1966, a statute emulated by many states. The purpose of the 1966 Act was to encourage Federal courts to release accused persons without requiring them to deal with bail bondsmen. Apparently, courts were to consider only whether pretrial release "will reasonably assure the appearance of the person for trial." No provision was made for confinement of an accused who might pose a "danger" to the community. The Act provided for alternative methods of assuring an appearance, including in-home detention and supervision by a designated person or organization.

Congress repealed the 1966 Bail Reform Act as part of its Comprehensive Crime Control Act of 1984, 18 U.S.C.A. §§ 3141–3150. The Bail Reform Act of 1984 was an important part of the comprehensive overhaul of Federal criminal law and is *much less generous* to defendants than the prior act. The most important changes are: 1) the explicit recognition that potential dangerousness to the community may be considered in pretrial release decisions; and 2) the possibility for preventive detention without bail. (So while it is the "Bail Reform Act" it is not reform in favor of defendants charged with a crime.).

The heart of the Bail Reform Act of 1984 is found in 18 U.S.C. § 3142, which proceeds in the following steps:

a. Court's Options:

The Act gives the court four options for a defendant who is bound over for trial. The court can:

(1) Release the defendant on personal recognizance or upon execution of an unsecured appearance bond;

(2) Release the defendant on a condition or combination of conditions, the violation of which will result in incarceration;

(3) If the defendant is on parole or subject to deportation, detain the defendant until he is processed; or

(4) Detain the defendant pending trial.

b. Release on personal recognizance or unsecured appearance bond:

Ostensibly this is the preferred procedure under the Bail Reform Act, and Section 3142(b) states that the court "shall order the pretrial release of the person on personal recognizance, or upon execution of an unsecured appearance bond in an amount specified by the court." But the Act contains a major exception: "unless the judicial officer determines that such release will not reasonably assure the appearance of the person as required or will endanger the safety of any other person or the community."

c. Release on conditions:

If the court determines that release on personal recognizance or on unsecured bond will not assure the defendant's appearance at trial or will endanger the safety of a person or the community, then conditions can be imposed on pretrial release. If the court decides to impose conditions, one that *must* be imposed is that the defendant "not commit a Federal, State, or local crime during the period of release." Conditions must also be set that will assure the defendant's appearance and the safety of other persons and the community. In setting conditions for appearance and safety, the court is instructed to impose the "least restrictive" conditions necessary to accomplish those objectives. The Act sets out a laundry list of possible conditions for release. The list is not intended to be exclusive or dispositive. The listed possible conditions are that the defendant:

(i) remain in the custody of a designated person, who agrees to assume supervision and to report any violation of a release condition to the court;

(ii) maintain employment, or, if unemployed, actively seek employment;

(iii) maintain or commence an educational program;

(iv) abide by specified restrictions on personal associations, place of abode, or travel;

(v) avoid all contact with an alleged victim of the crime and with any potential witness who may testify concerning the offense;

(vi) report on a regular basis to a designated law enforcement agency, pretrial services agency, or other agency;

(vii) comply with a specified curfew;

(viii) refrain from possessing a firearm, destructive device, or other dangerous weapon;

(ix) refrain from excessive use of alcohol, or any use of a narcotic drug or other controlled substance;

(x) undergo medical, psychological, or psychiatric treatment, including treatment for drug or alcohol dependency, and remain in a specified institution if required for that purpose;

(xi) execute an agreement to forfeit designated assets upon failing to appear as required;

(xii) execute a bail bond;

(xiii) return to custody for specified hours following release for employment, schooling, or the like; and

(xiv) "satisfy any other condition that is reasonably necessary to assure the appearance of the person as required and to assure the safety of any other person and the community."

The statute provides that the court "may not impose a financial condition that results in the pretrial detention of the person." That is, the court cannot impose a financial requirement for release that the defendant is not able to meet. See Wagenmann v. Adams, 829 F.2d 196 (1st Cir. 1987) (bail was unconstitutionally excessive when it was set at $500 when the court knew that he only had $480 on hand). If the defendant is going to be subject to pretrial detention, it must be upon findings, after a hearing, that he presents a flight or safety risk that no condition other than detention will reasonably alleviate (see below).

d. Pretrial Detention:

If the court finds that "no condition or combination of conditions will reasonably assure the appearance of the person as required and the safety of any other person and the community," then it must order the pretrial detention of the defendant, without bail. Preventive detention is only available, however, if the defendant is charged with a certain kind of crime; the possible crimes include crimes of violence, drug crimes, and other crimes designated by Congress.

In addition, if the defendant is charged with or has been previously convicted of certain specified crimes (including crimes of violence) within the past five years, then there is a "rebuttable presumption" that no condition or combination of conditions will reasonably assure the safety of any other person and the community. The statute also provides that there is a rebuttable presumption of both a flight and safety risk if the defendant has ever been convicted of a Federal drug crime with a maximum term of imprisonment of ten years or more. And the same rebuttable presumption applies to defendants charged with terrorism. The rebuttable presumption shifts the burden of production to the defendant to show that he does not pose a risk of flight or a safety risk. But "the burden of persuasion remains with the government." United States v. Hir, 517 F.3d 1081 (9th Cir. 2008).

The determination on pretrial detention is made after a hearing, at which the defendant has the right to counsel, including government-provided counsel if he is indigent. The defendant has the right to testify, to present witnesses, to cross-examine witnesses who appear at the hearing, and to present information by proffer or otherwise. The Federal Rules of Evidence do not apply at this hearing. Pretrial detention will be ordered if the government proves by a preponderance that the defendant is a flight risk; but if the ground of detention is that the defendant presents a safety risk, then the government must show this risk by clear and convincing evidence. 18 U.S.C. § 3142(f)(2)(B).

In determining risk of flight and risk to safety, the court is directed to consider 1) the nature and circumstances of the offense charged, including whether it is a crime of violence or a drug crime; 2) the strength of the evidence against the defendant (i.e., the stronger the evidence the greater the risks); 3) the defendant's character, including community ties and prior misconduct; and 4) specific dangers to any person that would be posed by the defendant's release.

There is little doubt that the 1984 legislation makes it more difficult for some defendants to obtain release pending trial. Before the 1984 Act, only about 2% of Federal defendants were detained pending trial. In 1990, the figure rose to 29% of all Federal defendants. The rate of detention in 1990 was 50% for those charged with violent crime, and 37% for those charged with drug crimes. Bureau of Justice Statistics, Pretrial Release of Federal Felony Defendants (1994). By 2005, 65.5% of defendants were detained pre-trial. Bureau of Justice Statistics, Federal Justice Statistics, 2005, Table 3.2.

It would be wrong to conclude, however, that the statute represents a uniformly negative attitude toward pretrial release. As noted above, no accused may be detained pending trial without findings by the judicial officer. A defendant may seek review of these findings. [§ 3145]. Most importantly, the statute explicitly provides that a financial condition may not be imposed if it results in the pretrial detention of the person. This means that, unless the judicial officer finds that no condition or conditions of release will provide that an accused will appear and will protect the community, the officer must provide for release of the accused.

Applying the Bail Reform Act of 1984

The Bail Reform Act of 1984 has raised a number of interpretive problems for the courts. One question is how a court is to assess the risk of flight. In United States v. Jessup, 757 F.2d 378 (1st Cir.1985), the court sustained the presumption in the Bail Reform Act of 1984 that a defendant charged with a serious drug offense poses a serious risk of flight. It concluded that Congress shifted only the burden of production with respect to the flight issue to the defendant and that the government continued to bear the burden of persuasion with respect to likelihood of flight. The court also concluded, however, that the presumption did not disappear when the defendant offered rebuttal evidence. Instead, it adopted a "middle ground" which requires judges and magistrates to consider Congress's finding that suspects charged with serious drug offenses pose special risks of flight and to weigh that finding when deciding whether the government has satisfied its persuasion burden. See also United States v. Xulam, 84 F.3d 441 (D.C.Cir.1996) (in non-drug cases, when the government seeks pretrial detention of a defendant on the ground that he poses a risk of flight, the standard it must satisfy is a preponderance of the evidence).

United States v. Abad, 350 F.3d 793 (8th Cir. 2003), provides a basic application of the Bail Reform Act's provisions on pretrial detention. Abad was charged with traveling in interstate commerce to have sex with a 13-year-old girl. He met the girl over the internet. This crime triggered the rebuttable presumption that the defendant presented a flight risk and presented a danger to the community (it is categorized as a crime of violence for purposes of the statutory presumption that the defendant presents a flight risk and a risk to the community). The defendant rebutted the presumption that he was a flight risk with letters from his parents and other members of the community, and with his parents' putting up their equity interest in their house as an assurance he would not flee. But this evidence served only to rebut the statutory presumption. The court found that the government had proved by a preponderance of the evidence that the defendant presented a flight risk that justified pretrial detention. The court reasoned as follows:

> Abad is not a United States citizen. Although Abad's family members are willing to pledge a $65,000 equity interest in the parents' home, such surety is insufficient to assure Abad's presence at trial. Abad faces a maximum sentence of 30 years, which reduces the significance of the surety amount and weighs strongly in favor of a finding Abad would be a flight risk. Although electronic surveillance is available, when considering all the factors at issue in the present case, there is insufficient evidence to assure Abad's appearance at trial.
>
> To counter the government's evidence regarding risk of flight, Abad offered five letters of support from family members and friends. However, none of the letters indicate the writers knew the nature of Abad's alleged crime. Two of the letters reference only the writers' familiarity with Abad's family rather than with Abad himself. Needless to say, these letters do not tip the scales when weighed against the government's damning evidence. Abad's family's

> willingness to supervise Abad while he is home is entitled to little weight, because Abad contacted the Iowa girl and engaged in web-cam sex with her while living at home with his family. Taking possession of Abad's passport has little flight deterrence considering the ease of travel to Mexico and Canada. Simply stated, we conclude Abad is a flight risk.

The *Abad* court also found that the government proved by clear and convincing evidence that the defendant presented a risk to the community that justified pretrial detention:

> Abad has no prior criminal history. However, the nature of the crime charged—sexual activity with a minor—weighs heavily against release. Strong evidence links Abad to this crime of violence. At the time of Abad's arrest, the police found a digital camera, condoms, KY Jelly, used contraceptive gels, and a dildo in Abad's hotel room. Abad admitted (1) he knew the girl was 13 years old, and he had met her in an Internet chat room for 13- and 14-year olds; (2) he engaged in telephone sex and web-cam sex with the girl before traveling to Iowa; and (3) he used a digital camera to take photos and video clips of the 13-year old girl masturbating and performing oral sex on Abad. The photos and video clips were found on the digital camera. Further, the government presented testimony Abad told the Iowa girl he previously, at the age of 22, had sex with a 15-year-old in Michigan. Based upon the evidence presented, we find the district court erred in ruling Abad is not a danger to the community. In particular, releasing Abad so he may return to his nursing position at Miami Children's Hospital is a clear abuse of discretion.

On the question of risk to the community, is the court saying that *anyone* charged with a child sex crime by definition presents a risk to the community warranting pretrial detention?

Risk to a Foreign Community?

In United States v. Hir, 517 F.3d 1081 (9th Cir. 2008), the defendant was charged with providing material support to a terrorist—his brother, who was wanted for terrorist acts in Asia. Hir had no prior record, and the government did not contend that he posed a threat to anyone in the United States. Nonetheless he was denied bail on the ground that he posed a threat to persons in Asia. The question for the court was whether the Bail Reform Act authorized pretrial detention for threats outside the country. The Act refers to threats to the "community"—but the court held that the relevant community need not be within the geographic bounds of the United States. The court reasoned that "[a]ny other interpretation would lead to an incongruous result: a court would be able to try a defendant under the laws of the United States for a crime the effects of which are felt abroad, but be unable to detain the defendant who committed the crime despite clear and convincing evidence that he continues to pose a danger to the same foreign community."

Prior History

How does the defendant's prior history factor into risk of flight or harm to the community? Courts under the Bail Reform Act understandably consider whether the defendant has a prior history of violent activity or prior flight. Does it also work the other way, so that a defendant's clean record must be considered as evidence that she is not a risk of flight or harm to the community?

This question was raised in *United States v. Mathis,* 963 F.3d 285 (2nd Cir. 2020), involving two lawyers who threw a Molotov cocktail into a vandalized police car during a demonstration against police brutality. The crime gave rise to the statutory presumption of no bail under the Bail Reform Act. The defendants sought to meet their burden of production by showing, among other things, that they had been law-abiding citizens and functioning lawyers, with no criminal history at the time of the demonstration. The government argued in response that it was the very fact of their lawfulness that required detention: because the defendants knew they had so much to lose by doing what they did, and yet did it anyway. The Magistrate Judge found the government's argument unpersuasive and granted bail in the amount of $250,000, along with house arrest and wearing of monitoring devices. The Court of Appeals affirmed, and addressed the relevance of prior history as follows:

> We are aware of no case where the fact that, prior to the offense charged, the defendants lived lives fully in accordance with the law, dedicated those lives to social betterment, and were employed in a profession that values ethics somehow militates *against* granting bail. If now a defendant's life history and characteristics can support detention, on the one hand, because that history demonstrates the defendant engaged in bad acts, and on the other hand, because the history is so spotless and impressive that the defendant should have "known better," the inquiry into a defendant's background may well become meaningless. We decline to endorse such a "heads I win, tails you lose" zero-sum analysis.

Drug Cases

The court in United States v. Rueben, 974 F.2d 580 (5th Cir.1992), set forth the standards for pretrial detention in drug cases as follows:

- probable cause of a serious drug crime creates a rebuttable presumption that no conditions of release exist which would assure the defendant's appearance and the safety of the community;

- where the defendant presents considerable evidence of longstanding ties to the community, the presumption of flight has been rebutted;
- the possibility of continued drug trafficking while on bail constitutes a safety risk to the community;
- for pretrial detention to be imposed, it is enough for the court to find either the lack of a reasonable assurance of the defendant's appearance, or a safety risk to others or the community;
- the rebuttable presumption against release shifts only the weight of producing evidence, not the burden of persuasion, but the mere production of some evidence does not completely rebut the presumption; and
- in making its ultimate determination, "the court may still consider the finding by Congress that drug offenders pose a special risk of flight and dangerousness to society."

In *Rueben*, the court held that the district court erred in releasing two drug defendants on a $100,000 unsecured bond. The court found that the defendants' "alleged family ties was hardly more than a reflection of the drug conspiracy itself." Similarly, the fact that one defendant owned a house "is not compelling as a tie to the community when its loss through forfeiture is a possibility because of its use in drug trafficking." Nor had the defendants presented any evidence to "indicate that they will not continue to engage in drug trafficking if released on bail pending trial."

Has the court in *Rueben* in effect established an irrebuttable presumption of detention in drug cases? See also United States v. Smith, 79 F.3d 1208 (D.C.Cir.1996) (indictment on drug charges creates a rebuttable presumption that no condition would reasonably assure the safety of the community; no error in ordering detention where the defendant was an "enforcer" in a drug conspiracy, and murdered a rival drug dealer in furtherance of the conspiracy); United States v. Cisneros, 328 F.3d 610 (10th Cir. 2003) (pretrial release properly denied where the defendant was charged with taking part in an international drug conspiracy, the defendant had the resources to abscond to Mexico, and the evidence suggested that the defendant was deeply involved in serious acts of violence). Compare United States v. Giampa, 755 F.Supp. 665 (W.D.Pa.1990) (presumption rebutted where drug defendant shows his long residence in the area, his close ties to his family, steady employment history, lack of resources or contacts that would enable him to flee the country with ease, and the fact that he had no record and did not appear to live the life of a serious drug dealer; court notes that the defendant was not the kind of "international narcotics trafficker" with whom Congress was most concerned when it enacted the Bail Reform Act).

Less Intrusive Alternatives

The ultimate statutory determination under the Bail Reform Act is whether "there are conditions of release that will reasonably assure the appearance of the [defendant] as required and the safety of any other person in the community." This statutory language is sometimes invoked by defendants to suggest less intrusive alternatives to pretrial detention. A typically suggested alternative is home detention and electronic monitoring. As to the effectiveness of this alternative to detention, consider the facts of United States v. Tortora, 922 F.2d 880 (1st Cir.1990):

> An alleged soldier in the Patriarca Family of the Mafia was indicted for violation of the RICO statute. His three predicate crimes in furtherance of the RICO enterprise were: extortion; violation of the Travel Act; and conspiracy to violate the Travel Act. Upon the grant of the government's motion for pretrial detention, the defendant proposed certain release conditions to assure the safety of the community. These conditions mandated, for example, that the defendant not violate the law, appear at scheduled proceedings, eschew possession of weapons and substance abuse, restrict his travel, etc. In granting the release order, the [district] court required the defendant to (1) remain at home twenty-four hours a day, except for a reasonable number of visits to doctors and lawyers, wearing an electronic bracelet; (2) refrain from communicating with any person not approved by the prosecutor and defense counsel; (3) meet with codefendants only in the presence of counsel for the purpose of preparing a defense; (4) allow only one telephone line into his residence, hooking it up to a pen register; and (5) post the residence—a house owned by his brother—as security.

The court of appeals vacated the order releasing Tortora. It first agreed with the district court that Tortora was properly classified as dangerous. The court reasoned that membership in an Organized Crime Organization was clearly relevant to dangerousness, rejecting Tortora's argument that such "associational ties" could not be considered. It concluded that as long as the defendant was judged as an individual, his devotion to the Mafia was important evidence of his dangerous character, especially where Tortora, at a ritualistic Mafia ceremony, "threatened to kill his brother if the latter posed a danger to any member of the organization." The court also rejected Tortora's argument that devotion to his family precluded a finding of dangerousness. It responded that in light of Tortora's oath of fealty to the Mafia, "there is every reason to believe that he will prefer Family over family."

The *Tortora* court next held that the release conditions were not adequate to assure the community's safety in view of the fact that virtually all of the conditions hinged upon the defendant's good faith compliance. As such they could be too easily manipulated or circumvented. For instance, electronic monitoring "cannot be expected to prevent a defendant from committing crimes or deter him from participating in felonious activity within the monitoring radius"; and pen registers could be evaded by "the surreptitious introduction into his home of a cellular telephone." The court concluded that the "honor-dependent" nature of the restrictions took on great significance where "little about the defendant or his history suggests that good faith will be forthcoming." The court rejected the argument that the conditions of release could be amended to eliminate the risk of danger to the community:

> Given the breadth of human imagination, it will always be possible to envision some set of release conditions which might reasonably assure the safety of the community. For instance, agents could be posted by the government to watch Tortora at all times to ensure that he remains compliant; the guards could search all visitors, dog Tortora's footsteps en route to all appointments, and otherwise act as private jailers. But the Bail Reform Act, as we read it, does not require release of a dangerous defendant if the only combination of conditions that would reasonably assure societal safety consists of heroic measures beyond those which can fairly be said to have been within Congress' contemplation.

Tortora argued that the release conditions proposed by him and adopted by the lower court were sufficient because the alternative was incarceration—and if kept in prison, he would have at least as much ability to commit crimes as he would have if released. The court viewed this argument as "perverse" and stated:

> The Bail Reform Act does not ordain that dangerousness upon release is to be measured relative to dangerousness if incarcerated, and for good reason: the ability of an incarcerated person to commit crimes while in jail is a problem for the Executive Branch to solve. The idea that someone who otherwise ought not to be released should be let loose by the courts because his jailers may not prevent him from committing crimes in prison comprises a classic non sequitur * * *.

See also United States v. Gotti, 776 F.Supp. 666 (E.D.N.Y.1991) (ordering pretrial detention and rejecting home detention as an alternative: "Home detention and electronic monitoring at best elaborately replicate a detention facility without the confidence of security such a facility instills."); United States v. Hir, 517 F.3d 1081 (9th Cir. 2008) (upholding an order rejecting bail for a defendant accused of sending assistance to his brother, a wanted terrorist; proposed limitations of in-house arrest and electronic monitoring were not sufficiently effective because assistance could continue through internet monetary transfers; other limitations, such as self-imposed limitations on computer use, were insufficient as they were dependent on good-faith compliance by the defendant).

The Right to a Prompt Hearing: United States v. Montalvo-Murillo

In United States v. Montalvo-Murillo, 495 U.S. 711 (1990), the government failed to comply with the provision in the Bail Reform Act of 1984 that a hearing to determine the propriety of pretrial release be held "immediately upon the person's first appearance before the judicial officer." The district court ultimately found that Montalvo-Murillo posed a risk of flight and a danger to the community, and that no condition of release could give reasonable assurances against these risks. The court nonetheless released Montalvo-Murillo due to the lack of a timely hearing. The government challenged the release order and argued that release was an unwarranted remedy for a violation of the prompt hearing requirement.

Justice Kennedy, writing for six Justices, agreed with the government. He acknowledged the importance of a prompt hearing, but asserted that "neither the timing requirements nor any other part of the Act can be read to require, or even suggest, that a timing error must result in release of a person who should otherwise be detained." The majority reasoned as follows:

> The safety of society does not become forfeit to the accident of noncompliance with statutory time limits where the Government is ready and able to come forward with the requisite showing to meet the burden of proof required by the statute. * * * An order of release in the face of the Government's ability to prove at once that detention is required by the law has neither causal nor proportional relation to any harm caused by the delay in holding the hearing.

Justice Kennedy concluded that release of Montalvo-Murillo was an unwarranted remedy because he had not been prejudiced by the delay:

> In this case, it is clear that the noncompliance with the timing requirement had no substantial influence on the outcome of the proceeding. Because respondent was dangerous and likely to flee, he would have been detained if his hearing had been held upon his first appearance rather than a few days later. On these facts, the detention was harmless.

Justice Stevens, joined by Justices Brennan and Marshall, dissented and argued that the majority had undervalued the importance of a prompt hearing on the propriety of pretrial detention.

Time Served and the Bail Reform Act: Reno v. Koray

Under the Bail Reform Act, it is possible that a defendant could be released pending trial and yet remain subject to substantial restrictions on liberty, such as confinement in a treatment center or under house arrest. Is such a defendant entitled to a reduction for pre-sentence "time served" if he is ultimately sentenced? Or must he actually be incarcerated to have credit for time served? This question is controlled by statute. 18 U.S.C. § 3585(b) provides that a defendant generally must "be given credit toward the service of a term of imprisonment for any time he has spent in official detention prior to the date the sentence commences." The limits of this provision in light of the Bail Reform Act are indicated by Reno v. Koray, 515 U.S. 50 (1995). Koray was convicted of money laundering. A Federal magistrate judge "released" him on bail, pending sentencing, pursuant to the Bail Reform Act. The "release" order required that Koray be confined to a community treatment center, where he stayed for 150 days. The Supreme Court, in an opinion by Chief Justice Rehnquist, held that since Koray was "released" by the magistrate judge's order under the terms of the Bail Reform Act, he could not be considered in "official detention" while confined in the treatment center so as to receive the credit provided by 18 U.S.C. § 3585(b). The Chief Justice reasoned that "under the language of the Bail Reform Act of 1984, a defendant suffers 'detention' only when committed to the custody of the Attorney General; a defendant admitted to bail on restrictive conditions, like respondent was, is 'released.' "

The Chief Justice recognized that a defendant "released" to a community treatment center "could be subject to restraints which do not materially differ from those imposed on a 'detained' defendant committed to the custody of the Attorney General, and thence assigned to a treatment center." But this did not change the result mandated by the statute. The latter defendant would be entitled to a credit while the former would not.

Justice Ginsburg wrote a concurring opinion in *Koray*. She agreed with the majority's statutory construction, but added that "Koray has not argued before us that he did not elect bail intelligently, i.e., with comprehension that time in the halfway house, unlike time in jail, would yield no credit against his eventual sentence." Justice Ginsburg would not foreclose the possibility that a defendant has a due process right to "notice and a comprehension check" before accepting the terms of release under the Bail Reform Act. Justice Stevens was the lone dissenter in *Koray*. Does a statutory scheme make sense where "release" and "detention" can result in similar deprivations of liberty? Does it make any sense that Koray might have been better off in jail for the time he was detained at the treatment center?

Application of the Bail Reform Act to Persons Charged with Acts of Terrorism

After the attacks of September 11, 2001, the Bail Reform Act has been used for preventive detention of a number of defendants charged with having ties to terrorism. In United States v. Goba, 240 F. Supp.2d 242 (S.D.N.Y. 2003), for example, the court denied four defendants' motions to revoke a pretrial detention order and found that the Government had demonstrated by clear and convincing evidence that defendants pose a danger to the community based on credible evidence that each defendant associated himself with al-Qaeda.

The Bail Reform Act is inapplicable to individuals detained as "enemy combatants" in Guantanamo Bay pursuant to a war powers rationale.

B. THE BAIL REFORM MOVEMENT

In recent years there has been increasing concern over the use of bail schedules that often keep individuals unable to make bail in pretrial detention despite the fact that they pose neither a danger of flight nor of harm to the community. Even in jurisdictions that purport to apply the principle that no one should be detained simply because of an inability to make bail, magistrates are prone to rely on bail schedules either because they lack sufficient information about individual defendants or they are concerned about being blamed if a person is released without bail and commits a crime.

The consequence is that pretrial incarceration is the norm, even for minor offenses. To take just one example: 60–80 percent of the people in Maine jails are there awaiting trial, and the majority of arrests every year are for misdemeanors. A 2015 survey of five jails by the Maine Judicial Branch found the average cash bail for misdemeanor offenses was $722 and the average length of pretrial detention for misdemeanor offenses was about a month. https://www.aclu.org/press-releases/bill-ending-cash-bail-minor-offenses-moves-out-maine-house-committee-majority-support.

The American Bar Association adopted the following resolution at its August 2017 annual meeting:

> RESOLVED, That the American Bar Association urges Federal, state, local, territorial, and tribal governments to adopt policies and procedures that:
>
> 1. favor release of defendants upon their own recognizance or unsecured bond;
> 2. require that a court determine that release on cash bail or secured bond is necessary to assure the defendant's

appearance and no other conditions will suffice for that purpose before requiring such bail or bond;

3. prohibit a judicial officer from imposing a financial condition of release that results in the pretrial detention of a defendant solely due to the defendant's inability to pay;

4. permit a court to order a defendant to be held without bail where public safety warrants pretrial detention and no conditions of pretrial release suffice, and require that the court state on the record the reasons for detention; and

5. bar the use of "bail schedules" that consider only the nature of the charged offense, and require instead that courts make bail and release determinations based upon individualized, evidence-based assessments that use objective verifiable release criteria that do not have a discriminatory or disparate impact based on race, ethnicity, religion, socio-economic status, disability, sexual orientation, or gender identification.

The accompanying report explained the need for the resolution:

* * *

Despite the ABA's insistence that pretrial detention should occur only in exceptional situations, large-scale pretrial confinement has continued unabated in this country since adoption of the ABA Standards in 2002. In 2015, almost eleven million people were admitted into a jail. Todd D. Minton & Zhen Zeng, U.S. Dep't of Justice, *Jail Inmates in 2015* at 2 (2016). Most of the people incarcerated in jails have not been convicted of the alleged crime that led to their confinement. They are simply awaiting a decision whether they will be charged with a crime or, if charged, their trial. These unconvicted individuals comprised over 62% of the people incarcerated in jails in 2015, up from 40% in 1983. Todd D. Minton & Zhen Zeng, U.S. Dep't of Justice, *Jail Inmates in 2015* at 5, Table 4 (2016); Allen J. Beck, U.S. Dep't of Justice, *Profile of Jail Inmates, 1989*, at 2 tbl. 1 (1991).

One of the chief reasons for the extensive incarceration of presumptively innocent people is the conditioning of release from jail (or not being booked into jail) on the meeting of financial requirements, whether in the form of a cash payment, the posting of property as collateral, or a surety bond from a commercial bail bondsman. * * *

As the Vera Institute of Justice recently reported, "Money, or the lack thereof, is now the most important factor in determining whether someone is held in jail pretrial." Ram Subramanian et al., Vera Inst. Of Justice, *Incarceration's Front Door: The Misuse of Jails in America* 29 (2015) . And therein lies the problem. Most of the people detained in jails are poor. Some manage to eventually procure the funds needed to post bail or pay a nonrefundable fee to a bail bonding company, though they have to endure days or weeks of incarceration in the meantime. Many others are unable to ever muster the financial resources needed to gain their freedom. In fact, statistics collected since the adoption of the ABA Standards have revealed that 90% of the individuals who never secure their release from jail while their criminal cases are being processed are not confined because they were denied bail due to being a flight risk or danger to the public. They are incarcerated simply because they could not muster the financial resources needed to secure their liberty. Brian A. Reaves, U.S. Dep't of Justice, *Felony Defendants in Large Urban Counties*, 2009, at 15 (2013).

* * *

An abundance of research conducted and knowledge amassed since the adoption of the ABA Standards in 2002 have now made it clear that financial conditions of release fail to protect individual or public safety. At best, in rare cases, financial conditions may be used in conjunction with an individualized assessment of risk and ability to pay.

The report emphasizes that "[t]he amount of money or property a person has is not an accurate predictor of the risk of danger that person poses to others or of the risk that he or she will not show up for a scheduled court proceeding." It explains that "researchers have now developed, and jurisdictions are increasingly employing, validated risk-assessment instruments to guide pretrial-release and detention decisions," and "[t]hese empirically-tested tools are much more accurate predictors of risk than financial bail, intuition, or professional judgments unguided by such risk-assessment instruments. Conference of State Court Administrators, *2012–2013 Policy Paper: Evidence-Based Pretrial Release* 6–7 (2012)."

The report describes "[n]ew research [that] has unveiled that when low- and moderate-risk people are detained in jail for more than a day, they are significantly more likely to engage in a future crime"; "[t]he trauma and stigma that people endure from being incarcerated pretrial"; and "[n]ew research * * * reveal[ing] that pretrial detention due to an inability to post bond has a pervasive and negative impact on the outcomes of criminal cases."

The report concludes that

> where these types of schedules represent a judicial determination that defendants charged with low-risk offenses ought to be released, the appropriate mechanisms are release on recognizance or unsecured appearance bonds. Otherwise, these low bail amounts simply serve as

an arrest fine or tax on those defendants who can make bail, while detaining those who can't.

The report ends with 10 key requirements for effective pretrial release and detention decision making.

The American Bar Association is not alone in urging for the reform of existing bail schemes. "Pretty much everyone who spends any time examining the American system of secured cash bail comes away with the same conclusion: It's unjust, expensive and ineffective." Editorial, Cash Bail's Lonely Defender, N.Y. Times, August 26, 2017, at A18. The bail industry has proved effective at lobbying legislatures and leaders of the industry "characterize their fight against ball reform as an all-out war." *Id.*

Concern about the unfairness of bail systems has been bipartisan. For example, Republican Senator Rand Paul and Democratic Senator Kamala Harris in 2017 proposed Federal legislation (S.1593), the Pretrial Integrity and Safety Act, which would set aside $10 million in Federal grant money to begin encouraging more states to drop or curtail cash bail systems and consider other factors when sorting out whether a defendant should be kept behind bars before trial. https://www.congress.gov/bill/115th-congress/senate-bill/1593/text.

For more information on efforts to reform or replace the system of cash bail, see Foderaro, New Jersey Alters its Bail System and Upends Legal Landscape, N.Y. Times, 2/7/2017, which notes that under an overhaul of New Jersey's bail system, which essentially eliminates cash bail at least for minor crimes, "judges are now considering defendant's flight risk and threat to public safety in deciding whether to detain them while they await trial. Otherwise, they are to be released, usually with certain conditions." The reform effort in New Jersey was spurred by findings that 39 percent of inmates were eligible to be released on bail but could not meet amounts as low as $2500. The bail bond industry is of course opposed, and cites public safety risks of releasing so many arrestees. But advocates of reform note that a system relying on cash bail does not guarantee safety, because those with some money—including drug dealers, etc.—can buy their freedom. New York now has a system similar to New Jersey's, essentially abolishing cash bail for minor crimes. Similarly, voters in New Mexico approved a constitutional amendment that allows judges to deny bail to defendants considered exceptionally dangerous, but otherwise permits pretrial release of nondangerous indigent offenders who cannot make bail. Other jurisdictions have altered or eliminated their money bail systems in recent years, including cities in Alabama, Georgia, and Maryland.

A new development intended to mitigate the adverse impact of bail decisions on the less wealthy is discussed in Jay Lambert & J. Vincent Aprile II, Bail Credit: An Innovative Way to Mitigate Oppressive Monetary Bail, 32 Criminal Justice 32 (Winter 2018). The innovation would permit pretrial detainees to earn the funds to meet their bail as they serve their pretrial confinement. An example is Kentucky Revised Statute 431.066, which was enacted in 2011, and provides that a court shall permit a defendant a credit of $100 per day as a payment toward the amount of the bail set for each day or a portion of a day that the defendant remains in jail prior to trial.

V. THE CONSTITUTIONALITY OF PREVENTIVE DETENTION

Preventive detention results in a loss of liberty, before an adjudication has been made that a person is guilty of a crime. How can this be squared with the detainee's right to due process? This question is explored in the following case.

UNITED STATES V. SALERNO

Supreme Court of the United States, 1987.
481 U.S. 739.

CHIEF JUSTICE REHNQUIST delivered the opinion of the Court.

The Bail Reform Act of 1984 allows a Federal court to detain an arrestee pending trial if the government demonstrates by clear and convincing evidence after an adversary hearing that no release conditions "will reasonably assure . . . the safety of any person and the community." The United States Court of Appeals for the Second Circuit struck down this provision of the Act as facially unconstitutional, because, in that court's words, this type of pretrial detention violates "substantive due process." * * * We hold that, as against the facial attack mounted by these respondents, the Act fully comports with constitutional requirements. We therefore reverse.

* * *

Responding to "the alarming problem of crimes committed by persons on release," Congress formulated the Bail Reform Act of 1984, as the solution to a bail crisis in the Federal courts. * * *

Respondents Anthony Salerno and Vincent Cafaro were arrested on March 21, 1986, after being charged in a 29-count indictment alleging various Racketeer Influenced and Corrupt Organizations Act (RICO) violations, mail and wire fraud offenses, extortion, and various criminal gambling violations. The RICO counts alleged 35 acts of racketeering activity, including fraud, extortion, gambling, and conspiracy to commit murder. At respondents' arraignment, the Government moved to have Salerno and Cafaro detained * * * on the ground that no condition of release would assure the safety of the community or any person. The District Court held a hearing at which the Government made a detailed proffer of evidence. The Government's case showed that Salerno was the "boss" of the Genovese Crime Family of La Cosa Nostra and that Cafaro was a "captain" in the Genovese Family. According to the Government's proffer, based in large part on conversations intercepted by a court-ordered wiretap, the two respondents had participated in wide-ranging conspiracies to aid their illegitimate enterprises through violent means. The Government also offered the testimony of two of its trial witnesses, who would assert that Salerno personally participated in two murder conspiracies. * * *

The District Court granted the Government's detention motion, concluding that the Government had established by clear and convincing evidence that no condition or combination of conditions of release would ensure the safety of the community or any person * * *.

Respondents appealed, contending that to the extent that the Bail Reform Act permits pretrial detention on the ground that the arrestee is likely to commit future crimes, it is unconstitutional on its face. Over a dissent, the United States Court of Appeals for the Second Circuit agreed. * * * It reasoned that our criminal law system holds persons accountable for past actions, not anticipated future actions. Although a court could detain an arrestee who threatened to flee before trial, such detention would be permissible because it would serve the basic objective of a criminal system—bringing the accused to trial. * * * The Court of Appeals also found our decision in Schall v. Martin, 467 U.S. 253 (1984), upholding postarrest pretrial detention of juveniles, inapposite because juveniles have a lesser interest in liberty than do adults. * * *

A facial challenge to a legislative Act is, of course, the most difficult challenge to mount successfully, since the challenger must establish that no set of circumstances exists under which the Act would be valid. The fact that the Bail Reform Act might operate unconstitutionally under some conceivable set of circumstances is insufficient to render it wholly invalid, since we have not recognized an "overbreadth" doctrine outside the limited context of the First Amendment. We think respondents have failed to shoulder their heavy burden to demonstrate that the Act is "facially" unconstitutional.

* * *

Respondents first argue that the Act violates substantive due process because the pretrial detention it authorizes constitutes impermissible punishment before trial. The Government, however, has never argued that pretrial detention could be upheld if it were "punishment." The Court of Appeals assumed that pretrial detention under the Bail Reform Act is regulatory, not penal, and we agree that it is.

* * * To determine whether a restriction on liberty constitutes impermissible punishment or permissible regulation, we first look to

legislative intent. Unless Congress expressly intended to impose punitive restrictions, the punitive/regulatory distinction turns on whether an alternative purpose to which the restriction] may rationally be connected is assignable for it, and whether it appears excessive in relation to the alternative purpose assigned to it.

We conclude that the detention imposed by the Act falls on the regulatory side of the dichotomy. The legislative history of the Bail Reform Act clearly indicates that Congress did not formulate the pretrial detention provisions as punishment for dangerous individuals. Congress instead perceived pretrial detention as a potential solution to a pressing societal problem. There is no doubt that preventing danger to the community is a legitimate regulatory goal.

Nor are the incidents of pretrial detention excessive in relation to the regulatory goal Congress sought to achieve. The Bail Reform Act carefully limits the circumstances under which detention may be sought to the most serious of crimes. See 18 U.S.C. § 3142(f)(detention hearings available if case involves crimes of violence, offenses for which the sentence is life imprisonment or death, serious drug offenses, or certain repeat offenders). The arrestee is entitled to a prompt detention hearing, and the maximum length of pretrial detention is limited by the stringent time limitations of the Speedy Trial Act. Moreover, as in Schall v. Martin, the conditions of confinement envisioned by the Act "appear to reflect the regulatory purposes relied upon by the government." As in *Schall* the statute at issue here requires that detainees be housed in a "facility separate, to the extent practicable, from persons awaiting or serving sentences or being held in custody pending appeal." We conclude, therefore, that the pretrial detention contemplated by the Bail Reform Act is regulatory in nature, and does not constitute punishment before trial in violation of the Due Process Clause.

The Court of Appeals nevertheless concluded that "the Due Process Clause prohibits pretrial detention on the ground of danger to the community as a regulatory measure, without regard to the duration of the detention." Respondents characterize the Due Process Clause as erecting an impenetrable "wall" in this area that "no governmental interest—rational, important, compelling or otherwise—may surmount."

We do not think the Clause lays down any such categorical imperative. We have repeatedly held that the government's regulatory interest in community safety can, in appropriate circumstances, outweigh an individual's liberty interest. For example, in times of war or insurrection, when society's interest is at its peak, the government may detain individuals whom the government believes to be dangerous. Even outside the exigencies of war, we have found that sufficiently compelling governmental interests can justify detention of dangerous persons. Thus, we have found no absolute constitutional barrier to detention of potentially dangerous resident aliens pending deportation proceedings. We have also held that the government may detain mentally unstable individuals who present a danger to the public, and dangerous defendants who become incompetent to stand trial. We have approved of postarrest regulatory detention of juveniles when they present a continuing danger to the community. Even competent adults may face substantial liberty restrictions as a result of the operation of our criminal justice system. If the police suspect an individual of a crime, they may arrest and hold him until a neutral magistrate determines whether probable cause exists. Finally, respondents concede and the Court of Appeals noted that an arrestee may be incarcerated until trial if he presents a risk of flight, or a danger to witnesses.

* * * Given the well-established authority of the government, in special circumstances, to restrain individuals' liberty prior to or even without criminal trial and conviction, we think that the present statute providing for pretrial detention on the basis of dangerousness must be evaluated in precisely the same manner that we evaluated the laws in the cases discussed above.

The government's interest in preventing crime by arrestees is both legitimate and compelling. * * * The Bail Reform Act * * * narrowly focuses on a particularly acute problem in which the government interests are overwhelming. The Act operates only on individuals who have been arrested for a specific category of extremely serious offenses. Congress specifically found that these individuals are far more likely to be responsible for dangerous acts in the community after arrest. Nor is the Act by any means a scattershot attempt to incapacitate those who are merely suspected of these serious crimes. The government must first of all demonstrate probable cause to believe that the charged crime has been committed by the arrestee, but that is not enough. In a full-blown adversary hearing, the government must convince a neutral decisionmaker by clear and convincing evidence that no conditions of release can reasonably assure the safety of the community or any person. * * * Under these narrow circumstances, society's interest in crime prevention is at its greatest.

On the other side of the scale, of course, is the individual's strong interest in liberty. We do not minimize the importance and fundamental nature of this right. But, as our cases hold, this right may, in circumstances where the government's interest is sufficiently weighty, be subordinated to the greater needs of society. * * * When the government proves by clear and convincing evidence that an arrestee presents an identified and articulable threat to an individual or the community, we believe that, consistent with the Due Process Clause, a court may disable the arrestee from executing that threat. * * *

Finally, we may dispose briefly of respondents' facial challenge to the procedures of the Bail Reform Act. To sustain them against such a challenge, we need only find them "adequate to authorize the pretrial detention of at least some [persons] charged with crimes," whether or not they might be insufficient in some particular circumstances. We think they pass that test. * * * Under the Bail Reform Act, the procedures by which a judicial officer evaluates the likelihood of future dangerousness are specifically designed to further the accuracy of that determination. Detainees have a right to counsel at the detention hearing. 18 U.S.C. § 3142(f). They may testify in their own behalf, present information by proffer or otherwise, and cross-examine witnesses who appear at the hearing. The judicial officer charged with the responsibility of determining the appropriateness of detention is guided by statutorily enumerated factors, which include the nature and the circumstances of the charges, the weight of the evidence, the history and characteristics of the putative offender, and the danger to the community. The government must prove its case by clear and convincing evidence. Finally, the judicial officer must include written findings of fact and a written statement of reasons for a decision to detain. The Act's review provisions provide for immediate appellate review of the detention decision.

We think these extensive safeguards suffice to repel a facial challenge. * * *

Respondents also contend that the Bail Reform Act violates the Excessive Bail Clause of the Eighth Amendment. The Court of Appeals did not address this issue because it found that the Act violates the Due Process Clause. We think that the Act survives a challenge founded upon the Eighth Amendment.

[The Court discusses both *Stack* and *Carlson* and concludes that "[w]hile we agree that a primary function of bail is to safeguard the courts' role in adjudicating the guilt or innocence of defendants, we reject the proposition that the Eighth Amendment categorically prohibits the government from pursuing other admittedly compelling interests through regulation of pretrial release."] * * * Nothing in the text of the Bail Clause limits permissible government considerations solely to questions of flight. The only arguable substantive limitation of the Bail Clause is that the government's proposed conditions of release or detention not be "excessive" in light of the perceived evil. Of course, to determine whether the government's response is excessive, we must compare that response against the interest the government seeks to protect by means of that response. Thus, when the government has admitted that its only interest is in preventing flight, bail must be set by a court at a sum designed to ensure that goal, and no more. We believe that when Congress has mandated detention on the basis of a compelling interest other than prevention of flight, as it has here, the Eighth Amendment does not require release on bail.

* * *

Reversed.

JUSTICE MARSHALL with whom JUSTICE BRENNAN joins, dissenting.

* * *

Throughout the world today there are men, women and children interned indefinitely, awaiting trials which may never come or which may be a mockery of the word, because their governments believe them to be "dangerous." Our Constitution, whose construction began two centuries ago, can shelter us forever from the evils of such unchecked power. Over two hundred years it has slowly, through our efforts, grown more durable, more expansive, and more just. But it cannot protect us if we lack the courage, and the self-restraint, to protect ourselves. Today a majority of the Court applies itself to an ominous exercise in demolition. Theirs is truly a decision which will go forth without authority, and come back without respect.

I dissent.

[The dissenting opinion of JUSTICE STEVENS is omitted.]

Unconstitutional Applications of Preventive Detention

The Court in *Salerno* left open the possibility that the Federal statute might be unconstitutionally applied. But after *Salerno*, courts have upheld lengthy pretrial detentions under the circumstances, upon a showing of risk of flight (by preponderance) or a risk to safety (by clear and convincing evidence). For example, in United States v. Infelise, 934 F.2d 103 (7th Cir.1991), the court held that continued detention for two years pending trial did not violate due process. The court noted that the Government cannot delay a trial in order to use preventive detention as a surrogate for punishment. But the court found the delay to be due to the complexity of the case, the presence of multiple defendants, and pre-trial motions by the defendants. In United States v. Millan, 4 F.3d 1038 (2d Cir.1993), the court upheld a 30 month pretrial detention of a defendant who was the head of a large heroin distribution network. It noted that the prosecution was not solely responsible for the delay in the trial, and that the evidence of risk of flight and dangerousness to the community was compelling. The court stated that "the constitutional limits on a detention period based on dangerousness to the community may be looser than the limits on a detention period based solely on risk of flight. In the former case, release risks injury to others, while in the latter case, release risks only the loss of a conviction." Do cases like these give defendants detained before trial a disincentive to file pretrial motions?

Is it possible for a pretrial detention to be so prolonged that it violates due process regardless of any risk of flight or danger to the community? In *Millan*, the court stated that the length of detention "will rarely by itself offend due process" and that the prospective detention of thirty months, "while weighing in favor of release, does not, standing alone, establish that pretrial confinement has exceeded constitutional limits." Rather, the court must balance "(i) the length of the detention; (ii) the extent of the prosecution's responsibility for the delay of the trial; and (iii) the strength of the evidence upon which the detention was based." Of course, the longer the detention, the more likely it is that some of the delay is attributable to the prosecution.

Constitutionality of Other Forms of Preventive Detention—Insanity Acquittees: Foucha v. Louisiana

Salerno was distinguished by the Court in Foucha v. Louisiana, 504 U.S. 71 (1992). Foucha was tried for a violent crime and was found not guilty by reason of insanity. Under Louisiana law he was committed to a psychiatric hospital for an indefinite period. Hospital officials subsequently recommended his release on the ground that he was not currently, and probably never had been, insane. However, Louisiana law provided that commitment would continue, even in the absence of mental illness, unless the detainee could prove that he was not dangerous to himself or others; and hospital officials, noting Foucha's "anti-social" personality, refused to attest to his non-dangerousness. The State relied heavily on *Salerno* to justify Foucha's continuing commitment on grounds of dangerousness, but a five-person majority, in an opinion by Justice White, held that the Louisiana scheme violated Foucha's right to due process. Justice White rejected *Salerno's* applicability in the following passage:

> Unlike the sharply focused scheme at issue in *Salerno,* the Louisiana scheme of confinement is not carefully limited. Under the state statute, Foucha is not now entitled to an adversary hearing at which the State must prove by clear and convincing evidence that he is demonstrably dangerous to the community. Indeed, the State need prove nothing to justify continued detention, for the statute places the burden on the detainee to prove that he is not dangerous. * * *
>
> It was emphasized in *Salerno* that the detention we found constitutionally permissible was strictly limited in duration. Here, in contrast, the State asserts that because Foucha once committed a criminal act and now has an antisocial personality that sometimes leads to aggressive conduct, a disorder for which there is no effective

treatment, he may be held indefinitely. This rationale would permit the State to hold indefinitely any other insanity acquittee not mentally ill who could be shown to have a personality disorder that may lead to criminal conduct. The same would be true of any convicted criminal, even though he has completed his prison term.

Justice O'Connor wrote a concurring opinion stating that under *Salerno* it might "be permissible for Louisiana to confine an insanity acquittee who has regained sanity if, unlike the situation in this case, the nature and duration of detention were tailored to reflect pressing public safety concerns related to the acquittee's continuing dangerousness."

Justice Thomas wrote a dissenting opinion and was joined by Chief Justice Rehnquist and Justice Scalia. He agreed that *Salerno* was readily distinguishable from the instant case, but argued that the distinction cut in favor of the Louisiana commitment scheme. He noted that insanity acquittees, unlike pretrial detainees subject to the Bail Reform Act, "have had their day in court. Although they have not been convicted of crimes, neither have they been exonerated * * *." Justice Kennedy also dissented in a separate opinion in which the Chief Justice joined.

Constitutionality of Other Forms of Preventive Detention—Sexual Predators: Kansas v. Hendricks

Responding to the rising public alarm over sex crimes, many states have enacted "sexual predator" laws. These laws typically allow preventive detention of defendants who have been convicted of sex crimes and have completed their sentences. The Supreme Court considered the constitutionality of preventive detention of sexual predators in Kansas v. Hendricks, 521 U.S. 346 (1997). Kansas's Sexually Violent Predator Act establishes procedures for the civil commitment of persons who, due to a "mental abnormality" or a "personality disorder," are likely to engage in "predatory acts of sexual violence." Kansas filed a petition under the Act to commit Hendricks, who had a long history of sexually molesting children and who was scheduled for release from prison after serving time for a series of convictions for sexual assault of minors. After Hendricks testified that he agreed with the state physician's diagnosis that he suffered from pedophilia and was not cured and that he continued to harbor sexual desires for children that he could not control when he got "stressed out," the jury determined by a preponderance of the evidence that he was a sexually violent predator. Finding that pedophilia qualifies as a mental abnormality under the Act, the court ordered him committed. On appeal, the State Supreme Court invalidated the Act on the ground that the precommitment condition of a "mental abnormality" did not satisfy what it perceived to be the "substantive" due process requirement that involuntary civil commitment must be predicated on a "mental illness" finding.

The Supreme Court reversed the State Supreme Court. The Justices unanimously agreed that civil detention of sex offenders, based on a finding of "mental abnormality", did not violate any guarantee of substantive due process. Justice Thomas, writing for five members of the Court on this question, stated as follows:

> The Court has recognized that an individual's constitutionally protected interest in avoiding physical restraint may be overridden even in the civil context. * * * We have consistently upheld such involuntary commitment statutes provided the confinement takes place pursuant to proper procedures and evidentiary standards. See Addington v. Texas, 441 U.S. 418 (1979). It thus cannot be said that the involuntary civil confinement of a limited subclass of dangerous persons is contrary to our understanding of ordered liberty.
>
> * * * A finding of dangerousness, standing alone, is ordinarily not a sufficient ground upon which to justify indefinite involuntary commitment. We have sustained civil commitment statutes when they have coupled proof of dangerousness with the proof of some additional factor, such as a "mental illness" or "mental abnormality." * * * These added statutory requirements serve to limit involuntary civil confinement to those who suffer from a volitional impairment rendering them dangerous beyond their control. The Kansas Act is plainly of a kind with these other civil commitment statutes: It requires a finding of future dangerousness, and then links that finding to the existence of a "mental abnormality" or "personality disorder" that makes it difficult, if not impossible, for the person to control his dangerous behavior. The precommitment requirement of a "mental abnormality" or "personality disorder" is consistent with the requirements of these other statutes that we have upheld in that it narrows the class of persons eligible for confinement to those who are unable to control their dangerousness.

Focusing on the facts of the case, the Court found that Hendricks' mental abnormality justified preventive detention:

> The mental health professionals who evaluated Hendricks diagnosed him as suffering from pedophilia, a condition the psychiatric profession itself classifies as a serious mental disorder. Hendricks even conceded that, when he becomes "stressed out," he cannot "control the urge" to molest children. This admitted lack of volitional control, coupled with a prediction of future dangerousness, adequately distinguishes Hendricks from other dangerous persons who are perhaps more properly dealt with exclusively through criminal proceedings. Hendricks' diagnosis as a pedophile, which qualifies as a "mental abnormality" under the Act, thus plainly suffices for due process purposes.

Justice Kennedy wrote a short concurring opinion. Justice Breyer, joined by Justices Stevens, Souter, and Ginsburg, dissented. He argued that the statute operated as an ex post facto law on Hendricks, because the State sought to punish him retroactively for an act that had been committed before the effective date of the statute. He agreed with Justice Thomas, however, that the civil commitment of sexually dangerous persons, on the basis of a finding of mental abnormality, did not violate the Due Process Clause.

If the sexual predator law were struck down, couldn't the state respond by imposing mandatory sentences of life in prison without parole for every person convicted of an act of sexual violence? Would it be a better system to confine such an offender in prison for life rather than in a hospital for treatment? See In re Blodgett, 510 N.W.2d 910 (Minn.1994) (upholding indefinite civil commitment of sexual predators: "If the state were denied the ability to hospitalize the sexual predator, rather than let the offender out on the street, the state will counter by increasing the length of the prison sentence. * * * Arguably, then, the question is not whether the sexual predator can be confined, but where? Should it be in prison or in a security hospital?").

Constitutionality of Other Forms of Preventive Detention— Persons Subject to Deportation: Zadvydas v. Davis

In Zadvydas v. Davis, 533 U.S. 678 (2001), the Court considered the plight of an undocumented person who was ordered removed from the United States but who could not be deported to a receiving country. A statute, 8 U.S.C. § 1231(a)(6), provides for detention for certain categories of undocumented individuals who have been ordered removed but who cannot be removed within 90 days of the deportation order. Those subject to continued detention those who are: inadmissible; criminal; or removable for certain national security or foreign relations reasons, as well as any anyone "who has been determined by the Attorney General to be a risk to the community or unlikely to comply with the order of removal." The statute states that an undocumented person who falls into one of these categories "may be detained beyond the removal period and, if released, shall be subject to [certain] terms of supervision."

The Government in *Zadvydas* argued that the statute means literally what it says and sets no limit on the length of time that a person subject to the statute may be detained if removal is not possible within 90 days. Justice Stevens, writing for five members of the Court, refused to read the statute to provide for indefinite detention, reasoning that to so read the statute would result in a serious constitutional question under the Due Process Clause. Justice Stevens discussed the constitutional concerns in the following passage:

> The civil confinement here at issue is not limited, but potentially permanent. The provision authorizing detention does not apply narrowly to "a small segment of particularly dangerous individuals," *Hendricks,* say suspected terrorists, but broadly to aliens ordered removed for many and various reasons, including tourist visa violations. And, once the flight risk justification evaporates, the only special circumstance present is the alien's removable status itself, which bears no relation to a detainee's dangerousness. * * * The serious constitutional problem arising out of a statute that, in these circumstances, permits an indefinite, perhaps permanent, deprivation of human liberty without any such protection is obvious.

The majority in *Zadvydas* construed the statute to avoid the constitutional problem that it perceived. It held that an undocumented person who is not removed within the 90-day period can bring a habeas corpus action to challenge his continued detention as unreasonable.

Justice Kennedy wrote a dissenting opinion joined by Chief Justice Rehnquist and joined in part by Justices Scalia and Thomas.

Constitutionality of Other Forms of Preventive Detention—Detention of Undocumented Persons During Removal Proceedings: Demore v. Kim

It might be important that *Zadvydas* was decided before the terrorist attacks of September 11, 2001. In Demore v. Kim, 538 U.S. 510 (2003), decided after those attacks, Chief Justice Rehnquist wrote for the Court as it distinguished *Zadvydas,* much to the chagrin of the dissenters. Kim, a citizen of the Republic of South Korea, entered the United States in 1984, at the age of six. After becoming a lawful permanent resident of the United States in 1986, he was convicted of first-degree burglary in state court in California in 1996 and a year later of "petty theft with priors." The Immigration and Naturalization Service (INS) charged Kim with being deportable from the United States in light of these convictions, and detained him pending his removal hearing. The Court held "that Congress, justifiably concerned that deportable criminal aliens who are not detained continue to engage in crime and fail to appear for their removal hearings in large numbers, may require that persons such as respondent be detained for the brief period necessary for their removal proceedings." Kim challenged his detention as a violation of due process because the INS made no determination that he posed either a danger to society or a flight risk.

The Court noted that Congress adopted a mandatory detention provision "against a backdrop of wholesale failure by the INS to deal with increasing rates of criminal activity by aliens," Congress had evidence that one of the major causes of the INS' failure to remove deportable criminals was the agency's failure to detain them during their deportation proceedings, and more than 20% of deportable criminals failed to appear for their removal hearings after their release.

Although it recognized that the Fifth Amendment entitles undocumented persons to due process of law in deportation proceedings, the Court reasoned that "in *Zadvydas*, the aliens challenging their detention following final orders of deportation were ones for whom removal was 'no longer practically attainable' " which meant that detention did not serve its purported immigration purpose. It found that the mandatory detention provision of "deportable criminal aliens *pending their removal proceedings* * * * necessarily serves the purpose of preventing deportable criminal aliens from fleeing prior to or during their removal proceedings, thus increasing the chance that, if ordered removed, the aliens will be successfully removed." The Court also relied on the fact that the period of detention at issue in *Zadvydas* was "indefinite" and "potentially permanent," while the detention involved in the present case is of a much shorter duration and in the majority of cases it lasts for less than the 90 days considered presumptively valid in *Zadvydas*.

Justice O'Connor, joined by Justices Scalia and Thomas, wrote a separate opinion contending that the Court had no jurisdiction over the case. She agreed, however, with the Court's resolution of the challenge on the merits. Justice Kennedy wrote a concurring opinion in which he opined that a lawful permanent resident like Kim "could be entitled to an individualized determination as to his risk of flight and dangerousness if the continued detention became unreasonable or unjustified.".

Justice Souter, joined by Justices Stevens and Ginsburg, dissented in relevant part and agreed with Kim's claim that "due process under the Fifth Amendment conditions a potentially lengthy detention on a hearing and an impartial decisionmaker's finding that detention is necessary to a governmental purpose." Justice Breyer also dissented in part on the ground that it was unclear whether Kim actually was deportable.

VI. SPECIAL PROBLEMS IN THE OPERATION OF BAIL

A. CAPITAL OFFENSES

The granting or denial of bail is traditionally a matter of judicial discretion where a capital offense is charged, but many states by statute prohibit bail for these offenses. A defendant charged with a capital crime may have an incentive to flee that is as great as anyone charged with a crime, and may be considered as belonging in the most dangerous category of offenders. This may explain why states have denied bail in capital cases.

B. JUVENILE OFFENDERS

In the legislative effort to afford complete treatment for juvenile offenders, many states do not provide a right to bail for juveniles charged with offenses that would be crimes if committed by an adult. The rationale is apparently that if the juvenile offender wants to be treated like an adult he has to take the bad with the good—he can only have bail if his offense is adjudicated as a crime. Some courts have noted the possibility of release into parental custody, and have held that the existence of such an option precludes bail, even in a case when the possibility is foreclosed by a judicial determination that release into parental custody would be inappropriate.

Other jurisdictions do use bail as a release mechanism for juveniles. On the same day in 2017 that the American Bar Association adopted its resolution on bail reform in criminal cases, it adopted a resolution that urged governmental entities to cease use of bail/bond in the juvenile justice system, and to utilize objective criteria that do not have a discriminatory or disparate impact, while ordering the least restrictive conditions of release. The report accompanying the resolution included the following:

> The policies that have led to an over reliance on collection of bail monies, and fines and fees to fund criminal justice are paralleled in juvenile justice. The consequences of these practices are exacerbated by a child's dependence on a parent or interested adult regarding indigence determinations as well as ability or willingness to post bond or pay fees and provide transport to court. In March of 2016 the Department of Justice issued recommendations to redress practices that disproportionally affect minority populations and poor communities. Bail orders and imposition of fees that cannot be paid foster class-driven preventive detention. The D.O.J. letter was directed at court systems to ensure "court systems at every level (emphasis included) of the justice system operate fairly and effectively." The D.O.J. letter stresses that all courts must inquire about a defendant's ability to pay in all contexts. Children, or their families, who are not able to post bond or pay fees penetrate more quickly into the juvenile and criminal justice systems, and the evidence suggests that this leads to increases in recidivism.

In Schall v. Martin, 467 U.S. 253 (1984), which the Court cited in *Salerno, supra*, the Court upheld a provision in the New York Family Court Act that authorized pretrial detention of an accused juvenile delinquent based on a finding that there is a "serious risk" that the child "may before the return date commit an act which if committed by an adult would constitute a crime." Justice Rehnquist wrote for the Court that "[t]he 'legitimate and compelling state interest' in protecting the community from crime cannot be doubted."

Justice Marshall, joined by Justices Brennan and Stevens, dissented and objected to the breadth of the statute: "The provision applies to all juveniles, regardless of their prior records or the severity of the offenses of which they are accused. The provision is not limited to the prevention of dangerous crimes; a prediction that a juvenile if released may commit a minor misdemeanor is sufficient to justify his detention."

C. BAIL AFTER CONVICTION

As early as 1894, the Supreme Court held that there is no constitutional right to bail pending appeal from a conviction. McKane v. Durston, 153 U.S. 684 (1894). The courts reason that "since there is no constitutional right to appeal, there is no constitutional right to be free pending appeal." United States v. Sine, 461 F.Supp. 565 (D.S.C.1978). The fundamental rights of the convicted defendant differ in other respects, as well. "[T]he presumption of innocence and the right to participate in the preparation of a defense to ensure a fair trial—are obviously not present where the defendant has already been convicted." Gallie v. Wainwright, 362 So.2d 936, 941 (Fla.1978). At the same time, the risk of flight is arguably greater for a defendant who has already been convicted and who may have little hope of a reversal. For these reasons, the standards for postconviction release are stricter, and different criteria may be applied from those used prior to trial. After conviction, the court may consider factors such as the likelihood of reversal, the substantiality of issues on appeal, the length of the sentence imposed, future dangerousness, and the seriousness of the conviction.

The Bail Reform Act of 1984 provides that a defendant may be released pending appeal only if: 1) the court finds "by clear and convincing evidence that the person is not likely to flee or pose a danger to the safety of any other person or the community", and 2) "the appeal is not for purpose of delay and raises a substantial question of law or fact likely to result in reversal or an order for a new trial." In addition, if the defendant has been convicted of a "crime of violence" he must show, in addition to the above factors, that there are "exceptional reasons" why detention is not appropriate. 18 U.S.C. §§ 3143(b)(2) and 3145(c).

Thus, Federal detention pending appeal is certainly the norm, as the definition of "crime of violence" is broad and "exceptional" circumstances are by definition rarely found. See United States v. Lea, 360 F.3d 401 (2d Cir. 2004) (bail should have been denied pending appeal because the defendant was convicted of a crime of violence—witness retaliation—and failed to show exceptional circumstances; exceptional circumstances exist where there is "a unique combination of circumstances giving rise to situations that are out of the ordinary"; there was nothing exceptional about the defendant's going to school, being employed, or being a first time offender).

The court in United States v. Koon, 6 F.3d 561 (9th Cir.1993), considered the "exceptional circumstances" language in an appeal by the two officers convicted in the beating of Rodney King (an African-American male beaten by police officers who were acquitted in a state prosecution before being convicted in a Federal civil rights prosecution). Officers Koon and Powell advanced several reasons in their request for release pending appeal which they argued qualified as "exceptional," including: their offense was "highly situational"; they had been acquitted in a state court before being prosecuted and convicted for the same activity in a Federal court; the victim's conduct contributed to the offense; there would be difficulty in assuring the officers' safety during detention pending appeal; and their sentences were relatively short in comparison to the relatively long process for appeal. But the court held that none of these reasons was "exceptional" because "each is an ordinary corollary of being a law enforcement officer convicted of violating another's civil rights." See also United States v. Little, 485 F.3d 1210 (8th Cir. 2007) (exceptional circumstances are those that are "clearly out of the ordinary, uncommon or rare"; bail pending appeal should have been denied because the defendant's cooperation and timely appearance at hearings, and the aggravated circumstances of his arrest, were not "exceptional circumstances").

CHAPTER 8

DISCOVERY

■ ■ ■

I. CRIMINAL DISCOVERY: UNLIKE CIVIL DISCOVERY

The Federal Rules of Civil Procedure marked an important change in the theory and practice of civil litigation. Before those Rules were adopted

> a diligent lawyer could come into court well prepared on his own case, but he was frequently in the dark as to the exact nature of his opponent's case, and consequently unprepared to meet it. Surprise was a legitimate trial tactic. A lawsuit was viewed as a game or joust in which counsel for each side strove mightily for his client, and the theory was that justice would emerge triumphant when the dust of combat settled in the judicial arena.

M. Green, The Business of the Trial Courts, in The Courts, the Public and the Law Explosion 7, 21–22 (1965).

This "sporting theory of justice" gave way to the belief that a trial should be a "quest for truth." The Federal Civil Rules, as well as the civil discovery rules in the states, provide opposing counsel and litigants with tools, such as depositions and interrogatories, for discovery of information prior to trial; they permit each party to discover much of the evidence that is in the exclusive control of the other.

In contrast, criminal discovery remains decidedly limited, at least at the Federal level—despite the almost universal condemnation of the "sporting theory" of litigation. This raises obvious questions: Are the arguments in favor of broad discovery for civil litigants any less persuasive in the criminal context? Is the "quest for truth" inherently different in civil and criminal cases? If not, are there countervailing considerations in criminal cases that justify a different approach to discovery?

Within the criminal law, the wide range of possible cases makes it difficult to predict the need for discovery or its possible abuses in particular cases. Opponents of discovery tend to focus on violent criminals, citing the danger of revealing prosecutorial information to them. Proponents of more liberal discovery often point to white collar crimes in order to align the accused with the civil defendant.

When a system of discovery is established, the most important issue is whether to presume that most defendants and most defense lawyers will abuse discovery or that most will use discovery as it should be used—i.e., to prepare for trial or plea negotiations.[1] Fundamentally, though, the question is whether there is anything in criminal discovery that justifies its closed nature. As the American College of Trial Lawyers has stated:

> It is anomalous that in civil cases, where generally only money is at stake, access to information is assured while, on the contrary, in criminal cases, where liberty is in issue, the defense is provided far less information.

Proposed Codification of Disclosure of Favorable Information under Federal Rules of Criminal Procedure 11 and 16, 41 Am. Crim. L.Rev. 93 (2003).

The Role of Constitutional Law

Most of the discovery questions considered in this chapter involve nonconstitutional issues. The Supreme Court has repeatedly stated that "there is no general constitutional right to discovery in a criminal case." Weatherford v. Bursey, 429 U.S. 545, 559 (1977). On the other hand, it is clear that constitutional considerations are implicated when a jurisdiction establishes a discovery system. Some sharing of information by the government may be necessary in order to guarantee a fair trial. And an accused may have to give the government notice of certain claims, if it is to have a fair chance to meet them. It may be impossible, however, to have a truly reciprocal discovery system in view of the fact that the accused has a privilege against self-incrimination and cannot be compelled to waive it as part of a discovery regime.

II. THE BASIC ISSUES

A. ARGUMENTS AGAINST BROAD CRIMINAL DISCOVERY

Arguments against broad criminal discovery focus primarily on the risks involved in giving the accused access to prosecutorial information.

---

[1] The federal discovery framework is discussed at some length herein. A number of states have used it as a model. But many states provide broader discovery for defendants than that granted in the Federal Rules of Criminal Procedure. The Department of Justice may view federal prosecutions as focused more than state counterparts on organized crime, gangs, terrorism and large-scale conspiracies, which might pose greater dangers (at least in some cases) to witnesses and evidence. But, there are a substantial number of drug, gun and immigration prosecutions that would not seem inherently more "dangerous" than many state cases. For decades the Department has opposed efforts to liberalize discovery through changes in the Federal Rules of Criminal Procedure or legislation. But there is some recent movement at the Federal level regarding discovery related to an expert's testimony. The amendment for providing greater discovery as to experts is discussed later in this Chapter.

Judge Learned Hand set the framework for such arguments in his oft-quoted opinion in United States v. Garsson, 291 F. 646, 649 (S.D.N.Y.1923):

> * * * Under our criminal procedure the accused has every advantage. While the prosecution is held rigidly to the charge, he need not disclose the barest outline of his defense. He is immune from question or comment on his silence; he cannot be convicted when there is the least fair doubt in the minds of any one of the twelve. Why in addition he should in advance have the whole evidence against him to pick over at his leisure, and make his defense, fairly or foully, I have never been able to see. * * * Our dangers do not lie in too little tenderness to the accused. Our procedure has been always haunted by the ghost of the innocent man convicted. It is an unreal dream.

This argument suggests that expansion of discovery for defendants would tip the balance too much on the side of the accused. Prosecutors already face a heavy burden of proof and the defendant has the benefit of a privilege against self-incrimination which allows her not to testify at all. Neither of these elements is found in a civil trial.

Opponents of discovery in criminal cases seem to argue that the accused can be treated poorly in some respects if she is treated well in other respects. But what does this say about our attitude toward constitutional rights? It is true that the defendant's right to invoke her privilege against self-incrimination makes it difficult for the prosecutor to gather evidence from a defendant in discovery. It is true that the restrictions on evidence-gathering attributable to the Fourth Amendment and the right to counsel under the Sixth Amendment sometimes impair the government's ability to gather evidence. But does this mean that defendants should not get information that might be necessary for them to prepare a defense or decide whether to enter into a plea agreement?

In a classic opinion, New Jersey Chief Justice Vanderbilt took a different tack from Judge Hand when he described the specific *dangers* that he perceived with rules providing for liberal discovery in criminal cases:

> In criminal proceedings long experience has taught the courts that often discovery will lead not to honest factfinding, but on the contrary to perjury and the suppression of evidence. Thus the criminal who is aware of the whole case against him will often procure perjured testimony in order to set up a false defense * * *. Another result of full discovery would be that the criminal defendant who is informed of the names of all of the State's witnesses may take steps to bribe or frighten them into giving perjured testimony or into absenting themselves so that they are unavailable to testify. Moreover, many witnesses, if they know that the defendant will have knowledge of their names prior to trial, will be reluctant to come forward with information during the investigation of the crime. * * * All these dangers are more inherent in

> criminal proceedings where the defendant has much more at stake, often his own life, than in civil proceedings.

State v. Tune, 13 N.J. 203, 210–11, 98 A.2d 881, 884 (1953).

The danger to witnesses might be the strongest argument against extensive discovery on behalf of criminal defendants. Whether the threat to witnesses and to the administration of justice is as great as the quote suggests is subject to fair debate, but many experienced prosecutors believe the threat to be real, at least in some cases. The question is whether this danger justifies a blanket limitation on discovery in virtually all criminal cases—or whether the solution is some protective order limiting discovery but only after a showing of a real risk by the government.

Another argument against broad defense discovery is that it will result in fishing expeditions into government records. This argument probably can be addressed by providing in discovery rules that only relevant information can be requested and by indicating the classes of information that generally should be discoverable. The use of protective orders and sanctions for discovery abuse can also go far to limit excessive discovery demands—as they do in civil cases. The fact that the same prosecutors' offices appear in all criminal cases means that they should be able to learn quickly what material courts will require them to turn over to defendants.

Case-by-Case Approach?

Is it necessary to take an all-or-nothing approach to discovery issues in criminal cases? Opponents of liberal discovery claim that it poses dangers, but surely they would concede that the dangers do not exist in all cases. Advocates of discovery reform argue that the dangers are overstated in the run of the mill case, but surely they would concede that danger is real in some cases. Why should a rule be written to deny or grant discovery for all criminal cases? It is possible, for example, either to presume that discovery is to be permitted, but to allow the government to oppose it in a particular case, or to presume that it is not to be permitted absent a showing by the defendant of specialized need.

B. ARGUMENTS FAVORING CRIMINAL DISCOVERY

Proponents of more liberal discovery emphasize the gravity of the liberty and reputation interests at stake in criminal cases. In a dissent in *Tune,* supra, State Supreme Court Justice (later United States Supreme Court Justice) Brennan answered Chief Justice Vanderbilt and said:

> It shocks my sense of justice that in these circumstances counsel for an accused facing a possible death sentence should be denied inspection of his confession which, were this a civil case, could not be denied.

In a later article, The Criminal Prosecution: Sporting Event or Quest for Truth?, 1963 Wash.U.L.Q. 279, Justice Brennan addressed the arguments against discovery. He pointed out that the privilege against self-incrimination has not prevented prosecutors from securing confessions or incriminating non-testimonial evidence from the criminally accused; that the best protections against manipulation and perjury are early exposure of the facts and emphasis on the ethical responsibilities of defense counsel; and that the trial judge can act to protect witnesses shown to be in danger. Justice Brennan and others have pointed out that, without discovery, indigent defendants are seriously handicapped in the preparation of a defense. In addition, as Dean Pye has noted:

> Most criminal cases result in a plea of guilty. The principal role of the capable advocate in many circumstances is to advise that his client plead guilty. For this advice to be meaningful, it must be based upon knowledge of the facts and the consequences. One of these consequences is the probability of conviction if the client goes to trial. It may be impossible for counsel to make any intelligent evaluation of the alternatives if he knows only what his client has told him and what he has discovered on his own.

The Defendant's Case for More Liberal Discovery, 33 F.R.D. 82, 83 (1963).

Finally, proponents seek to dispel the arguments against discovery by pointing to jurisdictions where broad discovery works. In many states there is an "open-file" policy—either in practice or by statute—without apparent detriment to the criminal justice process. See, e.g., Langrock, Vermont's Experiment in Criminal Discovery, 53 A.B.A.J. 732 (1967); Fletcher, Pretrial Discovery in State Criminal Cases, 12 Stan.L.Rev. 293 (1960). Even in Federal practice, many U.S. Attorneys provide broader discovery than the minimum required by the Federal Rules. Seventy-six percent of U.S. Attorneys who responded to an ABA survey stated that they provided "extensive informal discovery beyond the dictates" of the Federal Rules of Criminal Procedure. Middlekauf, What Practitioners Say About Broad Criminal Discovery, Criminal Justice, Spring 1994. This broader discovery has had no apparent deleterious effect, especially because U.S. Attorneys state that they do not grant additional discovery in cases where there is a substantial risk of witness intimidation.

III. DISCOVERY ON BEHALF OF THE DEFENDANT

A. THE STATE OF THE LAW

The federal system, like many of the states, grants only very limited discovery to criminal defendants. Fed.R.Crim.P. 16 is the basic rule providing for discovery in federal criminal cases. Subdivision (a)(1) of the

Rule sets forth seven categories of information that *must* be disclosed by the government "upon a defendant's request." They are:

(A) the defendant's own oral statements made in response to official interrogation, if the government intends to offer the statements at trial;

(B) the defendant's own written or recorded statements of which the government has custody;

(C) for organizational defendants, such as corporations, statements of agents that are legally attributable to the organization;

(D) the defendant's prior criminal record;

(E) documents and other tangible objects that are material to the defense, or intended for use by the government in its case in chief, or that were obtained from or belong to the defendant;

(F) reports of physical or mental examinations, as well as scientific tests, that are material to the defense or intended for use by the government in its case in chief; and

(G) a complete statement from an expert witness that describes the expert's opinion, the bases and reasons for those opinions, the witness's qualifications, a list of all publications authored in the previous 10 years, and a list of all other cases in which, during the previous four years, the witness has testified as an expert at trial or by deposition.[2]

By making discovery of certain materials a matter of right *upon request*, Rule 16 places primary responsibility on defense attorneys and prosecutors, instead of on the court.

By examining the rule's approach to various aspects of discovery and by comparing it to other approaches that have been recommended or adopted, we can outline the current state of discovery in most American criminal cases.

1. The Defendant's Statements

The Federal Rule gives the defendant the right to discover any oral statement made by the defendant in response to interrogation by a person known by the defendant to be a government agent; the defendant also has the right to discover any relevant written or recorded statement within the

---

[2] The text on expert disclosure describes the rule as of December 1, 2022. Before the 2022 amendment to Rule 16, the prosecution was required only to provide a summary of an expert's testimony. This meant that the expert who testified differently from the summary could not be impeached with it, because the summary was prepared by the prosecutor, not by the expert. Under the amendment, the expert must prepare and sign the report, so if the expert veers from the report at trial she can be impeached with her prior inconsistent statement. Moreover, the amendment requires the expert to disclose more information about her opinion than was previously the case.

custody or control of the government. The Rule provides a corresponding right to collective entities, such as corporations and labor organizations, to obtain the statements of their agents. The government must exercise due diligence in obtaining such statements upon request. Such discovery might not seem very controversial, but the fact that it has been so indicates the kind of opposition to defense discovery that has existed for some time.

The argument has been made that if the defendant's prior statements are disclosed, she can tailor her testimony at trial to eliminate any discrepancies and the prosecution will not be able to impeach her by way of prior inconsistent statements. This advantage, however, is already available for prosecution witnesses, who are "prepped" for cross-examination. Moreover, revealing prior incriminating statements may persuade the defendant to plead guilty and avoid trial—which provides an advantage not just for the defendant but for the system itself. Finally, the government will ordinarily offer the defendant's statements during its case-in-chief. So the defendant often will hear them before testifying anyway.

The importance to the defendant of discovery of her own statements is illustrated by United States v. Camargo-Vergara, 57 F.3d 993 (11th Cir.1995), where the defendant prepared a trial strategy emphasizing that he had no experience with drugs. In the middle of trial, the government called an agent who said that the defendant made a post-arrest statement to her that indicated substantial knowledge of the drug trade. This statement had not been disclosed previously to the defendant. The court found the non-disclosure a violation of Rule 16 and reversed the defendant's conviction, reasoning that the disclosure at trial "attacked the very foundation of the defense strategy." But didn't the defendant know that he had made this statement to the agent? And why is the court concerned about impairing a defense strategy that is belied by the facts? Does the defendant have the right to present a false defense?

What Is a "Statement"?

There has been some controversy over the meaning of the word "statement" in Rule 16. The difficulty arises where the defendant's words have been paraphrased or summarized in a writing. Must the writing be disclosed? The Jencks Act, discussed infra, defines statements of *government witnesses* discoverable for cross-examination purposes as:

> (1) a written statement made by said witness and signed or otherwise adopted or approved by him;
>
> (2) a stenographic, mechanical, electrical, or other recording, or a transcription thereof, which is a substantially verbatim recital of an oral statement made by said witness and recorded contemporaneously with the making of such oral statement; or

(3) a statement, however taken or recorded, or a transcription thereof, if any, made by said witness to a grand jury.

The courts have read the Jencks Act, 18 U.S.C. § 3500 (limiting disclosure of witness statements until after direct examination) to limit discovery to statements that reproduce exact words or are substantially verbatim. The drafters of Rule 16 provided no definition; but courts construe the term "statement" under Rule 16 in accordance with the Jencks Act definition. See United States v. Malone, 49 F.3d 393 (8th Cir.1995) (holding that the definition of "statement" under Rule 16 is the same as that under the Jencks Act: agent's notes of the defendant's interview do not qualify as Rule 16 material because the notes "constitute the agent's impression of his interview with Luckett, not a statement by Luckett"). Thus, police officers can avoid disclosure by summarizing a defendant's statements rather than taking them down verbatim.

Note that oral statements to be subject to discovery must be made "in response to interrogation by a person the defendant knew was a government agent." Thus, statements made by the defendant to undercover agents are not subject to disclosure, nor are oral statements made to those who are not government agents. See United States v. Siraj, 533 F.3d 99 (2nd Cir. 2008) (statements made by defendant to an undercover informant during the course of a conspiracy are not subject to disclosure under Rule 16(a)(1)). Can you figure out why the rule is drafted as it is?

2. Codefendants' Statements

Rule 16 does not require that a defendant be given a copy of a codefendant's statements. It can be argued that the defendant needs to know what a codefendant said in advance of trial in order to move for appropriate remedies such as severance or redaction of confessions. The Court in Bruton v. United States, 391 U.S. 123 (1968), held that it is constitutional error to hold a joint trial where one non-testifying codefendant has confessed and implicated another defendant, and the confession is used by the jury against that other defendant. It would make sense to require pre-trial disclosure in order to allow the defendant to implement *Bruton* rights and avoid the possibility that an inadmissible confession will find its way into evidence against him and result in a mistrial. It is true that under the Federal Rule each defendant could obtain her own statement and share it—but that depends on whether the defendants are making a common defense. In cases where the defendants are pointing fingers at each other, it would seem very helpful for a defendant to have pretrial access to inculpatory statements made by a codefendant, wouldn't it? Would any harm be done by providing for discovery directly by each defendant of all statements by all codefendants?

3. Discovery of Prior Criminal Records

As the Advisory Committee on the Federal Criminal Rules noted in its comment to Fed.R.Crim.P. 16(a):

> A defendant may be uncertain of the precise nature of his prior record and it seems therefore in the interest of efficient and fair administration to make it possible to resolve prior to trial any disputes as to the correctness of the relevant criminal record of the defendant.

Disclosure of prior convictions should enable the defendant to seek pretrial rulings on the admissibility of such convictions to impeach her if she should choose to testify. Rules like Fed.R.Evid. 609(a)(1), which permit the trial judge some discretion in admitting and rejecting some convictions as impeachment evidence, often invite pretrial motions, and these motions often save time once trial commences.

4. Documents and Tangible Objects

Rule 16 provides that the government must disclose upon request any material or data that it plans to use at trial, as well as any item that was obtained from or belongs to the defendant. More difficult to apply is the language in Rule 16(a)(1)(E)(i) requiring disclosure of items that are "material to preparing the defense." Consider United States v. Phillip, 948 F.2d 241 (6th Cir.1991). Phillip was on trial for murder and child abuse of one of his sons, Jamal. Jamal died after falling down a flight of stairs. The government contended that Phillip hit Jamal so hard that he fell down the steps. Phillip admitted that he had beaten Jamal for a period of weeks, but contended that Jamal had fallen down the steps accidentally while Phillip had his back turned. The government videotaped an interview with the defendant's six-year-old son, Roderick. Roderick stated that Phillip had not hit Jamal at the time of the dispute, but also stated that his mother had coached him; he also made several statements inculpating Phillip and describing acts of abuse. The court of appeals rejected Phillip's argument that the videotape was "material to preparing" his defense:

> Phillip asserts in conclusory fashion that access to the videotape * * * would have aided him in the preparation of his defense, but he does not state convincingly how the videotape would have assisted him. He does suggest that viewing the videotape would have allowed him to reach a more informed decision concerning whether or not to depose Roderick or to subpoena him as a defense witness. However, since Roderick was his son, Phillip was aware of Roderick's potential availability to testify concerning Phillip's battering of Jamal. Moreover, early access to the videotape certainly could not have enlightened Phillip with respect to the *wisdom* of deposing Roderick or calling him as a witness. * * * On the whole, the videotape is inculpatory in nature and reveals a highly impressionable young child

> making highly inconsistent statements within a short period of time. * * *
>
> [E]arly access to the videotape would have informed Phillip that if deposed or placed on the witness stand, Roderick might 1) make exculpatory statements, 2) make inculpatory statements, 3) make both exculpatory and inculpatory statements, and/or 4) have little memory of relevant events. After viewing the videotape, Phillip would have been in no better position to evaluate the wisdom of deposing Roderick or calling him as a witness. Accordingly, we conclude that the videotape was not material to the preparation of Phillip's defense * * *.

See also United States v. Stevens, 985 F.2d 1175 (2d Cir.1993) (document is not material to preparing the defense "merely because it would have persuaded the defendant from proffering easily impeached testimony"). Compare United States v. Cedano-Arellano, 332 F.3d 568 (9th Cir. 2003) (where the defendant was attacking the reliability of a drug-sniffing dog, the dog's training materials and certification records were material to preparing the defense, and should have been disclosed under Fed.R.Crim.P. 16(a)(1)(E)(i)).

Defenses Not Going to the Merits: United States v. Armstrong

In United States v. Armstrong, 517 U.S. 456 (1996), the defendants were African-Americans charged with crack cocaine offenses. They claimed that they were being prosecuted because of their race. The defendants argued that they were entitled under Rule 16(a)(1)(E) to discovery of documents relevant to their claim of selective prosecution, e.g., charging criteria, the number of unprosecuted crack violators who are white, etc. These materials were obviously not the property of the defendants. Nor did the government intend to use the documents at trial. Thus, discovery under Rule 16(a)(1)(E) hinged on whether materials supporting a claim of selective prosecution could be considered "material to preparing the defense."

The Court, in an opinion by Chief Justice Rehnquist, held that the term "material to preparing the defense" covered only those documents and objects that are responsive to the government's case-in-chief, i.e., those documents and objects that are *pertinent to the defendant's guilt or innocence.* The Chief Justice reasoned as follows:

> Respondents argue that the Rule applies because any claim that "results in nonconviction" if successful is a "defense" for the Rule's purposes, and a successful selective-prosecution claim has that effect.
>
> We reject this argument, because we conclude that in the context of Rule 16 "the defendant's defense" means the defendant's response

to the Government's case-in-chief. While it might be argued that as a general matter, the concept of a "defense" includes any claim that is a "sword," challenging the prosecution's conduct of the case, the term may encompass only the narrower class of "shield" claims, which refute the Government's arguments that the defendant committed the crime charged. Rule 16 * * * tends to support the "shield-only" reading. If "defense" means an argument in response to the prosecution's case-in-chief, there is a perceptible symmetry between documents "material to the preparation of the defendant's defense," and, in the very next phrase, documents "intended for use by the government as evidence in chief at the trial."

* * *

We hold that Rule 16(a) * * * authorizes defendants to examine Government documents material to the preparation of their defense against the Government's case-in-chief, but not to the preparation of selective-prosecution claims.

Justices Souter and Ginsburg concurred, with the reservation that the application of Rule 16(a)(1)(E) to *other* non-merits defenses (e.g., speedy trial, or affirmative defenses unrelated to the merits) had not been decided. Justice Stevens dissented on the ground that discovery was warranted under the district court's equitable power, but he agreed with the Chief Justice's Rule 16 analysis. Justice Breyer concurred in the judgment on the ground that a sufficient preliminary showing of selective prosecution had not been made in order to justify discovery. He disagreed, however, with the Chief Justice's construction of Rule 16, and argued that the Rule authorized discovery of any document material to dismissal of the prosecution on any grounds.

The Court in *Armstrong* did not hold that defendants *never* have a right to inspect documents and other information that pertain to matters other than the government's case-in-chief. Rather, the holding was that defendants are not *entitled* to these materials under Rule 16. A defendant is free to argue, for example, that notwithstanding Rule 16, discovery of certain materials is necessary to protect a constitutional right. This constitutional argument of selective prosecution was indeed made in *Armstrong,* but the Court held that mere allegations of selective prosecution are not enough to warrant discovery. See the discussion of this aspect of *Armstrong* in Chapter 6.

Fishing Expeditions

Under Rule 16(d)(1), the judge has discretion to quash discovery requests that are vague or overbroad. The courts are properly concerned with preventing "fishing expeditions" into the government's documents; thus it has been held that a request for "anything exculpatory" is equivalent to no request at all, and the "trial judge need not accord the slightest heed to such shotgun approach." United States v. Weiner, 578 F.2d 757 (9th Cir.1978).

Because documents cannot be intimidated and cannot easily be tampered with if the government retains the original, the fear of misuse by the defendant is not great. The limits of discovery here are to protect the government from having to respond to overbroad requests. If the documents would reveal the names of witnesses or other information not discoverable, such as work product, then they need not be disclosed.

Electronic Discovery

In many cases, electronically stored information (ESI) is critical to the success of an investigation and prosecution—and critical to the defense. The explosion of digital information over the last 20 years has created significant discovery problems, however. How much ESI is the government required to retain, search and produce?

Most courts have held that nothing about ESI requires the government to provide more information than is already required by Rule 16 and the Constitution. See United States v. Salyer, 271 F.R.D. 148 (E.D. Cal. 2010) (finding that defendant was only entitled to discovery of electronic materials relevant to mounting a defense and rejecting the defendant's "all documents civil type discovery request" for electronic data). Specifically, courts have typically rejected the premise that the electronic discovery rules found in the Federal Rules of Civil Procedure are applicable in criminal cases. See United States v. Warshak, 631 F.3d 266 (6th Cir. 2010) (finding no discovery violation in government production of data that was in an unsearchable format; concluding that the federal civil rule requiring electronic data to be turned over in a searchable form is not applicable to criminal cases).

If data is electronic, should the government have the obligation to turn over the metadata of the documents produced? "Metadata" is the data that provides information about how a document was generated, date, time, author, etc. The courts have not generally required the government to produce metadata in a criminal case (though production is required in civil cases), but it may be possible in some cases for the defendant to argue that disclosure of metadata is critical to the defense.

One of the problems of ESI is that there is so much of it—and much of it is duplicative, e.g., cloned emails. There is a risk with electronic data that the defendant will be the victim of a document dump—too much information. For example, in United States v. Graham, 2008 WL 2098044 (S.D.Ohio) the court found that the sheer volume of data produced by the government—combined with its erratic and unmanageable method of turning it over, prejudiced the defendants by the delay necessary to review all the material. Consequently the court found a violation of the Speedy Trial Act and dismissed the indictment. The *Graham* court likened the government in that case to "a restless volcano" that periodically "spewed forth" masses of electronic data. But see United States v. Qadri, 2010 WL 933752 (D. Haw.), where the government produced millions of electronic documents, 30 computer harddrives and three servers. The defendants argued that it was a document dump and moved to dismiss the indictment on Speedy Trial grounds. But the court denied the motion, finding that "the delays in this case may be attributed at least in part to the nature of e-discovery, the complex nature of the alleged crimes, and the necessity of coordinating various branches of government in the investigation." Of course, the appearance of a document dump will be mitigated if the material is produced in searchable form. See, e.g., United States v. Skilling, 554 F.3d 529 (5th Cir. 2009) (no discovery violation where government turned over electronic files related to Enron; the documentation was more than 700 million pages, but it was searchable).

For more on electronic discovery in criminal and civil cases, see Scheindlin, Capra, and the Sedona Conference, Electronic Discovery and Digital Evidence (2d. ed. West 2012).

Department of Justice Principles and Guidelines on Electronic Discovery, and New Criminal Rule 16.1

In 2012, the Department of Justice issued recommendations for ESI discovery in Federal criminal cases. It is a set of principles—based on cooperation by the parties—that is now being employed as guidance in many criminal cases. The principles are as follows:

Principle 1. Lawyers have a responsibility to have an adequate understanding of electronic discovery.

Principle 2. In the process of planning, producing, and resolving disputes about ESI discovery, the parties should include individuals with sufficient technical knowledge and experience regarding ESI.

Principle 3. At the outset of a case, the parties should meet and confer about the nature, volume, and mechanics of producing ESI discovery. Where the ESI discovery is particularly complex or produced on a rolling basis, an ongoing dialogue may be helpful.

Principle 4. The parties should discuss what formats of production are possible and appropriate, and what formats can be generated. Any format selected for producing discovery should maintain the ESI's integrity, allow for reasonable usability, reasonably limit costs, and, if possible, conform to industry standards for the format.

Principle 5. When producing ESI discovery, a party should not be required to take on substantial additional processing or format conversion costs and burdens beyond what the party has already done or would do for its own case preparation or discovery production.

Principle 6. Following meet and confer, the parties should notify the court of ESI discovery production issues or problems that they reasonably anticipate will significantly affect the handling of the case.

Principle 7. The parties should discuss ESI discovery transmission methods and media that promote efficiency, security, and reduced costs. The producing party should provide a general description and maintain a record of what was transmitted.

Principle 8. In multi-defendant cases, the defendants should authorize one or more counsel to act as the discovery coordinator(s) or seek appointment of a Coordinating Discovery Attorney.

Principle 9. The parties should make good faith efforts to discuss and resolve disputes over ESI discovery, involving those with the requisite technical knowledge when necessary, and they should consult with a supervisor, or obtain supervisory authorization, before seeking judicial resolution of an ESI discovery dispute or alleging misconduct, abuse, or neglect concerning the production of ESI.

Principle 10. All parties should limit dissemination of ESI discovery to members of their litigation team who need and are approved for access, and they should also take reasonable and appropriate measures to secure ESI discovery against unauthorized access or disclosure.

The DOJ concludes that the Guidelines "set forth a collaborative approach to ESI discovery involving mutual and interdependent responsibilities. The goal is to benefit all parties by making ESI discovery more efficient, secure, and less costly."

The "meet and confer" guideline (Principle 3) has been incorporated into a new Federal Rule of Criminal Procedure—Rule 16.1, effective December 1, 2019. The rule is in direct response to the rise of ESI, but it applies to all discovery. The new rule provides as follows:

> **(a) Discovery Conference.** No later than 14 days after the arraignment, the attorney for the government and the defendant's attorney must confer and try to agree on a timetable and procedures for pretrial disclosure under Rule 16.
>
> **(b) Request for Court Action.** After the discovery conference, one or both parties may ask the court to determine or modify the time, place, manner, or other aspects of disclosure to facilitate preparation for trial.

The Committee Note to the new Rule 16.1 has this to say about ESI:

> Because technology changes rapidly, the rule does not attempt to state specific requirements for the manner or timing of disclosure in

cases involving ESI. However, counsel should be familiar with best practices. For example, the Department of Justice, the Administrative Office of the U.S. Courts, and the Joint Working Group on Electronic Technology in the Criminal Justice System (JETWG) have published "Recommendations for Electronically Store Information (ESI) Discovery Production in Federal Criminal Cases" (2012).

5. Experts, Examinations, and Tests

Many jurisdictions, even those with restrictive discovery rules, require the government to disclose the results of examinations and tests such as autopsy reports, reports of medical or psychiatric examinations, blood tests, handwriting or fingerprinting comparisons, ballistic tests, and so forth. Because of its factual nature, such evidence is unlikely to be misused or distorted by disclosure. There is virtually no risk of witness intimidation. And the need for such discovery is apparent—it is practically impossible for the defense to test or rebut scientific or expert evidence without opportunities to examine that evidence before the trial. Federal Rule 16(a)(1)(F) requires disclosure of all such reports that are "material to preparing the defense" or that the government intends to use in its case-in-chief at trial.

Oral reports are not discoverable under Rule 16, as the Rule requires the government to "permit a defendant to inspect and to copy or photograph the results" and this cannot be done with oral reports. Professor Giannelli, in Criminal Discovery, Scientific Evidence, and DNA, 44 Vand.L.Rev. 791 (1991), notes that when the Rule was drafted in 1966, "most scientific evidence consisted of autopsy reports and crime laboratory reports." However, "today experts have developed many new categories of scientific evidence." Examples include expert testimony on DNA identification, blood spatter testimony, rape trauma syndrome, child sexual abuse accommodation syndrome, battered woman syndrome, and bite mark comparisons. "Neither custom nor regulation requires these experts to write reports. Indeed * * * the prosecution loses the element of surprise by preparing the report."

Discovery of Expert Methodology

The ability to challenge a scientific expert's report has become especially critical after the Supreme Court's decision in Daubert v. Merrell Dow Pharmaceuticals, Inc., 509 U.S. 579 (1993). In *Daubert*, the Court held that the trial court must act as a "gatekeeper" to assure that an expert's testimony is based on "good science" and comports with the scientific method. Obviously it is difficult for the defendant to challenge a prosecution expert's scientific reasoning if he has no prior information about the expert's basis, methodology, and conclusion.[3] Accordingly, Rule 16(a)(1)(G) was added shortly after *Daubert*, to provide that at the defendant's request, the government must provide a written summary of the testimony of any expert who the government intends to call in its case-in-chief. The summary must "describe the witness's opinions, the bases and the reasons for those opinions, and the witness's qualifications."

Note that the disclosure requirement applies to any witness that the government intends to call as an expert, even if the expert is not going to testify on a scientific subject. Discovery of the opinions of non-scientific experts is made more critical after the Supreme Court's decision in Kumho Tire Co. v. Carmichael, 526 U.S. 137 (1999). The Court in *Kumho* held that the *Daubert* gatekeeping requirement applies to non-scientific experts. Thus, the trial judge must determine that non-scientific experts are using a reliable methodology and are applying that methodology properly to the facts of the case. So it is crucial for defendants to obtain discovery of reports and opinions of non-scientific experts such as experts on handwriting identification and ballistics; only with advance notice can defendants make a proper challenge to the reliability of this expert testimony.

All that said, complaints have been made by defense counsel that disclosure of a "summary" of a witness's testimony is not very helpful, as it could end up being very general; and moreover a summary cannot be used to pin an expert witness down at trial, because the summary is not prepared by the expert herself, but rather by the prosecutor. Defense counsel have also complained that the discovery is often turned over too late to be useful at a *Daubert* hearing. A number of trial judges have joined in the complaint, noting that insufficient and untimely discovery makes it very difficult for a trial judge to act as an effective gatekeeper under *Daubert*. See Hon. Paul W. Grimm, Challenges Facing Judges Regarding Expert Evidence in Criminal Cases, 86 Fordham L. Rev. 1601 (2018):

> A final suggestion to make life easier for trial judges and counsel alike is a recommendation that the Criminal Rules Advisory Committee consider amending Rule 16 to enhance the Rule 16(a)(1)(G) and (b)(1)(C) expert disclosures. Specifically, the Committee should consider whether they should be made to more closely resemble the disclosures required in civil cases by Federal Rule of Civil Procedure 26(a)(2). At a minimum, Rule 16 disclosures should include (1) a complete statement of each opinion the expert will testify to, as well as the basis and reasons supporting them; (2) a summary of the facts or data considered (not just relied on) by the witness in forming her opinions; and (3) a description of the witness's qualifications. In addition, while less important, it would also bolster Rule 16 if the disclosures included a list of cases in the past four years where the

[3] For further discussion of *Daubert* and its progeny, see Capra, The *Daubert* Puzzle, 32 Ga.L.Rev. 699 (1998).

witness had testified (allowing counsel to read the prior testimony) and a copy of any exhibits that will be used by the expert in support of her testimony.

In response to these complaints, particularly of Judge Grimm, the Advisory Committee on Criminal Rules proposed amendments to Rule 16 that would require: 1) a statement from the expert, as opposed to a summary by the prosecutor; 2) a more detailed statement about the expert's methodology, basis, and qualifications, including a list of publications and of cases in which the expert testified; 3) disclosure that "must be sufficiently before trial to provide a fair opportunity for the defendant to meet the government's evidence." Unless something unforeseen arises, this amendment will go into effect in December, 2022.

It is hoped that more vigorous discovery will result in more effective challenges to prosecution experts, particularly with respect to forensic experts, who often provide overstated testimony—asserting that their discipline is "scientific" when in fact it is anecdotal. *See generally* President's Council of Advisors on Science & Technology, Forensic Science in Criminal Courts: Ensuring Scientific Validity of Feature-Comparison Methods. (2016), https://obamawhitehouse.archives.gov/sites/default/files/microsites/ostp/PCAST/pcast_forensic_science_report_final.pdf (concluding that forensic methods such as ballistics, fingerprint identification, and bitemark identification are not grounded in science but rather in subjective assessments of the examiners).

6. Names, Addresses, and Statements of Witnesses

Most of the states require advance disclosure of the names and the written or recorded statements of witnesses that the government intends to call. See Clennon, Pre-Trial Discovery of Witness Lists: A Modest Proposal to Improve the Administration of Justice in the Superior Court of the District of Columbia, 38 Cath.U.L.Rev. 641 (1989) (noting that "twenty-eight states grant the defendant as a matter of right pre-trial disclosure of the trial witnesses the prosecutor expects to call"). Some states by statute ban disclosure of witnesses' statements.

Federal courts require disclosure of witness statements, but *not in advance of their trial testimony.* The Jencks Act, 18 U.S.C.A. § 3500 requires disclosure of "statements" by government witnesses but only after they have testified on direct examination. The Jencks Act followed the Court's opinion in Jencks v. United States, 353 U.S. 657 (1957), where the Court exercised its supervisory power to require disclosure *during the trial* of the prior statements of prosecution witnesses.

Jencks Act Timing Issue

The *Jencks* Court rejected the notion that pretrial statements should only be made available where the defense could show a probable inconsistency between the witness's pretrial statements and his in-court testimony. The Court recognized that it would be very difficult for a defendant to prove that the statement was inconsistent without having access to the statement. The Jencks Act codified the *Jencks* Court's basic requirement that the government disclose pretrial statements made by its witnesses, whether or not the statements are inconsistent with trial testimony.[4] However, the *timing* of the disclosure requirement is critical. The Act *does not* provide for notification in advance of trial or even in advance of the witness's testimony. Rather, a statement covered by the Act must be disclosed, on the defendant's motion, *after* the witness testifies on direct examination. As one defense counsel has complained:

> The timing aspects of the Jencks Act [create] a dilemma for defense lawyers: either proceed without preparation or ask for a continuance in the middle of trial, which would be unfair to the jury and would understandably irritate them.

Cary, Exculpatory Evidence: A Call for Reform After the Unlawful Prosecution of Senator Ted Stevens, 36 Litigation 34 (2010).

Jencks Act Statements

"Statements" within the meaning of the Act include only 1) written statements approved by the witness; 2) stenographic or mechanical transcripts that purport to be almost verbatim accounts of oral statements; and 3) any statements, however recorded, made to a grand jury. If the information about a witness is not within those three categories, there is no obligation to disclose it at any time. See United States v. Farley, 2 F.3d 645 (6th Cir.1993) (a summary of a witness's account is not Jencks Act material unless it is a verbatim account or unless it has been adopted by the witness); United States v. Crowley, 285 F.3d 553 (7th Cir. 2002) ("The Jencks Act does not obligate the government to disclose investigative or trial preparation material; rather, it requires only the disclosure of pretrial statements a government witness signed, adopted, or otherwise approved.").

Also, a witness's prior statement need not be disclosed under the Jencks Act unless it relates to the subject matter of the witness's direct testimony. See United States v. Byrne, 83 F.3d 984 (8th Cir.1996) (where witness testifies to acts occurring during the conspiracy, there was no

---

[4] In Goldberg v. United States, 425 U.S. 94 (1976), the Court held that statements made to government lawyers otherwise producible under the Act are not barred from production by the work product doctrine.

violation of the Jencks Act when the government failed to disclose the witness's prior statement concerning acts committed before the conspiracy—this was collateral or background information that did not relate to the subject matter of the direct testimony). The Jencks Act provides for *in camera* review for the purpose of separating portions of statements relating to the witness's trial testimony from unrelated portions. Fed.R.Crim.P. 26.2, which was promulgated after the Jencks Act, largely tracks the provisions of the Act, with the exception that the Rule requires defense production of defense witness statements as well. See the discussion after United States v. Nobles, infra.

The Objections to Advance Disclosure of Witness Names and Statements

At one time, the Supreme Court proposed an amendment to Rule 16 that would have required the government to provide advance disclosure of names, addresses and prior statements of witnesses. The reasoning behind the amendment was that disclosure of witness names and statements is necessary so that defense counsel can prepare adequately to cross-examine witnesses and test their credibility. The Department of Justice vigorously opposed the amendment and mustered the support of numerous United States Attorneys, and the amendment was never adopted. A typical complaint was expressed by the United States Attorney for the Western District of Pennsylvania at the congressional hearings on the amendment:

> It seems clear that we have a hard enough time securing the cooperation of civilian witnesses who don't want to get involved without putting them in a situation in which, months before trial, they become subject to such degradation and harassment as may occur to an ingenious defendant, who will have far more to gain under the new rules than the present post-conviction satisfaction of revenge. Indeed, we are of the view that the law should not, in the name of "enlightened" discovery procedures, expose innocent members of the public, who have had the misfortune to be victims of or witnesses to criminal conduct, to the mercy of defendants any more than the confrontation clause presently requires.[5]

Are there more direct ways to eliminate the problems of witness intimidation and harassment perceived by the U.S. Attorney? Earl Silbert testified at the hearings and suggested the following alternative:

> Alternatively, we would recommend that in the event witness disclosure is to be permitted, some burden be placed on the party seeking disclosure to show a reasonable need for the information sought, and that whatever disclosure in this regard is permitted, no

[5] Statement of W. Vincent Rakestraw, Ass't Att'y Gen'l, in House Hearings on Federal Rules of Criminal Procedure, 93rd Cong., 2nd Sess. (1974).

> party be required to disclose earlier than three days in advance of trial. Finally, it is particularly critical that in this area the trial Court retain discretion as to whether or not to grant the discovery sought.

Would this have been a preferable approach?

Note that while there is no right to advance disclosure of a witness under Fed.R.Crim. 16, a court has discretion to order such disclosure in particular cases. See, e.g., United States v. W.R. Grace, 526 F.3d 499 (9th Cir. 2008) (en banc) (Rule 16 does not state that a court is *prohibited* from ordering advance disclosure of a witness; district court did not abuse discretion in requiring the government to provide a witness list, in light of the size and complexity of the case, which included charges reaching back 30 years, 200 proposed witnesses, and millions of pages of documents).

7. Grand Jury Minutes and Transcripts

Rule 16(a)(3) precludes defense discovery of grand jury proceedings, with two exceptions: 1) the defendant is entitled to a copy of his own grand jury testimony under Rule 16(a)(1)(B)(iii); and 2) the Jencks Act requires production of a trial witness's grand jury testimony after she has testified on direct examination. Also, of course, the prosecution is required to disclose any information obtained by the grand jury that is materially exculpatory to the defendant, as seen in the discussion of *Brady* rights, infra. But there is no right to more general disclosure of grand jury minutes and transcripts.

Once an indictment is returned, do arguments for secrecy still hold? Will secrecy protect the reputations of those accused? Will secrecy inhibit flight once a defendant is formally charged? Will secrecy protect the identity of witnesses who will appear at trial?

8. Work Product

Fed.R.Crim.P. 16(a)(2) protects against disclosure of "reports, memoranda, or other internal government documents made by an attorney for the government or other government agent in connection with investigating or prosecuting the case." What theory justifies protecting police or FBI reports under the Federal Rule? If it is true that the government has easier access to information than the defendant in many situations, why should that information not be shared with the defense?

Work product is one of those areas in which prosecutors complain that discovery would be one-sided, because the privilege against self-incrimination or the attorney-client privilege will in most cases bar the government from finding out what the defendant or her attorney has done to prepare a defense. Assume that the government could not force disclosure of much of the work product of the defense. Does that mean that one-sided disclosure of the government's work product is undesirable?

Remember that the government has the power of the grand jury and the subpoena power, so there is likely to be a lot of information that will be accessible to the government but not to the defendant.

B. MECHANISMS FOR DISCOVERY BY THE DEFENDANT

The predominant means for discovery in civil cases are depositions and interrogatories. In criminal cases the defense is not permitted to discover prosecutorial information through interrogatories, and if a bill of particulars is requested as a pretext for discovery, it is likely to be denied. See United States v. Livingstone, 576 F.3d 881 (8th Cir. 2009) (bill of particulars cannot be used to obtain witness testimony).

Depositions are authorized in criminal cases, but in most jurisdictions not a means of obtaining discovery. Rather, they are allowed only where necessary to preserve testimony for trial. Federal Rule 15 illustrates the restrictions on the use of depositions in federal criminal cases.

(a) When Taken.

> **(1) In General.** A party may move that a prospective witness be deposed in order to preserve testimony for trial. The court may grant the motion because of exceptional circumstances and in the interest of justice. If the court orders the deposition to be taken, it may also require the deponent to produce at the deposition any designated material that is not privileged, including any book, paper, document, record, recording, or data.

* * *

Assume that somehow a defendant learns the names of witnesses. There is little that she can do in most jurisdictions to compel the witnesses to talk with her or with counsel. It is true that the prosecutor cannot advise the witnesses not to talk with the defendant or with defense counsel. See, e.g., Gregory v. United States, 369 F.2d 185 (D.C.Cir.1966). But many witnesses may want to have nothing to do with the defense. Should there be some mechanism for the defense to find out what the witnesses know?

Two possibilities exist. The first is that a preliminary hearing can be made a discovery hearing in part, so that witnesses can be called by the defense. The trouble with this approach is that at the time the hearing is held, the defense may not know what questions to ask. More importantly, if the defense is not careful, it will preserve the testimony of an unfavorable witness who may become unavailable, and the witness's preliminary hearing testimony will be admitted at trial under a hearsay exception (see Fed.R.Evid. 804(b)(1), exception for prior testimony), even though the defense really did not effectively examine the witness. Also, early in the case, the defense may not have discovered the identities of all the witnesses. On the other hand, the advantage of the preliminary hearing approach is that discovery is conducted in one place, at one time, and under the supervision of the court. It should be noted that when an indictment is handed down, there generally is no right to a preliminary hearing.

The other alternative is the one used in civil cases: to allow depositions to be taken for discovery. Do you believe that such a rule would threaten legitimate government interests? Can you see why witnesses in criminal cases might be more reluctant to testify at all than witnesses in civil cases? If this is true, routine availability of depositions would mean that reluctant witnesses often would have to testify twice, once in a deposition and again at trial. Would it add substantially to the cost of criminal cases? In theory, it is easy to see why a jurisdiction might fear that permitting defendants to depose witnesses routinely might not only increase the cost of processing a criminal case, but might also slow down a process that is so heavily dependent on plea bargaining. In practice, however, some states have made depositions a standard part of criminal discovery without a breakdown in the system.[6]

IV. THE PROSECUTOR'S CONSTITUTIONAL DUTY TO DISCLOSE

A. THE *BRADY* RULE

The Supreme Court has established that, above and beyond the (minimal) obligations imposed by discovery rules, the prosecution has a *constitutional* duty to disclose certain exculpatory information to the defendant in advance of trial. The nature of the information required to be disclosed, and the scope of the prosecutor's obligation, are the subjects of this section.

Disclosure of False Evidence: Mooney v. Holohan and Its Progeny

The first case establishing a prosecutor's constitutional obligations in the discovery process was Mooney v. Holohan, 294 U.S. 103 (1935). The defendant sought habeas corpus relief, claiming "that the sole basis of his conviction was perjured testimony, which was knowingly used by the

[6] Jurisdictions that have permitted depositions in criminal cases appear to be staying with it. See, e.g., Florida Rule of Criminal Procedure 3.220 (a): "(a) Notice of Discovery. After the filing of the charging document, a defendant may elect to participate in the discovery process provided by these rules, including the taking of discovery depositions, by filing with the court and serving on the prosecuting attorney a "Notice of Discovery" which shall bind both the prosecution and defendant to all discovery procedures contained in these rules." Section 3.220 (b)(1)(A) obligates the prosecutor to provide a comprehensive witness list to a defendant who elects to participate in the discovery process, and section (s)(1)(A) requires the defendant to provide the prosecutor with a list of all witnesses the defense expects to call to testify. Thereafter, either party can depose witnesses.

prosecuting authorities in order to obtain that conviction and also that the prosecution knowingly suppressed evidence that the defense could have used to impeach the perjured testimony." The Court said that the Due Process Clause is violated if the government engages in "a deliberate deception of court and jury by the presentation of testimony known to be perjured." Seven years later, in Pyle v. Kansas, 317 U.S. 213 (1942), a habeas petitioner charged the prosecution with knowing use of perjured testimony and the deliberate suppression of evidence favorable to the defense by threats made to witnesses. The Court cited *Mooney* and held that the "allegations * * *, if proven, would entitle petitioner to release from his present custody."

Alcorta v. Texas, 355 U.S. 28 (1957), applied and invigorated the *Mooney* principle. The defendant was convicted of first degree murder; a defense claim of "sudden passion" was rejected after a witness answered the prosecutor's questions by saying that he had not kissed the defendant's wife (the victim) on the night of the murder and that he had only a casual relationship with her. Although the witness had previously told the prosecution that he had sexual intercourse with the victim on several occasions, the prosecution did not disclose this. The Supreme Court reversed because the prosecutor knowingly allowed an important witness to create a false impression at trial.

Napue v. Illinois, 360 U.S. 264 (1959), further developed the principle that prevents the prosecutor from knowingly presenting false evidence. There, the principal government witness testified that he had received no promises of special consideration in exchange for his testimony. The prosecutor elicited the information from the witness and made no effort to correct it, although he knew the testimony was false. The Court found that the resulting conviction was invalid.

Mandatory Disclosure of Materially Exculpatory Evidence: The Brady Rule

In 1963, the Court decided one of its most important disclosure cases, Brady v. Maryland, 373 U.S. 83. Brady and a companion, Boblit, were charged with first degree murder, a capital offense. Brady was tried first; he admitted participation in the crime, but claimed that Boblit did the actual killing. Prior to trial Brady's lawyer asked the prosecutor to allow him to see Boblit's statements. Several statements were shown to counsel, but one in which Boblit admitted the homicide was not revealed. The defense did not learn about that statement until after Brady's conviction and death sentence were affirmed. The Supreme Court found that the prosecutor has an obligation to disclose all materially exculpatory evidence, and that Boblit's admission would have had a material effect on Brady's death sentence. The Court declared that "[a] prosecution that withholds evidence on demand of an accused which, if made available, would tend to exculpate him or reduce the penalty helps shape a trial that bears heavily on the defendant. That casts the prosecutor in the role of an architect of a proceeding that does not comport with standards of justice * * *."

Knowledge Attributable to the Prosecutor: Giglio v. United States

In Giglio v. United States, 405 U.S. 150 (1972), the Court found a violation of due process when a key witness testified that he had not been given a deal for testifying for the government. Promises had in fact been made by a predecessor in the prosecutor's office and the trial attorney for the government did not know it. Even though the examining prosecutor was not aware that the witness's testimony was false, the Court reversed the conviction; it held that a promise by one attorney would be attributed to the government and suggested that procedures and regulations could be developed to avoid situations in which one prosecutor did not know what the other was doing.

Materiality and the Relevance of a Defense Request for Information: United States v. Agurs

The next case develops the *Brady* rule and answers important questions about the materiality of suppressed evidence and the relationship between a defense request for information and a prosecutor's suppression.

UNITED STATES V. AGURS

Supreme Court of the United States, 1976.
427 U.S. 97.

JUSTICE STEVENS delivered the opinion of the Court.

After a brief interlude in an inexpensive motel room, respondent repeatedly stabbed James Sewell, causing his death. She was convicted of second-degree murder. The question before us is whether the prosecutor's failure to provide defense counsel with certain background information about Sewell, which would have tended to support the argument that respondent acted in self-defense, deprived her of a fair trial under the rule of Brady v. Maryland.

* * *

At about 4:30 p.m. on September 24, 1971, respondent, who had been there before, and Sewell, registered in a motel as man and wife. * * * Sewell was wearing a bowie knife in a sheath, and carried another knife in his pocket. Less than two hours earlier, according to the testimony of his estranged wife, he had had $360 in cash on his person.

About 15 minutes later three motel employees heard respondent screaming for help. A forced entry into their room disclosed Sewell on top of respondent struggling for possession of the bowie knife. She was holding the knife; his bleeding hand grasped the blade; according to one witness he was trying to jam the blade into her chest. The employees separated the two and summoned the authorities. Respondent departed without comment before they arrived. Sewell was dead on arrival at the hospital.

Circumstantial evidence indicated that the parties had completed an act of intercourse, that Sewell had then gone to the bathroom * * * and that the struggle occurred upon his return. The contents of his pockets were in disarray on the dresser and no money was found; the jury may have inferred that respondent took Sewell's money and that the fight started when Sewell re-entered the room and saw what she was doing.

On the following morning respondent surrendered to the police. She was given a physical examination which revealed no cuts or bruises of any kind, except needle marks on her upper arm. An autopsy of Sewell disclosed that he had several deep stab wounds in his chest and abdomen, and a number of slashes on his arms and hands, characterized by the pathologist as "defensive wounds."

Respondent offered no evidence. Her sole defense was the argument made by her attorney that Sewell had initially attacked her with the knife, and that her actions had all been directed toward saving her own life. The support for this self-defense theory was based on the fact that she had screamed for help. Sewell was on top of her when help arrived, and his possession of two knives indicated that he was a violence-prone person. It took the jury about 25 minutes to elect a foreman and return a verdict.

Three months later defense counsel filed a motion for a new trial asserting that he had discovered (1) that Sewell had a prior criminal record that would have further evidenced his violent character; (2) that the prosecutor had failed to disclose this information to the defense; and (3) that a recent opinion of the United States Court of Appeals for the District of Columbia Circuit made it clear that such evidence was admissible even if not known to the defendant. Sewell's prior record included a plea of guilty to a charge of assault and carrying a deadly weapon in 1963, and another guilty plea to a charge of carrying a deadly weapon in 1971. Apparently both weapons were knives.

The Government opposed the motion, arguing that there was no duty to tender Sewell's prior record to the defense in the absence of an appropriate request * * * and that, in all events, it was not material.

The District Court denied the motion. * * * The Court of Appeals reversed.

* * *

The rule of Brady v. Maryland arguably applies in three quite different situations. Each involves the discovery, after trial, of information which had been known to the prosecution but unknown to the defense.

In the first situation, typified by Mooney v. Holohan, the undisclosed evidence demonstrates that the prosecution's case includes perjured testimony and that the prosecution knew, or should have known, of the perjury. In a series of subsequent cases, the Court has consistently held that a conviction obtained by the knowing use of perjured testimony is fundamentally unfair, and must be set aside if there is any reasonable likelihood that the false testimony could have affected the judgment of the jury. * * * In those cases the Court has applied a strict standard of materiality, not just because they involve prosecutorial misconduct, but more importantly because they involve a corruption of the truth-seeking function of the trial process. Since this case involves no misconduct, and since there is no reason to question the veracity of any of the prosecution witnesses, the test of materiality followed in the *Mooney* line of cases is not necessarily applicable to this case.

The second situation, illustrated by the *Brady* case itself, is characterized by a pretrial request for specific evidence. In that case defense counsel had requested the extrajudicial statements made by Brady's accomplice, one Boblit. This Court held that the suppression of one of Boblit's statements deprived Brady of due process, noting specifically that the statement had been requested and that it was "material." A fair analysis of the holding in *Brady* indicates that implicit in the requirement of materiality is a concern that the suppressed evidence might have affected the outcome of the trial.

* * *

In *Brady* the request was specific. It gave the prosecutor notice of exactly what the defense desired. Although there is, of course, no duty to provide defense counsel with unlimited discovery of everything known by the prosecutor, if the subject matter of such a request is material, or indeed if a substantial basis for claiming materiality exists, it is reasonable to require the prosecutor to respond either by furnishing the information or by submitting the problem to the trial judge. When the prosecutor receives a specific and relevant request, the failure to make any response is seldom, if ever, excusable.

In many cases, however, exculpatory information in the possession of the prosecutor may be unknown to defense counsel. In such a situation he may make no request at all, or possibly ask for "all *Brady* material" or for "anything exculpatory." Such a request really gives the prosecutor no better notice than if no request is made. If there is a duty to respond to a general request of that kind, it must derive from the obviously exculpatory character of certain evidence in the hands of the prosecutor. But if the evidence is so clearly supportive of a claim of innocence that it gives the prosecution notice of a duty to produce, that duty should equally arise even if no request is made. [W]e conclude that there is no significant difference between cases in which there has been merely a general request for exculpatory matter and cases, like the one we must now decide, in which there has been no request at all. The third situation in which the *Brady* rule arguably applies, typified by this case, therefore embraces the case in which only a general request for "*Brady* material" has been made.

We now consider whether the prosecutor has any constitutional duty to volunteer exculpatory matter to the defense, and if so, what standard of materiality gives rise to that duty.

* * *

The Court of Appeals appears to have assumed that the prosecutor has a constitutional obligation to disclose any information that might affect the jury's verdict. That statement of a constitutional standard of materiality approaches the "sporting theory of justice" which the Court expressly rejected in *Brady*. For a jury's appraisal of a case "might" be affected by an improper or trivial consideration as well as by evidence giving rise to a legitimate doubt on the issue of guilt. If everything that might influence a jury must be disclosed, the only way a prosecutor could discharge his constitutional duty would be to allow complete discovery of his files as a matter of routine practice.

Whether or not procedural rules authorizing such broad discovery might be desirable, the Constitution surely does not demand that much. * * * The mere possibility that an item of undisclosed information might have helped the defense, or might have affected the outcome of the trial, does not establish "materiality" in the constitutional sense.

Nor do we believe the constitutional obligation is measured by the moral culpability, or the willfulness, of the prosecutor. If evidence highly probative of innocence is in his file, he should be presumed to recognize its significance even if he has actually overlooked it. Conversely, if evidence actually has no probative significance at all, no purpose would be served by requiring a new trial simply because an inept prosecutor incorrectly believed he was suppressing a fact that would be vital to the defense. If the suppression of evidence results in constitutional error, it is because of the character of the evidence, not the character of the prosecutor.

* * * [T]here are situations in which evidence is obviously of such substantial value to the defense that elementary fairness requires it to be disclosed even without a specific request. For though the attorney for the

sovereign must prosecute the accused with earnestness and vigor, he must always be faithful to his client's overriding interest that "justice shall be done." He is the "servant of the law, the twofold aim of which is that guilt shall not escape or innocence suffer." Berger v. United States, 295 U.S. 78, 88. This description of the prosecutor's duty illuminates the standard of materiality that governs his obligation to disclose exculpatory evidence.

* * *

The proper standard of materiality must reflect our overriding concern with the justice of the finding of guilt.[a] Such a finding is permissible only if supported by evidence establishing guilt beyond a reasonable doubt. It necessarily follows that if the omitted evidence creates a reasonable doubt that did not otherwise exist, constitutional error has been committed. This means that the omission must be evaluated in the context of the entire record. If there is no reasonable doubt about guilt whether or not the additional evidence is considered, there is no justification for a new trial. On the other hand, if the verdict is already of questionable validity, additional evidence of relatively minor importance might be sufficient to create a reasonable doubt.

This statement of the standard of materiality describes the test which courts appear to have applied in actual cases although the standard has been phrased in different language. It is also the standard which the trial judge applied in this case. He evaluated the significance of Sewell's prior criminal record in the context of the full trial which he recalled in detail. Stressing in particular the incongruity of a claim that Sewell was the aggressor with the evidence of his multiple wounds and respondent's unscathed condition, the trial judge indicated his unqualified opinion that respondent was guilty. He noted that Sewell's prior record did not contradict any evidence offered by the prosecutor, and was largely cumulative of the evidence that Sewell was wearing a bowie knife in a sheath and carrying a second knife in his pocket when he registered at the motel.

Since the arrest record was not requested and did not even arguably give rise to any inference of perjury, since after considering it in the context of the entire record the trial judge remained convinced of respondent's guilt beyond a reasonable doubt, and since we are satisfied that his firsthand

[a] It has been argued that the standard should focus on the impact of the undisclosed evidence on the defendant's ability to prepare for trial, rather than the materiality of the evidence to the issue of guilt or innocence. See Note, The Prosecutor's Constitutional Duty to Reveal Evidence to the Defense, 74 Yale L.J. 136 (1964). Such a standard would be unacceptable for determining the materiality of what has been generally recognized as "*Brady* material" for two reasons. First, that standard would necessarily encompass incriminating evidence as well as exculpatory evidence, since knowledge of the prosecutor's entire case would always be useful in planning the defense. Second, such an approach would primarily involve an analysis of the adequacy of the notice given to the defendant by the State, and it has always been the Court's view that the notice component of due process refers to the charge rather than the evidentiary support for the charge.

appraisal of the record was thorough and entirely reasonable, we hold that the prosecutor's failure to tender Sewell's record to the defense did not deprive respondent of a fair trial as guaranteed by the Due Process Clause of the Fifth Amendment. * * *

JUSTICE MARSHALL with whom JUSTICE BRENNAN joins, dissenting.

* * *

* * * [The majority's] rule creates little, if any, incentive for the prosecutor conscientiously to determine whether his files contain evidence helpful to the defense. Indeed, the rule reinforces the natural tendency of the prosecutor to overlook evidence favorable to the defense, and creates an incentive for the prosecutor to resolve close questions of disclosure in favor of concealment.

* * * I would hold that the defendant in this case had the burden of demonstrating that there is a significant chance that the withheld evidence, developed by skilled counsel, would have induced a reasonable doubt in the minds of enough jurors to avoid a conviction. * * *

Refining the Test of Materiality: United States v. Bagley

Justice Blackmun wrote for the Court in United States v. Bagley, 473 U.S. 667 (1985), as the Court declined to overturn a conviction because of nondisclosure of exculpatory evidence. Bagley was charged with narcotics and firearms offenses and convicted in a bench trial only on the narcotics charges. Thereafter he learned that, despite his motion to discover any deals or promises between the government and its witnesses, the government had not disclosed that its two principal witnesses had signed contracts with the Bureau of Alcohol, Tobacco and Firearms to be paid for their undercover work. Although the trial judge ruled that the contracts would not have affected the outcome because the principal witnesses testified primarily concerning the firearms charges on which Bagley was acquitted, the court of appeals disagreed. The Supreme Court agreed with the trial judge and found that nondisclosure of impeachment evidence, like nondisclosure of other exculpatory evidence, requires reversal only if the evidence was material in the sense that it might have affected the outcome of the trial. No such showing was made on the facts of this case.

Justice Blackmun's opinion set forth a single "standard of materiality" applicable to nondisclosed exculpatory evidence. Justice Blackmun borrowed from the Court's ineffective assistance of counsel cases (discussed in Chapter 10) and derived the following standard:

> [Suppressed evidence] is material only if there is a reasonable probability that, had the evidence been disclosed to the defense, the result of the proceeding would have been different. A reasonable probability is a probability sufficient to undermine confidence in the outcome.

Justice Blackmun noted that this test was "sufficiently flexible" to cover no request, general request, and specific request cases.

In a part of the opinion joined only by Justice O'Connor, Justice Blackmun reasoned that "the more specifically the defense requests certain evidence * * * the more reasonable it is for the defense to assume from the nondisclosure that the evidence does not exist and to make pretrial and trial decisions on the basis of this assumption." Thus, specific request cases present special considerations in applying the single "reasonable probability" standard of materiality. The more specific the request, the more likely the suppression will be "material" in the *Brady* sense.

Justice White, joined by Chief Justice Burger and Justice Rehnquist, concurred in the judgment in *Bagley*. Although he expressed agreement with the single materiality standard developed by Justice Blackmun, he saw "no reason to attempt to elaborate on the relevance to the inquiry of the specificity of the defense's request for disclosure."

Justice Marshall, joined by Justice Brennan, dissented and argued that "when the Government withholds from a defendant evidence that might impeach the prosecution's *only witnesses,* that failure to disclose cannot be deemed harmless error." Justice Stevens, who authored *Agurs,* also dissented. He argued that, unlike *Agurs,* the instant case involved a specific request and that *Brady* requires reversal for failure to disclose evidence favorable to an accused upon a specific request if the evidence is material either to guilt or punishment. Thus, he would have remanded for a determination of whether there was "any reasonable likelihood" that the nondisclosure could have affected the judgment of the trier of fact.

Comments on Brady-Agurs-Bagley

Professor Stacy, in The Search for the Truth in Constitutional Criminal Procedure, 91 Colum.L.Rev. 1369, 1392 (1991), has this to say about the *Bagley* standard of materiality:

> The *Bagley* standard, which focuses on the likely impact of evidence on the ultimate result in the case, suffers from two interrelated deficiencies. The first problem is that the standard will frequently be misapplied. A prosecutor's lack of information about the planned defense and partisan inclinations impede her from making an accurate and objective assessment of the evidence's effect on the outcome. The second problem is that many misapplications of the

Bagley standard will never be detected and remedied. Because the prosecution has exclusive possession of the evidence subject to the duty to disclose and a clear incentive to withhold it, the defense or a court will sometimes never learn of evidence wrongly withheld.

In short, the Court has interpreted the prosecution's duty to disclose exculpatory evidence more narrowly than a true concern for accurate factfinding implies. For a Court genuinely interested in the search for the truth, neither the adversarial system, prosecutorial burdens, nor the constitutional text can justify the *Bagley* standard, which will result in important exculpatory evidence not being disclosed in a significant number of cases.

Can prosecutors refuse to turn over evidence that appears to be exculpatory but not sufficiently so to require a new trial under *Brady-Agurs-Bagley?* Should prosecutors be trusted with this authority? What would be wrong with requiring the prosecutor to turn over all evidence that a defense counsel would conclude *might tend* to exculpate the defendant?

Capra, Access to Exculpatory Evidence: Avoiding the Agurs Problems of Prosecutorial Discretion and Retrospective Review, 53 Ford.L.Rev. 391 (1984), argues that a per se right to an in camera hearing, at which the court would examine a prosecutor's files for *Brady* material, would be more effective than retrospective review of claims that exculpatory evidence was suppressed.

The Relevance of a Specific Request

While the combination of the Blackmun and White opinions in *Bagley* produce a single standard of materiality for all nondisclosure cases, *Bagley* leaves ambiguity about the relevance of a specific defense request for the evidence. In *Agurs,* Justice Stevens emphasized that the specific request increased the level of prosecutorial responsibility. In *Bagley,* Justice Blackmun emphasized the greater prejudicial impact of a denied specific request due to the possibility that defense counsel will be misled. Justice White thought it appropriate to leave the precise impact of a specific request for another day. Where a case involves a specific request, lower courts after *Bagley* have continued to take account of that factor, although not always stating why it is significant. See, e.g., Jean v. Rice, 945 F.2d 82 (4th Cir.1991) (recordings and reports indicating that the prosecution's star witness had been hypnotized were *Brady* material: "We are persuaded that the audio recordings and accompanying reports—twice requested—should have been disclosed to defense counsel."). As the Fifth Circuit stated in Lindsey v. King, 769 F.2d 1034 (5th Cir.1985): "Viewing the [*Bagley*] opinions as a whole, it is fair to say that all the participating Justices agreed on one thing at least: that reversal for suppression of evidence by the government is most likely where the request for it was specific."

B. APPLYING THE *BRADY* RULE

Fact-Intensive Applications: Three Illustrative Cases

The Court reaffirmed its *Brady-Agurs-Bagley* line of cases in Kyles v. Whitley, 514 U.S. 419 (1995), and applied those cases in an intensely fact-specific manner to reverse a conviction and death sentence. Kyles was convicted (after his first trial ended in a hung jury) of murdering a woman during the course of a robbery outside a grocery store. There was evidence that the killer left his car in the parking lot and drove away in the victim's car. The prosecution presented four eyewitnesses who identified Kyles unequivocally both before and at the trial. Kyles argued that an acquaintance, Beanie, committed the murders and framed him by planting the murder weapon (a gun) and the victim's purse and other items at Kyles's house. Beanie had originally approached the police with information that Kyles was the killer, and received a reward for his information. Beanie was not called by either side to testify at Kyles's trial. The prosecution suppressed many pieces of evidence, including: (1) pretrial statements from two of the eyewitnesses, which were markedly inconsistent with their later identifications, and one of which appeared to point to Beanie rather than Kyles as the perpetrator; (2) a series of statements by Beanie that were inconsistent and were ignored by the investigating officer; and (3) a police report indicating that Kyles's car was not on the list of cars found at the store shortly after the murder.

Justice Souter, writing for five Justices, made the following general points about the Court's *Brady-Agurs-Bagley* materiality standard:

> Four aspects of materiality under *Bagley* bear emphasis. * * * *Bagley's* touchstone of materiality is a "reasonable probability" of a different result, and the adjective is important. The question is not whether the defendant would more likely than not have received a different verdict with the evidence, but whether in its absence he received a fair trial, understood as a trial resulting in a verdict worthy of confidence. A "reasonable probability" of a different result is accordingly shown when the Government's evidentiary suppression "undermines confidence in the outcome of the trial."
>
> The second aspect of *Bagley* materiality bearing emphasis here is that it is not a sufficiency of evidence test. * * * The possibility of an acquittal on a criminal charge does not imply an insufficient evidentiary basis to convict. One does not show a *Brady* violation by demonstrating that some of the inculpatory evidence should have been excluded, but by showing that the favorable evidence could reasonably be taken to put the whole case in such a different light as to undermine confidence in the verdict.

Third, we note that * * * once a reviewing court applying *Bagley* has found constitutional error there is no need for further harmless-error review. Assuming arguendo that a harmless error enquiry were to apply, a *Bagley* error could not be treated as harmless, since "a reasonable probability that, had the evidence been disclosed to the defense, the result of the proceeding would have been different," necessarily entails the conclusion that the suppression must have had "substantial and injurious effect or influence in determining the jury's verdict." * * *

The fourth and final aspect of *Bagley* materiality to be stressed here is its definition in terms of suppressed evidence considered collectively, not item-by-item. * * * [T]he Constitution is not violated every time the government fails or chooses not to disclose evidence that might prove helpful to the defense. We have never held that the Constitution demands an open file policy * * *.

Justice Souter stressed that suppression of exculpatory evidence implicates *Brady* rights *even if the suppression is by police officers and the prosecutor is unaware of it.* He explained this point as follows:

* * * In the State's favor it may be said that no one doubts that police investigators sometimes fail to inform a prosecutor of all they know. But neither is there any serious doubt that procedures and regulations can be established to carry the prosecutor's burden and to insure communication of all relevant information on each case to every lawyer who deals with it. Since, then, the prosecutor has the means to discharge the government's *Brady* responsibility if he will, any argument for excusing a prosecutor from disclosing what he does not happen to know about boils down to a plea to substitute the police for the prosecutor, and even for the courts themselves, as the final arbiters of the government's obligation to ensure fair trials.

The State in *Kyles* argued that the *Brady-Bagley* standard of materiality should be made more rigorous (i.e., harder for the defendant to meet) because the current standard places a prosecutor in the uncomfortable position of having to predict the materiality of evidence before the trial. The State asked for "a certain amount of leeway in making a judgment call" as to the disclosure of any given piece of evidence. But the majority rejected the State's argument, and adhered to the *Brady-Bagley* standard of materiality, in the following analysis:

[W]ith or without more leeway, the prosecution cannot be subject to any disclosure obligation without at some point having the responsibility to determine when it must act. Indeed, even if due process were thought to be violated by every failure to disclose an item of exculpatory or impeachment evidence (leaving harmless error as the government's only fallback), the prosecutor would still be forced to make judgment calls about what would count as favorable evidence, owing to the very fact that the character of a piece of evidence as favorable will often turn on the context of the existing or potential evidentiary record. Since the prosecutor would have to exercise some judgment even if the State were subject to this most stringent disclosure obligation, it is hard to find merit in the State's complaint over the responsibility for judgment under the existing system, which does not tax the prosecutor with error for any failure to disclose, absent a further showing of materiality. * * *

> This means, naturally, that a prosecutor anxious about tacking too close to the wind will disclose a favorable piece of evidence. This is as it should be. Such disclosure will serve to justify trust in the prosecutor * * * [and] will tend to preserve the criminal trial, as distinct from the prosecutor's private deliberations, as the chosen forum for ascertaining the truth about criminal accusations. The prudence of the careful prosecutor should not therefore be discouraged.

Applying all these principles to the case, Justice Souter concluded that the cumulative effect of the suppressed evidence satisfied the materiality standard of *Brady-Agurs-Bagley*. In the majority's view, the suppressed evidence would have caused the jury to doubt the statements of two eyewitnesses, due to their inconsistent prior statements, and would further have caused the jury to doubt the integrity of the lead investigator, who trusted Beanie completely and never considered him as a suspect—even though Beanie's statements were often inconsistent and implausible. The majority concluded:

> [T]he question is not whether the State would have had a case to go to the jury if it had disclosed the favorable evidence, but whether we can be confident that the jury's verdict would have been the same. * * * But confidence that the verdict would have been unaffected cannot survive when suppressed evidence would have entitled a jury to find that the eyewitnesses were not consistent in describing the killer, that two out of the four eyewitnesses testifying were unreliable, that the most damning physical evidence was subject to suspicion [of having been planted], that the investigation that produced it was insufficiently probing, and that the principal police witness was insufficiently informed or candid.[7]

Justice Scalia, joined by Chief Justice Rehnquist and Justices Kennedy and Thomas, dissented in *Kyles*. The dissenters did not disagree with the majority's restatement of the principles derived from *Brady*, *Agurs* and *Bagley*. Rather, they argued that reversal was unwarranted because

[7] Justice Stevens wrote a short concurring opinion, defending the Court's role in engaging in fact-intensive review of capital cases, especially where the record points to the possibility that the defendant did not commit the crime.

the suppressed evidence, even considered cumulatively, was not materially exculpatory. Justice Scalia stated that even with the suppressed evidence, Kyles could not have overcome the implausibility of his own defense, which was that the witnesses misidentified him and that Beanie framed him. Justice Scalia explained as follows:

> [P]etitioner's theory was that he was the victim of a quadruple coincidence, in which four eyewitnesses to the crime mistakenly identified him as the murderer—three picking him out of a photo-array without hesitation, and all four affirming their identification in open court after comparing him with Beanie. The extraordinary mistake petitioner had to persuade the jury these four witnesses made was not simply to mistake the real killer, Beanie, for the very same innocent third party (hard enough to believe), but in addition to mistake him for the very man Beanie had chosen to frame—the last and most incredible level of coincidence. However small the chance that the jury would believe any one of those improbable scenarios, the likelihood that it would believe them all together is far smaller.

In Weary v. Cain, 577 U.S. 385 (2016) (per curiam), the Court vacated a capital conviction because of state prosecutors' failure to disclose material evidence. Nearly two years after a murder, a state prisoner, Scott, contacted authorities and implicated Weary in the murder. Scott changed his account of the crime four different times, and each version differed from the others in material ways. The Court described Scott as the state's star witness and observed that his trial testimony bore little resemblance to his original account. The state had no physical evidence linking Weary to the murder but it had another witness, Brown (also incarcerated at the time of Weary's trial), who testified that he saw Weary on the night of the murder with someone who looked like the victim. Brown had originally made a prior inconsistent statement to the police but recanted and agreed to testify ostensibly because he knew the victim's sister. The prosecutor told the jury that Brown had "no deal on the table."

Weary's defense was alibi. He claimed he was at a wedding reception 40 miles away at the time of the murder. His girlfriend, her sister, and her aunt corroborated his claim.

Post-trial proceedings revealed that police records showed that two of Scott's fellow inmates heard Scott make statements that cast doubt on his credibility. One inmate reported hearing Scott say that he wanted to make sure that Weary "gets the needle because he jacked over me." The other inmate told investigators that he had witnessed the murder, but recanted and revealed that Scott had told him what to say.

Weary's lawyers learned post-trial that Brown had twice sought a deal to reduce his sentence in exchange for his testimony against Weary, contrary to what the prosecutors suggested to the jury. They also learned that the medical records of one of the alleged participants in the murder according to Scott revealed that he had undergone surgery that would have disabled him from doing what Scott claimed he had done.

A state post-conviction court decided against Weary, but the Supreme Court summarily reversed. The Court emphasized that Weary was not required to show that it was more likely than not that he would have been acquitted had the suppressed evidence been disclosed; he had to show that the new evidence was sufficient to "undermine confidence" in the verdict.

Justice Alito, joined by Justice Thomas, dissented. He noted that the question whether the new evidence realistically could have changed the trial's outcome was an intensely factual question, expressed concern that the Court was deciding the case on the basis of a certiorari petition and the state's brief in opposition, and suggested it was more appropriate for a lower federal court to consider Weary's post-conviction claim in a habeas corpus proceeding.

In Turner v. United States, 137 S.Ct. 1885 (2017), Justice Breyer wrote for the Court as it held that, although the government withheld evidence from seven defendants tried together for the kidnaping, armed robbery, and murder of a woman in the District of Columbia, their convictions did not have to be set aside. The government did not contest that the withheld evidence was favorable to the defendants; nor did it contest that it suppressed the evidence. The issue before the Court was materiality.

The body of the victim was found inside an alley garage just a few blocks from her home. The government's theory at trial was that she was attacked by a large group of individuals, including the seven defendants. Its key witnesses were Alston and Bennett who confessed to participating in the murders and cooperated with the government in exchange for leniency. Both witnesses described members of the group pursuing the victim, shoving her into an alley, punching and kicking her, carrying her to a garage in the alley and moving her into the garage. The government also played a videotape of a recorded statement in which one defendant described the criminal activity. A jury convicted the seven defendants who were attacking their convictions and acquitted two others.

After their convictions became final, the defendants discovered the government had withheld the following evidence: (1) the government refused to disclose the names of two men seen by the vendor who discovered the body running into the alley, stopping near the garage while the vendor awaited the police, and then running away when an officer approached—and one of them was James McMillan, who lived in a house that opened in the back to a connecting alley and who was arrested in the weeks following the murder, but before the defendants' trial, for beating and robbing two women in the neighborhood; (2) Willie Luchie told police he was walking with three others through the alley around the time of the murder and heard several groans from the garage, one of the others said he heard moans, and two others heard nothing unusual; (3) Ammie Davis, who was arrested for disorderly conduct a few weeks after the murder told police that, while walking with a girlfriend, she saw another individual, James Blue, beat the victim to death in the alley and thereafter said she only saw Blue grab the victim and push her into the alley (Blue killed Davis before the defendant's trial in an unrelated drug dispute); (4) Carrie Eleby, who testified to hearing screams coming from where a "gang of boys" was beating someone near the garage was interviewed by the police along with a friend and both agreed that they heard Alston admit his involvement in robbing the victim, but the friend later recanted and said she just went along with what Eleby said; (5) Eleby told investigators she had been high on PCP; (6) a detective recorded in a note that Linda Jacobs, who was with Eleby at the time of the assault, vacillated about what she saw; and (7) a note indicated that the aunt of Maurice Thomas, a 14-year-old at the time of the murder who testified to recognizing six of the assailants, said she did not recall Maurice telling her anything like that.

The defendants argued that had they known of the identity of James McMillan and Luchie's statement about hearing groans they could have relied on the theory that the victim was killed by a single perpetrator, or two at most, rather than in a group attack. But, Justice Breyer reasoned that it was not reasonably probable that McMillan's identity and Luchie's ambiguous statement that he heard groans but saw no one could have led to a different result at trial given the testimony of Alston and Bennett, the videotaped statement, and the testimony of Thomas. He also reasoned that the undisclosed impeachment evidence was largely cumulative of evidence that the defendants had used at trial.

Justice Kagan, joined by Justice Ginsburg, dissented and pointed out that the actual trial involved 10 defendants accepting the government's theory that a gang had attacked the victim with each defendant claiming he was not part of the gang, which meant that the defendants undermined each other's arguments at every turn. She posited that had the defendants been aware of evidence suggesting that the murder was committed by someone else they might have vigorously disputed the government's gang attack theory and challenged the credibility of its investigation. She challenged the majority's "slam-dunk" description of the case and pointed out that there was no physical evidence tying any defendant to the crime, two key witnesses were testifying in exchange for favorable plea deals, two witnesses admitted they were high on PCP, and Thomas was an eighth grader whose aunt contradicted parts of his trial testimony.

Suppressed Evidence That Would Have Been Inadmissible at Trial: Wood v. Bartholemew

If the evidence suppressed by the prosecution would be inadmissible at the defendant's trial, could it ever be considered materially exculpatory? The Supreme Court considered this question in Wood v. Bartholomew, 516 U.S. 1 (1995), a per curiam opinion, in which exculpatory polygraph results were suppressed. Bartholomew admitted shooting a laundry attendant during a robbery, but claimed his gun accidentally discharged. This account was disputed by two prosecution witnesses, Bartholomew's brother Rodney and Rodney's girlfriend, who both claimed that Bartholomew told them that he intended to shoot the attendant. Both witnesses passed a polygraph examination on the questions regarding Bartholomew's intent to shoot the attendant, but Rodney was found to be deceptive when he denied all involvement in the crime. The court of appeals found that suppression of the polygraph results constituted a *Brady* violation, even though it recognized that polygraph evidence is not admissible for any purpose in Washington state courts. That court reasoned that if defense counsel had known about the polygraph results, he would have attacked Rodney's story more aggressively; that he "likely would have taken Rodney's deposition"; that in that deposition defense counsel "might well have succeeded in obtaining an admission that Rodney was lying about his participation in the crime"; and that defense counsel "would likely have uncovered a variety of conflicting statements which could have been used quite effectively in cross-examination at trial."

The Supreme Court rejected this reasoning as speculative and inconsistent with the *Brady-Agurs-Bagley* materiality requirement. The Court elaborated as follows:

> The information at issue here * * * is not "evidence" at all. Disclosure of the polygraph results, then, could have had no direct effect on the outcome of trial, because respondent could have made no mention of them either during argument or while questioning witnesses. To get around this problem, the Ninth Circuit reasoned that the information, had it been disclosed to the defense, might have led respondent's counsel to conduct additional discovery that might have led to some additional evidence that could have been utilized. Other than expressing a belief that in a deposition Rodney might have confessed to his involvement in the initial stages of the crime—a confession that itself would have been in no way inconsistent with respondent's guilt—the Court of Appeals did not specify what particular evidence it had in mind. Its judgment is based on mere speculation, in violation of the standards we have established.

The Court noted that Bartholemew's counsel, at the habeas hearing, testified that he made the strategic decision not to cross-examine Rodney aggressively at trial, for fear that Rodney would reiterate his brother's statement that he would "leave no witnesses." Thus, the lower court's judgment on what could have been done with the polygraph responses was inconsistent with the approach actually taken by Bartholemew's own trial counsel. Finally, the Court noted that the polygraph responses could not have been material in light of the overwhelming evidence of Bartholemew's guilt:

> To acquit of aggravated murder, the jury would have had to believe that respondent's single action revolver discharged accidently, not once but twice, by tragic coincidence depositing a bullet to the back of the victim's head, execution-style, as the victim lay face down on the floor. In the face of this physical evidence, as well as Rodney and Tracy's testimony * * * it should take more than supposition on the weak premises offered by respondent to undermine a court's confidence in the outcome.[8]

Does *Bartholomew* mean that inadmissible evidence can *never* be *Brady* material? See United States v. Salem, 578 F.3d 682 (7th Cir. 2009) (only admissible evidence can be "material" under *Brady*, because only admissible evidence could possibly lead to a different verdict). For a critique on limiting the *Brady* right to admissible evidence, see Ginsberg, Always Be Disclosing: The Prosecutor's Constitutional Duty to Divulge Inadmissible Evidence, 110 W.Va. L. Rev. 611 (2008).

Impeachment Evidence Found Material Under Brady: Smith v. Cain

In Smith v. Cain, 565 U.S. 73 (2012), Chief Justice Roberts wrote for an 8–1 Court, in a fact-intensive opinion, as it overturned a defendant's convictions on five first-degree murder counts due to a *Brady* violation in suppressing impeachment evidence. Boatner was the only eyewitness to the murders, and he identified the defendant as one of the perpetrators at trial. But he had told a detective on the night of the murders that he could not supply a description of the perpetrators other than that they were black males, and five days later he told the detective that he "could not ID anyone because [he] couldn't see faces" and "would not know them if [he] saw them." These statements were suppressed by the prosecution. No other witness and no physical evidence tied the defendant to the crime. The Chief Justice stated that the only question before the Court was whether the suppressed statements were "material" under *Brady*, and on that question wrote as follows:

> We have observed that evidence impeaching an eyewitness may not be material if the State's other evidence is strong enough to sustain

---

[8] Four Justices in *Bartholomew* dissented from the summary disposition of the case.

confidence in the verdict. That is not the case here. Boatner's testimony was the only evidence linking Smith to the crime. And Boatner's undisclosed statements directly contradict his testimony: Boatner told the jury that he had "[n]o doubt" that Smith was the gunman he stood "face to face" with on the night of the crime, but Ronquillo's notes show Boatner saying that he "could not ID anyone because [he] couldn't see faces" and "would not know them if [he] saw them." Boatner's undisclosed statements were plainly material.

The State and the dissent advance various reasons why the jury might have discounted Boatner's undisclosed statements. They stress, for example, that Boatner made other remarks on the night of the murder indicating that he could identify the first gunman to enter the house, but not the others. That merely leaves us to speculate about which of Boatner's contradictory declarations the jury would have believed. The State also contends that Boatner's statements made five days after the crime can be explained by fear of retaliation. Smith responds that the record contains no evidence of any such fear. Again, the State's argument offers a reason that the jury could have disbelieved Boatner's undisclosed statements, but gives us no confidence that it would have done so.

Justice Thomas dissented.

Impeachment Evidence That Does Not Raise a Reasonable Probability of a Different Result: Strickler v. Greene

In Strickler v. Greene, 527 U.S. 263 (1999), the Court considered the effect of suppressed impeachment evidence in a prosecution for capital murder. Strickler and Henderson abducted Whitlock at a shopping center and commandeered her car by striking a blow to her head with a 69-pound rock. There was abundant evidence connecting Strickler to the murder—among other things, he was seen driving the victim's car near the scene of the murder, he gave away some of the victim's valuables as presents, and both he and Henderson made inculpatory statements to friends. However, the only witness who testified to the abduction itself was a bystander named Stoltzfus. She gave detailed testimony indicating that Strickler took the lead in breaking into Whitlock's car and forcing her into the passenger seat, while Henderson and Strickler's girlfriend "hung back." Throughout her testimony, she referred to Strickler as "Mountain Man" and Henderson as "Shy Guy." She had no doubt about her testimony and offered that she had an excellent memory. In fact, however, Stoltzfus had been unable to identify Strickler during several meetings with a police officer, and indicated that she hadn't thought that the event she witnessed was very serious, in that it seemed like a college prank. This information about Stoltzfus' prior uncertainty was never disclosed to Strickler's defense counsel. Strickler was convicted and sentenced to death. In a separate trial, Henderson was also convicted, but did not receive a death sentence.

The District Court granted a writ of habeas corpus on Strickler's *Brady* claim. The Fourth Circuit reversed, finding no merit in the *Brady* claim on the ground that Stoltzfus' testimony related only to the abduction, and was therefore essentially irrelevant to the capital murder charges. The Supreme Court, in an opinion by Justice Stevens, agreed with the Fourth Circuit, though it found the *Brady* "prejudice" question much more difficult than had the Court of Appeals.

Justice Stevens analyzed the *Brady* "prejudice" claim in the following passage:

> The Court of Appeals' [ruling that the suppressed impeachment evidence was not "material"] rested on its conclusion that, without considering Stoltzfus' testimony, the record contained ample, independent evidence of guilt, as well as evidence sufficient to support the findings of vileness and future dangerousness that warranted the imposition of the death penalty. The standard used by that court was incorrect. As we made clear in *Kyles*, the materiality inquiry is not just a matter of determining whether, after discounting the inculpatory evidence in light of the undisclosed evidence, the remaining evidence is sufficient to support the jury's conclusions. Rather, the question is whether "the favorable evidence could reasonably be taken to put the whole case in such a different light as to undermine confidence in the verdict."
>
> * * *
>
> The District Court was surely correct that there is a reasonable *possibility* that either a total, or just a substantial, discount of Stoltzfus' testimony might have produced a different result, either at the guilt or sentencing phases. Petitioner did, for example, introduce substantial mitigating evidence about abuse he had suffered as a child at the hands of his stepfather. As the District Court recognized, however, petitioner's burden is to establish a reasonable *probability* of a different result.
>
> Even if Stoltzfus and her testimony had been entirely discredited, the jury might still have concluded that petitioner was the leader of the criminal enterprise because he was the one seen driving the car * * * near the location of the murder and the one who kept the car for the following week. In addition, [Strickler's girlfriend] testified that petitioner threatened Henderson with a knife later in the evening.
>
> * * *
>
> We recognize the importance of eyewitness testimony; Stoltzfus provided the only disinterested, narrative account of what transpired

on January 5, 1990. However, Stoltzfus' vivid description of the events at the mall was not the only evidence that the jury had before it. Two other eyewitnesses, the security guard and Henderson's friend, placed petitioner and Henderson at the Harrisonburg Valley Shopping Mall on the afternoon of Whitlock's murder. One eyewitness later saw petitioner driving Dean's car near the scene of the murder.

The record provides strong support for the conclusion that petitioner would have been convicted of capital murder and sentenced to death, even if Stoltzfus had been severely impeached. The jury was instructed on two predicates for capital murder: robbery with a deadly weapon and abduction with intent to defile. * * * [A]rmed robbery still would have supported the capital murder conviction. * * *

Petitioner also maintains that he suffered prejudice from the failure to disclose the Stoltzfus documents because her testimony impacted on the jury's decision to impose the death penalty. * * * With respect to the jury's discretionary decision to impose the death penalty, it is true that Stoltzfus described petitioner as a violent, aggressive person, but that portrayal surely was not as damaging as either the evidence that he spent the evening of the murder dancing and drinking * * * or the powerful message conveyed by the 69-pound rock that was part of the record before the jury. Notwithstanding the obvious significance of Stoltzfus' testimony, petitioner has not convinced us that there is a reasonable probability that the jury would have returned a different verdict if her testimony had been either severely impeached or excluded entirely.

Justice Souter, joined by Justice Kennedy, dissented in part in *Strickler*. He agreed with the Court that the suppressed impeachment information was not "material," in a *Brady* sense, to the defendant's guilt or innocence. But he argued that the impeachment material did create a reasonable probability that the jury would have recommended a life sentence rather than the death penalty. He explained as follows:

> I could not regard Stoltzfus's colorful testimony as anything but significant on the matter of sentence. It was Stoltzfus alone who described Strickler as the initiator of the abduction, as the one who broke into Whitlock's car, who beckoned his companions to follow him, and who violently subdued the victim while 'Shy Guy' sat in the back seat. The bare content of this testimony, important enough, was enhanced by one of the inherent hallmarks of reliability, as Stoltzfus confidently recalled detail after detail. The withheld documents would have shown, however, that many of the details Stoltzfus confidently mentioned on the stand * * * had apparently escaped her memory in her initial interviews with the police. Her persuasive account did not come, indeed, until after her recollection had been aided by further

conversations with the police and with the victim's boyfriend. I therefore have to assess the likely havoc that an informed cross-examiner could have wreaked upon Stoltzfus as adequate to raise a significant possibility of a different recommendation [of sentence], as sufficient to undermine confidence that the death recommendation would have been the choice. All it would have taken, after all, was one juror to hold out against death to preclude the recommendation actually given.

* * *

Professor Saltzburg, in Perjury and False Testimony: Should the Difference Matter So Much, 68 Fordham L. Rev. 1537 (2000), argues that Stoltzfus's trial testimony, which indicated confidence and certainty on her part, was amazingly inconsistent with what she told the Detective. The impression of confidence and certainty created by the prosecution appears to have been plainly false—something the *Strickler* Court largely ignored.

More Suppressed Impeachment Evidence: Banks v. Dretke

In Banks v. Dretke, 540 U.S. 668 (2004), the Court once again undertook a fact-intensive inquiry into whether a *Brady* violation occurred when impeachment evidence was suppressed. Banks was convicted of capital murder and sentenced to death. At the penalty phase, the jury was required to find that there was a probability that Banks would "commit criminal acts of violence that would constitute a continuing threat to society." As proof of this continuing dangerousness, the prosecution presented the testimony of Robert Farr. Farr testified that after the murder, he traveled with Banks to Dallas to retrieve Banks's gun, so that the gun could be used in a series of planned robberies. Farr testified that Banks promised to use the gun to "take care of it" if any problems arose during the robberies. On cross-examination, defense counsel asked Farr whether he had "ever taken any money from some police officers," or "given any police officers a statement." Farr answered "no" to both questions; he asserted that police officers had not promised him anything and that he had "talked to no one about this [case]" until a few days before trial. The prosecution also presented the testimony of Banks's brother-in-law, who testified that Banks had once struck him across the face with a gun and threatened to kill him.

The majority, in an opinion by Justice Ginsburg, ruled that the death penalty phase was tainted by a *Brady* error: the government had not disclosed that Farr had been paid $200 for his testimony, that Farr had instigated the adventure to retrieve the gun, and that Farr had conferred with the prosecutor in detail about the testimony. Justice Ginsburg found that the suppressed impeachment evidence was "material" for *Brady* purposes, reasoning as follows:

> Farr was paid for a critical role in the scenario that led to the indictment. * * * Farr, not Banks, initiated the proposal to obtain a gun to facilitate the commission of robberies. Had Farr not instigated, upon Deputy Sheriff Huff's request, the Dallas excursion to fetch Banks's gun, the prosecution would have had slim, if any, evidence that Banks planned to "continue" committing violent acts. Farr's admission of his instigating role, moreover, would have dampened the prosecution's zeal in urging the jury to bear in mind Banks's "planning and acquisition of a gun to commit robbery," or Banks's "planned violence."
>
> * * *
>
> Because Banks had no criminal record, Farr's testimony about Banks's propensity to commit violent acts was crucial to the prosecution. Without that testimony, the State could not have underscored, as it did three times in the penalty phase, that Banks would use the gun fetched in Dallas to "take care" of trouble arising during the robberies. The stress placed by the prosecution on this part of Farr's testimony, uncorroborated by any other witness, belies the State's suggestion that "Farr's testimony was adequately corroborated." The prosecution's penalty-phase summation, moreover, left no doubt about the importance the State attached to Farr's testimony. What Farr told the jury, the prosecution urged, was "of the utmost significance" to show "[Banks] is a danger to friends and strangers, alike."
>
> * * *
>
> At least as to the penalty phase, in sum, one can hardly be confident that Banks received a fair trial, given the jury's ignorance of Farr's true role in the investigation and trial of the case. On the record before us, one could not plausibly deny the existence of the requisite "reasonable probability of a different result" had the suppressed information been disclosed to the defense. * * *

Justice Thomas, joined by Justice Scalia, dissented on the question of *Brady* materiality. He concluded that there was no reasonable probability that the jury would have decided differently at the penalty phase if it had known about Farr's status as a paid informant and instigator.

> The jury knew that Banks had murdered a 16-year-old on a whim, had violently attacked and threatened a relative shortly before the murder, and was willing to assist another individual in committing armed robberies by providing the "means and possible death weapon" for these robberies. Even if the jury were to discredit entirely Farr's testimony that Banks was planning more robberies, in all likelihood the jury still would have found "beyond a reasonable doubt" that there

"[was] a probability that [Banks] would commit criminal acts of violence that would constitute a continuing threat to society."

Brady and Guilty Pleas: United States v. Ruiz

If the prosecutor has materially exculpatory evidence, must it be disclosed before the defendant enters into a guilty plea? Or is the *Brady* right simply a trial right? The question arises in the following procedural context: the defendant pleads guilty, later learns of exculpatory evidence that was suppressed, and moves to vacate his guilty plea as insufficiently knowing and voluntary.[9]

In United States v. Ruiz, 536 U.S. 622 (2002), the Court held that during guilty plea negotiations the government is not required to disclose information that could impeach government witnesses, nor information that could be used by the defendant to prove an affirmative defense.

Justice Breyer, writing for a unanimous Court, noted that "impeachment information is special in relation to the *fairness of a trial*, not in respect to whether a plea is *voluntary*." Justice Breyer expressed concern that requiring disclosure of impeachment information during guilty plea negotiations "could seriously interfere with the Government's interest in securing those guilty pleas that are factually justified, desired by defendants, and help to secure the efficient administration of justice." Specifically, early disclosure of impeachment evidence "could disrupt ongoing investigations and expose prospective witnesses to serious harm."

As to required disclosure of impeachment evidence, Justice Breyer concluded that it

> could force the Government to abandon its general practice of not disclosing to a defendant pleading guilty information that would reveal the identities of cooperating informants, undercover investigators, or other prospective witnesses. It could require the Government to devote substantially more resources to trial preparation prior to plea bargaining, thereby depriving the plea-bargaining process of its main resource-saving advantages. Or it could lead the Government instead to abandon its heavy reliance upon plea bargaining in a vast number—90% or more—of federal criminal cases. We cannot say that the Constitution's due process requirement demands so radical a change in the criminal justice process in order to achieve so comparatively small a constitutional benefit.

As to required disclosure of information bearing on an affirmative defense, the Court concluded as follows:

---

[9] See Chapter 9 for a more complete discussion of the voluntariness standards attendant to guilty pleas.

> We do not believe the Constitution here requires provision of this information to the defendant prior to plea bargaining—for most (though not all) of the reasons previously stated. That is to say, in the context of this agreement, the need for this information is more closely related to the *fairness* of a trial than to the *voluntariness* of the plea; the value in terms of the defendant's added awareness of relevant circumstances is ordinarily limited; yet the added burden imposed upon the Government by requiring its provision well in advance of trial (often before trial preparation begins) can be serious, thereby significantly interfering with the administration of the plea bargaining process.

The Court in *Ruiz* recognized the government's duty to disclose information bearing on the defendant's "factual innocence" during guilty plea negotiations, as well as a continuing duty to disclose such information throughout the plea proceedings. Indeed, the government recognized this obligation by including it in the plea agreement in *Ruiz*. See also Sanchez v. United States, 50 F.3d 1448 (9th Cir.1995) (guilty plea vacated because evidence material to innocence was suppressed, noting that otherwise "prosecutors may be tempted to deliberately withhold exculpatory information as part of an attempt to elicit guilty pleas").

What is the test of materiality in a guilty plea context? The court in *Sanchez,* supra declared that suppressed evidence is material if "there is a reasonable probability that but for the failure to disclose the *Brady* material, the defendant would have refused to plead and would have gone to trial." How is a court to determine this question? Does it rely on the defendant's assertions? On the power of the suppressed evidence? On a comparison between the deal that the defendant received and the sentence that he would have faced if convicted? See Miller v. Angliker, 848 F.2d 1312 (2d Cir.1988) (test of materiality, in the guilty plea context, is an objective one that centers on "the likely persuasiveness of the withheld information").

For a discussion of the relationship between *Brady* material and guilty pleas, see Lain, Accuracy Where It Matters: Brady v. Maryland in the Plea Bargaining Context, 80 Wash.U. L.Q. 1 (2002) (noting that "*Brady's* importance in the plea bargaining context is clear in part just because so many cases are resolved there"); Douglass, Fatal Attraction? The Uneasy Courtship of *Brady* and Plea Bargaining, 50 Emory L.J.437 (2001) ("If we are serious about better-informed guilty pleas, then we should address the problem when it matters most: before the plea.").

Disclosure of Evidence Without Indicating What Is Exculpatory

In some cases—particularly those involving electronic discovery—the government produces millions of documents to the defendant, and hidden in the haystack are some materially exculpatory documents. Has the prosecution satisfied its *Brady* obligations by such a production? In United States v. Skilling, 554 F.3d 529 (5th Cir. 2009), a prosecution of a high-ranking Enron executive, the government turned over millions of documents, and the defendant argued that the government should have identified the *Brady* material within the mountain of data. But the court rejected the defendant's argument. It stated that "[a]s a general rule, the government is under no duty to direct a defendant to exculpatory evidence within a larger mass of disclosed evidence." The court found that there would be a *Brady* violation if the prosecution was engaging in a document dump in an attempt to hide the exculpatory evidence. But in this case, all the data was electronic and provided in a searchable format. Thus, "the government was in no better position to locate any potentially exculpatory evidence than was Skilling." See also United States v. Ohle, 2011 WL 651849 (S.D.N.Y.) (where the government turned over seven million pages of documents, there was no *Brady* violation because the documents were in searchable form and so "the defendants were just as likely to uncover the purportedly exculpatory evidence as was the government").

"Materially Exculpatory Evidence" or "All Favorable Evidence"?

Brady does *not* require prosecutors to turn over every piece of evidence that might be considered favorable to the defense. The duty is to turn over "materially exculpatory" evidence. But is it a problem that the determination of what is "materially exculpatory" is left to the prosecutor? Wouldn't even a fair-minded prosecutor have a tendency to downplay the importance of evidence favorable to the defendant? For example, in Muhammad v. Kelly, 575 F.3d 359 (4th Cir. 2009), the prosecution of one of two defendants who tormented the D.C. metropolitan area by shooting innocent people from their automobile and who were referred to as "snipers," the government suppressed a number of documents favorable to the defense, such as an FBI analyst's report that the sniper committing the shootings was likely acting alone (whereas Muhammad was charged with having an accomplice). The court found that the report, while favorable, was not materially exculpatory because the language in the report was tentative and "did not definitively conclude that the killings were the work of a single shooter." Other favorable evidence that was suppressed was also found "cumulative" of evidence the defendant presented at trial and therefore not materially exculpatory. The court noted, however, that

> we by no means condone the action of the Commonwealth in this case. As a matter of practice, the prosecution should err on the side of disclosure, especially when a defendant is facing the specter of execution. When questioned at oral argument regarding why this information was withheld or why the Commonwealth did not take the

step of instituting an open-file policy, the Commonwealth had no explanation. Yet, at this stage of the process, we deal only with actions that were clear violations of the Constitution. While not admirable, the Commonwealth's actions did not violate the Constitution.

Many lawyers, judges, and academics have argued for a rule requiring the prosecutor to disclose all information that a *defense counsel might consider favorable* to the defense. That is, the prosecutor reviewing the evidence in the file should put on the defense counsel's hat and, from that perspective, disclose all the information that the defense counsel would find helpful.

The push for a broader rule of disclosure—mandated by rule, beyond the constitutional minimum set by *Brady*—was spurred by revelations that prosecutors in the corruption trial of Senator Ted Stevens had suppressed evidence about the star witness in the case. Prosecutors apparently acknowledged that the evidence might have helped the defense in attacking the witness's credibility, but didn't think that the evidence was important enough to be "materially exculpatory" under *Brady.* The presiding judge was so frustrated by the prosecutors' conduct that he wrote a letter to the Judicial Conference Advisory Committee on Criminal Rules, asking the Committee to amend Rule 16 to require the government to produce all favorable information to the defense.

The Department of Justice is opposed to amending Criminal Rule 16 to require the production of all favorable evidence. Assistant Attorney General Lanny Breuer, speaking in opposition to any rule amendment, stated that, notwithstanding the Stevens case, improper suppression by the government is infrequent. He noted that an internal DOJ review uncovered only 15 cases of misconduct over a nine-year period. He argued that eliminating the materiality standard "seriously comes into conflict" with victim rights, witness security and, in some cases, national security. In response, Senator Stevens' defense counsel, Brendan Sullivan, said in a statement that the materiality limitation "allows prosecutors to play games with their constitutional duties" and that "criminal trials are supposed to be a search for the truth, and there is no justification whatsoever for concealing any exculpatory information from the defense."

One of the problems of verifying Breuer's assertion that suppression is infrequent is that he is referring only to the cases in which improper suppression was *discovered.* But the very nature of suppression is that it is hard to discover. As then-Chief Judge Wolf wrote:

> The reported cases are not, however, a true measure of the scope of the problem [of prosecutorial suppression], which it is impossible to measure precisely. The defense is, by definition, unaware of exculpatory information that has not been provided by the government. Although some information of this nature comes to light

> by chance from time to time, it is reasonable to assume in other similar cases such information has never come to light. There is, however, no way to determine how frequently this occurs.

United States v. Jones, 620 F.Supp.2d 163 (D.Mass.2009) (an appendix to Judge Wolf's opinion cites 70 reported Federal decisions reversing convictions for violations of *Brady*).

Ultimately the Advisory Committee chose not to propose an amendment to Rule 16 that would require the prosecutor to turn over all evidence favorable to the defendant. The Committee withdrew from the field after the Justice Department made amendments to the United States Attorney's Manual that required U.S. Attorneys to make broader disclosure of evidence favorable to the defendant. See Section 9–500, "Policy Regarding Disclosure of Exculpatory and Impeachment Information." Judge Wolf, in *Jones,* argues that an internal guideline will do little to solve the problem of suppression, because it is not enforceable by the defendant, and so the remedy, if any, is prosecutorial discipline rather than reversal of an unjust conviction.

Given the difficulties of applying *Brady* and the likelihood that suppression will never be discovered, wouldn't it make sense to require the government to simply turn over its case file to the defendant—subject to culling work product and any information that would raise a security risk? See Cary, Exculpatory Evidence: A Call for Reform After the Unlawful Prosecution of Senator Ted Stevens, 36 Litigation 34 (2010) ("Changing to an open file discovery process would lead to fairer trials and to more guilty pleas when meritorious charges are supported by credible evidence. Moreover, open file discovery should actually relieve prosecutors of the burden of sifting through information to determine whether or not it is exculpatory. Honest prosecutors would no longer required to make judgment calls regarding what defendants and their counsel might find helpful.").

Congressional Legislation on the Prosecutor's Brady Obligation

In October, 2020, Congress enacted bipartisan legislation that added an emphasis of the prosecutor's *Brady* obligation as part of the Federal Rules of Criminal Procedure. The legislation, PL No. 116-182, 134 Stat. Ann. 894, added the following new subdivision to Fed. R. Crim.P. 5:

> **(f) Reminder of Prosecutorial Obligation.**
>
> **(1)** ***In general.*** In all criminal proceedings, on the first scheduled court date when both prosecutor and defense counsel are present, the judge shall issue an oral and written order to prosecution and defense counsel that confirms the disclosure obligation of the prosecutor under

> Brady v. Maryland, 373 U.S. 83 (1963) and its progeny, and the possible consequences of violating such order under applicable law.
>
> **(2) *Formation of order.*** Each judicial council in which a district court is located shall promulgate a model order for the purpose of paragraph (1) that the court may use as it determines appropriate.

What effect do you think this provision will have? Arguably it will provide a disincentive for the prosecutor to violate *Brady* because that would mean violating a court order—which could result in a finding of contempt, or a disciplinary action. It also brings the *Brady* obligation front and center for the court and the parties.

Here is the model order issued by the United States District Court for the Eastern District of Virginia pursuant to the new legislation:

> The Court ORDERS the United States to adhere to the disclosure obligations set forth in Brady v. Maryland, 373 U.S. 83 (1963) and its progeny. Brady v. Maryland instructs that "the suppression by the prosecution of evidence favorable to the accused" violated due process where the evidence is "material either to guilt or to punishment, irrespective of the good faith or the bad faith of the prosecution." 373 U.S. at 87. Failure to adhere to this requirement may result in serious consequences, up to and including vacating a conviction or disciplinary action against the prosecutor.

C. PRESERVING AND SEEKING OUT EXCULPATORY EVIDENCE

Brady prohibits the government from *suppressing* materially exculpatory evidence. But is there a constitutional right to have such evidence *preserved*? And how do you know if it was materially exculpatory unless it is preserved in the first place?

Justice Marshall wrote for a unanimous Supreme Court in California v. Trombetta, 467 U.S. 479 (1984), declaring that law enforcement officers are not required by the Due Process Clause to preserve breath samples of suspected drunk drivers for potential use by defendants at trial. A device called an Intoxilyzer was used to test these samples. Suspects, including those challenging the police procedures in the instant case, breathed into the device and infrared light sensed their blood alcohol level. California officers purge the device after each test, thus destroying the breath samples. Although the state health department had approved a kit which officers could use to preserve breath samples, it was not standard practice for officers to use the kit.

In his opinion in *Trombetta,* Justice Marshall declared that "[w]hatever duty the Constitution imposes on the States to preserve evidence, that duty must be limited to evidence that might be expected to play a significant role in the suspect's defense." The Court found that the chances were extremely low that preserved samples would have assisted defendants. Justice Marshall observed that the state had developed procedures to protect against machine malfunctions, and that some alternative attacks were possible when a defendant raised one of the limited number of claims available to challenge the functioning of a testing machine.

Chief Justice Rehnquist wrote for the Court in Arizona v. Youngblood, 488 U.S. 51 (1988), as it expanded upon *Trombetta* and held that "unless a criminal defendant can show bad faith on the part of the police, failure to preserve potentially useful evidence does not constitute a denial of due process of law." Youngblood was convicted of sexually assaulting a young boy. Although investigative authorities attempted to analyze semen obtained from the victim's clothing, they did not refrigerate the clothing and because of this they were unable to conduct an analysis. The Supreme Court found that the failure to preserve the evidence for testing was, at worst, negligent. The Chief Justice noted that there was no evidence that the police had any reason to believe that the semen samples might have exonerated the accused when they handled the clothing at the outset of the investigation. Nor was there any indication of bad faith on the part of the police. Indeed, the evidence, had it not been destroyed, could have helped the police to find the perpetrator, who at that point was unknown.

Chief Justice Rehnquist recognized that the *Brady* cases made the good or bad faith of the police irrelevant when material exculpatory evidence is *suppressed*, but he concluded that "the Due Process Clause requires a different result when we deal with the failure of the State to preserve evidentiary material of which no more can be said than that it could have been subjected to tests, the results of which might have exonerated the defendant." With suppression, the evidence still exists, so the court and the parties can determine whether it is materially exculpatory; but such is not the case with evidence that has been destroyed. The Chief Justice reasoned "that requiring a defendant to show bad faith on the part of the police both limits the extent of the police obligation to preserve evidence to reasonable bounds and confines it to that class of cases where the interests of justice most clearly require it, i.e., those cases in which the police themselves by their conduct indicate that the evidence could form a basis for exonerating the defendant." The Court noted that if evidence is destroyed and tests are not conducted, the defendant is free to argue to the finder of fact that the test might have been exculpatory, "but the police do not have a constitutional duty to perform any particular tests."

Justice Blackmun, joined by Justices Brennan and Marshall, dissented. He suggested that the bad faith test was less than clear and might create more questions than it answers. Justice Blackmun stated his due process test as follows: "[W]here no comparable evidence is likely to be available to the defendant, police must preserve physical evidence of a type that they reasonably should know has the potential, if tested, to reveal immutable characteristics of the criminal, and hence to exculpate a defendant charged with the crime."

See also United States v. Williams, 577 F.3d 878 (8th Cir. 2009), a felon-firearm possession case, in which the firearm was destroyed by the government before trial. The court found no due process violation. The court noted that the defendant could be found guilty even if the firearm was inoperable, so the condition of the firearm could not provide exculpatory evidence.

Is There a Duty to Seek out Exculpatory Evidence?

The Court in *Youngblood* clearly implies that while the prosecution has a duty to *disclose* exculpatory evidence, it has no duty to seek out or to investigate information that would lead to exculpatory evidence. That is, the government has no obligation to act as an investigator for the defense. If the government fails to follow leads, or to seek an alternative explanation for the crime, then the defendant is free to suggest to the trier of fact that it draw an adverse inference at trial—but he has no Due Process right to demand a certain investigation. See Fisher, "Just the Facts, Ma'am": Lying and the Omission of Exculpatory Evidence in Police Reports, 28 New Eng.L.Rev.1 (1993), for a discussion of this and other problems of police investigations that fail to develop exculpatory evidence.

D. DOES THE GOVERNMENT'S *BRADY* OBLIGATION CONTINUE TO APPLY AFTER THE DEFENDANT HAS BEEN CONVICTED?

DNA testing has been used in many cases to exonerate wrongfully convicted defendants. In District Attorney's Office for the Third Judicial District v. Osborne, 557 U.S. 52 (2009), a convicted defendant argued that he had a constitutional right to DNA testing that he claimed would exonerate him. The state had in fact conducted a rudimentary form of DNA testing before the trial; that test tended to include Osborne as a possible perpetrator in a sex crime, but it was not definitive. Osborne's counsel decided not to ask for a more sophisticated test to be done, fearing that it would further incriminate Osborne. Osborne was convicted and several years later brought a civil rights action against the state, alleging that he had a due process right to an even more sophisticated DNA test than was available at the time of his trial.

The lower court, in granting Osborne's demand for DNA testing, had relied on *Brady*. It reasoned that if the defendant had a constitutional right to exculpatory evidence *before* trial, he also had the right after conviction.

Chief Justice Roberts, writing for a 5–4 majority, rejected this reasoning in the following passage:

> The Court of Appeals went too far * * * in concluding that the Due Process Clause requires that certain familiar preconviction trial rights be extended to protect Osborne's postconviction liberty interest. After identifying Osborne's possible liberty interests, the court concluded that the State had an obligation to comply with the principles of Brady v. Maryland. In that case, we held that due process requires a prosecutor to disclose material exculpatory evidence to the defendant before trial. * * *
>
> A defendant proved guilty after a fair trial does not have the same liberty interests as a free man. At trial, the defendant is presumed innocent and may demand that the government prove its case beyond reasonable doubt. But once a defendant has been afforded a fair trial and convicted of the offense for which he was charged, the presumption of innocence disappears. * * *
>
> The State accordingly has more flexibility in deciding what procedures are needed in the context of postconviction relief. * * * Osborne's right to due process is not parallel to a trial right, but rather must be analyzed in light of the fact that he has already been found guilty at a fair trial, and has only a limited interest in postconviction relief. *Brady* is the wrong framework.
>
> Instead, the question is whether consideration of Osborne's claim within the framework of the State's procedures for postconviction relief "offends some principle of justice so rooted in the traditions and conscience of our people as to be ranked as fundamental," or "transgresses any recognized principle of fundamental fairness in operation." Federal courts may upset a State's postconviction relief procedures only if they are fundamentally inadequate to vindicate the substantive rights provided.

Chief Justice Roberts reviewed the state post-conviction procedures and saw "nothing inadequate about the procedures Alaska has provided to vindicate its state right to postconviction relief in general, and nothing inadequate about how those procedures apply to those who seek access to DNA evidence." Accordingly, the Court denied Osborne federal relief.

Justice Alito filed a concurring opinion in which Justice Kennedy, joined, and in which Justice Thomas joined in part. He argued that it would be inappropriate to allow Osborne to forego testing at trial and then to request a different test many years later. In Justice Alito's view, this would "allow prisoners to play games with the criminal justice system" because "with nothing to lose, the defendant could demand DNA testing in the hope that some happy accident—for example, degradation or contamination of the evidence—would provide the basis for postconviction relief."

Justice Stevens filed a dissenting opinion, joined by Justices Ginsburg and Breyer and by Justice Souter in part. Justice Stevens noted that no prisoner had ever obtained DNA evidence for testing in Alaska and that he had "grave doubts about the adequacy of the procedural protections" in state law. He noted that DNA testing in this case would cost the state nothing because Osborne had offered to pay for it. Justice Souter also filed a dissenting opinion, concluding that state officials had "demonstrated a combination of inattentiveness and intransigence that add up to procedural unfairness that violates the due process clause."

Ethical Responsibilities of Prosecutors

Wholly aside from constitutional obligations to permit DNA testing or to recognize *Brady* obligations post-conviction, prosecutors may have ethical obligations when they become aware that a defendant may have been wrongly convicted. For example, in 2008, the American Bar Association added Rules 3.8 (g) and (h) to its Model Rules of Professional Conduct.

Rule 3.8 Special Responsibilities of a Prosecutor

(g) When a prosecutor knows of new, credible and material evidence creating a reasonable likelihood that a convicted defendant did not commit an offense of which the defendant was convicted, the prosecutor shall:

(1) promptly disclose that evidence to an appropriate court or authority, and

(2) if the conviction was obtained in the prosecutor's jurisdiction,

(i) promptly disclose that evidence to the defendant unless a court authorizes delay, and

(ii) undertake further investigation, or make reasonable efforts to cause an investigation, to determine whether the defendant was convicted of an offense that the defendant did not commit.

(h) When a prosecutor knows of clear and convincing evidence establishing that a defendant in the prosecutor's jurisdiction was convicted of an offense that the defendant did not commit, the prosecutor shall seek to remedy the conviction.

V. DISCOVERY BY THE PROSECUTION

A. CONSTITUTIONAL IMPLICATIONS

Any attempt to force defendants to comply with government discovery requests runs into Fifth Amendment and due process concerns. The next case disposes of some of these.

WILLIAMS V. FLORIDA

Supreme Court of the United States, 1970.
399 U.S. 78.

JUSTICE WHITE delivered the opinion of the Court.

Prior to his trial for robbery in the State of Florida, petitioner filed a "Motion for a Protective Order," seeking to be excused from [a rule that] required a defendant, on written demand of the prosecuting attorney, to give notice in advance of trial if the defendant intends to claim an alibi, and to furnish the prosecuting attorney with information as to the place where he claims to have been and with the names and addresses of the alibi witnesses he intends to use. In his motion petitioner openly declared his intent to claim an alibi, but objected to the further disclosure requirements on the ground that the rule "compels the Defendant in a criminal case to be a witness against himself" in violation of his Fifth and Fourteenth Amendment rights. The motion was denied. * * * [The other aspect of the case involved a challenge to the six man jury provided by Florida. It also was unsuccessful. The jury issue is discussed in Chapter 10]. Petitioner was convicted as charged and was sentenced to life imprisonment. * * *

Florida's notice-of-alibi rule is in essence a requirement that a defendant submit to a limited form of pretrial discovery by the State whenever he intends to rely at trial on the defense of alibi. In exchange for the defendant's disclosure of the witnesses he proposes to use to establish that defense, the State in turn is required to notify the defendant of any witnesses it proposes to offer in rebuttal to that defense. * * * The threatened sanction for failure to comply is the exclusion at trial of the defendant's alibi evidence—except for his own testimony—or, in the case of the State, the exclusion of the State's evidence offered in rebuttal of the alibi.

In this case, following the denial of his Motion for a Protective Order, petitioner complied with the alibi rule and gave the State the name and address of one Mary Scotty. [The prosecution contacted Scotty and at trial, when she testified as an alibi witness, she was impeached with inconsistent statements she made to government investigators.]

We need not linger over the suggestion that the discovery permitted the State against petitioner in this case deprived him of "due process" or a "fair trial." Florida law provides for liberal discovery by the defendant against the State, and the notice-of-alibi rule is itself carefully hedged with reciprocal duties requiring state disclosure to the defendant. Given the ease with which an alibi can be fabricated, the State's interest in protecting itself against an eleventh-hour defense is both obvious and legitimate. * * * The adversary system of trial is hardly an end in itself; it is not yet a poker game in which players enjoy an absolute right always to conceal their cards until played. We find ample room in that system, at least as far as "due process" is concerned, for the instant Florida rule, which is designed to enhance the search for truth in the criminal trial by insuring both the defendant and the State ample opportunity to investigate certain facts crucial to the determination of guilt or innocence.

Petitioner's major contention is that he was "compelled * * * to be a witness against himself" contrary to the commands of the Fifth and Fourteenth Amendments because the notice-of-alibi rule required him to give the State the name and address of Mrs. Scotty in advance of trial and thus to furnish the State with information useful in convicting him. * * * Also, requiring him to reveal the elements of his defense is claimed to have interfered with his right to wait until after the State had presented its case to decide how to defend against it. We conclude, however, as has apparently every other court that has considered the issue, that the privilege against self-incrimination is not violated by a requirement that the defendant give notice of an alibi defense and disclose his alibi witnesses.

The defendant in a criminal trial is frequently forced to testify himself and to call other witnesses in an effort to reduce the risk of conviction. When he presents his witnesses, he must reveal their identity and submit them to cross-examination which in itself may prove incriminating or which may furnish the State with leads to incriminating rebuttal evidence. That the defendant faces such a dilemma demanding a choice between complete silence and presenting a defense has never been thought an invasion of the privilege against compelled self-incrimination. The pressures generated by the State's evidence may be severe but they do not vitiate the defendant's choice to present an alibi defense and witnesses to prove it, even though the attempted defense ends in catastrophe for the defendant. However, "testimonial" or "incriminating" the alibi defense proves to be, it cannot be considered "compelled" within the meaning of the Fifth and Fourteenth Amendments.

* * * We decline to hold that the privilege against compulsory self-incrimination guarantees the defendant the right to surprise the State with an alibi defense.

* * *

[JUSTICE BLACKMUN did not participate in the case. THE CHIEF JUSTICE filed a short concurring opinion on the alibi point. JUSTICE MARSHALL dissented on the jury issue, but concurred in the alibi ruling.]

JUSTICE BLACK, with whom JUSTICE DOUGLAS joins, concurring in part and dissenting in part.

* * *

On the surface this case involves only a notice-of-alibi provision, but in effect the decision opens the way for a profound change in one of the most important traditional safeguards of a criminal defendant. The rationale of today's decision is in no way limited to alibi defenses, or any other type or classification of evidence. The theory advanced goes at least so far as to permit the State to obtain under threat of sanction complete disclosure by the defendant in advance of trial of all evidence, testimony, and tactics he plans to use at that trial. In each case the justification will be that the rule affects only the "timing" of the disclosure, and not the substantive decision itself. * * *

Reciprocality Requirement

In Wardius v. Oregon, 412 U.S. 470 (1973), the Court struck down a notice of alibi provision that was not reciprocal—i.e., that did not require the prosecution to disclose in advance its rebuttal evidence. The Court suggested "that if there is to be any unbalance in discovery rights, it should work in the defendant's favor."

Other Notice Requirements

Besides a notice of alibi defense, the Federal Rules of Criminal Procedure also require the defendant to give advance notice of an insanity defense (Rule 12.2) and a notice of intent to assert "a defense of actual or believed exercise of public authority on behalf of a law enforcement agency or federal intelligence agency at the time of the alleged offense" (Rule 12.3). Failure to follow the notice requirements, without good cause, results in preclusion of witnesses who would testify to these defenses.

B. GENERAL DISCOVERY

The general federal discovery rule covering the defense is Rule 16(b), which provides for discovery of:

(A) documents and tangible objects within the control of the defendant and which the defendant intends to use in his case-in-chief;

(B) reports of examinations and tests within the control of the defendant and which the defendant either intends to use in his case-in-chief or which were prepared by a witness whom the defendant intends to call at trial; and

(C) a written statement of an expert that the defendant intends to call at trial, describing the opinions, bases, and qualifications of the expert. Protections are provided for privileged materials and work product. See Rule 16(b)(2).

The Federal Rule conditions government discovery of any of the above materials on a *prior request by the defendant* for discovery of similar information from the government and government compliance with that request.[10] By conditioning the government's right to discovery on a defense request, the Federal Rule is probably intended to avoid constitutional problems—essentially, asking the government for discovery is treated as a waiver of any constitutional right to protect one's own, related information.

The Federal Rule does not require disclosure of information that the defendant expects to use to impeach government witnesses (e.g., records of prior inconsistent statements). Disclosure encompasses only information within the categories above that is going to be used in the "case-in-chief." See United States v. Medearis, 380 F.3d 1049 (8th Cir. 2004) (defendant cannot be sanctioned for failing to disclose a letter that was admissible to impeach a government witness: "the requirement of reciprocal pre-trial disclosure under Rule 16(b)(1)(A) includes only documents which the defendant intends to introduce during his own case-in-chief.").

Justice Black in *Williams* was plainly correct in foreseeing that notice requirements would not be limited to alibi defenses. Mosteller, Discovery Against the Defense: Tilting the Adversarial Balance, 74 Cal.L.Rev. 1567 (1986), describes a discovery "revolution" in the states. Mosteller found that in addition to prosecutorial discovery with respect to alibi and insanity, which is available in the great majority of states, 25 states grant the prosecution an independent (non-reciprocal) right to discover at least one of the following: "defenses, witness names, statements of witnesses, reports of experts, or documents and tangible evidence." A number of states require broad defense disclosure upon a request for discovery from the prosecution. Twelve states give the prosecution an independent right to obtain the statements of all defense witnesses, and three more permit this discovery when the defendant seeks discovery from the government. Some states require a defendant to summarize the expected testimony of defense witnesses and to create a statement summarizing oral statements of witnesses. Other states require the defense to furnish the government with statements taken from government witnesses.

---

[10] The expert provision also comes into play if the defendant has given notice under Rule 12.2(b) of an intent to present expert testimony on the defendant's mental condition.

C. Sanctions for Nondisclosure

In Taylor v. Illinois, 484 U.S. 400 (1988) and Michigan v. Lucas, 500 U.S. 145 (1991), the Court considered whether it is constitutional for a trial court to preclude evidence proffered by criminal defendants who violate legitimate discovery obligations. In *Taylor,* defense counsel wilfully violated a state procedural rule by failing to identify a particular defense witness in response to a pretrial discovery request. The trial court sanctioned this violation by refusing to allow the undisclosed witness to testify. The Court rejected the argument that preclusion is never a permissible sanction for a discovery violation. The Court did not find it problematic to, in effect, sanction the defendant for his counsel's discovery violation; it reasoned that in most cases it would be quite difficult to determine whether the defense counsel or the defendant (or both) was responsible for the violation. Moreover, the Court did not consider it novel that a client would suffer due to the misstep of his counsel. Therefore, the trial court had discretion to determine whether to sanction defense counsel directly, or to use the sanction of preclusion. Justice Stevens wrote the majority opinion for six members of the Court. Justice Brennan, joined by Justices Marshall and Blackmun, dissented.

In *Lucas,* the defendant in a rape case proffered a defense of consent based in part upon the defendant's prior sexual relationship with the victim. The Michigan rape shield statute required that the defense give notice to the prosecution, within 10 days of the arraignment, of the intent to present evidence of past sexual conduct with the victim. The defendant did not comply with that notice requirement. As a discovery sanction, the trial court precluded any evidence of the sexual relationship at trial; but the State Supreme Court held that such preclusion violated the defendant's constitutional right to an effective defense. Justice O'Connor, writing for a majority of six justices, treated the case as presenting a limited question: whether the State Supreme Court had erred in adopting a per se rule that preclusion of evidence of a rape victim's prior sexual relationship with a criminal defendant violates the Constitution. The majority held that such a *per se* rule of unconstitutionality was inappropriate, because the notice requirement could serve a legitimate state purpose in some cases, and a defendant's violation of the notice requirement could be so egregious as to warrant the sanction of preclusion. The Court did not decide whether the Michigan notice period (the shortest in the nation, requiring notice to be given well before trial) was in fact "arbitrary or disproportionate" in light of the State's interests.

Justice O'Connor left room for a defendant to argue that a minimal violation of a notice requirement should result in some remedy short of preclusion of the evidence, e.g., a continuance, and implied that a rigid rule of preclusion might be unconstitutional in some circumstances. The Court remanded to determine whether preclusion was appropriate under the circumstances of the case. Justice Blackmun concurred in the judgment. Justice Stevens, joined by Justice Marshall, dissented, contending that the State Supreme Court had not in fact gone so far "as to adopt the per se straw man that the Court has decided to knock down today." In their view, the State Court had simply held that preclusion was unjustified under the circumstances.

Taylor and *Lucas* do not hold that exclusion of evidence is permitted every time the defense violates a discovery obligation. Those cases do hold that the Constitution does not absolutely prohibit the sanction of exclusion of defense-proffered evidence in all cases.

C. WORK PRODUCT PROTECTION

In the following case, the Court considers the possible need for discovery at trial to assist in the examination of witnesses. And it also addresses the basis for and scope of the work product immunity as it applies to criminal cases.

UNITED STATES V. NOBLES

Supreme Court of the United States, 1975.
422 U.S. 225.

JUSTICE POWELL delivered the opinion of the Court.

In a criminal trial, defense counsel sought to impeach the credibility of key prosecution witnesses by testimony of a defense investigator regarding statements previously obtained from the witnesses by the investigator. The question presented here is whether in these circumstances a federal trial court may compel the defense to reveal the relevant portions of the investigator's report for the prosecution's use in cross-examining him. The United States Court of Appeals for the Ninth Circuit concluded that it cannot. We granted certiorari, and now reverse.

* * *

Respondent was tried and convicted on charges arising from an armed robbery of a federally insured bank. The only significant evidence linking him to the crime was the identification testimony of two witnesses, a bank teller and a salesman who was in the bank during the robbery. Respondent offered an alibi but, as the Court of Appeals recognized, his strongest defense centered around attempts to discredit these eyewitnesses. Defense efforts to impeach them gave rise to the events that led to this decision.

In the course of preparing respondent's defense, an investigator for the defense interviewed both witnesses and preserved the essence of those conversations in a written report. When the witnesses testified for the prosecution, respondent's counsel relied on the report in conducting their cross-examination. Counsel asked the bank teller whether he recalled having told the investigator that he had seen only the back of the man he identified as respondent. The witness replied that he did not remember making such a statement. He was allowed, despite defense counsel's initial objection, to refresh his recollection by referring to a portion of the investigator's report. The prosecutor also was allowed to see briefly the relevant portion of the report. The witness thereafter testified that although the report indicated that he told the investigator he had seen only respondent's back, he in fact had seen more than that and continued to insist that respondent was the bank robber.

The other witness acknowledged on cross-examination that he too had spoken to the defense investigator. Respondent's counsel twice inquired whether he told the investigator that "all blacks looked alike" to him, and in each instance the witness denied having made such a statement. The prosecution again sought inspection of the relevant portion of the investigator's report, and respondent's counsel again objected. The court declined to order disclosure at that time, but ruled that it would be required if the investigator testified as to the witnesses' alleged statements from the witness stand. * * *

After the prosecution completed its case, respondent called the investigator as a defense witness. The court [ruled] that a copy of the report, inspected and edited *in camera,* would have to be submitted to Government counsel at the completion of the investigator's impeachment testimony. When respondent's counsel stated that he did not intend to produce the report, the court ruled that the investigator would not be allowed to testify about his interviews with the witnesses. [The court of appeals found reversible error in excluding the investigator's testimony.]

* * *

* * * Decisions of this Court repeatedly have recognized the federal judiciary's inherent power to require the prosecution to produce the previously recorded statements of its witnesses so that the defense may get the full benefit of cross-examination and the truth-finding process may be enhanced. Jencks v. United States. At issue here is whether, in a proper case, the prosecution can call upon that same power for production of witness statements that facilitate "full disclosure of all the [relevant] facts."

In this case, the defense proposed to call its investigator to impeach the identification testimony of the prosecution's eyewitnesses. * * * The investigator's contemporaneous report might provide critical insight into the issues of credibility that the investigator's testimony would raise. It could assist the jury in determining the extent to which the investigator's testimony actually discredited the prosecution's witnesses. * * *

It was therefore apparent to the trial judge that the investigator's report was highly relevant to the critical issue of credibility. * * * We must determine whether compelling its production was precluded by some privilege available to the defense in the circumstances of this case.

* * *

The Court of Appeals concluded that the Fifth Amendment renders criminal discovery "basically a one-way street." Like many generalizations in constitutional law, this one is too broad. The relationship between the accused's Fifth Amendment rights and the prosecution's ability to discover materials at trial must be identified in a more discriminating manner.

* * *

In this instance disclosure of the relevant portions of the defense investigator's report would not impinge on the fundamental values protected by the Fifth Amendment. The court's order was limited to statements allegedly made by third parties who were available as witnesses to both the prosecution and the defense. Respondent did not prepare the report, and there is no suggestion that the portions subject to the disclosure order reflected any information that he conveyed to the investigator. The fact that these statements of third parties were elicited by a defense investigator on respondent's behalf does not convert them into respondent's personal communications. Requiring their production from the investigator therefore would not in any sense compel respondent to be a witness against himself or extort communications from him.

* * *

The Court of Appeals also held that Fed.Rule Crim.Proc. 16 deprived the trial court of the power to order disclosure of the relevant portions of the investigator's report. * * *

Both the language and history of Rule 16 indicate that it addresses only pretrial discovery. * * *

* * * We conclude, therefore, that Rule 16 imposes no constraint on the District Court's power to condition the impeachment testimony of respondent's witness on the production of the relevant portions of his investigative report. * * *

Respondent contends further that the work-product doctrine exempts the investigator's report from disclosure at trial. While we agree that this doctrine applies to criminal litigation as well as civil, we find its protection unavailable in this case.

The work-product doctrine, recognized by this court in Hickman v. Taylor, 329 U.S. 495 (1947), reflects the strong "public policy underlying the orderly prosecution and defense of legal claims." * * * The Court therefore recognized a qualified privilege for certain materials prepared by an attorney "acting for his client in anticipation of litigation."

Although the work-product doctrine most frequently is asserted as a bar to discovery in civil litigation, its role in assuring the proper functioning of the criminal justice system is even more vital. The interests of society and the accused in obtaining a fair and accurate resolution of the question of guilt or innocence demand that adequate safeguards assure the thorough preparation and presentation of each side of the case.

At its core, the work-product doctrine shelters the mental processes of the attorney, providing a privileged area within which he can analyze and prepare his client's case. But the doctrine is an intensely practical one, grounded in the realities of litigation in our adversary system. One of those realities is that attorneys often must rely on the assistance of investigators and other agents in the compilation of materials in preparation for trial. It is therefore necessary that the doctrine protect material prepared by agents for the attorney as well as those prepared by the attorney himself. Moreover, the concerns reflected in the work-product doctrine do not disappear once trial has begun. Disclosure of an attorney's efforts at trial, as surely as disclosure during pretrial discovery, could disrupt the orderly development and presentation of his case. We need not, however, undertake here to delineate the scope of the doctrine at trial, for in this instance it is clear that the defense waived such right as may have existed to invoke its protections.

The privilege derived from the work-product doctrine is not absolute. Like other qualified privileges, it may be waived. Here respondent sought to adduce the testimony of the investigator and contrast his recollection of the contested statements with that of the prosecution's witnesses. Respondent, by electing to present the investigator as a witness, waived the privilege with respect to matters covered in his testimony.[a] Respondent can no more advance the work-product doctrine to sustain a unilateral testimonial use of work-product materials than he could elect to testify in his own behalf and thereafter assert his Fifth Amendment privilege to resist cross-examination on matters reasonably related to those brought out in direct examination.

* * *

Finally, our examination of the record persuades us that the District Court properly exercised its discretion in this instance. The court authorized no general "fishing expedition" into the defense files or indeed even into the defense investigator's report. Rather, its considered ruling was quite limited in scope, opening to prosecution scrutiny only the portion

[a] What constitutes a waiver with respect to work-product materials depends, of course, upon the circumstances. Counsel necessarily makes use throughout trial of the notes, documents, and other internal materials prepared to present adequately his client's case, and often relies on them in examining witnesses. When so used, there normally is no waiver. But where, as here, counsel attempts to make a testimonial use of these materials the normal rules of evidence come into play with respect to cross-examination and production of documents.

of the report that related to the testimony the investigator would offer to discredit the witnesses' identification testimony. * * *

The court's preclusion sanction was an entirely proper method of assuring compliance with its order. Respondent's argument that this ruling deprived him of the Sixth Amendment rights to compulsory process and cross-examination misconceives the issue. The District Court did not bar the investigator's testimony. It merely prevented respondent from presenting to the jury a partial view of the credibility issue by adducing the investigator's testimony and thereafter refusing to disclose the contemporaneous report that might offer further critical insights. * * *

JUSTICE DOUGLAS took no part in the consideration or decision of this case.

[JUSTICE WHITE's concurring opinion, which was joined by JUSTICE REHNQUIST, is omitted.]

NOTE ON NOBLES AND THE CRIMINAL RULES

The result in *Nobles* is formalized in Fed. R. Crim. P. 26.2, which provides in relevant part as follows:

> (a) MOTION TO PRODUCE. After a witness other than the defendant has testified on direct examination, the court, on motion of a party who did not call the witness, must order an attorney for the government or the defendant and the defendant's attorney to produce, for the examination and use of the moving party, any statement of the witness that is in their possession and that relates to the subject matter of the witness's testimony.

The Rule permits a trial court to inspect a statement to determine the parts that relate to the subject matter of the witness's testimony, to recess the proceedings to enable the party who receives a statement to examine it, and to strike testimony as a sanction for disobeying an order to produce. The Rule applies not only at trial, but also at a suppression hearing, a preliminary hearing, sentencing, a probation revocation proceeding, a pretrial detention proceeding, and in evidentiary hearings in collateral attack proceedings instituted by federal defendants.

CHAPTER 9

GUILTY PLEAS AND BARGAINING

■ ■ ■

I. THE GENERAL ISSUES

Once the determination to press charges is made and a case survives pre-trial motions or preliminary screening, the government becomes committed to the idea that the accused should be punished. The accused, even if innocent, must be concerned with how the case will ultimately be resolved. Questions like "Will I be convicted?" and "What kind of sentence will be imposed on me if I am convicted?" become increasingly important. Uncertainty about how these and other questions would be answered by going to trial often leads an accused to respond favorably to—or to initiate—"settlement" or "plea bargaining" discussions with the government. By agreeing to plead guilty the accused accepts punishment for some criminal activity. In exchange for this acceptance, the system—i.e., the prosecutor and the court—permits the accused to avoid some of the uncertainty endemic in any litigation system in which human beings must decide crucial questions of fact and law and often can exercise broad discretion in implementing social policy.

The extent to which negotiations actually take place, the nature of most agreements reached, the legitimacy of a bargained-for outcomes in criminal cases and the role of the various participants—i.e., the prosecutor, the trial judge, the defense counsel, the defendant, the victim, etc.—are all subjects that have been the subject of intense debate.

A. OVERVIEW OF THE PLEA BARGAINING SYSTEM

Although it is not possible in one chapter to capture all of the nuances of the debate, at least the surface of some of the principal issues can be scratched. This includes an overview of the system of plea bargaining, and some commentary from supporters and critics.

Prevalence (and Inevitability?) of Plea Bargaining

Almost all defendants charged with crime in the Federal and state systems end up pleading guilty rather than going to trial. See O'Hear, Plea Bargaining and Procedural Justice, 42 Ga. L. Rev. 409 (2008) ("Plea bargaining now dominates the day-to-day operation of the American criminal justice system; about ninety-five percent of convictions are obtained by way of a guilty plea. Indeed, despite the strenuous objections of prominent academic commentators, plea bargaining seems to be growing only more entrenched over time."). Justice Kennedy made this point for the Court in Lafler v. Cooper, 566 U.S. 166 (2012): "criminal justice today is for the most part a system of pleas, not a system of trials." Plea bargaining rates in many jurisdictions remain remarkably consistent. For example, the United States Sentencing Commission reports that 94.6% of Federal defendants pled guilty in 1999, and during the next decade the rate reached a high of 97.1 in 2002 and generally fell within the 94–97% range. From 2008 thru 2012, the cases disposed of by trial decreased each year to a low in 2012 of 3%. From 2012 thru 2016 the cases disposed of by trial declined each year to a low of 2.7% in 2016.

Plea bargaining is regulated only loosely by legal standards—it is essentially a marketplace for defendants and prosecutors, with sentencing parameters set by sentencing guidelines, statutory minimum sentences, and charging decisions, and governed by basic principles of contract. See Bibas, Regulating the Plea-Bargaining Market: From Caveat Emptor to Consumer Protection, 99 Cal. L.Rev. 1117 (2011) (noting that the Supreme Court has spent almost all its effort on regulating trials, while taking a laissez-faire attitude toward plea bargaining, resulting in "a free market that sometimes resemble[s] a Turkish bazaar.") Much of this Chapter considers whether this is any way to run a criminal justice system.

Professor Joseph Colquitt provides this overview of the plea bargaining process in Ad Hoc Plea Bargaining, 75 Tulane L.Rev. 695 (2001) (footnotes omitted):

> Plea bargaining typically is defined as an explicit or implicit exchange of concessions by the parties. Usually, the accused agrees to plead guilty and the government agrees to some form of reduction in charges or sentence. However, not all successful plea bargaining ends in a guilty plea. Some negotiations end in dismissal of the charges, perhaps after a deferral. Several types of negotiated settlements exist. First, the prosecution may agree to recommend to the court that one or more charges be dismissed in return for a plea of guilty by the defendant to another charge or other charges. The charges to which the defendant may agree to plead might include lesser offenses rather than the original charges. This approach is known as *charge bargaining*.
>
> Alternatively, the prosecution might agree simply to recommend a particular sentence in return for the plea. This approach frequently is called *sentence bargaining*. Sometimes the agreement includes both a reduction in the charge or a dismissal of other charges and a recommendation on the sentence. In all of these cases, in return for the prosecution's recommendation, the defendant waives the privilege

against self-incrimination and the right to a trial, including the attendant rights to confront accusers, to present witnesses on the question of guilt or innocence, and to testify in his or her own behalf.

* * *

[S]ome of plea bargaining's most resolute defenders believe that the court system needs plea bargaining in order to avoid a disastrous failure of the system as a result of the overwhelming number of cases that courts otherwise would have to try. * * * Moreover, bargaining reduces the time lag between the offense and the punishment, which potentially benefits not only the State, but also defendants, particularly those incarcerated. Reducing the time between crime and punishment also potentially enhances the deterrent effect of both conviction and punishment.

In addition to faster and more efficient case disposition, plea bargaining reduces costs, uncertainty, and risks. It allows courts and prosecutors to direct their resources more effectively, mitigates potentially severe punishment, provides flexibility, and, in the view of some, delivers justice. In sum, plea bargaining exists to a large extent because its supporters believe that the alternative, the criminal trial, is much more costly and time-consuming and no more likely to provide a just result.

Despite its widespread use and asserted benefits, the scheme is frequently criticized. * * * One of the principal arguments against plea bargaining is that those who plea bargain their cases are likely to be punished less severely than are those who insist on their constitutional right to trial. Some argue that the process abdicates control to the parties, relies too heavily on the prosecutor, or favors defense attorneys who carry favor with the prosecutor. Others fear that plea bargaining results in the conviction and punishment of innocent defendants at times. Some critics dislike the private, sometimes secret nature of the bargaining process or believe that the process causes the public to lose confidence in the criminal justice system.

* * *

In sum, many practitioners and scholars view plea bargaining as inevitable. Plea negotiation is simply too important and too ingrained in our criminal justice system to abandon it without identifying and providing a suitable replacement. That replacement has not been forthcoming, and it probably is the absence of a suitable replacement, rather than enthusiasm for plea bargaining, that supports its retention.

* * *

From time to time, the United States Department of Justice has also attempted to regulate or limit plea bargaining, but with very little success. For example, in September, 2003, Attorney General Ashcroft issued a memorandum to Federal prosecutors instructing them not to charge defendants with an eye toward plea bargaining. With few exceptions, prosecutors were instructed to pursue the toughest sentences possible under the Federal Sentencing Guidelines. The memo stated that prosecutors "must charge and pursue the most serious, readily provable offenses that are supported by the facts." The purpose of the policy was to assure consistency in charging decisions across the country. The exceptions to the "highest charge" policy were limited to: 1) cases in which problems with witnesses lead to a "post-indictment reassessment"; 2) cases in which the defendant decides to provide "substantial assistance" in prosecution of other criminals; and 3) "other exceptional circumstances" where a single case might place an extraordinary burden on a local U.S. attorney's office or reduce "the total number of cases disposed of by the office."

Professor George Fisher, in an op-ed piece in the New York Times, argued that Attorney General Ashcroft's new policy was doomed to fail. Fisher, A Practice as Old as Justice Itself, N.Y. Times, Sept. 28, 2003, at WK 11. He contended that plea bargaining reaches just results and that any attempt to regulate the practice simply drives it "underground." He elaborated as follows:

> * * * [P]lea bargaining will survive Mr. Ashcroft. Most prosecutors like plea bargaining; a sound bargain means an easy victory and more time to prosecute the next serious case.
>
> * * *
>
> Today the entire criminal justice system depends for its survival on plea bargaining. Last year 95 percent of criminal cases adjudicated in Federal courts ended with pleas of guilty or no contest. To try even one-quarter of all cases would mean five times as many trials, with a comparable increase in public expense. One wonders if Mr. Ashcroft wishes to preside over such an expansion.
>
> It's hardly likely. His new policy claiming to clamp down on plea bargaining leaves lots of bargaining room [given the built-in exceptions.] * * *
>
> And even if Mr. Ashcroft actually tries to limit plea bargaining, many judges will conspire with prosecutors to evade the rules. Judges know that the hundreds of new appointees needed to preside over an avalanche of new trials won't take the bench for years, if ever. * * * Defense lawyers will also help elude the policy. Private counsel often demand full payment up front and enjoy a rich payday when a case

ends in an effortless plea bargain. Public defenders have limited resources and know they cannot try all or most cases.

Cooperating Witnesses

As will be seen in this Chapter, a major reason that plea bargaining is here to stay is that prosecutors find it necessary to enter into cooperation agreements with criminals in order to get the testimony necessary to convict *other* criminals. Without plea bargaining—specifically the "carrots" of reduced charges and a further reduction in sentence for "substantial cooperation"—there would be little reason for criminal associates to "flip" and become a prosecution witness. Without turncoat witnesses, many prosecutions of major criminals would become virtually impossible.

Sentencing Differential Between Guilty Plea and Trial

It has been alleged that judges induce guilty pleas by imposing more severe sentences when a defendant chooses a trial rather than pleading guilty. Some studies suggest that differential sentencing exists at both the misdemeanor and felony levels.

There is disagreement as to the propriety of differential sentencing. Proponents believe leniency is proper for those who accept responsibility for their conduct by pleading guilty and contribute to the efficient and economical administration of the law. They assert that those submitting themselves to prompt correctional measures should be granted sentence concessions, and that differential sentences for those demanding trial is not undue punishment unless it is excessive. Those opposed believe that guilty pleas have no direct relevance to the appropriate disposition of an offender and that the constitutional right to trial should not be the cause of enhanced punishment.

Pleas by Innocent Defendants

Ronald F. Wright, in Trial Distortion and the End of Innocence in Federal Criminal Justice, 154 U. Pa. L. Rev 79 (2005), analyzes the relationship between acquittals and guilty plea rates in Federal criminal cases, and concludes that defendants who might have been acquitted at trial may nonetheless plead guilty because of a combination of stiff sentences imposed upon defendants who choose trial and the substantial discounts offered to defendants where the government's case is weak.

Supreme Court Support for Plea Bargaining: Brady v. United States

The leading case in the Supreme Court on plea bargaining is Brady v. United States, 397 U.S. 742 (1970). In *Brady,* the Court rejected the defendant's argument that a guilty plea is invalid "whenever motivated by the defendant's desire to accept the certainty or probability of a lesser penalty rather than face a wider range of possibilities extending from acquittal to conviction and a higher penalty authorized by law for the crime charged." The Court provided support for the system of plea bargaining as one based on "mutuality of advantage" and elaborated as follows:

> The issue we deal with is inherent in the criminal law and its administration because guilty pleas are not constitutionally forbidden, because the criminal law characteristically extends to judge or jury a range of choice in setting the sentence in individual cases, and because both the State and the defendant often find it advantageous to preclude the possibility of the maximum penalty authorized by law. For a defendant who sees slight possibility of acquittal, the advantages of pleading guilty and limiting the probable penalty are obvious—his exposure is reduced, the correctional processes can begin immediately, and the practical burdens of a trial are eliminated. For the State there are also advantages—the more promptly imposed punishment after an admission of guilt may more effectively attain the objectives of punishment; and with the avoidance of trial, scarce judicial and prosecutorial resources are conserved for those cases in which there is a substantial issue of the defendant's guilt or in which there is substantial doubt that the State can sustain its burden of proof.

B. ARGUMENTS IN FAVOR OF PLEA BARGAINING

Judge Easterbrook, in Plea Bargaining as Compromise, 101 Yale L.J. 1969 (1992), sets forth the following defense of plea bargaining, even though he recognizes that the system of plea bargaining is not as efficient as it might be:

> On the economic side, plea bargains do not represent Pareto improvements. Instead of engaging in trades that make at least one person better off and no one worse off, the parties dicker about how much worse off one side will be. In markets persons can borrow to take advantage of good deals or withdraw from the market, wait for a better offer, and lend their assets for a price in the interim. By contrast, both sides to a plea bargain operate under strict budget constraints, and they cannot bide their time. They bargain as bilateral monopolists (defendants can't shop in competitive markets for prosecutors) in the shadow of legal rules that work suspiciously like price controls. Judges, who do not join the bargaining, set the prices, increasingly by

reference to a table of punishments that looks like something the Office of Price Administration would have promulgated. Plea bargaining is to the sentencing guidelines as black markets are to price controls.

Black markets are better than no markets. Plea bargains are preferable to mandatory litigation—not because the analogy to contract is overpowering, but because compromise is better than conflict. * * * Defendants have many procedural and substantive rights. By pleading guilty, they sell these rights to the prosecutor, receiving concessions they esteem more highly than the rights surrendered. Rights that may be sold are more valuable than rights that must be consumed, just as money (which may be used to buy housing, clothing, or food) is more valuable to a poor person than an opportunity to live in public housing.

Defendants can use or exchange their rights, whichever makes them better off. So plea bargaining helps defendants. Forcing them to use their rights at trial means compelling them to take the risk of conviction or acquittal; risk-averse persons prefer a certain but small punishment to a chancy but large one. Defendants also get the process over sooner, and solvent ones save the expense of trial. Compromise also benefits prosecutors and society at large. In purchasing procedural entitlements with lower sentences, prosecutors buy that most valuable commodity, Time. With time they can prosecute more criminals.

* * *

Plea bargains are compromises. Autonomy and efficiency support them. "Imperfections" in bargaining reflect the imperfections of an anticipated trial. To improve plea bargaining, improve the process for deciding cases on the merits. When we deem that process adequate, there will be no reason to prevent the person most affected by the criminal process from improving his situation through compromise.

C. CRITIQUE OF PLEA BARGAINING

Professor Schulhofer, in Plea Bargaining as Disaster, 101 Yale L.J. 1979 (1992), argues that plea bargaining should be abolished because, among other things, it gives an innocent defendant a choice of pleading guilty and avoiding a trial—a choice that Professor Schulhofer argues should not be permitted:

> * * * [T]he innocent defendant, facing a small possibility of conviction on a serious charge, [often] considers it in his interest to accept conviction and a small penalty. The defendant's choice to plead guilty can be rational from his private perspective, but it imposes costs on society by undermining public confidence that criminal convictions

> reflect guilt beyond a reasonable doubt. An "efficient" system of voluntary contracting for pleas would convict large numbers of defendants who had a high probability of acquittal at trial; indeed, to the extent that innocent defendants are likely to be more risk averse than guilty ones, the former are likely to be overrepresented in the pool of "acquittable" defendants who are attracted by prosecutorial offers to plead guilty. To deal seriously with these problems we must consider complete abolition of plea bargaining. * * * The social interest in not punishing defendants who are factually innocent justifies a bar on compromise, low-sentence settlements, even if individual defendants would prefer to have that option.

Professor Schulhofer also argues that a system of plea bargaining imposes significant disadvantages on indigent defendants, because appointed counsel are underpaid, thus giving them an incentive to plead a case at the first opportunity, whether the plea agreement is fair or not. Abolishing plea bargaining would mean that an appointed attorney's performance would be more closely monitored:

> The single most serious agency problem on the defense side is that the attorney incurs a severe financial penalty if the case goes to trial. That prospect can powerfully skew his appraisal of the value of a prosecutor's plea offer and the advice he provides to his client. A prohibition on bargaining protects defendants who would accept a plea offer that was not in their interest, even if the attorney, once forced to trial, would give the same indifferent assistance that he would provide in plea negotiations.
>
> * * *
>
> The shift from plea bargaining to trial renders the attorney's performance highly visible to peers in the courtroom. This shift also enlarges both the attorney's formal legal obligations of effective assistance and the practical likelihood that they will be taken seriously. The institutional environment of the trial process thus limits the consequences of the agency problem in ways that are precluded when disposition occurs in a low-visibility plea. The visibility of trial also tends to generate pressure to alleviate the worst inadequacies of indigent defense funding. Indigents are far more likely to receive conscientious representation when cases are tried in open court than when the attorneys are permitted to settle on the basis of an uninformed guess about the likelihood of conviction.

Professor Schulhofer argues that one alternative for the current system of plea bargaining is a structured system in which defendants receive some automatic, non-negotiable concessions for pleading guilty.

> By abolishing bargaining but not abolishing concessions, a jurisdiction could retain control over its guilty plea rate and preserve its existing

> low level of resources committed to trials. * * * In such a system, the proportion of defendants pleading guilty would be similar to the present number, but the composition of the guilty plea pool presumably would change. Those who elect trial in the present system do not necessarily have the greatest chance of acquittal because such defendants are also the ones most likely to win the best sentence concessions in negotiation. Rather, those who now go to trial tend to be those who are least risk averse, a group that may include disproportionate numbers of those who are actually guilty. In contrast, in a system of nonnegotiable sentence concessions, defendants who elect trial are most likely to be those with the greatest likelihood of acquittal, a group that should include disproportionate numbers of the innocent. The normative premise of this approach is that the trial process, however infrequently used, should be reserved for cases where guilt is most in doubt.

As another alternative, Professor Schulhofer simply proposes that plea bargaining be abolished. He argues that a system without plea bargaining would provide greater protection for innocent defendants:

> Because processing each case would be more costly, and because innocents would be more difficult to convict, the prosecutor's incentives (both personal and public) to screen carefully at the charging stage would be enhanced. The total number of defendants charged might decrease if prosecutorial resources were held constant. But even if the number charged did not decline, the proportion of innocents in the pool of defendants would tend to decrease. * * * Because abolition would make it harder to convict the innocent, it would benefit defendants convicted in the plea bargaining process who would not be convicted, and perhaps would not even be charged, in a no-concessions world.

American jurisdictions that have attempted to ban or limit plea bargaining have found that it is difficult to do. This is not surprising. Prosecutors have limited resources and incentives to preserve them for cases that must be tried. See Langbein, Torture and Plea Bargaining, 46 Univ. Chi. L.Rev. 3 (1978) (arguing that the prosecutor has an incentive to coerce a guilty plea in order to avoid the panoply of rights that await the accused at a trial). Defendants have rights, as Judge Easterbrook explained, that they might find more valuable if waived than if exercised. Under-compensated defense counsel have incentives to encourage their clients to plead guilty. An over-burdened judiciary hardly yearns for more trials. So it appears that none of the participants in the criminal justice system are necessarily better off in a system that does not permit negotiations and plea bargains.

D. THE DISTINCTION BETWEEN REWARDING A GUILTY PLEA AND PUNISHING THE DECISION TO GO TO TRIAL

The trial judge in United States v. Medina-Cervantes, 690 F.2d 715 (9th Cir.1982), indicated concern that the defendant, convicted of entering the United States illegally and of reentering the United States after having been deported, was "thumbing his nose at our judicial system" by insisting on a trial and the exercise of the full panoply of trial rights. He imposed a fine that was intended to reimburse the government for the costs of the trial. The court of appeals stated that it did not doubt the good faith of the trial judge, but remanded for resentencing, observing that "[i]t is well settled that an accused may not be subjected to more severe punishment simply because he exercised his right to stand trial." It directed the trial judge to state the reasons for the sentence imposed upon remand.

Had the trial judge said nothing, and simply imposed a higher sentence after conviction within a permissible range, the court of appeals surely would have sustained the sentence. Once higher sentences are imposed, repeat players in the system know how it operates and will of course take into account a de facto higher sentence for going to trial. Do you think that a system that "encourages" pleas is likely to penalize those who insist on going to trial? Could a judge identify a lack of remorse as a basis for increasing the penalty? Should the judge do so? See Scott v. United States, 419 F.2d 264 (D.C.Cir.1969) (while a defendant may receive a longer sentence after going to trial, no part of that sentence can be attributable to punishing the defendant for having gone to trial).

Acceptance of Responsibility

These questions are not of merely theoretical interest. The United States Sentencing Guidelines [discussed in Chapter 11], which sentencing judges use as guidance, provide for a reduced sentence for defendants who accept responsibility for their criminal conduct. Section 3E1.1. Acceptance of responsibility does not require a guilty plea, but the Sentencing Commission envisioned, and the courts have held, that a defendant who goes to trial rarely will be able to qualify for the reduction.

Would the Guidelines be unconstitutional if they *conditioned* a reduction for acceptance of responsibility on a plea of guilty? See, e.g., United States v. White, 869 F.2d 822 (5th Cir.1989) (Section 3E1.1 does not impinge on defendant's Sixth Amendment right to trial: "It is not unconstitutional for the Government to bargain for a guilty plea in exchange for a reduced sentence. The fact that a more lenient sentence is imposed on a contrite defendant does not establish a corollary that those who elect to stand trial are penalized."). On questions of acceptance of responsibility and the effect on plea bargaining, see O'Hear, Remorse,

Cooperation, and "Acceptance of Responsibility": The Structure, Implementation, and Reform of Section 3E1.1 of the Federal Sentencing Guidelines, 91 Nw.U.L.Rev. 1507 (1997).

E. GUILTY PLEAS, CHARGING DECISIONS, AND MANDATORY MINIMUM SENTENCES

There can be circumstances in which the pressure on a Federal defendant to plead can be tremendous even without regard to the sentence reduction for acceptance of responsibility. This pressure results from two factors: (1) the existence of mandatory minimum sentencing statutes; and (2) the possibility of a reduction in sentence below a mandatory minimum for substantial assistance to the prosecution in the investigation and prosecution of other defendants.

Congress has enacted substantial mandatory minimum sentences for a number of crimes, particularly those involving drugs and firearms. The presence of a mandatory minimum penalty can produce great pressure on a defendant to plead guilty in order to escape the minimum. If a prosecutor is willing to charge under a non-mandatory or reduced-mandatory statute, the defendant may leap at a plea offer. See DeBenedectis, Mandatory Minimum Sentences Hit, A.B.A.J. Dec. 1991, p. 36 (noting that "mandatory minimums give Federal prosecutors wide discretion over sentencing through the crimes they charge and bargains they accept").

Should mandatory minimum penalties be permitted to go hand in hand with plea bargaining? If not, which should be abolished? For a discussion of the impact of mandatory minimum sentences on the decision to cooperate, see Richman, Cooperating Clients, 56 Ohio State L.J. 69 (1995). Professor Richman points out that clients are often caught between the pressures of severe sentencing under Federal law on the one hand, and defense counsel's financial, institutional, and emotional interest in preventing the client from cooperating with the government on the other.

As discussed in Chapter 11, infra, at various times inroads are made at the Federal level to reduce the use of mandatory minimums. See U.S. Orders More Steps to Curb Stiff Drug Sentences, N.Y. Times 8/20/2013, A18 ("The Obama Administration * * * expanded its effort to curtail severe penalties for low-level Federal drug offenses, ordering prosecutors to refile charges against defendants in pending cases and strip out any references to specific quantities of illicit substances that would trigger mandatory minimum sentencing laws."). Such inroads should make the plea bargaining system less coercive for some defendants. But they are not guaranteed to last—as illustrated by Attorney General Jeff Sessions' May 20, 2017 Memorandum for All Prosecutors ("it is a core principle that prosecutors should charge and pursue the most serious, readily provable offense,"; "[b]y definition, the most serious offenses are those that carry the most substantial guidelines sentence, including mandatory minimum sentences").

F. EFFICIENCY AT WHAT PRICE?

Plea bargaining is almost certain to produce disturbing results in some cases. Consider, for example, the following problem:

PROBLEM

A defendant is charged with first degree murder, and he pleads self-defense. The two witnesses for the state are the daughter and wife of the deceased. Both claim that the defendant fired a gun without provocation. At a preliminary hearing the magistrate judge believes that the question of sufficiency of the evidence to hold the defendant is a close one because the eyewitnesses are less believable than the defendant, but ultimately binds the defendant over because a jury could believe the wife and daughter and return a guilty verdict. The grand jury charges first degree murder.

Assume that the prosecutor says to the defense lawyer in the course of plea bargaining, "I agree with the magistrate. The greater probability is self-defense here, but I figure that there is about a 40% chance that the defendant will be convicted of first degree murder. This surely is a case of premeditated murder or self-defense. It was one or the other, pure and simple." The prosecutor goes on to say: "If I am right, the expected minimum penalty from your client's perspective is 40% multiplied by the minimum sentence he can receive which is twenty years, or 8 years as the bottom line. In other words, your client will be found innocent and serve no time in 6 out of 10 cases, and in 4 out of 10 cases your client will serve a minimum of twenty years. The way I see it the jury either believes my witnesses or yours and that kind of case is always unpredictable. Like the magistrate judge implied, reasonable juries have leeway in determining whom to believe. Since your client has a 40% chance of serving a minimum of 20 years, a conservative, but impartial, observer would say that your client should be looking to reduce his exposure to jail. Here is what I am prepared to do: I will let your client plead to negligent homicide and recommend a two year sentence. Because your client has no prior record, the court will probably accept that recommendation, though I cannot guarantee that." The defense lawyer takes this offer back to the client, who is afraid of the possibility of a minimum twenty year sentence.

If the defense lawyer agrees on the odds and so informs the defendant, should the defendant be permitted to plead to the negligent homicide charge? Does it matter that the defendant *could not possibly have committed negligent homicide* under either side's version of the facts? If a factual basis requirement is in effect, must there be a factual basis for negligent homicide, or is it sufficient that there is a basis for the greater offense? If a basis for the lesser offense must be shown, can the prosecutor ethically permit the defendant to state to the court a distorted version of the facts? Could the prosecutor put on only part of the state's evidence in an effort to create for the court an appearance of negligent homicide? If the answer to either or both of the last two questions is "no," what incentive does the system provide for anyone to challenge an improper plea?

If the illustration uses numbers that you believe are unrealistic, change them so that there is a 60% chance of conviction. Should the defendant accept an offer to plead to second degree murder with an 8-year sentence recommendation? Could a rational lawyer advise against such a plea? If you like plea bargaining, consider whether there is any prosecutorial offer that would be so coercive as to be unreasonable.

If you don't like plea bargaining, consider whether there is any offer that you would deem proper. Do you really want to force the defendant to go to trial in the examples offered here?

Inverted Sentencing

Another disturbing phenomenon of plea bargaining is that in multi-defendant cases, those more culpable might have a chance at receiving a lighter sentence than those less culpable. That is because prosecutors often need cooperation from some criminals in order to convict others, and plea bargaining is about the only tool that the prosecutor can legitimately employ to encourage cooperation. The incentives result in what Professor Richman terms "inverted sentencing": "The more serious the defendant's crimes, the lower the sentence—because the greater his wrongs, the more information and assistance he has to offer a prosecutor." Richman, Cooperating Clients, 56 Ohio St.L.J. 69 (1995). Judge Bright, dissenting in United States v. Griffin, 17 F.3d 269 (8th Cir.1994), had this to say about the phenomenon of inverted sentencing:

> What kind of a criminal justice system rewards the drug kingpin or near-kingpin who informs on all the criminal colleagues he or she has recruited, but sends to prison for years and years the least knowledgeable or culpable conspirator, one who knows very little about the conspiracy and is without information for the prosecution?

Is inverted sentencing an indictment of the plea bargaining system? Or is it an inevitable consequence of the prosecutor's need for cooperation from criminals? If plea bargaining were abolished, what incentive would a criminal have to cooperate with the government by giving away information about his confederates?

Three Strikes

In some jurisdictions a mandatory life sentence is imposed on a conviction for a specified felony if the defendant has been twice previously convicted of certain specified felonies. How do these "three strikes and you're out" provisions affect plea bargaining for the first, second, and third offenses? Is the bargaining dynamic different at each offense? Some states structure their three strikes laws so that the prosecution must charge a "strike" felony if the facts support it. In these states, will more defendants refuse to plead guilty and go to trial on the assumption that they have nothing to lose? Or can the parties work "underground" by fudging the facts and agreeing to a charge that does not qualify as a strike?

G. PROBLEMS OF OVERCHARGING

Timing Questions: Bordenkircher v. Hayes

Not all plea bargaining involves settlements that look like a wonderful deal for the defendant. Consider, for example, Bordenkircher v. Hayes, 434 U.S. 357 (1978). Hayes was indicted by a Kentucky grand jury on a charge of uttering a forged instrument in the amount of $88.30, an offense punishable by 2–10 years imprisonment. During pretrial negotiations, the prosecutor told Hayes that if he did not plead guilty and "save the court the inconvenience and necessity of a trial," the prosecutor would seek a new indictment under the then-existing Kentucky Habitual Criminal Act, which carried a mandatory life sentence. Hayes chose not to plead guilty, was indicted under the Act and received a life sentence. The Supreme Court affirmed, holding that the decision whether to charge an offense rests with prosecutors and grand juries, and it made no difference that the indictment on a more serious crime came after the defendant refused to bargain. The Court declared that "a rigid constitutional rule that would prohibit a prosecutor from acting forthrightly in his dealings with the defense could only invite unhealthy subterfuge that would drive the practice of plea bargaining back into the shadows from which it has so recently emerged." In sum, the Court concluded that "this case would be no different if the grand jury had indicted Hayes as a recidivist from the outset, and the prosecutor had offered to drop that charge as part of the plea bargain."

Justice Blackmun, joined by Justices Brennan and Marshall, dissented. He disagreed with the Court's analysis that the timing of the indictment made no difference and suggested that prior to *Hayes* the Court "ha[d] never openly sanctioned such deliberate overcharging or taken such a cynical view of the bargaining process." He added that "[e]ven if overcharging is to be sanctioned, there are strong reasons of fairness why the charge should be presented at the beginning of the bargaining process, rather than as a filliped thread at the end." Justice Powell also dissented on the ground that the prosecutor effectively conceded that his strategy did not reflect the public interest in an appropriate sentence, but simply a desire to avoid trial even if the means of doing so was the imposition of an unreasonable sentence.[1]

II. THE REQUIREMENTS FOR A VALID GUILTY PLEA

A. DISTINGUISHING BARGAINING FROM THE PLEA PROCEDURE

Courts tend to distinguish the bargaining that takes place, which is largely unregulated as Bordenkircher v. Hayes illustrates, from the procedures surrounding the judicial acceptance of a guilty plea. These procedures have grown more formal over time. See, e.g., United States v. Livorsi, 180 F.3d 76 (2d Cir.1999) ("we examine critically even slight procedural deficiencies to ensure that the defendant's guilty plea was a voluntary and intelligent choice, and that none of the defendant's substantial rights have been compromised"). The unanswered question is whether the formality provides realistic protection for defendants or only trappings to persuade the public that justice is being done.

B. THE REQUIREMENT OF SOME KIND OF A RECORD

The Boykin Requirements

In two cases decided in 1969, McCarthy v. United States, 394 U.S. 459, and Boykin v. Alabama, 395 U.S. 238, the Supreme Court made it clear that a valid guilty plea requires "an intentional relinquishment or abandonment of a known right or privilege." This is because a defendant who pleads guilty is giving up the constitutional right to a fair trial before a jury, the right to be proven guilty of all elements of the crime beyond a reasonable doubt, the right to silence, and the right to confront adverse witnesses. The Court said that "[c]onsequently, if a defendant's guilty plea is not equally voluntary and knowing, it has been obtained in violation of due process and is therefore void."

In *McCarthy,* the Court set aside the guilty plea of a defendant who had pleaded to one count of a three count indictment charging wilful and knowing attempts to evade Federal income tax payments. After discussing in dictum the constitutional requirements for a valid plea, the Court based its decision on Fed.R.Crim.P. 11, which sets forth procedural requirements for obtaining a valid guilty plea. The trial judge did not comply with the rule, because he failed both to ask the defendant whether he understood the nature of the charges against him and to inquire adequately into the

---

[1] In Corbitt v. New Jersey, 439 U.S. 212 (1978), the Court upheld a New Jersey statute that mandated life sentences for defendants convicted by a jury, but permitted lesser terms for those who pleaded guilty. The Court relied on Bordenkircher v. Hayes.

voluntariness of the plea. The Court concluded that the defendant had to be afforded the opportunity to plead anew. Rule 11 was viewed as an attempt to avoid post-plea hearings on waiver, and the Court refused to remand the case for such a hearing into the knowing and voluntary nature of McCarthy's plea.

Boykin v. Alabama overturned death sentences imposed on a 27 year old black man who pleaded guilty to five indictments charging common-law robbery. The Supreme Court said that "[i]t was error, plain on the face of the record, for the trial judge to accept petitioner's guilty plea without an affirmative showing that it was intelligent and voluntary." The Court held that it was impermissible to presume, on the basis of a silent record, a waiver of constitutional rights as important as the privilege against self-incrimination, trial by jury, and confrontation. Thus, there must be an affirmative indication on the record that the defendant made a knowing and voluntary waiver.

Application of Boykin

Boykin's requirement of an explicit record has been applied with some flexibility. Absence of an explicit record creates a *presumption* that the plea is invalid; but that presumption can be overcome by the government. See, e.g., United States v. Ferguson, 935 F.2d 862 (7th Cir.1991) (absence of transcript of guilty plea hearing is not fatal; the court relies on the custom, practice, and law applicable to guilty pleas in Illinois state courts, warranting a presumption that the defendant was informed of the necessary rights under *Boykin*).

Guilty Pleas Used for Enhancement of Sentence: Parke v. Raley

In Parke v. Raley, 506 U.S. 20 (1992), the Court considered the applicability of *Boykin* standards where guilty plea convictions are used to enhance punishment in subsequent cases. Raley was charged in 1986 with robbery and with being a repeat offender because he had pleaded guilty in 1979 and 1981 to two burglaries. Under Kentucky law, a presumption of regularity attaches to prior convictions resulting from guilty pleas, and an accused recidivist must produce evidence that his rights were infringed or that some other procedural irregularity occurred to render the conviction invalid. If the defendant produces such evidence, the burden shifts to the state to prove the actual validity of the prior conviction by a preponderance of the evidence. Raley argued that this procedure violated *Boykin* because it resulted in a presumption of a valid guilty plea from a silent record.

Justice O'Connor's opinion for the Court concluded that there was no tension between the Kentucky procedure and *Boykin*. She explained as follows:

Boykin involved direct review of a conviction allegedly based upon an uninformed guilty plea. Respondent, however, never appealed his earlier convictions. They became final years ago, and he now seeks to revisit the question of their validity in a separate recidivism proceeding. To import *Boykin's* presumption of invalidity into this very different context would, in our view, improperly ignore another presumption deeply rooted in our jurisprudence: the "presumption of regularity" that attaches to final judgments, even when the question is waiver of constitutional rights.

Justice O'Connor also rejected Raley's policy argument that it was unfair to place on the defendant the burden of producing evidence that prior guilty pleas are invalid. Raley contended that a defendant would find it inordinately difficult to obtain information concerning a dated guilty plea hearing. Justice O'Connor responded that a rule placing the entire burden on the state to prove the validity of a conviction would force the state "to expend considerable effort and expense attempting to reconstruct records from far-flung states where procedures are unfamiliar and memories are unreliable."

C. VOLUNTARY AND KNOWING PLEAS AND THE ADVANTAGES OF A COMPLETE RECORD

1. A Voluntary Plea

To be valid, a guilty plea must be voluntary; that is, it must not be the product of improper coercion by government officials. The standard of voluntariness is similar to that employed in connection with confessions, a standard that was examined in Chapter 3, supra. As the Supreme Court said in Brady v. United States, discussed supra, "the agents of the State may not produce a plea by actual or threatened physical harm or by mental coercion overbearing the will of the defendant." Thus, it is clear that if a defendant were threatened with physical torture or actually harmed as part of an effort to get him to plead guilty, any resulting plea would be involuntary. Of course most challenges to guilty pleas do not raise those kinds of claims. Unlike the interrogation process, the procedure for accepting pleas affords opportunities for trial judges to see whether a defendant is apparently exercising free will in choosing to plead. Still, some sophisticated questions of validity of guilty pleas have arisen under the rubric of voluntariness.

Package Deals

Suppose a prosecutor in a multi-defendant case proposes a global settlement: all the defendants can plead to specified crimes, but they must plead guilty as a group; if all the defendants do not agree, the deal is off.[2] Does a "wired" plea or "package deal" present a greater risk of coercion than an individual plea? In United States v. Pollard, 959 F.2d 1011 (D.C.Cir.1992), the defendant pleaded guilty to one count of conspiracy to deliver national defense information to the Government of Israel. He later claimed that the government coerced his guilty plea by linking his wife's plea to his own, especially as his wife was seriously ill at the time. But the court rejected his argument:

> To say that a practice is "coercive" or renders a plea "involuntary" means only that it creates improper pressure that would be likely to overbear the will of some innocent persons and cause them to plead guilty. Only physical harm, threats of harassment, misrepresentation, or promises that are by their nature improper as having no proper relationship to the prosecutor's business (e.g., bribes) render a guilty plea legally involuntary. * * *
>
> * * * We must be mindful * * * that if the judiciary were to declare wired pleas unconstitutional, the consequences would not be altogether foreseeable and perhaps would not be beneficial to defendants. Would Pollard, for instance, have been better off had he not been able to bargain to aid his wife? Would his wife have been better off? Would the bargaining take place in any event, but with winks and nods rather than in writing?
>
> Nor do we believe that Mrs. Pollard's medical condition makes an otherwise acceptable linkage of their pleas unconstitutional. The appropriate dividing line between acceptable and unconstitutional plea wiring does not depend upon the physical condition or personal circumstances of the defendant; rather, it depends upon the conduct of the government. Where, as here, the government had probable cause to arrest and prosecute both defendants in a related crime, and there is no suggestion that the government conducted itself in bad faith in an effort to generate additional leverage over the defendant, we think a wired plea is constitutional.

See also United States v. Mescual-Cruz, 387 F.3d 1 (1st Cir. 2004) (package plea not involuntary simply because a defendant is taking a higher sentence to get a lower sentence for a loved one: "If a defendant elects to sacrifice himself, that is his choice, and he cannot reverse it after he is dissatisfied with his sentence, or with other subsequent developments.").

Pollard considered the problem of a defendant "pressured" because of feelings toward the person with whom his plea is linked. The court in

[2] See Liebman and Snyder, Joint Guilty Pleas: "Group Justice" In Federal Plea Bargaining, N.Y.L.J., Sept.8, 1994, p.1, col.1 (noting that for the government, "group pleas dispose of cases in one fell swoop and thereby conserve scarce prosecutorial resources and, in some cases, avoid lengthy, costly or potentially embarrassing trials").

United States v. Caro, 997 F.2d 657 (9th Cir.1993), considered a different problem that might be created by wired pleas—the possibility of coercion by other defendants. Caro moved to set aside his guilty plea on the ground that he was pressured by his codefendants into going along with the package deal. At the hearing in which his plea was entered, the judge was never informed that Caro's plea was part of a group settlement. Judge Kozinski analyzed the problem as follows:

> Though package deal plea agreements are not per se impermissible, they pose an additional risk of coercion not present when the defendant is dealing with the government alone. Quite possibly, one defendant will be happier with the package deal than his codefendants; looking out for his own interests, the lucky one may try to force his codefendants into going along with the deal. * * * We * * * have recognized that the trial court should make a more careful examination of the voluntariness of a plea when it might have been induced by threats or promises from a third party. We make it clear today that, in describing a plea agreement * * * the prosecutor must alert the district court to the fact that codefendants are entering into a package deal.[3]

The court held that the trial court's error—really the prosecutor's error in failing to tell the judge that the pleas were "wired"—was not harmless. It vacated Caro's guilty plea and remanded. Compare United States v. Carr, 80 F.3d 413 (10th Cir.1996) (pressures of cohorts to accept a package deal "might have been palpable" to the defendant, but they did not vitiate the voluntariness of his plea because "it was still his choice to make").

Can the Defendant Voluntarily Waive the Right to Disclosure of Information That Could Be Used to Impeach Government Witnesses or for Affirmative Defenses? United States v. Ruiz

In the following case, the Court adhered to its position that the free market principles behind plea bargaining generally permit criminal defendants to voluntarily waive rights that could be invoked at trial. We examined this case briefly in Chapter 6, but its discussion of plea bargaining warrants additional attention here.

---

[3] Professor Green, in "Package" Plea Bargaining and the Prosecutor's Duty of Good Faith, 25 Crim.L.Bull. 507 (1989), argues that prosecutors who offer multi-defendant deals have an ethical responsibility to avoid overreaching.

UNITED STATES V. RUIZ

Supreme Court of the United States, 2002.
536 U.S. 622.

JUSTICE BREYER delivered the opinion of the Court.

In this case we primarily consider whether the Fifth and Sixth Amendments require Federal prosecutors, before entering into a binding plea agreement with a criminal defendant, to disclose "impeachment information relating to any informants or other witnesses." We hold that the Constitution does not require that disclosure.

* * *

After immigration agents found 30 kilograms of marijuana in Angela Ruiz's luggage, Federal prosecutors offered her what is known in the Southern District of California as a "fast track" plea bargain. That bargain—standard in that district—asks a defendant to waive indictment, trial, and an appeal. In return, the Government agrees to recommend to the sentencing judge a two-level departure downward from the otherwise applicable United States Sentencing Guidelines sentence. In Ruiz's case, a two-level departure downward would have shortened the ordinary Guidelines-specified 18-to-24-month sentencing range by 6 months, to 12-to-18 months.

The prosecutors' proposed plea agreement contains a set of detailed terms. Among other things, it specifies that "any [known] information establishing the factual innocence of the defendant" "has been turned over to the defendant," and it acknowledges the Government's "continuing duty to provide such information." At the same time it requires that the defendant "waiv[e] the right" to receive "impeachment information relating to any informants or other witnesses" as well as the right to receive information supporting any affirmative defense the defendant raises if the case goes to trial. Because Ruiz would not agree to this last-mentioned waiver, the prosecutors withdrew their bargaining offer. The Government then indicted Ruiz for unlawful drug possession. And despite the absence of any agreement, Ruiz ultimately pleaded guilty.

At sentencing, Ruiz asked the judge to grant her the same two-level downward departure that the Government would have recommended had she accepted the "fast track" agreement. The Government opposed her request, and the District Court denied it, imposing a standard Guideline sentence instead. [The Ninth Circuit vacated the sentencing decision, holding that Ruiz was entitled to disclosure of impeachment information at the guilty plea phase, and that the right could not be waived.]

* * *

In this case, the Ninth Circuit in effect held that a guilty plea is not "voluntary" (and that the defendant could not, by pleading guilty, waive his right to a fair trial) unless the prosecutors first made the same disclosure of material impeachment information that the prosecutors would have had to make had the defendant insisted upon a trial. We must decide whether the Constitution requires that preguilty plea disclosure of impeachment information. We conclude that it does not.

First, impeachment information is special in relation to the *fairness of a trial,* not in respect to whether a plea is *voluntary* ("knowing," "intelligent," and "sufficiently aware"). Of course, the more information the defendant has, the more aware he is of the likely consequences of a plea, waiver, or decision, and the wiser that decision will likely be. But the Constitution does not require the prosecutor to share all useful information with the defendant. And the law ordinarily considers a waiver knowing, intelligent, and sufficiently aware if the defendant fully understands the nature of the right and how it would likely apply *in general* in the circumstances—even though the defendant may not know the *specific detailed* consequences of invoking it. A defendant, for example, may waive his right to remain silent, his right to a jury trial, or his right to counsel even if the defendant does not know the specific questions the authorities intend to ask, who will likely serve on the jury, or the particular lawyer the State might otherwise provide.

* * *

Second, we have * * * found that the Constitution, in respect to a defendant's awareness of relevant circumstances, does not require complete knowledge of the relevant circumstances, but permits a court to accept a guilty plea, with its accompanying waiver of various constitutional rights, despite various forms of misapprehension under which a defendant might labor. See Brady v. United States (defendant "misapprehended the quality of the State's case", misapprehended "the likely penalties" and failed to "anticipate a change in the law regarding" relevant "punishments"); McMann v. Richardson, 397 U.S. 759, 770 (1970) (counsel "misjudged the admissibility" of a "confession"); United States v. Broce, 488 U.S. 563, 573 (1989) (counsel failed to point out a potential defense); Tollett v. Henderson, 411 U.S. 258, 267 (1973) (counsel failed to find a potential constitutional infirmity in grand jury proceedings). It is difficult to distinguish, in terms of importance, (1) a defendant's ignorance of grounds for impeachment of potential witnesses at a possible future trial from (2) the varying forms of ignorance at issue in these cases.

Third, due process considerations, the very considerations that led this Court to find trial-related rights to exculpatory and impeachment information, argue against the existence of the "right" that the Ninth Circuit found here. * * * [A]s the proposed plea agreement at issue here specifies, the Government will provide "any information establishing the factual innocence of the defendant" regardless. That fact, along with other guilty-plea safeguards, see Fed. Rule Crim. Proc. 11, diminishes the force of Ruiz's concern that, in the absence of impeachment information, innocent individuals, accused of crimes, will plead guilty.

At the same time, a constitutional obligation to provide impeachment information during plea bargaining, prior to entry of a guilty plea, could seriously interfere with the Government's interest in securing those guilty pleas that are factually justified, desired by defendants, and help to secure the efficient administration of justice. The Ninth Circuit's rule risks premature disclosure of Government witness information, which, the Government tells us, could "disrupt ongoing investigations" and expose prospective witnesses to serious harm. * * *

Consequently, the Ninth Circuit's requirement could force the Government to abandon its general practice of not disclosing to a defendant pleading guilty information that would reveal the identities of cooperating informants, undercover investigators, or other prospective witnesses. It could require the Government to devote substantially more resources to trial preparation prior to plea bargaining, thereby depriving the plea-bargaining process of its main resource-saving advantages. Or it could lead the Government instead to abandon its heavy reliance upon plea bargaining in a vast number—90% or more—of Federal criminal cases. We cannot say that the Constitution's due process requirement demands so radical a change in the criminal justice process in order to achieve so comparatively small a constitutional benefit.

* * *

[The opinion of JUSTICE THOMAS, concurring in the judgment, is omitted.]

Fast-Track Plea Bargaining

Ruiz was presented with a "fast-track" plea bargain, as described by Professor (now Judge) Bibas in Regulating the Plea-Bargaining Market: From Caveat Emptor to Consumer Protection, 99 Cal. L.Rev. 1117 (2011):

> Judicial districts * * * near the Mexican border have been overwhelmed with far more immigration and drug cases than they can handle. In response, Federal prosecutors in many of those districts developed fast-track plea-bargaining programs. The seminal program required defendants to waive indictment, forego motions, plead guilty immediately, waive presentence reports, stipulate to a particular sentence, agree to immediate sentencing, consent to deportation, and waive all sentencing and appeals. In exchange, prosecutors stipulated to sentences substantially below what defendants would have received after trial.

In light of the steep discount that Ruiz was offered under the fast-track program, is the Court's concern about burdens on the government of having to turn over impeachment evidence understandable? Did Ruiz get a fair exchange from the government for waiving access to impeachment evidence?

2. A Knowing Plea

Knowledge of the Elements of the Crime: Henderson v. Morgan

In Henderson v. Morgan, 426 U.S. 637 (1976), a 19 year old defendant, with substantially less than average intelligence, pleaded guilty to second degree murder after he was advised by counsel that a 25 year sentence would be imposed. The defendant had been indicted for first degree murder as a result of stabbing to death a woman who employed him while he was on release from a state school for the mentally disabled. The stabbing took place when she discovered him in her room at night trying to get his wages so that he could leave the premises unnoticed. The defendant was never informed that an intent to cause the victim's death was an element of second degree murder. The Court held the plea invalid, even though it assumed that the defendant's lawyers would have given the defendant the same advice—i.e., to plead guilty—and even if, having been informed of the elements of the crime, he would have pleaded anyway. The Court declared that a guilty plea cannot be valid unless the defendant knows the nature of the offense to which he pleads. In its footnote 18, the Court assumed that notice of a charge did not always require a description of every element of an offense, but said that "intent is such a critical element of the offense of second-degree murder that notice of that element is required."[4]

Applying Henderson v. Morgan

Defense counsel's assurance that she informed the defendant of the charges against him and the elements of those charges is enough to satisfy *Henderson*. The Supreme Court made this clear in Bradshaw v. Stumpf, 545 U.S. 175 (2005):

> While the court taking a defendant's plea is responsible for ensuring a record adequate for any review that may be later sought, we have never held that the judge must himself explain the elements of each charge to the defendant on the record. Rather, the constitutional prerequisites of a valid plea may be satisfied where the record accurately reflects that the nature of the charge and the

---

[4] Justice White, joined by Justices Stewart, Blackmun, and Powell, concurred and emphasized that the decision whether or not to plead to a specific offense is the defendant's alone, not his lawyer's. Justice Rehnquist, joined by Chief Justice Burger, dissented.

elements of the crime were explained to the defendant by his own, competent counsel. Where a defendant is represented by competent counsel, the court usually may rely on that counsel's assurance that the defendant has been properly informed of the nature and elements of the charge to which he is pleading guilty.

Henderson establishes that a defendant must know about the "crucial" elements of the offense to which the guilty plea is addressed, such as the requisite mental state. What else must a defendant know? Generally, a defendant must know the penalty that can be imposed. See, e.g., United States v. Goins, 51 F.3d 400 (4th Cir.1995) (guilty plea invalid where defendant was not made aware that he was subjecting himself to a mandatory minimum sentence of five years). Is a general idea of the maximum penalty enough? If the defendant is to understand the potential consequences of pleading, the general rule should be that a defendant must know whether several counts or indictments will produce concurrent or consecutive sentences. See ABA Standards, Pleas of Guilty, § 11–1.4 (requiring such an understanding).

On the other hand, a guilty plea can be sufficiently knowing even though the defendant has not been informed with precision of potential punishments under sentencing guidelines and without the defendant understanding the specifics of whether a sentencing judge might impose a sentence outside applicable guidelines. This is because, at the time of the plea allocution, the court "frequently has too little information available to provide defendant with an accurate sentencing range." United States v. Andrades, 169 F.3d 131 (2d Cir.1999).

Knowledge of Immigration Consequences: Padilla v. Kentucky

In Padilla v. Kentucky, 559 U.S. 356 (2010), the Court held that a defendant who is a noncitizen has a right to be told that he will be deported if he pleads guilty—without that information, the guilty plea is not a knowing one. The Court noted that "preserving the client's right to remain in the United States may be more important to the client than any potential jail sentence." The specific holding in *Padilla* was that defense counsel violated Padilla's constitutional right to effective counsel because he did not inform Padilla that the crime to which he pled guilty triggered automatic deportation under Federal law. The Court in *Padilla* noted that disclosure of immigration consequences could improve bargaining from both sides:

> [I]nformed consideration of possible deportation can only benefit both the State and noncitizen defendants during the plea-bargaining process. By bringing deportation consequences into this process, the defense and prosecution may well be able to reach agreements that better satisfy the interests of both parties. As in this case, a criminal

episode may provide the basis for multiple charges, of which only a subset mandate deportation following conviction. Counsel who possess the most rudimentary understanding of the deportation consequences of a particular criminal offense may be able to plea bargain creatively with the prosecutor in order to craft a conviction and sentence that reduce the likelihood of deportation, as by avoiding a conviction for an offense that automatically triggers the removal consequence. At the same time, the threat of deportation may provide the defendant with a powerful incentive to plead guilty to an offense that does not mandate that penalty in exchange for a dismissal of a charge that does.

Padilla is discussed more fully in the Chapter 10 materials on ineffective assistance of counsel.

Pleading to Something That Is Not a Crime: Bousley v. United States

The Court in Bousley v. United States, 523 U.S. 614 (1998), considered the problem of a defendant who pled guilty to a violation of a criminal statute that was later held not to cover his conduct. Bousley pleaded guilty to drug crimes, as well as to a violation of a Federal statute that prohibited "using" a firearm during the course of a drug transaction. At the time he pleaded guilty to the firearms offense, the local Federal courts had construed "using" expansively to cover basically any situation in which a defendant possessed a gun during the course of a drug offense. Bousley appealed his sentence, but did not challenge his guilty plea on direct appeal. His sentence was affirmed. Thereafter, the Supreme Court determined that the term "using" in the statute meant some kind of active use, such as brandishing or shooting. Bousley sought a writ of habeas corpus challenging the factual basis for his guilty plea on the ground that neither the "evidence" nor the "plea allocution" showed a "connection between the firearms in the bedroom of the house, and the garage, where the drug trafficking occurred."

The Supreme Court, in an opinion by Chief Justice Rehnquist for six Justices, held that Bousley would be entitled to a hearing on the merits of his challenge to his guilty plea if he could make the showing necessary to relieve the procedural default resulting from his failure to directly appeal his guilty plea. (On the question of procedural default, see the discussion of this case in Chapter 13). Addressing the question of whether Bousley's guilty plea could be considered valid under the circumstances, the Chief Justice declared:

> A plea of guilty is constitutionally valid only to the extent it is voluntary and intelligent. We have long held that a plea does not qualify as intelligent unless a criminal defendant first receives real notice of the true nature of the charge against him, the first and most

> universally recognized requirement of due process. [It is contended] that petitioner's plea was intelligently made because, prior to pleading guilty, he was provided with a copy of his indictment, which charged him with "using" a firearm. Such circumstances, standing alone, give rise to a presumption that the defendant was informed of the nature of the charge against him. Henderson v. Morgan. Petitioner nonetheless maintains that his guilty plea was unintelligent because the District Court subsequently misinformed him as to the elements of [the firearms] offense. In other words, petitioner contends that the record reveals that neither he, nor his counsel, nor the court correctly understood the essential elements of the crime with which he was charged. Were this contention proven, petitioner's plea would be * * * constitutionally invalid.

The Court remanded for a determination of whether Bousley could overcome his procedural default, whereupon he would receive a hearing on the merits of his invalid guilty plea claim.

Justice Stevens wrote a separate opinion concurring on the guilty plea question. He elaborated upon the Court's analysis in the following passage:

> [W]hen petitioner was advised by the trial judge, by his own lawyer, and by the prosecutor that mere possession of a firearm would support a conviction under [the firearms statute], he received critically incorrect legal advice. The fact that all of his advisers acted in good-faith reliance on existing precedent does not mitigate the impact of that erroneous advice. Its consequences for petitioner were just as severe, and just as unfair, as if the court and counsel had knowingly conspired to deceive him in order to induce him to plead guilty to a crime that he did not commit. Our cases make it perfectly clear that a guilty plea based on such misinformation is constitutionally invalid.

Justice Scalia, joined by Justice Thomas, dissented.

3. Competence to Plead Guilty

The validity of a guilty plea is also dependent on whether the defendant is *competent* to make a plea. That the "competence" factor is distinct from the "knowing and intelligent" factor was made plain by the Court in Godinez v. Moran, 509 U.S. 389 (1993). One question in *Moran* was whether the competency standard for pleading guilty is higher than the competency standard for standing trial. The competency standard for standing trial is met when the defendant is able to consult with his lawyer "with a reasonable degree of rational understanding" and has "a rational as well as factual understanding of the proceedings against him." Dusky v. United States, 362 U.S. 402 (1960). The lower court in *Moran* had held that this "rational understanding" test was insufficient to determine whether Moran was competent to plead guilty, because the decision to plead guilty required the appreciation of alternatives; that court concluded that a person cannot be competent to plead guilty unless he has the capacity to make a "reasoned choice" among the alternatives available to him.

The Supreme Court, in an opinion by Justice Thomas, rejected the lower court's position and held that the "rational understanding" test that defines competency to stand trial also defines competency to plead guilty. The Court found that the decisionmaking process attendant to standing trial was at least as complex and demanding as that required to plead guilty. Justice Thomas explained as follows:

> A defendant who stands trial is likely to be presented with choices that entail relinquishment of the same rights that are relinquished by a defendant who pleads guilty. * * * In consultation with his attorney, he may be called upon to decide, among other things, whether (and how) to put on a defense and whether to raise one or more affirmative defenses. In sum, all criminal defendants—not merely those who plead guilty—may be required to make important decisions once criminal proceedings have been initiated. And while the decision to plead guilty is undeniably a profound one, it is no more complicated than the sum total of decisions that a defendant may be called upon to make during the course of a trial. * * * This being so, we can conceive of no basis for demanding a higher level of competence for those defendants who plead guilty. If the *Dusky* standard is adequate for defendants who plead not guilty, it is necessarily adequate for those who plead guilty.

Justice Thomas stressed, however, that competence was not the only requirement for a valid guilty plea. He explained that a trial court must also "satisfy itself that the waiver of [the defendant's] constitutional rights is knowing and voluntary. In this sense there is a 'heightened' standard for pleading guilty, but it is not a heightened standard of competence."

Justice Kennedy, joined by Justice Scalia, concurred in part and in the judgment. He noted the difficulty that would result from applying different standards of competency at various stages of a criminal proceeding:

> The standard applicable at a given point in a trial could be difficult to ascertain. For instance, if a defendant decides to change his plea to guilty after a trial has commenced, one court might apply the competency standard for undergoing trial while another court might use the standard for pleading guilty. In addition, the subtle nuances among different standards are likely to be difficult to differentiate, as evidenced by the lack of any clear distinction between a "rational understanding" and a "reasoned choice" in this case.[5]

[5] Justice Blackmun, joined by Justice Stevens, dissented in *Moran*.

4. Waiver of the Right to Counsel at the Plea Hearing

An accused has a constitutional right to refuse counsel at trial and represent himself. [The right to self-representation is discussed in Chapter 10 of the Casebook.] It follows that the accused has the right to represent himself at a guilty plea hearing. But as with the right to counsel at trial, a waiver of the right to assistance of counsel during guilty plea proceedings must be knowing and voluntary. The Supreme Court, in Iowa v. Tovar, 541 U.S. 77 (2004), considered what warnings an accused must receive at a guilty plea hearing before a knowing and voluntary waiver of the right to counsel can be found. Justice Ginsburg, writing for the Court, posed the question as follows:

> This case concerns the extent to which a trial judge, before accepting a guilty plea from an uncounseled defendant, must elaborate on the right to representation.
>
> Beyond affording the defendant the opportunity to consult with counsel prior to entry of a plea and to be assisted by counsel at the plea hearing, must the court, specifically: (1) advise the defendant that waiving the assistance of counsel in deciding whether to plead guilty entails the risk that a viable defense will be overlooked; and (2) admonish the defendant that by waiving his right to an attorney he will lose the opportunity to obtain an independent opinion on whether, under the facts and applicable law, it is wise to plead guilty.

The Court held that neither of these warnings is mandated by the Sixth Amendment. Justice Ginsburg stated that a waiver of the right to counsel at the plea stage is sufficiently knowing "when the trial court informs the accused of the nature of the charges against him, of his right to be counseled regarding his plea, and of the range of allowable punishments attendant upon the entry of a guilty plea." The Court reasoned that the proposed warnings might actually be counterproductive.

> [T]he admonitions at issue might confuse or mislead a defendant more than they would inform him: The warnings * * * might be misconstrued as a veiled suggestion that a meritorious defense exists or that the defendant could plead to a lesser charge, when neither prospect is a realistic one. If a defendant delays his plea in the vain hope that counsel could uncover a tenable basis for contesting or reducing the criminal charge, the prompt disposition of the case will be impeded, and the resources of either the State (if the defendant is indigent) or the defendant himself (if he is financially ineligible for appointed counsel) will be wasted.

D. REGULATING GUILTY PLEAS UNDER FEDERAL RULE 11

1. Procedural Requirements of the Rule

Fed.R.Crim.P. 11 sets forth detailed procedural requirements to assure that defendants who plead guilty are informed of their rights and that the guilty plea is fairly rendered.[6] Subdivision (b)(1) provides that the court must address the defendant personally in open court and inform the defendant of, and determine that the defendant understands, the following:

(A) the government's right, in a prosecution for perjury or false statement, to use against the defendant any statement that the defendant gives under oath;

(B) the right to plead not guilty, or having already so pleaded, to persist in that plea;

(C) the right to a jury trial;

(D) the right to be represented by counsel—and if necessary have the court appoint counsel—at trial and at every other stage of the proceeding;

(E) the right at trial to confront and cross-examine adverse witnesses, to be protected from compelled self-incrimination, to testify and present evidence, and to compel the attendance of witnesses;

(F) the defendant's waiver of these trial rights if the court accepts a plea of guilty or nolo contendere;

(G) the nature of each charge to which the defendant is pleading;

(H) any maximum possible penalty, including imprisonment, fine, and term of supervised release;

(I) any mandatory minimum penalty;

(J) any applicable forfeiture;

(K) the court's authority to order restitution;

(L) the court's obligation to impose a special assessment;

(M) in determining a sentence, the court's obligation to calculate the applicable sentencing-guideline range and to consider that range, possible departures under the Sentencing Guidelines, and other sentencing factors under 18 U.S.C. § 3553(a);

---

[6] In United States v. Timmreck, 441 U.S. 780 (1979), Justice Stevens' opinion for a unanimous court established that a conviction based on a guilty plea cannot be collaterally attacked for a Rule 11 violation, unless the violation is constitutional or jurisdictional.

(N) the terms of any plea-agreement provision waiving the right to appeal or to collaterally attack the sentence; and

(O) that, if convicted, a defendant who is not a United States citizen may be removed from the United States, denied citizenship, and denied admission to the United States in the future.

Subdivision (b)(2) of Rule 11 requires the court to address the defendant in open court and "determine that the plea is voluntary and did not result from force, threats or promises (other than promises in a plea agreement)." See United States v. Smith, 184 F.3d 415 (5th Cir.1999) (Rule 11 violation found where judge did not specifically inform the defendant of the elements of the crime and did not personally ask the defendant if his plea was voluntary); United States v. Damon, 191 F.3d 561 (4th Cir. 1999) (Rule 11 violation found where the judge, after being informed that the defendant was under medication after a suicide attempt, failed to inquire into the effect that the medication may have had on the defendant's ability to make a voluntary plea and to understand the consequences: "The plea colloquy required by Rule 11 must be conducted with some flexibility. If a defendant's response to a court's question indicates the need for clarification, follow-up questions must be asked. Otherwise, the Rule 11 colloquy would be reduced to a formalistic ritual, stripped of its purpose.").

Rule 11(b)(3) provides that the court must assure itself that there is a *factual basis* for the guilty plea. See, e.g., United States v. Camacho, 233 F.3d 1308 (11th Cir. 2000) (district court satisfied its obligation of ensuring that there was an adequate factual basis for the defendant's guilty plea to a charge of possessing cocaine with intent to distribute, even though it did not explain or discuss directly the significance of the aiding and abetting theory set forth in the indictment; the court could conclude from the proffered facts that someone had knowingly possessed cocaine with intent to distribute and that the defendant had intentionally arranged for the acquisition of the cocaine, thereby committing an act that contributed to and furthered the unlawful possession).

Rule 11(c) provides that the prosecution and the defendant can enter into any of three agreements:

(A) an agreement not to bring or to dismiss charges;

(B) a recommendation, or an agreement not to oppose the defendant's request, to the judge, "that a particular sentence or sentencing range is appropriate"—with the understanding that the recommendation or request *does not bind the court*; or

(C) an agreement between the parties "that a specific sentence or sentencing range is the appropriate disposition of the case"—which binds the court once the court accepts the plea agreement.

Rule 11(c) provides further that the court "must not participate" in the discussions leading to a plea agreement.

2. The Role of the Court

The Judge's Power to Review the Agreement

The role of the trial judge in reviewing plea agreements is explained by the court in United States v. Bennett, 990 F.2d 998 (7th Cir.1993):

> If the plea agreement includes the dismissal of any charges (a type "A" plea agreement), or if the agreement includes a specific sentence (a type "C" plea agreement), the district court may accept or reject the plea agreement, or it may defer its decision regarding acceptance or rejection until it considers the presentence investigation report. In contrast, if the plea agreement includes sentencing recommendations or the government's promise not to oppose the defendant's sentencing requests (a type "B" plea agreement), the district court must advise the defendant of the nonbinding effect the recommendations have on the court and must also inform the defendant that he may not withdraw his guilty plea, even if the court does not adopt the recommendations. The district court does not need to make such an admonition when dealing with a type "A" or "C" plea agreement.

The court in *Bennett* found that the agreement in the case was a type "B" agreement, which did not bind the court in any respect. Thus, it refused to allow Bennett to vacate his plea when the court imposed a sentence significantly higher than that suggested in the agreement. If the agreement in *Bennett* had been a "C" agreement, the court could not have imposed a higher sentence than that agreed to between the parties. If the court objects to the terms of an "A" or "C" agreement, its only recourse is to *reject the agreement*, thus sending the prosecution and defendant back to the bargaining table.[7] See, e.g., United States v. Greener, 979 F.2d 517 (7th Cir.1992) (district court properly rejected a type "C" agreement where the sentence would not have sufficiently reflected the seriousness of the defendant's conduct); United States v. Brown, 331 F.3d 591 (8th Cir. 2003) (there is no absolute right to have a guilty plea accepted and a district court may reject a plea in the exercise of sound discretion).

Given the uncertain results, why would a defendant ever agree to a type "B" agreement? Isn't that just rolling the dice and hoping the judge is lenient? Do you think that the typical defendant really believes that the judge will not accept the recommendation? The defendant may well be

---

[7] A trial judge's blanket policy of rejecting plea agreements that permit a defendant charged with multiple counts to plead to only one was condemned in United States v. Miller, 722 F.2d 562 (9th Cir.1983). The court of appeals reasoned that trial judges must exercise their discretion in particular cases rather than establish blanket rules regarding acceptable pleas.

informed by counsel that judges accept recommendations almost all the time. This advice, while generally accurate, may cause a defendant to underestimate the risk of a plea. It is true that the defendant is protected if the judge fails to inform her of the fact that the judge may reject the recommendation. See United States v. Livorsi, 180 F.3d 76 (2d Cir.1999) (conviction vacated where defendant and prosecution reached a "B" agreement, and the judge failed to inform the defendant that such an agreement is not binding on the court). But, there is no protection for a defendant who relies on the informed prediction of counsel regarding a judge's likely action.

Intrusion into the Negotiations

Federal Rule 11(c) prohibits the judge from taking part in plea negotiations. The reasons for this rule are set forth in United States v. Barrett, 982 F.2d 193 (6th Cir.1992):

> When a judge becomes a participant in plea bargaining he brings to bear the full force and majesty of his office. His awesome power to impose a substantially longer or even maximum sentence in excess of that proposed is present whether referred to or not. * * *
>
> It is not only a court's sentencing power which gives coercive potential to its participation in the plea bargaining process, but also the court's control over the conduct of a trial. The defendant must view the judge as the individual who conducts the trial and whose rulings will affect what the jury is to consider in determining guilt or innocence. The defendant may be reluctant to reject such a proposition offered by one who wields such immediate power. * * * There is also a real danger that a judge's neutrality can be compromised.

See also United States v. Daigle, 63 F.3d 346 (5th Cir.1995) (judicial participation increases the possibility of coerced guilty pleas, and may impair judicial impartiality because the judge "seems more like an advocate for the agreement than a neutral arbiter if he joins the negotiations").

If the judge rejects a plea on the ground that it is too lenient, has she participated in the negotiations? If she rejects a plea and states what terms would be acceptable to her, has she participated in the negotiations? See United States v. Miles, 10 F.3d 1135 (5th Cir.1993) (plea vacated due to judicial participation, where the trial judge rejected a plea and suggested the terms that would be acceptable to him). If she rejects the plea *without* giving an explanation, is her action subject to attack as arbitrary? If she tells the defendant at a bail hearing, "you'd better see what you can get from the prosecutor because you have no defense as far as I can see," has she participated in the negotiations? If she tells the defendant, before the agreement is filed, that she accepts the government's recommendations in most cases, has she engaged in improper participation? See United States v. Daigle, 63 F.3d 346 (5th Cir.1995) (judge who so informs the defendant has improperly participated in negotiations).

Judge Rakoff has suggested that the rules should be changed to allow more participation of judges in the plea-bargaining process. He suggests the use of plea-bargaining conferences before the judge—a sealed proceeding in which judges would examine each party's position and recommend a non-binding plea bargain. The proposal

> provides a layer of review to protect the innocent from being pressured into pleading guilty, while potentially encouraging fairer plea bargains through the oversight of a neutral party. It creates a record of plea bargaining efforts, so there can be no uncertainty as to whether an offer was requested or ignored. Finally, it might help guilty people make a more informed choice about how to resolve their cases.

Murray, A Better Way to Plead Guilty, New York Times, p. A27, 1/23/2015.

Example of Improper Intrusions and the Need for a Harmless/Plain Error Review: United States v. Davila

In United States v. Davila, 569 U.S. 597 (2013), the Court unanimously found that a magistrate judge had violated Rule 11(c) by intruding into the defendant's guilty plea negotiations. The judge made the following statements to the defendant:

> "It might be a good idea for the Defendant to accept responsibility for his criminal conduct, to plead guilty, and go to sentencing with the best arguments still available without wasting the Court's time, [and] causing the Government to have to spend a bunch of money empanelling a jury to try an open and shut case."
>
> "[T]ry to understand, the Government, they have all of the marbles in this situation and they can file that . . . motion for a downward departure from the guidelines if they want to, you know, and the rules are constructed so that nobody can force them to file that motion for you. The only thing at your disposal that is entirely up to you is the two or three level reduction for acceptance of responsibility. That means you've got to go to the cross. You've got to tell the probation officer everything you did in this case regardless of how bad it makes you appear to be because that is the way you get that three-level reduction for acceptance, and believe me, Mr. Davila, someone with your criminal history needs a three-level reduction for acceptance. [The Sentencing Guidelines range would] probably be pretty bad because your criminal history score would be so high."

The *Davila* Court however, found that the judge's error under Rule 11(c) did not necessarily mandate the relief of vacating the guilty plea.

Justice Ginsburg, writing for the Court, found that a Rule 11(c) violation did not justify automatic relief, but rather was governed by the harmless and plain error provisions of Rule 11(h) [discussed immediately below.] The Court remanded for a determination of whether the judge's violation was harmless or plain error, with the focus being on whether the defendant would have pleaded guilty in any case. Justice Scalia, joined by Justice Thomas, wrote a short opinion concurring in part and concurring in the judgment.

3. Harmless Error and Plain Error

Fed.R.Crim.P. 11(h) provides that any error in obtaining the guilty plea under Rule 11 "that does not affect substantial rights" will be disregarded as harmless. This is the classic definition of harmless error that is also found in Fed.R.Crim.P. 52(a). But what if the defendant does not object to an error under Rule 11? Should the same harmless error standard apply as if he did? With respect to trial errors, Rule 52(b) provides that a defendant who fails to object has the burden of showing "plain error" that affected substantial rights. [See the discussion of plain error in Chapter 13]. But Rule 11(h) does not include a plain-error provision comparable to Rule 52(b).

The Court in United States v. Vonn, 535 U.S. 55 (2002), held that a defendant who does not object to an error under Rule 11 has the burden of showing "plain error." Justice Souter wrote for eight Justices. Justice Souter was not persuaded that there was any intent to differentiate by including a plain error provision in Rule 52 but not in Rule 11. He found that the lack of a plain error standard in Rule 11 would create an anomalous result, in that a defendant would be able to stand by and do nothing to correct an obvious Rule 11 error, and would lose nothing in doing so. The Court reasoned that Rule 52(b) implicitly applied to Rule 11 errors, and declared that the policy of the plain error rule is sound: "the value of finality requires defense counsel to be on his toes, not just the judge, and the defendant who just sits there when a mistake can be fixed cannot just sit there when he speaks up later on." Justice Stevens dissented from the Court's holding on plain error.

In United States v. Dominguez Benitez, 542 U.S. 74 (2004), the Court held that "a defendant who seeks reversal of his conviction after a guilty plea, on the ground that the district court committed plain error under Rule 11, must show a reasonable probability that, but for the error, he would not have entered the plea. A defendant must thus satisfy the judgment of the reviewing court, informed by the entire record, that the probability of a different result is sufficient to undermine confidence in the outcome of the proceeding."

E. GUILTY PLEA WITH A CLAIM OF INNOCENCE: *ALFORD* PLEAS

The Model Code of Pre-Arraignment Procedure § 350.4(4) provides that "[t]he court may accept the defendant's guilty plea even though the defendant does not admit that he is in fact guilty if the court finds that it is reasonable for someone in the defendant's position to plead guilty. The court shall advise the defendant that if he pleads guilty he will be treated as guilty whether he is guilty or not." This approach is consistent with North Carolina v. Alford, 400 U.S. 25 (1970).

Alford was indicted by North Carolina for the capital crime of first-degree murder. He pleaded guilty to second-degree murder, but at the plea hearing he took the stand and testified in part as follows:

> I pleaded guilty on second degree murder because they said there is too much evidence, but I ain't shot no man, but I take the fault for the other man. We never had an argument in our life and I just pleaded guilty because they said if I didn't they would gas me for it, and that is all.

Subsequently, Alford sought post-conviction relief on the ground that his plea was produced by fear and coercion. After noting that "[s]tate and lower Federal courts are divided upon whether a guilty plea can be accepted when it is accompanied by protestations of innocence and hence contains only a waiver of trial but no admission of guilt," the Court concluded that "[i]n view of the strong factual basis for the plea demonstrated by the State and Alford's clearly expressed desire to enter it despite his professed belief in his innocence, we hold that the trial judge did not commit constitutional error in accepting it."[8]

One of the reasons for sustaining the plea in *Alford* was the factual basis for it. Under Rule 11 there must always be a "factual basis" for the plea to be valid, but it is not necessary under the Rule that the defendant actually admit his guilt. See Cranford v. Lockhart, 975 F.2d 1347 (8th Cir.1992) (*Alford* plea upheld where information in prosecutor's file establishes a factual basis for the guilty plea).

In the Federal system, a defendant who enters an *Alford* plea is all but certain to be denied a reduction in sentence for acceptance of responsibility. See United States v. Harlan, 35 F.3d 176 (5th Cir.1994) ("A defendant's refusal to acknowledge essential elements of an offense is incongruous with the guideline's commentary that truthful admission of the conduct comprising an offense is relevant in determining whether a defendant qualifies for this reduction.").

---

[8] Justice Brennan, joined by Justices Douglas and Marshall, dissented. Justice Black concurred in "substantially all of the opinion in this case."

F. FACTUAL BASIS FOR PLEAS

The court's determination of the factual basis for a plea can help to assure that defendants who are innocent do not plead guilty. As stated above, Federal Rule 11(b)(3) requires the judge to determine that there is a factual basis for the plea. Such a factual basis can be found through statements by the defendant, factual assertions in the indictment, or information in the prosecutor's file. See generally United States v. Adams, 961 F.2d 505 (5th Cir.1992) (insufficient factual basis where the defendant did not admit facts in the plea colloquy, and no other factual information was provided; but the error was harmless because there was sufficient factual information in the presentence report filed after the plea was taken).

Lack of Factual Basis for a Forfeiture: Libretti v. United States

In Libretti v. United States, 516 U.S. 29 (1995), the defendant challenged a forfeiture order that was entered after he pleaded guilty to participating in a continuing criminal enterprise. He had stipulated to the terms of the forfeiture with the government when he entered into the plea agreement. But he argued that the stipulation was invalid because there was no factual basis for the forfeiture. In Libretti's view, Rule 11 prevented the entry of the forfeiture order because the trial judge had never determined that the forfeiture had a factual basis. But the Court, in an opinion by Justice O'Connor, rejected this argument and held that Rule 11 applies only to a "plea of guilty." She concluded that a "forfeiture provision embodied in a plea agreement is of an entirely different nature. Forfeiture is an element of the sentence imposed following conviction or, as here, a plea of guilty, and thus falls outside the scope of Rule 11." Justice Stevens dissented.

G. THE FINALITY OF GUILTY PLEAS

1. Withdrawal of a Plea

The criminal justice system abides and promotes plea bargaining because it is efficient. But in order to be efficient, plea bargains must carry some measure of finality. The system of plea bargaining could be disrupted if defendants could withdraw their pleas unilaterally and demand a trial. In effect this would create a system more inefficient than an "all trial" system. On the other hand, some safety valve must be in place to protect defendants from plea bargains that are completely unfair and unjust—especially considering that the performance of appointed counsel for indigents often leaves much to be desired, and there are a number of intricacies in the process that will be difficult for many defendants to understand, such as the rights being given up, the chances at trial, and possible sentencing ranges.

Fed.R.Crim.P. 11(d) provides that a court may allow the defendant to withdraw a guilty plea before sentence is imposed for any reason if the judge *has not yet accepted the plea.* But if the judge has accepted the plea, it may be withdrawn only if 1) the court has rejected the terms of the plea agreement, or 2) if the defendant provides the court with a "fair and just" reason for withdrawal. Courts are extremely reluctant to allow withdrawal of a guilty plea once the court accepts it, even if a sentence has not yet been imposed. See United States v. Goodson, 569 F.3d 379 (8th Cir. 2009) ("When a defendant has entered a knowing and voluntary guilty plea at a hearing at which he acknowledged the crime, the occasion for setting aside a guilty plea should seldom arise."); United States v. Hoke, 569 F.3d 718 (7th Cir. 2009) ("claims of innocence alone do not mandate permission to withdraw a plea"); United States v. Abreu, 964 F.2d 16 (D.C.Cir.1992) (presentence withdrawal of plea was properly denied where motion to withdraw was based upon the defendant's "reevaluation of the strength of the government's case").

Rule 11(e) prohibits the withdrawal of a guilty plea after sentence is imposed. Of course, if a guilty plea was not knowing and voluntary, then it can be vacated under the standards discussed earlier in this Chapter.

Withdrawal of Plea Before the Agreement Is Accepted: United States v. Hyde

As stated above, Rule 11 permits withdrawal of a guilty plea after it has been accepted by the court only "if the defendant can show a fair and just reason for requesting the withdrawal." In United States v. Hyde, 520 U.S. 670 (1997), a defendant reached a plea agreement with the government. At the guilty plea hearing, the defendant pleaded guilty to four counts of an eight-count indictment. The trial judge accepted the plea, but (as is common practice) the judge *deferred* decision on whether to accept the plea *agreement,* in which the government had agreed to dismiss the remaining four charges. So at this point the court had upheld the *defendant's* part of the agreement, while deferring consideration on the government's part of the agreement (as opposed to rejecting it). The defendant then sought to withdraw his plea—he did not proffer any "fair and just reason" for doing so. The lower court permitted the withdrawal, reasoning that a defendant has an absolute right to withdraw a guilty plea until it has been accepted; the agreement and the plea itself are inextricably intertwined; and the guilty plea is not really accepted until the agreement as a whole is accepted by the trial judge.

The Supreme Court, in a unanimous opinion by Chief Justice Rehnquist, rejected this reasoning and held that when a plea is accepted and the acceptance of the plea *agreement* deferred, the defendant cannot withdraw his plea unless he satisfies the "fair and just reason" requirement of Rule 11. The Chief Justice reasoned that if the defendant were permitted an absolute right to withdraw his plea after the court had actually accepted it, it would debase the judicial proceeding at which a defendant pleads and the court accepts his plea:

> After the defendant has sworn in open court that he actually committed the crimes, after he has stated that he is pleading guilty because he is guilty, after the court has found a factual basis for the plea, and after the court has explicitly announced that it accepts the plea, the Court of Appeals would allow the defendant to withdraw his guilty plea simply on a lark. * * * We think the Court of Appeals' holding would degrade the otherwise serious act of pleading guilty into something akin to a move in a game of chess.

The Chief Justice addressed the Court of Appeals' premise that a plea and a plea agreement are inextricably intertwined:

> The guilty plea and the plea agreement are "bound up together" in the sense that a *rejection* of the agreement simultaneously frees the defendant from his commitment to plead guilty. And since the guilty plea is but one side of the plea agreement, the plea is obviously not wholly independent of the agreement.
>
> But the Rules nowhere state that the guilty plea and the plea agreement must be treated identically. Instead, they explicitly envision a situation in which the defendant performs his side of the bargain (the guilty plea) before the Government is required to perform its side (here, the motion to dismiss four counts). If the court accepts the agreement and thus the Government's promised performance, then the contemplated agreement is complete and the defendant gets the benefit of his bargain. But if the court rejects the Government's promised performance, then the agreement is terminated and the defendant has the right to back out of his promised performance (the guilty plea), just as a binding contractual duty may be extinguished by the non-occurrence of a condition subsequent.

Thus, if the agreement were to be rejected by the judge, it would be void and the defendant would not have to worry about withdrawal. But the defendant could not, during the time between the Court's accepting the guilty plea and reviewing the terms of the agreement, move to withdraw the plea without providing a fair and just reason for doing so.

Constraints on Withdrawal and Poorly Advised Defendants

Professor Cook, in All Aboard! The Supreme Court, Guilty Pleas, and the Railroading of Criminal Defendants, 55 Colo. L. Rev. 863 (2004), argues that the strict limitations on withdrawal of guilty pleas, including the result in *Hyde*, lead to a system in which indigent and unschooled defendants are hoodwinked into harsh sentences and an unfair waiver of their right to a trial. He explains as follows:

> When a defendant enters a guilty plea and the court accepts that plea, the court has made a determination that the defendant has fully performed his contractual obligation. * * * [T]here is nothing more the defendant can do but wait for the promised return. Yet contrary to the law attendant to unilateral contracts, a defendant, despite having fully performed, is not entitled to demand performance under the contract. * * * To make a truly informed choice, the defendant should understand that when he enters a guilty plea prompted by the promises bandied before him in a plea agreement, that typically upon the conclusion of the Rule 11 hearing he essentially has no more of a plea deal than he did prior to the hearing. He needs to understand that * * * he is essentially binding himself to a guilt admission for a protracted period, and that he will not be entitled to any of the benefits under the contract until the court decides whether it will assent to the agreement.
>
> Unfortunately, few defendants are so aware. * * * [T]he bargaining system is coercive, resulting in plea dispositions that are uninformed and are of dubious contractual validity. This view is buttressed when considering the defendant populace, which is comparatively less resourceful than their prosecutorial and judicial counterparts. The Department of Justice has most recently indicated, for example, that among the federally convicted, over 70 percent had no more than a high school education, * * * and that in excess of 50 percent had appointed counsel. * * * The defendant is unaware that the contractual principles applicable in the free market are largely inapplicable in the criminal context and that his plea process will be governed by a uniquely crafted set of contractual rules designed to safeguard not his interests but those of the system's most influential participants. They are typically devoid of any knowledge that they are being asked to submit a binding guilty plea in the absence of an enforceable agreement, and that their ability to revoke and pursue other, more optimal strategies will be severely constricted.

Professor Cook suggests an amendment to Rule 11 that would allow the defendant a unilateral right to withdraw a guilty plea at any time up to the court's approval of all terms of the plea agreement. And if the judge rejects the agreement, the defendant's plea would be void in any case.

2. Breach of a Plea Agreement

Breach by the Prosecution: Santobello v. New York

A plea agreement between the government and the defendant, once approved, is treated as a contract and is enforceable under contract principles. The leading case on enforcement of plea agreements is Santobello v. New York, 404 U.S. 257 (1971). Charged with two gambling felonies, Santobello agreed to plead guilty to a lesser included offense and the prosecutor agreed to make no recommendation as to sentence. Thereafter, a second prosecutor took over the case and, ignorant of the terms of the bargain, made a sentence recommendation. In an opinion by Chief Justice Burger, the Court held that even an inadvertent breach of a plea agreement was unacceptable. The Court remanded to afford the state courts the option of allowing Santobello to withdraw the plea or to have a new sentencing proceeding before a different judge. Justice Marshall, joined by Justices Brennan and Stewart, agreed with the majority's finding of a breach, but argued that Santobello "must be permitted to withdraw his guilty plea." Justice Douglas said that "[i]n choosing a remedy, * * * a court ought to accord a defendant's preference considerable, if not controlling, weight inasmuch as the fundamental rights flouted by a prosecutor's breach of a plea bargain are those of the defendant, not of the state."

Remedies for Prosecutorial Breach

It is well-established after *Santobello* that the remedy for a breached plea agreement is for the court either to permit the plea to be withdrawn or to order specific performance of the agreement, and that the choice between these two remedies is "a discretionary one guided by the circumstances of the case." United States v. Palladino, 347 F.3d 29 (2d Cir. 2003). Thus, the choice of remedy is for *the court,* not the defendant. In *Palladino,* the prosecutor essentially promised not to ask for an enhanced sentence on the basis of certain evidence, and then did so at the sentencing hearing by introducing that evidence. The court found that the government breached the plea agreement and that under the circumstances, withdrawal of the plea was the correct remedy. It explained as follows:

> Specific performance in this case is rendered difficult by the fact that, on remand, the District Court cannot simply erase its knowledge that the Government has previously taken a position in favor of the imposition of the disputed * * * enhancement. Although remand to another judge for resentencing, pursuant to a new Presentence Report is possible, we believe that the plea agreement in this case is hopelessly tainted by the introduction of new evidence known to the Government at the time of the plea * * * that cannot be magically

erased or ignored on remand. On balance, we conclude that defendant should be permitted to withdraw his plea.

If a defendant manages to set aside a guilty plea and decides to go to trial, is the prosecutor entitled to charge a higher offense than the one to which the defendant pleaded? Most courts treat the abrogation of the plea as an erasure that allows both sides to proceed anew. See, e.g., United States ex rel. Williams v. McMann, 436 F.2d 103 (2d Cir.1970). However, the *Williams* court acknowledged that although general principles of fundamental fairness do not bar every prosecution, certain allegations such as prosecutorial vindictiveness could pose a reasonable challenge on the basis of due process. Nonetheless, "no presumption of vindictiveness arises when the prosecutor simply reinstates the indictment that was in effect before the plea agreement was entered." Taylor v. Kincheloe, 920 F.2d 599 (9th Cir.1990), citing Blackledge v. Perry, 417 U.S. 21 (1974). See Chapter 12 for a discussion of vindictive prosecution.

Is There a Breach?

Sometimes it is difficult to determine whether a plea agreement has been breached. For example, if a prosecutor agrees to drop two counts of a three count indictment in exchange for a plea to the remaining count, and the sentencing judge relies on the fact that three offenses were committed, has the bargain been breached? In deciding how to answer, would you view an objective or subjective test of the bargain as more appropriate?

The courts have held that any ambiguity in the terms of the agreement is to be construed against the government. See United States v. Palladino, 347 F.3d 29 (2d Cir. 2003) ("because the government ordinarily has certain awesome advantages in bargaining power, any ambiguities in the agreement must be resolved in favor of the defendant."). See also United States v. Hayes, 946 F.2d 230 (3d Cir.1991) (where government promised to "make no recommendation as to the specific sentence to be imposed" and then emphasized the seriousness of the offense at the sentencing hearing, the government breached the terms of the plea agreement); United States v. Johnson, 187 F.3d 1129 (9th Cir.1999) (where the plea agreement required the prosecution to recommend a certain sentence, the prosecutor violated the agreement by recommending the sentence and then introducing a victim impact statement: "We see no way to view the introduction of McDonald's statement other than as an attempt by the prosecutor to influence the court to give a higher sentence than the prosecutor's recommendation.").

Government Agreement to Recommend a Sentence

Questions of breach often arise when the government, as part of a plea agreement, agrees to recommend a certain sentence. Defendants often object that the government at the sentencing hearing might have recommended the agreed-upon sentence, but made clear to the judge that it was doing so only reluctantly, and wouldn't mind at all if the judge were to impose a higher sentence. Under such circumstances the Court in United States v. Benchimol, 471 U.S. 453 (1985), found no breach. The Court reasoned that the agreement called only for the prosecutor to *recommend* a certain sentence, and the prosecutor did make the recommendation—there was nothing in the agreement specifically requiring the prosecutor to make an *enthusiastic* recommendation. See also United States v. Johnson, 187 F.3d 1129 (9th Cir.1999) ("unless specifically required in the agreement, the government need not make the agreed-upon recommendation enthusiastically"). If you are defense counsel, do you insist on having the word "enthusiastic" added to the plea agreement before "recommendation"? How would a reviewing court decide whether the government's recommendation was enthusiastic?

Oral Promises

If the government is to be held to an obligation, it must be in the plea agreement. Thus, in United States v. Austin, 255 F.3d 593 (8th Cir. 2001), the defendant argued that the government breached its agreement when it sought a sentencing enhancement based on the defendant's leadership role in the offense. The defendant argued that the prosecutor had promised during negotiations not to seek such an enhancement. But the agreement itself was silent on the issue of enhancement, and a clause in the agreement provided that the agreement reflected "all promises, agreements, and conditions between the parties." The court therefore found that the government did not breach the agreement by arguing for enhancement at sentencing.

Cooperation Agreements

The question of prosecutorial breach becomes particularly difficult when the agreement imposes cooperation obligations on the defendant in exchange for the government's agreement to recommend a lesser sentence. Generally the prosecution prefers that its obligations under such an agreement remain vague, and contingent on its own view of the *quality* of the defendant's cooperation. When the defendant claims that the prosecution breached the agreement by failing to recommend a certain sentence or a sentence reduction, the prosecution often responds that its duty was contingent on the defendant's cooperation, and in its opinion the defendant failed to comply with his contractual obligations. Professor Richman, in Cooperating Clients, 56 Ohio St.L.J. 69 (1995), describes this phenomenon:

> Typically, the defendant will broadly promise to testify truthfully, and to truthfully disclose all information concerning matters covered by the government's inquiries. Any effort to bind a cooperator to a particular "story" would be unseemly, and probably illegal. The government will reserve for itself the right to determine, prior to sentencing, whether the defendant has in fact cooperated fully and told the truth. * * * If the government determines that a cooperator has not lived up to his obligations, it will * * * generally be able to prevent the sentencing judge from showing the defendant any significant leniency based on his cooperation.

Professor Richman notes that while a government's obligations under a cooperation agreement are thus difficult to enforce in court, there is some discipline that is imposed by the marketplace. "The prosecutor who mistreats snitches risks not being able to attract such assets in the future."

One defense attorney became so frustrated at what he perceived as a failure of a United States Attorney's office to live up to its obligations under a cooperation agreement, that he was moved to publish an open letter in a full-page advertisement in the National Law Journal:

> [Despite the client's cooperation], your office broke two written promises to make a 5K.1 motion [for reduction in sentence due to cooperation]. The reasons given by your office were pure bovine do-do. Even the district judge was appalled.
>
> During the sentence proceedings I stated that I was going to tell every defense lawyer in our nation not to enter any plea agreement with your office. Your office cannot be trusted. Your office cares nothing about promises and agreements. I am surprised that the eagle in the Great Seal of the United States didn't fly from the wall in horror. * * * Like some sleazy insurance company who refuses to pay the widow because it wants the premiums but doesn't want to honor its obligations, your office will go to any length to renege on its solemn promises.

Michael Metzger, Advertisement, Nat'l L.J., May 24, 1993, at 26. Metzger was complaining about the U.S. Attorney's office in the Southern District of Florida. If you were a defense attorney practicing in Miami, would this advertisement affect the advice that you would give to a client who seeks a benefit from cooperation? Can you write a cooperation agreement that would bind the prosecution to its promises?

For a case in which a breach was found when the government failed to move for a sentence reduction in a cooperation agreement, see United States v. Lukse, 286 F.3d 906 (6th Cir. 2002), where the government was required in the agreement to file a downward departure motion if the defendant provided the government with substantial assistance. At the sentencing hearing, the government conceded that the defendant *had* provided substantial assistance, but argued that the defendant had breached the agreement because he was caught smoking marijuana in jail after providing the assistance. Because the defendant made no promises in the agreement that were breached by this conduct, the agreement was found fully enforceable against the government. The court remanded and ordered the government to file a downward departure motion at a new sentencing proceeding.

Breach by the Defendant: Ricketts v. Adamson

In Ricketts v. Adamson, 483 U.S. 1 (1987), the Court held that the Double Jeopardy Clause did not bar a state from filing capital charges against a defendant who had entered a guilty plea in return for a specific prison term and subsequently violated the terms of the plea agreement. Adamson was one of three individuals charged with first-degree murder in the dynamiting of a reporter's car. He agreed to plead guilty to second-degree murder and to testify against the other defendants in exchange for a designated prison sentence. Although Adamson testified as promised and the other defendants were convicted, the State Supreme Court reversed the convictions and remanded their cases for new trials. Adamson's lawyer informed the prosecutor that Adamson would only testify at second trials if certain conditions were met, including his release from prison following his testimony. The state took the position that Adamson's refusal to testify would put him in breach of the agreement. Adamson nevertheless invoked his privilege against self-incrimination when called to testify at a pretrial proceeding. Thereafter, the state filed a new information and convicted Adamson of first-degree murder. He was sentenced to death. An en banc court of appeals found that Adamson was placed in jeopardy twice, but the Supreme Court disagreed.

Justice White wrote for the Court. The Court assumed that jeopardy attached when Adamson was sentenced pursuant to his guilty plea and that absent special circumstances, Adamson could not have been retried for first-degree murder. Justice White agreed with the state that special circumstances arose from the plea agreement which specifically provided that the entire agreement would be null and void if Adamson refused to testify. He was unimpressed with the court of appeals' reasoning that Adamson acted in good faith. Justice White concluded that Adamson knew that if he breached the agreement he could be retried, "it is incredible to believe that he did not anticipate that the extent of his obligation would be decided by a court," and the end "result was that respondent was returned to the position that he occupied prior to execution of the plea bargain; he stood charged with first-degree murder."

Justice White reasoned that it was "of no moment" that Adamson offered to comply with the agreement after the state supreme court decision interpreting it, since "[t]he parties did not agree that respondent would be relieved of the consequences of his refusal to testify if he were able to advance a colorable argument that a testimonial obligation was not owing." Justice White ended his opinion with the observation that "[t]he parties could have struck a different bargain, but permitting the State to enforce the agreement the parties actually made does not violate the Double Jeopardy Clause."

Justice Brennan, joined by Justices Marshall, Blackmun, and Stevens, dissented. He disagreed that Adamson ever breached the plea agreement and argued that, assuming such a breach occurred, Adamson never made a conscious decision to violate the agreement. Justice Brennan focused on the provision of the agreement stating that Adamson was to be sentenced at the conclusion of his promised testimony, and noted that Adamson was sentenced after he had provided extensive testimony. Thus, Justice Brennan found that Adamson reasonably could have concluded that he had met his contractual obligations.

3. Appeal and Collateral Attack

Jurisdictions that do not like to see guilty pleas withdrawn or vacated also do not like to see them challenged on appeal or collaterally attacked.[9] Thus, they generally establish a regime in which a voluntary and intelligent guilty plea is a waiver of all claims that the pleader has. The Supreme Court has promoted this approach in four cases: the *Brady* trilogy—Brady v. United States, 397 U.S. 742 (1970); McMann v. Richardson, 397 U.S. 759 (1970); Parker v. North Carolina, 397 U.S. 790 (1970)—and Tollett v. Henderson, 411 U.S. 258 (1973). We first examine the specific claims that are waived when a defendant pleads guilty.

The defendant in *Brady* was charged with kidnaping under a Federal statute that authorized the death penalty if a jury recommended it but not in a bench trial. Brady pleaded guilty when it appeared that the trial judge would not try the case without a jury, but Brady sought to challenge his guilty plea via habeas corpus on the ground that the statute unconstitutionally infringed his right to jury trial. The Supreme Court held that even if Brady would not have pleaded guilty but for the death penalty provision, he pleaded voluntarily and intelligently with the advice of counsel. Thus, he was not entitled to withdraw his plea collaterally, even if a Supreme Court decision rendered after his plea was entered suggested that the kidnaping statute was invalid in burdening the right to jury trial (i.e., even if the statute violated the Sixth Amendment). In *Parker,* the

[9] For a discussion of the defendant's right to appeal a guilty plea conviction see United States v. Melancon, 972 F.2d 566 (5th Cir.1992) (defendant may, as part of his plea agreement, waive the right to appeal his sentence; finding a knowing and intelligent waiver under the circumstances). Compare United States v. Padilla-Colon, 578 F.3d 23 (1st Cir. 2009) (statements by the court about appeal from the guilty plea were so misleading that they abrogated any waiver of the right to appeal).

Court reached a similar result with respect to a state court defendant who was charged with first-degree burglary and who pleaded guilty to avoid a possible jury-imposed death sentence.

The Court also said in *Parker* and in *McMann* that a defendant who pleaded guilty could not attack the plea in a subsequent collateral proceeding on the ground that it was motivated by a prior coerced confession (i.e., the plea resulted from a violation of the 5th or 14th Amendment).

Following this trilogy, the Court held in *Tollett* that a defendant who pleaded guilty to first-degree murder could not challenge in subsequent habeas corpus proceedings the racial composition of the grand jury that indicted him (i.e., the grand jury was selected in violation of Equal Protection).

The four cases appeared to hold that a guilty plea represents acceptance by a defendant of his conviction and that the conviction is valid unless the defendant was not adequately represented by counsel. But, the Court soon muddied the waters in Blackledge v. Perry, 417 U.S. 21 (1974), as it held that a prison inmate who pleaded guilty to a felony charge in a North Carolina court after seeking a trial de novo following a conviction on a misdemeanor charge could attack his plea on the ground that the prosecutor acted improperly in retaliating against the defendant by raising the charge to a felony from a misdemeanor (a vindictiveness claim discussed in Chapter 12, infra). Thereafter, the Court held in Menna v. New York, 423 U.S. 61 (1975), that a defendant who pleaded guilty did not lose the right to challenge the plea as a violation of double jeopardy rights. So, prosecutorial vindictiveness and double jeopardy claims are treated as unwaived.

The Court held in United States v. Broce, 488 U.S. 563 (1989), that defendants, who pleaded guilty to two separate counts charging bidrigging conspiracies, could not successfully move to vacate their sentences on the ground that they actually were involved in a single, large conspiracy. Justice Kennedy reasoned for the Court that the indictments charged two conspiracies and that the defendants conceded by their pleas that they committed two separate crimes. He observed that *Blackledge* and *Menna* were resolved on the basis of the existing record and did not require an inquiry into evidence outside the record; in contrast, the instant case involved indictments which on their face charged separate offenses—the only way to determine whether it was a single conspiracy would be to conduct a detailed inquiry into the facts. Does the distinction work? Does it explain the difference between waived and unwaived claims?

It is clear that the Supreme Court has attempted to promote plea bargaining. Yet, the Court has identified a narrow range of cases in which guilty pleas cannot bar a subsequent collateral attack. Can you draw from

Broce or from your own analysis of these cases any rule that would rationalize the cases?[10]

4. Conditional Pleas

Plea bargaining can be promoted if defendants who plead guilty are permitted to raise some particular kinds of post-plea claims. For example, Fed.R.Crim. P. 11(a)(2) provides that with the approval of the court and with the consent of the government, "a defendant may enter a conditional plea of guilty * * * reserving in writing the right to have an appellate court review an adverse determination of a specified pretrial motion." If the defendant prevails on appeal, he has the right to withdraw the plea. A typical example of the use of a conditional plea is where the defendant moves to suppress evidence on the ground that it was obtained as a result of an illegal search and seizure, and the court denies the motion to suppress. At that point, the defendant could go to trial to preserve the right to appeal the suppression motion, but this might make little sense to a defendant who is actually guilty. So the defendant pleads guilty on condition that he can appeal the judge's suppression ruling. Thus, a defendant need not go to trial just to preserve a search and seizure or confession challenge.[11] If the defendant prevails on appeal, he then withdraws the plea and it is up to the government to determine whether to proceed in the absence of the evidence.[12]

---

[10] For two attempts at stating such a rule, see Saltzburg, Pleas of Guilty and the Loss of Constitutional Rights: The Current Price of Pleading Guilty, 76 Mich.L.Rev. 1265 (1978); Westen, Away from Waiver: A Rationale for the Forfeiture of Constitutional Rights in Criminal Procedure, 75 Mich.L.Rev. 1214 (1977). See also Alschuler, The Supreme Court, the Defense Attorney, and the Guilty Plea, 47 U.Colo.L.Rev. 1 (1975); Dix, Waiver in Criminal Procedure: A Brief for More Careful Analysis, 55 Tex.L.Rev. 193 (1977).

[11] United States v. Burns, 684 F.2d 1066 (2d Cir.1982), urges trial courts to consent to the reservation of issues only where they can be reviewed without a full trial and are likely to be dispositive of the case.

[12] Note, Conditional Guilty Pleas, 93 Harv.L.Rev. (1980), argues that a defendant has a constitutional right to enter a conditional guilty plea.

CHAPTER 10

TRIAL AND TRIAL-RELATED RIGHTS

■ ■ ■

In the previous Chapter we found that almost all criminal prosecutions in the United States end in a guilty plea. Why, then, is it worth it to spend much time studying criminal trials? The answer is that trials and trial rights remain important because the decision to plead guilty or not is dependent on the parties' view of how a trial would unfold. Moreover, prosecutions of extremely serious or high-profile crimes usually do go to trial. Finally, the explication and development of constitutional rights at trial indicates our attitude toward civil rights in this country. So we proceed to an in-depth discussion of trial rights in America.

I. THE RIGHT TO A SPEEDY TRIAL

A. THE BACKGROUND OF AND POLICIES SUPPORTING THE RIGHT

The Sixth Amendment provides that "[i]n all criminal prosecutions, the accused shall enjoy the right to a speedy and public trial * * *" It is a guarantee of deliberate speed in the prosecution of a case and a protection against several evils associated with delayed litigation. The Supreme Court has long recognized that "[t]he right of a speedy trial is necessarily relative. It is consistent with delays and depends upon circumstances." Beavers v. Haubert, 198 U.S. 77 (1905). Careful analysis of the facts of each case, rather than bright line tests, has been, and is still, the preferred approach of the Court to constitutionally-based speedy trial claims.

Fundamental Right: Klopfer v. North Carolina

Klopfer v. North Carolina, 386 U.S. 213 (1967), established that the right to a speedy trial is fundamental and thus binding upon the states through the Due Process Clause of the Fourteenth Amendment. In *Klopfer*, the Court found a speedy trial violation when a Duke University professor, who was indicted for criminal trespass for participation in a sit-in at a restaurant, saw the prosecutor obtain a "nolle prosequi with leave" following a trial that ended in a hung jury. The nolle prosequi permitted the prosecutor to reinstate the case without further order. Because the procedure indefinitely prolonged the anxiety and concern accompanying public accusation, the Court found that it violated the defendant's right to a speedy trial.

Interests Protected by the Speedy Trial Right

There are three interests protected by the right to a speedy trial:

1. The interest of an accused person in avoiding prolonged detention prior to trial. Innocent persons are never compensated for the losses that result from such detention. Those who are convicted following trial may have been confined for long periods in inadequate jails. Some who receive probation would never have spent time incarcerated except for pretrial delay.

2. The interest of the accused in avoiding prolonged anxiety concerning the charges made and public suspicion while charges are pending.

3. The accused's interest in litigating a case before evidence disappears and memories fade.

Not all of these concerns are present in all cases, but they can be. See generally Godbold, Speedy Trial—Major Surgery for a National Ill, 24 Ala.L.Rev. 265 (1972).

Imprisonment on Other Offenses: Smith v. Hooey and Dickey v. Florida

In Smith v. Hooey, 393 U.S. 374 (1969), the Court held that speedy trial rights extend to people imprisoned on other offenses. The Court reasoned as follows:

> At first blush it might appear that a man already in prison under a lawful sentence is hardly in a position to suffer from "undue and oppressive incarceration prior to trial." But the fact is that delay in bringing such a person to trial on a pending charge may ultimately result in as much oppression as is suffered by one who is jailed without bail upon an untried charge. First, the possibility that the defendant already in prison might receive a sentence at least partially concurrent with the one he is serving may be forever lost if trial of the pending charge is postponed. Secondly, under procedures now widely practiced, the duration of his present imprisonment may be increased, and the conditions under which he must serve his sentence greatly worsened, by the pendency of another criminal charge outstanding against him.
>
> And while it might be argued that a person already in prison would be less likely than others to be affected by "anxiety and concern accompanying public accusation," there is reason to believe that an outstanding untried charge (of which even a convict may, of course, be

innocent) can have fully as depressive an effect upon a prisoner as upon a person who is at large.

* * *

Finally, * * * while "evidence and witnesses disappear, memories fade, and events lose their perspective," a man isolated in prison is powerless to exert his own investigative efforts to mitigate these erosive effects of the passage of time.

One year later, in Dickey v. Florida, 398 U.S. 30 (1970), the Court ordered a prosecution dismissed when a federal prisoner made persistent requests for a speedy trial on an armed robbery charge, and for seven years Florida took no action to bring him to trial. In the interim, potential defense witnesses had died or disappeared. Chief Justice Burger wrote the opinion for a unanimous court, stating that "[a]lthough a great many accused persons seek to put off the confrontation as long as possible, the right to a prompt inquiry into criminal charges is fundamental and the duty of the charging authority is to provide a prompt trial."

B. DELAY IN ARRESTING OR CHARGING THE DEFENDANT

Klopfer, *Smith*, and *Dickey* all wanted the charges brought against them disposed of promptly. But what if no formal charge or arrest is made against a person, and yet it is clear that one might be forthcoming at some future time? Presumably the suspect is concerned about the prosecution that is looming, but what protection, if any, can be claimed? That is the issue in the next two principal cases.

1. Speedy Trial Clause Analysis

UNITED STATES V. MARION

Supreme Court of the United States, 1971.
404 U.S. 307.

JUSTICE WHITE delivered the opinion of the Court.

This appeal requires us to decide whether dismissal of a federal indictment was constitutionally required by reason of a period of three years between the occurrence of the alleged criminal acts and the filing of the indictment.

* * *

Appellees * * * claim that their rights to a speedy trial were violated by the period of approximately three years between the end of the criminal scheme charged and the return of the indictment * * *. In our view, however, the Sixth Amendment speedy trial provision has no application until the putative defendant in some way becomes an "accused," an event that occurred in this case only when the appellees were indicted on April 21, 1970.

The Sixth Amendment provides that "[i]n all criminal prosecutions, the accused shall enjoy the right to a speedy and public trial * * *." On its face, the protection of the Amendment is activated only when a criminal prosecution has begun and extends only to those persons who have been "accused" in the course of that prosecution. * * *

It is apparent also that very little support for appellees' position emerges from a consideration of the purposes of the Sixth Amendment's speedy trial provision, a guarantee that this Court has termed "an important safeguard to prevent undue and oppressive incarceration prior to trial, to minimize anxiety and concern accompanying public accusation and to limit the possibilities that long delay will impair the ability of an accused to defend himself." Inordinate delay between arrest, indictment, and trial may impair a defendant's ability to present an effective defense. But the major evils protected against by the speedy trial guarantee exist quite apart from actual or possible prejudice to an accused's defense. * * * Arrest is a public act that may seriously interfere with the defendant's liberty, whether he is free on bail or not, and that may disrupt his employment, drain his financial resources, curtail his associations, subject him to public obloquy, and create anxiety in him, his family and his friends. * * * So viewed, it is readily understandable that it is either a formal indictment or information or else the actual restraints imposed by arrest and holding to answer a criminal charge that engage the particular protections of the speedy trial provision of the Sixth Amendment.

Invocation of the speedy trial provision thus need not await indictment, information, or other formal charge. But we decline to extend the reach of the amendment to the period prior to arrest. Until this event occurs, a citizen suffers no restraints on his liberty and is not the subject of public accusation; his situation does not compare with that of a defendant who has been arrested and held to answer. * * *

* * * [T]he applicable statute of limitations is the primary guarantee against bringing overly stale criminal charges. * * * These statutes provide predictability by specifying a limit beyond which there is an irrebuttable presumption that a defendant's right to a fair trial would be prejudiced. * * * There is thus no need to press the Sixth Amendment into service to guard against the mere possibility that pre-accusation delays will prejudice the defense in a criminal case since statutes of limitation already perform that function.

* * *

[JUSTICE DOUGLAS, joined by JUSTICES BRENNAN and MARSHALL concurred in the result on the ground that the case against the defendants was complex and required extensive investigation, so that the government's three-year delay in bringing the prosecution was permissible under the circumstances.]

Second Indictment: United States v. MacDonald

In United States v. MacDonald, 456 U.S. 1 (1982), charges were brought against the defendant for murdering his wife and children. Those charges were dismissed without prejudice. Four years later the defendant was indicted on the same murder charges. MacDonald alleged a speedy trial violation—arguing that the speedy trial clock started ticking upon the initial indictment. MacDonald contended that the long delay allowed the prosecution to refresh the memory of its witnesses, and the defense could not adequately probe the recollection of the witnesses whose memories were refreshed. But the Supreme Court rejected these concerns as irrelevant and held that the time between the dropping of charges and a later indictment does not count toward the speedy trial determination.

The *MacDonald* Court reasoned that the speedy trial guarantee is designed to "minimize the possibility of lengthy incarceration prior to trial" and that after charges are dismissed, the citizen, as in *Marion,* suffers no restraints on his liberty. Chief Justice Burger, writing for the majority, concluded that once charges are dismissed, "the formerly accused is, at most, in the same position as any other subject of a criminal investigation." Justice Marshall, joined by Justices Brennan and Blackmun dissented, arguing that MacDonald suffered continuous anxiety, disruption of employment, financial strain, and public obloquy while the same government that arrested him continued to investigate him from the time that formal charges were dropped in 1970 until he was indicted in 1975. Justice Stevens concurred in the judgment. He agreed with the dissenters that the Speedy Trial Clause applied, but he found no violation because the government had a need "to proceed cautiously and deliberately before making a final decision to prosecute for such a serious offense."

Inconsistent Attachment of Sixth Amendment Rights?

The Sixth Amendment begins "In all criminal prosecutions" and then lists the rights protected, including the right to speedy trial and the right to counsel. United States v. Gouveia (Chapter 5, supra), and Kirby v. Illinois (Chapter 4, supra) construe the term "criminal prosecutions" and conclude that the right to counsel does not begin until a formal charge has been filed. In contrast, *Marion* construes the term "criminal prosecutions" and holds that the right to speedy trial attaches at *arrest.* How can the same term mean something different depending on the right invoked?

2. Due Process Clause Analysis

UNITED STATES V. LOVASCO

Supreme Court of the United States, 1977.
431 U.S. 783.

JUSTICE MARSHALL delivered the opinion of the Court.

* * *

On March 6, 1975, respondent was indicted for possessing eight firearms stolen from the United States mails, and for dealing in firearms without a license. The offenses were alleged to have occurred between July 25 and August 31, 1973, more than 18 months before the indictment was filed. Respondent moved to dismiss the indictment due to the delay.

The District Court conducted a hearing on respondent's motion at which the respondent sought to prove that the delay was unnecessary and that it had prejudiced his defense. In an effort to establish the former proposition, respondent presented a Postal Inspector's report on his investigation that was prepared one month after the crimes were committed, and a stipulation concerning the post-report progress of the probe. The report stated, in brief, that within the first month of the investigation respondent had admitted to Government agents that he had possessed and then sold five of the stolen guns, and that the agents had developed strong evidence linking respondent to the remaining three weapons. The report also stated, however, that the agents had been unable to confirm or refute respondent's claim that he had found the guns in his car when he returned to it after visiting his son, a mail handler, at work. The stipulation into which the Assistant United States Attorney entered indicated that little additional information concerning the crimes was uncovered in the 17 months following the preparation of the Inspector's report.

To establish prejudice to the defense, respondent testified that he had lost the testimony of two material witnesses due to the delay. The first witness, Tom Stewart, died more than a year after the alleged crimes occurred. At the hearing respondent claimed that Stewart had been his source for two or three of the guns. The second witness, respondent's brother, died in April 1974, eight months after the crimes were completed. Respondent testified that his brother was present when respondent called Stewart to secure the guns, and witnessed all of respondent's sales. Respondent did not state how the witnesses would have aided the defense had they been willing to testify.

* * * [P]roof of prejudice is generally a necessary but not sufficient element of a due process claim, and * * * the due process inquiry must consider the reasons for the delay as well as the prejudice to the accused.

The Court of Appeals found that the sole reason for the delay here was a hope on the part of the Government that others might be discovered who may have participated in the theft. It concluded that this hope did not justify the delay, and therefore affirmed the dismissal of the indictment. But the Due Process Clause does not permit courts to abort criminal prosecutions simply because they disagree with a prosecutor's judgment as to when to seek an indictment. * * *

[P]rosecutors are under no duty to file charges as soon as probable cause exists but before they are satisfied they will be able to establish the suspect's guilt beyond a reasonable doubt. To impose such a duty would have a deleterious effect both upon the rights of the accused and upon the ability of society to protect itself. From the perspective of potential defendants, requiring prosecutions to commence when probable cause is established is undesirable because it would increase the likelihood of unwarranted charges being filed, and would add to the time during which defendants stand accused but untried. * * * From the perspective of law enforcement officials, a requirement of immediate prosecution upon probable cause is equally unacceptable because it could make obtaining proof of guilt beyond a reasonable doubt impossible by causing potentially fruitful sources of information to evaporate before they are fully exploited. And from the standpoint of the courts, such a requirement is unwise because it would cause scarce resources to be consumed on cases that prove to be insubstantial, or that involve only some of the responsible parties or some of the criminal acts. Thus, no one's interests would be well served by compelling prosecutors to initiate prosecutions as soon as they are legally entitled to do so.

It might be argued that once the Government has assembled sufficient evidence to prove guilt beyond a reasonable doubt, it should be constitutionally required to file charges promptly, even if its investigation of the entire criminal transaction is not complete. Adopting such a rule, however, would have many of the same consequences as adopting a rule requiring immediate prosecution upon probable cause.

First, compelling a prosecutor to file public charges as soon as the requisite proof has been developed against one participant on one charge would cause numerous problems in those cases in which a criminal transaction involves more than one person or more than one illegal act. In some instances, an immediate arrest or indictment would impair the prosecutor's ability to continue his investigation, thereby preventing society from bringing lawbreakers to justice. In other cases, the prosecutor would be able to obtain additional indictments despite an early prosecution, but the necessary result would be multiple trials involving a single set of facts. Such trials place needless burdens on defendants, law enforcement officials, and courts.

Second, insisting on immediate prosecution once sufficient evidence is developed to obtain a conviction would pressure prosecutors into resolving doubtful cases in favor of early—and possibly unwarranted—prosecutions. * * * In the instant case, for example, since respondent admitted possessing at least five of the firearms, the primary factual issue in dispute was whether respondent knew the guns were stolen * * *. Not surprisingly, the Postal Inspector's report contained no direct evidence bearing on this issue. The decision whether to prosecute, therefore, required a necessarily subjective evaluation of the strength of the circumstantial evidence available and the credibility of respondent's denial. * * * To avoid the risk that a subsequent indictment would be dismissed for preindictment delay, the prosecutor might feel constrained to file premature charges, with all the disadvantages that would entail.

Finally, requiring the Government to make charging decisions immediately upon assembling evidence sufficient to establish guilt would preclude the Government from giving full consideration to the desirability of not prosecuting in particular cases. The decision to file criminal charges, with the awesome consequences it entails, requires consideration of a wide range of factors in addition to the strength of the Government's case, in order to determine whether prosecution would be in the public interest. * * * [T]he instant case provides a useful illustration. Although proof of the identity of the mail thieves was not necessary to convict respondent of the possessory crimes with which he was charged, it might have been crucial in assessing respondent's culpability, as distinguished from his legal guilt. If, for example, further investigation were to show that respondent had no role in or advance knowledge of the theft and simply agreed, out of paternal loyalty, to help his son dispose of the guns once respondent discovered his son had stolen them, the United States Attorney might have decided not to prosecute, especially since at the time of the crime respondent was over 60 years old and had no prior criminal record. Requiring prosecution once the evidence of guilt is clear, however, could prevent a prosecutor from awaiting the information necessary for such a decision.

We would be most reluctant to adopt a rule which would have these consequences absent a clear constitutional command to do so. We can find no such command in the Due Process Clause of the Fifth Amendment. In our view, investigative delay is fundamentally unlike delay undertaken by the Government solely "to gain tactical advantage over the accused," precisely because investigative delay is not so one-sided. Rather than deviating from elementary standards of "fair play and decency," a prosecutor abides by them if he refuses to seek indictments until he is completely satisfied that he should prosecute and will be able promptly to establish guilt beyond a reasonable doubt. Penalizing prosecutors who defer action for these reasons would subordinate the goal of "orderly expedition" to that of "mere speed." * * * We therefore hold that to prosecute a defendant following investigative delay does not deprive him of due process, even if his defense might have been somewhat prejudiced by the lapse of time.

* * *

[The dissenting opinion of JUSTICE STEVENS is omitted.]

COMMENT ON LOVASCO

If *Lovasco* had come out the other way, consider the oddity of the arguments that the parties would have to make. The defendant would have to argue that his case was indictment-worthy—he would point to the strength of the evidence against him. Then he would have to turn around and argue, to prove prejudice, that his important witnesses had been lost, thus impairing his strong defense. The government would have to argue that its case was weak, justifying delay for more investigation. This all seems reason enough to reject the idea that pre-accusation delay is actionable in the absence of bad faith on the part of the government.

Dismissal of indictments for pre-accusation delay, in the absence of bad faith, would also raise separation of powers problems. For example, in United States v. Crouch, 84 F.3d 1497 (5th Cir.1996) (en banc), the defendants, who were charged with bank fraud, argued that their indictments should be dismissed due to pre-accusation delay of seven years. They attributed the delay in their case to "lack of manpower and the low priority which this investigation was assigned." This resulted from "the failure of the Executive Branch and the Department of Justice to request sufficient funding and to assign appropriate priorities." The court responded to these contentions as follows:

> What are we to make of all this? Are we to say that there would be no due process violation if the President had vigorously and timely requested additional funds to investigate and prosecute these cases, but Congress had refused? Or, that even so we will find a due process violation because Congress shouldn't have refused? Of course, funds must come from somewhere. Are we to say that such additional funding is better than increasing taxes or the deficit or decreasing funding for some other programs? Are we to judge whether financial institution fraud should be assigned a higher priority than drug or other offenses? It seems to us that all those decisions are quintessentially the business of either the legislative or the executive branch, or both, rather than the judiciary. * * *
>
> Accordingly, we * * * hold that for preindictment delay to violate the due process clause it must not only cause the accused substantial, actual prejudice, but the delay must also have been intentionally undertaken by the government for the purpose of gaining some tactical advantage over the accused in the contemplated prosecution or for some other impermissible, bad faith purpose.

It must be remembered that the limits of Due Process protection for pre-indictment delay are set within the premise that "[t]he primary safeguard against unreasonable prosecutorial delay is the statute of limitations, not the Constitution." United States v. Hagler, 700 F.3d 1091 (7th Cir. 2012). So for example, the defendant does not establish prejudice under the Due Process Clause simply because memories might have faded. That is so because "statutes of limitations reflect a legislative judgment that so long as prosecutions are brought within the designated timeframe, then, notwithstanding the possible loss of crucial evidence or failure of memory, a defendant will be able to adequately defend himself." Id. Moreover, faded recollection affects both prosecution and defense witnesses.

C. ASSESSING SPEEDY TRIAL CLAIMS

BARKER V. WINGO

Supreme Court of the United States, 1972.
407 U.S. 514.

JUSTICE POWELL delivered the opinion of the Court.

* * *

On July 20, 1958, in Christian County, Kentucky, an elderly couple was beaten to death by intruders wielding an iron tire tool. Two suspects, Silas Manning and Willie Barker, the petitioner, were arrested shortly thereafter. The grand jury indicted them on September 15. Counsel was appointed on September 17, and Barker's trial was set for October 21. The Commonwealth had a stronger case against Manning, and it believed that Barker could not be convicted unless Manning testified against him. Manning was naturally unwilling to incriminate himself. Accordingly, on October 23, the day Silas Manning was brought to trial, the Commonwealth sought and obtained the first of what was to be a series of 16 continuances of Barker's trial. Barker made no objection. By first convicting Manning, the Commonwealth would remove possible problems of self-incrimination and would be able to assure his testimony against Barker.

The Commonwealth encountered more than a few difficulties in its prosecution of Manning. The first trial ended in a hung jury. A second trial resulted in a conviction, but the Kentucky Court of Appeals reversed because of the admission of evidence obtained by an illegal search. At his third trial, Manning was again convicted, and the Court of Appeals again reversed because the trial court had not granted a change of venue. A fourth trial resulted in a hung jury. Finally, after five trials, Manning was convicted, in March 1962, of murdering one victim, and after a sixth trial, in December 1962, he was convicted of murdering the other.

The Christian County Circuit Court holds three terms each year—in February, June, and September. Barker's initial trial was to take place in the September term of 1958. The first continuance postponed it until the

February 1959 term. The second continuance was granted for one month only. Every term thereafter for as long as the Manning prosecutions were in process, the Commonwealth routinely moved to continue Barker's case to the next term. When the case was continued from the June 1959 term until the following September, Barker, having spent 10 months in jail, obtained his release by posting a $5,000 bond. He thereafter remained free in the community until his trial. Barker made no objection, through his counsel, to the first 11 continuances.

When on February 12, 1962, the Commonwealth moved for the twelfth time to continue the case until the following term, Barker's counsel filed a motion to dismiss the indictment. The motion to dismiss was denied two weeks later, and the Commonwealth's motion for a continuance was granted. The Commonwealth was granted further continuances in June 1962 and September 1962, to which Barker did not object.

In February 1963, the first term of court following Manning's final conviction, the Commonwealth moved to set Barker's trial for March 19. But on the day scheduled for trial, it again moved for a continuance until the June term. It gave as its reason the illness of the ex-sheriff who was the chief investigating officer in the case. To this continuance, Barker objected unsuccessfully.

The witness was still unable to testify in June, and the trial, which had been set for June 19, was continued again until the September term over Barker's objection. This time the court announced that the case would be dismissed for lack of prosecution if it were not tried during the next term. The final trial date was set for October 9, 1963. On that date, Barker again moved to dismiss the indictment, and this time specified that his right to a speedy trial had been violated. The motion was denied; the trial commenced with Manning as the chief prosecution witness; Barker was convicted and given a life sentence.

* * *

The right to a speedy trial is generically different from any of the other rights enshrined in the Constitution for the protection of the accused. * * * [T]here is a societal interest in providing a speedy trial which exists separate from, and at times in opposition to, the interests of the accused. The inability of courts to provide a prompt trial has contributed to a large backlog of cases in urban courts which, among other things, enables defendants to negotiate more effectively for pleas of guilty to lesser offenses and otherwise manipulate the system. In addition, persons released on bond for lengthy periods awaiting trial have an opportunity to commit other crimes. * * * Moreover, the longer an accused is free awaiting trial, the more tempting becomes his opportunity to jump bail and escape. Finally, delay between arrest and punishment may have a detrimental effect on rehabilitation.

If an accused cannot make bail, he is generally confined, as was Barker for 10 months, in a local jail. This contributes to the overcrowding and generally deplorable state of those institutions. Lengthy exposure to these conditions has a destructive effect on human character and makes the rehabilitation of the individual offender much more difficult. * * * Finally, lengthy pretrial detention is costly. * * * In addition, society loses wages which might have been earned, and it must often support families of incarcerated breadwinners.

A second difference between the right to speedy trial and the accused's other constitutional rights is that deprivation of the right may work to the accused's advantage. Delay is not an uncommon defense tactic. As the time between the commission of the crime and trial lengthens, witnesses may become unavailable or their memories may fade. If the witnesses support the prosecution, its case will be weakened, sometimes seriously so. And it is the prosecution which carries the burden of proof. Thus, unlike the right to counsel or the right to be free from compelled self-incrimination, deprivation of the right to speedy trial does not *per se* prejudice the accused's ability to defend himself.

Finally, and perhaps most importantly, the right to speedy trial is a more vague concept than other procedural rights. It is, for example, impossible to determine with precision when the right has been denied. * * * As a consequence, there is no fixed point in the criminal process when the State can put the defendant to the choice of either exercising or waiving the right to a speedy trial. * * *

The amorphous quality of the right also leads to the unsatisfactorily severe remedy of dismissal of the indictment when the right has been deprived. This is indeed a serious consequence because it means that a defendant who may be guilty of a serious crime will go free, without having been tried. Such a remedy is more serious than an exclusionary rule or a reversal for a new trial, but it is the only possible remedy.

* * *

Perhaps because the speedy trial right is so slippery, two rigid approaches are urged upon us as ways of eliminating some of the uncertainty which courts experience in protecting the right. The first suggestion is that we hold that the Constitution requires a criminal defendant to be offered a trial within a specified time period. * * *

But such a result would require this Court to engage in legislative or rulemaking activity, rather than in the adjudicative process to which we should confine our efforts. * * * We find no constitutional basis for holding that the speedy trial right can be quantified into a specified number of days or months. * * *

The second suggested alternative would restrict consideration of the right to those cases in which the accused has demanded a speedy trial. * * *

Such an approach, by presuming waiver of a fundamental right from inaction, is inconsistent with this Court's pronouncements on waiver of constitutional rights. * * *

The nature of the speedy trial right does make it impossible to pinpoint a precise time in the process when the right must be asserted or waived, but that fact does not argue for placing the burden of protecting the right solely on defendants. A defendant has no duty to bring himself to trial; the State has that duty as well as the duty of insuring that the trial is consistent with due process. Moreover, for the reasons earlier expressed, society has a particular interest in bringing swift prosecutions, and society's representatives are the ones who should protect that interest.

* * *

We reject, therefore, the rule that a defendant who fails to demand a speedy trial forever waives his right. This does not mean, however, that the defendant has no responsibility to assert his right. We think the better rule is that the defendant's assertion of or failure to assert his right to a speedy trial is one of the factors to be considered in an inquiry into the deprivation of the right. Such a formulation * * * allows the trial court to exercise a judicial discretion based on the circumstances * * *. It would permit, for example, a court to attach a different weight to a situation in which the defendant knowingly fails to object from a situation in which his attorney acquiesces in long delay without adequately informing his client, or from a situation in which no counsel is appointed. It would also allow a court to weigh the frequency and force of the objections as opposed to attaching significant weight to a purely *pro forma* objection.

* * * We have shown above that the right to a speedy trial is unique in its uncertainty as to when and under what circumstances it must be asserted or may be deemed waived. But the rule we announce today, which comports with constitutional principles, places the primary burden on the courts and the prosecutors to assure that cases are brought to trial. We hardly need add that if delay is attributable to the defendant, then his waiver may be given effect under standard waiver doctrine, the demand rule aside.

* * *

A balancing test necessarily compels courts to approach speedy trial cases on an *ad hoc* basis. We can do little more than identify some of the factors which courts should assess in determining whether a particular defendant has been deprived of his right. Though some might express them in different ways, we identify four such factors: Length of delay, the reason for the delay, the defendant's assertion of his right, and prejudice to the defendant.

The length of the delay is to some extent a triggering mechanism. Until there is some delay which is presumptively prejudicial, there is no necessity for inquiry into the other factors that go into the balance. Nevertheless, because of the imprecision of the right to speedy trial, the length of delay that will provoke such an inquiry is necessarily dependent upon the peculiar circumstances of the case. To take but one example, the delay that can be tolerated for an ordinary street crime is considerably less than for a serious, complex conspiracy charge.

Closely related to length of delay is the reason the government assigns to justify the delay. Here, too, different weights should be assigned to different reasons. A deliberate attempt to delay the trial in order to hamper the defense should be weighted heavily against the government. A more neutral reason such as negligence or overcrowded courts should be weighted less heavily but nevertheless should be considered since the ultimate responsibility for such circumstances must rest with the government rather than with the defendant. Finally, a valid reason, such as a missing witness, should serve to justify appropriate delay.

We have already discussed the third factor, the defendant's responsibility to assert his right. Whether and how a defendant asserts his right is closely related to the other factors we have mentioned. * * * The more serious the deprivation, the more likely a defendant is to complain. The defendant's assertion of his speedy trial right, then, is entitled to strong evidentiary weight in determining whether the defendant is being deprived of the right. We emphasize that failure to assert the right will make it difficult for a defendant to prove that he was denied a speedy trial.

A fourth factor is prejudice to the defendant. Prejudice, of course, should be assessed in the light of the interests of defendants which the speedy trial right was designed to protect. This Court has identified three such interests: (i) to prevent oppressive pretrial incarceration; (ii) to minimize anxiety and concern of the accused; and (iii) to limit the possibility that the defense will be impaired. Of these, the most serious is the last, because the inability of a defendant adequately to prepare his case skews the fairness of the entire system. If witnesses die or disappear during a delay, the prejudice is obvious. * * *

We have discussed previously the societal disadvantages of lengthy pretrial incarceration, but obviously the disadvantages for the accused who cannot obtain his release are even more serious. The time spent in jail awaiting trial has a detrimental impact on the individual. It often means loss of a job; it disrupts family life; and it enforces idleness. * * * Moreover, if a defendant is locked up, he is hindered in his ability to gather evidence, contact witnesses, or otherwise prepare his defense. * * * Finally, even if an accused is not incarcerated prior to trial, he is still disadvantaged by restraints on his liberty and by living under a cloud of anxiety, suspicion, and often hostility.

We regard none of the four factors identified above as either a necessary or sufficient condition to the finding of a deprivation of the right of speedy trial. Rather, they are related factors and must be considered together with such other circumstances as may be relevant.

* * *

The difficulty of the task of balancing these factors is illustrated by this case, which we consider to be close. It is clear that the length of delay between arrest and trial—well over five years—was extraordinary. Only seven months of that period can be attributed to a strong excuse, the illness of the ex-sheriff who was in charge of the investigation. Perhaps some delay would have been permissible under ordinary circumstances, so that Manning could be utilized as a witness in Barker's trial, but more than four years was too long a period, particularly since a good part of that period was attributable to the Commonwealth's failure or inability to try Manning under circumstances that comported with due process.

Two counterbalancing factors, however, outweigh these deficiencies. The first is that prejudice was minimal. Of course, Barker was prejudiced to some extent by living for over four years under a cloud of suspicion and anxiety. Moreover, although he was released on bond for most of the period, he did spend 10 months in jail before trial. But there is no claim that any of Barker's witnesses died or otherwise became unavailable owing to the delay. The trial transcript indicates only two very minor lapses of memory—one on the part of a prosecution witness—which were in no way significant to the outcome.

More important than the absence of serious prejudice, is the fact that Barker did not want a speedy trial. * * * Instead the record strongly suggests that while he hoped to take advantage of the delay in which he had acquiesced, and thereby obtain a dismissal of the charges, he definitely did not want to be tried.

* * *

The probable reason for Barker's attitude was that he was gambling on Manning's acquittal. The evidence was not very strong against Manning, as the reversals and hung juries suggest, and Barker undoubtedly thought that if Manning were acquitted, he would never be tried.

* * *

We do not hold that there may never be a situation in which an indictment may be dismissed on speedy trial grounds where the defendant has failed to object to continuances. There may be a situation in which the defendant was represented by incompetent counsel, was severely prejudiced, or even cases in which the continuances were granted *ex parte*. But barring extraordinary circumstances, we would be reluctant indeed to rule that a defendant was denied this constitutional right on a record that strongly indicates as does this one, that the defendant did not want a speedy trial. We hold, therefore, that Barker was not deprived of his due process right to a speedy trial.

The judgment of the Court of Appeals is affirmed.

JUSTICE WHITE, with whom JUSTICE BRENNAN joins, concurring.

Although the Court rejects petitioner's speedy trial claim * * *, it is apparent that had Barker not so clearly acquiesced in the major delays * * * the result would have been otherwise. * * *

Application of the Barker Test: Doggett v. United States

In Doggett v. United States, 505 U.S. 647 (1992), the Court applied and elaborated upon the *Barker* factors. It found that an 8 1/2 year-delay between Doggett's indictment and trial violated his Sixth Amendment right to a speedy trial, even though Doggett knew nothing about the indictment during that delay. Doggett was indicted on federal drug charges, but he left the country before he could be informed of the indictment. Two years after leaving, he returned to the United States, passed unhindered through Customs, married, went to college, found a job, lived openly under his own name, and engaged in no further criminal misconduct. Six years after his return, the Marshal's Service ran a credit check on several thousand people subject to outstanding arrest warrants and, within minutes, found where Doggett lived and worked. He was arrested within days of the credit check. Up to the time of his arrest, Doggett was never aware of the fact that he had been indicted more than eight years earlier.

Justice Souter wrote the majority opinion for five Justices. He addressed the first *Barker* factor—whether delay before trial was "uncommonly long"—as a "double enquiry." He explained as follows:

> Simply to trigger a speedy trial analysis, an accused must allege that the interval between accusation and trial has crossed the threshold dividing ordinary from "presumptively prejudicial" delay, * * *. If the accused makes this showing, the court must then consider, as one factor among several, the extent to which the delay stretches beyond the bare minimum needed to trigger judicial examination of the claim. This latter enquiry is significant to the speedy trial analysis

> because * * * the presumption that pretrial delay has prejudiced the accused intensifies over time.

So to trigger a *Barker* enquiry, the defendant must show that the delay was presumptively prejudicial. The *Doggett* majority stated that lower courts have generally undertaken the *Barker* enquiry when the period of postaccusation delay "approaches one year."[1] The Court therefore had no trouble finding that the "extraordinary" delay in Doggett's case was sufficient "to trigger the speedy trial enquiry."

As to the second *Barker* factor, concerning responsibility for the delay, Justice Souter relied on the findings of the lower court that the delay occurring after Doggett returned to the United States was attributable to the government. He concluded that "while the Government's lethargy may have reflected no more than Doggett's relative unimportance in the world of drug trafficking, it was still findable negligence, and the finding stands."

As to the third *Barker* factor, concerning the defendant's diligence in asserting his speedy trial rights, Justice Souter again relied on the findings of the lower court that Doggett was unaware of his indictment until he was arrested. Had that not been the case, the third factor would have been "weighed heavily against him." Thus, Justice Souter implied that a person who knows he is indicted, and who is at large, will lose his speedy trial claim because of his failure to timely assert it, even if he is not being diligently pursued by the authorities.

The fourth *Barker* factor, that of prejudice due to the delay, presented the most difficult problem for the majority, because Doggett was neither incarcerated nor aware of his indictment during the delay. Justice Souter noted that there was more to the "prejudice" factor than incarceration and anxiety over the indictment:

> We have observed in prior cases that unreasonable delay between formal accusation and trial threatens to produce more than one sort of harm, including * * * the possibility that the accused's defense will be impaired by dimming memories and loss of exculpatory evidence. * * * [T]he inability of a defendant adequately to prepare his case skews the fairness of the entire system.

After holding that the defendant could be prejudiced by the delay even though he was not incarcerated or under any anxiety during that time, the majority addressed the Government's argument that Doggett's claim should fail because he had "failed to make any affirmative showing that the delay weakened his ability to raise specific defenses, elicit specific testimony, or produce specific items of evidence." Justice Souter responded

---

[1] See also Joseph, Speedy Trial Rights in Application, 48 Fordham L.Rev. 611 (1980) (quoted in *Doggett*, noting a general consensus that a delay is presumptively prejudicial if it is longer than eight months, and that there is general agreement that a delay of less than five months is not presumptively prejudicial).

to this argument by stating that "consideration of prejudice is not limited to the specifically demonstrable" and that "affirmative proof of particularized prejudice is not essential to every speedy trial claim." He elaborated as follows:

> Our speedy trial standards recognize that pretrial delay is often both inevitable and wholly justifiable. The government may need time to collect witnesses against the accused, oppose his pretrial motions, or, if he goes into hiding, track him down. We attach great weight to such considerations when balancing them against the costs of going forward with a trial whose probative accuracy the passage of time has begun by degrees to throw into question. Thus, in this case, if the Government had pursued Doggett with reasonable diligence from his indictment to his arrest, his speedy trial claim would fail. * * *
>
> * * * [O]n the other hand, Doggett would prevail if he could show that the Government had intentionally held back in its prosecution of him to gain some impermissible advantage at trial. * * *
>
> Between diligent prosecution and bad-faith delay, official negligence in bringing an accused to trial occupies the middle ground. While not compelling relief in every case where bad-faith delay would make relief virtually automatic, neither is negligence automatically tolerable simply because the accused cannot demonstrate exactly how it has prejudiced him. * * *
>
> Although negligence is obviously to be weighed more lightly than a deliberate intent to harm the accused's defense, it still falls on the wrong side of the divide between acceptable and unacceptable reasons for delaying a criminal prosecution once it has begun. And such is the nature of the prejudice presumed that the weight we assign to official negligence compounds over time as the presumption of evidentiary prejudice grows. Thus, our toleration of such negligence varies inversely with its protractedness, and its consequent threat to the fairness of the accused's trial. * * *
>
> To be sure, to warrant granting relief, negligence unaccompanied by particularized trial prejudice must have lasted longer than negligence demonstrably causing such prejudice. But even so, the Government's egregious persistence in failing to prosecute Doggett is clearly sufficient.

Applying these factors, Justice Souter concluded that Doggett was entitled to dismissal of the indictment because the Government's negligence caused a delay "six times as long as that generally sufficient to trigger judicial review" and the presumption of prejudice was "neither extenuated, as by the defendant's acquiescence, nor persuasively rebutted."

Justice O'Connor wrote a short dissenting opinion in *Doggett*. She would have required a showing of actual prejudice. She also noted that "delay is a two-edged sword" because the Government bears the burden of proof beyond a reasonable doubt, and "the passage of time may make it difficult or impossible for the Government to carry this burden."

Justice Thomas, joined by Chief Justice Rehnquist and Justice Scalia, wrote a lengthy dissent in which he argued that the Speedy Trial Clause provides direct protection against only two "evils": 1) "oppressive and undue incarceration;" and 2) the "anxiety and concern accompanying public accusation." Because Doggett suffered neither of these burdens during the delay, Justice Thomas would have dismissed the speedy trial claim even if Doggett had proven that the passage of time had prejudiced his defense. In Justice Thomas's view, any possibility that a defendant may not be able to defend himself due to a pretrial delay was adequately protected by the Due Process Clause and by statutes of limitations.

Justice Thomas argued that the Speedy Trial Clause could not logically be concerned with prejudice to the defense resulting from pretrial delay. He explained as follows:

> [P]rejudice to the defense stems from the interval between crime and trial, which is quite distinct from the interval between accusation and trial. * * * A defendant prosecuted 10 years after a crime is just as hampered in his ability to defend himself whether he was indicted the week after the crime or the week before the trial—but no one would suggest that the Clause protects him in the latter situation, where the delay did not substantially impair his liberty, either through oppressive incarceration or the anxiety of known criminal charges. * * * The initiation of a formal criminal prosecution is simply irrelevant to whether the defense has been prejudiced by delay.

QUESTIONS AFTER DOGGETT

Who suffers more from a pretrial delay: a person who knows he is being investigated but has not been arrested, or a person like Doggett who has been indicted but knows nothing about it? If you think that a person who knows he is being investigated suffers more than a person like Doggett, does that mean that Justice Thomas is correct in concluding that *Barker's* fuzzy prejudice analysis is flawed? Or does it mean that the Court in *Marion* was wrong when it denied the protection of the Speedy Trial Clause to persons who have not yet been arrested or charged?

Justice O'Connor's point about the government's ability to prove its case being hampered by delay is made in Green, "Hare and Hounds": The Fugitive Defendant's Constitutional Right to be Pursued, 56 Brooklyn L.Rev. 439, 507 (1990) ("the passage of time is more likely to hurt the prosecution than the defense which, after all, has no obligation to call witnesses or present evidence, but need only, and in many cases does only, put the government to its proof").

Excusable Delay

Doggett holds that when the government has a good reason for a post-charge delay, the defendant's burden of showing prejudice is substantially increased. What constitutes excusable delay? In United States v. Vassell, 970 F.2d 1162 (2nd Cir.1992), the court held that a seven-month delay did not amount to a Speedy Trial Clause violation where the government spent most of that time trying to get Vassell's co-defendant to take a deal and testify against Vassell. The court stated:

> A guilty plea takes time to negotiate. A defendant may initially reject the plea offered by the government. Because prosecutors must obtain approval of a plea from their superiors, negotiations may drag on almost interminably. At some point the process may become so extreme as to prejudice co-defendants who are either not offered a plea, or who reject the plea offer. However, we are not called upon to establish a rigid time table prescribing how long the government may take to procure a guilty plea. Rather, consistent with the ad hoc balancing required by *Barker*, we hold only that a seven-month delay in a complex case is not transformed into a Sixth Amendment violation just because the government sought the delay to encourage a co-defendant to testify against a remaining defendant at trial.

In United States v. Loud Hawk, 474 U.S. 302 (1986), a majority of the Supreme Court concluded that "an interlocutory appeal by the Government [an appeal on a judge's ruling before a verdict has been rendered] ordinarily is a valid reason that justifies delay." Justice Powell's opinion observed that in assessing whether the delay is justifiable, the factors that might be examined "include the strength of the Government's position on the appealed issue, the importance of the issue in the posture of the case, and—in some cases—the seriousness of the crime." The opinion also stated that defendants ordinarily cannot use the delay caused by their *own* interlocutory appeals to support a speedy trial claim. Justice Marshall's dissenting opinion, joined by Justices Brennan, Blackmun, and Stevens, argued that the court of appeals, which took over five years to decide two interlocutory appeals, one of which was expedited, delayed a "patently unreasonable" amount of time and that the prosecutor's good faith could not discharge the responsibility of a court to decide an appeal within a reasonable period of time.

Defendant's Diligence

Under *Barker* and *Doggett,* a defendant's diligence in asserting his speedy trial right is a critical factor. A defendant who seeks to evade prosecution is unlikely to prevail on a speedy trial claim. In United States v. Aguirre, 994 F.2d 1454 (9th Cir.1993), Aguirre knew about his indictment during the five-year period before he was arrested. While the five-year delay was presumptively prejudicial under *Doggett*, the court noted that the government had diligently pursued the defendant during that period. Because the delay was not attributable to the government but to Aguirre's evasive actions, Aguirre was required to show prejudice, and this he could not do. But the court said that even if Aguirre had shown prejudice, his speedy trial claim would have been denied:

> Where, as here, the government diligently pursues the defendant and the defendant is aware that the government is trying to find him, even severe prejudice would still not be enough to tip the balance in his favor. Here Aguirre knew his charges were pending, but [chose not to appear]; the government, on the other hand, conducted a reasonably diligent investigation to find him. It's true that prejudice can arise with time, but it's equally true in situations like Aguirre's that the defendant, not the government, is in the best position to stop the clock and avoid the damage.

It goes without saying that to the extent the trial is delayed because the defendant is making pre-trial motions that are being considered and disposed of, this will not count against the government in the *Barker/Doggett* calculus. See United States v. Munoz-Amado, 182 F.3d 57 (1st Cir.1999) (rejecting a speedy trial claim and noting that the defendant "ignores the role his many pretrial motions played in causing the nineteen month delay between his indictment and the jury trial").

Delay and Prejudice

The Court in *Doggett* stated that, at some point, delay attributable to the government will be so extended that prejudice will be presumed—meaning that the defendant will not have to show, specifically, how he was prejudiced by the delay. The need to find prejudice thus diminishes as the delay mounts. The eight-year delay in *Doggett* went beyond the point of presumptive prejudice; but where is that point exactly? In United States v. Beamon, 992 F.2d 1009 (9th Cir.1993), the government was responsible for a 17 month delay. While this was long enough to trigger a *Barker-Doggett* inquiry, the court held that it was not long enough "to relieve the defendant of the burden of coming forward with any showing of actual prejudice." Thus forced to show prejudice, the defendant argued that the delay impaired his ability to negotiate a deal with the government. But the court held that "a diminished plea bargaining position does not amount to impairment of defense."[2] Because the defendant could not show that he

[2] For another case on the meaning of "prejudice" under *Barker* and *Doggett*, see United States v. Mundt, 29 F.3d 233 (6th Cir.1994) (in a tax prosecution, the defendant suffered no

suffered any form of prejudice in trial presentation, his appeal was dismissed.

Thus, under *Doggett*, the term "presumptive prejudice" has two distinct meanings. First, the delay must be so long as to trigger the *Barker-Doggett* inquiry in the first place. In this sense, the delay is presumptively prejudicial when it approaches one year. Second, if the delay is attributable to the government, it might be so long as to be presumptively prejudicial—meaning in this context that the defendant does not need to show specifically how the delay prejudiced him. In *Beamon*, the 17 month delay was presumptively prejudicial in the first (threshold, triggering) sense, but not in the second (balancing) sense. In *Doggett*, the delay was presumptively prejudicial as to both the threshold and the balancing inquiries. See also United States v. Brown, 169 F.3d 344 (6th Cir.1999) ("Given the extraordinary [five-year] delay in this case combined with the fact that the delay was attributable to the government's negligence in pursuing Brown, we conclude that the government did not sufficiently rebut the presumption that its delay did not prejudice Brown's case."); United States v. Graham, 128 F.3d 372 (6th Cir.1997) (eight year delay, much of it due to the trial court's failure to move discovery along and to appoint new counsel for one of the co-defendants; prejudice in *Barker-Doggett* balancing inquiry was presumed due to the length of the delay).

Delay Caused by Appointed Counsel Is Not Attributable to the State: Vermont v. Brillon

The *Barker* test for assessing whether the right to speedy trial is violated focuses in part on "the reason for delay." A speedy trial violation cannot be found unless the delay can be attributed to the state. What happens if the delay is attributable to defense counsel who was *appointed* by the state? In Vermont v. Brillon, 556 U.S. 81 (2009), the lower court found a speedy trial violation by attributing to the state the delays caused by the failure of Brillon's appointed counsel "to move his case forward." But the Supreme Court, in an opinion by Justice Ginsburg, held that "an assigned counsel's failure to move the case forward does not warrant attribution of delay to the state." While the Vermont Defender's office is funded by the State, Justice Ginsburg declared that "the individual counsel here acted only on behalf of Brillon, not the State." Justice Ginsburg noted the problems that would arise if delay by appointed counsel could be considered delay by the state:

> A contrary conclusion could encourage appointed counsel to delay proceedings by seeking unreasonable continuances, hoping thereby to obtain a dismissal of the indictment on speedy-trial grounds. Trial

---

prejudice from a long delay where his "position was and continues to be that he is not subject to the federal tax laws"; that defense is not dependent on witnesses or fresh recollections).

> courts might well respond by viewing continuance requests made by appointed counsel with skepticism, concerned that even an apparently genuine need for more time is in reality a delay tactic.

Justice Ginsburg noted however that "the general rule attributing to the defendant delay caused by assigned counsel is not absolute." Specifically, delay resulting from a "systemic breakdown in the public defender system" could be charged to the State. But Justice Ginsburg found "nothing in the record suggests, that institutional problems caused any part of the delay in Brillon's case."[3]

D. REMEDIES FOR SPEEDY TRIAL VIOLATIONS

In Strunk v. United States, 412 U.S. 434 (1973), the Court considered what remedies are available when the defendant's right to a speedy trial has been violated. The court of appeals had found a speedy trial violation, but declared that the "extreme" remedy of dismissal of the charges with prejudice was unwarranted. The court of appeals thought that a more appropriate remedy would be reduction in Strunk's sentence to compensate for the period of unnecessary delay. But Chief Justice Burger's opinion for a unanimous Court rejected this alternative. The Chief Justice wrote that "[i]n light of the policies which underlie the right to a speedy trial, dismissal must remain, as *Barker* noted, the only possible remedy."

Can you imagine situations in which you might find a speedy trial violation but *not* require dismissal? For example, if the only form of prejudice suffered by delay was incarceration, would it make sense to simply reduce the sentence of a defendant who was convicted after a delayed trial? Why is dismissal necessary in such a case?

If *Strunk* really means that there is only one remedy for all speedy trial violations and that remedy is the drastic one of dismissal, how likely is it that the courts will find speedy trial violations in the first place? Professor Arkin, in Speedy Criminal Appeal: A Right Without a Remedy, 74 Minn.L.Rev. 437, 482 (1990), argues that because of the extreme, exclusive remedy provided by *Barker* and *Strunk,* courts have "refused to find speedy trial violations except in the most outlandish cases" and that the *Barker-Strunk* remedy "effectively gutted the right."

E. THE RIGHT TO SPEEDY SENTENCING

In Betterman v. Montana, 578 U.S. 437 (2016), Justice Ginsburg wrote for the Court as it held that the Speedy Trial Clause does not apply to delayed sentencing. Betterman failed to appear in court on domestic relation charges. He pled guilty to bail-jumping and was jailed for over 14 months prior to sentencing due to delay in preparation of the pre-sentence

---

[3] Justice Breyer, joined by Justice Stevens, wrote a short dissent, arguing that the writ of certiorari should have been dismissed as improvidently granted.

report, the trial court's ruling on motions, and the trial court's setting a sentencing hearing. The Montana Supreme Court rejected Betterman's claim that his speedy trial right had been denied, and the U.S. Supreme Court agreed.

Justice Ginsburg described the three phases of criminal proceedings: the investigation and decision to charge a suspect, the disposition by trial or plea, and sentencing. She identified statutes of limitations as providing the primary protection against delay, with the Due Process Clause protecting against fundamentally unfair prosecutorial conduct; and the Speedy Trial Clause as providing the primary protection against delay in the second stage during which a defendant is presumed innocent until final disposition. She found that the Speedy Trial Clause was concerned with presumptively innocent individuals and that the Clause loses force upon conviction.

Because dismissal of charges is the remedy for a speedy trial violation, Justice Ginsburg found that such a remedy would be an unwarranted windfall for a convicted defendant whose sentence is delayed. She rejected Betterman's argument that, because guilty pleas are so prevalent, sentencing is the real forum for dispute resolution and the Clause should require speedy sentences. She observed that a central feature of contemporary sentences is preparation of pre-sentence reports that often will delay sentencing.

Justice Ginsburg pointed out that the inapplicability of the Speedy Trial Clause to sentencing did not mean that a defendant has no protection against undue delay. She pointed to court rules like Fed. Rule Crim. Proc. 32(b)(1), which directs the court to "impose sentence without unnecessary delay," and noted that a defendant "retains an interest in a sentencing proceeding that is fundamentally fair" and comports with due process.

Justice Thomas, joined by Justice Alito, concurred and agreed "with the Court that the Sixth Amendment's Speedy Trial Clause does not apply to sentencing proceedings, except perhaps to bifurcated sentencing proceedings where sentencing enhancements operate as functional elements of a greater offense" and with the Court's judgment not to elaborate on the role of the Due Process Clause in a case in which no due process claim was raised.

Justice Sotomayor also concurred and, after observing that the Court left open what a defendant might have to show to make out a Due Process Clause violation based on a delay in sentencing, suggested that "the *Barker* factors capture many of the concerns posed in the sentencing delay context and that because the *Barker* test is flexible, it will allow courts to take account of any differences between trial and sentencing delays."

Justice Thomas's concurrence responded to Justice Sotomayor's suggestion by saying he would not prejudge the matter and that the *Barker* factors "may not necessarily translate to the delayed sentencing context."

F. BEYOND THE CONSTITUTION: STATUTORY AND JUDICIAL TIME LIMITS

Although not required by the Sixth Amendment, a large number of jurisdictions have, by statute or court rule, set time limits for bringing cases to trial. The statutes and rules that have been adopted differ greatly, as each jurisdiction is free to set up any protective system that it wishes. Because of these statutes and rules, there has been a shift from constitutional litigation to statutory interpretation.

The Federal Speedy Trial Act

One important statute is the Speedy Trial Act of 1974. 18 U.S.C.A. §§ 3161–74. The Act provides definite time periods for bringing an accused to trial. The operation of the Speedy Trial Act was described by the Court in Zedner v. United States, 547 U.S. 489 (2006):

> [T]he Speedy Trial Act generally requires a trial to begin within 70 days of the filing of an information or indictment or the defendant's initial appearance, 18 U.S.C. § 3161(c)(1), but the Act recognizes that criminal cases vary widely and that there are valid reasons for greater delay in particular cases. To provide the necessary flexibility, the Act includes a long and detailed list of periods of delay that are excluded in computing the time within which trial must start. See § 3161(h). For example, the Act excludes "delay resulting from other proceedings concerning the defendant," § 3161(h)(1), "delay resulting from the absence or unavailability of the defendant or an essential witness," § 3161(h)(3), "delay resulting from the fact that the defendant is mentally incompetent or physically unable to stand trial," § 3161(h)(4), and "[a] reasonable period of delay when the defendant is joined for trial with a codefendant as to whom the time for trial has not run and no motion for severance has been granted," § 3161(h)(7).
>
> Much of the Act's flexibility is furnished by § 3161(h)(8), which governs ends-of-justice continuances * * *. This provision permits a district court to grant a continuance and to exclude the resulting delay if the court, after considering certain factors, makes on-the-record findings that the ends of justice served by granting the continuance outweigh the public's and defendant's interests in a speedy trial. This provision gives the district court discretion—within limits and subject to specific procedures—to accommodate limited delays for case-specific needs.

Dismissal with or Without Prejudice

If the applicable time limits of the Speedy Trial Act are not adhered to, charges against the defendant may be dismissed *either with or without prejudice*.[4] See 18 U.S.C.A. § 3162(a)(1)(2). The Court in *Zedner* described how the appropriate remedy is determined:

> In making that choice [between dismissal with or without prejudice], the court must take into account, among other things, "the seriousness of the offense; the facts and circumstances of the case which led to the dismissal; and the impact of a reprosecution on the administration of [the Act] and on the administration of justice." § 3162(a)(2).
>
> This scheme is designed to promote compliance with the Act without needlessly subverting important criminal prosecutions. The more severe sanction (dismissal with prejudice) is available for use where appropriate, and the knowledge that a violation could potentially result in the imposition of this sanction gives the prosecution a powerful incentive to be careful about compliance. The less severe sanction (dismissal without prejudice) lets the court avoid unduly impairing the enforcement of federal criminal laws—though even this sanction imposes some costs on the prosecution and the court, which further encourages compliance. When an indictment is dismissed without prejudice, the prosecutor may of course seek—and in the great majority of cases will be able to obtain—a new indictment, for even if "the period prescribed by the applicable statute of limitations has expired, a new indictment may be returned . . . within six calendar months of the date of the dismissal." § 3288.

In United States v. Taylor, 487 U.S. 326 (1988), the Supreme Court held that an indictment should have been dismissed *without* prejudice where the defendant failed to appear for his trial on federal narcotics charges, which was scheduled one day prior to expiration of the statutory period, and subsequently the government exceeded by 15 days the period permitted between the defendant's arrest and the filing of a superseding indictment. Justice Blackmun wrote for the court and reasoned that the statute provides no preference for whether a dismissal should be with or without prejudice; it permits district courts to exercise sound discretion. The Court noted that the statute sets forth specific factors—seriousness of the offense, facts and circumstances leading to dismissal, and the impact of a reprosecution on the speedy trial process and the administration of justice—as being "among others" that the Court may consider in ruling on a motion to dismiss. The Court determined that prejudice to the defendant was also a factor. It observed that the district court did not explain why these factors justified a dismissal with prejudice and that it had ignored

[4] Some states require dismissals to be with prejudice. See, e.g., Alaska Crim.R. 45(g); Wash. CrRLJ 3.3(h).

the "brevity of the delay" as well as Taylor's own "illicit contribution to the delay" (i.e., his failure to appear).

Where the defendant has already served a good part of his sentence by the time of appeal, the preferred remedy for a Speedy Trial Act violation is a dismissal of the indictment. The court applied this preference in United States v. Blackwell, 12 F.3d 44 (5th Cir.1994):

> [W]hile the maximum time of incarceration Blackwell could receive for committing the offense of impersonating a federal officer is three years, he has already been incarcerated for over two years. * * * [A] reprosecution would work a manifest injustice upon Blackwell, given the time he has already effectively "served" for this conviction which we reverse today due to the Speedy Trial Act violation in this case.

Time Limits of the Speedy Trial Act Cannot Be Waived Prospectively: Zedner v. United States

The Court in Zedner v. United States, 547 U.S. 489 (2006), considered the validity and relevance of the defendant's waiver of rights under the Speedy Trial Act. The defendant had asked for a long adjournment (which of course was excludible delay), but the trial court was concerned that the defendant might waive the right "only for so long as it is convenient for you to waive." So the trial judge said "if I am going to give you that long an adjournment, I will have to take a waiver for all time." After conferring with counsel, the defendant signed a waiver of speedy trial rights. After a variety of delays—including withdrawal of counsel, a competency determination, and a motion to dismiss for violation of the Speedy Trial Act—the trial finally began, six years after the defendant was indicted. Justice Alito, writing for the Court, declared that the protections of the Act are not prospectively waivable, most importantly because the Act protects more than the rights of the defendant:

> If the Act were designed solely to protect a defendant's right to a speedy trial, it would make sense to allow a defendant to waive the application of the Act. But the Act was designed with the public interest firmly in mind. That public interest cannot be served, the Act recognizes, if defendants may opt out of the Act entirely. * * * Because defendants may be content to remain on pretrial release, and indeed may welcome delay, it is unsurprising that Congress refrained from empowering defendants to make prospective waivers of the Act's application.

The Court distinguished waivers of a completed violation of the Act (for example, by simply not objecting), which are permitted by the Act, from prospective waivers, which are not:

It is significant that § 3162(a)(2) makes no mention of prospective waivers, and there is no reason to think that Congress wanted to treat prospective and retrospective waivers similarly. Allowing prospective waivers would seriously undermine the Act because there are many cases—like the case at hand—in which the prosecution, the defense, and the court would all be happy to opt out of the Act, to the detriment of the public interest. The sort of retrospective waiver allowed by § 3161(a)(2) does not pose a comparable danger because the prosecution and the court cannot know until the trial actually starts or the guilty plea is actually entered whether the defendant will forgo moving to dismiss. As a consequence, the prosecution and the court retain a strong incentive to make sure that the trial begins on time.

COVID-19, the Pandemic and Speedy Trial

Courts were forced by the COVID-19 pandemic to recognize that trials could not readily proceed without posing serious health threats to all participants and that most courtrooms were not easily adapted to account for social distancing. Thus, some courts suspended the Speedy Trial Act. For example, in United States v. Taylor, 2020 WL 7264070 (D.D.C. 2020), the court wrote:

> While many people have had their plans and living situations upended by the COVID-19 pandemic, few have suffered as much as those jail inmates whose pretrial detention has extended month after month. This case, unfortunately, provides a prime example. Although Defendants James Taylor, Darin Moore, Gabriel Brown, and John Sweeney were originally scheduled to be tried for first-degree murder and kidnapping on April 20, 2020, the pandemic forced this judicial district to postpone all approaching jury trials. The Chief Judge repeatedly extended the moratorium in the ensuing months, such that no trials have occurred since March 2020, and none may commence until—barring further extension—January 2021. Protesting this delay, Taylor moves to dismiss the indictment for violations of his rights under both the Speedy Trial Act and the Sixth Amendment. While sympathetic to Defendant's plight, the Court finds that neither right has been infringed. It will, accordingly, deny the Motion.

In United States v. Gomez, 2021 WL 3888252 (D. Utah 2021), the court entered the following order:

> This Order Continuing Trial and Excluding Time Under the Speedy Trial Act is entered in response to the outbreak of the Coronavirus Disease (COVID-19) in the District of Utah.
>
> On March 13, 2020, a National Emergency was declared in response to the nationwide outbreak, which the World Health Organization has declared a global pandemic.

> The court continues to monitor closely the state of the COVID-19 health crisis in Utah and around the nation. The number of Utahns receiving vaccines is falling even as daily cases of COVID-19 in Utah are increasing. Utah and the nation remain in the midst of the most serious global pandemic in over a century. Globally, it is estimated that more than 180 million people have been infected, and nearly 4,000,000 have died from the disease. The Judicial Conference of the United States has found that emergency conditions due to the national COVID-19 crisis have affected and continue to materially affect the functioning of the federal courts. State and federal courts are beginning to carefully move toward safe reopening as conditions in different regions of the country permit.
>
> The Centers for Disease Control and Prevention (CDC) continues to issue guidance to combat the spread of COVID-19 and to promote the health and well-being of the nation. This guidance includes recommendations that all Americans avoid close contact with others (*i.e.*, being within six feet), among other things. There are nationwide now over 38 million confirmed cases of Americans infected with COVID-19, resulting in over 630,000 deaths. Utah has now confirmed more than 458,000 cases, resulting in nearly 20,000 hospitalizations and slightly more than 2,600 deaths. COVID-19 test positivity rates remain above levels necessary to reduce community spread, and infection rates are climbing. Crucially, the Delta COVID variant is quickly spreading and is the dominant variant in Utah. The state has been trending in recent weeks towards greater infection and more serious disease, particularly among those who are not vaccinated. Vaccinations are proceeding in Utah but the percentage of vaccinated persons in Utah is less than neighboring states, and daily vaccine administrations are insufficient to reverse the current trends anytime soon.
>
> Taking into account all of the available and relevant data, including the numbers of daily new cases and hospitalizations, test positivity rates, ICU capacity in Utah hospitals, the availability of vaccines and the vaccination rates, the introduction and spread of several variants of the COVID-19 virus with unknown implications, as well as enhanced treatment capabilities for those infected with COVID-19, the court concludes the pandemic continues to present an ongoing health emergency in Utah.

Both of these orders were entered before the highly infectious omicron variant emerged.

II. JOINDER AND SEVERANCE

A. SOME GENERAL RULES AND PROBLEMS

The outcome of a criminal case can be affected by the number and nature of charges and defendants joined together. There was a time when the government could only charge one offense in an indictment and was greatly restricted in trying defendants jointly over objection. But that time is long past, largely because of the perceived economies of joinder in an era of scarce resources. In Richardson v. Marsh, 481 U.S. 200 (1987), Justice Scalia, writing for the Court, had this to say about the advantages of joining defendants:

> Joint trials play a vital role in the criminal justice system, accounting for almost one third of federal criminal trials in the past five years. Many joint trials—for example, those involving large conspiracies to import and distribute illegal drugs—involve a dozen or more codefendants. * * * It would impair both the efficiency and the fairness of the criminal justice system to require * * * that prosecutors bring separate proceedings, presenting the same evidence again and again, requiring victims and witnesses to repeat the inconvenience (and sometimes trauma) of testifying, and randomly favoring the last-tried defendants who have the advantage of knowing the prosecution's case beforehand. Joint trials generally serve the interests of justice by avoiding inconsistent verdicts and enabling more accurate assessment of relative culpability—advantages which sometimes operate to the defendant's benefit. Even apart from these tactical considerations, joint trials generally serve the interests of justice by avoiding the scandal and inequity of inconsistent verdicts.

Similar benefits—especially from the government's point of view—can flow from joining multiple counts against a single defendant. But there also are dangers when joinder is effected—most obviously, that defendants will suffer prejudice from the jury's possible tendency to merge defendants and charges into one big guilty verdict.

The Federal Rules of Criminal Procedure attempt to strike a balance of efficiency and fairness through three separate but related rules:

- Rule 8 governs the charges and defendants that can be joined. The Rule provides that charges against a single defendant can be joined if the offenses "are of the same or similar character or are based on the same act or transaction, or are connected with or constitute parts of a common scheme or plan." The Rule further provides that defendants can be joined "if they are alleged to have participated in the same act or transaction, or in the same series of acts or transactions, constituting an offense or offenses."

- Rule 13 permits the court to consolidate separate actions if they could have been joined under Rule 8.
- Rule 14 gives the court discretion to sever or to provide other relief if prejudice would result from joinder.

The principal arguments respecting joinder center around two competing assertions: (1) The defense contends that the government is seeking an unfair advantage by having charges combined in order to brand the defendant as a bad person, to show that "birds of a feather flock together," to reduce a jury's regret at convicting the defendant in a world of imperfect proof, or to establish a "where there's smoke, there's fire" attitude in the trier of fact.[5] (2) The government contends that the defense is trying to separate out issues to wear down the government, to compartmentalize a case in order to weaken it, to increase the odds that witnesses and evidence will become unavailable, or to increase the odds of winning at least one case.[6]

The competing policy considerations—efficiency in the presentation of evidence versus a fair trial on each charge made against a defendant—are best understood in the context of actual cases.

B. JOINDER OF CLAIMS

United States v. Holloway, 1 F.3d 307 (5th Cir.1993), illustrates a simple problem of joinder of claims. Holloway was identified as a culprit in two armed bank robberies. When he was arrested for these robberies, he was found to be carrying a firearm. Holloway had been convicted previously of a felony. The government joined the bank robbery counts with an additional count for felon firearm possession. The government never contended that the gun found on Holloway when he was arrested was the same gun used in the bank robberies. Holloway requested a severance of the felon firearm possession count from the other counts, but this was denied. The court of appeals, however, found that the firearms count was improperly joined under Rule 8(a), and therefore that the trial court abused its discretion in failing to sever it. The court analyzed the severance question in light of the standards of Rule 8(a):

> * * * Plainly speaking, we can see no basis for the United States Attorney to have included this weapons charge in the indictment in the first place unless he was seeking to get before the jury evidence that likely would be otherwise inadmissible, i.e., that Holloway was a convicted felon and that he had a weapon on his person when arrested. * * *

[5] Conversely, the defendant sometimes may want weak charges combined with strong ones in the hope that reasonable doubts as to the weak ones will carry over to the others.

[6] Usually the government wants to win at least one case. But defendants may believe that their best strategy is "divide and conquer."

> We thus conclude that this remote weapons charge should never have been joined with the other counts of Holloway's indictment in the first place. [By joining] the weapons charge with the robbery charges, the jury emphatically was told that Holloway was a bad and dangerous person "by his very nature" and that a felon who carried a gun was just the sort of character who was most likely to have committed the robberies charged in the indictment. In short, Holloway was unjustifiably tried, at least in part, on the basis of who he was, and not on the basis of the material evidence presented against him.

The *Holloway* court noted, however, that if evidence of the gun possession had been admissible as proof on the robbery charges, or if the gun had been used in the robbery, it would have been a different case and joinder would have been permitted.

Under Rule 404(b) of the Federal Rules of Evidence, evidence of the defendant's uncharged bad acts cannot be admitted to show he is a bad person, but they can be admitted where relevant to prove intent, knowledge, identity, or any other "non-character" issue.[7] Thus, if evidence of an uncharged criminal act would be admissible to prove a charged crime, there is no prejudice in joining charges for both crimes in a single trial. See United States v. Windom, 19 F.3d 1190 (7th Cir.1994) (gun charge was properly joined with a narcotics charge, "for the same reasons that allow the government to introduce weapons into evidence at narcotics trials"); United States v. Johnson, 462 F.3d 815 (8th Cir. 2006) (firearms charge was sufficiently related to narcotics charge, even though drug activity occurred on the streets and the gun was found in the defendant's girlfriend's apartment: "Johnson's firearms possession could be linked to his need to protect his ongoing distribution of illegal drugs" and so the charged were "part of a common scheme or plan."). Compare United States v. Randazzo, 80 F.3d 623 (1st Cir.1996) (charges of filing false tax returns could not be joined with charges for introducing misbranded or adulterated food into interstate commerce; crimes were completely unrelated and evidence as to one could not be admitted to prove the other).

It is notable that the trial court in *Holloway* failed to instruct the jury to refrain from using evidence concerning the firearms charge as proof on the robbery charge. Where the judge makes an effort to protect the defendant from prejudicial misjoinder, the risks of reversal are substantially diminished. See Leach v. Kolb, 911 F.2d 1249 (7th Cir.1990) (improper joinder of attempted murder, armed robbery, and attempted armed robbery charges arising from separate incidents did not deprive defendant of a fair trial, where evidence of the defendant's guilt on each charge was overwhelming, and the trial court gave explicit limiting

[7] Complete coverage of Rule 404(b) is left for a course in evidence. For an extensive discussion of that Rule, see Saltzburg, Martin and Capra, Federal Rules of Evidence Manual § 404.02 (12th ed. 2019).

instructions requiring the jury to determine guilt or innocence on each count without reference to guilt or innocence on other charged counts).

C. JOINDER OF DEFENDANTS

It is common to find joinder of defendants in several classes of cases, especially conspiracy cases. Generally, courts express sympathy for the plight of defendants joined in conspiracy cases, but find the Government interest in efficiency to be paramount. The general rule of thumb is that "persons who are indicted together should be tried together." United States v. O'Bryant, 998 F.2d 21 (1st Cir.1993). For example, in Schaffer v. United States, 362 U.S. 511 (1960), defendants were joined on the basis of a conspiracy charge, though the substantive counts charged each defendant with different acts of theft. At the close of the government's case, the trial court dismissed the conspiracy count for lack of proof. But the substantive counts were submitted to the jury and the defendants were convicted. The defendants argued that the only joinder "hook" was the conspiracy charge and once that was dismissed the cases should have been severed. The Supreme Court found, however, that the defendants had not suffered any prejudice warranting severance, because the proof at trial was "carefully compartmentalized" as to each defendant. It noted that, as of the beginning of the trial, the joinder was authorized by Rule 8(b), and it refused to adopt "a hard-and-fast formula that, when a conspiracy count fails, joinder [becomes] error as a matter of law." Justice Douglas, joined by Chief Justice Warren and Justices Black and Brennan, in dissent, found "implicit prejudice" in trying separate offenses in a joint trial, because "a subtle bond is likely to be created between the several defendants even though they have never met nor acted in unison."

Exculpatory Testimony from a Codefendant

Joinder of defendants may be improper where one or more of the defendants would, if separately tried, offer testimony that would exculpate the defendant who complains about joinder. The complaint is that the witness/codefendant will not testify if he is joined, for fear that he will injure his own defense. But in order to trigger severance on this ground, a defendant "must establish a bona fide need for the codefendant's testimony, the substance of the testimony, the exculpatory nature and effect of the testimony, and that the codefendant would in fact testify." United States v. Neal, 27 F.3d 1035 (5th Cir.1994) (severance should have been granted where codefendant would have taken the stand in a separate trial to exculpate the complaining defendants); United States v. Cobb, 185 F.3d 1193 (11th Cir.1999) (finding a "rare case" in which severance should have been granted, because the codefendant's testimony would have been critical to the defendant's defense, and the codefendant stated unequivocally that he would testify at the defendant's trial if his case were severed). Compare

United States v. Pursley, 577 F.3d 1204 (10th Cir.2009) (joint trial permissible where codefendant would only have made a conclusory statement that both defendants were innocent, and the codefendant would have been extensively impeached).

Disparity in the Evidence

Another, limited exception to the general rule of joinder is where there is a gross disparity in the evidence against the joined defendants. In these cases, "the danger is that the bit players may not be able to differentiate themselves in the jurors' minds from the stars." United States v. Zafiro, 945 F.2d 881 (7th Cir.1991), *aff'd* 506 U.S. 534 (1993). In order to obtain a severance on this ground, the defendant will have to show a disparity in the evidence so great that the jury will not be able to follow limiting instructions. See, e.g., United States v. Gonzalez, 933 F.2d 417 (7th Cir.1991) (some disparity between defendants is permissible if it is within the jury's capacity to follow the court's limiting instructions). Given the institutional interest in trying all participants in a crime together, the gross disparity argument is rarely successful. And it is particularly unlikely to be successful on appeal if the jury returned acquittals as to some defendants and/or some charges. See United States v. Neal, 27 F.3d 1035 (5th Cir.1994) ("the jury's not guilty verdicts as to some defendants demonstrate that the jurors followed the district court's instructions and considered the evidence separately as to each defendant").

It should be noted that not all defendants prefer to be tried separately. A gross disparity in evidence might result in lesser defendants being acquitted altogether when the cases against them suffer in comparison to other defendants. When a defense counsel concludes that a defendant might benefit from having counsel for other defendants make arguments or present evidence, defense counsel might make the reasonable choice to "lay low."

Finger-Pointing: Zafiro v. United States

Is severance required if defendants are "pointing fingers" at each other, such that if one defense is believed the other cannot be? This was the question in Zafiro v. United States, 506 U.S. 534 (1993), a case in which four defendants were tried for a narcotics conspiracy. Officers discovered a large amount of cocaine at a residence to which all four defendants were connected. Soto and Garcia argued lack of knowledge and that Martinez and Zafiro were the drug dealers. Martinez and Zafiro argued lack of knowledge and that Soto and Garcia were the drug dealers. Justice O'Connor, writing for eight members of the Court, held that all of the defendants were properly tried together. She declared that "[t]here is a preference in the federal system for joint trials of defendants who are indicted together" and rejected the defendants' proposed bright line test that severance is required whenever defendants have mutually antagonistic defenses. She concluded that severance might be required in only a few exceptional circumstances:

> Mutually antagonistic defenses are not prejudicial *per se.* Moreover, Rule 14 does not require severance even if prejudice is shown; rather, it leaves the tailoring of the relief to be granted, if any, to the district court's sound discretion.
>
> We believe that, when defendants properly have been joined under Rule 8(b), a district court should grant a severance under Rule 14 only if there is a serious risk that a joint trial would compromise a specific trial right of one of the defendants, or prevent the jury from making a reliable judgment about guilt or innocence. Such a risk might occur when evidence that the jury should not consider against a defendant and that would not be admissible if a defendant were tried alone is admitted against a codefendant. For example, evidence of a codefendant's wrongdoing in some circumstances erroneously could lead a jury to conclude that a defendant was guilty. When many defendants are tried together in a complex case and they have markedly different degrees of culpability, this risk of prejudice is heightened. Evidence that is probative of a defendant's guilt but technically admissible only against a codefendant also might present a risk of prejudice. Conversely, a defendant might suffer prejudice if essential exculpatory evidence that would be available to a defendant tried alone were unavailable in a joint trial.

Justice O'Connor noted that the defendants in *Zafiro* did not articulate any specific instances of prejudice, but merely argued that "the very nature of their defenses, without more, prejudiced them." She responded that "it is well settled that defendants are not entitled to severance merely because they may have a better chance of acquittal in separate trials."

The defendants in *Zafiro* argued that they suffered a risk of prejudice from the possibility that the jury could conclude, in light of the finger-pointing defenses, that *some* defendant must be guilty without regard to whether the evidence proved so beyond a reasonable doubt. But Justice O'Connor responded that "the short answer is that petitioners' scenario did not occur here" because the "Government argued that all four petitioners were guilty and offered sufficient evidence as to all four petitioners; the jury in turn found all four petitioners guilty of various offenses." She further stated that "even if there were some risk of prejudice, here it is of the type that can be cured with proper instructions." Justice O'Connor noted that the trial court instructed the jury to give separate consideration to each defendant, and also warned the jury that each defendant was entitled to have his or her case judged only on the basis of the evidence applicable to the individual defendant. She concluded that these instructions "sufficed to cure any possibility of prejudice."

Justice Stevens concurred in the judgment, observing that he did not share the majority's preference for joint trials. He pointed out two ways in which joinder is problematic in cases involving mutually antagonistic defenses:

> First, joinder may introduce what is in effect a second prosecutor into a case, by turning each codefendant into the other's most forceful adversary. Second, joinder may invite a jury confronted with two defendants, at least one of whom is almost certainly guilty, to convict the defendant who appears the more guilty of the two regardless of whether the prosecutor has proven guilt beyond a reasonable doubt as to that particular defendant.

D. MISJOINDER

Violation of Rule 8: United States v. Lane

The Supreme Court held in United States v. Lane, 474 U.S. 438 (1986), that misjoinder of counts in violation of Fed.R.Crim.P. 8(b) does not automatically compel reversal of convictions. A father and son were charged with various offenses arising out of an arson conspiracy. They persuaded a court of appeals that one count, brought solely against the father, was improperly joined with four counts naming them both and another count charging the son with perjury. The court of appeals concluded that misjoinder is prejudicial per se. Chief Justice Burger's opinion for the Court disagreed, reasoning that misjoinder surely can be harmless in light of decisions holding that even constitutional errors do not inevitably require reversal of convictions. The question in cases of misjoinder, then, is whether under Fed.R.Crim.P. 52(a) the error affected the "substantial rights" of a defendant.

The Bruton Problem

While the misjoinder in *Lane* was not of constitutional dimension, constitutional error can occur in a joint trial that would not arise if the defendants were tried separately. The predominant example is Bruton v. United States, 391 U.S. 123 (1968). The *Bruton* Court found constitutional error when Bruton's nontestifying codefendant made a post-custodial confession implicating both himself and Bruton, and this confession was admitted into evidence at the joint trial. The confession was admissible against the codefendant as a party admission, but it was inadmissible hearsay as to Bruton. The trial judge gave a limiting instruction that the statement could only be used against the codefendant. But the Court held that, in light of the "powerfully incriminating" nature of the confession, the instruction was insufficient to protect Bruton's constitutional right to confront his accuser.

The Court suggested separate trials to avoid a "*Bruton*" problem, but courts after *Bruton* have often used means short of separate trials to protect against the use of the confession of one codefendant against another. The Supreme Court has approved redaction of a confession as a permissible substitute for severance, so long as all reference to the existence of the non-confessing defendant is excised from the confession. See Richardson v. Marsh, 481 U.S. 200 (1987). In *Marsh,* the confession was redacted to refer only to the confessing codefendant and another perpetrator who had absconded. In contrast, in Gray v. Maryland, 523 U.S. 185 (1998), redaction was held insufficient to protect the defendant where the confession was changed, in essence, from "Gray and I did it" to "deleted and I did it." The *Gray* Court held that the redaction provided no protection, because the jury would know that "deleted" would have to be the other defendant sitting there at the trial.

Bruton has been held inapplicable to a bench trial of joined defendants, because the problem that the Court was concerned about in *Bruton* was the jury's inability to follow the judge's instruction not to use one codefendant's confession against another. Rogers v. McMackin, 884 F.2d 252 (6th Cir.1989). A *Bruton* violation can be harmless. Cruz v. New York, 481 U.S. 186 (1987).

III. CONSTITUTIONALLY BASED PROOF REQUIREMENTS

A. PROOF BEYOND A REASONABLE DOUBT GENERALLY

Constitutional Requirement: In re Winship

The Court in In re Winship, 397 U.S. 358 (1970), decided that the Due Process Clause requires the government in a criminal case to prove *every element* of the charged crime beyond a reasonable doubt. Samuel Winship, a 12-year-old boy, was brought before a juvenile court and charged with delinquency for taking $112 from a woman's pocketbook in a locker. The judge acknowledged that the conduct might not have been proved beyond a reasonable doubt, but determined that Winship could be adjudged a delinquent by a preponderance of the evidence. The Court in *Winship* held that the requirement of proof beyond a reasonable doubt is one of the "essentials of due process and fair treatment" required during the adjudicatory stage when a juvenile is charged with an act that would constitute a crime if committed by an adult. Justice Brennan's majority opinion traced the history of proof in American criminal trials and found "virtually unanimous" authority supporting the reasonable doubt standard for all elements of the crime. He concluded that the criminal defendant has a transcendent liberty interest in criminal trials that requires the narrowest margin for error.

> * * * [U]se of the reasonable-doubt standard is indispensable to command the respect and confidence of the community in applications of the criminal law. It is critical that the moral force of the criminal law not be diluted by a standard of proof that leaves people in doubt whether innocent men are being condemned. It is also important in our free society that every individual going about his ordinary affairs have confidence that his government cannot adjudge him guilty of a criminal offense without convincing a proper factfinder of his guilt with utmost certainty.
>
> Lest there remain any doubt about the constitutional stature of the reasonable-doubt standard, we explicitly hold that the Due Process Clause protects the accused against conviction except upon proof beyond a reasonable doubt of every fact necessary to constitute the crime with which he is charged.

Justice Harlan wrote an influential concurring opinion, stressing the policy arguments that support the reasonable doubt standard.

> [T]he choice of the standard for a particular variety of adjudication does, I think, reflect a very fundamental assessment of the comparative social costs of erroneous factual determinations. * * * [A] standard of proof represents an attempt to instruct the factfinder concerning the degree of confidence our society thinks he should have in the correctness of factual conclusions for a particular type of adjudication. Although the phrases "preponderance of the evidence" and "proof beyond a reasonable doubt" are quantitatively imprecise, they do communicate to the finder of fact different notions concerning the degree of confidence he is expected to have in the correctness of his factual conclusions.
>
> * * * If * * * the standard of proof for a criminal trial were a preponderance of the evidence rather than proof beyond a reasonable doubt, there would be a smaller risk of factual errors that result in freeing guilty persons, but a far greater risk of factual errors that result in convicting the innocent. Because the standard of proof affects the comparative frequency of these two types of erroneous outcomes, the choice of the standard to be applied in a particular kind of litigation should, in a rational world, reflect an assessment of the comparative social disutility of each.
>
> When one makes such an assessment, the reason for different standards of proof in civil as opposed to criminal litigation becomes apparent. In a civil suit between two private parties for money

damages, for example, we view it as no more serious in general for there to be an erroneous verdict in the defendant's favor than for there to be an erroneous verdict in the plaintiff's favor. * * *

In a criminal case, on the other hand, we do not view the social disutility of convicting an innocent man as equivalent to the disutility of acquitting someone who is guilty. * * *

In this context, I view the requirement of proof beyond a reasonable doubt in a criminal case as bottomed on a fundamental value determination of our society that it is far worse to convict an innocent man than to let a guilty man go free.

B. REASONABLE DOUBT AND JURY INSTRUCTIONS

"Presumed Innocent" Instructions

In Taylor v. Kentucky, 436 U.S. 478 (1978), the Court reversed a conviction where the judge refused to give a requested instruction that the defendant was presumed innocent. Later, however, in Kentucky v. Whorton, 441 U.S. 786 (1979), the Court held that a presumption of innocence instruction was not constitutionally required in every case. It stressed the facts of *Taylor,* where the trial judge's instructions were "spartan," the prosecutor made improper remarks, and the evidence against the defendant was weak. The Court concluded that the failure to give a requested instruction on the presumption of innocence "must be evaluated in light of the totality of the circumstances—including all the instructions to the jury, the arguments of counsel, whether the weight of the evidence was overwhelming, and other relevant factors—to determine whether the defendant received a constitutionally fair trial." See also United States v. Payne, 944 F.2d 1458 (9th Cir.1991) (underlying purposes of a presumption of innocence instruction were "served adequately by other instructions which squarely placed the burden on the government of proving its case beyond a reasonable doubt, defined beyond a reasonable doubt, and clearly confined the scope of the evidence properly before the jury").

Reasonable Doubt Instructions

What should the judge say to the jury about the meaning of reasonable doubt? The instruction in Cage v. Louisiana, 498 U.S. 39 (1990), defined reasonable doubt as one creating "a grave uncertainty" and "an actual substantial doubt." The trial court elaborated that a "moral certainty" was required to convict. The Supreme Court in a per curiam opinion held that the words "grave" and "substantial" "suggest a higher degree of doubt than is required for acquittal under the reasonable doubt standard." The Court concluded that the instruction was constitutionally defective; the references to the juries needing a grave and substantial doubt to acquit, combined with the reference to moral certainty, as opposed to evidentiary certainty, could have led a reasonable juror to find guilt on a lesser standard than that required by *Winship*.

In Sullivan v. Louisiana, 508 U.S. 275 (1993), the Court unanimously held that a constitutionally-defective reasonable doubt instruction cannot be harmless error. At Sullivan's trial, the judge gave a reasonable doubt instruction substantially identical to the instruction found defective in *Cage*. Justice Scalia, writing for the Court, stated that because of the instruction, Sullivan was deprived of his Sixth Amendment right to a jury verdict of guilt beyond a reasonable doubt. Under these circumstances, an appellate court cannot determine that the error was harmless, because "the wrong entity" would be judging the defendant guilty.

In the consolidated cases of Sandoval v. California and Victor v. Nebraska, 511 U.S. 1 (1994), the Court considered the constitutionality of two reasonable doubt instructions in light of *Cage*. In *Sandoval*, the trial court defined reasonable doubt as follows:

> It is not a mere possible doubt; because everything relating to human affairs, and depending on *moral evidence*, is open to some possible or imaginary doubt. It is that state of the case which, after the entire comparison and consideration of all the evidence, leaves the minds of the jurors in that condition that they cannot say they feel *an abiding conviction, to a moral certainty*, of the truth of the charge. [Emphasis added.]

Justice O'Connor, writing for the Court, found that while the instruction lacked clarity, there was no "reasonable likelihood" that the jury understood it to allow conviction to be based on proof less than the *Winship* standard. She rejected Sandoval's argument that the trial judge's reference to "moral certainty" would be understood by modern jurors to mean a standard of proof less stringent than that of reasonable doubt. She recognized that while the reference to moral certainty was "ambiguous in the abstract," the rest of the instruction sufficiently corrected any ambiguity by requiring "an abiding conviction" as to guilt. She stated that "we are satisfied that the reference to moral certainty, in conjunction with the abiding conviction language, impressed upon the factfinder the need to reach a subjective state of near certitude of the guilt of the accused."

While the Court found that the "moral certainty" language was not fatal, it stressed that it did not "condone the use of the phrase" and noted that the pattern jury instructions for federal courts do not refer to moral certainty.

The instruction defining reasonable doubt given by the trial court in *Victor* was as follows:

> Reasonable doubt is such a doubt as would cause a reasonable and prudent person, in one of the graver and more important transactions of life, to *pause and hesitate* before taking the represented facts as true and relying and acting thereon. It is such a doubt as will not permit you, after full, fair, and impartial consideration of all the evidence, to have an *abiding conviction, to a moral certainty,* of the guilt of the accused. At the same time, absolute or mathematical certainty is not required. You may be convinced of the truth of a fact beyond a reasonable doubt and yet be fully aware that possibly you may be mistaken. You may find an accused guilty upon the strong probabilities of the case, provided such probabilities are strong enough to exclude any doubt of his guilt that is reasonable. A reasonable doubt is an *actual and substantial doubt* arising from the evidence, or from the lack of evidence on the part of the state, *as distinguished from a doubt arising from mere possibility, from bare imagination, or from fanciful conjecture.* [Emphasis added.]

As with the instruction in *Sandoval,* Justice O'Connor found that the instruction in *Victor* adequately conveyed the concept of reasonable doubt to the jury. Justice O'Connor rejected Victor's argument that the reference to "substantial doubt" overstated the degree of doubt necessary for acquittal. She noted that the trial court had distinguished "substantial doubt" from "a doubt rising from mere possibility, from bare imagination, or from fanciful conjecture." This was enough to distinguish the instruction in *Victor* from that in *Cage,* where the "substantial doubt" language was also used. According to Justice O'Connor:

> This explicit distinction between a substantial doubt and a fanciful conjecture was not present in the *Cage* instruction. * * * [In *Cage*] we were concerned that the jury would interpret the term "substantial doubt" in parallel with the preceding reference to "grave uncertainty," leading to an overstatement of the doubt necessary to acquit. In the instruction given in Victor's case, the context makes clear that "substantial" is used in the sense of existence rather than magnitude of the doubt, so the same concern is not present.

Justice O'Connor noted in the alternative that the trial court's "hesitate to act" instruction cured whatever defect might have existed in the reference to substantial doubt. She concluded that "to the extent the word 'substantial' denotes the quantum of doubt necessary for acquittal, the hesitate to act standard gives a common-sense benchmark for just how substantial such a doubt must be."

Justice Kennedy wrote a short concurring opinion, in which he stated that a reference to moral certainty might once have made sense to jurors, but that it has "long since become archaic."

Justice Ginsburg wrote a concurring opinion, agreeing with the Court's suggestion that the term "moral certainty," "while not in itself so misleading as to render the instructions unconstitutional, should be avoided as an unhelpful way of explaining what reasonable doubt means." Unlike the Court, however, she also criticized the "hesitate to act" instruction as providing a "misplaced analogy." She reasoned that important decisions in one's life "generally involve a very heavy element of uncertainty and risk-taking" and thus are "wholly unlike the decisions jurors ought to make in criminal cases."[8]

Justice Ginsburg took issue with the statements of some federal circuit courts that a reasonable doubt instruction should *never* be given. See, e.g., United States v. Adkins, 937 F.2d 947 (4th Cir.1991) (arguing that such instructions "tend to impermissibly lessen the burden of proof"); Seventh Circuit Committee on Federal Jury Instructions ("The phrase 'reasonable doubt' is self-explanatory and is its own best definition. Further elaboration tends to misleading refinements which weaken and make imprecise the existing phrase."). See also Newman, Beyond Reasonable Doubt, 68 N.Y.U.L.Rev. 979 (1994) (arguing that the concept of reasonable doubt "will become less clear the more we explain it").

Justice Ginsburg noted studies indicating that "jurors are often confused about the meaning of reasonable doubt when that term is left undefined."

Justice Ginsburg approved of the reasonable doubt instruction proposed by the Federal Judicial Center. That instruction reads as follows:

> Proof beyond a reasonable doubt is proof that leaves you *firmly convinced* of the defendant's guilt. There are very few things in this world that we know with absolute certainty, and in criminal cases the law does not require proof that overcomes every possible doubt. If, based on your consideration of the evidence, you are firmly convinced that the defendant is guilty of the crime charged, you must find him guilty. If on the other hand, you think there is a *real possibility* that he is not guilty, you must give him the benefit of the doubt and find him not guilty. [Emphasis added.]

Justice Ginsburg concluded that the FJC instruction is "clear, straightforward and accurate" and that it avoids a choice between two potential sources of jury confusion: "on one hand, the confusions that may be caused by leaving reasonable doubt undefined, and on the other, the

---

8 See also Vargas v. Keane, 86 F.3d 1273 (2d Cir.1996) (Weinstein, J., concurring) (criticizing a "hesitate to act" instruction: "It could be misunderstood since many of us recognize that in the most important affairs of our lives—such as choice of mate, careers and conception—we tend to be largely emotional. Were we to require proof beyond a reasonable doubt that our important decisions are correct, few of us would marry, choose law as a career or have children. Most of us are probably comfortable with more risk-taking when making important personal decisions than we would be in declaring as criminals people who may be innocent.").

confusion that might be induced by the anachronism of 'moral certainty,' the misplaced analogy of 'hesitation to act,' or the circularity of 'doubt that is reasonable.' "

C. THE SCOPE OF THE REASONABLE DOUBT REQUIREMENT: WHAT IS AN ELEMENT OF THE CRIME?

Winship requires the government to prove all *elements* of the crime beyond a reasonable doubt. But does this leave the government with an unfettered discretion to determine just what the elements of a crime are? What if the government changes what was once an element of the crime into an affirmative defense—thus shifting the burden of proof? What if the government shifts what might be considered an element of the crime into a sentencing consideration, thus lessening the burden of proof? Does any of this violate *Winship*? These questions have been the subject of much Supreme Court and lower court case law.

1. Element of the Crime or Affirmative Defense?

Impermissible Burden-Shifting: Mullaney v. Wilbur

The Court's first attempt to identify *Winship's* scope came in Mullaney v. Wilbur, 421 U.S. 684 (1975). Maine required a defendant charged with murder to prove that he acted "in the heat of passion on sudden provocation" in order to reduce the homicide to manslaughter. Under the Maine system, the prosecutor had to show beyond a reasonable doubt that a homicide was both intentional and unlawful. Unless the defendant proved heat of passion or sudden provocation by a preponderance of the evidence, the defendant was convicted of murder. Justice Powell's majority opinion declared that "the Due Process Clause requires the prosecution to prove beyond a reasonable doubt the absence of the heat of passion or sudden provocation when the issue is properly presented in a homicide case."[9] In other words, the absence of heat of passion or provocation was an element of the crime, and could not be shifted to an affirmative defense. The Court reasoned as follows:

> [T]he criminal law of Maine, like that of other jurisdictions, is concerned not only with guilt or innocence in the abstract but also with the degree of criminal culpability. Maine has chosen to distinguish

[9] In contrast to the burden of persuasion is the burden of production. Many jurisdictions put the burden on a defendant to raise sufficient evidence to bring a defense into a case, at which time the prosecutor must disprove the defense beyond a reasonable doubt. Even if the Constitution permits a jurisdiction to impose the persuasion burden on a defendant, a jurisdiction may be satisfied with imposing the production burden instead. Whenever it is constitutional to put a burden of persuasion on a defendant, it will be constitutional to impose the lesser burden of production. *Mullaney* establishes that in some cases only a production burden may be imposed.

> those who kill in the heat of passion from those who kill in the absence of this factor. * * * By drawing this distinction, while refusing to require the prosecution to establish beyond a reasonable doubt the fact upon which it turns, Maine denigrates the interests found critical in *Winship*.
>
> * * *
>
> Moreover, if *Winship* were limited to those facts that constitute a crime as defined by state law, a State could undermine many of the interests that decision sought to protect without effecting any substantive change in its law. It would only be necessary to redefine the elements that constitute different crimes, characterizing them as factors that bear solely on the extent of punishment.

Justice Rehnquist, joined by Chief Justice Burger, concurred and noted that he saw no inconsistency between *Mullaney* and Leland v. Oregon, 343 U.S. 790 (1952) (upholding placement upon defendant of burden of persuasion beyond a reasonable doubt on issue of insanity).[10]

Flexibility to Determine Affirmative Defenses: Patterson v. New York

In Patterson v. New York, 432 U.S. 197 (1977), Justice White wrote for the majority as it upheld a New York statute that placed the burden on the defendant to prove extreme emotional disturbance by a preponderance of the evidence—after the prosecutor proved an intentional homicide beyond a reasonable doubt—in order to reduce second degree murder to manslaughter. After citing Leland v. Oregon, the majority reasoned as follows:

> Here, in revising its criminal code, New York provided the affirmative defense of extreme emotional disturbance, a substantially expanded version of the older heat-of-passion concept; but it was willing to do so only if the facts making out the defense were established by the defendant with sufficient certainty. The State was itself unwilling to undertake to establish the absence of those facts beyond a reasonable doubt, perhaps fearing that proof would be too difficult and that too many persons deserving treatment as murderers would escape that punishment if the evidence need merely raise a reasonable doubt about the defendant's emotional state. It has been said that the new criminal code of New York contains some 25

[10] In Rivera v. Delaware, 429 U.S. 877 (1976), over the dissent of Justice Brennan joined by Justice Marshall, the Court dismissed, for want of a substantial federal question, an appeal from the Delaware Supreme Court's holding that it was constitutional to put the burden of persuasion on insanity on the defendant. The federal Insanity Defense Reform Act—passed after the prosecution of John Hinckley for the attempted assassination of President Reagan—imposes the burden of persuasion of proving insanity on the defendant by clear and convincing evidence.

affirmative defenses which exculpate or mitigate but which must be established by the defendant to be operative. The Due Process Clause, as we see it, does not put New York to the choice of abandoning those defenses or undertaking to disprove their existence in order to convict of a crime which otherwise is within its constitutional powers to sanction by substantial punishment.

* * *

We thus decline to adopt as a constitutional imperative, operative countrywide, that a State must disprove beyond a reasonable doubt every fact constituting any and all affirmative defenses related to the culpability of an accused. * * *

Justice White noted that there are limits to shifting the burden of proof to the defendant—the state could not transmute what has *traditionally been an element of the crime* into an affirmative defense:

> It is not within the province of a legislature to declare an individual guilty or presumptively guilty of a crime. The legislature cannot validly command that the finding of an indictment, or mere proof of the identity of the accused, should create a presumption of the existence of all the facts essential to guilt.

In a footnote, Justice White quoted extensively from Chief Judge Breitel's concurring opinion in the New York Court of Appeals:

> Absent the affirmative defense, the crime of murder or manslaughter could legislatively be defined simply to require an intent to kill, unaffected by the spontaneity with which that intent is formed or the provocative or mitigating circumstances which should legally or morally lower the grade of crime. The placing of the burden of proof on the defense, with a lower threshold, however, is fair because of defendant's knowledge or access to the evidence other than his own on the issue. * * *
>
> In sum, the appropriate use of affirmative defenses enlarges the ameliorative aspects of a statutory scheme for the punishment of crime, rather than the other way around—a shift from primitive mechanical classifications based on the bare antisocial act and its consequences, rather than on the nature of the offender and the conditions which produce some degree of excuse for his conduct, the mark of an advanced criminology.

Thus, the Court reasoned that the state should be allowed to provide for affirmative defenses, because otherwise the state would simply legislate a single crime, making no attempt to differentiate levels of culpability. That would not be doing defendants any favors.

Justice Powell's dissent in *Patterson* was joined by Justices Brennan and Marshall. He argued that the distinction between the Maine law invalidated in *Mullaney* and the New York law upheld in *Patterson* was "formalistic rather than substantive."

After *Patterson*, can the state define murder as causing a death, and shift the burden of persuasion to the defendant to prove lack of intent? If not, why not? See also Mason v. Gramley, 9 F.3d 1345 (7th Cir.1993) (upholding Illinois murder statute, which requires the state to prove first degree murder, then permits the defendant to establish, by a preponderance, mitigating evidence to reduce the crime to second degree murder).[11]

For other Supreme Court cases involving the *Mullaney/Patterson* divide, see Martin v. Ohio, 480 U.S. 228 (1987) (upholding an Ohio rule placing the burden of persuasion on self-defense on the defendant); Montana v. Egelhoff, 518 U.S. 37 (1996) (upholding a state statute that prohibited the defendant from offering evidence of intoxication as a defense to the mental state necessary to commit homicide). In both *Martin* and *Egelhoff*, the Court relied on *Patterson* for the proposition that states are generally free to construct the elements of a crime.

Withdrawal from a Conspiracy as an Affirmative Defense: Smith v. United States

In Smith v. United States, 568 U.S. 106 (2013), the defendant was charged with conspiracy and claimed that he had withdrawn from it, and further that the date of his withdrawal meant that the statute of limitations had expired. The trial court instructed the jury that it had to find the defendant guilty of conspiracy beyond a reasonable doubt, but that the defendant had the burden of showing that he had withdrawn from the conspiracy. The defendant argued that this allocation of the burden of showing withdrawal violated his due process rights under *In re Winship* But the Court disagreed in a unanimous opinion by Justice Scalia. Justice Scalia relied on Patterson v. New York and declared as follows:

> The State is foreclosed from shifting the burden of proof to the defendant only when an affirmative defense does negate an element of the crime. Where instead it excuses conduct that would otherwise be punishable, but does not controvert any of the elements of the offense

[11] The Court relied heavily on *Patterson* in Medina v. California, 505 U.S. 437 (1992), as it upheld a state statute that established a presumption of competency to stand trial, and required the defendant to prove his incompetency by a preponderance of the evidence. Justice Kennedy wrote the opinion for the Court. He stated that under *Patterson*, it is appropriate to give "substantial deference to legislative judgments" allocating the burden of proof, because "the States have considerable expertise in matters of criminal procedure and the criminal process is grounded in centuries of common-law tradition."

itself, the Government has no constitutional duty to overcome the defense beyond a reasonable doubt.

Withdrawal does not negate an element of the conspiracy crimes charged here. * * * To convict a defendant of narcotics or RICO conspiracy, the Government must prove beyond a reasonable doubt that two or more people agreed to commit a crime covered by the specific conspiracy statute (that a conspiracy existed) and that the defendant knowingly and willfully participated in the agreement (that he was a member of the conspiracy). Far from contradicting an element of the offense, withdrawal presupposes that the defendant committed the offense. * * * Withdrawal terminates the defendant's liability for postwithdrawal acts of his co-conspirators, but he remains guilty of conspiracy.

* * *

Having joined forces to achieve collectively more evil than he could accomplish alone, Smith tied his fate to that of the group. His individual change of heart (assuming it occurred) could not put the conspiracy genie back in the bottle. We punish him for the havoc wreaked by the unlawful scheme, whether or not he remained actively involved. It is his withdrawal that must be active, and it was his burden to show that.

2. Element of the Crime or Sentencing Factor?

While the government has the burden of proving an element of the crime beyond a reasonable doubt, facts determined at sentencing have traditionally been subject to the preponderance of the evidence standard. For example, the defendant's criminal history is a sentencing factor, and the government need not prove that the defendant committed a prior crime beyond a reasonable doubt. The preponderance of the evidence standard is sufficient. [See Chapter 11 for a discussion of the standard of proof at sentencing].

Given the difference between the standard of proof at trial and sentencing, it is possible that a legislature might try to allocate certain facts to sentencing factors rather than to an element of the crime. Such a shift to sentencing factors implicates not only the reasonable doubt requirement of *Winship*, but also the defendant's constitutional right to a trial by jury on all elements of the crime. This is because sentencing factors are tried to the judge, not the jury.

In a series of important cases, the Court has sought to distinguish between what is a permissible sentencing factor and what must be an element of a crime. It is fair to state that the Court's journey down this path has been a winding one.

Preponderance of the Evidence at Sentencing: McMillan v. Pennsylvania

At issue in McMillan v. Pennsylvania, 477 U.S. 79 (1986), was a state statute providing that anyone convicted of certain enumerated felonies is subject to a mandatory minimum sentence of five years' imprisonment if the sentencing judge finds by a preponderance of the evidence that the defendant "visibly possessed a firearm" during the commission of the offense. If the aggravating factor of possessing a firearm were an element of the crime, it would of course have to be proven beyond a reasonable doubt—but the state chose instead to make it a sentencing factor.

The Court upheld the statute against a due process challenge. Justice Rehnquist wrote for the Court and argued that the state statute did not create a new offense, nor did it change the maximum punishment that could be imposed for an offense. Instead, it limited judicial discretion in sentencing. The Court found no problem with permitting a higher sentence to be based on proof of a fact by preponderance of the evidence, noting that the beyond the reasonable doubt standard had never been applied to sentencing factors. Justice Rehnquist stated that "*Patterson* stressed that in determining what facts must be proved beyond a reasonable doubt the state legislature's definition of the elements of the offense is usually dispositive," and that the Pennsylvania statute did not go beyond the minimal limitations set by *Patterson*: it did not create a presumption of guilt, and did not relieve the prosecution of its burden of proving guilt of the underlying crime.

Justice Stevens dissented, arguing that "the Due Process Clause requires proof beyond a reasonable doubt of conduct which exposes a criminal defendant to greater stigma or punishment * * *." Justice Marshall, joined by Justices Brennan and Blackmun, also dissented. He agreed with Justice Stevens that the Pennsylvania statute operated to create a special stigma and a special punishment upon a finding of specific conduct, and this was enough to mandate that the prosecution prove the conduct beyond a reasonable doubt.

Recidivism as a Sentencing Factor or as an Element of the Crime?

In Almendarez-Torres v. United States, 523 U.S. 224 (1998), the Court considered whether the defendant's prior conviction was an element of the crime or a sentencing factor. Almendarez-Torres was convicted under a statute with two provisions. The first provision prohibits a deported alien from returning to the United States, and authorizes a maximum prison term of two years. The second provision authorizes a maximum prison term of 20 years if the initial "deportation was subsequent to a conviction for commission of an aggravated felony." The defendant was convicted under the second provision and was sentenced to 85 months' imprisonment. The defendant argued that he could not be subject to such a serious sentence, as his indictment did not mention his aggravated felony convictions. Because an indictment must recite all elements of the crime charged, the defendant argued that he could not be convicted under the statute's second provision. The government argued that the second provision of the statute did not set forth a separate crime, but was rather a provision mandating an enhanced sentence for recidivism; thus, the first provision of the statute defined the elements of the crime, and the second provision established a *sentencing enhancement* for felons who committed the crime.

In a 5–4 decision written by Justice Breyer, the Court held that the legislature had the constitutional authority to treat recidivism as a sentencing factor rather than as an element of the crime. Therefore it was not necessary to include the defendant's prior felony record in the indictment. Justice Breyer concluded that "the sentencing factor at issue here—recidivism—is a traditional, if not the most traditional, basis for a sentencing court's increasing an offender's sentence. * * * [T]o hold that the Constitution requires that recidivism be deemed an element of petitioner's offense would mark an abrupt departure from a longstanding tradition of treating recidivism as going to the punishment only."

Justice Scalia, joined by Justices Stevens, Souter and Ginsburg, dissented. He contended that it would violate the defendant's right to jury trial to take from the jury factual issues that affect the penalty to which a defendant is exposed.

Facts That, if Found, Extend the Sentence Beyond the Statutory Maximum Penalty, Are Elements of the Crime: Apprendi v. New Jersey

In the following case, the Court limited *McMillan* to its facts, and established a broad principle that prohibits the state and federal governments from using sentencing enhancements to increase a sentence beyond the statutory maximum provided for the crime by the legislature. Where the fact supporting a sentencing enhancement is used in that way, it is an element of the crime that must be set forth in the indictment, and the defendant has the right to have the fact proved beyond a reasonable doubt to a jury.

APPRENDI V. NEW JERSEY

Supreme Court of the United States, 2000.
530 U.S. 466.

JUSTICE STEVENS delivered the opinion of the Court.

A New Jersey statute classifies the possession of a firearm for an unlawful purpose as a "second-degree" offense. Such an offense is punishable by imprisonment for between five years and 10 years. A separate statute, described by that State's Supreme Court as a "hate crime" law, provides for an "extended term" of imprisonment if the trial judge finds, by a preponderance of the evidence, that "[t]he defendant in committing the crime acted with a purpose to intimidate an individual or group of individuals because of race, color, gender, handicap, religion, sexual orientation or ethnicity." The extended term authorized by the hate crime law for second-degree offenses is imprisonment for between 10 and 20 years.

The question presented is whether the Due Process Clause of the Fourteenth Amendment requires that a factual determination authorizing an increase in the maximum prison sentence for an offense from 10 to 20 years be made by a jury on the basis of proof beyond a reasonable doubt.

[Apprendi pleaded guilty to a shooting, and at sentencing the government proffered evidence that the shooting was racially motivated. The sentencing court found evidence of racial bias by a preponderance of the evidence, and imposed an enhanced sentence on the basis of the hate crime law. That sentence was two years longer than the statutory maximum that Apprendi could have received for the crime to which he pled guilty. The sentence was upheld by the New Jersey court, which concluded that the state had the authority to define racial motivation as a sentencing factor rather than as an element of the crime.]

* * * The constitutional question * * * is whether the 12-year sentence imposed on count 18 was permissible, given that it was above the 10-year maximum for the offense charged in that count. The finding is legally significant because it increased—indeed, it doubled—the maximum range within which the judge could exercise his discretion, converting what otherwise was a maximum 10-year sentence on that count into a minimum sentence. * * * The question whether Apprendi had a constitutional right to have a jury find such bias on the basis of proof beyond a reasonable doubt is starkly presented.

* * *

[Justice Stevens reviewed the historical basis of the right to jury trial and the right to a beyond a reasonable doubt standard of proof as to all elements of the crime. He noted specifically that the right to jury trial was needed "to guard against a spirit of oppression and tyranny on the part of rulers, and as the great bulwark of our civil and political liberties."]

Any possible distinction between an "element" of a felony offense and a "sentencing factor" was unknown to the practice of criminal indictment, trial by jury, and judgment by court as it existed during the years surrounding our Nation's founding.

* * *

We do not suggest that trial practices cannot change in the course of centuries and still remain true to the principles that emerged from the Framers' fears "that the jury right could be lost not only by gross denial, but by erosion." But practice must at least adhere to the basic principles undergirding the requirements of trying to a jury all facts necessary to constitute a statutory offense, and proving those facts beyond reasonable doubt. * * *

Since *Winship*, we have made clear beyond peradventure that *Winship's* due process and associated jury protections extend, to some degree, "to determinations that [go] not to a defendant's guilt or innocence, but simply to the length of his sentence."

* * *

It was in McMillan v. Pennsylvania that this Court, for the first time, coined the term "sentencing factor" to refer to a fact that was not found by a jury but that could affect the sentence imposed by the judge. * * * We did not, however, there budge from the position that (1) constitutional limits exist to States' authority to define away facts necessary to constitute a criminal offense, and (2) that a state scheme that keeps from the jury facts that expose defendants to greater or additional punishment, may raise serious constitutional concern. As we explained:

> Section 9712 neither alters the maximum penalty for the crime committed nor creates a separate offense calling for a separate penalty; * * *. The statute gives no impression of having been tailored to permit the visible possession finding to be a tail which wags the dog of the substantive offense. * * *[a]

Finally, * * * Almendarez-Torres v. United States represents at best an exceptional departure from the historic practice that we have described. * * * [O]ur conclusion in *Almendarez-Torres* turned heavily upon the fact that the additional sentence to which the defendant was subject was "the prior commission of a serious crime." (explaining that "recidivism . . . is a

[a] The principal dissent accuses us of today "overruling *McMillan*." We do not overrule *McMillan*. We limit its holding to cases that do not involve the imposition of a sentence more severe than the statutory maximum for the offense established by the jury's verdict—a limitation identified in the *McMillan* opinion itself. * * *

traditional, if not the most traditional, basis for a sentencing Court's increasing an offender's sentence"). * * *

Even though it is arguable that *Almendarez-Torres* was incorrectly decided, and that a logical application of our reasoning today should apply if the recidivist issue were contested, Apprendi does not contest the decision's validity and we need not revisit it for purposes of our decision today to treat the case as a narrow exception to the general rule we recalled at the outset. * * *

In sum, our reexamination of our cases in this area, and of the history upon which they rely, confirms the opinion that we expressed in *Jones*. Other than the fact of a prior conviction, any fact that increases the penalty for a crime beyond the prescribed statutory maximum must be submitted to a jury, and proved beyond a reasonable doubt. * * *[b]

The New Jersey statutory scheme that Apprendi asks us to invalidate allows a jury to convict a defendant of a second-degree offense based on its finding beyond a reasonable doubt that he unlawfully possessed a prohibited weapon; after a subsequent and separate proceeding, it then allows a judge to impose punishment identical to that New Jersey provides for crimes of the first degree, based upon the judge's finding, by a preponderance of the evidence, that the defendant's "purpose" for unlawfully possessing the weapon was "to intimidate" his victim on the basis of a particular characteristic the victim possessed. In light of the constitutional rule explained above, and all of the cases supporting it, this practice cannot stand. * * * Just because the state legislature placed its hate crime sentence "enhancer" within the sentencing provisions of the criminal code does not mean that the finding of a biased purpose to intimidate is not an essential element of the offense. * * *

* * *

The New Jersey procedure challenged in this case is an unacceptable departure from the jury tradition that is an indispensable part of our criminal justice system. * * *

---

[b] The principal dissent would reject the Court's rule as a "meaningless formalism," because it can conceive of hypothetical statutes that would comply with the rule and achieve the same result as the New Jersey statute. While a State could, hypothetically, undertake to revise its entire criminal code in the manner the dissent suggests—extending all statutory maximum sentences to, for example, 50 years and giving judges guided discretion as to a few specially selected factors within that range—this possibility seems remote. Among other reasons, structural democratic constraints exist to discourage legislatures from enacting penal statutes that expose every defendant convicted of, for example, weapons possession, to a maximum sentence exceeding that which is, in the legislature's judgment, generally proportional to the crime. * * * Our rule ensures that a State is obliged to make its choices concerning the substantive content of its criminal laws with full awareness of the consequence, unable to mask substantive policy choices of exposing all who are convicted to the maximum sentence it provides. So exposed, the political check on potentially harsh legislative action is then more likely to operate.

* * *

JUSTICE SCALIA, concurring.

I feel the need to say a few words in response to Justice Breyer's dissent. It sketches an admirably fair and efficient scheme of criminal justice designed for a society that is prepared to leave criminal justice to the State. * * * The founders of the American Republic were not prepared to leave it to the State, which is why the jury-trial guarantee was one of the least controversial provisions of the Bill of Rights. It has never been efficient; but it has always been free.

As for fairness, which Justice Breyer believes "[i]n modern times," the jury cannot provide: I think it not unfair to tell a prospective felon that if he commits his contemplated crime he is exposing himself to a jail sentence of 30 years—and that if, upon conviction, he gets anything less than that he may thank the mercy of a tenderhearted judge * * *. Will there be disparities? Of course. But the criminal will never get more punishment than he bargained for when he did the crime, and his guilt of the crime (and hence the length of the sentence to which he is exposed) will be determined beyond a reasonable doubt by the unanimous vote of 12 of his fellow citizens.

In Justice Breyer's bureaucratic realm of perfect equity, by contrast, the facts that determine the length of sentence to which the defendant is exposed will be determined to exist (on a more-likely-than-not basis) by a single employee of the State. It is certainly arguable (Justice Breyer argues it) that this sacrifice of prior protections is worth it. But it is not arguable that, just because one thinks it is a better system, it must be, or is even more likely to be, the system envisioned by a Constitution that guarantees trial by jury. * * *

JUSTICE THOMAS, with whom JUSTICE SCALIA joins [in pertinent part] concurring.

* * *

[A] "crime" includes every fact that is by law a basis for imposing or increasing punishment (in contrast with a fact that mitigates punishment). Thus, if the legislature defines some core crime and then provides for increasing the punishment of that crime upon a finding of some aggravating fact—of whatever sort, including the fact of a prior conviction—the core crime and the aggravating fact together constitute an aggravated crime, just as much as grand larceny is an aggravated form of petit larceny. The aggravating fact is an element of the aggravated crime. * * *

[O]ne of the chief errors of *Almendarez-Torres*—an error to which I succumbed—was to attempt to discern whether a particular fact is traditionally (or typically) a basis for a sentencing court to increase an offender's sentence. * * * What matters is the way by which a fact enters into the sentence. If a fact is by law the basis for imposing or increasing punishment—for establishing or increasing the prosecution's entitlement—it is an element. * * *

* * *

JUSTICE O'CONNOR, with whom THE CHIEF JUSTICE, JUSTICE KENNEDY, and JUSTICE BREYER join, dissenting.

* * *

[Justice O'Connor accuses the majority of ignoring *Patterson,* which gave the states flexibility to define the elements of the crime.]

* * *

Any discussion of either the constitutional necessity or the likely effect of the Court's rule must begin, of course, with an understanding of what exactly that rule is. * * * In fact, there appear to be several plausible interpretations of the constitutional principle on which the Court's decision rests.

For example, under one reading, the Court appears to hold that the Constitution requires that a fact be submitted to a jury and proved beyond a reasonable doubt only if that fact, as a formal matter, extends the range of punishment beyond the prescribed statutory maximum. A State could, however, remove from the jury (and subject to a standard of proof below "beyond a reasonable doubt") the assessment of those facts that define narrower ranges of punishment, within the overall statutory range, to which the defendant may be sentenced. Thus, apparently New Jersey could cure its sentencing scheme, and achieve virtually the same results, by drafting its weapons possession statute in the following manner: First, New Jersey could prescribe, in the weapons possession statute itself, a range of 5 to 20 years' imprisonment for one who commits that criminal offense. Second, New Jersey could provide that only those defendants convicted under the statute who are found by a judge, by a preponderance of the evidence, to have acted with a purpose to intimidate an individual on the basis of race may receive a sentence greater than 10 years' imprisonment. * * * It is difficult to understand, and the Court does not explain, why the Constitution would require a state legislature to follow such a meaningless and formalistic difference in drafting its criminal statutes.

Under another reading of the Court's decision, it may mean only that the Constitution requires that a fact be submitted to a jury and proved beyond a reasonable doubt if it, as a formal matter, increases the range of punishment beyond that which could legally be imposed absent that fact.

A State could, however, remove from the jury (and subject to a standard of proof below "beyond a reasonable doubt") the assessment of those facts that, as a formal matter, decrease the range of punishment below that which could legally be imposed absent that fact. Thus, consistent with our decision in *Patterson*, New Jersey could cure its sentencing scheme, and achieve virtually the same results, by drafting its weapons possession statute in the following manner: First, New Jersey could prescribe, in the weapons possession statute itself, a range of 5 to 20 years' imprisonment for one who commits that criminal offense. Second, New Jersey could provide that a defendant convicted under the statute whom a judge finds, by a preponderance of the evidence, not to have acted with a purpose to intimidate an individual on the basis of race may receive a sentence no greater than 10 years' imprisonment. * * * Again, it is difficult to understand * * * why the Constitution would require a state legislature to follow such a meaningless and formalistic difference in drafting its criminal statutes.

If either of the above readings is all that the Court's decision means, the Court's principle amounts to nothing more than chastising the New Jersey Legislature for failing to use the approved phrasing in expressing its intent as to how unlawful weapons possession should be punished.

* * *

[Justice O'Connor expresses concern that the majority's decision could result in invalidating the Federal Sentencing Guidelines, under which sentences can be enhanced on the basis of judicial findings by a preponderance of the evidence. The Court takes up this point in United States v. Booker, infra.]

JUSTICE BREYER, with whom CHIEF JUSTICE REHNQUIST joins, dissenting.

The majority holds that the Constitution contains the following requirement: "any fact [other than recidivism] that increases the penalty for a crime beyond the prescribed statutory maximum must be submitted to a jury, and proved beyond a reasonable doubt." This rule would seem to promote a procedural ideal—that of juries, not judges, determining the existence of those facts upon which increased punishment turns. But the real world of criminal justice cannot hope to meet any such ideal. * * * There are, to put it simply, far too many potentially relevant sentencing factors to permit submission of all (or even many) of them to a jury. As the Sentencing Guidelines state the matter, "[a] bank robber with (or without) a gun, which the robber kept hidden (or brandished), might have frightened (or merely warned), injured seriously (or less seriously), tied up (or simply pushed) a guard, a teller or a customer, at night (or at noon), for a bad (or arguably less bad) motive, in an effort to obtain money for other crimes (or for other purposes), in the company of a few (or many) other robbers, for the first (or fourth) time that day, while sober (or under the influence of drugs or alcohol), and so forth." The Guidelines note that "a sentencing system tailored to fit every conceivable wrinkle of each case can become unworkable and seriously compromise the certainty of punishment and its deterrent effect." To ask a jury to consider all, or many, such matters would do the same.

At the same time, to require jury consideration of all such factors—say, during trial where the issue is guilt or innocence—could easily place the defendant in the awkward (and conceivably unfair) position of having to deny he committed the crime yet offer proof about how he committed it, e.g., "I did not sell drugs, but I sold no more than 500 grams." And while special postverdict sentencing juries could cure this problem, they have seemed (but for capital cases) not worth their administrative costs. * * *

* * * The majority raises no objection to traditional pre-Guidelines sentencing procedures under which judges, not juries, made the factual findings that would lead to an increase in an individual offender's sentence. How does a legislative determination differ in any significant way? For example, if a judge may on his or her own decide that victim injury or bad motive should increase a bank robber's sentence from 5 years to 10, why does it matter that a legislature instead enacts a statute that increases a bank robber's sentence from 5 years to 10 based on this same judicial finding?

* * *

I certainly do not believe that the present sentencing system is one of "perfect equity," and I am willing, consequently, to assume that the majority's rule would provide a degree of increased procedural protection in respect to those particular sentencing factors currently embodied in statutes. I nonetheless believe that any such increased protection provides little practical help and comes at too high a price.

* * *

NOTE ON APPRENDI

Professor Jacqueline Ross points out that the Court's ruling in *Apprendi* does not do defendants any favors. In fact, defendants may be put to added disadvantages after *Apprendi*, as Justice Breyer intimates in his dissent. Professor Ross elaborates as follows:

> Turning sentencing factors into offense elements to be tried to a jury will put defendants under pressure to produce evidence on an increasing range of issues. If the government must prove racial animus, drug amounts, relative culpability of different participants, or similar aggravating factors that may increase the maximum penalty for certain crimes, the government's presentation of evidence on these issues will put

> pressure on defendants to rebut the government's prima facie case by presenting their own evidence. Reallocating factual determinations from the sentencing judge to the jury in effect shifts the burden of production onto defendants, while the burden of proof remains formally on the government. * * * If he wishes to rebut the government's evidence on the disputed aggravating circumstances, a defendant may have to forego the benefits of the presumption of innocence (a) by presenting evidence and (b) by admitting some level of guilt or criminal involvement as the price of disagreeing with the degree of imputed culpability.
>
> For example, if the government were required to prove to the jury the amount of drugs sold by co-conspirators in furtherance of a narcotics conspiracy, government evidence that the conspirators sold at least 100 grams of heroin would potentially raise the maximum prison term from twenty to forty years' imprisonment. Defendants wanting to deny their identification as members of the conspiracy, or their presence at a drug transaction, may have to choose between presenting no evidence on the issue of drug amounts, in effect solidifying the often circumstantial inferences raised by the government's evidence, or producing evidence [of smaller than 100 gram drug amounts, which is] inconsistent with putting the government to its proof on the issues of defendant's identity and presence at the drug deal.

Ross, Unanticipated Consequences of Turning Sentencing Factors Into Offense Elements: The *Apprendi* Debate, 12 Federal Sentencing Reporter 197 (2000). As a juror, how would you react to the defendant's argument that "I wasn't there at the drug deal, but if I was there, the deal involved a lot less than 100 grams."?

Apprendi and Sentencing Factors That Do Not Increase the Minimum Penalty: Harris v. United States and Alleyne v. United States

Harris v. United States, 536 U.S. 545 (2002), involved a mandatory minimum sentencing provision—like that in *McMillan*. Harris was convicted of a narcotics violation. The statute called for a mandatory minimum of a five year sentence for drug trafficking, but if the defendant brandished a gun during the drug trafficking, the mandatory minimum was raised to seven years. The question of whether Harris brandished a gun was not addressed in the indictment and was not presented to the jury. Rather, the sentencing judge found by a preponderance of the evidence that Harris brandished a gun, and so employed the seven year mandatory minimum sentence. Harris's actual sentence was not more than he could have received just for drug trafficking—it did not go higher than the maximum sentence for drug trafficking. But a higher *floor* to the sentence was guaranteed by the judge's finding.

The Court found that the triggering of the mandatory minimum on the basis of a finding by the sentencing judge did not run afoul of *Apprendi*. Justice Kennedy, writing for the Court, declared as follows.

> *Apprendi* said that any fact extending the defendant's sentence beyond the maximum authorized by the jury's verdict would have been considered an element of an aggravated crime—and thus the domain of the jury—by those who framed the Bill of Rights. The same cannot be said of a fact increasing the mandatory minimum (but not extending the sentence beyond the statutory maximum), for the jury's verdict has authorized the judge to impose the minimum with or without the finding. As *McMillan* recognized, a statute may reserve this type of factual finding for the judge without violating the Constitution.

In Alleyne v. United States, 570 U.S. 99 (2013), the Court overruled Harris v. United States. Justice Thomas delivered an opinion which commanded five votes in part and four votes in part. Alleyne was subject to a mandatory minimum sentence if he "brandished" a firearm during his crime. The trial court treated the "brandishment" question as a sentencing factor and found by a preponderance of evidence that Alleyne had brandished a weapon. Alleyne received a 7-year sentence which comported with the mandatory minimum, but it was a sentence less than the maximum sentence that the defendant could have received for the crime. The core of the Court's holding is the following:

> *Harris* drew a distinction between facts that increase the statutory maximum and facts that increase only the mandatory minimum. We conclude that this distinction is inconsistent with our decision in Apprendi v. New Jersey, and with the original meaning of the Sixth Amendment. Any fact that, by law, increases the penalty for a crime is an "element" that must be submitted to the jury and found beyond a reasonable doubt. Mandatory minimum sentences increase the penalty for a crime. It follows, then, that any fact that increases the mandatory minimum is an "element" that must be submitted to the jury. Accordingly, *Harris* is overruled.

Justice Thomas discussed *McMillan* and *Apprendi* and, in a part of the opinion commanding five votes, he wrote that

> "[i]t is indisputable that a fact triggering a mandatory minimum alters the prescribed range of sentences to which a criminal defendant is exposed";
>
> "[i]t is impossible to dissociate the floor of a sentencing range from the penalty affixed to the crime";
>
> "[a] fact that increases a sentencing floor, thus, forms an essential ingredient of the offense";

"it is impossible to dispute that facts increasing the legally prescribed floor *aggravate* the punishment"; and

"because the fact of brandishing aggravates the legally prescribed range of allowable sentences, it constitutes an element of a separate, aggravated offense that must be found by the jury, regardless of what sentence the defendant *might* have received if a different range had been applicable."

Justice Sotomayor, joined by Justices Ginsburg and Kagan, agreed that both *Harris* and *McMillan* "were wrongly decided," and argued that *Apprendi* and other cases like Cunningham v. California and Blakely v. Washington, discussed infra, made *Harris* "even more of an outlier" and made it "appropriate for the Court to overrule *Harris* and to apply *Apprendi*'s basic jury-determination rule to mandatory minimum sentences in order to erase this anomaly in our case law."

Justice Breyer concurred in part and in the judgment. He had written in *Harris* that he could not distinguish it from *Apprendi* in terms of logic, expressed his continuing disagreement with *Apprendi*, and concluded that "[w]hile *Harris* has been the law for 11 years, *Apprendi* has been the law for even longer; and I think the time has come to end this anomaly in *Apprendi*'s application."

Chief Justice Roberts, joined by Justices Scalia and Kennedy, dissented and argued that

"the jury's verdict fully authorized the judge to impose a sentence of anywhere from five years to life in prison";

"[n]o additional finding of fact was 'essential' to any punishment within the range";

"[a]fter rendering the verdict, the jury's role was completed, it was discharged, and the judge began the process of determining where within that range to set Alleyne's sentence";

"[e]veryone agrees that in making that determination, the judge was free to consider any relevant facts about the offense and offender, including facts not found by the jury beyond a reasonable doubt";

Apprendi did not make it impermissible for judges to consider various factors relating to offense and offender;

"under the majority's rule, in the absence of a statutory mandatory minimum, there would have been no constitutional problem had the judge, exercising the discretion given him by the jury's verdict, decided that seven years in prison was the appropriate penalty for the crime *because of* his finding that the firearm had been brandished during the offense"; and

"[i]n my view, that is enough to resolve this case."

Justice Alito also dissented, arguing that if the Court were to reconsider existing precedent it should reconsider *Apprendi*, critiqued the historical analysis of the *Apprendi* majority, and concluded that "[t]he Court's decision creates a precedent about precedent that may have greater precedential effect than the dubious decisions on which it relies."

Apprendi and the Death Penalty: Ring v. Arizona

In Ring v. Arizona, 536 U.S. 584 (2002), the Court held that the Arizona capital sentencing statute was constitutionally infirm after *Apprendi*. Arizona provided that the judge would determine whether sufficient aggravating factors existed to justify the death penalty. Thus, if the judge found the factors to exist, she would impose a sentence—death—greater than that which could be authorized by the jury, because the jury's verdict could only justify a sentence of life imprisonment. Justice Ginsburg, writing for the Court, held that such a system could not be squared with *Apprendi*. She declared that "[c]apital defendants, no less than non-capital defendants * * * are entitled to a jury determination of any fact on which the legislature conditions an increase in their maximum punishment." Justice Ginsburg concluded as follows:

> The right to trial by jury guaranteed by the Sixth Amendment would be senselessly diminished if it encompassed the factfinding necessary to increase a defendant's sentence by two years, but not the factfinding necessary to put him to death. We hold that the Sixth Amendment applies to both.

The Court in *Ring* overruled its prior holding in Walton v. Arizona, 497 U.S. 639 (1990), which held that it was permissible for a judge to sentence the defendant to death on the basis of judicial findings of aggravating circumstances. The holding in *Walton* could not be squared with *Apprendi*.

Justice Scalia wrote a concurring opinion joined by Justice Thomas, in which he declared that "the accelerating propensity of both state and federal legislatures to adopt 'sentencing factors' determined by judges that increase punishment beyond what is authorized by the jury's verdict * * * cause me to believe that our people's traditional belief in the right of trial by jury is in perilous decline. That decline is bound to be confirmed, and indeed accelerated, by the repeated spectacle of a man's going to his death because *a judge* found that an aggravating factor existed. We cannot preserve our veneration for the protection of the jury in criminal cases if we render ourselves callous to the need for that protection by regularly imposing the death penalty without it."

Justice Kennedy wrote a short concurring opinion in *Ring* noting that while he disagreed with *Apprendi*, that case "is now the law, and its holding must be implemented in a principled way. * * * Justice Breyer concurred in the judgment, continuing to reject *Apprendi*, but concluding that jury sentencing in capital cases is mandated by the Eighth Amendment. Justice O'Connor wrote a dissenting opinion joined by Chief Justice Rehnquist. She agreed that *Walton* could not be squared with *Apprendi*. But forced to choose one case or the other to overrule, she would overrule *Apprendi*.

Application of Ring v. Arizona: Hurst v. Florida

In Hurst v. Florida, 577 U.S. 92 (2016), the Court reviewed a capital proceeding under Florida law, where state law provided that the death penalty was imposed by the judge, and the role of the jury was to provide an "advisory sentence" that the judge must accord great weight when imposing a sentence. To impose the death penalty, the judge was required to find facts that support the aggravating circumstances that warrant that punishment. The Court in *Hurst* found that this system ran afoul of the Sixth Amendment, according to the principles set forth in *Apprendi* and its progeny, including most importantly Ring v. Arizona. Justice Sotomayor, writing for the majority, declared as follows:

> The analysis the *Ring* Court applied to Arizona's sentencing scheme applies equally to Florida's. Like Arizona at the time of *Ring*, Florida does not require the jury to make the critical findings necessary to impose the death penalty. Rather, Florida requires a judge to find these facts. Although Florida incorporates an advisory jury verdict that Arizona lacked, we have previously made clear that this distinction is immaterial: "It is true that in Florida the jury recommends a sentence, but it does not make specific factual findings with regard to the existence of mitigating or aggravating circumstances and its recommendation is not binding on the trial judge. A Florida trial court no more has the assistance of a jury's findings of fact with respect to sentencing issues than does a trial judge in Arizona." Walton v. Arizona, 497 U.S. 639, 648 (1990).
>
> As with Timothy Ring, the maximum punishment Timothy Hurst could have received without any judge-made findings was life in prison without parole. As with Ring, a judge increased Hurst's authorized punishment based on her own factfinding. In light of *Ring*, we hold that Hurst's sentence violates the Sixth Amendment.

Justice Breyer concurred in the judgment.

Justice Alito dissented. He argued, as he had in previous cases, that *Apprendi* is inconsistent with the original understanding of the jury trial right. He also argued that the Arizona system gave the jury no fact finding role, whereas Florida permits a jury to recommend a death sentence only if it finds that the state has proved one or more aggravating factors beyond a reasonable doubt and has weighed aggravating and mitigating factors. He found this sufficient to distinguish *Ring*.

Application of Ring v. Arizona: Hurst v. Florida

In addition to aggravating factors, death penalty defendants have a constitutional right to present evidence of relevant mitigating factors. *See* Eddings v. Oklahoma, 455 U.S. 104 (1982); Lockett v. Ohio, 438 U.S. 586 (1978). Where trial courts err either in finding an aggravating factor or in failing to consider a relevant mitigating factor, it is not necessary to conduct a new sentencing hearing in front of a jury. Appellate courts may, instead, reweigh the sentence by disregarding any infirm aggravating factors and including any omitted mitigating factors. *See* McKinney v. Arizona, 140 S.Ct. 702 (2020); Clemons v. Mississippi, 494 U.S. 738 (1990).

Facts That Trigger Enhancement of a Sentence Under Mandatory Sentencing Guidelines Must Be Proved to a Jury: Blakely v. Washington

In Blakely v. Washington, 542 U.S. 296 (2004), the Court considered how *Apprendi* applied to a state sentencing scheme that allowed sentences to be enhanced on the basis of judicial findings pursuant to *mandatory sentencing guidelines*. Blakely entered a guilty plea admitting the elements of second-degree kidnaping and domestic-violence and firearm allegations, but no other relevant facts. The crimes to which he pleaded guilty called for a standard sentencing range, under the state's sentencing guidelines, of 49 to 53 months. The guidelines provided that a judge may impose a sentence above the standard range if the judge finds "substantial and compelling reasons justifying an exceptional sentence." The sentencing judge found, after a hearing, that the defendant had acted with deliberate cruelty, a statutorily enumerated ground for upward departure in domestic-violence cases. This finding resulted in the judge imposing an exceptional sentence of 90 months—37 months beyond the standard maximum. Blakely argued that this sentencing procedure deprived him of his constitutional right to have a jury determine beyond a reasonable doubt all facts legally essential to his sentence.

The State argued that *Apprendi* was inapplicable because the statute under which Blakely was convicted called for a sentence of up to 10 years, and he received a sentence within that range. Blakely argued that the effective sentencing range, for *Apprendi* purposes, was the sentencing *guideline* applicable to the crime, which topped out at 53 months. The Court sided with Blakely. Justice Scalia reasoned as follows:

> Our precedents make clear * * * that the "statutory maximum" for *Apprendi* purposes is the maximum sentence a judge may impose *solely on the basis of the facts reflected in the jury verdict or admitted by the defendant*. In other words, the relevant "statutory maximum" is not the maximum sentence a judge may impose after finding additional facts, but the maximum he may impose *without* any

additional findings. When a judge inflicts punishment that the jury's verdict alone does not allow, the jury has not found all the facts which the law makes essential to the punishment, and the judge exceeds his proper authority.

The judge in this case could not have imposed the exceptional 90-month sentence solely on the basis of the facts admitted in the guilty plea. Had the judge imposed the 90-month sentence solely on the basis of the plea, he would have been reversed. The "maximum sentence" is no more 10 years here than it was 20 years in *Apprendi* (because that is what the judge could have imposed upon finding a hate crime) * * *.

Justice Scalia spent some time explaining and defending the rationale of *Apprendi:*

Our commitment to *Apprendi* in this context reflects not just respect for longstanding precedent, but the need to give intelligible content to the right of jury trial. That right is no mere procedural formality, but a fundamental reservation of power in our constitutional structure. Just as suffrage ensures the people's ultimate control in the legislative and executive branches, jury trial is meant to ensure their control in the judiciary. * * * *Apprendi* carries out this design by ensuring that the judge's authority to sentence derives wholly from the jury's verdict. Without that restriction, the jury would not exercise the control that the Framers intended.

Those who would reject *Apprendi* are resigned to one of two alternatives. The first is that the jury need only find whatever facts the legislature chooses to label elements of the crime, and that those it labels sentencing factors—no matter how much they may increase the punishment—may be found by the judge. This would mean, for example, that a judge could sentence a man for committing murder even if the jury convicted him only of illegally possessing the firearm used to commit it—or of making an illegal lane change while fleeing the death scene. Not even *Apprendi*'s critics would advocate this absurd result. The jury could not function as circuitbreaker in the State's machinery of justice if it were relegated to making a determination that the defendant at some point did something wrong, a mere preliminary to a judicial inquisition into the facts of the crime the State *actually* seeks to punish.

The second alternative is that legislatures may establish legally essential sentencing factors *within limits*—limits crossed when, perhaps, the sentencing factor is a "tail which wags the dog of the substantive offense." *McMillan*. What this means in operation is that the law must not go *too far*—it must not exceed the judicial estimation of the proper role of the judge.

> * * * With *too far* as the yardstick, it is always possible to disagree with such judgments and never to refute them.
>
> Whether the Sixth Amendment incorporates this manipulable standard rather than *Apprendi*'s bright-line rule depends on the plausibility of the claim that the Framers would have left definition of the scope of jury power up to judges' intuitive sense of how far is *too far*. We think that claim not plausible at all, because the very reason the Framers put a jury-trial guarantee in the Constitution is that they were unwilling to trust government to mark out the role of the jury.

Justice O'Connor dissented in *Blakely,* in an opinion joined in whole by Justice Breyer and in pertinent part by Chief Justice Rehnquist and Justice Kennedy. She argued much as Justice Breyer had in *Apprendi* that requiring the jury to decide the many facts that go into sentencing decisions under guidelines regimes will probably make guidelines sentencing unworkable.

Justice Kennedy wrote a separate dissenting opinion, noting that while the majority struck down sentencing under a state system, its rationale was equally applicable to the Federal Sentencing Guidelines.

Justice Breyer also wrote a dissenting opinion in *Blakely* that was joined by Justice O'Connor. Justice Breyer addressed the rationale for permitting legislatures the leeway in identifying elements of the crime on the one hand and sentencing facts on the other:

> Why does the Sixth Amendment permit a jury trial right (in respect to a particular fact) to depend upon a legislative labeling decision, namely, the legislative decision to label the fact a *sentencing fact*, instead of an *element of the crime?* The answer is that the fairness and effectiveness of a sentencing system, and the related fairness and effectiveness of the criminal justice system itself, depends upon the legislature's possessing the constitutional authority (within due process limits) to make that labeling decision. To restrict radically the legislature's power in this respect, as the majority interprets the Sixth Amendment to do, prevents the legislature from seeking sentencing systems that are consistent with, and indeed may help to advance, the Constitution's greater fairness goals.
>
> To say this is not simply to express concerns about fairness to defendants. It is also to express concerns about the serious practical (or impractical) changes that the Court's decision seems likely to impose upon the criminal process; about the tendency of the Court's decision to embed further plea bargaining processes that lack transparency and too often mean nonuniform, sometimes arbitrary, sentencing practices; about the obstacles the Court's decision poses to legislative efforts to bring about greater uniformity between real criminal conduct and real punishment; and ultimately about the

limitations that the Court imposes upon legislatures' ability to make democratic legislative decisions. Whatever the faults of guidelines systems—and there are many—they are more likely to find their cure in legislation emerging from the experience of, and discussion among, all elements of the criminal justice community, than in a virtually unchangeable constitutional decision of this Court.

Applying Apprendi-Blakely to the Federal Sentencing Guidelines: United States v. Booker

Federal courts struggled to determine the precise impact of *Blakely* on the Federal Sentencing Guidelines, discussed fully in Chapter 11. In United States v. Booker, 543 U.S. 220 (2005), the Court in an opinion by Justice Stevens, held that the Federal Sentencing Guidelines are not distinguishable from the state guidelines found invalid in *Blakely*. That is, to the extent that the Federal Guidelines *require* the sentencing court to enhance a sentence beyond the guideline for the basic crime for which the defendant was convicted, on the basis of facts (other than prior convictions) found by the sentencing judge, then they violate the defendant's right to jury trial and the right to have the government prove all elements of the crime beyond a reasonable doubt.

But the most important part of Booker is the remedial opinion by Justice Breyer. There, a different majority of the Court found that the problem with the Guidelines is not that judges sentence on the basis of facts not found by the jury. Rather the problem is that those findings trigger *mandatory* enhancements, because the Guidelines had been construed up to then to bind district judges in their sentencing decisions. Under the remedial opinion, the Sentencing Guidelines become guidelines in the real sense. They are advisory only.

The remedial opinion, and the dissents to that opinion, are set forth in Chapter 11, as the matters discussed in those opinions delve deeply into the mechanics of the Sentencing Guidelines. This section describes the opinions discussing the applicability of *Apprendi* and *Blakely* to the Federal Sentencing Guidelines.

Justice Stevens found no relevant distinction between the State guidelines struck down in *Blakely* and the Federal Guidelines, as both require judges to impose a higher sentence than is applicable to the crime for which the defendant was convicted, on the basis of facts found by a district judge at sentencing. He noted that it was the mandatory aspect of the Guidelines that led to the constitutional problem. He explained as follows:

> If the Guidelines as currently written could be read as merely advisory provisions that recommended, rather than required, the selection of particular sentences in response to differing sets of facts,

their use would not implicate the Sixth Amendment. We have never doubted the authority of a judge to exercise broad discretion in imposing a sentence within a statutory range. Indeed, everyone agrees that the constitutional issues presented by these cases would have been avoided entirely if Congress had omitted * * * the provisions that make the Guidelines binding on district judges * * *. For when a trial judge exercises his discretion to select a specific sentence within a defined range, the defendant has no right to a jury determination of the facts that the judge deems relevant.

* * *

Booker's case illustrates the mandatory nature of the Guidelines. The jury convicted him of possessing at least 50 grams of crack based on evidence that he had 92.5 grams of crack in his duffel bag. * * * Booker's actual sentence, however, was 360 months, almost 10 years longer than the Guidelines range supported by the jury verdict alone. To reach this sentence, the judge found facts beyond those found by the jury: namely, that Booker possessed 566 grams of crack in addition to the 92.5 grams in his duffel bag. The jury never heard any evidence of the additional drug quantity, and the judge found it true by a preponderance of the evidence. Thus, just as in *Blakely*, "the jury's verdict alone does not authorize the sentence. The judge acquires that authority only upon finding some additional fact." There is no relevant distinction between the sentence imposed pursuant to the Washington statutes in *Blakely* and the sentences imposed pursuant to the Federal Sentencing Guidelines in these cases.

Justice Breyer (who played a major role in writing the Sentencing Guidelines), joined by the Chief Justice, Justice O'Connor, and Justice Kennedy, dissented. He reiterated the objections he made in both *Apprendi* and *Blakely*:

> * * * [T]he Court's Sixth Amendment decision would risk unwieldy trials, a two-tier jury system, a return to judicial sentencing discretion, or the replacement of sentencing ranges with specific mandatory sentences. The decision would pose a serious obstacle to congressional efforts to create a sentencing law that would mandate more similar treatment of like offenders, that would thereby diminish sentencing disparity, and that would consequently help to overcome irrational discrimination (including racial discrimination) in sentencing. These consequences would seem perverse when viewed through the lens of a Constitution that seeks a fair criminal process.
>
> The upshot is that the Court's Sixth Amendment decisions—*Apprendi, Blakely,* and today's—deprive Congress and state legislatures of authority that is constitutionally theirs. Congress' share of this joint responsibility has long included not only the power

to define crimes (by enacting statutes setting forth their factual elements) but also the power to specify sentences, whether by setting forth a range of individual-crime-related sentences (say, 0 to 10 years' imprisonment for bank robbery) or by identifying sentencing factors that permit or require a judge to impose higher or lower sentences in particular circumstances.

This last mentioned power is not absolute. * * * But the power does give Congress a degree of freedom (within constraints of fairness) to choose to characterize a fact as a "sentencing factor," relevant only to punishment, or as an element of a crime, relevant to guilt or innocence. The Court has rejected this approach apparently because it finds too difficult the judicial job of managing the "fairness" constraint, *i.e.*, of determining when Congress has overreached. But the Court has nowhere asked, "compared to what?" Had it done so, it could not have found the practical difficulty it has mentioned sufficient to justify the severe limits that its approach imposes upon Congress' legislative authority.

Justice Breyer also argued that the Federal Sentencing Guidelines were distinguishable from the Guidelines struck down in *Blakely*. This part of his argument presented a detailed analysis of the Federal Guidelines.

Ultimately, a majority of the Court, in an opinion on remedies for the Guidelines' unconstitutionality, found that the solution was not to strike down the Guidelines *in toto*, but rather to strike down those aspects of the Guidelines that made them *mandatory* on district judges. That remedial opinion, in an ironic twist, was authored by Justice Breyer.

State Sentencing Scheme Found Mandatory, Not Advisory: Cunningham v. California

In Cunningham v. California, 549 U.S. 270 (2007), Justice Ginsburg wrote for the Court as it found that California's determinate sentencing law (DSL) violated the *Apprendi* line of cases. Cunningham was tried and convicted of continuous sexual abuse of a child under the age of 14. The DSL provided that his offense was punishable by imprisonment for a lower term sentence of 6 years, a middle term sentence of 12 years, or an upper term sentence of 16 years, and that the trial judge was required to sentence Cunningham to the 12-year middle term unless the judge found one or more additional facts in aggravation. The judge conducted a post-trial hearing and found six aggravating circumstances and one mitigating factor. The judge found that the aggravators outweighed the mitigating factor and sentenced Cunningham to the upper term of 16 years.

The key provision of the California law for Justice Ginsburg was Penal Code § 1170(b), which provided that "the court shall order imposition of the middle term, unless there are circumstances in aggravation or mitigation of the crime."

Relying on *Blakely*, Justice Ginsburg wrote as follows:

> Under California's DSL, an upper term sentence may be imposed only when the trial judge finds an aggravating circumstance. An element of the charged offense, essential to a jury's determination of guilt, or admitted in a defendant's guilty plea, does not qualify as such a circumstance. Instead, aggravating circumstances depend on facts found discretely and solely by the judge. In accord with *Blakely*, therefore, the middle term prescribed in California's statutes, not the upper term, is the relevant statutory maximum. Because circumstances in aggravation are found by the judge, not the jury, and need only be established by a preponderance of the evidence, not beyond a reasonable doubt, the DSL violates *Apprendi*'s bright-line rule: Except for a prior conviction, "any fact that increases the penalty for a crime beyond the prescribed statutory maximum must be submitted to a jury, and proved beyond a reasonable doubt."

Justice Ginsburg concluded that "California's DSL does not resemble the advisory system the *Booker* Court had in view," because under California's system, judges are not free to exercise their "discretion to select a specific sentence within a defined range."

Justice Kennedy, joined by Justice Breyer, dissented and continued to attack the *Apprendi* reasoning.

Justice Alito, joined by the same two Justices, also dissented and argued as follows:

> The California sentencing law that the Court strikes down today is indistinguishable in any constitutionally significant respect from the advisory Guidelines scheme that the Court approved in United States v. Booker. Both sentencing schemes grant trial judges considerable discretion in sentencing; both subject the exercise of that discretion to appellate review for "reasonableness"; and both—the California law explicitly, and the federal scheme implicitly—require a sentencing judge to find some factor to justify a sentence above the minimum that could be imposed based solely on the jury's verdict. Because this Court has held unequivocally that the post-*Booker* federal sentencing system satisfies the requirements of the Sixth Amendment, the same should be true with regard to the California system. * * *

Apprendi and the Determination of Facts Necessary to Impose a Consecutive Sentence: Oregon v. Ice

Justice Ginsburg wrote for the Court in Oregon v. Ice, 555 U.S. 160 (2009), as it addressed this question: "When a defendant has been tried and convicted of multiple offenses, each involving discrete sentencing prescriptions, does the Sixth Amendment mandate jury determination of any fact declared necessary to the imposition of consecutive, in lieu of concurrent, sentences?" She answered the question by reference to historical practice and deference to state procedure:

> Most States continue the common-law tradition: They entrust to judges' unfettered discretion the decision whether sentences for discrete offenses shall be served consecutively or concurrently. In some States, sentences for multiple offenses are presumed to run consecutively, but sentencing judges may order concurrent sentences upon finding cause therefor. Other States, including Oregon, constrain judges' discretion by requiring them to find certain facts before imposing consecutive, rather than concurrent, sentences. It is undisputed that States may proceed on the first two tracks without transgressing the Sixth Amendment. The sole issue in dispute, then, is whether the Sixth Amendment, as construed in *Apprendi* and *Blakely*, precludes the mode of proceeding chosen by Oregon and several of her sister States. We hold, in light of historical practice and the authority of States over administration of their criminal justice systems, that the Sixth Amendment does not exclude Oregon's choice.

Justice Ginsburg looked to the historical role of the jury in sentencing, found that it differed greatly from the jury's role in determining guilt or innocence, and concluded that the concerns of *Apprendi* were not present:

> The historical record demonstrates that the jury played no role in the decision to impose sentences consecutively or concurrently. Rather, the choice rested exclusively with the judge. * * * The historical record further indicates that a judge's imposition of consecutive, rather than concurrent, sentences was the prevailing practice.
>
> In light of this history, legislative reforms regarding the imposition of multiple sentences do not implicate the core concerns that prompted our decision in *Apprendi*. * * *

Justice Scalia, joined by Chief Justice Roberts and Justices Souter and Thomas, dissented and argued that *Apprendi* clearly controlled the outcome:

> The rule of Apprendi v. New Jersey is clear: Any fact—other than that of a prior conviction—that increases the maximum punishment to which a defendant may be sentenced must be admitted by the defendant or proved beyond a reasonable doubt to a jury. Oregon's sentencing scheme allows judges rather than juries to find the facts necessary to commit defendants to longer prison sentences, and thus directly contradicts what we held eight years ago and have reaffirmed several times since.

Application of Apprendi to Criminal Fines: Southern Union Co. v. United States

A 6–3 majority of the Supreme Court held that *Apprendi* and its progeny apply to criminal fines in Southern Union Co. v. United States, 567 U.S. 343 (2012). A jury convicted Southern Union Company on one count of violating the Resource Conservation and Recovery Act of 1976 by knowingly storing liquid mercury at a subsidiary's facility "on or about September 19, 2002 to October 19, 2004." The statute makes violations punishable by a fine of not more than $50,000 for each day of violation. The probation office calculated a maximum fine of $38.1 million, on the basis that Southern Union violated the statute for *each* of the 762 days from September 19, 2002, through October 19, 2004. Southern Union contended that, based on the jury verdict and the district court's instructions, the jury necessarily found a violation for only one day within the period covered by the indictment. The district court held that *Apprendi* applied but concluded from the "content and context of the verdict all together" that the jury found a 762-day violation. It imposed a fine of $6 million and a "community service obligation" of $12 million. The First Circuit did not agree with the district court's analysis of the jury's verdict but affirmed the sentence on the ground that *Apprendi* did not apply to criminal fines—so the Government could, and did, prove by a preponderance of the evidence at sentencing that the storage occurred on each of the 762 days. The Supreme Court reversed.

Justice Sotomayor writing for the majority, discussed the *Apprendi* line of cases, and reasoned as follows:

> While the punishments at stake in those cases were imprisonment or a death sentence, we see no principled basis under *Apprendi* for treating criminal fines differently. *Apprendi*'s "core concern" is to reserve to the jury "the determination of facts that warrant punishment for a specific statutory offense." That concern applies whether the sentence is a criminal fine or imprisonment or death. Criminal fines, like these other forms of punishment, are penalties inflicted by the sovereign for the commission of offenses. Fines * * * are frequently imposed today, especially upon organizational defendants who cannot be imprisoned. And the amount of a fine, like the maximum term of imprisonment or eligibility for the death penalty, is often calculated by reference to particular facts. Sometimes, as here, the fact is the duration of a statutory violation; under other statutes it is the amount of the defendant's gain or the victim's loss, or some other factor. In all such cases, requiring juries to find beyond a reasonable doubt facts that determine the fine's maximum amount is necessary to implement *Apprendi*'s "animating principle": the

"preservation of the jury's historic role as a bulwark between the State and the accused at the trial for an alleged offense."

Justice Breyer, joined by Justices Kennedy and Alito, dissented. He reiterated previous arguments made in dissent in *Apprendi* cases and argued that applying *Apprendi* to fines would do no favors for criminal defendants:

> The consequence of the majority's holding, insisting that juries make such determinations, is likely to diminish the fairness of the criminal trial process. A defendant will not find it easy to show the jury at trial that (1) he committed no environmental crime, but (2) in any event, he committed the crime only on 20 days, not 30.

Apprendi Limitations as Applied to Supervised Release Revocation Proceedings: United States v. Haymond

In United States v. Haymond, 139 S.Ct. 2369 (2019), Justice Gorsuch wrote for a plurality that included Justices Ginsburg, Sotomayor and Kagan to hold that a judge could not increase a sentence because of additional conduct committed while on supervised release.

Justice Gorsuch summarized the facts:

> After a jury found Andre Haymond guilty of possessing child pornography in violation of federal law, the question turned to sentencing. The law authorized the district judge to impose a prison term of between zero and 10 years, and a period of supervised release of between 5 years and life. Because Mr. Haymond had no criminal history and was working to help support his mother who had suffered a stroke, the judge concluded that Mr. Haymond was "not going to get much out of being in prison" and sentenced him to a prison term of 38 months, followed by 10 years of supervised release.
>
> After completing his prison sentence, however, Mr. Haymond encountered trouble on supervised release. He sat for multiple polygraph tests in which he denied possessing or viewing child pornography, and each time the test indicated no deception. But when the government conducted an unannounced search of his computers and cellphone, it turned up 59 images that appeared to be child pornography. Based on that discovery, the government sought to revoke Mr. Haymond's supervised release and secure a new and additional prison sentence.
>
> A hearing followed before a district judge acting without a jury, and under a preponderance of the evidence rather than a reasonable doubt standard. In light of expert testimony regarding the manner in which cellphones can "cache" images without the user's knowledge, the judge found insufficient evidence to show that Mr. Haymond

knowingly possessed 46 of the images. At the same time, the judge found it more likely than not that Mr. Haymond knowingly downloaded and possessed the remaining 13 images.

With that, the question turned once more to sentencing. Under 18 U.S.C. § 3583(e)(3), enacted as part of the Sentencing Reform Act of 1984, a district judge who finds that a defendant has violated the conditions of his supervised release normally may (but is not required to) impose a new prison term up to the maximum period of supervised release authorized by statute for the defendant's original crime of conviction, subject to certain limits. Under that provision, the judge in this case would have been free to sentence Mr. Haymond to between zero and two additional years in prison.

But there was a complication. Under § 3583(k), added to the Act in 2003 and amended in 2006, if a judge finds by a preponderance of the evidence that a defendant on supervised release committed one of several enumerated offenses, including the possession of child pornography, the judge must impose an additional prison term of at least five years and up to life without regard to the length of the prison term authorized for the defendant's initial crime of conviction.

Because Mr. Haymond had committed an offense covered by § 3583(k), the judge felt bound to impose an additional prison term of at least five years. He did so, though, with reservations. It's one thing, Judge Terence Kern said, for a judge proceeding under a preponderance of the evidence standard to revoke a defendant's supervised release and order him to serve additional time in prison within the range already authorized by the defendant's original conviction; after all, the jury's verdict, reached under the reasonable doubt standard, permitted that much punishment. But the judge found it "repugnant" that a statute might impose a new and additional "mandatory five-year" punishment without those traditional protections. Were it not for § 3583(k)'s mandatory minimum, the judge added, he "probably would have sentenced in the range of two years or less."

On appeal to the Tenth Circuit, Mr. Haymond challenged both the factual support for his new punishment and its constitutionality. On the facts, the court of appeals held that the district court's findings against Mr. Haymond were clearly erroneous in certain respects. Even so, the court concluded, just enough evidence remained to sustain a finding that Mr. Haymond had knowingly possessed the 13 images at issue, in violation of § 3583(k). That left the question of the statute's constitutionality, and there the Tenth Circuit concluded that § 3583(k) violated the Fifth and Sixth Amendments. The court explained that a jury had convicted Mr. Haymond beyond a reasonable doubt of a crime

> carrying a prison term of zero to 10 years. Yet now Mr. Haymond faced a new potential prison term of five years to life. Because this new prison term included a new and higher mandatory minimum resting only on facts found by a judge by a preponderance of the evidence, the court held, the statute violated Mr. Haymond's right to trial by jury.
>
> By way of remedy, the court held the last two sentences of § 3583(k), which mandate a 5-year minimum prison term, "unconstitutional and unenforceable." The court then vacated Mr. Haymond's revocation sentence and remanded the case to the district court for resentencing without regard to those provisions. In effect, the court of appeals left the district court free to issue a new sentence under the preexisting statute governing most every other supervised release violation, § 3583(e). Following the Tenth Circuit's directions, the district court proceeded to resentence Mr. Haymond to time served, as he had already been detained by that point for approximately 28 months.

The plurality reasoned as follows:

> By now, the lesson for our case is clear. Based on the facts reflected in the jury's verdict, Mr. Haymond faced a lawful prison term of between zero and 10 years under § 2252(b)(2). But then a judge—acting without a jury and based only on a preponderance of the evidence—found that Mr. Haymond had engaged in additional conduct in violation of the terms of his supervised release. Under § 3583(k), that judicial factfinding triggered a new punishment in the form of a prison term of at least five years and up to life. So just like the facts the judge found at the defendant's sentencing hearing in *Alleyne*, the facts the judge found here increased "the legally prescribed range of allowable sentences" in violation of the Fifth and Sixth Amendments. In this case, that meant Mr. Haymond faced a minimum of five years in prison instead of as little as none. Nor did the absence of a jury's finding beyond a reasonable doubt only infringe the rights of the accused; it also divested the "people at large"—the men and women who make up a jury of a defendant's peers—of their constitutional authority to set the metes and bounds of judicially administered criminal punishments.

Justice Breyer concurred in the judgment. Although he was not in favor of "transplant[ing] the *Apprendi* line of cases to the supervised-release context," he agreed with the plurality that § 3583(k), is unconstitutional. He explained that "[r]evocation of supervised release is typically understood as part of the penalty for the initial offense"; "[t]he consequences that flow from violation of the conditions of supervised release are first and foremost considered sanctions for the defendant's "breach of trust" * * * not for the particular conduct triggering the revocation as if that conduct were being sentenced as new federal criminal conduct"; and therefore, "the consequences for violation of conditions of supervised release under § 3583(e), which governs most revocations, are limited by the severity of the original crime of conviction, not the conduct that results in revocation."

Justice Breyer found that § 3583(k) was difficult to reconcile with this understanding of supervised release and persuaded him that § 3583(k) was less like ordinary revocation and more like punishment for a new offense, to which the jury right would typically attach.

Justice Alito, joined by Chief Justice Roberts and Justices Thomas and Kavanaugh, dissented and analogized supervised release proceedings to parole revocation proceedings.

> I start with the proposition that the old federal parole system did not implicate the Sixth Amendment's jury trial right. A parole revocation proceeding was not a "criminal prosecution" within the meaning of the Sixth Amendment, and revocation did not result in a new sentence. When a prisoner was paroled, the Executive was simply exercising the authority conferred by law to grant the defendant a conditional release from serving part of the sentence imposed after a guilty verdict.
>
> Supervised release, for reasons already explained, is not fundamentally different and therefore should not be treated any differently for Sixth Amendment purposes. When a jury finds a federal defendant guilty of violating a particular criminal statute, the maximum period of confinement authorized is the maximum term of imprisonment plus the maximum term of supervised release. If a prisoner does not end up spending this full period in confinement, that is because service of part of the period is excused due to satisfactory conduct during the period of supervised release. Any other reading exalts form over substance in a way that has enormous consequences that cannot be justified on constitutional grounds.
>
> Once this is understood, it follows that the procedures that must be followed at a supervised-release revocation proceeding are the same that had to be followed at a parole revocation proceeding, and these were settled long ago. At a parole revocation hearing, the fundamental requisites of due process had to be observed, but a parolee did not have a right to a jury trial. Neither the Confrontation Clause nor the formal rules of evidence had to be followed. Due process did not require proof beyond a reasonable doubt as is necessary at trial * * * .

Justice Alito pointed out that the *Apprendi* line of cases required that a jury decide facts that increased the punishment for a crime, but supervised release revocation proceedings do not address the underlying criminal activity:

Here, the factual basis for revoking respondent's supervised release did not go * * * to what happened in the commission of the offense; it did not even relate to the commission of the offense. It had virtually nothing to do with the child-pornography offense that led to respondent's conviction, incarceration, and supervised release. The same would be true of a defendant convicted of burglary, arson, or any other crime: His failure to attend an employment class or to pass a drug test while on supervised release would have nothing to do with how he carried out those offenses. * * * Thus, no reasonable person would describe such postjudgment facts that go only to the administration of a previously imposed sentence as "ingredients" or "elements" of the charged offense. * * *

D. PROOF OF ALTERNATIVE MEANS OF COMMITTING A SINGLE CRIME

The requirement of proof beyond a reasonable doubt of all elements of a crime raises another question: whether it is constitutionally acceptable to define a "crime" so broadly as to permit jurors to reach one verdict based on any combination of alternative findings of fact. The Court considered this question in Schad v. Arizona, 501 U.S. 624 (1991). Schad was charged with first-degree murder. In Arizona, the crime of first-degree murder encompasses both premeditated murder and felony murder. At trial, the prosecutor advanced both premeditated and felony murder theories, and offered proof under both theories. The jury returned a general verdict of guilty of first degree murder. Schad complained that this procedure was invalid, because it excused the state from having to prove all of the elements of one specific crime beyond a reasonable doubt.

Justice Souter, writing for a plurality of four Justices, stated that it was constitutionally permissible to define first-degree murder in such a way that it could be committed by alternative means, so long as those means "reasonably reflect notions of equivalent blameworthiness or culpability." Justice Souter recognized that the Due Process Clause would not permit a state "to convict anyone under a charge of 'Crime' so generic that any combination of jury findings of embezzlement, reckless driving, murder, burglary, tax evasion, or littering, for example, would suffice for conviction." However, the Arizona statute did not create such a disparate collection of alternative means to commit first degree murder. Justice Souter concluded that felony murder and premeditated murder were of sufficient "moral equivalence" to be grouped together as two ways of committing the same crime, and that therefore the general verdict of guilt was constitutionally permissible.

Justice Souter found it highly relevant that many states have traditionally considered felony murder and premeditated murder as alternative means of committing first degree murder. He stated that the "historical and contemporary acceptance of Arizona's definition of the offense and verdict practice is a strong indication" that it did not violate due process, because "legal definitions, and the practices comporting with them, are unlikely to endure for long, or to retain wide acceptance, if they are at odds with notions of fairness and rationality sufficiently fundamental to be comprehended in due process."

Justice Scalia concurred in the judgment. In his view, the fact that the Arizona statutory definition of first-degree murder is traditionally and currently accepted in most states was dispositive of the due process issue. He concluded as follows:

> Submitting killing in the course of a robbery and premeditated killing to the jury under a single charge is not some novel composite that can be subjected to the indignity of fundamental fairness review. It was the norm when this country was founded, * * * and remains the norm today. Unless we are here to invent a Constitution rather than enforce one, it is impossible that a practice as old as the common law and still in existence in the vast majority of States does not provide that process which is due.

Justice White, joined by Justices Marshall, Blackmun, and Stevens, dissented. He noted that felony murder and premeditated murder contain separate elements of conduct and state of mind and argued that these elements could not "be mixed and matched at will." He asserted that "it is particularly fanciful to equate an intent to do no more than rob with a premeditated intent to murder."

The prosecution in *Schad* was required to prove all elements beyond a reasonable doubt, and the defendant was not required to prove anything. So how does the *Schad* issue relate to the *Mullaney-Patterson-Apprendi* line of cases, which deals with the state's power to define the elements of a crime? The answer lies in the possibility that by combining alternative theories of guilt, a prosecutor may manage to convict a defendant without proving beyond a reasonable doubt all of the elements of any one theory to a constitutionally adequate number of jurors. At the logical limit of the analysis, a prosecutor could argue twelve alternatives to a twelve-person jury and persuade only one juror beyond a reasonable doubt of each theory. Were the theories set forth in separate counts, a defendant would never be convicted. In fact, the vote would be 11–1 for acquittal on each count. But, by combining the theories, all twelve jurors would agree that the defendant is "guilty" of a "crime." All members of the Court in *Schad* agreed that at some point this tactic would be impermissible under the Due Process Clause. They disagreed, however, on where that point lies. Four Justices gave traditional and current acceptance significant weight, and one found traditional and current acceptance dispositive.

For a cogent criticism of *Schad,* see Howe, Jury Fact-Finding in Criminal Cases: Constitutional Limits on Factual Disagreements Among Convicting Jurors, 58 Missouri L.Rev.1 (1993).

Distinction Between Means and Elements: Richardson v. United States

Under *Schad*, the means by which a defendant commits a crime need not be proven beyond a reasonable doubt, if there are alternative means to commit the crime. Under *Winship,* the elements of the crime must be proven beyond a reasonable doubt. The distinction between means and elements is sometimes unclear. The Supreme Court encountered a problem of delineation between means and elements in Richardson v. United States, 526 U.S. 813 (1999). Richardson was convicted under the Continuing Criminal Enterprise statute. The statute defines "continuing criminal enterprise" (CCE) as involving a "violat[ion]" of the drug statutes where "such violation is a part of a continuing series of violations." The definitional problem arising under the statute was set forth in the majority opinion by Justice Breyer:

> The question before us arises out of the trial court's instruction about the statute's "series of violations" requirement. The judge rejected Richardson's proposal to instruct the jury that it must "unanimously agree on which three acts constituted [the] series of violations." Instead, the judge instructed the jurors that they "must unanimously agree that the defendant committed at least three federal narcotics offenses," while adding, "[y]ou do not . . . have to agree as to the particular three or more federal narcotics offenses committed by the defendant." * * *
>
> The question before us arises because a federal jury need not always decide unanimously which of several possible sets of underlying brute facts make up a particular element, say, which of several possible means the defendant used to commit an element of the crime. Schad v. Arizona. Where, for example, an element of robbery is force or the threat of force, some jurors might conclude that the defendant used a knife to create the threat; others might conclude he used a gun. But that disagreement—a disagreement about means—would not matter as long as all 12 jurors unanimously concluded that the Government had proved the necessary related element, namely that the defendant had threatened force.
>
> In this case, we must decide whether the statute's phrase "series of violations" refers to one element, namely a "series," in respect to which the "violations" constitute the underlying brute facts or means, or whether those words create several elements, namely the several "violations," in respect to each of which the jury must agree

> unanimously and separately. * * * If the statute creates a single element, a "series," in respect to which individual violations are but the means, then the jury need only agree that the defendant committed at least three of all the underlying crimes the Government has tried to prove. The jury need not agree about which three. On the other hand, if the statute makes each "violation" a separate element, then the jury must agree unanimously about which three crimes the defendant committed.

The majority held that the underlying illegal activity constituted an element of the crime, and not the means. Thus, the jury in order to convict the defendant would have to agree unanimously that the defendant committed at least three underlying drug transactions—*and* they would have to agree on the specific transactions in order for them to count toward the "series." Justice Breyer explained the majority's decision in the following passage:

> The CCE statute's breadth * * * argues against treating each individual violation as a means, for that breadth aggravates the dangers of unfairness that doing so would risk. Cf. Schad v. Arizona. The statute's word "violations" covers many different kinds of behavior of varying degrees of seriousness. * * * At the same time, the Government in a CCE case may well seek to prove that a defendant, charged as a drug kingpin, has been involved in numerous underlying violations. The first of these considerations increases the likelihood that treating violations simply as alternative means, by permitting a jury to avoid discussion of the specific factual details of each violation, will cover-up wide disagreement among the jurors about just what the defendant did, or did not, do. The second consideration significantly aggravates the risk (present at least to a small degree whenever multiple means are at issue) that jurors, unless required to focus upon specific factual detail, will fail to do so, simply concluding from testimony, say, of bad reputation, that where there is smoke there must be fire.
>
> Finally, this Court has indicated that the Constitution itself limits a State's power to define crimes in ways that would permit juries to convict while disagreeing about means, at least where that definition risks serious unfairness and lacks support in history or tradition. Schad v. Arizona, 501 U.S., at 632–633 (plurality opinion); id., at 651 (SCALIA, J., concurring) ("We would not permit . . . an indictment charging that the defendant assaulted either X on Tuesday or Y on Wednesday . . ."). We have no reason to believe that Congress intended to come close to, or to test, those constitutional limits when it wrote this statute.

Justice Kennedy, joined by Justices O'Connor and Ginsburg, dissented in *Richardson*. He argued that "[t]he CCE statute does not in any way implicate the suggestion in *Schad* that an irrational single crime consisting of, for instance, either robbery or failure to file a tax return would offend due process."

E. PRESUMPTIONS

An alternative to placing a burden of persuasion on a defendant in order to reduce the burden on the government of presenting evidence is to utilize a presumption or a judicially recognized inference.[12] Few aspects of procedural law can be more confusing than presumptions, as the word "presumption" is used to mean several different things in different contexts.

The following case illustrates how the Supreme Court has approached many criminal presumptions, and indicates the importance of jury instructions in assessing the permissibility of presumptions. The extensive footnotes provided by the Court are particularly helpful.

COUNTY COURT V. ALLEN

Supreme Court of the United States, 1979.
442 U.S. 140.

JUSTICE STEVENS delivered the opinion of the Court.

A New York statute provides that, with certain exceptions, the presence of a firearm in an automobile is presumptive evidence of its illegal possession by all persons then occupying the vehicle. The United States Court of Appeals for the Second Circuit held that respondents may challenge the constitutionality of this statute in a federal habeas corpus proceeding and that the statute is "unconstitutional on its face." * * *

Four persons, three adult males (respondents) and a 16-year-old girl (Jane Doe, who is not a respondent here), were jointly tried on charges that they possessed two loaded handguns, a loaded machinegun, and over a pound of heroin found in a Chevrolet in which they were riding when it was stopped for speeding * * *. The two large-caliber handguns, which together with their ammunition weighed approximately six pounds, were seen through the window of the car by the investigating police officer. They were positioned crosswise in an open handbag on either the front floor or the front seat of the car on the passenger side where Jane Doe was sitting. Jane Doe admitted that the handbag was hers. The machinegun and the heroin were discovered in the trunk after the police pried it open. The car had been borrowed from the driver's brother earlier that day; the key to the trunk

---

[12] In this section, the word "presumption" is used to cover situations in which the court instructs a jury that proof of one fact entitles the jury to infer, assume, or presume the existence of another fact.

could not be found in the car or on the person of any of its occupants, although there was testimony that two of the occupants had placed something in the trunk before embarking in the borrowed car. The jury convicted all four of possession of the handguns and acquitted them of possession of the contents of the trunk.

Counsel for all four defendants objected to the introduction into evidence of the two handguns, the machinegun, and the drugs, arguing that the State had not adequately demonstrated a connection between their clients and the contraband. The trial court overruled the objection, relying on the presumption of possession created by the New York statute. Because that presumption does not apply if a weapon is found "upon the person" of one of the occupants of the car, the three male defendants also moved to dismiss the charges relating to the handguns on the ground that the guns were found on the person of Jane Doe. * * *

At the close of the trial, the judge instructed the jurors that they were entitled to infer possession from the defendants' presence in the car. He did not make any reference to the "on the person" exception in his explanation of the statutory presumption, nor did any of the defendants object to this omission or request alternative or additional instructions on the subject.

* * *

Inferences and presumptions are a staple of our adversary system of factfinding. It is often necessary for the trier of fact to determine the existence of an element of the crime—that is, an "ultimate" or "elemental" fact—from the existence of one or more "evidentiary" or "basic" facts. The value of these evidentiary devices, and their validity under the Due Process Clause, vary from case to case, however, depending on the strength of the connection between the particular basic and elemental facts involved and on the degree to which the device curtails the factfinder's freedom to assess the evidence independently. Nonetheless, in criminal cases, the ultimate test of any device's constitutional validity in a given case remains constant; the device must not undermine the factfinder's responsibility at trial, based on evidence adduced by the State, to find the ultimate facts beyond a reasonable doubt.

The most common evidentiary device is the entirely permissive inference or presumption, which allows—but does not require—the trier of fact to infer the elemental fact from proof by the prosecutor of the basic one and that places no burden of any kind on the defendant. In that situation the basic fact may constitute prima facie evidence of the elemental fact. When reviewing this type of device, the Court has required the party challenging it to demonstrate its invalidity as applied to him. Because this permissive presumption leaves the trier of fact free to credit or reject the inference and does not shift the burden of proof, it affects the application of the "beyond a reasonable doubt" standard only if, under the facts of the case, there is no rational way the trier could make the connection permitted by the inference. For only in that situation is there any risk that an explanation of the permissible inference to a jury, or its use by a jury, has caused the presumptively rational factfinder to make an erroneous factual determination.

A mandatory presumption is a far more troublesome evidentiary device. For it may affect not only the strength of the "no reasonable doubt" burden but also the placement of that burden; it tells the trier that he or they must find the elemental fact upon proof of the basic fact, at least unless the defendant has come forward with some evidence to rebut the presumed connection between the two facts.[a] In this situation, the Court has generally examined the presumption on its face to determine the extent to which the basic and elemental facts coincide. To the extent that the trier of fact is forced to abide by the presumption, and may not reject it based on an independent evaluation of the particular facts presented by the State, the analysis of the presumption's constitutional validity is logically

---

[a] This class of more or less mandatory presumptions can be subdivided into two parts; presumptions that merely shift the burden of production to the defendant, following the satisfaction of which the ultimate burden of persuasion returns to the prosecution; and presumptions that entirely shift the burden of proof to the defendant. The mandatory presumptions examined by our cases have almost uniformly fit into the former subclass, in that they never totally removed the ultimate burden of proof beyond a reasonable doubt from the prosecution. E.g., Tot v. United States, 319 U.S. 463 (1943) [requiring a "rational connection between the fact proved and the ultimate fact presumed"].

To the extent that a presumption imposes an extremely low burden of production—e.g., being satisfied by "any" evidence—it may well be that its impact is no greater than that of a permissive inference, and it may be proper to analyze it as such.

In deciding what type of inference or presumption is involved in a case, the jury instructions will generally be controlling, although their interpretation may require recourse to the statute involved and the cases decided under it. * * *

The importance of focusing attention on the precise presentation of the presumption to the jury and the scope of that presumption is illustrated by a comparison of United States v. Gainey, 380 U.S. 63 (1965), with United States v. Romano, 382 U.S. 136 (1965). Both cases involved statutory presumptions based on proof that the defendant was present at the site of an illegal still. In *Gainey* the Court sustained a conviction "for carrying on" the business of the distillery in violation of 26 U.S.C. § 5601(a)(4), whereas in *Romano*, the Court set aside a conviction for being in "possession, or custody, or * * * control" of such a distillery in violation of § 5601(a)(1). The difference in outcome was attributable to two important differences between the cases. Because the statute involved in *Gainey* was a sweeping prohibition of almost any activity associated with the still, whereas the *Romano* statute involved only one narrow aspect of the total undertaking, there was a much higher probability that mere presence could support an inference of guilt in the former case than in the latter.

Of perhaps greater importance, however, was the difference between the trial judge's instructions to the jury in the two cases. In *Gainey*, the judge had explained that the presumption was permissive; it did not require the jury to convict the defendant even if it was convinced that he was present at the site. * * * In *Romano*, the trial judge told the jury that the defendant's presence at the still "shall be deemed sufficient evidence to authorize conviction." Although there was other evidence of guilt, that instruction authorized conviction even if the jury disbelieved all of the testimony except the proof of presence at the site. This Court's holding that the statutory presumption could not support the *Romano* conviction was thus dependent, in part, on the specific instructions given by the trial judge. Under those instructions it was necessary to decide whether, regardless of the specific circumstances of the particular case, the statutory presumption adequately supported the guilty verdict.

divorced from those facts and based on the presumption's accuracy in the run of cases.[b] It is for this reason that the Court has held it irrelevant in analyzing a mandatory presumption, but not in analyzing a purely permissive one, that there is ample evidence in the record other than the presumption to support a conviction.

* * *

The trial judge's instructions [in this case] make it clear that the presumption * * * gave rise to a permissive inference available only in certain circumstances, rather than a mandatory conclusion of possession, and that it could be ignored by the jury even if there was no affirmative proof offered by defendants in rebuttal. The judge explained that possession could be actual or constructive, but that constructive possession could not exist without the intent and ability to exercise control or dominion over the weapons. He also carefully instructed the jury that there is a mandatory presumption of innocence in favor of the defendants that controls unless it, as the exclusive trier of fact, is satisfied beyond a reasonable doubt that the defendants possessed the handguns in the manner described by the judge. In short, the instructions plainly directed the jury to consider all the circumstances tending to support or contradict the inference that all four occupants of the car had possession of the two loaded handguns and to decide the matter for itself without regard to how much evidence the defendants introduced.

* * *

As applied to the facts of this case, the presumption of possession is entirely rational. * * * [R]espondents were not hitch-hikers or other casual passengers, and the guns were neither a few inches in length nor out of respondents' sight. The argument against possession by any of the respondents was predicated solely on the fact that the guns were in Jane

---

[b] * * * [T]his point is illustrated by Leary v. United States, 395 U.S. 6 (1969). In that case, Dr. Timothy Leary, a professor at Harvard University, was stopped by customs inspectors in Laredo, Tex., as he was returning from the Mexican side of the international border. Marihuana seeds and a silver snuffbox filled with semirefined marihuana and three partially smoked marihuana cigarettes were discovered in his car. He was convicted of having knowingly transported marihuana which he knew had been illegally imported into this country in violation of 21 U.S.C. § 176a (1964 ed.) That statute included a mandatory presumption: "possession shall be deemed sufficient evidence to authorize conviction [for importation] unless the defendant explains his possession to the satisfaction of the jury." Leary admitted possession of the marihuana and claimed that he had carried it from New York to Mexico and then back.

* * *

Despite the fact that the defendant was well educated and had recently traveled to a country that is a major exporter of marihuana to this country, the Court found the presumption of knowledge of importation from possession irrational. It did so, not because Dr. Leary was unlikely to know the source of the marihuana, but instead because "a majority of possessors" were unlikely to have such knowledge. Because the jury had been instructed to rely on the presumption even if it did not believe the Government's direct evidence of knowledge of importation (unless, of course, the defendant met his burden of "satisfying" the jury to the contrary), the Court reversed the conviction.

Doe's pocketbook. But several circumstances * * * made it highly improbable that she was the sole custodian of those weapons.

Even if it was reasonable to conclude that she had placed the guns in her purse before the car was stopped by police, the facts strongly suggest that Jane Doe was not the only person able to exercise dominion over them. The two guns were too large to be concealed in her handbag. The bag was consequently open, and part of one of the guns was in plain view, within easy access of the driver of the car and even, perhaps, of the other two respondents who were riding in the rear seat.

Moreover, it is highly improbable that the loaded guns belonged to Jane Doe or that she was solely responsible for their being in her purse. As a 16-year-old girl in the company of three adult men she was the least likely of the four to be carrying one, let alone two, heavy handguns. It is far more probable that she relied on the pocketknife found in her brassiere for any necessary self-protection. Under these circumstances, it was not unreasonable for her counsel to argue and for the jury to infer that when the car was halted for speeding, the other passengers in the car anticipated the risk of a search and attempted to conceal their weapons in a pocketbook in the front seat. The inference is surely more likely than the notion that these weapons were the sole property of the 16-year-old girl.

Under these circumstances, the jury would have been entirely reasonable in rejecting the suggestion * * * that the handguns were in the sole possession of Jane Doe. Assuming that the jury did reject it, the case is tantamount to one in which the guns were lying on the floor or the seat of the car in plain view of the three other occupants of the automobile. In such a case, it is surely rational to infer that each of the respondents was fully aware of the presence of the guns and had both the ability and the intent to exercise dominion and control over the weapons.

JUSTICE POWELL, with whom JUSTICE BRENNAN, JUSTICE STEWART, and JUSTICE MARSHALL join, dissenting.

* * *

Undeniably, the presumption charged in this case encouraged the jury to draw a particular factual inference regardless of any other evidence presented: to infer that respondents possessed the weapons found in the automobile "upon proof of the presence of the machine gun and the hand weapon" and proof that respondents "occupied the automobile at the time such instruments were found." I believe that the presumption thus charged was unconstitutional because it did not fairly reflect what common sense and experience tell us about passengers in automobiles and the possession of handguns. People present in automobiles where there are weapons simply are not "more likely than not" the possessors of those weapons.

* * *

COMMENT ON PRESUMPTION CASES

The presumption cases establish three rules:

The first rule is that where the prosecution bears the burden of persuasion, a trial judge may not encourage the jury to make logical jumps not supported by the evidence. Otherwise the persuasion burden would be compromised.

The second rule, which would apply only where a persuasion burden could be shifted to a defendant, is that any "instruction must be a fair statement about evidence actually produced in the case." Saltzburg, Burdens of Persuasion in Criminal Cases: Harmonizing the Views of the Justices, 20 Am.Cr.L.Rev. 393 (1983).

The third rule is that any presumption that shifts to the defendant the burden of proof on an element of the crime is unconstitutional under *Winship*. That rule is applied in the cases immediately below.

Shifting the Burden on Intent: Sandstrom v. Montana and Francis v. Franklin

After deciding *Allen*, the Court held in Sandstrom v. Montana, 442 U.S. 510 (1979), that an instruction to the jury in a homicide case that "the law presumes that a person intends the ordinary consequences of his voluntary acts" violated the Constitution, because it may have removed from the prosecution some of its burden to prove beyond a reasonable doubt all elements of the crime charged. The Court observed that unlike in *Allen*, a reasonable jury could have interpreted the instruction as a legal command that was not rebuttable. Alternatively, the jury may have interpreted the instruction as a direction to find intent once voluntary action was proven unless the defendant proved the lack of intent. Finally, the jury could have read the instruction as authorizing it to draw a permissive inference. Because the first two interpretations would have shifted a constitutionally required burden from the prosecutor, and since the Court could not be sure how the jury treated the instruction, the Court found that reversal of the conviction was required.

Justice Brennan, who authored *Sandstrom*, wrote for five members of the Court in Francis v. Franklin, 471 U.S. 307 (1985), as it held invalid the following jury instruction:

> A crime is a violation of a statute of this State in which there shall be a union of joint operation of act or omission to act, and intention or criminal negligence. A person shall not be found guilty of any crime committed by misfortune or accident where it satisfactorily appears there was no criminal scheme or undertaking or intention or criminal

> negligence. *The acts of a person of sound mind and discretion are presumed to be the product of the person's will, but the presumption may be rebutted. A person of sound mind and discretion is presumed to intend the natural and probable consequences of his acts but the presumption may be rebutted.* A person will not be presumed to act with criminal intention but the trier of facts, that is, the jury, may find criminal intention upon a consideration of the words, conduct, demeanor, motive and all other circumstances connected with the act for which the accused is prosecuted. [Emphasis added.]

The defendant escaped from custody and attempted to obtain a car to speed his flight. He pounded on the door of a house until a 72-year-old resident opened the door. When the defendant pointed a gun and demanded the keys to the resident's car, the resident slammed the door and the gun fired and killed him. The defendant claimed that he did not intend to kill and that the firing was accidental. The jury found him guilty.

Justice Brennan began his analysis by restating the principles the Court had laid down for determining the constitutionality of presumptions:

> The court must determine whether the challenged portion of the instruction creates a mandatory presumption or merely a permissive inference. A mandatory presumption instructs the jury that it must infer the presumed fact if the State proves certain predicate facts. A permissive inference suggests to the jury a possible conclusion to be drawn if the State proves predicate facts, but does not require the jury to draw the conclusion.

Justice Brennan concluded that the challenged instruction created a mandatory presumption, because it was "cast in the language of command." The fact that the judge said the presumption "may be rebutted" did not affect the mandatory nature of the presumption itself. According to Justice Brennan, a mandatory rebuttable presumption can be just as constitutionally infirm as a mandatory irrebuttable presumption.

> A mandatory rebuttable presumption does not remove the presumed element from the case if the State proves the predicate facts, but it nonetheless relieves the State of the affirmative burden of persuasion on the presumed element by instructing the jury that it must find the presumed element unless the defendant persuades the jury not to make such a finding. A mandatory rebuttable presumption is perhaps less onerous from the defendant's perspective, but it is no less unconstitutional.

Justice Brennan reasoned that a reasonable jury could have concluded that it had to find an intent to kill unless the defendant persuaded it that intent should not be inferred.

Justice Powell dissented and argued that the combination of the trial court's instructions on reasonable doubt, the presumption of innocence, and interpretation of circumstantial evidence, and the portion of the challenged instructions stating that "criminal intention" cannot be presumed sufficiently removed any danger that a reasonable jury would have imposed a persuasion burden on the defendant. Justice Rehnquist also dissented, joined by the Chief Justice and Justice O'Connor. He suggested that instead of focusing on what a reasonable jury *might* have interpreted the instructions to mean, the Court should find it *likely* that a juror so understood the charge before finding constitutional error.[13]

Observations About Sandstrom and Francis

Sandstrom and *Francis* are cases in which the trial court impermissibly shifted a burden of persuasion through a jury instruction imposing a mandatory presumption. Remember, however, that such an impermissible shift can occur by way of statute as well. See Government of Virgin Islands v. Parrilla, 7 F.3d 1097 (3d Cir.1993) (statute criminalizing maiming, which provides that the infliction of injury is presumptive evidence of intent, constitutes an impermissible mandatory presumption, invalid on its face).

After *Sandstrom, Francis,* and *Allen,* why would a trial court choose to instruct the jury with a presumption, unless the defendant stipulated to it? If the presumption is mandatory, it runs the risk of violating *Winship* and *Mullaney.* If the instruction is permissive, it must be in accord with reason and common sense and as such it would seem to be superfluous to a jury of reasonable people.

The cases do leave a trial judge free, however, to instruct the jury that a given inference is permissible. Moreover, the prosecutor is entitled to mention to the jury during argument that the judge has informed the jury of a permissible inference, thereby seeking to take advantage of the judicial imprimatur placed upon the inference. Because a permissible inference instruction could have significant impact on a jury, most trial judges wisely avoid the use of the word "presumption" in criminal cases other than to refer to the presumption of innocence; the use of the word "presumption" is always risky, while a permissive instruction may have almost as much practical impact with almost no risk.

---

[13] See also United States v. Johnson, 71 F.3d 139 (4th Cir.1995) (defendant charged with armed robbery of a credit union; trial judge instructs jury that the institution was a credit union within the meaning of the statute; reversal required because the instruction was a mandatory, irrebuttable presumption, and the status of the victim institution as a credit union was an element of the crime).

IV. TRIAL BY JURY

A. THE FUNDAMENTAL RIGHT

Article III, Section 2, clause 3 of the Constitution provides that "[t]he trial of all Crimes, except in Cases of Impeachment, shall be by Jury; and such Trial shall be held in the State where the said Crimes shall have been committed; but when not committed within any State, the Trial shall be at such Place or Places as the Congress may by Law have directed." The Sixth Amendment is, in part, redundant; it provides that "[i]n all criminal prosecutions, the accused shall enjoy the right to a speedy and public trial, by an impartial jury of the State and district wherein the crime shall have been committed, which district shall have been previously ascertained by law * * *." Certainly, a right found in two places in the Constitution is likely to be regarded as fundamental. And that is just how the Supreme Court viewed it when it incorporated the Sixth Amendment through the Fourteenth and made it binding on the states.

Note that we have already discussed the right to a jury trial in one context—its interrelationship with the right to require the state to prove every element of the crime beyond a reasonable doubt. Thus, in *Apprendi, supra*, the Court held that the state violated both *Winship* and the constitutional right to a jury trial when it treated an element of a crime as a sentencing factor. The Court in *Apprendi* and its progeny emphasizes that the jury is a bulwark against government overreaching.

The importance of jury determination of all elements of the crime was set out forcefully in the following case.

DUNCAN V. LOUISIANA

Supreme Court of the United States, 1968.
391 U.S. 145.

JUSTICE WHITE delivered the opinion of the Court.

Appellant, Gary Duncan, was convicted of simple battery in the Twenty-fifth Judicial District Court of Louisiana. Under Louisiana law simple battery is a misdemeanor, punishable by a maximum of two years' imprisonment and a $300 fine. Appellant sought trial by jury, but because the Louisiana Constitution grants jury trials only in cases in which capital punishment or imprisonment at hard labor may be imposed, the trial judge denied the request. Appellant was convicted and sentenced to serve 60 days in the parish prison and pay a fine of $150. * * *

Appellant was 19 years of age when tried. While driving on Highway 23 in Plaquemines Parish on October 18, 1966, he saw two younger cousins engaged in a conversation by the side of the road with four white boys. Knowing his cousins, Negroes who had recently transferred to a formerly all-white high school, had reported the occurrence of racial incidents at the school, Duncan stopped the car, got out, and approached the six boys. At trial the white boys and a white onlooker testified, as did appellant and his cousins. The testimony was in dispute on many points, but the witnesses agreed that appellant and the white boys spoke to each other, that appellant encouraged his cousins to break off the encounter and enter his car, and that appellant was about to enter the car himself for the purpose of driving away with his cousins. The whites testified that just before getting in the car appellant slapped Herman Landry, one of the white boys, on the elbow. The Negroes testified that appellant had not slapped Landry, but had merely touched him. The trial judge concluded that the State had proved beyond a reasonable doubt that Duncan had committed simple battery, and found him guilty.

[The Court discusses its prior incorporation cases.]

* * * The claim before us is that the right to trial by jury guaranteed by the Sixth Amendment meets these tests. The position of Louisiana, on the other hand, is that the Constitution imposes upon the State no duty to give a jury trial in any criminal case, regardless of the seriousness of the crime or the size of the punishment which may be imposed. Because we believe that trial by jury in criminal cases is fundamental to the American scheme of justice, we hold that the Fourteenth Amendment guarantees a right of jury trial in all criminal cases which—were they to be tried in a federal court—would come within the Sixth Amendment's guarantee.

* * *

The guarantees of jury trial in the Federal and State Constitutions reflect a profound judgment about the way in which law should be enforced and justice administered. A right to a jury trial is granted to criminal defendants in order to prevent oppression by the Government. Those who wrote our constitutions knew from history and experience that it was necessary to protect against unfounded criminal charges brought to eliminate enemies and against judges too responsive to the voice of higher authority. * * * Providing an accused with the right to be tried by a jury of his peers gave him an inestimable safeguard against the corrupt or overzealous prosecutor and against the compliant, biased, or eccentric judge. If the defendant preferred the common-sense judgment of a jury to the more tutored but perhaps less sympathetic reaction of the single judge, he was to have it. Beyond this, the jury trial provisions in the Federal and State Constitutions reflect a fundamental decision about the exercise of official power—a reluctance to entrust plenary powers over the life and liberty of the citizen to one judge or to a group of judges. Fear of unchecked power, so typical of our State and Federal Governments in other respects, found expression in the criminal law in this insistence upon community participation in the determination of guilt or innocence. The deep commitment of the Nation to the right of jury trial in serious criminal cases as a defense against arbitrary law enforcement qualifies for protection under the Due Process Clause of the Fourteenth Amendment, and must therefore be respected by the States.

Of course jury trial has its weaknesses and the potential for misuse. We are aware of the long debate, especially in this century, among those who write about the administration of justice, as to the wisdom of permitting untrained laymen to determine the facts in civil and criminal proceedings. * * *

The State of Louisiana urges that holding that the Fourteenth Amendment assures a right to jury trial will cast doubt on the integrity of every trial conducted without a jury. Plainly, this is not the import of our holding. Our conclusion is that in the American States, as in the federal judicial system, a general grant of jury trial for serious offenses is a fundamental right, essential for preventing miscarriages of justice and for assuring that fair trials are provided for all defendants. We would not assert, however, that every criminal trial—or any particular trial—held before a judge alone is unfair or that a defendant may never be as fairly treated by a judge as he would be by a jury. Thus we hold no constitutional doubts about the practices common in both federal and state courts, of accepting waivers of jury trial and prosecuting petty crimes without extending a right to jury trial.

* * *

Louisiana's final contention is that even if it must grant jury trials in serious criminal cases, the conviction before us is valid and constitutional because here the petitioner was tried for simple battery and was sentenced to only 60 days in the parish prison. We are not persuaded. It is doubtless true that there is a category of petty crimes or offenses which is not subject to the Sixth Amendment jury trial provision and should not be subject to the Fourteenth Amendment jury trial requirement here applied to the States. Crimes carrying possible penalties up to six months do not require a jury trial if they otherwise qualify as petty offenses, Cheff v. Schnackenberg, 384 U.S. 373 (1966). But the penalty authorized for a particular crime is of major relevance in determining whether it is serious or not and may in itself, if severe enough, subject the trial to the mandates of the Sixth Amendment. * * * In the case before us the Legislature of Louisiana has made simple battery a criminal offense punishable by imprisonment for up to two years and a fine. The question, then, is whether a crime carrying such a penalty is an offense which Louisiana may insist on trying without a jury.

We think not. * * * Of course the boundaries of the petty offense category have always been ill-defined, if not ambulatory. * * * [I]t is necessary to draw a line in the spectrum of crime, separating petty from serious infractions. This process, although essential, cannot be wholly satisfactory, for it requires attaching different consequences to events which, when they lie near the line, actually differ very little.

* * * We need not, however, settle in this case the exact location of the line between petty offenses and serious crimes. It is sufficient for our purposes to hold that a crime punishable by two years in prison is, based on past and contemporary standards in this country, a serious crime and not a petty offense. Consequently, appellant was entitled to a jury trial and it was error to deny it.

* * *

[The concurring opinions of Justice Fortas, and Justice Black (who was joined by Justice Douglas), and the dissenting opinion by Justice Harlan, joined by Justice Stewart, are all omitted.]

NOTE ON THE DEFINITION OF PETTY OFFENSES

The Court clarified its definition of a "petty" offense—to which the right to jury trial does not extend—in Baldwin v. New York, 399 U.S. 66 (1970). In *Baldwin* the Court defined "petty" by considering the severity of the maximum penalty authorized by the legislature, and concluded that "no offense can be deemed petty for purposes of the right to trial by jury where imprisonment for more than six months is authorized."

Recall Scott v. Illinois, Chapter 5, supra, where the Court held that Scott was not entitled to appointed counsel because he was not imprisoned after his conviction. The offense for which Scott was convicted *authorized* imprisonment for up to a year. Apparently Scott had the right to a jury trial under *Baldwin*. Does it make sense to have a right to jury trial but no right to appointed counsel?

Joinder of Multiple Petty Offenses: Lewis v. United States

In Lewis v. United States, 518 U.S. 322 (1996), the defendant was charged with two misdemeanor counts of obstructing the mails. Each count carried a maximum prison term of six months, and thus each was a "petty offense" within the meaning of the Supreme Court's jury trial jurisprudence. However, the defendant could have been subject to consecutive sentences if convicted of both counts. The lower court denied the defendant's motion for a jury trial and also stated for the record that it would not impose a sentence of more than six months, even if the defendant were convicted of both counts.

Lewis appealed the denial of jury trial, arguing that petty offenses, when they are joined in a single trial, must be aggregated to determine the seriousness of the charges for purposes of the jury trial right. But the

Supreme Court rejected this aggregation argument in an opinion by Justice O'Connor. Justice O'Connor analyzed the problem as follows:

> The Sixth Amendment reserves the jury-trial right to defendants accused of serious crimes. * * * [W]e determine whether an offense is serious by looking to the judgment of the legislature, primarily as expressed in the maximum authorized term of imprisonment. Here, by setting the maximum authorized prison term at six months, the legislature categorized the offense of obstructing the mail as petty. The fact that the petitioner was charged with two counts of a petty offense does not revise the legislative judgment as to the gravity of that particular offense, nor does it transform the petty offense into a serious one, to which the jury-trial right would apply.
>
> * * *
>
> * * * As petitioner acknowledges, even if he were to prevail, the Government could properly circumvent the jury-trial right by charging the counts in separate informations and trying them separately.

Justice Kennedy, joined by Justice Breyer, concurred only in the judgment. He agreed that Lewis had no right to jury trial, but only because the lower court had stated that it would not sentence Lewis to more than six months even if he were convicted of both counts. In the absence of this self-imposed limitation, Justice Kennedy would have found a violation of the jury trial right. Justice Kennedy attacked the majority's analysis in the following passage:

> Providing a defendant with the right to be tried by a jury gives "him an inestimable safeguard against the corrupt or overzealous prosecutor and against the compliant, biased, or eccentric judge." These considerations all are present when a judge in a single case sends a defendant to prison for years, whether the sentence is the result of one serious offense or several petty offenses.
>
> On the Court's view of the case, however, there is no limit to the length of the sentence a judge can impose on a defendant without entitling him to a jury, so long as the prosecutor carves up the charges into segments punishable by no more than six months apiece. Prosecutors have broad discretion in framing charges, for criminal conduct often does not arrange itself in neat categories. In many cases, a prosecutor can choose to charge a defendant with multiple petty offenses rather than a single serious offense, and so prevent him under today's holding from obtaining a trial by jury while still obtaining the same punishment.[14]

---

[14] Justice Stevens wrote a short dissenting opinion in *Lewis*.

Penalties Other than Incarceration

Justice Marshall wrote for a unanimous Court in Blanton v. City of North Las Vegas, 489 U.S. 538 (1989), rejecting the jury trial claim of a defendant charged under Nevada law with driving under the influence (DUI). Under the Nevada law, a convicted defendant is subject to a minimum term of two days' imprisonment and a maximum term of six months' imprisonment. Alternatively, a trial court may order the defendant to perform 48 hours of community work while wearing distinctive garb identifying him as a DUI offender. A convicted defendant may also be fined from $200 to $1,000, he automatically loses his license for 90 days, and he must attend an alcohol abuse education class at his own expense. Blanton argued that all of these non-incarceration penalties made the crime sufficiently serious to require a jury trial.

Justice Marshall relied upon prior cases for the proposition that the primary emphasis in assessing the right to jury trial is on the maximum authorized term of incarceration. Although he recognized that a legislature's view of the seriousness of an offense might also be reflected in other penalties, he reasoned that incarceration is intrinsically different from other penalties and is the most powerful indication of whether an offense is "serious." Justice Marshall stated that penalties other than imprisonment were relevant to the jury trial right only if the defendant can demonstrate that "any additional statutory penalties, viewed in conjunction with the maximum authorized period of incarceration, are so severe that they clearly reflect a legislative determination that the offense in question is a 'serious' one." The Nevada penalties other than incarceration were not onerous enough to overcome the presumption that the offense was "petty."

The Court relied on its decision in *Blanton* in deciding United States v. Nachtigal, 507 U.S. 1 (1993) (per curiam). Nachtigal was charged with operating a motor vehicle in a national park while under the influence of alcohol. The maximum punishment was six months imprisonment and a $5,000 fine, and the sentencing court had the authority to impose a five year probationary sentence as an alternative to incarceration. A unanimous Supreme Court held that *Blanton* was controlling. The Court noted that "it is a rare case where a legislature packs an offense it deems serious with onerous penalties that nonetheless do not puncture the 6-month incarceration line." The Court reasoned that Congress limited penalties to six months and thereby made a legislative judgment as to the non-seriousness of such offenses, and that the possibility of a probationary sentence or a fine of $5,000 were not sufficiently severe to overcome the *Blanton* presumption.

B. WHAT THE JURY DECIDES

Are there any questions of fact that should or can be decided by the court rather than the jury? This question underlies much of the law concerning the use of presumptions, supra. Another important question, also previously discussed in this Chapter, under the *Apprendi* line of cases, is whether factual issues can be allocated to the judge rather than the jury as part of a sentencing determination.

We have seen that all elements of a crime must be left for the jury and must be proved beyond a reasonable doubt. When courts occasionally forget this principle, they are reminded by the Supreme Court. Thus, in United States v. Gaudin, 515 U.S. 506 (1995), the defendant was charged with violating 18 U.S.C. § 1001, which prohibits the making of false "material" statements to government agencies. The trial judge instructed the jury that the defendant's statements were material within the meaning of the statute. The Court, in a unanimous opinion by Justice Scalia, held that the question of materiality was for the jury. Therefore, the defendant's rights to jury trial and due process were violated when the judge rather than the jury decided whether the statements were material. Justice Scalia declared:

> The Constitution gives a criminal defendant the right to demand that a jury find him guilty of all the elements of the crime with which he is charged; one of the elements in the present case is materiality; respondent therefore had a right to have the jury decide materiality.

Justice Scalia rejected the government's argument that the Sixth Amendment permits judges to decide whether elements of the crime have been proved when those elements present mixed questions of law and fact. He noted that juries typically decide mixed questions of law and fact—including the ultimate question of whether the defendant is guilty of the crime charged.

If, however, an issue is collateral to the resolution of an element of the crime, it is generally resolved by the judge rather than the jury. For example, it is the judge who decides whether evidence was illegally obtained and should be excluded. Also, the admissibility of evidence is generally a question for the judge, while the jury decides the weight to be given to evidence that is admitted. See Federal Rule of Evidence 104.

C. REQUISITE FEATURES OF THE JURY

1. Size

WILLIAMS V. FLORIDA

Supreme Court of the United States, 1970.
399 U.S. 78.

JUSTICE WHITE delivered the opinion of the court.

[Williams filed a pretrial motion for a 12-person jury instead of the six-person jury provided by Florida law in all but capital cases. The motion was denied and Williams was convicted of robbery by a jury of six persons and sentenced to life imprisonment. In Part I of the opinion, the Court rejected Williams's attack on a state rule requiring the defendant to give notice of an alibi defense. See Chapter 8 for a discussion of that point.]

* * * The question in this case then is whether the constitutional guarantee of a trial by "jury" necessarily requires trial by exactly 12 persons, rather than some lesser number—in this case six. We hold that the 12-man panel is not a necessary ingredient of "trial by jury," and that respondent's refusal to impanel more than the six members provided for by Florida law did not violate petitioner's Sixth Amendment rights as applied to the States through the Fourteenth.

We had occasion in Duncan v. Louisiana to review briefly the oft-told history of the development of trial by jury in criminal cases. That history revealed a long tradition attaching great importance to the concept of relying on a body of one's peers to determine guilt or innocence as a safeguard against arbitrary law enforcement. That same history, however, affords little insight into the considerations that gradually led the size of that body to be generally fixed at 12. Some have suggested that the number 12 was fixed upon simply because that was the number of the presentment jury from the hundred, from which the petit jury developed. Other, less circular but more fanciful reasons for the number 12 have been given, "but they were all brought forward after the number was fixed," and rest on little more than mystical or superstitious insights into the significance of "12." Lord Coke's explanation that the "*number of twelve* is much respected *in holy writ,* as 12 *apostles,* 12 *stones,* 12 *tribes, etc.,*" is typical. In short, while sometime in the 14th century the size of the jury at common law came to be fixed generally at 12, that particular feature of the jury system appears to have been a historical accident, unrelated to the great purposes which gave rise to the jury in the first place. The question before us is whether this accidental feature of the jury has been immutably codified into our Constitution.

* * *

While "the intent of the Framers" is often an elusive quarry, the relevant constitutional history casts considerable doubt on the easy assumption in our past decisions that if a given feature existed in a jury at common law in 1789, then it was necessarily preserved in the Constitution. Provisions for jury trial were first placed in the Constitution in Article III's provision that "[t]he Trial of all Crimes * * * shall be by Jury; and such Trial shall be held in the State where the said Crimes shall have been committed." The "very scanty history [of this provision] in the records of the Constitutional Convention" sheds little light either way on the intended correlation between Article III's "jury" and the features of the jury at common law. Indeed, pending and after the adoption of the Constitution, fears were expressed that Article III's provision failed to preserve the common-law right to be tried by a "jury of the vicinage." That concern, as well as the concern to preserve the right to jury in civil as well as criminal cases, furnished part of the impetus for introducing amendments to the Constitution that ultimately resulted in the jury trial provisions of the Sixth and Seventh Amendments. As introduced by James Madison in the House, the Amendment relating to jury trial in criminal cases would have provided that:

> "The trial of all crimes * * * shall be by an impartial jury of free-holders of the vicinage, with the requisite of unanimity for conviction, of the right of challenge, and other accustomed requisites * * *."

The Amendment passed the House in substantially this form, but after more than a week of debate in the Senate it returned to the House considerably altered. * * * [The Court discusses more history, including appointment of a Conference committee.] The version that finally emerged from the Committee was the version that ultimately became the Sixth Amendment, ensuring an accused:

> "the right to a speedy and public trial, by an impartial jury of the State and district wherein the crime shall have been committed, which district shall have been previously ascertained by law * * *."

Gone were the provisions spelling out such common-law features of the jury as "unanimity," or "the accustomed requisites." And the "vicinage" requirement itself had been replaced by wording that reflected a compromise between broad and narrow definitions of that term, and that left Congress the power to determine the actual size of the "vicinage" by its creation of judicial districts.

Three significant features may be observed in this sketch of the background of the Constitution's jury trial provisions. First, even though the vicinage requirement was as much a feature of the common-law jury as was the 12-man requirement, the mere reference to "trial by jury" in Article III was not interpreted to include that feature. * * * Second, provisions that would have explicitly tied the "jury" concept to the "accustomed requisites" of the time were eliminated. * * * Finally, contemporary legislative and constitutional provisions indicate that where Congress wanted to leave no doubt that it was incorporating existing common-law features of the jury system, it knew how to use express language to that effect. * * *

* * * Nothing in this history suggests, then, that we do violence to the letter of the Constitution by turning to other than purely historical considerations to determine which features of the jury system, as it existed at common law, were preserved in the Constitution. The relevant inquiry, as we see it, must be the function that the particular feature performs and its relation to the purposes of the jury trial. Measured by this standard, the 12-man requirement cannot be regarded as an indispensable component of the Sixth Amendment.

The purpose of the jury trial, as we noted in *Duncan,* is to prevent oppression by the Government. * * * Given this purpose, the essential feature of a jury obviously lies in the interposition between the accused and his accuser of the commonsense judgment of a group of laymen, and in the community participation and shared responsibility that results from that group's determination of guilt or innocence. The performance of this role is not a function of the particular number of the body that makes up the jury. To be sure, the number should probably be large enough to promote group deliberation, free from outside attempts at intimidation, and to provide a fair possibility for obtaining a representative cross-section of the community. But we find little reason to think that these goals are in any meaningful sense less likely to be achieved when the jury numbers six, than when it numbers 12—particularly if the requirement of unanimity is retained. * * *

It might be suggested that the 12-man jury gives a defendant a greater advantage since he has more "chances" of finding a juror who will insist on acquittal and thus prevent conviction. But the advantage might just as easily belong to the State which also needs only one juror out of twelve insisting on guilt to prevent acquittal. What few experiments have occurred—usually in the civil area—indicate that there is no discernible difference between the results reached by the two different-sized juries. In short, neither currently available evidence nor theory suggests that the 12-man jury is necessarily more advantageous to the defendant than a jury composed of fewer members.

Similarly, while in theory the number of viewpoints represented on a randomly selected jury ought to increase as the size of the jury increases, in practice the difference between the 12-man and the six-man jury in terms of the cross-section of the community represented seems likely to be negligible. Even the 12-man jury cannot insure representation of every distinct voice in the community, particularly given the use of the peremptory challenge. * * *

* * *

[Justice Harlan, concurring in the result, reiterated his concern expressed in *Duncan*, that incorporation of the Sixth Amendment dilutes federal guarantees in order to reconcile the logic of "incorporation" with the reality of federalism.]

[The Chief Justice concurred. Justice Black and Justice Douglas concurred in part and dissented in part. Justice Marshall dissented in part. Justice Stewart concurred in the result. Justice Blackmun took no part in the decision of the case.]

BALLEW V. GEORGIA

Supreme Court of the United States, 1978.
435 U.S. 223.

JUSTICE BLACKMUN announced the judgment of the court and delivered an opinion in which JUSTICE STEVENS joined.

[Ballew was convicted on two misdemeanor counts of distributing obscene material by a five-person jury impaneled according to Georgia law. The opinion recites the facts and describes *Williams*].

When the Court in *Williams* permitted the reduction in jury size * * * it expressly reserved ruling on the issue whether a number smaller than six passed constitutional scrutiny. The Court refused to speculate when this so-called "slippery slope" would become too steep. We face now, however, the two-fold question whether a further reduction in the size of the state criminal trial jury does make the grade too dangerous, that is, whether it inhibits the functioning of the jury as an institution to a significant degree, and, if so, whether any state interest counterbalances and justifies the disruption so as to preserve its constitutionality.

Williams v. Florida * * * generated a quantity of scholarly work on jury size. These writings do not draw or identify a bright line below which the number of jurors would not be able to function as required by the standards enunciated in *Williams*. On the other hand, they raise significant questions about the wisdom and constitutionality of a reduction below six. We examine these concerns:

First, recent empirical data suggest that progressively smaller juries are less likely to foster effective group deliberation. At some point, this decline leads to inaccurate fact-finding and incorrect application of the common sense of the community to the facts. Generally, a positive correlation exists between group size and the quality of both group performance and group productivity. A variety of explanations have been offered for this conclusion. Several are particularly applicable in the jury setting. The smaller the group, the less likely are members to make critical contributions necessary for the solution of a given problem. Because most juries are not permitted to take notes, memory is important for accurate jury deliberations. As juries decrease in size, then, they are less likely to have members who remember each of the important pieces of evidence or argument. Furthermore, the smaller the group, the less likely it is to overcome the biases of its members to obtain an accurate result. When individual and group decisionmaking were compared, it was seen that groups performed better because prejudices of individuals were frequently counterbalanced, and objectivity resulted. Groups also exhibited increased motivation and self-criticism. All of these advantages, except, perhaps, self-motivation, tend to diminish as the size of the group diminishes. * * *

Second, the data now raise doubts about the accuracy of the results achieved by smaller and smaller panels. Statistical studies suggest that the risk of convicting an innocent person rises as the size of the jury diminishes * * *. [The studies posit that by considering the risk of not convicting a guilty party, an optimal jury size between six and eight is identified.] As the size diminished to five and below, the weighted sum of errors increased because of the enlarging risk of the conviction of innocent defendants.

Another doubt about progressively smaller juries arises from the increasing inconsistency that results from the decreases. [Several studies suggest that 12-person panels considering the same case will reach the same result, or compromise to the same result, with greater consistency than a six-person panel.]

Third, the data suggest that the verdicts of jury deliberation in criminal cases will vary as juries become smaller, and that the variance amounts to an imbalance to the detriment of one side, the defense. [The Court noted that hung juries will diminish because a person in the minority is less likely to have an ally on the six-person panel, and thus is less likely to speak up.]

Fourth, what has just been said about the presence of minority viewpoint as juries decrease in size foretells problems not only for jury decisionmaking, but also for the representation of minority groups in the community. * * * Further reduction in size will erect additional barriers to representation.

Fifth, several authors have identified in jury research methodological problems tending to mask differences in the operation of smaller and larger juries. Nationwide, however, these small percentages will represent a large number of cases. And it is with respect to those cases that the jury trial right has its greatest value. When the case is close, and the guilt or innocence of the defendant is not readily apparent, a properly functioning jury system will insure evaluation by the sense of the community and will also tend to insure accurate factfinding. * * *

* * *

While we adhere to, and reaffirm our holding in Williams v. Florida, these studies, most of which have been made since *Williams* was decided in 1970, lead us to conclude that the purpose and functioning of the jury in a criminal trial is seriously impaired, and to a constitutional degree, by a reduction in size to below six members. We readily admit that we do not pretend to discern a clear line between six members and five. But the assembled data raise substantial doubt about the reliability and appropriate representation of panels smaller than six. Because of the fundamental importance of the jury trial to the American system of criminal justice, any further reduction that promotes inaccurate and possibly biased decisionmaking, that causes untoward differences in verdicts, and that prevents juries from truly representing their communities, attains constitutional significance.

* * *

* * * We find no significant state advantage in reducing the number of jurors from six to five. * * *

[The concurring opinion of Justice Stevens is omitted.]

JUSTICE WHITE concurring in the judgment.

Agreeing that a jury of fewer than six persons would fail to represent the sense of the community and hence not satisfy the fair cross-section requirement of the Sixth and Fourteenth Amendments, I concur in the judgment of reversal.

JUSTICE POWELL, with whom THE CHIEF JUSTICE and MR. JUSTICE REHNQUIST join, concurring in the judgment.

I concur in the judgment, as I agree that use of a jury as small as five members, with authority to convict for serious offenses, involves grave questions of fairness. As the opinion of Mr. Justice Blackmun indicates, the line between five-and six-member juries is difficult to justify, but a line has to be drawn somewhere if the substance of jury trial is to be preserved.

* * * I have reservations as to the wisdom—as well as the necessity—of Mr. Justice Blackmun's heavy reliance on numerology derived from statistical studies. Moreover, neither the validity nor the methodology employed by the studies cited was subjected to the traditional testing mechanisms of the adversary process. The studies relied on merely represent unexamined findings of persons interested in the jury system.

For these reasons I concur only in the judgment.

JUSTICE BRENNAN, with whom JUSTICE STEWART and JUSTICE MARSHALL join.

I join Mr. Justice Blackmun's opinion insofar as it holds that the Sixth and Fourteenth Amendments require juries in criminal trials to contain more than five persons. * * *

2. Unanimity

RAMOS V. LOUISIANA

Supreme Court of the United States, 2020.
140 S.Ct. 1390.

JUSTICE GORSUCH delivered the opinion of the Court.

Accused of a serious crime, Evangelisto Ramos insisted on his innocence and invoked his right to a jury trial. Eventually, 10 jurors found the evidence against him persuasive. But a pair of jurors believed that the State of Louisiana had failed to prove Mr. Ramos's guilt beyond reasonable doubt; they voted to acquit.

In 48 States and federal court, a single juror's vote to acquit is enough to prevent a conviction. But not in Louisiana. Along with Oregon, Louisiana has long punished people based on 10-to-2 verdicts like the one here. So, instead of the mistrial he would have received almost anywhere else, Mr. Ramos was sentenced to life in prison without the possibility of parole.

Why do Louisiana and Oregon allow nonunanimous convictions? Though it's hard to say why these laws persist, their origins are clear. Louisiana first endorsed nonunanimous verdicts for serious crimes at a constitutional convention in 1898. According to one committee chairman, the avowed purpose of that convention was to "establish the supremacy of the white race," and the resulting document included many of the trappings of the Jim Crow era: a poll tax, a combined literacy and property ownership test, and a grandfather clause that in practice exempted white residents from the most onerous of these requirements.

Nor was it only the prospect of African-Americans voting that concerned the delegates. Just a week before the convention, the U.S. Senate passed a resolution calling for an investigation into whether Louisiana was systemically excluding African-Americans from juries. Seeking to avoid unwanted national attention, and aware that this Court would strike down any policy of overt discrimination against African-American jurors as a violation of the Fourteenth Amendment, the delegates sought to undermine African-American participation on juries in another way. With a careful eye on racial demographics, the convention delegates sculpted a "facially race-neutral" rule permitting 10-to-2 verdicts in order "to ensure that African-American juror service would be meaningless."

Adopted in the 1930s, Oregon's rule permitting nonunanimous verdicts can be similarly traced to the rise of the Ku Klux Klan and efforts to dilute "the influence of racial, ethnic, and religious minorities on Oregon juries." In fact, no one before us contests any of this; courts in both Louisiana and Oregon have frankly acknowledged that race was a motivating factor in the adoption of their States' respective nonunanimity rules.

We took this case to decide whether the Sixth Amendment right to a jury trial—as incorporated against the States by way of the Fourteenth Amendment—requires a unanimous verdict to convict a defendant of a serious offense. Louisiana insists that this Court has never definitively passed on the question and urges us to find its practice consistent with the Sixth Amendment. By contrast, the dissent doesn't try to defend Louisiana's law on Sixth or Fourteenth Amendment grounds; tacitly, it seems to admit that the Constitution forbids States from using nonunanimous juries. Yet, unprompted by Louisiana, the dissent suggests our precedent requires us to rule for the State anyway. What explains all this? To answer the puzzle, it's necessary to say a bit more about the merits of the question presented, the relevant precedent, and, at last, the consequences that follow from saying what we know to be true.

I

The Sixth Amendment promises that "[i]n all criminal prosecutions, the accused shall enjoy the right to a speedy and public trial, by an impartial jury of the State and district wherein the crime shall have been committed, which district shall have been previously ascertained by law." The Amendment goes on to preserve other rights for criminal defendants but says nothing else about what a "trial by an impartial jury" entails.

Still, the promise of a jury trial surely meant something—otherwise, there would have been no reason to write it down. Nor would it have made any sense to spell out the places from which jurors should be drawn if their powers as jurors could be freely abridged by statute. Imagine a constitution that allowed a "jury trial" to mean nothing but a single person rubberstamping convictions without hearing any evidence—but simultaneously insisting that the lone juror come from a specific judicial district "previously ascertained by law." And if that's not enough, imagine a constitution that included the same hollow guarantee twice—not only in the Sixth Amendment, but also in Article III. No: The text and structure of the Constitution clearly suggest that the term "trial by an impartial jury" carried with it some meaning about the content and requirements of a jury trial.

One of these requirements was unanimity. Wherever we might look to determine what the term "trial by an impartial jury trial" meant at the time of the Sixth Amendment's adoption—whether it's the common law, state practices in the founding era, or opinions and treatises written soon afterward—the answer is unmistakable. A jury must reach a unanimous verdict in order to convict.

The requirement of juror unanimity emerged in 14thcentury England and was soon accepted as a vital right protected by the common law. As Blackstone explained, no person could be found guilty of a serious crime unless "the truth of every accusation . . . should . . . be confirmed by the unanimous suffrage of twelve of his equals and neighbors, indifferently chosen, and superior to all suspicion." A " 'verdict, taken from eleven, was no verdict' " at all. This same rule applied in the young American States. Six State Constitutions explicitly required unanimity. Another four preserved the right to a jury trial in more general terms. But the variations did not matter much; consistent with the common law, state courts appeared to regard unanimity as an essential feature of the jury trial.

It was against this backdrop that James Madison drafted and the States ratified the Sixth Amendment in 1791. By that time, unanimous verdicts had been required for about 400 years. If the term "trial by an impartial jury" carried any meaning at all, it surely included a requirement as long and widely accepted as unanimity.

Influential, postadoption treatises confirm this understanding. For example, in 1824, Nathan Dane reported as fact that the U.S. Constitution required unanimity in criminal jury trials for serious offenses. A few years later, Justice Story explained in his Commentaries on the Constitution that "in common cases, the law not only presumes every man innocent, until he is proved guilty; but unanimity in the verdict of the jury is indispensable." Similar statements can be found in American legal treatises throughout the 19th century.

Nor is this a case where the original public meaning was lost to time and only recently recovered. This Court has, repeatedly and over many years, recognized that the Sixth Amendment requires unanimity. As early as 1898, the Court said that a defendant enjoys a "constitutional right to demand that his liberty should not be taken from him except by the joint action of the court and the unanimous verdict of a jury of twelve persons." A few decades later, the Court elaborated that the Sixth Amendment affords a right to "a trial by jury as understood and applied at common law, . . . includ[ing] all the essential elements as they were recognized in this country and England when the Constitution was adopted." And, the Court observed, this includes a requirement "that the verdict should be unanimous." In all, this Court has commented on the Sixth Amendment's unanimity requirement no fewer than 13 times over more than 120 years.

There can be no question either that the Sixth Amendment's unanimity requirement applies to state and federal criminal trials equally. This Court has long explained that the Sixth Amendment right to a jury trial is "fundamental to the American scheme of justice" and incorporated against the States under the Fourteenth Amendment. This Court has long explained, too, that incorporated provisions of the Bill of Rights bear the same content when asserted against States as they do when asserted against the federal government. So if the Sixth Amendment's right to a jury trial requires a unanimous verdict to support a conviction in federal court, it requires no less in state court.

II

A

How, despite these seemingly straightforward principles, have Louisiana's and Oregon's laws managed to hang on for so long? It turns out that the Sixth Amendment's otherwise simple story took a strange turn in 1972. That year, the Court confronted these States' unconventional schemes for the first time—in *Apodaca v. Oregon* and a companion case, *Johnson v. Louisiana*. Ultimately, the Court could do no more than issue a badly fractured set of opinions. Four dissenting Justices would not have hesitated to strike down the States' laws, recognizing that the Sixth Amendment requires unanimity and that this guarantee is fully applicable against the States under the Fourteenth Amendment. But a four-Justice plurality took a very different view of the Sixth Amendment. These Justices declared that the real question before them was whether unanimity serves an important "function" in "contemporary society." Then, having reframed the question, the plurality wasted few words before concluding that unanimity's costs outweigh its benefits in the modern era, so the Sixth Amendment should not stand in the way of Louisiana or Oregon.

The ninth Member of the Court adopted a position that was neither here nor there. On the one hand, Justice Powell agreed that, as a matter of "history and precedent, . . . the Sixth Amendment requires a unanimous jury verdict to convict." But, on the other hand, he argued that the Fourteenth Amendment does not render this guarantee against the federal government fully applicable against the States. In this way, Justice Powell doubled down on his belief in "dual-track" incorporation—the idea that a single right can mean two different things depending on whether it is being invoked against the federal or a state government.

Justice Powell acknowledged that his argument for dual-track incorporation came "late in the day." Late it was. The Court had already, nearly a decade earlier, "rejected the notion that the Fourteenth Amendment applies to the States only a 'watered-down, subjective version of the individual guarantees of the Bill of Rights.'" It's a point we've restated many times since, too, including as recently as last year. Still, Justice Powell frankly explained, he was "unwillin[g]" to follow the Court's precedents. So he offered up the essential fifth vote to uphold Mr. Apodaca's conviction—if based only on a view of the Fourteenth Amendment that he knew was (and remains) foreclosed by precedent. * * *

III

Louisiana's approach may not be quite as tough as trying to defend Justice Powell's dual-track theory of incorporation, but it's pretty close. How does the State deal with the fact this Court has said 13 times over 120 years that the Sixth Amendment does require unanimity? Or the fact that five Justices in *Apodaca* said the same? The best the State can offer is to suggest that all these statements came in dicta. But even supposing (without granting) that Louisiana is right and it's dicta all the way down, why would the Court now walk away from many of its own statements about the Constitution's meaning? And what about the prior 400 years of English and American cases requiring unanimity—should we dismiss all those as dicta too?

[The Court describes and rejects Louisiana's argument that the drafting history of the Sixth Amendment left unanimity behind, an argument similar to the one that prevailed in Williams v. Florida. The Court also rejects Louisiana's argument that unanimity is not important enough to be read as part of the Sixth Amendment.]

IV

A

[The Court rejects the dissent's argument that stare decisis requires adherence to *Apodaca*, notes that there was no majority for the proposition that unanimous juries are not part of the Sixth Amendment, and that Justice Powell's dual track theory of incorporation was rejected by the Court and continues to be rejected.]

B

1

There's another obstacle the dissent must overcome. Even if we accepted the premise that *Apodaca* established a precedent, no one on the Court today is prepared to say it was rightly decided, and *stare decisis* isn't supposed to be the art of methodically ignoring what everyone knows to be true. Of course, the precedents of this Court warrant our deep respect as embodying the considered views of those who have come before. But *stare decisis* has never been treated as "an inexorable command." And the doctrine is "at its weakest when we interpret the Constitution" because a mistaken judicial interpretation of that supreme law is often "practically impossible" to correct through other means. To balance these considerations, when it revisits a precedent this Court has traditionally considered "the quality of the decision's reasoning; its consistency with related decisions; legal developments since the decision; and reliance on the decision." In this case, each factor points in the same direction.

* * *

JUSTICE SOTOMAYOR, concurring.

[Justice Sotomayor joined all portions of the majority opinion reproduced above. She wrote separately on the question of *stare decisis* and to make clear that she is amenable to interpretive methods other than public meaning originalism.]

JUSTICE KAVANAUGH, concurring.

[Justice Kavanaugh joined all portions of the majority opinion reproduced above. He wrote separately on the question of *stare decisis*, describing a framework for its application in future cases.]

JUSTICE THOMAS, concurring.

[Justice Thomas did not join the majority opinion, but concurred in the judgment based on his view that the Privileges and Immunities clause of the Fourteenth Amendment made all provisions of the Bill of Rights enforceable against the states, including the unanimity requirement of the Sixth Amendment.]

JUSTICE ALITO, dissenting.

[Justice Alito dissented with Chief Justice Roberts and Justice Kagan on *stare decisis* grounds.]

QUESTIONS AFTER RAMOS V. LOUISIANA

In his majority opinion, Justice Gorsuch describes the Court's opinion in *Apodaca v. Oregon* as "badly fractured." There is some irony in that account given how fractured the Court's decision in *Ramos* itself is. Justices Sotomayor and Kavanaugh joined all parts of the majority opinion reproduced here, but declined to join another section in which Justice Gorsuch, with Justices Ginsburg and Breyer, addresses the dissenting justices' valuation of the precedential value of *Apodaca*. Another portion of Justice Gorsuch's opinion, addressing the retroactive application of *Ramos* to criminal convictions that are final, garnered support from Justices Ginsburg, Breyer, and Sotomayor, but not Justice Kavanaugh. In addition to these fractures in the majority,

Justice Alito took some umbrage in his dissenting opinion, criticizing both the tone of the majority opinion and its indictment of nonunanimous jury practices in Oregon and Louisiana as grounded in racism.

Ramos is also notable for Justice Gorsuch's full-throated originalism. Although Justice Sotomayor was careful in her concurring opinion to make clear that she is open to other modes of constitutional interpretation, the fact that she, Justice Ginsburg, Justice Breyer, and Justice Kavanaugh all signed-on to an opinion that rests entirely on an analysis of the Sixth Amendment's original public meaning highlights the ascendant influence of originalism on the Court—a trend likely to continue with Justice Barrett joining the Court. Notably, that analysis leads the Court to a result that most would regard as liberal or progressive in the context of contemporary political discourse. Of course, this is not the first time that a purportedly conservative Justice has deployed originalism to advance individual rights in the criminal procedure context. Justice Scalia's opinion in *Crawford v. Washington*, 541 U.S. 36 (2004), provides a ready example. So, too, his opinion in *Apprendi*, which provided Justice Gorsuch with the grounding for his plurality opinion in *Haymond*. Nevertheless, *Ramos* is significant for the fact that the Court's newest members signaled not only their sympathies with originalism, but neutrality with respect to results. In *Ramos*, method seems to drive the outcome.

In *Edwards v. Vannoy*, 141 S.Ct. 1547 (2021), the Court held that *Ramos* does not apply retroactively to cases on collateral review in federal courts.

3. The Interplay Between Size and Unanimity

Long before the *Ramos* decision, the Court analyzed the interplay between the constitutionally sufficient six-person jury, and the issue of unanimity, in Burch v. Louisiana, 441 U.S. 130 (1979). In an opinion by Justice Rehnquist, the Court held that "conviction by a nonunanimous six-person jury in a state criminal trial for a nonpetty offense deprives an accused of his constitutional right to trial by jury." The Court conceded that drawing lines was difficult, but found it essential to draw the line somewhere. It concluded that use of nonunanimous six-person juries violated the right to jury trial. There were no dissents.

D. JURY SELECTION AND COMPOSITION

1. The Jury Pool

The Sixth Amendment assures the defendant "an impartial jury of the State and district wherein the crime shall have been committed." This language, with its emphasis on both the impartial and community character of the jury, has served as a touchstone in the regulation of the pool from which the petit jury is drawn. (The body of candidates from which the petit jury is drawn is also known as the "venire"). Another constitutional regulation on selection of the jury pool is the Equal

Protection Clause, which prohibits exclusion from the jury pool on the basis of suspect classifications such as race.

In Glasser v. United States, 315 U.S. 60, 85–86 (1942), the Court observed as follows:

> [The jury selection process] must always accord with the fact that the proper functioning of the jury system, and, indeed, our democracy itself, requires that the jury be a "body truly representative of the community," and not the organ of any special group or class. If that requirement is observed, the officials charged with choosing federal jurors may exercise some discretion to the end that competent jurors may be called. But they must not allow the desire for competent jurors to lead them into selections which do not comport with the concept of the jury as a cross-section of the community.

Thus, the selection of the jury pool must be unbiased; it must generate a panel representing a cross-section of the community. Selection of jurors cannot violate principles of equal protection. And finally, each individual juror must be impartial, unbiased and free from outside influences.

2. The Fair Cross-Section Requirement and the Equal Protection Clause

Two Separate Rights

As stated above, there are two separate constitutional provisions that can impact the selection of the pool from which a jury is drawn. The Equal Protection Clause prohibits the selection or rejection of jurors on the basis of race, sex, or any other suspect classification. Application of equal protection standards to jury selection is similar to the equal protection law applied in other contexts. See, e.g., Castaneda v. Partida, 430 U.S. 482 (1977) (in order to establish a prima facie equal protection violation, the defendant "must show that the procedure employed resulted in substantial underrepresentation of his race or of the identifiable group to which he belongs"; the burden then shifts to the state to rebut the inference of discrimination by showing neutral selection criteria); United States v. Esquivel, 75 F.3d 545 (9th Cir.1996) (rejecting a challenge that selection of jury panel violated equal protection due to underrepresentation of Hispanics; defendant failed to show statistical disparity or intent to discriminate).[15] The Sixth Amendment independently requires that the jury be chosen from a fair cross-section of the community. The Supreme Court has used both constitutional protections to attempt to assure fair and representative jury selection procedures.

---

[15] Equal protection standards also regulate the use of peremptory challenges to prospective jurors. See the discussion of Batson v. Kentucky and its progeny, infra in this Chapter.

The goals of the two constitutional guarantees are somewhat different, though overlapping, in the context of selection of the jury pool. The goal of the Equal Protection Clause is of course to prevent government discrimination on the basis of race, sex, or other suspect classification. The goal of the fair cross-section requirement is to assure that the defendant get the benefit of a jury that is representative of the community. As one court put it, the purposes of the fair cross-section requirement include "ensuring that the common sense judgment of the community will act as a hedge against overzealous prosecutions; preserving public confidence in the criminal justice system; and furthering the notion that participation in the administration of justice is a part of one's civic responsibility." United States v. Raszkiewicz, 169 F.3d 459 (7th Cir.1999).

Early Cases Establishing the Rights

The first challenges to the selection of the jury developed under the rubric of the Equal Protection Clause, in response to race-related exclusions. In Strauder v. West Virginia, 100 U.S. 303 (1879), the Court struck down a state statute that excluded African-Americans from grand and petit jury service as violative of the Fourteenth Amendment's Equal Protection Clause.

The Court first recognized the impact of the exclusion of a non-race-related group in a civil case, Thiel v. Southern Pacific Co., 328 U.S. 217 (1946). The Court held that the systematic exclusion of daily wage earners from a federal court jury panel violated the fair cross-section requirement—no violation of equal protection could be found in the exclusion of daily wage earners as they were not a suspect class. See, e.g., United States v. Esquivel, 75 F.3d 545 (9th Cir.1996) (in contrast to an equal protection violation, "a prima facie case for establishing a Sixth Amendment, fair cross section violation does not require the appellant to prove discriminatory intent or require that the appellant be a member of the distinct, excluded group").

In *Thiel,* the jury commissioner and clerk used a city directory to identify and exclude daily wage earners from a federal court jury panel. The Court ruled that although a judge may exclude a person from jury service when participation entails a financial hardship, complete exclusion in the absence of such a finding is forbidden.

In Ballard v. United States, 329 U.S. 187 (1946), the Court held that the purposeful and systematic exclusion of women from both grand and petit juries in the district where an indictment was returned required its dismissal. The court exercised its supervisory power after concluding that the selection scheme departed from that which Congress adopted.

Fair Cross-Section Requirement Does Not Apply to Petit Jury

In recognizing the existence of cognizable classes other than race under the Fair Cross-Section Clause, the Court has been careful to delineate the scope of the defendant's challenge. Both *Thiel* and *Ballard* emphasized that a defendant has no right to challenge a particular jury as failing to represent all social, economic, and political groups. Rather, the defendant is restricted to challenging the selection *procedure* as systematically excluding a cognizable group. That is, the fair cross-section requirement is applicable to the jury *pool*, but not to the ultimate petit jury that hears the defendant's case. This was confirmed in Holland v. Illinois, 493 U.S. 474 (1990), where a five-person majority explicitly held that the fair cross-section requirement does not allow a defendant to attack the composition of the petit jury. Consequently, the Sixth Amendment did not protect the defendant, who was white, from the prosecutor's discriminatory use of peremptory challenges to exclude African-Americans from the petit jury. Justice Scalia, writing for the Court, stressed that it would be all but impossible to form a petit jury that mirrored a cross-section of the community. The impact of *Holland* has been severely curtailed, however, by the Court's use of the Equal Protection Clause to limit the exercise of peremptory challenges. Thus, the Equal Protection Clause, and not the Fair Cross-Section Clause, imposes restrictions on the composition of the petit jury. See the discussion of Batson v. Kentucky, infra.

Standing to Object to a Fair Cross-Section Violation

TAYLOR V. LOUISIANA

Supreme Court of the United States, 1975.
419 U.S. 522.

JUSTICE WHITE delivered the opinion of the Court.

[The Louisiana Code provided that a woman should not be selected for jury service unless she had previously filed a written declaration of her desire to be subject to jury service. Appellant, a male, alleged that the statute violated his Sixth and Fourteenth Amendment right to a jury drawn from a fair cross-section of the community.]

The Louisiana jury-selection system does not disqualify women from jury service, but in operation its conceded systematic impact is that only a very few women, grossly disproportionate to the number of eligible women in the community, are called for jury service. In this case, no women were on the venire from which the petit jury was drawn. * * *

The State first insists that Taylor, a male, has no standing to object to the exclusion of women from his jury. But Taylor's claim is that he was constitutionally entitled to a jury drawn from a venire constituting a fair

cross section of the community and that the jury that tried him was not such a jury by reason of the exclusion of women. Taylor was not a member of the excluded class; but there is no rule that claims such as Taylor presents may be made only by those defendants who are members of the group excluded from jury service. Taylor, in the case before us, was similarly entitled to tender and have adjudicated the claim that the exclusion of women from jury service deprived him of the kind of factfinder to which he was constitutionally entitled.

* * *

We accept the fair-cross-section requirement as fundamental to the jury trial guaranteed by the Sixth Amendment and are convinced that the requirement has solid foundation. The purpose of a jury is to guard against the exercise of arbitrary power—to make available the commonsense judgment of the community as a hedge against the overzealous or mistaken prosecutor and in preference to the professional or perhaps over-conditioned or biased response of a judge. This prophylactic vehicle is not provided if the jury pool is made up of only special segments of the populace or if large, distinctive groups are excluded from the pool. Community participation in the administration of the criminal law, moreover, is not only consistent with our democratic heritage but is also critical to public confidence in the fairness of the criminal justice system. * * *

We are also persuaded that the fair-cross-section requirement is violated by the systematic exclusion of women, who in the judicial district involved here amounted to 53% of the citizens eligible for jury service. This conclusion necessarily entails the judgment that women are sufficiently numerous and distinct from men and that if they are systematically eliminated from jury panels, the Sixth Amendment's fair-cross-section requirement cannot be satisfied. * * *

There remains the argument that women as a class serve a distinctive role in society and that jury service would so substantially interfere with that function that the state has ample justification for excluding women from service unless they volunteer, even though the result is that almost all jurors are men. * * *

The States are free to grant exemptions from jury service to individuals in case of special hardship or incapacity and to those engaged in particular occupations the uninterrupted performance of which is critical to the community's welfare. * * * A system excluding all women, however, is a wholly different matter. It is untenable to suggest these days that it would be a special hardship for each and every woman to perform jury service or that society cannot spare *any* women from their present duties. This may be the case with many, and it may be burdensome to sort out those who should be exempted from those who should serve. But that task is performed in the case of men, and the administrative convenience

in dealing with women as a class is insufficient justification for diluting the quality of community judgment represented by the jury in criminal trials.

* * *

Standards for Prima Facie Violation of the Fair Cross-Section Requirement: Duren v. Missouri

In Duren v. Missouri, 439 U.S. 357 (1979), the Court held that in order to establish a prima facie violation of the fair cross-section requirement, a defendant must show three things:

- the group excluded from the jury array is a distinctive group within the community;
- the representation of the group in the venire from which jurors are selected is not fair and reasonable in relation to the number of such persons in the community; and
- this underrepresentation is the result of a systematic exclusion of the group in the jury selection process.

If the defendant establishes these three factors, the burden shifts to the state to show that the inclusion of the underrepresented group would be "incompatible with a significant state interest."

The Court found that Duren had made out a prima facie case by showing that 54% of the adult inhabitants of the county were women, while only 15% of the persons placed on venires were women, and a woman could decline jury service by simply not reporting for jury duty while a man did not have the same option. Justice White, writing for the Court, stated that an exemption tailored to women who could not leave their children might effectuate a state interest sufficient to satisfy the fair cross-section requirement, but that no such limited exemption was operative in this case.

Distinctive Groups for Fair Cross-Section Purposes

What groups are distinctive under the fair cross-section requirement? After *Duren,* is a constitutional challenge alleging, for example, that blue collar workers are excluded from state juries likely to succeed? What about young adults? See Anaya v. Hansen, 781 F.2d 1 (1st Cir.1986) (neither young adults nor blue collar workers constituted a cognizable group for cross-section analysis).

The court in United States v. Fletcher, 965 F.2d 781 (9th Cir.1992), set forth a test, followed by many courts, for determining whether a group is "distinctive" under *Duren*:

> [A] defendant must show (1) that the group is defined and limited by some factor (i.e., that the group has a definite composition such as by

> race or sex); (2) that a common thread or basic similarity in attitude, ideas, or experience runs through the group; and (3) that there is a community of interests among members of the group such that the group's interest cannot be adequately represented if the group is excluded from the jury selection process.

Applying this three-factor test, the *Fletcher* court held that college students are not a distinctive group for fair cross-section purposes:

> The group of individuals we call "college students" is no more capable of fitting into a pigeon hole than the group we call "young adults." The group is not defined by any "limiting factor"—anyone may be a college student. Nor is there a common thread of "attitude" or "experience" that runs through the group, beyond the fact that every member spends a certain percentage of his or her time in a classroom. It is true that the privilege of a college education continues to be enjoyed only by a minority of our citizens. Nevertheless, the variety of groups that are represented in college classrooms is vast and growing, so that the economic, geographic, racial, sexual, political, and religious demographics of that minority are nearly as diverse as those of the nation itself. It is farfetched to suggest that the college experience could coalesce the diverse points of view that are the necessary product of such divergent experiences into a single "community of interest" that will go unrepresented on a jury if there are no "college students" among its members.

While college students do not have a sufficient community of interest to be distinctive, what about Grateful Dead fans? Liberal arts majors?

For other cases analyzing the distinctiveness of certain groups, see Brewer v. Nix, 963 F.2d 1111 (8th Cir.1992) (people over 65 are not a distinctive group for cross-section purposes); United States v. Raszkiewicz, 169 F.3d 459 (7th Cir.1999) (exclusion from jury venires of Native Americans who live on reservations did not violate the fair-cross section requirement because they are not a distinctive group); United States v. Barry, 71 F.3d 1269 (7th Cir.1995) (upholding exclusion from jury service of persons who have felony charges pending against them: "We are not convinced that alleged felons comprise a distinctive group. They have in common that they may have run afoul of the criminal justice system. However, there are many and varied ways to do that.").

Proper Sources for the Jury Pool

If a state can show a truly random selection process, and if the state uses a source (or sources) of jury names—e.g., driver's license lists as well as voting lists—that is likely to include most members of a community, most challenges to selection of the jury pool will be rejected.[16]

Contentions have been made that certain groups are especially likely not to register to vote and therefore that voter lists do not produce a cross-section of the community. However, as long as voter lists do not have racial identifications and are used as part of some non-discriminatory selection scheme, their use is likely to be sustained. See United States v. Lewis, 10 F.3d 1086 (4th Cir.1993) (use of voter lists is presumptively proper). In fact, underrepresentation should be rare if voting lists are used. But if a state refuses to follow clear, visible selection procedures, invalidation on fair cross-section grounds becomes more likely.[17]

3. Voir Dire and Court Control

Establishing a jury venire representing a fair cross-section of the community, and selected without violating principles of equal protection, is only the first stage in the jury selection procedure. The second stage, also regulated by these constitutional guarantees, is to assure that the actual trial jury is impartial and fairly chosen. Because preconceived notions about the case at issue threaten impartiality, each juror must be free of bias. Accordingly, in a process called voir dire—meaning "to speak the truth"—prospective jurors are subject to two kinds of challenges:

- An unlimited number of challenges based on a "narrowly specified, provable and legally cognizable basis of partiality"—i.e., challenges "for cause"; and
- A specified (by statute or rule) number of *peremptory* challenges, which at one time were exercised for any reason or no reason—though as we will see the use of peremptory challenges has been limited by Batson v. Kentucky and its progeny, infra.

Voir dire may be conducted in any of several methods: 1) by addressing all questions to the panel at one time, or by addressing each juror individually; 2) by having the judge put questions to the jurors or by allowing counsel to ask the questions; and 3) by allowing a broad inquiry into juror attitudes or by limiting the number and scope of questions that

[16] The Federal Jury Selection and Service Act of 1968, 28 U.S.C.A. §§ 1861–69, provides that Federal district courts must devise a plan for random selection of grand and petit jurors, and sets forth procedures for drawing names from a master wheel and summoning, qualifying, and impaneling jurors for service. The Act calls for the use of voter registration lists or lists of actual voters and "some other source or sources of names in addition to voter lists where necessary to foster the policy and protect the rights" set forth in the Act. The Act permits criminal defendants to move to dismiss the indictment or stay proceedings "on the ground of substantial failure to comply" with the provisions of the Act.

[17] Jurisdictions vary on whether a defendant has a right to inspect and copy jury lists. In Test v. United States, 420 U.S. 28 (1975), the Court held that a federal criminal defendant has the right to inspect in order to prepare challenges to petit and grand jury selection procedures. In some cases—e.g., treason or capital cases—statutes may require that the defendant be served with a list. See 18 U.S.C.A. § 3432.

may be asked to the narrow issues presented in a specific case. Voir dire vests broad authority in the trial judge.

The general practice in the federal system is for the judge to conduct the voir dire questioning of prospective jurors. See Fed.R.Crim.P. 24(a)(court *may* allow attorneys to question jurors). Some jurisdictions give parties or their counsel a right to conduct voir dire.

Court control over voir dire questioning became the usual practice in federal and some state courts after perceived abuses by counsel, including waste of time and inquiry into improper areas during voir dire examination. Some courts have questioned the practice of court control. For example, the court in United States v. Ible, 630 F.2d 389 (5th Cir.1980), stated that "the federal practice of almost exclusive voir dire examination by the court does not take into account the fact that it is parties, rather than the court, who have a full grasp of the nuances and the strength and weaknesses of the case." But the practice of court-controlled voir dire questioning remains the federal norm, with counsel left to making requests as to what questions to ask. See McMillion, Advocating Voir Dire Reform, 77 A.B.A.J., Nov. 1991, p. 114 (discussing legislation proposed in the Senate (but never enacted) to give attorneys a limited right to conduct questioning of jurors in the federal courts).

The judge has discretion to permit questions suggested by counsel for voir dire, and has the right to refuse to allow and to strike questions deemed irrelevant or inappropriate. The judge's determinations are fact-specific; they frequently turn on the particular aspects of the case to be tried. In most instances the appellate court will defer to the trial court, believing that the trial judge has a better feel than an appellate court for the need to put questions to prospective jurors. But the Constitution requires that some inquiries be made at the request of a defendant if necessary to assure an effective voir dire.

QUESTIONS CONCERNING RACIAL PREJUDICE: HAM V. SOUTH CAROLINA

In Ham v. South Carolina, 409 U.S. 524 (1973), a young, bearded African-American, active in the civil rights movement, was charged with possession of marijuana. He alleged, in defense, that police officials had framed him because of his civil rights activities. During voir dire, he requested that the trial judge ask four questions relating to potential juror prejudice: two related to prejudice against African-Americans, the third related to prejudice against individuals with beards, and the fourth related to pretrial publicity. The trial judge refused to ask any of the questions. The Supreme Court granted review to consider whether the refusal violated Ham's constitutional rights.

Justice Rehnquist, writing for the Court, declared as follows:

> [W]e think that the Fourteenth Amendment required the judge in this case to interrogate the jurors upon the subject of racial prejudice. South Carolina law permits challenges for cause, and authorizes the trial judge to conduct *voir dire* examination of potential jurors. The State having created this statutory framework for the selection of juries, the essential fairness required by the Due Process Clause of the Fourteenth Amendment requires that under the facts shown by this record the petitioner be permitted to have the jurors interrogated on the issue of racial bias.
>
> * * * [T]he trial judge was not required to put the question in any particular form, or to ask any particular number of questions on the subject, simply because requested to do so by petitioner. * * * In this context, either of the brief, general questions urged by the petitioner would appear sufficient to focus the attention of prospective jurors on any racial prejudice they might entertain.
>
> The third of petitioner's proposed questions was addressed to the fact that he wore a beard. While we cannot say that prejudice against people with beards might not have been harbored by one or more of the potential jurors in this case, this is the beginning and not the end of the inquiry as to whether the Fourteenth Amendment required the trial judge to interrogate the prospective jurors about such possible prejudice. Given the traditionally broad discretion accorded to the trial judge in conducting *voir dire,* and our inability to constitutionally distinguish possible prejudice against beards from a host of other possible similar prejudices, we do not believe the petitioner's constitutional rights were violated when the trial judge refused to put this question.

Inquiry into Racial Prejudice Not Automatically Required: Ristaino v. Ross

Ham's holding, that due process required the judge to inquire into the prospective jurors' possible racial prejudice, was distinguished in Ristaino v. Ross, 424 U.S. 589 (1976).

An African-American, charged in a state court with violent crimes against a white security guard, requested the trial court to ask during voir dire a question specifically directed to possible racial prejudice on the part of any prospective jurors. The trial court refused and was affirmed on appeal. The Supreme Court was reviewing a federal court of appeals' decision granting habeas relief on the basis of *Ham.* Justice Powell's opinion for the Court stated that:

> The Constitution does not always entitle a defendant to have questions posed during *voir dire* specifically directed to matters that conceivably might prejudice veniremen against him. *Voir dire* is

conducted under the supervision of the court, and a great deal must, of necessity, be left to its sound discretion. This is so because the determination of impartiality, in which demeanor plays such an important part, is particularly within the province of the trial judge. Thus, the State's obligation to the defendant to impanel an impartial jury generally can be satisfied by less than an inquiry into a specific prejudice feared by the defendant.

* * *

Justice Powell distinguished *Ham* as a case in which Ham's civil rights record and his claim to have been framed as a result of it meant that racial issues "were inextricably bound up with the conduct of the trial" and the defense he raised was "likely to intensify any prejudice that individual members of the jury might harbor."

Justice White concurred in the judgment. Justice Marshall, joined by justice Brennan, dissented and argued that "the Court emphatically confirms that the promises inherent in *Ham* * * * will not be fulfilled." Justice Stevens took no part in the case.

Limits on Mandatory Inquiry into Race: Rosales-Lopez v. United States

A divided Supreme Court held that there was no reversible error in a district court's refusal to voir dire prospective jurors on their racial prejudices in Rosales-Lopez v. United States, 451 U.S. 182 (1981). The defendant was a Mexican National charged with smuggling aliens into the United States. The trial judge asked jurors about attitudes toward "the alien problem" and aliens, but not about racial or ethnic prejudices. Justice White, writing for a plurality (Justices Stewart, Blackmun, and Powell) concluded that "it is usually best to allow the defendant * * * to have the inquiry into racial or ethnic prejudice pursued," but refused to require such an inquiry in all cases involving a defendant of a racial minority, reasoning that an inquiry into racial matters may create an impression that justice turns on race. The plurality said that prior federal cases invoking the Supreme Court's supervisory authority "fairly imply that federal trial courts must make such an inquiry when requested by a defendant accused of a violent crime and where the defendant and the victim are members of different racial or ethnic groups."

Justice Rehnquist, joined by Chief Justice Burger, concurred in the judgment, noting that the scope of voir dire was necessarily dependent on the discretion of trial judges. Justice Stevens, joined by Justices Brennan and Marshall, dissented and argued that "[m]uch as we wish it were otherwise, we should acknowledge the fact that there are many potential jurors who harbor strong prejudices against all members of certain racial, religious or ethnic groups for no reason other than hostility to the group as a whole."

Capital Defendants and Interracial Crime: Turner v. Murray

The Supreme Court departed from *Ristaino* in capital cases as it held in Turner v. Murray, 476 U.S. 28 (1986), that a death sentence was invalid where a trial judge refused an African-American defendant's request to question prospective jurors on racial prejudice in a prosecution charging him with murdering a white man. Justice White wrote for the Court as it held that "a capital defendant accused of an interracial crime is entitled to have prospective jurors informed of the race of the victim and questioned on the issue of racial bias." He noted that the trial judge retains discretion as to the form and number of questions, including whether to question jurors individually or collectively, and that a defendant cannot complain unless he has specifically asked for voir dire questions concerning race.

Voir Dire and the Need to Screen for Prejudicial Pretrial Publicity: Mu'Min v. Virginia

Chief Justice Rehnquist relied on *Ristaino* in his opinion for the Court in Mu'Min v. Virginia, 500 U.S. 415 (1991), holding that a state trial judge is not obliged to question prospective jurors individually about the contents of pretrial publicity to which they may have been exposed. Mu'Min was a state prisoner serving time for first-degree murder when he was charged with capital murder while on a work detail. The case was widely publicized, as it arose during the 1988 presidential campaign in which another case of a murder by a prisoner on furlough became an issue of national debate. Articles in the newspapers revealed details of the prior murder for which Mu'Min was incarcerated; the fact that the death penalty was unavailable at the time he committed the first murder; the denial of parole six times to Mu'Min; his confession to the crime charged; and criticism of the supervision of work gangs in Virginia.

As the Court had done in *Ristaino,* Chief Justice Rehnquist distinguished the requirements of the Due Process Clause concerning voir dire in state trials from the more extensive supervisory power of federal courts over federal trials. He reasoned that the need to weed out prejudicial pretrial publicity through voir dire was certainly no greater than the need to protect against racial or ethnic prejudice. He observed that if the effect of pretrial publicity must be the subject of inquiry, each juror would have to be voir dired individually, in order to prevent jurors from infecting each other with the publicity giving rise to the inquiry. In the Chief Justice's view, such a substantial burden on the system was not justified. He rejected the less burdensome alternative of written questions concerning the content of publicity to which each juror had been exposed, reasoning that written answers would not give counsel or the court access to the demeanor of jurors. Thus, because efforts to fully protect the defendant from jurors infected by pretrial publicity were too onerous, the Constitution did not require the court to take less effective efforts.

Justice O'Connor wrote a concurring opinion. She concluded that a trial judge could realistically assess whether jurors could be fair without knowing what each juror had heard about a case. Justice O'Connor agreed with Justice Marshall's dissenting view that the trial judge in this case could have done more, but ultimately concluded that "content" questions are not so indispensable to a fair trial that it violates the Constitution for a trial court to evaluate jurors without asking them.

Justice Marshall's dissenting opinion was joined by Justice Blackmun and Justice Stevens. His basic principle was that "[w]hen a prospective juror has been exposed to prejudicial pretrial publicity, a trial court cannot realistically assess the juror's impartiality without first establishing what the juror already has learned about the case."

Justice Kennedy also dissented. He contended that "the trial judge should have substantial discretion in conducting the voir dire, but, in my judgment, findings of impartiality must be based on something more than the mere silence of the individual in response to questions asked *en masse*."

Voir Dire and Jurors' Feelings About the Death Penalty: Morgan v. Illinois

The Court in Morgan v. Illinois, 504 U.S. 719 (1992), departed from its deferential analysis in *Mu'Min* when considering voir dire of jurors' views of the death penalty. Morgan was sentenced to death under an Illinois procedure that first required the jury unanimously to find at least one aggravating circumstance. After the jury determined that the defendant was death-eligible, it was instructed that it "should consider" all mitigating circumstances, and that it should impose the death sentence if "there are no mitigating factors sufficient to preclude" the death penalty in light of the aggravating factors.

During jury selection, Morgan requested that the judge ask prospective jurors whether they would automatically—regardless of any mitigating circumstances—impose the death penalty upon a finding that the defendant was death-eligible. The trial judge refused Morgan's request on the ground that each prospective juror had already been asked whether they would be able to follow the instructions on the law, and they were also asked whether they would be fair and impartial. Justice White, writing for the majority, found that this general questioning was insufficient under the Due Process Clause. He first noted the defendant's stake in voir dire:

> We deal here with petitioner's ability to exercise his * * * challenge for cause against those biased persons on the venire who as jurors would unwaveringly impose death after a finding of guilt. Were voir dire not available to lay bare the foundation of petitioner's challenge for cause against those prospective jurors who would always impose death following conviction, his right not to be tried by such jurors would be rendered * * * nugatory and meaningless * * *.

Justice White rejected the State's argument that general "fairness" and "follow the law" questions were sufficient to satisfy Morgan's right to inquire about a prospective juror's bias in favor of the death penalty:

> As to general questions of fairness and impartiality, such jurors could in all truth and candor respond affirmatively, personally confident that such dogmatic views are fair and impartial, while leaving the specific concern unprobed. * * * It may be that a juror could, in good conscience, swear to uphold that law and yet be unaware that maintaining such dogmatic beliefs about the death penalty would prevent him or her from doing so. A defendant on trial for his life must be permitted on voir dire to ascertain whether his prospective jurors function under such misconception. The risk that such jurors may have been empaneled in this case and infected petitioner's capital sentencing is unacceptable in light of the ease with which that risk could have been minimized.

Justice Scalia, joined by Chief Justice Rehnquist and Justice Thomas, dissented, accusing the majority of ignoring the deferential standard of review of voir dire in state courts, established in cases such as *Mu'Min.* He concluded that "[t]aking appropriate account of the opportunity for the trial court to observe and evaluate the demeanor of the veniremen, I see no basis for concluding that its finding that the 12 jurors were impartial was manifestly erroneous."

Voir Dire and the Federal Supervisory Power

As indicated in *Mu'Min,* the regulation of voir dire under the federal supervisory power is more rigorous than that required by the Constitution. Generally speaking, individual voir dire of jurors has been required in three situations in the Federal courts—although trial judges have significant discretion as to how to frame the questions. These three situations are:

- where a case has racial overtones;
- where the case involves matters concerning which the local community is known to harbor strong feelings, that may stop short of a need for a change of venue but may nonetheless affect the trial—such as child abuse or narcotics distribution; and

- where testimony from law enforcement agents is important in the case and might be overvalued.

See generally United States v. Contreras-Castro, 825 F.2d 185 (9th Cir.1987), where the trial court's failure to inquire about a bias in favor of law enforcement officers was held reversible error because the government's entire case rested on the testimony of government agents.

4. Challenges for Cause

The scope of voir dire, discussed above, is intricately related to the possibility of challenging prospective jurors for cause. The argument for expansive voir dire is that counsel needs information in order to make challenges for cause possible and meaningful.

The cognizable, specific biases that permit a challenge for cause are defined by statute. The typical statute permits such a challenge where the juror is of unsound mind or lacks the qualifications required by law; is related to a party; has served in a related case or on the indicting grand jury; or "is unable or unwilling to hear the case at issue fairly or impartially." ABA Standards for Criminal Justice, Trial by Jury 15–2.5 (1993). See 28 U.S.C. § 1866 (district court may exclude any person summoned for jury service "on the ground that such person may be unable to render impartial jury service").

a. Jurors Who Cannot Be Excused for Cause

Willingness and Ability to Follow Instructions as to the Death Penalty: Witherspoon v. Illinois and Adams v. Texas

Usually the question is whether a person *must* be excused for cause. However, one line of cases focuses on when persons may not be so excused. In Witherspoon v. Illinois, 391 U.S. 510 (1968), a statute provided that the prosecutor could challenge a juror for cause if the prospective juror stated "that he has conscientious scruples against capital punishment, or that he is opposed to the same." At Witherspoon's trial 47 veniremen, referred to by the trial court as "conscientious objectors," were successfully challenged on the basis of their negative attitude toward the death penalty. These jurors were not asked whether their scruples would invariably compel them to vote against capital punishment. Justice Stewart, writing for the Court, found that Witherspoon's death sentence was invalid because "in its role as arbiter of the punishment to be imposed, this jury fell woefully short of that impartiality to which the petitioner was entitled under the Sixth and Fourteenth Amendments." Justice Stewart reasoned as follows:

> A man who opposes the death penalty, no less than one who favors it, can make the discretionary judgment entrusted to him by the State and can thus obey the oath he takes as a juror. But a jury from which

> all such men have been excluded cannot perform the task demanded of it. * * *
>
> If the State had excluded only those prospective jurors who stated in advance of trial that they would not even consider returning a verdict of death, it could argue the resulting jury was simply neutral with respect to the penalty. But when it swept from the jury all who expressed conscientious or religious scruples against capital punishment and all who opposed it in principle, the State crossed the line of neutrality. In its quest for a jury capable of imposing the death penalty, the State produced a jury uncommonly willing to condemn a man to die. * * *
>
> [W]e hold that a sentence of death cannot be carried out if the jury that imposed or recommended it was chosen by excluding veniremen for cause simply because they voiced general objections to the death penalty or expressed conscientious or religious scruples against its infliction.

The Court in *Witherspoon* emphasized the narrowness of its holding. It did not prohibit the State from impanelling a "death-qualified" jury. It simply prohibited the exclusion for cause of a juror who expresses reservations about the death penalty but states that these reservations would not preclude a vote for the death penalty in the proper case.

In Adams v. Texas, 448 U.S. 38 (1980), the Court addressed a bifurcated Texas procedure in capital cases, in which the jury first considered the question of the defendant's guilt or innocence, and after a finding of guilt, heard evidence about mitigation or aggravation. The jury was required by statute to answer three specific questions concerning (1) whether the defendant's conduct causing the death at issue was deliberate, (2) whether the defendant's conduct in the future would constitute a continuing threat to society, and (3) whether his conduct in killing the victim was unreasonable in response to the victim's provocation, if any. A "Yes" answer to all three questions required the court to impose a death sentence, while "No" to a single one of the questions would have resulted in a life sentence. The trial judge had excluded from the jury a number of prospective jurors who were unwilling or unable to take an oath that the mandatory penalty of death or life imprisonment would not "affect [their] deliberations on any issue of fact." The resulting jury answered "Yes" to all three questions, and the court imposed a death sentence.

Justice White's opinion for the Court found that the Texas procedure violated *Witherspoon*. He explained as follows: "[T]he touchstone of the inquiry * * * was not whether putative jurors could and would follow their instructions and answer the posited questions in the affirmative if they honestly believed the evidence warranted it beyond reasonable doubt. Rather, the touchstone was whether the fact that the imposition of the death penalty would follow automatically from affirmative answers to the questions would have any effect at all on the jurors' performance of their duties. Such a test could, and did, exclude jurors who stated that they would be 'affected' by the possibility of the death penalty, but who apparently meant only that the potentially lethal consequences of their decision would invest their deliberations with greater seriousness and gravity or would involve them emotionally."

Death-Qualified Juries and Guilty Verdicts: Lockhart v. McCree and Buchanan v. Kentucky

In *Witherspoon,* the Court invalidated the defendant's death sentence, but it did not reverse the guilty verdict. The Court rejected the defendant's argument that a "death-qualified" jury would be biased in favor of the prosecution and therefore more likely to convict the defendant at the guilt phase. The basis for this rejection was that Witherspoon's empirical evidence was tentative and sketchy. The defendant in Lockhart v. McCree, 476 U.S. 162 (1986), made a similar argument with updated empirical evidence, and met a similar fate. The Court held that the Constitution does not prohibit the removal for cause, prior to the guilt phase of a bifurcated trial, of prospective jurors whose opposition to the death penalty is so strong that it would prevent or substantially impair the performance of their duties as jurors at the sentencing phase of the trial.

Writing for the Court, Justice Rehnquist refused to find that a jury is biased as to guilt when it is "death qualified." Justice Rehnquist reasoned that an impartial jury is one that will conscientiously apply the law and find the facts, and there was no showing that any of the twelve jurors in the case under review was partial. Justice Rehnquist stated that the removal of "*Witherspoon*-excludables"—those whose views against the death penalty would cause them to disregard the judge's instructions and refuse to return a capital sentence—serves the proper interest of attaining a jury that could impartially decide all of the issues in a case.

Justice Marshall, joined by Justices Brennan and Stevens, dissented. He argued that "the Court upholds a practice that allows a State a special advantage in those prosecutions where the charges are the most serious and the possible punishments, the most severe." The advantage is that "[t]he State's mere announcement that it intends to seek the death penalty if the defendant is found guilty of a capital offense will give the prosecution a license to empanel a jury especially likely to return that very verdict." Justice Blackmun concurred in the judgment without opinion.

Relying on *McCree,* the Supreme Court held, in Buchanan v. Kentucky, 483 U.S. 402 (1987), that a defendant as to whom the capital portion of an indictment was dismissed was not denied an impartial jury when he was tried together with another defendant facing a capital charge, by a jury from which prospective jurors unalterably opposed to the death penalty were excluded. Justice Blackmun's opinion for the Court reasoned that "*McCree* requires rejection of petitioner's claim that 'death qualification' violated his right to a jury selected from a representative cross-section of the community." He added that the state had not excluded the jurors opposed to the death penalty for arbitrary reasons unrelated to their ability to serve as jurors. Finally, he concluded that the state's interest in a joint trial is as compelling an interest as that recognized in *McCree* as sufficient to justify exclusion of jurors.

Justice Marshall, joined by Justices Brennan and Stevens, argued in dissent that the additional costs to a state of implementing a system of separate juries, or of providing alternate jurors who would replace those who opposed the death penalty after the guilt determination had been made, are minimal in comparison to a defendant's interest in an impartial jury at the guilt determination stage.

Limitation on Witherspoon: Wainwright v. Witt

The Court limited the impact of *Witherspoon* in Wainwright v. Witt, 469 U.S. 412 (1985). One of the prospective jurors in Witt's capital murder trial indicated that personal beliefs concerning the death penalty would "interfere" with her judging the guilt or innocence of the defendant. That juror was excluded for cause and Witt argued that *Witherspoon* was violated because the juror did not state that she would *automatically* vote against the death penalty, nor that she would be prevented from making an impartial decision as to guilt. Justice Rehnquist, writing for the Court, stated that *Witherspoon* did not require a "ritualistic adherence" to a requirement that a prospective juror make it "unmistakably clear that he would automatically vote against the death penalty." Justice Rehnquist set forth the following standard for determining whether a juror could be excluded for cause due to a negative attitude about the death penalty:

> [The] standard is whether the juror's views would prevent or substantially impair the performance of his duties as a juror in accordance with his instructions and his oath. * * * What common sense should have realized experience has proved: many veniremen simply cannot be asked enough questions to reach the point where their bias has been made "unmistakably clear"; these veniremen may not know how they will react when faced with imposing the death sentence, or may be unable to articulate, or may wish to hide their true feelings. Despite this lack of clarity in the printed record, however, there will be situations where the trial judge is left with the definite impression that a prospective juror would be unable to faithfully and impartially apply the law. * * * [T]his is why deference must be paid to the trial judge who sees and hears the juror.

Justice Rehnquist concluded that, giving proper deference to the trial judge, the juror in Witt's case was properly excused for cause.

Justice Stevens concurred in the judgment. Justice Brennan, joined by Justice Marshall, dissented and argued that "the inevitable result of the quest for such purity in the jury room in a capital case is not a neutral jury drawn from a fair cross-section of the community but a jury biased against the defendant, at least with respect to penalty, and a jury from which an identifiable segment of the community has been excluded."

Trial Court Discretion to Strike Jurors to Maintain a Death-Qualified Jury: Uttecht v. Brown

In Uttecht v. Brown, 551 U.S. 1 (2007), a 5–4 majority of the Court held that a trial judge did not violate *Witherspoon* and its progeny by excusing a juror for cause. The majority emphasized the deference owed to a trial judge who is called upon to screen jurors to determine whether they will give fair consideration to the state's argument in favor of the death penalty. Justice Kennedy's majority opinion found that the Court's decisions established four relevant principles:

> First, a criminal defendant has the right to an impartial jury drawn from a venire that has not been tilted in favor of capital punishment by selective prosecutorial challenges for cause. * * * Second, the State has a strong interest in having jurors who are able to apply capital punishment within the framework state law prescribes. * * * Third, to balance these interests, a juror who is substantially impaired in his or her ability to impose the death penalty under the state-law framework can be excused for cause; but if the juror is not substantially impaired, removal for cause is impermissible. * * * Fourth, in determining whether the removal of a potential juror would vindicate the State's interest without violating the defendant's right, the trial court makes a judgment based in part on the demeanor of the juror, a judgment owed deference by reviewing courts.

Justice Kennedy summarized the problems with the one juror that the defendant thought was erroneously struck for cause:

> Juror Z was examined on the seventh day of the voir dire and the fifth day of the death-qualification phase. The State argues that Juror Z was impaired not by his general outlook on the death penalty, but rather by his position regarding the specific circumstances in which the death penalty would be appropriate. The transcript of Juror Z's questioning reveals that, despite the preceding instructions and information, he had both serious misunderstandings about his responsibility as a juror and an attitude toward capital punishment that could have prevented him from returning a death sentence under the facts of this case.

Justice Stevens, joined by Justices Souter, Ginsburg and Breyer, dissented and contended that the majority mischaracterized Juror Z's stated attitude toward the death penalty.

Justice Breyer, joined by Justice Souter, wrote a separate, short dissent.

Effect of a Witherspoon Violation: Gray v. Mississippi

The Court found a *Witherspoon* violation in Gray v. Mississippi, 481 U.S. 648 (1987), and rejected the argument that exclusion of the juror was harmless error. In *Gray*, the prosecutor essentially argued that a *Witherspoon* violation was harmless because he would have exercised a peremptory strike on the juror if she had not been (improperly) excused for cause. But Justice Blackmun concluded that "[t]he nature of the jury selection process defies any attempt to establish that an erroneous *Witherspoon-Witt* exclusion of a juror is harmless."

Justice Blackmun was concerned with the practical implications of the prosecutor's argument that a *Witherspoon* violation should be deemed harmless whenever the prosecutor has an unexercised peremptory challenge that she said she would have exercised on the juror improperly excused for cause:

> The practical result of this unexercised peremptory argument would be to insulate jury-selection error from meaningful appellate review. By simply stating during voir dire that the State is prepared to exercise a peremptory challenge if the court denies its motion for cause, a prosecutor would ensure that a reviewing court would consider any erroneous exclusion harmless.

Justice Scalia, joined by Chief Justice Rehnquist and Justices White and O'Connor, dissented in *Gray*.

b. Jurors Who Must Be Excused for Cause

Courts often face the question of whether a juror *must* be excused for cause. It is fair to state that judges vary in aggressiveness in striking jurors for cause. Generally, the judge has considerable discretion in these matters, because it is the judge who sees and hears the suspect juror, and who knows the impact that any problems with the juror will have on the case.

The most frequently invoked grounds for excusal for cause are: 1) bias; 2) taint from trial publicity; 3) preconceived notions inconsistent with a presumption of innocence; 4) inability or refusal to follow instructions from the court. But with respect to these and other grounds, the question is not only whether some disability exists but whether the prospective juror, despite the disability, can fairly assess the evidence.

The following cases illustrate the kinds of challenges for cause that are attempted.

a. The defendant was convicted on two counts of aggravated bank robbery and attempted bank robbery. The government's case indicated that the defendant participated in three bank robberies and engaged in a shootout with police at a residence. During the voir dire, one venireman stated he was "not interested in convicting anybody," and when asked if he would be prejudiced against conviction, he said there was a "reasonable doubt in my mind, [and] it would take an awful lot." He was removed for cause, over the defendant's objection. The trial court thereafter denied the defendant's two motions to strike for cause. One was directed at a juror who was a senior vice-president of another bank and had previously served on a grand jury. The other was directed at a juror whose daughter had been robbed and raped. Both jurors said they believed they could give the defendant a fair trial.[18] The appellate court sustained the trial court's rulings as to all three prospective jurors. United States v. Young, 553 F.2d 1132 (8th Cir.1977).

b. The defendant was convicted for robbery and sentenced to twelve years' imprisonment. During the trial court voir dire, the following exchange took place.

Mr. Pickard (Defense Counsel): Has anybody been robbed? Due to the fact that you have recently been robbed do you think you might be a little bit more inclined to convict regardless of the evidence?

Juror Spencer: Yes sir, I probably would.

Mr. Pickard: You think you may be a little biased?

Juror Spencer: Yes sir.

Mr. Pickard: You're saying in all probability you wouldn't be able to give him a fair trial and view the evidence objectively?

Juror Spencer: Yes sir.

Mr. Pickard: We challenge for cause.

The Court: In spite of your experience a couple of weeks ago, could you still listen to the evidence that comes from this witness stand, and this evidence alone, and render a fair and impartial decision concerning the defendant, Beauford Harold Johnson?

Juror Spencer: Yes sir, I believe I could.

---

[18] One commentator has suggested that "[c]ourts, feeling helpless before questions of human psychology, are unable to decide whether a person can be fair in spite of having an opinion on the matter at issue—thus the technique of 'just asking her.' Once having asked, however, the court cannot easily impugn the credibility of a citizen who has professed her impartiality." B. Babcock, Voir Dire: Preserving "Its Wonderful Power", 27 Stan.L.Rev. 545, 550 (1975).

The Court: You wouldn't let that experience that you had affect you?

Juror Spencer: No sir.

The Court: Challenge denied.

Juror Spencer became the foreman of the jury. (Emphasis added.)

The appellate court sustained the trial court's denial of challenge. Johnson v. State, 356 So.2d 769 (Ala.Cr.App.1978).

c. Is a juror who is a county commissioner and also a part-time deputy sheriff subject to a challenge for cause? See State v. Radi, 176 Mont. 451, 578 P.2d 1169 (1978) (statute does not permit challenge). How does a decision like this affect the impartial appearance of the jury? In Dennis v. United States, 339 U.S. 162 (1950), the Court held that where the government was a party in a litigation, jurors could not be excused for cause merely because they were government employees. The Court stated that actual bias must be shown. Should the result in *Dennis* have been affected by the fact that the defendant was charged with failure to comply with a subpoena issued by the House Un-American Activities Committee? Would jurors who are government employees be less impartial in cases where the substantive offense is a wrong done to the government itself?

d. The defendant was charged with cocaine distribution. During jury selection, the court asked the prospective jurors whether they or anyone to whom they were close had any experience with illegal drugs. Juror Camacho responded affirmatively. She said that her ex-husband, the father of her five-year-old daughter, had both used and dealt cocaine during their marriage. His involvement in cocaine was one of the reasons for their divorce. Upon questioning by the court, Camacho admitted that the experience was painful. The court, apparently concerned by her answers, asked Camacho three times whether she could put her personal experience aside and serve impartially. Each time, she responded "I'll try."

The trial judge denied the defendant's motion to strike Camacho for cause. But the Court of Appeals reversed. It reasoned as follows:

> Camacho was asked three times whether she could be fair, and each time she responded equivocally. Not *once* did she affirmatively state that she could or would serve fairly or impartially. * * *
>
> * * * When a juror is unable to state that she will serve fairly and impartially despite being asked repeatedly for such assurances, we can have no confidence that the juror will put aside her biases or her prejudicial personal experiences and render a fair and impartial verdict. Given Camacho's responses to the court's questions and the similarity between her traumatic familial experience and the defendant's alleged conduct, we conclude that the failure to excuse her for cause * * * requires reversal.

United States v. Gonzalez, 214 F.3d 1109 (9th Cir. 2000). What if Camacho responded to the court's inquiries by saying "I am pretty sure I can" rather than "I'll try"? Must she be excused for cause?

e. Is the trial judge permitted to disqualify a juror for cause during the *deliberations*? Fed.R.Crim.P. 23(b) provides: "After a jury has retired to deliberate, the court may permit a jury of 11 persons to return a verdict, even without a stipulation by the parties, if the court finds good cause to excuse a juror." See United States v. Ruggiero, 928 F.2d 1289 (2d Cir.1991) (proper to excuse juror during deliberations when it was disclosed that the juror had been threatened by associates of the defendant). If the juror seems to have no grasp of the facts during deliberations, should or must he be struck for cause? See also United States v. Geffrard, 87 F.3d 448 (11th Cir.1996) (trial judge acted properly in excusing a juror for cause during the deliberations and proceeding to verdict with 11 jurors; the juror wrote a note to the judge which stated that she could not convict the defendants because of her beliefs in Swedenborgianism). Shouldn't jurors presenting these problems during deliberations have been rooted out during the voir dire process? Does this tell you anything about the voir dire process?

Jurors Who Will Never Consider Mitigating Evidence in a Capital Case: Morgan v. Illinois

Under *Witherspoon* and its progeny, the State is not permitted to exclude jurors for cause merely because they are reluctant to impose the death penalty, but the State is permitted to exclude jurors whose views against the death penalty would lead them to disregard the judge's instructions in the capital phase. The question in Morgan v. Illinois, 504 U.S. 719 (1992), was the reverse of *Witherspoon:* whether a juror *must* be excluded for cause if he would automatically *impose* the death penalty without regard to mitigating circumstances. Justice White, writing for the majority, held that the defendant had a due process right to have a prospective juror excused for cause if the juror would impose death regardless of the mitigating circumstances. He concluded that while the prosecutor has the right to seek a "death-qualified" jury, the defendant has the right to seek a "life-qualified" jury to assure that all jurors are actually impartial.

Justice Scalia, joined by Chief Justice Rehnquist and Justice Thomas, dissented. Justice Scalia distinguished *Witherspoon* on the ground that under Illinois law, a finding of aggravating circumstances must be considered by the jury, whereas the consideration of mitigating evidence "is left up to the judgment of each juror." He therefore concluded that a *Witherspoon*-excludible—one who says he will never vote for the death penalty and thus that he will never consider aggravating factors—is "saying that he will not apply the law" whereas the juror who says he will not consider mitigating evidence "is not promising to be lawless, since there is no case in which he is by law *compelled* to find a mitigating fact sufficiently mitigating." Is this persuasive, or is there a difference between saying an impartial juror must be willing to consider all evidence and not automatically reject a mitigating fact and saying that a juror is not compelled to find a mitigating fact?

Error by Failure to Excuse for Cause, Corrected by a Peremptory Challenge: Ross v. Oklahoma and Martinez-Salazar v. United States

In Ross v. Oklahoma, 487 U.S. 81 (1988), the defendant in a capital case challenged a juror who stated that he would automatically vote for capital punishment. Under *Morgan,* supra, that juror had to be excluded for cause—but the trial judge refused to disqualify the juror. The defendant then exercised a peremptory challenge to get the juror off the panel. On appeal, the state conceded that the juror should have been disqualified, but argued that the defendant's use of one of his nine peremptory challenges rectified the trial court's error. The defendant responded that he ultimately exhausted all of his peremptories, and would have used the one that he expended due to the trial court's error to excuse another juror who ultimately sat on his panel.

Chief Justice Rehnquist, writing for the Court, concluded that Ross had not been denied an impartial jury because the juror who would have automatically imposed the death penalty was "removed from the jury as effectively as if the trial court excused him for cause." The Chief Justice rejected the argument that the loss of a peremptory challenge constitutes a violation of the right to be tried by an impartial jury, reasoning that "peremptory challenges are not of constitutional dimension." He declared that the state may deny peremptory challenges altogether, and that Oklahoma had properly qualified its grant of such challenges "by the requirement that the defendant must use those challenges to cure erroneous refusal by the trial court to excuse jurors for cause." He concluded that Ross made no claim that any of the jurors who convicted him and sentenced him to death was biased or partial, and that an error with respect to a juror who did not sit did not mandate reversal.

Justice Marshall, joined by Justices Brennan, Blackmun, and Stevens, wrote that "[a] man's life is at stake," and "[w]e should not be playing games."

In United States v. Martinez-Salazar, 528 U.S. 304 (2000), a prospective juror indicated that he would favor the prosecution; he assumed "people are on trial because they did something wrong", though he understood the presumption of innocence "in theory". The defendant moved to strike the juror for cause, but the trial judge refused. So the defendant exercised a peremptory challenge to strike the juror. Eventually he expended all his peremptories. On appeal, the parties agreed that the juror should have been struck for cause. The defendant claimed a violation of Fed.R.Crim.P. 24(b), under which the defense was entitled to 10 peremptory challenges. He argued that he did not receive his full complement of peremptories, because he was forced to expend a challenge on a juror who should have been struck for cause.

The Supreme Court, in an opinion by Justice Ginsburg, held that Rule 24(b) was not violated. She reasoned that the trial court's mistake did not force the defendant to expend a peremptory challenge. She stated that a "hard choice is not the same as no choice" and concluded as follows:

> After objecting to the District Court's denial of his for-cause challenge, Martinez-Salazar had the option of letting Gilbert sit on the petit jury and, upon conviction, pursuing a Sixth Amendment challenge on appeal. Instead, Martinez-Salazar elected to use a challenge to remove Gilbert because he did not want Gilbert to sit on his jury. This was Martinez-Salazar's choice. * * * In choosing to remove Gilbert rather than taking his chances on appeal, Martinez-Salazar did not lose a peremptory challenge. Rather, he used the challenge in line with a principal reason for peremptories: to help secure the constitutional guarantee of trial by an impartial jury.

Justice Ginsburg observed that it would have been a different matter if the trial court's ruling resulted in the seating of any juror who should have been dismissed for cause. Justice Souter wrote a short concurring opinion. Justice Scalia, joined by Justice Kennedy, wrote a short opinion concurring in the judgment.

5. The Use of Peremptory Challenges

a. *The Purpose and Function of the Peremptory Challenge*

The Supreme Court has described the peremptory challenge as follows:

> The essential nature of the peremptory challenge is that it is one exercised without a reason stated, without inquiry, and without being subject to the court's control. While challenges for cause permit rejection of jurors on a narrowly specified, provable and legally cognizable basis of partiality, the peremptory permits rejection for a real or imagined partiality that is less easily designated or demonstrable.

Swain v. Alabama, 380 U.S. 202 (1965). The Court in *Swain* stated that the peremptory challenge serves salutary purposes in the adversary system:

> The function of the challenge is not only to eliminate extremes of partiality on both sides, but to assure the parties that the jurors before

whom they try the case will decide on the basis of the evidence placed before them, and not otherwise. * * * Indeed the very availability of peremptories allows counsel to ascertain the possibility of bias through probing questions on the *voir dire* and facilitates the exercise of challenges for cause by removing the fear of incurring a juror's hostility through examination and challenge for cause.

Another purpose for the peremptory is to encourage a litigant to accept the jury and its decision because it belongs to him in a vivid sense: he picked it and was able to exclude those he feared. See Babcock, Voir Dire: Preserving "Its Wonderful Power," 27 Stan.L.Rev. 545, 552 (1975). Finally, as Ross v. Oklahoma, supra, points out, the peremptory challenge serves as a "safety valve" when the trial judge erroneously refuses to excuse a juror for cause. But as the Court also noted in *Ross*, there is no constitutional right to a peremptory challenge.

Voir Dire and the Peremptory Challenge

The relationship between peremptory challenges and voir dire should be apparent. In cases like Mu'Min v. Virginia, supra, the defendant argues that extensive voir dire is essential not only to determine whether a juror should be excluded for cause, but also to give defense counsel the information necessary to decide whether to expend a peremptory. As you go through the materials on peremptory challenges, see if the Court has been consistent in protecting peremptories at the same time as it has, in cases like *Mu'Min*, accepted trial court limitations of voir dire. Can limitations on voir dire be justified by the fact that there is no constitutional right to a peremptory challenge given that there is a right to challenge jurors for cause (especially partiality)?

Number of Peremptories

In felony cases, Fed.R.Crim.P. 24(b) gives all of the defendants together ten peremptory challenges (20 in capital cases) and the prosecution six. Most states allocate equal numbers of challenges to prosecutors and defendants. In multiple defendant cases, the court will allocate challenges to defendants if they cannot agree on how to use them. Fed.R.Crim.P. 24(b) states that in multiple defendant cases the court may allow the parties additional peremptory challenges and may allow the defendants to exercise those challenges "separately or jointly."

Procedure for Exercising Peremptories

There are several different procedural approaches to the exercise of peremptory challenges. Some jurisdictions use the strike system, in which the parties get to see the entire panel and to strike the least desirable (from their viewpoints) jurors first. Some use the challenge system, where a party will not be sure who will take the seat of a challenged juror. In some courts, once a juror is "passed" (that is, not struck) the juror remains. Other courts permit challenges to any member of the panel until challenges are exhausted.

b. Constitutional Limits on Peremptory Challenges

While the peremptory challenge ostensibly allows the litigant to exclude a prospective juror on any grounds, the Equal Protection Clause imposes some limits on this choice. In Swain v. Alabama, supra, the defendant argued that the prosecutor exercised peremptories to exclude African-Americans from serving on petit juries. The Court held that if this allegation could be proven, the prosecutor's action would violate the Equal Protection Clause. However, in the Court's view, such a violation could not be proven by the discriminatory use of peremptory challenges in a single case. Rather, the defendant would have to show that the prosecutor "in case after case, whatever the circumstances" was responsible for the removal of prospective jurors who survived challenges for cause "with the result that no Negroes ever serve on petit juries."

It should be apparent that the proof requirement set forth in *Swain* is all but impossible to meet. See People v. Wheeler, 22 Cal.3d 258, 148 Cal.Rptr. 890, 583 P.2d 748 (1978) (noting that data on such practices is inaccessible, and that at the time a peremptory is exercised, trial judges would be reluctant to allow a continuance for an investigation into a pattern of discrimination in other cases). Moreover, *Swain* did nothing to protect the first several victims of discrimination in the use of peremptories. As the court in *Wheeler* stated, "each and every defendant, not merely the last in this artificial sequence," ought to be entitled to the same constitutional protection.

The following case reconsiders *Swain* and finds that its proof requirements are too stringent. Consider whom the Court is trying to protect and the costs involved in this protection?

BATSON V. KENTUCKY

Supreme Court of the United States, 1986.
476 U.S. 79.

JUSTICE POWELL delivered the opinion of the Court.

This case requires us to reexamine that portion of Swain v. Alabama, 380 U.S. 202 (1965), concerning the evidentiary burden placed on a criminal defendant who claims that he has been denied equal protection through the State's use of peremptory challenges to exclude members of his race from the petit jury.

* * *

Petitioner, a black man, was indicted in Kentucky on charges of second-degree burglary and receipt of stolen goods. * * * The prosecutor used his peremptory challenges to strike all four black persons on the venire, and a jury composed only of white persons was selected. Defense counsel moved to discharge the jury before it was sworn on the ground that the prosecutor's removal of the black veniremen violated petitioner's rights under the * * * Fourteenth Amendment to equal protection of the laws. * * * The judge then denied petitioner's motion * * *.

The jury convicted petitioner on both counts. * * * The Supreme Court of Kentucky affirmed. * * * We granted certiorari, and now reverse.

* * *

In Swain v. Alabama, this Court recognized that a "State's purposeful or deliberate denial to Negroes on account of race of participation as jurors in the administration of justice violates the Equal Protection Clause." * * * We reaffirm the principle today.

* * *

Purposeful racial discrimination in selection of the venire violates a defendant's right to equal protection because it denies him the protection that a trial by jury is intended to secure. * * * The petit jury has occupied a central position in our system of justice by safeguarding a person accused of crime against the arbitrary exercise of power by prosecutor or judge. Duncan v. Louisiana. Those on the venire must be "indifferently chosen," to secure the defendant's right under the Fourteenth Amendment to "protection of life and liberty against race or color prejudice."

Racial discrimination in selection of jurors harms not only the accused whose life or liberty they are summoned to try. Competence to serve as a juror ultimately depends on an assessment of individual qualifications and ability impartially to consider evidence presented at a trial. A person's race simply "is unrelated to his fitness as a juror." * * * [B]y denying a person participation in jury service on account of his race, the State unconstitutionally discriminated against the excluded juror.

The harm from discriminatory jury selection extends beyond that inflicted on the defendant and the excluded juror to touch the entire community. Selection procedures that purposefully exclude black persons from juries undermine public confidence in the fairness of our system of justice. * * *

* * * While decisions of this Court have been concerned largely with discrimination during selection of the venire, the principles announced there also forbid discrimination on account of race in selection of the petit jury. Since the Fourteenth Amendment protects an accused throughout the

proceedings bringing him to justice, the State may not draw up its jury lists pursuant to neutral procedures but then resort to discrimination at "other stages in the selection process."

Accordingly, the component of the jury selection process at issue here, the State's privilege to strike individual jurors through peremptory challenges, is subject to the commands of the Equal Protection Clause. Although a prosecutor ordinarily is entitled to exercise permitted peremptory challenges "for any reason at all, as long as that reason is related to his view concerning the outcome" of the case to be tried, the Equal Protection Clause forbids the prosecutor to challenge potential jurors solely on account of their race or on the assumption that black jurors as a group will be unable impartially to consider the State's case against a black defendant.

* * *

A number of lower courts following the teaching of *Swain* reasoned that proof of repeated striking of blacks over a number of cases was necessary to establish a violation of the Equal Protection Clause. Since this interpretation of *Swain* has placed on defendants a crippling burden of proof, prosecutors' peremptory challenges are now largely immune from constitutional scrutiny. For reasons that follow, we reject this evidentiary formulation as inconsistent with standards that have been developed since *Swain* for assessing a prima facie case under the Equal Protection Clause.

[Justice Powell discusses and relies on general equal protection cases outside the peremptory challenge context].

[S]ince *Swain,* we have recognized that a black defendant alleging that members of his race have been impermissibly excluded from the venire may make out a prima facie case of purposeful discrimination by showing that the totality of the relevant facts gives rise to an inference of discriminatory purpose. Once the defendant makes the requisite showing, the burden shifts to the State to explain adequately the racial exclusion. The State cannot meet this burden on mere general assertions that its officials did not discriminate or that they properly performed their official duties. Rather, the State must demonstrate that "permissible racially neutral selection criteria and procedures have produced the monochromatic result."[a]

---

[a] Our decisions concerning "disparate treatment" under Title VII of the Civil Rights Act of 1964 have explained the operation of prima facie burden of proof rules. See McDonnell Douglas Corp. v. Green, 411 U.S. 792 (1973); Texas Dept. of Community Affairs v. Burdine, 450 U.S. 248 (1981); United States Postal Service Board of Governors v. Aikens, 460 U.S. 711 (1983). The party alleging that he has been the victim of intentional discrimination carries the ultimate burden of persuasion.

* * *

[T]his Court has recognized that a defendant may make a prima facie showing of purposeful racial discrimination in selection of the venire by relying solely on the facts concerning its selection *in his case*. * * * "A single invidiously discriminatory governmental act" is not "immunized by the absence of such discrimination in the making of other comparable decisions." For evidentiary requirements to dictate that "several must suffer discrimination" before one could object, would be inconsistent with the promise of equal protection to all.

* * *

The standards for assessing a prima facie case in the context of discriminatory selection of the venire * * * support our conclusion that a defendant may establish a prima facie case of purposeful discrimination in selection of the petit jury solely on evidence concerning the prosecutor's exercise of peremptory challenges at the defendant's trial. To establish such a case, the defendant first must show that he is a member of a cognizable racial group, and that the prosecutor has exercised peremptory challenges to remove from the venire members of the defendant's race. Second, the defendant is entitled to rely on the fact, as to which there can be no dispute, that peremptory challenges constitute a jury selection practice that permits "those to discriminate who are of a mind to discriminate." Finally, the defendant must show that these facts and any other relevant circumstances raise an inference that the prosecutor used that practice to exclude the veniremen from the petit jury on account of their race. This combination of factors in the empaneling of the petit jury, as in the selection of the venire, raises the necessary inference of purposeful discrimination.

In deciding whether the defendant has made the requisite showing, the trial court should consider all relevant circumstances. For example, a "pattern" of strikes against black jurors included in the particular venire might give rise to an inference of discrimination. Similarly, the prosecutor's questions and statements during *voir dire* examination and in exercising his challenges may support or refute an inference of discriminatory purpose. These examples are merely illustrative. We have confidence that trial judges, experienced in supervising *voir dire,* will be able to decide if the circumstances concerning the prosecutor's use of peremptory challenges creates a prima facie case of discrimination against black jurors.

Once the defendant makes a prima facie showing, the burden shifts to the State to come forward with a neutral explanation for challenging black jurors. Though this requirement imposes a limitation in some cases on the full peremptory character of the historic challenge, we emphasize that the prosecutor's explanation need not rise to the level justifying exercise of a challenge for cause. But the prosecutor may not rebut the defendant's prima facie case of discrimination by stating merely that he challenged jurors of the defendant's race on the assumption—or his intuitive judgment—that they would be partial to the defendant because of their shared race. * * * The core guarantee of equal protection, ensuring citizens that their State will not discriminate on account of race, would be meaningless were we to approve the exclusion of jurors on the basis of such assumptions, which arise solely from the jurors' race. Nor may the prosecutor rebut the defendant's case merely by denying that he had a discriminatory motive * * *. If these general assertions were accepted as rebutting a defendant's prima facie case, the Equal Protection Clause would be but a vain and illusory requirement. The prosecutor therefore must articulate a neutral explanation related to the particular case to be tried. The trial court then will have the duty to determine if the defendant has established purposeful discrimination.

* * *

In this case, petitioner made a timely objection to the prosecutor's removal of all black persons on the venire. Because the trial court flatly rejected the objection without requiring the prosecutor to give an explanation for his action, we remand this case for further proceedings. If the trial court decides that the facts establish, prima facie, purposeful discrimination and the prosecutor does not come forward with a neutral explanation for his action, our precedents require that petitioner's conviction be reversed.

[Justice White's concurring opinion is omitted].

JUSTICE MARSHALL, concurring.

I join JUSTICE POWELL'S eloquent opinion for the Court, which takes a historic step toward eliminating the shameful practice of racial discrimination in the selection of juries. The Court's opinion cogently explains the pernicious nature of the racially discriminatory use of peremptory challenges, and the repugnancy of such discrimination to the Equal Protection Clause. * * * I nonetheless write separately to express my views. The decision today will not end the racial discrimination that peremptories inject into the jury-selection process. That goal can be accomplished only by eliminating peremptory challenges entirely.

* * *

* * * Merely allowing defendants the opportunity to challenge the racially discriminatory use of peremptory challenges in individual cases will not end the illegitimate use of the peremptory challenge.

* * * First, defendants cannot attack the discriminatory use of peremptory challenges at all unless the challenges are so flagrant as to

establish a prima facie case. * * * [W]here only one or two black jurors survive the challenges for cause, the prosecutor need have no compunction about striking them from the jury because of their race. Prosecutors are left free to discriminate against blacks in jury selection provided that they hold that discrimination to an "acceptable" level.

Second, when a defendant can establish a prima facie case, trial courts face the difficult burden of assessing prosecutors' motives. Any prosecutor can easily assert facially neutral reasons for striking a juror, and trial courts are ill equipped to second-guess those reasons. How is the court to treat a prosecutor's statement that he struck a juror because the juror had a son about the same age as defendant, or seemed "uncommunicative," or "never cracked a smile" and, therefore "did not possess the sensitivities necessary to realistically look at the issues and decide the facts in this case"? If such easily generated explanations are sufficient to discharge the prosecutor's obligation to justify his strikes on nonracial grounds, then the protection erected by the Court today may be illusory.

Nor is outright prevarication by prosecutors the only danger here. * * * A prosecutor's own conscious or unconscious racism may lead him easily to the conclusion that a prospective black juror is "sullen," or "distant," a characterization that would not have come to his mind if a white juror had acted identically. A judge's own conscious or unconscious racism may lead him to accept such an explanation as well supported. * * * Even if all parties approach the Court's mandate with the best of conscious intentions, that mandate requires them to confront and overcome their own racism on all levels—a challenge I doubt all of them can meet. * * *

The inherent potential of peremptory challenges to distort the jury process by permitting the exclusion of jurors on racial grounds should ideally lead the Court to ban them entirely from the criminal justice system. * * *

Some authors have suggested that the courts should ban prosecutors' peremptories entirely, but should zealously guard the defendant's peremptory as "essential to the fairness of trial by jury," and "one of the most important of the rights secured to the accused." I would not find that an acceptable solution. Our criminal justice system requires not only freedom from any bias against the accused, but also from any prejudice against his prosecution. Between him and the state the scales are to be evenly held. We can maintain that balance, not by permitting both prosecutor and defendant to engage in racial discrimination in jury selection, but by banning the use of peremptory challenges by prosecutors and by allowing the States to eliminate the defendant's peremptories as well.

* * *

[The concurring opinion of Justice Stevens, joined by Justice Brennan, and the concurring opinion of Justice O'Connor, are omitted.]

CHIEF JUSTICE BURGER, joined by JUSTICE REHNQUIST, dissenting.

* * *

Our system permits two types of challenges: challenges for cause and peremptory challenges. Challenges for cause obviously have to be explained; by definition, peremptory challenges do not. * * * Analytically, there is no middle ground: A challenge either has to be explained or it does not. It is readily apparent, then, that to permit inquiry into the basis for a peremptory challenge would force the peremptory challenge to collapse into the challenge for cause. * * *

* * *

Today we mark the return of racial differentiation as the Court accepts a positive evil for a perceived one. Prosecutors and defense attorneys alike will build records in support of their claims that peremptory challenges have been exercised in a racially discriminatory fashion by asking jurors to state their racial background and national origin for the record, despite the fact that such questions may be offensive to some jurors and thus are not ordinarily asked on voir dire. This process is sure to tax even the most capable counsel and judges since determining whether a prima facie case has been established will require a continued monitoring and recording of the "group" composition of the panel present and prospective.

* * *

JUSTICE Rehnquist, with whom THE CHIEF JUSTICE joins, dissenting.

* * *

In my view, there is simply nothing "unequal" about the State's using its peremptory challenges to strike blacks from the jury in cases involving black defendants, so long as such challenges are also used to exclude whites in cases involving white defendants, Hispanics in cases involving Hispanic defendants, Asians in cases involving Asian defendants, and so on. This case-specific use of peremptory challenges by the State does not single out blacks, or members of any other race for that matter, for discriminatory treatment. Such use of peremptories is at best based upon seat-of-the-pants instincts, which are undoubtedly crudely stereotypical and may in many cases be hopelessly mistaken. But as long as they are applied across-the-board to jurors of all races and nationalities, I do not see—and the Court most certainly has not explained—how their use violates the Equal Protection Clause.

* * *

OPEN QUESTIONS LEFT BY BATSON

Batson left a number of open questions, including:

- Is *Batson* applicable only to exclusion of African-Americans?
- Does *Batson* apply to discriminatory use of peremptories by parties other than the prosecutor?
- Must the defendant be a member of the excluded group?
- How does a party establish a prima facie case of racial discrimination in the exercise of peremptories?
- What kind of neutral explanation, short of a challenge for cause, will suffice?

The Court has decided several cases in an attempt to answer some of these questions.

Exclusion of Hispanic Jurors

The Court in Hernandez v. New York, 500 U.S. 352 (1991), held, not surprisingly, that Hispanics also have a right under the Equal Protection Clause to be free from discrimination in jury selection.

Standing to Assert a Batson Violation: Powers v. Ohio

In Powers v. Ohio, 499 U.S. 400 (1991), the defendant, a white man, alleged that the prosecutor exercised peremptory challenges to exclude African-American jurors on the basis of race. Powers was not asserting that his own equal protection rights were violated. Rather, he asserted that the equal protection rights of the jurors excluded on racial grounds were violated. The question boiled down to one of standing. In a 7–2 decision, the Court held that Powers had standing to bring an equal protection claim on behalf of the excluded African-American jurors. The case was remanded to determine whether the prosecutor had in fact excluded African-Americans on the basis of race.

The majority opinion, written by Justice Kennedy, downplayed the numerous references in *Batson* to the racial identity between the defendant and the excused prospective juror. Justice Kennedy asserted that "*Batson* was designed to serve multiple ends, only one of which was to protect individual defendants from discrimination in the selection of jurors. * * *

Batson recognized that a prosecutor's discriminatory use of peremptory challenges harms the excluded jurors and the community at large."[19]

Justice Kennedy noted three requirements for third party standing, based on the Court's previous cases: (1) the litigant must have suffered an "injury in fact;" (2) the litigant must have a "close relation to the third party;" and (3) there must exist some hindrance to the third party's ability to protect his or her own interests.

As to the first requirement of injury in fact, Justice Kennedy argued that a criminal defendant suffers from exclusion of jurors of a different race because "racial discrimination in the selection of jurors casts doubt on the integrity of the judicial process * * * and places the fairness of a criminal proceeding in doubt."

As to the second requirement of a close relationship between the litigant and the third party, the Court stated that "the excluded juror and the criminal defendant have a common interest in eliminating racial discrimination from the courtroom. * * * The rejected juror may lose confidence in the court and its verdicts, as may the defendant if his or her objections cannot be heard." Justice Kennedy also asserted that "*voir dire* permits a party to establish a relation, if not a bond of trust, with the jurors."

Concerning the third requirement for third party standing, the majority found that it was very unlikely that the excluded prospective juror would assert his or her own equal protection rights. Justice Kennedy noted that the barriers to bringing an individual action are "daunting," and concluded that "the reality is that a juror dismissed because of his race probably will leave the courtroom possessing little incentive to set in motion the arduous process needed to vindicate his own rights."

Justice Scalia, joined by Chief Justice Rehnquist, filed a stinging dissent. Justice Scalia contended that the majority had misapplied the holding and reasoning of *Batson* and stated that:

> This case * * * involves not a clarification of *Batson,* but the creation of an additional, *ultra-Batson* departure from established law. * * * Notwithstanding history, precedent, and the significant benefits of the peremptory challenge system, it is intolerably offensive for the State to imprison a person on the basis of a conviction rendered by a jury from which members of that person's minority race were carefully excluded. I am unmoved, however, and I think most Americans would be, by this white defendant's complaint that he was sought to be tried by an all-white jury * * *."

---

[19] Does this mean that the community at large has a cause of action when prospective jurors are excluded on account of race? What if a defendant intentionally decides not to object to race-based strikes? Does the defendant waive the community's right to challenge exclusion?

Recall that in Holland v. Illinois, supra, the Court held that a white defendant could not challenge the exclusion of African-Americans from the petit jury under the fair cross-section requirement of the Sixth Amendment. After *Powers,* does *Holland* have any practical effect?

Peremptory Strikes by Private Litigants: Edmonson v. Leesville Concrete Co.

After *Powers,* the fact that the objecting party is not of the same race as the excluded juror is irrelevant. However, in *Powers,* the party exercising the peremptory challenge was a government actor. If the party exercising the peremptory is a *private* actor, the issue is whether the challenge, even if racially discriminatory, constitutes state action. In Edmonson v. Leesville Concrete Co., 500 U.S. 614 (1991), the Court held that a private litigant in a civil case may not use peremptory challenges to exclude jurors on account of race. Justice Kennedy, writing for six members of the Court, found the necessary state action in the trial judge's excusing of the juror once a peremptory challenge is exercised: "By enforcing a discriminatory peremptory challenge, the court has not only made itself a party to the biased act, but has elected to place its power, property and prestige behind the alleged discrimination."

Justice O'Connor, joined by Chief Justice Rehnquist and Justice Scalia, dissented. She asserted that "not everything that happens in a courtroom is state action" and that "the peremptory is, by design, an enclave of private action in a government-managed proceeding." She concluded that "it is antithetical to the nature of our adversarial process * * * to say that a private attorney acting on behalf of a private client represents the government for constitutional purposes."

Peremptory Challenges by Criminal Defense Counsel: Georgia v. McCollum

In Georgia v. McCollum, 505 U.S. 42 (1992), two white defendants were charged with assault and battery of two African-Americans. The incident had sparked racial conflict in the community. The prosecution moved to prohibit the defendants from using their peremptory strikes in a racially discriminatory manner. This motion was denied by the Georgia trial and appellate courts.

Justice Blackmun wrote for the majority and relied heavily on *Edmonson.* He first found that "a criminal defendant's exercise of peremptory challenges in a racially discriminatory manner inflicts the harms addressed by *Batson.*" He noted that regardless of who exercises the challenge, the harm to the excluded juror is the same, in that the juror is "subjected to open and public racial discrimination." He also noted that the need for public confidence in the judicial system, addressed by *Batson* and

Edmonson, is at stake when a criminal defendant exercises a peremptory challenge on racial grounds, and especially so in cases involving race-related crimes. On this point, he concluded as follows:

> Be it at the hands of the State or the defense, if a court allows jurors to be excluded because of group bias, it is a willing participant in a scheme that could only undermine the very foundation of our system of justice—our citizens' confidence in it.

On the question of state action, Justice Blackmun concluded that no matter who exercises the peremptory, "the perception and the reality in a criminal trial will be that the court has excused jurors based on race, an outcome that will be attributed to the State."

Justice Blackmun further relied on *Edmonson* and *Powers* to conclude that the prosecution had third-party standing to assert the equal protection rights of jurors excluded on racial grounds. On this point he concluded that "the State's relation to potential jurors in this case is closer than the relationships approved in *Powers* and *Edmonson*" because "[a]s the representative of all its citizens, the State is the logical and proper party to assert the invasion of the constitutional rights of the excluded jurors in a criminal trial."

Finally, Justice Blackmun concluded that prohibiting a defendant from exercising race-based peremptory challenges does not violate any constitutional or other right afforded to criminal defendants.

Chief Justice Rehnquist wrote a short concurring opinion, stating that while he disagreed with *Edmonson,* it "controls the disposition of this case."

Justice Thomas concurred in the judgment. Like the Chief Justice, he agreed that *Edmonson* logically prohibited the exercise of race-based challenges by a criminal defendant. Having not been on the Court when the previous cases were decided, however, he took the opportunity to express his "general dissatisfaction with our continuing attempts to use the Constitution to regulate peremptory challenges." He asserted that "black criminal defendants will rue the day that this Court ventured down this road that inexorably will lead to the elimination of peremptory strikes." In his view, the Court had inverted its priorities and had "exalted the right of citizens to sit on juries over the rights of the criminal defendant, even though it is the defendant, not the jurors, who faces imprisonment or even death."

Justice O'Connor dissented from what she termed "the remarkable conclusion that criminal defendants being prosecuted by the State act on behalf of their adversary when they exercise peremptory challenges during jury selection."

Justice Scalia dissented in a separate opinion. He agreed with the Chief Justice and Justice Thomas that *Edmonson* logically applied to the exercise of race-based peremptory challenges by a criminal defendant. However, he asserted that "a bad decision should not be followed logically to its illogical conclusion." He argued that the Court should not, in the interest of promoting race relations, "use the Constitution to destroy the ages-old right of criminal defendants to exercise peremptory challenges as they wish, to secure a jury that they consider fair."

QUESTIONS AFTER MCCOLLUM

Would the result in *McCollum* have been different if the defendant had been African-American, and had exercised race-based peremptory challenges against prospective white jurors? The NAACP filed an amicus brief in *McCollum,* which argued that "whether white defendants can use peremptory challenges to purge minority jurors presents quite different issues from whether a minority defendant can strike majority group jurors." In his separate opinion, Justice Thomas commented that while this issue "technically remains open, it is difficult to see how the result could be different if the defendants here were black." The courts have read *McCollum* to prohibit minority defendants from challenging majority jurors on racial grounds. See, e.g., State v. Knox, 609 So.2d 803 (La.1992) (relying on *McCollum*, the court holds that the State "may properly object to a minority criminal defendant's racially discriminatory exercise of peremptory challenges" and "require the defendant to assert a racially neutral explanation for the peremptory challenge").

Applying Batson Beyond Racial Exclusions: J.E.B. v. Alabama

In J.E.B. v. Alabama, 511 U.S. 127 (1994), the Court extended *Batson* and held that the Equal Protection Clause prohibits the exercise of a peremptory challenge on the basis of the gender of a prospective juror. The case involved a child support action brought by the State against a father. The State used 9 of its 10 strikes to remove male jurors; as a result, all the selected jurors were female. Justice Blackmun, writing for five members of the Court, applied the "heightened scrutiny" test that the Court ordinarily applies to gender-based classifications in other contexts. Justice Blackmun stated that under that test, the question was whether gender-based peremptory challenges "substantially further the State's legitimate interest in achieving a fair and impartial trial." He found that gender-based challenges could not meet this strict test, because there was no correlation between sex and impartiality.

Justice Blackmun rejected the State's argument that the Equal Protection Clause was not violated in this case because it was men, and not women, who were excluded in the action. He reasoned as follows:

> All persons, when granted the opportunity to serve on a jury, have the right not to be excluded summarily because of discriminatory and

> stereotypical presumptions that reflect and reinforce patterns of historical discrimination. Striking individuals on the assumption that they hold particular views simply because of their gender is practically a brand upon them, affixed by law, an assertion of their inferiority.

Justice Blackmun also found it irrelevant that women and men, unlike racial minorities, are found in such numbers in the jury pool that they are likely to be represented on the jury even if each side uses all of its peremptory challenges on one gender or another. He explained as follows:

> Because the right to nondiscriminatory jury selection procedures belongs to the potential jurors, as well as to the litigants, the possibility that members of both genders will get on the jury despite the intentional discrimination is beside the point. The exclusion of even one juror for impermissible reasons harms that juror and undermines public confidence in the fairness of the system.

Justice Blackmun concluded the majority opinion by contending that it was of limited scope:

> Our conclusion that litigants may not strike potential jurors solely on the basis of gender does not imply the elimination of all peremptory challenges. * * * Parties still may remove jurors whom they feel might be less acceptable than others on the panel; gender simply may not serve as a proxy for bias. * * * Even strikes based on characteristics that are disproportionately associated with one gender could be appropriate, absent a showing of pretext.

As an explanation of the last sentence in the above quote, Justice Blackmun wrote the following footnote:

> For example, challenging all persons who have had military experience would disproportionately affect men at this time, while challenging all persons employed as nurses would disproportionately affect women. Without a showing of pretext, however, these challenges may well not be unconstitutional, since they are not gender or race-based.

Justice O'Connor wrote a reluctant concurring opinion, reasoning that the Court's *Batson* jurisprudence led to a conclusion that gender-biased peremptory challenges are unconstitutional. But she emphasized that "[i]n extending *Batson* to gender we have added an additional burden to the state and federal trial process, taken a step closer to eliminating the peremptory challenge, and diminished the ability of litigants to act on sometimes accurate gender-based assumptions about juror attitudes."

Chief Justice Rehnquist wrote a dissenting opinion in *J.E.B.*, arguing that "there are sufficient differences between race and gender discrimination such that the principle of *Batson* should not be extended to peremptory challenges to potential jurors based on sex." He declared that the "two sexes differ, both biologically and, to a diminishing extent, in experience. It is not merely stereotyping to say that these differences may produce a difference in outlook which is brought to the jury room."

Justice Scalia also dissented in an opinion joined by the Chief Justice and Justice Thomas. He declared as follows:

> In order, it seems to me, not to eliminate any real denial of equal protection, but simply to pay conspicuous obeisance to the equality of the sexes, the Court imperils a practice [the peremptory challenge] that has been considered an essential part of fair jury trial since the dawn of the common law. The Constitution of the United States neither requires nor permits this vandalizing of our people's traditions.

Prima Facie Case of Discrimination

What exactly constitutes a prima facie case of discrimination under *Batson?* What if a litigant strikes three of six prospective African-American jurors? What if five of six are struck, but the litigant still has a peremptory to use and does not use it against the sixth African-American? Is it relevant that the litigant exercised peremptory challenges against non-minorities? How important are the questions asked or suggested by counsel on voir dire? See generally United States v. Esparsen, 930 F.2d 1461 (10th Cir.1991) (courts have looked to questions asked on voir dire; the answers given by those jurors who were struck as compared to those who were not struck; the number of challenges used on a certain group; whether members of the group actually sat on the jury; whether the litigant had unexpended peremptories; the rate at which members of the group were struck compared to the rate at which non-members were struck; and other factors particular to the case).

While no single factor is usually dispositive, a prima facie case of discrimination will ordinarily be found if the litigant strikes *all* prospective jurors belonging to a protected group. As the court in *Esparsen* put it, "the striking of a single juror will not always constitute a prima facie case, but when no members of a racial group remain because of that strike, it does."

For other examples of a prima facie case of discrimination in the use of peremptories, see Morse v. Hanks, 172 F.3d 983 (7th Cir.1999) (prima facie case of discrimination found where the prosecutor struck the only African-American venireman on the panel, and the voir dire was perfunctory, giving no indication of any other reason to exercise a peremptory challenge: "It might be different, we think, if the excused black juror had given an answer that would expose a clear basis for the state to want to remove him from the pool."); United States v. Hughes, 864 F.2d 78 (8th Cir.1988) (questioning on voir dire did not reveal sufficient independent reasons, other than race, for the striking of two African-

Americans). The court in *Hughes* also found it relevant that there had been frequent charges of systematic exclusion of African-Americans from juries in the judicial district.

More Likely than Not Is Too Stringent a Standard for a Prima Facie Case: Johnson v. California

In Johnson v. California, 545 U.S. 162 (2005), the Court struck down a state procedure because it imposed too strict an evidentiary requirement on a party seeking to establish a *Batson* violation. The case involved a prosecutor who was accused of violating the Equal Protection Clause by striking African-Americans from the venire. The California rule required the defendant to show at the stage where a prima facie case must be shown that it was more likely than not that the prosecutor's peremptory challenges, if unexplained, were based on impermissible group bias. Justice Kennedy, writing for the Court, explained why this standard was too stringent.

> The issue in this case * * * concerns the scope of the first of three steps this Court enumerated in *Batson*, which together guide trial courts' constitutional review of peremptory strikes. Those three *Batson* steps should by now be familiar. First, the defendant must make out a prima facie case by showing that the totality of the relevant facts gives rise to an inference of discriminatory purpose. Second, once the defendant has made out a prima facie case, the burden shifts to the State to explain adequately the racial exclusion by offering permissible race-neutral justifications for the strikes. Third, if a race-neutral explanation is tendered, the trial court must then decide whether the opponent of the strike has proved purposeful racial discrimination.
>
> The question before us is whether *Batson* permits California to require at step one that "the objector must show that it is more likely than not the other party's peremptory challenges, if unexplained, were based on impermissible group bias." [W]e conclude that California's "more likely than not" standard is an inappropriate yardstick by which to measure the sufficiency of a prima facie case.
>
> We begin with *Batson* itself, which on its own terms provides no support for California's rule. There, we held that a prima facie case of discrimination can be made out by offering a wide variety of evidence, so long as the sum of the proffered facts gives "rise to an inference of discriminatory purpose." * * *
>
> Thus, in describing the burden-shifting framework, we assumed in *Batson* that the trial judge would have the benefit of all relevant circumstances, including the prosecutor's explanation, before deciding whether it was more likely than not that the challenge was improperly motivated. We did not intend the first step to be so onerous that a

defendant would have to persuade the judge—on the basis of all the facts, some of which are impossible for the defendant to know with certainty—that the challenge was more likely than not the product of purposeful discrimination. Instead, a defendant satisfies the requirements of *Batson's* first step by producing evidence sufficient to permit the trial judge to draw an inference that discrimination has occurred.

Justice Breyer wrote a short concurring opinion in *Johnson*. Justice Thomas wrote a short dissenting opinion.

Neutral Explanations: Purkett v. Elem

A *Batson* violation is not found every time that prima facie proof of a discriminatory peremptory challenge is established. A prima facie case of discrimination merely requires the party exercising the peremptory to provide a neutral explanation. The Court emphasized the minimal nature of the neutral explanation requirement in Purkett v. Elem, 514 U.S. 765 (1995), a per curiam opinion joined by seven Justices.

The prosecutor in Elem's trial excluded two African-American jurors, and offered as an explanation that they had long unkempt hair, a mustache, and a goatee-type beard. The Court of Appeals, on review of the denial of Elem's habeas petition, ordered that the writ be granted because of a *Batson* violation. The Court of Appeals reasoned that a prosecutor must give some explanation for exclusion that might be related to the prospective juror's performance in the case. It found that the prosecutor's explanations had nothing to do with juror performance and therefore were pretextual.

But the Supreme Court reversed, reasoning that the Court of Appeals had not properly applied the three-step analysis required by *Batson*. The Court explained that after a prima facie case is made and the prosecutor offers a race-neutral justification for a challenge, the trial court must decide in the final step whether the opponent of the strike has proven racial discrimination. The Court found that the Court of Appeals had conflated the second and third steps, reasoned that "to say that a trial judge may choose to disbelieve a silly or superstitious reason at step 3 is quite different from saying that a trial judge must terminate the inquiry at step 2 when the race-neutral reason is silly or superstitious," and explained that "[t]he latter violates the principle that the ultimate burden of persuasion regarding racial motivation rests with, and never shifts from, the opponent of the strike."

Because the prosecutor's explanation in *Purkett* was neutral—in that long, unkempt hair and mustaches and goatees are not indicative of a particular race—the Court held that the state had met its obligation under the second step of *Batson*. The state court had concluded that Elem failed to prove purposeful racial discrimination, and the Court remanded to allow the lower federal court to determine, on habeas review, whether the state court's conclusion was fairly supported by the record.[20]

Justice Stevens, joined by Justice Breyer, dissented. He contended that the Court had watered down the race-neutral explanation requirement of *Batson* to the point where it had no meaning at all. He elaborated as follows:

> In my opinion, preoccupation with the niceties of a three-step analysis should not foreclose meaningful judicial review of prosecutorial explanations that are entirely unrelated to the case to be tried. * * * The Court's unnecessary tolerance of silly, fantastic, and implausible explanations, together with its assumption that there is a difference of constitutional magnitude between a statement that "I had a hunch about this juror based on his appearance," and "I challenged this juror because he had a mustache," demeans the importance of the values vindicated by our decision in *Batson.*

Neutral Explanations and Bilingual Jurors: Hernandez v. New York

In Hernandez v. New York, 500 U.S. 352 (1991), the defendant claimed that the prosecutor struck Latino jurors on account of race. The prosecutor did not wait for the trial court's ruling on whether a prima facie case of discrimination had been established. Rather, the prosecutor defended his strikes on the ground that the prospective jurors were bilingual and many witnesses would be Spanish-speaking; therefore he "was very uncertain that they would be able to listen and follow the interpreter." The prosecutor based his assertion on the answers given by the prospective jurors to whether they could accept the interpreter as the final arbiter of what was said by the Spanish-speaking witnesses. According to the prosecutor, the excluded prospective jurors "looked away from me and said with some hesitancy that they would try * * * to follow the interpreter." The trial court and the State appellate courts found that this explanation was race-neutral and sufficient to rebut the defendant's prima facie case. The Supreme Court agreed, but there was no majority opinion.

Justice Kennedy wrote an opinion joined by Chief Justice Rehnquist, Justice White, and Justice Souter. Justice Kennedy found that the prosecutor's explanation "rested neither on the intention to exclude Latino or bilingual jurors, nor on stereotypical assumptions about Latinos or bilinguals." According to Justice Kennedy, the prosecutor properly divided jurors into two potential classes: "those whose conduct during *voir dire*

---

[20] On remand, the court of appeals found no *Batson* violation, reasoning that the prosecutor proffered reasons for striking the juror that were facially race-neutral, and the defendant made no attempt to persuade the state trial court that the prosecutor's reasons for striking the juror were pretextual. Elem v. Purkett, 64 F.3d 1195 (8th Cir.1995).

would persuade him they might have difficulty in accepting the translator's rendition of Spanish-language testimony and those potential jurors who gave no reason for such doubt. Each category would include both Latinos and non-Latinos."

Justice Kennedy recognized that the prosecutor's criterion for exclusion would have a disparate impact on prospective Latino jurors, because they were more likely to be fluent in Spanish than non-Latino jurors. He responded, however, that while disparate impact was relevant in determining whether the prosecutor acted with discriminatory intent, "it will not be conclusive in the preliminary race-neutrality step of the *Batson* inquiry. * * * Unless the government actor adopted a criterion with the intent of causing the impact asserted, that impact itself does not violate the principle of race-neutrality. Nothing in the prosecutor's explanation shows that he chose to exclude jurors * * * *because* he wanted to prevent bilingual Latinos from serving on the jury."[21]

Justice Kennedy cautioned that his opinion did not imply that the prosecutor had untrammeled discretion to exclude bilingual jurors. He noted that the case would be different if the prosecutor had merely stated that he did not want Spanish-speaking jurors.

Justice O'Connor, joined by Justice Scalia, concurred in the judgment. She agreed with much of Justice Kennedy's opinion, but felt that the plurality went "farther than it needs to in assessing the constitutionality of the prosecutor's asserted justification for his peremptory strikes." According to Justice O'Connor, "if the trial court believes the prosecutor's nonracial justification, and that finding is not clearly erroneous, that is the end of the matter." Justice O'Connor stressed that disparate impact was no substitute for a finding of intentional discrimination.

Justice Stevens, joined by Justices Marshall and Blackmun, dissented in *Hernandez*. He argued that the prosecutor's explanation was insufficient to overcome the prima facie case of discrimination because, among other things, "the justification would inevitably result in a disproportionate disqualification of Spanish-speaking venirepersons." According to Justice Stevens "an explanation that is race-neutral on its face is nonetheless unacceptable if it is merely a proxy for a discriminatory practice."

What limitations are placed on a prosecutor's explanation for exercising peremptory challenges after *Hernandez* and *Purkett?* Will a prosecutor who is intentionally discriminating on the basis of race always be able to assert some credible race-neutral explanation? For examples of explanations found race-neutral, see Jordan v. Lefevre, 293 F.3d 587 (2d

---

[21] See also United States v. Uwaezhoke, 995 F.2d 388 (3d Cir.1993) (in a drug prosecution, the prosecutor gave a neutral explanation when he excluded an African-American juror on the ground that she lived in public housing in Newark, an area known for drugs and crime; exclusion was permissible even though the prosecutor's justification resulted in a disparate impact on African-Americans).

Cir. 2002) (race-neutral explanation found where African-American juror did not know the occupations or whereabouts of her children, and prosecutor explained that she lacked the common sense he was looking for in a juror; it was also permissible to exclude an African-American juror who lived with her mother, worked only part-time, and spent the rest of her time watching television; the prosecutor explained that she seemed to lack both maturity and experience in making important decisions); Stubbs v. Gomez, 189 F.3d 1099 (9th Cir. 1999) (prosecutor's reasons for striking African-American juror were race-neutral under *Batson*: the prosecutor felt that the juror's demeanor and lack of eye contact showed disinterest in being a juror, and she had no employment record); United States v. Nichols, 937 F.2d 1257 (7th Cir.1991) (neutral explanation found where the prospective juror was young and living with a man to whom she was not married); United States v. Biaggi, 853 F.2d 89 (2d Cir.1988) (*Batson* limits exclusion of Italian-Americans, but prosecutor gave neutral explanation for exclusion; prospective jurors had displayed angry, arrogant, or flippant demeanors).

Commentators have argued that the Court has rendered *Batson* a nullity, because any prosecutor can come up with a facially neutral explanation for what is really a race-based challenge. See Cavise, The *Batson* Doctrine: The Supreme Court's Utter Failure to Meet the Challenge of Discrimination in Jury Selection, 1999 Wis.L.Rev. 501; Charlow, Tolerating Deception and Discrimination After *Batson*, 50 Stan.L.Rev. 9 (1997).

Fact-Intensive Reviews of Peremptory Challenges: Snyder v. Louisiana, Foster v. Chapman, and Flowers v. Mississippi

In Snyder v. Louisiana, 552 U.S. 472 (2008), the Supreme Court engaged in an extensive review of the facts surrounding jury selection in a case in which Snyder was convicted of first-degree murder and sentenced to death. Justice Alito wrote the opinion of the Court and found "the trial court committed clear error in its ruling on a *Batson* objection."

Justice Alito found the prosecutor's explanation for challenging an African-American juror to be unpersuasive. The prosecutor claimed that he struck a college senior who was attempting to fulfill his student-teaching obligation because he looked nervous and as a student teacher he might not want to miss class and therefore might vote for a lesser verdict to avoid a penalty phase. Justice Alito noted that the trial judge never made a determination as to demeanor and found that the nervousness explanation warranted no deference. He found that the explanation that the juror might want to go home early was belied by the fact that the trial was expected to be short and the prosecutor accepted white jurors who disclosed conflicting obligations as serious as the challenged juror. Justice Thomas, joined by Justice Scalia dissented and objected to the Court's second-guessing the state courts.

In Foster v. Chatman, 578 U.S. 488 (2016), Chief Justice Roberts wrote for the Court as it reversed lower federal courts who denied habeas relief to an African-American defendant convicted and sentenced to death in Georgia for the sexual assault and murder of a 79-year-old woman. The prosecutor had stricken all four qualified African-American jurors. During post-conviction proceedings the defendant had obtained documents pursuant to the state Open Records Act. They revealed, among other things, that the prosecutors had highlighted the names of the Black jurors on the jury venire list; a prosecutor had indicated in a note that one of the Black jurors might be okay if they were forced to pick a Black juror; a typed list of the qualified jurors who remained after voir dire had an N next to all qualified Black jurors; and a handwritten document titled "definite NO's" listed all Black jurors and only one other. The Court examined in detail the prosecutors' "neutral" explanation for the strikes and found as to two of the stricken jurors that the strikes "were motivated in substantial part by discriminatory intent" and "the focus on race in the prosecution's file plainly demonstrates a concerted effort to keep black jurors off the jury." Justice Alito filed an opinion concurring in the judgment. Justice Thomas dissented and argued that the Supreme Court of Georgia had properly analyzed the strikes and found them to have been race-neutral.

In Flowers v. Mississippi, 139 S.Ct. 2228 (2019), Justice Kavanaugh wrote for the Court as it reversed a defendant's conviction for murdering four people. He described the tortured history of the case:

> Flowers allegedly murdered four people in Winona, Mississippi. Flowers is black. He has been tried six separate times before a jury for murder. The same lead prosecutor represented the State in all six trials. In the initial three trials, Flowers was convicted, but the Mississippi Supreme Court reversed each conviction. In the first trial, Flowers was convicted, but the Mississippi Supreme Court reversed the conviction due to "numerous instances of prosecutorial misconduct." In the second trial, the trial court found that the prosecutor discriminated on the basis of race in the peremptory challenge of a black juror. The trial court seated the black juror. Flowers was then convicted, but the Mississippi Supreme Court again reversed the conviction because of prosecutorial misconduct at trial. In the third trial, Flowers was convicted, but the Mississippi Supreme Court yet again reversed the conviction, this time because the court concluded that the prosecutor had again discriminated against black prospective jurors in the jury selection process. * * * The fourth and fifth trials of Flowers ended in mistrials due to hung juries. In his sixth trial, which is the one at issue here, Flowers was convicted. The State

struck five of the six black prospective jurors. On appeal, Flowers argued that the State again violated *Batson* in exercising peremptory strikes against black prospective jurors. In a divided 5-to-4 decision, the Mississippi Supreme Court affirmed the conviction.

Justice Kavanaugh summarized the reasons for reversal:

> Four critical facts, taken together, require reversal. First, in the six trials combined, the State employed its peremptory challenges to strike 41 of the 42 black prospective jurors that it could have struck * * * . Second, in the most recent trial, the sixth trial, the State exercised peremptory strikes against five of the six black prospective jurors. Third, at the sixth trial, in an apparent effort to find pretextual reasons to strike black prospective jurors, the State engaged in dramatically disparate questioning of black and white prospective jurors. Fourth, the State then struck at least one black prospective juror, Carolyn Wright, who was similarly situated to white prospective jurors who were not struck by the State.

Justice Alito concurred and wrote: "Were it not for the unique combinations of circumstances present here, I would have no trouble affirming the decision of the Supreme Court of Mississippi, which conscientiously applied the legal standards applicable in less unusual cases. But viewing the totality of the circumstances present here, I agree with the Court that petitioner's capital conviction cannot stand."

Justice Thomas, joined in large part by Justice Gorsuch, dissented.

c. *The Future of Peremptory Challenges*

Justice Breyer has argued, as had Justice Marshall in *Batson*, that peremptory challenges should be abolished. See Miller-El v. Dretke, 545 U.S. 231 (2005) (concurring opinion). Justice Breyer contends that *Batson's* legal test is fraught with difficulty:

> At *Batson*'s first step, litigants remain free to misuse peremptory challenges as long as the strikes fall *below* the prima facie threshold level. At *Batson*'s second step, prosecutors need only tender a neutral reason, not a "persuasive, or even plausible" one. And most importantly, at step three, *Batson* asks judges to engage in the awkward, sometime hopeless, task of second-guessing a prosecutor's instinctive judgment—the underlying basis for which may be invisible even to the prosecutor exercising the challenge. * * * In such circumstances, it may be impossible for trial courts to discern if a "seat-of-the-pants" peremptory challenge reflects a "seat-of-the-pants" racial stereotype.

Justice Breyer notes the extensive literature concluding that *Batson* has been ineffective in eradicating discrimination in peremptory challenges:

> Given the inevitably clumsy fit between any objectively measurable standard and the subjective decisionmaking at issue, I am not surprised to find studies and anecdotal reports suggesting that, despite *Batson*, the discriminatory use of peremptory challenges remains a problem. See, *e.g.*, Baldus, Woodworth, Zuckerman, Weiner, & Broffitt, The Use of Peremptory Challenges in Capital Murder Trials: A Legal and Empirical Analysis, 3 U. Pa. J. Const. L. 3, 52–53, 73, n. 197 (2001) (in 317 capital trials in Philadelphia between 1981 and 1997, prosecutors struck 51% of black jurors and 26% of nonblack jurors; defense counsel struck 26% of black jurors and 54% of nonblack jurors; and race-based uses of prosecutorial peremptories declined by only 2% after *Batson*); Rose, The Peremptory Challenge Accused of Race or Gender Discrimination? Some Data from One County, 23 Law and Human Behavior 695, 698–699 (1999) (in one North Carolina county, 71% of excused black jurors were removed by the prosecution; 81% of excused white jurors were removed by the defense).

Justice Breyer further contends that *Batson's* promise will never be implemented so long as lawyers are trained and encouraged to rely on stereotypes in exercising peremptory challenges. He described examples of this stereotyping:

> [Despite *Batson*] the use of race-and gender-based stereotypes in the jury-selection process seems better organized and more systematized than ever before. For example, one jury-selection guide counsels attorneys to perform a "demographic analysis" that assigns numerical points to characteristics such as age, occupation, and marital status—in addition to race as well as gender. See V. Starr & McCormick, Jury Selection 193–200 (3d ed. 2001). Thus, in a hypothetical dispute between a white landlord and an African-American tenant, the authors suggest awarding two points to an African-American venire member while subtracting one point from her white counterpart. * * * [A] bar journal article counsels lawyers to "rate" potential jurors "demographically (age, gender, marital status, etc.) and mark who would be under stereotypical circumstances [their] natural *enemies* and *allies*." Drake, The Art of Litigating: Deselecting Jurors Like the Pros, 34 Md. Bar J. 18, 22 (Mar.–Apr. 2001). * * * These examples reflect a professional effort to fulfill the lawyer's obligation to help his or her client. Nevertheless, the outcome in terms of jury selection is the same as it would be were the motive less benign. And as long as that is so, the law's antidiscrimination command and a peremptory jury-selection system that permits or encourages the use of stereotypes work at cross-purposes.

Justice Breyer concludes as follows:

> I recognize that peremptory challenges have a long historical pedigree. They may help to reassure a party of the fairness of the jury. But [i]f used to express stereotypical judgments about race, gender, religion, or national origin, peremptory challenges betray the jury's democratic origins and undermine its representative function. The "scientific" use of peremptory challenges may also contribute to public cynicism about the fairness of the jury system and its role in American government. And, of course, the right to a jury free of discriminatory taint is constitutionally protected—the right to use peremptory challenges is not. * * * In light of the considerations I have mentioned, I believe it necessary to reconsider *Batson*'s test and the peremptory challenge system as a whole.

Consider also Judge Gee's comments about *Batson,* which were made in dissent in the court of appeals decision in *Edmonson,* 860 F.2d 1308 (5th Cir.1988), the case in which the Court ultimately extended *Batson* to civil cases:

> What remains after [*Batson*] is not the peremptory challenge which our procedure has known for decades—or not one which can be freely exercised against all jurors in all cases, at any rate. Justice Marshall would dispense with strikes entirely, and perhaps this will be the final outcome. In this much at least he is surely correct, that we must go on or backward; to stay here is to rest content with a strange procedural creature indeed: a challenge for semi-cause, * * * a skewed and curious device, exercisable without giving reasons in some cases but not in others, all depending on race.

England abolished peremptory challenges in 1988, and Canada abolished them in 2019. Arizona became the first state to abolish peremptory challenges effective January 1, 2022. Two judges on the Arizona Court of Appeals successfully filed a petition with the Arizona Supreme Court asking it to end the use of peremptory challenges.

For a view in favor of peremptory challenges, at least when exercised by criminal defendants, see Goldwasser, Limiting the Criminal Defendant's Use of Peremptory Challenges: On Symmetry and the Jury in a Criminal Trial, 102 Harv.L.Rev. 808 (1989).

E. PRESERVING THE INTEGRITY OF JURY DELIBERATIONS

Many devices are employed to assure that the jury process works as smoothly and as fairly as possible. Sometimes, however, efforts to protect the jury's deliberation process are in tension with the rights of the defendant or the interest in judicial efficiency.

1. Anonymous Juries

Ordinarily, the names of jurors are made known to counsel and the defendant during the voir dire process. However, in some cases prosecutors make the argument that juror anonymity is required to preserve the integrity of deliberations. For example, in United States v. Barnes, 604 F.2d 121 (2d Cir.1979), a divided court approved the trial judge's decision to keep the names and addresses of jurors secret from counsel and to bar defense counsel from inquiring into the jurors' ethnic and religious backgrounds. The defendant was charged with being a drug kingpin and the government made a preliminary showing that the defendant engaged in acts of violence and intimidation. The trial judge permitted an inquiry of prospective jurors only as to their county and length of residence and certain family history. The limitations on voir dire were intended to protect the jurors from harassment and threats to themselves and their families. In United States v. Tutino, 883 F.2d 1125 (2d Cir.1989), the judge ordered that the jury would remain anonymous in a trial alleging a heroin distribution conspiracy, when presented with the following submission from the government:

> The government requested an anonymous jury for five reasons: (1) the defendants faced serious penalties, including substantial prison terms and a possible parole revocation, and, according to the government, were therefore likely to bribe or threaten the jury; (2) [defendant] Tutino had attempted to tamper with a jury in a prior trial; (3) [defendants] Tutino and Guarino were known associates of organized crime figures; (4) Tutino had a prior extortion conviction and Guarino and [defendant] Larca had prior narcotics convictions; and (5) the jury had to be protected from the media.

In affirming the decision to use an anonymous jury, the court of appeals noted that the trial court issued instructions regarding the presumption of innocence more than once. The court believed that "these instructions were carefully framed to avoid any risk that the anonymous procedures would appear extraordinary or reflect adversely on the defendants." Do you believe that *any* instructions would suffice to protect the presumption of innocence when a jury is anonymous? Isn't the jury bound to think that there is a good reason why their names are not going to be made public?

There are limits, however, to ordering juror anonymity. For example, in United States v. Sanchez, 74 F.3d 562 (5th Cir.1996), the defendant, a police officer, was charged with coercing prostitutes to engage in sex acts with him. The trial judge ordered that the jury remain anonymous, reasoning that "I don't think there's anything more frightening to the populace than having a rogue cop on their hands." The court of appeals reversed the conviction. It noted that 1) the defendant was not involved in organized crime; 2) there was no evidence that the defendant had ever attempted to interfere with the judicial process; and 3) there was no indication that the case would receive extensive publicity that would enhance the possibility that the jurors' names would become public and expose them to intimidation or harassment. The court emphasized that anonymous juries are an extraordinary remedy that could only be used as a device of last resort. See also United States v. Wecht, 537 F.3d 222 (3rd Cir. 2008) (withholding names of jurors was error where the only unusual factor about the case was the local prominence of the defendant).

The *Sanchez* court held that the impermissible use of an anonymous jury can never be harmless and explained as follows:

> The defendant has a right to a jury of known individuals not just because information such as was redacted here yields valuable clues for purposes of jury selection, but also because the verdict is both personalized and personified when rendered by 12 known fellow citizens. [Unless strong factors supporting anonymity exist, the defendant] should receive a verdict not from anonymous decisionmakers, but from people he can name as responsible for their actions.

2. Protecting Against Judicial Influence on Jury Deliberations

Once the jury retires to deliberate, there is good reason to be concerned about any further contact with the judge.

Breaking a Deadlock: The Allen Charge

Assume that a jury has been deliberating for a day when it reports back that it is deadlocked. One possibility for the judge at this point is to consider granting a mistrial; but either or both parties might object to a mistrial for their own strategic reasons, and the judge is likely to be concerned about the substantial cost of a retrial. Therefore, the trial judge may want to encourage the jury to deliberate further in the hope of reaching a verdict. But just what should the judge tell the jury at this point? One jury charge was considered in Allen v. United States, 164 U.S. 492 (1896), and is commonly referred to as the "Allen charge" or the "dynamite" charge. The instruction provides as follows:

> In a large proportion of cases absolute certainty cannot be expected. Although your verdict must be the verdict of each of you individually and not a mere acquiescence in the conclusion of your fellows, yet you should examine the question submitted with candor and with a proper regard for and deference to the opinions of each other. It is your duty to decide the case if you can conscientiously do so. You should listen, with a disposition to be convinced, to each other's arguments. If much the larger number are for conviction, a dissenting juror should

consider whether his doubts are reasonable ones when they make no impression upon the minds of so many others, equally honest and equally intelligent. If, upon the other hand, the majority is for acquittal, the minority ought to ask themselves whether they might not reasonably doubt the correctness of a judgment which was not concurred in by the majority.

The concern with an *Allen*-type charge is that it will *coerce* the minority into agreeing with the majority, simply to reach a verdict. See, e.g., United States v. Robinson, 953 F.2d 433 (8th Cir.1992) (impermissible coercion where judge implied that deadlock would be wasteful and unpatriotic, and instructed the minority to give special consideration to the majority's position).

To limit the possibility of coercion, courts have generally required an *Allen* charge to include the following:

1) a recognition that a majority of jurors may favor acquittal;

2) a reminder that the government has the burden of proof beyond a reasonable doubt;

3) a statement that both the majority and the minority should reexamine their views;

4) a statement that no juror should abandon his or her conscientiously held view; and

5) a statement that the jury is free to deliberate as long as necessary.

These propositions go beyond the charge given in *Allen* itself, reproduced above. An instruction containing these five propositions is referred to as a "modified *Allen* charge." See United States v. Webb, 816 F.2d 1263 (8th Cir.1987) (finding reversible error where an *Allen* charge did not contain these five elements).

Courts have cautioned against an instruction that refers to the costs of a retrial, as this might pressure jurors to dispense with honestly-held views. United States v. Clinton, 338 F.3d 483 (6th Cir. 2003) (cautioning against such a statement, but noting that it didn't render the charge "coercive per se"). But courts have permitted an instruction stating that if the case is tried again "there is no reason to believe that any new evidence will be presented, or that the next twelve jurors will be any more conscientious or impartial than you are." See, e.g., Sixth Circuit Pattern Jury Instruction 9.04. Courts have generally not required the trial judge to instruct the jury that it is free to hang, i.e., that a deadlock is an acceptable resolution. United States v. Arpan, 887 F.2d 873 (8th Cir.1989) (en banc).

Even if a coercive deadlock charge is given, it does not necessarily mean that the verdict is tainted. Whether a coercive charge actually affected the jury depends on the circumstances. Thus, in United States v.

Ajiboye, 961 F.2d 892 (9th Cir.1992), the judge gave a deadlock instruction that did not include all the protective elements of a modified *Allen* charge. The defendant was tried on two counts, and the jury was deadlocked 9–3 for acquittal on one count and 9–3 for conviction on the other. After receiving the charge, the jury deliberated for two more days, and asked to review some of the evidence. The jury then returned a guilty verdict on both counts. The court found that the *Allen* charge did not coerce the jury into rendering guilty verdicts. Does the fact that the jury deliberated for two days after hearing the charge signify that it was not coercive? Would reversal have been likely if the jury deliberated only two hours after receiving the charge?

Successive Allen Charges

Some courts have found reversible error when the trial judge gives successive *Allen* charges—i.e., the jury reports a deadlock, a deadlock charge is given, the jury comes back deadlocked again, and the judge gives another deadlock charge. The concern is that the dissenting jurors are being worn down, and are getting the message that they will never be able to leave so long as they are deadlocked. This concern exists even if the charge contains the ameliorative language of a modified *Allen* charge. See United States v. Seawell, 550 F.2d 1159 (9th Cir.1977) (reversible error when successive *Allen* charges are given). However, even multiple *Allen* charges may be permissible, depending on the circumstances. Thus, in United States v. Nickell, 883 F.2d 824 (9th Cir.1989), the judge gave one modified *Allen* charge on Friday immediately before the jurors recessed for the weekend, and another when they resumed deliberations on Monday. The court found no error given that there were no deliberations between the two charges. See also United States v. Ruggiero, 928 F.2d 1289 (2d Cir.1991) ("we do not regard a repeated *Allen* charge as inevitably coercive").

Capital Punishment and the Allen Charge

The Supreme Court held, 5–3, in Lowenfield v. Phelps, 484 U.S. 231 (1988), that the trial judge did not act improperly in a capital case in giving a modified *Allen* charge during the sentencing phase of the case. When the jury indicated to the trial judge that it was unable to reach a decision on sentence, the judge gave each juror a piece of paper and asked each to indicate whether further deliberations would be helpful in obtaining a verdict. Eight jurors initially answered affirmatively, and three others subsequently indicated that they had misunderstood the question. The judge then asked each to indicate whether further deliberations would enable the jury to reach a verdict, and eleven jurors responded affirmatively. At this point, the judge told the jurors that they should consider each other's views with the objective of reaching a verdict without surrendering their honest beliefs in doing so, and that the court would impose a sentence of life imprisonment without possibility of probation, parole, or suspension of sentence if the jury failed to agree on a sanction. Shortly thereafter, the jury voted for the death penalty.

Chief Justice Rehnquist's majority opinion reasoned that the trial judge had not coerced the jury into reaching a decision and distinguished Brasfield v. United States, 272 U.S. 448 (1926), in which the Court had invoked its supervisory powers to condemn judicial inquiry into the numerical division of jurors. The Court also distinguished Jenkins v. United States, 380 U.S. 445 (1965), where the trial judge told the jury that "you have got to reach a decision in this case." Justice Marshall, joined by Justices Brennan and Stevens, dissented and argued that the two polls of the jury whittled the minority jurors from four to one. He condemned the fact that in the instant case, as in *Brasfield,* the jurors were asked to identify themselves by name in the polls. He also expressed doubts as to the wisdom of the *Allen* charge, especially in a case in which a hung jury would produce a life sentence rather than a new proceeding, and therefore the costs of a deadlock were not so substantial.

3. Protecting Against Jury Misconduct and Outside Influence

The conduct of individual jurors during the trial proceedings and deliberations must comport with the requirement of impartiality. The trial judge must deal with any particular action that could undermine a juror's impartiality. So for example, when jurors are exposed to highly inflammatory information that will not be brought out in evidence, and they can no longer remain impartial, they should be disqualified. See, e.g., United States v. Martinez, 14 F.3d 543 (11th Cir.1994) (juror saw newscast); People v. Honeycutt, 20 Cal.3d 150, 141 Cal.Rptr. 698, 570 P.2d 1050 (1977) (information and advice from an attorney friend of the foreman was prejudicial.) Even if the juror is adversely affected by events outside her control, she may have to be excused. See, e.g., United States v. Angulo, 4 F.3d 843 (9th Cir.1993) (juror excused after receiving threatening phone call).

Additionally, a juror must remain able and qualified to perform his duty. See United States v. Smith, 550 F.2d 277 (5th Cir.1977) (sleeping juror and juror whose conduct suggests that tampering has occurred are disqualified). Of course, the trial judge must be careful not to excuse a juror too quickly, and to excuse jurors in a way that does not prejudice either of the parties. See, e.g., United States v. Hernandez, 862 F.2d 17 (2d Cir.1988) (finding error in the trial court's decision to dismiss a juror where "the record seemed to reflect that the cause of the removal was as much to avoid a mistrial because of a hung jury as to excuse an incompetent juror").

The trial court has discretion in determining whether some development that might affect a juror is so substantial that a juror can no longer remain impartial. Thus, in Smith v. Phillips, 455 U.S. 209 (1982), the prosecutor learned during the trial that one juror's employment application was pending in his office, and the prosecutor did not disclose this fact to the court or the defense until after the jury returned its guilty verdict. The Supreme Court held that this development did not require a new trial under the circumstances. The Court observed that due process does not require a new trial every time a juror is placed in a potentially compromising situation The trial judge conducted a post-trial hearing and found that the juror was not actually biased, and this finding was entitled to deference, especially on habeas review.

Sequestration

During the course of trial, the judge has discretion to sequester the jury, i.e., to confine them, regulate access to media, prevent them from going home, etc. Some jurisdictions require sequestration, unless it is waived by the parties. See N.Y.C.P.L. § 310.10.

One famous trial lawyer believes that sequestration is usually prejudicial to the defendant:

> Every trial lawyer knows that a sequestered jury behaves radically differently from one whose members can go home at night. The jurors react to confinement with resentment. Sometimes they resent their captors. More often, they come to identify with the cops who are guarding them. And as the trial wears on, and the defense case threatens to lengthen their confinement, jurors begin to look at defense counsel with baleful eyes.

Tigar, Television and the Jury, Nat'l L.J., Aug. 21, 1995, p. A19.

Sequestration is ordinarily a response to the risk of prejudicial trial publicity. Is there a less onerous means of protecting the jurors from hearing about extrajudicial information? Would court orders preventing the jurors from reading newspapers, watching television, and accessing the internet be sufficient? Can we trust the jurors to close their eyes and ears and laptops if they are not sequestered?

Sequestration During Deliberations

It is more likely that a judge will exercise her discretion to sequester the jury once deliberations begin. The court in Hunley v. Godinez, 975 F.2d 316 (7th Cir.1992), considered a unique problem that arose with a jury that was sequestered during deliberations. The defendant was charged with murder and burglary, the prosecution contending that the murder occurred when the defendant was discovered by the victim while burgling her apartment. After the first day of deliberations, the jury stood 8 to 4 in favor of conviction. The jurors were then sequestered overnight in a hotel. That night, a burglar made an unforced entry into the rooms of four jurors, and stole several items. The jurors talked about the burglary among themselves the next day. The jury reached a guilty verdict after one hour of deliberation that day. Two of the four jurors who changed their minds from the previous day had been victims of the burglary. The trial judge held an in camera hearing, and each of the jurors said that the burglary had not affected their verdict. Nonetheless, the court of appeals reversed the conviction. It reasoned that "[t]he burglary placed the jurors in the shoes of the victim just before she was murdered." Obviously, the trial judge could not have prevented the burglary. Once it occurred, was there anything the judge could have done to assure fair deliberations? For example, would it have been sufficient if the judge permitted the jurors to take a day or two off and go home before returning to resume deliberations?

Ex Parte Communications with the Jury

In Rushen v. Spain, 464 U.S. 114 (1983), the Court denied relief to a petitioner who complained about ex parte communications between a trial judge and a juror. The juror had indicated to the judge that she was an acquaintance of a woman who had been murdered by one of the defense witnesses, although she expressed the view that she could be fair to the defendants. The lower courts had reasoned that the contact between judge and juror could not be deemed harmless, because no contemporaneous record had been made. But the Supreme Court ruled that the lower federal courts should have deferred to the "presumptively correct" state court finding that the jury's deliberations had not been affected by the ex parte contact. See also United States v. Strickland, 935 F.2d 822 (7th Cir.1991) (a juror acted improperly when he asked a question of a government witness outside of court; but this was not prejudicial because the witness did not answer, curative instructions were given, and the trial judge determined after questioning that the juror could remain impartial).

Evidentiary Limitations on Proof of Jury Misconduct: Tanner v. United States

The Supreme Court held, 5–4, in Tanner v. United States, 483 U.S. 107 (1987), that two defendants were properly denied a hearing concerning juror misconduct. The defendants called to the trial judge's attention one juror's statement that several jurors had consumed alcohol at lunch throughout the trial, causing them to sleep during the afternoons. The only other evidence offered in the trial court in support of a hearing was defense counsel's testimony that he had observed one of the jurors "in a sort of giggly mood" during the trial, something not called to the judge's attention.

While the case was pending on appeal, the defendants presented a second juror's affidavit indicating that numerous members of the jury, including the affiant, consumed alcohol during the trial and some jurors used illegal drugs.

Writing for the majority in *Tanner*, Justice O'Connor relied upon Rule 606(b) of the Federal Rules of Evidence, which generally prohibits an inquiry into the course of the jury's deliberations. Rule 606(b) does permit proof of "extraneous prejudicial information" that was brought to the jury's attention, and it also permits proof that an "outside influence was improperly brought to bear upon any juror." But Justice O'Connor declared that these exceptions did not apply to allegations of substance abuse by the jurors—rather, these exceptions covered matters such as threats or bribes to jurors from *outside sources*, or exposure to prejudicial trial publicity. Justice O'Connor also rejected the argument that the failure to inquire into juror intoxication denies a defendant a fair trial before an impartial and competent jury, reasoning that other aspects of the trial process—voir dire of jurors, observations by the trial judge and courtroom participants, and observations and reports by fellow jurors—are adequate to assure defendants fair trials.

Justice O'Connor expressed concern that routine impeachment of jury verdicts, by inquiring into what went on in the deliberations, would have a negative effect on finality and on the free flow of communications between jurors during deliberations.

Justice Marshall, joined by Justices Brennan, Blackmun, and Stevens, dissented. He concluded that "[e]very criminal defendant has a constitutional right to be tried by competent jurors," and that "[i]f, as charged, members of petitioners' jury were intoxicated as a result of their use of drugs and alcohol to the point of sleeping through material portions of the trial, the verdict in this case must be set aside." He concluded that voir dire of jurors prior to trial cannot disclose whether they will use drugs during the trial, and the type of misconduct alleged would not have been easily verified by courtroom personnel.

Examples of alleged jury misconduct that have been held immune from inquiry under Rule 606(b) after *Tanner* include:

- intimidation of one juror by another (United States v. Stansfield, 101 F.3d 909 (3d Cir.1996));
- unfair inferences drawn from the evidence (United States v. DiSalvo, 34 F.3d 1204 (3d Cir.1994));
- assumptions that if the defendant failed to take the stand, he must be guilty (United States v. Voigt, 877 F.2d 1465 (10th Cir.1989));

- a vote for conviction because extended deliberation would cut into the juror's vacation (United States v. Murphy, 836 F.2d 248 (6th Cir.1988)).

The court in United States v. Ruggiero, 56 F.3d 647, 652 (5th Cir.1995), summed it up by stating that Rule 606(b) bars juror testimony on "at least four topics: (1) the methods or arguments of the jury's deliberations, (2) the effect of any particular thing upon an outcome in the deliberations, (3) the mindset or emotions of any juror during deliberations, and (4) the testifying juror's own mental process during deliberations." See also United States v. Benally, 546 F.3d 1230 (10th Cir. 2008) (statements made by jurors during deliberations, indicating racial bias against the defendant, may not be introduced into evidence under the terms of Rule 606(b)).

But in Pena-Rodriguez v. Colorado, 137 S.Ct. 855 (2017), the Court found that an exception to the bar imposed by Rule 606(b) was required by the Sixth Amendment. The case involved racist statements made by a juror during deliberations: a juror stated that the defendant, a Hispanic, was likely to be guilty of the crime charged (accosting two women) because that was how Hispanic men acted. The Court held that applying Rule 606(b) to exclude a juror's statement about these racist comments violated the defendant's Sixth Amendment right to a fair trial. Justice Kennedy, writing for the Court, ruled as follows:

> [W]here a juror makes a clear statement that indicates he or she relied on racial stereotypes or animus to convict a criminal defendant, the Sixth Amendment requires that the no-impeachment rule give way in order to permit the trial court to consider the evidence of the juror's statement and any resulting denial of the jury trial guarantee.

Justice Kennedy emphasized, however, that "[n]ot every offhand comment indicating racial bias or hostility will justify setting aside the no-impeachment bar to allow further judicial inquiry. For the inquiry to proceed, there must be a showing that one or more jurors made statements exhibiting overt racial bias that cast serious doubt on the fairness and impartiality of the jury's deliberations and resulting verdict. To qualify, the statement must tend to show that racial animus was a significant motivating factor in the juror's vote to convict."

Justice Alito, joined by Chief Justice Roberts and Justice Thomas, dissented in *Pena-Rodriguez.* He argued that the majority's rule would undermine the finality of verdicts, that the rule could be expanded to allow proof of other forms of bias, and that the question of exceptions to Rule 606(b) is better left to rulemakers.

Lies on Voir Dire

Tanner states that the voir dire process is preferable to post-conviction review for determining whether jurors are competent and impartial. But what if the witness lies at the voir dire? In United States v. Colombo, 869 F.2d 149 (2d Cir.1989), the defendant submitted a post-conviction affidavit from an alternate juror, averring that a juror deliberately failed to reveal on voir dire that her brother-in-law was an attorney for the government. Her motivation for concealment was that she thought it would hurt her chances to sit on the case. The court held that if it could be shown that the juror's brother-in-law was a government attorney, "the conviction cannot stand, because such conduct obstructed the voir dire and indicated an impermissible partiality on the juror's part." The court rejected as irrelevant the argument that merely having a government attorney as a brother-in-law would not have been enough to challenge the juror for cause.

> The point is not that her relationship with her brother-in-law tainted the proceedings but that her willingness to lie about it exhibited an interest strongly suggesting partiality. * * * [C]ourts cannot administer justice in circumstances in which a juror can commit a federal crime in order to serve as a juror in a criminal case and do so with no fear of sanction so long as a conviction results.

See also Dyer v. Calderon, 151 F.3d 970 (9th Cir.1998) (en banc) (conviction must be reversed where juror lies in answering voir dire question as to whether a family member had ever been a victim of a crime: "[T]here is a fine line between being willing to serve and being anxious, between accepting the grave responsibility for passing judgment on a human life and being so eager that you court perjury to avoid being struck. The individual who lies in order to improve his chances of serving has too much of a stake in the matter to be considered indifferent.").

Should a conviction be automatically reversed whenever it is discovered that the juror told a lie on voir dire? See United States v. Langford, 990 F.2d 65 (2d Cir.1993), where a juror failed to admit that she had been arrested three times for prostitution fifteen years earlier. At the time of voir dire, the juror worked as a mental health assistant, had just taken a test to be a nurse, had a six-year-old daughter, and taught Sunday School. The court found that the juror had deliberately lied, but that her motivation was embarrassment. Unlike the juror in *Colombo*, she "had no interest in being on that particular jury." Accordingly, the defendant suffered no prejudice.

In Warger v. Shauers, 574 U.S. 40 (2014), the Court held that the fact that a juror lied during voir dire cannot be proved by comparing what she said during deliberations with what she said during voir dire. Rule 606(b), discussed *supra,* barred evidence of juror deliberations for this purpose. The case involved a crash involving a motorcycle and a truck after which the motorcycle rider sued the driver of the truck. During an extensive voir dire, all of the jurors, including the juror who became foreperson, claimed that they could be fair and impartial. After the jury found for the truck driver, one of the jurors submitted an affidavit saying that the foreperson said during deliberations that her daughter was at fault in an automobile accident in which a man died, and if her daughter had been sued it would have ruined her life. The Court held that statements made during jury deliberations were not a proper subject of post-verdict inquiry, but recognized that there were permissible other ways to prove that a juror was dishonest on voir dire (e.g., by relying on non-juror witnesses or documentary evidence that contradicts the juror's statements on voir dire).

4. The Use and Function of Alternate Jurors

Federal Rule of Criminal Procedure 24(c) provides that the court may empanel up to six alternate jurors, to provide for the possibility that one or more of the regular jurors may become unable or unqualified to serve as the trial progresses. The Federal Rule further provides that alternate jurors may be retained after the jury retires to consider its verdict; but the court must ensure that a retained alternate does not discuss the case with anyone until that alternate replaces a juror or is discharged. Thus, the alternate who is retained, but does not replace a juror, is not permitted to take part in the jury deliberations. The Federal Rule further provides that if "an alternate replaces a juror after deliberations have begun, the court must instruct the jury to begin its deliberations anew."

Some judges impanel a jury without telling the jurors who is an actual juror and who is an alternate. The theory is that this keeps the alternates as focused on the evidence as the actual jurors, which is important in any case in which a juror is excused and replaced by an alternate.

F. THE TRIAL JUDGE AND THE RIGHT TO JURY TRIAL

1. The Role of the Judge Generally

If the right to jury trial is to work as intended—i.e., to provide protection against eccentric, biased, overreaching or bureaucratic judges and public officials—it is necessary that the judge not take action that unduly invades the independence of the jury.

There is no doubt that judges have enormous powers reserved to them, powers that are exercised more or less independently of juries. For example, trial judges decide whether or not to accept guilty pleas and plea bargains; there is no right to jury trial on the advisability of any contract between the prosecutor and the defendant. Earlier in this Chapter, we saw that judges rule on questions of joinder and severance, that judges rule on speedy trial questions and that judges even control the selection process of the jury. Moreover, judges rule on the admissibility of evidence—the jury does not even hear evidence if one party objects and the judge finds it inadmissible. And judges of course have the power and duty to instruct the jury on the law. It is not difficult, then, to demonstrate that the meaningfulness of the jury trial right will depend in large part on the role played by the trial judge.

2. Selection of Judges

Who are these trial judges and how are they selected? Federal trial judges are, of course, nominated by the President and confirmed by the Senate, with life tenure as long as there is good behavior. State judges are selected by a variety of different methods; often they must win elections to continue in office. Proposals are often made to make judicial selection and retention decisions less political. But, in many states, political officials resist any attempt to limit the use of judicial positions as patronage or to remove the political constraints on the day-to-day actions of trial judges.

3. Challenges Against the Judge

Some jurisdictions recognize the potential impact that a judge can have on the ultimate disposition of any case, even one tried to a jury, by providing for a right of either the prosecution or defense to challenge one judge peremptorily—i.e., as a matter of right. See, e.g., Alaska Stat. 22.20.022. And all allow judges to be challenged for cause, although the standards by which such challenges are measured differ.

Where peremptory challenges of judges are permitted, can a judge be struck for discriminatory reasons? In People v. Williams, 8 Cal.App.4th 688, 10 Cal.Rptr.2d 873 (1992), the court held that the principles set forth in *Batson*, prohibiting discrimination in peremptory challenges of jurors, were applicable by analogy to peremptory challenges of judges.

Biased Judge: Bracy v. Gramley

A judge that is biased is subject to a challenge for cause. And if the bias is not discovered until after the verdict, the verdict is subject to reversal. See Ward v. Village of Monroeville, 409 U.S. 57 (1972) (traffic offense; judge not impartial where he is also the Mayor who is responsible for village finances); Tumey v. Ohio, 273 U.S. 510 (1927) (judge was paid only if the defendant was convicted).

In Bracy v. Gramley, 520 U.S. 899 (1997), Chief Justice Rehnquist wrote for the Court as it held that Bracy, who was convicted in state court of participation in an execution-style triple murder and sentenced to death, was entitled to discovery in his habeas corpus action challenging his conviction and sentence. The judge who had presided over Bracy's trial had been convicted of corruption and had been shown to have paid bribes to judges while a defense lawyer and to have received bribes as a judge. Bracy claimed that the judge might have been pro-prosecution in some cases, including his, to throw off suspicion that he was taking bribes from defense counsel and favoring their defendants. The lower courts found the claim speculative and denied discovery. The Chief Justice disagreed, stating that "the Due Process Clause clearly requires a fair trial in a fair tribunal, before a judge with no actual bias against the defendant or interest in the outcome of his particular case," and found that Bracy's trial judge "was shown to be thoroughly steeped in corruption through his public trial and conviction." The Chief Justice also observed that Bracy made specific allegations that his trial attorney, "a former associate of the corrupt judge in a law practice that was familiar and comfortable with corruption, may have agreed to take this capital case to trial quickly so that petitioner's conviction would deflect any suspicion the rigged * * * cases might attract."

NOTE ON BRACY

On remand, the Court of Appeals found that Bracy, after getting discovery, did not show that the judge was biased against him and that Bracy's claim was "hopelessly speculative."

> For all that appears, Maloney was a prosecution-minded judge for reasons unrelated to his taking bribes. That he would accept payment to acquit criminals does not imply any affection for criminal defendants or their lawyers such that he *must* have been acting against character when he ruled in favor of the prosecution in cases in which he was not bribed. That is a possibility, but no more than a possibility. Maloney's conduct was appalling, his character depraved, but the bridge to the trial of Bracy * * * is missing. He was certainly capable of dreaming up and acting on compensatory bias, but there is no evidence that he did.

Bracy v. Shomig, 248 F.3d 604 (7th Cir. 2001). See also Mann v. Thalacker, 246 F.3d 1092 (8th Cir. 2001) (due process did not require state trial judge to recuse himself in a bench trial on charges involving sexual abuse of a child, even though the judge had been sexually abused by his father when he was a child; the record did not reveal any statements or actions by the judge that indicated actual bias; and the judge's personal history did not make bias so likely that it should be presumed).

Judge with a Conflict of Interest Due to Previous Role as Prosecutor: Williams v. Pennsylvania

In Williams v. Pennsylvania, 579 U.S. 1 (2016), the Court held that the due process rights of a capital defendant were violated, when one of the Justices of the State Supreme Court who denied his *Brady* claim had previously served as the district attorney who made the decision on behalf of the state to seek the death penalty. The Court determined that the Due Process Clause required recusal of the State Supreme Court justice under these circumstances. Justice Kennedy, writing for five members of the Court, wrote that "[d]ue process guarantees an absence of actual bias on the part of a judge" and "[t]he due process guarantee that 'no man can be a judge in his own case' would have little substance if it did not disqualify a former prosecutor from sitting in judgment of a prosecution in which he or she had made a critical decision." Justice Kennedy found the conflict of interest to be particularly potent in this case because the *Brady* claim accused a prosecutor whom the state justice had previously supervised of suppressing materially exculpatory evidence.

Chief Justice Roberts, joined by Justice Alito, dissented. He argued the Due Process Clause was not violated because the state justice's decision—to seek the death penalty—was not related to the decision to reject the *Brady* claim. Justice Thomas wrote a separate dissent in which he argued that "the due process rights of the already convicted * * * do not include policing alleged violations of state codes of judicial ethics in postconviction proceedings."

Showing of Actual Bias Not Required: Rippo v. Baker

In the per curiam decision in Rippo v. Baker, 137 S.Ct. 905 (2017) the Court considered the defendant's claim of a due process violation because his trial judge was the target of a criminal investigation in which the District Attorney was taking part. The state courts ruled against the defendant on the ground that his allegations "did not support the assertion that the trial judge was actually biased [against him] in this case."

The Supreme Court remanded because the Nevada courts' requirement of showing "actual bias" was too strict. The Court explained as follows:

> Under our precedents, the Due Process Clause may sometimes demand recusal even when a judge has no actual bias. Recusal is required when, objectively speaking, the probability of actual bias on the part of the judge or decisionmaker is too high to be constitutionally tolerable. Our decision in *Bracy* is not to the contrary: Although we explained that the petitioner there had pointed to facts suggesting actual, subjective bias, we did not hold that a litigant must show as a matter of course that a judge was actually biased in the litigant's case—much less that he must do so when, as here, he does not allege a theory of "camouflaging bias." The Nevada Supreme Court did not ask the question our precedents require: whether, considering all the circumstances alleged, the risk of bias was too high to be constitutionally tolerable.

4. Limitations on Judicial Powers

Although it is clear that the trial judge can influence the outcome of a jury trial, the constitutional right to a jury trial means that there are some things that are beyond the power of trial judges.

No Directed Verdict of Guilt

One constitutionally-based rule is that the trial judge may not direct a verdict of guilty in a criminal jury trial, even if the defendant admits every material element of an offense. This is because a directed verdict deprives the defendant of the right to a jury trial. See Sullivan v. Louisiana, 508 U.S. 275 (1993) (recognizing that trial judges are constitutionally prohibited from directing a verdict against the defendant). Of course a trial judge has the power, and duty, to direct a verdict for the *defendant* if the evidence is insufficient to sustain a conviction. See Fed.R.Crim.P. 29.

Jury Nullification

Because a trial judge cannot direct a verdict against the defendant, and because the prosecution cannot appeal a not guilty verdict, the jury is essentially given the power to nullify the prosecution by refusing to convict even if there is evidence beyond a reasonable doubt that the defendant committed the crime with which he is charged. Examples of cases in which jury nullification might be a possibility include cases where abused wives have been charged with murdering their abusive husbands, as well as cases alleging drug possession or distribution of minor amounts of narcotics.

Jurors have the power to nullify, because the court cannot overturn a verdict of not guilty any more than the judge can direct a guilty verdict—to do so would violate the defendant's right to jury trial. But while jurors have the power to nullify, should they be informed of that power? Aren't jurors expected to follow the instructions of the trial judge, which tell them to convict if they find that the defendant has committed the charged crime beyond a reasonable doubt? Does nullification create chaos, or is the nullification power necessary to enforce the jury's role as the conscience of the community and the shield against abuse of power? See Weinstein, Considering Jury Nullification: When May and Should a Jury Reject the Law and Do Justice?, 30 Am.Crim.L.Rev. 239 (1993). For a history of jury nullification, see Clay S. Conrad, Jury Nullification: the Evolution of a Doctrine (2014).

The Second Circuit discussed the checkered history of jury nullification in United States v. Thomas, 116 F.3d 606 (2d Cir.1997):

> We are mindful that the term "nullification" can cover a number of distinct, though related, phenomena, encompassing in one word conduct that takes place for a variety of different reasons; jurors may

> nullify, for example, because of the identity of a party, a disapprobation of the particular prosecution at issue, or a more general opposition to the applicable criminal law or laws. We recognize, too, that nullification may at times manifest itself as a form of civil disobedience that some may regard as tolerable. The case of John Peter Zenger, the publisher of the New York Weekly Journal acquitted of criminal libel in 1735, and the nineteenth-century acquittals in prosecutions under the fugitive slave laws, are perhaps our country's most renowned examples of "benevolent" nullification. * * *
>
> [M]ore recent history presents numerous and notorious examples of jurors nullifying—cases that reveal the destructive potential of a practice Professor Randall Kennedy of the Harvard Law School has rightly termed a "sabotage of justice." Consider, for example, the two hung juries in the 1964 trials of Byron De La Beckwith in Mississippi for the murder of NAACP field secretary Medgar Evers, or the 1955 acquittal of J.W. Millam and Roy Bryant for the murder of fourteen-year-old Emmett Till—shameful examples of how nullification has been used to sanction murder and lynching.

The *Thomas* court emphasized that the trial judge must try to limit the possibility of jury nullification:

> * * * [T]he power of juries to "nullify" or exercise a power of lenity is just that—a power; it is by no means a right or something that a judge should encourage or permit if it is within his authority to prevent. * * * A jury has no more "right" to find a "guilty" defendant "not guilty" than it has to find a "not guilty" defendant guilty, and the fact that the former cannot be corrected by a court, while the latter can be, does not create a right out of the power to misapply the law. Such verdicts are lawless, a denial of due process and constitute an exercise of erroneously seized power. * * *
>
> Inasmuch as no juror has a right to engage in nullification—and, on the contrary, it is a violation of a juror's sworn duty to follow the law as instructed by the court—trial courts have the duty to forestall or prevent such conduct, whether by firm instruction or admonition or, where it does not interfere with guaranteed rights or the need to protect the secrecy of jury deliberations, by dismissal of an offending juror from the venire or the jury. * * * Accordingly, every day in courtrooms across the length and breadth of this country, jurors are dismissed from the venire "for cause" precisely because they are unwilling or unable to follow the applicable law. * * *
>
> So also, a presiding judge possesses both the responsibility and the authority to dismiss a juror whose refusal or unwillingness to follow the applicable law becomes known to the judge during the course of trial.

But how, exactly, is the judge to control the possibility of jury nullification once the jury has been empaneled? The facts of *Thomas* indicate the difficulty of the problem. After the jury retired to deliberate, the trial judge was informed by many of the jurors that Juror No. 5 was adamant in his opposition to a guilty verdict, rude to other jurors, and essentially refused to deliberate. There was a difference of views, however, on whether Juror No. 5 was basing his view on the evidence, or rather upon some moral objection to convicting the defendant. The trial court interviewed all the jurors in camera, and concluded that Juror No. 5 was purposely refusing to apply the law given in the judge's instructions, i.e., he was engaged in a personal act of nullification. So the juror was excused for cause, and the remainder of the jury found the defendant guilty.

The Second Circuit reversed in *Thomas*, despite its attack on jury nullification excerpted above. It noted that inquiries into jury nullification during deliberations were especially sensitive, and necessarily truncated, because of the need to protect jury secrecy, and to avoid intimidation of the jury. The court held that the trial court essentially did not have enough information to conclude, without any doubt, that Juror No. 5 was refusing to follow instructions or to consider the evidence. The court recognized, however, that the trial judge could not have obtained any more information without treading upon the secrecy of the jury deliberations. So essentially, the court held that a trial judge has a duty to inquire into allegations of juror nullification, but not to inquire so deeply that the judge would be able to find, without doubt, that a juror was actually engaged in nullification. The power to control jury nullification during deliberations was essentially limited to situations, undoubtedly rare, where the trial court asks jurors a few preliminary questions and a juror blurts out that he is engaged in nullification. The *Thomas* court summed up this way.

> Where the duty and authority to prevent defiant disregard of the law or evidence comes into conflict with the principle of secret jury deliberations, we are compelled to err in favor of the lesser of two evils—protecting the secrecy of jury deliberations at the expense of possibly allowing irresponsible juror activity. * * *
>
> We are required to vacate these judgments because the court dismissed Juror No. 5 largely on the ground that the juror was acting in purposeful disregard of the court's instructions on the law, when the record evidence raises a possibility that the juror was simply unpersuaded by the Government's case against the defendants.

So the bottom line is that a juror bent on nullification might not have a right to nullify, but basically has an unreviewable power to do so.

Is it a crime for a person to tell a prospective juror about the power to nullify? Julian Heicklen, a jury nullification advocate in the Southern District of New York, was prosecuted under 18 U.S.C. § 1504, which makes it a crime to "influence the action or decision" of a juror. He handed out pamphlets to prospective jurors telling them they could acquit a guilty defendant if they believed that "the government is just trying to flex its muscle by making an example out of the defendant." District Judge Kimba Wood dismissed the indictment, concluding that a person violates the jury tampering statute only when he knowingly tried to influence a juror's decision through a written communication "made in relation to a specific case pending before that juror." Benjamin Weiser, Jury Statute Not Violated by Protester, Judge Rules, N.Y. Times, April 19, 2012.

Racially-Based Jury Nullification

Marion Barry, the former Mayor of Washington, D.C., was caught on tape by federal agents while smoking crack cocaine. However, the African-American jury convicted Barry of only one minor count in a fourteen count indictment, despite the trial judge's post-verdict comment that he had "never seen a stronger government case." Was this an example of jury nullification? If so, should jury nullification by minority jurors be treated or considered differently from jury nullification in general? Professor Paul Butler, in Racially Based Jury Nullification: Black Power in the Criminal Justice System, 105 Yale L.J. 677 (1995), provides an argument in favor of race-based jury nullification:

> My thesis is that, for pragmatic and political purposes, the black community is better off when some nonviolent lawbreakers remain in the community rather than go to prison. The decision as to what kind of conduct by African-Americans ought to be punished is better made by African-Americans themselves, based on the costs and benefits to their community, than by the traditional criminal justice process, which is controlled by white lawmakers and white law enforcers. * * *

Applying this thesis to specific crimes, Professor Butler argues as follows:

> In cases involving violent *malum in se* crimes like murder, rape, and assault, jurors should consider the case strictly on the evidence presented, and, if they have no reasonable doubt that the defendant is guilty, they should convict. For nonviolent *malum in se* crimes such as theft or perjury, nullification is an option that the juror should consider, although there should be no presumption in favor of it. A juror might vote for acquittal, for example, when a poor woman steals from Tiffany's, but not when the same woman steals from her next door neighbor. Finally, in cases involving nonviolent, *malum prohibitum* offenses, including "victimless" crimes like narcotics offenses, there should be a presumption in favor of nullification.

Professor Nancy Marder, in The Myth of the Nullifying Jury, 93 Nw.U.L.Rev. 877 (1999), states that nullification can provide important benefits to the judicial system by operating as a device to curb overzealous prosecution or the application of bad laws. She takes issue, however, with Professor Butler's proposal for race-based nullification.

> Under Butler's proposal, the jury would become a mini-legislature in which jurors represent constituencies based on race and try to change social policy through their vote of not guilty. * * * Not only does Butler's plan for the jury compromise a basic tenet of due process—the need for an impartial decisionmaker—but it does so in a particularly cynical and divisive way. Butler's proposal is cynical because it seeks to replicate in the jury the politics of the legislature, in which politicians vote according to the interests of their constituents and because it reduces all African-American jurors to one view based upon their race. Butler's plan is divisive because it pits African-American jurors against jurors of all other races and backgrounds. * * *
>
> Finally, Butler's plan contains the seeds of its own undoing. If African-American jurors take Butler's advice seriously and vote to acquit in all cases of nonviolent African-American defendants as a way of protesting social conditions, then African-American jurors will no longer be seated on juries. Judges could excuse such jurors with for cause challenges on the theory that these jurors could not be impartial. * * *

Instructions on the Power to Nullify

United States v. Dougherty, 473 F.2d 1113 (D.C.Cir.1972), was a prosecution brought against Vietnam War protesters, who broke into property owned by Dow Chemical, the manufacturer of napalm. The defendants argued that the trial judge erred in refusing to instruct the jury that it had the power to nullify. Judge Leventhal responded that the jury should not be told that it may refuse to apply the law given it by the court. See also United States v. Trujillo, 714 F.2d 102 (11th Cir.1983) (defense counsel is not permitted to argue that the jury should nullify); United States v. Edwards, 101 F.3d 17 (2d Cir.1996) (defendant has no right to a jury instruction alerting jurors of the power to nullify, because this power is in contravention of their duty to follow jury instructions).

Commenting on the Evidence and Questioning Witnesses

Most states will not allow a trial judge to comment on the weight of the evidence or on the credibility of witnesses, although some of these states will allow the judge to sum up the evidence presented by both sides.

The federal courts and a minority of the states give much more power to the trial judge and allow comment and summation. But, they do not allow unlimited comment so that it is difficult to demarcate when the limits of permissible comment are exceeded and how much leeway the trial judge actually has. It appears that the practice is less expansive than the theory.

Virtually all jurisdictions allow the trial judge to call and to question witnesses, but none provides unlimited authority to the judge. See Federal Rule of Evidence 614. Again, drawing lines is difficult. See Saltzburg, Martin and Capra, Federal Rule of Evidence Manual § 614.02 (11th ed. 2015), for a discussion of the dangers of trial court questioning of witnesses, and the limitations imposed on the practice. The cases cited there indicate that trial judges are allowed to question witnesses to *clarify* matters, but must take care not to give the impression that they are taking sides in the case. See generally Saltzburg, The Unnecessarily Expanding Role of the American Trial Judge, 64 Va.L.Rev. 1 (1978).

Instructing the Jury

The most important aspect of judicial control may be the judge's instructions to the jury and responses to their inquiries after instructions are given. Since in most jurisdictions the judge instructs the jury on the law and binds them to follow the instructions, what the judge says is critical to the disposition of the case by the jurors. It is common to find provisions like Fed.R.Crim.P. 30, which requires the court to accept or reject proposed instructions by counsel before closing argument, and before the instructions as a whole are given.[22] The judge's choice of what to include in instructions might reflect to some extent the judge's views about certain witnesses and evidence, although the instructions will generally not name particular witnesses.

G. THE JURY VERDICT

Generally the verdict that the jury returns must be in writing. It must be returned by the jury in open court. See Fed.R.Crim.P. 31(a). "If there are multiple defendants, the jury may return a verdict at any time during its deliberations as to any defendant about whom it has agreed." Fed.R.Crim.P. 31(b). Some jurisdictions provide that unless the parties waive the right to a poll, the clerk will ask each juror individually whether the verdict announced is his or her verdict. Fed.R.Crim.P. 31(d) provides that after a verdict is returned and before the jury is excused, "the court must on a party's request, or may on its own, poll the jurors individually." See also United States v. Randle, 966 F.2d 1209 (7th Cir.1992) (reversible error to deny the defendant the opportunity to poll the jury). Verdicts are

[22] Aside from instructing the jurors on the law, the trial judge controls the jury in many ways. For example, some judges do not allow note-taking by jurors, while others do. See United States v. Maclean, 578 F.2d 64 (3d Cir.1978). Trial judges differ in their attitude toward questions by the jurors to witnesses during the trial. For a discussion of the case law, see Saltzburg, Martin & Capra, Federal Rules of Evidence Manual at § 611.02[4] (12th ed. 2019). For a suggested procedure, see Saltzburg, The Unnecessarily Expanding Role of the American Trial Judge, 64 Va.L.Rev. 1, 63–65 (1978).

usually general verdicts of guilty or not guilty on each count. In rare instances a special interrogatory is used.

Inconsistent Verdicts

Generally speaking, jury verdicts are valid even if they are inherently inconsistent. The idea is that the inconsistent jury may be attempting to mitigate the force of its verdicts—the jury may be engaging in a form of nullification, as they have the power to do. Of course, if a verdict is not supported by sufficient evidence, it is subject to attack on post-trial review; but sufficiency and inconsistency are not identical concepts.

Justice Rehnquist, writing for a unanimous Court in United States v. Powell, 469 U.S. 57 (1984), applied the general rule that a defendant convicted on one count of an indictment cannot attack the verdict as being inconsistent with acquittal on another count. Powell was charged on 15 federal counts involving narcotics offenses and was convicted of only three for using the telephone in connection with a cocaine conspiracy and possession charges. She was acquitted of the conspiracy itself and of possession with intent to distribute. The Court recognized that the verdict could not be reconciled, but reasoned that it is always uncertain why the jury returns such a verdict and that it is unclear "whose ox has been gored." Because the government may not appeal an inconsistent acquittal, the Court declined to give the defendant a new trial on the inconsistent conviction as a matter of course. Moreover, the Court expressed the view that inconsistent verdicts are often a matter of lenity and rejected as unworkable a rule that would permit criminal defendants to challenge verdicts by arguing that in particular cases they are not the product of lenity. The Court noted that the defendant received sufficient protection against jury irrationality "by the independent review of the sufficiency of the evidence undertaken by the trial and appellate courts." See also Dunn v. United States, 284 U.S. 390, 393 (1932) ("[c]onsistency in the verdict is not necessary").

In a footnote in *Powell,* Justice Rehnquist stated that "[n]othing in this opinion is intended to decide the proper resolution of a situation where a defendant is convicted of two crimes, where a guilty verdict on one count logically excludes a finding of guilt on the other." See State v. Moore, 458 N.W.2d 90 (Minn.1990) (vacating convictions for first degree murder and manslaughter because, as instructed, the jury necessarily found that the defendant's act was both intentional and reckless, mental states that are mutually exclusive).

Applying *Powell,* courts have held that a defendant can be properly convicted of conspiracy even if all of the other named co-conspirators are acquitted. See United States v. Zuniga-Salinas, 952 F.2d 876 (5th Cir.1992).

Although *Powell* holds that a defendant cannot set aside a conviction on the ground that a verdict is inconsistent, it does not address a situation in which a trial judge explicitly instructs a jury that its verdict need not be consistent. United States v. Moran-Toala, 726 F.3d 334 (2d Cir. 2013), addresses this and makes clear that inconsistent verdicts are tolerated because they often result from partial nullification that is unreviewable, but courts will not knowingly encourage nullification. If they do the encouragement is reviewable and may, as in the case of Moran-Toala, result in the setting aside of a conviction when it is too difficult to ascertain what the jury would have done absent the improper judicial encouragement.

Inconsistent Defenses

While verdicts can be inconsistent, does it follow that defendants ought to be allowed to assert inconsistent defenses, such as "I wasn't there and if I was, it was self-defense"? Or, "I didn't do it but if I did, I was entrapped"? In Mathews v. United States, 485 U.S. 58 (1988), Chief Justice Rehnquist wrote for the Court as it held that "even if the defendant denies one or more elements of the crime, he is entitled to an entrapment instruction whenever there is sufficient evidence from which a reasonable jury could find entrapment." The Court rejected the government's argument "that allowing a defendant to rely on inconsistent defenses will encourage perjury" and confuse a jury. Justice White, joined by Justice Blackmun, dissented.

Although a defendant is legally permitted to offer inconsistent defenses, as a matter of trial strategy defense counsel rarely want to be in the position of arguing inconsistent defenses because they are arguing against themselves—something that rarely is effective.

Use of Interrogatories

The question whether special interrogatories can and should be used in a criminal case is touched upon in United States v. Ruggiero, 726 F.2d 913 (2d Cir.1984). In a complicated prosecution for racketeering and other offenses, the government alleged various predicate acts to support its racketeering charges. (A minimum number of predicate acts must be proved to support a conviction.) The court found that one of the predicate acts alleged was improper as it could not support the charge. Because it was impossible to determine whether the jury relied upon this particular act in returning its guilty verdict on the racketeering charges, the court found that reversal was required. The majority opinion stated that "in a complex RICO [racketeering] trial such as this one, it can be extremely useful for a trial judge to request the jury to record their specific dispositions of the separate predicate acts charged, in addition to their verdict of guilt or innocence on the RICO charge."

Judge Newman wrote a separate opinion analyzing the subject of special interrogatories at greater length. He explained the reasons for judicial reluctance to use interrogatories in criminal cases:

> There is apprehension that eliciting "yes" or "no" answers to questions concerning the elements of an offense may propel a jury toward a logical conclusion of guilt, whereas a more generalized assessment might have yielded an acquittal. The possibility also exists that fragmenting a single count into the various ways an offense may be committed affords a divided jury an opportunity to resolve its differences to the defendant's disadvantage by saying "yes" to some means and "no" to others, although unified consideration of the count might have produced an acquittal or at least a hung jury.

Judge Newman noted that "[i]nterrogatories are especially objectionable when they make resolution of a single fact issue determinative of guilt or innocence, without regard to the elements of an offense, * * * or when their wording shifts the burden of proof to the defendant." On balance, he concluded that a trial judge "should have the discretion to use a jury interrogatory in cases where risk of prejudice to the defendant is slight and the advantage of securing particularized factfinding is substantial."

Lesser Included Offenses

The jury may find the defendant guilty of the crime charged or of any lesser included offense. The issue at trial is usually whether the defendant is entitled to a jury instruction on a lesser included offense.

In Schmuck v. United States, 489 U.S. 705 (1989), the Court adopted the "elements" test for determining whether a trial court must give a lesser included offense instruction under Fed.R.Crim.P. 31(c). Under this test, a lesser included offense is one in which each statutory element is also present in the more serious offense. For example, the elements required to prove involuntary manslaughter in most states are also required to prove the more serious offense of murder. Murder, of course, has additional elements, which is why manslaughter is referred to as "lesser included." The Court in *Schmuck* rejected the broader "inherent relationship" test, under which an offense is included within another when the facts proven at trial support the inference that the defendant committed the less serious offense, and an inherent relationship exists between the two offenses. Under this "inherent relationship" test, the lower court held that Schmuck was entitled to an instruction concerning odometer tampering, when he was charged with mail fraud arising from a scheme to sell cars with turned-back odometers. However, under the elements test, an instruction on odometer tampering was not required, because Schmuck could have been convicted of mail fraud without a showing that he actually turned back any odometers; thus, the elements of odometer tampering were not a "subset" of the elements of mail fraud.

In adopting the elements approach to Rule 31(c), the *Schmuck* Court noted that it was "grounded in the language and history of the Rule and provides greater certainty in its application." The Court also reasoned that the inherent relationship test may create notice problems where the prosecutor asks for a jury charge on an offense whose elements were not charged in the indictment. In contrast, the elements approach, which "involves a textual comparison of criminal statutes and does not depend on inferences that may be drawn from evidence introduced at trial * * * permits both sides to know in advance what jury instructions will be available and to plan their trial strategy accordingly." The Court found the inherent relationship approach to be "rife with the potential for confusion."

For an application of *Schmuck*, see Carter v. United States, 530 U.S. 255 (2000). Carter entered a bank, confronted an exiting customer, and pushed her back inside. She screamed, startling others in the bank. Undeterred, Carter ran inside and leaped over a counter and through one of the teller windows. A teller rushed into the manager's office. Meanwhile, Carter opened several teller drawers and emptied the money into a bag. After removing almost $16,000, he jumped back over the counter and fled. He was charged with violating 18 U.S.C. § 2113(a), which punishes "[w]hoever, by force and violence, or by intimidation, takes . . . any . . . thing of value [from a] bank." While not contesting the basic facts, Carter pleaded not guilty on the theory that he had not taken the bank's money "by force and violence, or by intimidation," as § 2113(a) requires. Before trial, he moved for a jury instruction on the offense described by § 2113(b) as a lesser included offense of the offense described by § 2113(a). Section 2113(b) entails less severe penalties than § 2113(a), punishing "[w]hoever takes and carries away, with intent to steal or purloin, any . . . thing of value exceeding $1,000 [from a] . . . bank." The District Court denied the motion. The jury, instructed on § 2113(a) alone, returned a guilty verdict.

The Supreme Court, in an opinion by Justice Thomas for five members of the Court, held that subsection (b) was not a lesser included offense of subsection (a), because it contains three elements that are not required by subsection (a). Justice Thomas applied a "textual comparison" of the elements of the two offenses and concluded as follows:

> First, whereas subsection (b) requires that the defendant act "with intent to steal or purloin," subsection (a) contains no similar requirement. Second, whereas subsection (b) requires that the defendant "tak[e] and carr[y] away" the property, subsection (a) only requires that the defendant "tak[e]" the property. Third, whereas the first paragraph of subsection (b) requires that the property have a

"value exceeding $1,000," subsection (a) contains no valuation requirement. These extra clauses in subsection (b) cannot be regarded as mere surplusage; they mean something.

Justice Ginsburg, joined by Justices Stevens, Souter and Breyer, dissented in *Carter*. She relied on common law traditions rather than strict textual comparison. She explained as follows:

> At common law, robbery meant larceny plus force, violence, or putting in fear. Because robbery was an aggravated form of larceny at common law, larceny was a lesser included offense of robbery. Congress, I conclude, did not depart from that traditional understanding when it rendered "Bank robbery and incidental crimes" federal offenses. Accordingly, I would hold that petitioner Carter is not prohibited as a matter of law from obtaining an instruction on bank larceny as a lesser included offense.[23]

H. WAIVER OF JURY TRIAL; TRIAL BY THE COURT

A defendant with a right to a jury trial might desire to be tried by a judge. Certain crimes—e.g., child abuse—may be difficult for lay jurors to view dispassionately. Defendants with prior records may believe that in reaching a decision on the merits of a case, a judge can discount prior convictions offered for impeachment purposes somewhat better than a jury can.

Jurisdictions differ on whether the defendant can waive a jury trial at all, on whether the prosecutor can force a jury trial when the defendant prefers a judge trial, and on whether the court can try a case with a jury when neither side wants one.

In Singer v. United States, 380 U.S. 24 (1965), the Supreme Court rebuffed a constitutional attack on Fed.R.Crim.P. 23(a), which permits the defendant to waive a jury trial only with the consent of both the government and the court. The Court rejected the argument that the Sixth Amendment's right to jury trial implies a correlative, unilateral right to waive a jury trial. The Court did say that it would not "assume that federal prosecutors would demand a jury trial for an ignoble purpose." And it left open the possibility that in some circumstances the defendant's reasons for wanting to avoid a jury would be so compelling that the government would deny "an impartial trial" if it insisted on a jury.[24] See also United States v.

[23] The concept of lesser included offense is also discussed in Chapter 12, in connection with double jeopardy rules.

[24] For a discussion of the proper procedure for a court to use in accepting a waiver of jury trial in federal court, see Marone v. United States, 10 F.3d 65 (2d Cir.1993) ("This court urges that at a minimum the district courts inform each defendant that a jury is composed of twelve members of the community, that the defendant may participate in the selection of the jurors, that the jury's verdict must be unanimous, and that a judge alone will decide guilt or innocence if the defendant waives the right to a jury trial.").

Clark, 943 F.2d 775 (7th Cir.1991) (no violation of the Constitution where "the result is simply that the defendant is subject to an impartial trial by jury—the very thing that the Constitution guarantees him"; in dictum, the court states that a defendant may have a right to a bench trial in a case involving "very complex facts").

Why would the prosecution ever object to the defendant's request for a bench trial?[25] Take the case of United States v. District Court for the Eastern District of California, 464 F.3d 1065 (9th Cir. 2006), where the defendants were charged with multiple counts arising out of the transport of young children in interstate commerce for the purpose of engaging in unlawful sexual acts. The facts involved ritualistic sexual abuse of children as young as seven. Defendants moved for a bench trial and the government opposed the motion. The trial judge granted the motion on the ground that "the heinous and repugnant conduct of the defendants * * * which will be vividly apparent to the jury from the evidence to be presented, would render it impossible that ordinary jurors would be able to dispassionately listen to and consider defendants' more technical arguments having to do with interstate commerce in defense to some of the charges." The government was so intent on a jury trial that it took an immediate appeal of the order and sought a writ of mandamus. The court of appeals granted the writ. The court noted that language in *Singer* implied that defendants might have a unilateral right to a bench trial in extreme circumstances, but found that "no United States Court of Appeals appears to have ever approved a defendant's waiver of a jury over the government's objection." The court concluded that while trying this case before a jury "is not without its challenges, we are confident that the able and experienced trial judge is fully capable of ensuring these defendants an impartial trial." The court noted that the trial judge could control prejudice in a number of ways, including extensive voir dire, exclusion of evidence as unduly prejudicial, exclusion of cumulative evidence, and instructions to the jury.

V. THE IMPARTIALITY OF THE TRIBUNAL AND THE INFLUENCE OF THE MEDIA

We have already seen one way of protecting against a biased jury—i.e., voir dire of prospective jurors in order to eliminate those whose partiality would threaten the integrity of the jury as factfinder. Another way of preventing or inhibiting jury bias is to control the flow of information to the potential pool of jurors in a community and, even more importantly, to control the flow of information to those selected as jurors.

[25] For a critical view of the Federal Rule, see Kurland, Providing a Defendant With a Unilateral Right to a Bench Trial: A Renewed Call to Amend Federal Rule of Criminal Procedure 23(a), 26 U.C.D.L.Rev. 309 (1993).

Whenever any government agency wants to control the flow of information to the public, it is likely to be resisted by the media and the public. Efforts to afford all parties a fair trial can threaten some of the interests served by a free press. How to accommodate the competing interests has become known as the "fair trial—free press" issue and is the subject of this section of the Chapter.

A. THE IMPACT OF MEDIA COVERAGE ON LITIGATION

1. Prejudicial Pretrial Publicity

Pervasive Prejudice: Irvin v. Dowd

In Irvin v. Dowd, 366 U.S. 717 (1961), a unanimous Supreme Court for the first time struck down a state conviction because pretrial publicity violated the defendant's right to a fair trial.[26] Irvin was convicted of murder and sentenced to death. The charge arose after six murders were committed in the vicinity of Evansville, Indiana. Police issued press releases saying that Irvin had confessed to murder. Although one change of venue was granted, it was from Evansville to an adjoining rural county that had received some of the publicity concerning the crimes and Irvin's arrest. A second change of venue was denied. Justice Clark's opinion for the Court stressed that the Constitution does not require a jury that is completely untouched by pretrial publicity:

> It is not required * * * that jurors be totally ignorant of the facts and issues involved. In these days of swift, widespread and diverse methods of communication, an important case can be expected to arouse the interest of the public in the vicinity, and scarcely any of those best qualified to serve as jurors will not have formed some impression or opinion as to the merits of the case. * * * To hold that the mere existence of any preconceived notion as to the guilt or innocence of the accused, without more, is sufficient to rebut the presumption of a prospective juror's impartiality would be to establish an impossible standard. It is sufficient if the juror can lay aside his impression or opinion and render a verdict based on the evidence presented in court.

The Court described the publicity that accompanied the case, and evaluated its effect on Irvin's trial, in the following passage:

> Here the build-up of prejudice is clear and convincing. * * * [A] barrage of newspaper headlines, articles, cartoons and pictures was unleashed against him during the six or seven months preceding his

[26] Prior to *Irvin*, the Court set aside a conviction in Marshall v. United States, 360 U.S. 310 (1959), under its supervisory powers because of news articles the jurors had read.

> trial. * * * [T]he newspapers in which the stories appeared were delivered regularly to approximately 95% of the dwellings in Gibson County and * * * in addition, the Evansville radio and TV stations, which likewise blanketed that county, also carried extensive newscasts covering the same incidents. These stories revealed the details of his background, including a reference to crimes committed when a juvenile, his convictions for arson almost 20 years previously, for burglary and by a court-martial on AWOL charges during the war. He was accused of being a parole violator. The headlines announced his police line-up identification, that he faced a lie detector test, had been placed at the scene of the crime and that the six murders were solved but petitioner refused to confess. Finally, they announced his confession to the six murders and the fact of his indictment for four of them in Indiana. * * * One story * * * characterized petitioner as remorseless and without conscience but also as having been found sane by a court-appointed panel of doctors. In many of the stories petitioner was described as the "confessed slayer of six," a parole violator and fraudulent-check artist.
>
> * * *
>
> Here the "pattern of deep and bitter prejudice" shown to be present throughout the community, was clearly reflected in the sum total of the voir dire examination of a majority of the jurors finally placed in the jury box. Eight out of the 12 thought petitioner was guilty. With such an opinion permeating their minds, it would be difficult to say that each could exclude this preconception of guilt from his deliberations. * * * With his life at stake, it is not requiring too much that petitioner be tried in an atmosphere undisturbed by so huge a wave of public passion and by a jury other than one in which two-thirds of the members admit, before hearing any testimony, to possessing a belief in his guilt.

Thus, the Court set aside the conviction. Justice Frankfurter's concurring opinion suggested both that the problem of undue publicity was not isolated in Evansville, and that its impact on the *Irvin* case was not atypical.

Televised Confession: Rideau v. Louisiana

The Court overturned another state conviction in Rideau v. Louisiana, 373 U.S. 723 (1963), a murder case in which Rideau's confession to police officers was heavily televised in the locality. His lawyers filed a motion for a change of venue, on the ground that he would be deprived of a fair trial because of the extensive airing of his confession. The motion was denied and Rideau was convicted and sentenced to death on the murder charge in the local trial court. Three members of the jury had stated on voir dire that they had seen and heard Rideau's confession at least once. Two members of the jury were deputy sheriffs of the locality. Rideau's counsel had requested that these jurors be excused for cause, having exhausted all peremptory challenges, but these challenges for cause had been denied by the trial judge.

The *Rideau* Court held that "it was a denial of due process of law to refuse the request for a change of venue, after the people of Calcasieu Parish had been exposed repeatedly and in depth to the spectacle of Rideau personally confessing in detail to the crimes with which he was later to be charged." The Court stated that the televised confession "in a very real sense *was* Rideau's trial—at which he pleaded guilty to murder," and that a later trial in a community so pervasively exposed to the confession "could be but a hollow formality." Justice Clark, joined by Justice Harlan, dissented, complaining that the defendant had not established any "substantial nexus" between the televised confession and any prejudice suffered at the trial.

QUESTIONS ABOUT RIDEAU

In *Rideau,* there was no indication that the confession was coerced, and therefore it was undoubtedly admissible against Rideau at trial. If the jurors would hear the confession at trial, what prejudice could Rideau have suffered from the pretrial publicity? Isn't the case really about the failure to strike the two law enforcement officers for cause?

If the facts of *Rideau* suffice to establish constitutional error, how many trials are tainted in these days of extensive media coverage of high profile trials—not to speak of widespread and real-time communications on Facebook and Twitter? Compare Fetterly v. Paskett, 163 F.3d 1144 (9th Cir.1998) (pretrial publicity not prejudicial where it focuses on facts and evidence that was ultimately presented at trial).

Questions about the impact of social media and other forms of communication about trials caused the American Bar Association to change the title of its Fair Trial-Free Press Standards to Fair Trial and Public Discourse when it adopted the 4th Edition of the Standards in 2013.

Extended Period of Time Between Publicity and the Trial: Patton v. Yount

Irvin and *Rideau* seem to indicate that the Court would find prejudicial pretrial publicity in a large number of cases. But the Court cut back in Patton v. Yount, 467 U.S. 1025 (1984), where it reinstated a state defendant's murder conviction that had been overturned due to prejudicial trial publicity. Justice Powell's opinion for the Court emphasized that the court of appeals' reliance on *Irvin* was misplaced because the trial in *Irvin* took place six or seven months after extensive publicity began, whereas

Yount was convicted in a second trial *four years* after most of the publicity occurred in connection with his first trial. That most jurors remembered the murder and surrounding publicity was not decisive. The Court stated that "[t]he relevant question is not whether the community remembered the case, but whether the jurors at Yount's trial had such fixed opinions that they could not judge impartially the guilt of the defendant." Justice Powell reasoned as follows:

> It is not unusual that one's recollection of the fact that a notorious crime was committed lingers long after the feelings of revulsion that create prejudice have passed. It would be fruitless to attempt to identify any particular lapse of time that in itself would distinguish the situation that existed in *Irvin*. But it is clear that the passage of time between a first and a second trial can be a highly relevant fact. In the circumstances of this case, we hold that it clearly rebuts any presumption of partiality or prejudice that existed at the time of the initial trial.

Justice Stevens, joined by Justice Brennan, dissented. Justice Marshall did not participate.

Deference to Trial Courts: Mu'Min v. Virginia

In Mu'Min v. Virginia, 500 U.S. 415 (1991), (discussed supra in the section on voir dire) the defendant was a state prisoner serving time for first-degree murder when he was charged with capital murder while on a work detail. The case was widely publicized. Articles in the newspapers revealed details of the prior murder for which Mu'Min was incarcerated, the fact that the death penalty was unavailable at the time of his earlier murder trial, the denial of parole six times to Mu'Min, his confession to the crime charged, and criticism of the supervision of work gangs in Virginia. Mu'Min claimed that the jurors could not be impartial in such a setting, despite the judge's finding on voir dire that the jurors had not been substantially affected by the publicity.

Chief Justice Rehnquist, writing for the Court, held that a trial court's finding of juror impartiality may be overturned only for manifest error. He stated that "particularly with respect to pretrial publicity, we think this primary reliance on the judgment of the trial court makes good sense. The judge of that court sits in the locale where the publicity is said to have had its effect, and brings to his evaluation of any such claim his own perception of the depth and extent of news stories that might influence a juror." This was so even though the judge in this case had not questioned jurors individually to determine whether they had been affected by pre-trial publicity.

The majority rejected Mu'Min's reliance on Irvin v. Dowd on the ground that the pretrial publicity in the instant case was not of the same kind or extent as in *Irvin*.

Justice O'Connor wrote a concurring opinion. She cited Patton v. Yount for the proposition that even jurors who had read about inadmissible confessions are not disqualified as a matter of law, and concluded that a trial judge could realistically assess whether jurors could be fair without knowing what each juror had heard about a case. Justices Marshall, Blackmun, Stevens, and Kennedy dissented.

Lower Court Cases

Generally speaking, the lower courts have been reluctant to find that prejudicial pretrial publicity has tainted a trial. See, e.g., Swindler v. Lockhart, 885 F.2d 1342 (8th Cir.1989) (substantial publicity, 98 out of 120 prospective jurors had heard about the case, no reversal); Simmons v. Lockhart, 814 F.2d 504 (8th Cir.1987) (55 of 56 members of the venire had heard about the case, but "[t]he accused is not entitled to an ignorant jury, just a fair one"); United States v. Lehder-Rivas, 955 F.2d 1510 (11th Cir.1992) (extensive media coverage describing the defendant as a "drug kingpin" and a "narco-terrorist"; but the trial judge conducted extensive voir dire and the jurors credibly asserted that they could remain impartial); United States v. Campa, 459 F.3d 1121 (11th Cir. 2006) (defendants charged with spying for Cuba, trial held in Miami; prejudicial publicity was not so great as to require change of venue, given the court's extensive voir dire and limiting instructions).

2. Television in the Courtroom

Televising criminal trials is controversial. Those who denigrate the practice argue among other things that television simply encourages the lawyers, and maybe the judge as well, to play to the cameras. Those who support cameras in the courtroom argue that television provides the public a crucial viewpoint into the workings of the criminal justice system. The Supreme Court has evaluated the effect of cameras in the courtroom on the right to fair trial in a number of cases.

Media Invades the Courtroom: Estes v. Texas

Billy Sol Estes was one of the first "subjects" of a high profile, televised trial. In Estes v. Texas, 381 U.S. 532 (1965), the Court held that Estes was denied a fair trial due to the pervasive and disruptive media presence in the courtroom. Justice Clark, writing for the Court, described the effect that the media had on the courtroom during both pre-trial hearings and at the trial:

> [A]t least 12 cameramen were engaged in the courtroom throughout the hearing taking motion and still pictures and televising the proceedings. * * * The trial witnesses present at the hearing, as well as the original jury panel, were undoubtedly made aware of the peculiar public importance of the case by the press and television coverage being provided, and by the fact that they themselves were televised live and their pictures rebroadcast on the evening show. * * *

The Court held that the First Amendment did not extend a right to the news media to televise from the courtroom, and that the disruption of the proceedings in this case created by television coverage required a new trial—even though Estes had not made a showing of actual prejudice. Justice Clark concluded with these critical comments about televised coverage of courtroom proceedings:

> [T]he chief function of our judicial machinery is to ascertain the truth. The use of television, however, cannot be said to contribute materially to this objective. Rather its use amounts to the injection of an irrelevant factor into court proceedings. In addition experience teaches that there are numerous situations in which it might cause actual unfairness—some so subtle as to defy detection by the accused or control by the judge. We enumerate some in summary:
>
> 1. The potential impact of television on the jurors is perhaps of the greatest significance. * * *
>
> 2. The quality of the testimony in criminal trials will often be impaired. * * * Embarrassment may impede the search for the truth, as may a natural tendency toward overdramatization. * * *
>
> * * *
>
> 3. A major aspect of the problem is the additional responsibilities the presence of television places on the trial judge. His job is to make certain that the accused receives a fair trial. This most difficult task requires his undivided attention. Still when television comes into the courtroom he must also supervise it. * * *
>
> * * *
>
> 4. Finally, we cannot ignore the impact of courtroom television on the defendant. * * * The inevitable close-ups of his gestures and expressions during the ordeal of his trial might well transgress his personal sensibilities, his dignity, and his ability to concentrate on the proceedings before him * * *. A defendant on trial for a specific crime is entitled to his day in court, not in a stadium, or a city or nationwide arena. * * *. Furthermore, telecasting may also deprive an accused of effective counsel. The distractions, intrusions into confidential attorney-client relationships and the temptation offered by television

to play to the public audience might often have a direct effect not only upon the lawyers, but the judge, the jury and the witnesses.

Chief Justice Warren, joined by Justices Douglas and Goldberg, wrote a concurring opinion concluding that "televising of criminal proceedings is inherently a denial of due process."

Justice Harlan wrote a separate opinion, agreeing with the Court that the First Amendment does not require that television be allowed in the courtroom, but disagreeing with the Court that televised proceedings were per se prohibited by the Constitution. He suggested a case-by-case approach. Justice Stewart's dissent, joined by Justices Black, Brennan, and White concluded that "in the present state of the art" televised judicial proceedings were unwise, but found no denial of Estes' constitutional rights. Justice White's short dissent noted that advances in technology might make televised judicial proceedings more acceptable. Justice Brennan's separate statement noted that because of Justice Harlan's vote, *Estes* could not be read as an absolute bar to televised trials.

In the following case, the Court clearly agreed with Justice Brennan's view that there is no bar on televised trials—thus allowing us all to watch the trials of George Zimmerman, Jody Arias, Casey Anthony, Derek Chauvin, Kyle Rittenhouse, the McMichaels and other "important" trials of the day.

CHANDLER V. FLORIDA

Supreme Court of the United States, 1981.
449 U.S. 560.

CHIEF JUSTICE BURGER delivered the opinion of the Court.

The question presented on this appeal is whether, consistent with constitutional guarantees, a state may provide for radio, television, and still photographic coverage of a criminal trial for public broadcast, notwithstanding the objection of the accused.

[The Florida Supreme Court established a pilot program permitting electronic media to cover all judicial proceedings, without reference to the consent of the participants. After the pilot program ended, the Florida Supreme Court sought comments and reviewed camera-in-the-courts projects in other states. The court concluded that "on balance there [was] more to be gained than lost by permitting electronic media coverage of judicial proceedings subject to standards for such coverage."]

The Florida court was of the view that because of the significant effect of the courts on the day-to-day lives of the citizenry, it was essential that the people have confidence in the process. It felt that broadcast coverage of trials would contribute to wider public acceptance and understanding of decisions. Consequently, * * * the Florida Supreme Court promulgated a revised Canon 3A(7). The canon provides:

> "Subject at all times to the authority of the presiding judge to (i) control the conduct of proceedings before the court, (ii) ensure decorum and prevent distractions, and (iii) ensure fair administration of justice in the pending cause, electronic media and still photography coverage of public judicial proceedings in the appellate and trial courts of this state shall be allowed in accordance with standards of conduct and technology promulgated by the Supreme Court of Florida."

* * *

[The defendants were Miami policemen charged with burglary. The case received extensive publicity.]

* * *

After several * * * fruitless attempts by the appellants to prevent electronic coverage of the trial, the jury was selected. At *voir dire*, the appellants' counsel asked each prospective juror whether he or she would be able to be "fair and impartial" despite the presence of a television camera during some, or all, of the trial. Each juror selected responded that such coverage would not affect his or her consideration in any way. A television camera recorded the *voir dire*.

A defense motion to sequester the jury because of the television coverage was denied by the trial judge. However, the court instructed the jury not to watch or read anything about the case in the media and suggested that jurors "avoid the local news and watch only the national news on television." * * *

A television camera was in place for one entire afternoon, during which the state presented the testimony of Sion, its chief witness. No camera was present for the presentation of any part of the case for the defense. The camera returned to cover closing arguments. Only two minutes and fifty-five seconds of the trial below were broadcast—and those depicted only the prosecution's side of the case.

The jury returned a guilty verdict on all counts. [The conviction was upheld on appeal.]

Appellants * * * argue that the televising of criminal trials is inherently a denial of due process, and they read *Estes* as announcing a *per se* constitutional rule to that effect.

* * *

An absolute constitutional ban on broadcast coverage of trials cannot be justified simply because there is a danger that, in some cases, prejudicial broadcast accounts of pretrial and trial events may impair the ability of jurors to decide the issue of guilt or innocence uninfluenced by extraneous matter. The risk of juror prejudice in some cases does not justify an absolute ban on news coverage of trials by the printed media; so also the risk of such prejudice does not warrant an absolute constitutional ban on all broadcast coverage. * * *

Not unimportant to the position asserted by Florida and other states is the change in television technology since 1962, when Estes was tried. It is urged, and some empirical data are presented, that many of the negative factors found in *Estes*—cumbersome equipment, cables, distracting lighting, numerous camera technicians—are less substantial factors today than they were at that time.

It is also significant that safeguards have been built into the experimental programs in state courts, and into the Florida program, to avoid some of the most egregious problems envisioned by the six opinions in the *Estes* case. Florida admonishes its courts to take special pains to protect certain witnesses—for example, children, victims of sex crimes, some informants, and even the very timid witness or party—from the glare of publicity and the tensions of being "on camera."

* * *

[A]t present no one has been able to present empirical data sufficient to establish that the mere presence of the broadcast media inherently has an adverse effect on that process. The appellants have offered nothing to demonstrate that their trial was subtly tainted by broadcast coverage—let alone that all broadcast trials would be so tainted.

* * *

To demonstrate prejudice in a specific case a defendant must show something more than juror awareness that the trial is such as to attract the attention of broadcasters.

* * *

[The Court affirmed the convictions.]

3. Protecting the Integrity of Judicial Proceedings

Circus Atmosphere: Sheppard v. Maxwell

The Supreme Court considered the effect of media coverage of a high-profile trial in Sheppard v. Maxwell, 384 U.S. 333 (1966). Sheppard was tried and convicted for murdering his wife. He claimed that she was killed by an intruder. Apparently because Sheppard was a well-to-do doctor, the case received substantial media coverage. (Yes, the case may well have been the model for the television series "The Fugitive" in which David

Janssen played Dr. Richard Kimble, and the movie "The Fugitive" in which Harrison Ford played the same role.)

In his opinion for the Court, Justice Clark noted the pervasive pre-trial publicity and the circus-type media coverage during the trial. Pretrial publicity included media coverage indicating that other suspects had been cleared and that the defendant had been having an affair. Newspapers called for Sheppard's arrest. The media invaded the courtroom. Pictures of the jury were published. During the nine week murder trial the courtroom "remained crowded to capacity with representatives of news media. Their movement in and out of the courtroom often caused so much confusion that, despite the loud-speaker system installed in the courtroom, it was difficult for the witnesses and counsel to be heard." Sheppard and counsel found it almost impossible to confer confidentially.

The *Sheppard* Court held that the trial judge's failure to control the media coverage of the judicial proceedings deprived Sheppard of his right to a fair trial, requiring a reversal of his conviction. Justice Clark emphasized that the trial court had substantial authority to control media coverage in order to protect the defendant's right to a fair trial, and that the trial court in *Sheppard* should have exercised this authority. The Court gave the following suggestions as to what could and should have been done:

> Bearing in mind the massive pretrial publicity, the judge should have adopted stricter rules governing the use of the courtroom by newsmen, as Sheppard's counsel requested. The number of reporters in the courtroom itself could have been limited at the first sign that their presence would disrupt the trial. They certainly should not have been placed inside the bar. Furthermore, the judge should have more closely regulated the conduct of newsmen in the courtroom. For instance, the judge belatedly asked them not to handle and photograph trial exhibits lying on the counsel table during recesses.
>
> Secondly, the court should have insulated the witnesses. All of the newspapers and radio stations apparently interviewed prospective witnesses at will, and in many instances disclosed their testimony. * * * Although the witnesses were barred from the courtroom during the trial the full verbatim testimony was available to them in the press. This completely nullified the judge's imposition of the rule [sequestering witnesses].
>
> Thirdly, the court should have made some effort to control the release of leads, information, and gossip to the press by police officers, witnesses, and the counsel for both sides. * * *

Justice Clark concluded that "where there is a reasonable likelihood that prejudicial news prior to trial will prevent a fair trial, the judge should continue the case until the threat abates, or transfer it to another county not so permeated with publicity." With respect to publicity during the proceedings, he concluded that "courts must take such steps by rule and regulation that will protect their processes from prejudicial outside interferences."

Gag Orders

Following the suggestion of the *Sheppard* Court, many judges in high profile cases have barred lawyers, their employees, law enforcement and court personnel, and witnesses from making extrajudicial statements prior to the entry of a verdict. An example arose in United States v. Cutler, 58 F.3d 825 (2d Cir.1995), where the lawyer for Mafia boss John Gotti, Bruce Cutler, was convicted of criminal contempt for violating a gag order entered in Gotti's murder prosecution. The order incorporated a local rule of court prohibiting statements from counsel that would create a reasonable likelihood of interfering with a fair trial. Despite the order, Cutler gave numerous interviews to the press and television. In these interviews, he claimed, among other things, that: the government was persecuting John Gotti; John Gotti was "anti-drugs" and a legitimate businessman; government witnesses were liars; and the Mafia does not exist. Cutler also mischaracterized important parts of the government's evidence.

Cutler argued that he did not violate the gag order because his statements were not reasonably likely to interfere with a fair trial. He contended that he was simply responding to the "veritable firestorm of anti-Gotti publicity." The court was not persuaded, however, by Cutler's "Uriah Heep pose." It stated that Cutler could be found in contempt for statements *likely* to impair a fair trial, even if the statements in fact had no effect. (Indeed, Cutler's p.r. campaign had no effect; almost all members of the venire panel had heard about Gotti, but apparently none had heard about Cutler's statements).

Cutler argued, finally, that he had not *willfully* violated the gag order. But the court found what it termed a "smoking gun" in a statement Cutler had made, while speaking at a seminar at Brooklyn Law School, about contacts with the press. At the seminar, Cutler said:

> I have honest reasons why I don't want to alienate [the press], that I want the prospective veniremen out there to feel that I mean what I say and say what I mean, and if that can spill over and help my client, then I feel it's important for me to do that.

The court upheld Cutler's sentence of 90 days' house arrest, three years' probation, and a six month suspension from the practice of law. It concluded as follows:

> In some quarters, doubtless, this affirmance will elicit thunderbolts that we are chilling effective advocacy. Obviously, that is neither our intention nor our result. The advocate is still entitled—

> indeed encouraged—to strike hard blows, but not unfair blows. Trial practice, whether civil or criminal, is not a contact sport. And its tactics do not include eye-gouging or shin-kicking.
>
> In this case, a conscientious trial judge tried mightily to limit the lawyers to press statements that were accurate and fair. The defendant's statements were dipped in venom and were deliberately couched to poison the well from which the jury would be selected. Such conduct goes beyond the pale, by any reasonable standard, and cannot be condoned under the rubric of "effective advocacy."

What kind of "fair blows" could Cutler have struck, given the anti-Gotti publicity that pervaded New York when the prosecution began? What's wrong with Cutler's desire to shape the opinions of the jury venire? It should be noted that the prosecutor gave an interview shortly after the indictment against Gotti was handed down. In the interview, he said that Gotti was "a murderer, not a folk hero," and expressed pleasure that the evidence he had was much stronger than the evidence in prior prosecutions in which Gotti had been acquitted. These statements were made before the trial judge imposed the gag order. Are they relevant to Cutler's contempt prosecution? Do you think the prosecutor would have been found guilty of criminal contempt if he had made those statements after the trial judge imposed a gag order?

Overbroad Gag Orders

United States v. Salameh, 992 F.2d 445 (2d Cir.1993), was a prosecution of defendants accused of bombing the World Trade Center. It was obviously a high profile case, and the judge was concerned about trial publicity in general and extrajudicial statements by lawyers in particular. So he imposed the following gag order:

> There will be no more statements in the press, on TV, in radio, or in any other electronic media, issued by either side or their agents. The next time I pick up a paper and see a quotation from any of you, you had best be prepared to have some money. The first fine will be $200. Thereafter, the fines will be squared.

After the order was entered, defense counsel had some questions for the judge about the scope of the order, such as, could counsel make a statement that his client had been tortured in Egypt? Could the lawyer talk to reporters about the client's background and family? The trial judge responded that the gag order applied to "what we are dealing with here."

The court of appeals vacated the gag order, on the ground that it violated the First Amendment principle that an order limiting speech "should be no broader than necessary to protect the integrity of the judicial system and the defendant's right to a fair trial." The court concluded as follows:

> The order imposed by the district court in the present case does not meet these standards. The restraint on the attorneys' speech is not narrowly tailored; rather, it is a blanket prohibition that extends to any statements that * * * may have something to do with the case. The court did not make a finding that alternatives to this blanket prohibition would be inadequate to protect defendants' rights to a fair trial before an impartial jury. * * * The record does not support a conclusion that no reasonable alternatives to a blanket prohibition exist.

Why was the order in *Salameh* any more problematic than the order at issue in *Cutler*, which prohibited counsel from making a statement that had a "reasonable likelihood of impairing a fair trial"? At least the order in *Salameh* had the virtue of clarity, did it not?

Ethical Proscriptions: Gentile v. State Bar of Nevada

To the extent that prejudicial trial publicity is caused by lawyers, codes of ethics impose limitations even if no gag order is in place. Rule 3.6 of the Model Rules of Professional Conduct makes disclosure of information by lawyers involved in a trial an ethical violation under some circumstances. These rules generally prohibit statements that create a reasonable likelihood of materially prejudicing the proceeding. See, e.g., United States v. Bingham, 769 F.Supp. 1039 (N.D.Ill.1991) (defense attorneys' conduct was referred to disciplinary committee, where attorneys criticized the empanelment of an anonymous jury in televised interviews the night before jury selection).

Like gag orders, lawyer disciplinary rules limiting speech raise First Amendment issues. In Gentile v. State Bar of Nevada, 501 U.S. 1030 (1991), the Supreme Court rebuffed a First Amendment challenge to a state disciplinary rule proscribing "an extrajudicial statement that a reasonable person would expect to be disseminated by means of media communication if the lawyer knows or reasonably should know that it will have a substantial likelihood of materially prejudicing an adjudicative proceeding." Chief Justice Rehnquist's opinion upholding this standard was joined by Justices White, O'Connor, Scalia, and Souter.

The case arose after cocaine and traveler's checks used in an undercover police operation were found missing from a vault, and an investigation led to the indictment of Gentile's client. Gentile held a press conference in which he suggested that the thief was a police officer, not his client, and that his client was not guilty. Gentile's main purpose in holding the press conference was to counter the adverse publicity that had been aired concerning his client. Gentile's client was ultimately acquitted.

Chief Justice Rehnquist's opinion for the Court on the relevant standard held that lawyers are entitled to less First Amendment protection than the press. The Chief Justice reasoned that "lawyers representing clients in pending cases are key participants in the criminal justice system, and the State may demand some adherence to the precepts of that system in regulating their speech as well as their conduct." He noted that a lawyer's extrajudicial statements can have significant impact on the trial "since lawyers' statements are likely to be received as especially authoritative." He concluded that the "substantial likelihood of material prejudice" test was an appropriate balance of the interests of the lawyer and the state, since it imposes "only narrow and necessary limitations on lawyers' speech," and "it merely postpones the attorney's comments until after the trial." A more rigorous "clear and present danger" standard was therefore not required.

Despite the Court's upholding the standard, Justice Kennedy wrote for the Court, joined by Justices Marshall, Blackmun, Stevens, and O'Connor, as it held that one aspect of the particular Nevada rule was void for vagueness. Consequently, the Court held that the rule could not support a reprimand of counsel for remarks made at a press conference following the indictment of his client.

Justice Kennedy found it unnecessary to address the constitutionality of the "substantial likelihood of material prejudice" standard, or to determine whether the First Amendment provides less protection for lawyers than for the press. He reasoned instead that the Nevada rule was vague because of its safe harbor provision, which set forth examples of some statements that would not violate the rule. He stated that a lawyer seeking to avail himself of the Nevada safe harbor provision "must guess at its contours." The safe harbor provision gave defense counsel the right to "explain the general nature of the defense" but "without elaboration." Justice Kennedy concluded that this provision was unconstitutionally vague because "general and elaboration are both classic terms of degree" with "no settled usage or tradition of interpretation in law." According to Justice Kennedy, Gentile was given "no principle for determining when his remarks pass from the safe harbor of the general to the forbidden sea of the elaborated." Justice Kennedy noted that Gentile had spent several hours researching the requirements of the Nevada rule, and that at his press conference his remarks were guarded and general. Still the Nevada courts had found that he violated the disciplinary rule. Justice Kennedy asserted that "the fact Gentile was found in violation of the Rules after studying them and making a conscious effort at compliance demonstrates that [the Nevada Rule] creates a trap for the wary as well as the unwary."

Justice O'Connor, who wrote a brief concurring opinion, agreed with Justice Kennedy's void for vagueness analysis. She also agreed, however, with Chief Justice Rehnquist's opinion that the "substantial likelihood of prejudice" standard set forth in the Nevada rule was indeed constitutional, even though it provided less protection to lawyers than the "clear and present danger" standard applicable to the press.

In the end, the Court invalidated the sanction imposed upon Gentile, indicated that state rules providing ambiguous examples may be invalidated as a result of vagueness, and yet upheld the standard that lawyers in pending cases may not make public comments when they know or should know that such comments will have a substantial likelihood of materially prejudicing an adjudicative proceeding.

B. CONTROLLING THE MEDIA'S IMPACT

Many participants in and observers of the criminal justice system have argued that undue or unfair media coverage can be remedied by limiting the information disseminated to the public. This can be accomplished in two ways: by controlling media access to information and by restricting what the media reports. The Supreme Court and lower courts have often been confronted with whether and under what circumstances media access to trials can be controlled consistently with the First Amendment and the defendant's Sixth Amendment right to a public trial.

1. Controlling Media Access to Criminal Proceedings

Pretrial Proceedings: Gannett Co., Inc. v. DePasquale

In Gannett Co., Inc. v. DePasquale, 443 U.S. 368 (1979), a state trial judge had granted two defendants' motions to exclude the press and public from a pretrial hearing on a motion to suppress confessions and physical evidence. The media challenged the judge's decision, which was upheld in the Supreme Court. The Court stated that the Framers of the Sixth Amendment did not intend "to create a constitutional right in strangers to attend a pretrial proceeding, when all that they actually did was to confer upon the accused an explicit right to demand a public trial." The Court also noted that, assuming the First Amendment granted a right of access to pretrial proceedings, the trial court had appropriately balanced the First Amendment interests with the defendant's right to be free from prejudicial pretrial publicity. Justice Powell's concurring opinion suggested that he would recognize some such right, but Justice Rehnquist's concurring opinion indicated that he thought the Court's prior decisions had rejected the idea that the First Amendment guaranteed access to government facilities. Chief Justice Burger also concurred, noting that a pretrial hearing was not a "trial" within the meaning of the Sixth Amendment. Justice Blackmun's dissenting opinion was joined by Justices Brennan, White and Marshall.

The result in *Gannett* was muddled. The Court had before it a pretrial proceeding, but the reasoning of the majority opinion restricting press access was not necessarily confined to such proceedings. Did *Gannett* mean to allow any and all exclusions of the media from any and all parts of trials? Subsequent case law has attempted to clarify the permissible limits on public access to criminal proceedings.

Limited Right of Access to Criminal Trials: Richmond Newspapers, Inc. v. Virginia

In Richmond Newspapers, Inc. v. Virginia, 448 U.S. 555 (1980), the Court held that the First Amendment does give the public and the media a limited right of access to criminal trials. Chief Justice Burger's plurality opinion commanded the most votes in the case. Only Justices White and Stevens joined the opinion, however. Justice Stevens also added a separate concurrence, and Justice White added a concurring statement. The Chief Justice distinguished *Gannett* as dealing with pretrial proceedings, looked to the history of American criminal trials, and found that they had long been conducted in public places in which the public and the media were welcome. He observed that the presence of the public added something of importance to the proceedings.

The Chief Justice concluded that the right of the public and the press to be present was not absolute and would give way to overriding governmental interests articulated in findings of a court. He suggested, however that alternatives must be explored before closure is ordered. Justice Brennan, joined by Justice Marshall, concurred in the judgment and would have held the underlying Virginia statute unconstitutional for giving trial judges too much discretion. Justice Brennan was reluctant to specify the countervailing government interests that might justify overriding the presumption of open trials. Justices Stewart and Blackmun wrote separate opinions concurring in the result. Justice Stewart distinguished the trial setting from places like jails not generally open to the public. Justice Rehnquist dissented. Justice Powell did not participate in the decision.

For cases applying *Richmond Newspapers*, see, e.g., People v. Martinez, 82 N.Y.2d 436, 604 N.Y.S.2d 932 (1993) (holding that the public may be excluded from testimony by an undercover informant, but only if a factual showing is made that continued confidentiality is necessary for the informant's safety or to preserve the integrity of an ongoing investigation); People v. Kin Kan, 78 N.Y.2d 54, 571 N.Y.S.2d 436 (1991) (error to exclude the public, including the defendant's family, during the testimony of the key cooperating witness-accomplice to the defendant's crime; the witness stated that he feared retaliation from testifying in open court, but not from the defendant's family, who knew him already anyway: "the expulsion of everyone during this accomplice's testimony was broader than constitutionally tolerable and constituted a violation of Kan's overriding right to a public trial").

One court has read *Richmond Newspapers* to articulate six societal interests advanced by open court proceedings. They are:

- promotion of informed discussion of governmental affairs by providing the public with the more complete understanding of the judicial system;
- promotion of the public perception of fairness which can be achieved only by permitting full public view of the proceedings;
- providing a significant community therapeutic value as an outlet for community concern, hostility and emotion;
- serving as a check on corrupt practices by exposing the judicial process to public scrutiny;
- enhancement of the performance of all involved; and
- discouragement of perjury.

United States v. Simone, 14 F.3d 833 (3d Cir.1994).

Closure to Protect Witnesses: Globe Newspaper Co. v. Superior Court

The Court relied on *Richmond Newspapers* in Globe Newspaper Co. v. Superior Court, 457 U.S. 596 (1982), to invalidate a state statute that required exclusion of the media and general public from the courtroom during the testimony of a sex offense victim under the age of 18. Justice Brennan's opinion for the Court observed that where "the State attempts to deny the right of access in order to inhibit the disclosure of sensitive information, it must be shown that the denial is necessitated by a compelling governmental interest, and is narrowly tailored to serve that interest." Although the Court agreed that safeguarding the physical and psychological well-being of a minor is a compelling state interest, it found that this could be accomplished on a case-by-case basis with the trial judge weighing "the minor victim's age, psychological maturity and understanding, the nature of the crime, the desires of the victim, and the interests of parents and relatives."[27] It rejected the assertion that the statute was necessary to encourage minor victims to come forward and to provide accurate testimony, saying that "[n]ot only is the claim speculative

[27] United States v. Sherlock, 962 F.2d 1349 (9th Cir.1989), upheld a trial court order excluding the defendant's family in a rape case. The victim, a child, became upset when the defendant's family began giggling and making faces at her during her testimony. The court held that a partial closure (excluding only certain people) was easier to justify than a total closure of a criminal proceeding.

in empirical terms, but it is also open to serious question as a matter of logic and common sense."

Chief Justice Burger, joined by Justice Rehnquist, dissented in *Globe Newspapers*. He argued that there was historical support for exclusion of the public from trials involving sexual assaults, particularly those against minors; that the law was a rational response to the undisputed problem of the underreporting of rapes and other sexual offenses; and that the states should have room to experiment before a court demands empirical data to justify a law permitting closure. Justice O'Connor concurred in the judgment, emphasizing that *Richmond Newspapers* applies only to criminal trials. Justice Stevens dissented on procedural grounds.

Globe Newspaper Co. answered some of the questions raised by *Richmond Newspapers*, but did not decide whether the First Amendment right of access applied in pretrial proceedings.

Closure of Voir Dire: Press Enterprise I

Richmond Newspapers was the authority that Chief Justice Burger cited in his opinion for the Court in Press-Enterprise Co. v. Superior Court, 464 U.S. 501 (1984) ("Press-Enterprise I"). The important facts were as follows: Jury selection in a capital prosecution for rape and murder took six weeks. Only three days of the voir dire of the jury was open to the public, because the trial judge was concerned about the privacy of the jurors. After the jury was selected, the trial judge denied a request by Press-Enterprise to release a transcript of the voir dire. A state appellate court sustained the trial judge and the state supreme court denied review.

Citing neither the First nor the Sixth Amendment, the Supreme Court stated that "how we allocate the 'right' to openness as between the accused and the public, or whether we view it as a component inherent in the system benefitting both, is not crucial. No right ranks higher than the right of the accused to a fair trial. But the primacy of the accused's right is difficult to separate from the right of everyone in the community to attend the voir dire which promotes fairness." It reasoned that openness has "a community therapeutic value" and that secret proceedings would deny an outlet for community reaction to serious crime.

Openness, while prized, was not absolutely required, however:

> The presumption of openness may be overcome only by an overriding interest based on findings that closure is essential to preserve higher values and is narrowly tailored to serve that interest. The interest is to be articulated along with findings specific enough that a reviewing court can determine whether the closure order was properly entered.

As an example of proper closure, the Court suggested that in a rape prosecution a prospective juror might privately inform the judge that she or a member of her family had been raped, but had declined to seek prosecution because of the associated emotional trauma. It also suggested that "[b]y requiring the prospective juror to make an affirmative request, the trial judge can ensure that there is in fact a valid basis for a belief that disclosure infringes a significant interest in privacy," and that "[w]hen limited closure is ordered, the constitutional values sought to be protected by holding open proceedings may be satisfied later by making a transcript of the closed proceedings available within a reasonable time, if the judge determines that disclosure can be accomplished while safeguarding the juror's valid privacy interests."

On the facts presented, the Court found that the closure order and the sealing of the transcript were unwarranted. It observed that there were less onerous alternatives than a total preclusion of media access to the voir dire transcript. For example, parts of the transcript might have been sealed and other parts disclosed; also, the judge could have considered revealing the substance of answers without disclosing the identity of jurors.

Justice Blackmun concurred, stating that he saw no need to decide whether privacy interests of jurors might outweigh a defendant's need for information about jurors. Justice Marshall, who concurred in the judgment, also expressed concern about denying the public and the press private information about jurors. Justice Stevens also concurred. He explicitly relied upon a First Amendment right of access.

Closure of Voir Dire Proceedings in a High Profile Trial—Martha Stewart

In ABC, Inc. v. Stewart, 360 F.3d 90 (2d Cir. 2004)—involving the prosecution of the television personality Martha Stewart—the trial judge barred the media from attending voir dire examinations of jurors, but provided that the voir dire transcripts would be released to the media with the names of the prospective jurors redacted. The trial judge was concerned that members of the media, in this high profile prosecution, would attempt to interview prospective jurors during jury selection. But the court of appeals found that the trial judge had erred under *Press Enterprise* because it had not made factual findings that its limitations on media access were "essential" to protect against juror interviews. There was no showing, for example, that any member of the media had ever attempted to interview a prospective juror. The court stated that "[t]he mere fact that the suit has been the subject of intense media coverage is not, however, sufficient to justify closure. To hold otherwise would render the First Amendment right of access meaningless; the very demand for openness would paradoxically defeat its availability."

Procedural Requirements for Determining the Propriety of Closure: Waller v. Georgia

In Waller v. Georgia, 467 U.S. 39 (1984), the Court considered the propriety of closure of a suppression hearing. An indictment charged a number of people with racketeering and other offenses. Prior to the trial of one group of defendants, a motion was made to suppress evidence obtained through wiretaps and searches of homes. The prosecution moved to have the suppression hearing closed to all persons other than those involved in the prosecution on the ground that the taps would "involve" some persons who were indicted but not on trial in this case and other persons not indicted at all. Over the objection of some defendants, the trial judge granted the motion. The suppression hearing lasted seven days, although only two and a half hours were devoted to playing tapes of intercepted conversations. The trial judge suppressed some, but not all, evidence. At trial the defendants were acquitted of racketeering and convicted on gambling charges. Thereafter, but before other persons named in the indictment were tried, a transcript of the suppression hearing was released. The Georgia Supreme Court found that the trial judge had properly balanced the defendants' right to a public hearing against the privacy rights of other persons. The United States Supreme Court disagreed.

Justice Powell, writing for the Court, stated that "there can be little doubt that the explicit Sixth Amendment right of the accused is no less protective than the implicit First Amendment right of the press and public." He also observed that "suppression hearings often are as important as the trial itself. In *Gannett*, as in many cases, the suppression hearing was the *only* trial, because the defendants thereafter pleaded guilty pursuant to a plea bargain." And he concluded that a suppression hearing often resembles a bench trial in which witnesses are sworn and testify, making the need for an open proceeding especially strong. Thus, the Court held "that under the Sixth Amendment any closure of a suppression hearing over the objections of the accused must meet the tests set out in *Press-Enterprise* and its predecessors."

The Court found that the trial judge erred in not considering alternatives to closing the entire hearing and in not requiring the government to provide more details about its need for closure. One option the Court cited was to close only the part of the hearing—e.g., the playing of the tapes—that jeopardized the interests articulated by the government. Rather than reverse the convictions, the Court remanded the case for a new suppression hearing to be conducted in accordance with the constitutional standards articulated in this and prior cases.

Lower courts have read *Waller* as articulating a four-prong test by which to assess the propriety of closure:

> (1) The party seeking to close the hearing must advance an overriding interest that is likely to be prejudiced; (2) the closure must be no broader than necessary to protect that interest; (3) the trial court must consider reasonable alternatives to closing the proceeding; and (4) the trial court must make findings adequate to support the closure.

People v. Kin Kan, 78 N.Y.2d 54, 571 N.Y.S.2d 436 (1991).

Sixth Amendment Limitation on Excluding the Public from Juror Voir Dire: Presley v. Georgia

In Presley v. Georgia, 558 U.S. 209 (2010) (per curiam), the defendant's uncle sought to sit in the courtroom during the voir dire of jurors, but the trial court determined that there were no seats available given the number of prospective jurors, and so excluded him from the courtroom. The defendant argued that his Sixth Amendment right to a public trial was violated, because the trial court failed to consider any alternatives that might accommodate the uncle. The Court observed that it held in *Press-Enterprise I* that the First Amendment right to a public trial in criminal cases extended to voir dire of prospective jurors and in *Waller* it held that the Sixth Amendment public trial right extended to a pretrial suppression hearing. The Court observed that "[t]he extent to which the First and Sixth Amendment public trial rights are coextensive is an open question, and it is not necessary here to speculate whether or in what circumstances the reach or protections of one might be greater than the other," but concluded that "there is no legitimate reason, at least in the context of juror selection proceedings, to give one who asserts a First Amendment privilege greater rights to insist on public proceedings than the accused has." The Court also concluded that "[t]rial courts are obligated to take every reasonable measure to accommodate public attendance at criminal trials," and "[n]othing in the record shows that the trial court could not have accommodated the public at Presley's trial." Justice Thomas, joined by Justice Scalia, dissented.

Preliminary Hearings: Press-Enterprise II

In Press-Enterprise Co. v. Superior Court, 478 U.S. 1 (1986) ("*Press-Enterprise II*"), Chief Justice Burger wrote for the majority as it concluded "that the qualified First Amendment right of access to criminal proceedings applies to preliminary hearings as they are conducted in California." He reasoned that preliminary hearings have usually been open, and that preliminary hearings are sufficiently like trials in California to justify the conclusion that public access is essential. Thus, the Chief Justice focused on two factors in determining the applicability of the First Amendment right of access to proceedings other than trials: 1) whether there has been a tradition of openness at such proceedings, and 2) whether the proceeding is "trial-like." Chief Justice Burger concluded that preliminary hearings may only be closed "if specific findings are made demonstrating that, first, there is a substantial probability that the defendant's right to a fair trial will be prejudiced by publicity that closure would prevent and, second, reasonable alternatives to closure cannot adequately protect the defendant's free trial rights."

Justice Stevens, joined in part by Justice Rehnquist, dissented. He challenged the reliance on the value of openness as proving too much, because the same argument could be made with respect to grand jury proceedings, even though these proceedings have historically been secret.[28]

See also United States v. Simone, 14 F.3d 833 (3d Cir.1994) (relying on *Press-Enterprise II* and holding that the First Amendment qualified right of access applies to a post-trial investigation of juror misconduct).

2. Change of Venue and Continuance

Media coverage of a crime is often the most intense and pervasive in the place where the crime occurred. And coverage often is greater immediately after a crime is committed or an arrest takes place than later. By transferring a case, or by continuing a trial until passions cool, some of the ill effects of pretrial publicity might be avoided.

Transfer of Venue

Fed.R.Crim.P. 21(a) provides that the court must transfer proceedings to another district upon the defendant's motion if the judge is "satisfied that so great a prejudice against the defendant exists in the transferring district that the defendant cannot obtain a fair and impartial trial there." In *Sheppard* the Court said that "where there is a *reasonable likelihood* that the prejudicial news prior to trial will prevent a fair trial, the judge should continue the case until the threat abates, or transfer it to another county not so permeated with publicity." (Emphasis added.) But most courts require much more than a reasonable likelihood of prejudice from pretrial publicity before transfer of venue is mandated. A defendant must ordinarily make a showing of *actual and substantial prejudice* before change of venue is required.

---

[28] *Press-Enterprise II* was found controlling in El Vocero de Puerto Rico v. Puerto Rico, 508 U.S. 147 (1993) (per curiam). Under Puerto Rican law, an accused felon is entitled to a hearing to determine if he shall be held for trial. Both sides may introduce evidence and cross-examine witnesses, and the defendant has the right to counsel. Puerto Rican law provided that the hearing is private unless the defendant requests otherwise. The Supreme Court held that the privacy provision of the Puerto Rican law was unconstitutional. As in *Press-Enterprise II,* the Court found that the Puerto Rican hearing was "sufficiently like a trial" to require public access. The Court rejected the notion that the unique history and traditions of Puerto Rican culture were at all relevant to whether the press and public could have access to the hearing. The Court concluded that any concerns that the defendant might not receive a fair trial must be addressed on a case-by-case basis.

An application of the actual and substantial prejudice standard is shown in United States v. Angiulo, 897 F.2d 1169 (1st Cir.1990), a widely publicized Mafia/RICO case, in which the court denied the defendant's motion for change of venue. The court, relying on Patton v. Yount, supra, held that the mere fact that a majority of the empaneled jurors had been exposed to the Patriarca-Angiulo names, or that some linked the Angiulo name with the Mafia, was not sufficient to support a finding of actual prejudice requiring a change of venue. The court deferred to the trial court's conclusion that the jurors could lay aside their impressions and render a verdict based on the evidence in court.

Because courts focus more on actual prejudice than on the likelihood of prejudice, it is common for the ruling on a change of venue motion to be reserved until jury selection, because it is then that the effect of trial publicity on potential jurors can be best assessed. But what happens then is predictable. Courts invest resources in voir dire of potential jurors, and the more they invest the more they want to get a return—to go ahead and try the case. It is the rare case in which a change of venue is granted once the jury is empaneled. The "solution" then becomes a set of stern jury instructions.

The hostility of some courts to change of venue motions can be attributed to feelings that trial at a distant location will burden witnesses, that the community in which the crime was committed has a substantial interest in seeing the law enforced against wrongdoers by means of the criminal justice system, and that a change of prosecutors might be required, which could be disruptive of legitimate interests of the government.[29] Courts may also be concerned that the selection of the transferee jurisdiction may be viewed as unfair to one side or the other. These interests in not changing venue are usually found to outweigh the benefits to the defendant of a venue change; less onerous alternatives such as careful voir dire and strong jury instructions are usually held sufficient to protect the defendant's interests, whether that is actually true or not.

Continuance

A continuance may be less disruptive than a change of venue, because it does not change the place where trial is held. In Patton v. Yount, supra, the Supreme Court emphasized that the passage of time would go far to dissipate the taint of prejudicial pretrial publicity. 18 U.S.C.A. § 316(b)(8)(A) indicates that a continuance can be granted if the judge determines that "the ends of justice served by taking such action outweigh

[29] Sometimes the government wants a change of venue despite the burden it may place on prosecutors. Because the defendant generally has a right to be tried in the jurisdiction where the crime was committed, courts are most reluctant to recognize change of venue requests by the government. See State v. Mendoza, 80 Wis.2d 122, 258 N.W.2d 260 (1977). Some states have upheld the prosecutor's right to seek a venue change. Others have limited the right to defendants.

the best interest of the public and the defendant in a speedy trial." What this apparently means is that the defendant's right to a speedy trial must be balanced against his right to a fair trial free of prejudicial publicity. Does that make any sense? Is a continuance a proper solution if the defendant is subject to pretrial incarceration?

VI. THE DEFENDANT'S RIGHT TO PARTICIPATE IN THE TRIAL

A. THE RIGHT OF THE DEFENDANT TO BE PRESENT

One aspect of the Sixth Amendment's right to a fair trial involves the defendant's right to be present during the trial. This right and its limits are discussed in the next case.

ILLINOIS V. ALLEN

Supreme Court of the United States, 1970.
397 U.S. 337.

JUSTICE BLACK delivered the opinion of the Court.

The Confrontation Clause of the Sixth Amendment to the United States Constitution provides that: "In all criminal prosecutions, the accused shall enjoy the right * * * to be confronted with the witnesses against him * * *." * * * One of the most basic of the rights guaranteed by the Confrontation Clause is the accused's right to be present in the courtroom at every stage of his trial. The question presented in this case is whether an accused can claim the benefit of this constitutional right to remain in the courtroom while at the same time he engages in speech and conduct which is so noisy, disorderly, and disruptive that it is exceedingly difficult or wholly impossible to carry on the trial.

[Allen was charged with armed robbery. He insisted on representing himself, but the trial judge assigned counsel to "sit in and protect the record" for Allen. During his voir dire of the first juror, Allen asked so many questions that the judge instructed him to limit himself to the juror's qualifications. Allen argued so much that the judge asked the assigned counsel to take over voir dire. The federal court of appeals, which held that Allen's rights were violated when he was removed from the courtroom following disruptive behavior described some of that behavior, beginning with Allen's threat to the judge: "When I go out for lunchtime, you're [the judge] going to be a corpse here." At that point he tore the file which his attorney had and threw the papers on the floor. The trial judge thereupon stated to the petitioner, "One more outbreak of that sort and I'll remove you from the courtroom." This warning had no effect on the petitioner. He continued to talk back to the judge, saying, "There's not going to be no trial, either. I'm going to sit here and you're going to talk and you can bring your shackles out and straight jacket and put them on me and tape my mouth, but it will do no good because there's not going to be no trial." After more abusive remarks by Allen, the trial judge ordered the trial to proceed in Allen's absence.]

It is essential to the proper administration of criminal justice that dignity, order, and decorum be the hallmarks of all court proceedings in our country. The flagrant disregard in the courtroom of elementary standards of proper conduct should not and cannot be tolerated. We believe trial judges confronted with disruptive, contumacious, stubbornly defiant defendants must be given sufficient discretion to meet the circumstances of each case. * * * We think there are at least three constitutionally permissible ways for a trial judge to handle an obstreperous defendant like Allen: (1) bind and gag him, thereby keeping him present; (2) cite him for contempt; (3) take him out of the courtroom until he promises to conduct himself properly.

* * *

Trying a defendant for a crime while he sits bound and gagged before the judge and jury would to an extent comply with that part of the Sixth Amendment's purposes that accords the defendant an opportunity to confront the witnesses at the trial. But even to contemplate such a technique, much less see it, arouses a feeling that no person should be tried while shackled and gagged except as a last resort. Not only is it possible that the sight of shackles and gags might have a significant effect on the jury's feelings about the defendant, but the use of this technique is itself something of an affront to the very dignity and decorum of judicial proceedings that the judge is seeking to uphold. Moreover, one of the defendant's primary advantages of being present at the trial, his ability to communicate with his counsel, is greatly reduced when the defendant is in a condition of total physical restraint. * * * However, in some situations which we need not attempt to foresee, binding and gagging might possibly be the fairest and most reasonable way to handle a defendant * * *.

* * *

Allen's behavior was clearly of such an extreme and aggravated nature as to justify either his removal from the courtroom or his total physical restraint. Prior to his removal he was repeatedly warned by the trial judge that he would be removed from the courtroom if he persisted in his unruly conduct, and * * * the record demonstrates that Allen would not have been at all dissuaded by the trial judge's use of his criminal contempt powers. Allen was constantly informed that he could return to the trial when he would agree to conduct himself in an orderly manner. Under these circumstances we hold that Allen lost his right guaranteed by the Sixth and Fourteenth Amendments to be present throughout his trial.

* * *

Shackling, Courtroom Security, and Prejudice to the Defendant

The Supreme Court held in Holbrook v. Flynn, 475 U.S. 560 (1986), that deployment of uniformed law enforcement officers in a courtroom during a trial for security reasons is not inherently prejudicial to a defendant. It found no denial of due process or equal protection when four uniformed state troopers sat in the spectator section of the courtroom behind the defense table. Justice Marshall's unanimous opinion for the Court stated that it would never be possible "to eliminate from trial procedures every reminder that the State has chosen to marshal its resources against a defendant to punish him for allegedly criminal conduct." According to Justice Marshall, the Due Process Clause prohibits only such procedures so inherently prejudicial that they "brand the defendant with an unmistakable mark of guilt." The use of security officers was not considered inherently prejudicial because "the presence of guards at a defendant's trial need not be interpreted as a sign that he is particularly dangerous or culpable." Justice Marshall concluded that four troopers, sitting in the first row of the spectator's section, "are unlikely to have been taken as a sign of anything other than a normal official concern for the safety and order of the proceedings." The Court distinguished Estelle v. Williams, 425 U.S. 501 (1976), where it had found a due process violation when the defendant was forced to wear prison garb at trial. Justice Marshall concluded that even if the presence of the guards was somewhat prejudicial, "sufficient cause for this level of security could be found in the State's need to maintain custody over defendants who had been denied bail after an individualized determination that their presence at trial could not otherwise be ensured." In contrast, there was no justifiable need in *Williams* to dress the defendant in prison garb for trial.

What about forcing the defendant to wear an electronic "stun belt" during trial proceedings? This can be hidden under the defendant's clothes, so it wouldn't seem to be the badge of guilt that the Court was concerned about in *Holbrook*. But the courts have been—understandably—wary, because of the possible psychological effects on the defendant. See Gonzalez v. Pliler, 341 F.3d 897 (9th Cir. 2003) (forcing defendant to wear an electronic "stun belt" during trial proceedings was improper where the only justification was that the court heard from the bailiff that the defendant had a "bit of an attitude"); United States v. Durham, 287 F.3d 1297 (11th Cir. 2002) (use of stun belt improper where court did not inquire into the possibility that the belt might be activated accidentally, and the defendant was already shackled during the trial).

Shackling at the Penalty Phase of a Capital Case: Deck v. Missouri

In Deck v. Missouri, 544 U.S. 622 (2005), Justice Breyer wrote for the Court as it considered the applicability of *Holbrook* and *Allen* to the practice of shackling capital defendants during the sentencing phase and held "that the Constitution forbids the use of visible shackles during the penalty phase, as it forbids their use during the guilt phase, *unless* that use is justified by an essential state interest—such as the interest in courtroom security—specific to the defendant on trial." The Court found that freedom from shackling in the absence of substantial government interests was grounded in three important considerations: 1) protecting the presumption of innocence; 2) protecting the right to confer with counsel; and 3) maintaining the dignity of the courtroom. But, the Court also recognized that "[t]here will be cases, of course, where these perils of shackling are unavoidable," and made clear that it did "not underestimate the need to restrain dangerous defendants to prevent courtroom attacks, or the need to give trial courts latitude in making individualized security determinations."

Justice Thomas, joined by Justice Scalia, dissented. He engaged in an extensive discussion of English common law and noted that the irons of that period were "heavy and painful" and thus raised concerns about torture. Justice Thomas argued that "[t]reating shackling at sentencing as inherently prejudicial ignores the commonsense distinction between a defendant who stands accused and a defendant who stands convicted," and "[c]apital sentencing jurors know that the defendant has been convicted of a dangerous crime" so that jurors are hardly "surprised at the sight of restraints." Is this persuasive? If a defendant is not shackled when guilt is determined but appears in shackles at sentencing, might the jury assume, incorrectly, that the defendant engaged in dangerous conduct after being convicted? If so, what impact is this likely to have on a sentencing recommendation?

Commenting on the Defendant's Presence at Trial: Portuondo v. Agard

Witnesses are often sequestered before they testify in a criminal trial. See Federal Rule of Evidence 615. Sequestration addresses the concern that if a witness knows the evidence already presented, he might tailor his testimony to fit that evidence. But a criminal defendant who chooses to testify cannot be sequestered, because he has a constitutional right to attend the trial. In Portuondo v. Agard, 529 U.S. 61 (2000), the prosecutor in summation sought to draw this fact to the jury's attention. The case required the jury to make a credibility judgment regarding both the defendant Agard and the victims. Although the more typical practice in federal court is to have the prosecution make the first closing argument and to make a rebuttal argument after the defense closes, apparently in this case each side had only one closing opportunity with the defense going first and the prosecutor (with the burden of persuasion) going last. The prosecutor argued as follows:

> You know, ladies and gentlemen, unlike all the other witnesses in this case the defendant has a benefit and the benefit that he has, unlike all the other witnesses, is he gets to sit here and listen to the testimony of all the other witnesses before he testifies. * * * That gives you a big advantage, doesn't it. You get to sit here and think what am I going to say and how am I going to say it? How am I going to fit it into the evidence? * * * He's a smart man. I never said he was stupid. . . . He used everything to his advantage.

Agard contended that the prosecutor's argument placed an impermissible burden on his right to be present at trial. The trial court rejected this claim, reasoning that Agard's status as the last witness in the case was simply a matter of fact. The Supreme Court, in an opinion by Justice Scalia for five Justices, agreed with the trial court. Justice Scalia concluded as follows:

> In sum, we see no reason to depart from the practice of treating testifying defendants the same as other witnesses. A witness's ability to hear prior testimony and to tailor his account accordingly, and the threat that ability presents to the integrity of the trial, are no different when it is the defendant doing the listening. Allowing comment upon the fact that a defendant's presence in the courtroom provides him a unique opportunity to tailor his testimony is appropriate—and indeed, given the inability to sequester the defendant, sometimes essential—to the central function of the trial, which is to discover the truth.

Justice Stevens, joined by Justice Breyer, concurred in the judgment in *Agard*. Justice Stevens found no constitutional violation in the prosecutor's tailoring argument. He wrote, however, to express his "disagreement with the Court's implicit endorsement of her summation" and concluded that such arguments should be discouraged as a matter of fair trial practice.

Justice Ginsburg, joined by Justice Souter, dissented in *Agard*. She focused on the fact that the prosecutor's tailoring argument was "generic", i.e., it could be applied in any case in which the defendant testified. Such an "automatic burden" on the defendant's credibility resulted, in her view, in an unfair penalty for the defendant's exercise of his constitutional right to be present.

For a discussion of the some of the implications of *Agard* on the admissibility of evidence and the possible use of the case to the benefit of the defense, see Saltzburg and Capra, The Unrecognized Right of Criminal

Defendants to Admit Their Own Pretrial Statements, 49 William & Mary L.Rev. 1991 (2008).

B. THE REQUIREMENT OF COMPETENCE TO STAND TRIAL

The premise of the constitutional right to be present is that the defendant has the right to participate in his own defense. Indeed, participation by the defendant is ordinarily essential to assure that witnesses are fully cross-examined, exculpatory facts are presented, and jurors are challenged when necessary, etc. But if the defendant is mentally incapable of participating in his defense, the right to be present is a nullity. Not surprisingly, then, the Supreme Court has often held that the Due Process Clause prohibits the criminal prosecution of a defendant who is not competent to stand trial. Drope v. Missouri, 420 U.S. 162 (1975); Pate v. Robinson, 383 U.S. 375 (1966).

In Dusky v. United States, 362 U.S. 402 (1960), the Court held that a defendant is competent to stand trial when he has "sufficient present ability to consult with his lawyer with a reasonable degree of rational understanding" and has a "rational as well as factual understanding of the proceedings against him." See also Drope v. Missouri, supra (a person "whose mental condition is such that he lacks the capacity to understand the nature and object of the proceedings against him, to consult with counsel, and to assist in preparing his defense may not be subjected to a trial").

A criminal prosecution must be delayed during the time that a defendant is incompetent, and a verdict rendered against an incompetent defendant is voidable. As a practical matter, it is often in the state's interest to press for a trial of a defendant whose claim of incompetency is questionable, and it is often in the defendant's interest to seek to delay such a trial in the hope that witnesses will become unavailable. Predictably, disputes arise on whether a defendant is actually incompetent, and whether the state can use certain methods to assure that the defendant is competent to stand trial.

Forced Medication to Assure Competence: Riggins v. Nevada

What should the state do if a defendant is only competent when taking medication and he refuses to take it? In Riggins v. Nevada, 504 U.S. 127 (1992), the defendant moved to terminate use of Mellaril, an anti-psychotic drug. His proposed defense at trial was insanity, and he argued that continued administration of the drug would deprive him of the right to show the jury his true mental state. The trial court held a hearing at which experts disagreed about whether Riggins would be competent to stand trial in the absence of medication. The experts also disagreed about the effects of the medication upon Riggins's demeanor at trial and upon his ability to participate in his defense. The trial court denied Riggins' motion. At the trial, Riggins testified while under medication. He was eventually convicted and sentenced to death.

The Supreme Court, in an opinion by Justice O'Connor, reversed the conviction. Justice O'Connor noted that a person has a liberty interest in being free from unwanted medication, citing Washington v. Harper, 494 U.S. 210 (1990). She recognized that the state could compel medication in certain circumstances—such as when the person presented a risk of harm to himself or to others—but concluded that the trial court had erred when it "allowed the administration of Mellaril to continue without making *any* determination of the need for this course or *any* findings about reasonable alternatives." She also noted that the trial court had not specifically acknowledged Riggins's liberty interest in freedom from unwanted anti-psychotic drugs. Relying on scientific literature, Justice O'Connor asserted that the side effects of Mellaril may have affected Riggins's demeanor, his testimony at trial, his ability to follow the proceedings, and his ability to communicate with counsel. She concluded that the forced medication created "a strong possibility that Riggins's defense was impaired due to the administration of Mellaril."

Justice O'Connor recognized that under *Holbrook* and *Allen,* "trial prejudice can sometimes be justified by an essential state interest." But because the record contained no finding that forced medication was necessary to accomplish an essential state policy, the majority held that there was no basis "for saying that the substantial probability of trial prejudice in this case was justified."

Justice Kennedy concurred in the judgment and argued that by forcing medication at trial, the state was "manipulating the evidence." He concluded that "if the State cannot render the defendant competent without involuntary medication, then it must resort to civil commitment, if appropriate, unless the defendant becomes competent through other means."

Justice Thomas, joined by Justice Scalia, dissented. He noted that the trial court had allowed defense experts to testify as to the effects of Mellaril on Riggins's demeanor, and that insofar as his ability to participate in his defense was concerned, "the record indicates that Riggins's mental capacity was *enhanced* by his administration of Mellaril." Accordingly, Justice Thomas concluded that Riggins had suffered no trial prejudice from the forced medication.

In Sell v. United States, 539 U.S. 166 (2003), the Court held that the Due Process Clause permits the Government to administer antipsychotic drugs to a mentally ill defendant facing serious criminal charges in order to render that defendant competent to stand trial—but only if the treatment is 1) medically appropriate; 2) substantially unlikely to have side effects that may undermine the fairness of the trial; and 3) necessary to further important governmental trial-related interests. The Court held that the defendant could not be ordered to take antipsychotic drugs solely to render him competent to stand trial without consideration of other factors.

Burden of Proof as to Competency: Medina v. California

The Court held in Medina v. California, 505 U.S. 437 (1992), that the Due Process Clause permits a state to allocate to the defendant the burden of proving that he is not competent to stand trial. On the basis of conflicting psychiatric testimony, Medina was found competent to stand trial under a state rule requiring that he show incompetence by a preponderance of the evidence. Medina was ultimately sentenced to death. Justice Kennedy wrote the majority opinion for five Justices. He asserted that the Due Process Clause does not "require a state to adopt one procedure over another on the basis that it may produce results more favorable to the accused." He concluded that "it is enough that the State affords the criminal defendant on whose behalf a plea of incompetence is asserted a reasonable opportunity to demonstrate that he is not competent to stand trial."

Justice Kennedy rejected the argument that the defendant's impairment may itself make it all but impossible to satisfy a burden of proof at the incompetency hearing. He explained that "although an impaired defendant might be limited in his ability to assist counsel in demonstrating incompetence, the defendant's inability to assist counsel can, in and of itself, constitute probative evidence of incompetence, and defense counsel will often have the best-informed view of the defendant's ability to participate in his defense."

Justice O'Connor, joined by Justice Souter, concurred in the judgment. Justice Blackmun dissented in an opinion joined by Justice Stevens. He concluded that the constitutional prohibition against convicting incompetent defendants is severely diminished "if the State is at liberty to go forward with a trial when the evidence of competency is inconclusive."

Does it really make much difference who has the burden of persuasion if the standard of proof is a preponderance of the evidence and the decision-maker is the trial judge? What is the likelihood that the judge will be in equipoise, which is the only time the burden is really meaningful?

Requiring the Defendant to Prove Competency by Clear and Convincing Evidence: Cooper v. Oklahoma

The State of Oklahoma sought to extend *Medina* in Cooper v. Oklahoma, 517 U.S. 348 (1996). The Oklahoma competency statute established a presumption that the defendant was competent to stand trial, and required the defendant to prove his incompetence by *clear and convincing evidence*. The trial court found it more likely than not that Cooper was incompetent, but nonetheless proceeded with the trial on the ground that Cooper had not shown incompetence by clear and convincing evidence. Cooper was convicted and sentenced to death, but his conviction was reversed in a unanimous opinion written by Justice Stevens.

Justice Stevens declared that the result in *Medina* (permitting the state to require the defendant to prove incompetence by a *preponderance* of the evidence) rested in part on the fact that the preponderance standard "affects the outcome only in a narrow class of cases where the evidence is in equipoise." In contrast, Oklahoma's practice of requiring the defendant to prove incompetence by clear and convincing evidence "poses a significant risk of an erroneous determination that the defendant is competent" and "affects a class of cases in which the defendant has already demonstrated that he is more likely than not incompetent."

Justice Stevens reasoned that a heightened standard of proof "does not decrease the risk of error, but simply reallocates that risk between the parties." Given the balance of interests at stake in the risk of a mistaken determination of a defendant's competence to stand trial, the Court found it unjust to allocate such a heavy burden to the defendant. The risk to the defendant of an erroneous determination of competence is that he will be unable to participate in his defense, thus impairing "the basic fairness of the trial itself." In contrast, the risk to the state of an erroneous determination of incompetence is "modest." While the state's interest in swift justice is implicated, the defendant can still be detained while incompetent, and a trial at a later date is possible if the defendant becomes competent.

C. THE RIGHT TO BE PRESENT AT ALL STAGES OF THE PROCEEDINGS

Fed.R.Crim.P. 43 provides that the defendant has the right to be present at the arraignment, at the plea, at every trial stage—including jury impanelment and the return of the verdict—and at sentencing. Rogers v. United States, 422 U.S. 35 (1975), indicates the importance of the words "every trial stage" in the Federal Rule. Rogers's conviction for threatening the President was overturned because the jury sent a note to the trial judge inquiring whether the court would "accept the Verdict—'Guilty as charged with extreme mercy of the Court,'" and the judge answered in the affirmative without notifying Rogers or his counsel. Despite the fact that Rogers did not know of the judge's action until after certiorari was granted and therefore never questioned it, the Court, in a unanimous opinion by Chief Justice Burger, concluded that Rule 43 was violated and that the error was not harmless.[30] The Court reasoned that the response that the judge gave the jury could have been improved considerably and might have induced unanimity among jury members.

Exclusion from Hearing on Competency of Witnesses: Kentucky v. Stincer

The Supreme Court held in Kentucky v. Stincer, 482 U.S. 730 (1987), that a defendant was not denied his right of confrontation when he was barred from an in-chambers hearing to determine the competency to testify of two minors who allegedly were sodomized by the defendant. Justice Blackmun reasoned in his majority opinion that there was no indication that the defendant's presence at the hearing would have promoted a more reliable competency determination. The defendant was represented at the hearing by counsel, who was permitted to question the victims on competency issues. After the judge found the victims to be competent, they testified in open court in the presence of the defendant and were asked by defense counsel questions about their memory and understanding of the difference between the truth and a lie.

Justice Blackmun declined to decide whether a competency hearing is a trial or pretrial proceeding and stated that "it is more useful to consider whether excluding the defendant from the hearing interferes with his opportunity for effective cross-examination." He emphasized that state law permitted the defendant to cross-examine the victims completely at trial and to address their competency, even to the point of repeating questions asked at the competency hearing.

Justice Blackmun placed great weight on the fact that at the competency hearing "[n]o question regarding the substantive testimony that the two girls would have given during trial was asked," and stated that "although a competency hearing in which a witness is asked to discuss upcoming substantive testimony might bear a substantial relationship to a defendant's opportunity better to defend himself at trial, that kind of inquiry is not before us in this case."

---

30 The Supreme Court reversed a court of appeals summarily in United States v. Gagnon, 470 U.S. 522 (1985), and found that four defendants waived a right to be present when a trial judge questioned a juror in chambers concerning his statement of concern to a bailiff about one defendant's drawing pictures of the jury. The Court held that the presence of counsel and the defendants was not necessary to ensure fundamental fairness and that the defendants waived any right to be present under Fed.R.Crim.P. 43 by not objecting to the procedure used by the trial judge.

Justice Marshall, joined by Justices Brennan and Stevens, dissented. Justice Marshall reasoned that "[p]hysical presence of the defendant enhances the reliability of the fact-finding process" and that "[i]t is both functionally inefficient and fundamentally unfair to attribute to the defendant's attorney complete knowledge of the facts which the trial judge, in the defendant's involuntary absence, deems relevant to the competency determination."

D. TRIAL IN ABSENTIA

Federal Rule 43(c) provides that a defendant loses his right to be present by disruptive conduct or by voluntarily absenting himself *after the trial starts.* In Crosby v. United States, 506 U.S. 255 (1993), Justice Blackmun wrote for a unanimous Court as it held that Rule 43 does not permit the trial *in absentia* of a defendant who absconds *prior* to trial and is absent at its beginning. Crosby, charged with mail fraud, was released on bond pending his trial. He failed to appear for trial while three codefendants and a pool of 54 jurors waited for him. The trial judge found that his absence was deliberate and that the trial should commence. The Supreme Court recognized that Rule 43 permits a trial to continue if a defendant absconds *after* it begins, but held that the Rule means what it says and that it does not permit a trial to be started when a defendant is absent.

Justice Blackmun stated that the distinction in the Rule between pretrial and mid-trial flight was not "so farfetched as to convince us that Rule 43 cannot mean what it says." He noted the following reasons for making such a distinction: 1) "the costs of suspending a proceeding already under way will be greater than the cost of postponing a trial not yet begun;" 2) "the defendant's initial presence assures that any waiver is indeed knowing," whereas it could not as easily be assumed that a defendant not yet at trial would know that a trial could occur in his absence; and 3) "a rule that allows an ongoing trial to continue when a defendant disappears deprives the defendant of the option of gambling on an acquittal knowing that he can terminate the trial if it seems that the verdict will go against him—an option that might otherwise appear preferable to the costly, perhaps unnecessary, path of becoming a fugitive from the outset." The Court did not decide whether trying Crosby *in absentia* violated his constitutional right to be present, as well as Rule 43.

VII. THE RIGHT TO EFFECTIVE ASSISTANCE OF COUNSEL

In Chapter 5 we saw that the accused is guaranteed the right to counsel. Here we examine the kind of counsel that the accused has a right to expect during the trial process.

A. INEFFECTIVENESS AND PREJUDICE

Although counsel is constitutionally required at trial and at many pre- and post-trial stages of a criminal prosecution, the quality of representation afforded defendants is uneven. A defendant who is acquitted has little reason to complain, even if her lawyer made serious errors at trial. But a defendant who is convicted may believe that her lawyer did not provide sufficiently competent representation. If so, she may challenge her conviction on the theory that she was denied "effective" assistance of counsel.

The notion that counsel must provide at least some minimal level of representation first appeared in Powell v. Alabama, 287 U.S. 45 (1932). Justice Sutherland's opinion concluded that the trial judge's failure to make an effective appointment of counsel resulted in the "denial of effective and substantial aid. * * * [D]efendants were not accorded the right of counsel in any substantial sense." The Court in *Powell* concluded that the right to counsel means the right to a reasonably effective counsel.

1. The *Strickland* Two-Pronged Test

In the following case, the Court set forth the standards that a defendant must meet to justify the reversal of a conviction or sentence for ineffective assistance of counsel.

STRICKLAND V. WASHINGTON

Supreme Court of the United States, 1984.
466 U.S. 668.

JUSTICE O'CONNOR delivered the opinion of the Court.

This case requires us to consider the proper standards for judging a criminal defendant's contention that the Constitution requires a conviction or death sentence to be set aside because counsel's assistance at the trial or sentencing was ineffective.

* * *

During a ten-day period in September 1976, respondent planned and committed three groups of crimes, which included three brutal stabbing murders, torture, kidnaping, severe assaults, attempted murders, attempted extortion, and theft. After his two accomplices were arrested, respondent surrendered to police and voluntarily gave a lengthy statement confessing to the third of the criminal episodes. The State of Florida indicted respondent for kidnaping and murder and appointed an experienced criminal lawyer to represent him.

Counsel actively pursued pretrial motions and discovery. He cut his efforts short, however, and he experienced a sense of hopelessness about the case, when he learned that, against his specific advice, respondent had also confessed to the first two murders. By the date set for trial, respondent was subject to indictment for three counts of first-degree murder and multiple counts of robbery, kidnapping for ransom, breaking and entering and assault, attempted murder, and conspiracy to commit robbery. Respondent waived his right to a jury trial, again acting against counsel's advice, and pleaded guilty to all charges, including the three capital murder charges.

In the plea colloquy, respondent told the trial judge that, although he had committed a string of burglaries, he had no significant prior criminal record and that at the time of his criminal spree he was under extreme stress caused by his inability to support his family. He also stated, however, that he accepted responsibility for the crimes. The trial judge told respondent that he had "a great deal of respect for people who are willing to step forward and admit their responsibility" but that he was making no statement at all about his likely sentencing decision.

Counsel advised respondent to invoke his right under Florida law to an advisory jury at his capital sentencing hearing. Respondent rejected the advice and waived the right. He chose instead to be sentenced by the trial judge without a jury recommendation.

In preparing for the sentencing hearing, counsel spoke with respondent about his background. He also spoke on the telephone with respondent's wife and mother, though he did not follow up on the one unsuccessful effort to meet with them. He did not otherwise seek out character witnesses for respondent. Nor did he request a psychiatric examination, since his conversations with his client gave no indication that respondent had psychological problems.

Counsel decided not to present and hence not to look further for evidence concerning respondent's character and emotional state. That decision reflected trial counsel's sense of hopelessness about overcoming the evidentiary effect of respondent's confessions to the gruesome crimes. It also reflected the judgment that it was advisable to rely on the plea colloquy for evidence about respondent's background and about his claim of emotional stress: the plea colloquy communicated sufficient information about these subjects, and by foregoing the opportunity to present new evidence on these subjects, counsel prevented the State from cross-examining respondent on his claim and from putting on psychiatric evidence of its own.

Counsel also excluded from the sentencing hearing other evidence he thought was potentially damaging. He successfully moved to exclude respondent's "rap sheet." Because he judged that a presentence report might prove more detrimental than helpful, as it would have included respondent's criminal history and thereby undermined the claim of no significant history of criminal activity, he did not request that one be prepared.

At the sentencing hearing, counsel's strategy was based primarily on the trial judge's remarks at the plea colloquy as well as on his reputation as a sentencing judge who thought it important for a convicted defendant to own up to his crime. Counsel argued that respondent's remorse and acceptance of responsibility justified sparing him from the death penalty. Counsel also argued that respondent had no history of criminal activity and that respondent committed the crimes under extreme mental or emotional disturbance, thus coming within the statutory list of mitigating circumstances. He further argued that respondent should be spared death because he had surrendered, confessed, and offered to testify against a co-defendant and because respondent was fundamentally a good person who had briefly gone badly wrong in extremely stressful circumstances. The State put on evidence and witnesses largely for the purpose of describing the details of the crimes. Counsel did not cross-examine the medical experts who testified about the manner of death of respondent's victims.

The trial judge found several aggravating circumstances with respect to each of the three murders. He found that all three murders were especially heinous, atrocious, and cruel, all involving repeated stabbings. All three murders were committed in the course of at least one other dangerous and violent felony, and since all involved robbery, the murders were for pecuniary gain. * * *

With respect to mitigating circumstances, the trial judge made the same findings for all three capital murders. First, although there was no admitted evidence of prior convictions, respondent had stated that he had engaged in a course of stealing. In any case, even if respondent had no significant history of criminal activity, the aggravating circumstances "would still clearly far outweigh" that mitigating factor. Second, the judge found that, during all three crimes, respondent was not suffering from extreme mental or emotional disturbance and could appreciate the criminality of his acts. Third, none of the victims was a participant in, or consented to, respondent's conduct. Fourth, respondent's participation in the crimes was neither minor nor the result of duress or domination by an accomplice. Finally, respondent's age (26) could not be considered a factor in mitigation, especially when viewed in light of respondent's planning of the crimes and disposition of the proceeds of the various accompanying thefts.

In short, the trial judge found numerous aggravating circumstances and no (or a single comparatively insignificant) mitigating circumstance. * * * He therefore sentenced respondent to death on each of the three counts of murder and to prison terms for the other crimes. The Florida Supreme Court upheld the convictions and sentences on direct appeal.

* * *

Respondent subsequently sought collateral relief in state court on numerous grounds, among them that counsel had rendered ineffective assistance at the sentencing proceeding. Respondent challenged counsel's assistance in six respects. He asserted that counsel was ineffective because he failed to move for a continuance to prepare for sentencing, to request a psychiatric report, to investigate and present character witnesses, to seek a presentence investigation report, to present meaningful arguments to the sentencing judge, and to investigate the medical examiner's reports or cross-examine the medical experts. In support of the claim, respondent submitted fourteen affidavits from friends, neighbors, and relatives stating that they would have testified if asked to do so. He also submitted one psychiatric report and one psychological report stating that respondent, though not under the influence of extreme mental or emotional disturbance, was "chronically frustrated and depressed because of his economic dilemma" at the time of his crimes.

The trial court denied relief without an evidentiary hearing, finding that the record evidence conclusively showed that the ineffectiveness claim was meritless. Four of the assertedly prejudicial errors required little discussion. First, there were no grounds to request a continuance, so there was no error in not requesting one when respondent pleaded guilty. Second, failure to request a presentence investigation was not a serious error because the trial judge had discretion not to grant such a request and because any presentence investigation would have resulted in admission of respondent's rap sheet and thus undermined his assertion of no significant history of criminal activity. Third, the argument and memorandum given to the sentencing judge were "admirable" in light of the overwhelming aggravating circumstances and absence of mitigating circumstances. Fourth, there was no error in failure to examine the medical examiner's reports or to cross-examine the medical witnesses testifying on the manner of death of respondent's victims, since respondent admitted that the victims died in the ways shown by the unchallenged medical evidence.

The trial court dealt at greater length with the two other bases for the ineffectiveness claim. The court pointed out that a psychiatric examination of respondent was conducted by state order soon after respondent's initial arraignment. That report states that there was no indication of major mental illness at the time of the crimes. Moreover, both the reports submitted in the collateral proceeding state that, although respondent was "chronically frustrated and depressed because of his economic dilemma," he was not under the influence of extreme mental or emotional disturbance. * * * Accordingly, counsel could reasonably decide not to seek psychiatric reports; indeed, by relying solely on the plea colloquy to support the emotional disturbance contention, counsel denied the State an opportunity to rebut his claim with psychiatric testimony. In any event, the aggravating circumstances were so overwhelming that no substantial prejudice resulted from the absence at sentencing of the psychiatric evidence offered in the collateral attack.

The court rejected the challenge to counsel's failure to develop and to present character evidence for much the same reasons. The affidavits submitted in the collateral proceeding showed nothing more than that certain persons would have testified that respondent was basically a good person who was worried about his family's financial problems. Respondent himself had already testified along those lines at the plea colloquy. Moreover, respondent's admission of a course of stealing rebutted many of the factual allegations in the affidavits. For those reasons, and because the sentencing judge had stated that the death sentence would be appropriate even if respondent had no significant prior criminal history, no substantial prejudice resulted from the absence at sentencing of the character evidence offered in the collateral attack.

* * *

The Florida Supreme Court affirmed the denial of relief.

Respondent next filed a petition for a writ of habeas corpus in the United States District Court for the Southern District of Florida. * * *

The District Court disputed none of the state court factual findings concerning trial counsel's assistance and made findings of its own that are consistent with the state court findings. * * * On the legal issue of ineffectiveness, the District Court concluded that, although trial counsel made errors in judgment in failing to investigate nonstatutory mitigating evidence further than he did, no prejudice to respondent's sentence resulted from any such error in judgment. * * *

[The Court of Appeals, en banc, reversed the judgment of the District Court and remanded].

* * *

The Sixth Amendment recognizes the right to the assistance of counsel because it envisions counsel's playing a role that is critical to the ability of the adversarial system to produce just results. An accused is entitled to be assisted by an attorney, whether retained or appointed, who plays the role necessary to ensure that the trial is fair.

For that reason, the Court has recognized that "the right to counsel is the right to the effective assistance of counsel." Government violates the right to effective assistance when it interferes in certain ways with the ability of counsel to make independent decisions about how to conduct the defense. See, e.g., Geders v. United States, 425 U.S. 80 (1976) (bar on attorney-client consultation during overnight recess); Herring v. New York, 422 U.S. 853 (1975) (bar on summation at bench trial); Brooks v.

Tennessee, 406 U.S. 605 (1972) (requirement that defendant be first defense witness); Ferguson v. Georgia, 365 U.S. 570 (1961) (bar on direct examination of defendant). Counsel, however, can also deprive a defendant of the right to effective assistance, simply by failing to render adequate legal assistance.

The Court has not elaborated on the meaning of the constitutional requirement of effective assistance in the latter class of cases—that is, those presenting claims of "actual ineffectiveness." In giving meaning to the requirement, however, we must take its purpose—to ensure a fair trial—as the guide. The benchmark for judging any claim of ineffectiveness must be whether counsel's conduct so undermined the proper functioning of the adversarial process that the trial cannot be relied on as having produced a just result.

The same principle applies to a capital sentencing proceeding such as that provided by Florida law. * * *

A convicted defendant's claim that counsel's assistance was so defective as to require reversal of a conviction or death sentence has two components. First, the defendant must show that counsel's performance was deficient. This requires showing that counsel made errors so serious that counsel was not functioning as the "counsel" guaranteed the defendant by the Sixth Amendment. Second, the defendant must show that the deficient performance prejudiced the defense. This requires showing that counsel's errors were so serious as to deprive the defendant of a fair trial, a trial whose result is reliable. Unless a defendant makes both showings, it cannot be said that the conviction or death sentence resulted from a breakdown in the adversary process that renders the result unreliable.

* * * When a convicted defendant complains of the ineffectiveness of counsel's assistance, the defendant must show that counsel's representation fell below an objective standard of reasonableness.

* * *

In any case presenting an ineffectiveness claim, the performance inquiry must be whether counsel's assistance was reasonable considering all the circumstances. * * * No particular set of detailed rules for counsel's conduct can satisfactorily take account of the variety of circumstances faced by defense counsel or the range of legitimate decisions regarding how best to represent a criminal defendant. Any such set of rules would interfere with the constitutionally protected independence of counsel and restrict the wide latitude counsel must have in making tactical decisions. Indeed, the existence of detailed guidelines for representation could distract counsel from the overriding mission of vigorous advocacy of the defendant's cause. * * *

Judicial scrutiny of counsel's performance must be highly deferential. It is all too tempting for a defendant to second-guess counsel's assistance after conviction or adverse sentence, and it is all too easy for a court, examining counsel's defense after it has proved unsuccessful, to conclude that a particular act or omission of counsel was unreasonable. A fair assessment of attorney performance requires that every effort be made to eliminate the distorting effects of hindsight, to reconstruct the circumstances of counsel's challenged conduct, and to evaluate the conduct from counsel's perspective at the time. Because of the difficulties inherent in making the evaluation, a court must indulge a strong presumption that counsel's conduct falls within the wide range of reasonable professional assistance; that is, the defendant must overcome the presumption that, under the circumstances, the challenged action might be considered sound trial strategy. There are countless ways to provide effective assistance in any given case. Even the best criminal defense attorneys would not defend a particular client in the same way.

* * *

These standards require no special amplification in order to define counsel's duty to investigate, the duty at issue in this case. As the Court of Appeals concluded, strategic choices made after thorough investigation of law and facts relevant to plausible options are virtually unchallengeable; and strategic choices made after less than complete investigation are reasonable precisely to the extent that reasonable professional judgments support the limitations on investigation. * * *

The reasonableness of counsel's actions may be determined or substantially influenced by the defendant's own statements or actions. Counsel's actions are usually based, quite properly, on informed strategic choices made by the defendant and on information supplied by the defendant. In particular, what investigation decisions are reasonable depends critically on such information. For example, when the facts that support a certain potential line of defense are generally known to counsel because of what the defendant has said, the need for further investigation may be considerably diminished or eliminated altogether. And when a defendant has given counsel reason to believe that pursuing certain investigations would be fruitless or even harmful, counsel's failure to pursue those investigations may not later be challenged as unreasonable.

* * *

An error by counsel, even if professionally unreasonable, does not warrant setting aside the judgment of a criminal proceeding if the error had no effect on the judgment. * * * Accordingly, any deficiencies in counsel's performance must be prejudicial to the defense in order to constitute ineffective assistance under the Constitution.

In certain Sixth Amendment contexts, prejudice is presumed. Actual or constructive denial of the assistance of counsel altogether is legally presumed to result in prejudice. So are various kinds of state interference with counsel's assistance. Prejudice in these circumstances is so likely that case by case inquiry into prejudice is not worth the cost. Moreover, such circumstances involve impairments of the Sixth Amendment right that are easy to identify and, for that reason and because the prosecution is directly responsible, easy for the government to prevent.

One type of actual ineffectiveness claim warrants a similar, though more limited, presumption of prejudice. In Cuyler v. Sullivan [discussed infra], the Court held that prejudice is presumed when counsel is burdened by an actual conflict of interest. In those circumstances, counsel breaches the duty of loyalty, perhaps the most basic of counsel's duties. Moreover, it is difficult to measure the precise effect on the defense of representation corrupted by conflicting interests. Given the obligation of counsel to avoid conflicts of interest and the ability of trial courts to make early inquiry in certain situations likely to give rise to conflicts, it is reasonable for the criminal justice system to maintain a fairly rigid rule of presumed prejudice for conflicts of interest. Even so, the rule is not quite the *per se* rule of prejudice that exists for the Sixth Amendment claims mentioned above. Prejudice is presumed only if the defendant demonstrates that counsel "actively represented conflicting interests" and "that an actual conflict of interest adversely affected his lawyer's performance."

Conflict of interest claims aside, actual ineffectiveness claims alleging a deficiency in attorney performance are subject to a general requirement that the defendant affirmatively prove prejudice. The government is not responsible for, and hence not able to prevent, attorney errors that will result in reversal of a conviction or sentence. Attorney errors come in an infinite variety and are as likely to be utterly harmless in a particular case as they are to be prejudicial. * * * Representation is an art, and an act or omission that is unprofessional in one case may be sound or even brilliant in another. * * *

It is not enough for the defendant to show that the errors had some conceivable effect on the outcome of the proceeding. Virtually every act or omission of counsel would meet that test, and not every error that conceivably could have influenced the outcome undermines the reliability of the result of the proceeding. Respondent suggests requiring a showing that the errors "impaired the presentation of the defense." That standard, however, provides no workable principle. * * *

On the other hand, we believe that a defendant need not show that counsel's deficient conduct more likely than not altered the outcome in the case. This outcome-determinative standard has several strengths. It defines the relevant inquiry in a way familiar to courts, though the inquiry, as is inevitable, is anything but precise. The standard also reflects the profound importance of finality in criminal proceedings. Moreover, it comports with the widely used standard for assessing motions for new trial based on newly discovered evidence. Nevertheless, the standard is not quite appropriate.

Even when the specified attorney error results in the omission of certain evidence, the newly discovered evidence standard is not an apt source from which to draw a prejudice standard for ineffectiveness claims. The high standard for newly discovered evidence claims presupposes that all the essential elements of a presumptively accurate and fair proceeding were present in the proceeding whose result is challenged. An ineffective assistance claim asserts the absence of one of the crucial assurances that the result of the proceeding is reliable, so finality concerns are somewhat weaker and the appropriate standard of prejudice should be somewhat lower. * * *

Accordingly, the appropriate test for prejudice finds its roots in the test for materiality of exculpatory information not disclosed to the defense by the prosecution * * *. The defendant must show that there is a reasonable probability that, but for counsel's unprofessional errors, the result of the proceeding would have been different. A reasonable probability is a probability sufficient to undermine confidence in the outcome.

* * *

When a defendant challenges a conviction, the question is whether there is a reasonable probability that, absent the errors, the factfinder would have had a reasonable doubt respecting guilt. When a defendant challenges a death sentence such as the one at issue in this case, the question is whether there is a reasonable probability that, absent the errors, the sentencer—including an appellate court, to the extent it independently reweighs the evidence—would have concluded that the balance of aggravating and mitigating circumstances did not warrant death.

* * *

Although we have discussed the performance component of an ineffectiveness claim prior to the prejudice component, there is no reason for a court deciding an ineffective assistance claim to approach the inquiry in the same order or even to address both components of the inquiry if the defendant makes an insufficient showing on one. * * *

* * *

Application of the governing principles is not difficult in this case. The facts as described above make clear that the conduct of respondent's counsel at and before respondent's sentencing proceeding cannot be found unreasonable. They also make clear that, even assuming the challenged conduct of counsel was unreasonable, respondent suffered insufficient prejudice to warrant setting aside his death sentence.

* * *

JUSTICE MARSHALL, **dissenting.**

* * *

My objection to the performance standard adopted by the Court is that it is so malleable that, in practice, it will either have no grip at all or will yield excessive variation in the manner in which the Sixth Amendment is interpreted and applied by different courts. * * *

* * * I agree that counsel must be afforded "wide latitude" when making "tactical decisions" regarding trial strategy, but many aspects of the job of a criminal defense attorney are more amenable to judicial oversight. For example, much of the work involved in preparing for a trial, applying for bail, conferring with one's client, making timely objections to significant, arguably erroneous rulings of the trial judge, and filing a notice of appeal if there are colorable grounds therefor could profitably be made the subject of uniform standards.

* * *

I object to the prejudice standard adopted by the Court for two independent reasons. First, it is often very difficult to tell whether a defendant convicted after a trial in which he was ineffectively represented would have fared better if his lawyer had been competent. Seemingly impregnable cases can sometimes be dismantled by good defense counsel. On the basis of a cold record, it may be impossible for a reviewing court confidently to ascertain how the government's evidence and arguments would have stood up against rebuttal and cross-examination by a shrewd, well prepared lawyer. The difficulties of estimating prejudice after the fact are exacerbated by the possibility that evidence of injury to the defendant may be missing from the record precisely because of the incompetence of defense counsel. * * *

Second and more fundamentally, the assumption on which the Court's holding rests is that the only purpose of the constitutional guarantee of effective assistance of counsel is to reduce the chance that innocent persons will be convicted. In my view, the guarantee also functions to ensure that convictions are obtained only through fundamentally fair procedures. * * *

* * *

[The separate opinion of Justice Brennan, concurring in part and dissenting in part, is omitted.]

2. Scope of the Right to Effective Assistance of Counsel

Questions have arisen on the extent of a defendant's right to effective assistance. Does it apply to retained counsel? Does it apply to later stages such as appeal and collateral attack?

Retained Counsel

In Cuyler v. Sullivan, 446 U.S. 335 (1980), the Court held that persons who retain counsel are entitled to the same standards of effectiveness as persons for whom the State appoints counsel. The Court reasoned that "[s]ince the State's conduct of a criminal trial itself implicates the State in the defendant's conviction, we see no basis for drawing a distinction between retained and appointed counsel that would deny equal justice to defendants who must choose their own lawyers."

First Appeal of Right: Evitts v. Lucey, Roe v. Flores-Ortega, and Garza v. Idaho

Justice Brennan wrote for the majority in Evitts v. Lucey, 469 U.S. 387 (1985), which holds that criminal defendants have the right to effective assistance of counsel on their first appeal of right. Lucey had been convicted of drug trafficking. He appealed, but his counsel failed to file a "statement of appeal," as required by state law, along with the appellate brief. For this reason, the state appellate courts refused to review the conviction. Justice Brennan reasoned that cases holding that a defendant has a right to counsel on a first appeal as of right dispositively established that a defendant also has a right to *effective* counsel on a first appeal as of right. The Court recognized that it had held that there is no constitutional right to appeal from a criminal conviction; however, the Court reasoned that "when a State opts to act in a field where its action has significant discretionary elements, it must nonetheless act in accord with the dictates of the Constitution—and, in particular, in accord with the Due Process Clause." Thus, because the state had instituted an appeal of right, it was required to comport with the constitutional standards for effective assistance of counsel. The Court affirmed lower court rulings requiring the state to release the defendant unless it either reinstated his appeal or granted him a new trial. Justice Rehnquist, joined by Chief Justice Burger, dissented. The Chief Justice added two short dissenting paragraphs of his own.

In Roe v. Flores-Ortega, 528 U.S. 470 (2000), the Court considered whether it was automatically ineffective assistance for counsel to fail to file a notice of appeal. The Court set forth the following standard:

> [C]ounsel has a constitutionally-imposed duty to consult with the defendant about an appeal when there is reason to think either (1) that

a rational defendant would want to appeal (for example, because there are non-frivolous grounds for appeal), or (2) that this particular defendant reasonably demonstrated to counsel that he was interested in appealing.

If counsel fails to comply with this standard, then the Court determined that prejudice would be found if the defendant can show that he would have filed an appeal if not for counsel's failure to file a notice. This standard does not require the defendant to show that his appeal would have been successful.

Justice Sotomayor wrote for the Court in *Garza v. Idaho*, 139 S.Ct. 738 (2019), as it held "that the presumption of prejudice recognized in *Flores-Ortega* applies regardless of whether the defendant has signed an appeal waiver." Garza pleaded guilty to two counts in an Idaho state court, signed appeal waivers, and was sentenced to prison. After sentencing he told his trial counsel he wanted to appeal and repeated his request that counsel file a notice of appeal several times. Counsel failed to do so, informing Garza that an appeal was "problematic" because he had waived his right to appeal. Garza filed a post-conviction petition in state court urging ineffective assistance of counsel. Despite the fact that 8 of 10 federal courts of appeal had held that *Flores-Ortega* applies regardless of whether the defendant has signed an appeal waiver, the Idaho Supreme Court found no prejudice because of the waiver.

Justice Sotomayor explained appeal waivers as follows:

> We begin with the term "appeal waivers." While the term is useful shorthand for clauses like those in Garza's plea agreements, it can misleadingly suggest a monolithic end to all appellate rights. In fact, however, no appeal waiver serves as an absolute bar to all appellate claims. As courts widely agree, a valid and enforceable appeal waiver only precludes challenges that fall within its scope. That an appeal waiver does not bar claims outside its scope follows from the fact that, "[a]lthough the analogy may not hold in all respects, plea bargains are essentially contracts." Puckett v. United States, 556 U.S. 129, 137 (2009).
>
> As with any type of contract, the language of appeal waivers can vary widely, with some waiver clauses leaving many types of claims unwaived. Additionally, even a waived appellate claim can still go forward if the prosecution forfeits or waives the waiver. Accordingly, a defendant who has signed an appeal waiver does not, in directing counsel to file a notice of appeal, necessarily undertake a quixotic or frivolous quest.
>
> Separately, all jurisdictions appear to treat at least some claims as unwaiveable. Most fundamentally, courts agree that defendants retain the right to challenge whether the waiver itself is valid and

enforceable—for example, on the grounds that it was unknowing or involuntary. Consequently, while signing an appeal waiver means giving up some, many, or even most appellate claims, some claims nevertheless remain.

Justice Sotomayor concluded that filing a notice of appeal is a ministerial burden on counsel given that the claims to be pursued may be vague when the notice is filed, so that great specificity is not required. She rejected Idaho's argument that Garza's counsel was entitled to make a strategic decision:

> Idaho maintains that the risk of breaching the defendant's plea agreement renders counsel's choice to override the defendant's instructions a strategic one. See *Strickland,* 466 U.S., at 690–691 ("[S]trategic choices made after thorough investigation of law and facts relevant to plausible options are virtually unchallengeable . . . "). That is not so. While we do not address what constitutes a defendant's breach of an appeal waiver or any responsibility counsel may have to discuss the potential consequences of such a breach, it should be clear from the foregoing that simply filing a notice of appeal does not necessarily breach a plea agreement, given the possibility that the defendant will end up raising claims beyond the waiver's scope. And in any event, the bare decision whether to appeal is ultimately the defendant's, not counsel's, to make. Where, as here, a defendant has expressly requested an appeal, counsel performs deficiently by disregarding the defendant's instructions.

Justice Sotomayor rejected Idaho's and the United States's (as amicus) argument that the presumption of prejudice did not apply because Garza had no right to appeal at all. "Garza did retain a right to his appeal; he simply had fewer possible claims than some other appellants." She also rejected the United States's argument that Garza should have to show a non-frivolous ground to support an appeal.

Justice Thomas, joined by Justice Gorsuch and in part by Justice Alito, dissented. He concluded that Garza's counsel acted reasonably. He distinguished *Flores-Ortega* as follows:

> The Court purports to follow *Flores-Ortega,* but glosses over the important factual and legal differences between that case and this one. The most obvious difference is also the most crucial: There was no appellate waiver in *Flores-Ortega.* The proximate cause of the defendant's failure to appeal in that case was his counsel's failure to file one. Not so here. Garza knowingly waived his appeal rights and never expressed a desire to withdraw his plea. It was thus Garza's agreement to waive his appeal rights, not his attorney's actions, that caused the forfeiture of his appeal. Thus, *Flores-Ortega* is inapposite.

Appeals Without Merit: Anders v. California

The Court in Anders v. California, 386 U.S. 738 (1967), determined how appointed counsel should proceed if she believes that an appeal lacks merit. The Court held that if, after a "conscientious examination" of the case, counsel finds an appeal to be "wholly frivolous," counsel should advise the court and request permission to withdraw. However, that request must be accompanied by a brief (now called an "*Anders* brief") "referring to anything in the record that might arguably support the appeal." If the court thereafter finds that there are non-frivolous arguments to be made, counsel must be appointed to bring the appeal. In McCoy v. Court of Appeals of Wisconsin, 486 U.S. 429 (1988), the Court upheld a state rule that required an *Anders* brief to include a discussion of why the appeal lacks merit. The Court noted that the point of an *Anders* brief is to inform the court that the defendant's right to counsel has been satisfied, and a requirement of stated reasons would further that goal. The Court rejected the argument that it would be unethical for counsel to explain why she thought the appeal was frivolous. It stated that "if an attorney can advise the court of his or her conclusion that an appeal is frivolous without impairment of the client's fundamental rights, it must follow that no constitutional deprivation occurs when the attorney explains the basis for that conclusion."[31]

Other Methods to Determine Whether an Appeal Is Frivolous: Smith v. Robbins

The Court in *Anders* required counsel who thought his client's appeal frivolous to file a brief with the court, directing the court to anything in the record "that might arguably support the appeal." After *Anders*, California instituted a different procedure for dealing with appeals that a lawyer believes to be without merit. In California, a lawyer who believes the client's appeal to be frivolous must file a brief with the court that summarizes the procedural and factual history of the case, with citations to the record. The lawyer also must attest that he has reviewed the record, explained his evaluation of the case to his client, provided the client with a copy of the brief, and informed the client of his right to file a pro se supplemental brief. The lawyer further requests that the court independently examine the record for arguable issues. Unlike under the *Anders* procedure, counsel neither explicitly states that his review has led him to conclude that an appeal would be frivolous nor requests leave to withdraw. Instead, he is silent on the merits of the case and expresses his availability to brief any issues on which the court might desire briefing.

---

[31] In Penson v. Ohio, 488 U.S. 75 (1988), the Court held that no showing of prejudice is required by a defendant whose counsel fails to file an *Anders* brief. The Court concluded that judicial scrutiny of the record is not an adequate substitute for a complete lack of counsel. It noted that "the denial of counsel in this case left petitioner completely without representation during the appellate court's actual decisional process."

The appellate court, upon receiving the brief, must conduct a review of the entire record. If the appellate court after its review of the record also finds the appeal to be frivolous, it may affirm. If, however, it finds an arguable (i.e., nonfrivolous) issue, it orders briefing on that issue.

In Smith v. Robbins, 528 U.S. 259 (2000), the majority in a 5–4 decision by Justice Thomas held that the California procedure provided sufficient protection of the defendant's constitutional right to effective assistance of counsel on the first appeal of right. While the procedure differed from that set forth in *Anders* (most importantly in the fact that a lawyer in California is not required to direct the court to matters that might arguably support the appeal), Justice Thomas stated that the *Anders* procedure is only one method of satisfying the Constitution's requirement for indigent criminal appeals; the States are free to adopt different procedures, so long as those procedures adequately safeguard a defendant's right to effective counsel on the first appeal. In Justice Thomas' view, the California procedure adequately assured that non-frivolous issues would be discovered and considered by counsel and the reviewing court.

Justice Souter, joined by Justice Stevens, Ginsburg, and Breyer, dissented. The dissenters complained that arguably non-frivolous issues on appeal would be unlikely to be discovered by the court, if counsel is not required to direct the court to those issues.

Subsequent Appeals and Collateral Attack

The right to effective assistance of counsel on appeal, of which *Anders* is a part, extends only to the first appeal of right. It is not applicable to any subsequent attacks on the judgment. This is because, as seen in Chapter 5, there is no constitutional right to counsel at these later stages. The Court has held that where there is no constitutional right to counsel, there can be no right to effective assistance of counsel. See Pennsylvania v. Finley, 481 U.S. 551 (1987) (no right to *Anders* brief in postconviction proceedings, therefore no claim of ineffective assistance of counsel is cognizable); Wainwright v. Torna, 455 U.S. 586 (1982) (no right to counsel at certiorari stage, therefore no claim of ineffective assistance can be asserted, even though defendant had retained counsel); Murray v. Giarratano, 492 U.S. 1 (1989) (no right to effective assistance of counsel in collateral attack of conviction of capital offense); Coleman v. Thompson, 501 U.S. 722 (1991) (no right to effective assistance of counsel on collateral attack even though the issues presented could not be addressed on direct review).

Strickland Procedures

Ordinarily, ineffectiveness claims are not considered on direct appeal, because the trial record and the appellate briefs rarely provide sufficient information with which to evaluate counsel's performance and its impact on the trial. For example, it is hard to determine whether counsel made a strategic decision to forego cross-examination of a witness simply by looking at the record; ordinarily it would be necessary to take testimony from counsel as to trial strategy. Thus, *Strickland* claims are almost always deferred to a collateral attack in which an evidentiary hearing is conducted—at which the defense counsel is a prime witness. See United States v. Bounds, 943 F.2d 541 (5th Cir.1991) (declining to address ineffectiveness claim on appeal, where the only information in the record is the defendant's own assertions in his brief).

3. Assessing Counsel's Effectiveness

In *Strickland*, the Court found that counsel was not constitutionally ineffective, because he undertook sufficient investigation, made reasonable strategic choices, and generally made the best out of a bad situation. *Strickland* was a fairly easy case, however, especially in light of the stringent standards imposed for proving counsel's ineffectiveness. Since *Strickland*, hundreds of dissatisfied defendants have charged that their counsel acted ineffectively. Federal and state courts have been required to apply the intentionally demanding *Strickland* standards to a wide variety of ineffectiveness claims.

Concerns About Prosecutorial Rebuttal: Darden v. Wainright

In Darden v. Wainwright, 477 U.S. 168 (1986), the Court held that a defendant convicted of murder and sentenced to death failed to demonstrate that his trial lawyers' performance fell below an objective standard of reasonableness. At the sentencing hearing, defense counsel failed to introduce any evidence in mitigation and relied solely on a simple plea for mercy from Darden himself. The Court, emphasizing the deference to defense counsel required by *Strickland,* noted several reasons why counsel may have made this strategic decision. If Darden's non-violence were introduced in mitigation, it would have opened the door to Darden's prior convictions. Any evidence of psychological impairment could have been rebutted by a state psychiatric report in which the expert concluded that Darden was a sociopath. Evidence that Darden was a family man could have been rebutted by his extramarital affairs. The Court concluded that Darden had failed to "overcome the presumption that, under the circumstances, the challenged action might be considered sound trial strategy." See also Stewart v. Dugger, 847 F.2d 1486 (11th Cir.1988) (counsel's decision to reargue innocence at capital sentencing hearing, rather than to present mitigating evidence, held reasonable strategy under *Strickland:* "Trial counsel cannot be faulted for attempting to make the best of a bad situation."). Compare Caro v. Calderon, 165 F.3d 1223 (9th Cir.1999) (failure to notify evaluating psychiatrist that defendant suffered organic brain damage from exposure to toxic chemicals was ineffective;

information was critical to a psychiatric analysis, and disclosure did not present a risk of prosecutorial rebuttal).

Failure to Investigate and Ignorance of the Law

The Court found that a lawyer who didn't know the law had acted ineffectively in Kimmelman v. Morrison, 477 U.S. 365 (1986). Justice Brennan's opinion for the Court noted that the defendant's trial counsel "failed to file a timely suppression motion, not due to strategic considerations, but because, until the day of trial, he was unaware of the search and of the State's intention to introduce the * * * evidence * * * because he had conducted no pretrial discovery." Counsel mistakenly believed that the State was required to turn over all inculpatory evidence to the defense.

Although the Court indicated that generally a reviewing court should assess counsel's overall performance in order to determine whether identified acts or omissions overcome the presumption that reasonable professional assistance was provided, it found that the total failure to conduct pretrial discovery was sufficient to justify the conclusion that the lawyer had not acted in accordance with standards of reasonable competence. Justice Brennan noted that "the justifications Morrison's attorney offered for his omission betray a startling ignorance of the law—or a weak attempt to shift blame for inadequate preparation," and that "such a complete lack of pre-trial preparation puts at risk both the defendant's right to meet the case of the prosecution and the reliability of the adversarial testing process." The Court remanded for an examination of possible prejudice. It noted that if the error alleged is counsel's failure to move to suppress evidence, the defendant must show both a reasonable probability of a successful suppression motion and a reasonable probability that without the suppressed evidence, the fact finder would have had a reasonable doubt as to guilt.

Justice Powell, joined by Chief Justice Burger and Justice Rehnquist, concurred in the judgment. He noted that a strong argument could be made that the admission of illegally seized but reliable evidence could not constitute prejudice—this is because the admission of illegally obtained evidence does not impeach the integrity of a guilty verdict.

In Hinton v. Alabama, 571 U.S. 263 (2014) (per curiam), the Court reversed a decision denying habeas corpus relief to a defendant convicted of two murders and sentenced to death. At trial, the prosecutor relied virtually exclusively on ballistics evidence to tie the defendant's gun to bullets used in the murders. Defense counsel (and the trial judge) mistakenly believed that the defense was only entitled to $500 per case (or $1,000 in total given that there were two homicide charges) to hire a defense expert. The defense could find only one expert who would testify for $1,000, his credentials were not strong, and cross-examination at trial cast doubt on whether his opinion that the bullets were not fired from the defendant's gun was reliable. Defense counsel was wrong about the limit on state-provided funds, because the law had changed and the defense was permitted to seek sufficient funds to hire an adequate expert. The state courts agreed that defense counsel failed the first prong of the *Strickland* test by being unfamiliar with and wrong on the law and thus failing to ask for sufficient funds to support the defense. The state court of appeals held that the defendant failed to show prejudice because the three experts who tested for the defendant during habeas proceedings testified to the same conclusion as the defense expert at trial. The Supreme Court found that this was an incorrect analysis because the jury might not have believed the expert at trial and said that "if there is a reasonable possibility that Hinton's attorney would have hired an expert who would have instilled in the jury a reasonable doubt as to Hinton's guilt had the attorney known that the statutory funding limit had been lifted, then Hinton was prejudiced by his lawyer's deficient performance and is entitled to a new trial."

In Wiggins v. Smith, 539 U.S. 510 (2003), Justice O'Connor wrote for the Court as it addressed both the duty to investigate in the context of a capital sentencing proceeding and the "prejudice" prong of *Strickland.*

Wiggins was convicted of murder and other offenses after police discovered 77-year-old Florence Lacs drowned in the bathtub of her ransacked apartment. Two Baltimore County public defenders represented him at trial and in the sentencing stage of his capital trial which resulted in conviction and a death sentence.

During post-conviction proceedings with new counsel, Wiggins alleged that his trial counsel were ineffective because they failed to investigate and present mitigating evidence of his dysfunctional background. He offered expert testimony from a licensed social worker certified as an expert by the court. The expert described Wiggins' severe physical and sexual abuse inflicted by his mother and various foster parents. The social worker relied on interviews with Wiggins and family members and reviewed state social services, medical, and school records.

During the postconviction proceedings, one of the trial counsel testified that, although the State made funds available to hire a social worker to prepare a social history, he did not recall retaining one. He explained that the trial strategy was to try the factual case and dispute whether Wiggins was directly responsible for the murder.

The state courts found no ineffectiveness, a federal district court granted a writ of habeas corpus, and the Fourth Circuit reversed and agreed with the state courts. The Supreme Court reversed the Fourth Circuit.

Justice O'Connor wrote that the question "is not whether counsel should have presented a mitigation case. Rather, we focus on whether the investigation supporting counsel's decision not to introduce mitigating evidence of Wiggins' background was itself reasonable."

She concluded that the investigation was not reasonable. Noting that trial counsel had available to them the written pre-sentence report in which Wiggins noted his "misery as a youth" and records kept by the Baltimore City Department of Social Services (DSS) documenting petitioner's various placements in the State's foster care system, Justice O'Connor found that "[c]ounsel's decision not to expand their investigation beyond the PSI and the DSS records fell short of the professional standards that prevailed in Maryland in 1989." She noted that the "acknowledged, standard practice in Maryland in capital cases at the time of Wiggins' trial included the preparation of a social history report" and funds were available to have such a report prepared.

Justice O'Connor also found that the scope of the investigation was also unreasonable in light of what counsel actually discovered in the DSS records, which included the following: "Petitioner's mother was a chronic alcoholic; Wiggins was shuttled from foster home to foster home and displayed some emotional difficulties while there; he had frequent, lengthy absences from school; and, on at least one occasion, his mother left him and his siblings alone for days without food."

The opinion emphasized that "*Strickland* does not require counsel to investigate every conceivable line of mitigating evidence no matter how unlikely the effort would be to assist the defendant at sentencing. Nor does *Strickland* require defense counsel to present mitigating evidence at sentencing in every case." But, in this case the Court found no reasonable explanation for not investigating mitigation and that there is "a reasonable probability that a competent attorney, aware of this history, would have introduced it at sentencing in an admissible form"; "given the strength of the available evidence, a reasonable attorney may well have chosen to prioritize the mitigation case over the direct responsibility challenge"; and "had the jury been confronted with this considerable mitigating evidence, there is a reasonable probability that it would have returned with a different sentence."

Justice Scalia, joined by Justice Thomas, dissented and argued that the court improperly chose to disbelieve Wiggins' trial counsel who testified under oath that he was aware of the basic features of Wiggins' troubled childhood that the Court claims he overlooked, and "even if this disbelief could plausibly be entertained, that would certainly not establish (as 28 U.S.C. § 2254(d) requires) that the Maryland Court of Appeals was unreasonable in believing it, and in therefore concluding that counsel adequately investigated Wiggins' background."

The Court relied on *Wiggins* in Porter v. McCollum, 558 U.S. 30 (2009) (per curiam). Porter was sentenced to death after a sentencing phase in which defense counsel failed to present any evidence of Porter's background—even though Porter was abused as a child, was shot at by his father, and suffered trauma from horrific battles in the Korean War. The Court had no trouble finding that defense counsel had conducted an insufficient investigation of Porter's background and consequently rendered ineffective assistance.

In Bobby v. Van Hook, 558 U.S. 4 (2009) (per curiam), the Court rejected the contention that counsel's duty to investigate under *Strickland* could be determined by ABA Guidelines for the Appointment and Performance of Defense Counsel in Death Penalty Cases (rev. ed. 2003). The Court described the ABA Guidelines on investigation of mitigating evidence as follows:

> [T]he Guidelines discuss the duty to investigate mitigating evidence in exhaustive detail, specifying what attorneys should look for, where to look, and when to begin. They include, for example, the requirement that counsel's investigation cover every period of the defendant's life from "the moment of conception," and that counsel contact "virtually everyone . . . who knew [the defendant] and his family" and obtain records "concerning not only the client, but also his parents, grandparents, siblings, and children."

The Court held that the Guidelines could not be read or applied to establish the minimum standard required by *Strickland.* It noted that *Strickland* stressed that

> American Bar Association standards and the like are only guides to what reasonableness means, not its definition. We have since regarded them as such. What we have said of state requirements is a fortiori true of standards set by private organizations: While States are free to impose whatever specific rules they see fit to ensure that criminal defendants are well represented, we have held that the Federal Constitution imposes one general requirement: that counsel make objectively reasonable choices.

In Rompilla v. Beard, 545 U.S. 374 (2005), the Court came close to saying that defense counsel has an obligation to engage in a detailed review of the case file for every conviction that the prosecution will seek to introduce, at least if the conviction is to be used in the penalty phase of a capital proceeding. Rompilla's counsel prepared for the capital phase, but did not review the case file of a prior criminal trial in which the defendant was convicted of a violent crime. That case file happened to have information concerning Rompilla's horrific childhood, mental illness and alcoholism, all of which would have been relevant to mitigation in the capital phase of the instant case. Most of this information was found in a transfer petition prepared by the Department of Corrections after Rompilla had been convicted. The mitigation evidence that counsel presented at trial was pretty thin: five of Rompilla's family members asked the jury for mercy, saying that they believed Rompilla was innocent and a good man; and Rompilla's son testified that he loved his father and would visit him in prison. The jury found that the aggravating factors (including prior violent felonies) outweighed the mitigating factors and sentenced Rompilla to death.

Justice Souter, writing for the Court, first noted that this was not a case in which defense counsel completely defaulted on their duty to investigate. The lawyers interviewed family members and reviewed reports by three mental health experts who gave opinions at the guilt phase. The Court held, however, that "the lawyers were deficient in failing to examine the court file on Rompilla's prior conviction." Justice Souter explained as follows:

> There is an obvious reason that the failure to examine Rompilla's prior conviction file fell below the level of reasonable performance. Counsel knew that the Commonwealth intended to seek the death penalty by proving Rompilla had a significant history of felony convictions indicating the use or threat of violence, an aggravator under state law. Counsel further knew that the Commonwealth would attempt to establish this history by proving Rompilla's prior conviction for rape and assault, and would emphasize his violent character by introducing a transcript of the rape victim's testimony given in that earlier trial. * * * It is also undisputed that the prior conviction file was a public document, readily available for the asking at the very courthouse where Rompilla was to be tried.

Justice Souter found that the failure to investigate the case file was prejudicial, because it happened to contain information that would have been very useful in mitigation.

Justice O'Connor wrote a concurring opinion emphasizing that the Court was not establishing a bright line rule that defense counsel must always investigate the case files for all of the defendant's prior convictions. She noted three factors that made defense counsel's failure to investigate unreasonable: 1) "Rompilla's attorneys knew that their client's prior conviction would be at the very heart of the prosecution's case"; 2) "In announcing an intention to introduce testimony about Rompilla's similar prior offense, the prosecutor put Rompilla's attorneys on notice that the prospective defense on mitigation [i.e., residual doubt] likely would be ineffective and counterproductive"; and 3) "the attorneys' * * * failure to obtain the crucial file was the result of inattention, not reasoned strategic judgment."

Justice Kennedy, joined by Chief Justice Rehnquist and Justices Scalia and Thomas, dissented.

Strategy or Not?

Strickland indicated that the performance prong will be satisfied if, using appropriate deference, counsel's actions fall within the realm of *reasonable trial strategy*. Most courts appear to bend over backwards to justify defense counsel's actions as proper strategy. See, e.g., Stringer v. Jackson, 862 F.2d 1108 (5th Cir.1988) (failure to present mitigating evidence was not ineffective); People v. Russell, 71 N.Y.2d 1016, 530 N.Y.S.2d 101 (1988) (failure to move to suppress evidence was a strategic decision); Brown v. Dixon, 891 F.2d 490 (4th Cir.1989) (not ineffective to argue inconsistent defenses); Rogers-Bey v. Lane, 896 F.2d 279 (7th Cir.1990) (proper strategy to inculpate the defendant in order to impeach a prosecution witness); United States v. Guerrero, 938 F.2d 725 (7th Cir.1991) (in light of overwhelming evidence of the defendant's involvement with narcotics, it was not ineffective to argue that the defendant was involved in a drug conspiracy different from that which was charged).

Consider the following cases and the judicial reactions to claims of trial strategy.

1. Martin was charged with sexual abuse of his two stepdaughters. He denied the charges, and claimed that he had a witness who would testify that the children had been encouraged to falsify their charges. Martin's counsel, appointed shortly before trial, filed a motion for a continuance, alleging that he was unprepared to try the case. This motion was denied. Counsel was convinced that the denial of a continuance was error. So he decided to "rely on his motion"; by design, he did not put on any proof in defense, and did not cross-examine or participate in the trial, other than to make an opening statement to the jury. This opening statement indicated that the defense was relying on its motion for continuance, and that the jury should not think "that my lack of participation is, uh, that I'm a dummy over here, and I don't know what's going on." The court of appeals stated that "even deliberate trial tactics may constitute ineffective assistance of counsel if they fall outside the wide range of professionally competent assistance." The court asserted that by calling the defendant and his witness to testify, the attorney could have presented a strong defense "without compromising" the motion for continuance. The court concluded that "the decision of Martin's attorney not to participate cannot be considered sound trial strategy," and that the failure of counsel to put on a defense was prejudicial as well. Martin v. Leech, 744 F.2d 1245 (6th Cir. 1984). Is the court second-guessing defense counsel? Is that permissible after *Strickland?*

See also United States v. Wolf, 787 F.2d 1094 (7th Cir.1986), where the court criticized defense counsel's "tactic of no objections" and held it ineffective:

> It is true that lawyers will frequently not object to objectionable questions, believing either that the witness will give an answer helpful to the defense (or at least not harmful to it) or that too-frequent objecting will irritate the jury or make it think the defendant is trying to hide the truth. But to have a *policy* of never objecting to improper questions is forensic suicide. It shifts the main responsibility for the defense from defense counsel to the judge.

Compare Warner v. Ford, 752 F.2d 622 (11th Cir.1985) (strategy of silence not ineffective in multi-defendant trial, where other defendants were defending aggressively and evidence against counsel's client was overwhelming; under these circumstances, it was reasonable to keep a "low profile").

In Woods v. Etherton, 578 U.S. 113 (2016) (per curiam), the defendant was convicted of drug offenses. At his trial the court admitted evidence of an anonymous tip to law enforcement that led to his arrest. The defendant was convicted and argued that his trial counsel was ineffective for failing to object to admission of the tip on the ground that it violated his right to confrontation. The court of appeals, on habeas review, agreed with the defendant—but the Supreme Court unanimously reversed and held that the court of appeals gave insufficient deference to the state court's determination that the anonymous tip was properly admitted for the non-hearsay purpose of explaining the context of the police investigation. Moreover, the Court concluded that "it would not be objectively unreasonable for a fair-minded judge to conclude" that the failure to raise the Confrontation claim "was not due to incompetence but because the facts of the tip were uncontested and in any event consistent with Etherton's defense"—that the drugs belonged to the passenger.

2. Willis was charged with murdering his son. At trial, the victim's wife testified that Willis came to his son's home to get a deer rifle. She then saw Willis shoot his son with a handgun. Willis denied this claim. No handgun was ever found or linked with the killing. No autopsy was ever performed. No bullet or bullet fragments were ever found. The medical examiner was unable to identify the caliber or type of gun used. Upon his arrest, Willis had stated with respect to his son "it was either him or me," and that statement was introduced at trial. The prosecution also introduced a trace metal test which showed that Willis had fired a gun on the day of his son's death. Willis' first trial ended in a deadlocked jury. He was convicted at the second trial. He claimed ineffective assistance because counsel failed to have an autopsy performed on the victim, which would have determined whether the victim was shot with a handgun. The court

held that the failure to obtain an autopsy was a "reasonable tactical decision" because counsel "decided that it was better for there to be uncertainty concerning the weapon used than to chance that an autopsy would reveal that a handgun was the murder weapon, thereby confirming the daughter-in-law's testimony." Willis v. Newsome, 771 F.2d 1445 (11th Cir.1985). Consider that defense counsel's explanation for making a certain decision is given at a hearing long after the trial, and that counsel has been charged at that point with ineffectiveness. Is there a risk that counsel will "color" his or her testimony under these circumstances, by providing a post hoc "strategy" that was never actually thought about at the time of trial?

3. John Wayne Gacy was a notorious mass murderer. At the penalty phase of his capital murder trial, defense counsel argued to the jury that Gacy should not be executed. The argument was not based on an appeal for mercy, nor on proof of mitigating circumstances. Rather, defense counsel argued "that Gacy should be sentenced to life imprisonment so that he could be studied to find out why he committed the murders." Is this "spare him for science" argument ineffective, or is it proper strategy? See Gacy v. Welborn, 994 F.2d 305 (7th Cir.1993) ("spare him for science" argument does not violate *Strickland* performance prong). See also Waters v. Thomas, 46 F.3d 1506 (11th Cir.1995), upholding a death sentence where a "spare him for science" argument was made. The court stated: "It was not unreasonable for counsel to have thought at least one juror in this case might have been persuaded that, given all the harm Waters had done it was time to get some good out of him, and that the way to do that was to keep him alive for study." The dissent in *Waters* stated that defense counsel "concluded the case for his client—not with a plea for mercy for a human being, but with a dehumanizing request to allow a specimen to be studied."

No Strategy at All

In some cases, counsel cannot even come up with a reason for acting (or not acting) as they did at trial. And in those cases courts have not been hesitant to find ineffectiveness. See, e.g., Jones v. Thigpen, 788 F.2d 1101 (5th Cir.1986) (no explanation for failure to argue mental retardation in mitigation at a capital sentencing hearing; defendant had an I.Q. of 41); Harding v. Davis, 878 F.2d 1341 (11th Cir.1989) (failure to object to judge's entry of directed guilty verdict—which deprived the defendant of his right to jury trial—is ineffective and per se prejudicial); Ouber v. Guarino, 293 F.3d 19 (2002) (no strategic reason for emphasizing in opening argument that the defendant would take the stand and tell her side of the story, and then not calling the defendant as a witness at trial).

Closing Argument: Yarborough v. Gentry

In *Yarborough v.* Gentry, 540 U.S. 1 (2003) (per curiam), the Court gave deference to defense counsel's strategy in making a closing argument. It is interesting to describe the facts to seasoned trial lawyers and ask their opinion about the effectiveness of counsel, which often results in a strong judgment of ineffectiveness. This is a reminder that the judges who rule on ineffectiveness claims are not all seasoned trial lawyers.

Gentry was convicted in a California state court of assault with a deadly weapon for stabbing his girlfriend. He claimed he stabbed her accidentally during a dispute with a drug dealer. The girlfriend testified at trial that she could not remember what happened, so the prosecution relied on her damaging preliminary hearing testimony. In her closing argument, the prosecutor expressed sympathy for the girlfriend's plight as a pregnant, drug-addicted mother of three and accused Gentry of telling the jury a "pack of lies."

Defense counsel responded with a closing argument that included the following statements:

> I don't know what happened. I can't tell you. And if I sit here and try to tell you what happened, I'm lying to you.
>
> I don't care that Tanaysha is pregnant. I don't care that she has three children. I don't know why that had to be brought out in closing. What does that have to do with this case?
>
> She was stabbed. The question is, did he intend to stab her? He said he did it by accident. If he's lying and you think he's lying then you have to convict him. If you don't think he's lying, bad person, lousy drug addict, stinking thief, jail bird, all that to the contrary, he's not guilty. It's as simple as that. I don't care if he's been in prison.
>
> I don't know if thievery and stabbing your girlfriend are all in the same pot. I don't know if just because of the fact that you stole some things in the past that means you must have stabbed your girlfriend. That sounds like a jump to me, but that's just [me]. * * *

After deliberating for about six hours, the jury convicted.

California appellate courts denied relief on direct appeal, as did a federal district court on habeas. But the Ninth Circuit held that Gentry was deprived of effective assistance of counsel. The Supreme Court disagreed and observed that there was double deference in this case: deference to the strategic judgment of defense counsel and deference on habeas to the judgment of the state courts. It reasoned that defense counsel made several key points during closing argument: the girlfriend's personal circumstances were irrelevant, Gentry's criminal history was irrelevant to guilt; and the jury, like the prosecutor and defense counsel had no personal knowledge of what happened and could only speculate. The Court recognized that defense counsel omitted facts that might have been favorable to the defense but opined that some of the omitted facts were ambiguous and it was not unreasonable to focus on a small number of key points.

The Court reasoned that, although the Ninth Circuit was concerned that defense counsel mentioned "a host of details that hurt his client's position, none of which mattered as a matter of law," defense counsel's tactic was not unreasonable because he "mentioned those details * * * precisely to remind the jury that they *were* legally irrelevant." The Court also reasoned that "there is nothing wrong with a rhetorical device that personalizes the doubts anyone but an eyewitness must necessarily have."

In the end, the Court concluded that "Gentry's lawyer was no Aristotle or even Clarence Darrow," but he was not ineffective.

Conceding Guilt in a Capital Prosecution: Florida v. Nixon and McCoy v. Louisiana

In Florida v. Nixon, 543 U.S. 175 (2004), Justice Ginsburg wrote for the Court as it refused to establish a per se rule prohibiting defense counsel from conceding the defendant's guilt in a capital prosecution in order "to concentrate the defense on establishing, at the penalty phase, cause for sparing the defendant's life." The Florida Supreme Court held that regardless of how gruesome a crime is and how strong the prosecution's case might be, any concession of guilt was prejudicial ineffective assistance of counsel unless made with the defendant's express consent. Justice Ginsburg rejected this rule and wrote that "[d]efense counsel undoubtedly has a duty to discuss potential strategies with the defendant," but counsel is not automatically barred from conceding guilt after explaining to the defendant that strategy and finding that the defendant neither consents nor objects to it. She reasoned that "[t]he reasonableness of counsel's performance, after consultation with the defendant yields no response, must be judged in accord with the inquiry generally applicable to ineffective-assistance-of-counsel claims: Did counsel's representation 'fall below an objective standard of reasonableness'?" She concluded that "[t]he Florida Supreme Court erred in applying, instead, a presumption of deficient performance, as well as a presumption of prejudice." The state gathered overwhelming evidence that Nixon had kidnaped Jeanne Bickner and then burned her alive. Nixon confessed to the crime in graphic detail.

Justice Ginsburg emphasized that Nixon persistently resisted answering questions from his counsel and the Court, and she concluded that although a concession of guilt "in a run-of-the-mine trial might present a closer question, the gravity of the potential sentence in a capital trial and the proceeding's two-phase structure vitally affect counsel's strategic calculus.

In McCoy v. Louisiana, 138 S.Ct. 1500 (2018), Justice Ginsburg wrote for the Court as it distinguished Florida v. Nixon:

> In the case now before us, in contrast to *Nixon*, the defendant vociferously insisted that he did not engage in the charged acts and adamantly objected to any admission of guilt. Yet the trial court permitted counsel, at the guilt phase of a capital trial, to tell the jury the defendant "committed three murders. . . . [H]e's guilty." We hold that a defendant has the right to insist that counsel refrain from admitting guilt, even when counsel's experienced-based view is that confessing guilt offers the defendant the best chance to avoid the death penalty. Guaranteeing a defendant the right "to have the *Assistance* of Counsel for *his* defence," the Sixth Amendment so demands. With individual liberty—and, in capital cases, life—at stake, it is the defendant's prerogative, not counsel's, to decide on the objective of his defense: to admit guilt in the hope of gaining mercy at the sentencing stage, or to maintain his innocence, leaving it to the State to prove his guilt beyond a reasonable doubt.

Justice Alito, joined by Justices Thomas and Gorsuch, dissented.

Ineffectiveness Charge Against a Lawyer Who Refuses to Bring a Defense That Is Likely to Fail: Knowles v. Mirzayance

In Knowles v. Mirzayance, 556 U.S. 111 (2009), the Court considered an ineffectiveness challenge to a defense lawyer's decision not to bring a claim at one phase of a trial, when that claim had already been rejected by the jury in an earlier phase. Justice Thomas, writing for the Court, recounted the facts:

> Mirzayance confessed that he stabbed his 19-year-old cousin nine times with a hunting knife and then shot her four times. At trial, he entered pleas of not guilty and not guilty by reason of insanity (NGI). Under California law, when both of these pleas are entered, the court must hold a bifurcated trial, with guilt determined during the first phase and the viability of the defendant's NGI plea during the second. During the guilt phase of Mirzayance's trial, he sought to avoid a conviction for first-degree murder by obtaining a verdict on the lesser included offense of second-degree murder. To that end, he presented medical testimony that he was insane at the time of the crime and was, therefore, incapable of the premeditation or deliberation necessary for a first-degree murder conviction. The jury nevertheless convicted Mirzayance of first-degree murder.

The trial judge set the NGI phase to begin the day after the conviction was entered but, on the advice of counsel, Mirzayance abandoned his NGI plea before it commenced. He would have borne the burden of proving his insanity during the NGI phase to the same jury that had just convicted him of first-degree murder.

Justice Thomas found that defense counsel was not unreasonable in recommending the withdrawal of a doomed defense even if it were the only available defense. He found "no prevailing professional norms that prevent counsel from recommending that a plea be withdrawn when it is almost certain to lose." He also found that, even if ineffectiveness could be shown, Mirzayance had not been prejudiced by the decision not to pursue the NGI defense.

Failure to Challenge a Widely Accepted Analysis That Is Later Discredited: Maryland v. Kulbicki

In Maryland v. Kulbicki, 577 U.S. 1 (2015) (per curiam), the Court summarily reversed the Maryland Court of Appeals' grant of habeas corpus relief from a state murder conviction. Kulbicki argued that his lawyers were ineffective for failing to challenge expert testimony that the bullet fragment found in the victim's brain matched a bullet fragment found in Kulbicki's truck. The expert employed the "comparative bullet lead analysis" (CBLA) that was widely used at the time of trial. Eleven years later, that process had fallen out of favor and was found by the courts to be not generally accepted by the scientific community. The Court held that "[c]ounsel did not perform deficiently by dedicating their time and focus to elements of the defense that did not involve poking methodological holes in a then-uncontroversial mode of ballistics analysis." The Court added that it was highly unlikely that due diligence would have uncovered an obscure report—prepared four years before the defendant's trial by the same FBI agent who testified for the State—suggesting that CBLA was an invalid way to compare bullet fragments. It concluded that the lower court had "demanded something close to 'perfect advocacy'—far more than the 'reasonable competence' the right to counsel guarantees."

4. The Impact of *AEDPA* on Ineffective Assistance Claims

Fact-Intensive Review Under AEDPA of Claim of Ineffectiveness for Failure to Investigate and Present Mitigating Evidence at the Penalty Phase: Cullen v. Pinholster

In Cullen v. Pinholster, 563 U.S. 170 (2011), the Court considered whether defense counsel at the penalty phase of a capital trial failed to conduct a sufficient investigation into possible mitigating evidence. Pinholster and others robbed and murdered a drug dealer. He was convicted of murder in the guilt phase. He was represented by appointed attorneys Brainard and Dettmar.

At the penalty phase the prosecution produced eight witnesses, who testified about Pinholster's history of threatening and violent behavior, including resisting arrest and assaulting police officers and involvement with juvenile gangs. The prosecution also offered evidence of a substantial prison disciplinary record. Defense counsel called only Pinholster's mother, who gave an account of Pinholster's troubled childhood and adolescent years, discussed Pinholster's siblings, and described Pinholster as "a perfect gentleman at home." Defense counsel did not call a psychiatrist, though they had consulted Dr. John Stalberg at least six weeks earlier. Dr. Stalberg noted Pinholster's "psychopathic personality traits," diagnosed him with antisocial personality disorder, and concluded that he "was not under the influence of extreme mental or emotional disturbance" at the time of the murders.

In his habeas case, Pinholster argued that Brainard and Dettmar had failed to adequately investigate and present mitigating evidence, including evidence of mental disorders. Pinholster contended that they should have pursued and presented additional evidence about: his family members and their criminal, mental, and substance abuse problems; his schooling; and his medical and mental health history, including his epileptic disorder. To support his allegation that his trial counsel had "no reasonable tactical basis" for the approach they took, Pinholster relied on statements his counsel made at trial. Counsel had moved to exclude the government's aggravating evidence, arguing that the government had failed to provide pretrial notice under the state statute. Dettmar stated on the record that because the State did not provide notice, he was "not presently prepared to offer anything by way of mitigation." In response to the trial court's inquiry as to whether a continuance might be helpful, Dettmar noted that the only mitigation witness he could think of was Pinholster's mother. Additional time, Dettmar stated, would not "make a great deal of difference."

The state courts rejected Pinholster's ineffectiveness claim, but Pinholster was successful in the Ninth Circuit in his habeas claim. The Supreme Court, in an opinion by Justice Thomas, reversed. In evaluating the ineffective investigation claim, Justice Thomas first emphasized the extremely deferential standard of review to be applied to state court decisions concerning ineffectiveness on habeas review. Justice Thomas concluded that defense counsel made a reasoned professional judgment that the best way to serve their client would be to rely on the fact that they never got the required notice and hope the judge would bar the state from putting on their aggravation witnesses; defense counsel were prepared, if their motion was denied, to present only Pinholster's mother in the penalty phase in an effort to create sympathy and utilize the "family sympathy" mitigation defense that had been used by other California attorneys.

Justice Thomas added that "[t]he record also shows that Pinholster's counsel confronted a challenging penalty phase with an unsympathetic client, which limited their feasible mitigation strategies." He concluded as follows:

> Given these impediments, it would have been a reasonable penalty-phase strategy to focus on evoking sympathy for Pinholster's mother. In fact, such a family sympathy defense is precisely how the State understood defense counsel's strategy. The prosecutor carefully opened her cross-examination of Pinholster's mother with, "I hope you understand I don't enjoy cross-examining a mother of anybody." And in her closing argument, the prosecutor attempted to undercut defense counsel's strategy by pointing out, "Even the most heinous person born, even Adolph Hitler[,] probably had a mother who loved him."

In short opinions, Justice Alito concurred in part and in the judgment, and Justice Breyer, concurred in part and dissented in part. Justice Sotomayor dissented in a lengthy opinion joined by Justices Ginsburg and Kagan. She stated as follows:

> The majority surmises that counsel decided on a strategy "to get the prosecution's aggravation witnesses excluded for lack of notice, and if that failed, to put on Pinholster's mother." This is the sort of post hoc rationalization for counsel's decisionmaking that contradicts the available evidence of counsel's actions that courts cannot indulge. The majority's explanation for counsel's conduct contradicts the best available evidence of counsel's actions: Dettmar's frank, contemporaneous statement to the trial judge that he "had not prepared any evidence by way of mitigation." The majority's conjecture that counsel had in fact prepared a mitigation defense, based primarily on isolated entries in counsel's billing records, requires it to assume that Dettmar was lying to the trial judge.

Application of Strickland—and AEDPA Standards of Deference—to Trial Counsel's Failure to Retain and Present a Forensic Expert: Harrington v. Richter

In Harrington v. Richter, 562 U.S. 86 (2011), the Court considered whether defense counsel had been ineffective for failure to investigate the possibility of presenting forensic expert testimony. The case was on habeas review from a state court decision finding no violation of the right to effective assistance of counsel.

Four men—Johnson, Richter, Branscombe and Klein—were smoking marijuana together. Klein and Johnson ended up each being shot twice. Johnson recovered; Klein died of his wounds. Johnson told investigators that he fell asleep and when he awoke he found Richter and Branscombe in his bedroom, at which point Branscombe shot him. Johnson heard more gunfire in the living room and the sound of his assailants leaving. He got up, found Klein bleeding on the living room couch, and called 911. A gun safe, a pistol, and $6,000 cash, all of which had been in the bedroom, were missing. Blood was found in the living room and the bedroom doorway, but investigators took only a few samples. Richter was tried for murder and related offenses. He contended that Branscombe was the shooter and that he was outside Johnson's house when he heard screams and gunshots and entered the house. A jury found him guilty.

In the state courts, Richter claimed his counsel was deficient for failing to present expert testimony on serology, pathology, and blood spatter patterns—testimony that, he argued, would disclose the source of the blood pool in the bedroom doorway. This, he contended, would bolster his theory of defense. The state courts denied relief but Harrington was successful in his habeas petition before the Ninth Circuit.

Justice Kennedy, writing for the Court, found that the Ninth Circuit erred by failing to give sufficient deference to the state court's determination that counsel was not ineffective for failing to pursue expert testimony on the blood found at the scene. As Justice Thomas had in *Pinholster*, Justice Kennedy noted that there was double deference at work: deference to the state court findings (reviewing whether "the state court's ruling on the claim being presented in federal court was so lacking in justification that there was an error well understood and comprehended in existing law beyond any possibility for fairminded disagreement") and also deference to counsel's strategic judgments.

Justice Kagan took no part in the decision. Justice Ginsburg wrote a short opinion concurring in the judgment.

5. Assessing Prejudice

In *Strickland,* the Court held that lower courts may proceed directly to the prejudice prong if that would dispose of the case, and thereby avoid having to evaluate defense counsel's performance. Many lower courts have done so. See, e.g., United States ex rel. Cross v. DeRobertis, 811 F.2d 1008 (7th Cir.1987) (performance issue requires "a particularly subtle assessment," so court proceeds directly to prejudice prong and rejects the defendant's claim). If it is important for courts to provide guidance on effectiveness standards, is it acceptable for a court to proceed directly to the prejudice prong of *Strickland?*

The Strength of the Case Against the Defendant

Concerning the prejudice prong of *Strickland,* it is obvious that the defendant is more likely to prove prejudice if the prosecution's evidence is weak. For example, in Atkins v. Attorney General of Alabama, 932 F.2d 1430 (11th Cir.1991), counsel failed to object to the introduction of a fingerprint card offered to make a comparison between Atkins's fingerprints and those found at the scene of the crime. The card included a printed notation of a prior arrest that would not have been admissible. The court found that the failure to object constituted ineffectiveness, and that without the error there was a reasonable probability that the outcome of the trial would have been different. Atkins's fingerprints had been found at the scene, but the victim testified that Atkins had worked for him at the house two days prior to the crime; no other physical evidence tied Atkins to the crime. The court asserted that "the introduction of a previous arrest can have an almost irreversible impact on the minds of the jurors" and that the evidence against Atkins was "not overwhelming." See also Hart v. Gomez, 174 F.3d 1067 (9th Cir.1999) (where trial was basically a credibility determination between the defendant's witness and the complainant, defense counsel's failure to introduce record evidence corroborating the defense witness' account was ineffective and prejudicial); Ouber v. Guarino, 293 F.3d 19 (1st Cir. 2002) (error in stating that defendant would testify and then not calling defendant was prejudicial; case had been tried twice previously and resulted in hung jury each time, when defendant testified in those trials).

The Strength of Evidence Not Presented

Where the error is in *not* presenting evidence, the prejudice inquiry will focus on the strength and persuasiveness of that evidence, as well as the strength and persuasiveness of other evidence on the point that was offered by the defendant. Thus, in Rompilla v. Beard, supra, the evidence of the defendant's horrific childhood was found by the Court to be very strong proof of mitigation, especially as compared to the relatively weak evidence on mitigation that was actually presented.

Prejudice Assessed at Time of Review: Lockhart v. Fretwell

In Lockhart v. Fretwell, 506 U.S. 364 (1993), the Court made it clear that prejudice under *Strickland* is not always found simply because effective assistance would have changed the outcome. Fretwell was tried for capital murder in an Arkansas state court. His trial counsel at the sentencing phase failed to object to the use of an aggravating factor that was unconstitutional under then-existing precedent of the United States Court of Appeals for the Eighth Circuit. The jury relied solely on this aggravating factor and sentenced Fretwell to death. Subsequent to Fretwell's trial, and in a different case, the Eighth Circuit Court of Appeals overruled its precedent and held that it was constitutional to use the Arkansas aggravating factor that had been relied upon by the jury in Fretwell's trial. Fretwell argued on habeas that trial counsel had acted ineffectively in failing to object to the use of the aggravating factor that the

Court of Appeals had originally (and as of the time of his trial) declared unconstitutional. He argued further that counsel's ineffectiveness prejudiced him, because if counsel had made the objection, the jury could not have used the aggravating factor at that time, and Fretwell could not have been sentenced to death.

Chief Justice Rehnquist wrote for seven Justices as the Court held that "counsel's failure to make an objection in a state criminal sentencing proceeding—an objection that would have been supported by a decision which subsequently was overruled—" could not constitute prejudice, because "the result of the sentencing proceeding * * * was rendered neither unreliable nor fundamentally unfair as a result of counsel's failure to make the objection." The Chief Justice reasoned that the right to effective assistance of counsel is intended to provide a fair trial. "Thus, an analysis focusing solely on mere outcome determination, without attention to whether the result of the proceeding was fundamentally unfair or unreliable, is defective. To set aside a conviction or sentence solely because the outcome would have been different but for counsel's error may grant the defendant a windfall to which the law does not entitle him."

The Chief Justice relied heavily on Nix v. Whiteside, 475 U.S. 157 (1986), where the Court held that the defendant was not prejudiced under *Strickland* when counsel refused to cooperate in presenting perjured testimony. Even though Whiteside might have swayed the jury with perjurious testimony, the Court in *Whiteside* held that "in judging prejudice and the likelihood of a different outcome, a defendant has no right to the luck of a lawless decisionmaker." The Chief Justice interpreted *Whiteside* as establishing that "sheer outcome determination" is not sufficient to make out a claim of prejudice under *Strickland.*

Justice O'Connor wrote a concurring opinion, describing the Court's holding as follows: "the court making the prejudice determination may not consider the effect of an objection it knows to be wholly meritless under current governing law, even if the objection might have been considered meritorious at the time of its omission." Justice Thomas also wrote a brief concurring opinion.

Justice Stevens, joined by Justice Blackmun, dissented and argued that "the Court today reaches the astonishing conclusion that deficient performance by counsel does not prejudice a defendant even when it results in the erroneous imposition of a death sentence," and "[t]he Court's aversion to windfalls seems to disappear * * * when the State is the favored recipient."

Prejudice Must Be Assessed by What Evidence—Including Damaging Evidence—Would Have Been Admitted Had Defense Counsel Acted Effectively: Wong v. Belmontes

In Wong v. Belmontes, 558 U.S. 15 (2009) (per curiam), the Court assumed that Belmontes's defense counsel had been ineffective at the capital phase of a state trial by failing to introduce some available mitigating evidence. But the Court held that in assessing prejudice, a reviewing court has to consider not only the evidence that counsel might have presented, but also the evidence that the government would introduce in response. Belmontes bludgeoned Steacy McConnell to death, striking her in the head 15 to 20 times with a steel dumbbell bar. At his capital trial the judge excluded evidence that Belmontes had murdered Jerry Howard execution-style, and had bragged about it. Evidence of the Howard murder was found not admissible, but the parties recognized that it might be admissible if Belmontes opened the door to it.

The Court found that some of the evidence that Belmontes argued should have been presented at the penalty phase might have been helpful for mitigation purposes but "would have triggered admission of the powerful Howard evidence in rebuttal. This evidence would have made a difference, but in the wrong direction for Belmontes." The Court gave the following example:

> [Belmontes] argues that the jury should have been told that he suffered an "extended bout with rheumatic fever," which led to "emotional instability, impulsivity, and impairment of the neurophysiological mechanisms for planning and reasoning." But the cold, calculated nature of the Howard murder and Belmontes' subsequent bragging about it would have served as a powerful counterpoint.
>
> The type of "more-evidence-is-better" approach advocated by Belmontes * * * might seem appealing—after all, what is there to lose? But here there was a lot to lose. A heavyhanded case to portray Belmontes in a positive light * * * would have invited the strongest possible evidence in rebuttal—the evidence that Belmontes was responsible for not one but two murders.

The Court criticized the Ninth Circuit, which found prejudice, for describing the aggravating evidence the State had as "scant." The Court observed this this description "misses *Strickland's* point that the reviewing court must consider all the evidence—the good and the bad—when evaluating prejudice. Here, the worst kind of bad evidence would have come in with the good."

Justice Stevens wrote a short concurring opinion.

Defense Counsel's Argument at the Penalty Phase of a Capital Trial, Stressing the Severity of the Crimes, Did Not Prejudice the Defendant: Smith v. Spisak

Justice Breyer wrote for the Court in Smith v. Spisak, 558 U.S. 139 (2010), as it reversed a grant of habeas corpus relief to a state defendant convicted of three murders and two attempted murders. The court of appeals had found ineffective assistance of counsel in the closing argument of Spisak's lawyer. Justice Breyer described that argument as follows:

> In his closing argument at the penalty phase, Spisak's counsel described Spisak's killings in some detail. He acknowledged that Spisak's admiration for Hitler inspired his crimes. He portrayed Spisak as "sick," "twisted," and "demented." And he said that Spisak was "never going to be any different." He then pointed out that all the experts had testified that Spisak suffered from some degree of mental illness. And, after a fairly lengthy and rambling disquisition about his own decisions about calling expert witnesses and preparing them, counsel argued that, even if Spisak was not legally insane so as to warrant a verdict of not guilty by reason of insanity, he nonetheless was sufficiently mentally ill to lessen his culpability to the point where he should not be executed. Counsel also told the jury that, when weighing Spisak's mental illness against the "substantial" aggravating factors present in the case, the jurors should draw on their own sense of "pride" for living in "a humane society" made up of "a humane people." That humanity, he said, required the jury to weigh the evidence "fairly" and to be "loyal to that oath" the jurors had taken to uphold the law.

Spisak argued that the closing argument was defective because: (1) It overly emphasized the gruesome nature of the killings; (2) it overly emphasized Spisak's threats to continue his crimes; (3) it understated the facts upon which the experts based their mental illness conclusions; (4) it said little or nothing about any other possible mitigating circumstance; and (5) it made no explicit request that the jury return a verdict against death. Justice Breyer responded that the Court would assume that the closing argument was inadequate, but that "[w]e nevertheless find no reasonable probability that a better closing argument without these defects would have made a significant difference." He went into detail about the evidence against Spisak and the testimony that he gave during the trial when called by defense counsel who was seeking to establish an insanity defense. Spisak described his crimes and testified that he would continue to commit such crimes if he could.

Justice Stevens, concurring in part and concurring in the judgment, wrote that "[i]t is difficult to convey how thoroughly egregious counsel's closing argument was without reproducing it in its entirety." He concluded that "counsel's argument grossly transgressed the bounds of what constitutionally competent counsel would have done in a similar situation," but "[i]n my judgment even the most skillful of closing arguments—even one befitting Clarence Darrow—would not have created a reasonable probability of a different outcome in this case."

Calling an Expert Who Testifies at the Capital Phase That the Defendant is Dangerous Because He Is Black: Buck v. Davis

In Buck v. Davis, 137 S.Ct. 759 (2017), the future dangerousness of the defendant was contested by the parties in the penalty phase of Buck's trial for capital murder. The defense counsel called a psychologist, who testified that Buck was unlikely to act violently in the future, because his violent acts were triggered by romantic relationships with women, which presumably he wouldn't have when imprisoned for life. But defense counsel also asked the expert about the assertion in his report regarding "statistical factors"—including an assertion that a black person (like Buck) is more likely to be dangerous than a white person. The expert then testified to this belief on both direct and cross-examination. Buck was sentenced to death.

The Supreme Court vacated the death sentence in an opinion by Chief Justice Roberts, on the ground that defense counsel's decision to invite the defense expert to testify about a supposed statistical connection between race and future dangerousness was ineffective and prejudicial. The Chief Justice easily found that the racial reference was objectively unreasonable and, as to the more difficult issue of prejudice, he observed that the state had to prove future dangerousness beyond a reasonable doubt, the brutality of the crime and lack of remorse did not necessarily prove that Buck would be dangerous in the future, and the most important evidence about future dangerousness came improperly from the defendant's expert.

Justice Thomas dissented, arguing that evidence of the heinousness of the crime and the defendant's clear lack of remorse were sufficient to support the jury's finding of future dangerousness.

"Significant" Prejudice Requirement Rejected: Glover v. United States

In Glover v. United States, 531 U.S. 198 (2001), Glover argued that his trial counsel was ineffective for failing to challenge a sentence that was allegedly set in violation of the Federal Sentencing Guidelines. The Court of Appeals assumed that counsel was ineffective, but denied relief on the ground that any ineffectiveness did not prejudice Glover within the meaning of *Strickland*. The Court of Appeals read the Supreme Court cases on prejudice to require a finding of "significant" prejudice. In this case, counsel's ineffectiveness resulted in an increased sentence somewhere between 6 and 21 months; the Court of Appeals did not view this increase as "significant".

The Supreme Court unanimously reversed in an opinion by Justice Kennedy. The Court assumed, as did the lower court, that counsel had been ineffective. Justice Kennedy criticized the lower court's analysis of prejudice in the following passage:

> Authority does not suggest that a minimal amount of additional time in prison cannot constitute prejudice. Quite to the contrary, our jurisprudence suggests that any amount of actual jail time has Sixth Amendment significance.
>
> The Seventh Circuit's rule is not well considered in any event, because there is no obvious dividing line by which to measure how much longer a sentence must be for the increase to constitute substantial prejudice.

Prejudice Due to Ineffectiveness on Appeal

How does the prejudice prong of *Strickland* apply to claims of ineffective assistance of counsel on appeal? In Lozada v. Deeds, 498 U.S. 430 (1991), the defendant alleged that his counsel failed to inform him of his right to appeal or of the procedures and time limitations for an appeal, and that counsel had misled him into thinking that his case had been forwarded to the public defender's office. The district court dismissed Lozada's habeas corpus petition on the ground that Lozada had not indicated what issues he would have raised on appeal and had not demonstrated that the appeal might have succeeded. Both the district court and the court of appeals denied a certificate of probable cause to appeal the denial of habeas relief under 28 U.S.C. § 2253. The Supreme Court in a per curiam opinion held that the certificate of probable cause should have been granted. The standard for granting such a certificate is that a court "could resolve the issues" in petitioner's favor. The Court held that Lozada had met that standard, because the issue of prejudice "could be resolved in a different manner than the one followed by the District Court."

Subsequently, in Roe v. Flores-Ortega, 528 U.S. 470 (2000), the Court considered the circumstances under which defense counsel's failure to file a notice of appeal would be prejudicial within the meaning of *Strickland*. The Court declared that "to show prejudice in these circumstances, a defendant must demonstrate that there is a reasonable probability that, but for counsel's deficient failure to consult with him about an appeal, he would have timely appealed." The defendant did not have to show that the appeal would be likely to result in a reversal of the conviction—though obviously the merits of an appeal bear somewhat on whether the defendant would have pursued it.

6. Per Se Ineffectiveness and Prejudice

In United States v. Cronic, 466 U.S. 648 (1984), the Court recognized that there might be some unusual, egregious, situations in which counsel's ineffectiveness and prejudice could be presumed and therefore reversal would be automatic. But the Court did not find such an extreme situation presented under the facts. Justice Stevens, writing for the Court, set forth the facts as follows:

> Respondent and two associates were indicted on mail fraud charges involving the transfer of over $9,400,000 in checks between banks in Tampa, Florida, and Norman, Oklahoma * * *. Shortly before the scheduled trial date, respondent's retained counsel withdrew. The court appointed a young lawyer with a real estate practice to represent respondent, but allowed him only 25 days for pretrial preparation, even though it had taken the Government over four and one-half years to investigate the case and it had reviewed thousands of documents during that investigation. The two codefendants agreed to testify for the Government; respondent was convicted on 11 of the 13 counts in the indictment and received a 25-year sentence.

Cronic argued that under these circumstances there was no way that counsel could have been effective, and therefore ineffectiveness and prejudice should be presumed without having to look at the record. Justice Stevens considered the possibility of automatic reversal:

> [B]ecause we presume that the lawyer is competent to provide the guiding hand that the defendant needs, the burden rests on the accused to demonstrate a constitutional violation. There are, however, circumstances that are so likely to prejudice the accused that the cost of litigating their effect in a particular case is unjustified.
>
> Most obvious, of course, is the complete denial of counsel. The presumption that counsel's assistance is essential requires us to conclude that a trial is unfair if the accused is denied counsel at a critical stage of his trial. Similarly, if counsel entirely fails to subject the prosecution's case to meaningful adversarial testing, then there has been a denial of Sixth Amendment rights that makes the adversary process itself presumptively unreliable. * * *
>
> Circumstances of that magnitude may be present on some occasions when although counsel is available to assist the accused during trial, the likelihood that any lawyer, even a fully competent one, could provide effective assistance is so small that a presumption of prejudice is appropriate without inquiry into the actual conduct of the trial. Powell v. Alabama, 287 U.S. 45 (1932), [set forth in Chapter 5] was such a case.

* * *

> But every refusal to postpone a criminal trial will not give rise to such a presumption. * * *

Justice Stevens found nothing so extreme in *Cronic* that would justify an automatic rule that counsel could not have been effective.

> Neither the period of time that the Government spent investigating the case, nor the number of documents that its agents reviewed during that investigation, is necessarily relevant to the question whether a competent lawyer could prepare to defend the case in 25 days. * * * In this case, the time devoted by the Government to the assembly, organization, and summarization of the thousands of written records * * * simplified the work of defense counsel in identifying and understanding the basic character of the defendants' scheme. * * *
>
> * * * [T]he only *bona fide* jury issue open to competent defense counsel on these facts was whether respondent acted with intent to defraud. When there is no reason to dispute the underlying historical facts, the period of 25 days to consider the question whether those facts justify an inference of criminal intent is not so short that it even arguably justifies a presumption that no lawyer could provide the respondent with the effective assistance of counsel required by the Constitution.
>
> That conclusion is not undermined by the fact that respondent's lawyer was young, that his principal practice was in real estate, or that this was his first jury trial. Every experienced criminal defense attorney once tried his first criminal case. Moreover, a lawyer's experience with real estate transactions might be more useful in preparing to try a criminal case involving financial transactions than would prior experience in handling, for example, armed robbery prosecutions. * * *

The Court in *Cronic* remanded for a determination of whether defense counsel's performance was in fact ineffective and prejudicial under the *Strickland* standards. Justice Marshall concurred in the judgment.

Note that the Court in *Cronic* did not hold that Cronic had received effective assistance of counsel. Rather, it rejected the per se rule of reversal applied by the lower court. On remand in *Cronic,* the court of appeals reviewed counsel's actual performance and held that it was ineffective and that Cronic was prejudiced. United States v. Cronic, 839 F.2d 1401 (10th Cir.1988). The court found that defense counsel ignored the issues of the defendant's intent and good faith, which were, as the Supreme Court had recognized, the only issues of dispute in the case. Cronic's attorney testified at the hearing on ineffectiveness that the defense he used was one seeking to "cloud the issues." The court held that "this cannot be a satisfactory explanation under *Strickland* or any other authority for a selection of a defense." The court also noted that defense counsel failed to object to evidence due to a misunderstanding of the statute under which Cronic was tried.

Denial of "Counsel" Within the Meaning of the Sixth Amendment

Cronic holds that in some limited cases, ineffectiveness and prejudice will be presumed without having to investigate counsel's performance. But it is clear that this rule of per se reversal is very narrow. If it did not apply under the facts of *Cronic,* where could it apply? Consider Solina v. United States, 709 F.2d 160 (2d Cir.1983), where the court concluded that per se reversal was required because defendant's trial counsel had held himself out as an attorney, but had never passed a bar exam. The evidence against Solina was overwhelming, and Solina could point to no error of judgment on the part of his counsel at trial. Yet the court reasoned as follows:

> The problem of representation by [one not admitted to the bar] is not simply one of competence * * * but that he was engaging in a crime. Such a person cannot be wholly free from fear of what might happen if a vigorous defense should lead the prosecutor or the trial judge to inquire into his background and discover his lack of credentials.

The court found that Solina had been denied "counsel," as that term is used in the Sixth Amendment, and that this total denial of counsel was per se prejudicial, as it was in Gideon v. Wainwright.

Solina preceded *Cronic,* but it has been followed by lower courts even after *Cronic.* See, e.g., United States v. Novak, 903 F.2d 883 (2d Cir.1990) (per se reversal where defense counsel had obtained admission to the bar by fraud). Compare Reese v. Peters, 926 F.2d 668 (7th Cir.1991) (*Solina* distinguished; no per se reversal where attorney's license had been suspended for failure to pay dues: "persons who obtain credentials by fraud, are classes apart from persons who satisfied the court of their legal skills but later ran afoul of some technical legal rule."). See also Pilchak v. Camper, 935 F.2d 145 (8th Cir.1991) (per se reversal where defense counsel was suffering from Alzheimer's disease at the time of trial).

Sleeping Defense Counsel

In Tippins v. Walker, 77 F.3d 682 (2d Cir.1996), Tippins argued for per se reversal of his conviction on the ground that his trial counsel slept through major portions of the trial. Testimony at the ineffectiveness hearing from the trial judge, court reporter, prosecutor, jurors and other defendants and defense counsel corroborated Tippins' account. Tippins' counsel slept every day of the trial; he could often be heard snoring; he slept through the testimony of several critical witnesses; and he was admonished by the trial judge for sleeping throughout the trial. The court held that this was a sufficient showing to trigger per se reversal under *Cronic.* It was careful to state, however, that not every instance of apparent sleeping on the part of defense counsel would be ineffective or cause for reversal. But the facts of this case were special:

> [T]he appearance of "sleeping" may cover a range of behavior. Lawyers may sometimes affect a drowsy or bored look to downplay an adversary's presentation of evidence. We are also mindful * * * that a per se rule would give unscrupulous attorneys a delayed-trigger weapon to be sprung at some later strategic phase of the proceeding if events developed very badly for a defendant. However, [the government] has not contended that Tirelli's sleeping was a charade or a tactical device. And it would be difficult for [the government] to make that claim, given the testimony that the trial prosecutor acknowledged his adversary's snoring by exchanging knowing looks with the court reporter. In any event, trial judges are well-positioned to detect, guard against, and penalize such a tactical abuse of the right to counsel.

Absence of Counsel for Ten Minutes During Presentation of Evidence Unrelated to the Defendant Is Not Clearly Per Se Prejudicial Under Cronic: Woods v. Donald

In Woods v. Donald, 575 U.S. 312 (2015) (per curiam), lower federal courts on habeas held that Donald was denied his right to effective assistance of counsel when his attorney was absent for approximately ten minutes during Donald's joint trial with two other defendants. The Supreme Court disagreed. Donald's defense counsel absented himself from the government's presentation of a chart chronicling phone calls that did not include Donald. Donald's attorney indicated before a recess that he had no "dog in this race" when the defense counsel for the other defendants objected to the government's introduction of the chart. Donald's lawyer returned after the trial was underway for approximately 10 minutes and the trial judge informed him that the focus had been on the chart. Donald's lawyer reiterated that he had no interest in that subject.

The Supreme Court stated it had "never addressed whether the rule announced in *Cronic* applies to testimony regarding codefendants' actions." It also concluded that "[w]ithin the contours of *Cronic,* a fair-minded jurist could conclude that a presumption of prejudice is not warranted by counsel's short absence during testimony about other defendants where that testimony was irrelevant to the defendant's theory of the case." The Court emphasized that its ruling was "only in the narrow context of federal habeas review" and expressed no view on the underlying Sixth Amendment question.

Counsel Present Only by Speakerphone: Wright v. Van Patten

In *Wright v. Van Patten,* 552 U.S. 120 (2008) (per curiam), a habeas petitioner argued that he was *per se* prejudiced when his counsel participated at his plea hearing only through a speakerphone. He contended that this amounted to a *virtual* absence of counsel and therefore counsel was automatically ineffective under *Cronic.* The government argued that counsel's effectiveness should be evaluated under the *Strickland* standard—and under that standard all parties agreed that the defendant could not prove ineffectiveness and prejudice. The state court had held that *Strickland* and not *Cronic* was applicable.

The Supreme Court held that "[n]o decision of this Court, * * * squarely addresses the issue in this case, or clearly establishes that *Cronic* should replace *Strickland* in this novel factual context," and it could not be said that the state court unreasonably applied clearly established Federal law—which is the standard for relief in habeas cases. Justice Stevens, the author of *Cronic,* reluctantly concurred in the judgment. He rued the fact that his opinion for the Court in *Cronic* did not make it clear that the *physical* presence of counsel at trial or a guilty plea hearing was critical.

Application of Per Se Prejudice Standard Not Warranted: Bell v. Cone

In Bell v. Cone, 535 U.S. 685 (2002), the Court found that defense counsel in a capital case did not perform so poorly as to justify a ruling of *per se* ineffectiveness and prejudice under *Cronic.* Chief Justice Rehnquist wrote the opinion for the Court. Cone was sentenced to death for murdering a couple after a two-day "crime rampage." He claimed, and the Court of Appeals found, that defense counsel was per se ineffective during the capital phase of the trial. The Chief Justice noted that the defense during the guilt phase was insanity and that defense counsel presented testimony from experts to support the defense, as well as testimony from witnesses that the defendant had suffered from drug use, trauma from his service in Vietnam, and depression from the deaths of his father and fiancée. The Chief Justice then observed that during the capital phase defense counsel called the jury's attention to the mitigating evidence already presented at the guilt phase of the trial and suggested that Cone was under the influence of extreme mental disturbance or duress, that he was an addict whose drug and other problems stemmed from the stress of his military service, and that he felt remorse.

The Supreme Court found no justification for per se reversal for ineffectiveness. Chief Justice Rehnquist stated that *Strickland,* and not

Cronic, was the relevant case for assessing counsel's performance in this case and that in this habeas case there was no showing of a clear case of ineffectiveness. The Chief Justice observed that defense counsel had offered substantial mitigating evidence in the guilt phase of the case and, once the junior prosecutor gave a low key closing argument, defense counsel might well have decided not to risk repeating the opening statement and giving the lead prosecutor, who was very effective, the chance to brand the defendant as a cold-blooded killer immediately before jury deliberations.

Justice Stevens dissented in *Cone*. He noted that counsel, subsequent to trial, was diagnosed with a mental illness that rendered him unfit to practice law and that apparently led to his suicide. Justice Stevens argued that counsel completely failed to present a defense at the capital phase, and therefore *Cronic's* per se reversal rule applied.

7. The Right to Effective Assistance of Counsel at the Guilty Plea Stage

More than 90% of criminal prosecutions end up in guilty pleas, so it is not surprising that the right to effective assistance of counsel has been applied to the guilty plea phase. See Hill v. Lockhart, 474 U.S. 52 (1985) (claims of ineffectiveness at the guilty plea stage governed by the *Strickland* two-pronged test). In the following case, the Court finds that counsel can be ineffective by failing to provide information that would be critical to a defendant's decision to accept or reject a plea offer.

The Duty to Inform the Defendant About Immigration Consequences of a Guilty Plea: Padilla v. Kentucky

PADILLA V. KENTUCKY

Supreme Court of the United States, 2010.
559 U.S. 356.

JUSTICE STEVENS delivered the opinion of the Court.

Petitioner Jose Padilla, a native of Honduras, has been a lawful permanent resident of the United States for more than 40 years. Padilla served this Nation with honor as a member of the U.S. Armed Forces during the Vietnam War. He now faces deportation after pleading guilty to the transportation of a large amount of marijuana in his tractor-trailer in the Commonwealth of Kentucky.

In this postconviction proceeding, Padilla claims that his counsel not only failed to advise him of this consequence prior to his entering the plea, but also told him that he "did not have to worry about immigration status since he had been in the country so long." Padilla relied on his counsel's erroneous advice when he pleaded guilty to the drug charges that made his deportation virtually mandatory. He alleges that he would have insisted on going to trial if he had not received incorrect advice from his attorney.

Assuming the truth of his allegations, the Supreme Court of Kentucky denied Padilla postconviction relief without the benefit of an evidentiary hearing. The court held that the Sixth Amendment's guarantee of effective assistance of counsel does not protect a criminal defendant from erroneous advice about deportation because it is merely a "collateral" consequence of his conviction. * * *

We granted certiorari to decide whether, as a matter of federal law, Padilla's counsel had an obligation to advise him that the offense to which he was pleading guilty would result in his removal from this country. We agree with Padilla that constitutionally competent counsel would have advised him that his conviction for drug distribution made him subject to automatic deportation. Whether he is entitled to relief depends on whether he has been prejudiced, a matter that we do not address.

* * *

The landscape of federal immigration law has changed dramatically over the last 90 years. While once there was only a narrow class of deportable offenses and judges wielded broad discretionary authority to prevent deportation, immigration reforms over time have expanded the class of deportable offenses and limited the authority of judges to alleviate the harsh consequences of deportation. The drastic measure of deportation or removal, is now virtually inevitable for a vast number of noncitizens convicted of crimes.

* * *

* * * Under contemporary law, if a noncitizen has committed a removable offense * * * his removal is practically inevitable * * * .

* * * These changes confirm our view that, as a matter of federal law, deportation is an integral part—indeed, sometimes the most important part—of the penalty that may be imposed on noncitizen defendants who plead guilty to specified crimes.

* * * The Supreme Court of Kentucky rejected Padilla's ineffectiveness claim on the ground that the advice he sought about the risk of deportation concerned only collateral matters, i.e., those matters not within the sentencing authority of the state trial court. * * * We, however, have never applied a distinction between direct and collateral consequences to define the scope of constitutionally "reasonable professional assistance" required under *Strickland*.

* * *

Deportation as a consequence of a criminal conviction is, because of its close connection to the criminal process, uniquely difficult to classify as either a direct or a collateral consequence. The collateral versus direct distinction is thus ill-suited to evaluating a *Strickland* claim concerning the specific risk of deportation. We conclude that advice regarding deportation is not categorically removed from the ambit of the Sixth Amendment right to counsel. *Strickland* applies to Padilla's claim.

* * *

In the instant case, the terms of the relevant immigration statute are succinct, clear, and explicit in defining the removal consequence for Padilla's conviction. Padilla's counsel could have easily determined that his plea would make him eligible for deportation simply from reading the text of the statute, which addresses not some broad classification of crimes but specifically commands removal for all controlled substances convictions except for the most trivial of marijuana possession offenses. Instead, Padilla's counsel provided him false assurance that his conviction would not result in his removal from this country. This is not a hard case in which to find deficiency * * *.

Immigration law can be complex, and it is a legal specialty of its own. * * * When the law is not succinct and straightforward * * * a criminal defense attorney need do no more than advise a noncitizen client that pending criminal charges may carry a risk of adverse immigration consequences. But when the deportation consequence is truly clear, as it was in this case, the duty to give correct advice is equally clear.

Accepting his allegations as true, Padilla has sufficiently alleged constitutional deficiency to satisfy the first prong of *Strickland.* * * *

We have given serious consideration to the concerns that the Solicitor General, respondent, and amici have stressed regarding the importance of protecting the finality of convictions obtained through guilty pleas. * * *

* * *

[A]lthough we must be especially careful about recognizing new grounds for attacking the validity of guilty pleas, in the 25 years since we first applied *Strickland* to claims of ineffective assistance at the plea stage, practice has shown that pleas are less frequently the subject of collateral challenges than convictions obtained after a trial. Pleas account for nearly 95% of all criminal convictions. But they account for only approximately 30% of the habeas petitions filed. The nature of relief secured by a successful collateral challenge to a guilty plea—an opportunity to withdraw the plea and proceed to trial—imposes its own significant limiting principle: Those who collaterally attack their guilty pleas lose the benefit of the bargain obtained as a result of the plea. Thus, a different calculus informs whether it is wise to challenge a guilty plea in a habeas proceeding because, ultimately, the challenge may result in a less favorable outcome for the defendant, whereas a collateral challenge to a conviction obtained after a jury trial has no similar downside potential.

Finally, informed consideration of possible deportation can only benefit both the State and noncitizen defendants during the plea-bargaining process. By bringing deportation consequences into this process, the defense and prosecution may well be able to reach agreements that better satisfy the interests of both parties. * * * Counsel who possess the most rudimentary understanding of the deportation consequences of a particular criminal offense may be able to plea bargain creatively with the prosecutor in order to craft a conviction and sentence that reduce the likelihood of deportation, as by avoiding a conviction for an offense that automatically triggers the removal consequence. At the same time, the threat of deportation may provide the defendant with a powerful incentive to plead guilty to an offense that does not mandate that penalty in exchange for a dismissal of a charge that does.

* * *

JUSTICE ALITO, with whom THE CHIEF JUSTICE joins, concurring in the judgment.

I concur in the judgment because a criminal defense attorney fails to provide effective assistance * * * if the attorney misleads a noncitizen client regarding the removal consequences of a conviction. In my view, such an attorney must (1) refrain from unreasonably providing incorrect advice and (2) advise the defendant that a criminal conviction may have adverse immigration consequences and that, if the alien wants advice on this issue, the alien should consult an immigration attorney.

* * *

[A] criminal defense attorney should not be required to provide advice on immigration law, a complex specialty that generally lies outside the scope of a criminal defense attorney's expertise. * * * [A]n alien defendant's Sixth Amendment right to counsel is satisfied if defense counsel advises the client that a conviction may have immigration consequences, that immigration law is a specialized field, that the attorney is not an immigration lawyer, and that the client should consult an immigration specialist if the client wants advice on that subject.

JUSTICE SCALIA, with whom JUSTICE THOMAS joins, dissenting.

* * *

There is no basis in text or in principle to extend the constitutionally required advice regarding guilty pleas beyond those matters germane to the criminal prosecution at hand—to wit, the sentence that the plea will produce, the higher sentence that conviction after trial might entail, and the chances of such a conviction. * * * Because the subject of the misadvice here was not the prosecution for which Jose Padilla was entitled to effective assistance of counsel, the Sixth Amendment has no application.

* * *

The Court's holding prevents legislation that could solve the problems addressed by today's opinions in a more precise and targeted fashion. * * *

Application of Strickland and AEDPA Review Standards to Counsel's Conduct When a Guilty Plea Is Entered Early in the Proceedings: Premo v. Moore

Justice Kennedy wrote for the Court in Premo v. Moore, 562 U.S. 115 (2011), as it considered the adequacy of representation in providing an assessment of a plea bargain without first seeking suppression of a confession assumed to have been improperly obtained. Moore and two others essentially kidnapped and murdered a man. Moore and one accomplice told Moore's brother and the accomplice's girlfriend about the crimes and later repeated their accounts during police interrogation. On the advice of counsel Moore agreed to plead no contest to felony murder in exchange for a sentence of 300 months, the minimum sentence allowed by law for the offense.

Moore later filed for postconviction relief in an Oregon state court, alleging that he had been denied his right to effective assistance of counsel because his lawyer had not filed a motion to suppress his confession to police in advance of the lawyer's advice that Moore considered before accepting the plea offer. The Oregon court held a hearing and concluded that a "motion to suppress would have been fruitless" in light of the other admissible confession by Moore, to which two witnesses could testify.

Counsel added at the hearing that he had made Moore aware of the possibility of being charged with aggravated murder, which carried a potential death sentence, as well as the possibility of a sentence of life imprisonment without parole. The intense and serious abuse to the victim before the shooting might well have led the State to insist on a strong response. In light of these facts the Oregon court concluded Moore had not established ineffective assistance of counsel under *Strickland.*

A federal district court denied habeas relief but the Ninth Circuit found that the state court's conclusion that counsel's action did not constitute ineffective assistance was an unreasonable application of clearly established law in light of *Strickland.* Justice Kennedy's opinion for the Court disagreed with the Ninth Circuit. He concluded that the Court of Appeals "was wrong to accord scant deference to counsel's judgment, and doubly wrong to conclude it would have been unreasonable to find that the defense attorney qualified as counsel for Sixth Amendment purposes."

Justice Kennedy noted that "[i]n the case of an early plea, neither the prosecution nor the defense may know with much certainty what course the case may take" so that "each side, of necessity, risks consequences that may arise from contingencies or circumstances yet unperceived." He reasoned that the prosecutors faced the cost of litigation and the risk of trying their case without Moore's confession to the police, which meant that Moore's counsel could reasonably believe that a swift plea bargain would allow Moore to take advantage of the State's aversion to these hazards." In the final analysis, he concluded that "Moore's counsel made a reasonable choice to opt for a quick plea bargain," and "[a]t the very least, the state court would not have been unreasonable to so conclude." With respect to prejudice, Justice Kennedy found that "[d]eference to the state court's prejudice determination is all the more significant in light of the uncertainty inherent in plea negotiations * * *." He explained that "[h]indsight and second guesses are also inappropriate, and often more so, where a plea has been entered without a full trial or, as in this case, even before the prosecution decided on the charges."

Justice Ginsburg concurred in the judgment on the ground that "[a]s Moore's counsel confirmed at oral argument, Moore never declared that, better informed, he would have resisted the plea bargain and opted for trial."

Justice Kagan took no part in the consideration or decision of this case.

Assessing Prejudice Where the Defendant, Through Counsel's Ineffectiveness, Is Not Informed of a Plea Bargain and Accepts a Less Favorable One: Missouri v. Frye

In the 2011 Term the Court decided two companion cases to determine whether and how a defendant could establish *Strickland* prejudice for bad (or no) advice given by his lawyer at the plea bargaining stage. The cases cover two fact situations: one where the defendant took a bad plea bargain (because he didn't know a better one was out there) and the other where the defendant rejected a good plea bargain on counsel's bad advice and was convicted at trial.

MISSOURI V. FRYE

Supreme Court of the United States, 2012.
566 U.S. 134.

JUSTICE KENNEDY delivered the opinion of the Court.

* * * This case arises in the context of claimed ineffective assistance that led to the lapse of a prosecution offer of a plea bargain, a proposal that

offered terms more lenient than the terms of the guilty plea entered later. The initial question is whether the constitutional right to counsel extends to the negotiation and consideration of plea offers that lapse or are rejected. If there is a right to effective assistance with respect to those offers, a further question is what a defendant must demonstrate in order to show that prejudice resulted from counsel's deficient performance. * * *

In August 2007, Respondent Galin Frye was charged with driving with a revoked license. Frye had been convicted for that offense on three other occasions, so the State of Missouri charged him with a class D felony, which carries a maximum term of imprisonment of four years.

On November 15, 2007, the prosecutor sent a letter to Frye's counsel offering a choice of two plea bargains. The prosecutor first offered to recommend a 3-year sentence if there was a guilty plea to the felony charge, without a recommendation regarding probation but with a recommendation that Frye serve 10 days in jail as so-called "shock" time. The second offer was to reduce the charge to a misdemeanor and, if Frye pleaded guilty to it, to recommend a 90-day sentence. The misdemeanor charge of driving with a revoked license carries a maximum term of imprisonment of one year. The letter stated both offers would expire on December 28. Frye's attorney did not advise Frye that the offers had been made.

Frye's preliminary hearing was scheduled for January 4, 2008. On December 30, 2007, less than a week before the hearing, Frye was again arrested for driving with a revoked license. [Frye pleaded guilty to the August charge.] There was no underlying plea agreement. The state trial court accepted Frye's guilty plea. The prosecutor recommended a 3-year sentence, made no recommendation regarding probation, and requested 10 days shock time in jail. The trial judge sentenced Frye to three years in prison.

Frye filed for postconviction relief in state court. He alleged his counsel's failure to inform him of the prosecution's plea offer denied him the effective assistance of counsel. At an evidentiary hearing, Frye testified he would have entered a guilty plea to the misdemeanor had he known about the offer.

[The Missouri appellate court found that Frye had established ineffectiveness and prejudice. To implement a remedy, the Missouri court held that Frye's guilty plea would be withdrawn, and gave Frye the option to either insist on a trial or to plead guilty to any offense the prosecutor deemed appropriate to charge.]

* * *

With respect to the right to effective counsel in plea negotiations, a proper beginning point is to discuss two cases from this Court considering the role of counsel in advising a client about a plea offer and an ensuing guilty plea: Hill v. Lockhart, 474 U.S. 52 (1985), and Padilla v. Kentucky.

* * * In the case now before the Court the State * * * points out that the legal question presented is different from that in *Hill* and *Padilla.* In those cases the claim was that the prisoner's plea of guilty was invalid because counsel had provided incorrect advice pertinent to the plea. In the instant case, by contrast, the guilty plea that was accepted, and the plea proceedings concerning it in court, were all based on accurate advice and information from counsel. * * *

To give further support to its contention that the instant case is in a category different from what the Court considered in *Hill* and *Padilla*, the State urges that there is no right to a plea offer or a plea bargain in any event. It claims Frye therefore was not deprived of any legal benefit to which he was entitled. Under this view, any wrongful or mistaken action of counsel with respect to earlier plea offers is beside the point.

* * * The State's contentions are neither illogical nor without some persuasive force, yet they do not suffice to overcome a simple reality. Ninety-seven percent of federal convictions and ninety-four percent of state convictions are the result of guilty pleas. The reality is that plea bargains have become so central to the administration of the criminal justice system that defense counsel have responsibilities in the plea bargain process, responsibilities that must be met to render the adequate assistance of counsel that the Sixth Amendment requires in the criminal process at critical stages. Because ours is for the most part a system of pleas, not a system of trials, it is insufficient simply to point to the guarantee of a fair trial as a backstop that inoculates any errors in the pretrial process. * * * In today's criminal justice system, therefore, the negotiation of a plea bargain, rather than the unfolding of a trial, is almost always the critical point for a defendant.

* * *

The inquiry then becomes how to define the duty and responsibilities of defense counsel in the plea bargain process. This is a difficult question. The art of negotiation is at least as nuanced as the art of trial advocacy and it presents questions farther removed from immediate judicial supervision. * * * The alternative courses and tactics in negotiation are so individual that it may be neither prudent nor practicable to try to elaborate or define detailed standards for the proper discharge of defense counsel's participation in the process.

This case presents neither the necessity nor the occasion to define the duties of defense counsel in those respects, however. Here the question is whether defense counsel has the duty to communicate the terms of a formal offer to accept a plea on terms and conditions that may result in a lesser sentence, a conviction on lesser charges, or both.

This Court now holds that, as a general rule, defense counsel has the duty to communicate formal offers from the prosecution to accept a plea on terms and conditions that may be favorable to the accused. Any exceptions to that rule need not be explored here, for the offer was a formal one with a fixed expiration date. When defense counsel allowed the offer to expire without advising the defendant or allowing him to consider it, defense counsel did not render the effective assistance the Constitution requires.

* * *

Here defense counsel did not communicate the formal offers to the defendant. As a result of that deficient performance, the offers lapsed. Under *Strickland,* the question then becomes what, if any, prejudice resulted from the breach of duty.

* * *

* * * In cases where a defendant complains that ineffective assistance led him to accept a plea offer as opposed to proceeding to trial, the defendant will have to show "a reasonable probability that, but for counsel's errors, he would not have pleaded guilty and would have insisted on going to trial." * * * In a case, such as this, where a defendant pleads guilty to less favorable terms and claims that ineffective assistance of counsel caused him to miss out on a more favorable earlier plea offer, *Strickland's* inquiry into whether "the result of the proceeding would have been different" requires looking not at whether the defendant would have proceeded to trial absent ineffective assistance but whether he would have accepted the offer to plead pursuant to the terms earlier proposed.

In order to complete a showing of *Strickland* prejudice, defendants who have shown a reasonable probability they would have accepted the earlier plea offer must also show that, if the prosecution had the discretion to cancel it or if the trial court had the discretion to refuse to accept it, there is a reasonable probability that neither the prosecution nor the trial court would have prevented the offer from being accepted or implemented. This further showing is of particular importance because a defendant has no right to be offered a plea, nor a federal right that the judge accept it. * * *

These standards must be applied to the instant case. * * * On this record, it is evident that Frye's attorney did not make a meaningful attempt to inform the defendant of a written plea offer before the offer expired. The Missouri Court of Appeals was correct that "counsel's representation fell below an objective standard of reasonableness."

* * *

There appears to be a reasonable probability Frye would have accepted the prosecutor's original offer of a plea bargain if the offer had been communicated to him, because he pleaded guilty to a more serious charge, with no promise of a sentencing recommendation from the prosecutor. It may be that in some cases defendants must show more than just a guilty plea to a charge or sentence harsher than the original offer. For example, revelations between plea offers about the strength of the prosecution's case may make a late decision to plead guilty insufficient to demonstrate, without further evidence, that the defendant would have pleaded guilty to an earlier, more generous plea offer if his counsel had reported it to him. Here, however, that is not the case. * * *

The Court of Appeals failed, however, to require Frye to show that the first plea offer, if accepted by Frye, would have been adhered to by the prosecution and accepted by the trial court. Whether the prosecution and trial court are required to do so is a matter of state law, and it is not the place of this Court to settle those matters. * * * In Missouri, it appears "a plea offer once accepted by the defendant can be withdrawn without recourse" by the prosecution. The extent of the trial court's discretion in Missouri to reject a plea agreement appears to be in some doubt.

* * * If * * * the prosecutor could have canceled the plea agreement, and if Frye fails to show a reasonable probability the prosecutor would have adhered to the agreement, there is no *Strickland* prejudice. Likewise, if the trial court could have refused to accept the plea agreement, and if Frye fails to show a reasonable probability the trial court would have accepted the plea, there is no *Strickland* prejudice. In this case, given Frye's new offense for driving without a license on December 30, 2007, there is reason to doubt that the prosecution would have adhered to the agreement or that the trial court would have accepted it at the January 4, 2008, hearing, unless they were required by state law to do so.

It is appropriate to allow the Missouri Court of Appeals to address this question in the first instance. * * *

JUSTICE SCALIA, with whom THE CHIEF JUSTICE, JUSTICE THOMAS, and JUSTICE ALITO join, dissenting.

* * *

Galin Frye's attorney failed to inform him about a plea offer, and Frye ultimately pleaded guilty without the benefit of a deal. Counsel's mistake did not deprive Frye of any substantive or procedural right; only of the opportunity to accept a plea bargain to which he had no entitlement in the first place. So little entitlement that, had he known of and accepted the bargain, the prosecution would have been able to withdraw it right up to the point that his guilty plea pursuant to the bargain was accepted.

* * *

While the inadequacy of counsel's performance in this case is clear enough, whether it was prejudicial (in the sense that the Court's new version of *Strickland* requires) is not. The Court's description of how that question is to be answered on remand is alone enough to show how unwise it is to constitutionalize the plea-bargaining process. Prejudice is to be determined, the Court tells us, by a process of retrospective crystal-ball gazing posing as legal analysis.

* * *

Assessing Prejudice When the Defendant, on Bad Advice, Rejects a Plea Bargain and Goes to Trial: Lafler v. Cooper

LAFLER V. COOPER

Supreme Court of the United States, 2012.
566 U.S. 156.

JUSTICE KENNEDY delivered the opinion of the Court.

In this case, as in Missouri v. Frye also decided today, a criminal defendant seeks a remedy when inadequate assistance of counsel caused nonacceptance of a plea offer and further proceedings led to a less favorable outcome. Here, the favorable plea offer was reported to the client but, on advice of counsel, was rejected. In *Frye* there was a later guilty plea. Here, after the plea offer had been rejected, there was a full and fair trial before a jury. After a guilty verdict, the defendant received a sentence harsher than that offered in the rejected plea bargain. [In the Supreme Court the state conceded that counsel had acted ineffectively, so the only question was prejudice.]

On the evening of March 25, 2003, respondent pointed a gun toward Kali Mundy's head and fired. From the record, it is unclear why respondent did this, and at trial it was suggested that he might have acted either in self-defense or in defense of another person. In any event the shot missed and Mundy fled. Respondent followed in pursuit, firing repeatedly. Mundy was shot in her buttock, hip, and abdomen but survived the assault.

Respondent was charged under Michigan law with assault with intent to murder, possession of a firearm by a felon, possession of a firearm in the commission of a felony, misdemeanor possession of marijuana, and for being a habitual offender. On two occasions, the prosecution offered to dismiss two of the charges and to recommend a sentence of 51 to 85 months for the other two, in exchange for a guilty plea. In a communication with the court respondent admitted guilt and expressed a willingness to accept the offer. Respondent, however, later rejected the offer on both occasions, allegedly after his attorney convinced him that the prosecution would be unable to establish his intent to murder Mundy because she had been shot below the waist. On the first day of trial the prosecution offered a significantly less favorable plea deal, which respondent again rejected. After trial, respondent was convicted on all counts and received a mandatory minimum sentence of 185 to 360 months' imprisonment. [The defendant's claims of ineffective assistance were rejected in the state courts but the lower federal court granted habeas relief.]

The question for this Court is how to apply *Strickland's* prejudice test where ineffective assistance results in a rejection of the plea offer and the defendant is convicted at the ensuing trial.

* * *

In Hill v. Lockhart, when evaluating the petitioner's claim that ineffective assistance led to the improvident acceptance of a guilty plea, the Court required the petitioner to show "that there is a reasonable probability that, but for counsel's errors, [the defendant] would not have pleaded guilty and would have insisted on going to trial."

In contrast to *Hill,* here the ineffective advice led not to an offer's acceptance but to its rejection. Having to stand trial, not choosing to waive it, is the prejudice alleged. In these circumstances a defendant must show that but for the ineffective advice of counsel there is a reasonable probability that the plea offer would have been presented to the court (i.e., that the defendant would have accepted the plea and the prosecution would not have withdrawn it in light of intervening circumstances), that the court would have accepted its terms, and that the conviction or sentence, or both, under the offer's terms would have been less severe than under the judgment and sentence that in fact were imposed. * * *

* * *

Even if a defendant shows ineffective assistance of counsel has caused the rejection of a plea leading to a trial and a more severe sentence, there is the question of what constitutes an appropriate remedy. That question must now be addressed.

* * *

The specific injury suffered by defendants who decline a plea offer as a result of ineffective assistance of counsel and then receive a greater sentence as a result of trial can come in at least one of two forms. In some cases, the sole advantage a defendant would have received under the plea is a lesser sentence. This is typically the case when the charges that would have been admitted as part of the plea bargain are the same as the charges the defendant was convicted of after trial. In this situation the court may conduct an evidentiary hearing to determine whether the defendant has shown a reasonable probability that but for counsel's errors he would have accepted the plea. If the showing is made, the court may exercise discretion in determining whether the defendant should receive the term of imprisonment the government offered in the plea, the sentence he received at trial, or something in between.

In some situations it may be that resentencing alone will not be full redress for the constitutional injury. If, for example, an offer was for a guilty plea to a count or counts less serious than the ones for which a defendant was convicted after trial, or if a mandatory sentence confines a judge's sentencing discretion after trial, a resentencing based on the conviction at trial may not suffice. In these circumstances, the proper exercise of discretion to remedy the constitutional injury may be to require the prosecution to reoffer the plea proposal. Once this has occurred, the judge can then exercise discretion in deciding whether to vacate the conviction from trial and accept the plea or leave the conviction undisturbed.

* * *

[Justice Kennedy applied the AEDPA standard to the decision of the Michigan Court of Appeals and found that it was "contrary to, or involved an unreasonable application of, clearly established Federal law, as determined by the Supreme Court of the United States." The state court failed to apply *Strickland* to the ineffective assistance of counsel claim.]

As to prejudice, respondent has shown that but for counsel's deficient performance there is a reasonable probability he and the trial court would have accepted the guilty plea. In addition, as a result of not accepting the plea and being convicted at trial, respondent received a minimum sentence 3 1/2 times greater than he would have received under the plea. The standard for ineffective assistance under *Strickland* has thus been satisfied.

As a remedy, the District Court ordered specific performance of the original plea agreement. The correct remedy in these circumstances, however, is to order the State to reoffer the plea agreement. Presuming respondent accepts the offer, the state trial court can then exercise its discretion in determining whether to vacate the convictions and resentence respondent pursuant to the plea agreement, to vacate only some of the convictions and resentence respondent accordingly, or to leave the convictions and sentence from trial undisturbed. Today's decision leaves open to the trial court how best to exercise that discretion in all the circumstances of the case.

* * *

JUSTICE SCALIA, with whom JUSTICE THOMAS joins, and with whom THE CHIEF JUSTICE joins in relevant part, dissenting.

* * * [T]he Court today opens a whole new field of constitutionalized criminal procedure: plea-bargaining law. The ordinary criminal process has become too long, too expensive, and unpredictable, in no small part as

a consequence of an intricate federal Code of Criminal Procedure imposed on the States by this Court in pursuit of perfect justice. The Court now moves to bring perfection to the alternative in which prosecutors and defendants have sought relief. * * *

In many—perhaps most—countries of the world, American-style plea bargaining is forbidden in cases as serious as this one, even for the purpose of obtaining testimony that enables conviction of a greater malefactor, much less for the purpose of sparing the expense of trial. * * *

In the United States, we have plea bargaining a-plenty, but until today it has been regarded as a necessary evil. * * *

Today, however, the Supreme Court of the United States elevates plea bargaining from a necessary evil to a constitutional entitlement. It is no longer a somewhat embarrassing adjunct to our criminal justice system; rather, as the Court announces in the companion case to this one, "it is the criminal justice system." Thus, even though there is no doubt that the respondent here is guilty of the offense with which he was charged; even though he has received the exorbitant gold standard of American justice—a full-dress criminal trial with its innumerable constitutional and statutory limitations upon the evidence that the prosecution can bring forward, and (in Michigan as in most States) the requirement of a unanimous guilty verdict by impartial jurors; the Court says that his conviction is invalid because he was deprived of his constitutional entitlement to plea-bargain.

* * *

[The dissenting opinion of Justice Alito is omitted.]

Counseling Client to Withdraw a Cooperation Agreement on the Basis of the Client's Protestation of Innocence: Burt v. Titlow

Justice Alito delivered the opinion of the Court in Burt v. Titlow, 571 U.S. 12 (2014), as the Court again emphasized the double deference due a state court holding that a defense lawyer was not ineffective. Titlow and her aunt murdered the aunt's husband by pouring vodka down his throat and smothering him with a pillow. Titlow, with the help of his lawyer, reached an agreement with state prosecutors to testify against the aunt, plead guilty to manslaughter, and receive a 7- to 15-year sentence. At a plea hearing, counsel confirmed that he had spent much time with Tidlow and that Tidlow understood that the evidence against her could support a conviction for first-degree murder. The trial court approved the plea bargain, but three days before the aunt's trial was to begin, Tidlow obtained a new lawyer, Toca, who helped her demand a three year rather than a seven year minimum sentence. The prosecutor refused the demand, Titlow withdrew her plea, and she acknowledged in open court that a first-degree murder charge could be reinstated. She was tried, a jury found her guilty of second-degree murder, and the judge imposed a 20–40 year sentence.

On direct appeal, Titlow argued that her new trial lawyer was ineffective because he had not taken time to learn the case and realize the strength of the state's evidence. The state appellate court found no ineffectiveness and that Toca advised Titlow to demand a lower sentence because she proclaimed her innocence. A federal district court denied relief, but the Sixth Circuit reversed and found that "the factual predicate for the state court's decision—that the withdrawal of the plea was based on respondent's assertion of innocence—was an unreasonable interpretation of the factual record.

The Supreme Court granted review and concluded that "the record readily supports the [State court's] factual finding that Toca advised withdrawal of the guilty plea only after respondent's proclamation of innocence."

Justice Sotomayor concurred on the ground that Titlow failed to overcome the presumptions that the new trial counsel performed effectively and that the state court ruled correctly. Justice Ginsburg concurred in the result, although she found "dubious the [State court's] conclusion that Toca acted reasonably in light of Titlow's protestations of innocence."

Reasonable Probability of Going to Trial Even Without a Strong Defense: Lee v. United States

Chief Justice Roberts wrote for the Court in Lee v. United States, 137 S.Ct. 1958 (2017), as it addressed a situation in which Lee, a non-citizen, was indicted on one count of possessing ecstasy with intent to distribute. He had lived for most of his life in the United States and feared that a criminal conviction might affect his status as a lawful permanent resident. Because his attorney assured him that the Government would not deport him if he pleaded guilty and because he had no real defense to the charge, he accepted a plea that carried a lesser prison sentence than he would have faced at trial. The advice was wrong, and Lee was subject to mandatory deportation from this country. He sought to vacate his conviction on the ground that he accepted the plea because he received ineffective assistance of counsel in violation of the Sixth Amendment.

Chief Justice Roberts stated that everyone agreed that that Lee received objectively unreasonable representation and the question was whether he could show prejudice. Lower federal courts denied relief on the ground that, without a defense at trial, Lee could not show prejudice. The Supreme Court disagreed.

The Chief Justice explained that "[w]hen a defendant alleges his counsel's deficient performance led him to accept a guilty plea rather than go to trial, we do not ask whether, had he gone to trial, the result of that trial 'would have been different' than the result of the plea bargain * * * because, while we ordinarily apply a strong presumption of reliability to judicial proceedings, we cannot accord any such presumption to judicial proceedings that never took place." He cited Hill v. Lockhart and further explained that "[w]e instead consider whether the defendant was prejudiced by the denial of the entire judicial proceeding to which he had a right."

Although the Chief Justice agreed with dissenters that a defendant must also show that he would have been better off going to trial when the defendant's decision about going to trial turns on his prospects of success and those are affected by the attorney's error, he reasoned that there are different types of errors. In Lee's case, the error had nothing to do with his trial chances; counsel's error affected Lee's understanding of the consequences of pleading guilty.

Chief Justice Roberts illustrated why a defendant with little chance of winning at trial might still choose trial over plea.

> [C]ommon sense (not to mention our precedent) recognizes that there is more to consider than simply the likelihood of success at trial. The decision whether to plead guilty also involves assessing the respective consequences of a conviction after trial and by plea. When those consequences are, from the defendant's perspective, similarly dire, even the smallest chance of success at trial may look attractive. For example, a defendant with no realistic defense to a charge carrying a 20-year sentence may nevertheless choose trial, if the prosecution's plea offer is 18 years. Here Lee alleges that avoiding deportation was *the* determinative factor for him; deportation after some time in prison was not meaningfully different from deportation after somewhat less time. He says he accordingly would have rejected any plea leading to deportation—even if it shaved off prison time—in favor of throwing a "Hail Mary" at trial.

The Chief Justice concluded that "[i]n the unusual circumstances of this case, we conclude that Lee has adequately demonstrated a reasonable probability that he would have rejected the plea had he known that it would lead to mandatory deportation," and "[w]e cannot agree that it would be irrational for a defendant in Lee's position to reject the plea offer in favor of trial."

The Court remanded for further proceedings.

Justice Thomas, joined in large part by Justice Alito, dissented and maintained his view that "the Sixth Amendment to the Constitution does not require counsel to provide accurate advice concerning the potential removal consequences of a guilty plea." He also challenged the prejudice standard adopted by the Court. Justice Alito did not participate in the decision.

8. Waiver of the Right to Effective Assistance

In Schriro v. Landrigan, 550 U.S. 465 (2007), Justice Thomas wrote for the Court as it held, in a habeas case, that a state court was not objectively unreasonably in finding that a criminal defendant had waived his right to challenge counsel's ineffectiveness by refusing to pursue the strategy urged by counsel.

Landrigan was convicted of murder and other offenses and sentenced to death. At his sentencing hearing, his counsel planned to call his ex-wife and birth mother as witnesses but both refused to testify and indicated that they did so at Landrigan's request. The trial judge inquired of both witnesses and Landrigan to confirm that he did not want them to testify. At the conclusion of the hearing, the trial judge asked Landrigan whether he had anything to say and he responded with a statement that concluded "I think if you want to give me the death penalty, just bring it right on. I'm ready for it." After his conviction and sentence were affirmed on direct appeal, Landrigan sought state habeas corpus relief and claimed ineffective assistance of counsel for failure to present mitigating evidence.

The same judge who presided at trial rejected Landrigan's habeas claim, finding that "[Landrigan] instructed his attorney not to present any evidence at the sentencing hearing, [so] it is difficult to comprehend how [Landrigan] can claim counsel should have presented other evidence at sentencing." Although Landrigan contended that he would have cooperated had mitigating evidence other than the testimony of the ex-wife and birth mother been presented, the judge concluded that Landrigan's "statements at sentencing belie his new-found sense of cooperation."

In rejecting the claim of ineffectiveness, Justice Thomas distinguished prior cases, including *Rompilla*, found that the Court had "never addressed a situation like this," and concluded "[i]n short, at the time of the Arizona postconviction court's decision, it was not objectively unreasonable for that court to conclude that a defendant who refused to allow the presentation of any mitigating evidence could not establish *Strickland* prejudice based on his counsel's failure to investigate further possible mitigating evidence."

Justice Stevens, joined by Justices Souter, Ginsburg and Breyer, dissented.

B. THE RIGHT TO CONFLICT-FREE REPRESENTATION

The right to effective assistance of counsel may be denied if defense counsel is operating under a conflict of interest, and as a result cannot or does not properly protect her client's interests. One situation of potential conflict arises when counsel represents multiple defendants. Codefendants may have divergent interests at all stages of a prosecution. A plea bargain advantageous to one defendant may produce testimony adverse to another defendant. Defendants may have inconsistent defenses, or wish to testify in ways that incriminate codefendants. See, e.g., United States v. Hall, 200 F.3d 962 (6th Cir. 2000) (conflict of interest where defense counsel represents two brothers, and one has a public authority defense while the other does not). Evidence inculpating one defendant might exculpate another, forcing counsel to make unsatisfactory choices in response to offered testimony. Separate counsel also might choose differing approaches to closing argument that one lawyer for multiple defendants might not be able to choose.

Conflicts also might arise because defense counsel has a personal interest that could be negatively affected by aggressive representation of the defendant. For example, in one notorious case, a defense counsel was representing the defendant in a felony prosecution and simultaneously having a sexual relationship with the defendant's wife. Counsel's ardor for the wife may well have dampened his ardor to have the defendant set free. See Hernandez v. State, 750 So.2d 50 (Fla.App. 1999).

Another possibility is that the interests of the defendant may be in conflict with the interests of defense counsel's client in another matter, or with the interests of a former client. For example, if counsel represents two defendants charged with the same crime in separate matters, the decision whether to call one defendant to testify in the other's trial may be impacted by counsel's conflicting loyalties. See, e.g., United States v. Elliot, 463 F.3d 858 (9th Cir. 2006) (conflict where two clients are separately tried for the same crime and their best defense is to shift blame to each other: "To represent Elliot adequately, Gordon needed to interview, aggressively examine, and possibly place blame on Hevia, all of which clashed with his attorney-client relationship with Hevia."). And the lawyer's duty to preserve the confidences and secrets of a former client may impair a current client's representation if the former client is called as a witness for the prosecution.

The rules adopted by the Supreme Court for assessing claims of defense counsel conflict of interest have been usefully summarized by the court in United States v. Kliti, 156 F.3d 150 (2d Cir.1998):

> A defendant's right to counsel under the Sixth Amendment includes the right to be represented by an attorney who is free from conflicts of interest. When the trial court knows or reasonably should know of the possibility of a conflict of interest, it has a threshold obligation to determine whether the attorney has an actual conflict, a potential conflict, or no conflict. In fulfilling this initial obligation to inquire into the existence of a conflict of interest, the trial court may

rely on counsel's representations. If a district court ignores a possible conflict and does not conduct this initial inquiry, reversal of a defendant's conviction is automatic. If, through this inquiry, the court determines that the attorney suffers from an actual or potential conflict of interest, the court has a "disqualification/waiver" obligation.

* * *

If the conflict is so severe that no rational defendant would waive it, the court must disqualify the attorney. If it is a lesser conflict, the court must conduct a * * * hearing to determine whether the defendant will knowingly and intelligently waive his right to conflict-free representation. (Before a defendant can knowingly and intelligently waive a conflict, the court must: (1) advise the defendant about potential conflicts; (2) determine whether the defendant understands the risks of those conflicts; and (3) give the defendant time to digest and contemplate the risks, with the aid of independent counsel if desired.)

1. The Duty of Court Inquiry

Per Se Reversal for Failure to Inquire into Joint Representation: Holloway v. Arkansas

In Holloway v. Arkansas, 435 U.S. 475 (1978), the Court made it clear that joint representation of codefendants by a single attorney is not a *per se* violation of the right to effective assistance of counsel. The Court noted that a common defense often gives strength against a common attack. Under some circumstances, however, joint representation may create a conflict that can deny a defendant effective assistance of counsel. In *Holloway,* the defense counsel made pretrial motions for appointment of separate counsel for each defendant because of possible conflicts of interest. The trial court denied the motion, and refused defense counsel's renewed request during the trial for separate counsel when the three codefendants each wished to testify. Counsel felt that he would be unable to examine or cross-examine any defendant to protect the interests of the others.

Without ever reaching the issue of whether there was an actual conflict of interest, the Supreme Court reversed the defendants' convictions. Reversal was required because the judge, after timely motions, erred in failing to "either appoint separate counsel, or to take adequate steps to ascertain whether the risk was too remote to warrant separate counsel." The Court held that in these circumstances, prejudice to the defendants must be presumed:

> Joint representation of conflicting interests is suspect because of what it tends to prevent the attorney from doing. For example, in this case it may well have precluded defense counsel for [one of the

> codefendants] from exploring possible plea negotiations and the possibility of an agreement to testify for the prosecution, provided a lesser charge or a favorable sentencing recommendation would be acceptable. Generally speaking a conflict may also prevent an attorney from challenging the admission of evidence prejudicial to one client but perhaps favorable to another, or from arguing at the sentencing hearing the relative involvement and culpability of his clients in order to minimize the culpability of one by emphasizing that of another. Examples can be readily multiplied. * * *
>
> [A] rule requiring a defendant to show that a conflict of interests—which he and his counsel tried to avoid by timely objections to the joint representation—prejudiced him in some specific fashion would not be susceptible to intelligent, evenhanded application. In the normal case where a harmless error rule is applied, the error occurs at trial and its scope is readily identifiable. * * * But in a case of joint representation of conflicting interests the evil * * * is in what the advocate finds himself compelled to *refrain* from doing, not only at trial but also as to possible pretrial plea negotiations and in the sentencing process. * * * Thus, an inquiry into a claim of harmless error here would require, unlike most cases, unguided speculation.

QUESTION ABOUT HOLLOWAY

Holloway was decided before *Strickland.* How does *Holloway's* rule of per se reversal square with *Strickland's* holding that a defendant must show that counsel was ineffective and that the ineffectiveness was prejudicial? In Selsor v. Kaiser, 22 F.3d 1029 (10th Cir.1994), the court concluded that the per se reversal rule of *Holloway* was unaffected by the Court's later requirement of a showing of prejudice in *Strickland.* It reasoned as follows:

> *Strickland's* requirement of a showing of actual conflict presupposes that trial courts conduct an appropriate inquiry when the defendant properly raises the issue. *Holloway,* however, addresses the situation where the trial court *fails* to make such inquiry in the face of the defendant's timely objection. As a result, the *Strickland* rule requiring a defendant to demonstrate an actual conflict of interest in order to obtain a presumption of prejudice is inapplicable in a *Holloway*-type case.

So *Holloway* is a limited exception to the *Strickland* case-by-case approach. Automatic reversal is required where 1) joint defendants are being represented by a single counsel; 2) defense counsel or the defendant raises the conflict issue with the court; and 3) the court fails even to conduct a hearing on the matter.

Federal Rule 44

Fed.R.Crim.P. 44 attempts to address the problem of joint representation and the need for a hearing which the Court was concerned with in *Holloway*:

Rule 44. Right to and Appointment of Counsel

* * *

> **(c)(2) Court's Responsibilities in Cases of Joint Representation.** The court must promptly inquire about the propriety of joint representation and must personally advise each defendant of the right to the effective assistance of counsel, including separate representation. Unless there is good cause to believe that no conflict of interest is likely to arise, the court must take appropriate measures to protect each defendant's right to counsel.

It should be apparent that Rule 44 does not address all the conflict situations that can arise in a criminal case. Rule 44 addresses only questions of multiple representation in the same criminal proceeding. So, for example, the Rule does not apply if defense counsel has previously represented a person who is now a government witness in the case against the defendant. It does not apply if the lawyer has a personal conflict. It does not apply if the lawyer is representing two related defendants in *separate* proceedings.

But these less obvious conflicts are in fact reviewed by the court at a hearing if they are raised with the court. Usually it is the government that raises such conflicts for the court to consider since the government does not want a potential ineffectiveness claim to linger in a case.

2. Active Conflict Impairing the Representation

A Different Kind of Prejudice Test: Cuyler v. Sullivan

In Cuyler v. Sullivan, 446 U.S. 335 (1980), the Court considered the propriety of relief where defense counsel operated under a conflict of interest that was not brought to the attention of the trial judge. Justice Powell's opinion for the Court rejected the petitioner's claim that *Holloway* requires a trial judge to inquire in every case into the propriety of joint representation, even in the absence of the defense's timely motion. He reasoned as follows:

> Defense counsel have an ethical obligation to avoid conflicting representations and to advise the court promptly when a conflict of interest arises during the course of a trial. Absent special circumstances, therefore, trial courts may assume that multiple

representation entails no conflict or that the lawyer and his clients knowingly accept such risk of conflict as may exist.

The Court recognized that multiple representation does give rise to a possibility of an improper conflict of interest and Justice Powell stated that a defendant "must have the opportunity to show that potential conflicts impermissibly imperil his right to a fair trial." But, "a defendant who raised no objection at trial must demonstrate that an actual conflict of interest adversely affected his lawyer's performance." Thus, the Court created a limited presumption of prejudice in cases where a defendant fails to make a timely objection to conflicted simultaneous representation: prejudice is presumed, but only if the defendant demonstrates that counsel "actively represented conflicting interests" and that "an actual conflict of interest adversely affected his lawyer's performance."[32]

The *Cuyler* prejudice standard applies when a defendant fails to bring a potential conflict to the trial court's attention. But it also applies when the defendant notifies the trial court of a potential conflict and the trial court, after a full hearing, finds that there is no actual or potential conflict and orders the multiple representation to continue. See Freund v. Butterworth, 165 F.3d 839 (11th Cir.1999) (en banc). *Holloway's* rule of per se reversal applies only when the court *refuses to hold a hearing* after the defense counsel brings a potential conflict to its attention.

Application of the Cuyler Standard: Burger v. Kemp

The Supreme Court found no ineffective assistance of counsel under the *Cuyler* standards in Burger v. Kemp, 483 U.S. 776 (1987), a capital case in which Burger and a codefendant were represented by law partners. The defendants were soldiers charged with the murder of a fellow soldier who worked part-time driving a taxi. Each defendant confessed, and Burger took military police to the place where the victim had been drowned. Leaphart, an experienced lawyer, was appointed to represent Burger, and he insisted that his law partner represent the codefendant. The two defendants were tried separately, and at their trials each defendant sought to avoid the death penalty by emphasizing the other's culpability. Burger was sentenced to death, and attacked his representation in a habeas corpus proceeding on the ground that Leaphart's partnership relationship created a conflict of interest for him.

Justice Stevens wrote for the Court and found that Burger was not entitled to relief. He conceded that "[t]here is certainly much substance to petitioner's argument that the appointment of two partners to represent

[32] When the Supreme Court remanded *Cuyler*, the court of appeals found that there was an actual conflict of interest that required reversal of Sullivan's conviction. Sullivan v. Cuyler, 723 F.2d 1077 (3d Cir.1983). Counsel, representing both a prospective witness and Sullivan, admitted at an evidentiary hearing that he did not call the witness on Sullivan's behalf because he had to take the witness's interests into account as well as those of Sullivan.

coindictees in their respective trials creates a possible conflict of interest that could prejudice either or both clients," and that "the risk of prejudice is increased when the two lawyers cooperate with one another in planning and conduct of trial strategy." He observed, however, that the Court's decisions do not presume prejudice in all cases, and he concluded that "the overlap of counsel, if any, did not so infect Leaphart's representation as to constitute an active representation of competing interests." Justice Stevens added that "[p]articularly in smaller communities where the supply of qualified lawyers willing to accept the demanding and unrewarding work of representing capital prisoners is extremely limited, the two defendants may actually benefit from the joint efforts of two partners who supplement one another in their preparation." Justice Stevens also emphasized that each defendant was tried separately, and that separate trials significantly reduce the risk of a conflict of interest. The Court declined to disturb the lower courts' findings that there was no actual conflict of interest.

Justice Stevens added that, even if an actual conflict had been established, counsel's advocacy was unaffected by it. He concluded that there was no evidence that the prosecutor would have been receptive to a plea bargain and no doubt that Leaphart sought to negotiate for a life sentence; there was no reason to believe that Leaphart attempted to protect the other defendant who was not on trial with Burger; and the decision not to offer mitigating evidence and open the door to cross-examination about Burger's background was not unreasonable even if it was erroneous.[33]

Relationship Between the Holloway Automatic Reversal Rule and the Cuyler Rule Regulating Active Representation of Conflicting Interests: Mickens v. Taylor

In Mickens v. Taylor, 535 U.S. 162 (2002), Justice Scalia wrote for the Court as it held that the *Holloway* rule—requiring automatic reversal when the trial court fails to inquire into a multiple representation conflict raised by defense counsel—does not apply when "the trial court fails to inquire into a potential conflict of interest about which it knew or reasonably should have known" but is not raised by defense counsel. The trial judge appointed Bryan Saunders counsel for a juvenile on assault and concealed weapons charges. Saunders met with the juvenile just once after being appointed and within days of that meeting, the juvenile was killed and Mickens was charged. The same judge appointed Saunders to represent Mickens approximately two weeks after appointing Saunders to represent the juvenile.

---

[33] Justice Blackmun filed a dissenting opinion, in which Justices Brennan and Marshall joined, and in which Justice Powell joined in part. Justice Powell filed a separate dissenting opinion, in which Justice Brennan joined.

Justice Scalia discussed *Cronic, Holloway,* and *Sullivan,* reminded that "*Holloway* * * * creates an automatic reversal rule only where defense counsel is forced to represent codefendants over his timely objection, unless the trial court has determined that there is no conflict," and contrasted the latter two cases: "* * * *Sullivan* addressed separately a trial court's duty to inquire into the propriety of a multiple representation, construing *Holloway* to require inquiry only when 'the trial court knows or reasonably should know that a particular conflict exists'—which is not to be confused with when the trial court is aware of a vague, unspecified possibility of conflict, such as that which 'inheres in almost every instance of multiple representation.' "

Justice Scalia rejected Mickens' argument for automatic reversal in a case in which a conflict existed but did not affect counsel's performance:

> Petitioner's proposed rule of automatic reversal when there existed a conflict that did not affect counsel's performance, but the trial judge failed to make the *Sullivan*-mandated inquiry, makes little policy sense. * * * The trial court's awareness of a potential conflict neither renders it more likely that counsel's performance was significantly affected nor in any other way renders the verdict unreliable. Nor does the trial judge's failure to make the *Sullivan*-mandated inquiry often make it harder for reviewing courts to determine conflict and effect, particularly since those courts may rely on evidence and testimony whose importance only becomes established at the trial.

Justice Scalia also rejected the argument that automatic reversal is an appropriate means of enforcing *Sullivan's* mandate of inquiry and suggested that "the *Sullivan* standard, which requires proof of effect upon representation but (once such effect is shown) presumes prejudice, already creates an 'incentive' to inquire into a potential conflict.

The Court affirmed the court of appeals' decision denying habeas corpus relief on the ground that Mickens was required and failed to establish that the conflict of interest adversely affected his counsel's performance.

Justice Kennedy, joined by Justice O'Connor wrote a concurring opinion in which he observed that

> the District Court conducted an evidentiary hearing on the conflict claim and issued a thorough opinion, which found that counsel's brief representation of the victim had no effect whatsoever on the course of petitioner's trial. * * * This conclusion is a good example of why a case-by-case inquiry is required, rather than simply adopting an automatic rule of reversal.

Justice Stevens dissented, arguing that Saunders had a duty to disclose to both Mickens and the trial court his prior representation of the juvenile, and that, having failed to do so, "[s]etting aside Mickens' conviction is the only remedy that can maintain public confidence in the fairness of the procedures employed in capital cases." Justice Breyer's dissent, joined by Justice Ginsburg, argued similarly that "the Commonwealth seeks to execute a defendant, having provided that defendant with a lawyer who, only yesterday, represented the victim," and "to carry out a death sentence so obtained would invariably diminish faith in the fairness and integrity of our criminal justice system."

Justice Souter also dissented and argued that "[s]ince the District Court in this case found that the state judge was on notice of a prospective potential conflict, this case calls for nothing more than the application of the prospective notice rule announced and exemplified by *Holloway* * * *."

COMMENT ON MICKENS

The Cuyler v. Sullivan standard requires the defendant to show that counsel made one decision that was due to a conflict of interest, i.e., one decision that was made because counsel was furthering another interest at the expense of the defendant. At that point, prejudice is presumed. It is a standard that is easier for defendant to meet than that employed in *Strickland*, which requires the court to look at the entire record to determine whether there is a reasonable probability that, if not for counsel's ineffectiveness, the outcome of the proceeding would have been different.

In *Mickens*, Justice Scalia avoids deciding whether the *Strickland* standard of prejudice governs conflict of interest challenges arising from some conflict other than multiple simultaneous representation. Other conflicts could include conflicts between the defendant's interests and the lawyer's personal interests, and conflicts arising from successive, rather than concurrent, representations (although the opinion explicitly takes no position on successive representations).

After *Mickens*, lower courts appear to be taking Justice Scalia's opinion as an indication that *Strickland,* and not *Cuyler*, governs conflict claims arising out of something other than multiple concurrent representation. For example, in Whiting v. Burt, 395 F.3d 602 (6th Cir. 2005), the defendant argued ineffective assistance of counsel on appeal, because his appellate counsel was also his trial counsel, and so could not be expected to raise any claims on appeal about his own ineffectiveness at trial. This conflict was not based on multiple representation, but rather on the lawyer's personal interest in not subjecting his own trial performance to a public self-critique. The court held that, after *Mickens*, every lower court has refused to apply the *Cuyler* standard outside the "concurrent joint representation context." The court reviewed for prejudice under *Strickland* and found none under the circumstances.

Conflict with the Attorney's Personal Interests

As noted above, in some cases counsel's personal interests may be in conflict with the duty of loyalty owed the client. United States v. Cancilla, 725 F.2d 867 (2d Cir.1984), is an example. Cancilla's counsel, while defending him, was engaged in criminal conduct with the defendant's coconspirators. The court reasoned that "with the similarity of counsel's criminal activities to Cancilla's schemes and the link between them, it must have occurred to counsel that a vigorous defense might uncover evidence or prompt testimony revealing his own crimes." See also United States ex rel. Duncan v. O'Leary, 806 F.2d 1307 (7th Cir.1986) (reversal where defense counsel is the prosecutor's campaign manager and the prosecutor is running on a "law and order" ticket).

In Winkler v. Keane, 7 F.3d 304 (2d Cir.1993), the court found an actual conflict of interest where counsel represented a criminal defendant on a contingent fee basis; under the agreement, defense counsel would receive a fee of $25,000, but only if the defendant was found not guilty. The court reasoned that counsel had "a disincentive to seek a plea agreement, or to put forth mitigating defenses that would result in conviction of a lesser included offense." But the court held that the conflict of interest did not adversely affect the defense, because the defendant steadfastly maintained his innocence throughout, rejected all attempts to plea bargain, and vetoed any attempt of defense counsel to argue the partial defense of intoxication. Thus, there was no reason to believe that defense counsel's representation would have been any different "if a proper fee arrangement had been utilized."

These cases strongly suggest that while operating under a conflict with personal interests is an act of ineffectiveness, the defendant must establish prejudice under *Strickland*. The more generous Cuyler v. Sullivan standard appears applicable, after *Mickens*, only to cases of multiple concurrent representation.

3. Waiver of the Right to Conflict-Free Counsel

The premise of Federal Rule 44 is that if the defendant is properly warned of the possible conflicts that could arise, then he can knowingly and voluntarily waive the right to conflict-free representation. Generally speaking, a knowing and voluntary waiver of conflict-free representation can be found if the trial court informs the defendant about the ways in which conflicted counsel can impair the representation—for example, that one client could shift blame to another, or testify against another, and defense counsel would be impaired in representing the multiple interests.

The trial court must assure itself that the defendant understands the consequences, and has made a rational decision to proceed with counsel despite the conflict. An example of a typical colloquy is found in United

States v. Flores, 5 F.3d 1070 (7th Cir.1993). In *Flores*, three defendants charged with major narcotics transactions had used a group of lawyers in previous brushes with the law. According to the court,

> like sick patients who call up longtime family doctors, they contacted attorneys who represented them before. Potential conflicts of interest arose, however, as the three defendants and their attorneys played a virtual musical chairs game of attorney-client relationships. The lawyers chosen to represent Flores and Fontanez, respectively Michael Green and Roberta Samotny, represented Rodriguez in prior, unrelated criminal proceedings. Further, Rodriguez's counsel, Glenn Seiden, initially represented Fontanez in the current case then switched to Rodriguez.

The government in *Flores* moved to disqualify all counsel, and the trial court held a Rule 44 hearing, at which the court asked the defendants and their respective attorneys about the alleged conflicts. The court questioned each attorney to make sure he or she had explained the problem to their respective clients. The court then asked each defendant if he wanted to continue with his current counsel and explained the possible conflicts. All three defendants on the record said they wanted to continue to retain their attorneys.

The trial court in *Flores* respected the expressed preferences of each defendant and declined the government's invitation to intrude into the defendants' counsel of choice. Each defendant subsequently appealed on the ground that they had not *knowingly* waived their right to conflict-free counsel. They argued that the district court failed to make a detailed inquiry into how the conflict of interest might relate to the individual defendants and noted that the defendants' answers were usually only one or two words. The court of appeals rejected these arguments and found that the colloquies were sufficient to establish a knowing waiver of conflict-free counsel.

It should be noted as a matter of practice that some judges require the defendant to articulate, in his own words, what counsel's conflict is, and how it could impair his representation. While the court in *Flores* found that this is not required, such a practice does help to assure that the defendant is making a knowing and intelligent waiver, or, to the contrary, could indicate that the defendant doesn't really know what he is giving up.

C. INEFFECTIVE ASSISTANCE WITHOUT FAULT ON THE PART OF DEFENSE COUNSEL

Impairing Defense Strategy

Governmental or prosecutorial action can deprive a defendant of effective assistance of counsel, by impairing the performance of even the best counsel. For example in Brooks v. Tennessee, 406 U.S. 605 (1972), a Tennessee rule required the defendant to testify as the first witness in the case or not at all. (This was an attempt to prevent the defendant from altering his testimony in the light of testimony provided by prosecution witnesses). The Court held that the rule violated the defendant's right to remain silent, and also deprived him of the aid of counsel in planning his defense, particularly in the decision to testify or remain silent.

> By requiring the accused and his lawyer to make that choice without an opportunity to evaluate the actual worth of their evidence, the state restricts the defense—particularly counsel—in the planning of its case. Furthermore, the penalty for not testifying first is to keep the defendant off the stand entirely, even though as a matter of professional judgment his lawyer might want to call him later in the trial. The accused is thereby deprived of the "guiding hand of counsel" in the timing of this critical element of his defense.

Similarly, in Herring v. New York, 422 U.S. 853 (1975), a New York statute giving a judge in a nonjury criminal trial the power to deny absolutely the opportunity for defense counsel to make a closing argument was held to be unconstitutional. New York denied Herring the effective assistance of counsel by permitting the judge to dispense with his counsel's summation.

Limiting Consultation Between Defendant and Counsel

In Geders v. United States, 425 U.S. 80 (1976), the defendant was prohibited from consulting with counsel during a 17-hour overnight recess between the direct and cross-examination of the defendant. Although recognizing the problem of "coached" witnesses, the Court decided that this method of preventing coaching violated the defendant's right to the effective assistance of counsel.

Justice Stevens wrote for a majority in Perry v. Leeke, 488 U.S. 272 (1989), as it distinguished *Geders* and held that a state trial judge did not commit constitutional error in declaring a 15 minute recess after the defendant's direct testimony in his murder trial and in ordering that the defendant talk to no one, including his lawyer, during the recess. Although Justice Stevens recognized that "[t]here is merit in petitioner's argument that a showing of prejudice is not an essential component of a violation of the rule announced in *Geders,*" he reasoned that "when a defendant becomes a witness, he has no constitutional right to consult with his lawyer while he is testifying." Justice Stevens recognized that nondiscussion orders can prevent coaching of witnesses that might interfere with the search for truth. He described *Geders* as a case involving an overnight recess in which matters that go beyond a defendant's own testimony would be discussed with counsel and stated that "in a short recess in which it is appropriate to presume that nothing but the testimony will be discussed, the testifying defendant does not have a constitutional right to advice."

Justice Marshall, joined by Justices Brennan and Blackmun, dissented. He argued that a defendant cannot be prevented from consulting with counsel during a recess and that the defendant was not arguing for a right to interrupt cross-examination in order to consult with his lawyer.

Interference with the Attorney-Client Relationship

State intrusion into attorney-client consultations can be a problem outside the trial context as well. The Supreme Court addressed one such problem in Weatherford v. Bursey, 429 U.S. 545 (1977). The defendant claimed a Sixth Amendment violation when an undercover agent and informant attended two meetings between the defendant and counsel; the undercover informant was ostensibly a codefendant. The Court concluded that despite this intrusion, the defendant received effective assistance of counsel. Those meetings resulted in no tainted evidence, and no communication of defense strategy to the government. Thus, there was no indication of prejudice that would require reversal. Justices Marshall and Brennan dissented, because they believed that when the prosecution acquires information about the defense, the fairness and integrity of the adversary system are impaired, so the intrusion cannot be harmless.

In United States v. Morrison, 449 U.S. 361 (1981), the Supreme Court unanimously concluded that "absent demonstrable prejudice, or substantial threat thereof, dismissal of the indictment is plainly inappropriate, even though the [Sixth Amendment] violation may have been deliberate." See also United States v. Noriega, 752 F.Supp. 1045 (S.D.Fla.1990), which held that despite outrageous, unconscionable conduct of law enforcement officers in eavesdropping on two conversations between the defendant and his counsel, dismissal of the prosecution was not warranted where there was no showing that trial strategy was revealed or that the defendant's ability to work in confidence with his attorney was impaired.

In Glebe v. Frost, 574 U.S. 21 (2014) (per curiam), a habeas petitioner relied on *Herring* to argue that per se reversible error occurred when the state trial court restricted defense counsel from making a particular argument in closing. Trial counsel wanted to argue to the jury in the alternative: 1) that the prosecution failed to prove that the defendant was an accomplice to robberies; and 2) that in committing the crime, the defendant was acting under duress. The trial judge insisted that defense counsel choose one argument or the other for closing, as the arguments were inconsistent. Defense counsel limited his closing argument to duress, and the defendant was convicted. On habeas review, Frost argued that the trial judge's restriction violated his right to effective counsel and that this violation was a "structural" error that could not be assessed for harmlessness. (See Chapter 13 for a discussion of structural errors).

Because the case was on habeas review, Frost was required to show not just that an error occurred but that the state court violated clearly established law as determined by the Supreme Court. 22 U.S.C. § 2254(d). The Court found that *Herring* did *not* clearly establish that a trial court was prohibited from requiring defense counsel to choose between inconsistent arguments.

D. THE PERJURY PROBLEM

When a defense attorney believes that her client is about to commit perjury, she faces a particularly difficult dilemma that bears on the right to effective assistance of counsel.

Applying Strickland to Client Perjury: Nix v. Whiteside

In Nix v. Whiteside, 475 U.S. 157 (1986), the defendant pleaded self-defense, but in his initial statement to defense counsel, he did not mention that the victim had a gun. In a later interview, the defendant stated that he now remembered that he saw the victim with "something metallic" in his hand. When challenged about the discrepancy by defense counsel, the defendant referred to a case in which an acquaintance was acquitted after testifying that his victim wielded a gun. In apparent comparison with that case, the defendant concluded: "If I don't say I saw a gun, I'm dead." The defense counsel told the client that any statement about a gun would be perjury; that if the defendant testified about a gun at trial, the lawyer would advise the court of the perjury, would probably be permitted to impeach the testimony, and would seek to withdraw. The client succumbed to the threats. He testified at trial that he believed the victim was reaching for a gun, but he had not seen one. The client challenged his second degree murder conviction on an ineffective assistance of counsel ground. Although the state courts commended the lawyer's integrity, a federal court of appeals granted habeas corpus relief.

The Supreme Court unanimously reversed in an opinion by Chief Justice Burger. He reasoned that no defendant has a right to commit perjury, therefore no defendant has a right to rely upon counsel to assist in the development of false testimony. The Court noted that under *Strickland,* the defendant must prove prejudice, and Whiteside "has no valid claim that confidence in the result of his trial has been diminished by his desisting from the contemplated perjury." Even if the jury would have been persuaded by the perjury, the Court concluded that under *Strickland,* "a defendant has no entitlement to the luck of a lawless decisionmaker."

Although lack of cognizable prejudice was enough to decide the case, the Chief Justice went further and held that Whiteside's counsel had not been ineffective in discouraging his client from committing perjury. He concluded that for the purposes of this case, effectiveness could be determined by reference to the prevailing rules of professional responsibility governing the conduct of lawyers. He noted that Disciplinary Rule 7–102(A)(4) of the ABA Code of Professional Responsibility (in effect in Iowa at that time) provided that a lawyer shall not "knowingly use perjured testimony or false evidence;" and that Rule 3.3 of the more recent Model Rules of Professional Conduct (in effect in almost all of the states, with some state-to-state variations) requires disclosure of client perjury to the tribunal as a last resort. The Chief Justice found that the prevailing ethical standards "confirm that the legal profession has accepted that an attorney's ethical duty to advance the interests of his client is limited by an equally solemn duty to comply with the law and standards of professional conduct.

Justice Brennan wrote an opinion concurring in the judgment. He agreed with the majority's analysis on the prejudice prong of *Strickland.* As to the performance prong, however, he argued that the Court "has no constitutional authority to establish rules of ethical conduct for lawyers practicing in the state courts," and that "the Court's essay regarding what constitutes the correct response to a criminal client's suggestion that he will perjure himself is pure discourse without force of law." Justice Blackmun wrote an opinion concurring in the judgment, joined by Justices Brennan, Marshall, and Stevens. He agreed that Whiteside had not shown prejudice from his lawyer's conduct, and saw no need to "grade counsel's performance." He argued, however, that the client perjury problem could not be solved by a simple reference to lawyers' ethics codes:

> Whether an attorney's response to what he sees as a client's command to commit perjury violates a defendant's Sixth Amendment rights may depend on many factors: how certain the attorney is that the proposed testimony is false, the stage of the proceedings at which the attorney discovers the plan, or the ways in which the attorney may be able to dissuade his client, to name just three. The complex interaction of factors, which is likely to vary from case to case, makes inappropriate a blanket rule that defense attorneys must reveal, or threaten to reveal, a client's anticipated perjury to the court. Except in the rarest of cases, attorneys who adopt the role of the judge or jury to determine the facts, pose a danger of depriving their clients of the zealous and loyal advocacy required by the Sixth Amendment.

Justice Stevens also wrote an opinion concurring in the judgment, emphasizing that it is often difficult to determine whether the client's proposed testimony is perjurious.

> A lawyer's certainty that a change in his client's recollection is a harbinger of intended perjury—as well as judicial review of such

apparent certainty—should be tempered by the realization that, after reflection, the most honest witness may recall (or sincerely believe he recalls) details that he previously overlooked.

Whiteside Was Too Easy

Assuming there was a real risk of perjury, *Whiteside* is an easy case. Most lawyers would think it entirely appropriate to try to discourage the client from a planned course of perjury. Indeed, discouragement of perjury is effective advocacy, because the jury may disbelieve the lie, the prosecutor may easily tear it apart on cross-examination, and the client may subject himself to a perjury charge. Moreover, if the trial judge believes that a defendant lied on the stand, this will be taken into account at sentencing. See United States v. Dunnigan, 507 U.S. 87 (1993) (discussing enhancement of sentences under the Federal Sentencing Guidelines if the court finds that the defendant lied while testifying). So it certainly makes sense to do everything reasonable to discourage a client from committing perjury on the witness stand.

HARDER QUESTIONS

The difficult questions, not presented by *Whiteside,* are three. First, what if the client refuses to be dissuaded from a course of perjury and demands to testify? Second, what if the client appears to have been dissuaded from testifying falsely, but then commits perjury after taking the stand? Third, what if the lawyer discovers *after* the testimony that the client has perjured himself? See Freedman, Client Confidences and Client Perjury: Some Unanswered Questions, 136 U.Pa.L.Rev. 1939 (1988) (arguing that all of these problems should be left to the adversary system and to cross-examination by the prosecutor). After *Whiteside,* the A.B.A. Standing Committee on Ethics issued Formal Opinion 87–353 (1987). That opinion provides that if the lawyer is convinced that a witness is going to commit perjury, and all discussions with the client fail, *then the lawyer must inform the court.* And if the lawyer discovers perjury after the fact but before the proceedings are terminated, the lawyer must inform the court as well. The opinion justifies this result as follows:

> [The] ethical rules clearly recognize that a lawyer representing a client who admits guilt in fact, but wants to plead not guilty and put the state to its proof, may assist the client in entering such a plea and vigorously challenge the state's case at trial through cross-examination, legal motions and argument to the jury. However, neither the adversary system nor the ethical rules permit the lawyer to participate in the corruption of the judicial process by assisting the client in the introduction of evidence the lawyer knows is false. * * *
>
> On the contrary, the lawyer, as an officer of the court, has a duty to prevent the perjury, and if the perjury has already been committed, to

> prevent its playing any part in the judgment of the court. This duty the lawyer owes the court is not inconsistent with any duty owed to the client. More particularly, it is not inconsistent with the lawyer's duty to preserve the client's confidences. For that duty is based on the lawyer's need for information from the client to obtain for the client all that the law and lawful process provide. Implicit in the promise of confidentiality is its nonapplicability where the client seeks the unlawful end of corrupting the judicial process by false evidence.

The ABA opinion emphasizes, however (as did the concurring opinions in *Whiteside*), that it is not for defense counsel to judge the client, and that the lawyer should not presume that the client is going to present perjured testimony simply because it is inconsistent with a previous statement.

> It must be emphasized that this opinion does not change the professional relationship the lawyer has with the client and require the lawyer now to judge, rather than represent, the client. The lawyer's obligation to disclose client perjury to the tribunal * * * is strictly limited by [Model] Rule 3.3 to the situation where the lawyer *knows* that the client has committed perjury, ordinarily based on admissions the client has made to the lawyer. (The Committee notes that some trial lawyers report that they have avoided the ethical dilemma posed by Rule 3.3 because they follow a practice of not questioning the client about the facts in the case and, therefore, never "know" that a client has given false testimony. Lawyers who engage in such practice may be violating their duties under Rule 3.3 and their obligation to provide competent representation under Rule 1.1.) * * *.

Can you think of anything more destructive to the attorney-client relationship than the lawyer ratting out her client? Why can't the perjury problem instead be handled through cross-examination by the prosecutor? When a District Attorney was asked what the defense lawyer should do when a client intends to commit perjury, he responded "Do me a favor. Let him try it." (Quoted in Freedman, Client Confidences and Client Perjury: Some Unanswered Questions, 136 U.Pa.L.Rev.1939 (1988)). Would most prosecutors respond the same way? See Saltzburg, Lawyers, Clients, and the Adversary System, 37 Mercer L.Rev. 674 (1986).

One problem with the ABA solution is that criminal defendants have a constitutional right to testify. They don't of course have a constitutional right to commit perjury; but perjury occurs only when the defendant actually testifies. What happens when defense counsel believes that the client is adamant about committing perjury, even after counsel gives the defendant *Whiteside* warnings. According to the ABA, counsel must now inform the trial judge that her client intends to commit perjury. But the trial judge cannot at this point, on defense counsel's word alone, prevent the defendant from testifying. To do so would risk almost certain reversal for violating the defendant's constitutional right to testify (because perjury has not been shown to a reviewing court's satisfaction). So the trial judge would have to hold some kind of hearing. At that hearing, the defendant will not admit that he is going to commit perjury if he is permitted to testify. The trial judge will be most reluctant to get into a quagmire of confidential communications between client and counsel in determining who is right about whether perjury is planned. It is very likely in most cases that a trial judge will be uncertain as to whether the defendant is going to commit perjury. The judge will not in these circumstances risk violating the constitutional right to testify by keeping the defendant off the stand. So in the vast majority of cases, defense counsel will have accomplished nothing by informing the tribunal of the client's planned perjury—the defendant will be permitted to testify anyway. The only thing accomplished is the destruction of the attorney-client relationship.

Compare the solution proposed by the A.B.A. Ethics Committee with that proposed by Professor Monroe Freedman, who addressed the perjury problem in Lawyer's Ethics in an Adversary System 31–37 (1985).

> In my opinion, the attorney's obligation in such a situation would be to advise the client that the proposed testimony is unlawful, but to proceed in the normal fashion in presenting the testimony and arguing the case to the jury if the client makes the decision to go forward. Any other course would be a betrayal of the assurances of confidentiality given by the attorney in order to induce the client to reveal everything, however damaging it might appear.

Professor Friedman argues that none of the other alternatives are workable. For example, the lawyer cannot effectively withdraw from the representation because

> [t]he client will then go to the nearest law office, realizing that the obligation of confidentiality is not what it has been represented to be, and withhold incriminating information or the fact of guilt from the new attorney. In terms of professional ethics, the practice of withdrawing from a case under such circumstances is difficult to defend, since the identical perjured testimony will ultimately be presented. Moreover, the new attorney will be ignorant of the perjury and therefore will be in no position to attempt to discourage the client from presenting it. Only the original attorney, who knows the truth, has that opportunity, but loses it in the very act of evading the ethical problem.

Professor Freedman describes the "Free Narrative" alternative, in which defense counsel lets the defendant tell his story on the stand, without asking questions and without referring to the statement in closing argument. He finds the free narrative solution unworkable:

> [E]xperienced trial attorneys have often noted that jurors assume that the defendant's lawyer knows the truth about the case, and that the jury will frequently judge the defendant by drawing inferences from the attorney's conduct in the case. There is, of course, only one inference that can be drawn if the defendant's own attorney turns his or her back on the defendant at the most critical point in the trial, and then, in closing

argument, sums up the case with no reference to the fact that the defendant has given exculpatory testimony.

Despite the rejection of the "free narrative" solution by the A.B.A., the Court in *Whiteside*, and Professor Freedman, the narrative "continues to be a commonly accepted method of dealing with client perjury." Shockley v. State, 565 A.2d 1373 (Del.1989) (holding that use of free narrative was ethically permissible and did not constitute ineffective assistance of counsel). See also Florida Bar v. Rubin, 549 So.2d 1000 (Fla.1989) (lawyer jailed for thirty days for refusing to defend client who intended to commit perjury; proper solution would have been to use a free narrative).

E. INEFFECTIVENESS AND SYSTEMS OF APPOINTED COUNSEL

Inadequate Funding

The overall quality and effectiveness of court-appointed attorneys may be limited by low compensation for services. For example, in South Carolina, a statute provided the following payment for appointed counsel in capital cases: $15/hour for in-court work, $10 for out-of-court time, with a $5,000 cap for trial work and a $2,500 cap for investigative and expert services. The South Carolina Supreme Court, in Bailey v. State, 309 S.C. 455, 424 S.E.2d 503 (1992), found that these statutory limits imposed a "gross and fundamental unfairness" on defense attorneys, and "do not provide compensation adequate to ensure effective assistance of counsel." The court remanded to determine what compensation would be reasonable. See also Smith v. New Hampshire, 118 N.H. 764, 394 A.2d 834 (1978) (invalidating similar statutory limits).

Cases like *Bailey* raise the question whether there are systemic flaws in the process of appointing counsel for indigents. Public defenders often have enormous caseloads and limited resources and might feel no choice but to choose to dispose of cases in ways that maximize the overall output of the agency rather than the welfare of any one client. See Miranda v. Clark County, Nevada, 319 F.3d 465 (9th Cir. 2003) (invalidating a rule adopted by the public defender that sharply curtailed the quality of appointed counsel if the defendant fails a polygraph examination—the policy was designed to give priority in allocation of scarce resources to innocent defendants, but this would violate the right to effective assistance of counsel for other defendants). Private appointed attorneys are often so poorly compensated that talented counsel are discouraged from taking on a representation; and even the best counsel might become so financially strapped to make it impractical, if not impossible, to put on an adequate defense.

Systematic Inadequacy in Capital Cases

Justice Blackmun, in his last term on the Court, took the occasion of the Court's denial of certiorari in a death penalty case to express concern about the system of appointed counsel in capital cases. Dissenting from denial of certiorari in McFarland v. Scott, 512 U.S. 1256 (1994), Justice Blackmun declared as follows:

> Without question, the principal failings of the capital punishment review process today are the inadequacy and inadequate compensation of counsel at trial and the unavailability of counsel in state post-conviction proceedings. The unique, bifurcated nature of capital trials and the special investigation into a defendant's personal history and background that may be required, the complexity and fluidity of the law, and the high, emotional stakes involved all make capital cases more costly and difficult to litigate than ordinary criminal trials. Yet, the attorneys assigned to represent indigent capital defendants at times are less qualified than those appointed in ordinary criminal cases. See Green, Lethal Fiction: The Meaning of "Counsel" in the Sixth Amendment, 78 Iowa L.Rev. 433, 434 (1993); Coyle et al., Fatal Defense, 12 Nat'l L.J. 30, 44 (June 11, 1990) (Capital-defense attorneys in eight States were disbarred, suspended, or disciplined at rates 3 to 46 times higher than the general attorney-discipline rates).
>
> * * * [C]ompensation for attorneys representing indigent capital defendants often is perversely low. Although a properly conducted capital trial can involve hundreds of hours of investigation, preparation, and lengthy trial proceedings, many States severely limit the compensation paid for capital defense. * * * See generally Klein, The Eleventh Commandment: Thou Shalt Not be Compelled to Render the Ineffective Assistance of Counsel, 68 Ind.L.J. 363, 364–375 (1993).
>
> Court-awarded funds for the appointment of investigators and experts often are either unavailable, severely limited, or not provided by state courts. As a result, attorneys appointed to represent capital defendants at the trial level frequently are unable to recoup even their overhead costs and out-of-pocket expenses, and effectively may be required to work at minimum wage or below while funding from their own pockets their client's defense. * * * The prospect that hours spent in trial preparation or funds expended hiring psychiatrists or ballistics experts will be uncompensated unquestionably chills even a qualified attorney's zealous representation of his client.
>
> The practical costs of such ad hoc systems of attorney selection and compensation are well documented. Capital defendants have been sentenced to death when represented by counsel who never bothered to read the state death penalty statute, e.g., Smith v. State, 581 So.2d 497 (Ala.Crim.App.1990), slept through or otherwise were not present

during trial, or failed to investigate or present any mitigating evidence at the penalty phase, Mitchell v. Kemp, 483 U.S. 1026 (1987) (Marshall, J., dissenting from denial of certiorari). * * * One Louisiana defendant was convicted of capital murder following a one-day trial and 20-minute penalty phase proceeding, in which his counsel stipulated to the defendant's age at the time of the crime and rested. State v. Messiah, 538 So.2d 175, 187 (La.1988). When asked to cite the criminal cases he knew, one defense attorney who failed to challenge his client's racially unrepresentative jury pool, could name only two cases: *Miranda* and *Dred Scott.* See Bright, Counsel for the Poor: The Death Sentence Not for the Worst Crime but for the Worst Lawyer, 103 Yale L.J. 1835, 1839.

Justice Blackmun contended that the *Strickland* test for reviewing the effectiveness of counsel provides insufficient protection for capital defendants, in light of the systemic underfunding and underregulation of appointed counsel in capital cases. He elaborated as follows:

> The impotence of the *Strickland* standard is perhaps best evidenced in the cases in which ineffective assistance claims have been denied. John Young, for example, was represented in his capital trial by an attorney who was addicted to drugs and who a few weeks later was incarcerated on federal drug charges. The Court of Appeals for the Eleventh Circuit rejected Young's ineffective assistance of counsel claim on federal habeas, Young v. Zant, 727 F.2d 1489 (11th Cir.1984), and this Court denied review. * * *
>
> Jesus Romero's attorney failed to present any evidence at the penalty phase and delivered a closing argument totaling 29 words. Although the attorney later was suspended on unrelated grounds, Romero's ineffective assistance claim was rejected by the Court of Appeals for the Fifth Circuit, Romero v. Lynaugh, 884 F.2d 871, 875 (1989), and this Court denied certiorari. Romero was executed in 1992. Larry Heath was represented on direct appeal by counsel who filed a 6-page brief before the Alabama Court of Criminal Appeals. The attorney failed to appear for oral argument before the Alabama Supreme Court and filed a brief in that court containing a 1-page argument and citing a single case. The Eleventh Circuit found no prejudice, Heath v. Jones, 941 F.2d 1126, 1131 (11th Cir.1991), and this Court denied review. Heath was executed in Alabama in 1992.
>
> James Messer, a mentally impaired capital defendant, was represented by an attorney who at the trial's guilt phase presented no defense, made no objections, and emphasized the horror of the capital crime in his closing statement. At the penalty phase, the attorney presented no evidence of mental impairment, failed to introduce other substantial mitigating evidence, and again repeatedly suggested in

closing that death was the appropriate punishment. The Eleventh Circuit refused to grant relief, Messer v. Kemp, 760 F.2d 1080 (11th Cir.1985), and this Court denied certiorari. Messer was executed in 1988. * * *

Justice Blackmun concluded with the hope that the system of appointed counsel in capital cases would be improved:

> Our system of justice is adversarial and depends for its legitimacy on the fair and adequate representation of all parties at all levels of the judicial process. * * * My 24 years of overseeing the imposition of the death penalty from this Court have left me in grave doubt whether this reliance is justified and whether the constitutional requirement of competent legal counsel for capital defendants is being fulfilled. * * * [W]e must have the courage to recognize the failings of our present system of capital representation and the conviction to do what is necessary to improve it.

Justice Blackmun's opinion was written before the Court's decisions in Wiggins v. Smith and Rompilla v. Beard, supra; in each of those cases, the Court vacated the death penalty because counsel had not been effective in the penalty phase. Does this mean that Justice Blackmun's concerns are now beginning to be addressed?

F. THE RIGHT TO COUNSEL OF CHOICE

Gideon guarantees an absolute right to counsel for all serious crimes. The Sixth Amendment also provides a right to counsel of one's own choosing. But that right is not absolute. Its most important limitation is that it is dependent on the ability to pay chosen counsel. The Supreme Court has held that so long as an indigent receives effective representation, he has no right to choose a particular counsel. In Morris v. Slappy, 461 U.S. 1 (1983), Slappy was appointed counsel whom he trusted, but that counsel became ill before trial, and another was substituted. Slappy argued that a continuance should have been granted until trusted counsel could return. He did not contend that substitute counsel was ineffective. Chief Justice Burger, writing for the Court, interpreted Slappy's request, and the lower court's holding, as assuming that the indigent had the right to a "meaningful attorney-client relationship." He rejected this argument in no uncertain terms.

> No authority was cited for this novel ingredient of the Sixth Amendment guarantee, and of course none could be. No court could possibly guarantee that a defendant will develop the kind of rapport with his attorney * * * that the Court of Appeals thought part of the Sixth Amendment guarantee of counsel.

See also United States v. Pina, 844 F.2d 1 (1st Cir.1988) (court has no obligation to appoint a lawyer outside the public defender's office, simply because the defendant believes that all lawyers from that office are incompetent).

For a proposal that the current indigent defense system should be replaced by a voucher program in which an indigent could select his own attorney, see Schulhofer and Friedman, Reforming Indigent Defense: How Free Market Principles Can Help to Fix a Broken System, Cato Institute Policy Analysis No. 666, September 1, 2010. The authors conclude as follows:

> [B]y denying freedom of choice to the indigent defendant in what will often be the most important matter of his lifetime, the current system presents a glaring breach of our ideas of personal autonomy and freedom from unwarranted government control. We conclude that present institutions for criminal defense ought to be replaced with a voucher system, in order to provide indigent defendants with freedom of choice and to provide attorneys with the same incentive to serve their clients that attorneys have always had when they represent clients other than the poor.

Violation of Right to Chosen Counsel Can Never Be Harmless: United States v. Gonzalez-Lopez

The right to pay for a particular counsel is grounded in personal autonomy: a defendant, whose liberty is at stake, should generally have the right to pick whomever he wants to assist him. In United States v. Gonzalez-Lopez, 548 U.S. 140 (2006), the Court considered whether the violation of the constitutional right to counsel of choice was subject to harmless error review. The trial court had denied the defendant the right to hire a lawyer from outside the state; the defendant then hired a different lawyer to defend him. The Court of Appeals found the denial to be a violation of the right to the defendant's constitutional right to counsel of choice; that ruling was not contested in the Supreme Court. The government did argue, however, that the defendant was required to show "prejudice" from the denial of his right to counsel of choice. The government relied on the cases requiring the defendant to show "prejudice" for a violation of the right to *effective* assistance of counsel, most notably Strickland v. Washington.

The Court, in an opinion by Justice Scalia for five Justices, held that a violation of the right to counsel of choice required automatic reversal; no showing of prejudice was necessary. Justice Scalia addressed the government's argument that a violation of the right to counsel of choice was not "complete" unless the defendant could show that substitute counsel prejudiced his defense; this argument was based on an analysis that the right to counsel of choice protects the right to a fair trial. Justice Scalia responded as follows:

> [The Sixth Amendment] commands, not that a trial be fair, but that a particular guarantee of fairness be provided—to wit, that the accused be defended by the counsel he believes to be best. * * * In sum, the right at stake here is the right to counsel of choice, not the right to a fair trial; and that right was violated because the deprivation of counsel was erroneous. No additional showing of prejudice is required to make the violation "complete."

Justice Scalia then distinguished the cases on effective assistance of counsel, requiring a showing of "prejudice" before reversal:

> [T]he requirement of showing prejudice in ineffectiveness claims stems from the very definition of the right at issue; it is not a matter of showing that the violation was harmless, but of showing that a violation of the right to effective representation *occurred*. A choice-of-counsel violation occurs *whenever* the defendant's choice is wrongfully denied. Moreover, if and when counsel's ineffectiveness "pervades" a trial, it does so * * * through identifiable mistakes. We can assess how those mistakes affected the outcome. To determine the effect of wrongful denial of choice of counsel, however, we would not be looking for mistakes committed by the actual counsel, but for differences in the defense that would have been made by the rejected counsel—in matters ranging from questions asked on *voir dire* and cross-examination to such intangibles as argument style and relationship with the prosecutors. * * * The difficulties of conducting the two assessments of prejudice are not remotely comparable.

Justice Alito, joined by Chief Justice Roberts, Justice Kennedy, and Justice Thomas, dissented. He argued that the majority's rule of automatic reversal created some "anomalous and unjustifiable consequences." He elaborated as follows:

> Suppose, for example, that a defendant is initially represented by an attorney who previously represented the defendant in civil matters and who has little criminal experience. Suppose that this attorney is erroneously disqualified and that the defendant is then able to secure the services of a nationally acclaimed and highly experienced criminal defense attorney who secures a surprisingly favorable result at trial—for instance, acquittal on most but not all counts. Under the majority's holding, the trial court's erroneous ruling automatically means that the Sixth Amendment was violated—even if the defendant makes no attempt to argue that the disqualified attorney would have done a better job.

1. Disqualification of Defendant's Counsel of Choice

If the defendant can afford to pay, there is a *qualified* right to retain counsel of choice. In Wheat v. United States, 386 U.S. 153 (1988), Chief

Justice Rehnquist wrote for the Court as it evaluated a district court's denial of Wheat's waiver of his right to conflict-free counsel and the court's refusal to permit a proposed substitution of attorneys.

Wheat was charged along with numerous others with participating in a farflung drug distribution conspiracy. One codefendant, Gomez-Barajas, was represented along with another, Bravo, by the same attorney, Iredale. Gomez-Barajas was tried first and acquitted on drug charges overlapping Wheat's. Gomez-Barajas sought to avoid a second trial on other charges and offered to plead guilty to tax evasion and illegal importation of merchandise. His plea was pending before the district court when Wheat's trial was to commence. Bravo, who apparently was a less significant defendant, pled guilty to one count of transporting approximately 2,400 pounds of marijuana.

Iredale, who had represented both of these defendants, notified the court that Wheat asked Iredale to try his case. The government raised with the court two possible conflicts: the court had not yet accepted the plea and sentencing arrangement negotiated between Gomez-Barajas and the Government, which meant that he could withdraw his plea and would be facing a trial represented by Iredale in which Wheat might be called as a government witness and Iredale would have already tried Wheat's case; and Iredale's representation of Bravo would directly affect Iredale's ability to represent Wheat because the government believed that the marijuana transported by Bravo was transferred to Wheat and the government asked Iredale to make Bravo available as a witness against Wheat in exchange for a change in the government's position as to Bravo's sentence.

Wheat responded to the government's concerns by emphasizing his right to have the counsel of his choice and noting that he, Gomez-Barajas, and Bravo all were willing to waive the right to conflict-free counsel. Wheat argued that, if called to testify against him, Bravo would simply say he did not know Wheat and had no dealings with him, and that in the unlikely event that Gomez-Barajas went to trial on tax evasion and illegal importation charges, Wheat would unlikely be a witness because he was not involved in those alleged crimes.

The trial court found for the Government and refused to permit Iredale to substitute in as Wheat's counsel. Wheat was convicted, the court of appeals affirmed the conviction, and the Supreme Court also affirmed. Chief Justice Rehnquist observed that the right to choose one's counsel is not absolute, noting as examples that a client who cannot afford a lawyer cannot insist on representation by that lawyer, and a client cannot generally compel a lawyer to accept a case.

The Chief Justice rejected Wheat's argument that he had the right to waive any conflict and observed that "[f]ederal courts have an independent interest in ensuring that criminal trials are conducted within the ethical standards of the profession and that legal proceedings appear fair to all who observe them," and "[n]ot only the interest of a criminal defendant but the institutional interest in the rendition of just verdicts in criminal cases may be jeopardized by unregulated multiple representation." He concluded that "[w]here a court justifiably finds an actual conflict of interest, there can be no doubt that it may decline a proffer of waiver, and insist that defendants be separately represented."

The Chief Justice recognized the difficulty that trial courts have in dealing with conflict waivers because "[u]nfortunately for all concerned, a district court must pass on the issue of whether or not to allow a waiver of a conflict of interest by a criminal defendant not with the wisdom of hindsight after the trial has taken place, but in the murkier pre-trial context when relationships between parties are seen through a glass, darkly"; and accordingly "the district court must be allowed substantial latitude in refusing waivers of conflicts of interest not only in those rare cases where an actual conflict may be demonstrated before trial, but in the more common cases where a potential for conflict exists which may or may not burgeon into an actual conflict as the trial progresses." He concluded that "[i]n the circumstances of this case, with the motion for substitution of counsel made so close to the time of trial the District Court relied on instinct and judgment based on experience in making its decision," and "[w]e do not think it can be said that the court exceeded the broad latitude which must be accorded it in making this decision."

Justice Marshall, joined by Justice Brennan, dissented, and argued that the conflict arguments were too speculative to deny Wheat the benefit of Iredale as his lawyer. He found the likelihood that Gomez-Barajas's plea agreement would be rejected to be small, and that even if he went to trial there was no indication that Wheat was a percipient witness to the remaining charges. He also found it unlikely that Bravo could identify Wheat so that Iredale's prior representation of Bravo was not a problem. Justice Stevens, joined by Justice Blackmun, also dissented.

Analysis of Wheat

Wheat is criticized in Green, "Through a Glass, Darkly": How the Court Sees Motions to Disqualify Criminal Defense Lawyers, 89 Colum.L.Rev. 1201 (1989). Among other criticisms, Professor Green notes that "the Court relied on an unwarranted assumption that if the defendant is willing to waive potential conflict of interest claims his attorney probably has not complied with the ethical standards governing the investigation and disclosure of potential conflicts."

Wheat is defended in Stuntz, Waiving Rights in Criminal Procedure, 75 Va.L.Rev. 761 (1989). Professor Stuntz argues that clients jointly represented by a single counsel may or may not have improper motives. It may be that joint counsel is retained to deter conspirators from cutting an individual deal and cooperating with the government. Thus, some defendants may be coerced into accepting a joint counsel relationship. On the other hand, it may be that the clients have proper motives—they all want the same lawyer because that lawyer is excellent. Stuntz argues that the capability of the lawyer is likely to be known by the trial judge; if the lawyer is known to be merely average, bad motives for the multiple representation can be inferred, and disqualification should be ordered because the client's waiver of conflict-free counsel is not really voluntary. Therefore a broad grant of discretion to the trial judge is necessary to allow the judge to separate good from bad motives in joint representation. Professor Stuntz's arguments are not borne out by the facts in *Wheat*, however, where it appeared that a number of the defendants came to Iredale fairly far along in the proceedings, because he had been so successful in defending other defendants. The trial judge specifically noted that Iredale was an excellent and highly successful defense attorney, and disqualified him nonetheless.

Another concern that might have animated the result in *Wheat* is that it is trial judges who see the defendant who is purporting to waive the right to conflict-free counsel. Conflicts of interest are complicated. How is the court to be sure that the defendant really understands what he is giving up? Especially with unsophisticated defendants, a trial judge might conclude that the defendant who says he wants to waive is in fact not making a truly knowing waiver. And because it is the trial judge who sees what is going on, appellate courts should be deferent to the trial judge's assessment and decision to override the defendant's "waiver." Otherwise the trial court will be whipsawed by granting the defendant's wish to proceed with counsel and then, on appeal, having the defendant argue that he did not really know what he was doing when he elected to go with conflicted counsel.

Cases Applying Wheat

After *Wheat*, appellate courts have usually upheld trial court disqualifications of defense counsel. For example, in United States v. Stites, 56 F.3d 1020 (9th Cir.1995), Stites and his sister Cheryl Dark were charged with RICO violations resulting from a scheme of insurance fraud. Stites fled the state, and Cheryl was represented by Juanita Brooks. Cheryl pleaded guilty and at the sentencing hearing, Brooks argued that Cheryl was a pawn of Stites; that Stites was "the mastermind," "a thief and a fraud," and a "cheap con artist." She added for good measure that "as an officer of the court and attorney myself, it makes me angry to see that people are able to so pervert our system of justice." Brooks won a light sentence for Dark. Two years later, Stites finally turned up for trial—and retained Brooks. When the prosecution objected, both Stites and Dark waived any conflict. But the trial judge—who happened to be the same judge who sentenced Dark—disqualified Brooks. The court of appeals upheld the disqualification. The court found that Brooks was properly disqualified because "[s]he could not, in the very same criminal prosecution, tell the court that Stites was a liar, a thief, and the mastermind of the massive fraud charged by the government and then represent the same person contending that he was innocent of the crimes charged." The court concluded as follows:

> Students of the classics may recall Cicero's comment that speeches at trials are for "the case and the occasion," they do not disclose "the man himself." But even if a certain insincerity may accompany the filling of an advocate's role, nothing in our professional ethics permits an advocate to tell a court one set of facts today and a contradictory set of facts tomorrow.

One of the more notable disqualifications of counsel occurred in the prosecution of former Mafia boss John Gotti. United States v. Locascio, 6 F.3d 924 (2d Cir.1993). The trial court disqualified Gotti's long-time counsel, Bruce Cutler, on two grounds: (1) the government had proof that Cutler served as house counsel to the Mafia, representing various conspirators who had not personally retained him—thus his representation would actually be proof of conspiratorial activity at trial; and (2) the government had tapes of conversations in which Cutler was present while criminal activity was being discussed—thus, in challenging the government's interpretation of the tapes, Cutler would be acting as an unsworn witness. The court of appeals upheld the disqualification, even though Gotti had waived his right to conflict-free counsel. The court noted in particular with respect to Cutler's status as an unsworn witness, that Gotti's waiver of conflict was irrelevant:

> When an attorney is an unsworn witness * * * the detriment is to the government, since the defendant gains an unfair advantage, and to the court, since the factfinding process is impaired. Waiver by the defendant is ineffective in such situations, since he is not the party prejudiced.
>
> * * * The government was legitimately concerned that, when Cutler argued before the jury for a particular interpretation of the tapes, his interpretation would be given added credibility due to his presence in the room when the statements were made. This would have given Gotti an unfair advantage, since Cutler would not have had to take an oath in presenting his interpretation, but could merely frame it in the form of legal argument.

See also United States v. Register, 182 F.3d 820 (11th Cir.1999) (no error in disqualifying counsel over the defendant's objections, where a government informant might testify that the defendant paid the attorney with drugs from the conspiracy: "It would have been virtually impossible for the attorney to question the informant without being concerned to a significant degree about his own interests rather than those of his client").

2. Rendering the Defendant Unable to Pay for Counsel of Choice

CAPLIN & DRYSDALE V. UNITED STATES

Supreme Court of the United States, 1989.
491 U.S. 617.

JUSTICE WHITE delivered the opinion of the Court.

We are called on to determine whether the federal drug forfeiture statute includes an exemption for assets that a defendant wishes to use to pay an attorney who conducted his defense in the criminal case where forfeiture was sought. Because we determine that no such exemption exists, we must decide whether that statute, so interpreted, is consistent with the Fifth and Sixth Amendments. We hold that it is.

[The defendant Reckmeyer was charged with running a massive drug importation and distribution scheme that was a continuing criminal enterprise (CCE), in violation of 21 U.S.C. § 848. The district court relied on the CCE statute and entered a restraining order forbidding the defendant to transfer any of the listed assets that were potentially forfeitable. The defendant had retained Caplin & Drysdale as counsel to represent him in grand jury investigations that resulted in the charges. The defendant moved to modify the restraining order to permit him to pay the law firm's fees and to exempt from any postconviction forfeiture order the assets that he intended to use to pay the firm. One week later, before the court ruled on the motion, the defendant pled guilty and agreed to forfeit all of the specified assets listed in the indictment. The district court entered an order forfeiting virtually all of the assets in the defendant's possession.

The law firm then filed a petition under a provision that permits third parties with an interest in forfeited property to ask the sentencing court for an adjudication of their rights to that property. The firm argued that a third party had a right to make claims against forfeited property if it was without cause to believe the property was subject to forfeiture at the time of a transaction and, alternatively, assets used to pay an attorney were exempt from forfeiture. The district court granted the firm's claim, and the court of appeals reversed in an en banc decision. The Supreme Court agreed with the court of appeals as to the firm's statutory argument in reliance on its decision in the companion case of United States v. Monsanto, 491 U.S. 600 (1989) (holding that the Comprehensive Forfeiture Act of 1984 (CFA), 21 U.S.C.S. § 853(a), clearly established that all of the assets of an accused are to be forfeited upon a finding of probable cause that they were the fruits of criminal activity and that the CFA made no allowances whatsoever for any discretionary release of funds by the courts to pay for an accused's attorney's fees).]

We therefore address petitioner's constitutional challenges to the forfeiture law. Petitioner contends that the statute infringes on criminal defendants' Sixth Amendment right to counsel of choice, and upsets the "balance of power" between the Government and the accused in a manner contrary to the Due Process Clause of the Fifth Amendment. We consider these contentions in turn.

* * *

Petitioner's first claim is that the forfeiture law makes impossible, or at least impermissibly burdens, a defendant's right "to select and be represented by one's preferred attorney." Petitioner does not, nor could it defensibly do so, assert that impecunious defendants have a Sixth Amendment right to choose their counsel. The Amendment guarantees defendants in criminal cases the right to adequate representation, but those who do not have the means to hire their own lawyers have no cognizable complaint so long as they are adequately represented by attorneys appointed by the courts. * * * The forfeiture statute does not prevent a defendant who has nonforfeitable assets from retaining any attorney of his choosing. Nor is it necessarily the case that a defendant who possesses nothing but assets the Government seeks to have forfeited will be prevented from retaining counsel of choice. Defendants like Reckmeyer may be able to find lawyers willing to represent them, hoping that their fees will be paid in the event of acquittal, or via some other means that a defendant might come by in the future. The burden placed on defendants by the forfeiture law is therefore a limited one.

Nonetheless, there will be cases where a defendant will be unable to retain the attorney of his choice, when that defendant would have been able to hire that lawyer if he had access to forfeitable assets * * *. It is in these cases, petitioner argues, that the Sixth Amendment puts limits on the forfeiture statute.

This submission is untenable. Whatever the full extent of the Sixth Amendment's protection of one's right to retain counsel of his choosing, that protection does not go beyond the individual's right to spend his own money to obtain the advice and assistance of counsel. A defendant has no Sixth Amendment right to spend another person's money for services rendered by an attorney, even if those funds are the only way that that defendant will be able to retain the attorney of his choice. A robbery suspect, for example, has no Sixth Amendment right to use funds he has stolen from a bank to retain an attorney to defend him if he is apprehended. The money, though in his possession, is not rightfully his; the Government does not violate the Sixth Amendment if it seizes the robbery proceeds and refuses to permit the defendant to use them to pay for his defense. * * *

* * *

There is no constitutional principle that gives one person the right to give another's property to a third party, even where the person seeking to complete the exchange wishes to do so in order to exercise a constitutionally protected right. * * *

Petitioner's "balancing analysis" to the contrary rests substantially on the view that the Government has only a modest interest in forfeitable assets that may be used to retain an attorney. Petitioner takes the position that, in large part, once assets have been paid over from client to attorney, the principal ends of forfeiture have been achieved: dispossessing a drug dealer or racketeer of the proceeds of his wrongdoing. We think that this view misses the mark for three reasons.

First, the Government has a pecuniary interest in forfeiture that goes beyond merely separating a criminal from his ill-gotten gains; that legitimate interest extends to recovering all forfeitable assets, for such assets are deposited in a Fund that supports law-enforcement efforts in a variety of important and useful ways. The sums of money that can be raised for law-enforcement activities this way are substantial,[a] and the Government's interest in using the profits of crime to fund these activities should not be discounted.

Second, the statute permits "rightful owners" of forfeited assets to make claims for forfeited assets before they are retained by the Government. The Government's interest in winning undiminished forfeiture thus includes the objective of returning property, in full, to those wrongfully deprived or defrauded of it. * * *

Finally * * * a major purpose motivating congressional adoption and continued refinement of the racketeer influenced and corrupt organizations (RICO) and CCE forfeiture provisions has been the desire to lessen the economic power of organized crime and drug enterprises. This includes the use of such economic power to retain private counsel. * * * The notion that the Government has a legitimate interest in depriving criminals of economic power, even insofar as that power is used to retain counsel of choice, may be somewhat unsettling. But when a defendant claims that he has suffered some substantial impairment of his Sixth Amendment rights by virtue of the seizure or forfeiture of assets in his possession, such a complaint is no more than the reflection of the harsh reality that the quality of a criminal defendant's representation frequently may turn on his ability to retain the best counsel money can buy. * * * [T]he Court of

---

[a] For example, just one of the assets which Reckmeyer agreed to forfeit, a parcel of land known as "Shelburne Glebe," was recently sold by federal authorities for $5.3 million. The proceeds of the sale will fund federal, state, and local law-enforcement activities.

Appeals put it aptly: "The modern day Jean Valjean must be satisfied with appointed counsel. Yet the drug merchant claims that his possession of huge sums of money . . . entitles him to something more. We reject this contention, and any notion of a constitutional right to use the proceeds of crime to finance an expensive defense."[b]

It is our view that there is a strong governmental interest in obtaining full recovery of all forfeitable assets, an interest that overrides any Sixth Amendment interest in permitting criminals to use assets adjudged forfeitable to pay for their defense. * * *

We therefore reject petitioner's claim of a Sixth Amendment right of criminal defendants to use assets that are the Government's—assets adjudged forfeitable, as Reckmeyer's were—to pay attorney's fees, merely because those assets are in their possession.[c] See also *Monsanto,* which rejects a similar claim with respect to pretrial orders and assets not yet judged forfeitable.

* * *

[b] We also reject the contention, advanced by amici, see, e.g., Brief for American Bar Association as Amicus Curiae 20–22, * * * that a type of "per se" ineffective assistance of counsel results—due to the particular complexity of RICO or drug-enterprise cases—when a defendant is not permitted to use assets in his possession to retain counsel of choice, and instead must rely on appointed counsel. If such an argument were accepted, it would bar the trial of indigents charged with such offenses, because those persons would have to rely on appointed counsel—which this view considers per se ineffective. * * *

[c] Petitioner advances * * * possible ethical conflicts created for lawyers defending persons facing forfeiture of assets in their possession.

Petitioner first notes the statute's exemption from forfeiture of property transferred to a bona fide purchaser who was "reasonably without cause to believe that the property was subject to forfeiture." This provision, it is said, might give an attorney an incentive not to investigate a defendant's case as fully as possible, so that the lawyer can invoke it to protect from forfeiture any fees he has received. Yet given the requirement that any assets which the Government wishes to have forfeited must be specified in the indictment, see Fed.Rule Crim.Proc. 7(c)(2), the only way a lawyer could be a beneficiary * * * would be to fail to read the indictment of his client. In this light, the prospect that a lawyer might find himself in conflict with his client, by seeking to take advantage of § 853(n)(6)(B), amounts to very little. * * *

The second possible conflict arises in plea bargaining: petitioner posits that a lawyer may advise a client to accept an agreement entailing a more harsh prison sentence but no forfeiture—even where contrary to the client's interests—in an effort to preserve the lawyer's fee. Following such a strategy, however, would surely constitute ineffective assistance of counsel. We see no reason why our cases such as Strickland v. Washington are inadequate to deal with any such ineffectiveness where it arises. * * *

Finally, petitioner argues that the forfeiture statute, in operation, will create a system akin to "contingency fees" for defense lawyers: only a defense lawyer who wins acquittal for his client will be able to collect his fees, and contingent fees in criminal cases are generally considered unethical. See ABA Model Rule of Professional Conduct 1.5(d)(2)(1983). But there is no indication here that petitioner, or any other firm, has actually sought to charge a defendant on a contingency basis; rather the claim is that a law firm's prospect of collecting its fee may turn on the outcome at trial. This, however, may often be the case in criminal defense work. Nor is it clear why permitting contingent fees in criminal cases—if that is what the forfeiture statute does—violates a criminal defendant's Sixth Amendment rights. The fact that a federal statutory scheme authorizing contingency fees—again, if that is what Congress has created in § 853 (a premise we doubt)—is at odds with model disciplinary rules or state disciplinary codes hardly renders the federal statute invalid.

JUSTICE BLACKMUN, with whom JUSTICES BRENNAN, MARSHALL and STEVENS join, dissenting.

* * *

Had it been Congress' express aim to undermine the adversary system as we know it, it could hardly have found a better engine of destruction than attorney's-fee forfeiture. The main effect of forfeitures under the Act, of course, will be to deny the defendant the right to retain counsel, and therefore the right to have his defense designed and presented by an attorney he has chosen and trusts. If the Government restrains the defendant's assets before trial, private counsel will be unwilling to continue, or to take on, the defense. Even if no restraining order is entered, the possibility of forfeiture after conviction will itself substantially diminish the likelihood that private counsel will agree to take the case.

* * *

Perhaps most troubling is the fact that forfeiture statutes place the Government in the position to exercise an intolerable degree of power over any private attorney who takes on the task of representing a defendant in a forfeiture case. * * * The Government will be ever tempted to use the forfeiture weapon against a defense attorney who is particularly talented or aggressive on the client's behalf—the attorney who is better than what, in the Government's view, the defendant deserves. * * *

The long-term effects of the fee-forfeiture practice will be to decimate the private criminal-defense bar. As the use of the forfeiture mechanism expands to new categories of federal crimes and spreads to the States, only one class of defendants will be free routinely to retain private counsel: the affluent defendant accused of a crime that generates no economic gain. As the number of private clients diminishes, only the most idealistic and the least skilled of young lawyers will be attracted to the field, while the remainder seek greener pastures elsewhere.

* * *

QUESTIONS ON CAPLIN

Hasn't the majority—by presuming the assets are ill-gotten and thus not the defendant's—begged the question? Maybe not, because according to the dissenters, it is the risk that assets will later be adjudicated forfeitable at trial that prevents the defendant from being able to retain an attorney, i.e., an attorney will not take the case given the risk that all of the assets will be forfeited at the end. Thus, even if the government only relied on *post-trial* forfeitures, defense counsel would be deterred from the representation due to the relation-back provision in the statute, which takes forfeited assets out of the hands of third parties.

Forfeiture Hearings Not Required After Indictment: Kaley v. United States

In Kaley v. United States, 571 U.S. 320 (2014), Justice Kagan wrote for the Court as it held that criminal defendants are not entitled to a hearing to contest a grand jury's finding of probable cause to believe they committed the crimes charged when they desire to challenge a pre-trial restraint on their property in order to use that property to hire counsel to defend them. Relying on the probable cause standard the Court established in *Monsanto*, the majority noted that pretrial restraint is permissible "based upon a finding of probable cause to believe that the property will ultimately be forfeitable." The finding has two parts: (1) that the defendant has committed a crime permitting forfeiture, and (2) the property at issue has the requisite connection to that crime. Justice Kagan noted that lower courts have generally permitted a hearing on the second part and have disagreed as to whether a hearing is permitted on the first part. Noting that a grand jury indictment "may do more than commence a criminal proceeding (with all the economic, reputational, and personal harm that entails)," she added that the indictment may also result in immediate deprivation of a defendant's freedom. The bottom line was that "[i]f judicial review of the grand jury's determination is not warranted (as we have so often held) to put a defendant on trial or place her in custody, then neither is it needed to freeze her property." The majority concluded that a judge's determination that there was no probable cause could create "legal dissonance" with the grand jury's indictment.

The defendants argued that the Court should apply the balancing test of Mathews v. Eldridge, 424 U.S. 319 (1976), to determine whether they should get a hearing. Justice Kagan responded that "[e]ven if *Mathews* applied here—even if, that is, its balancing inquiry were capable of trumping this Court's repeated admonitions that the grand jury's word is conclusive—the Kaleys still would not be entitled to the hearing they seek." She emphasized that "the Government has a substantial interest in freezing potentially forfeitable assists without an evidentiary hearing about the probable cause underlying criminal charges."

Chief Justice Roberts, joined by Justices Breyer and Sotomayor, dissented and began his opinion with these words: "An individual facing serious criminal charges brought by the United States has little but the Constitution and his attorney standing between him and prison. He might readily give all he owns to defend himself." The Chief Justice observed that *Monsanto* had left open the question whether the accused was entitled to a hearing before his property was restrained so that it could not be used to hire counsel and wrote that "[t]he possibility that a prosecutor could elect to hamstring his target by preventing him from paying his counsel of choice raises substantial concerns about the fairness of the entire proceeding."

The Chief Justice responded to the majority's analysis of *Mathews* by citing the important interests of defendants in a criminal proceeding, including the presumption of innocence and the choice of counsel "to vindicate that presumption by choosing the advocate that they believe will best defend them" which is "at the very core of the Sixth Amendment."

Freezing Untainted Assets That Would Be Used to Pay for Counsel: Luis v. United States

LUIS V. UNITED STATES

Supreme Court of the United States, 2016.
578 U.S. 5.

JUSTICE BREYER announced the judgment of the Court and delivered an opinion in which THE CHIEF JUSTICE, JUSTICE GINSBURG, and JUSTICE SOTOMAYOR join.

A federal statute provides that a court may freeze before trial certain assets belonging to a criminal defendant accused of violations of federal health care or banking laws. See 18 U.S.C. § 1345. Those assets include: (1) property "obtained as a result of" the crime, (2) property "traceable" to the crime, and (3) other "property of equivalent value." § 1345(a)(2). In this case, the Government has obtained a court order that freezes assets belonging to the third category of property, namely, property that is untainted by the crime, and that belongs fully to the defendant. That order, the defendant says, prevents her from paying her lawyer. She claims that insofar as it does so, it violates her Sixth Amendment "right . . . to have the Assistance of Counsel for [her] defence." We agree.

* * * In October 2012, a federal grand jury charged the petitioner, Sila Luis, with paying kickbacks, conspiring to commit fraud, and engaging in other crimes all related to health care. The Government claimed that Luis had fraudulently obtained close to $45 million, almost all of which she had already spent. Believing it would convict Luis of the crimes charged, and hoping to preserve the $2 million remaining in Luis' possession for payment of restitution and other criminal penalties (often referred to as criminal forfeitures, which can include innocent—not just tainted—assets, a point of critical importance here), the Government sought a pretrial order prohibiting Luis from dissipating her assets. And the District Court ultimately issued an order prohibiting her from "dissipating, or otherwise disposing of . . . assets, real or personal . . . up to the equivalent value of the proceeds of the Federal health care fraud ($45 million)."

The Government and Luis agree that this court order will prevent Luis from using her own untainted funds, *i.e.*, funds not connected with the crime, to hire counsel to defend her in her criminal case. * * * Although the District Court recognized that the order might prevent Luis from obtaining counsel of her choice, it held "that there is no Sixth Amendment right to use untainted, substitute assets to hire counsel."

The Eleventh Circuit upheld the District Court. We granted Luis' petition for certiorari.

* * *

No one doubts the fundamental character of a criminal defendant's Sixth Amendment right to the "Assistance of Counsel." [Justice Breyer cites and quotes from *Gideon v. Wainright.*]

Given the necessarily close working relationship between lawyer and client, the need for confidence, and the critical importance of trust, * * * the Court has held that the Sixth Amendment grants a defendant "a fair opportunity to secure counsel of his own choice." This "fair opportunity" for the defendant to secure counsel of choice has limits. A defendant has no right, for example, to an attorney who is not a member of the bar, or who has a conflict of interest due to a relationship with an opposing party. And an indigent defendant, while entitled to adequate representation, has no right to have the Government pay for his preferred representational choice.

We nonetheless emphasize that the constitutional right at issue here is fundamental: The Sixth Amendment guarantees a defendant the right to be represented by an otherwise qualified attorney whom that defendant can afford to hire.

The Government cannot, and does not, deny Luis' right to be represented by a qualified attorney whom she chooses and can afford. But the Government would undermine the value of that right by taking from Luis the ability to use the funds she needs to pay for her chosen attorney. The Government points out that, while freezing the funds may have this consequence, there are important interests on the other side of the legal equation: It wishes to guarantee that those funds will be available later to help pay for statutory penalties (including forfeiture of untainted assets) and restitution, should it secure convictions. And it points to two cases from this Court, *Caplin & Drysdale*, and [*United States v.*] *Monsanto*, which, in the Government's view, hold that the Sixth Amendment does not pose an obstacle to its doing so here. In our view, however, the nature of the assets at issue here differs from the assets at issue in those earlier cases. And that distinction makes a difference.

* * * The relevant difference consists of the fact that the property here is untainted; *i.e.*, it belongs to the defendant, pure and simple. In this respect it differs from a robber's loot, a drug seller's cocaine, a burglar's tools, or other property associated with the planning, implementing, or concealing of a crime. * * * The robber's loot belongs to the victim, not to the defendant. * * * The cocaine is contraband, long considered forfeitable

to the Government wherever found. * * * And title to property used to commit a crime (or otherwise "traceable" to a crime) often passes to the Government at the instant the crime is planned or committed. * * *

The property at issue here, however, is not loot, contraband, or otherwise "tainted." It belongs to the defendant. That fact undermines the Government's reliance upon precedent, for both *Caplin & Drysdale* and *Monsanto* relied critically upon the fact that the property at issue was "tainted," and that title to the property therefore had passed from the defendant to the Government before the court issued its order freezing (or otherwise disposing of) the assets.

* * *

The Court in those cases * * * acknowledged that whether property is "forfeitable" or subject to pretrial restraint under Congress' scheme is a nuanced inquiry that very much depends on who has the superior interest in the property at issue. * * *

The distinction * * * is thus an important one, not a technicality. It is the difference between what is yours and what is mine. In *Caplin & Drysdale* and *Monsanto*, the Government wanted to impose restrictions upon (or seize) property that the Government had probable cause to believe was the proceeds of, or traceable to, a crime. The relevant statute said that the Government took title to those tainted assets as of the time of the crime. And the defendants in those cases consequently had to concede that the disputed property was in an important sense the Government's at the time the court imposed the restrictions.

This is not to say that the Government "owned" the tainted property outright (in the sense that it could take possession of the property even before obtaining a conviction). Rather, it is to say that the Government even before trial had a "substantial" interest in the tainted property sufficient to justify the property's pretrial restraint. * * *

If we analogize to bankruptcy law, the Government [in *Caplin & Drysdale* and *Monsanto*] became something like a secured creditor with a lien on the defendant's tainted assets superior to that of most any other party. * * *

Here, by contrast, the Government seeks to impose restrictions upon Luis' *un*tainted property without any showing of any equivalent governmental interest in that property. Again, if this were a bankruptcy case, the Government would be at most an unsecured creditor. Although such creditors someday might collect from a debtor's general assets, they cannot be said to have any present claim to, or interest in, the debtor's property. * * * At least regarding her untainted assets, Luis can at this point reasonably claim that the property is still "mine," free and clear.

* * *

This distinction between (1) what is primarily "mine" (the defendant's) and (2) what is primarily "yours" (the Government's) does not by itself answer the constitutional question posed, for the law of property sometimes allows a person without a present interest in a piece of property to impose restrictions upon a current owner, say, to prevent waste. A holder of a reversionary interest, for example, can prevent the owner of a life estate from wasting the property. * * * The Government here seeks a somewhat analogous order, *i.e.*, an order that will preserve Luis' untainted assets so that they will be available to cover the costs of forfeiture and restitution if she is convicted, and if the court later determines that her tainted assets are insufficient or otherwise unavailable.

The Government finds statutory authority for its request in language authorizing a court to enjoin a criminal defendant from, for example, disposing of innocent "property of equivalent value" to that of tainted property. 18 U.S.C. § 1345(a)(2)(B)(i). * * *

[But] the nature of the competing interests argues against this kind of court order. On the one side we find, as we have previously explained, a Sixth Amendment right to assistance of counsel that is a fundamental constituent of due process of law. * * * The order at issue in this case would seriously undermine that constitutional right.

On the other side we find interests that include the Government's contingent interest in securing its punishment of choice (namely, criminal forfeiture) as well as the victims' interest in securing restitution (notably, from funds belonging to the defendant, not the victims). While these interests are important, to deny the Government the order it requests will not inevitably undermine them, for, at least sometimes, the defendant may possess other assets—say, "tainted" property—that might be used for forfeitures and restitution. Nor do the interests in obtaining payment of a criminal forfeiture or restitution order enjoy constitutional protection. Rather, despite their importance, compared to the right to counsel of choice, these interests would seem to lie somewhat further from the heart of a fair, effective criminal justice system.

* * *

[A]s a practical matter, to accept the Government's position could well erode the right to counsel to a considerably greater extent than we have so far indicated. To permit the Government to freeze Luis' untainted assets would unleash a principle of constitutional law that would have no obvious stopping place. The statutory provision before us authorizing the present restraining order refers only to "banking law violation[s]" and "Federal health care offense[s]." 18 U.S.C. § 1345(a)(2). But, in the Government's view, Congress could write more statutes authorizing pretrial restraints in cases involving other illegal behavior—after all, a broad range of such behavior can lead to postconviction forfeiture of untainted assets.

* * *

These defendants, rendered indigent, would fall back upon publicly paid counsel, including overworked and underpaid public defenders. As the Department of Justice explains, only 27 percent of county-based public defender offices have sufficient attorneys to meet nationally recommended caseload standards. And as one *amicus* points out, "[m]any federal public defender organizations and lawyers appointed under the Criminal Justice Act serve numerous clients and have only limited resources." The upshot is a substantial risk that accepting the Government's views would—by increasing the government-paid-defender workload—render less effective the basic right the Sixth Amendment seeks to protect.

* * * We add that the constitutional line we have drawn should prove workable. That line distinguishes between a criminal defendant's (1) tainted funds and (2) innocent funds needed to pay for counsel. We concede, as JUSTICE KENNEDY points out, that money is fungible; and sometimes it will be difficult to say whether a particular bank account contains tainted or untainted funds. But the law has tracing rules that help courts implement the kind of distinction we require in this case. * * * And those rules will likely also prevent Luis from benefiting from many of the money transfers and purchases JUSTICE KENNEDY describes.

Courts use tracing rules in cases involving fraud, pension rights, bankruptcy, trusts, etc. They consequently have experience separating tainted assets from untainted assets, just as they have experience determining how much money is needed to cover the costs of a lawyer.

* * *

For the reasons stated, we conclude that the defendant in this case has a Sixth Amendment right to use her own "innocent" property to pay a reasonable fee for the assistance of counsel. On the assumptions made here, the District Court's order prevents Luis from exercising that right. * * *

JUSTICE THOMAS, concurring in the judgment.

I agree with the plurality that a pretrial freeze of untainted assets violates a criminal defendant's Sixth Amendment right to counsel of choice. But * * * my reasoning rests strictly on the Sixth Amendment's text and common-law backdrop.

The Sixth Amendment provides important limits on the Government's power to freeze a criminal defendant's forfeitable assets before trial. And, constitutional rights necessarily protect the prerequisites for their exercise. The right "to have the Assistance of Counsel," U.S. Const., Amdt. 6, thus implies the right to use lawfully owned property to pay for an attorney. Otherwise the right to counsel—originally understood to protect only the right to hire counsel of choice—would be meaningless. History confirms this textual understanding. The common law limited pretrial asset restraints to tainted assets. Both this textual understanding and history establish that the Sixth Amendment prevents the Government from freezing untainted assets in order to secure a potential forfeiture. The freeze here accordingly violates the Constitution.

* * *

JUSTICE KENNEDY, with whom JUSTICE ALITO joins, dissenting.

The plurality and JUSTICE THOMAS find in the Sixth Amendment a right of criminal defendants to pay for an attorney with funds that are forfeitable upon conviction so long as those funds are not derived from the crime alleged. That unprecedented holding rewards criminals who hurry to spend, conceal, or launder stolen property by assuring them that they may use their own funds to pay for an attorney after they have dissipated the proceeds of their crime. * * * By granting a defendant a constitutional right to hire an attorney with assets needed to make a property-crime victim whole, the plurality and JUSTICE THOMAS ignore this Court's precedents and distort the Sixth Amendment right to counsel.

The result reached today makes little sense in cases that involve fungible assets preceded by fraud, embezzlement, or other theft. An example illustrates the point. Assume a thief steals $1 million and then wins another $1 million in a lottery. After putting the sums in separate accounts, he or she spends $1 million. If the thief spends his or her lottery winnings, the Government can restrain the stolen funds in their entirety. The thief has no right to use those funds to pay for an attorney. Yet if the thief heeds today's decision, he or she will spend the stolen money first; for if the thief is apprehended, the $1 million won in the lottery can be used for an attorney. This result is not required by the Constitution.

* * *

The true winners today are sophisticated criminals who know how to make criminal proceeds look untainted. They do so every day. * * * They structure their transactions to avoid triggering recordkeeping and reporting requirements. And they open bank accounts in other people's names and through shell companies, all to disguise the origins of their funds.

* * *

JUSTICE KAGAN, **dissenting.**

I find *United States* v. *Monsanto* a troubling decision. It is one thing to hold, as this Court did in *Caplin & Drysdale* that a convicted felon has no Sixth Amendment right to pay his lawyer with funds adjudged forfeitable. Following conviction, such assets belong to the Government, and "[t]here is no constitutional principle that gives one person the right to give another's property to a third party." But it is quite another thing to say that the Government may, prior to trial, freeze assets that a defendant needs to hire an attorney, based on nothing more than "probable cause to believe that the property will ultimately be proved forfeitable." At that time, the presumption of innocence still applies, and the Government's interest in the assets is wholly contingent on future judgments of conviction and forfeiture. * * *

But the correctness of *Monsanto* is not at issue today. Petitioner Sila Luis has not asked this Court either to overrule or to modify that decision; she argues only that it does not answer the question presented here. And because Luis takes *Monsanto* as a given, the Court must do so as well.

On that basis, I agree with the principal dissent that *Monsanto* controls this case. Because the Government has established probable cause to believe that it will eventually recover Luis's assets, she has no right to use them to pay an attorney. * * *

The plurality reaches a contrary result only by differentiating between the direct fruits of criminal activity and substitute assets that become subject to forfeiture when the defendant has run through those proceeds. But * * * the Government's and the defendant's respective legal interests in those two kinds of property, prior to a judgment of guilt, are exactly the same: The defendant maintains ownership of either type, with the Government holding only a contingent interest. * * *

3. Other Limitations on the Right to Counsel of Choice

There are other situations in which the right to chosen counsel has been trumped by a state interest. For example, if the defendant's chosen counsel is from out-of-state, counsel must apply for *pro hac vice* admission and be admitted by the court. In Leis v. Flynt, 439 U.S. 438 (1979), the Court held that the attorney had no due process right to be admitted *pro hac vice.* But the Court in *Leis* did not consider whether a criminal defendant's right to chosen counsel would be violated if out-of-state counsel is denied *pro hac vice* admission. Generally, courts have found that the state has a legitimate interest in regulating the practice of out-of-state lawyers who want to try cases in local courts, and that *pro hac vice* admission can be denied so long as the exclusion is not arbitrary. See Panzardi-Alvarez v. United States, 879 F.2d 975 (1st Cir.1989) (denial of *pro hac vice* admission does not violate right to chosen counsel where counsel had previously represented joint clients with conflicting interests). Compare Fuller v. Diesslin, 868 F.2d 604 (3d Cir.1989), where the trial court denied *pro hac vice* admission of the defendant's chosen counsel on the following grounds: 1) local lawyers were always better prepared on local practice rules; 2) out-of-state attorneys created delays due to traveling; and 3) there were many local attorneys who could effectively represent the defendant. The court of appeals found that the right to chosen counsel had been violated:

> [T]he trial court's wooden approach and its failure to make record-supported findings balancing the right to [chosen] counsel with the demands of the administration of justice resulted in an arbitrary denial [that] constituted per se constitutional error * * *. We conclude that [the argument that if there is adequate local counsel, then *pro hac vice* admission can be denied] is without merit, because it collapses the right to counsel of choice into the right to effective assistance of counsel. * * * [A]lthough the core value in the sixth amendment is effective assistance of counsel, the amendment also comprehends other related rights, such as the right to select and be represented by one's preferred attorney.

VIII. SELF-REPRESENTATION

A. THE CONSTITUTIONAL RIGHT

Although a defendant has a right to the assistance of counsel in all criminal prosecutions, sometimes she may prefer to defend herself. Beginning with the Judiciary Act of 1789, the right of self-representation in federal courts has been protected by statute. But California, where Anthony Faretta was convicted of grand theft, did not grant that right. It allowed a judge to appoint counsel over Faretta's objection and despite his knowing and voluntary waiver of his right to counsel.

FARETTA V. CALIFORNIA

Supreme Court of the United States, 1975.
422 U.S. 806.

JUSTICE STEWART delivered the opinion of the Court.

* * *

Anthony Faretta was charged with grand theft in an information filed in the Superior Court of Los Angeles County, Cal. At the arraignment, the Superior Court Judge assigned to preside at the trial appointed the public defender to represent Faretta. Well before the date of trial, however, Faretta requested that he be permitted to represent himself. Questioning by the judge revealed that Faretta had once represented himself in a criminal prosecution, that he had a high school education, and that he did not want to be represented by the public defender because he believed that that office was "very loaded down with * * * a heavy case load." The judge responded that he believed Faretta was "making a mistake" and emphasized that in further proceedings Faretta would receive no special favors. Nevertheless, after establishing that Faretta wanted to represent himself and did not want a lawyer, the judge, in a "preliminary ruling," accepted Faretta's waiver of the assistance of counsel. The judge indicated, however, that he might reverse this ruling if it later appeared that Faretta was unable adequately to represent himself.

Several weeks thereafter, but still prior to trial, the judge *sua sponte* held a hearing to inquire into Faretta's ability to conduct his own defense, and questioned him specifically about both the hearsay rule and the state law governing the challenge of potential jurors. After consideration of Faretta's answers, and observation of his demeanor, the judge ruled that Faretta had not made an intelligent and knowing waiver of his right to the assistance of counsel, and also ruled that Faretta had no constitutional right to conduct his own defense. The judge, accordingly, reversed his earlier ruling permitting self-representation and again appointed the public defender to represent Faretta. * * * Throughout the subsequent trial, the judge required that Faretta's defense be conducted only through the appointed lawyer from the public defender's office. At the conclusion of the trial, the jury found Faretta guilty as charged, and the judge sentenced him to prison.

[The appellate court affirmed Faretta's conviction.]

[The Court reviewed federal and state statutes according the right of self-representation, and decisions supporting such a right.]

* * * We confront here a nearly universal conviction, on the part of our people as well as our courts, that forcing a lawyer upon an unwilling defendant is contrary to his basic right to defend himself if he truly wants to do so.

This consensus is soundly premised. The right of self-representation finds support in the structure of the Sixth Amendment, as well as in the English and colonial jurisprudence from which the Amendment emerged.

* * *

The Sixth Amendment does not provide merely that a defense shall be made for the accused; it grants to the accused personally the right to make his defense. It is the accused, not counsel, who must be "informed of the nature and cause of the accusation," who must be "confronted with the witnesses against him," and who must be accorded "compulsory process for obtaining witnesses in his favor." Although not stated in the Amendment in so many words, the right to self-representation—to make one's own defense personally—is thus necessarily implied by the structure of the

Amendment. The right to defend is given directly to the accused; for it is he who suffers the consequences if the defense fails.

The counsel provision supplements this design. It speaks of the "assistance" of counsel, and an assistant, however expert, is still an assistant. The language and spirit of the Sixth Amendment contemplate that counsel, like the other defense tools guaranteed by the Amendment, shall be an aid to a willing defendant—not an organ of the State interposed between an unwilling defendant and his right to defend himself personally. To thrust counsel upon the accused, against his considered wish, thus violates the logic of the Amendment. In such a case, counsel is not an assistant, but a master; and the right to make a defense is stripped of the personal character upon which the Amendment insists. It is true that when a defendant chooses to have a lawyer manage and present his case, law and tradition may allocate to the counsel the power to make binding decisions of trial strategy in many areas. This allocation can only be justified, however, by the defendant's consent, at the outset, to accept counsel as his representative. An unwanted counsel "represents" the defendant only through a tenuous and unacceptable legal fiction. Unless the accused has acquiesced in such representation, the defense presented is not the defense guaranteed him by the Constitution, for, in a very real sense, it is not *his* defense.

* * *

[The Court explored in detail the historical development of the right to counsel in England and in the United States. It found that both English and colonial legal history support interpreting the Sixth Amendment to imply a right of self-representation].

There can be no blinking the fact that the right of an accused to conduct his own defense seems to cut against the grain of this Court's decisions holding that the Constitution requires that no accused can be convicted and imprisoned unless he has been accorded the right to the assistance of counsel. For it is surely true that the basic thesis of those decisions is that the help of a lawyer is essential to assure the defendant a fair trial. And a strong argument can surely be made that the whole thrust of those decisions must inevitably lead to the conclusion that a State may constitutionally impose a lawyer upon even an unwilling defendant.

But it is one thing to hold that every defendant, rich or poor, has the right to the assistance of counsel, and quite another to say that a State may compel a defendant to accept a lawyer he does not want. The value of state-appointed counsel was not unappreciated by the Founders, yet the notion of compulsory counsel was utterly foreign to them. And whatever else may be said of those who wrote the Bill of Rights, surely there can be no doubt that they understood the inestimable worth of free choice.

It is undeniable that in most criminal prosecutions defendants could better defend with counsel's guidance than by their own unskilled efforts. But where the defendant will not voluntarily accept representation by counsel, the potential advantage of a lawyer's training and experience can be realized, if at all, only imperfectly. To force a lawyer on a defendant can only lead him to believe that the law contrives against him. Moreover, it is not inconceivable that in some rare instances, the defendant might in fact present his case more effectively by conducting his own defense. Personal liberties are not rooted in the law of averages. The right to defend is personal. The defendant, and not his lawyer or the State, will bear the personal consequences of a conviction. It is the defendant, therefore, who must be free personally to decide whether in his particular case counsel is to his advantage. And although he may conduct his own defense ultimately to his own detriment, his choice must be honored out of "that respect for the individual which is the lifeblood of the law."[a]

* * *

When an accused manages his own defense, he relinquishes, as a purely factual matter, many of the traditional benefits associated with the right to counsel. For this reason, in order to represent himself, the accused must "knowingly and intelligently" forego those relinquished benefits. Although a defendant need not himself have the skill and experience of a lawyer in order competently and intelligently to choose self-representation, he should be made aware of the dangers and disadvantages of self-representation, so that the record will establish that he knows what he is doing and his choice is made with eyes open.

Here, weeks before trial, Faretta clearly and unequivocally declared to the trial judge that he wanted to represent himself and did not want counsel. The record affirmatively shows that Faretta was literate, competent, and understanding, and that he was voluntarily exercising his informed free will. The trial judge had warned Faretta that he thought it was a mistake not to accept the assistance of counsel, and that Faretta would be required to follow all the "ground rules" of trial procedure. We need make no assessment of how well or poorly Faretta had mastered the intricacies of the hearsay rule and the California code provisions that govern challenges of potential jurors on *voir dire*. For his technical legal knowledge, as such, was not relevant to an assessment of his knowing exercise of the right to defend himself.

---

[a] Of course, a State may—even over objection by the accused—appoint a "standby counsel" to aid the accused if and when the accused requests help, and to be available to represent the accused in the event that termination of the defendant's self-representation is necessary.

The right of self-representation is not a license to abuse the dignity of the courtroom. Neither is it a license not to comply with relevant rules of procedural and substantive law. Thus, whatever else may or may not be open to him on appeal, a defendant who elects to represent himself cannot thereafter complain that the quality of his own defense amounted to a denial of "effective assistance of counsel."

In forcing Faretta, under these circumstances, to accept against his will a state-appointed public defender, the California courts deprived him of his constitutional right to conduct his own defense. Accordingly, the judgment before us is vacated, and the case is remanded for further proceedings not inconsistent with this opinion.

CHIEF JUSTICE BURGER, with whom JUSTICE BLACKMUN and JUSTICE REHNQUIST join, dissenting.

* * *

This case * * * is an example of the judicial tendency to constitutionalize what is thought "good." That effort fails on its own terms here, because there is nothing desirable or useful in permitting every accused person, even the most uneducated and inexperienced, to insist upon conducting his own defense to criminal charges. Moreover, there is no constitutional basis for the Court's holding, and it can only add to the problems of an already malfunctioning criminal justice system. I therefore dissent.

The most striking feature of the Court's opinion is that it devotes so little discussion to the matter which it concedes is the core of the decision, that is, discerning an independent basis in the Constitution for the supposed right to represent oneself in a criminal trial. Its ultimate assertion that such a right is tucked between the lines of the Sixth Amendment is contradicted by the Amendment's language and its consistent judicial interpretation.

* * *

[Justice Blackmun also wrote a dissenting opinion in which the Chief Justice and Justice Rehnquist joined. He argued that the procedural problems spawned by the case "will far outweigh whatever tactical advantage the defendant may feel he has gained by electing to represent himself." Referring to the old proverb that "one who is his own lawyer has a fool for a client," Justice Blackmun opined that "the Court * * * now bestows a *constitutional* right on one to make a fool of himself."]

Defendant May Be Prohibited from Pro Se Representation if Not Competent to Conduct a Trial: Indiana v. Edwards

In Indiana v. Edwards, 554 U.S. 164 (2008), Justice Breyer wrote for the Court as it held that neither the Sixth Amendment nor *Faretta* barred a state from insisting that a defendant who is mentally competent to stand trial with counsel—but not mentally competent to conduct a trial himself—proceed to trial with counsel.

After Edwards was charged, issues as to his mental competency were ever-present. In extended proceedings, the trial judge found that the defendant was competent to stand trial under the *Dusky* standard, but that he suffered from schizophrenia. The trial judge concluded that "[w]ith these findings, he's competent to stand trial but I'm not going to find he's competent to defend himself." Counsel represented Edwards who was convicted.

Justice Breyer concluded that the Court's precedents did not provide a clear answer to Edwards' self-representation claim but that three factors supported permitting a state to compel a defendant who is competent to stand trial but not to represent himself to be tried with counsel.

> First, the Court's precedent, while not answering the question, points slightly in the direction of our affirmative answer. [T]he Court's "mental competency" cases set forth a standard that focuses directly upon a defendant's "present ability to consult with his lawyer." These standards assume representation by counsel and emphasize the importance of counsel. They thus suggest (though do not hold) that an instance in which a defendant who would choose to forgo counsel at trial presents a very different set of circumstances, which in our view, calls for a different standard.
>
> * * *
>
> Second, the nature of the problem before us cautions against the use of a single mental competency standard for deciding both (1) whether a defendant who is represented by counsel can proceed to trial and (2) whether a defendant who goes to trial must be permitted to represent himself. Mental illness itself is not a unitary concept. It varies in degree. It can vary over time. It interferes with an individual's functioning at different times in different ways. * * * In certain instances an individual may well be able to satisfy *Dusky's* mental competence standard, for he will be able to work with counsel at trial, yet at the same time he may be unable to carry out the basic tasks needed to present his own defense without the help of counsel.
>
> * * *
>
> Third, in our view, a right of self-representation at trial will not "affirm the dignity" of a defendant who lacks the mental capacity to conduct his defense without the assistance of counsel. To the contrary, given that defendant's uncertain mental state, the spectacle that could well result from his self-representation at trial is at least as likely to prove humiliating as ennobling. Moreover, insofar as a defendant's lack of capacity threatens an improper conviction or sentence, self-representation in that exceptional context undercuts the most basic of the Constitution's criminal law objectives, providing a fair trial. * * *

Indiana also argued a step further—it asked the Court overrule *Faretta.* The Court responded:

> * * * We decline to do so. We recognize that judges have sometimes expressed concern that *Faretta,* contrary to its intent, has led to trials that are unfair. But recent empirical research suggests that such instances are not common. See, *e.g.*, Hashimoto, Defending the Right of Self-Representation: An Empirical Look at the Pro Se Felony Defendant, 85 N. C. L. Rev. 423, 427, 447, 428 (2007) (noting that of the small number of defendants who chose to proceed *pro se*—"roughly 0.3% to 0.5%" of the total, state felony defendants in particular "appear to have achieved higher felony acquittal rates than their represented counterparts in that they were less likely to have been convicted of felonies"). At the same time, instances in which the trial's fairness is in doubt may well be concentrated in the 20 percent or so of self-representation cases where the mental competence of the defendant is also at issue. If so, today's opinion, assuring trial judges the authority to deal appropriately with cases in the latter category, may well alleviate those fair trial concerns.

Justice Scalia, joined by Justice Thomas, dissented and stated that "[i]n my view the Constitution does not permit a State to substitute its own perception of fairness for the defendant's right to make his own case before the jury—a specific right long understood as essential to a fair trial."

Knowing and Intelligent Waiver

In order to exercise the right of self-representation, a defendant must not only be competent; he must know and understand the consequences of waiving the assistance of counsel. See Godinez v. Moran, 509 U.S. 389 (1993) (besides finding competence, the trial court must also "satisfy itself that the waiver of his constitutional rights is knowing and voluntary."). A criminal defendant usually is untrained and unskilled in law and trial procedures. Studies indicate that representation by an attorney substantially improves an accused's chances of receiving a preliminary hearing and release on bail. A defendant represented by an attorney more frequently receives a jury trial, dismissal, or acquittal and, if convicted, more frequently receives a suspended sentence, a relatively short sentence, or probation. Should a defendant be advised of these and other dangers of self-representation before he waives the assistance of counsel? See United States v. Robinson, 913 F.2d 712 (9th Cir.1990) (for a knowing and intelligent waiver, "a criminal defendant must be aware of the nature of the charges against him, the possible penalties, and the dangers and disadvantages of self-representation").

A model inquiry for Federal District Judges to use with defendants who wish to proceed *pro se* is contained in 1 Bench Book for United States District Judges 1.02–2 to –5:

> When a defendant states that he wishes to represent himself, you should ask questions similar to the following:
>
> (a) Have you ever studied law?
>
> (b) Have you ever represented yourself or any other defendant in a criminal action?
>
> (c) You realize, do you not, that you are charged with these crimes: (Here state the crimes with which the defendant is charged.)
>
> (d) You realize, do you not, that if you are found guilty of the crime charged in Count I the court must impose an assessment of at least _______ and could sentence you to as much as _______ years in prison and fine you as much as $_______?
>
> (Then ask him a similar question with respect to each other crime with which he may be charged in the indictment or information.)
>
> (e) You realize, do you not, that if you are found guilty of more than one of those crimes this court can order that the sentences be served consecutively, that is, one after another?
>
> (f) You realize, do you not, that if you represent yourself, you are on your own? I cannot tell you how you should try your case or even advise you as to how to try your case.
>
> (g) Are you familiar with the Federal Rules of Evidence?
>
> (h) You realize, do you not, that the Federal Rules of Evidence govern what evidence may or may not be introduced at trial and, in representing yourself, you must abide by those rules?
>
> (i) Are you familiar with the Federal Rules of Criminal Procedure?
>
> (j) You realize, do you not, that those rules govern the way in which a criminal action is tried in federal court?
>
> (k) You realize, do you not, that if you decide to take the witness stand, you must present your testimony by asking questions of yourself? You cannot just take the stand and tell your story. You must proceed question by question through your testimony.
>
> (*l*) (Then say to the defendant something to this effect):
>
>> I must advise you that in my opinion you would be far better defended by a trained lawyer than you can be by yourself. I think it is unwise of you to try to represent yourself. You are not familiar with the law. You are not familiar with court procedure. You are

not familiar with the rules of evidence. I would strongly urge you not to try to represent yourself.

(m) Now, in light of the penalty that you might suffer if you are found guilty and in light of all of the difficulties of representing yourself, is it still your desire to represent yourself and to give up your right to be represented by a lawyer?

(n) Is your decision entirely voluntary on your part?

(*o*) If the answers to the two preceding questions are in the affirmative, [and in your opinion the waiver of counsel *is* knowing and voluntary,] you should then say something to the following effect:

> "I find that the defendant has knowingly and voluntarily waived his right to counsel. I will therefore permit him to represent himself."

(p) You should consider the appointment of standby counsel to assist the defendant and to replace him if the court should determine during trial that the defendant can no longer be permitted to represent himself.

Failure to conduct a waiver inquiry at least similar to that suggested in the Bench Book has been held reversible error. See United States v. McDowell, 814 F.2d 245 (6th Cir.1987); United States v. Balough, 820 F.2d 1485 (9th Cir.1987) (noting "limited exception" to per se reversal where the record on the whole reveals a knowing and intelligent waiver of counsel). See also Overton v. Mathes, 425 F.3d 518 (8th Cir. 2005) (no requirement to inform defendant that if he proceeds pro se, he will remain in leg restraints during the trial as a security measure).

Faretta Warning?

A defendant who invokes the right to self-representation is at the same time waiving the right to counsel. Conversely, invoking the right to counsel is at the same time waiving the right to self-representation. The defendant must receive detailed warnings, as discussed above, before a waiver of the right to counsel will be found. Is the defendant who invokes a right to counsel entitled to be notified of his right to proceed *pro se* before a waiver of *that* right can be found? In United States v. Martin, 25 F.3d 293 (6th Cir.1994), the court answered this question in the negative:

> While the right to self-representation is related to the right to counsel, [it] is grounded more in considerations of free choice than in fair trial concerns. Thus, the right to self-representation does not implicate constitutional fair trial concerns to the same extent as does an accused's right to counsel. As the constitutional basis of the right to self-representation does not require a knowing and intelligent waiver

> of that right, the district court need not advise a defendant of her right to proceed pro se prior to assertion of such a right.

Accord Munkus v. Furlong, 170 F.3d 980 (10th Cir.1999) (right to counsel is absolute while right to self-representation is subject to many conditions; given the constraints on the right to self-representation, a criminal defendant does not have to be informed of this right).

Requirement of Unequivocal Invocation

Courts have held that a defendant's waiver of the right to assistance of counsel must be "unequivocal." Courts are justifiably concerned that if the *Faretta* right is not clearly invoked, a defendant who ends up representing himself and losing will appeal on the ground that he never really waived his right to counsel. See United States v. Singleton, 107 F.3d 1091 (4th Cir.1997) (noting that a trial court evaluating a defendant's request to represent himself must "traverse a thin line between improperly allowing the defendant to proceed pro se, thereby violating his right to counsel, and improperly having the defendant proceed with counsel, thereby violating his right to self-representation"; noting also that "a skillful defendant could manipulate this dilemma to create reversible error.").

Courts have divided, however, about whether an unequivocal waiver is found when the defendant says that he wants to represent himself because he is in disagreement with defense counsel. Thus, in United States v. Mendez-Sanchez, 563 F.3d 935 (9th Cir. 2009), the court found that the defendant did not unequivocally waive his right to counsel and assert his right to self-representation when he stated that he wished to go to trial, but not with his appointed counsel, and when asked if he wished to represent himself, responded "that would be better than having one of these guys." Compare United States v. Volpontesta, 727 F.3d 666 (7th Cir. 2013), where the court found that

> the record shows that Volpontesta disagreed with his attorneys over trial strategy: specifically, their refusal to file certain motions they deemed frivolous, interview the large number of witnesses Volpontesta requested, and immediately provide Volpontesta with printed copies of discovery materials. The record indicates that Volpontesta's waiver of his right to counsel was a strategic decision he made so that he could pursue the case as he desired. We have held that a defendant's tactical decision to proceed pro se supports a finding of a knowing waiver. We find nothing in the context of Volpontesta's decision to represent himself that indicates that his waiver was anything but knowing and informed."

Of course, when the defendant's only choice is between self-representation and *incompetent* counsel, choice of *pro se* status does not indicate a voluntary waiver of the right to counsel, and reversal is required. Therefore, if the defendant states that he wishes to defend himself because he believes appointed counsel to be incompetent, the trial court must conduct a thorough inquiry into the allegations, and must appoint substitute counsel if the counsel has, up to that point, given ineffective representation under the standards of Strickland v. Washington. See United States v. Silkwood, 893 F.2d 245 (10th Cir.1989) (trial court erred when it failed to conduct inquiry to ensure that the defendant was not forced to make the "Hobson's choice * * * between incompetent or unprepared counsel and appearing *pro se*"); Crandell v. Bunnell, 144 F.3d 1213 (9th Cir.1998) (where counsel did nothing to prepare a defense for two months, his representation fell below an objective standard of reasonableness; the defendant's choice to represent himself, after the court refused to appoint substitute counsel, was therefore involuntary).

Remedy for a Faretta Violation

What is the remedy for the denial of the right to self-representation? Is reversal required even where counsel did a better job at trial than the defendant would have done? In McKaskle v. Wiggins, 465 U.S. 168 (1984), the Court held that the denial of the right to proceed *pro se* was a violation of the defendant's right to personal autonomy. It had nothing to do with the likelihood of a successful outcome at trial. The Court therefore concluded that "the right is either respected or denied; its deprivation cannot be harmless."

Thus, per se reversal is required for a violation of *Gideon,* and for the opposite violation of *Faretta.* Suppose that the defendant's *Faretta* rights are violated by the trial court's appointment of counsel over the defendant's explicit invocation of the right to represent himself. The conviction is therefore reversed. On retrial, the defendant changes his mind and *demands* counsel. Can the trial judge refuse this demand and require the defendant to represent himself, because that is what he wanted to do in the first place? Why should the state have to give him what he so strongly objected to in the first trial? In Johnstone v. Kelly, 812 F.2d 821 (2d Cir.1987), the court stated that counsel must be provided on retrial unless the defendant makes an unequivocal invocation of the right of self-representation. The court explained as follows:

> If Johnstone elects to be represented by counsel at a retrial, it is not quite true, as the State contends, that he will again receive what the State once provided him. Though the State previously provided him with counsel, it denied him the choice whether to have counsel or proceed *pro se.* It is that choice that must be accorded at a retrial * * *.

Right to Self-Representation in Death Penalty Proceedings

In United States v. Davis, 285 F.3d 378 (5th Cir. 2002), the defendant stated that he wanted to represent himself in the penalty phase of the capital trial. He stated that he didn't want to present mitigating evidence. The trial court found that his waiver of the right to counsel was unequivocal and was knowing and intelligent; but it concluded that the *Faretta* right to self-representation did not extend to the penalty phase, and that the defendant's interest in self-representation at that stage was outweighed by the Eighth Amendment requirement that the death penalty not be imposed arbitrarily and capriciously. Counsel was appointed over the defendant's wishes. But the Court of Appeals found this to be error. The court concluded as follows:

> *Faretta* teaches us that a right to self-representation is a personal right. It cannot be impinged upon merely because society, or a judge, may have a different opinion with the accused as to what type of evidence, if any, should be presented in a penalty trial.

The court noted information in the record that Davis was inviting the death penalty, but nonetheless concluded "that Davis has the right to conduct his penalty defense in the manner of his choosing for it is he who suffers the consequences if the defense fails." Does this mean that if the defendant simply wants to give up and be executed, he has the absolute right to do so? Does the right to self-representation justify a state-sponsored suicide?

B. LIMITS ON THE RIGHT OF SELF-REPRESENTATION

The Court in *Faretta* was careful to note that the right to self-representation is not absolute. It is fair to state that courts after *Faretta* have not given the right to self-representation preferred status. Many qualifications on the right have been found reasonable.

1. Timeliness

If the defendant waits until trial, or just before it, to invoke his right to self-representation, then the trial court has the discretion to deny it. See Horton v. Dugger, 895 F.2d 714 (11th Cir.1990) (request to proceed *pro se,* made on first day of trial, held untimely).

2. Disruption of the Court

The majority in *Faretta* recognized that "the right to self-representation is not a license to abuse the dignity of the courtroom." What type of acts can be considered so "obstructionist" that the right to self-representation is lost? In United States v. Flewitt, 874 F.2d 669 (9th Cir.1989), the trial court appointed counsel, against the Flewitts' wishes, because the Flewitts were unprepared at the time of trial, had made excessive and "poorly formulated" discovery motions, and had refused to cooperate with the government in utilizing discovery opportunities. On appeal, they argued that their right to self-representation had been violated, and the government argued that the Flewitts had lost their right due to their "obstructionist" tactics. The court found that the reference in *Faretta* to obstructionist tactics spoke of "disruption in the courtroom." The court noted that the Flewitts' pretrial activity may have been ill-advised and detrimental to them, but "that was their choice to make." Compare Savage v. Estelle, 924 F.2d 1459 (9th Cir.1990) (defendant with a severe speech impediment is found unable to "abide by rules of procedure and courtroom protocol"; therefore, the right to self-representation was properly denied); Overton v. Mathes, 425 F.3d 518 (8th Cir. 2005) (defendant who represents himself can still be shackled if that is a reasonable security measure).

Is the defendant "disruptive" when he makes ridiculous arguments in court, tries to introduce clearly irrelevant evidence, concocts outlandish defenses, and proffers long-winded questions on cross-examination? If such conduct at the trial is enough to be considered "disruptive" under *Faretta*, how many defendants will be permitted to invoke the right to self-representation?

3. Protection of Witnesses

In many cases, the defendant's self-representation is especially unsettling to prosecution witnesses. For example, in a case on Long Island where the defendant Colin Ferguson was tried for shooting commuters on a Long Island Railroad train, Ferguson demanded to represent himself. The shooting victims who survived were therefore subjected to the ordeal of having to be questioned directly in court by the very person who shot them. Can the interests of witnesses ever outweigh the defendant's qualified right to self-representation?

The Fourth Circuit, in Fields v. Murray, 49 F.3d 1024 (4th Cir.1995) (en banc), explored the limitations on a defendant's *Faretta* right to personally question witnesses in the context of a sex crimes prosecution. Fields sought to act, in his words, as "co-counsel" in order to question the alleged sex abuse victims himself, because he "firmly believed these kids cannot look me in the eye and lie to me." The state trial court did not permit Fields to personally cross-examine the young girls who were witnesses against him, but did permit him to write out his questions and give them to his appointed lawyer. Fields was convicted. His *Faretta* claim was rejected by the state appellate courts, on the ground that since he only wanted to cross-examine the prosecution witnesses, and not to represent himself in any other respect, he had failed to unequivocally invoke his right to self-representation.

On habeas review, the court of appeals agreed with the state courts that Field had not unequivocally invoked his right to self-representation. But the court held further that even if Fields had represented himself, he would have had no right under the circumstances to cross-examine the witnesses personally. The court relied on Maryland v. Craig, 497 U.S. 836 (1990), where the Supreme Court held that a defendant's right to face-to-face confrontation could be restricted where such confrontation would traumatize a child-witness. The court of appeals reasoned as follows:

> If a defendant's Confrontation Clause right can be limited in the manner provided in *Craig,* we have little doubt that a defendant's self-representation right can be similarly limited. While the Confrontation Clause right is guaranteed explicitly in the Sixth Amendment, * * * the self-representation right is only implicit in that Amendment. The self-representation right was only firmly established in 1975 in *Faretta,* and then only over the dissent of three justices. Moreover, it is universally recognized that the self-representation right is not absolute.
>
> The State's interest here in protecting child sexual abuse victims from the emotional trauma of being cross-examined by their alleged abuser is at least as great as, and likely greater than, the State's interest in *Craig* of protecting children from the emotional harm of merely having to testify in their alleged abuser's presence. We have little trouble determining, therefore, that the State's interest here was sufficiently important to outweigh Fields' right to cross-examine personally witnesses against him if denial of this cross-examination was necessary to protect the young girls from emotional trauma.

4. Standby Counsel

Faretta indicates that a court may appoint standby counsel, even over the defendant's objection, to aid the defendant and to be available to represent him if self-representation is for some reason terminated. The limits of standby counsel's role were explored in McKaskle v. Wiggins, 465 U.S. 168 (1984), where the Court found that advisory counsel's conduct did not unconstitutionally interfere with Wiggins' right to self-representation. Wiggins first waived his right to counsel, then requested counsel, and finally decided to represent himself. The trial court appointed two attorneys to advise him. Disagreements between counsel and Wiggins occurred and at times counsel quarreled openly with Wiggins. From time-to-time throughout the trial, Wiggins would give in and let standby counsel take over the defense.

Justice O'Connor wrote for the majority and stated that *Faretta* requires that a defendant be given more than just the chance to be heard along with others: he must be given control over the defense. *Faretta* held that the right to self-representation was based on two factors: first, the defendant has the right grounded in personal autonomy to choose to control his own defense; second, self-representation may in some cases be an effective strategy, because it would allow the jury to sympathize with a defendant matched up against overwhelming prosecutorial forces. So while the court has the power to appoint standby counsel against the defendant's wishes, that counsel cannot seize actual control over the defendant's case, or else the first, "core" aspect of the right to self-representation would be violated. And standby counsel cannot without the defendant's consent "destroy the jury's perception that the defendant is representing himself," or else the strategy aspect of the right to self-representation would be undermined. The Court stated that "participation by standby counsel outside the presence of the jury engages only the first of these two limitations." It further noted that "*Faretta* rights are adequately vindicated in proceedings outside the presence of the jury if the *pro se* defendant is allowed to address the court freely" and if "all disagreements between counsel and the *pro se* defendant are resolved in the defendant's favor whenever the matter is one that would normally be left to the discretion of counsel." It found that most of the incidents of which Wiggins complained occurred outside the jury's presence. And it emphasized that all conflicts between Wiggins and his counsel were resolved in Wiggins's favor, although it opined that several incidents in which counsel engaged in acrimonious exchanges with their client were "regrettable."

In dissent, Justice White, joined by Justices Brennan and Marshall, argued that the court of appeals correctly found that standby counsel continuously participated in the trial, disrupted the proceedings, and turned the trial into an ordeal for the jury. He expressed concern about the subtle influences that squabbles between counsel and client can have on the outcome of a case and about the defendant's (not the jury's) perception of fairness, observing that *Faretta* is premised on the importance of the appearance of justice to the accused.

It is worth noting that in later proceedings, Wiggins maintained that he was impermissibly *denied* his right to counsel at his trial, because he had not unequivocally invoked his right to self-representation. The court in Wiggins v. Procunier, 753 F.2d 1318 (5th Cir.1985), rejected his claim. This may give one some perspective on why courts require the right of self-representation to be unequivocally invoked?

Is standby counsel part of the right to effective assistance of counsel under the Sixth Amendment? In United States v. Pollani, 146 F.3d 269 (5th Cir.1998), the Court held that the trial court erred in allowing the defendant to proceed pro se, because the defendant had not unequivocally waived his right to counsel. The government responded that there was no error, because the trial court provided counsel—specifically, standby counsel to assist Pollani at the trial. But the court rejected the government's argument, stating that the appointment of standby counsel "is a tactic for assisting a pro se litigant in vindicating his Sixth Amendment right of self-representation, not a substitute for representation by counsel for a defendant who seeks to exercise his right to counsel."

For a discussion on standby counsel's proper role and how standby counsel can be most effective, see Poulin, The Role of Standby Counsel in Criminal Cases: In the Twilight Zone of the Criminal Justice System, 75 N.Y.U. L.Rev. 676 (2000).

5. Hybrid Counsel and Control of the Defense

Frequently a defendant wants to appear as "co-counsel" or to defend partially *pro se* and partially by counsel. The Court in *Wiggins* held that there is no constitutional right to "hybrid representation"; either the defendant could represent himself or cede control of the defense to counsel, but there is no constitutionally-required middle ground. But the *Wiggins* Court did state that a court could *permit* a hybrid relationship in the exercise of its discretion.

Only a few courts have exercised their discretion and permitted hybrid representation. See, e.g., State v. McCleary, 149 N.J.Super. 77, 373 A.2d 400 (1977). See also United States v. Turnbull, 888 F.2d 636 (9th Cir.1989) ("if the defendant assumes any of the 'core functions' of the lawyer, the hybrid scheme is acceptable only if the defendant has voluntarily waived counsel"). If the costs of the representation do not increase, what purpose, other than to discourage the exercise of *Faretta* rights, is served by denying hybrid representation? See generally Note, The Accused as Co-Counsel: The Case for the Hybrid Defense, 12 Valparaiso L.Rev. 329 (1978).

Ceding Control over the Defense

Unless hybrid representation is granted, a defendant who chooses the right to counsel over the right to self-representation gives up substantial control over the defense. Strategic choices are left to the lawyer; the lawyer can veto the client's wishes as to what defenses can be raised, what arguments will be made, how to cross-examine a witness, etc. See, e.g., United States v. Padilla, 819 F.2d 952 (10th Cir.1987), where the court found no constitutional violation even though counsel refused to structure a defense as the defendant directed. The court stated that "the Sixth Amendment provides no right to counsel blindly following a defendant's instructions."

There are three notable exceptions to counsel's control over the defense. It is ultimately the defendant's decision (1) whether to waive a jury trial, (2) whether to testify, and (3) whether to plead guilty. See, e.g., Stano v. Dugger, 921 F.2d 1125 (11th Cir.1991) (counsel cannot be deemed ineffective where defendant pleads guilty against counsel's advice). See also Rule 1.2 of the Model Rules of Professional Conduct (lawyer shall abide by client's decision "after consultation with the lawyer" as to these three matters).

In Jones v. Barnes, 463 U.S. 745 (1983), the Court held that the Sixth Amendment does not require appointed appellate counsel to raise all nonfrivolous claims on appeal. The Court reasoned that a contrary rule would seriously undermine "the ability of counsel to present the client's case in accord with counsel's professional evaluation." The Court stated that the right of personal autonomy recognized in *Faretta* did not extend to strategic choices once the right to counsel has been invoked. Justice Brennan, joined by Justice Marshall, dissented and argued that the defendant's right to "the assistance of counsel" requires that counsel raise all issues of arguable merit that his client insists upon raising. Justice Blackmun concurred in the result, reasoning that an attorney should, as an ethical, not a constitutional, requirement, raise all nonfrivolous claims upon which his client insists.

Retained Hybrid Counsel?

Does the defendant have the right to hybrid representation if he *retains* counsel? The Court in United States v. Singleton, 107 F.3d 1091 (4th Cir.1997), stated that there was no such right—if the defendant is asking for a constitutional right to control the "lawyer" aspects of the defense, then he must represent himself. The court reasoned as follows:

> A trial judge has broad supervisory power over his courtroom and may within that discretion insist that a trial before him, if orchestrated or guided by an attorney, be presented in accordance with the ethical, professional, and prudential rules of trial conduct. And in order to be so satisfied, the judge has discretion to insist that in the courtroom counsel, not the client, take over completely and act as the spokesperson of the defense's case. Thus, the district court, having properly recognized no constitutional right to have advisory counsel support Singleton in the courtroom during trial, had discretion, should Singleton have retained counsel, to insist that Singleton's case be presented in court either by his attorney or by himself, but not by a combination of the two.

6. Non-Lawyer Representation

A non-lawyer has the constitutional right to represent himself; but he has no constitutional right to have another person represent him if that person is not a lawyer. See, e.g., United States v. Turnbull, 888 F.2d 636 (9th Cir.1989) (" 'Counsel' means 'attorney' "). The reasoning of the court in United States v. Kelley, 539 F.2d 1199 (9th Cir.1976), is typical. Kelley wanted his friend Hurd, a roofer, to serve as trial counsel, but the district court denied that request. The court of appeals held that a defendant has no Sixth Amendment right to delegate his power of self-representation to a non-lawyer.

> The personal autonomy protected by the right of self-representation does not require that a delegation of this right to a non-lawyer be respected. It is true that autonomy is to some extent vindicated by allowing a right to be exercised by a designated proxy. However, such an interpretation of autonomy is at odds with the whole tenor of the *Faretta* opinion and runs counter to the competing institutional interest in seeing that justice is administered fairly and efficiently with the assistance of competent lawyers.

A judge may, in her discretion, permit hybrid representation, but may she allow representation by a layperson?[34] Some courts would say "no," out of concern about unauthorized practice of law. Should what some regard as monopolistic bar practices stand in the way of a defendant's choice of counsel?

7. Self-Representation on Appeal

Does a defendant have the right to proceed pro se on appeal? The Court answered "no" in Martinez v. Court of Appeal of California, 528 U.S. 152 (2000). Justice Stevens, writing for the Court, first distinguished the *Faretta* right to self-representation as grounded in the structure of the Sixth Amendment; he reasoned that Sixth Amendment rights are trial rights, and that the Amendment "does not include any right to appeal." Because the right to appeal is "a creature of statute," it followed that the Sixth Amendment "does not provide any basis for finding a right to self-representation on appeal."

Justice Stevens also noted that even at trial, the right to self-representation is not absolute. The autonomy-based right of self-representation is sometimes outweighed by "the government's interest in ensuring the integrity and efficiency of the trial." Justice Stevens applied this balancing of interests to the appellate context in the following passage:

> In the appellate context, the balance between the two competing interests surely tips in favor of the State. The status of the accused defendant, who retains a presumption of innocence throughout the trial process, changes dramatically when a jury returns a guilty verdict. * * * Considering the change in position from defendant to appellant, the autonomy interests that survive a felony conviction are less compelling than those motivating the decision in *Faretta*. Yet the overriding state interest in the fair and efficient administration of

---

[34] For an argument in favor of a defendant's right to elect lay representation, see Comment, The Criminal Defendant's Sixth Amendment Right to Lay Representation, 52 U.Chi.L.Rev. 460 (1985).

> justice remains as strong as at the trial level. Thus, the States are clearly within their discretion to conclude that the government's interests outweigh an invasion of the appellant's interest in self-representation.

Justice Stevens seemed to go out of his way to cast doubt on the wisdom of the *Faretta* decision, even as applied to trials. He criticized the *Faretta* Court's reliance on the historical grounding of the right to self-representation; he contended that self-representation was an absolute necessity in Colonial times, given the scarcity and widespread incompetence of counsel. But the original reasons for protecting the right to self-representation "do not have the same force when the availability of competent counsel for every indigent defendant has displaced the need—though not always the desire—for self-representation." Justice Stevens also stated that "[n]o one * * * attempts to argue as a rule pro se representation is wise, desirable or efficient" and that "it is representation by counsel that is the standard, not the exception."

Justice Kennedy wrote a short concurring opinion. Justice Breyer also concurred in a short opinion, noting that judges "have sometimes expressed dismay about the practical consequences" of *Faretta*. He cited United States v. Farhad, 190 F.3d 1097 (9th Cir. 1999), in which Judge Reinhardt stated that the right to self-representation frequently "conflicts squarely and inherently with the right to a fair trial." Justice Breyer stated, however, that he had "found no empirical research * * * that might help determine whether, in general, the right to represent oneself furthers, or inhibits, the Constitution's basic guarantee of fairness. And without some strong factual basis for believing that *Faretta's* holding has proved counterproductive in practice, we are not in a position to reconsider the constitutional assumptions that underlie that case."

Subsequently, in his opinion in Indiana v. Edwards, 554 U.S. 164 (2008), Justice Breyer wrote for the Court and explicitly declined to overrule *Faretta*. He expressed some hope that *Edwards*, discussed earlier in this Chapter, might ameliorate some of the practical problems courts have had in dealing with self-representation.

Justice Scalia concurred in the judgment. He objected to what he viewed as an inference in the majority opinion that *Faretta* itself was wrongly decided:

> I have no doubt that the Framers of our Constitution, who were suspicious enough of governmental power—including judicial power—that they insisted upon a citizen's right to be judged by an independent jury of private citizens, would not have found acceptable the compulsory assignment of counsel by the Government to plead a criminal defendant's case. * * *

That asserting the right of self-representation may often, or even usually, work to the defendant's disadvantage is no more remarkable—and no more a basis for withdrawing the right—than is the fact that proceeding without counsel in custodial interrogation, or confessing to the crime, usually works to the defendant's disadvantage. Our system of laws generally presumes that the criminal defendant, after being fully informed, knows his own best interests and does not need them dictated by the State. Any other approach is unworthy of a free people.

CHAPTER 11

SENTENCING

■ ■ ■

I. INTRODUCTION

A. THE IMPORTANCE OF SENTENCING

The most striking thing about the criminal process following a conviction is the relative absence of safeguards to assure evenhanded, fair, and accurate decisionmaking. Yet, the consequences of a sentence are obviously of critical importance. If too short or of the wrong type, it can deprive the law of its effectiveness and result in the premature release of a dangerous criminal. If too severe or improperly conceived, it can lead to injustice, sometimes grave injustice.

B. THE RESPONSIBILITY FOR SENTENCING

Who does sentencing in American courts? The usual answer is that in the federal courts and in most states, judges sentence convicted defendants, while in a small minority of jurisdictions the jury sentences those who are convicted.

But this is a most misleading answer, because the sentencing function hardly is confined to judges and juries. The prosecutor plainly has the power to affect the sentence that will be imposed on an offender through sentence and charge bargaining. Although the prosecutor never will pronounce the sentence in the sense of making it official, the power of the prosecutor to choose the charge upon which to proceed before a judge or jury and to press for either harsh or lenient treatment is substantial. And, of course, because most prosecutions end in a guilty plea, the sentencing power is in effect shifted to some extent to prosecutors (and defendants and their counsel) through plea bargaining.

Of course another source of responsibility for sentencing is the legislature. Because the legislature prescribes punishments and sentencing ranges, it can narrow the choices available to judges and juries. The legislature can also expand, contract or abolish parole schemes, and it can raise or lower overall punishment levels.

The United States Congress has acted in this area by imposing mandatory minimum sentences for a number of crimes (especially drug and firearms crimes). These mandatory minimums limit judicial discretion because they set a floor under which the judge cannot go. Correspondingly, they increase the opportunity of the prosecutor to exercise discretion and bargaining power—a prosecutor can assure that a defendant will avoid a mandatory minimum through charge bargaining.

C. THE DETERMINATION OF SENTENCES

How are sentences determined? For much of the 20th Century, American jurisdictions selected the penalty for any particular crime that the legislature, acting at the time a statute was enacted, thought appropriate. Little effort was made to make the punishments for different crimes consistent with one another or to explain how minimum and maximum punishments were chosen, and the range between the minimum and maximum often was considerable. In 1962, the Model Penal Code endeavored to fashion a more orderly system. It divided felonies into three degrees and specified two kinds of sentencing ranges for each degree—one for ordinary felony offenders, and one for persistent, professional, multiple, or especially dangerous offenders. Numerous states followed the lead of the Code and classified their crimes, although they may have used a different classification scheme than that proposed in the Code. But many jurisdictions have a variety of statutes enacted at different times that define crimes and prescribe punishment levels.

Indeterminate Sentencing

Whether a classification or a more ad hoc system is used to prescribe punishments, many state legislatures have left the sentencing judge (and in a minority of states the sentencing jury) with enormous flexibility in setting a sentence. Sentencing ranges for offenses are often wide, e.g., first degree murder might be punishable by 20 years to life, and arson by 5 to 20 years. If no plea bargain has been made or accepted, a judge doing the sentencing in these states has uncontrolled discretion to choose a sentence within the prescribed range.

The term "*indeterminate sentencing*" describes a scheme in which a prison sentence is subject to reconsideration by a parole or pardon board. Thus, a sentence of incarceration is not determinate because no one may know how much of a sentence a defendant will actually serve. Even in the most indeterminate system, however, there is an element of determinacy, because statutes usually prescribe when an offender becomes eligible for parole—e.g., after serving a quarter or a third of the imposed sentence. It should be noted that agencies like parole boards can protect a defendant to some extent from sentences that are too high, but they have no control over sentences that are too lenient.

Federal Rejection of Indeterminate Sentencing

The Sentencing Reform Act of 1984 established the U.S. Sentencing Commission. The Act and the Commission's Guidelines are discussed later in the Chapter. An important goal of the Guidelines is to limit disparity in sentencing. As will be discussed more fully below, the Guidelines limit the range of sentences based on a list of prescribed factors and considerations. But as we will see, today the Guidelines are advisory only, so judges retain some measure of discretion in setting the sentence. Still, the federal system remains a determinate sentencing system because the sentence imposed upon a defendant is the sentence the defendant actually will serve (although the defendant may get a minor reduction for "good time" or good behavior). There is no parole for those convicted and sentenced under the federal Guideline system.

For an analysis of the developments in American sentencing policy over more than four decades and some perspective on the future, see Michael Tonry, Sentencing in America, 1975–2025, 42 Crime and Justice 141 (2013).

D. CONSTITUTIONAL LIMITATIONS ON PUNISHMENT

The Constitution places a number of limitations on sentencing. The applicable rights include the Sixth Amendment right to jury trial and the Fifth and Fourteenth Amendment right to due process. These guarantees together prohibit the government from shifting elements of the crime (determined at trial beyond a reasonable doubt) to sentencing factors (determined by the sentencing judge by a preponderance of the evidence). These constitutional guarantees were discussed and applied in Apprendi v. New Jersey and subsequent cases that are discussed in detail in Chapter 10. But they are further developed here, with the focus on the impact of *Apprendi* on the Federal Sentencing Guidelines and on state guideline systems.

Other constitutional protections potentially applicable to sentencing are: 1) the Eighth Amendment; 2) the First Amendment; and 3) the Equal Protection Clause. Each will be discussed below after the discussion of the Sixth Amendment and Due Process Clause impact on sentencing.

1. Sentencing Enhancements, the Right to Jury Trial, and the Right to Due Process

Apprendi v. New Jersey and Blakely v. Washington

In Apprendi v. New Jersey, 530 U.S. 466 (2000), the Court held that the defendant's rights to jury trial and due process were violated when he received a sentence that was higher than the maximum sentence provided by the legislature for the crime of which he was convicted. The legislature authorized the enhancement on the basis of a finding by the sentencing judge. The Court stated that "other than the fact of a prior conviction, any fact that increases the penalty for a crime beyond the prescribed statutory maximum must be submitted to a jury, and proved beyond a reasonable doubt." The Court did not, however, challenge the traditional premise that sentencing courts were free to decide facts—and set a sentence on the basis of those facts—so long as the sentence is within the prescribed sentencing range set forth by the legislature for the crime of which the defendant was convicted. The problem in *Apprendi* was that the sentencing judge was *required* by the legislature to sentence beyond the prescribed range, on the basis of facts not determined by the jury.

Subsequently, in Blakely v. Washington, 542 U.S. 296 (2004), the Court struck down a sentencing guidelines system that required judges to enhance a sentence beyond the basic *guideline* applicable to the crime of which the defendant was convicted, on the basis of facts determined by the judge at sentencing and not the jury at trial. The sentence was within a broad statutory range, but the state had imposed mandatory sentencing guidelines to limit judicial discretion within that broad range. So the *Blakely* Court determined that it was the mandatory guidelines range, and not the broader sentencing range, that was relevant for *Apprendi* purposes. *Apprendi* and *Blakely* are discussed more fully in Chapter 10, in the section on constitutionally-based proof requirements.

Apprendi and the Federal Sentencing Guidelines: United States v. Booker

In United States v. Booker, 543 U.S. 220 (2005), the Court, in an opinion by Justice Stevens, held that the Federal Sentencing Guidelines were not distinguishable from the state guidelines found invalid in *Blakely*. That is, to the extent that the Federal Guidelines require the sentencing court to enhance a sentence beyond the guideline for the basic crime for which the defendant was convicted, on the basis of facts (other than prior convictions) found by the sentencing judge, they violate the defendant's right to jury trial and the right to have the government prove all elements of the crime beyond a reasonable doubt. This part of the *Booker* opinion is discussed after *Apprendi* in Chapter 10.

But the most important part of Booker is the remedial opinion by Justice Breyer, i.e., the determination of the appropriate remedy for the unconstitutionality of the Guidelines. Justice Breyer, who dissented from the decision finding the Guidelines unconstitutional, cobbled together a different majority of the Court, and found that the problem with the Guidelines is not that judges sentence on the basis of facts at sentencing. Rather the problem is that those findings trigger *mandatory* *enhancements*, because the Guidelines had been construed up to then to bind district judges in their sentencing decisions. The *Booker* "remedial" majority found that the proper remedy was not to strike down the Guidelines as a whole, but only those parts of the Guidelines that made enhancements mandatory on the basis of judicially-determined facts. Under the remedial opinion, the Sentencing Guidelines become guidelines in the real sense. They are advisory only.

Justice Breyer's opinion for the remedial majority, and portions of the dissenting opinions, are set forth in the section on the Sentencing Guidelines, later in this Chapter.

2. Eighth Amendment Limitations on Sentencing

The Eighth Amendment provides that "[e]xcessive bail shall not be required, nor excessive fines imposed, nor cruel and unusual punishments inflicted." Thus it has two clauses that are potentially relevant to sentencing. The application of the Excessive Fines Clause is considered later in this Chapter in the section on fines as an alternative or supplement to imprisonment. This section considers the limitations established by the Cruel and Unusual Punishment Clause.

Rummell v. Estelle

In Rummel v. Estelle, 445 U.S. 263 (1980), the defendant received a life sentence for obtaining $120.75 by false pretenses. That conviction was his third felony (the other two were fraudulent use of a credit card to obtain $80, and passing a forged check in the amount of $28.36). Justice Rehnquist's majority opinion concluded that it was unnecessary to decide whether a life sentence for a false pretenses conviction was itself cruel and unusual. He noted that the fact it was a third offense, and the possibility of parole after 12 years, made the punishment justifiable and not necessarily as severe as it might first appear. Justice Powell dissented and was joined by Justices Brennan, Marshall, and Stevens. He argued that the possibility of parole should not be considered in deciding the cruel and unusual punishment question because it was not guaranteed, and that the penalty for the offense was unconstitutionally disproportionate in view of the nonviolent nature of the offenses.

Three-Pronged Test for Disproportionality: Solem v. Helm

The Court departed somewhat from *Rummel* in Solem v. Helm, 463 U.S. 277 (1983), as it struck down a life sentence without parole for a seventh nonviolent felony. Helm's crimes were relatively petty and nonviolent (e.g., burglary and driving under the influence). His seventh crime was uttering a "no account" check for $100. Because of his criminal record, Helm was subject to South Dakota's recidivist statute, resulting in a life sentence without parole.

Justice Powell, writing for the Court, rejected the state's argument that the Eighth Amendment proportionality principle was completely inapplicable to felony prison sentences. He explained as follows:

> The constitutional language itself suggests no exception for imprisonment. We have recognized that the Eighth Amendment imposes "parallel limitations" on bail, fines, and other punishments, and the text is explicit that bail and fines may not be excessive. It would be anomalous indeed if the lesser punishment of a fine and the greater punishment of death were both subject to proportionality analysis, but the intermediate punishment of imprisonment were not. * * *
>
> In sum, we hold as a matter of principle that a criminal sentence must be proportionate to the crime for which the defendant has been convicted. Reviewing courts, of course, should grant substantial deference to the broad authority that legislatures necessarily possess in determining the types and limits of punishments for crimes, as well as to the discretion that trial courts possess in sentencing convicted criminals. But no penalty is *per se* constitutional.

Justice Powell declared that proportionality review should be guided by three "objective" factors:

> First, we look to the gravity of the offense and the harshness of the penalty. * * * Of course, a court must consider the severity of the penalty in deciding whether it is disproportionate.
>
> Second, it may be helpful to compare the sentences imposed on other criminals in the same jurisdiction. If more serious crimes are subject to the same penalty, or to less serious penalties, that is some indication that the punishment at issue may be excessive. * * *
>
> Third, courts may find it useful to compare the sentences imposed for commission of the same crime in other jurisdictions. * * *

Applying the three-pronged test to Helm's life sentence without parole, the Court found it constitutionally disproportionate:

> Helm's crime was "one of the most passive felonies a person could commit." It involved neither violence nor threat of violence to any person. * * * His prior offenses, although classified as felonies, were all relatively minor. All were nonviolent and none was a crime against a person. * * * Barring executive clemency, Helm will spend the rest of his life in the state penitentiary. This sentence is far more severe than the life sentence we considered in Rummel v. Estelle. Rummel was likely to have been eligible for parole within 12 years of his initial

confinement, a fact on which the Court relied heavily. * * * Helm has been treated in the same manner as, or more severely than, criminals who have committed far more serious crimes. * * * Helm could not have received such a severe sentence in 48 of the 50 States.

Chief Justice Burger, joined by Justices White, Rehnquist, and O'Connor, dissented in *Solem*. The dissenters objected to the majority's three-pronged test. The Chief Justice viewed the test as unduly intrusive into legislative judgments, and impermissibly subjective:

> By asserting the power to review sentences of imprisonment for excessiveness the Court launches into uncharted and unchartable waters. Today it holds that a sentence of life imprisonment, without the possibility of parole, is excessive punishment for a seventh allegedly "nonviolent" felony. How about the eighth "nonviolent" felony? The ninth? The twelfth? Suppose one offense was a simple assault? Or selling liquor to a minor? Or statutory rape? Or price-fixing? The permutations are endless and the Court's opinion is bankrupt of realistic guiding principles. * * * I can see no limiting principle in the Court's holding.[1]

Limiting Proportionality Review: Harmelin v. Michigan

The Court substantially limited the application of the *Solem* three-factor test of disproportionality in Harmelin v. Michigan, 501 U.S. 957 (1991), although there was no majority opinion for the Court. Harmelin received a life sentence without parole for possession of 672 grams of cocaine. The Michigan statute was unique in the United States in the severity of punishment for possession of large amounts of cocaine. Moreover, the statute prescribed the same penalty, life without parole, for possession as well as for distribution of a large amount of cocaine. Harmelin argued that under the *Solem* three-factor test, his sentence was constitutionally disproportionate.

The Scalia Opinion in Harmelin

Justice Scalia, joined by Chief Justice Rehnquist, engaged in an extensive historical analysis and concluded that "there is no proportionality requirement in the Eighth Amendment." Justice Scalia noted that the proportionality principle in the Eighth Amendment is derived from the term "excessive"; but the term "excessive" is used in the Amendment in reference to bail and to fines, and is pointedly not used to modify the term "punishment."

---

[1] On remand, Helm received a 20 year sentence. Is it constitutionally valid? Would 25 years have been too much?

Justice Scalia concluded that *Solem* should be overruled. He argued that the *Solem* factors were indeterminate and led to judicial subjectivity.

Justice Scalia recognized that the Court had previously invalidated death sentences because of disproportionality. He stated, however, that proportionality review "is one of several respects in which we have held that death is different, and have imposed protections that the Constitution nowhere else provides."

The Kennedy Opinion in Harmelin

Justice Kennedy, joined by Justices O'Connor and Souter, stated that "stare decisis counsels our adherence to the narrow proportionality principle that has existed in our Eighth Amendment jurisprudence for 80 years." Justice Kennedy concluded that the Eighth Amendment "forbids only extreme sentences that are grossly disproportionate to the crime." He stated that the second and third factors of *Solem*—which mandate an intra- and inter-jurisdictional comparative analysis—are appropriate "only in the rare case in which a threshold comparison of the crime committed and the sentence imposed leads to an inference of gross disproportionality."

In Justice Kennedy's view, a comparative analysis was not required for Harmelin's sentence, because life imprisonment without parole was not grossly disproportionate to the crime. Justice Kennedy emphasized the pernicious effects of the drug epidemic, and stated that "the Michigan Legislature could with reason conclude that the threat imposed to the individual and society by possession of this large an amount of cocaine—in terms of violence, crime, and social displacement—is momentous enough to warrant the deterrence and retribution of a life sentence without parole."

The White Dissent in Harmelin

Justice White, joined by Justices Marshall, Blackmun, and Stevens, dissented. Justice White reasoned that the Framers would not have included an excessive fines clause in the Eighth Amendment (which specifically refers to proportionality) without also intending to prevent excessive sentences that could be imposed in lieu of fines. He argued that Justice Scalia's view failed to explain why the words "cruel and unusual punishment" would impose a proportionality requirement in capital cases but not in noncapital cases. He contended that the *Solem* analysis "has worked well in practice" and stated that "Justice Kennedy's abandonment of the second and third factors set forth in *Solem* makes any attempt at an objective proportionality analysis futile."

The Mandatory Sentencing Issue in Harmelin

Harmelin also attacked the constitutionality of his sentence on the ground that, even if it was not disproportionate, it was cruel and unusual to impose a mandatory life sentence without any consideration of mitigating factors. Justice Scalia, writing for five members of the Court on this question, held that if a sentence is not otherwise cruel and unusual, it cannot become so simply because it is mandatory. Justice Scalia recognized that in capital cases, the Eighth Amendment requires individualized sentencing and consideration of all relevant mitigating evidence. He stated, however, that "we have drawn the line of required individualized sentencing at capital cases, and see no basis for extending it further." Justices White, Marshall, Blackmun, and Stevens did not find it necessary to consider Harmelin's mandatory sentencing issue in light of their view that the sentence was constitutionally disproportionate.

Three Strikes Legislation: California v. Ewing

In the following case, the Court applies its *Rummel-Harmelin* line of Eighth Amendment jurisprudence to the California "Three Strikes" law.

EWING V. CALIFORNIA

Supreme Court of the United States, 2003.
538 U.S. 11.

JUSTICE O'CONNOR announced the judgment of the Court and delivered an opinion in which THE CHIEF JUSTICE and JUSTICE KENNEDY join.

In this case, we decide whether the Eighth Amendment prohibits the State of California from sentencing a repeat felon to a prison term of 25 years to life under the State's "Three Strikes and You're Out" law.

* * *

California's three strikes law reflects a shift in the State's sentencing policies toward incapacitating and deterring repeat offenders who threaten the public safety. * * * Between 1993 and 1995, 24 States and the Federal Government enacted three strikes laws. Though the three strikes laws vary from State to State, they share a common goal of protecting the public safety by providing lengthy prison terms for habitual felons.

* * * If the defendant has two or more prior "serious" or "violent" felony convictions, he must receive "an indeterminate term of life imprisonment." Defendants sentenced to life under the three strikes law become eligible for parole on a date calculated by reference to a "minimum term" * * *.

[Ewing was convicted of stealing three golf clubs from a pro shop. He had previously convicted of three burglaries and a robbery. His prior record made him subject to the three strikes law and he was given a sentence from 25 years to life for the stealing conviction.]

* * *

The Eighth Amendment, which forbids cruel and unusual punishments, contains a narrow proportionality principle that applies to noncapital sentences. We have most recently addressed the proportionality principle as applied to terms of years in a series of cases beginning with Rummel v. Estelle.

[Justice O'Connor discusses the facts and analyses in Rummel v. Estelle and Solem v. Helm. She noted that Justice Kennedy's opinion in *Harmelin* was the controlling opinion for determining whether a sentence is disproportionate under the Eighth Amendment—as it was the most limited opinion on which the majority of justices could agree.]

* * * Though three strikes laws may be relatively new, our tradition of deferring to state legislatures in making and implementing such important policy decisions is longstanding.

* * *

When the California Legislature enacted the three strikes law, it made a judgment that protecting the public safety requires incapacitating criminals who have already been convicted of at least one serious or violent crime. Nothing in the Eighth Amendment prohibits California from making that choice. * * * Recidivism has long been recognized as a legitimate basis for increased punishment.

California's justification is no pretext. Recidivism is a serious public safety concern in California and throughout the Nation. * * *

The State's interest in deterring crime also lends some support to the three strikes law. We have long viewed both incapacitation and deterrence as rationales for recidivism statutes. Four years after the passage of California's three strikes law, the recidivism rate of parolees returned to prison for the commission of a new crime dropped by nearly 25 percent.

[Justice O'Connor also cites statistics indicating that the three strikes law has led parolees to leave California, which was a "positive development."]

To be sure, California's three strikes law has sparked controversy. Critics have doubted the law's wisdom, cost-efficiency, and effectiveness in reaching its goals. This criticism is appropriately directed at the legislature, which has primary responsibility for making the difficult policy choices that underlie any criminal sentencing scheme. We do not sit as a "superlegislature" to second-guess these policy choices. * * *

* * *

Against this backdrop, we consider Ewing's claim that his three strikes sentence of 25 years to life is unconstitutionally disproportionate to his offense * * *. We first address the gravity of the offense compared to the harshness of the penalty. At the threshold, we note that Ewing incorrectly frames the issue. * * * Even standing alone, Ewing's theft should not be taken lightly. His crime was certainly not one of the most passive felonies a person could commit. * * * Theft of $1,200 in property is a felony under federal law, and in the vast majority of States. * * *

In weighing the gravity of Ewing's offense, we must place on the scales not only his current felony, but also his long history of felony recidivism. Any other approach would fail to accord proper deference to the policy judgments that find expression in the legislature's choice of sanctions. * * * His prior "strikes" were serious felonies including robbery and three residential burglaries. To be sure, Ewing's sentence is a long one. But it reflects a rational legislative judgment, entitled to deference, that offenders who have committed serious or violent felonies and who continue to commit felonies must be incapacitated. * * * Ewing's is not "the rare case in which a threshold comparison of the crime committed and the sentence imposed leads to an inference of gross disproportionality." *Harmelin* (Kennedy, J., concurring in part and concurring in judgment).

We hold that Ewing's sentence of 25 years to life in prison, imposed for the offense of felony grand theft under the three strikes law, is not grossly disproportionate and therefore does not violate the Eighth Amendment's prohibition on cruel and unusual punishments. * * *

JUSTICE SCALIA, concurring in the judgment.

In my concurring opinion in Harmelin v. Michigan, I concluded that the Eighth Amendment's prohibition of "cruel and unusual punishments" was aimed at excluding only certain *modes* of punishment, and was not a "guarantee against disproportionate sentences." Out of respect for the principle of *stare decisis*, I might nonetheless accept the contrary holding of Solem v. Helm—that the Eighth Amendment contains a narrow proportionality principle—if I felt I could intelligently apply it. This case demonstrates why I cannot.

Proportionality—the notion that the punishment should fit the crime—is inherently a concept tied to the penological goal of retribution. It becomes difficult even to speak intelligently of "proportionality," once deterrence and rehabilitation are given significant weight—not to mention giving weight to the purpose of California's three strikes law: incapacitation. * * * Perhaps the plurality should revise its terminology, so that what it reads into the Eighth Amendment is not the unstated proposition that all punishment should be reasonably proportionate to the gravity of the offense, but rather the unstated proposition that all punishment should reasonably pursue the multiple purposes of the criminal law. That formulation would make it clearer than ever, of course, that the plurality is not applying law but evaluating policy.

Because I agree that petitioner's sentence does not violate the Eighth Amendment's prohibition against cruel and unusual punishments, I concur in the judgment.

JUSTICE THOMAS, concurring in the judgment.

I agree with JUSTICE SCALIA'S view that the proportionality test announced in Solem v. Helm, is incapable of judicial application. Even were *Solem*'s test perfectly clear, however, I would not feel compelled by *stare decisis* to apply it. In my view, the Cruel and Unusual Punishments Clause of the Eighth Amendment contains no proportionality principle.

Because the plurality concludes that petitioner's sentence does not violate the Eighth Amendment's prohibition on cruel and unusual punishments, I concur in the judgment.

JUSTICE STEVENS, with whom JUSTICE SOUTER, JUSTICE GINSBURG and JUSTICE BREYER join, dissenting.

* * *

* * * I think it clear that the Eighth Amendment's prohibition of "cruel and unusual punishments" expresses a broad and basic proportionality principle that takes into account all of the justifications for penal sanctions. It is this broad proportionality principle that would preclude reliance on any of the justifications for punishment to support, for example, a life sentence for overtime parking.

JUSTICE BREYER, with whom JUSTICE STEVENS, JUSTICE SOUTER, and JUSTICE GINSBURG join, dissenting.

* * *

Ewing's sentence on its face imposes one of the most severe punishments available upon a recidivist who subsequently engaged in one of the less serious forms of criminal conduct. I do not deny the seriousness of shoplifting, which an *amicus curiae* tells us costs retailers in the range of $30 billion annually. But consider that conduct in terms of the factors that this Court mentioned in *Solem*—the "harm caused or threatened to the victim or society," the "absolute magnitude of the crime," and the offender's "culpability." In respect to all three criteria, the sentence-triggering behavior here ranks well toward the bottom of the criminal conduct scale. * * *[2]

Life Without Parole Sentence Imposed on a Person Who Was Less than 18 at the Time of the Crime: Graham v. Florida and Miller v. Alabama

In the cases of Graham v. Florida, 560 U.S. 48 (2010), and Miller v. Alabama, 567 U.S. 460 (2012), the Court held that the Eighth Amendment imposed limitations on life without parole sentences for defendants who were under 18 years old when they committed the crime charged. *Graham* involved a defendant who, when 16 years old, committed a violent robbery of a restaurant—and while on probation for that crime, committed an armed robbery of a private home. He was sentenced to life without parole. Justice Kennedy, writing for the Court, applied his own "controlling" opinion in *Harmelin,* and stated categorically that the Eighth Amendment "prohibits the imposition of a life without parole sentence on a juvenile offender who did not commit homicide." Justice Kennedy relied on the following principles for this conclusion:

- while many jurisdictions statutorily permit sentences like that in this case, "an examination of *actual* sentencing practices * * * discloses a consensus" against the use of life without parole sentences for juveniles who did not commit homicide.
- "parts of the brain involved in behavior control continue to mature through late adolescence" and "because juveniles have lessened culpability they are less deserving of the most severe punishments."
- "defendants who do not kill, intend to kill, or foresee that life will be taken are categorically less deserving of the most serious forms of punishment than are murderers."
- "life without parole sentences share some characteristics with death sentences that are shared by no other sentences" as the sentence "deprives the convict of the most basic liberties without giving hope of restoration, except perhaps by executive clemency—the remote possibility of which does not mitigate the harshness of the sentence."

---

[2] See also the companion case of Lockyer v. Andrade, 538 U.S. 63 (2003), rejecting an Eighth Amendment challenge to a sentence of two consecutive terms of 25 years to life for stealing videotapes worth about $150 from two stores. Andrade had been convicted previously of three counts of residential burglary. The Supreme Court, in an opinion by Justice O'Connor for five members of the Court, held that the state court's interpretation of the Eighth amendment was neither "contrary to" nor "an unreasonable application of clearly established federal law"—which are the relevant standards for reviewing state court determinations on habeas corpus review.

- "Life without parole is an especially harsh punishment for a juvenile" because "a juvenile offender will on average serve more years and a greater percentage of his life in prison than an adult offender."
- "retribution does not justify imposing the second most severe penalty on the less culpable juvenile nonhomicide offender."
- "Deterrence does not justify the sentence either" because "juveniles' lack of maturity and underdeveloped sense of responsibility often result in impetuous and ill-considered actions and decisions" so "they are less likely to take a possible punishment into consideration when making decisions."
- "incapacitation may be a legitimate penological goal sufficient to justify life without parole in other contexts" but it is dependent on an assumption that the defendant is incorrigible, and "incorrigibility is inconsistent with youth. * * * A life without parole sentence improperly denies the juvenile offender a chance to demonstrate growth and maturity."
- "A sentence of life imprisonment without parole * * * cannot be justified by the goal of rehabilitation. The penalty forswears altogether the rehabilitative ideal."

Justice Kennedy clarified that the Court was not precluding the possibility that a person who committed a nonhomicide crime as a juvenile might spend his life in prison.

> A state is not required to guarantee eventual freedom to a juvenile convicted of a nonhomicide crime. What the State must do, however, is give defendants like Graham some meaningful opportunity to obtain release based on demonstrated maturity and rehabilitiation.

Chief Justice Roberts wrote a lengthy opinion concurring in the judgment in *Graham*. He agreed that Graham's sentence was cruel and unusual, because it failed under the *Harmelin* factors: Graham was less culpable and his crime less serious than other adult defendants who received sentences of life without parole, in both Florida and other jurisdictions. But the Chief Justice objected to the Court's bright-line rule, because it "ignores the fact that some nonhomicide crimes * * * are especially heinous and grotesque, and thus may be deserving of more severe punishment."

Justice Thomas dissented in *Graham* in an opinion joined in full by Justice Scalia and in part by Justice Alito. Justices Thomas and Scalia reiterated their position that the Cruel and Unusual Punishments clause was not originally understood to provide proportionality in sentencing. The three dissenters contended that the majority of states permit life without parole sentences for nonhomicide convictions of juveniles. They concluded as follows:

> The fact that the Court categorically prohibits life without parole sentences for juvenile nonhomicide offenders in the face of an overwhelming legislative majority in favor of leaving that sentencing option available under certain cases simply illustrates how far beyond any cognizable constitutional principle the Court has reached to ensure that its own sense of morality and retributive justice pre-empts that of the people and their representatives.

Justice Alito wrote a short dissenting opinion in *Graham.*

In Miller v. Alabama, the Court considered the constitutionality of *mandatory* life without parole sentences for juveniles convicted of homicide. The Court was reviewing two cases in which 14-year-olds were convicted of murder and sentenced to a mandatory term of life without parole. The Court, in an opinion by Justice Kagan for five Justices, held that the Eighth Amendment forbids a sentencing scheme that *mandates* life without parole sentences for juvenile homicide offenders. Justice Kagan essentially found that the analysis in *Graham*—particularly its reliance on the fact that juveniles were less culpable than adults and a life without parole sentence is more serious because of its comparative length—applied equally to juvenile homicide offenders. She explained as follows:

> Mandatory life without parole for a juvenile precludes consideration of his chronological age and its hallmark features—among them, immaturity, impetuosity, and failure to appreciate risks and consequences. It prevents taking into account the family and home environment that surrounds him—and from which he cannot usually extricate himself—no matter how brutal or dysfunctional. It neglects the circumstances of the homicide offense, including the extent of his participation in the conduct and the way familial and peer pressures may have affected him. Indeed, it ignores that he might have been charged and convicted of a lesser offense if not for incompetencies associated with youth—for example, his inability to deal with police officers or prosecutors (including on a plea agreement) or his incapacity to assist his own attorneys.

Justice Kagan summed up and noted that the Court had not held that life without parole could *never* be imposed on a juvenile who committed a homicide:

> We therefore hold that the Eighth Amendment forbids a sentencing scheme that mandates life in prison without possibility of parole for juvenile offenders. By making youth (and all that accompanies it) irrelevant to imposition of that harshest prison sentence, such a scheme poses too great a risk of disproportionate punishment. Because that holding is sufficient to decide these cases,

we do not consider [the] alternative argument that the Eighth Amendment requires a categorical bar on life without parole for juveniles, or at least for those 14 and younger. But given all we have said * * * about children's diminished culpability and heightened capacity for change, we think appropriate occasions for sentencing juveniles to this harshest possible penalty will be uncommon. * * * Although we do not foreclose a sentencer's ability to make that judgment in homicide cases, we require it to take into account how children are different, and how those differences counsel against irrevocably sentencing them to a lifetime in prison.

Chief Justice Roberts dissented in *Miller,* in an opinion joined by Justices Scalia, Thomas, and Alito. His major argument was that the punishment could not be cruel and unusual under the Eighth Amendment because it was not unusual:

The parties agree that nearly 2,500 prisoners are presently serving life sentences without the possibility of parole for murders they committed before the age of 18. The Court accepts that over 2,000 of those prisoners received that sentence because it was mandated by a legislature. And it recognizes that the Federal Government and most States impose such mandatory sentences. Put simply, if a 17-year-old is convicted of deliberately murdering an innocent victim, it is not "unusual" for the murderer to receive a mandatory sentence of life without parole. That reality should preclude finding that mandatory life imprisonment for juvenile killers violates the Eighth Amendment.

Justice Thomas wrote a separate dissenting opinion joined by Justice Scalia, and Justice Alito wrote a dissent joined by Justice Scalia.

Life Without Parole Sentence Without a Finding of Impossibility of Rehabilitation: Jones v. Mississippi

In Jones v. Mississippi, 141 S.Ct. 1307 (2021), the Could held that the Eighth Amendment requires neither an explicit or implicit finding of permanent incorrigibility before sentencing a juvenile offender to life without parole. In an opinion written by Justice Kavanaugh, the Court held that discretionary sentencing systems that provide the opportunity for courts to take account of an offender's youth and attendant circumstances are both "constitutionally necessary and constitutionally sufficient." The Court left to state courts and legislators the task of imposing additional sentencing limits in cases involving defendants under 18 at the time of the crime.

Justice Thomas wrote a concurring opinion in *Jones* arguing that Miller v. Louisiana should not be applied retroactively to cases on collateral review, as it was in this case. Justice Sotomayor wrote a dissenting opinion joined by Justices Breyer and Kagan, arguing that the majority had given short shrift to *Miller v. Alabama*. In her view, *Miller* requires a sentencing judge to make an explicit finding that a juvenile offender is "one of those rare children whose crimes reflect irreparable corruption" before imposing a sentence of life without parole.

NOTE ON THE DEATH PENALTY

As the Court recognized in *Harmelin*, the Eighth Amendment does impose proportionality limitations on the use of the death penalty. The complexities of the death penalty are often considered in a separate law school course. A full treatment of the Supreme Court's complicated jurisprudence on the subject is beyond the scope of this Book. What follows is a short summary of the framework that the Court has established for regulating the death penalty under the Eighth Amendment.

1. A death sentence cannot be imposed arbitrarily. Furman v. Georgia, 408 U.S. 238 (1972). The Eighth Amendment requires each defendant to be considered individually, and that the death penalty be "narrowed" to apply only to those who truly merit such severe and final punishment. Gregg v. Georgia, 428 U.S. 153 (1976) (statute upheld where it provided that the sentencer could not impose a death sentence without stating in writing that it found an aggravating circumstance beyond a reasonable doubt).

2. A death sentence cannot be imposed on the basis of aggravating circumstances that are vague, overbroad, or ill-defined. See Maynard v. Cartwright, 486 U.S. 356 (1988), where the Court struck down death sentences based on a finding that the defendant had committed a murder in an "especially heinous, atrocious or cruel" manner. The Court held that this aggravating circumstance was impermissibly broad and vague. It did not sufficiently channel the sentencer's discretion, and thus presented the risk of arbitrary enforcement of the death penalty. Overbroad statutory aggravators can be "narrowed", however, by judicial construction that provides more definition.

3. Another line of cases concerns a different "narrowing" principle—that the death penalty should only be applied to the most egregious types of crime. See, e.g., Enmund v. Florida, 458 U.S. 782 (1982) (capital sanction for aiding and abetting a murder without regard to the intent of the defendant was cruel and unusual punishment); Coker v. Georgia, 433 U.S. 584 (1977) (rape not resulting in death could not be punished by death).

4. The *Furman-Gregg* line of cases deals with arbitrary imposition of the death penalty. The concern is that the sentencer will have too much discretion to choose among similarly situated defendants. The solution to the *Gregg* problem is to control the sentencer by guiding discretion through particularized aggravating circumstances that control the sentencing determination. In Lockett v. Ohio, 438 U.S. 586 (1978), the Court expressed a different concern about the death penalty—that the sentencer would not consider the individual *mitigating* characteristics of each defendant. *Lockett* requires that a defendant in a capital sentencing proceeding must have

reasonably free reign to introduce, *and to require the sentencer to consider*, relevant evidence in mitigation of a death sentence. The Court declared that the sentencer "in all but the rarest kind of capital case, [must] not be precluded from considering *as a mitigating factor*, any aspect of a defendant's character or record and any of the circumstances of the offense that the defendant proffers as a basis for a sentence less than death." However, the state is permitted to structure the sentencer's consideration of mitigating evidence in reasonable ways. Compare Saffle v. Parks, 494 U.S. 484 (1990) (no Eighth Amendment violation in permitting judge to instruct jury to caution against giving undue sympathy to the defendant), with McKoy v. North Carolina, 494 U.S. 433 (1990) (Eighth Amendment prohibits a state from requiring mitigating circumstances to be found unanimously).

Justice Stevens provides a useful summary of the Court's death penalty jurisprudence in his opinion in Graham v. Collins, 506 U.S. 461 (1993):

> [T]he Court's capital punishment cases have erected four important safeguards against arbitrary imposition of the death penalty. First, * * * we have concluded that death is an impermissible punishment for certain offenses. Specifically, neither the crime of rape nor the crime of unintentional homicide * * * may now support a death sentence. See Enmund v. Florida; Coker v. Georgia.
>
> Second, as a corollary to the proportionality requirement, the Court has demanded that the States narrow the class of individuals eligible for the death penalty, either through statutory definitions of capital murder, or through statutory specification of aggravating circumstances. This narrowing requirement, like the categorical exclusion of the offense of rape, has significantly minimized the risk of racial bias in the sentencing process. * * *
>
> Third, the Court has condemned the use of aggravating factors so vague that they actually enhance the risk that unguided discretion will control the sentencing determination. See, e.g., Maynard v. Cartwright (invalidating "especially heinous, atrocious, or cruel" aggravating circumstance); Godfrey v. Georgia (invalidating "outrageously or wantonly vile, horrible or inhuman" aggravating circumstance). An aggravating factor that invites a judgment as to whether a murder committed by a member of another race is especially "heinous" or "inhuman" may increase, rather than decrease, the chance of arbitrary decisionmaking, by creating room for the influence of personal prejudices. * * *
>
> Finally, at the end of the process, when dealing with the narrow class of offenders deemed death-eligible, we insist that the sentencer be permitted to give effect to all relevant mitigating evidence offered by the defendant, in making the final sentencing determination. See, e.g., Lockett v. Ohio. * * * [O]nce the class of death-eligible offenders is

sufficiently narrowed, consideration of relevant, individual mitigating circumstances in no way compromises the rationalizing principle of Furman v. Georgia. To the contrary, the requirement that sentencing decisions be guided by consideration of relevant mitigating evidence reduces still further the chance that the decision will be based on irrelevant factors such as race. *Lockett* itself illustrates this point. A young black woman, Lockett was sentenced to death because the Ohio statute "did not permit the sentencing judge to consider, as mitigating factors, her character, prior record, age, lack of specific intent to cause death, and her relatively minor part in the crime." When such relevant facts are excluded from the sentencing determination, there is more, not less, reason to believe that the sentencer will be left to rely on irrational considerations like racial animus.

There is much more to the Court's death penalty jurisprudence than this thumbnail sketch can provide. For more on this difficult subject, see the Symposium on the death penalty, 83 Cornell L.Rev. 1431–1820 (1998); Steiker and Steiker, Sober Second Thoughts: Reflections on Two Decades of Constitutional Regulation of Capital Punishment, 109 Harv.L.Rev. 355 (1995); Sundby, The *Lockett* Paradox: Reconciling Guided Discretion and Unguided Mitigation in Capital Sentencing, 38 UCLA L.Rev. 1147 (1991).

For other developments in death penalty jurisprudence, *see, e.g.,* Atkins v. Virginia, 536 U.S. 304 (2002) (execution of a mentally retarded defendant is a cruel and unusual punishment prohibited by the Eighth Amendment); Ring v. Arizona, 536 U.S. 584 (2002) (Sixth Amendment right to jury trial requires that statutory aggravating factors must be determined by the jury, not the judge); Roper v. Simmons, 534 U.S. 551 (2005) (Eighth Amendment prohibits execution of a person who was under 18 years old at the time of the crime).

3. The First Amendment

Enhancement for Hate Crimes: Wisconsin v. Mitchell

In Wisconsin v. Mitchell, 508 U.S. 476 (1993), the Court explored the extent of First Amendment limitations on punishment. Mitchell, an African-American, was convicted of aggravated battery for his part in the beating of a young white boy. The maximum sentence for aggravated battery was two years' imprisonment. However, the jury found that Mitchell intentionally selected his victim on account of the victim's race. Under a Wisconsin "hate crime" law, this finding resulted in an enhanced sentence of up to seven years' imprisonment; Mitchell received a four-year prison term for the aggravated battery. Mitchell argued that the enhancement statute violated his First Amendment rights because it resulted in punishment for his bigoted beliefs. But his argument was rejected by a unanimous Court in an opinion by Chief Justice Rehnquist.

The Chief Justice noted that "[t]raditionally, sentencing judges have considered a wide variety of factors in addition to evidence bearing on guilt in determining what sentence to impose," and that the defendant's "motive for committing the offense is one important factor." He observed that the First Amendment would prohibit a sentencer from taking a defendant's "abstract beliefs" into consideration in imposing a sentence. However, he declared that the enhancement of Mitchell's sentence was not based merely on his abstract beliefs. Rather, Mitchell received an enhanced sentence because Wisconsin had made an assessment that *conduct* motivated by racial animus was more harmful than conduct that was not.

Mitchell also argued that the enhancement statute was unconstitutional because it chilled free speech. His argument proceeded as follows: the prosecution may use statements made by the defendant on occasions unrelated to the crime charged (e.g., at meetings), in order to prove a racial animus in committing the charged crime; therefore, a person concerned about the possibility of an enhanced sentence, should they commit a crime in the future, would have to refrain from expressing ideas reflecting a racial bias. The Court rejected Mitchell's argument, concluding that the "chill" he envisioned was "attenuated and unlikely." The Chief Justice also declared that the First Amendment "does not prohibit the evidentiary use of speech to establish the elements of a crime or to prove motive or intent."

4. The Equal Protection Clause

Individual sentencing determinations are rarely the subject of equal protection claims—if for no other reason than they would be virtually impossible to prove. Some broad attacks have been launched at certain statutes or guidelines that are perceived to have a disproportionate effect on racial minorities. One target of attack was the federal statute and accompanying Sentencing Guideline providing for a far higher sentence for crack distribution than for distribution of a similar amount of powder cocaine. The equal protection arguments were addressed in United States v. Thurmond, 7 F.3d 947 (10th Cir.1993), a case in which the defendants were sentenced to 87 months and 97 months of imprisonment respectively, for distributing six grams of crack cocaine:

> Defendants argue that their national statistics, which indicate that 95% of federal cocaine base prosecutions are brought against African-Americans while 40% of federal cocaine powder prosecutions are brought against whites, are so stark, that this case is one of those rare cases * * * wherein statistical evidence alone is enough to prove that Congress had a racially discriminatory purpose in enacting the provisions, as well as in leaving them intact. * * *

* * *

However, * * * there is ample evidence of Congress's reasons, other than race, for providing harsher penalties for offenses involving cocaine base. * * * [T]he government offered evidence that Congress provided for enhanced penalties for cocaine base offenses because cocaine base (1) has a more rapid onset of action, (2) is more potent, (3) is more highly addictive, (4) is less expensive than cocaine powder, and (5) has widespread availability. [Citing to legislative history]. * * * Finally, cocaine base is simply a different drug than cocaine powder, with a different chemical composition; as a result, Congress can justifiably provide for different penalties for each. Therefore, because reasons exist, other than race, for enhanced penalties for cocaine base offenses, we conclude that Defendants' statistics of disproportionate impact are not sufficient * * * to demonstrate that Congress or the Sentencing Commission had a discriminatory purpose * * *.

After the Court's decision in United States v. Booker, supra, the Sentencing Guidelines are advisory and not mandatory. So a sentencing court is not *required* to sentence more severely for crack than powder. The Supreme Court has made it clear that sentencing judges may depart from the crack guideline. Kimbrough v. United States, 552 U.S. 85 (2007). Moreover, the disparity has been lessened by subsequent amendments to the Guidelines, and by the Fair Sentencing Act of 2010 (Public Law 111–220), signed into law by President Obama on August 3, 2010 (reducing the disparity between the amount of crack cocaine and powder cocaine needed to trigger certain United States federal criminal penalties from a 100:1 weight ratio to an 18:1 weight ratio and eliminating the five-year mandatory minimum sentence for simple possession of crack cocaine).

E. SENTENCING ALTERNATIVES OTHER THAN INCARCERATION

What sentencing options other than traditional imprisonment are available? The answer is that a number of options exist; some are substitutes for imprisonment, and others amount to punishment in addition to imprisonment.

1. Fines and Forfeitures

Problems in Using a Fine as a Sanction

One of the most familiar alternatives is the fine. But there are several problems with the fine as a sanction. One problem is that it works better for middle-class or wealthier defendants than poorer defendants. Should ability to pay dictate the choice between jail and an alternative such as a fine? Should a fine be added to a prison sentence as punishment simply because the defendant can afford to pay it?

Another problem is that judges often are not well enough informed about a defendant's ability to pay or to earn money to arrive at a realistic fine. Many defendants find that they are unable to pay the fine that the judge sets. A related problem is what to do with the defendant who attempts to pay the fine, but is unable to do so. A further problem is designating the kinds of offenses that are appropriately punished by fines. Is it ever appropriate to respond to violent crime with a fine? Are fines more appropriate for nonviolent theft crimes? Another issue is that the proceeds of a fine go to the government, usually to defray the expenses of law enforcement. Is there a concern that the government may have an economic incentive to seek an unduly harsh fine? Finally, there is the question whether corporations should be penalized by fine in a different and harsher manner than natural persons, on the ground that corporations cannot be incarcerated. See 18 U.S.C. § 3571(c) and (d), providing that an organizational defendant that has been found guilty of a felony may be sentenced to pay a maximum statutory fine of not more than the greater of $500,000, twice the gross gain, or twice the gross loss.

Indigents and Fines

Williams v. Illinois, 399 U.S. 235 (1970), and Tate v. Short, 401 U.S. 395 (1971), protect indigents against oppressive fine systems. In *Williams,* the Court held that an indigent defendant was denied equal protection when he was imprisoned beyond the maximum term authorized by statute because of an inability to pay a fine and court costs. Tate v. Short held that an indigent defendant could not be imprisoned for failure to pay a fine when the state statute made traffic offenses punishable by fine only. Thus, imposing a fine is not the problem—imprisonment for inability to pay the fine is the problem.

The Supreme Court again considered the permissible treatment of indigents unable to pay fines in Bearden v. Georgia, 461 U.S. 660 (1983). Bearden was convicted of burglary and theft. Under the state's first offender statute, the trial judge did not enter a judgment of guilt, but deferred further proceedings and sentenced Bearden to three years on probation for the burglary charge and a concurrent one year on probation for the theft charge. As a condition of probation he ordered Bearden to pay a $500 fine and $250 restitution. Bearden borrowed $200 to make the initial payments required by the order, but was unable to make further payments. Subsequently, the court revoked Bearden's probation for failure to pay the balance of the fine and restitution, entered a judgment of conviction, and sentenced him to serve the remaining portion of the probationary period (more than two years) in prison.

Justice O'Connor's opinion for the Court observed that "[a] defendant's poverty in no way immunizes him from punishment." Thus, a state court may consider a defendant's entire background including employment and financial resources in arriving at a sentence. She reasoned further that a state could imprison a probationer who wilfully refused to pay a fine or restitution or to make bona fide efforts to seek employment or borrow money to pay a fine; but that "if the probationer has made all reasonable efforts to pay the fine or restitution, and yet cannot do so through no fault of his own, it is fundamentally unfair to revoke probation automatically without considering whether adequate alternative methods of punishing the defendant are available." Alternatives might include an extension of time to make payments, a reduction of the fine, or a requirement of some form of public service.

Justice White, joined by Chief Justice Burger and Justices Powell and Rehnquist, concurred in the judgment. He argued that nothing in the Constitution prohibited a state from making "a good-faith effort to impose a jail sentence that in terms of the state's sentencing objectives will be roughly equivalent to the fine and restitution that the defendant failed to pay." He found no such effort by the trial court in this case.

Forfeiture of the Proceeds of Crime

A variation on the fine is forfeiture of property used in or the proceeds of criminal activity. Many federal and state laws provide for forfeiture upon conviction, and other statutes provide for civil forfeiture, which does not require a conviction. Congress has provided that a court must order forfeiture where appropriate in addition to imposing other sanctions upon a defendant. 18 U.S.C. § 3554. As part of its Comprehensive Crime Control Act of 1984, Congress enacted the Comprehensive Forfeiture Act of 1984, which expands the forfeiture provisions in racketeering and drug cases. See 28 U.S.C. § 881. For a discussion of how these forfeiture provisions operate, see Caplin & Drysdale v. United States, discussed in Chapter 10.

The government's economic interest in forfeiture is undeniable. At the federal level, all assets seized by the Department of Justice go into its Asset Forfeiture Fund, which the Attorney General is authorized to use for law enforcement purposes. 28 U.S.C. § 524(c). This has led Attorneys General in recent years to urge United States attorneys to increase the volume of forfeitures in order to meet the Department of Justice's annual budget target. As one court put it: "Forfeitures, in effect, impose an impressive levy on wrongdoers to finance, in part, the law enforcement efforts of both the state and national governments." United States v. Real Property Located in El Dorado, 59 F.3d 974 (9th Cir.1995).

Constitutional Limitations on Forfeiture: Alexander v. United States

In Alexander v. United States, 509 U.S. 544 (1993), the Court considered some constitutional questions arising from an application of the RICO forfeiture statute, 18 U.S.C. § 1963. Alexander was found guilty of 17 counts of obscenity and three counts of violating RICO, arising from the sale of obscene magazines and tapes. Alexander owned more than a dozen stores and theaters dealing in sexually explicit materials; the jury found that four magazines and three videotapes sold through Alexander's retail stores were obscene. Alexander was sentenced to six years in prison, fined $100,000, and ordered to pay the costs of prosecution, incarceration, and supervised release. The District Court then reconvened the same jury and conducted a forfeiture proceeding pursuant to 18 U.S.C. § 1963(a)(2). At this proceeding, the government sought forfeiture of the entirety of Alexander's interest in the stores and theaters. The jury found that Alexander had an interest in 10 pieces of commercial real estate and 31 current or former businesses, all of which had been used to conduct his racketeering enterprise. The District Court ultimately ordered Alexander to forfeit his wholesale and retail businesses, and all the assets thereof, as well as almost $9 million dollars acquired through racketeering activity.

Alexander argued that the forfeiture order, considered together with his six-year prison term and $100,000 fine, was disproportionate to the gravity of his offenses and thus violated the Eighth Amendment. The lower court dismissed this claim by reasoning that the Eighth Amendment does not require any proportionality review of a sentence less than life imprisonment without the possibility of parole. But the Chief Justice rejected the lower court's analysis as misdirected to the Cruel and Unusual Punishments Clause of the Eighth Amendment, whereas Alexander's claim was more properly based in the Excessive Fines Clause. The Chief Justice explained as follows:

> Unlike the Cruel and Unusual Punishments Clause, which is concerned with matters such as the duration or conditions of confinement, the Excessive Fines Clause limits the Government's power to extract payments, whether in cash or kind, as punishment for some offense. The in personam criminal forfeiture at issue here is clearly a form of monetary punishment no different, for Eighth Amendment purposes, from a traditional "fine."

The Court remanded for a determination of whether the forfeiture in combination with the other penalties was constitutionally disproportionate under the Excessive Fines Clause. On remand, the court of appeals found no constitutional infirmity in the forfeiture. It distinguished forfeiture of the proceeds of a crime from property that is used for criminal activity. The forfeiture of proceeds from an illegal enterprise "is not considered punishment subject to the excessive fines analysis because the forfeiture of proceeds simply deprives the owner of the fruits of his criminal activity." The court found that the amount of proceeds from Alexander's racketeering activity amounted to almost $9 million; that amount was excluded from the proportionality analysis. The remainder of the property forfeited was found to be not disproportionate in light of Alexander's racketeering crimes. United States v. Alexander, 108 F.3d 853 (8th Cir.1997).

Excessive Forfeiture: United States v. Bajakajian

In United States v. Bajakajian, 524 U.S. 321 (1998), the Court struck down a criminal forfeiture of assets as excessive under the Eighth Amendment. Justice Thomas wrote the majority opinion for five members of the Court. Bajakajian was found trying to leave the country with more than $350,000. He was charged with, and pled guilty to, failure to report the currency. The government sought forfeiture of all the currency, under a statute permitting forfeiture of property "involved" in a criminal offense. The majority found that forfeiture of the entire amount was disproportionate to Bajakajian's offense. Justice Thomas analyzed the proportionality question in the following passage:

> Respondent's crime was solely a reporting offense. It was permissible to transport the currency out of the country so long as he reported it. * * * Furthermore, as the District Court found, respondent's violation was unrelated to any other illegal activities. The money was the proceeds of legal activity and was to be used to repay a lawful debt. Whatever his other vices, respondent does not fit into the class of persons for whom the statute was principally designed: He is not a money launderer, a drug trafficker, or a tax evader. And under the Sentencing Guidelines, the maximum sentence that could have been imposed on respondent was six months, while the maximum fine was $5,000. Such penalties confirm a minimal level of culpability.
>
> The harm that respondent caused was also minimal. Failure to report his currency affected only one party, the Government, and in a relatively minor way. There was no fraud on the United States, and respondent caused no loss to the public fisc. Had his crime gone undetected, the Government would have been deprived only of the information that $357,144 had left the country. * * * There is no inherent proportionality in such a forfeiture. * * *

Justice Kennedy, joined by Chief Justice Rehnquist and Justices O'Connor and Scalia, dissented. He argued that the forfeiture of the entire sum of smuggled cash was a reasonable means of deterring criminals such as money launderers and drug dealers.

Proportionality Limitations on In Rem Forfeitures: Austin v. United States

Austin v. United States, 509 U.S. 602 (1993), dealt with a type of forfeiture known as *in rem*, i.e., a forfeiture proceeding brought against the property rather than against the owner. After a state court sentenced Austin on his guilty plea to one count of possessing cocaine with intent to distribute, the United States filed an in rem civil forfeiture action against his mobile home and auto body shop under 21 U.S.C. § 881, which provides for the forfeiture of property used, or intended to be used, to facilitate the commission of certain drug-related crimes. The government presented evidence that Austin had brought two ounces of cocaine from his mobile home to his body shop in order to consummate a pre-arranged sale there. The lower court ordered the properties to be forfeited to the government. Austin objected that forfeiture of the properties, in light of the relatively minor offense, constituted a violation of the Eighth Amendment's Excessive Fines Clause. The lower court rejected this argument and on the ground that when the proceeding is in rem—against the property rather than its owner—the guilt or innocence of the owner is "constitutionally irrelevant" and therefore such a forfeiture could not be considered excessive in relationship to any offense.

The Supreme Court, in an opinion by Justice Blackmun, rejected the lower court's reasoning and held that the forfeiture *was* subject to review for proportionality under the Excessive Fines Clause. Justice Blackmun noted that the text of the Eighth Amendment contained no specific limitation to criminal cases—unlike the Sixth Amendment, for example.

Justice Blackmun further stressed that—whatever the status of in rem forfeiture under the common-law—the statutory forfeiture provisions applicable to drug cases provide an "innocent owner" defense. He reasoned that these exemptions "serve to focus the provisions on the culpability of the owner in a way that makes them look more like punishment, not less" and concluded that the inclusion of innocent owner defenses revealed a "congressional intent to punish only those involved in drug trafficking." In other words, the statutory "in rem" forfeiture at issue in *Austin* was operating against the owner, not just against the property.

The Court remanded to determine whether the forfeiture was constitutionally excessive in light of the offense. It refused to set forth a particular test for determining proportionality in forfeiture actions. Justice Kennedy, joined by Chief Justice Rehnquist and Justice Thomas, wrote an opinion concurring in part and in the judgment.[3]

---

[3] See Bennis v. Michigan, 516 U.S. 442 (1996) (forfeiture of automobile was permissible even though the owner was unaware of illegal activity occurring in the automobile).

Excessive Fines Clause Binding on the States: Timbs v. Indiana

In *Timbs v. Indiana*, 139 S.Ct. 1682 (2019), the Court held that the Eighth Amendment prohibition on excessive fines was binding on the States, because it had been incorporated through the Fourteenth Amendment. The Court's extensive incorporation analysis is discussed in Chapter 1.

2. Probation

Another alternative to incarceration is probation—called "supervised release" in the federal system. Probation means that a prison sentence is held in abeyance in whole or in part, and the defendant is released subject to terms and conditions. If the defendant fails to meet those conditions, then the sentence can be reinstated upon proof by a preponderance of evidence at a probation revocation hearing. Familiar conditions for probation are that the probationer meet his family obligations, pay a fine if possible, keep a job, undergo medical (including psychiatric) treatment, submit to drug testing, follow a prescribed course of study or training, report regularly to a probation officer, remain within a specified geographical area and, most importantly, refrain from further criminal conduct. Community service requirements may also be imposed. See generally United States v. Smith, 332 F.3d 455 (7th Cir. 2003) ("A district court may impose special conditions of supervised release that it deems appropriate so long as the conditions are reasonably related to: 1) the nature and circumstances of the offense and the history and characteristics of the defendant; 2) the need for the sentence imposed to afford adequate deterrence to criminal conduct; 3) the need to protect the public from further crimes of the defendant; and 4) the need to provide the defendant with needed educational or vocational training, medical care or other correctional treatment in the most effective manner.").

More controversial conditions are those that call upon probationers to forego personal liberties that the unconvicted citizen may claim under the Bill of Rights. For example, in United States v. Smith, 972 F.2d 960 (8th Cir.1992), the court imposed as a condition of supervised release that "the defendant shall not cause the conception of another child other than to his wife, unless he can demonstrate he is fully providing support to the three children presently in existence, and the two en ventre sa mere." The sentencing judge was concerned that the defendant if released would father children who would not be supported and sustained. But the court of appeals held that the sentencing court had no authority to impose that condition. Under the Federal Probation Act, 18 U.S.C. § 3563, conditions imposed on liberty or property must be reasonably necessary to foster rehabilitation of the defendant or the protection of the public. The court held that restricting Smith's right to have offspring did not meet this test, and also noted that the right to have children is a "sensitive and important area of human rights." What conditions should the court have imposed to allay its concerns? Compare United States v. Zobel, 696 F.3d 558 (6th Cir. 2012) (blanket prohibition on pornography use was valid where there was evidence that the defendant's self-professed addiction to pornography caused an increased risk of recidivism for the crime for which he was convicted—coercing and enticing a minor to engage in sexual activity); United States v. Tome, 611 F.3d 1371 (11th Cir. 2010) (ban on internet access as a condition for supervised release of defendant convicted of possession of child pornography was valid where the defendant had violated the terms of his prior supervised release by using the internet to communicate with sex offenders).

If the judge cannot impose what she feels to be effective conditions, she can presumably deny probation and incarcerate the defendant. Is this a better result for the defendant?

Whatever conditions may be imposed, they must be sufficiently clear so that the person on supervised release will know when he violates them. Thus, in United States v. Reeves, 591 F.3d 77 (2d Cir. 2010), the defendant pled guilty to child pornography charges, and received a term of imprisonment and supervised release. The judge imposed a condition on supervised release requiring Reeves to "Notify the Probation Department when he establishes a significant romantic relationship and inform the other party of his prior criminal history concerning his sentencing offenses." The court of appeals found that the condition, triggered by a "significant romantic relationship," was void for vagueness under the Due Process Clause:

> What makes a relationship "romantic," let alone "significant" in its romantic depth, can be the subject of endless debate * * *. for some, it would involve the exchange of gifts, such as flowers or chocolates; for others, it would depend on acts of physical intimacy; and for still others, all of these elements could be present yet the relationship, without a promise of exclusivity, would not be "significant." The history of romance is replete with precisely these blurred lines and misunderstandings. See, e.g. Wolfgang Amadeus Mozart, *The Marriage of Figaro* (1786); Jane Austen, *Mansfield Park* (1814); *When Harry Met Sally* (Columbia Pictures, 1989); *He's Just Not That Into You* (Flower Films 2009).

The trial judge usually has broad discretion to select a probation period. In United States v. Thomas, 934 F.2d 840 (7th Cir.1991), the defendant thought the conditions and length of the imposed probation to be onerous and argued that he had an absolute right to reject probation and opt for a prison sentence—which would not have been as long as the probation period. The court of appeals held that the defendant had no such option. It reasoned that it is the court, not the defendant, who is given the task of determining the sentence for a crime.

3. Restitution

A third alternative to incarceration (or a penalty in addition to incarceration) is restitution. There has been increasing concern in the United States with the plight of victims of crime. So it is not surprising that courts are ordering more defendants to make financial restitution to victims. The Victim and Witness Protection Act of 1982 ("VWPA") provided two new sections on restitution, 18 U.S.C.A. §§ 3663 and 3664, which authorize restitution for victims of certain offenses and require a court to justify a sentence that does not include restitution. 18 U.S.C.A. § 3664(c) requires that the defendant and the government be informed of provisions of the presentence report relating to restitution. The prosecution must bear the burden of persuasion as to the victim's loss, while the defendant has the burden of persuasion as to his financial resources.

Congress again demonstrated its concern for crime victims and its interest in promoting restitution in the Sentencing Reform Act of 1984. The Act recognizes that restitution may be a condition of probation, 18 U.S.C. § 3563, provides that a defendant may have to give notice to victims of fraud or deception in connection with sentencing, 18 U.S.C. § 3555, provides that a court may order portions of a fine remitted if a defendant makes restitution, 18 U.S.C. § 3572, and states that restitution may be imposed in addition to other sanctions, 18 U.S.C. § 3556. As part of the Comprehensive Crime Control Act of 1984, Congress also enacted the Victims of Crime Act of 1984, which creates a crime victims fund and provides for crime victim compensation.

In 1996 Congress enacted the Mandatory Victim's Restitution Act (MVRA). The MVRA further amended 18 U.S.C. §§ 3663 and 3664, and added new section 3663A, all with the view to fortifying the remedy of restitution for victims of crime. The VWPA provided a presumption in favor of restitution. The MVRA goes much further by providing that restitution is *mandatory* for crimes of violence, offenses against property, and for the crime of tampering with consumer products. With respect to these crimes, an order of restitution is mandatory even if the defendant has no ability to pay. See, e.g., United States v. Nichols, 169 F.3d 1255 (10th Cir.1999) (upholding order requiring defendant, convicted of conspiracy to bomb the Federal building Oklahoma City, to pay restitution in the amount of $14.5 million: "The district court was not required to consider Mr. Nichols' financial condition under 18 U.S.C. 3664(f)(1)(A)."). The Act does provide, however, that an indigent defendant cannot be incarcerated "solely on the basis of inability" to make restitution payments. And for the crimes not covered by the MVRA amendments, a restitution order must be structured within the defendant's ability to pay. See United States v. Dunigan, 163 F.3d 979 (6th Cir.1999) (defendant convicted of defrauding the United States; restitution order in the amount of $311,000 was vacated because defendant was indigent).

The MVRA specifically provides for restitution to victims who suffer bodily injury, essentially applying tort damages principles. See, e.g., United States v. Cienfuegos, 462 F.3d 1160 (9th Cir. 2006) (manslaughter victim's estate is entitled to a restitution award for future lost income). Another innovation of the MVRA is to provide restitution for drug crimes. The money is allocated 65% to the government's crime assistance fund, and 35% to a fund for substance abuse block grants. The Act also contains special provisions for compensation of victims of terrorism.

The MVRA requires restitution even where counts involving injured victims are dismissed at trial, so long as the defendant has been convicted of a crime triggering restitution, and the trial judge finds causation. See United States v. Edwards, 728 F.3d 1286 (11th Cir. 2013) ("While a conviction is required to trigger restitution under the MVRA, once the defendant is convicted, a court may order restitution for acts of related conduct for which the defendant was not convicted * * * so long as the injury is related to an offense of which the defendant was convicted.").

In Lagos v. United States, 138 S.Ct. 1684 (2018), Justice Breyer wrote for a unanimous Court rejecting lower courts' analyses of the provision of the MVRA requiring defendants to "reimburse the victim for * * * expenses incurred during participation in the investigation or prosecution of the offense or attendance at proceedings related to the Offense." Lagos pled guilty to using a company he controlled to defraud a lender of tens of millions of dollars. When the lender became aware of the scheme and Lagos's company went bankrupt, the lender spent nearly $5 million dollars to conduct a private investigation and to participate as a party in the bankruptcy proceedings. The expenditures included legal, accounting and consulting fees. At sentencing the district court required Lagos to reimburse the lender for these expenditures, and the Fifth Circuit affirmed. Justice Breyer concluded that the words "investigation" and "proceedings" in the Act are limited to government investigations and criminal proceedings and do not include private investigations and civil or bankruptcy proceedings.

Restitution for Victims of Child Pornography: Paroline v. United States

Congress enacted the Mandatory Restitution for Sexual Exploitation of Children Act—18 U.S.C. § 2259—as a special provision to protect and compensate children who are the subjects of sexual abuse, including the abuse of appearing in child pornography. The Act provides that a defendant convicted of an offense of sexual exploitation of a child must provide restitution of "the full amount of the victim's losses."

In Paroline v. United States, 572 U.S. 434 (2014), the Court considered whether restitution to victims of child pornography requires proof that the defendant proximately caused the victim's injury. Paroline pleaded guilty to possessing child pornography, including two images of "Amy" being sexually abused by her uncle when she was a child. Amy sought restitution for the psychological harm she suffered from knowing that the pictures of her were being seen by thousands of people over the Internet. The Court, in an opinion by Justice Kennedy for five Justices, read the restitution statute to require a showing by the government that the defendant proximately caused the victim's injuries. The Court rejected the victim's argument that every possessor should be responsible for the entirety of her damages as too extreme a position, especially in light of the purposes of imposing restitution as a part of a criminal punishment. Justice Kennedy elaborated as follows:

> The striking outcome of this reasoning—that each possessor of the victim's images would bear the consequences of the acts of the many thousands who possessed those images—illustrates why the Court has been reluctant to adopt aggregate causation logic in an incautious manner, especially in interpreting criminal statutes where there is no language expressly suggesting Congress intended that approach. * * *
>
> Contrary to the victim's suggestion, this is not akin to a case in which a "gang of ruffians" collectively beats a person, or in which a woman is "gang raped by five men on one night or by five men on five sequential nights." First, this case does not involve a set of wrongdoers acting in concert; for Paroline had no contact with the overwhelming majority of the offenders for whose actions the victim would hold him accountable. Second, adopting the victim's approach would make an individual possessor liable for the combined consequences of the acts of not just 2, 5, or even 100 independently acting offenders; but instead, a number that may reach into the tens of thousands.
>
> It is unclear whether it could ever be sensible to embrace the fiction that this victim's entire losses were the "proximate result," of a single possessor's offense. Paroline's contribution to the causal process underlying the victim's losses was very minor, both compared to the combined acts of all other relevant offenders, and in comparison to the contributions of other individual offenders, particularly distributors (who may have caused hundreds or thousands of further viewings) and the initial producer of the child pornography. Congress gave no indication that it intended its statute to be applied in the expansive manner the victim suggests, a manner contrary to the bedrock principle that restitution should reflect the consequences of the

defendant's own conduct, not the conduct of thousands of geographically and temporally distant offenders acting independently, and with whom the defendant had no contact.

The reality is that the victim's suggested approach would amount to holding each possessor of her images liable for the conduct of thousands of other independently acting possessors and distributors, with no legal or practical avenue for seeking contribution. That approach is so severe it might raise questions under the Excessive Fines Clause of the Eighth Amendment.

The victim (and the government) in *Paroline* argued that under a strict requirement of proximate cause, the victim would never be able to recover *anything* from an individual wrongdoer, because the victim's damages stemmed from the fact that there was an entire market of individuals accessing the offensive pictures over the Internet. Justice Kennedy was sympathetic to this argument, and essentially crafted a compromise approach—between the victim's position that each user should be liable for all of her injuries and the defendant's position that the victim could not recover anything from a single user because the harm was coming from the market. Justice Kennedy set forth the Court's position in the following passage:

> In this special context, where it can be shown both that a defendant possessed a victim's images and that a victim has outstanding losses caused by the continuing traffic in those images but where it is impossible to trace a particular amount of those losses to the individual defendant by recourse to a more traditional causal inquiry, a court applying 18 U.S.C. § 2259 should order restitution in an amount that comports with the defendant's relative role in the causal process that underlies the victim's general losses. The amount would not be severe in a case like this, given the nature of the causal connection between the conduct of a possessor like Paroline and the entirety of the victim's general losses from the trade in her images, which are the product of the acts of thousands of offenders. It would not, however, be a token or nominal amount. The required restitution would be a reasonable and circumscribed award imposed in recognition of the indisputable role of the offender in the causal process underlying the victim's losses and suited to the relative size of that causal role. This would serve the twin goals of helping the victim achieve eventual restitution for all her child-pornography losses and impressing upon offenders the fact that child-pornography crimes, even simple possession, affect real victims.

Chief Justice Roberts, joined by Justices Scalia and Thomas, "regretfully" dissented in *Paroline*. The Chief Justice contended that Congress had not authorized the majority's compromise approach to assessing restitution for victims of child pornography. In his view, "the restitution statute that Congress wrote for child pornography offenses makes it impossible to award relief" for damages caused by viewing the pictures of the victim over the Internet—because the statute requires proof of damage by a preponderance of the evidence. The Chief Justice concluded that it could not be possible to show that Paroline caused Amy any damage by a preponderance, because even without his viewing, Amy would have suffered the same damages from viewing by thousands of others. The Chief Justice concluded as follows:

> The Court's decision today means that Amy will not go home with nothing. But it would be a mistake for that salutary outcome to lead readers to conclude that Amy has prevailed or that Congress has done justice for victims of child pornography. The statute as written allows no recovery; we ought to say so, and give Congress a chance to fix it.

Justice Sotomayor wrote a separate dissent in *Paroline*. She argued that the statute should be read to allow apportionment of a victim's damages, and that each convicted defendant should have a payment schedule imposed in light of that defendant's financial circumstances.

4. Youth Offenders

Special detention provisions are often made for juvenile offenders. One statutory scheme was the Federal Youth Corrections Act, which provided the trial judge with special sentencing options for offenders under 22 years of age. Although the result of sentencing under the Act could have been a longer sentence than would be served by an adult, there was greater emphasis on treatment under the Act. In the Comprehensive Crime Control Act of 1984, Congress decided to replace the Youth Corrections Act with its general guideline approach to sentencing. In United States v. R.L.C., 503 U.S. 291 (1992), the Court held that the maximum permissible sentence in federal juvenile-delinquency proceedings must be limited to that which could have been imposed upon an adult under the Sentencing Guidelines.

What is often a crucial question for a juvenile charged with a crime is whether he will be treated as a "child" or as an adult. Perhaps no advantage is more significant than the limit on incarceration to a designated age. If a person is transferred to the typical criminal court, the potential range of prison sentences may increase, so the transfer decision is of critical importance. 18 U.S.C. § 5032 provides that if a person between 15 and 18 commits a federal crime, he can be tried as an adult "in the interest of justice." In determining whether trying the defendant as an adult is in the interest of justice, the judge must consider the defendant's age and social background, the nature of the offense, any prior acts of delinquency, the juvenile's intellectual development and emotional maturity, the nature of past treatment efforts, if any, and the juvenile's response to such treatment, and the availability of juvenile programs. See United States v. Nelson, 68 F.3d 583 (2d Cir.1995) (trial court erred in refusing to try the defendant as an adult, where he was 19 at the time of trial, charged with murder, and had committed previous acts of delinquency).

5. Insanity Acquittees and Civil Commitment

In the Insanity Defense Reform Act of 1984 ("IDRA"), Congress made insanity an affirmative defense, created a special verdict of "not guilty only by reason of insanity" ("NGI"), and established a comprehensive civil commitment procedure. See 18 U.S.C. §§ 17, 4241–4247. Under that procedure, a defendant found NGI is held in custody pending a court hearing, which must occur within 40 days of the verdict. At the conclusion of the hearing, the court determines whether the defendant should be hospitalized or released. Provisions similar to IDRA exist in many states.

One question arising under IDRA is whether the defendant has the right to have the jury instructed that an NGI verdict will result in his involuntary commitment. In Shannon v. United States, 512 U.S. 573 (1994), Shannon argued that such an instruction was necessary to prevent a possible misconception among the jurors that he would be quickly set free after an NGI verdict. But the trial court refused to give the instruction and Shannon was found guilty.

The Supreme Court, in an opinion written by Justice Thomas for seven members of the Court, held that Shannon had no right to an instruction concerning the consequences of an NGI verdict. Justice Thomas relied on the "well established" principle that "when a jury has no sentencing function, it should be admonished to reach its verdict without regard to what sentence might be imposed." He argued that "providing jurors sentencing information invites them to ponder matters that are not within their province, distracts them from their factfinding responsibilities, and creates a strong possibility of confusion."

Justice Thomas noted, however, that a clarifying instruction about an NGI verdict might be required if "a witness or prosecutor states in the presence of the jury that a particular defendant would 'go free' if found NGI." Justice Stevens, joined by Justice Blackmun, dissented in *Shannon*. He contended that "[t]here is no reason to keep this information from the jurors and every reason to make them aware of it."

II. GUIDELINES SENTENCING

A. THE PERCEIVED NEED FOR CONSISTENCY IN SENTENCING

Judge Marvin Frankel conducted a study of sentencing and published his results in 1972. See Frankel, Criminal Sentences: Law Without Order.

In that influential study, Judge Frankel found significant disparities in federal sentencing decisions. He attributed the disparities to "the almost wholly unchecked and sweeping powers we give to judges in the fashioning of sentences"—powers that Judge Frankel himself had exercised and found "terrifying and intolerable for a society that professes devotion to the rule of law." The solution, for Judge Frankel, was "concrete agreement on concrete factors capable of being stated, discussed and thought about in the style of a legal system for rational people rather than a lottery." He posited the possibility of "scientific sentencing." Judge Frankel's views eventually bore fruit in Congress, with a statute sponsored by Senators Kennedy and Thurmond, designed to replace "our haphazard approach to sentencing." It should not be surprising that a statutory scheme that appealed to both liberals and conservatives and to both Democrats and Republicans had several rationales. One was the importance of avoiding unwarranted disparities in sentencing. Another was the desire to promote "truth in sentencing" (meaning that a 15-year sentence should really mean 15 years rather than release on parole after 5).

Professor Robinson provides the following perspective about the move away from discretionary sentencing and toward guidelines sentencing:

> Although almost ubiquitous in state and federal systems by the 1960's, the indeterminate sentence became the subject of intense criticism. Prisoners complained of the uncertainty of their situation and disparate sentences proposed by judges. Law and order advocates worried about the possibility of quick parole. Libertarians expressed concern with the length of time inmates spent prior to parole. Social scientists complained about the lack of empirical support for the proposition that prisons were rehabilitative institutions. Other critics pointed out that prison behavior correlated poorly with post-release recidivism and that the best predictors were factors known at the time of the original sentences. Thus, if guidelines could be directed at the courts, rather than the parole boards, the uncertainty and potential deceptiveness of indeterminate sentences could be avoided.

Robinson, The Decline and Potential Collapse of Federal Guideline Sentencing, 74 Wash.U.L.Q 881 (1996).

The Sentencing Reform Act of 1984 made a number of important changes in Federal sentencing. Among other changes, the Act 1) classifies federal criminal offenses and designates the sentencing range for the new classes; 2) states the purposes to be served by any sentence; 3) establishes a Sentencing Commission to promulgate guidelines binding on sentencing courts; 4) and requires judges to give reasons for sentencing.[4]

[4] In Mistretta v. United States, 488 U.S. 361 (1989), the defendant argued that Congress, in the Sentencing Reform Act, had delegated excessive power to the Sentencing Commission to

The Reform Act abolishes parole in the Federal system. The rationale for abolishing parole is that the discretion exercised by parole boards was one of the major causes of disparity in sentencing. As Professor Robinson, supra, puts it:

> To achieve the goal of minimizing judge-created disparities, the danger of merely shifting discretion from the district court judges to other actors in the criminal justice process had to be faced. One such actor was the United States Parole Commission, which had authority to release inmates prior to completion of their maximum terms of confinement. The Sentencing Reform Act addressed this problem by abolishing parole for persons sentenced under the guidelines to be established by the Sentencing Commission.

The Goals of the Sentencing Commission

The U.S. Sentencing Commission found that adoption of guidelines satisfactory to legislators, prosecutors, defense lawyers, and judges was no simple task. After the circulation of various drafts and extensive debate within the Commission, the Commission finally agreed to the following principles:

> (1) Similar offense categories—e.g., for various kinds of fraud—would be grouped together under a single generic heading.
>
> (2) The base sentence for each offense would be determined by a discussion process, *"anchored, but not bound by,"* estimates of the average time served in past years by offenders convicted of that offense and the percentage of offenders given a non-incarceration sentence.
>
> (3) For articulated policy reasons—e.g., to increase deterrence—sentences could be raised or lowered with respect to past practice.
>
> (4) Base offense sentences would be modified by a set of specific offense characteristics that would be determined by looking to past sentencing practices, statutory aggravating or mitigating factors, factors that are taken into consideration in similar offenses, the vulnerability of victims, the offender's role in an offense, acceptance of responsibility, and the criminal history of the offender.

Thus, the Commission began with past practice, emphasized the importance of rationalizing sentences, and adopted an approach that focuses on the charges actually brought and the real offense behavior of the offender. It decided that conspiracies and attempts would generally be treated the same as the object offense, with a modest downward adjustment.

---

establish Guidelines. But the Court rejected this argument in an 8–1 decision, with Justice Scalia dissenting.

B. HOW THE FEDERAL SENTENCING GUIDELINES WORK

The process of sentencing under the Federal Guidelines has been described succinctly as follows:

> Under the federal guidelines, sentences are based on a mathematical equation that begins with an offense level depending on its seriousness. Murder, for instance, is at level 43, while robbery is at 20, altering or removing a motor vehicle identification number is at level 8 and obscenity is at 6.
>
> That offense level is then reduced or increased depending on factors such as a defendant's criminal history, level of cooperation, use of a deadly weapon and role in the offense. Other key factors are the quantities of drugs or money involved, injury to a victim and vulnerability of the victim.
>
> The sum of factors leads to a box on a grid that suggests a sentencing range such as 0 to 6 months at the low end or 292 to 365 months at the high end.

Pines, After Five Years, No One Loves Federal Sentencing Guidelines, N.Y.L.J., November 4, 1992, p. 3.

It is critical to note, as you proceed through these materials, that the Guidelines are only *advisory*. While sentencing courts are required to calculate the Guidelines sentence, they are not bound by the Guidelines. They can diverge from the Guidelines to adjust for various factors to be discussed below. See United States v. Booker, infra (holding that Sentencing Guidelines are advisory, not mandatory).

Base Offense Level

To understand how the Guidelines work as an advisory source for the sentence imposed by the court, it is useful to consider a hypothetical case.[5] Suppose that a defendant is convicted of obstruction of justice. The Guidelines describe offenses generically and contain an index indicating which Guidelines cover various code sections. Obstruction of justice is governed by Guideline § 2J1.2. The base offense level is 14 (raised from 12 after the Enron scandal); but the level increases to 16 if the obstruction involved destruction or alteration of either a substantial number of records or an especially probative record. (Similarly, with drug crimes, the base

[5] Citations to and quotations of particular Guidelines in the following discussion may not be definitive at the time you read this. The Sentencing Commission has amended the Guidelines hundreds of times since 1984. The discussion that follows is therefore intended merely to give you a general impression of how the Guidelines work.

offense level increases as the quantity increases, and with financial crimes the base level increases as the amount of loss to victims increases.)

Relevant Conduct

Section 1B1.3 of the Guidelines provides that the sentencing range is based not only on evidence with which the defendant was convicted, but also on evidence that is *related* to the conduct forming the basis of the conviction. See, e.g., United States v. Santiago, 906 F.2d 867 (2d Cir.1990) (in a drug distribution case, quantities and types of drugs not specified in the count of conviction are to be included in determining the base offense level if they were part of the same course of conduct or part of a common scheme or plan as the count of conviction; the sentencing court properly considered previous, uncharged sales to the same buyer). "Relevant conduct" is to be proven to the sentencing judge by a preponderance of the evidence—*not* beyond a reasonable doubt. United States v. Mourning, 914 F.2d 699 (5th Cir.1990) (trial court properly considered uncharged acts of money laundering, proven by a preponderance of the evidence). Thus, in our obstruction of justice hypothetical, if the government could show by a preponderance that the defendant engaged in related acts of fraud or perjury, these acts would be considered in setting the base offense level. And they would *count as much for sentencing purposes as the acts for which the defendant was convicted.*

Adjustments

The Guidelines call for certain adjustments of a sentence from the base offense level. There are victim-related adjustments—e.g., a two-level increase when the victim is especially vulnerable, § 3A1.1, or a three-level increase when the victim is a government official or employee. § 3A1.2. See, e.g., United States v. Wright, 160 F.3d 905 (2d Cir.1998) (two-step upward adjustment upheld under vulnerable victim provision, based on defendant's embezzlement of funds from mentally disabled individuals). Adjustments are provided when the defendant had an aggravating role (two to four-level upward adjustment) or mitigating role (two to four-level decrease) in an offense. §§ 3B1.1, 3B1.2. The offense level is increased by two levels if the defendant is found to have "abused a position of public or private trust * * * in a manner that significantly facilitated the commission or concealment of the offense." § 3B1.3. That same Guideline provides a two-level increase if the defendant committed the crime by exploiting a "special skill." See, e.g., United States v. Smith, 332 F.3d 455 (7th Cir. 2003) (conviction for theft of interstate freight raised by two levels because the defendant exploited his "special skills" in operating a tractor-trailer). Another adjustment increases punishment by two levels for obstruction of justice with respect to the investigation or prosecution of the offense charged. § 3C1.1. See United States v. Thompson, 944 F.2d 1331 (7th Cir.1991) (enhancement for obstruction of justice not permitted under the Guidelines where the defendant merely denies wrongdoing); United States v. Dunnigan, 507 U.S. 87 (1993) (upward adjustment where the court finds that the defendant committed perjury while testifying at trial).

If the defendant is convicted on several counts, the calculation is usually made separately for each count, and a set of rules is applied to the totality. But there are special rules that aggregate some conduct. §§ 3D1.1–3D1.5. Assume, for example, that a securities fraud defendant was convicted of defrauding three victims whose estimated losses were $250,000, $100,000, and $500,000. For crimes in which offense level is determined primarily on the basis of the amount of the loss, the three estimated losses are added together for a total of $850,000, increasing the punishment above the base offense level.

Acceptance of Responsibility

The final determinant of the offense level is the defendant's acceptance of responsibility. § 3E1.1. A defendant who clearly demonstrates recognition and affirmative acceptance of personal responsibility for his crime may receive a reduction of two levels. The defendant receives a further one level reduction if his offense level is 16 or above and his acceptance of responsibility includes assistance to the government in the investigation or prosecution of his own misconduct. Thus, if the obstruction of justice defendant cooperates with the government and promises to institute corrective measures, his level might drop from 14 to 12. It could not drop to 11, however, even if he supplies the government complete information concerning his involvement in the crime, or promptly notifies the government of his intent to plead guilty (because the offense level started below 16). See, e.g., United States v. Phillip, 948 F.2d 241 (6th Cir.1991) (defendant not entitled to reduction for acceptance of responsibility where he gave a false alibi to the investigating officers); United States v. Burns, 925 F.2d 18 (1st Cir.1991) (defendant who enters *Alford* plea—pleading guilty while protesting his innocence—is not entitled to reduction for acceptance of responsibility under the Guidelines); United States v. Boos, 329 F.3d 907 (7th Cir. 2003) (defendant who pleaded guilty to drug activity was not entitled to reduction for acceptance of responsibility under the Guidelines, where the sentencing judge enhanced the sentence for obstruction of justice).

Criminal History Category

Once the offense level is fixed, the sentencing judge, with the assistance of the probation officer, must determine the defendant's criminal history. §§ 4A1.1–4A1.3. Criminal history points are determined by a defendant's prior convictions. Three points are allocated, for example, for each prior sentence of imprisonment exceeding one year and one month, and two points are added for each sentence of imprisonment of at least 60 days but less than one year and one month. Some offenses are excluded, and time periods are designated to exclude stale convictions. Special provision is made for "career offenders"—i.e., defendants who were at least 18 at the time they commit the crime of conviction, which is a crime of violence or trafficking in a controlled substance, and who had at least two prior felony convictions for violent crimes or trafficking in controlled substances. § 4B1.1.

Using this formula, an obstruction of justice defendant with no prior criminal record would have a criminal history of 0. A prior conviction for a non-violent crime would put him in category I.

Using the 258-Box Sentencing Grid

Using the sentencing table, and assuming no prior criminal history, an obstruction of justice defendant convicted of one count involving extensive destruction of documents, but who was able to obtain all possible credit for acceptance of responsibility, would fall within a guideline for offense level 13 calling for a sentence of 12–18 months.

If instead of no criminal record, a defendant had a category III criminal record, the sentence for a level 13 offense increases to 18–24 months and for a level 16 offense to 30–37 months. Defendants in the worst criminal category (VI) would face a Guideline of 33–41 months at level 13 and 51–63 months at level 16.

Each row of the sentencing table contains levels that overlap with the levels in the preceding and succeeding rows. By overlapping the levels, the Commission intended to discourage unnecessary litigation. Both the prosecutor and the defendant are expected to realize that the difference between one level and another will not necessarily make a difference in sentencing.

Authorized Departures

The Guidelines contain a section on "departures." They authorize departures from the Guidelines when a defendant has provided substantial assistance to authorities (downward departure), death or serious injury has resulted from conduct (upward departure), the defendant's conduct was unusually extreme or cruel (upward departure), and in unusual circumstances not otherwise covered by the Guidelines. §§ 5K1, 5K2. See, e.g., United States v. Orchard, 332 F.3d 1133 (8th Cir. 2003) (the defendant was convicted of knowingly distributing a controlled substance analogue to a person under 21; the seriousness of the psychological harm to victim, the defendant's abuse of a relationship of trust, and his facilitation of a sex crime on the victim justified an upward departure); United States v. Phillip, 948 F.2d 241 (6th Cir.1991) (three-level upward departure under § 5K2.8 for extreme cruelty inflicted by the defendant on his four-year-old son); United States v. Williams, 937 F.2d 979 (5th Cir.1991) (defendant's advantageous social background does not justify an upward departure).

The Guidelines departure system was intended to be limited. But those limitations are no longer binding on sentencing courts after *Booker*, because the Guidelines are now advisory, not mandatory.

The Effect of Mandatory Minimum Sentences on Guidelines Sentencing

The Sentencing Guidelines establish sentencing ranges to be considered by judges. But Congress has set mandatory minimum sentences for certain crimes—especially drug and firearms offenses—and has required that these sentences be incorporated into the Guidelines structure. What this means is that if the Guidelines calculation is lower than the minimum sentence statutorily provided, the mandatory minimum controls. In these circumstances, mandatory minimum sentences operate to limit judicial discretion in favor of an across-the-board result.

In 1991, the Sentencing Commission released a report concluding that mandatory minimum sentences clash with the concept of sentencing guidelines, lead to unduly harsh sentences, and are responsible for increased racial disparities in sentencing. See McMillion, Hard Time, A.B.A.J., March, 1993, p. 100. See also Hansen, Mandatories Going, Going, Gone, ABAJ, April, 1999, p. 14 ("More and more people who once supported mandatory minimums have realized that they have done nothing to reduce crime or put big-time drug dealers out of business. What they have done, critics say, is fill prisons with young, nonviolent, low-level drug offenders serving long sentences at enormous and growing cost to taxpayers.").

The Sentencing Commission issued a 2011 report on federal mandatory minimums, and its most recent report on mandatory minimums, Overview of Mandatory Minimum Penalties in the Federal Criminal Justice System (2017), revealed that more than one-fifth of federal offenders sentenced in fiscal year 2016 were convicted of an offense carrying a mandatory minimum penalty; their average sentence was nearly four times the average sentence for offenders whose offense did not carry a mandatory minimum; and 55.7% of federal inmates in federal custody were convicted of an offense carrying a mandatory minimum penalty.

Justice Kennedy, in a speech before the American Bar Association in 2003, made a point of criticizing mandatory minimums as 1) often leading to harsh results that have no relation to the actual facts of a particular case; and 2) allowing prosecutors, by charging decisions, to control the sentencing system. Justice Breyer added to the chorus in his concurring opinion in Harris v. United States, 536 U.S. 545 (2002):

> Mandatory minimum statutes are fundamentally inconsistent with Congress' simultaneous effort to create a fair, honest, and rational sentencing system through the use of Sentencing Guidelines. Unlike Guideline sentences, statutory mandatory minimums generally deny the judge the legal power to depart downward, no matter how unusual the special circumstances that call for leniency. They rarely reflect an effort to achieve sentencing proportionality—a key element of sentencing fairness that demands that the law punish a drug "kingpin" and a "mule" differently. They transfer sentencing power to prosecutors, who can determine sentences through the charges they decide to bring, and who thereby have reintroduced much of the sentencing disparity that Congress created Guidelines to eliminate. They rarely are based upon empirical study. And there is evidence that they encourage subterfuge, leading to more frequent downward departures (on a random basis), thereby making them a comparatively ineffective means of guaranteeing tough sentences.

The chorus of criticism of mandatory minimum sentences, especially in drug cases, led the Obama administration to prohibit the practice of prosecutors charging drug crimes calling for mandatory minimum sentences when the defendant is a low-level drug offender. As reported by the New York Times, 9/23/13 at page A8:

> The Justice Department Policy follows efforts pioneered in conservative-leaning Texas and South Carolina to control soaring taxpayer money that is spent to incarcerate huge numbers of nonviolent offenders. * * * Mr. Holder [the Attorney General] has repeatedly criticized the moral impact of the nation's high incarceration rate, emphasizing that while the United States has only 5 percent of the world's population, it has 25 percent of its prisoners.

Attorney General Eric Holder set forth the Obama Administration's policy in a May 19, 2010 Memorandum to All Federal Prosecutors. But Attorney General Jeff Sessions abandoned the Obama administration's policy in a May 10, 2016 Memorandum For All Federal Prosecutors.

The First Step Act: An Attempt to Reduce the Effect of Mandatory Minimums

In 2018, the President signed into law the First Step Act (FSA) (P.L. 115–391). The act was the culmination of a bi-partisan effort to alleviate some of the harsh effects of mandatory minimum sentences in drug cases. The FSA modifies mandatory minimum sentences for some drug traffickers with prior drug convictions by increasing the threshold for prior convictions that count toward triggering higher mandatory minimums for repeat offenders: reducing the 20-year mandatory minimum (applicable where the offender has one prior qualifying conviction) to a 15-year mandatory minimum; and reducing a life-in-prison mandatory minimum (applicable where the offender has two or more prior qualifying convictions) to a 25-year mandatory minimum. The FSA also expands the number of defendants who may be eligible for "safety valve" relief. Prior to the First Step Act, only defendants with one "criminal history point" could receive sentences below the mandatory minimums, but under the Act, defendants with up to four points (depending on the type of offense) may be eligible.

C. CRITICISM OF MANDATORY FEDERAL SENTENCING GUIDELINES

As promulgated in the Sentencing Reform Act, 18 U.S.C. § 3553(b) provided that courts "shall" impose a sentence under the Guidelines. For 20 years, the "Guidelines" were a misnomer. They were in fact mandatory rules that substantially limited judicial discretion in sentencing. Many judges and commentators viewed the mandatory Guidelines as a failure. Some of the major criticisms were:

- In the desire to bring mathematical precision to sentencing, the Guidelines turned judges into accountants, and turned sentencing proceedings into highly technical and burdensome ordeals for all concerned.
- The Guidelines when mandatory replaced the discretion of an unbiased judge with the charging discretion of a prosecutor who is, obviously, an advocate for the government.
- The Guidelines were (and remain, though only in an advisory capacity) unduly harsh, especially in drug cases.[6]
- The Guidelines punish equally for charged conduct and uncharged "relevant conduct" even though the latter need only be proven by a preponderance of the evidence.
- In drug cases, the Guidelines use weight of the drug as a surrogate for culpability, when that may not always be the case.
- In monetary cases, the Guidelines use amount of loss as a surrogate for culpability, when that may not always be the case.

The following is a small sampling of some of the criticism of the Guidelines during the time that they were mandatory:

[6] See Richman, Cooperating Clients, 56 Ohio St.L.J. 69 (1995) (citing federal statistics showing a significant increase in both incarceration and in the average length of prison sentences since 1984, and an increase in mean prison terms for drug offenses from 27 months to 67 months).

Judge Edwards, concurring in United States v. Harrington, 947 F.2d 956 (D.C.Cir.1991):

> [T]he Guidelines do not, by any stretch of the imagination, ensure uniformity in sentencing. Assistant U.S. Attorneys have been heard to say, with open candor, that there are many "games to be played," both in charging defendants and in plea bargaining, to circumvent the Guidelines. Because of this reality, sentences under the Guidelines often bear no relationship to what the Sentencing Commission may have envisioned as appropriate to any given case.
>
> The first "game" to be played under the Guidelines occurs in connection with the charging decision. The confluence of the Guidelines' restriction of judicial discretion and the enactment of mandatory minimum sentences for many drug crimes has placed enormous power in the hands of the AUSA, effectively replacing judicial discretion over sentencing with prosecutorial discretion. * * *
>
> The second disparity-creating game to be played—this one by prosecutors and defense attorneys in collaboration—is the plea bargaining process. By offering a plea, defense counsel may be able to cut a deal with the prosecutor to "bend the rules." However, whether the rules actually get bent may depend upon the luck of the draw in judicial assignment: if the trial judge is willing to look the other way, the facts can be manipulated and the Guidelines ignored because no appeal will be taken by the prosecutor.
>
> * * *
>
> Perhaps most importantly, the Probation Officer determines and evaluates the defendant's "relevant conduct"—that is, conduct (often uncharged) that is related to, but not part of, the offense for which conviction has been sought. This determination can have a substantial impact on the applicable sentencing range.
>
> * * *

Judge Bright, concurring in United States v. Baker, 961 F.2d 1390 (8th Cir.1992), a case in which the court upheld a sentence of almost 20 years for a "career offender" convicted of cocaine distribution and money laundering:

> This sentence demonstrates yet again the vagaries of Guideline sentencing. A similar offender, who would have been under age eighteen when the prior offenses occurred, would not be a career offender, and would not have received this lengthy sentence but one no longer than eleven years and five months. This sort of gross disparity in sentencing often occurs under the Guidelines. * * * This

case is another example of rigid guidelines sentencing producing inequity and injustice in sentencing, and demonstrates a need for the reformation, if not the abolishment, of Guideline sentencing.

Professor Raeder, Gender and Sentencing: Single Moms, Battered Women, and Other Sex-Based Anomalies in the Gender-Free World of the Federal Sentencing Guidelines, 20 Pepp.L.Rev. 905 (1993):

> [T]he Guidelines explicitly mandate that sex is not relevant in the determination of a sentence. However, such legislated equality poses difficulties for many women whose criminal behavior and history, as well as family responsibilities, cannot easily be shoehorned into a punitive pro-prison model for sentencing males assumed to be violent and/or major drug dealers. For example, female offenders are often mothers who have sole or primary responsibility for the care of their children, a consideration virtually ignored by the current Guidelines. Many women * * * may find themselves involved in criminal activity because of social and cultural pressures or occasionally as a result of more obvious means of coercion such as battering. Harsh mandatory minimums combined with the inflexible Guidelines regime result in lengthy incarceration of such women whose actual role in drug cases is often quite limited.

For more judicial commentary on the mandatory Guidelines, see United States v. Concepcion, 983 F.2d 369 (2d Cir.1992) (Newman, J., concurring) (complaining that because the Guidelines treat relevant conduct equally with conduct that is the subject of the conviction, the defendant who was charged with two crimes, and acquitted of one, received the same sentence as if he were convicted of both!); Bonin v. Calderon, 59 F.3d 815 (9th Cir.1995) (Kozinski, J., concurring) (criticizing the fact that the Guidelines often provide harsher sentences for small-time drug offenders than for murderers and rapists).

D. SUPREME COURT CONSTRUCTION OF THE FEDERAL SENTENCING GUIDELINES

1. Guidelines as Advisory, Not Mandatory: United States v. Booker

The *Booker* opinion comes in two parts, with different majorities for each part. In the first part—which might be called the *Apprendi* part—the majority opinion, written by Justice Stevens, holds that the Sentencing Guidelines violate the defendant's rights to jury trial and due process to the extent they require the sentencing judge to increase the sentence beyond that applicable to the crime for which the defendant was convicted, on the basis of facts found by the judge, not the jury. The Guidelines therefore violated the defendant's right to a jury trial on the facts used by the judge to increase the sentence; and they violated the due process right to a determination of all elements of the crime beyond a reasonable doubt, because sentencing facts are determined by the lesser standard of proof by preponderance of the evidence. United States v. Booker, 543 U.S. 220 (2005).

Justice Stevens focused on the fact that the Guidelines as written *required* an enhancement of the sentence, beyond that applicable to the crime found by the jury, on the basis of facts found by the judge by a preponderance of the evidence at sentencing. He explained as follows:

> If the Guidelines as currently written could be read as merely advisory provisions that recommended, rather than required, the selection of particular sentences in response to differing sets of facts, their use would not implicate the Sixth Amendment. We have never doubted the authority of a judge to exercise broad discretion in imposing a sentence within a statutory range. Indeed, everyone agrees that the constitutional issues presented by these cases would have been avoided entirely if Congress had omitted * * * provisions that make the Guidelines binding on district judges; it is that circumstance that makes the Court's answer to the second question presented possible. For when a trial judge exercises his discretion to select a specific sentence within a defined range, the defendant has no right to a jury determination of the facts that the judge deems relevant.
>
> The Guidelines as written, however, are not advisory; they are mandatory and binding on all judges. While subsection (a) of § 3553 of the sentencing statute lists the Sentencing Guidelines as one factor to be considered in imposing a sentence, subsection (b) directs that the court "*shall* impose a sentence of the kind, and within the range" established by the Guidelines, subject to departures in specific, limited cases.

How to Solve the Constitutional Infirmity in the Guidelines?

After a majority in *Booker* held that the Guidelines can operate to deprive the accused of the right to jury trial and the right to a determination of all elements of the crime beyond a reasonable doubt, the question was, what to do about it? Five members of the Court, in an opinion by Justice Breyer, held that the proper solution—the one most in accord with Congress's intent when it set up the system of Sentencing Guidelines—was to ***invalidate the statutory provisions that made the Guidelines mandatory***. If the Guidelines are only advisory, then, as Justice Stevens recognized in the excerpt above, they could not violate

Apprendi—because then sentencing would be based on judicial discretion, and the Court has always accepted the premise that the exercise of judicial discretion to set a sentence does not violate the defendant's constitutional rights to jury trial or due process. The problem with the Guidelines was that Congress *required* sentencing courts to increase the sentence beyond the sentencing range for the crime found by the jury, on the basis of facts found at sentencing by a preponderance of the evidence.

Both Justice Stevens and Justice Breyer recognize a constitutional distinction between (1) finding facts that increase a sentencing range set by a legislature or sentencing commission (a task for juries), and (2) exercising judgment based on the consideration of relevant sentencing factors (a task for judges). See generally Berman, Conceptualizing *Booker*, 38 Ariz. St. L.J. 387, 406–14 (2006), for a discussion of this distinction.

In order to understand Justice Breyer's opinion for the "remedial" majority, you need to review the statute that establishes the system of Federal Sentencing Guidelines. That statute is 18 U.S.C. § 3553. Subdivision (a) provides as follows:

> (a) Factors to be considered in imposing a sentence.—The court shall impose a sentence sufficient, but not greater than necessary, to comply with the purposes set forth in paragraph (2) of this subsection. The court, in determining the particular sentence to be imposed, shall consider—
>
> (1) the nature and circumstances of the offense and the history and characteristics of the defendant;
>
> (2) the need for the sentence imposed—
>
> (A) to reflect the seriousness of the offense, to promote respect for the law, and to provide just punishment for the offense;
>
> (B) to afford adequate deterrence to criminal conduct;
>
> (C) to protect the public from further crimes of the defendant; and
>
> (D) to provide the defendant with needed educational or vocational training, medical care, or other correctional treatment in the most effective manner;
>
> (3) the kinds of sentences available;
>
> (4) the kinds of sentence and the sentencing range established for—
>
> (A) the applicable category of offense committed by the applicable category of defendant as set forth in the guidelines—

(i) issued by the Sentencing Commission * * * subject to any amendments made to such guidelines by act of Congress; and

(ii) that * * * are in effect on the date the defendant is sentenced; or

(B) in the case of a violation of probation or supervised release, the applicable guidelines or policy statements issued by the Sentencing Commission * * * taking into account any amendments made to such guidelines or policy statements by act of Congress * * *;

(5) any pertinent policy statement—

(A) issued by the Sentencing Commission * * * subject to any amendments made to such policy statement by act of Congress * * *; and

(B) that * * * is in effect on the date the defendant is sentenced.

(6) the need to avoid unwarranted sentence disparities among defendants with similar records who have been found guilty of similar conduct; and

(7) the need to provide restitution to any victims of the offense.

So section 3553(a) sets forth a grab bag of factors—including a reference to the Guidelines—that the court is to take into account. Looking only to this subdivision, it would appear that judges have a lot of discretion to set a sentence, after considering broad factors, and that the Guidelines are only one source for setting a reasonable sentence.

But subdivision (b)(1) of section 3553 required that the sentencing court adhere to the Guidelines.

(b) Application of guidelines in imposing a sentence.—(1) In general.—* * * the court *shall* impose a sentence of the kind, and within the range, referred to in subsection (a)(4) unless the court finds that there exists an aggravating or mitigating circumstance of a kind, or to a degree, not adequately taken into consideration by the Sentencing Commission in formulating the guidelines that should result in a sentence different from that described. In determining whether a circumstance was adequately taken into consideration, the court shall consider only the sentencing guidelines, policy statements, and official commentary of the Sentencing Commission. * * *

The *Booker* Court was essentially left with two alternatives: 1) it could require that the Guidelines system of judicial factfinding be scrapped, replacing it with a system requiring juries to find all of the facts that are relevant to sentencing enhancements; or 2) it could invalidate the provisions that require mandatory adherence to the Guidelines, thus returning to judicial discretion in sentencing that all members of the Court had found acceptable. The remedial majority chose the latter option. The dissenters opted for the former.

The Remedial Majority Opinion in Booker

Justice Breyer started with a concise statement of the remedial holding:

> We answer the question of remedy by finding the provision of the federal sentencing statute that makes the Guidelines mandatory, 18 USC § 3553(b)(1), incompatible with today's constitutional holding. We conclude that this provision must be severed and excised, as must one other statutory section, § 3742(e), which depends upon the Guidelines' mandatory nature. [Section 3742 covers appeal, and will be discussed below.] So modified, the Federal Sentencing Act makes the Guidelines effectively advisory. It requires a sentencing court to consider Guidelines ranges, see 18 USC § 3553(a)(4), but it permits the court to tailor the sentence in light of other statutory concerns as well, see § 3553(a).

Justice Breyer described the task at hand:

> We answer the remedial question by looking to legislative intent. We seek to determine what Congress would have intended in light of the Court's constitutional holding. In this instance, we must determine which of the two following remedial approaches is the more compatible with the legislature's intent as embodied in the 1984 Sentencing Act.

Justice Breyer found that making the Guidelines advisory was more consistent with congressional intent in establishing the Guidelines system than a system depending on jury determination of sentencing factors. He argued that a system based on jury determination of all the facts that could increase a sentence beyond a base offense level would increase sentencing disparity—a result that Congress (which passed the Sentencing Reform Act to *cure* sentencing disparities) would not have accepted. He explained as follows:

> Congress' basic statutory goal—a system that diminishes sentencing disparity—depends for its success upon judicial efforts to determine, and to base punishment upon, the *real conduct* that underlies the crime of conviction. * * * Judges have long looked to real conduct when sentencing. Federal judges have long relied upon a presentence report, prepared by a probation officer, for information (often unavailable until *after* the trial) relevant to the manner in which the convicted offender committed the crime of conviction.

> Congress expected this system to continue. * * *
>
> To engraft the Court's constitutional requirement onto the sentencing statutes, however, would destroy the system. It would prevent a judge from relying upon a presentence report for factual information, relevant to sentencing, uncovered after the trial. In doing so, it would, even compared to pre-Guidelines sentencing, weaken the tie between a sentence and an offender's real conduct. It would thereby undermine the sentencing statute's basic aim of ensuring similar sentences for those who have committed similar crimes in similar ways.
>
> * * *
>
> Congress' basic goal in passing the Sentencing Act was to move the sentencing system in the direction of increased uniformity. That uniformity does not consist simply of similar sentences for those convicted of violations of the same statute * * *. It consists, more importantly, of similar relationships between sentences and real conduct, relationships that Congress' sentencing statutes helped to advance * * *.

Justice Breyer also argued that a system requiring jury determination of all facts pertinent to sentencing enhancements would be unworkable—and Congress obviously wanted a workable system of sentencing.

> How would courts and counsel work with an indictment and a jury trial that involved not just whether a defendant robbed a bank but also how? Would the indictment have to allege, in addition to the elements of robbery, whether the defendant possessed a firearm, whether he brandished or discharged it, whether he threatened death, whether he caused bodily injury, whether any such injury was ordinary, serious, permanent or life threatening, whether he abducted or physically restrained anyone, whether any victim was unusually vulnerable, how much money was taken, and whether he was an organizer, leader, manager, or supervisor in a robbery gang? If so, how could a defendant mount a defense against some or all such specific claims should he also try simultaneously to maintain that the Government's evidence failed to place him at the scene of the crime? * * * How could a judge expect a jury to work with the Guidelines' definitions of, say, "relevant conduct" * * * ? How would a jury measure "loss" in a securities fraud case—a matter so complex as to lead the Commission to instruct judges to make "only . . . a reasonable estimate"? § 2B1.1, comment., n. 3(C). How would the court take account, for punishment purposes, of a defendant's contemptuous behavior at trial—a matter that the Government could not have charged in the indictment? § 3C1.1.

Justice Breyer then turned to what had to be done to make the Guidelines advisory rather than mandatory:

> Most of the statute is perfectly valid. See, *e.g.*, 18 USC § 3551 (describing authorized sentences as probation, fine, or imprisonment); § 3552 (presentence reports); § 3554 (forfeiture); § 3555 (notification to the victims); § 3583 (supervised release). And we must refrain from invalidating more of the statute than is necessary. Indeed, we must retain those portions of the Act that are (1) constitutionally valid, (2) capable of functioning independently, and (3) consistent with Congress' basic objectives in enacting the statute.
>
> Application of these criteria indicates that we must sever and excise two specific statutory provisions: the provision that requires sentencing courts to impose a sentence within the applicable Guidelines range (in the absence of circumstances that justify a departure), see 18 USC § 3553(b)(1), and the provision that sets forth standards of review on appeal, including *de novo* review of departures from the applicable Guidelines range, see § 3742(e) [which provides that the court of appeals must reverse a sentencing decision that was "imposed as a result of an incorrect application of the sentencing guidelines."] With these two sections excised (and statutory cross-references to the two sections consequently invalidated), the remainder of the Act satisfies the Court's constitutional requirements.

Justice Breyer described how sentencing would work in the absence of these mandatory provisions—noting most importantly that the Guidelines sentence must be calculated in every sentencing.

> The remainder of the Act functions independently. Without the "mandatory" provision, the Act nonetheless requires judges to take account of the Guidelines together with other sentencing goals. See 18 USC § 3553(a). The Act nonetheless requires judges to consider the Guidelines "sentencing range established for . . . the applicable category of offense committed by the applicable category of defendant," § 3553(a)(4), the pertinent Sentencing Commission policy statements, the need to avoid unwarranted sentencing disparities, and the need to provide restitution to victims, §§ 3553(a)(1), (3), (5)–(7). And the Act nonetheless requires judges to impose sentences that reflect the seriousness of the offense, promote respect for the law, provide just punishment, afford adequate deterrence, protect the public, and effectively provide the defendant with needed educational or vocational training and medical care. § 3553(a)(2).
>
> Moreover, despite the absence of § 3553(b)(1), the Act continues to provide for appeals from sentencing decisions (irrespective of whether the trial judge sentences within or outside the Guidelines range in the exercise of his discretionary power under § 3553(a)). See § 3742(a) (appeal by defendant); § 3742(b) (appeal by Government). We concede that the excision of § 3553(b)(1) requires the excision of a different,

appeals-related section, namely § 3742(e), which sets forth standards of review on appeal. That section contains critical cross-references to the (now-excised) § 3553(b)(1) and consequently must be severed and excised for similar reasons

Having struck the standard for appellate review, Justice Breyer recognized that it was necessary to determine what standard would apply. He reached the following conclusion:

> Excision of § 3742(e), however, does not pose a critical problem for the handling of appeals. That is because, as we have previously held, a statute that does not *explicitly* set forth a standard of review may nonetheless do so *implicitly*. We infer appropriate review standards from related statutory language, the structure of the statute, and the "sound administration of justice." And in this instance those factors, in addition to the past two decades of appellate practice in cases involving departures, imply a practical standard of review already familiar to appellate courts: review for "unreasonable[ness]." 18 USC § 3742(e)(3).

Justice Breyer concluded as follows on the future of sentencing after *Booker:*

> [T]he Sentencing Commission remains in place, writing Guidelines, collecting information about actual district court sentencing decisions, undertaking research, and revising the Guidelines accordingly. The district courts, while not bound to apply the Guidelines, must consult those Guidelines and take them into account when sentencing. The courts of appeals review sentencing decisions for unreasonableness. These features of the remaining system, while not the system Congress enacted, nonetheless continue to move sentencing in Congress' preferred direction, helping to avoid excessive sentencing disparities while maintaining flexibility sufficient to individualize sentences where necessary. We can find no feature of the remaining system that tends to hinder, rather than to further, these basic objectives.

Dissents from the Booker Remedial Opinion

Justice Stevens, joined by Justices Souter and Scalia, took issue with the majority's contention that jury determination of sentencing facts would be unworkable. He elaborated as follows:

> * * * [T]he majority argues that my remedy would make sentencing proceedings far too complex. But of the very small number of cases in which a Guidelines sentence would implicate the Sixth Amendment * * * most involve drug quantity determinations, firearm enhancements, and other factual findings that can readily be made by

juries. I am not blind to the fact that some cases, such as fraud prosecutions, would pose new problems for prosecutors and trial judges. In such cases, I am confident that federal trial judges, assisted by capable prosecutors and defense attorneys, could have devised appropriate procedures to impose the sentences the Guidelines envision in a manner that is consistent with the Sixth Amendment. We have always trusted juries to sort through complex facts in various areas of law. This may not be the most efficient system imaginable, but the Constitution does not permit efficiency to be our primary concern.

Justice Scalia dissented and argued that the system of appellate review left by the majority's opinion would lead to uncertainty and to disparity in sentencing—results clearly contrary to Congress's intent in the Sentencing Reform Act.

What I anticipate will happen is that "unreasonableness" review will produce a discordant symphony of different standards, varying from court to court and judge to judge, giving the lie to the remedial majority's sanguine claim that no feature of its avant-garde Guidelines system will tend to hinder the avoidance of excessive sentencing disparities.

Justice Thomas wrote a separate dissent, arguing that the mandatory application of the Guidelines was constitutional in a number of situations (e.g., where the sentence stayed within the Guideline for the base offense level, or where the Guideline controlled a *downward* adjustment of a sentence). He concluded that "the majority, by facially invalidating the statute, also invalidates these unobjectionable applications of the statute and thereby ignores the longstanding distinction between as-applied and facial challenges."

2. Application of Advisory Guidelines After *Booker*

The remedial opinion in *Booker* emphasizes that the Guidelines remain critical to sentencing determinations. The Guidelines *must still be considered* in setting a reasonable sentence. The circuit courts after *Booker* have clearly stated that sentencing courts must determine what the Guideline sentence is, in the same way as they did before *Booker*. See generally United States v. Crosby, 397 F.3d 103 (2d Cir. 2005). A sentencing court that does not compute the Guidelines sentence will be reversed for unreasonableness, without regard to the length of the sentence. See United States v. McVay, 447 F.3d 1348 (11th Cir. 2006) ("Before we conduct a reasonableness review of the ultimate sentence imposed, we must first determine whether the district court correctly interpreted and applied the Guidelines to calculate the appropriate advisory Guidelines range. It is only after a district court correctly calculates the Guidelines range, which it still must do after *Booker*, that it may consider imposing a more severe or lenient sentence."); United States v. Johnson, 467 F.3d 559 (6th Cir. 2006) ("Although no longer bound by the Guidelines, district courts are still required to consider the applicable Guideline range along with the other statutory factors.").

It is also important to note that factfinding by the sentencing court has not been altered by *Booker*. The Second Circuit in *Crosby* held that judicial factfinding should proceed as previously; now that the Guidelines are advisory only, there can be no Sixth Amendment objection to judicial factfinding, even where it is used to increase a sentence. And there can be no complaint that the district judge, in making sentencing decisions, is deciding facts by a *preponderance of the evidence* rather than beyond a reasonable doubt. The problem with the Guidelines was that judicial factfinding occurred within the context of a mandatory sentencing scheme. As the Third Circuit explained in United States v. Grier, 449 F.3d 558 (3d Cir. 2006):

> There can be no question, in light of the holding of *Booker*, and the reasoning of *Apprendi*, that the right to proof beyond a reasonable doubt does not apply to facts relevant to enhancements under an advisory Guidelines regime. Like the right to jury trial, the right to proof beyond a reasonable doubt attaches only when the facts at issue have the effect of increasing the maximum punishment to which the defendant is exposed. The advisory Guidelines do not have this effect. They require the district judge to make findings of fact, but none of these alters the judge's final sentencing authority. They merely inform the judge's broad discretion.

Guidelines Entitled to "Great Weight" After Booker?

How much weight should be given to the advisory Guidelines after *Booker*? In United States v. Wilson, 355 F.Supp.2d 1269 (D.Utah 2005), Judge Cassell concluded that "considerable weight should be given to the Guidelines in determining what sentence to impose."

Judge Cassell argued that the Guidelines are the best expression of Congress's intent in setting an appropriate sentence under Section 3553. He further argued—relying on opinion polls and social science data—that the Guidelines generally achieve the goals of "just punishment" and "deterrence" that still bind the federal courts after *Booker*. Judge Cassell concluded that the most important reason for applying the Guidelines was to assure uniformity of sentencing after *Booker*. He elaborated as follows:

> The only way of avoiding gross disparities in sentencing from judge-to judge and district-to-district is for sentencing courts to apply some uniform measure in all cases. The only standard currently available is the Sentencing Guidelines. If each district judge follows his or her own views of "just punishment" and "adequate deterrence,"

> the result will be a system in which prison terms will depend on "what the judge ate for breakfast" on the day of sentencing and other irrelevant factors. * * * It would, in short, be a return to the pre-Guidelines days, which produced astounding disparities among the sentences that were imposed on defendants convicted of the same offense with similar backgrounds with different judicial districts across the country—and even among different judges in the same district.

Other courts have argued that to give the Guidelines heavy weight would be improper after *Booker*, because it would essentially make the Guidelines mandatory, which is prohibited by the *Booker* merits opinion. One leading proponent of this view is Judge Adelman in United States v. Ranum, 353 F.Supp.2d 984 (E.D.Wis.2005). The court in *Ranum* stated that after *Booker*, sentencing courts are required to *consult* the Guidelines, but they are also required to consider the factors set forth in 18 U.S.C. 3553(a) as well. The court contended that some of those statutory factors actually conflict with the Guidelines. For example, section 3553(a) states that the court must consider the characteristics and history of the defendant; but under the Guidelines, the defendant's character and background are generally irrelevant, and the only history that can be considered is criminal history. The court declared that "in every case, courts must now consider all of the § 3553(a) factors, not just the guidelines. And where the guidelines conflict with other factors set forth in § 3553(a), courts will have to resolve the conflicts."

The defendant in *Ranum* was a bank official who made unauthorized loans to a start-up corporation, GLC, and lied to the bank about it. His actions were not motivated by personal profit. The court found that the Guidelines called for a sentence of 37–46 months. The defendant argued for a period of home confinement. The court decided that the appropriate sentence was imprisonment for a year and a day.

Judge Adelman argued that a strict application of the Guidelines might lead to an inappropriate sentence because the Guidelines for monetary crimes are driven almost exclusively by the amount of loss.

> One of the primary limitations of the guidelines, particularly in white-collar cases, is their mechanical correlation between loss and offense level. For example, the guidelines treat a person who steals $100,000 to finance a lavish lifestyle the same as someone who steals the same amount to pay for an operation for a sick child. It is true that * * * from the victim's perspective the loss is the same no matter why it occurred. But from the standpoint of personal culpability, there is a significant difference. In the present case, defendant did not act for personal gain. He made loans outside his authority and was reckless with his employer's money. But that is not the same as stealing it.

Thus, due to the nature of the case, I found the guideline range, which depended so heavily on the loss amount, greater than necessary.

Ultimately, Judge Adelman found that "in order to promote respect for the law and in recognition of the significant loss to the bank, * * * defendant had to be confined for a significant period of time" but that "the sentence called for by the guidelines, 37–46 months, was much greater than necessary to satisfy the purposes of sentencing set forth in § 3553(a)" because that range "does not properly account for defendant's absence of interest in personal gain, * * * for defendant's otherwise outstanding character and for the significant benefits to family members resulting from his presence." He concluded that a sentence of twelve months and one day, followed by five years of supervised release, "was sufficient to promote respect for the law and account for defendant's serious abuse of trust over an extended period of time."

So after *Booker*, federal sentencing courts must tread the line between *excessive* reliance on the Guidelines (which will in effect make them mandatory and thus in violation of the *Booker* merits opinion) and *insufficient* reliance on the Guidelines (which could lead to unbridled discretion and disparity in sentencing). See, e.g., United States v. Zavala, 443 F.3d 1165 (9th Cir. 2006) (district court erred by treating the Guidelines sentence as the "presumptive" sentence after *Booker*, from which it would depart only if the defendant provided satisfactory reasons: "The court's approach brings us perilously close to the mandatory Guidelines regime squarely rejected by the Supreme Court in *Booker*.").

Sentencing Disparity After Booker?

Professor Ryan Scott evaluated post-*Booker* sentencing decisions in the District of Massachusetts and came to the following conclusions:

> Analysis of those sentences reveals a clear increase in inter-judge disparity * * *. In cases not governed by a mandatory minimum, the court's three most lenient judges have imposed average sentences of 25.5 months or less, while its two most severe judges have imposed average sentences of 51.4 months or more.
>
> Similarly, the * * * data reveal that some judges have taken advantage of their enhanced discretion to depart from the Guidelines to a far greater extent than others. Two judges * * * continue to impose below-Guidelines sentences at essentially the same rate as before *Booker*, as little as 16% of the time. But four other judges * * * now sentence below the guideline range at triple or quadruple their pre-*Booker* rates, as much as 53% of the time.

Scott, Inter-Judge Sentencing Disparity After *Booker*: A First Look, 63 Stan. L.Rev. 1 (2010). See also Memorandum of Department of Justice to the Sentencing Commission, 6/28/2010 ("More and more, we are receiving reports from our prosecutors that in many federal courts, a defendant's sentence will largely be determined by the judicial assignment of the case.").

Disagreement with Guidelines Policy: Kimbrough v. United States

In the following case, the Court emphasizes that sentencing courts have discretion, under the *Booker* regime of advisory guidelines, to disagree with a policy decision upon which a guideline is based.

KIMBROUGH V. UNITED STATES

Supreme Court of the United States, 2007.
552 U.S. 85.

JUSTICE GINSBURG delivered the opinion of the Court.

This Court's remedial opinion in United States v. Booker instructed district courts to read the United States Sentencing Guidelines as "effectively advisory." In accord with 18 U.S.C. § 3553(a), the Guidelines, formerly mandatory, now serve as one factor among several courts must consider in determining an appropriate sentence. *Booker* further instructed that "reasonableness" is the standard controlling appellate review of the sentences district courts impose.

Under the statute criminalizing the manufacture and distribution of crack cocaine, 21 U.S.C. § 841, and the relevant Guidelines prescription, § 2D1.1, a drug trafficker dealing in crack cocaine is subject to the same sentence as one dealing in 100 times more powder cocaine. [This disparity was subsequently reduced to 18:1 by the Fair Sentencing Act of 2010]. The question here presented is whether, as the Court of Appeals held in this case, "a sentence . . . outside the guidelines range is per se unreasonable when it is based on a disagreement with the sentencing disparity for crack and powder cocaine offenses." We hold that, under *Booker*, the cocaine Guidelines, like all other Guidelines, are advisory only, and that the Court of Appeals erred in holding the crack/powder disparity effectively mandatory. A district judge must include the Guidelines range in the array of factors warranting consideration. The judge may determine, however, that, in the particular case, a within-Guidelines sentence is "greater than necessary" to serve the objectives of sentencing. 18 U.S.C. § 3553(a). In making that determination, the judge may consider the disparity between the Guidelines' treatment of crack and powder cocaine offenses.

* * *

[P]etitioner Derrick Kimbrough was indicted * * * and charged with four offenses: conspiracy to distribute crack and powder cocaine; possession with intent to distribute more than 50 grams of crack cocaine; possession with intent to distribute powder cocaine; and possession of a firearm in furtherance of a drug-trafficking offense. Kimbrough pleaded guilty to all four charges.

Under the relevant statutes, Kimbrough's plea subjected him to an aggregate sentence of 15 years to life in prison: 10 years to life for the three drug offenses, plus a consecutive term of 5 years to life for the firearm offense. In order to determine the appropriate sentence within this statutory range, the District Court first calculated Kimbrough's sentence under the advisory Sentencing Guidelines. Kimbrough's guilty plea acknowledged that he was accountable for 56 grams of crack cocaine and 92.1 grams of powder cocaine. This quantity of drugs yielded a base offense level of 32 for the three drug charges. See United States Sentencing Commission, Guidelines Manual § 2D1.1(c). Finding that Kimbrough, by asserting sole culpability for the crime, had testified falsely at his codefendant's trial, the District Court increased his offense level to 34. See § 3C1.1. In accord with the presentence report, the court determined that Kimbrough's criminal history category was II. An offense level of 34 and a criminal history category of II yielded a Guidelines range of 168 to 210 months for the three drug charges. The Guidelines sentence for the firearm offense was the statutory minimum, 60 months. See USSG § 2K2.4(b). Kimbrough's final advisory Guidelines range was thus 228 to 270 months, or 19 to 22.5 years.

A sentence in this range, in the District Court's judgment, would have been "greater than necessary" to accomplish the purposes of sentencing set forth in 18 U.S.C. § 3553(a). As required by § 3553(a), the court took into account the "nature and circumstances" of the offense and Kimbrough's "history and characteristics." The court also commented that the case exemplified the "disproportionate and unjust effect that crack cocaine guidelines have in sentencing." In this regard, the court contrasted Kimbrough's Guidelines range of 228 to 270 months with the range that would have applied had he been accountable for an equivalent amount of powder cocaine: 97 to 106 months, inclusive of the 5-year mandatory minimum for the firearm charge, see USSG § 2D1.1(c). Concluding that the statutory minimum sentence was "clearly long enough" to accomplish the objectives listed in § 3553(a), the court sentenced Kimbrough to 15 years, or 180 months, in prison plus 5 years of supervised release. [The Fourth Circuit reversed.]

Although chemically similar, crack and powder cocaine are handled very differently for sentencing purposes. The 100-to-1 ratio [under the Guidelines applicable at the time of Kimbrough's sentencing] yields sentences for crack offenses three to six times longer than those for powder offenses involving equal amounts of drugs. This disparity means that a major supplier of powder cocaine may receive a shorter sentence than a low-level dealer who buys powder from the supplier but then converts it to crack.

* * *

[T]he Government argues that if district courts are * * * permitted to vary from the Guidelines based on their disagreement with the crack/powder disparity, "defendants with identical real conduct will receive markedly different sentences, depending on nothing more than the particular judge drawn for sentencing." * * * [I]t is unquestioned that uniformity remains an important goal of sentencing. As we explained in *Booker*, however, * * * some departures from uniformity were a necessary cost of the remedy we adopted. * * *

Moreover, to the extent that the Government correctly identifies risks of "unwarranted sentence disparities" within the meaning of 18 U.S.C. § 3553(a)(6), the proper solution is not to treat the crack/powder ratio as mandatory. Section 3553(a)(6) directs district courts to consider the need to avoid unwarranted disparities—along with other § 3553(a) factors—when imposing sentences. * * * To reach an appropriate sentence, these disparities must be weighed against the other § 3553(a) factors and any unwarranted disparity created by the crack/powder ratio itself.

* * *

While rendering the Sentencing Guidelines advisory, we have nevertheless preserved a key role for the Sentencing Commission. * * * [D]istrict courts must treat the Guidelines as the starting point and the initial benchmark. * * *

We have accordingly recognized that, in the ordinary case, the Commission's recommendation of a sentencing range will reflect a rough approximation of sentences that might achieve § 3553(a)'s objectives. The sentencing judge, on the other hand, has greater familiarity with the individual case and the individual defendant before him than the Commission or the appeals court. He is therefore in a superior position to find facts and judge their import under § 3553(a) in each particular case. In light of these discrete institutional strengths, a district court's decision to vary from the advisory Guidelines may attract greatest respect when the sentencing judge finds a particular case outside the "heartland" to which the Commission intends individual Guidelines to apply. On the other hand, while the Guidelines are no longer binding, closer review may be in order when the sentencing judge varies from the Guidelines based solely on the judge's view that the Guidelines range fails properly to reflect § 3553(a) considerations even in a mine-run case.

The crack cocaine Guidelines, however, present no occasion for elaborative discussion of this matter because those Guidelines do not exemplify the Commission's exercise of its characteristic institutional role.

In formulating Guidelines ranges for crack cocaine offenses, * * * the Commission looked to the mandatory minimum sentences set [by Congress], and did not take account of empirical data and national experience. Indeed, the Commission itself has reported that the crack/powder disparity produces disproportionately harsh sanctions * * *. Given all this, it would not be an abuse of discretion for a district court to conclude when sentencing a particular defendant that the crack/powder disparity yields a sentence greater than necessary to achieve § 3553(a)'s purposes, even in a mine-run case.

* * *

Taking account of the foregoing discussion in appraising the District Court's disposition in this case, we conclude that the 180-month sentence imposed on Kimbrough should survive appellate inspection. The District Court began by properly calculating and considering the advisory Guidelines range. It then addressed the relevant § 3553(a) factors. First, the court considered "the nature and circumstances" of the crime, see 18 U.S.C. § 3553(a)(1), which was an unremarkable drug-trafficking offense. * * * Second, the court considered Kimbrough's "history and characteristics." § 3553(a)(1). The court noted that Kimbrough had no prior felony convictions, that he had served in combat during Operation Desert Storm and received an honorable discharge from the Marine Corps, and that he had a steady history of employment.

Furthermore, the court alluded to the Sentencing Commission's reports criticizing the 100-to-1 ratio, noting that the Commission "recognizes that crack cocaine has not caused the damage that the Justice Department alleges it has." Comparing the Guidelines range to the range that would have applied if Kimbrough had possessed an equal amount of powder, the court suggested that the 100-to-1 ratio itself created an unwarranted disparity within the meaning of § 3553(a). Finally, the court did not purport to establish a ratio of its own. Rather, it appropriately framed its final determination in line with § 3553(a)'s overarching instruction to "impose a sentence sufficient, but not greater than necessary" to accomplish the sentencing goals advanced in § 3553(a)(2). * * *

The ultimate question in Kimbrough's case is whether the sentence was reasonable—*i.e.*, whether the District Judge abused his discretion in determining that the § 3553(a) factors supported a sentence of [15 years] and justified a substantial deviation from the Guidelines range. The sentence the District Court imposed on Kimbrough was 4.5 years below the bottom of the Guidelines range. But in determining that 15 years was the appropriate prison term, the District Court properly homed in on the particular circumstances of Kimbrough's case and accorded weight to the

Sentencing Commission's consistent and emphatic position that the crack/powder disparity is at odds with § 3553(a). * * *

[The concurring opinion of Justice Scalia is omitted.]

JUSTICE THOMAS, dissenting.

I continue to disagree with the remedy fashioned in *United States* v. *Booker*. The Court's post-*Booker* sentencing cases illustrate why the remedial majority in *Booker* was mistaken to craft a remedy far broader than necessary to correct constitutional error. The Court is now confronted with a host of questions about how to administer a sentencing scheme that has no basis in the statute. Because the Court's decisions in this area are necessarily grounded in policy considerations rather than law, I respectfully dissent.

* * *

[The dissenting opinion of Justice Alito is omitted.]

Rehabilitation and Guidelines Sentencing: Tapia v. United States

In Tapia v. United States, 564 U.S. 319 (2011), Justice Kagan wrote for a unanimous court as it held that 18 U.S.C. 3582(a), a part of the Sentencing Reform Act, does not permit a sentencing court to impose or lengthen a prison term in order to foster a defendant's rehabilitation. The statute provides as follows:

> The court, in determining whether to impose a term of imprisonment, and, if a term of imprisonment is to be imposed, in determining the length of the term, shall consider the factors set forth in section 3553(a) to the extent that they are applicable, recognizing that imprisonment is not an appropriate means of promoting correction and rehabilitation.

The Court found that the language of the statute clearly supported its holding, but added the following: "A court commits no error by discussing the opportunities for rehabilitation within prison or the benefits of specific treatment or training programs. To the contrary, a court properly may address a person who is about to begin a prison term about these important matters. And * * * a court may urge the BOP [Bureau of Prisons] to place an offender in a prison treatment program."

Appellate Review of Advisory Guidelines Sentences

After *Booker*, appellate courts are to review sentences for "reasonableness" as opposed to strict adherence to the Guidelines. One question for the appellate courts was whether a sentence within the Guidelines range is "presumptively" reasonable. The Supreme Court answered that question in the next case.

RITA V. UNITED STATES

Supreme Court of the United States, 2007.
551 U.S. 338.

JUSTICE BREYER delivered the opinion of the Court.

The federal courts of appeals review federal sentences and set aside those they find "unreasonable." Several Circuits have held that, when doing so, they will presume that a sentence imposed within a properly calculated United States Sentencing Guidelines range is a reasonable sentence. The most important question before us is whether the law permits the courts of appeals to use this presumption. We hold that it does.

* * *

The basic crime in this case concerns two false statements which Victor Rita, the petitioner, made under oath to a federal grand jury. * * * Rita [was charged] with perjury, making false statements, and obstructing justice, and, after a jury trial, obtained convictions on all counts.

* * *

The parties subsequently proceeded to sentencing. Initially, a probation officer, with the help of the parties, and after investigating the background both of the offenses and of the offender, prepared a presentence report. * * * Ultimately, the report calculates the Guidelines sentencing range. The Guidelines specify for base level 20, criminal history category I, a sentence of 33-to-41 months' imprisonment. The report adds that there "appears to be no circumstance or combination of circumstances that warrant a departure from the prescribed sentencing guidelines."

* * *

At the sentencing hearing, both Rita and the Government presented their sentencing arguments. * * * Rita argued for a sentence outside (and lower than) the recommended Guidelines 33-to-41 month range.

The judge made clear that Rita's argument for a lower sentence could take either of two forms. First, Rita might argue *within the Guidelines' framework,* for a departure from the applicable Guidelines range on the ground that his circumstances present an "atypical case" that falls outside the "heartland" to which the United States Sentencing Commission intends each individual Guideline to apply. USSG § 5K2.0(a)(2). Second, Rita might argue that, independent of the Guidelines, application of the sentencing factors set forth in 18 U.S.C. § 3553(a) warrants a lower sentence. See *Booker*.

Thus, the judge asked Rita's counsel, "Are you going to put on evidence to show that [Rita] should be getting a downward departure, or under 3553, your client would be entitled to a different sentence than he should get under sentencing guidelines?" And the judge later summarized:

> "You're asking for a departure from the guidelines or a sentence under 3553 that is lower than the guidelines, and here are the reasons:
>
> "One, he is a vulnerable defendant because he's been involved in [government criminal justice] work which has caused people to become convicted criminals who are in prison and there may be retribution against him.
>
> "Two, his military experience. . . ."

Counsel agreed, while adding that Rita's poor physical condition constituted a third reason. And counsel said that he rested his claim for a lower sentence on "just [those] three" special circumstances, "physical condition, vulnerability in prison and the military service." * * *

After hearing * * * arguments, the judge concluded that he was "unable to find that the [report's recommended] sentencing guideline range . . . is an inappropriate guideline range for that, and under 3553 . . . the public needs to be protected if it is true, and I must accept as true the jury verdict." The court concluded: "So the Court finds that it is appropriate to enter" a sentence at the bottom of the Guidelines range, namely a sentence of imprisonment "for a period of 33 months."

* * *

On appeal, Rita argued that his 33-month sentence was "unreasonable" because (1) it did not adequately take account of "the defendant's history and characteristics," and (2) it "is greater than necessary to comply with the purposes of sentencing set forth in 18 U.S.C. § 3553(a)(2)." The Fourth Circuit * * * stated that "a sentence imposed within the properly calculated Guidelines range . . . is presumptively reasonable." * * * The Fourth Circuit then rejected Rita's arguments and upheld the sentence.

* * *

The first question is whether a court of appeals may apply a presumption of reasonableness to a district court sentence that reflects a proper application of the Sentencing Guidelines. We conclude that it can.

* * *

For one thing, the presumption is not binding. * * * Rather, the presumption reflects the fact that, by the time an appeals court is considering a within-Guidelines sentence on review, *both* the sentencing judge and the Sentencing Commission will have reached the *same* conclusion as to the proper sentence in the particular case. That double determination significantly increases the likelihood that the sentence is a reasonable one.

Further, the presumption reflects the nature of the Guidelines-writing task that Congress set for the Commission and the manner in which the Commission carried out that task. * * * The upshot is that the sentencing statutes envision both the sentencing judge and the Commission as carrying out the same basic § 3553(a) objectives, the one, at retail, the other at wholesale.

* * * The Commission, in describing its Guidelines-writing efforts, * * * says that it has tried to embody in the Guidelines the factors and considerations set forth in § 3553(a). * * * Rather than choose among differing practical and philosophical objectives, the Commission took an "empirical approach," beginning with an empirical examination of 10,000 presentence reports setting forth what judges had done in the past and then modifying and adjusting past practice in the interests of greater rationality, avoiding inconsistency, complying with congressional instructions, and the like.

* * *

The result is a set of Guidelines that seek to embody the § 3553(a) considerations, both in principle and in practice. * * * [I]t is fair to assume that the Guidelines, insofar as practicable, reflect a rough approximation of sentences that might achieve § 3553(a)'s objectives.

[T]he courts of appeals' "reasonableness" presumption, rather than having independent legal effect, simply recognizes the real-world circumstance that when the judge's discretionary decision accords with the Commission's view of the appropriate application of § 3553(a) in the mine run of cases, it is probable that the sentence is reasonable. * * *

We repeat that the presumption before us is an *appellate* court presumption. * * * The sentencing judge, as a matter of process, will normally begin by considering the presentence report and its interpretation of the Guidelines. He may hear arguments by prosecution or defense that the Guidelines sentence should not apply, perhaps because (as the Guidelines themselves foresee) the case at hand falls outside the "heartland" to which the Commission intends individual Guidelines to apply, perhaps because the Guidelines sentence itself fails properly to reflect § 3553(a) considerations, or perhaps because the case warrants a different sentence regardless. * * * In determining the merits of these arguments, the sentencing court does not enjoy the benefit of a legal presumption that the Guidelines sentence should apply.

* * *

A nonbinding appellate presumption that a Guidelines sentence is reasonable does not *require* the sentencing judge to impose that sentence.

Still less does it *forbid* the sentencing judge from imposing a sentence higher than the Guidelines provide for the jury-determined facts standing alone. * * *

In the present case the sentencing judge's statement of reasons was brief but legally sufficient. * * * The record makes clear that the sentencing judge listened to each argument. The judge considered the supporting evidence. The judge was fully aware of defendant's various physical ailments and imposed a sentence that takes them into account. The judge understood that Rita had previously worked in the immigration service where he had been involved in detecting criminal offenses. And he considered Rita's lengthy military service, including over 25 years of service, both on active duty and in the Reserve, and Rita's receipt of 35 medals, awards, and nominations.

The judge then simply found these circumstances insufficient to warrant a sentence lower than the Guidelines range of 33 to 45 months. * * * He immediately added that he found that the 33-month sentence at the bottom of the Guidelines range was "appropriate." He must have believed that there was not much more to say.

* * *

We turn to the final question: Was the Court of Appeals, after applying its presumption, legally correct in holding that Rita's sentence (a sentence that applied, and did not depart from, the relevant sentencing Guideline) was not "unreasonable"? In our view, the Court of Appeals' conclusion was lawful.

As we previously said, the crimes at issue are perjury and obstruction of justice. In essence those offenses involved the making of knowingly false, material statements under oath before a grand jury, thereby impeding its criminal investigation. The Guidelines provide for a typical such offense a base offense level of 20, 6 levels below the level provided for a simple violation of the crime being investigated (here the unlawful importation of machineguns). The offender, Rita, has no countable prior offenses and consequently falls within criminal history category I. The intersection of base offense level 20 and criminal history category I sets forth a sentencing range of imprisonment of 33 to 45 months.

Rita argued at sentencing that his circumstances are special. He based this argument upon his health, his fear of retaliation, and his prior military record. His sentence explicitly takes health into account by seeking assurance that the Bureau of Prisons will provide appropriate treatment. The record makes out no special fear of retaliation, asserting only that the threat is one that any former law enforcement official might suffer. Similarly, though Rita has a lengthy and distinguished military record, he did not claim at sentencing that military service should ordinarily lead to a sentence more lenient than the sentence the Guidelines impose. Like the

District Court and the Court of Appeals, we simply cannot say that Rita's special circumstances are special enough that, in light of § 3553(a), they require a sentence lower than the sentence the Guidelines provide.

* * * [The concurring opinion of Justice Stevens, joined in part by Justice Ginsburg, is omitted.]

JUSTICE SCALIA, with whom JUSTICE THOMAS joins, concurring in part and concurring in the judgment.

* * *

I believe it is possible to give some effect to the *Booker* remedial opinion and the purposes that it sought to serve while still avoiding the constitutional defect identified in the *Booker* merits opinion. Specifically, I would limit reasonableness review to the sentencing *procedures* mandated by statute.

* * *

JUSTICE SOUTER, dissenting.

[Justice Souter conducts a lengthy description of the *Apprendi* line of cases.]

If district judges treated the now-discretionary Guidelines simply as worthy of consideration but open to rejection in any given case, the *Booker* remedy would threaten a return to the old sentencing regime and would presumably produce the apparent disuniformity that convinced Congress to adopt Guidelines sentencing in the first place. But if sentencing judges attributed substantial gravitational pull to the now-discretionary Guidelines, if they treated the Guidelines result as persuasive or presumptively appropriate, the *Booker* remedy would in practical terms preserve the very feature of the Guidelines that threatened to trivialize the jury right. For a presumption of Guidelines reasonableness would tend to produce Guidelines sentences almost as regularly as mandatory Guidelines had done, with judges finding the facts needed for a sentence in an upper subrange. This would open the door to undermining *Apprendi* itself, and this is what has happened today. * * * [I]t seems fair to ask just what has been accomplished in real terms by all the judicial labor imposed by *Apprendi* and its associated cases.

* * *

Review of Outside-Guidelines Sentences for Reasonableness: Gall v. United States

In Gall v. United States, 552 U.S. 38 (2007), Justice Stevens wrote for the Court as it addressed an issue left open in *Rita*: whether sentences *outside* the Guidelines are presumptively *un*reasonable.

Gall was found guilty of conspiracy to distribute the drug "ecstasy." The probation officer calculated the Guideline sentencing range as 30 to 37 months of imprisonment. The District Judge sentenced Gall to probation for a term of 36 months and, in doing so, made a lengthy statement on the record and filed a detailed sentencing memorandum explaining his decision—noting that Gall had reformed, and citing a number of personal factors in his favor. The Court of Appeals held that a sentence outside of the Guidelines range must be supported by a justification that "is proportional to the extent of the difference between the advisory range and the sentence imposed." That court characterized the difference between a sentence of probation and the bottom of Gall's advisory Guidelines range of 30 months as "extraordinary" because it amounted to "a 100% downward variance," and held that such a variance must be supported by extraordinary circumstances not present in the case.

Justice Stevens found that the Court of Appeals' rule was inappropriately rigid and it had erred in essentially establishing a presumption of unreasonableness for outside-Guidelines sentences. He elaborated as follows:

> In reviewing the reasonableness of a sentence outside the Guidelines range, appellate courts may * * * take the degree of variance into account and consider the extent of a deviation from the Guidelines. We reject, however, an appellate rule that requires "extraordinary" circumstances to justify a sentence outside the Guidelines range. We also reject the use of a rigid mathematical formula that uses the percentage of a departure as the standard for determining the strength of the justifications required for a specific sentence.
>
> * * *
>
> [B]oth the exceptional circumstances requirement and the rigid mathematical formulation reflect a practice—common among courts that have adopted "proportional review"—of applying a heightened standard of review to sentences outside the Guidelines range. This is inconsistent with the rule that the abuse-of-discretion standard of review applies to appellate review of all sentencing decisions—whether inside or outside the Guidelines range.

Justice Stevens then explained the proper operation of sentencing by the trial court, and reasonableness review, after *Booker:*

As we explained in *Rita*, a district court should begin all sentencing proceedings by correctly calculating the applicable Guidelines range. As a matter of administration and to secure nationwide consistency, the Guidelines should be the starting point and the initial benchmark. The Guidelines are not the only consideration, however. Accordingly, * * * the district judge should then consider all of the § 3553(a) factors to determine whether they support the sentence requested by a party. In so doing, he may not presume that the Guidelines range is reasonable. He must make an individualized assessment based on the facts presented. If he decides that an outside-Guidelines sentence is warranted, he must consider the extent of the deviation and ensure that the justification is sufficiently compelling to support the degree of the variance. We find it uncontroversial that a major departure should be supported by a more significant justification than a minor one. After settling on the appropriate sentence, he must adequately explain the chosen sentence to allow for meaningful appellate review and to promote the perception of fair sentencing.

Regardless of whether the sentence imposed is inside or outside the Guidelines range, the appellate court must review the sentence under an abuse-of-discretion standard. It must first ensure that the district court committed no significant procedural error, such as failing to calculate (or improperly calculating) the Guidelines range, treating the Guidelines as mandatory, failing to consider the § 3553(a) factors, selecting a sentence based on clearly erroneous facts, or failing to adequately explain the chosen sentence—including an explanation for any deviation from the Guidelines range. Assuming that the district court's sentencing decision is procedurally sound, the appellate court should then consider the substantive reasonableness of the sentence imposed under an abuse-of-discretion standard. * * * If the sentence is within the Guidelines range, the appellate court may, but is not required to, apply a presumption of reasonableness. But if the sentence is outside the Guidelines range, the court may not apply a presumption of unreasonableness. It may consider the extent of the deviation, but must give due deference to the district court's decision that the § 3553(a) factors, on a whole, justify the extent of the variance. The fact that the appellate court might reasonably have concluded that a different sentence was appropriate is insufficient to justify reversal of the district court.

Justice Stevens concluded that although the court of appeals "believed that the circumstances presented here were insufficient to sustain such a marked deviation from the Guidelines range," it was "not for the Court of Appeals to decide *de novo* whether the justification for a variance is sufficient or the sentence reasonable," and "[o]n abuse-of-discretion review, the Court of Appeals should have given due deference to the District Court's reasoned and reasonable decision that the § 3553(a) factors, on the whole, justified the sentence."

Justice Scalia wrote a concurring opinion in which he stated that "substantive-reasonableness review is inherently flawed" but recognized the *stare decisis* effect of the statutory holding of *Rita*. He observed that "[t]he highly deferential standard adopted by the Court today will result in far fewer unconstitutional sentences than the proportionality standard employed by the Eighth Circuit."

Justice Souter also concurred and wrote that "I continue to think that the best resolution of the tension between substantial consistency throughout the system and the right of jury trial would be a new Act of Congress: reestablishing a statutory system of mandatory sentencing guidelines (though not identical to the original in all points of detail), but providing for jury findings of all facts necessary to set the upper range of sentencing discretion."

Justice Thomas dissented and "would affirm the judgment of the Court of Appeals because the District Court committed statutory error when it departed below the applicable Guidelines range."

Justice Alito also dissented and argued that "a district court must give the policy decisions that are embodied in the Sentencing Guidelines at least some significant weight in making a sentencing decision" because if those policies are rejected there will, over time, be significant disparity in sentencing—contrary to the intent of Congress, which the remedial opinion in *Booker* purported to implement.

Trial Court's Explanation of a Guideline Reduction or Sentence Modification: Chavez-Mesa v. United States

In *Chavez-Meza v. United States*, 138 S.Ct. 1959 (2018), the Court held that a district judge who originally sentenced the defendant to the bottom of his Guideline range (135–168 months) for possessing methamphetamine with intent to distribute adequately explained the reasons for imposing a *revised* sentence of 114 months—after the Sentencing Commission lowered the relevant Guideline range to 108 to 135 months.

Justice Breyer wrote for the majority. He relied on *Rita v. United States*, 551 U.S. 338 (2007), in which the Court set forth the explanation requirement at sentencing, and concluded that "[a]t bottom, the sentencing judge need only set forth enough to satisfy the appellate court that he has considered the parties' arguments and has a reasoned basis for exercising his own legal decisionmaking authority." The government argued that this was a sentence modification and "this fact alone should secure it a virtually automatic victory." Justice Breyer found that it was unnecessary to go so far. He concluded that "[e]ven assuming (purely for argument's sake) district courts have equivalent duties when initially sentencing a defendant and when later modifying the sentence, what the District Court did here was sufficient."

Finally, Justice Breyer indicated that the Court was not saying that a sentence modification never requires a more detailed explanation than was provided in this case, and explained that "under different facts and a different record, the district court's use of a barebones form order in response to a motion like petitioner's would be inadequate."

Justice Kennedy, joined by Justices Kagan and Sotomayor, dissented.

Appellate Court May Not Increase a Sentence in the Absence of a Government Appeal: Greenlaw v. United States

In Greenlaw v. United States, 554 U.S. 237 (2008), the defendant appealed from his sentence, and the government filed no cross-appeal. The court of appeals rejected the defendant's challenge to his sentence and then proceeded *sua sponte* to determine whether the defendant's sentence was too low. Relying on the doctrine of plain error, the court of appeals entered an order increasing the defendant's sentence by 15 years. The Supreme Court, in an opinion by Justice Ginsburg for six Justices, held that the court of appeals could not use the plain error doctrine to increase a sentence from which the government had not appealed.

Justice Ginsburg relied on 18 U.S.C. § 3742(b), which provides that the government may not appeal a sentence "without the personal approval of the Attorney General, the Solicitor General, or a deputy solicitor general designated by the Solicitor General." She declared that "Congress, in § 3742(b), has accorded to the top representatives of the United States in litigation the prerogative to seek or forgo appellate correction of sentencing errors, however plain they may be. That measure should garner the Judiciary's full respect."

Justice Alito, joined by Justices Breyer and Stevens, dissented. He argued that § 3742(b) "does not apportion authority over sentencing appeals between the Executive and Judicial Branches. By its terms, § 3742(b) simply apportions that authority *within* an executive department."

Sentencing Under a Guideline That Advises a Greater Sentence than the Guideline Existing When the Crime Was Committed: Peugh v. United States

In Peugh v. United States, 569 U.S. 530 (2013), the defendant committed a crime in 1999 but he was not caught, convicted and sentenced until 2009. The Sentencing Guideline applicable to his crime has changed in the interim—it has become more severe. Peugh argued that sentencing him under the later Guideline would violate the Ex Post Facto Clause, which prohibits application of a law in a criminal case that "changes the punishment, and inflicts a greater punishment, than the law annexed to the crime, when committed." Calder v. Bull, 3 U.S. 386 (1798). The Supreme Court, in an opinion by Justice Sotomayor, agreed.

The government's major contention against the Ex Post Facto claim was that after *Booker,* the Sentencing Guidelines are merely advisory—therefore there was no "law" that required a harsher sentence to be imposed. But Justice Sotomayor disagreed. She reasoned that while the Guidelines are advisory, they impose constraints that were sufficient to constitute a real risk that Peugh's sentence would be harsher than that imposed under the then-mandatory but less harsh Guideline in 1999. She noted that the Guidelines after *Booker* "impose a series of requirements on sentencing courts that cabin the exercise of [judicial] discretion. Common sense indicates that in general, this system will steer district courts to more within-Guidelines sentences." Justice Sotomayor noted that as a matter of fact, most sentences after *Booker* have fallen within the Guidelines.

Justice Sotomayor concluded that "[t]he federal system adopts procedural measures intended to make the Guidelines the lodestone of sentencing. A retrospective increase in the Guidelines range applicable to a defendant creates a sufficient risk of a higher sentence to constitute an ex post facto violation."

Justice Thomas dissented in an opinion joined by the Chief Justice and Justice Scalia, and in part by Justice Alito.

Incorrect Sentencing That Ends up to Be in the Correct Guidelines Range: Molina-Martinez v. United States

In Molina-Martinez v. United States, 578 U.S. 189 (2016), the Court considered a situation in which the trial court applied an incorrect Guidelines range—higher than the applicable one. But the sentence actually fell within the range for the right Guideline. The government argued that the defendant was not entitled to relief, but the Court in an opinion by Justice Kennedy, found that "in most cases, when a district court adopts an incorrect Guidelines range, there is a reasonable probability that the defendant's sentence would be different absent the error." Justice Kennedy declared that "[f]rom the centrality of the Guidelines in the sentencing process it must follow that, when the defendant shows that the district court used an incorrect range, he should not be barred from relief on appeal simply because there is no other evidence that the sentencing outcome would have been different had the correct range been used." Justice Kennedy found it notable that the sentencing judge in this case had expressed an interest in sentencing at the lower end of the (incorrect) Guideline that the court applied, while if the correct Guideline had been applied, the lower end of sentencing would have resulted in a sentence several months shorter than the one that the defendant received.

Justice Kennedy observed that "[t]here may be instances when, despite application of an erroneous Guidelines range, a reasonable probability of prejudice does not exist." He elaborated as follows:

> The record in a case may show, for example, that the district court thought the sentence it chose was appropriate irrespective of the Guidelines range. Judges may find that some cases merit a detailed explanation of the reasons the selected sentence is appropriate. And that explanation could make it clear that the judge based the sentence he or she selected on factors independent of the Guidelines. The Government remains free to point to parts of the record—including relevant statements by the judge—to counter any ostensible showing of prejudice the defendant may make. Where, however, the record is silent as to what the district court might have done had it considered the correct Guidelines range, the court's reliance on an incorrect range in most instances will suffice to show an effect on the defendant's substantial rights.

Justice Alito, joined by Justice Thomas, concurred in the judgment in *Molina-Martinez.*

Considering Post-Sentence Rehabilitation When a Sentence Is Vacated on Appeal: Pepper v. United States

In Pepper v. United States, 562 U.S. 476 (2011), the Court considered whether the Sentencing Guidelines allow a district court, when called on to resentence a defendant, to further reduce the sentence on the basis of post-sentence rehabilitation. The Court, in an opinion by Justice Sotomayor, held that when a defendant's sentence has been set aside on appeal, a district court at resentencing may consider evidence of the defendant's postsentencing rehabilitation, and such evidence may, in appropriate cases, support a downward variance from the now-advisory Guidelines range. She explained as follows:

> This Court has long recognized that sentencing judges "exercise a wide discretion" in the types of evidence they may consider when imposing sentence and that "[h]ighly relevant-if not essential-to [the] selection of an appropriate sentence is the possession of the fullest information possible concerning the defendant's life and characteristics." Williams v. New York, 337 U.S. 241 (1949). Congress codified this principle at 18 U.S.C. § 3661, which provides that "[n]o limitation shall be placed on the information" a sentencing court may consider "concerning the [defendant's] background, character, and

conduct," and at § 3553(a), which sets forth certain factors that sentencing courts must consider, including "the history and characteristics of the defendant," § 3553(a)(1).

Justice Sotomayor emphasized that Pepper's post-sentencing rehabilitation was plainly relevant to the § 3553 sentencing factors:

> Most fundamentally, evidence of Pepper's conduct since his release from custody in June 2005 provides the most up-to-date picture of Pepper's "history and characteristics." § 3553(a)(1). At the time of his initial sentencing in 2004, Pepper was a 25-year-old drug addict who was unemployed, estranged from his family, and had recently sold drugs as part of a methamphetamine conspiracy. By the time of his second resentencing in 2009, Pepper had been drug-free for nearly five years, had attended college and achieved high grades, was a top employee at his job slated for a promotion, had re-established a relationship with his father, and was married and supporting his wife's daughter. There is no question that this evidence of Pepper's conduct since his initial sentencing constitutes a critical part of the "history and characteristics" of a defendant that Congress intended sentencing courts to consider. § 3553(a).
>
> Pepper's postsentencing conduct also sheds light on the likelihood that he will engage in future criminal conduct, a central factor that district courts must assess when imposing sentence. See §§ 3553(a)(2)(B)–(C). As recognized by Pepper's probation officer, Pepper's steady employment, as well as his successful completion of a 500-hour drug treatment program and his drug-free condition, also suggest a diminished need for "educational or vocational training . . . or other correctional treatment." § 3553(a)(2)(D). Finally, Pepper's exemplary postsentencing conduct may be taken as the most accurate indicator of his present purposes and tendencies and significantly to suggest the period of restraint and the kind of discipline that ought to be imposed upon him.

Justice Breyer wrote a separate opinion concurring in part and in the judgment.

Justice Alito also wrote a separate opinion, concurring in part, concurring in the judgment in part, and dissenting in part. Justice Alito criticized the majority's reliance on *Williams* as a justification for considering post-sentencing rehabilitation.

> Anyone familiar with the history of criminal sentencing in this country cannot fail to see the irony in the Court's praise for the sentencing scheme exemplified by Williams v. New York, 337 U.S. 241 (1949). By the time of the enactment of the Sentencing Reform Act in 1984, this scheme had fallen into widespread disrepute. Under this system, each federal district judge was free to implement his or her individual

sentencing philosophy, and therefore the sentence imposed in a particular case often depended heavily on the spin of the wheel that determined the judge to whom the case was assigned.

Some language in today's opinion reads like a paean to that old regime, and I fear that it may be interpreted as sanctioning a move back toward the system that prevailed prior to 1984. If that occurs, I suspect that the day will come when the irrationality of that system is once again seen, and perhaps then the entire *Booker* line of cases will be reexamined.

Justice Thomas dissented, basically continuing his objection to the Court's remedial opinion in *Booker*. Justice Kagan took no part in the decision in *Pepper*.

Sentencing Guidelines Cannot Be Subject to Void-for-Vagueness Challenges: Beckles v. United States

In Beckles v. United States, 137 S.Ct. 886 (2017), the defendant was found eligible for a sentencing enhancement under the Guidelines because he was a career offender and his offense qualified as a "crime of violence." The Guidelines definition of "crime of violence" tracked a federal penal statute that the Supreme Court had previously found to be void-for-vagueness under the Due Process Clause. The defendant relied on the Supreme Court's striking down the penal statute as a basis for attack under the Sentencing Guidelines. But the Supreme Court held that Sentencing Guidelines (unlike penal statutes) cannot be subject to void-for-vagueness challenges. Justice Thomas, writing for seven Justices, reasoned that allowing a void for vagueness challenge was inconsistent with Supreme Court precedent upholding essentially unlimited sentencing discretion. He explained as follows:

> The limited scope of the void-for-vagueness doctrine in this context is rooted in the history of federal sentencing. Instead of enacting specific sentences for particular federal crimes, Congress historically permitted district courts wide discretion to decide whether the offender should be incarcerated and for how long. * * *
>
> Yet in the long history of discretionary sentencing, this Court has "never doubted the authority of a judge to exercise broad discretion in imposing a sentence within a statutory range." United States v. Booker; see also, e.g., *Apprendi* ("[N]othing in this history suggests that it is impermissible for judges to exercise discretion . . . in imposing a judgment within the range prescribed by statute").
>
> More specifically, our cases have never suggested that a defendant can successfully challenge as vague a sentencing statute conferring discretion to select an appropriate sentence from within a statutory

> range, even when that discretion is unfettered. * * * Indeed, no party to this case suggests that a system of purely discretionary sentencing could be subject to a vagueness challenge.

Turning specifically to the Guidelines, Justice Thomas concluded that a void-for-vagueness challenge was inapt because the Guidelines are, after *Booker,* discretionary and not binding.

> Because they merely guide the district courts' discretion, the Guidelines are not amenable to a vagueness challenge. As discussed above, the system of purely discretionary sentencing that predated the Guidelines was constitutionally permissible. If a system of unfettered discretion is not unconstitutionally vague, then it is difficult to see how the present system of guided discretion could be.

Justice Thomas closed by emphasizing that the Guidelines are not free from all constitutional concerns. He noted some limitations:

> Our holding today does not render the advisory Guidelines immune from constitutional scrutiny. This Court held in *Peugh,* for example, that a "retrospective increase in the Guidelines range applicable to a defendant" violates the Ex Post Facto Clause." But the void-for-vagueness and ex post facto inquiries are analytically distinct. Our ex post facto cases have focused on whether a change in law creates a significant risk of a higher sentence. A retroactive change in the Guidelines creates such a risk because sentencing decisions are anchored by the Guidelines, which establish the framework for sentencing. In contrast, the void-for-vagueness doctrine requires a different inquiry. The question is whether a law regulating private conduct by fixing permissible sentences provides notice and avoids arbitrary enforcement by clearly specifying the range of penalties available.
>
> * * *
>
> Finally, our holding today also does not render sentencing procedures entirely immune from scrutiny under the due process clause. See, e.g., Townsend v. Burke, 334 U.S. 736, 741 (1948) (holding that due process is violated when a court relies on "extensively and materially false" evidence to impose a sentence on an uncounseled defendant).

Justices Ginsburg and Sotomayor concurred only in the judgment. They argued that the Guideline under which Beckles was sentenced was not in fact constitutionally vague, so it was unnecessary to reach the broad holding that the majority did. Justice Sotomayor wrote separately to argue that the Guidelines should be subject to scrutiny as void-for-vagueness. She concluded that "[i]t violates the Due Process Clause to condemn someone to prison on the basis of a sentencing rule so shapeless as to resist interpretation. But the Court's decision today permits exactly that result."

3. The Principle of Relevant Conduct

Relevant Conduct and Subsequent Convictions: Witte v. United States

As discussed above, the Sentencing Guidelines assess the now-advisory sentence on the basis not only of the charge for which the defendant is convicted, but also on the basis of relevant uncharged conduct. If a defendant ends up with a longer sentence because the judge relies on uncharged "relevant conduct," what happens if the defendant is subsequently convicted of that uncharged conduct? Does he, in effect, get sentenced twice for the same conduct? This question arose in Witte v. United States, 515 U.S. 389 (1995), where Witte pleaded guilty to a marijuana offense. His uncharged cocaine transactions were considered as relevant conduct, and he received a longer sentence for the marijuana offense than he would otherwise have received. He was then charged with the cocaine transactions. He moved to dismiss the charges on double jeopardy grounds. The Court, in an opinion by Justice O'Connor, rejected Witte's double jeopardy attack, reasoning that he had not been punished previously for the cocaine transactions. Those transactions were simply a basis for "a stiffened penalty for the [marijuana] crime, which is considered to be an aggravated offense because a repetitive one."

4. Reductions for Substantial Assistance to the Government

Substantial Assistance Motions: Wade v. United States

Sentencing Guideline 5K1.1 provides for a possible reduction in sentence if the government files a motion to reduce the sentence on the basis of the defendant's substantial assistance in the prosecution of other defendants. In Wade v. United States, 504 U.S. 181 (1992), the Court held that a reduction for substantial assistance was, by the terms of the Guideline, contingent on a Government motion. Thus, at least under the Guidelines, the district court has no discretion to reduce the sentence for the defendant's assistance in other cases, unless the prosecution moves for such a reduction. The Court stated that the Government's decision not to make a substantial-assistance motion was reviewable only under two limited conditions: 1) if the prosecutor was acting pursuant to an unconstitutional motive such as to discriminate on the basis of race or religion; or 2) if the prosecutor's decision was totally arbitrary.

After *Booker,* however, district courts are not bound by the Guidelines—they are only advisory. So can a judge take account of the defendant's cooperation, even in the absence of a government motion, in reaching a sentence below the Guidelines? A fair reading of *Booker* would indicate that the sentencing judge can consider cooperation and sentence below the Guidelines range, without having to wait for a government motion, and can also reduce the sentence below the recommendation of the government if it does make a 5K1.1 motion. Of course, the ultimate sentence reached would have to be reasonable under Section 3553(a). See United States v. Saenz, 428 F.3d 1159 (8th Cir. 2005) (sentencing court can depart below government's recommended reduction, but in this case the reduction was unreasonable because the court was operating under a presumption that timely and truthful cooperation always warrants a reduction of more than 50 percent).

Substantial Assistance Motions and Mandatory Minimums: Melendez v. United States

In Melendez v. United States, 518 U.S. 120 (1996), the defendant entered into a plea agreement in which the government agreed to make a substantial assistance motion for reduction of the applicable Guideline sentence. As discussed above, such a motion is provided for under § 5K1.1 of the Guidelines. However, the defendant pleaded guilty to a drug crime that was also subject to a mandatory minimum sentence of 10 years. The government moved, in accordance with the agreement, for a reduction of the applicable sentence under the Guidelines, which would have resulted in a sentence of less than 10 years. The government did not move, as it could have done, for a departure from the statutory minimum—there was no requirement in the agreement that the government make such a motion. The sentencing court held itself bound by the statutory minimum, and sentenced the defendant to 10 years.

Justice Thomas, writing for the Court, held that the trial court acted appropriately. Justice Thomas relied on 18 U.S.C. § 3553(e), which requires a specific government motion to depart from an applicable mandatory minimum sentence on the basis of the defendant's substantial assistance. Justice Thomas referred to this system as "binary." Thus, if the defendant is to receive a reduction from an applicable statutory minimum as well as from the Sentencing Guideline, the government must specifically move for reduction from both—and defense counsel must seek an agreement from the government for two substantial assistance motions rather than being content with one.

As a result of 18 U.S.C. § 3553(e), mandatory minimum statutes increase the prosecutor's bargaining power. Because a sentencing judge can apply the 18 U.S.C. § 3553(a) factors to reach an appropriate sentence in every case in which no mandatory minimum statute applies, the threat to charge an offense governed by a mandatory minimum statute can be a powerful incentive for a defendant to plead guilty to a charge the prosecutor will accept that is not governed by such a statute.

E. SENTENCING DEVELOPMENTS IN THE STATES

Both before and after the adoption of federal sentencing guidelines, there has been a move in many states toward some form of determinate sentencing. This move often reflected cynicism toward the concept of parole and doubts about the ability of prisons to rehabilitate inmates. Truth in sentencing is frequently the mantra of sentencing advocates who believe that offenders and the public should know how long the offender will serve at the time the sentence is imposed.

Not all truth in sentencing states are alike. Most states use between 75% and 85% of a pre-determined "benchmark" as their standard to implement a truth in sentencing program, but the states differ in how they implement the program. For example, Virginia requires a mandatory 85% of an offender's effective sentence (which is the imposed sentence minus any suspended portion) to be served. Thus, judges in Virginia retain some freedom to individualize sentences at the time of sentencing. Other states—Utah, for example—have guideline sentencing and require an offender to serve 85% of a guideline sentence before any release is considered.

Some states—Florida and North Carolina, for example—have abolished parole completely. Other states retain some form of parole system. It may be misleading, however, to view the abolition of parole as meaning that offenders will serve their entire sentences in prison. In Virginia, for example, it is very common for judges to suspend large parts of a sentence of incarceration, which results in an offender serving a determinate time in prison and then being under supervision for the suspended portion of incarceration. The difference between this and parole is that the *judge* makes the decision to suspend a sentence at the time of sentencing, rather than having a parole board make a decision after sentence is imposed. But, the resulting punishment may be a shorter period of incarceration followed by a longer period of supervision, which may resemble a parole system and may be quite similar to a probationary system.

All states with guidelines appear to have the same basic goals: to reduce sentencing disparity and provide guidance to judges as to appropriate sentences for particular crimes and types of offenders. As in the federal system, most state jurisdictions with guidelines have made some effort to examine the pre-guideline sentences imposed by all judges in a state and to tailor the guidelines to the average or typical sentence previously imposed.

In drafting guidelines some sentencing commissions have considered the effect of sentences on prison populations. This may be viewed as consistent with the basic goal of reducing disparity. It may also be necessary for a state to consider adjusting some guidelines downward if the state desires to raise sentences for some violent offenders without creating additional prison space.

Of course, after *Apprendi* and *Blakely,* if Guidelines are mandatory, they run afoul of the Sixth Amendment and due process if they require a court to enhance a sentence on the basis of facts found by a judge at sentencing, and the enhancement takes it above the maximum provided for the base offense. For a discussion of how advisory guidelines can and do work in the states, see Pfaff, The Continued Vitality of Structured Sentencing After *Blakely*: The Effectiveness of Voluntary Guidelines, 54 U.C.L.A. L. Rev. 235 (2006).

In Cunningham v. California, 549 U.S. 270 (2007), the Court held that the California Determinative Sentencing Law violated *Apprendi* because it required a trial judge to impose a sentence in a higher sentencing category, upon the basis of certain aggravating facts found by the judge. Justice Ginsburg, writing for the six-person majority, declared as follows:

> Under California's DSL, an upper term sentence may be imposed only when the trial judge finds an aggravating circumstance. An element of the charged offense, essential to a jury's determination of guilt, or admitted in a defendant's guilty plea, does not qualify as such a circumstance. Instead, aggravating circumstances depend on facts found discretely and solely by the judge. In accord with *Blakely*, therefore, the middle term prescribed in California's statutes [for the crime charged and proved to the jury], not the upper term, is the relevant statutory maximum. Because circumstances in aggravation are found by the judge, not the jury, and need only be established by a preponderance of the evidence, not beyond a reasonable doubt, the DSL violates *Apprendi*'s bright-line rule: Except for a prior conviction, "any fact that increases the penalty for a crime beyond the prescribed statutory maximum must be submitted to a jury, and proved beyond a reasonable doubt."

Justice Kennedy (joined by Justice Breyer) and Justice Alito (joined by Justices Kennedy and Breyer) dissented.

In Oregon v. Ice, 555 U.S. 160 (2009), the Court upheld a state law allowing the judge to impose consecutive, rather than concurrent, sentences after finding certain facts. The Court distinguished *Apprendi* as a case involving "sentencing for a discrete crime, not—as here—for multiple offenses different in character or committed at different times."

III. SENTENCING PROCEDURES

A. GENERAL PROCEDURES

One might suppose that a part of the criminal justice system as important as sentencing would carry with it extensive procedural protections to guard against abuse of authority. But that supposition would be largely unfounded. Due process rights in sentencing have been hard to establish since 1949 when the Supreme Court decided the next case, the one to which Justice Alito referred in his separate opinion in *Pepper*.

WILLIAMS V. NEW YORK

Supreme Court of the United States, 1949.
337 U.S. 241.

JUSTICE BLACK delivered the opinion of the court.

A jury in a New York state court found appellant guilty of murder in the first degree. The jury recommended life imprisonment, but the trial judge imposed sentence of death. In giving his reason for imposing the death sentence the judge discussed in open court the evidence upon which the jury had convicted stating that this evidence had been considered in the light of additional information obtained through the court's "Probation Department, and through other sources." * * *

The Court of Appeals of New York affirmed the conviction and sentence over the contention that * * * "the sentence of death was based upon information supplied by witnesses with whom the accused had not been confronted and as to whom he had no opportunity for cross-examination or rebuttal" [and accordingly was in violation of due process].

* * * The record shows a carefully conducted trial lasting more than two weeks in which appellant was represented by three appointed lawyers who conducted his defense with fidelity and zeal. The evidence proved a wholly indefensible murder committed by a person engaged in a burglary. * * *

The case presents a serious and difficult question. The question relates to the rules of evidence applicable to the manner in which a judge may obtain information to guide him in the imposition of sentence upon an already convicted defendant. * * * To aid a judge in exercising * * * discretion intelligently the New York procedural policy encourages him to consider information about the convicted person's past life, health, habits, conduct, and mental and moral propensities. The sentencing judge may consider such information even though obtained outside the courtroom from persons whom a defendant has not been permitted to confront or cross-examine. It is the consideration of information obtained by a sentencing judge in this manner that is the basis for appellant's broad constitutional challenge * * *.

Tribunals passing on the guilt of a defendant always have been hedged in by strict evidentiary procedural limitations. But both before and since the American colonies became a nation, courts in this country and in England practiced a policy under which a sentencing judge could exercise a wide discretion in the sources and types of evidence used to assist him in determining the kind and extent of punishment to be imposed within limits fixed by law. Out-of-court affidavits have been used frequently, and of course in the smaller communities sentencing judges naturally have in mind their knowledge of the personalities and backgrounds of convicted offenders. * * *

In addition to the historical basis for different evidentiary rules governing trial and sentencing procedures there are sound practical reasons for the distinction. In a trial before verdict the issue is whether a defendant is guilty of having engaged in certain criminal conduct of which he has been specifically accused. Rules of evidence have been fashioned for criminal trials which narrowly confine the trial contest to evidence that is strictly relevant to the particular offense charged. * * * A sentencing judge, however, is not confined to the narrow issue of guilt. * * * Highly relevant—if not essential—to his selection of an appropriate sentence is the possession of the fullest information possible concerning the defendant's life and characteristics. And modern concepts individualizing punishment have made it all the more necessary that a sentencing judge not be denied an opportunity to obtain pertinent information by a requirement of rigid adherence to restrictive rules of evidence properly applicable to the trial.

* * * We must recognize that most of the information now relied upon by judges to guide them in the intelligent imposition of sentences would be unavailable if information were restricted to that given in open court by witnesses subject to cross-examination. And the modern probation report draws on information concerning every aspect of a defendant's life. The type and extent of this information make totally impractical if not impossible open court testimony with cross-examination. * * *

* * * New York criminal statutes set wide limits for maximum and minimum sentences. Under New York statutes a state judge cannot escape his grave responsibility of fixing sentence. In determining whether a defendant shall receive a one-year minimum or a twenty-year maximum sentence, we do not think the Federal Constitution restricts the view of the sentencing judge to the information received in open court.

* * *

[The dissenting opinion of JUSTICE MURPHY is omitted.]

Pre-Sentence Reports and the Sentencing Guidelines

Fed.R.Cr.P. 32 requires that a presentence report inform the defendant of the guidelines that govern his case and of pertinent policy statements by the Sentencing Commission. Ordinarily the presentence report is prepared by a probation officer. The goal of Rule 32 is to focus "on preparation of the presentence report as a means of identifying and narrowing the issues to be decided at the sentencing hearing." Advisory Committee's Note to 1994 amendment to Rule 32. Some of the procedural requirements in the Rule are:

(1) defense counsel is entitled to notice and a reasonable opportunity to be present at any interview of the defendant conducted by the probation officer who is preparing the presentence report;

(2) the probation officer must present the presentence report to the parties not later than 35 days before the sentencing hearing, in order to provide additional time for the parties and the probation officer to attempt to resolve any objections to the report;

(3) parties must provide the probation officer with a written list of objections to the presentence report within 14 days of receiving it;

(4) the probation officer must meet with the defendant, defense counsel, and an attorney for the Government, in order to go over objections to the report and to arrange for additional investigation and revisions to the report if necessary; and

(5) the sentencing court may treat the presentencing report as its findings of fact, except for material subject to the parties' unresolved objections.

The Court's opinion in United States v. Booker, which held that the Sentencing Guidelines are advisory and not mandatory, did not render presentence reports irrelevant or unhelpful. After *Booker,* sentencing courts still must determine the Guidelines sentence and must consider it as a factor among others listed in Section 3553(a). So sentencing courts still rely on presentence reports in determining the Guidelines sentence. Moreover, presentence reports have been expanded to assist the court in considering Section 3553(a) factors that had not previously been considered relevant to Guidelines sentencing, e.g., rehabilitation, personal circumstances of the defendant, etc.

Rule 32 Notice Requirement Does Not Apply to Court's Decision to Consider a Sentence Outside the Guidelines: Irizzary v. United States

Federal Rule 32(h) states that "[b]efore the court may depart from the applicable sentencing range on a ground not identified for departure either in the presentence report or in a party's prehearing submission, the court must give the parties reasonable notice that it is contemplating such a departure." In Irizarry v. United States, 553 U.S. 708 (2008), the Court held that this notice requirement does not apply to the sentencing court's consideration of whether to impose a sentence *outside the Guidelines*, which were made advisory in United States v. Booker. Justice Stevens, writing for the Court, found that the notice requirement was not appropriate as applied to the consideration of sentences outside the Guidelines after *Booker*. He explained that when the Guidelines were mandatory, the defendant needed notice of an anticipated departure in order to be able to have meaningful input into the sentencing decision. But "faced with advisory Guidelines, neither the Government nor the defendant may place the same degree of reliance on the type of expectancy that gave rise to a special need for notice."

Justice Stevens concluded as follows:

> Sound practice dictates that judges in all cases should make sure that the information provided to the parties in advance of the hearing, and in the hearing itself, has given them an adequate opportunity to confront and debate the relevant issues. We recognize that there will be some cases in which the factual basis for a particular sentence will come as a surprise to a defendant or the Government. The more appropriate response to such a problem is not to extend the reach of Rule 32(h)'s notice requirement categorically, but rather for a district judge to consider granting a continuance when a party has a legitimate basis for claiming that the surprise was prejudicial.

Justice Thomas concurred. Justice Breyer, joined by Justices Kennedy, Souter and Ginsburg dissented. The dissenters argued that a notice requirement would provide an important procedural safeguard and would help to assure the effective advocacy made all the more important after the Court's decision in *Booker*.

Preponderance of the Evidence

Factual determinations in sentencing are by a preponderance of the evidence rather than beyond a reasonable doubt. The Court in United States v. Watts, 519 U.S. 148 (1997), held that defendants can be sentenced under the Guidelines on the basis of relevant conduct for which they have been acquitted, so long as the conduct is shown at sentencing by a preponderance of the evidence. Courts after *Booker* have held that *Watts* is still the rule for assessing relevant conduct as part of an advisory Guidelines sentence. The court in United States v. Magallanez, 408 F.3d 672 (10th Cir. 2005) explains *Watts* and its applicability post-*Booker*, as follows:

The decision in *Watts* was predicated on the rationale that "different standards of proof . . . govern at trial and sentencing." An acquittal by the jury proves only that the defendant was not guilty beyond a reasonable doubt. Both before and under the Guidelines, facts relevant to sentencing have generally been found by a preponderance of the evidence. A jury verdict of acquittal on related conduct, therefore, "does not prevent the sentencing court from considering conduct underlying the acquitted charge, so long as that conduct has been proved by a preponderance of the evidence."

* * * Applying the logic of *Watts* to the Guidelines system as modified by *Booker*, we conclude that when a district court makes a determination of sentencing facts by a preponderance test under the now-advisory Guidelines, it is not bound by jury determinations reached through application of the more onerous reasonable doubt standard. In this respect, the prior Guidelines scheme is unchanged by the seeming revolution of *Booker*.

Consideration of Prior Convictions at the Sentencing Proceeding

In many cases, the prosecution offers evidence of the defendant's prior convictions at the sentencing proceeding. Under the Federal Sentencing Guidelines, a defendant's prior convictions, both state and federal, are relevant to the criminal history category that is part of the sentencing matrix. Moreover, many specific sentencing statutes provide for enhancement if the defendant has been convicted of certain specified state or federal crimes.

One question that arises with the use of these prior convictions for sentencing purposes is whether the defendant has a right to challenge their validity at the sentencing proceeding. This is a particular problem in federal sentencing proceedings where the defendant wishes to attack prior state convictions. For example, in Custis v. United States, 511 U.S. 485 (1994), the defendant was given an enhanced sentence under the Armed Career Criminal Act (18 U.S.C. § 924(e)) on the basis of having three previous state convictions "for a violent felony or a serious drug offense." At the sentencing hearing, Custis sought to attack his prior state convictions collaterally on the ground that one was based on an invalid guilty plea and another was tainted by ineffective assistance of counsel.

The Court, in an opinion by Chief Justice Rehnquist, held that Custis had no statutory or constitutional right to collaterally attack a prior state conviction at his federal sentencing hearing. The only exception would be if the state conviction was obtained in the complete absence of counsel in violation of Gideon v. Wainwright. The Chief Justice distinguished a collateral attack for absence of counsel from a collateral attack for an invalid guilty plea or ineffective assistance of counsel, on the basis that a *Gideon* defect is "jurisdictional" while the other defects are not. He expressed concern about upsetting the finality of convictions, and about the costliness of having to investigate the effectiveness of counsel or the voluntariness of a guilty plea in a long-completed state proceeding. Justice Souter, joined by Justices Blackmun and Stevens, dissented in *Custis.* He saw no constitutional distinction between a collateral attack based on the absence of counsel and a collateral attack based on ineffective assistance of counsel or an invalid guilty plea.

Use of Hearsay at Sentencing Under the Guidelines

Williams permitted the use of hearsay by a sentencing judge. Should the rationale of *Williams* apply to guidelines sentencing? In United States v. Silverman, 976 F.2d 1502 (6th Cir.1992), the court held that the right to confrontation was not applicable to sentencing proceedings involving disputed facts under the Federal Sentencing Guidelines. Thus, the sentencing court is permitted to use hearsay in assessing a sentence under the Guidelines. The court rejected the contention that sentencing under the Guidelines is substantially different from the discretionary sentencing procedures reviewed in *Williams.* The court asserted that procedural requirements for establishing the "factual basis of sentencing, akin to the real offense aspects of pre-guideline sentencing, continue from former sentencing practices." It concluded that "[s]o long as the evidence in the presentence report bears some minimal indicia of reliability in respect of defendant's right to due process, the district court may still continue to consider and rely on hearsay evidence without any confrontation requirement." See also United States v. Petty, 982 F.2d 1365 (9th Cir.1993) (joining all other circuits in holding that the Confrontation Clause does not apply to Guidelines sentencing and declaring that "the procedural protections afforded a convicted defendant at sentencing are traditionally less stringent than the protections afforded a presumptively innocent defendant at trial").

Courts have held that *Booker* has not changed the traditional rule that a sentencing court can rely on hearsay in assessing facts, and that the defendant still has no right to confrontation at a sentencing proceeding. The rationale is that *Booker* simply made the Guidelines advisory; there was no intent and no reason to alter the accepted rules of factual determinations by sentencing courts. See United States v. Umana, 750 F.3d 320 (4th Cir. 2014) ("We conclude that *Williams* squarely disposes of Umana's argument that the Sixth Amendment right to confrontation should apply to capital sentencing."); United States v. Brown, 430 F.3d 942 (8th Cir. 2005) (sentencing court can rely on hearsay in determining sentence after *Booker:* "In determining the appropriate guidelines sentencing range to be considered as a factor under § 3553(a), we see nothing in *Booker* that would require the court to determine the sentence in any manner other than the way the sentence would have been determined pre-*Booker*."); United States v. Luciano, 414 F.3d 174 (1st Cir. 2005) (*Booker* did not alter the view that there is no Sixth Amendment right to confront witnesses during the sentencing phase.). See also Fed.R.Evid. 1101 (Evidence Rules, other than privilege, are not applicable to sentencing proceedings).

B. PAROLE AND PROBATION PROCEDURES

1. Probation and Parole Denials; Classification Decisions

When a trial judge considers whether to impose probation—either in addition to or in lieu of a sentence of incarceration—the *Williams* attitude toward procedural rights prevails. In People v. Edwards, 18 Cal.3d 796, 135 Cal.Rptr. 411, 557 P.2d 995 (1976), for example, the court held that a trial judge need not state reasons for denying probation. But parole is a different concept altogether. The parole board makes a determination whether someone who has been sentenced should be released before the sentence is fully served (though as we have seen, this is no longer the case in the federal system and in those states that have abolished parole). For some time courts differed over the question of what, if any, procedural protections are constitutionally required in parole-release decisionmaking. The threshold question was whether a constitutionally protected liberty interest was at stake; if so, then certain procedural protections would be constitutionally mandated under the Due Process Clause. The Supreme Court considered the due process questions in a series of cases.

In Greenholtz v. Inmates, 442 U.S. 1 (1979), Chief Justice Burger wrote for the Court that the possibility of parole does not by itself create an entitlement to due process protections, but that some parole systems, including Nebraska's which was at issue in the case, create legitimate expectations of release that require some procedural protections. The decision required some opportunity for the parole applicant to be heard and some indication of the reasons why parole is not granted. Justice Marshall's dissenting opinion was joined by Justices Brennan and Stevens. Justice Powell agreed with these dissenters that parole decisionmaking triggered due process safeguards, but was unwilling to provide as many safeguards as the others would have. However, he concluded that Nebraska provided an inadequate opportunity for prisoners to present information to parole authorities. The Court relied upon *Greenholtz* in Board of Pardons v. Allen, 482 U.S. 369 (1987), which held, 6–3, that Montana parole law created a liberty interest. Justice O'Connor, joined Chief Justice Rehnquist and Justice Scalia, dissented.

No constitutionally protected expectancy interest was found in an explicitly discretionary pardon system despite the frequency with which pardons were granted. Connecticut Bd. of Pardons v. Dumschat, 452 U.S. 458 (1981). See also Jago v. Van Curen, 454 U.S. 14 (1981) (inmate told that he was being paroled had no protected interest that was violated when parole was rescinded before release from custody).

2. Probation and Parole Revocations

MORRISSEY V. BREWER

Supreme Court of the United States, 1972.
408 U.S. 471.

CHIEF JUSTICE BURGER delivered the opinion of the Court.

[Morrisey and Booher both were paroled from Iowa state prisons. Each subsequently had his parole revoked because of violations of parole conditions, and each sued, challenging the revocation procedures. One principal line of attack was that the absence of a revocation hearing violated due process.]

To accomplish the purpose of parole, those who are allowed to leave prison early are subjected to specified conditions for the duration of their terms. These conditions restrict their activities substantially beyond the ordinary restrictions imposed by law on an individual citizen. * * *

It has been estimated that 35–45% of all parolees are subjected to revocation and return to prison. Sometimes revocation occurs when the parolee is accused of another crime; it is often preferred to a new prosecution because of the procedural ease of recommitting the individual on the basis of a lesser showing by the State.

Implicit in the system's concern with parole violations is the notion that the parolee is entitled to retain his liberty as long as he substantially abides by the conditions of his parole. The first step in a revocation decision thus involves a wholly retrospective factual question: whether the parolee has in fact acted in violation of one or more conditions of his parole. Only if it is determined that the parolee did violate the conditions does the second question arise: should the parolee be recommitted to prison or should other steps be taken to protect society and improve chances of rehabilitation? The first step is relatively simple; the second is more complex. The second question involves the application of expertise by the parole authority in making a prediction as to the ability of the individual to live in society without committing antisocial acts. This part of the decision, too, depends on facts, and therefore it is important for the Board to know not only that some violation was committed but also to know accurately how many and how serious the violations were. Yet this second step, deciding what to do about the violation once it is identified, is not purely factual but also predictive and discretionary.

If a parolee is returned to prison, he often receives no credit for the time "served" on parole. Thus the returnee may face a potential of substantial imprisonment.

* * *

We begin with the proposition that the revocation of parole is not part of a criminal prosecution and thus the full panoply of rights due a defendant in such a proceeding does not apply to parole revocations. * * * Revocation deprives an individual not of the absolute liberty to which every citizen is entitled, but only of the conditional liberty properly dependent on observance of special parole restrictions.

We turn therefore to the question whether the requirements of due process in general apply to parole revocations. * * *

* * * The liberty of a parolee enables him to do a wide range of things open to persons who have never been convicted of any crime. * * * Though the State properly subjects him to many restrictions not applicable to other citizens, his condition is very different from that of confinement in a prison. * * *

We see, therefore, that the liberty of a parolee, although indeterminate, includes many of the core values of unqualified liberty and its termination inflicts a "grievous loss" on the parolee and often on others. * * * Its termination calls for some orderly process, however informal.

Turning to the question what process is due, we find that the State's interests are several. The State has found the parolee guilty of a crime against the people. * * * Given the previous conviction and the proper imposition of conditions, the State has an overwhelming interest in being able to return the individual to imprisonment without the burden of a new adversary criminal trial if in fact he has failed to abide by the conditions of his parole.

Yet the State has no interest in revoking parole without some informal procedural guarantees. * * * [We are not] persuaded by the argument that revocation is so totally a discretionary matter that some form of hearing would be administratively intolerable. A simple factual hearing will not interfere with the exercise of discretion. * * *

* * * What is needed is an informal hearing structured to assure that the finding of a parole violation will be based on verified facts and that the exercise of discretion will be informed by an accurate knowledge of the parolee's behavior.

* * *

We now turn to the nature of the process that is due, bearing in mind that the interest of both State and parolee will be furthered by an effective but informal hearing. In analyzing what is due, we see two important stages in the typical process of parole revocation.

(a) Arrest of Parolee and Preliminary Hearing. * * *

In our view due process requires that after the arrest, the determination that reasonable grounds exist for revocation of parole should be made by someone not directly involved in the case. * * * The officer directly involved in making recommendations cannot always have complete objectivity in evaluating them. * * *

This independent officer need not be a judicial officer. The granting and revocation of parole are matters traditionally handled by administrative officers. * * * It will be sufficient, therefore, in the parole revocation context, if an evaluation of whether reasonable cause exists to believe that conditions of parole have been violated is made by someone such as a parole officer other than the one who has made the report of parole violations or has recommended revocation. * * *

With respect to the preliminary hearing before this officer, the parolee should be given notice that the hearing will take place and that its purpose is to determine whether there is probable cause to believe he has committed a parole violation. The notice should state what parole violations have been alleged. At the hearing the parolee may appear and speak in his own behalf; he may bring letters, documents, or individuals who can give relevant information to the hearing officer. On request of the parolee, persons who have given adverse information on which parole revocation is to be based are to be made available for questioning in his presence. However, if the hearing officer determines that the informant would be subjected to risk of harm if his identity were disclosed, he need not be subjected to confrontation and cross-examination.

The hearing officer * * * should determine whether there is probable cause to hold the parolee for the final decision of the parole board on revocation. Such a determination would be sufficient to warrant the parolee's continued detention and return to the state correctional institution pending the final decision. * * *

(b) The Revocation Hearing. There must also be an opportunity for a hearing, if it is desired by the parolee, prior to the final decision on revocation by the parole authority. This hearing must be the basis for more than determining probable cause; it must lead to a final evaluation of any contested relevant facts and consideration of whether the facts as determined warrant revocation. The parolee must have an opportunity to be heard and to show, if he can, that he did not violate the conditions, or, if he did, that circumstances in mitigation suggest the violation does not warrant revocation. The revocation hearing must be tendered within a reasonable time after the parolee is taken into custody. A lapse of two months, as the State suggests occurs in some cases, would not appear to be unreasonable.

* * * Our task is limited to deciding the minimum requirements of due process. They include (a) written notice of the claimed violations of parole; (b) disclosure to the parolee of evidence against him; (c) opportunity to be heard in person and to present witnesses and documentary evidence; (d) the right to confront and cross-examine adverse witnesses (unless the hearing officer specifically finds good cause for not allowing confrontation); (e) a "neutral and detached" hearing body such as a traditional parole board, members of which need not be judicial officers or lawyers; and (f) a written statement by the factfinders as to the evidence relied on and reasons for revoking parole. We emphasize that there is no thought to equate this second stage of parole revocation to a criminal prosecution in any sense; it is a narrow inquiry; the process should be flexible enough to consider evidence including letters, affidavits, and other material that would not be admissible in an adversary criminal trial.

We do not reach or decide the question whether the parolee is entitled to the assistance of retained counsel or to appointed counsel if he is indigent.

We have no thought to create an inflexible structure for parole revocation procedures. The few basic requirements set out above, which are applicable to future revocations of parole, should not impose a great burden on any State's parole system. * * *

[JUSTICE BRENNAN, joined by JUSTICE MARSHALL, concurred in the result. He expressed his view that prisoners who can afford to retain and wish to retain counsel must be permitted to do so. He left open the question of whether counsel must be appointed for indigents. JUSTICE DOUGLAS dissented in part; although his view was not very different from the majority's, he would not as readily allow revocation upon a preliminary showing.]

Procedural Protections at a Probation Revocation Proceeding: Gagnon v. Scarpelli

In Gagnon v. Scarpelli, 411 U.S. 778 (1973), decided the year after Morrisey v. Brewer, Justice Powell wrote for the Court as it addressed what protections an individual was entitled to in a probation revocation proceeding. Gagnon pleaded guilty to a state charge of armed robbery, the trial judge sentenced him to 15 years' imprisonment, and the judge then suspended the sentence, placed Gagnon on probation for 7 years. After he was arrested for burglary, the state revoked his probation because of the burglary arrest without affording him either a hearing or counsel. Gagnon began serving his 15 year sentence and sought federal habeas corpus relief on the ground that the revocation of his probation without affording him a hearing or counsel was a denial of due process. The district court and the court of appeals agreed with him.

The Court affirmed in part, reversed in part, and remanded the case. Justice Powell's opinion for a unanimous Court held that Gagnon was entitled to both a preliminary hearing to determine whether there was probable cause to believe that he had violated his probation and a final hearing prior to the ultimate decision whether his probation should be revoked. Justice Powell wrote for eight Justices as the Court held that the state was not under a constitutional duty to provide counsel for indigents in all probation revocation cases, but that the state authority charged with responsibility for administering the probation system must use sound discretion to decide on the need for counsel on a case-by-case basis, and certain general guidelines as to whether the assistance of counsel was constitutionally necessary should be applied in the first instance by those charged with conducting the revocation hearing.

Justice Douglas dissented in part on the ground that since Gagnon claimed that his confession of the burglary had been made under coercion, due process required the appointment of counsel.

Consideration of Alternatives: Black v. Romano

A unanimous Supreme Court held in Black v. Romano, 471 U.S. 606 (1985), that the Due Process Clause does not require a sentencing court to indicate that it has considered alternatives to incarceration before revoking probation. Romano pleaded guilty to two counts of transferring and selling a controlled substance. The trial judge imposed two concurrent twenty-year sentences, suspended execution of the sentences, and placed Romano on probation for five years. Two months later Romano was arrested for leaving the scene of an accident after he had run over a pedestrian. The trial judge held a probation revocation hearing during which no suggestion was made by Romano or his two lawyers that an alternative to incarceration be considered. Instead, Romano's argument was that he had not violated his probation conditions.

Justice O'Connor's opinion for the Court analyzed *Morrissey* and *Gagnon* and concluded that although the Court did "not question the desirability of considering possible alternatives to imprisonment before probation is revoked," the "decision to revoke probation is generally predictive and subjective in nature" and "incarceration for violation of a probation condition is not constitutionally limited to circumstances where that sanction represents the only means of promoting the State's interest in punishment and deterrence." A statement of reasons for revocation is not required because "[t]he written statement required by *Gagnon* and *Morrissey* helps to insure accurate factfinding with respect to any alleged violation and provides an adequate basis for review to determine if the decision rests on permissible grounds supported by the evidence."

3. The Relationship Between Supervised Release and Imprisonment

In Johnson v. United States, 529 U.S. 694 (2000), the defendant was convicted on a number of narcotics and firearm counts. He was sentenced to a lengthy prison term on all these sentences, as well as a mandatory 3-year term of supervised release on the narcotics offenses. But because the firearms offenses were based on an incorrect interpretation of the law, they were vacated, and the court reduced the prison sentence. By the time this happened, Johnson had already served 30 months longer than the valid sentence. He was immediately released, and filed a motion to have his term of supervised release reduced by the amount of extra prison time he had served. The district court's refusal to grant this motion was upheld in a unanimous opinion written by Justice Kennedy. The Court held that a period of supervised release is not altered by the fact that a defendant serves excess prison time.

Justice Kennedy parsed 18 U.S.C. § 3624(e), the statutory provision governing the time at which a period of supervised release can begin. That statute provides explicitly that the term of supervised release "commences on the day the person is released from imprisonment." Justice Kennedy reasoned that "released" means what it says, and to say that Johnson "was released while still imprisoned diminishes the concept the word intends to convey."

Justice Kennedy also noted that beginning the period of supervised release upon actual release from imprisonment is consistent with Congress's purpose in establishing a system of supervised release. He observed that "Congress intended supervised release to assist individuals in their transition to community life. Supervised release fulfills rehabilitative ends, distinct from those served by incarceration." Therefore, it would be error to treat time in prison as interchangeable with a period of supervised release.

4. Probation and Parole Officers

In many jurisdictions, probation and parole revocations are common, in part because supervising officers are often rated on the basis of how many revocations they make. Many officers operate on a "trail 'em and jail 'em" system. In 2004, the ABA Justice Kennedy Commission, recommended a different approach to parole and probation revocation that was approved by the ABA House of Delegates:

> The Commission makes one recommendation concerning probation and parole: i.e., develop graduated sanctions for probation

> and parole violations that result in incarceration only when a probation or parole violator has committed a new crime or poses a serious danger to the community.
>
> * * * Hundreds of thousands of individuals on parole or probation are incarcerated each year for some type of violation of parole or probation. Many of these violations are "technical"—i.e., they do not reflect commission of a new crime or a threat to the community. The revolving door in which inmates are released to the community, returned to prison, released to the community, etc. is most evident in California, but it is also a problem in other jurisdictions. * * *
>
> * * *
>
> The [California] Little Hoover Commission concludes that a number of alternatives would be cost-effective and protect public safety:
>
> - Establish clear, transparent and binding guidelines for parole revocation
> - Work with police chiefs and sheriffs to develop a range of sanctions for violations
> - Include as sanctions community-based alternatives for "technical violations" (e.g., drug treatment, home monitoring, curfews)
> - Identify the serious violations justifying a return to prison;
> - Lower the revocation sentences based on offender risk assessments; and
> - Provide short term incarceration in community correctional facilities as an alternative.
>
> One way for jurisdictions to improve their parole and probation revocation decision-making is to utilize risk assessment tools. Washington and Oregon are two states that have taken the lead in using risk assessments in their criminal justice systems. Under its Offender Accountability Act, Washington classifies offenders according to the risk they pose of re-offending in the future and the amount of harm they have caused in the past. By classifying offenders by risk, Washington can devote more resources on higher-risk offenders and spend less on lower-risk offenders. * * * Jurisdictions may find that risk assessments offer useful data in deciding whether to incarcerate a parole or probation violator.

A successor to the ABA Justice Kennedy Commission, the ABA Commission on Effective Criminal Sanctions, developed another resolution to reform parole and probation revocation decisions that was approved by the ABA House of Delegates: "That the American Bar Association urges federal, state, territorial and local governments, to create standards for the performance of probation or parole officers that will consider, in addition to other appropriate factors, the number of individuals under an officer's supervision who successfully complete supervision, as well as those whose probation or parole is appropriately revoked, taking into account the nature of the officer's caseload." The report accompanying the resolution explains the goal:

> If parole and probation officers are empowered and encouraged to utilize sanctions other than outright revocation when offenders violate the conditions of supervision, if they are permitted to focus their energy on offenders who need the most help, and if an important factor in assessing the performance of officers is their success in helping offenders reintegrate, there is a greater opportunity to enhance public safety by enabling offenders to overcome addictions, find housing, receive job training and placement assistance, and other services. Public safety must remain the central responsibility of parole and probation agencies, but it is not enhanced by taking offenders whose behavior could be modified and recycling them in and out of prison without providing them the tools they need to change.

CHAPTER 12

DOUBLE JEOPARDY

■ ■ ■

I. INTRODUCTION

The Double Jeopardy Clause of the Fifth Amendment provides: "[N]or shall any person be subject for the same offense to be twice put in jeopardy of life or limb." Made applicable to the states in Benton v. Maryland, 395 U.S. 784 (1969), the clause provides three basic related protections:

> It protects against a second prosecution for the same offense after acquittal. It protects against a second prosecution for the same offense after conviction. And it protects against multiple punishments for the same offense.

North Carolina v. Pearce, 395 U.S. 711, 717 (1969). As you will see, the case law on the Double Jeopardy Clause seeks to balance the defendant's interest in finality and the government's interest in having one fair opportunity to prosecute and convict.

The Double Jeopardy Clause is not easily understood. Although its history suggests some answers to a few questions, most hard questions were not debated, perhaps not even contemplated, during the drafting and discussion of the Bill of Rights and the Fourteenth Amendment. And when the words of the Double Jeopardy Clause are parsed, it appears that the language offers few clues to the intent of its drafters.

II. THE EFFECT OF AN ACQUITTAL

If the defendant is "acquitted" the government cannot bring a second prosecution on the theory that the acquittal was mistaken. And the government may not appeal from an acquittal or legal rulings that produced the acquittal, even if there was error. In Sanabria v. United States, 437 U.S. 54 (1978), for example, the trial court erroneously excluded evidence of the alleged crime and then granted an acquittal based on the insufficiency of the remaining evidence. The Double Jeopardy Clause barred retrial.

It follows that if a jury acquits a defendant, the trial judge cannot grant the government a second trial, even if the judge believes the jury erred badly or was engaged in nullifying the court's instructions.

Given the preclusive effect of an acquittal, it is important to know what constitutes an acquittal—that is, to know when the government can appeal an adverse ruling or dismissal of a case on the ground that the trial court did something other than acquit the defendant. The Supreme Court considered these questions in United States v. Scott.

UNITED STATES V. SCOTT

Supreme Court of the United States, 1978.
437 U.S. 82.

JUSTICE REHNQUIST delivered the opinion of the Court.

[The defendant moved to dismiss a count against him on grounds of preindictment delay. The trial court granted the motion. The government sought to appeal the dismissal, but the Court of Appeals, relying on United States v. Jenkins, 420 U.S. 358 (1975), concluded that any further prosecution was barred by the Double Jeopardy Clause, due to the trial court's dismissal.] We now reverse.

* * * The Court has long taken the view that the United States has no right of appeal in a criminal case, absent explicit statutory authority. [Under the Criminal Appeals Act the government may appeal] "except that no appeal shall lie where the Double Jeopardy Clause of the United States Constitution prohibits further prosecution." 18 U.S.C.A. § 3731. * * *

* * * "Congress [in the Criminal Appeals Act] intended to remove all statutory barriers to Government appeals and to allow appeals whenever the Constitution would permit." United States v. Wilson, 420 U.S. 332, 337 (1975). * * * A detailed canvass of the history of the double jeopardy principles in English and American law led us to conclude that the Double Jeopardy Clause was primarily "directed at the threat of multiple prosecutions," and posed no bar to Government appeals "where those appeals would not require a new trial." We accordingly held in *Jenkins*, that, whether or not a dismissal of an indictment after jeopardy had attached amounted to an acquittal on the merits, the Government had no right to appeal, because "further proceedings of some sort, devoted to the resolution of factual issues going to the elements of the offense charged, would have been required upon reversal and remand."[a]

---

[a] The rule established in *Wilson* and *Jenkins* was later described in the following terms:

"[D]ismissals (as opposed to mistrials) if they occurred at a stage of the proceeding after which jeopardy had attached, but prior to the factfinder's conclusion as to guilt or innocence, were final so far as the accused defendant was concerned and could not be appealed by the Government because retrial was barred by double jeopardy. This made the issue of double jeopardy turn very largely on temporal considerations—if the Court granted an order of dismissal during the factfinding stage of the proceedings, the defendant could not be reprosecuted, but if the dismissal came later, he could." Lee v. United States, 432 U.S. 23, 36 (1977) (Rehnquist, J., concurring).

[Editor's Note: In *Lee*, a defendant, after the prosecutor's opening statement, moved to dismiss an information because it failed to allege specific intent. Following a two hour trial, the court noted

If *Jenkins* is a correct statement of the law, the judgment of the Court of Appeals relying on that decision, as it was bound to do, would in all likelihood have to be affirmed. Yet, though our assessment of the history and meaning of the Double Jeopardy Clause in *Wilson, Jenkins,* and Serfass v. United States, 420 U.S. 377 (1975),[b] occurred only three Terms ago, our vastly increased exposure to the various facets of the Double Jeopardy Clause has now convinced us that *Jenkins* was wrongly decided. It placed an unwarrantedly great emphasis on the defendant's right to have his guilt decided by the first jury empaneled to try him so as to include those cases where the defendant himself seeks to terminate the trial before verdict on grounds unrelated to factual guilt or innocence. We have therefore decided to overrule *Jenkins*, and thus to reverse the judgment of the Court of Appeals in this case.[c]

The origin and history of the Double Jeopardy Clause are hardly a matter of dispute. The constitutional provision had its origin in the three common-law pleas of *autrefois acquit, autrefois convict,* and pardon. These three pleas prevented the retrial of a person who had previously been acquitted, convicted, or pardoned for the same offense. As this Court has described the purpose underlying the prohibition against double jeopardy:

> "The underlying idea, one that is deeply ingrained in at least the Anglo-American system of jurisprudence, is that the State with all its resources and power should not be allowed to make repeated attempts to convict an individual for an alleged offense, thereby subjecting him to embarrassment, expense and ordeal and compelling him to live in a continuing state of anxiety and insecurity, as well as enhancing the possibility that even though innocent he may be found guilty." *Green* [v. United States, 355 U.S. 184] at 187–188.

These historical purposes are necessarily general in nature, and their application has come to abound in often subtle distinctions which cannot

---

that the defendant had been proved guilty beyond a reasonable doubt, but granted the motion to dismiss the information. Subsequently, the defendant was charged again with the same crime and convicted. The Court held that retrial was not barred by the double jeopardy clause. The Court reasoned that the trial court granted the motion to dismiss in contemplation of a second prosecution, and that it was permissible under the circumstances to delay a ruling on the motion to dismiss until the trial was completed.]

[b] [Editor's Note: In *Serfass*, the Court held that the government could appeal a *pre-trial* dismissal of an indictment, because the defendant, having never been subjected to factfinding on the guilt and innocence question, could be tried if the trial judge erred in dismissing the indictment.]

[c] [Editor's Note: The appellate scheme in the Federal courts is described in this opinion. Note that there can be no appeal in circumstances where new trial court proceedings would be necessary for there to be a valid conviction and those proceedings are barred by the Double Jeopardy Clause. For purposes of this chapter, it is not critical to master the Federal statute governing appeals; it is sufficient to remember that when the Supreme Court holds that there can be no appeal because of the double jeopardy clause, the Supreme Court is saying that there can be no further trial proceedings. The Court would say the same thing if the government tried to bring a second action instead of appealing, and the defendant complained.]

by any means all be traced to the original three common-law pleas referred to above.

* * *

[In] United States v. Ball, 163 U.S. 662 (1896), the Court established principles that have been adhered to ever since. Three persons had been tried together for murder; two were convicted, the other acquitted. This Court reversed the convictions, finding the indictment fatally defective, whereupon all three defendants were tried again. This time all three were convicted and they again sought review here. This Court held that the Double Jeopardy Clause precluded further prosecution of the defendant who had been *acquitted* at the original trial but that it posed no such bar to the prosecution of those defendants who had been *convicted* in the earlier proceeding. The Court disposed of their objection almost peremptorily:

> "Their plea of former conviction cannot be sustained, because upon a writ of error sued out by themselves the judgment and sentence against them were reversed, and the indictment ordered to be dismissed. * * * [I]t is quite clear that a defendant, who procures a judgment against him upon an indictment to be set aside, may be tried anew upon the same indictment, or upon another indictment, for the same offence of which he had been convicted."

Although *Ball* firmly established that a successful appeal of a conviction precludes a subsequent plea of double jeopardy, the opinion shed no light on whether a judgment of acquittal could be reversed on appeal consistently with the Double Jeopardy Clause. * * *

* * * [I]n Fong Foo v. United States, 369 U.S. 141 (1962), this Court reviewed the issuance of a writ of mandamus by the Court of Appeals for the First Circuit instructing a District Court to vacate certain judgments of acquittal. Although indicating its agreement with the Court of Appeals that the judgments had been entered erroneously, this Court nonetheless held that a second trial was barred by the Double Jeopardy Clause. Only last Term, this Court relied upon these precedents in United States v. Martin Linen Supply Co., 430 U.S. 564 (1977), and held that the Government could not appeal the granting of a motion to acquit pursuant to Fed.Rule Crim.Proc. 29 where a second trial would be required upon remand.[d] The Court * * * stated: "Perhaps the most fundamental rule in the history of double jeopardy jurisprudence has been that a verdict of acquittal * * * could not be reviewed, on error or otherwise, without putting [a defendant] twice in jeopardy, and thereby violating the Constitution."

These, then, at least, are two venerable principles of double jeopardy jurisprudence. The successful appeal of a judgment of conviction, on any

[d] [Editor's Note: In *Martin* the jury was hopelessly deadlocked and was discharged. Subsequently, the trial judge entered a judgment of acquittal. The Court held that any retrial would violate the Double Jeopardy Clause.]

ground other than the insufficiency of the evidence to support the verdict, poses no bar to further prosecution on the same charge. A judgment of acquittal, whether based on a jury verdict of not guilty or on a ruling by the court that the evidence is insufficient to convict, may not be appealed and terminates the prosecution when a second trial would be necessitated by a reversal.

* * * [T]he law attaches particular significance to an acquittal. To permit a second trial after an acquittal, however mistaken the acquittal may have been, would present an unacceptably high risk that the Government, with its vastly superior resources, might wear down the defendant so that even though innocent he may be found guilty. On the other hand, to require a criminal defendant to stand trial again after he has successfully invoked a statutory right of appeal to upset his first conviction is not an act of governmental oppression of the sort against which the Double Jeopardy Clause was intended to protect.

* * *

Although the primary purpose of the Double Jeopardy Clause was to protect the integrity of a final judgment, this Court has also developed a body of law guarding the separate but related interest of a defendant in avoiding multiple prosecutions even where no final determination of guilt or innocence has been made. Such interests may be involved in two different situations: the first, in which the trial judge declares a mistrial; the second, in which the trial judge terminates the proceedings favorably to the defendant on a basis not related to factual guilt or innocence.

* * *

When a trial court declares a mistrial, it all but invariably contemplates that the prosecutor will be permitted to proceed anew notwithstanding the defendant's plea of double jeopardy. Such a motion may be granted upon the initiative of either party or upon the court's own initiative. The fact that the trial judge contemplates that there will be a new trial is not conclusive on the issue of double jeopardy; in passing on the propriety of a declaration of mistrial granted at the behest of the prosecutor or on the court's own motion, this Court has balanced "the valued right of a defendant to have his trial completed by the particular tribunal summoned to sit in judgment on him," Downum v. United States, 372 U.S. 734, 736 (1963), against the public interest in insuring that justice is meted out to offenders.

Our very first encounter with this situation came in United States v. Perez, 9 Wheat. 579 (1824), in which the trial judge had on his own motion declared a mistrial because of the jury's inability to reach a verdict. The Court said that trial judges might declare mistrials "whenever, in their opinion, taking all the circumstances into consideration, there is a manifest necessity for the act, or the ends of public justice would otherwise be defeated." In our recent decision in Arizona v. Washington, 434 U.S. 497 (1978), we reviewed this Court's attempts to give content to the term "manifest necessity." That case, like *Downum*, supra, arose from a motion of the prosecution for a mistrial, and we noted that the trial court's discretion must be exercised with a careful regard for the interests first described in United States v. Perez.

Where, on the other hand, a *defendant* successfully seeks to avoid his trial prior to its conclusion by a motion for mistrial, the Double Jeopardy Clause is not offended by a second prosecution. * * * Such a motion by the defendant is deemed to be a deliberate election on his part to forego his valued right to have his guilt or innocence determined before the first trier of fact. * * *[e]

* * *

We turn now to the relationship between the Double Jeopardy Clause and reprosecution of a defendant who has successfully obtained not a mistrial but a termination of the trial in his favor before any determination of factual guilt or innocence. * * *

In the present case, the District Court's dismissal of the first count of the indictment was based upon a claim of preindictment delay and not on the court's conclusion that the Government had not produced sufficient evidence to establish the guilt of the defendant. Respondent Scott points out quite correctly that he had moved to dismiss the indictment on this ground prior to trial, and that had the District Court chosen to grant it at that time the Government could have appealed the ruling under our holding in Serfass v. United States, 420 U.S. 377 (1975). He also quite correctly points out that jeopardy had undeniably "attached" at the time the District Court terminated the trial in his favor; since a successful Government appeal would require further proceedings in the District Court leading to a factual resolution of the issue of guilt or innocence, *Jenkins* bars the Government's appeal. However, our growing experience with Government appeals convinces us that we must re-examine the rationale of *Jenkins* in light of *Lee, Martin Linen*, and other recent expositions of the Double Jeopardy Clause.

* * * It is quite true that the Government with all its resources and power should not be allowed to make repeated attempts to convict an individual for an alleged offense. * * *

But that situation is obviously a far cry from the present case, where the Government was quite willing to continue with its production of evidence to show the defendant guilty before the jury first empaneled to try him, but the defendant elected to seek termination of the trial on grounds

[e] [Editor's Note: But see the limited exception to this principle, established in the later case of Oregon v. Kennedy, discussed infra.]

unrelated to guilt or innocence. This is scarcely a picture of an all-powerful state relentlessly pursuing a defendant who had either been found not guilty or who had at least insisted on having the issue of guilt submitted to the first trier of fact. It is instead a picture of a defendant who chooses to avoid conviction and imprisonment, not because of his assertion that the Government has failed to make out a case against him, but because of a legal claim that the Government's case against him must fail even though it might satisfy the trier of fact that he was guilty beyond a reasonable doubt.

We have previously noted that "the trial judge's characterization of his own action cannot control the classification of the action." Despite respondent's contentions, an appeal is not barred simply because a ruling in favor of a defendant "is based upon facts outside the face of the indictment," or because it "is granted on the ground * * * that the defendant simply cannot be convicted of the offense charged." Rather, a defendant is acquitted only when "the ruling of the judge, whatever its label, actually represents a resolution [in the defendant's favor], correct or not, of some or all of the factual elements of the offense charged." Where the court, before the jury returns a verdict, enters a judgment of acquittal pursuant to Fed.Rule Crim.Proc. 29, appeal will be barred only when "it is plain that the District Court * * * evaluated the Government's evidence and determined that it was legally insufficient to sustain a conviction."

* * *

We think that in a case such as this the defendant, by deliberately choosing to seek termination of the proceedings against him on a basis unrelated to factual guilt or innocence of the offense of which he is accused, suffers no injury cognizable under the Double Jeopardy Clause if the Government is permitted to appeal from such a ruling of the trial court in favor of the defendant. * * * [I]n the present case, respondent successfully avoided * * * a submission of the first count of the indictment [to the jury] by persuading the trial court to dismiss it on a basis which did not depend on guilt or innocence. He was thus neither acquitted nor convicted, because he himself successfully undertook to persuade the trial court not to submit the issue of guilt or innocence to the jury which had been empaneled to try him.

* * * [W]here the defendant, instead of obtaining a reversal of his conviction on appeal, obtains the termination of the proceedings against him in the trial court without any finding by a court or jury as to his guilt or innocence [h]e has not been "deprived" of his valued right to go to the first jury; only the public has been deprived of its valued right to one complete opportunity to convict those who have violated its laws. No interest protected by the Double Jeopardy Clause is invaded when the

Government is allowed to appeal and seek reversal of such a midtrial termination of the proceedings in a manner favorable to the defendant.[f]

* * *

JUSTICE BRENNAN, with whom JUSTICE WHITE, JUSTICE MARSHALL, and JUSTICE STEVENS join, dissenting.

* * *

It is manifest that the reasons that bar a retrial following an acquittal are equally applicable to a final judgment entered on a ground "unrelated to factual innocence." The heavy personal strain of the second trial is the same in either case. So too is the risk that, though innocent, the defendant may be found guilty at a second trial. If the appeal is allowed in either situation, the Government will, following any reversal, not only obtain the benefit of the favorable appellate ruling but also be permitted to shore up any other weak points of its case and obtain all the other advantages at the second trial that the Double Jeopardy Clause was designed to forbid.

[The dissenters also objected to the difficulties in applying the Court's approach. They questioned the difference between a dismissal based on the defenses of insanity and entrapment and a dismissal for pre-indictment delay. The decision, in their view, needlessly complicates an area of law which was "crystal clear."]

Entry of a Judgment of Acquittal

If a trial judge enters a judgment of acquittal, before the jury reaches a verdict, that determination is final. United States v. Martin Linen Supply, 430 U.S. 564 (1977), so indicates. In fact, it holds that a judgment of acquittal following a mistrial is as final as a directed verdict.[1]

[f] We should point out that it is entirely possible for a trial court to reconcile the public interest in the Government's right to appeal from an erroneous conclusion of law with the defendant's interest in avoiding a second prosecution. In *Wilson*, supra, the court permitted the case to go to the jury, which returned a verdict of guilty, but it subsequently dismissed the indictment for preindictment delay on the basis of evidence adduced at trial. More recently in United States v. Ceccolini, 435 U.S. 268 (1978), we described similar action with approval: "The District Court had sensibly first made its finding on the factual question of guilt or innocence, and then ruled on the motion to suppress; a reversal of these rulings would require no further proceedings in the District Court, but merely a reinstatement of the finding of guilt."

We, of course, do not suggest that a midtrial dismissal of a prosecution, in response to a defense motion on grounds unrelated to guilt or innocence, is necessarily improper. Such rulings may be necessary to terminate proceedings marred by fundamental error. But where a defendant prevails on such a motion, he takes the risk that an appellate court will reverse the trial court.

[1] Compare *Martin Linen Supply* with United States v. Sanford, 429 U.S. 14 (1976) (no double jeopardy problem where trial court dismissed indictment after mistrial was declared, even though the court's determination was based on evidence presented at trial). See also United States v. Maddox, 944 F.2d 1223 (6th Cir.1991) (no double jeopardy violation where the trial judge granted a post-trial motion for acquittal, then changed his mind and reinstated the conviction;

In Smalis v. Pennsylvania, 476 U.S. 140 (1986), Justice White wrote for a unanimous Court as it found that a husband and wife, charged with various crimes in connection with a fire in a building they owned that killed two tenants, were acquitted for double jeopardy purposes when a state trial judge sustained a motion to dismiss at the close of the prosecution's case in a bench trial. The state trial judge in so ruling determined that the state's evidence was insufficient to establish factual guilt, so the Double Jeopardy Clause barred a post-judgment appeal by the government. Even if the state trial court was incorrect about the sufficiency of the evidence, jeopardy had attached and was terminated by the acquittal. The Court held that an acquittal would be found not only where the judge assessed the evidence as a matter of credibility and found it insufficient, but also where the judge determined that evidence was insufficient "as a matter of law." For a discussion of *Smalis* and other cases concerning government appeals, see Strazzella, The Relationship of Double Jeopardy to Prosecution Appeals, 73 Notre Dame L.Rev. 1 (1997).

In Price v. Vincent, 538 U.S. 634 (2003), the Court distinguished *Smalis* and *Martin Linen* and held that a trial judge's ruling was not sufficiently final to terminate jeopardy. The defendant was charged with murder. At the close of the government's case, defense counsel moved for a directed verdict of acquittal as to first degree murder, arguing that there was insufficient evidence of deliberation and premeditation. The trial judge stated:

> "My impression at this time is that there's not been shown premeditation or planning in the, in the alleged slaying. That what we have at the very best is Second Degree Murder. . . . I think that Second Degree Murder is an appropriate charge as to the defendants. Okay."

The prosecutor asked to make a brief statement regarding first-degree murder, but the defendant objected, arguing that his motion for directed verdict had been granted, and that further consideration of that charge would violate the Double Jeopardy Clause. The trial judge responded that he had "granted a motion" but had not directed a verdict. The judge noted that the jury had not been informed of his statements, and that his language indicated that he was going to reserve a ruling on the matter. Subsequently, the trial judge submitted the charge of first-degree murder to the jury and the defendant was convicted on that charge. The state courts, on review, concluded that the trial judge's comments on the directed verdict motion were not sufficiently final to constitute a judgment of acquittal terminating jeopardy.

The defendant sought habeas corpus relief, arguing that his rights under the Double Jeopardy Clause had been violated. Chief Justice

---

Martin Linen distinguished as a case in which the jury never reached a verdict, and therefore further proceedings would have been necessary).

Rehnquist, in an opinion for a unanimous Court, noted first that to obtain habeas relief the petitioner must show that the state court's adjudication of his claim was "contrary to, or involved an unreasonable application of, clearly established Federal law, as determined by the Supreme Court of the United States." [See the discussion of the standard of review of a state conviction on a collateral attack in Chapter 13]. Thus, if reasonable minds could differ about whether the state courts were correct in finding insufficient finality to the trial court's ruling in this case, habeas relief must be denied. On the question of finality, the Court noted that in *Smalis* and *Martin Linen*, unlike in the present case, "the trial courts not only rendered statements of clarity and finality but also entered formal orders from which appeals were taken." No such order was entered in the instant case. Under these circumstances, the Michigan courts were not unreasonable in concluding that the trial judge's oral ruling was insufficiently final to terminate jeopardy.

Acquittal for Failure to Prove an Element That the Government Never Had to Prove: Evans v. Michigan

In Evans v. Michigan, 568 U.S. 313 (2013), Justice Sotomayor wrote for the Court as it held that double jeopardy barred retrial of a defendant where the trial court entered a directed verdict of acquittal, based upon its view that the State had not provided sufficient evidence of a particular element of the offense—even though that element was not actually required to be proven under the applicable law. Evans was charged with burning "other real property." The State's evidence at trial suggested that Evans had burned down an unoccupied house. At the close of the State's case Evans moved for a directed verdict of acquittal, citing pattern jury instructions which indicated that an element of the crime for which he was charged is that the real property had to be a dwelling house. The trial court granted the directed verdict on that ground. On appeal by the government, all parties agreed that the trial court was wrong on the law—no proof that the property was a dwelling house was required. The appellate court rejected the defendant's argument that a retrial was barred by the Double Jeopardy Clause.

Justice Sotomayor relied on Arizona v. Rumsey, 467 U.S. 203 (1984), in which the trial court, sitting as sentencer in a capital case involving a murder committed during a robbery, mistakenly held that Arizona's statutory aggravating factor describing killings for pecuniary gain was limited to murders for hire. In *Rumsey,* the Court had held that a judicial acquittal premised upon a "misconstruction" of a criminal statute is an "acquittal on the merits . . . [that] bars retrial." Justice Sotomayor concluded that there was "no meaningful constitutional distinction between a trial court's 'misconstruction' of a statute and its erroneous addition of a statutory element."

Justice Sotomayor reasoned that "[t]he law attaches particular significance to an acquittal, so a merits-related ruling concludes proceedings absolutely." In this case, she found that the judge, albeit erroneously, had made a merits-based ruling. She rejected alternative arguments made by the State:

> [T]he State suggests that because Evans induced the trial court's error, he should not be heard to complain when that error is corrected and the State wishes to retry him. But we have recognized that "most judgments of acquittal result from defense motions," so "to hold that a defendant waives his double jeopardy protection whenever a trial court error in his favor on a midtrial motion leads to an acquittal would undercut the adversary assumption on which our system of criminal justice rests, and would vitiate one of the fundamental rights established by the Fifth Amendment." *Sanabria*, 437 U.S., at 78. It is true that when a defendant persuades the court to declare a mistrial, jeopardy continues and retrial is generally allowed. But in such circumstances the defendant consents to a disposition that contemplates reprosecution, whereas when a defendant moves for acquittal he does not.
>
> * * *

Justice Sotomayor rejected the government's argument to reconsider its double jeopardy cases involving judicial acquittals, including *Scott, supra*. She made clear that states do not have to permit certain types of trial court rulings:

> First, we have no reason to believe the existing rules have become so unworkable as to justify overruling precedent. The distinction drawn in *Scott* has stood the test of time, and we expect courts will continue to have little difficulty in distinguishing between those rulings which relate to the ultimate question of guilt or innocence and those which serve other purposes.
>
> * * *
>
> Finally, the State and the United States object that this rule denies the prosecution a full and fair opportunity to present its evidence to the jury, while the defendant reaps a "windfall" from the trial court's unreviewable error. But sovereigns are hardly powerless to prevent this sort of situation * * *. Nothing obligates a jurisdiction to afford its trial courts the power to grant a midtrial acquittal, and at least two States disallow the practice. Many jurisdictions, including the Federal system, allow or encourage their courts to defer consideration of a motion to acquit until after the jury returns a verdict, which mitigates double jeopardy concerns [because appellate reversal of the trial court's dismissal simply allows the jury verdict to

be reinstated]. See Fed. Rule Crim. Proc. 29(b). * * * But having chosen to vest its courts with the power to grant midtrial acquittals, the State must bear the corresponding risk that some acquittals will be granted in error.

Justice Alito dissented, arguing that "[f]or no good reason, the Court deprives the State of Michigan of its right to have one fair opportunity to convict petitioner, " and would have held "that double jeopardy protection is not triggered by a judge's erroneous preverdict ruling that creates an 'element' out of thin air and then holds that the element is not satisfied."

Is the Jury's Announcement That It Is Unanimous Against Guilt on One Count—but Deadlocked on Others—an Acquittal on That Count?: Blueford v. Arkansas

In Blueford v. Arkansas, 566 U.S. 599 (2012), the Court reviewed a capital case in which the jury reported to the judge that it 1) was unanimous against guilt on charges of capital murder and first degree murder, 2) was deadlocked on manslaughter, and 3) had not voted on negligent homicide. The court declared a mistrial. Before the Supreme Court, all agreed that the defendant could be retried on charges of manslaughter and negligent homicide. But Blueford argued that the Double Jeopardy Clause prohibited retrial on capital and first degree murder, as he had been "acquitted" on those charges.

Chief Justice Roberts, writing for the Court, held that Blueford had not been acquitted of the most serious charges for Double Jeopardy purposes. He reasoned as follows:

> When the foreperson told the court how the jury had voted on each offense, the jury's deliberations had not yet concluded. The jurors in fact went back to the jury room to deliberate further, even after the foreperson had delivered her report. When they emerged a half hour later, the foreperson stated only that they were unable to reach a verdict. She gave no indication whether it was still the case that all 12 jurors believed Blueford was not guilty of capital or first-degree murder, that 9 of them believed he was guilty of manslaughter, or that a vote had not been taken on negligent homicide. The fact that deliberations continued after the report deprives that report of the finality necessary to constitute an acquittal on the murder offenses.

Justice Sotomayor, joined by Justices Ginsburg and Kagan, dissented in *Blueford*. She stated as follows:

> Here, the trial judge instructed Blueford's jury to consider the offenses in order, from the charged offense of capital murder to the lesser included offenses of first-degree murder, manslaughter, and negligent homicide. The judge told the jury to proceed past capital

murder only upon a unanimous finding of a "reasonable doubt" as to that offense—that is, upon an acquittal. * * *

In this context, the forewoman's announcement in open court that the jury was "unanimous against" conviction on capital and first-degree murder was an acquittal for double jeopardy purposes. * * * That acquittal cannot be reconsidered without putting Blueford twice in jeopardy.

Reversal of a Judgment of Acquittal During the Trial: Smith v. Massachusetts

In Smith v. Massachusetts, 554 U.S. 442 (2005), the trial court, midway through a jury trial, granted Smith's motion for acquittal on one of the three offenses with which he was charged. The judge found that the government presented insufficient evidence on that count. Later in the trial, after Smith rested his case, the judge reconsidered and changed his mind about the acquittal. The jury was never informed of the acquittal and Smith was eventually convicted of all three charges.

The Court, in an opinion by Justice Scalia, found that the Double Jeopardy Clause prevented the trial judge from reversing his order of acquittal during the trial. He reasoned as follows:

> [W]hen, as here, the trial has proceeded to the defendant's presentation of his case, the possibility of prejudice arises. The seeming dismissal may induce a defendant to present a defense to the undismissed charges when he would be better advised to stand silent. Many jurisdictions still follow the traditional rule that after trial or on appeal, sufficiency-of-the-evidence challenges are reviewed on the basis of the *entire* trial record, even if the defendant moved for acquittal when the prosecution rested and the court erroneously denied that motion. In these jurisdictions, the defendant who puts on a case runs the risk that he will bolster the Government case enough for it to support a verdict of guilty. The defendant's evidence may lay the foundation for otherwise inadmissible evidence in the Government's initial presentation or provide corroboration for essential elements of the Government's case. In all jurisdictions, moreover, false assurance of acquittal on one count may induce the defendant to present defenses to the remaining counts that are inadvisable—for example, a defense that entails admission of guilt on the acquitted count.
>
> The Double Jeopardy Clause's guarantee cannot be allowed to become a potential snare for those who reasonably rely upon it. If, after a facially unqualified midtrial dismissal of one count, the trial has proceeded to the defendant's introduction of evidence, the acquittal must be treated as final, unless the availability of reconsideration has

been plainly established by pre-existing rule or case authority expressly applicable to midtrial rulings on the sufficiency of the evidence. That requirement was not met here. * * *

Justice Ginsburg, joined by Chief Justice Roberts and Justices Kennedy and Breyer, dissented in *Smith*. She stated that "Smith was subjected to a single, unbroken trial proceeding in which he was denied no opportunity to air his defense before presentation of the case to the jury. I would not deny prosecutors in such circumstances, based on a trial judge's temporary error, *one* full and fair opportunity to present the State's case."

Acquittal After a Jury Convicts

If a judge waits until after a jury convicts to enter a judgment of acquittal, may the government appeal that ruling? A footnote in *Scott* suggests that an appeal in those circumstances is permissible. The lower courts have agreed, reasoning that if the government is successful on appeal, the verdict can simply be reinstated and further proceedings are unnecessary. See United States v. Maddox, 944 F.2d 1223 (6th Cir.1991). You can see in the Supreme Court decisions suggesting that waiting until a jury verdict is rendered avoids some double jeopardy problems.

Dismissal When the Government Refuses to Participate in the Trial After the Jury Has Been Empaneled: Martinez v. Illinois

In Martinez v. Illinois, 527 U.S. 833 (2014), the defendant was charged with aggravated battery and mob action against two individuals whom the prosecution had difficulty in getting to trial. On the morning of trial, the victims were nowhere to be found. The trial judge offered to delay swearing in the jurors until a complete jury had been empaneled and to give the prosecution the opportunity to have the jury sworn or to dismiss its case. The state filed a written motion for a continuance on the ground it could not proceed without the victims. The judge denied it and offered to delay the trial for several more hours if that would help the prosecution. After the prosecution made clear that the whereabouts of the victims were "unknown," the judge swore in the jury and invited the prosecution to call its first witness. The prosecution declined to present any evidence. The defendant moved for a directed not-guilty verdict, which the judge granted. The state appealed and the Illinois Supreme Court held that Martinez was never at risk of conviction and jeopardy never attached.

The Court reversed in a per curiam opinion in which it said that "[t]here are few if any rules of criminal procedure clearer than the rule that jeopardy attaches when the jury is empaneled and sworn." The Court held that there was no doubt that Martinez's jeopardy ended in a manner that barred his retrial, as the trial judge granted the motion for a directed finding of not guilty and "[t]hat is a textbook acquittal." It stated that it had "never suggested that jeopardy may not have attached where, under the circumstances of a particular case, the defendant was not genuinely at risk of conviction."

III. ABORTED PROCEEDINGS

A. THE RIGHT TO A DETERMINATION FROM THE FIRST JURY IMPANELED

As noted earlier, the Double Jeopardy Clause is derived from English law, which provided that a defendant was put in jeopardy only after a conviction or an acquittal. The protection was afforded to a defendant only after a complete trial. The notion that a defendant may be put in jeopardy in a prosecution that does not terminate in a conviction or acquittal was incorporated gradually into the Double Jeopardy Clause. The Court determined that the defendant's interest in finality could be undermined if the prosecution could terminate a trial before the verdict, and institute a new proceeding. This protection, like other double jeopardy guarantees, becomes operative when jeopardy "attaches."

In Crist v. Bretz, 437 U.S. 28 (1978), the Court held that jeopardy attaches when the jury is impaneled and sworn. The Court reasoned that the impaneled-and-sworn rule of attachment reflects and protects the defendant's interest in retaining a chosen jury, which the Court found to be one of the core principles of double jeopardy protection. See United States v. Juarez-Fierro, 935 F.2d 672 (5th Cir.1991) (pre-voir dire oath to the venire does not constitute attachment of jeopardy; a jury is not empaneled until all parties have exercised their challenges, and jurors have been selected to serve on the petit jury). In a non-jury trial, jeopardy attaches when the court begins to hear evidence.

B. MISTRIAL DECLARED OVER THE DEFENDANT'S OBJECTION

The following cases consider when a retrial is permissible following a mistrial. The next case discusses the major prior cases on the subject.

1. The Requirement of Manifest Necessity for a Mistrial Granted over the Defendant's Objection

ILLINOIS V. SOMERVILLE

Supreme Court of the United States, 1973.
410 U.S. 458.

JUSTICE REHNQUIST delivered the opinion of the Court.

We must here decide whether declaration of a mistrial over the defendant's objection, because the trial court concluded that the indictment was insufficient to charge a crime, necessarily prevents a State from subsequently trying the defendant under a valid indictment. We hold that the mistrial met the "manifest necessity" requirement of our cases, since the trial court could reasonably have concluded that the "ends of public justice" would be defeated by having allowed the trial to continue. Therefore, the Double Jeopardy Clause of the Fifth Amendment, made applicable to the States through the Due Process Clause of the Fourteenth Amendment, did not bar retrial under a valid indictment.

[The defendant was indicted for theft. After the jury was sworn, but before any evidence was presented, the trial court granted the State's motion for a mistrial despite the defendant's objection, because the indictment was fatally defective for failure to allege the requisite intent. After a new trial and conviction, the defendant sought a writ of habeas corpus. He alleged that the new trial violated his rights under the Double Jeopardy Clause.]

The fountainhead decision construing the Double Jeopardy Clause in the context of a declaration of a mistrial over a defendant's objection is United States v. Perez, 9 Wheat. 579 (1824). Mr. Justice Story, writing for a unanimous Court, set forth the standards for determining whether a retrial, following a declaration of a mistrial over a defendant's objection, constitutes double jeopardy within the meaning of the Fifth Amendment. In holding that the failure of the jury to agree on a verdict of either acquittal or conviction did not bar retrial of the defendant, Mr. Justice Story wrote:

> We think that in all cases of this nature, the law has invested Courts of justice with the authority to discharge a jury from giving any verdict, whenever, in their opinion, taking all the circumstances into consideration, there is a manifest necessity for the act, or the ends of public justice would otherwise be defeated. They are to exercise a sound discretion on the subject; and it is impossible to define all the circumstances, which would render it proper to interfere. To be sure, the power ought to be used with the greatest caution, under urgent circumstances, and for very plain and obvious causes * * *.

This formulation, consistently adhered to by this Court in subsequent decisions, abjures the application of any mechanical formula by which to judge the propriety of declaring a mistrial in the varying and often unique situations arising during the course of a criminal trial. The broad discretion reserved to the trial judge in such circumstances has been consistently reiterated in decisions of this Court. * * *

While virtually all of the cases turn on the particular facts and thus escape meaningful categorization, it is possible to distill from them a general approach, premised on the "public justice" policy enunciated in United States v. Perez, to situations such as that presented by this case. A trial judge properly exercises his discretion to declare a mistrial if an impartial verdict cannot be reached, or if a verdict of conviction could be reached but would have to be reversed on appeal due to an obvious procedural error in the trial. If an error would make reversal on appeal a certainty, it would not serve "the ends of public justice" to require that the Government proceed with its proof when, if it succeeded before the jury, it would automatically be stripped of that success by an appellate court. * * * While the declaration of a mistrial on the basis of a rule or a defective procedure that would lend itself to prosecutorial manipulation would involve an entirely different question, such was not the situation * * * in the instant case.

In Downum v. United States [372 U.S. 734 (1963)], the defendant was charged with six counts of mail theft, and forging and uttering stolen checks. A jury was selected and sworn in the morning, and instructed to return that afternoon. When the jury returned, the Government moved for the discharge of the jury on the ground that a key prosecution witness, for two of the six counts against defendant, was not present. The prosecution knew, prior to the selection and swearing of the jury, that this witness could not be found and had not been served with a subpoena. The trial judge discharged the jury over the defendant's motions to dismiss two counts for failure to prosecute and to continue the other four. This Court, in reversing the convictions on the ground of double jeopardy * * * held that the second prosecution constituted double jeopardy, because the absence of the witness and the reason therefore did not there justify, in terms of "manifest necessity," the declaration of a mistrial.

In United States v. Jorn [400 U.S. 470 (1971)], the Government called a taxpayer witness in a prosecution for wilfully assisting in the preparation of fraudulent income tax returns. Prior to his testimony, defense counsel suggested he be warned of his constitutional right against compulsory self-incrimination. The trial judge warned him of his rights, and the witness stated that he was willing to testify and that the Internal Revenue Service agent who first contacted him warned him of his rights. The trial judge, however, did not believe the witness' declaration that the IRS had so warned him, and refused to allow him to testify until after he had consulted with an attorney. After learning from the Government that the remaining four witnesses were "similarly situated," and after surmising that they, too, had not been properly informed of their rights, the trial judge declared a mistrial to give the witnesses the opportunity to consult with attorneys. In sustaining a plea in bar of double jeopardy to an attempted second trial of the defendant, the plurality opinion of the Court, emphasizing the importance to the defendant of proceeding before the first jury sworn, concluded:

> It is apparent from the record that no consideration was given to the possibility of a trial continuance; indeed, the trial judge acted so abruptly in discharging the jury that, had the prosecutor been disposed to suggest a continuance, or the defendant to object to the discharge of the jury, there would have been no opportunity to do so. When one examines the circumstances surrounding the discharge of this jury, it seems abundantly apparent that the trial judge made no effort to exercise a sound discretion to assure that, taking all the circumstances into account, there was a manifest necessity for the *sua sponte* declaration of this mistrial.

* * *

[The Court rejected Somerville's argument that any trial on a defective indictment precludes retrial, and then considered whether the circumstances of the case justified the mistrial.]

In the instant case, the trial judge terminated the proceeding because a defect was found to exist in the indictment that was, as a matter of Illinois law, not curable by amendment. The Illinois courts have held that even after a judgment of conviction has become final, the defendant may be released on habeas corpus, because the defect in the indictment deprives the trial court of "jurisdiction." * * * The trial judge was faced with a situation * * * in which a procedural defect might or would preclude the public from either obtaining an impartial verdict or keeping a verdict of conviction if its evidence persuaded the jury. If a mistrial were constitutionally unavailable in situations such as this, the State's policy could only be implemented by conducting a second trial after verdict and reversal on appeal, thus wasting time, energy, and money for all concerned. Here, the trial judge's action was a rational determination designed to implement a legitimate state policy, with no suggestion that the implementation of that policy in this manner could be manipulated so as to prejudice the defendant. * * * Given the established standard of discretion * * *, we cannot say that the declaration of a mistrial was not required by "manifest necessity" or the "ends of public justice."

Our decision in *Jorn*, relied upon by the court below and respondent, does not support the opposite conclusion. * * * That opinion dealt with action by a trial judge that can fairly be described as erratic. The Court held that the lack of apparent harm to the defendant from the declaration of a mistrial did not itself justify the mistrial, and concluded that there was no "manifest necessity" for the mistrial, as opposed to less drastic alternatives. The Court emphasized that the absence of any manifest need for the mistrial had deprived the defendant of his right to proceed before the first jury, but it did not hold that that right may never be forced to yield, as in this case, to "the public's interest in fair trials designed to end in just judgments." * * *.

The determination by the trial court to abort a criminal proceeding where jeopardy has attached is not one to be lightly undertaken, since the interest of the defendant in having his fate determined by the jury first impaneled is itself a weighty one. Nor will the lack of demonstrable additional prejudice preclude the defendant's invocation of the double jeopardy bar in the absence of some important countervailing interest of proper judicial administration. But where the declaration of a mistrial implements a reasonable state policy and aborts a proceeding that at best would have produced a verdict that could have been upset at will by one of the parties, the defendant's interest in proceeding to verdict is outweighed by the competing and equally legitimate demand for public justice.

[Justice White, joined by Justices Douglas and Brennan, dissented. Relying on *Downum* and *Jorn,* Justice White argued that even when prosecutorial misconduct consists of a mistake or oversight, the defendant's interest in having the trial completed by the first tribunal prevails. This should be true even when no specific prejudice to the defendant is shown. In this case, the reason for the mistrial was the state's error.

Justice Marshall dissented separately. Also relying on *Downum* and *Jorn,* he argued that the court's "balancing" approach underemphasized the defendant's interest in continuing with the trial. Continuation, under the circumstances of the case, was a viable alternative to a mistrial in his view.]

NOTE ON THE IMPACT OF SOMERVILLE

Somerville generally has been considered a retreat from the heightened scrutiny of mistrials granted without the defendant's consent in *Downum* and *Jorn*. It is clear that after *Somerville,* the term "manifest necessity" is no longer an accurate description of what constitutes a proper ground for a mistrial sufficient to allow a new trial. It is more like "reasonable cause." See United States v. Toribio-Lugo, 376 F.3d 33 (1st Cir. 2004) (In assessing "manifest necessity," an appellate court's inquiry "inevitably reduces to whether the district judge's declaration of a mistrial was reasonably necessary under all the circumstances."). Is there really ever a "manifest necessity" to abort a trial because of a defective indictment when the defect could have been noticed by the prosecutor or the court and corrected before jeopardy attached?

Trial Court's Declaring Mistrial Was Not an Unreasonable Application of Manifest Necessity Standard: Renico v. Lett

In Renico v. Lett, 559 U.S. 766 (2010), the Court reviewed a habeas claim in which the petitioner argued that the trial court declared a mistrial without "manifest necessity" and therefore his retrial violated Double Jeopardy. Because the case was on habeas, the standard of review for the trial court's decision was extremely deferential. The question was not whether the trial court erred but whether its ruling was an unreasonable application of clearly established Supreme Court law. The trial judge granted a mistrial in a murder case in which the foreperson of the jury told the judge, in response to a question after the jury sent seven notes to the judge, that the jury would not be unanimous. Chief Justice Roberts noted that "the jury only deliberated for four hours, its notes were arguably ambiguous, the trial judge's initial question to the foreperson was imprecise, and the judge neither asked for elaboration of the foreperson's answers nor took any other measures to confirm the foreperson's prediction that a unanimous verdict would not be reached."

Nonetheless, the Chief Justice found that the trial court's grant of a mistrial was not an unreasonable application of the Supreme Court cases (the standard for review on habeas). The Chief Justice reasoned as follows:

> Since *Perez*, we have clarified that the "manifest necessity" standard "cannot be interpreted literally," and that a mistrial is appropriate when there is a "high degree" of necessity. * * * In particular, the trial judge's decision to declare a mistrial when he considers the jury deadlocked is accorded great deference by a reviewing court. * * *
>
> The reasons for allowing the trial judge to exercise broad discretion are especially compelling in cases involving a potentially deadlocked jury. There, the justification for deference is that the trial court is in the best position to assess all the factors which must be considered in making a necessarily discretionary determination whether the jury will be able to reach a just verdict if it continues to deliberate. In the absence of such deference, trial judges might otherwise employ coercive means to break the apparent deadlock, thereby creating a significant risk that a verdict may result from pressures inherent in the situation rather than the considered judgment of all the jurors.

Justice Stevens, joined by Justices Sotomayor and Breyer, dissented in *Renico*. She failed to see how the trial court's "abrupt" action could be considered "sound discretion" under any standard of review.

2. Manifest Necessity as a Flexible Test

ARIZONA V. WASHINGTON

Supreme Court of the United States, 1978.
434 U.S. 497.

JUSTICE STEVENS delivered the opinion of the Court.

An Arizona trial judge granted the prosecutor's motion for a mistrial predicated on improper and prejudicial comment during defense counsel's opening statement. * * *. The questions presented are whether the record reflects the kind of "necessity" for the mistrial ruling that will avoid a valid plea of double jeopardy, and if so, whether the plea must nevertheless be allowed because the Arizona trial judge did not fully explain the reasons for his mistrial ruling.

* * *

In 1971 respondent was found guilty of murdering a hotel night clerk. In 1973, the Superior Court of Pima County, Ariz., ordered a new trial because the prosecutor had withheld exculpatory evidence from the defense. * * *

Respondent's second trial began in January 1975. During the *voir dire* examination of prospective jurors, the prosecutor made reference to the fact that some of the witnesses whose testimony the jurors would hear had testified in proceedings four years earlier. Defense counsel told the prospective jurors "that there was evidence hidden from [respondent] at the last trial." In his opening statement, he made this point more forcefully:

> "You will hear testimony that notwithstanding the fact that we had a trial in May of 1971 in this matter, that the prosecutor hid those statements and didn't give those to the lawyer for George saying the man was Spanish speaking, didn't give those statements at all, hid them.
>
> "You will hear that that evidence was suppressed and hidden by the prosecutor in that case. You will hear that that evidence was purposely withheld. You will hear that because of the misconduct of the County Attorney at that time and because he withheld evidence, that the Supreme Court of Arizona granted a new trial in this case."

[The prosecutor moved for a mistrial, because there was no theory on which the prior suppression of evidence and granting of a new trial could be admissible, and the prejudice to the jury could not be repaired by any cautionary instruction. The judge granted the motion, but did not expressly find that there was "manifest necessity" for a mistrial, and did not expressly state that he had considered and found alternative solutions to be inadequate.]

Because jeopardy attaches before the judgment becomes final, the constitutional protection * * * embraces the defendant's "valued right to have his trial completed by a particular tribunal." The reasons why this "valued right" merits constitutional protection are worthy of repetition. Even if the first trial is not completed, a second prosecution may be grossly unfair. It increases the financial and emotional burden on the accused, prolongs the period in which he is stigmatized by an unresolved accusation of wrongdoing, and may even enhance the risk that an innocent defendant may be convicted. * * *

Unlike the situation in which the trial has ended in an acquittal or conviction, retrial is not automatically barred when a criminal proceeding is terminated without finally resolving the merits of the charges against the accused. Because of the variety of circumstances that may make it necessary to discharge a jury before a trial is concluded, and because those circumstances do not invariably create unfairness to the accused, his valued right to have the trial concluded by a particular tribunal is sometimes subordinate to the public interest in affording the prosecutor one full and fair opportunity to present his evidence to an impartial jury. Yet in view of the importance of the right, and the fact that it is frustrated by any mistrial, the prosecutor must shoulder the burden of justifying the mistrial if he is to avoid the double jeopardy bar. * * * The prosecutor must demonstrate "manifest necessity" for any mistrial declared over the objection of the defendant.

The words "manifest necessity" * * * do not describe a standard that can be applied mechanically or without attention to the particular problem confronting the trial judge. Indeed, it is manifest that the key word "necessity" cannot be interpreted literally; instead, contrary to the teaching of Webster, we assume that there are degrees of necessity and we require a "high degree" before concluding that a mistrial is appropriate.

The question whether that "high degree" has been reached is answered more easily in some kinds of cases than in others. At one extreme are cases in which a prosecutor requests a mistrial in order to buttress weaknesses in his evidence. * * * Thus, the strictest scrutiny is appropriate when the basis for the mistrial is the unavailability of critical prosecution evidence,[a] or when there is reason to believe that the prosecutor is using the superior resources of the State to harass or to achieve a tactical advantage over the accused.

At the other extreme is the mistrial premised upon the trial judge's belief that the jury is unable to reach a verdict, long considered the classic

[a] If, for example, a prosecutor proceeds to trial aware that key witnesses are not available to give testimony and a mistrial is later granted for that reason, a second prosecution is barred. Downum v. United States, 372 U.S. 734. The prohibition against double jeopardy unquestionably "forbids the prosecutor to use the first proceeding as a trial run of his case." Note, Twice in Jeopardy, 75 Yale L.J. 262, 287–288 (1965).

basis for a proper mistrial. * * * This rule accords recognition to society's interest in giving the prosecution one complete opportunity to convict those who have violated its laws.

* * * [T]here are especially compelling reasons for allowing the trial judge to exercise broad discretion in deciding whether or not "manifest necessity" justifies a discharge of the jury. * * * If retrial of the defendant were barred whenever an appellate court views the "necessity" for a mistrial differently from the trial judge, there would be a danger that the latter, cognizant of the serious societal consequences of an erroneous ruling, would employ coercive means to break the apparent deadlock. * * *

We are persuaded that, along the spectrum of trial problems which may warrant a mistrial and which vary in their amenability to appellate scrutiny, the difficulty which led to the mistrial in this case also falls in an area where the trial judge's determination is entitled to special respect.

In this case the trial judge ordered a mistrial because the defendant's lawyer made improper and prejudicial remarks during his opening statement to the jury. * * * We therefore start from the premise that defense counsel's comment was improper and may have affected the impartiality of the jury.

We recognize that the extent of the possible bias cannot be measured, and that the District Court was quite correct in believing that some trial judges might have proceeded with the trial after giving the jury appropriate cautionary instructions. In a strict, literal sense, the mistrial was not "necessary." Nevertheless, the overriding interest in the evenhanded administration of justice requires that we accord the highest degree of respect to the trial judge's evaluation of the likelihood that the impartiality of one or more jurors may have been affected by the improper comment.

* * * We are * * * persuaded by the record that the trial judge acted responsibly and deliberately, and accorded careful consideration to respondent's interest in having the trial concluded in a single proceeding. * * * Neither party has a right to have his case decided by a jury which may be tainted by bias; in these circumstances, "the public's interest in fair trials designed to end in just judgments" must prevail over the defendant's "valued right" to have his trial concluded before the first jury impaneled.

* * *

One final matter requires consideration. The absence of an explicit finding of "manifest necessity" appears to have been determinative for the District Court and may have been so for the Court of Appeals. If those courts regarded that omission as critical, they required too much. Since the record provides sufficient justification for the state-court ruling, the failure to explain that ruling more completely does not render it constitutionally defective.

* * *

[Justice White argued in dissent that the case should have been remanded to the district court for a new determination of manifest necessity for the mistrial. Justice Marshall, joined by Justice Brennan, dissented on the ground that a finding of manifest necessity must be explicit, rather than implied from the record.]

Applying the Manifest Necessity Test

One court has set forth helpful standards for determining whether a mistrial was granted out of manifest necessity:

> The Supreme Court and appellate courts have relied on four indicators in determining whether the trial court abused its discretion. Has the trial judge (1) heard the opinions of the parties about the propriety of the mistrial, (2) considered the alternatives to a mistrial and chosen the alternative least harmful to a defendant's rights, (3) acted deliberately instead of abruptly, and (4) properly determined that the defendant would benefit from the declaration of mistrial? If a district court engages in this type of effort, it is much more likely to have exercised sound discretion in concluding that manifest necessity for a mistrial existed.

United States v. Elliot, 463 F.3d 858 (9th Cir.2006).

Deadlocked Juries: Blueford v. Arkansas

In Arizona v. Washington, the Court indicated that great deference should be given to a judge's determination to declare a mistrial when the jury appears deadlocked. The subsequent decision in Renico v. Lett supra, reaffirms that standard of extreme deference. Similarly, in Blueford v. Arkansas, supra, the Court rejected the defendant's argument that the trial judge abused discretion in granting a mistrial on all counts when the jury reported that it had agreed to acquit on some counts but disagreed on others. Chief Justice Roberts analyzed Blueford's "manifest necessity" attack in the following passage:

> Blueford * * * accepts that a second trial on manslaughter and negligent homicide would pose no double jeopardy problem. He contends, however, that there was no necessity for a mistrial on capital and first-degree murder, given the foreperson's report that the jury had voted unanimously against guilt on those charges. According to Blueford, the court at that time should have taken "some action," whether through partial verdict forms or other means, to allow the

jury to give effect to those votes, and then considered a mistrial only as to the remaining charges.

We reject that suggestion. We have never required a trial court, before declaring a mistrial because of a hung jury, to consider any particular means of breaking the impasse—let alone to consider giving the jury new options for a verdict. As permitted under Arkansas law, the jury's options in this case were limited to two: either convict on one of the offenses, or acquit on all. The instructions explained those options in plain terms, and the verdict forms likewise contemplated no other outcome. * * * When the foreperson disclosed the jury's votes on capital and first-degree murder, the trial court did not abuse its discretion by refusing to add another option—that of acquitting on some offenses but not others. That, however, is precisely the relief Blueford seeks—relief the Double Jeopardy Clause does not afford him.

C. MISTRIAL DECLARED UPON DEFENDANT'S MOTION

Goading the Defendant into Moving for a Mistrial: Oregon v. Kennedy

Under what circumstances, if any, can the defendant who *moves* for a mistrial invoke double jeopardy protections against a retrial? This question was considered in Oregon v. Kennedy, 456 U.S. 667 (1982). After defense counsel had brought out during cross-examination of the state's expert witness that the expert had previously filed a criminal complaint against the defendant, the prosecutor suggested on redirect examination that the reason for the filing was that the defendant was "a crook." Kennedy moved for a mistrial, and the trial court granted Kennedy's motion. When the state sought to retry Kennedy, he moved to dismiss the charges because of double jeopardy. Justice Rehnquist, writing for the Court, concluded that a retrial was not barred. He reasoned as follows:

> Where the trial is terminated over the objection of the defendant, the classical test for lifting the double jeopardy bar to a second trial is the "manifest necessity" standard * * *. But in the case of a mistrial declared at the behest of the defendant, quite different principles come into play. Here the defendant himself has elected to terminate the proceedings against him, and the manifest necessity standard has no place in the application of the Double Jeopardy Clause. * * *
>
> Our cases, however, have indicated that even where the defendant moves for a mistrial, there is a narrow exception to the rule that the Double Jeopardy Clause is no bar to retrial. * * *

> Since one of the principal threads making up the protection embodied in the Double Jeopardy Clause is the right of the defendant to have his trial completed before the first jury empaneled to try him, it may be wondered as a matter of original inquiry why the defendant's election to terminate the first trial by his own motion should not be deemed a renunciation of that right for all purposes. We have recognized, however, that there would be great difficulty in applying such a rule where the prosecutor's actions giving rise to the mistrial were done in order to goad the defendant into requesting a mistrial. In such a case, the defendant's valued right to complete his trial before the first jury would be a hollow shell if the inevitable motion for mistrial were held to prevent a later invocation of the bar of double jeopardy in all circumstances. But the precise phrasing of the circumstances which *will* allow a defendant to interpose the defense of double jeopardy * * * have been stated with less than crystal clarity * * *.

Justice Rehnquist rejected the argument that double jeopardy should apply whenever the prosecutor's conduct at the first trial indicated "overreaching." He argued that such a test offered "virtually no standards" for application. He opted for an approach that examined the intent of the prosecutor:

> [A] standard that examines the intent of the prosecutor, though certainly not entirely free from practical difficulties, is a manageable standard to apply. It merely calls for the court to make a finding of fact. Inferring the existence or nonexistence of intent from objective facts and circumstances is a familiar process in our criminal justice system. * * *
>
> * * * Only where the governmental conduct in question is intended to "goad" the defendant into moving for a mistrial may a defendant raise the bar of double jeopardy. * * *

Justice Powell's concurring opinion emphasized that a court determining the intent of the prosecutor "should rely primarily upon the objective facts and circumstances of the particular case." He noted that in the instant case, the prosecutor had made only a single comment, and that the prosecutor was surprised by and resisted the defendant's motion for a mistrial. Justice Stevens, joined by Justices Brennan, Marshall, and Blackmun, concurred in the judgment. He argued that "[i]t is almost inconceivable that a defendant could prove that the prosecutor's deliberate misconduct was motivated by an intent to provoke a mistrial," and asserted that an "overreaching" standard was preferable even though it would be a "rare and compelling case" in which retrial would be barred.[2]

---

[2] When Oregon v. Kennedy returned to state court, the state supreme court relied upon the state constitution to find that Kennedy's rights were violated. State v. Kennedy, 295 Or. 260, 666

For an application of *Kennedy*, see United States v. Curry, 328 F.3d 970 (8th Cir. 2003) (mistrial granted on defendant's motion because the prosecutor suppressed impeachment evidence and made improper comments during closing argument; but retrial was not barred because the prosecutor did not engage in this conduct with the intent to goad the defendant into declaring a mistrial).

The Rationale of Oregon v. Kennedy

Judge Easterbrook, writing for the court in United States v. Jozwiak, 954 F.2d 458 (7th Cir.1992), provides an excellent explanation and application of Oregon v. Kennedy. Judge Easterbrook set forth the facts of *Jozwiak* as follows:

> Nine of the twenty-six defendants in this case charging a conspiracy to distribute cocaine went to trial on November 4, 1991. A prosecutor—whose first trial this was—told the jury during his opening statement that five of the original defendants were cooperating with the government and would appear as witnesses and that four others had also pleaded guilty. The mention that some of the defendants had entered pleas of guilty led the defendants to seek a mistrial. A senior prosecutor from the United States Attorney's office confessed error and apologized. As everyone wanted a mistrial, the district judge sent the jury home. There was no point conducting a long trial with a built-in error.
>
> All nine defendants then insisted that the double jeopardy clause bars further prosecution. The district court denied the motion, observing that the defendants had requested the mistrial.

The defendants requested a hearing to probe the prosecutor's intent, but the trial judge denied the request. Judge Easterbrook analyzed the double jeopardy question and the applicability of Oregon v. Kennedy while distinguishing between an intent to goad and an intent to win:

> Any search for steps intended to goad defendants into seeking mistrials encounters a problem. Because intent is a matter of characterization, you cannot even know what indicia to look for unless you know the direction toward which the (forbidden) intent would be bent. Prosecutors intend to secure convictions, intend to secure all advantages the adversary system allows. An overstep (sometimes even a correct step) may lead to howls from the defense, and next to an argument that the overstep was intended to goad the adversary into howling. Yet a search for intent that leads only to a conclusion that the prosecutor wanted to win is pointless. We must be looking for intent to

P.2d 1316 (1983). It reasoned that retrial should be barred when the prosecution "either intends or is indifferent to the resulting mistrial or reversal."

do something that undercuts the interests protected by the double jeopardy clause. *Kennedy* distinguishes intent to improve the chance that the trier of fact will return a favorable decision from the forbidden intent to avoid decision by the trier of fact.

Judge Easterbrook provided a rule of thumb for determining prosecutorial intent in these murky circumstances:

> A defendant's interest in preserving the benefits of a trial that has been going well enables us to distinguish these two characterizations of prosecutorial intent. Only a prosecutor who thinks the trial is going sour—or who seeks to get just far enough into the trial to preview the defense—would want to precipitate a mistrial. Otherwise the mistrial means a waste for both sides, injuring the prosecutor along with the defense. (Trying one defendant twice means, for a prosecutor with limited resources, letting some other defendant go.) Unless there is reason to believe that the prosecutor set out to rescue a case on the path to acquittal or filch a road map of the defense, a court may cut off the inquiry; whatever may have been in the prosecutor's head was not the kind of intent with which the Double Jeopardy Clause is concerned.

Applying these standards to the facts, Judge Easterbrook concluded that the prosecutor had no intent to goad the defendant into asking for a mistrial when he referred, in opening argument, to the fact that some of the conspirators had entered guilty pleas.

> The prosecutor's case against these nine defendants was not going downhill; it was not going, period. It ended within minutes after the prosecutor rose to speak. * * * Defense counsel did not tip their hands; they barely had time to tip their hats. Scuttling a trial at dockside poses few if any risks to the defendant's legitimate interests.

Why Should the Defendant's Motion Make a Difference?

As we have seen, if the prosecution moves for a mistrial, double jeopardy bars a new trial unless the "manifest necessity" standard is met. However, if the defendant moves for a mistrial, double jeopardy only bars a new trial in the very rare case in which the prosecutor has intentionally goaded the defendant into moving for a mistrial. Why should it matter, for double jeopardy purposes, whether it is the prosecutor or the defendant who moves for the mistrial? Judge Easterbrook, in Miller v. Indiana Dept. of Corrections, 75 F.3d 330 (7th Cir.1996), posits that if double jeopardy would routinely bar a retrial whenever the defendant moved for a mistrial in good faith, such a rule would in the long run harm defendants. He reasoned that the threat of double jeopardy in such circumstances would mean that "judges would be even more reluctant to grant mistrials than they are already."

IV. THE CONVICTED DEFENDANT APPEALS

May a defendant who successfully appeals a conviction be retried? Ball v. United States, 163 U.S. 662 (1896), mentioned in *Scott* and discussed in the following case, established that a retrial following a reversal of a conviction is generally permissible. In the next case, the Court considered whether a defendant may be retried when the appellate reversal is based on insufficiency of the evidence rather than on trial error.

A. INSUFFICIENT EVIDENCE TO CONVICT

BURKS V. UNITED STATES

Supreme Court of the United States, 1978.
437 U.S. 1.

CHIEF JUSTICE BURGER delivered the opinion of the Court.

We granted certiorari to resolve the question of whether an accused may be subjected to a second trial when conviction in a prior trial was reversed by an appellate court solely for lack of sufficient evidence to sustain the jury's verdict.

* * *

Petitioner Burks was tried in the United States District Court for the crime of robbing a Federally insured bank by use of a dangerous weapon * * *. Burks' principal defense was insanity.

[Burks moved for acquittal at trial, on grounds that the government had not shown a culpable mental state. The trial court denied the motion. But the court of appeals found that there was insufficient evidence of the necessary mental state, and reversed the conviction. The Court of Appeals, rather than terminating the case, remanded to the District Court for a determination of whether a directed verdict of acquittal should be entered or a new trial ordered.]

It is unquestionably true that the Court of Appeals' decision "represented a resolution, correct or not, of some or all of the factual elements of the offense charged." United States v. Martin Linen Supply Co., 430 U.S. 564, 571 (1977). By deciding that the Government had failed to come forward with sufficient proof of petitioner's capacity to be responsible for criminal acts, that court was clearly saying that Burks' criminal culpability had not been established. If the District Court had so held in the first instance, as the reviewing court said it should have done, a judgment of acquittal would have been entered and, of course, petitioner could not be retried for the same offense. Consequently * * * it should make no difference that the *reviewing* court, rather than the trial court, determined the evidence to be insufficient. The appellate decision unmistakably meant that the District Court had erred in failing to grant a judgment of acquittal. To hold otherwise would create a purely arbitrary distinction between those in petitioner's position and others who would enjoy the benefit of a correct decision by the District Court.

* * *

Nonetheless, * * * our past holdings do not appear consistent with what we believe the Double Jeopardy Clause commands. A close reexamination of those precedents, however, persuades us that they have not properly construed the Clause, and accordingly should no longer be followed.

[Reconsideration of the prior cases involved an examination of Ball v. United States, 163 U.S. 662 (1896), which permitted a new trial when the accused successfully sought review of a conviction.]

Ball came before the Court twice, the first occasion being on writ of error from Federal convictions for murder. On this initial review, those defendants who had been found guilty obtained a reversal of their convictions due to a fatally defective indictment. On remand after appeal, the trial court dismissed the flawed indictment and proceeded to retry the defendants on a new indictment. They were again convicted and the defendants came once more to this Court, arguing that their second trial was barred because of former jeopardy. The Court rejected this plea in a brief statement * * *. The reversal in *Ball* was therefore based not on insufficiency of evidence but rather on trial error, i.e., failure to dismiss a faulty indictment. * * * We have no doubt that *Ball* was correct in allowing a new trial to rectify *trial error* * * *.

* * * In short, reversal for trial error, as distinguished from evidentiary insufficiency, does not constitute a decision to the effect that the government has failed to prove its case. As such, it implies nothing with respect to the guilt or innocence of the defendant. Rather, it is a determination that a defendant has been convicted through a judicial process which is defective in some fundamental respect, e.g., incorrect receipt or rejection of evidence, incorrect instructions, or prosecutorial misconduct. When this occurs, the accused has a strong interest in obtaining a fair readjudication of his guilt free from error, just as society maintains a valid concern for insuring that the guilty are punished. * * *

The same cannot be said when a defendant's conviction has been overturned due to a failure of proof at trial, in which case the prosecution cannot complain of prejudice, for it has been given one fair opportunity to offer whatever proof it could assemble. Moreover, such an appellate reversal means that the government's case was so lacking that it should not have even been *submitted* to the jury. Since we necessarily afford absolute finality to a jury's *verdict* of acquittal—no matter how erroneous its decision—it is difficult to conceive how society has any greater interest in retrying a defendant when, on review, it is decided as a matter of law that the jury could not properly have returned a verdict of guilty.

* * *

In our view it makes no difference that a defendant has sought a new trial as one of his remedies, or even as the sole remedy. It cannot be meaningfully said that a person "waives" his right to a judgment of acquittal by moving for a new trial. * * * Since we hold today that the Double Jeopardy Clause precludes a second trial once the reviewing court has found the evidence legally insufficient, the only "just" remedy available for that court is the direction of a judgment of acquittal. To the extent that our prior decisions suggest that by moving for a new trial, a defendant waives his right to a judgment of acquittal on the basis of evidentiary insufficiency, those cases are overruled.

* * *

MR. JUSTICE BLACKMUN took no part in the consideration or decision of this case.

Burks Applied: Hudson v. Louisiana

Hudson v. Louisiana, 450 U.S. 40 (1981), held that *Burks* applied when a second trial was held after the trial judge at the first trial granted a motion for a new trial on the ground that the evidence was insufficient to support the jury's guilty verdict. The basis for the trial judge's ruling was insufficiency of the evidence, and under *Burks,* that ruling terminates the proceedings.

B. INSUFFICIENT EVIDENCE AND TRIAL COURT ERROR

Erroneously Admitted Evidence: Lockhart v. Nelson

Does *Burks* apply when the evidence actually introduced at trial is sufficient to sustain the convictions, but the legally competent evidence—excluding from consideration evidence erroneously admitted by the trial court—is insufficient? The Court in Lockhart v. Nelson, 488 U.S. 33 (1988), answered that *Burks* does not apply and that the defendant can be retried after a successful appeal. The prosecutor used Nelson's prior convictions at a sentencing hearing, to prove that Nelson should receive an enhanced sentence as a habitual offender. This was error under state law as to one of the convictions, for which Nelson had been pardoned. On habeas review, the district court found the sentence invalid. The State announced its intention to resentence Nelson as a habitual offender, by using a prior conviction not offered or admitted at the initial sentencing hearing. Nelson interposed a claim of double jeopardy. Chief Justice Rehnquist, writing for the Court, concluded that the *Burks* exception was inapplicable and that Nelson's resentencing would not implicate Double Jeopardy concerns.

> *Burks* was based on the view that an appellate court's reversal for insufficiency of the evidence is in effect a determination that the government's case against the defendant was so lacking that the trial court should have entered a judgment of acquittal, rather than submitting the case to the jury. * * *
>
> *Burks* was careful to point out that a reversal based solely on evidentiary insufficiency has fundamentally different implications * * * than a reversal based on such ordinary "trial errors" as the incorrect receipt or rejection of evidence. While the former is in effect a finding that the government has failed to prove its case against the defendant, the latter implies nothing with respect to the guilt or innocence of the defendant, but is simply a determination that he has been convicted through a judicial *process* which is defective in some fundamental respect.

Justice Marshall, joined by Justices Brennan and Blackmun, dissented. Justice Marshall argued that if the State had produced a "blank piece of paper" at the sentencing hearing "no one would doubt that Arkansas had produced insufficient evidence and that the Double Jeopardy Clause barred retrial." He concluded that "there is no constitutionally significant difference between that hypothetical and this case."

Charged with the Wrong Crime: Montana v. Hall

In Montana v. Hall, 481 U.S. 400 (1987), the Court summarily reversed a state supreme court decision that a defendant whose conviction was overturned could not be retried on another charge. Hall was originally charged with sexual assault of the daughter of his ex-wife. He successfully moved to dismiss the charge, persuading the trial court that he could only be prosecuted for incest. After his conviction for incest, he persuaded the state supreme court that the incest statute did not apply on the facts of the case because the statute had not been in effect on the date of the charged criminal act. That court concluded that Hall could not be retried on the original charge because sexual assault and incest were the same offense, so that a retrial after a conviction for committing a nonexistent crime (incest under these circumstances) would violate double jeopardy. The Supreme Court disagreed, finding no constitutional bar to Hall's reprosecution for sexual assault, because a reversal of a conviction on grounds other than insufficiency of the evidence—such as, in this case, a "defect in the charging instrument"—does not bar a retrial. Justice Marshall dissented from the summary handling of the case, and Justice Stevens filed a separate dissent suggesting that the state supreme court may have rested its decision on state law. See also United States v. Dalton,

990 F.2d 1166 (10th Cir.1993) (new trial permitted where defendant's conviction was reversed because the statute under which he was charged had been implicitly repealed; reversal was due to a "defect in the charging instrument," not insufficiency of evidence).

Reversal of Convictions Rendered Against the Weight of the Evidence: Tibbs v. Florida

In Tibbs v. Florida, 457 U.S. 31 (1982), the Supreme Court held 5–4 that a defendant could be retried after an appellate court overturned an initial conviction on the ground that it was *against the weight* of the evidence. Writing for the majority, Justice O'Connor reasoned that "[a] reversal based on the weight of the evidence * * * can occur only after the State both has presented sufficient evidence to support conviction and has persuaded the jury to convict. The reversal simply affords the defendant a second opportunity to seek a favorable judgment." That is, there is a distinction between a reversal based on *insufficiency* of the evidence and a reversal of a guilty verdict against the weight of the evidence—under applicable legal standards, the prosecution's case is stronger in the latter instance, indeed it is legally sufficient to support a conviction.

Justice White's dissent in *Tibbs*, joined by Justices Brennan, Marshall, and Blackmun, argued that whether a reversal is based on insufficiency or weight of the evidence, a retrial gives the prosecution a second chance to do what it was unable to do in the first trial—i.e., put on stronger evidence. The dissenters suggested that appellate judges, when deciding that a conviction should be reversed, might use weight-of-the-evidence reasoning to permit retrial where it ought to be prohibited under *Burks*. In response, the majority observed that "trial and appellate judges commonly distinguish between the weight and the sufficiency of the evidence. We have no reason to believe that today's decision will erode the demonstrated ability of judges to distinguish legally insufficient evidence from evidence that rationally supports a verdict."

For more on the distinction between a verdict based on insufficient evidence and a verdict against the weight of the evidence, see section II. B. of Chapter 13.

C. TRIAL DE NOVO AND CONTINUING JEOPARDY

Two-Tiered System: Justices v. Lydon

The Court distinguished *Burks* in Justices v. Lydon, 466 U.S. 294 (1984). Lydon was arrested after breaking into an automobile in Boston. Under state procedure, Lydon had a right to choose a jury trial or an initial trial to the bench. An acquittal before either a judge or a jury would have been final; but a guilty verdict was final only if rendered by a jury; a defendant who elected a bench trial had an absolute right to a trial de novo if convicted.

Lydon, like most Massachusetts defendants, opted for the bench trial. (Why not?). He was convicted. He then requested a trial de novo to a jury, but he attempted in state court, and then in Federal court, to bar the second trial on the ground that there had been insufficient evidence to warrant a conviction in the bench trial. He claimed that *Burks* barred retrial. The Court disagreed.

Justice White wrote for the Court and recognized that *Burks* prohibited a second trial after a court found that a conviction was based on insufficient evidence. However, under the Massachusetts system, no such determination had been made. The policies underlying *Burks* did not apply, he said, because this was not a case in which the prosecution had an incentive to offer a weak case first, in order to discover the defendant's evidence and theories, since an acquittal would be a final victory for the defendant; and the prosecutor received no education as to how to present a better case from reviewing judges, since there had been no review. Justice White explained that the two-tiered option granted to a defendant offered benefits not generally available in a single-tiered system. He noted that if the defendant were convicted on insufficient evidence at the trial de novo, *Burks* would apply at that point.

Event Necessary to Terminate Jeopardy: Richardson v. United States

Justice Rehnquist relied on the Court's reasoning in *Lydon* in his majority opinion in Richardson v. United States, 468 U.S. 317 (1984). The Court held that a defendant was not placed in jeopardy twice when a mistrial was declared due to a genuine jury deadlock, Richardson's motion for judgment of acquittal was denied, and the trial judge scheduled a second trial. The Court held that the defendant had never been acquitted. As it had in *Lydon,* the Court read *Burks* as holding only that "once a defendant obtained an unreversed * * * ruling that the Government had failed to introduce sufficient evidence to convict him at trial, a second trial was barred by the Double Jeopardy Clause." Examining Richardson's claim, the Court said that "[w]here, as here, there has been only a mistrial resulting from a hung jury, *Burks* simply does not require that an appellate court rule on the sufficiency of the evidence because retrial might be barred by the Double Jeopardy Clause." The Court found that the declaration of a mistrial was not the equivalent of an acquittal, it did not terminate jeopardy, and that "[r]egardless of the sufficiency of the evidence at petitioner's first trial, he has no valid double jeopardy claim to prevent his retrial." Justice Brennan, joined by Justice Marshall, dissented. He agreed with the majority that a new trial is not barred simply because a jury could not reach a verdict, but urged that "[w]hen the prosecution has failed to present constitutionally sufficient evidence, it cannot complain of unfairness in being denied a second chance, and the interests in finality, shared by the defendant and society, strongly outweigh the reasons for a retrial."

V. MULTIPLE PROSECUTIONS OF CONVICTED DEFENDANTS

A. THE SAME OFFENSE

Double jeopardy bars not only the retrial of a defendant who is acquitted; it also bars the reprosecution of a defendant who has already been convicted of the same offense. Here the policies are obvious. The defendant may be forced to defend, but not repetitively. Once the government gets the conviction it originally sought or loses at trial on a charge, further proceedings might well be vexatious, and the proceedings will certainly subject the defendant to the inconvenience, anxiety and expense of having to defend again. Thus, there is no doubt that after a valid conviction or acquittal, the *same offense* cannot be prosecuted again. But what constitutes the same offense?

Lesser Included Offenses: Brown v. Ohio and the Blockburger Test

In Brown v. Ohio, 432 U.S. 161 (1977), the defendant stole a car in East Cleveland, Ohio. Nine days later, he was arrested in another city and charged with joyriding. He pled guilty and served his sentence. After his release, he was returned to East Cleveland and charged with auto theft and joyriding. He pled guilty to auto theft, but reserved his double jeopardy claim for a motion to withdraw his plea. The court overruled his double jeopardy objection and sentenced him. The Supreme Court concluded that the conviction violated the Double Jeopardy Clause, because joyriding is a lesser included offense of auto theft under Ohio law. The Court applied the test of different offenses that was established in Blockburger v. United States, 284 U.S. 299 (1932), for the purpose of determining whether it is permissible to cumulate punishment. It found no reason to apply different tests to multiple trials and multiple punishments. The Court noted that "[w]here the judge is forbidden to impose cumulative punishment for two crimes at the end of a single proceeding, the prosecutor is forbidden to strive for the same result in successive proceedings." Under *Blockburger,* the test for the same offense is whether *each statutory provision contains an element that the other does not*. Because the Ohio statute under which Brown was convicted defined auto theft as joyriding with the intent to permanently deprive the owner of possession, the only difference in proof between the two crimes was the intent. (i.e., only one crime—auto theft—required something that the other—joy riding—did not; put another way, auto theft is joy riding with something extra—the intent to permanently deprive the owner of possession).

The government argued that Brown could be tried twice because the second charge covered a different *part* of the joy ride than that considered in the first trial. But the Court disagreed. The nine-day joyride could not be divided into a series of temporal or spatial units, because Ohio law did not create separate offenses for each day someone was joyriding. After nine days the joyriding was still going on. Justices Blackmun, Burger, and Rehnquist argued in dissent that Brown committed a separate offense when he operated the car nine days after stealing it.

It is important under *Blockburger* that *each* statutory crime must require an element that the other does not for there to be separate offenses. In Illinois v. Vitale, 447 U.S. 410 (1980), the Court considered whether a driver of an automobile that struck and killed two children could be prosecuted for involuntary manslaughter, following his conviction for failing to reduce speed to avoid the collision. The Court remanded the case for further development of state law, observing that "if manslaughter by automobile does not always entail proof of a failure to slow, then the two offenses are not the 'same' under the *Blockburger* test," but cautioning also that if the state would "find it necessary to prove a failure to slow or to rely on conduct necessarily involving such failure" Vitale's double jeopardy claim "would be substantial." Four dissenters argued that no further proceedings were appropriate. The decisions in *Grady* and *Dixon*, discussed below, deal with the Court's cautionary statement.

The Grady v. Corbin "Same Conduct" Test

The Court held that the *Blockburger* test of "same offense" was not sufficient to protect double jeopardy rights in Grady v. Corbin, 495 U.S. 508 (1990)—though the holding proved to be short-lived, as demonstrated in *Dixon*, infra. Justice Brennan, writing for a five-Justice majority in *Grady*, stated that "the Double Jeopardy Clause bars a subsequent prosecution if, to establish an essential element of an offense charged in that prosecution, the government will prove *conduct* that constitutes an offense for which the defendant has already been prosecuted."(Emphasis added). The case involved Corbin, who was at fault in a car accident resulting in fatal injuries, and was also intoxicated. He was served with traffic tickets charging him with the misdemeanor of driving while intoxicated and with failing to keep right of the median. He pleaded guilty to the two traffic tickets, with the presiding judge being unaware of the fatality stemming from the accident. Thereafter he was indicted for reckless manslaughter, second-degree vehicular manslaughter, and criminally negligent homicide, third-degree reckless assault, and driving while intoxicated.

Justice Brennan held that a trial on manslaughter and homicide charges was barred by the Double Jeopardy Clause, if the government sought to prove the crimes through evidence of drunk driving or failure to keep to the right of the median. He recognized that the prosecution for these crimes would not be barred under the *Blockburger* test, because each of the minor crimes to which Corbin pled guilty contained elements that the more serious crimes did not, and vice versa. (For example, reckless manslaughter does not include an element of driving, or driving while intoxicated, and driving while intoxicated does not contain an element of reckless disregard for human life). Justice Brennan argued, however, that the *Blockburger* test was insufficient to protect against the risk of multiple prosecutions:

> If *Blockburger* constituted the entire double jeopardy inquiry in the context of successive prosecutions, the State could try Corbin in four consecutive trials: for failure to keep right of the median, for driving while intoxicated, for assault, and for homicide. The State could improve its presentation of proof with each trial, assessing which witnesses gave the most persuasive testimony, which documents had the greatest impact, which opening and closing arguments most persuaded the jurors. Corbin would be forced either to contest each of these trials or to plead guilty to avoid the harassment and expense.

Justice Brennan applied the "same conduct" test to Corbin's situation, and held that prosecution on the serious charges was barred, because the state had admitted that it would use the conduct for which he was convicted (i.e., driving carelessly and while drunk) to prove the more serious charges.

Justice O'Connor wrote a dissent. Justice Scalia also wrote a dissent, in which Chief Justice Rehnquist and Justice Kennedy joined. Justice Scalia "would adhere to the *Blockburger* rule that successive prosecutions under two different statutes do not constitute double jeopardy if each statutory crime contains an element that the other does not, regardless of the overlap between the proof required for each prosecution in the particular case." He argued that the "same conduct" test was an impermissible expansion from the common-law jurisprudence that spawned the Double Jeopardy Clause, and that it was inconsistent with precedent, which had relied solely on the *Blockburger* test.

Return to the Blockburger Test

The expansive *Grady* test was not the law for long. Only three years later, the Court, in the following case, overruled *Grady* and returned to the *Blockburger* test as the sole benchmark for determining the permissibility of successive prosecutions. However, there was dispute among the Justices as to how to apply *Blockburger*.

UNITED STATES V. DIXON

Supreme Court of the United States, 1993.
509 U.S. 688.

JUSTICE SCALIA announced the judgment of the Court and delivered the opinion of the Court with respect to Parts I, II, and IV, and an opinion with respect to Parts III and V, in which JUSTICE KENNEDY joins.

In both of these cases, respondents were tried for criminal contempt of court for violating court orders that prohibited them from engaging in conduct that was later the subject of a criminal prosecution. We consider whether the subsequent criminal prosecutions are barred by the Double Jeopardy Clause.

I

Respondent Alvin Dixon was arrested for second-degree murder and was released on bond. * * * Dixon's release form specified that he was not to commit "any criminal offense," and warned that any violation of the conditions of release would subject him "to revocation of release, an order of detention, and prosecution for contempt of court."

While awaiting trial, Dixon was arrested and indicted for possession of cocaine with intent to distribute. The court issued an order requiring Dixon to show cause why he should not be held in contempt or have the terms of his pretrial release modified. At the show-cause hearing, four police officers testified to facts surrounding the alleged drug offense; Dixon's counsel cross-examined these witnesses and introduced other evidence. The court concluded that the Government had established "beyond a reasonable doubt that [Dixon] was in possession of drugs and that those drugs were possessed with the intent to distribute." The court therefore found Dixon guilty of criminal contempt under D.C.Code Ann. § 23–1329(c) * * *. Dixon was sentenced to 180 days in jail. He later moved to dismiss the cocaine indictment on double jeopardy grounds; the trial court granted the motion.

Respondent Michael Foster's route to this Court is similar. Based on Foster's alleged physical attacks upon her in the past, Foster's estranged wife Ana obtained a civil protection order (CPO) in Superior Court of the District of Columbia. The order, to which Foster consented, required that he not "molest, assault, or in any manner threaten or physically abuse" Ana Foster * * *.

Over the course of eight months, Ana Foster filed three separate motions to have her husband held in contempt for numerous violations of the CPO. Of the 16 alleged episodes, the only charges relevant here are three separate instances of threats (on November 12, 1987, and March 26 and May 17, 1988) and two assaults (on November 6, 1987, and May 21, 1988), in the most serious of which Foster "threw [his wife] down basement stairs, kicking her body[,] * * * pushed her head into the floor causing head injuries, [and Ana Foster] lost consciousness."

After issuing a notice of hearing and ordering Foster to appear, the court held a 3-day bench trial. Counsel for Ana Foster * * * prosecuted the action * * *. As to the assault charges, the court stated that Ana Foster would have "to prove as an element, first that there was a Civil Protection Order, and then [that] . . . the assault as defined by the criminal code, in fact occurred." * * * The court found Foster guilty beyond a reasonable doubt of four counts of criminal contempt including the November 6, 1987 and May 21, 1988 assaults, but acquitted him on other counts, including the March 26 alleged threats. He was sentenced to an aggregate 600 days' imprisonment.

The United States Attorney's Office later obtained an indictment charging Foster with simple assault on or about November 6, 1987 (Count I, violation of § 22–504); threatening to injure another on or about November 12, 1987, and March 26 and May 17, 1988 (Counts II–IV, violation of § 22–2307); and assault with intent to kill on or about May 21, 1988 (Count V, violation of § 22–501). Ana Foster was the complainant in all counts; the first and last counts were based on the events for which Foster had been held in contempt, and the other three were based on the alleged events for which Foster was acquitted of contempt. Like Dixon, Foster filed a motion to dismiss, claiming a double jeopardy bar to all counts, and also collateral estoppel as to Counts II–IV. The trial court denied the double-jeopardy claim and did not rule on the collateral-estoppel assertion.

The Government appealed the double jeopardy ruling in *Dixon,* and Foster appealed the trial court's denial of his motion. The District of Columbia Court of Appeals * * * relying on our recent decision in Grady v. Corbin, ruled that both subsequent prosecutions were barred by the Double Jeopardy Clause. In its petition for certiorari, the Government presented the sole question "[w]hether the Double Jeopardy Clause bars prosecution of a defendant on substantive criminal charges based upon the same conduct for which he previously has been held in criminal contempt of court."

II

* * *

We recently held in *Grady* that in addition to passing the *Blockburger* test, a subsequent prosecution must satisfy a "same-conduct" test to avoid the double jeopardy bar. The *Grady* test provides that, "if, to establish an essential element of an offense charged in that prosecution, the government will prove conduct that constitutes an offense for which the defendant has already been prosecuted," a second prosecution may not be had.

III

* * *

The first question before us today is whether *Blockburger* analysis permits subsequent prosecution in [the] criminal contempt context, where judicial order has prohibited criminal act. If it does, we must then proceed to consider whether *Grady* also permits it.

We begin with *Dixon.* The statute applicable in Dixon's contempt prosecution provides that "[a] person who has been conditionally released . . . and who has violated a condition of release shall be subject to . . . prosecution for contempt of court." * * *

In this situation, in which the contempt sanction is imposed for violating the order through commission of the incorporated drug offense, the later attempt to prosecute Dixon for the drug offense resembles the situation that produced our judgment of double jeopardy in Harris v. Oklahoma, 433 U.S. 682 (1977) (*per curiam*). There we held that a subsequent prosecution for robbery with a firearm was barred by the Double Jeopardy Clause, because the defendant had already been tried for felony-murder based on the same underlying felony. We have described our terse *per curiam* in *Harris* as standing for the proposition that, for double jeopardy purposes, "the crime generally described as felony murder" is not "a separate offense distinct from its various elements." Illinois v. Vitale, 447 U.S. 410, 420–421 (1980). So too here, the "crime" of violating a condition of release cannot be abstracted from the "element" of the violated condition. The *Dixon* court order incorporated the entire governing criminal code in the same manner as the *Harris* felony-murder statute incorporated the several enumerated felonies. Here, as in *Harris,* the underlying substantive criminal offense is "a species of lesser-included offense."

* * * Because Dixon's drug offense did not include any element not contained in his previous contempt offense, his subsequent prosecution violates the Double Jeopardy Clause.

The foregoing analysis obviously applies as well to Count I of the indictment against Foster, charging assault in violation of § 22–504, based on the same event that was the subject of his prior contempt conviction for violating the provision of the CPO forbidding him to commit simple assault under § 22–504. The subsequent prosecution for assault fails the *Blockburger* test, and is barred.

* * *

The remaining four counts in *Foster*, assault with intent to kill (Count V; § 22–501) and threats to injure or kidnap (Counts II–IV; § 22–2307), are not barred under *Blockburger*. As to Count V: Foster's conduct on May 21, 1988 was found to violate the Family Division's order that he not "molest, assault, or in any manner threaten or physically abuse" his wife. At the contempt hearing, the court stated that Ana Foster's attorney, who prosecuted the contempt, would have to prove first, knowledge of a CPO, and second, a willful violation of one of its conditions, here simple assault as defined by the criminal code. On the basis of the same episode, Foster was then indicted for violation of § 22–501, which proscribes assault with intent to kill. Under governing law, that offense requires proof of specific intent to kill; simple assault does not. Similarly, the contempt offense required proof of knowledge of the CPO, which assault with intent to kill does not. Applying the *Blockburger* elements test, the result is clear: These crimes were different offenses and the subsequent prosecution did not violate the Double Jeopardy Clause.

Counts II, III, and IV of Foster's indictment are likewise not barred. These charged Foster under § 22–2307 (forbidding anyone to "threate[n] * * * to kidnap any person or to injure the person of another or physically damage the property of any person") for his alleged threats on three separate dates. Foster's contempt prosecution included charges that, on the same dates, he violated the CPO provision ordering that he not "in any manner threaten" Ana Foster. Conviction of the contempt required willful violation of the CPO—which conviction under § 22–2307 did not; and conviction under § 22–2307 required that the threat be a threat to kidnap, to inflict bodily injury, or to damage property—which conviction of the contempt (for violating the CPO provision that Foster not "in any manner threaten") did not. Each offense therefore contained a separate element, and the *Blockburger* test for double jeopardy was not met.

IV

Having found that at least some of the counts at issue here are not barred by the *Blockburger* test, we must consider whether they are barred by the new, additional double jeopardy test we announced three Terms ago in Grady v. Corbin. They undoubtedly are * * *.

We have concluded, however, that *Grady* must be overruled. Unlike *Blockburger* analysis, whose definition of what prevents two crimes from being the "same offence," U.S. Const., Amdt. 5, has deep historical roots and has been accepted in numerous precedents of this Court, *Grady* lacks constitutional roots. The "same-conduct" rule it announced is wholly inconsistent with earlier Supreme Court precedent and with the clear common-law understanding of double jeopardy. See, e.g., Gavieres v. United States, 220 U.S., at 345 (in subsequent prosecution, "[w]hile it is true that the conduct of the accused was one and the same, two offenses resulted, each of which had an element not embraced in the other"). We need not discuss the many proofs of these statements, which were set forth at length in the *Grady* dissent. See 495 U.S., at 526 (Scalia, J., dissenting). * * *

* * * *Grady* * * * has already proved unstable in application. Less than two years after it came down, in United States v. Felix, 503 U.S. 378 (1992), we were forced to recognize a large exception to it. There we concluded that a subsequent prosecution for conspiracy to manufacture, possess, and distribute methamphetamine was not barred by a previous conviction for attempt to manufacture the same substance. We offered as a justification for avoiding a "literal" (i.e., faithful) reading of *Grady* "longstanding authority" to the effect that prosecution for conspiracy is not precluded by prior prosecution for the substantive offense. Of course the very existence of such a large and longstanding "exception" to the *Grady* rule gave cause for concern that the rule was not an accurate expression of the law. This "past practice" excuse is not available to support the ignoring of *Grady* in the present case, since there is no Supreme Court precedent even discussing this fairly new breed of successive prosecution (criminal contempt for violation of a court order prohibiting a crime, followed by prosecution for the crime itself).

A hypothetical based on the facts in *Harris* reinforces the conclusion that *Grady* is a continuing source of confusion and must be overruled. Suppose the State first tries the defendant for felony-murder, based on robbery, and then indicts the defendant for robbery with a firearm in the same incident. Absent *Grady,* our cases provide a clear answer to the double-jeopardy claim in this situation. Under *Blockburger,* the second prosecution is not barred—as it clearly was not barred at common law * * *.[a]

Having encountered today yet another situation in which the pre-*Grady* understanding of the Double Jeopardy Clause allows a second trial, though the "same-conduct" test would not, we think it time to acknowledge what is now, three years after *Grady,* compellingly clear: the case was a mistake. We do not lightly reconsider a precedent, but, because *Grady* contradicted an "unbroken line of decisions," contained "less than accurate"

---

[a] * * * Justice Souter's concern that prosecutors will bring separate prosecutions in order to perfect their case seems unjustified. They have little to gain and much to lose from such a strategy. Under Ashe v. Swenson, 397 U.S. 436 (1970), an acquittal in the first prosecution might well bar litigation of certain facts essential to the second one—though a conviction in the first prosecution would not excuse the Government from proving the same facts the second time. Surely, moreover, the Government must be deterred from abusive, repeated prosecutions of a single offender for similar offenses by the sheer press of other demands upon prosecutorial and judicial resources. Finally, even if Justice Souter's fear were well founded, no double-jeopardy bar short of a same-transaction analysis will eliminate this problem; but that interpretation of the Double Jeopardy Clause has been soundly rejected, and would require overruling numerous precedents, the latest of which is barely a year old * * *.

historical analysis, and has produced "confusion,"[b] we do so here. Although stare decisis is the "preferred course" in constitutional adjudication, "when governing decisions are unworkable or are badly reasoned, this Court has never felt constrained to follow precedent." We would mock stare decisis and only add chaos to our double jeopardy jurisprudence by pretending that *Grady* survives when it does not.

CHIEF JUSTICE REHNQUIST, with whom JUSTICE O'CONNOR and JUSTICE THOMAS join, concurring in part and dissenting in part.

* * * I do not join Part III of Justice Scalia's opinion because I think that none of the criminal prosecutions in this case were barred under *Blockburger*. I must then confront the expanded version of double jeopardy embodied in *Grady*. For the reasons set forth in the *Grady* dissent, and in Part IV of the Court's opinion, I, too, think that *Grady* must be overruled. I therefore join Parts I, II, and IV of the Court's opinion, and write separately to express my disagreement with Justice Scalia's application of *Blockburger* in Part III.

In my view, *Blockburger*'s same-elements test requires us to focus not on the terms of the particular court orders involved, but on the elements of contempt of court in the ordinary sense. Relying on *Harris,* a three-paragraph *per curiam* in an unargued case, Justice Scalia concludes otherwise today, and thus incorrectly finds * * * that the subsequent prosecutions of Dixon for drug distribution and of Foster for assault violated the Double Jeopardy Clause. * * * Because the generic crime of contempt of court has different elements than the substantive criminal charges in this case, I believe that they are separate offenses under *Blockburger*. I would therefore limit *Harris* to the context in which it arose: where the crimes in question are analogous to greater and lesser included offenses. The crimes at issue here bear no such resemblance.

[In *Blockburger*] we stated that two offenses are different for purposes of double jeopardy if "each *provision* requires proof of a fact which the other does not." Applying this test to the offenses at bar, it is clear that the elements of the governing contempt *provision* are entirely different from the elements of the substantive crimes. Contempt of court comprises two elements: (i) a court order made known to the defendant, followed by (ii) willful violation of that order. Neither of those elements is necessarily satisfied by proof that a defendant has committed the substantive offenses of assault or drug distribution. Likewise, no element of either of those

[b] See, e.g., Sharpton v. Turner, 964 F.2d 1284, 1287 (CA2) (*Grady* formulation "has proven difficult to apply" and "whatever difficulties we have previously encountered in grappling with the *Grady* language have not been eased by" *Felix*); Ladner v. Smith, 941 F.2d 356, 362, 364 (C.A.5 1991) (a divided court adopts a four-part test for application of *Grady* and notes that *Grady,* "even if carefully analyzed and painstakingly administered, is not easy to apply"). * * *

substantive offenses is necessarily satisfied by proof that a defendant has been found guilty of contempt of court.

* * * Justice Scalia * * * concludes that *Harris* somehow requires us to look to the facts that must be proven under the particular court orders in question (rather than under the general law of criminal contempt) in determining whether contempt and the related substantive offenses are the same for double jeopardy purposes. This interpretation of *Harris* is both unprecedented and mistaken.

* * * By focusing on the facts needed to show a violation of the specific court orders involved in this case, and not on the generic elements of the crime of contempt of court, Justice Scalia's double-jeopardy analysis bears a striking resemblance to that found in *Grady*—not what one would expect in an opinion that overrules *Grady*.

* * *

The following analogy * * * helps illustrate the absurd results that Justice Scalia's *Harris/Blockburger* analysis could in theory produce. Suppose that the offense in question is failure to comply with a lawful order of a police officer, and that the police officer's order was, "Don't shoot that man." Under Justice Scalia's flawed reading of *Harris,* the elements of the offense of failure to obey a police officer's lawful order would include, for purposes of *Blockburger*'s same-elements test, the elements of, perhaps, murder or manslaughter, in effect converting those felonies into a lesser included offense of the crime of failure to comply with a lawful order of a police officer.

* * *

[The short opinion by Justice White joined by Justices Stevens and Souter, concurring in the judgment and dissenting in part, is omitted. Justice White disagreed with the Court's overruling of *Grady*.]

JUSTICE SOUTER, with whom JUSTICE STEVENS joins, concurring in the judgment in part and dissenting in part.

* * *

If a separate prosecution were permitted for every offense arising out of the same conduct, the government could manipulate the definitions of offenses, creating fine distinctions among them and permitting a zealous prosecutor to try a person again and again for essentially the same criminal conduct. * * *

* * * Whatever may have been the merits of the debate in *Grady,* the decision deserves more respect than it receives from the Court today. Although adherence to precedent is not rigidly required in constitutional

cases, any departure from the doctrine of *stare decisis* demands special justification.

The search for any justification fails to reveal that *Grady*'s conclusion was either "unsound in principle," or "unworkable in practice." *Grady*'s rule is straightforward, and a departure from it is not justified by the fact that two Court of Appeals decisions have described it as difficult to apply. * * * The protection of the Double Jeopardy Clause against successive prosecutions is not so fragile that it can be avoided by finely drafted statutes and carefully planned prosecutions.

* * *

[Justice Blackmun's opinion, concurring in the judgment in part and dissenting in part, is omitted.]

QUESTION AFTER DIXON

In civil cases, the plaintiff is required by the doctrine of res judicata to join in one case all claims against a single defendant arising from the same transaction. See Restatement, Second of Judgments, § 24 (1980). Why should we demand any less of a prosecutor?

Dispute About the Blockburger Test

The Justices in *Dixon*, especially Justice Scalia and Chief Justice Rehnquist, disagree on how to apply the *Blockburger* test. In determining the elements of two crimes, do you look at the statute itself (the Rehnquist view) or to the factual allegations in the indictment, at least when the crime covers a wide range of conduct (the Scalia view)? The different approaches are discussed by the court in United States v. Liller, 999 F.2d 61 (2d Cir.1993). Liller was charged with interstate transportation of a stolen firearm, and was acquitted, apparently on the basis of his testimony that he had taken the gun from its owner in order to prevent her from committing suicide. The government then discovered that Liller had been convicted of felonies under a different name. Liller was then charged with being a felon in possession of a firearm—the same firearm that was the subject of the first prosecution. The district court dismissed the indictment, relying on *Grady*; but by the time the case reached the Second Circuit, *Dixon* had been decided. The court analyzed the double jeopardy question as follows:

> While the District Court's application of *Grady* to the facts of the pending case would present several interesting questions, the analysis after *Dixon* is straightforward. Normally we would apply *Blockburger* by examining the facts required to be proved for conviction under the provisions supporting Liller's prior and pending charges. However, in certain circumstances, including where one of the statute covers a

> broad range of conduct, it is appropriate under *Blockburger* to examine the allegations of the indictment rather than only the terms of the statutes. * * * [I]n *Dixon*, at least four Justices, see (Scalia, J., joined by Kennedy, J.) (White, J., joined by Stevens, J.), and perhaps five, see (Souter, J., joined by Stevens, J.), examined the content of the particular Court order violated by the defendants rather than the more general statutory elements of the criminal contempt provision under which they were charged. But see (Rehnquist, C.J., joined by O'Connor, J., and Thomas, J.).

The *Liller* court found that it did not have to decide whether the more narrow "elements" test or the broader "facts in the indictment" test of *Blockburger* was controlling:

> In this case, whether we examine only the statutes or broaden the inquiry to include the facts alleged in the indictments, Liller's offenses are separate. Only the new charge under [the felon-firearm-possession statute] requires proof that the possessor is a felon, and only the old charge * * * requires proof that the firearm was stolen and was transported interstate. Thus, each charge requires proof of a fact not required for the other. Therefore, the Double Jeopardy Clause does not bar the Government from prosecuting Liller for possession of a firearm by a felon despite his prior prosecution for transporting the same weapon in interstate commerce knowing it was stolen.

See also United States v. Bennett, 44 F.3d 1364 (8th Cir.1995) ("[W]e note that courts are split on whether the test is to be applied by looking solely to the statutory elements of the offense, or by going beyond the statute and looking at the underlying facts or averments in the indictment" and that there is "disagreement on this issue among members of the Supreme Court").

Chief Justice Rehnquist accuses Justice Scalia of resurrecting *Grady* by employing a "facts of the indictment" approach to the *Blockburger* test. Is this a fair criticism? What is the difference between a "facts of the indictment" approach and the *Grady* "same conduct" test? Should the Court be concerned that a "statutory elements" test might allow the government to charge a defendant with violation of a broad statute in one prosecution, and violations of more narrow statutes in successive prosecutions, even though the conduct at issue is identical in all cases?

Application of Blockburger to Criminal Enterprises: Rutledge v. United States

The Court applied the *Blockburger* test to a case of conspiracy and continuing criminal enterprise in Rutledge v. United States, 517 U.S. 292 (1996). The defendant was convicted of a conspiracy to distribute controlled substances in violation of 21 U.S.C. § 846, and one count of conducting a continuing criminal enterprise (CCE) "in concert" with others in violation of 21 U.S.C. § 848. Rutledge contended that the conspiracy count was a lesser included offense of the CCE count, and that therefore he had been punished twice for the same offense. The Supreme Court agreed. Justice Stevens, writing for a unanimous Court, reasoned that the elements of conspiracy were precisely the same as the "in concert" element of CCE. Thus, proof of the CCE offense requires proof of a conspiracy that would also violate 21 U.S.C. § 846. While the CCE offense required proof of several elements other than conspiracy (such as the derivation of substantial income), the *Blockburger* test requires that *each* crime contain an element that the other does not. Accordingly, one of the defendant's convictions was unauthorized punishment, and had to be vacated.

Guilty Plea Problems Under the Blockburger Test

However the *Blockburger* test is conceived, it obviously gives the prosecution a good deal of discretion in bringing successive prosecutions on related conduct. There are a lot of criminal statutes out there, with different elements, that could cover some aspect of a defendant's pattern of criminal conduct. Professor Richman, in Bargaining About Future Jeopardy, 49 Vand. L.Rev. 1181 (1996), notes the problems created by the *Blockburger* test that must be encountered by defendants who are engaged in bargaining with prosecutors.

> Consider the plight of a savings and loan executive who finds herself facing a Federal indictment in one district, charging her with several offenses relating to a fraudulent loan scheme. She would like to dispose of the pending charges but worries that whatever sentencing concessions she gains in exchange for her guilty plea would be effectively nullified if she were prosecuted for the other loan scams she engineered, some of which involved real estate in other Federal districts. The pending indictment—and her limited knowledge of the investigation—give her no reason to think that the government knows of these other crimes. Yet she cannot be sure of what the future will hold. Should she bring the uncharged crimes to the government's attention and seek to reach a global settlement, or should she discount the value of the sentencing concessions offered on the pending indictment? If she fails to volunteer this information, to what extent would a plea agreement reached with respect to the charged counts bar the government from prosecuting on the uncharged counts?
>
> This dilemma is not confined to the white-collar context. Consider the drug defendant charged with a single count of narcotics distribution who, upon arrest, confesses to having sold cocaine on thirty other occasions at the same street corner.

In neither case will the Double Jeopardy Clause, as currently interpreted [in *Blockburger*], be of much help.

Professor Richman concludes that because *Blockburger* provides so little in the way of protection against multiple prosecutions, defendants in the plea bargaining process may be forced to disclose information to the prosecution that they would not otherwise wish to without some corresponding concessions. He criticizes a system "that frequently works to extract private information from defendants as the price of repose."

Remedy for Multiple Prosecutions in Violation of the Double Jeopardy Clause: Morris v. Mathews

In Morris v. Mathews, 475 U.S. 237 (1986), the Court found that the defendant was not prejudiced by a double jeopardy violation in a second prosecution. The defendant pleaded guilty to aggravated robbery of a bank. Subsequently, he was charged with and convicted of aggravated murder, which was defined as causing the death of another while fleeing immediately after committing aggravated robbery. A state appellate court concluded that the Double Jeopardy Clause barred the conviction for aggravated murder. But that court held that the jury had properly found the defendant guilty of murder (a crime not barred by the Double Jeopardy Clause), and it reduced his sentence accordingly.

Justice White's opinion for the Court reasoned that "when a jeopardy-barred conviction is reduced to a conviction for a lesser included offense which is not jeopardy-barred, the burden shifts to the defendant to demonstrate a reasonable probability that he would not have been convicted of the non-jeopardy-barred offense absent the presence of the jeopardy-barred offense."[3] He added that "[t]o prevail in a case like this, the defendant must show that, but for the improper inclusion of the jeopardy-barred charge, the result of the proceeding would have been different." The Court remanded the case for a determination of whether the result would have been different if the defendant had been tried only on the lesser offense.

Justice Blackmun, joined by Justice Powell, concurred in the judgment. He argued that the usual harmless error test should apply and that reversal should be required unless the error was harmless beyond a reasonable doubt.

Justice Brennan dissented. He agreed with Justice Blackmun's argument that the harmless error test should apply, but found the error

---

[3] He cited *Strickland v. Washington,* an ineffective assistance of counsel case, discussed in connection with Chapter 10. Justice White explained that a reasonable probability is one that is "sufficient to undermine confidence in the outcome."

not harmless beyond a reasonable doubt. Justice Marshall also agreed that the harmless error test should apply and that the error was not harmless.

B. DEFENSE RESPONSIBILITY FOR MULTIPLE TRIALS

Opposing Joinder of Charges: Jeffers v. United States

The constitutional limitation on multiple prosecutions does not apply if the defendant is responsible for the multiplicity. In Jeffers v. United States, 432 U.S. 137 (1977), the defendant was charged with conspiracy to distribute drugs and with engaging in a continuing criminal enterprise to violate the drug laws. Jeffers opposed a government motion to consolidate the indictments. He moved for a severance, arguing that he would be prejudiced by joinder because much of the evidence that would be admitted against him on the conspiracy charge would be inadmissible in his trial for conducting a continuing criminal enterprise. The trial court granted a severance and he was tried on the conspiracy charge. Jenkins maintained that his subsequent prosecution for engaging in a continuing criminal enterprise violated the Double Jeopardy Clause because the conspiracy charge was a lesser included offense. The Supreme Court rejected the claim, reasoning that the defendant was responsible for the multiplicity of which he complained.

Defense Agreement to Sever Charges: Currier v. Virginia

In Currier v. Virginia, 138 S.Ct. 2144 (2018), the defendant was worried that the prosecution would introduce prejudicial but probative evidence against him on one count that could infect the jury's deliberations on others. To address the problem, he agreed to sever the charges and hold two trials instead of one. But after the first trial finished in an acquittal, the defendant argued that proceeding with the second would violate his right against double jeopardy. The question for the Court was whether a defendant who agrees to have the charges against him considered in two trials later can successfully argue that the second trial offends the Fifth Amendment's Double Jeopardy Clause.

Justice Gorsuch, writing for the majority, relied on Jeffers v. United States, *supra.*

> In *Jeffers v. United States,* 432 U.S. 137 (1977), the defendant sought separate trials on each of the counts against him to reduce the possibility of prejudice. The court granted his request. After the jury convicted the defendant in the first trial of a lesser-included offense, he argued that the prosecution could not later try him for a greater offense. In any other circumstance the defendant likely would have had a good argument. Historically, courts have treated greater and

> lesser-included offenses as the same offense for double jeopardy purposes, so a conviction on one normally precludes a later trial on the other. But, *Jeffers* concluded, it's different when the defendant consents to two trials where one could have done. If a single trial on multiple charges would suffice to avoid a double jeopardy complaint, "there is no violation of the Double Jeopardy Clause when [the defendant] elects to have the . . . offenses tried separately and persuades the trial court to honor his election." 432 U.S., at 152.
>
> What was true in *Jeffers*, we hold, can be no less true here. * * * Nor does anything in *Jeffers* suggest that the outcome should be different if the first trial yielded an acquittal rather than a conviction when a defendant consents to severance. [A]s a general rule, the Double Jeopardy Clause protects against a second prosecution for the same offense after conviction as well as against a second prosecution for the same offense after acquittal. Because the Clause applies equally in both situations, consent to a second trial should in general have equal effect in both situations. * * * [A] defendant's consent dispels any specter of double jeopardy abuse that holding two trials might otherwise present. This Court's teachings are consistent and plain: the Clause, which guards against Government oppression, does not relieve a defendant from the consequences of his voluntary choice.

Currier argued that he had no real choice but to agree to sever the charges, because it he hadn't, the evidence offered as to one charge would be prejudicial as to the others. Justice Gorsuch addressed that argument as follows:

> Mr. Currier faced a lawful choice between two courses of action that each bore potential costs and rationally attractive benefits. It might have been a hard choice. But litigants every day face difficult decisions. Whether it's the defendant who finds himself in the shoes of Jeffers * * * and forced to choose between allowing an imperfect trial to proceed or seeking a second that promises its own risks. Or whether it's the defendant who must decide between exercising his right to testify in his own defense or keeping impeachment evidence of past bad acts from the jury.

Justice Kennedy wrote a concurring opinion. Justices Ginsburg, Breyer, Kagan and Sotomayor dissented in *Currier,* but on a separate issue—whether the government should have been collaterally estopped from litigating certain issues of fact that were resolved favorably to *Currier* in the first prosecution. That discussion in *Currier* will be addressed later in this Chapter.

Guilty Plea to a Lesser Offense over Government Objection: Ohio v. Johnson

If a trial judge accepts a guilty plea to a lesser offense over the objection of a prosecutor who seeks to convict on a greater offense, the fact that the trial judge dismisses the greater charges does not bar reprosecution on those charges. So the Supreme Court held in Ohio v. Johnson, 467 U.S. 493 (1984).

Johnson was charged with four offenses, including murder. He offered to plead guilty to involuntary manslaughter and grand theft, but not to murder and aggravated robbery. The trial judge accepted his offer and dismissed the remaining charges on the ground that to prosecute him on these charges would place him in jeopardy twice. The prosecutor objected to this procedure and appealed from the dismissals. The Supreme Court, in an opinion by Justice Rehnquist, rejected the claim that the Constitution barred a trial on the more serious charges. It was the defendant who made the choice, over government objection, to split the offenses.

C. SUBSEQUENT DEVELOPMENTS AND JEOPARDY

Continuing Violations: Garrett v. United States

In Garrett v. United States, 471 U.S. 773 (1985), the Court held that a defendant who had pleaded guilty to importing marijuana could be prosecuted thereafter and punished for engaging in a "continuing criminal enterprise," even though the marijuana importation to which he had pleaded was used as evidence of the enterprise. The enterprise charged had not been completed when the defendant was indicted for importing marijuana. The Court stated that "one who insists that the music stop and the piper be paid at a particular point must at least have stopped dancing himself before he may seek such an accounting." See also United States v. Paternostro, 966 F.2d 907 (5th Cir.1992) (permissible to bring multiple prosecutions for violating the terms of a Corps of Engineers use permit, because the defendant continued to violate the terms after his conviction, and thus the violation was a continuing one; citing *Garrett*, the court stated that "[i]n this case, Paternostro has not stopped dancing").

Post-Charge Changes of Fact

In Diaz v. United States, 223 U.S. 442 (1912), the defendant was convicted of assault and battery. Then his victim died. He was then tried for homicide, and moved to dismiss the charges on double jeopardy grounds. But the Court held that the homicide prosecution was permissible, because the government could not possibly have brought homicide charges in the original prosecution.

D. SENTENCING ENHANCEMENTS AND SUBSEQUENT PROSECUTION

If criminal conduct is used to enhance a sentence, can that same conduct be charged in a subsequent prosecution? This question was addressed by the Court in Witte v. United States, 515 U.S. 389 (1995). After Witte pleaded guilty to a Federal marijuana charge, a presentence report calculated the base offense level under the Sentencing Guidelines by aggregating the total quantity of drugs involved not only in Witte's offense of conviction but also in uncharged cocaine transactions in which he had engaged with several coconspirators. Under the Sentencing Guidelines, the sentencing range for a particular offense is determined on the basis of all "relevant conduct" in which the defendant was engaged, not just the conduct underlying the offense of conviction. See Sentencing Guidelines, § 1B1.3; see also the discussion in Chapter 11. Witte's resulting sentencing range on the marijuana offense was higher than it would have been if only the drugs involved in his conviction had been considered, but it still fell within the scope of the legislatively authorized penalty. The district court accepted the presentence report's calculation in sentencing Witte, concluding that the other offenses were part of a continuing conspiracy that should be taken into account under the Guidelines as "relevant conduct." When Witte was subsequently indicted for conspiring and attempting to import cocaine, he moved to dismiss the charges, arguing that he had already been punished for those offenses because that cocaine had been considered as "relevant conduct" at his marijuana sentencing.

The Supreme Court, in an opinion by Justice O'Connor, held that the Double Jeopardy Clause would not prevent prosecution of Witte for the subsequently charged cocaine offenses, because he had not been *prosecuted* for those offenses previously. The prior sentence was imposed only for the marijuana offense for which Witte was convicted. Consideration of uncharged relevant conduct was not prosecution for that conduct, but rather a basis for "a stiffened penalty for the [charged] crime, which is considered to be an aggravated offense because a repetitive one."

Justice Stevens dissented in *Witte*. He argued that from the defendant's point of view, it was clear that he was being punished twice for the relevant conduct used to enhance his sentence on the marijuana conviction.

VI. MULTIPLE PUNISHMENTS IN A SINGLE CASE

A. PROHIBITION ON TWO PUNISHMENTS WHEN ONLY ONE IS AUTHORIZED

So far we have considered the application of the Double Jeopardy Clause to multiple actions brought against the defendant for the "same offence." Another line of cases indicates that the Double Jeopardy Clause has some relevance when the defendant is subject to multiple *punishments* for the same offense *in a single case.* However, if there is no multiple prosecution, only multiple punishment, the reach of the Double Jeopardy Clause is limited—the Clause does not *prohibit* the legislature from imposing multiple punishments for a single course of conduct. Rather, it prohibits the prosecution from charging and the *court* from sentencing a defendant to multiple punishments in the absence of statutory authorization.

The limitations on multiple punishments in a single case were first explored by the Court in Ex parte Lange, 85 U.S. (18 Wall.) 163 (1873). Lange was sentenced to both a fine and imprisonment for the same conduct. After Lange fully paid the fine, the judge realized that the statute allowed only a fine *or* imprisonment. He vacated the sentence and imposed a new sentence of imprisonment. But since the defendant had suffered complete punishment for the crime by paying the fine, the Supreme Court held that no further punishment could be imposed. To do so would be outside the punishment authorized by the legislature. Thus the Double Jeopardy Clause in this context works as a means of keeping sentencing courts within the range authorized by the legislature.

The Court distinguished *Lange* in Jones v. Thomas, 491 U.S. 376 (1989). Thomas had been convicted of attempted robbery and of first-degree felony murder for a killing during the commission of a felony and was sentenced to 15 years and life respectively, with the 15 years to be served first. He sought state postconviction relief, arguing that the legislature did not authorize separate punishment for the enhanced murder and the underlying felony. After the state supreme court accepted this argument in another case, the Governor commuted Thomas's sentence, and he remained in custody pursuant to the murder conviction with credit for the time served on the underlying felony. The Supreme Court held that the Double Jeopardy Clause did not require that Thomas be released simply because he had completed his sentence on the underlying felony offense.

Justice Kennedy wrote for the Court and acknowledged that the Double Jeopardy Clause protects against "additions to a sentence in a subsequent proceeding that upset a defendant's legitimate expectation of finality." He nonetheless concluded that the state had properly cured the double jeopardy problem, because the defendant was, in effect, being subject to a single prison sentence (for the murder) that was authorized by the legislature. He distinguished *Lange* as involving more punishment than the legislature authorized. Justice Scalia, joined by Justices Stevens, Brennan and Marshall, dissented.

B. LEGISLATIVE INTENT TO IMPOSE MULTIPLE PUNISHMENTS FOR THE SAME OFFENSE

The protection against multiple punishments for the same offense is directed against prosecutors and trial courts, not against legislators. If a legislature decides that it wants a robber or burglar to serve twice as much time for an offense, it can increase the maximum sentence (and raise the minimum also, if necessary)—subject to the Eighth Amendment's almost-nonexistent proportionality requirements. But a prosecutor who wants someone to serve more time than the legislature has prescribed may try to join multiple charges for the same offense.

Generally, a legislature that establishes a hierarchy of lesser and greater offenses increases the punishment for each greater offense. The increased punishment represents punishment for the additional elements that distinguish the greater from the lesser offense. For example, if the legislature imposes a five year sentence for robbery and a ten year sentence for armed robbery, it can reasonably be assumed that the armed robbery penalty includes the robbery penalty, and adds on five years for the use of a weapon. Courts properly assume that prosecutors and trial courts cannot add together sentences for greater and lesser offenses, because to do so would constitute double-counting.

While there is a presumption that the legislature did not intend multiple punishment for the same conduct, the Supreme Court has emphasized that a legislature may provide separate, cumulative penalties for the same offense if it wishes to do so. It is a matter of legislative intent.

Felony Murder and the Underlying Felony: Whalen v. United States

In Whalen v. United States, 445 U.S. 684 (1980), Justice Stewart's opinion for the Court held that the Federal defendant was improperly sentenced when he was given one sentence for felony (first-degree) murder and another for the underlying offense of rape. Justice Stewart found that Congress had not authorized multiple sentences for these crimes. He stated that "[t]he Double Jeopardy Clause at the very least precludes Federal courts from imposing consecutive sentences unless authorized by Congress to do so. * * * If a Federal court exceeds its own authority by imposing multiple punishments not authorized by Congress, it violates not only the specific guarantee against double jeopardy, but also the constitutional principle of separation of powers in a manner that trenches particularly harshly on individual liberty." Separate opinions by Justice Blackmun and Justice White emphasized that their votes turned solely on the intent of Congress, not on double jeopardy principles—though that is really the same thing in this branch of Double Jeopardy law. Justice Rehnquist dissented and was joined by Chief Justice Burger.

Conspiracy to Import and Conspiracy to Distribute: Albernaz v. United States

In Albernaz v. United States, 450 U.S. 333 (1981), the defendants received consecutive sentences for conspiracy to import and conspiracy to distribute marijuana. Both convictions were under the Comprehensive Drug Abuse and Control Act of 1970. The lower court focused on Congressional intent and found no double jeopardy problem, reasoning that "the Double Jeopardy Clause imposes no limits on Congress' power to define the allowable unit of prosecution and punishment, at least so long as all charges are brought in a single proceeding." The Supreme Court affirmed this analysis, saying that "the question of what punishments are constitutionally permissible is not different from the question of what punishment the Legislative Branch intended to be imposed." Justice Stewart, joined by Justices Marshall and Stevens, concurred in the judgment.

Overcoming the Presumption That Multiple Punishments for the Same Offense Are Not Intended: Missouri v. Hunter

In the context of multiple punishments in a single prosecution (as opposed to multiple prosecutions in cases like *Dixon*), the *Blockburger* test has been used by the Court as a tool to divine legislative intent. As discussed above, the *Blockburger* test provides that offenses are separate if each contains an element that the other does not. If two offenses are the same offense under this test, the Court indulges a *presumption* that the legislature did not intend for multiple punishments to be imposed. However, the Court in Missouri v. Hunter, 459 U.S. 359 (1983), held that *Blockburger* is, in this context, merely a rule of statutory construction—the presumption can be overcome by a clear showing that the legislature in fact intended multiple punishments. The Court stated that where "a legislature specifically authorizes cumulative punishments under two statutes, regardless of whether those two statutes proscribe the same conduct under *Blockburger,* a court's task of statutory construction is at an end" and cumulative punishments can be imposed so long as it is done in a single trial.

Hunter was convicted of first degree robbery of a grocery store (which meant that he used a deadly weapon in the robbery) and also of armed criminal action (which meant that he committed a felony with a deadly weapon). The lower court held that the state legislature intended to provide two punishments for what it found to be the same offense. Writing for the majority, Chief Justice Burger observed that Hunter had not been subjected to two trials, only to two punishments. He reasoned that there is nothing in the Double Jeopardy Clause to prohibit a state from punishing conduct by means of cumulative statutes, and that it was clear that the legislature intended to do so in this case. Justice Marshall, joined by Justice Stevens, dissented. The dissent argued that where multiple charges for the same conduct are brought, the prosecution obtains an unfair advantage because a jury is more likely to convict on one count, even as a compromise; that several convictions, rather than one, mean greater collateral consequences for the defendant; and that the stigma resulting from more than one conviction for the same conduct would be excessive.

Charged with Two, Sentenced for One: Ball v. United States

Chief Justice Burger wrote for the Court in Ball v. United States, 470 U.S. 856 (1985), as it found that Congress did not intend that a felon could be convicted and concurrently sentenced for both receiving a firearm and possessing it in violation of Federal law. The Court concluded, however, that a defendant could be *charged* with two of the same offenses in a single prosecution. Should the defendant be found guilty of both, the trial judge could solve the double jeopardy problem by entering a judgment as to only one offense. Justice Stevens concurred in the judgment. He suggested that the Court correctly held that the defendant's conduct supported a conviction under either statute but not both, but it was unnecessary for the Court to decide whether a defendant could be charged with the two offenses as long as he was convicted of only one. He added that "I see no reason why this Court should go out of its way to encourage prosecutors to tilt the scales of justice against the defendant by employing such tactics."

VII. DOUBLE JEOPARDY AND SENTENCING

A. GOVERNMENT APPEALS OF SENTENCES

Seeking a Harsher Sentence: United States v. DiFrancesco

Justice Blackmun wrote for the majority in United States v. DiFrancesco, 449 U.S. 117 (1980), upholding the government's right to appeal the *sentence* imposed upon a "dangerous special offender." The majority said that the prohibition against multiple *trials* is the controlling constitutional principle in double jeopardy cases and that the prohibition on appellate review of acquittals is based on the fact that a second trial is necessary if relief is granted. In contrast, appellate review of sentencing need not require a second trial. Moreover, the majority noted that "the pronouncement of sentence has never carried the finality that attaches to an acquittal." The Court also observed that the defendant is not subjected to multiple sentences when resentenced following an appeal, because the defendant understands that an initial sentence is not final. Justice Brennan, joined by Justices White, Marshall, and Stevens, dissented and argued that "most defendants are more concerned with how much time they must spend in prison than with whether their record shows a conviction" and that the anxiety associated with multiple trials is equally present when the government can take an appeal from sentencing. Justice Stevens also filed a separate dissent.

B. CAPITAL SENTENCES

Death Is Different: Bullington v. Missouri

The Supreme Court distinguished *DiFrancesco* in Bullington v. Missouri, 451 U.S. 430 (1981), and held that it would violate the Double Jeopardy Clause to impose a death penalty at a second trial when the jury in the first trial (in which the prosecution had the burden in the separate sentencing proceeding of proving certain elements beyond a reasonable doubt) returned a verdict of life imprisonment. The Court noted that the capital sentencing procedure was more like a trial on guilt or innocence than are most sentencing proceedings and that the prior jury determination was tantamount to an acquittal on the death sentence. Four dissenters argued that the purpose of double jeopardy protection is to protect the innocent from wrongful conviction and that sentencing procedures present no danger of convicting the innocent.

Trial Court Error in Favor of the Defendant: Arizona v. Rumsey

Bullington proved to be controlling in Arizona v. Rumsey, 467 U.S. 203 (1984), as the Supreme Court held that a state judge's erroneous finding that there were no aggravating factors warranting capital punishment had the same effect as an "acquittal"—so the state supreme court violated the Double Jeopardy Clause when it remanded a defendant's case back for resentencing and a death sentence was then imposed. Like Missouri, Arizona placed on the prosecution the burden of proving aggravating circumstances beyond a reasonable doubt. The Court declined to distinguish the jury findings in Bullington's case from the Arizona judge's findings in *Rumsey*. Even though the state supreme court held that the trial judge had erred as a matter of law in construing one of the statutory aggravating circumstances and thus prejudiced the government, the Supreme Court held that "[r]eliance on an error of law * * * does not change the double jeopardy effects of a judgment that amounts to an acquittal on the merits." Justice O'Connor wrote for the Court. Justice Rehnquist dissented and was joined by Justice White.

Review of Individual Issues After a Death Sentence Is Imposed: Poland v. Arizona

The Supreme Court distinguished *Bullington* and *Rumsey* in Poland v. Arizona, 476 U.S. 147 (1986). The defendants were convicted of robbing a bank van and killing its guards. The trial court, making the same error as in *Rumsey*, found that the offense was not committed for "pecuniary gain," because the statutory aggravating circumstance applied only to contract killings. But, the court found that the crime was committed in "an especially heinous" manner, which was a specified aggravating circumstance, and imposed death sentences. On appeal, the state supreme court, reversing and remanding on another ground, held both that there was insufficient evidence of heinousness and that the trial judge erred in ruling that the crime was not for pecuniary gain under the statute.

Justice White's majority opinion found that both *Bullington* and *Rumsey* involved the equivalent of acquittals during sentencing, while there was no finding in the instant case that the prosecution failed to prove its case. The Court rejected the argument that a capital sentencer's failure to find a particular aggravating circumstance constitutes an acquittal of that circumstance for double jeopardy purposes and held instead that the proper inquiry is whether the sentencer or reviewing court has decided that the prosecution has failed to prove that death is an appropriate sentence. Thus, the Court ruled that the state supreme court acted properly in reviewing the "pecuniary gain" ruling by the trial judge and in permitting the judge to consider this aggravating circumstance once again upon retrial.

Justice Marshall, joined by Justices Brennan and Blackmun, dissented and argued that the only difference between this case and *Rumsey* was that the sentencing judge made two errors of state law while the *Rumsey* judge made only one. The dissent reasoned that the state supreme court effectively held that the defendants were entitled to acquittals on the only aggravating circumstance that the trial court found to have been validly proved.

Capital Sentencing Proceeding Is Not a Successive Prosecution: Schiro v. Farley

The Court once again distinguished *Bullington* in Schiro v. Farley, 510 U.S. 222 (1994). Schiro admitted to raping and killing a woman and was subsequently charged in separate counts with intentional murder and felony murder. The State sought the death penalty for the felony murder count. The State of Indiana, where Schiro was tried, does not require a showing of intent to kill for felony murder. The jury was given verdict forms for both charges and found Schiro guilty of felony murder, but not intentional murder. The trial judge at the capital phase nonetheless sentenced Schiro to death on the basis of the aggravating circumstance that Schiro had "intentionally" murdered his victim. In the Supreme Court, Schiro argued that imposing the death sentence, on the basis of the intentional murder aggravating circumstance, violated the Double Jeopardy Clause. He reasoned that the sentencing proceeding became a successive prosecution for intentional murder, in light of the jury's failure to find an intent to kill at trial.

Justice O'Connor, writing for seven members of the Court, rejected Schiro's argument and concluded that an initial sentencing proceeding cannot constitute a successive prosecution for purposes of the Double Jeopardy Clause. She distinguished *Bullington* as follows:

> In *Bullington* we recognized the general rule that "the Double Jeopardy Clause imposes no absolute prohibition against the imposition of a harsher sentence at retrial." Nonetheless, we recognized a narrow exception to this general principle because the capital sentencing scheme at issue "differed significantly from those employed in any of the Court's cases where the Double Jeopardy Clause has been held inapplicable to sentencing." Because the capital sentencing proceeding "was itself a trial on the issue of punishment," requiring a defendant to submit to a second, identical proceeding was tantamount to permitting a second prosecution of an acquitted defendant.
>
> This case is manifestly different. Neither the prohibition against a successive trial on the issue of guilt, nor the *Bullington* prohibition against a second capital sentencing proceeding, is implicated here—the State did not reprosecute Schiro for intentional murder, nor did it force him to submit to a second death penalty hearing. It simply conducted a single sentencing hearing in the course of a single prosecution. The state is entitled to "one fair opportunity" to prosecute a defendant, and that opportunity extends not only to prosecution at the guilt phase, but also to present evidence at an ensuing sentencing proceeding.

Justice Blackmun, in dissent, argued that the "sentencing proceeding at issue here is indistinguishable from that confronted in *Bullington*." Justice Stevens wrote a separate dissent in which Justice Blackmun joined.

Jury Deadlock on the Death Penalty and Death Penalty Imposed on a Retrial: Sattazahn v. Pennsylvania

The Court applied its *Bullington-Rumsey* line of cases in Sattazahn v. Pennsylvania, 537 U.S. 101 (2003), and found that the state could permissibly impose the death penalty on a retrial, after the defendant appealed a conviction in which life imprisonment was imposed. The jury at Sattazahn's first trial convicted him of first degree murder but then deadlocked on the death penalty. Under Pennsylvania law, if the jury deadlocks on a penalty of death, the judge must sentence the defendant to life imprisonment. Sattazahn appealed his conviction, alleging that the jury in the guilt phase had received improper instructions on certain matters. The state court agreed with Sattazahn, reversing his conviction and remanding. On retrial, the defendant was found guilty; the state again sought the death penalty, and this time (in part based on facts not presented previously) the jury unanimously agreed on a death sentence.

Justice Scalia, joined by Chief Justice Rehnquist and Justice Thomas, and in most respects by Justice O'Connor and Justice Kennedy, reasoned that Satterzahn's double jeopardy rights were not violated because he had never been "acquitted" of a death sentence. Justice Scalia addressed the defendant's argument that a jury deadlock should trigger double jeopardy protection in the death penalty context:

> Under the *Bullington* line of cases * * *, the touchstone for double-jeopardy protection in capital-sentencing proceedings is whether there has been an "acquittal." Petitioner here cannot establish that the jury or the court "acquitted" him during his first capital-sentencing proceeding. As to the jury: The verdict form returned by the foreman stated that the jury deadlocked 9-to-3 on whether to impose the death penalty; it made no findings with respect to the alleged aggravating circumstance. That result—or more appropriately, that non-result—cannot fairly be called an acquittal "based on findings sufficient to establish legal entitlement to the life sentence." *Rumsey.*

The entry of a life sentence by the judge was not "acquittal," either. Justice Scalia noted that under the Pennsylvania's sentencing scheme, the court has no discretion once it finds that the jury is deadlocked. The court makes no factual findings, it must enter a life sentence. Justice Scalia concluded that a "default judgment does not trigger a double jeopardy bar to the death penalty upon retrial."

Justice Ginsburg, joined by Justices Stevens, Souter and Breyer, dissented. She argued that the policies of the Double Jeopardy Clause are at stake when the defendant is sentenced to life imprisonment rather than death and is then subject to the death penalty on retrial. She explained as follows:

I would decide the double jeopardy issue in Sattazahn's favor [because the] Court's holding confronts defendants with a perilous choice * * *. Under the Court's decision, if a defendant sentenced to life after a jury deadlock chooses to appeal her underlying conviction, she faces the possibility of death if she is successful on appeal but convicted on retrial. If, on the other hand, the defendant loses her appeal, or chooses to forgo an appeal, the final judgment for life stands. In other words, a defendant in Sattazahn's position must relinquish either her right to file a potentially meritorious appeal, or her state-granted entitlement to avoid the death penalty.

C. RESENTENCING FOLLOWING PARTIAL REVERSAL

The Supreme Court cited *DiFrancesco* in its per curiam opinion in Pennsylvania v. Goldhammer, 474 U.S. 28 (1985), which held that the Double Jeopardy Clause did not prevent a state court from resentencing a defendant after some of his convictions had been overturned on appeal. Goldhammer had been convicted on 56 counts of forgery and 56 counts of theft, but he was sentenced to 2–5 years on a single theft count and five years of probation on a single forgery count with sentence on all other counts suspended. The state supreme court overturned 34 of the theft convictions, including the one count on which Goldhammer had been sentenced to prison, because the statute of limitations had run. The Supreme Court remanded the case for a determination of whether state law permitted resentencing.

VIII. COLLATERAL ESTOPPEL

Closely related to the double jeopardy prohibition against retrial after an acquittal is the bar to relitigation of any ultimate fact determined in favor of the defendant in a prior prosecution. In the following case—which holds that the rule of collateral estoppel is a constitutional requirement of the Double Jeopardy Clause—note what the prosecutor was trying to do.

ASHE V. SWENSON

Supreme Court of the United States, 1970.
397 U.S. 436.

JUSTICE STEWART delivered the opinion of the Court.

* * *

Sometime in the early hours of the morning of January 10, 1960, six men were engaged in a poker game in the basement of the home of John Gladson at Lee's Summit, Missouri. Suddenly three or four masked men, armed with a shotgun and pistols, broke into the basement and robbed each of the poker players of money and various articles of personal property. The robbers—and it has never been clear whether there were three or four of them—then fled in a car belonging to one of the victims of the robbery. Shortly thereafter the stolen car was discovered in a field, and later that morning three men were arrested by a state trooper while they were walking on a highway not far from where the abandoned car had been found. The petitioner was arrested by another officer some distance away.

The four were subsequently charged with seven separate offenses—the armed robbery of each of the six poker players and the theft of the car. In May 1960 the petitioner went to trial on the charge of robbing Donald Knight, one of the participants in the poker game. At the trial the State called Knight and three of his fellow poker players as prosecution witnesses. Each of them described the circumstances of the holdup and itemized his own individual losses. The proof that an armed robbery had occurred and that personal property had been taken from Knight as well as from each of the others was unassailable. * * * But the State's evidence that the petitioner had been one of the robbers was weak. Two of the witnesses thought that there had been only three robbers altogether, and could not identify the petitioner as one of them. Another of the victims, who was the petitioner's uncle by marriage, said that at the "patrol station" he had positively identified each of the other three men accused of the holdup, but could say only that the petitioner's voice "sounded very much like" that of one of the robbers. The fourth participant in the poker game did identify the petitioner, but only by his "size and height, and his actions."

The cross-examination of these witnesses was brief, and it was aimed primarily at exposing the weakness of their identification testimony. Defense counsel made no attempt to question their testimony regarding the holdup itself or their claims as to their losses. * * *

The trial judge instructed the jury that if it found that the petitioner was one of the participants in the armed robbery, the theft of "any money" from Knight would sustain a conviction. He also instructed the jury that if the petitioner was one of the robbers, he was guilty under the law even if he had not personally robbed Knight. The jury—though not instructed to elaborate upon its verdict—found the petitioner "not guilty due to insufficient evidence."

Six weeks later the petitioner was brought to trial again, this time for the robbery of another participant in the poker game, a man named Roberts. The petitioner filed a motion to dismiss, based on his previous acquittal. The motion was overruled, and the second trial began. The witnesses were for the most part the same, though this time their testimony was substantially stronger on the issue of the petitioner's identity. For example, two witnesses who at the first trial had been wholly unable to identify the petitioner as one of the robbers, now testified that his features, size, and mannerisms matched those of one of their assailants.

Another witness who before had identified the petitioner only by his size and actions now also remembered him by the unusual sound of his voice. The State further refined its case at the second trial by declining to call one of the participants in the poker game whose identification testimony at the first trial had been conspicuously negative. The case went to the jury on instructions virtually identical to those given at the first trial. This time the jury found the petitioner guilty, and he was sentenced to a 35-year term in the state penitentiary.

* * *

"Collateral estoppel" is an awkward phrase, but it stands for an extremely important principle in our adversary system of justice. It means simply that when an issue of ultimate fact has once been determined by a valid and final judgment, that issue cannot again be litigated between the same parties in any future lawsuit. * * *

The Federal decisions have made clear that the rule of collateral estoppel in criminal cases is not to be applied with the hypertechnical and archaic approach of a 19th century pleading book, but with realism and rationality. Where a previous judgment of acquittal was based upon a general verdict, as is usually the case, this approach requires a court to "examine the record of a prior proceeding, taking into account the pleadings, evidence, charge, and other relevant matter, and conclude whether a rational jury could have grounded its verdict upon an issue other than that which the defendant seeks to foreclose from consideration." * * * Any test more technically restrictive would, of course, simply amount to a rejection of the rule of collateral estoppel in criminal proceedings, at least in every case where the first judgment was based upon a general verdict of acquittal.

Straightforward application of the Federal rule to the present case can lead to but one conclusion. For the record is utterly devoid of any indication that the first jury could rationally have found that an armed robbery had not occurred, or that Knight had not been a victim of that robbery. The single rationally conceivable issue in dispute before the jury was whether the petitioner had been one of the robbers. And the jury by its verdict found that he had not. The Federal rule of law, therefore, would make a second prosecution for the robbery of Roberts wholly impermissible.

The ultimate question to be determined, then, is whether this established rule of Federal law is embodied in the Fifth Amendment guarantee against double jeopardy. We do not hesitate to hold that it is. For whatever else that constitutional guarantee may embrace, it surely protects a man who has been acquitted from having to "run the gantlet" a second time.

The question is not whether Missouri could validly charge the petitioner with six separate offenses for the robbery of the six poker players. It is not whether he could have received a total of six punishments if he had been convicted in a single trial of robbing the six victims. It is simply whether, after a jury determined by its verdict that the petitioner was not one of the robbers, the State could constitutionally hale him before a new jury to litigate that issue again.

After the first jury had acquitted the petitioner of robbing Knight, Missouri could certainly not have brought him to trial again upon that charge. * * * The situation is constitutionally no different here, even though the second trial related to another victim of the same robbery. For the name of the victim, in the circumstances of this case, had no bearing whatever upon the issue of whether the petitioner was one of the robbers.

In this case the State in its brief has frankly conceded that following the petitioner's acquittal, it treated the first trial as no more than a dry run for the second prosecution: "No doubt the prosecutor felt the state had a provable case on the first charge and, when he lost, he did what every good attorney would do—he refined his presentation in light of the turn of events at the first trial." But this is precisely what the constitutional guarantee forbids.

[The concurring opinions by Justice Black (joined by Justice Harlan), and by Justice Brennan (joined by Justices Douglas and Marshall), are omitted, as is the dissenting opinion by Chief Justice Burger.]

The Problem of General Verdicts

Ashe provides some protection for a defendant who is acquitted and then subject to prosecution on a crime that is related, but not the "same offence." However, collateral estoppel (or, more descriptively, issue preclusion) applies only to facts that were actually and necessarily decided by the jury in the defendant's favor. Juries usually return general verdicts in criminal cases. The defense of collateral estoppel may not be available because any number of issues might have been the basis for the acquittal; what issues the jury necessarily decided often cannot be determined.

The Court in *Ashe* suggests a functional approach to determine what the jury decided. An example of that approach is found in Wright v. Whitley, 11 F.3d 542 (5th Cir.1994). Wright was charged with a firearm offense based on an alleged gunfight in which he participated in March 1986. He testified that he was unarmed, and presented corroborating witnesses. The jury acquitted. Subsequently, Wright was indicted for a triple murder by firearm, occurring in May 1986. The court held that the first acquittal had no preclusive effect on any issue in the second prosecution. The fact that Wright was unarmed in one conflagration was not determinative of whether he possessed a firearm two months later.

Compare United States v. Seley, 957 F.2d 717 (9th Cir.1992), where the defendant was acquitted of knowingly importing marijuana across the border. The court held that the government was precluded from proving in a subsequent prosecution that the defendant was involved in a conspiracy to import that same marijuana.

Application of Ashe When There Is an Acquittal on Some Counts and a Deadlock on Others: Yeager v. United States

In Yeager v. United States, 557 U.S. 10 (2009), the defendant, a former Enron executive, was charged with a number of counts of fraud and a number of counts of insider trading. The theory of prosecution was that Yeager had deceived the public about an Enron project in order to inflate the value of Enron stock, and then sold his own stock on the basis of inside information. At his trial, the jury acquitted him of the fraud counts but hung on the insider trading counts. The government sought to reprosecute him on the insider trading counts and the defendant, citing *Ashe,* argued that the government was collaterally estopped due to the acquittal on the fraud counts. He argued that the jury by acquitting him of fraud had necessarily decided that he did not possess material inside information. The Court of Appeals disagreed. It reasoned that if the jury had actually found that he had no inside information, then it would not have hung on the insider trading counts. Since the jury hung, it could not be concluded that they necessarily found that the defendant had no inside information.

The question for the Supreme Court was whether a hung verdict is relevant to a court's determination of what was actually decided when the defendant was acquitted on other charges. The Court, in an opinion by Justice Stevens, found that a juror deadlock on a count could not be considered in the collateral estoppel analysis. Justice Stevens reasoned as follows:

> A hung count is not a relevant part of the record of the prior proceeding. Because a jury speaks only through its verdict, its failure to reach a verdict cannot—by negative implication—yield a piece of information that helps put together the trial puzzle. * * * A host of reasons—sharp disagreement, confusion about the issues, exhaustion after a long trial, to name but a few—could work alone or in tandem to cause a jury to hang. To ascribe meaning to a hung count would presume an ability to identify which factor was at play in the jury room. But that is not reasoned analysis; it is guesswork. Such conjecture about possible reasons for a jury's failure to reach a decision should play no part in assessing the legal consequences of a unanimous verdict that the jurors did return.
>
> A contrary conclusion would require speculation into what transpired in the jury room. Courts properly avoid such explorations

> into the jury's sovereign space, and for good reason. The jury's deliberations are secret and not subject to outside examination. If there is to be an inquiry into what the jury decided, the evidence should be confined to the points in controversy on the former trial, to the testimony given by the parties, and to the questions submitted to the jury for their consideration.
>
> Accordingly, we hold that the consideration of hung counts has no place in the issue-preclusion analysis. Indeed, if it were relevant, the fact that petitioner has already survived one trial should be a factor cutting in favor of, rather than against, applying a double jeopardy bar. * * * Thus, if the possession of insider information was a critical issue of ultimate fact in all of the charges against petitioner, a jury verdict that necessarily decided that issue in his favor protects him from prosecution for any charge for which that is an essential element.

The Court remanded for a determination of whether the acquittal on the fraud charges was preclusive on the factual issues contested on the insider trading charges.

Justice Scalia, joined by Justices Thomas and Alito, dissented. He first criticized *Ashe* as improperly extending Double Jeopardy protection beyond its historic origins:

> This case would be easy indeed if our cases had adhered to the Clause's original meaning. The English common-law pleas of auterfoits acquit and auterfoits convict, on which the Clause was based, barred only repeated "prosecution for the same identical act and crime." As described by Sir Matthew Hale, "a man acquitted for stealing [a] horse" could be later "arraigned and convict[ed] for stealing the saddle, tho both were done at the same time." Under the common-law pleas, the jury's acquittal of Yeager on the fraud counts would have posed no bar to further prosecution for the distinct crimes of insider trading and money laundering.
>
> * * * In *Ashe* the Court departed from the original meaning of the Double Jeopardy Clause, holding that it precludes successive prosecutions on distinct crimes when facts essential to conviction of the second crime have necessarily been resolved in the defendant's favor by a verdict of acquittal of the first crime.

Justice Scalia argued that even under *Ashe,* there was no clear determination that precluded retrial on the insider trading counts:

> There is no clear, unanimous jury finding here. In the unusual situation in which a factual finding upon which an acquittal must have been based would also logically require an acquittal on the hung count, all that can be said for certain is that the conflicting dispositions are irrational—the result of mistake, compromise, or lenity. It is at least

as likely that the irrationality consisted of failing to make the factual finding necessary to support the acquittal as it is that the irrationality consisted of failing to adhere to that factual finding with respect to the hung count.

Justice Alito wrote a separate dissenting opinion joined by Justices Scalia and Thomas.

Identity of Party Requirement

Only a party to the prior criminal proceeding may take advantage of the issue preclusion rule against the government in criminal cases. A unanimous Court in Standefer v. United States, 447 U.S. 10 (1980), held that a defendant accused of aiding and abetting the commission of a Federal offense may be convicted after the named principal has been acquitted of that offense. Chief Justice Burger's opinion rejected the attempt to extend the concept of "nonmutual collateral estoppel," developed in civil cases, into constitutional criminal procedure. Among the special attributes of criminal cases relied upon were the following: the government's limited discovery rights; the impossibility of a directed verdict for the government; the limitations on the government's right to appeal; the existence of exclusionary rules that may exclude evidence as to one defendant but not another; and the government's interest in enforcement of the criminal law.

Non-parties cannot be bound by a prior adjudication of facts. See Vestal, Issue Preclusion and Criminal Prosecutions, 65 Iowa L.Rev. 281 (1980). So, for example, the suppression of evidence in a state prosecution does not automatically prevent the United States from using that evidence in a Federal proceeding against the same defendant. "Since the United States was not a party to the state action, and had no way of making its views on the issue known to the state judge, it cannot be fairly considered to have had its day in court." United States v. Davis, 906 F.2d 829 (2d Cir.1990). The same principles would apply to a subsequent prosecution in a different state.

Issue Preclusion Applied Against the Accused?

Courts have held that issue preclusion cannot be used by the government to preclude an accused from relitigating a fact found against him in a prior criminal proceeding. See, e.g., United States v. Harnage, 976 F.2d 633 (11th Cir.1992). The reasoning is that the use of issue preclusion against the accused would violate his constitutional right to a jury trial in the later prosecution. United States v. Pelullo, 14 F.3d 881 (3d Cir.1994) ("applying collateral estoppel against the defendant in a criminal case interferes with the power of the jury to determine every element of the crime, impinging upon the accused's right to a jury trial").

Relitigation of Facts Offered as Uncharged Misconduct: Dowling v. United States

In Dowling v. United States, 493 U.S. 342 (1990), the Court refused to apply the collateral estoppel doctrine when facts underlying an acquittal were used as evidence of uncharged misconduct in a subsequent prosecution. Dowling was charged with bank robbery. On the issue of identification, the prosecution offered evidence that the defendant had participated in a different robbery—one that was conducted similarly to the robbery with which Dowling was charged. Evidence of the prior robbery was admitted under Federal Rule of Evidence 404(b), which permits proof of the defendant's uncharged misconduct when offered to show intent, knowledge, identity, or any purpose other than to show that the defendant is a bad person. Dowling had been acquitted of the prior robbery. He argued that admitting evidence of the robbery at the later trial was prohibited by *Ashe*. Justice White's majority opinion distinguished *Ashe* on the ground that Dowling's prior acquittal "did not determine the ultimate issue in the present case." The Court further noted that, to introduce evidence of an unrelated crime, the prosecution was not required to show that the defendant committed that crime beyond a reasonable doubt. Under the Federal Rules of Evidence, similar act evidence is admissible if the jury could reasonably conclude by a preponderance of the evidence that the act occurred and the defendant was the actor.

Justice Brennan, joined by Justices Marshall and Stevens, dissented. Justice Brennan argued that the majority took insufficient account of the burdens imposed upon a defendant if facts are relitigated in a subsequent criminal prosecution.

Collateral Estoppel in a Criminal Case is Narrower than in a Civil Case, Because it is Limited to a Trial on the Same Offense: Currier v. Virginia

In Currier v. Virginia, 138 S.Ct. 2144 (2018), the Court considered the following facts: Currier was charged with burglary, grand larceny, and unlawful possession of a firearm by a felon (the prior felony was for burglary and grand larceny). Currier was concerned that evidence to prove the firearm count would be unduly prejudicial to the grand larceny and burglary charges, because the government was required to prove up the felony, and so the jury would hear that he was previously convicted of exactly the same crimes before. In this situation, Virginia allows the defendant to opt for separate trials—which Currier did. The burglary and grand larceny charges were tried first, and Currier was acquitted. He then argued that in the firearm prosecution, the government should be barred from introducing any evidence about the burglary or grand larceny. He relied on preclusion principles that are applicable to civil cases. In essence he argued that Ashe v. Swenson should be extended to prevent the parties from retrying any issue or introducing any evidence about a previously tried issue, whether or not it involved the same offense.

Justice Gorsuch, in a plurality opinion joined by the Chief Justice and Justices Thomas and Alito, refused to apply the rule of collateral estoppel as broadly as Currier requested. Justice Gorsuch reasoned as follows:

> Mr. Currier's problems begin with the text of the Double Jeopardy Clause. As we've seen, the Clause speaks not about prohibiting the relitigation of issues or evidence but offenses. [In this case the firearms charge was a separate offense from the burglary and grand larceny charges.] * * *
>
> What problems the text suggests, the original public understanding of the Fifth Amendment confirms. The Double Jeopardy Clause took its cue from English common law pleas that prevented courts from retrying a criminal defendant previously acquitted or convicted of the crime in question. * * * Of course, *Ashe* later pressed *Blockburger's* boundaries by suggesting that, in narrow circumstances, the retrial of an issue can be considered tantamount to the retrial of an offense. But, as we've seen, even there a court's ultimate focus remains on the practical identity of offenses, and the only available remedy is the traditional double jeopardy bar against the retrial of the same offense—not a bar against the relitigation of issues or evidence. Even at the outer reaches of our double jeopardy jurisprudence, then, this Court has never sought to regulate the retrial of issues or evidence in the name of the Double Jeopardy Clause.

Justice Gorsuch relied on *Dowling,* in which the Court "declined to extend *Ashe* to exclude in all circumstances, as the defendant would have it, relevant and probative evidence that is otherwise admissible under the Rules of Evidence simply because it relates to alleged criminal conduct for which a defendant has been acquitted." He concluded that "if a second trial is permissible, the admission of evidence at that trial is governed by normal evidentiary rules—not by the terms of the Double Jeopardy Clause."

Justice Gorsuch noted that even in civil cases, issue preclusion does not bar the relitigation of issues when "[t]he party against whom preclusion is sought could not, as a matter of law, have obtained review of the judgment in the initial action." In this case, the government could not obtain review of the acquittal on the grand larceny and burglary charges, leading Justice Gorsuch to conclude that "a faithful application of civil preclusion principles in our case and others like it might actually militate *against* finding preclusion."

Justice Gorsuch concluded as follows:

> The fact is, civil preclusion principles and double jeopardy are different doctrines, with different histories, serving different purposes. Historically, both claim and issue preclusion have sought to "promot[e] judicial economy by preventing needless litigation." That interest may make special sense in civil cases where often only money is at stake. But the Double Jeopardy Clause and the common law principles it built upon govern *criminal* cases and concern more than efficiency. They aim instead, as we've seen, to balance vital interests against abusive prosecutorial practices with consideration to the public's safety. The Clause's terms and history simply do not contain the rights Mr. Currier seeks.
>
> Nor are we at liberty to rewrite those terms or that history. While the growing number of criminal offenses in our statute books may be cause for concern, no one should expect (or want) judges to revise the Constitution to address every social problem they happen to perceive. The proper authorities, the States and Congress, are empowered to adopt new laws or rules experimenting with issue or claim preclusion in criminal cases if they wish. In fact, some States have already done so. On these matters, the Constitution dictates no answers but entrusts them to a self-governing people to resolve.

Justice Kennedy wrote a concurring opinion in which he declined to join the plurality's discussion of issue preclusion. In his view, the fact that Currier requested separate trials ended all Double Jeopardy questions:

> The end result is that when a defendant's voluntary choices lead to a second prosecution he cannot later use the Double Jeopardy Clause, whether thought of as protecting against multiple trials or the relitigation of issues, to forestall that second prosecution. The extent of the Double Jeopardy Clause protections discussed and defined in *Ashe* need not be reexamined here; for, whatever the proper formulation and implementation of those rights are, they can be lost when a defendant agrees to a second prosecution.

Justice Ginsburg dissented in an opinion joined by Justices Breyer, Sotomayor, and Kagan. Justice Ginsburg stated that "the plurality would take us back to the days before the Court recognized issue preclusion as a constitutionally grounded component of the Double Jeopardy Clause."

Use of Acquitted Conduct for Sentencing Purposes

Under the "relevant conduct" provisions of the Federal Sentencing Guidelines the district court considers all of the defendant's criminal acts that were part of the offense of conviction, whether those acts were the basis of the conviction or not. All that is required is that the government prove that the relevant conduct occurred by a preponderance of the evidence. Suppose the defendant is charged in a multiple count indictment. He is acquitted on some counts and convicted on others. Assume further that while the government could not prove the acquitted counts beyond a reasonable doubt, it can prove them by a preponderance of the evidence. Under these circumstances, the advisory Guidelines sentence includes consideration of the acquitted conduct; and indeed the Guidelines provide that the acquitted conduct is given *the same weight in sentencing* as the conduct for which the defendant was convicted. See United States v. Concepcion, 983 F.2d 369 (2d Cir.1992) (defendant acquitted on one count and convicted on another receives the same sentence as if he had been convicted of both).

In the per curiam opinion in United States v. Watts, 519 U.S. 148 (1997), the Court relied on *Dowling* and *Ashe* and held that it was permissible for defendants to be sentenced in part on the basis of conduct for which they had been acquitted. Watts was charged with drug and firearms offenses. He was convicted of the former and acquitted of the latter. But the trial judge, using the preponderance of the evidence standard mandated by the Federal Sentencing Guidelines, found by a preponderance that Watts had possessed guns in connection with the drug offenses, and added two points to his base offense level for the Guidelines sentence. The Court found that this did not violate the Double Jeopardy Clause, because "sentencing enhancements do not punish a defendant for crimes of which he was not convicted, but rather increase his sentence because of the manner in which he committed the crime of conviction." The Court also noted that an acquittal could have no preclusive effect on a sentencing determination, because of the lesser standard of proof involved in sentencing. Justice Stevens dissented.

IX. DUAL SOVEREIGNS

The Double Jeopardy Clause prohibits successive prosecutions only if brought by the same "sovereign." The dual sovereignty doctrine is well-explained by the court in United States v. Davis, 906 F.2d 829 (2d Cir.1990):

> The states and the national government are distinct political communities, drawing their separate sovereign power from different sources, each from the organic law that established it. Each has the power, inherent in any sovereign, independently to determine what shall be an offense against its authority and to punish such offenses. When a single act violates the laws of two sovereigns, the wrongdoer has committed two distinct offenses. See generally United States v. Wheeler, 435 U.S. 313 (1978).

> In practice, successive prosecutions for the same conduct remain rarities. In the normal exercise of prosecutorial discretion, one sovereign usually defers to the other. * * * However, this is no limitation on the government's sovereign right to vindicate its interests and values, and nothing prevents a Federal prosecution whenever the state proceeding has not adequately protected the Federal interest.
>
> The only legally binding exception to the dual sovereignty doctrine is a narrow one carved out by the Supreme Court in Bartkus v. Illinois, 359 U.S. 121 (1959). Successive prosecutions will be barred where one prosecuting sovereign can be said to be acting as a "tool" of the other, or where one prosecution is merely a "sham and a cover" for another. Except for this extraordinary type of case, successive state and Federal prosecutions may, in fact as well as form, be brought by different sovereigns and the outcome in a state proceeding is not binding upon the later prosecution.

As implied by the discussion in *Davis,* the dual sovereignty principle also allows two different states to prosecute the defendant for the same conduct. Heath v. Alabama, 474 U.S. 82 (1985) (discussed below). Also, it does not matter that the defendant is acquitted by one sovereign, because another sovereign is not bound by the prior adjudication. See Bartkus v. Illinois, 359 U.S. 121 (1959) (upholding state conviction for robbery where defendant had been acquitted of Federal charges stemming from the same robbery)Federal.

Adhering to the Dual Sovereignty Doctrine: Gamble v. United States

In the following case, the Court considered whether to abrogate the Dual Sovereignty doctrine.

GAMBLE V. UNITED STATES

Supreme Court of the United States, 2019.
139 S.Ct. 1960.

JUSTICE ALITO delivered the opinion of the Court.

We consider in this case whether to overrule a longstanding interpretation of the Double Jeopardy Clause of the Fifth Amendment. That Clause provides that no person may be "twice put in jeopardy" "for the same offence." Our double jeopardy case law is complex, but at its core, the Clause means that those acquitted or convicted of a particular "offence" cannot be tried a second time for the same "offence." But what does the Clause mean by an "offence"?

We have long held that a crime under one sovereign's laws is not "the same offence" as a crime under the laws of another sovereign. Under this "dual-sovereignty" doctrine, a State may prosecute a defendant under state law even if the Federal Government has prosecuted him for the same conduct under a Federal statute.

Or the reverse may happen, as it did here. Terance Gamble, convicted by Alabama for possessing a firearm as a felon, now faces prosecution by the United States under its own felon-in-possession law. Attacking this second prosecution on double jeopardy grounds, Gamble asks us to overrule the dual-sovereignty doctrine. He contends that it departs from the founding-era understanding of the right enshrined by the Double Jeopardy Clause. But the historical evidence assembled by Gamble is feeble; pointing the other way are the Clause's text, other historical evidence, and 170 years of precedent. Today we affirm that precedent, and with it the decision below.

I

In November 2015, a local police officer in Mobile, Alabama, pulled Gamble over for a damaged headlight. Smelling marijuana, the officer searched Gamble's car, where he found a loaded 9-mm handgun. Since Gamble had been convicted of second-degree robbery, his possession of the handgun violated an Alabama law providing that no one convicted of "a crime of violence" "shall own a firearm or have one in his or her possession." After Gamble pleaded guilty to this state offense, Federal prosecutors indicted him for the same instance of possession under a Federal law—one forbidding those convicted of "a crime punishable by imprisonment for a term exceeding one year . . . to ship or transport in interstate or foreign commerce, or possess in or affecting commerce, any firearm or ammunition." 18 U.S.C. § 922(g)(1).

Gamble moved to dismiss on one ground: The Federal indictment was for "the same offence" as the one at issue in his state conviction and thus exposed him to double jeopardy. But because this Court has long held that two offenses "are *not* the 'same offence' " for double jeopardy purposes if "prosecuted by different sovereigns," *Heath v. Alabama*, 474 U.S. 82, 92 (1985), the District Court denied Gamble's motion to dismiss. * * * We granted certiorari to determine whether to overturn that doctrine.

II

Gamble contends that the Double Jeopardy Clause must forbid successive prosecutions by different sovereigns because that is what the founding-era common law did. * * * [W]e review the Clause's text and some of the cases Gamble asks us to overturn.

A

We start with the text of the Fifth Amendment. Although the dual-sovereignty rule is often dubbed an "exception" to the double jeopardy right, it is not an exception at all. On the contrary, it follows from the text that defines that right in the first place. "[T]he language of the Clause . . . protects individuals from being twice put in jeopardy 'for the same *offence*,' not for the same *conduct* or *actions*" * * *. As originally understood, then, an "offence" is defined by a law, and each law is defined by a sovereign. So where there are two sovereigns, there are two laws, and two "offences." * * *

We see no reason to abandon the sovereign-specific reading of the phrase "same offence," from which the dual-sovereignty rule immediately follows.

B

Our cases * * * reveal how fidelity to the Double Jeopardy Clause's text does more than honor the formal difference between two distinct criminal codes. It honors the substantive differences between the interests that two sovereigns can have in punishing the same act.

[Justice Alito discusses cases from the early 1800's establishing that "offences" are tied to the particular sovereign.]

We cemented that foundation 70 years after the last of those antebellum cases, in a decision upholding a Federal prosecution that followed one by a State. See United States v. Lanza, 260 U.S. 377, 382 (1922) ("[A]n act denounced as a crime by both national and state sovereignties is an offense against the peace and dignity of both and may be punished by each"). And for decades more, we applied our precedent without qualm or quibble. When petitioners in 1959 asked us twice to reverse course, we twice refused, finding "[n]o consideration or persuasive reason not presented to the Court in the prior cases" for disturbing our "firmly established" doctrine. Abbate v. United States, 359 U.S. 187, 195; see also Bartkus v. Illinois, 359 U.S. 121. And then we went on enforcing it, adding another six decades of cases to the doctrine's history. See, e.g., Puerto Rico v. Sánchez Valle, [136 S.Ct. 1863] 2016); Heath v. Alabama, 474 U.S. 82 (1985); United States v. Wheeler, 435 U.S. 313 (1978); Rinaldi v. United States, 434 U.S. 22 (1977) (per curiam).

C

We briefly address two objections to this analysis.

First, the dissents contend that our dual-sovereignty rule errs in treating the Federal and State *Governments* as two separate sovereigns when in fact sovereignty belongs to the people. This argument is based on a non sequitur. Yes, our Constitution rests on the principle that the people are sovereign, but that does not mean that they have conferred all the attributes of sovereignty on a single government. Instead, the people, by adopting the Constitution, " 'split the atom of sovereignty.' " Alden v. Maine, 527 U.S. 706, 751 (1999). * * *

It is true that the Republic is " 'ONE WHOLE,' " *post*, at 3 (opinion of GINSBURG, J.) (quoting The Federalist No. 82, p. 493 (C. Rossiter ed. 1961) (A. Hamilton)). But there is a difference between the whole and a single part, and that difference underlies decisions as foundational to our legal system as McCulloch v. Maryland, 4 Wheat. 316 (1819). There, in terms so directly relevant as to seem presciently tailored to answer this very objection, Chief Justice Marshall distinguished precisely between "the people of a State" and "[t]he people of all the States"; between the "sovereignty which the people of a single state possess" and the sovereign powers "conferred by the people of the United States on the government of the Union"; and thus between "the action of a part" and "the action of the whole." In short, *McCulloch*'s famous holding that a State may not tax the national bank rested on a recognition that the States and the Nation have different "interests" and "right[s]." One strains to imagine a clearer statement of the premises of our dual-sovereignty rule, or a more authoritative source. The United States is a *Federal* republic; it is not, contrary to JUSTICE GORSUCH's suggestion, a unitary state like the United Kingdom.

Gamble and the dissents lodge a second objection to this line of reasoning. They suggest that because the division of Federal and state power was meant to promote liberty, it cannot support a rule that exposes Gamble to a second sentence. This argument fundamentally misunderstands the governmental structure established by our Constitution. Our Federal system advances individual liberty in many ways. Among other things, it limits the powers of the Federal Government and protects certain basic liberties from infringement. But because the powers of the Federal Government and the States often overlap, allowing both to regulate often results in two layers of regulation. Taxation is an example that comes immediately to mind. It is also not at all uncommon for the Federal Government to permit activities that a State chooses to forbid or heavily restrict—for example, gambling and the sale of alcohol. And a State may choose to legalize an activity that Federal law prohibits, such as the sale of marijuana. So while our system of Federalism is fundamental to the protection of liberty, it does not always maximize individual liberty at the expense of other interests. * * *

III

* * *

IV

* * * Gamble contends that recent changes—one doctrinal, one practical—blunt the force of *stare decisis* here. They do not.

A

* * * In Gamble's telling, the recognition of the Double Jeopardy Clause's incorporation against the States, see Benton v. Maryland, 395 U.S. 784, 794 (1969), washed away any theoretical foundation for the dual-sovereignty rule. But this incorporation-changes-everything argument trades on a false analogy.

The analogy Gamble draws is to the evolution of our doctrine on the Fourth Amendment right against unreasonable searches and seizures. We have long enforced this right by barring courts from relying on evidence gathered in an illegal search. Thus, in Weeks v. United States, 232 U.S. 383, 391–393 (1914), the Court held that Federal prosecutors could not rely on the fruits of an unreasonable search undertaken by Federal agents. But what if state or local police conducted a search that would have violated the Fourth Amendment if conducted by Federal agents? Before incorporation, the state search would not have violated the Federal Constitution, so Federal law would not have barred admission of the resulting evidence in a state prosecution. But by the very same token, under what was termed "the silver-platter doctrine," state authorities could hand such evidence over to *Federal* prosecutors for use in a Federal case.

Once the Fourth Amendment was held to apply to the States as well as the Federal Government, however, the silver-platter doctrine was scuttled. See Elkins v. United States, 364 U.S. 206 (1960); Wolf v. Colorado, 338 U.S. 25 (1949). Now the fruits of unreasonable state searches are inadmissible in Federal and state courts alike.

Gamble contends that the incorporation of the Double Jeopardy Clause should likewise end the dual-sovereignty rule, but his analogy fails. The silver-platter doctrine was based on the fact that the state searches to which it applied did not at that time violate Federal law. Once the Fourth Amendment was incorporated against the States, the status of those state searches changed. Now they did violate Federal law, so the basis for the silver-platter doctrine was gone.

By contrast, the premises of the dual-sovereignty doctrine have survived incorporation intact. Incorporation meant that the States were now required to abide by this Court's interpretation of the Double Jeopardy Clause. But that interpretation has long included the dual-sovereignty doctrine, and there is no logical reason why incorporation should change it. After all, the doctrine rests on the fact that only same-sovereign successive prosecutions are prosecutions for the "same offense"—and that is just as true after incorporation as before.

B

If incorporation is the doctrinal shift that Gamble invokes to justify a departure from precedent, the practical change he cites is the proliferation of Federal criminal law. Gamble says that the resulting overlap of Federal and criminal codes heightens the risk of successive prosecutions under state and Federal law for the same criminal conduct. Thus, Gamble contends, our precedent should yield to "far-reaching systemic and structural changes" that make our "earlier error all the more egregious and harmful." But unlike Gamble's appeal to incorporation, this argument obviously assumes that the dual-sovereignty doctrine was legal error from the start. So the argument is only as strong as Gamble's argument about the original understanding of double jeopardy rights, an argument that we have found wanting.

* * * Eliminating the dual-sovereignty rule would do little to trim the reach of Federal criminal law, and it would not even prevent many successive state and Federal prosecutions for the same criminal conduct unless we also overruled the long-settled rule that an "offence" for double jeopardy purposes is defined by statutory elements, not by what might be described in a looser sense as a unit of criminal conduct. See Blockburger v. United States, 284 U.S. 299 (1932). Perhaps believing that two revolutionary assaults in the same case would be too much, Gamble has not asked us to overrule *Blockburger* along with the dual-sovereignty rule.

* * *

The judgment of the Court of Appeals for the Eleventh Circuit is affirmed.

JUSTICE THOMAS, concurring.

* * * The founding generation foresaw very limited potential for overlapping criminal prosecutions by the States and the Federal Government. The Founders therefore had no reason to address the double jeopardy question that the Court resolves today. Given their understanding of Congress' limited criminal jurisdiction and the absence of an analogous dual-sovereign system in England, it is difficult to conclude that the People who ratified the Fifth Amendment understood it to prohibit prosecution by a State and the Federal Government for the same offense. And, of course, we are not entitled to interpret the Constitution to align it with our personal sensibilities about "unjust" prosecutions. * * *

JUSTICE GINSBURG, dissenting.

* * * Instead of frittering away Gamble's liberty upon a metaphysical subtlety, two sovereignties, I would hold that the Double Jeopardy Clause

bars successive prosecutions for the same offense by parts of the whole USA.

* * *

Justification for the separate-sovereigns doctrine centers on the word "offence": An "offence," the argument runs, is the violation of a sovereign's law, the United States and each State are separate sovereigns, ergo successive state and Federal prosecutions do not place a defendant in "jeopardy . . . for the same offence."

This compact syllogism is fatally flawed. The United States and its constituent States, unlike foreign nations, are "kindred systems," "parts of ONE WHOLE." The Federalist No. 82, p. 493 (C. Rossiter ed. 1961) (A. Hamilton). They compose one people, bound by an overriding Federal Constitution. Within that "WHOLE," the Federal and State Governments should be disabled from accomplishing together "what neither government [could] do alone—prosecute an ordinary citizen twice for the same offence." Amar & Marcus, Double Jeopardy Law After Rodney King, 95 Colum. L. Rev. 1, 2 (1995).

The notion that the Federal Government and the States are separate sovereigns overlooks a basic tenet of our Federal system. The doctrine treats *governments* as sovereign, with state power to prosecute carried over from years predating the Constitution. In the system established by the Federal Constitution, however, ultimate sovereignty resides in the *governed*. * * * States may be separate, but their populations are part of the people composing the United States.

In our "compound republic," the division of authority between the United States and the States was meant to operate as "a double security [for] the rights of the people." The Federalist No. 51, at 323 (J. Madison).

The separate-sovereigns doctrine, however, scarcely shores up people's rights. Instead, it invokes Federalism to withhold liberty.

It is the doctrine's premise that each government has—and must be allowed to vindicate—a distinct interest in enforcing its own criminal laws. That is a peculiar way to look at the Double Jeopardy Clause, which by its terms safeguards the "person" and restrains the government. * * *

* * *

The Court regards incorporation as immaterial because application of the Double Jeopardy Clause to the States did not affect comprehension of the word "offence" to mean the violation of one sovereign's law. But the Court attributed a separate-sovereigns meaning to "offence" at least in part because the Double Jeopardy Clause did not apply to the States. Incorporation of the Clause should prompt the Court to consider the protection against double jeopardy from the defendant's perspective and to ask why each of two governments within the United States should be permitted to try a defendant once for the same offense when neither could try him or her twice.

* * *

The expansion of Federal criminal law has exacerbated the problems created by the separate-sovereigns doctrine. Ill effects of the doctrine might once have been tempered by the limited overlap between Federal and state criminal law. * * *

* * *

Against all this, there is little to be said for keeping the separate-sovereigns doctrine.

* * *

JUSTICE GORSUCH, dissenting.

A free society does not allow its government to try the same individual for the same crime until it's happy with the result. Unfortunately, the Court today endorses a colossal exception to this ancient rule against double jeopardy. My colleagues say that the Federal government and each State are "separate sovereigns" entitled to try the same person for the same crime. So if all the might of one "sovereign" cannot succeed against the presumptively free individual, another may insist on the chance to try again. And if both manage to succeed, so much the better; they can add one punishment on top of the other. But this "separate sovereigns exception" to the bar against double jeopardy finds no meaningful support in the text of the Constitution, its original public meaning, structure, or history. Instead, the Constitution promises all Americans that they will never suffer double jeopardy. I would enforce that guarantee.

* * * We know that the framers didn't conceive of the term "same offence" in some technical way as referring only to the same statute. And if double jeopardy prevents *one* government from prosecuting a defendant multiple times for the same offense under the banner of separate statutory labels, on what account can it make a difference when *many* governments collectively seek to do the same thing?

The government identifies no evidence suggesting that the framers understood the term "same offence" to bear such a lawyerly sovereign-specific meaning. * * *

Imagine trying to explain the Court's separate sovereigns rule to a criminal defendant, then or now. Yes, you were sentenced to state prison for being a felon in possession of a firearm. And don't worry—the State can't prosecute you again. But a Federal prosecutor *can* send you to prison again for exactly the same thing. What's more, that Federal prosecutor may work hand-in-hand with the same state prosecutor who already went after you. They can share evidence and discuss what worked and what didn't the first time around. And the Federal prosecutor can pursue you even if you were *acquitted* in the state case. None of that offends the Constitution's plain words protecting a person from being placed "twice . . . in jeopardy of life or limb" for "the same offence." Really?

* * *

Enforcing the Constitution always bears its costs. But when the people adopted the Constitution and its Bill of Rights, they thought the liberties promised there worth the costs. It is not for this Court to reassess this judgment to make the prosecutor's job easier. Nor is there any doubt that the benefits the framers saw in prohibiting double prosecutions remain real, and maybe more vital than ever, today. When governments may unleash all their might in multiple prosecutions against an individual, exhausting themselves only when those who hold the reins of power are content with the result, it is "the poor and the weak," and the unpopular and controversial, who suffer first—and there is nothing to stop them from being the last. The separate sovereigns exception was wrong when it was invented, and it remains wrong today.

I respectfully dissent.

The Petite Policy

In Abbate v. United States, 359 U.S. 187 (1959), the Court upheld a Federal prosecution following a state conviction based upon the same criminal act. The Court expressed concern that without the dual sovereignty doctrine, one sovereign, acting quickly, could hinder the law enforcement efforts of another.

Shortly after the decision in *Abbate*, the Justice Department established the "Petite Policy" of not prosecuting an individual after a state prosecution for the same act, unless there are "compelling interests of Federal law enforcement" at stake. The policy is set forth in the United States Attorneys' Manual, § 9–2.031, which provides, among other things:

> This policy precludes the initiation or continuation of a Federal prosecution, following a prior state or Federal prosecution based on substantially the same act(s) or transaction(s) unless three substantive prerequisites are satisfied: first, the matter must involve a substantial Federal interest; second, the prior prosecution must have left that interest demonstrably unvindicated; and third, applying the same test that is applicable to all Federal prosecutions, the government must believe that the defendant's conduct constitutes a Federal offense, and that the admissible evidence probably will be

sufficient to obtain and sustain a conviction by an unbiased trier of fact. In addition, there is a procedural prerequisite to be satisfied, that is, the prosecution must be approved by the appropriate Assistant Attorney General.[4]

Was the Federal prosecution in *Gamble* consistent with the *Petite* policy? Here is Justice Ginsburg's account of the matter in her dissenting opinion in *Gamble:*

> Terance Martez Gamble pleaded guilty in Alabama state court to both possession of a firearm by a person convicted of "a crime of violence" and drug possession, and was sentenced to ten years' imprisonment, all but one year suspended. Apparently regarding Alabama's sentence as too lenient, Federal prosecutors pursued a parallel charge, possession of a firearm by a convicted felon, in violation of Federal law. Gamble again pleaded guilty and received nearly three more years in prison.

If the Federal prosecutor thought that the state sentence was too lenient, it could be concluded, in accordance with the Petite policy factors, that the matter must involve a substantial Federal interest (prosecuting firearms violations); that the prior prosecution must have left that interest demonstrably unvindicated (sentence too lenient); and third, the admissible evidence probably would be sufficient to obtain and sustain a conviction by an unbiased trier of fact (he pled guilty before, presumably in the face of some evidence). But if this relatively garden variety case is sufficient to satisfy the Petite policy, then it is pretty clear that this policy is not much of a bar on Federal overreaching.

Municipality Is Not a Separate Sovereign: Waller v. Florida

In Waller v. Florida, 397 U.S. 387 (1970), the Court held that, for double jeopardy purposes, a municipality was not a separate sovereign from the state of which it is a part. The defendant, who removed a mural from a wall in the St. Petersburg city hall, was convicted in municipal court of violating a city ordinance prohibiting destruction of city property and of disorderly breach of the peace. The State of Florida subsequently charged him with grand larceny. The Court refused to permit successive municipality-state prosecutions, and analogized the relationship to that of the Federal government and a Federal territory.[5]

---

[4] The court held in United States v. Renfro, 620 F.2d 569 (6th Cir.1980), that the decision whether or not to prosecute after a state prosecution was left to the United States Attorney, and a defendant could not challenge the government's failure to comply with its Petite policy. See also United States v. Lester, 992 F.2d 174 (8th Cir.1993) (Petite policy does not grant substantive rights to the defendant).

[5] In United States v. Wheeler, 435 U.S. 313 (1978), Federal prosecution of a Native American for statutory rape was permitted even though he had been convicted of a lesser offense by a tribal court.

The States as Dual Sovereigns: Heath v. Alabama

In Heath v. Alabama, 474 U.S. 82 (1985), the Supreme Court affirmed an Alabama capital murder conviction of a man who had pleaded guilty in Georgia to murder based on the same homicide. Heath hired two men to kill his wife. The men kidnapped her in Alabama and apparently killed her in Georgia. Heath pleaded guilty in Georgia and received a life sentence. Thereafter, Alabama indicted him and convicted him of a murder during a kidnaping.

Justice O'Connor wrote for the Court and stated that "in applying the dual sovereignty doctrine * * * the crucial determination is whether the two entities that seek successively to prosecute a defendant for the same course of conduct can be termed separate sovereigns. This determination turns on whether the two entities draw their authority to punish the offender from distinct sources of power." She concluded that "it is the presence of independent authority to prosecute, not the relation between the States and the Federal Government in our Federalist system, that constitutes the basis for the dual sovereignty doctrine." She concluded that "[t]he States are no less sovereign with respect to each other than they are with respect to the Federal Government."

Justice O'Connor asserted that "to deny a State its power to enforce its criminal laws because another state won the race to the courthouse would be a shocking and untoward deprivation of the historic right and obligation of the States to maintain peace and order within their confines." She stated that "a State's interest in vindicating its sovereign authority through enforcement of its laws by definition can never be satisfied by another State's enforcement of its own laws."

Justice Marshall, joined by Justice Brennan, dissented and argued that the fact that the Federal government and the states have differing interests in criminal prosecutions does not necessarily mean that two states have differing interests in prosecuting the same crime. He argued that "in contrast to the Federal-state context, barring the second prosecution would still permit one government to act upon the broad range of sovereign concerns that have been reserved to the States by the Constitution."

Heath's Supreme Court lawyer has criticized the reasoning of the Supreme Court. See Allen & Ratnaswamy, Heath v. Alabama: A Case Study of Doctrine and Rationality in the Supreme Court, 76 J.Crim.L. & Crim. 801 (1985). The article predicts that ambitious prosecutors will abuse the authority conferred upon them in noteworthy cases in order to further their political advancement.

The United States and Puerto Rico: Dual Sovereigns?

In Commonwealth of Puerto Rico v. Sanchez Valle, 579 U.S. 59 (2016), Justice Kagan wrote for the Court as it held that Puerto Rico and the United States are not separate sovereigns for purposes of the Double Jeopardy Clause. Therefore the defendant could not be prosecuted by Puerto Rico and the Federal government for the same offense. Justice Kagan explained how the Court determines whether jurisdictions are separate sovereigns:

> Whether two prosecuting entities are dual sovereigns in the double jeopardy context * * * depends on whether they draw their authority to punish the offender from distinct sources of power. The inquiry is thus historical, not functional—looking at the deepest wellsprings, not the current exercise, of prosecutorial authority. If two entities derive their power to punish from wholly independent sources (imagine here a pair of parallel lines), then they may bring successive prosecutions. Conversely, if those entities draw their power from the same ultimate source (imagine now two lines emerging from a common point, even if later diverging), then they may not.

Justice Kagan concluded that Puerto Rico's authority to establish and enforce criminal laws came from Congress. Justice Ginsburg, joined by Justice Thomas, concurred and suggested that the Court should at some point examine whether parts of the United States should be considered separate sovereigns. Justice Thomas concurred in part and in the judgment, indicating his disagreement with the Court's analysis of successive prosecutions involving Indian tribes. Justice Breyer, joined by Justice Sotomayor, dissented, and argued that Congress was not the source of prosecutorial power for Puerto Rico.

Joint Efforts in the War on Drugs

State and Federal law enforcement often act jointly in combating the drug trade, for example through the auspices of a joint task force. Apparently this cooperation has not resulted in any limitation on the power of both sovereigns to prosecute the same defendant for the same drug activity. Professor Sandra Guerra, in The Myth of Dual Sovereignty: Multijurisdictional Drug Law Enforcement and Double Jeopardy, 73 No.Car.L.Rev. 1159 (1995), found over 100 Federal drug prosecutions in the previous 20 years that took place after a state prosecution on the same conduct. She draws the following conclusions:

> [T]he dual sovereignty doctrine rests on a Federalist theory that envisions two separate and independent sovereigns, each of which has its respective laws that reflect its unique priorities and interests. The doctrine shows respect for each sovereign's right to vindicate its own

interests without interference from another sovereign. The irony lies in the fact that it is precisely in drug cases where this theory least reflects reality. In drug cases, multijurisdictional drug task forces bring the sovereigns together in a united effort against a common foe. * * * To insist that the cooperating governments make a choice of forum for criminal prosecutions resulting from their joint efforts would neither infringe the sovereign rights of the participating governments, nor create incentives for defendants to race to the courthouse of the jurisdiction offering the best plea bargain.

X. CONTROLS ON JUDICIAL AND PROSECUTORIAL VINDICTIVENESS

In the cases that follow, the Court holds that the Double Jeopardy Clause is not applicable to control judicial vindictiveness in sentencing or prosecutorial vindictiveness in charging. However, the Due Process Clause is held to impose some limitations on those practices.

A. JUDICIAL VINDICTIVENESS

NORTH CAROLINA V. PEARCE

Supreme Court of the United States, 1969.
395 U.S. 711.

JUSTICE STEWART delivered the opinion of the Court.

When at the behest of the defendant a criminal conviction has been set aside and a new trial ordered, to what extent does the Constitution limit the imposition of a harsher sentence after conviction upon retrial? That is the question presented by these two cases.

In No. 413 the respondent Pearce was convicted in a North Carolina court upon a charge of assault with intent to commit rape. The trial judge sentenced him to prison for a term of 12 to 15 years. Several years later he initiated a state post-conviction proceeding which culminated in the reversal of his conviction by the Supreme Court of North Carolina, upon the ground that an involuntary confession had unconstitutionally been admitted in evidence against him. He was retried, convicted, and sentenced by the trial judge to an eight-year prison term, which, when added to the time Pearce had already spent in prison, the parties agree amounted to a longer total sentence than that originally imposed. * * *

In No. 418 the respondent Rice pleaded guilty in an Alabama trial court to four separate charges of second-degree burglary. He was sentenced to prison terms aggregating 10 years. Two and one-half years later the judgments were set aside in a state * * * proceeding, upon the ground that Rice had not been accorded his constitutional right to counsel. He was retried upon three of the charges, convicted, and sentenced to prison on terms aggregating 25 years. No credit was given for the time he had spent in prison on the original judgments.

* * *

The problem before us involves * * * the constitutional limitations upon the imposition of a more severe punishment after conviction for the same offense upon retrial. * * *

* * *

Long-established constitutional doctrine makes clear that * * * the guarantee against double jeopardy imposes no restrictions upon the length of a sentence imposed upon reconviction. * * * [I]t has been settled that this constitutional guarantee imposes no limitations whatever upon the power to *retry* a defendant who has succeeded in getting his first conviction set aside. * * * And * * * it has been settled that a corollary of the power to retry a defendant is the power, upon the defendant's reconviction, to impose whatever sentence may be legally authorized, whether or not it is greater than the sentence imposed after the first conviction. * * *

Although the rationale for this well-established part of our constitutional jurisprudence has been variously verbalized, it rests ultimately upon the premise that the original conviction has, at the defendant's behest, been wholly nullified and the slate wiped clean. As to whatever punishment has actually been suffered under the first conviction, that premise is, of course, an unmitigated fiction * * *. But, so far as the conviction itself goes, and that part of the sentence that has not yet been served, it is no more than a simple statement of fact to say that the slate *has* been wiped clean. The conviction *has* been set aside, and the unexpired portion of the original sentence will never be served. A new trial may result in an acquittal. But if it does result in a conviction, we cannot say that the constitutional guarantee against double jeopardy of its own weight restricts the imposition of an otherwise lawful single punishment for the offense in question. * * *

[The Court rejected an argument that the Equal Protection Clause forbids the imposition of a more severe sentence upon retrial.]

To say that there exists no absolute constitutional bar to the imposition of a more severe sentence upon retrial is not, however, to end the inquiry. There remains for consideration the impact of the Due Process Clause of the Fourteenth Amendment.

It can hardly be doubted that it would be a flagrant violation of the Fourteenth Amendment for a state trial court to follow an announced practice of imposing a heavier sentence upon every reconvicted defendant for the explicit purpose of punishing the defendant for his having succeeded in getting his original conviction set aside. Where, as in each of the cases before us, the original conviction has been set aside because of a constitutional error, the imposition of such a punishment, penalizing those who choose to exercise constitutional rights, would be patently unconstitutional. And the very threat inherent in the existence of such a punitive policy would, with respect to those still in prison, serve to chill the exercise of basic constitutional rights. But even if the first conviction has been set aside for nonconstitutional error, the imposition of a penalty upon the defendant for having successfully pursued a statutory right of appeal or collateral remedy would be no less a violation of due process of law. * * *

Due process of law, then, requires that vindictiveness against a defendant for having successfully attacked his first conviction must play no part in the sentence he receives after a new trial. And since the fear of such vindictiveness may unconstitutionally deter a defendant's exercise of the right to appeal or collaterally attack his first conviction, due process also requires that a defendant be freed of apprehension of such a retaliatory motivation on the part of the sentencing judge.

In order to assure the absence of such a motivation, we have concluded that whenever a judge imposes a more severe sentence upon a defendant after a new trial, the reasons for his doing so must affirmatively appear. Those reasons must be based upon objective information concerning identifiable conduct on the part of the defendant occurring after the time of the original sentencing proceeding. And the factual data upon which the increased sentence is based must be made part of the record, so that the constitutional legitimacy of the increased sentence may be fully reviewed on appeal.

We dispose of the two cases before us in the light of these conclusions. In No. 418 Judge Johnson noted that "the State of Alabama offers no evidence attempting to justify the increase in Rice's original sentences * * *." He found it "shocking that the State of Alabama has not attempted to explain or justify the increase in Rice's punishment—in these three cases, over threefold." And he found that "the conclusion is inescapable that the State of Alabama is punishing petitioner Rice for his having exercised his post-conviction right of review * * *." In No. 413 the situation is not so dramatically clear. Nonetheless, the fact remains that neither at the time the increased sentence was imposed upon Pearce, nor at any stage in this habeas corpus proceeding, has the State offered any reason or justification for that sentence beyond the naked power to impose it.

[The Court upheld the relief granted to Pearce and Rice by the lower courts. Justices Douglas and Marshall concurred, but would have held that the Double Jeopardy Clause bars a higher penalty upon reconviction in every case. Justice Harlan's separate opinion largely agreed with the view of Justices Douglas and Marshall.

Justice Black wrote a concurring and dissenting opinion. He concluded that due process prohibited a higher sentence imposed on appeal for the purpose of punishing a defendant for appealing, but that the detailed procedure mandated by the Court was not required. Justice White wrote an opinion concurring in part.]

Determining Vindictiveness After Pearce

That *Pearce* was decided as a due process and not a double jeopardy case is of great importance. As we will see, the more flexible due process approach produced subsequent rulings that narrowed the potential reach of *Pearce*, rulings that would have been more difficult had *Pearce* rested on the more absolutist double jeopardy language of the Fifth Amendment.

More Convictions in the Interim: Wasman v. United States

The Supreme Court explained in Wasman v. United States, 468 U.S. 559 (1984), that *Pearce* did not prevent imposing a higher sentence upon reconviction of a defendant who had been convicted of additional offenses between the first and second trials. The trial judge who sentenced Wasman carefully explained that he gave him a greater sentence after the second trial than he had after the first because of these additional defenses. The Court found this explanation sufficient to rebut the presumption of vindictiveness established by *Pearce*.

Trial After a Guilty Plea: Alabama v. Smith

In Alabama v. Smith, 490 U.S. 794 (1989), the defendant pled guilty and was sentenced; he appealed to have his guilty plea vacated and was successful. He was then tried on the original charges before the judge who had sentenced him under the vacated guilty plea. He was found guilty after trial, and the judge imposed a sentence more severe than the one he rendered after the guilty plea. Chief Justice Rehnquist, writing for eight Justices, held that the *Pearce* presumption of vindictiveness does not apply when a sentence imposed after a trial is greater than that previously imposed after a guilty plea that was subsequently found invalid.

The Court asserted that the *Pearce* presumption should apply only to circumstances where there is "a reasonable likelihood that the increase in sentence is the product of actual vindictiveness." The Chief Justice stated that "when a greater penalty is imposed after trial than was imposed after a prior guilty plea, the increase in sentence is not more likely than not attributable to the vindictiveness on the part of the sentencing judge." He reasoned that "[e]ven when the same judge imposes both sentences, the relevant sentencing information available to the judge after the plea will usually be considerably less than that available after a trial," and "after trial, the factors that may have indicated leniency as consideration for the guilty plea are no longer present." The Court distinguished *Pearce* as a situation in which the sentencing judge, who presided at both trials, could be "expected to operate in the context of roughly the same sentencing considerations after the second trial as he does after the first; any unexplained change in the sentence is therefore subject to a presumption of vindictiveness." Justice Marshall dissented.

B. PROSECUTORIAL VINDICTIVENESS

Prosecutor's Conduct After the Defendant Exercises the Right to Appeal: Blackledge v. Perry

The court found prosecutorial vindictiveness and, accordingly, a due process violation in Blackledge v. Perry, 417 U.S. 21 (1974). Perry, an inmate in a North Carolina prison, was involved in a fight with another inmate and was charged with misdemeanor assault with a deadly weapon. After he was convicted in the lower trial court, he appealed as of right to the higher trial court where he was entitled to a trial de novo. After the filing of the notice of appeal, the prosecutor obtained an indictment from a grand jury, charging Perry with felonious assault with intent to kill or inflict serious bodily injury. Perry pleaded guilty to the felony charge and received a sentence that was greater than that imposed by the lower trial court on the misdemeanor conviction. The Supreme Court held that a person who is convicted of an offense and who has an opportunity for a trial de novo has a right to avail himself of the opportunity without apprehension that the prosecutor will substitute a more serious charge for the one brought in the lower court. The Court found that where a prosecutor brings more serious charges after a trial has been completed, a presumption of vindictiveness arises. The Court reasoned as follows:

> A prosecutor clearly has a considerable stake in discouraging [appeals which] will clearly require increased expenditures of prosecutorial resources before the defendant's conviction becomes final, and may even result in a formerly convicted defendant going free. And, if the prosecutor has the means readily at hand to discourage such appeals—by "upping the ante" through a felony indictment * * * the state can insure that only the most hardy defendants will brave the hazards of a de novo trial.
>
> There is, of course, no evidence that the prosecutor in this case acted in bad faith or maliciously in seeking a felony indictment against Perry. The rationale of [*Pearce*], however, was not grounded upon the proposition that actual retaliatory motivation must inevitably exist. Rather, we emphasized that since the fear of such vindictiveness may unconstitutionally deter a defendant's exercise of the right to appeal

> * * * due process also requires that a defendant be freed of apprehension of such a retaliatory motivation on the part of the sentencing judge. We think it clear that the same considerations apply here.

The Court noted that the presumption of vindictiveness would be overcome if the State could show "that it was impossible to proceed on the more serious charge at the outset" and cited Diaz v. United States, 223 U.S. 442 (1912), discussed supra. In *Diaz,* the Double Jeopardy Clause was held not to bar a later murder trial where the victim did not die until after the defendant's trial for assault and battery. See also United States v. York, 933 F.2d 1343 (7th Cir.1991), where the defendant was subjected to an additional charge of obstruction of justice after a successful appeal of his murder conviction. The court found that the testimony required to support the obstruction charge came from the defendant's son, who had expressed an unwillingness to testify against his father at the first trial. When the son changed his mind and approached the authorities two years later, the prosecution could not be presumed vindictive when it added the obstruction charge.[6]

Prosecutor's Conduct After the Defendant Invokes a Trial Right: United States v. Goodwin

In United States v. Goodwin, 454 U.S. 1138 (1982), the Court distinguished *Blackledge* and refused to apply a presumption of vindictiveness to a prosecutor's decisions in the pretrial setting. Goodwin was charged with several misdemeanors, including assault, following an incident in which a police officer stopped his car for speeding. After he invoked his right to a jury trial, an Assistant United States Attorney obtained a four count indictment against Goodwin that included a felony charge of forcibly assaulting a Federal officer. Goodwin was convicted on the felony count and one misdemeanor count. The Supreme Court, in an opinion by Justice Stevens, held that the Due Process Clause does not prohibit the government from bringing more serious charges against a defendant after he has exercised his right to jury trial. Distinguishing *Pearce* and *Blackledge* as decisions reflecting "a recognition by the Court of the institutional bias inherent in the judicial system against the retrial of issues that have already been decided," Justice Stevens's opinion reasoned as follows:

---

[6] The Court found that *Blackledge* clearly controlled in Thigpen v. Roberts, 468 U.S. 27 (1984). The defendant was convicted in a lower level court of several misdemeanors, he sought a de novo trial in a higher level court, and he was indicted for a felony offense arising out of the same conduct. Finding that the same prosecutor was involved in both prosecutions, the Court stated that it "need not determine the correct rule when two independent prosecutors are involved." It observed that the *Blackledge* presumption of vindictiveness is rebuttable, but that no attempt at rebuttal had been made in the lower courts.

> There is good reason to be cautious before adopting an inflexible presumption of prosecutorial vindictiveness in a pre-trial setting. In the course of preparing for trial, the prosecutor may uncover additional information that suggests a basis for further prosecution or he simply may come to realize that information possessed by the State has a broader significance. At this stage of the proceedings, the prosecutor's assessment of the proper extent of prosecution may not have crystallized. In contrast, once a trial begins—and certainly by the time a conviction has been obtained—it is much more likely that the State has discovered and assessed all of the information against an accused and has made a determination, on the basis of that information, of the extent to which he should be prosecuted. Thus, a change in the charging decision made after an initial trial is completed is much more likely to be improperly motivated than is a pretrial decision.

Although Justice Stevens declined to adopt a presumption of vindictiveness in the circumstances presented, he stated that "we of course do not foreclose the possibility that a defendant in an appropriate case might prove objectively that the prosecutor's decision was motivated by a desire to punish him for doing something that the law plainly allowed him to do." Justice Blackmun would have presumed vindictiveness but found that the prosecutor's reasons for seeking a felony indictment adequately rebutted the presumption. Justice Brennan, joined by Justice Marshall, dissented.

Applications of Goodwin

The lower courts have rarely found prosecutorial vindictiveness. For example, in United States v. Sinigaglio, 942 F.2d 581 (9th Cir.1991), the court stated that "when increased charges are filed in the routine course of prosecutorial review or as a result of continuing investigation, there is no realistic likelihood of prosecutorial abuse, and therefore no appearance of vindictive prosecution arises merely because the prosecutor's action was taken after a defense right was exercised." It has also been held that the increase in charges due to the prosecutor's discovery of a new law does not warrant a presumption of vindictiveness. United States v. Austin, 902 F.2d 743 (9th Cir.1990). In United States v. Muldoon, 931 F.2d 282 (4th Cir.1991), the court held that a presumption of vindictiveness "does not arise from plea negotiations when the prosecutor threatens to bring additional charges if the accused refuses to plead guilty to pending charges. The Due Process Clause does not bar the prosecutor from carrying out his threat." See also United States v. Williams, 47 F.3d 658 (4th Cir.1995) (no presumption of vindictiveness where prosecutor increases the charges when the defendant refuses to become a cooperating witness and undercover informant).

XI. CIVIL PENALTIES AS PUNISHMENT

In several cases, the Court has considered whether civil sanctions may constitute "punishment" under the Double Jeopardy Clause. If a civil sanction triggers the Double Jeopardy Clause, the state cannot bring multiple actions to enforce both the civil sanction and a criminal sanction for the same conduct.

Does the Double Jeopardy Clause Regulate Civil Penalties? United States v. Halper

The first in the line of cases was United States v. Halper, 490 U.S. 435 (1989). The facts involved a manager of a medical service company who was convicted of submitting 65 false claims for government reimbursement and fined $5,000. Thereafter, the government sought summary judgment under the False Claims Act, which provided for a civil penalty of $2,000 on each claim, as well as a penalty for twice the amount of the government's actual damages of $585 and the costs of the action. Thus, the government sought a sanction of $130,000 for a $585 fraud.

Justice Blackmun wrote as follows:

> What we announce now is a rule for the rare case, the case such as the one before us, where a fixed-penalty provision subjects a prolific but small-gauge offender to a sanction overwhelmingly disproportionate to the damages he has caused. The rule is one of reason: Where a defendant previously has sustained a criminal penalty and the civil penalty sought in the subsequent proceeding bears no rational relation to the goal of compensating the Government for its loss, but rather appears to qualify as "punishment" in the plain meaning of the word, then the defendant is entitled to an accounting of the Government's damages and costs to determine if the penalty sought in fact constitutes a second punishment. * * *

The scope of *Halper* was potentially broad. Criminal law violators often suffer substantial civil sanctions for the same conduct. For example, a defendant convicted of drunk driving will often lose his license; a lawyer convicted of stealing from clients will usually be disbarred; and a defendant convicted of a drug crime may also face civil charges for failure to pay taxes. Are all of these civil consequences barred by the Double Jeopardy Clause after the criminal conviction? (Or vice versa—will the imposition of these civil sanctions bar subsequent criminal prosecution?) In subsequent cases, the Court has taken pains to shy away from the implication in *Halper* that the Double Jeopardy Clause imposes some significant limitation on civil penalties. Indeed, less than a decade after deciding *Halper*, the Court would decide that the decision was a mistake, as explained below.

Civil In Rem Forfeiture: United States v. Ursery

In United States v. Ursery, 518 U.S. 267 (1996), the Court held that civil in rem forfeitures generally do not constitute punishment within the meaning of the Double Jeopardy Clause. *Ursery* involved an attempt to forfeit property in two cases, after the respective property owners had been convicted of criminal offenses. In one case, the government sought forfeiture of the proceeds of drug and money-laundering activity that was the subject of the criminal prosecution. In the other case, the government sought forfeiture of the house of a person convicted of marijuana offenses. In this latter case, the government argued that the house was used as an instrumentality of the crime for which the defendant had been convicted.

Chief Justice Rehnquist, writing for the Court, relied heavily on previous cases involving civil in rem forfeitures and noted the precedent indicating "a sharp distinction between in rem civil forfeitures and in personam civil penalties such as fines: Though the latter could, in some circumstances, be punitive, the former could not."

Applying the "non-punitive" presumption to the in rem forfeitures at issue, the Chief Justice found no violation of the Double Jeopardy Clause. The claimants had not come close to establishing the "clearest proof" that the forfeitures were punitive rather than civil in nature. While "perhaps having punitive aspects" the forfeiture statutes at issue served significant nonpunitive goals, such as: encouraging property owners to use their property legally; abating a nuisance; and preventing drug dealers and money launderers from profiting. The Court also noted that the procedural requirements for establishing forfeitability in the relevant statutes tracked civil rather than criminal law. For example, the government was not required to establish scienter for purposes of civil in rem forfeiture. The Court also disregarded the fact that forfeiture statutes serve a deterrent purpose, reasoning that deterrence is a proper motive of both civil and criminal laws.

Justice Kennedy wrote a concurring opinion in *Ursery*. Justice Scalia, joined by Justice Thomas, concurred in the judgment. Justice Stevens concurred in part and dissented in part.

Repudiating Halper: Hudson v. United States

The Court repudiated the *Halper* analysis in Hudson v. United States, 522 U.S. 93 (1997). The Office of the Comptroller of the Currency (OCC) imposed monetary penalties and occupational debarment on Hudson, a bank official, for violating Federal banking laws by making improper loans. When the Government later indicted Hudson for essentially the same conduct, he moved to dismiss under the Double Jeopardy Clause. The Court of Appeals rejected the double jeopardy claims; it applied *Halper* and concluded that the monetary and other penalties were not disproportionate to the harm caused by Hudson and so were not punishment. The Supreme Court, in an opinion by Chief Justice Rehnquist, affirmed the result reached by the Court of Appeals but rejected the *Halper* analysis.

The Chief Justice's analysis of the relationship between ostensibly civil penalties and the Double Jeopardy Clause proceeded as follows:

> Whether a particular punishment is criminal or civil is, at least initially, a matter of statutory construction. A court must first ask whether the legislature, "in establishing the penalizing mechanism, indicated either expressly or impliedly a preference for one label or the other." [United States v.] Ward, 448 U.S. at 248. Even in those cases where the legislature "has indicated an intention to establish a civil penalty, we have inquired further whether the statutory scheme was so punitive either in purpose or effect," as to "transform what was clearly intended as a civil remedy into a criminal penalty,"
>
> In making this latter determination, the factors listed in Kennedy v. Mendoza-Martinez, 372 U.S. 144 (1963), provide useful guideposts, including: (1) "whether the sanction involves an affirmative disability or restraint"; (2) "whether it has historically been regarded as a punishment"; (3) "whether it comes into play only on a finding of scienter"; (4) "whether its operation will promote the traditional aims of punishment—retribution and deterrence"; (5) "whether the behavior to which it applies is already a crime"; (6) "whether an alternative purpose to which it may rationally be connected is assignable for it"; and (7) "whether it appears excessive in relation to the alternative purpose assigned." It is important to note, however, that "these factors must be considered in relation to the statute on its face," and "only the clearest proof" will suffice to override legislative intent and transform what has been denominated a civil remedy into a criminal penalty.
>
> Our opinion in United States v. Halper marked the first time we applied the Double Jeopardy Clause to a sanction without first determining that it was criminal in nature. * * *
>
> The analysis applied by the *Halper* Court deviated from our traditional double jeopardy doctrine in two key respects. First, the *Halper* Court bypassed the threshold question: whether the successive punishment at issue is a "criminal" punishment. Instead, it focused on whether the sanction, regardless of whether it was civil or criminal, was so grossly disproportionate to the harm caused as to constitute "punishment." In so doing, the Court elevated a single *Kennedy* factor—whether the sanction appeared excessive in relation to its nonpunitive purposes—to dispositive status. But as we emphasized in *Kennedy* itself, no one factor should be considered controlling as they "may often point in differing directions." The second significant departure in *Halper*

was the Court's decision to "assess the character of the actual sanctions imposed," rather than, as *Kennedy* demanded, evaluating the "statute on its face" to determine whether it provided for what amounted to a criminal sanction.

> We believe that *Halper's* deviation from longstanding double jeopardy principles was ill considered. As subsequent cases have demonstrated, *Halper's* test for determining whether a particular sanction is "punitive," and thus subject to the strictures of the Double Jeopardy Clause, has proved unworkable. We have since recognized that all civil penalties have some deterrent effect. See United States v. Ursery. If a sanction must be "solely" remedial (i.e., entirely nondeterrent) to avoid implicating the Double Jeopardy Clause, then no civil penalties are beyond the scope of the Clause. Under *Halper's* method of analysis, a court must also look at the "sanction actually imposed" to determine whether the Double Jeopardy Clause is implicated. Thus, it will not be possible to determine whether the Double Jeopardy Clause is violated until a defendant has proceeded through a trial to judgment. But in those cases where the civil proceeding follows the criminal proceeding, this approach flies in the face of the notion that the Double Jeopardy Clause forbids the government from even attempting a second time to punish criminally.

Applying "traditional double jeopardy principles" to the facts, the Chief Justice found that the OCC penalties and debarment sanctions were clearly civil rather than criminal, and therefore the subsequent prosecution of Hudson did not violate the Double Jeopardy Clause. The monetary penalties were explicitly designated as civil, and the fact that debarment proceedings were conducted administratively was a strong indication that they were civil rather than criminal. The Chief Justice also noted "that there is little evidence, much less the clearest proof that we require, suggesting that either OCC money penalties or debarment sanctions are so punitive in form and effect as to render them criminal despite Congress' intent to the contrary." Neither money penalties nor debarment have historically been viewed as punishment. Nor did the sanctions involve an "affirmative disability or restraint," as that term is normally understood. * * * Furthermore, neither sanction came into play only on a finding of scienter. The regulatory provisions under which the monetary penalties were imposed allow for the assessment of a penalty against any person "who violates" any of the underlying banking statutes, without regard to the violator's state of mind.

The Chief Justice recognized that imposing monetary penalties and debarment sanctions will deter others from engaging in similar conduct, a traditional goal of criminal punishment. "But the mere presence of this purpose is insufficient to render a sanction criminal, as deterrence may serve civil as well as criminal goals." The Chief Justice noted that the monetary and debarment sanctions, "while intended to deter future wrongdoing, also serve to promote the stability of the banking industry. To hold that the mere presence of a deterrent purpose renders such sanctions criminal for double jeopardy purposes would severely undermine the Government's ability to engage in effective regulation of institutions such as banks."

Justice Stevens concurred in the judgment. He found it unnecessary to consider the viability of *Halper,* because even if the civil sanctions were punishment, the statute under which they were imposed did not constitute the "same offense" as the criminal charges. Justices Souter, and Justice Breyer joined by Justice Ginsburg, also wrote separate opinions concurring in the judgment.

CHAPTER 13

POST-CONVICTION CHALLENGES

■ ■ ■

I. INTRODUCTION

Because of the Double Jeopardy Clause and the constitutional right to a jury trial, the prosecutor generally will be unable to seek review of an acquittal. The criminal defendant who is convicted has greater opportunities to challenge the trial court's judgment.[1] This Chapter addresses the opportunities most likely to be made available in the typical criminal case.

Three types of post-conviction proceedings will be examined in this Chapter: 1) motions made in the trial court after a conviction, 2) direct appellate review of convictions, and 3) collateral attacks on convictions. We assume that everyone has a basic familiarity with the following facts: criminal cases are tried in both federal and state courts; an appeal of one sort or another generally is provided a convicted defendant; the defendant may raise claims concerning almost any trial errors, defects in trial procedure, problems with the substantive law or the overall fairness of the results on appeal; but crowded appellate courts may screen some appeals and decide them on the basis of written briefs, reserving oral argument for special cases. Questions concerning the right to counsel and to the effective assistance of counsel in post-conviction proceedings are addressed in Chapters 5 and 10. Appellate review of sentences is examined in Chapter 11 and also touched upon in Chapter 12.

II. GROUNDS FOR DIRECT ATTACKS ON A CONVICTION

If the defendant has been convicted, there are two procedural avenues by which he can attack the judgment "directly": through motions to the trial judge or by way of direct appeal. This section considers some possible grounds for a direct attack, and some defenses that the government might have against a remedy that would vacate the judgment.

---

[1] As noted in the previous chapter on double jeopardy, not all government appeals are constitutionally barred. Generally, if the prosecutor is not challenging an acquittal or seeking a second adjudication on the guilt-innocence question, the Constitution will not stand in the way of an appeal. While Congress has acted to open the doors to government appeals virtually to the limits of the Constitution in 18 U.S.C.A. § 3731, not all states permit the government such review.

A. INSUFFICIENT EVIDENCE

1. The General Standard

A defendant may move during trial or after a verdict is returned for an acquittal on the ground that the evidence is insufficient to sustain a conviction. Federal Rule of Criminal Procedure 29 indicates the opportunities available to a defendant to make and repeat such a motion. The same legal standard is used in judging post-verdict as mid-trial motions. The general rule is that a guilty verdict can only stand if there is sufficient evidence to convince a reasonable jury of guilt beyond a reasonable doubt of all necessary elements of the government's case. See United States v. Ramirez, 362 F.3d 521 (8th Cir. 2004) ("While the evidence need not preclude every outcome other than guilty, we consider whether it would be sufficient to convince a reasonable jury beyond a reasonable doubt."). After In re Winship, discussed in Chapter 10, this standard of review is probably required by the Constitution. When the burden of persuasion as to a defense is placed upon the defendant, a guilty verdict will be set aside if no reasonable jury could have rejected the defendant's evidence, when measured under the appropriate standard of proof. For example, if a defendant bears the burden of proving insanity by a preponderance of the evidence, a jury verdict of guilty will be set aside if the defendant's evidence is so strong that any *reasonable* jury would have found the proof of insanity to be preponderant.

Review by Trial Judge for Insufficiency

The standard for review by a trial judge upon a motion for acquittal is well-stated by the court in United States v. Mariani, 725 F.2d 862 (2d Cir.1984):

> When a defendant moves for a judgment of acquittal, the court must determine whether upon the evidence, giving full play to the right of the jury to determine credibility, weigh the evidence, and draw justifiable inferences of fact, a reasonable mind might fairly conclude guilt beyond a reasonable doubt. If it concludes that upon the evidence there must be such a doubt in a reasonable mind, it must grant the motion; or, to state it another way, if there is no evidence upon which a reasonable mind might fairly conclude guilt beyond a reasonable doubt, the motion must be granted. If it concludes that either of the two results, a reasonable doubt or no reasonable doubt, is fairly possible, it must let the jury decide the matter.

Timing of a Motion for Acquittal

Fed.R.Crim.P. 29 provides, as does the law of most states, that a motion for judgment of acquittal must be granted after the evidence of either side is concluded if the evidence against the defendant is insufficient to warrant conviction. If the defendant makes a motion for acquittal at the close of the government's case, the trial court may reserve a ruling on the motion until the end of the case. If the defendant, after making the motion, puts on evidence, the trial court in subsequently ruling on the motion for acquittal is to consider only the evidence presented as of the time "the ruling was reserved." Rule 29(b). Therefore, the defendant who puts on evidence after the judge reserves a ruling on the motion avoids the risk that the evidence and the government's rebuttal will be considered as favorable to the government for purposes of the dismissal motion. That is, the defendant does not waive the right to have the acquittal motion judged solely on the basis of the government's evidence, without reference to the evidence offered after the government rests. While Rule 29 specifically limits only the trial court and not the appellate court, the Advisory Committee's comment to the Rule states that "in reviewing a trial court's ruling, the appellate court would be similarly limited" to the evidence presented as of the time the motion was made.

Fed.R.Crim.P. 29(c) provides that a motion for judgment of acquittal can be made after the jury returns a verdict, but it sets a time limit for such a motion—it must be made "within 7 days after a guilty verdict or after the court discharges the jury, whichever is later." In Carlisle v. United States, 517 U.S. 416 (1996), the defendant's motion for acquittal was made 8 days after the jury was discharged. The Court, in an opinion by Justice Scalia, held that the district court has no jurisdiction to entertain a motion for acquittal made outside the time limit of Rule 29(c)—even if the defendant is innocent. Justice Scalia declared that the Rule is "plain and unambiguous" and that there is "simply no room in the text * * * for the granting of an untimely post-verdict motion for judgment of acquittal, regardless of whether the motion is accompanied by a claim of legal innocence, is filed before sentencing, or was filed late because of attorney error." Justice Souter wrote a short concurring opinion, as did Justice Ginsburg, joined by Justices Souter and Breyer. Justice Ginsburg argued that the Rule 29 time bar might be lifted if defense counsel were somehow misled by the trial court. But Carlisle's counsel was not misled; rather, he neglected to follow plain instructions as set forth in the Rule. She also observed that Carlisle was not bereft of protection at this point, because he could still challenge his conviction on appeal, and could also bring a collateral attack on grounds of ineffective assistance of counsel.

Justice Stevens, joined by Justice Kennedy, dissented in *Carlisle*. He contended that there was nothing in Rule 29(c) that "withdraws the court's pre-existing authority to refrain from entering judgment of conviction against a defendant whom it knows to be legally innocent."

2. The Standard of Appellate Review of Sufficiency of the Evidence

Rational Trier of Fact Test: Jackson v. Virginia

At one time, there was a tendency among appellate courts to uphold verdicts supported by *any* evidence. Only "no evidence" cases produced reversals. But in Jackson v. Virginia, 443 U.S. 307 (1979), the Supreme Court rejected the "no evidence" test. Writing for the Court, Justice Stewart opined that the "no evidence" rule was inadequate to protect against misapplication of the proof beyond a reasonable doubt requirement, and that the critical question on review of a criminal conviction is whether the record evidence could reasonably support a finding of guilt beyond a reasonable doubt. Justice Stewart elaborated on the appropriate test for review of sufficiency claims:

> After *Winship* the critical inquiry on review of the sufficiency of the evidence to support a criminal conviction must be not simply to determine whether the jury was properly instructed, but to determine whether the record evidence could reasonably support a finding of guilt beyond a reasonable doubt. But this inquiry does not require a court to ask itself whether *it* believes that the evidence at the trial established guilt beyond a reasonable doubt. Instead, the relevant question is whether, after viewing the evidence in the light most favorable to the prosecution, *any* rational trier of fact could have found the essential elements of the crime beyond a reasonable doubt. This familiar standard gives full play to the responsibility of the trier of fact fairly to resolve conflicts in the testimony, to weigh the evidence, and to draw reasonable inferences from basic facts to ultimate facts. * * * The criterion thus impinges upon jury discretion only to the extent necessary to guarantee the fundamental protection of due process of law.[2]

Thus, the standard for appellate review of sufficiency of the evidence under *Jackson* is the same as the standard used by the trial court in ruling on a motion for acquittal.

Ironically, Jackson, who was convicted of first degree murder, did not benefit from his victory on the legal standard of sufficiency. Jackson was convicted of premeditated murder and claimed that he shot the victim by accident. The Court found that because Jackson, among other things, admitted firing several shots into the ground and reloading his gun before killing the deceased, a rational trier of fact could have found beyond a reasonable doubt that the killing was premeditated.

---

[2] Justice Stevens dissented and was joined by Chief Justice Burger and Justice Rehnquist. Justice Powell did not participate.

Jackson was a habeas corpus case, but the standards set forth in *Jackson* apply to direct appeals as well. See, e.g., United States v. Aina-Marshall, 336 F.3d 167 (2d Cir. 2003) ("A defendant challenging a conviction based on insufficient evidence bears a heavy burden. * * * A conviction will be affirmed so long as any rational trier of fact could have found the essential elements of the crime beyond a reasonable doubt.").

As discussed later in this Chapter, changes in federal habeas corpus law have made it especially difficult to win a *Jackson* challenge in a federal habeas proceeding. See Coleman v. Johnson, *infra.*

Application of Jackson: Wright v. West

In Wright v. West, 505 U.S. 277 (1992), West was convicted of grand larceny on the basis of possession of stolen goods. The theft occurred several weeks before the items were found in West's house; only a few of the stolen items were found there; West had made no attempt to conceal the items; and West testified that he had bought the items at a flea market. West challenged his conviction on sufficiency grounds, arguing that his was a "mere possession" case, and that a rational trier of fact could not conclude that West had the intent to commit grand larceny. The court of appeals held in favor of West, but the Supreme Court concluded that the lower court had misapplied the standards of *Jackson* in reversing West's conviction.

Justice Thomas, in a plurality opinion joined by Chief Justice Rehnquist and Justice Scalia, concluded that "the case against West was strong." He stressed the following points: 1) over 15 of the stolen items were recovered from West's home; 2) West had failed to offer specific information about how he came to possess the stolen items, saying only that he frequently bought and sold items at various flea markets; 3) West contradicted himself repeatedly on the witness stand as to where he had bought the stolen goods; 4) West had no explanation whatsoever for the presence of some of the stolen goods in his home; 5) West failed to produce any other supporting evidence, such as testimony of the person from whom he claimed to have purchased some of the goods, even though he stated that he had known this person for years; and 6) the jury was entitled to disbelieve West's "uncorroborated and confused" testimony, and "was further entitled to consider whatever it concluded to be perjured testimony as affirmative evidence of guilt."

Justice Thomas concluded as follows:

> In *Jackson,* we emphasized repeatedly the deference owed to the trier of fact and, correspondingly, the sharply limited nature of constitutional sufficiency review. We said that "all of the evidence is to be considered in the light most favorable to the prosecution"; that the prosecution need not affirmatively "rule out every hypothesis except that of guilt"; and that a reviewing court "faced with a record of

historical facts that supports conflicting inferences must presume—even if it does not appear affirmatively in the record—that the trier of fact resolved any such conflicts in favor of the prosecution, and must defer to that resolution." Under these standards, we think it clear that the trial record contained sufficient evidence to support West's conviction.[3]

For other examples of appellate review of sufficiency challenges, see United States v. Jackson, 368 F.3d 59 (2d Cir. 2004) (defendant convicted of felon-firearm-possession; conviction reversed because of insufficient evidence that the defendant was a felon; the government offered a conviction entered against "Aaron Jackson", but there are many Aaron Jacksons, and the government "offered no evidence that the two Aaron Jacksons were of the same race, or of similar height, coloring, fingerprint configuration, or even general physical description."); United States v. Ramirez, 362 F.3d 521 (8th Cir. 2004) (driver of car contended he did not know that drugs were in the car; appellate court finds sufficient evidence: "The circumstances surrounding the traffic stop and Ramirez's trip, including documents found inside the truck and his inconsistent and improbable explanations for his trip; his lies regarding his plans to meet his uncle; * * * his implausible trial testimony; and expert testimony concerning the methods used by drug traffickers, when considered together" provided sufficient evidence of the defendant's knowing participation in drug trafficking).

More on Deference to Jury Determinations: Cavazos v. Smith

The Court repeated its emphasis in Wright v. West on deference to jury verdicts in a per curiam summary disposition in Cavazos v. Smith, 565 U.S. 1 (2011), where it reversed a Ninth Circuit opinion granting habeas relief to a state defendant convicted in a case involving "shaken baby syndrome." The Court noted that the fact that the government's evidence and theory might be disputed is no reason to overturn a jury verdict. In the case, there were affirmative indications of trauma that supported the government's experts' opinion that the death occurred from sudden tearing of the brainstem caused by shaking—even though the experts were unable to identify the precise point of the tearing. Three dissenters protested the summary disposition.

---

[3] Justices White, O'Connor, Blackmun, Stevens, and Kennedy all concurred in the judgment, in three separate opinions. They all agreed that under *Jackson,* there was sufficient evidence to convince a rational factfinder of West's guilt beyond a reasonable doubt. Justice Souter also concurred in the judgment, but did not reach the sufficiency issue.

Two Layers of Deference to Jury Determinations on Habeas Review: Coleman v. Johnson and Parker v. Matthews

In Coleman v. Johnson, 566 U.S. 650 (2012) (per curiam), the Court once again considered and applied the standard for reviewing habeas claims challenging the sufficiency of evidence at a state trial. Johnson was convicted of being an accomplice and conspirator in the murder of a victim killed by a shotgun blast to the chest. Johnson's convictions were affirmed in state court, and a federal district court denied relief before the Third Circuit held that the evidence at trial was insufficient to support Johnson's conviction under the standard set forth in Jackson v. Virginia.

The Supreme Court observed that *Jackson* claims "face a high bar in federal habeas proceedings because they are subject to two layers of judicial deference." As to the first layer, the Court noted its instruction from Cavazos v. Smith, supra: "it is the responsibility of the jury—not the court—to decide what conclusions should be drawn from evidence admitted at trial. A reviewing court may set aside the jury's verdict on the ground of insufficient evidence only if no rational trier of fact could have agreed with the jury." Thus, the first layer of deference is appellate deference to jury findings. The second level is federal habeas deference to state court decisions. A federal court may not overturn a state court's finding of sufficient evidence merely because the federal court disagrees with the finding; a federal court may only overturn a state court finding if it is "objectively unreasonable."

The trial evidence left little doubt that Johnson, along with the shooter, intended to confront the victim, but the Third Circuit (contrary to the state courts) found insufficient evidence that Johnson shared the shooter's intent to kill the victim. Reviewing the record, the Supreme Court concluded that the state appellate court's ruling finding sufficient evidence was entitled to greater deference than the Third Circuit gave it.

Court Reviewing Sufficiency of the Evidence Must Consider All Evidence Admitted at Trial, Even if Erroneously: McDaniel v. Brown

In McDaniel v. Brown, 558 U.S. 120 (2010), the Court considered whether, in reviewing a conviction for sufficiency of evidence, the reviewing court must consider evidence that was admitted in error. Brown was convicted of sexual assault, and challenged the verdict for sufficiency, but also argued that DNA evidence was unreliable and therefore erroneously admitted. Brown did not, however, dispute the fact that the evidence presented at trial was sufficient. Under these circumstances, the Court in a per curiam opinion ruled that there could be no relief under *Jackson* for insufficiency. The Court explained as follows:

An appellate court's reversal for insufficiency of the evidence is in effect a determination that the government's case against the defendant was so lacking that the trial court should have entered a judgment of acquittal. Because reversal for insufficiency of the evidence is equivalent to a judgment of acquittal, such a reversal bars a retrial. To make the analogy complete between a reversal for insufficiency of the evidence and the trial court's granting a judgment of acquittal, a reviewing court must consider all of the evidence admitted by the trial court, regardless whether that evidence was admitted erroneously.

Assessment of Sufficiency Where the Jury Instructions Add an Extra Element to the Crime: Musacchio v. United States

In Musacchio v. United States, 577 U.S. 237 (2016), the trial judge misinstructed the jury that it had to find two facts rather than one: the instruction was that the jury had to find that the defendant intentionally accessed a computer without authorization *and* exceeded authorized use, whereas the statute under which Musacchio was charged makes it a crime if a person "intentionally accesses a computer without authorization *or* exceeds authorized use." The Government failed to object to the trial court's jury instruction that, in essence, erroneously added an element that it had to prove. The defendant was nonetheless convicted, and appealed on grounds of insufficient evidence. One question for the Supreme Court was whether the sufficiency review would have to evaluate the evidence in light of the elements of the crime, or instead in light of all the elements provided in the jury instruction. The Court, in a unanimous opinion written by Justice Thomas, ruled that a sufficiency challenge must be assessed against the elements of the charged crime, not against the elements set forth in an erroneously heightened jury instruction. He reasoned as follows:

> When a jury finds guilt after being instructed on all elements of the charged crime plus one more element, the jury has made all the findings that due process requires. If a jury instruction requires the jury to find guilt on the elements of the charged crime, a defendant will have had a meaningful opportunity to defend against the charge. And if the jury instruction requires the jury to find those elements "beyond a reasonable doubt," the defendant has been accorded the procedure that this Court has required to protect the presumption of innocence. The Government's failure to introduce evidence of an additional element does not implicate the principles that sufficiency review protects.

General Verdict with Insufficient Evidence on One Ground: Griffin v. United States

Is reversal required when a defendant is charged with multiple acts or means of committing a crime in a single count, and the evidence is insufficient as to one of the acts or means? In Griffin v. United States, 502 U.S. 46 (1991), the Court relied on the common-law rule that a general verdict is valid so long as it is legally supportable on any one of the submitted grounds—"even though that gave no assurance that a valid ground, rather than an invalid one, was actually the basis for the jury's action."

Griffin was charged, with others, in a conspiracy that was alleged to have two objects: (1) impairing the efforts of the Internal Revenue Service to ascertain income taxes (the "IRS object"); and (2) impairing the efforts of the Drug Enforcement Administration to ascertain forfeitable assets (the "DEA object"). The evidence introduced at trial implicated Griffin's codefendants in both conspiratorial objects, but it did not sufficiently connect Griffin with the DEA object. The trial court over objection instructed the jury that it could return a guilty verdict if it found Griffin to have participated in either one of the two objects of the conspiracy. The jury returned a general verdict of guilty. The court of appeals found the evidence tying Griffin to the DEA object insufficient, but nonetheless affirmed Griffin's conviction on the ground that sufficient evidence existed to tie her to the IRS object. Griffin argued that this result violated her right to due process, because the jury might not actually have found her guilty of the IRS crime. But the Supreme Court disagreed in an opinion by Justice Scalia.

Justice Scalia recognized that despite the general common-law rule upholding an ambiguous general verdict, the Court had held in Stromberg v. California, 283 U.S. 359 (1931), that "where a provision of the Constitution forbids conviction on a particular ground, the constitutional guarantee is violated by a general verdict that may have rested on that ground." He also recognized that in Yates v. United States, 354 U.S. 298 (1957), the Court used a similar principle to void a conviction in which one means alleged in a single count was insufficient in law because barred by the statute of limitations. But Justice Scalia found these precedents to be exceptions to the general rule, and inapposite to a case where one of the objects in a single count was void not because of a legal error but rather due to factual insufficiency. He explained the *Stromberg-Yates* exception, and distinguished it from the general rule, as follows:

> Jurors are not generally equipped to determine whether a particular theory of conviction submitted to them is contrary to law—whether, for example, the action in question is protected by the Constitution, is time barred, or fails to come within the statutory

definition of the crime. When, therefore, jurors have been left the option of relying upon a legally inadequate theory, there is no reason to think that their own intelligence and expertise will save them from that error. Quite the opposite is true, however, when they have been left the option of relying upon a factually inadequate theory, since jurors *are* well equipped to analyze the evidence. * * *

Thus, the Court found it fair to presume from the general verdict that the jury convicted on the factually sufficient ground.[4] Compare United States v. Garcia, 992 F.2d 409 (2d Cir.1993) (*Griffin* distinguished where three legal theories were submitted to the jury, and two of them were legally erroneous: "If the challenge is evidentiary, as long as there was sufficient evidence to support one of the theories presented, then the verdict should be affirmed. However, if the challenge is legal and any of the theories was legally insufficient, then the verdict must be reversed.").

B. MOTION FOR NEW TRIAL

Federal Rule of Criminal Procedure 33, providing for a new trial on motion "if the interest of justice so requires," affords another avenue for direct attack on a conviction. Note that, as was true of motions for acquittal, post-verdict new trial motions are defendants' remedies.

One might expect that the same trial judge who erred once is unlikely to be quick to change her mind, but it sometimes happens. The trial judge knows that it is likely that a convicted defendant will appeal, and the post-trial motion enables the trial judge to correct any error that an appellate court would correct. In close cases, the trial judge has authority to grant a new trial even if an appellate court, acting on the basis of a cold record, would not, because the trial judge is well situated to see or feel the prejudicial impact of an error that on paper does not appear to be significant.

One ground on which a motion for a new trial might be granted is that the trial judge is convinced that a verdict is against the weight of the evidence. "Against the weight of the evidence" is not the same as "insufficient evidence." The standards governing a trial judge's ruling on a motion for a new trial on "weight of the evidence" grounds are well-stated by the court in United States v. Martinez, 763 F.2d 1297 (11th Cir.1985):

On a motion for judgment of acquittal, the court must view the evidence in the light most favorable to the verdict, and, under that light, determine whether the evidence is sufficient to support the verdict. Thus * * * the court assumes the truth of the evidence offered by the prosecution. On a motion for a new trial based on the weight of the evidence, the court need not view the evidence in the light most

---

[4] Justice Blackmun concurred in the judgment. Justice Thomas did not participate.

favorable to the verdict. It may weigh the evidence and consider the credibility of the witnesses. If the court concludes that despite the abstract sufficiency of the evidence to sustain the verdict, the evidence preponderates sufficiently heavily against the verdict that a serious miscarriage of justice may have occurred, it may set aside the verdict, grant a new trial, and submit the issues for determination by another jury.

* * * While the district court's discretion is quite broad, there are limits to it. The court may not reweigh the evidence and set aside the verdict simply because it feels some other result would be more reasonable. The evidence must preponderate heavily against the verdict, such that it would be a miscarriage of justice to let the verdict stand. Motions for new trials based on weight of the evidence are not favored. Courts are to grant them sparingly and with caution, doing so only in those really exceptional cases.

Applying these principles trial courts, generally speaking, have granted new trial motions on weight of the evidence only where the credibility of the government's witnesses has been impeached and the government's case has been marked by uncertainties and discrepancies.

C. NEWLY DISCOVERED EVIDENCE CLAIMS

Judges are understandably reluctant to overturn verdicts supported by sufficient evidence to prove guilt beyond a reasonable doubt. If courts readily accepted newly discovered evidence claims, litigants who discovered that a tactical judgment made in one trial did not work would ask for another chance to litigate, and litigation finality interests would be undermined. The line between discovery of new evidence and discovery of new theories of how to use evidence is fuzzy, but rarely must it be sharpened in light of the reluctance of courts to take seriously either claim.

Requirements for a Newly Discovered Evidence Claim

A defendant must meet a four prong test before a court will grant him a retrial based on any newly discovered evidence. As stated in United States v. Lenz, 577 F.3d 377 (1st Cir.2009), the defendant must establish the following:

(1) the evidence was unknown or unavailable at the time of the trial;

(2) the evidence could not have been discovered earlier with due diligence;

(3) the evidence is material and not merely cumulative or impeaching; and

(4) the evidence would probably result in an acquittal upon retrial.

In *Lenz,* the court concluded that a witness's newfound willingness to corroborate the defendant's story was not newly discovered evidence: "Whether or not a witness will testify truthfully is simply not 'evidence' that can be used as a basis to invoke Rule 33 of the Federal Rules of Criminal Procedure." See also United States v. Gonzalez, 933 F.2d 417 (7th Cir.1991) (defendants were not entitled to a new trial on the basis of newly discovered evidence where the evidence would merely impeach a government witness's testimony that he had never had anything to do with cocaine, and evidence of the defendants' guilt was overwhelming).

Newly Discovered vs. Newly Available

There is a distinction between newly *discovered* and newly *available* evidence. Evidence is not "new" merely because it has been generated after the conviction. For example, in Harris v. Vasquez, 913 F.2d 606 (9th Cir.1990), a death penalty case, the court concluded that the defendant's new psychiatric reports did not justify another penalty hearing. Because defense counsel possessed evidence of the defendant's brain damage at the original hearing, and no new psychiatric techniques or theories were alleged to have arisen in the interim, the court concluded that the new reports were not new evidence but merely new opinions from new psychiatrists.

New Forensic Techniques: District Attorney's Office v. Osborne

Advances in forensic testing techniques have occasionally given rise to newly discovered evidence claims—e.g., exculpatory DNA tests. But they are not always successful. When the forensic testing is conducted long after the crime, it will sometimes be insufficiently conclusive to show that the defendant would probably be acquitted on retrial. See Dumond v. Lockhart, 911 F.2d 104 (8th Cir.1990), where the court held that evidence of a genetic marker test done on a semen sample, showing that the sample was unlikely to be the defendant's, was newly discovered evidence. Yet the defendant's motion for a new trial was found properly denied because it was not likely that the evidence would produce an acquittal on retrial.

In District Attorney's Office for the Third Judicial District v. Osborne, 557 U.S. 52 (2009), a convicted defendant argued that he had a constitutional right to DNA testing that he claimed would provide newly discovered evidence to exonerate him. The state had in fact conducted a rudimentary form of DNA testing before the trial; that test tended to include Osborne as a possible perpetrator in a sex crime, but it was not definitive. Osborne's counsel decided not to ask for a more sophisticated test to be done, fearing that it would further incriminate Osborne. Osborne was convicted and several years later brought a civil rights action against the state, alleging that he had a due process right to an even more sophisticated DNA test than was available at the time of his trial.

In a 5–4 opinion, the Court held that convicted defendants have no freestanding due process right to DNA testing. Chief Justice Roberts, writing for the majority, declared as follows:

> DNA testing has an unparalleled ability both to exonerate the wrongly convicted and to identify the guilty. It has the potential to significantly improve both the criminal justice system and police investigative practices. The Federal Government and the States have recognized this, and have developed special approaches to ensure that this evidentiary tool can be effectively incorporated into established criminal procedure—usually but not always through legislation.
>
> Against this prompt and considered response, the respondent, William Osborne, proposes a different approach: the recognition of a freestanding and far-reaching constitutional right of access to this new type of evidence. The nature of what he seeks is confirmed by his decision to file this lawsuit in federal court under 42 U. S. C. § 1983, not within the state criminal justice system. This approach would take the development of rules and procedures in this area out of the hands of legislatures and state courts shaping policy in a focused manner and turn it over to federal courts applying the broad parameters of the Due Process Clause. There is no reason to constitutionalize the issue in this way. Because the decision below would do just that, we reverse.

Chief Justice Roberts noted that the defendant's right to obtain evidence after trial is more circumscribed than the right to exculpatory evidence before or during trial:

> Osborne's right to due process is not parallel to a trial right, but rather must be analyzed in light of the fact that he has already been found guilty at a fair trial, and has only a limited interest in postconviction relief. *Brady* is the wrong framework.
>
> Instead, the question is whether consideration of Osborne's claim within the framework of the State's procedures for postconviction relief "offends some principle of justice so rooted in the traditions and conscience of our people as to be ranked as fundamental," or "transgresses any recognized principle of fundamental fairness in operation." Federal courts may upset a State's postconviction relief procedures only if they are fundamentally inadequate to vindicate the substantive rights provided.
>
> We see nothing inadequate about the procedures Alaska has provided to vindicate its state right to postconviction relief in general, and nothing inadequate about how those procedures apply to those who seek access to DNA evidence. Alaska provides a substantive right

to be released on a sufficiently compelling showing of new evidence that establishes innocence. It exempts such claims from otherwise applicable time limits. The State provides for discovery in postconviction proceedings, and has—through judicial decision—specified that this discovery procedure is available to those seeking access to DNA evidence. These procedures are not without limits. The evidence must indeed be newly available to qualify under Alaska's statute, must have been diligently pursued, and must also be sufficiently material. These procedures are similar to those provided for DNA evidence by federal law and the law of other States, see, e.g., 18 U. S. C. § 3600(a), and they are not inconsistent with the "traditions and conscience of our people" or with "any recognized principle of fundamental fairness."

Justice Alito filed a concurring opinion in which Justice Kennedy, joined, and in which Justice Thomas joined in part. He argued that it would be inappropriate to allow Osborne to forego testing at trial and then to request a different test many years later. In Justice Alito's view, this would "allow prisoners to play games with the criminal justice system" because "with nothing to lose, the defendant could demand DNA testing in the hope that some happy accident—for example, degradation or contamination of the evidence—would provide the basis for postconviction relief."

Justice Stevens filed a dissenting opinion, joined by Justices Ginsburg and Breyer and by Justice Souter in part. Justice Stevens argued that the state had no legitimate interest in denying the test, because Osborne had agreed to pay for it; and the state's interest in finality could not outweigh a plausible claim of innocence.

Justice Souter also filed a dissenting opinion, concluding that state officials had "demonstrated a combination of inattentiveness and intransigence that add up to procedural unfairness that violates the due process clause."

Second Thoughts of Witnesses and Jurors

Once a verdict is rendered and judgment is imposed, experienced judges know that the participants in the trial process might have second thoughts after sending a person to prison, or even to death. Most second thoughts, when raised as grounds for reversal due to newly discovered evidence, are treated as routine and ignored. See, e.g., Mastrian v. McManus, 554 F.2d 813 (8th Cir.1977) (recantation by star witness does not warrant new trial). For example, jurors generally cannot attack their verdicts by raising questions about the quality of the deliberations or the firmness of their votes. See Fed.R.Evid. 606(b). Similarly, witnesses who recant their trial testimony and change stories are viewed with utmost suspicion, not only because of the commonness of feelings of remorse, but also because of a judicial fear that improper post-trial influence may be encouraged by ready judicial acceptance of recantations. Third party confessions exculpating the defendant, which are viewed with suspicion even if offered during a trial, see, e.g., Fed.R.Evid. 804(b)(3), are scrutinized with great care. See, e.g., United States v. Kamel, 965 F.2d 484 (7th Cir.1992) (third party "repeatedly and firmly denied involvement in the crime for a period of three years. [The third party's] purported confession, coming after his conviction and shortly before sentencing, when he has relatively little to lose by accepting sole responsibility * * * is far less credible.").

Time Limits

The Advisory Committee on Criminal Rules had suggested that newly discovered evidence motions could be made "at any time before or after final judgment," but the Federal Rule (Rule 33(b)(1)) imposes a three-year time limit. See Herrera v. Collins, 506 U.S. 390 (1993), upholding, against a constitutional attack, a Texas procedure that requires a new trial motion based on newly discovered evidence to be made within 30 days of judgment.

D. THE EFFECT OF AN ERROR ON THE VERDICT

1. Harmless Error

If constitutional error has occurred at a trial (e.g., introduction of a confession in violation of the Sixth Amendment), should reversal be automatic? The next case considers this question.

CHAPMAN V. CALIFORNIA

Supreme Court of the United States, 1967.
386 U.S. 18.

JUSTICE BLACK delivered the opinion of the Court.

[At a murder trial the prosecutor commented on Chapman's failure to testify and the trial court told the jury it could draw adverse inferences from his silence. The comment and the instruction violated Chapman's privilege against self-incrimination under Griffin v. California, 380 U.S. 609 (1965). The California Supreme Court held that the error was harmless. Justice Black indicated at the outset of his opinion that two questions were presented: (1) whether a *Griffin* error could ever be harmless, and (2) if so, was the error harmless in this case? Justice Black also stated as an introductory point that the effect of a constitutional error on a state proceeding is a question of federal law.]

We are urged by petitioners to hold that all federal constitutional errors, regardless of the facts and circumstances, must always be deemed harmful. Such a holding, as petitioners correctly point out, would require an automatic reversal of their convictions and make further discussion unnecessary. We decline to adopt any such rule. All 50 States have harmless-error statutes or rules, and the United States long ago through its Congress established for its courts the rule that judgments shall not be reversed for "errors or defects which do not affect the substantial rights of the parties." 28 U.S.C.A. § 2111. * * * All of these rules, state or federal, serve a very useful purpose insofar as they block setting aside convictions for small errors or defects that have little, if any, likelihood of having changed the result of the trial. We conclude that there may be some constitutional errors which in the setting of a particular case are so unimportant and insignificant that they may, consistent with the Federal Constitution, be deemed harmless, not requiring the automatic reversal of the conviction.

* * *

In fashioning a harmless-constitutional-error rule, we must recognize that harmless-error rules can work very unfair and mischievous results when, for example, highly important and persuasive evidence, or argument, though legally forbidden, finds its way into a trial in which the question of guilt or innocence is a close one. What harmless-error rules all aim at is a rule that will save the good in harmless-error practices while avoiding the bad, so far as possible.

[Justice Black refers to Fahy v. Connecticut, 375 U.S. 85, where the Court, construing the harmless error statute, said: "The question is whether there is a reasonable possibility that the evidence complained of might have contributed to the conviction."] Although our prior cases have indicated that there are some constitutional rights so basic to a fair trial that their infraction can never be treated as harmless error,[a] this statement in *Fahy* itself belies any belief that all trial errors which violate the Constitution automatically call for reversal. At the same time, however, like the federal harmless-error statute, it emphasizes an intention not to treat as harmless those constitutional errors that "affect substantial rights" of a party. An error in admitting plainly relevant evidence which possibly influenced the jury adversely to a litigant cannot, under *Fahy*, be conceived of as harmless. Certainly error, constitutional error, in illegally admitting highly prejudicial evidence or comments, casts on someone other than the person prejudiced by it a burden to show that it was harmless. * * * We, therefore, do no more than adhere to the meaning of our *Fahy* case when we hold, as we now do, that before a federal constitutional error can be held harmless, the court must be able to declare a belief that it was harmless beyond a reasonable doubt. While appellate courts do not ordinarily have the original task of applying such a test, it is a familiar

[a] See, e.g., Payne v. Arkansas, 356 U.S. 560 (coerced confession); Gideon v. Wainwright, 372 U.S. 335 (right to counsel); Tumey v. Ohio, 273 U.S. 510 (impartial judge).

standard to all courts, and we believe its adoption will provide a more workable standard, although achieving the same result as that aimed at in our *Fahy* case.

* * *

[The Court went on to hold that the error was not harmless. Justice Stewart concurred in the result and opted for automatic reversal for *Griffin* violations. Justice Harlan dissented on the ground that application of a state harmless error rule was an independent state ground barring Supreme Court review.]

Errors Subject to the Chapman Analysis

The Court has invoked *Chapman* in several cases to hold errors harmless. See Harrington v. California, 395 U.S. 250 (1969) (holding harmless the improper introduction of confessions of non-testifying codefendants); Milton v. Wainwright, 407 U.S. 371 (1972) (declaring that any error in obtaining statements of accused in violation of right to counsel was harmless). The harmless error rule applies to all Fourth Amendment violations as well; see the discussion of the exclusionary rule in Chapter 2.[5]

Harmless Error Review as a Way to Avoid Ruling on the Merits of the Constitutional Challenge

Note that a court may refuse to consider the merits of a constitutional claim on the ground that, even if error, it would be harmless in any event. This use of harmless error as merits-avoidance is taken to task by Professor Kamin in Harmless Error and the Rights/Remedies Split, 88 Va. L.Rev. 1 (2002). Professor Kamin argues that excessive use of the harmless error rule will fail to deter official misconduct. He therefore suggests that the "harmlessness of an alleged error should never be used as a threshold question; that is, courts should determine whether or not the conduct alleged was error, and should turn to the impact of that error only after determining that it occurred." Professor Kamins also suggests that "where a state official should have known that her conduct was error, the state should be denied the benefit of the harmless error rule." He concludes that "it is only by applying the harmless error rule in these ways * * * that the rule can be kept from stifling the development of constitutional law and can become a tool for changing the behaviors of prosecutors and law enforcement."

---

[5] The harmless error rule employed in habeas corpus cases is stricter (i.e., reversal less likely) than the *Chapman* standard that is applied to constitutional errors on direct review. See the discussion of habeas corpus later in this Chapter.

Constitutional Errors Not Subject to Harmless Error Review

The Supreme Court has held that most constitutional violations are subject to the harmless error rule, but, as it recognized in the footnote in *Chapman,* some errors can never be harmless. The question is how to determine which errors can be harmless and which cannot.

The errors that the Court has held can never be harmless include: (1) total deprivation of the right to counsel (*Gideon,* cited in the footnote in *Chapman*); (2) a biased judge (Tumey v. Ohio, cited in the footnote in *Chapman*); (3) unlawful exclusion of members of the defendant's race from the grand jury (Vasquez v. Hillery, 474 U.S. 254 (1986)); (4) violation of the right to a public trial (Waller v. Georgia, 467 U.S. 39 (1984)); (5) violation of the right of self-representation (McKaskle v. Wiggins, discussed in Chapter 10); (6) improper exclusion of a juror who is reluctant to impose the death penalty (Gray v. Mississippi, discussed in Chapter 10); (7) improper instruction on the prosecution's burden of proof (Sullivan v. Louisiana, discussed infra); (8) improper denial of the defendant's right to chosen counsel (United States v. Gonzalez-Lopez, infra); and (9) defense counsel's concession of guilt at trial over the defendant's objection (McCoy v. Louisiana, infra).

In addition, harmless error analysis cannot apply if a new trial would in itself be the harm. Thus, violations of the right to speedy trial and a multiple prosecution in violation of the Double Jeopardy Clause will never be harmless error. Finally, some errors require a showing of prejudice before a constitutional violation can even be found. This is so, for example, under the *Strickland* standard for ineffective assistance of counsel and under the *Brady* standard for disclosure of exculpatory evidence by the prosecution. In these two areas, a court that finds a constitutional violation has by definition determined that the error is harmful, and the *Chapman* standard becomes superfluous. See Capra, Access to Exculpatory Evidence: Avoiding the *Agurs* Problems of Prosecutorial Discretion and Retrospective Review, 53 Ford.L.Rev. 391 (1984); Kyles v. Whitley, discussed in Chapter 8 (harmless error analysis redundant after *Brady* violation has been found).

Involuntary Confessions: Arizona v. Fulminante

In Arizona v. Fulminante, 499 U.S. 279 (1991), the Court retreated from the *Chapman* footnote insofar as it implied that admission of an involuntary confession could never be harmless error. Chief Justice Rehnquist, writing for five members of the Court, explained the *Chapman* footnote as a "historical reference."

The Chief Justice distinguished a trial error—"error which occurred during the presentation of the case to the jury, and which may therefore be quantitatively assessed in the context of other evidence presented in order to determine whether its admission was harmless beyond a reasonable doubt"—from an error that is not subject to such an assessment, "a structural defect affecting the framework in which the trial proceeds." A structural defect can never be harmless, because by definition the error infects the entirety of the trial. In contrast, a trial error can be harmless, because it is a more discrete violation and its harm can be more easily pinpointed. According to the majority, admission of an involuntary confession falls into the category of trial error, while total deprivation of counsel as in *Gideon,* or a biased judge as in *Tumey,* falls into the category of structural defect.

For purposes of harmless error analysis, the Chief Justice saw no reason to distinguish admission of coerced confessions from admissions of confessions obtained in violation of the defendant's Sixth Amendment rights or in violation of *Miranda.* As the Court had already found that these violations could be harmless, the Chief Justice concluded that admission of a coerced confession could also be harmless. The Chief Justice noted, however, that due to the substantial impact that a confession has on the trial, it would be the rare case in which admission of a coerced confession would be harmless on the facts. On the merits, the Court found that the admission of Fulminante's involuntary confession was not harmless error.

QUESTIONS ABOUT FULMINANTE

Chief Justice Rehnquist's reference to "structural" error requires a determination of which errors affect an entire trial. In some instances, there is structural error even if a trial was arguably "fair." Consider the defendant who is deprived of the right to proceed *pro se.* It is no answer to say that at his trial, his counsel performed very well and the evidence against him was overwhelming. The right to self-representation is not based upon an effective defense and a correct verdict, but rather upon personal autonomy. Whether or not a violation of this right can be labeled a structural defect, the harmless error rule cannot apply because harmlessness as to the verdict is irrelevant to the wrong suffered. A similar example is the denial of the accused's right to counsel of choice, discussed infra.

Is it possible that the application of the harmless error standard to coerced confessions will make a reviewing court more likely to find certain police tactics impermissible? Is anyone better off when a court holds that a confession was coerced but that its introduction at trial is harmless, where if automatic reversal were required, a court concerned about the cost of retrial might hold the confession voluntary?

Error in a Burden of Proof Instruction: Sullivan v. Louisiana

In Sullivan v. Louisiana, 508 U.S. 275 (1993), the Court unanimously held that a constitutionally deficient beyond-a-reasonable-doubt instruction can never be harmless error. At Sullivan's trial, the judge gave an instruction as to reasonable doubt that was virtually identical to the instruction held constitutionally defective in Cage v. Louisiana, 498 U.S. 39 (1990) (instruction defining reasonable doubt in terms of grave and substantial doubt suggests "a higher degree of doubt than is required for acquittal under the reasonable doubt standard"). The state appellate court determined that the evidence against Sullivan was overwhelming and that therefore the erroneous instruction was harmless beyond a reasonable doubt.

Justice Scalia, writing for the Court, noted that the Sixth Amendment right to jury trial means an entitlement to a jury verdict; so, for example, the trial judge may not direct a verdict for the State, no matter how overwhelming the evidence. Justice Scalia explained why, under *Chapman,* an erroneous reasonable doubt instruction could not be harmless:

> Harmless-error review looks, we have said, to the basis on which "the jury actually rested its verdict." The inquiry, in other words, is not whether, in a trial that occurred without the error, a guilty verdict would surely have been rendered, but whether the guilty verdict actually rendered in *this* trial was surely unattributable to the error. This must be so, because to hypothesize a guilty verdict that was never in fact rendered—no matter how inescapable the findings to support that verdict might be—would violate the jury trial guarantee.
>
> Once the proper role of an appellate court engaged in the *Chapman* inquiry is understood, the illogic of harmless-error review in the present case becomes evident. Since there has been no jury verdict within the meaning of the Sixth Amendment, the entire premise of *Chapman* review is simply absent. * * * There is no *object,* so to speak, upon which harmless-error scrutiny can operate. * * * The Sixth Amendment requires more than appellate speculation about a hypothetical jury's action, or else directed verdicts for the State would be sustainable on appeal; it requires an actual jury verdict of guilty.

Justice Scalia distinguished cases where the trial court gives an erroneous instruction that erects a presumption regarding an element of the offense that might affect the jury's finding of a predicate fact (e.g., that malice can be presumed if the jury finds that the defendant possessed a deadly weapon). See Yates v. Evatt, 500 U.S. 391 (1991) (erroneous burden-shifting presumption can be assessed for harmlessness). While such an instruction may impermissibly ease the State's burden of having to prove all elements of the offense, the jury is still instructed that it must find the existence of the predicate facts supporting the presumption beyond a reasonable doubt. In contrast, where the instructional error consists of a misdescription of the burden of proof, this "vitiates *all* of the jury's findings," and a reviewing court can only engage in "pure speculation," which would mean that "the wrong entity judges the defendant guilty."

Erroneous Instructions on the Elements of a Crime: Neder v. United States

The trial judge in Neder v. United States, 527 U.S. 1 (1999) erroneously instructed the jury that it would not have to decide whether Neder's false statements on tax forms were "material." In the trial judge's view, the question of materiality was for the judge, not the jury. Neder was convicted. The instruction was error because materiality is an element of the crime of tax fraud, and therefore the question of materiality was for the jury. On appeal, the government agreed with the defendant that the erroneous instruction was error, but argued that the error was harmless. Neder argued that depriving the jury of the power to decide an element of the crime can never be harmless. The Supreme Court, in an opinion by Chief Justice Rehnquist, held that such an error was subject to harmless error review. He analyzed the harmless error question in the following passage:

> Unlike such defects as the complete deprivation of counsel or trial before a biased judge, an instruction that omits an element of the offense does not necessarily render a criminal trial fundamentally unfair or an unreliable vehicle for determining guilt or innocence. * * * In fact, as this case shows, quite the opposite is true: Neder was tried before an impartial judge, under the correct standard of proof and with the assistance of counsel; a fairly selected, impartial jury was instructed to consider all of the evidence and argument in respect to Neder's defense against the tax charges. Of course, the court erroneously failed to charge the jury on the element of materiality, but that error did not render Neder's trial "fundamentally unfair," as that term is used in our cases.

The Chief Justice distinguished *Sullivan* on the ground that a defective instruction as to one element of a crime did not vitiate *all* of the jury's findings. He concluded as follows:

> The omitted element was materiality. Petitioner underreported $5 million on his tax returns, and did not contest the element of materiality at trial. Petitioner does not suggest that he would introduce any evidence bearing upon the issue of materiality if so allowed. Reversal without any consideration of the effect of the error upon the verdict would send the case back for retrial—a retrial not

> focused at all on the issue of materiality, but on contested issues on which the jury was properly instructed. We do not think the Sixth Amendment requires us to veer away from settled precedent to reach such a result.

Justice Stevens concurred in the judgment in *Neder*. Justice Scalia, joined by Justices Souter and Ginsburg, dissented. He noted that cases such as *Sullivan* indicate that if the entire case is taken away from the jury, this cannot be harmless error. If that is so, how could it be harmless error to take an element of the case away from the jury? Justice Scalia stated that

> we do not know, when the Court's opinion is done, how many elements can be taken away from the jury with impunity, so long as appellate judges are persuaded that the defendant is surely guilty. What if, in the present case, besides keeping the materiality issue for itself, the District Court had also refused to instruct the jury to decide whether the defendant signed his tax return? If Neder had never contested that element of the offense, and the record contained a copy of his signed return, would his conviction be automatically reversed in that situation but not in this one, even though he would be just as obviously guilty? We do not know. We know that all elements cannot be taken from the jury, and that one can. How many is too many (or perhaps what proportion is too high) remains to be determined by future improvisation.

Apprendi Violations Can Be Harmless: Washington v. Recuenco

In Apprendi v. New Jersey, discussed in Chapters 10 and 11, the Court held that the Sixth Amendment was violated when the defendant received a sentence beyond the statutory maximum on the basis of facts proven to the judge at sentencing, but not to the jury. In Washington v. Recuenco, 548 U.S. 212 (2006), the Court held that *Apprendi* violations are not "structural" and are subject to harmless error review. Justice Thomas, writing for six members of the Court, relied heavily on Neder v. United States; as in *Neder* an issue was taken from the jury and given to the judge (the difference in *Apprendi* being that the issue was decided by the judge at sentencing rather than at trial). Justice Thomas reasoned as follows:

> The only difference between this case and *Neder* is that in *Neder*, the prosecution failed to prove the element of materiality to the jury beyond a reasonable doubt, while here the prosecution failed to prove the sentencing factor of "armed with a firearm" to the jury beyond a reasonable doubt. Assigning this distinction constitutional significance cannot be reconciled with our recognition in *Apprendi* that elements and sentencing factors must be treated the same for Sixth Amendment purposes.

The Court remanded for a determination of whether the error was harmless. Justice Kennedy wrote a short concurring opinion emphasizing that the Court was not revisiting the merits of its *Apprendi* jurisprudence. Justice Stevens wrote a short dissent, contending that the Court should never have taken the case because the state court's decision could have been based on its own constitution. Justice Ginsburg wrote a separate dissenting opinion joined by Justice Stevens.

Automatic Reversal for Violation of the Right to Counsel of Choice: United States v. Gonzalez-Lopez

In United States v. Gonzalez-Lopez, 548 U.S. 140 (2006), the Court held that the violation of the constitutional right to counsel of choice can never be harmless. The trial court had denied the defendant the right to hire a lawyer from outside the state; the defendant then hired a different lawyer to defend him. The Court of Appeals found the denial to be a violation of the right to the defendant's constitutional right to counsel of choice; that ruling was not contested in the Supreme Court. The government did contend, however, that the defendant was required to show "prejudice" from the denial of his right to counsel of choice. But the Court, in an opinion by Justice Scalia for five Justices, held that no showing of prejudice was required. He noted that any prejudice inquiry would be "speculative" because "[d]ifferent attorneys will pursue different strategies with regard to investigation and discovery, development of the theory of defense, selection of the jury, presentation of the witnesses, and style of witness examination and jury argument. And the choice of attorney will affect whether and on what terms the defendant cooperates with the prosecution, plea bargains, or decides instead to go to trial."

Justice Alito, joined by Chief Justice Roberts, Justice Kennedy, and Justice Thomas, dissented. He argued that the majority's rule of automatic reversal was anomalous because "a defendant who is erroneously required to go to trial with a second-choice attorney is automatically entitled to a new trial even if this attorney performed brilliantly."

Defense Counsel's Conceding Guilt over the Defendant's Objection Is a Structural Error: McCoy v. Louisiana

The defendant in *McCoy v. Louisiana*, 138 S.Ct. 1500 (2018), was tried for capital murder. All the evidence indicated that he committed the murders. But the defendant steadfastly denied committing the murders, and blamed it all on a far-flung conspiracy against him. He testified to that effect at trial. Trial counsel chose, as a matter of strategy—and over McCoy's strenuous objections—to concede that the defendant did the killings, but to argue that he did not have the requisite mental state to commit murder, given his serious mental and emotional issues. McCoy was convicted of murder and sentenced to death.

The Supreme Court, in an opinion by Justice Ginsburg for six Justices, held that defense counsel has no authority under the Sixth Amendment to concede guilt over the objection of the defendant. That is because the decision whether or not to contest guilt is a matter of personal autonomy and a decision to be made by the client. [The Court's discussion of this point is set out in Chapter Ten.]

The Court further found that when defense counsel does make such an argument, it constitutes a structural error, not susceptible to harmless error review. Justice Ginsburg explained the Court's ruling on structural error as follows:

> Because a client's autonomy, not counsel's competence, is in issue, we do not apply our ineffective-assistance-of-counsel jurisprudence to McCoy's claim. To gain redress for attorney error, a defendant ordinarily must show prejudice. Here, however, the violation of McCoy's protected autonomy right was complete when the court allowed counsel to usurp control of an issue within McCoy's sole prerogative.
>
> Violation of a defendant's Sixth Amendment-secured autonomy ranks as error of the kind our decisions have called "structural"; when present, such an error is not subject to harmless-error review. * * * An error may be ranked structural, we have explained, "if the right at issue is not designed to protect the defendant from erroneous conviction but instead protects some other interest," such as "the fundamental legal principle that a defendant must be allowed to make his own choices about the proper way to protect his own liberty." An error might also count as structural when its effects are too hard to measure, as is true of the right to counsel of choice, or where the error will inevitably signal fundamental unfairness, as we have said of a judge's failure to tell the jury that it may not convict unless it finds the defendant's guilt beyond a reasonable doubt.
>
> Under at least the first two rationales, counsel's admission of a client's guilt over the client's express objection is error structural in kind. Such an admission blocks the defendant's right to make the fundamental choices about his own defense. And the effects of the admission would be immeasurable, because a jury would almost certainly be swayed by a lawyer's concession of his client's guilt. McCoy must therefore be accorded a new trial without any need first to show prejudice.

Justice Alito, joined by Justices Thomas and Gorsuch, dissented.

Breach of Plea Agreement Is Not a Structural Error Justifying Automatic Relief: Puckett v. United States

In Puckett v. United States, 556 U.S. 129 (2009), Puckett entered into a plea agreement in which the government agreed to support a reduction of Puckett's sentence for acceptance of responsibility. But at the sentencing proceeding the government opposed a sentence reduction on those grounds. Yet Puckett's counsel did not object to, or even mention, the government's breach of its plea agreement. On appeal Puckett raised the issue of breach, but the reviewing court found that he had forfeited his claim of error. It reviewed for plain error and found none—specifically finding that the error did not affect Puckett's substantial rights because the sentencing court indicated that it would not reduce his sentence in any case.

In the Supreme Court, Puckett argued that the plain error standard was inappropriate because a breach of a plea agreement amounts to a "structural error"—rendering it unnecessary to show prejudice and mandating automatic relief. But the Supreme Court, in an opinion by Justice Scalia, rejected this argument. Justice Scalia declared as follows:

> [B]reach of a plea deal is not a "structural" error as we have used that term. * * * A plea breach does not "necessarily render a criminal trial fundamentally unfair or an unreliable vehicle for determining guilt or innocence," Neder v. United States; it does not "defy analysis by harmless-error standards" by affecting the entire adjudicatory framework; and the "difficulty of assessing the effect of the error," United States v. Gonzalez-Lopez, is no greater with respect to plea breaches at sentencing than with respect to other procedural errors at sentencing, which are routinely subject to harmlessness review.

Justice Souter, joined by Justice Stevens, dissented.

Improper Denial of a Peremptory Challenge Is Not Automatically Reversible: Rivera v. Illinois

The defendant in Rivera v. Illinois, 556 U.S. 148 (2009), exercised a peremptory challenge at trial. The trial judge denied the challenge and seated the juror (who ended up serving as foreperson). The trial judge concluded that the defendant struck the juror on impermissible grounds under *Batson*. Rivera was convicted and appealed on the ground that he had a proper reason for striking the juror. The appellate court agreed, but nonetheless affirmed the conviction, on the ground that the trial court's error in seating the juror was harmless: Rivera conceded that the jury (including the juror he sought to strike) was unbiased. Rivera argued, however, that automatic reversal was necessary because it was impossible to tell whether the outcome would have been different had the juror been struck.

The Court, in a unanimous opinion by Justice Ginsburg, held that an improper denial of a peremptory strike did not warrant an automatic reversal. Justice Ginsburg emphasized that the defendant has no constitutional right to a peremptory challenge, and concluded as follows:

> If a defendant is tried before a qualified jury composed of individuals not challengeable for cause, the loss of a peremptory challenge due to a state court's good-faith error is not a matter of federal constitutional concern. Rather, it is a matter for the State to address under its own laws.

Overview on Structural Error: Weaver v. Massachusetts

The Court in Weaver v. Massachusetts, 137 S.Ct. 1899 (2017) (per curiam) considered whether a structural error must result in automatic reversal when the error was not raised until the defendant complained about it on collateral attack in the form of an ineffective assistance of counsel claim. The ineffective assistance claim was that defense counsel failed to object to the exclusion of the public during two days of jury selection.

Justice Kennedy, writing for six members of the Court, held that when a structural error is raised collaterally as a ground for ineffective assistance, the defendant must show prejudice under *Strickland.* He first laid out an overview of the Court's case law on structural error; he noted that the Court had found three different types of errors that it has defined as structural:

> First, an error has been deemed structural in some instances if the right at issue is not designed to protect the defendant from erroneous conviction but instead protects some other interest. This is true of the defendant's right to conduct his own defense, which, when exercised, "usually increases the likelihood of a trial outcome unfavorable to the defendant." McKaskle v. Wiggins, 465 U.S. 168, 177, n. 8 (1984). * * *
>
> Second, an error has been deemed structural if the effects of the error are simply too hard to measure. For example, when a defendant is denied the right to select his or her own attorney, the precise effect of the violation cannot be ascertained. * * *
>
> Third, an error has been deemed structural if the error always results in fundamental unfairness. For example, if an indigent defendant is denied an attorney or if the judge fails to give a reasonable-doubt instruction, the resulting trial is always a fundamentally unfair one. See Gideon v. Wainwright, 372 U.S. 335, 343–345 (1963) (right to an attorney); Sullivan v. Louisiana, 508 U.S.

275, 279 (1993) (right to a reasonable-doubt instruction). It therefore would be futile for the government to try to show harmlessness.

These categories are not rigid. In a particular case, more than one of these rationales may be part of the explanation for why an error is deemed to be structural. For these purposes, however, one point is critical: An error can count as structural even if the error does not lead to fundamental unfairness in every case.

Next, Justice Kennedy evaluated the right to a public trial [discussed in Chapter Ten] and why the deprivation of that right is a structural error; but also why it is not the type of structural error that always leads to fundamental unfairness:

> [A] violation of the right to a public trial is a structural error. It is relevant to determine why that is so. In particular, the question is whether a public-trial violation counts as structural because it always leads to fundamental unfairness or for some other reason.

Justice Kennedy concluded that its public trial jurisprudence [discussed in Chapter Ten] provide "that courtroom closure is to be avoided, but that there are some circumstances when it is justified"; "although the public-trial right is structural, it is subject to exceptions"; and "in some cases an unlawful closure might take place and yet the trial still will be fundamentally fair from the defendant's standpoint."

Justice Kennedy found a critical difference between structural errors raised at the time of trial or direct review, and those raised in the course of an ineffective counsel claim:

> [W]hen a defendant objects to a courtroom closure, the trial court can either order the courtroom opened or explain the reasons for keeping it closed. When a defendant first raises the closure in an ineffective-assistance claim, however, the trial court is deprived of the chance to cure the violation either by opening the courtroom or by explaining the reasons for closure.
>
> Furthermore, when state or federal courts adjudicate errors objected to during trial and then raised on direct review, the systemic costs of remedying the error are diminished to some extent. That is because, if a new trial is ordered on direct review, there may be a reasonable chance that not too much time will have elapsed for witness memories still to be accurate and physical evidence not to be lost. * * *
>
> When an ineffective-assistance-of-counsel claim is raised in postconviction proceedings, the costs and uncertainties of a new trial are greater because more time will have elapsed in most cases. The finality interest is more at risk, * * * and direct review often has given at least one opportunity for an appellate review of trial proceedings. * * *

Justice Kennedy found that Weaver "offered no evidence or legal argument establishing prejudice in the sense of a reasonable probability of a different outcome but for counsel's failure to object," and further that he had not "shown that counsel's failure to object rendered the trial fundamentally unfair."

Justice Thomas, joined by Justice Gorsuch, wrote a short concurring opinion, stating that there were open questions as to two of the Court's assumptions: that the right to a public trial extends to jury selection, and that *Strickland* prejudice can be found by errors that lead to fundamental unfairness.

Justice Alito, joined by Justice Thomas, concurred in the judgment, seeing the case as presenting a straightforward application of *Strickland* prejudice requirements. He concluded that "in order to obtain relief under *Strickland,* Weaver must show that the result of his trial was unreliable. He could do so by demonstrating a reasonable likelihood that his counsel's error affected the verdict. Alternatively, he could establish that the error falls within the very short list of errors for which prejudice [under *Strickland*] is presumed. Weaver has not attempted to make either argument, so his claim must be rejected."

Justice Breyer, joined by Justice Kagan, dissented in *Weaver.* He argued that all structural errors require automatic reversal and therefore could not be evaluated under *Strickland* prejudice standards.

Harmlessness Standard for Non-Constitutional Error: The Kotteakos-Lane Rule

In Kotteakos v. United States, 328 U.S. 750 (1946), the Court established a test of harmlessness for trial errors of a *nonconstitutional* dimension: reversal is not required if the federal appellate court "is sure that the error did not influence the jury or had but very slight effect." Put the other way, reversal is required for a non-constitutional error if it "had substantial and injurious effect or influence in determining the jury's verdict." United States v. Lane, 474 U.S. 438 (1986) (applying the *Kotteakos* standard to a misjoinder under Fed.R.Crim.P. 8(b)). See also Fed.R.Crim.P. 52(a) (an error that does not affect "substantial rights must be disregarded.").

The *Kotteakos-Lane* standard is clearly less protective of defendants than the harmless error rule applied to constitutional errors under *Chapman.* See United States v. Owens, 789 F.2d 750 (9th Cir.1986) (if admission of prior identification was merely a violation of the hearsay rule, it was harmless under the *Kotteakos-Lane* standard; but if admission also violated the defendant's constitutional right to confrontation, the error was harmful under the *Chapman* standard and reversal was required).

If you read federal cases from different circuits, you undoubtedly will find varying statements of the standard for harmless nonconstitutional error. Some examples are found in Saltzburg, Capra & Martin, 1 Federal Rules of Evidence Manual § 103.03[1][d] (12th ed. 2019). State courts, although bound to apply *Chapman* to constitutional errors, are free to adopt their own harmless error standards for nonconstitutional errors.

2. Plain Error

The harmless error standards discussed above are applied when the defendant makes a timely and specific objection at trial. A more stringent standard for reversal is applied when the defendant fails to make an objection at trial, and then argues on appeal that the trial court was in error. The appellate court in such a situation reviews for "plain error." The rationale for the more stringent standard is that if a defendant does not properly object at trial, he deprives the trial judge of the opportunity to focus on the problem and perhaps correct the error at that point. The distinction between harmful error and plain error is set forth in Federal Rule of Criminal Procedure 52, which states as follows:

> **(a) Harmless Error.** Any error, defect, irregularity or variance that does not affect substantial rights must be disregarded.
>
> **(b) Plain Error.** A plain error that affects substantial rights may be considered even though it was not brought to the court's attention.

Thus, Rule 52(a), by negative implication, states that reversal is required if the error affected substantial rights.[6] However, if the defendant did not bring the error to the attention of the court, then a reversal *may* be granted under Rule 52(b) if the error affected substantial rights.

Application of the Plain Error Standard: United States v. Olano

The Supreme Court had occasion to review the concept of "plain error," and its distinction from harmful error, in United States v. Olano, 507 U.S. 725 (1993). The Court held that the presence of alternate jurors during deliberations was not, under the circumstances of the case, an error that the court of appeals was authorized to correct under Fed.R.Crim.P. 52(b). The defendants had not objected to the presence of the alternate jurors during the deliberations, even though this practice at the time violated the plain terms of Fed.R.Crim.P. 24(c). [The current Rule 24 allows the court to retain alternate jurors even after the jury retires to deliberate although

[6] This is the harmless error standard applied for non-constitutional errors. For constitutional errors on direct review, the more defendant-friendly *Chapman* standard requires reversal unless the error was harmless beyond a reasonable doubt.

the alternates cannot participate in deliberations unless they actually replace regular jurors].

Writing for the Court, Justice O'Connor reasoned that Rule 52(b) "defines a single category of forfeited-but-reversible error." She identified *three conditions* on a court's power to reverse because of errors that were not properly preserved for review in the trial court:

1. There must be an error, i.e., a deviation from a legal rule *absent a waiver* by a defendant. Justice O'Connor distinguished waiver of a right from forfeiture of a right, stating that "[w]hereas forfeiture is the failure to make the timely assertion of a right, waiver is the intentional relinquishment of a known right." Thus, if the defendant knowingly and voluntarily waives a right—such as the right to a jury trial—there is no error in the proceedings and the plain error rule is inapplicable. If, on the other hand, the defendant fails to object to an erroneous ruling by the trial court, then the plain error standard is applicable.

2. The error must be plain, which means it must be clear or obvious—so obvious that the judge should have seen it even though it was not flagged by defense counsel.

3. The plain error must affect substantial rights, which means that it must have been prejudicial in the sense of affecting the outcome of the case.

Justice O'Connor emphasized that the language of Rule 52(b) is permissive, not mandatory. She stated that "the Court of Appeals should correct a plain forfeited error affecting substantial rights if the error seriously affects the fairness, integrity or public reputation of judicial proceedings." However, a "plain error affecting substantial rights, does not, without more" mandate reversal, "for otherwise the discretion afforded by Rule 52(b) would be rendered illusory."

So in essence there is a fourth requirement for plain error reversal—the error must seriously affect the fairness, integrity or public reputation of judicial proceedings.

Justice O'Connor compared Rule 52(a), which defines harmless error, with Rule 52(b). She concluded that the rules were different in the manner in which they allocated the burden of persuasion in showing prejudice. She analyzed the difference between the rules as follows:

> When the defendant has made a timely objection to an error and Rule 52(a) applies, the Court of Appeals normally engages in a specific analysis of the District Court record—a so-called "harmless error" inquiry—to determine whether the error was prejudicial. Rule 52(b) normally requires the same kind of inquiry, with one important difference: It is the defendant rather than the Government who bears the burden of persuasion with respect to prejudice. In most cases, the

Court of Appeals cannot correct the forfeited error unless the defendant shows that the error was prejudicial. This burden-shifting is dictated by a subtle but important difference in language between the two parts of Rule 52: while Rule 52(a) precludes error-correction only if the error "does *not* affect substantial rights" (emphasis added), Rule 52(b) authorizes no remedy unless the error *does* "affec[t] substantial rights."

Justice O'Connor left open the possibility that "[t]here may be a special category of forfeited errors that can be corrected regardless of their effect on the outcome," and declined to address the errors that should be presumed prejudicial. She concluded that normally, the defendant must make a "specific showing of prejudice" under Rule 52(b).

In *Olano,* the Court held that the defendants had failed to show that their substantial rights had been affected by any error. Justice O'Connor noted that the trial judge instructed the alternates that they were not to participate in deliberations, and that the defendants had made no showing that the presence of the alternates affected deliberations in any way.[7]

Plain Error in Guidelines Sentencing: Rosales-Mireles v. United States

In *Rosales-Mireles v. United States,* 138 S.Ct. 1897 (2018), Justice Sotomayor wrote for seven justices as the Court held that a miscalculation of a Guidelines sentencing range that has been determined to be plain and to affect a defendant's substantial rights calls for a court of appeals to exercise its discretion under Rule 52(b) to vacate the defendant's sentence in the ordinary case.

Rosales-Mireles pled guilty to illegal reentry into the United States. The Probation Office mistakenly counted a state misdemeanor conviction twice in calculating the Guidelines range, and its presentence report yielded a Guidelines range of 77 to 96 months when the correctly calculated range would have been 70 to 87 months. Rosales-Mireles did not object to the error in the District Court, which relied on the miscalculated Guidelines range to sentence him to 78 months of imprisonment. He challenged the incorrect Guidelines range for the first time on appeal. The Fifth Circuit found that the error was plain and affected Rosales-Mireles' substantial rights but declined to remand the case because he had not established that the error would seriously affect the fairness, integrity, or public reputation of judicial proceedings because neither the error nor the resulting sentence "would shock the conscience."

[7] Justice Kennedy wrote a short concurring opinion. Justice Stevens, joined by Justices White and Blackmun, dissented.

Justice Sotomayor set forth the four requirements that must be met before an error is declared to be plain: (1) the error must not have been intentionally relinquished or abandoned; (2) it must be plain (i.e., clear or obvious); (3) it must have affected the defendant's substantial rights; and (4) the error must seriously affect the fairness, integrity, or public reputation of judicial proceedings. The Court's focus was on the fourth prong.

Justice Sotomayor reasoned that (a) district judges have ultimate responsibility to apply the Guidelines correctly, but the Guidelines are sufficiently complex that judges sometimes make mistakes; (b) the Court in *Olano* rejected a rule that would have called for relief only "in those circumstances in which a miscarriage of justice would otherwise result"—i.e., where a defendant is actually innocent—so that the Fifth Circuit's rule was also unduly restrictive; (c) "[w]hen a defendant is sentenced under an incorrect Guidelines range—whether or not the defendant's ultimate sentence falls within the correct range—the error itself can, and most often will, be sufficient to show a reasonable probability of a different outcome absent the error"; and (d) "[t]he risk of unnecessary deprivation of liberty particularly undermines the fairness, integrity, or public reputation of judicial proceedings in the context of a plain Guidelines error because of the role the district court plays in calculating the range and the relative ease of correcting the error."

Justice Thomas, joined by Justice Alito, dissented. He agreed with the conclusion that the Fifth Circuit's rule was unduly narrow, but concluded that the Court's broad statement that Guidelines errors will ordinarily satisfy the fourth prong of plain-error review contravened precedents establishing that this prong must be applied on a case-specific and fact-intensive basis.

Error "Plain" at the Time of Appellate Review: Johnson v. United States

Can an error be "plain" when the trial court rules correctly at the time of trial, but then the law changes while the case is on direct appeal? This was one of the questions in Johnson v. United States, 520 U.S. 461 (1997). At Johnson's trial for perjury, the trial judge rather than the jury decided the question of whether Johnson's false statement to a grand jury was "material." This practice was in accord with circuit precedent at the time. However, in United States v. Gaudin, 515 U.S. 506 (1995), the Court held that the jury and not the judge must decide whether a false statement is material in cases such as Johnson's. *Gaudin* was decided after Johnson's trial, but while Johnson's case was on direct appeal—therefore *Gaudin* was applicable retroactively to Johnson's case. (See the discussion on retroactivity in Chapter 1). However, Johnson had not objected at trial to the trial judge taking the materiality question away from the jury. Indeed, Johnson complained at trial about the prosecution's proffer of evidence of materiality; he argued that the evidence was irrelevant, on the ground that materiality was a question for the judge rather than the jury.

Chief Justice Rehnquist, writing for a unanimous Court, noted that because of *Gaudin*, an "error" had occurred at Johnson's trial. He also noted, however, that because *Gaudin* was decided after Johnson's trial, it was difficult to determine whether the error complained of was "plain" within the meaning of *Olano*:

> In the case with which we are faced today, the error is certainly clear under "current law," but it was by no means clear at the time of trial.
>
> The Government contends that for an error to be "plain," it must have been so both at the time of trial and at the time of appellate consideration. In this case, it says, petitioner should have objected to the court's deciding the issue of materiality, even though near-uniform precedent both from this Court and from the Courts of Appeals held that course proper. Petitioner, on the other hand, urges that such a rule would result in counsel's inevitably making a long and virtually useless laundry list of objections to rulings that were plainly supported by existing precedent. We agree with petitioner on this point, and hold that in a case such as this—where the law at the time of trial was settled and clearly contrary to the law at the time of appeal—it is enough that an error be "plain" at the time of appellate consideration. * * * The second part of the *Olano* test is therefore satisfied.

It must be remembered, though, that under *Olano* plain error does not give rise to relief unless the error affected "substantial rights" and "seriously affects the fairness, integrity or public reputation of judicial proceedings." The Chief Justice concluded that it was not necessary to decide whether the error at Johnson's trial affected substantial rights, because it was clear that the error did not affect the fairness or integrity of the proceedings. He found that the evidence indicating that statements were material was "overwhelming," and that the question of materiality was "essentially uncontroverted at trial and remains so on appeal." Therefore, "no miscarriage of justice will occur if we do not notice the error."

Plain Error Review of an Apprendi Violation: United States v. Cotton

In Apprendi v. New Jersey, 530 U.S. 466 (2000), the Court held that "[o]ther than the fact of a prior conviction, any fact that increases the penalty for a crime beyond the prescribed statutory maximum must be submitted to a jury, and proved beyond a reasonable doubt." [*Apprendi* is set forth in full in the Chapter 10 discussion of constitutionally-based proof requirements]. In federal prosecutions, such facts must also be charged in the indictment. In United States v. Cotton, 535 U.S. 625 (2002), the Court reviewed an *Apprendi* violation for plain error. The defendants in *Cotton* received a sentence beyond the statutory maximum, after the trial judge (rather than the jury) found that the drug offenses involved more than 50 grams of cocaine base. The indictment made no allegation as to any amount of drugs. The government conceded that the defendants' enhanced sentence was erroneous under *Apprendi*, but pointed out that the defendants had failed to raise the *Apprendi* argument before the district court.

The Supreme Court, in an opinion by Chief Justice Rehnquist, held that the defendants were not entitled to relief because they could not meet their burden of showing plain error under the circumstances. Chief Justice Rehnquist concluded that the error did not seriously affect the fairness, integrity, or public reputation of judicial proceedings. He explained as follows:

> The evidence that the conspiracy involved at least 50 grams of cocaine base was overwhelming and essentially uncontroverted. Much of the evidence implicating respondents in the drug conspiracy revealed the conspiracy's involvement with far more than 50 grams of cocaine base. Baltimore police officers made numerous state arrests and seizures between February 1996 and April 1997 that resulted in the seizure of 795 ziplock bags and clear bags containing approximately 380 grams of cocaine base. A federal search of respondent Jovan Powell's residence resulted in the seizure of 51.3 grams of cocaine base. A cooperating co-conspirator testified at trial that he witnessed respondent Hall cook one-quarter of a kilogram of cocaine powder into cocaine base. Another cooperating co-conspirator testified at trial that she was present in a hotel room where the drug operation bagged one kilogram of cocaine base into ziplock bags. Surely the grand jury, having found that the conspiracy existed, would have also found that the conspiracy involved at least 50 grams of cocaine base.

Plain Error Review of Failure to Obtain a Knowing and Intelligent Guilty Plea: United States v. Dominguez-Benitez

As discussed in Chapter 9, Fed.R.Crim.P. 11 sets forth procedural requirements that the court must follow to obtain a valid guilty plea. These requirements are to ensure that the defendant knows the rights he is giving up by pleading guilty and foregoing a trial. In United States v. Dominguez-Benitez, 542 U.S. 74 (2004), the Court considered how a violation of the Rule 11 requirements are to be reviewed for plain error. The parties in *Dominguez-Benitez* entered into the kind of plea in which the government agrees to make a sentencing recommendation, but the court is not bound to accept it. Fed.R.Crim. P. 11(c)(3)(B). Under Rule 11, the defendant entering into such an agreement must be warned that he cannot withdraw his guilty plea if the court refuses to go along with the Government's recommendations. Dominguez-Benitez was not so warned, and he received a sentence much higher than he expected under the agreement. But he never made a timely objection. On appeal, he argued that he should be allowed to withdraw his plea because of plain error.

Justice Souter, writing for the Court, analyzed the function of plain error review for an alleged error in following the procedural requirements of Rule 11.

> [T]he burden of establishing entitlement to relief for plain error is on the defendant claiming it, and for several reasons, we think that burden should not be too easy for defendants in Dominguez's position. First, the standard should enforce the policies that underpin Rule 52(b) generally, to encourage timely objections and reduce wasteful reversals by demanding strenuous exertion to get relief for unpreserved error. Second, it should respect the particular importance of the finality of guilty pleas, which usually rest, after all, on a defendant's profession of guilt in open court, and are indispensable in the operation of the modern criminal justice system. And, in this case, these reasons are complemented by the fact, worth repeating, that the violation claimed was of Rule 11, not of due process.
>
> We hold, therefore, that a defendant who seeks reversal of his conviction after a guilty plea, on the ground that the district court committed plain error under Rule 11, must show a reasonable probability that, but for the error, he would not have entered the plea. A defendant must thus satisfy the judgment of the reviewing court, informed by the entire record, that the probability of a different result is "sufficient to undermine confidence in the outcome" of the proceeding.

The Court remanded for a determination of whether the defendant could prove plain error. It noted that relevant factors would include the difference between the sentence the defendant received and the sentence he anticipated under the agreement; the strength of the evidence that could have been presented at trial; and "any record evidence tending to show that a misunderstanding was inconsequential to a defendant's decision, or evidence indicating the relative significance of other facts that may have borne on his choice regardless of any Rule 11 error."

Plain Error Standard Applies to Forfeited Objection on Breach of Plea Agreement: Puckett v. United States

In Puckett v. United States, 556 U.S. 129 (2009), Puckett argued that the plain error standard was inappropriate when the error was the breach of a plea agreement. But the Court, in an opinion by Justice Scalia, disagreed. Justice Scalia reviewed the plain error doctrine, and in the following passage found it applicable:

> If an error is not properly preserved, appellate-court authority to remedy the error (by reversing the judgment, for example, or ordering a new trial) is strictly circumscribed. There is good reason for this; anyone familiar with the work of courts understands that errors are a constant in the trial process, that most do not much matter, and that a reflexive inclination by appellate courts to reverse because of unpreserved error would be fatal.
>
> This limitation on appellate-court authority serves to induce the timely raising of claims and objections, which gives the district court the opportunity to consider and resolve them. That court is ordinarily in the best position to determine the relevant facts and adjudicate the dispute. In the case of an actual or invited procedural error, the district court can often correct or avoid the mistake so that it cannot possibly affect the ultimate outcome. And of course the contemporaneous-objection rule prevents a litigant from "sandbagging" the court—remaining silent about his objection and belatedly raising the error only if the case does not conclude in his favor.
>
> * * *
>
> The real question in this case is not whether plain-error review applies when a defendant fails to preserve a claim that the Government defaulted on its plea-agreement obligations, but rather what conceivable reason exists for disregarding its evident application. Such a breach is undoubtedly a violation of the defendant's rights, but the defendant has the opportunity to seek vindication of those rights in district court; if he fails to do so, Rule 52(b) as clearly sets forth the consequences for that forfeiture as it does for all others.

Justice Souter, joined by Justice Stevens, dissented.

"Any Possibility" Test Is Too Permissive for Plain Error Review: United States v. Marcus

In United States v. Marcus, 560 U.S. 258 (2010), the Court was reviewing a Second Circuit decision conducting plain error review of a claim that Marcus did not raise at trial. Marcus was convicted of sex trafficking. On appeal, for the first time, he argued that some of his conduct preceded the statute under which he was convicted, and therefore his conviction violated the Ex Post Facto Clause of the Constitution. The Government argued that because some of the conduct was conceded to be after the statute went into effect, there was no error that affected Marcus's substantial rights. Justice Breyer, writing for the Court, rejected the Second Circuit's ruling that it must recognize a "plain error" if there is "any possibility," however remote, that a jury convicted a defendant exclusively on the basis of actions taken before enactment of the statute that made those actions criminal. He concluded that a "plain error" must affect substantial rights and therefore be prejudicial and "seriously affect[ ] the fairness, integrity, or public reputation of judicial proceedings.". Justice Breyer noted that there is an exception permitting plain error review for "structural" errors, but concluded that the Ex Post Facto error was not structural.

Justice Stevens dissented in *Marcus*. He contended that the Court's plain error jurisprudence was too formalistic:

> In our attempt to clarify Rule 52(b), we have, I fear, both muddied the waters and lost sight of the wisdom embodied in the Rule's spare text. Errors come in an endless variety of shapes and sizes. Because error-free trials are so rare, appellate courts must repeatedly confront the question whether a trial judge's mistake was harmless or warrants reversal. * * * This Court's ever more intensive efforts to rationalize plain-error review may have been born of a worthy instinct. But they have trapped the appellate courts in an analytic maze that, I have increasingly come to believe, is more liable to frustrate than to facilitate sound decisionmaking.

Justice Sotomayor did not participate in the decision in *Marcus*.

Appellate Court May Not Invoke Plain Error to Increase a Sentence in the Absence of a Government Appeal: Greenlaw v. United States

In Greenlaw v. United States, 554 U.S. 237 (2008), the defendant appealed from his sentence, and the government filed no cross-appeal. The court of appeals rejected the defendant's challenge to his sentence and then proceeded *sua sponte* to determine whether the defendant's sentence was too low. Relying on the doctrine of plain error, the court of appeals entered an order increasing the defendant's sentence by 15 years. The Supreme Court, in an opinion by Justice Ginsburg for six Justices, held that the court of appeals could not use the plain error doctrine to increase a sentence from which the government had not appealed.

Justice Ginsburg relied on 18 U.S.C. § 3742(b), which provides that the government may not appeal a sentence "without the personal approval of the Attorney General, the Solicitor General, or a deputy solicitor general designated by the Solicitor General." She declared that "Congress, in § 3742(b), has accorded to the top representatives of the United States in litigation the prerogative to seek or forgo appellate correction of sentencing errors, however plain they may be. That measure should garner the Judiciary's full respect." Justice Alito, joined by Justices Breyer and Stevens, dissented.

E. DISENTITLEMENT FROM THE RIGHT TO APPEAL

The Fugitive Dismissal Rule: Ortega-Rodriguez v. United States

If a defendant flees during the pendency of his appeal, the appellate court has the authority to dismiss the appeal. See Molinaro v. New Jersey, 396 U.S. 365 (1970). This "fugitive dismissal" rule is based upon two justifications: 1) the appellate court should not render a judgment that may prove unenforceable; and 2) a defendant who takes flight disentitles himself from the right to call upon the resources of the appellate court.

In Ortega-Rodriguez v. United States, 507 U.S. 234 (1993), the Court considered whether the justifications behind the fugitive dismissal rule apply when a defendant flees the jurisdiction of a district court and is recaptured *before* he invokes the jurisdiction of the appellate court. The Court, in a 5–4 decision, held that "when a defendant's flight and recapture occur before appeal, the defendant's former fugitive status may well lack the kind of connection to the appellate process that would justify an appellate sanction of dismissal."

Justice Stevens pointed out that the enforceability concerns behind the fugitive dismissal rule are not applicable to a defendant who has been returned before the appellate process has begun. He further claimed that flight while the case is pending in the district court was a sign of disrespect for the authority of that court, not of the appellate court; therefore the disentitlement justification of the fugitive dismissal rule would ordinarily not apply to pre-appeal flight, and the defendant's act of flight "is best sanctioned by the district court itself."

The Court refused, however, to adopt a bright-line rule that pre-appeal flight could never result in dismissal of an appeal. Justice Stevens noted that "some actions by a defendant, though they occur while his case is before the district court, might have an impact on the appellate process sufficient to warrant an appellate sanction." For example, the government may be prejudiced in locating witnesses for retrial if the appeal is significantly delayed; or the appellate court may be inconvenienced due to the inability to consolidate the fugitive defendant's appeal with other related appeals. The Court ruled that if such circumstances existed, "a dismissal rule could properly be applied." The Court remanded the case to determine whether the defendant's pre-appeal flight imposed consequences on the appellate system sufficient to justify dismissal of his appeal.

Chief Justice Rehnquist, joined by Justices White, O'Connor, and Thomas, dissented. He stated that "there is as much of a chance that flight will disrupt the proper functioning of the appellate process if it occurs before the court of appeals obtains jurisdiction as there is if it occurs after the court of appeals obtains jurisdiction."

III. COLLATERAL ATTACK

A. REMEDIES GENERALLY

1. Collateral Attacks

After new trial motions have been rejected and all appeals are exhausted—or lost, perhaps for failure to comply with an appellate rule, such as a time limit on filing a notice of appeal—a defendant has a natural incentive to attempt additional attacks on the conviction.

Post-conviction remedies after an appeal, of which habeas corpus is the most common, known as *collateral* remedies, "providing an avenue for upsetting judgments that have become otherwise final." Mackey v. United States, 401 U.S. 667 (1971) (Harlan, J., separate opinion). They are not designed to substitute for direct review of convictions, nor can all the questions properly subject to appeal be raised collaterally. Because collateral attacks collide with principles of finality, there are substantial limitations imposed on persons who want to bring such attacks.

2. Coram Nobis

One rarely used form of collateral attack is for the petitioner to obtain a writ of coram nobis. This is a remedy of last resort, available only to one otherwise remediless. Given the availability of a habeas corpus petition for those in custody, the coram nobis remedy has only very limited applicability. See Lowery v. United States, 956 F.2d 227 (11th Cir.1992) (coram nobis relief is not available where the defendant is still in custody and can petition for habeas relief). As the court in Telink, Inc. v. United States, 24 F.3d 42 (9th Cir.1994), put it:

> The writ of error coram nobis affords a remedy to attack an unconstitutional or unlawful conviction in cases when the petitioner has already served a sentence. The petition fills a very precise gap in federal criminal procedure. A convicted defendant in federal custody may petition to have a sentence or conviction vacated, set aside or corrected under the federal habeas statute, 28 U.S.C. § 2255. However, if the sentence has been served, there is no statutory basis to remedy the lingering collateral consequences of the unlawful conviction. Recognizing this statutory gap, the Supreme Court has held that the common law petition for writ of error coram nobis is available in such situations * * *.

Availability of the Writ of Coram Nobis in Federal Courts: United States v. Morgan and Korematsu v. United States

The Supreme Court held in United States v. Morgan, 346 U.S. 502 (1954) that the writ of coram nobis is available in federal courts. After

Morgan was convicted in federal court and served his sentence, he was convicted in a state court and sentenced to a longer term as a second offender on the basis of the federal conviction. Collateral attack on the federal conviction under 28 U.S.C.A. § 2255, discussed infra, was not possible because Morgan was not in federal custody. But the Court held that an attack in the nature of coram nobis—in *Morgan* the challenge was that he had not been represented by counsel—was available. The burden of proving a right to relief was placed upon the convicted person. The Court stated that the grant of relief "should be allowed through this extraordinary remedy only under circumstances compelling such action to achieve justice."

Subsequently the Court recognized "the obvious fact of life that most criminal convictions do in fact entail adverse collateral legal consequences." Sibron v. New York, 392 U.S. 40, 55 (1968). Coram nobis, in the absence of other remedies, will allow a convicted person to attempt to avoid these consequences—for example, disentitlement from the right to vote.

One of the most celebrated uses of the writ of coram nobis is Korematsu v. United States, 584 F.Supp. 1406 (N.D.Cal.1984), in which the court vacated the notorious conviction of an American citizen of Japanese ancestry for being in a place where all persons of Japanese ancestry had been excluded following the declaration of war by the United States against Japan in 1941. The conviction had been sustained by the Supreme Court in 1944. 323 U.S. 214 (1944). The district court relied upon a Report of the Commission on Wartime Relocation and Internment of Civilians (1982), which concluded that military necessity did not warrant the exclusion and detention of ethnic Japanese. It also relied upon internal government documents that demonstrated that the government knowingly withheld information from the courts when they were considering the critical question of military necessity in this case.

3. Habeas Corpus

Habeas corpus is a collateral remedy for those who are in custody; the petitioner seeks a writ to be served against the official holding him in custody—usually the warden. The justification for the writ is that some error occurred that makes the custody illegal.

History of the Great Writ

"The early function of the writ of habeas corpus, say from 1150, was simply to get an unwilling party into court regardless of the kind of case involved." R. Sokol, Federal Habeas Corpus § B, at 4. It did not begin a proceeding; rather, it assured that once a proceeding was otherwise begun, it would not be futile because of the absence of a party. In the fourteenth century, the writ, in addition to its earlier function, also became an independent action to test the cause of a detention. With the development of this aspect of the writ, it took its place in the struggle between the common-law and the chancery courts. "Time and again * * * the common-law judges through habeas corpus released from custody persons committed by other courts," and thus undercut the authority of the Chancellor. D. Meador, Habeas Corpus and Magna Carta: Dualism of Power and Liberty 12 (1966).

Darnel's Case, 3 St.Trials 1, arose in 1627 and probably accounts significantly for the development of the writ. Darnel and four other knights were sent to prison for refusing to "loan" money to a demanding monarch. They sought habeas corpus to inquire into the power of the monarch to imprison them. Unsuccessful though they were, they invoked the concept of "due process of law," and they relied on Magna Carta in a way that led parliament to modify the decision by providing in its Petition of Right that no person should be imprisoned without being charged in some way that allowed an opportunity for an answer. The writ of habeas corpus became the established vehicle for challenging confinement as denying due process of law. In the famous decision in Bushell's Case, 124 Eng.Rep. 1006, 6 St.Trials 999 (1670), the court utilized habeas corpus to order the release of a juror committed for contempt for returning a not guilty verdict in the trial of William Penn and others. A century later Blackstone would call the writ "the most celebrated in the English law."

Following English common-law, the writ of habeas corpus became a part of American law. See generally Oaks, Habeas Corpus in the States—1776–1865, 32 U.Chi.L.Rev. 243 (1965). At the time of the constitutional convention, 4 of the 12 states with written constitutions had provisions regarding habeas corpus. In Article I of the Constitution, which sets forth the powers of Congress and restrictions upon those powers, clause 2 of section 9 provides that "[t]he Privilege of the Writ of Habeas Corpus shall not be suspended, unless when in Cases of Rebellion or Invasion the public Safety may require it."

Congressional Power to Restrict Habeas Corpus

It is unclear how far Congress can go in restricting the habeas corpus power of federal courts. If, for example, Congress did not authorize lower federal courts to hear any habeas corpus cases, would the anti-suspension clause be violated? Under the Constitution, Congress need not create federal courts at all. This might suggest that no habeas power necessarily must be placed in lower courts. See generally Developments in the Law—Federal Habeas Corpus, 83 Harv.L.Rev. 1038, 1049–50, 1263–66 (1970). Some suggestions have been made that even without statutory authority federal courts could grant writs of habeas corpus. See, e.g., Chafee, The

Most Important Human Right in the Constitution, 32 B.U.L.Rev. 143 (1952).

Until 2006, no serious effort had been made by Congress to strip federal courts of habeas corpus jurisdiction. Indeed, as will be seen below, Congress has passed statutes that authorize collateral attack by a petition for habeas corpus. But in the Military Commissions Act of 2006, Congress did purport to deny habeas jurisdiction over a certain set of claims of detained persons who were alleged to be enemy combatants after 9/11. The Military Commissions Act expressly provided that "[n]o court, justice, or judge shall have jurisdiction to hear or consider an application for a writ of habeas corpus filed by or on behalf of an alien detained by the United States who has been determined by the United States to have been properly detained as an enemy combatant or is awaiting such determination."

In Boumediene v. Bush, 553 U.S. 723 (2008), a five-Justice majority invalidated the provision of the Military Commissions Act that purported to deprive the federal courts of habeas jurisdiction over the proceedings against alleged enemy combatants. The Court held that this provision of the Military Commissions Act operated as a suspension of the writ of habeas corpus. The Court rejected the government's argument that the alternative procedures provided by the Act were the functional equivalent of the habeas remedy.

State Habeas Provisions

At one time the Supreme Court granted certiorari to decide whether states are obliged under the Federal Constitution to provide persons convicted in state court with some post-conviction process to correct judgments of conviction obtained in violation of federal law. But the Court remanded the case to the Nebraska Supreme Court when the state legislature passed a post-conviction statute. Case v. Nebraska, 381 U.S. 336 (1965). Since then, all states have recognized some form of post-conviction attack after direct appeal in the state courts has been exhausted. See generally Whitmore v. State, 299 Ark. 55, 771 S.W.2d 266 (1989), for a discussion of the costs of allowing state post-conviction proceedings and the problems involved in integrating state and federal post-conviction proceedings.

In state habeas proceedings, state law governs the extent to which claims can be raised and the procedures that must be followed in raising the claims. If a convicted person wins collateral relief in state court, further proceedings will be unnecessary. But failure to win in state court often will not bar a subsequent federal action to set aside a state conviction.

The remainder of this Chapter will focus on federal actions and two basic questions: (1) What issues should be cognizable in collateral actions? (2) Should it matter (and if so, why) whether the collateral action is brought by a person convicted in a state or federal court? Because this material involves, in part, complex questions of federal-state relations, only the surface is scratched here.

B. FEDERAL HABEAS CORPUS: THE PROCEDURAL FRAMEWORK

1. The Statutes

Federal habeas corpus remedies are available to challenge convictions rendered by both state and federal courts. The challenge must be brought by a person in custody—that person, who was originally the defendant in a criminal proceeding, is the "petitioner" in the habeas proceeding. The petitioner files a civil action in federal court, seeking a writ of habeas corpus on the ground that he is in custody in violation of federal law. Generally speaking, petitions for habeas corpus filed by state prisoners are governed by 28 U.S.C. § 2254 and are often referred to as section 2254 actions. Petitions in the nature of habeas corpus filed by federal prisoners are governed by 28 U.S.C. § 2255 and are often referred to as section 2255 actions.

In 1996 the President signed into law the Antiterrorism and Effective Death Penalty Act (hereinafter referred to as AEDPA). AEDPA imposes significant limitations on the habeas corpus remedy in federal courts. Some of these limitations are directed specifically to state death-row claimants, and are conditioned on the state's implementation of a mechanism for appointing competent counsel for state post-conviction proceedings. Other limitations are directed more generally toward any state claimant seeking relief in the federal district court under the provisions of 28 U.S.C. § 2254. Limitations similar to these are imposed by AEDPA on federal prisoners seeking collateral relief under 28 U.S.C. § 2255.

What follows are the statutory provisions that are pertinent to the habeas corpus remedy, as amended by AEDPA. *AEDPA amendments are italicized.*

Section 2241

28 U.S.C.A. § 2241 et seq. sets forth the powers of federal judges to issue writs of habeas corpus and identifies the courts from which it may be sought.

§ 2241. Power to Grant Writ

(a) Writs of habeas corpus may be granted by the Supreme Court, any justice thereof, the district courts and any circuit judge within their respective jurisdictions. The order of a circuit judge shall be entered in the records of the district court of the district wherein the restraint complained of is had.

(b) The Supreme Court, any justice thereof, and any circuit judge may decline to entertain an application for a writ of habeas corpus and may transfer the application for hearing and determination to the district court having jurisdiction to entertain it.

(c) The writ of habeas corpus shall not extend to a prisoner unless—

(1) He is in custody under or by color of the authority of the United States or is committed for trial before some court thereof; or

(2) He is in custody for an act done or omitted in pursuance of an Act of Congress, or an order, process, judgment or decree of a court or judge of the United States; or

(3) He is in custody in violation of the Constitution or laws or treaties of the United States; * * *

* * *

Section 2244

Section 2244, as amended by AEDPA, essentially provides that a habeas petitioner gets one collateral attack. Successive petitions are virtually always to be dismissed. It also provides for a statute of limitations on habeas petitions.

28 U.S.C. § 2244. Finality of Determination

(a) No circuit or district judge shall be required to entertain an application for a writ of habeas corpus to inquire into the detention of a person pursuant to a judgment of a court of the United States if it appears that the legality of such detention has been determined by a judge or court of the United States on a prior application for a writ of habeas corpus *except as provided in Section 2255.*

(b)(1) A claim presented in a second or successive Habeas Corpus application under section 2254 that was presented in a prior application shall be dismissed.

(2) A claim presented in a second or successive Habeas Corpus application under section 2254 that was not presented in a prior application shall be dismissed unless—

(A) The applicant shows that the claim relies on a new rule of Constitutional law, made retroactive to cases on collateral review by the Supreme Court, that was previously unavailable; or

(B)(i) the factual predicate for the claim could not have been discovered previously through the exercise of due diligence; and

(ii) the facts underlying the claim, if proven and viewed in light of the evidence as a whole, would be sufficient to establish by clear and convincing evidence that, but for constitutional error, no reasonable factfinder would have found the applicant guilty of the underlying offense.

(3)(A) Before a second or successive application permitted by this section is filed in the district court, the applicant shall move in the appropriate court of appeals for an order authorizing the district court to consider the application.

(B) A motion in the court of appeals for an order authorizing the district court to consider a second or successive application shall be determined by a three-judge panel of the court of appeals.

(C) The court of appeals may authorize the filing of a second or successive application only if it determines that the application makes a prima facie showing that the application satisfies the requirements of this subsection.

(D) The court of appeals shall grant or deny the authorization to file a second or successive application not later than 30 days after the filing of the motion.

(E) The grant or denial of an authorization by a court of appeals to file a second or successive application shall not be appealable and shall not be the subject of a petition for rehearing or for a Writ of Certiorari.

(4) A district court shall dismiss any claim presented in a second or successive application that the court of appeals has authorized to be filed unless the applicant shows that the claim satisfies the requirements of this section.

(c) In a habeas corpus proceeding brought in behalf of a person in custody pursuant to the judgment of a State court, a prior judgment of the Supreme Court of the United States on an appeal or review by a writ of certiorari at the instance of the prisoner of the decision of such State court, shall be conclusive as to all issues of fact or law with respect to an asserted denial of a Federal right which constitutes ground for discharge in a habeas corpus proceeding, actually adjudicated by the Supreme Court therein, unless the applicant for the writ of habeas corpus shall plead and the court shall find the existence of a material and controlling fact which did not appear in the record of the proceeding in the Supreme Court and the court shall further find that

the applicant for the writ of habeas corpus could not have caused such fact to appear in such record by the exercise of reasonable diligence.

(d)(1) A 1-year period of limitation shall apply to an application for a writ of habeas corpus by a person in custody pursuant to the judgment of a State court. The limitation period shall run from the latest of—

(A) the date on which the judgment became final by the conclusion of direct review or the expiration of the time for seeking such review;

(B) the date on which the impediment to filing an application created by State action in violation of the Constitution or laws of the United States is removed, if the applicant was prevented from filing by such State action;

(C) the date on which the constitutional right asserted was initially recognized by the Supreme Court, if the right has been newly recognized by the Supreme Court and made retroactively applicable to cases on collateral review; or

(D) the date on which the factual predicate of the claim or claims presented could have been discovered through the exercise of due diligence.

(2) The time during which a properly filed application for State post-conviction or other collateral review with respect to the pertinent judgment or claim is pending shall not be counted toward any period of limitation under this subsection.

Section 2253

Section 2253 limits the right of appeal from a district court's denial of a writ of habeas corpus.

28 U.S.C. § 2253. Appeal

(a) In a habeas corpus proceeding or a proceeding under section 2255 before a district judge, the final order shall be subject to review, on appeal, by the court of appeals for the circuit in which the proceeding is held.

(b) There shall be no right of appeal from a final order in a proceeding to test the validity of a warrant to remove to another district or place for commitment or trial a person charged with a criminal offense against the United States, or to test the validity of such person's detention pending removal proceedings.

(c)(1) Unless a circuit justice or judge issues a certificate of appealability, an appeal may not be taken to the court of appeals from—

(A) the final order in a habeas corpus proceeding in which the detention complained of arises out of process issued by a State court; or

(B) the final order in a proceeding under section 2255.

(2) A certificate of appealability may issue under paragraph (1) only if the applicant has made a substantial showing of the denial of a constitutional right.

(3) The certificate of appealability under paragraph (1) shall indicate which specific issue or issues satisfy the showing required by paragraph (2).

Section 2254

Section 2254 is the basic section governing review of state court convictions by a federal district court in a habeas corpus action. The AEDPA requires federal courts to give substantial deference to state court determinations of federal law. And it requires the petitioner to exhaust state remedies before seeking a habeas corpus petition in federal court. It also limits the ability of a state petitioner to receive an evidentiary hearing in the federal court.

28 U.S.C. § 2254. State Custody; Remedies in Federal Courts

(a) The Supreme Court, a Justice thereof, a circuit judge, or a district court shall entertain an application for a writ of habeas corpus in behalf of a person in custody pursuant to the judgment of a State court only on the ground that he is in custody in violation of the Constitution or laws or treaties of the United States.

(b)*(1) An application for a writ of habeas corpus on behalf of a person in custody pursuant to the judgment of a State court shall not be granted unless it appears that—*

(A) the applicant has exhausted the remedies available in the courts of the State; or

(B)(i) there is an absence of available State corrective process; or

(ii) circumstances exist that render such process ineffective to protect the rights of the applicant.

(2) An application for a writ of habeas corpus may be denied on the merits, notwithstanding the failure of the applicant to exhaust the remedies available in the courts of the State.

(3) A State shall not be deemed to have waived the exhaustion requirement or be estopped from reliance upon the requirement

unless the State, through counsel, expressly waives the requirement.

(c) An applicant shall not be deemed to have exhausted the remedies available in the courts of the State, within the meaning of this section, if he has the right under the law of the State to raise, by any available procedure, the question presented.

(d) An application for a writ of habeas corpus on behalf of a person in custody pursuant to the judgment of a State court shall not be granted with respect to any claim that was adjudicated on the merits in State court proceedings unless the adjudication of the claim—

(1) resulted in a decision that was contrary to, or involved an unreasonable application of, clearly established Federal law, as determined by the Supreme Court of the United States; or

(2) resulted in a decision that was based on an unreasonable determination of the facts in light of the evidence presented in the State court proceeding.

(e)*(1) In a proceeding instituted by an application for a writ of habeas corpus by a person in custody pursuant to the judgment of a State court, a determination of a factual issue made by a State court shall be presumed to be correct. The applicant shall have the burden of rebutting the presumption of correctness by clear and convincing evidence.*

(2) If the applicant has failed to develop the factual basis of a claim in State court proceedings, the court shall not hold an evidentiary hearing on the claim unless the applicant shows that—

(A) the claim relies on—

(i) a new rule of constitutional law, made retroactive to cases on collateral review by the Supreme Court, that was previously unavailable; or

(ii) a factual predicate that could not have been previously discovered through the exercise of due diligence; and

(B) the facts underlying the claim would be sufficient to establish by clear and convincing evidence that but for constitutional error, no reasonable factfinder would have found the applicant guilty of the underlying offense; and

(f) If the applicant challenges the sufficiency of the evidence adduced in such State court proceeding to support the State court's determination of a factual issue made therein, the applicant, if able, shall produce that part of the record pertinent to a determination of the sufficiency of the evidence to support such determination. If the applicant, because of indigency or other reason is unable to produce such part of the record, then the State shall produce such part of the record and the Federal court shall direct the State to do so by order directed to an appropriate State official. If the State cannot provide such pertinent part of the record, then the court shall determine under the existing facts and circumstances what weight shall be given to the State court's factual determination.

(g) A copy of the official records of the State court, duly certified by the clerk of such court to be a true and correct copy of a finding, judicial opinion, or other reliable written indicia showing such a factual determination by the State court shall be admissible in the Federal court proceeding.

(h) Except as provided in section 408 of the Controlled Substances Act, in all proceedings brought under this section, and any subsequent proceedings on review, the court may appoint counsel for an applicant who is or becomes financially unable to afford counsel, except as provided by a rule promulgated by the Supreme Court pursuant to statutory authority. * * *

(i) The ineffectiveness or incompetence of counsel during Federal or State collateral post-conviction proceedings shall not be a ground for relief in a proceeding arising under section 2254.

Section 2255

Section 2255 is the main provision regulating habeas petitions by those who have been convicted in federal court. The AEDPA imposes a one-year statute of limitations on such petitions, and generally precludes successive petitions.

28 U.S.C. § 2255. Federal Custody; Remedies on Motion Attacking Sentence

A prisoner in custody under sentence of a court established by Act of Congress claiming the right to be released upon the ground that the sentence was imposed in violation of the Constitution or laws of the United States, or that the court was without jurisdiction to impose such sentence, or that the sentence was in excess of the maximum authorized by law, or is otherwise subject to collateral attack, may move the court which imposed the sentence to vacate, set aside or correct the sentence.

Unless the motion and the files and records of the case conclusively show that the prisoner is entitled to no relief, the court shall cause notice thereof to be served upon the United States attorney, grant a prompt hearing thereon, determine the issues and make findings of fact and conclusions of law with respect thereto. If the court finds that the judgment was rendered without jurisdiction, or that the sentence imposed was not authorized by law or otherwise open to collateral attack, or that there has been such a denial or infringement of the constitutional rights of the prisoner as to render the judgment vulnerable to collateral attack, the court shall vacate and set the judgment aside and shall discharge the prisoner or resentence him or grant a new trial or correct the sentence as may appear appropriate.

A court may entertain and determine such motion without requiring the production of the prisoner at the hearing.

An appeal may be taken to the court of appeals from the order entered on the motion as from the final judgment on application for a writ of habeas corpus.

An application for a writ of habeas corpus in behalf of a prisoner who is authorized to apply for relief by motion pursuant to this section, shall not be entertained if it appears that the applicant has failed to apply for relief, by motion, to the court which sentenced him, or that such court has denied him relief, unless it also appears that the remedy by motion is inadequate or ineffective to test the legality of his detention.

A 1-year period of limitation shall apply to a motion under this section. The limitation period shall run from the latest of—

(1) the date on which the judgment of conviction becomes final;

(2) the date on which the impediment to making a motion created by governmental action in violation of the Constitution or laws of the United States is removed, if the movant was prevented from making a motion by such governmental action;

(3) the date on which the right asserted was initially recognized by the Supreme Court, if that right has been newly recognized by the Supreme Court and made retroactively applicable to cases on collateral review; or

(4) the date on which the facts supporting the claim or claims presented could have been discovered through the exercise of due diligence.

Except as provided in section 408 of the Controlled Substances Act, in all proceedings brought under this section, and any subsequent proceedings on review, the court may appoint counsel, except as provided by a rule promulgated by the Supreme Court pursuant to statutory authority. * * *

A second or successive motion must be certified as provided in section 2244 by a panel of the appropriate court of appeals to contain—

(1) newly discovered evidence that, if proven and viewed in light of the evidence as a whole, would be sufficient to establish by clear and convincing evidence that no reasonable factfinder would have found the movant guilty of the offense; or

(2) a new rule of constitutional law, made retroactive to cases on collateral review by the Supreme Court, that was previously unavailable.

Sections 2261–68

28 U.S.C. §§ 2261–68 are provisions added by AEDPA to limit collateral attacks by state death row inmates. Among other things, these sections: 1) limit the ability of death row inmates to obtain more than one stay of execution; 2) generally preclude considerations of claims that were not heard in state court because of the petitioner's failure to comply with a state procedural rule; 3) provide a "rocket docket" for expedited consideration of death penalty claims on habeas. To invoke these provisions, the state must prove that it has established "by statute, rule of its court of last resort, or by another agency authorized by State law, a mechanism for the appointment, compensation, and payment of reasonable litigation expenses of competent counsel in State post-conviction proceedings brought by indigent prisoners whose capital convictions and sentences have been upheld on direct appeal to the court of last resort in the State or have otherwise become final for State law purposes. The rule of court or statute must provide standards of competency for the appointment of such counsel."

2. General Principles Concerning Habeas Relief After AEDPA

The innovations of AEDPA have raised some important questions about the extent of habeas corpus relief.

a. Statute of Limitations

AEDPA imposes a statute of limitations for habeas corpus petitions: for most petitioners a petition must be filed within one year after the conviction becomes final., There is potentially an even stricter period for death row petitioners—if it is determined, under criteria provided in the statute, that the state provides competent counsel for state post-conviction proceedings, then a death row claimant must file a habeas petition within 180 days of the date his conviction becomes final, with a possible 30-day extension for cause. In Lonchar v. Thomas, 517 U.S. 314 (1996), the Court—applying pre-AEDPA law—held that there was no time limitation on an initial habeas petition, other than the equitable principle of laches. The Court in *Lonchar* declined to dismiss an initial petition filed just before the petitioner was scheduled to be executed six years after his conviction became final. But under the AEDPA, such a petition would have to be dismissed as untimely.[8]

Note that the limitations period in AEDPA is tolled in section 2254 actions for the time taken to pursue state collateral relief. See Carey v. Saffold, 536 U.S. 214 (2002) (petition for state collateral review in California was "pending" in the time between the lower state court's decision and the filing of a new petition in a higher court, tolling the period for filing a federal habeas petition). See also Duncan v. Walker, 533 U.S. 167 (2001) (action for federal relief does not toll the AEDPA statute of limitations; section 2254 refers only to "state" collateral proceedings as tolling the limitations period).

Equitable Tolling: Holland v. Florida

In Holland v. Florida, 560 U.S. 631 (2010), the Court in an opinion by Justice Breyer held that the timeliness provision of AEDPA is subject to equitable tolling. While there is nothing in AEDPA about equitable tolling, Justice Breyer noted that the limitations period of AEDPA is not jurisdictional and stated that "a nonjurisdictional federal statute of limitations is ordinarily subject to a rebuttable presumption of equitable tolling." In the case of AEDPA, "the presumption's strength is reinforced by the fact that equitable principles have traditionally governed the substantive law of habeas corpus." Justice Breyer concluded as follows:

> The importance of the Great Writ, the only writ explicitly protected by the Constitution, Art. I, § 9, cl. 2, along with congressional efforts to harmonize the new statute with prior law, counsels hesitancy before interpreting AEDPA's statutory silence as indicating a congressional intent to close courthouse doors that a strong equitable claim would ordinarily keep open.

Justice Breyer stated that a petitioner is entitled to equitable tolling "only if he shows (1) that he has been pursuing his rights diligently, and (2) that some extraordinary circumstance stood in his way and prevented timely filing." Under the facts presented in *Holland,* the Court found that the limitations period was equitably tolled because Holland's lawyer (Collins)

[8] In Day v. McDonough, 547 U.S. 198 (2006), the Court held that a district court has the authority to raise an untimeliness defense *sua sponte,* but only in "exceptional circumstances." Thereafter in Wood v. Milyard, 566 U.S. 463 (2012), the Court held that an appellate court has a similar authority to raise an untimely defense *sua sponte,* but stated that the authority was somewhat more narrow than the district court's because the appellate court must consider the fact that the district court has already expended time and consideration on the merits.

failed to file Holland's petition on time despite Holland's many letters that repeatedly emphasized the importance of his doing so. Collins apparently did not do the research necessary to find out the proper filing date, despite Holland's letters that went so far as to identify the applicable legal rules. Collins failed to inform Holland in a timely manner about the crucial fact that the Florida Supreme Court had decided his case, again despite Holland's many pleas for that information. And Collins failed to communicate with his client over a period of years, despite various pleas from Holland that Collins respond to his letters.

Justice Scalia, joined by Justice Thomas, dissented in *Holland.* Justice Alito wrote an opinion concurring in part and concurring in the judgment.

Relation Back: Mayle v. Felix

In Mayle v. Felix, 545 U.S. 644 (2005), the Court held that an amended habeas petition does not relate back (and thereby avoid AEDPA's one-year time limit) when it asserts a new ground for relief supported by facts that differ in both time and type from those set forth in the original timely pleading. The Court applied the relation-back provision of Rule 15(c)(2) of the Federal Rules of Civil Procedure (because habeas petitions are civil cases). The Court concluded that a limitation on relation-back principles was necessary to accommodate the intent of AEDPA which emphasized the importance of finality and federalism. Justice Souter, joined by Justice Stevens, dissented.

b. Effect on Supreme Court's Appellate Jurisdiction: Felker v. Turpin

AEDPA requires dismissal of a claim presented in a state prisoner's federal habeas application if the claim was also presented in a prior application. The Act also compels dismissal of a claim that could have been but was not presented in a prior federal application, unless certain extremely rigorous conditions are met. These limitations are directed at the perceived problem of successive habeas petitions. To effectuate these strict standards, the Act creates a "gatekeeping" mechanism, under which a petitioner must move in the court of appeals for leave to file a second or successive habeas application in the district court. A three-judge panel then determines whether the petitioner has made a prima facie showing that the strict substantive requirements for successive applications have been met. The Act further declares that a panel's grant or denial of authorization to file "shall not be appealable and shall not be the subject of a petition for . . . writ of certiorari." Thus, the Act limits the appellate jurisdiction of the Supreme Court over successive habeas applications.

In Felker v. Turpin, 518 U.S. 651 (1996), the Court unanimously rejected a constitutional attack on this statutory limitation of Supreme Court appellate jurisdiction. Chief Justice Rehnquist, writing for the Court, declared that AEDPA did not alter the Supreme Court's power to exercise *original* jurisdiction over a habeas petition, as provided for by 28 U.S.C. §§ 2241 and 2254. (It should be noted, however, that the Supreme Court has not granted relief on original jurisdiction over a habeas petition in more than 100 years.) On the jurisdictional question, Chief Justice Rehnquist concluded as follows:

> The critical language of Article III, § 2, of the Constitution provides that, apart from several classes of cases specifically enumerated in this Court's original jurisdiction, "in all the other Cases . . . the supreme Court shall have appellate Jurisdiction, both as to Law and Fact, with such Exceptions, and under such Regulations as the Congress shall make." Previous decisions construing this clause have said that while our appellate powers "are given by the constitution," "they are limited and regulated by the [Judiciary Act of 1789], and by such other acts as have been passed on the subject." [AEDPA] does remove our authority to entertain an appeal or a petition for a writ of certiorari to review a decision of a court of appeals exercising its "gatekeeping" function over a second petition. But since it does not repeal our authority to entertain a petition for habeas corpus, there can be no plausible argument that the Act has deprived this Court of appellate jurisdiction in violation of Article III, § 2.

On the merits, the Court refused, as an exercise of its original jurisdiction, to entertain Felker's claim for habeas relief on a successive petition. Felker challenged his conviction on the grounds of a *Brady* violation and an erroneous instruction on reasonable doubt. The Chief Justice set forth the standards for original jurisdiction, and the resolution of Felker's claims, in the following passage:

> [W]e now dispose of the petition for an original writ of habeas corpus. Our Rule 20.4(a) delineates the standards under which we grant such writs:
>
> > "* * * To justify the granting of a writ of habeas corpus, the petitioner must show exceptional circumstances warranting the exercise of the Court's discretionary powers and must show that adequate relief cannot be obtained in any other form or from any other court. These writs are rarely granted."
>
> Reviewing petitioner's claims here, they do not materially differ from numerous other claims made by successive habeas petitioners which we have had occasion to review on stay applications to this Court. Neither of them satisfies the requirements of the relevant

provisions of the [AEDPA], let alone the requirement that there be "exceptional circumstances" justifying the issuance of the writ.

c. *Certificate of Appealability*

The AEDPA limits the right to appeal from a district court's denial of a state defendant's petition for a writ of habeas corpus. The Act requires that the petitioner must obtain a "certificate of appeal" from a circuit judge. In Slack v. McDaniel, 529 U.S. 473 (2000), the Court set forth the standard that circuit judges are to apply in deciding whether to issue a certificate of appealability. It declared as follows:

> Where a district court has rejected the constitutional claims on the merits, the showing required to satisfy § 2253(c) is straightforward: The petitioner must demonstrate that reasonable jurists would find the district court's assessment of the constitutional claims debatable or wrong. The issue becomes somewhat more complicated where, as here, the district court dismisses the petition based on procedural grounds. We hold as follows: When the district court denies a habeas petition on procedural grounds without reaching the prisoner's underlying constitutional claim, a COA should issue when the prisoner shows, at least, that jurists of reason would find it debatable whether the petition states a valid claim of the denial of a constitutional right and that jurists of reason would find it debatable whether the district court was correct in its procedural ruling. This construction gives meaning to Congress' requirement that a prisoner demonstrate substantial underlying constitutional claims and is in conformity with the meaning of the "substantial showing" standard * * * adopted by Congress in AEDPA. Where a plain procedural bar is present and the district court is correct to invoke it to dispose of the case, a reasonable jurist could not conclude either that the district court erred in dismissing the petition or that the petitioner should be allowed to proceed further. In such a circumstance, no appeal would be warranted.

See also Miller-El v. Cockrell, 537 U.S. 322 (2003) (finding that the petitioner met the *Slack* standard by providing circumstantial evidence that the prosecutor excused jurors on racial grounds in violation of Batson v. Kentucky, and remanding for a hearing of the appeal on the merits).

3. Factual Findings and Mixed Questions of Law and Fact

In a Section 2254 action, what deference does a federal court owe to the state court's determinations of law and fact? Before AEDPA, the Court had held that federal habeas courts were not required to defer to a state court's interpretations of federal law, nor to mixed questions of fact and law. See, e.g., Miller v. Fenton, 474 U.S. 104 (1985) (state court's decision that a confession was voluntary is a mixed question of fact and law which federal courts do not presume to be correct).

But as amended by AEDPA, section 2254 requires habeas courts to give substantial deference to *all* state court rulings in the case. AEDPA makes no definite distinction, in terms of deference, between questions of law and mixed questions of law and fact. The pertinent provision states as follows:

(d) An application for a writ of habeas corpus on behalf of a person in custody pursuant to the judgment of a State court shall not be granted with respect to any claim that was adjudicated on the merits in State court proceedings unless the adjudication of the claim—

> (1) resulted in a decision that was contrary to, or involved an unreasonable application of, clearly established Federal law, as determined by the Supreme Court of the United States; or
>
> (2) resulted in a decision that was based on an unreasonable determination of the facts in light of the evidence presented in the State court proceeding.

Guidelines on the Deferential Standard of Review in Section 2254(d): Williams v. Taylor

In Williams v. Taylor, 529 U.S. 362 (2000), the Court construed section 2254(d) as amended by the AEDPA, and set forth the standard for federal review of state court determinations, as mandated by that section. The case involved a claim on habeas that Williams's counsel had been ineffective at the penalty phase of his capital trial by failing to introduce evidence that Williams had been abused as a child and had a learning disability. The State Supreme Court, applying Strickland v. Washington and subsequent Supreme Court cases, rejected Williams's ineffectiveness claim on the ground that Williams had not been prejudiced. Justice O'Connor, writing for the Court, analyzed the standard of review under AEDPA in the following passage:

> [F]or Williams to obtain federal habeas relief, he must first demonstrate that his case satisfies the condition set by § 2254(d)(1). That provision modifies the role of federal habeas courts in reviewing petitions filed by state prisoners.
>
> * * *
>
> The word "contrary" is commonly understood to mean "diametrically different," "opposite in character or nature," or "mutually opposed." The text of § 2254(d)(1) therefore suggests that the state court's decision must be substantially different from the relevant precedent of this Court. * * * A state-court decision will

certainly be contrary to our clearly established precedent if the state court applies a rule that contradicts the governing law set forth in our cases. Take, for example, our decision in Strickland v. Washington. If a state court were to reject a prisoner's claim of ineffective assistance of counsel on the grounds that the prisoner had not established by a preponderance of the evidence that the result of his criminal proceeding would have been different, that decision would be "diametrically different," "opposite in character or nature," and "mutually opposed" to our clearly established precedent because we held in *Strickland* that the prisoner need only demonstrate a "reasonable probability that . . . the result of the proceeding would have been different." A state-court decision will also be contrary to this Court's clearly established precedent if the state court confronts a set of facts that are materially indistinguishable from a decision of this Court and nevertheless arrives at a result different from our precedent. Accordingly, in either of these two scenarios, a federal court will be unconstrained by § 2254(d)(1) because the state-court decision falls within that provision's "contrary to" clause.

On the other hand, a run-of-the-mill state-court decision applying the correct legal rule from our cases to the facts of a prisoner's case would not fit comfortably within § 2254(d)(1)'s "contrary to" clause. Assume, for example, that a state-court decision on a prisoner's ineffective-assistance claim correctly identifies *Strickland* as the controlling legal authority and, applying that framework, rejects the prisoner's claim. Quite clearly, the state-court decision would be in accord with our decision in *Strickland* as to the legal prerequisites for establishing an ineffective-assistance claim, even assuming the federal court considering the prisoner's habeas application might reach a different result applying the *Strickland* framework itself. * * * Although the state-court decision may be contrary to the federal court's conception of how *Strickland* ought to be applied in that particular case, the decision is not "mutually opposed" to *Strickland* itself.

So a state court decision cannot be overturned on habeas simply because it is incorrect—under the "contrary to" clause, the state court decision must be diametrically opposed to Supreme Court precedent in order to justify habeas relief.

Justice O'Connor next construed the "unreasonable application" clause of § 2254(d)(1):

First, a state-court decision involves an unreasonable application of this Court's precedent if the state court identifies the correct governing legal rule from this Court's cases but unreasonably applies it to the facts of the particular state prisoner's case. Second, a state-court decision also involves an unreasonable application of this Court's precedent if the state court either unreasonably extends a legal principle from our precedent to a new context where it should not apply or unreasonably refuses to extend that principle to a new context where it should apply.

A state-court decision that correctly identifies the governing legal rule but applies it unreasonably to the facts of a particular prisoner's case certainly would qualify as a decision "involv[ing] an unreasonable application of . . . clearly established Federal law."

Justice O'Connor noted that some lower courts had defined "unreasonable application of law" by determining whether any reasonable jurist would agree with the state court's determination—if so, this would preclude habeas relief. Justice O'Connor, however, rejected the "reasonable jurist" standard:

Defining an "unreasonable application" by reference to a "reasonable jurist" * * * is of little assistance to the courts that must apply § 2254(d)(1) and, in fact, may be misleading. Stated simply, a federal habeas court making the "unreasonable application" inquiry should ask whether the state court's application of clearly established federal law was objectively unreasonable. The federal habeas court should not transform the inquiry into a subjective one by resting its determination instead on the simple fact that at least one of the Nation's jurists has applied the relevant federal law in the same manner the state court did in the habeas petitioner's case. * * *

The term "unreasonable" is no doubt difficult to define. That said, it is a common term in the legal world and, accordingly, federal judges are familiar with its meaning. For purposes of today's opinion, the most important point is that an unreasonable application of federal law is different from an incorrect application of federal law. * * * In § 2254(d)(1), Congress specifically used the word "unreasonable," and not a term like "erroneous" or "incorrect." Under § 2254(d)(1)'s "unreasonable application" clause, then, a federal habeas court may not issue the writ simply because that court concludes in its independent judgment that the relevant state-court decision applied clearly established federal law erroneously or incorrectly. Rather, that application must also be unreasonable.

Justice O'Connor concluded as follows:

In sum, § 2254(d)(1) places a new constraint on the power of a federal habeas court to grant a state prisoner's application for a writ of habeas corpus with respect to claims adjudicated on the merits in state court. * * * Under the "contrary to" clause, a federal habeas court may grant the writ if the state court arrives at a conclusion opposite to that reached by this Court on a question of law or if the state court decides a case differently than this Court has on a set of materially indistinguishable facts. Under the "unreasonable application" clause, a federal habeas court may grant the writ if the state court identifies the correct governing legal principle from this Court's decisions but unreasonably applies that principle to the facts of the prisoner's case.

On the merits, a majority of the *Williams* Court held that the state court's decision was both "contrary to" and an "unreasonable application" of *Strickland*. The state court held that the *Strickland* prejudice prong did not focus on what the outcome might have been had defense counsel acted effectively—when in fact that is the very focus of the prejudice prong. The state court also ignored the impact that the substantial mitigating evidence might have had on the jury at the penalty phase.

Application of Deferential AEDPA Standards of Review and Rejection of Relief for "Unreasonable Failure to Extend" Existing Precedent: White v. Woodall

In White v. Woodall, 572 U.S. 415 (2014), Justice Scalia wrote for the Court as it reversed the Sixth Circuit's grant of habeas relief to a state court defendant who brutally raped, slashed with a box cutter, and drowned a 16-year-old high-school student. The defendant pled guilty to murder, rape, and kidnaping, and was sentenced to death. The Kentucky Supreme Court affirmed the sentence, and the U. S. Supreme Court denied certiorari. Ten years later, the Sixth Circuit granted habeas relief on the ground that the state court had misapplied federal law.

At the penalty-phase trial, Woodall called character witnesses but declined to testify himself. Defense counsel asked the trial judge to instruct the jury that "[a] defendant is not compelled to testify and the fact that the defendant did not testify should not prejudice him in any way." The trial judge denied the request, and the Kentucky Supreme Court affirmed that denial. A federal district court ruled that the state judge's denial Woodard his Fifth Amendment self-incrimination right, and the Sixth Circuit agreed.

Justice Scalia examined the Court's precedents to find that Carter v. Kentucky, 450 U.S. 288 (1981), held that a non-inference instruction is required at the guilt stage of a case; Estelle v. Smith, 451 U.S. 454 (1981), concerned the introduction at the penalty phase of the results of an involuntary, un-*Mirandized* pretrial psychiatric examination; and Mitchell v. United States, 526 U.S. 314 (1999), disapproved a trial judge's drawing of an adverse inference from the defendant's silence at sentencing "with regard to factual determinations respecting the circumstances and details of the crime." From this he concluded that "[i]t is clear that the Kentucky Supreme Court's conclusion is not 'contrary to' the actual holding of any of these cases and did not amount to "an unreasonable application of" those cases." Justice Scalia noted that "*Mitchell* itself leaves open the possibility that some inferences might permissibly be drawn from a defendant's penalty-phase silence" and "suggests that *some* actual inferences might be permissible at the penalty phase."

Justice Scalia rejected the lower courts reasoning that Kentucky was "unreasonable in refusing to extend the governing legal principle to a context in which the principle should have controlled" and made clear that the AEDPA "does not require state courts to *extend* that precedent or license federal courts to treat the failure to do so as error." He identified "[t]he critical point" as being "relief is available under § 2254(d)(1)'s unreasonable-application clause if, and only if, it is so obvious that a clearly established rule applies to a given set of facts that there could be no fairminded disagreement on the question."

Justice Breyer, joined by Justices Ginsburg and Sotomayor, dissented and argued that *Carter* and *Estelle* "clearly establish that a criminal defendant is entitled to a requested no-adverse-inference instruction in the penalty phase of a capital trial."

4. Retroactivity

As discussed in Chapter 1, in a habeas action, a state court's determination of federal law is assessed as of the time the state conviction was finalized (i.e., direct review is over). Once the defendant's conviction has been finalized, he is not entitled to subsequent changes in legal doctrine that might work to his advantage. The Court established this principle in Teague v. Lane, set forth as a principal case in Chapter 1. The AEDPA essentially codified Teague v. Lane in section 2254(d), set forth above. The AEDPA's innovation is to treat the *Teague* concept not as one of retroactive application, but rather as a matter of deference to state court determinations. If the petitioner argues that a new rule should work to his benefit, this argument would be dismissed because new section 2254(d) requires a federal court to defer to a state court's determination of "clearly established" federal law. Arguing for a new rule on habeas is by definition prohibited because the state court decision is judged by whether it was contrary to clearly established law *at the time of the state court ruling.*

C. CLAIMS COGNIZABLE IN COLLATERAL PROCEEDINGS

Section 2254(a) makes it clear that a district court can only entertain an application for habeas corpus relief on behalf of a state prisoner if the prisoner alleges that state custody "is in violation of the Constitution or laws or treaties of the United States." In almost every case the prisoner claims that the state conviction was obtained in violation of the federal Constitution. Section 2255 allows an attack on a federal conviction alleged to be in violation of the Constitution or laws of the United States and adds other grounds for attack. But not every claim of a violation of federal law is cognizable on habeas. If that were so, the collateral remedy might serve as a substitute for appeal.

1. Non-Constitutional Claims

Federal Defendants

The courts have limited section 2255 relief to "substantial" violations of federal law that have resulted in significant harm to the petitioner. See Hill v. United States, 368 U.S. 424 (1962) (defendant denied opportunity to make a statement before sentencing; no attack permitted); United States v. Timmreck, 441 U.S. 780 (1979) (technical violation of rule establishing procedures for accepting guilty pleas; no attack permitted). As the Court in *Hill* put it, habeas review for federal statutory violations is not available for federal defendants under section 2255 unless the statutory violation qualifies as a "fundamental defect which inherently results in a complete miscarriage of justice, or an omission inconsistent with the rudimentary demands of fair procedure."

The Court applied the principles of *Hill* and *Timmreck* in Peguero v. United States, 526 U.S. 23 (1999). Peguero sought habeas relief from a federal conviction because the district court at sentencing failed to inform him of his right to appeal the sentence. This failure to notify was a violation of Fed.R.Crim.P. 32(a)(2). The Court, in an opinion by Justice Kennedy, relied on *Hill* and *Timmreck* and declared that as a general rule, "a court's failure to give a defendant advice required by the Federal Rules is a sufficient basis for collateral relief only when the defendant is prejudiced by the court's error." In this case, no prejudice could be found, because Peguero in fact had full knowledge of his right to appeal the sentence. Accordingly, he was not entitled to habeas relief.

State Defendants

In Reed v. Farley, 512 U.S. 339 (1994), the Court extended the "fundamental defect" test of *Hill* to claims of federal statutory violations brought by state defendants under section 2254. The statutory violation at issue in *Reed* concerned the Interstate Agreement on Detainers ("IAD"), a compact among 48 States, the District of Columbia, and the Federal Government. Article IV(c) of the IAD provided, among other things, that the trial of a prisoner transferred from one participating jurisdiction to another must commence within 120 days of the prisoner's arrival in the receiving State, and directed dismissal with prejudice when trial does not occur within the time prescribed. Reed's trial did not begin within this time limit. The trial court denied Reed's petition for discharge on the ground that the judge had previously been unaware of the 120-day limitation and that Reed had not earlier objected to the trial date or requested a speedier trial. Reed was convicted, and after unsuccessful appeals in the Indiana courts, he petitioned for a federal writ of habeas corpus under section 2254.

Justice Ginsburg, in an opinion for five Justices, rejected Reed's argument that the "fundamental defect" standard of *Hill* should not be applicable to habeas claims of state defendants brought under section 2254. She analyzed the issue as follows:

> [I]t is scarcely doubted that, at least where mere statutory violations are at issue, § 2255 was intended to mirror § 2254 in operative effect. Far from suggesting that the *Hill* standard is inapplicable to § 2254 cases, our decisions assume that *Hill* controls collateral review—under both §§ 2254 and 2255—when a federal statute, but not the Constitution, is the basis for the postconviction attack. * * *
>
> We see no reason to afford habeas review to a state prisoner like Reed, who let a time clock run without alerting the trial court, yet deny collateral review to a federal prisoner similarly situated.

The question remained whether the statutory violation suffered by Reed (i.e., the violation of the time limits of the IAD) rose to the level of a "fundamental defect" under *Hill*. Five members of the Court concluded that there was no "fundamental defect," but there was no majority opinion on this point. Justice Ginsburg, joined by Chief Justice Rehnquist and Justice O'Connor on this question, emphasized that Reed had not asserted his rights under the IAD in a timely manner. She did not, however, preclude the possibility that some violation of the IAD might be cognizable on section 2254 habeas review under the "fundamental defect" standard. She noted that the IAD's purpose of providing a nationally uniform means of transferring prisoners between jurisdictions "would be undermined if a State's courts resisted steadfast enforcement, with total insulation from § 2254 review."

Justice Scalia, in an opinion joined by Justice Thomas, concurred in Justice Ginsburg's determination that the "fundamental defect" standard was applicable to claims brought for federal statutory violations by state defendants under section 2254. He concurred only in the result, however, on the question of whether the IAD violation suffered by Reed rose to the level of a "fundamental defect." He argued, more broadly than Justice Ginsburg, that a violation of the IAD could never result in a "fundamental defect" warranting habeas review, and he implied even more broadly that there could never be a federal statutory violation that would justify review under the "fundamental defect" standard.

Justice Blackmun dissented in *Reed* in an opinion joined by Justices Stevens, Kennedy, and Souter. He argued that the "fundamental defect" test of *Hill* was too stringent to be applied to federal statutory claims brought by state prisoners under section 2254. He reasoned that section 2255 actions "cover the ground already covered by federal courts" and so error should be egregious before collateral relief is granted. In contrast " a primary purpose of § 2254 is to provide a federal forum to review a state prisoner's claimed violations of federal law." Thus, "where no federal court previously has addressed the § 2254 petitioner's federal claims, there is less reason to sift these claims through so fine a screen" as *Hill* provides.

State Law Violations as Due Process Violations: Estelle v. McGuire

Federal due process claims are clearly cognizable under §§ 2254 and 2255. State defendants are often therefore tempted to characterize a violation of some state law as tantamount to a due process violation. This ploy is not often successful, however. For example, in Estelle v. McGuire, 502 U.S. 62 (1991), McGuire was convicted in state court of the murder of his infant daughter. At the trial, the state offered medical evidence indicating that the infant had suffered severe injuries several weeks before her death. This evidence was offered to prove "battered child syndrome." The Ninth Circuit granted McGuire's habeas petition, reasoning that evidence of the child's prior injury was incorrectly admitted under the California rules of evidence, and that the violation of a California rule of evidence also violated McGuire's due process rights.

The Supreme Court, in an opinion by Chief Justice Rehnquist, held that the alleged error did not "rise to the level of a due process violation" and reversed the grant of habeas relief. The Chief Justice concluded that "it is not the province of a federal habeas court to reexamine state court determinations on state law questions," and that "in conducting habeas review, a federal court is limited to deciding whether a conviction violated the Constitution, laws, or treaties of the United States." Thus it was irrelevant that the evidence of prior injuries may have been inadmissible under state law. The only question was whether admission of the evidence violated McGuire's right to due process, and the Court held that it did not. The Chief Justice reasoned that the prior injuries were admissible even if they were not linked to McGuire, because they tended to show that the infant's death "was the result of an intentional act by *someone,* and not an accident." As the evidence met the low threshold of relevance, any due process inquiry was at an end. The Chief Justice stated that "we need not explore further the apparent assumption of the court of appeals that it is a violation of the due process guaranteed by the Fourteenth Amendment for evidence that is not relevant to be received at a criminal trial."

2. Constitutional Claims Generally

From the foregoing it is apparent that federal habeas review is generally limited to constitutional claims. The next question is whether all constitutional claims can be raised in § 2254 and § 2255 proceedings. On the face of the statutes, the answer might appear to be "yes," but that would not be a correct statement of the current state of the law. Nor would it reflect the status of the writ through most of its history.

In the early days, the writ was used most frequently to attack the jurisdiction of the court imposing judgment. However, in cases like Ex parte Lange, 85 U.S. (18 Wall.) 163 (1873) (permitting a challenge to a court's authority to impose sentence) and Ex parte Siebold, 100 U.S. 371 (1879) (permitting a challenge to the constitutionality of a statute), the writ was used more broadly for consideration of constitutional claims on the merits.

Consideration of Constitutional Claims: Brown v. Allen

In Brown v. Allen, 344 U.S. 443 (1953), claims of racial injustice in the South were at the heart of three consolidated cases involving collateral attacks on state convictions. Brown, convicted of rape and sentenced to death, alleged racial discrimination in the selection of the grand and petit juries and also the use of a coerced confession. Speller, also convicted of rape and sentenced to death, charged racial discrimination in the selection of the jury array in his case. Bernie and Lloyd Daniels were sentenced to death upon convictions for murder. They claimed that coerced confessions were used against them, that the procedure to determine the voluntariness of their confessions was invalid, and that there was racial bias in the selection of both grand and petit juries. Justice Reed delivered the opinion of the Court on most issues. The Reed opinion assumed that the lower federal courts had the power to issue writs of habeas corpus, even though there was no allegation of a jurisdictional defect in the state proceedings: "A way is left open to redress violations of the Constitution." The Court considered the merits of the Brown and Speller claims in affirming the denial of habeas corpus relief. But it held the Daniels's claims were barred because of the noncompliance with state procedures and the failure to file a timely appeal: "A failure to use a state's available remedy in the absence of some interference or incapacity * * * bars federal habeas corpus."

After Brown v. Allen, it appeared that all constitutional claims were cognizable in habeas corpus cases. No Justice actually argued otherwise in *Brown*. Kaufman v. United States, 394 U.S. 217 (1969), established that the same scope of review was available to § 2255 litigants.

Fourth Amendment Claims Not Cognizable on Habeas: Stone v. Powell

In the landmark case of Stone v. Powell, 428 U.S. 465 (1976), the Court held that Fourth Amendment claims are generally not cognizable on habeas review. Justice Powell, writing for the Court, reasoned that the primary purpose of the Fourth Amendment exclusionary rule is deterrence of illegal police conduct; as such, the rule operates to exclude reliable evidence and has nothing to do with protecting innocent people from unjust convictions, which is the goal of the writ. Justice Powell concluded that the benefits of extending the exclusionary rule to collateral review of Fourth Amendment claims were outweighed by the costs—not only the costs of losing reliable evidence, but also the dislocation costs associated with upsetting finalized criminal convictions and thereby increasing (1) the prosecutorial burdens on the government, (2) the sense of frustration of state and federal judges whose decisions are set aside, and (3) the general uncertainty costs associated with non-final judgments. Justice Powell concluded as follows:

> [W]here the State has provided an opportunity for full and fair litigation of a Fourth Amendment claim, a state prisoner may not be granted federal habeas relief on the ground that evidence obtained in an unconstitutional search or seizure was introduced at his trial. In this context the contribution of the exclusionary rule, if any, to the effectuation of the Fourth Amendment is minimal and the societal costs of the application of the rule persist with special force.

Justice Brennan, joined by Justice Marshall, dissented. He urged that the Court was rewriting jurisdictional statutes, those governing § 2254 and § 2255 cases, and arrogating Congressional power to itself. Justice White also dissented and argued that "[u]nder the amendments to the habeas corpus statute, which * * * represented an effort by Congress to lend a modicum of finality to state criminal judgments, I cannot distinguish between Fourth Amendment and other constitutional issues."

Full and Fair Opportunity

It is truly a rare case in which a state fails to meet the *Stone* requirement that it provide a full and fair opportunity for litigation of Fourth Amendment claims. The requirement has been held to mean that on factual issues the defendant had an opportunity to offer evidence, and that some appellate review was provided. See generally Willett v. Lockhart, 37 F.3d 1265 (8th Cir.1994) (en banc) (the only questions after *Stone* are whether the state has provided any corrective procedures at all, and whether an "unconscionable procedural breakdown" prevented the petitioner from using the corrective mechanism). The question is not whether state courts applied the Fourth Amendment correctly, but whether they provided sufficient *process* for the defendant to get some consideration of his Fourth Amendment claim. See also Capellan v. Riley, 975 F.2d 67 (2d Cir.1992) (summary affirmance of Fourth Amendment ruling, which was probably wrong on the merits, did not constitute an unconscionable breakdown in the state appellate process; claim barred on habeas).

Ineffective Assistance of Counsel: Kimmelman v. Morrison

In Kimmelman v. Morrison, 477 U.S. 365 (1986), Justice Brennan wrote for the Court as it held that Stone v. Powell did not bar a habeas petitioner from claiming ineffective assistance of counsel based upon his trial counsel's failure to file a timely motion to suppress evidence. The Court declined "to hold either that the guarantee of effective assistance of counsel belongs solely to the innocent or that it attaches only to matters affecting the determination of actual guilt." Justice Brennan reasoned as follows:

> Were we to extend *Stone* and hold that criminal defendants may not raise ineffective assistance claims that are based primarily on incompetent handling of Fourth Amendment issues on federal habeas, we would deny most defendants whose trial attorneys performed incompetently in this regard the opportunity to vindicate their right to effective trial counsel. We would deny all defendants whose appellate counsel performed inadequately with respect to Fourth Amendment issues the opportunity to protect their right to effective appellate counsel. * * * Thus, we cannot say, as the Court was able to say in *Stone,* that restriction of federal habeas review would not severely interfere with the protection of the constitutional right asserted by the habeas petitioner.

Justice Brennan also noted that unlike Fourth Amendment claims, there is usually no full and fair opportunity to bring ineffective assistance claims at trial or on direct review.

It should be noted that *Kimmelman* creates an anomaly when juxtaposed with *Stone.* If two defendants have the same meritorious Fourth Amendment claim, and both are prejudiced by the admission of the tainted evidence at trial, the defendant with the incompetent lawyer can reap the benefit of exclusion on habeas while the defendant with the competent lawyer cannot. See Friedman, A Tale of Two Habeas, 73 Minn.L.Rev. 247 (1988).

Miranda Claims: Withrow v. Williams

In Withrow v. Williams, 507 U.S. 680 (1993), the Court held that "*Stone*'s restriction on the exercise of federal habeas jurisdiction does not extend to a state prisoner's claim that his conviction rests on statements obtained in violation of the safeguards mandated by Miranda v. Arizona." Justice Souter wrote for the Court and began by noting that "*Stone's* limitation on federal habeas relief was not jurisdictional in nature, but rested on prudential concerns counseling against the application of the Fourth Amendment exclusionary rule on collateral review." He stressed that cases decided after *Stone* had read that case narrowly:

> Over the years, we have repeatedly declined to extend the rule in *Stone* beyond its original bounds. In Jackson v. Virginia, 443 U.S. 307 (1979), for example, we denied a request to apply *Stone* to bar habeas reconsideration of a Fourteenth Amendment due process claim of insufficient evidence to support a state conviction. We stressed that the issue was "central to the basic question of guilt or innocence," unlike a claim that a state court had received evidence in violation of the Fourth Amendment exclusionary rule, and we found that to review such a claim on habeas imposed no great burdens on the federal courts.

Justice Souter concluded that with respect to *Miranda* claims, "the argument for extending *Stone* again falls short." He explained this conclusion by stressing the difference between Fourth Amendment claims and *Miranda* claims:

> [T]he *Mapp* rule "is not a personal constitutional right," but serves to deter future constitutional violations; * * * the exclusion of evidence at trial can do nothing to remedy the completed and wholly extrajudicial Fourth Amendment violation. Nor can the *Mapp* rule be thought to enhance the soundness of the criminal process by improving the reliability of evidence introduced at trial. * * *
>
> *Miranda* differs from *Mapp* in both respects. * * * [I]n protecting a defendant's Fifth Amendment privilege against self-incrimination *Miranda* safeguards a fundamental *trial* right. * * *
>
> Nor does the Fifth Amendment "trial right" protected by *Miranda* serve some value necessarily divorced from the correct ascertainment of guilt. * * * By bracing against the possibility of unreliable statements in every instance of in-custody interrogation, *Miranda* serves to guard against the use of unreliable statements at trial.

Justice Souter also noted that barring *Miranda* claims on habeas "would not significantly benefit the federal courts in their exercise of habeas jurisdiction, or advance the cause of federalism in any substantial way." Justice Souter explained this assertion as follows:

> [E]liminating habeas review of *Miranda* issues would not prevent a state prisoner from simply converting his barred *Miranda* claim into a due process claim that his conviction rested on an involuntary confession. * * *

> If that is so, the federal courts would certainly not have heard the last of *Miranda* on collateral review. Under the due process approach, * * * courts look to the totality of circumstances to determine whether a confession was voluntary. Those potential circumstances * * * include the failure of police to advise the defendant of his rights to remain silent and to have counsel present during custodial interrogation. We could lock the front door against *Miranda,* but not the back.

Justice O'Connor, joined by the Chief Justice, dissented on the *Stone* issue and reasoned that confessions obtained in violation of *Miranda* are not necessarily untrustworthy. She recognized that reversal of a conviction on direct review because of a violation of the *Miranda* rule may be "an acceptable sacrifice for the deterrence and respect for constitutional values that the *Miranda* rule brings." But she concluded that "once a case is on collateral review, the balance between the costs and benefits shifts; the interests of federalism, finality, and fairness compel *Miranda*'s exclusion from habeas."

Justice Scalia, joined by Justice Thomas, also dissented on the *Stone* issue. Justice Scalia argued broadly that "[p]rior opportunity to litigate an issue should be an important equitable consideration in *any* habeas case, and should ordinarily preclude the court from reaching the merits of a claim, unless it goes to the fairness of the trial process or to the accuracy of the ultimate result."

D. LIMITATIONS ON OBTAINING HABEAS RELIEF

Even if the petitioner's claim is cognizable in a federal habeas proceeding, there are several important procedural limitations that must be overcome before habeas relief can be granted.

1. The Custody Requirement

Whether relief is sought under § 2254 or under § 2255, the applicant must be in custody. "Custody" is a term of art. Clearly if the petitioner is incarcerated at the time the habeas relief is sought, as a result of the conviction that he is challenging, he is in custody for purposes of the habeas statutes. But difficult questions arise if the petitioner has been released, or if he has completed his sentence for one crime and is serving a sentence on another.

In 1963, the Court found that parole was a custody status. Jones v. Cunningham, 371 U.S. 236 (1963). Subsequently, in Peyton v. Rowe, 391 U.S. 54 (1968), the Court held that habeas corpus could be used by a prisoner serving one sentence who wished to attack a consecutive sentence. In Carafas v. LaVallee, 391 U.S. 234 (1968), the Court held that a petitioner was in custody within the meaning of the statutes when he was incarcerated at the time the petition was filed, but released before his case was heard on the merits by the Supreme Court. Thus, discharge of a prisoner once properly before the court will not result in a finding of "no custody." The Court in *Carafas* noted that because of his conviction, the petitioner "cannot engage in certain businesses; he cannot serve as an official of a labor union for a specified period of time; he cannot vote in any election held in New York State; he cannot serve as a juror. Because of these disabilities or burdens which may flow from petitioner's conviction, he has a substantial stake in the judgment of conviction which survives the satisfaction of the sentence imposed on him."

Subsequently, the Court found custody in Hensley v. Municipal Court, 411 U.S. 345 (1973), where a defendant sentenced to prison for one year had his sentence stayed pending appellate and post-conviction attacks. After *Hensley,* release on bail has been held to constitute custody for purposes of federal habeas corpus. See. e.g., Campbell v. Shapp, 521 F.2d 1398 (3d Cir.1975). If a person is in custody in one jurisdiction and wishes to attack a conviction mandating future custody in another jurisdiction, Braden v. 30th Judicial Circuit Ct., 410 U.S. 484 (1973), suggests that any "detainer" or formal demand for custody by the expectant jurisdiction is "custody." In sum, "custody" is found even where the defendant is not incarcerated on the conviction he is challenging, so long as he is still suffering some significant harm from that conviction.

Collateral Harm and Mootness

In Lane v. Williams, 455 U.S. 624 (1982), the Court found that two defendants were not in custody for purposes of the habeas statutes. They pleaded guilty to burglary charges; each was incarcerated, released on parole, found to be a parole violator, and reincarcerated. When parole was revoked each challenged his guilty plea on the ground that he had not known of the mandatory parole requirement when he pleaded. But before the case reached the Supreme Court, each was released from custody. Because the parole terms had expired, Justice Stevens's opinion for the Court concluded that the case was moot. "No civil disabilities such as those present in *Carafas* result from a finding that an individual has violated parole. At most, certain non-statutory consequences may occur; employment prospects, or the sentence imposed in a future criminal proceeding, could be affected." Justice Marshall, joined by Justices Brennan and Blackmun, dissented, arguing that federal courts should presume the existence of collateral consequences to avoid the necessity of predicting how a state might use a conviction or parole revocation in future proceedings.

The Court reaffirmed the Lane v. Williams mootness principle in Spencer v. Kemna, 523 U.S. 1 (1998). Spencer's parole was revoked due to charges that he committed a rape. He attacked the parole revocation unsuccessfully in state courts, then brought a habeas proceeding. Largely due to state delay, the habeas petition was not considered until after Spencer's sentence had expired and he was released. Relying heavily on Lane v. Williams, the Court, in an opinion by Justice Scalia for eight Justices, held that the habeas petition was moot. The Court declared: "We adhere to the principles announced in *Lane*, and decline to presume that collateral consequences adequate to meet Article III's injury-in-fact requirement resulted from petitioner's parole revocation."

The Court rejected, as speculative, all the collateral harms asserted by Spencer. Spencer argued (1) that his parole revocation could be used to his detriment in a future parole proceeding; (2) that the revocation could be used to increase his sentence in a future sentencing proceeding should he violate the law and be caught and convicted; (3) that the parole revocation could be used to impeach him should he appear as a witness in future proceedings; and (4) that it could be used directly against him should he appear as a defendant in a criminal proceeding. According to the Court, none of these asserted harms were concrete enough to create a case or controversy.

Finally, Justice Scalia rejected the notion that an exception to the mootness limitation should apply when the delay leading to mootness is caused by the State. He reasoned as follows:

> [M]ootness, however it may have come about, simply deprives us of our power to act; there is nothing for us to remedy, even if we were disposed to do so. * * * As for petitioner's concern that law enforcement officials and district judges will repeat with impunity the mootness-producing abuse that he alleges occurred here: We are confident that, as a general matter, district courts will prevent dilatory tactics by the litigants and will not unduly delay their own rulings; and that, where appropriate, corrective mandamus will issue from the courts of appeals.

Justice Stevens dissented.

Custody and AEDPA

As seen above, custody questions have usually arisen after the petitioner has been released and is arguing that his conviction is causing him some collateral harm. AEDPA has put a damper on such claims by imposing a one-year statute of limitations on habeas petitions. The year basically runs from the date on which a conviction becomes final. It is the rare habeas petitioner who has been freed from incarceration and yet is still arguably in custody within the one year AEDPA statutory period. It appears that many of the difficult custody questions have evaporated under AEDPA.

2. Exhaustion of State Remedies

A petitioner challenging a state conviction on habeas must establish that he has exhausted his state remedies before proceeding to federal court. The exhaustion requirement originated in Ex parte Royall, 117 U.S. 241 (1886), and it is now codified in 28 U.S.C.A. § 2254(b)–(c).

The Purpose of the Exhaustion Requirement

The exhaustion requirement is rooted in federal-state comity. It allows the states the first opportunity to apply controlling legal principles to the facts bearing on the constitutional claim of a defendant in a state criminal action. It thereby preserves for state courts a role in the application and enforcement of federal law and prevents interruption of state adjudication by federal habeas proceedings. Consequently, it is not enough that the petitioner has *been* to the state courts; he must have presented there the same ground he seeks to advance in his federal habeas corpus petition. See Byrnes v. Vose, 969 F.2d 1306 (1st Cir.1992) ("considerations of comity require that state courts be afforded the opportunity, in the first instance, to correct a constitutional violation before a federal court intervenes").

Which "Grounds" Have Been Exhausted?

Disputes arise when the petitioner's argument on habeas is different from that made in the state courts. The petitioner might argue that he exhausted his "claim" and the government argues that the claim he is making now was never made below. The petitioner's response is essentially "I did make that claim, and the state courts rejected it; I just made the claim in different words than I am using now." How to resolve this dispute?

The Court in Picard v. Connor, 404 U.S. 270, 278 (1971) provided the following basic definition: "the substance of a federal habeas corpus claim must first be presented to the state courts." Connor challenged the legality of an indictment, which had originally named John Doe, and then was amended to name him. In the state courts, he contended that the amending procedure did not comply with the Massachusetts statute, and therefore that he had not been lawfully indicted. In his habeas petition, he alleged a violation of equal protection. Justice Black, writing for the Court, concluded that the equal protection claim had not been exhausted in the state courts. He stated as follows:

> We emphasize that the federal claim must be fairly presented to the state courts. If the exhaustion doctrine is to prevent unnecessary conflict between courts equally bound to guard and protect rights secured by the Constitution, it is not sufficient merely that the federal habeas applicant has been through the state courts. The rule would

> serve no purpose if it could be satisfied by raising one claim in the state courts and another in the federal courts. * * *
>
> Until he reached this Court, respondent never contended that the method by which he was brought to trial denied him equal protection of the laws. * * * To be sure, respondent presented all the facts. Yet the constitutional claim * * * in those facts was never brought to the attention of the state courts. * * * [We] do not imply that respondent could have raised the equal protection claim only by citing book and verse on the federal constitution. We simply hold that the substance of a federal habeas corpus claim must first be presented to the state courts. The claim that an indictment is invalid is not the substantial equivalent of a claim that it results in an unconstitutional discrimination.

In Duncan v. Henry, 513 U.S. 364 (1995), Henry was convicted in a state court for child molestation, and on his state appeal he argued that the admission of testimony concerning an uncharged act of molestation was a violation of the California evidence code and was also a "miscarriage of justice" under the California Constitution. The state appellate courts denied relief. Subsequently, in his federal habeas petition, Henry argued that admitting the challenged testimony caused a fundamentally unfair trial, violating his federal due process rights. Relying on *Picard*, the Court, in a per curiam opinion, held that Henry had not exhausted that federal claim in the state courts. The Court concluded that Henry "did not apprise the state court of his claim that the evidentiary ruling of which he complained was not only a violation of state law, but denied him the due process of law guaranteed by the Fourteenth Amendment." While recognizing that the state law "miscarriage of justice" claim and the federal law "fundamental fairness" claim were *similar*, the Court stated that "mere similarity of claims is insufficient to exhaust." The Court noted that the state appellate court had "confined its analysis to the application of state law."

Justice Stevens dissented, accusing the majority of imposing "an exact labeling requirement." He called the majority's opinion "hypertechnical and unwise" because the state and Federal claims were substantially similar. Justice Stevens argued that where the state court has already denied a claim of fundamental unfairness, "nothing is to be gained by requiring the prisoner to present the same claim under a different label to the same courts that have already found it insufficient."

Mixed Petitions: Rose v. Lundy

What if a habeas petition contains a number of claims, some of which have been considered and denied by the state courts, and some of which have not? Such petitions are referred to as "mixed petitions"—containing both exhausted and unexhausted claims.

AEDPA provides that a district court faced with a mixed petition has three options:

1) it can dismiss the entire petition without prejudice, requiring the petitioner to exhaust the unexhausted claims in state court—this procedure was set forth by the Court in the pre-AEDPA case of Rose v. Lundy, 455 U.S. 509 (1982);

2) if the exhausted claims lack merit, the court can consider and dismiss them on the merits, then dismiss the unexhausted claims without prejudice so that the petitioner can bring them to state court; or

3) in limited circumstances discussed infra, the court can enter a stay until the petitioner gets a state resolution on the unexhausted claims.

Under AEDPA, the district court does not have discretion to *grant* relief on the merits of exhausted claims that are included in mixed petitions. It only has discretion to deny relief on the merits.

As the Court in Rose v. Lundy made clear, the exhaustion requirement does not *preclude* habeas review; it merely *delays* habeas review. The exhaustion requirement is therefore unlike other limitations on collateral review (discussed later in this Chapter) such as the bar of procedural default in the state court, or the related bar of adequate state ground, both of which prevent claims from *ever* being heard on habeas.

Exhaustion and Multiple Habeas Petitions

What happens if a petitioner wants to split his claims, i.e., pursue the exhausted claims right now in federal court, then bring another habeas petition on the remaining claims once they were exhausted in the state court? This does not work, because the petitioner would run afoul of the severe limitations on successive habeas petitions that are found in AEDPA. See Burris v. Parke, 72 F.3d 47 (7th Cir.1995) ("A prisoner who decides to proceed only with his exhausted claims and deliberately sets aside his unexhausted claims risks dismissal of subsequent federal petitions.").

What happens if a habeas petition is dismissed because it contains unexhausted claims, then the petitioner exhausts the claims in state court and brings another federal habeas petition? Is this petition of now-exhausted claims considered "successive," and thus dismissed, within the meaning of AEDPA? In Stewart v. Martinez-Villareal, 523 U.S. 637 (1998), the Court, in an opinion by Chief Justice Rehnquist, held that such a petition setting forth claims previously dismissed as unexhausted could not be considered "successive" within the meaning of AEDPA, and therefore such a petition could be considered on the merits. The Chief Justice declared that "[t]o hold otherwise would mean that a dismissal of a first habeas petition for technical procedural reasons would bar the prisoner from ever obtaining federal habeas review." Justice Scalia and Justice Thomas dissented.

Mixed Petitions and the Statute of Limitations: Pliler v. Ford

In Pliler v. Ford, 542 U.S. 225 (2004), the Court considered the relationship between a mixed petition and the one-year statute of limitations applicable to habeas petitions under AEDPA. Justice Thomas, writing for the Court, noted the interplay:

> The combined effect of *Rose* and AEDPA's limitations period is that if a petitioner comes to federal court with a mixed petition toward the end of the limitations period, a dismissal of his mixed petition could result in the loss of all of his claims—including those already exhausted—because the limitations period could expire during the time a petitioner returns to state court to exhaust his unexhausted claims.

The case involved whether federal courts were required to notify pro se petitioners of this risk. The Court held that such notification was not required. Justice Thomas declared as follows:

> District judges have no obligation to act as counsel or paralegal to *pro se* litigants. * * * Explaining the details of federal habeas procedure and calculating statutes of limitations are tasks normally and properly performed by trained counsel as a matter of course. Requiring district courts to advise a *pro se* litigant in such a manner would undermine district judges' role as impartial decisionmakers.

Justices Ginsburg and Breyer dissented.

Staying a Mixed Petition to Allow Unexhausted Claims to Be Presented to the State Court: Rhines v. Weber

In Rhines v. Weber, 544 U.S. 269 (2005), the Court held that a federal court can, in narrow circumstances, enter a stay on a mixed petition; the stay will allow the petitioner to present his unexhausted claims to the state court in the first instance, and then to return to federal court for review of his perfected petition. The stay will protect the petitioner from having the AEDPA limitations period expire. Justice O'Connor, writing for the Court, noted that the "stay-and-abeyance" procedure was justified in certain cases because without it a petitioner with mixed claims would risk dismissal of the unexhausted claims due to the statute of limitations provision added by AEDPA. But the Court emphasized that the stay-and-abeyance procedure could be used only in limited circumstances. Justice O'Connor explained as follows:

> Because granting a stay effectively excuses a petitioner's failure to present his claims first to the state courts, stay and abeyance is only appropriate when the district court determines there was good cause for the petitioner's failure to exhaust his claims first in state court. Moreover, even if a petitioner had good cause for that failure, the district court would abuse its discretion if it were to grant him a stay when his unexhausted claims are plainly meritless.
>
> Even where stay and abeyance is appropriate, the district court's discretion in structuring the stay is limited by the timeliness concerns reflected in AEDPA. A mixed petition should not be stayed indefinitely. * * * [N]ot all petitioners have an incentive to obtain federal relief as quickly as possible. In particular, capital petitioners might deliberately engage in dilatory tactics to prolong their incarceration and avoid execution of the sentence of death. * * * Thus, district courts should place reasonable time limits on a petitioner's trip to state court and back. And if a petitioner engages in abusive litigation tactics or intentional delay, the district court should not grant him a stay at all.
>
> On the other hand, it likely would be an abuse of discretion for a district court to deny a stay and to dismiss a mixed petition if the petitioner had good cause for his failure to exhaust, his unexhausted claims are potentially meritorious, and there is no indication that the petitioner engaged in intentionally dilatory litigation tactics. * * * In such a case, the petitioner's interest in obtaining federal review of his claims outweighs the competing interests in finality and speedy resolution of federal petitions. For the same reason, if a petitioner presents a district court with a mixed petition and the court determines that stay and abeyance is inappropriate, the court should allow the petitioner to delete the unexhausted claims and to proceed with the exhausted claims if dismissal of the entire petition would unreasonably impair the petitioner's right to obtain federal relief.

Justice Stevens, joined by Justices Ginsburg and Breyer, wrote a one-sentence concurring opinion. Justice Souter, joined by Justices Ginsburg and Breyer, wrote a short opinion concurring in part and concurring in the judgment.

Procedural Bars and Exhaustion of Claims

A petition is not a "mixed" petition within the meaning of Rose v. Lundy if the unexhausted claims are procedurally barred on other grounds. For example, if a petitioner fails to make an objection in the trial court, and state rules of procedure treat that failure as barring consideration on appeal, the defendant's claim is probably procedurally barred from consideration on habeas. (See the discussion of state procedural bars later in this Chapter). If the unexhausted claim is procedurally barred, "exhaustion is not possible because the state court would find the claims procedurally defaulted. The district court may not go to the merits of the barred claims, but must decide the merits of the claims that are exhausted and not barred." Toulson v. Beyer, 987 F.2d 984 (3d Cir.1993).

Waiver by the State

Before AEDPA, the state's failure to invoke the exhaustion requirement constituted a waiver and allowed the federal court to review an unexhausted claim. Granberry v. Greer, 481 U.S. 129 (1987). But this is no longer the case. Under the AEDPA the exhaustion requirement is not waived unless expressly by the state through counsel.

The Futility Exception to the Exhaustion Requirement

A habeas petitioner is not required to exhaust his claims in the state court if to do so would be futile—this futility exception, which was established by case law, has been retained in AEDPA. A good example of the futility exception is Harris v. DeRobertis, 932 F.2d 619 (7th Cir.1991). The district court dismissed Harris's habeas petition, holding that Harris had not exhausted the state post-conviction remedy established by an Illinois statute. Harris had failed to assert his constitutional claim in his state appeal. An Illinois statute allowed claims such as Harris's to be brought on collateral attack; but if the proceedings were commenced more than ten years after final judgment the petitioner had to prove that the delay was for some reason other than "culpable negligence." Harris's petition was filed twenty years after his conviction. The district court held that Harris could have tried to invoke the state remedy by demonstrating a lack of culpable negligence, and therefore his claim was unexhausted. The court of appeals disagreed. It noted that the Illinois statute had been in effect for more than forty years, and in that time "the Illinois courts have failed to produce even a single published opinion in which the court found a lack of culpable negligence." Based on the Illinois case law, the court found that "the culpable negligence standard is an exceptional means of relief which will be unavailable to virtually all prisoners." The court concluded as follows:

> We believe the better approach is to forego resort to the Illinois post-conviction process if a petition would be untimely, absent judicial precedent indicating that the culpable negligence exception would be met. Such a holding avoids the "merry-go-round procedure" * * * by which prisoners are shuttled back and forth between the state and

federal courts before any decision on the merits is ever reached in order to exhaust meaningless remedies.

Inexhaustible State Review and the Exhaustion Requirement: Castille v. Peoples

Suppose the state provides for collateral review without limitation as to number of petitions or the time in which they may be brought. Would it follow that a federal habeas petition could never be brought because the state post-conviction remedy is *never exhausted*? The Court in Castille v. Peoples, 489 U.S. 346 (1989), addressed this question. Justice Scalia wrote for a unanimous Court as follows:

> Title 28 U.S.C. § 2254(c) provides that a claim shall not be deemed exhausted so long as a petitioner "has the right under the law of the State to raise, by any available procedure, the question presented." Read narrowly, this language appears to preclude a finding of exhaustion if there exists any possibility of further state-court review. We have, however, expressly rejected such a construction, holding instead that once the state courts have ruled upon a claim, it is not necessary for the petitioner to ask the state for collateral relief, based upon the same evidence and issues already decided by direct review. It would be inconsistent * * * to mandate recourse to state collateral review whose results have effectively been predetermined, or permanently to bar from federal habeas prisoners in States whose post-conviction procedures are technically inexhaustible.
>
> Thus, the rule is that state collateral review is relevant for exhaustion purposes only if direct appeal has been bypassed and only if the collateral review process is meaningful and not itself inexhaustible.

Exhaustion and Discretionary Review in the State Supreme Court: O'Sullivan v. Boerckel

If the habeas petitioner has failed to include a constitutional claim in his petition for leave to appeal to the state supreme court, must the claim be dismissed in a federal habeas action for lack of exhaustion? This was the question addressed by the Court in O'Sullivan v. Boerckel, 526 U.S. 838 (1999). Boerckel appealed his state conviction to an intermediate appellate court, asserting six constitutional claims. After the claims were denied, Boerckel sought leave to appeal to the Supreme Court of Illinois. Review in that Court, as in the United States Supreme Court, is discretionary. In his motion, Boerckel included only three of his constitutional claims. He then sought habeas review for the three claims that he did not include in his petition to the Illinois Supreme Court. If Boerckel was required to bring those claims before the Illinois Supreme Court in order to satisfy the exhaustion requirement, his habeas petition would have to be dismissed. Moreover, it would have to be dismissed with prejudice, because the time to bring those claims to the Illinois Supreme Court had long since run out—meaning that he had committed a procedural default disentitling him from habeas review. However, if the exhaustion doctrine did not require him to bring those claims to the Illinois Supreme Court, then there was no bar to hearing them on habeas.

The Supreme Court, in an opinion by Justice O'Connor for six Justices, held that Boerckel had failed to exhaust his claims when he failed to bring them before the Illinois Supreme Court for discretionary review. She analyzed the rationale and application of the exhaustion requirement as follows:

> Because the exhaustion doctrine is designed to give the state courts a full and fair opportunity to resolve federal constitutional claims before those claims are presented to the federal courts, we conclude that state prisoners must give the state courts one full opportunity to resolve any constitutional issues by invoking one complete round of the State's established appellate review process. Here, Illinois's established, normal appellate review procedure is a two-tiered system. Comity, in these circumstances, dictates that Boerckel use the State's established appellate review procedures before he presents his claims to a federal court.

Boerckel argued that if he were forced to bring all his constitutional claims before the Illinois Supreme Court, that Court would be inundated by claims that it could not meaningfully review and would have no interest in reviewing—thus undercutting the very comity interests that are behind the exhaustion requirement. Justice O'Connor responded to this argument in the following passage:

> We acknowledge that the rule we announce today—requiring state prisoners to file petitions for discretionary review when that review is part of the ordinary appellate review procedure in the State—has the potential to increase the number of filings in state supreme courts. We also recognize that this increased burden may be unwelcome in some state courts because the courts do not wish to have the opportunity to review constitutional claims before those claims are presented to a federal habeas court. * * * In this regard, we note that nothing in our decision today requires the exhaustion of any specific state remedy when a State has provided that that remedy is unavailable. * * * We hold today only that the creation of a discretionary review system does not, without more, make review in the Illinois Supreme Court unavailable.

Justice Souter concurred in *Boerckel*, noting that a state can avoid a flood of appeals to its State Supreme Court by making it plain "that it does not wish to require such applications before its petitioners may seek federal habeas relief." Justice Stevens, joined by Justices Ginsburg and Breyer, dissented in *Boerckel*. Justice Stevens concluded that the majority's application of the exhaustion requirement to state appellate court discretionary review "will impose unnecessary burdens on habeas petitioners; it will delay the completion of litigation that is already more protracted than it should be; and, most ironically, it will undermine federalism by thwarting the interests of those state supreme courts that administer discretionary dockets."

Justice Breyer wrote a separate dissenting opinion in *Boerckel*, joined by Justice Ginsburg. He noted that discretionary review is rarely granted by any of the State Supreme Courts, and "would presume, on the basis of Illinois's own rules and related statistics, and in the absence of any clear legal expression to the contrary, that Illinois does not mind if a state prisoner does not ask its Supreme Court for discretionary review prior to seeking habeas relief in federal court."

3. Procedural Default

Procedural default means that the habeas petitioner failed to comply with a rule of procedure during the trial or direct appeal. Like the exhaustion requirement, the procedural default doctrine is rooted in principles of federalism and comity. If the habeas remedy were always available despite the transgression of a state procedural rule, then state procedures—such as the requirement of a timely objection and the requirement of a timely notice of appeal—could be routinely disregarded. State defendants might not worry about complying if they could always seek habeas relief. Unlike the exhaustion requirement, however, which merely *delays* a collateral attack, the procedural default doctrine *precludes* it. The question, then, is whether and under what circumstances a habeas petitioner can be excused from a procedural default that was made in the state courts.

While the bar of procedural default is usually applied against state defendants, it is also applicable to federal defendants seeking habeas relief under section 2255. The reason is obvious: if the defendant violated a procedural rule that would bar *direct* review in the federal appellate court—such as failure to file timely notice of appeal—it would undermine that rule to excuse that default and allow collateral relief. This result is not, of course, due to federalism, but rather due to the respect for federal rules of procedure.

a. Deliberate Bypass

In Fay v. Noia, 372 U.S. 391 (1963), the Court created a very permissive test for lifting a state procedural bar to habeas relief. Noia brought a habeas petition, arguing that the confession admitted against him at trial was coerced. However, Noia had not brought an appeal on this or any other issue in the state courts; he had failed to a file a timely notice of appeal. Justice Brennan, writing for the Court, held that a procedural bar would be lifted unless it could be shown that the petitioner had *deliberately bypassed* a state procedural rule. Justice Brennan argued that lifting a procedural bar in all other cases—including where the default was caused by inadvertence or neglect—was necessary to effectuate federal interests. He asserted that petitioners would be unlikely to flaunt state procedural requirements and that state interests would not be unduly impaired. He reasoned as follows:

> A man under conviction for crime has an obvious inducement to do his very best to keep his state remedies open, and not stake his all on the outcome of a federal habeas proceeding which, in many respects, may be less advantageous to him than a state court proceeding. And if because of inadvertence or neglect he runs afoul of a state procedural requirement, and thereby forfeits his state remedies, * * * those consequences should be sufficient to vindicate the State's valid interest in orderly procedure.

Justice Clark dissented in *Fay,* contending that a deliberate bypass test was insufficient to protect legitimate interests of the states in their procedural rules. He argued that the majority had in effect substituted federal habeas corpus review for an appeal in state court. Justice Harlan also dissented in an opinion joined by Justices Clark and Stewart. He contended that the deliberate bypass standard "amounts to no limitation at all."

b. A Required Showing of Cause and Prejudice

Soon the Court began to cut back on Fay v. Noia, and ultimately it was overruled. In Francis v. Henderson, 425 U.S. 536 (1976), the petitioner challenged the make-up of his grand jury; but he had failed to comply with a state rule of procedure requiring that an objection to the composition of the grand jury must be made by motion prior to trial. The Court expressed deference to state procedures and held that habeas corpus relief was barred. It distinguished *Fay* as a case where the petitioner had defaulted on his entire appeal (by failing to file a timely notice of appeal) rather than a specific claim.

The majority in *Francis* stated that the procedural bar could be lifted only if the petitioner 1) could show good "cause" (i.e., a legitimate excuse) for the procedural default, and 2) could establish that the alleged violation of federal law had actually prejudiced his case.[9] *Francis* paved the way for the next case.

---

[9] Justices Marshall and Stevens did not participate. Justice Brennan dissented.

WAINWRIGHT V. SYKES

Supreme Court of the United States, 1977.
433 U.S. 72.

JUSTICE REHNQUIST delivered the opinion of the Court.

[Sykes was convicted of murder. At his trial, his confession was admitted. Sykes did not object and made no *Miranda* argument. Nor did he contend the confession was inadmissible in his appeals to the state courts. He then sought federal habeas relief, arguing that his *Miranda* rights were violated and his confession was erroneously admitted. The district court granted habeas relief (finding no deliberate bypass) and the court of appeals affirmed.]

To the extent that the dicta of Fay v. Noia may be thought to have laid down an all-inclusive rule rendering state timely objection rules ineffective to bar review of underlying federal claims in federal habeas proceedings—absent a "knowing waiver" or a "deliberate bypass" of the right to so object—its effect was limited by *Francis*, which applied a different rule and barred a habeas challenge to the makeup of a grand jury. Petitioner Wainwright in this case urges that we further confine its effect by applying the principle enunciated in *Francis* to a claimed error in the admission of a defendant's confession.

* * *

* * * [I]t has been the rule that the federal habeas petitioner who claims he is detained pursuant to a final judgment of a state court in violation of the United States Constitution is entitled to have the federal habeas court make its own independent determination of his federal claim, without being bound by the determination on the merits of that claim reached in the state proceedings. This rule * * * is in no way changed by our holding today. Rather, we deal only with contentions of federal law which were *not* resolved on the merits in the state proceeding due to respondent's failure to raise them there as required by state procedure. We leave open for resolution in future decisions the precise definition of the "cause"-and-"prejudice" standard, and note here only that it is narrower than the standard set forth in dicta in Fay v. Noia, which would make federal habeas review generally available to state convicts absent a knowing and deliberate waiver of the federal constitutional contention. It is the sweeping language of Fay v. Noia, going far beyond the facts of the case eliciting it, which we today reject.

The reasons for our rejection of it are several. The contemporaneous-objection rule itself is by no means peculiar to Florida, and deserves greater respect than *Fay* gives it, both for the fact that it is employed by a coordinate jurisdiction within the federal system and for the many interests which it serves in its own right. A contemporaneous objection enables the record to be made with respect to the constitutional claim when the recollections of witnesses are freshest, not years later in a federal habeas proceeding. It enables the judge who observed the demeanor of those witnesses to make the factual determinations necessary for properly deciding the federal constitutional question. * * *

We think that the rule of Fay v. Noia, broadly stated, may encourage "sandbagging" on the part of defense lawyers, who may take their chances on a verdict of not guilty in a state trial court with the intent to raise their constitutional claims in a federal habeas court if their initial gamble does not pay off. The refusal of federal habeas courts to honor contemporaneous-objection rules may also make state courts themselves less stringent in their enforcement. Under the rule of Fay v. Noia, state appellate courts know that a federal constitutional issue raised for the first time in the proceeding before them may well be decided in any event by a federal *habeas* tribunal. Thus, their choice is between addressing the issue notwithstanding the petitioner's failure to timely object, or else face the prospect that the federal habeas court will decide the question without the benefit of their views.

* * *

We believe that the adoption of the *Francis* rule in this situation will have the salutary effect of making the state trial on the merits the "main event," so to speak, rather than a "tryout on the road" for what will later be the determinative federal habeas hearing. * * * If a criminal defendant thinks that an action of the state trial court is about to deprive him of a federal constitutional right there is every reason for his following state procedure in making known his objection.

The "cause"-and-"prejudice" exception of the *Francis* rule will afford an adequate guarantee, we think, that the rule will not prevent a federal habeas court from adjudicating for the first time the federal constitutional claim of a defendant who in the absence of such an adjudication will be the victim of a miscarriage of justice. Whatever precise content may be given those terms by later cases, we feel confident in holding without further elaboration that they do not exist here. Respondent has advanced no explanation whatever for his failure to object at trial, and, as the proceeding unfolded, the trial judge is certainly not to be faulted for failing to question the admission of the confession himself. The other evidence of guilt presented at trial, moreover, was substantial to a degree that would negate any possibility of actual prejudice resulting to the respondent from the admission of his inculpatory statement.

* * *

[The concurring opinions of CHIEF JUSTICE BURGER and JUSTICE STEVENS are omitted].

[The opinion of JUSTICE WHITE, concurring in the judgment, is omitted].

JUSTICE BRENNAN, with whom JUSTICE MARSHALL joins, dissenting.

* * *

Punishing a lawyer's unintentional errors by closing the federal courthouse door to his client is both a senseless and misdirected method of deterring the slighting of state rules. It is senseless because unplanned and unintentional action of any kind generally is not subject to deterrence * * * . And it is a misdirected sanction because even if the penalization of incompetence or carelessness will encourage more thorough legal training and trial preparation, the habeas applicant, as opposed to his lawyer, hardly is the proper recipient of such a penalty. * * *

Fay Overruled: Coleman v. Thompson

The Court finally overruled Fay v. Noia and its deliberate bypass standard in Coleman v. Thompson, 501 U.S. 722 (1991). Cases such as *Sykes* had limited *Fay* to its facts, so that the deliberate bypass standard essentially applied only when a state prisoner defaulted his entire appeal. That was the situation in *Coleman*, where the prisoner, by filing a late notice of appeal, defaulted his entire state post-conviction remedy. Justice O'Connor, writing for six members of the Court, recognized that the error in filing a late notice was "inadvertent" and the State conceded that Coleman had not deliberately bypassed his state post-conviction review. The Court nonetheless held that Coleman's habeas petition was barred in the absence of a showing of cause and prejudice. Justice O'Connor reasoned that the cause and prejudice standard was more compatible with interests of comity and finality than the deliberate bypass standard. She concluded as follows:

> In all cases in which a state prisoner has defaulted his federal claims in state court pursuant to an independent and adequate state procedural rule, federal habeas review of the claims is barred unless the prisoner can demonstrate cause for the default and actual prejudice as a result of the alleged violation of federal law, or demonstrate that failure to consider the claims will result in a fundamental miscarriage of justice. *Fay* was based on a conception of federal/state relations that undervalued the importance of state procedural rules. The several cases after *Fay* that applied the cause and prejudice standard to a variety of state procedural defaults represent a different view. We now recognize the important interest in finality served by state procedural rules, and the significant harm to

the States that results from the failure of federal courts to respect them.

Justices Blackmun, Stevens, and Marshall dissented.

Cause and Prejudice for Federal Habeas Petitioners: United States v. Frady

United States v. Frady, 456 U.S. 152 (1982), holds that on collateral attack under § 2255 a petitioner convicted in federal court may not rely on the "plain error" doctrine of Fed.R.Crim.P. 52(b) to challenge an error as to which there was a procedural default. Frady, convicted in federal court of a vicious killing in 1963, moved to vacate his sentence on the ground that the jury instructions erroneously equated intent with malice and told the jury that the law presumes malice from the use of a weapon. He did not object to the instructions at trial. For the majority, Justice O'Connor wrote that the plain error standard, which is applicable on direct review and "was intended to afford a means for the prompt redress of miscarriages of justice," "is out of place when a prisoner launches a collateral attack against a criminal conviction after society's legitimate interest in the finality of the judgment has been perfected by the expiration of the time allowed for direct review or by the affirmance of the conviction on appeal." To prevail, Frady would have to meet the stricter standards of cause and prejudice under Wainwright v. Sykes. (Stricter even than the plain error standard, which is really saying something).

The *Frady* majority found, without reaching the question of cause, that Frady could not show prejudice. The Court noted that Frady had admitted the killing for which he had been convicted. Justice O'Connor stated that prejudice does not follow simply from the fact that a jury instruction was erroneous. Rather, prejudice must be evaluated by the effect of the error in the context of the whole trial. She concluded that a petitioner must show that errors at the trial "worked to his *actual* and substantial disadvantage, infecting his entire trial with error of constitutional dimensions." Frady had failed to contradict strong evidence in the record that he had acted with malice, and therefore the instruction was not prejudicial.[10]

Federal Defendant's Failure to Raise an Ineffective Assistance Claim on Direct Appeal; Is That a Procedural Default?: Massaro v. United States

In Massaro v. United States, 538 U.S. 500 (2003), the Court considered whether a federal defendant had procedurally defaulted an ineffective assistance of counsel claim by failing to assert it on direct review of his

[10] Justice Stevens concurred. Justice Blackmun concurred in the judgment. Justice Brennan dissented. Chief Justice Burger and Justice Marshall did not participate.

conviction. Justice Kennedy, writing for the Court, noted as "background" the general rule that claims not raised on direct appeal may not be raised on collateral review unless the petitioner shows cause and prejudice. But he found an exception to that general requirement for claims of ineffective assistance of counsel at trial. He noted that claims of ineffective assistance of counsel are not ordinarily—and not efficiently—made on direct review because a factual record of counsel's performance was never developed at trial. He explained as follows:

> Under Strickland v. Washington [discussed in Chapter 10], a defendant claiming ineffective counsel must show that counsel's actions were not supported by a reasonable strategy and that the error was prejudicial. The evidence introduced at trial, however, will be devoted to issues of guilt or innocence, and the resulting record in many cases will not disclose the facts necessary to decide either prong of the *Strickland* analysis. If the alleged error is one of commission, the record may reflect the action taken by counsel but not the reasons for it. * * * The trial record may contain no evidence of alleged errors of omission, much less the reasons underlying them. And evidence of alleged conflicts of interest might be found only in attorney-client correspondence or other documents that, in the typical criminal trial, are not introduced. Without additional factual development, moreover, an appellate court may not be able to ascertain whether the alleged error was prejudicial.

Justice Kennedy also noted that "[s]ubjecting ineffective-assistance claims to the usual cause-and-prejudice rule also would create perverse incentives for counsel on direct appeal. To ensure that a potential ineffective assistance claim is not waived—and to avoid incurring a claim of ineffective counsel at the appellate stage—counsel would be pressured to bring claims of ineffective trial counsel, regardless of merit." Justice Kennedy concluded as follows:

> We do not hold that ineffective-assistance claims must be reserved for collateral review. There may be cases in which trial counsel's ineffectiveness is so apparent from the record that appellate counsel will consider it advisable to raise the issue on direct appeal. There may be instances, too, when obvious deficiencies in representation will be addressed by an appellate court *sua sponte*. * * * We do hold that failure to raise an ineffective-assistance-of-counsel claim on direct appeal does not bar the claim from being brought in a later, appropriate [collateral] proceeding.

c. *The Meaning of "Cause and Prejudice"*

An Objection That Could Have Been Brought: Engle v. Isaac

One of the Court's first attempts to explain the "cause" part of the cause and prejudice standard is Engle v. Isaac, 456 U.S. 107 (1982). The Court in *Engle* held that three habeas corpus petitioners could not collaterally challenge jury instructions given in a state criminal proceeding. The petitioners contended that Ohio had impermissibly shifted the burden of persuasion on self-defense issues to them, but none had objected at trial to the trial court's instructions. Without reaching the question of prejudice, the *Engle* Court found that there was no good cause for the petitioners' failure to object to the instructions in the state trial. The petitioners contended that their failure to raise the claim should be excused because the legal basis for an objection to the instructions was "novel" or unknown to them at the time of their trial. There was no clearly established law on point. But Justice O'Connor found that the basis of petitioners' constitutional claim (i.e., impermissible burden-shifting) had been apparent since *In re Winship,* decided before the petitioners were tried. (The Court in *Winship* held that due process requires the prosecution to prove every element of the crime beyond a reasonable doubt.)

The petitioners argued that the failure to invoke *Winship* had been justifiable, because *Winship* concerned the prosecution's burden to prove the *elements* of the crime, and did not specifically consider whether it was permissible to allocate to the defendant the burden of proof on affirmative defenses. But Justice O'Connor rejected this argument. She noted that *Winship* had been relied on by some lawyers making similar claims at that time. Thus, it could not be said that the petitioners had "lacked the tools to construct" an argument based on *Winship,* and consequently there was no good cause for failing to bring the argument. So long as the claim was "reasonably available" at the time of trial, there was no cause for the petitioners' failure to comply with the state's contemporary objection requirement. Justice O'Connor recognized that not "every astute counsel" would have made a constitutional objection in these circumstances. However, she concluded that the Constitution "does not insure that defense counsel will recognize and raise every constitutional claim."

Finally, Justice O'Connor rejected the petitioners' argument that an objection would have been "futile," because Ohio courts had routinely given the instruction shifting the burden of proving self-defense to the defendant. She stated that "the futility of presenting an objection to the state courts cannot alone constitute cause for a failure to object at trial." Justice O'Connor reasoned that a contemporary objection was required because "a state court that has previously rejected a constitutional argument may decide, upon reflection, that the contention is valid." Thus, the question for determining cause is not whether an objection would be "futile" but rather whether the objection was "reasonably available."[11]

Failure to Bring a Novel Claim as "Cause": Reed v. Ross

The Court examined the concept of "cause" again in Reed v. Ross, 468 U.S. 1 (1984). Ross was convicted of first-degree murder in 1969, *prior* to the Supreme Court's holding in *Winship* that the Due Process Clause requires the state to prove beyond a reasonable doubt all of the elements necessary to constitute the crime with which a defendant is charged. (Thus, the case differed from *Engle*, where *Winship* had already been decided at the time of the state trial). Jury instructions had imposed upon Ross the burden of showing that he lacked malice and that he acted in self-defense. Ross did not properly object to the instructions. Ross then sought federal habeas corpus relief.

The Supreme Court held, 5–4, in an opinion by Justice Brennan, that Ross had established cause for his failure to challenge the instructions. The state conceded that Ross had been prejudiced by the claimed violation—challenging only whether there was cause—so the Court concluded that the state procedural bar was lifted.

On the question of cause, Justice Brennan stated that "[c]ounsel's failure to raise a claim for which there was no reasonable basis in existing law does not seriously implicate any of the concerns that might otherwise require deference to a State's procedural bar" and that "if we were to hold that the novelty of a constitutional question does not give rise to cause for counsel's failure to raise it, we might actually disrupt state-court proceedings by encouraging defense counsel to include any and all remotely plausible constitutional claims that could, some day, gain recognition." The Court held, therefore, "that where a constitutional claim is so novel that its legal basis is not reasonably available to counsel, a defendant has cause for his failure to raise the claim in accordance with applicable state procedures." Justice Brennan concluded as follows:

> Whether an attorney had a reasonable basis for pressing a claim challenging a practice that this Court has arguably sanctioned depends on how direct this Court's sanction of the prevailing practice had been, how well entrenched the practice was in the relevant jurisdiction at the time of defense counsel's failure to challenge it, and how strong the available support is from sources opposing the prevailing practice.

Applying those standards to Ross's case, the Court looked to the law as it existed prior to *Winship* and found only scant, indirect support for the

[11] Justice Blackmun concurred in the result without opinion. Justice Stevens concurred in part and dissented in part in a brief opinion. Justice Brennan, joined by Justice Marshall, dissented.

challenge that Ross mounted in his habeas corpus petition. So while Ross's claim of error was similar to that of the petitioners in *Engle,* those petitioners had the benefit of *Winship* in constructing their arguments at trial, while Ross did not. Therefore, Ross had cause for his procedural fault while the petitioners in *Engle* did not.

Justice Rehnquist dissented, joined by Chief Justice Burger and Justices Blackmun and O'Connor. He noted that the equating of novelty of claims with cause not to bring them "pushes the Court into a conundrum which it refuses to recognize. The more novel a claimed constitutional right, the more unlikely a violation of that claimed right undercut the fundamental fairness of the trial." In Justice Rehnquist's view, the majority's construction meant that if there was "cause" for not bringing a novel claim, there would by definition not be prejudice.

The Reed-Engle/AEDPA Whipsaw

Reed v. Ross holds that if a development in the law could not have been reasonably anticipated by the petitioner, then there is cause for not invoking the rule in the state proceedings. But can the petitioner then rely on that rule in habeas proceedings to show a violation of the Constitution? Recall the discussion of nonretroactivity of new rules on habeas, and particularly Teague v. Lane, in Chapter 1. Under *Teague,* new rules are generally inapplicable to habeas cases. A new rule is defined as any rule as to which reasonable minds could have differed before it was adopted, i.e., a rule that was not dictated by existing precedent. That standard was codified in AEDPA, which essentially prohibits federal courts from finding constitutional error if the state courts reasonably construed then-existing federal law as determined by the Supreme Court. How can the petitioner establish cause on grounds of "novelty" and yet argue that the state court decision was completely unreasonable because it failed to consider an admittedly novel federal claim? The "whipsaw" effect of *Ross* and the *Teague* principle is described by Professor Arkin in The Prisoner's Dilemma: Life in the Lower Federal Courts After Teague v. Lane, 69 No.Car.L.Rev. 371, 408 (1991):

> [I]f a petitioner is able to show that his claim is based on a "new" rule of law, the habeas court will excuse his state procedural default, assuming petitioner can show actual prejudice. But, having shown that the rule under which he seeks relief was not available to him at the time he should have raised it in the state courts, the petitioner may well have won the battle under *Wainwright* [v. Sykes] only to lose the war to *Teague.* Under most circumstances, the petitioner will have just shown that the very rule under which he seeks relief is not retroactive * * *.

See also Hopkinson v. Shillinger, 888 F.2d 1286 (10th Cir.1989) ("a holding that a claim is so novel that there is no reasonably available basis for it, thus establishing cause, must also mean that the claim was too novel to be dictated by past precedent").

Unavailability of Facts as Cause: Amadeo v. Zant

The *Ross* "reasonable availability" definition of cause can still have utility where the failure to assert a claim is due to a lack of *facts* that were not reasonably available to the defendant at the time of the state proceedings. A unanimous Supreme Court held in Amadeo v. Zant, 486 U.S. 214 (1988), that a state defendant who was convicted of murder and sentenced to death showed cause for a late challenge to the racial composition of the grand jury. The petitioner demonstrated that local officials had concealed a handwritten memorandum from the District Attorney to jury commissioners, which indicated that underrepresentation of black members of the grand jury was intentional. The memorandum was discovered by a lawyer in a civil suit challenging voting procedures. Amadeo's lawyer relied upon the report on direct appeal, but the state supreme court found that the challenge to the grand jury's composition came too late under state procedures.

Justice Marshall wrote for the Court as it found cause for the procedural default because the factual basis for the equal protection claim had been suppressed by the state. In articulating the meaning of "cause," the Court cited *Ross* and concluded as follows:

> If the District Attorney's memorandum was not reasonably discoverable because it was concealed by Putnam County officials, and if that concealment, rather than tactical considerations, was the reason for the failure of petitioner's lawyers to raise the jury challenge in the trial court, then petitioner established cause to excuse his procedural default under this Court's precedents.

Attorney Error Is Not Cause Unless It Constitutes Ineffective Assistance: Murray v. Carrier and Smith v. Murray

In Murray v. Carrier, 477 U.S. 478 (1986), Justice O'Connor wrote for the Court as it held that a federal habeas petitioner cannot show cause for a procedural default by establishing that competent defense counsel's failure to raise a claim of error was inadvertent rather than deliberate. In a rape and abduction case, the defendant's trial counsel had twice unsuccessfully requested an opportunity to review the victim's statements. Counsel failed to attack the trial judge's rulings in his petition for appeal, thus defaulting under a state court rule limiting judicial consideration on appeal to errors raised in the petition. The Court held that this failure to comply with the state procedure barred federal habeas corpus review even if it resulted from ignorance or inadvertence. Justice O'Connor wrote that "we discern no inequity in requiring [the defendant] to bear the risk of attorney error that results in a procedural default" by "counsel whose performance is not constitutionally ineffective." To establish cause for a procedural default, a prisoner must ordinarily "show that some objective factor external to the defense impeded counsel's efforts to comply with the State's procedural rule." Justice O'Connor elaborated as follows:

> Without attempting an exhaustive catalog * * *, we note that a showing that the factual or legal claim was not reasonably available to counsel * * *, or that some interference by officials * * * made compliance impracticable, would constitute cause under this standard.
>
> Similarly, if the procedural default is the result of ineffective assistance of counsel, the Sixth Amendment itself requires that responsibility for the default be imputed to the State [and it is therefore] cause for a procedural default.

Justice Stevens, joined by Justice Blackmun, concurred in the judgment. He argued that the cause and prejudice formula "is not dispositive when the fundamental fairness of a prisoner's conviction is at issue" and advocated an "overall inquiry into justice." Justice O'Connor responded that the Stevens approach would actually replace the cause requirement with a manifest injustice standard. She observed that the relationship of this standard to prejudice was uncertain. But in recognition of the fact that the cause and prejudice standard might produce a miscarriage of justice in some cases, Justice O'Connor stated that "in an extraordinary case, where a constitutional violation has probably resulted in the conviction of one who is actually innocent, a federal habeas corpus court may grant the writ even in the absence of a showing of cause for the procedural default." The Court remanded for an inquiry into whether the victim's statements contained material that would establish the defendant's innocence.

Justice Brennan, joined by Justice Marshall, dissented and argued that the cause and prejudice limitation, a judicial form of abstention not required by the language of the habeas corpus statute, should permit federal consideration of claims not raised because of inadvertence or ignorance.

Decided with Murray v. Carrier was Smith v. Murray, 477 U.S. 527 (1986), a capital case. Once again Justice O'Connor found no cause for a procedural default. A psychiatrist who examined Smith was called to testify by the state at the sentencing phase of the trial. He described, over Smith's objection, an incident that Smith had related to him. On appeal, Smith's counsel did not claim error in the use of the testimony, and so the claim was procedurally defaulted. In his habeas corpus petition, Smith claimed that the use of the statements violated his constitutional rights under the Fifth and Sixth Amendments. Justice O'Connor found that a deliberate decision had been made not to put the claim before the state supreme court and that, even if the decision was made out of ignorance of the claim's strength, this was not sufficient to demonstrate cause. She also concluded that the application of the cause and prejudice standard would not result in a fundamental miscarriage of justice, because "the alleged constitutional error neither precluded the development of true facts nor resulted in the admission of false ones."

Justice Stevens dissented in *Smith*, joined in full by Justices Marshall and Blackmun, and in part by Justice Brennan. He disagreed with the idea that only a claim implicating "actual innocence" could rise to the level of a miscarriage of justice, and argued that accuracy is not the only value protected by the Constitution.

Attorney Abandonment as Cause and Prejudice: Maples v. Thomas

In Maples v. Thomas, 565 U.S. 266 (2012), a state prisoner's pro bono attorneys left the law firm representing him without notifying either him or the court, thus causing him to miss the deadline for filing a notice of appeal in his state post-conviction case. The Court found that under these circumstances the prisoner demonstrated "cause" that excused the procedural default. Justice Ginsburg, writing for a seven-Justice majority, noted that "under agency principles, a client cannot be charged with the acts or omissions of an attorney who has abandoned him. Nor can a client be faulted for failing to act on his own behalf when he lacks reason to believe his attorneys of record, in fact, are not representing him." Reviewing the circumstances, the Court found that the prisoner's attorneys of record had abandoned him, thereby supplying the "extraordinary circumstances beyond his control" necessary to lift the state procedural bar to his federal petition. Justice Ginsburg concluded as follows:

> Through no fault of his own, Maples lacked the assistance of any authorized attorney during the 42 days Alabama allows for noticing an appeal from a trial court's denial of postconviction relief. As just observed, he had no reason to suspect that, in reality, he had been reduced to pro se status. Maples was disarmed by extraordinary circumstances quite beyond his control. He has shown ample cause, we hold, to excuse the procedural default into which he was trapped when counsel of record abandoned him without a word of warning.

Justice Alito, in a concurring opinion, summarized the confluence of eight factors that prevented the petitioner from filing the notice:

> Unbeknownst to petitioner, he was effectively deprived of legal representation due to the combined effect of no fewer than eight unfortunate events: (1) the departure from their law firm of the two

young lawyers who appeared as counsel of record in his state postconviction proceeding; (2) the acceptance by these two attorneys of new employment that precluded them from continuing to represent him; (3) their failure to notify petitioner of their new situation; (4) their failure to withdraw as his counsel of record; (5) the apparent failure of the firm that they left to monitor the status of petitioner's case when these attorneys departed; (6) when notice of the decision denying petitioner's request for state postconviction relief was received in that firm's offices, the failure of the firm's mail room to route that important communication to either another member of the firm or to the departed attorneys' new addresses; (7) the failure of the clerk's office to take any action when the envelope containing that notice came back unopened; and (8) local counsel's very limited conception of the role that he was obligated to play in petitioner's representation.

Justice Alito concluded that "[w]hat occurred here was not a predictable consequence of the Alabama system but a veritable perfect storm of misfortune, a most unlikely combination of events that, without notice, effectively deprived petitioner of legal representation. Under these unique circumstances, I agree that petitioner's procedural default is overcome."

Justice Scalia, joined by Justice Thomas, dissented on the ground that, although a procedural default may be excused when it is attributable to abandonment by his attorney, the petitioner failed to prove abandonment.

No Cause Based on Ineffectiveness of Counsel, Where There Is No Constitutional Right to Counsel: Coleman v. Thompson, Martinez v. Ryan, and Davila v. Davis

Carrier held that constitutionally ineffective assistance of counsel would establish the "cause" requirement that is part of the showing necessary to excuse a procedural default. In Coleman v. Thompson, 501 U.S. 722 (1991), Coleman had been convicted of capital murder; his direct appeals had been unsuccessful; he brought a petition in state court for relief under the *state* habeas corpus provisions; this petition was denied, and Coleman's counsel failed to file a notice of appeal from the denial. The failure to file the notice of appeal imposed a procedural bar to further relief. Coleman argued that his counsel's failure constituted ineffective assistance, and that the procedural bar was therefore lifted after Murray v. Carrier. Justice O'Connor, writing for the Court, rejected this argument. She relied on the line of right to counsel cases (discussed in Chapters 5 and 10), which hold that the defendant has no constitutional right to appointed counsel beyond the first appeal of right. She reasoned that because Coleman had no constitutional right to counsel in the state habeas proceedings, there could be no claim of constitutionally ineffective counsel.

She concluded that "Coleman must bear the risk of attorney error that results in a procedural default."

Justice O'Connor also rejected the argument that cause to excuse a procedural default should be found whenever counsel was so ineffective as to violate the standards of Strickland v. Washington (discussed in Chapter 10), even though no Sixth Amendment claim is possible because the ineffectiveness did not occur at a stage of the proceedings in which there is a constitutional right to counsel. She stated that this argument "is inconsistent not only with the language of *Carrier,* but the logic of that opinion as well." She reasoned that "cause" must be something "external to the petitioner, something that cannot be fairly attributed to him." She asserted that the only type of attorney error for which the State must take responsibility independent of the petitioner is where the Sixth Amendment has been violated, i.e., where ineffectiveness occurs before or during the trial or in the first appeal. She explained as follows:

> Where a petitioner defaults a claim as a result of the denial of the right to effective assistance of counsel, the State, which is responsible for the denial as a constitutional matter, must bear the cost of any resulting default and the harm to state interests that federal habeas review entails. A different allocation of costs is appropriate in those circumstances where the State has no responsibility to ensure that the petitioner was represented by competent counsel. As between the State and the petitioner, it is the petitioner who must bear the burden of a failure to follow state procedural rules.

Justice Blackmun, joined by Justices Marshall and Stevens in dissent, attacked the majority's holding as "patently unfair." He argued that to permit a procedural default to preclude habeas review, when it was caused by attorney error egregious enough to constitute ineffective assistance of counsel, "in no way serves the State's interest in preserving the integrity of its rules and proceedings."

The alleged failure of counsel in *Coleman* was on *appeal* from an initial-review collateral proceeding, and in that initial proceeding the prisoner's claims had been addressed by the state habeas trial court. Subsequently, the Court in Martinez v. Ryan, 566 U.S. 1 (2012), modified "the unqualified statement in *Coleman* that an attorney's ignorance or inadvertence in a postconviction proceeding does not qualify as cause to excuse a procedural default." The Court, in an opinion by Justice Kennedy, qualified *Coleman* by recognizing "a narrow exception":

> Inadequate assistance of counsel at *initial-review* collateral proceedings may establish cause for a prisoner's procedural default of a claim of ineffective assistance at trial." (Emphasis added).

The Court explained that in *Coleman,* the substantive claim had already been addressed at the initial state collateral proceeding. In contrast, the substantive claim of the petitioner in *Martinez*—ineffective assistance of counsel at trial—had never been heard. Justice Kennedy explained as follows:

> Where, as here, the initial-review collateral proceeding is the first designated proceeding for a prisoner to raise a claim of ineffective assistance at trial, the collateral proceeding is in many ways the equivalent of a prisoner's direct appeal as to the ineffective-assistance claim. This is because the state habeas court looks to the merits of the claim of ineffective assistance, no other court has addressed the claim, and defendants pursuing first-tier review are generally ill equipped to represent themselves because they do not have a brief from counsel or an opinion of the court addressing their claim of error.
>
> Justice Kennedy concluded as follows:
>
> [W]hen a State requires a prisoner to raise an ineffective-assistance-of-trial-counsel claim in a collateral proceeding, a prisoner may establish cause for a default of an ineffective-assistance claim in two circumstances. The first is where the state courts did not appoint counsel in the initial-review collateral proceeding for a claim of ineffective assistance at trial. The second is where appointed counsel in the initial-review collateral proceeding, where the claim should have been raised, was ineffective under the standards of Strickland v. Washington. To overcome the default, a prisoner must also demonstrate that the underlying ineffective-assistance-of-trial-counsel claim is a substantial one, which is to say that the prisoner must demonstrate that the claim has some merit.

Justice Scalia, joined by Justice Thomas, dissented, objecting to the modification of *Coleman,* on the ground that the majority had made "a radical alteration of our habeas jurisprudence that will impose considerable economic costs on the States and further impair their ability to provide justice in a timely fashion."

In Davila v. Davis, 137 S.Ct. 2058 (2017), the Court held that *Coleman* and not *Martinez* applied to a default of a claim allegedly caused by ineffectiveness of appellate counsel in state post-conviction proceedings. Therefore the defendant's procedural default—failure to raise a claim on appeal—was not excused and habeas relief was not available to him. The Court held that the *Martinez* Court provided a limited exception to the *Coleman* rule that precludes a finding of cause when counsel was ineffective in failing to raise the claim. The Court in *Martinez* did not intend to replace *Coleman* in the context of appellate ineffectiveness. Justice Thomas wrote the opinion for five Members of the Court. Justice Breyer, joined by Justices Ginsburg, Sotomayor, and Kagan, dissented.

Cause and Prejudice in the Context of a Brady Violation: Strickler v. Greene

The Court considered how the cause and prejudice standards apply to *Brady* violations in Strickler v. Greene, 527 U.S. 263 (1999). One of the major prosecution witnesses in Strickler's capital murder trial had made several statements to police that were flatly inconsistent with her very evocative and detailed trial testimony. The prosecutor had an open file policy, but despite this, the witness's pretrial statements were not turned over to the defense. Defense counsel, in light of the open file policy, made no pretrial request for *Brady* material. Nor did defense counsel pursue a *Brady* claim at trial or on state appellate and collateral review—this was understandable, however, because defense counsel had no reason to think that any exculpatory information had been suppressed.

Strickler conceded that he had procedurally defaulted the *Brady* claim; but he argued that the very suppression of the witness's statements constituted cause. As to prejudice, he argued that in order for information to be "material" under *Brady*, it has to be information strong enough to undermine confidence in the outcome of the trial. (See Chapter 8, supra, for a full discussion of this standard). So if suppression of information violates *Brady*, it should by definition satisfy the standard for "prejudice" under the procedural default doctrine.

Justice Stevens, writing for the Court, agreed in principle with Strickler that the factors supporting the finding of a *Brady* violation could also be the factors that would lead to a finding of cause. He focused on three factors in the case at bar:

> The documents were suppressed by the Commonwealth; the prosecutor maintained an open file policy; and trial counsel were not aware of the factual basis for the claim. The first and second factors—i.e., the non-disclosure and the open file policy—are both fairly characterized as conduct attributable to the State that impeded trial counsel's access to the factual basis for making a *Brady* claim. As we explained in Murray v. Carrier it is just such factors that ordinarily establish the existence of cause for a procedural default.

Justice Stevens found it unnecessary to decide, however, whether "cause" for a procedural default would be found if the prosecutor did not maintain an open file policy, and the defendant failed to make a *Brady* request before trial or a *Brady* claim on state court appeal.

On the question of prejudice, Justice Stevens agreed with Strickler that suppressing information important enough to rise to the level of *Brady* material would by definition satisfy the standard for prejudice under the procedural default doctrine. On the merits, however, the Court found that the suppression of the witness's statements did not constitute a *Brady* violation. Justice Stevens found that Strickler could not show that there was "a reasonable probability that his conviction or sentence would have been different had these materials been disclosed. He therefore cannot show materiality under *Brady* or prejudice from his failure to raise the claim earlier."

d. The Actual Innocence Exception to the Cause and Prejudice Requirement

The Court in *Smith* and *Carrier* acknowledged that a procedural default could be lifted even in the absence of cause and prejudice, if the petitioner can show "actual innocence." This exception to the cause and prejudice requirement was described by the court in Johnson v. Singletary, 940 F.2d 1540 (11th Cir.1991) (en banc):

> [A]lthough factual inaccuracy in the guilt or sentencing context may well be *necessary* to a claim of actual innocence, factual inaccuracy is not *sufficient* unless the inaccuracy demonstrates, at least colorably, that the petitioner is * * * ineligible for either an adjudication of guilt or the sentence imposed. If prejudicial factual inaccuracy alone is enough to warrant review of a defaulted claim, then the actual innocence standard is meaningless.

Actual Innocence and the Death Penalty: Sawyer v. Whitley

In Sawyer v. Whitley, 505 U.S. 333 (1992), the Court applied the "actual innocence" exception to the cause and prejudice requirement in the context of a challenge to the death penalty. Chief Justice Rehnquist, writing for the Court, stated that in a habeas challenge to a death penalty, the petitioner will establish "actual innocence" only if he shows "by clear and convincing evidence that but for a constitutional error, no reasonable juror would have found the petitioner eligible for the death penalty under the applicable state law."

Sawyer and his accomplice Lane brutally murdered a woman; they beat her, scalded her with water, poured lighter fluid on her, and ignited the fluid. The victim died of her injuries two months later. At the sentencing phase, Sawyer's sister testified to Sawyer's mistreatment as a child. The jury found aggravating factors—that Sawyer was engaged in aggravated arson and that the murder was committed in an especially atrocious manner. It found no mitigating factors and sentenced Sawyer to death.

Sawyer brought two claims on habeas, both of which were procedurally barred, and neither of which satisfied the cause and prejudice requirement. One claim, a *Brady* claim, concerned exculpatory evidence relating to Sawyer's role in the offense, including evidence impeaching the credibility of a star prosecution witness, and an affidavit claiming that a child who witnessed the event had stated that Sawyer's accomplice had poured lighter fluid on the victim and ignited it, and that Sawyer had tried to stop him. The second claim was that Sawyer's trial lawyer had erred in failing to introduce at the sentencing phase the medical records from Sawyer's stays as a teenager in two mental hospitals.

The Chief Justice determined that there were three possible ways in which "actual innocence" might be defined in the death penalty context. The "strictest definition" would be to require the petitioner to show that the constitutional error negated an essential element of the capital offense of which he was convicted. The Chief Justice rejected this definition because the Court in Smith v. Murray had "suggested a more expansive meaning to the term of actual innocence in a capital case than simply innocence of the capital offense itself."

The "most lenient of the three possibilities" would be to allow the showing of actual innocence to extend to three factors: 1) the elements of the crime; 2) the existence of all aggravating factors; and 3) mitigating evidence "which bore, not on the defendant's eligibility to receive the death penalty, but only on the ultimate discretionary decision between the death penalty and life imprisonment." Put another way, "actual innocence" would be found under this view if the sentencer was presented with "a factually inaccurate sentencing profile." The Chief Justice rejected this definition, however, as too permissive. He reasoned that under this test, "actual innocence amounts to little more than what is already required to show prejudice." The majority therefore opted for a middle ground, and defined "innocent of the death penalty" as allowing a showing not only pertaining to innocence of the capital crime itself, but also permitting "a showing that there was no aggravating circumstance or that some other condition of eligibility had not been met." The Court noted that this test "hones in on the objective factors or conditions which must be shown to exist before a defendant is eligible to have the death penalty imposed." The Chief Justice concluded as follows:

> [T]he "actual innocence" requirement must focus on those elements which render a defendant eligible for the death penalty, and not on additional mitigating evidence which was prevented from being introduced as a result of claimed constitutional error.

Applying this test to Sawyer's claims, Chief Justice Rehnquist found that the medical records that Sawyer's attorney failed to introduce were not pertinent to actual innocence, as they were in the nature of mitigating evidence and so did not affect his death-eligibility. The fact that Sawyer had spent time in mental hospitals as a teenager was not relevant to an aggravating factor nor to an element of the crime.

As to the *Brady* material, the affidavit relating the statement of the child-eyewitness—to the effect that Sawyer had tried to stop the burning of the victim—was pertinent both to the crime and to the aggravating factor of arson. The Court concluded, however, that the affidavit, "in view of all the other evidence in the record, does not show that no rational juror would find that petitioner committed both of the aggravating circumstances found by the jury." The Court noted that the murder was atrocious and cruel "based on the undisputed evidence of torture before the jury quite apart from the arson" and that at any rate a reasonable juror could have discredited the affidavit in light of the other evidence. Thus, Sawyer had not established clear and convincing proof of his ineligibility for the death penalty.

Justice Stevens, joined by Justices Blackmun and O'Connor, concurred in the judgment. While agreeing that Sawyer had failed to establish "actual innocence," Justice Stevens took issue with the majority's definition of that standard. He argued that the majority's clear and convincing evidence standard imposed too severe a burden on the capital defendant. Justice Stevens found "no basis for requiring a federal court to be virtually certain that the defendant is actually ineligible for the death penalty, before merely entertaining his claim."

Justice Blackmun wrote a separate opinion concurring in the judgment. He launched a broad attack on the Court's habeas corpus jurisprudence. He criticized the "actual innocence" exception as assuming erroneously "that the only value worth protecting through federal habeas review is the accuracy and reliability of the guilt determination." He elaborated as follows:

> The accusatorial system of justice adopted by the Founders affords a defendant certain process-based protections that do not have accuracy of truth-finding as their primary goal. These protections * * * are debased, and indeed, rendered largely irrelevant, in a system that values the accuracy of the guilt determination above individual rights. Nowhere is this single-minded focus on actual innocence more misguided than in a case where a defendant alleges a constitutional error in the sentencing phase of a capital trial.

Actual Innocence of the Crime Itself: Schlup v. Delo

The Court distinguished *Sawyer,* and applied a more permissive standard to claims of actual innocence of the crime itself (as opposed to the death penalty), in Schlup v. Delo, 513 U.S. 298 (1995). Schlup was subject to the cause and prejudice requirements, which would have barred his *Brady* and *Strickland* claims. He argued, however, that the bar should be lifted because he had discovered new evidence that established his innocence of the crime. The lower courts held that Schlup's new evidence did not provide "clear and convincing" proof of his innocence as required by *Sawyer*. But the Supreme Court, in an opinion by Justice Stevens for a five-person majority, held that *Sawyer* was limited to challenges to the petitioner's sentence, and that "actual innocence" claims must be treated more permissively when the petitioner's challenge is to the conviction itself.

Justice Stevens explained the need to provide a more permissive standard of proof to claims of innocence of the crime:

> Claims of actual innocence pose less of a threat to scarce judicial resources and to principles of finality and comity than do claims that focus solely on the erroneous imposition of the death penalty. Though challenges to the propriety of imposing a sentence of death are routinely asserted in capital cases, experience has taught us that a substantial claim that constitutional error has caused the conviction of an innocent person is extremely rare. To be credible, such a claim requires petitioner to support his allegations of constitutional error with new reliable evidence—whether it be exculpatory scientific evidence, trustworthy eyewitness accounts, or critical physical evidence—that was not presented at trial. Because such evidence is obviously unavailable in the vast majority of cases, claims of actual innocence are rarely successful. * * *
>
> Of greater importance, the individual interest in avoiding injustice is most compelling in the context of actual innocence. The quintessential miscarriage of justice is the execution of a person who is entirely innocent. * * *
>
> The overriding importance of this greater individual interest merits protection by imposing a somewhat less exacting standard of proof on a habeas petitioner alleging a fundamental miscarriage of justice than on one alleging that his sentence is too severe. * * * Though the *Sawyer* standard was fashioned to reflect the relative importance of a claim of an erroneous sentence, application of that standard to petitioners such as Schlup would give insufficient weight to the correspondingly greater injustice that is implicated by a claim of actual innocence.

Justice Stevens concluded that in order to lift a procedural bar relating to a conviction as opposed to a sentence, in the absence of cause and prejudice, "the petitioner must show that it is more likely than not that no reasonable juror would have convicted him in the light of the new evidence." He noted that a habeas petitioner "is thus required to make a stronger showing than that needed to establish prejudice" but that, at the same time, the showing of "more likely than not" imposes a lower burden of proof than the "clear and convincing" standard required under *Sawyer*. The Court remanded for a determination of whether Schlup's new evidence met the more permissive standard.

Chief Justice Rehnquist wrote a dissenting opinion joined by Justices Kennedy and Thomas. The Chief Justice complained that the Court had added to the complexity of habeas corpus jurisprudence by creating two standards of proof for "actual innocence"—one for attacks on a conviction and one for attacks on a sentence. Justice Scalia wrote a separate dissent joined by Justice Thomas.

Actual Innocence and an Untimely Petition: McQuiggin v. Perkins

In McQuiggin v. Perkins, 569 U.S. 383 (2013), the Court held that the "actual innocence" exception serves as a gateway through which a petitioner may pass whether the impediment is a procedural bar, as it was in Schlup v. Delo, or expiration of the AEDPA statute of limitations—as in this case, where the petitioner filed a habeas petition (alleging ineffective assistance of trial counsel) more than 11 years after his conviction became final. Justice Ginsburg, for five members of the Court, found no reason to distinguish between the statute of limitations and any other procedural bar when the petitioner could show actual innocence. Justice Ginsburg emphasized, however, that

> tenable actual-innocence gateway pleas are rare: a petitioner does not meet the threshold requirement unless he persuades the district court that, in light of the new evidence, no juror, acting reasonably, would have voted to find him guilty beyond a reasonable doubt. And in making an assessment of the kind *Schlup* envisioned, the timing of the petition is a factor bearing on the reliability of the evidence purporting to show actual innocence.

Justice Scalia filed a dissenting opinion joined in full by Chief Justice Roberts and Justice Thomas, and joined in part by Justice Alito. Justice Scalia argued that the AEDPA statute of limitations did not provide for an actual innocence exception. He concluded as follows:

> "Actual innocence" has, until today, been an exception only to judge-made, prudential barriers to habeas relief, or as a means of channeling judges' statutorily conferred discretion not to apply a procedural bar. * * * Where Congress has erected a constitutionally valid barrier to habeas relief, a court cannot decline to give it effect.

Actual Innocence and Invalid Guilty Pleas: Bousley v. United States

The Court in Bousley v. United States, 523 U.S. 614 (1998), considered whether the actual innocence exception could apply to a procedurally defaulted attack on the validity of a guilty plea. Bousley pleaded guilty to drug crimes, as well as to a violation of a federal statute that prohibited "using" a firearm during the course of a drug transaction. At the time he pleaded guilty to the firearms offense, the local federal courts had construed "using" expansively, to cover basically any situation in which a defendant possessed a gun during the course of a drug offense. Bousley appealed his sentence, but did not challenge his guilty plea on direct appeal. His sentence was affirmed. Thereafter, the Supreme Court determined that the term "using" in the statute meant some kind of active use, such as brandishing or, of course, shooting. Bousley sought a writ of habeas corpus challenging the factual basis for his guilty plea to the firearms charge, on the ground that neither the "evidence" nor the "plea allocution" showed a "connection between the firearms in the bedroom of the house, and the garage, where the drug trafficking occurred."

The Supreme Court, in an opinion by Chief Justice Rehnquist for six Justices, held that Bousley would be entitled to a hearing on the merits of his involuntary guilty plea claim, if he could make the showing necessary to relieve the procedural default resulting from his failure to appeal his guilty plea. While he could not establish "cause" and "prejudice" under the circumstances, the Court held that Bousley would be entitled to relief if he could establish actual innocence. However, the Court noted that the question of actual innocence was somewhat different in the context of an attack on a guilty plea. The Chief Justice elaborated:

> It is important to note in this regard that "actual innocence" means factual innocence, not mere legal insufficiency. In other words, the Government is not limited to the existing record to rebut any showing that petitioner might make. Rather, on remand, the Government should be permitted to present any admissible evidence of petitioner's guilt * * *. In cases where the Government has forgone more serious charges in the course of plea bargaining, petitioner's showing of actual innocence must also extend to those charges.

The Chief Justice rejected the argument made by Justice Scalia, in dissent, that the actual innocence inquiry will be unduly complicated by the absence of a trial transcript in the guilty plea context. He found this concern "overstated," because in federal courts, where this case arose, "guilty pleas must be accompanied by proffers, recorded verbatim on the record, demonstrating a factual basis for the plea."

Justice Stevens wrote a separate opinion dissenting from the majority's application of the actual innocence standard. He argued that it was unnecessary for Bousley to establish actual innocence, because under the Supreme Court's subsequent construction of the firearms statute, he had never been found guilty of any criminal conduct. This in itself was enough to require that his guilty plea be vacated.

Justice Scalia, joined by Justice Thomas, dissented. He asked: "How is the court to determine 'actual innocence' upon our remand in the present case, where conviction was based upon an admission of guilt? Presumably the defendant will introduce evidence (perhaps nothing more than his own testimony) showing that he did not 'use' a firearm in committing the crime to which he pleaded guilty, and the Government, eight years after the fact, will have to find and produce witnesses saying that he did. This seems to me not to remedy a miscarriage of justice, but to produce one."

4. Adequate and Independent State Grounds

A federal court is precluded from considering a habeas petition from a state prisoner—absent cause and prejudice or actual innocence—if the state decision rests on an adequate and independent state ground, such as a state procedural bar. The Supreme Court has stated that "in the habeas context, the application of the independent and adequate state ground doctrine is grounded in concerns of comity and federalism" and that without this doctrine "habeas petitioners would be able to avoid the exhaustion requirement by defaulting their federal claims in state court." Coleman v. Thompson, 501 U.S. 722 (1991).

The Court has recognized that it is often difficult to determine whether a state court has in fact relied on an adequate and independent state ground that would preclude review of any constitutional claim. In Harris v. Reed, 489 U.S. 255 (1989), the Court established the following presumption:

> When a state court decision fairly appears to rest primarily on federal law, or to be interwoven with federal law, and when the adequacy and independence of any possible state law ground is not clear from the face of the opinion, we will accept as the most reasonable explanation that the state court decided the case the way it did because it believed that federal law required it to do so.

Thus, *Harris* requires the state court to make a plain statement that the ruling is based on state law, where it could fairly construed as resting on either federal or state law. But subsequent cases have found an adequate state ground in the absence of a plain statement.

Adequate State Ground Without an Explicit Statement: Coleman v. Thompson

The question in Coleman v. Thompson, 501 U.S. 722 (1991), was whether an adequate and independent state ground could be found in a state appellate court's summary order of dismissal. Coleman brought a state habeas proceeding alleging various federal constitutional errors. The trial court denied relief. Coleman's notice of appeal to the Virginia Supreme Court from the trial court's decision was untimely under Virginia law. The Commonwealth moved to dismiss the appeal on the sole ground that it was untimely. The Virginia Supreme Court delayed ruling on the motion to dismiss, and consequently briefs on both the motion and the merits were filed. Six months later, stating that it had considered all the briefs, the Virginia Supreme Court summarily granted the motion to dismiss the appeal and dismissed the petition for appeal. So the question was whether the Virginia court relied on the procedural bar to dismiss the action (in which case habeas relief would be denied), or relied instead on its interpretation of Coleman's constitutional claim.

Justice O'Connor, writing for the Court, found that the summary order rested on the adequate and independent state ground, i.e., the state law allowing dismissal of an appeal that was untimely filed. She rejected, for two reasons, Coleman's argument that the state court should be required to state explicitly that it is relying on an independent state ground in order to preclude federal habeas review. First, she asserted that an absolute requirement of an explicit statement misreads *Harris*, which requires an explicit statement only upon a predicate finding that the state decision "must fairly appear to rest primarily on federal law or to be interwoven with federal law." Second, the proposal for a per se plain statement rule would "greatly and unacceptably expand the risk" that federal habeas courts would review state decisions that were in fact based on adequate and independent state grounds.

Justice O'Connor explained that where it does not fairly appear that the state court decision is based primarily on federal grounds, "it is simply not true that the most reasonable explanation is that the state judgment rested on federal grounds," and that a conclusive presumption to that effect "is simply not worth the cost in the loss of respect for the State that such a rule would entail." She concluded that "we will not impose on state courts the responsibility for using particular language in every case in which a state prisoner presents a federal claim * * * in order that federal courts might not be bothered with reviewing state law and the record in the case." Rather, federal courts on habeas must consider the nature of the disposition and the surrounding circumstances of the order to determine whether the state court relied on an adequate state ground.

On the facts, the Court found that the Virginia Supreme Court's summary order did not "fairly appear" to rest on or to be interwoven with federal law. Justice O'Connor noted that the summary order granted the Commonwealth's motion to dismiss, which was based solely upon Coleman's failure to meet the time requirements for a notice of appeal. Federal law was not mentioned in the order. She recognized that the Virginia Supreme Court's explicit consideration of briefs discussing the merits "adds some ambiguity," but concluded that this did not override the "explicit grant of a dismissal motion based solely on procedural grounds."

Justice White wrote a concurring opinion in *Coleman*, emphasizing that he was not convinced that the Virginia Supreme Court followed a practice of waiving a procedural bar when constitutional issues are at stake.

Justice Blackmun, joined by Justices Marshall and Stevens, filed a lengthy dissent, criticizing the Court's "crusade to erect petty procedural barriers in the path of any state prisoner seeking review of his federal constitutional claims." He argued that the Court "is creating a Byzantine morass of arbitrary, unnecessary and unjustifiable impediments to the vindication of federal rights" and "subordinates fundamental constitutional rights to mere utilitarian interests."

Note that on the habeas corpus flow chart, the Court's finding that Virginia relied on a state rule to dismiss the appeal does not end the case. Rather, it means that the state applied a procedural bar. Coleman could still have his habeas petition heard—but only if he could establish cause and prejudice or actual innocence. As discussed above, Coleman could not do so. If the state procedural bar had not been applied, then Virginia would have ruled on the constitutional claims, there would have been no procedural defaults, and Coleman's habeas petition would have been heard.

Coleman and the Plain Statement Rule

After *Coleman,* is there anything left of the Harris v. Reed "plain statement" rule? Consider the views of Judge Williams, concurring in Young v. Herring, 938 F.2d 543 (5th Cir.1991) (en banc).

> [The plain statement] requirement is to be applied narrowly—only in those cases where the state court considers both the procedural bar and explicitly the federal constitutional issue on the merits. The fact that the [state] court is fully aware of the presence of the federal constitutional issue is not enough even though the court does not clearly and expressly rely upon the procedural bar.

State Ground That Is Not Adequate

A state procedural bar will be deemed "adequate" to preclude habeas review only if it is *regularly followed* and *firmly established* in practice. See James v. Kentucky, 466 U.S. 341 (1984), where the defendant asked the judge to admonish the jury not to draw an inference from his failure to testify. The judge refused the request, and James appealed the refusal. The state supreme court held that a request for an admonition was not adequate to preserve a claim on appeal for a failure to give an instruction. But the U.S. Supreme Court stated that "for federal constitutional purposes, James adequately invoked his substantive right to jury guidance." The Court held that "Kentucky's distinction between admonitions and instructions is not the sort of firmly established and regularly followed state practice that can prevent implementation of federal constitutional rights."

In Ford v. Georgia, 498 U.S. 411 (1991), a unanimous Supreme Court held that a state procedural rule could not be applied retroactively to prevent federal review of a constitutional claim. Justice Souter's opinion for the Court concluded that a rule unannounced at the time of petitioner's trial by definition could not have been firmly established at that time, and was thus "inadequate to serve as an independent state ground within the meaning of *James*." See also Johnson v. Mississippi, 486 U.S. 578 (1988) (no adequate state ground where Mississippi law did not consistently require a claim such as the defendant's to be asserted on direct appeal).

Discretionary Rules as Adequate State Grounds: Beard v. Kindler

In Beard v. Kindler, 558 U.S. 53 (2009), the Court considered whether a discretionary state rule could ever be an adequate state ground, the violation of which would preclude federal habeas review of a state conviction. Kindler challenged his Pennsylvania state court conviction, but the state court exercised its discretion under the state's "fugitive dismissal rule" to dismiss the challenge because he had fled to Canada. Chief Justice Roberts, writing for the Court, set forth the issue:

> "Is a state procedural rule automatically 'inadequate' under the adequate-state-grounds doctrine—and therefore unenforceable on federal habeas corpus review—because the state rule is discretionary rather than mandatory?"

The Court answered that question in the negative. The Chief Justice explained the result as follows:

> We have framed the adequacy inquiry by asking whether the state rule in question was "firmly established and regularly followed." We hold that a discretionary state procedural rule can serve as an adequate ground to bar federal habeas review. * * * [A] discretionary rule can be "firmly established" and "regularly followed"—even if the appropriate exercise of discretion may permit consideration of a federal claim in some cases but not others.
>
> A contrary holding would pose an unnecessary dilemma for the States: States could preserve flexibility by granting courts discretion to excuse procedural errors, but only at the cost of undermining the finality of state court judgments. Or States could preserve the finality of their judgments by withholding such discretion, but only at the cost of precluding any flexibility in applying the rules.
>
> We are told that, if forced to choose, many States would opt for mandatory rules to avoid the high costs that come with plenary federal

> review. That would be unfortunate in many cases, as discretionary rules are often desirable. * * * The result would be particularly unfortunate for criminal defendants, who would lose the opportunity to argue that a procedural default should be excused through the exercise of judicial discretion.

Justice Alito took no part in the consideration of the case. Justice Kennedy, joined by Justice Thomas, wrote a concurring opinion.

Flexible Rules as Adequate State Grounds: Walker v. Martin

Most states set determinate time limits for collateral relief applications. But some like California apply a general "reasonableness standard" to judge whether a petition is timely filed. In Walker v. Martin, 562 U.S. 307 (2011), Martin raised claims on state collateral review five years after his conviction. The California Supreme Court denied relief on the ground that Martin was not reasonably timely under the state case law. The Supreme Court, in a unanimous opinion by Justice Ginsburg, held that California's timeliness requirement qualified as an independent state ground adequate to bar habeas corpus relief in federal court. Justice Ginsburg concluded that California's time rule, although discretionary and flexible, met the Beard v. Kindler "firmly established" criterion. The California Supreme Court framed the requirement in a trilogy of cases, instructing habeas petitioners to allege with specificity the absence of substantial delay, good cause for delay, or eligibility for one of four exceptions to the time bar. And California's case law made it plain that Martin's nearly five-year delay was "substantial." Justice Ginsburg observed that state ground may be found inadequate when a court has exercised its discretion in a surprising or unfair manner, but Martin made no such contention here.

"Exorbitant" Application of an Adequate State Ground: Lee v. Kemna

In Lee v. Kemna, 534 U.S. 362 (2002), the Court recognized the possibility of "exceptional cases in which exorbitant application of a generally sound rule renders the state ground inadequate to stop consideration of a federal question" on habeas review. Lee, being tried for murder in Missouri, had produced alibi witnesses from California who would have testified that Lee was with them in California on the day of the murder. When it came time to present the witnesses, however, on the third day of trial, they were not in court and Lee's counsel did not know where they were. He asked for a day's continuance so that he could locate the witnesses, and assured the court that the witnesses had not left the jurisdiction because they had business to attend to locally. The trial judge refused to continue the trial, because he wanted to be with his daughter (who was having surgery) the next day, and had other trials to attend to after that. Lee presented no witnesses and was convicted. He brought a habeas petition, arguing that the trial court's refusal to grant a continuance violated his due process rights, and he presented affidavits from the alibi witnesses stating that they were not in the courtroom on the third day of trial because they had been informed by court personnel that they would not be testifying that day.

The state appellate court refused to consider the merits of Lee's due process argument, relying on a procedural bar: Missouri rules of procedure that require a motion for continuance to be submitted in writing with a supporting affidavit. The question for the Supreme Court was whether this procedural bar prohibited a habeas action in the absence of a showing of cause and prejudice or actual innocence.

Justice Ginsburg, writing for six Justices, declared that this case fit into the "limited category" of exceptional cases in which a generally sound state rule of procedure must be found inadequate. She summarized as follows:

> [W]hen the trial judge denied Lee's motion, he stated a reason that could not have been countered by a perfect motion for continuance. The judge said he could not carry the trial over until the next day because he had to be with his daughter in the hospital; the judge further informed counsel that another scheduled trial prevented him from concluding Lee's case on the following business day. Although the judge hypothesized that the witnesses had "abandoned" Lee, he had not a scintilla of evidence or a shred of information on which to base this supposition. * * * Lee's predicament, from all that appears, was one Missouri courts had not confronted before. * * * [A]nd most important, given the realities of trial, Lee substantially complied with Missouri's key Rule.

Justice Kennedy, joined by Justices Scalia and Thomas, dissented. Justice Kennedy argued that a regularly followed state rule had previously been found inadequate "only when the state had no legitimate interest in the rule's enforcement." The need to provide regulations on possibly spurious motions for continuance meant that the Missouri rules were "adequate" within the meaning of Supreme Court jurisprudence.

5. Successive Petitions; Abuse of the Writ

Even before enactment of AEDPA, successive habeas petitions—serial collateral attacks on the same judgment—ordinarily constituted "abuse of the writ," which generally precluded review regardless of the merits of the subsequent petitions. In McCleskey v. Zant, 499 U.S. 467 (1991), the Court held that a petitioner must ordinarily bring all claims in a single petition. Justice Kennedy wrote the opinion for six members of the Court.

Justice Kennedy accepted McCleskey's argument that the comity notions behind the procedural default doctrine were not applicable to successive federal habeas petitions. He responded as follows:

> Nonetheless, the doctrines of procedural default and abuse of the writ are both designed to lessen the injury to a State that results through reexamination of a state conviction on a ground that the State did not have the opportunity to address at a prior, appropriate time; and both doctrines seek to vindicate the State's interest in the finality of its criminal judgments.

The common purposes of "abuse of the writ" and "procedural default" led the Court in *McCleskey* to hold that a successive habeas petition could be entertained only if the petitioner could show cause and prejudice for failing to bring all claims together in a single petition, or, failing that, if he could show that the successive petition established his actual innocence.

Effect of AEDPA

AEDPA limits the use of successive petitions even further than the Court had done in *McCleskey*. The *McCleskey* Court held that a showing of cause and prejudice, or actual innocence, would permit a successive petition. AEDPA, in contrast, provides for absolute dismissal of claims identical to those previously brought (no exceptions), and dismissal of new claims with two minor exceptions: 1) if they are based on a new rule made retroactive to habeas cases by the Supreme Court (which essentially can never happen), or 2) if the claims were not included in the initial petition due to an unavailable factual predicate (as with the suppression of information that occurred in Amadeo v. Zant, supra). Moreover, assuming that one of these causes are shown, the petitioner then has to show by clear and convincing evidence that no reasonable factfinder could have convicted him. Thus, there is no actual innocence exception to excuse the cause requirement—the petitioner must establish not only cause, but also a standard of prejudice more rigorous than the actual innocence exception to the cause and prejudice requirement had been, i.e., clear and convincing evidence that but for the constitutional violation, no reasonable factfinder could have convicted the petitioner. Finally, the petitioner must obtain clearance from a three-member panel of the court of appeals (which must be satisfied of a prima facie case) before a successive petition can even be brought.

In Felker v. Turpin, 518 U.S. 651 (1996), the petitioner argued that the above provisions operate as a "suspension" of the writ of habeas corpus, in violation of Article I, section 9 of the Constitution. That clause provides that "the Privilege of the Writ of Habeas Corpus shall not be suspended, unless when in Cases of Rebellion or Invasion the public Safety may require it." But the Suspension Clause argument was unanimously rejected in an opinion by Chief Justice Rehnquist who viewed the statute as "a modified res judicata rule, a restraint on what is called in habeas corpus practice 'abuse of the writ.' "

Premature Claims and Successive Petitions: Stewart v. Martinez-Villareal

In Stewart v. Martinez-Villareal, 523 U.S. 637 (1998), Martinez brought a habeas petition challenging his capital conviction. The petition contained a number of claims; one claim was that Martinez was incompetent and therefore could not be executed. Such a claim is called a "*Ford*" claim, after Ford v. Wainwright, 477 U.S. 399 (1986) (holding that the Eight Amendment prohibits the execution of an incompetent person). The lower courts held that the *Ford* claim was procedurally premature, and the remaining claims were eventually dismissed on the merits. When the state proceeded to set a date certain for the execution, Martinez sought to reopen his *Ford* claim. The state argued that this was a successive petition, barred by the terms of AEDPA. But the Supreme Court, in an opinion by Chief Justice Rehnquist, held that the incompetence claim could not be treated as a successive petition because "[t]here was only one application for habeas relief, and the District Court ruled (or should have ruled) on each claim at the time it became ripe"; therefore the petitioner had the right to have it considered on the merits. The Chief Justice noted that if the government were correct, "the implications for habeas practice would be far-reaching and seemingly perverse" because "a dismissal of a first habeas petition for technical procedural reasons would bar the prisoner from ever obtaining federal habeas review."

Justices Scalia and Thomas dissented; each wrote separate opinions joined by the other. Both opinions made the point that however "perverse" the result, the plain meaning of AEDPA was that the revival of a petition dismissed or deferred on procedural grounds constitutes a successive petition, and is therefore prohibited, subject to the two very limited exceptions not at issue in this case.

Note that the *Martinez* rule would also apply in situations where a habeas claim is dismissed because the petitioner has not exhausted state remedies. If the petitioner then goes to state court and exhausts his remedies, but gets no relief, he can then refile his habeas petition. Such a petition is not "successive" within the meaning of AEDPA, because, like Martinez, the petitioner never had his claims considered on the merits by the federal court. But it would be subject to another pitfall—the AEDPA statute of limitations. See the discussion of mixed petitions earlier in this Chapter.

6. Newly Discovered Evidence

Chief Justice Rehnquist wrote for the Court in Herrera v. Collins, 506 U.S. 390 (1993), as it rejected a habeas corpus challenge to a death penalty conviction based upon a claim of newly discovered evidence purporting to demonstrate innocence. Herrera was convicted of killing two police officers. He was identified by an eyewitness and in a dying declaration made by one of the officers. A note written by Herrera, implicating him in one of the murders, was found on his person when he was arrested. Forensic evidence also connected him to the crimes. Herrera filed a habeas corpus petition in state court. He did not contend that an error had been made at his trial. Rather, he contended that he had discovered new evidence proving that his brother Raul had actually killed the officers. He supported the petition with affidavits of Raul's lawyer and former cellmate, both relating inculpatory statements made by Raul, as well as an affidavit from Raul's son who purported to be an eyewitness to his father's murder of the officers. These affidavits were inconsistent with some details about the murders. Herrera's petition was filed 10 years after his conviction, and eight years after Raul's death.

Herrera's state habeas petition was dismissed as untimely by the Texas courts. He then filed a federal habeas petition asserting "that the Eighth and Fourteenth Amendments to the United States Constitution prohibit the execution of a person who is innocent of the crime for which he was convicted." In rejecting this assertion, the Chief Justice reasoned that innocence "must be determined in some sort of a judicial proceeding" and that when a defendant has been afforded a fair trial "and convicted of the offense for which he was charged, the presumption of innocence disappears." He stated that the writ of habeas corpus was not an appropriate vehicle for assessing factual innocence, in the absence of a claim of a constitutional violation in the proceeding—and Herrera made no such claim:

> Claims of actual innocence based on newly discovered evidence have never been held to state a ground for federal habeas relief absent an independent constitutional violation occurring in the underlying state criminal proceeding. * * * This rule is grounded in the principle that federal habeas courts sit to ensure that individuals are not imprisoned in violation of the Constitution—not to correct errors of fact.

Herrera relied on Sawyer v. Whitley, supra, where the Court held that a habeas petitioner who procedurally defaulted his claim may still have his federal constitutional claims heard if he makes a proper showing of actual innocence. But the Chief Justice distinguished *Sawyer* on the ground that it "makes clear that a claim of actual innocence is not itself a constitutional claim, but instead a gateway through which a habeas petitioner must pass to have his otherwise barred constitutional claim considered on the merits." The Chief Justice concluded that the "actual innocence" exception set forth in *Sawyer* did not extend to "freestanding claims of actual innocence." Compare Schlup v. Delo, 513 U.S. 298 (1995) (petitioner can rely on newly discovered evidence to establish actual innocence, where he claims—unlike Herrera—that there was a constitutional error at his trial).

In denying habeas relief, the Court relied on the fact that Herrera was not "left without a forum to raise his actual innocence claim." The Court noted that under Texas law, Herrera could seek executive clemency, and stated that clemency "is deeply rooted in our Anglo-American tradition of law, and is the historic remedy for preventing miscarriage of justice where judicial process has been exhausted."

Ultimately, the Court found it unnecessary to reach the question whether federal habeas relief would *ever* be available to prevent the execution of an innocent person when there is no possible state relief. The Chief Justice assumed *arguendo* that the Constitution prohibited such an execution; but he stated that, even if that were so, a defendant who claimed actual innocence after an error-free trial would have to make an "extraordinarily high" showing that the newly discovered evidence proved his innocence. This high threshold was required due to the "very disruptive effect that entertaining claims of actual innocence would have on the need for finality in capital cases, and the enormous burden that having to retry cases based on often stale evidence would place on the States."

The Court found that Herrera had not come close to satisfying an "extraordinarily high" threshold of proof of actual innocence. The Chief Justice stated that the evidence presented against Herrera at trial was strong, and that his purported evidence of innocence consisted of inconsistent and suspiciously-timed affidavits implicating a person who was now dead. He concluded that "coming 10 years after petitioner's trial, this showing of innocence falls far short of that which would have to be made in order to trigger the sort of constitutional claim which we have assumed, *arguendo,* to exist."

Justice O'Connor, joined by Justice Kennedy, wrote a concurring opinion and stated that she could "not disagree with the fundamental legal principle that executing the innocent is inconsistent with the Constitution." However, she found that Herrera was not "an innocent man on the verge of execution. He is instead a legally guilty one who, refusing to accept the jury's verdict, demands a hearing in which to have his culpability determined once again."

Justice Scalia, joined by Justice Thomas, concurred and argued that "[t]here is no basis in text, tradition, or even in contemporary practice (if that were enough) for finding in the Constitution a right to demand judicial consideration of newly discovered evidence of innocence brought forward after conviction."

Justice White concurred in the judgment. He assumed that a persuasive showing of actual innocence would bar execution, but found that Herrera had not made a sufficient showing of his innocence.

Justice Blackmun, joined by Justices Stevens and in large part by Justice Souter, dissented. He argued that the Eighth Amendment and the Due Process Clause forbid the execution of a person who can prove his innocence with newly discovered evidence. Justice Blackmun contended that the remedy of executive clemency is not adequate to satisfy the Constitution, because that remedy is too idiosyncratic and politicized to protect against the execution of an innocent person. He would "hold that, to obtain relief on a claim of actual innocence, the petitioner must show that he probably is innocent."

7. Limitations on Obtaining a Hearing

What happens if a habeas petitioner claims that constitutional error occurred at his state trial, but the argument of error is dependent on a factual predicate that remains undeveloped? For example, if the defendant argues that the prosecutor exercised peremptory challenges in a discriminatory manner, certain factual issues will be important, e.g., how many were struck, who were they, what was said on voir dire, what rationale did the prosecutor give for striking the juror, etc.

If the facts supporting a habeas claim were not developed in the state court, the petitioner will need to move for an evidentiary hearing to develop his claims. However, if the petitioner should have developed the facts in the state system, and failed to do so, a question similar to that discussed in Wainwright v. Sykes, supra, arises—why should the petitioner be permitted an evidentiary hearing if he failed to develop the necessary facts in the state proceeding? Such a petitioner would seem to have run aground on a state procedural bar.

In Keeney v. Tamayo-Reyes, 504 U.S. 1 (1992), the Court relied on its procedural default cases such as Wainwright v. Sykes to hold that a petitioner who could have developed facts in the state proceeding but failed to do so could be denied an evidentiary hearing in federal court (and thus, as a practical matter, denied habeas relief on the merits) unless he could establish "cause and prejudice" for the failure to develop the facts below. Tamayo-Reyes had pleaded nolo contendere to a charge of first-degree manslaughter. In his habeas action, he argued that his plea was not knowing and intelligent because his translator had not translated accurately and completely for him the *mens rea* element of the crime. He also contended that he did not understand the purposes of the plea form and the plea hearing, and that he thought he was agreeing to be tried for manslaughter rather than agreeing to plead guilty. The merits of his claim were obviously fact-dependent, but his counsel had failed to develop the necessary facts in state collateral proceedings. Justice White, writing for the Court, declared that "encouraging the full factual development in state court of a claim that state courts committed constitutional error advances comity by allowing a coordinate jurisdiction to correct its own errors in the first instance." He concluded that the state court "is the appropriate forum for resolution of factual issues in the first instance, and creating incentives for the deferral of factfinding to later federal-court proceedings can only degrade the accuracy and efficiency of judicial proceedings. This is fully consistent with and gives meaning to the requirement of exhaustion."

AEDPA Limitations on Obtaining a Hearing: Williams v. Taylor and Schriro v. Landrigan

After AEDPA, there are only a few reasons for which a habeas court can hold a factfinding hearing; the standards set forth in *Tamayo-Reyes* are restricted even further. As amended by AEDPA, 28 U.S.C. § 2254(e)(2)—the provision that controls whether a habeas petitioner may receive an evidentiary hearing in federal district court on claims that were not developed in the state court—provides as follows:

> If the applicant has failed to develop the factual basis of a claim in State court proceedings, the court shall not hold an evidentiary hearing on the claim unless the applicant shows that—
>
> (A) the claim relies on—
>
> (i) a new rule of constitutional law, made retroactive to cases on collateral review by the Supreme Court, that was previously unavailable; or
>
> (ii) a factual predicate that could not have been previously discovered through the exercise of due diligence; and
>
> (B) the facts underlying the claim would be sufficient to establish by clear and convincing evidence that but for constitutional error, no reasonable factfinder would have found the applicant guilty of the underlying offense.

The Court construed the AEDPA provisions concerning hearings in Williams v. Taylor, 529 U.S. 420 (2000). In his habeas petition, Williams sought an evidentiary hearing to develop three claims: 1) a claim under *Brady* that the prosecution failed to disclose a psychological report on the prosecution's star witness; 2) a claim that a juror had lied on voir dire by failing to disclose a source of bias; and 3) a related claim that the prosecutor committed misconduct because he knew that the juror was biased and failed to disclose that fact.

In the Supreme Court, Williams conceded that he could not satisfy the stringent standards for relief set forth in subdivision (B) of the statute (i.e., clear and convincing evidence of actual innocence). Resolution of the right to an evidentiary hearing therefore depended on whether Williams had "failed to develop" the basis of the factual claim in state court. The parties agreed that the facts necessary to support Williams's habeas claims had *not* been developed in the state court. Williams argued, however, that he had not *failed* to develop the claims, because he was *unable* to pursue the claims during the state court proceeding, i.e., he was not at fault. The government argued for a no-fault interpretation of the statutory term "failed", i.e., if the claims were not developed in the state court—no matter the reason—then there is no right to an evidentiary hearing to develop the claims in the federal district court.

The Court, in a unanimous opinion by Justice Kennedy, rejected the government's strict construction of the AEDPA term "failed", and held that the term "failed to develop" requires some "lack of diligence" on the petitioner's part. Justice Kennedy explained this ruling in the following passage:

> In its customary and preferred sense, "fail" connotes some omission, fault, or negligence on the part of the person who has failed to do something. To say a person has failed in a duty implies he did not take the necessary steps to fulfill it. He is, as a consequence, at fault and bears responsibility for the failure. In this sense, a person is not at fault when his diligent efforts to perform an act are thwarted, for example, by the conduct of another or by happenstance. * * * We conclude Congress used the word "failed" in the sense just described. * * *

Justice Kennedy explained that the statute required the defendant and counsel to pursue factfinding with "diligence" in the state court:

> For state courts to have their rightful opportunity to adjudicate federal rights, the prisoner must be diligent in developing the record and presenting, if possible, all claims of constitutional error. * * * Federal courts sitting in habeas are not an alternative forum for trying facts and issues which a prisoner made insufficient effort to pursue in state proceedings. Yet comity is not served by saying a prisoner "has failed to develop the factual basis of a claim" where he was unable to develop his claim in state court despite diligent effort. In that circumstance, an evidentiary hearing is not barred by § 2254(e)(2).

Justice Kennedy then applied the "diligence" test to the facts of the case. He found that Williams had not been diligent in pursuing his *Brady* claim, because the witness's psychological history had been disclosed at that witness's sentencing proceeding, well in time for Williams to use it in his state proceedings. Williams and his counsel were thus aware of the report and yet took no steps to have it produced. In contrast, Williams was *not* at fault for failing to develop the claim of juror bias and the related claim of prosecutorial misconduct in not disclosing it. The juror had misrepresented her background in answering a question on voir dire. There was no reason for Williams or his counsel to believe that the juror and the prosecutor were hiding anything. The Court noted that it would be "surprised, to say the least, if a district court familiar with the standards of trial practice were to hold that in all cases diligent counsel must check public records containing personal information pertaining to each and every juror."

In Schriro v. Landrigan, 550 U.S. 465 (2007), the Court found that a district court had not abused its discretion in refusing to grant a habeas petitioner's request for an evidentiary hearing to develop the facts supporting defense counsel's alleged ineffectiveness at a capital sentencing proceeding. Justice Thomas, writing for five members of the Court, found that the record in the instant case demonstrated that the defendant himself objected to pursuing any avenues of mitigating evidence.

Justice Stevens, joined by Justices Souter, Ginsburg and Breyer, dissented. He argued that the record was not as clear as the majority would have it, and that at any rate defense counsel's effectiveness was not dependent on the defendant's willingness to agree to foregoing favorable evidence.

8. Harmless Error in Habeas Corpus Cases

A Less Onerous Standard of Harmlessness for the State to Meet: Brecht v. Abrahamson

In Brecht v. Abrahamson, 507 U.S. 619 (1993), the Court considered the standard that should be applied by a federal habeas court in assessing whether a constitutional error in a state court was harmless. The state urged as a standard that an error should be presumed harmless unless it had a "substantial and injurious effect on the verdict." This standard, which is employed by the Court for review of non-constitutional error on direct review, is referred to as the "*Kotteakos*" standard. See Kotteakos v. United States, 328 U.S. 750 (1946). The *Kotteakos* standard is less onerous for the state to meet—the error is less likely to create a reversal—than is the "harmless beyond a reasonable doubt" standard applied by the Court to constitutional errors on direct review. The more stringent test of harmlessness—understandably advocated by the petitioner in *Brecht*—is known as the "*Chapman*" standard. See Chapman v. California, discussed earlier in this Chapter in the section on harmless error on direct review.

The 5–4 majority in *Brecht* held that the *Chapman* standard was too stringent to be applied in a collateral attack of a state court conviction and that the more permissive *Kotteakos* test applied. The Court concluded that the "*Kotteakos* harmless-error standard is better tailored to the nature and purpose of collateral review than the *Chapman* standard, and application of a less onerous harmless-error standard on habeas promotes the considerations underlying our habeas jurisprudence."

Writing for the majority, Chief Justice Rehnquist emphasized the difference between collateral review and direct appeal:

> The reason most frequently advanced in our cases for distinguishing between direct and collateral review is the State's interest in the finality of convictions that have survived direct review within the state court system. We have also spoken of comity and federalism. * * * Finally, we have recognized that liberal allowance of the writ degrades the prominence of the trial itself, and at the same time encourages habeas petitioners to relitigate their claims on collateral review.
>
> * * * State courts are fully qualified to identify constitutional error and evaluate its prejudicial effect on the trial process under *Chapman,* and state courts often occupy a superior vantage point from which to evaluate the effect of trial error. For these reasons, it scarcely seems logical to require federal habeas courts to engage in the identical approach to harmless-error review that *Chapman* requires state courts to engage in on direct review.

The Chief Justice emphasized the following costs of "overturning final and presumptively correct convictions on collateral review because the State cannot prove that an error is harmless under *Chapman*":

1) the State's interest in finality and in sovereignty over criminal matters is undermined;

2) granting habeas relief "merely because there is a reasonable possibility that trial error contributed to the verdict is at odds with the historic meaning of habeas corpus—to afford relief to those whom society has grievously wronged"; and

3) the State suffers "social costs" due to the necessity to retry a case after a significant passage of time.

The Chief Justice was careful to note that the *Kotteakos* standard would be applied only to constitutional errors of the "trial type." If the constitutional error is "structural" in the sense that it tainted the entirety of the trial, then per se reversal is required whether the error is discovered on direct or habeas review. See the discussion earlier in this Chapter about errors that cannot be harmless.

Justice Stevens filed a concurring opinion in which he emphasized that, even under *Kotteakos,* the reviewing court must make a *de novo* examination of the trial record. He also emphasized that the reviewing court must focus on the effect of the error, not on whether it thinks that a defendant would have been convicted absent the error. He concluded that "the way we phrase the governing standard is far less important than the quality of the judgment with which it is applied."

Justice White dissented, joined by Justice Blackmun and in substantial part by Justice Souter. He argued that the *Chapman* standard was essential to the safeguard of constitutional rights. Justice O'Connor dissented in a separate opinion in which she argued that "the harmless-error standard is crucial to our faith in the accuracy of the outcome" of a state proceeding.

Burden of Proof as to Harmlessness: O'Neal v. McAninch

Who bears the burden on the harmlessness question in habeas cases? Must the defendant show that the error was harmful, or must the state show that the error was harmless? In O'Neal v. McAninch, 513 U.S. 432 (1995), the Court held that where a judge has "grave doubt" as to whether an error was harmless or not under the *Kotteakos* standard, the petitioner is entitled to habeas relief. Justice Breyer, writing for six Justices, defined "grave doubt" as arising when, "in the judge's mind, the matter is so evenly balanced that he feels himself in virtual equipoise as to the harmlessness of the error." Where "grave doubt" as to harmlessness exists, "the uncertain judge should treat the error, not as if it were harmless, but as if it affected the verdict."

Justice Breyer reasoned that allowing the petitioner to win in cases of "grave doubt" as to harmlessness was a result that was consistent with other harmless-error cases such as *Kotteakos* and *Chapman,* where the Court imposed the burden of showing harmlessness on the government. He contended that a rule "denying the writ in cases of grave uncertainty, would virtually guarantee that many, in fact, will be held in unlawful custody—contrary to the writ's most basic traditions and purposes." Justice Breyer recognized the state's interest in finality but declared that "this interest is somewhat diminished by the legal circumstance that the State normally bears responsibility for the error that infected the initial trial."

Justice Thomas, joined by Chief Justice Rehnquist and Justice Scalia, dissented. He argued that the burden should be placed on the petitioner, as it was the petitioner who was bringing the action. He emphasized that the habeas petitioner "comes to federal court as a plaintiff" and so "he naturally should be expected to bear the risk of failure of proof or persuasion." Justice Thomas also noted the limited impact that the majority's decision would have, because "cases in which habeas courts are in equipoise on the issue of harmlessness are astonishingly rare."